The THOMPSON

Exhaustive

TOPICAL BIBLE

The
THOMPSON
Exhaustive
TOPICAL
BIBLE
King James Version

Frank Charles Thompson

Compiled and Edited by

Paul M. Hillman

John Stephen Jauchen

B. B. KIRKBRIDE BIBLE CO., INC.
INDIANAPOLIS, INDIANA
U.S.A.

The Thompson Exhaustive Topical Bible
Copyright © 1997 by B. B. Kirkbride Bible Co., Inc.
ISBN: 0-88707-320-4

Requests for information should be addressed to:
B. B. Kirkbride Bible Co., Inc.
P. O. Box 606
Indianapolis, IN 46206

All Scripture quotations are taken from the King James Version of the Bible.

Printed in the United States of America

97 98 99 00 01/ DK / 10 9 8 7 6 5 4 3 2 1

Cover Designed by Michael B. Gage

CONTENTS

FOREWORD

The Topical Bible is the most overlooked volume in the library of biblical reference books, yet it is one of the most useful and flexible resources for general biblical study. Further, while the names associated with other standard resources abound—Cruden, Young, and Strong in concordances; Smith, Hastings, and Tenney in dictionaries; Halley and Unger in handbooks—Nave has had a near monopoly on Topical Bibles for more than a century. But that will change with the appearance of the *Thompson Exhaustive Topical Bible.*

The twentieth century has seen more Bible translation activity than any century since the flurry of translations from Tyndale to King James in 1525 through 1611. This century is characterized as much, however, by the Study Bible: a translation accompanied by features designed to assist the reader in researching and interpreting the text. Two Study Bibles introduced at the beginning of the century set the standards for all the versions that followed—and both remain in print and best-sellers. The *Scofield Reference Bible*, first published in 1909, established the model of a commentary-style, doctrinally-oriented Study Bible. The *Thompson Chain-Reference Bible*, introduced in 1908, pioneered the self-study Bible without commentary, by surrounding the biblical text with a library of features that guided the user through countless hours of personal discovery.

The most significant feature of the *Thompson Chain-Reference Bible* is its unique chain-reference system. Rather than sprinkling the margins of the Bible with disjointed cross-references, Thompson developed a well-defined system of thousands of biblical references organized under more than four thousand biblical subjects. These topics and the chain references appear in a topical index in all editions of the *Thompson Chain-Reference Bible.*

Editors Paul Hillman and John Jauchen have expertly drawn on the massive resources of Thompson's chain-reference system and formatted them according to the model suggested by Thompson's own topical Bible section to produce the *Thompson Exhaustive Topical Bible.* Herein the reader will find more than 9,200 biblical topics and subtopics containing tens of thousands of biblical references. The novice Bible student will easily find definitions of biblical words, character studies of biblical personalities, and the most significant references to the most important biblical subjects. Pastors and teachers will discover a wealth of materials for expository preaching, devotionals, thematic studies, character sketches, and doctrinal teaching.

Nave's Topical Bible was edited into a Study Bible format shortly after the appearance of the original *Thompson Chain-Reference Bible*. It is fitting for Thompson's Study Bible to be reformatted into a reference book. And where there is room in the marketplace and on every serious student's bookshelf for more than one Bible translation, so there is room for more than one Topical Bible—and great value in the use of both Nave's and Thompson's works. As the editor of the Zondervan *NIV Nave's Topical Bible*, I strongly recommend the *Thompson Exhaustive Topical Bible* to all students of God's Word.

—John R. Kohlenberger III

INTRODUCTION

All Bible topics, great and small, wise and wonderful, are part of the *Thompson Exhaustive Topical Bible*. A topical Bible is an idea book about people, places, events, objects, and doctrines. It illustrates and associates. For example, the *Thompson* gives over 100 illustrations of miraculous events under Miracles with citations about death-defying bones, floating axheads, and tax-paying fish. The topic Sin has over 90 subtopics, or associations, explaining every facet of the subject from its birth in Eden to its defeat at Calvary. The *Thompson* is a massive storehouse of ideas, words, phrases, and much more. Those who draw from that treasury will think about God and his Word in new ways.

FEATURES *(see the chart on next page)*

Main Entries

The *Thompson Exhaustive Topical Bible* contains more than 9200 biblical topics and subtopics. Find in alphabetical order almost any Bible subject, including many contemporary topics.

Definition Entries

Topics difficult to understand are defined and explained. There are more than 2000 definitions and explanations of topics.

Verse Entries

Verses are either cited by reference or by full text, with almost 31,000 verses printed in full.

Outline Entries

In addition to three levels of subheads, there are over 4000 special outline entries in SMALL CAPITALS. These special outlines are a unique feature. They are valuable resources for teaching, preaching, and devotional studies..

Cross-reference Entries

Cross-references point to parallel, associative, or contrasting topics. For instance, after the entry Poverty there are the following nine cross-references: avarice, covetousness, greed, justice, kindness, oppression, partiality, poor, and riches. The cross-reference *poor* is parallel and the cross-reference *riches* is contrasting; the rest are associative. Dr. Thompson often studied a topic by analyzing its opposite, or contrasting viewpoint (see the list on pages 13–14). In his original work he compiled verses on such opposites as Abundance and Want, Blessings and Afflictions, Cheerfulness and Despondency, Comfort and Misery, and many others. Cross-references are idea amplifiers. Use them to expand any concept.

Bible Book Entries

There is information on all sixty-six books of the Bible. Most entries give the author, date written, purpose, to whom written, main theme, key words, and key verses.

Main Topic Heading Definition of Heading	**FRIENDSHIP**, *a relationship marked by knowledge, trust, and appreciation*
Subtopic Heading	***1. Characteristics***
Outline Heading Verse Reference Verse Text	PROFITABLE **Ec 4:9–10** Two *are* better than one; because they have a good reward for their labour. For if they fall, the one will lift up his fellow: but woe to him *that* is alone when he falleth; for *he hath* not another to help him up.
	2. Examples of True
Verse List	1 S 18:1; 20:4, 41; 23:16; 2 S 1:26; 9:7; 15:21, 37; 19:31, 38; 1 K 4:5; 5:1; Jb 2:11; Lu 11:5; 2 Co 2:13; Ph 2:25, 27; 2 Ti 1:4, 16; 3 Jn 13–14
Cross-Reference	*See* **FRIENDLESSNESS**

Contemporary Issues Entries

The genius of the Bible is that it speaks across time. See what the Bible has to say about Abortion by reading the cross-referenced topic Babies. Look up the verses under the topic Homosexuality. Get the Bible's view of capital punishment by scanning the topic Death Penalty. Check out the topic Business for a biblical philosophy of work life.

Biographical Entries

Bible characters are often given special treatment with extended outlines and helpful facts about their lives. See the entry on Elijah as an example. There are also helpful general biographical categories such as the entry Women.

Geographical Entries

Most of the entries for major places in the Bible have information about their history and importance.

Theological Entries

This is one of the strong features of this unique volume. There are major entries on Angels, God, Christ, Future Life, Holy Spirit, Judgments, Salvation, Satan, and Sin.

SPECIAL USES

For Devotions

Pick a topic and study it. Select the key texts and read the context where needed. Observe each text, especially its relationship to the topic and its distinctive teaching. Make a personal application. What does it mean to me?

Your topical devotional studies can be a week or a year. Everyday for a week study one of the seven responsibilities of Christians in section 5 of the topic Seven. Each Sunday meditate on two names of Christ from the list of 104 names under Titles and Names and spend a year thinking about Jesus.

For Teaching and Preaching Topically

Do a Sunday school lesson on faith and choose from one of the 13 subtopics in the *Thompson* under Faith, such as subtopic 10 on how faith is tested. Study the examples under this subtopic in context and get the class to share examples of how their own faith has been tested.

Preach for several months on faith by using material from the 13 subtopics. The first sermon might be from subtopic 5 on faith in Christ; another might use subtopic 4 on victorious faith. Other subjects in the series might be obstacles to faith from subtopic 10 or instances of little faith from subtopic 9.

For Teaching and Preaching Biographically

Use the outline under the topic John the Baptist for a lesson. Talk about the characteristics of his life, such as self-denial, courage, obedience, humility, holiness, and zeal.

Preach a whole series on women of the Bible. Note the seventeen women mentioned as notable in subtopic 10 under Women. Start with Eve and her sin and finish with Lydia and her salvation.

HISTORY

The desire to see the Bible in fresh ways was the starting point for the topical works of Orville James Nave and Frank Charles Thompson. Both began their studies of Bible topics in the late 1800s. Nave's work, developed over fourteen years, was eventually published as *Nave's Topical Bible* in 1896. Although the word *Bible* was in the title, it was not a Bible. The word emphasized the completeness of the work and the many Bible verses quoted.

Frank Charles Thompson began his original research in 1890 and his *Thompson Chain-Reference Bible* was published in 1908. It differed from Nave's volume in that it was actually a Bible and not a reference book. Thompson linked his topics to the Bible text with his chain-reference numbers. Although the topical studies done by Nave and Thompson have been the standards in the twentieth century, Thompson's

work has only been accessible to those who use his study Bible. Now his monumental work is available to all Bible students in this easy-to-use reference book.

OTHER RESOURCES

Thompson Chain-Reference Bible

This is the sum of Dr. Thompson's study of Bible topics and is available in four Bible versions: King James, New American Standard, New King James, and the New International. The *Thompson Exhaustive Topical Bible* in the King James Version can profitably be used with the *KJV Thompson Chain-Reference Bible*. The topics from the *Topical Bible* can easily be found in the General Index of the *Thompson Chain-Reference Bible*. In the General Index are found the chain-reference numbers that will guide the user into the biblical context for many of the topics. The many additional resources in the *Thompson Chain-Reference Bible,* such as character studies, Bible harmonies, maps, charts, and archaeological studies, will greatly supplement any topical study.

Thompson Multi-Media on CD-Rom

This has all the resources of the *Thompson Chain-Reference Bible* and many more features. Search on any word, topic, or phrase, and you can retrieve Strong's Hebrew or Greek root words, and then actually hear them and other words pronounced. Many topics can be further studied in *Matthew Henry's Concise Commentary* or *Easton's Bible Dictionary*. Parallel analysis of topics is available through six translations of the Bible. Colorful maps and hundreds of photographs from the Middle East inform and delight the user.

ABBREVIATIONS

OLD TESTAMENT

Genesis	Ge	2 Chronicles	2 Chr	Daniel	Da
Exodus	Ex	Ezra	Ezr	Hosea	Ho
Leviticus	Le	Nehemiah	Ne	Joel	Jl
Numbers	Nu	Esther	Est	Amos	Am
Deuteronomy	De	Job	Jb	Obadiah	Obad
Joshua	Jos	Psalms	Ps	Jonah	Jona
Judges	Jud	Proverbs	Pr	Micah	Mi
Ruth	Ru	Ecclesiastes	Ec	Nahum	Na
1 Samuel	1 S	Song of Solomon	Song	Habakkuk	Hab
2 Samuel	2 S	Isaiah	Is	Zephaniah	Zep
1 Kings	1 K	Jeremiah	Je	Haggai	Hag
2 Kings	2 K	Lamentations	Lam	Zechariah	Zec
1 Chronicles	1 Chr	Ezekiel	Eze	Malachi	Mal

NEW TESTAMENT

Matthew	Mt	Ephesians	Ep	Hebrews	He
Mark	Mk	Philippians	Ph	James	Ja
Luke	Lu	Colossians	Col	1 Peter	1 Pe
John	Jn	1 Thessalonians	1 Th	2 Peter	2 Pe
Acts	Ac	2 Thessalonians	2 Th	1 John	1 Jn
Romans	Ro	1 Timothy	1 Ti	2 John	2 Jn
1 Corinthians	1 Co	2 Timothy	2 Ti	3 John	3 Jn
2 Corinthians	2 Co	Titus	Tit	Jude	Jude
Galatians	Ga	Philemon	Phm	Revelation	Re

CONTRASTING TOPICS

One of the strengths of Thompson's topical study was his analysis of opposite concepts. In the *Thompson Chain-Reference Bible* each topic and its opposite are treated under one heading. In the *Thompson Exhaustive Topical Bible* all topics are listed alphabetically, so the user should look up in alphabetical order all topics given below. A thorough study of the following pairs will greatly enhance a Bible student's understanding of God's Word.

Abundance—Want	Goodness—Evil
Associations—Separation	Gratitude—Ingratitude
Blessings—Afflictions	Haste—Delay
Catholicity—Bigotry	Health—Disease
Certainties—Uncertainties	Hearing—Deafness
Cheerfulness—Despondency	Honor—Dishonor
Cleansing—Defilement	Hope—Despair
Comfort—Misery	Humility—Pride
Commendation—Reproof	Immaturity—Maturity
Consecration—Backsliding	Immortality—Mortality
Contentment—Discontentment	Immutability—Mutability
Courage—Fear	Innocence—Guilt
Courtesy—Discourtesy	Invitations—Warnings
Discernment—Dullness	Joy—Sorrow
Earnestness—Indifference	Justice—Injustice
Encouragement—Discouragement	Kindness—Cruelty
Enduring—Transient	Knowledge—Ignorance
Exaltation—Abasement	Liberty—Bondage
Expectation—Disappointment	Life—Death
Faith—Unbelief	Light—Darkness
Faithfulness—Unfaithfulness	Love—Hatred
Fellowship—Estrangement	Meekness—Retaliation
Friendship—Friendlessness	Memories—Oblivion
Fruitfulness—Unfruitfulness	Mercy—Unmercifulness
Fullness—Emptiness	Obedience—Disobedience
Gain—Loss	Patience—Impatience
Giving—Greed	Peace—War
God—Satan	Perfection—Imperfection

Poverty—Riches
Power—Weakness
Purity—Impurity
Prosperity—Adversity
Prudence—Rashness
Quietness—Tumults
Readiness—Unreadiness
Reception—Rejection
Remembrance—Forgetfulness
Repentance—Impenitence
Resurrection—Death
Rest—Unrest
Revelations—Mysteries
Reward—Punishment
Righteous—Wicked
Righteousness—Unrighteousness
Salvation—Condemnation
Satisfaction—Dissatisfaction

Saviour—Sin
Security—Insecurity
Self-Abasement—Self-Exaltation
Self-Denial—Self-Indulgence
Showers—Drought
Silence—Speech
Simplicity—Duplicity
Steadfastness—Instability
Stewardship—Ownership
Submission—Self-Will
Sympathy—Pitilessness
Thankfulness—Thanklessness
Truth—Deception
Unity—Strife
Unselfishness—Selfishness
Unworldliness—Worldliness
Vision—Blindness
Wisdom—Folly

A

AARON, *son of Amram, the first high priest*

Ex 4:14; 5:20; 6:20; 7:1, 7, 12; 12:1; 16:34; 17:12; 19:24; 24:14; 28:1, 12; 30:10; 32:2–4; Le 10:6; Nu 12:1; 16:11; 17:3; 20:12, 25, 28; 26:59; 27:13; 33:38; De 10:6; 32:50; 1 Chr 6:3, 49; 23:13; 2 Chr 13:10; Ezr 7:5; Ps 77:20; 99:6; 105:26; 106:16; 133:2; Mi 6:4; Lu 1:5; Ac 7:40; He 5:4

MADE SPOKESMAN FOR MOSES

Ex 7:1 And the LORD said unto Moses, See, I have made thee a god to Pharaoh: and Aaron thy brother shall be thy prophet.

WITH HUR, SUPPORTS MOSES' HANDS DURING A BATTLE

Ex 17:12 But Moses' hands *were* heavy; and they took a stone, and put *it* under him, and he sat thereon; and Aaron and Hur stayed up his hands, the one on the one side, and the other on the other side; and his hands were steady until the going down of the sun.

MADE HIGH PRIEST

Ex 28:1 And take thou unto thee Aaron thy brother, and his sons with him, from among the children of Israel, that he may minister unto me in the priest's office, *even* Aaron, Nadab and Abihu, Eleazar and Ithamar, Aaron's sons.

BROKE THE COVENANT AND MADE THE GOLDEN CALF

Ex 32:2–4 And Aaron said unto them, Break off the golden earrings, which *are* in the ears of your wives, of your sons, and of your daughters, and bring *them* unto me.

And all the people brake off the golden earrings which *were* in their ears, and brought *them* unto Aaron.

And he received *them* at their hand, and fashioned it with a graving tool, after he had made it a molten calf: and they said, These *be* thy gods, O Israel, which brought thee up out of the land of Egypt.

EXCLUDED FROM THE PROMISED LAND

Nu 20:12 And the LORD spake unto Moses and Aaron, Because ye believed me not, to sanctify me in the eyes of the children of Israel, therefore ye shall not bring this congregation into the land which I have given them.

DIED ON MT HOR

Nu 20:28 And Moses stripped Aaron of his garments, and put them upon Eleazar his sons; and Aaron died there in the top of the mount: and Moses and Eleazar came down from the mount.

AB *See* **MONTHS**

ABANA *See* **RIVERS**

ABARIM

De 32:49

See **MOUNTAINS AND HILLS**

ABASEMENT, *degradation, humiliation*

1. Of the Proud Foretold

Ge 3:14; 43:28; Le 26:19; Nu 12:11; 22:31; De 9:3; Jud 8:16; 1 S 2:7, 36; 28:20; 2 S 22:28, 39; 1 K 20:20, 32; 2 K 13:7; 19:28; 2 Chr 12:8; Ne 6:16; Jb 8:22; 20:7; 30:7; 40:12; Ps 7:5; 9:20; 55:23; 71:24; 72:9; 81:15; 83:10; 101:5; 107:11; 119:118; Pr 15:25; 16:18; 21:22; 25:7; 29:23; Is 2:12; 3:17; 10:6; 14:10; 22:18; 23:9; 25:5, 11; 29:3; 37:29; Je 48:25; 49:16; 50:32; Lam 1:9; 2:2; 5:16; Eze 21:26; 25:4; 26:16, 20; 28:9; 29:15; 30:6; 31:13, 18; 32:18, 25, 28; Da 4:23 Da 4:37; 7:12; 11:4; Ho 4:7;

7:12; Am 7:17; 9:2; Obad 4; Mi 7:17; Na 3:6, 18; Zec 9:6; 10:11; Mal 2:3, 9; 4:1; Mt 23:12; Lu 1:52; 10:15; 13:30; 14:9; 15:15; 18:14; Re 18:2

2. Examples

PHARAOH

Ex 15:4 Pharaoh's chariots and his host hath he cast into the sea: his chosen captains also are drowned in the Red sea.

SENNACHERIB

2 Chr 32:21 And the LORD sent an angel, which cut off all the mighty men of valour, and the leaders and captains in the camp of the king of Assyria. So he returned with shame of face to his own land. And when he was come into the house of his god, they that came forth of his own bowels slew him there with the sword.

HAMAN

Est 7:9 And Harbonah, one of the chamberlains, said before the king, Behold also, the gallows fifty cubits high, which Haman had made for Mordecai, who had spoken good for the king, standeth in the house of Haman. Then the king said, Hang him thereon.

NEBUCHADNEZZAR

Da 4:33 The same hour was the thing fulfilled upon Nebuchadnezzar: and he was driven from men, and did eat grass as oxen, and his body was wet with the dew of heaven, till his hairs were grown like eagles' *feathers,* and his nails like birds' *claws.*

BELSHAZZAR

Da 5:28 Peres; Thy kingdom is divided, and given to the Medes and Persians.

NINEVEH

Zep 2:15 This *is* the rejoicing city that dwelt carelessly, that said in her heart, I *am,* and *there is* none beside me: how is she become a desolation, a place for beasts to lie down in! every one that passeth by her shall hiss, *and* wag his hand.

3. Humbling of the Proud

Ge 50:17; Ex 8:8; 9:28; 10:16; 11:8; 12:32; 1 S 19:24; 2 S 19:18; 21:21; 22:48; 1 K 1:53; 13:6; Est 6:12; 7:7; Jb 9:13; 12:21, 24; 24:24; 26:12; 34:24; Ps 2:9; 18:27; 20:8; 59:11; 75:7; 76:12; 106:43; 107:40; Pr 14:18; 15:25; 16:18; Is 2:11; 5:15; 10:4, 12, 33; 14:5, 11, 25; 19:4; 22:18; 23:9; 24:4, 21; 25:10; 26:5; 28:3; 29:20; 40:23; 41:25; 43:14; 47:1; 49:23; 60:14; 63:6; Je 13:18; 22:23; 36:30; 46:12; 48:18; 49:15; 50:36; 51:25; Lam 1:1; Eze 7:24; 17:24; 28:17; 29:5; 30:18; 31:11; 32:12; Da 4:31; 5:21; 11:14; Jl 3:11; Obad 8; Na 3:10; Hab 2:16; Zep 2:10; Zec 9:5; Mt 11:23; Lu 1:51; 14:9, 11; Ac 9:8; 16:39; Ja 4:6; Re 3:9

See **EXALTATION**

ABBA *See* **GOD, HOLY SPIRIT**

ABDON *See* **ISRAEL**

ABED-NEGO, *one of the Hebrew children delivered from the fiery furnace*

Da 1:7; 2:17, 49; 3:12, 23, 30

ABEL, *son of Adam, slain by Cain*

Ge 4:2, 8; Mt 23:35; Lu 11:51; He 11:4; 12:24

ABEL-BETH-MAACHAH, *meadow of the house of oppression*

This was an ancient fortified city in the extreme north of Palestine that played an important, although tragic, role in ancient Bible times. It was to this city that Joab pursued Sheba, the rebel leader, as he fled there for refuge. A "wise woman" of the city tossed the rebel's head over the wall and thereby saved the city (2 S 20:14–22). It was taken by the Syrians under Ben-hadad in the ninth century B.C. (1 K 15:20) and later by the Assyrians under Tiglath-pileser III in 734 B.C. (2 K 15:29).

ABIATHAR, *high priest, son of Ahimelech*

1 S 22:20; 23:6; 2 S 8:17; 15:29; 1 K 1:7; 2:22, 26, 27; 4:4; 1 Chr 15:11; 18:16; 24:6; 27:34; Mk 2:26

ABIB   *See* MONTHS

ABIDING IN CHRIST

SPIRITUAL FRUITFULNESS

Jn 15:5 I am the vine, ye *are* the branches: He that abideth in me, and I in him, the same bringeth forth much fruit: for without me ye can do nothing.

ANSWERED PRAYER

Jn 15:7 If ye abide in me, and my words abide in you, ye shall ask what ye will, and it shall be done unto you.

PEACE IN THE STORM

Jn 16:33 These things I have spoken unto you, that in me ye might have peace. In the world ye shall have tribulation: but be of good cheer; I have overcome the world.

NEW LIFE

2 Co 5:17 Therefore if any man *be* in Christ, *he is* a new creature: old things are passed away; behold, all things are become new.

ROBE OF RIGHTEOUSNESS

Ph 3:9 And be found in him, not having mine own righteousness, which is of the law, but that which is through the faith of Christ, the righteousness which is of God by faith:

See CHRIST

ABIGAIL, *wife of Nabal, becomes David's wife*

1 S 25:3; 27:3; 30:5; 2 S 2:2; 3:3; 1 Chr 3:1

ABIHU, *son of Aaron, offers strange fire and is smitten of God*

Ex 6:23; 24:9; 28:1; Le 10:1; Nu 3:4; 26:61; 1 Chr 24:1

ABIGAIL   *See* WOMEN

ABIJAM, *or Abijah, king of Judah*

1 K 14:31; 15:1; 2 Chr 11:20, 22; 12:16; 13:4; 14:1; Mt 1:7

See ISRAEL

ABIMELECH, *king of Gerar, reproves Abraham*

Ge 20:2; 21:22, 32; 26:1, 26

See ISRAEL

ABINADAB, *receives the ark from the Philistines*

1 S 7:1; 2 S 6:3; 1 Chr 13:7

ABISHAI, *son of David's sister, Zeruiah*

1 S 26:6; 2 S 2:18; 3:30; 10:10; 16:9; 18:2; 19:21; 20:6; 21:17; 23:18; 1 Chr 11:20; 18:12; 19:11

ABNER, *son of Ner, cousin of Saul and captain of his host*

1 S 14:51; 17:55; 20:25; 26:5, 7, 14; 2 S 2:8, 14, 31; 3:6, 27; 1 K 2:32

ABOMINATIONS, *things hateful to God*

De 7:25 The graven images of their gods shall ye burn with fire: thou shalt not desire the silver or gold *that is* on them, nor take *it* unto thee, lest thou be snared therein: for it *is* an abomination to the LORD thy God.

De 18:12 For all that do these things *are* an abomination unto the LORD: and because of these abominations the LORD thy God doth drive them out from before thee.

De 25:16 For all that do such things, *and* all that do unrighteously, *are* an abomination unto the LORD thy God.

Pr 6:16 These six *things* doth the LORD hate: yea, seven *are* an abomination unto him:

Pr 11:20 They that are of a froward heart *are* abomination to the LORD: but *such as are* upright in *their* way *are* his delight.

Pr 12:22 Lying lips *are* abomination to the LORD: but they that deal truly *are* his delight.

Pr 21:27 The sacrifice of the wicked *is* abomination: how much more, *when* he bringeth it with a wicked mind?

Pr 28:9 He that turneth away his ear from hearing the law, even his prayer *shall be* abomination.

Je 16:18 And first I will recompense their iniquity and their sin double;

because they have defiled my land, they have filled mine inheritance with the carcases of their detestable and abominable things.

Je 44:4 Howbeit I sent unto you all my servants the prophets, rising early and sending *them,* saying, Oh, do not this abominable thing that I hate.

Eze 7:9 And mine eye shall not spare, neither will I have pity: I will recompense thee according to thy ways and thine abominations *that* are in the midst of thee; and ye shall know that I *am* the LORD that smiteth.

Lu 16:15 And he said unto them, Ye are they which justify yourselves before men; but God knoweth your hearts: for that which is highly esteemed among men is abomination in the sight of God.

Re 17:5 And upon her forehead *was* a name written, MYSTERY, BABYLON THE GREAT, THE MOTHER OF HARLOTS AND ABOMINATIONS OF THE EARTH.

Re 21:27 And there shall in no wise enter into it any thing that defileth, neither *whatsoever* worketh abomination, or *maketh* a lie: but they which are written in the Lamb's book of life.

See **SIN**

ABOMINATION OF DESOLATION, *an act of profanity predicted by Jesus to introduce the Antichrist*

Da 9:27 And he shall confirm the covenant with many for one week: and in the midst of the week he shall cause the sacrifice and the oblation to cease, and for the overspreading of abominations he shall make *it* desolate, even until the consummation, and that determined shall be poured upon the desolate.

Da 11:31 And arms shall stand on his part, and they shall pollute the sanctuary of strength, and shall take away the daily *sacrifice,* and they shall place the abomination that maketh desolate.

Da 12:11 And from the time *that* the daily *sacrifice* shall be taken away, and the abomination that maketh deso-

late set up, *there shall be* a thousand two hundred and ninety days.

Mt 24:15 When ye therefore shall see the abomination of desolation, spoken of by Daniel the prophet, stand in the holy place, (whoso readeth, let him understand:)

Mk 13:14 But when ye shall see the abomination of desolation, spoken of by Daniel the prophet, standing where it ought not, (let him that readeth understand,) then let them that be in Judaea flee to the mountains:

See **SECOND COMING**

ABORTION   *See* **BABIES**

ABRAHAM, *or Abram, son of Terah, father of the chosen family*

While living with his father in Haran, he received a message from the Lord calling him to separate himself from his old associations and go to a new country. He was promised divine favor, a great posterity, and the blessing of his obedience on all families of the earth. He obeyed the call and became the leader of all pilgrims who seek a city whose builder and maker is God (He 11:8–10).

Ge 11:27, 31; 12:1, 4; 13:1, 8, 9, 12; 14:14, 19, 20, 23; 15:1; 16:3; 17:1, 18:10, 23–33; 20:1; 21:2; 22:1; 23:2; 24:1, 25:1, 8; 49:31; 1 Chr 1:27; 2 Chr 20:7; Ne 9:7; Ps 105:6; Is 51:2; Mt 1:2; 3:9; 8:11; 22:32; Mk 12:26; Lu 1:73; 3:34, 13:16, 28; 20:37, Jn 8:39, 56; Ac 3:13, 7:2, 32; 13:26; Ro 4:3; 9:7; 11:1; Ga 3:6, 7, 16; 4:22, He 6:13, 11:8, 17, Ja 2:21, 23, 1 Pe 3:6

1. Main Events and Experiences

a. The divine call (Ge 12:1)

b. The covenant (Ge 12:2–3; 17:1–6)

c.. The delay in the fulfillment of the promise of a son (Ge 12:4; 21:5)

d. His great mistake (Ge 16:3)

e. His great intercession (Ge 18:23–32)

f. The fulfillment of his hopes in the birth of Isaac (Ge 21:5)

g. His severe test (Ge 22:1–2)

h. His remarkable faith and obedience (Ge 22:3–10)

i. His greatest need supplied (Ge 22:11–13)

2. Characteristics of Life

OBEDIENCE—LEFT HOME AND FRIENDS AT THE CALL OF GOD

Ge 12:4 So Abram departed, as the LORD had spoken unto him; and Lot went with him: and Abram *was* seventy and five years old when he departed out of Haran.

UNSELFISHNESS—GAVE LOT THE FIRST CHOICE OF THE LAND

Ge 13:9 *Is* not the whole land before thee? separate thyself, I pray thee, from me: if *thou wilt take* the left hand, then I will go to the right; or if *thou depart* to the right hand, then I will go to the left.

COURAGE—DEFEATED THE ROBBER KINGS

Ge 14:14 And when Abram heard that his brother was taken captive, he armed his trained *servants,* born in his own house, three hundred and eighteen, and pursued *them* unto Dan.

BENEVOLENCE—GAVE TITHES TO MELCHIZEDEK, THE PRIEST

Ge 14:20 And blessed be the most high God, which hath delivered thine enemies into thy hand. And he gave him tithes of all.

INCORRUPTIBILITY—REFUSED TO RECEIVE GIFTS FOR SERVICE RENDERED

Ge 14:23 That I will not *take* from a thread even to a shoelatchet, and that I will not take any thing that *is* thine, lest thou shouldest say, I have made Abram rich:

MIGHTY IN PRAYER

Ge 18:23–33 And Abraham drew near, and said, Wilt thou also destroy the righteous with the wicked?

Peradventure there be fifty righteous within the city: wilt thou also destroy and not spare the place for the fifty righteous that *are* therein?

That be far from thee to do after this manner, to slay the righteous with the wicked: and that the righteous should be as the wicked, that be far from thee: Shall not the Judge of all the earth do right?

And the LORD said, If I find in Sodom fifty righteous within the city, then I will spare all the place for their sakes.

And Abraham answered and said, Behold now, I have taken upon me to speak unto the LORD, which *am but* dust and ashes:

Peradventure there shall lack five of the fifty righteous: wilt thou destroy all the city for *lack of* five? And he said, If I find there forty and five, I will not destroy *it.*

And he spake unto him yet again, and said, Peradventure there shall be forty found there. And he said, I will not do it for forty's sake.

And he said *unto him,* Oh let not the LORD be angry, and I will speak: Peradventure there shall thirty be found there. And he said, I will not do *it,* if I find thirty there.

And he said, Behold now, I have taken upon me to speak unto the LORD: Peradventure there shall be twenty found there. And he said, I will not destroy *it* for twenty's sake.

And he said, Oh let not the LORD be angry, and I will speak yet but this once: Peradventure ten shall be found there. And he said, I will not destroy *it* for ten's sake.

And the LORD went his way, as soon as he had left communing with Abraham: and Abraham returned unto his place.

WONDERFUL IN FAITH—WAS WILLING TO OFFER UP HIS ONLY SON, ISAAC

He 11:17 By faith Abraham, when he was tried, offered up Isaac: and he that had received the promises offered up his only begotten *son,*

ABRAHAM'S BOSOM

See **PARADISE**

ABSALOM, *the son of David*

2 S 3:3, 13:1, 23, 29, 37, 14:25, 15:2–3, 13, 14; 16:15; 17:1; 18:9, 14, 33; 1 K 1:6; 1 Chr 3:2; 2 Chr 11:20

BORN OF A POLYGAMOUS MARRIAGE

2 S 3:3 And his second, Chileab, of Abigail the wife of Nabal the Carmelite; and the third, Absalom the son of Maacah the daughter of Talmai king of Geshur;

MURDERS HIS BROTHER

2 S 13:29 And the servants of Absalom did unto Amnon as Absalom had commanded. Then all the king's sons arose, and every man gat him up upon his mule, and fled.

AN EXILE FROM HOME

2 S 13:37 But Absalom fled, and went to Talmai, the son of Ammihud, king of Geshur. And *David* mourned for his son every day.

RENOWNED FOR HIS BEAUTY

2 S 14:25 But in all Israel there was none to be so much praised as Absalom for his beauty: from the sole of his foot even to the crown of his head there was no blemish in him.

THE DESIGNING POLITICIAN

2 S 15:2 And Absalom rose up early, and stood beside the way of the gate: and it was so, that when any man that had a controversy came to the king for judgment, then Absalom called unto him, and said, Of what city *art* thou? And he said, Thy servant is of one of the tribes of Israel.

CONSPIRES AGAINST HIS FATHER, DAVID

2 S 15:13 And there came a messenger to David, saying, The hearts of the men of Israel are after Absalom.

COMES TO AN UNTIMELY END

2 S 18:9 And Absalom met the servants of David. And Absalom rode upon a mule, and the mule went under the thick boughs of a great oak, and his head caught hold of the oak, and he was taken up between the heaven and the earth; and the mule that *was* under him went away.

See **YOUNG PEOPLE**

ABSTAIN, *commands to avoid certain evils*

Ac 15:20; 1 Th 4:3; 5:22; 1 Pe 2:11

See **EVIL**

ABSTINENCE *See* **DRUNKENNESS, WINE**

ABUNDANCE, *SPIRITUAL*

Ps 34:10; 36:8; 37:11; 85:12; 116:7; 119:17; 142:7; Song 5:1; Mt 13:12; 25:29; Mk 4:24; Lu 6:38; 8:18; 14:22; 18:30; 19:26; Jn 10:10; Ro 5:17; 2 Co 4:15; 9:8; Ep 1:8; 3:20

ABUNDANT JOYS

Ps 36:8 They shall be abundantly satisfied with the fatness of thy house; and thou shalt make them drink of the river of thy pleasures.

ABUNDANT LIFE

Jn 10:10 The thief cometh not, but for to steal, and to kill, and to destroy: I am come that they might have life, and that they might have *it* more abundantly.

ABUNDANT GRACE

2 Co 9:8 And God *is* able to make all grace abound toward you; that ye, always having all sufficiency in all *things,* may abound to every good work:

ABUNDANT POWER

Ep 3:20 Now unto him that is able to do exceeding abundantly above all that we ask or think, according to the power that worketh in us,

ABUNDANT SUPPLIES

Ph 4:19 But my God shall supply all your need according to his riches in glory by Christ Jesus.

ABUNDANT ENTRANCE

2 Pe 1:11 For so an entrance shall be ministered unto you abundantly into the everlasting kingdom of our Lord and Saviour Jesus Christ.

See **WANT**

ABUSE *See* **DRUNKENNESS, FAMILY, EMPLOYERS, FOOD, WINE**

ACACIA WOOD, *used in the construction of the tabernacle*

Le 26:20, 26; De 28:53; 32:24; 2 S 24:13; Ps 107:34; Is 3:1; 51:19; Je 14:12, 16; 15:2; 16:4; 19:9; 21:7; 24:10; 27:8; 32:24, 36; 34:17; 38:2; 42:16; 44:12; 52:6; Lam 5:10; Eze 4:16; 5:12, 16; 6:12; 14:21; Re 18:8

ACCEPTANCE, *benefactors of God's grace and mercy*

Ac 18:27; 19:21; Ro 15:26; 16:5; 1 Co 16:15; 2 Co 1:1; 9:2; 11:10; 1 Th 1:8

See **REJECTION**

ACCESS, *into God's presence*

Ex 19:24 And the LORD said unto him, Away, get thee down, and thou shalt come up, thou, and Aaron with thee: but let not the priests and the people break through to come up unto the LORD, lest he break forth upon them.

Ex 20:21 And the people stood afar off, and Moses drew near unto the thick darkness where God *was.*

Ps 15:1 LORD, who shall abide in thy tabernacle? who shall dwell in thy holy hill?

Ps 24:3–4 Who shall ascend into the hill of the LORD? or who shall stand in his holy place?

He that hath clean hands, and a pure heart; who hath not lifted up his soul unto vanity, nor sworn deceitfully.

Ps 118:19 Open to me the gates of righteousness: I will go into them, *and* I will praise the LORD:

Ps 140:13 Surely the righteous shall give thanks unto thy name: the upright shall dwell in thy presence.

Is 26:2 Open ye the gates, that the righteous nation which keepeth the truth may enter in.

Is 60:11 Therefore thy gates shall be open continually; they shall not be shut day nor night; that *men* may bring unto thee the forces of the Gentiles, and *that* their kings *may be* brought.

Jn 10:9 I am the door: by me if any man enter in, he shall be saved, and shall go in and out, and find pasture.

Jn 14:6 Jesus saith unto him, I am the way, the truth, and the life: no man cometh unto the Father, but by me.

Ro 5:2 By whom also we have access by faith into this grace wherein we stand, and rejoice in hope of the glory of God.

Ep 2:18 For through him we both have access by one Spirit unto the Father.

Ep 3:12 In whom we have boldness and access with confidence by the faith of him.

He 10:19 Having therefore, brethren, boldness to enter into the holiest by the blood of Jesus,

1 Pe 3:12 For the eyes of the Lord *are* over the righteous, and his ears *are open* unto their prayers: but the face of the Lord *is* against them that do evil.

Re 3:8 I know thy works: behold, I have set before thee an open door, and no man can shut it: for thou hast a little strength, and hast kept my word, and hast not denied my name.

See **EXCLUSION**

ACCUMULATION *See* **RICHES**

ACELDAMA, *or the Potter's Field*

This place reminds us of the tragic occasion when Judas sold the Lord for thirty pieces of silver, then in the agony of his soul returned the money and went and hanged himself Mt 27:6-8. On the east end of the southern slope of the Valley of Hinnom is a rugged, rocky area of about two acres, which since Jerome's time (A.D. 400) has been known as the Potter's Field.

ACHAIA, *a region of Greece*

Ac 18:27; 19:21; Ro 15:26; 16:5; 1 Co 16:15; 2 Co 1:1; 9:2; 11:10; 1 Th 1:8

ACHAN, *hid a wedge of gold*

Jos 7:1, 20, 25; 22:20; 1 Chr 2:7

ACHISH, *king of Gath*

1 S 21:10; 27:2; 28:1; 29:6; 1 K 2:39

ACHOR, *valley of, Achan slain there*

Jos 7:26; 15:7; Is 65:10; Ho 2:15

ACRE, *or Acco*

It was known as Acco in Old Testament times (Jud 1:31) and was called Ptolemais in the New Testament. It lies at the north end of the curving beach of the Bay of Acre and is now called Acre. The place is filled with historic associations reaching back to the days before the children of Israel were in Palestine. It is mentioned as a place of importance in the writings of the Assyrians, Egyptians, Maccabeans, Greeks, Romans, Crusaders, and in the time of Napoleon and later. The Christian world remembers it as the place where Paul, on his final journey to Jerusalem, stayed with the brethren (Ac 21:7).

ACTIVITY, *EVIL, contrary to the holiness of a righteous God*

Ps 12:8 The wicked walk on every side, when the vilest men are exalted.

Ps 55:10 Day and night they go about it upon the walls thereof: mischief also and sorrow *are* in the midst of it.

Pr 1:16 For their feet run to evil, and make haste to shed blood.

Pr 4:16 For they sleep not, except they have done mischief; and their sleep is taken away, unless they cause *some* to fall.

Pr 6:18 An heart that deviseth wicked imaginations, feet that be swift in running to mischief,

Is 59:7 Their feet run to evil, and they make haste to shed innocent blood: their thoughts *are* thoughts of iniquity; wasting and destruction *are* in their paths.

Je 2:23 How canst thou say, I am not polluted, I have not gone after Baalim? see thy way in the valley, know what thou hast done: *thou art* a swift dromedary traversing her ways;

Mi 2:1 Woe to them that devise iniquity, and work evil upon their beds! when the morning is light, they practise it, because it is in the power of their hand.

Ro 3:15 Their feet *are* swift to shed blood:

1 Pe 5:8 Be sober, be vigilant; because your adversary the devil, as a roaring lion, walketh about, seeking whom he may devour:

1. By Evil People

Mi 7:3 That they may do evil with both hands earnestly, the prince asketh, and the judge *asketh* for a reward; and the great *man,* he uttereth his mischievous desire: so they wrap it up.

Mt 23:15 Woe unto you, scribes and Pharisees, hypocrites! for ye compass sea and land to make one proselyte, and when he is made, ye make him twofold more the child of hell than yourselves.

Ac 9:2 And desired of him letters to Damascus to the synagogues, that if he found any of this way, whether they were men or women, he might bring them bound unto Jerusalem.

Ac 22:4 And I persecuted this way unto the death, binding and delivering into prisons both men and women.

Ac 26:11 And I punished them oft in every synagogue, and compelled *them* to blaspheme; and being exceedingly mad against them, I persecuted *them* even unto strange cities.

Ga 1:13 For ye have heard of my conversation in time past in the Jews' religion, how that beyond measure I persecuted the church of God, and wasted it:

Ph 3:6 Concerning zeal, persecuting the church; touching the righteousness which is in the law, blameless.

2. By Busybodies

Ne 6:19 Also they reported his good deeds before me, and uttered my words to him. *And* Tobiah sent letters to put me in fear.

Est 3:4 Now it came to pass, when they spake daily unto him, and he hearkened not unto them, that they told Haman, to see whether Mordecai's matters would stand: for he had told them that he *was* a Jew.

Pr 17:9 He that covereth a transgression seeketh love; but he that repeateth a matter separateth *very* friends.

2 Th 3:11 For we hear that there are some which walk among you disorderly, working not at all, but are busybodies.

1 Ti 5:13 And withal they learn *to be* idle, wandering about from house to house; and not only idle, but tattlers also and busybodies, speaking things which they ought not.

1 Pe 4:15 But let none of you suffer as a murderer, or *as* a thief, or *as* an evildoer, or as a busybody in other men's matters.

ACTS

Author: Luke, the beloved physician. The book is in some sense a sequel to the Gospel of Luke and is addressed to the same unknown person, Theophilus (1:1).

Date Written: Probably prior to Paul's trial (A.D. 62).

Purpose: To document the growth of the early church.

To Whom Written: Specifically, Theophilus (1:1). Also to believers throughout history who would know their "roots" and to unbelievers who sincerely seek to know the historical basis behind Christianity's early rapid expansion.

Main Theme: The history of the development of the early church from the Ascension of Christ to Paul's imprisonment at Rome and the opening of his ministry there. Many Bible students see in the book the formal beginning of the dispensation of the Holy Spirit. The departing Christ makes the announcement of a great campaign of world-wide missions through human agency under the power of the Spirit (1:8).

Key Words: Holy Spirit and the Church.

Key Verses: 1:8; 2:42–47.

ADAM, *created in the image of God*

Ge 1:26 And God said, Let us make man in our image, after our likeness: and let them have dominion over the fish of the sea, and over the fowl of the air, and over the cattle, and over all the earth, and over every creeping thing that creepeth upon the earth.

Ge 2:19 And out of the ground the LORD God formed every beast of the field, and every fowl of the air; and brought *them* unto Adam to see what he would call them: and whatsoever Adam called every living creature, that *was* the name thereof.

Ge 2:23 And Adam said, This *is* now bone of my bones, and flesh of my flesh: she shall be called Woman, because she was taken out of Man.

Ge 3:8 And they heard the voice of the LORD God walking in the garden in the cool of the day: and Adam and his wife hid themselves from the presence of the LORD God amongst the trees of the garden.

Ge 3:17 And unto Adam he said, Because thou hast hearkened unto the voice of thy wife, and hast eaten of the tree, of which I commanded thee, saying, Thou shalt not eat of it: cursed *is* the ground for thy sake; in sorrow shalt thou eat *of* it all the days of thy life;

Ge 5:5 And all the days that Adam lived were nine hundred and thirty years: and he died.

1 Co 15:22 For as in Adam all die, even so in Christ shall all be made alive.

1 Ti 2:13 For Adam was first formed, then Eve.

ADAR *See* MONTHS

ADDERS *See* REPTILES

ADDICTION *See* HINDRANCE, LIBERTY, POWER

ADMONITION

Jos 22:5 But take diligent heed to do the commandment and the law, which Moses the servant of the LORD charged you, to love the LORD your God, and to walk in all his ways, and to keep his commandments, and to cleave unto him, and to serve him with all your heart and with all your soul.

Ro 15:14 And I myself also am persuaded of you, my brethren, that ye also are full of goodness, filled with all knowledge, able also to admonish one another.

1 Co 4:14 I write not these things to shame you, but as my beloved sons I warn *you*.

Ep 6:4 And, ye fathers, provoke not your children to wrath: but bring them up in the nurture and admonition of the Lord.

Col 3:16 Let the word of Christ dwell in you richly in all wisdom; teaching and admonishing one another in psalms and hymns and spiritual songs, singing with grace in your hearts to the Lord.

1 Th 5:14 Now we exhort you, brethren, warn them that are unruly, comfort the feebleminded, support the weak, be patient toward all *men*.

2 Th 3:15 Yet count *him* not as an enemy, but admonish *him* as a brother.

Tit 3:10 A man that is an heretick after the first and second admonition reject;

See WARNINGS

ADONIJAH, *son of David*

2 S 3:4; 1 K 1:5, 41; 2:13; 1 Chr 3:2

ADOPTION *See* FAMILY, GOD, HOLY SPIRIT

ADORNING *See* APPAREL

ADULLAM

This is a city about midway between Bethlehem and Gath, first mentioned in Genesis 38:1 as the home of Hirah the Adullamite. The king of Adullam fought unsuccessfully in the coalition against the invading Israelites (Jos 12:15), and Abullam was given to the tribe of Judah (Jos 15:35). David used a cave near Adullam as his secret headquarters when hiding from Saul (1 S 22:1). Rehoboam fortified the city in his attempts to halt the invasion of Pharoah Shishak in the early tenth century B.C. (2 Chr 11:7).

1 S 22:1; 2 S 23:13; 1 Chr 11:15; Mi 1:15

See CITIES

ADULTERY, *sexual infidelity by a married person*

Ex 20:14 Thou shalt not commit adultery.

Le 20:10 And the man that committeth adultery with *another* man's wife, *even he* that committeth adultery with his neighbour's wife, the adulterer and the adulteress shall surely be put to death.

Jb 24:15 The eye also of the adulterer waiteth for the twilight, saying, No eye shall see me: and disguiseth *his* face.

1 Co 6:9 Know ye not that the unrighteous shall not inherit the kingdom of God? Be not deceived: neither fornicators, nor idolaters, nor adulterers, nor effeminate, nor abusers of themselves with mankind,

2 Pe 2:14 Having eyes full of adultery, and that cannot cease from sin; beguiling unstable souls: an heart they have exercised with covetous practices; cursed children:

See SEX

ADVENT *See* FUTURE LIFE

ADVERSARY *See* ENEMIES, SATAN

ADVERSITY, *sometimes the result of sin and folly*

Le 26:16 I also will do this unto you; I will even appoint over you terror, consumption, and the burning ague, that shall consume the eyes, and cause sorrow of heart: and ye shall sow your seed in vain, for your enemies shall eat it.

Le 26:22 I will also send wild beasts among you, which shall rob you of your children, and destroy your cattle, and make you few in number; and your *high* ways shall be desolate.

De 28:31 Thine ox *shall be* slain before thine eyes, and thou shalt not eat thereof: thine ass *shall be* violently taken away from before thy face, and shall not be restored to thee: thy sheep *shall be* given unto thine enemies, and thou shalt have none to rescue *them*.

De 28:48 Therefore shalt thou serve thine enemies which the Lord shall send against thee, in hunger, and in thirst, and in nakedness, and in want of all *things:* and he shall put a yoke of iron upon thy neck, until he have destroyed thee.

De 28:65 And among these nations shalt thou find no ease, neither shall the sole of thy foot have rest: but the Lord shall give thee there a trembling heart, and failing of eyes, and sorrow of mind:

De 31:17 Then my anger shall be kindled against them in that day, and I will forsake them, and I will hide my face from them, and they shall be devoured, and many evils and troubles shall befall them; so that they will say in that day, Are not these evils come upon us, because our God *is* not among us?

De 32:24 *They shall be* burnt with hunger, and devoured with burning heat, and with bitter destruction: I will also send the teeth of beasts upon them, with the poison of serpents of the dust.

Jud 6:4 And they encamped against them, and destroyed the increase of the earth, till thou come unto Gaza, and left no sustenance for Israel, neither sheep, nor ox, nor ass.

1 S 4:21 And she named the child Ichabod, saying, The glory is departed from Israel: because the ark of God was taken, and because of her father in law and her husband.

2 K 6:25 And there was a great famine in Samaria: and, behold, they besieged it, until an ass's head was *sold* for fourscore *pieces* of silver, and the fourth part of a cab of dove's dung for five *pieces* of silver.

2 K 8:12 And Hazael said, Why weepeth my lord? And he answered, Because I know the evil that thou wilt do unto the children of Israel: their strong holds wilt thou set on fire, and their young men wilt thou slay with the sword, and wilt dash their children, and rip up their women with child.

2 Chr 15:6 And nation was destroyed of nation, and city of city: for God did vex them with all adversity.

2 Chr 24:20 And the Spirit of God came upon Zechariah the son of Jehoiada the priest, which stood above the people, and said unto them, Thus saith God, Why transgress ye the commandments of the Lord, that ye cannot prosper? because ye have forsaken the Lord, he hath also forsaken you.

2 Chr 29:8 Wherefore the wrath of the Lord was upon Judah and Jerusalem, and he hath delivered them to trouble, to astonishment, and to hissing, as ye see with your eyes.

Ezr 9:7 Since the days of our fathers *have* we *been* in a great trespass unto this day; and for our iniquities have we, our kings, and *our* priests, been delivered into the hand of the kings of the lands, to the sword, to captivity, and to a spoil, and to confusion of face, as *it is* this day.

Ezr 9:13 And after all that is come upon us for our evil deeds, and for our great trespass, seeing that thou our God hast punished us less than our iniquities *deserve,* and hast given us *such* deliverance as this;

Ps 16:4 Their sorrows shall be multiplied *that* hasten *after* another *god:* their drink offerings of blood will I not offer, nor take up their names into my lips.

Ps 32:10 Many sorrows *shall be* to the wicked: but he that trusteth in the LORD, mercy shall compass him about.

Ps 107:17 Fools because of their transgression, and because of their iniquities, are afflicted.

Pr 24:22 For their calamity shall rise suddenly; and who knoweth the ruin of them both?

Is 8:22 And they shall look unto the earth; and behold trouble and darkness, dimness of anguish; and *they shall be* driven to darkness.

Is 17:14 And behold at eveningtide trouble; *and* before the morning he *is* not. This *is* the portion of them that spoil us, and the lot of them that rob us.

Is 22:5 For *it is* a day of trouble, and of treading down, and of perplexity by the Lord GOD of hosts in the valley of vision, breaking down the walls, and of crying to the mountains.

Is 51:21 Therefore hear now this, thou afflicted, and drunken, but not with wine:

Is 65:15 And ye shall leave your name for a curse unto my chosen: for the Lord GOD shall slay thee, and call his servants by another name:

Je 2:37 Yea, thou shalt go forth from him, and thine hands upon thine head: for the LORD hath rejected thy confidences, and thou shalt not prosper in them.

Je 10:21 For the pastors are become brutish, and have not sought the LORD: therefore they shall not prosper, and all their flocks shall be scattered.

Je 14:18 If I go forth into the field, then behold the slain with the sword! and if I enter into the city, then behold them that are sick with famine! yea, both the prophet and the priest go about into a land that they know not.

Je 22:30 Thus saith the LORD, Write ye this man childless, a man *that* shall not prosper in his days: for no man of his seed shall prosper, sitting upon the throne of David, and ruling any more in Judah.

Je 48:16 The calamity of Moab *is* near to come, and his affliction hasteth fast.

Je 48:38 *There shall be* lamentation generally upon all the housetops of Moab, and in the streets thereof: for I have broken Moab like a vessel wherein *is* no pleasure, saith the LORD.

Lam 1:2 She weepeth sore in the night, and her tears *are* on her cheeks: among all her lovers she hath none to comfort *her:* all her friends have dealt treacherously with her, they are become her enemies.

Lam 1:12 *Is it* nothing to you, all ye that pass by? behold, and see if there be any sorrow like unto my sorrow, which is done unto me, wherewith the LORD hath afflicted *me* in the day of his fierce anger.

Lam 1:20 Behold, O LORD; for I *am* in distress: my bowels are troubled; mine heart is turned within me; for I have grievously rebelled: abroad the sword bereaveth, at home *there is* as death.

See **MISERY, FAMINE, PROSPERITY, WANT**

ADVICE *See* **COUNSEL**

ADVOCATES *See* **COURTS**

AFFECTIONS *See* **DESIRE**

AFFLICTIONS, *suffering, pain, distress*

Ex 3:7 And the LORD said, I have surely seen the affliction of my people which *are* in Egypt, and have heard their cry by reason of their taskmasters; for I know their sorrows;

Job 14:1 Man *that is* born of a woman is of few days, and full of trouble.

Ps 119:50 This *is* my comfort in my affliction: for thy word hath quickened me.

Ps 119:143 Trouble and anguish have taken hold on me: *yet* thy commandments *are* my delights.

Is 63:9 In all their affliction he was afflicted, and the angel of his presence saved them: in his love and in his pity he redeemed them; and he bare them, and carried them all the days of old.

Ro 8:18 For I reckon that the sufferings of this present time *are* not worthy *to be compared* with the glory which shall be revealed in us.

2 Co 4:8 *We are* troubled on every side, yet not distressed; *we are* perplexed, but not in despair;

1. Blessings in Disguise

Ex 1:12 But the more they afflicted them, the more they multiplied and grew. And they were grieved because of the children of Israel.

Jb 5:17 Behold, happy *is* the man whom God correcteth: therefore despise not thou the chastening of the Almighty:

Jb 23:10 But he knoweth the way that I take: *when* he hath tried me, I shall come forth as gold.

Jb 34:31 Surely it is meet to be said unto God, I have borne *chastisement,* I will not offend *any more:*

Jb 36:8 And if *they be* bound in fetters, *and* be holden in cords of affliction;

Ps 78:34 When he slew them, then they sought him: and they returned and enquired early after God.

Ps 119:67 Before I was afflicted I went astray: but now have I kept thy word.

Ec 7:2 *It is* better to go to the house of mourning, than to go to the house of feasting: for that is the end of all men; and the living will lay *it* to his heart.

Da 4:36 At the same time my reason returned unto me; and for the glory of my kingdom, mine honour and brightness returned unto me; and my counsellors and my lords sought unto me; and I was established in my kingdom, and excellent majesty was added unto me.

Jona 2:2 And said, I cried by reason of mine affliction unto the LORD, and he heard me; out of the belly of hell cried I, *and* thou heardest my voice.

Zec 13:9 And I will bring the third part through the fire, and will refine them as silver is refined, and will try them as gold is tried: they shall call on my name, they shall say, The LORD *is* my God.

2 Co 4:17 For our light affliction, which is but for a moment, worketh for us a far more exceeding *and* eternal weight of glory;

He 12:11 Now no chastening for the present seemeth to be joyous, but grievous: nevertheless afterward it yieldeth the peaceable fruit of righteousness unto them which are exercised thereby.

Re 7:14 And I said unto him, Sir, thou knowest. And he said to me, These are they which came out of great tribulation, and have washed their robes, and made them white in the blood of the Lamb.

2. From God

Ge 15:13 And he said unto Abram, Know of a surety that thy seed shall be a stranger in a land *that is* not theirs, and shall serve them; and they shall afflict them four hundred years;

De 8:5 Thou shalt also consider in thine heart, that, as a man chasteneth his son, *so* the LORD thy God chasteneth thee.

Ru 1:20 And she said unto them, Call me not Naomi, call me Mara: for the Almighty hath dealt very bitterly with me.

1 K 2:26 And unto Abiathar the priest said the king, Get thee to Anathoth, unto thine own fields; for thou *art* worthy of death: but I will not at this time put thee to death, because thou barest the ark of the LORD God before David my father, and because thou hast been afflicted in all wherein my father was afflicted.

Jb 6:4 For the arrows of the Almighty *are* within me, the poison whereof drinketh up my spirit: the terrors of God do set themselves in array against me.

Jb 16:12 I was at ease, but he hath broken me asunder: he hath also taken *me* by my neck, and shaken me to pieces, and set me up for his mark.

Ps 66:11 Thou broughtest us into the net; thou laidst affliction upon our loins.

Ps 90:7 For we are consumed by thine anger, and by thy wrath are we troubled.

Ps 102:9–10 For I have eaten ashes like bread, and mingled my drink with weeping,

Because of thine indignation and thy wrath: for thou hast lifted me up, and cast me down.

Ps 132:1 LORD, remember David, *and* all his afflictions:

Lam 1:9 Her filthiness *is* in her skirts; she remembereth not her last end; therefore she came down wonderfully: she had no comforter. O LORD, behold my affliction: for the enemy hath magnified *himself.*

Eze 24:16 Son of man, behold, I take away from thee the desire of thine eyes with a stroke: yet neither shalt thou mourn nor weep, neither shall thy tears run down.

Am 3:6 Shall a trumpet be blown in the city, and the people not be afraid? shall there be evil in a city, and the LORD hath not done *it?*

2 Co 8:2 How that in a great trial of affliction the abundance of their joy and their deep poverty abounded unto the riches of their liberality.

2 Co 12:7 And lest I should be exalted above measure through the abundance of the revelations, there was given to me a thorn in the flesh, the messenger of Satan to buffet me, lest I should be exalted above measure.

He 11:37 They were stoned, they were sawn asunder, were tempted, were slain with the sword: they wandered about in sheepskins and goatskins; being destitute, afflicted, tormented;

3. Of Ministers and Prophets

Eze 24:18; 1 Co 4:11; 2 Co 1:6; 6:5; 11:23; 12:7; 1 Th 3:3

4. Sometimes Prolonged

Jb 7:19; Ps 6:3; 13:1; 35:17; 74:10; 79:5; 80:4; 89:46; 90:13; 94:3; 119:84; Is 64:12; Lam 5:20; Da 8:13; Hab 1:2; Zec 1:12; Lu 6:49; Re 6:10

5. True Believers Do Not Faint

Jb 4:5 But now it is come upon thee, and thou faintest; it toucheth thee, and thou art troubled.

2 Co 4:1 Therefore seeing we have this ministry, as we have received mercy, we faint not;

2 Co 4:16 For which cause we faint not; but though our outward man perish, yet the inward *man* is renewed day by day.

Ga 6:9 And let us not be weary in well doing: for in due season we shall reap, if we faint not.

Ep 3:13 Wherefore I desire that ye faint not at my tribulations for you, which is your glory.

He 12:5 And ye have forgotten the exhortation which speaketh unto you as unto children, My son, despise not thou the chastening of the Lord, nor faint when thou art rebuked of him:

Re 2:3 And hast borne, and hast patience, and for my name's sake hast laboured, and hast not fainted.

6. Cup of Suffering

Job 9:18 He will not suffer me to take my breath, but filleth me with bitterness.

Ps 60:3 Thou hast shewed thy people hard things: thou hast made us to drink the wine of astonishment.

Ps 73:10 Therefore his people return hither: and waters of a full *cup* are wrung out to them.

Ps 80:5 Thou feedest them with the bread of tears; and givest them tears to drink in great measure.

Ps 102:9 For I have eaten ashes like bread, and mingled my drink with weeping,

Lam 3:15 He hath filled me with bitterness, he hath made me drunken with wormwood.

Mt 20:22 But Jesus answered and said, Ye know not what ye ask. Are ye able to drink of the cup that I shall drink of, and to be baptized with the baptism that I am baptized with? They say unto him, We are able.

Mt 26:39 And he went a little farther, and fell on his face, and prayed, saying, O my Father, if it be possible, let this cup pass from me: nevertheless not as I will, but as thou *wilt.*

Mt 27:34 They gave him vinegar to drink mingled with gall: and when he had tasted *thereof,* he would not drink.

Mark 5:26 And had suffered many things of many physicians, and had spent all that she had, and was nothing bettered, but rather grew worse,

Mark 10:38 But Jesus said unto them, Ye know not what ye ask: can ye drink of the cup that I drink of? and be baptized with the baptism that I am baptized with?

Mark 14:36 And he said, Abba, Father, all things *are* possible unto thee; take away this cup from me: nevertheless not what I will, but what thou wilt.

Lu 22:42 Saying, Father, if thou be willing, remove this cup from me: nevertheless not my will, but thine, be done.

John 18:11 Then said Jesus unto Peter, Put up thy sword into the sheath: the cup which my Father hath given me, shall I not drink it?

7. Its Refining Influence

Jb 23:10 But he knoweth the way that I take: *when* he hath tried me, I shall come forth as gold.

Ps 66:10 For thou, O God, hast proved us: thou hast tried us, as silver is tried.

Pr 3:12 For whom the LORD loveth he correcteth; even as a father the son *in whom* he delighteth.

Is 1:25 And I will turn my hand upon thee, and purely purge away thy dross, and take away all thy tin:

Is 48:10 Behold, I have refined thee, but not with silver; I have chosen thee in the furnace of affliction.

Je 9:7 Therefore thus saith the LORD of hosts, Behold, I will melt them, and try them; for how shall I do for the daughter of my people?

Eze 22:20 *As* they gather silver, and brass, and iron, and lead, and tin, into the midst of the furnace, to blow the fire upon it, to melt *it;* so will I gather *you* in mine anger and in my fury, and I will leave *you there,* and melt you.

Zec 13:9 And I will bring the third part through the fire, and will refine them as silver is refined, and will try them as gold is tried: they shall call on my name, and I will hear them: I will

say, It *is* my people: and they shall say, The LORD *is* my God.

Mal 3:3 And he shall sit *as* a refiner and purifier of silver: and he shall purify the sons of Levi, and purge them as gold and silver, that they may offer unto the LORD an offering in righteousness.

1 Pe 1:7 That the trial of your faith, being much more precious than of gold that perisheth, though it be tried with fire, might be found unto praise and honour and glory at the appearing of Jesus Christ:

1 Pe 4:12 Beloved, think it not strange concerning the fiery trial which is to try you, as though some strange thing happened unto you:

8. Chastisement

Le 26:29 And ye shall eat the flesh of your sons, and the flesh of your daughters shall ye eat.

De 8:5 Thou shalt also consider in thine heart, that, as a man chasteneth his son, *so* the LORD thy God chasteneth thee.

Jb 33:19 He is chastened also with pain upon his bed, and the multitude of his bones with strong *pain:*

Jb 36:9 Then he sheweth them their work, and their transgressions that they have exceeded.

Ps 6:1 O LORD, rebuke me not in thine anger, neither chasten me in thy hot displeasure.

Ps 94:12 Blessed *is* the man whom thou chastenest, O LORD, and teachest him out of thy law;

Pr 3:11–12 My son, despise not the chastening of the LORD; neither be weary of his correction:

For whom the LORD loveth he correcteth; even as a father the son *in whom* he delighteth.

Je 10:24 O LORD, correct me, but with judgment; not in thine anger, lest thou bring me to nothing.

Lam 3:32 But though he cause grief, yet will he have compassion according to the multitude of his mercies.

Eze 22:21 Yea, I will gather you, and blow upon you in the fire of my wrath, and ye shall be melted in the midst thereof.

Eze 39:28 Then shall they know that I *am* the LORD their God, which caused them to be led into captivity among the heathen: but I have gathered them unto their own land, and have left none of them any more there.

Jn 15:2 Every branch in me that beareth not fruit he taketh away: and every *branch* that beareth fruit, he purgeth it, that it may bring forth more fruit.

1 Co 11:32 But when we are judged, we are chastened of the Lord, that we should not be condemned with the world.

He 12:5 And ye have forgotten the exhortation which speaketh unto you as unto children, My son, despise not thou the chastening of the Lord, nor faint when thou art rebuked of him:

Re 3:19 As many as I love, I rebuke and chasten: be zealous therefore, and repent.

9. Waters of Affliction

Ps 42:7; 69:1, 15; 73:10; 88:7; 124:4; Is 30:20; 43:2; Je 8:14; Lam 3:54; Jona 2:5

10. Tribulation

De 4:30 When thou art in tribulation, and all these things are come upon thee, *even* in the latter days, if thou turn to the LORD thy God, and shalt be obedient unto his voice;

Ps 102:4 My heart is smitten, and withered like grass; so that I forget to eat my bread.

Mt 24:21 For then shall be great tribulation, such as was not since the beginning of the world to this time, no, nor ever shall be.

Jn 16:33 These things I have spoken unto you, that in me ye might have peace. In the world ye shall have tribulation: but be of good cheer; I have overcome the world.

Ac 14:22 Confirming the souls of the disciples, *and* exhorting them to continue in the faith, and that we must through much tribulation enter into the kingdom of God.

Ro 5:3 And not only *so*, but we glory in tribulations also: knowing that tribulation worketh patience;

1 Th 3:4 For verily, when we were with you, we told you before that we should suffer tribulation; even as it came to pass, and ye know.

Re 2:9 I know thy works, and tribulation, and poverty, (but thou art rich) and *I know* the blasphemy of them which say they are Jews, and are not, but *are* the synagogue of Satan.

Re 7:14 And I said unto him, Sir, thou knowest. And he said to me, These are they which came out of great tribulation, and have washed their robes, and made them white in the blood of the Lamb.

See **DELAY, DISCOURAGEMENT, TESTS**

AFTERWARDS, *specific references to*

Ps 73:24; Pr 20:17; Mt 25:11; Jn 13:36; 1 Co 15:46; Ga 3:23; He 12:11, 17

AGATE See **STONES**

AGE, *OLD*

1. For the Righteous

PROMISED TO ABRAHAM

Ge 15:15 And thou shalt go to thy fathers in peace; thou shalt be buried in a good old age.

PRAYER CONCERNING

Ps 71:9 Cast me not off in the time of old age; forsake me not when my strength faileth.

CROWN OF GLORY

Pr 16:31 The hoary head *is* a crown of glory, *if* it be found in the way of righteousness.

Pr 20:29 The glory of young men *is* their strength: and the beauty of old men *is* the grey head.

STARTS IN YOUTH

Ec 12:1 Remember now thy Creator in the days of thy youth, while the evil days come not, nor the years draw nigh, when thou shalt say, I have no pleasure in them;

DIVINE PRESENCE IN

Is 46:4 And *even* to *your* old age I *am* he; and *even* to hoar hairs will I carry *you:* I have made, and I will bear; even I will carry, and will deliver *you.*

RULES OF CONDUCT

Tit 2:2–3 That the aged men be sober, grave, temperate, sound in faith, in charity, in patience.

The aged women likewise, that *they be* in behaviour as becometh holiness, not false accusers, not given to much wine, teachers of good things;

2. Vigorous

MOSES

De 34:7 And Moses *was* an hundred and twenty years old when he died: his eye was not dim, nor his natural force abated.

CALEB

Jos 14:11 As yet I *am as* strong this day as *I was* in the day that Moses sent me: as my strength *was* then, even so *is* my strength now, for war, both to go out, and to come in.

ANNA

Lu 2:36 And there was one Anna, a prophetess, the daughter of Phanuel, of the tribe of Aser: she was of a great age and had lived with an husband seven years from her virginity;

3. Feebleness

1 K 1:1; Ps 71:9; Ec 12:3, 5; Zec 8:4; He 11:21

4. Gray Hair

1 S 12:2; Jb 15:10; Pr 16:31; 20:29; Ec 12:5; Ho 7:9

5. Dimness of Vision

Ge 27:1, 23; 48:10; 1 S 3:2; 4:15; 1 K 14:4; Ec 12:3

AGRICULTURE, *the cultivation of soil, production of crops, and the raising of livestock*

Ge 2:15; 3:23; 4:2; 9:20; 26:12; Ex 23:10; Le 25:3, 22; 2 S 9:10; 1 K 19:19;

1 Chr 4:23; 27:26; 2 Chr 26:10; Jb 1:14; Ps 107:37; Pr 12:11; 28:19; Ec 5:9; Is 17:11; 28:24; 37:30; Mt 13:4; 1 Co 9:10

1. First Human Occupation

Ge 2:15; 3:23

2. Seedtime and Harvest Promised

Ge 8:22

3. People Engaged in Agriculture

a. Examples

ABEL

Ge 4:2 And she again bare his brother Abel. And Abel was a keeper of sheep, but Cain was a tiller of the ground.

NOAH

Ge 9:20 And Noah began *to be* an husbandman, and he planted a vineyard:

ELISHA

1 K 19:19 So he departed thence plowing *with* twelve yoke *of oxen* before him, and he with the twelfth: and Elijah passed by him, and cast his mantle upon him.

DAVID

1 Chr 27:26 And over them that did the work of the field for tillage of the ground *was* Ezri the son of Chelub:

UZZIAH

2 Chr 26:10 Also he built towers in the desert, and digged many wells: for he had much cattle, both in the low country, and in the plains: husbandmen *also,* and vine dressers in the mountains, and in Carmel: for he loved husbandry.

THE RICH MAN

Lu 12:16 And he spake a parable unto them, saying, The ground of a certain rich man brought forth plentifully:

b. Called Husbandmen

Ge 9:20; 2 Chr 26:10; Je 31:24; 51:23; 52:16; Jl 1:11; Am 5:16; Zec 13:5; Mt

21:33; 24:18; Mk 12:2; Lu 15:25; 20:14, 16; 2 Ti 2:6; Ja 5:7

4. Operations

a. Gleaning

Le 19:10; 23:22; De 24:19; Ru 2:2, 8, 23; Is 17:6

b. Harrowing

Jb 39:10

c. Harvesting

Ge 8:22; 47:24; Ex 23:16; Le 19:9; De 24:19; Jud 15:1; Ru 1:22; 2:23; 1 S 6:13; 8:12; 12:17; 2 S 21:9; 2 K 4:18; Jb 24:6; Ps 129:7; Pr 10:5; 26:1; 27:25; Is 37:30; Je 5:24; Am 4:7; Mk 4:29; Jn 4:35

d. Irrigating

De 11:10; Ec 2:6; Is 58:11

e. Mowing

Ps 72:6; 129:7; Am 7:1

f. Planting

Pr 31:16; Is 44:14

g. Plowing

1 K 19:19; Jb 1:14; Lu 9:62; 17:7; 1 Co 9:10

h. Reaping

Le 19:9; 23:10, 22; 25:5

i. Binding

Ge 37:7; Mt 13:30

j. Sowing

Ec 11:4; Is 32:20; Mt 13:3

k. Threshing

Jud 6:11; Ru 3:2; 1 Chr 21:20; Is 28:27, 28; 1 Co 9:9

l. Winnowing

Ru 3:2; Mt 3:12

5. Products

a. Barley

Ex 9:31; Le 27:16; Nu 5:15; Ru 1:22; 3:17; 2 S 14:30; 17:28; 21:9; 1 K 4:28;

2 K 4:42; 1 Chr 11:13; 2 Chr 2:10, 15; Jb 31:40; Is 28:25; Je 41:8; Eze 4:9; 45:13; Ho 3:2; Jl 1:11

b. Grain

Ge 41:5, 49, 57; 42:19, 26; 43:2; 47:14; Le 2:14; Nu 18:27; De 14:23; 16:13; 23:25; 25:4; 28:51; Jos 5:11; Ru 3:7; 2 Chr 31:5; 32:28; Ne 5:2; 10:39; 13:5; Ps 65:9; 72:16; Is 17:5; Ho 14:7; Jl 2:19; Hag 1:11; Zec 9:17; Mt 12:1; Mk 2:23; 4:28; Lu 6:1; Jn 12:24; Ac 7:12

c. Increase

Ge 1:11; 26:12; 41:47; 47:24; Le 25:7; 26:4; De 14:22, 28; 16:15; 28:4; Ps 67:6; 85:12; 107:37; Pr 3:9; Is 30:23; 55:10; Eze 34:27; 36:30; 48:18; Ho 2:22; Jl 2:22; Zec 8:12; Mk 4:28; Lu 12:16; He 6:7; Ja 5:7, 18

6. Foes

a. Barrenness of Soil

Ge 4:12; 42:12; Le 26:20; De 11:17; 28:18, 38; 29:23; 2 K 2:19; Jb 31:40; Is 5:10; 32:13; 34:13; Je 8:13; 12:4; Ho 8:7; Mi 6:15; Hab 3:17; Hag 1:6, 10; 2:16

b. Blasting of Crops

De 28:22; 1 K 8:37; 2 Chr 6:28; Am 4:9; Hag 2:17

c. Drought See **DROUGHT**

d. Frost See **WEATHER**

e. Caterpillars See **INSECTS**

f. Grasshoppers See **INSECTS**

g. Locusts See **INSECTS**

h. Palmerworm, possibly caterpillar.

See **INSECTS**

7. Made Difficult by Sin
Ge 3:17–18; Ge 5:29

8. Other Topics

a. Barns

Jb 39:12; Pr 3:10; Hag 2:19; Mt 6:26; Lu 12:18, 24

b. Sickles

De 16:9; 23:25; Je 50:16; Jl 3:13; Mk 4:29; Re 14:14

c. Threshing-floors

Ge 50:10; Nu 15:20; Jud 6:37; Ru 3:2, 6; 1 S 23:1; 2 S 6:6; 24:16; 1 Chr 13:9; 21:15, 18; 2 Chr 3:1; Je 51:33; Ho 9:2; Mi 4:12

d. Gardens

Ge 2:8; 1 K 21:2; Ne 3:15; Est 7:7; Ec 2:5; Song 4:12; 5:1; Is 51:3; 58:11; Je 31:12

e. Oliveyards

Jos 24:13; 1 S 8:14; 2 K 5:26; Ne 5:11; 9:25

f. Orchards

Ec 2:5; Song 4:13

g. Plants

Ps 128:3; 144:12; Is 5:7; 53:2; Jona 4:6; Mt 15:13

h. Pruning

Le 25:3; Is 5:6; Jn 15:2

i. Pruning Hooks

Is 18:5; Jl 3:10

j. Vineyards

Ex 22:5; 23:11; Le 19:10; 25:3; De 6:11; 20:6; 22:9; 23:24; 24:21; Jud 9:27; 14:5; 15:5; 1 S 8:15; 1 K 21:1; 1 Chr 27:27; Ne 5:11; Pr 31:16; Ec 2:4; Is 37:30; 65:21; Je 39:10; Am 9:14

k. Winepress

De 15:14; Jud 6:11; 2 K 6:27; Ne 13:15; Jb 24:11; Pr 3:10; Is 5:2; 63:3; Ho 9:2; Hag 2:16; Mt 21:33; Mk 12:1

9. Fruit

Ge 1:11; Le 19:25; 27:30; Nu 13:26; De 33:14; 2 S 16:1; Am 8:1–2; Mt 21:19; Mk 12:2

a. Apples

Pr 25:11; Song 2:5; Jl 1:12

b. Figs

Nu 13:23; 20:5; 1 S 25:18; 2 K 20:7; Ne 13:15; Is 34:4; Je 24:1

c. Grapes

Ge 40:11; Le 19:10; 25:5; Nu 6:3; 13:20, 23; De 23:24; 24:21; Je 31:29; Eze 18:2; Ho 9:10; Mt 7:16; Lu 6:44

d. Pomegranates

Ex 28:33; 39:24; Nu 13:23; 20:5; 1 S 14:2; 1 K 7:18, 20, 42; 2 Chr 3:16; 4:13; Song 6:7; Je 52:22; Jl 1:12; Hag 2:19

e. Cucumbers

Nu 11:5; Is 1:8

AHA, *a term of derision*

Ps 35:21; 40:15; 70:3; Eze 25:3; 26:2; 36:2; Mk 15:29

AHAB, *king of Israel, son of Omri*

1 K 16:29–33; 17:1; 18:5, 44; 19:1; 20:2; 21:2, 4, 7, 22, 25, 26; 22:3, 20, 28–29, 37, 51; 2 K 10:1, 10; 2 1 Chr 18:3; 21:6; 22:8; Mi 6:16

ESTABLISHED IDOLATRY

1 K 16:30–33 And Ahab the son of Omri did evil in the sight of the LORD above all that *were* before him.

And it came to pass, as if it had been a light thing for him to walk in the sins of Jeroboam the son of Nebat, that he took to wife Jezebel the daughter of Ethbaal king of the Zidonians, and went and served Baal, and worshipped him.

And he reared up an altar for Baal in the house of Baal, which he had built in Samaria.

And Ahab made a grove; and Ahab did more to provoke the LORD God of Israel to anger than all the kings of Israel that were before him.

WAS WEAK-MINDED

1 K 21:4 And Ahab came into his house heavy and displeased because of the word which Naboth the Jezreelite had spoken to him: for he had said, I will not give thee the inheritance of my fathers. And he laid him down upon his bed, and turned away his face, and would eat no bread.

THE TOOL OF HIS WIFE JEZEBEL

1 K 21:7 And Jezebel his wife said unto him, Dost thou now govern the kingdom of Israel? arise, *and* eat bread, and let thine heart be merry: I will give thee the vineyard of Naboth the Jezreelite.

1 K 21:25 But there was none like unto Ahab, which did sell himself to work wickedness in the sight of the LORD, whom Jezebel his wife stirred up.

DOOM FORETOLD BY ELIJAH

1 K 21:22 And will make thine house like the house of Jeroboam the son of Nebat, and like the house of Baasha the son of Ahijah, for the provocation wherewith thou hast provoked *me* to anger, and made Israel to sin.

DOOM FORETOLD BY MICAIAH

1 K 22:28 And Micaiah said, If thou return at all in peace, the LORD hath not spoken by me. And he said, Hearken, O people, every one of you.

See **HUMILITY, ISRAEL**

AHAZ, *king of Judah, son of Jotham*

2 K 15:38; 16:2, 8, 19; 20:11; 1 Chr 3:13; 2 Chr 28:1, 27; 29:19; Is 1:1; 7:1, 12; 14:28; 38:8; Ho 1:1; Mi 1:1; Mt 1:9

See **ISRAEL**

AHAZIAH, *king of Judah, also called Azariah, or Jehoahaz, son of*

2 K 8:25; 9:16, 23, 27; 10:13; 1 K 22:40, 51; 2 K 1:2, 17; 2 Chr 20:35

See **ISRAEL**

AHIJAH, *the Shilonite, a prophet*

1 K 11:29; 12:15; 14:4, 18; 15:29; 2 Chr 9:29; 10:15

AHIMAAZ, *high priest, son of Zadok*

2 S 15:36; 17:17; 18:19, 28; 1 Chr 6:8

AHIMELECH, *high priest, son of Ahitub*

1 S 21:1; 22:9, 16

AHITHOPHEL, *David's counsellor*

2 S 15:12, 31; 16:15, 23; 17:1, 14, 23; 1 Chr 27:33

AI, *a city of Canaan captured by Joshua*

Ge 12:8; 13:3; Jos 7:2; 8:1, 12; 10:1; 12:9; Ezr 2:28; Ne 7:32; Je 49:3

AIJALON, *or Ajalon, a city of refuge*

Jos 10:12; 19:42; 21:24; Jud 1:35; 12:12; 1 S 14:31; 1 Chr 6:69; 8:13; 2 Chr 11:10; 28:18

AILMENTS, *sicknesses and disabilities*

Mk 5:25; 9:22; Lu 8:43; 13:11; Jn 5:5; 9:1; Ac 3:2; 4:22; 9:33; 14:8

See **SICKNESS**

AIR

Ac 22:23; 1 Co 9:26; 14:9; Ep 2:2; 1 Th 4:17

ALABASTER, *a kind of marble*

Est 1:6; Mt 26:7; Mk 14:3; Lu 7:37

ALCOHOL *See* **DRUNKENNESS, WINE**

ALEXANDRIA, *a city of Egypt*

Ac 6:9; 18:24; 27:6; 28:11

ALLIANCES, *EVIL, treaties, covenants, associations contrary to God's will*

1. By God's People

1 K 3:1; 15:19; 20:34; 22:4; 2 K 3:7; 2 Chr 16:3; 18:1; 20:35; Is 7:2; 30:2; 31:1; Je 2:25; Ho 8:9; 12:1

2. By Heathen Nations

Jos 9:2; 10:5, 33; 11:5; Jud 3:13; 6:3, 33; 2 S 10:6, 16; 1 K 20:1, 16; Ne 4:8; Ps 2:2; 48:4; 56:6; 83:5; 94:21; 140:2; Is 8:10; Mi 4:11; Zec 12:3; Ac 4:26

See **ASSOCIATIONS**

ALLUREMENTS *See* **SIN**

ALMOND *See* **TREES**

ALMSGIVING

Le 25:35; De 15:7, 11; Est 9:22; Ps 112:9; Pr 22:9; 31:20; Is 58:7; Eze 18:7, 16; Mt 6:1; 19:21; Mk 10:21; Lu 6:30; 11:41;

12:33; 18:22; 19:8; Ac 3:2; 9:36; 10:4, 31; 24:17; Ro 15:26; 1 Co 13:3; 2 Co 8:4; 9:9, 12; Ga 2:10; 1 Jn 3:17

See **GIVING**

ALOES See **TREES**

ALPHA, *first letter of the Greek alphabet, a name applied to Christ*
Re 1:8, 11; 21:6; 22:13

ALTARS, *elevated places, often made of dirt or stone, on which sacrifices were presented to God, incense burned, or before which ceremonies were enacted*

1. Built for Worship

Ge 8:20 And Noah builded an altar unto the Lord; and took of every clean beast, and of every clean fowl, and offered burnt offerings on the altar.

Ge 12:7 And the Lord appeared unto Abram, and said, Unto thy seed will I give this land: and there builded he an altar unto the Lord, who appeared unto him.

Ge 13:4 Unto the place of the altar, which he had made there at the first: and there Abram called on the name of the Lord.

Ge 13:18 Then Abram removed *his* tent, and came and dwelt in the plain of Mamre, which *is* in Hebron, and built there an altar unto the Lord.

Ge 22:9 And they came to the place which God had told him of; and Abraham built an altar there, and laid the wood in order, and bound Isaac his son, and laid him on the altar upon the wood.

Ge 26:25 And he builded an altar there, and called upon the name of the Lord and pitched his tent there: and there Isaac's servants digged a well.

Ge 33:20 And he erected there an altar, and called it El-elohe-Israel.

Ge 35:7 And he built there an altar, and called the place El-beth-el: because there God appeared unto him, when he fled from the face of his brother.

Ex 17:15 And Moses built an altar, and called the name of it Jehovah-nissi:

Ex 24:4 And Moses wrote all the words of the Lord, and rose up early in the morning, and builded an altar under the hill, and twelve pillars, according to the twelve tribes of Israel.

Jos 8:30 Then Joshua built an altar unto the Lord God of Israel in mount Ebal,

Jud 6:26 And build an altar unto the Lord thy God upon the top of this rock, in the ordered place, and take the second bullock, and offer a burnt sacrifice with the wood of the grove which thou shalt cut down.

1 S 14:35 And Saul built an altar unto the Lord: the same was the first altar that he built unto the Lord.

2 S 24:25 And David built there an altar unto the Lord, and offered burnt offerings and peace offerings. So the Lord was intreated for the land, and the plague was stayed from Israel.

1 K 18:32 And with the stones he built an altar in the name of the Lord: and he made a trench about the altar, as great as would contain two measures of seed.

Is 19:19 In that day shall there be an altar to the Lord in the midst of the land of Egypt, and a pillar at the border thereof to the Lord.

Mt 23:18 And, Whosoever shall swear by the altar, it is nothing; but whosoever sweareth by the gift that is upon it, he is guilty.

2. Laws Regarding

Ex 20:24; De 27:5; Jos 8:31; Eze 43:13, 18, 26; He 13:10

3. Brazen, *or altar of burnt offering*

Ex 27:1, 7; 29:13, 36; 30:18, 28; 31:9; 35:16; 38:1, 4, 30; 39:39; 40:6, 10, 29; Le 1:7; 4:7, 18, 25, 30, 34; 6:13; 7:5; 9:7; 16:20, 33; Nu 4:13; 7:1, 11, 84, 88; 16:38; 18:7, 17; De 12:27; Jos 22:29; 1 K 1:50; 2:29; 8:64; 2 K 16:14; 1 Chr 6:49; 16:40; 21:29; 2 Chr 1:5; 4:1; 7:7; 15:8; 29:18; 33:16; 35:16; Eze 9:2; 40:46; 43:16

4. Of Incense

Ex 30:1, 27; 31:8; 35:15; 37:25; 39:38; 40:5, 26; Le 4:7, 18; 1 K 6:22; 7:48; 1 Chr 6:49; 28:18; 2 Chr 4:19; 26:19; Lu 1:11; Re 8:3; 9:13

See **WORSHIP, WORSHIPERS**

ALTRUISM

See **HELPER, LOVE, KINDNESS**

AMALEK, *a descendant of Esau*

Ge 14:7; 36:12; Ex 17:8; Nu 13:29; 14:43; 24:20; De 25:17, 19; Jud 5:14; 6:3, 33; 12:15; 1 S 14:48; 15:3; 28:18; 30:1; 2 S 1:1; 8:12; 1 Chr 4:43; Ps 83:7

AMASA, *Absalom's general*

2 S 17:25; 19:13; 20:4, 12; 1 K 2:5, 32; 2 K 14:1, 5, 8; 1 Chr 2:17

AMAZIAH, *king of Judah, son of Joash*

1 Chr 3:12; 2 Chr 24:27; 25:5, 21, 27

See **ISRAEL**

AMBASSADORS *See* **NATIONS**

AMBITION, *striving for things*

1. Holy

Lu 13:24 Strive to enter in at the strait gate: for many, I say unto you, will seek to enter in, and shall not be able.
1 Co 9:24 Know ye not that they which run in a race run all, but one receiveth the prize? So run, that ye may obtain.
1 Co 12:31 But covet earnestly the best gifts: and yet shew I unto you a more excellent way.
1 Co 14:1 Follow after charity, and desire spiritual *gifts*, but rather that ye may prophesy.
1 Co 14:12 Even so ye, forasmuch as ye are zealous of spiritual *gifts*, seek that ye may excel to the edifying of the church.
Ph 3:13 Brethren, I count not myself to have apprehended: but *this* one thing *I do*, forgetting those things which are behind, and reaching forth unto those things which are before,

1 Ti 3:1 This *is* a true saying, If a man desire the office of a bishop, he desireth a good work.

2. Worldly

PEOPLE AFTER THE FLOOD
Ge 11:4

ABSALOM
2 S 15:1–2, 4

ADONIJAH
1 K 1:5; 2 K 14:10; Ps 49:11; Is 14:13; Is 22:16; Hab 2:5

THE MOTHER OF JAMES AND JOHN
Mt 20:21; Lu 11:43

THE DISCIPLES
Lu 22:24

THE JEWS
Jn 5:44; 2 Th 2:4

See **PRIDE**

AMBUSH

Jos 8:2, 12; Jud 9:25, 34, 43; 16:2; 20:29, 37; 2 S 5:23; 2 K 7:12; 1 Chr 14:14; 2 Chr 13:13; 20:22; Je 51:12

AMEN, *a form of assent*

De 27:15; Ne 5:13; 2 Co 1:20; Re 1:18; 22:20

AMETHYST *See* **STONES**

AMMONITES, *descendants of Lot*

Ge 19:38; De 2:19; 23:3; Jud 10:7, 17; 11:4, 30; 1 S 14:47; 2 S 8:12; 10:3; 23:37; 2 K 24:2; 1 Chr 19:1, 6, 11; 2 Chr 20:1, 23; 26:8; 27:5; Ezr 9:1; Ne 2:10; 4:3; Ps 83:7; Is 11:14; Je 25:21; 27:3; 40:11; 41:10, 15; 49:1; Eze 21:20, 28; 25:2, 10; Da 11:41; Am 1:13

AMON, *a son of Manasseh*

2 K 21:19, 23; 2 Chr 33:21, 22; Mt 1:10

See **ISRAEL**

AMORITES, *descendants of Canaan*

Ge 10:16; 14:7; 15:16; 48:22; Ex 3:17; 13:5; 23:23; 34:11; Nu 13:29; 21:13, 21, 25, 31; 22:2; 32:33; De 1:4, 20, 44; 3:2, 8; 4:47; 20:17; 31:4; Jos 2:10; 5:1; 9:1, 10; 10:6; 11:3; 12:2, 8; 13:4, 21; 24:8, 12, 18; Jud 1:34, 36; 6:10; 10:8; 11:21; 2 S 21:2; 1 K 9:20; 21:26; 2 K 21:11; 1 Chr 1:14; 2 Chr 8:7; Ezr 9:1; Eze 16:3, 45; Am 2:9

AMOS

1. Person, *a prophet of Israel*

Amos 1:1; 7:8, 14; 8:2

2. Book

Author: Amos. His name means "burden" or "burden-bearer." He was a citizen of Tekoa in the tribe of Judah. A herdsman and a grower of sycamore figs (7:14), Amos received a clear call from God (7:15). In spite of attempts to silence him (7:10–13), he clearly communicated his message.

Date Written: Approximately 755 B.C. to 750 B.C. during the reigns of Jeroboam II in Israel and Uzziah in Judah.

Purpose: To pronounce God's righteous judgment on his unrighteous people.

To Whom Written: The Northern Kingdom (Israel).

Main Themes: The style is simple but picturesque. The book abounds in striking metaphors.

(1) The straining of God's mercy by sinners compared to the overloading of a wagon (2:13).

(2) The pressure of duty upon the prophet compared to the roaring of a lion in his ears (3:8).

(3) The narrow escape of a remnant of Israel compared to a shepherd recovering two legs or the piece of an ear from a lion (3:12).

(4) The scarcity of God's Word compared to a famine in the natural world (8:11–12).

Key Word: Judgment.

Key Verses: 3:1–2; 8:11–12.

AMUSEMENTS, *pleasurable diversions*

Ex 32:6; Jud 16:25; 2 S 2:14; Am 6:5

Of Children

Jb 21:11; Zec 8:5; Mt 11:16–17

ANANIAS, *Yahweh has dealt graciously*

1. High Priest

Ac 23:2; 24:1; 25:2

2. Husband of Sapphira

Ac 5:1

3. Of Damascus

Ac 9:10; 22:12

ANARCHY *See* **REBELLION**

ANATHEMA *See* **CURSE**

ANATHOTH

The home of Abiathar the priest (1 K 2:26) and of Jeremiah the prophet (Je 1:1, 32:7–9) was located about three miles northeast of Jerusalem.

ANCHORS

Ac 27:29; He 6:19

ANDREW, *the apostle*

BROTHER OF PETER

Mt 4:18 And Jesus, walking by the sea of Galilee, saw two brethren, Simon called Peter, and Andrew his brother, casting a net into the sea: for they were fishers.

ORIGINALLY A DISCIPLE OF JOHN THE BAPTIST

Jn 1:35 Again the next day after John stood, and two of his disciples;

Jn 1:40 One of the two which heard John *speak*, and followed him, was Andrew, Simon Peter's brother.

SPENT A DAY IN CHRIST'S HOME

Jn 1:39 He saith unto them, Come and see. They came and saw where he dwelt, and abode with him that day: for it was about the tenth hour.

RESPONDED IMMEDIATELY WHEN CALLED

Mt 4:19–20 And he saith unto them, Follow me, and I will make you fishers of men.

And they straightway left *their* nets, and followed him.

BROUGHT PETER TO CHRIST

Jn 1:42 And he brought him to Jesus. And when Jesus beheld him, he said, Thou art Simon the son of Jona: thou shalt be called Cephas, which is by interpretation, A stone.

PROMPT TO HELP

Jn 6:8–9 One of his disciples, Andrew, Simon Peter's brother, saith unto him,

There is a lad here, which hath five barley loaves, and two small fishes: but what are they among so many?

Jn 12:21–22 The same came therefore to Philip, which was of Bethsaida of Galilee, and desired him, saying, Sir, we would see Jesus.

Philip cometh and telleth Andrew: and again Andrew and Philip tell Jesus.

ANGEL OF THE LORD, *a heavenly being sent by God to deal with humans as His personal agent. Many identify Old Testament appearances to be the Christ of the New Testament.*

Ge 16:7 And the angel of the LORD found her by a fountain of water in the wilderness, by the fountain in the way to Shur.

Ge 16:10 And the angel of the LORD said unto her, I will multiply thy seed exceedingly, that it shall not be numbered for multitude.

Ge 22:15 And the angel of the LORD called unto Abraham out of heaven the second time,

Ex 14:19 And the angel of God, which went before the camp of Israel, removed and went behind them; and the pillar of the cloud went from before their face, and stood behind them:

Nu 22:23 And the ass saw the angel of the LORD standing in the way, and his sword drawn in his hand: and the ass turned aside out of the way, and went into the field: and Balaam smote the ass, to turn her into the way.

Jud 2:1 And an angel of the LORD came up from Gilgal to Bochim, and said, I made you to go up out of Egypt, and have brought you unto the land which I sware unto your fathers; and I said, I will never break my covenant with you.

Jud 13:3 And the angel of the LORD appeared unto the woman, and said unto her, Behold now, thou *art* barren, and bearest not: but thou shalt conceive, and bear a son.

Is 63:9 In all their affliction he was afflicted, and the angel of his presence saved them: in his love and in his pity he redeemed them; and he bare them, and carried them all the days of old.

Mt 28:2 And, behold, there was a great earthquake: for the angel of the Lord descended from heaven, and came and rolled back the stone from the door, and sat upon it.

Ac 8:26 And the angel of the Lord spake unto Philip, saying, Arise, and go toward the south unto the way that goeth down from Jerusalem unto Gaza, which is desert.

Ac 27:23 For there stood by me this night the angel of God, whose I am, and whom I serve,

ANGEL REAPERS, *end-time heavenly harvesters of God, spoken of by Jesus*

Mt 13:30 Let both grow together until the harvest: and in the time of harvest I will say to the reapers, Gather ye together first the tares, and bind them in bundles to burn them: but gather the wheat into my barn.

Mt 13:39 The enemy that sowed them is the devil; the harvest is the end of the world; and the reapers are the angels.

Mt 13:49 So shall it be at the end of the world: the angels shall come forth, and sever the wicked from among the just,

Mk 13:27 And then shall he send his angels, and shall gather together his elect from the four winds, from the uttermost part of the earth to the uttermost part of heaven.

ANGELS, *messengers, most often in Scripture spiritual or superhuman beings*

1. Ministering

Ge 16:7 And the angel of the LORD found her by a fountain of water in the wilderness, by the fountain in the way to Shur.

Ge 19:16 And while he lingered, the men laid hold upon his hand, and upon the hand of his wife, and upon the hand of his two daughters; the LORD being merciful unto him: and they brought him forth, and set him without the city.

Ge 21:17 And God heard the voice of the lad; and the angel of God called Hagar out of heaven, and said unto her, What aileth thee, Hagar? fear not; for God hath heard the voice of the lad where he *is.*

Ge 22:11 And the angel of the LORD called unto him out of heaven, and said, Abraham, Abraham: and he said, Here *am* I.

Ge 28:12 And he dreamed, and behold a ladder set up on the earth, and the top of it reached to heaven: and behold the angels of God ascending and descending on it.

Ex 14:19 And the angel of God, which went before the camp of Israel, removed and went behind them; and the pillar of the cloud went from before their face, and stood behind them:

Ex 23:20 Behold, I send an Angel before thee, to keep thee in the way, and to bring thee into the place which I have prepared.

1 K 19:5 And as he lay and slept under a juniper tree, behold, then an angel touched him, and said unto him, Arise *and* eat.

Ps 34:7 The angel of the LORD encampeth round about them that fear him, and delivereth them.

Ps 91:11 For he shall give his angels charge over thee, to keep thee in all thy ways.

Is 63:9 In all their affliction he was afflicted, and the angel of his presence saved them: in his love and in his pity he redeemed them; and he bare them, and carried them all the days of old.

Da 3:28 *Then* Nebuchadnezzar spake, and said, Blessed *be* the God of Shadrach, Meshach, and Abed-nego, who hath sent his angel, and delivered his servants that trusted in him, and have changed the king's word, and yielded their bodies, that they might not serve nor worship any god, except their own God.

Da 6:22 My God hath sent his angel, and hath shut the lions' mouths, that they have not hurt me: forasmuch as before him innocency was found in me; and also before thee, O king, have I done no hurt.

Mt 4:11 Then the devil leaveth him, and, behold, angels came and ministered unto him.

Mt 18:10 Take heed that ye despise not one of these little ones; for I say unto you, That in heaven their angels do always behold the face of my Father which is in heaven.

Mk 1:13 And he was there in the wilderness forty days, tempted of Satan; and was with the wild beasts; and the angels ministered unto him.

Lu 4:10 For it is written, He shall give his angels charge over thee, to keep thee:

Lu 16:22 And it came to pass, that the beggar died, and was carried by the angels into Abraham's bosom: the rich man also died, and was buried;

Lu 22:43 And there appeared an angel unto him from heaven, strengthening him.

Ac 5:19 But the angel of the LORD by night opened the prison doors, and brought them forth, and said,

Ac 12:7 And, behold, the angel of the Lord came upon *him,* and a light shined in the prison: and he smote Peter on the side, and raised him up, saying, Arise up quickly. And his chains fell off from *his* hands.

Ac 27:23 For there stood by me this night the angel of God, whose I am, and whom I serve,

He 1:14 Are they not all ministering spirits, sent forth to minister for them who shall be heirs of salvation?

2. Appearing

Ge 18:2 And he lift up his eyes and looked, and, lo, three men stood by him: and when he saw *them,* he ran to meet them from in the tent door, and bowed himself toward the ground,

Ge 22:11 And the angel of the LORD called unto him out of heaven, and said, Abraham, Abraham: and he said, Here *am* I.

Ge 22:15 And the angel of the LORD called unto Abraham out of heaven the second time,

Ge 31:11 And the angel of God spake unto me in a dream, *saying,* Jacob: And I said, Here *am* I.

Ge 32:1 And Jacob went on his way, and the angels of God met him.

Ex 3:2 And the angel of the LORD appeared unto him in a flame of fire out of the midst of a bush: and he looked, and, behold, the bush burned with fire, and the bush *was* not consumed.

Nu 22:31 Then the LORD opened the eyes of Balaam, and he saw the angel of the LORD standing in the way, and his sword drawn in his hand: and he bowed down his head, and fell flat on his face.

Jos 5:13 And it came to pass, when Joshua was by Jericho, that he lifted up his eyes and looked, and, behold, there stood a man over against him with his sword drawn in his hand: and Joshua went unto him, and said unto him, *Art* thou for us, or for our adversaries?

Jud 2:1 And an angel of the LORD came up from Gilgal to Bochim, and said, I made you to go up out of Egypt, and have brought you unto the land which I sware unto your fathers; and I said, I will never break my covenant with you.

Jud 6:11 And there came an angel of the LORD, and sat under an oak which *was* in Ophrah, that *pertained* unto Joash the Abi-ezrite: and his son Gideon threshed wheat by the winepress, to hide *it* from the Midianites.

Jud 13:3 And the angel of the LORD appeared unto the woman, and said unto her, Behold now, thou *art* barren, and bearest not: but thou shalt conceive, and bear a son.

Jud 13:9 And God hearkened to the voice of Manoah; and the angel of God came again unto the woman as she sat in the field: but Manoah her husband *was* not with her.

Jud 13:13 And the angel of the LORD said unto Manoah, Of all that I said unto the woman let her beware.

2 S 24:17 And David spake unto the LORD when he saw the angel that smote the people, and said, Lo, I have sinned, and I have done wickedly: but these sheep, what have they done? let thine hand, I pray thee, be against me, and against my father's house.

1 K 19:7 And the angel of the LORD came again the second time, and touched him, and said, Arise *and* eat; because the journey *is* too great for thee.

2 K 1:3 But the angel of the LORD said to Elijah the Tishbite, Arise, go up to meet the messengers of the king of Samaria, and say unto them, *Is it* not because *there is* not a God in Israel, *that* ye go to enquire of Baal-zebub the god of Ekron?

2 K 1:15 And the angel of the LORD said unto Elijah, Go down with him: be not afraid of him. And he arose, and went down with him unto the king.

1 Chr 21:16 And David lifted up his eyes, and saw the angel of the LORD stand between the earth and the heaven, having a drawn sword in his hand stretched out over Jerusalem. Then David and the elders *of Israel,* who *were* clothed in sackcloth, fell upon their faces.

1 Chr 21:20 And Ornan turned back, and saw the angel; and his four sons with him hid themselves. Now Ornan was threshing wheat.

Da 4:13 I saw in the visions of my head upon my bed, and, behold, a watcher and an holy one came down from heaven;

Da 8:15 And it came to pass, when I, *even* I Daniel, had seen the vision, and sought for the meaning, then, behold, there stood before me as the appearance of a man.

Da 10:5 Then I lifted up mine eyes, and looked, and behold a certain man clothed in linen, whose loins *were* girded with fine gold of Uphaz:

Da 12:5 Then I Daniel looked, and, behold, there stood other two, the one on this side of the bank of the river, and the other on that side of the bank of the river.

Zec 1:9 Then said I, O my lord, what *are* these? And the angel that talked with me said unto me, I will shew thee what these *be*.

Zec 2:3 And, behold, the angel that talked with me went forth, and another angel went out to meet him,

Zec 4:1 And the angel that talked with me came again, and waked me, as a man that is wakened out of his sleep,

Mt 1:20 But while he thought on these things, behold, the angel of the Lord appeared unto him in a dream, saying, Joseph, thou son of David, fear not to take unto thee Mary thy wife: for that which is conceived in her is of the Holy Ghost.

Mt 2:13 And when they were departed, behold, the angel of the Lord appeareth to Joseph in a dream, saying, Arise, and take the young child and his mother, and flee into Egypt, and be thou there until I bring thee word: for Herod will seek the young child to destroy him.

Mt 2:19 But when Herod was dead, behold an angel of the Lord appeareth in a dream to Joseph in Egypt,

Mt 28:2 And, behold, there was a great earthquake: for the angel of the Lord descended from heaven, and came and rolled back the stone from the door, and sat upon it.

Mk 16:5 And entering into the sepulchre, they saw a young man sitting on the right side, clothed in a long white garment; and they were affrighted.

Lu 1:11 And there appeared unto him an angel of the Lord standing on the right side of the altar of incense.

Lu 1:28 And the angel came in unto her, and said, Hail, *thou that art* highly favoured, the Lord *is* with thee: blessed *art* thou among women.

Lu 2:9 And, lo, the angel of the Lord came upon them, and the glory of the Lord shone round about them: and they were sore afraid.

Lu 24:4 And it came to pass, as they were much perplexed thereabout, behold, two men stood by them in shining garments:

Lu 24:23 And when they found not his body, they came, saying, that they had also seen a vision of angels, which said that he was alive.

Jn 20:12 And seeth two angels in white sitting, the one at the head, and the other at the feet, where the body of Jesus had lain.

Ac 1:10 And while they looked stedfastly toward heaven as he went up, behold, two men stood by them in white apparel;

Ac 8:26 And the angel of the Lord spake unto Philip, saying, Arise, and go toward the south unto the way that goeth down from Jerusalem unto Gaza, which is desert.

Ac 10:3 He saw in a vision evidently about the ninth hour of the day an angel of God coming in to him, and saying unto him, Cornelius.

Ac 10:22 And they said, Cornelius the centurion, a just man, and one that feareth God, and of good report among all the nation of the Jews, was warned from God by an holy angel to send for thee into his house, and to hear words of thee.

Ac 10:30 And Cornelius said, Four days ago I was fasting until this hour; and at the ninth hour I prayed in my house, and, behold, a man stood before me in bright clothing,

Ac 11:13 And he shewed us how he had seen an angel in his house, which stood and said unto him, Send men to Joppa, and call for Simon, whose surname is Peter;

Ac 12:7 And, behold, the angel of the Lord came upon *him,* and a light shined in the prison: and he smote Peter on the side, and raised him up, saying, Arise up quickly. And his chains fell off from *his* hands.

Ac 27:23 For there stood by me this night the angel of God, whose I am, and whom I serve,

He 13:2 Be not forgetful to entertain strangers: for thereby some have entertained angels unawares.

3. Waiting on Christ

Da 7:10 A fiery stream issued and came forth from before him: thousand thousands ministered unto him, and ten thousand times ten thousand stood before him: the judgment was set, and the books were opened.

Mt 13:41 The Son of man shall send forth his angels, and they shall gather out of his kingdom all things that offend, and them which do iniquity;

Mt 16:27 For the Son of man shall come in the glory of his Father with his angels; and then he shall reward every man according to his works.

Mt 24:31 And he shall send his angels with a great sound of a trumpet, and they shall gather together his elect from the four winds, from one end of heaven to the other.

Mt 25:31 When the Son of man shall come in his glory, and all the holy angels with him, then shall he sit upon the throne of his glory:

Mt 26:53 Thinkest thou that I cannot now pray to my Father, and he shall presently give me more than twelve legions of angels?

Mk 8:38 Whosoever therefore shall be ashamed of me and of my words in this adulterous and sinful generation; of him also shall the Son of man be ashamed, when he cometh in the glory of his Father with the holy angels.

Lu 2:13 And suddenly there was with the angel a multitude of the heavenly host praising God, and saying,

Lu 9:26 For whosoever shall be ashamed of me and of my words, of him shall the Son of man be ashamed, when he shall come in his own glory, and in his Father's, and of the holy angels.

Lu 22:43 And there appeared an angel unto him from heaven, strengthening him.

Jn 1:51 And he saith unto him, Verily, verily, I say unto you, Hereafter ye shall see heaven open, and the angels of God ascending and descending upon the Son of man.

2 Th 1:7 And to you who are troubled rest with us, when the Lord Jesus shall be revealed from heaven with his mighty angels,

He 1:6 And again, when he bringeth in the firstbegotten into the world, he saith, And let all the angels of God worship him.

Re 1:1 The Revelation of Jesus Christ, which God gave unto him, to shew unto his servants things which must shortly come to pass; and he sent and signified it by his angel unto his servant John:

Re 5:11 And I beheld, and I heard the voice of many angels round about the throne and the beasts and the elders: and the number of them was ten thousand times ten thousand, and thousands of thousands;

4. Executing the Judgments of God

Ge 19:1 And there came two angels to Sodom at even; and Lot sat in the gate of Sodom: and Lot seeing them rose up to meet them; and he bowed himself with his face toward the ground;

Nu 22:22 And God's anger was kindled because he went: and the angel of the LORD stood in the way for an adversary against him. Now he was riding upon his ass, and his two servants were with him.

Jud 5:23 Curse ye Meroz, said the angel of the LORD, curse ye bitterly the inhabitants thereof; because they came not to the help of the LORD, to the help of the LORD against the mighty.

2 S 24:16 And when the angel stretched out his hand upon Jerusalem to destroy it, the LORD repented him of the evil, and said to the angel that destroyed the people, It is enough: stay now thine hand. And the angel of the LORD was by the threshingplace of Araunah the Jebusite.

2 K 19:35 And it came to pass that night, that the angel of the LORD went out, and smote in the camp of the Assyrians an hundred fourscore and five thousand: and when they arose

early in the morning, behold, they *were* all dead corpses.

1 Chr 21:15 And God sent an angel unto Jerusalem to destroy it: and as he was destroying, the LORD beheld, and he repented him of the evil, and said to the angel that destroyed, It is enough, stay now thine hand. And the angel of the LORD stood by the threshingfloor of Ornan the Jebusite.

2 Chr 32:21 And the LORD sent an angel, which cut off all the mighty men of valour, and the leaders and captains in the camp of the king of Assyria. So he returned with shame of face to his own land. And when he was come into the house of his god, they that came forth of his own bowels slew him there with the sword.

Ps 35:5 Let them be as chaff before the wind: and let the angel of the LORD chase *them*.

Ps 78:49 He cast upon them the fierceness of his anger, wrath, and indignation, and trouble, by sending evil angels *among them*.

Is 37:36 Then the angel of the LORD went forth, and smote in the camp of the Assyrians a hundred and fourscore and five thousand: and when they arose early in the morning, behold, they *were* all dead corpses.

Ac 12:23 And immediately the angel of the Lord smote him, because he gave not God the glory: and he was eaten of worms, and gave up the ghost.

5. Fallen

Jb 4:18 Behold, he put no trust in his servants; and his angels he charged with folly:

Mt 25:41 Then shall he say also unto them on the left hand, Depart from me, ye cursed, into everlasting fire, prepared for the devil and his angels:

2 Pe 2:4 For if God spared not the angels that sinned, but cast *them* down to hell, and delivered *them* into chains of darkness, to be reserved unto judgment;

Jude 6 And the angels which kept not their first estate, but left their own habitation, he hath reserved in ever-lasting chains under darkness unto the judgment of the great day.

Re 12:9 And the great dragon was cast out, that old serpent, called the Devil, and Satan, which deceiveth the whole world: he was cast out into the earth, and his angels were cast out with him.

6. In Heaven

Ps 103:20 Bless the LORD, ye his angels, that excel in strength, that do his commandments, hearkening unto the voice of his word.

Mt 22:30 For in the resurrection they neither marry, nor are given in marriage, but are as the angels of God in heaven.

Mk 12:25 For when they shall rise from the dead, they neither marry, nor are given in marriage; but are as the angels which are in heaven.

Lu 1:19 And the angel answering said unto him, I am Gabriel, that stand in the presence of God; and am sent to speak unto thee, and to shew thee these glad tidings.

Lu 12:8 Also I say unto you, Whosoever shall confess me before men, him shall the Son of man also confess before the angels of God:

Lu 15:10 Likewise, I say unto you, there is joy in the presence of the angels of God over one sinner that repenteth.

Lu 20:36 Neither can they die any more: for they are equal unto the angels; and are the children of God, being the children of the resurrection.

He 12:22 But ye are come unto mount Sion, and unto the city of the living God, the heavenly Jerusalem, and to an innumerable company of angels,

2 Pe 2:11 Whereas angels, which are greater in power and might, bring not railing accusation against them before the Lord.

Re 8:2 And I saw the seven angels which stood before God; and to them were given seven trumpets.

Re 12:7 And there was war in heaven: Michael and his angels fought against the dragon; and the dragon fought and his angels,

Re 14:17 And another angel came out of the temple which is in heaven, he also having a sharp sickle.

Re 18:1 And after these things I saw another angel come down from heaven, having great power; and the earth was lightened with his glory.

Re 20:1 And I saw an angel come down from heaven, having the key of the bottomless pit and a great chain in his hand.

7. Of the Churches

Re 1:20 The mystery of the seven stars which thou sawest in my right hand, and the seven golden candlesticks. The seven stars are the angels of the seven churches: and the seven candlesticks which thou sawest are the seven churches.

Re 2:1 Unto the angel of the church of Ephesus write; These things saith he that holdeth the seven stars in his right hand, who walketh in the midst of the seven golden candlesticks;

Re 2:8 And unto the angel of the church in Smyrna write; These things saith the first and the last, which was dead, and is alive;

Re 2:12 And to the angel of the church in Pergamos write; These things saith he which hath the sharp sword with two edges;

Re 2:18 And unto the angel of the church in Thyatira write; These things saith the Son of God, who hath his eyes like unto a flame of fire, and his feet *are* like fine brass;

Re 3:1 And unto the angel of the church in Sardis write; These things saith he that hath the seven Spirits of God, and the seven stars; I know thy works, that thou hast a name that thou livest, and art dead.

Re 3:7 And to the angel of the church in Philadelphia write; These things saith he that is holy, he that is true, he that hath the key of David, he that openeth, and no man shutteth; and shutteth, and no man openeth;

Re 3:14 And unto the angel of the church of the Laodiceans write; These things saith the Amen, the faithful and true witness, the beginning of the creation of God;

ANGER, *wrath, ire, indignation*

1. God's

Ex 4:14 And the anger of the LORD was kindled against Moses, and he said, *Is* not Aaron the Levite thy brother? I know that he can speak well. And also, behold, he cometh forth to meet thee: and when he seeth thee, he will be glad in his heart.

Nu 11:1 And *when* the people complained, it displeased the LORD: and the LORD heard *it;* and his anger was kindled; and the fire of the LORD burnt among them, and consumed *them that were* in the uttermost parts of the camp.

Nu 12:9 And the anger of the LORD was kindled against them; and he departed.

Nu 14:11 And the LORD said unto Moses, How long will this people provoke me? and how long will it be ere they believe me, for all the signs which I have shewed among them?

Nu 22:22 And God's anger was kindled because he went: and the angel of the LORD stood in the way for an adversary against him. Now he was riding upon his ass, and his two servants *were* with him.

Nu 25:3 And Israel joined himself unto Baal-peor: and the anger of the LORD was kindled against Israel.

Nu 32:13 And the LORD's anger was kindled against Israel, and he made them wander in the wilderness forty years, until all the generation, that had done evil in the sight of the LORD, was consumed.

De 9:20 And the LORD was very angry with Aaron to have destroyed him: and I prayed for Aaron also the same time.

Jos 7:1 But the children of Israel committed a trespass in the accursed thing: for Achan, the son of Carmi, the son of Zabdi, the son of Zerah, of the tribe of Judah, took of the accursed thing: and the anger of the LORD was kindled against the children of Israel.

Jud 2:14 And the anger of the LORD was hot against Israel, and he delivered them into the hands of spoilers that spoiled them, and he sold them into the hands of their enemies round about, so that they could not any longer stand before their enemies.

2 S 24:1 And again the anger of the LORD was kindled against Israel, and he moved David against them to say, Go, number Israel and Judah.

1 K 14:15 For the LORD shall smite Israel, as a reed is shaken in the water, and he shall root up Israel out of this good land, which he gave to their fathers, and shall scatter them beyond the river, because they have made their groves, provoking the LORD to anger.

1 K 15:30 Because of the sins of Jeroboam which he sinned, and which he made Israel sin, by his provocation wherewith he provoked the LORD God of Israel to anger.

1 K 16:2 Forasmuch as I exalted thee out of the dust, and made thee prince over my people Israel; and thou hast walked in the way of Jeroboam, and hast made my people Israel to sin, to provoke me to anger with their sins;

1 K 16:26 For he walked in all the way of Jeroboam the son of Nebat, and in his sin wherewith he made Israel to sin, to provoke the LORD God of Israel to anger with their vanities.

1 K 16:33 And Ahab made a grove; and Ahab did more to provoke the LORD God of Israel to anger than all the kings of Israel that were before him.

1 K 22:53 For he served Baal, and worshipped him, and provoked to anger the LORD God of Israel, according to all that his father had done.

2 K 13:3 And the anger of the LORD was kindled against Israel, and he delivered them into the hand of Hazael king of Syria, and into the hand of Ben-hadad the son of Hazael, all *their* days.

2 K 17:11 And there they burnt incense in all the high places, as *did* the heathen whom the LORD carried away before them; and wrought wicked things to provoke the LORD to anger:

2 K 23:19 And all the houses also of the high places that *were* in the cities of Samaria, which the kings of Israel had made to provoke *the* LORD to anger,

Josiah took away, and did to them according to all the acts that he had done in Bethel.

1 Chr 13:10 And the anger of the LORD was kindled against Uzza, and he smote him, because he put his hand to the ark: and there he died before God.

2 Chr 28:25 And in every several city of Judah he made high places to burn incense unto other gods, and provoked to anger the LORD God of his fathers.

Ps 7:11 God judgeth the righteous, and God is angry *with the wicked* every day.

Ps 27:9 Hide not thy face *far* from me; put not thy servant away in anger: thou hast been my help; leave me not, neither forsake me, O God of my salvation.

Is 1:4 Ah sinful nation, a people laden with iniquity, a seed of evildoers, children that are corrupters: they have forsaken the LORD, they have provoked the Holy One of Israel unto anger, they are gone away backward.

Ho 12:14 Ephraim provoked *him* to anger most bitterly: therefore shall he leave his blood upon him, and his reproach shall his Lord return unto him.

2. Human

2 K 5:11 But Naaman was wroth, and went away, and said, Behold, I thought, He will surely come out to me, and stand, and call on the name of the LORD his God, and strike his hand over the place, and recover the leper.

Ne 4:7 But it came to pass, *that* when Sanballat, and Tobiah, and the Arabians, and the Ammonites, and the Ashdodites, heard that the walls of Jerusalem were made up, *and* that the breaches began to be stopped, then they were very wroth,

Est 1:12 But the queen Vashti refused to come at the king's commandment by *his* chamberlains: therefore was the king very wroth, and his anger burned in him.

Ps 37:8 Cease from anger, and forsake wrath: fret not thyself in any wise to do evil.

Pr 14:17 *He that is* soon angry dealeth foolishly: and a man of wicked devices is hated.

Pr 16:32 *He that is* slow to anger *is* better than the mighty; and he that ruleth his spirit than he that taketh a city.

Pr 19:11 The discretion of a man deferreth his anger; and *it is* his glory to pass over a transgression.

Pr 22:24 Make no friendship with an angry man; and with a furious man thou shalt not go:

Pr 27:4 Wrath *is* cruel, and anger *is* outrageous; but who *is* able to stand before envy?

Ec 7:9 Be not hasty in thy spirit to be angry: for anger resteth in the bosom of fools.

Mt 5:22 But I say unto you, That whosoever is angry with his brother without a cause shall be in danger of the judgment: and whosoever shall say to his brother, Raca, shall be in danger of the council: but whosoever shall say, Thou fool, shall be in danger of hell fire.

Col 3:8 But now ye also put off all these; anger, wrath, malice, blasphemy, filthy communication out of your mouth.

Tit 1:7 For a bishop must be blameless, as the steward of God; not selfwilled, not soon angry, not given to wine, no striker, not given to filthy lucre;

Ja 1:19 Wherefore, my beloved brethren, let every man be swift to hear, slow to speak, slow to wrath:

3. Easily Kindled

2 Chr 28:9 But a prophet of the LORD was there, whose name *was* Oded: and he went out before the host that came to Samaria, and said unto them, Behold, because the LORD God of your fathers was wroth with Judah, he hath delivered them into your hand, and ye have slain them in a rage *that* reacheth up unto heaven.

Pr 25:28 He that *hath* no rule over his own spirit *is like* a city *that is* broken down, *and* without walls.

Pr 29:22 An angry man stirreth up strife, and a furious man aboundeth in transgression.

Da 3:19 Then was Nebuchadnezzar full of fury, and the form of his visage was changed against Shadrach, Meshach, and Abed-nego: *therefore* he spake, and commanded that they should heat the furnace one seven times more than it was wont to be heated.

Lu 23:5 And they were the more fierce, saying, He stirreth up the people, teaching throughout all Jewry, beginning from Galilee to this place.

Jn 10:31 Then the Jews took up stones again to stone him.

Ac 7:57 Then they cried out with a loud voice, and stopped their ears, and ran upon him with one accord,

Ac 22:23 And as they cried out, and cast off *their* clothes, and threw dust into the air,

Ac 26:11 And I punished them oft in every synagogue, and compelled *them* to blaspheme; and being exceedingly mad against them, I persecuted *them* even unto strange cities.

See **WRATH**

ANIMALS

1. Clean and Unclean

Ge 6:20; 30:32; 31:18; 46:32; 47:16; Ex 9:4; 10:26; Le 1:2; 11:1–47, 29; Nu 32:1, 4; De 2:35; 3:7, 19; 14:3–20, 5; Jos 8:27; 11:14; 14:4; 21:2; Ps 148:10; Eze 39:18; Jona 4:11; 1 Co 15:39

2. Names

a. Apes

1 K 10:22; 2 Chr 9:21

b. Asses, Donkeys, Beasts of Burden

Ge 22:3; 36:24; 44:13; 47:17; Ex 34:20; Nu 22:28; 31:39, 45; De 22:10; Jud 5:10; 10:4; 1 S 9:3, 20; 1 Chr 5:21; Ezr 2:67; Mt 21:2

c. Bears

1 S 17:34; 2 S 17:8; 2 K 2:24; Pr 17:12; 28:15; Is 11:7; Da 7:5

d. Behemoth

Jb 40:15

e. Birds See **BIRDS**

f. Boars

Ps 80:13

g. Bullocks

Ex 29:1, 11, 36; Le 1:5; 4:4, 14; 8:14, 17; 9:4, 18; 16:3, 11, 27; 22:23, 27; 23:18; Nu 7:15, 27, 39, 45, 63, 81, 87; 8:8, 12; 15:8, 11, 24; 23:2, 29; 28:11, 19, 27; 29:2, 8, 13, 17, 23, 27, 32, 36; De 15:19; 17:1; Jud 6:25; 1 S 1:24; 1 K 18:23, 33; 2 Chr 13:9; 29:21; 30:24; 35:7; Ezr 6:9, 17; 7:17; 8:35; Jb 42:8; Ps 51:19; 66:15; Eze 43:21, 25; 45:18, 22; 46:7

h. Calves

Ge 18:7; 1 S 28:24; Am 6:4; Lu 15:23, 30

i. Camels

Ge 12:16; 24:10, 19, 61; 30:43; 31:17; 32:15; Ex 9:3; Le 11:4; De 14:7; Jud 6:5; 7:12; 8:21, 26; 1 S 27:9; 30:17; 1 Chr 5:21; 12:40; 27:30; 2 Chr 9:1; 14:15; Ezr 2:67; Ne 7:69; Jb 1:3, 17; Is 60:6; Je 49:29; Eze 25:5; Mt 19:24; 23:24

j. Cattle

Ge 1:25; 2:20; 7:14; 8:17; 9:10; 41:3, 19; Ex 20:10; Nu 35:3; Am 4:1

k. Chameleon

Le 11:30

l. Conies, rock rabbits

Le 11:5; De 14:7; Ps 104:18; Pr 30:26

m. Deer

De 14:5; 2 S 2:18; 22:34; 1 K 4:23; 1 Chr 12:8; Ps 42:1; Pr 5:19; 6:5; Is 35:6; Je 14:5; Lam 1:6

n. Dogs

Ex 22:31; De 23:18; 1 K 14:11; 16:4; 21:23; 22:38; 2 K 8:13; 9:10; Jb 30:1; Ps 59:6; Pr 26:17; Ec 9:4; Lu 16:21

A Term of Reproach: Ps 22:16; Mt 7:6; 15:26; Mk 7:27; Ph 3:2; Re 22:15

o. Dragons, a reptile-like monster, used figuratively of Satan

De 32:33; Ps 74:13; 91:13; Is 34:13; Je 51:34, 37; Mi 1:8; Mal 1:3

p. Dromedaries, Camels, used as beasts of burden

Is 60:6; Je 2:23

q. Elephants

1 K 10:22; Jb 40:15

r. Ferret

Le 11:30

s. Fish See **FISH**

t. Foxes

Jud 15:4; Ne 4:3; Song 2:15; Lam 5:18; Mt 8:20

u. Frogs

Ex 8:2; Ps 78:45; 105:30; Re 16:13

v. Goats

Ge 15:9; 30:32; 32:14; Ex 12:5; Le 1:10; 3:12; 4:24, 28; 5:6; 9:3, 15; 16:8, 15, 21, 27; 22:27; 23:19; Nu 7:16, 23, 28, 35, 40, 46, 65, 82; 15:24, 27; 18:17; 28:15, 22, 30; 29:5, 19, 22, 28, 31, 38; De 14:4; Jud 13:19; 1 S 25:2; 2 Chr 29:21, 23; Ezr 6:17; Eze 43:25; 45:23

w. Greyhounds

Pr 30:31

x. Heifers

Ge 15:9; Nu 19:2, 17; De 21:3; He 9:13, 17

y. Hen

Mt 23:37; Lu 13:34

z. Horses

Ge 47:17; Ex 9:Ge 47:3; De 17:16; Jos 11:4; 2 S 8:4; 1 K 4:26, 28; 10:25, 28; 20:25; 2 K 7:14; 10:2; 23:11; 2 Chr 1:16; 9:25; 25:28; Ezr 2:66; Ne 7:68; Est 8:10, 10; Jb 39:19; Ps 32:9; 33:17; Pr 21:31; Is 2:7; 31:1, 3; Je 50:37; Eze 23:23; 26:11;

27:14; 38:15; Mi 5:10; Na 3:2; Ja 3:3; Re
18:13

aa. Insects See **INSECTS**

bb. Kine, Cows
Ge 32:15; De 7:13; 1 S 6:7

cc. Lambs
Ge 22:8; Ex 12:3, 21; 13:13; 29:39;
34:20; Le 3:7; 4:32; 5:6; 9:3; 12:6; 14:10,
13, 24; 22:23; 23:12, 18; Nu 6:12; 7:15,
23, 27, 35, 39, 41, 45, 65, 83, 87; 15:5,
11; 28:3, 9, 11, 19, 27; 29:2, 8, 13, 17,
23, 27, 32, 36; 2 Chr 29:21; 35:7; Ezr
6:9, 17; 8:35; Eze 45:15; 46:4, 13, 15

dd. Leopards
Song 4:8; Is 11:6; Je 5:6; 13:23; Da 7:6;
Ho 13:7; Hab 1:8

ee. Lions
Jud 14:5; 1 S 17:34; 2 S 23:20; 1 K 13:24;
20:36; 2 K 17:25; 1 Chr 11:22; Jb 4:10;
38:39; Ps 104:21; Ec 9:4; Is 11:7; Da
6:16, 19; Am 3:4; Na 2:11; He 11:33

ff. Lizards
Le 11:30

gg. Mice
Le 11:29; 1 S 6:4; Is 66:17

hh. Mules
2 S 13:29; 18:9; 1 K 1:33; Ps 32:9; Zec
14:15

ii. Oxen
Ex 21:28; 22:1; 23:4; Le 2:1; 25:4; Lu
13:15; Jn 2:15; Ac 14:13; 1 Co 9:9; 1 Ti
5:18

jj. Pygarg, Ibex, wild goat
De 14:5

kk. Rams
Ge 15:9; 22:13; Ex 29:15, 20; Le 5:15,
18; 6:6; 8:18; 9:18; 19:21; 23:18; Nu 5:8;
6:14; 7:17, 21, 29, 33, 41, 47, 51, 63, 83,
87; 15:6, 11; 23:2, 29; 28:11, 20, 27;
29:2, 8, 13, 17, 23, 27, 32, 37; Eze 46:4

ll. Reptiles See **REPTILES**

mm. Serpents See **REPTILES**

nn. Sheep
Ge 4:4; 12:16; 21:27; 29:3; 30:32; 32:14;
Ex 9:3; 12:5; 34:19; Le 1:10; 22:21, 27;
27:26; Nu 18:17; 31:28, 36, 43; 32:24;
De 14:4; 15:19; 17:1; 18:3, 4; 32:14; Jos
7:24; 1 S 25:2; 1 K 4:23; 8:63; 1 Chr
5:21; 2 Chr 7:5; 14:15; 15:11; 30:24; Jb
1:3, 16; 42:12; Ps 8:7; 65:13; Mt 12:11;
Jn 2:15

oo. Snail
Le 11:30; Ps 58:8

pp. Swine, Pigs
Le 11:7; De 14:8; Is 65:4; 66:17; Mt 7:6;
8:30; Mk 5:11, 14; Lu 8:32; 15:15; 2 Pe
2:22

qq. Unicorn, Wild Ox
Nu 23:22; De 33:17; Jb 39:9; Ps 29:6; Is
34:7

rr. Weasel
Le 11:29

ss. Wolves
Eze 22:27; Zep 3:3; Mt 7:15; 10:16; Lu
10:3; Jn 10:12; Ac 20:29

ANNA See WOMEN

ANNAS, *high priest*
Lu 3:2; Jn 18:13; Ac 4:6

ANOINTING, *to apply oil as a sign of
consecration*

1. Of Objects
Ex 29:36 And thou shalt offer every
day a bullock *for* a sin offering for
atonement: and thou shalt cleanse the
altar, when thou hast made an atonement for it, and thou shalt anoint it,
to sanctify it.
Ex 30:26 And thou shalt anoint the
tabernacle of the congregation therewith, and the ark of the testimony,
Ex 40:10 And thou shalt anoint the
altar of the burnt offering, and all his
vessels, and sanctify the altar: and it
shall be an altar most holy.

Le 8:11 And he sprinkled thereof upon the altar seven times, and anointed the altar and all his vessels, both the laver and his foot, to sanctify them.

Nu 7:1 And it came to pass on the day that Moses had fully set up the tabernacle, and had anointed it, and sanctified it, and all the instruments thereof, both the altar and all the vessels thereof, and had anointed them, and sanctified them;

2. Of Persons

Le 8:30 And Moses took of the anointing oil, and of the blood which *was* upon the altar, and sprinkled *it* upon Aaron, *and* upon his garments, and upon his sons, and upon his sons' garments with him; and sanctified Aaron, *and* his garments, and his sons, and his sons' garments with him.

1 S 10:1 Then Samuel took a vial of oil, and poured *it* upon his head, and kissed him, and said, *Is it* not because the LORD hath anointed thee *to be* captain over his inheritance?

1 S 16:13 Then Samuel took the horn of oil, and anointed him in the midst of his brethren: and the Spirit of the LORD came upon David from that day forward. So Samuel rose up, and went to Ramah.

1 K 1:39 And Zadok the priest took an horn of oil out of the tabernacle, and anointed Solomon. And they blew the trumpet; and all the people said, God save king Solomon.

1 K 19:16 And Jehu the son of Nimshi shalt thou anoint *to be* king over Israel: and Elisha the son of Shaphat of Abel-meholah shalt thou anoint *to be* prophet in thy room.

2 K 9:3 Then take the box of oil, and pour *it* on his head, and say, Thus saith the LORD, I have anointed thee king over Israel. Then open the door, and flee, and tarry not.

2 K 11:12 And he brought forth the king's son, and put the crown upon him, and *gave him* the testimony; and they made him king, and anointed him; and they clapped their hands, and said, God save the king.

2 K 23:30 And his servants carried him in a chariot dead from Megiddo, and brought him to Jerusalem, and buried him in his own sepulchre. And the people of the land took Jehoahaz the son of Josiah, and anointed him, and made him king in his father's stead.

Mt 6:17 But thou, when thou fastest, anoint thine head, and wash thy face;

2 Co 1:21 Now he which stablisheth us with you in Christ, and hath anointed us, *is* God;

3. Of Guests *See* **SOCIAL DUTIES, FUNCTIONS**

4. With Oil

Ru 3:3 Wash thyself therefore, and anoint thee, and put thy raiment upon thee, and get thee down to the floor: *but* make not thyself known unto the man, until he shall have done eating and drinking.

Ps 92:10 But my horn shalt thou exalt like *the horn of* an unicorn: I shall be anointed with fresh oil.

Ec 9:8 Let thy garments be always white; and let thy head lack no ointment.

Is 57:9 And thou wentest to the king with ointment, and didst increase thy perfumes, and didst send thy messengers far off, and didst debase *thyself even* unto hell.

Am 6:6 That drink wine in bowls, and anoint themselves with the chief ointments: but they are not grieved for the affliction of Joseph.

Mi 6:15 Thou shalt sow, but thou shalt not reap; thou shalt tread the olives, but thou shalt not anoint thee with oil; and sweet wine, but shalt not drink wine.

5. As a Remedy

Is 1:6 From the sole of the foot even unto the head *there is* no soundness in it; *but* wounds, and bruises, and putrifying sores: they have not been closed, neither bound up, neither mollified with ointment.

Mk 6:13 And they cast out many devils, and anointed with oil many that were sick, and healed *them.*

Lu 10:34 And went to *him*, and bound up his wounds, pouring in oil and wine, and set him on his own beast, and brought him to an inn, and took care of him.

Ja 5:14 Is any sick among you? let him call for the elders of the church; and let them pray over him, anointing him with oil in the name of the Lord:

Re 3:18 I counsel thee to buy of me gold tried in the fire, that thou mayest be rich; and white raiment, that thou mayest be clothed, and *that* the shame of thy nakedness do not appear; and anoint thine eyes with eyesalve, that thou mayest see.

6. Figurative

2 Co 1:21 Now he which stablisheth us with you in Christ, and hath anointed us, *is* God;

1 Jn 2:20 But ye have an unction from the Holy One, and ye know all things.

1 Jn 2:27 But the anointing which ye have received of him abideth in you, and ye need not that any man teach you: but as the same anointing teacheth you of all things, and is truth, and is no lie, and even as it hath taught you, ye shall abide in him.

ANTICHRIST, *opposer of Christ*

2 Th 2:3 Let no man deceive you by any means: for *that day shall not come,* except there come a falling away first, and that man of sin be revealed, the son of perdition;

1 Jn 2:18 Little children, it is the last time: and as ye have heard that antichrist shall come, even now are there many antichrists; whereby we know that it is the last time.

1 Jn 4:3 And every spirit that confesseth not that Jesus Christ is come in the flesh is not of God: and this is that *spirit* of antichrist, whereof ye have heard that it should come; and even now already is it in the world.

2 Jn 7 For many deceivers are entered into the world, who confess not that Jesus Christ is come in the flesh. This is a deceiver and an antichrist.

See **CHRIST**

ANTIOCH, *cities named after Antiochus, a Syrian king; each founded by Seleucus Nicator (312–280 B.C.)*

This is the name of several ancient cities of the Seleucid kings. This entry discusses the Antioch where the followers of Christ were first called Christians (Ac 11:26). It is located about three hundred miles north of Jerusalem on the west bank of the Orontes River (Antioch of Syria). In ancient times it was called "The Queen of the East" because of the beauty of its surroundings, the importance of its commerce, and its strategic location on intersecting caravan routes.

1. A City in Syria

Ac 6:5; 11:19, 22, 26; 13:1; 14:26; 15:22, 30; 18:22; Ga 2:11

2. A City in Pisidia

Ac 13:14; 14:19; 2 Ti 3:11

ANTS   *See* **INSECTS**

ANXIETY

Lu 12:11–12 And when they bring you unto the synagogues, and *unto* magistrates, and powers, take ye no thought how or what thing ye shall answer, or what ye shall say:

For the Holy Ghost shall teach you in the same hour what ye ought to say.

Lu 12:25 And which of you with taking thought can add to his stature one cubit?

Lu 12:26 If ye then be not able to do that thing which is least, why take ye thought for the rest?

1 Co 7:32 But I would have you without carefulness. He that is unmarried careth for the things that belong to the Lord, how he may please the Lord:

Ph 4:6 Be careful for nothing; but in every thing by prayer and supplication with thanksgiving let your requests be made known unto God.

1 Pe 5:7 Casting all your care upon him; for he careth for you.

APATHY   *See* **INDIFFERENCE**

APES   *See* **ANIMALS**

APOSTASY, *abandonment of one's faith, especially in God*

1. Warnings

Ex 34:15; Le 17:7; 20:5; De 8:19; 31:16, 20; Is 48:8; Je 2:21; Eze 18:24; Mt 24:10; 26:15; Lu 11:26; 14:30; 2 Th 2:3; 1 Ti 1:19; 4:1; 5:12; 2 Ti 4:4; He 3:12; 10:26; 2 Pe 2:21; 3:17

2. Examples

Ex 32:1, 23; De 9:16; 13:13; 17:3; 29:18; 31:29; 32:18; Jud 2:12, 17; 3:6; 5:8; 8:33; 2 Chr 7:22; 24:18; 25:20; 28:23; Ne 9:26; Is 59:13; Je 2:5, 11, 25; 3:8, 20; 7:9; 18:15; 32:33; Eze 5:6; 8:16; 20:32; 23:30, 35; 36:20; 44:10; Ho 2:5, 13; 5:7; 7:13; 9:1; Ac 7:39; 19:13; 2 Ti 4:10; He 6:6; 1 Jn 2:19

3. Reversion to Judaism, *first-century backsliding*

Ac 15:1, 5; 21:24; Ga 2:4, 12, 14; 3:3; 4:9–10, 21; 5:2; 6:12

APOSTLES, *ones sent out*

Lu 17:5 And the apostles said unto the Lord, Increase our faith.

Lu 22:14 And when the hour was come, he sat down, and the twelve apostles with him.

Ac 1:13 And when they were come in, they went up into an upper room, where abode both Peter, and James, and John, and Andrew, Philip, and Thomas, Bartholomew, and Matthew, James *the son* of Alphaeus, and Simon Zelotes, and Judas *the brother* of James.

Ac 1:26 And they gave forth their lots; and the lot fell upon Matthias; and he was numbered with the eleven apostles.

1 Co 4:9 For I think that God hath set forth us the apostles last, as it were appointed to death: for we are made a spectacle unto the world, and to angels, and to men.

1 Co 9:1 Am I not an apostle? am I not free? have I not seen Jesus Christ our Lord? are not ye my work in the Lord?

2 Co 11:5 For I suppose I was not a whit behind the very chiefest apostles.

Ep 2:20 And are built upon the foundation of the apostles and prophets, Jesus Christ himself being the chief corner *stone;*

1. Names

Mt 10:2 Now the names of the twelve apostles are these; The first, Simon, who is called Peter, and Andrew his brother; James *the son* of Zebedee, and John his brother;

Mt 28:16 Then the eleven disciples went away into Galilee, into a mountain where Jesus had appointed them.

Mk 3:16 And Simon he surnamed Peter;

Mk 4:10 And when he was alone, they that were about him with the twelve asked of him the parable.

Mk 6:7 And he called *unto him* the twelve, and began to send them forth by two and two; and gave them power over unclean spirits;

Mk 6:30 And the apostles gathered themselves together unto Jesus, and told him all things, both what they had done, and what they had taught.

Mk 9:35 And he sat down, and called the twelve, and saith unto them, If any man desire to be first, *the same* shall be last of all, and servant of all.

Mk 10:32 And they were in the way going up to Jerusalem; and Jesus went before them: and they were amazed; and as they followed, they were afraid. And he took again the twelve, and began to tell them what things should happen unto him,

Mk 10:46 And they came to Jericho: and as he went out of Jericho with his disciples and a great number of people, blind Bartimaeus, the son of Timaeus, sat by the highway side begging.

Mk 11:11 And Jesus entered into Jerusalem, and into the temple: and when he had looked round about upon all things, and now the eventide was come, he went out unto Bethany with the twelve.

Mk 14:17 And in the evening he cometh with the twelve.

Lu 6:13–14 And when it was day, he called *unto him* his disciples: and of them he chose twelve, whom also he named apostles;

Simon, (whom he also named Peter,) and Andrew his brother, James and John, Philip and Bartholomew,

Lu 8:1 And it came to pass afterward, that he went throughout every city and village, preaching and shewing the glad tidings of the kingdom of God: and the twelve *were* with him,

Lu 9:12 And when the day began to wear away, then came the twelve, and said unto him, Send the multitude away, that they may go into the towns and country round about, and lodge, and get victuals: for we are here in a desert place.

Lu 22:3 Then entered Satan into Judas surnamed Iscariot, being of the number of the twelve.

Lu 22:11 And ye shall say unto the goodman of the house, The Master saith unto thee, Where is the guestchamber, where I shall eat the passover with my disciples?

Jn 2:12 After this he went down to Capernaum, he, and his mother, and his brethren, and his disciples: and they continued there not many days.

Jn 4:8 (For his disciples were gone away unto the city to buy meat.)

Jn 6:3 And Jesus went up into a mountain, and there he sat with his disciples.

Jn 6:67 Then said Jesus unto the twelve, Will ye also go away?

Jn 17:6 I have manifested thy name unto the men which thou gavest me out of the world: thine they were, and thou gavest them me; and they have kept thy word.

Jn 18:1 When Jesus had spoken these words, he went forth with his disciples over the brook Cedron, where was a garden, into the which he entered, and his disciples.

Ac 1:13 And when they were come in, they went up into an upper room, where abode both Peter, and James, and John, and Andrew, Philip, and Thomas, Bartholomew, and Matthew, James *the son* of Alphaeus, and Simon Zelotes, and Judas *the brother* of James.

Ac 5:34 Then stood there up one in the council, a Pharisee, named Gamaliel, a doctor of the law, had in reputation among all the people, and

commanded to put the apostles forth a little space;

Ac 6:2 Then the twelve called the multitude of the disciples *unto them,* and said, It is not reason that we should leave the word of God, and serve tables.

Ac 9:27 But Barnabas took him, and brought *him* to the apostles, and declared unto them how he had seen the Lord in the way, and that he had spoken to him, and how he had preached boldly at Damascus in the name of Jesus.

Ac 11:1 And the apostles and brethren that were in Judaea heard that the Gentiles had also received the word of God.

Ac 15:22 Then pleased it the apostles and elders, with the whole church, to send chosen men of their own company to Antioch with Paul and Barnabas; *namely,* Judas surnamed Barsabas, and Silas, chief men among the brethren:

1 Co 9:5 Have we not power to lead about a sister, a wife, as well as other apostles, and *as* the brethren of the Lord, and Cephas?

1 Co 12:28 And God hath set some in the church, first apostles, secondarily prophets, thirdly teachers, after that miracles, then gifts of healings, helps, governments, diversities of tongues.

1 Co 15:5 And that he was seen of Cephas, then of the twelve:

Ep 2:20 And are built upon the foundation of the apostles and prophets, Jesus Christ himself being the chief corner *stone;*

2 Pe 1:1 Simon Peter, a servant and an apostle of Jesus Christ, to them that have obtained like precious faith with us through the righteousness of God and our Saviour Jesus Christ:

2 Pe 3:2 That ye may be mindful of the words which were spoken before by the holy prophets, and of the commandment of us the apostles of the Lord and Saviour:

Jude 17 But, beloved, remember ye the words which were spoken before of the apostles of our Lord Jesus Christ;

Re 18:20 Rejoice over her, *thou* heaven, and *ye* holy apostles and prophets; for God hath avenged you on her.

Re 21:14 And the wall of the city had twelve foundations, and in them the names of the twelve apostles of the Lamb.

2. Called to Special Work

Is 56:10 His watchmen *are* blind: they are all ignorant, they *are* all dumb dogs, they cannot bark; sleeping, lying down, loving to slumber.

Je 23:1 Woe be unto the pastors that destroy and scatter the sheep of my pasture! saith the LORD.

Eze 3:17 Son of man, I have made thee a watchman unto the house of Israel: therefore hear the word at my mouth, and give them warning from me.

Mk 1:17 And Jesus said unto them, Come ye after me, and I will make you to become fishers of men.

Mk 1:20 And straightway he called them: and they left their father Zebedee in the ship with the hired servants, and went after him.

Mk 2:14 And as he passed by, he saw Levi the *son* of Alphaeus sitting at the receipt of custom, and said unto him, Follow me. And he arose and followed him.

Lu 6:13 And when it was day, he called *unto him* his disciples: and of them he chose twelve, whom also he named apostles;

Jn 1:43 The day following Jesus would go forth into Galilee, and findeth Philip, and saith unto him, Follow me.

Ac 20:17 And from Miletus he sent to Ephesus, and called the elders of the church.

Ac 22:21 And he said unto me, Depart: for I will send thee far hence unto the Gentiles.

1 Co 2:1 And I, brethren, when I came to you, came not with excellency of speech or of wisdom, declaring unto you the testimony of God.

2 Co 6:1 We then, *as* workers together *with him*, beseech *you* also that ye receive not the grace of God in vain.

1 Ti 3:1 This *is* a true saying, If a man desire the office of a bishop, he desireth a good work.

1 Ti 6:11 But thou, O man of God, flee these things; and follow after righteousness, godliness, faith, love, patience, meekness.

2 Ti 2:1 Thou therefore, my son, be strong in the grace that is in Christ Jesus.

2 Ti 4:1 I charge *thee* therefore before God, and the Lord Jesus Christ, who shall judge the quick and the dead at his appearing and his kingdom;

APOTHECARIES *See* ARTS AND CRAFTS

APPAREL

1. Physical

a. Ornaments

Ex 33:4; Is 3:18, 20; Je 2:32; 4:30; Eze 16:11; 23:40; 1 Pe 3:3; Re 18:16

b. Bracelets

Ge 24:22, 30, 47; 38:18; Ex 35:22; Nu 31:50; 2 S 1:10; Is 3:19; Eze 16:11; 23:42

c. Chains as ornaments

Ge 41:42; Jud 8:26; Pr 1:9; Song 1:10; Is 3:19; Eze 16:11; Da 5:7, 16, 29

d. Earrings

Ge 35:4; Ex 32:2; 35:22; Nu 31:50; Jud 8:24; Jb 42:11; Pr 25:12; Eze 16:12; Ho 2:13

e. Rings

Ge 24:22, 30, 47; 41:42; Ex 35:22; Est 3:10; 8:2, 8; Is 3:21; Lu 15:22; Ja 2:2

f. Jewels

Ge 24:53; Ex 3:22; 11:2; 12:35; 35:22; Nu 31:50; 1 S 6:8, 15; Jb 28:17; Pr 11:22; Is 61:10; Eze 16:12

1). Discarded

Ge 35:4; Ex 33:4; 1 Pe 3:3

2). Brought as Offerings to God

Ex 35:22; Nu 31:50

2. Spiritual

Ps 45:13 The king's daughter *is* all glorious within: her clothing *is* of wrought gold.

Pr 1:9 For they *shall be* an ornament of grace unto thy head, and chains about thy neck.

Pr 4:9 She shall give to thine head an ornament of grace: a crown of glory shall she deliver to thee.

Song 1:10 Thy cheeks are comely with rows *of jewels,* thy neck with chains *of gold.*

Is 61:10 I will greatly rejoice in the LORD, my soul shall be joyful in my God; for he hath clothed me with the garments of salvation, he hath covered me with the robe of righteousness, as a bridegroom decketh *himself* with ornaments, and as a bride adorneth *herself* with her jewels.

1 Pe 3:4 But *let it be* the hidden man of the heart, in that which is not corruptible, *even the ornament* of a meek and quiet spirit, which is in the sight of God of great price.

Re 21:2 And I John saw the holy city, new Jerusalem, coming down from God out of heaven, prepared as a bride adorned for her husband.

3. The Robe of Righteousness

2 Chr 6:41 Now therefore arise, O LORD God, into thy resting place, thou, and the ark of thy strength: let thy priests, O LORD God, be clothed with salvation, and let thy saints rejoice in goodness.

Jb 29:14 I put on righteousness, and it clothed me: my judgment *was* as a robe and a diadem.

Ps 132:16 I will also clothe her priests with salvation: and her saints shall shout aloud for joy.

Is 52:1 Awake, awake; put on thy strength, O Zion; put on thy beautiful garments, O Jerusalem, the holy city: for henceforth there shall no more come into thee the uncircumcised and the unclean.

Is 59:17 For he put on righteousness as a breastplate, and an helmet of salvation upon his head; and he put on the garments of vengeance *for* clothing, and was clad with zeal as a cloke.

Is 61:10 I will greatly rejoice in the LORD, my soul shall be joyful in my God; for he hath clothed me with the garments of salvation, he hath covered me with the robe of righteousness, as a bridegroom decketh *himself* with ornaments, and as a bride adorneth *herself* with her jewels.

Eze 16:10 I clothed thee also with broidered work, and shod thee with badgers' skin, and I girded thee about with fine linen, and I covered thee with silk.

Zec 3:4 And he answered and spake unto those that stood before him, saying, Take away the filthy garments from him. And unto him he said, Behold, I have caused thine iniquity to pass from thee, and I will clothe thee with change of raiment.

Mt 22:11 And when the king came in to see the guests, he saw there a man which had not on a wedding garment.

Lu 15:22 But the father said to his servants, Bring forth the best robe, and put *it* on him; and put a ring on his hand, and shoes on *his* feet:

Re 19:8 And to her was granted that she should be arrayed in fine linen, clean and white: for the fine linen is the righteousness of saints.

4. White Raiment

2 Chr 5:12 Also the Levites *which were* the singers, all of them of Asaph, of Heman, of Jeduthun, with their sons and their brethren, *being* arrayed in white linen, having cymbals and psalteries and harps, stood at the east end of the altar, and with them an hundred and twenty priests sounding with trumpets:)

Eze 16:13 Thus wast thou decked with gold and silver; and thy raiment *was of* fine linen, and silk, and broidered work; thou didst eat fine flour, and honey, and oil: and thou wast exceeding beautiful, and thou didst prosper into a kingdom.

Mt 17:2 And was transfigured before them: and his face did shine as the sun, and his raiment was white as the light.

Re 3:5 He that overcometh, the same shall be clothed in white raiment; and I will not blot out his name out of the book of life, but I will confess his name before my Father, and before his angels.

Re 3:18 I counsel thee to buy of me gold tried in the fire, that thou mayest be rich; and white raiment, that thou mayest be clothed, and *that* the shame of thy nakedness do not appear; and anoint thine eyes with eyesalve, that thou mayest see.

Re 4:4 And round about the throne *were* four and twenty seats: and upon the seats I saw four and twenty elders sitting, clothed in white raiment; and they had on their heads crowns of gold.

Re 7:9 After this I beheld, and, lo, a great multitude, which no man could number, of all nations, and kindreds, and people, and tongues, stood before the throne, and before the Lamb, clothed with white robes, and palms in their hands;

Re 7:13 And one of the elders answered, saying unto me, What are these which are arrayed in white robes? and whence came they?

Re 19:8 And to her was granted that she should be arrayed in fine linen, is the righteousness of saints.

See **DRESS**

APPEAL

1. To God

Ge 31:50; De 4:26; 30:19; 31:28; Jud 11:10, 27; 1 S 12:5; Jb 16:19; Je 42:5; Mi 1:2; Mal 2:14; Ro 1:9; 2 Co 1:23; 11:31; 12:19; Ga 1:20; Ph 1:8; 1 Th 2:5

2. Earnest

1 K 22:16; 2 Chr 18:15; Mt 26:63; Mk 5:7; Ac 19:13

APPEARANCES

1. Deceitful

1 S 9:2; 16:6; 2 S 14:25; Mk 11:13

2. Outward

1 S 16:7 But the LORD said unto Samuel, Look not on his countenance, or on the height of his stature; because I have refused him: for *the LORD seeth* not as man seeth; for man looketh on the outward appearance, but the LORD looketh on the heart.

Ps 147:10 He delighteth not in the strength of the horse: he taketh not pleasure in the legs of a man.

Mt 23:27 Woe unto you, scribes and Pharisees, hypocrites! for ye are like unto whited sepulchres, which indeed appear beautiful outward, but are within full of dead *men's* bones, and of all uncleanness.

Jn 7:24 Judge not according to the appearance, but judge righteous judgment.

2 Co 5:12 For we commend not ourselves again unto you, but give you occasion to glory on our behalf, that ye may have somewhat to *answer* them which glory in appearance, and not in heart.

2 Co 10:7 Do ye look on things after the outward appearance? If any man trust to himself that he is Christ's, let him of himself think this again, that, as he *is* Christ's, even so *are* we Christ's.

3. Divine

Ge 12:7 And the LORD appeared unto Abram, and said, Unto thy seed will I give this land: and there builded he an altar unto the LORD, who appeared unto him.

Ge 17:1 And when Abram was ninety years old and nine, the LORD appeared to Abram, and said unto him, I *am* the Almighty God; walk before me, and be thou perfect.

Ge 18:1 And the LORD appeared unto him in the plains of Mamre: and he sat in the tent door in the heat of the day;

Ge 26:2 And the LORD appeared unto him, and said, Go not down into Egypt; dwell in the land which I shall tell thee of:

Ge 35:7 And he built there an altar, and called the place El-beth-el: because there God appeared unto him, when he fled from the face of his brother.

Ge 35:9 And God appeared unto Jacob again, when he came out of Padan-aram, and blessed him.

Ex 3:16 Go, and gather the elders of Israel together, and say unto them, The LORD God of your fathers, the God of Abraham, of Isaac, and of Jacob, appeared unto me, saying, I have surely visited you, and *seen* that which is done to you in Egypt:

1 K 3:5 In Gibeon the LORD appeared to Solomon in a dream by night: and God said, Ask what I shall give thee.

1 K 9:2 That the LORD appeared to Solomon the second time, as he had appeared unto him at Gibeon.

1 K 11:9 And the LORD was angry with Solomon, because his heart was turned from the LORD God of Israel, which had appeared unto him twice,

2 Chr 3:1 Then Solomon began to build the house of the LORD at Jerusalem in mount Moriah, where *the LORD* appeared unto David his father, in the place that David had prepared in the threshingfloor of Ornan the Jebusite.

Mi 1:3 For, behold, the LORD cometh forth out of his place, and will come down, and tread upon the high places of the earth.

Hab 3:3 God came from Teman, and the Holy One from mount Paran. Selah. His glory covered the heavens, and the earth was full of his praise.

Ac 7:2 And he said, Men, brethren, and fathers, hearken; The God of glory appeared unto our father Abraham, when he was in Mesopotamia, before he dwelt in Charran,

APPETITE *See* **DISEASE**

APPLE *See* **TREES**

APPOLLOS, *an eloquent Jew of Alexandria, who preached Christ with great zeal and power*

MIGHTY IN THE SCRIPTURES

Ac 18:24–25 And a certain Jew named Apollos, born at Alexandria, an eloquent man, *and* mighty in the scriptures, came to Ephesus. This man

was instructed in the way of the Lord; and being fervent in the spirit, he spake and taught diligently the things of the Lord, knowing only the baptism of John.

INSTRUCTED BY AQUILA AND PRISCILLA

Ac 18:26 And he began to speak boldly in the synagogue: whom when Aquila and Priscilla had heard, they took him unto *them,* and expounded unto him the way of God more perfectly.

POPULAR IN CORINTH

1 Co 1:11–12 For it hath been declared unto me of you, my brethren, by them *which are of the house* of Chloe, that there are contentions among you. Now this I say, that every one of you saith, I am of Paul; and I of Apollos; and I of Cephas; and I of Christ.

1 Co 3:4–6 For while one saith, I am of Paul; and another, I *am* of Apollos; are ye not carnal? Who then is Paul, and who *is* Apollos, but ministers by whom ye believed, even as the Lord gave to every man? I have planted, Apollos watered; but God gave the increase.

HESITATED TO RETURN TO CORINTH

1 Co 16:12 As touching *our* brother Apollos, I greatly desired him to come unto you with the brethren: but his will was not at all to come at this time; but he will come when he shall have convenient time.

APRON, *a garment worn over the front part of the body*

Ge 3:7; Ac 19:12

AQUILA AND PRISCILLA, *coworkers with Paul*

Ac 18:2, 18, 26; Ro 16:3; 1 Co 16:19; 2 Ti 4:19

ARABIANS, *descendants of Ishmael*

Ge 25:13; 2 Chr 9:14; 17:11; 22:1; 26:7; Ne 2:19; 4:7; 6:1; Eze 27:21; Ac 2:11

ARARAT

ARARAT, *mountain in Armenia*
Ge 8:4; Je 51:27

See **MOUNTAINS AND HILLS**

ARBITRATION   See **COURTS**

ARCHANGEL, *ruling angel, identified by Jude as Michael*
1 Th 4:16; Jude 9

ARCHERS, *those shooting with bows and arrows*
Ge 21:20; 1 S 31:3; 1 Chr 8:40; 10:3; 2 Chr 35:23

ARISTARCHUS, *a fellow worker of Paul*
Ac 19:29; 20:4; 27:2; Col 4:10; Phm 24

ARK

1. Noah's
Ge 6:14; 7:1, 18; 8:1, 4, 16; Mt 24:38; Lu 17:27; He 11:7; 1 Pe 3:20

See **DELUGE**

2. Of Bulrushes
Ex 2:3

3. Of the Covenant
Ex 25:10 And they shall make an ark *of* shittim wood: two cubits and a half *shall be* the length thereof, and a cubit and a half the breadth thereof, and a cubit and a half the height thereof.

Ex 25:16 And thou shalt put into the ark the testimony which I shall give thee.

Ex 26:33 And thou shalt hang up the vail under the taches, that thou mayest bring in thither within the vail the ark of the testimony: and the vail shall divide unto you between the holy *place* and the most holy.

Ex 30:26 And thou shalt anoint the tabernacle of the congregation therewith, and the ark of the testimony,

Ex 37:1 And Bezaleel made the ark *of* shittim wood: two cubits and a half *was* the length of it, and a cubit and a half the breadth of it, and a cubit and a half the height of it:

Nu 4:5 And when the camp setteth forward, Aaron shall come, and his sons, and they shall take down the covering vail, and cover the ark of testimony with it:

Nu 10:35 And it came to pass, when the ark set forward, that Moses said, Rise up, LORD, and let thine enemies be scattered; and let them that hate thee flee before thee.

De 10:8 At that time the LORD separated the tribe of Levi, to bear the ark of the covenant of the LORD, to stand before the LORD to minister unto him, and to bless in his name, unto this day.

De 31:26 Take this book of the law, and put it in the side of the ark of the covenant of the LORD your God, that it may be there for a witness against thee.

Jos 3:15 And as they that bare the ark were come unto Jordan, and the feet of the priests that bare the ark were dipped in the brim of the water, (for Jordan overfloweth all his banks all the time of harvest,)

Jos 4:11 And it came to pass, when all the people were clean passed over, that the ark of the LORD passed over, and the priests, in the presence of the people.

Jos 6:11 So the ark of the LORD compassed the city, going about *it* once: and they came into the camp, and lodged in the camp.

Jos 7:6 And Joshua rent his clothes, and fell to the earth upon his face before the ark of the LORD until the eventide, he and the elders of Israel, and put dust upon their heads.

Jud 20:27 And the children of Israel enquired of the LORD, (for the ark of the covenant of God *was* there in those days,

1 S 4:3 And when the people were come into the camp, the elders of Israel said, Wherefore hath the LORD smitten us to day before the Philistines? Let us fetch the ark of the covenant of the LORD out of Shiloh unto us, that, when it cometh among us, it may save us out of the hand of our enemies.

1 S 4:11 And the ark of God was taken; and the two sons of Eli, Hophni and Phinehas, were slain.

1 S 4:18 And it came to pass, when he made mention of the ark of God, that he fell from off the seat backward by the side of the gate, and his neck brake, and he died: for he was an old man, and heavy. And he had judged Israel forty years.

1 S 5:1 And the Philistines took the ark of God, and brought it from Ebenezer unto Ashdod.

1 S 6:1 And the ark of the LORD was in the country of the Philistines seven months.

1 S 7:1 And the men of Kirjath-jearim came, and brought up the ark of the LORD, and brought it into the house of Abinadab in the hill, and sanctified Eleazar his son to keep the ark of the LORD.

1 S 14:18 And Saul said unto Ahiah, Bring hither the ark of God. For the ark of God was at that time with the children of Israel.

2 S 6:2 And David arose, and went with all the people that *were* with him from Baale of Judah, to bring up from thence the ark of God, whose name is called by the name of the LORD of hosts that dwelleth *between* the cherubims.

2 S 6:6 And when they came to Nachon's threshingfloor, Uzzah put forth *his hand* to the ark of God, and took hold of it; for the oxen shook *it*.

2 S 6:11 And the ark of the LORD continued in the house of Obed-edom the Gittite three months: and the LORD blessed Obed-edom, and all his household.

2 S 6:17 And they brought in the ark of the LORD, and set it in his place, in the midst of the tabernacle that David had pitched for it: and David offered burnt offerings and peace offerings before the LORD.

2 S 15:24 And lo Zadok also, and all the Levites *were* with him, bearing the ark of the covenant of God: and they set down the ark of God; and Abiathar went up, until all the people had done passing out of the city.

1 K 8:6 And the priests brought in the ark of the covenant of the LORD unto his place, into the oracle of the house, to the most holy *place, even* under the wings of the cherubims.

1 K 8:9 *There was* nothing in the ark save the two tables of stone, which Moses put there at Horeb, when the LORD made *a covenant* with the children of Israel, when they came out of the land of Egypt.

1 Chr 6:31 And these *are they* whom David set over the service of song in the house of the LORD, after that the ark had rest.

1 Chr 16:1 So they brought the ark of God, and set it in the midst of the tent that David had pitched for it: and they offered burnt sacrifices and peace offerings before God.

1 Chr 16:37 So he left there before the ark of the covenant of the LORD Asaph and his brethren, to minister before the ark continually, as every day's work required:

2 Chr 5:5 And they brought up the ark, and the tabernacle of the congregation, and all the holy vessels that *were* in the tabernacle, these did the priests and the Levites bring up.

2 Chr 35:3 And said unto the Levites that taught all Israel, which were holy unto the LORD, Put the holy ark in the house which Solomon the son of David king of Israel did build; *it shall not be* a burden upon *your* shoulders: serve now the LORD your God, and his people Israel,

Je 3:16 And it shall come to pass, when ye be multiplied and increased in the land, in those days, saith the LORD, they shall say no more, The ark of the covenant of the LORD: neither shall it come to mind: neither shall they remember it; neither shall they visit *it;* neither shall *that* be done any more.

He 9:4 Which had the golden censer, and the ark of the covenant overlaid round about with gold, wherein *was* the golden pot that had manna, and Aaron's rod that budded, and the tables of the covenant;

Re 11:19 And the temple of God was opened in heaven, and there was seen in his temple the ark of his testament: and there were lightnings, and voices, and thunderings, and an earthquake, and great hail.

ARM

1. Divine, Powerful

Ex 6:6; 15:16; De 4:34; 5:15; 7:19; 9:29; 11:2; 26:8; 33:27; 1 K 8:42; 2 K 17:36; 2 Chr 6:32; Jb 40:9; Ps 44:3; 77:15; 89:10, 13; 98:1; 136:12; Is 30:30; 33:2; 51:5; 52:10; 53:1; 59:16; 62:8; 63:5, 12; Je 21:5; 27:5; 32:17, 21; Eze 20:34; Lu 1:51; Ac 13:17

2. Everlasting

De 33:27; Is 46:4; Mk 10:16

See **POWER**

ARMAGEDDON

Re 16:16

ARMENIA, *a country east of Asia Minor*

2 K 19:37; Is 37:38; Je 51:27

ARMOUR, *to protect the body in war*

1 S 17:5, 38; 31:9; 2 S 2:21; 2 K 3:21; Eze 38:4; Lu 11:22

See **SHIELDS**

ARMOURBEARERS, *people selected by prominent officers to carry armour, stand by in danger, and carry out orders*

Jud 9:54; 1 S 14:1, 7, 14; 16:21; 17:7; 31:4; 2 S 23:37; 1 Chr 10:4; 11:39

ARMY *See* WAR

ARNON, *a river east of Jordan*

Nu 21:13, 26; 22:36; De 2:24, 36; 3:8; 4:48; Jos 12:1; 13:9, 16; Jud 11:13, 18

See **RIVERS**

ARROGANCE, *haughtiness*

1 S 2:3; 2 S 3:8; 1 K 12:14; 2 K 18:20, 33; 2 Chr 10:14; 32:14; Ps 12:4; 17:10; 73:8; 94:4; Pr 8:13; 21:24; Is 13:11; 37:12; Je 48:29; Da 3:15; Jn 5:12; 7:48; 9:34; 18:35; 19:10

See **PRIDE**

ARROWS

1. Physical

1 S 20:20, 37; 2 K 13:15; 1 Chr 12:2; Jb 41:28; Je 51:11; Eze 39:9

2. Spiritual

De 32:23, 42; 2 S 22:15; Jb 6:4; 16:13; Ps 7:13; 18:14; 21:12; 38:2; 45:5; 64:7; 77:17; 144:6; Je 50:25; Lam 2:4; 3:13; Eze 5:16; Hab 3:11; Zec 9:14

See **JUDGMENTS**

ARTS AND CRAFTS, *skills used for economic, cultural, and religious purposes*

a. Apothecaries (perfumers)

Ex 30:25, 35; 37:29; 2 Chr 16:14; Ne 3:8

b. Bakers

Ge 18:6; Ge 40:1, 16; 41:10; Ex 16:23; Le 2:4; 6:21; 26:26; Nu 11:8; 1 S 8:13; 1 S 28:24; 2 S 13:8; 1 K 19:6; Is 44:15; Je 37:21; Ho 7:4

c. Baking

d. Barbers

Is 7:20; Eze 5:1

e. Boatbuilders

1 K 9:7

f. Braziers

Ge 4:22

g. Brickmakers

Ge 11:3; Ex 5:7

h. Calkers

Eze 27:9

i. Carpenters

2 S 5:11; 2 K 12:11; 22:6; 1 Chr 14:1; 2 Chr 24:12; Is 41:7; 44:13; Je 24:1; 29:2; Zec 1:20; Mt 13:55; Mk 6:3

j. Carvers

Ex 31:5; 35:33; 1 K 6:18, 29; Ps 74:6

k. Confectioners, *blenders of candies and preserves, spices, and medicines*

1 S 8:13

l. Coppersmiths
2 Ti 4:14

m. Dyers, those who color cloth
Ex 25:5; 26:14; Eze 23:15

n. Embalmers
See **DEATH**

o. Embroiderers
Ex 26:1, 36; 28:6, 39; 35:35; 36:37;
38:18, 23; 39:29; Ps 45:14; Eze 27:7, 16

p. Engravers
Ex 28:11, 21, 36; 35:35; 38:23; 39:6, 14,
30; 2 Chr 2:7, 14; Zec 3:9; 2 Co 3:7

q. Fishermen
Mt 4:18; Mk 1:16; Lu 5:2

r. Founders
Jud 17:4

*s. Fullers, cleaners or dyers of cloth or
garments*
2 K 18:17; Mk 9:3

t. Gardeners
Je 29:5; Jn 20:15

u. Goldsmiths
2 Chr 2:7, 14; Ne 3:8, 31; Is 40:19; 41:7;
46:6

v. Masons
2 K 12:12; 22:6; 1 Chr 14:1; 22:2; 2 Chr
24:12; Ezr 3:7

w. Masterworkers
1 Co 3:10

x. Molders of metals
Ex 32:4; 1 K 7:15, 23; 2 Chr 4:17

y. Needleworkers
Ex 26:36; 28:39; Jud 5:30; Ps 45:14

z. Painters
Je 22:14

aa. Porters, door or gate keepers
2 S 18:26; 2 K 7:11; 1 Chr 9:17, 22;
15:18; 16:42; 23:5; 26:1, 12, 19; 2 Chr

8:14; 23:4, 19; 31:14; 35:15; Ezr 2:42,
70; 7:7, 24; 10:24; Ne 7:1, 45, 73; 10:28;
11:19; 12:25, 45; 13:5

bb. Potters
Is 64:8; Je 18:2; Ro 9:21; Re 2:27

cc. Refiners of metals
1 Chr 28:18; Mal 3:2, 3

dd. Sewers
Ge 3:7; Ec 3:7; Eze 13:18; Mk 2:21

ee. Silversmiths
Jud 17:4; Ac 19:24

ff. Smelters
Jb 28:2

gg. Smiths, workers in metals
1 S 13:19; 2 K 24:14; Is 44:12; 54:16; Je
24:1; 29:2

*hh. Spinners, producers of yarn at a
spindle*
Ex 35:25; Pr 31:19

ii. Stonecutters
Ex 31:5; 1 Chr 22:15

jj. Tailors
Ex 28:3

kk. Tanners
Ac 9:43

ll. Tentmakers
Ac 18:3; 1 Th 2:9

mm. Weavers
Ex 28:32; 35:35; 2 K 23:7; Is 19:9

nn. Workers in metals
Ex 31:4; 1 Chr 22:15–16; Is 40:19

ASA, *king of Judah, son of Abijah*
1 K 15:8, 16; 16:8, 15, 23, 29; 22:43;
2 Chr 14:2, 13; 16:7, 13; Je 41:9; Mt 1:8
See **ISRAEL**

ASAHEL, *brother of Joab*
2 S 2:18, 23; 3:27; 23:24; 1 Chr 11:26;
27:7

ASAPH, *a musician*

1 Chr 6:39; 9:15; 15:17; 16:5; 25:1; 26:1; 2 Chr 5:12; 20:14; 29:13; 35:15; Ezr 2:41; Ne 7:44; 11:22; 12:35, 46

ASCENSION *See* **CHRIST**

ASCETICISM, *philosophy that teaches that one can reach a higher spiritual state through extreme self-denial and self-discipline*

Mt 3:4; 9:14; 11:18; 19:12; Mk 1:6; 2:18; Lu 1:80; 5:33; 7:25, 33; Col 2:23; 1 Ti 4:3

1. Exemplified in Celibacy

Je 16:2; Mt 19:10; 1 Co 7:8, 27, 38; 1 Ti 4:3; Re 14:4

2. Practiced by the Nazarites

Nu 6:2–3, 13, 20; Jud 13:5, 7; 16:17; 1 S 1:11; Lam 4:7; Am 2:11; Lu 1:15; Ac 21:24

ASH *See* **TREES**

ASHDOD, *or Azotus, a city of the Philistines*

The military pride of the Philistines, this city was located on a low rounded hill nine miles north of ancient Ashkelon and three and a half miles southeast of the modern Jewish city of Ashdod. The mound occupies an area of more than 120 acres, which consists of a well-defined acropolis and a lower city. When the Philistines captured the ark of the covenant of the Lord, they brought it here and placed it in the house (temple) of Dagon. The next morning the people were deeply impressed when they found Dagon fallen upon his face before the ark of God (1 S 5:1–5). Isaiah reports (Is 20:1) that Sargon the king of Assyria sent his army commander (the Tartan) to take the city of Ashdod in 713 B.C.

Jos 11:22; 1 S 5:1; 6:17; 2 Chr 26:6; Ne 4:7; 13:23; Is 20:1; Je 25:20; Am 1:8; 3:9; Zep 2:4; Zec 9:6

ASHER, *son of Jacob*

Ge 30:13; 35:26; 46:17; 49:20; Nu 1:13, 40; 2:27; 10:26; 13:13; 26:44; 34:27; De 33:24; Jos 17:10; 19:24, 31, 34; 21:6, 30;

Jud 1:31; 5:17; 6:35; 1 Chr 6:62, 74; 7:30; 2 Chr 30:11; Eze 48:3, 34; Re 7:6

ASHES, *of burnt offerings*

Le 4:12; 6:11; Nu 19:9; He 9:13

ASHKELON, *or Askelon, a city of the Philistines*

Jud 1:18; 14:19; 1 S 6:17; 2 S 1:20; Je 25:20; 47:5; Am 1:8; Zep 2:4; Zec 9:5

ASHTAROTH, *common name in various forms among many ancient Middle Eastern peoples for a mother goddess of fertility, love, and war*

1. City of Bashan

De 1:4; Jos 9:10; 12:4; 13:12, 31; 1 Chr 6:71

2. Or Ashtoreth, *a heathen goddess*

See **GODS, WORSHIP**

ASIA, *a district of Asia Minor*

Ac 2:9; 6:9; 16:6; 19:10, 22, 27; 20:4, 16; 21:27; 27:2; 1 Co 16:19; 2 Co 1:8; 2 Ti 1:15; 1 Pe 1:1; Re 1:11

ASPS

De 32:33; Jb 20:16; Is 11:8; Ro 3:13

See **REPTILES**

ASSASSINATION *See* **NATION**

ASSAULT

Ex 21:15, 18–19, 22–27, De 17:8; Mt 5:39

ASSEMBLY, *the meeting of the early Christians*

De 31:12; Ps 111:1; Mt 18:20; Lu 24:33; Jn 20:19; Ac 1:4, 14; 2:1; 4:31; 14:27; 15:25; 16:13; 20:7; 28:23; 1 Co 5:4; 11:33; 14:23; Ja 2:2

ASSOCIATIONS, *EVIL, relationships contrary to God's revealed will*

1. Warnings

Ex 23:2 Thou shalt not follow a multitude to *do* evil; neither shalt thou speak in a cause to decline after many to wrest *judgment*:

Ex 23:33 They shall not dwell in thy land, lest they make thee sin against me: for if thou serve their gods, it will surely be a snare unto thee.

Ex 34:12 Take heed to thyself, lest thou make a covenant with the inhabitants of the land whither thou goest, lest it be for a snare in the midst of thee:

Jud 14:11 And it came to pass, when they saw him, that they brought thirty companions to be with him.

2 Chr 18:2 And after *certain* years he went down to Ahab to Samaria. And Ahab killed sheep and oxen for him in abundance, and for the people that *he had* with him, and persuaded him to go up *with him* to Ramoth-gilead.

Jb 34:8 Which goeth in company with the workers of iniquity, and walketh with wicked men.

Ps 1:1 Blessed *is* the man that walketh not in the counsel of the ungodly, nor standeth in the way of sinners, nor sitteth in the seat of the scornful.

Ps 26:5 I have hated the congregation of evildoers; and will not sit with the wicked.

Pr 1:15 My son, walk not thou in the way with them; refrain thy foot from their path:

Pr 4:14 Enter not into the path of the wicked, and go not in the way of evil *men.*

Pr 22:24 Make no friendship with an angry man; and with a furious man thou shalt not go:

Pr 23:6 Eat thou not the bread of *him that hath* an evil eye, neither desire thou his dainty meats:

Pr 24:1 Be not thou envious against evil men, neither desire to be with them.

1 Co 5:9 I wrote unto you in an epistle not to company with fornicators:

2 Co 6:14 Be ye not unequally yoked together with unbelievers: for what fellowship hath righteousness with unrighteousness? and what communion hath light with darkness?

2 Jn 10 If there come any unto you, and bring not this doctrine, receive him not into *your* house, neither bid him God speed:

2. Results

MISERY

Nu 33:55 But if ye will not drive out the inhabitants of the land from before you; then it shall come to pass, that those which ye let remain of them *shall be* pricks in your eyes, and thorns in your sides, and shall vex you in the land wherein ye dwell.

Jud 16:4 And it came to pass afterward, that he loved a woman in the valley of Sorek, whose name *was* Delilah.

APOSTASY

1 K 11:2 Of the nations *concerning* which the LORD said unto the children of Israel, Ye shall not go in to them, neither shall they come in unto you: *for* surely they will turn away your heart after their gods: Solomon clave unto these in love.

DIVINE WRATH

2 Chr 19:2 And Jehu the son of Hanani the seer went out to meet him, and said to king Jehoshaphat, Shouldest thou help the ungodly, and love them that hate the LORD? therefore is wrath upon thee from before the LORD.

Ezr 9:14 Should we again break thy commandments, and join in affinity with the people of these abominations? wouldest not thou be angry with us till thou hadst consumed *us,* so that *there should be* no remnant nor escaping?

Pr 13:20 He that walketh with wise *men* shall be wise: but a companion of fools shall be destroyed.

PARENTAL SHAME

Pr 28:7 Whoso keepeth the law *is* a wise son: but he that is a companion of riotous *men* shameth his father.

DENIAL OF CHRIST

Jn 18:17 Then saith the damsel that kept the door unto Peter, Art not thou also *one* of this man's disciples? He saith, I am not.

Jn 18:25 And Simon Peter stood and warmed himself. They said therefore unto him, Art not thou also *one* of his disciples? He denied *it,* and said, I am not.

DEFILEMENT

1 Co 15:33 Be not deceived: evil communications corrupt good manners.

See **ALLIANCES, EVIL, SEPARATION**

ASSURANCE, *SPIRITUAL*

Col 2:2 That their hearts might be comforted, being knit together in love, and unto all riches of the full assurance of understanding, to the acknowledgement of the mystery of God, and of the Father, and of Christ;

1 Th 1:5 For our gospel came not unto you in word only, but also in power, and in the Holy Ghost, and in much assurance; as ye know what manner of men we were among you for your sake.

2 Ti 1:12 For the which cause I also suffer these things: nevertheless I am not ashamed: for I know whom I have believed, and am persuaded that he is able to keep that which I have committed unto him against that day.

He 10:22 Let us draw near with a true heart in full assurance of faith, having our hearts sprinkled from an evil conscience, and our bodies washed with pure water.

1 Jn 2:3 And hereby we do know that we know him, if we keep his commandments.

1 Jn 3:19 And hereby we know that we are of the truth, and shall assure our hearts before him.

1 Jn 4:13 Hereby know we that we dwell in him, and he in us, because he hath given us of his Spirit.

1 Jn 5:10 He that believeth on the Son of God hath the witness in himself: he that believeth not God hath made him a liar; because he believeth not the record that God gave of his Son.

See **SECURITY**

ASSYRIA, *kingdom founded by Asshur and Nimrod*

Ge 2:14; 10:11; 25:18; 2 K 15:19; 17:3, 6, 23; 18:9; 1 Chr 5:26; 2 Chr 30:6; Ps 83:8; Is 7:20; 10:5; 14:25; 19:23; 30:31; 31:8; 36:1; Eze 23:12; 31:3; Je 50:17; Mi 5:6

ASTONISHMENT, *surprise*

1 S 10:11 And it came to pass, when all that knew him beforetime saw that, behold, he prophesied among the prophets, then the people said one to another, What *is* this *that* is come unto the son of Kish? *Is* Saul also among the prophets?

Is 52:14 As many were astonied at thee; his visage was so marred more than any man, and his form more than the sons of men:

Da 3:24 Then Nebuchadnezzar the king was astonied, and rose up in haste, *and* spake, and said unto his counsellors, Did not we cast three men bound into the midst of the fire? They answered and said unto the king, True, O king.

Mt 7:28 And it came to pass, when Jesus had ended these sayings, the people were astonished at his doctrine:

Mt 8:27 But the men marvelled, saying, What manner of man is this, that even the winds and the sea obey him!

Mt 9:8 But when the multitudes saw *it,* they marvelled, and glorified God, which had given such power unto men.

Mt 9:33 And when the devil was cast out, the dumb spake: and the multitudes marvelled, saying, It was never so seen in Israel.

Mt 12:23 And all the people were amazed, and said, Is not this the son of David?

Mt 13:54 And when he was come into his own country, he taught them in their synagogue, insomuch that they were astonished, and said, Whence hath this *man* this wisdom, and *these* mighty works?

Mt 15:31 Insomuch that the multitude wondered, when they saw the dumb to speak, the maimed to be whole, the lame to walk, and the blind to see: and they glorified the God of Israel.

Mt 19:25 When his disciples heard *it,* they were exceedingly amazed, saying, Who then can be saved?

Mt 21:20 And when the disciples saw *it,* they marvelled, saying, How soon is the fig tree withered away!

Mt 22:22 When they had heard *these words,* they marvelled, and left him, and went their way.

Mt 22:33 And when the multitude heard *this,* they were astonished at his doctrine.

Mt 27:14 And he answered him to never a word; insomuch that the governor marvelled greatly.

Mk 1:22 And they were astonished at his doctrine: for he taught them as one that had authority, and not as the scribes.

Mk 1:27 And they were all amazed, insomuch that they questioned among themselves, saying, What thing is this? what new doctrine *is* this? for with authority commandeth he even the unclean spirits, and they do obey him.

Mk 2:12 And immediately he arose, took up the bed, and went forth before them all; insomuch that they were all amazed, and glorified God, saying, We never saw it on this fashion.

Mk 4:41 And they feared exceedingly, and said one to another, What manner of man is this, that even the wind and the sea obey him?

Mk 5:20 And he departed, and began to publish in Decapolis how great things Jesus had done for him: and all *men* did marvel.

Mk 5:42 And straightway the damsel arose, and walked; for she was *of the age* of twelve years. And they were astonished with a great astonishment.

Mk 6:2 And when the sabbath day was come, he began to teach in the synagogue: and many hearing *him* were astonished, saying, From whence hath this *man* these things? and what wisdom *is* this which is given unto him, that even such mighty works are wrought by his hands?

Mk 6:51 And he went up unto them into the ship; and the wind ceased: and they were sore amazed in themselves beyond measure, and wondered.

Mk 7:37 And were beyond measure astonished, saying, He hath done all things well: he maketh both the deaf to hear, and the dumb to speak.

Mk 10:24 And the disciples were astonished at his words. But Jesus answereth again, and saith unto them, Children, how hard is it for them that trust in riches to enter into the kingdom of God!

Mk 10:26 And they were astonished out of measure, saying among themselves, Who then can be saved?

Mk 11:18 And the scribes and chief priests heard *it,* and sought how they might destroy him: for they feared him, because all the people was astonished at his doctrine.

Mk 12:17 And Jesus answering said unto them, Render to Caesar the things that are Caesar's, and to God the things that are God's. And they marvelled at him.

Mk 15:5 But Jesus yet answered nothing; so that Pilate marvelled.

Mk 16:8 And they went out quickly, and fled from the sepulchre; for they trembled and were amazed: neither said they any thing to any *man;* for they were afraid.

Lu 2:18 And all they that heard *it* wondered at those things which were told them by the shepherds.

Lu 2:33 And Joseph and his mother marvelled at those things which were spoken of him.

Lu 2:48 And when they saw him, they were amazed: and his mother said unto him, Son, why hast thou thus dealt with us? behold, thy father and I have sought thee sorrowing.

Lu 4:22 And all bare him witness, and wondered at the gracious words which proceeded out of his mouth. And they said, Is not this Joseph's son?

Lu 4:32 And they were astonished at his doctrine: for his word was with power.

Lu 4:36 And they were all amazed, and spake among themselves, saying,

What a word *is* this! for with authority and power he commandeth the unclean spirits, and they come out.

Lu 5:9 For he was astonished, and all that were with him, at the draught of the fishes which they had taken:

Lu 5:26 And they were all amazed, and they glorified God, and were filled with fear, saying, We have seen strange things to day.

Lu 8:25 And he said unto them, Where is your faith? And they being afraid wondered, saying one to another, What manner of man is this! for he commandeth even the winds and water, and they obey him.

Lu 8:56 And her parents were astonished: but he charged them that they should tell no man what was done.

Lu 9:43 And they were all amazed at the mighty power of God. But while they wondered every one at all things which Jesus did, he said unto his disciples,

Lu 11:14 And he was casting out a devil, and it was dumb. And it came to pass, when the devil was gone out, the dumb spake; and the people wondered.

Lu 18:26 And they that heard *it* said, Who then can be saved?

Lu 20:26 And they could not take hold of his words before the people: and they marvelled at his answer, and held their peace.

Lu 24:12 Then arose Peter, and ran unto the sepulchre; and stooping down, he beheld the linen clothes laid by themselves, and departed, wondering in himself at that which was come to pass.

Jn 4:27 And upon this came his disciples, and marvelled that he talked with the woman: yet no man said, What seekest thou? or, Why talkest thou with her?

Jn 5:20 For the Father loveth the Son, and sheweth him all things that himself doeth: and he will shew him greater works than these, that ye may marvel.

Jn 7:15 And the Jews marvelled, saying, How knoweth this man letters, having never learned?

Jn 7:21 Jesus answered and said unto them, I have done one work, and ye all marvel.

Jn 9:8 The neighbours therefore, and they which before had seen him that he was blind, said, Is not this he that sat and begged?

Jn 9:30 The man answered and said unto them, Why herein is a marvellous thing, that ye know not from whence he is, and *yet* he hath opened mine eyes.

Ac 2:7 And they were all amazed and marvelled, saying one to another, Behold, are not all these which speak Galilaeans?

Ac 2:12 And they were all amazed, and were in doubt, saying one to another, What meaneth this?

Ac 3:10 And they knew that it was he which sat for alms at the Beautiful gate of the temple: and they were filled with wonder and amazement at that which had happened unto him.

Ac 8:13 Then Simon himself believed also: and when he was baptized, he continued with Philip, and wondered, beholding the miracles and signs which were done.

Ac 9:6 And he trembling and astonished said, Lord, what wilt thou have me to do? And the Lord *said* unto him, Arise, and go into the city, and it shall be told thee what thou must do.

Ac 10:45 And they of the circumcision which believed were astonished, as many as came with Peter, because that on the Gentiles also was poured out the gift of the Holy Ghost.

Ac 12:16 But Peter continued knocking: and when they had opened *the door*, and saw him, they were astonished.

ATHALIAH, *a wicked queen*

2 K 8:26; 11:1, 3, 13, 16; 2 Chr 22:2; 23:12, 21

See **ISRAEL**

ATHEISM, *denial of the existence of God*

2 K 18:30 Neither let Hezekiah make you trust in the Lord, saying, The Lord will surely deliver us, and this city shall not be delivered into the hand of the king of Assyria.

2 K 18:35 Who *are* they among all the gods of the countries, that have delivered their country out of mine hand, that the LORD should deliver Jerusalem out of mine hand?

2 K 19:10 Thus shall ye speak to Hezekiah king of Judah, saying, Let not thy God in whom thou trustest deceive thee, saying, Jerusalem shall not be delivered into the hand of the king of Assyria.

Jb 31:28 This also *were* an iniquity *to be punished by* the judge: for I should have denied the God *that is* above.

Ps 10:4 The wicked, through the pride of his countenance, will not seek *after God:* God *is* not in all his thoughts.

Ps 14:1 The fool hath said in his heart, *There is* no God. They are corrupt, they have done abominable works, *there is* none that doeth good.

Ps 36:1 The transgression of the wicked saith within my heart, *that there is* no fear of God before his eyes.

Ps 42:10 *As* with a sword in my bones, mine enemies reproach me; while they say daily unto me, Where *is* thy God?

Ps 53:1 To the chief Musician upon Mahalath, Maschil, A *Psalm* of David. The fool hath said in his heart, *There is* no God. Corrupt are they, and have done abominable iniquity: *there is* none that doeth good.

Ps 94:7 Yet they say, The LORD shall not see, neither shall the God of Jacob regard *it.*

Ps 115:2 Wherefore should the heathen say, Where *is* now their God?

Pr 30:9 Lest I be full, and deny *thee,* and say, Who *is* the LORD? or lest I be poor, and steal, and take the name of my God *in vain.*

Is 29:15 Woe unto them that seek deep to hide their counsel from the LORD, and their works are in the dark, and they say, Who seeth us? and who knoweth us?

Is 36:18 *Beware* lest Hezekiah persuade you, saying, The LORD will deliver us. Hath any of the gods of the nations delivered his land out of the hand of the king of Assyria?

Je 5:12 They have belied the LORD, and said, *It is* not he; neither shall evil come upon us; neither shall we see sword nor famine:

Eze 8:13 He said also unto me, Turn thee yet again, *and* thou shalt see greater abominations that they do.

Mi 7:10 Then *she that is* mine enemy shall see *it,* and shame shall cover her which said unto me, Where is the LORD thy God? mine eyes shall behold her: now shall she be trodden down as the mire of the streets.

Ro 1:28 And even as they did not like to retain God in *their* knowledge, God gave them over to a reprobate mind, to do those things which are not convenient;

1 Jn 2:22 Who is a liar but he that denieth that Jesus is the Christ? He is antichrist, that denieth the Father and the Son.

See **DESPISERS, GODLESSNESS, SCOFFERS**

ATHENS, *a city in Greece*

One of the greatest cultural centers of Paul's day, it grew up around a 520-foot-high rocky plateau called the Acropolis. On this elevated area stood the many columned Parthenon (a widely famous architectural wonder) and so many other sacred edifices that the place was called "the many-templed Acropolis." To the north of the Acropolis was the celebrated civic center and marketplace, known as the Agora, where people not only traded, but also visited and discussed questions of interest at the time. To the northwest there extended out from the Acropolis, on a somewhat lower level, a rocky hill called the Areopagus (Hill of Ares) or Mars' Hill. Here the councils and the High Court met, although the actual site of the council meetings has been increasingly questioned.

Both of these well-known places were familiar to Paul. In the marketplace he reasoned with those who happened to be present, among whom were some Stoics and Epicureans. They regarded him with curiosity as "a proclaimer of strange deities" (Ac 17:17–18). So they brought him up the hill to speak before an informal session of the supreme court. Standing in the midst of the Areopagus before these well-educated Greeks and Romans, Paul took as his topic "the unknown God" and delivered one of the most dynamic messages of all time. Some mocked, some were deeply impressed and wanted to hear more, while others were converted then and there (Ac 17:22–34; cf. 1 Th 3:1).

ATONEMENT, *the covering over of sin, accomplished through the work of Christ on the Cross*

1. Doctrine

Ex 30:15 The rich shall not give more, and the poor shall not give less than half a shekel, when *they* give an offering unto the LORD, to make an atonement for your souls.

Ex 32:30 And it came to pass on the morrow, that Moses said unto the people, Ye have sinned a great sin: and now I will go up unto the LORD; peradventure I shall make an atonement for your sin.

Le 1:4 And he shall put his hand upon the head of the burnt offering; and it shall be accepted for him to make atonement for him.

Le 4:20 And he shall do with the bullock as he did with the bullock for a sin offering, so shall he do with this: and the priest shall make an atonement for them, and it shall be forgiven them.

Le 4:26 And he shall burn all his fat upon the altar, as the fat of the sacrifice of peace offerings: and the priest shall make an atonement for him as concerning his sin, and it shall be forgiven him.

Le 4:31 And he shall take away all the fat thereof, as the fat is taken away from off the sacrifice of peace offerings; and the priest shall burn *it* upon the altar for a sweet savour unto the LORD; and the priest shall make an atonement for him, and it shall be forgiven him.

Le 4:35 And he shall take away all the fat thereof, as the fat of the lamb is taken away from the sacrifice of the peace offerings; and the priest shall burn them upon the altar, according to the offerings made by fire unto the LORD: and the priest shall make an atonement for his sin that he hath committed, and it shall be forgiven him.

Le 5:6 And he shall bring his trespass offering unto the LORD for his sin which he hath s flock, a lamb or a kid of the goats, for a sin offering; and the priest shall make an atonement for him concerning his sin.

Le 5:10 And he shall offer the second *for* a burnt offering, according to the manner: and the priest shall make an atonement for him for his sin which he hath sinned, and it shall be forgiven him.

Le 5:13 And the priest shall make an atonement for him as touching his sin that he hath sinned in one of these, and it shall be forgiven him: and *the remnant* shall be the priest's, as a meat offering.

Le 5:16 And he shall make amends for the harm that he hath done in the holy thing, and shall add the fifth part thereto, and give it unto the priest: and the priest shall make an atonement for him with the ram of the trespass offering, and it shall be forgiven him.

Le 5:18 And he shall bring a ram without blemish out of the flock, with thy estimation, for a trespass offering, unto the priest: and the priest shall make an atonement for him concerning his ignorance wherein he erred and wist *it* not, and it shall be forgiven him.

Le 6:7 And the priest shall make an atonement for him before the LORD: and it shall be forgiven him for any thing of all that he hath done in trespassing therein.

Le 7:7 As the sin offering *is,* so *is* the trespass offering: *there is* one law for them: the priest that maketh atonement therewith shall have *it.*

Le 8:34 As he hath done this day, *so* the LORD hath commanded to do, to make an atonement for you.

Le 9:7 And Moses said unto Aaron, Go unto the altar, and offer thy sin offering, and thy burnt offering, and make an atonement for thyself, and for the people: and offer the offering of the people, and make an atonement for them; as the LORD command.

Le 10:17 Wherefore have ye not eaten the sin offering in the holy place, seeing it *is* most holy, and *God* hath given it you to bear the iniquity of the congregation, to make atonement for them before the LORD?

Le 12:7 Who shall offer it before the LORD, and make an atonement for her; and she shall be cleansed from the issue of her blood. This *is* the law for her that hath born a male or a female.

Le 14:18 And the remnant of the oil that *is* in the priest's hand he shall pour upon the head of him that is to be cleansed: and the priest shall make an atonement for him before the LORD.

Le 14:21 And if he *be* poor, and cannot get so much; then he shall take one lamb *for* a trespass offering to be waved, to make an atonement for him, and one tenth deal of fine flour mingled with oil for a meat offering, and a log of oil;

Le 14:29 And the rest of the oil that *is* in the priest's hand he shall put upon the head of him that is to be cleansed, to make an atonement for him before the LORD.

Le 14:53 But he shall let go the living bird out of the city into the open fields, and make an atonement for the house: and it shall be clean.

Le 15:15 And the priest shall offer them, the one *for* a sin offering, and the other *for* a burnt offering; and the priest shall make an atonement for him before the LORD for his issue.

Le 15:30 And the priest shall offer the one *for* a sin offering, and the other *for* a burnt offering; and the priest shall make an atonement for her before the LORD for the issue of her uncleanness.

Le 16:6 And Aaron shall offer his bullock of the sin offering, which *is* for himself, and make an atonement for himself, and for his house.

Le 16:10 But the goat, on which the lot fell to be the scapegoat, shall be presented alive before the LORD, to make an atonement with him, *and* to let him go for a scapegoat into the wilderness.

Le 16:16 And he shall make an atonement for the holy *place,* because of the uncleanness of the children of Israel, and because of their transgressions in all their sins: and so shall he do for the tabernacle of the congregation, that remaineth among them in the midst of their uncleanness.

Le 16:24 And he shall wash his flesh with water in the holy place, and put on his garments, and come forth, and offer his burnt offering, and the burnt offering of the people, and make an atonement for himself, and for the people.

Le 16:33 And he shall make an atonement for the holy sanctuary, and he shall make an atonement for the tabernacle of the congregation, and for the altar, and he shall make an atonement for the priests, and for all the people of the congregation.

Le 17:11 For the life of the flesh *is* in the blood: and I have given it to you upon the altar to make an atonement for your souls: for it *is* the blood *that* maketh an atonement for the soul.

Le 19:22 And the priest shall make an atonement for him with the ram of the trespass offering before the LORD for his sin which he hath done: and the sin which he hath done shall be forgiven him.

Nu 5:8 But if the man have no kinsman to recompense the trespass unto, let the trespass be recompensed unto the LORD, *even* to the priest; beside the ram of the atonement, whereby an atonement shall be made for him.

Nu 6:11 And the priest shall offer the one for a sin offering, and the other for a burnt offering, and make an atonement for him, for that he sinned by the dead, and shall hallow his head that same day.

Nu 8:12 And the Levites shall lay their hands upon the heads of the bullocks: and thou shalt offer the one *for* a sin offering, and the other *for* a burnt offering, unto the LORD, to make an atonement for the Levites.

Nu 8:21 And the Levites were purified, and they washed their clothes; and Aaron offered them *as* an offering before the LORD; and Aaron made an atonement for them to cleanse them.

Nu 15:25 And the priest shall make an atonement for all the congregation of the children of Israel, and it shall be forgiven them; for it is ignorance: and they shall bring their offering, a sacrifice made by fire unto the LORD, and their sin offering before the LORD, for their ignorance:

Nu 15:28 And the priest shall make an atonement for the soul that sinneth ignorantly, when he sinneth by ignorance before the LORD, to make an atonement for him; and it shall be forgiven him.

Nu 16:46 And Moses said unto Aaron, Take a censer, and put fire therein from off the altar, and put on incense, and go quickly unto the congregation, and make an atonement for them: for there is wrath gone out from the LORD; the plague is begun.

Nu 16:47 And Aaron took as Moses commanded, and ran into the midst of the congregation; and, behold, the plague was begun among the people: and he put on incense, and made an atonement for the people.

Nu 25:13 And he shall have it, and his seed after him, *even* the covenant of an everlasting priesthood; because he was zealous for his God, and made an atonement for the children of Israel.

Nu 28:30 *And* one kid of the goats, to make an atonement for you.

Nu 31:50 We have therefore brought an oblation for the LORD, what every man hath gotten, of jewels of gold, chains, and bracelets, rings, earrings, and tablets, to make an atonement for our souls before the LORD.

2 Chr 29:24 And the priests killed them, and they made reconciliation with their blood upon the altar, to make an atonement for all Israel: for the king commanded *that* the burnt offering and the sin offering *should be made* for all Israel.

Ne 10:33 For the shewbread, and for the continual meat offering, and for the continual burnt offering, of the sabbaths, of the new moons, for the set feasts, and for the holy *things,* and for the sin offerings to make an atonement for Israel, and *for* all the work of the house of our God.

Eze 45:20 And so thou shalt do the seventh *day* of the month for every one

that erreth, and for *him that is* simple: so shall ye reconcile the house.

Mt 26:28 For this is my blood of the new testament, which is shed for many for the remission of sins.

Ro 5:11 And not only *so,* but we also joy in God through our Lord Jesus Christ, by whom we have now received the atonement.

2. Day of

Ex 30:10 And Aaron shall make an atonement upon the horns of it once in a year with the blood of the sin offering of atonements: once in the year shall he make atonement upon it throughout your generations: it *is* most holy unto the LORD.

Le 16:30 For on that day shall *the priest* make an atonement for you, to cleanse you, *that* ye may be clean from all your sins before the LORD.

Le 23:27 Also on the tenth *day* of this seventh month *there shall be* a day of atonement: it shall be an holy convocation unto you; and ye shall afflict your souls, and offer an offering made by fire unto the LORD.

Nu 29:7 And ye shall have on the tenth *day* of this seventh month an holy convocation; and ye shall afflict your souls: ye shall not do any work *therein:*

He 9:7 But into the second *went* the high priest alone once every year, not without blood, which he offered for himself, and *for* the errors of the people:

See **BLOOD, RECONCILIATION, REDEMPTION**

ATTENDANCE *See* **SYNAGOGUES**

ATTITUDES *See* **SEVEN**

ATTRACTION, DIVINE, the appeal of *the love and beauty of God*

1. Spiritual

Song 1:4 Draw me, we will run after thee: the king hath brought me into his chambers: we will be glad and rejoice in thee, we will remember thy love more than wine: the upright love thee.

Je 31:3 The LORD hath appeared of old unto me, *saying,* Yea, I have loved thee with an everlasting love: therefore with lovingkindness have I drawn thee.

Ho 11:4 I drew them with cords of a man, with bands of love: and I was to them as they that take off the yoke on their jaws, and I laid meat unto them.

Jn 6:44 No man can come to me, except the Father which hath sent me draw him: and I will raise him up at the last day.

Jn 12:32 And I, if I be lifted up from the earth, will draw all *men* unto me.

2. For Christ

Mal 3:1 Behold, I will send my messenger, and he shall prepare the way before me: and the LORD, whom ye seek, shall suddenly come to his temple, even the messenger of the covenant, whom ye delight in: behold, he shall come, saith the LORD of hosts.

Mk 1:37 And when they had found him, they said unto him, All *men* seek for thee.

Lu 4:42 And when it was day, he departed and went into a desert place: and the people sought him, and came unto him, and stayed him, that he should not depart from them.

Lu 19:3 And he sought to see Jesus who he was; and could not for the press, because he was little of stature.

Jn 6:24 When the people therefore saw that Jesus was not there, neither his disciples, they also took shipping, and came to Capernaum, seeking for Jesus.

Jn 12:21 The same came therefore to Philip, which was of Bethsaida of Galilee, and desired him, saying, Sir, we would see Jesus.

See **CHRIST**

AUTHORITY, *rule, dominion, power*

1. Of Christ
See **CHRIST**

2. Of the Church
See **CHURCH**

AVARICE, *greed*

1. Results

FAMILY TROUBLE
Pr 15:27 He that is greedy of gain troubleth his own house; but he that hateth gifts shall live.

DISAPPOINTMENT
Ec 5:10 He that loveth silver shall not be satisfied with silver; nor he that loveth abundance with increase: this *is* also vanity.

FOLLY
Je 17:11 As the partridge sitteth *on eggs*, and hatcheth *them* not; *so* he that getteth riches, and not by right, shall leave them in the midst of his days, and at his end shall be a fool.

APOSTASY
1 Ti 6:10 For the love of money is the root of all evil: which while some coveted after, they have erred from the faith, and pierced themselves through with many sorrows.

MISERY
Ja 5:3 Your gold and silver is cankered; and the rust of them shall be a witness against you, and shall eat your flesh as it were fire. Ye have heaped treasure together for the last days.

2. Examples

ACHAN
Jos 7:21 When I saw among the spoils a goodly Babylonish garment, and two hundred shekels of silver, and a wedge of gold of fifty shekels weight, then I coveted them, and took them; and, behold, they *are* hid in the earth in the midst of my tent, and the silver under it.

THE JEWS
Is 56:11 Yea, *they are* greedy dogs *which* can never have enough, and they *are* shepherds *that* cannot understand: they all look to their own way, every one for his gain, from his quarter.

Am 2:7 That pant after the dust of the earth on the head of the poor, and turn aside the way of the meek: and a man and his father will go in unto the *same* maid, to profane my holy name:

Mi 3:11 The heads thereof judge for reward, and the priests thereof teach for hire, and the prophets thereof divine for money: yet will they lean upon the LORD, and say, *Is* not the LORD among us? none evil can come upon us.

THE PEOPLE OF TYRE

Zec 9:3 And Tyrus did build herself a strong hold, and heaped up silver as the dust, and fine gold as the mire of the streets.

JUDAS

Mt 26:15 And said *unto them,* What will ye give me, and I will deliver him unto you? And they covenanted with him for thirty pieces of silver.

Mt 26:16 And from that time he sought opportunity to betray him.

Jn 12:6 This he said, not that he cared for the poor; but because he was a thief, and had the bag, and bare what was put therein.

THE MASTERS OF THE PHILIPPIAN DAMSEL

Ac 16:19 And when her masters saw that the hope of their gains was gone, they caught Paul and Silas, and drew *them* into the marketplace unto the rulers,

GOVERNOR FELIX

Ac 24:26 He hoped also that money should have been given him of Paul that he might loose him: wherefore he sent for him the oftener, and communed with him.

BALAAM

2 Pe 2:15 Which have forsaken the right way, and are gone astray, following the way of Balaam *the son* of Bosor, who loved the wages of unrighteousness;

AVENGER, *of blood*

Nu 35:12, 19; De 19:6, 12; Jos 20:3, 9; 2 S 3:27; 14:7, 11; Ac 7:24; Ro 12:19

AWAKENING, *DIVINE, figurative*

Jb 8:6; Ps 7:6; 35:23; 44:23; 59:4; 73:20; 78:65; 80:2; 119:126; Is 33:10; Is 42:14; Is 51:9; Zep 3:8; Zec 2:13

AWAKENINGS *and religious reforms, spiritual movements marked by return to God*

1 K 18:39 And when all the people saw *it,* they fell on their faces: and they said, The LORD, he *is* the God; the LORD, he *is* the God.

2 Chr 30:11 Nevertheless divers of Asher and Manasseh and of Zebulun humbled themselves, and came to Jerusalem.

Ezr 10:1 Now when Ezra had prayed, and when he had confessed, weeping and casting himself down before the house of God, there assembled unto him out of Israel a very great congregation of men and women and children: for the people wept very sore.

Eze 16:61 Then thou shalt remember thy ways, and be ashamed, when thou shalt receive thy sisters, thine elder and thy younger: and I will give them unto thee for daughters, but not by thy covenant.

Jona 3:5 So the people of Nineveh believed God, and proclaimed a fast, and put on sackcloth, from the greatest of them even to the least of them.

Zec 8:21 And the inhabitants of one *city* shall go to another, saying, Let us go speedily to pray before the LORD, and to seek the LORD of hosts: I will go also.

Mk 1:5 And there went out unto him all the land of Judaea, and they of Jerusalem, and were all baptized of him in the river of Jordan, confessing their sins.

Lu 3:10 And the people asked him, saying, What shall we do then?

Lu 7:29 And all the people that heard *him,* and the publicans, justified God, being baptized with the baptism of John.

Jn 4:29 Come, see a man, which told me all things that ever I did: is not this the Christ?

Jn 4:39 And many of the Samaritans of that city believed on him for the saying of the woman, which testified, He told me all that ever I did.

Ac 2:41 Then they that gladly received his word were baptized: and the same day there were added *unto them* about three thousand souls.

Ac 8:6 And the people with one accord gave heed unto those things which Philip spake, hearing and seeing the miracles which he did.

Ac 9:35 And all that dwelt at Lydda and Saron saw him, and turned to the Lord.

Ac 11:21 And the hand of the Lord was with them: and a great number believed, and turned unto the Lord.

Ac 13:48 And when the Gentiles heard this, they were glad, and glorified the word of the Lord: and as many as were ordained to eternal life believed.

Ac 17:4 And some of them believed, and consorted with Paul and Silas; and of the devout Greeks a great multitude, and of the chief women not a few.

Ac 18:8 And Crispus, the chief ruler of the synagogue, believed on the Lord with all his house; and many of the Corinthians hearing believed, and were baptized.

Ac 19:18 And many that believed came, and confessed, and shewed their deeds.

1. Examples

UNDER SAMUEL
1 S 7:5–6

ELIJAH
1 K 18:21–40

HEZEKIAH
2 Chr 30:1–27

EZRA
Ezr 10:1–44

JOHN THE BAPTIST
Lu 3:2–14

CHRIST AT SAMARIA
Jn 4:28–42; Ac 2:1–47; 8:5–8

PETER AT LYDDA
Ac 9:35

PAUL AT ANTIOCH, SYRIA
Ac 11:21

PAUL AT ANTIOCH, PISIDIA
Ac 13:48

PAUL AT CORINTH
Ac 18:8

PAUL AT EPHESUS
Ac 19:18–20

2. Revivals

Is 35:6 Then shall the lame *man* leap as an hart, and the tongue of the dumb sing: for in the wilderness shall waters break out, and streams in the desert.

Lam 3:40 Let us search and try our ways, and turn again to the Lord.

Ho 6:2 After two days will he revive us: in the third day he will raise us up, and we shall live in his sight.

Ho 14:2 Take with you words, and turn to the Lord: say unto him, Take away all iniquity, and receive *us* graciously: so will we render the calves of our lips.

a. Sought

Ps 51:13 *Then* will I teach transgressors thy ways; and sinners shall be converted unto thee.

Ps 80:7 Turn us again, O God of hosts, and cause thy face to shine; and we shall be saved.

Ps 85:6 Wilt thou not revive us again: that thy people may rejoice in thee?

Is 32:15 Until the spirit be poured upon us from on high, and the wilderness be a fruitful field, and the fruitful field be counted for a forest.

Hab 3:2 O LORD, I have heard thy speech, *and* was afraid: O LORD, revive thy work in the midst of the years, in the midst of the years make known; in wrath remember mercy.

b. Examples

1 S 7:4 Then the children of Israel did put away Baalim and Ashtaroth, and served the LORD only.

1 K 18:39 And when all the people saw *it,* they fell on their faces: and they said, The LORD, he *is* the God; the LORD, he *is* the God.

2 Chr 30:11 Nevertheless divers of Asher and Manasseh and of Zebulun humbled themselves, and came to Jerusalem.

Zec 8:21 And the inhabitants of one *city* shall go to another, saying, Let us go speedily to pray before the LORD, and to seek the LORD of hosts: I will go also.

Ac 2:41 Then they that gladly received his word were baptized: and the same day there were added *unto them* about three thousand souls.

Ac 8:6 And the people with one accord gave heed unto those things which Philip spake, hearing and seeing the miracles which he did.

c. General References

Ps 80:18 So will not we go back from thee: quicken us, and we will call upon thy name.

Ps 119:25 My soul cleaveth unto the dust: quicken thou me according to thy word.

Ps 119:40 Behold, I have longed after thy precepts: quicken me in thy righteousness.

Ps 119:50 This *is* my comfort in my affliction: for thy word hath quickened me.

Ps 119:88 Quicken me after thy lovingkindness; so shall I keep the testimony of thy mouth.

Ps 119:149 Hear my voice according unto thy lovingkindness: O LORD, quicken me according to thy judgment.

Ps 143:11 Quicken me, O LORD, for thy name's sake: for thy righteousness' sake bring my soul out of trouble.

Hab 3:2 O LORD, I have heard thy speech, *and* was afraid: O LORD, revive thy work in the midst of the years, in the midst of the years make known; in wrath remember mercy.

Zec 4:1 And the angel that talked with me came again, and waked me, as a man that is wakened out of his sleep,

Jn 5:21 For as the Father raiseth up the dead, and quickeneth *them;* even so the Son quickeneth whom he will.

Jn 6:63 It is the spirit that quickeneth; the flesh profiteth nothing: the words that I speak unto you, *they* are spirit, and *they* are life.

Col 2:13 And you, being dead in your sins and the uncircumcision of your flesh, hath he quickened together with him, having forgiven you all trespasses;

3. Religious Reforms

a. Leaders

ASA

1 K 15:12 And he took away the sodomites out of the land, and removed all the idols that his fathers had made.

JEHU

2 K 10:27 And they brake down the image of Baal, and brake down the house of Baal, and made it a draught house unto this day.

JEHOIADA

2 K 11:18 And all the people of the land went into the house of Baal, and brake it down; his altars and his images brake they in pieces thoroughly, and slew Mattan the priest of Baal before the altars. And the priest appointed officers over the house of the LORD.

JOSIAH

2 K 23:4 And the king commanded Hilkiah the high priest, and the priests of the second order, and the keepers of the door, to bring forth out of the temple of the LORD all the vessels that were made for Baal, and for the grove, and for all the host of heaven: and he burned them without Jerusalem in the fields of Kidron, and carried the ashes of them unto Bethel.

JEHOSHAPHAT

2 Chr 19:3 Nevertheless there are good things found in thee, in that thou hast taken away the groves out of the land, and hast prepared thine heart to seek God.

HEZEKIAH

2 Chr 31:1 Now when all this was finished, all Israel that were present went out to the cities of Judah, and brake the images in pieces, and cut down the groves, and threw down the high places and the altars out of all Judah and Benjamin, in Ephraim also and Manasseh, until they had utterly destroyed them all. Then all the children of Israel returned, every man to his possession, into their own cities.

MANASSEH

2 Chr 33:15 And he took away the strange gods, and the idol out of the house of the LORD, and all the altars that he had built in the mount of the house of the LORD, and in Jerusalem, and cast *them* out of the city.

EZRA

Ezr 10:3 Now therefore let us make a covenant with our God to put away all the wives, and such as are born of them, according to the counsel of my lord, and of those that tremble at the commandment of our God; and let it be done according to the law.

NEHEMIAH

Ne 13:19 And it came to pass, that when the gates of Jerusalem began to be dark before the sabbath, I commanded that the gates should be shut, and charged that they should not be opened till after the sabbath: and *some* of my servants set I at the gates, *that* there should no burden be brought in on the sabbath day.

b. Idols Put Away

Ge 35:2; Jos 24:14, 23; Jud 10:16; 1 S 7:3; 12:10; 1 K 15:12; 2 K 3:2; 23:24;

2 Chr 14:5; 15:8; 33:15; Is 2:20; 17:8; 30:22; 31:7; Je 4:1; Eze 36:25; 37:23; Ho 2:17; 14:3, 8; 1 Th 1:9

c. The Temple Cleansed

2 K 23:4; 2 Chr 29:5, 15; 34:8; Ne 13:9; Da 8:14; Mt 21:12; Mk 11:15; Lu 19:45; Jn 2:15

4. Iconoclasm

a. Idols to Be Destroyed

Ex 23:24; 34:13; Nu 33:52; De 7:5, 25; 12:3; Jud 6:25; 1 Chr 14:12; Is 2:18; 30:22; Je 43:13

b. Examples

Ex 32:20; De 9:21; Jud 2:2; 6:28; 2 S 5:21; 1 K 15:13; 2 K 10:26; 11:18; 18:4; 23:6, 14; 2 Chr 14:3; 15:16; 23:17; 31:1; 33:15; 34:4; Is 27:9; 37:19; Eze 6:6; Mi 1:7

AWE *See* **REVERENCE**

AXES, *tools used for cutting trees and chopping wood*

De 19:5; Jud 9:48; 1 S 13:20; 2 S 12:31; 1 K 6:7; 2 K 6:5; Ps 74:5; Mt 3:10

AZARIAH, *strengthened by Jehovah*

1. The Prophet

2 Chr 15:1–19

2. The High Priest

1 Chr 6:10; 2 Chr 19:11

3. A High Priest in Hezekiah's Reign

2 Chr 31:10

See **ISRAEL**

AZEKAH, *a city of Judah*

Jos 10:10; 15:35; 1 S 17:1; 2 Chr 11:9; Ne 11:30; Je 34:7

AZOTUS

See **ASHDOD**

B

BAASHA, *king of Israel*

1 K 15:16, 27, 34; 21:22; 2 K 9:9; 2 Chr 16:1; Je 41:9

See **ISRAEL**

BABBLING, *condemned*

Pr 23:29; 1 Ti 6:20; 2 Ti 2:16

BABEL, *TOWER OF, became a symbol of disobedience and pride*

Ge 11:9

BABIES

1. Value

Ps 139:13–16 For thou hast possessed my reins: thou hast covered me in my mother's womb.

I will praise thee; for I am fearfully and wonderfully made: marvellous are thy works; and that my soul knoweth right well.

My substance was not hid from thee, when I was made in secret, and curiously wrought in the lowest parts of the earth.

Thine eyes did see my substance, yet being unperfect; and in thy book all my members were written, which in continuance were fashioned, when as yet there was none of them.

Ec 11:5 As thou knowest not what is the way of the spirit, nor how the bones do grow in the womb of her that is with child: even so thou knowest not the works of God who maketh all.

2. Death

Ex 21:22 If men strive, and hurt a woman with child, so that her fruit depart from her, and yet no mischief follow: he shall be surely punished, according as the woman's husband will lay upon him; and he shall pay as the judges determine.

2 K 8:12 And Hazael said, Why weepeth my lord? And he answered, Because I know the evil that thou wilt do unto the children of Israel: their strong holds wilt thou set on fire, and their young men wilt thou slay with the sword, and wilt dash their children, and rip up their women with child.

Am 1:13 Thus saith the LORD; For three transgressions of the children of Ammon, and for four, I will not turn away the punishment thereof; because they have ripped up the women with child of Gilead, that they might enlarge their border:

Mt 2:16 Then Herod, when he saw that he was mocked of the wise men, was exceeding wroth, and sent forth, and slew all the children that were in Bethlehem, and in all the coasts thereof, from two years old and under, according to the time which he had diligently enquired of the wise men.

BABYLON, *gate of god; a city-state in the plain of Shinar*

Babylon, the mightiest metropolis of the ancient world, was located on the Euphrates River, about fifty miles south of Baghdad, Iraq. The Babylonian city was largely built by the efforts of Hammurabi (1728–1686 B.C.) and Nebuchadnezzar II (604–562 B.C.). It declined with the fall of Nebuchadnezzar, fell to a lower level under Belshazzar, and came to ruin when Xerxes, the Persian king, destroyed it in 478 B.C. The entire site lies within the suburbs of modern Baghdad.

Ge 10:10; 2 K 17:24, 30; 20:14; 24:1, 15; 25:1, 7, 13, 22; 2 Chr 36:10; Ezr 2:1; 5:12, 17; 7:6; 8:1; Ne 7:6; 13:6; Ps 87:4; Is 14:4; 39:1, 3; Je 27:18; 28:3; 29:4; 34:1; 51:8; Eze 12:13; 17:16; Da 3:1; 4:29; Zec 6:10; Mt 1:12; 1 Pe 5:13

1. Prophecies

Ps 137:8; Is 13:19; 14:12, 22; 21:9; 43:14; 47:1; 48:14; Je 21:2; 25:12; 50:1, 13, 23, 39; 51:1, 29, 37, 55, 60, 64

2. The Great

Re 14:8; 16:19; 17:5; 18:2

BACKBITING See SPEECH

BACKSLIDING, *reverting to sin and wrongdoing*

1. Results

SELFISH ABSORPTION

Pr 14:14; Is 1:4; Je 14:7; Ho 11:7

RELIGIOUS INDIFFERENCE

Mt 24:12

UNFITNESS FOR THE KINGDOM

Lu 9:62; Ga 1:6

BONDAGE TO FORMS

Ga 4:9

DIVINE DISPLEASURE

He 10:38; 2 Pe 2:20

LOSS OF SPIRITUAL ENTHUSIASM

Re 2:4

2. Produces

ABSENCE OF SPIRITUAL LEADERS

Ex 32:1 And when the people saw that Moses delayed to come down out of the mount, the people gathered themselves together unto Aaron, and said unto him, Up, make us gods, which shall go before us; for *as for* this Moses, the man that brought us up out of the land of Egypt, we wot not what is become of him.

Ex 32:8 They have turned aside quickly out of the way which I commanded them: they have made them a molten calf, and have worshipped it, and have sacrificed thereunto, and said, These *be* thy gods, O Israel, which have brought thee up out of the land of Egypt.

1 S 15:11 It repenteth me that I have set up Saul *to be* king: for he is turned back from following me, and hath not performed my commandments. And it grieved Samuel; and he cried unto the LORD all night.

EVIL ASSOCIATIONS

1 K 11:4 For it came to pass, when Solomon was old, *that* his wives turned away his heart after other gods: and his heart was not perfect with the LORD his God, as *was* the heart of David his father.

WORLDLY SUCCESS

2 Chr 25:2 And he did *that which was* right in the sight of the LORD, but not with a perfect heart.

2 Chr 25:14 Now it came to pass, after that Amaziah was come from the slaughter of the Edomites, that he brought the gods of the children of Seir, and set them up *to be* his gods, and bowed down himself before them, and burned incense unto them.

Ps 78:57 But turned back, and dealt unfaithfully like their fathers: they were turned aside like a deceitful bow.

Ho 6:4 O Ephraim, what shall I do unto thee? O Judah, what shall I do unto thee? for your goodness *is* as a morning cloud, and as the early dew it goeth away.

Zep 1:6 And them that are turned back from the LORD; and *those* that have not sought the LORD, nor enquired for him.

SHALLOWNESS

Lu 8:13 They on the rock *are they,* which, when they hear, receive the word with joy; and these have no root, which for a while believe, and in time of temptation fall away.

EMPTINESS OF LIFE

Lu 11:24 When the unclean spirit is gone out of a man, he walketh through dry places, seeking rest; and finding none, he saith, I will return unto my house whence I came out.

Lu 11:25 And when he cometh, he findeth *it* swept and garnished.

Lu 11:26 Then goeth he, and taketh *to him* seven other spirits more wicked than himself; and they enter in, and dwell there: and the last *state* of that man is worse than the first.

LACK OF SPIRITUAL INSIGHT

Jn 6:63 It is the spirit that quickeneth; the flesh profiteth nothing: the words that I speak unto you, *they* are spirit, and *they* are life.

Jn 6:64 But there are some of you that believe not. For Jesus knew from the beginning who they were that believed not, and who should betray him.

Jn 6:66 From that *time* many of his disciples went back, and walked no more with him.

1 Ti 5:15 For some are already turned aside after Satan.

LOVE OF THE WORLD

2 Ti 4:10 For Demas hath forsaken me, having loved this present world, and is departed unto Thessalonica; Crescens to Galatia, Titus unto Dalmatia.

See **APOSTASY, CONSECRATION**

BADGERS' SKINS, *one of the coverings of the tabernacle*

Ex 25:5; 26:14; 35:7, 23; 36:19; 39:34; Nu 4:6, 10, 14, 25; Eze 16:10

BAKERS *See* **ARTS AND CRAFTS**

BALAAM, *a heathen diviner who lived at Pethor*

FAMOUS

Nu 22:5–6 He sent messengers therefore unto Balaam the son of Beor to Pethor, which *is* by the river of the land of the children of his people, to call him, saying, Behold, there is a people come out from Egypt: behold, they cover the face of the earth, and they abide over against me:

Come now therefore, I pray thee, curse me this people; for they *are* too mighty for me: peradventure I shall prevail, *that* we may smite them, and *that* I may drive them out of the land:

for I wot that he whom thou blessest *is* blessed, and he whom thou cursest is cursed.

SELF-WILLED

Nu 22:21–22 And Balaam rose up in the morning, and saddled his ass, and went with the princes of Moab.

And God's anger was kindled because he went: and the angel of the LORD stood in the way for an adversary against him. Now he was riding upon his ass, and his two servants *were* with him.

SAVED FROM DESTRUCTION

Nu 22:33 And the ass saw me, and turned from me these three times: unless she had turned from me, surely now also I had slain thee, and saved her alive.

DOUBLE-MINDED

Nu 23–24

SENT HOME

Nu 24:10 And Balak's anger was kindled against Balaam, and he smote his hands together: and Balak said unto Balaam, I called thee to curse mine enemies, and, behold, thou hast altogether blessed *them* these three times.

AN EVIL COUNSELLOR

Nu 31:16 Behold, these caused the children of Israel, through the counsel of Balaam, to commit trespass against the LORD in the matter of Peor, and there was a plague among the congregation of the LORD.

BESETTING SIN

2 Pe 2:15 Which have forsaken the right way, and are gone astray, following the way of Balaam *the son* of Bosor, who loved the wages of unrighteousness;

BALAK, *king of Moab*

Nu 22:2; Jos 24:9; Jud 11:25

BALANCES, DIVINE, *the fairness of God*

Jb 31:6; Ps 62:9; Pr 16:2, 11; Is 40:12; Da 5:27; Re 6:5

BALDNESS

Le 13:40; 21:5; De 14:1; 2 K 2:23; Is 3:24; 15:2; Je 48:37; Eze 7:18; 27:31; 29:18; Am 8:10; Mi 1:16

BALM, *a fragrant balsam*

Ge 37:25; 43:11; Je 8:22; 46:11; 51:8; Eze 27:17

BANNERS

Ps 20:5; 60:4; Song 2:4; 6:4; Is 13:2

BANISHMENT *See* NATION

BAPTISM *See* CHURCH

BARABBAS, *a robber released instead of Christ*

Mt 27:16, 17, 20, 26; Mk 15:7; Lu 23:18; Jn 18:40

BARAK, *a judge*

Jud 4:6; 5:1, 15; He 11:32

BARBARIANS, *foreigners*

Ac 28:4; Ro 1:14; 1 Co 14:11; Col 3:11

See KINDNESS

BARBERS *See* ARTS AND CRAFTS

BARLEY *See* AGRICULTURE

BARNABAS, *Paul's companion*

Ac 4:36–37; 9:27; 11:22–24, 25–26, 30; 12:25; 13:1, 2, 50; 14:12, 20; 15:22, 25, 36, 39; 1 Co 9:6; Ga 2:1, 9, 13; Col 4:10

SYMPATHY

Ac 4:36–37 And Joses, who by the apostles was surnamed Barnabas, (which is, being interpreted, The son of consolation,) a Levite, *and* of the country of Cyprus,

Having land, sold *it,* and brought the money, and laid *it* at the apostles' feet.

BROADMINDEDNESS

Ac 9:26–27 And when Saul was come to Jerusalem, he assayed to join himself to the disciples: but they were all afraid of him, and believed not that he was a disciple.

But Barnabas took him, and brought *him* to the apostles, and declared unto them how he had seen the Lord in the way, and that he had spoken to him, and how he had preached boldly at Damascus in the name of Jesus.

GIFT OF EXHORTATION

Ac 11:23 Who, when he came, and had seen the grace of God, was glad, and exhorted them all, that with purpose of heart they would cleave unto the Lord.

SPIRIT FILLED

Ac 11:24 For he was a good man, and full of the Holy Ghost and of faith: and much people was added unto the Lord.

INSPIRING INFLUENCE

Ac 11:25–26 Then departed Barnabas to Tarsus, for to seek Saul:

And when he had found him, he brought him unto Antioch. And it came to pass, that a whole year they assembled themselves with the church, and taught much people. And the disciples were called Christians first in Antioch.

TRUSTWORTHY

Ac 11:30 Which also they did, and sent it to the elders by the hands of Barnabas and Saul.

ATTRACTIVE APPEARANCE

Ac 14:12 And they called Barnabas, Jupiter; and Paul, Mercurius, because he was the chief speaker.

ADAPTED TO MISSIONARY WORK

Ac 13:2 As they ministered to the Lord, and fasted, the Holy Ghost said, Separate me Barnabas and Saul for the work whereunto I have called them.

SELF-SUPPORTING

1 Co 9:6 Or I only and Barnabas, have not we power to forbear working?

BARNS *See* AGRICULTURE

BARREL, *vessel used for keeping flour*
1 K 17:12; 18:33

BARRENNESS *See* **FAMILY**

BARTHOLOMEW, *an apostle, perhaps another name for Nathanael*
Mt 10:3; Mk 3:18; Lu 6:14; Jn 1:48; 21:2; Ac 1:13

BARTIMEUS, *a blind beggar healed by Christ*
Mk 10:46; Lu 18:35

BARUCH, *writes Jeremiah's prophecy*
Je 32:12; 36:4, 10, 32; 43:3, 6

BARZILLAI, *a friend of David*
2 S 17:27; 19:31; 1 K 2:7; Ezr 2:61; Ne 7:63

BASE FELLOWS, *wicked persons, sons of Belial*
De 13:13; Jud 9:4; 11:3; 19:22; 20:13; 1 S 2:12; 10:27; 25:3, 17, 25; 30:22; 2 S 3:34; 20:1; 1 K 21:10; 2 Chr 13:7; Jb 30:8

See **EVIL**

BASHAN, *a region east of the river Jordan*
Nu 21:33; 32:33; De 1:4; 3:1, 10; 4:43; Jos 12:4; 13:12, 30; 17:1, 5; 22:7; 1 K 4:13; 2 K 10:33; 1 Chr 5:11, 23; Ps 68:15, 22; Is 2:13; 33:9; Je 22:20; 50:19; Eze 27:6; Am 4:1; Mi 7:14; Na 1:4; Zec 11:2

See **MOUNTAINS AND HILLS**

BASINS, *basons, rounded vessels that held water used in the tabernacle and the temple*
Ex 27:3; 38:3; Nu 4:14; 1 K 7:40, 50; 1 Chr 28:17; 2 Chr 4:8; Ezr 1:10; 8:27

BASKETS, *containers of different sizes, shapes, and construction used for transporting burdens, including people*
Ge 40:16; Ex 29:3, 32; Le 8:2; Nu 6:15; De 26:2; 28:17; 2 K 10:7; Je 24:1; Am 8:2; Mt 14:20; 15:37; 16:10; Mk 6:43; 8:8; Ac 9:25; 2 Co 11:33

BATHS, *a measure*
1 K 7:26, 38; 2 Chr 4:5; Ezr 7:22; Is 5:10; Eze 45:11

BATH-SHEBA, *or Bath-shua, wife of Uriah, becomes David's wife*
2 S 11:3, 27; 1 K 1:11, 31; 2:13; 1 Chr 3:5; Mt 1:6

BATTERING-RAMS, *simple war machines, long enough to need one to two hundred men, whose object it was to make a breach in the wall of a beleaguered town*
Eze 4:2; 21:22; 26:9

BAY *See* **TREES**

BEARD
Le 14:9; 19:27; 21:5; 1 S 21:13; 2 S 10:4; 19:24; Ezr 9:3; Ps 133:2; Is 7:20; 15:2; Eze 5:1

BEARS *See* **ANIMALS**

BEATINGS *See* **NATION**

BEATITUDES, *blessings*

1. Blessed Ones

Nu 24:9 He couched, he lay down as a lion, and as a great lion: who shall stir him up? Blessed *is* he that blesseth thee, and cursed is he that curseth thee.

Ru 2:20 And Naomi said unto her daughter in law, Blessed *be* he of the LORD, who hath not left off his kindness to the living and to the dead. And Naomi said unto her, The man *is* near of kin unto us, one of our next kinsmen.

Ps 1:1 Blessed *is* the man that walketh not in the counsel of the ungodly, nor standeth in the way of sinners, nor sitteth in the seat of the scornful.

Ps 2:12 Kiss the Son, lest he be angry, and ye perish *from* the way, when his wrath is kindled but a little. Blessed *are* all they that put their trust in him.

Ps 21:6 For thou hast made him most blessed for ever: thou hast made him exceeding glad with thy countenance.

Ps 32:1 Blessed *is he whose* transgression *is* forgiven, *whose* sin *is* covered.

Ps 40:4 Blessed *is* that man that maketh the LORD his trust, and respecteth not the proud, nor such as turn aside to lies.

Ps 41:1 Blessed *is* he that considereth the poor: the LORD will deliver him in time of trouble.

Ps 65:4 Blessed *is the man whom* thou choosest, and causest to approach *unto thee, that* he may dwell in thy courts: we shall be satisfied with the goodness of thy house, *even* of thy holy temple.

Ps 84:4 Blessed *are* they that dwell in thy house: they will be still praising thee. Selah.

Ps 84:12 O LORD of hosts, blessed *is* the man that trusteth in thee.

Ps 89:15 Blessed *is* the people that know the joyful sound: they shall walk, O LORD, in the light of thy countenance.

Ps 106:3 Blessed *are* they that keep judgment, *and* he that doeth righteousness at all times.

Ps 112:1 Praise ye the LORD. Blessed *is* the man *that* feareth the LORD, *that* delighteth greatly in his commandments.

Ps 115:15 Ye *are* blessed of the LORD which made heaven and earth.

Ps 119:1 Blessed *are* the undefiled in the way, who walk in the law of the LORD.

Ps 127:5 Happy *is* the man that hath his quiver full of them: they shall not be ashamed, but they shall speak with the enemies in the gate.

Ps 128:1 Blessed *is* every one that feareth the LORD; that walketh in his ways.

Pr 8:32 Now therefore hearken unto me, O ye children: for blessed *are they that* keep my ways.

Is 32:20 Blessed *are* ye that sow beside all waters, that send forth *thither* the feet of the ox and the ass.

Is 56:2 Blessed *is* the man *that* doeth this, and the son of man *that* layeth hold on it; that keepeth the sabbath from polluting it, and keepeth his hand from doing any evil.

Je 17:7 Blessed *is* the man that trusteth in the LORD, and whose hope the LORD is.

Da 12:12 Blessed *is* he that waiteth, and cometh to the thousand three hundred and five and thirty days.

Mal 3:12 And all nations shall call you blessed: for ye shall be a delightsome land, saith the LORD of hosts.

Mt 11:6 And blessed is *he,* whosoever shall not be offended in me.

Mt 24:46 Blessed *is* that servant, whom his lord when he cometh shall find so doing.

Lu 1:28 And the angel came in unto her, and said, Hail, *thou that art* highly favoured, the Lord *is* with thee: blessed *art* thou among women.

Lu 1:45 And blessed *is* she that believed: for there shall be a performance of those things which were told her from the Lord.

Lu 6:22 Blessed are ye, when men shall hate you, and when they shall separate you *from their company,* and shall reproach *you,* and cast out your name as evil, for the Son of man's sake.

Lu 7:23 And blessed is *he,* whosoever shall not be offended in me.

Lu 11:28 But he said, Yea rather, blessed *are* they that hear the word of God, and keep it.

Lu 12:37 Blessed *are* those servants, whom the lord when he cometh shall find watching: verily I say unto you, that he shall gird himself, and make them to sit down to meat, and will come forth and serve them.

Lu 12:43 Blessed *is* that servant, whom his lord when he cometh shall find so doing.

Jn 13:17 If ye know these things, happy are ye if ye do them.

Jn 20:29 Jesus saith unto him, Thomas, because thou hast seen me, thou hast believed: blessed *are* they that have not seen, and *yet* have believed.

Ro 4:7 *Saying,* Blessed *are* they whose iniquities are forgiven, and whose sins are covered.

Ja 1:12 Blessed *is* the man that endureth temptation: for when he is tried, he shall receive the crown of life, which the Lord hath promised to them that love him.

Re 1:3 Blessed *is* he that readeth, and they that hear the words of this prophecy, and keep those things which are written therein: for the time *is* at hand.

Re 14:13 And I heard a voice from heaven saying unto me, Write, Blessed *are* the dead which die in the Lord from henceforth: Yea, saith the Spirit, that they may rest from their labours; and their works do follow them.

Re 19:9 And he saith unto me, Write, Blessed *are* they which are called unto the marriage supper of the Lamb. And he saith unto me, These are the true sayings of God.

Re 20:6 Blessed and holy *is* he that hath part in the first resurrection: on such the second death hath no power, but they shall be priests of God and of Christ, and shall reign with him a thousand years.

Re 22:7 Behold, I come quickly: blessed is he that keepeth the sayings of the prophecy of this book.

Re 22:14 Blessed *are* they that do his commandments, that they may have right to the tree of life, and may enter in through the gates into the city.

2. Beatitudes of Christ

1ST STEP, HUMILITY, *conscious need*

Mt 5:3 Blessed *are* the poor in spirit: for theirs is the kingdom of heaven.

2ND STEP, PENITENCE, *mourning for sin*

Mt 5:4 Blessed *are* they that mourn: for they shall be comforted.

3RD STEP, MEEKNESS, *marking the birth of a new spirit*

Mt 5:5 Blessed *are* the meek: for they shall inherit the earth.

4TH STEP, SPIRITUAL APPETITE, *signifying growth*

Mt 5:6 Blessed *are* they which do hunger and thirst after righteousness: for they shall be filled.

5TH STEP, MERCIFULNESS, *an attribute of God, indicating further advance*

Mt 5:7 Blessed *are* the merciful: for they shall obtain mercy.

6TH STEP, HEART PURITY, *marking the attainment of higher attitudes, where comes the vision of God*

Mt 5:8 Blessed *are* the pure in heart: for they shall see God.

7TH STEP, PEACEMAKING, *a Christlike influence, calming the storms of life*

Mt 5:9 Blessed *are* the peacemakers: for they shall be called the children of God.

8TH STEP, THE SUMMIT, *suffering for Christ, standing beside the prophets and martyrs*

Mt 5:10–12 Blessed *are* they which are persecuted for righteousness' sake: for theirs is the kingdom of heaven.

Blessed are ye, when *men* shall revile you, and persecute *you*, and shall say all manner of evil against you falsely, for my sake.

Rejoice, and be exceeding glad: for great *is* your reward in heaven: for so persecuted they the prophets which were before you.

See **BLESSINGS**

BEAUTY, *that which attracts, pleases, and satisfies*

1. Physical

a. Examples

Ge 6:2; 12:11, 14; 24:16; 26:7; 29:17; De 21:11; Jud 15:2; 1 S 16:12; 25:3; 2 S 11:2; 13:1; 14:25, 27; 1 K 1:4; Est 1:11; 2:7, 15; Jb 42:15; Ps 45:11; Da 1:4, 15; Ac 7:20

b. Vanity

Ps 39:11; 49:14; Pr 11:22; 31:30; Is 3:17, 24; 28:1; Lam 4:7

c. Of Nature

Ps 19:1; Ec 3:11; Is 35:1; Ho 14:6; Mt 6:28–29

See **NATURE**

2. Spiritual

a. Described

Ps 149:4 For the LORD taketh pleasure in his people: he will beautify the meek with salvation.

Song 1:14 My beloved *is* unto me *as* a cluster of camphire in the vineyards of En-gedi.

Song 4:1 Behold, thou *art* fair, my love; behold, thou *art* fair; thou *hast* doves' eyes within thy locks: thy hair *is* as a flock of goats, that appear from mount Gilead.

Song 6:1 Whither is thy beloved gone, O thou fairest among women? whither is thy beloved turned aside? that we may seek him with thee.

Song 6:4 Thou *art* beautiful, O my love, as Tirzah, comely as Jerusalem, terrible as *an army* with banners.

Song 6:10 Who *is* she *that* looketh forth as the morning, fair as the moon, clear as the sun, *and* terrible as *an army* with banners?

Song 7:1 How beautiful are thy feet with shoes, O prince's daughter! the joints of thy thighs *are* like jewels, the work of the hands of a cunning workman.

Eze 16:14 And thy renown went forth among the heathen for thy beauty: for it *was* perfect through my comeliness, which I had put upon thee, saith the Lord GOD.

Ep 5:27 That he might present it to himself a glorious church, not having spot, or wrinkle, or any such thing; but that it should be holy and without blemish.

1 Pe 3:4 But *let it be* the hidden man of the heart, in that which is not corruptible, *even the ornament* of a meek and quiet spirit, which is in the sight of God of great price.

b. Christlikeness

Ro 8:29 For whom he did foreknow, he also did predestinate *to be* conformed to the image of his Son, that he might be the firstborn among many brethren.

1 Co 15:49 And as we have borne the image of the earthy, we shall also bear the image of the heavenly.

2 Co 3:18 But we all, with open face beholding as in a glass the glory of the Lord, are changed into the same image from glory to glory, *even* as by the Spirit of the Lord.

Ph 3:21 Who shall change our vile body, that it may be fashioned like unto his glorious body, according to the working whereby he is able even to subdue all things unto himself.

Col 3:10 And have put on the new *man,* which is renewed in knowledge after the image of him that created him:

2 Pe 1:4 Whereby are given unto us exceeding great and precious promises: that by these ye might be partakers of the divine nature, having escaped the corruption that is in the world through lust.

1 Jn 3:2 Beloved, now are we the sons of God, and it doth not yet appear what we shall be: but we know that, when he shall appear, we shall be like him; for we shall see him as he is.

BEDS

De 3:11; Est 1:6; Pr 7:17; 22:27; Song 3:7; Mt 10:25; 12:27; Mk 3:22; Lu 11:15, 18

BEER-SHEBA, *a city on the southern frontier of Palestine*

Beer-Sheba (*well of the oath*) was the center of patriarchal life. Its name originated from the oath between Abraham and Abimelech, King of Gerar. The town was an important stopping point on the main trade-route to Egypt, which led some to conclude that Abraham made his living as a trader. There are wells in this area, two of them ancient. The wells are circular, with the largest one 12.5 feet in diameter and about 40 feet deep today. Many herds of camel, cattle, and sheep still drink there from troughs made of hewn stone and cement. The town, forty-eight miles southwest of Jerusalem, marked the southern boundary of Israelite territory in the Old Testament (Jud 20:1; 1 S 3:20). Its idolatrous high places were destroyed by Josiah (2 K 23:8).

Ge 21:31, 33; 22:19; 26:23, 33; 28:10; 46:1, 5; Jos 15:28; 19:2; Jud 20:1; 1 S 8:2; 2 S 17:11; 1 K 4:25; 1 Chr 4:28; 21:2; 2 Chr 19:4; 30:5; Ne 11:27; Am 5:5

See **CITIES**

BEES See **INSECTS**

BEGGARS, *those who solicited alms publicly, often going door to door*
1 S 2:8; Ps 37:25; 109:10; Pr 20:4; Lu 18:35

Examples
Mk 10:46; Lu 16:20; Jn 9:8; Ac 3:2

BEHEADING See **NATION**

BEHEMOTH See **ANIMALS**

BELLS
Ex 28:33; 39:25; Zec 14:20

BELSHAZZAR, *king of Babylon*
Da 5:1; 7:1

BENAIAH, *a captain of David's army*
2 S 8:18; 23:20; 1 K 1:10, 32, 36; 2:29; 4:4; 1 Chr 11:22; 18:17; 27:5, 34

BENEDICTIONS, *a form of public worship, adding God's promise of blessing*

1. Apostolic
Ro 16:20 And the God of peace shall bruise Satan under your feet shortly. The grace of our Lord Jesus Christ *be* with you. Amen.
2 Co 13:14 The grace of the Lord Jesus Christ, and the love of God, and the communion of the Holy Ghost, *be* with you all. Amen.
2 Th 3:18 The grace of our Lord Jesus Christ *be* with you all. Amen.
Jude 24 Now unto him that is able to keep you from falling, and to present *you* faultless before the presence of his glory with exceeding joy,
Re 22:21 The grace of our Lord Jesus Christ *be* with you all. Amen.

2. Old Testament Examples
Le 9:22 And Aaron lifted up his hand toward the people, and blessed them, and came down from offering of the sin offering, and the burnt offering, and peace offerings.
Nu 6:23 Speak unto Aaron and unto his sons, saying, On this wise ye shall bless the children of Israel, saying unto them,
De 21:5 And the priests the sons of Levi shall come near; for them the LORD thy God hath chosen to minister unto him, and to bless in the name of the LORD; and by their word shall every controversy and every stroke be *tried:*
Jos 22:6 So Joshua blessed them, and sent them away: and they went unto their tents.
1 S 1:17 Then Eli answered and said, Go in peace: and the God of Israel grant *thee* thy petition that thou hast asked of him.
2 S 6:18 And as soon as David had made an end of offering burnt offerings and peace offerings, he blessed the people in the name of the LORD of hosts.
1 K 8:55 And he stood, and blessed all the congregation of Israel with a loud voice, saying,
1 Chr 16:2 And when David had made an end of offering the burnt offerings and the peace offerings, he blessed the people in the name of the LORD.
2 Chr 30:27 Then the priests the Levites arose and blessed the people: and their voice was heard, and their prayer came *up* to his holy dwelling place, *even* unto heaven.

3. Other Passages
Nu 6:24–26 The LORD bless thee, and keep thee:
The LORD make his face shine upon thee, and be gracious unto thee.
The LORD life up his countenance upon thee, and give thee peace.
Ep 3:20–21 Now unto him that is able to do exceeding abundantly above all that we ask or think, according to the power that worketh in us,
Unto him *be* glory in the church by Christ Jesus throughout all ages, world without end. Amen.
1 Ti 1:17 Now unto the King eternal, immortal, invisible, the only wise

God, *be* honour and glory for ever and ever. Amen.

He 13:20–21 Now the God of peace, that brought again from the dead our Lord Jesus, that great shepherd of the sheep, through the blood of the everlasting covenant,

Make you perfect in every good work to do his will, working in you that which is well-pleasing in his sight, through Jesus Christ; to whom *be* glory for ever and ever. Amen.

1 Pe 5:10–11 But the God of all grace, who hath called us unto his eternal glory by Christ Jesus, after that ye have suffered a while, make you perfect, stablish, strengthen, settle *you*.

To him *be* glory and dominion for ever and ever. Amen.

BENEFICENCE *See* **GOODNESS, KINDNESS**

BENEVOLENCE, *good will, kindness, charity*

1. The Duty

MOSES' INJUNCTION

De 15:12 *And* if thy brother, an Hebrew man, or an Hebrew woman, be sold unto thee, and serve thee six years; then in the seventh year thou shalt let him go free from thee.

De 15:13 And when thou sendest him out free from thee, thou shalt not let him go away empty:

De 15:14 Thou shalt furnish him liberally out of thy flock, and out of thy floor, and out of thy winepress: *of that* wherewith the Lord thy God hath blessed thee thou shalt give unto him.

Ne 8:10 Then he said unto them, Go your way, eat the fat, and drink the sweet, and send portions unto them for whom nothing is prepared: for *this* day *is* holy unto our Lord: neither be ye sorry; for the joy of the Lord is your strength.

THE WISE MAN'S ADVICE

Pr 25:21 If thine enemy be hungry, give him bread to eat; and if he be thirsty, give him water to drink:

Ec 11:1 Cast thy bread upon the waters: for thou shalt find it after many days.

THE PROPHET'S WORDS

Is 58:7 *Is it* not to deal thy bread to the hungry, and that thou bring the poor that are cast out to thy house? when thou seest the naked, that thou cover him; and that thou hide not thyself from thine own flesh?

CHRIST'S COMMANDS

Mt 5:42 Give to him that asketh thee, and from him that would borrow of thee turn not thou away.

Lu 3:11 He answereth and saith unto them, He that hath two coats, let him impart to him that hath none; and he that hath meat, let him do likewise.

Lu 12:33 Sell that ye have, and give alms; provide yourselves bags which wax not old, a treasure in the heavens that faileth not, where no thief approacheth, neither moth corrupteth.

PAUL'S EXHORTATION

Ac 20:35 I have shewed you all things, how that so labouring ye ought to support the weak, and to remember the words of the Lord Jesus, how he said, It is more blessed to give than to receive.

Ro 12:13 Distributing to the necessity of saints; given to hospitality.

Ga 6:10 As we have therefore opportunity, let us do good unto all *men*, especially unto them who are of the household of faith.

1 Ti 6:18 That they do good, that they be rich in good works, ready to distribute, willing to communicate;

He 13:16 But to do good and to communicate forget not: for with such sacrifices God is well pleased.

2. Results

2 Chr 31:10 And Azariah the chief priest of the house of Zadok answered him, and said, Since *the people* began to bring the offerings into the house of the Lord, we have had enough to eat, and have left plenty: for the Lord hath blessed his people; and that which is left *is* this great store.

Ps 112:9 He hath dispersed, he hath given to the poor; his righteousness endureth for ever; his horn shall be exalted with honour.

Pr 11:25 The liberal soul shall be made fat: and he that watereth shall be watered also himself.

Pr 22:9 He that hath a bountiful eye shall be blessed; for he giveth of his bread to the poor.

Is 32:8 But the liberal deviseth liberal things; and by liberal things shall he stand.

Is 32:20 Blessed *are* ye that sow beside all waters, that send forth *thither* the feet of the ox and the ass.

Is 58:10 And *if* thou draw out thy soul to the hungry, and satisfy the afflicted soul; then shall thy light rise in obscurity, and thy darkness *be* as the noonday:

Mal 3:10 Bring ye all the tithes into the storehouse, that there may be meat in mine house, and prove me now herewith, saith the LORD of hosts, if I will not open you the windows of heaven, and pour you out a blessing, that *there shall* not *be room* enough *to receive it.*

Lu 6:38 Give, and it shall be given unto you; good measure, pressed down, and shaken together, and running over, shall men give into your bosom. For with the same measure that ye mete withal it shall be measured to you again.

2 Co 9:6 But this *I say,* He which soweth sparingly shall reap also sparingly; and he which soweth bountifully shall reap also bountifully.

2 Co 9:9 (As it is written, He hath dispersed abroad; he hath given to the poor: his righteousness remaineth for ever.

3. Examples

BOAZ

Ru 2:15 And when she was risen up to glean, Boaz commanded his young men, saying, Let her glean even among the sheaves, and reproach her not:

WIDOW OF ZAREPHATH

1 K 17:15 And she went and did according to the saying of Elijah: and she, and he, and her house, did eat *many* days.

ELISHA

2 K 6:22 And he answered, Thou shalt not smite *them:* wouldest thou smite those whom thou hast taken captive with thy sword and with thy bow? set bread and water before them, that they may eat and drink, and go to their master.

THE CHILDREN OF EPHRAIM

2 Chr 28:15 And the men which were expressed by name rose up, and took the captives, and with the spoil clothed all that were naked among them, and arrayed them, and shod them, and gave them to eat and to drink, and anointed them, and carried all the feeble of them upon asses, and brought them to Jericho, the city of palm trees, to their brethren: then they returned to Samaria.

JOB

Jb 29:16 I *was* a father to the poor: and the cause *which* I knew not I searched out.

THE INHABITANTS OF TEMA

Is 21:14 The inhabitants of the land of Tema brought water to him that was thirsty, they prevented with their bread him that fled.

THE GOOD SAMARITAN

Lu 10:34–35 And went to *him,* and bound up his wounds, pouring in oil and wine, and set him on his own beast, and brought him to an inn, and took care of him.

And on the morrow when he departed, he took out two pence, and gave *them* to the host, and said unto him, Take care of him; and whatsoever thou spendest more, when I come again, I will repay thee.

See **GIVING**

BENHADAD, *son of the god Hadad*

1. King of Syria

1 K 15:18; 2 Chr 16:2

2. King of Syria in the Time of Ahab

1 K 20:1–43; 2 K 5:6–7

3. Son of Hazael

2 K 13:3; Am 1:4

BENJAMIN, *son of Jacob*

Ge 35:18; 42:4, 36; 43:15, 34; 45:12, 22; 46:19, 21; 49:27; Ex 1:3; Nu 1:11, 36; 2:22; 10:24; 13:9; 26:38; 34:21; Jos 18:11, 20; 21:4; Jud 20:14; 1 S 9:1; 2 S 23:29; 1 Chr 7:6; 8:1, 40; 9:3, 7; 12:29; 27:12; Ne 11:7, 31; Ps 68:27; Eze 48:22, 32; Ac 13:21; Ro 11:1; Ph 3:5; Re 7:8

BEREA, *a city of Macedonia*

Ac 17:10, 13; 20:4

BEREAVEMENT *See* **DEATH**

BERYL *See* **STONES**

BETH-ABARA, *a place near Jordan where John baptized*

Jud 7:24; Jn 1:28; 10:40

BETHANY, *a village east of Jerusalem*

Bethany, the home of Mary, Martha, and Lazarus, is now called el-Azariyeh ("The Place of Lazarus"). It is located two miles east of Jerusalem (Jn 11:1, 18), on the eastern slope of the Mount of Olives.

Mt 21:2, 17; 26:6; Mk 11:11; 14:3; Lu 10:38; 19:29; 24:50; Jn 11:18; 12:1

See **CITIES**

BETH-AVEN, *a town east of Beth-el*

Jos 7:2; 18:12; 1 S 13:5; 14:23; Ho 4:15; 5:8; 10:5

See **CITIES**

BETH-EL, *the house of God, a town 12 miles north of Jerusalem*

Beth-el (*house of God*) is mentioned more in the Old Testament than any city except Jerusalem. It is the site where Abraham built his second altar (Ge 12:8); where Jacob had his vision

of angels ascending and descending on a heavenly ladder (Ge 28:11–22); and where after twenty years Jacob returned, according to his vow, to set up an altar. He called the place Beth-el "because there God had revealed Himself to him" (Ge 35:2–7). Jeroboam desecrated the place by setting up a calf-god of gold. The Syrian general Baccides fortified the city (1 Maccabees 9:50) and it was captured by the Roman general Vespian in A.D. 69, according to Josephus. The city was destroyed during the Arab conquest in the seventh century.

Ge 12:8; 13:3; 28:19; 31:13; 35:1, 6, 15; 48:3; Jos 8:12; 12:16; 16:2; 18:13, 22; Jud 1:22; 4:5; 21:19; 1 S 7:16; 10:3; 13:2; 30:27; 1 K 12:29; 13:1; 2 K 2:2, 23; 10:29; 17:28; 23:4, 15; 1 Chr 7:28; 2 Chr 13:19; Ezr 2:28; Ne 7:32; 11:31; Am 3:14; 5:6

See **CITIES, MOUNTAINS AND HILLS**

BETH-HORON, *upper and nether, two towns of Palestine*

Jos 10:10; 1 S 13:18; 1 K 9:17; 1 Chr 6:68; 7:24; 2 Chr 8:5; 25:13

See **CITIES**

BETH-LEHEM, *a city of Judah*

Beth-lehem, the city of David, lies five miles south of Jerusalem. Near here Rachel was buried, Ruth gleaned in Boaz' field, David was anointed king, Christ was born, and the magi came from the east seeking the Savior.

Ge 48:7; Jos 19:15; Jud 12:10; Ru 1:19; 2:4; 4:11; 1 S 16:4; 17:15; 20:6; 2 S 2:32; 23:15; 1 Chr 11:16; 2 Chr 11:6; Ezr 2:21; Ne 7:26; Je 41:17; Mi 5:2; Mt 2:1, 5, 8, 16; Lu 2:4, 11, 15; Jn 7:42

See **CITIES, CHRIST**

BETH-PEOR, *a city of Moab*

De 3:29; 4:46; 34:6; Jos 13:20

See **CITIES**

BETH-SHAN(*BETH-SHEAN*)

Located at the east end of the Valley of Jezreel on the south bank of the river Jalud, this city guarded the highway between the valleys of Jezreel and the Jordan. It was, therefore, of strategic importance. It could not be overthrown by the invading Israelites (Jos 17:11–12) and was the site where Saul's body would be displayed (1 S 31:10–12). By Solomon's time it was firmly in Israelite hands (1 K 4:12).

See **CITIES**

BETH-SHEMESH

Beth-Shemesh (the house of the sun) is situated twenty-four miles west of Jerusalem, on a hill spur overlooking the Valley of Sorek in the Shephelah. It was important because it was a Levitical city (Jos 21:16) and a frontier post between Judah and the Philistines. It was here that the ark of the covenant was returned after it had long been in possession of the Philistines.

See **CITIES**

BETHESDA

This was a spring-fed pool surrounded by five porches where Jesus healed the man who had been sick for thirty-eight years (Jn 5:2–9).

BETHPHAGE, *a village near Jerusalem*
Mt 21:1; Mk 11:1; Lu 19:29

See **CITIES**

BETHSAIDA, *of Galilee, home of Philip*
Mt 11:21; Mk 6:45; 8:22; Lu 9:10; 10:13; Jn 1:44; 12:21

See **PHILIP**

BETRAYAL, *of men into the hands of their enemies*
Jud 14:17; 16:18; Ps 41:9; 55:12; Je 9:4; Mi 7:6; Zec 13:6; Mt 10:21; 17:22; 20:18; 24:10; 26:2, 16, 21, 49; Mk 3:19; 13:12; 14:10, 18, 41

BETROTHALS, *similar to an engagement period, bound by official ceremonies of commitment*
Ge 29:11–20, 19; De 20:7; Jud 14:1–10; 1 S 18:17; Mt 1:18; Lu 1:26–27

BEZALEEL, *inspired with skill to construct the tabernacle*
Ex 31:2; 35:30; 36:1; 37:1; 38:22; 2 Chr 1:5

BIBLE See **WORD OF GOD**

BIGOTRY

JEALOUSY OF OTHER WORKERS

Mk 9:38 And John answered him, saying, Master, we saw one casting out devils in thy name, and he followeth not us: and we forbad him, because he followeth not us.

EXCLUSION OF THE YOUNG

Mk 10:13 And they brought young children to him, that he should touch them: and *his* disciples rebuked those that brought *them.*

REJECTION OF CHRIST

Lu 9:53 And they did not receive him, because his face was as though he would go to Jerusalem.

CRITICISM OF CHRIST

Lu 19:7 And when they saw *it,* they all murmured, saying, That he was gone to be guest with a man that is a sinner.

PERSECUTION OF THE SAINTS

Ac 26:11 And I punished them oft in every synagogue, and compelled *them* to blaspheme; and being exceedingly mad against them, I persecuted *them* even unto strange cities.

See **CATHOLICITY, EXCLUSIVENESS, PREJUDICE**

BIND See **AGRICULTURE**

BIRDS, *warm-blooded animals with feathers and wings; symbols of objects of God's meticulous concern*

1. God's Care
De 22:6; Mt 6:26; Lu 12:6

2. Their Nests
Ps 84:3; 104:17; Is 34:15; Mt 8:20

3. Their Singing

Ps 104:12; Ec 12:4; Song 2:12

4. Their Names

a. Cormorants

Le 11:17; De 14:17; Is 34:11; Zep 2:14

b. Doves

Ge 8:8; Ps 55:6; 68:13; Song 6:9; Eze 7:16; Mt 3:16; 10:16; 21:12; Lu 3:22

c. Eagles

Ex 19:4; De 14:12; 32:11; 2 S 1:23; Jb 9:26; 39:27; Pr 23:5; 30:19; Is 40:31; Je 48:40; Eze 17:3; Obad 4; Hab 1:8; Lu 17:37

d. Hawks

Le 11:16; De 14:15; Jb 39:26

e. Ostriches

Jb 39:13–14; Lam 4:3

f. Owls

Le 11:16–17; De 14:15–16; Ps 102:6; Is 34:11, 14–15

g. Peacocks

1 K 10:22; 2 Chr 9:21; Jb 39:13

h. Pelicans

Le 11:18; De 14:17; Ps 102:6

i. Pigeons

Ge 15:9; Le 1:14; 5:7; 12:6, 8; 14:22, 30; 15:14, 29; Nu 6:10; Lu 2:24

j. Quails

Ex 16:13; Nu 11:31–32; Ps 105:40

k. Ravens

Ge 8:7; De 14:14; 1 K 17:4; Jb 38:41; Ps 147:9; Pr 30:17; Is 34:11; Lu 12:24

l. Sparrows

Ps 84:3; 102:7; Mt 10:29; Lu 12:6

m. Storks

Le 11:19; De 14:18; Ps 104:17; Je 8:7; Zec 5:9

n. Swallows

Ps 84:3; Is 38:14; Je 8:7

o. Turtledoves

Ge 15:9; Le 1:14; 5:7; 12:6, 8; 14:22, 30; 15:14, 29; Nu 6:10; Ps 74:19; Lu 2:24

p. Vultures

Le 11:14; De 14:13–14

BIRTH   *See* **CHILDREN, FAMILY**

BIRTHDAYS

See **SOCIAL FUNCTIONS**

BISHOPS   *See* **CHURCH**

BITTERNESS, *symbolic of affliction, misery, servitude; often producing pain, sorrow, or grief*

De 29:18 Lest there should be among you man, or woman, or family, or tribe, whose heart turneth away this day from the LORD our God, to go *and* serve the gods of these nations; lest there should be among you a root that beareth gall and wormwood;
De 32:32 For their vine *is* of the vine of Sodom, and of the fields of Gomorrah: their grapes *are* grapes of gall, their clusters *are* bitter:
Je 4:18 Thy way and thy doings have procured these *things* unto thee; this *is* thy wickedness, because it is bitter, because it reacheth unto thine heart.
Ac 8:23 For I perceive that thou art in the gall of bitterness, and *in* the bond of iniquity.
Ro 3:14 Whose mouth *is* full of cursing and bitterness:
Ep 4:31 Let all bitterness, and wrath, and anger, and clamour, and evil speaking, be put away from you, with all malice:
He 12:15 Looking diligently lest any man fail of the grace of God; lest any root of bitterness springing up trouble *you,* and thereby many be defiled;
Ja 3:14 But if ye have bitter envying and strife in your hearts, glory not, and lie not against the truth.

BLACKNESS, *figurative, evil or sin*

Is 50:3; Je 8:21; Jl 2:6; Na 2:10

BLASPHEMY, *speaking evil of deity*

1. Against God

Le 24:11, 16, 23; 2 K 18:33; 19:6, 22; 2 Chr 32:16; Ps 74:10, 18; Is 3:8; 36:20; 37:4, 6, 23; 52:5; 65:7; Je 12:8; Eze 20:27; 35:12; Da 7:25; 11:36; Mt 12:31; Mk 3:28; 7:22; Ac 13:45; 18:6; Col 3:8; 1 Ti 1:20; 6:1; 2 Ti 3:2; Ja 2:7; Jude 15; Re 13:1, 5; 16:11, 21

2. Against Christ

Mt 9:34 But the Pharisees said, He casteth out devils through the prince of the devils.

Mt 12:24 But when the Pharisees heard *it,* they said, This *fellow* doth not cast out devils, but by Beelzebub the prince of the devils.

Mk 3:30 Because they said, He hath an unclean spirit.

Lu 11:15 But some of them said, He casteth out devils through Beelzebub the chief of the devils.

Lu 22:65 And many other things blasphemously spake they against him.

Ja 2:7 Do not they blaspheme that worthy name by the which ye are called?

See **CURSING**

BLESSINGS, *expressions or acts of well-being directed toward another*

1. Explanation

a. Temporal from God

Ge 24:35 And the LORD hath blessed my master greatly; and he is become great: and he hath given him flocks, and herds, and silver, and gold, and menservants, and maidservants, and camels, and asses.

Ge 26:12 Then Isaac sowed in that land, and received in the same year an hundredfold: and the LORD blessed him.

De 16:17 Every man *shall give* as he is able, according to the blessing of the LORD thy God which he hath given thee.

De 29:5 And I have led you forty years in the wilderness: your clothes are not waxen old upon you, and thy shoe is not waxen old upon thy foot.

2 S 6:11 And the ark of the LORD continued in the house of Obed-edom the Gittite three months: and the LORD blessed Obed-edom, and all his household.

1 K 3:13 And I have also given thee that which thou hast not asked, both riches, and honour: so that there shall not be any among the kings like unto thee all thy days.

2 Chr 32:29 Moreover he provided him cities, and possessions of flocks and herds in abundance: for God had given him substance very much.

Ps 65:9 Thou visitest the earth, and waterest it: thou greatly enrichest it with the river of God, *which* is full of water: thou preparest them corn, when thou hast so provided for it.

Ps 68:19 Blessed *be* the LORD, *who* daily loadeth us *with benefits, even* the God of our salvation. Selah.

Ps 107:38 He blesseth them also, so that they are multiplied greatly; and suffereth not their cattle to decrease.

Ps 144:13 *That* our garners *may be* full, affording all manner of store: *that* our sheep may bring forth thousands and ten thousands in our streets:

Je 27:6 And now have I given all these lands into the hand of Nebuchadnezzar the king of Babylon, my servant; and the beasts of the field have I given him also to serve him.

Ac 14:17 Nevertheless he left not himself without witness, in that he did good, and gave us rain from heaven, and fruitful seasons, filling our hearts with food and gladness.

2 Co 9:10 Now he that ministereth seed to the sower both minister bread for *your* food, and multiply your seed sown, and increase the fruits of your righteousness;)

1 Ti 6:17 Charge them that are rich in this world, that they be not highminded, nor trust in uncertain riches, but in the living God, who giveth us richly all things to enjoy;

See **PLENTY, PROVIDENCE**

b. Temporal and Spiritual Promised

Ge 22:17 That in blessing I will bless thee, and in multiplying I will multiply thy seed as the stars of the heaven, and as the sand which *is* upon the sea shore; and thy seed shall possess the gate of his enemies;

Ex 23:25 And ye shall serve the LORD your God, and he shall bless thy bread, and thy water; and I will take sickness away from the midst of thee.

Le 26:4 Then I will give you rain in due season, and the land shall yield her increase, and the trees of the field shall yield their fruit.

Nu 10:32 And it shall be, if thou go with us, yea, it shall be, that what goodness the LORD shall do unto us, the same will we do unto thee.

De 28:2 And all these blessings shall come on thee, and overtake thee, if thou shalt hearken unto the voice of the LORD thy God.

Ps 81:16 He should have fed them also with the finest of the wheat: and with honey out of the rock should I have satisfied thee.

Ps 103:1 Bless the LORD, O my soul: and all that is within me, *bless* his holy name.

Pr 28:20 A faithful man shall abound with blessings: but he that maketh haste to be rich shall not be innocent.

Is 30:23 Then shall he give the rain of thy seed, that thou shalt sow the ground withal; and bread of the increase of the earth, and it shall be fat and plenteous: in that day shall thy cattle feed in large pastures

Jl 2:26 And ye shall eat in plenty, and be satisfied, and praise the name of the LORD your God, that hath dealt wondrously with you: and my people shall never be ashamed.

Am 9:13 Behold, the days come, saith the LORD, that the plowman shall overtake the reaper, and the treader of grapes him that soweth seed; and the mountains shall drop sweet wine, and all the hills shall melt.

Zec 10:1 Ask ye of the LORD rain in the time of the latter rain; *so* the LORD shall make bright clouds, and give them showers of rain, to every one grass in the field.

Mal 3:10 Bring ye all the tithes into the storehouse, that there may be meat in mine house, and prove me now herewith, saith the LORD of hosts, if I will not open you the windows of heaven, and pour you out a blessing, that *there shall* not *be room* enough *to receive it.*

Mt 6:33 But seek ye first the kingdom of God, and his righteousness; and all these things shall be added unto you.

Lu 18:30 Who shall not receive manifold more in this present time, and in the world to come life everlasting.

See **BENEVOLENCE, FULLNESS, OBEDIENCE, PROSPERITY**

c. The Blessing of God upon His People

De 23:5 Nevertheless the LORD thy God would not hearken unto Balaam; but the LORD thy God turned the curse into a blessing unto thee, because the LORD thy God loved thee.

2 S 7:29 Therefore now let it please thee to bless the house of thy servant, that it may continue for ever before thee: for thou, O LORD God, hast spoken *it:* and with thy blessing let the house of thy servant be blessed for ever.

Jb 42:11 Then came there unto him all his brethren, and all his sisters, and all they that had been of his acquaintance before, and did eat bread with him in his house: and they bemoaned him, and comforted him over all the evil that the LORD had brought upon him: every man also gave him a piece of money, and every one an earring of gold.

Ps 3:8 Salvation *belongeth* unto the LORD: thy blessing *is* upon thy people. Selah.

Ps 24:5 He shall receive the blessing from the LORD, and righteousness from the God of his salvation.

Ps 129:8 Neither do they which go by say, The blessing of the LORD *be* upon you: we bless you in the name of the LORD.

Ps 133:3 As the dew of Hermon, *and as the dew* that descended upon the mountains of Zion: for there the LORD commanded the blessing, *even* life for evermore.

Ps 134:3 The LORD that made heaven and earth bless thee out of Zion.

Pr 10:22 The blessing of the LORD, it maketh rich, and he addeth no sorrow with it.

Eze 44:30 And the first of all the firstfruits of all *things,* and every oblation of all, of every *sort* of your oblations, shall be the priest's: ye shall also give unto the priest the first of your dough, that he may cause the blessing to rest in thine house.

1 Pe 3:9 Not rendering evil for evil, or railing for railing: but contrariwise blessing; knowing that ye are thereunto called, that ye should inherit a blessing.

d. Pronounced by the Lord

Ge 1:28 And God blessed them, and God said unto them, Be fruitful, and multiply, and replenish the earth, and subdue it: and have dominion over the fish of the sea, and over the fowl of the air, and over every living thing that moveth upon the earth.

Ge 9:1 And God blessed Noah and his sons, and said unto them, Be fruitful, and multiply, and replenish the earth.

Ge 12:2 And I will make of thee a great nation, and I will bless thee, and make thy name great; and thou shalt be a blessing:

Ge 17:20 And as for Ishmael, I have heard thee: Behold, I have blessed him, and will make him fruitful, and will multiply him exceedingly; twelve princes shall he beget, and I will make him a great nation.

Ge 32:29 And Jacob asked *him,* and said, Tell *me,* I pray thee, thy name. And he said, Wherefore *is* it *that* thou dost ask after my name? And he blessed him there.

Lu 1:28 And the angel came in unto her, and said, Hail, *thou that art* highly favoured, the LORD *is* with thee: blessed *art* thou among women.

e. Pronounced by Men

Ge 24:31 And he said, Come in, thou blessed of the LORD; wherefore standest thou without? for I have prepared the house, and room for the camels.

Ge 27:10 And thou shalt bring *it* to thy father, that he may eat, and that he may bless thee before his death.

Ge 27:27 And he came near, and kissed him: and he smelled the smell of his raiment, and blessed him, and said, See, the smell of my son *is* as the smell of a field which the LORD hath blessed:

Ge 28:1 And Isaac called Jacob, and blessed him, and charged him, and said unto him, Thou shalt not take a wife of the daughters of Canaan.

Ge 48:16 The Angel which redeemed me from all evil, bless the lads; and let my name be named on them, and the name of my fathers Abraham and Isaac; and let them grow into a multitude in the midst of the earth.

Jos 14:13 And Joshua blessed him, and gave unto Caleb the son of Jephunneh Hebron for an inheritance.

Jos 22:6 So Joshua blessed them, and sent them away: and they went unto their tents.

Ru 1:8 And Naomi said unto her two daughters in law, Go, return each to her mother's house: the LORD deal kindly with you, as ye have dealt with the dead, and with me.

Ru 2:12 The LORD recompense thy work, and a full reward be given thee of the LORD God of Israel, under whose wings thou art come to trust.

Ru 2:19 And her mother in law said unto her, Where hast thou gleaned to day? and where wroughtest thou? blessed be he that did take knowledge of thee. And she shewed her mother in law with whom she had wrought, and said, The man's name with whom I wrought to day *is* Boaz.

Ru 4:11 And all the people that *were* in the gate, and the elders, said, *We are* witnesses. The LORD make the woman that is come into thine house like Rachel and like Leah, which two did build the house of Israel: and do thou worthily in Ephratah, and be famous in Bethlehem:

1 S 2:20 And Eli blessed Elkanah and his wife, and said, The LORD give thee seed of this woman for the loan which is lent to the LORD. And they went unto their own home.

2 S 13:25 And the king said to Absalom, Nay, my son, let us not all now go, lest we be chargeable unto thee. And he pressed him: howbeit he would not go, but blessed him.

1 K 8:14 And the king turned his face about, and blessed all the congregation of Israel: (and all the congregation of Israel stood;)

2 Chr 31:8 And when Hezekiah and the princes came and saw the heaps, they blessed the LORD, and his people Israel.

Lu 2:34 And Simeon blessed them, and said unto Mary his mother, Behold, this *child* is set for the fall and rising again of many in Israel; and for a sign which shall be spoken against;

He 7:1 For this Melchisedec, king of Salem, priest of the most high God, who met Abraham returning from the slaughter of the kings, and blessed him;

See **FAVOR**

2. Delayed Blessings Test Faith

BIRTH OF A SON

Ge 15:4 And, behold, the word of the LORD *came* unto him, saying, This shall not be thine heir; but he that shall come forth out of thine own bowels shall be thine heir.

MANY YEARS WAITING

Ge 21:2 For Sarah conceived, and bare Abraham a son in his old age, at the set time of which God had spoken to him.

SACRIFICE PROVIDED

Ge 22:8 And Abraham said, My son, God will provide himself a lamb for a burnt offering: so they went both of them together.

MESSIAH

Ge 3:15 And I will put enmity between thee and the woman, and between thy seed and her seed; it shall bruise thy head, and thou shalt bruise his heel.

Lu 2:30 For mine eyes have seen thy salvation,

HEALING

Mt 15:28 Then Jesus answered and said unto her, O woman, great *is* thy faith: be it unto thee even as thou wilt. And her daughter was made whole from that very hour.

RELIEF AND RESURRECTION

Jn 11:6 When he had heard therefore that he was sick, he abode two days still in the same place where he was.

Jn 11:32 Then when Mary was come where Jesus was, and saw him, she fell down at his feet, saying unto him, Lord, if thou hadst been here, my brother had not died.

Jn 11:43–44 And when he thus had spoken, he cried with a loud voice, Lazarus, come forth.

And he that was dead came forth, bound hand and foot with graveclothes: and his face was bound about with a napkin. Jesus saith unto them, Loose him, and let him go.

GIFT OF THE SPIRIT

Lu 24:49 And, behold, I send the promise of my Father upon you: but tarry ye in the city of Jerusalem, until ye be endued with power from on high.

DELIVERANCE

Ac 12:7 And, behold, the angel of the Lord came upon *him,* and a light shined in the prison: and he smote Peter on the side, and raised him up, saying, Arise up quickly. And his chains fell off from *his* hands.

ESCAPE

Ac 27:44 And the rest, some on boards, and some on *broken pieces* of the ship. And so it came to pass, that they escaped all safe to land.

See **AFFLICTIONS, DELAY, WAITING**

3. Universal

ETERNAL LIFE—IF ANY MAN EAT OF THIS
BREAD, HE WILL LIVE FOREVER

Jn 6:51 I am the living bread which
came down from heaven: if any man
eat of this bread, he shall live for ever:
and the bread that I will give is my
flesh, which I will give for the life of
the world.

SPIRITUAL KNOWLEDGE—IF ANY MAN WILL
DO HIS WILL, HE SHALL KNOW OF THE
DOCTRINE

Jn 7:17 If any man will do his will, he
shall know of the doctrine, whether it
be of God, or *whether* I speak of myself.

SALVATION—BY ME IF ANY MAN ENTER IN,
HE SHALL BE SAVED

Jn 10:9 I am the door: by me if any
man enter in, he shall be saved, and
shall go in and out, and find pasture.

WISDOM—IF ANY OF YOU LACK WISDOM,
LET HIM ASK OF GOD

Ja 1:5 If any of you lack wisdom, let
him ask of God, that giveth to all *men*
liberally, and upbraideth not; and it
shall be given him.

DIVINE FELLOWSHIP—IF ANY MAN HEAR MY
VOICE AND OPEN THE DOOR, I WILL COME IN
TO HIM

Re 3:20 Behold, I stand at the door,
and knock: if any man hear my voice,
and open the door, I will come in to
him, and will sup with him, and he
with me.

See **LOVE, SALVATION**

BLINDNESS, *inability to see in the
physical or spiritual realm*

1. Physical

Le 19:14; De 27:18; Jb 29:15; Lu 18:35

See **INFIRMITIES**

2. Spiritual

a. Examples

Jb 5:14 They meet with darkness in
the daytime, and grope in the noonday as in the night.

Is 59:10 We grope for the wall like the
blind, and we grope as if *we had* no
eyes: we stumble at noonday as in the
night; *we are* in desolate places as dead
men.

Mt 6:23 But if thine eye be evil, thy
whole body shall be full of darkness.
If therefore the light that is in thee be
darkness, how great *is* that darkness!

Mt 15:14 Let them alone: they be
blind leaders of the blind. And if the
blind lead the blind, both shall fall
into the ditch.

Mt 23:19 *Ye* fools and blind: for
whether *is* greater, the gift, or the altar
that sanctifieth the gift?

2 Co 3:14 But their minds were
blinded: for until this day remaineth
the same vail untaken away in the
reading of the old testament; which
vail is done away in Christ.

2 Co 4:4 In whom the god of this
world hath blinded the minds of them
which believe not, lest the light of the
glorious gospel of Christ, who is the
image of God, should shine unto
them.

Ep 4:18 Having the understanding
darkened, being alienated from the
life of God through the ignorance that
is in them, because of the blindness of
their heart:

2 Pe 1:9 But he that lacketh these
things is blind, and cannot see afar off,
and hath forgotten that he was purged
from his old sins.

1 Jn 2:11 But he that hateth his
brother is in darkness, and walketh in
darkness, and knoweth not whither
he goeth, because that darkness hath
blinded his eyes.

See **VISION**

b. Inflicted

Ex 7:3; De 29:4; Jos 11:20; Jb 12:24; Ps
69:23; Is 6:10; 19:14; 29:10; 44:18; Je
13:16; Mk 4:12; Jn 12:40; Ro 11:8, 25;
2 Th 2:11

BLOOD, *life-fluid of the body; in ancient thought, closely associated with the soul*

1. Of Christ See CHRIST

2. Sprinkled

Ex 12:7, 22; 24:8; 29:16, 21; Le 1:5, 11; 3:2, 8, 13; 4:6, 17; 5:9; 7:2; 8:19, 24, 30; 9:12, 18; 14:7, 51; 16:14, 19; 17:6; Nu 18:17; 19:4; 2 Chr 29:22; 30:16; 35:11; Eze 43:20; 45:19; He 9:19; 11:28; 12:24; 1 Pe 1:2

3. Innocent

Le 19:16; De 19:10; 21:8; 1 S 19:5; 2 S 4:11; 1 K 2:31; 2 K 9:26; 21:16; 24:4; Ps 94:21; 106:38; Pr 6:17; 28:17; Is 59:7; Je 2:34; 7:6; 19:4; 22:3, 17; 26:15; Lam 4:13; Eze 22:3; Jl 3:19; Jona 1:14; Hab 2:17; Mt 23:30; 27:4

4. Forbidden to Be Eaten

Ge 9:4; Le 3:17; 7:26; 17:10, 14; 19:26; De 12:16, 23; 15:23; 1 S 14:32, 34; Eze 33:25; Ac 15:20, 29; 21:25

5. Upon Men

Ge 42:22; Le 20:11, 16, 27; Jos 2:19; Jud 9:24; 2 S 1:16; 3:29; 1 K 2:5, 33; Ps 51:14; Je 2:34; 51:35; Eze 18:13; 23:45; 33:6; Ho 12:14; Mt 23:35; 27:25; Lu 11:50; Ac 5:28; 18:6

6. Of Sacrifices, *typical of the blood of Christ*

SHELTERING

Ex 12:13 And the blood shall be to you for a token upon the houses where ye *are:* and when I see the blood, I will pass over you, and the plague shall not be upon you to destroy *you,* when I smite the land of Egypt.

ATONING

Ex 30:10 And Aaron shall make an atonement upon the horns of it once in a year with the blood of the sin offering of atonements: once in the year shall he make atonement upon it throughout your generations: it *is* most holy unto the LORD.

Le 17:11 For the life of the flesh *is* in the blood: and I have given it to you upon the altar to make an atonement for your souls: for it *is* the blood *that* maketh an atonement for the soul.

LIBERATING

Zec 9:11 As for thee also, by the blood of thy covenant I have sent forth thy prisoners out of the pit wherein *is* no water.

SECURING PARDON

He 9:7 But into the second *went* the high priest alone once every year, not without blood, which he offered for himself, and *for* the errors of the people:

CLEANSING

He 9:22 And almost all things are by the law purged with blood; and without shedding of blood is no remission.

See CHRIST

7. Applied to Persons

Ex 29:20; Le 8:23; 14:14, 25

BLUE

Ex 26:4, 36; 27:16; 28:8, 15, 31; 35:23, 35; 36:11, 35; 38:18; 39:1, 5, 22, 31; Nu 4:6, 9, 12; 15:38; 2 Chr 2:7, 14; 3:14; Est 1:6; Eze 27:7

BOARS See ANIMALS

BOASTERS

1. Examples

Ex 15:9; Jud 9:38; 1 S 14:12; 17:10, 44; 1 K 20:10; 2 K 18:23, 34; 19:12; 2 Chr 25:19; 32:13; Ps 12:4; 73:9; 75:4; Is 10:11; 36:8, 19; 37:11; Je 48:14; Eze 35:13; Da 3:15; 7:8, 20; Zep 2:8; Mt 23:30; 26:33; Mk 14:29; Ac 5:36; 8:9; Ro 1:30; 2 Ti 3:2; 2 Pe 2:18; Jude 16; Re 13:5

2. Folly

Ps 10:3; 49:6–7; 52:1; 94:4; Pr 20:14; 25:14; 27:1; Mt 26:35; Ro 11:18; 1 Co 4:7; Ja 3:5; 4:16

BOATBUILDING See ARTS AND CRAFTS

BOAZ, *husband of Ruth, David's progenitor*

Ru 2:4; 4:13; 1 Chr 2:11; Mt 1:5; Lu 3:32

See **KINDNESS**

BODY

1. Human, not to be disfigured

Le 19:28; 21:5; De 14:1; 1 Co 6:15; 1 Th 5:23

See **MUTILATION**

2. Spiritual, resurrected

1 Co 15:44 It is sown a natural body; it is raised a spiritual body. There is a natural body, and there is a spiritual body.

1 Co 15:49 And as we have borne the image of the earthy, we shall also bear the image of the heavenly.

2 Co 5:2 For in this we groan, earnestly desiring to be clothed upon with our house which is from heaven:

Ph 3:21 Who shall change our vile body, that it may be fashioned like unto his glorious body, according to the working whereby he is able even to subdue all things unto himself.

Col 3:4 When Christ, *who is* our life, shall appear, then shall ye also appear with him in glory.

See **RESURRECTION**

BOILS *See* **DISEASE, MIRACLES**

BOLDNESS, *courage*

Jb 11:15 For then shalt thou lift up thy face without spot; yea, thou shalt be stedfast, and shalt not fear:

Ep 3:12 In whom we have boldness and access with confidence by the faith of him.

1 Ti 3:13 For they that have used the office of a deacon well purchase to themselves a good degree, and great boldness in the faith which is in Christ Jesus.

He 4:16 Let us therefore come boldly unto the throne of grace, that we may obtain mercy, and find grace to help in time of need.

He 10:19 Having therefore, brethren, boldness to enter into the holiest by the blood of Jesus,

1 Jn 4:17 Herein is our love made perfect, that we may have boldness in the day of judgment: because as he is, so are we in this world.

Examples

Da 3:16 Shadrach, Meshach, and Abed-nego, answered and said to the king, O Nebuchadnezzar, we *are* not careful to answer thee in this matter.

Mk 15:43 Joseph of Arimathaea, an honourable counsellor, which also waited for the kingdom of God, came, and went in boldly unto Pilate, and craved the body of Jesus.

Ac 4:13 Now when they saw the boldness of Peter and John, and perceived that they were unlearned and ignorant men, they marvelled; and they took knowledge of them, that they had been with Jesus.

Ac 4:31 And when they had prayed, the place was shaken where they were assembled together; and they were all filled with the Holy Ghost, and they spake the word of God with boldness.

Ac 9:29 And he spake boldly in the name of the Lord Jesus, and disputed against the Grecians: but they went about to slay him.

Ac 14:3 Long time therefore abode they speaking boldly in the Lord, which gave testimony unto the word of his grace, and granted signs and wonders to be done by their hands.

Ac 19:8 And he went into the synagogue, and spake boldly for the space of three months, disputing and persuading the things concerning the kingdom of God.

Ac 28:31 Preaching the kingdom of God, and teaching those things which concern the Lord Jesus Christ, with all confidence, no man forbidding him.

2 Co 3:12 Seeing then that we have such hope, we use great plainness of speech:

1 Th 2:2 But even after that we had suffered before, and were shamefully entreated, as ye know, at Philippi, we were bold in our God to speak unto you the gospel of God with much contention.

See **COURAGE, WITNESSES**

BONDAGE

1. Physical

a. Of Israel

See **ISRAEL**

b. General Statements

Ge 21:10; Ex 12:44; 21:2; Le 19:20; 25:39, 42; Jos 9:23; 1 K 9:21; Est 7:4; 1 Co 7:21; Ga 4:31

See **CAPTIVES**

2. Spiritual

a. Of Sin

Pr 5:22 His own iniquities shall take the wicked himself, and he shall be holden with the cords of his sins.

Is 28:22 Now therefore be ye not mockers, lest your bands be made strong: for I have heard from the Lord God of hosts a consumption, even determined upon the whole earth.

Je 13:23 Can the Ethiopian change his skin, or the leopard his spots? *then* may ye also do good, that are accustomed to do evil.

Jn 8:34 Jesus answered them, Verily, verily, I say unto you, Whosoever committeth sin is the servant of sin.

Ac 8:23 For I perceive that thou art in the gall of bitterness, and *in* the bond of iniquity.

Ro 6:16 Know ye not, that to whom ye yield yourselves servants to obey, his servants ye are to whom ye obey; whether of sin unto death, or of obedience unto righteousness?

Ro 7:23 But I see another law in my members, warring against the law of my mind, and bringing me into captivity to the law of sin which is in my members.

2 Ti 2:26 And *that* they may recover themselves out of the snare of the devil, who are taken captive by him at his will.

2 Pe 2:19 While they promise them liberty, they themselves are the ser-

vants of corruption: for of whom a man is overcome, of the same is he brought in bondage.

b. Sold under Sin

1 K 21:20; 2 K 17:17; Is 50:1; 52:3; Ro 7:14

See **LIBERTY, SIN**

BONNETS   *See* **DRESS**

BOOKS, *God's record of human dealings, originated and supervised by God*

1. Book of Judgment

Da 7:10 A fiery stream issued and came forth from before him: thousand thousands ministered unto him, and ten thousand times ten thousand stood before him: the judgment was set, and the books were opened.

Re 20:12 And I saw the dead, small and great, stand before God; and the books were opened: and another book was opened, which is *the book* of life: and the dead were judged out of those things which were written in the books, according to their works.

2. Book of the Law

De 31:26 Take this book of the law, and put it in the side of the ark of the covenant of the LORD your God, that it may be there for a witness against thee.

Jos 1:8 This book of the law shall not depart out of thy mouth; but thou shalt meditate therein day and night, that thou mayest observe to do according to all that is written therein: for then thou shalt make thy way prosperous, and then thou shalt have good success.

2 K 22:8 And Hilkiah the high priest said unto Shaphan the scribe, I have found the book of the law in the house of the LORD. And Hilkiah gave the book to Shaphan, and he read it.

2 K 23:2 And the king went up into the house of the LORD, and all the men of Judah and all the inhabitants of Jerusalem with him, and the priests, and the prophets, and all the people, both small and great: and he read in their ears all the words of the book of the covenant which was found in the house of the LORD.

2 Chr 17:9 And they taught in Judah, and *had* the book of the law of the LORD with them, and went about throughout all the cities of Judah, and taught the people.

Ne 8:8 So they read in the book in the law of God distinctly, and gave the sense, and caused *them* to understand the reading.

Ne 8:18 Also day by day, from the first day unto the last day, he read in the book of the law of God. And they kept the feast seven days; and on the eighth day *was* a solemn assembly, according unto the manner.

Ga 3:10 For as many as are of the works of the law are under the curse: for it is written, Cursed *is* every one that continueth not in all things which are written in the book of the law to do them.

3. Book of Life

Ex 32:33 And the LORD said unto Moses, Whosoever hath sinned against me, him will I blot out of my book.

Ps 56:8 Thou tellest my wanderings: put thou my tears into thy bottle: *are they* not in thy book?

Ps 69:28 Let them be blotted out of the book of the living, and not be written with the righteous.

Ps 87:6 The LORD shall count, when he writeth up the people, that this man was born there. Selah.

Is 4:3 And it shall come to pass, *that he that is* left in Zion, and *he that* remaineth in Jerusalem, shall be called holy, *even* every one that is written among the living in Jerusalem:

Da 7:10 A fiery stream issued and came forth from before him: thousand thousands ministered unto him, and ten thousand times ten thousand stood before him: the judgment was set, and the books were opened.

Da 12:1 And at that time shall Michael stand up, the great prince which standeth for the children of thy people: and there shall be a time of trouble, such as never was since there was a

nation *even* to that same time: and at that time thy people shall be delivered, every one that shall be found written in the book.

Mal 3:16 Then they that feared the LORD spake often one to another: and the LORD hearkened, and heard *it*, and a book of remembrance was written before him for them that feared the LORD, and that thought upon his name.

Lu 10:20 Notwithstanding in this rejoice not, that the spirits are subject unto you; but rather rejoice, because your names are written in heaven.

Ph 4:3 And I intreat thee also, true yokefellow, help those women which laboured with me in the gospel, with Clement also, and *with* other my fellowlabourers, whose names *are* in the book of life.

He 12:23 To the general assembly and church of the firstborn, which are written in heaven, and to God the Judge of all, and to the spirits of just men made perfect,

Re 3:5 He that overcometh, the same shall be clothed in white raiment; and I will not blot out his name out of the book of life, but I will confess his name before my Father, and before his angels.

Re 13:8 And all that dwell upon the earth shall worship him, whose names are not written in the book of life of the Lamb slain from the foundation of the world.

Re 17:8 The beast that thou sawest was, and is not; and shall ascend out of the bottomless pit, and go into perdition: and they that dwell on the earth shall wonder, whose names were not written in the book of life from the foundation of the world, when they behold the beast that was, and is not, and yet is.

Re 20:12 And I saw the dead, small and great, stand before God; and the books were opened: and another book was opened, which is *the book* of life: and the dead were judged out of those things which were written in the books, according to their works.

Re 21:27 And there shall in no wise enter into it any thing that defileth, neither *whatsoever* worketh abomination, or *maketh* a lie: but they which are written in the Lamb's book of life.

Re 22:19 And if any man shall take away from the words of the book of this prophecy, God shall take away his part out of the book of life, and out of the holy city, and *from* the things which are written in this book.

4. Writings

Ex 17:14; Nu 5:23; 21:14; Jb 19:23; Ec 12:12; Is 30:8; Je 30:2; 32:12; 36:11, 18; 51:60; Jn 21:25; Ac 19:19; 2 Ti 4:13; Re 5:1; 10:2

BOOTHS, *made of boughs as a shelter*

Ge 33:17; Le 23:42; Ne 8:14; Jona 4:5; Mk 9:5; Lu 9:33

BORROWING *See* **CREDIT SYSTEM**

BOTTLES, *wineskins*

Ge 21:14; Jud 4:19; 1 S 1:24; 10:3; 25:18; 2 S 16:1; Ps 56:8; 119:83; Mt 9:17; Mk 2:22

BOWLS, *vessels, the earliest made of wood and shells of larger nuts*

Ex 25:29; 37:16; Nu 4:7; 7:19, 31, 37, 43, 61, 79, 85; 2 K 12:13; 25:15; 1 Chr 28:17; Am 6:6; Zec 9:15; Re 5:8; 15:7; 16:1; 17:1

BOWS, *weapons of ancient warfare*

Ge 27:3; 1 S 18:4; 2 S 1:18; 1 K 22:34; 2 K 9:24; 13:15; 1 Chr 5:18; 12:2; 2 Chr 17:17; 26:14; Ne 4:13; Ps 78:9; Is 5:28; Je 46:9; 50:29, 42; Ho 7:16; Zec 10:4; Re 6:2

BOX *See* **TREES**

BOZRAH, *a city of Edom*

Is 34:6; Je 48:24; 49:13, 22; Am 1:12

BRACELETS *See* **APPAREL**

BRANDS, *symbolic of salvation from destruction*

Am 4:11; Zec 3:2; 1 Co 3:15; Jude 23

BRASS, *an alloy of copper and zinc with other metals in lesser amounts*

Ge 4:22; Ex 25:3; 26:11, 37; 27:2, 10, 17; 30:18; 35:24; 36:18, 38; 38:3, 11, 17, 19, 29; Jos 6:19; 1 S 17:5; 2 S 8:8; 21:16; 1 K 7:14, 27, 47; 2 K 25:13; 1 Chr 18:8; 22:3, 14; 29:2; 2 Chr 4:9, 18; 12:10; Jb 28:2; 41:27; Je 52:17; Eze 27:13; Da 2:35; Re 18:12

BRAZEN SERPENT, *made by Moses*

Nu 21:9; 2 K 18:4; Jn 3:14

BRAZIERS *See* **ARTS AND CRAFTS**

BREAD, *sometimes used in broad sense to include all food; specifically that which is baked into loaves*

1. Baking *See* **ARTS AND CRAFTS**

2. Staff of Life

Ge 41:54; 47:15; Je 52:6; Eze 4:16; 5:16; 14:13

3. Breaking

Mt 14:19 And he commanded the multitude to sit down on the grass, and took the five loaves, and the two fishes, and looking up to heaven, he blessed, and brake, and gave the loaves to *his* disciples, and the disciples to the multitude.

Lu 24:30 And it came to pass, as he sat at meat with them, he took bread, and blessed *it*, and brake, and gave to them.

Lu 24:35 And they told what things *were done* in the way, and how he was known of them in breaking of bread.

Ac 2:42 And they continued stedfastly in the apostles' doctrine and fellowship, and in breaking of bread, and in prayers.

Ac 20:11 When he therefore was come up again, and had broken bread, and eaten, and talked a long while, even till break of day, so he departed.

Ac 27:35 And when he had thus spoken, he took bread, and gave thanks to God in presence of them all: and when he had broken *it*, he began to eat.

4. Unleavened

Ge 19:3; Ex 12:8, 15, 18, 39; 13:6–7; 23:15; 29:2, 23; 34:18; Le 6:16; 8:2, 26; 23:6; Nu 6:15; 9:11; 28:17; De 16:3, 8; Jos 5:11; Jud 6:19; 1 S 28:24; 2 K 23:9; Ezr 6:22; Eze 45:21; Lu 22:7; 1 Co 5:8

BREAKFAST *See* FOOD

BREASTPLATE, *armour; an official piece of dress for the High Priest*

1. Of the Priests

Ex 25:7; 28:4, 15, 24, 28; 29:5; 35:9, 27; 39:8, 15; Le 8:8

2. Figurative

Is 59:17; Ep 6:14; 1 Th 5:8

BREATH

1. Of God

Ex 15:8; 2 S 22:16; 2 K 19:7; Jb 4:9; 12:10; 15:30; 32:8; 34:14; 37:10; Ps 18:15; Is 11:4; 30:28, 33; 40:7, 24; Ho 13:15; Hag 1:9

2. Of Life

Ge 2:7 And the LORD God formed man *of* the dust of the ground, and breathed into his nostrils the breath of life; and man became a living soul.

Ge 6:17 And, behold, I, even I, do bring a flood of waters upon the earth, to destroy all flesh, wherein *is* the breath of life, from under heaven; *and* every thing that *is* in the earth shall die.

Ge 7:22 All in whose nostrils *was* the breath of life, of all that *was* in the dry *land,* died.

Job 27:3 All the while my breath *is* in me, and the spirit of God *is* in my nostrils;

Job 33:4 The Spirit of God hath made me, and the breath of the Almighty hath given me life.

Ec 3:19 For that which befalleth the sons of men befalleth beasts; even one thing befalleth them: as the one dieth, so dieth the other; yea, they have all one breath; so that a man hath no preeminence above a beast: for all *is* vanity.

Is 2:22 Cease ye from man, whose breath *is* in his nostrils: for wherein is he to be accounted of?

Is 42:5 Thus saith God the LORD, he that created the heavens, and stretched them out; he that spread forth the earth, and that which cometh out of it; he that giveth breath unto the people upon it, and spirit to them that walk therein:

Lam 4:20 The breath of our nostrils, the anointed of the LORD, was taken in their pits, of whom we said, Under his shadow we shall live among the heathen.

Eze 37:5 Thus saith the Lord GOD unto these bones; Behold, I will cause breath to enter into you, and ye shall live:

Eze 37:9 Then said he unto me, Prophesy unto the wind, prophesy, son of man, and say to the wind, Thus saith the Lord GOD; Come from the four winds, O breath, and breathe upon these slain, that they may live.

Da 5:23 But hast lifted up thyself against the Lord of heaven; and they have brought the vessels of his house before thee, and thou, and thy lords, thy wives, and thy concubines, have drunk wine in them; and thou hast praised the gods of silver, and gold, of brass, iron, wood, and stone, which see not, nor hear, nor know: and the God in whose hand thy breath *is,* and whose *are* all thy ways, hast thou not glorified:

Ac 17:25 Neither is worshipped with men's hands, as though he needed any thing, seeing he giveth to all life, and breath, and all things;

BRETHREN, *of Christ*

Mt 12:46; 13:55; Mk 3:31; 6:3; Lu 8:20; Jn 2:12; 7:3, 5; Ac 1:14; 1 Co 9:5; Ga 1:19

BRIBERY *See* NATION

BRICKS, *made from clay*

Ge 11:3; Ex 1:14; 5:8; Is 65:3

BRICK-MAKERS *See* ARTS AND CRAFTS

BRIDEGROOM

De 24:5; Jud 14:11; Ps 19:5; Je 16:9; 25:10; 33:11; Jl 2:16; Mt 25:10; Jn 2:9; Re 18:23

See **CHRIST**

BRIDLE, *used to control an animal*

Ps 32:9; Pr 26:3; Re 14:20

BRIERS, *thorny plants or bushes*

Is 5:6; 55:13; Eze 2:6; Mi 7:4

BRIMSTONE, *sulphur*

Ge 19:24; De 29:23; Jb 18:15; Ps 11:6; Is 30:33; 34:9; Eze 38:22; Lu 17:29; Re 9:17; 19:20

See **JUDGMENTS**

BROOKS, *small freshwater streams*

Nu 13:23; 21:14, 24; De 2:13; 1 S 30:9; 2 S 15:23; 1 K 17:3; 18:5, 40; 1 Chr 11:32; Ps 83:9; Jn 18:1

BROTHEL See **SEX**

BROTHER, *fellow Christian*

Mt 12:50; Ac 9:17; 21:20; 22:13; Ro 16:23; 1 Co 7:12; 2 Co 1:1; 8:18; Ep 6:21; Col 1:1; 4:7; He 13:23; 2 Pe 3:15; Re 1:9

See **BRETHREN**

BUL See **MONTHS**

BULLOCKS See **ANIMALS**

BULRUSHES, *reeds, broad blades of grass growing in wet places*

Ex 2:3; Jb 8:11; Is 18:2; 35:7; 58:5

BURDENS, *physical or emotional difficulties, responsibilities or duties*

1. Physical

Nu 11:11; 2 Co 5:4; Re 2:24

2. Prophetic

2 K 9:25; Is 13:1; 14:28; 15:1; 17:1; 19:1; 21:1, 11; 23:1; Je 23:33; Eze 12:10; Na 1:1; Hab 1:1; Zec 9:1; 12:1; Mal 1:1

BURIAL CEREMONIES See **DEAD**

BURNING See **NATION**

BURNING BUSH, *seen by Moses*

De 24:5; Jud 14:11; Ps 19:5; Je 16:9; 25:10; 33:11; Jl 2:16; Mt 25:10; Jn 2:9; Re 18:23

BURNT OFFERINGS

See **OFFERINGS**

BUSINESS

1. Cares and Troubles

NEGLECT OF DUTY

1 K 20:39 And as the king passed by, he cried unto the king: and he said, Thy servant went out into the midst of the battle; and, behold, a man turned aside, and brought a man unto me, and said, Keep this man: if by any means he be missing, then shall thy life be for his life, or else thou shalt pay a talent of silver.

1 K 20:40 And as thy servant was busy here and there, he was gone. And the king of Israel said unto him, So *shall* thy judgment *be;* thyself hast decided *it.*

A RESTLESS LIFE

Ps 39:6 Surely every man walketh in a vain shew: surely they are disquieted in vain: he heapeth up *riches,* and knoweth not who shall gather them.

DISAPPOINTMENT

Ec 2:20 Therefore I went about to cause my heart to despair of all the labour which I took under the sun.

SLEEPLESSNESS

Ec 5:12 The sleep of a labouring man *is* sweet, whether he eat little or much: but the abundance of the rich will not suffer him to sleep.

PRESUMPTION

Lu 12:17–18 And he thought within himself, saying, What shall I do, because I have no room where to bestow my fruits?

And he said, This will I do: I will pull down my barns, and build greater; and there will I bestow all my fruits and my goods.

Lu 12:20 But God said unto him, *Thou* fool, this night thy soul shall be required of thee: then whose shall those things be, which thou hast provided?

2. Engagements

Mt 22:4–5; Lu 14:16–20

3. Life, instructions for work

a. Merchandise

Ne 10:31; 13:16; Eze 27:16, 34; Jn 2:16; Re 18:12

b. Goods

Ge 14:16; 31:18; Nu 31:9; Ezr 1:6; Ne 9:25; Mk 13:15; Lu 12:18; 15:12; 17:31

c. Barter

Ge 47:17; 1 K 5:10; 2 Chr 1:16; Ho 3:2

d. Trading

Ge 34:10; 42:34; 47:16; De 2:6, 28; 1 K 10:15; Pr 20:14; Eze 17:4; 27:12; Lu 17:28; 19:15; 1 Co 7:30

e. Merchants

Ge 37:25; 1 K 10:15; Ne 13:20; Jb 41:6; Is 23:2, 8; Eze 27:23, 36; 38:13; Na 3:16; Zep 1:11; Re 18:11

4. Vices, ungodliness in the marketplace

a. Broken Trust

Le 6:2 If a soul sin, and commit a trespass against the LORD, and lie unto his neighbour in that which was delivered him to keep, or in fellowship, or in a thing taken away by violence, or hath deceived his neighbour;

Song 1:6 Look not upon me, because I *am* black, because the sun hath looked upon me: my mother's children were angry with me; they made me the keeper of the vineyards; *but* mine own vineyard have I not kept.

Eze 16:17 Thou hast also taken thy fair jewels of my gold and of my silver, which I had given thee, and madest to thyself images of men, and didst commit whoredom with them,

Lu 16:12 And if ye have not been faithful in that which is another man's, who shall give you that which is your own?

b. Dishonesty

Le 6:2 If a soul sin, and commit a trespass against the LORD, and lie unto his neighbour in that which was delivered him to keep, or in fellowship, or in a thing taken away by violence, or hath deceived his neighbour;

Le 19:35 Ye shall do no unrighteousness in judgment, in meteyard, in weight, or in measure.

De 25:13 Thou shalt not have in thy bag divers weights, a great and a small.

Ps 37:21 The wicked borroweth, and payeth not again: but the righteous sheweth mercy, and giveth.

Pr 11:1 A false balance *is* abomination to the LORD: but a just weight *is* his delight.

Pr 20:10 Divers weights, *and* divers measures, both of them *are* alike abomination to the LORD.

Pr 20:14 *It is* naught, *it is* naught, saith the buyer: but when he is gone his way, then he boasteth.

Pr 20:23 Divers weights *are* an abomination unto the LORD; and a false balance *is* not good.

Pr 21:6 The getting of treasures by a lying tongue *is* a vanity tossed to and fro of them that seek death.

Je 17:11 As the partridge sitteth *on eggs,* and hatcheth *them* not; *so* he that getteth riches, and not by right, shall leave them in the midst of his days, and at his end shall be a fool.

Je 22:13 Woe unto him that buildeth his house by unrighteousness, and his chambers by wrong; *that* useth his neighbour's service without wages, and giveth him not for his work;

Ho 12:7 *He is* a merchant, the balances of deceit *are* in his hand: he loveth to oppress.

Am 8:5 Saying, When will the new moon be gone, that we may sell corn? and the sabbath, that we may set forth wheat, making the ephah small, and the shekel great, and falsifying the balances by deceit?

Mi 6:11 Shall I count *them* pure with the wicked balances, and with the bag of deceitful weights?

c. Extortion

Ne 5:10 I likewise, *and* my brethren, and my servants, might exact of them money and corn: I pray you, let us leave off this usury.

Is 10:2 To turn aside the needy from judgment, and to take away the right from the poor of my people, that widows may be their prey, and *that* they may rob the fatherless!

Is 16:4 Let mine outcasts dwell with thee, Moab; be thou a covert to them from the face of the spoiler: for the extortioner is at an end, the spoiler ceaseth, the oppressors are consumed out of the land.

Eze 22:12 In thee have they taken gifts to shed blood; thou hast taken usury and increase, and thou hast greedily gained of thy neighbours by extortion, and hast forgotten me, saith the Lord GOD.

Eze 45:9 Thus saith the Lord GOD; Let it suffice you, O princes of Israel: remove violence and spoil, and execute judgment and justice, take away your exactions from my people, saith the Lord GOD.

Am 5:11 Forasmuch therefore as your treading *is* upon the poor, and ye take from him burdens of wheat: ye have built houses of hewn stone, but ye shall not dwell in them; ye have planted pleasant vineyards, but ye shall not drink wine of them.

Mt 18:28 But the same servant went out, and found one of his fellow-servants, which owed him an hundred pence: and he laid hands on him, and took *him* by the throat, saying, Pay me that thou owest.

Mt 23:14 Woe unto you, scribes and Pharisees, hypocrites! for ye devour widows' houses, and for a pretence make long prayer: therefore ye shall receive the greater damnation.

Mt 23:25 Woe unto you, scribes and Pharisees, hypocrites! for ye make clean the outside of the cup and of the platter, but within they are full of extortion and excess.

Lu 3:13 And he said unto them, Exact no more than that which is appointed you.

1 Co 5:10 Yet not altogether with the fornicators of this world, or with the covetous, or extortioners, or with idolaters; for then must ye needs go out of the world.

1 Co 6:10 Nor thieves, nor covetous, nor drunkards, nor revilers, nor extortioners, shall inherit the kingdom of God.

See **ROBBERY**

d. Fraud

Le 19:13 Thou shalt not defraud thy neighbour, neither rob *him*: the wages of him that is hired shall not abide with thee all night until the morning.

Je 6:14 They have healed also the hurt *of the daughter* of my people slightly, saying, Peace, peace; when *there is* no peace.

Je 8:10 Therefore will I give their wives unto others, *and* their fields to them that shall inherit *them*: for every one from the least even unto the greatest is given to covetousness, from the prophet even unto the priest every one dealeth falsely.

Je 22:13 Woe unto him that buildeth his house by unrighteousness, and his chambers by wrong; *that* useth his neighbour's service without wages, and giveth him not for his work;

Am 8:6 That we may buy the poor for silver, and the needy for a pair of shoes; *yea,* and sell the refuse of the wheat?

Mark 10:19 Thou knowest the commandments, Do not commit adultery, Do not kill, Do not steal, Do not bear false witness, Defraud not, Honour thy father and mother.

1 Co 6:8 Nay, ye do wrong, and defraud, and that *your* brethren.

1 Th 4:6 That no *man* go beyond and defraud his brother in *any* matter: because that the Lord *is* the avenger of all such, as we also have forewarned you and testified.

Ja 5:4 Behold, the hire of the labourers who have reaped down your fields, which is of you kept back by fraud, crieth: and the cries of them which have reaped are entered into the ears of the Lord of sabaoth.

See **DECEPTION**

e. Unjust Gain

Le 6:4 Then it shall be, because he hath sinned, and is guilty, that he shall restore that which he took violently away, or the thing which he hath deceitfully gotten, or that which was delivered him to keep, or the lost thing which he found,

1 K 21:16 And it came to pass, when Ahab heard that Naboth was dead, that Ahab rose up to go down to the vineyard of Naboth the Jezreelite, to take possession of it.

Job 20:15 He hath swallowed down riches, and he shall vomit them up again: God shall cast them out of his belly.

Ps 37:16 A little that a righteous man hath *is* better than the riches of many wicked.

Ps 62:10 Trust not in oppression, and become not vain in robbery: if riches increase, set not your heart *upon them.*

Pr 10:2 Treasures of wickedness profit nothing: but righteousness delivereth from death.

Pr 13:11 Wealth *gotten* by vanity shall be diminished: but he that gathereth by labour shall increase.

Pr 15:6 In the house of the righteous *is* much treasure: but in the revenues of the wicked is trouble.

Pr 16:8 Better *is* a little with righteousness than great revenues without right.

Pr 20:14 *It is* naught, *it is* naught, saith the buyer: but when he is gone his way, then he boasteth.

Pr 21:6 The getting of treasures by a lying tongue *is* a vanity tossed to and fro of them that seek death.

Pr 22:16 He that oppresseth the poor to increase his *riches, and* he that giveth to the rich, *shall* surely *come* to want.

Pr 28:8 He that by usury and unjust gain increaseth his substance, he shall gather it for him that will pity the poor.

Is 33:15 He that walketh righteously, and speaketh uprightly; he that despiseth the gain of oppressions, that shaketh his hands from holding of bribes, that stoppeth his ears from hearing of blood, and shutteth his eyes from seeing evil;

Is 56:11 Yea, *they are* greedy dogs *which* can never have enough, and they *are* shepherds *that* cannot understand: they all look to their own way, every one for his gain, from his quarter.

Je 5:27 As a cage is full of birds, so *are* their houses full of deceit: therefore they are become great, and waxen rich.

Je 17:11 As the partridge sitteth *on eggs,* and hatcheth *them* not; *so* he that getteth riches, and not by right, shall leave them in the midst of his days, and at his end shall be a fool.

Je 22:13 Woe unto him that buildeth his house by unrighteousness, and his chambers by wrong; *that* useth his neighbour's service without wages, and giveth him not for his work;

Eze 18:13 Hath given forth upon usury, and hath taken increase: shall he then live? he shall not live: he hath done all these abominations; he shall surely die; his blood shall be upon him.

Eze 22:13 Behold, therefore I have smitten mine hand at thy dishonest gain which thou hast made, and at thy blood which hath been in the midst of thee.

Eze 22:27 Her princes in the midst thereof *are* like wolves ravening the prey, to shed blood, *and* to destroy souls, to get dishonest gain.

Mi 6:10 Are there yet the treasures of wickedness in the house of the wicked, and the scant measure *that is* abominable?

Hab 2:6 Shall not all these take up a parable against him, and a taunting proverb against him, and say, Woe to him that increaseth *that which is* not his! how long? and to him that ladeth himself with thick clay!

Mt 27:3 Then Judas, which had betrayeth him, when he saw that he was condemned, repented himself, and brought again the thirty pieces of silver to the chief priests and elders,

Ac 16:16 And it came to pass, as we went to prayer, a certain damsel possessed with a spirit of divination met us, which brought her masters much gain by soothsaying:

Ac 16:19 And when her masters saw that the hope of their gains was gone, they caught Paul and Silas, and drew *them* into the marketplace unto the rulers,

1 Co 5:11 But now I have written unto you not to keep company, if any man that is called a brother be a fornicator, or covetous, or an idolater, or a railer, or a drunkard, or an extortioner; with such an one no not to eat.

Ja 5:4 Behold, the hire of the labourers who have reaped down your fields, which is of you kept back by fraud, crieth: and the cries of them which have reaped are entered into the ears of the Lord of sabaoth.

See **GREED, POOR**

f. Slothfulness

Jud 18:9 And they said, Arise, that we may go up against them: for we have seen the land, and, behold, it *is* very good: and *are* ye still? be not slothful to go, *and* to enter to possess the land.

Pr 6:9 How long wilt thou sleep, O sluggard? when wilt thou arise out of thy sleep?

Pr 10:4 He becometh poor that dealeth *with* a slack hand: but the hand of the diligent maketh rich.

Pr 12:24 The hand of the diligent shall bear rule: but the slothful shall be under tribute.

Pr 12:27 The slothful *man* roasteth not that which he took in hunting: but the substance of a diligent man *is* precious.

Pr 18:9 He also that is slothful in his work is brother to him that is a great waster.

Pr 19:15 Slothfulness casteth into a deep sleep; and an idle soul shall suffer hunger.

Pr 21:25 The desire of the slothful killeth him; for his hands refuse to labour.

Pr 22:13 The slothful *man* saith, *There is* a lion without, I shall be slain in the streets.

Pr 24:30–31 I went by the field of the slothful, and by the vineyard of the man void of understanding;

And, lo, it was all grown over with thorns, *and* nettles had covered the face thereof, and the stone wall thereof was broken down.

Pr 26:13 The slothful *man* saith, *There is* a lion in the way; a lion *is* in the streets.

Ec 4:5 The fool foldeth his hands together, and eateth his own flesh.

Ec 10:18 By much slothfulness the building decayeth; and through idleness of the hands the house droppeth through.

Is 56:10 His watchmen *are* blind: they are all ignorant, they *are* all dumb dogs, they cannot bark; sleeping, lying down, loving to slumber.

Am 6:4 That lie upon beds of ivory, and stretch themselves upon their couches, and eat the lambs out of the flock, and the calves out of the midst of the stall;

Mt 20:3 And he went out about the third hour, and saw others standing idle in the marketplace,

Mt 25:18 But he that had received one went and digged in the earth, and hid his lord's money.

Mt 25:26 His lord answered and said unto him, *Thou* wicked and slothful servant, thou knewest that I reap where I sowed not, and gather where I have not strawed:

Lu 11:7 And he from within shall answer and say, Trouble me not: the door is now shut, and my children are with me in bed; I cannot rise and give thee.

Lu 19:20 And another came, saying, Lord, behold, *here is* thy pound, which I have kept laid up in a napkin:

Ro 12:11 Not slothful in business; fervent in spirit; serving the Lord;

2 Th 3:11 For we hear that there are some which walk among you disorderly, working not at all, but are busybodies.

1 Ti 5:13 And withal they learn *to be* idle, wandering about from house to house; and not only idle, but tattlers also and busybodies, speaking things which they ought not.

Tit 1:12 One of themselves, *even* a prophet of their own, said, The Cretians *are* alway liars, evil beasts, slow bellies.

He 6:12 That ye be not slothful, but followers of them who through faith and patience inherit the promises.

See **POVERTY**

5. Virtues

a. Diligence

Ezr 7:23 Whatsoever is commanded by the God of heaven, let it be diligently done for the house of the God of heaven: for why should there be wrath against the realm of the king and his sons?

Ne 4:23 So neither I, nor my brethren, nor my servants, nor the men of the guard which followed me, none of us put off our clothes, *saving that* every one put them off for washing.

Ne 5:16 Yea, also I continued in the work of this wall, neither bought we any land: and all my servants *were* gathered thither unto the work.

Pr 10:4 He becometh poor that dealeth *with* a slack hand: but the hand of the diligent maketh rich.

Pr 13:4 The soul of the sluggard desireth, and *hath* nothing: but the soul of the diligent shall be made fat.

Pr 22:29 Seest thou a man diligent in his business? he shall stand before kings; he shall not stand before mean *men.*

Ro 12:8 Or he that exhorteth, on exhortation: he that giveth, *let him do it* with simplicity; he that ruleth, with diligence; he that sheweth mercy, with cheerfulness.

He 6:11 And we desire that every one of you do shew the same diligence to the full assurance of hope unto the end:

2 Pe 1:10 Wherefore the rather, brethren, give diligence to make your calling and election sure: for if ye do these things, ye shall never fall:

2 Pe 3:14 Wherefore, beloved, seeing that ye look for such things, be diligent that ye may be found of him in peace, without spot, and blameless.

b. Fidelity

Ge 39:6 And he left all that he had in Joseph's hand; and he knew not ought he had, save the bread which he did eat. And Joseph was *a goodly person,* and well favoured.

2 K 12:15 Moreover they reckoned not with the men, into whose hand they delivered the money to be bestowed on workmen: for they dealt faithfully.

2 Chr 34:12 And the men did the work faithfully: and the overseers of them *were* Jahath and Obadiah, the Levites, of the sons of Merari; and Zechariah and Meshullam, of the sons of the Kohathites, to set *it* forward; and *other of* the Levites, all that could skill of instruments of musick.

Ne 13:13 And I made treasurers over the treasuries, Shelemiah the priest, and Zadok the scribe, and of the Levites, Pedaiah: and next to them *was* Hanan the son of Zaccur, the son of Mattaniah: for they were counted faithful, and their office *was* to distribute unto their brethren.

Da 6:4 Then the presidents and princes sought to find occasion against Daniel concerning the kingdom; but they could find none occasion nor fault; forasmuch as he *was* faithful, neither was there any error or fault found in him.

1 Co 4:2 Moreover it is required in stewards, that a man be found faithful.

He 3:5 And Moses verily *was* faithful in all his house, as a servant, for a testimony of those things which were to be spoken after;

c. Honesty

Le 19:36 Just balances, just weights, a just ephah, and a just hin, shall ye have: I *am* the LORD your God, which brought you out of the land of Egypt.

De 25:15 *But* thou shalt have a perfect and just weight, a perfect and just measure shalt thou have: that thy days may be lengthened in the land which the LORD thy God giveth thee.

2 K 12:15 Moreover they reckoned not with the men, into whose hand they delivered the money to be bestowed on workmen: for they dealt faithfully.

Pr 11:1 A false balance *is* abomination to the LORD: but a just weight *is* his delight.

Ro 12:17 Recompense to no man evil for evil. Provide things honest in the sight of all men.

Ro 13:8 Owe no man any thing, but to love one another: for he that loveth another hath fulfilled the law.

2 Co 8:21 Providing for honest things, not only in the sight of the Lord, but also in the sight of men.

Ph 4:8 Finally, brethren, whatsoever things are true, whatsoever things *are* honest, whatsoever things *are* just, whatsoever things *are* pure, whatsoever things *are* lovely, whatsoever things *are* of good report; if *there be* any virtue, and if *there be* any praise, think on these things.

d. Giving of Just Weights

Le 19:36 Just balances, just weights, a just ephah, and a just hin, shall ye have: I *am* the LORD your God, which brought you out of the land of Egypt.

De 25:13 Thou shalt not have in thy bag divers weights, a great and a small.

Pr 11:1 A false balance *is* abomination to the LORD: but a just weight *is* his delight.

Pr 16:11 A just weight and balance *are* the LORD's: all the weights of the bag *are* his work.

Pr 20:10 Divers weights, *and* divers measures, both of them *are* alike abomination to the LORD.

Eze 45:10 Ye shall have just balances, and a just ephah, and a just bath.

Ho 12:7 *He is* a merchant, the balances of deceit *are* in his hand: he loveth to oppress.

Am 8:5 Saying, When will the new moon be gone, that we may sell corn? and the sabbath, that we may set forth wheat, making the ephah small, and the shekel great, and falsifying the balances by deceit?

Mi 6:11 Shall I count *them* pure with the wicked balances, and with the bag of deceitful weights?

See **JUSTICE**

e. Industry

1). Commended

Ge 2:15 And the LORD God took the man, and put him into the garden of Eden to dress it and to keep it.

Ge 24:20 And she hasted, and emptied her pitcher into the trough, and ran again unto the well to draw *water,* and drew for all his camels.

Pr 6:6 Go to the ant, thou sluggard; consider her ways, and be wise:

Pr 10:5 He that gathereth in summer *is* a wise son: *but* he that sleepeth in harvest *is* a son that causeth shame.

Pr 12:11 He that tilleth his land shall be satisfied with bread: but he that followeth vain *persons is* void of understanding.

Pr 13:11 Wealth *gotten* by vanity shall be diminished: but he that gathereth by labour shall increase.

Pr 20:13 Love not sleep, lest thou come to poverty; open thine eyes, *and* thou shalt be satisfied with bread.

Pr 31:13 She seeketh wool, and flax, and worketh willingly with her hands.

Ro 12:11 Not slothful in business; fervent in spirit; serving the Lord;

1 Ti 5:8 But if any provide not for his own, and specially for those of his own house, he hath denied the faith, and is worse than an infidel.

2). Examples

Ge 31:40 *Thus* I was; in the day the drought consumed me, and the frost by night; and my sleep departed from mine eyes.

Ru 2:17 So she gleaned in the field until even, and beat out that she had gleaned: and it was about an ephah of barley.

1 K 11:28 And the man Jeroboam *was* a mighty man of valour: and Solomon seeing the young man that he was industrious, he made him ruler over all the charge of the house of Joseph.

Ne 4:21 So we laboured in the work: and half of them held the spears from the rising of the morning till the stars appeared.

Pr 31:27 She looketh well to the ways of her household, and eateth not the bread of idleness.

Ac 18:3 And because he was of the same craft, he abode with them, and wrought: for by their occupation they were tentmakers.

1 Co 4:12 And labour, working with our own hands: being reviled, we bless; being persecuted, we suffer it:

f. Integrity

1). General

Ex 18:21 Moreover thou shalt provide out of all the people able men, such as fear God, men of truth, hating covetousness; and place *such* over them, *to be* rulers of thousands, *and* rulers of hundreds, rulers of fifties, and rulers of tens:

Ps 41:12 And as for me, thou upholdest me in mine integrity, and settest me before thy face for ever.

Pr 11:3 The integrity of the upright shall guide them: but the perverseness of transgressors shall destroy them.

Pr 19:1 Better *is* the poor that walketh in his integrity, than *he that is* perverse in his lips, and is a fool.

Pr 20:7 The just *man* walketh in his integrity: his children *are* blessed after him.

2). Examples

Ge 14:23 That I will not *take* from a thread even to a shoelatchet, and that I will not take any thing that *is* thine, lest thou shouldest say, I have made Abram rich:

Nu 16:15 And Moses was very wroth, and said unto the LORD, Respect not thou their offering: I have not taken one ass from them, neither have I hurt one of them.

1 S 12:4 And they said, Thou hast not defrauded us, nor oppressed us,

neither hast thou taken ought of any man's hand.

2 S 18:12 And the man said unto Joab, Though I should receive a thousand *shekels* of silver in mine hand, yet would I not put forth mine hand against the king's son: for in our hearing the king charged thee and Abishai and Ittai, saying, Beware that none *touch* the young man Absalom.

1 K 13:8 And the man of God said unto the king, If thou wilt give me half thine house, I will not go in with thee, neither will I eat bread nor drink water in this place:

2 K 5:16 But he said, *As* the LORD liveth, before whom I stand, I will receive none. And he urged him to take *it;* but he refused.

2 K 12:15 Moreover they reckoned not with the men, into whose hand they delivered the money to be bestowed on workmen: for they dealt faithfully.

2 K 22:7 Howbeit there was no reckoning made with them of the money that was delivered into their hand, because they dealt faithfully.

Ne 5:15 But the former governors that *had been* before me were chargeable unto the people, and had taken of them bread and wine, beside forty shekels of silver; yea, even their servants bare rule over the people: but so did not I, because of the fear of God.

2 Co 7:2 Receive us; we have wronged no man, we have corrupted no man, we have defrauded no man.

He 13:18 Pray for us: for we trust we have a good conscience, in all things willing to live honestly.

BUTLERS, *cupbearers*

Ge 40:1, 9; 41:9; 1 K 10:5; 2 Chr 9:4; Ne 1:11

BUTTER, *curds and cream*

Ge 18:8; De 32:14; Jud 5:25; 2 S 17:29; Jb 29:6; Pr 30:33; Is 7:15, 22

C

CAESAR AUGUSTUS, *Roman emperor during half the lifetime of Christ*
Lu 2:1

CAESAR CLAUDIUS, *Roman emperor (A.D. 37–A.D. 54)*
Ac 11:28; 18:2

CAESAR NERO, *Roman emperor before whom Paul appeared during his first imprisonment in Rome; he persecuted Christians and Paul and Peter are supposed to have suffered martyrdom under his command*
Ac 25:21; 26:32; 27:24; 28:19; Ph 4:22

CAESAR TIBERIUS, *Roman emperor (A.D. 14–A.D. 37)*
Lu 3:1; 20:24; 23:2; Jn 19:12

CAESAREA, *a seaport of Palestine*
Caesarea, also called Caesarea Maritima or Caesarea Palestinae, was the Roman capital of Judea in the time of Christ and Paul. It was located by the sea, thirty-two miles north of Joppa and about sixty miles northwest of Jerusalem. Herod the Great began to build the New Testament city in 25 B.C. and completed it in 13 B.C. At the dedication in 12 B.C., he named it Caesarea in honor of Augustus Caesar and made it the Roman capital of Judea. It was a busy seaport with a mammoth harbor and a great commercial center. It was constructed so well and on such a magnificent plan that it was frequently called "Little Rome." It was the home of Philip the evangelist (Ac 8:40; 21:8) and the place where Cornelius was converted (Ac 10). Paul was imprisoned here for two years, during which time he appeared before Felix, Festus, and King Agrippa before being sent on to Rome (Ac 23–26).

CAESAREA PHILIPPI, *a town in north Palestine*
Caesarea Philippi was a town located at the southwest foot of Mount Hermon, where a sparkling stream, the most eastern source of the Jordan River, rushes out from a cave at the base of a great cliff. Being well-watered, it is one of the most beautiful places in all the Holy Land. In Old Testament times it had a shrine dedicated to Baal (Jos 11:17); while later the Greeks built a shrine to Pan, the god of nature, and called the place Paneas (the city of Pan). In 20 B.C. Herod the Great built a white marble temple here and dedicated it to Augustus Caesar. After Herod's death, his son Herod Philip enlarged the town and named it Caesarea to complete the honor to Augustus. By the first century A.D. it was called Caesarea Philippi to distinguish it from the better-known capital and seaport Caesarea Maritima on the coast. It was on the way to this area of natural beauty that Jesus asked his disciples, "Whom do men say that I the Son of man am?" and Simon Peter made the great declaration, "Thou art the Christ, the Son of the living God" (Mt 16:13–16; Mk 8:27–30).

CAIAPHAS, *high priest in the time of Christ*
Mt 26:3, 57; Lu 3:2; Jn 11:49; 18:14, 24; Ac 4:6

CAIN, *son of Adam*
Ge 4:2–3, 5–9, 14–16; He 11:4; 1 Jn 3:12; Jude 11

BROUGHT AN OFFERING

Ge 4:3 And in process of time it came to pass, that Cain brought of the fruit of the ground an offering unto the LORD.

JEALOUS

Ge 4:5 But unto Cain and to his offering he had not respect. And Cain was very wroth, and his countenance fell.

HARDENED, *under divine reproof*

Ge 4:6–7 And the LORD said unto Cain, Why art thou wroth? and why is thy countenance fallen? If thou doest well, shalt thou not be accepted? and if thou doest not well, sin lieth at the door. And unto thee *shall be* his desire, and thou shalt rule over him.

THE FIRST MURDERER

Ge 4:8 And Cain talked with Abel his brother: and it came to pass, when they were in the field, that Cain rose up against Abel his brother, and slew him.

IRREVERENT AND SELFISH

Ge 4:9 And the LORD said unto Cain, Where *is* Abel thy brother? And he said, I know not: *Am* I my brother's keeper?

LOST THE DIVINE FAVOR

Ge 4:14–16 Behold, thou hast driven me out this day from the face of the earth; and from thy face shall I be hid; and I shall be a fugitive and a vagabond in the earth; and it shall come to pass, *that* every one that findeth me shall slay me. And the LORD said unto him, Therefore whosoever slayeth Cain, vengeance shall be taken on him sevenfold. And the LORD set a mark upon Cain, lest any finding him should kill him. And Cain went out from the presence of the LORD, and dwelt in the land of Nod, on the east of Eden.

See **YOUNG PEOPLE**

CAKES, *bread, often made from unleavened dough and baked on hot sand or flat stones*

2 S 6:19; 1 K 19:6; Ho 7:8

CALAH

The city lies about twenty miles south of Nineveh on the east bank of the Tigris River, just north of the point where the Upper Zab River joins the Tigris. According to Genesis 10:11 it was first built by Nimrod, and the biblical association has remained in its modern name—Nimrod.

CALDRON, *large kettle*

1 S 2:14; 2 Chr 35:13; Jb 41:20; Je 52:17–18; Eze 11:7; Mi 3:3

CALEB, *son of Jephunneh*

Nu 13:6, 30; 14:6–9, 24, 30, 37; 26:65; 32:12; 34:19; De 1:36; Jos 14:6, 10–14; 15:13–14; 21:12; Jud 1:15; 1 S 25:3; 1 Chr 2:42; 4:15; 6:56

ONE OF THE TWELVE SPIES

Nu 13:6 Of the tribe of Judah, Caleb the son of Jephunneh.

COURAGEOUS

Nu 13:30 And Caleb stilled the people before Moses, and said, Let us go up at once, and possess it; for we are well able to overcome it.

Nu 14:6–9 And Joshua the son of Nun, and Caleb the son of Jephunneh, *which were* of them that searched the land, rent their clothes:

And they spake unto all the company of the children of Israel, saying, The land, which we passed through to search it, *is* an exceeding good land.

If the LORD delight in us, then he will bring us into this land, and give it us; a land which floweth with milk and honey.

Only rebel not ye against the LORD, neither fear ye the people of the land; for they *are* bread for us: their defence is departed from them, and the LORD *is* with us: fear them not.

PRESERVED WHEN OTHER SPIES PERISHED

Nu 14:37–38 Even those men that did bring up the evil report upon the land, died by the plague before the LORD.

But Joshua the son of Nun, and Caleb the son of Jephunneh, *which were* of the men that went to search the land, lived *still*.

CONSECRATED TO GOD

De 1:36 Save Caleb the son of Jephunneh; he shall see it, and to him will I give the land that he hath trodden upon, and to his children, because he hath wholly followed the LORD.

VIGOROUS AND FAITHFUL IN OLD AGE

Jos 14:10–14 And now, behold, the LORD hath kept me alive, as he said, these forty and five years, even since the LORD spake this word unto Moses, while *the children of* Israel wandered in the wilderness: and now, lo, I *am* this day fourscore and five years old.

As yet I *am as* strong this day as *I was* in the day that Moses sent me: as my strength *was* then, even so *is* my strength now, for war, both to go out, and to come in.

Now therefore give me this mountain, whereof the LORD spake in that day; for thou heardest in that day how the Anakims *were* there, and *that* the cities *were* great *and* fenced: if so be the LORD *will be* with me, then I shall be able to drive them out, as the LORD said.

And Joshua blessed him, and gave unto Caleb the son of Jephunneh Hebron for an inheritance.

Hebron therefore became the inheritance of Caleb the son of Jephunneh the Kenezite unto this day, because that he wholly followed the LORD God of Israel.

INVINCIBLE, *drove out the giants from his inheritance*

Jos 15:14 And Caleb drove thence the three sons of Anak, Sheshai, and Ahiman, and Talmai, the children of Anak.

CALKERS See ARTS AND CRAFTS

CALL, *DIVINE, God's invitation to people*

1. To Repentance and Righteousness

Ge 3:9 And the LORD God called unto Adam, and said unto him, Where *art* thou?

2 Chr 30:10 So the posts passed from city to city through the country of Ephraim and Manasseh even unto Zebulun: but they laughed them to scorn, and mocked them.

Pr 1:24 Because I have called, and ye refused; I have stretched out my hand, and no man regarded;

Pr 9:3 She hath sent forth her maidens: she crieth upon the highest places of the city,

Is 22:12 And in that day did the Lord GOD of hosts call to weeping, and to mourning, and to baldness, and to girding with sackcloth:

Is 65:1 I am sought of *them that* asked not *for me;* I am found of *them that* sought me not: I said, Behold me, behold me, unto a nation *that* was not called by my name.

Je 3:7 And I said after she had done all these *things,* Turn thou unto me. But she returned not. And her treacherous sister Judah saw *it.*

Je 6:16 Thus saith the LORD, Stand ye in the ways, and see, and ask for the old paths, where is the good way, and walk therein, and ye shall find rest for your souls. But they said, We will not walk *therein.*

Je 7:3 Thus saith the LORD of hosts, the God of Israel, Amend your ways and your doings, and I will cause you to dwell in this place.

Je 7:13 And now, because ye have done all these works, saith the LORD, and I spake unto you, rising up early and speaking, but ye heard not; and I called you, but ye answered not;

Je 7:27 Therefore thou shalt speak all these words unto them; but they will not hearken to thee: thou shalt also call unto them; but they will not answer thee.

Je 11:6 Then the LORD said unto me, Proclaim all these words in the cities of Judah, and in the streets of Jerusalem, saying, Hear ye the words of this covenant, and do them.

Je 25:3 From the thirteenth year of Josiah the son of Amon king of Judah, even unto this day, that *is* the three and twentieth year, the word of the LORD hath come unto me, and I have spoken unto you, rising early and speaking; but ye have not hearkened.

Je 26:5 To hearken to the words of my servants the prophets, whom I sent unto you, both rising up early, and sending *them,* but ye have not hearkened;

Je 29:19 Because they have not hearkened to my words, saith the LORD, which I sent unto them by my servants the prophets, rising up early and sending *them;* but ye would not hear, saith the LORD.

Je 35:15 I have sent also unto you all my servants the prophets, rising up early and sending *them,* saying, Return ye now every man from his evil way, and amend your doings, and go not after other gods to serve them, and ye shall dwell in the land which I have given to you and to your fathers: but ye have not inclined your ear, nor hearkened unto me.

Je 35:17 Therefore thus saith the LORD God of hosts, the God of Israel; Behold, I will bring upon Judah and upon all the inhabitants of Jerusalem all the evil that I have pronounced against them: because I have spoken unto them, but they have not heard; and I have called unto them, but they have not answered.

Je 44:4 Howbeit I sent unto you all my servants the prophets, rising early and sending *them,* saying, Oh, do not this abominable thing that I hate.

Eze 18:30 Therefore I will judge you, O house of Israel, every one according to his ways, saith the Lord GOD. Repent, and turn *yourselves* from all your transgressions; so iniquity shall not be your ruin.

Eze 33:11 Say unto them, *As* I live, saith the Lord GOD, I have no pleasure in the death of the wicked; but that the wicked turn from his way and live: turn ye, turn ye from your evil ways; for why will ye die, O house of Israel?

Da 9:10 Neither have we obeyed the voice of the LORD our God, to walk in his laws, which he set before us by his servants the prophets.

Ho 6:1 Come, and let us return unto the LORD: for he hath torn, and he will heal us; he hath smitten, and he will bind us up.

Ho 12:10 I have also spoken by the prophets, and I have multiplied visions, and used similitudes, by the ministry of the prophets.

Jl 2:12 Therefore also now, saith the LORD, turn ye *even* to me with all your heart,g, and with weeping, and with mourning:

Jl 2:32 And it shall come to pass, *that* whosoever shall call on the name of the LORD shall be delivered: for in mount Zion and in Jerusalem shall be deliverance, as the LORD hath said, and in the remnant whom the LORD shall call.

Mi 6:9 The LORD's voice crieth unto the city, and *the man of* wisdom shall see thy name: hear ye the rod, and who hath appointed it.

Zep 2:3 Seek ye the LORD, all ye meek of the earth, which have wrought his judgment; seek righteousness, seek meekness: it may be ye shall be hid in the day of the LORD's anger.

Zec 1:3 Therefore say thou unto them, Thus saith the LORD of hosts; Turn ye unto me, saith the LORD of hosts, and I will turn unto you, saith the LORD of hosts.

Zec 7:7 *Should ye* not *hear* the words which the LORD hath cried by the former prophets, when Jerusalem was inhabited and in prosperity, and the cities thereof round about her, when *men* inhabited the south and the plain?

Mt 8:21 And another of his disciples said unto him, Lord, suffer me first to go and bury my father.

Mt 9:13 But go ye and learn what *that* meaneth, I will have mercy, and not sacrifice: for I am not come to call the righteous, but sinners to repentance.

Mt 20:16 So the last shall be first, and the first last: for many be called, but few chosen.

Mt 21:36 Again, he sent other servants more than the first: and they did unto them likewise.

Mt 22:3 And sent forth his servants to call them that were bidden to the wedding: and they would not come.

Mt 23:34 Wherefore, behold, I send unto you prophets, and wise men, and scribes: and *some of them* ye shall kill and crucify; and some of them shall ye scourge in your synagogues, and persecute *them* from city to city:

Mk 2:17 When Jesus heard *it*, he saith unto them, They that are whole have no need of the physician, but they that are sick: I came not to call the righteous, but sinners to repentance.

Lu 5:32 I came not to call the righteous, but sinners to repentance.

Lu 9:59 And he said unto another, Follow me. But he said, Lord, suffer me first to go and bury my father.

Lu 11:49 Therefore also said the wisdom of God, I will send them prophets and apostles, and *some* of them they shall slay and persecute:

Lu 14:17 And sent his servant at supper time to say to them that were bidden, Come; for all things are now ready.

Lu 19:5 And when Jesus came to the place, he looked up, and saw him, and said unto him, Zacchaeus, make haste, and come down; for to day I must abide at thy house.

Ro 8:30 Moreover whom he did predestinate, them he also called: and whom he called, them he also justified: and whom he justified, them he also glorified.

1 Co 1:2 Unto the church of God which is at Corinth, to them that are sanctified in Christ Jesus, called *to be* saints, with all that in every place call upon the name of Jesus Christ our Lord, both theirs and ours:

1 Co 1:9 God *is* faithful, by whom ye were called unto the fellowship of his Son Jesus Christ our Lord.

2 Co 5:20 Now then we are ambassadors for Christ, as though God did beseech *you* by us: we pray *you* in Christ's stead, be ye reconciled to God.

He 3:7 Wherefore (as the Holy Ghost saith, To day if ye will hear his voice,

He 3:15 While it is said, To day if ye will hear his voice, harden not your hearts, as in the provocation.

1 Pe 2:9 But ye *are* a chosen generation, a royal priesthood, an holy nation, a peculiar people; that ye should shew forth the praises of him who hath called you out of darkness into his marvellous light:

Re 2:5 Remember therefore from whence thou art fallen, and repent, and do the first works; or else I will come unto thee quickly, and will remove thy candlestick out of his place, except thou repent.

Re 3:20 Behold, I stand at the door, and knock: if any man hear my voice, and open the door, I will come in to him, and will sup with him, and he with me.

Re 19:9 And he saith unto me, Write, Blessed *are* they which are called unto the marriage supper of the Lamb. And he saith unto me, These are the true sayings of God.

See **DISCIPLESHIP**

2. Call to Leadership

ABRAHAM
Ge 12:1

MOSES
Ex 3:10; 28:1;31:2

GIDEON
Jud 6:14

ELISHA
1 K 19:19

ISAIAH
Is 6:8

PAUL
Ac 26:16

See **MINISTERS**

3. Universality

Is 45:22 Look unto me, and be ye saved, all the ends of the earth: for I *am* God, and *there is* none else.

Is 55:1 Ho, every one that thirsteth, come ye to the waters, and he that hath no money; come ye, buy, and eat; yea, come, buy wine and milk without money and without price.

Mt 22:9 Go ye therefore into the highways, and as many as ye shall find, bid to the marriage.

Jn 7:37 In the last day, that great *day* of the feast, Jesus stood and cried, saying, If any man thirst, let him come unto me, and drink.

Ro 10:12 For there is no difference between the Jew and the Greek: for the same Lord over all is rich unto all that call upon him.

1 Ti 2:4 Who will have all men to be saved, and to come unto the knowledge of the truth.

Re 22:17 And the Spirit and the bride say, Come. And let him that heareth say, Come. And let him that is athirst come. And whosoever will, let him take the water of life freely.

See **SALVATION**

4. Refused

Ps 81:11 But my people would not hearken to my voice; and Israel would none of me.

Pr 1:24 Because I have called, and ye refused; I have stretched out my hand, and no man regarded;

Is 65:12 Therefore will I number you to the sword, and ye shall all bow down to the slaughter: because when I called, ye did not answer; when I spake, ye did not hear; but did evil before mine eyes, and did choose *that* wherein I delighted not.

Is 66:4 I also will choose their delusions, and will bring their fears upon them; because when I called, none did answer; when I spake, they did not hear: but they did evil before mine eyes, and chose *that* in which I delighted not.

Je 7:13 And now, because ye have done all these works, saith the LORD, and I spake unto you, rising up early and speaking, but ye heard not; and I called you, but ye answered not;

Je 44:5 But they hearkened not, nor inclined their ear to turn from their wickedness, to burn no incense unto other gods.

Eze 33:4 Then whosoever heareth the sound of the trumpet, and taketh not warning; if the sword come, and take him away, his blood shall be upon his own head.

Ho 9:17 My God will cast them away, because they did not hearken unto him: and they shall be wanderers among the nations.

Ho 11:2 *As* they called them, so they went from them: they sacrificed unto Baalim, and burned incense to graven images.

Mt 22:3 And sent forth his servants to call them that were bidden to the wedding: and they would not come.

Jn 5:40 And ye will not come to me, that ye might have life.

Ro 10:21 But to Israel he saith, All day long I have stretched forth my hands unto a disobedient and gainsaying people.

See **IMPENITENCE**

5. To Decision

De 30:15 See, I have set before thee this day life and good, and death and evil;

Jos 24:15 And if it seem evil unto you to serve the LORD, choose you this day whom ye will serve; whether the gods which your fathers served that *were* on the other side of the flood, or the gods of the Amorites, in whose land ye dwell: but as for me and my house, we will serve the LORD.

Ru 1:15 And she said, Behold, thy sister in law is gone back unto her people, and unto her gods: return thou after thy sister in law.

1 K 18:21 And Elijah came unto all the people, and said, How long halt ye between two opinions? if the LORD *be* God, follow him: but if Baal, *then* follow him. And the people answered him not a word.

Jb 34:4 Let us choose to us judgment: let us know among ourselves what *is* good.

Je 21:8 And unto this people thou shalt say, Thus saith the LORD; Behold, I set before you the way of life, and the way of death.

Je 38:21 But if thou refuse to go forth, this *is* the word that the LORD hath shewed me:

Mt 27:17 Therefore when they were gathered together, Pilate said unto them, Whom will ye that I release unto you? Barabbas, or Jesus which is called Christ?

Mt 27:21 The governor answered and said unto them, Whether of the twain will ye that I release unto you? They said, Barabbas.

Mk 10:21 Then Jesus beholding him loved him, and said unto him, One thing thou lackest: go thy way, sell whatsoever thou hast, and give to the poor, and thou shalt have treasure in heaven: and come, take up the cross, and follow me.

Mk 15:12 And Pilate answered and said again unto them, What will ye then that I shall do *unto him* whom ye call the King of the Jews?

Lu 16:13 No servant can serve two masters: for either he will hate the one, and love the other; or else he will hold to the one, and despise the other. Ye cannot serve God and mammon.

Lu 18:22 Now when Jesus heard these things, he said unto him, Yet lackest thou one thing: sell all that thou hast, and distribute unto the poor, and thou shalt have treasure in heaven: and come, follow me.

Jn 6:67 Then said Jesus unto the twelve, Will ye also go away?

2 Co 6:2 (For he saith, I have heard thee in a time accepted, and in the day of salvation have I succoured thee: behold, now *is* the accepted time; behold, now *is* the day of salvation.)

See **CHOICE, EXHORTATIONS**

CALLING, *a sense of divine appointment*

Jl 2:32 And it shall come to pass, *that* whosoever shall call on the name of the Lord shall be delivered: for in mount Zion and in Jerusalem shall be deliverance, as the Lord hath said, and in the remnant whom the Lord shall call.

1 Co 1:24 But unto them which are called, both Jews and Greeks, Christ the power of God, and the wisdom of God.

1 Co 1:26 For ye see your calling, brethren, how that not many wise

men after the flesh, not many mighty, not many noble, *are called:*

Ep 1:18 The eyes of your understanding being enlightened; that ye may know what is the hope of his calling, and what the riches of the glory of his inheritance in the saints,

Ep 4:1 I therefore, the prisoner of the Lord, beseech you that ye walk worthy of the vocation wherewith ye are called,

Ph 3:14 I press toward the mark for the prize of the high calling of God in Christ Jesus.

1 Th 2:12 That ye would walk worthy of God, who hath called you unto his kingdom and glory.

2 Th 2:14 Whereunto he called you by our gospel, to the obtaining of the glory of our Lord Jesus Christ.

2 Ti 1:9 Who hath saved us, and called *us* with an holy calling, not according to our works, but according to his own purpose and grace, which was given us in Christ Jesus before the world began,

He 3:1 Wherefore, holy brethren, partakers of the heavenly calling, consider the Apostle and High Priest of our profession, Christ Jesus;

1 Pe 5:10 But the God of all grace, who hath called us unto his eternal glory by Christ Jesus, after that ye have suffered a while, make you perfect, stablish, strengthen, settle *you.*

2 Pe 1:10 Wherefore the rather, brethren, give diligence to make your calling and election sure: for if ye do these things, ye shall never fall:

CALVARY, *MOUNT, place of Christ's crucifixion*

Calvary, or Golgotha is known as *the skull* or *place of a skull.* Both names—the first derived from Latin and the latter from Aramaic—refer to the place where Christ was crucified (Mt 27:33; Lu 23:33). Whether it was called "the skull" because it was a place of execution (a place where skulls were found) or because the site resembled a skull is a matter of conjecture, although the first explanation is the most likely. The Scriptures indicate that the crucifixion occurred outside the city walls on a promontory that could be seen from a distance. It was fairly near a city gate and near a roadway that evidently passed through the gate and on by the place of execution (Jn 19:20; He 13:12; Lu 23:49; Mt 27:39). John states that the tomb was in a garden (Jn 19:41).

See **CHRIST, SUFFERING**

CALVES *See* **ANIMALS**

CAMELS *See* **ANIMALS**

CANA, *a town of Galilee*
Cana of Galilee, the village where Jesus performed His first miracle, has been traditionally identified with Kefr Kenna, about four miles northeast of Nazareth. This is on the road to Capernaum. It is blessed with vineyards, orchards of fig trees, and an abundance of water (cf. Jn 2:1; 4:46; 21:2).

See **HOSPITALITY**

CANAAN, *son of Ham*

1. Person
Ge 9:18, 22, 25, 27; 10:6, 15–18

2. Land, *later known as Palestine*

a. Promised to Abraham
Ge 11:31 And Terah took Abram his son, and Lot the son of Haran his son's son, and Sarai his daughter in law, his son Abram's wife; and they went forth with them from Ur of the Chaldees, to go into the land of Canaan; and they came unto Haran, and dwelt there.
Ge 12:5 And Abram took Sarai his wife, and Lot his brother's son, and all their substance that they had gathered, and the souls that they had gotten in Haran; and they went forth to go into the land of Canaan; and into the land of Canaan they came.
Ge 13:12 Abram dwelled in the land of Canaan, and Lot dwelled in the cities of the plain, and pitched *his* tent toward Sodom.
Ge 16:3 And Sarai Abram's wife took Hagar her maid the Egyptian, after Abram had dwelt ten years in the land

of Canaan, and gave her to her husband Abram to be his wife.
Ge 17:8 And I will give unto thee, and to thy seed after thee, the land wherein thou art a stranger, all the land of Canaan, for an everlasting possession; and I will be their God.
Ge 42:5 And the sons of Israel came to buy *corn* among those that came: for the famine was in the land of Canaan.
Ge 49:30 In the cave that *is* in the field of Machpelah, which *is* before Mamre, in the land of Canaan, which Abraham bought with the field of Ephron the Hittite for a possession of a buryingplace.
Ex 6:4 And I have also established my covenant with them, to give them the land of Canaan, the land of their pilgrimage, wherein they were strangers.
Ex 15:15 Then the dukes of Edom shall be amazed; the mighty men of Moab, trembling shall take hold upon them; all the inhabitants of Canaan shall melt away.
Nu 32:32 We will pass over armed before the LORD into the land of Canaan, that the possession of our inheritance on this side Jordan *may be* ours.
Jos 5:12 And the manna ceased on the morrow after they had eaten of the old corn of the land; neither had the children of Israel manna any more; but they did eat of the fruit of the land of Canaan that year.
1 Chr 16:18 Saying, Unto thee will I give the land of Canaan, the lot of your inheritance;
Is 8:8 And he shall pass through Judah; he shall overflow and go over, he shall reach *even* to the neck; and the stretching out of his wings shall fill the breadth of thy land, O Immanuel.
Eze 37:25 And they shall dwell in the land that I have given unto Jacob my servant, wherein your fathers have dwelt; and they shall dwell therein, *even* they, and their children, and their children's children for ever: and my servant David *shall be* their prince for ever.
Ac 7:11 Now there came a dearth over all the land of Egypt and Cha-

naan, and great affliction: and our fathers found no sustenance.

b. Fruitful Land

Ge 41:47; Ex 3:8, 17; 13:5; 33:3; Le 20:24; 25:19; 26:5; Nu 13:27; 14:7; 16:14; De 1:25; 3:25; 6:3; 8:8; 11:9; 26:9, 15; 27:3; 31:20; 33:28; Jos 5:12; 24:13; Jud 18:10; 1 K 14:15; Ezr 9:12; Ne 9:25, 35; Is 36:17; Je 2:7; 11:5; 32:22; Eze 17:5; 20:6, 15; Da 8:9; Jl 3:18; Mal 3:12; He 6:7

c. Polluted by Sin

Le 18:25; 19:29; Nu 35:34; Ps 106:38; Is 24:5; Je 2:7; 3:2; 16:18; Eze 22:24; 36:18; 39:14; Am 7:17; Mi 2:10

See **POLLUTIONS**

d. Heathen Cast Out

Ex 23:27; 32:34; 33:2; 34:11, 24; Le 18:24; 20:23; Nu 24:8, 24; 32:39; 33:52; De 2:12; 4:38; 6:19; 7:1, 22; 9:4; 11:23; 12:29; 18:12; 19:1; 31:3; 33:27; Jos 3:10; 8:1; 13:6, 12; 23:5, 9; 24:12, 18; Jud 6:9; 11:23; 1 K 21:26; 2 K 16:3; 17:8; 21:2; 1 Chr 17:21; 2 Chr 20:7; 28:3; 33:2, 9; Ne 9:24; Ps 18:42; 44:2; 78:55; 80:8; 105:44; 111:6; 135:12; 136:21; Is 16:2; Ac 7:45; 13:19

e. Wars of Extermination

Ex 23:24; Nu 21:2, 35; 31:7, 17; De 2:21, 34; 3:3, 6; 7:2, 16, 23; 9:3; 13:15; 20:13, 17; 25:19; 31:5; Jos 6:21; 8:22; 9:24; 10:20, 28, 33, 39; 11:8, 11; Jud 4:16; 21:11; 1 S 14:36; 15:3, 8, 18; 27:9, 11; 1 K 11:15; 2 K 10:11, 17; 2 Chr 25:12; Is 14:22; Je 46:28; Na 3:3; Zep 1:3; 2:5; 3:6

See **DESTRUCTION**

f. Ancient Names

HOLY LAND

Zec 2:12 And the LORD shall inherit Judah his portion in the holy land, and shall choose Jerusalem again.

IMMANUEL'S LAND

Is 8:8 And he shall pass through Judah; he shall overflow and go over, he shall reach *even* to the neck; and the stretching out of his wings shall fill the breadth of thy land, O Immanuel.

LAND OF ISRAEL

1 S 13:19 Now there was no smith found throughout all the land of Israel: for the Philistines said, Lest the Hebrews make *them* swords or spears:

LAND OF THE HEBREWS

Ge 40:15 For indeed I was stolen away out of the land of the Hebrews: and here also have I done nothing that they should put me into the dungeon.

LAND OF THE JEWS

Ac 10:39 And we are witnesses of all things which he did both in the land of the Jews, and in Jerusalem; whom they slew and hanged on a tree:

LAND OF PROMISE

He 11:9 By faith he sojourned in the land of promise, as *in* a strange country, dwelling in tabernacles with Isaac and Jacob, the heirs with him of the same promise:

PALESTINA

Ex 15:14 The people shall hear, *and* be afraid: sorrow shall take hold on the inhabitants of Palestina.

PLEASANT LAND

Da 8:9 And out of one of them came forth a little horn, which waxed exceeding great, toward the south, and toward the east, and toward the pleasant *land*.

THE LORD'S LAND

Ho 9:3 They shall not dwell in the LORD's land; but Ephraim shall return to Egypt, and they shall eat unclean *things* in Assyria.

g. Description

Ge 13:10; De 8:7; 11:11

h. Division

Jos 14:1; 1 K 4:7; 11:35; Lu 3:1

CANAANITES, *descendants of Canaan*

Ge 10:18; 12:6; 13:7; 15:21; 38:2; 50:11; Ex 3:17; 13:5; 23:28; 33:2; 34:11; Nu 13:29; 14:25, 43; 21:1; 33:40; De 1:7; 7:1; 11:30; Jos 3:10; 5:1; 11:3; 13:4; 16:10; 17:12, 18; 24:11; Jud 1:5, 17, 27; 3:3; 2 S 24:7; 1 K 9:16; Ne 9:8, 24

CANDLE, *lamp*

Jb 18:6; 21:17; Ps 18:28; Pr 20:27; Mt 5:15; Lu 11:33; 15:8

CANDLESTICK, *lampstand*

Le 24:4; Nu 3:31; 4:9; 8:2; 1 K 7:49; 1 Chr 28:15; 2 Chr 4:7, 20; 13:11; Je 52:19; Zec 4:2; He 9:2; Re 1:12; 2:5; 11:4

See **LIGHT**

CANE, *sweet, or calamus*

Ex 30:23; Song 4:14; Is 43:24; Je 6:20; Eze 27:19

CANKERWORM, *locust*

Jl 1:4; 2:25; Na 3:15

See **INSECTS**

CANNIBALISM, *eating of human flesh by other humans*

Le 26:29; De 28:53; 2 K 6:28; Je 19:9; Lam 2:20; 4:10; Eze 5:10

CAPERNAUM, *a city near the Sea of Galilee*

Capernaum was located on the northwest shore of the Sea of Galilee at a place now called Tell Hum. It was the chief commercial and social center of this area during the ministry of Jesus. Here, on the great highway between Syria and Palestine, the custom taxes were collected and a Roman garrison stationed. Jesus came here after leaving Nazareth, and Peter's home became His headquarters. Here He called Matthew from tax collection, taught and preached, and did many miracles. Christ predicted Capernaum's downfall (Mt 11:23–24), and today its scattered heaps of black basalt building stones extend for a mile along the shore of the sea.

Mt 4:13; 8:5; 9:1; 11:23; 17:24; Mk 1:21; 2:1; 9:33; Lu 4:23, 31; 7:1; 10:15; Jn 2:12; 4:46; 6:17, 24, 59

See **CITIES**

CAPITAL PUNISHMENT

See **DEATH PENALTY, NATION**

CAPTAINS, *of the host*

Nu 31:14, 48, 54; De 1:15; 20:9; 29:10; Jud 4:2; 1 S 8:12; 14:50; 17:18; 18:13; 22:2; 2 S 18:1; 23:19; 1 K 9:22; 16:16; 22:32; 2 K 1:11; 9:5; 10:25; 11:9, 15; 25:8; 1 Chr 11:11, 21; 12:14, 34; 28:1; 2 Chr 23:14; Is 3:3; Je 42:1; Eze 23:23; Da 3:2

CAPTIVES, *of war*

Ge 14:12; 34:29; Nu 21:1, 29; 31:9; De 20:14; 21:11; 1 S 30:2; 2 K 5:2; 25:6; 1 Chr 5:21; 18:4; 2 Chr 28:8, 15; Ezr 10:6; Ne 1:11; Ps 137:3; Is 49:25; Je 28:4; 29:4; 41:10; 48:46; 52:15; Da 2:25; 11:8; Obad 20; Hab 1:9

See **WAR**

CAPTIVITY *See* **ISRAEL**

CARAVANS, *company of travelers united most often for mutual protection*

Ge 24:10, 63; 37:25; 46:6; 50:9; 1 K 10:2; 2 K 8:9; 2 Chr 9:1; Ezr 8:31; Is 21:13

CARBUNCLE *See* **STONES**

CARE *See* **CHURCH, FAMILY, WORLD**

CARMEL *See* **MOUNTAINS AND HILLS**

CARNALITY, *of the flesh, at enmity with God*

Ge 25:34 Then Jacob gave Esau bread and pottage of lentiles; and he did eat and drink, and rose up, and went his way: thus Esau despised *his* birthright. **Ex 16:3** And the children of Israel said unto them, Would to God we had died by the hand of the LORD in the land of Egypt, when we sat by the flesh pots, *and* when we did eat bread to the full; for ye have brought us forth into this wilderness, to kill this whole assembly with hunger.

Nu 11:4 And the mixt multitude that *was* among them fell a lusting: and the children of Israel also wept again, and said, Who shall give us flesh to eat?

Ps 78:18 And they tempted God in their heart by asking meat for their lust.

Ps 106:14 But lusted exceedingly in the wilderness, and tempted God in the desert.

Zec 11:16 For, lo, I will raise up a shepherd in the land, *which* shall not visit those that be cut off, neither shall seek the young one, nor heal that that is broken, nor feed that that standeth still: but he shall eat the flesh of the fat, and tear their claws in pieces.

Jn 6:26 Jesus answered them and said, Verily, verily, I say unto you, Ye seek me, not because ye saw the miracles, but because ye did eat of the loaves, and were filled.

Ro 7:23 But I see another law in my members, warring against the law of my mind, and bringing me into captivity to the law of sin which is in my members.

Ro 8:5 For they that are after the flesh do mind the things of the flesh; but they that are after the Spirit the things of the Spirit.

Ga 5:13 For, brethren, ye have been called unto liberty; only *use* not liberty for an occasion to the flesh, but by love serve one another.

1 Jn 2:16 For all that *is* in the world, the lust of the flesh, and the lust of the eyes, and the pride of life, is not of the Father, but is of the world.

CARPENTERS See **ARTS AND CRAFTS**

CARTS, *wheeled vehicles used for transporting people and goods*

Ge 45:19, 27; 46:5; Nu 7:3; 1 S 6:7; 2 S 6:3; 1 Chr 13:7

CARVING See **ARTS AND CRAFTS**

CASSIA, *a fragrant spice*

Ex 30:24; Ps 45:8; Eze 27:19

CASTAWAYS, *SPIRITUAL*

Ge 3:24; 2 K 17:23; Ps 5:10; 51:11; 89:38; Je 22:28; Jona 2:4; Mt 5:13; 7:23; 8:12; 12:32; 13:42, 48; 22:13; 25:30; Lu 9:25; 14:35; Jn 15:6; Ro 11:22; 1 Co 9:27; Re 2:5

CASTLES, *or forts*

Nu 31:10; 1 Chr 6:54; 11:7; 2 Chr 17:12; 27:4; Ac 23:10, 32

CATERPILLARS (caterpillers)

See **INSECTS**

CATHOLICITY, *liberality of sentiment*

Mark 2:15 And it came to pass, that, as Jesus sat at meat in his house, many publicans and sinners sat also together with Jesus and his disciples: for there were many, and they followed him.

Mark 9:39 But Jesus said, Forbid him not: for there is no man which shall do a miracle in my name, that can lightly speak evil of me.

Lu 5:27 And after these things he went forth, and saw a publican, named Levi, sitting at the receipt of custom: and he said unto him, Follow me.

Lu 7:5 For he loveth our nation, and he hath built us a synagogue.

Lu 9:50 And Jesus said unto him, Forbid *him* not: for he that is not against us is for us.

Ac 8:14 Now when the apostles which were at Jerusalem heard that Samaria had received the word of God, they sent unto them Peter and John:

Ac 8:25 And they, when they had testified and preached the word of the Lord, returned to Jerusalem, and preached the gospel in many villages of the Samaritans.

Ac 9:27 But Barnabas took him, and brought *him* to the apostles, and declared unto them how he had seen the Lord in the way, and that he had spoken to him, and how he had preached boldly at Damascus in the name of Jesus.

Ac 10:28 And he said unto them, Ye know how that it is an unlawful thing for a man that is a Jew to keep company, or come unto one of another nation; but God hath shewed me that I should not call any man common or unclean.

Ac 10:47 Can any man forbid water, that these should not be baptized, which have received the Holy Ghost as well as we?

Ac 11:18 When they heard these things, they held their peace, and glorified God, saying, Then hath God also to the Gentiles granted repentance unto life.

Ac 15:10 Now therefore why tempt ye God, to put a yoke upon the neck of the disciples, which neither our fathers nor we were able to bear?

Ac 15:19 Wherefore my sentence is, that we trouble not them, which from among the Gentiles are turned to God:

Ac 26:29 And Paul said, I would to God, that not only thou, but also all that hear me this day, were both almost, and altogether such as I am, except these bonds.

Ro 1:14 I am debtor both to the Greeks, and to the Barbarians; both to the wise, and to the unwise.

Ro 15:7 Wherefore receive ye one another, as Christ also received us to the glory of God.

1 Co 9:20 And unto the Jews I became as a Jew, that I might gain the Jews; to them that are under the law, as under the law, that I might gain them that are under the law;

Ga 2:9 And when James, Cephas, and John, who seemed to be pillars, perceived the grace that was given unto me, they gave to me and Barnabas the right hands of fellowship; that we *should go* unto the heathen, and they unto the circumcision.

Ga 3:28 There is neither Jew nor Greek, there is neither bond nor free, there is neither male nor female: for ye are all one in Christ Jesus.

See **BIGOTRY**

CATTLE *See* **ANIMALS**

CAVES, *an opening on a hill or mountain, often used for refuge, shelter, or a burial place*

Ge 19:30; 23:9, 19; 25:9; 49:30; 50:13; Jos 10:16; Jud 6:2; 1 S 13:6; 22:1; 24:3; 2 S 23:13; 1 K 18:4; 19:9; 1 Chr 11:15; Eze 33:27; Jn 11:38; He 11:38

CEDAR, *lumber*

Le 14:4, 49; Nu 19:6; 2 S 7:2; 1 K 6:9, 15, 18, 36; 7:2, 12; 1 Chr 22:4; Song 1:17; 8:9; Je 22:14; Zep 2:14

See **TREES**

CENSERS, *used in religious service*

Le 16:12; Nu 4:14; 16:6, 17, 37, 46; 1 K 7:50; 2 Chr 4:22; Eze 8:11; He 9:4; Re 8:3

CENTURIONS, *Roman officers over one hundred men*

Mt 8:5, 9; 27:54; Mk 15:39, 44; Lu 7:2; Ac 10:1, 22; 21:32; 22:25; 23:17; 24:23; 27:1, 11, 43; 28:16

CERTAINTIES, *beliefs settled, unquestioned, beyond a doubt*

1. Comforting, *seven that encourage the believer*

SURE PROMISES

1 K 8:56 Blessed *be* the LORD, that hath given rest unto his people Israel, according to all that he promised: there hath not failed one word of all his good promise, which he promised by the hand of Moses his servant.

SURE FOUNDATIONS

Is 28:16 Therefore thus saith the Lord God, Behold, I lay in Zion for a foundation a stone, a tried stone, a precious corner *stone,* a sure foundation: he that believeth shall not make haste.

SURE REWARD

Mt 10:42 And whosoever shall give to drink unto one of these little ones a cup of cold *water* only in the name of a disciple, verily I say unto you, he shall in no wise lose his reward.

ASSURED ACCEPTANCE

Jn 6:37 All that the Father giveth me shall come to me; and him that cometh to me I will in no wise cast out.

DIVINE LOVE

Ro 8:38–39 For I am persuaded, that neither death, nor life, nor angels, nor principalities, nor powers, nor things present, nor things to come,

Nor height, nor depth, nor any other creature, shall be able to separate us from the love of God, which is in Christ Jesus our Lord.

ASSURED IMMORTALITY

2 Co 5:1 For we know that if our earthly house of *this* tabernacle were dissolved, we have a building of God, an house not made with hands, eternal in the heavens.

ETERNAL ANCHORAGE

He 6:19 Which *hope* we have as an anchor of the soul, both sure and stedfast, and which entereth into that within the veil;

2. Sobering, seven that confront the unrepentant

CERTAINTY OF EXPOSURE

Nu 32:23 But if ye will not do so, behold, ye have sinned against the LORD: and be sure your sin will find you out.

CERTAINTY OF DISAPPOINTMENT

De 32:32 For their vine *is* of the vine of Sodom, and of the fields of Gomorrah: their grapes *are* grapes of gall, their clusters *are* bitter:

CERTAINTY OF LEAVING EARTHLY POSSESSIONS

1 Ti 6:7 For we brought nothing into *this* world, *and it is* certain we can carry nothing out.

CERTAINTY OF DEATH

Ec 8:8 *There is* no man that hath power over the spirit to retain the spirit; neither *hath he* power in the day of death: and *there is* no discharge in *that* war; neither shall wickedness deliver those that are given to it.

CERTAINTY OF JUDGMENT

Ec 12:14 For God shall bring every work into judgment, with every secret thing, whether *it be* good, or whether *it be* evil.

CERTAINTY OF SEPARATION FROM THE RIGHTEOUS

Mt 25:31–33 When the Son of man shall come in his glory, and all the holy angels with him, then shall he sit upon the throne of his glory:

And before him shall be gathered all nations: and he shall separate them one from another, as a shepherd divideth *his* sheep from the goats:

And he shall set the sheep on his right hand, but the goats on the left.

CERTAINTY OF BANISHMENT FROM THE DIVINE PRESENCE

2 Th 1:9 Who shall be punished with everlasting destruction from the presence of the Lord, and from the glory of his power;

See **ASSURANCE, SECURITY, UNCERTAINTIES**

CHAINS *See* **APPAREL**

CHALCEDONY *See* **STONES**

CHALDEANS, *an ancient race*

Eze 23:23; Da 2:2; 3:8; 4:7; 5:7

CHAMBERLAINS, *a chief steward in the royal court*

2 K 23:11; Ac 12:20; Ro 16:23

CHAMELEONS *See* **REPTILES**

CHARACTER *See* **DISCIPLESHIP, EVIL, FAITH, WICKED**

CHARIOTS, *a horse-drawn, wheeled vehicle of war*

1. Used in War

Ex 14:7; Jos 11:4; 17:16; 24:6; Jud 1:19; 4:3, 13; 1 S 8:11; 13:5; 2 S 1:6; 8:4; 10:18; 1 K 1:5; 9:19; 10:26; 20:1, 25; 22:32; 2 K 6:14; 8:21; 10:2; 19:23; 1 Chr

18:4; 19:6, 18; 2 Chr 1:14; 9:25; 12:3; 14:9; 35:24; Ps 20:7; Song 1:9; Is 2:7; 21:7; 22:7; 31:1; 36:9; 37:24; 43:17; Je 4:13; 46:9; 47:3; 50:37; 51:21; Eze 23:24; 26:7, 10; Da 11:40; Jl 2:5; Na 2:4, 13; 3:2; Re 9:9

2. Used in Traveling

Ge 41:43; 46:29; 50:9; Ex 14:17; 1 K 12:18; 18:44; 2 K 5:9; 9:16; Song 3:9; Je 17:25; Ac 8:29, 38

3. Of God, figurative

2 K 2:11; 6:17; 7:6; Jb 25:3; Ps 68:17; 104:3; Is 13:4; 66:15; Hab 3:8

CHARITABLENESS See KINDNESS, LOVE

CHASTISEMENT See AFFLICTIONS, PUNISHMENT

CHASTITY See ADULTERY, MARRIAGE, SELF-CONTROL

CHEBAR See RIVERS

CHEERFULNESS

Jb 9:27 If I say, I will forget my complaint, I will leave off my heaviness, and comfort *myself:*

Pr 15:13 A merry heart maketh a cheerful countenance: but by sorrow of the heart the spirit is broken.

Pr 17:22 A merry heart doeth good *like* a medicine: but a broken spirit drieth the bones.

Jn 16:33 These things I have spoken unto you, that in me ye might have peace. In the world ye shall have tribulation: but be of good cheer; I have overcome the world.

Ac 27:25 Wherefore, sirs, be of good cheer: for I believe God, that it shall be even as it was told me.

Ac 27:36 Then were they all of good cheer, and they also took *some* meat.

See **DESPONDENCY**

CHEESE, prepared from the pressed curd of milk

1 S 17:18; 2 S 17:29; Jb 10:10

CHERUB, cherubim, angelic beings

Ge 3:24 So he drove out the man; and he placed at the east of the garden of Eden Cherubim, and a flaming sword which turned every way, to keep the way of the tree of life.

Ex 25:18–19 And thou shalt make two cherubims *of* gold, *of* beaten work shalt thou make them, in the two ends of the mercy seat.

And make one cherub on the one end, and the other cherub on the other end: *even* of the mercy seat shall ye make the cherubims on the two ends thereof.

Ex 36:8 And every wise hearted man among them that wrought the work of the tabernacle made ten curtains *of* fine twined linen, and blue, and purple, and scarlet: *with* cherubims of cunning work made he them.

Ex 37:9 And the cherubims spread out *their* wings on high, *and* covered with their wings over the mercy seat, with their faces one to another; *even* to the mercy seatward were the faces of the cherubims.

Nu 7:89 And when Moses was gone into the tabernacle of the congregation to speak with him, then he heard the voice of one speaking unto him from off the mercy seat that *was* upon the ark of testimony, from between the two cherubims: and he spake unto him.

1 S 4:4 So the people sent to Shiloh, that they might bring from thence the ark of the covenant of the Lord of hosts, which dwelleth *between* the cherubims: and the two sons of Eli, Hophni and Phinehas, *were* there with the ark of the covenant of God.

2 S 6:2 And David arose, and went with all the people that *were* with him from Baale of Judah, to bring up from thence the ark of God, whose name is called by the name of the Lord of hosts that dwelleth *between* the cherubims.

1 K 6:23 And within the oracle he made two cherubims *of* olive tree, *each* ten cubits high.

1 K 6:25 And the other cherub *was* ten cubits: both the cherubims *were* of one measure and one size.

1 K 6:32 The two doors also *were of* olive tree; and he carved upon them carvings of cherubims and palm trees and open flowers, and overlaid *them* with gold, and spread gold upon the cherubims, and upon the palm trees.

1 K 6:35 And he carved *thereon* cherubims and palm trees and open flowers: and covered *them* with gold fitted upon the carved work.

1 K 7:36 For on the plates of the ledges thereof, and on the borders thereof, he graved cherubims, lions, and palm trees, according to the proportion of every one, and additions round about.

1 K 8:6 And the priests brought in the ark of the covenant of the LORD unto his place, into the oracle of the house, to the most holy *place, even* under the wings of the cherubims.

2 K 19:15 And Hezekiah prayed before the LORD, and said, O LORD God of Israel, which dwellest *between* the cherubims, thou art the God, *even* thou alone, of all the kingdoms of the earth: thou hast made heaven and earth.

1 Chr 13:6 And David went up, and all Israel, to Baalah, *that is,* to Kirjath-jearim, which *belonged* to Judah, to bring up thence the ark of God the LORD, that dwelleth *between* the cherubims, whose name is called *on it.*

1 Chr 28:18 And for the altar of incense refined gold by weight; and gold for the pattern of the chariot of the cherubims, that spread out *their wings,* and covered the ark of the covenant of the LORD.

2 Chr 3:11 And the wings of the cherubims *were* twenty cubits long: one wing *of the one cherub was* five cubits, reaching to the wall of the house: and the other wing *was likewise* five cubits, reaching to the wing of the other cherub.

2 Chr 5:7 And the priests brought in the ark of the covenant of the LORD unto his place, to the oracle of the house, into the most holy *place, even* under the wings of the cherubims:

Ps 80:1 Give ear, O Shepherd of Israel, thou that leadest Joseph like a flock; thou that dwellest *between* the cherubims, shine forth.

Ps 99:1 The LORD reigneth; let the people tremble: he sitteth *between* the cherubims; let the earth be moved.

Is 37:16 O LORD of hosts, God of Israel, that dwellest *between* the cherubims, thou *art* the God, *even* thou alone, of all the kingdoms of the earth: thou hast made heaven and earth.

Eze 9:3 And the glory of the God of Israel was gone up from the cherub, whereupon he was, to the threshold of the house. And he called to the man clothed with linen, which *had* the writer's inkhorn by his side;

Eze 10:1 Then I looked, and, behold, in the firmament that was above the head of the cherubims there appeared over them as it were a sapphire stone, as the appearance of the likeness of a throne.

Eze 10:5 And the sound of the cherubims' wings was heard *even* to the outer court, as the voice of the Almighty God when he speaketh.

Eze 10:7 And *one* cherub stretched forth his hand from between the cherubims unto the fire that *was* between the cherubims, and took *thereof,* and put *it* into the hands of *him that was* clothed with linen: who took *it,* and went out.

Eze 10:15 And the cherubims were lifted up. This *is* the living creature that I saw by the river of Chebar.

Eze 10:20 This *is* the living creature that I saw under the God of Israel by the river of Chebar; and I knew that they *were* the cherubims.

Eze 11:22 Then did the cherubims lift up their wings, and the wheels beside them; and the glory of the God of Israel *was* over them above.

Eze 28:14 Thou *art* the anointed cherub that covereth; and I have set thee *so:* thou wast upon the holy mountain of God; thou hast walked up and down in the midst of the stones of fire.

Eze 41:18 And *it was* made with cherubims and palm trees, so that a palm tree *was* between a cherub and a cherub; and *every* cherub had two faces;

Eze 41:25 And *there were* made on them, on the doors of the temple, cherubims and palm trees, like as *were* made upon the walls; and *there were* thick planks upon the face of the porch without.

He 9:5 And over it the cherubims of glory shadowing the mercyseat; of which we cannot now speak particularly.

CHESTNUT *See* TREES

CHESTS, *a box for storage, for money*

CHILDHOOD

DEPENDENCE

Nu 11:12 Have I conceived all this people? have I begotten them, that thou shouldest say unto me, Carry them in thy bosom, as a nursing father beareth the sucking child, unto the land which thou swarest unto their fathers?

CREDULITY

Pr 14:15 The simple believeth every word: but the prudent *man* looketh well to his going.

FOOLISHNESS

Pr 22:15 Foolishness *is* bound in the heart of a child; *but* the rod of correction shall drive it far from him.

LOVE OF AMUSEMENT

Zec 8:5 And the streets of the city shall be full of boys and girls playing in the streets thereof.

PETTY COMPLAINTS

Mt 11:17 And saying, We have piped unto you, and ye have not danced; we have mourned unto you, and ye have not lamented.

NEED OF RULERS

Ga 4:2 But is under tutors and governors until the time appointed of the father.

FICKLENESS

Ep 4:14 That we *henceforth* be no more children, tossed to and fro, and carried about with every wind of doctrine, by the sleight of men, *and* cunning craftiness, whereby they lie in wait to deceive;

IGNORANCE

He 5:12 For when for the time ye ought to be teachers, ye have need that one teach you again which *be* the first principles of the oracles of God; and are become such as have need of milk, and not of strong meat.

WEAK DIGESTION

He 5:13 For every one that useth milk *is* unskilful in the word of righteousness: for he is a babe.

See **FAMILY**

CHILDISHNESS, *immature and without understanding*

Pr 22:15 Foolishness *is* bound in the heart of a child; *but* the rod of correction shall drive it far from him.

Je 4:22 For my people *is* foolish, they have not known me; they *are* sottish children, and they have none understanding: they *are* wise to do evil, but to do good they have no knowledge.

Ho 7:11 Ephraim also is like a silly dove without heart: they call to Egypt, they go to Assyria.

1 Co 13:11 When I was a child, I spake as a child, I understood as a child, I thought as a child: but when I became a man, I put away childish things.

CHILDLIKENESS, *an essential element in the Christian life*

Ps 131:2 Surely I have behaved and quieted myself, as a child that is weaned of his mother: my soul *is* even as a weaned child.

Mt 19:14 But Jesus said, Suffer little children, and forbid them not, to come unto me: for of such is the kingdom of heaven.

Mk 9:36 And he took a child, and set him in the midst of them: and when he had taken him in his arms, he said unto them,

Mk 10:15 Verily I say unto you, Whosoever shall not receive the kingdom of God as a little child, he shall not enter therein.

Lu 18:16–17 But Jesus called them *unto him*, and said, Suffer little children to come unto me, and forbid them not: for of such is the kingdom of God.

Verily I say unto you, Whosoever shall not receive the kingdom of God as a little child shall in no wise enter therein.

Jn 13:33 Little children, yet a little while I am with you. Ye shall seek me: and as I said unto the Jews, Whither I go, ye cannot come; so now I say to you.

1 Co 14:20 Brethren, be not children in understanding: howbeit in malice be ye children, but in understanding be men.

1 Pe 2:2 As newborn babes, desire the sincere milk of the word, that ye may grow thereby:

1 Jn 2:1 My little children, these things write I unto you, that ye sin not. And if any man sin, we have an advocate with the Father, Jesus Christ the righteous:

1 Jn 2:12 I write unto you, little children, because your sins are forgiven you for his name's sake.

See **FAITH**

CHILDREN, *offspring, descendants*

1. The Gift of God

Ge 30:2 And Jacob's anger was kindled against Rachel: and he said, *Am* I in God's stead, who hath withheld from thee the fruit of the womb?

Ge 30:6 And Rachel said, God hath judged me, and hath also heard my voice, and hath given me a son: therefore called she his name Dan.

Ge 33:5 And he lifted up his eyes, and saw the women and the children; and said, Who *are* those with thee? And he said, The children which God hath graciously given thy servant.

Ge 48:9 And Joseph said unto his father, They *are* my sons, whom God hath given me in this *place*. And he said, Bring them, I pray thee, unto me, and I will bless them.

Jos 24:3 And I took your father Abraham from the other side of the flood, and led him throughout all the land of Canaan, and multiplied his seed, and gave him Isaac.

1 S 2:21 And the Lord visited Hannah, so that she conceived, and bare three sons and two daughters. And the child Samuel grew before the Lord.

1 Chr 26:5 Ammiel the sixth, Issachar the seventh, Peulthai the eighth: for God blessed him.

1 Chr 28:5 And of all my sons, (for the Lord hath given me many sons,) he hath chosen Solomon my son to sit upon the throne of the kingdom of the Lord over Israel.

Jb 1:2 And there were born unto him seven sons and three daughters.

Ps 113:9 He maketh the barren woman to keep house, *and to be* a joyful mother of children. Praise ye the Lord.

Ps 127:3 Lo, children *are* an heritage of the Lord: *and* the fruit of the womb *is* his reward.

Is 8:18 Behold, I and the children whom the Lord hath given me *are* for signs and for wonders in Israel from the Lord of hosts, which dwelleth in mount Zion.

Lu 1:58 And her neighbours and her cousins heard how the Lord had shewed great mercy upon her; and they rejoiced with her.

2. Esteemed Highly

Ge 1:28 And God blessed them, and God said unto them, Be fruitful, and multiply, and replenish the earth, and subdue it: and have dominion over the fish of the sea, and over the fowl of the air, and over every living thing that moveth upon the earth.

Ge 5:29 And he called his name Noah, saying, This *same* shall comfort us concerning our work and toil of our hands, because of the ground which the Lord hath cursed.

Jud 11:34 And Jephthah came to Mizpeh unto his house, and, behold, his daughter came out to meet him with timbrels and with dances: and she *was his* only child; beside her he had neither son nor daughter.

Ru 4:15 And he shall be unto thee a restorer of *thy* life, and a nourisher of thine old age: for thy daughter in law, which loveth thee, which is better to thee than seven sons, hath born him.

Ps 127:4 As arrows *are* in the hand of a mighty man; so *are* children of the youth.

Ps 127:5 Happy *is* the man that hath his quiver full of them: they shall not be ashamed, but they shall speak with the enemies in the gate.

Ps 128:3 Thy wife *shall be* as a fruitful vine by the sides of thine house: thy children like olive plants round about thy table.

Ps 144:12 That our sons *may be* as plants grown up in their youth; *that* our daughters *may be* as corner stones, polished *after* the similitude of a palace:

Pr 4:3 For I was my father's son, tender and only *beloved* in the sight of my mother.

Pr 17:6 Children's children *are* the crown of old men; and the glory of children *are* their fathers.

Ec 6:3 If a man beget an hundred *children,* and live many years, so that the days of his years be many, and his soul be not filled with good, and also *that* he have no burial; I say, *that* an untimely birth *is* better than he.

Zec 8:5 And the streets of the city shall be full of boys and girls playing in the streets thereof.

Mt 19:14 But Jesus said, Suffer little children, and forbid them not, to come unto me: for of such is the kingdom of heaven.

Jn 16:21 A woman when she is in travail hath sorrow, because her hour is come: but as soon as she is delivered of the child, she remembereth no more the anguish, for joy that a man is born into the world.

3. Exhortations

Ps 34:11 Come, ye children, hearken unto me: I will teach you the fear of the LORD.

Ps 148:12 Both young men, and maidens; old men, and children:

Pr 10:1 A wise son maketh a glad father: but a foolish son *is* the heaviness of his mother.

Pr 20:11 Even a child is known by his doings, whether his work *be* pure, and whether *it be* right.

Pr 23:22 Hearken unto thy father that begat thee, and despise not thy mother when she is old.

Pr 27:11 My son, be wise, and make my heart glad, that I may answer him that reproacheth me.

Ec 12:1 Remember now thy Creator in the days of thy youth, while the evil days come not, nor the years draw nigh, when thou shalt say, I have no pleasure in them;

Eze 20:18 But I said unto their children in the wilderness, Walk ye not in the statutes of your fathers, neither observe their judgments, nor defile yourselves with their idols:

Mk 7:10 For Moses said, Honour thy father and thy mother; and, Whoso curseth father or mother, let him die the death:

Ep 6:1 Children, obey your parents in the Lord: for this is right.

Ep 6:2–3 Honour thy father and mother; (which is the first commandment with promise;)

That it may be well with thee, and thou mayest live long on the earth.

Col 3:20 Children, obey *your* parents in all things: for this is well pleasing unto the Lord.

1 Ti 5:4 But if any widow have children or nephews, let them learn first to shew piety at home, and to requite their parents: for that is good and acceptable before God.

4. Present at Worship

Jos 8:35 There was not a word of all that Moses commanded, which Joshua read not before all the congregation of Israel, with the women, and the little ones, and the strangers that were conversant among them.

2 Chr 20:13 And all Judah stood before the LORD, with their little ones, their wives, and their children.

Ezr 8:21 Then I proclaimed a fast there, at the river of Ahava, that we might afflict ourselves before our God, to seek of him a right way for us, and for our little ones, and for all our substance.

Ne 12:43 Also that day they offered great sacrifices, and rejoiced: for God had made them rejoice with great joy: the wives also and the children rejoiced: so that the joy of Jerusalem was heard even afar off.

Mt 21:15 And when the chief priests and scribes saw the wonderful things that he did, and the children crying in the temple, and saying, Hosanna to the Son of David; they were sore displeased,

5. Ungrateful

Ex 21:15 And he that smiteth his father, or his mother, shall be surely put to death.

Le 20:9 For every one that curseth his father or his mother shall be surely put to death: he hath cursed his father or his mother; his blood *shall be* upon him.

De 21:18 If a man have a stubborn and rebellious son, which will not obey the voice of his father, or the voice of his mother, and *that,* when they have chastened him, will not hearken unto them:

Pr 19:26 He that wasteth *his* father, *and* chaseth away *his* mother, *is* a son that causeth shame, and bringeth reproach.

Pr 28:24 Whoso robbeth his father or his mother, and saith, *It is* no transgression; the same *is* the companion of a destroyer.

Pr 30:11 *There is* a generation *that* curseth their father, and doth not bless their mother.

Pr 30:17 The eye *that* mocketh at *his* father, and despiseth to obey *his* mother, the ravens of the valley shall pick it out, and the young eagles shall eat it.

Eze 22:7 In thee have they set light by father and mother: in the midst of thee have they dealt by oppression with the stranger: in thee have they vexed the fatherless and the widow.

Mi 7:6 For the son dishonoureth the father, the daughter riseth up against her mother, the daughter in law against her mother in law; a man's enemies *are* the men of his own house.

Mk 7:11 But ye say, If a man shall say to his father or mother, *It is* Corban, that is to say, a gift, by whatsoever thou mightest be profited by me; *he shall be free.*

6. Helpful

THE CHILD SAMUEL, *assists Eli*

1 S 2:18 But Samuel ministered before the LORD, *being* a child, girded with a linen ephod.

A BOY, *waits upon David and Jonathan*

1 S 20:36 And he said unto his lad, Run, find out now the arrows which I shoot. *And* as the lad ran, he shot an arrow beyond him.

A LITTLE MAID, *who aided Naaman in securing his health*

2 K 5:2 And the Syrians had gone out by companies, and had brought away captive out of the land of Israel a little maid; and she waited on Naaman's wife.

2 K 5:3 And she said unto her mistress, Would God my lord *were* with the prophet that *is* in Samaria! for he would recover him of his leprosy.

A CHILD KING

2 Chr 24:1 Joash *was* seven years old when he began to reign, and he reigned forty years in Jerusalem. His mother's name also *was* Zibiah of Beer-sheba.

THE BOY CHRIST, *about his Father's business*

Lu 2:49 And he said unto them, How is it that ye sought me? wist ye not that I must be about my Father's business?

THE LAD, *giving his lunch to help feed the multitude*

Jn 6:9 There is a lad here, which hath five barley loaves, and two small fishes: but what are they among so many?

7. Vices

2 K 2:23; Jb 19:18; 30:12; Is 3:5

8. Special Promises

REVERENT CHILDREN

De 5:16 Honour thy father and thy mother, as the LORD thy God hath commanded thee; that thy days may be prolonged, and that it may go well with thee, in the land which the LORD thy God giveth thee.

FORSAKEN CHILDREN

Ps 27:10 When my father and my mother forsake me, then the LORD will take me up.

EARLY SEEKERS

Pr 8:17 I love them that love me; and those that seek me early shall find me.

OBEDIENT CHILDREN

Pr 8:32 Now therefore hearken unto me, O ye children: for blessed *are they that* keep my ways.

LAMBS OF THE FLOCK

Is 40:11 He shall feed his flock like a shepherd: he shall gather the lambs with his arm, and carry *them* in his bosom, *and* shall gently lead those that are with young.

LITTLE CHILDREN

Mk 10:14 But when Jesus saw *it,* he was much displeased, and said unto them, Suffer the little children to come unto me, and forbid them not: for of such is the kingdom of God.

CHILDREN OF BELIEVERS

Ac 2:39 For the promise is unto you, and to your children, and to all that are afar off, *even* as many as the Lord our God shall call.

THE COMMANDMENT WITH PROMISE

Ep 6:2 Honour thy father and mother; (which is the first commandment with promise;)

9. Good Children, *of Good Parentage*

ISAAC

Ge 22:7 And Isaac spake unto Abraham his father, and said, My father: and he said, Here *am* I, my son. And he said, Behold the fire and the wood: but where *is* the lamb for a burnt offering?

JEPHTHAH'S DAUGHTER

Jud 11:36 And she said unto him, My father, *if* thou hast opened thy mouth unto the LORD, do to me according to that which hath proceeded out of thy mouth; forasmuch as the LORD hath taken vengeance for thee of thine enemies, *even* of the children of Ammon.

SAMUEL

1 S 2:26 And the child Samuel grew on, and was in favour both with the LORD, and also with men.

JOHN THE BAPTIST

Lu 1:80 And the child grew, and waxed strong in spirit, and was in the deserts till the day of his shewing unto Israel.

THE BOY JESUS

Lu 2:49 And he said unto them, How is it that ye sought me? wist ye not that I must be about my Father's business?

TIMOTHY

2 Ti 1:5 When I call to remembrance the unfeigned faith that is in thee, which dwelt first in thy grandmother Lois, and thy mother Eunice; and I am persuaded that in thee also.

2 Ti 3:15 And that from a child thou hast known the holy scriptures, which are able to make thee wise unto salvation through faith which is in Christ Jesus.

10. Good Children of Wicked

2 K 12:2; 18:3; 22:2; 2 Chr 34:3

11. Naming

Ge 4:25; 5:3, 29; 16:15; 21:3; 30:8; 35:18; 38:3, 30; 41:51; Ex 2:10, 22; Jud 13:24; Ru 4:17; 1 S 1:20; 4:21; 1 Chr 2:9; 4:9; 22:9; Jb 42:14; Is 8:3; Ho 1:4, 9; Mt 1:23, 25; Lu 1:60; 2:21

12. Adoption

Ge 15:3 And Abram said, Behold, to me thou hast given no seed: and, lo, one born in my house is mine heir.

Ge 48:5 And now thy two sons, Ephraim and Manasseh, which were born unto thee in the land of Egypt before I came unto thee into Egypt, *are* mine; as Reuben and Simeon, they shall be mine.

Ge 48:16 The Angel which redeemed me from all evil, bless the lads; and let my name be named on them, and the name of my fathers Abraham and Isaac; and let them grow into a multitude in the midst of the earth.

Ex 2:10 And the child grew, and she brought him unto Pharaoh's daughter, and he became her son. And she called his name Moses: and she said, Because I drew him out of the water.

Est 2:7 And he brought up Hadassah, that *is,* Esther, his uncle's daughter: for she had neither father nor mother, and the maid *was* fair and beautiful; whom Mordecai, when her father and mother were dead, took for his own daughter.

Est 2:15 Now when the turn of Esther, the daughter of Abihail the uncle of Mordecai, who had taken her for his daughter, was come to go in unto the king, she required nothing but what Hegai the king's chamberlain, the keeper of the women, appointed. And Esther obtained favour in the sight of all them that looked upon her.

Ac 7:21 And when he was cast out, Pharaoh's daughter took him up, and nourished him for her own son.

13. Births Foretold

Ge 16:11; 17:16; 18:10; Jud 13:3, 7; 1 S 1:17; 2:20; 1 K 13:2; 2 K 4:16; Is 9:6; Mt 1:21; Lu 1:13, 31; Ro 9:9; Ga 4:23; He 11:18

14. Birthright

Ge 25:31; 27:36; 43:33; 48:22; De 21:16; 1 Chr 5:1; 2 Chr 21:3; He 12:16

15. Dishonoring Parents

BY STUBBORNNESS AND SENSUALITY

De 21:20 And they shall say unto the elders of his city, This our son *is* stubborn and rebellious, he will not obey our voice; *he is* a glutton, and a drunkard.

BY LACK OF RESPECT

De 27:16 Cursed *be* he that setteth light by his father or his mother. And all the people shall say, Amen.

BY DESPISING THEIR MOTHER

Pr 15:20 A wise son maketh a glad father: but a foolish man despiseth his mother.

BY CURSING THEIR FATHER

Pr 30:11 *There is* a generation *that* curseth their father, and doth not bless their mother.

BY STRIFE IN THE HOUSEHOLD

Mi 7:6 For the son dishonoureth the father, the daughter riseth up against her mother, the daughter in law against her mother in law; a man's enemies *are* the men of his own house.

BY FAILURE IN PROVIDING FOR

Mk 7:11 But ye say, If a man shall say to his father or mother, *It is* Corban, that is to say, a gift, by whatsoever thou mightest be profited by me; *he shall be free.*

BY DISOBEDIENCE

2 Ti 3:2 For men shall be lovers of their own selves, covetous, boasters, proud, blasphemers, disobedient to parents, unthankful, unholy,

See **FAMILY, PARENTS**

CHOICE, *a selection*

1. Evil

Ge 13:11 Then Lot chose him all the plain of Jordan; and Lot journeyed east: and they separated themselves the one from the other.

Jb 36:21 Take heed, regard not iniquity: for this hast thou chosen rather than affliction.

Pr 1:29 For that they hated knowledge, and did not choose the fear of the LORD:

Is 65:12 Therefore will I number you to the sword, and ye shall all bow down to the slaughter: because when I called, ye did not answer; when I spake, ye did not hear; but did evil before mine eyes, and did choose *that* wherein I delighted not.

Is 66:3 He that killeth an ox *is as if* he slew a man; he that sacrificeth a lamb, *as if* he cut off a dog's neck; he that offereth an oblation, *as if he offered* swine's blood; he that burneth incense, *as if* he blessed an idol. Yea, they have chosen their own ways, and their soul delighteth in their abominations.

Mt 27:21 The governor answered and said unto them, Whether of the twain will ye that I release unto you? They said, Barabbas.

2. Wise

JOSHUA

Jos 24:15 And if it seem evil unto you to serve the LORD, choose you this day whom ye will serve; whether the gods which your fathers served that *were* on the other side of the flood, or the gods of the Amorites, in whose land ye dwell: but as for me and my house, we will serve the LORD.

RUTH

Ru 1:16 And Ruth said, Intreat me not to leave thee, *or* to return from following after thee: for whither thou goest, I will go; and where thou lodgest, I will lodge: thy people *shall be* my people, and thy God my God:

SOLOMON

1 K 3:9 Give therefore thy servant an understanding heart to judge thy people, that I may discern between good and bad: for who is able to judge this thy so great a people?

THE PSALMIST

Ps 119:30 I have chosen the way of truth: thy judgments have I laid *before me*.

Ps 119:173 Let thine hand help me; for I have chosen thy precepts.

Mi 4:5 For all people will walk every one in the name of his god, and we will walk in the name of the LORD our God for ever and ever.

MARY

Lu 10:42 But one thing is needful: and Mary hath chosen that good part, which shall not be taken away from her.

MOSES

He 11:25 Choosing rather to suffer affliction with the people of God, than to enjoy the pleasures of sin for a season;

CHRIST

1. Divinity, *fully God*

a. Scriptural Testimony

1). God's Own Words

Is 9:6 For unto us a child is born, unto us a son is given: and the government shall be upon his shoulder: and his name shall be called Wonderful, Counsellor, The mighty God, The everlasting Father, The Prince of Peace.

Mt 22:43 He saith unto them, How then doth David in spirit call him Lord, saying,

Mt 27:43 He trusted in God; let him deliver him now, if he will have him: for he said, I am the Son of God.

Mk 1:1 The beginning of the gospel of Jesus Christ, the Son of God;

Mk 4:38 And he was in the hinder part of the ship, asleep on a pillow:

and they awake him, and say unto him, Master, carest thou not that we perish?

2). Testimony of the Apostles

Mt 1:23 Behold, a virgin shall be with child, and shall bring forth a son, and they shall call his name Emmanuel, which being interpreted is, God with us.

Mt 16:16 And Simon Peter answered and said, Thou art the Christ, the Son of the living God.

Jn 1:1–2 In the beginning was the Word, and the Word was with God, and the Word was God.

Jn 9:33 If this man were not of God, he could do nothing.

Ro 1:4 And declared *to be* the Son of God with power, according to the spirit of holiness, by the resurrection from the dead:

Ro 9:5 Whose *are* the fathers, and of whom as concerning the flesh Christ *came,* who is over all, God blessed for ever. Amen.

2 Co 4:4 In whom the god of this world hath blinded the minds of them which believe not, lest the light of the glorious gospel of Christ, who is the image of God, should shine unto them.

Col 1:15 Who is the image of the invisible God, the firstborn of every creature:

Col 2:9 For in him dwelleth all the fulness of the Godhead bodily.

1 Ti 3:16 And without controversy great is the mystery of godliness: God was manifest in the flesh, justified in the Spirit, seen of angels, preached unto the Gentiles, believed on in the world, received up into glory.

1 Ti 6:15 Which in his times he shall shew, *who is* the blessed and only Potentate, the King of kings, and Lord of lords;

He 1:3 Who being the brightness of *his* glory, and the express image of his person, and upholding all things by the word of his power, when he had by himself purged our sins, sat down on the right hand of the Majesty on high;

Re 19:16 And he hath on *his* vesture and on his thigh a name written, KING OF KINGS, AND LORD OF LORDS.

3). The Father Bears Witness

Ps 2:7 I will declare the decree: the LORD hath said unto me, Thou *art* my Son; this day have I begotten thee.

Mt 3:17 And lo a voice from heaven, saying, This is my beloved Son, in whom I am well pleased.

Mt 17:5 While he yet spake, behold, a bright cloud overshadowed them: and behold a voice out of the cloud, which said, This is my beloved Son, in whom I am well pleased; hear ye him.

Mk 1:11 And there came a voice from heaven, *saying,* Thou art my beloved Son, in whom I am well pleased.

Mk 9:7 And there was a cloud that overshadowed them: and a voice came out of the cloud, saying, This is my beloved Son: hear him.

Lu 3:22 And the Holy Ghost descended in a bodily shape like a dove upon him, and a voice came from heaven, which said, Thou art my beloved Son; in thee I am well pleased.

Lu 9:35 And there came a voice out of the cloud, saying, This is my beloved Son: hear him.

Jn 1:33 And I knew him not: but he that sent me to baptize with water, the same said unto me, Upon whom thou shalt see the Spirit descending, and remaining on him, the same is he which baptizeth with the Holy Ghost.

Jn 5:32 There is another that beareth witness of me; and I know that the witness which he witnesseth of me is true.

Jn 5:37 And the Father himself, which hath sent me, hath borne witness of me. Ye have neither heard his voice at any time, nor seen his shape.

Jn 8:18 I am one that bear witness of myself, and the Father that sent me beareth witness of me.

Jn 8:54 Jesus answered, If I honour myself, my honour is nothing: it is my Father that honoureth me; of whom ye say, that he is your God:

Jn 12:28 Father, glorify thy name. Then came there a voice from heaven, *saying,* I have both glorified *it,* and will glorify *it* again.

Jn 15:26 But when the Comforter is come, whom I will send unto you from the Father, *even* the Spirit of truth, which proceedeth from the Father, he shall testify of me:

Ac 2:22 Ye men of Israel, hear these words; Jesus of Nazareth, a man approved of God among you by miracles and wonders and signs, which God did by him in the midst of you, as ye yourselves also know:

He 1:5 For unto which of the angels said he at any have I begotten thee? And again, I will be to him a Father, and he shall be to me a Son?

He 2:4 God also bearing *them* witness, both with signs and wonders, and with divers miracles, and gifts of the Holy Ghost, according to his own will?

2 Pe 1:17 For he received from God the Father honour and glory, when there came such a voice to him from the excellent glory, This is my beloved Son, in whom I am well pleased.

1 Jn 5:9 If we receive the witness of men, the witness of God is greater: for this is the witness of God which he hath testified of his Son.

4). Seven Scriptural Witnesses

JOHN THE BAPTIST

Jn 1:34 And I saw, and bare record that this is the Son of God.

THE WORKS OF CHRIST

Jn 5:36 But I have greater witness than *that* of John: for the works which the Father hath given me to finish, the same works that I do, bear witness of me, that the Father hath sent me.

THE FATHER

Jn 5:37 And the Father himself, which hath sent me, hath borne witness of me. Ye have neither heard his voice at any time, nor seen his shape.

THE OLD TESTAMENT

Jn 5:39 Search the scriptures; for in them ye think ye have eternal life: and they are they which testify of me.

JESUS CHRIST HIMSELF

Jn 8:14 Jesus answered and said unto them, Though I bear record of myself, *yet* my record is true: for I know whence I came, and whither I go; but ye cannot tell whence I come, and whither I go.

THE HOLY SPIRIT

Jn 15:26 But when the Comforter is come, whom I will send unto you from the Father, *even* the Spirit of truth, which proceedeth from the Father, he shall testify of me:

BELIEVERS

Jn 15:27 And ye also shall bear witness, because ye have been with me from the beginning.

5). Evil Spirits Confess His Divinity

Mt 8:29 And, behold, they cried out, saying, What have we to do with thee, Jesus, thou Son of God? art thou come hither to torment us before the time?

Mk 1:24 Saying, Let *us* alone; what have we to do with thee, thou Jesus of Nazareth? art thou come to destroy us? I know thee who thou art, the Holy One of God.

Mk 3:11 And unclean spirits, when they saw him, fell down before him, and cried, saying, Thou art the Son of God.

Mk 5:7 And cried with a loud voice, and said, What have I to do with thee, Jesus, *thou* Son of the most high God? I adjure thee by God, that thou torment me not.

Lu 4:34 Saying, Let *us* alone; what have we to do with thee, *thou* Jesus of Nazareth? art thou come to destroy us? I know thee who thou art; the Holy One of God.

Lu 4:41 And devils also came out of many, crying out, and saying, Thou art Christ the Son of God. And he rebuking *them* suffered them not to speak: for they knew that he was Christ.

Lu 8:28 When he saw Jesus, he cried out, and fell down before him, and with a loud voice said, What have I to do with thee, Jesus, *thou* Son of God most high? I beseech thee, torment me not.

Ac 16:17 The same followed Paul and us, and cried, saying, These men are the servants of the most high God, which shew unto us the way of salvation.

Ac 19:15 And the evil spirit answered and said, Jesus I know, and Paul I know; but who are ye?

Ja 2:19 Thou believest that there is one God; thou doest well: the devils also believe, and tremble.

b. Divine NamesAscribed to Christ

1). Beloved Son

Is 42:1 Behold my servant, whom I uphold; mine elect, *in whom* my soul delighteth; I have put my spirit upon him: he shall bring forth judgment to the Gentiles.

Is 49:5 And now, saith the LORD that formed me from the womb *to be* his servant, to bring Jacob again to him, Though Israel be not gathered, yet shall I be glorious in the eyes of the LORD, and my God shall be my strength.

Is 53:10 Yet it pleased the LORD to bruise him; he hath put *him* to grief: when thou shalt make his soul an offering for sin, he shall see *his* seed, he shall prolong *his* days, and the pleasure of the LORD shall prosper in his hand.

Mt 3:17 And lo a voice from heaven, saying, This is my beloved Son, in whom I am well pleased.

Mt 12:18 Behold my servant, whom I have chosen; my beloved, in whom my soul is well pleased: I will put my spirit upon him, and he shall shew judgment to the Gentiles.

Mt 17:5 While he yet spake, behold, a bright cloud overshadowed them: and behold a voice out of the cloud, which said him.

Mt 21:37 But last of all he sent unto them his son, saying, They will reverence my son.

Mk 1:11 And there came a voice from heaven, *saying,* Thou art my beloved Son, in whom I am well pleased.

Mk 12:6 Having yet therefore one son, his wellbeloved, he sent him also last unto them, saying, They will reverence my son.

Lu 3:22 And the Holy Ghost descended in a bodily shape like a dove upon him, and a voice came from heaven, which said, Thou art my beloved Son; in thee I am well pleased.

Lu 9:35 And there came a voice out of the cloud, saying, This is my beloved Son: hear him.

Lu 20:13 Then said the lord of the vineyard, What shall I do? I will send my beloved son: it may be they will reverence *him* when they see him.

Jn 1:14 And the Word was made flesh, and dwelt among us, (and we beheld his glory, the glory as of the only begotten of the Father,) full of grace and truth.

Jn 1:18 No man hath seen God at any time; the only begotten Son, which is in the bosom of the Father, he hath declared *him.*

Jn 3:16 For God so loved the world, that he gave his only begotten Son, that whosoever believeth in him should not perish, but have everlasting life.

Jn 3:35 The Father loveth the Son, and hath given all things into his hand.

Jn 5:20 For the Father loveth the Son, and sheweth him all things that himself doeth: and he will shew him greater works than these, that ye may marvel.

Jn 5:32 There is another that beareth witness of me; and I know that the witness which he witnesseth of me is true.

Jn 6:27 Labour not for the meat which perisheth, but for that meat which endureth unto everlasting life, which the Son of man shall give unto you: for him hath God the Father sealed.

Jn 8:18 I am one that bear witness of myself, and the Father that sent me beareth witness of me.

Jn 10:17 Therefore doth my Father love me, because I lay down my life, that I might take it again.

Jn 15:9 As the Father hath loved me, so have I loved you: continue ye in my love.

Jn 17:24 Father, I will that they also, whom thou hast given me, be with me where I am; that they may behold my glory, which thou hast given me: for thou lovedst me before the foundation of the world.

Ac 3:13 The God of Abraham, and of Isaac, and of Jacob, the God of our fathers, hath glorified his Son Jesus; whom ye delivered up, and denied him in the presence of Pilate, when he was determined to let *him* go.

Ac 4:27 For of a truth against thy holy child Jesus, whom thou hast anointed, both Herod, and Pontius Pilate, with the Gentiles, and the people of Israel, were gathered together,

Ac 13:33 God hath fulfilled the same unto us their children, in that he hath raised up Jesus again; as it is also written in the second psalm, Thou art my Son, this day have I begotten thee.

Ro 1:3 Concerning his Son Jesus Christ our Lord, which was made of the seed of David according to the flesh;

Ro 8:3 For what the law could not do, in that it was weak through the flesh, God sending his own Son in the likeness of sinful flesh, and for sin, condemned sin in the flesh:

Ro 8:32 He that spared not his own Son, but delivered him up for us all, how shall he not with him also freely give us all things?

Ga 1:16 To reveal his Son in me, that I might preach him among the heathen; immediately I conferred not with flesh and blood:

Ep 1:6 To the praise of the glory of his grace, wherein he hath made us accepted in the beloved.

Col 1:13 Who hath delivered us from the power of darkness, and hath translated *us* into the kingdom of his dear Son:

Col 1:19 For it pleased *the Father* that in him should all fulness dwell;

He 1:5 For unto which of the angels said he at any time, Thou art my Son, this day have I begotten thee? And again, I will be to him a Father, and he shall be to me a Son?

He 5:5 So also Christ glorified not himself to be made an high priest; but he that said unto him, Thou art my Son, to day have I begotten thee.

He 5:8 Though he were a Son, yet learned he obedience by the things which he suffered;

1 Pe 2:4 To whom coming, *as unto* a living stone, disallowed indeed of men, but chosen of God, *and* precious,

2 Pe 1:17 For he received from God the Father honour and glory, when there came such a voice to him from the excellent glory, This is my beloved Son, in whom I am well pleased.

1 Jn 4:9 In this was manifested the love of God toward us, because that God sent his only begotten Son into the world, that we might live through him.

2 Jn 3 Grace be with you, mercy, *and* peace, from God the Father, and from the Lord Jesus Christ, the Son of the Father, in truth and love.

2). Son of God

Ps 2:7 I will declare the decree: the LORD hath said unto me, Thou *art* my Son; this day have I begotten thee.

Mt 2:15 And was there until the death of Herod: that it might be fulfilled which was spoken of the Lord by the prophet, saying, Out of Egypt have I called my son.

Mt 3:17 And lo a voice from heaven, saying, This is my beloved Son, in whom I am well pleased.

Mt 4:3 And when the tempter came to him, he said, If thou be the Son of God, command that these stones be made bread.

Mt 4:6 And saith unto him, If thou be the Son of God, cast thyself down: for it is written, He shall give his angels charge concerning thee: and in *their* hands they shall bear thee up, lest at any time thou dash thy foot against a stone.

Mt 8:29 And, behold, they cried out, saying, What have we to do with thee, Jesus, thou Son of God? art thou come hither to torment us before the time?

Mt 11:27 All things are delivered unto me of my Father: and no man knoweth the Son, but the Father; neither knoweth any man the Father, save the Son, and *he* to whomsoever the Son will reveal *him*.

Mt 14:33 Then they that were in the ship came and worshipped him, saying, Of a truth thou art the Son of God.

Mt 17:5 While he yet spake, behold, a bright cloud overshadowed them: and behold a voice out of the cloud, which said, This is my beloved Son, in whom I am well pleased; hear ye him.

Mt 26:53 Thinkest thou that I cannot now pray to my Father, and he shall presently give me more than twelve legions of angels?

Mt 26:63 But Jesus held his peace. And the high priest answered and said unto him, I adjure thee by the living God, that thou tell us whether thou be the Christ, the Son of God.

Mt 27:43 He trusted in God; let him deliver him now, if he will have him: for he said, I am the Son of God.

Mt 27:54 Now when the centurion, and they that were with him, watching Jesus, saw the earthquake, and those things that were done, they feared greatly, saying, Truly this was the Son of God.

Mk 1:1 The beginning of the gospel of Jesus Christ, the Son of God;

Mk 9:7 And there was a cloud that overshadowed them: and a voice came out of the cloud, saying, This is my beloved Son: hear him.

Mk 14:62 And Jesus said, I am: and ye shall see the Son of man sitting on the right hand of power, and coming in the clouds of heaven.

Mk 15:39 And when the centurion, which stood over against him, saw that he so cried out, and gave up the ghost, he said, Truly this man was the Son of God.

Lu 1:32 He shall be great, and shall be called the Son of the Highest: and the Lord God shall give unto him the throne of his father David:

Lu 1:35 And the angel answered and said unto her, The Holy Ghost shall come upon thee, and the power of the Highest shall overshadow thee: there-

fore also that holy thing which shall be born of thee shall be called the Son of God.

Lu 4:3 And the devil said unto him, If thou be the Son of God, command this stone that it be made bread.

Lu 4:9 And he brought him to Jerusalem, and set him on a pinnacle of the temple, and said unto him, If thou be the Son of God, cast thyself down from hence:

Lu 8:28 When he saw Jesus, he cried out, and fell down before him, and with a loud voice said, What have I to do with thee, Jesus, *thou* Son of God most high? I beseech thee, torment me not.

Lu 22:70 Then said they all, Art thou then the Son of God? And he said unto them, Ye say that I am.

Jn 1:34 And I saw, and bare record that this is the Son of God.

Jn 1:49 Nathanael answered and saith unto him, Rabbi, thou art the Son of God; thou art the King of Israel.

Jn 3:18 He that believeth on him is not condemned: but he that believeth not is condemned already, because he hath not believed in the name of the only begotten Son of God.

Jn 5:25 Verily, verily, I say unto you, The hour is coming, and now is, when the dead shall hear the voice of the Son of God: and they that hear shall live.

Jn 9:35 Jesus heard that they had cast him out; and when he had found him, he said unto him, Dost thou believe on the Son of God?

Jn 10:36 Say ye of him, whom the Father hath sanctified, and sent into the world, Thou blasphemest; because I said, I am the Son of God?

Jn 11:4 When Jesus heard *that,* he said, This sickness is not unto death, but for the glory of God, that the Son of God might be glorified thereby.

Jn 11:27 She saith unto him, Yea, Lord: I believe that thou art the Christ, the Son of God, which should come into the world.

Jn 17:1 These words spake Jesus, and lifted up his eyes to heaven, and said, Father, the hour is come; glorify thy

Son, that thy Son also may glorify thee:

Jn 20:31 But these are written, that ye might believe that Jesus is the Christ, the Son of God; and that believing ye might have life through his name.

Ac 9:20 And straightway he preached Christ in the synagogues, that he is the Son of God.

Ac 13:33 God hath fulfilled the same unto us their children, in that he hath raised up Jesus again; as it is also written in the second psalm, Thou art my Son, this day have I begotten thee.

Ro 1:4 And declared *to be* the Son of God with power, according to the spirit of holiness, by the resurrection from the dead:

2 Co 1:19 For the Son of God, Jesus Christ, who was preached among you by us, *even* by me and Silvanus and Timotheus, was not yea and nay, but in him was yea.

Ga 2:20 I am crucified with Christ: nevertheless I live; yet not I, but Christ liveth in me: and the life which I now live in the flesh I live by the faith of the Son of God, who loved me, and gave himself for me.

1 Th 1:10 And to wait for his Son from heaven, whom he raised from the dead, *even* Jesus, which delivered us from the wrath to come.

He 1:2 Hath in these last days spoken unto us by *his* Son, whom he hath appointed heir of all things, by whom also he made the worlds;

He 3:6 But Christ as a son over his own house; whose house are we, if we hold fast the confidence and the rejoicing of the hope firm unto the end.

He 4:14 Seeing then that we have a great high priest, that is passed into the heavens, Jesus the Son of God, let us hold fast *our* profession.

He 7:3 Without father, without mother, without descent, having neither beginning of days, nor end of life; but made like unto the Son of God; abideth a priest continually.

He 7:28 For the law maketh men high priests which have infirmity; but the word of the oath, which was since the law, *maketh* the Son, who is consecrated for evermore.

He 10:29 Of how much sorer punishment, suppose ye, shall he be thought worthy, who hath trodden under foot the Son of God, and hath counted the blood of the covenant, wherewith he was sanctified, an unholy thing, and hath done despite unto the Spirit of grace?

1 Jn 1:3 That which we have seen and heard declare we unto you, that ye also may have fellowship with us: and truly our fellowship *is* with the Father, and with his Son Jesus Christ.

1 Jn 1:7 But if we walk in the light, as he is in the light, we have fellowship one with another, and the blood of Jesus Christ his Son cleanseth us from all sin.

1 Jn 3:8 He that committeth sin is of the devil; for the devil sinneth from the beginning. For this purpose the Son of God was manifested, that he might destroy the works of the devil.

1 Jn 3:23 And this is his commandment, That we should believe on the name of his Son Jesus Christ, and love one another, as he gave us commandment.

1 Jn 4:10 Herein is love, not that we loved God, but that he loved us, and sent his Son *to be* the propitiation for our sins.

1 Jn 4:15 Whosoever shall confess that Jesus is the Son of God, God dwelleth in him, and he in God.

1 Jn 5:5 Who is he that overcometh the world, but he that believeth that Jesus is the Son of God?

1 Jn 5:13 These things have I written unto you that believe on the name of the Son of God; that ye may know that ye have eternal life, and that ye may believe on the name of the Son of God.

1 Jn 5:20 *And* we know that the Son of God is come, and hath given us an understanding, that we may know him that is true, and we are in him that is true, *even* in his Son Jesus Christ. This is the true God, and eternal life.

Re 2:18 And unto the angel of the church in Thyatira write; These things saith the Son of God, who hath his eyes like unto a flame of fire, and his feet *are* like fine brass;

3). King of Kings

De 10:17 For the LORD your God *is* God of gods, and LORD of lords, a great God, a mighty, and a terrible, which regardeth not persons, nor taketh reward:

Jos 22:22 The LORD God of gods, the LORD God of gods, he knoweth, and Israel he shall know; if *it be* in rebellion, or if in transgression against the LORD, (save us not this day,)

Jb 12:18 He looseth the bond of kings, and girdeth their loins with a girdle.

Ps 24:7 Lift up your heads, O ye gates; and be ye lift up, ye everlasting doors; and the King of glory shall come in.

Ps 72:11 Yea, all kings shall fall down before him: all nations shall serve him.

Ps 136:3 O give thanks to the LORD of lords: for his mercy *endureth* for ever.

Zec 6:5 And the angel answered and said unto me, These *are* the four spirits of the heavens, which go forth from standing before the LORD of all the earth.

1 Ti 6:15 Which in his times he shall shew, *who is* the blessed and only Potentate, the King of kings, and Lord of lords;

Re 1:5 And from Jesus Christ, *who is* the faithful witness, *and* the first begotten of the dead, and the prince of the kings of the earth. Unto him that loved us, and washed us from our sins in his own blood,

Re 17:14 These shall make war with the Lamb, and the Lamb shall overcome them: for he is Lord of lords, and King of kings: and they that are with him *are* called, and chosen, and faithful.

Re 19:12 His eyes *were* as a flame of fire, and on his head *were* many crowns; and he had a name written, that no man knew, but he himself.

Re 19:16 And he hath on *his* vesture and on his thigh a name written, KING OF KINGS, AND LORD OF LORDS.

c. Special Marks of Divinity

1). His Pre-existence

Is 9:7 Of the increase of *his* government and peace *there shall be* no end, upon the throne of David, and upon his kingdom, to order it, and to establish it with judgment and with justice from henceforth even for ever. The zeal of the LORD of hosts will perform this.

Is 53:10 Yet it pleased the LORD to bruise him; he hath put *him* to grief: when thou shalt make his soul an offering for sin, he shall see *his* seed, he shall prolong *his* days, and the pleasure of the LORD shall prosper in his hand.

Mi 5:2 But thou, Bethlehem Ephratah, *though* thou be little among the thousands of Judah, *yet* out of thee shall he come forth unto me *that is* to be ruler in Israel; whose goings forth *have been* from of old, from everlasting.

Lu 24:5 And as they were afraid, and bowed down *their* faces to the earth, they said unto them, Why seek ye the living among the dead?

Jn 1:1 In the beginning was the Word, and the Word was with God, and the Word was God.

Jn 1:2 The same was in the beginning with God.

Jn 1:15 John bare witness of him, and cried, saying, This was he of whom I spake, He that cometh after me is preferred before me: for he was before me.

Jn 1:30 This is he of whom I said, After me cometh a man which is preferred before me: for he was before me.

Jn 6:62 *What* and if ye shall see the Son of man ascend up where he was before?

Jn 8:58 Jesus said unto them, Verily, verily, I say unto you, Before Abraham was, I am.

Jn 12:34 The people answered him, We have heard out of the law that Christ abideth for ever: and how sayest thou, The Son of man must be lifted up? who is this O Father, glorify thou me with thine own self with the glory which I had with thee before the world was.

Jn 17:24 Father, I will that they also, whom thou hast given me, be with me where I am; that they may behold my glory, which thou hast given me: for thou lovedst me before the foundation of the world.

Ro 6:9 Knowing that Christ being raised from the dead dieth no more; death hath no more dominion over him.

Col 1:17 And he is before all things, and by him all things consist.

He 1:11 They shall perish; but thou remainest; and they all shall wax old as doth a garment;

He 7:3 Without father, without mother, without descent, having neither beginning of days, nor end of life; but made like unto the Son of God; abideth a priest continually.

He 7:16 Who is made, not after the law of a carnal commandment, but after the power of an endless life.

He 7:25 Wherefore he is able also to save them to the uttermost that come unto God by him, seeing he ever liveth to make intercession for them.

He 13:8 Jesus Christ the same yesterday, and to day, and for ever.

1 Pe 1:20 Who verily was foreordained before the foundation of the world, but was manifest in these last times for you,

1 Jn 1:1 That which was from the beginning, which we have heard, which we have seen with our eyes, which we have looked upon, and our hands have handled, of the Word of life;

1 Jn 2:13 I write unto you, fathers, because ye have known him *that is* from the beginning. I write unto you, young men, because ye have overcome the wicked one. I write unto you, little children, because ye have known the Father.

Re 1:11 Saying, I am Alpha and Omega, the first and the last: and, What thou seest, write in a book, and send *it* unto the seven churches which are in Asia; unto Ephesus, and unto Smyrna, and unto Pergamos, and unto Thyatira, and unto Sardis, and unto Philadelphia, and unto Laodicea.

Re 1:14 His head and *his* hairs *were* white like wool, as white as snow; and his eyes *were* as a flame of fire;

Re 1:17 And when I saw him, I fell at his feet as dead. And he laid his right hand upon me, saying unto me, Fear not; I am the first and the last:

Re 2:8 And unto the angel of the church in Smyrna write; These things saith the first and the last, which was dead, and is alive;

Re 3:14 And unto the angel of the church of the Laodiceans write; These things saith the Amen, the faithful and true witness, the beginning of the creation of God;

Re 22:13 I am Alpha and Omega, the beginning and the end, the first and the last.

See **IMMUTABILITY**

2). His Authority

Mt 5:22 But I say unto you, That whosoever is angry with his brother without a cause shall be in danger of the judgment: and whosoever shall say to his brother, Raca, shall be in danger of the council: but whosoever shall say, Thou fool, shall be in danger of hell fire.

Mt 5:28 But I say unto you, That whosoever looketh on a woman to lust after her hath committed adultery with her already in his heart.

Mt 5:44 But I say unto you, Love your enemies, bless them that curse you, do good to them that hate you, and pray for them which despitefully use you, and persecute you;

Mt 6:29 And yet I say unto you, That even Solomon in all his glory was not arrayed like one of these.

Mt 7:29 For he taught them as *one* having authority, and not as the scribes.

Mt 9:6 But that ye may know that the Son of man hath power on earth to forgive sins, (then saith he to the sick of the palsy,) Arise, take up thy bed, and go unto thine house.

Mt 9:24 He said unto them, Give place: for the maid is not dead, but sleepeth. And they laughed him to scorn.

Mt 12:31 Wherefore I say unto you, All manner of sin and blasphemy shall be forgiven unto men: but the blasphemy *against* the *Holy* Ghost shall not be forgiven unto men.

Mt 14:19 And he commanded the multitude to sit down on the grass, and took the five loaves, and the two fishes, and looking up to heaven, he blessed, and brake, and gave the loaves to *his* disciples, and the disciples to the multitude.

Mt 15:35 And he commanded the multitude to sit down on the ground.

Mt 16:19 And I will give unto thee the keys of the kingdom of heaven: and whatsoever thou shalt bind on earth shall be bound in heaven: and whatsoever thou shalt loose on earth shall be loosed in heaven.

Mt 21:12 And Jesus went into the temple of God, and cast out all them that sold and bought in the temple, and overthrew the tables of the money-changers, and the seats of them that sold doves,

Mt 21:23 And when he was come into the temple, the chief priests and the elders of the people came unto him as he was teaching, and said, By what authority doest thou these things? and who gave thee this authority?

Mt 28:18 And Jesus came and spake unto them, saying, All power is given unto me in heaven and in earth.

Mk 1:22 for he taught them as one that had authority, and not as the scribes.

Mk 1:27 And they were all amazed, insomuch that they questioned among themselves, saying, What thing is this? what new doctrine *is* this? for with authority commandeth he even the unclean spirits, and they do obey him.

Mk 2:11 I say unto thee, Arise, and take up thy bed, and go thy way into thine house.

Mk 3:3 And he saith unto the man which had the withered hand, Stand forth.

Mk 5:8 For he said unto him, Come out of the man, *thou* unclean spirit.

Mk 5:41 And he took the damsel by the hand, and said unto her, Talitha cumi; which is, being interpreted, Damsel, I say unto thee, arise.

Mk 7:14 And when he had called all the people *unto him,* he said unto them, Hearken unto me every one *of you,* and understand:

Mk 9:7 And there was a cloud that overshadowed them: and a voice came out of the cloud, saying, This is my beloved Son: hear him.

Mk 9:25 When Jesus saw that the people came running together, he rebuked the foul spirit, saying unto him, *Thou* dumb and deaf spirit, I charge thee, come out of him, and enter no more into him.

Mk 11:16 And would not suffer that any man should carry *any* vessel through the temple.

Mk 11:28 And say unto him, By what authority doest thou these things? and who gave thee this authority to do these things?

Lu 4:36 And they were all amazed, and spake among themselves, saying, What a word *is* this! for with authority and power he commandeth the unclean spirits, and they come out.

Lu 5:24 But that ye may know that the Son of man hath power upon earth to forgive sins, (he said unto the sick of the palsy,) I say unto thee, Arise, and take up thy couch, and go into thine house.

Lu 6:27 But I say unto you which hear, Love your enemies, do good to them which hate you,

Lu 15:7 I say unto you, that likewise joy shall be in heaven over one sinner that repenteth, more than over ninety and nine just persons, which need no repentance.

Lu 18:14 I tell you, this man went down to his house justified *rather* than himself shall be abased; and he that humbleth himself shall be exalted.

Lu 19:45 And he went into the temple, and began to cast out them that sold therein, and them that bought;

Lu 20:2 And spake unto him, saying, Tell us, by what authority doest thou these things? or who is he that gave thee this authority?

Jn 5:11 He answered them, He that made me whole, the same said unto me, Take up thy bed, and walk.

Jn 5:27 And hath given him authority to execute judgment also, because he is the Son of man.

Jn 7:46 The officers answered, Never man spake like this man.

Ac 3:22 For Moses truly said unto the fathers, A prophet shall the Lord your God raise up unto you of your brethren, like unto me; him shall ye hear in all things whatsoever he shall say unto you.

1 Co 5:4 In the name of our Lord Jesus Christ, when ye are gathered together, and my spirit, with the power of our Lord Jesus Christ,

Re 3:7 And to the angel of the church in Philadelphia write; These things saith he that is holy, he that is true, he that hath the key of David, he that openeth, and no man shutteth; and shutteth, and no man openeth;

3). His Foreknowledge

Mt 26:12 For in that she hath poured this ointment on my body, she did *it* for my burial.

Mt 26:21 And as they did eat, he said, Verily I say unto you, that one of you shall betray me.

Mt 26:25 Then Judas, which betrayed him, answered and said, Master, is it I? He said unto him, Thou hast said.

Mt 26:34 Jesus said unto him, Verily I say unto thee, That this night, before the cock crow, thou shalt deny me thrice.

Mt 26:45 Then cometh he to his disciples, and saith unto them, Sleep on now, and take *your* rest: behold, the hour is at hand, and the Son of man is betrayed into the hands of sinners.

Mk 10:33 *Saying,* Behold, we go up to Jerusalem; and the Son of man shall be delivered unto the chief priests, and unto the scribes; and they shall condemn him to death, and shall deliver him to the Gentiles:

Mk 13:2 And Jesus answering said unto him, Seest thou these great buildings? there shall not be left one stone upon another, that shall not be thrown down.

Mk 13:23 But take ye heed: behold, I have foretold you all things.

Mk 14:13 And he sendeth forth two of his disciples, and saith unto them, Go ye into the city, and there shall meet you a man bearing a pitcher of water: follow him.

Mk 14:18 And as they sat and did eat, Jesus said, Verily I say unto you, One of you which eateth with me shall betray me.

Mk 14:30 And Jesus saith unto him, Verily I say unto thee, That this day, *even* in this night, before the cock crow twice, thou shalt deny me thrice.

Mk 14:42 Rise up, let us go; lo, he that betrayeth me is at hand.

Mk 14:72 And the second time the cock crew. And Peter called to mind the word that Jesus said unto him, Before the cock crow twice, thou shalt deny me thrice. And when he thought thereon, he wept.

Lu 13:32 And he said unto them, Go ye, and tell that fox, Behold, I cast out devils, and I do cures to day and to morrow, and the third *day* I shall be perfected.

Lu 18:31 Then he took unto them, Behold, we go up to Jerusalem, and all things that are written by the prophets concerning the Son of man shall be accomplished.

Lu 19:43 For the days shall come upon thee, that thine enemies shall cast a trench about thee, and compass thee round, and keep thee in on every side,

Lu 22:16 For I say unto you, I will not any more eat thereof, until it be fulfilled in the kingdom of God.

Lu 22:34 And he said, I tell thee, Peter, the cock shall not crow this day, before that thou shalt thrice deny that thou knowest me.

Jn 6:64 But there are some of you that believe not. For Jesus knew from the beginning who they were that believed not, and who should betray him.

Jn 13:1 Now before the feast of the passover, when Jesus knew that his hour was come that he should depart out of this world unto the Father, having loved his own which were in the world, he loved them unto the end.

Jn 13:11 For he knew who should betray him; therefore said he, Ye are not all clean.

Jn 13:19 Now I tell you before it come, that, when it is come to pass, ye may believe that I am *he*.

Jn 13:38 Jesus answered him, Wilt thou lay down thy life for my sake? Verily, verily, I say unto thee, The cock shall not crow, till thou hast denied me thrice.

Jn 14:29 And now I have told you before it come to pass, that, when it is come to pass, ye might believe.

Jn 16:4 But these things have I told you, that when the time shall come, ye may remember that I told you of them. And these things I said not unto you at the beginning, because I was with you.

Jn 18:4 Jesus therefore, knowing all things that should come upon him, went forth, and said unto them, Whom seek ye?

Jn 19:28 After this, Jesus knowing that all things were now accomplished, that the scripture might be fulfilled, saith, I thirst.

Jn 21:18 Verily, verily, I say unto thee, When thou wast young, thou girdedst thyself, and walkedst whither thou wouldest: but when thou shalt be old, thou shalt stretch forth thy hands, and another shall gird thee, and carry *thee* whither thou wouldest not.

See **FOREKNOWLEDGE**

a). Predicts His Own Sufferings

Is 52:14 As many were astonied at thee; his visage was so marred more than any man, and his form more than the sons of men:

Da 9:26 And after threescore and two weeks shall Messiah be cut off, but not for himself: and the people of the prince that shall come shall destroy the city and the sanctuary; and the end thereof *shall be* with a flood, and unto the end of the war desolations are determined.

Mt 12:40 For as Jonas was three days and three nights in the whale's belly; so shall the Son of man be three days and three nights in the heart of the earth.

Mt 17:12 But I say unto you, That Elias is come already, and they knew him not, but have done unto him whatsoever they listed. Likewise shall also the Son of man suffer of them.

Mt 17:23 And they shall kill him, and the third day he shall be raised again. And they were exceeding sorry.

Mt 20:18 Behold, we go up to Jerusalem; and the Son of man shall be betrayed unto the chief priests and unto the scribes, and they shall condemn him to death,

Mt 26:2 Ye know that after two days is *the feast of* the passover, and the Son of man is betrayed to be crucified.

Mt 26:24 The Son of man goeth as it is written of him: but woe unto that man by whom the Son of man is betrayed! it had been good for that man if he had not been born.

Mt 26:54 But how then shall the scriptures be fulfilled, that thus it must be?

Mk 8:31 And he began to teach them, that the Son of man must suffer many things, and be rejected of the elders, and *of* the chief priests, and scribes, and be killed, and after three days rise again.

Mk 9:12 And he answered and told them, Elias verily cometh first, and restoreth all things; and how it is written of the Son of man, that he must suffer many things, and be set at nought.

Mk 9:31 For he taught his disciples, and said unto them, The Son of man is delivered into the hands of men, and they shall kill him; and after that he is killed, he shall rise the third day.

Mk 10:32–33 And they were in the way going up to Jerusalem; and Jesus went before them: and they were amazed; and as they followed, they were afraid. And he took again the twelve, and began to tell them what things should happen unto him,

Saying, Behold, we go up to Jerusalem; and the Son of man shall be delivered unto the chief priests, and unto the scribes; and they shall condemn him to death, and shall deliver him to the Gentiles:

Mk 14:18 And as they sat and did eat, Jesus said, Verily I say unto you, One of you which eateth with me shall betray me.

Lu 9:22 Saying, The Son of man must suffer many things, and be rejected of the elders and chief priests and scribes, and be slain, and be raised the third day.

Lu 9:44 Let these sayings sink down into your ears: for the Son of man shall be delivered into the hands of men.

Lu 12:50 But I have a baptism to be baptized with; and how am I straitened till it be accomplished!

Lu 13:32 And he said unto them, Go ye, and tell that fox, Behold, I cast out devils, and I do cures to day and to morrow, and the third *day* I shall be perfected.

Lu 17:25 But first must he suffer many things, and be rejected of this generation.

Lu 18:32 For he shall be delivered unto the Gentiles, and shall be mocked, and spitefully entreated, and spitted on:

Lu 22:15 And he said unto them, With desire I have desired to eat this passover with you before I suffer:

Lu 22:22 And truly the Son of man goeth, as it was determined: but woe unto that man by whom he is betrayed!

Lu 22:37 For I say unto you, that this that is written must yet be accomplished in me, And he was reckoned among the transgressors: for the things concerning me have an end.

Lu 24:7 Saying, The Son of man must be delivered into the hands of sinful men, and be crucified, and the third day rise again.

Lu 24:26 Ought not Christ to have suffered these things, and to enter into his glory?

Lu 24:46 And said unto them, Thus it is written, and thus it behoved Christ to suffer, and to rise from the dead the third day:

Jn 2:19 Jesus answered and said unto them, Destroy this temple, and in three days I will raise it up.

Jn 3:14 And as Moses lifted up the serpent in the wilderness, even so must the Son of man be lifted up:

Jn 8:28 Then said Jesus unto them, When ye have lifted up the Son of man, then shall ye know that I am *he*, and *that* I do nothing of myself; but as my Father hath taught me, I speak these things.

Jn 18:32 That the saying of Jesus might be fulfilled, which he spake, signifying what death he should die.

See **SUFFERING**

b). Foretells His Departure

Mt 9:15 And Jesus said unto them, Can the children of the bridechamber mourn, as long as the bridegroom is with them? but the days will come, when the bridegroom shall be taken from them, and then shall they fast.

Mt 23:39 For I say unto you, Ye shall not see me henceforth, till ye shall say, Blessed *is* he that cometh in the name of the Lord.

Mt 26:11 For ye have the poor always with you; but me ye have not always.

Mk 2:20 But the days will come, when the bridegroom shall be taken away from them, and then shall they fast in those days.

Mk 14:7 For ye have the poor with you always, and whensoever ye will ye may do them good: but me ye have not always.

Mk 14:21 The Son of man indeed goeth, as it is written of him: but woe to that man by whom the Son of man is betrayed! good were it for that man if he had never been born.

Lu 5:35 But the days will come, when the bridegroom shall be taken away from them, and then shall they fast in those days.

Lu 13:35 Behold, your house is left unto you desolate: and verily I say unto you, Ye shall not see me, until *the time* come when ye shall say, Blessed *is* he that cometh in the name of the Lord.

Lu 19:12 He said therefore, A certain nobleman went into a far country to receive for himself a kingdom, and to return.

Jn 7:33 Then said Jesus unto them, Yet a little while am I with you, and *then* I go unto him that sent me.

Jn 8:21 Then said Jesus again unto them, I go my way, and ye shall seek me, and shall die in your sins: whither I go, ye cannot come.

Jn 12:8 For the poor always ye have with you; but me ye have not always.

Jn 12:35 Then Jesus said unto them, Yet a little while is the light with you. Walk while ye have the light, lest darkness come upon you: for he that walketh in darkness knoweth not whither he goeth.

Jn 13:33 Little children, yet a little while I am with you. Ye shall seek me: and as I said unto the Jews, Whither I go, ye cannot come; so now I say to you.

Jn 14:19 Yet a little while, and the world seeth me no more; but ye see me: because I live, ye shall live also.

Jn 14:28 Ye have heard how I said unto you, I go away, and come *again* unto you. If ye loved me, ye would rejoice, because I said, I go unto the Father: for my Father is greater than I.

Jn 16:5 But now I go my way to him that sent me; and none of you asketh me, Whither goest thou?

Jn 16:10 Of righteousness, because I go to my Father, and ye see me no more;

Jn 16:16 A little while, and ye shall not see me: and again, a little while, and ye shall see me, because I go to the Father.

Jn 16:28 I came forth from the Father, and am come into the world: again, I leave the world, and go to the Father.

Jn 17:11 And now I am no more in the world, but these are in the world, and I come to thee. Holy Father, keep through thine own name those whom thou hast given me, that they may be one, as we *are.*

4). His Lordship

Mt 12:8 For the Son of man is Lord even of the sabbath day.

Mk 2:28 Therefore the Son of man is Lord also of the sabbath.

Lu 1:43 And whence *is* this to me, that the mother of my Lord should come to me?

Lu 1:76 And thou, child, shalt be called the prophet of the Highest: for thou shalt go before the face of the Lord to prepare his ways;

Lu 6:5 And he said unto them, That the Son of man is Lord also of the sabbath.

Jn 13:14 If I then, *your* Lord and Master, have washed your feet; ye also ought to wash one another's feet.

Jn 20:13 And they say unto her, Woman, why weepest thou? She saith unto them, Because they have taken away my Lord, and I know not where they have laid him.

Ac 2:36 Therefore let all the house of Israel know assuredly, that God hath made that same Jesus, whom ye have crucified, both Lord and Christ.

Ac 5:31 Him hath God exalted with his right hand *to be* a Prince and a Saviour, for to give repentance to Israel, and forgiveness of sins.

Ac 10:36 The word which *God* sent unto the children of Israel, preaching peace by Jesus Christ: (he is Lord of all:)

Ro 10:9 That if thou shalt confess with thy mouth the Lord Jesus, and shalt believe in thine heart that God hath raised him from the dead, thou shalt be saved. For to this end Christ both died, and rose, and revived, that he might be Lord both of the dead and living.

1 Co 1:9 God *is* faithful, by whom ye were called unto the fellowship of his Son Jesus Christ our Lord.

1 Co 2:8 Which none of the princes of this world knew: for had they known *it,* they would not have crucified the Lord of glory.

1 Co 8:6 But to us *there is but* one God, the Father, of whom *are* all things, and we in him; and one Lord Jesus Christ, by whom *are* all things, and we by him.

1 Co 12:3 Wherefore I give you to understand, that no man speaking by the Spirit of God calleth Jesus accursed: and *that* no man can say that Jesus is the Lord, but by the Holy Ghost.

1 Co 12:5 And there are differences of administrations, but the same Lord.

1 Co 15:47 The first man *is* of the earth, earthy: the second man *is* the Lord from heaven.

2 Co 1:3 Blessed *be* God, even the Father of our Lord Jesus Christ, the Father of mercies, and the God of all comfort;

2 Co 4:5 For we preach not ourselves, but Christ Jesus the Lord; and ourselves your servants for Jesus' sake.

Ga 1:3 Grace *be* to you and peace from God the Father, and *from* our Lord Jesus Christ,

Ga 6:14 But God forbid that I should glory, save in the cross of our Lord Jesus Christ, by whom the world is crucified unto me, and I unto the world.

Ep 1:3 Blessed *be* the God and Father of our Lord Jesus Christ, who hath blessed us with all spiritual blessings in heavenly *places* in Christ:

Ep 3:11 According to the eternal purpose which he purposed in Christ Jesus our Lord:

Ep 4:5 One Lord, one faith, one baptism,

Ep 5:20 Giving thanks always for all things unto God and the Father in the name of our Lord Jesus Christ;

Ph 2:11 And *that* every tongue should confess that Jesus Christ *is* Lord, to the glory of God the Father.

1 Th 3:11 Now God himself and our Father, and our Lord Jesus Christ, direct our way unto you.

2 Th 1:1 Paul, and Silvanus, and Timotheus, unto the church of the Thessalonians in God our Father and the Lord Jesus Christ:

2 Th 2:16 Now our Lord Jesus Christ himself, and God, even our Father, which hath loved us, and hath given *us* everlasting consolation and good hope through grace,

1 Ti 1:2 Unto Timothy, *my* own son in the faith: Grace, mercy, *and* peace,

from God our Father and Jesus Christ our Lord.

1 Pe 1:3 Blessed *be* the God and Father of our Lord Jesus Christ, which according to his abundant mercy hath begotten us again unto a lively hope by the resurrection of Jesus Christ from the dead,

2 Pe 1:2 Grace and peace be multiplied unto you through the knowledge of God, and of Jesus our Lord,

Jude 17 But, beloved, remember ye the words which were spoken before of the apostles of our Lord Jesus Christ;

5). His Preeminence

Song 5:10 My beloved *is* white and ruddy, the chiefest among ten thousand.

Is 52:13 Behold, my servant shall deal prudently, he shall be exalted and extolled, and be very high.

Is 55:4 Behold, I have given him *for* a witness to the people, a leader and commander to the people.

Mt 3:11 I indeed baptize you with water unto repentance: but he that cometh after me is mightier than I, whose shoes I am not worthy to bear: he shall baptize you with the Holy Ghost, and *with* fire:

Mt 12:6 But I say unto you, That in this place is *one* greater than the temple.

Mt 12:41 The men of Nineveh shall rise in judgment with this generation, and shall condemn it: because they repented at the preaching of Jonas; and, behold, a greater than Jonas *is* here.

Mt 12:42 The queen of the south shall rise up in the judgment with this generation, and shall condemn it: for she came from the uttermost parts of the earth to hear the wisdom of Solomon; and, behold, a greater than Solomon *is* here.

Mk 1:7 And preached, saying, There cometh one mightier than I after me, the latchet of whose shoes I am not worthy to stoop down and unloose.

Lu 3:16 John answered, saying unto *them* all, I indeed baptize you with water; but one mightier than I cometh, the latchet of whose shoes I am not worthy to unloose: he shall baptize you with the Holy Ghost and with fire:

Lu 11:32 The men of Nineveh shall rise up in the judgment with this generation, and shall condemn it: for they repented at the preaching of Jonas; and, behold, a greater than Jonas *is* here.

Jn 1:15 John bare witness of him, and cried, saying, This was he of whom I spake, He that cometh after me is preferred before me: for he was before me.

Jn 1:27 He it is, who coming after me is preferred before me, whose shoe's latchet I am not worthy to unloose.

Jn 3:31 He that cometh from above is above all: he that is of the earth is earthly, and speaketh of the earth: he that cometh from heaven is above all.

Jn 4:12 Art thou greater than our father Jacob, which gave us the well, and drank thereof himself, and his children, and his cattle?

Jn 8:53 Art thou greater than our father Abraham, which is dead? and the prophets are dead: whom makest thou thyself?

Jn 13:13 Ye call me Master and Lord: and ye say well; for so I am.

Ac 2:36 Therefore let all the house of Israel know assuredly, that God hath made that same Jesus, whom ye have crucified, both Lord and Christ.

Ac 13:25 And as John fulfilled his course, he said, Whom think ye that I am? I am not *he*. But, behold, there cometh one after me, whose shoes of *his* feet I am not worthy to loose.

Ro 14:9 For to this end Christ both died, and rose, and revived, that he might be Lord both of the dead and living.

Ep 1:21 Far above all principality, and power, and might, and dominion, and every name that is named, not only in this world, but also in that which is to come:

Col 1:18 And he is the head of the body, the church: who is the beginning, the firstborn from the dead; that in all *things* he might have the preeminence.

Col 2:10 And ye are complete in him, which is the head of all principality and power:

He 1:4 Being made so much better than the angels, as he hath by inheritance obtained a more excellent name than they.

He 1:9 Thou hast loved righteousness, and hated iniquity, therefore God, *even* thy God, hath anointed thee with the oil of gladness above thy fellows.

He 3:3 For this *man* was counted worthy of more glory than Moses, inasmuch as he who hath builded the house hath more honour than the house.

He 7:22 By so much was Jesus made a surety of a better testament.

He 8:6 But now hath he obtained a more excellent ministry, by how much also he is the mediator of a better covenant, which was established upon better promises.

1 Pe 3:22 Who is gone into heaven, and is on the right hand of God; angels and authorities and powers being made subject unto him.

Re 1:11 Saying, I am Alpha and Omega, the first and the last: and, What thou seest, write in a book, and send *it* unto the seven churches which are in Asia; unto Ephesus, and unto Smyrna, and unto Pergamos, and unto Thyatira, and unto Sardis, and unto Philadelphia, and unto Laodicea.

6). His Dominion

Nu 24:19 Out of Jacob shall come he that shall have dominion, and shall destroy him that remaineth of the city.

Ps 72:8 He shall have dominion also from sea to sea, and from the river unto the ends of the earth.

Ps 110:2 The Lord shall send the rod of thy strength out of Zion: rule thou in the midst of thine enemies.

Is 9:6 For unto us a child is born, unto us a son is given: and the government shall be upon his shoulder: and his name shall be called Wonderful, Counsellor, The mighty God, The everlasting Father, The Prince of Peace.

Is 9:7 Of the increase of *his* government and peace *there shall be* no end, upon the throne of David, and upon his kingdom, to order it, and to establish it with judgment and with justice from henceforth even for ever. The zeal of the Lord of hosts will perform this.

Is 40:10 Behold, the LORD God will come with strong *hand,* and his arm shall rule for him: behold, his reward *is* with him, and his work before him.

Da 4:3 How great *are* his signs! and how mighty *are* his wonders! his kingdom *is* an everlasting kingdom, and his dominion *is* from generation to generation.

Da 7:14 And there was given him dominion, and glory, and a kingdom, that all people, nations, and languages, should serve him: his dominion *is* an everlasting dominion, which shall not pass away, and his kingdom *that* which shall not be destroyed.

Zec 9:10 And I will cut off the chariot from Ephraim, and the horse from Jerusalem, and the battle bow shall be cut off: and he shall speak peace unto the heathen: and his dominion *shall be* from sea *even* to sea, and from river *even* to the ends of the earth.

Mt 2:6 And thou Bethlehem, in the land of Juda, art not the least among the princes of Juda: for out of thee shall come a Governor, that shall rule my people Israel.

Mt 8:27 But the men marvelled, saying, What manner of man is this, that even the winds and the sea obey him!

Mt 8:32 And he said unto them, Go. And when they were come out, they went into the herd of swine: and, behold, the whole herd of swine ran violently down a steep place into the sea, and perished in the waters.

Mt 11:27 All things are delivered unto me of my Father: and no man knoweth the Son, but the Father; neither knoweth any man the Father, save the Son, and *he* to whomsoever the Son will reveal *him.*

Mt 13:41 The Son of man shall send forth his angels, and they shall gather out of his kingdom all things that offend, and them which do iniquity;

Mt 28:18 And Jesus came and spake unto them, saying, All power is given unto me in heaven and in earth.

Mk 1:25 And Jesus rebuked him, saying, Hold thy peace, and come out of him.

Mk 1:27 And they were all amazed, insomuch that they questioned among themselves, saying, What thing is this? what new doctrine *is* this? for with authority commandeth he even the unclean spirits, and they do obey him.

Mk 2:28 Therefore the Son of man is Lord also of the sabbath.

Mk 3:11 And unclean spirits, when they saw him, fell down before him, and cried, saying, Thou art the Son of God.

Mk 4:39 And he arose, and rebuked the wind, and said unto the sea, Peace, be still. And the wind ceased, and there was a great calm.

Mk 5:9 And he asked him, What *is* thy name? And he answered, saying, My name *is* Legion: for we are many.

Mk 5:12 And all the devils besought him, saying, Send us into the swine, that we may enter into them.

Mk 6:48 And he saw them toiling in rowing; for the wind was contrary unto them: and about the fourth watch of the night he cometh unto them, walking upon the sea, and would have passed by them.

Mk 9:25 When Jesus saw that the people came running together, he rebuked the foul spirit, saying unto him, *Thou* dumb and deaf spirit, I charge thee, come out of him, and enter no more into him.

Mk 11:21 And Peter calling to remembrance saith unto him, Master, behold, the fig tree which thou cursedst is withered away.

Lu 4:35 And Jesus rebuked him, saying, Hold thy peace, and come out of him. And when the devil had thrown him in the midst, he came out of him, and hurt him not.

Lu 4:41 And devils also came out of many, crying out, and saying, Thou art Christ the Son of God. And he rebuking *them* suffered them not to speak: for they knew that he was Christ.

Lu 6:5 And he said unto them, That the Son of man is Lord also of the sabbath.

Lu 7:7 Wherefore neither thought I myself worthy to come unto thee: but say in a word, and my servant shall be healed.

Lu 7:14 And he came and touched the bier: and they that bare *him* stood still. And he said, Young man, I say unto thee, Arise.

Lu 8:24 And they came to him, and awoke him, saying, Master, master, we perish. Then he arose, and rebuked the wind and the raging of the water: and they ceased, and there was a calm.

Lu 8:29 (For he had commanded the unclean spirit to come out of the man. For oftentimes it had caught him: and he was kept bound with chains and in fetters; and he brake the bands, and was driven of the devil into the wilderness.)

Lu 8:32 And there was there an herd of many swine feeding on the mountain: and they besought him that he would suffer them to enter into them. And he suffered them.

Lu 9:1 Then he called his twelve disciples together, and gave them power and authority over all devils, and to cure diseases.

Lu 9:42 And as he was yet a coming, the devil threw him down, and tare *him*. And Jesus rebuked the unclean spirit, and healed the child, and delivered him again to his father.

Lu 10:17 And the seventy returned again with joy, saying, Lord, even the devils are subject unto us through thy name.

Lu 10:22 All things are delivered to me of my Father: and no man knoweth who the Son is, but the Father; and who the Father is, but the Son, and *he* to whom the Son will reveal *him*.

Lu 11:22 But when a stronger than he shall come upon him, and overcome him, he taketh from him all his armour wherein he trusted, and divideth his spoils.

Jn 3:30 He must increase, but I *must* decrease.

Jn 3:35 The Father loveth the Son, and hath given all things into his hand.

Jn 6:19 So when they had rowed about five and twenty or thirty furlongs, they see Jesus walking on the sea, and drawing nigh unto the ship: and they were afraid.

Jn 13:3 Jesus knowing that the Father had given all things into his hands, and that he was come from God, and went to God;

Ro 9:5 Whose *are* the fathers, and of whom as concerning the flesh Christ *came,* who is over all, God blessed for ever. Amen.

1 Co 15:25 For he must reign, till he hath put all enemies under his feet.

Ep 1:22 And hath put all *things* under his feet, and gave him *to be* the head over all *things* to the church,

Ph 2:10 That at the name of Jesus every knee should bow, of *things* in heaven, and *things* in earth, and *things* under the earth;

He 1:8 But unto the Son he saith, Thy throne, O God, *is* for ever and ever: a sceptre of righteousness *is* the sceptre of thy kingdom.

1 Pe 3:22 Who is gone into heaven, and is on the right hand of God; angels and authorities and powers being made subject unto him.

1 Pe 4:11 If any man speak, *let him speak* as the oracles of God; if any man minister, *let him do it* as of the ability which God giveth: that God in all things may be glorified through Jesus Christ, to whom be praise and dominion for ever and ever. Amen.

Re 11:15 And the seventh angel sounded; and there were great voices in heaven, saying, The kingdoms of this world are become *the kingdoms* of our Lord, and of his Christ; and he shall reign for ever and ever.

See **POWER**

7.) His Exaltation to Heavenly Places

Is 52:13 Behold, my servant shall deal prudently, he shall be exalted and extolled, and be very high.

Is 53:12 Therefore will I divide him *a portion* with the great, and he shall divide the spoil with the strong; because he hath poured out his soul unto death: and he was numbered with the transgressors; and he bare the sin of many, and made intercession for the transgressors.

Da 7:14 And there was given him dominion, and glory, and a kingdom, that all people, nations, and languages, should serve him: his dominion *is* an everlasting dominion, which shall not pass away, and his kingdom *that* which shall not be destroyed.

Mt 19:28 And Jesus said unto them, Verily I say unto you, That ye which have followed me, in the regeneration when the Son of man shall sit in the throne of his glory, ye also shall sit upon twelve thrones, judging the twelve tribes of Israel.

Mt 21:42 Jesus saith unto them, Did ye never read in the scriptures, The stone which the builders rejected, the same is become the head of the corner: this is the Lord's doing, and it is marvellous in our eyes?

Mt 22:44 The Lord said unto my Lord, Sit thou on my right hand, till I make thine enemies thy footstool?

Mt 23:39 For I say unto you, Ye shall not see me henceforth, till ye shall say, Blessed *is* he that cometh in the name of the Lord.

Mt 24:30 And then shall appear the sign of the Son of man in heaven: and then shall all the tribes of the earth mourn, and they shall see the Son of man coming in the clouds of heaven with power and great glory.

Mt 26:64 Jesus saith unto him, Thou hast said: nevertheless I say unto you, Hereafter shall ye see the Son of man sitting on the right hand of power, and coming in the clouds of heaven.

Mk 12:10 And have ye not read this scripture; The stone which the builders rejected is become the head of the corner:

Mk 16:19 So then after the Lord had spoken unto them, he was received up into heaven, and sat on the right hand of God.

Lu 1:32 He shall be great, and shall be called the Son of the Highest: and the Lord God shall give unto him the throne of his father David:

Lu 13:35 Behold, your house is left unto you desolate: and verily I say unto you, Ye shall not see me, until *the time* come when ye shall say, Blessed *is* he that cometh in the name of the Lord.

Lu 19:15 And it came to pass, that when he was returned, having received the kingdom, then he commanded these servants to be called unto him, to whom he had given the money, that he might know how much every man had gained by trading.

Lu 21:27 And then shall they see the Son of man coming in a cloud with power and great glory.

Lu 22:29 And I appoint unto you a kingdom, as my Father hath appointed unto me;

Lu 22:69 Hereafter shall the Son of man sit on the right hand of the power of God.

Ac 2:33 Therefore being by the right hand of God exalted, and having received of the Father the promise of the Holy Ghost, he hath shed forth this, which ye now see and hear.

Ac 2:36 Therefore let all the house of Israel know assuredly, that God hath made that same Jesus, whom ye have crucified, both Lord and Christ.

Ac 5:31 Him hath God exalted with his right hand *to be* a Prince and a Saviour, for to give repentance to Israel, and forgiveness of sins.

Ac 7:55 But he, being full of the Holy Ghost, looked up stedfastly into heaven, and saw the glory of God, and Jesus standing on the right hand of God,

Ro 8:34 Who *is* he that condemneth? *It is* Christ that died, yea rather, that is risen again, who is even at the right hand of God, who also maketh intercession for us.

1 Co 15:27 For he hath put all things under his feet. But when he saith, all things are put under *him, it is* manifest that he is excepted, which did put all things under him.

Ep 1:20 Which he wrought in Christ, when he raised him from the dead, and set *him* at his own right hand in the heavenly *places*.

Ep 4:10 He that descended is the same also that ascended up far above all heavens, that he might fill all things.)

Ph 2:9 Wherefore God also hath highly exalted him, and given him a name which is above every name:

Col 3:1 If ye then be risen with Christ, seek those things which are above, where Christ sitteth on the right hand of God.

He 1:3 Who being the brightness of *his* glory, and the express image of his person, and upholding all things by the word of his power, when he had by himself purged our sins, sat down on the right hand of the Majesty on high;

He 1:9 Thou hast loved righteousness, and hated iniquity; therefore God, *even* thy God, hath anointed thee with the oil of gladness above thy fellows.

He 2:9 But we see Jesus, who was made a little lower than the angels for the suffering of death, crowned with glory and honour; that he by the grace of God should taste death for every man.

He 7:26 For such an high priest became us, *who is* holy, harmless, undefiled, separate from sinners, and made higher than the heavens;

He 8:1 Now of the things which we have spoken *this is* the sum: We have such an high priest, who is set on the right hand of the throne of the Majesty in the heavens;

He 10:12 But this man, after he had offered one sacrifice for sins for ever, sat down on the right hand of God;

He 12:2 Looking unto Jesus the author and finisher of *our* faith; who for the joy that was set before him endured the cross, despising the shame, and is set down at the right hand of the throne of God.

1 Pe 2:7 Unto you therefore which believe *he is* precious: but unto them which be disobedient, the stone which the builders disallowed, the same is made the head of the corner,

1 Pe 3:22 Who is gone into heaven, and is on the right hand of God; angels and authorities and powers being made subject unto him.

Re 3:21 To him that overcometh will I grant to sit with me in my throne, even as I also overcame, and am set down with my Father in his throne.

Re 5:12 Saying with a loud voice, Worthy is the Lamb that was slain to receive power, and riches, and wisdom, and strength, and honour, and glory, and blessing.

Re 22:3 There shall be no more curse: but the throne of God and of the Lamb shall be in it; and his servants shall serve him:

See **GOD**

2. His Humanity, *fully man*

a. Manifested in the Incarnation

Is 7:14 Therefore the LORD himself shall give you a sign; Behold, a virgin shall conceive, and bear a son, and shall call his name Immanuel.

Is 9:6 For unto us a child is born, unto us a son is given: and the government shall be upon his shoulder: and his name shall be called Wonderful, Counsellor, The mighty God, The everlasting Father, The Prince of Peace.

Is 11:1 And there shall come forth a rod out of the stem of Jesse, and a Branch shall grow out of his roots:

Is 49:1 Listen, O isles, unto me; and hearken, ye people, from far; The LORD hath called me from the womb; from the bowels of my mother hath he made mention of my name.

Mt 1:18 Now the birth of Jesus Christ was on this wise: When as his mother Mary was espoused to Joseph, before they came together, she was found with child of the Holy Ghost.

Mt 1:23 Behold, a virgin shall be with child, and shall bring forth a son, and they shall call his name Emmanuel, which being interpreted is, God with us.

Lu 1:31 And, behold, thou shalt conceive in thy womb, and bring forth a son, and shalt call his name Jesus.

Lu 1:35 And the angel answered and said unto her, The Holy Ghost shall come upon thee, and the power of the Highest shall overshadow thee: therefore also that holy thing which shall be born of thee shall be called the Son of God.

Lu 2:7 And she brought forth her firstborn son, and wrapped him in swaddling clothes, and laid him in a manger; because there was no room for them in the inn.

Jn 1:10 He was in the world, and the world was made by him, and the world knew him not.

Jn 1:14 And the Word was made flesh, and dwelt among us, (and we beheld his glory, the glory as of the only begotten of the Father,) full of grace and truth.

Jn 16:28 I came forth from the Father, and am come into the world: again, I leave the world, and go to the Father.

Ac 2:30 Therefore being a prophet, and knowing that God had sworn with an oath to him, that of the fruit of his loins, according to the flesh, he would raise up Christ to sit on his throne;

Ro 1:3 Concerning his Son Jesus Christ our Lord, which was made of the seed of David according to the flesh;

Ro 8:3 For what the law could not do, in that it was weak through the flesh, God sending his own Son in the likeness of sinful flesh, and for sin, condemned sin in the flesh:

Ro 9:5 Whose *are* the fathers, and of whom as concerning the flesh Christ *came,* who is over all, God blessed for ever. Amen.

Ga 4:4 But when the fulness of the time was come, God sent forth his Son, made of a woman, made under the law,

Ph 2:7 But made himself of no reputation, and took upon him the form of a servant, and was made in the likeness of men:

1 Ti 3:16 And without controversy great is the mystery of godliness: God was manifest in the flesh, justified in the Spirit, seen of angels, preached unto the Gentiles, believed on in the world, received up into glory.

He 2:14 Forasmuch then as the children are partakers of flesh and blood, he also himself likewise took part of the same; that through death he might destroy him that had the power of death, that is, the devil;

He 5:7 Who in the days of his flesh, when he had offered up prayers and supplications with strong crying and tears unto him that was able to save him from death, and was heard in that he feared;

He 7:14 For *it is* evident that our Lord sprang out of Juda; of which tribe Moses spake nothing concerning priesthood.

He 10:20 By a new and living way, which he hath consecrated for us, through the veil, that is to say, his flesh;

1 Pe 1:20 Who verily was foreordained before the foundation of the world, but was manifest in these last times for you,

1 Jn 1:2 (For the life was manifested, and we have seen *it,* and bear witness, and shew unto you that eternal life, which was with the Father, and was manifested unto us;)

1 Jn 4:2 Hereby know ye the Spirit of God: Every spirit that confesseth that Jesus Christ is come in the flesh is of God:

1 Jn 5:20 *And* we know that the Son of God is come, and hath given us an understanding, that we may know him that is true, and we are in him that is true, *even* in his Son Jesus Christ. This is the true God, and eternal life.

2 Jn 7 For many deceivers are entered into the world, who confess not that Jesus Christ is come in the flesh. This is a deceiver and an antichrist.

b. Shared the Common Experiences of Humanity

Mt 4:2 And when he had fasted forty days and forty nights, he was afterward an hungred.

Mt 8:24 And, behold, there arose a great tempest in the sea, insomuch that the ship was covered with the waves: but he was asleep.

Mt 21:18 Now in the morning as he returned into the city, he hungered.

Mt 26:37 And he took with him Peter and the two sons of Zebedee, and began to be sorrowful and very heavy.

Mt 26:42 He went away again the second time, and prayed, saying, O my Father, if this cup may not pass away from me, except I drink it, thy will be done.

Mk 4:38 And he was in the hinder part of the ship, asleep on a pillow: and they awake him, and say unto him, Master, carest thou not that we perish?

Mk 11:12 And on the morrow, when they were come from Bethany, he was hungry:

Mk 14:34 And saith unto them, My soul is exceeding sorrowful unto death: tarry ye here, and watch.

Lu 2:40 And the child grew, and waxed strong in spirit, filled with wisdom: and the grace of God was upon him.

Lu 2:52 And Jesus increased in wisdom and stature, and in favour with God and man.

Lu 4:2 Being forty days tempted of the devil. And in those days he did eat nothing: and when they were ended, he afterward hungered.

Lu 8:23 But as they sailed he fell asleep: and there came down a storm of wind on the lake; and they were filled *with water,* and were in jeopardy.

Lu 9:58 And Jesus said unto him, Foxes have holes, and birds of the air *have* nests; but the Son of man hath not where to lay *his* head.

Lu 24:39 Behold my hands and my feet, that it is I myself: handle me, and see; for a spirit hath not flesh and bones, as ye see me have.

Jn 4:6 Now Jacob's well was there. Jesus therefore, being wearied with *his* journey, sat thus on the well: *and* it was about the sixth hour.

Jn 12:27 Now is my soul troubled; and what shall I say? Father, save me from this hour: but for this cause came I unto this hour.

Jn 21:13 Jesus then cometh, and taketh bread, and giveth them, and fish likewise.

c. Called the Son of Man

Da 7:13 I saw in the night visions, and, behold, *one* like the Son of man came with the clouds of heaven, and came to the Ancient of days, and they brought him near before him.

Mt 8:20 And Jesus saith unto him, The foxes have holes, and the birds of the air *have* nests; but the Son of man hath not where to lay *his* head.

Mt 9:6 But that ye may know that the Son of man hath power on earth to forgive sins, (then saith he to the sick of the palsy,) Arise, take up thy bed, and go unto thine house.

Mt 11:19 The Son of man came eating and drinking, and they say, Behold a man gluttonous, and a winebibber, a friend of publicans and sinners. But wisdom is justified of her children.

Mt 12:8 For the Son of man is Lord even of the sabbath day.

Mt 12:32 And whosoever speaketh a word against the Son of man, it shall be forgiven him: but whosoever speaketh against the Holy Ghost, it shall not be forgiven him, neither in this world, neither in the *world* to come.

Mt 12:40 For as Jonas was three days and three nights in the whale's belly; so shall the Son of man be three days and three nights in the heart of the earth.

Mt 13:37 He answered and said unto them, He that soweth the good seed is the Son of man;

Mt 13:41 The Son of man shall send forth his angels, and they shall gather out of his kingdom all things that offend, and them which do iniquity;

Mt 16:13 When Jesus came into the coasts of Caesarea Philippi, he asked his disciples, saying, Whom do men say that I the Son of man am?

Mt 16:28 Verily I say unto you, There be some standing here, which shall not taste of death, till they see the Son of man coming in his kingdom.

Mt 17:22 And while they abode in Galilee, Jesus said unto them, The Son of man shall be betrayed into the hands of men:

Mt 18:11 For the Son of man is come to save that which was lost.

Mt 19:28 And Jesus said unto them, Verily I say unto you, That ye which have followed me, in the regeneration when the Son of man shall sit in the throne of his glory, ye also shall sit upon twelve thrones, judging the twelve tribes of Israel.

Mt 20:28 Even as the Son of man came not to be ministered unto, but to minister, and to give his life a ransom for many.

Mt 24:27 For as the lightning cometh out of the east, and shineth even unto the west; so shall also the coming of the Son of man be.

Mt 24:37 But as the days of Noe *were,* so shall also the coming of the Son of man be.

Mt 24:44 Therefore be ye also ready: for in such an hour as ye think not the Son of man cometh.

Mt 26:2 Ye know that after two days is *the feast of* the passover, and the Son of man is betrayed to be crucified.

Mt 26:64 Jesus saith unto him, Thou hast said: nevertheless I say unto you, Hereafter shall ye see the Son of man sitting on the right hand of power, and coming in the clouds of heaven.

Mk 2:28 Therefore the Son of man is Lord also of the sabbath.

Mk 8:38 Whosoever therefore shall be ashamed of me and of my words in this adulterous and sinful generation; of him also shall the Son of man be ashamed, when he cometh in the glory of his Father with the holy angels.

Mk 9:9 And as they came down from the mountain, he charged them that they should tell no man what things they had seen, till the Son of man were risen from the dead.

Mk 9:31 For he taught his disciples, and said unto them, The Son of man is delivered into the hands of men, and they shall kill him; and after that he is killed, he shall rise the third day.

Mk 10:33 *Saying,* Behold, we go up to Jerusalem; and the Son of man shall be delivered unto the chief priests, and unto the scribes; and they shall condemn him to death, and shall deliver him to the Gentiles:

Mk 10:45 For even the Son of man came not to be ministered unto, but to minister, and to give his life a ransom for many.

Mk 13:26 And then shall they see the Son of man coming in the clouds with great power and glory.

Mk 14:21 The Son of man indeed goeth, as it is written of him: but woe to that man by whom the Son of man is betrayed! good were it for that man if he had never been born.

Mk 14:41 And he cometh the third time, and saith unto them, Sleep on now, and take *your* rest: it is enough, the hour is come; behold, the Son of man is betrayed into the hands of sinners.

Mk 14:62 And Jesus said, I am: and ye shall see the Son of man sitting on the right hand of power, and coming in the clouds of heaven.

Lu 5:24 But that ye may know that the Son of man hath power upon earth to forgive sins, (he said unto the sick of the palsy,) I say unto thee, Arise, and take up thy couch, and go into thine house.

Lu 6:5 And he said unto them, That the Son of man is Lord also of the sabbath.

Lu 7:34 The Son of man is come eating and drinking; and ye say, Behold a gluttonous man, and a winebibber, a friend of publicans and sinners!

Lu 9:22 Saying, The Son of man must suffer many things, and be rejected of the elders and chief priests and scribes, and be slain, and be raised the third day.

Lu 9:44 Let these sayings sink down into your ears: for the Son of man shall be delivered into the hands of men.

Lu 9:56 For the Son of man is not come to destroy men's lives, but to save *them*. And they went to another village.

Lu 11:30 For as Jonas was a sign unto the Ninevites, so shall also the Son of man be to this generation.

Lu 12:8 Also I say unto you, Whosoever shall confess me before men, him shall the Son of man also confess before the angels of God:

Lu 17:22 And he said unto the disciples, The days will come, when ye shall desire to see one of the days of the Son of man, and ye shall not see *it*.

Lu 18:8 I tell you that he will avenge them speedily. Nevertheless when the Son of man cometh, shall he find faith on the earth?

Lu 18:31 Then he took *unto him* the twelve, and said unto them, Behold, we go up to Jerusalem, and all things that are written by the prophets concerning the Son of man shall be accomplished.

Lu 21:36 Watch ye therefore, and pray always, that ye may be accounted worthy to escape all these things that shall come to pass, and to stand before the Son of man.

Lu 22:69 Hereafter shall the Son of man sit on the right hand of the power of God.

Lu 24:7 Saying, The Son of man must be delivered into the hands of sinful men, and be crucified, and the third day rise again.

Jn 1:51 And he saith unto him, Verily, verily, I say unto you, Hereafter ye shall see heaven open, and the angels of God ascending and descending upon the Son of man.

Jn 3:13 And no man hath ascended up to heaven, but he that came down from heaven, *even* the Son of man which is in heaven.

Jn 5:27 And hath given him authority to execute judgment also, because he is the Son of man.

Jn 6:53 Then Jesus said unto them, Verily, verily, I say unto you, Except ye eat the flesh of the Son of man, and drink his blood, ye have no life in you.

Jn 8:28 Then said Jesus unto them, When ye have lifted up the Son of man, then shall ye know that I am *he*, and *that* I do nothing of myself; but as my Father hath taught me, I speak these things.

Jn 12:23 And Jesus answered them, saying, The hour is come, that the Son of man should be glorified.

Jn 12:34 The people answered him, We have heard out of the law that Christ abideth for ever: and how sayest thou, The Son of man must be lifted up? who is this Son of man?

Jn 13:31 Therefore, when he was gone out, Jesus said, Now is the Son of man glorified, and God is glorified in him.

Ac 7:56 And said, Behold, I see the heavens opened, and the Son of man standing on the right hand of God.

Re 1:13 And in the midst of the seven candlesticks *one* like unto the Son of man, clothed with a garment down to the foot, and girt about the paps with a golden girdle.

Re 14:14 And I looked, and behold a white cloud, and upon the cloud *one* sat like unto the Son of man, having on his head a golden crown, and in his hand a sharp sickle.

d. Called Son of David

Mt 1:1 The book of the generation of Jesus Christ, the son of David, the son of Abraham.

Mt 9:27 And when Jesus departed thence, two blind men followed him, crying, and saying, *Thou* Son of David, have mercy on us.

Mt 12:23 And all the people were amazed, and said, Is not this the son of David?

Mt 15:22 And, behold, a woman of Canaan came out of the same coasts, and cried unto him, saying, Have mercy on me, O Lord, *thou* Son of David; my daughter is grievously vexed with a devil.

Mt 20:31 And the multitude rebuked them, because they should hold their peace: but they cried the more, saying, Have mercy on us, O Lord, *thou* Son of David.

Mt 21:9 And the multitudes that went before, and that followed, cried, saying, Hosanna to the Son of David: Blessed *is* he that cometh in the name of the Lord; Hosanna in the highest.

Mt 21:15 And when the chief priests and scribes saw the wonderful things that he did, and the children crying in the temple, and saying, Hosanna to the Son of David; they were sore displeased,

Mt 22:42 Saying, What think ye of Christ? whose son is he? They say unto him, *The Son* of David.

Mk 10:47 And when he heard that it was Jesus of Nazareth, he began to cry out, and say, Jesus, *thou* Son of David, have mercy on me.

Mk 10:48 And many charged him that he should hold his peace: but he cried the more a great deal, *Thou* Son of David, have mercy on me.

Mk 12:35 And Jesus answered and said, while he taught in the temple, How say the scribes that Christ is the Son of David?

Lu 1:69 And hath raised up an horn of salvation for us in the house of his servant David;

Lu 18:38 And he cried, saying, Jesus, *thou* Son of David, have mercy on me.

Lu 20:41 And he said unto them, How say they that Christ is David's son?

Jn 7:42 Hath not the scripture said, That Christ cometh of the seed of David, and out of the town of Bethlehem, where David was?

Ro 1:3 Concerning his Son Jesus Christ our Lord, which was made of the seed of David according to the flesh;

Ro 15:12 And again, Esaias saith, There shall be a root of Jesse, and he that shall rise to reign over the Gentiles; in him shall the Gentiles trust.

2 Ti 2:8 Remember that Jesus Christ of the seed of David was raised from the dead according to my gospel:

Re 5:5 And one of the elders saith unto me, Weep not: behold, the Lion of the tribe of Juda, the Root of David, hath prevailed to open the book, and to loose the seven seals thereof.

Re 22:16 I Jesus have sent mine angel to testify unto you these things in the churches. I am the root and the offspring of David, *and* the bright and morning star.

3. *His Life*, the Messiah

a. His Anointing

Ps 45:7 Thou lovest righteousness, and hatest wickedness: therefore God, thy God, hath anointed thee with the oil of gladness above thy fellows.

Ps 132:10 For thy servant David's sake turn not away the face of thine anointed.

Is 61:1 The Spirit of the Lord GOD *is* upon me; because the LORD hath anointed me to preach good tidings unto the meek; he hath sent me to bind up the brokenhearted, to proclaim liberty to the captives, and the opening of the prison to *them that are* bound;

Da 9:24 Seventy weeks are determined upon thy people and upon thy holy city, to finish the transgression, and to make an end of sins, and to make reconciliation for iniquity, and to bring in everlasting righteousness, and to seal up the vision and prophecy, and to anoint the most Holy.

Lu 4:18 The Spirit of the Lord is upon me, because he hath anointed me to preach the gospel to the poor; he hath sent me to heal the brokenhearted, to preach deliverance to the captives, and recovering of sight to the blind, to set at liberty them that are bruised,

Ac 4:27 For of a truth against thy holy child Jesus, whom thou hast anointed, both Herod, and Pontius Pilate, with the Gentiles, and the people of Israel, were gathered together,

Ac 10:38 How God anointed Jesus of Nazareth with the Holy Ghost and with power: who went about doing good, and healing all that were oppressed of the devil; for God was with him.

He 1:9 Thou hast loved righteousness, and hated iniquity; therefore God, *even* thy God, hath anointed thee with the oil of gladness above thy fellows.

b. His Ascension

Ps 68:18 Thou hast ascended on high, thou hast led captivity captive: thou hast received gifts for men; yea, *for* the rebellious also, that the LORD God might dwell *among them.*

Mk 16:19 So then after the Lord had spoken unto them, he was received up into heaven, and sat on the right hand of God.

Lu 9:51 And it came to pass, when the time was come that he should be received up, he stedfastly set his face to go to Jerusalem,

Lu 24:51 And it came to pass, while he blessed them, he was parted from them, and carried up into heaven.

Jn 6:62 *What* and if ye shall see the Son of man ascend up where he was before?

Jn 7:33 Then said Jesus unto them, Yet a little while am I with you, and *then* I go unto him that sent me.

Jn 13:3 Jesus knowing that the Father had given all things into his hands, and that he was come from God, and went to God;

Jn 14:28 Ye have heard how I said unto you, I go away, and come *again* unto you. If ye loved me, ye would rejoice, because I said I go unto the Father: for my Father is greater than I.

Jn 16:10 Of righteousness, because I go to my Father, and ye see me no more;

Jn 16:16 A little while, and ye shall not see me: and again, a little while, and ye shall see me, because I go to the Father.

Jn 16:28 I came forth from the Father, and am come into the world: again, I leave the world, and go to the Father.

Jn 17:11 And now I am no more in the world, but these are in the world, and I come to thee. Holy Father, keep through thine own name those whom thou hast given me, that they may be one, as we *are.*

Jn 17:13 And now come I to thee; and these things I speak in the world, that they might have my joy fulfilled in themselves.

Jn 20:17 Jesus saith unto her, Touch me not; for I am not yet ascended to my Father: but go to my brethren, and say unto them, I ascend unto my Father, and your Father; and *to* my God, and your God.

Ac 1:2 Until the day in which he was taken up, after that he through the Holy Ghost had given commandments unto the apostles whom he had chosen:

Ac 1:9 And when he had spoken these things, while they beheld, he was taken up; and a cloud received him out of their sight.

Ac 1:22 Beginning from the baptism of John, unto that same day that he was taken up from us, must one be ordained to be a witness with us of his resurrection.

Ac 3:21 Whom the heaven must receive until the times of restitution of all things, which God hath spoken by the mouth of all his holy prophets since the world began.

Ep 4:8 Wherefore he saith, When he ascended up on high, he led captivity captive, and gave gifts unto men.

1 Ti 3:16 And without controversy great is the mystery of godliness: God was manifest in the flesh, justified in the Spirit, seen of angels, preached unto the Gentiles, believed on in the world, received up into glory.

He 4:14 Seeing then that we have a great high priest, that is passed into the heavens, Jesus the Son of God, let us hold fast *our* profession.

He 6:20 Whither the forerunner is for us entered, *even* Jesus, made an high priest for ever after the order of Melchisedec.

He 8:1 Now of the things which we have spoken *this is* the sum: We have such an high priest, who is set on the right hand of the throne of the Majesty in the heavens;

He 9:12 Neither by the blood of goats and calves, but by his own blood he entered in once into the holy place, having obtained eternal redemption *for us.*

He 9:24 For Christ is not entered into the holy places made with hands, *which are* the figures of the true; but into heaven itself, now to appear in the presence of God for us:

1 Pe 3:22 Who is gone into heaven, and is on the right hand of God; angels and authorities and powers being made subject unto him.

c. His Blood

Ex 12:13 And the blood shall be to you for a token upon the houses where ye *are:* and when I see the blood, I will pass over you, and the plague shall not be upon you to destroy *you,* when I smite the land of Egypt.

Zec 13:1 In that day there shall be a fountain opened to the house of David and to the inhabitants of Jerusalem for sin and for uncleanness.

Mt 26:28 For this is my blood of the new testament, which is shed for many for the remission of sins.

Mk 14:24 And he said unto them, This is my blood of the new testament, which is shed for many.

Lu 22:20 Likewise also the cup after supper, saying, This cup *is* the new testament in my blood, which is shed for you.

Jn 6:55–56 For my flesh is meat indeed, and my blood is drink indeed.

He that eateth my flesh, and drinketh my blood, dwelleth in me, and I in him.

Jn 19:34 But one of the soldiers with a spear pierced his side, and forthwith came there out blood and water.

Ac 20:28 Take heed therefore unto yourselves, and to all the flock, over the which the Holy Ghost hath made you overseers, to feed the church of God, which he hath purchased with his own blood.

Ro 3:25 Whom God hath set forth *to be* a propitiation through faith in his blood, to declare his righteousness for the remission of sins that are past, through the forbearance of God;

Ro 5:9 Much more then, being now justified by his blood, we shall be saved from wrath through him.

1 Co 10:16 The cup of blessing which we bless, is it not the communion of the blood of Christ? The bread which

we break, is it not the communion of the body of Christ?

1 Co 11:25 After the same manner also *he took* the cup, when he had supped, saying, This cup is the new testament in my blood: this do ye, as oft as ye drink *it,* in remembrance of me.

Ep 1:7 In whom we have redemption through his blood, the forgiveness of sins, according to the riches of his grace;

Ep 2:13 But now in Christ Jesus ye who sometimes were far off are made nigh by the blood of Christ.

Col 1:14 In whom we have redemption through his blood, *even* the forgiveness of sins:

Col 1:20 And, having made peace through the blood of his cross, by him to reconcile all things unto himself; by him, *I say,* whether *they be* things in earth, or things in heaven.

He 1:3 Who being the brightness of *his* glory, and the express image of his person, and upholding all things by the word of his power, when he had by himself purged our sins, sat down on the right hand of the Majesty on high;

He 9:12 Neither by the blood of goats and calves, but by his own blood he entered in once into the holy place, having obtained eternal redemption *for us.*

He 9:14 How much more shall the blood of Christ, who through the eternal Spirit offered himself without spot to God, purge your conscience from dead works to serve the living God?

He 10:19 Having therefore, brethren, boldness to enter into the holiest by the blood of Jesus,

He 10:29 Of how much sorer punishment, suppose ye, shall he be thought worthy, who hath trodden under foot the Son of God, and hath counted the blood of the covenant, wherewith he was sanctified, an unholy thing, and hath done despite unto the Spirit of grace?

He 12:24 And to Jesus the mediator of the new covenant, and to the blood of *that of* Abel.

He 13:12 Wherefore Jesus also, that he might sanctify the people with his own blood, suffered without the gate.

He 13:20 Now the God of peace, that brought again from the dead our Lord Jesus, that great shepherd of the sheep, through the blood of the everlasting covenant,

1 Pe 1:2 Elect according to the foreknowledge of God the Father, through sanctification of the Spirit, unto obedience and sprinkling of the blood of Jesus Christ: Grace unto you, and peace, be multiplied.

1 Pe 1:18–19 Forasmuch as ye know that ye were not redeemed with corruptible things, *as* silver and gold, from your vain conversation *received* by tradition from your fathers;

But with the precious blood of Christ, as of a lamb without blemish and without spot:

1 Jn 1:7 But if we walk in the light, as he is in the light, we have fellowship one with another, and the blood of Jesus Christ his Son cleanseth us from all sin.

1 Jn 5:6 This is he that came by water and blood, *even* Jesus Christ; not by water only, but by water and blood. And it is the Spirit that beareth witness, because the Spirit is truth.

Re 1:5 And from Jesus Christ, *who is* the faithful witness, *and* the first begotten of the dead, and the prince of the kings of the earth. Unto him that loved us, and washed us from our sins in his own blood,

Re 5:9 And they sung a new song, saying, Thou art worthy to take the book, and to open the seals thereof: for thou wast slain, and hast redeemed us to God by thy blood out of every kindred, and tongue, and people, and nation;

Re 7:14 And I said unto him, Sir, thou knowest. And he said to me, These are they which came out of great tribulation, and have washed their robes, and made them white in the blood of the Lamb.

Re 12:11 And they overcame him by the blood of the Lamb, and by the word of their testimony; and they loved not their lives unto the death.

Re 19:13 And he *was* clothed with a vesture dipped in blood: and his name is called The Word of God.

See **BLOOD**

d. His Creation

Jn 1:3 All things were made by him; and without him was not any thing made that was made.

Jn 1:10 He was in the world, and the world was made by him, and the world knew him not.

1 Co 8:6 But to us *there is but* one God, the Father, of whom *are* all things, and we in him; and one Lord Jesus Christ, by whom *are* all things, and we by him.

Ep 3:9 And to make all *men* see what *is* the fellowship of the mystery, which from the beginning of the world hath been hid in God, who created all things by Jesus Christ:

Col 1:16 For by him were all things created, that are in heaven, and that are in earth, visible and invisible, whether *they be* thrones, or dominions, or principalities, or powers: all things were created by him, and for him:

He 1:1–2 God, who at sundry times and in divers manners spake in time past unto the fathers by the prophets,

Hath in these last days spoken unto us by *his* Son, whom he hath appointed heir of all things, by whom also he made the worlds;

He 1:10 And, Thou, Lord, in the beginning hast laid the foundation of the earth; and the heavens are the works of thine hands:

He 3:3 For this *man* was counted worthy of more glory than Moses, inasmuch as he who hath builded the house hath more honour than the house.

Re 3:14 And unto the angel of the church of the Laodiceans write; These things saith the Amen, the faithful and true witness, the beginning of the creation of God;

See **CREATOR**

e. His Cries

Mt 27:46 And about the ninth hour Jesus cried with a loud voice, saying, Eli, Eli, lama sabachthani? that is to say, My God, my God, why hast thou forsaken me?

Mt 27:50 Jesus, when he had cried again with a loud voice, yielded up the ghost.

Mk 15:37 And Jesus cried with a loud voice, and gave up the ghost.

Lu 8:8 And other fell on good ground, and sprang up, and bare fruit an hundredfold. And when he had said these things, he cried, He that hath ears to hear, let him hear.

Lu 23:46 And when Jesus had cried with a loud voice, he said, Father, into thy hands I commend my spirit: and having said thus, he gave up the ghost.

Jn 7:28 Then cried Jesus in the temple as he taught, saying, Ye both know me, and ye know whence I am: and I am not come of myself, but he that sent me is true, whom ye know not.

Jn 7:37 In the last day, that great *day* of the feast, Jesus stood and cried, saying, If any man thirst, let him come unto me, and drink.

Jn 11:43 And when he thus had spoken, he cried with a loud voice, Lazarus, come forth.

Jn 12:44 Jesus cried and said, He that believeth on me, believeth not on me, but on him that sent me.

f. His Appearance

SEEN AT THE TRANSFIGURATION

Mk 9:2–3 And after six days Jesus taketh *with him* Peter, and James, and John, and leadeth them up into an high mountain apart by themselves: and he was transfigured before them.

And his raiment became shining, exceeding white as snow; so as no fuller on earth can white them.

AS PORTRAYED BY HIMSELF

Jn 1:51 And he saith unto him, Verily, verily, I say unto you, Hereafter ye shall see heaven open, and the angels of God ascending and descending upon the Son of man.

APPEARED AT PAUL'S CONVERSION

Ac 9:4–5 And he fell to the earth, and heard a voice saying unto him, Saul, Saul, why persecutest thou me?

And he said, Who art thou, Lord? And the Lord said, I am Jesus whom thou persecutest: *it is* hard for thee to kick against the pricks.

DESCRIBED BY THE REVELATOR

Re 1:13–16 And in the midst of the seven candlesticks *one* like unto the Son of man, clothed with a garment down to the foot, and girt about the paps with a golden girdle.

His head and *his* hairs *were* white like wool, as white as snow; and his eyes *were* as a flame of fire;

And his feet like unto fine brass, as if they burned in a furnace; and his voice as the sound of many waters.

And he had in his right hand seven stars: and out of his mouth went a sharp twoedged sword: and his countenance *was* as the sun shineth in his strength.

Re 14:14 And I looked, and behold a white cloud, and upon the cloud one sat like unto the Son of man, having on his head a golden crown, and in his hand a sharp sickle.

Re 19:11–12 And I saw heaven opened, and behold a white horse; and he that sat upon him *was* called Faithful and True, and in righteousness he doth judge and make war.

His eyes *were* as a flame of fire, and on his head *were* many crowns; and he had a name written, that no man knew, but he himself.

g. His Glory

Is 63:1 Who *is* this that cometh from Edom, with dyed garments from Bozrah? this *that is* glorious in his apparel, travelling in the greatness of his strength? I that speak in righteousness, mighty to save.

Da 7:14 And there was given him dominion, and glory, and a kingdom, that all people, nations, and languages, should serve him: his dominion *is* an everlasting dominion, which shall not pass away, and his kingdom *that* which shall not be destroyed.

Zec 6:13 Even he shall build the temple of the LORD; and he shall bear the glory, and shall sit and rule upon his throne; and he shall be a priest upon his throne: and the counsel of peace shall be between them both.

Mt 16:27 For the Son of man shall come in the glory of his Father with his angels; and then he shall reward every man according to his works.

Mt 19:28 And Jesus said unto them, Verily I say unto you, That ye which have followed me, in the regeneration when the Son of man shall sit in the throne of his glory, ye also shall sit upon twelve thrones, judging the twelve tribes of Israel.

Mt 24:30–31 And then shall appear the sign of the Son of man in heaven: and then shall all the tribes of the earth mourn, and they shall see the Son of man coming in the clouds of heaven with power and great glory.

And he shall send his angels with a great sound of a trumpet, and they shall gather together his elect from the four winds, from one end of heaven to the other.

Mt 26:64 Jesus saith unto him, Thou hast said: nevertheless I say unto you, Hereafter shall ye see the Son of man sitting on the right hand of power, and coming in the clouds of heaven.

Mk 8:38 Whosoever therefore shall be ashamed of me and of my words in this adulterous and sinful generation; of him also shall the Son of man be ashamed, when he cometh in the glory of his Father with the holy angels.

Mk 13:26 And then shall they see the Son of man coming in the clouds with great power and glory.

Mk 14:62 And Jesus said, I am: and ye shall see the Son of man sitting on the right hand of power, and coming in the clouds of heaven.

Lu 3:16 John answered, saying unto *them* all, I indeed baptize you with water; but one mightier than I cometh, the latchet of whose shoes I am not worthy to unloose: he shall baptize you with the Holy Ghost and with fire:

Lu 9:26 For whosoever shall be ashamed of me and of my words, of him shall the Son of man be ashamed, when he shall come in his own glory, and *in his* Father's, and of the holy angels.

Lu 9:32 But Peter and they that were with him were heavy with sleep: and when they were awake, they saw his glory, and the two men that stood with him.

Lu 21:27 And then shall they see the Son of man coming in a cloud with power and great glory.

Lu 24:26 Ought not Christ to have suffered these things, and to enter into his glory.

Jn 1:14 And the Word was made flesh, and dwelt among us, (and we beheld his glory, the glory as of the only begotten of the Father,) full of grace and truth.

Jn 1:51 And he saith unto him, Verily, verily, I say unto you, Hereafter ye shall see heaven open, and the angels of God ascending and descending upon the Son of man.

Jn 2:11 This beginning of miracles did Jesus in Cana of Galilee, and manifested forth his glory; and his disciples believed on him.

Jn 12:41 These things said Esaias, when he saw his glory, and spake of him.

Jn 13:32 If God be glorified in him, God shall also glorify him in himself, and shall straightway glorify him.

Jn 17:5 And now, O Father, glorify thou me with thine own self with the glory which I had with thee before the world was.

Jn 17:22 And the glory which thou gavest me I have given them; that they may be one, even as we are one:

Jn 17:24 Father, I will that they also, whom thou hast given me, be with me where I am; that they may behold my glory, which thou hast given me: for thou lovedst me before the foundation of the world.

2 Th 1:10 When he shall come to be glorified in his saints, and to be admired in all them that believe (because our testimony among you was believed) in that day.

2 Th 2:14 Whereunto he called you by our gospel, to the obtaining of the glory of our Lord Jesus Christ.

He 1:3 Who being the brightness of *his* glory, and the express image of his person, and upholding all things by the word of his power, when he had by himself purged our sins, sat down on the right hand of the Majesty on high;

He 3:3 For this *man* was counted worthy of more glory than Moses, inasmuch as he who hath builded the house hath more honour than the house.

1 Pe 1:11 Searching what, or what manner of time the Spirit of Christ which was in them did signify, when it testified beforehand the sufferings of Christ, and the glory that should follow.

1 Pe 1:21 Who by him do believe in God, that raised him up from the dead, and gave him glory; that your faith and hope might be in God.

1 Pe 4:13 But rejoice, inasmuch as ye are partakers of Christ's sufferings; that, when his glory shall be revealed, ye may be glad also with exceeding joy.

2 Pe 3:18 But grow in grace, and *in* the knowledge of our Lord and Saviour Jesus Christ. To him *be* glory both now and for ever. Amen.

Re 5:12 Saying with a loud voice, Worthy is the Lamb that was slain to receive power, and riches, and wisdom, and strength, and honour, and glory, and blessing.

MANIFESTED, *at His Second Coming*

Mt 16:27 For the Son of man shall come in the glory of his Father with his angels; and then he shall reward every man according to his works.

SHARED, *by believers*

Mt 19:28 And Jesus said unto them, Verily I say unto you, That ye which have followed me, in the regeneration when the Son of man shall sit in the throne of his glory, ye also shall sit

upon twelve thrones, judging the twelve tribes of Israel.

Mt 24:30 And then shall appear the sign of the Son of man in heaven: and then shall all the tribes of the earth mourn, and they shall see the Son of man coming in the clouds of heaven with power and great glory.

BEHELD, *upon the Mount*

Lu 9:32 But Peter and they that were with him were heavy with sleep: and when they were awake, they saw his glory, and the two men that stood with him.

REVEALED, *in the Incarnation*

Jn 1:14 And the Word was made flesh, and dwelt among us, (and we beheld his glory, the glory as of the only begotten of the Father,) full of grace and truth.

POSSESSED, *before the foundation of the world*

Jn 17:5 And now, O Father, glorify thou me with thine own self with the glory which I had with thee before the world was.

Jn 17:24 Father, I will that they also, whom thou hast given me, be with me where I am; that they may behold my glory, which thou hast given me: for thou lovedst me before the foundation of the world.

He 3:3 For this *man* was counted worthy of more glory than Moses, inasmuch as he who hath builded the house hath more honour than the house.

ASCRIBED, *by the heavenly host*

Re 5:12 Saying with a loud voice, Worthy is the Lamb that was slain to receive power, and riches, and wisdom, and strength, and honour, and glory, and blessing.

See **GLORY**

h. His Mission

Mt 5:17 Think not that I am come to destroy the law, or the prophets: I am not come to destroy, but to fulfil.

Mt 9:12-13 But when Jesus heard *that,* he said unto them, They that be whole need not a physician, but they that are sick.

But go ye and learn what *that* meaneth, I will have mercy, and not sacrifice: for I am not come to call the righteous, but sinners to repentance.

Mt 10:34 Think not that I am come to send peace on earth: I came not to send peace, but a sword.

Mt 12:18 Behold my servant, whom I have chosen; my beloved, in whom my soul is well pleased: I will put my spirit upon him, and he shall shew judgment to the Gentiles.

Mt 18:11 For the Son of man is come to save that which was lost.

Mt 20:28 Even as the Son of man came not to be ministered unto, but to minister, and to give his life a ransom for many.

Mk 1:38 And he said unto them, Let us go into the next towns, that I may preach there also: for therefore came I forth.

Mk 2:17 When Jesus heard *it,* he saith unto them, They that are whole have no need of the physician, but they that are sick: I came not to call the righteous, but sinners to repentance.

Lu 4:43 And he said unto them, I must preach the kingdom of God to other cities also: for therefore am I sent.

Lu 5:31 And Jesus answering said unto them, They that are whole need not a physician; but they that are sick.

Lu 9:56 For the Son of man is not come to destroy men's lives, but to save *them.* And they went to another village.

Lu 12:14 And he said unto him, Man, who made me a judge or a divider over you?

Lu 12:49 I am come to send fire on the earth; and what will I, if it be already kindled?

Lu 15:4 What man of you, having an hundred sheep, if he lose one of them, doth not leave the ninety and nine in the wilderness, and go after that which is lost, until he find it?

Lu 19:10 For the Son of man is come to seek and to save that which was lost.

Lu 20:13 Then said the lord of the vineyard, What shall I do? I will send my beloved son: it may be they will reverence *him* when they see him.

Jn 3:17 For God sent not his Son into the world to condemn the world; but that the world through him might be saved.

Jn 6:39 And this is the Father's will which hath sent me, that of all which he hath given me I should lose nothing, but should raise it up again at the last day.

Jn 8:15 Ye judge after the flesh; I judge no man.

Jn 9:39 And Jesus said, For judgment I am come into this world, that they which see not might see; and that they which see might be made blind.

Jn 10:10 The thief cometh not, but for to steal, and to kill, and to destroy: I am come that they might have life, and that they might have *it* more abundantly.

Jn 12:27 Now is my soul troubled; and what shall I say? Father, save me from this hour: but for this cause came I unto this hour.

Jn 12:47 And if any man hear my words, and believe not, I judge him not: for I came not to judge the world, but to save the world.

Jn 18:37 Pilate therefore said unto him, Art thou a king then? Jesus answered, Thou sayest that I am a king. To this end was I born, and for this cause came I into the world, that I should bear witness unto the truth. Every one that is of the truth heareth my voice.

1 Ti 1:15 This *is* a faithful saying, and worthy of all acceptation, that Christ Jesus came into the world to save sinners; of whom I am chief.

He 2:14 Forasmuch then as the children are partakers of flesh and blood, he also himself likewise took part of the same; that through death he might destroy him that had the power of death, that is, the devil;

1 Jn 3:5 And ye know that he was manifested to take away our sins; and in him is no sin.

1 Jn 3:8 He that committeth sin is of the devil; for the devil sinneth from the beginning. For this purpose the Son of God was manifested, that he might destroy the works of the devil.

1 Jn 4:14 And we have seen and do testify that the Father sent the Son *to be* the Saviour of the world.

i. His Oneness with the Father

Mk 9:37 Whosoever shall receive one of such children in my name, receiveth me: and whosoever shall receive me, receiveth not me, but him that sent me.

Jn 1:18 No man hath seen God at any time; the only begotten Son, which is in the bosom of the Father, he hath declared *him*.

Jn 5:19 Then answered , verily, I say unto you, The Son can do nothing of himself, but what he seeth the Father do: for what things soever he doeth, these also doeth the Son likewise.

Jn 5:30 I can of mine own self do nothing: as I hear, I judge: and my judgment is just; because I seek not mine own will, but the will of the Father which hath sent me.

Jn 6:57 As the living Father hath sent me, and I live by the Father: so he that eateth me, even he shall live by me.

Jn 8:16 And yet if I judge, my judgment is true: for I am not alone, but I and the Father that sent me.

Jn 8:29 And he that sent me is with me: the Father hath not left me alone; for I do always those things that please him.

Jn 10:30 I and *my* Father are one.

Jn 10:38 But if I do, though ye believe not me, believe the works: that ye may know, and believe, that the Father is in me, and I in him.

Jn 12:45 And he that seeth me seeth him that sent me.

Jn 14:7 If ye had known me, ye should have known my Father also: and from henceforth ye know him, and have seen him.

Jn 14:10 Believest thou not that I am in the Father, and the Father in me?

the words that I speak unto you I speak not of myself: but the Father that dwelleth in me, he doeth the works.

Jn 14:20 At that day ye shall know that I *am* in my Father, and ye in me, and I in you.

Jn 15:23 He that hateth me hateth my Father also.

Jn 16:15 All things that the Father hath are mine: therefore said I, that he shall take of mine, and shall shew *it* unto you.

Jn 17:10–11 And all mine are thine, and thine are mine; and I am glorified in them.

And now I am no more in the world, but these are in the world, and I come to thee. Holy Father, keep through thine own name those whom thou hast given me, that they may be one, as we *are*.

Jn 17:21–22 That they all may be one; as thou, Father, *art* in me, and I in thee, that they also may be one in us: that the world may believe that thou hast sent me.

And the glory which thou gavest me I have given them; that they may be one, even as we are one:

Ac 10:38 How God anointed Jesus of Nazareth with the Holy Ghost and with power: who went about doing good, and healing all that were oppressed of the devil; for God was with him.

1 Co 3:23 And ye are Christ's; and Christ *is* God's.

2 Co 5:19 To wit, that God was in Christ, reconciling the world unto himself, not imputing their trespasses unto them; and hath committed unto us the word of reconciliation.

Ph 2:6 Who, being in the form of God, thought it not robbery to be equal with God:

2 Jn 9 Whosoever transgresseth, and abideth not in the doctrine of Christ, hath not God. He that abideth in the doctrine of Christ, he hath both the Father and the Son.

j. His Righteousness

Ps 24:5 He shall receive the blessing from the LORD, and righteousness from the God of his salvation.

Is 45:24 Surely, shall *one* say, in the LORD have I righteousness and strength: *even* to him shall *men* come; and all that are incensed against him shall be ashamed.

Is 53:11 He shall see of the travail of his soul, *and* shall be satisfied: by his knowledge shall my righteous servant justify many; for he shall bear their iniquities.

Is 54:17 No weapon that is formed against thee shall prosper; and every tongue *that* shall rise against thee in judgment thou shalt condemn. This *is* the heritage of the servants of the LORD, and their righteousness *is* of me, saith the LORD.

Da 9:24 Seventy weeks are determined upon thy people and upon thy holy city, to finish the transgression, and to make an end of sins, and to make reconciliation for iniquity, and to bring in everlasting righteousness, and to seal up the vision and prophecy, and to anoint the most Holy.

Ro 5:19 For as by one man's disobedience many were made sinners, so by the obedience of one shall many be made righteous.

Ro 10:4 For Christ *is* the end of the law for righteousness to every one that believeth.

1 Co 1:30 But of him are ye in Christ Jesus, who of God is made unto us wisdom, and righteousness, and sanctification, and redemption:

Ph 3:9 And be found in him, not having mine own righteousness, which is of the law, but that which is through the faith of Christ, the righteousness which is of God by faith:

Col 1:22 In the body of his flesh through death, to present you holy and unblameable and unreproveable in his sight:

See **RIGHTEOUSNESS**

k. His Seven Last Sayings, on the Cross

Mt 27:46 And about the ninth hour Jesus cried with a loud voice, saying, Eli, Eli, lama sabachthani? that is to say, My God, my God, why hast thou forsaken me?

Mk 15:34 And at the ninth hour Jesus cried with a loud voice, saying, Eloi, Eloi, lama sabachthani? which is, being interpreted, My God, my God, why hast thou forsaken me?

Lu 23:34 Then said Jesus, Father, forgive them; for they know not what they do. And they parted his raiment, and cast lots.

Lu 23:43 And Jesus said unto him, Verily I say unto thee, To day shalt thou be with me in paradise.

Lu 23:46 And when Jesus had cried with a loud voice, he said, Father, into thy hands I commend my spirit: and having said thus, he gave up the ghost.

Jn 19:27–28 Then saith he to the disciple, Behold thy mother! And from that hour that disciple took her unto his own *home.*

After this, Jesus knowing that all things were now accomplished, that the scripture might be fulfilled, saith, I thirst.

Jn 19:30 When Jesus therefore had received the vinegar, he said, It is finished: and he bowed his head, and gave up the ghost.

l. His Transfiguration

Mt 17:2 And was transfigured before them: and his face did shine as the sun, and his raiment was white as the light.

Mk 9:2 And after six days Jesus taketh *with him* Peter, and James, and John, and leadeth them up into an high mountain apart by themselves: and he was transfigured before them.

Lu 9:29 And as he prayed, the fashion of his countenance was altered, and his raiment *was* white *and* glistering.

2 Pe 1:18 And this voice which came from heaven we heard, when we were with him in the holy mount.

m. His Witness to the Truth

Is 55:4 Behold, I have given him *for* a witness to the people, a leader and commander to the people.

Mt 12:18 Behold my servant, whom I have chosen; my beloved, in whom my soul is well pleased: I will put my spirit upon him, and he shall shew judgment to the Gentiles.

Jn 1:18 No man hath seen God at any time; the only begotten Son, which is in the bosom of the Father, he hath declared *him*.

Jn 3:11 Verily, verily, I say unto thee, We speak that we do know, and testify that we have seen; and ye receive not our witness.

Jn 3:32 And what he hath seen and heard, that he testifieth; and no man receiveth his testimony.

Jn 8:14 Jesus answered and said unto them, Though I bear record of myself, *yet* my record is true: for I know whence I came, and whither I go; but ye cannot tell whence I come, and whither I go.

Jn 17:6 I have manifested thy name unto the men which thou gavest me out of the world: thine they were, and thou gavest them me; and they have kept thy word.

Jn 17:26 And I have declared unto them thy name, and will declare *it:* that the love wherewith thou hast loved me may be in them, and I in them.

Jn 18:37 Pilate therefore said unto him, Art thou a king then? Jesus answered, Thou sayest that I am a king. To this end was I born, and for this cause came I into the world, that I should bear witness unto the truth. Every one that is of the truth heareth my voice.

1 Ti 6:13 I give thee charge in the sight of God, who quickeneth all things, and *before* Christ Jesus, who before Pontius Pilate witnessed a good confession;

Re 1:5 And from Jesus Christ, *who is* the faithful witness, *and* the first begotten of the dead, and the prince of the kings of the earth. Unto him that loved us, and washed us from our sins in his own blood,

Re 3:14 And unto the angel of the church of the Laodiceans write; These things saith the Amen, the faithful and true witness, the beginning of the creation of God;

n. His Personal Appearance

Ps 45:2 Thou art fairer than the children of men: grace is poured into thy lips: therefore God hath blessed thee for ever.

Song 5:16 His mouth *is* most sweet: yea, he *is* altogether lovely. This *is* my beloved, and this *is* my friend, O daughters of Jerusalem.

Is 52:14 As many were astonied at thee; his visage was so marred more than any man, and his form more than the sons of men:

Is 53:2 For he shall grow up before him as a tender plant, and as a root out of a dry ground: he hath no form nor comeliness; and when we shall see him, *there is* no beauty that we should desire him.

Da 7:9 I beheld till the thrones were cast down, and the Ancient of days did sit, whose garment *was* white as snow, and the hair of his head like the pure wool: his throne *was like* the fiery flame, *and* his wheels *as* burning fire.

Mt 17:2 And was transfigured before them: and his face did shine as the sun, and his raiment was white as the light.

Re 1:14 His head and *his* hairs *were* white like wool, as white as snow; and his eyes *were* as a flame of fire;

Re 14:3 And he that sat was to look upon like a jasper and a sardine stone: and *there was* a rainbow round about the throne, in sight like unto an emerald.

o. His Names

1). Branch

Is 4:2 In that day shall the branch of the Lord be beautiful and glorious, and the fruit of the earth *shall be* excellent and comely for them that are escaped of Israel.

Is 11:1 And there shall come forth a rod out of the stem of Jesse, and a Branch shall grow out of his roots:

Je 23:5 Behold, the days come, saith the Lord, that I will raise unto David a righteous Branch, and a King shall reign and prosper, and shall execute judgment and justice in the earth.

Je 33:15 In those days, and at that time, will I cause the Branch of righteousness to grow up unto David; and he shall execute judgment and righteousness in the land.

Zec 3:8 Hear now, O Joshua the high priest, thou, and thy fellows that sit before thee: for they *are* men wondered at: for, behold, I will bring forth my servant the BRANCH.

Zec 6:12 And speak unto him, saying, Thus speaketh the LORD of hosts, saying, Behold the man whose name *is* The BRANCH; and he shall grow up out of his place, and he shall build the temple of the LORD:

2). Cornerstone

Ps 118:22 The stone *which* the builders refused is become the head *stone* of the corner.

Is 28:16 Therefore thus saith the Lord GOD, Behold, I lay in Zion for a foundation a stone, a tried stone, a precious corner *stone,* a sure foundation: he that believeth shall not make haste.

Zec 3:9 For behold the stone I have laid before Joshua; upon one stone *shall be* seven eyes: behold, I will engrave the graving thereof, saith the LORD of hosts, and I will remove the iniquity of that land in one day.

Zec 10:4 Out of him came forth the corner, out of him the nail, out of him the battle bow, out of him every oppressor together.

Mt 21:42 Jesus saith unto them, Did ye never read in the scriptures, The stone which the builders rejected, the same is become the head of the corner: this is the Lord's doing, and it is marvellous in our eyes?

Mk 12:10 And have ye not read this scripture; The stone which the builders rejected is become the head of the corner:

Lu 20:17 And he beheld them, and said, What is this then that is written, The stone which the builders rejected, the same is become the head of the corner?

Ac 4:11 This is the stone which was set at nought of you builders, which is become the head of the corner.

1 Co 3:11 For other foundation can no man lay than that is laid, which is Jesus Christ.

Ep 2:20 And are built upon the foundation of the apostles and prophets, Jesus Christ himself being the chief corner *stone;*

1 Pe 2:6 Wherefore also it is contained in the scripture, Behold, I lay in Sion a chief corner stone, elect, precious: and he that believeth on him shall not be confounded.

3). Master

Mal 1:6 A son honoureth *his* father, and a servant his master: if then I *be* a father, where *is* mine honour? and if I *be* a master, where *is* my fear? saith the LORD of hosts unto you, O priests, that despise my name. And ye say, Wherein have we despised thy name?

Mt 10:24 The disciple is not above *his* master, nor the servant above his lord.

Lu 5:5 And Simon answering said unto him, Master, we have toiled all the night, and have taken nothing: nevertheless at thy word I will let down the net.

Lu 8:24 And they came to him, and awoke him, saying, Master, master, we perish. Then he arose, and rebuked the wind and the raging of the water: and they ceased, and there was a calm.

Lu 8:45 And Jesus said, Who touched me? When all denied, Peter and they that were with him said, Master, the multitude throng thee and press *thee,* and sayest thou, Who touched me?

Lu 9:33 And it came to pass, as they departed from him, Peter said unto Jesus, Master, it is good for us to be here: and let us make three tabernacles; one for thee, and one for Moses, and one for Elias: not knowing what he said.

Lu 9:49 And John answered and said, Master, we saw one casting out devils in thy name; and we forbad him, because he followeth not with us.

Lu 13:25 When once the master of the house is risen up, and hath shut to the door, and ye begin to stand without, and to knock at the door, saying,

Lord, Lord, open unto us; and he shall answer and say unto you, I know you not whence ye are.

Jn 13:13 Ye call me Master and Lord: and ye say well; for so I am.

Ep 6:9 And, ye masters, do the same things unto them, forbearing threatening: knowing that your Master also is in heaven; neither is there respect of persons with him.

Col 4:1 Masters, give unto *your* servants that which is just and equal; knowing that ye also have a Master in heaven.

4). Messenger

Is 42:6 I the LORD have called thee in righteousness, and will hold thine hand, and will keep thee, and give thee for a covenant of the people, for a light of the Gentiles;

Is 48:16 Come ye near unto me, hear ye this; I have not spoken in secret from the beginning; from the time that it was, there *am* I: and now the Lord GOD, and his Spirit, hath sent me.

Zec 2:11 And many nations shall be joined to the LORD in that day, and shall be my people: and I will dwell in the midst of thee, and thou shalt know that the LORD of hosts hath sent me unto thee.

Zec 6:15 And they *that are* far off shall come and build in the temple of the LORD, and ye shall know that the LORD of hosts hath sent me unto you. And *this* shall come to pass, if ye will diligently obey the voice of the LORD your God.

Mal 3:1 Behold, I will send my messenger, and he shall prepare the way before me: and the LORD, whom ye seek, shall suddenly come to his temple, even the messenger of the covenant, whom ye delight in: behold, he shall come, saith the LORD of hosts.

Mt 21:37 But last of all he sent unto them his son, saying, They will reverence my son.

Mk 9:37 Whosoever shall receive one of such children in my name, receiveth me: and whosoever shall receive me, receiveth not me, but him that sent me.

Mk 12:6 Having yet therefore one son, his wellbeloved, he sent him also last unto them, saying, They will reverence my son.

Lu 4:43 And he said unto them, I must preach the kingdom of God to other cities also: for therefore am I sent.

Lu 9:48 And said unto them, Whosoever shall receive this child in my name receiveth me: and whosoever shall receive me receiveth him that sent me: for he that is least among you all, the same shall be great.

Lu 10:16 He that heareth you heareth me; and he that despiseth you despiseth me; and he that despiseth me despiseth him that sent me.

Lu 20:13 Then said the lord of the vineyard, What shall I do? I will send my beloved son: it may be they will reverence *him* when they see him.

Jn 3:17 For God sent not his Son into the world to condemn the world; but that the world through him might be saved.

Jn 3:34 For he whom God hath sent speaketh the words of God: for God giveth not the Spirit by measure *unto him*.

Jn 5:23 That all *men* should honour the Son, even as they honour the Father. He that honoureth not the Son honoureth not the Father which hath sent him.

Jn 5:30 I can of mine own self do nothing: as I hear, I judge: and my judgment is just; because I seek not mine own will, but the will of the Father which hath sent me.

Jn 5:36 But I have greater witness than *that* of John: for the works which the Father hath given me to finish, the same works that I do, bear witness of me, that the Father hath sent me.

Jn 5:43 I am come in my Father's name, and ye receive me not: if another shall come in his own name, him ye will receive.

Jn 6:29 Jesus answered and said unto them, This is the work of God, that ye believe on him whom he hath sent.

Jn 6:38 For I came down from heaven, not to do mine own will, but the will of him that sent me.

Jn 6:44 No man can come to me, except the Father which hath sent me draw him: and I will raise him up at the last day.

Jn 6:57 As the living Father hath sent me, and I live by the Father: so he that eateth me, even he shall live by me.

Jn 7:16 Jesus answered them, and said, My doctrine is not mine, but his that sent me.

Jn 7:29 But I know him: for I am from him, and he hath sent me.

Jn 8:17 It is also written in your law, that the testimony of two men is true.

Jn 8:29 And he that sent me is with me: the Father hath not left me alone; for I do always those things that please him.

Jn 8:42 Jesus said unto them, If God were your Father, ye would love me: for I proceeded forth and came from God; neither came I of myself, but he sent me.

Jn 9:4 I must work the works of him that sent me, while it is day: the night cometh, when no man can work.

Jn 10:36 Say ye of him, whom the Father hath sanctified, and sent into the world, Thou blasphemest; because I said, I am the Son of God?

Jn 11:42 And I knew that thou hearest me always: but because of the people which stand by I said it, that they may believe that thou hast sent me.

Jn 12:44 Jesus cried and said, He that believeth on me, believeth not on me, but on him that sent me.

Jn 12:49 For I have not spoken of myself; but the Father which sent me, he gave me a commandment, what I should say, and what I should speak.

Jn 13:3 Jesus knowing that the Father had given all things into his hands, and that he was come from God, and went to God;

Jn 13:20 Verily, verily, I say unto you, He that receiveth whomsoever I send receiveth me; and he that receiveth me receiveth him that sent me.

Jn 14:24 He that loveth me not keepeth not my sayings: and the word which ye hear is not mine, but the Father's which sent me.

Jn 16:5 But now I go my way to him that sent me; and none of you asketh me, Whither goest thou?

Jn 16:28 I came forth from the Father, and am come into the world: again, I leave the world, and go to the Father.

Jn 17:3 And this is life eternal, that they might know thee the only true God, and Jesus Christ, who thou hast sent.

Jn 17:8 For I have given unto them the words which thou gavest me; and they have received *them,* and have known surely that I came out from thee, and they have believed that thou didst send me.

Jn 17:18 As thou hast sent me into the world, even so have I also sent them into the world.

Jn 17:21 That they all may be one; as thou, Father, *art* in me, and I in thee, that they also may be one in us: that the world may believe that thou hast sent me.

Jn 17:25 O righteous Father, the world hath not known thee: but I have known thee, and these have known that thou hast sent me.

Jn 20:21 Then said Jesus to them again, Peace *be* unto you: as *my* Father hath sent me, even so send I you.

Ac 3:26 Unto you first God, having raised up his Son Jesus, sent him to bless you, in turning away every one of you from his iniquities.

Ro 8:3 For what the law could not do, in that it was weak through the flesh, God sending his own Son in the likeness of sinful flesh, and for sin, condemned sin in the flesh:

Ga 4:4 But when the fulness of the time was come, God sent forth his Son, made of a woman, made under the law,

1 Jn 4:10 Herein is love, not that we loved God, but that he loved us, and sent his Son *to be* the propitiation for our sins.

5). Messiah

Da 9:25 Know therefore and understand, *that* from the going forth of the commandment to restore and to build Jerusalem unto the Messiah the Prince *shall be* seven weeks, and threescore and two weeks: the street shall be built again, and the wall, even in troublous times.

Mt 11:3 And said unto him, Art thou he that should come, or do we look for another?

Mt 12:23 And all the people were amazed, and said, Is not this the son of David?

Mt 16:16 And Simon Peter answered and said, Thou art the Christ, the Son of the living God.

Mt 26:63 But Jesus held his peace. And the high priest answered and said unto him, I adjure thee by the living God, that thou tell us whether thou be the Christ, the Son of God.

Mk 8:29 And he saith unto them, But whom say ye that I am? And Peter answereth and saith unto him, Thou art the Christ.

Mk 14:61 But he held his peace, and answered nothing. Again the high priest asked him, and said unto him, Art thou the Christ, the Son of the Blessed?

Lu 2:11 For unto you is born this day in the city of David a Saviour, which is Christ the Lord.

Lu 2:26 And it was revealed unto him by the Holy Ghost, that he should not see death, before he had seen the Lord's Christ.

Lu 4:41 And devils also came out of many, crying out, and saying, Thou art Christ the Son of God. And he rebuking *them* suffered them not to speak: for they knew that he was Christ.

Lu 7:19 And John calling *unto him* two of his disciples sent *them* to Jesus, saying, Art thou he that should come? or look we for another?

Lu 9:20 He said unto them, But whom say ye that I am? Peter answering said, The Christ of God.

Lu 22:67 Art thou the Christ? tell us. And he said unto them, If I tell you, ye will not believe:

Lu 24:21 But we trusted that it had been he which should have redeemed Israel: and beside all this, to day is the third day since these things were done.

Lu 24:26 Ought not Christ to have suffered these things, and to enter into his glory?

Jn 1:41 He first findeth his own brother Simon, and saith unto him, We have found the Messias, which is, being interpreted, the Christ.

Jn 4:26 Jesus saith unto her, I that speak unto thee am *he*.

Jn 6:14 Then those men, when they had seen the miracle that Jesus did, said, This is of a truth that prophet that should come into the world.

Jn 6:69 And we believe and are sure that thou art that Christ, the Son of the living God.

Jn 7:41 Others said, This is the Christ. But some said, Shall Christ come out of Galilee?

Jn 8:24 I said therefore unto you, that ye shall die in your sins: for if ye believe not that I am *he*, ye shall die in your sins.

Jn 8:28 Then said Jesus unto them, When ye have lifted up the Son of man, then shall ye know that I am *he*, and *that* I do nothing of myself; but as my Father hath taught me, I speak these things.

Jn 9:37 And Jesus said unto him, Thou hast both seen him, and it is he that talketh with thee.

Jn 11:27 She saith unto him, Yea, Lord: I believe that thou art the Christ, the Son of God, which should come into the world.

Jn 13:19 Now I tell you before it come, that, when it is come to pass, ye may believe that I am *he*.

Jn 20:31 But these are written, that ye might believe that Jesus is the Christ, the Son of God; and that believing ye might have life through his name.

Ac 2:36 Therefore let all the house of Israel know assuredly, that God hath made that same Jesus, whom ye have crucified, both Lord and Christ.

Ac 4:26 The kings of the earth stood up, and the rulers were gathered together against the Lord, and against his Christ.

Ac 9:20 And straightway he preached Christ in the synagogues, that he is the Son of God.

Ac 9:22 But Saul increased the more in strength, and confounded the Jews which dwelt at Damascus, proving that this is very Christ.

Ac 17:3 Opening and alleging, that Christ must needs have suffered, and risen again from the dead; and that this Jesus, whom I preach unto you, is Christ.

Ac 18:5 And when Silas and Timotheus were come from Macedonia, Paul was pressed in the spirit, and testified to the Jews *that* Jesus *was* Christ.

Ac 18:28 For he mightily convinced the Jews, *and that* publickly, shewing by the scriptures that Jesus was Christ.

1 Jn 2:22 Who is a liar but he that denieth that Jesus is the Christ? He is antichrist, that denieth the Father and the Son.

1 Jn 5:1 Whosoever believeth that Jesus is the Christ is born of God: and every one that loveth him that begat loveth him also that is begotten of him.

6). Morning Star

Nu 24:17 I shall see him, but not now: I shall behold him, but not nigh: there shall come a Star out of Jacob, and a Sceptre shall rise out of Israel, and shall smite the corners of Moab, and destroy all the children of Sheth.

2 Pe 1:19 We have also a more sure word of prophecy; whereunto ye do well that ye take heed, as unto a light that shineth in a dark place, until the day dawn, and the day star arise in your hearts:

Re 2:28 And I will give him the morning star.

Re 22:16 I Jesus have sent mine angel to testify unto you these things in the churches. I am the root and the offspring of David, *and* the bright and morning star.

7). Prophet

De 18:15 The LORD thy God will raise up unto thee a Prophet from the midst of thee, of thy brethren, like unto me; unto him ye shall hearken;

De 18:18 I will raise them up a Prophet from among their brethren,

like unto thee, and will put my words in his mouth; and he shall speak unto them all that I shall command him.

Mt 21:11 And the multitude said, This is Jesus the prophet of Nazareth of Galilee.

Mt 21:46 But when they sought to lay hands on him, they feared the multitude, because they took him for a prophet.

Mt 23:36 Verily I say unto you, All these things shall come upon this generation.

Mt 24:2 And Jesus said unto them, See ye not all these things? verily I say unto you, There shall not be left here one stone upon another, that shall not be thrown down.

Mt 24:25 Behold, I have told you before.

Mt 24:34 Verily I say unto you, This generation shall not pass, till all these things be fulfilled.

Mt 26:64 Jesus saith unto him, Thou hast said: nevertheless I say unto you, Hereafter shall ye see the Son of man sitting on the right hand of power, and coming in the clouds of heaven.

Mt 26:75 And Peter remembered the word of Jesus, which said unto him, Before the cock crow, thou shalt deny me thrice. And he went out, and wept bitterly.

Mk 2:20 But the days will come, when the bridegroom shall be taken away from them, and then shall they fast in those days.

Mk 6:15 Others said, That it is Elias. And others said, That it is a prophet, or as one of the prophets.

Mk 8:28 And they answered, John the Baptist: but some *say,* Elias; and others, One of the prophets.

Mk 13:2 And Jesus answering said unto him, Seest thou these great buildings? there shall not be left one stone upon another, that shall not be thrown down.

Mk 13:30 Verily I say unto you, that this generation shall not pass, till all these things be done.

Mk 14:62 And Jesus said, I am: and ye shall see the Son of man sitting on the right hand of power, and coming in the clouds of heaven.

Lu 4:18 The Spirit of the Lord is upon me, because he hath anointed me to preach the gospel to the poor; he hath sent me to heal the brokenhearted, to preach deliverance recovering of sight to the blind, to set at liberty them that are bruised,

Lu 5:35 But the days will come, when the bridegroom shall be taken away from them, and then shall they fast in those days.

Lu 7:16 And there came a fear on all: and they glorified God, saying, That a great prophet is risen up among us; and, That God hath visited his people.

Lu 7:39 Now when the Pharisee which had bidden him saw *it,* he spake within himself, saying, This man, if he were a prophet, would have known who and what manner of woman *this is* that toucheth him: for she is a sinner.

Lu 13:33 Nevertheless I must walk to day, and to morrow, and the *day* following: for it cannot be that a prophet perish out of Jerusalem.

Lu 21:32 Verily I say unto you, This generation shall not pass away, till all be fulfilled.

Lu 22:69 Hereafter shall the Son of man sit on the right hand of the power of God.

Lu 23:30 Then shall they begin to say to the mountains, Fall on us; and to the hills, Cover us.

Lu 24:6 He is not here, but is risen: remember how he spake unto you when he was yet in Galilee,

Lu 24:19 And he said unto them, What things? And they said unto him, Concerning Jesus of Nazareth, which was a prophet mighty in deed and word before God and all the people:

Lu 24:44 And he said unto them, These *are* the words which I spake unto you, while I was yet with you, that all things must be fulfilled, which were written in the law of Moses, and *in* the prophets, and *in* the psalms, concerning me.

Jn 4:19 The woman saith unto him, Sir, I perceive that thou art a prophet.

Jn 6:14 Then those men, when they had seen the miracle that Jesus did, said, This is of a truth that prophet that should come into the world.

Jn 7:40 Many of the people therefore, when they heard this saying, said, Of a truth this is the Prophet.

Jn 9:17 They say unto the blind man again, What sayest thou of him, that he hath opened thine eyes? He said, He is a prophet.

Jn 14:29 And now I have told you before it come to pass, that, when it is come to pass, ye might believe.

Jn 16:4 But these things have I told you, that when the time shall come, ye may remember that I told you of them. And these things I said not unto you at the beginning, because I was with you.

Jn 21:18 Verily, verily, I say unto thee, When thou wast young, thou girdedst thyself, and walkedst whither thou wouldest: but when thou shalt be old, thou shalt stretch forth thy hands, and another shall gird thee, and carry *thee* whither thou wouldest not.

Ac 3:22 For Moses truly said unto the fathers, A prophet shall the Lord your God raise up unto you of your brethren, like unto me; him shall ye hear in all things whatsoever he shall say unto you.

Ac 7:37 This is that Moses, which said unto the children of Israel, A prophet shall the Lord your God raise up unto you of your brethren, like unto me; him shall ye hear.

8). Rock of Offense

Ps 118:22 The stone *which* the builders refused is become the head *stone* of the corner.

Is 8:14 And he shall be for a sanctuary; but for a stone of stumbling and for a rock of offence to both the houses of Israel, for a gin and for a snare to the inhabitants of Jerusalem.

Je 6:21 Therefore thus saith the LORD, Behold, I will lay stumblingblocks before this people, and the fathers and the sons together shall fall upon them; the neighbour and his friend shall perish.

Eze 3:20 Again, When a righteous man doth turn from his righteousness, and commit iniquity, and I lay a stumblingblock before him, he shall die: because thou hast not given him warning, he shall die in his sin, and his righteousness which he hath done shall not be remembered; but his blood will I require at thine hand.

Mt 11:6 And blessed is *he,* whosoever shall not be offended in me.

Mt 13:57 And they were offended in him. But Jesus said unto them, A prophet is not without honour, save in his own country, and in his own house.

Mt 15:12 Then came his disciples, and said unto him, Knowest thou that the Pharisees were offended, after they heard this saying?

Mt 21:42 Jesus saith unto them, Did ye never read in the scriptures, The stone which the builders rejected, the same is become the head of the corner: this is the Lord's doing, and it is marvellous in our eyes?

Mt 26:31 Then saith Jesus unto them, All ye shall be offended because of me this night: for it is written, I will smite the shepherd, and the sheep of the flock shall be scattered abroad.

Mk 6:3 Is not this the carpenter, the son of Mary, the brother of James, and Joses, and of Juda, and Simon? and are not his sisters here with us? And they were offended at him.

Mk 12:10 And have ye not read this scripture; The stone which the builders rejected is become the head of the corner:

Mk 14:27 And Jesus saith unto them, All ye shall be offended because of me this night: for it is written, I will smite the shepherd, and the sheep shall be scattered.

Lu 2:34 And Simeon blessed them, and said unto Mary his mother, Behold, this *child* is set for the fall and rising again of many in Israel; and for a sign which shall be spoken against;

Lu 7:23 And blessed is *he,* whosoever shall not be offended in me.

Jn 6:61 When Jesus knew in himself that his disciples murmured at it, he said unto them, Doth this offend you?

Jn 7:12 And there was much murmuring among the people concerning him: for some said, He is a good man: others said, Nay; but he deceiveth the people.

Ro 9:32 Wherefore? Because *they sought it* not by faith, but as it were by the works of the law. For they stumbled at that stumblingstone;

1 Co 1:23 But we preach Christ crucified, unto the Jews a stumblingblock, and unto the Greeks foolishness;

1 Pe 2:8 And a stone of stumbling, and a rock of offence, *even to them* which stumble at the word, being disobedient: whereunto also they were appointed.

9). The True Vine

Jn 15:1 I am the true vine, and my Father is the husbandman.

10). The Word

Jn 1:1 In the beginning was the Word, and the Word was with God, and the Word was God.

Jn 1:14 And the Word was made flesh, and dwelt among us, (and we beheld his glory, the glory as of the only begotten of the Father,) full of grace and truth.

1 Jn 1:1 That which was from the beginning, which we have heard, which we have seen with our eyes, which we have looked upon, and our hands have handled, of the Word of life;

1 Jn 5:7 For there are three that bear record in heaven, the Father, the Word, and the Holy Ghost: and these three are one.

Re 19:13 And he *was* clothed with a vesture dipped in blood: and his name is called The Word of God.

See **TITLES AND NAMES**

4. His Attitude toward Children

GENTLE

Is 40:11 He shall feed his flock like a shepherd: he shall gather the lambs with his arm, and carry *them* in his bosom, *and* shall gently lead those that are with young.

PROMISES A REWARD FOR KINDNESS TO

Mt 10:42 And whosoever shall give to drink unto one of these little ones a cup of cold *water* only in the name of a disciple, verily I say unto you, he shall in no wise lose his reward.

USED A CHILD AS AN EXAMPLE

Mt 18:2 And Jesus called a little child unto him, and set him in the midst of them,

DECLARED THAT A CHILDLIKE SPIRIT IS ABSOLUTELY ESSENTIAL IN RELIGION

Mt 18:3–4 And said, Verily I say unto you, Except ye be converted, and become as little children, ye shall not enter into the kingdom of heaven.

Whosoever therefore shall humble himself as this little child, the same is greatest in the kingdom of heaven.

WARNED AGAINST DESPISING

Mt 18:10 Take heed that ye despise not one of these little ones; for I say unto you, That in heaven their angels do always behold the face of my Father which is in heaven.

COMMANDS RECEPTION OF

Mk 9:37 Whosoever shall receive one of such children in my name, receiveth me: and whosoever shall receive me, receiveth not me, but him that sent me.

SAID, "SUFFER THE LITTLE CHILDREN TO COME UNTO ME,"

Mk 10:14 But when Jesus saw *it,* he was much displeased, and said unto them, Suffer the little children to come unto me, and forbid them not: for of such is the kingdom of God.

OBSERVED THE CHILDREN AT PLAY

Mt 11:16 But whereunto shall I liken this generation? It is like unto children sitting in the markets, and calling unto their fellows,

COMMANDED THAT THEY SHOULD BE FED SPIRITUAL FOOD

Jn 21:15 So when they had dined, Jesus saith to Simon Peter, Simon, *son of* Jonas, lovest thou me more than these? He saith unto him, Yea, Lord; thou knowest that I love thee. He saith unto him, Feed my lambs.

5. His Attractiveness

Mt 8:1 When he was come down from the mountain, great multitudes followed him.

Mt 8:18 Now when Jesus saw great multitudes about him, he gave commandment to depart unto the other side.

Mt 12:15 But when Jesus knew *it,* he withdrew himself from thence: and great multitudes followed him, and he healed them all;

Mt 13:2 And great multitudes were gathered together unto him, so that he went into a ship, and sat; and the whole multitude stood on the shore.

Mt 15:32 Then Jesus called his disciples *unto him,* and said, I have compassion on the multitude, because they continue with me now three days, and have nothing to eat: and I will not send them away fasting, lest they faint in the way.

Mt 19:2 And great multitudes followed him; and he healed them there.

Mk 1:36 And Simon and they that were with him followed after him.

Mk 1:45 But he went out, and began to publish *it* much, and to blaze abroad the matter, insomuch that Jesus could no more openly enter into the city, but was without in desert places: and they came to him from every quarter.

Mk 3:8 And from Jerusalem, and from Idumaea, and *from* beyond Jordan; and they about Tyre and Sidon, a great multitude, when they had heard what great things he did, came unto him.

Mk 5:2 And when he was come out of the ship, immediately there met him out of the tombs a man with an unclean spirit,

Mk 5:6 But when he saw Jesus afar off, he ran and worshipped him,

Mk 6:33 And the people saw them departing, and many knew him, and ran afoot thither out of all cities, and outwent them, and came together unto him.

Lu 4:20 And he closed the book, and he gave *it* again to the minister, and sat down. And the eyes of all them that were in the synagogue were fastened on him.

Lu 4:42 And when it was day, he departed and went into a desert place: and the people sought him, and came unto him, and stayed him, that he should not depart from them.

Lu 6:17 And he came down with them, and stood in the plain, and the company of his disciples, and a great multitude of people out of all Judaea and Jerusalem, and from the sea coast of Tyre and Sidon, which came to hear him, and to be healed of their diseases;

Lu 8:38 Now the man out of whom the devils were departed besought him that he might be with him: but Jesus sent him away, saying,

Lu 9:37 And it came to pass, that on the next day, when they were come down from the hill, much people met him.

Jn 12:32 And I, if I be lifted up from the earth, will draw all *men* unto me.

See **ATTRACTION**

6. His Composure

Mt 26:50 And Jesus said unto him, Friend, wherefore art thou come? Then came they, and laid hands on Jesus, and took him.

Mt 26:62 And the high priest arose, and said unto him, Answerest thou nothing? what *is it which* these witness against thee?

Mk 4:39 And he arose, and rebuked the wind, and said unto the sea, Peace, be still. And the wind ceased, and there was a great calm.

Mk 5:39 And when he was come in, he saith unto them, Why make ye this ado, and weep? the damsel is not dead, but sleepeth.

Lu 13:33 Nevertheless I must walk to day, and to morrow, and the *day* following: for it cannot be that a prophet perish out of Jerusalem.

Lu 23:28 But Jesus turning unto them said, Daughters of Jerusalem, weep not

for me, but weep for yourselves, and for your children.

Jn 13:31 Therefore, when he was gone out, Jesus said, Now is the Son of man glorified, and God is glorified in him.

Jn 18:4 Jesus therefore, knowing all things that should come upon him, went forth, and said unto them, Whom seek ye?

Jn 18:8 Jesus answered, I have told you that I am *he:* if therefore ye seek me, let these go their way:

Jn 19:11 Jesus answered, Thou couldest have no power *at all* against me, except it were given thee from above: therefore he that delivered me unto thee hath the greater sin.

See **COMPOSURE**

7. His Power over Death

FORETOLD BY THE PROPHETS

Is 25:8 He will swallow up death in victory; and the Lord GOD will wipe away tears from off all faces; and the rebuke of his people shall he take away from off all the earth: for the LORD hath spoken *it.*

Ac 2:27 Because thou wilt not leave my soul in hell, neither wilt thou suffer thine Holy One to see corruption.

DEFIED DEATH TO HOLD HIM

Jn 10:17–18 Therefore doth my Father love me, because I lay down my life, that I might take it again.

No man taketh it from me, but I lay it down of myself. I have power to lay it down, and I have power to take it again. This commandment have I received of my Father.

SUBMITTED TO THE STROKE OF DEATH FOR OUR SINS

1 Co 15:4 And that he was buried, and that he rose again the third day according to the scriptures:

THREE TIMES HE ENTERED THE REALMS OF DEATH AND RESCUED VICTIMS

Mt 9:25 But when the people were put forth, he went in, and took her by the hand, and the maid arose.

Lu 7:14–15 And he came and touched the bier: and they that bare *him* stood still. And he said, Young man, I say unto thee, Arise.

And he that was dead sat up, and began to speak. And he delivered him to his mother.

Jn 11:43–44 And when he thus had spoken, he cried with a loud voice, Lazarus, come forth.

And he that was dead came forth, bound hand and foot with graveclothes: and his face was bound about with a napkin. Jesus saith unto them, Loose him, and let him go.

DEMONSTRATED HIS VICTORY BY HIS OWN RESURRECTION

Ro 1:4 And declared *to be* the Son of God with power, according to the spirit of holiness, by the resurrection from the dead:

CARRIES THE KEYS OF THE GRAVE IN HIS GIRDLE

Re 1:18 I *am* he that liveth, and was dead; and, behold, I am alive for evermore, Amen; and have the keys of hell and of death.

WILL CALL ALL MEN FROM DEATH'S DOMAIN

Jn 5:28–29 Marvel not at this: for the hour is coming, in the which all that are in the graves shall hear his voice,

And shall come forth; they that have done good, unto the resurrection of life; and they that have done evil, unto the resurrection of damnation.

WILL COMPLETELY DESTROY DEATH AT LAST

1 Co 15:25–26 For he must reign, till he hath put all enemies under his feet.

The last enemy *that* shall be destroyed *is* death.

8. His Accusers

ACCUSED OF KEEPING BAD COMPANY

Mt 9:11 And when the Pharisees saw *it,* they said unto his disciples, Why eateth your Master with publicans and sinners?

ACCUSED OF GLUTTONY AND INTEMPERANCE

Mt 11:19 The Son of man came eating and drinking, and they say, Behold a man gluttonous, and a winebibber, a friend of publicans and sinners. But wisdom is justified of her children.

ACCUSED OF BLASPHEMY

Mt 26:65 Then the high priest rent his clothes, saying, He hath spoken blasphemy; what further need have we of witnesses? behold, now ye have heard his blasphemy.

ACCUSED OF INSANITY

Mk 3:21 And when his friends heard *of it,* they went out to lay hold on him: for they said, He is beside himself.

ACCUSED OF BEING POSSESSED WITH DEVILS

Jn 7:20 The people answered and said, Thou hast a devil: who goeth about to kill thee?

ACCUSED OF BREAKING THE SABBATH

Jn 9:16 Therefore said some of the Pharisees, This man is not of God, because he keepeth not the sabbath day. Others said, How can a man that is a sinner do such miracles? And there was a division among them.

Jn 10:20 And many of them said, He hath a devil, and is mad; why hear ye him?

ACCUSED OF TREASON

Jn 19:12 And from thenceforth Pilate sought to release him: but the Jews cried out, saying, If thou let this man go, thou art not Caesar's friend: whosoever maketh himself a king speaketh against Caesar.

9. His Liberating Power, means to ultimate freedom

Lu 11:14 And he was casting out a devil, and it was dumb. And it came to pass, when the devil was gone out, the dumb spake; and the people wondered.

Jn 8:32 And ye shall know the truth, and the truth shall make you free.

Jn 8:36 If the Son therefore shall make you free, ye shall be free indeed.

Ro 7:25 I thank God through Jesus Christ our Lord. So then with the mind I myself serve the law of God; but with the flesh the law of sin.

Ro 8:2 For the law of the Spirit of life in Christ Jesus hath made me free from the law of sin and death.

Ro 8:21 Because the creature itself also shall be delivered from the bondage of corruption into the glorious liberty of the children of God.

Ga 5:1 Stand fast therefore in the liberty wherewith Christ hath made us free, and be not entangled again with the yoke of bondage.

10. His Light

Nu 24:17 I shall see him, but not now: I shall behold him, but not nigh: there shall come a Star out of Jacob, and a Sceptre shall rise out of Israel, and shall smite the corners of Moab, and destroy all the children of Sheth.

Is 9:2 The people that walked in darkness have seen a great light: they that dwell in the land of the shadow of death, upon them hath the light shined.

Is 30:26 Moreover the light of the moon shall be as the light of the sun, and the light of the sun shall be sevenfold, as the light of seven days, in the day that the LORD bindeth up the breach of his people, and healeth the stroke of their wound.

Is 42:6 I the LORD have called thee in righteousness, and will hold thine hand, and will keep thee, and give thee for a covenant of the people, for a light of the Gentiles;

Is 49:6 And he said, It is a light thing that thou shouldest be my servant to raise up the tribes of Jacob, and to restore the preserved of Israel: I will also give thee for a light to the Gentiles, that thou mayest be my salvation unto the end of the earth.

Mal 4:2 But unto you that fear my name shall the Sun of righteousness arise with healing in his wings; and ye shall go forth, and grow up as calves of the stall.

Mt 4:16 The people which sat in darkness saw great light; and to them which sat in the region and shadow of death light is sprung up.

Mt 17:2 And was transfigured before them: and his face did shine as the sun, and his raiment was white as the light.

Lu 1:79 To give light to them that sit in darkness and *in* the shadow of death, to guide our feet into the way of peace.

Lu 2:32 A light to lighten the Gentiles, and the glory of thy people Israel.

Jn 1:4 In him was life; and the life was the light of men.

Jn 1:9 *That* was the true Light, which lighteth every man that cometh into the world.

Jn 3:19 And this is the condemnation, that light is come into the world, and men loved darkness rather than light, because their deeds were evil.

Jn 8:12 Then spake Jesus again unto them, saying, I am the light of the world: he that followeth me shall not walk in darkness, but shall have the light of life.

Jn 9:5 As long as I am in the world, I am the light of the world.

Jn 12:35 Then Jesus said unto them, Yet a little while is the light with you. Walk while ye have the light, lest darkness come upon you: for he that walketh in darkness knoweth not whither he goeth.

John 12:46 I am come a light into the world, that whosoever believeth on me should not abide in darkness.

Ac 22:6 And it came to pass, that, as I made my journey, and was come nigh unto Damascus about noon, suddenly there shone from heaven a great light round about me.

Ac 26:23 That Christ should suffer, *and* that he should be the first that should rise from the dead, and should shew light unto the people, and to the Gentiles.

2 Co 3:14 But their minds were blinded: for until this day remaineth the same vail untaken away in the reading of the old testament; which *vail* is done away in Christ.

2 Co 4:6 For God, who commanded the light to shine out of darkness, hath shined in our hearts, to *give* the light of the knowledge of the glory of God in the face of Jesus Christ.

Ep 5:14 Wherefore he saith, Awake thou that sleepest, and arise from the dead, and Christ shall give thee light.

1 Jn 1:5 This then is the message which we have heard of him, and declare unto you, that God is light, and in him is no darkness at all.

1 Jn 2:8 Again, a new commandment I write unto you, which thing is true in him and in you: because the darkness is past, and the true light now shineth.

Re 1:16 And he had in his right hand seven stars: and out of his mouth went a sharp twoedged sword: and his countenance *was* as the sun shineth in his strength.

Re 21:23 And the city had no need of the sun, neither of the moon, to shine in it: for the glory of God did lighten it, and the Lamb *is* the light thereof.

Re 22:16 I Jesus have sent mine angel to testify unto you these things in the churches. I am the root and the offspring of David, *and* the bright and morning star.

See **TITLES AND NAMES**

11. His Preciousness

THE FAIREST AMONG TEN THOUSAND

Song 5:10 My beloved is white and ruddy, the chiefest among ten thousand.

A JEWEL BEYOND COMPARE

Mt 13:46 Who, when he had found one pearl of great price, went and sold all that he had, and bought it.

THE ONLY SAVIOUR

Ac 4:12 Neither is there salvation in any other: for there is none other name under heaven given among men, whereby we must be saved.

THE ONLY FOUNDATION

1 Co 3:11 For other foundation can no man lay than that is laid, which is Jesus Christ.

PAUL'S ESTIMATE OF

Ph 3:8 Yea doubtless, and I count all things *but* loss for the excellency of the knowledge of Christ Jesus my Lord: for whom I have suffered the loss of all things, and do count them *but* dung, that I may win Christ,

PRICELESS TO BELIEVERS

1 Pe 2:7 Unto you therefore which believe *he is* precious: but unto them which be disobedient, the stone which the builders disallowed, the same is made the head of the corner,

12. His Prayers

AT HIS BAPTISM

Lu 3:21 Now when all the people were baptized, it came to pass, that Jesus also being baptized, and praying, the heaven was opened,

BEFORE CALLING THE TWELVE APOSTLES

Lu 6:12 And it came to pass in those days, that he went out into a mountain to pray, and continued all night in prayer to God.

WHEN THE PEOPLE WOULD CROWN HIM

Jn 6:15 When Jesus therefore perceived that they would come and take him by force, to make him a king, he departed again into a mountain himself alone.

AT HIS TRANSFIGURATION

Lu 9:29 And as he prayed, the fashion of his countenance was altered, and his raiment *was* white *and* glistering.

HIS FAREWELL PRAYER

Jn 17:1 These words spake Jesus, and lifted up his eyes to heaven, and said, Father, the hour is come; glorify thy Son, that thy Son also may glorify thee:

ON THE CROSS FOR HIS ENEMIES

Lu 23:34 Then said Jesus, Father, forgive them; for they know not what they do. And they parted his raiment, and cast lots.

See **PRAYER**

13. His Service

Is 42:1 Behold my servant, whom I uphold; mine elect, *in whom* my soul delighteth; I have put my spirit upon him: he shall bring forth judgment to the Gentiles.

Is 49:3 And said unto me, Thou *art* my servant, O Israel, in whom I will be glorified.

Mt 12:18 Behold my servant, whom I have chosen; my beloved, in whom my soul is well pleased: I will put my spirit upon him, and he shall shew judgment to the Gentiles.

Mk 10:45 For even the Son of man came not to be ministered unto, but to minister, and to give his life a ransom for many.

Lu 12:37 Blessed *are* those servants, whom the lord when he cometh shall find watching: verily I say unto you, that he shall gird himself, and make them to sit down to meat, and will come forth and serve them.

Lu 22:27 For whether *is* greater, he that sitteth at meat, or he that serveth? *is* not he that sitteth at meat? but I am among you as he that serveth.

Jn 13:4–5 He riseth from supper, and laid aside his garments; and took a towel, and girded himself.

After that he poureth water into a bason, and began to wash the disciples' feet, and to wipe *them* with the towel wherewith he was girded.

Ph 2:7 But made himself of no reputation, and took upon him the form of a servant, and was made in the likeness of men:

14. His Spirit

DIVINE

Is 11:2 And the spirit of the LORD shall rest upon him, the spirit of wisdom and understanding, the spirit of counsel and might, the spirit of knowledge and of the fear of the LORD;

WISE

Is 11:3 And shall make him of quick understanding in the fear of the LORD: and he shall not judge after the sight of his eyes, neither reprove after the hearing of his ears:

JUST AND FEARLESS

Is 11:4 But with righteousness shall he judge the poor, and reprove with equity for the meek of the earth: and he shall smite the earth with the rod of his mouth, and with the breath of his lips shall he slay the wicked.

FAITHFUL

Is 11:5 And righteousness shall be the girdle of his loins, and faithfulness the girdle of his reins.

TENDER

Is 40:11 He shall feed his flock like a shepherd: he shall gather the lambs with his arm, and carry *them* in his bosom, *and* shall gently lead those that are with young.

QUIET

Is 42:2 He shall not cry, nor lift up, nor cause his voice to be heard in the street.

GENTLE

Is 42:3 A bruised reed shall he not break, and the smoking flax shall he not quench: he shall bring forth judgment unto truth.

PERSEVERING

Is 42:4 He shall not fail nor be discouraged, till he have set judgment in the earth: and the isles shall wait for his law.

LIBERATING

Is 61:1 The Spirit of the Lord GOD *is* upon me; because the LORD hath anointed me to preach good tidings unto the meek; he hath sent me to bind up the brokenhearted, to proclaim liberty to the captives, and the opening of the prison to *them that are* bound;

SAVING

Is 63:1 Who *is* this that cometh from Edom, with dyed garments from Bozrah? this *that is* glorious in his apparel, travelling in the greatness of his strength? I that speak in righteousness, mighty to save.

COMPASSIONATE

Mt 9:36 But when he saw the multitudes, he was moved with compassion on them, because they fainted, and were scattered abroad, as sheep having no shepherd.

MEEK AND LOWLY

Mt 11:29 Take my yoke upon you, and learn of me; for I am meek and lowly in heart: and ye shall find rest unto your souls.

LONGSUFFERING

Lu 9:55–56 But he turned, and rebuked them, and said, Ye know not what manner of spirit ye are of.

For the Son of man is not come to destroy men's lives, but to save *them.* And they went to another village.

FORGIVING

Lu 23:34 Then said Jesus, Father, forgive them; for they know not what they do. And they parted his raiment, and cast lots.

ZEALOUS

Ac 10:38 How God anointed Jesus of Nazareth with the Holy Ghost and with power: who went about doing good, and healing all that were oppressed of the devil; for God was with him.

BURDEN-BEARING

Ga 6:2 Bear ye one another's burdens, and so fulfil the law of Christ.

LOVING

Ep 5:2 And walk in love, as Christ also hath loved us, and hath given himself for us an offering and a sacrifice to God for a sweetsmelling savour.

15. His Sufferings

Ge 3:15 And I will put enmity between thee and the woman, and between thy seed and her seed; it shall bruise thy head, and thou shalt bruise his heel.

Ps 69:20 Reproach hath broken my heart; and I am full of heaviness: and I looked *for some* to take pity, but *there* was none; and for comforters, but I found none.

Is 50:6 I gave my back to the smiters, and my cheeks to them that plucked off the hair: I hid not my face from shame and spitting.

Is 53:5 But he *was* wounded for our transgressions, *he was* bruised for our iniquities: the chastisement of our peace *was* upon him; and with his stripes we are healed.

Is 53:10 Yet it pleased the LORD to bruise him; he hath put *him* to grief: when thou shalt make his soul an offering for sin, he shall see *his* seed, he shall prolong *his* days, and the pleasure of the LORD shall prosper in his hand.

Zec 13:6 And *one* shall say unto him, What *are* these wounds in thine hands? Then he shall answer, *Those* with which I was wounded *in* the house of my friends.

Mt 26:31 Then saith Jesus unto them, All ye shall be offended because of me this night: for it is written, I will smite the shepherd, and the sheep of the flock shall be scattered abroad.

Mt 26:38 Then saith he unto them, My soul is exceeding sorrowful, even unto death: tarry ye here, and watch with me.

Mt 27:26 Then released he Barabbas unto them: and when he had scourged Jesus, he delivered *him* to be crucified.

Mt 27:29 And when they had platted a crown of thorns, they put *it* upon his head, and a reed in his right hand: and they bowed the knee before him, and mocked him, saying, Hail, King of the Jews!

Mt 27:46 And about the ninth hour Jesus cried with a loud voice, saying, Eli, Eli, lama sabachthani? that is to say, My God, my God, why hast thou forsaken me?

Mk 14:27 And Jesus saith unto them, All ye shall be offended because of me this night: for it is written, I will smite the shepherd, and the sheep shall be scattered.

Mk 14:34 And saith unto them, My soul is exceeding sorrowful unto death: tarry ye here, and watch.

Mk 15:17 And they clothed him with purple, and platted a crown of thorns, and put it about his *head,*

Mk 15:34 And at the ninth hour Jesus cried with a loud voice, saying, Eloi, Eloi, lama sabachthani? which is, being interpreted, My God, my God, why hast thou forsaken me?

Lu 22:44 And being in an agony he prayed more earnestly: and his sweat was as it were great drops of blood falling down to the ground.

Lu 22:63 And the men that held Jesus mocked him, and smote *him.*

Jn 12:27 Now is my soul troubled; and what shall I say? Father, save me from this hour: but for this cause came I unto this hour.

Jn 19:2 And the soldiers platted a crown of thorns, and put *it* on his head, and they put on him a purple robe,

Jn 19:37 And again another scripture saith, They shall look on him whom they pierced.

Ac 3:18 But those things, which God before had shewed by the mouth of all his prophets, that Christ should suffer, he hath so fulfilled.

Ac 17:3 Opening and alleging, that Christ must needs have suffered, and risen again from the dead; and that this Jesus, whom I preach unto you, is Christ.

Ac 26:23 That Christ should suffer, *and* that he should be the first that should rise from the dead, and should shew light unto the people, and to the Gentiles.

He 2:10 For it became him, for whom *are* all things, and by whom *are* all things, in bringing many sons unto glory, to make the captain of their salvation perfect through sufferings.

He 5:8 Though he were a Son, yet learned he obedience by the things which he suffered;

He 12:3 For consider him that endured such contradiction of sinners against himself, lest ye be wearied and faint in your minds.

He 13:12 Wherefore Jesus also, that he might sanctify the people with his own blood, suffered without the gate.

1 Pe 1:11 Searching what, or what manner of time the Spirit of Christ which was in them did signify, when it testified beforehand the sufferings of Christ, and the glory that should follow.

1 Pe 2:21 For even hereunto were ye called: because Christ also suffered for us, leaving us an example, that ye should follow his steps:

1 Pe 3:18 For Christ also hath once suffered for sins, the just for the unjust, that he might bring us to God, being put to death in the flesh, but quickened by the Spirit:

1 Pe 4:1 Forasmuch then as Christ hath suffered for us in the flesh, arm yourselves likewise with the same mind: for he that hath suffered in the flesh hath ceased from sin;

1 Pe 5:1 The elders which are among you I exhort, who am also an elder, and a witness of the sufferings of Christ, and also a partaker of the glory that shall be revealed:

Re 19:13 And he *was* clothed with a vesture dipped in blood: and his name is called The Word of God.

Re 19:15 And out of his mouth goeth a sharp sword, that with it he should smite the nations: and he shall rule them with a rod of iron: and he treadeth the winepress of the fierceness and wrath of Almighty God.

a. Sorrowful

Is 53:3 He is despised and rejected of men; a man of sorrows, and acquainted with grief: and we hid as it were *our* faces from him; he was despised, and we esteemed him not.

Mt 17:12 But I say unto you, That Elias is come already, and they knew him not, but have done unto him whatsoever they listed. Likewise shall also the Son of man suffer of them.

Mt 21:39 And they caught him, and cast *him* out of the vineyard, and slew *him.*

Mt 26:38 Then saith he unto them, My soul is exceeding sorrowful, even unto death: tarry ye here, and watch with me.

Mt 27:31 And after that they had mocked him, they took the robe off from him, and put his own raiment on him, and led him away to crucify *him*.

Mt 27:46 And about the ninth hour Jesus cried with a loud voice, saying, Eli, Eli, lama sabachthani? that is to say, My God, my God, why hast thou forsaken me?

Mk 7:34 And looking up to heaven, he sighed, and saith unto him, Ephphatha, that is, Be opened.

Mk 8:12 And he sighed deeply in his spirit, and saith, Why doth this generation seek after a sign? verily I say unto you, There shall no sign be given unto this generation.

Mk 14:33 And he taketh with him Peter and James and John, and began to be sore amazed, and to be very heavy;

Lu 19:41 And when he was come near, he beheld the city, and wept over it,

Jn 11:33 When Jesus therefore saw her weeping, and the Jews also weeping which came with her, he groaned in the spirit, and was troubled,

Jn 11:35 Jesus wept.

Jn 12:27 Now is my soul troubled; and what shall I say? Father, save me from this hour: but for this cause came I unto this hour.

Jn 13:21 When Jesus had thus said, he was troubled in spirit, and testified, and said, Verily, verily, I say unto you, that one of you shall betray me.

b. Despised

Ps 22:6 But I *am* a worm, and no man; a reproach of men, and despised of the people.

Is 49:7 Thus saith the LORD, the Redeemer of Israel, *and* his Holy One, to him whom man despiseth, to him whom the nation abhorreth, to a servant of rulers, Kings shall see and arise, princes also shall worship, because of the LORD that is faithful, *and* the Holy One of Israel, and he shall choose thee.

Is 53:3 He is despised and rejected of men; a man of sorrows, and acquainted with grief: and we hid as it were *our* faces from him; he was despised, and we esteemed him not.

Mt 9:24 He said unto them, Give place: for the maid is not dead, but sleepeth. And they laughed him to scorn.

Mt 10:25 It is enough for the disciple that he be as his master, and the servant as his lord. If they have called the master of the house Beelzebub, how much more *shall they call* them of his household?

Mt 13:55 Is not this the carpenter's son? is not his mother called Mary? and his brethren, James, and Joses, and Simon, and Judas?

Mt 26:55 In that same hour said Jesus to the multitudes, Are ye come out as against a thief with swords and staves for to take me? I sat daily with you teaching in the temple, and ye laid no hold on me.

Mt 27:22 Pilate saith unto them, What shall I do then with Jesus which is called Christ? *They* all say unto him, Let him be crucified.

Mt 27:30 And they spit upon him, and took the reed, and smote him on the head.

Mt 27:40 And saying, Thou that destroyest the temple, and buildest *it* in three days, save thyself. If thou be the Son of God, come down from the cross.

Mk 6:3 Is not this the carpenter, the son of Mary, the brother of James, and Joses, and of Juda, and Simon? and are not his sisters here with us? And they were offended at him.

Mk 15:29–30 And they that passed by railed on him, wagging their heads, and saying, Ah, thou that destroyest the temple, and buildest *it* in three days,

Save thyself, and come down from the cross.

Lu 4:22 And all bare him witness, and wondered at the gracious words which proceeded out of his mouth. And they said, Is not this Joseph's son?

Lu 10:16 He that heareth you heareth me; and he that despiseth you despiseth me; and he that despiseth me despiseth him that sent me.

Lu 16:14 And the Pharisees also, who were covetous, heard all these things: and they derided him.

Lu 22:64 And when they had blindfolded him, they struck him on the face, and asked him, saying, Prophesy, who is it that smote thee?

Jn 6:42 And they said, Is not this Jesus, the son of Joseph, whose father and mother we know? how is it then that he saith, I came down from heaven?

Jn 7:20 The people answered and said, Thou hast a devil: who goeth about to kill thee?

Jn 7:27 Howbeit we know this man whence he is: but when Christ cometh, no man knoweth whence he is.

Jn 7:48 Have any of the rulers or of the Pharisees believed on him?

Jn 8:49 Jesus answered, I have not a devil; but I honour my Father, and ye do dishonour me.

Jn 9:29 We know that God spake unto Moses: *as for* this *fellow,* we know not from whence he is.

Jn 10:20 And many of them said, He hath a devil, and is mad; why hear ye him?

He 6:6 If they shall fall away, to renew them again unto repentance; seeing they crucify to themselves the Son of God afresh, and put *him* to an open shame.

c. Humiliated

Is 53:2 For he shall grow up before him as a tender plant, and as a root out of a dry ground: he hath no form nor comeliness; and when we shall see him, *there is* no beauty that we should desire him.

Is 53:9 And he made his grave with the wicked, and with the rich in his death; because he had done no violence, neither *was any* deceit in his mouth.

Mt 8:20 And Jesus saith unto him, The foxes have holes, and the birds of the air *have* nests; but the Son of man hath not where to lay *his* head.

Mt 27:28 And they stripped him, and put on him a scarlet robe.

Mt 27:38 Then were there two thieves crucified with him, one on the right hand, and another on the left.

Mk 1:13 And he was there in the wilderness forty days, tempted of Satan; and was with the wild beasts; and the angels ministered unto him.

Mk 14:48 And Jesus answered and said unto them, Are ye come out, as against a thief, with swords and *with* staves to take me?

Mk 15:17 And they clothed him with purple, and platted a crown of thorns, and put it about his *head,*

Mk 15:27 And with him they crucify two thieves; the one on his right hand, and the other on his left.

Lu 2:7 And she brought forth her firstborn son, and wrapped him in swaddling clothes, and laid him in a manger; because there was no room for them in the inn.

Lu 2:12 And this *shall be* a sign unto you; Ye shall find the babe wrapped in swaddling clothes, lying in a manger.

Lu 9:58 And Jesus said unto him, Foxes have holes, and birds of the air *have* nests; but the Son of man hath not where to lay *his* head.

Lu 22:37 For I say unto you that this that is written must yet be accomplished in me, And he was reckoned among the transgressors: for the things concerning me have an end.

Lu 22:52 Then Jesus said unto the chief priests, and captains of the temple, and the elders, which were come to him, Be ye come out, as against a thief, with swords and staves?

Lu 22:65 And many other things blasphemously spake they against him.

Lu 23:33 And when they were come to the place, which is called Calvary, there they crucified him, and the malefactors, one on the right hand, and the other on the left.

Jn 19:3 And said, Hail, King of the Jews! and they smote him with their hands.

Jn 19:18 Where they crucified him, and two others with him, on either side one, and Jesus in the midst.

Ac 8:33 In his humiliation his judgment was taken away: and who shall declare his generation? for his life is taken from the earth.

2 Co 8:9 For ye know the grace of our Lord Jesus Christ, that, though he was rich, yet for your sakes he became poor, that ye through his poverty might be rich.

Ph 2:7–8 But made himself of no reputation, and took upon him the form of a servant, and was made in the likeness of men:

And being found in fashion as a man, he humbled himself, and became obedient unto death, even the death of the cross.

He 2:9 But we see Jesus, who was made a little lower than the angels for the suffering of death, crowned with glory and honour; that he by the grace of God should taste death for every man.

He 2:17 Wherefore in all things it behoved him to be made like unto *his* brethren, that he might be a merciful and faithful high priest in things *pertaining* to God, to make reconciliation for the sins of the people.

d. Mocked

Mt 27:29 And when they had platted a crown of thorns, they put *it* upon his head, and a reed in his right hand: and they bowed the knee before him, and mocked him, saying, Hail, King of the Jews!

Mt 27:41 Likewise also the chief priests mocking *him,* with the scribes and elders, said,

Lu 22:63 And the men that held Jesus mocked him, and smote *him.*

Lu 23:11 And Herod with his men of war set him at nought, and mocked *him,* and arrayed him in a gorgeous robe, and sent him again to Pilate.

Lu 23:36 And the soldiers also mocked him, coming to him, and offering him vinegar,

e. Reviled

Ps 22:7 All they that see me laugh me to scorn: they shoot out the lip, they shake the head *saying,*

Mt 27:39 And they that passed by reviled him, wagging their heads,

Mk 15:32 Let Christ the King of Israel descend now from the cross, that we may see and believe. And they that were crucified with him reviled him.

Lu 23:39 And one of the malefactors which were hanged railed on him, saying, If thou be Christ, save thyself and us.

f. Crucified

Ps 22:16 For dogs have compassed me: the assembly of the wicked have inclosed me: they pierced my hands and my feet.

Zec 12:10 And I will pour upon the house of David, and upon the inhabitants of Jerusalem, the spirit of grace and of supplications: and they shall look upon me whom they have pierced, and they shall mourn for him, as one mourneth for *his* only *son,* and shall be in bitterness for him, as one that is in bitterness for *his* firstborn.

Mt 20:19 And shall deliver him to the Gentiles to mock, and to scourge, and to crucify *him:* and the third day he shall rise again.

Mt 21:39 And they caught him, and cast *him* out of the vineyard, and slew *him.*

Mt 23:34 Wherefore, behold, I send unto you prophets, and wise men, and scribes: and *some* of them ye shall kill and crucify; and *some* of them shall ye scourge in your synagogues, and persecute *them* from city to city:

Mt 26:2 Ye know that after two days is *the feast of* the passover, and the Son of man is betrayed to be crucified.

Mt 27:22 Pilate saith unto them, What shall I do then with Jesus which is called Christ? *They* all say unto him, Let him be crucified.

Mt 27:26 Then released he Barabbas unto them: and when he had scourged Jesus, he delivered *him* to be crucified.

Mt 27:35 And they crucified him, and parted his garments, casting lots: that it might be fulfilled which was spoken by the prophet, They parted my garments among them, and upon my vesture did they cast lots.

Mt 28:5 And the angel answered and said unto the women, Fear not ye: for

I know that ye seek Jesus, which was crucified.

Mk 8:31 And he began to teach them, that the Son of man must suffer many things, and be rejected of the elders, and of the chief priests, and scribes, and be killed, and after three days rise again.

Mk 10:34 And they shall mock him, and shall scourge him, and shall spit upon him, and shall kill him: and the third day he shall rise again.

Mk 12:8 And they took him, and killed him, and cast him out of the vineyard.

Mk 15:24 And when they had crucified him, they parted his garments, casting lots upon them, what every man should take.

Mk 16:6 And he saith unto them, Be not affrighted: Ye seek Jesus of Nazareth, which was crucified: he is risen; he is not here: behold the place where they laid him.

Lu 18:32 For he shall be delivered unto the Gentiles, and shall be mocked, and spitefully entreated, and spitted on:

Lu 20:15 So they cast him out of the vineyard, and killed him. What therefore shall the lord of the vineyard do unto them?

Lu 23:33 And when they were come to the place, which is called Calvary, there they crucified him, and the malefactors, one on the right hand, and the other on the left.

Lu 24:7 Saying, The Son of man must be delivered into the hands of sinful men, and be crucified, and the third day rise again.

Lu 24:20 And how the chief priests and our rulers delivered him to be condemned to death, and have crucified him.

Jn 3:14 And as Moses lifted up the serpent in the wilderness, even so must the Son of man be lifted up:

Jn 12:33 This he what death he should die.

Jn 19:18 Where they crucified him, and two others with him, on either side one, and Jesus in the midst.

Jn 19:23 Then the soldiers, when they had crucified Jesus, took his gar-

ments, and made four parts, to every soldier a part; and also his coat: now the coat was without seam, woven from the top throughout.

Ac 2:23 Him, being delivered by the determinate counsel and foreknowledge of God, ye have taken, and by wicked hands have crucified and slain:

Ac 3:15 And killed the Prince of life, whom God hath raised from the dead; whereof we are witnesses.

Ac 4:10 Be it known unto you all, and to all the people of Israel, that by the name of Jesus Christ of Nazareth, whom ye crucified, whom God raised from the dead, even by him doth this man stand here before you whole.

Ac 5:30 The God of our fathers raised up Jesus, whom ye slew and hanged on a tree.

Ac 7:52 Which of the prophets have not your fathers persecuted? and they have slain them which shewed before of the coming of the Just One; of whom ye have been now the betrayers and murderers:

Ac 10:39 And we are witnesses of all things which he did both in the land of the Jews, and in Jerusalem; whom they slew and hanged on a tree:

1 Co 1:13 Is Christ divided? was Paul crucified for you? or were ye baptized in the name of Paul?

1 Co 2:8 Which none of the princes of this world knew: for had they known it, they would not have crucified the Lord of glory.

2 Co 13:4 For though he was crucified through weakness, yet he liveth by the power of God. For we also are weak in him, but we shall live with him by the power of God toward you.

1 Th 2:15 Who both killed the Lord Jesus, and their own prophets, and have persecuted us; and they please not God, and are contrary to all men:

He 2:9 But we see Jesus, who was made a little lower than the angels for the suffering of death, crowned with glory and honour; that he by the grace of God should taste death for every man.

Ja 5:6 Ye have condemned and killed the just; and he doth not resist you.

Re 11:8 And their dead bodies *shall lie* in the street of the great city, which spiritually is called Sodom and Egypt, where also our Lord was crucified.

16. His Task

Jn 4:34 Jesus saith unto them, My meat is to do the will of him that sent me, and to finish his work.

Jn 5:36 But I have greater witness than *that* of John: for the works which the Father hath given me to finish, the same works that I do, bear witness of me, that the Father hath sent me.

Jn 9:4 I must work the works of him that sent me, while it is day: the night cometh, when no man can work.

Jn 17:4 I have glorified thee on the earth: I have finished the work which thou gavest me to do.

Jn 19:30 When Jesus therefore had received the vinegar, he said, It is finished: and he bowed his head, and gave up the ghost.

CHRISTIANS

Ac 11:26 And when he had found him, he brought him unto Antioch. And it came to pass, that a whole year they assembled themselves with the church, and taught much people. And the disciples were called Christians first in Antioch.

Ac 15:17 That the residue of men might seek after the Lord, and all the Gentiles, upon whom my name is called, saith the Lord, who doeth all these things.

Ac 26:28 Then Agrippa said unto Paul, Almost thou persuadest me to be a Christian.

Ac 28:22 But we desire to hear of thee what thou thinkest: for as concerning this sect, we know that every where it is spoken against.

2 Ti 2:19 Nevertheless the foundation of God standeth sure, having this seal, The Lord knoweth them that are his. And, Let every one that nameth the name of Christ depart from iniquity.

Ja 2:7 Do not they blaspheme that worthy name by the which ye are called?

1 Pe 4:16 Yet if *any man suffer* as a Christian, let him not be ashamed; but let him glorify God on this behalf.

CHRISTIANITY, *characteristics of true*

A NEW BIRTH

Jn 3:5 Jesus answered, Verily, verily, I say unto thee, Except a man be born of water and *of* the Spirit, he cannot enter into the kingdom of God.

A GROWTH

2 Pe 3:18 But grow in grace, and *in* the knowledge of our Lord and Saviour Jesus Christ. To him *be* glory both now and for ever. Amen.

A NEW DRESS

Is 61:10 I will greatly rejoice in the LORD, my soul shall be joyful in my God; for he hath clothed me with the garments of salvation, he hath covered me with the robe of righteousness, as a bridegroom decketh *himself* with ornaments, and as a bride adorneth *herself* with her jewels.

A RADIANT LIFE

Mt 5:16 Let your light so shine before men, that they may see your good works, and glorify your Father which is in heaven.

A CHARACTER BUILDING

Mt 7:24 Therefore whosoever heareth these sayings of mine, and doeth them, I will liken him unto a wise man, which built his house upon a rock:

A FELLOWSHIP

Lu 24:32 And they said one to another, Did not our heart burn within us, while he talked with us by the way, and while he opened to us the scriptures?

A SONSHIP

Jn 1:12 But as many as received him, to them gave he power to become the sons of God, *even* to them that believe on his name:

AN EDUCATION

Jn 8:31–32 Then said Jesus to those Jews which believed on him, If ye continue in my word, *then* are ye my disciples indeed;

And ye shall know the truth, and the truth shall make you free.

A SERVICE

1 Ti 6:18 That they do good, that they be rich in good works, ready to distribute, willing to communicate;

A SACRIFICE

Ro 12:1 I beseech you therefore, brethren, by the mercies of God, that ye present your bodies a living sacrifice, holy, acceptable unto God, *which is* your reasonable service.

A WALK

Col 2:6 As ye have therefore received Christ Jesus the Lord, *so* walk ye in him:

A WARFARE

1 Ti 6:12 Fight the good fight of faith, lay hold on eternal life, whereunto thou art also called, and hast professed a good profession before many witnesses.

A RACE

He 12:1 Wherefore seeing we also are compassed about with so great a cloud of witnesses, let us lay aside every weight, and the sin which doth so easily beset us, and let us run with patience the race that is set before us,

A VICTORY

1 Jn 5:4 For whatsoever is born of God overcometh the world: and this is the victory that overcometh the world, *even* our faith.

AN ASSURANCE OF IMMORTALITY

Jn 17:3 And this is life eternal, that they might know thee the only true God, and Jesus Christ, whom thou hast sent.

CHRISTS, *impostors*

Mt 24:5, 24; Mk 13:6, 22; Lu 21:8; Jn 5:43

CHRONICLES

1. FIRST

Author: Uncertain, thought to have been edited by Ezra.

Date Written: Most likely edited between 450 B.C. and 430 B.C., though probably written during, or shortly after, the captivity.

Distinctive Features: 1 Chronicles deals almost exclusively with the history of Judah and takes the story through the death of David. The spiritual element in the history is more emphasized than in the other historical books.

Purpose: To highlight the righteous kings of Judah and expose the sins of the evil ones, demonstrating each one's lasting influence upon the worship life of God's people.

To Whom Written: The nation of Israel.

Main Themes: Desire of David to build temple, and sovereignty of God.

Key Words: Temple, House of God, The House of the Lord.

Key Verses: 4:9–10; 5:20; 11:14; 12:18; 14:2, 10, 14–15.

2. SECOND

Author: Uncertain, thought to have been edited by Ezra.

Date Written: Most likely edited between 450 B.C. and 430 B.C., though probably written during, or shortly after, the captivity.

Distinctive Features: 2 Chronicles deals almost exclusively with the history of Judah and takes the story from the reign of Solomon to the restoration decree. The spiritual element in the history is more emphasized than in the other historical books.

Purpose: To highlight the righteous kings of Judah and expose the sins of the evil ones, demonstrating each one's lasting influence upon the worship life of God's people.

To Whom Written: The nation of Israel.

Main Themes: The Davidic line, temple, and the priesthood.

Key Words: Temple, House of God, The House of the Lord.

Key Verses: 7:14-16.

CHISLEU *See* **MONTHS**

CHRYSOLITE *See* **STONES**

CHRYSOPRASUS *See* **STONES**

CHURCH, *the "called out" ones, body of believers*

1. Called the Body of Christ

Ro 12:5 So we, *being* many, are one body in Christ, and every one members one of another.

1 Co 10:17 For we *being* many are one bread, *and* one body: for we are all partakers of that one bread.

1 Co 12:13 For by one Spirit are we all baptized into one body, whether *we be* Jews or Gentiles, whether *we be* bond or free; and have been all made to drink into one Spirit.

1 Co 12:27 Now ye are the body of Christ, and members in particular.

Ep 1:23 Which is his body, the fulness of him that filleth all in all.

Ep 2:16 And that he might reconcile both unto God in one body by the cross, having slain the enmity thereby:

Ep 3:6 That the Gentiles should be fellowheirs, and of the same body, and partakers of his promise in Christ by the gospel:

Ep 4:4 *There is* one body, and one Spirit, even as ye are called in one hope of your calling;

Ep 4:12 For the perfecting of the saints, for the work of the ministry, for the edifying of the body of Christ:

Ep 4:16 From whom the whole body fitly joined together and compacted by that which every joint supplieth, according to the effectual working in the measure of every part, maketh increase of the body unto the edifying of itself in love.

Ep 5:23 For the husband is the head of the wife, even as Christ is the head of the church: and he is the saviour of the body.

Ep 5:30 For we are members of his body, of his flesh, and of his bones.

Col 1:18 And he is the head of the body, the church: who is the beginning, the firstborn from the dead; that in all *things* he might have the preeminence.

Col 1:24 Who now rejoice in my sufferings for you, and fill up that which is behind of the afflictions of Christ in my flesh for his body's sake, which is the church:

Col 2:19 And not holding the Head, from which all the body by joints and bands having nourishment ministered, and knit together, increaseth with the increase of God.

Col 3:15 And let the peace of God rule in your hearts, to the which also ye are called in one body; and be ye thankful.

2. Compared to a Building

Mt 16:18 And I say also unto thee, That thou art Peter, and upon this rock I will build my church; and the gates of hell shall not prevail against it.

Ro 15:20 Yea, so have I strived to preach the gospel, not where Christ was named, lest I should build upon another man's foundation:

1 Co 3:10 According to the grace of God which is given unto me, as a wise masterbuilder, I have laid the foundation, and another buildeth thereon. But let every man take heed how he buildeth thereupon.

Ep 2:21 In whom all the building fitly framed together groweth unto an holy temple in the Lord:

1 Ti 3:15 But if I tarry long, that thou mayest know how thou oughtest to behave thyself in the house of God, which is the church of the living God, the pillar and ground of the truth.

He 3:4 For every house is builded by some *man*; but he that built all things *is* God.

He 10:21 And *having* an high priest over the house of God;

1 Pe 2:5 Ye also, as lively stones, are built up a spiritual house, an holy priesthood, to offer up spiritual sacrifices, acceptable to God by Jesus Christ.

See **TEMPLES**

3. Its Government

Ac 15:6 And the apostles and elders came together for to consider of this matter.

Ac 15:28 For it seemed good to the Holy Ghost, and to us, to lay upon you no greater burden than these necessary things;

1 Co 7:17 But as God hath distributed to every man, as the Lord hath called every one, so let him walk. And so ordain I in all churches.

1 Co 11:34 And if any man hunger, let him eat at home; that ye come not together unto condemnation. And the rest will I set in order when I come.

1 Ti 3:5 (For if a man know not how to rule his own house, how shall he take care of the church of God?)

1 Ti 5:1 Rebuke not an elder, but intreat *him* as a father; *and* the younger men as brethren;

4. Its Preciousness

a. Israel, pictures God's love

De 32:10 He found him in a desert land, and in the waste howling wilderness; he led him about, he instructed him, he kept him as the apple of his eye.

Is 43:4 Since thou wast precious in my sight, thou hast been honourable, and I have loved thee: therefore will I give men for thee, and people for thy life.

Is 49:16 Behold, I have graven thee upon the palms of *my* hands; thy walls *are* continually before me.

Is 62:3 Thou shalt also be a crown of glory in the hand of the LORD, and a royal diadem in the hand of thy God.

Zec 2:8 For thus saith the LORD of hosts; After the glory hath he sent me unto the nations which spoiled you:

for he that toucheth you toucheth the apple of his eye.

Zec 9:16 And the LORD their God shall save them in that day as the flock of his people: for they *shall be as* the stones of a crown, lifted up as an ensign upon his land.

Mal 3:17 And they shall be mine, saith the LORD of hosts, in that day when I make up my jewels; and I will spare them, as a man spareth his own son that serveth him.

b. Believers, show Christ's love

Ac 20:28 Take heed therefore unto yourselves, and to all the flock, over the which the Holy Ghost hath made you overseers, to feed the church of God, which he hath purchased with his own blood.

1 Co 10:32 Give none offence, neither to the Jews, nor to the Gentiles, nor to the church of God:

Ep 5:25 Husbands, love your wives, even as Christ also loved the church, and gave himself for it;

Ep 5:29 For no man ever yet hated his own flesh; but nourisheth and cherisheth it, even as the Lord the church:

Col 1:24 Who now rejoice in my sufferings for you, and fill up that which is behind of the afflictions of Christ in my flesh for his body's sake, which is the church:

See **MARRIAGE**

5. Love for

Ro 15:23 But now having no more place in these parts, and having a great desire these many years to come unto you;

2 Co 7:3 I speak not *this* to condemn *you:* for I have said before, that ye are in our hearts to die and live with *you.*

2 Co 13:9 For we are glad, when we are weak, and ye are strong: and this also we wish, *even* your perfection.

Ep 1:15 Wherefore I also, after I heard of your faith in the Lord Jesus, and love unto all the saints,

Ph 1:7 Even as it is meet for me to think this of you all, because I have you in my heart; inasmuch as both in my bonds, and in the defence and confirmation of the gospel, ye all are partakers of my grace.

Ph 1:24 Nevertheless to abide in the flesh *is* more needful for you.

Ph 2:12 Wherefore, my beloved, as ye have always obeyed, not as in my presence only, but now much more in my absence, work out your own salvation with fear and trembling.

Ph 4:1 Therefore, my brethren dearly beloved and longed for, my joy and crown, so stand fast in the Lord, *my* dearly beloved.

Col 1:4 Since we heard of your faith in Christ Jesus, and of the love *which ye have* to all the saints,

1 Th 2:8 So being affectionately desirous of you, we were willing to have imparted unto you, not the gospel of God only, but also our own souls, because ye were dear unto us.

1 Th 2:17 But we, brethren, being taken from you for a short time in presence, not in heart, endeavoured the more abundantly to see your face with great desire.

1 Th 3:6 But now when Timotheus came from you unto us, and brought us good tidings of your faith and charity, and that ye have good remembrance of us always, desiring greatly to see us, as we also *to see* you:

2 Th 1:3 We are bound to thank God always for you, brethren, as it is meet, because that your faith groweth exceedingly, and the charity of every one of you all toward each other aboundeth;

Phm 1:5 Hearing of thy love and faith, which thou hast toward the Lord Jesus, and toward all saints;

He 6:9 But, beloved, we are persuaded better things of you, and things that accompany salvation, though we thus speak.

1 Pe 1:22 Seeing ye have purified your souls in obeying the truth through the Spirit unto unfeigned love of the brethren, *see that ye* love one another with a pure heart fervently:

1 Pe 2:17 Honour all *men*. Love the brotherhood. Fear God. Honour the king.

1 Jn 3:14 We know that we have passed from death unto life, because we love the brethren. He that loveth not *his* brother abideth in death.

1 Jn 5:2 By this we know that we love the children of God, when we love God, and keep his commandments.

2 Jn 5 And now I beseech thee, lady, not as though I wrote a new commandment unto thee, but that which we had from the beginning, that we love one another.

6. Divinely Instituted

Ep 2:20 And are built upon the foundation of the apostles and prophets, Jesus Christ himself being the chief corner *stone;*

1 Th 1:1 Paul, and Silvanus, and Timotheus, unto the church of the Thessalonians *which is* in God the Father and *in* the Lord Jesus Christ: Grace *be* unto you, and peace, from God our Father, and the Lord Jesus Christ.

1 Ti 3:15 But if I tarry long, that thou mayest know how thou oughtest to behave thyself in the house of God, which is the church of the living God, the pillar and ground of the truth.

7. Paul's Care

Ac 20:31 Therefore watch, and remember, that by the space of three years I ceased not to warn every one night and day with tears.

1 Co 7:32 But I would have you without carefulness. He that is unmarried careth for the things that belong to the Lord, how he may please the Lord:

1 Co 12:25 That there should be no schism in the body; but *that* the members should have the same care one for another.

1 Co 15:10 But by the grace of God I am what I am: and his grace *which was* bestowed upon me was not in vain; but I laboured more abundantly than they all: yet not I, but the grace of God which was with me.

1 Co 16:24 My love *be* with you all in Christ Jesus. Amen.

2 Co 7:12 Wherefore, though I wrote unto you, *I did it* not for his cause that had done the wrong, nor for his cause that suffered wrong, but that our care for you in the sight of God might appear unto you.

2 Co 8:16 But thanks *be* to God, which put the same earnest care into the heart of Titus for you.

2 Co 11:28 Beside those things that are without, that which cometh upon me daily, the care of all the churches.

2 Co 12:20 For I fear, lest, when I come, I shall not find you such as I would, and *that* I shall be found unto you such as ye would not: lest *there be* debates, envyings, wraths, strifes, backbitings, whisperings, swellings, tumults:

Ga 4:11 I am afraid of you, lest I have bestowed upon you labour in vain.

1 Th 3:5 For this cause, when I could no longer forbear, I sent to know your faith, lest by some means the tempter have tempted you, and our labour be in vain.

1 Th 3:10 Night and day praying exceedingly that we might see your face, and might perfect that which is lacking in your faith?

1 Ti 3:5 (For if a man know not how to rule his own house, how shall he take care of the church of God?)

See **SOLICITUDE**

8. Additions

ON THE DAY OF PENTECOST

Ac 2:41 Then they that gladly received his word were baptized: and the same day there were added *unto them* about three thousand souls.

DAILY ADDITIONS

Ac 2:47 Praising God, and having favour with all the people. And the Lord added to the church daily such as should be saved.

NUMBER INCREASED AFTER PENTECOST

Ac 4:4 Howbeit many of them which heard the word believed; and the number of the men was about five thousand.

STEADY GROWTH OF THE CHURCH

Ac 5:14 And believers were the more added to the Lord, multitudes both of men and women.)

PRIESTS JOIN THE DISCIPLES

Ac 6:7 And the word of God increased; and the number of the disciples multiplied in Jerusalem greatly; and a great company of the priests were obedient to the faith.

Ac 9:31 Then had the churches rest throughout all Judaea and Galilee and Samaria, and were edified; and walking in the fear of the Lord, and in the comfort of the Holy Ghost, were multiplied.

IN ANTIOCH

Ac 11:21 And the hand of the Lord was with them: and a great number believed, and turned unto the Lord.

Ac 11:24 For he was a good man, and full of the Holy Ghost and of faith: and much people was added unto the Lord.

UNDER PAUL'S PREACHING

Ac 14:1 And it came to pass in Iconium, that they went both together into the synagogue of the Jews, and so spake, that a great multitude both of the Jews and also of the Greeks believed.

Ac 16:5 And so were the churches established in the faith, and increased in number daily.

Ac 17:4 And some of them believed, and consorted with Paul and Silas; and of the devout Greeks a great multitude, and of the chief women not a few.

Ac 18:8 And Crispus, the chief ruler of the synagogue, believed on the Lord with all his house; and many of the Corinthians hearing believed, and were baptized.

9. Strife

Is 58:4 Behold, ye fast for strife and debate, and to smite with the fist of wickedness: ye shall not fast as *ye do this* day, to make your voice to be heard on high.

Ac 6:1 And in those days, when the number of the disciples was multiplied, there arose a murmuring of the Grecians against the Hebrews, because their widows were neglected in the daily ministration.

Ac 15:2 When therefore Paul and Barnabas had no small dissension and disputation with them, they determined that Paul and Barnabas, and certain other of them, should go up to Jerusalem unto the apostles and elders about this question.

Ac 15:7 And when there had been much disputing, Peter rose up, and said unto them, Men *and* brethren, ye know how that a good while ago God made choice among us, that the Gentiles by my mouth should hear the word of the gospel, and believe.

1 Co 1:11 For it hath been declared unto me of you, my brethren, by them *which are of the house* of Chloe, that there are contentions among you.

1 Co 3:3 For ye are yet carnal: for whereas *there is* among you envying, and strife, and divisions, are ye not carnal, and walk as men?

1 Co 6:6 But brother goeth to law with brother, and that before the unbelievers.

1 Co 11:18 For first of all, when ye come together in the church, I hear that there be divisions among you; and I partly believe it.

2 Co 12:20 For I fear, lest, when I come, I shall not find you such as I would, and *that* I shall be found unto you such as ye would not: lest *there be* debates, envyings, wraths, strifes, backbitings, whisperings, swellings, tumults:

Ga 5:15 But if ye bite and devour one another, take heed that ye be not consumed one of another.

Ph 4:2 I beseech Euodias, and beseech Syntyche, that they be of the same mind in the Lord.

See **STRIFE**

10. Its Head, Christ

Ho 1:11 Then shall the children of Judah and the children of Israel be gathered together, and appoint them-selves one head, and they shall come up out of the land: for great *shall be* the day of Jezreel.

1 Co 11:3 But I would have you know, that the head of every man is Christ; and the head of the woman *is* the man; and the head of Christ *is* God.

Ep 1:22 And hath put all *things* under his feet, and gave him *to be* the head over all *things* to the church,

Ep 4:15 But speaking the truth in love, may grow up into him in all things, which is the head, *even* Christ:

Ep 5:23 For the husband is the head of the wife, even as Christ is the head of the church: and he is the saviour of the body.

Col 1:18 And he is the head of the body, the church: who is the beginning, the firstborn from the dead; that in all *things* he might have the preeminence.

Col 2:19 And not holding the Head, from which all the body by joints and bands having nourishment ministered, and knit together, increaseth with the increase of God.

1 Pe 2:7 Unto you therefore which believe *he is* precious: but unto them which be disobedient, the stone which the builders disallowed, the same is made the head of the corner,

a. The Church as Bride

Song 4:1 Behold, thou *art* fair, my love; behold, thou *art* fair; thou *hast* doves' eyes within thy locks: thy hair *is* as a flock of goats, that appear from mount Gilead.

Song 4:9 Thou hast ravished my heart, my sister, *my* spouse; thou hast ravished my heart with one of thine eyes, with one chain of thy neck.

Song 6:3 I *am* my beloved's, and my beloved *is* mine: he feedeth among the lilies.

Song 7:10 I *am* my beloved's, and his desire *is* toward me.

Is 62:5 For *as* a young man marrieth a virgin, *so* shall thy sons marry thee: and *as* the bridegroom rejoiceth over the bride, *so* shall thy God rejoice over thee.

Ro 7:4 Wherefore, my brethren, ye also are become dead to the law by the body of Christ; that ye should be married to another, *even* to him who is raised from the dead, that we should bring forth fruit unto God.

2 Co 11:2 For I am jealous over you with godly jealousy: for I have espoused you to one husband, that I may present *you as* a chaste virgin to Christ.

Re 19:7 Let us be glad and rejoice, and give honour to him: for the marriage of the Lamb is come, and his wife hath made herself ready.

Re 21:2 And I John saw the holy city, new Jerusalem, coming down from God out of heaven, prepared as a bride adorned for her husband.

Re 21:9 And there came unto me one of the seven angels which had the seven vials full of the seven last plagues, and talked with me, saying, Come hither, I will shew thee the bride, the Lamb's wife.

Re 22:17 And the Spirit and the bride say, Come. And let him that heareth say, Come. And let him that is athirst come. And whosoever will, let him take the water of life freely.

See **MARRIAGE**

b. United

Jn 17:21 That they all may be one; as thou, Father, *art* in me, and I in thee, that they also may be one in us: that the world may believe that thou hast sent me.

Ro 6:5 For if we have been planted together in the likeness of his death, we shall be also *in the likeness of his* resurrection:

Ro 7:4 Wherefore, my brethren, ye also are become dead to the law by the body of Christ; that ye should be married to another, *even* to him who is raised from the dead, that we should bring forth fruit unto God.

Ro 8:1 *There is* therefore now no condemnation to them which are in Christ Jesus, who walk not after the flesh, but after the Spirit.

1 Co 6:15 Know ye not that your bodies are the members of Christ?

shall I then take the members of Christ, and make *them* the members of an harlot? God forbid.

1 Co 6:17 But he that is joined unto the Lord is one spirit.

2 Co 11:2 For I am jealous over you with godly jealousy: for I have espoused you to one husband, that I may present *you as* a chaste virgin to Christ.

Ep 5:30 For we are members of his body, of his flesh, and of his bones.

He 2:11 For both he that sanctifieth and they who are sanctified *are* all of one: for which cause he is not ashamed to call them brethren,

1 Jn 2:24 Let that therefore abide in you, which ye have heard from the beginning. If that which ye have heard from the beginning shall remain in you, ye also shall continue in the Son, and in the Father.

1 Jn 5:20 *And* we know that the Son of God is come, and hath given us an understanding, that we may know him that is true, and we are in him that is true, *even* in his Son Jesus Christ. This is the true God, and eternal life.

See **ABIDING IN CHRIST, FELLOWSHIP**

11. The Family of God

a. Adoption of Believers

Ge 17:7 And I will establish my covenant between me and thee and thy seed after thee in their generations for an everlasting covenant, to be a God unto thee, and to thy seed after thee.

Ex 4:22 And thou shalt say unto Pharaoh, Thus saith the LORD, Israel *is* my son, *even* my firstborn:

Ex 6:7 And I will take you to me for a people, and I will be to you a God: and ye shall know that I *am* the LORD your God, which bringeth you out from under the burdens of the Egyptians.

Ex 34:9 And he said, If now I have found grace in thy sight, O LORD, let my LORD, I pray thee, go among us; for it *is* a stiffnecked people; and pardon our iniquity and our sin, and take us for thine inheritance.

Le 11:45 For I *am* the LORD that bringeth you up out of the land of Egypt, to be your God: ye shall therefore be holy, for I *am* holy.

Nu 6:27 And they shall put my name upon the children of Israel; and I will bless them.

Nu 15:41 I *am* the LORD your God, which brought you out of the land of Egypt, to be your God: I *am* the LORD your God.

De 14:2 for thou *art* an holy people unto the LORD thy God, and the LORD hath chosen thee to be a peculiar people unto himself, above all the nations that *are* upon the earth.

De 26:18 And the LORD hath avouched thee this day to be his peculiar people, as he hath promised thee, and that *thou* shouldest keep all his commandments;

De 27:9 And Moses and the priests the Levites spake unto all Israel, saying, Take heed, and hearken, O Israel; this day thou art become the people of the LORD thy God.

2 S 7:14 I will be his father, and he shall be my son. If he commit iniquity, I will chasten him with the rod of men, and with the stripes of the children of men.

2 S 7:24 For thou hast confirmed to thyself thy people Israel *to be* a people unto thee for ever: and thou, LORD, art become their God.

1 Chr 17:13 I will be his father, and he shall be my son: and I will not take my mercy away from him, as I took *it* from *him* that was before thee:

1 Chr 17:22 For thy people Israel didst thou make thine own people for ever; and thou, LORD, becamest their God.

1 Chr 22:10 He shall build an house for my name; and he shall be my son, and I *will be* his father; and I will establish the throne of his kingdom over Israel for ever.

1 Chr 28:6 And he said unto me, Solomon thy son, he shall build my house and my courts: for I have chosen him *to be* my son, and I will be his father.

Ps 89:27 Also I will make him *my* firstborn, higher than the kings of the earth.

Is 19:25 Whom the LORD of hosts shall bless, saying, Blessed *be* Egypt my people, and Assyria the work of my hands, and Israel mine inheritance.

Is 43:1 But now thus saith the LORD that created thee, O Jacob, and he that formed thee, O Israel, Fear not: for I have redeemed thee, I have called *thee* by thy name; thou *art* mine.

Is 63:16 Doubtless thou *art* our father, though Abraham be ignorant of us, and Israel acknowledge us not: thou, O LORD, *art* our father, our redeemer; thy name *is* from everlasting.

Je 15:16 Thy words were found, and I did eat them; and thy word was unto me the joy and rejoicing of mine heart: for I am called by thy name, O LORD God of hosts.

Je 31:1 At the same time, saith the LORD, will I be the God of all the families of Israel, and they shall be my people.

Je 31:9 They shall come with weeping, and with supplications will I lead them: I will cause them to walk by the rivers of waters in a straight way, wherein they shall not stumble: for I am a father to Israel, and Ephraim *is* my firstborn.

Je 31:20 *Is* Ephraim my dear son? *is he* a pleasant child? for since I spake against him, I do earnestly remember him still: therefore my bowels are troubled for him; I will surely have mercy upon him, saith the LORD.

Je 31:33 But this *shall be* the covenant that I will make with the house of Israel; After those days, saith the LORD, I will put my law in their inward parts, and write it in their hearts; and will be their God, and they shall be my people.

Eze 11:20 That they may walk in my statutes, and keep mine ordinances, and do them: and they shall be my people, and I will be their God.

Eze 16:8 Now when I passed by thee, and looked upon thee, behold, thy time *was* the time of love; and I spread my skirt over thee, and covered thy nakedness: yea, I sware unto thee, and entered into a covenant with thee, saith the Lord GOD, and thou becamest mine.

Eze 34:24 And I the LORD will be their God, and my servant David a prince among them; I the LORD have spoken *it.*

Eze 34:31 And ye my flock, the flock of my pasture, *are* men, *and* I *am* your God, saith the Lord GOD.

Ho 1:10 Yet the number of the children of Israel shall be as the sand of the sea, which cannot be measured nor numbered; and it shall come to pass, *that* in the place where it was said unto them, Ye *are* not my people, *there* it shall be said unto them, Ye *are* the sons of the living God.

Ho 2:23 And I will sow her unto me in the earth; and I will have mercy upon her that had not obtained mercy; and I will say to *them which were* not my people, Thou *art* my people; and they shall say, *Thou art* my God.

Ho 11:1 When Israel *was* a child, then I loved him, and called my son out of Egypt.

Jn 1:12 But as many as received him, to them gave he power to become the sons of God, *even* to them that believe on his name:

Ro 8:15 For ye have not received the spirit of bondage again to fear; but ye have received the Spirit of adoption, whereby we cry, Abba, Father.

Ro 9:4 Who are Israelites; to whom *pertaineth* the adoption, and the glory, and the covenants, and the giving of the law, and the service *of God,* and the promises;

Ro 9:8 That is, They which are the children of the flesh, these *are* not the children of God: but the children of the promise are counted for the seed.

Ro 9:25 As he saith also in Osee, I will call them my people, which were not my people; and her beloved, which was not beloved.

Ro 11:17 And if some of the branches be broken off, and thou, being a wild olive tree, wert graffed in among them, and with them partakest of the root and fatness of the olive tree;

2 Co 6:18 And will be a Father unto you, and ye shall be my sons and daughters, saith the Lord Almighty.

Ga 3:26 For ye are all the children of God by faith in Christ Jesus.

Ga 4:5 To redeem them that were under the law, that we might receive the adoption of sons.

Ga 4:6 And because ye are sons, God hath sent forth the Spirit of his Son into your hearts, crying, Abba, Father.

Ep 1:5 Having predestinated us unto the adoption of children by Jesus Christ to himself, according to the good pleasure of his will,

Ep 2:19 Now therefore ye are no more strangers and foreigners, but fellowcitizens with the saints, and of the household of God;

He 2:13 And again, I will put my trust in him. And again, Behold I and the children which God hath given me.

He 8:10 For this *is* the covenant that I will make with the house of Israel after those days, saith the Lord; I will put my laws into their mind, and write them in their hearts: and I will be to them a God, and they shall be to me a people:

1 Pe 2:10 Which in time past *were* not a people, but *are* now the people of God: which had not obtained mercy, but now have obtained mercy.

1 Jn 3:1 Behold, what manner of love the Father hath bestowed upon us, that we should be called the sons of God: therefore the world knoweth us not, because it knew him not.

See **FAMILY**

b. Its Spiritual Relationships

BASED ON OBEDIENCE

Mt 12:50 For whosoever shall do the will of my Father which is in heaven, the same is my brother, and sister, and mother.

Lu 8:21 And he answered and said unto them, My mother and my brethren are these which hear the word of God, and do it.

HEIRS WITH CHRIST

Ro 8:17 And if children, then heirs; heirs of God, and joint-heirs with Christ; if so be that we suffer with *him,* that we may be also glorified together.

Ro 9:26 And it shall come to pass, *that* in the place where it was said unto them, Ye *are* not my people; there shall they be called the children of the living God.

Ro 16:13 Salute Rufus chosen in the Lord, and his mother and mine.

1 Co 4:17 For this cause have I sent unto you Timotheus, who is my beloved son, and faithful in the Lord, who shall bring you into remembrance of my ways which be in Christ, as I teach every where in every church.

ALL BARRIERS BROKEN DOWN

Ep 2:19 Now therefore ye are no more strangers and foreigners, but fellowcitizens with the saints, and of the household of God;

SAINTS IN HEAVEN AND EARTH UNITED

Ep 3:15 Of whom the whole family in heaven and earth is named,

RECOGNIZED BY CHRIST

He 2:11 For both he that sanctifieth and they who are sanctified *are* all of one: for which cause he is not ashamed to call them brethren,

c. Known as Brethren

Mt 12:49 And he stretched forth his hand toward his disciples, and said, Behold my mother and my brethren!

Mt 23:8 But be not ye called Rabbi: for one is your Master, *even* Christ; and all ye are brethren.

Mt 25:40 And the King shall answer and say unto them, Verily I say unto you, Inasmuch as ye have done *it* unto one of the least of these my brethren, ye have done *it* unto me.

Mt 28:10 Then said Jesus unto them, Be not afraid: go tell my brethren that they go into Galilee, and there shall they see me.

Mk 3:35 For whosoever shall do the will of God, the same is my brother, and my sister, and mother.

Lu 8:21 And he answered and said unto them, My mother and my brethren are these which hear the word of God, and do it.

Jn 20:17 Jesus saith unto her, Touch me not; for I am not yet ascended to my Father: but go to my brethren, and say unto them, I ascend unto my Father, and your Father; and *to* my God, and your God.

Jn 21:23 Then went this saying abroad among the brethren, that that disciple should not die: yet Jesus said not unto him, He shall not die; but, If I will that he tarry till I come, what *is that* to thee?

Ac 9:30 *Which* when the brethren knew, they brought him down to Caesarea, and sent him forth to Tarsus.

Ac 10:23 Then called he them in, and lodged *them.* And on the morrow Peter went away with them, and certain brethren from Joppa accompanied him.

Ac 11:1 And the apostles and brethren that were in Judaea heard that the Gentiles had also received the word of God.

Ac 11:29 Then the disciples, every man according to his ability, determined to send relief unto the brethren which dwelt in Judaea:

Ac 12:17 But he, beckoning unto them with the hand to hold their peace, declared unto them how the Lord had brought him out of the prison. And he said, Go shew these things unto James, and to the brethren. And he departed, and went into another place.

Ac 14:2 But the unbelieving Jews stirred up the Gentiles, and made their minds evil affected against the brethren.

Ac 15:3 And being brought on their way by the church, they passed through Phenice and Samaria, declaring the conversion of the Gentiles: and they caused great joy unto all the brethren.

Ac 15:36 And some days after Paul said unto Barnabas, Let us go again and visit our brethren in every city where we have preached the word of the Lord, *and see* how they do.

Ac 16:40 And they went out of the prison, and entered into *the house of* Lydia and when they had seen the brethren, they comforted them, and departed.

Ac 18:18 And Paul *after this* tarried *there* yet a good while, and then took his leave of the brethren, and sailed thence into Syria, and with him Priscilla and Aquila; having shorn *his* head in Cenchrea: for he had a vow.

Ac 28:14 Where we found brethren, and were desired to tarry with them seven days: and so we went toward Rome.

Ro 7:1 Know ye not, brethren, (for I speak to them that know the law,) how that the law hath dominion over a man as long as he liveth?

Ro 8:29 For whom he did foreknow, he also did predestinate *to be* conformed to the image of his Son, that he might be the firstborn among many brethren.

Ro 12:10 *Be* kindly affectioned one to another with brotherly love; in honour preferring one another;

Ro 15:14 And I myself also am persuaded of you, my brethren, that ye also are full of goodness, filled with all knowledge, able also to admonish one another.

Ro 16:14 Salute Asyncritus, Phlegon, Hermas, Patrobas, Hermes, and the brethren which are with them.

1 Co 1:10 Now I beseech you, brethren, by the name of our Lord Jesus Christ, that ye all speak the same thing, and *that* there be no divisions among you; but *that* ye be perfectly joined together in the same mind and in the same judgment.

1 Co 2:1 And I, brethren, when I came to you, came not with excellency of speech or of wisdom, declaring unto you the testimony of God.

1 Co 3:1 And I, brethren, could not speak unto you as unto spiritual, but as unto carnal, *even* as unto babes in Christ.

1 Co 6:8 Nay, ye do wrong, and defraud, and that *your* brethren.

1 Co 8:12 But when ye sin so against the brethren, and wound their weak conscience, ye sin against Christ.

1 Co 10:1 Moreover, brethren, I would not that ye should be ignorant, how that all our fathers were under the cloud, and all passed through the sea;

1 Co 10:14 Wherefore, my dearly beloved, flee from idolatry.

1 Co 14:26 How is it then, brethren? when ye come together, every one of you hath a psalm, hath a doctrine, hath a tongue, hath a revelation, hath an interpretation. Let all things be done unto edifying.

1 Co 15:6 After that, he was seen of above five hundred brethren at once; of whom the greater part remain unto this present, but some are fallen asleep.

1 Co 15:58 Therefore, my beloved brethren, be ye stedfast, unmovable, always abounding in the work of the Lord, forasmuch as ye know that your labour is not in vain in the Lord.

1 Co 16:11 Let no man therefore despise him: but conduct him forth in peace, that he may come unto me: for I look for him with the brethren.

1 Co 16:20 All the brethren greet you. Greet ye one another with an holy kiss.

2 Co 2:13 I had no rest in my spirit, because I found not Titus my brother: but taking my leave of them, I went from thence into Macedonia.

2 Co 8:23 Whether *any do enquire* of Titus, *he is* my partner and fellow-helper concerning you: or our brethren *be enquired of, they are* the messengers of the churches, *and* the glory of Christ.

Ga 1:2 And all the brethren which are with me, unto the churches of Galatia:

Ga 3:15 Brethren, I speak after the manner of men; Though *it be* but a man's covenant, yet *if it be* confirmed, no man disannulleth, or addeth thereto.

Ga 4:12 Brethren, I beseech you, be as I *am;* for I *am* as ye *are:* ye have not injured me at all.

Ga 5:11 And I, brethren, if I yet preach circumcision, why do I yet suffer persecution? then is the offence of the cross ceased.

Ga 6:1 Brethren, if a man be over-taken in a fault, ye which are spiritual, restore such an one in the spirit of meekness; considering thyself, lest thou also be tempted.

Ga 6:18 Brethren, the grace of our Lord Jesus Christ *be* with your spirit. Amen.

Ph 1:14 And many of the brethren in the Lord, waxing confident by my bonds, are much more bold to speak the word without fear.

Ph 2:25 Yet I supposed it necessary to send to you Epaphroditus, my brother, and companion in labour, and fellow soldier, but your messenger, and he that ministered to my wants.

Ph 3:1 Finally, my brethren, rejoice in the Lord. To write the same things to you, to me indeed *is* not grievous, but for you *it is* safe.

Ph 4:21 Salute every saint in Christ Jesus. The brethren which are with me greet you.

Col 1:2 To the saints and faithful brethren in Christ which are at Colosse: Grace *be* unto you, and peace, from God our Father and the Lord Jesus Christ.

Col 4:9 With Onesimus, a faithful and beloved brother, who is *one* of you. They shall make known unto you all things which *are done* here.

1 Th 1:4 Knowing, brethren beloved, your election of God.

1 Th 2:1 For yourselves, brethren, know our entrance in unto you, that it was not in vain:

1 Th 2:14 For ye, brethren, became followers of the churches of God which in Judaea are in Christ Jesus: for ye also have suffered like things of your own countrymen, even as they *have* of the Jews:

1 Th 4:10 And indeed ye do it toward all the brethren which are in all Macedonia: but we beseech you, brethren, that ye increase more and more;

1 Th 5:4 But ye, brethren, are not in darkness, that that day should overtake you as a thief.

1 Th 5:27 I charge you by the Lord that this epistle be read unto all the holy brethren.

2 Th 2:13 But we are bound to give thanks alway to God for you, brethren beloved of the Lord, because God hath from the beginning chosen you to salvation through sanctification of the Spirit and belief of the truth:

2 Th 3:1 Finally, brethren, pray for us, that the word of the Lord may have *free* course, and be glorified, even as *it is* with you:

1 Ti 5:1 Rebuke not an elder, but intreat *him* as a father; *and* the younger men as brethren;

1 Ti 6:2 And they that have believing masters, let them not despise *them,* because they are brethren; but rather do *them* service, because they are faithful and beloved, partakers of the benefit. These things teach and exhort.

2 Ti 4:21 Do thy diligence to come before winter. Eubulus greeteth thee, and Pudens, and Linus, and Claudia, and all the brethren.

Phm 1:16 Not now as a servant, but above a servant, a brother beloved, specially to me, but how much more unto thee, both in the flesh, and in the Lord?

He 2:11 For both he that sanctifieth and they who are sanctified *are* all of one: for which cause he is not ashamed to call them brethren,

He 2:17 Wherefore in all things it behoved him to be made like unto *his* brethren, that he might be a merciful and faithful high priest in things *pertaining* to God, to make reconciliation for the sins of the people.

He 3:1 Wherefore, holy brethren, partakers of the heavenly calling, consider the Apostle and High Priest of our profession, Christ Jesus;

Ja 1:2 My brethren, count it all joy when ye fall into divers temptations;

Ja 2:1 My brethren, have not the faith of our Lord Jesus Christ, *the Lord* of glory, with respect of persons.

Ja 4:11 Speak not evil one of another, brethren. He that speaketh evil of *his* brother, and judgeth his brother, speaketh evil of the law, and judgeth the law: but if thou judge the law, thou art not a doer of the law, but a judge.

3 Jn 5 Beloved, thou doest faithfully whatsoever thou doest to the brethren, and to strangers;

Re 12:10 And I heard a loud voice saying in heaven, Now is come salvation, and strength, and the kingdom of our God, and the power of his Christ: for the accuser of our brethren is cast down, which accused them before our God day and night.

Re 19:10 And I fell at his feet to worship him. And he said unto me, See *thou do it* not: I am thy fellowservant, and of thy brethren that have the testimony of Jesus: worship God: for the testimony of Jesus is the spirit of prophecy.

Re 22:9 Then saith he unto me, See *thou do it* not: for I am thy fellowservant, and of thy brethren the prophets, and of them which keep the sayings of this book: worship God.

12. Special Titles of Members

a. Children of God

De 14:1 Ye *are* the children of the LORD your God: ye shall not cut yourselves, nor make any baldness between your eyes for the dead.

Ps 82:6 I have said, Ye *are* gods; and all of you *are* children of the most High.

Mt 5:9 Blessed *are* the peacemakers: for they shall be called the children of God.

Mt 5:45 That ye may be the children of your Father which is in heaven: for he maketh his sun to rise on the evil and on the good, and sendeth rain on the just and on the unjust.

Mt 13:38 The field is the world; the good seed are the children of the kingdom; but the tares are the children of the wicked *one;*

Mk 2:19 And Jesus said unto them, Can the children of the bridechamber fast, while the bridegroom is with them? as long as they have the bridegroom with them, they cannot fast.

Lu 5:34–35 And he said unto them, Can ye make the children of the bridechamber fast, while the bridegroom is with them?

But love ye your enemies, and do good, and lend, hoping for nothing again; and your reward shall be great, and ye shall be the children of the Highest: for he is kind unto the unthankful and *to* the evil.

Lu 20:36 Neither can they die any more: for they are equal unto the angels; and are the children of God, being the children of the resurrection.

Jn 11:52 And not for that nation only, but that also he should gather together in one the children of God that were scattered abroad.

Jn 12:36 While ye have light, believe in the light, that ye may be the children of light. These things spake Jesus, and departed, and did hide himself from them.

Ro 8:16 The Spirit itself beareth witness with our spirit, that we are the children of God:

Ro 8:21 Because the creature itself also shall be delivered from the bondage of corruption into the glorious liberty of the children of God.

Ro 9:8 That is, They which are the children of the flesh, these *are* not the children of God: but the children of the promise are counted for the seed.

Ro 9:26 And it shall come to pass, *that* in the place where it was said unto them, Ye *are* not my people; there shall they be called the children of the living God.

Ga 3:26 For ye are all the children of God by faith in Christ Jesus.

Ep 1:5 Having predestinated us unto the adoption of children by Jesus Christ to himself, according to the good pleasure of his will,

Ep 2:19 Now therefore ye are no more strangers and foreigners, but fellowcitizens with the saints, and of the household of God;

1 Jn 3:10 In this the children of God are manifest, and the children of the devil: whosoever doeth not righteousness is not of God, neither he that loveth not his brother.

1 Jn 4:4 Ye are of God, little children, and have overcome them: because greater is he that is in you, than he that is in the world.

1 Jn 5:2 By this we know that we love the children of God, when we love God, and keep his commandments.

1 Jn 5:19 And we know that we are of God, and the whole world lieth in wickedness.

b. Heirs of God

Lu 15:31 And he said unto him, Son, thou art ever with me, and all that I have is thine.

Ro 4:13 For the promise, that he should be the heir of the world, *was* not to Abraham, or to his seed, through the law, but through the righteousness of faith.

Ro 8:17 And if children, then heirs; heirs of God, and joint-heirs with Christ; if so be that we suffer with *him,* that we may be also glorified together.

Ga 3:29 And if ye *be* Christ's, then are ye Abraham's seed, and heirs according to the promise.

Ga 4:7 Wherefore thou art no more a servant, but a son; and if a son, then an heir of God through Christ.

Ep 3:6 That the Gentiles should be fellowheirs, and of the same body, and partakers of his promise in Christ by the gospel:

Tit 3:7 That being justified by his grace, we should be made heirs according to the hope of eternal life.

He 1:14 Are they not all ministering spirits, sent forth to minister for them who shall be heirs of salvation?

He 6:17 Wherein God, willing more abundantly to shew unto the heirs of promise the immutability of his counsel, confirmed *it* by an oath:

He 11:7 By faith Noah, being warned of God of things not seen as yet, moved with fear, prepared an ark to the saving of his house; by the which he condemned the world, and became heir of the righteousness which is by faith.

Ja 2:5 Hearken, my beloved brethren, Hath not God chosen the poor of this world rich in faith, and heirs of the kingdom which he hath promised to them that love him?

1 Pe 1:4 To an inheritance incorruptible, and undefiled, and that fadeth not away, reserved in heaven for you,

1 Pe 3:7 Likewise, ye husbands, dwell with *them* according to knowledge, giving honour unto the wife, as unto the weaker vessel, and as being heirs together of the grace of life; that your prayers be not hindered.

Re 21:7 He that overcometh shall inherit all things; and I will be his God, and he shall be my son.

c. Sons of God

2 S 7:14 I will be his father, and he shall be my son. If he commit iniquity, I will chasten him with the rod of men, and with the stripes of the children of men:

Ho 1:10 Yet the number of the children of Israel shall be as the sand of the sea, which cannot be measured nor numbered; and it shall come to pass, *that* in the place where it was said unto them, Ye *are* not my people, *there* it shall be said unto them, *Ye are* the sons of the living God.

Jn 1:12 But as many as received him, to them gave he power to become the sons of God, *even* to them that believe on his name:

Ro 8:14 For as many as are led by the Spirit of God, they are the sons of God.

Ro 8:19 For the earnest expectation of the creature waiteth for the manifestation of the sons of God.

2 Co 6:18 And will be a Father unto you, and ye shall be my sons and daughters, saith the Lord Almighty.

Ga 4:7 Wherefore thou art no more a servant, but a son; and if a son, then an heir of God through Christ.

Ph 2:15 That ye may be blameless and harmless, the sons of God, without rebuke, in the midst of a crooked and perverse nation, among whom ye shine as lights in the world;

He 2:10 For it became him, for whom *are* all things, and by whom *are* all things, in bringing many sons unto glory, to make the captain of their salvation perfect through sufferings.

He 12:7 If ye endure chastening, God dealeth with you as with sons; for what son is he whom the father chasteneth not?

1 Jn 3:1 Behold, what manner of love the Father hath bestowed upon us, that we should be called the sons of God: therefore the world knoweth us not, because it knew him not.

Re 21:7 He that overcometh shall inherit all things; and I will be his God, and he shall be my son.

d. Children of Light

Mt 5:15 Neither do men light a candle, and put it under a bushel, but on a candlestick; and it giveth light unto all that are in the house.

Lu 16:8 And the lord commended the unjust steward, because he had done wisely: for the children of this world are in their generation wiser than the children of light.

Jn 3:21 But he that doeth truth cometh to the light, that his deeds may be made manifest, that they are wrought in God.

Jn 12:36 While ye have light, believe in the light, that ye may be the children of light. These things spake Jesus, and departed, and did hide himself from them.

Ep 5:8 For ye were sometimes darkness, but now *are ye* light in the Lord: walk as children of light:

Col 1:12 Giving thanks unto the Father, which hath made us meet to be partakers of the inheritance of the saints in light:

1 Th 5:5 Ye are all the children of light, and the children of the day: we are not of the night, nor of darkness.

See **TITLES AND NAMES**

13. Compared to a Flock

a. Scattered by Persecution and False Shepherds

Je 23:2 Therefore thus saith the LORD God of Israel against the pastors that feed my people; Ye have scattered my flock, and driven them away, and have not visited them: behold, I will visit upon you the evil of your doings, saith the LORD.

Eze 34:12 As a shepherd seeketh out his flock in the day that he is among his sheep *that are* scattered; so will I seek out my sheep, and will deliver them out of all places where they have been scattered in the cloudy and dark day.

Mt 9:36 But when he saw the multitudes, he was moved with compassion on them, because they fainted, and were scattered abroad, as sheep having no shepherd.

Mt 26:31 Then saith Jesus unto them, All ye shall be offended because of me this night: for it is written, I will smite the shepherd, and the sheep of the flock shall be scattered abroad.

Jn 10:12 But he that is an hireling, and not the shepherd, whose own the sheep are not, seeth the wolf coming, and leaveth the sheep, and fleeth: and the wolf catcheth them, and scattereth the sheep.

Jn 16:32 Behold, the hour cometh, yea, is now come, that ye shall be scattered, every man to his own, and shall leave me alone: and yet I am not alone, because the Father is with me.

Ac 8:1 And Saul was consenting unto his death. And at that time there was a great persecution against the church which was at Jerusalem; and they were all scattered abroad throughout the regions of Judaea and Samaria, except the apostles.

b. Ministers as Shepherds

Je 3:15 And I will give you pastors according to mine heart, which shall feed you with knowledge and understanding.

Je 23:4 And I will set up shepherds over them which shall feed them: and they shall fear no more, nor be dismayed, neither shall they be lacking, saith the LORD.

1 Pe 5:2 Feed the flock of God which is among you, taking the oversight *thereof*, not by constraint, but willingly; not for filthy lucre, but of a ready mind;

See **MINISTERS**

14. Its Government and Discipline

a. Authority

Je 1:10 See, I have this day set thee over the nations and over the kingdoms, to root out, and to pull down, and to destroy, and to throw down, to build, and to plant.

Je 6:27 I have set thee *for* a tower *and* a fortress among my people, that thou mayest know and try their way.

Eze 2:4 For *they are* impudent children and stiffhearted. I do send thee unto them; and thou shalt say unto them, Thus saith the Lord GOD.

Eze 3:8 Behold, I have made thy face strong against their faces, and thy forehead strong against their foreheads.

Eze 32:18 Son of man, wail for the multitude of Egypt, and cast them down, *even* her, and the daughters of the famous nations, unto the nether parts of the earth, with them that go down into the pit.

Mt 16:19 And I will give unto thee the keys of the kingdom of heaven: and whatsoever thou shalt bind on earth shall be bound in heaven: and whatsoever thou shalt loose on earth shall be loosed in heaven.

Mt 18:18 Verily I say unto you, Whatsoever ye shall bind on earth shall be bound in heaven: and whatsoever ye shall loose on earth shall be loosed in heaven.

Jn 20:23 Whose soever sins ye remit, they are remitted unto them; *and* whose soever *sins* ye retain, they are retained.

Ac 16:4 And as they went through the cities, they delivered them the decrees for to keep, that were ordained of the apostles and elders which were at Jerusalem.

1 Co 4:21 What will ye? shall I come unto you with a rod, or in love, and *in* the spirit of meekness?

1 Co 5:3 For I verily, as absent in body, but present in spirit, have judged already, as though I were present, *concerning* him that hath so done this deed,

1 Co 7:17 But as God hath distributed to every man, as the Lord hath called every one, so let him walk. And so ordain I in all churches.

1 Co 11:34 And if any man hunger, let him eat at home; that ye come not together unto condemnation. And the rest will I set in order when I come.

1 Co 14:37 If any man think himself to be a prophet, or spiritual, let him acknowledge that the things that I write unto you are the commandments of the Lord.

1 Co 16:1 Now concerning the collection for the saints, as I have given order to the churches of Galatia, even so do ye.

2 Co 1:23–24 Moreover I call God for a record upon my soul, that to spare you I came not as yet unto Corinth.

Not for that we have dominion over your faith, but are helpers of your joy: for by faith ye stand.

2 Co 10:8 For though I should boast somewhat more of our authority, which the Lord hath given us for edification, and not for your destruction, I should not be ashamed:

2 Co 13:2 I told you before, and foretell you, as if I were present, the second time; and being absent now I write to them which heretofore have sinned, and to all other, that, if I come again, I will not spare:

2 Co 13:10 Therefore I write these things being absent, lest being present I should use sharpness, according to the power which the Lord hath given me to edification, and not to destruction.

1 Ti 1:20 Of whom is Hymenaeus and Alexander; whom I have delivered unto Satan, that they may learn not to blaspheme.

Tit 2:15 These things speak, and exhort, and rebuke with all authority. Let no man despise thee.

Phm 8 Wherefore, though I might be much bold in Christ to enjoin thee that which is convenient,

He 13:17 Obey them that have the rule over you, and submit yourselves: for they watch for your souls, as they that must give account, that they may do it with joy, and not with grief: for that *is* unprofitable for you.

He 13:24 Salute all them that have the rule over you, and all the saints. They of Italy salute you.

2 Pe 3:2 That ye may be mindful of the words which were spoken before by the holy prophets, and of the commandment of us the apostles of the Lord and Saviour:

3 Jn 10 Wherefore, if I come, I will remember his deeds which he doeth, prating against us with malicious words: and not content therewith, neither doth he himself receive the brethren, and forbiddeth them that would, and casteth *them* out of the church.

See **SUBMISSION**

b. Discipline

Mt 13:29 But he said, Nay; lest while ye gather up the tares, ye root up also the wheat with them.

Mt 18:17 And if he shall neglect to hear them, tell *it* unto the church: but if he neglect to hear the church, let him be unto thee as an heathen man and a publican.

1 Co 5:5 To deliver such an one unto Satan for the destruction of the flesh, that the spirit may be saved in the day of the Lord Jesus.

1 Co 5:12–13 For what have I to do to judge them also that are without? do not ye judge them that are within?

But them that are without God judgeth. Therefore put away from among yourselves that wicked person.

2 Co 2:6 Sufficient to such a man is this punishment, which *was inflicted* of many.

2 Co 7:11 For behold this selfsame thing, that ye sorrowed after a godly sort, what carefulness it wrought in you, yea, *what* clearing of yourselves, yea, *what* indignation, yea, *what* fear, yea, *what* vehement desire, yea *what* zeal, yea, *what* revenge! In all *things* ye have approved yourselves to be clear in this matter.

2 Co 10:6 And having in a readiness to revenge all disobedience, when your obedience is fulfilled.

2 Co 13:2 I told you before, and foretell you, as if I were present, the second time; and being absent now I write to them which heretofore have sinned, and to all other, that, if I come again, I will not spare:

2 Co 13:10 Therefore I write these things being absent, lest being present

I should use sharpness, according to the power which the Lord hath given me to edification, and not to destruction.

Ga 5:12 I would they were even cut off which trouble you.

1 Ti 1:20 Of whom is Hymenaeus and Alexander; whom I have delivered unto Satan, that they may learn not to blaspheme.

Tit 3:10 A man that is an heretick after the first and second admonition reject;

Re 2:2 I know thy works, and thy labour, and thy patience, and how thou canst not bear them which are evil: and thou hast tried them which say they are apostles, and are not, and hast found them liars:

c. Government

Ac 15:6 And the apostles and elders came together for to consider of this matter.

Ac 15:28 For it seemed good to the Holy Ghost, and to us, to lay upon you no greater burden than these necessary things;

1 Co 7:17 But as God hath distributed to every man, as the Lord hath called every one, so let him walk. And so ordain I in all churches.

1 Co 11:34 And if any man hunger, let him eat at home; that ye come not together unto condemnation. And the rest will I set in order when I come.

1 Ti 3:5 (For if a man know not how to rule his own house, how shall he take care of the church of God?)

1 Ti 5:1 Rebuke not an elder, but intreat *him* as a father; *and* the younger men as brethren;

d. Excommunication

Ex 12:15 Seven days shall ye eat unleavened bread; even the first day ye shall put away leaven out of your houses: for whosoever eateth leavened bread from the first day until the seventh day, that soul shall be cut off from Israel.

Ex 12:19 Seven days shall there be no leaven found in your houses: for whosoever eateth that which is leavened, even that soul shall be cut off from the congregation of Israel, whether he be a stranger, or born in the land.

Ex 30:33 Whosoever compoundeth *any* like it, or whosoever putteth *any* of it upon a stranger, shall even be cut off from his people.

Ex 30:38 Whosoever shall make like unto that, to smell thereto, shall even be cut off from his people.

Le 7:20 But the soul that eateth *of* the flesh of the sacrifice of peace offerings, that *pertain* unto the LORD, having his uncleanness upon him, even that soul shall be cut off from his people.

Le 7:27 Whatsoever soul *it be* that eateth any manner of blood, even that soul shall be cut off from his people.

Le 17:4 And bringeth it not unto the door of the tabernacle of the congregation, to offer an offering unto the LORD before the tabernacle of the LORD; blood shall be imputed unto that man; he hath shed blood; and that man shall be cut off from among his people:

Le 17:9 And bringeth it not unto the door of the tabernacle of the congregation, to offer it unto the LORD; even that man shall be cut off from among his people.

Le 17:14 For *it is* the life of all flesh; the blood of it *is* for the life thereof: therefore I said unto the children of Israel, Ye shall not eat the blood of no manner of flesh: for the life of all flesh *is* the blood thereof: whosoever eateth it shall be cut off.

Le 22:3 Say unto them, Whosoever *he be* of all your seed among your generations, that goeth unto the holy things, which the children of Israel hallow unto the LORD, having his uncleanness upon him, that soul shall be cut off from my presence: I *am* the LORD.

Le 23:29 For whatsoever soul *it be* that shall not be afflicted in that same day, he shall be cut off from among his people.

Nu 9:13 But the man that *is* clean, and is not in a journey, and forbeareth to keep the passover, even the same soul shall be cut off from among his people: because he brought not the

offering of the LORD in his appointed season, that man shall bear his sin.

Nu 19:13 Whosoever toucheth the dead body of any man that is dead, and purifieth not himself, defileth the tabernacle of the LORD; and that soul shall be cut off from Israel: because the water of separation was not sprinkled upon him, he shall be unclean; his uncleanness *is* yet upon him.

Nu 19:20 But the man that shall be unclean, and shall not purify himself, that soul shall be cut off from among the congregation, because he hath defiled the sanctuary of the LORD: the water of separation hath not been sprinkled upon him; he *is* unclean.

Lu 6:22 Blessed are ye, when men shall hate you, and when they shall separate you *from their company,* and shall reproach *you,* and cast out your name as evil, for the Son of man's sake.

Jn 9:22 These *words* spake his parents, because they feared the Jews: for the Jews had agreed already, that if any man did confess that he was Christ, he should be put out of the synagogue.

Jn 9:34 They answered and said unto him, Thou wast altogether born in sins, and dost thou teach us? And they cast him out.

Jn 12:42 Nevertheless among the chief rulers also many believed on him; but because of the Pharisees they did not confess *him,* lest they should be put out of the synagogue:

Jn 16:2 They shall put you out of the synagogues: yea, the time cometh, that whosoever killeth you will think that he doeth God service.

1 Co 5:5 To deliver such an one unto Satan for the destruction of the flesh, that the spirit may be saved in the day of the Lord Jesus.

15. Officers

a. Deacons

Ac 6:3 Wherefore, brethren, look ye out among you seven men of honest report, full of the Holy Ghost and wisdom, whom we may appoint over this business.

Ph 1:1 Paul and Timotheus, the servants of Jesus Christ, to all the saints in Christ Jesus which are at Philippi, with the bishops and deacons:

1 Ti 3:8 Likewise *must* the deacons *be* grave, not doubletongued, not given to much wine, not greedy of filthy lucre;

b. Elders

Ac 11:30 Which also they did, and sent it to the elders by the hands of Barnabas and Saul.

Ac 14:23 And when they had ordained them elders in every church, and had prayed with fasting, they commended them to the Lord, on whom they believed.

Ac 15:2 When therefore Paul and Barnabas had no small dissension and disputation with them, they determined that Paul and Barnabas, and certain other of them, should go up to Jerusalem unto the apostles and elders about this question.

Ac 15:22 Then pleased it the apostles and elders, with the whole church, to send chosen men of their own company to Antioch with Paul and Barnabas; *namely,* Judas surnamed Barsabas, and Silas, chief men among the brethren:

Ac 16:4 And as they went through the cities, they delivered them the decrees for to keep, that were ordained of the apostles and elders which were at Jerusalem.

Ac 20:17 And from Miletus he sent to Ephesus, and called the elders of the church.

Ac 21:18 And the *day* following Paul went in with us unto James; and all the elders were present.

1 Ti 5:17 Let the elders that rule well be counted worthy of double honour, especially they who labour in the word and doctrine.

Tit 1:5 For this cause left I thee in Crete, that thou shouldest set in order the things that are wanting, and ordain elders in every city, as I had appointed thee:

Ja 5:14 Is any sick among you? let him call for the elders of the church;

and let them pray over him, anointing him with oil in the name of the Lord:

1 Pe 5:1 The elders which are among you I exhort, who am also an elder, and a witness of the sufferings of Christ, and also a partaker of the glory that shall be revealed:

2 Jn 1 The elder unto the elect lady and her children, whom I love in the truth; and not I only, but also all they that have known the truth;

c. Bishops, or Overseers

Ph 1:1 Paul and Timotheus, the servants of Jesus Christ, to all the saints in Christ Jesus which are at Philippi, with the bishops and deacons:

1 Ti 3:1 This *is* a true saying, If a man desire the office of a bishop, he desireth a good work.

Tit 1:7 For a bishop must be blameless, as the steward of God; not selfwilled, not soon angry, not given to wine, no striker, not given to filthy lucre;

See **LEADER**

16. Its Sacraments

a. Baptism

1). Of Believers

Mt 28:19 Go ye therefore, and teach all nations, baptizing them in the name of the Father, and of the Son, and of the Holy Ghost:

Mk 16:16 He that believeth and is baptized shall be saved; but he that believeth not shall be damned.

Jn 3:5 Jesus answered, Verily, verily, I say unto thee, Except a man be born of water and *of* the Spirit, he cannot enter into the kingdom of God.

Jn 3:22 After these things came Jesus and his disciples into the land of Judaea; and there he tarried with them, and baptized.

Jn 4:2 (Though Jesus himself baptized not, but his disciples,)

Ac 2:38 Then Peter said unto them, Repent, and be baptized every one of you in the name of Jesus Christ for the remission of sins, and ye shall receive the gift of the Holy Ghost.

Ac 10:48 And he commanded them to be baptized in the name of the Lord. Then prayed they him to tarry certain days.

Ac 22:16 And now why tarriest thou? arise, and be baptized, and wash away thy sins, calling on the name of the Lord.

2). Significance

Ro 6:3 Know ye not, that so many of us as were baptized into Jesus Christ were baptized into his death?

1 Co 1:13 Is Christ divided? was Paul crucified for you? or were ye baptized in the name of Paul?

1 Co 12:13 For by one Spirit are we all baptized into one body, whether *we be* Jews or Gentiles, whether *we be* bond or free; and have been all made to drink into one Spirit.

Ga 3:27 For as many of you as have been baptized into Christ have put on Christ.

Col 2:12 Buried with him in baptism, wherein also ye are risen with *him* through the faith of the operation of God, who hath raised him from the dead.

He 6:2 Of the doctrine of baptisms, and of laying on of hands, and of resurrection of the dead, and of eternal judgment.

1 Pe 3:21 The like figure whereunto *even* baptism doth also now save us (not the putting away of the filth of the flesh, but the answer of a good conscience toward God,) by the resurrection of Jesus Christ:

3). Examples

BELIEVERS AT PENTECOST

Ac 2:41 Then they that gladly received his word were baptized: and the same day there were added *unto them* about three thousand souls.

CONVERTS IN SAMARIA

Ac 8:12 But when they believed Philip preaching the things concerning the kingdom of God, and the name of Jesus Christ, they were baptized, both men and women.

THE ETHIOPIAN EUNUCH

Ac 8:38 And he commanded the chariot to stand still: and they went down both into the water, both Philip and the eunuch; and he baptized him.

SAUL OF TARSUS

Ac 9:18 And immediately there fell from his eyes as it had been scales: and he received sight forthwith, and arose, and was baptized.

LYDIA OF THYATIRA

Ac 16:15 And when she was baptized, and her household, she besought *us,* saying, If ye have judged me to be faithful to the Lord, come into my house, and abide *there.* And she constrained us.

PHILIPPIAN JAILER AND HOUSEHOLD

Ac 16:33 And he took them the same hour of the night, and washed *their* stripes; and was baptized, he and all his, straightway.

BELIEVERS IN CORINTH

Ac 18:8 And Crispus, the chief ruler of the synagogue, believed on the Lord with all his house; and many of the Corinthians hearing believed, and were baptized.

EPHESIAN DISCIPLES

Ac 19:5 When they heard *this,* they were baptized in the name of the Lord Jesus.

4). Of Christ

Mt 3:13 Then cometh Jesus from Galilee to Jordan unto John, to be baptized of him.

Mk 1:9 And it came to pass in those days, that Jesus came from Nazareth of Galilee, and was baptized of John in Jordan.

Lu 3:21 Now when all the people were baptized, it came to pass, that Jesus also being baptized, and praying, the heaven was opened,

Jn 3:23 And John also was baptizing in Aenon near to Salim, because there was much water there: and they came, and were baptized.

1 Jn 5:6 This is he that came by water and blood, *even* Jesus Christ; not by water only, but by water and blood. And it is the Spirit that beareth witness, because the Spirit is truth.

5). By John the Baptist

Mt 3:6 And were baptized of him in Jordan, confessing their sins.

Mt 3:11 I indeed baptize you with water unto repentance: but he that cometh after me is mightier than I, whose shoes I am not worthy to bear: he shall baptize you with the Holy Ghost, and *with* fire:

Mt 21:25 The baptism of John, whence was it? from heaven, or of men? And they reasoned with themselves, saying, If we shall say, From heaven; he will say unto us, Why did ye not then believe him?

Mk 1:4 John did baptize in the wilderness, and preach the baptism of repentance for the remission of sins.

Mk 1:8 I indeed have baptized you with water: but he shall baptize you with the Holy Ghost.

Mk 11:30 The baptism of John, was *it* from heaven, or of men? answer me.

Lu 3:3 And he came into all the country about Jordan, preaching the baptism of repentance for the remission of sins;

Lu 3:7 Then said he to the multitude that came forth to be baptized of him, O generation of vipers, who hath warned you to flee from the wrath to come?

Lu 3:12 Then came also publicans to be baptized, and said unto him, Master, what shall we do?

Lu 3:16 John answered, saying unto *them* all, I indeed baptize you with water; but one mightier than I cometh, the latchet of whose shoes I am not worthy to unloose: he shall baptize you with the Holy Ghost and with fire:

Lu 7:29 And all the people that heard *him,* and the publicans, justified God, being baptized with the baptism of John.

Lu 20:4 The baptism of John, was it from heaven, or of men?

Jn 1:26 John answered them, saying, I baptize with water: but there standeth one among you, whom ye know not;

Jn 1:31 And I knew him not: but that he should be made manifest to Israel, therefore am I come baptizing with water.

Jn 3:23 And John also was baptizing in Aenon near to Salim, because there was much water there: and they came, and were baptized.

Jn 10:40 And went away again beyond Jordan into the place where John at first baptized; and there he abode.

Ac 1:5 For John truly baptized with water; but ye shall be baptized with the Holy Ghost not many days hence.

Ac 1:22 Beginning from the baptism of John, unto that same day that he was taken up from us, must one be ordained to be a witness with us of his resurrection.

Ac 10:37 That word, *I say,* ye know, which was published throughout all Judaea, and began from Galilee, after the baptism which John preached;

Ac 11:16 Then remembered I the word of the Lord, how that he said, John indeed baptized with water; but ye shall be baptized with the Holy Ghost.

Ac 13:24 When John had first preached before his coming the baptism of repentance to all the people of Israel.

Ac 18:25 This man was instructed in the way of the Lord; and being fervent in the spirit, he spake and taught diligently the things of the Lord, knowing only the baptism of John.

Ac 19:3 And he said unto them, Unto what then were ye baptized? And they said, Unto John's baptism.

b. The Lord's Supper

Mt 26:26 And as they were eating, Jesus took bread, and blessed *it,* and brake *it,* and gave *it* to the disciples, and said, Take, eat; this is my body.

Mk 14:22 And as they did eat, Jesus took bread, and blessed, and brake *it,* and gave to them, and said, Take, eat: this is my body.

Lu 22:19 And he took bread, and gave thanks, and brake *it,* and gave unto them, saying, This is my body which is given for you: this do in remembrance of me.

1 Co 10:16 The cup of blessing which we bless, is it not the communion of the blood of Christ? The bread which we break, is it not the communion of the body of Christ?

1 Co 10:21 Ye cannot drink the cup of the Lord, and the cup of devils: ye cannot be partakers of the Lord's table, and of the table of devils.

1 Co 11:20 When ye come together therefore into one place, *this* is not to eat the Lord's supper.

1 Co 11:23 For I have received of the Lord that which also I delivered unto you, That the Lord Jesus the *same* night in which he was betrayed took bread:

17. Metaphors

1—A BUILDING

1 Co 3:9 For we are labourers together with God: ye are God's husbandry, *ye are* God's building.

CHRIST THE BUILDER

Mt 16:18 And I say also unto thee, That thou art Peter, and upon this rock I will build my church; and the gates of hell shall not prevail against it.

CHRIST THE CORNERSTONE

Ep 2:19–20 Now therefore ye are no more strangers and foreigners, but fellowcitizens with the saints, and of the household of God;

And are built upon the foundation of the apostles and prophets, Jesus Christ himself being the chief corner *stone;*

2—A LIVING BODY

1 Co 12:27 Now ye are the body of Christ, and members in particular.

CHRIST THE HEAD

Col 2:19 And not holding the Head, from which all the body by joints and bands having nourishment minis-tered, and knit together, increaseth with the increase of God.

3—A FLOCK

Lu 12:32 Fear not, little flock; for it is your Father's good pleasure to give you the kingdom.

CHRIST THE SHEPHERD

Jn 10:11 I am the good shepherd: the good shepherd giveth his life for the sheep.

4—A BRIDE

Re 21:2 And I John saw the holy city, new Jerusalem, coming down from God out of heaven, prepared as a bride adorned for her husband.

CHRIST THE BRIDEGROOM

Jn 3:29 He that hath the bride is the bridegroom: but the friend of the bridegroom, which standeth and heareth him, rejoiceth greatly because of the bridegroom's voice: this my joy therefore is fulfilled.

5—BRANCHES OF THE VINE

Jn 15:2 Every branch in me that beareth not fruit he taketh away: and every *branch* that beareth fruit, he purgeth it, that it may bring forth more fruit.

6—A TEMPLE

1 Co 3:16 Know ye not that ye are the temple of God, and *that* the Spirit of God dwelleth in you?

CHRIST THE HIGH PRIEST

He 4:15 For we have not an high priest which cannot be touched with the feeling of our infirmities; but was in all points tempted like as *we are,* yet without sin.

18. Church Order, rules and disciplines designed to ensure smooth and effective operation of local assemblies

1 Co 7:17 But as God hath distributed to every man, as the Lord hath called every one, so let him walk. And so ordain I in all churches.

1 Co 11:34 And if any man hunger, let him eat at home; that ye come not together unto condemnation. And the rest will I set in order when I come.
1 Co 14:23 If therefore the whole church be come together into one place, and all speak with tongues, and there come in *those that are* unlearned, or unbelievers, will they not say that ye are mad?
1 Co 14:40 Let all things be done decently and in order.

19. Seven Churches in Asia

Re 1:4, 11, 20; 2:7, 11, 17, 29; 3:1, 6–7, 13, 22

CILICIA, *a province of Asia Minor*

Ac 6:9; 15:23, 41; 21:39; 22:3; 23:34; 27:5; Ga 1:21

CINNAMON, *a spice*

Ex 30:23; Pr 7:17; Song 4:14; Re 18:13

CIRCUMCISION, *cutting away the foreskin, performed on all Hebrew males on the eighth day*

Ge 17:10, 14, 23; 21:4; 34:15, 22; Ex 4:25; 12:44; Le 12:3; Jos 5:3, 7; Lu 1:59; 2:21; Jn 7:22; Ac 7:8; 15:1; 16:3; 21:21; Ro 2:25; 3:1; 4:11; 1 Co 7:18; Ga 2:3; 5:2; 6:12; Ph 3:5

1. Spiritual

De 10:16; 30:6; Je 4:4; 9:26; Eze 44:9; Ac 7:51; Ro 2:29; Col 2:11

2. Name, given to the Jews

Ac 10:45; 11:2; Ro 3:30; 4:9; 15:8; Ga 2:8, 9, 12; Ep 2:11; Ph 3:3; Col 4:11

CISTERNS, *reservoirs dug out for the collection of water*

2 K 18:31; 2 Chr 26:10; Ec 12:6; Je 2:13; 14:3

CITIES, *permanent settlements*

As centers of commerce and culture, cities have always been places for God's people to use or lose their faith. The most important city in the Bible is Jerusalem, but many others are significant in God's dealings with mankind.

Ge 11:4; 18:24; 41:48; 47:21; Le 25:29; Nu 13:28; 31:10; 32:16; De 6:10; 13:12; 21:2; Jos 11:21; 16:9; 21:2; 24:13; Jud 21:23; 2 K 13:25; Ps 55:9; Mi 5:14

1. Fenced, fortified

Nu 32:17; De 3:5; 9:1; Jos 10:20; 19:35; 1 S 6:18; 2 K 3:19; 10:2; 18:13; 2 Chr 12:4; 14:6; 17:2, 19; 19:5; 21:3; 32:1; 33:14; Je 5:17; 34:7; Ho 8:14; Zep 1:16

2. Of Refuge

Ex 21:13; Nu 35:6, 13, 26; De 4:42; 19:3; Jos 20:2, 9; 21:13, 21, 27, 32, 38; 1 Chr 6:57, 67; He 6:18

CITIZENS, ROMAN, *those who can claim protection from Rome*

Ac 16:37, 38; 21:39; 22:25; 23:27; 25:10

CIVIC DUTIES   See NATION

CIVIL SERVICE   See NATION

CLAUDIUS LYSIAS, *a Roman military officer*

Ac 21:33; 22:24; 23:10, 26

CLAY, *man in the hands of God*

Jb 10:9; 33:6; Ps 33:15; Is 29:16; 45:9; 64:8; Je 18:6; 43:9; Da 2:34; Jn 9:6; Ro 9:21

CLEANLINESS, *purity*

1. Commanded

Ge 35:2; Ex 30:19; Le 13:6, 34, 58; 14:9; Nu 8:7; Ru 3:3; Mt 6:17; He 10:22

2. Examples

Ge 18:4; 43:24; Ex 2:5; 19:14; 2 S 12:20; Ne 4:23; Mk 7:3

CLEANSING, *being washed, purified*

1. Ceremonial

Ex 19:10; 30:20; 40:12, 31; Le 8:6; 13:35; 14:8, 17, 52; 15:6, 10, 13, 22, 27; 16:4, 24, 26; 17:15; 22:6; Nu 8:6, 15; 19:7, 19; De 23:11; 2 Chr 30:17; Ezr 6:20; Ne 12:30; 13:22; Eze 39:16; 43:20; 44:26; Mk 1:44; 7:3; Lu 5:14; 17:14; He 9:10

2. Spiritual, Prescribed

2 K 5:14 Then went he down, and dipped himself seven times in Jordan, according to the saying of the man of God: and his flesh came again like unto the flesh of a little child, and he was clean.

2 Chr 34:5 And he burnt the bones of the priests upon their altars, and cleansed Judah and Jerusalem.

Is 1:16 Wash you, make you clean; put away the evil of your doings from before mine eyes; cease to do evil;

Je 4:4 Circumcise yourselves to the LORD, and take away the foreskins of your heart, ye men of Judah and inhabitants of Jerusalem: lest my fury come forth like fire, and burn that none can quench it, because of the evil of your doings.

Je 4:14 O Jerusalem, wash thine heart from wickedness, that thou mayest be saved. How long shall thy vain thoughts lodge within thee?

Ac 22:16 And now why tarriest thou? arise, and be baptized, and wash away thy sins, calling on the name of the Lord.

1 Co 5:7 Purge out therefore the old leaven, that ye may be a new lump, as ye are unleavened. For even Christ our passover is sacrificed for us:

2 Co 7:1 Having therefore these promises, dearly beloved, let us cleanse ourselves from all filthiness of the flesh and spirit, perfecting holiness in the fear of God.

2 Ti 2:21 If a man therefore purge himself from these, he shall be a vessel unto honour, sanctified, and meet for the master's use, and prepared unto every good work.

Ja 4:8 Draw nigh to God, and he will draw nigh to you. Cleanse your hands, ye sinners; and purify your hearts, ye double minded.

1 Jn 3:3 And every man that hath this hope in him purifieth himself, even as he is pure.

3. Spiritual, Promised

2 K 5:10 And Elisha sent a messenger unto him, saying, Go and wash in the Jordan seven times, and thy flesh shall come again to thee, and thou shalt be clean.

Ps 65:3 Iniquities prevail against me: as for our transgressions, thou shalt purge them away.

Is 1:18 Come now, and let us reason together, saith the LORD: though your sins be as scarlet, they shall be as white as snow; though they be red like crimson, they shall be as wool.

Eze 36:25 Then will I sprinkle clean water upon you, and ye shall be clean: from all your filthiness, and from all your idols, will I cleanse you.

Zec 13:1 In that day there shall be a fountain opened to the house of David and to the inhabitants of Jerusalem for sin and for uncleanness.

Mal 3:3 And he shall sit as a refiner and purifier of silver: and he shall purify the sons of Levi, and purge them as gold and silver, that they may offer unto the LORD an offering in righteousness.

Ep 5:25–26 Husbands, love your wives, even as Christ also loved the church, and gave himself for it;

That he might sanctify and cleanse it with the washing of water by the word,

Tit 3:5 Not by works of righteousness which we have done, but according to his mercy he saved us, by the washing of regeneration, and renewing of the Holy Ghost;

He 9:14 How much more shall the blood of Christ, who through the eternal Spirit offered himself without spot to God, purge your conscience from dead works to serve the living God?

1 Jn 1:7 But if we walk in the light, as he is in the light, we have fellowship one with another, and the blood of Jesus Christ his Son cleanseth us from all sin.

Re 1:5 And from Jesus Christ, who is the faithful witness, and the first begotten of the dead, and the prince of the kings of the earth. Unto him that loved us, and washed us from our sins in his own blood,

4. Requests

Ps 19:12 Who can understand *his* errors? cleanse thou me from secret *faults.*

Ps 51:2 Wash me throughly from mine iniquity, and cleanse me from my sin.

Ps 51:7 Purge me with hyssop, and I shall be clean: wash me, and I shall be whiter than snow.

Ps 79:9 Help us, O God of our salvation, for the glory of thy name: and deliver us, and purge away our sins, for thy name's sake.

Jn 13:9 Simon Peter saith unto him, Lord, not my feet only, but also *my* hands and *my* head.

5. Examples

Is 6:7 And he laid *it* upon my mouth, and said, Lo, this hath touched thy lips; and thine iniquity is taken away, and thy sin purged.

Eze 16:9 Then washed I thee with water; yea, I throughly washed away thy blood from thee, and I anointed thee with oil.

Zec 3:4 And he answered and spake unto those that stood before him, saying, Take away the filthy garments from him. And unto him he said, Behold, I have caused thine iniquity to pass from thee, and I will clothe thee with change of raiment.

Jn 15:3 Now ye are clean through the word which I have spoken unto you.

1 Co 6:11 And such were some of you: but ye are washed, but ye are sanctified, but ye are justified in the name of the Lord Jesus, and by the Spirit of our God.

Re 7:14 And I said unto him, Sir, thou knowest. And he said to me, These are they which came out of great tribulation, and have washed their robes, and made them white in the blood of the Lamb.

See **DEFILEMENT**

CLEOPAS, *a disciple to whom Jesus appeared after his resurrection*

Lu 24:18

CLOAKS See **DRESS**

CLOSET, *room*

Jl 2:16; Mt 6:6; Lu 12:3

CLOTH, *woven material, used primarily for covering*

Mt 9:16; 27:59; Mk 14:51

CLOTHING See **DRESS**

CLOUD, *appearance of the Lord in*

Ex 19:9, 16; 34:5; Nu 11:25; 12:5; De 4:11; 5:22; Jb 26:9; Ps 18:11; 97:2; Eze 1:4; 10:4; Na 1:3; Mt 17:5; Mk 9:7; Lu 9:34; 21:27; Ac 1:9; Re 1:7; 11:12; 14:14

See **WEATHER**

COATS See **DRESS**

COCK

Mt 26:34, 74; Mk 14:68; Lu 22:60; Jn 13:38

See **ANIMALS**

COCKATRICE, *adder*

See **REPTILES**

COLD See **WEATHER**

COLLECTIONS, *offerings*

1 Co 16:1; 2 Chr 24:6

See **GIVING, KINDNESS, LOVE, POOR, RICHES**

COLOSSIANS

Author: The apostle Paul.

Date Written: Probably written from Rome between A.D. 60 and 64.

Purpose:

(1) General, a message of goodwill to exhort and edify believers.

(2) Special, to counteract doctrinal errors growing out of the mixture of Judaistic teaching combined with the vagaries of oriental and philosophic speculation. These heresies tended to obscure the divine glory of Christ.

To Whom Written: The church in Colosse, a city of Asia Minor.

Main Themes: The epistle resembles Ephesians, both in thought and language, yet has a distinct message of its own. In Ephesians Paul dwells on the thought of the church as the body of Christ, while in Colossians he emphasizes Christ as the head of the church. The warning against trusting in worldly wisdom that appears in 1 Corinthians reappears in Colossians.

Key Words: Christ the Head of All (2:10).

Key Verses: 2:9–10.

COMFORT, *to console in time of grief or fear*

1. From God

Jb 15:11 *Are* the consolations of God small with thee? is there any secret thing with thee?

Ps 71:21 Thou shalt increase my greatness, and comfort me on every side.

Ps 86:17 Shew me a token for good; that they which hate me may see *it*, and be ashamed: because thou, LORD, hast holpen me, and comforted me.

Ps 94:19 In the multitude of my thoughts within me thy comforts delight my soul.

Ps 119:50 This *is* my comfort in my affliction: for thy word hath quickened me.

Ps 119:76 Let, I pray thee, thy merciful kindness be for my comfort, according to thy word unto thy servant.

Ps 147:3 He healeth the broken in heart, and bindeth up their wounds.

Is 12:1 And in that day thou shalt say, O LORD, I will praise thee: though thou wast angry with me, thine anger is turned away, and thou comfortedst me.

Is 49:13 Sing, O heavens; and be joyful, O earth; and break forth into singing, O mountains: for the LORD hath comforted his people, and will have mercy upon his afflicted.

Is 51:3 For the LORD shall comfort Zion: he will comfort all her waste places; and he will make her wilderness like Eden, and her desert like the garden of the LORD; joy and gladness shall be found therein, thanksgiving, and the voice of melody.

Is 51:12 I, *even* I, *am* he that comforteth you: who *art* thou, that thou shouldest be afraid of a man *that* shall die, and of the son of man *which* shall be made as grass;

Is 52:9 Break forth into joy, sing together, ye waste places of Jerusalem: for the LORD hath comforted his people, he hath redeemed Jerusalem.

Is 54:11 O thou afflicted, tossed with tempest, *and* not comforted, behold, I will lay thy stones with fair colors, and lay thy foundations with sapphires.

Is 61:2 To proclaim the acceptable year of the LORD, and the day of vengeance of our God; to comfort all that mourn;

Is 66:13 As one whom his mother comforteth, so will I comfort you; and ye shall be comforted in Jerusalem.

Je 31:13 Then shall the virgin rejoice in the dance, both young men and old together: for I will turn their mourning into joy, and will comfort them, and make them rejoice from their sorrow.

Eze 14:22 Yet, behold, therein shall be left a remnant that shall be brought forth, *both* sons and daughters: behold, they shall come forth unto you, and ye shall see their way and their doings: and ye shall be comforted concerning the evil that I have brought upon Jerusalem, *even* concerning all that I have brought upon it.

Ho 2:14 Therefore, behold, I will allure her, and bring her into the wilderness, and speak comfortably unto her.

Zec 1:13 And the LORD answered the angel that talked with me *with* good words *and* comfortable words.

Zec 1:17 Cry yet, saying, Thus saith the LORD of hosts; My cities through prosperity shall yet be spread abroad; and the LORD shall yet comfort Zion, and shall yet choose Jerusalem.

Ro 15:5 Now the God of patience and consolation grant you to be likeminded one toward another according to Christ Jesus:

2 Co 1:3 Blessed *be* God, even the Father of our Lord Jesus Christ, the Father of mercies, and the God of all comfort;

2 Co 7:6 Nevertheless God, that comforteth those that are cast down, comforted us by the coming of Titus;

2 Th 2:16 Now our Lord Jesus Christ himself, and God, even our Father, which hath loved us, and hath given *us* everlasting consolation and good hope through grace,

2 Th 2:17 Comfort your hearts, and stablish you in every good word and work.

See **ASSURANCE, SECURITY**

2. From Christ

Mt 9:22 But Jesus turned him about, and when he saw her, he said, Daughter, be of good comfort; thy faith hath made thee whole. And the woman was made whole from that hour.

Mt 14:27 But straightway Jesus spake unto them, saying, Be of good cheer; it is I; be not afraid.

Mk 5:34 And he said unto her, Daughter, thy faith hath made thee whole; go in peace, and be whole of thy plague.

Mk 5:36 As soon as Jesus heard the word that was spoken, he saith unto the ruler of the synagogue, Be not afraid, only believe.

Mk 6:50 For they all saw him, and were troubled. And immediately he talked with them, and saith unto them, Be of good cheer: it is I; be not afraid.

Lu 4:18 The Spirit of the Lord is upon me, because he hath anointed me to preach the gospel to the poor; he hath sent me to heal the brokenhearted, to preach deliverance to the captives, and recovering of sight to the blind, to set at liberty them that are bruised,

Lu 7:13 And when the Lord saw her, he had compassion on her, and said unto her, Weep not.

Lu 8:48 And he said unto her, Daughter, be of good comfort: thy faith hath made thee whole; go in peace.

Lu 8:52 And all wept, and bewailed her: but he said, Weep not; she is not dead, but sleepeth.

Lu 24:38 And he said unto them, Why are ye troubled? and why do thoughts arise in your hearts?

Jn 6:20 But he saith unto them, It is I; be not afraid.

Jn 14:1 Let not your heart be troubled: ye believe in God, believe also in me.

Jn 14:18 I will not leave you comfortless: I will come to you.

Jn 14:27 Peace I leave with you, my peace I give unto you: not as the world giveth, give I unto you. Let not your heart be troubled, neither let it be afraid.

Jn 16:22 And ye now therefore have sorrow: but I will see you again, and your heart shall rejoice, and your joy no man taketh from you.

Jn 16:33 These things I have spoken unto you, that in me ye might have peace. In the world ye shall have tribulation: but be of good cheer; I have overcome the world.

2 Co 1:5 For as the sufferings of Christ abound in us, so our consolation also aboundeth by Christ.

Ph 2:1 If *there be* therefore any consolation in Christ, if any comfort of love, if any fellowship of the Spirit, if any bowels and mercies,

2 Th 2:16 Now our Lord Jesus Christ himself, and God, even our Father, which hath loved us, and hath given *us* everlasting consolation and good hope through grace,

See **CHRIST, WORD OF GOD**

3. Duty of Administering

Is 40:1 Comfort ye, comfort ye my people, saith your God.

Ac 16:40 And they went out of the prison, and entered into *the house of* Lydia and when they had seen the brethren, they comforted them, and departed.

1 Co 14:3 But he that prophesieth speaketh unto men *to* edification, and exhortation, and comfort.

1 Co 14:31 For ye may all prophesy one by one, that all may learn, and all may be comforted.

2 Co 1:4 Who comforteth us in all our tribulation, that we may be able to comfort them which are in any trouble, by the comfort wherewith we ourselves are comforted of God.

2 Co 2:7 So that contrariwise ye *ought* rather to forgive *him,* and comfort *him,* lest perhaps such a one should be swallowed up with overmuch sorrow.

2 Co 7:7 And not by his coming only, but by the consolation wherewith he was comforted in you, when he told us your earnest desire, your mourning, your fervent mind toward me; so that I rejoiced the more.

Ep 6:22 Whom I have sent unto you for the same purpose, that ye might know our affairs, and *that* he might comfort your hearts.

Col 2:2 That their hearts might be comforted, being knit together in love, and unto all riches of the full assurance of understanding, to the acknowledgement of the mystery of God, and of the Father, and of Christ;

Col 4:8 Whom I have sent unto you for the same purpose, that he might know your estate, and comfort your hearts;

1 Th 2:11 As ye know how we exhorted and comforted and charged every one of you, as a father *doth* his children,

1 Th 3:2 And sent Timotheus, our brother, and minister of God, and our fellowlabourer in the gospel of Christ, to establish you, and to comfort you concerning your faith:

1 Th 4:18 Wherefore comfort one another with these words.

1 Th 5:11 Wherefore comfort yourselves together, and edify one another, even as also ye do.

1 Th 5:14 Now we exhort you, brethren, warn them that are unruly, comfort the feebleminded, support the weak, be patient toward all *men.*

4. Examples

Ge 37:35 And all his sons and all his daughters rose up to comfort him; but he refused to be comforted; and he said, For I will go down into the grave unto my son mourning. Thus his father wept for him.

Ge 50:21 Now therefore fear ye not: I will nourish you, and your little ones. And he comforted them, and spake kindly unto them.

Ru 2:13 Then she said, Let me find favour in thy sight, my lord; for that thou hast comforted me, and for that thou hast spoken friendly unto thine handmaid, though I be not like unto one of thine handmaidens.

1 S 1:8 Then said Elkanah her husband to her, Hannah, why weepest thou? and why eatest thou not? and why is thy heart grieved? *am* not I better to thee than ten sons?

2 S 10:2 Then said David, I will shew kindness unto Hanun the son of Nahash, as his father shewed kindness unto me. And David sent to comfort him by the hand of his servants for his father. And David's servants came into the land of the children of Ammon.

2 S 12:24 And David comforted Bath-sheba his wife, and went in unto her, and lay with her: and she bare a son, and he called his name Solomon: and the LORD loved him.

1 Chr 7:22 And Ephraim their father mourned many days, and his brethren came to comfort him.

1 Chr 19:2 And David said, I will shew kindness unto Hanun the son of Nahash, because his father shewed kindness to me. And David sent messengers to comfort him concerning his father. So the servants of David came into the land of the children of Ammon to Hanun, to comfort him.

Jb 2:11 Now when Job's three friends heard of all this evil that was come upon him, they came every one from his own place; Eliphaz the Temanite, and Bildad the Shuhite, and Zophar the Naamathite: for they had made an appointment together to come to mourn with him and to comfort him.

Jb 42:11 Then came there unto him all his brethren, and all his sisters, and all they that had been of his acquaintance before, and did eat bread with him in his house: and they bemoaned him, and comforted him over all the evil that the LORD had brought upon him: every man also gave him a piece of money, and every one an earring of gold.

Eze 14:23 And they shall comfort you, when ye see their ways and their doings: and ye shall know that I have not done without cause all that I have done in it, saith the Lord GOD.

Jn 11:19 And many of the Jews came to Martha and Mary, to comfort them concerning their brother.

Jn 11:31 The Jews then which were with her in the house, and comforted her, when they saw Mary, that she rose up hastily and went out, followed her, saying, She goeth unto the grave to weep there.

Ac 20:10 And Paul went down, and fell on him, and embracing *him* said, Trouble not yourselves; for his life is in him.

1 Th 4:13 But I would not have you to be ignorant, brethren, concerning them which are asleep, that ye sorrow not, even as others which have no hope.

5. Special Passages

Jb 5:19 He shall deliver thee in six troubles: yea, in seven there shall no evil touch thee.

Jb 11:16 Because thou shalt forget *thy* misery, *and* remember *it* as waters *that* pass away:

Ps 27:5 For in the time of trouble he shall hide me in his pavilion: in the secret of his tabernacle shall he hide me; he shall set me up upon a rock.

Ps 30:5 For his anger *endureth but* a moment; in his favour is life: weeping may endure for a night, but joy *cometh* in the morning.

Ps 42:5 Why art thou cast down, O my soul? and why *art* thou disquieted in me? hope thou in God: for I shall yet praise him *for* the help of his countenance.

Ps 103:13 Like as a father pitieth *his* children, *so* the LORD pitieth them that fear him.

Ps 119:50 This *is* my comfort in my affliction: for thy word hath quickened me.

Ps 138:7 Though I walk in the midst of trouble, thou wilt revive me: thou shalt stretch forth thine hand against the wrath of mine enemies, and thy right hand shall save me.

Is 46:4 And *even* to *your* old age I *am* he; and *even* to hoar hairs will I carry *you:* I have made, and I will bear; even I will carry, and will deliver *you.*

Is 61:3 To appoint unto them that mourn in Zion, to give unto them beauty for ashes, the oil of joy for mourning, the garment of praise for the spirit of heaviness; that they might be called trees of righteousness, the planting of the LORD, that he might be glorified.

Is 63:9 In all their affliction he was afflicted, and the angel of his presence saved them: in his love and in his pity he redeemed them; and he bare them, and carried them all the days of old.

Mt 5:4 Blessed *are* they that mourn: for they shall be comforted.

Jn 14:1 Let not your heart be troubled: ye believe in God, believe also in me.

Ro 8:28 And we know that all things work together for good to them that love God, to them who are the called according to *his* purpose.

Ro 15:4 For whatsoever things were written aforetime were written for our learning, that we through patience and comfort of the scriptures might have hope.

1 Th 3:7 Therefore, brethren, we were comforted over you in all our affliction and distress by your faith:

1 Th 4:13 But I would not have you to be ignorant, brethren, concerning them which are asleep, that ye sorrow not, even as others which have no hope.

See **MISERY, PROMISES**

COMFORTLESS

De 28:32; Jb 21:34; Ps 77:2; Ec 4:1; Is 51:19; Je 16:7; Lam 1:2, 9, 17, 21; Na 3:7

COMMANDS, *divine, reflecting God's holiness and for man's highest good*

1. Of God

Ex 4:6 And the LORD said furthermore unto him, Put now thine hand into thy bosom. And he put his hand into his bosom: and when he took it out, behold, his hand *was* leprous as snow.

Ex 6:11 Go in, speak unto Pharaoh king of Egypt, that he let the children of Israel go out of his land.

Ex 7:19 And the LORD spake unto Moses, Say unto Aaron, Take thy rod, and stretch out thine hand upon the waters of Egypt, upon their streams, upon their rivers, and upon their ponds, and upon all their pools of water, that they may become blood; and *that* there may be blood throughout all the land of Egypt, both in *vessels of* wood, and in *vessels of* stone.

Ex 8:5 And the LORD spake unto Moses, Say unto Aaron, Stretch forth thine hand with thy rod over the streams, over the rivers, and over the ponds, and cause frogs to come up upon the land of Egypt.

Ex 8:16 And the LORD said unto Moses, Say unto Aaron, Stretch out thy rod, and smite the dust of the land, that it may become lice throughout all the land of Egypt.

Ex 9:8 And the LORD said unto Moses and unto Aaron, Take to you handfuls of ashes of the furnace, and let Moses sprinkle it toward the heaven in the sight of Pharaoh.

Ex 10:12 And the LORD said unto Moses, Stretch out thine hand over the land of Egypt for the locusts, that they may come up upon the land of Egypt, and eat every herb of the land, *even* all that the hail hath left.

Ex 11:2 Speak now in the ears of the people, and let every man borrow of his neighbour, and every woman of her neighbour, jewels of silver, and jewels of gold.

Ex 12:3 Speak ye unto all the congregation of Israel, saying, In the tenth *day* of this month they shall take to them every man a lamb, according to the house of *their* fathers, a lamb for an house:

Ex 16:16 This *is* the thing which the LORD hath commanded, Gather of it every man *according to* his eating, an omer for every man, according to the number of your persons; take ye every man for *them* which *are* in his tents.

Ex 19:21 And the LORD said unto Moses, Go down, charge the people, lest they break through unto the LORD to gaze, and many of them perish.

Ex 40:1 And the LORD spake unto Moses, saying,

Le 4:1 And the LORD spake unto Moses, saying,

Le 7:36 Which the LORD commanded to be given them of the children of Israel, in the day that he anointed them, *by* a statute for ever throughout their generations.

Le 7:38 Which the LORD commanded Moses in mount Sinai, in the day that he commanded the children of Israel to offer their oblations unto the LORD, in the wilderness of Sinai.

Le 8:35 Therefore shall ye abide *at* the door of the tabernacle of the congregation day and night seven days, and keep the charge of the LORD, that ye die not: for so I am commanded.

Le 9:7 And Moses said unto Aaron, Go unto the altar, and offer thy sin offering, and thy burnt offering, and make an atonement for thyself, and for the people: and offer the offering of the people, and make an atonement for them; as the LORD commanded.

Le 10:8 And the LORD spake unto Aaron, saying,

Le 10:13 And ye shall eat it in the holy place, because it *is* thy due, and thy sons' due, of the sacrifices of the LORD made by fire: for so I am commanded.

Le 14:1 And the LORD spake unto Moses, saying,

Le 17:2 Speak unto Aaron, and unto his sons, and unto all the children of Israel, and say unto them; This *is* the thing which the LORD hath commanded, saying,

Nu 1:2 Take ye the sum of all the congregation of the children of Israel, after their families, by the house of their fathers, with the number of *their* names, every male by their polls;

Nu 4:41 These *are* they that were numbered of the families of the sons of Gershon, of all that might do service in the tabernacle of the congregation, whom Moses and Aaron did number according to the commandment of the LORD.

Nu 9:2 Let the children of Israel also keep the passover at his appointed season.

Nu 33:2 And Moses wrote their goings out according to their journeys by the commandment of the LORD: and these *are* their journeys according to their goings out.

Nu 34:2 Command the children of Israel, and say unto them, When ye come into the land of Canaan; (this is the land that shall fall unto you for an inheritance, *even* the land of Canaan with the coasts thereof:)

Nu 35:2 Command the children of Israel, that they give unto the Levites of the inheritance of their possession cities to dwell in; and ye shall give *also* unto the Levites suburbs for the cities round about them.

Nu 36:2 And they said, The LORD commanded my lord to give the land for an inheritance by lot to the children of Israel: and my lord was commanded by the LORD to give the inheritance of Zelophehad our brother unto his daughters.

Nu 36:6 This is the thing which the LORD doth command concerning the daughters of Zelophehad, saying, Let them marry to whom they think best; only to the family of the tribe of their father shall they marry.

De 1:3 And it came to pass in the fortieth year, in the eleventh month, on the first *day* of the month, *that* Moses spake unto the children of Israel, according unto all that the LORD had given him in commandment unto them;

De 24:8 Take heed in the plague of leprosy, that thou observe diligently, and do according to all that the priests the Levites shall teach you: as I commanded them, so ye shall observe to do.

Jos 4:16 Command the priests that bear the ark of the testimony, that they come up out of Jordan.

Jos 6:3 And ye shall compass the city, all *ye* men of war, *and* go round about the city once. Thus shalt thou do six days.

Jos 21:3 And the children of Israel gave unto the Levites out of their inheritance, at the commandment of the LORD, these cities and their suburbs.

Jud 20:23 (And the children of Israel went up and wept before the LORD until even, and asked counsel of the LORD, saying, Shall I go up again to battle against the children of Benjamin my brother? And the LORD said, Go up against him.)

1 S 15:18 And the LORD sent thee on a journey, and said, Go and utterly destroy the sinners the Amalekites, and fight against them until they be consumed.

1 S 23:2 Therefore David enquired of the LORD, saying, Shall I go and smite these Philistines? And the LORD said unto David, Go, and smite the Philistines, and save Keilah.

1 K 13:17 For it was said to me by the word of the LORD, Thou shalt eat no bread nor drink water there, nor turn again to go by the way that thou camest.

Je 42:19 The LORD hath said concerning you, O ye remnant of Judah; Go ye not into Egypt: know certainly that I have admonished you this day.

John 12:50 And I know that his commandment is life everlasting: whatsoever I speak therefore, even as the Father said unto me, so I speak.

Ac 13:47 For so hath the Lord commanded us, *saying,* I have set thee to be a light of the Gentiles, that thou shouldest be for salvation unto the ends of the earth.

2. Of Christ

Mt 11:1 And it came to pass, when Jesus had made an end of commanding his twelve disciples, he departed thence to teach and to preach in their cities.

Mt 12:13 Then saith he to the man, Stretch forth thine hand. And he stretched *it* forth; and it was restored whole, like as the other.

Mt 26:27 And he took the cup, and gave thanks, and gave *it* to them, saying, Drink ye all of it;

Mt 28:20 Teaching them to observe all things whatsoever I have commanded you: and, lo, I am with you alway, *even* unto the end of the world. Amen.

Mark 2:9 Whether is it easier to say to the sick of the palsy, *Thy* sins be forgiven thee; or to say, Arise, and take up thy bed, and walk?

Mark 3:3 And he saith unto the man which had the withered hand, Stand forth.

Mark 3:5 And when he had looked round about on them with anger, being grieved for the hardness of their hearts, he saith unto the man, Stretch forth thine hand. And he stretched *it* out: and his hand was restored whole as the other.

Mark 14:15 And he will shew you a large upper room furnished *and* prepared: there make ready for us.

Lu 5:4 Now when he had left speaking, he said unto Simon, Launch out into the deep, and let down your nets for a draught.

Lu 6:8 But he knew their thoughts, and said to the man which had the withered hand, Rise up, and stand forth in the midst. And he arose and stood forth.

Lu 22:12 And he shall shew you a large upper room furnished: there make ready.

Lu 22:19 And he took bread, and gave thanks, and brake *it,* and gave unto them, saying, This is my body which is given for you: this do in remembrance of me.

John 13:34 A new commandment I give unto you, That ye love one another; as I have loved you, that ye also love one another.

John 14:15 If ye love me, keep my commandments.

John 14:21 He that hath my commandments, and keepeth them, he it is that loveth me: and he that loveth me shall be loved of my Father, and I will love him, and will manifest myself to him.

John 15:10 If ye keep my commandments, ye shall abide in my love; even as I have kept my Father's commandments, and abide in his love.

John 15:14 Ye are my friends, if ye do whatsoever I command you.

John 15:17 These things I command you, that ye love one another.

Ac 1:2 Until the day in which he was taken up, after that he through the Holy Ghost had given commandments unto the apostles whom he had chosen:

Ac 10:42 And he commanded us to preach unto the people, and to testify that it is he which was ordained of God *to be* the Judge of quick and dead.

Tit 1:3 But hath in due times manifested his word through preaching, which is committed unto me according to the commandment of God our Saviour;

2 Pe 3:2 That ye may be mindful of the words which were spoken before by the holy prophets, and of the commandment of us the apostles of the Lord and Saviour:

1 John 2:4 He that saith, I know him, and keepeth not his commandments, is a liar, and the truth is not in him.

1 John 3:23 And this is his commandment, That we should believe on the name of his Son Jesus Christ, and love one another, as he gave us commandment.

1 John 4:21 And this commandment have we from him, That he who loveth God love his brother also.

2 John 1:6 And this is love, that we walk after his commandments. This is the commandment, That, as ye have heard from the beginning, ye should walk in it.

3. Judge Not

Eze 16:52 Thou also, which hast judged thy sisters, bear thine own shame for thy sins that thou hast committed more abominable than they: they are more righteous than thou: yea, be thou confounded also, and bear thy shame, in that thou hast justified thy sisters.

Mt 7:1 Judge not, that ye be not judged.

Ro 2:1 Therefore thou art inexcusable, O man, whosoever thou art that judgest: for wherein thou judgest another, thou condemnest thyself; for thou that judgest doest the same things.

Ro 14:4 Who art thou that judgest another man's servant? to his own master he standeth or falleth. Yea, he shall be holden up: for God is able to make him stand.

Ro 14:13 Let us not therefore judge one another any more: but judge this rather, that no man put a stumbling-block or an occasion to fall in *his* brother's way.

1 Co 4:5 Therefore judge nothing before the time, until the Lord come, who both will bring to light the hidden things of darkness, and will make manifest the counsels of the hearts: and then shall every man have praise of God.

Ja 4:12 There is one lawgiver, who is able to save and to destroy: who art thou that judgest another?

See **WORD OF GOD**

COMMANDMENTS *See* **LAW, WORD OF GOD**

COMMENDATION, *of persons by Christ*

THE SYROPHENICIAN WOMAN

Mt 15:28 Then Jesus answered and said unto her, O woman, great *is* thy faith: be it unto thee even as thou wilt. And her daughter was made whole from that very hour.

MARY OF BETHANY

Mk 14:6 And Jesus said, Let her alone; why trouble ye her? she hath wrought a good work on me.

A CENTURION

Lu 7:9 When Jesus heard these things, he marvelled at him, and turned him about, and said unto the people that followed him, I say unto you, I have not found so great faith, no, not in Israel.

JOHN THE BAPTIST

Lu 7:28 For I say unto you, Among those that ere is not a greater prophet than John the Baptist: but he that is least in the kingdom of God is greater than he.

A POOR WIDOW

Lu 21:3 And he said, Of a truth I say unto you, that this poor widow hath cast in more than they all:

See **ENCOURAGEMENT, REPROOF**

COMPANIONSHIP, *friendship, fellowship, close association*

1. Good Company

Ps 119:63 I *am* a companion of all *them* that fear thee, and of them that keep thy precepts.

Pr 2:20 That thou mayest walk in the way of good *men,* and keep the paths of the righteous.

Pr 13:20 He that walketh with wise *men* shall be wise: but a companion of fools shall be destroyed.

1 Co 5:11 But now I have written unto you not to keep company, if any man that is called a brother be a fornicator, or covetous, or an idolater, or a railer, or a drunkard, or an extortioner; with such an one no not to eat.

Ep 5:7 Be not ye therefore partakers with them.

2 Th 3:14 And if any man obey not our word by this epistle, note that man, and have no company with him, that he may be ashamed.

2. Comfort and Help

SEEN *in God's original plan*

Ge 2:18 And the LORD God said, *It is* not good that the man should be alone; I will make him an help meet for him.

ILLUSTRATED *in the life of Moses*

Nu 10:31 And he said, Leave us not, I pray thee; forasmuch as thou knowest how we are to encamp in the wilderness, and thou mayest be to us instead of eyes.

EMPHASIZED *by Solomon*

Ec 4:9 Two *are* better than one; because they have a good reward for their labour.

APPRECIATED *by Christ*

Mt 26:37 And he took with him Peter and the two sons of Zebedee, and began to be sorrowful and very heavy.

SHOWN *by the sending forth of the disciples two by two*

Lu 10:1 After these things the Lord appointed other seventy also, and sent them two and two before his face into every city and place, whither he himself would come.

RECOGNIZED *by Paul in his missionary work*

Ac 13:2 As they ministered to the Lord, and fasted, the Holy Ghost said, Separate me Barnabas and Saul for the work whereunto I have called them.

3. Desired

Mt 26:37; Ac 28:15; 2 Co 7:6; Ph 2:26; 2 Ti 4:9, 21; Tit 3:12; Phm 13

See **ENEMIES, FRIENDSHIP**

COMPASSION, *sharing the suffering of another*

1. Of God

Ge 16:11 And the angel of the LORD said unto her, Behold, thou *art* with child, and shalt bear a son, and shalt call his name Ishmael; because the LORD hath heard thy affliction.

Ge 21:17 And God heard the voice of the lad; and the angel of God called Hagar out of heaven, and said unto her, What aileth thee, Hagar? fear not; for God hath heard the voice of the lad where he *is*.

Ge 31:42 Except the God of my father, the God of Abraham, and the fear of Isaac, had been with me, surely thou hadst sent me away now empty. God hath seen mine affliction and the labour of my hands, and rebuked *thee* yesternight.

Ex 3:7 And the LORD said, I have surely seen the affliction of my people which *are* in Egypt, and have heard their cry by reason of their taskmasters; for I know their sorrows;

Ex 4:31 And the people believed: and when they heard that the LORD had visited the children of Israel, and that he had looked upon their affliction, then they bowed their heads and worshipped.

Ex 16:4 Then said the LORD unto Moses, Behold, I will rain bread from heaven for you; and the people shall go out and gather a certain rate every day, that I may prove them, whether they will walk in my law, or no.

Nu 11:17 And I will come down and talk with thee there: and I will take of the spirit which *is* upon thee, and will put *it* upon them; and they shall bear the burden of the people with thee, that thou bear it not thyself alone.

De 10:10 And I stayed in the mount, according to the first time, forty days and forty nights; and the LORD hearkened unto me at that time also, *and* the LORD would not destroy thee.

De 13:17 And there shall cleave nought of the cursed thing to thine hand: that the LORD may turn from the fierceness of his anger, and shew thee mercy, and have compassion upon thee, and multiply thee, as he hath sworn unto thy fathers;

De 26:7 And when we cried unto the LORD God of our fathers, the LORD heard our voice, and looked on our affliction, and our labour, and our oppression:

De 30:3 That then the LORD thy God will turn thy captivity, and have compassion upon thee, and will return and gather thee from all the nations, whither the LORD thy God hath scattered thee.

Jud 2:18 And when the LORD raised them up judges, then the LORD was with the judge, and delivered them out of the hand of their enemies all the days of the judge: for it repented the LORD because of their groanings by reason of them that oppressed them and vexed them.

Jud 10:16 And they put away the strange gods from among them, and served the LORD: and his soul was grieved for the misery of Israel.

1 S 9:16 To morrow about this time I will send thee a man out of the land of Benjamin, and thou shalt anoint him *to be* captain over my people Israel, that he may save my people out of the hand of the Philistines: for I have looked upon my people, because their cry is come unto me.

2 K 13:23 And the LORD was gracious unto them, and had compassion on them, and had respect unto them, because of his covenant with Abraham, Isaac, and Jacob, and would not destroy them, neither cast he them from his presence as yet.

2 K 14:26 For the LORD saw the affliction of Israel, *that it was* very bitter: for *there was* not any shut up, nor any left, nor any helper for Israel.

1 Chr 21:15 And God sent an angel unto Jerusalem to destroy it: and as he was destroying, the LORD beheld, and he repented him of the evil, and said to the angel that destroyed, It is enough, stay now thine hand. And the angel of the LORD stood by the threshingfloor of Ornan the Jebusite.

2 Chr 36:15 And the LORD God of their fathers sent to them by his messengers, rising up betimes, and sending; because he had compassion on his people, and on his dwelling place:

Ezr 9:9 For we *were* bondmen; yet our God hath not forsaken us in our bondage, but hath extended mercy unto us in the sight of the kings of Persia, to give us a reviving, to set up the house of our God, and to repair the desolations thereof, and to give us a wall in Judah and in Jerusalem.

Ne 9:9 And didst see the affliction of our fathers in Egypt, and heardest their cry by the Red sea;

Ne 9:27 Therefore thou deliveredst them into the hand of their enemies, who vexed them: and in the time of their trouble, when they cried unto thee, thou heardest *them* from heaven; and according to thy manifold mercies thou gavest them saviours, who saved them out of the hand of their enemies.

Jb 36:5 Behold, God *is* mighty, and despiseth not *any: he is* mighty in strength *and* wisdom.

Ps 6:8 Depart from me, all ye workers of iniquity; for the LORD hath heard the voice of my weeping.

Ps 22:24 For he hath not despised nor abhorred the affliction of the af-flicted; neither hath he hid his face from him; but when he cried unto him, he heard.

Ps 31:7 I will be glad and rejoice in thy mercy: for thou hast considered my trouble; thou hast known my soul in adversities;

Ps 31:22 For I said in my haste, I am cut off from before thine eyes: nevertheless thou heardest the voice of my supplications when I cried unto thee.

Ps 78:38 But he, *being* full of compassion, forgave *their* iniquity, and destroyed *them* not: yea, many a time turned he his anger away, and did not stir up all his wrath.

Ps 79:11 Let the sighing of the prisoner come before thee; according to the greatness of thy power preserve thou those that are appointed to die;

Ps 86:15 But thou, O Lord, *art* a God full of compassion, and gracious, longsuffering, and plenteous in mercy and truth.

Ps 102:20 To hear the groaning of the prisoner; to loose those that are appointed to death;

Ps 106:44 Nevertheless he regarded their affliction, when he heard their cry:

Ps 107:19 Then they cry unto the LORD in their trouble, *and* he saveth them out of their distresses.

Ps 111:4 He hath made his wonderful works to be remembered: the LORD *is* gracious and full of compassion.

Ps 145:8 The LORD *is* gracious, and full of compassion; slow to anger, and of great mercy.

Is 12:1 And in that day thou shalt say, O LORD, I will praise thee: though thou wast angry with me, thine anger is turned away, and thou comfortedst me.

Is 14:1 For the LORD will have mercy on Jacob, and will yet choose Israel, and set them in their own land: and the strangers shall be joined with them, and they shall cleave to the house of Jacob.

Is 30:18 And therefore will the LORD wait, that he may be gracious unto you, and therefore will he be exalted, that he may have mercy upon you: for the LORD is a God of judgment: blessed *are* all they that wait for him.

Is 48:9 For my name's sake will I defer mine anger, and for my praise will I refrain for thee, that I cut thee not off.

Is 63:15 Look down from heaven, and behold from the habitation of thy holiness and of thy glory: where *is* thy zeal and thy strength, the sounding of thy bowels and of thy mercies toward me? are they restrained?

Je 12:15 And it shall come to pass, after that I have plucked them out I will return, and have compassion on them, and will bring them again, every man to his heritage, and every man to his land.

Je 31:20 *Is* Ephraim my dear son? *is he* a pleasant child? for since I spake against him, I do earnestly remember him still: therefore my bowels are troubled for him; I will surely have mercy upon him, saith the LORD.

Lam 3:22 *It is of* the LORD's mercies that we are not consumed, because his compassions fail not.

Lam 3:32 But though he cause grief, yet will he have compassion according to the multitude of his mercies.

Lam 3:57 Thou drewest near in the day *that* I called upon thee: thou saidst, Fear not.

Eze 6:8 Yet will I leave a remnant, that ye may have *some* that shall escape the sword among the nations, when ye shall be scattered through the countries.

Eze 16:6 And when I passed by thee, and saw thee polluted in thine own blood, I said unto thee *when thou wast* in thy blood, Live; yea, I said unto thee *when thou wast* in thy blood, Live.

Eze 34:16 I will seek that which was lost, and bring again that which was driven away, and will bind up *that which was* broken, and will strengthen that which was sick: but I will destroy the fat and the strong; I will feed them with judgment.

Ho 11:4 I drew them with cords of a man, with bands of love: and I was to them as they that take off the yoke on their jaws, and I laid meat unto them.

Ho 11:9 I will not execute the fierceness of mine anger, I will not return to destroy Ephraim: for I *am* God, and not man; the Holy One in the midst of thee: and I will not enter into the city.

Jl 2:13 And rend your heart, and not your garments, and turn unto the LORD your God: for he *is* gracious and merciful, slow to anger, and of great kindness, and repenteth him of the evil.

Jl 2:18 Then will the LORD be jealous for his land, and pity his people.

Mi 7:19 He will turn again, he will have compassion upon us; he will subdue our iniquities; and thou wilt cast all their sins into the depths of the sea.

Mt 24:22 And except those days should be shortened, there should no flesh be saved: but for the elect's sake those days shall be shortened.

Mk 5:19 Howbeit Jesus suffered him not, but saith unto him, Go home to thy friends, and tell them how great things the Lord hath done for thee, and hath had compassion on thee.

Mk 13:20 And except that the Lord had shortened those days, no flesh should be saved: but for the elect's sake, whom he hath chosen, he hath shortened the days.

Lu 15:20 And he arose, and came to his father. But when he was yet a great way off, his father saw him, and had compassion, and ran, and fell on his neck, and kissed him.

Ac 7:34 I have seen, I have seen the affliction of my people which is in Egypt, and I have heard their groaning, and am come down to deliver them. And now come, I will send thee into Egypt.

Ac 9:12 And hath seen in a vision a man named Ananias coming in, and putting *his* hand on him, that he might receive his sight.

Ro 9:15 For he saith to Moses, I will have mercy on whom I will have mercy, and I will have compassion on whom I will have compassion.

Ja 5:11 Behold, we count them happy which endure. Ye have heard of the patience of Job, and have seen the end of the Lord; that the Lord is very pitiful, and of tender mercy.

Re 2:24 But unto you I say, and unto the rest in Thyatira, as many as have not this doctrine, and which have not known the depths of Satan, as they speak; I will put upon you none other burden.

2. Of Christ

FOR THE MULTITUDE

Mt 9:36 But when he saw the multitudes, he was moved with compassion on them, because they fainted, and were scattered abroad, as sheep having no shepherd.

Mt 14:14 And Jesus went forth, and saw a great multitude, and was moved with compassion toward them, and he healed their sick.

Mt 15:32 Then Jesus called his disciples *unto him,* and said, I have compassion on the multitude, because they continue with me now three days, and have nothing to eat: and I will not send them away fasting, lest they faint in the way.

FOR THE UNFORTUNATE

Mt 20:34 So Jesus had compassion *on them,* and touched their eyes: and immediately their eyes received sight, and they followed him.

FOR JERUSALEM

Mt 23:37 O Jerusalem, Jerusalem, *thou* that killest the prophets, and stonest them which are sent unto thee, how often would I have gathered thy children together, even as a hen gathereth her chickens under *her* wings, and ye would not!

FOR THE LEPER

Mk 1:41 And Jesus, moved with compassion, put forth *his* hand, and touched him, and saith unto him, I will; be thou clean.

FOR THE BEREAVED

Lu 7:13 And when the Lord saw her, he had compassion on her, and said unto her, Weep not.

Jn 11:35 Jesus wept.

3. Of Humans

PHARAOH'S DAUGHTER

Ex 2:6 And when she had opened *it,* she saw the child: and, behold, the babe wept. And she had compassion on him, and said, This *is one* of the Hebrews' children.

CERTAIN LEADERS IN ISRAEL

2 Chr 28:15 And the men which were expressed by name rose up, and took the captives, and with the spoil clothed all that were naked among them, and arrayed them, and shod them, and gave them to eat and to drink, and anointed them, and carried all the feeble of them upon asses, and brought them to Jericho, the city of palm trees, to their brethren: then they returned to Samaria.

JOB

Jb 29:13 The blessing of him that was ready to perish came upon me: and I caused the widow's heart to sing for joy.

THE GOOD SAMARITAN

Lu 10:33 But a certain Samaritan, as he journeyed, came where he was: and when he saw him, he had compassion *on him,*

THE PHILIPPIAN JAILER

Ac 16:33 And he took them the same hour of the night, and washed *their* stripes; and was baptized, he and all his, straightway.

THE BARBARIANS

Ac 28:2 And the barbarous people shewed us no little kindness: for they kindled a fire, and received us every one, because of the present rain, and because of the cold.

He 10:34 For ye had compassion of me in my bonds, and took joyfully the spoiling of your goods, knowing in yourselves that ye have in heaven a better and an enduring substance.

See **LOVE, SYMPATHY**

COMPOSURE

Mt 24:6 And ye shall hear of wars and rumours of wars: see that ye be not troubled: for all *these things* must come to pass, but the end is not yet.

Lu 24:38 And he said unto them, Why are ye troubled? and why do thoughts arise in your hearts?

Jn 14:1 Let not your heart be troubled: ye believe in God, believe also in me.

Ac 20:24 But none of these things move me, neither count I my life dear unto myself, so that I might finish my course with joy, and the ministry, which I have received of the Lord Jesus, to testify the gospel of the grace of God.

2 Th 1:7 And to you who are troubled rest with us, when the Lord Jesus shall be revealed from heaven with his mighty angels,

2 Th 2:2 That ye be not soon shaken in mind, or be troubled, neither by spirit, nor by word, nor by letter as from us, as that the day of Christ is at hand.

1 Pe 3:14 But and if ye suffer for righteousness' sake, happy *are ye:* and be not afraid of their terror, neither be troubled;

See **PEACE**

CONCEIT, *an exaggerated opinion of oneself*

1 S 17:44; 1 K 2:15; Est 6:6; Jb 12:2; 15:8; 32:13; Pr 3:7; 12:15; 18:12; 23:4; 26:5, 12; 28:11; Ec 7:16; Is 5:21; 10:13; 19:11; Je 8:8; Eze 28:3; Mk 8:32; Jn 9:41; Ro 1:22; 11:25; 12:3, 16; 1 Co 3:18; 8:2; Ga 6:3

CONCEPTION

Ge 4:1, 17, 25; 16:4; 21:2; 25:21; 29:32; 30:5, 17, 23; 38:3, 18; Ex 2:2; Jud 13:5; Ru 4:13; 1 S 1:20; 2:21; 2 S 11:5; 2 K 4:17; 1 Chr 7:23; Is 8:3; Ho 1:3, 8; Mt 1:18; Lu 1:24, 36; He 11:11

CONCUBINES *See* **FAMILY**

CONDEMNATION

Is 50:9 Behold, the Lord God will help me; who *is* he *that* shall condemn me?

lo, they all shall wax old as a garment; the moth shall eat them up.

Lu 6:37 Judge not, and ye shall not be judged: condemn not, and ye shall not be condemned: forgive, and ye shall be forgiven:

Jn 3:18 He that believeth on him is not condemned: but he that believeth not is condemned already, because he hath not believed in the name of the only begotten Son of God.

Jn 5:24 Verily, verily, I say unto you, He that heareth my word, and believeth on him that sent me, hath everlasting life, and shall not come into condemnation; but is passed from death unto life.

Ro 8:1 *There is* therefore now no condemnation to them which are in Christ Jesus, who walk not after the flesh, but after the Spirit.

Ro 8:34 Who *is* he that condemneth? *It is* Christ that died, yea rather, that is risen again, who is even at the right hand of God, who also maketh intercession for us.

1 Jn 3:21 Beloved, if our heart condemn us not, *then* have we confidence toward God.

See **SALVATION**

CONDESCENSION, *DIVINE, God's entrance to the human realm*

Ex 19:11 And be ready against the third day: for the third day the LORD will come down in the sight of all the people upon mount Sinai.

Ex 20:22 And the LORD said unto Moses, Thus thou shalt say unto the children of Israel, Ye have seen that I have talked with you from heaven.

Nu 11:17 And I will come down and talk with thee there: and I will take of the spirit which *is* upon thee, and will put *it* upon them; and they shall bear the burden of the people with thee, that thou bear it not thyself alone.

De 18:18 I will raise them up a Prophet from among their brethren, like unto thee, and will put my words in his mouth; and he shall speak unto them all that I shall command him.

De 34:6 And he buried him in a valley in the land of Moab, over against

Beth-peor: but no man knoweth of his sepulchre unto this day.

Jud 6:18 Depart not hence, I pray thee, until I come unto thee, and bring forth my present, and set *it* before thee. And he said, I will tarry until thou come again.

Jud 6:40 And God did so that night: for it was dry upon the fleece only, and there was dew on all the ground.

2 S 7:7 In all *the places* wherein I have walked with all the children of Israel spake I a word with any of the tribes of Israel, whom I commanded to feed my people Israel, saying, Why build ye not me an house of cedar?

2 Chr 6:18 But will God in very deed dwell with men on the earth? behold, heaven and the heaven of heavens cannot contain thee; how much less this house which I have built!

Ne 9:13 Thou camest down also upon mount Sinai, and spakest with them from heaven, and gavest them right judgments, and true laws, good statutes and commandments:

Ps 40:1 I waited patiently for the LORD; and he inclined unto me, and heard my cry.

Ps 102:19 For he hath looked down from the height of his sanctuary; from heaven did the LORD behold the earth;

Ps 113:6 Who humbleth *himself* to behold *the things that are* in heaven, and in the earth!

Ps 136:23 Who remembered us in our low estate: for his mercy *endureth* for ever:

Ps 138:6 Though the LORD *be* high, yet hath he respect unto the lowly: but the proud he knoweth afar off.

Is 57:15 For thus saith the high and lofty One that inhabiteth eternity, whose name *is* Holy; I dwell in the high and holy *place,* with him also *that is* of a contrite and humble spirit, to revive the spirit of the humble, and to revive the heart of the contrite ones.

Zec 9:10 And I will cut off the chariot from Ephraim, and the horse from Jerusalem, and the battle bow shall be cut off: and he shall speak peace unto the heathen: and his dominion *shall be* from sea *even* to sea, and from river *even* to the ends of the earth.

Mt 9:11 And when the Pharisees saw *it,* they said unto his disciples, Why eateth your Master with publicans and sinners?

Mt 21:7 And brought the ass, and the colt, and put on them their clothes, and they set *him* thereon.

Mk 2:16 And when the scribes and Pharisees saw him eat with publicans and sinners, they said unto his disciples, How is it that he eateth and drinketh with publicans and sinners?

Lu 1:19 And the angel answering said unto him, I am Gabriel, that stand in the presence of God; and am sent to speak unto thee, and to shew thee these glad tidings.

Lu 1:48 For he hath regarded the low estate of his handmaiden: for, behold, from henceforth all generations shall call me blessed.

Lu 5:30 But their scribes and Pharisees murmured against his disciples, saying, Why do ye eat and drink with publicans and sinners?

Lu 15:2 And the Pharisees and scribes murmured, saying, This man receiveth sinners, and eateth with them.

Lu 19:5 And when Jesus came to the place, he looked up, and saw him, and said unto him, Zacchaeus, make haste, and come down; for to day I must abide at thy house.

Lu 24:39 Behold my hands and my feet, that it is I myself: handle me, and see; for a spirit hath not flesh and bones, as ye see me have.

Lu 24:42 And they gave him a piece of a broiled fish, and of an honeycomb.

Jn 13:4 He riseth from supper, and laid aside his garments; and took a towel, and girded himself.

Jn 20:20 And when he had so said, he shewed unto them *his* hands and his side. Then were the disciples glad, when they saw the Lord.

Jn 20:27 Then saith he to Thomas, reach hither thy finger, and behold my hands; and reach hither thy hand, and thrust *it* into my side: and be not faithless, but believing.

He 2:17 Wherefore in all things it behoved him to be made like unto *his* brethren, that he might be a merciful and faithful high priest in things *pertaining* to God, to make reconciliation for the sins of the people.

Re 21:3 And I heard a great voice out of heaven saying, Behold, the tabernacle of God *is* with men, and he will dwell with them, and they shall be his people, and God himself shall be with them, *and be* their God.

See **CHRIST**

CONDUCT

1. Advice

Ps 50:23 Whoso offereth praise glorifieth me: and to him that ordereth *his* conversation *aright* will I shew the salvation of God.

Ph 1:27 Only let your conversation be as it becometh the gospel of Christ: that whether I come and see you, or else be absent, I may hear of your affairs, that ye stand fast in one spirit, with one mind striving together for the faith of the gospel;

1 Ti 4:12 Let no man despise thy youth; but be thou an example of the believers, in word, in conversation, in charity, in spirit, in faith, in purity.

Ja 3:13 Who *is* a wise man and endued with knowledge among you? let him shew out of a good conversation his works with meekness of wisdom.

1 Pe 2:12 Having your conversation honest among the Gentiles: that, whereas they speak against you as evildoers, they may by *your* good works, which they shall behold, glorify God in the day of visitation.

1 Pe 3:16 Having a good conscience; that, whereas they speak evil of you, as of evildoers, they may be ashamed that falsely accuse your good conversation in Christ.

2 Pe 3:11 *Seeing* then *that* all these things shall be dissolved, what manner *of persons* ought ye to be in *all* holy conversation and godliness,

2. Behavior

1 S 18:14 And David behaved himself wisely in all his ways; and the LORD *was* with him.

1 S 18:30 Then the princes of the Philistines went forth: and it came to pass, after they went forth, *that* David behaved himself more wisely than all the servants of Saul; so that his name was much set by.

Ps 101:2 I will behave myself wisely in a perfect way. O when wilt thou come unto me? I will walk within my house with a perfect heart.

1 Co 13:5 Doth not behave itself unseemly, seeketh not her own, is not easily provoked, thinketh no evil;

2 Co 1:12 For our rejoicing is this, the testimony of our conscience, that in simplicity and godly sincerity, not with fleshly wisdom, but by the grace of God, we have had our conversation in the world, and more abundantly to you-ward.

Ph 1:10 That ye may approve things that are excellent; that ye may be sincere and without offence till the day of Christ;

1 Th 2:10 Ye *are* witnesses, and God *also,* how holily and justly and unblameably we behaved ourselves among you that believe:

2 Th 3:7 For yourselves know how ye ought to follow us: for we behaved not ourselves disorderly among you;

1 Ti 3:2 A bishop then must be blameless, the husband of one wife, vigilant, sober, of good behaviour, given to hospitality, apt to teach;

1 Ti 3:15 But if I tarry long, that thou mayest know how thou oughtest to behave thyself in the house of God, which is the church of the living God, the pillar and ground of the truth.

Tit 2:3 The aged women likewise, that *they be* in behaviour as becometh holiness, not false accusers, not given to much wine, teachers of good things;

1 Pe 1:15 But as he which hath called you is holy, so be ye holy in all manner of conversation;

1 Pe 3:2 While they behold your chaste conversation *coupled* with fear.

3. Blamelessness

Ge 6:9 These *are* the generations of Noah: Noah was a just man *and* perfect in his generations, *and* Noah walked with God.

1 S 19:4 And Jonathan spake good of David unto Saul his father, and said unto him, Let not the king sin against his servant, against David; because he hath not sinned against thee, and because his works *have been* to thee-ward very good:

1 S 29:6 Then Achish called David, and said unto him, Surely, *as* the LORD liveth, thou hast been upright, and thy going out and thy coming in with me in the host *is* good in my sight: for I have not found evil in thee since the day of thy coming unto me unto this day: nevertheless the lords favour thee not.

Mt 12:5 Or have ye not read in the law, how that on the sabbath days the priests in the temple profane the sabbath, and are blameless?

Lu 1:6 And they were both righteous before God, walking in all the commandments and ordinances of the Lord blameless.

1 Co 1:8 Who shall also confirm you unto the end, *that ye may be* blameless in the day of our Lord Jesus Christ.

2 Co 6:3 Giving no offence in any thing, that the ministry be not blamed:

2 Co 8:20 Avoiding this, that no man should blame us in this abundance which is administered by us:

Ep 1:4 According as he hath chosen us in him before the foundation of the world, that we should be holy and without blame before him in love:

Ph 2:15 That ye may be blameless and harmless, the sons of God, without rebuke, in the midst of a crooked and perverse nation, among whom ye shine as lights in the world;

Ph 3:6 Concerning zeal, persecuting the church; touching the righteousness which is in the law, blameless.

Col 1:22 In the body of his flesh through death, to present you holy and unblameable and unreproveable in his sight:

1 Th 2:10 Ye *are* witnesses, and God *also*, how holily and justly and unblameably we behaved ourselves among you that believe:

1 Th 3:13 To the end he may stablish your hearts unblameable in holiness before God, even our Father, at the coming of our Lord Jesus Christ with all his saints.

1 Th 5:23 And the very God of peace sanctify you wholly; and *I pray God* your whole spirit and soul and body be preserved blameless unto the coming of our Lord Jesus Christ.

1 Ti 3:2 A bishop then must be blameless, the husband of one wife, vigilant, sober, of good behaviour, given to hospitality, apt to teach;

1 Ti 3:10 And let these also first be proved; then let them use the office of a deacon, being *found* blameless.

1 Ti 5:7 And these things give in charge, that they may be blameless.

Tit 1:6 If any be blameless, the husband of one wife, having faithful children not accused of riot or unruly.

2 Pe 3:14 Wherefore, beloved, seeing that ye look for such things, be diligent that ye may be found of him in peace, without spot, and blameless.

4. Harmlessness

Mt 10:16 Behold, I send you forth as sheep in the midst of wolves: be ye therefore wise as serpents, and harmless as doves.

Ro 16:19 For your obedience is come abroad unto all *men.* I am glad therefore on your behalf: but yet I would have you wise unto that which is good, and simple concerning evil.

Ph 1:10 That ye may approve things that are excellent; that ye may be sincere and without offence till the day of Christ;

Ph 2:15 That ye may be blameless and harmless, the sons of God, without rebuke, in the midst of a crooked and perverse nation, among whom ye shine as lights in the world;

He 7:26 For such an high priest became us, *who is* holy, harmless, undefiled, separate from sinners, and made higher than the heavens;

5. Exhortations

Ex 23:7 Keep thee far from a false matter; and the innocent and righteous slay thou not: for I will not justify the wicked.

De 4:9 Only take heed to thyself, and keep thy soul diligently, lest thou forget the things which thine eyes have seen, and lest they depart from thy heart all the days of thy life: but teach them thy sons, and thy sons' sons;

De 23:9 When the host goeth forth against thine enemies, then keep thee from every wicked thing.

Ps 18:23 I was also upright before him, and I kept myself from mine iniquity.

Pr 4:23 Keep thy heart with all diligence; for out of it *are* the issues of life.

Pr 16:17 The highway of the upright *is* to depart from evil: he that keepeth his way preserveth his soul.

Ac 15:29 That ye abstain from meats offered to idols, and from blood, and from things strangled, and from fornication: from which if ye keep yourselves, ye shall do well. Fare ye well.

Ac 21:25 As touching the Gentiles which believe, we have written *and* concluded that they observe no such thing, save only that they keep themselves from *things* offered to idols, and from blood, and from strangled, and from fornication.

1 Ti 4:16 Take heed unto thyself, and unto the doctrine; continue in them: for in doing this thou shalt both save thyself, and them that hear thee.

1 Ti 5:22 Lay hands suddenly on no man, neither be partaker of other men's sins: keep thyself pure.

Ja 1:27 Pure religion and undefiled before God and the Father is this, To visit the fatherless and widows in their affliction, *and* to keep himself unspotted from the world.

1 Jn 5:18 We know that whosoever is born of God sinneth not; but he that is begotten of God keepeth himself, and that wicked one toucheth him not.

1 Jn 5:21 Little children, keep yourselves from idols. Amen.

Jude 21 Keep yourselves in the love of God, looking for the mercy of our Lord Jesus Christ unto eternal life.

CONFECTIONERS

See **ARTS AND CRAFTS**

CONFESSION OF FAITH, *verbal allegiance to the inner commitment*

1. The Duty

Mt 10:32 Whosoever therefore shall confess me before men, him will I confess also before my Father which is in heaven.

Lu 8:39 Return to thine own house, and shew how great things God hath done unto thee. And he went his way, and published throughout the whole city how great things Jesus had done unto him.

Lu 12:8 Also I say unto you, Whosoever shall confess me before men, him shall the Son of man also confess before the angels of God:

Ro 10:9 That if thou shalt confess with thy mouth the Lord Jesus, and shalt believe in thine heart that God hath raised him from the dead, thou shalt be saved.

Ph 2:11 And *that* every tongue should confess that Jesus Christ *is* Lord, to the glory of God the Father.

1 Jn 2:23 Whosoever denieth the Son, the same hath not the Father: *(but) he that acknowledgeth the Son hath the Father also.*

1 Jn 4:15 Whosoever shall confess that Jesus is the Son of God, God dwelleth in him, and he in God.

2. Seven Remarkable Confessions

PETER

Mt 16:16 And Simon Peter answered and said, Thou art the Christ, the Son of the living God.

NATHANAEL

Jn 1:49 Nathanael answered and saith unto him, Rabbi, thou art the Son of God; thou art the King of Israel.

THE WOMAN OF SAMARIA

Jn 4:29 Come, see a man, which told me all things that ever I did: is not this the Christ?

PETER'S SECOND CONFESSION

Jn 6:69 And we believe and are sure that thou art that Christ, the Son of the living God.

MARTHA

Jn 11:27 She saith unto him, Yea, Lord: I believe that thou art the Christ, the Son of God, which should come into the world.

THOMAS

Jn 20:28 And Thomas answered and said unto him, My Lord and my God.

THE ETHIOPIAN EUNUCH

Ac 8:37 And Philip said, If thou believest with all thine heart, thou mayest. And he answered and said, I believe that Jesus Christ is the Son of God.

CONFIDENCE

Ge 24:7 The LORD God of heaven, which took me from my father's house, and from the land of my kindred, and which spake unto me, and that sware unto me, saying, Unto thy seed will I give this land; he shall send his angel before thee, and thou shalt take a wife unto my son from thence.

Ge 24:40 And he said unto me, The LORD, before whom I walk, will send his angel with thee, and prosper thy way; and thou shalt take a wife for my son of my kindred, and of my father's house:

Ge 48:21 And Israel said unto Joseph, Behold, I die: but God shall be with you, and bring you again unto the land of your fathers.

Ge 50:24 And Joseph said unto his brethren, I die: and God will surely visit you, and bring you out of this land unto the land which he sware to Abraham, to Isaac, and to Jacob.

Nu 14:8 If the LORD delight in us, then he will bring us into this land, and give it us; a land which floweth with milk and honey.

Jos 14:12 Now therefore give me this mountain, whereof the LORD spake in that day; for thou heardest in that day how the Anakims were there, and that the cities were great and fenced: if so be the LORD will be with me, then I shall be able to drive them out, as the LORD said.

Jud 3:28 And he said unto them, Follow after me: for the LORD hath delivered your enemies the Moabites into your hand. And they went down after him, and took the fords of Jordan toward Moab, and suffered not a man to pass over.

Jud 4:14 And Deborah said unto Barak, Up; for this is the day in which the LORD hath delivered Sisera into thine hand: is not the LORD gone out before thee? So Barak went down from mount Tabor, and ten thousand men after him.

Jud 7:15 And it was so, when Gideon heard the telling of the dream, and the interpretation thereof, that he worshipped, and returned into the host of Israel, and said, Arise; for the LORD hath delivered into your hand the host of Midian.

Jud 11:24 Wilt not thou possess that which Chemosh thy god giveth thee to possess? So whomsoever the LORD our God shall drive out from before us, them will we possess.

1 S 14:10 But if they say thus, Come up unto us; then we will go up: for the LORD hath delivered them into our hand: and this shall be a sign unto us.

1 S 17:37 David said moreover, The LORD that delivered me out of the paw of the lion, and out of the paw of the bear, he will deliver me out of the hand of this Philistine. And Saul said unto David, Go, and the LORD be with thee.

2 S 15:25 And the king said unto Zadok, Carry back the ark of God into the city: if I shall find favour in the eyes of the LORD, he will bring me again, and shew me both it, and his habitation:

2 S 22:19 They prevented me in the day of my calamity: but the LORD was my stay.

2 S 24:14 And David said unto Gad, I am in a great strait: let us fall now into the hand of the LORD; for his mercies are great: and let me not fall into the hand of man.

2 Chr 13:12 And, behold, God himself is with us for *our* captain, and his priests with sounding trumpets to cry alarm against you. O children of Israel, fight ye not against the LORD God of your fathers; for ye shall not prosper.

2 Chr 13:18 Thus the children of Israel were brought under at that time, and the children of Judah prevailed, because they relied upon the LORD God of their fathers.

2 Chr 14:11 And Asa cried unto the LORD his God, and said, LORD, *it is* nothing with thee to help, whether with many, or with them that have no power: help us, O LORD our God; for we rest on thee, and in thy name we go against this multitude. O LORD, thou *art* our God; let not man prevail against thee.

2 Chr 16:8 Were not the Ethiopians and the Lubims a huge host, with very many chariots and horsemen? yet, because thou didst rely on the LORD, he delivered them into thine hand.

2 Chr 18:4 And Jehoshaphat said unto the king of Israel, Enquire, I pray thee, at the word of the LORD to day.

2 Chr 20:4 And Judah gathered themselves together, to ask *help* of the LORD: even out of all the cities of Judah they came to seek the LORD.

2 Chr 32:11 Doth not Hezekiah persuade you to give over yourselves to die by famine and by thirst, saying, The LORD our God shall deliver us out of the hand of the king of Assyria?

Ne 2:20 Then answered I them, and said unto them, The God of heaven, he will prosper us; therefore we his servants will arise and build: but ye have no portion, nor right, nor memorial, in Jerusalem.

Ps 3:6 I will not be afraid of ten thousands of people, that have set *themselves* against me round about.

Ps 16:6 The lines are fallen unto me in pleasant *places;* yea, I have a goodly heritage.

Ps 20:7 Some *trust* in chariots, and some in horses: but we will remember the name of the LORD our God.

Ps 22:5 They cried unto thee, and were delivered: they trusted in thee, and were not confounded.

Ps 23:4 Yea, though I walk through the valley of the shadow of death, I will fear no evil: for thou *art* with me; thy rod and thy staff they comfort me.

Ps 27:3 Though an host should encamp against me, my heart shall not fear: though war should rise against me, in this *will* I *be* confident.

Ps 27:13 *I had fainted,* unless I had believed to see the goodness of the LORD in the land of the living.

Ps 31:6 I have hated them that regard lying vanities: but I trust in the LORD.

Ps 40:3 And he hath put a new song in my mouth, *even* praise unto our God: many shall see *it,* and fear, and shall trust in the LORD.

Ps 46:2 Therefore will not we fear, though the earth be removed, and though the mountains be carried into the midst of the sea;

Ps 55:23 But thou, O God, shalt bring them down into the pit of destruction: bloody and deceitful men shall not live out half their days; but I will trust in thee.

Ps 56:4 In God I will praise his word, in God I have put my trust; I will not fear what flesh can do unto me.

Ps 60:12 Through God we shall do valiantly: for he *it is that* shall tread down our enemies.

Ps 71:1 In thee, O LORD, do I put my trust: let me never be put to confusion.

Ps 102:13 Thou shalt arise, *and* have mercy upon Zion: for the time to favour her, yea, the set time, is come.

Ps 108:13 Through God we shall do valiantly: for he *it is that* shall tread down our enemies.

Ps 118:6 The LORD *is* on my side; I will not fear: what can man do unto me?

Ps 118:10 All nations compassed me about: but in the name of the LORD will I destroy them.

Ps 124:1 If *it had not been* the LORD who was on our side, now may Israel say;

Ps 138:8 The LORD will perfect *that which* concerneth me: thy mercy, O

LORD, *endureth* for ever: forsake not the works of thine own hands.

Pr 3:26 For the LORD shall be thy confidence, and shall keep thy foot from being taken.

Is 12:2 Behold, God *is* my salvation; I will trust, and not be afraid: for the LORD JEHOVAH *is* my strength and *my* song; he also is become my salvation.

Is 37:14 And Hezekiah received the letter from the hand of the messengers, and read it: and Hezekiah went up unto the house of the LORD, and spread it before the LORD.

Is 49:4 Then I said, I have laboured in vain, I have spent my strength for nought, and in vain: *yet* surely my judgment *is* with the LORD, and my work with my God.

Je 20:11 But the LORD *is* with me as a mighty terrible one: therefore my persecutors shall stumble, and they shall not prevail: they shall be greatly ashamed; for they shall not prosper: *their* everlasting confusion shall never be forgotten.

Da 3:17 If it be *so,* our God whom we serve is able to deliver us from the burning fiery furnace, and he will deliver *us* out of thine hand, O king.

Da 6:16 Then the king commanded, and they brought Daniel, and cast *him* into the den of lions. *Now* the king spake and said unto Daniel, Thy God whom thou servest continually, he will deliver thee.

Hab 3:18 Yet I will rejoice in the LORD, I will joy in the God of my salvation.

Zec 12:5 And the governors of Judah shall say in their heart, The inhabitants of Jerusalem *shall be* my strength in the LORD of hosts their God.

Lu 23:46 And when Jesus had cried with a loud voice, he said, Father, into thy hands I commend my spirit: and having said thus, he gave up the ghost.

Ac 27:34 Wherefore I pray you to take *some* meat: for this is for your health: for there shall not an hair fall from the head of any of you.

Ro 4:20 He staggered not at the promise of God through unbelief; but was strong in faith, giving glory to God;

Ro 8:31 What shall we then say to these things? If God *be* for us, who *can be* against us?

2 Co 1:11 Ye also helping together by prayer for us, that for the gift *bestowed* upon us by the means of many persons thanks may be given by many on our behalf.

2 Co 3:4 And such trust have we through Christ to God-ward:

2 Co 4:14 Knowing that he which raised up the Lord Jesus shall raise up us also by Jesus, and shall present *us* with you.

Ph 1:6 Being confident of this very thing, that he which hath begun a good work in you will perform *it* until the day of Jesus Christ:

Ph 2:24 But I trust in the Lord that I also myself shall come shortly.

2 Th 3:4 And we have confidence in the Lord touching you, that ye both do and will do the things which we command you.

2 Ti 4:18 And the Lord shall deliver me from every evil work, and will preserve *me* unto his heavenly kingdom: to whom *be* glory for ever and ever. Amen.

He 11:11 Through faith also Sara herself received strength to conceive seed, and was delivered of a child when she was past age, because she judged him faithful who had promised.

He 11:19 Accounting that God *was* able to raise *him* up, even from the dead; from whence also he received him in a figure.

He 13:6 So that we may boldly say, The Lord *is* my helper, and I will not fear what man shall do unto me.

1 Pe 3:5 For after this manner in the old time the holy women also, who trusted in God, adorned themselves, being in subjection unto their own husbands:

See **DOUBT**

CONFISCATION *See* **NATION**

CONFLAGRATIONS, *burnings*

Ge 19:28; Jos 6:24; 8:20, 28; 11:13; Jud 18:27; 20:40, 48; 1 S 30:1; 1 K 9:16; 2 K 25:9; 2 Chr 36:19; Jb 1:16; Je 17:27; 52:13; Eze 24:9

See **FIRE**

CONFLICT

1. Characteristics

AN INWARD BATTLE

Ro 7:23 But I see another law in my members, warring against the law of my mind, and bringing me into captivity to the law of sin which is in my members.

SPIRITUAL WEAPONS

2 Co 10:4 (For the weapons of our warfare *are* not carnal, but mighty through God to the pulling down of strong holds;)

INVISIBLE FOES

Ep 6:12 For we wrestle not against flesh and blood, but against principalities, against powers, against the rulers of the darkness of this world, against spiritual wickedness in high *places.*

YOUNG SOLDIERS ENLISTED

1 Ti 1:18 This charge I commit unto thee, son Timothy, according to the prophecies which went before on thee, that thou by them mightest war a good warfare;

A FIGHT OF FAITH

1 Ti 6:12 Fight the good fight of faith, lay hold on eternal life, whereunto thou art also called, and hast professed a good profession before many witnesses.

ENTIRE CONSECRATION DEMANDED

2 Ti 2:4 No man that warreth entangleth himself with the affairs of *this* life; that he may please him who hath chosen him to be a soldier.

He 10:32 But call to remembrance the former days, in which, after ye were illuminated, ye endured a great fight of afflictions;

Re 12:17 And the dragon was wroth with the woman, and went to make war with the remnant of her seed, which keep the commandments of God, and have the testimony of Jesus Christ.

2. Exhortations

De 11:8 Therefore shall ye keep all the commandments which I command you this day, that ye may be strong, and go in and possess the land, whither ye go to possess it;

Jos 1:6 Be strong and of a good courage: for unto this people shalt thou divide for an inheritance the land, which I sware unto their fathers to give them.

Jos 17:15 And Joshua answered them, If thou *be* a great people, *then* get thee up to the wood *country,* and cut down for thyself there in the land of the Perizzites and of the giants, if mount Ephraim be too narrow for thee.

1 K 2:2 I go the way of all the earth: be thou strong therefore, and shew thyself a man;

2 Chr 15:7 Be ye strong therefore, and let not your hands be weak: for your work shall be rewarded.

Is 35:4 Say to them *that are* of a fearful heart, Be strong, fear not: behold, your God will come *with* vengeance, *even* God *with* a recompence; he will come and save you.

Is 52:1 Awake, awake; put on thy strength, O Zion; put on thy beautiful garments, O Jerusalem, the holy city: for henceforth there shall no more come into thee the uncircumcised and the unclean.

Hag 2:4 Yet now be strong, O Zerubbabel, saith the LORD; and be strong, O Joshua, son of Josedech, the high priest; and be strong, all ye people of the land, saith the LORD, and work: for *I am* with you, saith the LORD of hosts:

Zec 8:9 Thus saith the LORD of hosts; Let your hands be strong, ye that hear in these days these words by the mouth of the prophets, which *were* in the day *that* the foundation of the house of the LORD of hosts was laid, that the temple might be built.

1 Co 16:13 Watch ye, stand fast in the faith, quit you like men, be strong.

Ep 6:10 Finally, my brethren, be strong in the Lord, and in the power of his might.

2 Ti 2:1 Thou therefore, my son, be strong in the grace that is in Christ Jesus.

See **ARMOUR, PEACE, PROTECTION**

CONFORMITY *See* **WORLDLINESS**

CONGREGATION, *assembly*

Ex 12:6; 16:2, 9; 17:1; 35:1, 20; Le 4:13; 9:5; 16:17, 33; 24:14; Nu 13:26; 14:1, 35; 15:15, 24; 16:9, 21, 41, 46; 20:8, 27; 27:21; 31:12, 27; De 23:1; 29:10; Jos 9:18; 20:6; 22:12; 24:1; 1 Chr 29:10, 20; 2 Chr 7:8; 23:3; 29:23; 30:25; Ne 8:17

The Assembling of

Le 8:3; Nu 1:18; 8:9; De 5:1; Jos 8:32; 18:1; 23:2; Jud 20:1; 1 S 7:6; 10:17; 1 K 8:5, 22; 2 K 23:2; 1 Chr 13:5; 15:3; 2 Chr 5:3; 10:3; 15:9; 30:13; 34:30; 35:18; Ezr 3:1; 9:4; 10:1, 9; Ps 40:9; 68:10; Jl 1:14; 2:16; Mi 2:5

CONJUGAL LOVE *See* **FAMILY**

CONQUESTS, *of the heathen by Israel*

Nu 21:24, 32, 35; 32:39; 33:53; De 2:36; 3:4; 9:3; 11:23; 29:8; Jos 6:20; 8:24; 10:28, 39; 11:8, 17, 23; 12:7; 18:1; 19:47; 24:8; Jud 1:8, 25, 35; 3:30; 4:16, 24; 8:28; 9:45; 11:21, 33; 18:27; 1 S 7:13; 2 K 14:7; 1 Chr 18:1; 19:19; 22:18; 2 Chr 8:3; 27:5; Ps 18:37; Is 41:15; Jl 3:8; Mi 4:13; Zep 2:9; He 11:33

See **WAR**

CONSCIENCE

Ac 23:1 And Paul, earnestly beholding the council, said, Men *and* brethren, I have lived in all good conscience before God until this day.

Ro 2:15 Which shew the work of the law written in their hearts, their conscience also bearing witness, and *their* thoughts the mean while accusing or else excusing one another;)

Ro 13:5 Wherefore *ye* must needs be subject, not only for wrath, but also for conscience sake.

1 Co 8:7 Howbeit *there is* not in every man that knowledge: for some with conscience of the idol unto this hour eat *it* as a thing offered unto an idol; and their conscience being weak is defiled.

1 Co 10:25 Whatsoever is sold in the shambles, *that* eat, asking no question for conscience sake:

2 Co 5:11 Knowing therefore the terror of the Lord, we persuade men; but we are made manifest unto God; and I trust also are made manifest in your consciences.

He 9:14 How much more shall the blood of Christ, who through the eternal Spirit offered himself without spot to God, purge your conscience from dead works to serve the living God?

He 10:22 Let us draw near with a true heart in full assurance of faith, having our hearts sprinkled from an evil conscience, and our bodies washed with pure water.

1. Good

Ac 24:16 And herein do I exercise myself, to have always a conscience void of offence toward God, and *toward* men.

Ro 9:1 I say the truth in Christ, I lie not, my conscience also bearing me witness in the Holy Ghost,

2 Co 1:12 For our rejoicing is this, the testimony of our conscience, that in simplicity and godly sincerity, not with fleshly wisdom, but by the grace of God, we have had our conversation in the world, and more abundantly to you-ward.

1 Ti 1:5 Now the end of the commandment is charity out of a pure heart, and *of* a good conscience, and *of* faith unfeigned:

1 Ti 1:19 Holding faith, and a good conscience; which some having put away concerning faith have made shipwreck:

1 Ti 3:9 Holding the mystery of the faith in a pure conscience.

2 Ti 1:3 I thank God, whom I serve from *my* forefathers with pure conscience, that without ceasing I have remembrance of thee in my prayers night and day;

He 13:18 Pray for us: for we trust we have a good conscience, in all things willing to live honestly.

1 Pe 2:19 For this *is* thankworthy, if a man for conscience toward God endure grief, suffering wrongfully.

1 Pe 3:16 Having a good conscience; that, whereas they speak evil of you, as of evildoers, they may be ashamed that falsely accuse your good conversation in Christ.

1 Pe 3:21 The like figure whereunto *even* baptism doth also now save us (not the putting away of the filth of the flesh, but the answer of a good conscience toward God,) by the resurrection of Jesus Christ:

2. Guilty

JOSEPH'S BRETHREN

Ge 42:21 Then they said to one another, "We *are* truly guilty concerning our brother, for we saw the anguish of his soul when he pleaded with us, and we would not hear; therefore this distress has come upon us."

PHARAOH

Ex 9:27 And Pharaoh sent, and called for Moses and Aaron, and said unto them, I have sinned this time: the Lord *is* righteous, and I and my people *are* wicked.

EZRA

Ezr 9:6 And said, O my God, I am ashamed and blush to lift up my face to thee, my God: for our iniquities are increased over *our* head, and our trespass is grown up unto the heavens.

THE PSALMIST

Ps 40:12 For innumerable evils have compassed me about: mine iniquities have taken hold upon me, so that I am not able to look up; they are more than the hairs of mine head: therefore my heart faileth me.

BELSHAZZAR

Da 5:6 Then the king's countenance was changed, and his thoughts troubled him, so that the joints of his loins were loosed, and his knees smote one against another.

THE SCRIBES AND PHARISEES

Jn 8:9 And they which heard *it,* being convicted by *their own* conscience, went out one by one, beginning at the eldest, *even* unto the last: and Jesus was left alone, and the woman standing in the midst.

See **CONDEMNATION, SIN**

CONSECRATION, *the act of setting apart as sacred*

1. Personal

Ex 32:29 For Moses had said, Consecrate yourselves to day to the Lord, even every man upon his son, and upon his brother; that he may bestow upon you a blessing this day.

1 Chr 29:5 The gold for *things* of gold, and the silver for *things* of silver, and for all manner of work *to be made* by the hands of artificers. And who *then* is willing to consecrate his service this day unto the Lord?

Pr 23:26 My son, give me thine heart, and let thine eyes observe my ways.

Ro 12:1 I beseech you therefore, brethren, by the mercies of God, that ye present your bodies a living sacrifice, holy, acceptable unto God, *which is* your reasonable service.

2 Ti 2:21 If a man therefore purge himself from these, he shall be a vessel unto honour, sanctified, and meet for the master's use, *and* prepared unto every good work.

2. Examples

Jud 5:2 Praise ye the Lord for the avenging of Israel, when the people willingly offered themselves.

2 Chr 17:16 And next him *was* Amasiah the son of Zichri, who willingly offered himself unto the Lord; and with him two hundred thousand mighty men of valour.

Ps 40:7 Then said I, Lo, I come: in the volume of the book *it is* written of me,

Is 6:8 Also I heard the voice of the Lord, saying, Whom shall I send, and who will go for us? Then said I, Here *am* I; send me.

Ac 6:4 But we will give ourselves continually to prayer, and to the ministry of the word.

2 Co 8:5 And *this they did,* not as we hoped, but first gave their own selves to the Lord, and unto us by the will of God.

Ph 3:8 Yea doubtless, and I count all things *but* loss for the excellency of the knowledge of Christ Jesus my Lord: for whom I have suffered the loss of all things, and do count them *but* dung, that I may win Christ,

See **BACKSLIDING, OBEDIENCE**

3. To Special Religious Work

Ex 29:9 And thou shalt gird them with girdles, Aaron and his sons, and put the bonnets on them: and the priest's office shall be theirs for a perpetual statute: and thou shalt consecrate Aaron and his sons.

Le 8:12 And he poured of the anointing oil upon Aaron's head, and anointed him, to sanctify him.

Nu 3:3 These *are* the names of the sons of Aaron, the priests which were anointed, whom he consecrated to minister in the priest's office.

Nu 16:9 *Seemeth it but* a small thing unto you, that the God of Israel hath separated you from the congregation of Israel, to bring you near to himself to do the service of the tabernacle of the LORD, and to stand before the congregation to minister unto them?

Nu 27:23 And he laid his hands upon him, and gave him a charge, as the LORD commanded by the hand of Moses.

2 Chr 5:11 And it came to pass, when the priests were come out of the holy *place:* (for all the priests *that were* present were sanctified, *and* did not *then* wait by course:

Ac 6:6 Whom they set before the apostles: and when they had prayed, they laid *their* hands on them.

Ac 13:3 And when they had fasted and prayed, and laid *their* hands on them, they sent *them* away.

See **ANOINTING**

4. Entire

CALEB AND JOSHUA

Nu 32:12 Save Caleb the son of Jephunneh the Kenezite, and Joshua the son of Nun: for they have wholly followed the LORD.

JOSIAH AND HIS SUBJECTS

2 K 23:3 And the king stood by a pillar, and made a covenant before the LORD, to walk after the LORD, and to keep his commandments and his testimonies and his statutes with all *their* heart and all *their* soul, to perform the words of this covenant that were written in this book. And all the people stood to the covenant.

2 K 23:25 And like unto him was there no king before him, that turned to the LORD with all his heart, and with all his soul, and with all his might, according to all the law of Moses; neither after him arose there *any* like him.

JUDAH UNDER KING ASA

2 Chr 15:15 And all Judah rejoiced at the oath: for they had sworn with all their heart, and sought him with their whole desire; and he was found of them: and the LORD gave them rest round about.

PAUL THE APOSTLE

Ph 3:7–8 But what things were gain to me, those I counted loss for Christ.

Yea doubtless, and I count all things *but* loss for the excellency of the knowledge of Christ Jesus my Lord: for whom I have suffered the loss of all things, and do count them *but* dung, that I may win Christ,

1 Th 5:23 And the very God of peace sanctify you wholly; and *I pray God* your whole spirit and soul and body be preserved blameless unto the coming of our Lord Jesus Christ.

CONSISTENCY　See **LIFE**

CONSPIRACY, connivance

Ex 23:2; 32:4; Le 5:1; 20:4; Jud 9:24; 1 K 21:11; Ps 50:18; Pr 24:24; 28:4; 29:24; Je 5:31; 44:15; Mk 14:11; Ac 22:20; Ro 1:32; 2 Jn 11

CONSTANCY See GOD

CONSTITUTION See NATION

CONSUMPTION See DISEASE

CONTACT

1. Personal

JEHONADAB'S, by Jehu

2 K 10:15 And when he was departed thence, he lighted on Jehonadab the son of Rechab *coming* to meet him: and he saluted him, and said to him, Is thine heart right, as my heart *is* with thy heart? And Jehonadab answered, It is. If it be, give *me* thine hand. And he gave *him* his hand; and he took him up to him into the chariot.

THE LITTLE MAID'S, by Jesus

Mt 9:25 But when the people were put forth, he went in, and took her by the hand, and the maid arose.

THE DEMONIAC'S, by Jesus

Mk 9:27 But Jesus took him by the hand, and lifted him up; and he arose.

THE LAME MAN'S, by Peter

Ac 3:7 And he took him by the right hand, and lifted *him* up: and immediately his feet and ankle bones received strength.

DORCAS'S, by Peter in restoring life

Ac 9:41 And he gave her *his* hand, and lifted her up, and when he had called the saints and widows, presented her alive.

2. The Church, like salt, saves by contact

Mt 5:13 Ye are the salt of the earth: but if the salt have lost his savour, wherewith shall it be salted? it is thenceforth good for nothing, but to be cast out, and to be trodden under foot of men.

Mk 9:50 Salt *is* good: but if the salt have lost his saltness, wherewith will ye season it? Have salt in yourselves, and have peace one with another.

Lu 14:34 Salt *is* good: but if the salt have lost his savour, wherewith shall it be seasoned?

3. In Raising the Dead

1 K 17:21–22; 2 K 4:34–35

4. With Christ

a. People Who Touched Christ

Mt 9:20 And, behold, a woman, which was diseased with an issue of blood twelve years, came behind *him,* and touched the hem of his garment:

Mt 14:35 And when the men of that place had knowledge of him, they sent out into all that country round about, and brought unto him all that were diseased;

Mt 14:36 And besought him that they might only touch the hem of his garment: and as many as touched were made perfectly whole.

Mk 3:10 For he had healed many; insomuch that they pressed upon him for to touch him, as many as had plagues.

Mk 5:27 When she had heard of Jesus, came in the press behind, and touched his garment.

Mk 5:30 And Jesus, immediately knowing in himself that virtue had gone out of him, turned him about in the press, and said, who touched my clothes?

Mk 6:56 And whithersoever he entered, into villages, or cities, or country, they laid the sick in the streets, and besought him that they might touch if it were but the border of his garment: and as many as touched him were made whole.

Lu 6:19 And the whole multitude sought to touch him: for there went virtue out of him, and healed *them* all.

Lu 8:44 Came behind *him,* and touched the border of his garment: and immediately her issue of blood stanched.

b. People Whom Christ Touched

THE CLEANSING TOUCH

Mt 8:3 And Jesus put forth *his* hand, and touched him, saying, I will; be thou clean. And immediately his leprosy was cleansed.

THE QUIETING TOUCH

Mt 8:15 And he touched her hand, and the fever left her: and she arose, and ministered unto them.

THE ILLUMINATING TOUCH

Mt 9:29–30 Then touched he their eyes, saying, According to your faith be it unto you.

And their eyes were opened; and Jesus straitly charged them, saying, See *that* no man know *it*.

THE REASSURING TOUCH

Mt 17:7 And Jesus came and touched them, and said, Arise, and be not afraid.

Mt 20:34 So Jesus had compassion *on them*, and touched their eyes: and immediately their eyes received sight, and they followed him.

THE LIBERATING TOUCH

Mk 7:33 And he took him aside from the multitude, and put his fingers into his ears, and he spit, and touched his tongue;

Mk 7:35 And straightway his ears were opened, and the string of his tongue was loosed, and he spake plain.

THE TOUCH UPON CHILDHOOD

Mk 10:13 And they brought young children to him, that he should touch them: and *his* disciples rebuked those that brought *them*.

Mk 10:16 And he took them up in his arms, put *his* hands upon them, and blessed them.

THE HEALING TOUCH

Lu 22:51 And Jesus answered and said, Suffer ye thus far. And he touched his ear, and healed him.

5. With Impurity, *caused uncleanness; due to association with certain foods, contact with dead bodies, or certain bodily conditions and diseases*

a. Contaminates

Le 5:2; 15:5, 11, 21, 27; 22:4; Nu 19:13, 22; Is 52:11; Lam 4:14; Hag 2:13; Lu 7:39

b. Forbidden

Ge 3:3; Nu 16:26; Ps 125:3; Is 52:11; 2 Co 6:17; Col 2:21

See **ASSOCIATIONS, SEPARATION**

CONTEMPT, *for the righteous*

Ge 16:4; Ex 2:14; 1 S 10:27; 14:11; 17:28, 43; 25:10; 2 S 5:6; 6:20; 16:13; Ne 2:19; 4:3; Jb 12:5; Ps 31:18; 80:6; 119:22; 123:4; Pr 11:12; 18:3; Mt 13:55; Jn 7:47; 9:34; Ac 17:18

See **WICKED**

CONTENTMENT

Ex 2:21 And Moses was content to dwell with the man: and he gave Moses Zipporah his daughter.

2 K 4:13 And he said unto him, Say now unto her, Behold, thou hast been careful for us with all this care; what *is* to be done for thee? wouldest thou be spoken for to the king, or to the captain of the host? And she answered, I dwell among mine own people.

Pr 15:16 Better *is* little with the fear of the LORD than great treasure and trouble therewith.

Mk 6:10 And he said unto them, In what place soever ye enter into an house, there abide till ye depart from that place.

Lu 3:14 And the soldiers likewise demanded of him, saying, And what shall we do? And he said unto them, Do violence to no man, neither accuse *any* falsely; and be content with your wages.

1 Co 7:24 Brethren, let every man, wherein he is called, therein abide with God.

Ph 2:14 Do all things without murmurings and disputings:

Ph 4:11 Not that I speak in respect of want: for I have learned, in whatsoever state I am, *therewith* to be content.

1 Ti 6:6 But godliness with contentment is great gain.

1 Ti 6:8 And having food and raiment let us be therewith content.

He 13:5 *Let your* conversation *be* without covetousness; *and be* content with such things as ye have: for he hath said, I will never leave thee, nor forsake thee.

See **DISCONTENTMENT**

CONTRACTS, *agreements or compacts between two or more parties*

1. Binding Force
Ga 3:15

2. Examples
Ge 21:27; 23:20; Ru 4:7–8; 1 K 5:8–11

See **COVENANTS, REAL ESTATE**

CONVERSATION, *spiritual*

USED IN EVERYDAY LIFE

De 6:7 And thou shalt teach them diligently unto thy children, and shalt talk of them when thou sittest in thine house, and when thou walkest by the way, and when thou liest down, and when thou risest up.

De 11:19 And ye shall teach them your children, speaking of them when thou sittest in thine house, and when thou walkest by the way, when thou liest down, and when thou risest up.

CONCERNING THE THINGS OF GOD

Ps 145:11 They shall speak of the glory of thy kingdom, and talk of thy power;

THE HABIT OF THE SAINTS

Mal 3:16 Then they that feared the LORD spake often one to another: and the LORD hearkened, and heard *it,* and a book of remembrance was written before him for them that feared the LORD, and that thought upon his name.

THE TOPIC

Lu 24:13–14 And, behold, two of them went that same day to a village called Emmaus, which was from Jerusalem *about* threescore furlongs.

And they talked together of all these things which had happened.

EXPRESSING RELIGIOUS FERVENCY

Lu 24:32 And they said one to another, Did not our heart burn within us, while he talked with us by the way, and while he opened to us the scriptures?

EXPRESSED IN MUSIC

Ep 5:19 Speaking to yourselves in psalms and hymns and spiritual songs, singing and making melody in your heart to the Lord;

CONVERSION

DIVINE LAW THE AGENT

Ps 19:7 The law of the LORD *is* perfect, converting the soul: the testimony of the LORD *is* sure, making wise the simple.

JOYFUL BELIEVERS USED AS INSTRUMENTS

Ps 51:12–13 Restore unto me the joy of thy salvation; and uphold me *with thy* free spirit.

Then will I teach transgressors thy ways; and sinners shall be converted unto thee.

ESSENTIAL FOR ENTRANCE
INTO GOD'S KINGDOM

Mt 18:3 And said, Verily I say unto you, Except ye be converted, and become as little children, ye shall not enter into the kingdom of heaven.

PREPARES FOR CHRISTIAN SERVICE

Lu 22:32 But I have prayed for thee, that thy faith fail not: and when thou art converted, strengthen thy brethren.

ENJOINED UPON ALL

Ac 3:19 Repent ye therefore, and be converted, that your sins may be blotted out, when the times of refreshing shall come from the presence of the Lord;

THE SUPREME TASK OF THE CHURCH

Ja 5:19–20 Brethren, if any of you do err from the truth, and one convert him;

Let him know, that he which converteth the sinner from the error of his way shall save a soul from death, and shall hide a multitude of sins.

1. Instances

KING SAUL

1 S 10:9 And it was *so,* that when he had turned his back to go from Samuel, God gave him another heart: and all those signs came to pass that day.

ZACCHEUS

Lu 19:9 And Jesus said unto him, This day is salvation come to this house, forsomuch as he also is a son of Abraham.

ETHIOPIAN EUNUCH

Ac 8:37 And Philip said, If thou believest with all thine heart, thou mayest. And he answered and said, I believe that Jesus Christ is the Son of God.

SAUL OF TARSUS

Ac 9:6 And he trembling and astonished said, Lord, what wilt thou have me to do? And the Lord *said* unto him, Arise, and go into the city, and it shall be told thee what thou must do.

ROMAN PROCONSUL

Ac 13:12 Then the deputy, when he saw what was done, believed, being astonished at the doctrine of the Lord.

LYDIA

Ac 16:14 And a certain woman named Lydia, a seller of purple, of the city of Thyatira, which worshipped God, heard *us:* whose heart the Lord opened, that she attended unto the things which were spoken of Paul.

PHILIPPIAN JAILER

Ac 16:33–34 And he took them the same hour of the night, and washed *their* stripes; and was baptized, he and all his, straightway.

And when he had brought them into his house, he set meat before them, and rejoiced, believing in God with all his house.

2. Transformations

PETER, THE PROFANE FISHERMAN

Ac 5:15 Insomuch that they brought forth the sick into the streets, and laid *them* on beds and couches, that at the least the shadow of Peter passing by might overshadow some of them.

THE RESTLESS DEMONIAC

Mk 5:15 And they come to Jesus, and see him that was possessed with the devil, and had the legion, sitting, and clothed, and in his right mind: and they were afraid.

JOHN THE VINDICTIVE JEW

1 Jn 4:7 Beloved, let us love one another: for love is of God; and every one that loveth is born of God, and knoweth God.

THE WOMAN OF SAMARIA

Jn 4:29 Come, see a man, which told me all things that ever I did: is not this the Christ?

SAUL, THE BLOODTHIRSTY PERSECUTOR

Ac 21:13 Then Paul answered, What mean ye to weep and to break mine heart? for I am ready not to be bound only, but also to die at Jerusalem for the name of the Lord Jesus.

THE COLD-HEARTED PHILIPPIAN JAILER

Ac 16:33 And he took them the same hour of the night, and washed *their* stripes; and was baptized, he and all his, straightway

See **SALVATION**

CONVICTION OF SIN

UNREST

Ps 32:3 When I kept silence, my bones waxed old through my roaring all the day long.

BURDEN OF SOUL

Ps 38:4 For mine iniquities are gone over mine head: as an heavy burden they are too heavy for me.

MISERY

Ps 51:3 For I acknowledge my transgressions: and my sin *is* ever before me.

Ps 73:21 Thus my heart was grieved, and I was pricked in my reins.

Jn 16:8 And when he is come, he will reprove the world of sin, and of righteousness, and of judgment:

STING OF CONSCIENCE

Ac 2:37 Now when they heard *this,* they were pricked in their heart, and said unto Peter and to the rest of the apostles, Men *and* brethren, what shall we do?

Ac 16:29 Then he called for a light, and sprang in, and came trembling, and fell down before Paul and Silas,

TERROR

Ac 24:25 And as he reasoned of righteousness, temperance, and judgment to come Felix trembled, and answered, Go thy way for this time; when I have a convenient season, I will call for thee.

See **GUILT, HOLY SPIRIT, REPENTANCE**

CONVOCATION, *general assembly of the Israelites*

Ex 12:16; Le 23:3, 21, 27, 35; Nu 28:18, 25, 26; 29:1, 7, 12, 35

See **CONGREGATION**

COOKING See **FOOD**

COOPERATION, *working together toward a common goal*

1. Essential to Success

TO SUSTAIN IN TIMES OF WEAKNESS

Ex 17:12 But Moses' hands *were* heavy; and they took a stone, and put *it* under him, and he sat thereon; and Aaron and Hur stayed up his hands, the one on the one side, and the other on the other side; and his hands were steady until the going down of the sun.

TO GIVE SUCCESS IN BATTLE

Jud 20:11 So all the men of Israel were gathered against the city, knit together as one man.

TO RAISE COURAGE FOR THE CONFLICT

1 S 14:6–7 And Jonathan said to the young man that bare his armour, Come, and let us go over unto the garrison of these uncircumcised: it may be that the LORD will work for us: for *there is* no restraint to the LORD to save by many or by few.

And his armourbearer said unto him, Do all that *is* in thine heart: turn thee; behold, I *am* with thee according to thy heart.

TO INSPIRE IMPROVEMENT

2 K 6:1–3 And the sons of the prophets said unto Elisha, Behold now, the place where we dwell with thee is too strait for us.

Let us go, we pray thee, unto Jordan, and take thence every man a beam, and let us make us a place there, where we may dwell. And he answered, Go ye.

And one said, Be content, I pray thee, and go with thy servants. And he answered, I will go.

TO ENCOURAGE REFORMS

1 Chr 12:38 All these men of war, that could keep rank, came with a perfect heart to Hebron, to make David king over all Israel: and all the rest also of Israel *were* of one heart to make David king.

TO CARRY THROUGH GREAT UNDERTAKINGS

Ne 4:16–17 And it came to pass from that time forth, *that* the half of my servants wrought in the work, and the other half of them held both the spears, the shields, and the bows, and the habergeons; and the rulers *were* behind all the house of Judah.

They which builded on the wall, and they that bare burdens, with those that laded, *every one* with one of his hands wrought in the work, and with the other *hand* held a weapon.

TO GIVE ADDED POWER IN PRAYER

Mt 18:19 Again I say unto you, That if two of you shall agree on earth as touching any thing that they shall ask, it shall be done for them of my Father which is in heaven.

TO BRING MEN TO CHRIST

Mk 2:3 And they come unto him, bringing one sick of the palsy, which was borne of four.

Mk 6:7 And he called *unto him* the twelve, and began to send them forth by two and two; and gave them power over unclean spirits;

Ph 1:27 Only let your conversation be as it becometh the gospel of Christ: that whether I come and see you, or else be absent, I may hear of your affairs, that ye stand fast in one spirit, with one mind striving together for the faith of the gospel;

2. Exemplified in Marriage

Ge 2:18 And the Lord God said, *It is* not good that the man should be alone; I will make him an help meet for him.

Pr 31:12–13 She will do him good and not evil all the days of her life.

She seeketh wool, and flax, and worketh willingly with her hands.

1 Pe 3:7 Likewise, ye husbands, dwell with *them* according to knowledge, giving honour unto the wife, as unto the weaker vessel, and as being heirs together of the grace of life; that your prayers be not hindered.

See **MARRIAGE, STRIFE**

3. Seen in the Divine Plan

MOSES AND AARON

Ex 4:16 And he shall be thy spokesman unto the people: and he shall be, *even* he shall be to thee instead of a mouth, and thou shalt be to him instead of God.

CALEB AND JOSHUA

Nu 14:6 And Joshua the son of Nun, and Caleb the son of Jephunneh, *which were* of them that searched the land, rent their clothes:

ELIJAH AND ELISHA

2 K 2:6 And Elijah said unto him, Tarry, I pray thee, here; for the Lord hath sent me to Jordan. And he said, *As* the Lord liveth, and *as* thy soul liveth, I will not leave thee. And they two went on.

SEVENTY SENT FORTH TWO BY TWO

Lu 10:1 After these things the Lord appointed other seventy also, and sent them two and two before his face into every city and place, whither he himself would come.

PAUL AND BARNABAS

Ac 13:2 As they ministered to the Lord, and fasted, the Holy Ghost said, Separate me Barnabas and Saul for the work whereunto I have called them.

PAUL AND SILAS

Ac 15:40 And Paul chose Silas, and departed, being recommended by the brethren unto the grace of God.

COPPERSMITHS *See* ARTS AND CRAFTS

CORAL, *rocklike structures formed by sea organisms, considered as precious stones by the Hebrews*

Jb 28:18; Eze 27:16

COPULATION *See* ADULTERY, SEX

CORDS, *small rope*

Ex 35:18; 39:40; Nu 3:26, 37; Jos 2:15; Jud 15:13; 16:12; Jb 39:10; 41:1

CORINTH, *a city of Achaia*

Corinth, a proud and wealthy city of the ancient world, was located on the four-mile-wide strip of land that linked the southern Peloponnesus with the mainland of Greece. Being on the north-south highway and having the two thriving seaports of Cenchraea on the east and Lechaeum on the west, it was literally "at the meeting of the ways." It easily became the greatest commercial center of Greece and was the head of the Achaean League. Around it were fertile lands on which were grown olives, grapes, dates, and many other familiar fruits. Paul came to Corinth about A.D. 50 and stayed a year and a half (Ac 18), supporting himself by tent-making. By his preaching and teaching he converted both Jews and Greeks and gathered together the Corinthian church, to which he later wrote two epistles.

Ac 18:1; 19:1; 1 Co 1:2; 2 Co 1:1, 23; 2 Ti 4:20

See **PAUL**

CORINTHIANS

1. FIRST

Author: The apostle Paul.

Date Written: A.D. 56, from Ephesus (16:5–8) on his third missionary journey.

Purpose: To purify the church from divisions and immorality. The church at Corinth was founded by Paul on his second missionary journey. It had become infected with the evils surrounding it in a licentious city. The Greeks were proud of their learning and philosophy but at the same time were addicted to gross immorality. They were especially fond of oratory. It is apparent that Apollos, an eloquent Christian Jew, had come to Corinth and captured the imaginations of the Greek Christians (Acts 18:24–28). This fact led to the drawing of comparisons between him, with his silver tongue, and other religious leaders, especially to the discredit of Paul, whose bodily presence seems to have

been unimpressive (2 Co 10:10). This probably is a clue to the schisms in the church (1:11–13).

Paul's primary aim was to combat the worldliness that had crept into the church, and the sectarianism that was divisive.

To Whom Written: The church in Corinth (1:2).

Main Theme: Unified and pure living in the midst of an impure world.

Key Word: Love (13).

Key Verses: showing the false conceptions of the ministry: 1:12-17; 3:4–7, 21–22; 4:6–7.

2. SECOND

Author: The apostle Paul.

Date Written: Late in A.D. 56, from Macedonia, probably Philippi.

Purpose: To expose "deceitful workers" and to defend Paul's apostolic authority.

To Whom Written: The church in Corinth (1:1).

Main Theme: This is somewhat hidden, but it is quite apparent that Paul had in mind the vindication of his apostleship when he wrote this book. Both epistles to the Corinthians indicate that there was an element in this church that tended to discredit his ministry and authority. This tendency is shown in the texts of the key passages below.

Key Words: Apostle (1:1, 12:12) and Ambassadors of Jesus Christ (5:20).

Key Verses: 3:1; 5:12; 7:2; 10:2-3; 11:5–6; 12:11; 13:3.

CORMORANTS *See* **BIRDS**

CORNELIUS, *a godly Roman centurion*

BENEVOLENCE, PRAYERFULNESS

Ac 10:2 A devout *man,* and one that feared God with all his house, which gave much alms to the people, and prayed to God alway.

OBEDIENCE

Ac 10:7–8 And when the angel which spake unto Cornelius was departed, he called two of his household servants, and a devout soldier of them that waited on him continually;

And when he had declared all *these* things unto them, he sent them to Joppa.

SPIRITUAL WORK

Ac 10:24 And the morrow after they entered into Caesarea. And Cornelius waited for them, and had called together his kinsmen and near friends.

SPIRITUAL RECEPTIVITY

Ac 10:33 Immediately therefore I sent to thee; and thou hast well done that thou art come. Now therefore are we all here present before God, to hear all things that are commanded thee of God.

CORNET *See* MUSIC

CORONATIONS *See* NATION

CORRECTION *See* PARENTS

CORRUPTION

1. Physical

Ge 3:19 In the sweat of thy face shalt thou eat bread, till thou return unto the ground; for out of it wast thou taken: for dust thou *art,* and unto dust shalt thou return.

Jb 7:5 My flesh is clothed with worms and clods of dust; my skin is broken, and become loathsome.

Jb 13:28 And he, as a rotten thing, consumeth, as a garment that is moth eaten.

Jb 17:14 I have said to corruption, Thou *art* my father: to the worm, *Thou art* my mother, and my sister.

Jb 19:26 And *though* after my skin *worms* destroy this *body,* yet in my flesh shall I see God:

Jb 21:26 They shall lie down alike in the dust, and the worms shall cover them.

Jb 24:20 The womb shall forget him; the worm shall feed sweetly on him;

he shall be no more remembered; and wickedness shall be broken as a tree.

Ps 16:10 For thou wilt not leave my soul in hell; neither wilt thou suffer thine Holy One to see corruption.

Ps 49:9 That he should still live for ever, *and* not see corruption.

Ps 104:29 Thou hidest thy face, they are troubled: thou takest away their breath, they die, and return to their dust.

Ps 119:25 My soul cleaveth unto the dust: quicken thou me according to thy word.

Ps 146:4 His breath goeth forth, he returneth to his earth; in that very day his thoughts perish.

Ec 3:20 All go unto one place; all are of the dust, and all turn to dust again.

Ec 12:7 Then shall the dust return to the earth as it was: and the spirit shall return unto God who gave it.

Is 14:11 Thy pomp is brought down to the grave, *and* the noise of thy viols: the worm is spread under thee, and the worms cover thee.

Jn 11:39 Jesus said, Take ye away the stone. Martha, the sister of him that was dead, saith unto him, Lord, by this time he stinketh: for he hath been *dead* four days.

Ac 2:27 Because thou wilt not leave my soul in hell, neither wilt thou suffer thine Holy One to see corruption.

Ac 13:36 For David, after he had served his own generation by the will of God, fell on sleep, and was laid unto his fathers, and saw corruption:

1 Co 15:42 So also *is* the resurrection of the dead. It is sown in corruption; it is raised in incorruption:

1 Co 15:50 Now this I say, brethren, that flesh and blood cannot inherit the kingdom of God; neither doth corruption inherit incorruption.

See **DEATH**

2. Moral

Ge 6:12 And God looked upon the earth, and, behold, it was corrupt; for all flesh had corrupted his way upon the earth.

Le 19:29 Do not prostitute thy daughter, to cause her to be a whore;

lest the land fall to whoredom, and the land become full of wickedness.

De 4:16 Lest ye corrupt *yourselves,* and make you a graven image, the similitude of any figure, the likeness of male or female,

Jud 2:19 And it came to pass, when the judge was dead, *that* they returned, and corrupted *themselves* more than their fathers, in following other gods to serve them, and to bow down unto them; they ceased not from their own doings, nor from their stubborn way.

2 K 21:6 And he made his son pass through the fire, and observed times, and used enchantments, and dealt with familiar spirits and wizards: he wrought much wickedness in the sight of the Lord, to provoke *him* to anger.

2 K 23:7 And he brake down the houses of the sodomites, that *were* by the house of the Lord, where the women wove hangings for the grove.

2 Chr 33:6 And he caused his children to pass through the fire in the valley of the son of Hinnom: also he observed times, and used enchantments, and used witchcraft, and dealt with a familiar spirit, and with wizards: he wrought much evil in the sight of the Lord, to provoke him to anger.

2 Chr 36:8 Now the rest of the acts of Jehoiakim, and his abominations which he did, and that which was found in him, behold, they *are* written in the book of the kings of Israel and Judah: and Jehoiachin his son reigned in his stead.

Ezr 9:11 Which thou hast commanded by thy servants the prophets, saying, The land, unto which ye go to possess it, is an unclean land with the filthiness of the people of the lands, with their abominations, which have filled it from one end to another with their uncleanness.

Ne 1:7 We have dealt very corruptly against thee, and have not kept the commandments, nor the statutes, nor the judgments, which thou commandedst thy servant Moses.

Jb 22:5 *Is* not thy wickedness great? and thine iniquities infinite?

Ps 14:1 The fool hath said in his heart, *There is* no God. They are corrupt, they have done abominable works, *there is* none that doeth good.

Ps 53:1 The fool hath said in his heart, *There is* no God. Corrupt are they, and have done abominable iniquity: *there is* none that doeth good.

Ps 55:11 Wickedness *is* in the midst thereof: deceit and guile depart not from her streets.

Ps 58:3 The wicked are estranged from the womb: they go astray as soon as they be born, speaking lies.

Is 1:6 From the sole of the foot even unto the head *there is* no soundness in it; *but* wounds, and bruises, and putrifying sores: they have not been closed, neither bound up, neither mollified with ointment.

Is 28:8 For all tables are full of vomit *and* filthiness, *so that there is* no place *clean.*

Je 5:28 They are waxen fat, they shine: yea, they overpass the deeds of the wicked: they judge not the cause, the cause of the fatherless, yet they prosper; and the right of the needy do they not judge.

Je 6:28 They *are* all grievous revolters, walking with slanders: *they are* brass and iron; they *are* all corrupters.

Eze 7:23 Make a chain: for the land is full of bloody crimes, and the city is full of violence.

Mi 6:12 For the rich men thereof are full of violence, and the inhabitants thereof have spoken lies, and their tongue *is* deceitful in their mouth.

Zep 3:7 I said, Surely thou wilt fear me, thou wilt receive instruction; so their dwelling should not be cut off, howsoever I punished them: but they rose early, *and* corrupted all their doings.

Mt 23:28 Even so ye also outwardly appear righteous unto men, but within ye are full of hypocrisy and iniquity.

Lu 11:39 And the Lord said unto him, Now do ye Pharisees make clean the outside of the cup and the platter; but your inward part is full of ravening and wickedness.

See **NATION, SIN**

COUNSEL, *advice, direction*

1. Its Importance

Jud 19:30 And it was so, that all that saw it said, There was no such deed done nor seen from the day that the children of Israel came up out of the land of Egypt unto this day: consider of it, take advice, and speak *your minds.*

Jud 20:7 Behold, ye *are* all children of Israel; give here your advice and counsel.

1 S 5:8 They sent therefore and gathered all the lords of the Philistines unto them, and said, What shall we do with the ark of the God of Israel? And they answered, Let the ark of the God of Israel be carried about unto Gath. And they carried the ark of the God of Israel about *thither.*

2 S 16:20 Then said Absalom to Ahithophel, Give counsel among you what we shall do.

2 S 17:5 Then said Absalom, Call now Hushai the Archite also, and let us hear likewise what he saith.

1 K 1:12 Now therefore come, let me, I pray thee, give thee counsel, that thou mayest save thine own life, and the life of thy son Solomon.

2 K 6:8 Then the king of Syria warred against Israel, and took counsel with his servants, saying, In such and such a place *shall be* my camp.

1 Chr 27:32 Also Jonathan David's uncle was a counsellor, a wise man, and a scribe: and Jehiel the son of Hachmoni *was* with the king's sons:

2 Chr 20:21 And when he had consulted with the people, he appointed singers unto the LORD, and that should praise the beauty of holiness, as they went out before the army, and to say, Praise the LORD; for his mercy *endureth* for ever.

2 Chr 30:2 For the king had taken counsel, and his princes, and all the congregation in Jerusalem, to keep the passover in the second month.

2 Chr 32:3 He took counsel with his princes and his mighty men to stop the waters of the fountains which *were* without the city: and they did help him.

Ezr 10:8 And that whosoever would not come within three days, according to the counsel of the princes and the elders, all his substance should be forfeited, and himself separated from the congregation of those that had been carried away.

Pr 11:14 Where no counsel *is,* the people fall: but in the multitude of counsellors *there is* safety.

Pr 12:15 The way of a fool *is* right in his own eyes: but he that hearkeneth unto counsel *is* wise.

Pr 13:10 Only by pride cometh contention: but with the well advised *is* wisdom.

Pr 15:22 Without counsel purposes are disappointed: but in the multitude of counsellors they are established.

Pr 19:20 Hear counsel, and receive instruction, that thou mayest be wise in thy latter end.

Pr 20:5 Counsel in the heart of man *is like* deep water; but a man of understanding will draw it out.

Pr 20:18 *Every* purpose is established by counsel: and with good advice make war.

Pr 22:20 Have not I written to thee excellent things in counsels and knowledge,

Pr 27:9 Ointment and perfume rejoice the heart: so *doth* the sweetness of a man's friend by hearty counsel.

Ec 4:13 Better *is* a poor and a wise child than an old and foolish king, who will no more be admonished.

Is 16:3 Take counsel, execute judgment; make thy shadow as the night in the midst of the noonday; hide the outcasts; bewray not him that wandereth.

Is 45:21 Tell ye, and bring *them* near; yea, let them take counsel together: who hath declared this from ancient time? *who* hath told it from that time? *have* not I the LORD? and *there is* no God else beside me; a just God and a Saviour; *there is* none beside me.

Lu 14:31 Or what king, going to make war against another king, sitteth not down first, and consulteth whether he be able with ten thousand to meet him that cometh against him with twenty thousand?

1 Co 7:25 Now concerning virgins I have no commandment of the LORD: yet I give my judgment, as one that hath obtained mercy of the LORD to be faithful.

2. Good Examples

Ge 31:16 For all the riches which God hath taken from our father, that *is* ours, and our children's: now then, whatsoever God hath said unto thee, do.

Ge 41:35 And let them gather all the food of those good years that come, and lay up corn under the hand of Pharaoh, and let them keep food in the cities.

Ex 10:7 And Pharaoh's servants said unto him, How long shall this man be a snare unto us? let the men go, that they may serve the LORD their God: knowest thou not yet that Egypt is destroyed?

Ex 18:19 Hearken now unto my voice, I will give thee counsel, and God shall be with thee: Be thou for the people to God-ward, that thou mayest bring the causes unto God:

Nu 13:30 And Caleb stilled the people before Moses, and said, Let us go up at once, and possess it; for we are well able to overcome it.

De 1:14 And ye answered me, and said, The thing which thou hast spoken is good *for us* to do.

1 S 14:36 And Saul said, Let us go down after the Philistines by night, and spoil them until the morning light, and let us not leave a man of them. And they said, Do whatsoever seemeth good unto thee. Then said the priest, Let us draw near hither unto God.

1 S 16:16 Let our lord now command thy servants, *which are* before thee, to seek out a man, *who is* a cunning player on an harp: and it shall come to pass, when the evil spirit from God

is upon thee, that he shall play with his hand, and thou shalt be well.

1 S 25:33 And blessed *be* thy advice, and blessed *be* thou, which hast kept me this day from coming to *shed* blood, and from avenging myself with mine own hand.

2 S 17:14 And Absalom and all the men of Israel said, The counsel of Hushai the Archite *is* better than the counsel of Ahithophel. For the LORD had appointed to defeat the good counsel of Ahithophel, to the intent that the LORD might bring evil upon Absalom.

2 S 17:16 Now therefore send quickly, and tell David, saying, Lodge not this night in the plains of the wilderness, but speedily pass over; lest the king be swallowed up, and all the people that *are* with him.

2 S 19:7 Now therefore arise, go forth, and speak comfortably unto thy servants: for I swear by the LORD, if thou go not forth, there will not tarry one with thee this night: and that will be worse unto thee than all the evil that befell thee from thy youth until now.

2 S 20:22 Then the woman went unto all the people in her wisdom. And they cut off the head of Sheba the son of Bichri, and cast *it* out to Joab. And he blew a trumpet, and they retired from the city, every man to his tent. And Joab returned to Jerusalem unto the king.

2 S 24:3 And Joab said unto the king, Now the LORD thy God add unto the people, how many soever they be, an hundredfold, and that the eyes of my lord the king may see *it:* but why doth my lord the king delight in this thing?

1 K 12:7 And they spake unto him, saying, If thou wilt be a servant unto this people this day, and wilt serve them, and answer them, and speak good words to them, then they will be thy servant for ever.

2 K 5:13 And his servants came near, and spake unto him, and said, My father, *if* the prophet had bid thee *do some* great thing, wouldest thou not have done *it?* how much rather then, when he saith to thee, Wash, and be clean?

2 K 14:10 Thou hast indeed smitten Edom, and thine heart hath lifted thee up: glory *of this*, and tarry at home: for why shouldest thou meddle to *thy* hurt, that thou shouldest fall, *even* thou, and Judah with thee?

1 Chr 21:3 And Joab answered, The LORD make his people an hundred times so many more as they *be:* but, my lord the king, *are* they not all my lord's servants? why then doth my lord require this thing? why will he be a cause of trespass to Israel?

2 Chr 10:7 And they spake unto him, saying, If thou be kind to this people, and please them, and speak good words to them, they will be thy servants for ever.

2 Chr 25:19 Thou sayest, Lo, thou hast smitten the Edomites; and thine heart lifteth thee up to boast: abide now at home; why shouldest thou meddle to *thine* hurt, that thou shouldest fall, *even* thou, and Judah with thee?

2 Chr 28:13 And said unto them, Ye shall not bring in the captives hither: for whereas we have offended against the LORD *already,* ye intend to add *more* to our sins and to our trespass: for our trespass is great, and *there is* fierce wrath against Israel.

Jb 29:21 Unto me *men* gave ear, and waited, and kept silence at my counsel.

Pr 1:5 A wise *man* will hear, and will increase learning; and a man of understanding shall attain unto wise counsels:

Ec 9:17 The words of wise *men are* heard in quiet more than the cry of him that ruleth among fools.

Je 38:15 Then Jeremiah said unto Zedekiah, If I declare *it* unto thee, wilt thou not surely put me to death? and if I give thee counsel, wilt thou not hearken unto me?

Da 2:14 Then Daniel answered with counsel and wisdom to Arioch the captain of the king's guard, which was gone forth to slay the wise *men* of Babylon:

Da 4:27 Wherefore, O king, let my counsel be acceptable unto thee, and break off thy sins by righteousness, and thine iniquities by shewing mercy to the poor; if it may be a lengthening of thy tranquility.

Mt 27:19 When he was set down on the judgment seat, his wife sent unto him, saying, Have thou nothing to do with that just man: for I have suffered many things this day in a dream because of him.

Ac 5:35 And said unto them, Ye men of Israel, take heed to yourselves what ye intend to do as touching these men.

Ac 15:19 Wherefore my sentence is, that we trouble not them, which from among the Gentiles are turned to God:

Ac 19:36 Seeing then that these things cannot be spoken against, ye ought to be quiet, and to do nothing rashly.

Ac 27:10 And said unto them, Sirs, I perceive that this voyage will be with hurt and much damage, not only of the lading and ship, but also of our lives.

Ac 27:21 But after long abstinence Paul stood forth in the midst of them, and said, Sirs, ye should have hearkened unto me, and not have loosed from Crete, and to have gained this harm and loss.

2 Co 8:10 And herein I give *my* advice: for this is expedient for you, who have begun before, not only to do, but also to be forward a year ago.

Re 3:18 I counsel thee to buy of me gold tried in the fire, that thou mayest be rich; and white raiment, that thou mayest be clothed, and *that* the shame of thy nakedness do not appear; and anoint thine eyes with eyesalve, that thou mayest see.

3. Evil Examples

Nu 31:16 Behold, these caused the children of Israel, through the counsel of Balaam, to commit trespass against the LORD in the matter of Peor, and there was a plague among the congregation of the LORD.

1 S 24:4 And the men of David said unto him, Behold the day of which the LORD said unto thee, Behold, I will deliver thine enemy into thine hand, that thou mayest do to him as it shall seem good unto thee. Then David arose, and cut off the skirt of Saul's robe privily.

2 S 13:5 And Jonadab said unto him, Lay thee down on thy bed, and make thyself sick: and when thy father cometh to see thee, say unto him, I pray thee, let my sister Tamar come, and give me meat, and dress the meat in my sight, that I may see *it,* and eat *it* at her hand.

2 S 16:21 And Ahithophel said unto Absalom, Go in unto thy father's concubines, which he hath left to keep the house; and all Israel shall hear that thou art abhorred of thy father: then shall the hands of all that *are* with thee be strong.

1 K 12:10 And the young men that were grown up with him spake unto him, saying, Thus shalt thou speak unto this people that spake unto thee, saying, Thy father made our yoke heavy, but make thou *it* lighter unto us; thus shalt thou say unto them, My little *finger* shall be thicker than my father's loins.

1 K 12:28 Whereupon the king took counsel, and made two calves *of* gold, and said unto them, It is too much for you to go up to Jerusalem: behold thy gods, O Israel, which brought thee up out of the land of Egypt.

1 K 21:15 And it came to pass, when Jezebel heard that Naboth was stoned, and was dead, that Jezebel said to Ahab, Arise, take possession of the vineyard of Naboth the Jezreelite, which he refused to give thee for money: for Naboth is not alive, but dead.

2 Chr 10:10 And the young men that were brought up with him spake unto him, saying, Thus shalt thou answer the people that spake unto thee, saying, Thy father made our yoke heavy, but make thou *it* somewhat lighter for us; thus shalt thou say unto them, My little *finger* shall be thicker than my father's loins.

2 Chr 22:3 He also walked in the ways of the house of Ahab: for his mother was his counsellor to do wickedly.

2 Chr 22:5 He walked also after their counsel, and went with Jehoram the son of Ahab king of Israel to war against Hazael king of Syria at Ramoth-gilead: and the Syrians smote Joram.

2 Chr 25:17 Then Amaziah king of Judah took advice, and sent to Joash, the son of Jehoahaz, the son of Jehu, king of Israel, saying, Come, let us see one another in the face.

Est 1:16 And Memucan answered before the king and the princes, Vashti the queen hath not done wrong to the king only, but also to all the princes, and to all the people that *are* in all the provinces of the king Ahasuerus.

Est 3:9 If it please the king, let it be written that they may be destroyed: and I will pay ten thousand talents of silver to the hands of those that have the charge of the business, to bring *it* into the king's treasuries.

Est 5:14 Then said Zeresh his wife and all his friends unto him, Let a gallows be made of fifty cubits high, and to morrow speak thou unto the king that Mordecai may be hanged thereon: then go thou in merrily with the king unto the banquet. And the thing pleased Haman; and he caused the gallows to be made.

Jb 2:9 Then said his wife unto him, Dost thou still retain thine integrity? curse God, and die.

Jb 21:16 Lo, their good *is* not in their hand: the counsel of the wicked is far from me.

Jb 22:18 Yet he filled their houses with good *things:* but the counsel of the wicked is far from me.

Ps 1:1 Blessed *is* the man that walketh not in the counsel of the ungodly, nor standeth in the way of sinners, nor sitteth in the seat of the scornful.

Ps 2:2 The kings of the earth set themselves, and the rulers take counsel together, against the LORD, and against his anointed, *saying,*

Ps 5:10 Destroy thou them, O God; let them fall by their own counsels; cast them out in the multitude of their transgressions; for they have rebelled against thee.

Ps 83:3 They have taken crafty counsel against thy people, and consulted against thy hidden ones.

Pr 12:5 The thoughts of the righteous *are* right: *but* the counsels of the wicked *are* deceit.

Is 30:1 Woe to the rebellious children, saith the Lord, that take counsel, but not of me; and that cover with a covering, but not of my spirit, that they may add sin to sin:

Eze 11:2 Then said he unto me, Son of man, these *are* the men that devise mischief, and give wicked counsel in this city:

Da 6:8 Now, O king, establish the decree, and sign the writing, that it be not changed, according to the law of the Medes and Persians, which altereth not.

Mi 6:16 For the statutes of Omri are kept, and all the works of the house of Ahab, and ye walk in their counsels; that I should make thee a desolation, and the inhabitants thereof an hissing: therefore ye shall bear the reproach of my people.

Na 1:11 There is *one* come out of thee, that imagineth evil against the Lord, a wicked counsellor.

Mk 6:24 And she went forth, and said unto her mother, What shall I ask? And she said, The head of John the Baptist.

Jn 18:14 Now Caiaphas was he, which gave counsel to the Jews, that it was expedient that one man should die for the people.

Ac 27:42 And the soldiers' counsel was to kill the prisoners, lest any of them should swim out, and escape.

4. Divine

Ps 16:7 I will bless the Lord, who hath given me counsel: my reins also instruct me in the night seasons.

Ps 32:8 I will instruct thee and teach thee in the way which thou shalt go: I will guide thee with mine eye.

Ps 33:11 The counsel of the Lord standeth for ever, the thoughts of his heart to all generations.

Ps 73:24 Thou shalt guide me with thy counsel, and afterward receive me *to* glory.

Ps 106:13 They soon forgat his works; they waited not for his counsel:

Ps 107:11 Because they rebelled against the words of God, and contemned the counsel of the most High:

Pr 1:26 I also will laugh at your calamity; I will mock when your fear cometh;

Pr 8:14 Counsel *is* mine, and sound wisdom: I *am* understanding; I have strength.

Pr 24:6 For by wise counsel thou shalt make thy war: and in multitude of counsellors *there is* safety.

Is 11:2 And the spirit of the Lord shall rest upon him, the spirit of wisdom and understanding, the spirit of counsel and might, the spirit of knowledge and of the fear of the Lord;

Is 28:29 This also cometh forth from the Lord of hosts, *which* is wonderful in counsel, *and* excellent in working.

Is 46:10 Declaring the end from the beginning, and from ancient times *the things* that are not *yet* done, saying, My counsel shall stand, and I will do all my pleasure:

Je 23:22 But if they had stood in my counsel, and had caused my people to hear my words, then they should have turned them from their evil way, and from the evil of their doings.

Je 32:19 Great in counsel, and mighty in work: for thine eyes *are* open upon all the ways of the sons of men: to give every one according to his ways, and according to the fruit of his doings:

Lu 12:58 When thou goest with thine adversary to the magistrate, *as thou art* in the way, give diligence that thou mayest be delivered from him; lest he hale thee to the judge, and the judge deliver thee to the officer, and the officer cast thee into prison.

Re 3:18 I counsel thee to buy of me gold tried in the fire, that thou mayest be rich; and white raiment, that thou mayest be clothed, and *that* the shame of thy nakedness do not appear; and anoint thine eyes with eyesalve, that thou mayest see.

COUNSELORS

2 S 16:23 And the counsel of Ahithophel, which he counselled in those days, *was* as if a man had enquired at the oracle of God: so *was* all the counsel of Ahithophel both with David and with Absalom.

2 S 17:11 Therefore I counsel that all Israel be generally gathered unto thee, from Dan even to Beer-sheba, as the sand that *is* by the sea for multitude; and that thou go to battle in thine own person.

1 K 12:6 And king Rehoboam consulted with the old men, that stood before Solomon his father while he yet lived, and said, How do ye advise that I may answer this people?

1 Chr 13:1 And David consulted with the captains of thousands and hundreds, *and* with every leader.

1 Chr 27:33 And Ahithophel *was* the king's counsellor: and Hushai the Archite *was* the king's companion:

2 Chr 10:6 And king Rehoboam took counsel with the old men that had stood before Solomon his father while he yet lived, saying, What counsel give ye *me* to return answer to this people?

Ezr 7:14 Forasmuch as thou art sent of the king, and of his seven counsellors, to enquire concerning Judah and Jerusalem, according to the law of thy God which *is* in thine hand;

Ne 11:24 And Pethahiah the son of Meshezabeel, of the children of Zerah the son of Judah, *was* at the king's hand in all matters concerning the people.

Est 1:13 Then the king said to the wise men, which knew the times, (for so *was* the king's manner toward all that knew law and judgment:

Pr 11:14 Where no counsel *is,* the people fall: but in the multitude of counsellors *there is* safety.

Pr 15:22 Without counsel purposes are disappointed: but in the multitude of counsellors they are established.

Pr 24:6 For by wise counsel thou shalt make thy war: and in multitude of counsellors *there is* safety.

Is 1:26 And I will restore thy judges as at the first, and thy counsellors as at the beginning: afterward thou shalt be called, The city of righteousness, the faithful city.

Is 3:3 The captain of fifty, and the honourable man, and the counsellor, and the cunning artificer, and the eloquent orator.

Da 3:2 Then Nebuchadnezzar the king sent to gather together the princes, the governors, and the captains, the judges, the treasurers, the counsellors, the sheriffs, and all the rulers of the provinces, to come to the dedication of the image which Nebuchadnezzar the king had set up.

COURAGE, *bravery*

1. Prescribed

Nu 13:20 And what the land *is,* whether it *be* fat or lean, whether there be wood therein, or not. And be ye of good courage, and bring of the fruit of the land. Now the time *was* the time of the firstripe grapes.

De 31:6 Be strong and of a good courage, fear not, nor be afraid of them: for the LORD thy God, he *it is* that doth go with thee; he will not fail thee, nor forsake thee.

Jos 1:6 Be strong and of a good courage: for unto this people shalt thou divide for an inheritance the land, which I sware unto their fathers to give them.

Jos 10:25 And Joshua said unto them, Fear not, nor be dismayed, be strong and of good courage: for thus shall the LORD do to all your enemies against whom ye fight.

Jos 23:6 Be ye therefore very courageous to keep and to do all that is written in the book of the law of Moses, that ye turn not aside therefrom *to* the right hand or *to* the left;

2 S 10:12 Be of good courage, and let us play the men for our people, and for the cities of our God: and the LORD do that which seemeth him good.

1 Chr 19:13 Be of good courage, and let us behave ourselves valiantly for our people, and for the cities of our

God: and let the LORD do *that which is* good in his sight.

1 Chr 22:13 Then shalt thou prosper, if thou takest heed to fulfil the statutes and judgments which the LORD charged Moses with concerning Israel: be strong, and of good courage; dread not, nor be dismayed.

1 Chr 28:20 And David said to Solomon his son, Be strong and of good courage, and do *it:* fear not, nor be dismayed: for the LORD God, *even* my God, *will be* with thee; he will not fail thee, nor forsake thee, until thou hast finished all the work for the service of the house of the LORD.

2 Chr 19:11 And, behold, Amariah the chief priest is over you in all matters of the LORD; and Zebadiah the son of Ishmael, the ruler of the house of Judah, for all the king's matters: also the Levites *shall be* officers before you. Deal courageously, and the LORD shall be with the good.

2 Chr 32:7 Be strong and courageous, be not afraid nor dismayed for the king of Assyria, nor for all the multitude that *is* with him: for *there be* more with us than with him:

Ezr 10:4 Arise; for *this* matter *belongeth* unto thee: we also *will be* with thee: be of good courage, and do *it.*

Ph 1:28 And in nothing terrified by your adversaries: which is to them an evident token of perdition, but to you of salvation, and that of God.

2. Examples

Jos 14:12 Now therefore give me this mountain, whereof the LORD spake in that day; for thou heardest in that day how the Anakims *were* there, and *that* the cities *were* great *and* fenced: if so be the LORD *will be* with me, then I shall be able to drive them out, as the LORD said.

Jud 5:18 Zebulun and Naphtali *were* a people *that* jeoparded their lives unto the death in the high places of the field.

JONATHAN

1 S 14:6 And Jonathan said to the young man that bare his armour, Come, and let us go over unto the garrison of these uncircumcised: it may be that the LORD will work for us: for *there is* no restraint to the LORD to save by many or by few.

DAVID

1 S 17:32 And David said to Saul, Let no man's heart fail because of him; thy servant will go and fight with this Philistine.

2 S 12:7 And Nathan said to David, Thou *art* the man. Thus saith the LORD God of Israel, I anointed thee king over Israel, and I delivered thee out of the hand of Saul;

1 K 21:20 And Ahab said to Elijah, Hast thou found me, O mine enemy? And he answered, I have found *thee:* because thou hast sold thyself to work evil in the sight of the LORD.

1 K 22:14 And Micaiah said, *As* the LORD liveth, what the LORD saith unto me, that will I speak.

2 K 3:14 And Elisha said, *As* the LORD of hosts liveth, before whom I stand, surely, were it not that I regard the presence of Jehoshaphat the king of Judah, I would not look toward thee, nor see thee.

See **DAVID**

NEHEMIAH

Ne 6:11 And I said, Should such a man as I flee? and who *is there,* that, *being* as I *am,* would go into the temple to save his life? I will not go in.

See **NEHEMIAH**

THE THREE CAPTIVES

Da 3:16–17 Shadrach, Meshach, and Abed-nego, answered and said to the king, O Nebuchadnezzar, we *are* not careful to answer thee in this matter.

If it be *so,* our God whom we serve is able to deliver us from the burning fiery furnace, and he will deliver *us* out of thine hand, O king.

DANIEL

Da 6:10 Now when Daniel knew that the writing was signed, he went into his house; and his windows being open in his chamber toward Jerusalem, he kneeled upon his knees three times a day, and prayed, and gave thanks before his God, as he did aforetime.

See **DANIEL**

JOHN

Mt 14:4 For John said unto him, It is not lawful for thee to have her.

CHRIST

Jn 19:10–11 Then saith Pilate unto him, Speakest thou not unto me? knowest thou not that I have power to crucify thee, and have power to release thee?

Jesus answered, Thou couldest have no power *at all* against me, except it were given thee from above: therefore he that delivered me unto thee hath the greater sin.
Ac 4:20 For we cannot but speak the things which we have seen and heard.
Ac 7:51 Ye stiffnecked and uncircumcised in heart and ears, ye do always resist the Holy Ghost: as your fathers *did*, so *do* ye.

See **FEAR**

COURTESY, *gracious politeness*

Ge 24:18; Mt 10:12; Lu 7:6; Ac 26:3; 27:3; 28:7; 1 Co 10:27; 11:33; Col 4:6; 1 Ti 5:1; 1 Pe 3:8

See **DISCOURTESY**

COURTS, *judicial assemblies*

1. Sanhedrin, *the supreme council, or court, of the Jewish nation*

Nu 11:16, 24; Eze 8:11; Mt 2:4; 5:22; 10:17; 26:3, 59; 27:1, 7, 62; 28:11; Mk 13:9; 14:53, 55; 15:1; Lu 23:13, 50; 24:20; Jn 11:47; Ac 4:6, 15; 5:21; 6:12; 22:30; 23:1, 6, 20, 28; 24:20

2. Other Courts

a. Inferior
Ex 18:21–22; De 1:15–16; De 17:9

b. Superior
Ex 18:13–26

c. Circuit
1 S 7:15–16

d. Roman
Mt 27:11; Ac 25:6

3. Related Topics

a. Places of holding courts
De 21:19; 25:7; Jud 4:5

b. Sentences
De 17:8–11

c. Appeals
Ac 25:11

d. Contempt
De 17:12

e. Corruption
Is 10:1–2; Mi 7:3; Zep 3:3

f. Laws for judges
Le 19:15; De 16:18–19

g. Litigation to be avoided
Pr 25:8; Mt 5:25, 40; 1 Co 6:1

h. Perjury condemned
Le 6:3; 19:12; Ne 5:13; Ps 24:4; Je 5:2; 7:9; Eze 16:59; 17:18; Ho 10:4; Zec 5:4; 8:17; Mal 3:5; Mt 5:33; 1 Ti 1:10

i. Advocates

1). The accused
Je 26:11–15; Jn 18:33–37

2). Professional
Ac 24:1

j. Examination of Prisoners
Jud 8:14; Jn 18:33

k. Prisoners maltreated
Jn 18:22; Ac 22:24

I. Witnesses, needed to convict

Nu 35:30; De 17:6; 19:15; Ru 4:9; Ps 40:10; Is 8:2; Je 32:12; Mt 18:16; Jn 8:17; 2 Co 13:1; 1 Ti 5:19; He 10:28; 1 Jn 5:9

COURTSHIP, *period before betrothal*

Ge 29:11–20; Jud 14:1–10

COVENANTS, *agreements, contracts*

1. Everlasting

Ge 8:21 And the LORD smelled a sweet savour; and the LORD said in his heart, I will not again curse the ground any more for man's sake; for the imagination of man's heart *is* evil from his youth; neither will I again smite any more every thing living, as I have done.

Ge 9:16 And the bow shall be in the cloud; and I will look upon it, that I may remember the everlasting covenant between God and every living creature of all flesh that *is* upon the earth.

Ge 17:7 And I will establish my covenant between me and thee and thy seed after thee in their generations for an everlasting covenant, to be a God unto thee, and to thy seed after thee.

Ge 17:13 He that is born in thy house, and he that is bought with thy money, must needs be circumcised: and my covenant shall be in your flesh for an everlasting covenant.

Ge 17:19 And God said, Sarah thy wife shall bear thee a son indeed; and thou shalt call his name Isaac: and I will establish my covenant with him for an everlasting covenant, *and* with his seed after him.

Ex 31:16 Wherefore the children of Israel shall keep the sabbath, to observe the sabbath throughout their generations, *for* a perpetual covenant.

Le 24:8 Every sabbath he shall set it in order before the LORD continually, *being taken* from the children of Israel by an everlasting covenant.

Nu 18:19 All the heave offerings of the holy things, which the children of Israel offer unto the LORD, have I given thee, and thy sons and thy daughters with thee, by a statute for ever: it is a covenant of salt for ever before the LORD unto thee and to thy seed with thee.

2 S 23:5 Although my house *be* not so with God; yet he hath made with me an everlasting covenant, ordered in all *things,* and sure: for *this is* all my salvation, and all *my* desire, although he make *it* not to grow.

1 Chr 16:17 And hath confirmed the same to Jacob for a law, *and* to Israel *for* an everlasting covenant,

1 Chr 17:14 But I will settle him in mine house and in my kingdom for ever: and his throne shall be established for evermore.

2 Chr 13:5 Ought ye not to know that the LORD God of Israel gave the kingdom over Israel to David for ever, *even* to him and to his sons by a covenant of salt?

Ps 74:20 Have respect unto the covenant: for the dark places of the earth are full of the habitations of cruelty.

Ps 89:34 My covenant will I not break, nor alter the thing that is gone out of my lips.

Ps 105:10 And confirmed the same unto Jacob for a law, *and* to Israel *for* an everlasting covenant:

Ps 111:9 He sent redemption unto his people: he hath commanded his covenant for ever: holy and reverend *is* his name.

Is 24:5 The earth also is defiled under the inhabitants thereof; because they have transgressed the laws, changed the ordinance, broken the everlasting covenant.

Is 54:10 For the mountains shall depart, and the hills be removed; but my kindness shall not depart from thee, neither shall the covenant of my peace be removed, saith the LORD that hath mercy on thee.

Is 55:3 Incline your ear, and come unto me: hear, and your soul shall live; and I will make an everlasting covenant with you, *even* the sure mercies of David.

Is 61:8 For I the LORD love judgment, I hate robbery for burnt offering; and I will direct their work in truth, and I will make an everlasting covenant with them.

Je 32:40 And I will make an everlasting covenant with them, that I will not turn away from them, to do them good; but I will put my fear in their hearts, that they shall not depart from me.

Je 33:20 Thus saith the LORD; If ye can break my covenant of the day, and my covenant of the night, and that there should not be day and night in their season;

Eze 16:60 Nevertheless I will remember my covenant with thee in the days of thy youth, and I will establish unto thee an everlasting covenant.

Eze 37:26 Moreover I will make a covenant of peace with them; it shall be an everlasting covenant with them: and I will place them, and multiply them, and will set my sanctuary in the midst of them for evermore.

He 13:20 Now the God of peace, that brought again from the dead our Lord Jesus, that great shepherd of the sheep, through the blood of the everlasting covenant,

2. Divine

Ge 12:3 And I will bless them that bless thee, and curse him that curseth thee: and in thee shall all families of the earth be blessed.

Ge 17:2 And I will make my covenant between me and thee, and will multiply thee exceedingly.

Ex 6:4 And I have also established my covenant with them, to give them the land of Canaan, the land of their pilgrimage, wherein they were strangers.

Nu 25:12 Wherefore say, Behold, I give unto him my covenant of peace:

Jud 2:1 And an angel of the LORD came up from Gilgal to Bochim, and said, I made you to go up out of Egypt, and have brought you unto the land which I sware unto your fathers; and I said, I will never break my covenant with you.

2 S 7:12 And when thy days be fulfilled, and thou shalt sleep with thy fathers, I will set up thy seed after thee, which shall proceed out of thy bowels, and I will establish his kingdom.

2 Chr 21:7 Howbeit the LORD would not destroy the house of David, because of the covenant that he had made with David, and as he promised to give a light to him and to his sons for ever.

Ps 89:28 My mercy will I keep for him for evermore, and my covenant shall stand fast with him.

Is 59:21 As for me, this *is* my covenant with them, saith the LORD; My spirit that *is* upon thee, and my words which I have put in thy mouth, shall not depart out of thy mouth, nor out of the mouth of thy seed, nor out of the mouth of thy seed's seed, saith the LORD, from henceforth and for ever.

Je 33:21 *Then* may also my covenant be broken with David my servant, that he should not have a son to reign upon his throne; and with the Levites the priests, my ministers.

Ac 3:25 Ye are the children of the prophets, and of the covenant which God made with our fathers, saying unto Abraham, And in thy seed shall all the kindreds of the earth be blessed.

Ga 3:8 And the scripture, foreseeing that God would justify the heathen through faith, preached before the gospel unto Abraham, *saying,* In thee shall all nations be blessed.

He 8:9 Not according to the covenant that I made with their fathers in the day when I took them by the hand to lead them out of the land of Egypt; because they continued not in my covenant, and I regarded them not, saith the LORD.

3. God and Man

Ge 14:22; 28:21; Ex 19:8; 24:3, 7; De 5:27; 29:12; Jos 24:18, 24; 2 K 11:17; 23:3; 2 Chr 5:10; 15:12; 23:16; 29:10; 34:31; Ezr 10:3; Ne 9:38; 10:29; Ps 119:8, 106; Je 11:3, 10; 34:13, 18; 42:6; 50:5; Eze 20:37; Hag 2:5; Zec 11:10

4. Human

Ge 21:23, 27; 24:9; 26:31; 30:34; 31:44; Jos 2:14; 1 S 18:3; 20:8, 16; 23:18; 2 S 3:21; 5:3; 21:7; 1 K 5:12; 20:34; 2 K 11:4, 17; 1 Chr 11:3; 2 Chr 23:1; Je 34:8; Eze 17:13

5. New

De 29:14 Neither with you only do I make this covenant and this oath;

Je 3:16 And it shall come to pass, when ye be multiplied and increased in the land, in those days, saith the LORD, they shall say no more, The ark of the covenant of the LORD: neither shall it come to mind: neither shall they remember it; neither shall they visit *it*; neither shall *that* be done any more.

Je 31:31 Behold, the days come, saith the LORD, that I will make a new covenant with the house of Israel, and with the house of Judah:

Mt 26:28 For this is my blood of the new testament, which is shed for many for the remission of sins.

Mk 14:24 And he said unto them, This is my blood of the new testament, which is shed for many.

Lu 22:20 Likewise also the cup after supper, saying, This cup *is* the new testament in my blood, which is shed for you.

Ro 11:27 For this *is* my covenant unto them, when I shall take away their sins.

1 Co 11:25 After the same manner also *he took* the cup, when he had supped, saying, This cup is the new testament in my blood: this do ye, as oft as ye drink *it*, in remembrance of me.

2 Co 3:6 Who also hath made us able ministers of the new testament; not of the letter, but of the spirit: for the letter killeth, but the spirit giveth life.

He 7:22 By so much was Jesus made a surety of a better testament.

He 8:8 For finding fault with them, he saith, Behold, the days come, saith the Lord, when I will make a new covenant with the house of Israel and with the house of Judah:

He 8:10 For this *is* the covenant that I will make with the house of Israel after those days, saith the Lord; I will put my laws into their mind, and write them in their hearts: and I will be to them a God, and they shall be to me a people:

He 9:15 And for this cause he is the mediator of the new testament, that by means of death, for the redemption of the transgressions *that were* under the first testament, they which are called might receive the promise of eternal inheritance.

He 10:16 This *is* the covenant that I will make with them after those days, saith the Lord, I will put my laws into their hearts, and in their minds will I write them;

He 12:24 And to Jesus the mediator of the new covenant, and to the blood of sprinkling, that speaketh better things than *that of* Abel.

See **CONTRACTS**

COVETOUSNESS, *greed, avarice*

1. Condemned

Ex 20:17 Thou shalt not covet thy neighbour's house, thou shalt not covet thy neighbour's wife, nor his manservant, nor his maidservant, nor his ox, nor his ass, nor any thing that *is* thy neighbour's.

Ps 10:3 For the wicked boasteth of his heart's desire, and blesseth the covetous, *whom* the LORD abhorreth.

Pr 28:16 The prince that wanteth understanding *is* also a great oppressor: *but* he that hateth covetousness shall prolong *his* days.

Je 6:13 For from the least of them even unto the greatest of them every one *is* given to covetousness; and from the prophet even unto the priest every one dealeth falsely.

Eze 33:31 And they come unto thee as the people cometh, and they sit before thee as my people, and they hear thy words, but they will not do them: for with their mouth they shew much love, *but* their heart goeth after their covetousness.

Mi 2:2 And they covet fields, and take *them* by violence; and houses, and take *them* away: so they oppress a man and his house, even a man and his heritage.

Hab 2:9 Woe to him that coveteth an evil covetousness to his house, that he may set his nest on high, that he may be delivered from the power of evil!

Lu 12:15 And he said unto them, Take heed, and beware of covetousness: for a man's life consisteth not in the abundance of the things which he possesseth.

Ep 5:3 But fornication, and all uncleanness, or covetousness, let it not be once named among you, as becometh saints;

Col 3:5 Mortify therefore your members which are upon the earth; fornication, uncleanness, inordinate affection, evil concupiscence, and covetousness, which is idolatry:

1 Ti 3:3 Not given to wine, no striker, not greedy of filthy lucre; but patient, not a brawler, not covetous;

He 13:5 *Let your* conversation *be* without covetousness; *and be* content with such things as ye have: for he hath said, I will never leave thee, nor forsake thee.

2. Natural Results

OPPRESSION

Ge 31:41 Thus have I been twenty years in thy house; I served thee fourteen years for thy two daughters, and six years for thy cattle: and thou hast changed my wages ten times.

THEFT

Jos 7:21 When I saw among the spoils a goodly Babylonish garment, and two hundred shekels of silver, and a wedge of gold of fifty shekels weight, then I coveted them, and took them; and, behold, they *are* hid in the earth in the midst of my tent, and the silver under it.

DISOBEDIENCE

1 S 15:9 But Saul and the people spared Agag, and the best of the sheep, and of the oxen, and of the fatlings, and the lambs, and all *that was* good, and would not utterly destroy them: but every thing *that was* vile and refuse, that they destroyed utterly.

ROBBERY

1 K 20:6 Yet I will send my servants unto thee to morrow about this time, and they shall search thine house, and the houses of thy servants; and it shall be, *that* whatsoever is pleasant in thine eyes, they shall put *it* in their hand, and take *it* away.

MEANNESS

1 K 21:2 And Ahab spake unto Naboth, saying, Give me thy vineyard, that I may have it for a garden of herbs, because it *is* near unto my house: and I will give thee for it a better vineyard than it; *or,* if it seem good to thee, I will give thee the worth of it in money.

UNSCRUPULOUSNESS

2 K 5:20 But Gehazi, the servant of Elisha the man of God, said, Behold, my master hath spared Naaman this Syrian, in not receiving at his hands that which he brought: but, *as* the LORD liveth, I will run after him, and take somewhat of him.

SCOFFING

Lu 16:14 And the Pharisees also, who were covetous, heard all these things: and they derided him.

See **AVARICE, GREED**

COWARDICE

Nu 13:33 And there we saw the giants, the sons of Anak, *which come* of the giants: and we were in our own sight as grasshoppers, and so we were in their sight.

Nu 14:1 And all the congregation lifted up their voice, and cried; and the people wept that night.

Jos 7:5 And the men of Ai smote of them about thirty and six men: for they chased them *from* before the gate *even* unto Shebarim, and smote them in the going down: wherefore the hearts of the people melted, and became as water.

Jud 7:3 Now therefore go to, proclaim in the ears of the people, saying, Whosoever *is* fearful and afraid, let him return and depart early from mount Gilead. And there returned of the people twenty and two thousand; and there remained ten thousand.

1 S 17:24 And all the men of Israel, when they saw the man, fled from him, and were sore afraid.

1 S 18:29 And Saul was yet the more afraid of David; and Saul became David's enemy continually.

2 S 15:14 And David said unto all his servants that *were* with him at Jerusalem, Arise, and let us flee; for we shall not *else* escape from Absalom: make speed to depart, lest he overtake us suddenly, and bring evil upon us, and smite the city with the edge of the sword.

Ps 78:9 The children of Ephraim, *being* armed, *and* carrying bows, turned back in the day of battle.

Mt 26:56 But all this was done, that the scriptures of the prophets might be fulfilled. Then all the disciples forsook him, and fled.

See **COURAGE, FEAR**

COWS *See* **ANIMALS**

CRAFTINESS *See* **DECEPTION**

CREATOR, *originator, architect, designer*

Ge 1:1 In the beginning God created the heaven and the earth.

Ge 1:20 And God said, Let the waters bring forth abundantly the moving creature that hath life, and fowl *that* may fly above the earth in the open firmament of heaven.

Ge 2:3 And God blessed the seventh day, and sanctified it: because that in it he had rested from all his work which God created and made.

Ex 20:11 For *in* six days the LORD made heaven and earth, the sea, and all that in them *is,* and rested the seventh day: wherefore the LORD blessed the sabbath day, and hallowed it.

Ex 31:17 It *is* a sign between me and the children of Israel for ever: for *in* six days the LORD made heaven and earth, and on the seventh day he rested, and was refreshed.

1 S 2:8 He raiseth up the poor out of the dust, *and* lifteth up the beggar from the dunghill, to set *them* among princes, and to make them inherit the throne of glory: for the pillars of the earth *are* the LORD's, and he hath set the world upon them.

2 K 19:15 And Hezekiah prayed before the LORD, and said, O LORD God of Israel, which dwellest *between* the cherubims, thou art the God, *even* thou alone, of all the kingdoms of the earth: thou hast made heaven and earth.

2 K 19:25 Hast thou not heard long ago *how* I have done it, *and* of ancient times that I have formed it? now have I brought it to pass, that thou shouldest be to lay waste fenced cities *into* ruinous heaps.

1 Chr 16:26 For all the gods of the people *are* idols: but the LORD made the heavens.

2 Chr 2:12 Huram said moreover, Blessed *be* the LORD God of Israel, that made heaven and earth, who hath given to David the king a wise son, endued with prudence and understanding, that might build an house for the LORD, and an house for his kingdom.

Ne 9:6 Thou, *even* thou, *art* LORD alone; thou hast made heaven, the heaven of heavens, with all their host, the earth, and all *things* that *are* therein, the seas, and all that *is* therein, and thou preservest them all; and the host of heaven worshippeth thee.

Jb 9:9 Which maketh Arcturus, Orion, and Pleiades, and the chambers of the south.

Jb 12:9 Who knoweth not in all these that the hand of the LORD hath wrought this?

Jb 26:7 He stretcheth out the north over the empty place, *and* hangeth the earth upon nothing.

Jb 26:13 By his spirit he hath garnished the heavens; his hand hath formed the crooked serpent.

Jb 35:10 But none saith, Where *is* God my maker, who giveth songs in the night;

Jb 38:4 Where wast thou when I laid the foundations of the earth? declare, if thou hast understanding.

Jb 40:15 Behold now behemoth, which I made with thee; he eateth grass as an ox.

Ps 8:3 When I consider thy heavens, the work of thy fingers, the moon and the stars, which thou hast ordained;

Ps 24:2 For he hath founded it upon the seas, and established it upon the floods.

Ps 33:6 By the word of the LORD were the heavens made; and all the host of them by the breath of his mouth.

Ps 74:17 Thou hast set all the borders of the earth: thou hast made summer and winter.

Ps 89:11 The heavens *are* thine, the earth also *is* thine: *as for* the world and the fulness thereof, thou hast founded them.

Ps 90:2 Before the mountains were brought forth, or ever thou hadst formed the earth and the world, even from everlasting to everlasting, thou *art* God.

Ps 95:5 The sea *is* his, and he made it: and his hands formed the dry *land.*

Ps 96:5 For all the gods of the nations *are* idols: but the LORD made the heavens.

Ps 102:25 Of old hast thou laid the foundation of the earth: and the heavens *are* the work of thy hands.

Ps 104:5 *Who* laid the foundations of the earth, *that* it should not be removed for ever.

Ps 115:15 Ye *are* blessed of the LORD which made heaven and earth.

Ps 119:90 Thy faithfulness *is* unto all generations: thou hast established the earth, and it abideth.

Ps 121:2 My help *cometh* from the LORD, which made heaven and earth.

Ps 124:8 Our help *is* in the name of the LORD, who made heaven and earth.

Ps 134:3 The LORD that made heaven and earth bless thee out of Zion.

Ps 136:5 To him that by wisdom made the heavens: for his mercy *endureth* for ever.

Ps 146:6 Which made heaven, and earth, the sea, and all that therein *is:* which keepeth truth for ever:

Ps 148:5 Let them praise the name of the LORD: for he commanded, and they were created.

Pr 3:19 The LORD by wisdom hath founded the earth; by understanding hath he established the heavens.

Pr 8:26 While as yet he had not made the earth, nor the fields, nor the highest part of the dust of the world.

Pr 16:4 The LORD hath made all *things* for himself: yea, even the wicked for the day of evil.

Pr 26:10 The great *God* that formed all *things* both rewardeth the fool, and rewardeth transgressors.

Pr 30:4 Who hath ascended up into heaven, or descended? who hath gathered the wind in his fists? who hath bound the waters in a garment? who hath established all the ends of the earth? what *is* his name, and what *is* his son's name, if thou canst tell?

Ec 3:11 He hath made every *thing* beautiful in his time: also he hath set the world in their heart, so that no man can find out the work that God maketh from the beginning to the end.

Is 37:16 O LORD of hosts, God of Israel, that dwellest *between* the cherubims, thou *art* the God, *even* thou alone, of all the kingdoms of the earth: thou hast made heaven and earth.

Is 40:12 Who hath measured the waters in the hollow of his hand, and meted out heaven with the span, and comprehended the dust of the earth in a measure, and weighed the mountains in scales, and the hills in a balance?

Is 40:22 *It is* he that sitteth upon the circle of the earth, and the inhabitants thereof *are* as grasshoppers; that stretcheth out the heavens as a curtain, and spreadeth them out as a tent to dwell in:

Is 40:28 Hast thou not known? hast thou not heard, that the everlasting God, the LORD, the Creator of the ends of the earth, fainteth not, neither is weary? *there is* no searching of his understanding.

Is 42:5 Thus saith God the LORD, he that created the heavens, and stretched them out; he that spread forth the earth, and that which cometh out of it; he that giveth breath unto the people upon it, and spirit to them that walk therein:

Is 44:24 Thus saith the LORD, thy redeemer, and he that formed thee from the womb, I *am* the LORD that maketh all *things;* that stretcheth forth the heavens alone; that spreadeth abroad the earth by myself;

Is 45:12 I have made the earth, and created man upon it: I, *even* my hands, have stretched out the heavens, and all their host have I commanded.

Is 45:18 For thus saith the LORD that created the heavens; God himself that formed the earth and made it; he hath established it, he created it not in vain, he formed it to be inhabited: I *am* the LORD; and *there is* none else.

Is 48:13 Mine hand also hath laid the foundation of the earth, and my right hand hath spanned the heavens: *when* I call unto them, they stand up together.

Is 57:16 For I will not contend for ever, neither will I be always wroth: for the spirit should fail before me, and the souls *which* I have made.

Is 66:2 For all those *things* hath mine hand made, and all those *things* have been, saith the LORD: but to this *man* will I look, *even* to *him that is* poor and of a contrite spirit, and trembleth at my word.

Je 10:12 He hath made the earth by his power, he hath established the world by his wisdom, and hath stretched out the heavens by his discretion.

Je 10:16 The portion of Jacob *is* not like them: for he *is* the former of all *things;* and Israel *is* the rod of his inheritance: The LORD of hosts *is* his name.

Je 14:22 Are there *any* among the vanities of the Gentiles that can cause rain? or can the heavens give showers? *art* not thou he, O LORD our God?

therefore we will wait upon thee: for thou hast made all these *things.*

Je 27:5 I have made the earth, the man and the beast that *are* upon the ground, by my great power and by my outstretched arm, and have given it unto whom it seemed meet unto me.

Je 31:35 Thus saith the LORD, which giveth the sun for a light by day, *and* the ordinances of the moon and of the stars for a light by night, which divideth the sea when the waves thereof roar; The LORD of hosts *is* his name:

Je 32:17 Ah Lord GOD! behold, thou hast made the heaven and the earth by thy great power and stretched out arm, *and* there is nothing too hard for thee:

Je 33:2 Thus saith the LORD the maker thereof, the LORD that formed it, to establish it; the LORD *is* his name;

Je 38:16 So Zedekiah the king sware secretly unto Jeremiah, saying, *As* the LORD liveth, that made us this soul, I will not put thee to death, neither will I give thee into the hand of these men that seek thy life.

Je 51:15 He hath made the earth by his power, he hath established the world by his wisdom, and hath stretched out the heaven by his understanding.

Je 51:19 The portion of Jacob *is* not like them; for he *is* the former of all things: and *Israel is* the rod of his inheritance: the LORD of hosts *is* his name.

Am 4:3 For, lo, he that formeth the mountains, and createth the wind, and declareth unto man what *is* his thought, that maketh the morning darkness, and treadeth upon the high places of the earth, The LORD, The God of hosts, *is* his name.

Am 5:8 *Seek him* that maketh the seven stars and Orion, and turneth the shadow of death into the morning, and maketh the day dark with night: that calleth for the waters of the sea, and poureth them out upon the face of the earth: The LORD *is* his name:

Am 9:6 *It is* he that buildeth his stories in the heaven, and hath founded his troop in the earth; he that calleth for the waters of the sea, and poureth them out upon the face of the earth: The LORD *is* his name.

Jona 1:9 And he said unto them, I *am* an Hebrew; and I fear the LORD, the God of heaven, which hath made the sea and the dry *land.*

Zec 12:1 The burden of the word of the LORD for Israel, saith the LORD, which stretcheth forth the heavens, and layeth the foundation of the earth, and formeth the spirit of man within him.

Mk 13:19 For *in* those days shall be affliction, such as was not from the beginning of the creation which God created unto this time, neither shall be.

Ac 4:24 And when they heard that, they lifted up their voice to God with one accord, and said, Lord, thou *art* God, which hast made heaven, and earth, and the sea, and all that in them is:

Ac 7:50 Hath not my hand made all these things?

Ac 14:15 And saying, Sirs, why do ye these things? We also are men of like passions with you, and the living God, which made heaven, and earth, and the sea, and all things that are therein:

Ac 17:24 God that made the world and all things therein, seeing that he is Lord of heaven and earth, dwelleth not in temples made with hands;

Ro 11:36 For of him, and through him, and to him, *are* all things: to whom *be* glory for ever. Amen.

1 Co 8:6 But to us *there is but* one God, the Father, of whom *are* all things, and we in him; and one Lord Jesus Christ, by whom *are* all things, and we by him.

1 Co 15:38 But God giveth it a body as it hath pleased him, and to every seed his own body.

Ep 3:9 And to make all *men* see what *is* the fellowship of the mystery, which from the beginning of the world hath been hid in God, who created all things by Jesus Christ:

1 Ti 4:3 Forbidding to marry, *and commanding* to abstain from meats, which God hath created to be received with thanksgiving of them which believe and know the truth.

1 Ti 6:13 I give thee charge in the sight of God, who quickeneth all things, and *before* Christ Jesus, who before Pontius Pilate witnessed a good confession;

He 1:10 And, Thou, Lord, in the beginning hast laid the foundation of the earth; and the heavens are the works of thine hands:

He 2:10 For it became him, for whom *are* all things, and by whom *are* all things, in bringing many sons unto glory, to make the captain of their salvation perfect through sufferings.

He 3:4 For every house is builded by some *man;* but he that built all things *is* God.

He 11:3 Through faith we understand that the worlds were framed by the word of God, so that things which are seen were not made of things which do appear.

2 Pe 3:5 For this they willingly are ignorant of, that by the word of God the heavens were of old, and the earth standing out of the water and in the water:

Re 4:11 Thou art worthy, O Lord, to receive glory and honour and power: for thou hast created all things, and for thy pleasure they are and were created.

Re 10:6 And sware by him that liveth for ever and ever, who created heaven, and the things that therein are, and the earth, and the things that therein are, and the sea, and the things which are therein, that there should be time no longer:

Re 14:7 Saying with a loud voice, Fear God, and give glory to him; for the hour of his judgment is come: and worship him that made heaven, and earth, and the sea, and the fountains of waters.

1. Of Universe

See **NATURE**

2. Of Man

Ge 1:26 And God said, Let us make man in our image, after our likeness: and let them have dominion over the fish of the sea, and over the fowl of the air, and over the cattle, and over all the earth, and over every creeping thing that creepeth upon the earth.

Ge 2:7 And the LORD God formed man *of* the dust of the ground, and breathed into his nostrils the breath of life; and man became a living soul.

Ge 5:2 Male and female created he them; and blessed them, and called their name Adam, in the day when they were created.

De 4:32 For ask now of the days that are past, which were before thee, since the day that God created man upon the earth, and *ask* from the one side of heaven unto the other, whether there hath been *any such thing* as this great thing *is,* or hath been heard like it?

De 32:6 Do ye thus requite the LORD, O foolish people and unwise? *is* not he thy father *that* hath bought thee? hath he not made thee, and established thee?

De 32:18 Of the Rock *that* begat thee thou art unmindful, and hast forgotten God that formed thee.

Jb 4:17 Shall mortal man be more just than God? shall a man be more pure than his maker?

Jb 10:8 Thine hands have made me and fashioned me together round about; yet thou dost destroy me.

Jb 31:15 Did not he that made me in the womb make him? and did not one fashion us in the womb?

Jb 32:22 For I know not to give flattering titles; *in so doing* my maker would soon take me away.

Jb 33:4 The Spirit of God hath made me, and the breath of the Almighty hath given me life.

Jb 34:19 *How much less to him* that accepteth not the persons of princes, nor regardeth the rich more than the poor? for they all *are* the work of his hands.

Ps 8:5 For thou hast made him a little lower than the angels, and hast crowned him with glory and honour.

Ps 22:9 But thou *art* he that took me out of the womb: thou didst make me hope *when I was* upon my mother's breasts.

Ps 71:6 By thee have I been holden up from the womb: thou art he that

took me out of my mother's bowels: my praise *shall be* continually of thee.

Ps 86:9 All nations whom thou hast made shall come and worship before thee, O LORD; and shall glorify thy name.

Ps 94:9 He that planted the ear, shall he not hear? he that formed the eye, shall he not see?

Ps 95:6 O come, let us worship and bow down: let us kneel before the LORD our maker.

Ps 100:3 Know ye that the LORD he *is* God: *it is* he *that* hath made us, and not we ourselves; *we are* his people, and the sheep of his pasture.

Ps 119:73 Thy hands have made me and fashioned me: give me understanding, that I may learn thy commandments.

Ps 139:13 For thou hast possessed my reins: thou hast covered me in my mother's womb.

Ps 149:2 Let Israel rejoice in him that made him: let the children of Zion be joyful in their King.

Pr 20:12 The hearing ear, and the seeing eye, the LORD hath made even both of them.

Pr 22:2 The rich and poor meet together: the LORD *is* the maker of them all.

Ec 12:1 Remember now thy Creator in the days of thy youth, while the evil days come not, nor the years draw nigh, when thou shalt say, I have no pleasure in them;

Ec 12:7 Then shall the dust return to the earth as it was: and the spirit shall return unto God who gave it.

Is 19:25 Whom the LORD of hosts shall bless, saying, Blessed *be* Egypt my people, and Assyria the work of my hands, and Israel mine inheritance.

Is 27:11 When the boughs thereof are withered, they shall be broken off: the women come, *and* set them on fire: for it *is* a people of no understanding: therefore he that made them will not have mercy on them, and he that formed them will shew them no favour.

Is 29:23 But when he seeth his children, the work of mine hands, in the midst of him, they shall sanctify my name, and sanctify the Holy One of Jacob, and shall fear the God of Israel.

Is 41:4 Who hath wrought and done *it,* calling the generations from the beginning? I the LORD, the first, and with the last; I *am* he.

Is 42:5 Thus saith God the LORD, he that created the heavens, and stretched them out; he that spread forth the earth, and that which cometh out of it; he that giveth breath unto the people upon it, and spirit to them that walk therein:

Is 43:1 But now thus saith the LORD that created thee, O Jacob, and he that formed thee, O Israel, Fear not: for I have redeemed thee, I have called *thee* by thy name; thou *art* mine.

Is 43:7 *Even* every one that is called by my name: for I have created him for my glory, I have formed him; yea, I have made him.

Is 43:15 I *am* the LORD, your Holy One, the creator of Israel, your King.

Is 44:2 Thus saith the LORD that made thee, and formed thee from the womb, *which* will help thee; Fear not, O Jacob, my servant; and thou, Jesurun, whom I have chosen.

Is 44:21 Remember these, O Jacob and Israel; for thou *art* my servant: I have formed thee; thou *art* my servant: O Israel, thou shalt not be forgotten of me.

Is 45:12 I have made the earth, and created man upon it: I, *even* my hands, have stretched out the heavens, and all their host have I commanded.

Is 51:13 And forgettest the LORD thy maker, that hath stretched forth the heavens, and laid the foundations of the earth; and the oppressor, as if he were ready to destroy? and where *is* the fury of the oppressor?

Is 54:16 Behold, I have created the smith that bloweth the coals in the fire, and that bringeth forth an instrument for his work; and I have created the waster to destroy.

Is 64:8 But now, O LORD, thou *art* our father; we *are* the clay, and thou our potter; and we all *are* the work of thy hand.

Je 1:5 Before I formed thee in the belly I knew thee; and before thou camest forth out of the womb I sanctified thee, *and* I ordained thee a prophet unto the nations.

Je 27:5 I have made the earth, the man and the beast that *are* upon the ground, by my great power and by my outstretched arm, and have given it unto whom it seemed meet unto me.

Zec 12:1 The burden of the word of the LORD for Israel, saith the LORD, which stretcheth forth the heavens, and layeth the foundation of the earth, and formeth the spirit of man within him.

Mal 2:10 Have we not all one father? hath not one God created us? why do we deal treacherously every man against his brother, by profaning the covenant of our fathers?

Mt 19:4 And he answered and said unto them, Have ye not read, that he which made *them* at the beginning made them male and female,

Mk 10:6 But from the beginning of the creation God made them male and female.

Lu 3:38 Which was *the son* of Enos, which was *the son* of Seth, which was *the son* of Adam, which was *the son* of God.

Lu 11:40 *Ye* fools, did not he that made that which is without make that which is within also?

Ac 17:26 And hath made of one blood all nations of men for to dwell on all the face of the earth, and hath determined the times before appointed, and the bounds of their habitation;

1 Co 11:12 For as the woman *is* of the man, even so *is* the man also by the woman; but all things of God.

2 Co 5:5 Now he that hath wrought us for the selfsame thing *is* God, who also hath given unto us the earnest of the Spirit.

Ga 1:15 But when it pleased God, who separated me from my mother's womb, and called *me* by his grace,

He 2:7 Thou madest him a little lower than the angels; thou crownedst him with glory and honour, and didst set him over the works of thy hands:

1 Pe 4:19 Wherefore let them that suffer according to the will of God commit the keeping of their souls *to him* in well doing, as unto a faithful Creator.

See **GOD**

3. Christ See **CHRIST**

4. Holy Spirit

Ge 1:2 And the earth was without form, and void; and darkness *was* upon the face of the deep. And the Spirit of God moved upon the face of the waters.

Jb 26:13 By his spirit he hath garnished the heavens; his hand hath formed the crooked serpent.

Jb 33:4 The Spirit of God hath made me, and the breath of the Almighty hath given me life.

Ps 104:30 Thou sendest forth thy spirit, they are created: and thou renewest the face of the earth.

CREDIT SYSTEM

1. Borrowing

Ex 22:14 And if a man borrow *ought* of his neighbour, and it be hurt, or die, the owner thereof *being* not with it, he shall surely make *it* good.

2 K 4:3 Then he said, Go, borrow thee vessels abroad of all thy neighbours, *even* empty vessels; borrow not a few.

2 K 6:5 But as one was felling a beam, the axe head fell into the water: and he cried, and said, Alas, master! for it was borrowed.

Ps 37:21 The wicked borroweth, and payeth not again: but the righteous sheweth mercy, and giveth.

Pr 22:7 The rich ruleth over the poor, and the borrower *is* servant to the lender.

Mt 5:42 Give to him that asketh thee, and from him that would borrow of thee turn not thou away.

2. Lending

De 15:8 But thou shalt open thine hand wide unto him, and shalt surely lend him sufficient for his need, *in that* which he wanteth.

Ps 37:26 *He is* ever merciful, and lendeth; and his seed *is* blessed.

Ps 112:5 A good man sheweth favour, and lendeth: he will guide his affairs with discretion.

Mt 5:42 Give to him that asketh thee, and from him that would borrow of thee turn not thou away.

Lu 6:35 But love ye your enemies, and do good, and lend, hoping for nothing again; and your reward shall be great, and ye shall be the children of the Highest: for he is kind unto the unthankful and *to* the evil.

3. Creditors

De 24:6 No man shall take the nether or the upper millstone to pledge: for he taketh *a man's* life to pledge.

2 K 4:1 Now there cried a certain woman of the wives of the sons of the prophets unto Elisha, saying, Thy servant my husband is dead; and thou knowest that thy servant did fear the LORD: and the creditor is come to take unto him my two sons to be bondmen.

Jb 24:3 They drive away the ass of the fatherless, they take the widow's ox for a pledge.

Mt 18:24 And when he had begun to reckon, one was brought unto him, which owed him ten thousand talents.

4. Debts

NOT TO BE REPUDIATED

2 K 4:7 Then she came and told the man of God. And he said, Go, sell the oil, and pay thy debt, and live thou and thy children of the rest.

SECURED BY MORTGAGES

Ne 5:3 *Some* also there were that said, We have mortgaged our lands, vineyards, and houses, that we might buy corn, because of the dearth.

INSOLVENCY

Mt 18:24–25 And when he had begun to reckon, one was brought unto him, which owed him ten thousand talents.

But forasmuch as he had not to pay, his lord commanded him to be sold, and his wife, and children, and all that he had, and payment to be made.

FRAUD

Lu 16:5–6 So he called every one of his lord's debtors *unto him,* and said unto the first, How much owest thou unto my lord?

And he said, An hundred measures of oil. And he said unto him, Take thy bill, and sit down quickly, and write fifty.

OBLIGATION TO PAY

Ro 13:8 Owe no man any thing, but to love one another: for he that loveth another hath fulfilled the law.

5. *Pledges*, security for debt

Ex 22:26 If thou at all take thy neighbour's raiment to pledge, thou shalt deliver it unto him by that the sun goeth down:

De 24:6 No man shall take the nether or the upper millstone to pledge: for he taketh *a man's* life to pledge.

Jb 22:6 For thou hast taken a pledge from thy brother for nought, and stripped the naked of their clothing.

Jb 24:3 They drive away the ass of the fatherless, they take the widow's ox for a pledge.

Am 2:8 And they lay *themselves* down upon clothes laid to pledge by every altar, and they drink the wine of the condemned in the house of their god.

6. *Sureties*, endorsements

Jb 17:3 Lay down now, put me in a surety with thee; who *is* he *that* will strike hands with me?

Pr 6:1–2 My son, if thou be surety for thy friend, *if* thou hast stricken thy hand with a stranger,

Thou art snared with the words of thy mouth, thou art taken with the words of thy mouth.

Pr 11:15 He that is surety for a stranger shall smart *for it:* and he that hateth suretiship is sure.

Pr 17:18 A man void of understanding striketh hands, *and* becometh surety in the presence of his friend.

Pr 20:16 Take his garment that is surety *for* a stranger: and take a pledge of him for a strange woman.

Pr 22:26 Be not thou *one* of them that strike hands, *or* of them that are sureties for debts.

Pr 27:13 Take his garment that is surety for a stranger, and take a pledge of him for a strange woman.

7. *Usury*

Ex 22:25 If thou lend money to *any of* my people *that is* poor by thee, thou shalt not be to him as an usurer, neither shalt thou lay upon him usury.

Le 25:36 Take thou no usury of him, or increase: but fear thy God; that thy brother may live with thee.

Ne 5:7 Then I consulted with myself, and I rebuked the nobles, and the rulers, and said unto them, Ye exact usury, every one of his brother. And I set a great assembly against them.

Ps 15:5 *He that* putteth not out his money to usury, nor taketh reward against the innocent. He that doeth these *things* shall never be moved.

Pr 28:8 He that by usury and unjust gain increaseth his substance, he shall gather it for him that will pity the poor.

Eze 18:8 He *that* hath not given forth upon usury, neither hath taken any increase, *that* hath withdrawn his hand from iniquity, hath executed true judgment between man and man,

See **BUSINESS**

CREDULITY, *credence, assurance*

Ge 3:6; Jos 9:14; Pr 14:15; 17:4; Mt 24:5, 23; Ac 8:10; 1 Jn 4:1

See **ASSURANCE**

CREEPING THINGS, *land animals created by God on the sixth day*

Ge 1:26, 30; 6:20; 7:14; 8:17; Le 5:2; 11:20, 29, 42; 22:5; De 14:19; 1 K 4:33;

Ps 104:25; 148:10; Eze 8:10; 38:20; Ho 2:18; Hab 1:14; Ac 10:12; 11:6; Ro 1:23

See **ANIMALS**

CREMATION *See* **DEAD**

CRETE, *Candia, an island in the Mediterranean Sea*

Ac 2:11; 27:7, 7, 12, 21; Tit 1:5, 5

CRIMSON, *a deep red color*

2 Chr 2:7; 3:14; Is 1:18; Je 4:30

CROSSBEARING, *commanded of disciples*

Mt 10:38 And he that taketh not his cross, and followeth after me, is not worthy of me.

Mt 16:24 Then said Jesus unto his disciples, If any *man* will come after me, let him deny himself, and take up his cross, and follow me.

Mk 8:34 And when he had called the people *unto him* with his disciples also, he said unto them, Whosoever will come after me, let him deny himself, and take up his cross, and follow me.

Mk 10:21 Then Jesus beholding him loved him, and said unto him, One thing thou lackest: go thy way, sell whatsoever thou hast, and give to the poor, and thou shalt have treasure in heaven: and come, take up the cross, and follow me.

Lu 9:23 And he said to *them* all, If any *man* will come after me, let him deny himself, and take up his cross daily, and follow me.

Lu 14:27 And whosoever doth not bear his cross, and come after me, cannot be my disciple.

See **DISCIPLESHIP**

CROSS OF CHRIST, *the symbol of shame, humiliation, and forgiveness*

1. An Instrument of Death

Mt 27:32 And as they came out, they found a man of Cyrene, Simon by name: him they compelled to bear his cross.

Mk 15:21 And they compel one Simon a Cyrenian, who passed by, com-

ing out of the country, the father of Alexander and Rufus, to bear his cross.

Lu 23:26 And as they led him away, they laid hold upon one Simon, a Cyrenian, coming out of the country, and on him they laid the cross, that he might bear *it* after Jesus.

Jn 19:17 And he bearing his cross went forth into a place called *the place* of a skull, which is called in the Hebrew Golgotha:

Ph 2:8 And being found in fashion as a man, he humbled himself, and became obedient unto death, even the death of the cross.

He 12:2 Looking unto Jesus the author and finisher of *our* faith; who for the joy that was set before him endured the cross, despising the shame, and is set down at the right hand of the throne of God.

2. A Symbol of Doctrine

ITS MESSAGE

1 Co 1:17 For Christ sent me not to baptize, but to preach the gospel: not with wisdom of words, lest the cross of Christ should be made of none effect.

ITS GLORY

Ga 6:14 But God forbid that I should glory, save in the cross of our Lord Jesus Christ, by whom the world is crucified unto me, and I unto the world.

ITS RECONCILIATION

Ep 2:16 And that he might reconcile both unto God in one body by the cross, having slain the enmity thereby:

ITS ENEMIES

Ph 3:18 (For many walk, of whom I have told you often, and now tell you even weeping, *that they are* the enemies of the cross of Christ:

ITS PEACE

Col 1:20 And, having made peace through the blood of his cross, by him to reconcile all things unto himself; by him, *I say*, whether *they be* things in earth, or things in heaven.

ITS ACCOMPLISHMENT

Col 2:14 Blotting out the handwriting of ordinances that was against us, which was contrary to us, and took it out of the way, nailing it to his cross;

See **BLOOD, REDEMPTION**

CROWN OF GLORY   See **REWARD**

CROWN OF LIFE   See **REWARD**

CROWN OF RIGHTEOUSNESS
See **REWARD**

CROWNS, *head ornaments worn as symbols of sovereignty, position, power or reward*

1. Literal

Le 8:9 And he put the mitre upon his head; also upon the mitre, *even* upon his forefront, did he put the golden plate, the holy crown; as the LORD commanded Moses.

2 S 1:10 So I stood upon him, and slew him, because I was sure that he could not live after that he was fallen: and I took the crown that *was* upon his head, and the bracelet that *was* on his arm, and have brought them hither unto my lord.

2 S 12:30 And he took their king's crown from off his head, the weight whereof *was* a talent of gold with the precious stones: and it was *set* on David's head. And he brought forth the spoil of the city in great abundance.

2 K 11:12 And he brought forth the king's son, and put the crown upon him, and *gave him* the testimony; and they made him king, and anointed him; and they clapped their hands, and said, God save the king.

Est 1:11 To bring Vashti the queen before the king with the crown royal, to shew the people and the princes her beauty: for she *was* fair to look on.

Est 8:15 And Mordecai went out from the presence of the king in royal apparel of blue and white, and with a great crown of gold, and with a gar-

ment of fine linen and purple: and the city of Shushan rejoiced and was glad.

Mt 27:29 And when they had platted a crown of thorns, they put *it* upon his head, and a reed in his right hand: and they bowed the knee before him, and mocked him, saying, Hail, King of the Jews!

Re 4:10 The four and twenty elders fall down before him that sat on the throne, and worship him that liveth for ever and ever, and cast their crowns before the throne, saying,

2. Figurative

Ps 8:5 For thou hast made him a little lower than the angels, and hast crowned him with glory and honour.

Ps 21:3 For thou preventest him with the blessings of goodness: thou settest a crown of pure gold on his head.

Ps 103:4 Who redeemeth thy life from destruction; who crowneth thee with lovingkindness and tender mercies;

Pr 4:9 She shall give to thine head an ornament of grace: a crown of glory shall she deliver to thee.

Pr 12:4 A virtuous woman *is* a crown to her husband: but she that maketh ashamed *is* as rottenness in his bones.

Pr 16:31 The hoary head *is* a crown of glory, *if* it be found in the way of righteousness.

Pr 17:6 Children's children *are* the crown of old men; and the glory of children *are* their fathers.

3. Spiritual

See **FUTURE LIFE, REWARD**

CRUELTY, *causing pain and suffering*

Ge 49:5; Ex 21:20; De 25:18; 2 K 15:16; Jb 6:27; 24:21; Ps 27:12; Pr 11:17; Is 13:18; 33:1; Je 50:42; 52:10; Da 2:5; Mt 21:35

1. Examples

Ge 37:24; Ex 1:22; 5:14; Jud 1:6; 9:18, 24, 49; 16:21; 1 S 11:2; 2 S 12:31; 2 K 8:12; 25:7; Je 38:6; 39:6; Da 3:20; Am 1:13; Mt 2:16; 27:26; Mk 6:25; Lu 10:30; 20:12; Jn 18:22; 19:2, 32; Ac 16:24; 22:24; 27:42

2. To Animals

Nu 22:25, 27; 2 S 8:4; 1 Chr 18:4; Pr 12:10

See **EVIL, KINDNESS**

CRUSES, *jars, jugs, small vessels for holding liquids*

1 S 26:11, 16; 1 K 14:3; 17:12; 19:6; 2 K 2:20

CRYING, *pleas for help*

Mt 14:30 But when he saw the wind boisterous, he was afraid; and beginning to sink, he cried, saying, Lord, save me.

Mt 15:22 And, behold, a woman of Canaan came out of the same coasts, and cried unto him, saying, Have mercy on me, O Lord, *thou* Son of David; my daughter is grievously vexed with a devil.

Mt 15:25 Then came she and worshipped him, saying, Lord, help me.

Mt 17:15 Lord, have mercy on my son: for he is lunatick, and sore vexed: for ofttimes he falleth into the fire, and oft into the water.

Mt 20:30 And, behold, two blind men sitting by the way side, when they heard that Jesus passed by, cried out, saying, Have mercy on us, O Lord, *thou* Son of David.

Mk 7:26 The woman was a Greek, a Syrophenician by nation; and she besought him that he would cast forth the devil out of her daughter.

Mk 10:47 And when he heard that it was Jesus of Nazareth, he began to cry out, and say, Jesus, *thou* Son of David, have mercy on me.

Lu 17:12–13 And as he entered into a certain village, there met him ten men that were lepers, which stood afar off:
And they lifted up *their* voices, and said, Jesus, Master, have mercy on us.

Lu 18:38 And he cried, saying, Jesus, *thou* Son of David, have mercy on me.

See **WEEPING**

CRYSTAL See **STONES**

CUBITS, *measures of length*

Ge 6:16; Ex 26:2; 27:9; 36:9; 37:1; 38:1, 18; Nu 35:5; De 3:11; 1 K 6:2; 7:32; 2 Chr 3:4; Ezr 6:3; Eze 40:5, 21, 47; 41:10, 13; 42:4; 43:13; 47:3; Da 3:1; Zec 5:2; Mt 6:27; Lu 12:25; Re 21:17

See **WEIGHTS AND MEASURES**

CUCUMBERS

Nu 11:5; Is 1:8

See **AGRICULTURE**

CUMMIN, *a plant*

Is 28:25, 27

CUPS, *drinking vessels*

Ge 40:11; 44:2, 17; 2 S 12:3; Je 52:19; Mk 7:4

CURE, *treatment of disease*

1. Physicians

Ge 50:2; 2 Chr 16:12; Jb 13:4; Je 8:22; Mt 9:12; Mk 2:17; 5:26; Lu 4:23; 5:31; 8:43; Col 4:14

2. Medicine

Pr 17:22; Je 8:22; 30:13; 46:11; Eze 47:12

3. Remedies

2 K 20:7; Is 1:6; 38:21; Lu 10:34; 1 Ti 5:23; Ja 5:14

a. Anointing with Oil

Mk 6:13; Ja 5:14

b. Ointment

Is 1:6

c. Poultices

2 K 20:7

4. Treatment of Fractures

Eze 30:21

5. Treatment of Wounds

Is 1:6; Lu 10:34

6. Disinfection

Le 14:41; 15:5

7. Quarantine

Le 13:4, 21, 26, 31, 33, 46, 50; 14:8, 38; Nu 5:2; 12:15; 31:19; 2 K 7:3; 15:5; 2 Chr 26:21; Lu 17:12

8. Miraculous Disappearance of Disease

Mt 8:3, 13; 9:7, 22; 15:28; 17:18; 20:34; Mk 1:31, 42; 2:12; 5:29, 42; 7:35; Lu 5:13, 25; 8:47; 18:42; Jn 4:53; Ac 3:8; 9:18

See **SICKNESS**

CURIOSITY, *inquisitiveness*

1. Examples of Idle

THE MEN OF BETH-SHEMESH, *desired to see inside the Ark*

1 S 6:19 And he smote the men of Beth-shemesh, because they had looked into the ark of the LORD, even he smote of the people fifty thousand and threescore and ten men: and the people lamented, because the LORD had smitten *many* of the people with a great slaughter.

HEROD

Lu 9:9 And Herod said, John have I beheaded: but who is this, of whom I hear such things? And he desired to see him.

THE LEVITE

Lu 10:32 And likewise a Levite, when he was at the place, came and looked *on him,* and passed by on the other side.

THE JEWS WHO CAME TO SEE LAZARUS

Jn 12:9 Much people of the Jews therefore knew that he was there: and they came not for Jesus' sake only, but that they might see Lazarus also, whom he had raised from the dead.

THE ATHENIANS

Ac 17:21 (For all the Athenians and strangers which were there spent their time in nothing else, but either to tell, or to hear some new thing.)

2. Leads to the Desire for Signs

Ex 7:9; Jud 6:17, 37; 2 K 20:8; Is 7:11; 38:22; Mt 12:38; 16:1; 24:3; 27:42; Mk 8:11; 15:32, 36; Lu 4:23; 11:16, 29; 16:30; 21:7; 23:8; Jn 2:18; 4:48; 6:30; 20:25

See **QUESTIONS**

CURSE

Ge 3:14 And the LORD God said unto the serpent, Because thou hast done this, thou *art* cursed above all cattle, and above every beast of the field; upon thy belly shalt thou go, and dust shalt thou eat all the days of thy life:

Ge 3:17 And unto Adam he said, Because thou hast hearkened unto the voice of thy wife, and hast eaten of the tree, of which I commanded thee, saying, Thou shalt not eat of it: cursed *is* the ground for thy sake; in sorrow shalt thou eat *of* it all the days of thy life;

Ge 4:11 And now *art* thou cursed from the earth, which hath opened her mouth to receive thy brother's blood from thy hand;

Ge 5:29 And he called his name Noah, saying, This *same* shall comfort us concerning our work and toil of our hands, because of the ground which the LORD hath cursed.

Nu 5:21 Then the priest shall charge the woman with an oath of cursing, and the priest shall say unto the woman, The LORD make thee a curse and an oath among thy people, when the LORD doth make thy thigh to rot, and thy belly to swell;

De 11:28 And a curse, if ye will not obey the commandments of the LORD your God, but turn aside out of the way which I command you this day, to go after other gods, which ye have not known.

De 27:15 Cursed *be* the man that maketh *any* graven or molten image, an abomination unto the LORD, the work of the hands of the craftsman, and putteth *it* in *a* secret *place.* And all the people shall answer and say, Amen.

De 28:16 Cursed *shalt* thou *be* in the city, and cursed *shalt* thou *be* in the field.

De 28:45 Moreover all these curses shall come upon thee, and shall pursue thee, and overtake thee, till thou be destroyed; because thou hearkenedst not unto the voice of the LORD thy God, to keep his commandments and his statutes which he commanded thee:

De 29:20 The LORD will not spare him, but then the anger of the LORD and his jealousy shall smoke against that man, and all the curses that are written in this book shall lie upon him, and the LORD shall blot out his name from under heaven.

De 29:27 And the anger of the LORD was kindled against this land, to bring upon it all the curses that are written in this book:

De 30:7 And the LORD thy God will put all these curses upon thine enemies, and on them that hate thee, which persecuted thee.

Jos 6:26 And Joshua adjured *them* at that time, saying, Cursed *be* the man before the LORD, that riseth up and buildeth this city Jericho: he shall lay the foundation thereof in his firstborn, and in his youngest *son* shall he set up the gates of it.

Jud 5:23 Curse ye Meroz, said the angel of the LORD, curse ye bitterly the inhabitants thereof; because they came not to the help of the LORD, to the help of the LORD against the mighty.

2 Chr 34:24 Thus saith the LORD, Behold, I will bring evil upon this place, and upon the inhabitants thereof, *even* all the curses that are written in the book which they have read before the king of Judah:

Ps 119:21 Thou hast rebuked the proud *that are* cursed, which do err from thy commandments.

Pr 3:33 The curse of the LORD *is* in the house of the wicked: but he blesseth the habitation of the just.

Is 24:6 Therefore hath the curse devoured the earth, and they that dwell therein are desolate: therefore the inhabitants of the earth are burned, and few men left.

Is 65:20 There shall be no more thence an infant of days, nor an old man that hath not filled his days: for the child shall die an hundred years old; but the sinner *being* an hundred years old shall be accursed.

Je 11:3 And say thou unto them, Thus saith the LORD God of Israel; Cursed *be* the man that obeyeth not the words of this covenant,

Lam 3:65 Give them sorrow of heart, thy curse unto them.

Da 9:11 Yea, all Israel have transgressed thy law, even by departing, that they might not obey thy voice; therefore the curse is poured upon us, and the oath that *is* written in the law of Moses the servant of God, because we have sinned against him.

Zec 5:3 Then said he unto me, This *is* the curse that goeth forth over the face of the whole earth: for every one that stealeth shall be cut off *as* on this side according to it; and every one that sweareth shall be cut off *as* on that side according to it.

Mal 1:14 But cursed *be* the deceiver, which hath in his flock a male, and voweth, and sacrificeth unto the LORD a corrupt thing: for I *am* a great King, saith the LORD of hosts, and my name *is* dreadful among the heathen.

Mal 3:9 Ye *are* cursed with a curse: for ye have robbed me, *even* this whole nation.

Mal 4:6 And he shall turn the heart of the fathers to the children, and the heart of the children to their fathers, lest I come and smite the earth with a curse.

Mt 21:19 And when he saw a fig tree in the way, he came to it, and found nothing thereon, but leaves only, and said unto it, Let no fruit grow on thee henceforward for ever. And presently the fig tree withered away.

Mk 11:14 And Jesus answered and said unto it, No man eat fruit of thee hereafter for ever. And his disciples heard *it*.

Ro 5:16 And not as *it was* by one that sinned, *so is* the gift: for the judgment *was* by one to condemnation, but the free gift *is* of many offences unto justification.

Ro 8:22 For we know that the whole creation groaneth and travaileth in pain together until now.

Ga 3:10 For as many as are of the works of the law are under the curse: for it is written, Cursed *is* every one that continueth not in all things which are written in the book of the law to do them.

Re 22:3 And there shall be no more curse: but the throne of God and of the Lamb shall be in it; and his servants shall serve him:

CURSING, *rendering of several Hebrew and Greek words; sometimes divine maledictions, other times predictions by holy men; also, prohibited expressions against parents and God*

Nu 22:6 Come now therefore, I pray thee, curse me this people; for they *are* too mighty for me: peradventure I shall prevail, *that* we may smite them, and *that* I may drive them out of the land: for I wot that he whom thou blessest *is* blessed, and he whom thou cursest is cursed.

Ps 10:7 His mouth is full of cursing and deceit and fraud: under his tongue *is* mischief and vanity.

Ps 59:12 *For* the sin of their mouth *and* the words of their lips let them even be taken in their pride: and for cursing and lying *which* they speak.

Ps 109:17 As he loved cursing, so let it come unto him: as he delighted not in blessing, so let it be far from him.

Ec 7:22 For oftentimes also thine own heart knoweth that thou thyself likewise hast cursed others.

Is 8:21 And they shall pass through it, hardly bestead and hungry: and it shall come to pass, that when they shall be hungry, they shall fret themselves, and curse their king and their God, and look upward.

Je 23:10 For the land is full of adulterers; for because of swearing the land mourneth; the pleasant places of the wilderness are dried up, and their course is evil, and their force *is* not right.

Ro 3:14 Whose mouth *is* full of cursing and bitterness:

Ja 3:9 Therewith bless we God, even the Father; and therewith curse we men, which are made after the similitude of God.

1. Examples

Ge 9:25 And he said, Cursed *be* Canaan; a servant of servants shall he be unto his brethren.

Le 24:11 And the Israelitish woman's son blasphemed the name *of the LORD,* and cursed. And they brought him unto Moses: (and his mother's name *was* Shelomith, the daughter of Dibri, of the tribe of Dan:)

Jud 9:27 And they went out into the fields, and gathered their vineyards, and trode *the grapes,* and made merry, and went into the house of their god, and did eat and drink, and cursed Abimelech.

1 S 17:43 And the Philistine said unto David, *Am* I a dog, that thou comest to me with staves? And the Philistine cursed David by his gods.

2 S 16:5 And when king David came to Bahurim, behold, thence came out a man of the family of the house of Saul, whose name *was* Shimei, the son of Gera: he came forth, and cursed still as he came.

2 S 16:13 And as David and his men went by the way, Shimei went along on the hill's side over against him, and cursed as he went, and threw stones at him, and cast dust.

2 S 19:19 And said unto the king, Let not my lord impute iniquity unto me, neither do thou remember that which thy servant did perversely the day that my lord the king went out of Jerusalem, that the king should take it to his heart.

Jb 31:30 Neither have I suffered my mouth to sin by wishing a curse to his soul.

Mt 26:74 Then began he to curse and to swear, *saying,* I know not the man. And immediately the cock crew.

Mk 14:71 But he began to curse and to swear, *saying,* I know not this man of whom ye speak.

2. Of Parents

Ex 21:17 And he that curseth his father, or his mother, shall surely be put to death.

Le 20:9 For every one that curseth his father or his mother shall be surely put to death: he hath cursed his father or his mother; his blood *shall be* upon him.

Pr 20:20 Whoso curseth his father or his mother, his lamp shall be put out in obscure darkness.

Pr 30:11 *There is* a generation *that* curseth their father, and doth not bless their mother.

Mt 15:4 For God commanded, saying, Honour thy father and mother: and, He that curseth father or mother, let him die the death.

Mk 7:10 For Moses said, Honour thy father and thy mother; and, Whoso curseth father or mother, let him die the death:

3. Forbidden

Le 19:14 Thou shalt not curse the deaf, nor put a stumblingblock before the blind, but shalt fear thy God: I *am* the LORD.

Le 24:15 And thou shalt speak unto the children of Israel, saying, Whosoever curseth his God shall bear his sin.

Nu 23:11 And Balak said unto Balaam, What hast thou done unto me? I took thee to curse mine enemies, and, behold, thou hast blessed *them* altogether.

Ps 109:28 Let them curse, but bless thou: when they arise, let them be ashamed; but let thy servant rejoice.

Ec 10:20 Curse not the king, no not in thy thought; and curse not the rich in thy bedchamber: for a bird of the air shall carry the voice, and that which hath wings shall tell the matter.

Lu 6:28 Bless them that curse you, and pray for them which despitefully use you.

Ro 12:14 Bless them which persecute you: bless, and curse not.

Ja 3:10 Out of the same mouth proceedeth blessing and cursing. My brethren, these things ought not so to be.

See **BLESSINGS**

CURTAINS, *of the tabernacle*

Ex 26:1; 36:9; 2 S 7:2; 1 Chr 17:1

CYMBALS *See* **MUSIC**

CYPRESS *See* **TREES**

CYPRUS, *an island in the Mediterranean*

Ac 4:36; 11:19–20; 13:4; 15:39; 21:3, 16; 27:4

CYRENE, *a city in Libya*

Mt 27:32 And as they came out, they found a man of Cyrene, Simon by name: him they compelled to bear his cross.

Ac 2:10 Phrygia, and Pamphylia, in Egypt, and in the parts of Libya about Cyrene, and strangers of Rome, Jews and proselytes,

Ac 11:20 And some of them were men of Cyprus and Cyrene, which, when they were come to Antioch, spake unto the Grecians, preaching the Lord Jesus.

See **CITIES**

CYRUS, *king of Persia*

2 Chr 36:22; Ezr 1:1; 3:7; 4:3; 5:13; 6:3; Is 44:28; 45:1; Da 1:21; 10:1

D

DAMASCUS, *a city of Syria*

Damascus, "the Pearl of the East," is said to be the oldest city in the world with a continuous history. Its permanency is attributed to the fact that it is located within a 60,000–acre plain (2,260 feet above sea level) that is one of the most fertile oases of the world. The city and surrounding plain owe their life and prosperity to the Abana and Pharpar rivers of biblical fame (2 K 5:12). In addition to being the capital of modern Syria, the city was also a former capital of the Kingdom of Aram, alternately an enemy or ally of Israel until subdued and annexed by Assyria in 732 B.C.

Ancient Damascus lies under the old section of the modern city. Excavations of the ancient city have only penetrated to the Roman period (63 B.C.–A.D. 70). New Testament Damascus is in the southeast section of the modern city. Its streets were arrayed in a typical Hellenistic grid that can be seen as the basis of the modern streets. A fifty-foot-wide street with colonnades has been excavated; it is probably the "street called Straight" where Ananias was told to go to find Paul (Ac 9:11.

Ge 14:15; 15:2; 2 S 8:6; 1 K 11:24; 19:15; 20:34; 2 K 5:12; 8:7; 14:28; 16:9; 1 Chr 18:5; 2 Chr 16:2; 24:23; 28:5; Song 7:4; Is 7:8; 10:9; 17:1; Je 49:23; Eze 27:18; 47:16; 48:1; Am 1:3; 5:27; Zec 9:1; Ac 9:2, 8, 19; 22:6, 11; 26:12, 20; 2 Co 11:32; Ga 1:17

See CITIES, PAUL

DAN

1. Son of Jacob

Ge 30:6; 35:25; 46:23; 49:16; Ex 1:4; Nu 1:12; 26:42; De 33:22; Eze 48:32

2. Town

The name of Dan is first mentioned in the Bible in Genesis 14:14; its earlier name was Laish (Jud 18:29). Jeroboam, shortly after establishing the northern kingdom, built a pagan sanctuary in Dan in which was placed a golden calf (1 K 12:28–30).

Ge 14:14; Jos 19:47; Jud 13:25; 18:27, 29; 2 S 17:11; 1 K 4:25; 12:29; 15:20; 1 Chr 21:2; 2 Chr 30:5

See CITIES

3. Tribe

Nu 1:39; 2:25; 10:25; 13:12; 34:22; Jos 19:40, 48; 21:5, 23; Jud 18:1, 22, 30; 1 Chr 27:22; Eze 48:1

DANCING, *moving to music, leaping or skipping about excitedly*

1. Examples

Ex 32:19; Jud 11:34; 21:21; 1 S 30:16; Jb 21:11; Ec 3:4; Je 31:4; Lam 5:15; Mt 11:17; 14:6; Mk 6:22

2. Before the Lord

Ex 15:20; 1 S 18:6; 2 S 6:14; 1 Chr 15:29; Ps 30:11; 149:3; 150:4

DANIEL

1. Person, *one of the greater prophets*

Nothing is known of his family, but he is thought to have been of noble descent (Da 1:3). H e was carried captive to Babylon during the reign of Jehoiakim (1:2). He, and three companions, because of their special qualifications were selected to be trained for the king's service (1:3–4).

There is a marked resemblance between Daniel's career and that of Joseph. Both were carried captive in youth, were model young men, and found employment in a king's court.

Both were unjustly persecuted, their hardships becoming stepping stones to honor, and through the interpretation of dreams were exalted to rulership. Both lived pure lives in the midst of corrupt courts and died in foreign lands.

Daniel, like Moses, was both a statesman and a prophet. As a prophet he was given a telescopic vision that had a longer range than that of most of the prophets. He saw beyond the coming of Christ and beheld his enthronement as King of kings. He is particularly a prophet of the last days.
Eze 14:14 Though these three men, Noah, Daniel, and Job, were in it, they should deliver *but* their own souls by their righteousness, saith the Lord God.

Eze 28:3 Behold, thou *art* wiser than Daniel; there is no secret that they can hide from thee:

Da 1:6 Now among these were of the children of Judah, Daniel, Hananiah, Mishael, and Azariah:

Da 2:14 Then Daniel answered with counsel and wisdom to Arioch the captain of the king's guard, which was gone forth to slay the wise *men* of Babylon:

Da 2:17–18 Then Daniel went to his house, and made the thing known to Hananiah, Mishael, and Azariah, his companions:

That they would desire mercies of the God of heaven concerning this secret; that Daniel and his fellows should not perish with the rest of the wise *men* of Babylon.

Da 5:17 Then Daniel answered and said before the king, Let thy gifts be to thyself, and give thy rewards to another; yet I will read the writing unto the king, and make known to him the interpretation.

Da 5:22–23 And thou his son, O Belshazzar, hast not humbled thine heart, though thou knewest all this;

But hast lifted up thyself against the Lord of heaven; and they have brought the vessels of his house before thee, and thou, and thy lords, thy wives, and thy concubines, have drunk wine in them; and thou hast

praised the gods of silver, and gold, of brass, iron, wood, and stone, which see not, nor hear, nor know: and the God in whose hand thy breath *is,* and whose *are* all thy ways, hast thou not glorified:

Da 6:04 Then the presidents and princes sought to find occasion against Daniel concerning the kingdom; but they could find none occasion nor fault; forasmuch as he *was* faithful, neither was there any error or fault found in him.

Da 6:10 Now when Daniel knew that the writing was signed, he went into his house; and his windows being open in his chamber toward Jerusalem, he kneeled upon his knees three times a day, and prayed, and gave thanks before his God, as he did aforetime.

Da 6:21 Then said Daniel unto the king, O king, live for ever.

Da 7:9–12 I beheld till the thrones were cast down, and the Ancient of days did sit, whose garment *was* white as snow, and the hair of his head like the pure wool: his throne *was like* the fiery flame, *and* his wheels *as* burning fire.

A fiery stream issued and came forth from before him: thousand thousands ministered unto him, and ten thousand times ten thousand stood before him: the judgment was set, and the books were opened.

I beheld then because of the voice of the great words which the horn spake: I beheld *even* till the beast was slain, and his body destroyed, and given to the burning flame.

As concerning the rest of the beasts, they had their dominion taken away: yet their lives were prolonged for a season and time.

Da 9:2 In the first year of his reign I Daniel understood by books the number of the years, whereof the word of the Lord came to Jeremiah the prophet, that he would accomplish seventy years in the desolations of Jerusalem.

Da 10:5–6 Then I lifted up mine eyes, and looked, and behold a certain man clothed in linen, whose loins *were* girded with fine gold of Uphaz:

His body also *was* like the beryl, and his face as the appearance of lightning, and his eyes as lamps of fire, and his arms and his feet like in colour to polished brass, and the voice of his words like the voice of a multitude.

Da 10:17 For how can the servant of this my lord talk with this my lord? for as for me, straightway there remained no strength in me, neither is there breath left in me.

Da 12:4 But thou, O Daniel, shut up the words, and seal the book, *even* to the time of the end: many shall run to and fro, and knowledge shall be increased.

Mk 13:14 But when ye shall see the abomination of desolation, spoken of by Daniel the prophet, standing where it ought not, (let him that readeth understand,) then let them that be in Judaea flee to the mountains:

2. Book

Author: Daniel, like Ezekiel, was a captive in Babylon. He was brought before King Nebuchadnezzar while young and trained in the Chaldean language and sciences (1:17–18). His career resembled that of Joseph. Promoted to the highest office in the realm (2:48), he maintained his spiritual life in the midst of a heathen court (6:10).

Date Written: Before 530 B.C. The book records the events of Daniel's lifetime, beginning with his teenage years in 605 B.C.

Purpose: To give hope to God's people by revealing God's sovereign program for them, even during Gentile domination. God's eternal program will not be deterred.

To Whom Written: Jewish exiles in Babylon and God's people everywhere.

Main Theme: The sovereignty of God over the affairs of people in all ages. The pagan kings' confessions of this fact constitute significant verses of this book: 2:47; 4:37; 6:26.

Key Words: God's Eternal Kingdom.
Key Verses: 2:20–22, 44.

DARIUS, *name given to three 5th–6th century B.C. rulers of world powers who significantly affected the nation of Israel*

1. Median King of Persia

Da 5:31; 6:1, 25; 9:1

2. Emancipator of Israel

Ezr 4:24; 5:6; 6:1, 13; Hag 1:1, 15; 2:10; Zec 1:1

3. King of Persia

Ne 12:22

DARKNESS, *absence of light*

1. Physical

Ge 1:2, 18; Jb 3:6; 38:19; Ps 104:20; Am 4:13

2. Supernatural

Ex 10:22 And Moses stretched forth his hand toward heaven; and there was a thick darkness in all the land of Egypt three days:

Ps 105:28 He sent darkness, and made it dark; and they rebelled not against his word.

Jl 3:15 The sun and the moon shall be darkened, and the stars shall withdraw their shining.

Mt 27:45 Now from the sixth hour there was darkness over all the land unto the ninth hour.

Re 6:12 And I beheld when he had opened the sixth seal, and, lo, there was a great earthquake; and the sun became black as sackcloth of hair, and the moon became as blood;

3. Figurative

Jb 18:5 Yea, the light of the wicked shall be put out, and the spark of his fire shall not shine.

Pr 20:20 Whoso curseth his father or his mother, his lamp shall be put out in obscure darkness.

Am 5:20 *Shall* not the day of the LORD *be* darkness, and not light? even very dark, and no brightness in it?

Mi 3:6 Therefore night *shall be* unto you, that ye shall not have a vision; and it shall be dark unto you, that ye shall not divine; and the sun shall go down over the prophets, and the day shall be dark over them.

Mt 8:12 But the children of the kingdom shall be cast out into outer darkness: there shall be weeping and gnashing of teeth.

Mt 22:13 Then said the king to the servants, Bind him hand and foot, and take him away, and cast *him* into outer darkness; there shall be weeping and gnashing of teeth.

2 Pe 2:17 These are wells without water, clouds that are carried with a tempest; to whom the mist of darkness is reserved for ever.

Jude 6 And the angels which kept not their first estate, but left their own habitation, he hath reserved in everlasting chains under darkness unto the judgment of the great day.

4. Spiritual

1 S 3:1 And the child Samuel ministered unto the LORD before Eli. And the word of the LORD was precious in those days; *there was* no open vision.

Jb 5:14 They meet with darkness in the daytime, and grope in the noonday as in the night.

Jb 18:6 The light shall be dark in his tabernacle, and his candle shall be put out with him.

Ps 107:10 Such as sit in darkness and in the shadow of death, *being* bound in affliction and iron;

Is 9:2 The people that walked in darkness have seen a great light: they that dwell in the land of the shadow of death, upon them hath the light shined.

Is 49:9 That thou mayest say to the prisoners, Go forth; to them that *are* in darkness, Shew yourselves. They shall feed in the ways, and their pastures *shall be* in all high places.

Mi 3:6 Therefore night *shall be* unto you, that ye shall not have a vision; and it shall be dark unto you, that ye

shall not divine; and the sun shall go down over the prophets, and the day shall be dark over them.

Zec 14:6 And it shall come to pass in that day, *that* the light shall not be clear, *nor* dark:

Mt 6:23 But if thine eye be evil, thy whole body shall be full of darkness. If therefore the light that is in thee be darkness, how great *is* that darkness!

Jn 1:5 And the light shineth in darkness; and the darkness comprehended it not.

Jn 3:19 And this is the condemnation, that light is come into the world, and men loved darkness rather than light, because their deeds were evil.

Ro 13:12 The night is far spent, the day is at hand: let us therefore cast off the works of darkness, and let us put on the armour of light.

Ep 5:8 For ye were sometimes darkness, but now *are ye* light in the Lord: walk as children of light:

1 Th 5:4 But ye, brethren, are not in darkness, that that day should overtake you as a thief.

5. Walking in Darkness

De 28:29 And thou shalt grope at noonday, as the blind gropeth in darkness, and thou shalt not prosper in thy ways: and thou shalt be only oppressed and spoiled evermore, and no man shall save *thee*.

Ps 35:6 Let their way be dark and slippery: and let the angel of the LORD persecute them.

Ps 82:5 They know not, neither will they understand; they walk on in darkness: all the foundations of the earth are out of course.

Pr 2:13 Who leave the paths of uprightness, to walk in the ways of darkness;

Pr 4:19 The way of the wicked *is* as darkness: they know not at what they stumble.

Is 59:9 Therefore is judgment far from us, neither doth justice overtake us: we wait for light, but behold obscurity; for brightness, *but* we walk in darkness.

Je 23:12 Wherefore their way shall be unto them as slippery *ways* in the darkness: they shall be driven on, and fall therein: for I will bring evil upon them, *even* the year of their visitation, saith the LORD.

Zep 1:17 And I will bring distress upon men, that they shall walk like blind men, because they have sinned against the LORD: and their blood shall be poured out as dust, and their flesh as the dung.

Mt 15:14 Let them alone: they be blind leaders of the blind. And if the blind lead the blind, both shall fall into the ditch.

Jn 11:10 But if a man walk in the night, he stumbleth, because there is no light in him.

1 Jn 1:6 If we say that we have fellowship with him, and walk in darkness, we lie, and do not the truth:

See **EVIL, LIGHT**

DATHAN AND ABIRAM, *destroyed for their rebellion*
Nu 16:1, 12, 27; 26:9; De 11:6

DAUGHTERS OF PHILIP *See* **WOMEN, YOUNG PEOPLE**

DAVID, *king and poet*
Ru 4:22; De 17:17; 1 S 13:14; 16:12–13; 17:14, 34–36, 40, 50; 18:1, 29; 2 S 5:7, 13; 7:5; 11:1–15; 12:1–31; 18:33; 23:1; 24:1; 1 K 1:1; 2:10; 15:5; 1 Chr 2:15; 3:1; 10:14; 17:1; 23:1; 28:3; 29:26; 2 Chr 6:6; 35:4; Ezr 8:20; Ne 12:46; Ps 8:1; 19:1; 23:1; 51:1–19; 72:20; 89:20; 132:10; Pr 1:1; Is 55:3; Eze 37:24; Mt 1:6; 22:45; Mk 2:25; Lu 2:4; 3:31; Jn 7:42; Ac 2:25, 29; 7:45; 13:22; Ro 4:6; 11:9; He 11:32

1. His Early Life

Spent on his father's farm at Bethlehem; he was the youngest of eight sons.
1 S 16:10–11

As a shepherd he showed great courage in protecting the flock.
1 S 17:34–36

He was divinely chosen to succeed King Saul and quietly anointed by the prophet Samuel.
1 S 16:12–13

2. His Service under Saul

He became the king's harpist.
1 S 16:14–23

After remaining at court for a time he returns to the farm.
1 S 17:15

He next appears as champion of Israel and kills the giant, Goliath, which results in a great victory for God's people.
1 S 17:25–53

This heroic feat wins the admiration of Jonathan, the king's son, but the praises of the people given to David arouse the hatred of Saul.
1 S 18:1–9

Soon David is compelled to flee for his life.
1 S 19

3. As a Fugitive

The magnanimous intercession of Jonathan, securing David's temporary restoration to the king's favor.
1 S 19:4–7

The generosity of David in twice sparing his enemy's life.
1 S 24:1–15; 26:1–20

4. As a King

After the death of Saul, the tribe of Judah anoints him as king and he reigns seven years in Hebron.
2 S 5:1–5

At the death of Ishbosheth, the son of Saul, David becomes king of all Israel.
2 S 5:3

5. His Later Years

The capture of Jerusalem and the establishment of the capitol there.

2 S 5:7

The bringing of the ark to Jerusalem.
2 S 6:1–11; 1 Chr 15:1–29

The military victories and enlargement of the kingdom.
2 S 8, 10

His sin against Uriah, the Hittite.
2 S 11–12

His penitence.
Ps 51

Absalom's rebellion against his father.
2 S 15–18

David's preparation for building the temple.
1 Chr 22:5, 14; 29:2

6. His Last Days

He appoints his son, Solomon, as his successor.
1 K 1:11–39

Gives him a solemn charge.
1 K 2:1–9

He dies.
1 Chr 29:26–28

See **YOUNG PEOPLE**

DAWN, *SPIRITUAL, the coming of Christ*

Is 21:12 The watchman said, The morning cometh, and also the night: if ye will enquire, enquire ye: return, come.

Is 30:26 Moreover the light of the moon shall be as the light of the sun, and the light of the sun shall be sevenfold, as the light of seven days, in the day that the LORD bindeth up the breach of his people, and healeth the stroke of their wound.

Is 60:1 Arise, shine; for thy light is come, and the glory of the LORD is risen upon thee.

Is 60:3 And the Gentiles shall come to thy light, and kings to the brightness of thy rising.

Ho 6:3 Then shall we know, *if* we follow on to know the LORD: his going forth is prepared as the morning; and he shall come unto us as the rain, as the latter *and* former rain unto the earth.

Mal 4:2 But unto you that fear my name shall the Sun of righteousness arise with healing in his wings; and ye shall go forth, and grow up as calves of the stall.

Lu 1:78 Through the tender mercy of our God; whereby the dayspring from on high hath visited us,

Ro 13:12 The night is far spent, the day is at hand: let us therefore cast off the works of darkness, and let us put on the armour of light.

2 Pe 1:19 We have also a more sure word of prophecy; whereunto ye do well that ye take heed, as unto a light that shineth in a dark place, until the day dawn, and the day star arise in your hearts:

1 Jn 2:8 Again, a new commandment I write unto you, which thing is true in him and in you: because the darkness is past, and the true light now shineth.

See **FUTURE LIFE**

DAY, *period of light between sunrise and sunset; also, a twenty-four hour period*

Ge 1:5; 8:22; Ps 19:2; 74:16; Je 33:20; Am 5:8

DAY OF THE LORD, *an eschatological term referring to the day when Jehovah would put Israel at the head of the nations*

Jb 24:1 Why, seeing times are not hidden from the Almighty, do they that know him not see his days?

Is 22:5 For *it is* a day of trouble, and of treading down, and of perplexity by the Lord GOD of hosts in the valley of vision, breaking down the walls, and of crying to the mountains.

Eze 13:5 Ye have not gone up into the gaps, neither made up the hedge for the house of Israel to stand in the battle in the day of the LORD.

Am 5:20 *Shall* not the day of the LORD *be* darkness, and not light? even very dark, and no brightness in it?

Obad 15 For the day of the LORD *is* near upon all the heathen: as thou hast done, it shall be done unto thee: thy reward shall return upon thine own head.

Zep 1:7 Hold thy peace at the presence of the Lord GOD: for the day of the LORD *is* at hand: for the LORD hath prepared a sacrifice, he hath bid his guests.

Zep 2:3 Seek ye the LORD, all ye meek of the earth, which have wrought his judgment; seek righteousness, seek meekness: it may be ye shall be hid in the day of the LORD's anger.

Zec 14:1 Behold, the day of the LORD cometh, and thy spoil shall be divided in the midst of thee.

Mal 4:5 Behold, I will send you Elijah the prophet before the coming of the great and dreadful day of the LORD:

Ro 2:16 In the day when God shall judge the secrets of men by Jesus Christ according to my gospel.

1 Co 1:8 Who shall also confirm you unto the end, *that ye may be* blameless in the day of our Lord Jesus Christ.

1 Co 3:13 Every man's work shall be made manifest: for the day shall declare it, because it shall be revealed by fire; and the fire shall try every man's work of what sort it is.

1 Co 5:5 To deliver such an one unto Satan for the destruction of the flesh, that the spirit may be saved in the day of the Lord Jesus.

2 Co 1:14 As also ye have acknowledged us in part, that we are your rejoicing, even as ye also *are* ours in the day of the Lord Jesus.

Ph 1:6 Being confident of this very thing, that he which hath begun a good work in you will perform *it* until the day of Jesus Christ:

Ph 2:16 Holding forth the word of life; that I may rejoice in the day of Christ, that I have not run in vain, neither laboured in vain.

1 Th 5:2 For yourselves know perfectly that the day of the Lord so cometh as a thief in the night.

2 Pe 3:10 But the day of the Lord will come as a thief in the night; in the which the heavens shall pass away with a great noise, and the elements shall melt with fervent heat, the earth also and the works that are therein shall be burned up.

1. The Last, or Great, Day

Jb 21:30 That the wicked is reserved to the day of destruction? they shall be brought forth to the day of wrath.

Ps 98:9 Before the LORD; for he cometh to judge the earth: with righteousness shall he judge the world, and the people with equity.

Ps 110:5 The LORD at thy right hand shall strike through kings in the day of his wrath.

Pr 11:4 Riches profit not in the day of wrath: but righteousness delivereth from death.

Is 2:12 For the day of the LORD of hosts *shall be* upon every *one that is* proud and lofty, and upon every *one that is* lifted up; and he shall be brought low:

Is 13:13 Therefore I will shake the heavens, and the earth shall remove out of her place, in the wrath of the LORD of hosts, and in the day of his fierce anger.

Is 34:8 For *it is* the day of the LORD's vengeance, *and* the year of recompences for the controversy of Zion.

Is 61:2 To proclaim the acceptable year of the LORD, and the day of vengeance of our God; to comfort all that mourn;

Je 25:33 And the slain of the LORD shall be at that day from *one* end of the earth even unto the *other* end of the earth: they shall not be lamented, neither gathered, nor buried; they shall be dung upon the ground.

Je 30:7 Alas! for that day *is* great, so that none *is* like it: it *is* even the time of Jacob's trouble; but he shall be saved out of it.

Je 46:10 For this *is* the day of the Lord GOD of hosts, a day of vengeance, that he may avenge him of his adversaries: and the sword shall devour, and it shall be satiate and made drunk with their blood: for the Lord GOD of hosts hath a sacrifice in the north country by the river Euphrates.

Eze 7:19 They shall cast their silver in the streets, and their gold shall be removed: their silver and their gold shall not be able to deliver them in the day of the wrath of the LORD: they shall not satisfy their souls, neither fill their bowels: because it is the stumblingblock of their iniquity.

Jl 2:1 Blow ye the trumpet in Zion, and sound an alarm in my holy mountain: let all the inhabitants of the land tremble: for the day of the LORD cometh, for *it is* nigh at hand;

Jl 2:11 And the LORD shall utter his voice before his army: for his camp *is* very great: for *he is* strong that executeth his word: for the day of the LORD *is* great and very terrible; and who can abide it?

Jl 2:31 The sun shall be turned into darkness, and the moon into blood, before the great and the terrible day of the LORD come.

Jl 3:14 Multitudes, multitudes in the valley of decision: for the day of the LORD *is* near in the valley of decision.

Zep 1:14 The great day of the LORD *is* near, *it is* near, and hasteth greatly, *even* the voice of the day of the LORD: the mighty man shall, the day cometh, that shall burn as an oven; and all the proud, yea, and all that do wickedly, shall be stubble: and the day that cometh shall burn them up, saith the LORD of hosts, that it shall leave them neither root nor branch.

Mt 7:22 Many will say to me in that day, Lord, Lord, have we not prophesied in thy name? and in thy name have cast out devils? and in thy name done many wonderful works?

Lu 17:30 Even thus shall it be in the day when the Son of man is revealed.

Jn 12:48 He that rejecteth me, and receiveth not my words, hath one that judgeth him: the word that I have spoken, the same shall judge him in the last day.

Ac 2:20 The sun shall be turned into darkness, and the moon into blood, before that great and notable day of the Lord come:

Ro 2:5 But after thy hardness and impenitent heart treasurest up unto thyself wrath against the day of wrath and revelation of the righteous judgment of God;

2 Ti 1:12 For the which cause I also suffer these things: nevertheless I am not ashamed: for I know whom I have believed, and am persuaded that he is able to keep that which I have committed unto him against that day.

2 Ti 1:18 The Lord grant unto him that he may find mercy of the Lord in that day: and in how many things he ministered unto me at Ephesus, thou knowest very well.

2 Ti 4:8 Henceforth there is laid up for me a crown of righteousness, which the Lord, the righteous judge, shall give me at that day: and not to me only, but unto all them also that love his appearing.

He 10:25 Not forsaking the assembling of ourselves together, as the manner of some *is;* but exhorting *one another:* and so much the more, as ye see the day approaching.

Jude 6 And the angels which kept not their first estate, but left their own habitation, he hath reserved in everlasting chains under darkness unto the judgment of the great day.

Re 6:17 For the great day of his wrath is come; and who shall be able to stand?

Re 16:14 For they are the spirits of devils, working miracles, *which* go forth unto the kings of the earth and of the whole world, to gather them to the battle of that great day of God Almighty.

2. Day of Visitation

Ex 32:34 Therefore now go, lead the people unto *the place* of which I have spoken unto thee: behold, mine Angel shall go before thee: nevertheless in the day when I visit I will visit their sin upon them.

Nu 16:29 If these men die the common death of all men, or if they be visited after the visitation of all men; *then* the LORD hath not sent me.

Jb 31:14 What then shall I do when God riseth up? and when he visiteth, what shall I answer him?

Jb 35:15 But now, because *it is* not *so,* he hath visited in his anger; yet he knoweth *it* not in great extremity:

Ps 37:13 The LORD shall laugh at him: for he seeth that his day is coming.

Ps 50:3 Our God shall come, and shall not keep silence: a fire shall devour before him, and it shall be very tempestuous round about him.

Ps 59:5 Thou therefore, O LORD God of hosts, the God of Israel, awake to visit all the heathen: be not merciful to any wicked transgressors. Selah.

Is 3:18 In that day the LORD will take away the bravery of *their* tinkling ornaments *about their feet,* and *their* cauls, and *their* round tires like the moon,

Is 10:3 And what will ye do in the day of visitation, and in the desolation *which* shall come from far? to whom will ye flee for help? and where will ye leave your glory?

Is 13:6 Howl ye; for the day of the LORD *is* at hand; it shall come as a destruction from the Almighty.

Is 13:9 Behold, the day of the LORD cometh, cruel both with wrath and fierce anger, to lay the land desolate: and he shall destroy the sinners thereof out of it.

Is 24:22 And they shall be gathered together, *as* prisoners are gathered in the pit, and shall be shut up in the prison, and after many days shall they be visited.

Is 26:21 For, behold, the LORD cometh out of his place to punish the inhabitants of the earth for their iniquity: the earth also shall disclose her blood, and shall no more cover her slain.

Is 29:6 Thou shalt be visited of the LORD of hosts with thunder, and with earthquake, and great noise, with storm and tempest, and the flame of devouring fire.

Is 63:4 For the day of vengeance *is* in mine heart, and the year of my redeemed is come.

Je 5:9 Shall I not visit for these *things?* saith the LORD: and shall not my soul be avenged on such a nation as this?

Je 5:29 Shall I not visit for these *things?* saith the LORD: shall not my soul be avenged on such a nation as this?

Je 6:15 Were they ashamed when they had committed abomination? nay, they were not at all ashamed, neither could they blush: therefore they shall fall among them that fall: at the time *that* I visit them they shall be cast down, saith the LORD.

Je 9:9 Shall I not visit them for these *things?* saith the LORD: shall not my soul be avenged on such a nation as this?

Je 10:15 They *are* vanity, *and* the work of errors: in the time of their visitation they shall perish.

Je 14:10 Thus saith the LORD unto this people, Thus have they loved to wander, they have not refrained their feet, therefore the LORD doth not accept them; he will now remember their iniquity, and visit their sins.

Je 23:2 Therefore thus saith the LORD God of Israel against the pastors that feed my people; Ye have scattered my flock, and driven them away, and have not visited them: behold, I will visit upon you the evil of your doings, saith the LORD.

Je 23:12 Wherefore their way shall be unto them as slippery *ways* in the darkness: they shall be driven on, and fall therein: for I will bring evil upon them, *even* the year of their visitation, saith the LORD.

Je 46:21 Also her hired men *are* in the midst of her like fatted bullocks; for they also are turned back, *and* are fled away together: they did not stand, because the day of their calamity was come upon them, *and* the time of their visitation.

Je 47:4 Because of the day that cometh to spoil all the Philistines, *and* to cut off from Tyrus and Zidon every helper that remaineth: for the LORD will spoil the Philistines, the remnant of the country of Caphtor.

Je 48:45 They that fled stood under the shadow of Heshbon because of the force: but a fire shall come forth out of Heshbon, and a flame from the midst of Sihon, and shall devour the corner of Moab, and the crown of the head of the tumultuous ones.

Je 49:8 Flee ye, turn back, dwell deep, O inhabitants of Dedan; for I will bring the calamity of Esau upon him, the time *that* I will visit him.

Je 50:27 Slay all her bullocks; let them go down to the slaughter: woe unto them! for their day is come, the time of their visitation.

Je 51:18 They *are* vanity, the work of errors: in the time of their visitation they shall perish.

Je 51:47 Therefore, behold, the days come, that I will do judgment upon the graven images of Babylon: and her whole land shall be confounded, and all her slain shall fall in the midst of her.

Lam 1:21 They have heard that I sigh: *there is* none to comfort me: all mine enemies have heard of my trouble; they are glad that thou hast done *it:* thou wilt bring the day *that* thou hast called, and they shall be like unto me.

Eze 7:7 The morning is come unto thee, O thou that dwellest in the land: the time is come, the day of trouble *is* near, and not the sounding again of the mountains.

Eze 12:23 Tell them therefore, Thus saith the Lord GOD; I will make this proverb to cease, and they shall no more use it as a proverb in Israel; but say unto them, The days are at hand, and the effect of every vision.

Eze 21:25 And thou, profane wicked prince of Israel, whose day is come, when iniquity *shall have* an end,

Eze 21:29 Whiles they see vanity unto thee, whiles they divine a lie unto thee, to bring thee upon the necks of *them that are* slain, of the wicked, whose day is come, when their iniquity *shall have* an end.

Eze 22:4 Thou art become guilty in thy blood that thou hast shed; and hast defiled thyself in thine idols which thou hast made; and thou hast caused thy days to draw near, and art come *even* unto thy years: therefore have I made thee a reproach unto the heathen, and a mocking to all countries.

Eze 22:14 Can thine heart endure, or can thine hands be strong, in the days that I shall deal with thee? I the LORD have spoken *it,* and will do *it.*

Eze 30:3 For the day *is* near, even the day of the LORD *is* near, a cloudy day; it shall be the time of the heathen.

Eze 39:8 Behold, it is come, and it is done, saith the Lord GOD; this *is* the day whereof I have spoken.

Ho 1:4 And the LORD said unto him, Call his name Jezreel; for yet a little *while,* and I will avenge the blood of Jezreel upon the house of Jehu, and will cause to cease the kingdom of the house of Israel.

Ho 5:9 Ephraim shall be desolate in the day of rebuke: among the tribes of Israel have I made known that which shall surely be.

Ho 8:13 They sacrifice flesh *for* the sacrifices of mine offerings, and *eat it;* but the LORD accepteth them not; now will he remember their iniquity, and visit their sins: they shall return to Egypt.

Ho 9:7 The days of visitation are come, the days of recompence are come; Israel shall know *it:* the prophet *is* a fool, the spiritual man *is* mad, for the multitude of thine iniquity, and the great hatred.

Jl 1:15 Alas for the day! for the day of the LORD *is* at hand, and as a destruction from the Almighty shall it come.

Am 3:14 That in the day I shall visit the transgressions of Israel upon him I will also visit the altars of Bethel: and the horns of the altar shall be cut off, and fall to the ground.

Am 5:18 Woe unto you that desire the day of the LORD! to what end *is* it for you? the day of the LORD *is* darkness, and not light.

Am 8:9 And it shall come to pass in that day, saith the Lord GOD, that I will cause the sun to go down at noon, and I will darken the earth in the clear day:

Mi 7:4 The best of them *is* as a brier: the most upright *is sharper* than a thorn hedge: the day of thy watchmen *and* thy visitation cometh; now shall be their perplexity.

Mt 22:11 And when the king came in to see the guests, he saw there a man which had not on a wedding garment:

Lu 19:44 And shall lay thee even with the ground, and thy children within thee; and they shall not leave in thee one stone upon another; because thou knewest not the time of thy visitation.

1 Pe 2:12 Having your conversation honest among the Gentiles: that, whereas they speak against you as evildoers, they may by *your* good works, which they shall behold, glorify God in the day of visitation.

See **JUDGMENT**

DAY OF PREPARATION, *the day before a Sabbath or the day prior to a feast*

Mt 27:62; Mk 15:42; Lu 23:54; Jn 19:14, 31, 42

DAYS

1. Last

Ge 49:1; Is 2:2; Da 2:28; 10:14; 12:9; Ho 3:5; Mi 4:1; Jn 11:24; Ac 2:17; 1 Ti 4:1; 2 Ti 3:1; Ja 5:3; 2 Pe 3:3; 1 Jn 2:18

2. Dark, *figurative*

2 S 22:29 For thou *art* my lamp, O Lord: and the Lord will lighten my darkness.

Jb 19:8 He hath fenced up my way that I cannot pass, and he hath set darkness in my paths.

Jb 30:26 When I looked for good, then evil came *unto me:* and when I waited for light, there came darkness.

Ps 88:6 Thou hast laid me in the lowest pit, in darkness, in the deeps.

Ps 88:8 Thou hast put away mine acquaintance far from me; thou hast made me an abomination unto them: *I am* shut up, and I cannot come forth.

Ec 11:8 But if a man live many years, *and* rejoice in them all; yet let him remember the days of darkness; for they shall be many. All that cometh *is* vanity.

Is 24:11 *There is* a crying for wine in the streets; all joy is darkened, the mirth of the land is gone.

Mi 7:8 Rejoice not against me, O mine enemy: when I fall, I shall arise; when I sit in darkness, the Lord *shall be* a light unto me.

Mk 2:20 But the days will come, when the bridegroom shall be taken away from them, and then shall they fast in those days.

Lu 22:53 When I was daily with you in the temple, ye stretched forth no hands against me: but this is your hour, and the power of darkness.

Lu 24:17 And he said unto them, What manner of communications *are* these that ye have one to another, as ye walk, and are sad?

Jn 8:12 Then spake Jesus again unto them, saying, I am the light of the world: he that followeth me shall not walk in darkness, but shall have the light of life.

Jn 16:20 Verily, verily, I say unto you, That ye shall weep and lament, but the world shall rejoice: and ye shall be sorrowful, but your sorrow shall be turned into joy.

Ac 27:20 And when neither sun nor stars in many days appeared, and no small tempest lay on *us,* all hope that we should be saved was then taken away.

DAY'S JOURNEY, *eighteen or twenty miles*

Ex 3:18; 1 K 19:4; Jona 3:4; Lu 2:44

DEAD

1. Preparation for Burial

Mt 26:12; 27:59; Jn 11:44; Ac 9:37

a. Embalming

Ge 50:2, 26; 2 Chr 16:14; Mk 16:1; Lu 24:1; Jn 19:40

b. Graveclothes

Mt 27:59; Mk 15:46; Lu 23:53; Jn 11:44; 19:40; 20:7; Ac 5:6

c. Cremation

Jos 7:25; 1 S 31:12; 2 K 23:20; Am 2:1; 6:10

d. Burial Ceremonies

Ge 50:10; Je 34:5

2. Bodies

a. Jewish Laws

Le 10:6; 21:1, 11; 22:4; Nu 5:2; 6:6; 9:6; 19:11, 16; 31:19; De 21:23; Eze 44:25; Hag 2:13

b. Unburied

Ge 40:19; Le 26:30; De 28:26; 1 S 31:8; 1 K 14:11; 16:4; 21:24; 2 K 9:10, 37; Jb 27:19; Ps 79:2; Ec 6:3; Is 5:25; 14:19; Je 7:33; 8:2; 9:22; 14:16; 16:4; 19:7; 25:33; 34:20; 36:30; Eze 39:4; Am 8:3; Re 11:9

c. Burial

Ge 23:19; 25:9; 35:29; 50:13; Nu 20:1; 33:4; De 10:6; 34:6; Jos 24:30, 32; Jud 2:9; 8:32; 10:2; 12:7, 12; 2 S 2:5; 3:32; 4:12; 21:14; 1 K 2:34; 11:15, 43

3. Burial Places

a. Sepulchres

Ge 23:6; De 34:6; 2 S 4:12; 17:23; 21:14; 2 K 9:28; 13:21; 21:26; 2 Chr 16:14; 28:27; 32:33; Is 22:16; 53:9; Mt 23:29; 27:60; 28:1; Mk 5:2; 6:29; 15:46; 16:2; Lu 11:48; 23:53; 24:1; Jn 11:38; 19:41

b. Attachment to the Burial Places of "The Fathers"

Ge 49:29; 50:25; Ne 2:3

4. Tombstones

Ge 35:20; 2 K 23:17

See **DEATH**

DEAD IN SIN, *the state of the sinner*

Pr 21:16 The man that wandereth out of the way of understanding shall remain in the congregation of the dead.

Is 59:10 We grope for the wall like the blind, and we grope as if *we had* no eyes: we stumble at noonday as in the night; *we are* in desolate places as dead *men.*

Eze 37:1 The hand of the LORD was upon me, and carried me out in the spirit of the LORD, and set me down in the midst of the valley which *was* full of bones,

Mt 8:22 But Jesus said unto him, Follow me; and let the dead bury their dead.

Lu 15:32 It was meet that we should make merry, and be glad: for this thy brother was dead, and is alive again; and was lost, and is found.

Jn 6:53 Then Jesus said unto them, Verily, verily, I say unto you, Except ye eat the flesh of the Son of man, and drink his blood, ye have no life in you.

2 Co 5:14 For the love of Christ constraineth us; because we thus judge, that if one died for all, then were all dead:

Ep 2:1 And you *hath he quickened,* who were dead in trespasses and sins;

Ep 5:14 Wherefore he saith, Awake thou that sleepest, and arise from the dead, and Christ shall give thee light.

Col 2:13 And you, being dead in your sins and the uncircumcision of your flesh, hath he quickened together with him, having forgiven you all trespasses;

1 Ti 5:6 But she that liveth in pleasure is dead while she liveth.

Re 3:1 And unto the angel of the church in Sardis write; These things saith he that hath the seven Spirits of God, and the seven stars; I know thy works, that thou hast a name that thou livest, and art dead.

DEAD SEA, *also called Salt Sea, or Sea of Arabah*

Ge 14:3; Nu 34:3, 12; De 3:17; 4:49; Jos 3:16; 12:3; 15:2, 5; 18:19; Jl 2:20; Zec 14:8

DEAFNESS, *inability to hear*

1. Natural

Le 19:14; 2 S 19:35; Ec 12:4; Mt 11:5; Mk 7:32; 9:25; Lu 7:22

2. Spiritual

Is 6:10 Make the heart of this people fat, and make their ears heavy, and shut their eyes; lest they see with their eyes, and hear with their ears, and understand with their heart, and convert, and be healed.

Je 6:10 To whom shall I speak, and give warning, that they may hear? behold, their ear *is* uncircumcised, and they cannot hearken: behold, the word of the LORD is unto them a reproach; they have no delight in it.

Eze 12:2 Son of man, thou dwellest in the midst of a rebellious house, which have eyes to see, and see not; they have ears to hear, and hear not: for they *are* a rebellious house.

Zec 7:11 But they refused to hearken, and pulled away the shoulder, and stopped their ears, that they should not hear.

Mt 13:15 For this people's heart is waxed gross, and *their* ears are dull of hearing, and their eyes they have closed; lest at any time they should see with *their* eyes, and hear with *their* ears, and should understand with *their* heart, and should be converted, and I should heal them.

Ac 28:26 Saying, Go unto this people, and say, Hearing ye shall hear, and shall not understand; and seeing ye shall see, and not perceive:

2 Ti 4:4 And they shall turn away *their* ears from the truth, and shall be turned unto fables.

See **HEARING, IMPENITENCE, INDIFFERENCE, UNBELIEF**

DEATH, *physical and spiritual*

1. Its Universality

Ge 5:5 And all the days that Adam lived were nine hundred and thirty years: and he died.

Ge 9:29 And all the days of Noah were nine hundred and fifty years: and he died.

Ge 36:33 And Bela died, and Jobab the son of Zerah of Bozrah reigned in his stead.

Ge 47:29 And the time drew nigh that Israel must die: and he called his son Joseph, and said unto him, If now I have found grace in thy sight, put, I pray thee, thy hand under my thigh, and deal kindly and truly with me; bury me not, I pray thee, in Egypt:

Ge 48:21 And Israel said unto Joseph, Behold, I die: but God shall be with you, and bring you again unto the land of your fathers.

Ge 50:24 And Joseph said unto his brethren, I die: and God will surely visit you, and bring you out of this land unto the land which he sware to Abraham, to Isaac, and to Jacob.

Ex 1:6 And Joseph died, and all his brethren, and all that generation.

Ex 12:30 And Pharaoh rose up in the night, he, and all his servants, and all the Egyptians; and there was a great cry in Egypt; for *there was* not a house where *there was* not one dead.

Nu 17:12 And the children of Israel spake unto Moses, saying, Behold, we die, we perish, we all perish.

Nu 20:28 And Moses stripped Aaron of his garments, and put them upon Eleazar his son; and Aaron died there in the top of the mount: and Moses and Eleazar came down from the mount.

Nu 27:13 And when thou hast seen it, thou also shalt be gathered unto thy people, as Aaron thy brother was gathered.

De 10:6 And the children of Israel took their journey from Beeroth of the children of Jaakan to Mosera: there Aaron died, and there he was buried; and Eleazar his son ministered in the priest's office in his stead.

Jos 23:14 And, behold, this day I *am* going the way of all the earth: and ye know in all your hearts and in all your souls, that not one thing hath failed of all the good things which the LORD your God spake concerning you; all are come to pass unto you, *and* not one thing hath failed thereof.

Jud 2:10 And also all that generation were gathered unto their fathers: and there arose another generation after them, which knew not the LORD, nor yet the works which he had done for Israel.

1 S 26:10 David said furthermore, *As* the LORD liveth, the LORD shall smite him; or his day shall come to die; or he shall descend into battle, and perish.

2 S 7:12 And when thy days be fulfilled, and thou shalt sleep with thy fathers, I will set up thy seed after thee, which shall proceed out of thy bowels, and I will establish his kingdom.

2 S 12:23 But now he is dead, wherefore should I fast? can I bring him back again? I shall go to him, but he shall not return to me.

2 S 14:14 For we must needs die, and *are* as water spilt on the ground, which cannot be gathered up again; neither doth God respect *any* person: yet doth he devise means, that his banished be not expelled from him.

1 K 2:2 I go the way of all the earth: be thou strong therefore, and shew thyself a man;

1 Chr 17:11 And it shall come to pass, when thy days be expired that thou must go *to be* with thy fathers, that I will raise up thy seed after thee, which shall be of thy sons; and I will establish his kingdom.

Jb 3:19 The small and great are there; and the servant *is* free from his master.

Jb 4:20 They are destroyed from morning to evening: they perish for ever without any regarding *it.*

Jb 14:12 So man lieth down, and riseth not: till the heavens *be* no more, they shall not awake, nor be raised out of their sleep.

Jb 17:16 They shall go down to the bars of the pit, when *our* rest together *is* in the dust.

Jb 21:25 And another dieth in the bitterness of his soul, and never eateth with pleasure.

Jb 21:33 The clods of the valley shall be sweet unto him, and every man shall draw after him, as *there are* innumerable before him.

Jb 30:23 For I know *that* thou wilt bring me *to* death, and *to* the house appointed for all living.

Ps 22:29 All *they that be* fat upon earth shall eat and worship: all they that go down to the dust shall bow before him: and none can keep alive his own soul.

Ps 49:10 For he seeth *that* wise men die, likewise the fool and the brutish person perish, and leave their wealth to others.

Ps 49:19 He shall go to the generation of his fathers; they shall never see light.

Ps 82:7 But ye shall die like men, and fall like one of the princes.

Ps 89:48 What man *is he that* liveth, and shall not see death? shall he deliver his soul from the hand of the grave? Selah.

Ps 90:3 Thou turnest man to destruction; and sayest, Return, ye children of men.

Ec 2:16 For *there is* no remembrance of the wise more than of the fool for ever; seeing that which now *is* in the days to come shall all be forgotten. And how dieth the wise *man?* as the fool.

Ec 3:2 A time to be born, and a time to die; a time to plant, and a time to pluck up *that which is* planted;

Ec 3:19 For that which befalleth the sons of men befalleth beasts; even one thing befalleth them: as the one dieth, so dieth the other; yea, they have all one breath; so that a man hath no preeminence above a beast: for all *is* vanity.

Ec 6:6 Yea, though he live a thousand years twice *told,* yet hath he seen no good: do not all go to one place?

Ec 7:2 *It is* better to go to the house of mourning, than to go to the house of feasting: for that is the end of all men; and the living will lay *it* to his heart.

Ec 8:8 *There is* no man that hath power over the spirit to retain the spirit; neither *hath he* power in the day of death: and *there is* no discharge in *that* war; neither shall wickedness deliver those that are given to it.

Ec 9:3 This *is* an evil among all *things* that are done under the sun, that *there is* on: yea, also the heart of the sons of men is full of evil, and madness is in their heart while they live, and after that *they go* to the dead.

Is 14:18 All the kings of the nations, *even* all of them, lie in glory, every one in his own house.

Is 38:1 In those days was Hezekiah sick unto death. And Isaiah the prophet the son of Amoz came unto him, and said unto him, Thus saith the LORD, Set thine house in order: for thou shalt die, and not live.

Je 9:21 For death is come up into our windows, *and* is entered into our palaces, to cut off the children from without, *and* the young men from the streets.

Eze 31:14 To the end that none of all the trees by the waters exalt themselves for their height, neither shoot up their top among the thick boughs, neither their trees stand up in their height, all that drink water: for they are all delivered unto death, to the nether parts of the earth, in the midst of the children of men, with them that go down to the pit.

Eze 32:22 Asshur *is* there and all her company: his graves *are* about him: all of them slain, fallen by the sword:

Zec 1:5 Your fathers, where *are* they? and the prophets, do they live for ever?

Mt 22:27 And last of all the woman died also.

Mk 12:22 And the seven had her, and left no seed: last of all the woman died also.

Lu 20:32 Last of all the woman died also.

Jn 6:49 Your fathers did eat manna in the wilderness, and are dead.

Ac 2:29 Men *and* brethren, let me freely speak unto you of the patriarch David, that he is both dead and buried, and his sepulchre is with us unto this day.

Ro 5:12 Wherefore, as by one man sin entered into the world, and death by sin; and so death passed upon all men, for that all have sinned:

1 Co 15:22 For as in Adam all die, even so in Christ shall all be made alive.

He 7:23 And they truly were many priests, because they were not suffered to continue by reason of death:

He 9:27 And as it is appointed unto men once to die, but after this the judgment:

Ja 4:14 Whereas ye know not what *shall be* on the morrow. For what *is* your life? It is even a vapour, that appeareth for a little time, and then vanisheth away.

2 Pe 1:14 Knowing that shortly I must put off *this* my tabernacle, even as our Lord Jesus Christ hath shewed me.

Re 6:8 And I looked, and behold a pale horse: and his name that sat on him was Death, and Hell followed with him. And power was given unto them over the fourth part of the earth, to kill with sword, and with hunger, and with death, and with the beasts of the earth.

See **JUDGMENTS**

2. Compared to Sleep

De 31:16; 1 K 14:20, 31; 15:8, 24; 22:40; 2 K 20:21; 21:18; 2 Chr 12:16; 21:1; 26:23; 27:9; 32:33; 33:20; Jb 7:21; Da 12:2; Mk 5:39; Lu 8:52; Jn 11:11; Ac 13:36; 1 Co 15:6; 1 Th 4:13

3. Vanquished

See **FUTURE LIFE**

4. Of the Righteous

DESIRED

Nu 23:10 Who can count the dust of Jacob, and the number of the fourth *part* of Israel? Let me die the death of the righteous, and let my last end be like his!

FEARLESS

Ps 23:4 Yea, though I walk through the valley of the shadow of death, I will fear no evil: for thou *art* with me; thy rod and thy staff they comfort me.

PRECIOUS

Ps 116:15 Precious in the sight of the LORD *is* the death of his saints.

HOPEFUL

Pr 14:32 The wicked is driven away in his wickedness: but the righteous hath hope in his death.

TRIUMPHANT

Lu 16:22 And it came to pass, that the beggar died, and was carried by the angels into Abraham's bosom: the rich man also died, and was buried;

DIVINE

Ro 14:8 For whether we live, we live unto the Lord; and whether we die, we die unto the Lord: whether we live therefore, or die, we are the Lord's.

RESULTS IN GAIN

Ph 1:21 For to me to live *is* Christ, and to die *is* gain.

INVOLVES FAITH

He 11:13 These all died in faith, not having received the promises, but having seen them afar off, and were persuaded of *them,* and embraced *them,* and confessed that they were strangers and pilgrims on the earth.

BLESSED

Re 14:13 And I heard a voice from heaven saying unto me, Write, Blessed *are* the dead which die in the Lord from henceforth: Yea, saith the Spirit, that they may rest from their labours; and their works do follow them.

5. Relief from Trouble

See **DESPAIR**

6. Spiritual

Ge 2:17 But of the tree of the knowledge of good and evil, thou shalt not eat of it: for in the day that thou eatest thereof thou shalt surely die.

Ge 3:3 But of the fruit of the tree which *is* in the midst of the garden, God hath said, Ye shall not eat of it, neither shall ye touch it, lest ye die.

Pr 8:36 But he that sinneth against me wrongeth his own soul: all they that hate me love death.

Pr 14:27 The fear of the LORD *is* a fountain of life, to depart from the snares of death.

Pr 15:10 Correction *is* grievous unto him that forsaketh the way: *and* he that hateth reproof shall die.

Eze 18:20 The soul that sinneth, it shall die. The son shall not bear the iniquity of the father, neither shall the father bear the iniquity of the son: the righteousness of the righteous shall be upon him, and the wickedness of the wicked shall be upon him.

Eze 33:12 Therefore, thou son of man, say unto the children of thy people, The righteousness of the righteous shall not deliver him in the day of his transgression: as for the wickedness of the wicked, he shall not fall thereby in the day that he turneth from his wickedness; neither shall the righteous be able to live for his *righteousness* in the day that he sinneth.

Ro 6:23 For the wages of sin *is* death; but the gift of God *is* eternal life through Jesus Christ our Lord.

Ro 8:6 For to be carnally minded *is* death; but to be spiritually minded *is* life and peace.

Ja 1:15 Then when lust hath conceived, it bringeth forth sin: and sin, when it is finished, bringeth forth death.

Ja 5:20 Let him know, that he which converteth the sinner from the error of his way shall save a soul from death, and shall hide a multitude of sins.

Re 21:8 But the fearful, and unbelieving, and the abominable, and murderers, and whoremongers, and sorcerers, and idolaters, and all liars, shall have their part in the lake which burneth with fire and brimstone: which is the second death.

7. Of the Wicked

Ps 37:36; Pr 5:23; Ec 8:10; Is 17:14; Je 16:4; Eze 18:23; Lu 12:20

8. Of Christ

See **CHRIST**

9. Preparation

2 K 20:1; Ec 9:10; 11:8; Mt 24:44; Lu 2:29; 12:35; Jn 9:4; 2 Co 5:8; 1 Pe 1:17

10. No One Exempt

JOB ACKNOWLEDGES HIS MORTALITY

Jb 30:23 For I know *that* thou wilt bring me *to* death, and *to* the house appointed for all living.

WISE AND FOOLISH ALIKE WILL DIE

Ps 49:10 For he seeth *that* wise men die, likewise the fool and the brutish person perish, and leave their wealth to others.

RESISTANCE IS VAIN

Ec 8:8 *There is* no man that hath power over the spirit to retain the spirit; neither *hath he* power in the day of death: and *there is* no discharge in *that* war; neither shall wickedness deliver those that are given to it.

ALL DIE BECAUSE ALL SIN

Ro 5:12 Wherefore, as by one man sin entered into the world, and death by sin; and so death passed upon all men, for that all have sinned:

TWO HAVE ESCAPED

2 K 2:11 And it came to pass, as they still went on, and talked, that, behold, *there appeared* a chariot of fire, and horses of fire, and parted them both asunder; and Elijah went up by a whirlwind into heaven.

He 11:5 By faith Enoch was translated that he should not see death; and was not found, because God had translated him: for before his translation he had this testimony, that he pleased God.

11. Translations, *a way of entering eternity without experiencing death*

ENOCH

Ge 5:24 And Enoch walked with God: and he *was* not; for God took him.

ELIJAH

2 K 2:11 And it came to pass, as they still went on, and talked, that, behold, *there appeared* a chariot of fire, and horses of fire, and parted them both asunder; and Elijah went up by a whirlwind into heaven.

See **LIFE, RESURRECTION**

DEATH PENALTY

1. For Capital Offences

Ge 9:6 Whoso sheddeth man's blood, by man shall his blood be shed: for in the image of God made he man.

Ex 2:15 Now when Pharaoh heard this thing, he sought to slay Moses. But Moses fled from the face of Pharaoh, and dwelt in the land of Midian: and he sat down by a well.

Ex 21:14 But if a man come presumptuously upon his neighbour, to slay him with guile; thou shalt take him from mine altar, that he may die.

Ex 21:29 But if the ox were wont to push with his horn in time past, and it hath been testified to his owner, and he hath not kept him in, but that he hath killed a man or a woman; the ox shall be stoned, and his owner also shall be put to death.

Ex 22:20 He that sacrificeth unto *any* god, save unto the LORD only, he shall be utterly destroyed.

Ex 35:2 Six days shall work be done, but on the seventh day there shall be to you an holy day, a sabbath of rest to the LORD: whosoever doeth work therein shall be put to death.

Le 20:10 And the man that committeth adultery with *another* man's wife, *even he* that committeth adultery with his neighbour's wife, the adulterer and the adulteress shall surely be put to death.

De 13:9 But thou shalt surely kill him; thine hand shall be first upon him to put him to death, and afterwards the hand of all the people.

De 17:12 And the man that will do presumptuously, and will not hearken unto the priest that standeth to minister there before the LORD thy God, or unto the judge, even that man shall die: and thou shalt put away the evil from Israel.

De 21:21 And all the men of his city shall stone him with stones, that he die: so shalt thou put evil away from among you; and all Israel shall hear, and fear.

Ec 3:3 A time to kill, and a time to heal; a time to break down, and a time to build up;

Mt 15:4 For God commanded, saying, Honour thy father and mother: and, He that curseth father or mother, let him die the death.

Re 13:10 He that leadeth into captivity shall go into captivity: he that killeth with the sword must be killed with the sword. Here is the patience and the faith of the saints.

2. Examples

Le 10:2 And there went out fire from the LORD, and devoured them, and they died before the LORD.

Le 16:1 And the LORD spake unto Moses after the death of the two sons of Aaron, when they offered before the LORD, and died;

Le 24:16 And he that blasphemeth the name of the LORD, he shall surely be put to death, *and* all the congregation shall certainly stone him: as well the stranger, as he that is born in the land, when he blasphemeth the name *of the LORD,* shall be put to death.

Nu 15:36 And all the congregation brought him without the camp, and stoned him with stones, and he died; as the LORD commanded Moses.

Nu 16:32 And the earth opened her mouth, and swallowed them up, and their houses, and all the men that *appertained* unto Korah, and all *their* goods.

Nu 18:3 And they shall keep thy charge, and the charge of all the tabernacle: only they shall not come nigh the vessels of the sanctuary and the altar, that neither they, nor ye also, die.

De 11:6 And what he did unto Dathan and Abiram, the sons of Eliab, the son of Reuben: how the earth opened her mouth, and swallowed them up, and their households, and their tents, and all the substance that *was* in their possession, in the midst of all Israel:

De 24:7 If a man be found stealing any of his brethren of the children of Israel, and maketh merchandise of him, or selleth him; then that thief shall die; and thou shalt put evil away from among you.

Jos 7:25 And Joshua said, Why hast thou troubled us? the LORD shall trouble thee this day. And all Israel stoned him with stones, and burned them with fire, after they had stoned them with stones.

2 K 9:33 And he said, Throw her down. So they threw her down: and

some of her blood was sprinkled on the wall, and on the horses: and he trode her under foot.

2 Chr 23:15 So they laid hands on her; and when she was come to the entering of the horse gate by the king's house, they slew her there.

Est 7:10 So they hanged Haman on the gallows that he had prepared for Mordecai. Then was the king's wrath pacified.

Ac 5:5 And Ananias hearing these words fell down, and gave up the ghost: and great fear came on all them that heard these things.

Ac 12:23 And immediately the angel of the Lord smote him, because he gave not God the glory: and he was eaten of worms, and gave up the ghost.

DEATHS FORETOLD

Ge 3:19; Ex 11:5; Nu 20:24; 27:13; 31:2; De 4:22; 31:14; 32:50; 1 S 2:34; 28:19; 2 S 12:14; 1 K 14:12; 2 K 1:4; 7:2; 8:10; 19:7; 20:1; Je 28:16; Eze 11:10; 17:16; Mk 14:8; Ac 5:9; 2 Pe 1:14

DEBORAH, *a judge of Israel*

SUMMONS BARAK TO DELIVER ISRAEL

Jud 4:6

AGREES TO ACCOMPANY HIM TO BATTLE

Jud 4:9

INSPIRES HIM TO ACTION

Jud 4:14

SINGS A PAEAN OF VICTORY

Jud 5:1–31

REBUKES THE INDIFFERENCE OF THE TRIBES

Jud 5:16, 17, 23

See **ISRAEL, WOMEN**

DEBTORS

Ro 1:14 I am debtor both to the Greeks, and to the Barbarians; both to the wise, and to the unwise.

Ps 116:12 What shall I render unto the LORD *for* all his benefits toward me?

1 Co 4:7 For who maketh thee to differ *from another?* and what hast thou that thou didst not receive? now if thou didst receive *it,* why dost thou glory, as if thou hadst not received *it?*

1 Co 6:20 For ye are bought with a price: therefore glorify God in your body, and in your spirit, which are God's.

1 Jn 3:16 Hereby perceive we the love *of God,* because he laid down his life for us: and we ought to lay down *our* lives for the brethren.

DECALOGUE, *the Ten Commandments*

Ex 20:1; 32:16; 34:1, 28; De 4:13; 5:7; 10:4; Jos 8:32; Ps 78:5; Ho 8:12; Mt 5:21; Lu 18:20; Ro 9:4; Ga 3:17

See **TABLETS**

DECAPOLIS, *ten cities near the Sea of Galilee*

Mt 4:25; Mk 5:20; 7:31

DECEPTION, *causing people to believe a lie*

1. Religious Persons Guilty

Ge 12:13; 20:2; 26:7; 27:19; 31:35; Jud 4:20; 16:7, 11; 1 S 21:2, 8; 27:10; 2 S 15:34; 16:18; 17:20; 18:29; 1 K 13:18; 22:15; 2 K 6:19; 8:10; 10:18; Je 38:27; Mt 26:74

2. Examples

Ge 3:4; 29:23; 34:13; Jos 7:11; 9:4, 9, 12; Jud 3:20; 1 S 19:17; 20:29; 28:12; 2 S 13:6; 2 K 5:22; 2 Chr 18:11; Je 12:6; 27:14; 41:6; Mt 2:8

3. The Wicked Guilty

THEIR WORDS

Ps 36:3 The words of his mouth *are* iniquity and deceit: he hath left off to be wise, *and* to do good.

THEIR COUNSELS

Pr 12:5 The thoughts of the righteous *are* right: *but* the counsels of the wicked *are* deceit.

THEIR KISSES

Pr 27:6 Faithful *are* the wounds of a friend; but the kisses of an enemy *are* deceitful.

THEIR HOUSES

Je 5:27 As a cage is full of birds, so *are* their houses full of deceit: therefore they are become great, and waxen rich.

THEIR HEARTS

Mk 7:22 Thefts, covetousness, wickedness, deceit, lasciviousness, an evil eye, blasphemy, pride, foolishness:

4. Its Prevalence

Ps 116:11 I said in my haste, All men *are* liars.

Pr 20:17 Bread of deceit *is* sweet to a man; but afterwards his mouth shall be filled with gravel.

Is 28:15 Because ye have said, We have made a covenant with death, and with hell are we at agreement; when the overflowing scourge shall pass through, it shall not come unto us: for we have made lies our refuge, and under falsehood have we hid ourselves:

Je 9:5 And they will deceive every one his neighbour, and will not speak the truth: they have taught their tongue to speak lies, *and* weary themselves to commit iniquity.

Je 17:9 The heart *is* deceitful above all *things,* and desperately wicked: who can know it?

Mi 6:12 For the rich men thereof are full of violence, and the inhabitants thereof have spoken lies, and their tongue *is* deceitful in their mouth.

Na 3:1 Woe to the bloody city! it is all full of lies *and* robbery; the prey departeth not;

Ro 3:13 Their throat *is* an open sepulchre; with their tongues they have used deceit; the poison of asps *is* under their lips:

5. The Work of Deceivers

2 Chr 18:5 Therefore the king of Israel gathered together of prophets four hundred men, and said unto them, Shall we go to Ramoth-gilead to battle, or shall I forbear? And they said, Go up; for God will deliver *it* into the king's hand.

Pr 12:20 Deceit *is* in the heart of them that imagine evil: but to the counsellors of peace *is* joy.

Je 14:13 Then said I, Ah, Lord God! behold, the prophets say unto them, Ye shall not see the sword, neither shall ye have famine; but I will give you assured peace in this place.

Je 27:14 Therefore hearken not unto the words of the prophets that speak unto you, saying, Ye shall not serve the king of Babylon: for they prophesy a lie unto you.

Je 28:11 And Hananiah spake in the presence of all the people, saying, Thus saith the Lord; Even so will I break the yoke of Nebuchadnezzar king of Babylon from the neck of all nations within the space of two full years. And the prophet Jeremiah went his way.

Je 29:21 Thus saith the Lord of hosts, the God of Israel, of Ahab the son of Kolaiah, and of Zedekiah the son of Maaseiah, which prophesy a lie unto you in my name; Behold, I will deliver them into the hand of Nebuchadrezzar king of Babylon; and he shall slay them before your eyes;

Je 29:31 Send to all them of the captivity, saying, Thus saith the Lord concerning Shemaiah the Nehelamite; Because that Shemaiah hath prophesied unto you, and I sent him not, and he caused you to trust in a lie:

Eze 13:4 O Israel, thy prophets are like the foxes in the deserts.

Eze 13:22 Because with lies ye have made the heart of the righteous sad, whom I have not made sad; and strengthened the hands of the wicked, that he should not return from his wicked way, by promising him life:

Eze 22:28 And her prophets have daubed them with untempered *morter,* seeing vanity, and divining lies unto them, saying, Thus saith the Lord God, when the Lord hath not spoken.

Da 2:9 But if ye will not make known unto me the dream, *there is but* one

decree for you: for ye have prepared lying and corrupt words to speak before me, till the time be changed: therefore tell me the dream, and I shall know that ye can shew me the interpretation thereof.

Zec 10:2 For the idols have spoken vanity, and the diviners have seen a lie, and have told false dreams; they comfort in vain: therefore they went their way as a flock, they were troubled, because *there was* no shepherd.

Mt 24:11 And many false prophets shall rise, and shall deceive many.

Mt 24:24 For there shall arise false Christs, and false prophets, and shall shew great signs and wonders; insomuch that, if *it were* possible, they shall deceive the very elect.

Mt 28:14 And if this come to the governor's ears, we will persuade him, and secure you.

Mk 13:6 For many shall come in my name, saying, I am *Christ;* and shall deceive many.

Ac 8:9 But there was a certain man, called Simon, which beforetime in the same city used sorcery, and bewitched the people of Samaria, giving out that himself was some great one:

Ac 19:13 Then certain of the vagabond Jews, exorcists, took upon them to call over them which had evil spirits the name of the Lord Jesus, saying, We adjure you by Jesus whom Paul preacheth.

Ac 20:30 Also of your own selves shall men arise, speaking perverse things, to draw away disciples after them.

Ro 16:18 For they that are such serve not our Lord Jesus Christ, but their own belly; and by good words and fair speeches deceive the hearts of the simple.

2 Co 2:17 For we are not as many, which corrupt the word of God: but as of sincerity, but as of God, in the sight of God speak we in Christ.

2 Co 11:13 For such *are* false apostles, deceitful workers, transforming themselves into the apostles of Christ.

Ga 1:7 Which is not another; but there be some that trouble you, and would pervert the gospel of Christ.

Ga 3:1 O foolish Galatians, who hath bewitched you, that ye should not obey the truth, before whose eyes Jesus Christ hath been evidently set forth, crucified among you?

Ep 4:14 That we *henceforth* be no more children, tossed to and fro, and carried about with every wind of doctrine, by the sleight of men, *and* cunning craftiness, whereby they lie in wait to deceive;

Ph 1:16 The one preach Christ of contention, not sincerely, supposing to add affliction to my bonds:

Col 2:4 And this I say, lest any man should beguile you with enticing words.

Col 2:18 Let no man beguile you of your reward in a voluntary humility and worshipping of angels, intruding into those things which he hath not seen, vainly puffed up by his fleshly mind,

2 Ti 2:18 Who concerning the truth have erred, saying that the resurrection is past already; and overthrow the faith of some.

2 Ti 3:13 But evil men and seducers shall wax worse and worse, deceiving, and being deceived.

Tit 1:10 For there are many unruly and vain talkers and deceivers, specially they of the circumcision:

2 Pe 2:3 And through covetousness shall they with feigned words make merchandise of you: whose judgment now of a long time lingereth not, and their damnation slumbereth not.

2 Pe 2:17 These are wells without water, clouds that are carried with a tempest; to whom the mist of darkness is reserved for ever.

1 Jn 2:18 Little children, it is the last time: and as ye have heard that antichrist shall come, even now are there many antichrists; whereby we know that it is the last time.

1 Jn 2:26 These *things* have I written unto you concerning them that seduce you.

1 Jn 4:5 They are of the world: therefore speak they of the world, and the world heareth them.

2 Jn 7 For many deceivers are entered into the world, who confess not that Jesus Christ is come in the flesh. This is a deceiver and an antichrist.

Jude 4 For there are certain men crept in unawares, who were before of old ordained to this condemnation, ungodly men, turning the grace of our God into lasciviousness, and denying the only Lord God, and our Lord Jesus Christ.

Re 2:2 I know thy works, and thy labour, and thy patience, and how thou canst not bear them which are evil: and thou hast tried them which say they are apostles, and are not, and hast found them liars:

Re 18:23 And the light of a candle shall shine no more at all in thee; and the voice of the bridegroom and of the bride shall be heard no more at all in thee: for thy merchants were the great men of the earth; for by thy sorceries were all nations deceived.

See **SIN, TRUTH**

DECISION *See* **INVITATION**

DECLARATION OF GOOD

1. Different Forms

Ps 100:2; 145:11; 147:1; Lu 6:38; 9:23; Ph 4:6

2. Required by Christ

Mt 9:28; 16:15; Mk 9:33; 10:51; Lu 8:45; 24:17; Jn 5:6; 21:15

DEDICATION

1. Of the Tabernacle

Ex 40:1–38; Jn 10:22

2. Of Solomon's Temple

1 K 8:1–66

3. Of the Wall of Jerusalem

Ne 12:27

DEEP, *the sea*

Ge 1:2; Ps 42:7; 104:6; 107:24; Is 51:10; 63:13; Hab 3:10; 2 Co 11:25

DEEPER LIFE

Ps 1:2 But his delight *is* in the law of the LORD; and in his law doth he meditate day and night.

Da 2:22 He revealeth the deep and secret things: he knoweth what *is* in the darkness, and the light dwelleth with him.

Lu 6:48 He is like a man which built an house, and digged deep, and laid the foundation on a rock: and when the flood arose, the stream beat vehemently upon that house, and could not shake it: for it was founded upon a rock.

Lu 10:39 And she had a sister called Mary, which also sat at Jesus' feet, and heard his word.

1 Co 2:10 But God hath revealed *them* unto us by his Spirit: for the Spirit searcheth all things, yea, the deep things of God.

Ep 3:18–19 May be able to comprehend with all saints what *is* the breadth, and length, and depth, and height;

And to know the love of Christ, which passeth knowledge, that ye might be filled with all the fulness of God.

Ph 4:8 Finally, brethren, whatsoever things are true, whatsoever things *are* honest, whatsoever things *are* just, whatsoever things *are* pure, whatsoever things *are* lovely, whatsoever things *are* of good report; if *there be* any virtue, and if *there be* any praise, think on these things.

Col 3:3 For ye are dead, and your life is hid with Christ in God.

DEER *See* ANIMALS

DEFENDER

1. Christ

OF LITTLE CHILDREN

Mt 19:13–14 Then were there brought unto him little children, that he should put *his* hands on them, and pray: and the disciples rebuked them.

But Jesus said, Suffer little children, and forbid them not, to come unto me: for of such is the kingdom of heaven.

A SINFUL WOMAN

Lu 7:44–48 And he turned to the woman, and said unto Simon, Seest thou this woman? I entered into thine house, thou gavest me no water for my feet: but she hath washed my feet with tears, and wiped *them* with the hairs of her head.

Thou gavest me no kiss: but this woman since the time I came in hath not ceased to kiss my feet.

My head with oil thou didst not anoint: but this woman hath anointed my feet with ointment.

Wherefore I say unto thee, Her sins, which are many, are forgiven; for she loved much: but to whom little is forgiven, *the same* loveth little.

And he said unto her, Thy sins are forgiven.

Jn 8:3 And the scribes and Pharisees brought unto him a woman taken in adultery; and when they had set her in the midst,

A WEAK WOMAN

Lu 13:11 And, behold, there was a woman which had a spirit of infirmity eighteen years, and was bowed together, and could in no wise lift up *herself*.

MARY OF BETHANY

Jn 12:3 Then took Mary a pound of ointment of spikenard, very costly, and anointed the feet of Jesus, and wiped his feet with her hair: and the house was filled with the odour of the ointment.

THE FRIGHTENED DISCIPLES

Jn 18:8 Jesus answered, I have told you that I am *he:* if therefore ye seek me, let these go their way:

2. Of Faith

Ga 2:11 But when Peter was come to Antioch, I withstood him to the face, because he was to be blamed.

Ga 2:14 But when I saw that they walked not uprightly according to the truth of the gospel, I said unto Peter before *them* all, If thou, being a Jew, livest after the manner of Gentiles, and not as do the Jews, why compellest thou the Gentiles to live as do the Jews?

Ph 1:7 Even as it is meet for me to think this of you all, because I have you in my heart; inasmuch as both in my bonds, and in the defence and confirmation of the gospel, ye all are partakers of my grace.

Ph 1:17 But the other of love, knowing that I am set for the defence of the gospel.

Ph 1:27 Only let your conversation be as it becometh the gospel of Christ: that whether I come and see you, or else be absent, I may hear of your affairs, that ye stand fast in one spirit, with one mind striving together for the faith of the gospel;

Tit 1:13 This witness is true. Wherefore rebuke them sharply, that they may be sound in the faith;

Jude 3 Beloved, when I gave all diligence to write unto you of the common salvation, it was needful for me to write unto you, and exhort *you* that ye should earnestly contend for the faith which was once delivered unto the saints.

See **COURAGE**

DEFILEMENT, *impurity*

1. Of Sin

Le 16:16 And he shall make an atonement for the holy *place,* because of the uncleanness of the children of Israel, and because of their transgressions in all their sins: and so shall he do for the tabernacle of the congregation, that remaineth among them in the midst of their uncleanness.

Le 16:19 And he shall sprinkle of the blood upon it with his finger seven times, and cleanse it, and hallow it from the uncleanness of the children of Israel.

Le 18:24 Defile not ye yourselves in any of these things: for in all these the nations are defiled which I cast out before you:

Le 18:30 Therefore shall ye keep mine ordinance, that *ye* commit not *any one* of these abominable customs, which were committed before you, and that ye defile not yourselves therein: I *am* the LORD your God.

Le 19:31 Regard not them that have familiar spirits, neither seek after wizards, to be defiled by them: I *am* the LORD your God.

Le 20:3 And I will set my face against that man, and will cut him off from among his people; because he hath given of his seed unto Molech, to defile my sanctuary, and to profane my holy name.

Nu 5:20 But if thou hast gone aside *to another* instead of thy husband, and if thou be defiled, and some man have lain with thee beside thine husband:

Nu 5:29 This *is* the law of jealousies, when a wife goeth aside *to another* instead of her husband, and is defiled;

Nu 6:9 And if any man die very suddenly by him, and he hath defiled the head of his consecration; then he shall shave his head in the day of his cleansing, on the seventh day shall he shave it.

Nu 35:34 Defile not therefore the land which ye shall inhabit, wherein I dwell: for I the LORD dwell among the children of Israel.

Ne 13:29 Remember them, O my God, because they have defiled the priesthood, and the covenant of the priesthood, and of the Levites.

Ps 106:39 Thus were they defiled with their own works, and went a whoring with their own inventions.

Pr 30:12 *There is* a generation *that are* pure in their own eyes, and *yet* is not washed from their filthiness.

Is 24:5 The earth also is defiled under the inhabitants thereof; because they have transgressed the laws, changed the ordinance, broken the everlasting covenant.

Is 28:8 For all tables are full of vomit *and* filthiness, *so that there is* no place *clean.*

Is 59:3 For your hands are defiled with blood, and your fingers with iniquity; your lips have spoken lies, your tongue hath muttered perverseness.

Je 2:7 And I brought you into a plentiful country, to eat the fruit thereof and the goodness thereof; but when ye entered, ye defiled my land, and made mine heritage an abomination.

Je 3:2 Lift up thine eyes unto the high places, and see where thou hast not been lien with. In the ways hast thou sat for them, as the Arabian in the wilderness; and thou hast polluted the land with thy whoredoms and with thy wickedness.

Je 3:9 And it came to pass through the lightness of her whoredom, that she defiled the land, and committed adultery with stones and with stocks.

Je 16:18 And first I will recompense their iniquity and their sin double; because they have defiled my land, they have filled mine inheritance with the carcases of their detestable and abominable things.

Lam 4:14 They have wandered *as* blind *men* in the streets, they have polluted themselves with blood, so that men could not touch their garments.

Eze 20:7 Then said I unto them, Cast ye away every man the abominations of his eyes, and defile not yourselves with the idols of Egypt: I *am* the LORD your God.

Eze 20:18 But I said unto their children in the wilderness, Walk ye not in the statutes of your fathers, neither observe their judgments, nor defile yourselves with their idols:

Eze 20:30 Wherefore say unto the house of Israel, Thus saith the Lord GOD; Are ye polluted after the manner of your fathers? and commit ye whoredom after their abominations?

Eze 20:43 And there shall ye remember your ways, and all your doings, wherein ye have been defiled; and ye shall lothe yourselves in your own sight for all your evils that ye have committed.

Eze 22:4 Thou art become guilty in thy blood that thou hast shed; and hast defiled thyself in thine idols which thou hast made; and thou hast caused thy days to draw near, and art

come *even* unto thy years: therefore have I made thee a reproach unto the heathen, and a mocking to all countries.

Eze 23:7 Thus she committed her whoredoms with them, with all them *that were* the chosen men of Assyria, and with all on whom she doted: with all their idols she defiled herself.

Eze 23:13 Then I saw that she was defiled, *that* they *took* both one way,

Eze 28:18 Thou hast defiled thy sanctuaries by the multitude of thine iniquities, by the iniquity of thy traffick; therefore will I bring forth a fire from the midst of thee, it shall devour thee, and I will bring thee to ashes upon the earth in the sight of all them that behold thee.

Eze 36:17 Son of man, when the house of Israel dwelt in their own land, they defiled it by their own way and by their doings: their way was before me as the uncleanness of a removed woman.

Eze 43:8 In their setting of their threshold by my thresholds, and their post by my posts, and the wall between me and them, they have even defiled my holy name by their abominations that they have committed: wherefore I have consumed them in mine anger.

Ho 5:3 I know Ephraim, and Israel is not hid from me: for now, O Ephraim, thou committest whoredom, *and* Israel is defiled.

Ho 6:10 I have seen an horrible thing in the house of Israel: there *is* the whoredom of Ephraim, Israel is defiled.

Zec 3:3 Now Joshua was clothed with filthy garments, and stood before the angel.

Zec 13:1 In that day there shall be a fountain opened to the house of David and to the inhabitants of Jerusalem for sin and for uncleanness.

Mt 15:11 Not that which goeth into the mouth defileth a man; but that which cometh out of the mouth, this defileth a man.

Mk 7:15 There is nothing from without a man, that entering into him can defile him: but the things which come out of him, those are they that defile the man.

Mk 7:23 All these evil things come from within, and defile the man.

Jn 13:10 Jesus saith to him, He that is washed needeth not save to wash *his* feet, but is clean every whit: and ye are clean, but not all.

Ro 1:26 For this cause God gave them up unto vile affections: for even their women did change the natural use into that which is against nature:

1 Co 3:17 If any man defile the temple of God, him shall God destroy; for the temple of God is holy, which *temple* ye are.

2 Co 7:1 Having therefore these promises, dearly beloved, let us cleanse ourselves from all filthiness of the flesh and spirit, perfecting holiness in the fear of God.

Ep 5:5 For this ye know, that no whoremonger, nor unclean person, nor covetous man, who is an idolater, hath any inheritance in the kingdom of Christ and of God.

Tit 1:15 Unto the pure all things *are* pure: but unto them that are defiled and unbelieving *is* nothing pure; but even their mind and conscience is defiled.

He 12:15 Looking diligently lest any man fail of the grace of God; lest any root of bitterness springing up trouble *you,* and thereby many be defiled;

Ja 3:6 And the tongue *is* a fire, a world of iniquity: so is the tongue among our members, that it defileth the whole body, and setteth on fire the course of nature; and it is set on fire of hell.

2 Pe 2:22 But it is happened unto them according to the true proverb, The dog *is* turned to his own vomit again; and the sow that was washed to her wallowing in the mire.

Jude 7 Even as Sodom and Gomorrha, and the cities about them in like manner, giving themselves over to fornication, and going after strange flesh, are set forth for an example, suffering the vengeance of eternal fire.

Re 2:20 Notwithstanding I have a few things against thee, because thou sufferest that woman Jezebel, which calleth herself a prophetess, to teach and to seduce my servants to commit fornication, and to eat things sacrificed unto idols.

Re 21:27 And there shall in no wise enter into it any thing that defileth, neither *whatsoever* worketh abomination, or *maketh* a lie: but they which are written in the Lamb's book of life.

2. *Ceremonial*

Le 5:2; 11:43, 44; 13:46; 15:2, 31; 21:4; Nu 5:2; 19:11; Jn 18:28

See **CLEANSING, SIN**

DEGRADATION, *of God's people*

Ex 32:25 And when Moses saw that the people *were* naked; (for Aaron had made them naked unto *their* shame among their enemies:)

Pr 14:34 Righteousness exalteth a nation: but sin *is* a reproach to any people.

Is 3:8 For Jerusalem is ruined, and Judah is fallen: because their tongue and their doings *are* against the LORD, to provoke the eyes of his glory.

Is 52:2 Shake thyself from the dust; arise, *and* sit down, O Jerusalem: loose thyself from the bands of thy neck, O captive daughter of Zion.

Eze 16:6 And when I passed by thee, and saw thee polluted in thine own blood, I said unto thee *when thou wast* in thy blood, Live; yea, I said unto thee *when thou wast* in thy blood, Live.

Eze 20:31 For when ye offer your gifts, when ye make your sons to pass through the fire, ye pollute yourselves with all your idols, even unto this day: and shall I be enquired of by you, O house of Israel? *As* I live, saith the Lord GOD, I will not be enquired of by you.

2 Pe 2:22 But it is happened unto them according to the true proverb, The dog *is* turned to his own vomit again; and the sow that was washed to her wallowing in the mire.

See **ISRAEL, SIN, WICKED**

DELAY

Sometimes Results in Death

THE EGYPTIANS, *in attempting to escape God's judgments*

Ex 14:24–25 And it came to pass, that in the morning watch the LORD looked unto the host of the Egyptians through the pillar of fire and of the cloud, and troubled the host of the Egyptians,

And took off their chariot wheels, that they drave them heavily: so that the Egyptians said, Let us flee from the face of Israel; for the LORD fighteth for them against the Egyptians.

ISRAEL, *in seeking to enter the Promised Land*

Nu 14:40–41 And they rose up early in the morning, and gat them up into the top of the mountain, saying, Lo, we *be here,* and will go up unto the place which the LORD hath promised: for we have sinned.

And Moses said, Wherefore now do ye transgress the commandment of the LORD? but it shall not prosper.

Nu 14:44–45 But they presumed to go up unto the hill top: nevertheless the ark of the covenant of the LORD, and Moses, departed not out of the camp.

Then the Amalekites came down, and the Canaanites which dwelt in that hill, and smote them, and discomfited them, *even* unto Hormah.

SAUL, *in repenting his disobedience*

1 S 15:24–26 And Saul said unto Samuel, I have sinned: for I have transgressed the commandment of the LORD, and thy words: because I feared the people, and obeyed their voice.

Now therefore, I pray thee, pardon my sin, and turn again with me, that I may worship the LORD.

And Samuel said unto Saul, I will not return with thee: for thou hast rejected the word of the LORD, and the LORD hath rejected thee from being king over Israel.

ISRAEL, *in repenting of sin*

Je 8:20 The harvest is past, the summer is ended, and we are not saved.

THE FOOLISH VIRGINS, *in preparing for the coming of the Bridegroom*

Mt 25:11–12 Afterward came also the other virgins, saying, Lord, Lord, open to us.

But he answered and said, Verily I say unto you, I know you not.

JUDAS, *in repenting his betrayal of Christ*

Mt 27:3 Then Judas, which had betrayeth him, when he saw that he was condemned, repented himself, and brought again the thirty pieces of silver to the chief priests and elders,

THOSE KNOCKING AT THE CLOSED DOOR

Lu 13:25 When once the master of the house is risen up, and hath shut to the door, and ye begin to stand without, and to knock at the door, saying, Lord, Lord, open unto us; and he shall answer and say unto you, I know you not whence ye are:

ESAU, *in repenting the sale of his birthright*

He 12:17 For ye know how that afterward, when he would have inherited the blessing, he was rejected: for he found no place of repentance, though he sought it carefully with tears.

See **HASTE, WAITING**

DELILAH *See* **WOMEN**

DELIVERANCE, *the state of being released, set free, rescued*

1. Of Israel

Ge 15:14; 45:7; Ex 3:8; 6:6; 12:27, 42; 13:3; 14:13, 30; 18:4, 9; 20:2; 32:11; Le 25:42; 26:13; Nu 14:13; De 4:20, 34, 37; 5:6, 15; 6:12, 23; 7:8, 19; 8:14; 13:5, 10; 15:15; 16:1; Jos 24:5, 10; Jud 2:18; 6:9; 1 S 7:10; 10:18; 12:8; 14:15; 2 S 7:23; 1 Chr 11:14; 17:21; 2 Chr 14:12; 20:22; 32:21; Ezr 8:31; 9:13; Ne 9:28; Ps 22:4; 78:42; 81:7; 106:10; 107:6, 20; 114:1; 124:7; 136:24; Pr 11:21; Is 9:4; 14:3, 29; Je 2:20; 11:4; 30:8; Eze 20:6, 10; Am 4:11; Mi 6:4; Hab 3:13; Zec 3:4; 9:11

2. Divine

LOT

Ge 19:16 And while he lingered, the men laid hold upon his hand, and upon the hand of his wife, and upon the hand of his two daughters; the LORD being merciful unto him: and they brought him forth, and set him without the city.

DAVID

1 S 17:37 David said moreover, The LORD that delivered me out of the paw of the lion, and out of the paw of the bear, he will deliver me out of the hand of this Philistine. And Saul said unto David, Go, and the LORD be with thee.

THE HEBREW CHILDREN

Da 3:27 And the princes, governors, and captains, and the king's counsellors, being gathered together, saw these men, upon whose bodies the fire had no power, nor was an hair of their head singed, neither were their coats changed, nor the smell of fire had passed on them.

DANIEL

Da 6:22 My God hath sent his angel, and hath shut the lions' mouths, that they have not hurt me: forasmuch as before him innocency was found in me; and also before thee, O king, have I done no hurt.

JONAH

Jona 1:17 Now the LORD had prepared a great fish to swallow up Jonah. And Jonah was in the belly of the fish three days and three nights.

THE APOSTLES

Ac 5:18–19 And laid their hands on the apostles, and put them in the common prison.

But the angel of the Lord by night opened the prison doors, and brought them forth, and said,

PETER

Ac 12:7 And, behold, the angel of the Lord came upon *him,* and a light shined in the prison: and he smote Peter on the side, and raised him up, saying, Arise up quickly. And his chains fell off from *his* hands.

PAUL AND SILAS

Ac 16:26 And suddenly there was a great earthquake, so that the foundations of the prison were shaken: and immediately all the doors were opened, and every one's bands were loosed.

SHIPWRECKED PASSENGERS

Ac 27:44 And the rest, some on boards, and some on *broken pieces* of the ship. And so it came to pass, that they escaped all safe to land.

3. Promised for Believers

2 S 22:17 He sent from above, he took me; he drew me out of many waters;

2 S 22:49 And that bringeth me forth from mine enemies: thou also hast lifted me up on high above them that rose up against me: thou hast delivered me from the violent man.

1 K 20:28 And there came a man of God, and spake unto the king of Israel, and said, Thus saith the LORD, Because the Syrians have said, The LORD *is* God of the hills, but he *is* not God of the valleys, therefore will I deliver all this great multitude into thine hand, and ye shall know that I *am* the LORD.

Jb 5:19 He shall deliver thee in six troubles: yea, in seven there shall no evil touch thee.

Jb 33:28 He will deliver his soul from going into the pit, and his life shall see the light.

Jb 42:10 And the LORD turned the captivity of Job, when he prayed for his friends: also the LORD gave Job twice as much as he had before.

Ps 18:17 He delivered me from my strong enemy, and from them which hated me: for they were too strong for me.

Ps 86:13 For great *is* thy mercy toward me: and thou hast delivered my soul from the lowest hell.

Ps 91:3 Surely he shall deliver thee from the snare of the fowler, *and* from the noisome pestilence.

Ps 102:20 To hear the groaning of the prisoner; to loose those that are appointed to death;

Ps 107:14 He brought them out of darkness and the shadow of death, and brake their bands in sunder.

Ps 116:8 For thou hast delivered my soul from death, mine eyes from tears, *and* my feet from falling.

Is 46:4 And *even* to *your* old age I *am* he; and *even* to hoar hairs will I carry *you:* I have made, and I will bear; even I will carry, and will deliver *you.*

Eze 33:5 He heard the sound of the trumpet, and took not warning; his blood shall be upon him. But he that taketh warning shall deliver his soul.

1 Co 10:13 There hath no temptation taken you but such as is common to man: but God *is* faithful, who will not suffer you to be tempted above that ye are able; but will with the temptation also make a way to escape, that ye may be able to bear *it.*

2 Co 1:10 Who delivered us from so great a death, and doth deliver: in whom we trust that he will yet deliver *us;*

2 Ti 4:18 And the Lord shall deliver me from every evil work, and will preserve *me* unto his heavenly kingdom: to whom *be* glory for ever and ever. Amen.

He 2:15 And deliver them who through fear of death were all their lifetime subject to bondage.

2 Pe 2:9 The Lord knoweth how to deliver the godly out of temptations, and to reserve the unjust unto the day of judgment to be punished:

4. Sought by the Psalmist

Ge 32:11; Jud 10:15; 1 S 12:10; 2 K 19:19; 1 Chr 16:35; Ps 6:4; 7:2; 17:13; 22:20; 25:20; 31:1, 15; 35:17; 40:13; 43:1; 44:26; 59:2; 69:14; 70:1; 71:4; 79:9; 108:6; 109:21; 116:4; 119:134, 153, 170; 120:2; 140:1; 142:7; 143:9; 144:7, 11; Lu 11:4; 22:42; Ro 15:31; 2 Th 3:2

See **PROMISES, PROVIDENCE, TEMPTATION**

DELIVERER

Jud 7:14 And his fellow answered and said, This *is* nothing else save the sword of Gideon the son of Joash, a man of Israel: *for* into his hand hath God delivered Midian, and all the host.

Jud 8:34 And the children of Israel remembered not the LORD their God, who had delivered them out of the hands of all their enemies on every side:

Jud 10:12 The Zidonians also, and the Amalekites, and the Maonites, did oppress you; and ye cried to me, and I delivered you out of their hand.

Jud 11:21 And the LORD God of Israel delivered Sihon and all his people into the hand of Israel, and they smote them: so Israel possessed all the land of the Amorites, the inhabitants of that country.

Jud 12:3 And when I saw that ye delivered *me* not, I put my life in my hands, and passed over against the children of Ammon, and the LORD delivered them into my hand: wherefore then are ye come up unto me this day, to fight against me?

Jud 20:28 And Phinehas, the son of Eleazar, the son of Aaron, stood before it in those days,) saying, Shall I yet again go out to battle against the children of Benjamin my brother, or shall I cease? And the LORD said, Go up; for to morrow I will deliver them into thine hand.

1 S 9:16 To morrow about this time I will send thee a man out of the land of Benjamin, and thou shalt anoint him *to be* captain over my people Israel, that he may save my people out of the hand of the Philistines: for I have looked upon my people, because their cry is come unto me.

1 S 14:12 And the men of the garrison answered Jonathan and his armourbearer, and said, Come up to us, and we will shew you a thing. And Jonathan said unto his armourbearer, Come up after me: for the LORD hath delivered them into the hand of Israel.

1 S 17:37 David said moreover, The LORD that delivered me out of the paw of the lion, and out of the paw of the bear, he will deliver me out of the hand of this Philistine. And Saul said unto David, Go, and the LORD be with thee.

1 S 17:46 This day will the LORD deliver thee into mine hand; and I will smite thee, and take thine head from thee; and I will give the carcases of the host of the Philistines this day unto the fowls of the air, and to the wild beasts of the earth; that all the earth may know that there is a God in Israel.

1 S 24:15 The LORD therefore be judge, and judge between me and thee, and see, and plead my cause, and deliver me out of thine hand.

1 S 26:24 And, behold, as thy life was much set by this day in mine eyes, so let my life be much set by in the eyes of the LORD, and let him deliver me out of all tribulation.

2 S 4:9 And David answered Rechab and Baanah his brother, the sons of Rimmon the Beerothite, and said unto them, As the LORD liveth, who hath redeemed my soul out of all adversity,

2 S 18:28 And Ahimaaz called, and said unto the king, All is well. And he fell down to the earth upon his face before the king, and said, Blessed *be* the LORD thy God, which hath delivered up the men that lifted up their hand against my lord the king.

2 S 22:2 And he said, The LORD *is* my rock, and my fortress, and my deliverer;

2 S 22:18 He delivered me from my strong enemy, *and* from them that hated me: for they were too strong for me.

2 S 22:49 And that bringeth me forth from mine enemies: thou also hast lifted me up on high above them that rose up against me: thou hast delivered me from the violent man.

2 K 17:39 But the LORD your God ye shall fear; and he shall deliver you out of the hand of all your enemies.

2 K 18:32 Until I come and take you away to a land like your own land, a land of corn and wine, a land of bread and vineyards, a land of oil olive and of honey, that ye may live, and not die: and hearken not unto Hezekiah, when he persuadeth you, saying, The LORD will deliver us.

2 K 19:19 Now therefore, O LORD our God, I beseech thee, save thou us out of his hand, that all the kingdoms of the earth may know that thou *art* the LORD God, *even* thou only.

2 Chr 16:8 Were not the Ethiopians and the Lubims a huge host, with very many chariots and horsemen? yet, because thou didst rely on the LORD, he delivered them into thine hand.

Jb 5:15 But he saveth the poor from the sword, from their mouth, and from the hand of the mighty.

Ps 18:2 The LORD *is* my rock, and my fortress, and my deliverer; my God, my strength, in whom I will trust; my buckler, and the horn of my salvation, *and* my high tower.

Ps 18:17 He delivered me from my strong enemy, and from them which hated me: for they were too strong for me.

Ps 18:43 Thou hast delivered me from the strivings of the people; *and* thou hast made me the head of the heathen: a people *whom* I have not known shall serve me.

Ps 18:50 Great deliverance giveth he to his king; and sheweth mercy to his anointed, to David, and to his seed for evermore.

Ps 22:5 They cried unto thee, and were delivered: they trusted in thee, and were not confounded.

Ps 34:4 I sought the LORD, and he heard me, and delivered me from all my fears.

Ps 34:17 *The righteous* cry, and the LORD heareth, and delivereth them out of all their troubles.

Ps 54:7 For he hath delivered me out of all trouble: and mine eye hath seen *his desire* upon mine enemies.

Ps 55:18 He hath delivered my soul in peace from the battle *that was* against me: for there were many with me.

Ps 56:13 For thou hast delivered my soul from death: *wilt* not *thou deliver* my feet from falling, that I may walk before God in the light of the living?

Ps 68:20 *He that is* our God *is* the God of salvation; and unto God the L ORD *belong* the issues from death.

Ps 69:14 Deliver me out of the mire, and let me not sink: let me be delivered from them that hate me, and out of the deep waters.

Ps 71:2 Deliver me in thy righteousness, and cause me to escape: incline thine ear unto me, and save me.

Ps 106:43 Many times did he deliver them; but they provoked *him* with their counsel, and were brought low for their iniquity.

Ps 107:2 Let the redeemed of the L ORD say so, whom he hath redeemed from the hand of the enemy;

Ps 109:31 For he shall stand at the right hand of the poor, to save *him* from those that condemn his soul.

Ps 129:4 The L ORD *is* righteous: he hath cut asunder the cords of the wicked.

Ps 144:10 *It is he* that giveth salvation unto kings: who delivereth David his servant from the hurtful sword.

Is 38:17 Behold, for peace I had great bitterness: but thou hast in love to my soul *delivered it* from the pit of corruption: for thou hast cast all my sins behind thy back.

Is 46:4 And *even* to *your* old age I *am* he; and *even* to hoar hairs will I carry *you:* I have made, and I will bear; even I will carry, and will deliver *you.*

Je 1:8 Be not afraid of their faces: for I *am* with thee to deliver thee, saith the L ORD.

Je 31:11 For the L ORD hath redeemed Jacob, and ransomed him from the hand of *him that was* stronger than he.

Eze 13:23 Therefore ye shall see no more vanity, nor divine divinations: for I will deliver my people out of your hand: and ye shall know that I *am* the L ORD.

Eze 34:12 As a shepherd seeketh out his flock in the day that he is among his sheep *that are* scattered; so will I seek out my sheep, and will deliver them out of all places where they have been scattered in the cloudy and dark day.

Da 3:17 If it be *so,* our God whom we serve is able to deliver us from the

burning fiery furnace, and he will deliver *us* out of thine hand, O king.

Da 3:25 He answered and said, Lo, I see four men loose, walking in the midst of the fire, and they have no hurt; and the form of the fourth is like the Son of God.

Da 3:29 Therefore I make a decree, That every people, nation, and language, which speak any thing amiss against the God of Shadrach, Mechach, and Abed-nego, shall be cut in pieces, and their houses shall be made a dunghill: because there is no other God that can deliver after this sort.

Da 6:16 Then the king commanded, and they brought Daniel, and cast *him* into the den of lions. *Now* the king spake and said unto Daniel, Thy God whom thou servest continually, he will deliver thee.

Da 6:27 He delivereth and rescueth, and he worketh signs and wonders in heaven and in earth, who hath delivered Daniel from the power of the lions.

Mi 5:6 And they shall waste the land of Assyria with the sword, and the land of Nimrod in the entrances thereof: thus shall he deliver *us* from the Assyrian, when he cometh into our land, and when he treadeth within our borders.

Mt 6:13 And lead us not into temptation, but deliver us from evil: For thine is the kingdom, and the power, and the glory, for ever. Amen.

Mt 14:31 And immediately Jesus stretched forth *his* hand, and caught him, and said unto him, O thou of little faith, wherefore didst thou doubt?

Mt 26:53 Thinkest thou that I cannot now pray to my Father, and he shall presently give me more than twelve legions of angels?

Lu 1:69 And hath raised up an horn of salvation for us in the house of his servant David;

Lu 1:74 That he would grant unto us, that we being delivered out of the hand of our enemies might serve him without fear,

Lu 18:8 I tell you that he will avenge them speedily. Nevertheless when the

Son of man cometh, shall he find faith on the earth?

Ac 5:23 Saying, The prison truly found we shut with all safety, and the keepers standing without before the doors: but when we had opened, we found no man within.

Ac 26:17 Delivering thee from the people, and *from* the Gentiles, unto whom now I send thee,

2 Co 1:10 Who delivered us from so great a death, and doth deliver: in whom we trust that he will yet deliver *us;*

2 Ti 3:11 Persecutions, afflictions, which came unto me at Antioch, at Iconium, at Lystra; what persecutions I endured: but out of *them* all the Lord delivered me.

2 Ti 4:18 And the Lord shall deliver me from every evil work, and will preserve *me* unto his heavenly kingdom: to whom *be* glory for ever and ever. Amen.

He 2:15 And deliver them who through fear of death were all their lifetime subject to bondage.

2 Pe 2:7 And delivered just Lot, vexed with the filthy conversation of the wicked:

See **GOD**

DELUGE, *the Great Flood*

Ge 6:7, 17; 7:4, 11, 17; 9:11; 11:10; Jb 12:15; 22:16; Is 54:9; Eze 38:22; Mt 24:38; Lu 17:27; He 11:7; 1 Pe 3:20; 2 Pe 2:5; 3:6

DELUSIONS

THINKING THAT SIN WILL GIVE FULLNESS OF LIFE

Ge 3:5–6 For God doth know that in the day ye eat thereof, then your eyes shall be opened, and ye shall be as gods, knowing good and evil.

And when the woman saw that the tree *was* good for food, and that it *was* pleasant to the eyes, and a tree to be desired to make *one* wise, she took of the fruit thereof, and did eat, and gave also unto her husband with her; and he did eat.

TRUSTING IN RACIAL CONNECTIONS FOR SALVATION

Mt 3:9 And think not to say within yourselves, We have Abraham to *our* father: for I say unto you, that God is able of these stones to raise up children unto Abraham.

USING VAIN REPETITIONS IN PRAYER

Mt 6:7 But when ye pray, use not vain repetitions, as the heathen *do:* for they think that they shall be heard for their much speaking.

SELF-CONFIDENCE

Mt 26:33 Peter answered and said unto him, Though all *men* shall be offended because of thee, *yet* will I never be offended.

BUILDING ON THE SAND

Mt 7:26 And every one that heareth these sayings of mine, and doeth them not, shall be likened unto a foolish man, which built his house upon the sand:

Lu 6:49 But he that heareth, and doeth not, is like a man that without a foundation built an house upon the earth; against which the stream did beat vehemently, and immediately it fell; and the ruin of that house was great.

TRUSTING IN RICHES

Lu 12:19 And I will say to my soul, Soul, thou hast much goods laid up for many years; take thine ease, eat, drink, *and* be merry.

THINKING THE DEITY IS REPRESENTED BY IDOLS

Ac 17:29 Forasmuch then as we are the offspring of God, we ought not to think that the Godhead is like unto gold, or silver, or stone, graven by art and man's device.

THINKING THAT THERE IS PLENTY OF TIME

Ac 24:25 And as he reasoned of righteousness, temperance, and judgment to come Felix trembled, and answered, Go thy way for this time;

when I have a convenient season, I will call for thee.

Ga 6:3 For if a man think himself to be something, when he is nothing, he deceiveth himself.

1 Ti 6:5 Perverse disputings of men of corrupt minds, and destitute of the truth, supposing that gain is godliness: from such withdraw thyself.

PRESUMING UPON UNCHANGING
CONDITIONS

Ja 4:13–14 Go to now, ye that say, To day or to morrow we will go into such a city, and continue there a year, and buy and sell, and get gain:

Whereas ye know not what *shall be* on the morrow. For what *is* your life? It is even a vapour, that appeareth for a little time, and then vanisheth away.

DEMAS, *one of Paul's co-laborers*

Col 4:14; 2 Ti 4:10; Phm 24

DEMONIACS, *people possessed by evil spirits*

Mt 4:24; 8:28; 9:32; 12:22; 15:22; 17:15; Mk 1:23, 32; 5:2; 9:17; Lu 4:33; 8:2, 27; 9:39; Ac 5:16

DEMONS, *wicked beings under Satan's domain*

Jud 9:23 Then God sent an evil spirit between Abimelech and the men of Shechem; and the men of Shechem dealt treacherously with Abimelech:

1 S 16:15 And Saul's servants said unto him, Behold now, an evil spirit from God troubleth thee.

Mt 12:45 Then goeth he, and taketh with himself seven other spirits more wicked than himself, and they enter in and dwell there: and the last *state* of that man is worse than the first. Even so shall it be also unto this wicked generation.

Mk 1:26 And when the unclean spirit had torn him, and cried with a loud voice, he came out of him.

Mk 5:9 And he asked him, What *is* thy name? And he answered, saying, My name *is* Legion: for we are many.

Mk 7:30 And when she was come to her house, she found the devil gone

out, and her daughter laid upon the bed.

Mk 9:17 And one of the multitude answered and said, Master, I have brought unto thee my son, which hath a dumb spirit;

Mk 16:9 Now when *Jesus* was risen early the first *day* of the week, he appeared first to Mary Magdalene, out of whom he had cast seven devils.

Lu 10:19 Behold, I give unto you power to tread on serpents and scorpions, and over all the power of the enemy: and nothing shall by any means hurt you.

Ac 8:7 For unclean spirits, crying with loud voice, came out of many that were possessed *with them:* and many taken with palsies, and that were lame, were healed.

Ac 19:13 Then certain of the vagabond Jews, exorcists, took upon them to call over them which had evil spirits the name of the Lord Jesus, saying, We adjure you by Jesus whom Paul preacheth.

Ep 6:12 For we wrestle not against flesh and blood, but against principalities, against powers, against the rulers of the darkness of this world, against spiritual wickedness in high *places.*

1 Ti 4:1 Now the Spirit speaketh expressly, that in the latter times some shall depart from the faith, giving heed to seducing spirits, and doctrines of devils;

Ja 2:19 Thou believest that there is one God; thou doest well: the devils also believe, and tremble.

Re 16:14 For they are the spirits of devils, working miracles, *which* go forth unto the kings of the earth and of the whole world, to gather them to the battle of that great day of God Almighty.

Cast Out of

1 S 16:23 And it came to pass, when the *evil* spirit from God was upon Saul, that David took an harp, and played with his hand: so Saul was refreshed, and was well, and the evil spirit departed from him.

Mt 8:32 And he said unto them, Go. And when they were come out, they went into the herd of swine: and, behold, the whole herd of swine ran violently down a steep place into the sea, and perished in the waters.

Mt 9:33 And when the devil was cast out, the dumb spake: and the multitudes marvelled, saying, It was never so seen in Israel.

Mt 10:8 Heal the sick, cleanse the lepers, raise the dead, cast out devils: freely ye have received, freely give.

Mt 12:28 But if I cast out devils by the Spirit of God, then the kingdom of God is come unto you.

Mt 15:28 Then Jesus answered and said unto her, O woman, great *is* thy faith: be it unto thee even as thou wilt. And her daughter was made whole from that very hour.

Mt 17:18 And Jesus rebuked the devil; and he departed out of him: and the child was cured from that very hour.

Mk 1:26 And when the unclean spirit had torn him, and cried with a loud voice, he came out of him.

Mk 1:34 And he healed many that were sick of divers diseases, and cast out many devils; and suffered not the devils to speak, because they knew him.

Lu 8:2 And certain women, which had been healed of evil spirits and infirmities, Mary called Magdalene, out of whom went seven devils,

Ac 5:16 There came also a multitude *out* of the cities round about unto Jerusalem, bringing sick folks, and them which were vexed with unclean spirits: and they were healed every one.

Ac 16:18 And this did she many days. But Paul, being grieved, turned and said to the spirit, I command thee in the name of Jesus Christ to come out of her. And he came out the same hour.

Ac 19:12 So that from his body were brought unto the sick handkerchiefs or aprons, and the diseases departed from them, and the evil spirits went out of them.

See **SPIRITS**

DEMONSTRATION

1 S 17:46 This day will the LORD deliver thee into mine hand; and I will smite thee, and take thine head from thee; and I will give the carcases of the host of the Philistines this day unto the fowls of the air, and to the wild beasts of the earth; that all the earth may know that there is a God in Israel.

1 K 18:38 Then the fire of the LORD fell, and consumed the burnt sacrifice, and the wood, and the stones, and the dust, and licked up the water that *was* in the trench.

Mt 9:5 For whether is easier, to say, *Thy* sins be forgiven thee; or to say, Arise, and walk?

Mt 27:54 Now when the centurion, and they that were with him, watching Jesus, saw the earthquake, and those things that were done, they feared greatly, saying, Truly this was the Son of God.

Mk 2:10 But that ye may know that the Son of man hath power on earth to forgive sins, (he saith to the sick of the palsy,)

Lu 1:44 For, lo, as soon as the voice of thy salutation sounded in mine ears, the babe leaped in my womb for joy.

Lu 5:23 Whether is easier, to say, Thy sins be forgiven thee; or to say, Rise up and walk?

Jn 4:53 So the father knew that *it was* at the same hour, in the which Jesus said unto him, Thy son liveth: and himself believed, and his whole house.

Jn 6:13 Therefore they gathered *them* together, and filled twelve baskets with the fragments of the five barley loaves, which remained over and above unto them that had eaten.

Jn 20:27 Then saith he to Thomas, reach hither thy finger, and behold my hands; and reach hither thy hand, and thrust *it* into my side: and be not faithless, but believing.

Ac 9:22 But Saul increased the more in strength, and confounded the Jews which dwelt at Damascus, proving that this is very Christ.

Re 2:23 And I will kill her children with death; and all the churches shall know that I am he which searcheth the reins and hearts: and I will give unto every one of you according to your works.

DENIAL OF CHRIST, *verbal rejection of allegiance to Christ*

Mt 10:33 But whosoever shall deny me before men, him will I also deny before my Father which is in heaven.

Mt 26:34 Jesus said unto him, Verily I say unto thee, That this night, before the cock crow, thou shalt deny me thrice.

Mt 26:69–70 Now Peter sat without in the palace: and a damsel came unto him, saying, Thou also wast with Jesus of Galilee.

But he denied before *them* all, saying, I know not what thou sayest.

Mt 26:74 Then began he to curse and to swear, *saying*, I know not the man. And immediately the cock crew.

Mk 8:38 Whosoever therefore shall be ashamed of me and of my words in this adulterous and sinful generation; of him also shall the Son of man be ashamed, when he cometh in the glory of his Father with the holy angels.

Mk 14:30 And Jesus saith unto him, Verily I say unto thee, That this day, *even* in this night, before the cock crow twice, thou shalt deny me thrice.

Mk 14:68 But he denied, saying, I know not, neither understand I what thou sayest. And he went out into the porch; and the cock crew.

Lu 9:26 For whosoever shall be ashamed of me and of my words, of him shall the Son of man be ashamed, when he shall come in his own glory, and *in his* Father's, and of the holy angels.

Lu 12:9 But he that denieth me before men shall be denied before the angels of God.

Lu 22:34 And he said, I tell thee, Peter, the cock shall not crow this day, before that thou shalt thrice deny that thou knowest me.

Lu 22:57 And he denied him, saying, Woman, I know him not.

Jn 13:38 Jesus answered him, Wilt thou lay down thy life for my sake? Verily, verily, I say unto thee, The cock shall not crow, till thou hast denied me thrice.

Jn 18:17 Then saith the damsel that kept the door unto Peter, Art not thou also *one* of this man's disciples? He saith, I am not.

Jn 18:25 And Simon Peter stood and warmed himself. They said therefore unto him, Art not thou *it,* and said, I am not.

Ac 3:14 But ye denied the Holy One and the Just, and desired a murderer to be granted unto you;

1 Ti 5:8 But if any provide not for his own, and specially for those of his own house, he hath denied the faith, and is worse than an infidel.

2 Ti 2:12 If we suffer, we shall also reign with *him:* if we deny *him,* he also will deny us:

Tit 1:16 They profess that they know God; but in works they deny *him,* being abominable, and disobedient, and unto every good work reprobate.

2 Pe 2:1 But there were false prophets also among the people, even as there shall be false teachers among you, who privily shall bring in damnable heresies, even denying the Lord that bought them, and bring upon themselves swift destruction.

1 Jn 2:22 Who is a liar but he that denieth that Jesus is the Christ? He is antichrist, that denieth the Father and the Son.

1 Jn 4:3 And every spirit that confesseth not that Jesus Christ is come in the flesh is not of God: and this is that *spirit* of antichrist, whereof ye have heard that it should come; and even now already is it in the world.

2 Jn 7 For many deceivers are entered into the world, who confess not that Jesus Christ is come in the flesh. This is a deceiver and an antichrist.

Jude 4 For there are certain men crept in unawares, who were before of old ordained to this condemnation, ungodly men, turning the grace of our God into lasciviousness, and denying the only Lord God, and our Lord Jesus Christ.

See **CHRIST**

DENS, *lairs of wild beasts, holes of a poisonous reptile, or caves used for hiding*

Jud 6:2; Jb 37:8; 38:40; Ps 104:22; Je 7:11; Da 6:7; He 11:38

DEPARTURE

From Worldy Associations

Eze 3:22 And the hand of the LORD was there upon me; and he said unto me, Arise, go forth into the plain, and I will there talk with thee.

Mt 14:23 And when he had sent the multitudes away, he went up into a mountain apart to pray: and when the evening was come, he was there alone.

Mt 15:29 And Jesus departed from thence, and came nigh unto the sea of Galilee; and went up into a mountain, and sat down there.

Mt 17:1 And after six days Jesus taketh Peter, James, and John his brother, and bringeth them up into an high mountain apart,

Mt 20:17 And Jesus going up to Jerusalem took the twelve disciples apart in the way, and said unto them,

Mk 6:31 And he said unto them, Come ye yourselves apart into a desert place, and rest a while: for there were many coming and going, and they had no leisure so much as to eat.

Mk 7:24 And from thence he arose, and went into the borders of Tyre and Sidon, and entered into an house, and would have no man know *it:* but he could not be hid.

Lu 9:10 And the apostles, when they were returned, told him all that they had done. And he took them, and went aside privately into a desert place belonging to the city called Bethsaida.

Lu 22:41 And he was withdrawn from them about a stone's cast, and kneeled down, and prayed,

See **SOLITUDE**

DEPRAVITY *See* SIN

DERISION, *scoffing, ridicule*

2 S 16:6; 2 K 18:27; Jb 12:5; 17:2; 30:1; Ps 22:7; 35:21; 42:10; 44:13; 69:12; 79:4; 80:6; 109:25; 119:51; Je 20:7; 48:26; Lam 3:14, 63; Eze 36:3; Hab 1:10; Mt 27:43; Mk 15:19; Lu 16:14; 23:35; Jn 19:3

DESERTS, *vast barren isolated places*

Ex 5:3; Mt 14:15; Mk 6:32, 35; Lu 1:80; 4:42; 9:10, 12; Ac 8:26

Notable

Ex 19:2; 23:31; Nu 20:1; 1 S 23:24; 2 S 2:24

DESIRE, *want, wish, passion*

1. Evil

Nu 11:4 And the mixt multitude that *was* among them fell a lusting: and the children of Israel also wept again, and said, Who shall give us flesh to eat?

Ps 106:14 But lusted exceedingly in the wilderness, and tempted God in the desert.

Pr 21:10 The soul of the wicked desireth evil: his neighbour findeth no favour in his eyes.

Pr 30:15 The horseleach hath two daughters, *crying,* Give, give. There are three *things that are* never satisfied, *yea,* four *things* say not, *It is* enough:

Ho 7:7 They are all hot as an oven, and have devoured their judges; all their kings are fallen: *there is* none among them that calleth unto me.

Mi 7:3 That they may do evil with both hands earnestly, the prince asketh, and the judge *asketh* for a reward; and the great *man,* he uttereth his mischievous desire: so they wrap it up.

Hab 2:5 Yea also, because he transgresseth by wine, *he is* a proud man, neither keepeth at home, who enlargeth his desire as hell, and *is* as death, and cannot be satisfied, but gathereth unto him all nations, and heapeth unto him all people:

Mk 4:19 And the cares of this world, and the deceitfulness of riches, and the lusts of other things entering in, choke the word, and it becometh unfruitful.

Ro 7:8 But sin, taking occasion by the commandment, wrought in me all manner of concupiscence. For without the law sin *was* dead.

1 Co 10:6 Now these things were our examples, to the intent we should not lust after evil things, as they also lusted.

Ep 2:3 Among whom also we all had our conversation in times past in the lusts of our flesh, fulfilling the desires of the flesh and of the mind; and were by nature the children of wrath, even as others.

1 Ti 6:9 But they that will be rich fall into temptation and a snare, and *into* many foolish and hurtful lusts, which drown men in destruction and perdition.

2 Ti 4:3 For the time will come when they will not endure sound doctrine; but after their own lusts shall they heap to themselves teachers, having itching ears;

Ja 1:14 But every man is tempted, when he is drawn away of his own lust, and enticed.

Ja 4:2 Ye lust, and have not: ye kill, and desire to have, and cannot obtain: ye fight and war, yet ye have not, because ye ask not.

2 Pe 1:4 Whereby are given unto us exceeding great and precious promises: that by these ye might be partakers of the divine nature, having escaped the corruption that is in the world through lust.

2 Pe 3:3 Knowing this first, that there shall come in the last days scoffers, walking after their own lusts,

1 Jn 2:16 For all that *is* in the world, the lust of the flesh, and the lust of the eyes, and the pride of life, is not of the Father, but is of the world.

Jude 16 These are murmurers, complainers, walking after their own lusts; and their mouth speaketh great swelling *words,* having men's persons in admiration because of advantage.

2. Spiritual

Ex 33:18 And he said, I beseech thee, shew me thy glory.

De 18:6 And if a Levite come from any of thy gates out of all Israel, where he sojourned, and come with all the desire of his mind unto the place which the Lord shall choose;

1 S 7:2 And it came to pass, while the ark abode in Kirjath-jearim, that the time was long; for it was twenty years: and all the house of Israel lamented after the Lord.

2 S 23:5 Although my house *be* not so with God; yet he hath made with me an everlasting covenant, ordered in all *things,* and sure: for *this is* all my salvation, and all *my* desire, although he make *it* not to grow.

2 K 2:9 And it came to pass, when they were gone over, that Elijah said unto Elisha, Ask what I shall do for thee, before I be taken away from thee. And Elisha said, I pray thee, let a double portion of thy spirit be upon me.

2 Chr 1:11 And God said to Solomon, Because this was in thine heart, and thou hast not asked riches, wealth, or honour, nor the life of thine enemies, neither yet hast asked long life; but hast asked wisdom and knowledge for thyself, that thou mayest judge my people, over whom I have made thee king:

2 Chr 15:15 And all Judah rejoiced at the oath: for they had sworn with all their heart, and sought him with their whole desire; and he was found of them: and the Lord gave them rest round about.

Ne 1:11 O Lord, I beseech thee, let now thine ear be attentive to the prayer of thy servant, and to the prayer of thy servants, who desire to fear thy name: and prosper, I pray thee, thy servant this day, and grant him mercy in the sight of this man. For I was the king's cupbearer.

Jb 23:3 Oh that I knew where I might find him! *that* I might come *even* to his seat!

Ps 21:2 Thou hast given him his heart's desire, and hast not withholden the request of his lips. Selah.

Ps 27:4 One *thing* have I desired of the Lord, that will I seek after; that I may dwell in the house of the Lord all the days of my life, to behold the beauty of the Lord, and to enquire in his temple.

Ps 37:4 Delight thyself also in the LORD; and he shall give thee the desires of thine heart.

Ps 38:9 LORD, all my desire *is* before thee; and my groaning is not hid from thee.

Ps 42:1 As the hart panteth after the water brooks, so panteth my soul after thee, O God.

Ps 51:2 Wash me throughly from mine iniquity, and cleanse me from my sin.

Ps 63:1 O God, thou *art* my God; early will I seek thee: my soul thirsteth for thee, my flesh longeth for thee in a dry and thirsty land, where no water is;

Ps 73:25 Whom have I in heaven *but thee?* and *there is* none upon earth *that* I desire beside thee.

Ps 84:2 My soul longeth, yea, even fainteth for the courts of the LORD: my heart and my flesh crieth out for the living God.

Ps 90:16 Let thy work appear unto thy servants, and thy glory unto their children.

Ps 101:2 I will behave myself wisely in a perfect way. O when wilt thou come unto me? I will walk within my house with a perfect heart.

Ps 118:19 Open to me the gates of righteousness: I will go into them, *and* I will praise the LORD:

Ps 119:20 My soul breaketh for the longing *that it hath* unto thy judgments at all times.

Ps 119:40 Behold, I have longed after thy precepts: quicken me in thy righteousness.

Ps 119:81 My soul fainteth for thy salvation: *but* I hope in thy word.

Ps 119:131 I opened my mouth, and panted: for I longed for thy commandments.

Ps 130:6 My soul *waiteth* for the LORD more than they that watch for the morning: *I say, more than* they that watch for the morning.

Ps 143:6 I stretch forth my hands unto thee: my soul *thirsteth* after thee, as a thirsty land. Selah.

Pr 10:24 The fear of the wicked, it shall come upon him: but the desire of the righteous shall be granted.

Pr 11:23 The desire of the righteous *is* only good: *but* the expectation of the wicked *is* wrath.

Song 1:7 Tell me, O thou whom my soul loveth, where thou feedest, where thou makest *thy flock* to rest at noon: for why should I be as one that turneth aside by the flocks of thy companions?

Song 2:5 Stay me with flagons, comfort me with apples: for I *am* sick of love.

Song 5:8 I charge you, O daughters of Jerusalem, if ye find my beloved, that ye tell him, that I *am* sick of love.

Song 8:1 O that thou *wert* as my brother, that sucked the breasts of my mother! *when* I should find thee without, I would kiss thee; yea, I should not be despised.

Is 26:9 With my soul have I desired thee in the night; yea, with my spirit within me will I seek thee early: for when thy judgments *are* in the earth, the inhabitants of the world will learn righteousness.

Is 64:1 Oh that thou wouldest rend the heavens, that thou wouldest come down, that the mountains might flow down at thy presence,

Mt 5:6 Blessed *are* they which do hunger and thirst after righteousness: for they shall be filled.

Mt 13:17 For verily I say unto you, That many prophets and righteous *men* have desired to see *those things* which ye see, and have not seen *them;* and to hear *those things* which ye hear, and have not heard *them.*

Mk 5:18 And when he was come into the ship, he that had been possessed with the devil prayed him that he might be with him.

Mk 11:24 Therefore I say unto you, What things soever ye desire, when ye pray, believe that ye receive *them,* and ye shall have *them.*

Lu 1:53 He hath filled the hungry with good things; and the rich he hath sent empty away.

Lu 2:46 And it came to pass, that after three days they found him in the temple, sitting in the midst of the doctors, both hearing them, and asking them questions.

Lu 5:1 And it came to pass, that, as the people pressed upon him to hear the word of God, he stood by the lake of Gennesaret,

Lu 6:21 Blessed *are ye* that hunger now: for ye shall be filled. Blessed *are ye* that weep now: for ye shall laugh.

Lu 10:24 For I tell you, that many prophets and kings have desired to see those things which ye see, and have not seen *them;* and to hear those things which ye hear, and have not heard *them.*

Lu 15:17 And when he came to himself, he said, How many hired servants of my father's have bread enough and to spare, and I perish with hunger!

Jn 6:34 Then said they unto him, LORD, evermore give us this bread.

Jn 9:36 He answered and said, Who is he, LORD, that I might believe on him?

Ac 8:36 And as they went on *their* way, they came unto a certain water: and the eunuch said, See, *here is* water; what doth hinder me to be baptized?

1 Co 7:34 There is difference *also* between a wife and a virgin. The unmarried woman careth for the things of the Lord, that she may be holy both in body and in spirit: but she that is married careth for the things of the world, how she may please *her* husband.

1 Co 14:1 Follow after charity, and desire spiritual *gifts,* but rather that ye may prophesy.

2 Co 5:2 For in this we groan, earnestly desiring to be clothed upon with our house which is from heaven:

2 Co 7:11 For behold this selfsame thing, that ye sorrowed after a godly sort, what carefulness it wrought in you, yea, *what* clearing of yourselves, yea, *what* indignation, yea, *what* fear, yea, *what* vehement desire, yea, *what* zeal, yea, *what* revenge! In all *things* ye have approved yourselves to be clear in this matter.

Ph 3:12 Not as though I had already attained, either were already perfect: but I follow after, if that I may apprehend that for which also I am apprehended of Christ Jesus.

He 11:16 But now they desire a better *country,* that is, an heavenly: where-fore God is not ashamed to be called their God: for he hath prepared for them a city.

1 Pe 2:2 As newborn babes, desire the sincere milk of the word, that ye may grow thereby:

Re 22:17 And the Spirit and the bride say, Come. And let him that heareth say, Come. And let him that is athirst come. And whosoever will, let him take the water of life freely.

3. Spiritual Thirst

Jb 23:3 Oh that I knew where I might find him! *that* I might come *even* to his seat!

Ps 42:2 My soul thirsteth for God, for the living God: when shall I come and appear before God?

Ps 63:1 O God, thou *art* my God; early will I seek thee: my soul thirsteth for thee, my flesh longeth for thee in a dry and thirsty land, where no water is;

Ps 119:174 I have longed for thy salvation, O LORD; and thy law *is* my delight.

Ps 143:6 I stretch forth my hands unto thee: my soul *thirsteth* after thee, as a thirsty land. Selah.

Is 26:8 Yea, in the way of thy judgments, O LORD, have we waited for thee; the desire of *our* soul *is* to thy name, and to the remembrance of thee.

Am 8:11 Behold, the days come, saith the Lord GOD, that I will send a famine in the land, not a famine of bread, nor a thirst for water, but of hearing the words of the LORD:

DESOLATION, *as a result of sin*

1. Of Israel

Le 26:32; Jud 5:6; 2 K 22:19; 2 Chr 30:7; Ne 2:17; Ps 79:1; 80:12; 89:40; Is 1:8; 3:6; 5:5; 6:11; 7:23; 10:3; 17:9; 24:12; 27:10; 32:14; 33:8; 51:19; 64:12; Je 2:15; 4:7, 27; 6:8; 7:34; 9:11; 10:22, 25; 12:7, 11; 18:16; 19:8; 22:5; 25:9, 18; 26:9; 32:43; 33:10; 34:22; 44:2, 6; Lam 1:1, 4; 3:47; 5:18; Eze 5:14; 6:6, 14; 12:19; 14:15; 15:8; 19:13; 20:26; 23:33; 25:3; 33:24, 28; 36:4; Da 9:18; Ho 2:3, 12; 13:16; Jl 1:10, 17; 2:3; Am 7:9; Mi

3:12; 6:16; 7:13; Zep 1:13; Zec 7:14; Mt 23:38; Lu 13:35

2. Of Heathen Nations

Is 13:9, 20, 22; 14:23; 15:1; 16:9; 17:1; 19:7; 23:1, 14; 24:1; 34:10; 42:15; Je 25:12, 38; 46:19; 48:9, 34; 49:2, 13, 17, 20, 33; 50:3, 13, 23, 39; 51:26, 37, 62; Eze 25:13; 26:5; 29:9, 12; 30:7, 14; 32:15; 35:3, 15; Jl 3:19; Mi 1:6; Na 2:10; 3:7; Zep 2:4, 9, 13; 3:6; Zec 9:5; Re 18:19

3. Of the Wicked

Le 26:22; Jos 8:28; Jb 15:28, 34; Ps 34:21; 40:14–15; 69:25; 73:19; 109:10; Pr 3:25; Is 3:26; 5:9; 24:6; 47:11; 59:11; 60:12; Lam 4:5; 5:3; Eze 7:27; 26:14, 19; 29:10; 31:12; 33:29; 35:14; Ho 4:3; 5:9; 9:6; Mi 6:13; Zep 2:15; Mt 23:38; Ac 1:20; Re 18:22

See **ABOMINATION OF DESOLATION**

DESPAIR, *loss of hope; overcome with a sense of futility*

Ex 6:9 And Moses spake so unto the children of Israel: but they hearkened not unto Moses for anguish of spirit, and for cruel bondage.

De 28:34 So that thou shalt be mad for the sight of thine eyes which thou shalt see.

De 28:66 And thy life shall hang in doubt before thee; and thou shalt fear day and night, and shalt have none assurance of thy life:

Jb 7:6 My days are swifter than a weaver's shuttle, and are spent without hope.

Ps 88:15 I *am* afflicted and ready to die from *my* youth up: *while* I suffer thy terrors I am distracted.

Lam 3:18 And I said, My strength and my hope is perished from the LORD:

Eze 37:11 Then he said unto me, Son of man, these bones are the whole house of Israel: behold, they say, Our bones are dried, and our hope is lost: we are cut off for our parts.

Ac 27:20 And when neither sun nor stars in many days appeared, and no small tempest lay on *us,* all hope that we should be saved was then taken away.

Re 9:6 And in those days shall men seek death, and shall not find it; and shall desire to die, and death shall flee from them.

1. Leads to the Desire for Death

Ex 16:3; Nu 11:15; 14:2; 20:3; Jud 9:54; 16:30; 1 S 31:4; 1 K 19:4; 1 Chr 10:4; Jb 3:11, 21; 6:9; 7:15; 14:13; Je 8:3; 20:17; Jona 4:3; 2 Co 5:2; Re 9:6

2. Leads to Suicide

1 S 31:4; 2 S 17:23; 1 K 16:18; 1 Chr 10:4; Mt 27:5; Ac 1:18; 16:27

See **DESPONDENCY, HOPE**

DESPISERS, *those who look down on others with contempt or disdain*
Pr 1:30; 9:8; Mt 7:6; Ac 13:41; Ro 2:4; 2 Ti 3:3; He 10:28; 2 Pe 2:10

DESPONDENCY

MOSES

Nu 11:15 And if thou deal thus with me, kill me, I pray thee, out of hand, if I have found favour in thy sight; and let me not see my wretchedness.

JOSHUA

Jos 7:7 And Joshua said, Alas, O LORD God, wherefore hast thou at all brought this people over Jordan, to deliver us into the hand of the Amorites, to destroy us? would to God we had been content, and dwelt on the other side Jordan!

ELIJAH

1 K 19:4 But he himself went a day's journey into the wilderness, and came and sat down under a juniper tree: and he requested for himself that he might die; and said, It is enough; now, O LORD, take away my life; for I *am* not better than my fathers.

Jb 10:1 My soul is weary of my life; I will leave my complaint upon myself; I will speak in the bitterness of my soul.

Ps 31:10 For my life is spent with grief, and my years with sighing: my strength faileth because of mine iniquity, and my bones are consumed.

DAVID

Ps 42:6 O my God, my soul is cast down within me: therefore will I remember thee from the land of Jordan, and of the Hermonites, from the hill Mizar.

Ps 69:2 I sink in deep mire, where *there is* no standing: I am come into deep waters, where the floods overflow me.

Ps 73:16 When I thought to know this, it *was* too painful for me;

Ps 137:1 By the rivers of Babylon, there we sat down, yea, we wept, when we remembered Zion.

JEREMIAH

Je 15:10 Woe is me, my mother, that thou hast borne me a man of strife and a man of contention to the whole earth! I have neither lent on usury, nor men have lent to me on usury; *yet* every one of them doth curse me.

Mi 7:1 Woe is me! for I am as when they have gathered the summer fruits, as the grapegleanings of the vintage: *there is* no cluster to eat: my soul desired the firstripe fruit.

Lu 24:17 And he said unto them, What manner of communications *are* these that ye have one to another, as ye walk, and are sad?

See **AFFLICTIONS, CHEERFULNESS**

DESTRUCTION

1. Sudden

See **INSECURITY**

2. Complete

Ge 6:7, 13, 17; 7:4; 19:13; Ex 17:14; Le 26:38; Nu 24:20; De 4:26; 6:15; 7:4, 23; 9:25; 12:2; 13:15; 20:16; 28:45, 62; 1 K 20:42; 2 K 21:13; 1 Chr 4:41; 2 Chr 14:13; 25:16; 36:17; Jb 20:26; 21:20; Ps 2:9; 5:6; 28:5; 36:12; 37:38; 52:5; 73:18, 27; 92:7; 106:11, 23; 110:6; 139:19; Pr 1:27, 32; 10:29; 13:13; 15:24; 21:15 ; Is 1:28; 9:14; 13:6; 14:23; 23:11; 24:3, 12; 28:22; 30:14; 34:2; Je 4:20; 5:10; 6:12, 26; 7:20; 12:17; 13:14; 19:11; 22:7; 25:9; 46:20; 48:3, 8, 42; 51:3, 22, 40, 54; Lam 2:8; 3:47, 66; Eze 7:25; 9:6;

13:14; 16:41; 21:32; 23:25; 25:7, 13; 26:4, 17, 21; 27:27, 36; 28:16, 19; 30:8; 32:9; Ho 7:13; 10:8; 11:6; Jl 1:15; Am 1:7; 9:1, 8; Obad 9, 18; Na 2:13; Zep 1:2; 2:5, 9; Hag 2:22; Zec 12:9; Mal 4:1 Mt 21:44; 22:7; Mk 12:9; Lu 3:9; 19:44; 2 Th 1:9; Ja 4:12; 2 Pe 2:12; Re 11:18; 18:21

3. Examples

Ge 7:21; 34:29; Ex 14:28; Nu 21:3; De 2:34; 3:6; Jos 2:10; 6:21; 8:26; 10:1, 28, 35, 39; 11:12, 20; 24:8; Jud 1:17; 18:27; 20:48; 1 S 5:9; 15:8; Ps 9:5; Is 25:2; Lam 2:22; 4:10; Am 2:9; Zep 3:6; Lu 17:29

See **THREATENINGS**

DETERIORATION, *a tendency of the sinful life*

Is 1:22 Thy silver is become dross, thy wine mixed with water:

Is 3:12 *As for* my people, children *are* their oppressors, and women rule over them. O my people, they which lead thee cause *thee* to err, and destroy the way of thy paths.

Je 6:28 They *are* all grievous revolters, walking with slanders: *they are* brass and iron; they *are* all corrupters.

Je 7:26 Yet they hearkened not unto me, nor inclined their ear, but hardened their neck: they did worse than their fathers.

Je 16:12 And ye have done worse than your fathers; for, behold, ye walk every one after the imagination of his evil heart, that they may not hearken unto me:

Lam 4:1 How is the gold become dim! *how* is the most fine gold changed! the stones of the sanctuary are poured out in the top of every street.

Eze 5:6 And she hath changed my judgments into wickedness more than the nations, and my statutes more than the countries that *are* round about her: for they have refused my judgments and my statutes, they have not walked in them.

Eze 16:47 Yet hast thou not walked after their ways, nor done after their abominations: but, as *if that were* a very little *thing,* thou wast corrupted more than they in all thy ways.

Ho 13:2 And now they sin more and more, and have made them molten images of their silver, *and* idols according to their own understanding, all of it the work of the craftsmen: they say of them, Let the men that sacrifice kiss the calves.

Lu 11:26 Then goeth he, and taketh *to him* seven other spirits more wicked than himself; and they enter in, and dwell there: and the last *state* of that man is worse than the first.

2 Ti 3:13 But evil men and seducers shall wax worse and worse, deceiving, and being deceived.

2 Pe 2:20 For if after they have escaped the pollutions of the world through the knowledge of the Lord and Saviour Jesus Christ, they are again entangled therein, and overcome, the latter end is worse with them than the beginning.

See **WANDERERS**

DEUTERONOMY

Name: Derived from two Greek words, "deuteros," meaning second, and "nomos," law.

Author: Moses (commonly accepted). The final chapter was probably recorded by Joshua.

Date Written: 1407–1406 B.C.

Purpose: The former generation of Israel had died in the wilderness; hence it was important that the law should be repeated and expounded to the new generation before they entered the Promised Land.

To Whom Written: The children of Israel, the generation which would enter and conquer the Promised Land.

Main Theme: A rehearsal of the laws proclaimed at Sinai, with a call to obedience, interspersed with a review of the experiences of the old generation. The divine requirement of obedience is highlighted (10:12–13).

Key Word: Remember. It is frequently repeated throughout the entire book.

Key Verses: 6:1–4.

DEVIL *See* **DESIRE**

DEVOTIONAL LIFE, *cultivating a personal relationship with God*

1. Morning Devotions

Ge 22:2–3 And he said, Take now thy son, thine only *son* Isaac, whom thou lovest, and get thee into the land of Moriah; and offer him there for a burnt offering upon one of the mountains which I will tell thee of.

And Abraham rose up early in the morning, and saddled his ass, and took two of his young men with him, and Isaac his son, and clave the wood for the burnt offering, and rose up, and went unto the place of which God had told him.

Ge 28:16 And Jacob awaked out of his sleep, and he said, Surely the LORD is in this place; and I knew *it* not.

Ge 28:18 And Jacob rose up early in the morning, and took the stone that he had put *for* his pillows, and set it up *for* a pillar, and poured oil upon the top of it.

Ex 24:4 And Moses wrote all the words of the LORD, and rose up early in the morning, and builded an altar under the hill, and twelve pillars, according to the twelve tribes of Israel.

Jud 21:4 And it came to pass on the morrow, that the people rose early, and built there an altar, and offered burnt offerings and peace offerings.

1 S 1:19 And they rose up in the morning early, and worshipped before the LORD, and returned, and came to their house to Ramah: and Elkanah knew Hannah his wife; and the LORD remembered her.

2 Chr 29:20 Then Hezekiah the king rose early, and gathered the rulers of the city, and went up to the house of the LORD.

Jb 1:5 And it was so, when the days of *their* feasting were gone about, that Job sent and sanctified them, and rose up early in the morning, and offered burnt offerings *according* to the number of them all: for Job said, It may be that my sons have sinned, and cursed God in their hearts. Thus did Job continually.

Ps 57:8 Awake up, my glory; awake, psaltery and harp: I *myself* will awake early.

Ps 119:147 I prevented the dawning of the morning, and cried: I hoped in thy word.

Song 7:12 Let us get up early to the vineyards; let us see if the vine flourish, *whether* the tender grape appear, *and* the pomegranates bud forth: there will I give thee my loves.

Mt 28:1 In the end of the sabbath, as it began to dawn toward the first *day* of the week, came Mary Magdalene and the other Mary to see the sepulchre.

Mk 1:35 And in the morning, rising up a great while before day, he went out, and departed into a solitary place, and there prayed.

Lu 21:38 And all the people came early in the morning to him in the temple, for to hear him.

Lu 24:1 Now upon the first *day* of the week, very early in the morning, they came unto the sepulchre, bringing the spices which they had prepared, and certain *others* with them.

Jn 8:2 And early in the morning he came again into the temple, and all the people came unto him; and he sat down, and taught them.

Ac 5:21 And when they heard *that,* they entered into the temple early in the morning, and taught. But the high priest came, and they that were with him, and called the council together, and all the senate of the children of Israel and sent to the prison to have them brought.

2. *Prayerfulness*

Ge 4:26 And to Seth, to him also there was born a son; and he called his name Enos: then began men to call upon the name of the LORD.

Ge 12:8 And he removed from thence unto a mountain on the east of Bethel, and pitched his tent, *having* Bethel on the west, and Hai on the east: and there he builded an altar unto the LORD, and called upon the name of the LORD.

Ge 21:33 And *Abraham* planted a grove in Beer-sheba, and called there on the name of the LORD, the everlasting God.

Ge 25:22 And the children struggled together within her; and she said, If *it be* so, why *am* I thus? And she went to enquire of the LORD.

Ge 26:25 And he builded an altar there, and called upon the name of the LORD and pitched his tent there: and there Isaac's servants digged a well.

Ge 32:9 And Jacob said, O God of my father Abraham, and God of my father Isaac, the LORD which saidst unto me, Return unto thy country, and to thy kindred, and I will deal well with thee:

Ex 5:22 And Moses returned unto the LORD, and said, LORD, wherefore hast thou *so* evil entreated this people? why *is* it *that* thou hast sent me?

Jud 13:8 Then Manoah intreated the LORD, and said, O my LORD, let the man of God which thou didst send come again unto us, and teach us what we shall do unto the child that shall be born.

Jud 15:18 And he was sore athirst, and called on the LORD, and said, Thou hast given this great deliverance into the hand of thy servant: and now shall I die for thirst, and fall into the hand of the uncircumcised?

1 S 2:1 And Hannah prayed, and said, My heart rejoiceth in the LORD, mine horn is exalted in the LORD: my mouth is enlarged over mine enemies; because I rejoice in thy salvation.

1 S 8:6 But the thing displeased Samuel, when they said, Give us a king to judge us. And Samuel prayed unto the LORD.

1 S 23:10 Then said David, O LORD God of Israel, thy servant hath certainly heard that Saul seeketh to come to Keilah, to destroy the city for my sake.

2 S 7:27 For thou, O LORD of hosts, God of Israel, hast revealed to thy servant, saying, I will build thee an house: therefore hath thy servant found in his heart to pray this prayer unto thee.

2 S 22:4 I will call on the LORD, *who is* worthy to be praised: so shall I be saved from mine enemies.

1 K 22:5 And Jehoshaphat said unto the king of Israel, Enquire, I pray thee, at the word of the LORD to day.

2 K 4:33 He went in therefore, and shut the door upon them twain, and prayed unto the LORD.

2 K 6:17 And Elisha prayed, and said, LORD, I pray thee, open his eyes, that he may see. And the LORD opened the eyes of the young man; and he saw: and, behold, the mountain *was* full of horses and chariots of fire round about Elisha.

2 K 19:14 And Hezekiah received the letter of the hand of the messengers, and read it: and Hezekiah went up into the house of the LORD, and spread it before the LORD.

2 K 20:2 Then he turned his face to the wall, and prayed unto the LORD, saying,

1 Chr 4:10 And Jabez called on the God of Israel, saying, Oh that thou wouldest bless me indeed, and enlarge my coast, and that thine hand might be with me, and that thou wouldest keep *me* from evil, that it may not grieve me! And God granted him that which he requested.

1 Chr 17:25 For thou, O my God, hast told thy servant that thou wilt build him an house: therefore thy servant hath found *in his heart* to pray before thee.

2 Chr 32:24 In those days Hezekiah was sick to the death, and prayed unto the LORD: and he spake unto him, and he gave him a sign.

2 Chr 34:21 Go, enquire of the LORD for me, and for them that are left in Israel and in Judah, concerning the words of the book that is found: for great *is* the wrath of the LORD that is poured out upon us, because our fathers have not kept the word of the LORD, to do after all that is written in this book.

Ne 1:5 And said, I beseech thee, O LORD God of heaven, the great and terrible God, that keepeth covenant and mercy for them that love him and observe his commandments:

Ne 2:4 Then the king said unto me, For what dost thou make request? So I prayed to the God of heaven.

Ne 4:9 Nevertheless we made our prayer unto our God, and set a watch against them day and night, because of them.

Jb 9:15 Whom, though I were righteous, *yet* would I not answer, *but* I would make supplication to my judge.

Jb 16:20 My friends scorn me: *but* mine eye poureth out *tears* unto God.

Jb 22:27 Thou shalt make thy prayer unto him, and he shall hear thee, and thou shalt pay thy vows.

Jb 23:4 I would order *my* cause before him, and fill my mouth with arguments.

Ps 4:1 Hear me when I call, O God of my righteousness: thou hast enlarged me *when I was* in distress; have mercy upon me, and hear my prayer.

Ps 5:3 My voice shalt thou hear in the morning, O LORD; in the morning will I direct *my prayer* unto thee, and will look up.

Ps 17:6 I have called upon thee, for thou wilt hear me, O God: incline thine ear unto me, *and hear* my speech.

Ps 18:3 I will call upon the LORD, *who is worthy* to be praised: so shall I be saved from mine enemies.

Ps 25:1 Unto thee, O LORD, do I lift up my soul.

Ps 27:4 One *thing* have I desired of the LORD, that will I seek after; that I may dwell in the house of the LORD all the days of my life, to behold the beauty of the LORD, and to enquire in his temple.

Ps 30:8 I cried to thee, O LORD; and unto the LORD I made supplication.

Ps 31:17 Let me not be ashamed, O LORD; for I have called upon thee: let the wicked be ashamed, *and* let them be silent in the grave.

Ps 42:8 *Yet* the LORD will command his lovingkindness in the daytime, and in the night his song *shall be* with me, *and* my prayer unto the God of my life.

Ps 55:17 Evening, and morning, and at noon, will I pray, and cry aloud: and he shall hear my voice.

Ps 69:13 But as for me, my prayer *is* unto thee, O LORD, *in* an acceptable time: O God, in the multitude of thy mercy hear me, in the truth of thy salvation.

Ps 80:18 So will not we go back from thee: quicken us, and we will call upon thy name.

Ps 86:1 Bow down thine ear, O LORD, hear me: for I *am* poor and needy.

Ps 88:1 O LORD God of my salvation, I have cried day *and* night before thee:

Ps 88:9 Mine eye mourneth by reason of affliction: LORD, I have called daily upon thee, I have stretched out my hands unto thee.

Ps 99:6 Moses and Aaron among his priests, and Samuel among them that call upon his name; they called upon the LORD, and he answered them.

Ps 109:4 For my love they are my adversaries: but I *give myself unto* prayer.

Ps 116:2 Because he hath inclined his ear unto me, therefore will I call upon *him* as long as I live.

Ps 116:13 I will take the cup of salvation, and call upon the name of the LORD.

Ps 119:62 At midnight I will rise to give thanks unto thee because of thy righteous judgments.

Ps 119:147 I prevented the dawning of the morning, and cried: I hoped in thy word.

Ps 140:6 I said unto the LORD, Thou *art* my God: hear the voice of my supplications, O LORD.

Ps 141:1 LORD, I cry unto thee: make haste unto me; give ear unto my voice, when I cry unto thee.

Ps 141:5 Let the righteous smite me; *it shall be* a kindness: and let him reprove me; *it shall be* an excellent oil, *which* shall not break my head: for yet my prayer also *shall be* in their calamities.

Ps 143:1 Hear my prayer, O LORD, give ear to my supplications: in thy faithfulness answer me, *and* in thy righteousness.

Is 19:20 And it shall be for a sign and for a witness unto the LORD of hosts in the land of Egypt: for they shall cry unto the LORD because of the oppressors, and he shall send them a saviour, and a great one, and he shall deliver them.

Is 38:2 Then Hezekiah turned his face toward the wall, and prayed unto the LORD,

Je 18:19 Give heed to me, O LORD, and hearken to the voice of them that contend with me.

Je 26:19 Did Hezekiah king of Judah and all Judah put him at all to death? did he not fear the LORD, and besought the LORD, and the LORD, repented him of the evil which he had pronounced against them? Thus might we procure great evil against our souls.

Je 32:16 Now when I had delivered the evidence of the purchase unto Baruch the son of Neriah, I prayed unto the LORD, saying,

Lam 3:55 I called upon thy name, O LORD, out of the low dungeon.

Da 6:11 Then these men assembled, and found Daniel praying and making supplication before his God.

Da 6:13 Then answered they and said before the king, That Daniel, which *is* of the children of the captivity of Judah, regardeth not thee, O king, nor the decree that thou hast signed, but maketh his petition three times a day.

Da 9:3 And I set my face unto the LORD God, to seek by prayer and supplications, with fasting, and sackcloth, and ashes:

Da 9:17 Now therefore, O our God, hear the prayer of thy servant, and his supplications, and cause thy face to shine upon thy sanctuary that is desolate, for the LORD's sake.

Zec 8:21 And the inhabitants of one *city* shall go to another, saying, Let us go speedily to pray before the LORD, and to seek the LORD of hosts: I will go also.

Zec 12:10 And I will pour upon the house of David, and upon the inhabitants of Jerusalem, the spirit of grace and of supplications: and they shall look upon me whom they have pierced, and they shall mourn for him, as one mourneth for *his* only *son,* and shall be in bitterness for him, as one that is in bitterness for *his* firstborn.

Zec 13:9 And I will bring the third part through the fire, and will refine them as silver is refined, and will try them as gold is tried: they shall call on my name, and I will hear them: I will say, It *is* my people: and they shall say, The LORD *is* my God

Mk 1:35 And in the morning, rising up a great while before day, he went out, and departed into a solitary place, and there prayed.

Mk 14:32 And they came to a place which was named Gethsemane: and he saith to his disciples, Sit ye here, while I shall pray.

Lu 2:37 And she *was* a widow of about fourscore and four years, which departed not from the temple, but served *God* with fastings and prayers night and day.

Lu 9:18 And it came to pass, as he was alone praying, his disciples were with him: and he asked them, saying, Whom say the people that I am?

Lu 11:1 And it came to pass, that, as he was praying in a certain place, when he ceased, one of his disciples said unto him, Lord, teach us to pray, as John also taught his disciples.

Lu 18:10 Two men went up into the temple to pray; the one a Pharisee, and the other a publican.

Ac 1:24 And they prayed, and said, Thou, Lord, which knowest the hearts of all *men,* shew whether of these two thou hast chosen,

Ac 2:42 And they continued stedfastly in the apostles' doctrine and fellowship, and in breaking of bread, and in prayers.

Ac 6:4 But we will give ourselves continually to prayer, and to the ministry of the word.

Ac 9:11 And the Lord *said* unto him, Arise, and go into the street which is called Straight, and enquire in the house of Judas for *one* called Saul, of Tarsus: for, behold, he prayeth,

Ac 10:2 A devout *man,* and one that feared God with all his house, which gave much alms to the people, and prayed to God alway.

Ac 10:9 On the morrow, as they went on their journey, and drew nigh unto the city, Peter went up upon the housetop to pray about the sixth hour:

Ac 11:5 I was in the city of Joppa praying: and in a trance I saw a vision, A certain vessel descend, as it had been a great sheet, let down from heaven by four corners; and it came even to me:

Ac 14:23 And when they had ordained them elders in every church, and had prayed with fasting, they commended them to the Lord, on whom they believed.

Ac 16:25 And at midnight Paul and Silas prayed, and sang praises unto God: and the prisoners heard them.

Ac 20:36 And when he had thus spoken, he kneeled down, and prayed with them all.

Ac 22:17 And it came to pass, that, when I was come again to Jerusalem, even while I prayed in the temple, I was in a trance;

Ac 28:8 And it came to pass, that the father of Publius lay sick of a fever and of a bloody flux: to whom Paul entered in, and prayed, and laid his hands on him, and healed him.

Ro 1:10 Making request, if by any means now at length I might have a prosperous journey by the will of God to come unto you.

1 Co 1:2 Unto the church of God which is at Corinth, to them that are sanctified in Christ Jesus, called *to be* saints, with all that in every place call upon the name of Jesus Christ our Lord, both theirs and ours:

1 Th 3:10 Night and day praying exceedingly that we might see your face, and might perfect that which is lacking in your faith?

1 Ti 5:5 Now she that is a widow indeed, and desolate, trusteth in God, and continueth in supplications and prayers night and day.

2 Ti 1:3 I thank God, whom I serve from *my* forefathers with pure conscience, that without ceasing I have remembrance of thee in my prayers night and day;

Phm 1:4 I thank my God, making mention of thee always in my prayers,

3. Prayer Three Times a Day

Ps 55:17 Evening, and morning, and at noon, will I pray, and cry aloud: and he shall hear my voice.

Da 6:10 Now when Daniel knew that the writing was signed, he went into his house; and his windows being open in his chamber toward Jerusalem, he kneeled upon his knees three times a day, and prayed, and gave thanks before his God, as he did aforetime.

4. All-Night Prayers

Ge 32:24 And Jacob was left alone; and there wrestled a man with him until the breaking of the day.

1 S 15:11 It repenteth me that I have set up Saul *to be* king: for he is turned back from following me, and hath not performed my commandments. And it grieved Samuel; and he cried unto the LORD all night.

Ps 55:17 Evening, and morning, and at noon, will I pray, and cry aloud: and he shall hear my voice.

Ps 119:62 At midnight I will rise to give thanks unto thee because of thy righteous judgments.

Mt 26:36 Then cometh Jesus with them unto a place called Gethsemane, and saith unto the disciples, Sit ye here, while I go and pray yonder.

Lu 6:12 And it came to pass in those days, that he went out into a mountain to pray, and continued all night in prayer to God.

Ac 16:25 And at midnight Paul and Silas prayed, and sang praises unto God: and the prisoners heard them.

See **FELLOWSHIP, MIND, PRAYER**

DEVOUTNESS *See* **CONSECRATION, FAMILY**

DEW *See* **WEATHER**

DIAMONDS *See* **STONES**

DIBON, *a town of Moab*

Dibon, once the capital of Moab, is located on a highway three miles north of the river Arnon. Israel captured Dibon (Nu 21:21–30) and it was assigned to Reuben (Nu 32:3–5; Jos

13:15–23). Later the Israelites served Moab for about eighteen years (Jud 3:12–30). David conquered Moab (2 S 8:2), but it was likely that Moab attained independence again with the death of Solomon. The Lord intervened against the Moabites when they invaded Judah (2 Chr 20:1–30), and Omri ultimately forced Moab to pay heavy tribute (2 K 3:4). When Mesha revolted upon the death of Ahab, Jehoram and Jehoshaphat's coalition probably seized Dibon but failed to conquer the inhabitants of Moab (1 K 22:47; 2 K 3:4–27).

See **CITIES**

DILEMMA

De 28:29 And thou shalt grope at noonday, as the blind gropeth in darkness, and thou shalt not prosper in thy ways: and thou shalt be only oppressed and spoiled evermore, and no man shall save *thee*.

Ps 107:27 They reel to and fro, and stagger like a drunken man, and are at their wit's end.

Mt 27:22 Pilate saith unto them, What shall I do then with Jesus which is called Christ? *They* all say unto him, Let him be crucified.

Lu 12:17 And he thought within himself, saying, What shall I do, because I have no room where to bestow my fruits?

Lu 16:3 Then the steward said within himself, What shall I do? for my lord taketh away from me the stewardship: I cannot dig; to beg I am ashamed.

Jn 12:35 Then Jesus said unto them, Yet a little while is the light with you. Walk while ye have the light, lest darkness come upon you: for he that walketh in darkness knoweth not whither he goeth.

Ac 4:16 Saying, What shall we do to these men? for that indeed a notable miracle hath been done by them *is* manifest to all them that dwell in Jerusalem; and we cannot deny *it*.

Ac 5:24 Now when the high priest and the captain of the temple and the chief priests heard these things, they doubted of them whereunto this would grow.

DINNER See FOOD

DISAPPOINTMENT, of the sinful life

Ge 27:34; De 28:30, 39; Jb 5:5; 11:20; 17:11; 20:18; 27:17; 30:26; 31:8; Ps 109:11; 112:10; Pr 5:10; 10:3; 11:7; Ec 2:20; 6:2; Is 17:11; 26:18; 62:8; Je 2:13; 5:17; 8:15; 12:13; 14:19; Ho 2:7, 12; 4:10; 8:7; Am 5:11; Mi 1:12; 6:15; Zep 1:13; Hag 1:6, 9; 2:16; Mt 20:10

See **DESPAIR, DESPONDENCY, DISCOURAGEMENT, EXPECTATION**

DISCERNMENT

1 K 3:9 Give therefore thy servant an understanding heart to judge thy people, that I may discern between good and bad: for who is able to judge this thy so great a people?

Pr 1:2 To know wisdom and instruction; to perceive the words of understanding;

Pr 21:11 When the scorner is punished, the simple is made wise: and when the wise is instructed, he receiveth knowledge.

Is 7:15 Butter and honey shall he eat, that he may know to refuse the evil, and choose the good.

Is 11:3 And shall make him of quick understanding in the fear of the LORD: and he shall not judge after the sight of his eyes, neither reprove after the hearing of his ears:

Eze 40:4 And the man said unto me, Son of man, behold with thine eyes, and hear with thine ears, and set thine heart upon all that I shall shew thee; for to the intent that I might shew *them* unto thee *art* thou brought hither: declare all that thou seest to the house of Israel.

Da 5:12 Forasmuch as an excellent spirit, and knowledge, and understanding, interpreting of dreams, and shewing of hard sentences, and dissolving of doubts, were found in the same Daniel, whom the king named Belteshazzar: now let Daniel be called, and he will shew the interpretation.

1 Co 2:14 But the natural man receiveth not the things of the Spirit of God: for they are foolishness unto him: neither can he know *them*, because they are spiritually discerned.

He 5:14 But strong meat belongeth to them that are of full age, *even* those who by reason of use have their senses exercised to discern both good and evil.

See **DULLNESS, WISDOM**

DISCIPLE

1. Beloved, John

Jn 13:23; 19:26; 20:2; 21:7, 20

2. Empowered

Mk 3:15 And to have power to heal sicknesses, and to cast out devils:

Mk 6:7 And he called *unto him* the twelve, and began to send them forth by two and two; and gave them power over unclean spirits;

Lu 10:19 Behold, I give unto you power to tread on serpents and scorpions, and over all the power of the enemy: and nothing shall by any means hurt you.

Lu 12:12 For the Holy Ghost shall teach you in the same hour what ye ought to say.

Ac 4:33 And with great power gave the apostles witness of the resurrection of the Lord Jesus: and great grace was upon them all.

Ac 6:10 And they were not able to resist the wisdom and the spirit by which he spake.

DISCIPLESHIP

1. Conditions

Mt 4:20; 9:9; 10:38; 16:24; 27:57; Mk 1:18; 2:14; 8:34; 10:21, 28; Lu 5:11, 28; 9:23, 59; 14:26, 33; 18:22, 28; Jn 8:12, 31; 13:35; 15:8; 21:19; 1 Pe 2:21

SELF-DENIAL

Mt 16:24 Then said Jesus unto his disciples, If any *man* will come after me, let him deny himself, and take up his cross, and follow me.

RENUNCIATION OF FAMILY

Lu 14:26 If any *man* come to me, and hate not his father, and mother, and wife, and children, and brethren, and sisters, yea, and his own life also, he cannot be my disciple.

LEAVING ALL

Lu 14:33 So likewise, whosoever he be of you that forsaketh not all that he hath, he cannot be my disciple.

STEADFASTNESS

Jn 8:31 Then said Jesus to those Jews which believed on him, If ye continue in my word, *then* are ye my disciples indeed;

FRUITFULNESS

Jn 15:8 Herein is my Father glorified, that ye bear much fruit; so shall ye be my disciples.

2. Examples

Mt 5:15; Mk 4:21; Lu 8:16; 11:33; Jn 3:1–2; 7:13, 50; 12:42; 19:38

3. Blessings

SPIRITUAL KNOWLEDGE

Ho 6:3 Then shall we know, *if* we follow on to know the LORD: his going forth is prepared as the morning; and he shall come unto us as the rain, as the latter *and* former rain unto the earth.

Lu 14:27 And whosoever doth not bear his cross, and come after me, cannot be my disciple.

SPIRITUAL LIGHT

Jn 8:12 Then spake Jesus again unto them, saying, I am the light of the world: he that followeth me shall not walk in darkness, but shall have the light of life.

GUIDANCE OF THE STILL SMALL VOICE

Jn 10:27 My sheep hear my voice, and I know them, and they follow me:

HEAVENLY HONOR

Jn 12:26 If any man serve me, let him follow me; and where I am, there shall also my servant be: if any man serve me, him will *my* Father honour.

Jn 21:22 Jesus saith unto him, If I will that he tarry till I come, what *is that* to thee? follow thou me.

Ep 5:1 Be ye therefore followers of God, as dear children;

A DIVINE EXAMPLE

1 Pe 2:21 For even hereunto were ye called: because Christ also suffered for us, leaving us an example, that ye should follow his steps:

Re 14:4 These are they which were not defiled with women; for they are virgins. These are they which follow the Lamb whithersoever he goeth. These were redeemed from among men, *being* the firstfruits unto God and to the Lamb.

DISCONTENTMENT

Ex 2:24 And God heard their groaning, and God remembered his covenant with Abraham, with Isaac, and with Jacob.

Nu 11:12 Have I conceived all this people? have I begotten them, that thou shouldest say unto me, Carry them in thy bosom, as a nursing father beareth the sucking child, unto the land which thou swarest unto their fathers?

Jb 6:2 O that my grief were throughly weighed, and my calamity laid in the balances together!

Jb 7:11 Therefore I will not refrain my mouth; I will speak in the anguish of my spirit; I will complain in the bitterness of my soul.

Jb 9:17 For he breaketh me with a tempest, and multiplieth my wounds without cause.

Jb 9:22 This *is* one *thing*, therefore I said *it*, He destroyeth the perfect and the wicked.

Jb 10:1 My soul is weary of my life; I will leave my complaint upon myself; I will speak in the bitterness of my soul.

Jb 23:2 Even to day *is* my complaint bitter: my stroke is heavier than my groaning.

Ps 22:1 My God, my God, why hast thou forsaken me? *why art thou so* far from helping me, *and from* the words of my roaring?

Ps 55:2 Attend unto me, and hear me: I mourn in my complaint, and make a noise;

Ps 77:3 I remembered God, and was troubled: I complained, and my spirit was overwhelmed. Selah.

Ps 88:6 Thou hast laid me in the lowest pit, in darkness, in the deeps.

Ps 142:2 I poured out my complaint before him; I shewed before him my trouble.

Je 15:18 Why is my pain perpetual, and my wound incurable, *which* refuseth to be healed? wilt thou be altogether unto me as a liar, *and as* waters *that* fail?

Hab 1:3 Why dost thou shew me iniquity, and cause *me* to behold grievance? for spoiling and violence *are* before me: and there are *that* raise up strife and contention.

Hab 1:13 *Thou art* of purer eyes than to behold evil, and canst not look on iniquity: wherefore lookest thou upon them that deal treacherously, *and* holdest thy tongue when the wicked devoureth *the man that is* more righteous than he?

He 12:11 Now no chastening for the present seemeth to be joyous, but grievous: nevertheless afterward it yieldeth the peaceable fruit of righteousness unto them which are exercised thereby.

See **CONTENTMENT**

DISCOURAGEMENT

De 13:4; 1 K 14:8; Ps 63:8; 94:15; Pr 15:9; 21:21; Is 51:1; Je 2:2; Ho 6:3; 11:10; Mt 4:19, 22; 10:38; 19:28; 20:34; Mk 1:17, 20; 2:15; 3:7; 6:1; 10:52; 15:41; Lu 9:57; 14:27; 18:28, 43; Jn 1:37; 8:12; 10:4, 27; 12:26; 21:22; Ep 5:1; Ph 3:12; 1 Pe 2:21; Re 14:4; 19:14

See **ENCOURAGEMENT**

DISCOURTESY

NABAL

1 S 25:3 Now the name of the man *was* Nabal; and the name of his wife *was* Abigail: and *she was* a woman of good

understanding, and of a beautiful countenance: but the man *was* churlish and evil in his doings; and he *was* of the house of Caleb.

REHOBOAM

1 K 12:13 And the king answered the people roughly, and forsook the old men's counsel that they gave him;

THE RICH

Pr 18:23 The poor useth intreaties; but the rich answereth roughly.

SIMON

Lu 7:44 And he turned to the woman, and said unto Simon, Seest thou this woman? I entered into thine house, thou gavest me no water for my feet: but she hath washed my feet with tears, and wiped *them* with the hairs of her head.

MARTHA

Lu 10:40 But Martha was cumbered about much serving, and came to him, and said, Lord, dost thou not care that my sister hath left me to serve alone? bid her therefore that she help me.

THE WOMAN OF SAMARIA

Jn 4:9 Then saith the woman of Samaria unto him, How is it that thou, being a Jew, askest drink of me, which am a woman of Samaria? for the Jews have no dealings with the Samaritans.

See **COURTESY**

DISCRETION, *prudence, cautious reserve*

Ge 32:7 Then Jacob was greatly afraid and distressed: and he divided the people that *was* with him, and the flocks, and herds, and the camels, into two bands;

Ge 32:20 And say ye moreover, Behold, thy servant Jacob *is* behind us. For he said, I will appease him with the present that goeth before me, and afterward I will see his face; peradventure he will accept of me.

Ge 41:33 Now therefore let Pharaoh look out a man discreet and wise, and set him over the land of Egypt.

Ge 41:39 And Pharaoh said unto Joseph, Forasmuch as God hath shewed thee all this, *there is* none so discreet and wise as thou *art:*

1 S 18:5 And David went out whithersoever Saul sent him, *and* behaved himself wisely: and Saul set him over the men of war, and he was accepted in the sight of all the people, and also in the sight of Saul's servants.

1 S 25:18 Then Abigail made haste, and took two hundred loaves, and two bottles of wine, and five sheep ready dressed, and five measures of parched *corn,* and an hundred clusters of raisins, and two hundred cakes of figs, and laid *them* on asses.

1 Chr 12:32 And of the children of Issachar, *which were men* that had understanding of the times, to know what Israel ought to do; the heads of them *were* two hundred; and all their brethren *were* at their commandment.

2 Chr 11:23 And he dealt wisely, and dispersed of all his children throughout all the countries of Judah and Benjamin, unto every fenced city: and he gave them victual in abundance. And he desired many wives.

Ezr 8:18 And by the good hand of our God upon us they brought us a man of understanding, of the sons of Mahli, the son of Levi, the son of Israel; and Sherebiah, with his sons and his brethren, eighteen;

Ps 112:5 A good man sheweth favour, and lendeth: he will guide his affairs with discretion.

Pr 1:4 To give subtilty to the simple, to the young man knowledge and discretion.

Pr 2:11 Discretion shall preserve thee, understanding shall keep thee:

Pr 3:21 My son, let not them depart from thine eyes: keep sound wisdom and discretion:

Pr 5:2 That thou mayest regard discretion, and *that* thy lips may keep knowledge.

Pr 16:20 He that handleth a matter wisely shall find good: and whoso trusteth in the LORD, happy *is* he.

Pr 19:11 The discretion of a man deferreth his anger; and *it is* his glory to pass over a transgression.

Is 28:26 For his God doth instruct him to discretion, *and* doth teach him.

Da 6:3 Then this Daniel was preferred above the presidents and princes, because an excellent spirit *was* in him; and the king thought to set him over the whole realm.

Mt 27:19 When he was set down on the judgment seat, his wife sent unto him, saying, Have thou nothing to do with that just man: for I have suffered many things this day in a dream because of him.

Mk 12:34 And when Jesus saw that he answered discreetly, he said unto him, Thou art not far from the kingdom of God. And no man after that durst ask him *any question.*

Tit 2:5 *To be* discreet, chaste, keepers at home, good, obedient to their own husbands, that the word of God be not blasphemed.

Leads to Tactfulness

Jud 8:2 And he said unto them, What have I done now in comparison of you? *Is* not the gleaning of the grapes of Ephraim better than the vintage of Abi-ezer?

2 S 2:5 And David sent messengers unto the men of Jabesh-gilead, and said unto them, Blessed *be* ye of the LORD, that ye have shewed this kindness unto your lord, *even* unto Saul, and have buried him.

Ac 23:6 But when Paul perceived that the one part were Sadducees, and the other Pharisees, he cried out in the council, Men *and* brethren, I am a Pharisee, the son of a Pharisee: of the hope and resurrection of the dead I am called in question.

2 Co 6:3 Giving no offence in any thing, that the ministry be not blamed:

See **WISDOM**

DISEASE

1. Boils

Ex 9:9; Le 13:18; 2 K 20:7; Jb 2:7; Is 38:21

2. Epilepsy

Mt 4:24; 17:14–15

3. Fever

Le 26:16; De 28:22; Jb 30:30; Ps 38:7; Mk 1:30; Lu 4:38; Jn 4:52; Ac 28:8

4. Insanity

Da 4:33; Mt 4:24; 17:15

5. Leprosy

Le 13:2, 9, 15, 20, 25, 27, 30, 42, 52; 14:2, 32, 34, 57; De 24:8; 2 Chr 26:19; Mt 8:4; Mk 1:44

6. Loss of Appetite

1 S 1:7; 28:23; 2 S 12:17; 1 K 21:4; Jb 6:7; 33:20; Ps 102:4; 107:18

7. Palsy

Mt 4:24; 8:6; 9:2; Mk 2:4; Lu 5:18; Ac 8:7; 9:33

8. Ague, *a fever marked by chills and sweating*

Le 26:16

9. Consumption

Le 26:16; De 28:22

10. Dropsy, *excess accumulation of fluid in connective tissue*

Lu 14:2

11. Dysentery

Ac 28:8

12. Emerods, *hemorrhoids*

De 28:27; 1 S 5:6

13. Issue of Blood

Mt 9:20

14. Itch

De 28:27

15. Sun-stroke

2 K 4:18–19; Is 49:10

16. Ulcers

Is 1:6; Lu 16:20

See **HEALTH, SICKNESS**

DISFIGUREMENT *See* BEAUTY

DISGUISES

Ge 27:16; 38:14; 1 S 28:8; 1 K 14:2, 6; 20:38; 22:30; 2 Chr 18:29; 35:22; Jb 24:15

DISHONOR

2 K 19:21 This *is* the word that the LORD hath spoken concerning him; The virgin the daughter of Zion hath despised thee, *and* laughed thee to scorn; the daughter of Jerusalem hath shaken her head at thee.

2 Chr 21:20 Thirty and two years old was he when he began to reign, and he reigned in Jerusalem eight years, and departed without being desired. Howbeit they buried him in the city of David, but not in the sepulchres of the kings.

2 Chr 24:25 And when they were departed from him, (for they left him in great diseases,) his own servants conspired against him for the blood of the sons of Jehoiada the priest, and slew him on his bed, and he died: and they buried him in the city of David, but they buried him not in the sepulchres of the kings.

Est 3:2 And all the king's servants, that *were* in the king's gate, bowed, and reverenced Haman: for the king had so commanded concerning him. But Mordecai bowed not, nor did *him* reverence.

Est 5:9 Then went Haman forth that day joyful and with a glad heart: but when Haman saw Mordecai in the king's gate, that he stood not up, nor moved for him, he was full of indignation against Mordecai.

Jb 5:3 I have seen the foolish taking root: but suddenly I cursed his habitation.

Jb 27:23 *Men* shall clap their hands at him, and shall hiss him out of his place.

Ps 52:6 The righteous also shall see, and fear, and shall laugh at him:

Pr 12:8 A man shall be commended according to his wisdom: but he that is of a perverse heart shall be despised.

Pr 14:17 *He that is* soon angry dealeth foolishly: and a man of wicked devices is hated.

Pr 24:24 He that saith unto the wicked, Thou *art* righteous; him shall the people curse, nations shall abhor him:

Is 66:24 And they shall go forth, and look upon the carcases of the men that have transgressed against me: for their worm shall not die, neither shall their fire be quenched; and they shall be an abhorring unto all flesh.

Je 4:30 And *when* thou *art* spoiled, what wilt thou do? Though thou clothest thyself with crimson, though thou deckest thee with ornaments of gold, though thou rentest thy face with painting, in vain shalt thou make thyself fair; *thy* lovers will despise thee, they will seek thy life.

Da 4:32–33 And they shall drive thee from men, and thy dwelling *shall be* with the beasts of the field: they shall make thee to eat grass as oxen, and seven times shall pass over thee, until thou know that the most High ruleth in the kingdom of men, and giveth it to whomsoever he will.

The same hour was the thing fulfilled upon Nebuchadnezzar: and he was driven from men, and did eat grass as oxen, and his body was wet with the dew of heaven, till his hairs were grown like eagles' *feathers,* and his nails like birds' *claws.*

Da 12:2 And many of them that sleep in the dust of the earth shall awake, some to everlasting life, and some to shame *and* everlasting contempt.

Obad 2 Behold, I have made thee small among the heathen: thou art greatly despised.

Na 3:19 *There is* no healing of thy bruise; thy wound is grievous: all that hear the bruit of thee shall clap the hands over thee: for upon whom hath not thy wickedness passed continually?

Mal 1:4 Whereas Edom saith, We are impoverished, but we will return and build the desolate places; thus saith the LORD of hosts, They shall build, but I will throw down; and they shall call them, The border of wickedness, and, The people against whom the LORD hath indignation for ever.

See **HONOR**

DISMISSALS

Of the Needy by the Disciples

Mt 14:15 And when it was evening, his disciples came to him, saying, This is a desert place, and the time is now past; send the multitude away, that they may go into the villages, and buy themselves victuals.

Mt 15:23 But he answered her not a word. And his disciples came and besought him, saying, Send her away; for she crieth after us.

Mk 6:36 Send them away, that they may go into the country round about, and into the villages, and buy themselves bread: for they have nothing to eat.

Mk 10:13 And they brought young children to him, that he should touch them: and *his* disciples rebuked those that brought *them.*

Mk 10:48 And many charged him that he should hold his peace: but he cried the more a great deal, *Thou* Son of David, have mercy on me.

Lu 9:12 And when the day began to wear away, then came the twelve, and said unto him, Send the multitude away, that they may go into the towns and country round about, and lodge, and get victuals: for we are here in a desert place.

Lu 18:15 And they brought unto him also infants, that he would touch them: but when *his* disciples saw *it,* they rebuked them.

Lu 18:39 And they which went before rebuked him, that he should hold his peace: but he cried so much the more, *Thou* Son of David, have mercy on me.

DISOBEDIENCE

1. Penalty

De 11:28; 1 S 12:15; 28:18; 1 K 13:21; Je 12:17; Ep 5:6; 2 Th 1:8–9; He 2:2–3

2. Examples

Ge 3:11 And he said, Who told thee that thou *wast* naked? Hast thou eaten of the tree, whereof I commanded thee that thou shouldest not eat?

Ge 19:26 But his wife looked back from behind him, and she became a pillar of salt.

Le 10:1 And Nadab and Abihu, the sons of Aaron, took either of them his censer, and put fire therein, and put incense thereon, and offered strange fire before the LORD, which he commanded them not.

Nu 20:11 And Moses lifted up his hand, and with his rod he smote the rock twice: and the water came out abundantly, and the congregation drank, and their beasts *also*.

Jos 7:1 But the children of Israel committed a trespass in the accursed thing: for Achan, the son of Carmi, the son of Zabdi, the son of Zerah, of the tribe of Judah, took of the accursed thing: and the anger of the LORD was kindled against the children of Israel.

1 S 13:13 And Samuel said to Saul, Thou hast done foolishly: thou hast not kept the commandment of the LORD thy God, which he commanded thee: for now would the LORD have established thy kingdom upon Israel for ever.

Jona 1:3 But Jonah rose up to flee unto Tarshish from the presence of the LORD, and went down to Joppa; and he found a ship going to Tarshish: so he paid the fare thereof, and went down into it, to go with them unto Tarshish from the presence of the LORD.

Zep 3:2 She obeyed not the voice; she received not correction; she trusted not in the LORD; she drew not near to her God.

Lu 6:49 But he that heareth, and doeth not, is like a man that without a foundation built an house upon the earth; against which the stream did beat vehemently, and immediately it fell; and the ruin of that house was great.

He 3:18 And to whom sware he that they should not enter into his rest, but to them that believed not?

See **OBEDIENCE**

DISOWNED, *BY CHRIST*

Mt 7:23 And then will I profess unto them, I never knew you: depart from me, ye that work iniquity.

Mt 25:12 But he answered and said, Verily I say unto you, I know you not.

Mk 8:38 Whosoever therefore shall be ashamed of me and of my words in this adulterous and sinful generation; of him also shall the Son of man be ashamed, when he cometh in the glory of his Father with the holy angels.

Lu 9:26 For whosoever shall be ashamed of me and of my words, of him shall the Son of man be ashamed, when he shall come in his own glory, and *in his* Father's, and of the holy angels.

Lu 12:9 But he that denieth me before men shall be denied before the angels of God.

DISPENSATION, *period of time*

1. Described

Mt 11:11 Verily I say unto you, Among them that are born of women there hath not risen a greater than John the Baptist: notwithstanding he that is least in the kingdom of heaven is greater than he.

2 Co 3:11 For if that which is done away *was* glorious, much more that which remaineth *is* glorious.

He 7:19 For the law made nothing perfect, but the bringing in of a better hope *did;* by the which we draw nigh unto God.

He 8:6 But now hath he obtained a more excellent ministry, by how much also he is the mediator of a better covenant, which was established upon better promises.

He 9:23 *It was* therefore necessary that the patterns of things in the heavens should be purified with these; but the heavenly things themselves with better sacrifices than these.

He 11:40 God having provided some better thing for us, that they without us should not be made perfect.

He 12:22 But ye are come unto mount Sion, and unto the city of the living God, the heavenly Jerusalem, and to an innumerable company of angels,

He 12:27 And this *word*, Yet once more, signifieth the removing of those things that are shaken, as of things that are made, that those things which cannot be shaken may remain.

2. Specified

BETTER REVELATION

He 1:1–4 God, who at sundry times and in divers manners spake in time past unto the fathers by the prophets,

Hath in these last days spoken unto us by *his* Son, whom he hath appointed heir of all things, by whom also he made the worlds;

Who being the brightness of *his* glory, and the express image of his person, and upholding all things by the word of his power, when he had by himself purged our sins, sat down on the right hand of the Majesty on high;

Being made so much better than the angels, as he hath by inheritance obtained a more excellent name than they.

BETTER HOPE

He 7:19 For the law made nothing perfect, but the bringing in of a better hope *did;* by the which we draw nigh unto God.

BETTER PRIESTHOOD

He 7:20–28 And inasmuch as not without an oath *he was made priest:*

(For those priests were made without an oath; but this with an oath by him that said unto him, The Lord sware and will not repent, Thou *art* a priest for ever after the order of Melchisedec:)

By so much was Jesus made a surety of a better testament.

And they truly were many priests, because they were not suffered to continue by reason of death:

But this *man*, because he continueth ever, hath an unchangeable priesthood.

Wherefore he is able also to save them to the uttermost that come unto God by him, seeing he ever liveth to make intercession for them.

For such an high priest became us, *who is* holy, harmless, undefiled, separate from sinners, and made higher than the heavens;

Who needeth not daily, as those high priests, to offer up sacrifice, first for his own sins, and then for the people's: for this he did once, when he offered up himself.

For the law maketh men high priests which have infirmity; but the word of the oath, which was since the law, *maketh* the Son, who is consecrated for evermore.

BETTER COVENANT AND PROMISES

He 8:6 But now hath he obtained a more excellent ministry, by how much also he is the mediator of a better covenant, which was established upon better promises.

BETTER SACRIFICES

He 9:23 *It was* therefore necessary that the patterns of things in the heavens should be purified with these; but the heavenly things themselves with better sacrifices than these.

BETTER POSSESSIONS

He 10:34 For ye had compassion of me in my bonds, and took joyfully the spoiling of your goods, knowing in yourselves that ye have in heaven a better and an enduring substance.

BETTER COUNTRY

He 11:16 But now they desire a better *country*, that is, an heavenly: wherefore God is not ashamed to be called their God: for he hath prepared for them a city.

BETTER RESURRECTION

He 11:35 Women received their dead raised to life again: and others were tortured, not accepting deliverance; that they might obtain a better resurrection:

DISPERSION, *scattering*

1. Of the Nations after the Flood

Ge 9:19; 10:5, 32; 11:8; De 32:8; Je 49:32, 36; Eze 29:12; 30:23, 26; Am 9:9

2. Of the Jews

Le 26:33, 41; De 4:27; 28:25, 64; 30:1; 32:26; Ne 1:8; Est 3:8; Ps 44:11; 106:27; Is 11:12; Je 8:3; 9:16; 15:4; 16:13; 17:4; 18:17; 24:9; 29:18; 32:37; 34:17; 44:1; Lam 1:3; Eze 5:10; 6:8; 11:16; 12:15; 17:21; 20:23; 22:15; 34:6, 12; 36:19; Da 9:7; Ho 9:17; Jl 3:2; Zep 3:10; Zec 2:6; 7:14; 10:9; Jn 7:35; 11:52; Ac 2:6; Ja 1:1

3. Of the Early Disciples

Zec 13:7; Mt 26:31; Mk 14:27; Ac 8:1, 4; 11:19

DISPLAY, *outward show, especially of riches*

2 K 20:13; Est 1:4; 5:11; Ps 39:6; Is 39:2; Ho 2:13; Mk 12:38; Lu 20:46; Ac 25:23

In Religious Service

2 K 10:16; Mt 6:2, 5, 16; 23:5

DISPLEASURE, *God's reaction to sin*

Ex 33:5; Le 20:23; Nu 11:1; De 9:19; 1 S 13:14; 15:11, 35; 2 S 11:27; 1 Chr 21:7; 2 Chr 26:18; Ps 2:5; 5:4; 6:2; 38:1; 60:1; 78:21; 88:7; 106:40; Pr 24:18; Is 9:17; 27:11; 59:15; 63:10; Je 16:13; 21:9; 51:25; Eze 5:8; 13:8; 21:3; 23:18; 26:3; 30:22; 34:10; 38:3; Ho 2:4; 9:15; 13:7; Am 6:8; Na 2:13; 3:5; Zec 1:2, 15; Mal 1:10; Mk 10:14; Ro 8:8; 1 Co 10:5; 1 Th 2:15; He 3:10, 17; 8:9; 10:38

DISSATISFACTION

Nu 11:20 *But* even a whole month, until it come out at your nostrils, and it be loathsome unto you: because that ye have despised the LORD which *is* among you, and have wept before him, saying, Why came we forth out of Egypt?

De 32:32 For their vine *is* of the vine of Sodom, and of the fields of Gomorrah: their grapes *are* grapes of gall, their clusters *are* bitter:

1 K 20:43 And the king of Israel went to his house heavy and displeased, and came to Samaria.

Ps 59:15 Let them wander up and down for meat, and grudge if they be not satisfied.

Ec 2:11 Then I looked on all the works that my hands had wrought, and on the labour that I had laboured to do: and, behold, all *was* vanity and vexation of spirit, and *there was* no profit under the sun.

Ec 2:18 Yea, I hated all my labour which I had taken under the sun: because I should leave it unto the man that shall be after me.

Ec 5:16 And this also *is* a sore evil, *that* in all points as he came, so shall he go: and what profit hath he that hath laboured for the wind?

Ec 6:9 Better *is* the sight of the eyes than the wandering of the desire: this *is* also vanity and vexation of spirit.

Is 8:21 And they shall pass through it, hardly bestead and hungry: and it shall come to pass, that when they shall be hungry, they shall fret themselves, and curse their king and their God, and look upward.

Is 29:8 It shall even be as when an hungry *man* dreameth, and, behold, he eateth; but he awaketh, and his soul is empty: or as when a thirsty man dreameth, and, behold, he drinketh; but he awaketh, and, behold, *he is* faint, and his soul hath appetite: so shall the multitude of all the nations be, that fight against mount Zion.

Is 44:20 He feedeth on ashes: a deceived heart hath turned him aside, that he cannot deliver his soul, nor say, *Is there* not a lie in my right hand?

Is 57:10 Thou art wearied in the greatness of thy way; *yet* saidst thou not, There is no hope: thou hast found the life of thine hand; therefore thou wast not grieved.

Lu 1:53 He hath filled the hungry with good things; and the rich he hath sent empty away.

Lu 15:14 And when he had spent all, there arose a mighty famine in that land; and he began to be in want.

Jn 14:27 Peace I leave with you, my peace I give unto you: not as the world giveth, give I unto you. Let not your heart be troubled, neither let it be afraid.

Re 18:14 And the fruits that thy soul lusted after are departed from thee, and all things which were dainty and goodly are departed from thee, and thou shalt find them no more at all.

See **SATISFACTION**

DISTAFF, *part of a spindle*

Ex 35:25; Pr 31:19

DIVORCE See **FAMILY**

DIVINATION, *obtaining secret knowledge, especially of the future, a pagan counterpart of prophecy*

Ge 44:5, 15; Nu 22:7; 23:23; 24:1; De 18:10, 14; 1 S 6:2; 2 K 17:17; Is 44:25; Je 14:14; 27:9; 29:8; Eze 12:24; 13:6, 23; 21:21; Zec 10:2; Ac 16:16

DIVINITY, *CHRIST'S*

1. Acknowledged

BY PETER

Mt 16:16 And Simon Peter answered and said, Thou art the Christ, the Son of the living God.

BY DEMONS

Mk 5:7 And cried with a loud voice, and said, What have I to do with thee, Jesus, *thou* Son of the most high God? I adjure thee by God, that thou torment me not.

BY THE CENTURION

Mk 15:39 And when the centurion, which stood over against him, saw that he so cried out, and gave up the ghost, he said, Truly this man was the Son of God.

BY NATHANAEL

Jn 1:49 Nathanael answered and saith unto him, Rabbi, thou art the Son of God; thou art the King of Israel.

BY THE SAMARITANS

Jn 4:42 And said unto the woman, Now we believe, not because of thy saying: for we have heard *him* ourselves, and know that this is indeed the Christ, the Saviour of the world.

BY MARTHA

Jn 11:27 She saith unto him, Yea, Lord: I believe that thou art the Christ, the Son of God, which should come into the world.

BY THOMAS

Jn 20:28 And Thomas answered and said unto him, My Lord and my God.

2. Challenged

BY SATAN

Mt 4:3 And when the tempter came to him, he said, If thou be the Son of God, command that these stones be made bread.

Mt 4:6 And saith unto him, If thou be the Son of God, cast thyself down: for it is written, He shall give his angels charge concerning thee: and in *their* hands they shall bear thee up, lest at any time thou dash thy foot against a stone.

BY SCRIBES AND PHARISEES

Lu 5:21 And the scribes and the Pharisees began to reason, saying, Who is this which speaketh blasphemies? Who can forgive sins, but God alone?

BY THE JEWISH PEOPLE

Jn 5:18 Therefore the Jews sought the more to kill him, because he not only had broken the sabbath, but said also that God was his Father, making himself equal with God.

Jn 8:53 Art thou greater than our father Abraham, which is dead? and the prophets are dead: whom makest thou thyself?

Jn 10:33 The Jews answered him, saying, For a good work we stone thee not; but for blasphemy; and because that thou, being a man, makest thyself God.

BY THE SCRIBES AND ELDERS

Lu 20:1–2 And it came to pass, *that* on one of those days, as he taught the people in the temple, and preached the gospel, the chief priests and the scribes came upon *him* with the elders,

And spake unto him, saying, Tell us, by what authority doest thou these things? or who is he that gave thee this authority?

BY THE RABBLE

Mt 27:39–40 And they that passed by reviled him, wagging their heads,

And saying, Thou that destroyest the temple, and buildest *it* in three days, save thyself. If thou be the Son of God, come down from the cross.

BY THE RULERS

Lu 23:35 And the people stood beholding. And the rulers also with them derided *him*, saying, He saved others; let him save himself, if he be Christ, the chosen of God.

BY THE SOLDIERS

Lu 23:36–37 And the soldiers also mocked him, coming to him, and offering him vinegar,

And saying, If thou be the king of the Jews, save thyself.

BY ONE OF THE THIEVES

Lu 23:39 And one of the malefactors which were hanged railed on him, saying, If thou be Christ, save thyself and us.

BY THE CHIEF PRIESTS

Mk 15:31–32 Likewise also the chief priests mocking said among themselves with the scribes, He saved others; himself he cannot save.

Let Christ the King of Israel descend now from the cross, that we may see and believe. And they that were crucified with him reviled him.

DIVISIONS, *disunity*

Mk 3:24 And if a kingdom be divided against itself, that kingdom cannot stand.

Lu 11:17 But he, knowing their thoughts, said unto them, Every kingdom divided against itself is brought to desolation; and a house *divided* against a house falleth.

1 Co 1:10 Now I beseech you, brethren, by the name of our Lord Jesus Christ, that ye all speak the same thing, and *that* there be no divisions among you; but *that* ye be perfectly joined together in the same mind and in the same judgment.

1 Co 3:3 For ye are yet carnal: for whereas *there is* among you envying, and strife, and divisions, are ye not carnal, and walk as men?

1 Co 11:18 For first of all, when ye come together in the church, I hear that there be divisions among you; and I partly believe it.

See **STRIFE**

DOCTRINE, *teaching*

1. False

Pr 19:27 Cease, my son, to hear the instruction *that causeth* to err from the words of knowledge.

Is 32:6 For the vile person will speak villany, and his heart will work iniquity, to practise hypocrisy, and to utter error against the LORD, to make empty the soul of the hungry, and he will cause the drink of the thirsty to fail.

Je 23:16 Thus saith the LORD of hosts, Hearken not unto the words of the prophets that prophesy unto you: they make you vain: they speak a vision of their own heart, *and* not out of the mouth of the LORD.

Je 23:32 Behold, I *am* against them that prophesy false dreams, saith the LORD, and do tell them, and cause my people to err by their lies, and by their lightness; yet I sent them not, nor commanded them: therefore they shall not profit this people at all, saith the LORD.

Eze 13:10 Because, even because they have seduced my people, saying,

Peace; and *there was* no peace; and one built up a wall, and, lo, others daubed it with untempered *morter:*

Eze 22:28 And her prophets have daubed them with untempered *morter,* seeing vanity, and divining lies unto them, saying, Thus saith the Lord GOD, when the LORD hath not spoken.

Mt 4:6 And saith unto him, If thou be the Son of God, cast thyself down: for it is written, He shall give his angels charge concerning thee: and in *their* hands they shall bear thee up, lest at any time thou dash thy foot against a stone.

Mt 16:12 Then understood they how that he bade *them* not beware of the leaven of bread, but of the doctrine of the Pharisees and of the Sadducees.

Mk 7:7 Howbeit in vain do they worship me, teaching *for* doctrines the commandments of men.

Mk 8:15 And he charged them, saying, Take heed, beware of the leaven of the Pharisees, and *of* the leaven of Herod.

Lu 12:1 In the mean time, when there were gathered together an innumerable multitude of people, insomuch that they trode one upon another, he began to say unto his disciples first of all, Beware ye of the leaven of the Pharisees, which is hypocrisy.

Ac 20:30 Also of your own selves shall men arise, speaking perverse things, to draw away disciples after them.

2 Co 11:4 For if he that cometh preacheth another Jesus, whom we have not preached, or *if* ye receive another spirit, which ye have not received, or another gospel, which ye have not accepted, ye might well bear with *him.*

Ga 5:9 A little leaven leaveneth the whole lump.

Ga 5:20 Idolatry, witchcraft, hatred, variance, emulations, wrath, strife, seditions, heresies,

Ep 5:6 Let no man deceive you with vain words: for because of these things cometh the wrath of God upon the children of disobedience.

Col 2:8 Beware lest any man spoil you through philosophy and vain deceit, after the tradition of men, after the rudiments of the world, and not after Christ.

1 Ti 1:3 As I besought thee to abide still at Ephesus, when I went into Macedonia, that thou mightest charge some that they teach no other doctrine,

1 Ti 4:1 Now the Spirit speaketh expressly, that in the latter times some shall depart from the faith, giving heed to seducing spirits, and doctrines of devils;

1 Ti 6:20 O Timothy, keep that which is committed to thy trust, avoiding profane *and* vain babblings, and oppositions of science falsely so called:

2 Ti 2:17 And their word will eat as doth a canker: of whom is Hymenaeus and Philetus;

Tit 3:10 A man that is an heretick after the first and second admonition reject;

He 13:9 Be not carried about with divers and strange doctrines. For *it is* a good thing that the heart be established with grace; not with meats, which have not profited them that have been occupied therein.

2 Pe 2:1 But there were false prophets also among the people, even as there shall be false teachers among you, who privily shall bring in damnable heresies, even denying the Lord that bought them, and bring upon themselves swift destruction.

2 Pe 3:17 Ye therefore, beloved, seeing ye know *these things* before, beware lest ye also, being led away with the error of the wicked, fall from your own stedfastness.

Re 2:14 But I have a few things against thee, because thou hast there them that hold the doctrine of Balaam, who taught Balac to cast a stumblingblock before the children of Israel, to eat things sacrificed unto idols, and to commit fornication.

2. Good

De 32:2 My doctrine shall drop as the rain, my speech shall distil as the dew, as the small rain upon the tender herb, and as the showers upon the grass:

Pr 4:2 For I give you good doctrine, forsake ye not my law.

Mt 7:28 And it came to pass, when Jesus had ended these sayings, the people were astonished at his doctrine:

Ro 6:17 But God be thanked, that ye were the servants of sin, but ye have obeyed from the heart that form of doctrine which was delivered you.

1 Th 2:3 For our exhortation *was* not of deceit, nor of uncleanness, nor in guile:

1 Ti 4:6 If thou put the brethren in remembrance of these things, thou shalt be a good minister of Jesus Christ, nourished up in the words of faith and of good doctrine, whereunto thou hast attained.

1 Ti 6:3 If any man teach otherwise, and consent not to wholesome words, *even* the words of our Lord Jesus Christ, and to the doctrine which is according to godliness;

Tit 1:9 Holding fast the faithful word as he hath been taught, that he may be able by sound doctrine both to exhort and to convince the gainsayers.

Tit 2:1 But speak thou the things which become sound doctrine:

Tit 2:7 In all things shewing thyself a pattern of good works: in doctrine *shewing* uncorruptness, gravity, sincerity,

See **DECEPTION, HERESY, TEACHERS**

DOERS, *the obedient*

De 26:14 I have not eaten thereof in my mourning, neither have I taken away *ought* thereof for *any* unclean *use,* nor given *ought* thereof for the dead: *but* I have hearkened to the voice of the LORD my God, *and* have done according to all that thou hast commanded me.

2 Chr 34:31 And the king stood in his place, and made a covenant before the LORD, to walk after the LORD, and to keep his commandments, and his testimonies, and his statues, with all his heart, and with all his soul, to perform

the words of the covenant which are written in this book.

Eze 18:21 But if the wicked will turn from all his sins that he hath committed, and keep all my statutes, and do that which is lawful and right, he shall surely live, he shall not die.

Eze 33:19 But if the wicked turn from his wickedness, and do that which is lawful and right, he shall live thereby.

Mt 7:21 Not every one that saith unto me, Lord, Lord, shall enter into the kingdom of heaven; but he that doeth the will of my Father which is in heaven.

Mt 12:50 For whosoever shall do the will of my Father which is in heaven, the same is my brother, and sister, and mother.

Lu 6:47 Whosoever cometh to me, and heareth my sayings, and doeth them, I will shew you to whom he is like:

Jn 13:17 If ye know these things, happy are ye if ye do them.

Ro 2:13 (For not the hearers of the law *are* just before God, but the doers of the law shall be justified.

Ja 1:22 But be ye doers of the word, and not hearers only, deceiving your own selves.

Ja 4:11 Speak not evil one of another, brethren. He that speaketh evil of *his* brother, and judgeth his brother, speaketh evil of the law, and judgeth the law: but if thou judge the law, thou art not a doer of the law, but a judge.

1 Jn 2:17 And the world passeth away, and the lust thereof: but he that doeth the will of God abideth for ever.

Re 22:14 Blessed *are* they that do his commandments, that they may have right to the tree of life, and may enter in through the gates into the city.

DOGS *See* **ANIMALS**

DOOR, *a metaphor for Christ*

Jn 10:7 Then said Jesus unto them again, Verily, verily, I say unto you, I am the door of the sheep.

Jn 14:6 Jesus saith unto him, I am the way, the truth, and the life: no man cometh unto the Father, but by me.

Ro 5:2 By whom also we have access by faith into this grace wherein we stand, and rejoice in hope of the glory of God.

Ep 2:18 For through him we both have access by one Spirit unto the Father.

He 9:8 The Holy Ghost this signifying, that the way into the holiest of all was not yet made manifest, while as the first tabernacle was yet standing:

He 10:19–20 Having therefore, brethren, boldness to enter into the holiest by the blood of Jesus,

By a new and living way, which he hath consecrated for us, through the veil, that is to say, his flesh;

See **TITLES AND NAMES**

DONKEYS See **ANIMALS**

DOORKEEPERS, *those who guard doors and gates in temples, walled cities, and buildings*

2 K 25:18; 1 Chr 9:19; 15:23; Ps 84:10; Jn 18:17; Ac 12:13

DORCAS, *a benevolent woman of Joppa*

Ac 9:36

See **WOMEN**

DOTHAN, *a district and town near Samaria*

It was here that Joseph was thrown into a well and later sold by his brothers to a passing caravan of Ishmaelites and Midianites (Ge 37:17–28). It was also the place Elisha told his servant, "Fear not, for they that *be* with us *are* more than they that *be* with them" (2 K 6:13–23), after which Elisha's servant saw the mountain full of horses and chariots of fire.

See **CITIES**

DOUBLE-MINDEDNESS

2 K 17:33 They feared the LORD, and served their own gods, after the manner of the nations whom they carried away from thence.

1 Chr 12:33 Of Zebulun, such as went forth to battle, expert in war, with all instruments of war, fifty thousand, which could keep rank: *they were* not of double heart.

Zep 1:4–5 I will also stretch out mine hand upon Judah, and upon all the inhabitants of Jerusalem; and I will cut off the remnant of Baal from this place, *and* the name of the Chemarims with the priests;

And them that worship the host of heaven upon the housetops; and them that worship *and* that swear by the LORD, and that swear by Malcham;

Lu 16:13 No servant can serve two masters: for either he will hate the one, and love the other; or else he will hold to the one, and despise the other. Ye cannot serve God and mammon.

1 Co 10:21 Ye cannot drink the cup of the Lord, and the cup of devils: ye cannot be partakers of the Lord's table, and of the table of devils.

Ja 1:8 A double minded man is unstable in all his ways.

Ja 4:8 Draw nigh to God, and he will draw nigh to you. Cleanse *your* hands, *ye* sinners; and purify *your* hearts, *ye* double minded.

See **DECEPTION, MIND**

DOUBT, *disbelief, distrust, uncertain, skeptical*

1. Rebuked by Christ

PETER SINKING IN THE SEA

Mt 14:31 And immediately Jesus stretched forth *his* hand, and caught him, and said unto him, O thou of little faith, wherefore didst thou doubt?

Mt 16:8 *Which* when Jesus perceived, he said unto them, O ye of little faith, why reason ye among yourselves, because ye have brought no bread?

THE DISCIPLES POWERLESS TO HEAL

Mt 17:17 Then Jesus answered and said, O faithless and perverse generation, how long shall I be with you? how long shall I suffer you? bring him hither to me.

THE DISCIPLES IN THE STORM

Mk 4:40 And he said unto them, Why are ye so fearful? how is it that ye have no faith?

THE TWO ON THE WAY TO EMMAUS

Lu 24:25 Then he said unto them, O fools, and slow of heart to believe all that the prophets have spoken:

Jn 20:27 Then saith he to Thomas, reach hither thy finger, and behold my hands; and reach hither thy hand, and thrust *it* into my side: and be not faithless, but believing.

2. Momentary Doubts

ABRAHAM, *as to the inheritance of Canaan*

Ge 15:8 And he said, Lord GOD, whereby shall I know that I shall inherit it?

GIDEON, *as to victory over Midian*

Jud 6:17 And he said unto him, If now I have found grace in thy sight, then shew me a sign that thou talkest with me.

JOHN THE BAPTIST, *as to whether Jesus was the Messiah*

Mt 11:3 And said unto him, Art thou he that should come, or do we look for another?

SOME OF THE DISCIPLES

Mt 28:17 And when they saw him, they worshipped him: but some doubted.

MARTHA, *as to the resurrection of Lazarus*

Jn 11:39 Jesus said, Take ye away the stone. Martha, the sister of him that was dead, saith unto him, Lord, by this time he stinketh: for he hath been *dead* four days.

THOMAS, *as to the resurrection of Christ*

Jn 20:25 The other disciples therefore said unto him, We have seen the Lord. But he said unto them, Except I shall see in his hands the print of the nails, and put my finger into the print of the nails, and thrust my hand into his side, I will not believe.

EARLY CHRISTIANS, *as to the deliverance of Peter*

Ac 12:14-15 And when she knew Peter's voice, she opened not the gate for gladness, but ran in, and told how Peter stood before the gate.

And they said unto her, Thou art mad. But she constantly affirmed that it was even so. Then said they, It is his angel

See **FAITH**

DOUGH, *mixture of ingredients used to bake bread and other pastries*

Ex 12:34; Nu 15:20; Ne 10:37; Je 7:18; Eze 44:30; Ho 7:4

DOVES *See* **BIRDS**

DOWRY, *given to brides*

Ge 30:20; 34:12; Ex 22:17; Jos 15:18; Jud 1:14; 1 S 18:25

DRAGONS *See* **ANIMALS, REPTILES**

DREAMS, *thoughts and mental images experienced during sleep, often conveying a revelatory message in biblical literature*

Ge 20:3, 6; 31:11, 24; Nu 12:6; Jb 7:14; 33:15; Ec 5:3, 7; Je 23:28; 29:8; Jl 2:28; Ac 2:17

1. Notable

Ge 28:12; 37:5, 9; 40:5, 16; 41:1, 11, 17; 42:9; Jud 7:13; 1 K 3:5, 15; Da 2:1; 4:5; Mt 1:20; 2:12, 13, 19, 22; 27:19

2. Interpretation

Ge 40:8, 12, 18; 41:12, 25; Jud 7:14; Da 1:17; 2:4, 28, 36, 45; 4:20, 24

DRESS, *attire, clothing*

1. Special Counsel

De 22:5, 11; Ec 9:8; Eze 44:17; Zep 1:8; Mt 6:25, 28; Lu 12:23; 1 Ti 2:9; 1 Pe 3:3

2. Futility of Adornment

Is 3:16, 18–24; Mt 6:25, 28–29; Mk 1:6; 1 Pe 3:3–4

3. Clothing

Ge 3:21; 27:15; 2 S 1:24; Pr 27:26; Da 5:29; Mt 3:4; Mk 1:6; 12:38; Ac 9:39; Ja 2:3

a. Costly Apparel

Ge 37:23; 41:42; Jud 8:26; 2 S 1:24; 13:18; 1 K 10:5; 22:10; 2 Chr 18:9; Est 5:1; 6:8; 8:15; Ps 45:13; Pr 31:22; Is 3:22–23; Je 4:30; Eze 16:10; 23:12; 26:16; 27:24; Da 5:7, 16; Zep 1:8; Mt 11:8; Lu 7:25; 16:19; Ac 12:21; 1 Ti 2:9; Ja 2:2; Re 17:4; 18:16

b. Coats

Ge 37:3, 23, 33; Ex 28:40; 29:5, 8; 40:14; Le 8:7, 13; Da 3:21; Mt 10:10; Mk 6:9; Lu 6:29; Jn 19:23; Ac 9:39

c. Mantles

1 K 19:13; 2 K 2:8, 13; Ezr 9:3; Jb 1:20

d. Robes

1 S 18:4; 2 S 13:18

e. Sandals

Mk 6:9; Ac 12:8

4. Cloaks

a. Garments

Mt 5:40; Lu 6:29; 2 Ti 4:13

b. Figurative

Mt 7:15; 1 Th 2:5; 1 Pe 2:16

5. Garments of Priests

Ex 28:2, 42; 29:5, 21, 29; 31:10; 35:19; 39:1, 27, 41; 40:13; Le 6:10; 8:2, 7, 30; 16:4, 23, 32; 21:10; Nu 20:26; Ezr 2:69; 3:10; Ne 7:70; Ps 133:2; Eze 42:14; 44:17; Zec 3:5

Bonnets

Ex 28:40; 29:9; 39:28; Le 8:13; Eze 44:18

See **APPAREL**

DRINK See **MILK, WATER, WINE**

DRINK OFFERINGS See **OFFERINGS**

DROPSY See **DISEASE**

DROSS, *used to describe the wicked*

Ps 119:119; Pr 25:4; Is 1:22, 25; Je 6:30; Eze 22:18; Da 5:28

See **WICKED**

DROUGHT, SPIRITUAL

2 Chr 6:26; Jb 20:17; Ps 63:1; 68:6; Is 1:30; 5:13; 41:17; Je 17:6; Eze 19:13; Ho 2:3; Am 8:13

See **SHOWERS, WEATHER**

DRUNKENNESS, *the state of being inebriated*

1. Warnings

Pr 20:1 Wine *is* a mocker, strong drink *is* raging: and whosoever is deceived thereby is not wise.

Pr 23:20 Be not among winebibbers; among riotous eaters of flesh:

Pr 23:29–31 Who hath woe? who hath sorrow? who hath contentions? who hath babbling? who hath wounds without cause? who hath redness of eyes?

They that tarry long at the wine; they that go to seek mixed wine.

Look not thou upon the wine when it is red, when it giveth his colour in the cup, *when* it moveth itself aright.

Ec 10:17 Blessed *art* thou, O land, when thy king *is* the son of nobles, and thy princes eat in due season, for strength, and not for drunkenness!

Is 5:11 Woe unto them that rise up early in the morning, *that* they may follow strong drink; that continue until night, *till* wine inflame them!

Is 28:1 Woe to the crown of pride, to the drunkards of Ephraim, whose glorious beauty is a fading flower, which *are* on the head of the fat valleys of them that are overcome with wine!

Na 1:10 For while *they be* folden together *as* thorns, and while they are drunken *as* drunkards, they shall be devoured as stubble fully dry.

Hab 2:15 Woe unto him that giveth his neighbour drink, that puttest thy bottle to *him,* and makest *him* drunken also, that thou mayest look on their nakedness!

Lu 21:34 And take heed to yourselves, lest at any time your hearts be overcharged with surfeiting, and drunkenness, and cares of this life, and so that day come upon you unawares.

Ro 13:13 Let us walk honestly, as in the day; not in rioting and drunkenness, not in chambering and wantonness, not in strife and envying.

1 Co 6:10 Nor thieves, nor covetous, nor drunkards, nor revilers, nor extortioners, shall inherit the kingdom of God.

Ep 5:18 And be not drunk with wine, wherein is excess; but be filled with the Spirit;

1 Th 5:7 For they that sleep sleep in the night; and they that be drunken are drunken in the night.

2. Examples

NOAH

Ge 9:21 And he drank of the wine, and was drunken; and he was uncovered within his tent.

NABAL

1 S 25:36 And Abigail came to Nabal; and, behold, he held a feast in his house, like the feast of a king; and Nabal's heart *was* merry within him, for he *was* very drunken: wherefore she told him nothing, less or more, until the morning light.

URIAH

2 S 11:13 And when David had called him, he did eat and drink before him; and he made him drunk: and at even he went out to lie on his bed with the servants of his lord, but went not down to his house.

ELAH

1 K 16:9 And his servant Zimri, captain of half *his* chariots, conspired against him, as he was in Tirzah, drinking himself drunk in the house of Arza steward of *his* house in Tirzah.

BEN HADAD

1 K 20:16 And they went out at noon. But Ben-hadad *was* drinking himself drunk in the pavilions, he and the kings, the thirty and two kings that helped him.

AHASUERUS

Est 1:10 On the seventh day, when the heart of the king was merry with wine, he commanded Mehuman, Biztha, Harbona, Bigtha, and Abagtha, Zethar, and Carcas, the seven chamberlains that served in the presence of Ahasuerus the king,

WATCHMEN OF ISRAEL

Is 56:12 Come ye, *say they*, I will fetch wine, and we will fill ourselves with strong drink; and to morrow shall be as this day, *and* much more abundant.

KINGS OF ISRAEL

Ho 7:5 In the day of our king the princes have made *him* sick with bottles of wine; he stretched out his hand with scorners.

OTHER EXAMPLES

Jl 3:3 And they have cast lots for my people; and have given a boy for an harlot, and sold a girl for wine, that they might drink.

Lu 12:45 But and if that servant say in his heart, My lord delayeth his coming; and shall begin to beat the menservants and maidens, and to eat and drink, and to be drunken;

1 Co 11:21 For in eating every one taketh before *other* his own supper: and one is hungry, and another is drunken.

3. Drunkards

1 K 20:16 And they went out at noon. But Ben-hadad *was* drinking himself drunk in the pavilions, he and the kings, the thirty and two kings that helped him.

Ps 69:12 They that sit in the gate speak against me; and I *was* the song of the drunkards.

Pr 23:21 For the drunkard and the glutton shall come to poverty: and drowsiness shall clothe *a man* with rags.

Pr 23:30 They that tarry long at the wine; they that go to seek mixed wine.

Pr 26:9 *As* a thorn goeth up into the hand of a drunkard, so *is* a parable in the mouth of fools.

Is 5:11 Woe unto them that rise up early in the morning, *that* they may follow strong drink; that continue until night, *till* wine inflame them!

Is 5:22 Woe unto *them that are* mighty to drink wine, and men of strength to mingle strong drink:

Is 28:3 The crown of pride, the drunkards of Ephraim, shall be trodden under feet:

Jl 1:5 Awake, ye drunkards, and weep; and howl, all ye drinkers of wine, because of the new wine; for it is cut off from your mouth.

Na 1:10 For while *they be* folden together *as* thorns, and while they are drunken *as* drunkards, they shall be devoured as stubble fully dry.

See **TEMPERANCE, WINE**

DRY PLACES, *literal and spiritual*

Ex 15:22; 17:1; Nu 20:2; 21:5; 33:14; 2 K 3:9; Ps 68:6; Pr 30:16; Is 1:30; Je 14:3; 17:6

DULCIMER *See* **MUSIC**

DULLNESS, *spiritual unresponsiveness and disinterest*

1. Condemned

Nu 22:34; De 29:4; Jb 33:14; Ps 92:6; Pr 17:10; 27:22; 28:5; 29:19; Is 26:10; 40:21; 44:19; 47:7; 48:8; Je 7:28; 10:14; 51:17; Eze 12:2; Mk 4:12; Lu 12:56; Jn 3:11; 8:43; Ro 3:11; 1 Co 2:14; 11:29; He 5:11

2. Examples

Jb 32:9; Ps 82:5; Is 5:12; 56:11; Eze 33:5; Da 12:10; Ho 7:2; Mi 4:12; Mt 13:13; 16:3; 26:61; 27:47; Mk 14:5; Jn 1:5; 2:20; 4:10; 6:52; 7:35; 8:22, 27; 10:6; 12:29; Ac 28:27; Ro 1:31; 2 Ti 3:7

3. Of Israel

De 32:28; Ne 9:17; Ps 106:7; Is 1:3; 27:11; 29:11; 42:20; 53:1; Je 4:22; Mt 12:7; 17:12; Lu 8:10; 19:44; Ac 7:25; 1 Co 14:21; 2 Co 3:15

4. Of the Disciples

Mt 15:16; 16:7, 11; 26:9; Mk 4:13; 6:52; 7:18; 8:16, 21; 9:32; 16:14; Lu 9:32, 45; 18:34; 24:11, 25; Jn 4:33; 12:16; 14:9; 16:18; 20:9

5. Understanding

Jn 2:20; 3:4; 4:11, 33; 6:52; 11:12

See **DISCERNMENT, INDIFFERENCE**

DUPLICITY

1. Dissimulation

1 S 21:13 And he changed his behaviour before them, and feigned himself mad in their hands, and scrabbled on the doors of the gate, and let his spittle fall down upon his beard.

2 S 14:2 And Joab sent to Tekoah, and fetched thence a wise woman, and said unto her, I pray thee, feign thyself to be a mourner, and put on now mourning apparel, and anoint not thyself with oil, but be as a woman that had a long time mourned for the dead:

2 K 10:19 Now therefore call unto me all the prophets of Baal, all his servants, and all his priests; let none be wanting: for I have a great sacrifice *to do* to Baal; whosoever shall be wanting, he shall not live. But Jehu did *it* in subtilty, to the intent that he might destroy the worshippers of Baal.

Pr 26:24 He that hateth dissembleth with his lips, and layeth up deceit within him;

Mt 2:8 And he sent them to Bethlehem, and said, Go and search diligently for the young child; and when ye have found *him,* bring me word again, that I may come and worship him also.

Lu 20:20 And they watched *him,* and sent forth spies, which should feign themselves just men, that they might take hold of his words, that so they might deliver him unto the power and authority of the governor.

Ac 23:15 Now therefore ye with the council signify to the chief captain that he bring him down unto you to morrow, as though ye would enquire something more perfectly concerning him: and we, or ever he come near, are ready to kill him.

Ga 2:13 And the other Jews dissembled likewise with him; insomuch that Barnabas also was carried away with their dissimulation.

2. Craftiness

Ge 3:1 Now the serpent was more subtil than any beast of the field which the Lord God had made. And he said unto the woman, Yea, hath God said, Ye shall not eat of every tree of the garden?

Ge 25:31 And Jacob said, Sell me this day thy birthright.

Ge 27:16 And she put the skins of the kids of the goats upon his hands, and upon the smooth of his neck:

Ge 27:35 And he said, Thy brother came with subtilty, and hath taken away thy blessing.

Ge 29:27 Fulfil her week, and we will give thee this also for the service which thou shalt serve with me yet seven other years.

Ge 30:38 And he set the rods which he had pilled before the flocks in the gutters in the watering troughs when the flocks came to drink, that they should conceive when they came to drink.

Ge 37:31 And they took Joseph's coat, and killed a kid of the goats, and dipped the coat in the blood;

Ex 1:10 Come on, let us deal wisely with them; lest they multiply, and it come to pass, that, when there falleth out any war, they join also unto our enemies, and fight against us, and so get them up out of the land.

Jos 9:4 They did work wilily, and went and made as if they had been ambassadors, and took old sacks upon their asses, and wine bottles, old, and rent, and bound up;

Jud 3:19 But he himself turned again from the quarries that were by Gilgal, and said, I have a secret errand unto thee, O king: who said, Keep silence. And all that stood by him went out from him.

Jud 9:2 Speak, I pray you, in the ears of all the men of Shechem, Whether is better for you, either that all the sons of Jerubbaal, which are threescore and ten persons, reign over you, or that one reign over you? remember also that I am your bone and your flesh.

Jud 16:5 And the lords of the Philistines came up unto her, and said unto her, Entice him, and see wherein his great strength lieth, and by what means we may prevail against him, that we may bind him to afflict him: and we will give thee every one of us eleven hundred pieces of silver.

1 S 18:21 And Saul said, I will give him her, that she may be a snare to him, and that the hand of the Philistines may be against him. Wherefore Saul said to David, Thou shalt this day be my son in law in the one of the twain.

2 S 13:3 But Amnon had a friend, whose name was Jonadab, the son of Shimeah David's brother: and Jonadab was a very subtil man.

2 S 15:3 And Absalom said unto him, See, thy matters are good and right; but there is no man deputed of the king to hear thee.

2 Chr 16:3 There is a league between me and thee, as there was between my father and thy father: behold, I have sent thee silver and gold; go, break thy league with Baasha king of Israel, that he may depart from me.

Ne 6:2 That Sanballat and Geshem sent unto me, saying, Come, let us meet together in some one of the villages in the plain of Ono. But they thought to do me mischief.

Ne 6:8 Then I sent unto him, saying, There are no such things done as thou sayest, but thou feignest them out of thine own heart.

Jb 15:5 For thy mouth uttereth thine iniquity, and thou choosest the tongue of the crafty.

Ps 10:9 He lieth in wait secretly as a lion in his den: he lieth in wait to catch the poor: he doth catch the poor, when he draweth him into his net.

Ps 35:20 For they speak not peace: but they devise deceitful matters against them that are quiet in the land.

Ps 83:3 They have taken crafty counsel against thy people, and consulted against thy hidden ones.

Da 8:25 And through his policy also he shall cause craft to prosper in his hand; and he shall magnify *himself* in his heart, and by peace shall destroy many: he shall also stand up against the Prince of princes; but he shall be broken without hand.

Da 11:23 And after the league *made* with him he shall work deceitfully: for he shall come up, and shall become strong with a small people.

Mt 2:4 And when he had gathered all the chief priests and scribes of the people together, he demanded of them where Christ should be born.

Mt 26:4 And consulted that they might take Jesus by subtilty, and kill *him*.

Mk 12:14 And when they were come, they say unto him, Master, we know that thou art true, and carest for no man: for thou regardest not the person of men, but teachest the way of God in truth: Is it lawful to give tribute to Caesar, or not?

Mk 14:1 After two days was *the feast of* the passover, and of unleavened bread: and the chief priests and the scribes sought how they might take him by craft, and put *him* to death.

Lu 16:4 I am resolved what to do, that, when I am put out of the stewardship, they may receive me into their houses.

Lu 16:8 And the lord commended the unjust steward, because he had done wisely: for the children of this world are in their generation wiser than the children of light.

Lu 20:23 But he perceived their craftiness, and said unto them, Why tempt ye me?

Lu 22:6 And he promised, and sought opportunity to betray him unto them in the absence of the multitude.

Jn 19:12 And from thenceforth Pilate sought to release him: but the Jews cried out, saying, If thou let this man go, thou art not Caesar's friend: whosoever maketh himself a king speaketh against Caesar.

Ac 7:18 Till another king arose, which knew not Joseph.

Ep 4:14 That we *henceforth* be no more children, tossed to and fro, and carried about with every wind of doctrine, by the sleight of men, *and* cunning craftiness, whereby they lie in wait to deceive;

3. Crookedness

De 32:5 They have corrupted themselves, their spot *is* not *the spot* of his children: *they are* a perverse and crooked generation.

Ps 125:5 As for such as turn aside unto their crooked ways, the Lord shall lead them forth with the workers of iniquity: *but* peace *shall be* upon Israel.

Pr 2:15 Whose ways *are* crooked, and *they* froward in their paths:

Pr 21:8 The way of man *is* froward and strange: but *as for* the pure, his work *is* right.

Is 59:8 The way of peace they know not; and *there is* no judgment in their goings: they have made them crooked paths: whosoever goeth therein shall not know peace.

See **DECEPTION, SIMPLICITY**

DUST, *common in countries suffering from severe droughts, combined with violent winds can produce desolating storms*

1. Basic Ingredient of Humanity

Ge 2:7; 3:19; 18:27; Jb 4:19; 10:9; 33:6; 34:15; Ps 22:15; 90:3; 103:14; Ec 3:20; 12:7

See **DEATH**

2. Thrown or Shaken off in Anger

Mt 10:14; Mk 6:11; Lu 9:5; 10:11; Ac 13:51; 18:6

3. Placed on the Head as a Sign of Grief

Jos 7:6; 1 S 4:12; 2 S 1:2; 13:19; 15:32; Ne 9:1; Jb 2:12; Lam 2:10; Eze 27:30; Re 18:19

DUTY, *task*

1. Daily

GATHERING THE MANNA

Ex 16:4 Then said the LORD unto Moses, Behold, I will rain bread from heaven for you; and the people shall go out and gather a certain rate every day, that I may prove them, whether they will walk in my law, or no.

1 Chr 16:37 So he left there before the ark of the covenant of the LORD Asaph and his brethren, to minister before the ark continually, as every day's work required:

2 Chr 8:14 And he appointed, according to the order of David his father, the courses of the priests to their service, and the Levites to their charges, to praise and minister before the priests, as the duty of every day required: the porters also by their courses at every gate: for so had David the man of God commanded.

Ezr 3:4 They kept also the feast of tabernacles, as *it is* written, and *offered* the daily burnt offerings by number, according to the custom, as the duty of every day required;

READING OF THE WORD

Ne 8:18 Also day by day, from the first day unto the last day, he read in the book of the law of God. And they kept the feast seven days; and on the eighth day *was* a solemn assembly, according unto the manner.

PERFORMING OF VOWS

Ps 61:8 So will I sing praise unto thy name for ever, that I may daily perform my vows.

PRAYER

Ps 88:9 Mine eye mourneth by reason of affliction: LORD, I have called daily upon thee, I have stretched out my hands unto thee.

Ps 145:2 Every day will I bless thee; and I will praise thy name for ever and ever.

WATCHFULNESS

Pr 8:34 Blessed *is* the man that heareth me, watching daily at my gates, waiting at the posts of my doors.

CROSS-BEARING

Lu 9:23 And he said to *them* all, If any *man* will come after me, let him deny himself, and take up his cross daily, and follow me.

EXHORTATION

He 3:13 But exhort one another daily, while it is called To day; lest any of you be hardened through the deceitfulness of sin.

2. Of Ministers

Is 58:1 Cry aloud, spare not, lift up thy voice like a trumpet, and shew my people their transgression, and the house of Jacob their sins.

Is 62:6 I have set watchmen upon thy walls, O Jerusalem, *which* shall never hold their peace day nor night: ye that make mention of the LORD, keep not silence,

Eze 4:4 Lie thou also upon thy left side, and lay the iniquity of the house of Israel upon it: *according* to the number of the days that thou shalt lie upon it thou shalt bear their iniquity.

Mt 28:19 Go ye therefore, and teach all nations, baptizing them in the name of the Father, and of the Son, and of the Holy Ghost:

Mk 16:15 And he said unto them, Go ye into all the world, and preach the gospel to every creature.

Jn 21:16 He saith to him again the second time, Simon, *son* of Jonas, lovest thou me? He saith unto him, Yea, Lord; thou knowest that I love thee. He saith unto him, Feed my sheep.

Ac 5:20 Go, stand and speak in the temple to the people all the words of this life.

Ac 6:4 But we will give ourselves continually to prayer, and to the ministry of the word.

Ac 14:22 Confirming the souls of the disciples, *and* exhorting them to continue in the faith, and that we must through much tribulation enter into the kingdom of God.

Ac 20:28 Take heed therefore unto yourselves, and to all the flock, over the which the Holy Ghost hath made you overseers, to feed the church of God, which he hath purchased with his own blood.

Ro 12:6–8 Having then gifts differing according to the grace that is given to us, whether prophecy, *let us prophesy* according to the proportion of faith;

Or ministry, *let us wait* on *our* ministering: or he that teacheth, on teaching;

Or he that exhorteth, on exhortation: he that giveth, *let him do it* with simplicity; he that ruleth, with diligence; he that sheweth mercy, with cheerfulness.

Ep 3:9 And to make all *men* see what *is* the fellowship of the mystery, which from the beginning of the world hath been hid in God, who created all things by Jesus Christ:

1 Ti 4:6 If thou put the brethren in remembrance of these things, thou shalt be a good minister of Jesus Christ, nourished up in the words of faith and of good doctrine, whereunto thou hast attained.

2 Ti 1:6 Wherefore I put thee in remembrance that thou stir up the gift of God, which is in thee by the putting on of my hands.

2 Ti 2:15 Study to shew thyself approved unto God, a workman that needeth not to be ashamed, rightly dividing the word of truth.

Tit 1:5 For this cause left I thee in Crete, that thou shouldest set in order the things that are wanting, and ordain elders in every city, as I had appointed thee:

1 Pe 5:2 Feed the flock of God which is among you, taking the oversight *thereof,* not by constraint, but willingly; not for filthy lucre, but of a ready mind;

2 Pe 1:12 Wherefore I will not be negligent to put you always in remembrance of these things, though ye know *them,* and be established in the present truth.

3. To the weak

Eze 34:4 The diseased have ye not strengthened, neither have ye healed that which was sick, neither have ye bound up *that which was* broken, neither have ye brought again that which was driven away, neither have ye sought that which was lost; but with force and with cruelty have ye ruled them.

Eze 34:21 Because ye have thrust with side and with shoulder, and pushed all the diseased with your horns, till ye have scattered them abroad;

Mt 10:42 And whosoever shall give to drink unto one of these little ones a cup of cold *water* only in the name of a disciple, verily I say unto you, he shall in no wise lose his reward.

Mt 18:6 But whoso shall offend one of these little ones which believe in me, it were better for him that a millstone were hanged about his neck, and *that* he were drowned in the depth of the sea.

Mt 18:10 Take heed that ye despise not one of these little ones; for I say unto you, That in heaven their angels do always behold the face of my Father which is in heaven.

Mt 25:35–36 For I was an hungred, and ye gave me meat: I was thirsty, and ye gave me drink: I was a stranger, and ye took me in:

Naked, and ye clothed me: I was sick, and ye visited me: I was in prison, and ye came unto me.

Mt 25:45 Then shall he answer them, saying, Verily I say unto you, Inasmuch as ye did *it* not to one of the least of these, ye did *it* not to me.

Mk 9:42 And whosoever shall offend one of *these* little ones that believe in me, it is better for him that a millstone were hanged about his neck, and he were cast into the sea.

Lu 9:48 And said unto them, Whosoever shall receive this child in my name receiveth me: and whosoever shall receive me receiveth him that sent me: for he that is least among you all, the same shall be great.

Lu 15:14 And when he had spent all, there arose a mighty famine in that land; and he began to be in want.

Lu 17:2 It were better for him that a millstone were hanged about his neck, and he cast into the sea, than that he should offend one of these little ones.

Jn 21:15 So when they had dined, Jesus saith to Simon Peter, Simon, *son of* Jonas, lovest thou me more than these? He saith unto him, Yea, Lord; thou knowest that I love thee. He saith unto him, Feed my lambs.

Ac 20:35 I have shewed you all things, how that so labouring ye ought to support the weak, and to remember the words of the Lord Jesus, how he said, It is more blessed to give than to receive.

Ro 14:1 Him that is weak in the faith receive ye, *but* not to doubtful disputations.

Ro 14:15 But if thy brother be grieved with *thy* meat, now walkest thou not charitably. Destroy not him with thy meat, for whom Christ died.

Ro 14:21 *It is* good *any thing* whereby thy brother stumbleth, or is offended, or is made weak.

Ro 15:1 We then that are strong ought to bear the infirmities of the weak, and not to please ourselves.

1 Co 8:11 And through thy knowledge shall the weak brother perish, for whom Christ died?

1 Co 9:22 To the weak became I as weak, that I might gain the weak: I am made all things to all *men,* that I might by all means save some.

1 Co 10:28 But if any man say unto you, This is offered in sacrifice unto idols, eat not for his sake that shewed it, and for conscience sake: for the earth *is* the Lord's, and the fulness thereof:

1 Co 12:25 That there should be no schism in the body; but *that* the members should have the same care one for another.

1 Co 14:16 Else when thou shalt bless with the spirit, how shall he that occupieth the room of the unlearned say Amen at thy giving of thanks, seeing he understandeth not what thou sayest?

2 Co 2:7 So that contrariwise ye *ought* rather to forgive *him,* and comfort *him,* lest perhaps such a one should be swallowed up with overmuch sorrow.

Ga 6:1 Brethren, if a man be overtaken in a fault, ye which are spiritual, restore such an one in the spirit of meekness; considering thyself, lest thou also be tempted.

1 Th 5:14 Now we exhort you, brethren, warn them that are unruly, comfort the feebleminded, support the weak, be patient toward all *men.*

He 12:13 And make straight paths for your feet, lest that which is lame be turned out of the way; but let it rather be healed.

Jude 22 And of some have compassion, making a difference:

See **HELPER**

4. Threefold

a. Appropriation

Ps 116:13 I will take the cup of salvation, and call upon the name of the LORD.

Pr 4:13 Take fast hold of instruction; let *her* not go: keep her; for she *is* thy life.

Is 27:5 Or let him take hold of my strength, *that* he may make peace with me; *and* he shall make peace with me.

Lu 19:13 And he called his ten servants, and delivered them ten pounds, and said unto them, Occupy till I come.

Jn 6:54 Whoso eateth my flesh, and drinketh my blood, hath eternal life; and I will raise him up at the last day.

Re 22:17 And the Spirit and the bride say, Come. And let him that heareth say, Come. And let him that is athirst come. And whosoever will, let him take the water of life freely.

b. Formation

Ex 25:40 And look that thou make *them* after their pattern, which was shewed thee in the mount.

Jn 13:15 For I have given you an example, that ye should do as I have done to you.

Ro 12:2 And be not conformed to this world: but be ye transformed by the renewing of your mind, that ye may prove what is that good, and acceptable, and perfect, will of God.

2 Co 3:18 But we all, with open face beholding as in a glass the glory of the Lord, are changed into the same image from glory to glory, *even* as by the Spirit of the Lord.

1 Pe 1:14–15 As obedient children, not fashioning yourselves according to the former lusts in your ignorance:

But as he which hath called you is holy, so be ye holy in all manner of conversation;

c. Donation

Mt 10:8 Heal the sick, cleanse the lepers, raise the dead, cast out devils: freely ye have received, freely give.

Mt 16:25 For whosoever will save his life shall lose it: and whosoever will lose his life for my sake shall find it.

Lu 3:11 He answereth and saith unto them, He that hath two coats, let him impart to him that hath none; and he that hath meat, let him do likewise.

Ac 20:35 I have shewed you all things, how that so labouring ye ought to support the weak, and to remember the words of the Lord Jesus, how he said, It is more blessed to give than to receive.

1 Pe 4:10 As every man hath received the gift, *even so* minister the same one to another, as good stewards of the manifold grace of God.

5. The Pressure

IT BURNS LIKE AN INWARD FIRE

Je 20:9 Then I said, I will not make mention of him, nor speak any more in his name. But *his word* was in mine heart as a burning fire shut up in my bones, and I was weary with forbearing, and I could not *stay*.

IT CALLS LIKE THE VOICE OF A LION

Am 3:8 The lion hath roared, who will not fear? the Lord GOD hath spoken, who can but prophesy?

IT BINDS THE SOUL TO ITS TASK

Lu 12:50 But I have a baptism to be baptized with; and how am I straitened till it be accomplished!

IT URGES TO HASTE

Jn 9:4 I must work the works of him that sent me, while it is day: the night cometh, when no man can work.

IT MAKES THE MESSAGE IMPERATIVE

Ac 4:20 For we cannot but speak the things which we have seen and heard.

Ac 18:5 And when Silas and Timotheus were come from Macedonia, Paul was pressed in the spirit, and testified to the Jews *that* Jesus *was* Christ.

Ac 20:22 And now, behold, I go bound in the spirit unto Jerusalem, not knowing the things that shall befall me there:

IT RESULTS IN PREACHING

1 Co 9:16 For though I preach the gospel, I have nothing to glory of: for necessity is laid upon me; yea, woe is unto me, if I preach not the gospel!

See **SELF-SACRIFICE, SERVICE**

DYEING, *of garments*

DYERS *See* **ARTS AND CRAFTS**

DYSENTERY

Ex 25:5; 26:14; Is 63:1

See **DISEASE**

E

EAGLES *See* **BIRDS**

EARLY RISING

Ge 19:27; 20:8; 21:14; 26:31; Ex 8:20; 9:13; 34:4; Jos 3:1; 6:12, 15; 7:16; 8:10, 14; Jud 6:38; 7:1; 19:5; Ru 3:14; 1 S 5:4; 9:26; 15:12; 17:20; 29:11; 2 K 3:22; 6:15; 2 Chr 20:20; Pr 31:15; Da 6:19; Mk 16:2; Jn 20:1

1. For Devotions

See **DEVOTIONAL LIFE**

2. To Do Evil

Ex 32:6; Nu 14:40; Jb 24:13–14; Is 5:11; Zep 3:7

EARNESTNESS, *wholeheartedness*

IN LOVE

De 6:5 And thou shalt love the LORD thy God with all thine heart, and with all thy soul, and with all thy might.
De 30:2 And shalt return unto the LORD thy God, and shalt obey his voice according to all that I command thee this day, thou and thy children, with all thine heart, and with all thy soul;

IN OBEDIENCE

Ps 119:2 Blessed *are* they that keep his testimonies, *and that* seek him with the whole heart.
Ps 119:34 Give me understanding, and I shall keep thy law; yea, I shall observe it with *my* whole heart.

IN TRUST

Pr 3:5 Trust in the LORD with all thine heart; and lean not unto thine own understanding.

IN PRAYER

Je 29:13 And ye shall seek me, and find *me*, when ye shall search for me with all your heart.

IN REPENTANCE

Jl 2:12 Therefore also now, saith the LORD, turn ye *even* to me with all your heart, and with fasting, and with weeping, and with mourning:
Mt 22:37 Jesus said unto him, Thou shalt love the LORD thy God with all thy heart, and with all thy soul, and with all thy mind.
Ac 8:37 And Philip said, If thou believest with all thine heart, thou mayest. And he answered and said, I believe that Jesus Christ is the Son of God.

1. Crying to God

Ge 32:9 And Jacob said, O God of my father Abraham, and God of my father Isaac, the LORD which saidst unto me, Return unto thy country, and to thy kindred, and I will deal well with thee:
Ex 2:23 And it came to pass in process of time, that the king of Egypt died: and the children of Israel sighed by reason of the bondage, and they cried, and their cry came up unto God by reason of the bondage.
Ex 8:12 And Moses and Aaron went out from Pharaoh: and Moses cried unto the LORD because of the frogs which he had brought against Pharaoh.
Ex 8:30 And Moses went out from Pharaoh, and intreated the LORD.
Ex 14:10 And when Pharaoh drew nigh, the children of Israel lifted up their eyes, and, behold, the Egyptians marched after them; and they were sore afraid: and the children of Israel cried out unto the LORD.
Ex 15:25 And he cried unto the LORD; and the LORD shewed him a tree, *which* when he had cast into the waters, the waters were made sweet: there he made for them a statute and an ordinance, and there he proved them,

Ex 17:4 And Moses cried unto the LORD, saying, What shall I do unto this people? they be almost ready to stone me.

Ex 22:23 If thou afflict them in any wise, and they cry at all unto me, I will surely hear their cry;

Ex 22:27 For that *is* his covering only, it *is* his raiment for his skin: wherein shall he sleep? and it shall come to pass, when he crieth unto me, that I will hear; for I *am* gracious.

Nu 20:16 And when we cried unto the LORD, he heard our voice, and sent an angel, and hath brought us forth out of Egypt: and, behold, we *are* in Kadesh, a city in the uttermost of thy border:

De 15:9 Beware that there be not a thought in thy wicked heart, saying, The seventh year, the year of release, is at hand; and thine eye be evil against thy poor brother, and thou givest him nought; and he cry unto the LORD against thee, and it be sin unto thee.

De 24:15 At his day thou shalt give *him* his hire, neither shall the sun go down upon it; for he *is* poor, and setteth his heart upon it: lest he cry against thee unto the LORD, and it be sin unto thee.

De 26:7 And when we cried unto the LORD God of our fathers, the LORD heard our voice, and looked on our affliction, and our labour, and our oppression:

Jos 24:7 And when they cried unto the LORD, he put darkness between you and the Egyptians, and brought the sea upon them, and covered them; and your eyes have seen what I have done in Egypt: and ye dwelt in the wilderness a long season.

Jud 3:9 And when the children of Israel cried unto the LORD, the LORD raised up a deliverer to the children of Israel, who delivered them, *even* Othniel the son of Kenaz, Caleb's younger brother.

Jud 3:15 But when the children of Israel cried unto the LORD, the LORD raised them up a deliverer, Ehud the son of Gera, a Benjamite, a man lefthanded: and by him the children of Israel sent a present unto Eglon the king of Moab.

Jud 4:3 And the children of Israel cried unto the LORD: for he had nine hundred chariots of iron; and twenty years he mightily oppressed the children of Israel.

Jud 6:7 And it came to pass, when the children of Israel cried unto the LORD because of the Midianites,

Jud 10:10 And the children of Israel cried unto the LORD, saying, We have sinned against thee, both because we have forsaken our God, and also served Baalim.

Jud 20:23 (And the children of Israel went up and wept before the LORD until even, and asked counsel of the LORD, saying, Shall I go up again to battle against the children of Benjamin my brother? And the LORD said, Go up against him.)

1 S 1:10 And she *was* in bitterness of soul, and prayed unto the LORD, and wept sore.

1 S 7:9 And Samuel took a sucking lamb, and offered *it for* a burnt offering wholly unto the LORD: and Samuel cried unto the LORD for Israel; and the LORD heard him.

1 S 12:8 When Jacob was come into Egypt, and your fathers cried unto the LORD, then the LORD sent Moses and Aaron, which brought forth your fathers out of Egypt, and made them dwell in this place.

1 S 12:10 And they cried unto the LORD, and said, We have sinned, because we have forsaken the LORD, and have served Baalim and Ashtaroth: but now deliver us out of the hand of our enemies, and we will serve thee.

1 S 15:11 It repenteth me that I have set up Saul *to be* king: for he is turned back from following me, and hath not performed my commandments. And it grieved Samuel; and he cried unto the LORD all night.

2 S 22:7 In my distress I called upon the LORD, and cried to my God: and he did hear my voice out of his temple, and my cry *did enter* into his ears.

1 K 8:28 Yet have thou respect unto the prayer of thy servant, and to his supplication, O LORD my God, to hearken unto the cry and to the prayer, which thy servant prayeth before thee to day:

1 K 8:47 Yet if they shall bethink themselves in the land whither they were carried captives, and repent, and make supplication unto thee in the land of them that carried them captives, saying, We have sinned, and have done perversely, we have committed wickedness;

1 K 17:20 And he cried unto the LORD, and said, O LORD my God, hast thou also brought evil upon the widow with whom I sojourn, by slaying her son?

2 K 20:11 And Isaiah the prophet cried unto the LORD: and he brought the shadow ten degrees backward, by which it had gone down in the dial of Ahaz.

1 Chr 5:20 And they were helped against them, and the Hagarites were delivered into their hand, and all that were with them: for they cried to God in the battle, and he was intreated of them; because they put their trust in him.

2 Chr 13:14 And when Judah looked back, behold, the battle was before and behind: and they cried unto the LORD, and the priests sounded with the trumpets.

2 Chr 14:11 And Asa cried unto the LORD his God, and said, LORD, it is nothing with thee to help, whether with many, or with them that have no power: help us, O LORD our God; for we rest on thee, and in thy name we go against this multitude. O LORD, thou art our God; let not man prevail against thee.

2 Chr 32:20 And for this cause Hezekiah the king, and the prophet Isaiah the son of Amoz, prayed and cried to heaven.

Ne 9:4 Then stood up upon the stairs, of the Levites, Jeshua, and Bani, Kadmiel, Shebaniah, Bunni, Sherebiah, Bani, and Chenani, and cried with a loud voice unto the LORD their God.

Ne 9:27 Therefore thou deliveredst them into the hand of their enemies, who vexed them: and in the time of their trouble, when they cried unto thee, thou heardest them from heaven; and according to thy manifold mercies thou gavest them saviours, who saved them out of the hand of their enemies.

Est 9:31 To confirm these days of Purim in their times appointed, according as Mordecai the Jew and Esther the queen had enjoined them, and as they had decreed for themselves and for their seed, the matters of the fastings and their cry.

Ps 3:4 I cried unto the LORD with my voice, and he heard me out of his holy hill. Selah.

Ps 5:2 Hearken unto the voice of my cry, my King, and my God: for unto thee will I pray.

Ps 17:1 Hear the right, O LORD, attend unto my cry, give ear unto my prayer, that goeth not out of feigned lips.

Ps 18:6 In my distress I called upon the LORD, and cried unto my God: he heard my voice out of his temple, and my cry came before him, even into his ears.

Ps 22:2 O my God, I cry in the daytime, but thou hearest not; and in the night season, and am not silent.

Ps 28:1 Unto thee will I cry, O LORD my rock; be not silent to me: lest, if thou be silent to me, I become like them that go down into the pit.

Ps 30:2 O LORD my God, I cried unto thee, and thou hast healed me.

Ps 34:6 This poor man cried, and the LORD heard him, and saved him out of all his troubles.

Ps 35:1 Plead my cause, O LORD, with them that strive with me: fight against them that fight against me.

Ps 39:12 Hear my prayer, O LORD, and give ear unto my cry; hold not thy peace at my tears: for I am a stranger with thee, and a sojourner, as all my fathers were.

Ps 55:1 Give ear to my prayer, O God; and hide not thyself from my supplication.

Ps 56:9 When I cry unto thee, then shall mine enemies turn back: this I know; for God is for me.

Ps 57:2 I will cry unto God most high; unto God that performeth *all things* for me.

Ps 61:2 From the end of the earth will I cry unto thee, when my heart is overwhelmed: lead me to the rock *that* is higher than I.

Ps 66:17 I cried unto him with my mouth, and he was extolled with my tongue.

Ps 69:16 Hear me, O LORD; for thy lovingkindness *is* good: turn unto me according to the multitude of thy tender mercies.

Ps 77:1 I cried unto God with my voice, *even* unto God with my voice; and he gave ear unto me.

Ps 81:7 Thou calledst in trouble, and I delivered thee; I answered thee in the secret place of thunder: I proved thee at the waters of Meribah. Selah.

Ps 83:1 Keep not thou silence, O God: hold not thy peace, and be not still, O God.

Ps 86:3 Be merciful unto me, O Lord: for I cry unto thee daily.

Ps 88:1 O LORD God of my salvation, I have cried day *and* night before thee:

Ps 88:13 But unto thee have I cried, O LORD; and in the morning shall my prayer prevent thee.

Ps 102:1 Hear my prayer, O LORD, and let my cry come unto thee.

Ps 106:44 Nevertheless he regarded their affliction, when he heard their cry:

Ps 107:6 Then they cried unto the LORD in their trouble, *and* he delivered them out of their distresses.

Ps 107:13 Then they cried unto the LORD in their trouble, *and* he saved them out of their distresses.

Ps 107:19 Then they cry unto the LORD in their trouble, *and* he saveth them out of their distresses.

Ps 116:4 Then called I upon the name of the LORD; O LORD, I beseech thee, deliver my soul.

Ps 118:5 I called upon the LORD in distress: the LORD answered me, *and set me* in a large place.

Ps 119:145 I cried with *my* whole heart; hear me, O LORD: I will keep thy statutes.

Ps 119:169 Let my cry come near before thee, O LORD: give me understanding according to thy word.

Ps 120:1 In my distress I cried unto the LORD, and he heard me.

Ps 130:1 Out of the depths have I cried unto thee, O LORD.

Ps 141:1 LORD, I cry unto thee: make haste unto me; give ear unto my voice, when I cry unto thee.

Ps 142:1 I cried unto the LORD with my voice; with my voice unto the LORD did I make my supplication.

Is 19:20 And it shall be for a sign and for a witness unto the LORD of hosts in the land of Egypt: for they shall cry unto the LORD because of the oppressors, and he shall send them a saviour, and a great one, and he shall deliver them.

Is 26:16 LORD, in trouble have they visited thee, they poured out a prayer *when* thy chastening *was* upon them.

Lam 2:18 Their heart cried unto the Lord, O wall of the daughter of Zion, let tears run down like a river day and night: give thyself no rest; let not the apple of thine eye cease.

Lam 3:56 Thou hast heard my voice: hide not thine ear at my breathing, at my cry.

Eze 9:8 And it came to pass, while they were slaying them, and I was left, that I fell upon my face, and cried, and said, Ah Lord GOD! wilt thou destroy all the residue of Israel in thy pouring out of thy fury upon Jerusalem?

Eze 11:13 And it came to pass, when I prophesied, that Pelatiah the son of Benaiah died. Then fell I down upon my face, and cried with a loud voice, and said, Ah Lord GOD! wilt thou make a full end of the remnant of Israel?

Joel 1:14 Sanctify ye a fast, call a solemn assembly, gather the elders *and* all the inhabitants of the land *into* the house of the LORD your God, and cry unto the LORD,

Joel 1:19 O LORD, to thee will I cry: for the fire hath devoured the pastures of the wilderness, and the flame hath burned all the trees of the field.

Jona 1:14 Wherefore they cried unto the LORD, and said, We beseech thee,

O LORD, we beseech thee, let us not perish for this man's life, and lay not upon us innocent blood: for thou, O LORD, hast done as it pleased thee.

Jona 2:2 And said, I cried by reason of mine affliction unto the LORD, and he heard me; out of the belly of hell cried I, *and* thou heardest my voice.

Hab 1:2 O LORD, how long shall I cry, and thou wilt not hear! *even* cry out unto thee *of* violence, and thou wilt not save!

Mt 24:20 But pray ye that your flight be not in the winter, neither on the sabbath day:

Lu 18:7 And shall not God avenge his own elect, which cry day and night unto him, though he bear long with them?

He 5:7 Who in the days of his flesh, when he had offered up prayers and supplications with strong crying and tears unto him that was able to save him from death, and was heard in that he feared;

2. Seven Earnest Pleas

THE CRY FOR HELP (JACOB)

Ge 32:26 And he said, Let me go, for the day breaketh. And he said,

THE CRY OF INTERCESSION (MOSES)

Ex 32:31–32 And Moses returned unto the LORD, and said, Oh, this people have sinned a great sin, and have made them gods of gold.

Yet now, if thou wilt forgive their sin—; and if not, blot me, I pray thee, out of thy book which thou hast written.

THE CRY FOR WISDOM (SOLOMON)

1 K 3:7–9 And now, O LORD my God, thou hast made thy servant king instead of David my father: and I *am but* a little child: I know not *how* to go out or come in.

And thy servant *is* in the midst of thy people which thou hast chosen, a great people, that cannot be numbered nor counted for multitude.

Give therefore thy servant an understanding heart to judge thy people, that I may discern between good and

bad: for who is able to judge this thy so great a people?

THE CRY FOR CLEANSING (DAVID)

Ps 51:1–2 Have mercy upon me, O God, according to thy lovingkindness: according unto the multitude of thy tender mercies blot out my transgressions.

Wash me throughly from mine iniquity, and cleanse me from my sin.

THE CRY OF THE DYING SOUL (PENITENT THIEF)

Lu 23:42 And he said unto Jesus, Lord, remember me when thou comest into thy kingdom.

THE CRY FOR SALVATION (PHILIPPIAN JAILER)

Ac 16:30 And brought them out, and said, Sirs, what must I do to be saved?

THE CRY FOR DELIVERANCE (PAUL)

2 Co 12:8–9 For this thing I besought the Lord thrice, that it might depart from me.

And he said unto me, My grace is sufficient for thee: for my strength is made perfect in weakness. Most gladly therefore will I rather glory in my infirmities, that the power of Christ may rest upon me.

See **INDIFFERENCE**

EARRINGS *See* APPAREL

EARTH

Ge 1:1, 10; 8:22; 10:25; 2 S 22:8; Jb 26:7; 38:18; Ps 24:1; Is 6:3; Zec 12:1

EARTHQUAKES

Ex 19:18; 1 S 14:15; 2 S 22:8; 1 K 19:11; Jb 9:6; Ps 18:7; 46:3; 60:2; 68:8; 77:18; 97:4; 114:7; Is 13:13; 24:19; 29:6; Je 4:24; Eze 38:19; Jl 2:10; 3:16; Am 1:2; Hab 3:10; Zec 14:5; Mt 24:7; 27:51; 28:2; Mk 13:8; Lu 21:11; Ac 16:26; Re 6:12; 8:5; 11:13, 19; 16:18

EASTER, *celebration day of Christ's resurrection*

Ac 12:4

EATING *See* FOOD

EBAL *See* **MOUNTAINS AND HILLS**

EBENEZER, *a place near Mizpah*
1 S 4:1; 5:1; 7:12

EBER, *or Heber, a descendant of Shem*
Ge 10:21

ECCLESIASTES

Name: Borrowed from the Septuagint. In the Hebrew Bible it is called "Koheleth." The meaning of this word is somewhat disputed, but it is rendered in the English version Preacher, or one who addresses an assembly.

Author: Uncertain, but is commonly ascribed to Solomon (1:1–2). Many of the experiences related seem to correspond to those likely to have happened in his life, judging from the bare outline of his history found in the Bible.

Date Written: Late in Solomon's life, probably around 935 B.C.

Purpose: To report the author's finding about the ultimate meaning in life. "To fear God and keep His commandments" (12:3) is man's source of highest satisfaction and fulfillment.

To Whom Written: To those who seek meaning and significance in life, especially young people.

Main Theme: Life without God leads to emptiness, futility, and lack of significant meaning.

Key Words: Vanity and Under the Sun.

Key Verse: 12:13.

ECLIPSE, *a time of darkness*
Is 13:10; 24:23; Eze 32:7; Jl 2:10, 31; 3:15; Am 8:9; Mt 24:29; Mk 13:24; Ac 2:20; Re 6:12

EDEN, *the garden in which God placed Adam and Eve*
Ge 2:8; 3:23; 4:16; Is 51:3; Eze 28:13; 31:9, 16; 36:35; Jl 2:3

EDIFICATION, *the building up of believers*

Ac 18:23 And after he had spent some time *there,* he departed, and went over *all* the country of Galatia and Phrygia in order, strengthening all the disciples.

Ac 18:27 And when he was disposed to pass into Achaia, the brethren wrote, exhorting the disciples to receive him: who, when he was come, helped them much which had believed through grace:

Ro 14:19 Let us therefore follow after the things which make for peace, and things wherewith one may edify another.

Ro 15:2 Let every one of us please *his* neighbour for *his* good to edification.

1 Co 8:1 Now as touching things offered unto idols, we know that we all have knowledge. Knowledge puffeth up, but charity edifieth.

1 Co 14:3 But he that prophesieth speaketh unto men *to* edification, and exhortation, and comfort.

1 Co 14:26 How is it then, brethren? when ye come together, every one of you hath a psalm, hath a doctrine, hath a tongue, hath a revelation, hath an interpretation. Let all things be done unto edifying.

2 Co 10:8 For though I should boast somewhat more of our authority, which the Lord hath given us for edification, and not for your destruction, I should not be ashamed:

2 Co 12:19 Again, think ye that we excuse ourselves unto you? we speak before God in Christ: but *we do* all things, dearly beloved, for your edifying.

Ep 4:12 For the perfecting of the saints, for the work of the ministry, for the edifying of the body of Christ:

Ep 4:29 Let no corrupt communication proceed out of your mouth, but that which is good to the use of edifying, that it may minister grace unto the hearers.

EDOMITES, *descendants of Esau*
Ge 36:9, 43; Nu 20:18; De 2:4; 23:7; Jud 11:17; 1 S 14:47; 21:7; 2 S 8:14; 1 K

11:1; 1 Chr 18:12; 2 Chr 21:8; 28:17; Ps 83:6; 137:7; Je 49:7; Eze 25:12; 32:29; Da 11:41; Am 1:11; Obad 1; Mal 1:4

EFFEMINACY, *men having the characteristics generally associated with women*

Is 19:16; Je 48:41; 50:37; 51:30; Na 3:13; 1 Co 11:14

EFFORT

MONEY FOR TAXES

Mt 17:27 Notwithstanding, lest we should offend them, go thou to the sea, and cast an hook, and take up the fish that first cometh up; and when thou hast opened his mouth, thou shalt find a piece of money: that take, and give unto them for me and thee.

HEALING OF WITHERED HAND

Mk 3:5 And when he had looked round about on them with anger, being grieved for the hardness of their hearts, he saith unto the man, Stretch forth thine hand. And he stretched *it* out: and his hand was restored whole as the other.

GREAT DRAUGHT OF FISH

Lu 5:4 Now when he had left speaking, he said unto Simon, Launch out into the deep, let down your nets for a draught.

HEALING OF PALSY

Lu 5:24 But that ye may know that the Son of man hath power upon earth to forgive sins, (he said unto the sick of the palsy,) I say unto thee, Arise, and take up thy couch, and go into thine house.

HEALING OF LEPROSY

Lu 17:14 And when he saw *them,* he said unto them, Go shew yourselves unto the priests. And it came to pass, that, as they went, they were cleansed.

WINE FOR WEDDING

Jn 2:7 Jesus saith unto them, Fill the waterpots with water. And they filled them up to the brim.

WATER OF SALVATION

Jn 4:16 Jesus saith unto her, Go, call thy husband, and come hither.

ABILITY TO WALK

Jn 5:8 Jesus saith unto him, Rise, take up thy bed, and walk.

EYESIGHT

Jn 9:7 And said unto him, Go, wash in the pool of Siloam, (which is by interpretation, Sent.) He went his way therefore, and washed, and came seeing.

RAISING OF A BROTHER FROM THE DEAD

Jn 11:39 Jesus said, Take ye away the stone. Martha, the sister of him that was dead, saith unto him, Lord, by this time he stinketh: for he hath been *dead* four days.

EGGS

De 22:6; Jb 39:14; Is 10:14; 59:5; Lu 11:12

EGYPT

Ge 12:10; 26:2; 37:28; 39:1; 42:1; 46:3; 50:14; Ex 1:1; 4:19; 12:40; 13:17; 19:1; Nu 1:1; 20:15; 33:1; De 26:5; 29:2; 34:11; Jos 24:4; 1 S 2:27; 12:8; 15:7; 1 K 11:40; 2 K 18:21; 25:26; 2 Chr 10:2; Ps 105:23; Is 19:1; 20:5; 30:2; 31:1; 36:6; 45:14; Je 2:18, 36; 41:17; 42:14; 44:8, 14; Eze 17:15; 29:2, 6, 16; 30:6; Ho 7:11; Mi 7:15; Mt 2:14; Ac 7:6, 12, 15; 13:17

EHUD, *one of the judges*

Jud 3:15, 20, 26; 4:1

See **ISRAEL**

EKRON, *a city of the Philistines*

Jos 13:3; 15:11, 46; Jud 1:18; 1 S 5:10; 6:16; 7:14; 17:52; 2 K 1:2, 6; Je 25:20; Am 1:8; Zep 2:4; Zec 9:5

ELAH, *a king of Israel*

1 K 16:8; 2 K 9:31

See **ISRAEL**

ELAM, *a district southeast of Mesopotamia*

Ge 14:1; Is 21:2; 22:6; Je 25:25; 49:34, 38; Eze 32:24; Ac 2:9

ELATH, *a city of Idumea*

De 2:8; 1 K 9:26; 2 Chr 8:17

ELDERS, *those chosen to fulfill official positions within the community of faith*

1. Governmental

Ge 50:7; Ex 3:16; 4:29; 12:21; 17:5; 18:12; 19:7; 24:1, 9, 14; Le 4:15; 9:1; Nu 11:16, 25, 30; 16:25; 31:26; De 5:23; 19:12; 21:2; 25:7; 27:1; 29:10; 31:9, 28; Jos 8:10, 33; 20:4; 23:2; 24:1, 31; Jud 2:7; 21:16; Ru 4:2, 9; 1 S 4:3; 8:4; 11:3; 16:4; 2 S 3:17; 17:4; 19:11; 1 K 8:1, 3; 20:7; 21:8; 2 K 10:1; 23:1; 1 Chr 11:3; 15:25; 21:16; 2 Chr 5:2; 34:29; Ezr 5:5; 6:8; 10:8, 14; Ps 107:32; Pr 31:23; Je 19:1; 26:17; Lam 2:10; 4:16; 5:14; Eze 8:1, 12; 9:6; 14:1; 20:1; Jl 1:14; 2:16; Re 7:13

2. Jewish

Mt 15:2; 21:23; 26:3, 57; 27:1, 20; 28:12; Mk 7:5; 8:31; 11:27; 14:43; 15:1; Lu 7:3; 20:1; 22:52, 66; Ac 4:5, 8; 6:12; 22:5; 23:14; 24:1; 25:15

3. Christian *See* **CHURCH**

ELEAZAR, *a high priest*

Ex 6:23; 28:1; Nu 3:2, 32; 4:16; 16:37; 20:26; 26:1, 60, 63; 27:2; 31:12, 26, 41; 32:2, 28; 34:17; De 10:6; Jos 14:1; 17:4; 19:51; 21:1; 22:32; 24:33; Jud 20:28; 1 Chr 6:3, 50; 9:20; 24:1

ELECTION, *of God's people*

Ex 6:7; De 4:37; 7:6; Mt 25:34; Jn 15:16; Ga 4:30; Ep 1:4; 1 Pe 1:2

ELEPHANTS *See* **ANIMALS**

ELI, *a judge and high priest*

TENDERNESS WITH CHILD

1 S 3:6

SPIRITUAL PERCEPTION

1 S 3:8

SUBMISSION

1 S 3:18

SPIRITUAL SOLICITUDE

1 S 4:13

UNFAITHFULNESS TO STEWARDSHIP

1 S 2:29–36

PARENTAL INDULGENCE

1 S 3:13

See **ISRAEL**

ELIAB, *David's eldest brother*

1 S 16:6; 17:13, 28; 1 Chr 27:18; 2 Chr 11:18

ELIAKIM, *son of Hilkiah*

2 K 18:18; Is 22:20; 36:3, 22

ELIEZER, *Abraham's steward*

Ge 15:2

ELIJAH, *the prophet*

1. His life

HIS ORIGIN AND APPEARANCE

Nothing is known of his parentage. He is one of the most unique and dramatic characters of Bible history. Rugged in appearance and dress, he is a prototype of John the Baptist (2 K 1:8; Mt 3:4).

THE MAIN EVENTS

First Scene. His unheralded appearance before the idolatrous king Ahab to announce a prolonged drought (1 K 17:1).

Second Scene. In the wilderness by the brook Cherith, where he has gone by divine command to depend for his food on supplies brought by unclean birds (1 K 17:2–6). Here his faith is tested when the brook dries up (v. 7).

Third Scene. At Zarephath. Outside the famine-stricken city, a widow is gathering sticks to cook her last meal. The prophet is sent to widow to be fed (1 K 17:8–9). On arrival he begs for a drink of water and a piece of bread, but she tells him that her supplies are reduced to a handful of meal and a little oil in a cruse (v. 12). Then comes the divine, "Do not fear," and the promise of plentiful supplies to the end of the famine (vv. 13–14).

Fourth Scene. In the loft, at the widow's home at Zarephath. The strain of the famine has been too great for her son, and he lies dead before the prophet. By a mighty struggle in prayer, Elijah brings the boy to life again (1 K 17:17–24).

Fifth Scene. False prophets summoned. Elijah suddenly appears before King Ahab and commands him to summon the false prophets to Mount Carmel (1 K 18:17–19).

Sixth Scene. On Mount Carmel. The prophet calls the people to a decision concerning God and challenges the prophets of Baal to a fiery test (1 K 18:20–24). The failure of the false prophets (vv. 26–29). After the prayer of Elijah the divine fire descends and consumes his sacrifice (vv. 30–38). The verdict of the people that Jehovah is the true God, and the destruction of the false prophets (vv. 39–40).

Seventh Scene. The end of the drought. Elijah's prayer for rain. The coming of the storm. The prophet runs before the king to the entrance of Jezreel (1 K 18:41–46).

Eighth Scene. The prophet under a juniper tree in the wilderness, having fled from the wrath of Queen Jezebel. Discouraged and exhausted, he desires to die, but is fed by an angel, and journeys on to Mount Horeb (1 K 19:1–8).

Ninth Scene. The prophet pours out his complaint to the Lord. He is given a new and better revelation of the divine character and methods (1 K 19:9–13. He is commanded to anoint two prospective kings and his own successor (vv. 15–17).

Tenth Scene. On a farm at Abel-meholah. Elijah finds Elisha plowing and casts his own mantle on him to indicate that this farmer is called to be his successor (1 K 19:19–21).

Eleventh Scene. In the vineyard of Naboth. The prophet finds King Ahab come to take possession of the inheri-

tance which the king murdered Naboth to obtain. Elijah pronounces an awful doom on the wicked king and his wife (1 K 21:17–24).

Twelfth Scene. Two companies of soldiers are sent by the king of Samaria to capture the prophet and he calls down fire from heaven and destroys them (2 K 1:1–12); later he announces the doom of the idolatrous king (v. 16).

Thirteenth Scene. The last journey of Elijah. Accompanied by Elisha, he travels through the country until they reach the Jordan river, where Elijah smites the waters with his mantle and the two pass over on dry ground. As they stand conversing Elisha makes his farewell request. Suddenly a chariot of fire separates the two friends, and Elijah is taken up by a whirlwind into heaven (2 K 2:1–11).

Post Mortem Scene. On the mount of transfiguration Elijah reappears with Moses and talks with Christ (Mt 17:3).

2. Prophecies

1 K 17:1; 21:19–24; 2 K 1:2–17; 9:25–37; 2 Chr 21:12–15

ELIMELECH, *father-in-law of Ruth*
Ru 1:2; 2:3; 4:3

ELIPHAZ, *the Temanite*
Jb 2:11; 4:1

ELISHA, *successor of the prophet Elijah*

1. Resemblance to Elijah
There is a striking resemblance between the life of Elisha and that of Elijah. Not only do their names sound alike, but the main events of their lives run in much the same channels. They are twin figures in Hebrew history.

2. The Two Prophets in Parallel. Both . . .

a. Strike the waters of the river Jordan and pass over on dry ground (2 K 2:8, 14).

b. Bring waters of refreshment in times of drought (1 K 18:41–45; 2 K 3:9–20).

c. Increase a widow's store of food (1 K 17:10–16; 2 K 4:1–7).

d. Raise only sons to life (1 K 17:17–24; 2 K 4:18–35).

e. Perform miracles for persons outside the boundaries of Israel (1 K 17:9–16; 2 K 5:1–15).

f. Pronounce sentences on kings (1 K 21:19–22; 2 K 8:7–10).

g. Call down vengeance on unbelievers (2 K 1:9–12; 2:23–25).

In spite of the points of resemblance between the miracles performed by the two prophets, Elisha was not a mere echo of his fiery predecessor. There was a marked difference between the temperaments of the two men, and their general attitude toward society.

Elijah was a solitary figure like John the Baptist. His life was largely spent in an unavailing struggle with the evils of his times, and he had his periods of great depression.

Not so Elisha. His gift of "a double portion of the Spirit" enabled him to lead a triumphant life as he mingled with his fellow men.

We have no record that he ever complained of his lot, fled from his enemies, or lost his courage.

Even on his death bed he seemed to be full of power as he gave commands to a king.

His reception of a double portion of the Spirit is demonstrated by the fact that he lived a victorious life and also that he performed a greater number of miracles than any other prophet except Moses.

ELIZABETH, *the mother of John the Baptist*

Lu 1:5, 24, 36, 57

See **WOMEN**

ELKANAH, *the father of Samuel*

1 S 1:1, 4, 23; 2:20

ELON   *See* **ISRAEL**

ELUL   *See* **MONTHS**

EMANCIPATION

Le 25:10, 41; 2 Chr 36:23; Ezr 1:3; Ps 146:7; Is 61:1; Je 34:9

EMBALMING   *See* **DEAD**

EMBROIDERY   *See* **ARTS AND CRAFTS**

EMERALDS   *See* **STONES**

EMERODS   *See* **DISEASE**

EMMAUS, *a village near Jerusalem*

On the day of Jesus' resurrection, two of the disciples were on their way from Jerusalem to Emmaus when the risen Christ joined them on their journey (Lu 24:13–35).

See **CITIES**

EMPLOYEES, *servants*

1. Faithful

Ex 21:5 And if the servant shall plainly say, I love my master, my wife, and my children; I will not go out free:

Ps 123:2 Behold, as the eyes of servants *look* unto the hand of their masters, *and* as the eyes of a maiden unto the hand of her mistress; so our eyes *wait* upon the LORD our God, until that he have mercy upon us.

Pr 17:2 A wise servant shall have rule over a son that causeth shame, and shall have part of the inheritance among the brethren.

Pr 25:13 As the cold of snow in the time of harvest, *so is* a faithful messenger to them that send him: for he refresheth the soul of his masters.

Pr 27:18 Whoso keepeth the fig tree shall eat the fruit thereof: so he that waiteth on his master shall be honoured.

Mt 24:45 Who then is a faithful and wise servant, whom his lord hath made ruler over his household, to give them meat in due season?

2. Duties

OBEDIENCE

Ep 6:5 Servants, be obedient to them that are *your* masters according to the flesh, with fear and trembling, in singleness of your heart, as unto Christ;

FAITHFULNESS

Col 3:22 Servants, obey in all things *your* masters according to the flesh; not with eyeservice, as menpleasers; but in singleness of heart, fearing God:

RESPECT FOR MASTERS

1 Ti 6:1 Let as many servants as are under the yoke count their own masters worthy of all honour, that the name of God and *his* doctrine be not blasphemed.

DESIRE TO PLEASE

Tit 2:9 *Exhort* servants to be obedient unto their own masters, *and* to please *them* well in all *things;* not answering again;

PATIENCE IN HARD PLACES

1 Pe 2:18 Servants, *be* subject to *your* masters with all fear; not only to the good and gentle, but also to the froward.

See **HUMILITY, SERVANTS**

EMPLOYERS, *masters*

1. Duties

PROMPT PAYMENT OF WAGES

De 24:15 At his day thou shalt give *him* his hire, neither shall the sun go down upon it; for he *is* poor, and setteth his heart upon it: lest he cry against thee unto the LORD, and it be sin unto thee.

CONSIDERATION FOR EMPLOYEES

Jb 31:13–14 If I did despise the cause of my manservant or of my maidservant, when they contended with me;
What then shall I do when God riseth up? and when he visiteth, what shall I answer him?

REFRAINING FROM THREATS

Ep 6:9 And, ye masters, do the same things unto them, forbearing threatening: knowing that your Master also is in heaven; neither is there respect of persons with him.

JUST DEALING

Col 4:1 Masters, give unto *your* servants that which is just and equal; knowing that ye also have a Master in heaven.

2. Sins Regarding Wages

DELAYING PAYMENT

Le 19:13 Thou shalt not defraud thy neighbour, neither rob *him:* the wages of him that is hired shall not abide with thee all night until the morning.
De 24:15 At his day thou shalt give *him* his hire, neither shall the sun go down upon it; for he *is* poor, and setteth his heart upon it: lest he cry against thee unto the LORD, and it be sin unto thee.

EXACTING SERVICE WITHOUT WAGES

Je 22:13 Woe unto him that buildeth his house by unrighteousness, and his chambers by wrong; *that* useth his neighbour's service without wages, and giveth him not for his work;

FAILING TO PAY A LIVING WAGE

Mal 3:5 And I will come near to you to judgment; and I will be a swift witness against the sorcerers, and against the adulterers, and against false swearers, and against those that oppress the hireling in *his* wages, the widow, and the fatherless, and that turn aside the stranger *from his right,* and fear not me, saith the LORD of hosts..
Lu 3:14 And the soldiers likewise demanded of him, saying, And what shall we do? And he said unto them, Do violence to no man, neither accuse *any* falsely; and be content with your wages.

FRAUDULENT WITHHOLDING OF WAGES

Ja 5:4 Behold, the hire of the labourers who have reaped down your fields, which is of you kept back by fraud, crieth:o the ears of the Lord of sabaoth.

3. Good Examples
Ge 18:19 For I know him, that he will command his children and his household after him, and they shall keep the way of the LORD, to do justice and judgment; that the LORD may bring upon Abraham that which he hath spoken of him.
Ge 35:2 Then Jacob said unto his household, and to all that *were* with him, Put away the strange gods that *are* among you, and be clean, and change your garments:
Jos 24:15 And if it seem evil unto you to serve the LORD, choose you this day whom ye will serve; whether the gods which your fathers served that *were* on the other side of the flood, or the gods of the Amorites, in whose land ye dwell: but as for me and my house, we will serve the LORD.
Lu 7:2-3 And a certain centurion's servant, who was dear unto him, was sick, and ready to die.
And when he heard of Jesus, he sent unto him the elders of the Jews, beseeching him that he would come and heal his servant.
Ac 10:2 A devout *man,* and one that feared God with all his house, which gave much alms to the people, and prayed to God alway.

4. Bad Examples
Ge 16:6 But Abram said unto Sarai, Behold, thy maid *is* in thy hand; do to her as it pleaseth thee. And when Sarai dealt hardly with her, she fled from her face.
Ge 31:7 And your father hath deceived me, and changed my wages ten times; but God suffered him not to hurt me.
Ge 39:20 And Joseph's master took him, and put him into the prison, a place where the king's prisoners *were* bound: and he was there in the prison.
Ex 1:13 And the Egyptians made the children of Israel to serve with rigour:
1 S 30:13 And David said unto him, To whom *belongest* thou? and whence

art thou? And he said, I *am* a young man of Egypt, servant to an Amalekite; and my master left me, because three days agone I fell sick.

5. Overseers
Ge 39:4 And Joseph found grace in his sight, and he served him: and he made him overseer over his house, and all that he had he put into his hand.
1 Chr 9:29 *Some* of them also *were* appointed to oversee the vessels, and all the instruments of the sanctuary, and the fine flour, and the wine, and the oil, and the frankincense, and the spices.
2 Chr 2:18 And he set threescore and ten thousand of them *to be* bearers of burdens, and fourscore thousand *to be* hewers in the mountain, and three thousand and six hundred overseers to set the people a work.
2 Chr 34:17 And they have gathered together the money that was found in the house of the LORD, and have delivered it into the hand of the overseers, and to the hand of the workmen.

See **BUSINESS, SERVANTS**

EMPTINESS, *vanity*

1. Of the Worldly Life
2 K 17:15 And they rejected his statutes, and his covenant that he made with their fathers, and his testimonies which he testified against them; and they followed vanity, and became vain, and went after the heathen that *were* round about them, *concerning* whom the LORD had charged them, that they should not do like them.
Job 7:16 I loathe *it;* I would not live alway: let me alone; for my days *are* vanity.
Job 15:31 Let not him that is deceived trust in vanity: for vanity shall be his recompence.
Ps 4:2 O ye sons of men, how long *will ye turn* my glory into shame? *how long* will ye love vanity, *and* seek after leasing? Selah.
Ps 39:11 When thou with rebukes dost correct man for iniquity, thou

makest his beauty to consume away like a moth: surely every man *is* vanity. Selah.

Ps 62:9 Surely men of low degree *are* vanity, *and* men of high degree *are* a lie: to be laid in the balance, they *are* altogether *lighter* than vanity.

Ps 89:47 Remember how short my time is: wherefore hast thou made all men in vain?

Ps 119:37 Turn away mine eyes from beholding vanity; *and* quicken thou me in thy way.

Pr 21:6 The getting of treasures by a lying tongue *is* a vanity tossed to and fro of them that seek death.

Pr 22:8 He that soweth iniquity shall reap vanity: and the rod of his anger shall fail.

Ec 1:2 Vanity of vanities, saith the Preacher, vanity of vanities; all *is* vanity.

Ec 1:14 I have seen all the works that are done under the sun; and, behold, all *is* vanity and vexation of spirit.

Ec 2:1 I said in mine heart, Go to now, I will prove thee with mirth, therefore enjoy pleasure: and, behold, this also *is* vanity.

Ec 2:11 Then I looked on all the works that my hands had wrought, and on the labour that I had laboured to do: and, behold, all *was* vanity and vexation of spirit, and *there was* no profit under the sun.

Ec 2:17 Therefore I hated life; because the work that is wrought under the sun is grievous unto me: for all *is* vanity and vexation of spirit.

Ec 2:26 For *God* giveth to a man that *is* good in his sight wisdom, and knowledge, and joy: but to the sinner he giveth travail, to gather and to heap up, that he may give to *him that is* good before God. This also *is* vanity and vexation of spirit.

Ec 4:4 Again, I considered all travail, and every right work, that for this a man is envied of his neighbour. This *is* also vanity and vexation of spirit.

Ec 4:16 *There is* no end of all the people, *even* of all that have been before them: they also that come after shall not rejoice in him. Surely this also *is* vanity and vexation of spirit.

Ec 11:8 But if a man live many years, *and* rejoice in them all; yet let him remember the days of darkness; for they shall be many. All that cometh *is* vanity.

Ec 11:10 Therefore remove sorrow from thy heart, and put away evil from thy flesh: for childhood and youth *are* vanity.

Ec 12:8 Vanity of vanities, saith the preacher; all *is* vanity.

Eze 13:8 Therefore thus saith the Lord GOD; Because ye have spoken vanity, and seen lies, therefore, behold, I *am* against you, saith the Lord GOD.

Ep 4:17 This I say therefore, and testify in the Lord, that ye henceforth walk not as other Gentiles walk, in the vanity of their mind,

2. No Satisfaction in Temporal Things

Pr 27:20 Hell and destruction are never full; so the eyes of man are never satisfied.

Ec 1:8 All things *are* full of labour; man cannot utter *it:* the eye is not satisfied with seeing, nor the ear filled with hearing.

Ec 4:8 There is one *alone,* and *there is* not a second; yea, he hath neither child nor brother: yet *is there* no end of all his labour; neither is his eye satisfied with riches; neither *saith he,* For whom do I labour, and bereave my soul of good? This *is* also vanity, yea, it *is* a sore travail.

Ec 5:10 He that loveth silver shall not be satisfied with silver; nor he that loveth abundance with increase: this *is* also vanity.

Ec 6:3 If a man beget an hundred *children,* and live many years, so that the days of his years be many, and his soul be not filled with good, and also *that* he have no burial; I say, *that* an untimely birth *is* better than he.

Ec 6:7 All the labour of man *is* for his mouth, and yet the appetite is not filled.

Is 9:20 And he shall snatch on the right hand, and be hungry; and he shall eat on the left hand, and they shall not be satisfied: they shall eat every man the flesh of his own arm:

Is 29:8 It shall even be as when an hungry *man* dreameth, and, behold, he eateth; but he awaketh, and his soul is empty: or as when a thirsty man dreameth, and, behold, he drinketh; but he awaketh, and, behold, *he is* faint, and his soul hath appetite: so shall the multitude of all the nations be, that fight against mount Zion.

Is 55:2 Wherefore do ye spend money for *that which is* not bread? and your labour for *that which* satisfieth not? hearken diligently unto me, and eat ye *that which is* good, and let your soul delight itself in fatness.

Is 65:13 Therefore thus saith the Lord God, Behold, my servants shall eat, but ye shall be hungry: behold, my servants shall drink, but ye shall be thirsty: behold, my servants shall rejoice, but ye shall be ashamed:

Eze 7:19 They shall cast their silver in the streets, and their gold shall be removed: their silver and their gold shall not be able to deliver them in the day of the wrath of the Lord: they shall not satisfy their souls, neither fill their bowels: because it is the stumblingblock of their iniquity.

Ho 4:10 For they shall eat, and not have enough: they shall commit whoredom, and shall not increase: because they have left off to take heed to the Lord.

Ho 12:1 Ephraim feedeth on wind, and followeth after the east wind: he daily increaseth lies and desolation; and they do make a covenant with the Assyrians, and oil is carried into Egypt.

Mi 6:14 Thou shalt eat, but not be satisfied; and thy casting down *shall be* in the midst of thee; and thou shalt take hold, but shalt not deliver; and *that* which thou deliverest will I give up to the sword.

Hab 2:5 Yea also, because he transgresseth by wine, *he is* a proud man, neither keepeth at home, who enlargeth his desire as hell, and *is* as death, and cannot be satisfied, but gathereth unto him all nations, and heapeth unto him all people:

Hag 1:6 Ye have sown much, and bring in little; ye eat, but ye have not enough; ye drink, but ye are not filled with drink; ye clothe you, but there is none warm; and he that earneth wages earneth wages *to put it* into a bag with holes.

Lu 15:14 And when he had spent all, there arose a mighty famine in that land; and he began to be in want.

John 4:13 Jesus answered and said unto her, Whosoever drinketh of this water shall thirst again:

Ja 4:2 Ye lust, and have not: ye kill, and desire to have, and cannot obtain: ye fight and war, yet ye have not, because ye ask not.

Re 18:14 And the fruits that thy soul lusted after are departed from thee, and all things which were dainty and goodly are departed from thee, and thou shalt find them no more at all.

3. Peril of an Empty Heart

Mt 12:43–45

See **FULLNESS, PEACE, SATISFACTION**

ENCOURAGEMENT

Ex 14:13 And Moses said unto the people, Fear ye not, stand still, and see the salvation of the Lord, which he will shew to you to day: for the Egyptians whom ye have seen to day, ye shall see them again no more for ever.

2 Chr 35:2 And he set the priests in their charges, and encouraged them to the service of the house of the Lord,

Pr 12:25 Heaviness in the heart of man maketh it stoop: but a good word maketh it glad.

Is 35:3 Strengthen ye the weak hands, and confirm the feeble knees.

Is 41:13 For I the Lord thy God will hold thy right hand, saying unto thee, Fear not; I will help thee.

Da 5:10 *Now* the queen, by reason of the words of the king and his lords, came into the banquet house: *and* the queen spake and said, O king, live for ever: let not thy thoughts trouble thee, nor let thy countenance be changed:

Mt 9:2 And, behold, they brought to him a man sick of the palsy, lying on a bed: and Jesus seeing their faith said unto the sick of the palsy; Son, be of good cheer; thy sins be forgiven thee.

Mt 14:27 But straightway Jesus spake unto them, saying, Be of good cheer; it is I; be not afraid.

Mt 17:7 And Jesus came and touched them, and said, Arise, and be not afraid.

Mk 16:6 And he saith unto them, Be not affrighted: Ye seek Jesus of Nazareth, which was crucified: he is risen; he is not here: behold the place where they laid him.

Lu 24:38 And he said unto them, Why are ye troubled? and why do thoughts arise in your hearts?

Ac 23:11 And the night following the Lord stood by him, and said, Be of good cheer, Paul: for as thou hast testified of me in Jerusalem, so must thou bear witness also at Rome.

Ac 27:22 And now I exhort you to be of good cheer: for there shall be no loss of *any man's* life among you, but of the ship.

See **DISCOURAGEMENT**

ENDOR, *a town west of the Jordan*
Jos 17:11; 1 S 28:7; Ps 83:10

ENDURING, *things that abide*

DIVINE SUPPLIES

1 K 19:8 And he arose, and did eat and drink, and went in the strength of that meat forty days and forty nights unto Horeb the mount of God.

SPIRITUAL FOOD

Jn 6:27 Labour not for the meat which perisheth, but for that meat which endureth unto everlasting life, which the Son of man shall give unto you: for him hath God the Father sealed.

SPIRITUAL WORKS

1 Co 3:14 If any man's work abide which he hath built thereupon, he shall receive a reward.

THE THREE GRACES

1 Co 13:13 And now abideth faith, hope, charity, these three; but the greatest of these *is* charity.

THE UNSEEN THINGS

2 Co 4:18 While we look not at the things which are seen, but at the things which are not seen: for the things which are seen *are* temporal; but the things which are not seen *are* eternal.

THE SPIRITUAL KINGDOM

He 12:27 And this *word*, Yet once more, signifieth the removing of those things that are shaken, as of things that are made, that those things which cannot be shaken may remain.
1 Pe 1:25 But the word of the Lord endureth for ever. And this is the word which by the gospel is preached unto you.

See **TRANSIENT**

ENEMIES, *foes, opponents*

1. Of Believers Are Defeated

1 S 12:11; Ezr 8:31; Ps 18:48; Is 62:8; Lu 1:71

2. Of God Are Punished

Ex 15:6, 9; 17:16; Nu 10:35; 32:21; De 32:27, 41; Jos 11:5; Jud 5:31; 1 S 2:10; 28:16; 30:26; 2 S 12:14; Jb 19:11; Ps 2:2; 21:8; 37:20; 66:3; 68:1, 21; 74:4, 23; 78:66; 81:15; 83:2; 89:10, 51; 92:9; 97:3; 139:20; Is 1:24; 26:11; 37:28; 42:13; 66:6; Na 1:2, 8; Mt 13:28; Lu 19:27; 20:43; Jn 15:24; Ac 5:39; Col 1:21; Ja 4:4

See **WICKED**

EN-GEDI, *spring of young goat*

1. Or Hazezon Tamar, a city of Judah

Ge 14:7; Jos 15:62; 1 S 23:29; 24:1; 2 Chr 20:2; Song 1:14; Eze 47:10

2. Wilderness

1 S 23:29; 24:1

3. Cave
1 S 24:3

ENGRAVING *See* ARTS AND CRAFTS

ENLARGEMENT

1. Spiritual
See **GROWTH**

2. National, of Israel
Ex 23:31; 34:24; De 12:20

ENLIGHTENMENT
Jb 33:30 To bring back his soul from the pit, to be enlightened with the light of the living.

Ps 18:28 For thou wilt light my candle: the LORD my God will enlighten my darkness.

Ps 25:15 Mine eyes *are* ever toward the LORD; for he shall pluck my feet out of the net.

Ps 119:130 The entrance of thy words giveth light; it giveth understanding unto the simple.

Pr 29:13 The poor and the deceitful man meet together: the LORD lighteneth both their eyes.

Is 29:18 And in that day shall the deaf hear the words of the book, and the eyes of the blind shall see out of obscurity, and out of darkness.

Is 30:26 Moreover the light of the moon shall be as the light of the sun, and the light of the sun shall be sevenfold, as the light of seven days, in the day that the LORD bindeth up the breach of his people, and healeth the stroke of their wound.

Is 60:19 The sun shall be no more thy light by day; neither for brightness shall the moon give light unto thee: but the LORD shall be unto thee an everlasting light, and thy God thy glory.

Ac 26:18 To open their eyes, *and* to turn *them* from darkness to light, and *from* the power of Satan unto God, that they may receive forgiveness of sins, and inheritance among them which are sanctified by faith that is in me.

2 Co 4:6 For God, who commanded the light to shine out of darkness, hath shined in our hearts, to *give* the light of the knowledge of the glory of God in the face of Jesus Christ.

Ep 1:18 The eyes of your understanding being enlightened; that ye may know what is the hope of his calling, and what the riches of the glory of his inheritance in the saints,

1 Pe 2:9 But ye *are* a chosen generation, a royal priesthood, an holy nation, a peculiar people; that ye should shew forth the praises of him who hath called you out of darkness into his marvellous light:

See **UNDERSTANDING**

ENOCH, *the father of Methuselah*

WALKING WITH GOD
Ge 5:24 And Enoch walked with God: and he *was* not; for God took him.

PLEASING GOD
He 11:5 By faith Enoch was translated that he should not see death; and was not found, because God had translated him: for before his translation he had this testimony, that he pleased God.

WITNESSING FOR GOD
Jude 14 And Enoch also, the seventh from Adam, prophesied of these, saying, Behold, the Lord cometh with ten thousands of his saints,

ENON, *a place where John baptized*
Jn 3:23

ENTHUSIASM *See* EARNESTNESS

ENVY, *jealousy, strife, covetousness*

1. Forbidden
Ps 37:1; 49:16; Pr 3:31; 14:30; 23:17; 24:1, 19; Eze 31:9; Ro 1:29; 13:13; 1 Co 13:4; Ga 5:26; 1 Ti 6:4; Tit 3:3; Ja 3:14, 16; 1 Pe 2:1

2. Examples

Ge 4:5; 26:14; 30:1; 31:1; 37:3–5, 11; Nu 16:3; Est 5:13; Ps 73:3; 106:16; 112:10; Ec 4:4; Eze 35:11; Da 6:4; Mt 27:18; Mk 15:10; Ac 13:45; 17:5; 1 Co 3:3; Ga 5:21; 1 Jn 3:12

EPAPHRAS, *a companion of Paul*

Col 1:7; 4:12; Phm 23

EPAPHRODITUS, *a fellow-laborer with Paul*

Ph 2:25; 4:18

EPHAH, *a measure*

Ex 16:36; Le 5:11; 6:20; 19:36; Jud 6:19; Ru 2:17; 1 S 1:24; Eze 45:11, 24; 46:11; Am 8:5

See **WEIGHTS AND MEASURES**

EPHESIANS

Author: The apostle Paul.

Date Written: Probably written at Rome between A.D. 60 and 64.

Purpose: To show believers their position in Christ and encourage them to walk accordingly.

To Whom Written: The church in Ephesus. Paul's ministry at Ephesus is given in Acts:

(1) His first visit (Ac 18:18–21).

(2) His second visit, when the Holy Spirit is given to believers (Ac 19:2–7).

(3) His continuance of the work with remarkable success (Ac 19:9–20).

(4) His conflict with the silversmiths (Ac 19:23–41).

(5) His address to the Ephesian elders (Ac 20:17–35).

Main Theme: The converted Jews in the early churches were inclined to be exclusive and to separate themselves from their Gentile brethren. This condition in the church at Ephesus may have been the historical occasion that led to the writing of this epistle. The unity of the church, especially between Jew and Gentile believers, is the keynote of the book.

Key Words:

(1) Together

(2) One

(3) In Christ (1:1, 3, 6, 12, 15, 20; 2:10, 13; 3:11; 4:21).

(4) In Heavenly Places (1:3, 20; 2:6; 3:10).

(5) Riches of Grace (1:7; 2:7); of Glory (1:18; 3:16); of Christ (3:8).

Key Verses: 1:10; 2:6, 14–22; 4:3–16 (especially 4:13).

EPHESUS, *a city of Asia Minor*

Ephesus, once the commercial, political, and religious center of western Asia, was located near where the Cayester and the Meander rivers enter the Aegean Sea. Paul labored here for three years and laid the foundation for one of the strongest Christian churches of the first century. So effective was his ministry that magicians confessed and disclosed their practices and brought their books of magic for burning (Ac 19:18–19). The worship of Artemis was threatened, which prompted Demetrius the silversmith to stir up a riot against Paul (Ac 19:24–38). Timothy and John the Beloved carried on the work here and in the other six churches of this area (see Re 2–3).

Ac 18:19, 24; 19:1, 17, 26; 20:16; 1 Co 15:32; 16:8; Ep 1:1; 1 Ti 1:3; 2 Ti 1:18; 4:12; Re 1:11; 2:1

See **CITIES, PAUL**

EPHOD, *vestment worn by the high priest*

Ex 25:7; 28:4, 12, 25; 29:5; 35:9, 27; 39:2, 7, 18, 22; Le 8:7; Jud 8:27; 17:5; 18:14; 1 S 2:18, 28; 14:3; 21:9; 22:18; 23:6, 9; 30:7; 2 S 6:14; 1 Chr 15:27; Ho 3:4

See **PRIESTS**

EPHRAIM, *fruitful*

1. Son of Joseph

Ge 41:52; 46:20; 48:5, 14, 17; Nu 1:10; 26:35; Jos 14:4; 16:4; Jud 5:14; 1 Chr 7:20; Ps 60:7

2. Tribe

Nu 1:33; 2:18; 10:22; 13:8; 34:24; De 33:17; Jos 16:5; 21:5, 20; Jud 1:22, 29; 8:1; 12:1; 1 S 1:1; 2 S 2:9; 1 Chr 6:66; 12:30; 27:10, 14, 20; 2 Chr 15:9; 28:7; 30:18; Is 7:9; 11:13; Eze 48:6

3. Town

2 S 13:23; Jn 11:54

See **CITIES**

4. A Gate of Jerusalem

Ne 8:16; 12:39

See **ISRAEL**

EPILEPSY *See* **DISEASE**

EQUITY

De 10:17 For the LORD your God *is* God of gods, and Lord of lords, a great God, a mighty, and a terrible, which regardeth not persons, nor taketh reward:

Ps 17:2 Let my sentence come forth from thy presence; let thine eyes behold the things that are equal.

Ps 18:25 With the merciful thou wilt shew thyself merciful; with an upright man thou wilt shew thyself upright;

Ps 98:9 Before the LORD; for he cometh to judge the earth: with righteousness shall he judge the world, and the people with equity.

Ps 99:4 The king's strength also loveth judgment; thou dost establish equity, thou executest judgment and righteousness in Jacob.

Is 11:4 But with righteousness shall he judge the poor, and reprove with equity for the meek of the earth: and he shall smite the earth with the rod of his mouth, and with the breath of his lips shall he slay the wicked.

Eze 18:29 Yet saith the house of Israel, The way of the Lord is not equal. O house of Israel, are not my ways equal? are not your ways unequal?

Eze 33:17 Yet the children of thy people say, The way of the Lord is not equal: but as for them, their way is not equal.

Mt 20:13 But he answered one of them, and said, Friend, I do thee no wrong: didst not thou agree with me for a penny?

Ep 6:9 And, ye masters, do the same things unto them, forbearing threatening: knowing that your Master also is in heaven; neither is there respect of persons with him.

ERASTUS, *a Christian convert*

Ac 19:22; Ro 16:23; 2 Ti 4:20

ESAU, *eldest son of Isaac*

A HUNTER

Ge 25:27 And the boys grew: and Esau was a cunning hunter, a man of the field; and Jacob *was* a plain man, dwelling in tents.

IMPULSIVE, DOMINATED BY APPETITE

Ge 25:32 And Esau said, Behold, I *am* at the point to die: and what profit shall this birthright do to me?

MADE A BAD BARGAIN

Ge 25:33 And Jacob said, Swear to me this day; and he sware unto him: and he sold his birthright unto Jacob.

LACKED APPRECIATION
FOR HIGHER THINGS

Ge 25:34 Then Jacob gave Esau bread and pottage of lentiles; and he did eat and drink, and rose up, and went his way: thus Esau despised *his* birthright.

MARRIED HEATHEN WIVES

Ge 26:34 And Esau was forty years old when he took to wife Judith the daughter of Beeri the Hittite, and Bashemath the daughter of Elon the Hittite:

LOST HIS BLESSING

Ge 27:38 And Esau said unto his father, Hast thou but one blessing, my father? bless me, *even* me also, O my father. And Esau lifted up his voice, and wept.

REPENTED TOO LATE

He 12:16–17 Lest there *be* any fornicator, or profane person, as Esau, who for one morsel of meat sold his birthright.

For ye know how that afterward, when he would have inherited the blessing, he was rejected: for he found no place of repentance, though he sought it carefully with tears.

See **YOUNG PEOPLE**

ESHCOL, *a fruitful valley*
Nu 13:23; 32:9; De 1:24

ESHTAOL, *a town of Judah*
Jos 15:33; 18:41; Jud 13:25; 16:31

See **CITIES**

ESTHER, *the queen, wife of Ahasuerus*

1. Person
Est 2:7, 17; 4:14–16; 5:8; 7:6; 8:3–6

2. Book
Author: Unknown.

Canonicity: The right of the book to a place in the Scripture canon has been greatly disputed. The name of God does not appear in it, while a heathen king is referred to over one hundred and fifty times. There is no allusion to prayer or spiritual service of any kind, with the possible exception of fasting.

Date Written: Sometime between 464 B.C. and 435 B.C.(?).

Purpose: To document and demonstrate God's sovereign care of his people, especially for those who remain within Gentile communities.

To Whom Written: Jewish people everywhere, especially for those scattered among the nations of the world.

Main Theme: The deliverance of the Jews by Queen Esther. Without a doubt the book occupies its place in God's Word because of its hidden teaching of an overshadowing providence in connection with God's people and the certainty of retribution overtaking their enemies.

Key Word: Providence.

Key Verse: 4:14.

See **WOMEN, YOUNG PEOPLE**

ESTRANGEMENT
Ps 58:3 The wicked are estranged from the womb: they go astray as soon as they be born

Is 50:1 Thus saith the LORD, Where *is* the bill of your mother's divorcement, whom I have put away? or which of my creditors *is it* to whom I have sold you? Behold, for your iniquities have ye sold yourselves, and for your transgressions is your mother put away.

Je 2:5 Thus saith the LORD, What iniquity have your fathers found in me, that they are gone far from me, and have walked after vanity, and are become vain?

Eze 14:5 That I may take the house of Israel in their own heart, because they are all estranged from me through their idols.

Eze 44:10 And the Levites that are gone away far from me, when Israel went astray, which went astray away from me after their idols; they shall even bear their iniquity.

Eze 44:15 But the priests the Levites, the sons of Zadok, that kept the charge of my sanctuary when the children of Israel went astray from me, they shall come near to me to minister unto me, and they shall stand before me to offer unto me the fat and the blood, saith the Lord GOD:

Eze 48:11 *It shall be* for the priests that are sanctified of the sons of Zadok; which have kept my charge, which went not astray when the children of Israel went astray, as the Levites went astray.

Mt 15:8 This people draweth nigh unto me with their mouth, and honoureth me with *their* lips; but their heart is far from me.

Ep 2:12 That at that time ye were without Christ, being aliens from the commonwealth of Israel, and strangers from the covenants of promise, having no hope, and without God in the world:

Ep 4:18 Having the understanding darkened, being alienated from the life of God through the ignorance that is in them, because of the blindness of their heart:

See **FELLOWSHIP**

ETERNAL *See* **CHRIST, DEATH, GLORY, GOD, HOPE, KINGDOM, LIFE, PUNISHMENT**

ETERNAL FIRE, *place of judgment*

See **FIRE, JUDGMENTS**

ETHANIM, *seventh month, October*

Le 23:24; 25:9; 1 K 8:2; Ezr 3:1

See **MONTHS**

ETHIOPIA, *or Cush*

Nu 12:1; Est 1:1; 8:9; Jb 28:19; Ps 68:31; 87:4; Is 18:1; 20:3; 37:9; 43:3; 45:14; Eze 29:10; 30:4; 38:5; Na 3:9; Ac 8:27

EUNICE, *mother of Timothy*

Ac 16:1; 2 Ti 1:5

EUNUCHS, *castrated*

De 23:1; 2 K 20:18; Est 1:10; 2:21; 4:5; 6:2, 14; Is 39:7; 56:3; Je 29:2; 38:7; 41:16; Da 1:3, 9; Mt 19:12; Ac 8:27

EUPHRATES, *a river*

Ge 2:14; 15:18; De 1:7; 11:24; Jos 1:4; 2 S 8:3; 2 K 23:29; 24:7; 1 Chr 5:9; 18:3; 2 Chr 35:20; Je 13:4; 46:10; 51:63; Re 9:14; 16:12

See **RIVERS**

EVANGELISM, *helping people make contact with Jesus, sharing the good news*

THE SICK

Mt 4:24 And his fame went throughout all Syria: and they brought unto him all sick people that were taken with divers diseases and torments, and those which were possessed with devils, and those which were lunatick, and those that had the palsy; and he healed them.

Mt 8:16 When the even was come, they brought unto him many that were possessed with devils: and he cast out the spirits with *his* word, and healed all that were sick:

THE INSANE

Mt 9:32 As they went out, behold, they brought to him a dumb man possessed with a devil.

THOSE IGNORED

Mk 9:17–20 And one of the multitude answered and said, Master, I have brought unto thee my son, which hath a dumb spirit;

And wheresoever he taketh him, he teareth him: and he foameth, and gnasheth with his teeth, and pineth away: and I spake to thy disciples that they should cast him out; and they could not.

He answereth him, and saith, O faithless generation, how long shall I be with you? how long shall I suffer you? bring him unto me.

And they brought him unto him: and when he saw him, straightway the spirit tare him; and he fell on the ground, and wallowed foaming.

THE HELPLESS

Lu 5:18–19 And, behold, men brought in a bed a man which was taken with a palsy: and they sought *means* to bring him in, and to lay *him* before him.

And when they could not find by what *way* they might bring him in because of the multitude, they went upon the housetop, and let him down through the tiling with *his* couch into the midst before Jesus.

THE BLIND

Lu 18:40 And Jesus stood, and commanded him to be brought unto him: and when he was come near, he asked him,

THE SEEKERS

Jn 1:41–42 He first findeth his own brother Simon, and saith unto him, We have found the Messias, which is, being interpreted, the Christ.

And he brought him to Jesus. And when Jesus beheld him, he said, Thou art Simon the son of Jona: thou shalt be called Cephas, which is by interpretation, A stone.

Jn 12:20–22 And there were certain Greeks among them that came up to worship at the feast:

The same came therefore to Philip, which was of Bethsaida of Galilee, and desired him, saying, Sir, we would see Jesus.

Philip cometh and telleth Andrew: and again Andrew and Philip tell Jesus.

THE DOUBTERS

Jn 1:45–46 Philip findeth Nathanael, and saith unto him, We have found him, of whom Moses in the law, and the prophets, did write, Jesus of Nazareth, the son of Joseph.

And Nathanael said unto him, Can there any good thing come out of Nazareth? Philip saith unto him, Come and see.

THE SINFUL, *wrong reason of Pharisees produces right results*

Jn 8:3 And the scribes and Pharisees brought unto him a woman taken in adultery; and when they had set her in the midst,

THE SORROWING

Jn 11:28 And when she had so said, she went her way, and called Mary her sister secretly, saying, The Master is come, and calleth for thee.

See **WITNESSES**

EVANGELISTS, *proclaimers of the Good News*

Ac 21:8; Ep 4:11; 2 Ti 4:5

EVE, *the female counterpart of Adam*

Ge 2:22; 3:1, 6, 20; 2 Co 11:3; 1 Ti 2:13

See **WOMEN**

EVENTS, *sudden*

Ec 9:12; Da 4:31; Mal 3:1; Mt 24:27, 50; Mk 13:36; Lu 2:13; 12:46; 17:24; Ac 2:2; 9:3; 16:26; 1 Co 15:52; Re 2:5, 16; 3:3

EVERLASTING *See* **FIRE, LIFE, PUNISHMENT**

EVIL

1. Its Roots

Is 5:24; Ho 9:16; Mal 4:1; Mt 3:10; Jude 12

2. Examples

Pr 6:10; Ec 10:1; Song 2:15; 1 Co 5:6

3. To Be Put Away

De 13:5 And that prophet, or that dreamer of dreams, shall be put to death; because he hath spoken to turn *you* away from the LORD your God, which brought you out of the land of Egypt, and redeemed you out of the house of bondage, to thrust thee out of the way which the LORD thy God commanded thee to walk in. So shalt thou put the evil away from the midst of thee.

De 17:7 The hands of the witnesses shall be first upon him to put him to death, and afterward the hands of all the people. So thou shalt put the evil away from among you.

De 17:12 And the man that will do presumptuously, and will not hearken unto the priest that standeth to minister there before the LORD thy God, or unto the judge, even that man shall die: and thou shalt put away the evil from Israel.

De 19:13 Thine eye shall not pity him, but thou shalt put away *the guilt of* innocent blood from Israel, that it may go well with thee.

De 19:19 Then shall ye do unto him, as he had thought to have done unto his brother: so shalt thou put the evil away from among you.

De 21:21 And all the men of his city shall stone him with stones, that he die: so shalt thou put evil away from among you; and all Israel shall hear, and fear.

De 22:21 Then they shall bring out the damsel to the door of her father's house, and the men of her city shall stone her with stones that she die: because she hath wrought folly in Israel, to play the whore in her father's house: so shalt thou put evil away from among you.

De 24:7 If a man be found stealing any of his brethren of the children of Israel, and maketh merchandise of him, or selleth him; then that thief shall die; and thou shalt put evil away from among you.

Jud 20:13 Now therefore deliver *us* the men, the children of Belial, which *are* in Gibeah, that we may put them to death, and put away evil from Israel. But the children of Benjamin would not hearken to the voice of their brethren the children of Israel:

Jb 22:23 If thou return to the Almighty, thou shalt be built up, thou shalt put away iniquity far from thy tabernacles.

Ec 11:10 Therefore remove sorrow from thy heart, and put away evil from thy flesh: for childhood and youth *are* vanity.

Eze 14:6 Therefore say unto the house of Israel, Thus saith the Lord GOD; Repent, and turn *yourselves* from your idols; and turn away your faces from all your abominations.

Eze 43:9 Now let them put away their whoredom, and the carcases of their kings, far from me, and I will dwell in the midst of them for ever.

1 Co 5:13 But them that are without God judgeth. Therefore put away from among yourselves that wicked person.

Col 3:8 But now ye also put off all these; anger, wrath, malice, blasphemy, filthy communication out of your mouth.

1 Pe 2:1 Wherefore laying aside all malice, and all guile, and hypocrisies, and envies, and all evil speakings,

4. Its Fullness

Ge 15:16 But in the fourth generation they shall come hither again: for the iniquity of the Amorites *is* not yet full.

Ec 9:3 This *is* an evil among all *things* that are done under the sun, that *there is* one event unto all: yea, also the heart of the sons of men is full of evil, and madness is in their heart while they live, and after that *they go* to the dead.

Mt 23:31–32 Wherefore ye be witnesses unto yourselves, that ye are the children of them which killed the prophets.

Fill ye up then the measure of your fathers.

Ac 13:10 And said, O full of all subtilty and all mischief, *thou* child of the devil, *thou* enemy of all righteousness, wilt thou not cease to pervert the right ways of the Lord?

Ro 1:29 Being filled with all unrighteousness, fornication, wickedness, covetousness, maliciousness; full of envy, murder, debate, deceit, malignity; whisperers,

1 Th 2:16 Forbidding us to speak to the Gentiles that they might be saved, to fill up their sins alway: for the wrath is come upon them to the uttermost.

Re 17:4 And the woman was arrayed in purple and scarlet colour, and decked with gold and precious stones and pearls, having a golden cup in her hand full of abominations and filthiness of her fornication:

5. United

Ex 16:2 And the whole congregation of the children of Israel murmured against Moses and Aaron in the wilderness:

Mt 8:34 And, behold, the whole city came out to meet Jesus: and when they saw him, they besought *him* that he would depart out of their coasts.

Ac 17:6 And when they found them not, they drew Jason and certain brethren unto the rulers of the city, crying, These that have turned the world upside down are come hither also;

Re 17:13 These have one mind, and shall give their power and strength unto the beast.

See **SIN, WICKED**

EVILDOERS, *those who practice malice, enemies of God*

1. Warnings

De 4:25 When thou shalt beget children, and children's children, and ye shall have remained long in the land, and shall corrupt *yourselves*, and make a graven image, *or* the likeness of any *thing*, and shall do evil in the sight of the LORD thy God, to provoke him to anger:

Jud 3:12 And the children of Israel did evil again in the sight of the LORD: and the LORD strengthened Eglon the king of Moab against Israel, because they had done evil in the sight of the LORD.

2 S 3:39 And I *am* this day weak, though anointed king; and these men the sons of Zeruiah *be* too hard for me: the LORD shall reward the doer of evil according to his wickedness.

Jb 8:20 Behold, God will not cast away a perfect *man,* neither will he help the evil doers:

Ps 5:6 Thou shalt destroy them that speak leasing: the LORD will abhor the bloody and deceitful man.

Ps 34:16 The face of the LORD *is* against them that do evil, to cut off the remembrance of them from the earth.

Ps 37:1 Fret not thyself because of evildoers, neither be thou envious against the workers of iniquity.

Ps 37:9 For evildoers shall be cut off: but those that wait upon the LORD, they shall inherit the earth.

Ps 92:9 For, lo, thine enemies, O LORD, for, lo, thine enemies shall perish; all the workers of iniquity shall be scattered.

Ps 94:16 Who will rise up for me against the evildoers? *or* who will stand up for me against the workers of iniquity?

Ps 119:115 Depart from me, ye evildoers: for I will keep the commandments of my God.

Ps 125:5 As for such as turn aside unto their crooked ways, the LORD shall lead them forth with the workers of iniquity: *but* peace *shall be* upon Israel.

Pr 10:29 The way of the LORD *is* strength to the upright: but destruction *shall be* to the workers of iniquity.

Pr 21:15 *It is* joy to the just to do judgment: but destruction *shall be* to the workers of iniquity.

Is 1:4 Ah sinful nation, a people laden with iniquity, a seed of evildoers, children that are corrupters: they have forsaken the LORD, they have provoked the Holy One of Israel unto anger, they are gone away backward.

Is 9:17 Therefore the Lord shall have no joy in their young men, neither shall have mercy on their fatherless and widows: for every one is an hypocrite and an evildoer, and every mouth speaketh folly. For all this his anger is not turned away, but his hand *is* stretched out still.

Is 13:11 And I will punish the world for *their* evil, and the wicked for their iniquity; and I will cause the arrogancy of the proud to cease, and will lay low the haughtiness of the terrible.

Is 14:20 Thou shalt not be joined with them in burial, because thou hast destroyed thy land, *and* slain thy people: the seed of evildoers shall never be renowned.

Is 31:2 Yet he also *is* wise, and will bring evil, and will not call back his words: but will arise against the house of the evildoers, and against the help of them that work iniquity.

Je 4:4 Circumcise yourselves to the LORD, and take away the foreskins of your heart, ye men of Judah and inhabitants of Jerusalem: lest my fury come forth like fire, and burn that none can quench *it,* because of the evil of your doings.

Je 20:13 Sing unto the LORD, praise ye the LORD: for he hath delivered the soul of the poor from the hand of evildoers.

Je 21:12 O house of David, thus saith the LORD; Execute judgment in the morning, and deliver *him that is* spoiled out of the hand of the oppressor, lest my fury go out like fire, and burn that none can quench *it,* because of the evil of your doings.

Je 23:14 I have seen also in the prophets of Jerusalem an horrible thing: they commit adultery, and walk in lies: they strengthen also the hands of evildoers, that none doth return from his wickedness: they are all of them unto me as Sodom, and the inhabitants thereof as Gomorrah.

Je 29:23 Because they have committed villany in Israel, and have committed adultery with their neighbours' wives, and have spoken lying words in my name, which I have not commanded them; even I know, and *am* a witness, saith the LORD.

Eze 18:18 *As for* his father, because he cruelly oppressed, spoiled his brother by violence, and did *that* which *is* not good among his people, lo, even he shall die in his iniquity.

Ho 9:15 All their wickedness *is* in Gilgal: for there I hated them: for the wickedness of their doings I will drive them out of mine house, I will love them no more: all their princes *are* revolters.

Ro 13:4 For he is the minister of God to thee for good. But if thou do that which is evil, be afraid; for he beareth not the sword in vain: for he is the minister of God, a revenger to *execute* wrath upon him that doeth evil.

Ph 3:2 Beware of dogs, beware of evil workers, beware of the concision.

1 Ti 1:9 Knowing this, that the law is not made for a righteous man, but for the lawless and disobedient, for the ungodly and for sinners, for unholy and profane, for murderers of fathers and murderers of mothers, for manslayers,

1 Pe 4:15 But let none of you suffer as a murderer, or *as* a thief, or *as* an evildoer, or as a busybody in other men's matters.

2. Examples

Nu 32:13 And the LORD's anger was kindled against Israel, and he made them wander in the wilderness forty years, until all the generation, that had done evil in the sight of the LORD, was consumed.

De 9:18 And I fell down before the LORD, as at the first, forty days and forty nights: I did neither eat bread, nor drink water, because of all your sins which ye sinned, in doing wickedly in the sight of the LORD, to provoke him to anger.

Jud 2:11 And the children of Israel did evil in the sight of the LORD, and served Baalim:

Jud 3:7 And the children of Israel did evil in the sight of the LORD, and forgat the LORD their God, and served Baalim and the groves.

Jud 4:1 And the children of Israel again did evil in the sight of the LORD, when Ehud was dead.

Jud 6:1 And the children of Israel did evil in the sight of the LORD: and the LORD delivered them into the hand of Midian seven years.

Jud 10:6 And the children of Israel did evil again in the sight of the LORD, and served Baalim, and Ashtaroth, and the gods of Syria, and the gods of Zidon, and the gods of Moab, and the gods of the children of Ammon, and forsook the LORD, and served not him.

Jud 13:1 And the children of Israel did evil again in the sight of the LORD; and the LORD delivered them into the hand of the Philistines forty years.

1 S 2:23 And he said unto them, Why do ye such things? for I hear of your evil dealings by all this people.

1 S 15:19 Wherefore then didst thou not obey the voice of the LORD, but didst fly upon the spoil, and didst evil in the sight of the LORD?

2 S 12:9 Wherefore hast thou despised the commandment of the LORD, to do evil in his sight? thou hast killed Uriah the Hittite with the sword, and hast taken his wife *to be* thy wife, and hast slain him with the sword of the children of Ammon.

1 K 11:5 For Solomon went after Ashtoreth the goddess of the Zidonians, and after Milcom the abomination of the Ammonites.

1 K 11:33 Because that they have forsaken me, and have worshipped Ashtoreth the goddess of the Zidonians, Chemosh the god of the Moabites, and Milcom the god of the children of Ammon, and have not walked in my ways, to do *that which is* right in mine eyes, and *to keep* my statutes and my judgments, as *did* David his father.

1 K 14:9 But hast done evil above all that were before thee: for thou hast gone and made thee other gods, and molten images, to provoke me to anger, and hast cast me behind thy back:

1 K 14:22 And Judah did evil in the sight of the LORD, and they provoked him to jealousy with their sins which they had committed, above all that their fathers had done.

1 K 15:26 And he did evil in the sight of the LORD, and walked in the way of his father, and in his sin wherewith he made Israel to sin.

1 K 15:34 And he did evil in the sight of the LORD, and walked in the way of Jeroboam, and in his sin wherewith he made Israel to sin.

1 K 16:7 And also by the hand of the prophet Jehu the son of Hanani came the word of the LORD against Baasha, and against his house, even for all the evil that he did in the sight of the LORD, in provoking him to anger with the work of his hands, in being like the house of Jeroboam; and because he killed him.

1 K 16:19 For his sins which he sinned in doing evil in the sight of the LORD, in walking in the way of Jeroboam, and in his sin which he did, to make Israel to sin.

1 K 16:25 But Omri wrought evil in the eyes of the LORD, and did worse than all that *were* before him.

1 K 16:30 And Ahab the son of Omri did evil in the sight of the LORD above all that *were* before him.

1 K 21:11 And the men of his city, *even* the elders and the nobles who were the inhabitants in his city, did as Jezebel had sent unto them, *and* as it *was* written in the letters which she had sent unto them.

1 K 22:52 And he did evil in the sight of the LORD, and walked in the way of his father, and in the way of his mother, and in the way of Jeroboam the son of Nebat, who made Israel to sin:

2 K 3:2 And he wrought evil in the sight of the LORD; but not like his father, and like his mother: for he put away the image of Baal that his father had made.

2 K 8:18 And he walked in the way of the kings of Israel, as did the house of Ahab: for the daughter of Ahab was his wife: and he did evil in the sight of the LORD.

2 K 8:27 And he walked in the way of the house of Ahab, and did evil in the sight of the LORD, as *did* the house of Ahab: for he *was* the son in law of the house of Ahab.

2 K 13:2 And he did *that which was* evil in the sight of the LORD, and fol-

lowed the sins of Jeroboam the son of Nebat, which made Israel to sin; he departed not therefrom.

2 K 13:11 And he did *that which was* evil in the sight of the LORD; he departed not from all the sins of Jeroboam the son of Nebat, who made Israel sin: *but* he walked therein.

2 K 14:24 And he did *that which was* evil in the sight of the LORD: he departed not from all the sins of Jeroboam the son of Nebat, who made Israel to sin.

2 K 15:9 And he did *that which was* evil in the sight of the LORD, as his fathers had done: he departed not from the sins of Jeroboam the son of Nebat, who made Israel to sin.

2 K 15:18 And he did *that which was* evil in the sight of the LORD: he departed not all his days from the sins of Jeroboam the son of Nebat, who made Israel to sin.

2 K 15:24 And he did *that which was* evil in the sight of the LORD: he departed not from the sins of Jeroboam the son of Nebat, who made Israel to sin.

2 K 15:28 And he did *that which was* evil in the sight of the LORD: he departed not from the sins of Jeroboam the son of Nebat, who made Israel to sin.

2 K 17:2 And he did *that which was* evil in the sight of the LORD, but not as the kings of Israel that were before him.

2 K 17:11 And there they burnt incense in all the high places, as *did* the heathen whom the LORD carried away before them; and wrought wicked things to provoke the LORD to anger:

2 K 21:2 And he did *that which was* evil in the sight of the LORD, after the abominations of the heathen, whom the LORD cast out before the children of Israel.

2 K 21:15 Because they have done *that which was* evil in my sight, and have provoked me to anger, since the day their fathers came forth out of Egypt, even unto this day.

2 K 21:20 And he did *that which was* evil in the sight of the LORD, as his father Manasseh did.

2 K 23:32 And he did *that which was* evil in the sight of the LORD, according to all that his fathers had done.

2 K 23:37 And he did *that which was* evil in the sight of the LORD, according to all that his fathers had done.

2 K 24:9 And he did *that which was* evil in the sight of the LORD, according to all that his father had done.

2 K 24:19 And he did *that which was* evil in the sight of the LORD, according to all that Jehoiakim had done.

1 Chr 2:3 The sons of Judah; Er, and Onan, and Shelah: *which* three were born unto him of the daughter of Shua the Canaanitess. And Er, the firstborn of Judah, was evil in the sight of the LORD; and he slew him.

2 Chr 12:14 And he did evil, because he prepared not his heart to seek the LORD.

2 Chr 21:6 And he walked in the way of the kings of Israel, like as did the house of Ahab: for he had the daughter of Ahab to wife: and he wrought *that which was* evil in the eyes of the LORD.

2 Chr 22:4 Wherefore he did evil in the sight of the LORD like the house of Ahab: for they were his counsellors after the death of his father to his destruction.

2 Chr 28:1 Ahaz *was* twenty years old when he began to reign, and he reigned sixteen years in Jerusalem: but he did not *that which was* right in the sight of the LORD, like David his father:

2 Chr 28:19 For the LORD brought Judah low because of Ahaz king of Israel; for he made Judah naked, and transgressed sore against the LORD.

2 Chr 33:2 But did *that which was* evil in the sight of the LORD, like unto the abominations of the heathen, whom the LORD had cast out before the children of Israel.

2 Chr 33:22 But he did *that which was* evil in the sight of the LORD, as did Manasseh his father: for Amon sacrificed unto all the carved images which Manasseh his father had made, and served them;

2 Chr 36:5 Jehoiakim *was* twenty and five years old when he began to reign, and he reigned eleven years in Jerusalem: and he did *that which was* evil in the sight of the LORD his God.

2 Chr 36:9 Jehoiachin *was* eight years old when he began to reign, and he reigned three months and ten days in Jerusalem: and he did *that which was* evil in the sight of the LORD.

2 Chr 36:12 And he did *that which was* evil in the sight of the LORD his God, *and* humbled not himself before Jeremiah the prophet *speaking* from the mouth of the LORD.

Ne 9:28 But after they had rest, they did evil again before thee: therefore leftest thou them in the hand of their enemies, so that they had the dominion over them: yet when they returned, and cried unto thee, thou heardest *them* from heaven; and many times didst thou deliver them according to thy mercies;

Ne 13:17 Then I contended with the nobles of Judah, and said unto them, What evil thing *is* this that ye do, and profane the sabbath day?

Is 3:8 For Jerusalem is ruined, and Judah is fallen: because their tongue and their doings *are* against the LORD, to provoke the eyes of his glory.

Is 65:12 Therefore will I number you to the sword, and ye shall all bow down to the slaughter: because when I called, ye did not answer; when I spake, ye did not hear; but did evil before mine eyes, and did choose *that* wherein I delighted not.

Is 66:4 I also will choose their delusions, and will bring their fears upon them; because when I called, none did answer; when I spake, they did not hear: but they did evil before mine eyes, and chose *that* in which I delighted not.

Je 5:6 Wherefore a lion out of the forest shall slay them, *and* a wolf of the evenings shall spoil them, a leopard shall watch over their cities: every one that goeth out thence shall be torn in pieces: because their transgressions are many, *and* their backslidings are increased.

Je 7:30 For the children of Judah have done evil in my sight, saith the LORD: they have set their abominations in the house which is called by my name, to pollute it.

Je 9:3 And they bend their tongues *like* their bow *for* lies: but they are not valiant for the truth upon the earth; for they proceed from evil to evil, and they know not me, saith the LORD.

Je 11:17 For the LORD of hosts, that planted thee, hath pronounced evil against thee, for the evil of the house of Israel and of the house of Judah, which they have done against themselves to provoke me to anger in offering incense unto Baal.

Je 18:10 If it do evil in my sight, that it obey not my voice, then I will repent of the good, wherewith I said I would benefit them.

Je 32:30 For the children of Israel and the children of Judah have only done evil before me from their youth: for the children of Israel have only provoked me to anger with the work of their hands, saith the LORD.

Je 38:9 My lord the king, these men have done evil in all that they have done to Jeremiah the prophet, whom they have cast into the dungeon; and he is like to die for hunger in the place where he is: for *there is* no more bread in the city.

Je 44:9 Have ye forgotten the wickedness of your fathers, and the wickedness of the kings of Judah, and the wickedness of their wives, and your own wickedness, and the wickedness of your wives, which they have committed in the land of Judah, and in the streets of Jerusalem?

Je 52:2 And he did *that which was* evil in the eyes of the LORD, according to all that Jehoiakim had done.

Eze 20:43 And there shall ye remember your ways, and all your doings, wherein ye have been defiled; and ye shall lothe yourselves in your own sight for all your evils that ye have committed.

Eze 33:26 Ye stand upon your sword, ye work abomination, and ye defile every one his neighbour's wife: and shall ye possess the land?

Eze 39:23 And the heathen shall know that the house of Israel went into captivity for their iniquity: be-

cause they trespassed against me, therefore hid I my face from them, and gave them into the hand of their enemies: so fell they all by the sword.

Ho 6:7 But they like men have transgressed the covenant: there have they dealt treacherously against me.

Mi 3:4 Then shall they cry unto the LORD, but he will not hear them: he will even hide his face from them at that time, as they have behaved themselves ill in their doings.

2 Ti 4:14 Alexander the coppersmith did me much evil: the Lord reward him according to his works:

See **JUDGMENTS, WICKED**

EXALTATION, *elevation, glorification*

1. Of Christ

See **CHRIST**

2. Of God

Ex 15:2, 21; 18:11; 1 Chr 29:11; Ne 9:5; Jb 11:8; 22:12; Ps 21:13; 46:10; 47:9; 57:11; 82:1; 92:8; 97:9; 99:5; 108:5; 113:4; 118:28; 136:2; 138:6; Is 2:11; 5:16; 6:1; 12:4; 25:1; 30:18; 33:5, 10; Eze 38:23; 39:21; Da 2:47; Mal 1:5; 1 Co 15:28; Ep 4:6

See **GOD**

3. Of the Saints

De 26:19 And to make thee high above all nations which he hath made, in praise, and in name, and in honour; and that thou mayest be an holy people unto the LORD thy God, as he hath spoken.

Jos 3:7 And the LORD said unto Joshua, This day will I begin to magnify thee in the sight of all Israel, that they may know that, as I was with Moses, so I will be with thee.

Jos 4:14 On that day the LORD magnified Joshua in the sight of all Israel; and they feared him, as they feared Moses, all the days of his life.

1 S 2:8 He raiseth up the poor out of the dust, *and* lifteth up the beggar from the dunghill, to set *them* among princes, and to make them inherit the throne of glory: for the pillars of the earth *are* the LORD's, and he hath set the world upon them.

2 Chr 24:16 And they buried him in the city of David among the kings, because he had done good in Israel, both toward God, and toward his house.

2 Chr 32:33 And Hezekiah slept with his fathers, and they buried him in the chiefest of the sepulchres of the sons of David: and all Judah and the inhabitants of Jerusalem did him honour at his death. And Manasseh his son reigned in his stead.

Est 9:4 For Mordecai *was* great in the king's house, and his fame went out throughout all the provinces: for this man Mordecai waxed greater and greater.

Jb 22:29 When *men* are cast down, then thou shalt say, *There is* lifting up; and he shall save the humble person.

Ps 71:21 Thou shalt increase my greatness, and comfort me on every side.

Ps 91:14 Because he hath set his love upon me, therefore will I deliver him: I will set him on high, because he hath known my name.

Ps 107:41 Yet setteth he the poor on high from affliction, and maketh *him* families like a flock.

Ps 113:7 He raiseth up the poor out of the dust, *and* lifteth the needy out of the dunghill;

Ps 132:12 If thy children will keep my covenant and my testimony that I shall teach them, their children shall also sit upon thy throne for evermore.

Ps 145:14 The LORD upholdeth all that fall, and raiseth up all *those that be* bowed down.

Is 33:16 He shall dwell on high: his place of defence *shall be* the munitions of rocks: bread shall be given him; his waters *shall be* sure.

Is 52:2 Shake thyself from the dust; arise, *and* sit down, O Jerusalem: loose thyself from the bands of thy neck, O captive daughter of Zion.

Is 58:14 Then shalt thou delight thyself in the LORD; and I will cause thee to ride upon the high places of the earth, and feed thee with the heritage

of Jacob thy father: for the mouth of the LORD hath spoken *it.*

Da 2:48 Then the king made Daniel a great man, and gave him many great gifts, and made him ruler over the whole province of Babylon, and chief of the governors over all the wise *men* of Babylon.

Da 12:3 And they that be wise shall shine as the brightness of the firmament; and they that turn many to righteousness as the stars for ever and ever.

Hab 3:19 The LORD God *is* my strength, and he will make my feet like hinds' *feet,* and he will make me to walk upon mine high places. To the chief singer on my stringed instruments.

Mt 19:28 And Jesus said unto them, Verily I say unto you, That ye which have followed me, in the regeneration when the Son of man shall sit in the throne of his glory, ye also shall sit upon twelve thrones, judging the twelve tribes of Israel.

Lu 19:17 And he said unto him, Well, thou good servant: because thou hast been faithful in a very little, have thou authority over ten cities.

1 Co 6:2 Do ye not know that the saints shall judge the world? and if the world shall be judged by you, are ye unworthy to judge the smallest matters?

1 Pe 5:6 Humble yourselves therefore under the mighty hand of God, that he may exalt you in due time:

Re 3:21 To him that overcometh will I grant to sit with me in my throne, even as I also overcame, and am set down with my Father in his throne.

Re 5:10 And hast made us unto our God kings and priests: and we shall reign on the earth.

Re 11:12 And they heard a great voice from heaven saying unto them, Come up hither. And they ascended up to heaven in a cloud; and their enemies beheld them.

Re 20:4 And I saw thrones, and they sat upon them, and judgment was given unto them: and *I saw* the souls of them that were beheaded for the witness of Jesus, and for the word of

God, and which had not worshipped the beast, neither his image, neither had received *his* mark upon their foreheads, or in their hands; and they lived and reigned with Christ a thousand years.

4. From God

See **ABASEMENT, HONOR, REVERSALS**

EXAMPLE, *pattern*

1. Of Christ to Be Followed

Mt 3:15; 10:25; 11:29; 16:24; Mk 8:34; Lu 6:40; 9:23; 14:27; Jn 13:15; 21:19; Ro 13:14; 15:3, 5; 1 Co 11:1; 2 Co 10:1; Ph 2:5; Col 3:13; He 3:1; 12:2; 1 Pe 2:21; 4:1; 1 Jn 2:6

2. Of Evil to Be Shunned

Le 18:3 After the doings of the land of Egypt, wherein ye dwelt, shall ye not do: and after the doings of the land of Canaan, whither I bring you, shall ye not do: neither shall ye walk in their ordinances.

Le 20:23 And ye shall not walk in the manners of the nation, which I cast out before you: for they committed all these things, and therefore I abhorred them.

De 7:4 For they will turn away thy son from following me, that they may serve other gods: so will the anger of the LORD be kindled against you, and destroy thee suddenly.

De 12:30 Take heed to thyself that thou be not snared by following them, after that they be destroyed from before thee; and that thou enquire not after their gods, saying, How did these nations serve their gods? even so will I do likewise.

De 18:9 When thou art come into the land which the LORD thy God giveth thee, thou shalt not learn to do after the abominations of those nations.

1 K 15:3 And he walked in all the sins of his father, which he had done before him: and his heart was not perfect with the LORD his God, as the heart of David his father.

1 K 15:34 And he did evil in the sight of the LORD, and walked in the way of Jeroboam, and in his sin wherewith he made Israel to sin.

1 K 16:7 And also by the hand of the prophet Jehu the son of Hanani came the word of the LORD against Baasha, and against his house, even for all the evil that he did in the sight of the LORD, in provoking him to anger with the work of his hands, in being like the house of Jeroboam; and because he killed him.

1 K 22:53 For he served Baal, and worshipped him, and provoked to anger the LORD God of Israel, according to all that his father had done.

2 K 8:27 And he walked in the way of the house of Ahab, and did evil in the sight of the LORD, as *did* the house of Ahab: for he *was* the son in law of the house of Ahab.

2 K 10:31 But Jehu took no heed to walk in the law of the LORD God of Israel with all his heart: for he departed not from the sins of Jeroboam, which made Israel to sin.

2 K 14:24 And he did *that which was* evil in the sight of the LORD: he departed not from all the sins of Jeroboam the son of Nebat, who made Israel to sin.

2 K 15:18 And he did *that which was* evil in the sight of the LORD: he departed not all his days from the sins of Jeroboam the son of Nebat, who made Israel to sin.

2 K 15:24 And he did *that which was* evil in the sight of the LORD: he departed not from the sins of Jeroboam the son of Nebat, who made Israel to sin.

2 K 16:2 Twenty years old *was* Ahaz when he began to reign, and reigned sixteen years in Jerusalem, and did not *that which was* right in the sight of the LORD his God, like David his father.

2 K 17:21 For he rent Israel from the house of David; and they made Jeroboam the son of Nebat king: and Jeroboam drave Israel from following the LORD, and made them sin a great sin.

1 Chr 10:5 And when his armour-bearer saw that Saul was dead, he fell likewise on the sword, and died.

2 Chr 12:1 And it came to pass, when Rehoboam had established the kingdom, and had strengthened himself, he forsook the law of the LORD, and all Israel with him.

Pr 22:24–25 Make no friendship with an angry man; and with a furious man thou shalt not go:

Lest thou learn his ways, and get a snare to thy soul.

Eze 20:18 But I said unto their children in the wilderness, Walk ye not in the statutes of your fathers, neither observe their judgments, nor defile yourselves with their idols:

He 4:11 Let us labour therefore to enter into that rest, lest any man fall after the same example of unbelief.

He 12:15 Looking diligently lest any man fail of the grace of God; lest any root of bitterness springing up trouble *you*, and thereby many be defiled;

2 Pe 2:1 But there were false prophets also among the people, even as there shall be false teachers among you, who privily shall bring in damnable heresies, even denying the Lord that bought them, and bring upon themselves swift destruction.

2 Pe 3:17 Ye therefore, beloved, seeing ye know *these things* before, beware lest ye also, being led away with the error of the wicked, fall from your own stedfastness.

3. Of Good to Be Sought

Jud 7:17 And he said unto them, Look on me, and do likewise: and, behold, when I come to the outside of the camp, it shall be *that,* as I do, so shall ye do.

1 K 22:43 And he walked in all the ways of Asa his father; he turned not aside from it, doing *that which was* right in the eyes of the LORD: nevertheless the high places were not taken away; *for* the people offered and burnt incense yet in the high places.

2 K 18:3 And he did *that which was* right in the sight of the LORD, according to all that David his father did.

2 K 22:2 And he did *that which was* right in the sight of the LORD, and walked in all the way of David his father, and turned not aside to the right hand or to the left.

2 Chr 29:2 And he did *that which was* right in the sight of the LORD, according to all that David his father had done.

Pr 2:20 That thou mayest walk in the way of good *men,* and keep the paths of the righteous.

Jn 13:15 For I have given you an example, that ye should do as I have done to you.

Ac 27:35 And when he had thus spoken, he took bread, and gave thanks to God in presence of them all: and when he had broken *it,* he began to eat.

1 Co 8:13 Wherefore, if meat make my brother to offend, I will eat no flesh while the world standeth, lest I make my brother to offend.

2 Co 8:8 I speak not by commandment, but by occasion of the forwardness of others, and to prove the sincerity of your love.

1 Th 1:7 So that ye were ensamples to all that believe in Macedonia and Achaia.

2 Th 3:9 Not because we have not power, but to make ourselves an ensample unto you to follow us.

1 Ti 4:12 Let no man despise thy youth; but be thou an example of the believers, in word, in conversation, in charity, in spirit, in faith, in purity.

Tit 2:7 In all things shewing thyself a pattern of good works: in doctrine *shewing* uncorruptness, gravity, sincerity,

He 6:12 That ye be not slothful, but followers of them who through faith and patience inherit the promises.

He 11:4 By faith Abel offered unto God a more excellent sacrifice than Cain, by which he obtained witness that he was righteous, God testifying of his gifts: and by it he being dead yet speaketh.

He 13:7 Remember them which have the rule over you, who have spoken unto you the word of God: whose faith follow, considering the end of *their* conversation.

Ja 5:10 Take, my brethren, the prophets, who have spoken in the name of the Lord, for an example of suffering affliction, and of patience.

1 Pe 2:21 For even hereunto were ye called: because Christ also suffered for us, leaving us an example, that ye should follow his steps:

1 Pe 5:3 Neither as being lords over *God's* heritage, but being ensamples to the flock.

4. Of Paul to Be Esteemed

Ac 20:35; 1 Co 4:16; 7:7; 11:1; Ga 4:12; Ph 1:14; 2:2; 3:17; 4:9; 1 Th 1:6; 2:10; 2 Th 3:7; 1 Ti 1:16; 2 Ti 1:13; 3:10

5. Of Parents to Be Honored

See **FAMILY, PARENTS**

6. Of Leaders to Be Followed

MOSES

Ex 14:13 And Moses said unto the people, Fear ye not, stand still, and see the salvation of the LORD, which he will shew to you to day: for the Egyptians whom ye have seen to day, ye shall see them again no more for ever.

GIDEON

Jud 7:17 And he said unto them, Look on me, and do likewise: and, behold, when I come to the outside of the camp, it shall be *that,* as I do, so shall ye do.

JONATHAN

1 S 14:6-7 And Jonathan said to the young man that bare his armour, Come, and let us go over unto the garrison of these uncircumcised: it may be that the LORD will work for us: for *there is* no restraint to the LORD to save by many or by few.

And his armourbearer said unto him, Do all that *is* in thine heart: turn thee; behold, I *am* with thee according to thy heart.

DAVID

1 S 17:50-52 So David prevailed over the Philistine with a sling and with a stone, and smote the Philistine, and slew him; but *there was* no sword in the hand of David.

Therefore David ran, and stood upon the Philistine, and took his sword, and drew it out of the sheath thereof, and slew him, and cut off his head therewith. And when the Philistines saw their champion was dead, they fled.

And the men of Israel and of Judah arose, and shouted, and pursued the Philistines, until thou come to the valley, and to the gates of Ekron. And the wounded of the Philistines fell down by the way to Shaaraim, even unto Gath, and unto Ekron.

PAUL

Ac 27:35-36 And when he had thus spoken, he took bread, and gave thanks to God in presence of them all: and when he had broken *it,* he began to eat.

Then were they all of good cheer, and they also took *some* meat.

CHRIST

He 12:3 For consider him that endured such contradiction of sinners against himself, lest ye be wearied and faint in your minds.

See **ASSOCIATIONS, CHRIST, INFLUENCE, LEADER**

EXCELLENCIES, *DIVINE*

Jb 37:23; Ps 8:1, 9; Is 12:5; 28:29; 35:2; Zec 9:17

See **GLORY, GOD**

EXCESS, *unbalanced life style*

Ge 9:22 And Ham, the father of Canaan, saw the nakedness of his father, and told his two brethren without.

1 K 20:16 And they went out at noon. But Ben-hadad *was* drinking himself drunk in the pavilions, he and the kings, the thirty and two kings that helped him.

Pr 23:20 Be not among winebibbers; among riotous eaters of flesh:

Pr 23:30 They that tarry long at the wine; they that go to seek mixed wine.

Pr 28:7 Whoso keepeth the law *is* a wise son: but he that is a companion of riotous *men* shameth his father.

Is 5:22 Woe unto *them that are* mighty to drink wine, and men of strength to mingle strong drink:

Is 28:7 But they also have erred through wine, and through strong drink are out of the way; the priest and the prophet have erred through strong drink, they are swallowed up of wine, they are out of the way through strong drink; they err in vision, they stumble *in* judgment.

Is 56:12 Come ye, *say they,* I will fetch wine, and we will fill ourselves with strong drink; and to morrow shall be as this day, *and* much more abundant.

Da 5:1 Belshazzar the king made a great feast to a thousand of his lords, and drank wine before the thousand.

Ho 3:1 Then said the Lord unto me, Go yet, love a woman beloved of *her* friend, yet an adulteress, according to the love of the Lord toward the children of Israel, who look to other gods, and love flagons of wine.

Am 4:1 Hear this word, ye kine of Bashan, that *are* in the mountain of Samaria, which oppress the poor, which crush the needy, which say to their masters, Bring, and let us drink.

Am 6:6 That drink wine in bowls, and anoint themselves with the chief ointments: but they are not grieved for the affliction of Joseph.

Mt 23:25 Woe unto you, scribes and Pharisees, hypocrites! for ye make clean the outside of the cup and of the platter, but within they are full of extortion and excess.

Lu 15:13 And not many days after the younger son gathered all together, and took his journey into a far country, and there wasted his substance with riotous living.

Lu 21:34 And take heed to yourselves, lest at any time your hearts be overcharged with surfeiting, and drunkenness, and cares of this life, and so that day come upon you unawares.

Ga 5:21 Envyings, murders, drunkenness, revellings, and such like: of the which I tell you before, as I have also told *you* in time past, that they which do such things shall not inherit the kingdom of God.

Ep 5:18 And be not drunk with wine, wherein is excess; but be filled with the Spirit;

1 Pe 4:3 For the time past of *our* life may suffice us to have wrought the will of the Gentiles, when we walked in lasciviousness, lusts, excess of wine, revellings, banquetings, and abominable idolatries:

2 Pe 2:13 And shall receive the reward of unrighteousness, *as* they that count it pleasure to riot in the daytime. Spots *they are* and blemishes, sporting themselves with their own deceivings while they feast with you;

See **SIN, TEMPERANCE**

EXCLUSION, *shut out, kept from entering*

1. From Canaan

Nu 14:23, 30; 20:12, 24; 26:65; 36; Ps 95:11; Eze 13:9; 20:15, 38; 33:25; Ho 9:3; He 3:11, 19; 4:6

2. From the Kingdom of Heaven

Ge 3:23 Therefore the LORD God sent him forth from the garden of Eden, to till the ground from whence he was taken.

Jb 13:16 He also *shall be* my salvation: for an hypocrite shall not come before him.

Is 35:8 And an highway shall be there, and a way, and it shall be called The way of holiness; the unclean shall not pass over it; but it *shall be* for those: the wayfaring men, though fools, shall not err *therein.*

Is 52:1 Awake, awake; put on thy strength, O Zion; put on thy beautiful garments, O Jerusalem, the holy city: for henceforth there shall no more come into thee the uncircumcised and the unclean.

Mt 5:20 For I say unto you, That except your righteousness shall exceed *the righteousness* of the scribes and Pharisees, ye shall in no case enter into the kingdom of heaven.

Mt 18:3 And said, Verily I say unto you, Except ye be converted, and become as little children, ye shall not enter into the kingdom of heaven.

Mt 25:10 And while they went to buy, the bridegroom came; and they that were ready went in with him to the marriage: and the door was shut.

Mk 10:15 Verily I say unto you, Whosoever shall not receive the kingdom of God as a little child, he shall not enter therein.

Lu 13:28 There shall be weeping and gnashing of teeth, when ye shall see Abraham, and Isaac, and Jacob, and all the prophets, in the kingdom of God, and you *yourselves* thrust out.

1 Co 6:9 Know ye not that the unrighteous shall not inherit the kingdom of God? Be not deceived: neither fornicators, nor idolaters, nor adulterers, nor effeminate, nor abusers of themselves with mankind,

1 Co 15:50 Now this I say, brethren, that flesh and blood cannot inherit the kingdom of God; neither doth corruption inherit incorruption.

Ga 5:21 Envyings, murders, drunkenness, revellings, and such like: of the which I tell you before, as I have also told *you* in time past, that they which do such things shall not inherit the kingdom of God.

Ep 5:5 For this ye know, that no whoremonger, nor unclean person, nor covetous man, who is an idolater, hath any inheritance in the kingdom of Christ and of God.

Re 21:27 And there shall in no wise enter into it any thing that defileth, neither *whatsoever* worketh abomination, or *maketh* a lie: but they which are written in the Lamb's book of life.

Re 22:15 For without *are* dogs, and sorcerers, and whoremongers, and murderers, and idolaters, and whosoever loveth and maketh a lie.

3. From Holy Places

Le 21:17; Nu 1:51; 3:10, 38; 4:20; 16:40; 17:13; 18:3, 4, 7, 22; De 23:2; 2 Chr 23:19; 26:20; Ne 7:65; 13:1; Eze 44:9, 13; Jl 3:17; Zec 14:21; He 9:8

EXCLUSIVENESS, *a form of elitism*

Ge 43:32; Lu 5:30; 9:49; Jn 4:9; Ac 10:28

See **ASSOCIATIONS**

EXCOMMUNICATION

See **CHURCH**

EXCUSES

1. To Justify Wrongdoing

Ge 3:12; Ex 32:24; 1 S 13:12; 1 S 15:21

2. For the Neglect of Duty

PERSONAL INCOMPETENCY

Ex 3:11 And Moses said unto God, Who *am* I, that I should go unto Pharaoh, and that I should bring forth the children of Israel out of Egypt?

Ex 4:1 And Moses answered and said, But, behold, they will not believe me, nor hearken unto my voice: for they will say, The LORD hath not appeared unto thee.

Ex 4:10 And Moses said unto the LORD, O my Lord, I *am* not eloquent, neither heretofore, nor since thou hast spoken unto thy servant: but I *am* slow of speech, and of a slow tongue.

LACK OF SOCIAL POSITION

Jud 6:15 And he said unto him, Oh my Lord, wherewith shall I save Israel? behold, my family is poor in Manasseh, and I *am* the least in my father's house.

DIFFICULTIES OF THE UNDERTAKING

Pr 22:13 The slothful *man* saith, *There is* a lion without, I shall be slain in the streets.

PERSONAL WEAKNESS

Je 1:6–7 Then said I, Ah, Lord GOD! behold, I cannot speak: for I *am* a child.

But the LORD said unto me, Say not, I *am* a child: for thou shalt go to all that I shall send thee, and whatsoever I command thee thou shalt speak.

THE HARDNESS OF THE MASTER

Mt 25:24–25 Then he which had received the one talent came and said, Lord, I knew thee that thou art an hard man, reaping where thou hast not sown, and gathering where thou hast not strawed:

And I was afraid, and went and hid thy talent in the earth: lo, *there* thou hast *that is* thine.

NO NEED DISCOVERED

Mt 25:44–45 Then shall they also answer him, saying, Lord, when saw we thee an hungred, or athirst, or a stranger, or naked, or sick, or in prison, and did not minister unto thee?

Then shall he answer them, saying, Verily Inasmuch as ye did *it* not to one of the least of these, ye did *it* not to me.

PRESSURE OF BUSINESS

Lu 14:18–20 And they all with one *consent* began to make excuse. The first said unto him, I have bought a piece of ground, and I must needs go and see it: I pray thee have me excused.

And another said, I have bought five yoke of oxen, and I go to prove them: I pray thee have me excused.

And another said, I have married a wife, and therefore I cannot come.

See **JUDGMENTS, JUSTICE**

EXECUTIONERS, *those who administer capital punishment*

Je 39:9; Da 2:14–15, 24; Mk 6:27

EXERCISE, SPIRITUAL, *discipline of a godly life*

Mt 25:16 Then he that had received the five talents went and traded with the same, and made *them* other five talents.

Mt 25:27 Thou oughtest therefore to have put my money to the exchang-

ers, and *then* at my coming I should have received mine own with usury.

1 Ti 4:7 But refuse profane and old wives' fables, and exercise thyself *rather* unto godliness.

2 Ti 1:6 Wherefore I put thee in remembrance that thou stir up the gift of God, which is in thee by the putting on of my hands.

See **DEVOTIONAL LIFE, DISCIPLESHIP, WORD OF GOD**

EXHORTATIONS, *urgent appeals*

1. Duty of Giving

Ac 20:2; 1 Ti 4:13; 6:2; 2 Ti 4:2; Tit 1:9; 2:15; He 3:13; 10:25; 2 Pe 3:1

2. Examples

1 K 8:61; Je 38:20; 44:7; Ho 12:6; Hag 1:5; 2:4; Lu 3:7, 18; Ac 2:40; 11:23; 13:15; 14:15, 22; 15:32; Ro 12:8; 15:15; 1 Co 14:3; 2 Co 5:11; 6:1; 9:5; Ep 4:1, 17; 1 Th 2:3, 11; 4:1; 5:14; 2 Th 3:12; 1 Ti 2:1; He 6:11; 12:1; 13:22; 1 Pe 5:1, 12; 2 Pe 1:13; Jude 3

3. Special

a. To Avoid Various Forms of Evil

Pr 4:15; Ro 16:17; 1 Ti 6:20; 2 Ti 2:16, 23; Tit 3:9

b. To Choose between Good and Evil

Ex 32:26; De 30:19; Jos 24:15; 1 K 18:21

See **CHOICE**

c. To Hearken to Admonition

De 4:1; 5:1; 6:4; 9:1; 13:18; 15:5; 18:15; 26:14; 27:9; Jos 3:9; Jud 3:4; 1 S 15:1; 2 Chr 20:15, 20; Jb 34:2, 10; Ps 49:1; 50:7; 78:1; 81:8; Pr 7:24; 22:17; Is 1:2, 10; 18:3; 28:14, 23; 32:9; 33:13; 34:1; 42:18, 23; 44:1; 46:3, 12; 48:1, 12, 16; 49:1; 51:1, 4; 55:2; 66:5; Je 2:4; 5:21; 6:17; 7:2; 9:20; 10:1; 13:15; 17:20; 19:3; 22:2; 31:10; 35:13; 42:15; Eze 6:3; 16:35; 20:47; 25:3; 34:7; 37:4; 40:4; 44:5; Ho 4:1; 5:1; Jl 1:2; Am 3:1; 4:1; 7:16; Mi 1:2; 3:1, 9; 6:1; Zec 3:8; Mt 13:9; 15:10; Mk 4:3, 9; 7:14; 12:29; Lu 9:44; Ac 2:14, 22; 7:2; Ja 2:5

See **HEARING**

d. To Hold Fast the Good

1 Th 5:21; 2 Th 2:15; 2 Ti 3:14; Tit 1:9; He 3:6; 4:14; 10:23; Re 2:13, 25; 3:3

See **STEADFASTNESS**

e. To Redeem the Time

Ps 90:12; Ec 12:1; 1 Co 7:29; Ep 5:16; Col 4:5

See **TIME**

EXODUS

Author And Central Character: Moses.

Date Written: 1447–1410 B.C.

Purpose: To be a permanent reminder of God's redemptive act on Passover night and of his care and direction during his people's wilderness wanderings on the way to Canaan.

To Whom Written: Each new generation of the people of Israel.

Main Theme: The history of Israel from the death of Joseph to the erection of the tabernacle.

Key Word: Deliverance.

Key Verses: 12:40–43.

EXPECTATION, *the state of waiting*

1. Of the Righteous

1 K 18:43; Ps 9:18; 62:5; 123:2; 130:5; Pr 23:18; 24:14; Hab 2:3; Lu 2:38; 12:36; 23:51; Ac 3:5; Ro 8:25; 1 Co 1:7; Ph 1:20; 1 Th 1:10; Tit 2:13; He 9:28; 11:13; 2 Pe 3:12; Jude 21

2. Of the Wicked

Pr 10:28; 11:7, 23; Is 20:6; 59:11; Je 8:15; Zec 9:5; Ac 12:11

See **DISAPPOINTMENT**

EYES

Ps 119:37; Pr 4:25; Is 33:15; Mt 5:29

See **LUST**

EZEKIEL

1. Person, *the prophet*

Eze 1:1

2. Book

Author: Ezekiel, whose name means "God strengthens."

Date Written: Probably recorded over the 22-year ministry of the prophet and completed around 565 B.C.

Purpose: To relate a sovereign, holy God's condemnation of sinful ways and his continuing efforts to restore his people. He wants them to know that he is the Lord.

To Whom Written: Jewish exiles in Babylon and God's people everywhere.

Main Themes: This prophecy, like Daniel and Revelation, might be termed a mystery book. It contains much imagery that is difficult to interpret. Nevertheless, many of its teachings are clear and of the highest value. Two primary themes stand out: condemnation (1–32) and consolation (33–48).

Key Words: "I am the LORD."

Key Verses: 36:24–26.

EZION GABER, *a city near the Red Sea*

Ezion Gaber was a camping place of the Israelites on their journey from Egypt to Canaan (Nu 33:35), and later the naval port of King Solomon (1 K 9:26; 2 Chr 8:17).

EZRA

1. Person, *the scribe*

Ezr 7:1, 10, 11, 13–26, 25; 8:21–22; 10:1, 2–5, 6–7, 10, 16; Ne 8:1–9; 12:1, 26, 36

2. Book

Author: Unknown. It is generally conceded that Ezra was not the author of the entire book but may have been the compiler of those portions that he did not write. He was a Jewish exile in Babylon of priestly descent (7:1–6).

Date Written: Around 450 B.C.

Purpose: To document the faithfulness of God, who kept his promise, sovereignly protected his people during their captivity, and returned them to their land.

To Whom Written: The restored remnant in Jerusalem and future generations.

Main Themes: The return of the Jews from the Babylonian captivity, the rebuilding of the temple, and the inauguration of social and religious reforms.

Key Words: Word of God. The power of the Word of God in human life. Referred to as the "word of the Lord" (1:1; 9:4); "law of Moses" (3:2; 6:18; 7:6); "commandments" (6:14; 10:3, 5); "law of the Lord" (7:10, 14).

Key Verses: 1:3, 7:10.

See **NEHEMIAH**

F

FABLES

1 Ti 1:4; 4:7; 2 Ti 4:4; Tit 1:14; 2 Pe 1:16

FACE

1. *God's Hidden*, *on account of sin*

Ge 4:14; Le 17:10; 23:3, 6; 26; Ps 34:16; 44:24; 69:17; 88:14; 102:2; 143:7; Pr 1:28; Is 1:15; 8:17; 54:8; 57:17; 59:2; 64:7; Je 11:14; 18:17; 21:10; 33:5; 44:11; Lam 3:44; Eze 7:22; 14:8; 39:23; Mi 3:4; 1 Pe 3:12

2. *God's Shining*, *reflections of glory*

Ex 34:30, 35; Jud 13:6; Ec 8:1; Da 1:15; 10:6; Mt 5:15; 17:2; 28:3; Lu 9:29; Ac 6:15; 2 Co 3:7; Re 10:1

FAILURE, *SPIRITUAL*

Mt 7:27 And the rain descended, and the floods came, and the winds blew, and beat upon that house; and it fell: and great was the fall of it.

Mt 17:16 And I brought him to thy disciples, and they could not cure him.

Lu 14:30 Saying, This man began to build, and was not able to finish.

1 Co 3:15 If any man's work shall be burned, he shall suffer loss: but he himself shall be saved; yet so as by fire.

He 4:6 Seeing therefore it remaineth that some must enter therein, and they to whom it was first preached entered not in because of unbelief:

FAINTHEARTEDNESS, *lacking conviction, cowardly, timid*

Le 26:36; Nu 13:31; 14:3; De 1:28; 20:8; Jud 4:8; 7:3; 1 S 13:7; 2 S 4:1; 1 K 20:4; 22:30; 2 K 10:4; Ne 6:10; Jb 23:15; Pr 24:10; Is 7:4; 19:16; 30:17; 36:11; Je 41:18; 49:23; Lam 5:17; Eze 21:7; Mt 25:25; Ga 6:12

See **COURAGE**

FAITH, *belief, trust, confidence, reliance*

1 K 20:14 And Ahab said, By whom? And he said, Thus saith the LORD, *Even* by the young men of the princes of the provinces. Then he said, Who shall order the battle? And he answered, Thou.

Ps 56:3 What time I am afraid, I will trust in thee.

Ps 106:12 Then believed they his words; they sang his praise.

Lu 17:5 And the apostles said unto the Lord, Increase our faith.

Lu 18:8 I tell you that he will avenge them speedily. Nevertheless when the Son of man cometh, shall he find faith on the earth?

Ac 6:5 And the saying pleased the whole multitude: and they chose Stephen, a man full of faith and of the Holy Ghost, and Philip, and Prochorus, and Nicanor, and Timon, and Parmenas, and Nicolas a proselyte of Antioch:

Ac 11:24 For he was a good man, and full of the Holy Ghost and of faith: and much people was added unto the Lord.

Ro 1:8 First, I thank my God through Jesus Christ for you all, that your faith is spoken of throughout the whole world.

Ro 1:12 That is, that I may be comforted together with you by the mutual faith both of you and me.

Ro 10:17 So then faith *cometh* by hearing, and hearing by the word of God.

Ro 14:23 And he that doubteth is damned if he eat, because *he eateth* not of faith: for whatsoever *is* not of faith is sin.

1 Co 2:5 That your faith should not stand in the wisdom of men, but in the power of God.

1 Co 12:9 To another faith by the same Spirit; to another the gifts of healing by the same Spirit;

1 Co 13:7 Beareth all things, believeth all things, hopeth all things, endureth all things.

1 Co 13:13 And now abideth faith, hope, charity, these three; but the greatest of these *is* charity.

2 Co 4:13 We having the same spirit of faith, according as it is written, I believed, and therefore have I spoken; we also believe, and therefore speak;

2 Co 5:7 (For we walk by faith, not by sight:)

2 Co 8:7 Therefore, as ye abound in every *thing, in* faith, and utterance, and knowledge, and *in* all diligence, and *in* your love to us, *see* that ye abound in this grace also.

Ga 5:6 For in Jesus Christ neither circumcision availeth any thing, nor uncircumcision; but faith which worketh by love.

Col 2:5 For though I be absent in the flesh, yet am I with you in the spirit, joying and beholding your order, and the stedfastness of your faith in Christ.

1 Th 3:5 For this cause, when I could no longer forbear, I sent to know your faith, lest by some means the tempter have tempted you, and our labour be in vain.

1 Th 3:6 But now when Timotheus came from you unto us, and brought us good tidings of your faith and charity, and that ye have good remembrance of us always, desiring greatly to see us, as we also *to see* you:

1 Th 4:14 For if we believe that Jesus died and rose again, even so them also which sleep in Jesus will God bring with him.

2 Th 1:3 We are bound to thank God always for you, brethren, as it is meet, because that your faith groweth exceedingly, and the charity of every one of you all toward each other aboundeth;

1 Ti 1:5 Now the end of the commandment is charity out of a pure heart, and *of* a good conscience, and *of* faith unfeigned:

1 Ti 3:13 For they that have used the office of a deacon well purchase to themselves a good degree, and great boldness in the faith which is in Christ Jesus.

2 Ti 1:5 When I call to remembrance the unfeigned faith that is in thee, which dwelt first in thy grandmother Lois, and thy mother Eunice; and I am persuaded that in thee also.

2 Ti 2:22 Flee also youthful lusts: but follow righteousness, faith, charity, peace, with them that call on the Lord out of a pure heart.

He 11:1 Now faith is the substance of things hoped for, the evidence of things not seen.

He 11:39 And these all, having obtained a good report through faith, received not the promise:

Ja 2:17 Even so faith, if it hath not works, is dead, being alone.

2 Pe 1:1 Simon Peter, a servant and an apostle of Jesus Christ, to them that have obtained like precious faith with us through the righteousness of God and our Saviour Jesus Christ:

2 Pe 1:5 And beside this, giving all diligence, add to your faith virtue; and to virtue knowledge;

1 Jn 5:4 For whatsoever is born of God overcometh the world: and this is the victory that overcometh the world, *even* our faith.

Re 2:19 I know thy works, and charity, and service, and faith, and thy patience, and thy works; and the last *to be* more than the first.

1. Prescribed

ASSURES SUCCESS

2 Chr 20:20 And they rose early in the morning, and went forth into the wilderness of Tekoa: and as they went forth, Jehoshaphat stood and said, Hear me, O Judah, and ye inhabitants of Jerusalem; Believe in the LORD your God, so shall ye be established; believe his prophets, so shall ye prosper.

Mk 11:22 And Jesus answering saith unto them, Have faith in God.

Lu 8:50 But when Jesus heard *it,* he answered him, saying, Fear not: believe only, and she shall be made whole.

A FUNDAMENTAL DUTY

Jn 6:28 Then said they unto him, What shall we do, that we might work the works of God?

Jn 6:29 Jesus answered and said unto them, This is the work of God, that ye believe on him whom he hath sent.

Jn 20:27 Then saith he to Thomas, reach hither thy finger, and behold my hands; and reach hither thy hand, and thrust *it* into my side: and be not faithless, but believing.

A DEFENSIVE WEAPON

Ep 6:16 Above all, taking the shield of faith, wherewith ye shall be able to quench all the fiery darts of the wicked.

1 Th 5:8 But let us, who are of the day, be sober, putting on the breastplate of faith and love; and for an helmet, the hope of salvation.

1 Ti 1:19 Holding faith, and a good conscience; which some having put away concerning faith have made shipwreck:

1 Ti 6:12 Fight the good fight of faith, lay hold on eternal life, whereunto thou art also called, and hast professed a good profession before many witnesses.

He 10:22 Let us draw near with a true heart in full assurance of faith, having our hearts sprinkled from an evil conscience, and our bodies washed with pure water.

AN INDISPENSABLE ELEMENT IN RELIGION

He 11:6 But without faith *it is* impossible to please *him:* for he that cometh to God must believe that he is, and *that* he is a rewarder of them that diligently seek him.

ESSENTIAL IN PRAYER

Ja 1:5 If any of you lack wisdom, let him ask of God, that giveth to all *men* liberally, and upbraideth not; and it shall be given him.

Ja 1:6 But let him ask in faith, nothing wavering. For he that wavereth is like a wave of the sea driven with the wind and tossed.

SHOULD BE UNITED WITH LOVE

1 Jn 3:23 And this is his commandment, That we should believe on the name of his Son Jesus Christ, and love one another, as he gave us commandment.

2. Justification

Jos 6:25 And Joshua saved Rahab the harlot alive, and her father's household, and all that she had; and she dwelleth in Israel *even* unto this day; because she hid the messengers, which Joshua sent to spy out Jericho.

Hab 2:4 Behold, his soul *which* is lifted up is not upright in him: but the just shall live by his faith.

Ac 15:9 And put no difference between us and them, purifying their hearts by faith.

Ro 1:17 For therein is the righteousness of God revealed from faith to faith: as it is written, The just shall live by faith.

Ro 3:26 To declare, *I say,* at this time his righteousness: that he might be just, and the justifier of him which believeth in Jesus.

Ro 4:3 For what saith the scripture? Abraham believed God, and it was counted unto him for righteousness.

Ro 5:1 Therefore being justified by faith, we have peace with God through our LORD Jesus Christ:

Ro 10:6 But the righteousness which is of faith speaketh on this wise, Say not in thine heart, Who shall ascend into heaven? (that is, to bring Christ down *from above:*)

2 Co 1:24 Not for that we have dominion over your faith, but are helpers of your joy: for by faith ye stand.

Ga 2:16 Knowing that a man is not justified by the works of the law, but by the faith of Jesus Christ, even we have believed in Jesus Christ, that we might be justified by the faith of Christ, and not by the works of the law: for by the works of the law shall no flesh be justified.

Ga 3:6 Even as Abraham believed God, and it was accounted to him for righteousness.

Ga 3:11 But that no man is justified by the law in the sight of God, *it is* evident: for, The just shall live by faith.

Ga 3:24 Wherefore the law was our schoolmaster *to bring us* unto Christ, that we might be justified by faith.

Ep 3:17 That Christ may dwell in your hearts by faith; that ye, being rooted and grounded in love,

Ph 3:9 And be found in him, not having mine own righteousness, which is of the law, but that which is through the faith of Christ, the righteousness which is of God by faith:

He 10:38 Now the just shall live by faith: but if *any man* draw back, my soul shall have no pleasure in him.

He 11:4 By faith Abel offered unto God a more excellent sacrifice than Cain, by which he obtained witness that he was righteous, God testifying of his gifts: and by it he being dead yet speaketh.

3. Blessings

Nu 21:9 And Moses made a serpent of brass, and put it upon a pole, and it came to pass, that if a serpent had bitten any man, when he beheld the serpent of brass, he lived.

Jos 10:12 Then spake Joshua to the LORD in the day when the LORD delivered up the Amorites before the children of Israel, and he said in the sight of Israel, Sun, stand thou still upon Gibeon; and thou, Moon, in the valley of Ajalon.

2 K 2:10 And he said, Thou hast asked a hard thing: *nevertheless,* if thou see me *when I am* taken from thee, it shall be so unto thee; but if not, it shall not be so.

Is 7:9 And the head of Ephraim *is* Samaria, and the head of Samaria *is* Remaliah's son. If ye will not believe, surely ye shall not be established.

Da 6:23 Then was the king exceeding glad for him, and commanded that they should take Daniel up out of the den. So Daniel was taken up out of the den, and no manner of hurt was found

upon him, because he believed in his God.

Mt 8:13 And Jesus said unto the centurion, Go thy way; and as thou hast believed, so be it done unto thee. And his servant was healed in the selfsame hour.

Mt 9:2 And, behold, they brought to him a man sick of the palsy, lying on a bed: and Jesus seeing their faith said unto the sick of the palsy; Son, be of good cheer; thy sins be forgiven thee.

Mt 9:22 But Jesus turned him about, and when he saw her, he said, Daughter, be of good comfort; thy faith hath made thee whole. And the woman was made whole from that hour.

Mt 9:29 Then touched he their eyes, saying, According to your faith be it unto you.

Mt 9:30 And their eyes were opened; and Jesus straitly charged them, saying, See *that* no man know *it.*

Mt 17:20 And Jesus said unto them, Because of your unbelief: for verily I say unto you, If ye have faith as a grain of mustard seed, ye shall say unto this mountain, Remove hence to yonder place; and it shall remove; and nothing shall be impossible unto you.

Mt 21:21 Jesus answered and said unto them, Verily I say unto you, If ye have faith, and doubt not, ye shall not only do this *which is done* to the fig tree, but also if ye shall say unto this mountain, Be thou removed, and be thou cast into the sea; it shall be done.

Mk 9:23 Jesus said unto him, If thou canst believe, all things *are* possible to him that believeth.

Mk 11:23 For verily I say unto you, That whosoever shall say unto this mountain, Be thou removed, and be thou cast into the sea; and shall not doubt in his heart, but shall believe that those things which he saith shall come to pass; he shall have whatsoever he saith.

Lu 1:45 And blessed *is* she that believed: for there shall be a performance of those things which were told her from the Lord.

Lu 8:48 And he said unto her, Daughter, be of good comfort: thy faith hath made thee whole; go in peace.

Lu 17:6 And the Lord said, If ye had faith as a grain of mustard seed, ye might say unto this sycamine tree, Be thou plucked up by the root, and be thou planted in the sea; and it should obey you.

Lu 17:19 And he said unto him, Arise, go thy way: thy faith hath made thee whole.

Lu 18:42 And Jesus said unto him, Receive thy sight: thy faith hath saved thee.

Jn 9:7 And said unto him, Go, wash in the pool of Siloam, (which is by interpretation, Sent.) He went his way therefore, and washed, and came seeing.

Jn 9:11 He answered and said, A man that is called Jesus made clay, and anointed mine eyes, and said unto me, Go to the pool of Siloam, and wash: and I went and washed, and I received sight.

Jn 11:40 Jesus saith unto her, Said I not unto thee, that, if thou wouldest believe, thou shouldest see the glory of God?

Ac 3:16 And his name through faith in his name hath made this man strong, whom ye see and know: yea, the faith which is by him hath given him this perfect soundness in the presence of you all.

Ga 3:2 This only would I learn of you, Received ye the Spirit by the works of the law, or by the hearing of faith?

He 11:19 Accounting that God *was* able to raise *him* up, even from the dead; from whence also he received him in a figure.

Ja 5:15 And the prayer of faith shall save the sick, and the Lord shall raise him up; and if he have committed sins, they shall be forgiven him.

4. Victorious

ABRAHAM

Ge 22:8 And Abraham said, My son, God will provide himself a lamb for a burnt offering: so they went both of them together.

Ro 4:20 He staggered not at the promise of God through unbelief; but

was strong in faith, giving glory to God;

CALEB

Jos 14:12 Now therefore give me this mountain, whereof the LORD spake in that day; for thou heardest in that day how the Anakims *were* there, and *that* the cities *were* great *and* fenced: if so be the LORD *will be* with me, then I shall be able to drive them out, as the LORD said.

JONATHAN

1 S 14:6 And Jonathan said to the young man that bare his armour, Come, and let us go over unto the garrison of these uncircumcised: it may be that the LORD will work for us: for *there is* no restraint to the LORD to save by many or by few.

DAVID

1 S 17:37 David said moreover, The LORD that delivered me out of the paw of the lion, and out of the paw of the bear, he will deliver me out of the hand of this Philistine. And Saul said unto David, Go, and the LORD be with thee.

JEHOSHAPHAT

2 Chr 20:12 O our God, wilt thou not judge them? for we have no might against this great company that cometh against us; neither know we what to do: but our eyes *are* upon thee.

HEZEKIAH

2 Chr 32:8 With him *is* an arm of flesh; but with us *is* the LORD our God to help us, and to fight our battles. And the people rested themselves upon the words of Hezekiah king of Judah.

JOB

Jb 19:25 For I know *that* my redeemer liveth, and *that* he shall stand at the latter *day* upon the earth:

THE THREE HEBREW CAPTIVES

Da 3:17 If it be *so*, our God whom we serve is able to deliver us from the burning fiery furnace, and he will deliver *us* out of thine hand, O king.

PAUL

Ac 27:25 Wherefore, sirs, be of good cheer: for I believe God, that it shall be even as it was told me.

THE ANCIENT WORTHIES

He 11:33 Who through faith subdued kingdoms, wrought righteousness, obtained promises, stopped the mouths of lions,

See **CONFIDENCE, TRUST**

5. Faith in Christ, *secures salvation*

Jos 2:21 And she said, According unto your words, so *be* it. And she sent them away, and they departed: and she bound the scarlet line in the window.

Jona 3:5 So the people of Nineveh believed God, and proclaimed a fast, and put on sackcloth, from the greatest of them even to the least of them.

Mt 21:32 For John came unto you in the way of righteousness, and ye believed him not: but the publicans and the harlots believed him: and ye, when ye had seen *it,* repented not afterward, that ye might believe him.

Mk 16:16 He that believeth and is baptized shall be saved; but he that believeth not shall be damned.

Lu 7:50 And he said to the woman, Thy faith hath saved thee; go in peace.

Jn 2:23 Now when he was in Jerusalem at the passover, in the feast in his name, when they saw the miracles which he did.

Jn 3:15 That whosoever believeth in him should not perish, but have eternal life.

Jn 3:18 He that believeth on him is not condemned: but he that believeth not is condemned already, because he hath not believed in the name of the only begotten Son of God.

Jn 3:36 He that believeth on the Son hath everlasting life: and he that believeth not the Son shall not see life; but the wrath of God abideth on him.

Jn 4:41 And many more believed because of his own word;

Jn 5:24 Verily, verily, I say unto you, He that heareth my word, and believeth on him that sent me, hath everlasting life, and shall not come into condemnation; but is passed from death unto life.

Jn 6:40 And this is the will of him that sent me, that every one which seeth the Son, and believeth on him, may have everlasting life: and I will raise him up at the last day.

Jn 6:47 Verily, verily, I say unto you, He that believeth on me hath everlasting life.

Jn 9:35 Jesus heard that they had cast him out; and when he had found him, he said unto him, Dost thou believe on the Son of God?

Jn 11:25 Jesus said unto her, I am the resurrection, and the life: he that believeth in me, though he were dead, yet shall he live:

Jn 12:46 I am come a light into the world, that whosoever believeth on me should not abide in darkness.

Jn 16:27 For the Father himself loveth you, because ye have loved me, and have believed that I came out from God.

Jn 20:31 But these are written, that ye might believe that Jesus is the Christ, the Son of God; and that believing ye might have life through his name.

Ac 4:4 Howbeit many of them which heard the word believed; and the number of the men was about five thousand.

Ac 8:37 And Philip said, If thou believest with all thine heart, thou mayest. And he answered and said, I believe that Jesus Christ is the Son of God.

Ac 10:43 To him give all the prophets witness, that through his name whosoever believeth in him shall receive remission of sins.

Ac 13:39 And by him all that believe are justified from all things, from which ye could not be justified by the law of Moses.

Ac 13:48 And when the Gentiles heard this, they were glad, and glorified the word of the Lord: and as many as were ordained to eternal life believed.

Ac 16:31 And they said, Believe on the Lord Jesus Christ, and thou shalt be saved, and thy house.

Ac 19:4 Then said Paul, John verily baptized with the baptism of repentance, saying unto the people, that they should believe on him which should come after him, that is, on Christ Jesus.

Ac 20:21 Testifying both to the Jews, and also to the Greeks, repentance toward God, and faith toward our Lord Jesus Christ.

Ac 24:24 And after certain days, when Felix came with his wife Drusilla, which was a Jewess, he sent for Paul, and heard him concerning the faith in Christ.

Ac 26:18 To open their eyes, *and* to turn *them* from darkness to light, and *from* the power of Satan unto God, that they may receive forgiveness of sins, and inheritance among them which are sanctified by faith that is in me.

Ro 1:16 For I am not ashamed of the gospel of Christ: for it is the power of God unto salvation to every one that believeth; to the Jew first, and also to the Greek.

Ro 3:22 Even the righteousness of God *which is* by faith of Jesus Christ unto all and upon all them that believe: for there is no difference:

Ro 3:25 Whom God hath set forth *to be* a propitiation through faith in his blood, to declare his righteousness for the remission of sins that are past, through the forbearance of God;

Ro 3:28 Therefore we conclude that a man is justified by faith without the deeds of the law.

Ro 4:24 But for us also, to whom it shall be imputed, if we believe on him that raised up Jesus our Lord from the dead;

Ro 9:33 As it is written, Behold, I lay in Sion a stumblingstone and rock of offence: and whosoever believeth on him shall not be ashamed.

Ro 10:9 That if thou shalt confess with thy mouth the Lord Jesus, and shalt believe in thine heart that God hath raised him from the dead, thou shalt be saved.

Ro 10:10 For with the heart man believeth unto righteousness; and with the mouth confession is made unto salvation.

Ro 11:20 Well; because of unbelief they were broken off, and thou standest by faith. Be not highminded, but fear:

Ga 2:20 I am crucified with Christ: nevertheless I live; yet not I, but Christ liveth in me: and the life which I now live in the flesh I live by the faith of the Son of God, who loved me, and gave himself for me.

Ga 3:14 That the blessing of Abraham might come on the Gentiles through Jesus Christ; that we might receive the promise of the Spirit through faith.

Ga 3:22 But the scripture hath concluded all under sin, that the promise by faith of Jesus Christ might be given to them that believe.

Ep 1:12 That we should be to the praise of his glory, who first trusted in Christ.

Ep 1:15 Wherefore I also, after I heard of your faith in the Lord Jesus, and love unto all the saints,

Ep 2:8 For by grace are ye saved through faith; and that not of yourselves: *it is* the gift of God:

Ep 3:12 In whom we have boldness and access with confidence by the faith of him.

Col 1:4 Since we heard of your faith in Christ Jesus, and of the love *which ye have* to all the saints,

Col 2:12 Buried with him in baptism, wherein also ye are risen with *him* through the faith of the operation of God, who hath raised him from the dead.

2 Th 2:13 But we are bound to give thanks alway to God for you, brethren beloved of the Lord, because God hath from the beginning chosen you to salvation through sanctification of the Spirit and belief of the truth:

1 Ti 1:16 Howbeit for this cause I obtained mercy, that in me first Jesus Christ might shew forth all longsuffering, for a pattern to them which should hereafter believe on him to life everlasting.

1 Ti 4:10 For therefore we both labour and suffer reproach, because we trust in the living God, who is the Saviour of all men, specially of those that believe.

2 Ti 1:13 Hold fast the form of sound words, which thou hast heard of me, in faith and love which is in Christ Jesus.

2 Ti 3:15 And that from a child thou hast known the holy scriptures, which are able to make thee wise unto salvation through faith which is in Christ Jesus.

Tit 1:1 Paul, a servant of God, and an apostle of Jesus Christ, according to the faith of God's elect, and the acknowledging of the truth which is after godliness;

Phm 5 Hearing of thy love and faith, which thou hast toward the Lord Jesus, and toward all saints;

He 3:14 For we are made partakers of Christ, if we hold the beginning of our confidence stedfast unto the end;

He 6:1 Therefore leaving the principles of the doctrine of Christ, let us go on unto perfection; not laying again the foundation of repentance from dead works, and of faith toward God,

He 6:12 That ye be not slothful, but followers of them who through faith and patience inherit the promises.

He 10:39 But we are not of them who draw back unto perdition; but of them that believe to the saving of the soul.

He 11:31 By faith the harlot Rahab perished not with them that believed not, when she had received the spies with peace.

He 12:2 Looking unto Jesus the author and finisher of *our* faith; who for the joy that was set before him endured the cross, despising the shame, and is set down at the right hand of the throne of God.

1 Pe 1:5 Who are kept by the power of God through faith unto salvation ready to be revealed in the last time.

1 Pe 1:9 Receiving the end of your faith, *even* the salvation of *your* souls.

1 Jn 5:1 Whosoever believeth that Jesus is the Christ is born of God: and every one that loveth him that begat

loveth him also that is begotten of him.

1 Jn 5:5 Who is he that overcometh the world, but he that believeth that Jesus is the Son of God?

1 Jn 5:10 He that believeth on the Son of God hath the witness in himself: he that believeth not God hath made him a liar; because he believeth not the record that God gave of his Son.

Re 14:12 Here is the patience of the saints: here *are* they that keep the commandments of God, and the faith of Jesus.

6. Exceptional Examples

THE LEPER

Mt 8:2 And, behold, there came a leper and worshipped him, saying, Lord, if thou wilt, thou canst make me clean.

THE CENTURION

Mt 8:10 When Jesus heard *it,* he marvelled, and said to them that followed, Verily I say unto you, I have not found so great faith, no, not in Israel.

THE RULER

Mt 9:18 While he spake these things unto them, behold, there came a certain ruler, and worshipped him, saying, My daughter is even now dead: but come and lay thy hand upon her, and she shall live.

THE BLIND MAN

Mt 9:28 And when he was come into the house, the blind men came to him: and Jesus saith unto them, Believe ye that I am able to do this? They said unto him, Yea, Lord.

THE DISEASED

Mt 14:36 And besought him that they might only touch the hem of his garment: and as many as touched were made perfectly whole.

THE SYROPHENICIAN WOMAN

Mt 15:28 Then Jesus answered and said unto her, O woman, great *is* thy faith: be it unto thee even as thou wilt.

And her daughter was made whole from that very hour.

THE AFFLICTED WOMAN

Mk 5:28 For she said, If I may touch but his clothes, I shall be whole.

7. Special Promises

SOUL REST

He 4:3 For we which have believed do enter into rest, as he said, As I have sworn in my wrath, if they shall enter into my rest: although the works were finished from the foundation of the world.

SPIRITUAL INHERITANCE

Ja 2:5 Hearken, my beloved brethren, Hath not God chosen the poor of this world rich in faith, and heirs of the kingdom which he hath promised to them that love him?

SPIRITUAL FOUNDATION

1 Pe 2:6 Wherefore also it is contained in the scripture, Behold, I lay in Sion a chief corner stone, elect, precious: and he that believeth on him shall not be confounded.

SPIRITUAL ASSURANCE

1 Jn 5:14 And this is the confidence that we have in him, that, if we ask any thing according to his will, he heareth us:

8. Reasons to Believe

Ex 4:5 That they may believe that the LORD God of their fathers, the God of Abraham, the God of Isaac, and the God of Jacob, hath appeared unto thee.

Ex 16:6 And Moses and Aaron said unto all the children of Israel, At even, then ye shall know that the LORD hath brought you out from the land of Egypt:

Ex 19:9 And the LORD said unto Moses, Lo, I come unto thee in a thick cloud, that the people may hear when I speak with thee, and believe thee for ever. And Moses told the words of the people unto the LORD.

Is 41:20 That they may see, and know, and consider, and understand together, that the hand of the LORD hath done this, and the Holy One of Israel hath created it.

Is 43:10 Ye *are* my witnesses, saith the LORD, and my servant whom I have chosen: that ye may know and believe me, and understand that I *am* he: before me there was no God formed, neither shall there be after me.

Jn 1:7 The same came for a witness, to bear witness of the Light, that all *men* through him might believe.

Jn 11:15 And I am glad for your sakes that I was not there, to the intent ye may believe; nevertheless let us go unto him.

Jn 11:42 And I knew that thou hearest me always: but because of the people which stand by I said *it,* that they may believe that thou hast sent me.

Jn 13:19 Now I tell you before it come, that, when it is come to pass, ye may believe that I am *he.*

Jn 14:29 And now I have told you before it come to pass, that, when it is come to pass, ye might believe.

Jn 17:21 That they all may be one; as thou, Father, *art* in me, and I in thee, that they also may be one in us: that the world may believe that thou hast sent me.

Jn 19:35 And he that saw *it* bare record, and his record is true: and he knoweth that he saith true, that ye might believe.

Jn 20:31 But these are written, that ye might believe that Jesus is the Christ, the Son of God; and that believing ye might have life through his name.

9. Instances of Little Faith

Mt 6:30 Wherefore, if God so clothe the grass of the field, which to day is, and to morrow is cast into the oven, *shall he* not much more *clothe* you, O ye of little faith?

Mt 8:26 And he saith unto them, Why are ye fearful, O ye of little faith? Then he arose, and rebuked the winds and the sea; and there was a great calm.

Mt 14:31 And immediately Jesus stretched forth *his* hand, and caught him, and said unto him, O thou of little faith, wherefore didst thou doubt?

Mt 16:8 *Which* when Jesus perceived, he said unto them, O ye of little faith, why reason ye among yourselves, because ye have brought no bread?

10. Faith Tested

Ge 22:2 And he said, Take now thy son, thine only *son* Isaac, whom thou lovest, and get thee into the land of Moriah; and offer him there for a burnt offering upon one of the mountains which I will tell thee of.

Ex 17:1 And all the congregation of the children of Israel journeyed from the wilderness of Sin, after their journeys, according to the commandment of the LORD, and pitched in Rephidim: and *there was* no water for the people to drink.

Jos 6:3 And ye shall compass the city, all *ye* men of war, *and* go round about the city once. Thus shalt thou do six days.

Jud 7:7 And the LORD said unto Gideon, By the three hundred men that lapped will I save you, and deliver the Midianites into thine hand: and let all the *other* people go every man unto his place.

1 K 17:9 Arise, get thee to Zarephath, which *belongeth* to Zidon, and dwell there: behold, I have commanded a widow woman there to sustain thee.

1 K 17:13 And Elijah said unto her, Fear not; go *and* do as thou hast said: but make me thereof a little cake first, and bring *it* unto me, and after make for thee and for thy son.

2 K 3:16 And he said, Thus saith the LORD, Make this valley full of ditches.

2 K 4:3 Then he said, Go, borrow thee vessels abroad of all thy neighbours, *even* empty vessels; borrow not a few.

Mt 9:28 And when he was come into the house, the blind men came to him: and Jesus saith unto them, Believe ye that I am able to do this? They said unto him, Yea, Lord.

Mk 7:27 But Jesus said unto her, Let the children first be filled: for it is not meet to take the children's bread, and to cast *it* unto the dogs.

He 11:8 By faith Abraham, when he was called to go out into a place which he should after receive for an inheritance, obeyed; and he went out, not knowing whither he went.

He 11:17 By faith Abraham, when he was tried, offered up Isaac: and he that had received the promises offered up his only begotten *son,*

He 11:36 And others had trial of *cruel* mockings and scourgings, yea, moreover of bonds and imprisonment:

Ja 1:3 Knowing *this,* that the trying of your faith worketh patience.

1 Pe 1:7 That the trial of your faith, being much more precious than of gold that perisheth, though it be tried with fire, might be found unto praise and honour and glory at the appearing of Jesus Christ:

11. Honored by Christ

Mk 1:41 And Jesus, moved with compassion, put forth *his* hand, and touched him, and saith unto him, I will; be thou clean.

Mk 2:5 When Jesus saw their faith, he said unto the sick of the palsy, Son, thy sins be forgiven thee.

Mk 5:34 And he said unto her, Daughter, thy faith hath made thee whole; go in peace, and be whole of thy plague.

Mk 7:29 And he said unto her, For this saying go thy way; the devil is gone out of thy daughter.

Mk 10:52 And Jesus said unto him, Go thy way; thy faith hath made thee whole. And immediately he received his sight, and followed Jesus in the way.

Lu 7:10 And they that were sent, returning to the house, found the servant whole that had been sick.

Lu 17:14 And when he saw *them,* he said unto them, Go shew yourselves unto the priests. And it came to pass, that, as they went, they were cleansed.

Jn 4:51 And as he was now going down, his servants met him, and told *him,* saying, Thy son liveth.

Jn 9:7 And said unto him, Go, wash in the pool of Siloam, (which is by interpretation, Sent.) He went his way therefore, and washed, and came seeing.

Ac 14:9 The same heard Paul speak: who stedfastly beholding him, and perceiving that he had faith to be healed,

12. Believers

Ps 56:11 In God have I put my trust: I will not be afraid what man can do unto me.

Jn 2:22 When therefore he was risen from the dead, his disciples remembered that he had said this unto them; and they believed the scripture, and the word which Jesus had said.

Jn 4:53 So the father knew that *it was* at the same hour, in the which Jesus said unto him, Thy son liveth: and himself believed, and his whole house.

Jn 7:31 And many of the people believed on him, and said, When Christ cometh, will he do more miracles than these which this *man* hath done?

Jn 8:30 As he spake these words, many believed on him.

Jn 10:42 And many believed on him there.

Jn 12:42 Nevertheless among the chief rulers also many believed on him; but because of the Pharisees they did not confess *him,* lest they should be put out of the synagogue:

Jn 17:8 For I have given unto them the words which thou gavest me; and they have received *them,* and have known surely that I came out from thee, and they have believed that thou didst send me.

Ac 9:42 And it was known throughout all Joppa; and many believed in the Lord.

Ac 16:34 And when he had brought them into his house, he set meat before them, and rejoiced, believing in God with all his house.

Ac 17:12 Therefore many of them believed; also of honourable women which were Greeks, and of men, not a few.

Ac 19:18 And many that believed came, and confessed, and shewed their deeds.

Ac 24:14 But this I confess unto thee, that after the way which they call heresy, so worship I the God of my fathers, believing all things which are written in the law and in the prophets:

Ro 4:18 Who against hope believed in hope, that he might become the father of many nations; according to that which was spoken, So shall thy seed be.

2 Ti 1:12 For the which cause I also suffer these things: nevertheless I am not ashamed: for I know whom I have believed, and am persuaded that he is able to keep that which I have committed unto him against that day.

13. Its Obstacles

LACK OF SYMPATHY

Mt 15:23 But he answered her not a word. And his disciples came and besought him, saying, Send her away; for she crieth after us.

Mk 10:13 And they brought young children to him, that he should touch them: and *his* disciples rebuked those that brought *them.*

DISCOURAGING CIRCUMSTANCES

Lu 5:18–19 And, behold, men brought in a bed a man which was taken with a palsy: and they sought *means* to bring him in, and to lay *him* before him.

And when they could not find by what *way* they might bring him in because of the multitude, they went upon the housetop, and let him down through the tiling with *his* couch into the midst before Jesus.

UNBELIEVING FRIENDS

Mk 5:35 While he yet spake, there came from the ruler of the synagogue's *house certain* which said, Thy daughter is dead: why troublest thou the Master any further?

SCOFFERS

Jn 9:24 Then again called they the man that was blind, and said unto him, Give God the praise: we know that this man is a sinner.

DIVINE DELAYS

Jn 11:3–6 Therefore his sisters sent unto him, saying, Lord, behold, he whom thou lovest is sick.

When Jesus heard *that,* he said, This sickness is not unto death, but for the glory of God, that the Son of God might be glorified thereby.

Now Jesus loved Martha, and her sister, and Lazarus.

When he had heard therefore that he was sick, he abode two days still in the same place where he was.

See **UNBELIEF**

FAITHFULNESS

1. Of God

Ge 9:15 And I will remember my covenant, which *is* between me and you and every living creature of all flesh; and the waters shall no more become a flood to destroy all flesh.

Ge 18:19 For I know him, that he will command his children and his household after him, and they shall keep the way of the LORD, to do justice and judgment; that the LORD may bring upon Abraham that which he hath spoken of him.

Ge 21:1 And the LORD visited Sarah as he had said, and the LORD did unto Sarah as he had spoken.

Ge 24:27 And he said, Blessed *be* the LORD God of my master Abraham, who hath not left destitute my master of his mercy and his truth: I *being* in the way, the LORD led me to the house of my master's brethren.

Ge 28:15 And, behold, I *am* with thee, and will keep thee in all *places* whither thou goest, and will bring thee again into this land; for I will not leave thee, until I have done *that* which I have spoken to thee of.

Ge 50:24 And Joseph said unto his brethren, I die: and God will surely visit you, and bring you out of this land unto the land which he sware to Abraham, to Isaac, and to Jacob.

Ex 2:24 And God heard their groaning, and God remembered his covenant with Abraham, with Isaac, and with Jacob.

Ex 6:5 And I have also heard the groaning of the children of Israel, whom the Egyptians keep in bondage; and I have remembered my covenant.

Ex 8:13 And the LORD did according to the word of Moses; and the frogs died out of the houses, out of the villages, and out of the fields.

De 4:31 (For the LORD thy God *is* a merciful God;) he will not forsake thee, neither destroy thee, nor forget the covenant of thy fathers which he sware unto them.

De 7:9 Know therefore that the LORD thy God, he *is* God, the faithful God, which keepeth covenant and mercy with them that love him and keep his commandments to a thousand generations;

De 9:5 Not for thy righteousness, or for the uprightness of thine heart, dost thou go to possess their land: but for the wickedness of these nations the LORD thy God doth drive them out from before thee, and that he may perform the word which the LORD sware unto thy fathers, Abraham, Isaac, and Jacob.

De 10:22 Thy fathers went down into Egypt with threescore and ten persons; and now the LORD thy God hath made thee as the stars of heaven for multitude.

De 26:3 And thou shalt go unto the priest that shall be in those days, and say unto him, I profess this day unto the LORD thy God, that I am come unto the country which the LORD sware unto our fathers for to give us.

Jos 1:3 Every place that the sole of your foot shall tread upon, that have I given unto you, as I said unto Moses.

Jos 14:10 And now, behold, the LORD hath kept me alive, as he said, these forty and five years, even since the LORD spake this word unto Moses, while *the children of* Israel wandered in the wilderness: and now, lo, I *am* this day fourscore and five years old.

Jos 21:45 There failed not ought of any good thing which the LORD had spoken unto the house of Israel; all came to pass.

1 S 12:22 For the LORD will not forsake his people for his great name's sake: because it hath pleased the LORD to make you his people.

2 S 7:21 For thy word's sake, and according to thine own heart, hast thou done all these great things, to make thy servant know *them.*

1 K 8:15 And he said, Blessed *be* the LORD God of Israel, which spake with his mouth unto David my father, and hath with his hand fulfilled *it,* saying,

1 K 8:23 And he said, LORD God of Israel, *there is* no God like thee, in heaven above, or on earth beneath, who keepest covenant and mercy with thy servants that walk before thee with all their heart:

1 K 8:56 Blessed *be* the LORD, that hath given rest unto his people Israel, according to all that he promised: there hath not failed one word of all his good promise, which he promised by the hand of Moses his servant.

2 K 8:19 Yet the LORD would not destroy Judah for David his servant's sake, as he promised him to give him alway a light, *and* to his children.

2 K 13:23 And the LORD was gracious unto them, and had compassion on them, and had respect unto them, because of his covenant with Abraham, Isaac, and Jacob, and would not destroy them, neither cast he them from his presence as yet.

1 Chr 28:20 And David said to Solomon his son, Be strong and of good courage, and do *it:* fear not, nor be dismayed: for the LORD God, *even* my God, *will be* with thee; he will not fail thee, nor forsake thee, until thou hast finished all the work for the service of the house of the LORD.

2 Chr 6:4 And he said, Blessed *be* the LORD God of Israel, who hath with his hands fulfilled *that* which he spake with his mouth to my father David, saying,

2 Chr 6:14 And said, O LORD God of Israel, *there is* no God like thee in the heaven, nor in the earth; which keepest covenant, and *shewest* mercy unto thy servants, that walk before thee with all their hearts:

2 Chr 21:7 Howbeit the LORD would not destroy the house of David, because of the covenant that he had made with David, and as he promised to give a light to him and to his sons for ever.

Ne 1:5 And said, I beseech thee, O LORD God of heaven, the great and terrible God, that keepeth covenant and mercy for them that love him and observe his commandments:

Ne 9:8 And foundest his heart faithful before thee, and madest a covenant with him to give the land of the Canaanites, the Hittites, the Amorites, and the Perizzites, and the Jebusites, and the Girgashites, to give *it, I say,* to his seed, and hast performed thy words; for thou *art* righteous:

Ne 9:32 Now therefore, our God, the great, the mighty, and the terrible God, who keepest covenant and mercy, let not all the trouble seem little before thee, that hath come upon us, on our kings, on our princes, and on our priests, and on our prophets, and on our fathers, and on all thy people, since the time of the kings of Assyria unto this day.

Ps 9:10 And they that know thy name will put their trust in thee: for thou, LORD, hast not forsaken them that seek thee.

Ps 36:5 Thy mercy, O LORD, *is* in the heavens; *and* thy faithfulness *reacheth* unto the clouds.

Ps 40:10 I have not hid thy righteousness within my heart; I have declared thy faithfulness and thy salvation: I have not concealed thy lovingkindness and thy truth from the great congregation.

Ps 71:22 I will also praise thee with the psaltery, *even* thy truth, O my God: unto thee will I sing with the harp, O thou Holy One of Israel.

Ps 77:8 Is his mercy clean gone for ever? doth *his* promise fail for evermore?

Ps 88:11 Shall thy lovingkindness be declared in the grave? or thy faithfulness in destruction?

Ps 89:1 I will sing of the mercies of the Lord for ever: with my mouth will I make known thy faithfulness to all generations.

Ps 89:24 But my faithfulness and my mercy *shall be* with him: and in my name shall his horn be exalted.

Ps 89:33 Nevertheless my lovingkindness will I not utterly take from him, nor suffer my faithfulness to fail.

Ps 92:2 To shew forth thy lovingkindness in the morning, and thy faithfulness every night,

Ps 98:3 He hath remembered his mercy and his truth toward the house of Israel: all the ends of the earth have seen the salvation of our God.

Ps 105:8 He hath remembered his covenant for ever, the word *which* he commanded to a thousand generations.

Ps 105:42 For he remembered his holy promise, *and* Abraham his servant.

Ps 106:45 And he remembered for them his covenant, and repented according to the multitude of his mercies.

Ps 111:5 He hath given meat unto them that fear him: he will ever be mindful of his covenant.

Ps 119:65 Thou hast dealt well with thy servant, O Lord, according unto thy word.

Ps 119:90 Thy faithfulness *is* unto all generations: thou hast established the earth, and it abideth.

Ps 119:138 Thy testimonies *that* thou hast commanded *are* righteous and very faithful.

Ps 132:11 The Lord hath sworn *in* truth unto David; he will not turn from it; Of the fruit of thy body will I set upon thy throne.

Ps 143:1 Hear my prayer, O Lord, give ear to my supplications: in thy faithfulness answer me, *and* in thy righteousness.

Is 25:1 O Lord, thou *art* my God; I will exalt thee, I will praise thy name; for thou hast done wonderful *things; thy* counsels of old *are* faithfulness *and* truth.

Is 44:26 That confirmeth the word of his servant, and performeth the coun-

sel of his messengers; that saith to Jerusalem, Thou shalt be inhabited; and to the cities of Judah, Ye shall be built, and I will raise up the decayed places thereof:

Is 49:7 Thus saith the Lord, the Redeemer of Israel, *and* his Holy One, to him whom man despiseth, to him whom the nation abhorreth, to a servant of rulers, Kings shall see and arise, princes also shall worship, because of the Lord that is faithful, *and* the Holy One of Israel, and he shall choose thee.

Je 33:14 Behold, the days come, saith the Lord, that I will perform that good thing which I have promised unto the house of Israel and to the house of Judah.

Je 33:21 *Then* may also my covenant be broken with David my servant, that he should not have a son to reign upon his throne; and with the Levites the priests, my ministers.

Je 33:26 Then will I cast away the seed of Jacob, and David my servant, so that I will not take *any* of his seed *to be* rulers over the seed of Abraham, Isaac, and Jacob: for I will cause their captivity to return, and have mercy on them.

Lam 3:23 *They are* new every morning: great *is* thy faithfulness.

Eze 16:60 Nevertheless I will remember my covenant with thee in the days of thy youth, and I will establish unto thee an everlasting covenant.

Eze 36:36 Then the heathen that are left round about you shall know that I the Lord build the ruined *places, and* plant that that was desolate: I the Lord have spoken *it,* and I will do *it.*

Eze 37:14 And shall put my spirit in you, and ye shall live, and I shall place you in your own land: then shall ye know that I the Lord have spoken *it,* and performed *it,* saith the Lord.

Da 9:4 And I prayed unto the Lord my God, and made my confession, and said, O Lord, the great and dreadful God, keeping the covenant and mercy to them that love him, and to them that keep his commandments;

Ho 2:20 I will even betroth thee unto me in faithfulness: and thou shalt know the LORD.

Mi 7:20 Thou wilt perform the truth to Jacob, *and* the mercy to Abraham, which thou hast sworn unto our fathers from the days of old.

Zep 3:5 The just LORD *is* in the midst thereof; he will not do iniquity: every morning doth he bring his judgment to light, he faileth not; but the unjust knoweth no shame.

Zec 8:8 And I will bring them, and they shall dwell in the midst of Jerusalem: and they shall be my people, and I will be their God, in truth and in righteousness.

Lu 1:55 As he spake to our fathers, to Abraham, and to his seed for ever.

Lu 1:72 To perform the mercy *promised* to our fathers, and to remember his holy covenant;

1 Co 1:9 God *is* faithful, by whom ye were called unto the fellowship of his Son Jesus Christ our Lord.

1 Co 10:13 There hath no temptation taken you but such as is common to man: but God *is* faithful, who will not suffer you to be tempted above that ye are able; but will with the temptation also make a way to escape, that ye may be able to bear *it*.

2 Co 1:18 But *as* God *is* true, our word toward you was not yea and nay.

2 Co 1:20 For all the promises of God in him *are* yea, and in him Amen, unto the glory of God by us.

He 6:18 That by two immutable things, in which *it was* impossible for God to lie, we might have a strong consolation, who have fled for refuge to lay hold upon the hope set before us:

He 11:11 Through faith also Sara herself received strength to conceive seed, and was delivered of a child when she was past age, because she judged him faithful who had promised.

1 Pe 4:19 Wherefore let them that suffer according to the will of God commit the keeping of their souls *to him* in well doing, as unto a faithful Creator.

2 Pe 3:9 The Lord is not slack concerning his promise, as some men count slackness; but is longsuffering to us-ward, not willing that any should perish, but that all should come to repentance.

2. Of Christ

Is 11:6 The wolf also shall dwell with the lamb, and the leopard shall lie down with the kid; and the calf and the young lion and the fatling together; and a little child shall lead them.

Mk 16:7 But go your way, tell his disciples and Peter that he goeth before you into Galilee: there shall ye see him, as he said unto you.

1 Th 5:24 Faithful *is* he that calleth you, who also will do *it*.

2 Th 3:3 But the Lord is faithful, who shall stablish you, and keep *you* from evil.

2 Ti 2:13 If we believe not, *yet* he abideth faithful: he cannot deny himself.

He 2:17 Wherefore in all things it behoved him to be made like unto *his* brethren, that he might be a merciful and faithful high priest in things *pertaining* to God, to make reconciliation for the sins of the people.

He 3:2 Who was faithful to him that appointed him, as also Moses *was faithful* in all his house.

He 10:23 Let us hold fast the profession of *our* faith without wavering; (for he is faithful that promised;)

Re 1:5 And from Jesus Christ, *who is* the faithful witness, *and* the first begotten of the dead, and the prince of the kings of the earth. Unto him that loved us, and washed us from our sins in his own blood,

Re 19:11 And I saw heaven opened, and behold a white horse; and he that sat upon him *was* called Faithful and True, and in righteousness he doth judge and make war.

See **UNFAITHFULNESS**

FAITHFUL SAYINGS, *words that are true*

1 Ti 1:15; 3:1; 4:9; 2 Ti 2:11; Tit 3:8

See **VERILY**

FALL, OF ADAM, *first man's choice to disobey God, thereby allowing the entrance of sin to contaminate the entire human race*

Ge 3:6; Is 43:27; Ro 5:12, 17; 1 Co 15:21; 1 Ti 2:14

FALSEHOOD, *lying*

1. Warnings

Le 19:11 Ye shall not steal, neither deal falsely, neither lie one to another.
Ps 5:6 Thou shalt destroy them that speak leasing: the LORD will abhor the bloody and deceitful man.
Ps 7:14 Behold, he travaileth with iniquity, and hath conceived mischief, and brought forth falsehood.
Ps 31:18 Let the lying lips be put to silence; which speak grievous things proudly and contemptuously against the righteous.
Ps 101:7 He that worketh deceit shall not dwell within my house: he that telleth lies shall not tarry in my sight.
Ps 120:2 Deliver my soul, O LORD, from lying lips, *and* from a deceitful tongue.
Pr 12:22 Lying lips *are* abomination to the LORD: but they that deal truly *are* his delight.
Pr 17:7 Excellent speech becometh not a fool: much less do lying lips a prince.
Pr 19:9 A false witness shall not be unpunished, and he that speaketh lies shall perish.
Pr 21:6 The getting of treasures by a lying tongue *is* a vanity tossed to and fro of them that seek death.
Je 7:28 But thou shalt say unto them, This *is* a nation that obeyeth not the voice of the LORD their God, nor receiveth correction: truth is perished, and is cut off from their mouth.
Col 3:9 Lie not one to another, seeing that ye have put off the old man with his deeds;

Re 21:8 But the fearful, and unbelieving, and the abominable, and murderers, and whoremongers, and sorcerers, and idolaters, and all liars, shall have their part in the lake which burneth with fire and brimstone: which is the second death.

2. Liars Condemned

Ps 63:11 But the king shall rejoice in God; every one that sweareth by him shall glory: but the mouth of them that speak lies shall be stopped.
Pr 19:5 A false witness shall not be unpunished, and *he that* speaketh lies shall not escape.
Pr 19:9 A false witness shall not be unpunished, and he that speaketh lies shall perish.
Pr 24:28 Be not a witness against thy neighbour without cause; and deceive *not* with thy lips.
Is 44:25 That frustrateth the tokens of the liars, and maketh diviners mad; that turneth wise *men* backward, and maketh their knowledge foolish;
1 Jn 2:22 Who is a liar but he that denieth that Jesus is the Christ? He is antichrist, that denieth the Father and the Son.
Re 21:8 But the fearful, and unbelieving, and the abominable, and murderers, and whoremongers, and sorcerers, and idolaters, and all liars, shall have their part in the lake which burneth with fire and brimstone: which is the second death.
Re 22:15 For without *are* dogs, and sorcerers, and whoremongers, and murderers, and idolaters, and whosoever loveth and maketh a lie.

3. Examples

Ge 3:4 And the serpent said unto the woman, Ye shall not surely die:
Ge 4:9 And the Lord said unto Cain, Where *is* Abel thy brother? And he said, I know not: *Am* I my brother's keeper?
Ge 18:15 Then Sarah denied, saying, I laughed not; for she was afraid. And he said, Nay; but thou didst laugh.
Ge 27:24 And he said, *Art* thou my very son Esau? And he said, I *am*.

Ge 37:20 Come now therefore, and let us slay him, and cast him into some pit, and we will say, Some evil beast hath devoured him: and we shall see what will become of his dreams.

Ge 37:32 And they sent the coat of *many* colours, and they brought *it* to their father; and said, This have we found: know now whether it *be* thy son's coat or no.

Ge 39:17 And she spake unto him according to these words, saying, The Hebrew servant, which thou hast brought unto us, came in unto me to mock me:

Ex 8:32 And Pharaoh hardened his heart at this time also, neither would he let the people go.

Le 6:3 Or have found that which was lost, and lieth concerning it, and sweareth falsely; in any of all these that a man doeth, sinning therein:

Jos 2:4 And the woman took the two men, and hid them, and said thus, There came men unto me, but I wist not whence they *were:*

2 K 5:22 And he said, All *is* well. My master hath sent me, saying, Behold, even now there be come to me from mount Ephraim two young men of the sons of the prophets: give them, I pray thee, a talent of silver, and two changes of garments.

2 K 5:25 But he went in, and stood before his master. And Elisha said unto him, Whence *comest thou,* Gehazi? And he said, Thy servant went no whither.

Jb 13:4 But ye *are* forgers of lies, ye *are* all physicians of no value.

Ps 58:3 The wicked are estranged from the womb: they go astray as soon as they be born, speaking lies.

Is 57:11 And of whom hast thou been afraid or feared, that thou hast lied, and hast not remembered me, nor laid *it* to thy heart? have not I held my peace even of old, and thou fearest me not?

Is 59:3 For your hands are defiled with blood, and your fingers with iniquity; your lips have spoken lies, your tongue hath muttered perverseness.

Je 28:3 Within two full years will I bring again into this place all the vessels of the Lord's house, that Nebuchadnezzar king of Babylon took away from this place, and carried them to Babylon:

Je 29:23 Because they have committed villany in Israel, and have committed adultery with their neighbours' wives, and have spoken lying words in my name, which I have not commanded them; even I know, and *am* a witness, saith the Lord.

Eze 13:19 And will ye pollute me among my people for handfuls of barley and for pieces of bread, to slay the souls that should not die, and to save the souls alive that should not live, by your lying to my people that hear *your* lies?

Eze 21:29 Whiles they see vanity unto thee, whiles they divine a lie unto thee, to bring thee upon the necks of *them that are* slain, of the wicked, whose day is come, when their iniquity *shall have* an end.

Mt 26:70 But he denied before *them* all, saying, I know not what thou sayest.

Mt 26:74 Then began he to curse and to swear, *saying,* I know not the man. And immediately the cock crew.

Mt 28:13 Saying, Say ye, His disciples came by night, and stole him *away* while we slept.

Mk 14:71 But he began to curse and to swear, *saying,* I know not this man of whom ye speak.

Lu 22:57 And he denied him, saying, Woman, I know him not.

Jn 8:44 Ye are of your father the devil, and the lusts of *your* father ye will do. He was a murderer from the beginning, and abode not in the truth, because there is no truth in him. When he speaketh a lie, he speaketh of his own: for he is a liar, and the father of it.

Ac 5:8 And Peter answered unto her, Tell me whether ye sold the land for so much? And she said, Yea, for so much.

Ac 24:6 Who also hath gone about to profane the temple: whom we took, and would have judged according to our law.

See **DECEPTION, TRUTH**

FAME, *well-known*

Nu 16:2; Jos 6:27; 1 S 9:6; 2 S 7:9; 8:13; 23:18; 1 K 4:31; 10:1, 24; 1 Chr 11:20; 12:30; 14:17; 17:8; 2 Chr 9:1, 6; 26:8, 15; 32:23; Est 9:4; Da 5:14; Mt 4:24; 9:26, 31; Mk 1:28; 2:1; 3:8; 6:14; Lu 4:14, 37; 5:15; 7:17; 23:8

FAMILY

1. Cares

SERVANTS' ILLS

Mt 8:6 And saying, Lord, my servant lieth at home sick of the palsy, grievously tormented.

CHILDREN'S SICKNESS

Mt 15:22 And, behold, a woman of Canaan came out of the same coasts, and cried unto him, saying, Have mercy on me, O Lord, *thou* Son of David; my daughter is grievously vexed with a devil.

ENTERTAINMENT OF GUESTS

Lu 10:40 But Martha was cumbered about much serving, and came to him, and said, Lord, dost thou not care that my sister hath left me to serve alone? bid her therefore that she help me.

HOSPITALITY

Lu 11:5–6 And he said unto them, Which of you shall have a friend, and shall go unto him at midnight, and say unto him, Friend lend me three loaves;

For a friend of mine in his journey is come to me, and I have nothing to set before him?

RESPONSIBILITY FOR HUSBAND OR WIFE

Lu 14:20 And another said, I have married a wife, and therefore I cannot come.

1 Co 7:33 But he that is married careth for the things that are of the world, how he may please *his* wife.

PROVIDING FOR THE FAMILY

1 Ti 5:8 But if any provide not for his own, and specially for those of his own house, he hath denied the faith, and is worse than an infidel.

2. Joys

CONJUGAL LOVE

Ge 24:67 And Isaac brought her into his mother Sarah's tent, and took Rebekah, and she became his wife; and he loved her: and Isaac was comforted after his mother's *death.*

BIRTH OF CHILDREN

Ge 21:6 And Sarah said, God hath made me to laugh, *so that* all that hear will laugh with me.

CHILDREN IN THE HOME

Jb 29:5 When the Almighty *was* yet with me, *when* my children *were* about me;

Ps 127:4–5 As arrows *are* in the hand of a mighty man; so *are* children of the youth.

Happy *is* the man that hath his quiver full of them: they shall not be ashamed, but they shall speak with the enemies in the gate.

BEING A WIFE AND MOTHER

Pr 31:28 Her children arise up, and call her blessed; her husband *also*, and he praiseth her.

POSSESSION OF A HOME

Mi 4:4 But they shall sit every man under his vine and under his fig tree; and none shall make *them* afraid: for the mouth of the LORD of hosts hath spoken *it.*

3. Trouble

a. Examples

SARAH AND HAGAR

Ge 16:5 And Sarai said unto Abram, My wrong *be* upon thee: I have given my maid into thy bosom; and when she saw that she had conceived, I was despised in her eyes: the LORD judge between me and thee.

REBEKAH AND HER DAUGHTERS-IN-LAW

Ge 26:34 And Esau was forty years old when he took to wife Judith the daughter of Beeri the Hittite, and Bashemath the daughter of Elon the Hittite:

Ge 26:35 Which were a grief of mind unto Isaac and to Rebekah.

Ge 27:46 And Rebekah said to Isaac, I am weary of my life because of the daughters of Heth: if Jacob take a wife of the daughters of Heth, such as these *which are* of the daughters of the land, what good shall my life do me?

JACOB AND ESAU

Ge 27:41 And Esau hated Jacob because of the blessing wherewith his father blessed him: and Esau said in his heart, The days of mourning for my father are at hand; then will I slay my brother Jacob.

JOSEPH AND HIS BRETHREN

Ge 37:4 And when his brethren saw that their father loved him more than all his brethren, they hated him, and could not speak peaceably unto him.

MOSES, AARON, AND MIRIAM

Nu 12:1 And Miriam and Aaron spake against Moses because of the Ethiopian woman whom he had married: for he had married an Ethiopian woman.

DAVID AND HIS WIFE

2 S 6:16 And as the ark of the LORD came into the city of David, Michal Saul's daughter looked through a window, and saw king David leaping and dancing before the LORD; and she despised him in her heart.

DAVID AND HIS HOUSEHOLD

2 S 12:11 Thus saith the LORD, Behold, I will raise up evil against thee out of thine own house, and I will take thy wives before thine eyes, and give *them* unto thy neighbour, and he shall lie with thy wives in the sight of this sun.

AHASUERUS AND VASHTI

Est 1:12 But the queen Vashti refused to come at the king's commandment by *his* chamberlains: therefore was the king very wroth, and his anger burned in him.

b. Causes

HATRED

Ge 27:41

ENVY

Ge 37:11

UNGRATEFUL CHILDREN

De 21:20; 2 S 15:6

UNWORTHY HUSBANDS

1 S 25:25

AVARICE

Pr 15:27

CONTENTIOUS WIVES

Pr 21:19

SLOTHFULNESS

Ec 10:18

CHILDLESSNESS, *regarded as a misfortune*

Ge 11:30; 15:2; 16:1; 25:21; 29:31; 30:1; Le 20:20; Nu 3:4; Jud 13:2; 1 S 1:2, 5; 2 S 6:23; 2 K 4:14; 1 Chr 2:30; Jb 18:19; Pr 30:16; Je 22:30; Ho 9:11; Mt 22:25; Mk 12:19; Lu 1:7, 25, 36; 20:29; Ac 7:5

FRATRICIDE

Ge 4:8; Jud 9:5; 2 S 13:28; 1 K 2:25; 2 Chr 21:4; Is 19:2; Mt 10:21; Mk 13:12

See **CHILDREN, HUSBANDS, PARENTS, WIVES**

FAMINE, *a drastic and far-reaching shortage of food*

1. Prophesied

Ge 41:27, 54; 42:5; 2 K 8:1; 1 Chr 21:12; 2 Chr 6:28; Je 11:22; 29:17; Eze 7:15; 12:19; 14:13; Hab 3:17; Mt 24:7; Mk 13:8; Lu 21:11; Ac 11:28; Re 6:8

2. Examples

Ge 12:10; 26:1; 43:1; 45:6; 47:4, 13, 20; Ru 1:1; 2 S 21:1; 1 K 8:37; 17:12; 18:2; 2 K 4:38; 6:25; 7:4; 25:3; Ne 5:3; Ps 105:16; Je 38:9; Lam 2:12; 4:4; Jl 1:17; Am 4:6; Lu 4:25; Ac 7:11; Re 6:6

3. Threatened

Le 26:26; De 28:53; Je 14:16; Eze 4:16; 5:12; 6:12; Re 18:8

FANATICISM

THE PROPHETS OF BAAL

1 K 18:28 And they cried aloud, and cut themselves after their manner with knives and lancets, till the blood gushed out upon them.

THE JEWS AGAINST CHRIST

Jn 19:15 But they cried out, Away with *him,* away with *him,* crucify him. Pilate saith unto them, Shall I crucify your King? The chief priests answered, We have no king but Caesar.

THE JEWS IN STONING STEPHEN

Ac 7:57 Then they cried out with a loud voice, and stopped their ears, and ran upon him with one accord,

SAUL IN PERSECUTING THE CHURCH

Ac 9:1 And Saul, yet breathing out threatenings and slaughter against the disciples of the Lord, went unto the high priest,

THE JEWS IN THEIR RAGE AGAINST PAUL

Ac 21:36 For the multitude of the people followed after, crying, Away with him.

Ac 22:23 And as they cried out, and cast off *their* clothes, and threw dust into the air,

FAREWELLS

Ru 1:14; Lu 9:61; Ac 18:21; 20:1, 38; 21:6; 2 Co 13:11

FARMER *See* AGRICULTURE

FARMING *See* AGRICULTURE

FARTHING, *a piece of money*

Mt 5:26; 10:29; Mk 12:42; Lu 12:6

See **WEIGHTS AND MEASURES**

FASTING, *going without drink and/or food for a period of time and for a stated purpose*

Ps 35:13 But as for me, when they were sick, my clothing *was* sackcloth: I humbled my soul with fasting; and my prayer returned into mine own bosom.

Ps 69:10 When I wept, *and chastened* my soul with fasting, that was to my reproach.

Is 58:3 Wherefore have we fasted, *say they,* and thou seest not? *wherefore* have we afflicted our soul, and thou takest no knowledge? Behold, in the day of your fast ye find pleasure, and exact all your labours.

Je 14:12 When they fast, I will not hear their cry; and when they offer burnt offering and an oblation, I will not accept them: but I will consume them by the sword, and by the famine, and by the pestilence.

Zec 7:5 Speak unto all the people of the land, and to the priests, saying, When ye fasted and mourned in the fifth and seventh *month,* even those seventy years, did ye at all fast unto me, *even* to me?

Mt 9:15 And Jesus said unto them, Can the children of the bridechamber mourn, as long as the bridegroom is with them? but the days will come, when the bridegroom shall be taken from them, and then shall they fast.

1. Commanded

Jl 1:14 Sanctify ye a fast, call a solemn assembly, gather the elders *and* all the inhabitants of the land *into* the house of the LORD your God, and cry unto the LORD,

Jl 2:12 Therefore also now, saith the LORD, turn ye *even* to me with all your heart, and with fasting, and with weeping, and with mourning:

Mt 6:17–18 But thou, when thou fastest, anoint thine head, and wash thy face;

That thou appear not unto men to fast, but unto thy Father which is in secret: and thy Father, which seeth in secret, shall reward thee openly.

1 Co 7:5 Defraud ye not one the other, except *it be* with consent for a time, that ye may give yourselves to fasting and prayer; and come together again, that Satan tempt you not for your incontinency.

2. Examples

MOSES

Ex 34:28; Jud 20:26

ISRAEL

1 S 7:6; 20:34; 28:20; 31:13; 2 S 1:12; 3:35; 12:16

ELIJAH

1 K 19:8; 1 Chr 10:12

EZRA

Ezr 10:6; Ne 9:1; Da 6:18

DANIEL

Da 10:3; Mt 4:2

CHRIST

Lu 4:1–2; 18:12

PAUL

Ac 9:9; 10:30

LEADERS IN THE CHURCH AT ANTIOCH

Ac 13:2–3

PAUL AND BARNABAS

Ac 14:23

See **DISCIPLESHIP**

FAT, *to be burned in every sacrificial offering*

1. Offered in Sacrifice

Ex 23:18; 29:13, 22; Le 1:8; 3:4, 10, 15; 4:8, 19, 26, 31; 7:3; 8:16; 9:10, 20; 10:15; 16:25; 17:6; Nu 18:17; 1 S 2:16; 2 Chr 7:7; 29:35; 35:14; Is 43:24; Eze 44:7, 15

2. Eating Prohibited

Le 3:17; 7:23

See **OFFERINGS**

FATHER *See* **FAMILY, GOD**

FATHERHOOD OF GOD, *nourisher, protector*

1 Chr 17:13 I will be his father, and he shall be my son: and I will not take my mercy away from him, as I took *it* from *him* that was before thee:

1 Chr 29:10 Wherefore David blessed the Lord before all the congregation: and David said, Blessed *be* thou, Lord God of Israel our father, for ever and ever.

Ps 68:5 A father of the fatherless, and a judge of the widows, *is* God in his holy habitation.

Ps 89:26 He shall cry unto me, Thou *art* my father, my God, and the rock of my salvation.

Is 63:16 Doubtless thou *art* our father, though Abraham be ignorant of us, and Israel acknowledge us not: thou, O Lord, *art* our father, our redeemer; thy name *is* from everlasting.

Is 64:8 But now, O Lord, thou *art* our father; we *are* the clay, and thou our potter; and we all *are* the work of thy hand.

Je 3:4 Wilt thou not from this time cry unto me, My father, thou art the guide of my youth?

Je 3:19 But I said, How shall I put thee among the children, and give thee a pleasant land, a goodly heritage of the hosts of nations? and I said, Thou shalt call me, My father; and shalt not turn away from me.

Je 31:9 They shall come with weeping, and with supplications will I lead them: I will cause them to walk by the rivers of waters in a straight way, wherein they shall not stumble: for I am a father to Israel, and Ephraim *is* my firstborn.

Mt 5:16 Let your light so shine before men, that they may see your good works, and glorify your Father which is in heaven.

Mt 6:1 Take heed that ye do not your alms before men, to be seen of them:

otherwise ye have no reward of your Father which is in heaven.

Mt 6:9 After this manner therefore pray ye: Our Father which art in heaven, Hallowed be thy name.

Mt 6:18 That thou appear not unto men to fast, but unto thy Father which is in secret: and thy Father, which seeth in secret, shall reward thee openly.

Mt 6:26 Behold the fowls of the air: for they sow not, neither do they reap, nor gather into barns; yet your heavenly Father feedeth them. Are ye not much better than they?

Mt 7:11 If ye then, being evil, know how to give good gifts unto your children, how much more shall your Father which is in heaven give good things to them that ask him?

Mt 12:50 For whosoever shall do the will of my Father which is in heaven, the same is my brother, and sister, and mother.

Mt 13:43 Then shall the righteous shine forth as the sun in the kingdom of their Father. Who hath ears to hear, let him hear.

Mt 16:17 And Jesus answered and said unto him, Blessed art thou, Simon Barjona: for flesh and blood hath not revealed it unto thee, but my Father which is in heaven.

Mt 18:10 Take heed that ye despise not one of these little ones; for I say unto you, That in heaven their angels do always behold the face of my Father which is in heaven.

Mt 18:35 So likewise shall my heavenly Father do also unto you, if ye from your hearts forgive not every one his brother their trespasses.

Mk 13:32 But of that day and that hour knoweth no man, no, not the angels which are in heaven, neither the Son, but the Father.

Lu 11:2 And he said unto them, When ye pray, say, Our Father which art in heaven, Hallowed be thy name. Thy kingdom come. Thy will be done, as in heaven, so in earth.

Lu 12:32 Fear not, little flock; for it is your Father's good pleasure to give you the kingdom.

Lu 15:17 And when he came to himself, he said, How many hired servants of my father's have bread enough and to spare, and I perish with hunger!

Jn 16:25 These things have I spoken unto you in proverbs: but the time cometh, when I shall no more speak unto you in proverbs, but I shall shew you plainly of the Father.

Jn 20:17 Jesus saith unto her, Touch me not; for I am not yet ascended to my Father: but go to my brethren, and say unto them, I ascend unto my Father, and your Father; and to my God, and your God.

Ro 8:15 For ye have not received the spirit of bondage again to fear; but ye have received the Spirit of adoption, whereby we cry, Abba, Father.

Ro 15:6 That ye may with one mind and one mouth glorify God, even the Father of our Lord Jesus Christ.

1 Co 1:3 Grace be unto you, and peace, from God our Father, and from the Lord Jesus Christ.

2 Co 1:3 Blessed be God, even the Father of our Lord Jesus Christ, the Father of mercies, and the God of all comfort;

2 Co 6:18 And will be a Father unto you, and ye shall be my sons and daughters, saith the Lord Almighty.

Ga 1:4 Who gave himself for our sins, that he might deliver us from this present evil world, according to the will of God and our Father:

Ga 4:6 And because ye are sons, God hath sent forth the Spirit of his Son into your hearts, crying, Abba, Father.

Ep 1:2 Grace be to you, and peace, from God our Father, and from the Lord Jesus Christ.

Ep 1:17 That the God of our Lord Jesus Christ, the Father of glory, may give unto you the spirit of wisdom and revelation in the knowledge of him:

Ep 3:14 For this cause I bow my knees unto the Father of our Lord Jesus Christ,

Ep 5:20 Giving thanks always for all things unto God and the Father in the name of our Lord Jesus Christ;

Ph 4:20 Now unto God and our Father be glory for ever and ever. Amen.

Col 1:3 We give thanks to God and the Father of our Lord Jesus Christ, praying always for you,

Col 1:12 Giving thanks unto the Father, which hath made us meet to be partakers of the inheritance of the saints in light:

1 Th 3:11 Now God himself and our Father, and our Lord Jesus Christ, direct our way unto you.

2 Th 1:1 Paul, and Silvanus, and Timotheus, unto the church of the Thessalonians in God our Father and the Lord Jesus Christ:

2 Th 2:16 Now our Lord Jesus Christ himself, and God, even our Father, which hath loved us, and hath given *us* everlasting consolation and good hope through grace,

1 Ti 1:2 Unto Timothy, *my* own son in the faith: Grace, mercy, *and* peace, from God our Father and Jesus Christ our Lord.

Tit 1:4 To Titus, *mine* own son after the common faith: Grace, mercy, *and* peace, from God the Father and the Lord Jesus Christ our Saviour.

1 Pe 1:17 And if ye call on the Father, who without respect of persons judgeth according to every man's work, pass the time of your sojourning *here* in fear:

1 Jn 2:13 I write unto you, fathers, because ye have known him *that is* from the beginning. I write unto you, young men, because ye have overcome the wicked one. I write unto you, little children, because ye have known the Father.

1 Jn 3:1 Behold, what manner of love the Father hath bestowed upon us, that we should be called the sons of God: therefore the world knoweth us not, because it knew him not.

Jude 1 Jude, the servant of Jesus Christ, and brother of James, to them that are sanctified by God the Father, and preserved in Jesus Christ, *and* called:

God the Father of All

De 32:6 Do ye thus requite the LORD, O foolish people and unwise? *is* not he thy father *that* hath bought thee? hath

he not made thee, and established thee?

Is 45:11 Thus saith the LORD, the Holy One of Israel, and his Maker, Ask me of things to come concerning my sons, and concerning the work of my hands command ye me.

Mal 2:10 Have we not all one father? hath not one God created us? why do we deal treacherously every man against his brother, by profaning the covenant of our fathers?

Mt 23:9 And call no *man* your father upon the earth: for one is your Father, which is in heaven.

Ro 3:29 *Is he* the God of the Jews only? *is he* not also of the Gentiles? Yes, of the Gentiles also:

1 Co 8:6 But to us *there is but* one God, the Father, of whom *are* all things, and we in him; and one Lord Jesus Christ, by whom *are* all things, and we by him.

Ep 4:6 One God and Father of all, who *is* above all, and through all, and in you all.

He 12:9 Furthermore we have had fathers of our flesh which corrected *us,* and we gave *them* reverence: shall we not much rather be in subjection unto the Father of spirits, and live?

1 Jn 5:7 For there are three that bear record in heaven, the Father, the Word, and the Holy Ghost: and these three are one.

FAULTFINDING

1. Of Others

Jos 22:16 Thus saith the whole congregation of the LORD, What trespass *is* this that ye have committed against the God of Israel, to turn away this day from following the LORD, in that ye have builded you an altar, that ye might rebel this day against the LORD?

Jb 1:9 Then Satan answered the LORD, and said, Doth Job fear God for nought?

Jb 2:5 But put forth thine hand now, and touch his bone and his flesh, and he will curse thee to thy face.

Ps 15:3 *He that* backbiteth not with his tongue, nor doeth evil to his neighbour, nor taketh up a reproach against his neighbour.

Is 29:20–21 For the terrible one is brought to nought, and the scorner is consumed, and all that watch for iniquity are cut off:

That make a man an offender for a word, and lay a snare for him that reproveth in the gate, and turn aside the just for a thing of nought.

Mt 7:4 Or how wilt thou say to thy brother, Let me pull out the mote out of thine eye; and, behold, a beam *is* in thine own eye?

Jn 1:46 And Nathanael said unto him, Can there any good thing come out of Nazareth? Philip saith unto him, Come and see.

Ac 28:4 And when the barbarians saw the *venomous* beast hang on his hand, they said among themselves, No doubt this man is a murderer, whom, though he hath escaped the sea, yet vengeance suffereth not to live.

1 Ti 6:4 He is proud, knowing nothing, but doting about questions and strifes of words, whereof cometh envy, strife, railings, evil surmisings,

2. Of Christ

Mt 9:11; 12:2; 15:2; Mk 2:7, 16, 18, 24; 7:2; 14:4; Lu 5:21, 30; 6:2; 7:34, 39, 49; 10:40; 13:14; 15:2; 19:7, 39; Jn 6:41; Ac 11:2

FAULTLESSNESS, *without sin, perfect*

1 S 12:5; 29:3; Da 6:4; Lu 23:4, 14; Jn 18:38; 19:6; Jude 24; Re 14:5

FAVOR, DIVINE, *God's approval*

1. Examples

Ge 4:4 And Abel, he also brought of the firstlings of his flock and of the fat thereof. And the LORD had respect unto Abel and to his offering:

Ge 6:8 But Noah found grace in the eyes of the LORD.

Ge 12:3 And I will bless them that bless thee, and curse him that curseth thee: and in thee shall all families of the earth be blessed.

Ge 39:21 But the LORD was with Joseph, and shewed him mercy, and gave him favour in the sight of the keeper of the prison.

Ex 2:25 And God looked upon the children of Israel, and God had respect unto *them*.

Ex 33:12 And Moses said unto the LORD, See, thou sayest unto me, Bring up this people: and thou hast not let me know whom thou wilt send with me. Yet thou hast said, I know thee by name, and thou hast also found grace in my sight.

1 S 2:26 And the child Samuel grew on, and was in favour both with the LORD, and also with men.

2 K 13:23 And the LORD was gracious unto them, and had compassion on them, and had respect unto them, because of his covenant with Abraham, Isaac, and Jacob, and would not destroy them, neither cast he them from his presence as yet.

Jb 33:26 He shall pray unto God, and he will be favourable unto him: and he shall see his face with joy: for he will render unto man his righteousness.

Ps 21:6 For thou hast made him most blessed for ever: thou hast made him exceeding glad with thy countenance.

Pr 3:4 So shalt thou find favour and good understanding in the sight of God and man.

Pr 8:35 For whoso findeth me findeth life, and shall obtain favour of the LORD.

Pr 12:2 A good *man* obtaineth favour of the LORD: but a man of wicked devices will he condemn.

Pr 16:7 When a man's ways please the LORD, he maketh even his enemies to be at peace with him.

Pr 18:22 *Whoso* findeth a wife findeth a good *thing*, and obtaineth favour of the LORD.

Eze 36:37 Thus saith the Lord GOD; I will yet *for* this be enquired of by the house of Israel, to do *it* for them; I will increase them with men like a flock.

Lu 1:30 And the angel said unto her, Fear not, Mary: for thou hast found favour with God.

Lu 2:52 And Jesus increased in wisdom and stature, and in favour with God and man.

Ac 7:46 Who found favour before God, and desired to find a tabernacle for the God of Jacob.

2. Invoked

Ge 43:29; Ex 33:13; Nu 6:25; Ps 4:6; 31:16; 67:1; 80:3, 19; 106:4; 119:135; Is 33:2; Da 9:17

See **BENEDICTIONS**

3. Promised to Saints

Ps 85:1 LORD, thou hast been favourable unto thy land: thou hast brought back the captivity of Jacob.

Ps 89:17 For thou *art* the glory of their strength: and in thy favour our horn shall be exalted.

Is 30:18 And therefore will the LORD wait, that he may be gracious unto you, and therefore will he be exalted, that he may have mercy upon you: for the LORD *is* a God of judgment: blessed *are* all they that wait for him.

Is 60:10 And the sons of strangers shall build up thy walls, and their kings shall minister unto thee: for in my wrath I smote thee, but in my favour have I had mercy on thee.

Is 62:4 Thou shalt no more be termed Forsaken; neither shall thy land any more be termed Desolate: but thou shalt be called Hephzi-bah, and thy land Beulah: for the LORD delighteth in thee, and thy land shall be married.

Is 65:19 And I will rejoice in Jerusalem, and joy in my people: and the voice of weeping shall be no more heard in her, nor the voice of crying.

Je 32:41 Yea, I will rejoice over them to do them good, and I will plant them in this land assuredly with my whole heart and with my whole soul.

Ho 1:10 Yet the number of the children of Israel shall be as the sand of the sea, which cannot be measured nor numbered; and it shall come to pass, *that* in the place where it was said unto them, Ye *are* not my people, *there* it shall be said unto them, *Ye are* the sons of the living God.

Am 5:15 Hate the evil, and love the good, and establish judgment in the gate: it may be that the LORD God of hosts will be gracious unto the remnant of Joseph.

Zep 3:17 The LORD thy God in the midst of thee *is* mighty; he will save, he will rejoice over thee with joy; he will rest in his love, he will joy over thee with singing.

1 Co 4:5 Therefore judge nothing before the time, until the Lord come, who both will bring to light the hidden things of darkness, and will make manifest the counsels of the hearts: and then shall every man have praise of God.

See **OBEDIENCE, PROMISES**

4. Possessed by Pleasing God

RENDERS LIFE SECURE

Pr 16:7 When a man's ways please the LORD, he maketh even his enemies to be at peace with him.

A CHARACTERISTIC OF CHRIST

Mt 3:17 And lo a voice from heaven, saying, This is my beloved Son, in whom I am well pleased.

Jn 8:29 And he that sent me is with me: the Father hath not left me alone; for I do always those things that please him.

THE AIM OF THE TRUE MINISTER

1 Th 2:4 But as we were allowed of God to be put in trust with the gospel, even so we speak; not as pleasing men, but God, which trieth our hearts.

THE CHRISTIAN'S DUTY

1 Th 4:1 Furthermore then we beseech you, brethren, and exhort *you* by the Lord Jesus, that as ye have received of us how ye ought to walk and to please God, *so* ye would abound more and more.

ENOCH'S EXAMPLE

He 11:5 By faith Enoch was translated that he should not see death; and was not found, because God had translated him: for before his translation he had this testimony, that he pleased God.

THROUGH BENEVOLENCE

He 13:16 But to do good and to communicate forget not: for with such sacrifices God is well pleased.

1 Jn 3:22 And whatsoever we ask, we receive of him, because we keep his commandments, and do those things that are pleasing in his sight.

See **ACCEPTANCE**

FEAR, *result of estrangement from God*

Ge 3:8 And they heard the voice of the LORD God walking in the garden in the cool of the day: and Adam and his wife hid themselves from the presence of the LORD God amongst the trees of the garden.

Ge 3:10 And he said, I heard thy voice in the garden, and I was afraid, because I *was* naked; and I hid myself.

Ge 42:28 And he said unto his brethren, My money is restored; and, lo, *it is* even in my sack: and their heart failed *them,* and they were afraid, saying one to another, What *is* this *that* God hath done unto us?

Ge 43:18 And the men were afraid, because they were brought into Joseph's house; and they said, Because of the money that was returned in our sacks at the first time are we brought in; that he may seek occasion against us, and fall upon us, and take us for bondmen, and our asses.

Ge 45:3 And Joseph said unto his brethren, I *am* Joseph; doth my father yet live? And his brethren could not answer him; for they were troubled at his presence.

Ge 50:15 And when Joseph's brethren saw that their father was dead, they said, Joseph will peradventure hate us, and will certainly requite us all the evil which we did unto him.

Ex 2:14 And he said, Who made thee a prince and a judge over us? intendest thou to kill me, as thou killedst the Egyptian? And Moses feared, and said, Surely this thing is known.

Ex 14:25 And took off their chariot wheels, that they drave them heavily: so that the Egyptians said, Let us flee from the face of Israel; for the LORD fighteth for them against the Egyptians.

Le 26:17 And I will set my face against you, and ye shall be slain before your enemies: they that hate you shall reign over you; and ye shall flee when none pursueth you.

Le 26:36 And upon them that are left *alive* of you I will send a faintness into their hearts in the lands of their enemies; and the sound of a shaken leaf shall chase them; and they shall flee, as fleeing from a sword; and they shall fall when none pursueth.

Nu 16:34 And all Israel that *were* round about them fled at the cry of them: for they said, Lest the earth swallow us up *also.*

Nu 17:12 And the children of Israel spake unto Moses, saying, Behold, we die, we perish, we all perish.

De 28:65 And among these nations shalt thou find no ease, neither shall the sole of thy foot have rest: but the LORD shall give thee there a trembling heart, and failing of eyes, and sorrow of mind:

1 Chr 21:20 And Ornan turned back, and saw the angel; and his four sons with him hid themselves. Now Ornan was threshing wheat.

1 Chr 21:30 But David could not go before it to enquire of God: for he was afraid because of the sword of the angel of the LORD.

2 Chr 18:29 And the king of Israel said unto Jehoshaphat, I will disguise myself, and will go to the battle; but put thou on thy robes. So the king of Israel disguised himself; and they went to the battle.

Ezr 10:9 Then all the men of Judah and Benjamin gathered themselves together unto Jerusalem within three days. It *was* the ninth month, on the twentieth *day* of the month; and all the people sat in the street of the house of God, trembling because of *this* matter, and for the great rain.

Est 7:6 And Esther said, The adversary and enemy *is* this wicked Haman. Then Haman was afraid before the king and the queen.

Jb 13:11 Shall not his excellency make you afraid? and his dread fall upon you?

Jb 15:24 Trouble and anguish shall make him afraid; they shall prevail against him, as a king ready to the battle.

Jb 18:11 Terrors shall make him afraid on every side, and shall drive him to his feet.

Jb 22:10 Therefore snares *are* round about thee, and sudden fear troubleth thee;

Ps 53:5 There were they in great fear, *where* no fear was: for God hath scattered the bones of him that encampeth *against* thee: thou hast put *them* to shame, because God hath despised them.

Pr 28:1 The wicked flee when no man pursueth: but the righteous are bold as a lion.

Is 2:10 Enter into the rock, and hide thee in the dust, for fear of the LORD, and for the glory of his majesty.

Is 2:19 And they shall go into the holes of the rocks, and into the caves of the earth, for fear of the LORD, and for the glory of his majesty, when he ariseth to shake terribly the earth.

Is 13:8 And they shall be afraid: pangs and sorrows shall take hold of them; they shall be in pain as a woman that travaileth: they shall be amazed one at another; their faces *shall be as* flames.

Is 24:17 Fear, and the pit, and the snare, *are* upon thee, O inhabitant of the earth.

Is 33:14 The sinners in Zion are afraid; fearfulness hath surprised the hypocrites. Who among us shall dwell with the devouring fire? who among us shall dwell with everlasting burnings?

Is 66:4 I also will choose their delusions, and will bring their fears upon them; because when I called, none did answer; when I spake, they did not hear: but they did evil before mine eyes, and chose *that* in which I delighted not.

Je 36:16 Now it came to pass, when they had heard all the words, they were afraid both one and other, and said unto Baruch, We will surely tell the king of all these words.

Eze 32:10 Yea, I will make many people amazed at thee, and their kings shall be horribly afraid for thee, when I shall brandish my sword before them; and they shall tremble at *every* moment, every man for his own life, in the day of thy fall.

Da 5:6 Then the king's countenance was changed, and his thoughts troubled him, so that the joints of his loins were loosed, and his knees smote one against another.

Da 10:7 And I Daniel alone saw the vision: for the men that were with me saw not the vision; but a great quaking fell upon them, so that they fled to hide themselves.

Ho 10:8 The high places also of Aven, the sin of Israel, shall be destroyed: the thorn and the thistle shall come up on their altars; and they shall say to the mountains, Cover us; and to the hills, Fall on us.

Mi 7:17 They shall lick the dust like a serpent, they shall move out of their holes like worms of the earth: they shall be afraid of the LORD our God, and shall fear because of thee.

Mt 24:30 And then shall appear the sign of the Son of man in heaven: and then shall all the tribes of the earth mourn, and they shall see the Son of man coming in the clouds of heaven with power and great glory.

Mt 28:4 And for fear of him the keepers did shake, and became as dead *men.*

Mk 5:15 And they come to Jesus, and see him that was possessed with the devil, and had the legion, sitting, and clothed, and in his right mind: and they were afraid.

Jn 19:8 When Pilate therefore heard that saying, he was the more afraid;

Ac 8:24 Then answered Simon, and said, Pray ye to the Lord for me, that none of these things which ye have spoken come upon me.

Ac 16:29 Then he called for a light, and sprang in, and came trembling, and fell down before Paul and Silas,

Ac 22:9 And they that were with me saw indeed the light, and were afraid;

but they heard not the voice of him that spake to me.

Ac 22:29 Then straightway they departed from him which should have examined him: and the chief captain also was afraid, after he knew that he was a Roman, and because he had bound him.

1 Co 15:56 The sting of death *is* sin; and the strength of sin *is* the law.

He 10:27 But a certain fearful looking for of judgment and fiery indignation, which shall devour the adversaries.

1 Jn 4:18 There is no fear in love; but perfect love casteth out fear: because fear hath torment. He that feareth is not made perfect in love.

Re 6:15 And the kings of the earth, and the great men, and the rich men, and the chief captains, and the mighty men, and every bondman, and every free man, hid themselves in the dens and in the rocks of the mountains;

Re 11:11 And after three days and an half the Spirit of life from God entered into them, and they stood upon their feet; and great fear fell upon them which saw them.

Re 11:13 And the same hour was there a great earthquake, and the tenth part of the city fell, and in the earthquake were slain of men seven thousand: and the remnant were affrighted, and gave glory to the God of heaven.

1. Terror of the Wicked

Ge 4:14 Behold, thou hast driven me out this day from the face of the earth; and from thy face shall I be hid; and I shall be a fugitive and a vagabond in the earth; and it shall come to pass, *that* every one that findeth me shall slay me.

Ex 12:33 And the Egyptians were urgent upon the people, that they might send them out of the land in haste; for they said, We *be* all dead *men.*

Ex 15:16 Fear and dread shall fall upon them; by the greatness of thine arm they shall be *as* still as a stone; till thy people pass over, O LORD, till the people pass over, *which* thou hast purchased.

Le 26:36 And upon them that are left *alive* of you I will send a faintness into their hearts in the lands of their enemies; and the sound of a shaken leaf shall chase them; and they shall flee, as fleeing from a sword; and they shall fall when none pursueth.

Nu 22:3 And Moab was sore afraid of the people, because they *were* many: and Moab was distressed because of the children of Israel.

De 5:25 Now therefore why should we die? for this great fire will consume us: if we hear the voice of the LORD our God any more, then we shall die.

De 28:10 And all people of the earth shall see that thou art called by the name of the LORD; and they shall be afraid of thee.

De 28:66 And thy life shall hang in doubt before thee; and thou shalt fear day and night, and shalt have none assurance of thy life:

De 32:25 The sword without, and terror within, shall destroy both the young man and the virgin, the suckling *also* with the man of gray hairs.

De 34:12 And in all that mighty hand, and in all the great terror which Moses shewed in the sight of all Israel.

Jos 5:1 And it came to pass, when all the kings of the Amorites, which *were* on the side of Jordan westward, and all the kings of the Canaanites, which *were* by the sea, heard that the LORD had dried up the waters of Jordan from before the children of Israel, until we were passed over, that their heart melted, neither was there spirit in them any more, because of the children of Israel.

Jos 7:9 For the Canaanites and all the inhabitants of the land shall hear *of it,* and shall environ us round, and cut off our name from the earth: and what wilt thou do unto thy great name?

Jud 7:21 And they stood every man in his place round about the camp: and all the host ran, and cried, and fled.

1 S 5:10 Therefore they sent the ark of God to Ekron. And it came to pass, as the ark of God came to Ekron, that the Ekronites cried out, saying, They have brought about the ark of the God of Israel to us, to slay us and our people.

1 S 14:15 And there was trembling in the host, in the field, and among all the people: the garrison, and the spoilers, they also trembled, and the earth quaked: so it was a very great trembling.

1 S 25:37 But it came to pass in the morning, when the wine was gone out of Nabal, and his wife had told him these things, that his heart died within him, and he became *as* a stone.

1 S 28:20 Then Saul fell straightway all along on the earth, and was sore afraid, because of the words of Samuel: and there was no strength in him; for he had eaten no bread all the day, nor all the night.

2 S 22:46 Strangers shall fade away, and they shall be afraid out of their close places.

1 K 1:50 And Adonijah feared because of Solomon, and arose, and went, and caught hold on the horns of the altar.

1 K 2:28 Then tidings came to Joab: for Joab had turned after Adonijah, though he turned not after Absalom. And Joab fled unto the tabernacle of the LORD, and caught hold on the horns of the altar.

2 K 7:6 For the Lord had made the host of the Syrians to hear a noise of chariots, and a noise of horses, *even* the noise of a great host: and they said one to another, Lo, the king of Israel hath hired against us the kings of the Hittites, and the kings of the Egyptians, to come upon us.

2 K 25:26 And all the people, both small and great, and the captains of the armies, arose, and came to Egypt: for they were afraid of the Chaldees.

Job 4:14 Fear came upon me, and trembling, which made all my bones to shake.

Jb 15:21 A dreadful sound *is* in his ears: in prosperity the destroyer shall come upon him.

Jb 18:11 Terrors shall make him afraid on every side, and shall drive him to his feet.

Jb 20:25 It is drawn, and cometh out of the body; yea, the glittering sword

cometh out of his gall: terrors *are* upon him.

Jb 27:20 Terrors take hold on him as waters, a tempest stealeth him away in the night.

Jb 31:23 For destruction *from* God *was* a terror to me, and by reason of his highness I could not endure.

Ps 14:5 There were they in great fear: for God *is* in the generation of the righteous.

Ps 18:45 The strangers shall fade away, and be afraid out of their close places.

Ps 48:6 Fear took hold upon them there, *and* pain, as of a woman in travail.

Ps 65:8 They also that dwell in the uttermost parts are afraid at thy tokens: thou makest the outgoings of the morning and evening to rejoice.

Ps 73:19 How are they *brought* into desolation, as in a moment! they are utterly consumed with terrors.

Pr 1:27 When your fear cometh as desolation, and your destruction cometh as a whirlwind; when distress and anguish cometh upon you.

Pr 10:24 The fear of the wicked, it shall come upon him: but the desire of the righteous shall be granted.

Is 2:19 And they shall go into the holes of the rocks, and into the caves of the earth, for fear of the LORD, and for the glory of his majesty, when he ariseth to shake terribly the earth.

Is 13:7 Therefore shall all hands be faint, and every man's heart shall melt:

Is 13:14 And it shall be as the chased roe, and as a sheep that no man taketh up: they shall every man turn to his own people, and flee every one into his own land.

Is 30:17 One thousand *shall flee* at the rebuke of one; at the rebuke of five shall ye flee: till ye be left as a beacon upon the top of a mountain, and as an ensign on an hill.

Is 31:9 And he shall pass over to his strong hold for fear, and his princes shall be afraid of the ensign, saith the LORD, whose fire *is* in Zion, and his furnace in Jerusalem.

Is 33:14 The sinners in Zion are afraid; fearfulness hath surprised the hypocrites. Who among us shall dwell with the devouring fire? who among us shall dwell with everlasting burnings?

Je 6:24 We have heard the fame thereof: our hands wax feeble: anguish hath taken hold of us, *and* pain, as of a woman in travail.

Je 15:8 Their widows are increased to me above the sand of the seas: I have brought upon them against the mother of the young men a spoiler at noonday: I have caused *him* to fall upon it suddenly, and terrors upon the city.

Je 20:4 For thus saith the LORD, Behold, I will make thee a terror to thyself, and to all thy friends: and they shall fall by the sword of their enemies, and thine eyes shall behold *it:* and I will give all Judah into the hand of the king of Babylon, and he shall carry them captive into Babylon, and shall slay them with the sword.

Je 30:5 For thus saith the LORD; We have heard a voice of trembling, of fear, and not of peace.

Je 46:5 Wherefore have I seen them dismayed *and* turned away back? and their mighty ones are beaten down, and are fled apace, and look not back: *for* fear *was* round about, saith the LORD.

Je 48:41 Kerioth is taken, and the strong holds are surprised, and the mighty men's hearts in Moab at that day shall be as the heart of a woman in her pangs.

Je 48:43 Fear, and the pit, and the snare, *shall be* upon thee, O inhabitant of Moab, saith the LORD.

Je 49:5 Behold, I will bring a fear upon thee, saith the Lord GOD of hosts, from all those that be about thee; and ye shall be driven out every man right forth; and none shall gather up him that wandereth.

Je 49:22 Behold, he shall come up and fly as the eagle, and spread his wings over Bozrah: and at that day shall the heart of the mighty men of Edom be as the heart of a woman in her pangs.

Je 49:29 Their tents and their flocks shall they take away: they shall take to themselves their curtains, and all their vessels, and their camels; and they shall cry unto them, Fear *is* on every side.

Je 50:43 The king of Babylon hath heard the report of them, and his hands waxed feeble: anguish took hold of him, *and* pangs as of a woman in travail.

Je 51:32 And that the passages are stopped, and the reeds they have burned with fire, and the men of war are affrighted.

Lam 2:22 Thou hast called as in a solemn day my terrors round about, so that in the day of the LORD's anger none escaped nor remained: those that I have swaddled and brought up hath mine enemy consumed.

Lam 3:47 Fear and a snare is come upon us, desolation and destruction.

Eze 21:12 Cry and howl, son of man: for it shall be upon my people, it *shall be* upon all the princes of Israel: terrors by reason of the sword shall be upon my people: smite therefore upon *thy* thigh.

Eze 26:16 Then all the princes of the sea shall come down from their thrones, and lay away their robes, and put off their broidered garments: they shall clothe themselves with trembling; they shall sit upon the ground, and shall tremble at *every* moment, and be astonished at thee.

Eze 26:21 I will make thee a terror, and thou *shalt be* no *more:* though thou be sought for, yet shalt thou never be found again, saith the Lord GOD.

Eze 32:10 Yea, I will make many people amazed at thee, and their kings shall be horribly afraid for thee, when I shall brandish my sword before them; and they shall tremble at *every* moment, every man for his own life, in the day of thy fall.

Eze 32:23 Whose graves are set in the sides of the pit, and her company is round about her grave: all of them slain, fallen by the sword, which caused terror in the land of the living.

Eze 32:32 For I have caused my terror in the land of the living: and he shall be laid in the midst of the uncircumcised with *them that are* slain with the sword, *even* Pharaoh and all his multitude, saith the Lord GOD.

Da 5:6 Then the king's countenance was changed, and his thoughts troubled him, so that the joints of his loins were loosed, and his knees smote one against another.

Ho 10:5 The inhabitants of Samaria shall fear because of the calves of Beth-aven: for the people thereof shall mourn over it, and the priests thereof *that* rejoiced on it, for the glory thereof, because it is departed from it.

Joel 2:6 Before their face the people shall be much pained: all faces shall gather blackness.

Na 2:10 She is empty, and void, and waste: and the heart melteth, and the knees smite together, and much pain *is* in all loins, and the faces of them all gather blackness.

Zep 1:10 And it shall come to pass in that day, saith the LORD, *that there shall be* the noise of a cry from the fish gate, and an howling from the second, and a great crashing from the hills.

Mt 8:33 And they that kept them fled, and went their ways into the city, and told every thing, and what was befallen to the possessed of the devils.

Mt 28:4 And for fear of him the keepers did shake, and became as dead *men.*

Mk 5:14 And they that fed the swine fled, and told *it* in the city, and in the country. And they went out to see what it was that was done.

Lu 8:34 When they that fed *them* saw what was done, they fled, and went and told *it* in the city and in the country.

Lu 21:26 Men's hearts failing them for fear, and for looking after those things which are coming on the earth: for the powers of heaven shall be shaken.

Re 6:16 And said to the mountains and rocks, Fall on us, and hide us from the face of him that sitteth on the throne, and from the wrath of the Lamb:

Re 11:11 And after three days and an half the Spirit of life from God entered into them, and they stood upon their feet; and great fear fell upon them which saw them.

2. The Divine Presence, *a source of fear to the wicked*

See **PRESENCE**

3. Heathen Nations

Ge 35:5; Ex 12:33; 15:16; 23:27; De 28:10; Jos 2:9, 11; 5:1; 9:9, 24; 10:2; Jud 7:14; 1 S 5:7, 10; 18:12; 2 K 1:13; 17:32; 2 Chr 14:14; 17:10; 20:29; Jb 13:11; Ps 48:5; 65:8; 76:8; 102:15; 105:38; Is 19:1; 25:3; 33:3; 41:5; 59:19; Je 33:9; Eze 27:35; 30:9, 13; 32:32; 38:20; Mi 7:17; Mt 25:25; 27:54; Lu 8:37; Ac 19:17

See **COURAGE**

FEAR OF GOD, *reverence*

1. Prescribed

Ge 20:11 And Abraham said, Because I thought, Surely the fear of God *is* not in this place; and they will slay me for my wife's sake.

Ex 20:20 And Moses said unto the people, Fear not: for God is come to prove you, and that his fear may be before your faces, that ye sin not.

Le 19:14 Thou shalt not curse the deaf, nor put a stumblingblock before the blind, but shalt fear thy God: I *am* the LORD.

Le 19:32 Thou shalt rise up before the hoary head, and honour the face of the old man, and fear thy God: I *am* the LORD.

Le 25:17 Ye shall not therefore oppress one another; but thou shalt fear thy God: for I *am* the LORD your God.

Le 25:36 Take thou no usury of him, or increase: but fear thy God; that thy brother may live with thee.

Le 25:43 Thou shalt not rule over him with rigour; but shalt fear thy God.

De 2:25 This day will I begin to put the dread of thee and the fear of thee upon the nations *that are* under the whole heaven, who shall hear report of thee, and shall tremble, and be in anguish because of thee.

De 4:10 *Specially* the day that thou stoodest before the LORD thy God in Horeb, when the LORD said unto me, Gather me the people together, and I will make them hear my words, that they may learn to fear me all the days that they shall live upon the earth, and *that* they may teach their children.

De 5:29 O that there were such an heart in them, that they would fear me, and keep all my commandments always, that it might be well with them, and with their children for ever!

De 6:2 That thou mightest fear the LORD thy God, to keep all his statutes and his commandments, which I command thee, thou, and thy son, and thy son's son, all the days of thy life; and that thy days may be prolonged.

De 6:13 Thou shalt fear the LORD thy God, and serve him, and shalt swear by his name.

De 6:24 And the LORD commanded us to do all these statutes, to fear the LORD our God, for our good always, that he might preserve us alive, as *it is* at this day.

De 8:6 Therefore thou shalt keep the commandments of the LORD thy God, to walk in his ways, and to fear him.

De 10:12 And now, Israel, what doth the LORD thy God require of thee, but to fear the LORD thy God, to walk in all his ways, and to love him, and to serve the LORD thy God with all thy heart and with all thy soul,

De 10:20 Thou shalt fear the LORD thy God; him shalt thou serve, and to him shalt thou cleave, and swear by his name.

De 11:25 There shall no man be able to stand before you: *for* the LORD your God shall lay the fear of you and the dread of you upon all the land that ye shall tread upon, as he hath said unto you.

De 13:4 Ye shall walk after the LORD your God, and fear him, and keep his commandments, and obey his voice, and ye shall serve him, and cleave unto him.

De 13:11 And all Israel shall hear, and fear, and shall do no more any such wickedness as this is among you.

De 14:23 And thou shalt eat before the LORD thy God, in the place which he shall choose to place his name there, the tithe of thy corn, of thy wine, and of thine oil, and the firstlings of thy herds and of thy flocks; that thou mayest learn to fear the LORD thy God always.

De 17:19 And it shall be with him, and he shall read therein all the days of his life: that he may learn to fear the LORD his God, to keep all the words of this law and these statutes, to do them:

De 28:58 If thou wilt not observe to do all the words of this law that are written in this book, that thou mayest fear this glorious and fearful name, THE LORD THY GOD;

De 31:12 Gather the people together, men, and women, and children, and thy stranger that *is* within thy gates, that they may hear, and that they may learn, and fear the LORD your God, and observe to do all the words of this law:

Jos 4:24 That all the people of the earth might know the hand of the LORD, that it *is* mighty: that ye might fear the LORD your God for ever.

Jos 24:14 Now therefore fear the LORD, and serve him in sincerity and in truth: and put away the gods which your fathers served on the other side of the flood, and in Egypt; and serve ye the LORD.

1 S 4:7 And the Philistines were afraid, for they said, God is come into the camp. And they said, Woe unto us! for there hath not been such a thing heretofore.

1 S 11:7 And he took a yoke of oxen, and hewed them in pieces, and sent *them* throughout all the coasts of Israel by the hands of messengers, saying, Whosoever cometh not forth after Saul and after Samuel, so shall it be done unto his oxen. And the fear of the LORD fell on the people, and they came out with one consent.

1 S 12:24 Only fear the LORD, and serve him in truth with all your heart:

for consider how great *things* he hath done for you.

2 S 23:3 The God of Israel said, the Rock of Israel spake to me, He that ruleth over men *must be* just, ruling in the fear of God.

1 K 8:40 That they may fear thee all the days that they live in the land which thou gavest unto our fathers.

1 K 8:43 Hear thou in heaven thy dwelling place, and do according to all that the stranger calleth to thee for: that all people of the earth may know thy name, to fear thee, as *do* thy people Israel; and that they may know that this house, which I have builded, is called by thy name.

2 K 4:1 Now there cried a certain woman of the wives of the sons of the prophets unto Elisha, saying, Thy servant my husband is dead; and thou knowest that thy servant did fear the LORD: and the creditor is come to take unto him my two sons to be bondmen.

2 K 17:28 Then one of the priests whom they had carried away from Samaria came and dwelt in Bethel, and taught them how they should fear the LORD.

2 K 17:36 But the LORD, who brought you up out of the land of Egypt with great power and a stretched out arm, him shall ye fear, and him shall ye worship, and to him shall ye do sacrifice.

2 K 17:39 But the LORD your God ye shall fear; and he shall deliver you out of the hand of all your enemies.

1 Chr 16:25 For great *is* the LORD, and greatly to be praised: he also *is* to be feared above all gods.

1 Chr 16:30 Fear before him, all the earth: the world also shall be stable, that it be not moved.

2 Chr 6:31 That they may fear thee, to walk in thy ways, so long as they live in the land which thou gavest unto our fathers.

2 Chr 6:33 Then hear thou from the heavens, *even* from thy dwelling place, and do according to all that the stranger calleth to thee for; that all people of the earth may know thy name, and fear thee, as *doth* thy people Israel, and

may know that this house which I have built is called by thy name.

2 Chr 19:7 Wherefore now let the fear of the LORD be upon you; take heed and do *it:* for *there is* no iniquity with the LORD our God, nor respect of persons, nor taking of gifts.

Ne 5:9 Also I said, It *is* not good that ye do: ought ye not to walk in the fear of our God because of the reproach of the heathen our enemies?

Est 8:17 And in every province, and in every city, whithersoever the king's commandment and his decree came, the Jews had joy and gladness, a feast and a good day. And many of the people of the land became Jews; for the fear of the Jews fell upon them.

Jb 4:6 Is not *this* thy fear, thy confidence, thy hope, and the uprightness of thy ways?

Jb 23:15 Therefore am I troubled at his presence: when I consider, I am afraid of him.

Jb 25:2 Dominion and fear *are* with him, he maketh peace in his high places.

Jb 28:28 And unto man he said, Behold, the fear of the Lord, that *is* wisdom; and to depart from evil *is* understanding.

Jb 37:24 Men do therefore fear him: he respecteth not any *that are* wise of heart.

Ps 2:11 Serve the LORD with fear, and rejoice with trembling.

Ps 9:20 Put them in fear, O LORD: *that* the nations may know themselves to *be but* men. Selah.

Ps 19:9 The fear of the LORD *is* clean, enduring for ever: the judgments of the LORD *are* true *and* righteous altogether.

Ps 22:23 Ye that fear the LORD, praise him; all ye the seed of Jacob, glorify him; and fear him, all ye the seed of Israel.

Ps 33:8 Let all the earth fear the LORD: let all the inhabitants of the world stand in awe of him.

Ps 33:18 Behold, the eye of the LORD *is* upon them that fear him, upon them that hope in his mercy;

Ps 34:9 O fear the Lord, ye his saints: for *there is* no want to them that fear him.

Ps 34:11 Come, ye children, hearken unto me: I will teach you the fear of the Lord.

Ps 61:5 For thou, O God, hast heard my vows: thou hast given *me* the heritage of those that fear thy name.

Ps 76:7 Thou, *even* thou, *art* to be feared: and who may stand in thy sight when once thou art angry?

Ps 76:11 Vow, and pay unto the Lord your God: let all that be round about him bring presents unto him that ought to be feared.

Ps 85:9 Surely his salvation *is* nigh them that fear him; that glory may dwell in our land.

Ps 89:7 God is greatly to be feared in the assembly of the saints, and to be had in reverence of all *them that are* about him.

Ps 96:4 For the Lord *is* great, and greatly to be praised: he *is* to be feared above all gods.

Ps 96:9 O worship the Lord in the beauty of holiness: fear before him, all the earth.

Ps 103:11 For as the heaven is high above the earth, *so* great is his mercy toward them that fear him.

Ps 111:10 The fear of the Lord *is* the beginning of wisdom: a good understanding have all they that do *his commandments:* his praise endureth for ever.

Ps 115:13 He will bless them that fear the Lord, *both* small and great.

Ps 119:120 My flesh trembleth for fear of thee; and I am afraid of thy judgments.

Ps 128:1 Blessed *is* every one that feareth the Lord; that walketh in his ways.

Ps 130:4 But *there is* forgiveness with thee, that thou mayest be feared.

Ps 135:20 Bless the Lord, O house of Levi: ye that fear the Lord, bless the Lord.

Pr 2:5 Then shalt thou understand the fear of the Lord, and find the knowledge of God.

Pr 3:7 Be not wise in thine own eyes: fear the Lord, and depart from evil.

Pr 8:13 The fear of the Lord *is* to hate evil: pride, and arrogancy, and the evil way, and the froward mouth, do I hate.

Pr 9:10 The fear of the Lord *is* the beginning of wisdom: and the knowledge of the holy *is* understanding.

Pr 10:27 The fear of the Lord prolongeth days: but the years of the wicked shall be shortened.

Pr 14:2 He that walketh in his uprightness feareth the Lord: but *he that is* perverse in his ways despiseth him.

Pr 14:16 A wise *man* feareth, and departeth from evil: but the fool rageth, and is confident.

Pr 14:26 In the fear of the Lord *is* strong confidence: and his children shall have a place of refuge.

Pr 15:16 Better *is* little with the fear of the Lord than great treasure and trouble therewith.

Pr 15:33 The fear of the Lord *is* the instruction of wisdom; and before honour *is* humility.

Pr 16:6 By mercy and truth iniquity is purged: and by the fear of the Lord *men* depart from evil.

Pr 19:23 The fear of the Lord *tendeth* to life: and *he that hath it* shall abide satisfied; he shall not be visited with evil.

Pr 22:4 By humility *and* the fear of the Lord *are* riches, and honour, and life.

Pr 23:17 Let not thine heart envy sinners: but *be thou* in the fear of the Lord all the day long.

Pr 24:21 My son, fear thou the Lord and the king: *and* meddle not with them that are given to change:

Pr 28:14 Happy *is* the man that feareth alway: but he that hardeneth his heart shall fall into mischief.

Pr 31:30 Favour *is* deceitful, and beauty *is* vain: *but* a woman *that* feareth the Lord, she shall be praised.

Ec 3:14 I know that, whatsoever God doeth, it shall be for ever: nothing can be put to it, nor any thing taken from it: and God doeth *it*, that *men* should fear before him.

Ec 5:7 For in the multitude of dreams and many words *there are* also *divers* vanities: but fear thou God.

Ec 7:18 *It is* good that thou shouldest take hold of this; yea, also from this withdraw not thine hand: for he that feareth God shall come forth of them all.

Ec 8:12 Though a sinner do evil an hundred times, and his *days* be prolonged, yet surely I know that it shall be well with them that fear God, which fear before him:

Ec 12:13 Let us hear the conclusion of the whole matter: Fear God, and keep his commandments: for this *is* the whole *duty* of man.

Is 8:13 Sanctify the Lord of hosts himself; and *let* him *be* your fear, and *let* him *be* your dread.

Is 11:2 And the spirit of the Lord shall rest upon him, the spirit of wisdom and understanding, the spirit of counsel and might, the spirit of knowledge and of the fear of the Lord;

Is 19:16 In that day shall Egypt be like unto women: and it shall be afraid and fear because of the shaking of the hand of the Lord of hosts, which he shaketh over it.

Is 29:23 But when he seeth his children, the work of mine hands, in the midst of him, they shall sanctify my name, and sanctify the Holy One of Jacob, and shall fear the God of Israel.

Is 33:6 And wisdom and knowledge shall be the stability of thy times, *and* strength of salvation: the fear of the Lord *is* his treasure.

Is 66:2 For all those *things* hath mine hand made, and all those *things* have been, saith the Lord: but to this *man* will I look, *even* to *him that is* poor and of a contrite spirit, and trembleth at my word.

Is 66:5 Hear the word of the Lord, ye that tremble at his word; your brethren that hated you, that cast you out for my name's sake, said, Let the Lord be glorified: but he shall appear to your joy, and they shall be ashamed.

Je 2:19 Thine own wickedness shall correct thee, and thy backslidings shall reprove thee: know therefore and see that *it is* an evil *thing* and bitter, that thou hast forsaken the Lord thy God, and that my fear *is* not in thee, saith the Lord God of hosts.

Je 10:7 Who would not fear thee, O King of nations? for to thee doth it appertain: forasmuch as among all the wise *men* of the nations, and in all their kingdoms, *there is* none like unto thee.

Je 48:43 Fear, and the pit, and the snare, *shall be* upon thee, O inhabitant of Moab, saith the Lord.

Da 6:26 I make a decree, That in every dominion of my kingdom men tremble and fear before the God of Daniel: for he is the living God, and stedfast for ever, and his kingdom *that* which shall not be destroyed, and his dominion *shall be even* unto the end.

Jona 1:10 Then were the men exceedingly afraid, and said unto him, Why hast thou done this? For the men knew that he fled from the presence of the Lord, because he had told them.

Hab 3:16 When I heard, my belly trembled; my lips quivered at the voice: rottenness entered into my bones, and I trembled in myself, that I might rest in the day of trouble: when he cometh up unto the people, he will invade them with his troops.

Zep 3:7 I said, Surely thou wilt fear me, thou wilt receive instruction; so their dwelling should not be cut off, howsoever I punished them: but they rose early, *and* corrupted all their doings.

Mal 2:5 My covenant was with him of life and peace; and I gave them to him *for* the fear wherewith he feared me, and was afraid before my name.

Mt 10:28 And fear not them which kill the body, but are not able to kill the soul: but rather fear him which is able to destroy both soul and body in hell.

Lu 12:5 But I will forewarn you whom ye shall fear: Fear him, which after he hath killed hath power to cast into hell; yea, I say unto you, Fear him.

Lu 23:40 But the other answering rebuked him, saying, Dost not thou fear God, seeing thou art in the same condemnation?

Ro 11:20 Well; because of unbelief they were broken off, and thou standest by faith. Be not highminded, but fear:

2 Co 5:11 Knowing therefore the terror of the Lord, we persuade men; but we are made manifest unto God; and I trust also are made manifest in your consciences.

1 Pe 1:17 And if ye call on the Father, who without respect of persons judgeth according to every man's work, pass the time of your sojourning *here* in fear:

1 Pe 2:17 Honour all *men*. Love the brotherhood. Fear God. Honour the king.

Re 14:7 Saying with a loud voice, Fear God, and give glory to him; for the hour of his judgment is come: and worship him that made heaven, and earth, and the sea, and the fountains of waters.

2. Promises

1 S 12:14 If ye will fear the LORD, and serve him, and obey his voice, and not rebel against the commandment of the LORD, then shall both ye and also the king that reigneth over you continue following the LORD your God:

Ps 25:12 What man *is* he that feareth the LORD? him shall he teach in the way *that* he shall choose.

Ps 31:19 *Oh* how great *is* thy goodness, which thou hast laid up for them that fear thee; *which* thou hast wrought for them that trust in thee before the sons of men!

Ps 103:13 Like as a father pitieth *his* children, *so* the LORD pitieth them that fear him.

Ps 147:11 The LORD taketh pleasure in them that fear him, in those that hope in his mercy.

Pr 1:7 The fear of the LORD *is* the beginning of knowledge: *but* fools despise wisdom and instruction.

Is 50:10 Who *is* among you that feareth the LORD, that obeyeth the voice of his servant, that walketh *in* darkness, and hath no light? let him trust in the name of the LORD, and stay upon his God.

Je 5:22 Fear ye not me? saith the LORD: will ye not tremble at my presence, which have placed the sand *for* the bound of the sea by a perpetual decree, that it cannot pass it: and though the waves thereof toss themselves, yet can they not prevail; though they roar, yet can they not pass over it?

Mal 3:16 Then they that feared the LORD spake often one to another: and the LORD hearkened, and heard *it*, and a book of remembrance was written before him for them that feared the LORD, and that thought upon his name.

Lu 1:50 And his mercy *is* on them that fear him from generation to generation.

Ac 10:35 But in every nation he that feareth him, and worketh righteousness, is accepted with him.

3. Examples

Ge 20:8 Therefore Abimelech rose early in the morning, and called all his servants, and told all these things in their ears: and the men were sore afraid.

Ezr 7:23 Whatsoever is commanded by the God of heaven, let it be diligently done for the house of the God of heaven: for why should there be wrath against the realm of the king and his sons?

Ne 5:15 But the former governors that *had been* before me were chargeable unto the people, and had taken of them bread and wine, beside forty shekels of silver; yea, even their servants bare rule over the people: but so did not I, because of the fear of God.

Jb 1:8 And the LORD said unto Satan, Hast thou considered my servant Job, that *there is* none like him in the earth, a perfect and an upright man, one that feareth God, and escheweth evil?

Jona 1:9 And he said unto them, I *am* an Hebrew; and I fear the LORD, the God of heaven, which hath made the sea and the dry *land*.

Jona 1:16 Then the men feared the LORD exceedingly, and offered a sacrifice unto the LORD, and made vows.

Ac 5:11 And great fear came upon all the church, and upon as many as heard these things.

Ac 9:31 Then had the churches rest throughout all Judaea and Galilee and Samaria, and were edified; and walking in the fear of the Lord, and in the comfort of the Holy Ghost, were multiplied.

Ac 10:2 A devout *man,* and one that feared God with all his house, which gave much alms to the people, and prayed to God alway.

Ep 5:21 Submitting yourselves one to another in the fear of God.

Re 15:4 Who shall not fear thee, O Lord, and glorify thy name? for *thou* only *art* holy: for all nations shall come and worship before thee; for thy judgments are made manifest.

See **BLESSINGS, OBEDIENCE, PROMISES**

FEARLESSNESS

Jb 5:21 Thou shalt be hid from the scourge of the tongue: neither shalt thou be afraid of destruction when it cometh.

Ps 3:6 I will not be afraid of ten thousands of people, that have set *themselves* against me round about.

Ps 27:3 Though an host should encamp against me, my heart shall not fear: though war should rise against me, in this *will I be* confident.

Ps 46:2 Therefore will not we fear, though the earth be removed, and though the mountains be carried into the midst of the sea;

Ps 49:5 Wherefore should I fear in the days of evil, *when* the iniquity of my heels shall compass me about?

Ps 91:5 Thou shalt not be afraid for the terror by night; *nor* for the arrow *that* flieth by day;

Ps 112:8 His heart *is* established, he shall not be afraid, until he see *his desire* upon his enemies.

Ps 118:6 The LORD *is* on my side; I will not fear: what can man do unto me?

Pr 3:24 When thou liest down, thou shalt not be afraid: yea, thou shalt lie down, and thy sleep shall be sweet.

Is 8:12 Say ye not, A confederacy, to all *them to* whom this people shall say, A confederacy; neither fear ye their fear, nor be afraid.

Is 12:2 Behold, God *is* my salvation; I will trust, and not be afraid: for the LORD Jehovah *is* my strength and *my* song; he also is become my salvation.

Lu 1:74 That he would grant unto us, that we being delivered out of the hand of our enemies might serve him without fear,

2 Ti 1:7 For God hath not given us the spirit of fear; but of power, and of love, and of a sound mind.

1 Jn 4:18 There is no fear in love; but perfect love casteth out fear: because fear hath torment. He that feareth is not made perfect in love.

See **COURAGE**

FEAR OF MAN, *an evidence of lack of trust in God*

Ge 12:12 Therefore it shall come to pass, when the Egyptians shall see thee, that they shall say, This *is* his wife: and they will kill me, but they will save thee alive.

De 1:17 Ye shall not respect persons in judgment; *but* ye shall hear the small as well as the great; ye shall not be afraid of the face of man; for the judgment *is* God's: and the cause that is too hard for you, bring *it* unto me, and I will hear it.

1 S 13:12 Therefore said I, The Philistines will come down now upon me to Gilgal, and I have not made supplication unto the LORD: I forced myself therefore, and offered a burnt offering.

1 S 15:24 And Saul said unto Samuel, I have sinned: for I have transgressed the commandment of the LORD, and thy words: because I feared the people, and obeyed their voice.

2 S 3:11 And he could not answer Abner a word again, because he feared him.

1 K 18:14 And now thou sayest, Go, tell thy lord, Behold, Elijah *is here:* and he shall slay me.

2 K 18:14 And Hezekiah king of Judah sent to the king of Assyria to Lachish, saying, I have offended; return from me: that which thou puttest on me will I bear. And the king of Assyria appointed unto Hezekiah king of Judah three hundred talents of silver and thirty talents of gold.

Ps 18:4 The sorrows of death compassed me, and the floods of ungodly men made me afraid.

Pr 25:26 A righteous man falling down before the wicked *is as* a troubled fountain, and a corrupt spring.

Pr 29:25 The fear of man bringeth a snare: but whoso putteth his trust in the LORD shall be safe.

Is 7:2 And it was told the house of David, saying, Syria is confederate with Ephraim. And his heart was moved, and the heart of his people, as the trees of the wood are moved with the wind.

Is 57:11 And of whom hast thou been afraid or feared, that thou hast lied, and hast not remembered me, nor laid *it* to thy heart? have not I held my peace even of old, and thou fearest me not?

Je 1:8 Be not afraid of their faces: for I *am* with thee to deliver thee, saith the LORD.

Je 26:21 And when Jehoiakim the king, with all his mighty men, and all the princes, heard his words, the king sought to put him to death: but when Urijah heard it, he was afraid, and fled, and went into Egypt;

Je 38:19 And Zedekiah the king said unto Jeremiah, I am afraid of the Jews that are fallen to the Chaldeans, lest they deliver me into their hand, and they mock me.

Je 42:11 Be not afraid of the king of Babylon, of whom ye are afraid; be not afraid of him, saith the LORD: for I *am* with you to save you, and to deliver you from his hand.

Eze 2:6 And thou, son of man, be not afraid of them, neither be afraid of their words, though briers and thorns *be* with thee, and thou dost dwell among scorpions: be not afraid of their words, nor be dismayed at their looks, though they *be* a rebellious house.

Mt 26:56 But all this was done, that the scriptures of the prophets might be fulfilled. Then all the disciples forsook him, and fled.

Lu 12:4 And I say unto you my friends, Be not afraid of them that kill the body, and after that have no more that they can do.

Jn 7:13 Howbeit no man spake openly of him for fear of the Jews.

Jn 9:22 These *words* spake his parents, because they feared the Jews: for the Jews had agreed already, that if any man did confess that he was Christ, he should be put out of the synagogue.

Jn 12:42 Nevertheless among the chief rulers also many believed on him; but because of the Pharisees they did not confess *him,* lest they should be put out of the synagogue:

Jn 19:38 And after this Joseph of Arimathaea, being a disciple of Jesus, but secretly for fear of the Jews, besought Pilate that he might take away the body of Jesus: and Pilate gave *him* leave. He came therefore, and took the body of Jesus.

Ga 2:12 For before that certain came from James, he did eat with the Gentiles: but when they were come, he withdrew and separated himself, fearing them which were of the circumcision.

See **TRUST**

FEAR NOTS, *seven reasons for encouragement*

BLESSINGS IN THE JOURNEY OF LIFE

Ge 26:24 And the LORD appeared unto him the same night, and said, I *am* the God of Abraham thy father: fear not, for I *am* with thee, and will bless thee, and multiply thy seed for my servant Abraham's sake.

Nu 21:34 And the LORD said unto Moses, Fear him not: for I have delivered him into thy hand, and all his people, and his land; and thou shalt do to him as thou didst unto Sihon king of the Amorites, which dwelt at Heshbon.

Jud 6:23 And the LORD said unto him, Peace *be* unto thee; fear not: thou shalt not die.

SUPPLIES IN FAMINE

1 K 17:13 And Elijah said unto her, Fear not; go *and* do as thou hast said: but make me thereof a little cake first, and bring *it* unto me, and after make for thee and for thy son.

PROTECTION IN PERIL

2 K 6:16 And he answered, Fear not: for they that *be* with us *are* more than they that *be* with them.

STRENGTH IN WEAKNESS

Is 41:10 Fear thou not; for I *am* with thee: be not dismayed; for I *am* thy God: I will strengthen thee; yea, I will help thee; yea, I will uphold thee with the right hand of my righteousness.

COMPANIONSHIP IN TRIAL

Is 43:1 But now thus saith the LORD that created thee, O Jacob, and he that formed thee, O Israel, Fear not: for I have redeemed thee, I have called *thee* by thy name; thou *art* mine.

Is 43:2–3 When thou passest through the waters, I *will be* with thee; and through the rivers, they shall not overflow thee: when thou walkest through the fire, thou shalt not be burned; neither shall the flame kindle upon thee.

For I *am* the LORD thy God, the Holy One of Israel, thy Saviour: I gave Egypt *for* thy ransom, Ethiopia and Seba for thee.

OVERSHADOWING CARE

Mt 10:30 But the very hairs of your head are all numbered.

Mt 10:31 Fear ye not therefore, ye are of more value than many sparrows.

Mt 28:5 And the angel answered and said unto the women, Fear not ye: for I know that ye seek Jesus, which was crucified.

Lu 12:32 Fear not, little flock; for it is your Father's good pleasure to give you the kingdom.

LIFE BEYOND THE GRAVE

Re 1:17 And when I saw him, I fell at his feet as dead. And he laid his right hand upon me, saying unto me, Fear not; I am the first and the last:

Re 1:18 I *am* he that liveth, and was dead; and, behold, I am alive for evermore, Amen; and have the keys of hell and of death.

See **PROMISES**

FEASTS *See* **FESTIVALS**

FEET, *of wicked, intentioned toward evil*

Pr 1:16; 6:18; Is 59:7; Ro 3:15

FELIX, *a Roman governor of Judea*

Ac 23:24, 33; 24:3, 10, 22, 24; 25:14

FELLOW, *a term of reproach*

1 S 21:15; 25:21; 29:24; 1 K 22:27; 2 Chr 18:26; Mt 12:24; 26:61; Lu 23:2; Jn 9:29; Ac 22:22

FELLOWSHIP

1. Social

Est 1:9 Also Vashti the queen made a feast for the women *in* the royal house which *belonged* to king Ahasuerus.

Lu 10:7 And in the same house remain, eating and drinking such things as they give: for the labourer is worthy of his hire. Go not from house to house.

Lu 14:8 When thou art bidden of any *man* to a wedding, sit not down in the highest room; lest a more honourable man than thou be bidden of him;

Lu 14:12 Then said he also to him that bade him, When thou makest a dinner or a supper, call not thy friends, nor thy brethren, neither thy kinsmen, nor *thy* rich neighbours; lest they also bid thee again, and a recompence be made thee.

Lu 15:9 And when she hath found *it*, she calleth *her* friends and *her* neighbours together, saying, Rejoice with me; for I have found the piece which I had lost.

Lu 15:25 Now his elder son was in the field: and as he came and drew nigh to the house, he heard musick and dancing.

Jn 2:2 And both Jesus was called, and his disciples, to the marriage.

Jn 12:2 There they made him a supper; and Martha served: but Lazarus was one of them that sat at the table with him.

1 Co 10:27 If any of them that believe not bid you *to a feast,* and ye be disposed to go; whatsoever is set before you, eat, asking no question for conscience sake.

2. *Spiritual, intimacy with God*

a. With Christ

FOUND IN SPIRITUAL ASSEMBLIES
Mt 18:20 For where two or three are gathered together in my name, there am I in the midst of them.

IN THE COMMUNION OF SAINTS
Lu 24:15 And it came to pass, that, while they communed *together* and reasoned, Jesus himself drew near, and went with them.

WARMS THE HEART
Lu 24:32 And they said one to another, Did not our heart burn within us, while he talked with us by the way, and while he opened to us the scriptures?

LEAVES ITS IMPRESS UPON THE LIFE
Ac 4:13 Now when they saw the boldness of Peter and John, and perceived that they were unlearned and ignorant men, they marvelled; and they took knowledge of them, that they had been with Jesus.

BELIEVERS CALLED TO
1 Co 1:9 God *is* faithful, by whom ye were called unto the fellowship of his Son Jesus Christ our Lord.

TESTIMONY AN AID TO
1 Jn 1:3 That which we have seen and heard declare we unto you, that ye also may have fellowship with us: and truly our fellowship *is* with the Father, and with his Son Jesus Christ.

SPIRITUAL RECEPTIVITY THE CONDITION OF
Re 3:20 Behold, I stand at the door, and knock: if any man hear my voice, and open the door, I will come in to him, and will sup with him, and he with me.

b. *Moses' Fellowship with God*

Ge 17:3; 31:5; Ex 19:3, 20; 20:21; 24:2, 11; 25:22; 29:42; 30:36; 31:18; 33:9; 34:34; Le 1:1; 26:12; Nu 12:8; De 5:31; Eze 3:22; Re 21:3

c. *Walking with God*

Ge 5:22 And Enoch walked with God after he begat Methuselah three hundred years, and begat sons and daughters:

Ge 5:24 And Enoch walked with God: and he *was* not; for God took him.

Ge 6:9 These *are* the generations of Noah: Noah was a just man *and* perfect in his generations, *and* Noah walked with God.

De 5:33 Ye shall walk in all the ways which the LORD your God hath commanded you, that ye may live, and *that it may be* well with you, and *that* ye may prolong *your* days in the land which ye shall possess.

De 19:9 If thou shalt keep all these commandments to do them, which I command thee this day, to love the LORD thy God, and to walk ever in his ways; then shalt thou add three cities more for thee, beside these three:

De 26:17 Thou hast avouched the LORD this day to be thy God, and to walk in his ways, and to keep his statutes, and his commandments, and his judgments, and to hearken unto his voice:

De 28:9 The LORD shall establish thee an holy people unto himself, as he hath sworn unto thee, if thou shalt keep the commandments of the LORD thy God, and walk in his ways.

De 30:16 In that I command thee this day to love the LORD thy God, to walk in his ways, and to keep his commandments and his statutes and his judgments, that thou mayest live and multiply: and the LORD thy God shall bless thee in the land whither thou goest to possess it.

1 K 8:58 That he may incline our hearts unto him, to walk in all his ways, and to keep his commandments, and his statutes, and his judgments, which he commanded our fathers.

2 K 23:3 And the king stood by a pillar, and made a covenant before the LORD, to walk after the LORD, and to keep his commandments and his testimonies and his statutes with all *their* heart and all *their* soul, to perform the words of this covenant that were written in this book. And all the people stood to the covenant.

2 Chr 6:31 That they may fear thee, to walk in thy ways, so long as they live in the land which thou gavest unto our fathers.

2 Chr 34:31 And the king stood in his place, and made a covenant before the LORD, to walk after the LORD, and to keep his commandments, and his testimonies, and his statutes, with all his heart, and with all his soul, to perform the words of the covenant which are written in this book.

Ps 81:13 Oh that my people had hearkened unto me, *and* Israel had walked in my ways!

Ps 89:15 Blessed *is* the people that know the joyful sound: they shall walk, O LORD, in the light of thy countenance.

Ps 119:3 They also do no iniquity: they walk in his ways.

Am 3:3 Can two walk together, except they be agreed?

Mi 4:5 For all people will walk every one in the name of his god, and we will walk in the name of the LORD our God for ever and ever.

Zec 10:12 And I will strengthen them in the LORD; and they shall walk up and down in his name, saith the LORD.

Mal 2:6 The law of truth was in his mouth, and iniquity was not found in his lips: he walked with me in peace and equity, and did turn many away from iniquity.

Ep 5:8 For ye were sometimes darkness, but now *are ye* light in the Lord: walk as children of light:

Re 3:4 Thou hast a few names even in Sardis which have not defiled their garments; and they shall walk with me in white: for they are worthy.

See **ESTRANGEMENT, FRIENDSHIP**

FERRET *See* **ANIMALS**

FESTIVALS, *Hebrew, joyful occasions, celebrated by the entire congregation, for the purposes of fellowship and worship*

Ex 23:14; 34:23; Le 23:2, 37, 44; Nu 15:3; 29:39; 1 K 9:25; 1 Chr 23:31; 2 Chr 2:4; 8:13; 31:3; Ezr 3:5; Ne 10:33; Is 1:14; 30:29; 33:20; Lam 1:4; 2:6; Eze 36:38; 45:17; 46:9, 11; Ho 2:11; 9:5; Na 1:15; Zec 8:19; Mal 2:3; Mt 26:2; Lu 2:41; Jn 4:45; 5:1; Ac 18:21; Col 2:16

FESTUS, *a Roman governor of Judea*

Ac 24:27; 25:1, 9, 12, 24; 26:24, 32

FETTERS, *anything which restricts or restrains, specifically designed for prisoners*

Jud 16:21; 2 K 25:7; 2 Chr 33:11; 36:6; Ps 149:8; Je 39:7; 52:11; Eze 19:9; Na 3:10; Mk 5:4

Good Men Bound

Jb 36:8; Ps 105:18; Je 40:1; Eze 3:25; Da 3:20; Mt 27:2; Mk 6:17; 15:1; Jn 18:12; Ac 12:6; 16:24; 20:23; 21:33; 22:25; 28:20; Ph 1:7, 13; Phm 9; He 10:34; 13:3

FEVER *See* **DISEASE**

FIDELITY, *faithfulness, loyalty, trustworthiness*

1. In Business *See* **BUSINESS**

2. To God

Nu 12:7 My servant Moses *is* not so, who *is* faithful in all mine house.

Nu 14:24 But my servant Caleb, because he had another spirit with him, and hath followed me fully, him will I bring into the land whereinto he went; and his seed shall possess it.

1 K 19:18 Yet I have left *me* seven thousand in Israel, all the knees which have not bowed unto Baal, and every mouth which hath not kissed him.

Ne 7:2 That I gave my brother Hanani, and Hananiah the ruler of the palace, charge over Jerusalem: for he *was* a faithful man, and feared God above many.

Ne 12:45 And both the singers and the porters kept the ward of their God, and the ward of the purification, according to the commandment of David, *and* of Solomon his son.

Ps 119:93 I will never forget thy precepts: for with them thou hast quickened me.

Ho 11:12 Ephraim compasseth me about with lies, and the house of Israel with deceit: but Judah yet ruleth with God, and is faithful with the saints.

1 Co 4:17 For this cause have I sent unto you Timotheus, who is my beloved son, and faithful in the Lord, who shall bring you into remembrance of my ways which be in Christ, as I teach every where in every church.

Col 1:7 As ye also learned of Epaphras our dear fellowservant, who is for you a faithful minister of Christ;

Col 4:9 With Onesimus, a faithful and beloved brother, who is *one* of you. They shall make known unto you all things which *are done* here.

Re 17:14 These shall make war with the Lamb, and the Lamb shall overcome them: for he is Lord of lords, and King of kings: and they that are with him *are* called, and chosen, and faithful.

3. Its Rewards

Ps 31:23 O love the LORD, all ye his saints: *for* the LORD preserveth the faithful, and plentifully rewardeth the proud doer.

Mt 24:45 Who then is a faithful and wise servant, whom his lord hath made ruler over his household, to give them meat in due season?

Lu 19:17 And he said unto him, Well, thou good servant: because thou hast been faithful in a very little, have thou authority over ten cities.

Re 2:10 Fear none of those things which thou shalt suffer: behold, the devil shall cast *some* of you into prison, that ye may be tried; and ye shall have tribulation ten days: be thou faithful unto death, and I will give thee a crown of life.

Re 3:10 Because thou hast kept the word of my patience, I also will keep thee from the hour of temptation, which shall come upon all the world, to try them that dwell upon the earth.

Re 20:4 And I saw thrones, and they sat upon them, and judgment was given unto them: and *I saw* the souls of them that were beheaded for the witness of Jesus, and for the word of God, and which had not worshipped the beast, neither his image, neither had received *his* mark upon their foreheads, or in their hands; and they lived and reigned with Christ a thousand years.

4. In Keeping God's Covenant

Ge 17:9 And God said unto Abraham, Thou shalt keep my covenant therefore, thou, and thy seed after thee in their generations.

Ex 19:5 Now therefore, if ye will obey my voice indeed, and keep my covenant, then ye shall be a peculiar treasure unto me above all people: for all the earth *is* mine:

De 33:9 Who said unto his father and to his mother, I have not seen him; neither did he acknowledge his brethren, nor knew his own children: for they have observed thy word, and kept thy covenant.

Jos 4:12 And the children of Reuben, and the children of Gad, and half the tribe of Manasseh, passed over armed before the children of Israel, as Moses spake unto them:

Jos 22:3 Ye have not left your brethren these many days unto this day, but have kept the charge of the commandment of the LORD your God.

1 Chr 16:15 Be ye mindful always of his covenant; the word *which* he commanded to a thousand generations;

2 Chr 34:32 And he caused all that were present in Jerusalem and Benjamin to stand *to it*. And the inhabitants of Jerusalem did according to the covenant of God, the God of their fathers.

Ps 103:17–18 But the mercy of the LORD *is* from everlasting to everlasting upon them that fear him, and his righteousness unto children's children;

To such as keep his covenant, and to those that remember his commandments to do them.

Ps 132:12 If thy children will keep my covenant and my testimony that I shall teach them, their children shall also sit upon thy throne for evermore.

Is 56:4 For thus saith the LORD unto the eunuchs that keep my sabbaths, and choose *the things* that please me, and take hold of my covenant;

Da 9:4 And I prayed unto the LORD my God, and made my confession, and said, O Lord, the great and dreadful God, keeping the covenant and mercy to them that love him, and to them that keep his commandments;

FIGHTING

2 Chr 13:12 And, behold, God himself is with us for *our* captain, and his priests with sounding trumpets to cry alarm against you. O children of Israel, fight ye not against the LORD God of your fathers; for ye shall not prosper.

Mt 27:64 Command therefore that the sepulchre be made sure until the third day, lest his disciples come by night, and steal him away, and say unto the people, He is risen from the dead: so the last error shall be worse than the first.

Ac 5:39 But if it be of God, ye cannot overthrow it; lest haply ye be found even to fight against God.

Ac 23:9 And there arose a great cry: and the scribes *that were* of the Pharisees' part arose, and strove, saying, We find no evil in this man: but if a spirit or an angel hath spoken to him, let us not fight against God.

See **GOD**

FIGS *See* **AGRICULTURE, TREES**

FILTHINESS

Ge 19:5 And they called unto Lot, and said unto him, Where *are* the men which came in to thee this night? bring them out unto us, that we may know them.

Ezr 9:11 Which thou hast commanded by thy servants the prophets, saying, The land, unto which ye go to possess it, is an unclean land with the filthiness of the people of the lands, with their abominations, which have filled it from one end to another with their uncleanness.

Ps 53:3 Every one of them is gone back: they are altogether become filthy; *there is* none that doeth good, no, not one.

Ho 4:13 They sacrifice upon the tops of the mountains, and burn incense upon the hills, under oaks and poplars and elms, because the shadow thereof *is* good: therefore your daughters shall commit whoredom, and your spouses shall commit adultery.

Ho 6:9 And as troops of robbers wait for a man, *so* the company of priests murder in the way by consent: for they commit lewdness.

Mt 23:27 Woe unto you, scribes and Pharisees, hypocrites! for ye are like unto whited sepulchres, which indeed appear beautiful outward, but are within full of dead *men's* bones, and of all uncleanness.

Ro 6:19 I speak after the manner of men because of the infirmity of your flesh: for as ye have yielded your members servants to uncleanness and to iniquity unto iniquity; even so now yield your members servants to righteousness unto holiness.

Ep 5:4 Neither filthiness, nor foolish talking, nor jesting, which are not convenient: but rather giving of thanks.

Ja 1:21 Wherefore lay apart all filthiness and superfluity of naughtiness, and receive with meekness the engrafted word, which is able to save your souls.

2 Pe 2:10 But chiefly them that walk after the flesh in the lust of uncleanness, and despise government. Presumptuous *are they,* selfwilled, they are not afraid to speak evil of dignities.

See **SIN, WICKED**

FINGER OF GOD, *symbolism for God's detailed interaction with His creation*

Ex 8:19; 31:18; 32:16; De 9:10; Ps 8:3; Da 5:5; Lu 11:20

See **GOD**

FIR *See* **TREES**

FIRE

1. Eternal

Is 1:31 And the strong shall be as tow, and the maker of it as a spark, and they shall both burn together, and none shall quench *them*.

Is 33:14 The sinners in Zion are afraid; fearfulness hath surprised the hypocrites. Who among us shall dwell with the devouring fire? who among us shall dwell with everlasting burnings?

Is 34:10 It shall not be quenched night nor day; the smoke thereof shall go up for ever: from generation to generation it shall lie waste; none shall pass through it for ever and ever.

Is 66:24 And they shall go forth, and look upon the carcases of the men that have transgressed against me: for their worm shall not die, neither shall their fire be quenched; and they shall be an abhorring unto all flesh.

Da 7:11 I beheld then because of the voice of the great words which the horn spake: I beheld *even* till the beast was slain, and his body destroyed, and given to the burning flame.

Mt 3:12 Whose fan *is* in his hand, and he will throughly purge his floor, and gather his wheat into the garner; but he will burn up the chaff with unquenchable fire.

Mt 13:42 And shall cast them into a furnace of fire: there shall be wailing and gnashing of teeth.

Mt 18:8 Wherefore if thy hand or thy foot offend thee, cut them off, and cast *them* from thee: it is better for thee to enter into life halt or maimed, rather than having two hands or two feet to be cast into everlasting fire.

Mt 25:41 Then shall he say also unto them on the left hand, Depart from me, ye cursed, into everlasting fire, prepared for the devil and his angels:

Mk 9:44 Where their worm dieth not, and the fire is not quenched.

Re 14:10 The same shall drink of the wine of the wrath of God, which is poured out without mixture into the cup of his indignation; and he shall be tormented with fire and brimstone in the presence of the holy angels, and in the presence of the Lamb:

Re 20:10 And the devil that deceived them was cast into the lake of fire and brimstone, where the beast and the false prophet *are*, and shall be tormented day and night for ever and ever.

Re 20:15 And whosoever was not found written in the book of life was cast into the lake of fire.

Re 21:8 But the fearful, and unbelieving, and the abominable, and murderers, and whoremongers, and sorcerers, and idolaters, and all liars, shall have their part in the lake which burneth with fire and brimstone: which is the second death.

2. Sent by God

Ge 15:17 And it came to pass, that, when the sun went down, and it was dark, behold a smoking furnace, and a burning lamp that passed between those pieces.

Ex 3:2 And the angel of the LORD appeared unto him in a flame of fire out of the midst of a bush: and he looked, and, behold, the bush burned with fire, and the bush *was* not consumed.

Le 9:24 And there came a fire out from before the LORD, and consumed upon the altar the burnt offering and the fat: *which* when all the people saw, they shouted, and fell on their faces.

1 K 18:24 And call ye on the name of your gods, and I will call on the name of the LORD: and the God that answereth by fire, let him be God. And all the people answered and said, It is well spoken.

1 K 18:38 Then the fire of the LORD fell, and consumed the burnt sacrifice, and the wood, and the stones, and the dust, and licked up the water that *was* in the trench.

1 Chr 21:26 And David built there an altar unto the LORD, and offered burnt offerings and peace offerings, and called upon the LORD; and he answered him from heaven by fire upon the altar of burnt offering.

2 Chr 7:1 Now when Solomon had made an end of praying, the fire came down from heaven, and consumed the burnt offering and the sacrifices; and the glory of the LORD filled the house.

3. Used as Divine Judgment

Ge 19:24 Then the LORD rained upon Sodom and upon Gomorrah brimstone and fire from the LORD out of heaven;

Le 10:2 And there went out fire from the LORD, and devoured them, and they died before the LORD.

Nu 11:1 And *when* the people complained, it displeased the LORD: and the LORD heard *it;* and his anger was kindled; and the fire of the LORD burnt among them, and consumed *them that were* in the uttermost parts of the camp.

Nu 16:35 And there came out a fire from the LORD, and consumed the two hundred and fifty men that offered incense.

2 S 23:7 But the man *that* shall touch them must be fenced with iron and the staff of a spear; and they shall be utterly burned with fire in the *same* place.

2 K 1:10 And Elijah answered and said to the captain of fifty, If I *be* a man of God, then let fire come down from heaven, and consume thee and thy fifty. And there came down fire from heaven, and consumed him and his fifty.

Ps 18:8 There went up a smoke out of his nostrils, and fire out of his mouth devoured: coals were kindled by it.

Ps 106:18 And a fire was kindled in their company; the flame burned up the wicked.

Ps 140:10 Let burning coals fall upon them: let them be cast into the fire; into deep pits, that they rise not up again.

Is 1:31 And the strong shall be as tow, and the maker of it as a spark, and they shall both burn together, and none shall quench *them.*

Is 9:18 For wickedness burneth as the fire: it shall devour the briers and thorns, and shall kindle in the thickets of the forest, and they shall mount up *like* the lifting up of smoke.

Is 31:9 And he shall pass over to his strong hold for fear, and his princes shall be afraid of the ensign, saith the LORD, whose fire *is* in Zion, and his furnace in Jerusalem.

Is 33:12 And the people shall be as the burnings of lime: *as* thorns cut up shall they be burned in the fire.

Is 34:10 It shall not be quenched night nor day; the smoke thereof shall go up for ever: from generation to generation it shall lie waste; none shall pass through it for ever and ever.

Je 7:20 Therefore thus saith the Lord GOD; Behold, mine anger and my fury shall be poured out upon this place, upon man, and upon beast, and upon the trees of the field, and upon the fruit of the ground; and it shall burn, and shall not be quenched.

Je 11:16 The LORD called thy name, A green olive tree, fair, *and* of goodly fruit: with the noise of a great tumult he hath kindled fire upon it, and the branches of it are broken.

Je 15:14 And I will make *thee* to pass with thine enemies into a land *which* thou knowest not: for a fire is kindled in mine anger, *which* shall burn upon you.

Je 17:27 But if ye will not hearken unto me to hallow the sabbath day, and not to bear a burden, even entering in at the gates of Jerusalem on the sabbath day; then will I kindle a fire in the gates thereof, and it shall devour the palaces of Jerusalem, and it shall not be quenched.

Je 21:10 For I have set my face against this city for evil, and not for good, saith the LORD: it shall be given into the hand of the king of Babylon, and he shall burn it with fire.

Lam 4:11 The LORD hath accomplished his fury; he hath poured out his fierce anger, and hath kindled a fire in Zion, and it hath devoured the foundations thereof.

Eze 30:8 And they shall know that I *am* the LORD, when I have set a fire in Egypt, and *when* all her helpers shall be destroyed.

Jl 2:3 A fire devoureth before them; and behind them a flame burneth: the land *is* as the garden of Eden before them, and behind them a desolate wilderness; yea, and nothing shall escape them.

Am 5:6 Seek the LORD, and ye shall live; lest he break out like fire in the house of Joseph, and devour *it,* and *there be* none to quench *it* in Bethel.

Zec 11:1 Open thy doors, O Lebanon, that the fire may devour thy cedars.

2 Th 1:8 In flaming fire taking vengeance on them that know not God, and that obey not the gospel of our Lord Jesus Christ:

2 Pe 3:10 But the day of the Lord will come as a thief in the night; in the which the heavens shall pass away with a great noise, and the elements shall melt with fervent heat, the earth also and the works that are therein shall be burned up.

4. As a Purifier

Nu 31:23 Every thing that may abide the fire, ye shall make *it* go through the fire, and it shall be clean: nevertheless it shall be purified with the water of separation: and all that abideth not the fire ye shall make go through the water.

Is 6:6 Then flew one of the seraphims unto me, having a live coal in his hand, *which* he had taken with the tongs from off the altar:

Eze 22:20 *As* they gather silver, and brass, and iron, and lead, and tin, into the midst of the furnace, to blow the fire upon it, to melt *it;* so will I gather *you* in mine anger and in my fury, and I will leave *you there,* and melt you.

Zec 13:9 And I will bring the third part through the fire, and will refine them as silver is refined, and will try them as gold is tried: they shall call on my name, and I will hear them: I will

say, It *is* my people: and they shall say, The LORD *is* my God.

Mal 3:2 But who may abide the day of his coming? and who shall stand when he appeareth? for he *is* like a refiner's fire, and like fullers' sope:

1 Co 3:13 Every man's work shall be made manifest: for the day shall declare it, because it shall be revealed by fire; and the fire shall try every man's work of what sort it is.

1 Pe 1:7 That the trial of your faith, being much more precious than of gold that perisheth, though it be tried with fire, might be found unto praise and honour and glory at the appearing of Jesus Christ:

5. A Symbol of God's Presence and Power

De 4:36 Out of heaven he made thee to hear his voice, that he might instruct thee: and upon earth he shewed thee his great fire; and thou heardest his words out of the midst of the fire.

1 K 19:12 And after the earthquake a fire; *but* the LORD *was* not in the fire: and after the fire a still small voice.

Ps 50:3 Our God shall come, and shall not keep silence: a fire shall devour before him, and it shall be very tempestuous round about him.

Ps 97:3 A fire goeth before him, and burneth up his enemies round about.

Is 10:17 And the light of Israel shall be for a fire, and his Holy One for a flame: and it shall burn and devour his thorns and his briers in one day;

Is 66:15 For, behold, the LORD will come with fire, and with his chariots like a whirlwind, to render his anger with fury, and his rebuke with flames of fire.

Eze 1:13 As for the likeness of the living creatures, their appearance *was* like burning coals of fire, *and* like the appearance of lamps: it went up and down among the living creatures; and the fire was bright, and out of the fire went forth lightning.

Mi 1:4 And the mountains shall be molten under him, and the valleys shall be cleft, as wax before the fire, *and* as the

Ac 2:3 And there appeared unto them cloven tongues like as of fire, and it sat upon each of them.

Ac 7:30 And when forty years were expired, there appeared to him in the wilderness of mount Sina an angel of the Lord in a flame of fire in a bush.

He 12:29 For our God *is* a consuming fire.

6. Inward

KINDLED BY MEDITATION

Ps 39:3 My heart was hot within me, while I was musing the fire burned: *then* spake I with my tongue,

MAKES THE MESSAGE INEVITABLE

Je 20:9 Then I said, I will not make mention of him, nor speak any more in his name. But *his word* was in mine heart as a burning fire shut up in my bones, and I was weary with forbearing, and I could not *stay*.

CHRIST CAME TO IGNITE

Lu 12:49 I am come to send fire on the earth; and what will I if it be already kindled?

DIVINE FELLOWSHIP LIGHTS

Lu 24:32 And they said one to another, Did not our heart burn within us, while he talked with us by the way, and while he opened to us the scriptures?

See **JUDGMENTS**

FIRMAMENT, *or heavens*

Ge 1:6; Ps 19:1; Eze 1:22, 23; Da 12:3

See **CREATOR**

FIRSTFRUITS   *See* **STEWARDSHIP**

FISH, *created on the fifth day*

Ge 1:21; Ex 7:21; Le 11:9; Nu 11:5, 22; 1 K 4:33; Ps 8:8; Eze 29:4; 38:20; Jona 1:17; Hab 1:14; Mt 7:10; Mk 8:7; Lu 24:42; Jn 21:6, 9, 13

Miraculous Draughts

Mt 17:27; Lu 5:6, 9; Jn 21:6

See **MIRACLES**

FISHERMEN   *See* **ARTS AND CRAFTS**

FLATTERY, *excessive and false praise*

1. Warnings

Jb 32:21; Ps 5:9; 12:3; Pr 2:16; 5:3; 6:24; 7:5, 21; 20:19; 23:8; 24:24; 26:28; 27:14; 28:23; 29:5; Mt 22:16; Lu 6:26; 1 Th 2:5

2. Examples

Jud 8:18; 2 S 14:17; 19:27; Da 11:21, 32; Mk 12:14; Lu 20:21; Ac 12:22; 24:2

See **SPEECH**

FLAX, *a plant whose bark can be used to make linen*

Ex 9:31; Jos 2:6; Jud 15:14; Pr 31:13; Is 19:9; Eze 40:3

FLEAS   *See* **INSECTS**

FLESH, *the carnal nature of humanity*

Ge 6:3 And the Lord said, My spirit shall not always strive with man, for that he also *is* flesh: yet his days shall be an hundred and twenty years.

Ro 7:18 For I know that in me (that is, in my flesh,) dwelleth no good thing: for to will is present with me; but *how* to perform that which is good I find not.

Ro 7:25 I thank God through Jesus Christ our Lord. So then with the mind I myself serve the law of God; but with the flesh the law of sin.

Ro 8:8 So then they that are in the flesh cannot please God.

Ro 8:13 For if ye live after the flesh, ye shall die: but if ye through the Spirit do mortify the deeds of the body, ye shall live.

1 Co 15:50 Now this I say, brethren, that flesh and blood cannot inherit the kingdom of God; neither doth corruption inherit incorruption.

Ga 5:17 For the flesh lusteth against the Spirit, and the Spirit against the flesh: and these are contrary the one to the other: so that ye cannot do the things that ye would.

Ga 6:8 For he that soweth to his flesh shall of the flesh reap corruption; but he that soweth to the Spirit shall of the Spirit reap life everlasting.

1 Jn 2:16 For all that *is* in the world, the lust of the flesh, and the lust of the eyes, and the pride of life, is not of the Father, but is of the world.

See **SIN**

FLESHHOOKS, *meat forks used by Levites and priests*

Ex 27:3; 38:3; Nu 4:14; 1 S 2:13; 2 Chr 4:16

FLIES *See* **INSECTS, MIRACLES**

FLINT, *a very hard stone*

Is 5:28; 50:7; Eze 3:9; Zec 7:12

FLOOD *See* **DELUGE**

FLOUR, *ground grain for making bread*

Ex 29:2; Le 2:2; 5:11; 6:15, 20; 7:12; 23:13, 17; 24:5; Nu 7:13, 25, 37, 43, 61, 79; 8:8; 15:4, 9; 28:5, 9, 13, 20, 28; 29:3, 14; Jud 6:19; 1 S 28:24; 2 S 13:8; 17:28; 1 K 4:22; 1 Chr 9:29; 23:29; Eze 16:13; 46:14

See **FOOD**

FLOWERS, *term applied to floral ornaments found on temple pieces*

Nu 17:8; Is 35:1; Mt 6:29; Lu 12:27

See **AGRICULTURE**

FLUTES *See* **MUSIC**

FOLDS, *an enclosure for sheep and other domestic animals*

Nu 32:24; Ps 50:9; Is 13:20; Je 23:3–4; Eze 34:14; Mi 2:12; Zep 2:6; Jn 10:16

FOLLY

2 Chr 10:8 But he forsook the counsel which the old men gave him, and took counsel with the young men that were brought up with him, that stood before him.

Jb 17:10 But as for you all, do ye return, and come now: for I cannot find one wise *man* among you.

Ps 49:13 This their way *is* their folly: yet their posterity approve their sayings. Selah.

Pr 14:8 The wisdom of the prudent *is* to understand his way: but the folly of fools *is* deceit.

Pr 15:14 The heart of him that hath understanding seeketh knowledge: but the mouth of fools feedeth on foolishness.

Pr 18:13 He that answereth a matter before he heareth *it*, it *is* folly and shame unto him.

Pr 26:11 As a dog returneth to his vomit, *so* a fool returneth to his folly.

Ec 2:13 Then I saw that wisdom excelleth folly, as far as light excelleth darkness.

Ec 10:1 Dead flies cause the ointment of the apothecary to send forth a stinking savour: *so doth* a little folly him that is in reputation for wisdom *and* honour.

1 Co 3:19 For the wisdom of this world is foolishness with God. For it is written, He taketh the wise in their own craftiness.

Tit 3:3 For we ourselves also were sometimes foolish, disobedient, deceived, serving divers lusts and pleasures, living in malice and envy, hateful, *and* hating one another.

1. Fools

ATHEISM

Ps 53:1 The fool hath said in his heart, *There is* no God. Corrupt are they, and have done abominable iniquity: *there is* none that doeth good.

SLANDER

Pr 10:18 He that hideth hatred *with* lying lips, and he that uttereth a slander, *is* a fool.

MOCKING AT SIN

Pr 14:9 Fools make a mock at sin: but among the righteous *there is* favour.

DESPISING INSTRUCTION

Pr 15:5 A fool despiseth his father's instruction: but he that regardeth reproof is prudent.

CONTENTIOUSNESS

Pr 18:6 A fool's lips enter into contention, and his mouth calleth for strokes.

MEDDLESOMENESS

Pr 20:3 *It is* an honour for a man to cease from strife: but every fool will be meddling.

SELF-CONFIDENCE

Pr 28:26 He that trusteth in his own heart is a fool: but whoso walketh wisely, he shall be delivered.

Ec 7:9 Be not hasty in thy spirit to be angry: for anger resteth in the bosom of fools.

DISHONESTY

Je 17:11 As the partridge sitteth *on eggs,* and hatcheth *them* not; *so* he that getteth riches, and not by right, shall leave them in the midst of his days, and at his end shall be a fool.

Mt 7:26 And every one that heareth these sayings of mine, and doeth them not, shall be likened unto a foolish man, which built his house upon the sand:

HYPOCRISY

Lu 11:39–40 And the Lord said unto him, Now do ye Pharisees make clean the outside of the cup and the platter; but your inward part is full of ravening and wickedness.

Ye fools, did not he that made that which is without make that which is within also?

Lu 12:20 But God said unto him, *Thou* fool, this night thy soul shall be required of thee: then whose shall those things be, which thou hast provided?

Ro 1:22 Professing themselves to be wise, they became fools,

Ep 5:15 See then that ye walk circumspectly, not as fools, but as wise,

2. Deceives the Simple

Pr 1:4 To give subtilty to the simple, to the young man knowledge and discretion.

Pr 1:22 How long, ye simple ones, will ye love simplicity? and the scorners delight in their scorning, and fools hate knowledge?

Pr 7:7 And beheld among the simple ones, I discerned among the youths, a young man void of understanding,

Pr 8:5 O ye simple, understand wisdom: and, ye fools, be ye of an understanding heart.

Pr 9:13 A foolish woman *is* clamorous: *she is* simple, and knoweth nothing.

Pr 14:15 The simple believeth every word: but the prudent *man* looketh well to his going.

Pr 14:18 The simple inherit folly: but the prudent are crowned with knowledge.

Pr 15:21 Folly *is* joy to *him that is* destitute of wisdom: but a man of understanding walketh uprightly.

Pr 19:25 Smite a scorner, and the simple will beware: and reprove one that hath understanding, *and* he will understand knowledge.

Pr 21:11 When the scorner is punished, the simple is made wise: and when the wise is instructed, he receiveth knowledge.

Pr 22:3 A prudent *man* foreseeth the evil, and hideth himself: but the simple pass on, and are punished.

Pr 27:12 A prudent *man* foreseeth the evil, *and* hideth himself; *but* the simple pass on, *and* are punished.

Ho 7:11 Ephraim also is like a silly dove without heart: they call to Egypt, they go to Assyria.

Lu 11:40 *Ye* fools, did not he that made that which is without make that which is within also?

3. Sure to Manifest Itself

Pr 12:16 A fool's wrath is presently known: but a prudent *man* covereth shame.

Pr 12:23 A prudent man concealeth knowledge: but the heart of fools proclaimeth foolishness.

Pr 13:16 Every prudent *man* dealeth with knowledge: but a fool layeth open *his* folly.

Pr 14:33 Wisdom resteth in the heart of him that hath understanding: but *that which is* in the midst of fools is made known.

Pr 15:2 The tongue of the wise useth knowledge aright: but the mouth of fools poureth out foolishness.

Pr 18:2 A fool hath no delight in understanding, but that his heart may discover itself.

Pr 29:11 A fool uttereth all his mind: but a wise *man* keepeth it in till afterwards.

Ec 5:3 For a dream cometh through the multitude of business; and a fool's voice *is known* by multitude of words.

Ec 10:3 Yea also, when he that is a fool walketh by the way, his wisdom faileth *him,* and he saith to every one *that* he *is* a fool.

See **PRUDENCE, WISDOM**

FOOD

*1. **Physical**, essential for physical growth*

a. From God

Ge 1:29; 2:16; 3:2; 6:21; 9:3; 28:20; Ex 16:8; De 10:18; Ru 1:6; 1 K 19:6; Jb 36:31; 40:20; Ps 78:24; 103:5; 104:14; 111:5; 136:25; 145:15; Eze 48:18; Jl 2:26; Mt 14:15; Lu 8:55; 11:3; Jn 6:31; Ac 9:19; 14:17; 27:35; 1 Ti 6:8

b. Kinds Prohibited by Mosaic Law

Ge 3:3; 9:4; Ex 22:31; Le 11:4, 42; 19:23; 22:8; De 14:3, 10; Jud 13:4, 14; Eze 4:14; 44:31; Ho 9:3; Ac 11:6, 8

c. Varieties

Ge 18:8; Le 11:3; De 32:14; 1 S 17:17; 25:18; 30:12; 2 S 6:19; 16:2; Pr 27:27; Jn 21:9

d. List of Articles

Ge 18:6; Ex 13:6; 1 S 17:17; Jn 6:7

e. Sumptuous

Pr 23:3; Am 6:4; Lu 16:19

f. Meals

1). Breakfast

Jud 19:5; Jn 21:9

2). Mid-day Repast

Ge 43:16; Jn 4:6, 31

3). Evening Meal

Ge 24:33; Lu 24:29–30

g. Admonitions

Ps 141:4; Pr 23:1–2; 24:13; 25:27; Da 1:8; Zec 7:6; Lu 10:8; 12:22; 1 Co 10:25, 31; 1 Ti 4:4

h. Blessings (Grace) before Meals

1 S 9:13; Mt 14:19; 15:36; 26:26, 27; Mk 6:41; 8:6; 14:23; Lu 9:16; 22:17; 24:30; Jn 6:11; Ac 27:35; Ro 14:6; 1 Co 10:30; 11:24

*2. **Spiritual**, essential for spiritual growth*

a. Prepared in Abundance for Believers

De 32:14; Ps 23:5; Pr 9:2; Song 2:4; Is 25:6; Mt 22:4; Mk 14:22; Lu 12:37; 14:16; 15:23; 22:30; Re 19:9

b. Christ, the Bread of Life

Ex 16:15; Jos 5:12; Mt 26:26; Mk 14:22; Jn 6:32–35, 48, 49–51, 58; 1 Co 11:24; He 6:4

*3. **Worldly***

Lu 15:16

FOOLS *See* **FOLLY, WISDOM**

FOOTSTOOL

*1. **Of Christ***

Ps 110:1; Mt 22:44; Mk 12:36; Lu 20:43; Ac 2:35; He 1:13; 10:13

*2. **Of God***

1 Chr 28:2; Ps 99:5; Is 66:1; Lam 2:1; Eze 43:7; Mt 5:35; Ac 7:49

See **JUDGMENTS**

FORBEARANCE, *a holding back, delaying*

*1. **Divine***

Ge 18:32 And he said, Oh let not the Lord be angry, and I will speak yet but this once: Peradventure ten shall be found there. And he said, I will not destroy *it* for ten's sake.

Ne 9:30 Yet many years didst thou forbear them, and testifiedst against them by thy spirit in thy prophets: yet would they not give ear: therefore gavest thou them into the hand of the people of the lands.

Ps 103:8 The LORD *is* merciful and gracious, slow to anger, and plenteous in mercy.

Is 57:11 And of whom hast thou been afraid or feared, that thou hast lied, and hast not remembered me, nor laid *it* to thy heart? have not I held my peace even of old, and thou fearest me not?

Eze 16:60 Nevertheless I will remember my covenant with thee in the days of thy youth, and I will establish unto thee an everlasting covenant.

Eze 20:17 Nevertheless mine eye spared them from destroying them, neither did I make an end of them in the wilderness.

Ho 11:9 I will not execute the fierceness of mine anger, I will not return to destroy Ephraim: for I *am* God, and not man; the Holy One in the midst of thee: and I will not enter into the city.

Jona 4:11 And should not I spare Nineveh, that great city, wherein are more than sixscore thousand persons that cannot discern between their right hand and their left hand; and *also* much cattle?

Mk 12:5 And again he sent another; and him they killed, and many others; beating some, and killing some.

Ac 17:30 And the times of this ignorance God winked at; but now commandeth all men every where to repent:

Ro 2:4 Or despisest thou the riches of his goodness and forbearance and longsuffering; not knowing that the goodness of God leadeth thee to repentance?

Ro 3:25 Whom God hath set forth *to be* a propitiation through faith in his blood, to declare his righteousness for the remission of sins that are past, through the forbearance of God;

Ro 10:21 But to Israel he saith, All day long I have stretched forth my hands unto a disobedient and gainsaying people.

2 Pe 3:9 The Lord is not slack concerning his promise, as some men count slackness; but is longsuffering to us-ward, not willing that any should perish, but that all should come to repentance.

2. Prescribed

1 S 24:7 So David stayed his servants with these words, and suffered them not to rise against Saul. But Saul rose up out of the cave, and went on *his* way.

1 S 24:10 Behold, this day thine eyes have seen how that the LORD had delivered thee to day into mine hand in the cave: and *some* bade *me* kill thee: but *mine eye* spared thee; and I said, I will not put forth mine hand against my lord; for he *is* the LORD's anointed.

1 S 26:11 The LORD forbid that I should stretch forth mine hand against the LORD's anointed: but, I pray thee, take thou now the spear that *is* at his bolster, and the cruse of water, and let us go.

1 Co 13:7 Beareth all things, believeth all things, hopeth all things, endureth all things.

Ep 4:2 With all lowliness and meekness, with longsuffering, forbearing one another in love;

Ep 6:9 And, ye masters, do the same things unto them, forbearing threatening: knowing that your Master also is in heaven; neither is there respect of persons with him.

Col 3:13 Forbearing one another, and forgiving one another, if any man have a quarrel against any: even as Christ forgave you, so also *do* ye.

3. Human

Pr 12:16 A fool's wrath is presently known: but a prudent *man* covereth shame.

Pr 17:9 He that covereth a transgression seeketh love; but he that repeateth a matter separateth *very* friends.

Mt 7:3 And why beholdest thou the mote that is in thy brother's eye, but considerest not the beam that is in thine own eye?

Ro 15:1 We then that are strong ought to bear the infirmities of the weak, and not to please ourselves.

Ga 6:1 Brethren, if a man be overtaken in a fault, ye which are spiritual, restore such an one in the spirit of meekness; considering thyself, lest thou also be tempted.

1 Pe 4:8 And above all things have fervent charity among yourselves: for charity shall cover the multitude of sins.

See **GOD, PATIENCE**

FOREKNOWLEDGE

Is 7:16 For before the child shall know to refuse the evil, and choose the good, the land that thou abhorrest shall be forsaken of both her kings.

Is 16:14 But now the LORD hath spoken, saying, Within three years, as the years of an hireling, and the glory of Moab shall be contemned, with all that great multitude; and the remnant *shall be* very small *and* feeble.

Is 41:23 Shew the things that are to come hereafter, that we may know that ye *are* gods: yea, do good, or do evil, that we may be dismayed, and behold *it* together.

Is 42:9 Behold, the former things are come to pass, and new things do I declare: before they spring forth I tell you of them.

Is 46:10 Declaring the end from the beginning, and from ancient times *the things* that are not *yet* done, saying, My counsel shall stand, and I will do all my pleasure:

Da 2:28 But there is a God in heaven that revealeth secrets, and maketh known to the king Nebuchadnezzar what shall be in the latter days. Thy dream, and the visions of thy head upon thy bed, are these;

Ho 5:9 Ephraim shall be desolate in the day of rebuke: among the tribes of Israel have I made known that which shall surely be.

Mt 24:36 But of that day and hour knoweth no *man,* no, not the angels of heaven, but my Father only.

Ac 3:18 But those things, which God before had shewed by the mouth of all his prophets, that Christ should suffer, he hath so fulfilled.

Ac 15:18 Known unto God are all his works from the beginning of the world.

Ro 8:29 For whom he did foreknow, he also did predestinate *to be* conformed to the image of his Son, that he might be the firstborn among many brethren.

Ro 11:2 God hath not cast away his people which he foreknew. Wot ye not what the scripture saith of Elias? how he maketh intercession to God against Israel, saying,

1 Pe 1:2 Elect according to the foreknowledge of God the Father, through sanctification of the Spirit, unto obedience and sprinkling of the blood of Jesus Christ: Grace unto you, and peace, be multiplied.

See **FORETHOUGHT, GOD**

FORESTS, *sometimes used symbolically to denote a city, kingdom, or even a picture of unfruitfulness, in contrast to a cultivated field or vineyard*

2 S 18:6; 2 K 19:23; 2 Chr 27:4; Ne 2:8; Ps 50:10; Is 44:14; Je 10:3; 46:23; Eze 20:46; 34:25; 39:10

FORETHOUGHT, *planning ahead*

Ge 41:34 Let Pharaoh do *this,* and let him appoint officers over the land, and take up the fifth part of the land of Egypt in the seven plenteous years.

1 K 18:5 And Ahab said unto Obadiah, Go into the land, unto all fountains of water, and unto all brooks: peradventure we may find grass to save the horses and mules alive, that we lose not all the beasts.

Pr 6:8 Provideth her meat in the summer, *and* gathereth her food in the harvest.

Pr 22:3 A prudent *man* foreseeth the evil, and hideth himself: but the simple pass on, and are punished.

Pr 24:27 Prepare thy work without, and make it fit for thyself in the field; and afterwards build thine house.

Lu 12:33 Sell that ye have, and give alms; provide yourselves bags which wax not old, a treasure in the heavens that faileth not, where no thief approacheth, neither moth corrupteth.

Lu 14:28 For which of you, intending to build a tower, sitteth not down first, and counteth the cost, whether he have *sufficient* to finish *it?*

See **FOREKNOWLEDGE**

FORGETFULNESS, *living as though God did not exist*

1. Warnings

NEED FOR WATCHFULNESS

De 4:9 Only take heed to thyself, and keep thy soul diligently, lest thou forget the things which thine eyes have seen, and lest they depart from thy heart all the days of thy life: but teach them thy sons, and thy sons' sons;

FOLLOWS PROSPERITY

De 6:10 And it shall be, when the LORD thy God shall have brought thee into the land which he sware unto thy fathers, to Abraham, to Isaac, and to Jacob, to give thee great and goodly cities, which thou buildedst not,

De 6:12 *Then* beware lest thou forget the LORD, which brought thee forth out of the land of Egypt, from the house of bondage.

De 8:11 Beware that thou forget not the LORD thy God, in not keeping his commandments, and his judgments, and his statutes, which I command thee this day:

Jud 8:34 And the children of Israel remembered not the LORD their God, who had delivered them out of the hands of all their enemies on every side:

LEADS TO DOOM

Ps 9:17 The wicked shall be turned into hell, *and* all the nations that forget God.

Ps 50:22 Now consider this, ye that forget God, lest I tear *you* in pieces, and *there be* none to deliver.

Ps 78:11 And forgat his works, and his wonders that he had shewed them.

Is 17:10 Because thou hast forgotten the God of thy salvation, and hast not been mindful of the rock of thy strength, therefore shalt thou plant pleasant plants, and shalt set it with strange slips:

BEGETS MORAL COWARDICE

Is 51:13

And forgettest the LORD thy maker, that hath stretched forth the heavens, and laid the foundations of the earth; and hast feared continually every day because of the fury of the oppressor, as if he were ready to destroy? and where *is* the fury of the oppressor?

ENDS IN BITTER TEARS

Je 3:21 A voice was heard upon the high places, weeping *and* supplications of the children of Israel: for they have perverted their way, *and* they have forgotten the LORD their God.

He 2:1 Therefore we ought to give the more earnest heed to the things which we have heard, lest at any time we should let *them* slip.

2. Memorials

THE PASSOVER

Ex 12:14

THE LAYING UP OF THE MANNA

Ex 16:32

THE STONES OF THE EPHOD

Ex 28:12

THE FRINGES ON THE GARMENTS

Nu 15:39

THE BRAZEN CENSERS

Nu 16:40

THE TWELVE STONES FROM JORDAN

Jos 4:7

JOSHUA'S STONE OF MEMORIAL

Jos 24:27

THE LORD'S SUPPER

Lu 22:19; Ac 10:4

See **REMEMBRANCE**

FORGIVENESS, *a pardon*

1. Divine Promised

Ex 34:7 Keeping mercy for thousands, forgiving iniquity and transgression and sin, and that will by no means clear *the guilty;* visiting the iniquity of the fathers upon the children, and upon the children's children, unto the third and to the fourth *generation.*

Le 4:20 And he shall do with the bullock as he did with the bullock for a sin offering, so shall he do with this: and the priest shall make an atonement for them, and it shall be forgiven them.

Le 4:26 And he shall burn all his fat upon the altar, as the fat of the sacrifice of peace offerings: and the priest shall make an atonement for him as concerning his sin, and it shall be forgiven him.

Le 4:31 And he shall take away all the fat thereof, as the fat is taken away from off the sacrifice of peace offerings; and the priest shall burn *it* upon the altar for a sweet savour unto the LORD; and the priest shall make an atonement for him, and it shall be forgiven him.

Le 4:35 And he shall take away all the fat thereof, as the fat of the lamb is taken away from the sacrifice of the peace offerings; and the priest shall burn them upon the altar, according to the offerings made by fire unto the LORD: and the priest shall make an atonement for his sin that he hath committed, and it shall be forgiven him.

Le 5:10 And he shall offer the second *for* a burnt offering, according to the manner: and the priest shall make an atonement for him for his sin which he hath sinned, and it shall be forgiven him.

Le 5:13 And the priest shall make an atonement for him as touching his sin that he hath sinned in one of these, and it shall be forgiven him: and *the remnant* shall be the priest's, as a meat offering.

Le 5:16 And he shall make amends for the harm that he hath done in the holy thing, and shall add the fifth part thereto, and give it unto the priest: and the priest shall make an atonement for him with the ram of the trespass offering, and it shall be forgiven him.

Le 5:18 And he shall bring a ram without blemish out of the flock, with thy estimation, for a trespass offering, unto the priest: and the priest shall make an atonement for him concerning his ignorance wherein he erred and wist *it* not, and it shall be forgiven him.

Le 6:7 And the priest shall make an atonement for him before the LORD: and it shall be forgiven him for any thing of all that he hath done in trespassing therein.

Le 19:22 And the priest shall make an atonement for him with the ram of the trespass offering before the LORD for his sin which he hath done: and the sin which he hath done shall be forgiven him.

Nu 14:18 The LORD *is* longsuffering, and of great mercy, forgiving iniquity and transgression, and by no means clearing *the guilty,* visiting the iniquity of the fathers upon the children unto the third and fourth *generation.*

Nu 15:25 And the priest shall make an atonement for all the congregation of the children of Israel, and it shall be forgiven them; for it is ignorance: and they shall bring their offering, a sacrifice made by fire unto the LORD, and their sin offering before the LORD, for their ignorance:

Nu 15:28 And the priest shall make an atonement for the soul that sinneth ignorantly, when he sinneth by ignorance before the LORD, to make an atonement for him; and it shall be forgiven him.

De 21:8 Be merciful, O LORD, unto thy people Israel, whom thou hast redeemed, and lay not innocent blood unto thy people of Israel's charge. And the blood shall be forgiven them.

1 K 8:34 Then hear thou in heaven, and forgive the sin of thy people Israel, and bring them again unto the land which thou gavest unto their fathers.

2 Chr 7:14 If my people, which are called by my name, shall humble themselves, and pray, and seek my face, and turn from their wicked ways; then will I hear from heaven, and will forgive their sin, and will heal their land.

Ne 9:17 And refused to obey, neither were mindful of thy wonders that thou didst among them; but hardened their necks, and in their rebellion appointed a captain to return to their bondage: but thou *art* a God ready to pardon, gracious and merciful, slow to anger, and of great kindness, and forsookest them not.

Ps 32:1 Blessed *is he whose* transgression *is* forgiven, *whose* sin *is* covered.

Ps 65:3 Iniquities prevail against me: *as for* our transgressions, thou shalt purge them away.

Ps 103:3 Who forgiveth all thine iniquities; who healeth all thy diseases;

Ps 130:4 But *there is* forgiveness with thee, that thou mayest be feared.

Is 1:18 Come now, and let us reason together, saith the LORD: though your sins be as scarlet, they shall be as white as snow; though they be red like crimson, they shall be as wool.

Is 6:7 And he laid *it* upon my mouth, and said, Lo, this hath touched thy lips; and thine iniquity is taken away, and thy sin purged.

Is 33:24 And the inhabitant shall not say, I am sick: the people that dwell therein *shall be* forgiven *their* iniquity.

Je 3:12 Go and proclaim these words toward the north, and say, Return, thou backsliding Israel, saith the LORD; *and* I will not cause mine anger to fall upon you: for I *am* merciful, saith the LORD, *and* I will not keep *anger* for ever.

Je 31:34 And they shall teach no more every man his neighbour, and every man his brother, saying, Know the LORD: for they shall all know me, from the least of them unto the greatest of them, saith the LORD; for I will forgive their iniquity, and I will remember their sin no more.

Je 36:3 It may be that the house of Judah will hear all the evil which I purpose to do unto them; that they may return every man from his evil way; that I may forgive their iniquity and their sin.

Eze 18:22 All his transgressions that he hath committed, they shall not be mentioned unto him: in his righteousness that he hath done he shall live.

Eze 33:16 None of his sins that he hath committed shall be mentioned unto him: he hath done that which is lawful and right; he shall surely live.

Da 9:9 To the Lord our God *belong* mercies and forgivenesses, though we have rebelled against him;

Zec 3:4 And he answered and spake unto those that stood before him, saying, Take away the filthy garments from him. And unto him he said, Behold, I have caused thine iniquity to pass from thee, and I will clothe thee with change of raiment.

Mt 6:14 For if ye forgive men their trespasses, your heavenly Father will also forgive you:

Mt 12:31 Wherefore I say unto you, All manner of sin and blasphemy shall be forgiven unto men: but the blasphemy *against* the *Holy* Ghost shall not be forgiven unto men.

Mk 3:28 Verily I say unto you, All sins shall be forgiven unto the sons of men, and blasphemies wherewith soever they shall blaspheme:

Mk 11:25 And when ye stand praying, forgive, if ye have ought against any: that your Father also which is in heaven may forgive you your trespasses.

Lu 7:42 And when they had nothing to pay, he frankly forgave them both. Tell me therefore, which of them will love him most?

Lu 11:4 And forgive us our sins; for we also forgive every one that is indebted to us. And lead us not into temptation; but deliver us from evil.

Ac 5:31 Him hath God exalted with his right hand *to be* a Prince and a

Saviour, for to give repentance to Israel, and forgiveness of sins.

Ac 8:22 Repent therefore of this thy wickedness, and pray God, if perhaps the thought of thine heart may be forgiven thee.

Ac 13:38 Be it known unto you therefore, men *and* brethren, that through this man is preached unto you the forgiveness of sins:

Ac 26:18 To open their eyes, *and* to turn *them* from darkness to light, and *from* the power of Satan unto God, that they may receive forgiveness of sins, and inheritance among them which are sanctified by faith that is in me.

Ro 4:7 *Saying,* Blessed *are* they whose iniquities are forgiven, and whose sins are covered.

Ep 1:7 In whom we have redemption through his blood, the forgiveness of sins, according to the riches of his grace;

Col 1:14 In whom we have redemption through his blood, *even* the forgiveness of sins:

He 8:12 For I will be merciful to their unrighteousness, and their sins and their iniquities will I remember no more.

Ja 5:15 And the prayer of faith shall save the sick, and the Lord shall raise him up; and if he have committed sins, they shall be forgiven him.

1 Jn 1:9 If we confess our sins, he is faithful and just to forgive us *our* sins, and to cleanse us from all unrighteousness.

2. Human Commanded

Ge 50:17 So shall ye say unto Joseph, Forgive, I pray thee now, the trespass of thy brethren, and their sin; for they did unto thee evil: and now, we pray thee, forgive the trespass of the servants of the God of thy father. And Joseph wept when they spake unto him.

Pr 19:11 The discretion of a man deferreth his anger; and *it is* his glory to pass over a transgression.

Mt 6:14 For if ye forgive men their trespasses, your heavenly Father will also forgive you:

Mt 18:21 Then came Peter to him, and said, Lord, how oft shall my brother sin against me, and I forgive him? till seven times?

Mt 18:35 So likewise shall my heavenly Father do also unto you, if ye from your hearts forgive not every one his brother their trespasses.

Mk 11:25 And when ye stand praying, forgive, if ye have ought against any: that your Father also which is in heaven may forgive you your trespasses.

Lu 6:37 Judge not, and ye shall not be judged: condemn not, and ye shall not be condemned: forgive, and ye shall be forgiven:

Lu 11:4 And forgive us our sins; for we also forgive every one that is indebted to us. And lead us not into temptation; but deliver us from evil.

Lu 17:4 And if he trespass against thee seven times in a day, and seven times in a day turn again to thee, saying, I repent; thou shalt forgive him.

2 Co 2:7 So that contrariwise ye *ought* rather to forgive *him,* and comfort *him,* lest perhaps such a one should be swallowed up with overmuch sorrow.

Ep 4:26 Be ye angry, and sin not: let not the sun go down upon your wrath:

Ep 4:32 And be ye kind one to another, tenderhearted, forgiving one another, even as God for Christ's sake hath forgiven you.

Col 3:13 Forbearing one another, and forgiving one another, if any man have a quarrel against any: even as Christ forgave you, so also *do* ye.

3. Examples of Human

Ge 33:4 And Esau ran to meet him, and embraced him, and fell on his neck, and kissed him: and they wept.

Ge 45:5 Now therefore be not grieved, nor angry with yourselves, that ye sold me hither: for God did send me before you to preserve life.

Ge 45:15 Moreover he kissed all his brethren, and wept upon them: and after that his brethren talked with him.

2 S 19:23 Therefore the king said unto Shimei, Thou shalt not die. And the king sware unto him.

1 K 1:53 So king Solomon sent, and they brought him down from the altar. And he came and bowed himself to king Solomon: and Solomon said unto him, Go to thine house.

Mt 18:27 Then the lord of that servant was moved with compassion, and loosed him, and forgave him the debt.

Mt 18:32 Then his lord, after that he had called him, said unto him, O thou wicked servant, I forgave thee all that debt, because thou desiredst me:

Ac 7:60 And he kneeled down, and cried with a loud voice, Lord, lay not this sin to their charge. And when he had said this, he fell asleep.

2 Co 2:10 To whom ye forgive any thing, I *forgive* also: for if I forgave any thing, to whom I forgave *it,* for your sakes *forgave I it* in the person of Christ;

2 Ti 4:16 At my first answer no man stood with me, but all *men* forsook me: *I pray God* that it may not be laid to their charge.

4. Examples of Divine

See **PENITENCE, REPENTANCE, RESTORATION, SIN**

FORSAKING

1. Christ

Mt 19:22; 26:56; Jn 6:66; 13:30; 1 Ti 5:11; 1 Jn 2:19

2. God

Ex 34:16; Nu 32:15; De 29:18; 31:16; 32:15; Jos 24:20; Jud 2:12; 10:10; 1 K 9:6; 1 Chr 28:9; 2 Chr 7:19; 15:2; 34:25; Ezr 8:22; Jb 21:14; 34:27; Ps 73:27; 89:30; 106:39; Is 1:4, 28; 59:13; Je 1:16; 2:13; 5:7, 19; 15:6; 16:11; 17:5; 22:9; Eze 6:9; 14:7; Ho 2:5; Ro 1:25; 2 Pe 2:15

See **GOD**

Examples

Ex 32:8; Nu 14:43; De 28:20; 29:25; 31:18; Jud 8:33; 10:6, 13; 1 S 8:8; 10:19;

12:10; 28:7; 1 K 9:9; 11:9, 33; 14:9; 18:18; 2 K 17:7, 16; 21:22; 22:17; 1 Chr 5:25; 10:14; 2 Chr 12:1; 13:11; 21:10; 24:20, 24; 25:27; 28:6; 29:6; Ezr 9:10; Ps 16:4; Is 1:21; 17:10; 31:1; 43:22; 65:11; Je 2:17, 31; 17:13; 19:4; Eze 23:5; Da 9:5; Ho 1:2; 4:12; 5:7; 7:13; Zep 3:2; Mal 3:7

See **ESTRANGEMENT, WANDERERS**

FORSAKEN, *the righteous apparently*

Ps 22:1; 42:9; 74:1; 77:7–8; 88:14; Is 49:14; 54:07; Mt 27:46

FORTRESSES, *places of safety, refuge*

Jud 9:46, 51; 2 S 5:9; 2 K 25:1; Is 17:3; 25:12; Eze 21:22; 33:27; Da 11:7; Ho 10:14; Mi 7:11–12

FOUNDERS *See* ARTS AND CRAFTS

FOUNTAIN OF LIFE, *symbol of divine life*

Ps 36:9; 87:7; Pr 10:11; 13:14; 14:27; 16:22; Je 2:13; Zec 13:1; Re 7:17

See **WATER**

FOXES *See* ANIMALS

FRAILTY, *human weakness*

1 S 20:3 And David sware moreover, and said, Thy father certainly knoweth that I have found grace in thine eyes; and he saith, Let not Jonathan know this, lest he be grieved: but truly *as* the Lord liveth, and *as* thy soul liveth, *there is* but a step between me and death.

Jb 4:20 They are destroyed from morning to evening: they perish for ever without any regarding *it.*

Jb 13:25 Wilt thou break a leaf driven to and fro? and wilt thou pursue the dry stubble?

Jb 17:1 My breath is corrupt, my days are extinct, the graves *are ready* for me.

Ps 38:10 My heart panteth, my strength faileth me: as for the light of mine eyes, it also is gone from me.

Ps 39:4 Lord, make me to know mine end, and the measure of my days, what it *is; that* I may know how frail I *am.*

Ps 49:12 Nevertheless man *being* in honour abideth not: he is like the beasts *that* perish.

Ps 78:39 For he remembered that they *were but* flesh; a wind that passeth away, and cometh not again.

Ps 90:6 In the morning it flourisheth, and groweth up; in the evening it is cut down, and withereth.

Ps 103:14 For he knoweth our frame; he remembereth that we *are* dust.

Ps 141:7 Our bones are scattered at the grave's mouth, as when one cutteth and cleaveth *wood* upon the earth.

Is 2:22 Cease ye from man, whose breath *is* in his nostrils: for wherein is he to be accounted of?

Is 38:12 Mine age is departed, and is removed from me as a shepherd's tent: I have cut off like a weaver my life: he will cut me off with pining sickness: from day *even* to night wilt thou make an end of me.

Is 40:6 The voice said, Cry. And he said, What shall I cry? All flesh *is* grass, and all the goodliness thereof *is* as the flower of the field:

Is 40:30 Even the youths shall faint and be weary, and the young men shall utterly fall:

Is 64:6 But we are all as an unclean *thing,* and all our righteousnesses *are* as filthy rags; and we all do fade as a leaf; and our iniquities, like the wind, have taken us away.

Je 9:23 Thus saith the Lord, Let not the wise *man* glory in his wisdom, neither let the mighty *man* glory in his might, let not the rich *man* glory in his riches:

Mt 28:4 And for fear of him the keepers did shake, and became as dead *men.*

2 Co 5:4 For we that are in *this* tabernacle do groan, being burdened: not for that we would be unclothed, but clothed upon, that mortality might be swallowed up of life.

Ja 1:10 But the rich, in that he is made low: because as the flower of the grass he shall pass away.

Ja 4:14 Whereas ye know not what *shall be* on the morrow. For what *is* your life? It is even a vapour, that appeareth for a little time, and then vanisheth away.

1 Pe 1:24 For all flesh *is* as grass, and all the glory of man as the flower of grass. The grass withereth, and the flower thereof falleth away:

See **LIFE, MORTALITY**

FRANKINCENSE, *a plant used as a constituent of a sacred incense*

Ex 30:34; Le 2:1, 15; 5:11; 6:15; 24:7; Nu 5:15; Ne 13:5, 9; Song 3:6; 4:6, 14; Mt 2:11; Re 18:13

FRATRICIDE *See* **FAMILY**

FRIENDLESSNESS

Jb 17:3; 19:13; Ps 31:11; 38:11; 69:8; 88:8, 18; 142:4; Pr 19:7; Ec 4:10; Na 3:7; Mk 14:48, 50; Lu 15:16; 16:20, 21; Jn 5:7; 2 Ti 4:16

FRIENDSHIP, *a relationship marked by knowledge, trust, and appreciation*

1. Characteristics

TRUE AND UNCHANGEABLE
Pr 17:17 A friend loveth at all times, and a brother is born for adversity.

THE DESIRE FOR MANY FRIENDS PERILOUS
Pr 18:24 A man *that hath* friends must shew himself friendly: and there is a friend *that* sticketh closer than a brother.

OLD FRIENDS TO BE CHERISHED
Pr 27:10 Thine own friend, and thy father's friend, forsake not; neither go into thy brother's house in the day of thy calamity: *for* better *is* a neighbour *that is* near than a brother far off.

STIMULATING
Pr 27:17 Iron sharpeneth iron; so a man sharpeneth the countenance of his friend.

PROFITABLE
Ec 4:9–10 Two *are* better than one; because they have a good reward for their labour.

For if they fall, the one will lift up his fellow: but woe to him *that is* alone when he falleth; for *he hath* not another to help him up.

CHRIST'S PREEMINENT

Jn 15:13–14 Greater love hath no man than this, that a man lay down his life for his friends.

Ye are my friends, if ye do whatsoever I command you.

2. Examples of True

1 S 18:1; 20:4, 41; 23:16; 2 S 1:26; 9:7; 15:21, 37; 19:31, 38; 1 K 4:5; 5:1; Jb 2:11; Lu 11:5; 2 Co 2:13; Ph 2:25, 27; 2 Ti 1:4, 16; 3 Jn 13–14

RUTH

Ru 1:16 And Ruth said, Intreat me not to leave thee, *or* to return from following after thee: for whither thou goest, I will go; and where thou lodgest, I will lodge: thy people *shall be* my people, and thy God my God:

JONATHAN

1 S 20:17 And Jonathan caused David to swear again, because he loved him: for he loved him as he loved his own soul.

2 S 15:21 And Ittai answered the king, and said, *As* the LORD liveth, and *as* my lord the king liveth, surely in what place my lord the king shall be, whether in death or life, even there also will thy servant be.

ELISHA

2 K 2:2 And Elijah said unto Elisha, Tarry here, I pray thee; for the LORD hath sent me to Bethel. And Elisha said *unto him,* As the LORD liveth, and as thy soul liveth, I will not leave thee. So they went down to Bethel.

MARY MAGDALENE AND OTHER WOMEN

Mt 27:55–56 And many women were there beholding afar off, which followed Jesus from Galilee, ministering unto him:

Among which was Mary Magdalene, and Mary the mother of James and Joses, and the mother of Zebedee's children.

Mt 28:1 In the end of the sabbath, as it began to dawn toward the first *day* of the week, came Mary Magdalene and the other Mary to see the sepulchre.

THOMAS

Jn 11:16 Then said Thomas, which is called Didymus, unto his fellow-disciples, Let us also go, that we may die with him.

CHRIST

Jn 13:1 Now before the feast of the passover, when Jesus knew that his hour was come that he should depart out of this world unto the Father, having loved his own which were in the world, he loved them unto the end.

PRISCILLA AND AQUILA

Ro 16:4 Who have for my life laid down their own necks: unto whom not only I give thanks, but also all the churches of the Gentiles.

ONESIPHORUS

2 Ti 1:16 The Lord give mercy unto the house of Onesiphorus; for he oft refreshed me, and was not ashamed of my chain:

See **FAITHFULNESS**

3. Among Believers

1 Chr 12:39 And there they were with David three days, eating and drinking: for their brethren had prepared for them.

Ps 119:63 I *am* a companion of all *them* that fear thee, and of them that keep thy precepts.

Pr 18:24 A man *that hath* friends must shew himself friendly: and there is a friend *that* sticketh closer than a brother.

Da 8:13 Then I heard one saint speaking, and another saint said unto that certain *saint* which spake, How long *shall be* the vision *concerning* the daily *sacrifice,* and the transgression of desolation, to give both the sanctuary and the host to be trodden under foot?

Zec 3:10 In that day, saith the LORD of hosts, shall ye call every man his neighbour under the vine and under the fig tree.

Mal 3:16 Then they that feared the LORD spake often one to another: and the LORD hearkened, and heard *it*, and a book of remembrance was written before him for them that feared the LORD, and that thought upon his name.

Lu 24:15 And it came to pass, that, while they communed *together* and reasoned, Jesus himself drew near, and went with them.

Ac 2:42 And they continued stedfastly in the apostles' doctrine and fellowship, and in breaking of bread, and in prayers.

Ro 1:12 That is, that I may be comforted together with you by the mutual faith both of you and me.

Ph 1:5 For your fellowship in the gospel from the first day until now;

Ph 2:17 Yea, and if I be offered upon the sacrifice and service of your faith, I joy, and rejoice with you all.

Ph 2:28 I sent him therefore the more carefully, that, when ye see him again, ye may rejoice, and that I may be the less sorrowful.

1 Jn 1:7 But if we walk in the light, as he is in the light, we have fellowship one with another, and the blood of Jesus Christ his Son cleanseth us from all sin.

4. Divine, *our highest honor—to know God*

a. Of Christ

Jn 11:5 Now Jesus loved Martha, and her sister, and Lazarus.

Jn 11:35–36 Jesus wept.

Then said the Jews, Behold how he loved him!

Jn 13:23 Now there was leaning on Jesus' bosom one of his disciples, whom Jesus loved.

Jn 15:15 Henceforth I call you not servants; for the servant knoweth not what his lord doeth: but I have called you friends; for all things that I have heard of my Father I have made known unto you.

b. Of God

Ex 33:11 And the LORD spake unto Moses face to face, as a man speaketh unto his friend. And he turned again into the camp: but his servant Joshua, the son of Nun, a young man, departed not out of the tabernacle.

Nu 12:8 With him will I speak mouth to mouth, even apparently, and not in dark speeches; and the similitude of the LORD shall he behold: wherefore then were ye not afraid to speak against my servant Moses?

De 34:10 And there arose not a prophet since in Israel like unto Moses, whom the LORD knew face to face,

2 Chr 20:7 *Art* not thou our God, *who* didst drive out the inhabitants of this land before thy people Israel, and gavest it to the seed of Abraham thy friend for ever?

Ja 2:23 And the scripture was fulfilled which saith, Abraham believed God, and it was imputed unto him for righteousness: and he was called the Friend of God.

See **CHRIST, GOD**

c. Of Sinners

Mt 11:19 The Son of man came eating and drinking, and they say, Behold a man gluttonous, and a winebibber, a friend of publicans and sinners. But wisdom is justified of her children.

Mk 2:17 When Jesus heard *it,* he saith unto them, They that are whole have no need of the physician, but they that are sick: I came not to call the righteous, but sinners to repentance.

Lu 7:39 Now when the Pharisee which had bidden him saw *it,* he spake within himself, saying, This man, if he were a prophet, would have known who and what manner of woman *this is* that toucheth him: for she is a sinner.

Lu 19:7 And when they saw *it,* they all murmured, saying, That he was gone to be guest with a man that is a sinner.

Jn 8:10–11 When Jesus had lifted up himself, and saw none but the woman, he said unto her, Woman, where are those thine accusers? hath no man condemned thee?

She said, No man, Lord. And Jesus said unto her, Neither do I condemn thee: go, and sin no more.

Ro 5:8 But God commendeth his love toward us, in that, while we were yet sinners, Christ died for us.

1 Ti 1:15 This *is* a faithful saying, and worthy of all acceptation, that Christ Jesus came into the world to save sinners; of whom I am chief.

5. Inner Circle, *of the disciples*

AT THE MAID'S BEDSIDE

Mk 5:37 And he suffered no man to follow him, save Peter, and James, and John the brother of James.

AT GETHSEMANE

Mt 26:37 And he took with him Peter and the two sons of Zebedee, and began to be sorrowful and very heavy.

AT THE TRANSFIGURATION

Mk 9:2 And after six days Jesus taketh *with him* Peter, and James, and John, and leadeth them up into an high mountain apart by themselves: and he was transfigured before them.

See **FRIENDLESSNESS**

FREEDOM *See* LIBERTY

FREEWILL OFFERINGS

See **OFFERINGS**

FRINGES *See* REMEMBRANCE

FROGS *See* MIRACLES, REPTILES

FROST *See* WEATHER

FROWARDNESS, *disobedience, extreme stubbornness*

Ps 101:4; Pr 2:12; 3:32; 4:24; 8:13; 10:31; 11:20; 17:20; 21:8; 22:5

See **WICKED**

FRUGALITY, *thrift, extreme care with money*

Ge 41:35, 36; Pr 21:20; Mt 15:37; Mk 8:8; Lu 15:8; Jn 6:12

See **BUSINESS**

FRUIT

1. Sinful, *life-traits characterized by evil, due to alienation from God*

BITTER

De 32:32 For their vine *is* of the vine of Sodom, and of the fields of Gomorrah: their grapes *are* grapes of gall, their clusters *are* bitter:

NATURAL

Is 5:2 And he fenced it, and gathered out the stones thereof, and planted it with the choicest vine, and built a tower in the midst of it, and also made a winepress therein: and he looked that it should bring forth grapes, and it brought forth wild grapes.

SELFISH

Ho 10:1 Israel *is* an empty vine, he bringeth forth fruit unto himself: according to the multitude of his fruit he hath increased the altars; according to the goodness of his land they have made goodly images.

DECEITFUL

Ho 10:13 Ye have plowed wickedness, ye have reaped iniquity; ye have eaten the fruit of lies: because thou didst trust in thy way, in the multitude of thy mighty men.

CORRUPT

Mt 7:17 Even so every good tree bringeth forth good fruit; but a corrupt tree bringeth forth evil fruit.

FLESHLY, ADULTERY, FORNICATION, UNCLEANNESS, LASCIVIOUSNESS

Ga 5:19–21 Now the works of the flesh are manifest, which are *these*; Adultery, fornication, uncleanness, lasciviousness,

Idolatry, witchcraft, hatred, variance, emulations, wrath, strife, seditions, heresies,

Envyings, murders, drunkenness, revellings, and such like: of the which I tell you before, as I have also told *you* in time past, that they which do such things shall not inherit the kingdom of God.

2. Spiritual, *results of the Holy Spirit's indwelling presence*

a. Characteristics

PRODUCED IN ALL PERIODS OF LIFE

Ps 92:13–14 Those that be planted in the house of the LORD shall flourish in the courts of our God.

They shall still bring forth fruit in old age; they shall be fat and flourishing;

PERENNIAL

Eze 47:12 And by the river upon the bank thereof, on this side and on that side, shall grow all trees for meat, whose leaf shall not fade, neither shall the fruit thereof be consumed: it shall bring forth new fruit according to his months, because their waters they issued out of the sanctuary: and the fruit thereof shall be for meat, and the leaf thereof for medicine.

GROWN ONLY IN GOOD GROUND

Mt 13:8 But other fell into good ground, and brought forth fruit, some an hundredfold, some sixtyfold, some thirtyfold.

VARIETIES

Ga 5:22–23 But the fruit of the Spirit is love, joy, peace, longsuffering, gentleness, goodness, faith,

Meekness, temperance: against such there is no law.

WITHOUT DEFECT

Ep 5:9 (For the fruit of the Spirit is in all goodness and righteousness and truth;)

Ph 1:11 Being filled with the fruits of righteousness, which are by Jesus Christ, unto the glory and praise of God.

THE PRODUCT OF HEAVENLY WISDOM

Ja 3:17 But the wisdom that is from above is first pure, then peaceable, gentle, *and* easy to be intreated, full of mercy and good fruits, without partiality, and without hypocrisy.

b. Conditions for Growing

CONTACT WITH THE LIVING WATER

Ps 1:3 And he shall be like a tree planted by the rivers of water, that bringeth forth his fruit in his season; his leaf also shall not wither; and whatsoever he doeth shall prosper.

SPIRITUAL RECEPTIVITY

Mt 13:23 But he that received seed into the good ground is he that heareth the word, and understandeth *it;* which also beareth fruit, and bringeth forth, some an hundredfold, some sixty, some thirty.

DEATH OF THE OLD LIFE

Jn 12:24 Verily, verily, I say unto you, Except a corn of wheat fall into the ground and die, it abideth alone: but if it die, it bringeth forth much fruit.

CHASTENING, OR PRUNING

Jn 15:2 Every branch in me that beareth not fruit he taketh away: and every *branch* that beareth fruit, he purgeth it, that it may bring forth more fruit.

ABIDING IN CHRIST

Jn 15:5 I am the vine, ye *are* the branches: He that abideth in me, and I in him, the same bringeth forth much fruit: for without me ye can do nothing.

Ro 6:22 But now being made free from sin, and become servants to God, ye have your fruit unto holiness, and the end everlasting life.

He 12:11 Now no chastening for the present seemeth to be joyous, but grievous: nevertheless afterward it yieldeth the peaceable fruit of righteousness unto them which are exercised thereby.

c. Examples

Song 7:1 How beautiful are thy feet with shoes, O prince's daughter! the joints of thy thighs *are* like jewels, the work of the hands of a cunning workman.

Ro 5:3–4 And not only *so,* but we glory in tribulations also: knowing that tribulation worketh patience;

And patience, experience; and experience, hope:

2 Co 6:6 By pureness, by knowledge, by longsuffering, by kindness, by the Holy Ghost, by love unfeigned,

2 Co 8:7 Therefore, as ye abound in every *thing, in* faith, and utterance, and knowledge, and *in* all diligence, and *in* your love to us, *see* that ye abound in this grace also.

2 Pe 1:5–7 And beside this, giving all diligence, add to your faith virtue; and to virtue knowledge;

And to knowledge temperance; and to temperance patience; and to patience godliness;

And to godliness brotherly kindness; and to brotherly kindness charity.

3. Test of Its Worth

Mt 3:8 Bring forth therefore fruits meet for repentance:

Mt 7:16 Ye shall know them by their fruits. Do men gather grapes of thorns, or figs of thistles?

Mt 7:19–20 Every tree that bringeth not forth good fruit is hewn down, and cast into the fire.

Wherefore by their fruits ye shall know them.

Lu 13:7 Then said he unto the dresser of his vineyard, Behold, these three years I come seeking fruit on this fig tree, and find none: cut it down; why cumbereth it the ground?

Jn 15:8 Herein is my Father glorified, that ye bear much fruit; so shall ye be my disciples.

Ph 4:17 Not because I desire a gift: but I desire fruit that may abound to your account.

See **TREE OF LIFE**

FRUITFULNESS

1. Spiritual

Ge 49:22 Joseph *is* a fruitful bough, *even* a fruitful bough by a well; *whose* branches run over the wall:

Is 5:2 And he fenced it, and gathered out the stones thereof, and planted it with the choicest vine, and built a tower in the midst of it, and also made a winepress therein: and he looked that it should bring forth grapes, and it brought forth wild grapes.

Mt 3:8 Bring forth therefore fruits meet for repentance:

Mt 13:26 But when the blade was sprung up, and brought forth fruit, then appeared the tares also.

Mt 21:34 And when the time of the fruit drew near, he sent his servants to the husbandmen, that they might receive the fruits of it.

Mt 21:41 They say unto him, He will miserably destroy those wicked men, and will let out *his* vineyard unto other husbandmen, which shall render him the fruits in their seasons.

Mt 21:43 Therefore say I unto you, The kingdom of God shall be taken from you, and given to a nation bringing forth the fruits thereof.

Mt 25:20 And so he that had received five talents came and brought other five talents, saying, Lord, thou deliveredst unto me five talents: behold, I have gained beside them five talents more.

Mk 4:8 And other fell on good ground, and did yield fruit that sprang up and increased; and brought forth, some thirty, and some sixty, and some an hundred.

Lu 3:8 Bring forth therefore fruits worthy of repentance, and begin not to say within yourselves, We have Abraham to *our* father: for I say unto you, That God is able of these stones to raise up children unto Abraham.

Lu 8:15 But that on the good ground are they, which in an honest and good heart, having heard the word, keep *it,* and bring forth fruit with patience.

Lu 13:7 Then said he unto the dresser of his vineyard, Behold, these three years I come seeking fruit on this fig tree, and find none: cut it down; why cumbereth it the ground?

Lu 20:10 And at the season he sent a servant to the husbandmen, that they should give him of the fruit of the vineyard: but the husbandmen beat him, and sent *him* away empty.

Jn 15:8 Herein is my Father glorified, that ye bear much fruit; so shall ye be my disciples.

Jn 15:16 Ye have not chosen me, but I have chosen you, and ordained you, that ye should go and bring forth fruit, and *that* your fruit should remain: that whatsoever ye shall ask of the Father in my name, he may give it you.

Ro 7:4 Wherefore, my brethren, ye also are become dead to the law by the body of Christ; that ye should be married to another, *even* to him who is raised from the dead, that we should bring forth fruit unto God.

2 Co 9:10 Now he that ministereth seed to the sower both minister bread for *your* food, and multiply your seed sown, and increase the fruits of your righteousness;)

Ph 1:11 Being filled with the fruits of righteousness, which are by Jesus Christ, unto the glory and praise of God.

Ph 4:17 Not because I desire a gift: but I desire fruit that may abound to your account.

Col 1:10 That ye might walk worthy of the Lord unto all pleasing, being fruitful in every good work, and increasing in the knowledge of God;

Tit 3:14 And let ours also learn to maintain good works for necessary uses, that they be not unfruitful.

He 6:7 For the earth which drinketh in the rain that cometh oft upon it, and bringeth forth herbs meet for them by whom it is dressed, receiveth blessing from God:

2 Pe 1:8 For if these things be in you, and abound, they make *you that ye shall* neither *be* barren nor unfruitful in the knowledge of our Lord Jesus Christ.

2. *Degrees*, *fruit, more fruit, much fruit*

Da 4:12 The leaves thereof *were* fair, and the fruit thereof much, and in it *was* meat for all: the beasts of the field had shadow under it, and the fowls of the heaven dwelt in the boughs thereof, and all flesh was fed of it.

Mt 13:8 But other fell into good ground, and brought forth fruit, some an hundredfold, some sixtyfold, some thirtyfold.

Jn 15:2 Every branch in me that beareth not fruit he taketh away: and every *branch* that beareth fruit, he purgeth it, that it may bring forth more fruit.

Ja 3:17 But the wisdom that is from above is first pure, then peaceable, gentle, *and* easy to be intreated, full of mercy and good fruits, without partiality, and without hypocrisy.

Re 22:2 In the midst of the street of it, and on either side of the river, *was there* the tree of life, which bare twelve *manner* of fruits, *and* yielded her fruit every month: and the leaves of the tree *were* for the healing of the nations.

See **UNFRUITFULNESS**

FUGITIVES, *a runaway, refugee*

Ge 4:4; 16:6; Ex 2:15; 14:5; De 23:15; Jud 9:21; 11:3; 1 S 19:18; 21:10; 2 S 13:34; 1 K 2:39; 11:17, 40; 12:2; 20:30; 2 Chr 10:2; 25:27; Je 39:4; 48:19; Eze 17:21; Ho 12:12; Mt 2:13; Ac 7:29; He 11:38

See **HELPER, HELPLESSNESS**

FULFILLMENT OF PROHECY

See **PROPHECY**

FULLERS *See* **ARTS AND CRAFTS**

FULLNESS

1. *Spiritual*, *satisfaction of our deepest needs*

Ps 23:5 Thou preparest a table before me in the presence of mine enemies: thou anointest my head with oil; my cup runneth over.

Ps 81:10 I *am* the LORD thy God, which brought thee out of the land of Egypt: open thy mouth wide, and I will fill it.

Pr 8:21 That I may cause those that love me to inherit substance; and I will fill their treasures.

Pr 28:25 He that is of a proud heart stirreth up strife: but he that putteth his trust in the LORD shall be made fat.

Is 66:11 That ye may suck, and be satisfied with the breasts of her consolations; that ye may milk out, and be delighted with the abundance of her glory.

Eze 34:14 I will feed them in a good pasture, and upon the high mountains of Israel shall their fold be: there shall they lie in a good fold, and *in* a fat pasture shall they feed upon the mountains of Israel.

Mal 3:10 Bring ye all the tithes into the storehouse, that there may be meat in mine house, and prove me now herewith, saith the LORD of hosts, if I will not open you the windows of heaven, and pour you out a blessing, that *there shall* not *be room* enough *to receive it.*

Mt 5:6 Blessed *are* they which do hunger and thirst after righteousness: for they shall be have I spoken unto you, that my joy might remain in you, and *that* your joy might be full.

Ro 15:29 And I am sure that, when I come unto you, I shall come in the fulness of the blessing of the gospel of Christ.

Ep 3:19 And to know the love of Christ, which passeth knowledge, that ye might be filled with all the fulness of God.

Ep 5:18 And be not drunk with wine, wherein is excess; but be filled with the Spirit;

Col 1:9 For this cause we also, since the day we heard *it*, do not cease to pray for you, and to desire that ye might be filled with the knowledge of his will in all wisdom and spiritual understanding;

2. Of Christ, *the possession of every true believer*

Jn 1:16 And of his fulness have all we received, and grace for grace.

Ep 1:22–23 And hath put all *things* under his feet, and gave him *to be* the head over all *things* to the church,
Which is his body, the fulness of him that filleth all in all.

Ep 4:13 Till we all come in the unity of the faith, and of the knowledge of the Son of God, unto a perfect man, unto the measure of the stature of the fulness of Christ:

Col 1:19 For it pleased *the Father* that in him should all fulness dwell;

Col 2:9 For in him dwelleth all the fulness of the Godhead bodily.

See **EMPTINESS**

FULLNESS OF TIME, *God's appointed time when everything is ready*

Jos 6:16; Da 9:24; Mk 1:15; Lu 2:6; 21:24; Jn 7:8, 30; Ro 5:6; Ga 4:4; Ep 1:10; 1 Ti 2:6; 6:15; Tit 1:3; He 1:2; 9:10, 26; 1 Pe 1:20; Re 1:3

See **TIME**

FUTURE LIFE

1. Things Eliminated

NO MORE SEA

Re 21:1 And I saw a new heaven and a new earth: for the first heaven and the first earth were passed away; and there was no more sea.

NO SORROW

Re 21:4 And God shall wipe away all tears from their eyes; and there shall be no more death, neither sorrow, nor crying, neither shall there be any more pain: for the former things are passed away.

NO CRYING

Re 21:4 And God shall wipe away all tears from their eyes; and there shall be no more death, neither sorrow, nor crying, neither shall there be any more pain: for the former things are passed away.

NO PAIN

Re 21:4 And God shall wipe away all tears from their eyes; and there shall be no more death, neither sorrow, nor crying, neither shall there be any more pain: for the former things are passed away.

NO CURSE

Re 22:3 And there shall be no more curse: but the throne of God and of the Lamb shall be in it; and his servants shall serve him:

NO NIGHT

Re 22:5 And there shall be no night there; and they need no candle, neither light of the sun; for the Lord God giveth them light: and they shall reign for ever and ever.

NO DEATH

Re 21:4 And God shall wipe away all tears from their eyes; and there shall be no more death, neither sorrow, nor crying, neither shall there be any more pain: for the former things are passed away.

2. Death Vanquished

Is 25:8 He will swallow up death in victory; and the Lord GOD will wipe away tears from off all faces; and the rebuke of his people shall he take away from off all the earth: for the LORD hath spoken *it*.

Ho 13:14 I will ransom them from the power of the grave; I will redeem them from death: O death, I will be thy plagues; O grave, I will be thy destruction: repentance shall be hid from mine eyes.

Mt 12:40 For as Jonas was three days and three nights in the whale's belly; so shall the Son of man be three days and three nights in the heart of the earth.

Mk 5:42 And straightway the damsel arose, and walked; for she was *of the age* of twelve years. And they were astonished with a great astonishment.

Ro 6:9 Knowing that Christ being raised from the dead dieth no more;

death hath no more dominion over him.

1 Co 15:26 The last enemy *that* shall be destroyed *is* death.

1 Co 15:54 So when this corruptible shall have put on incorruption, and this mortal shall have put on immortality, then shall be brought to pass the saying that is written, Death is swallowed up in victory.

2 Ti 1:10 But is now made manifest by the appearing of our Saviour Jesus Christ, who hath abolished death, and hath brought life and immortality to light through the gospel:

He 2:14 Forasmuch then as the children are partakers of flesh and blood, he also himself likewise took part of the same; that through death he might destroy him that had the power of death, that is, the devil;

Re 1:18 I *am* he that liveth, and was dead; and, behold, I am alive for evermore, Amen; and have the keys of hell and of death.

Re 20:14 And death and hell were cast into the lake of fire. This is the second death.

Re 21:4 And God shall wipe away all tears from their eyes; and there shall be no more death, neither sorrow, nor crying, neither shall there be any more pain: for the former things are passed away.

3. Saints Glorified

Eze 34:29 And I will raise up for them a plant of renown, and they shall be no more consumed with hunger in the land, neither bear the shame of the heathen any more.

Mt 13:43 Then shall the righteous shine forth as the sun in the kingdom of their Father. Who hath ears to hear, let him hear.

Lu 9:30–31 And, behold, there talked with him two men, which were Moses and Elias:

Who appeared in glory, and spake of his decease which he should accomplish at Jerusalem.

Ro 8:17 And if children, then heirs; heirs of God, and joint-heirs with Christ; if so be that we suffer with *him*, that we may be also glorified together.

1 Co 15:43 It is sown in dishonour; it is raised in glory: it is sown in weakness; it is raised in power:

1 Co 15:51 Behold, I shew you a mystery; We shall not all sleep, but we shall all be changed,

1 Co 15:54 So when this corruptible shall have put on incorruption, and this mortal shall have put on immortality, then shall be brought to pass the saying that is written, Death is swallowed up in victory.

Ep 2:6 And hath raised *us* up together, and made *us* sit together in heavenly *places* in Christ Jesus:

Ph 1:23 For I am in a strait betwixt two, having a desire to depart, and to be with Christ; which is far better:

Ph 3:21 Who shall change our vile body, that it may be fashioned like unto his glorious body, according to the working whereby he is able even to subdue all things unto himself.

Col 3:4 When Christ, *who is* our life, shall appear, then shall ye also appear with him in glory.

2 Th 2:14 Whereunto he called you by our gospel, to the obtaining of the glory of our Lord Jesus Christ.

He 2:10 For it became him, for whom *are* all things, and by whom *are* all things, in bringing many sons unto glory, to make the captain of their salvation perfect through sufferings.

1 Pe 1:7 That the trial of your faith, being much more precious than of gold that perisheth, though it be tried with fire, might be found unto praise and honour and glory at the appearing of Jesus Christ:

1 Pe 4:13 But rejoice, inasmuch as ye are partakers of Christ's sufferings; that, when his glory shall be revealed, ye may be glad also with exceeding joy.

1 Pe 5:1 The elders which are among you I exhort, who am also an elder, and a witness of the sufferings of Christ, and also a partaker of the glory that shall be revealed:

Jude 24 Now unto him that is able to keep you from falling, and to present *you* faultless before the presence of his glory with exceeding joy,

Re 7:9 After this I beheld, and, lo, a great multitude, which no man could number, of all nations, and kindreds, and people, and tongues, stood before the throne, and before the Lamb, clothed with white robes, and palms in their hands;

Re 7:15 Therefore are they before the throne of God, and serve him day and night in his temple: and he that sitteth on the throne shall dwell among them.

Re 14:1 And I looked, and, lo, a Lamb stood on the mount Sion, and with him an hundred forty *and* four thousand, having his Father's name written in their foreheads.

Re 22:5 And there shall be no night there; and they need no candle, neither light of the sun; for the Lord God giveth them light: and they shall reign for ever and ever.

4. Glory Endless

Ps 73:24 Thou shalt guide me with thy counsel, and afterward receive me *to* glory.

Ps 84:11 For the LORD God *is* a sun and shield: the LORD will give grace and glory: no good *thing* will he withhold from them that walk uprightly.

Ro 2:7 To them who by patient continuance in well doing seek for glory and honour and immortality, eternal life:

Ro 8:18 For I reckon that the sufferings of this present time *are* not worthy *to be compared* with the glory which shall be revealed in us.

Ro 8:30 Moreover whom he did predestinate, them he also called: and whom he called, them he also justified: and whom he justified them he also glorified.

2 Co 4:17 For our light affliction, which is but for a moment, worketh for us a far more exceeding *and* eternal weight of glory;

Ep 1:18 The eyes of your understanding being enlightened; that ye may know what is the hope of his calling, and what the riches of the glory of his inheritance in the saints,

2 Ti 2:10 Therefore I endure all things for the elect's sakes, that they may also obtain the salvation which is in Christ Jesus with eternal glory.

1 Pe 5:1 The elders which are among you I exhort, who am also an elder, and a witness of the sufferings of Christ, and also a partaker of the glory that shall be revealed:

1 Pe 5:10 But the God of all grace, who hath called us unto his eternal glory by Christ Jesus, after that ye have suffered a while, make you perfect, stablish, strengthen, settle *you*.

5. Joy in Christ's Presence

Ps 16:11 Thou wilt shew me the path of life: in thy presence *is* fulness of joy; at thy right hand *there are* pleasures for evermore.

Mt 17:4 Then answered Peter, and said unto Jesus, Lord, it is good for us to be here: if thou wilt, let us make here three tabernacles; one for thee, and one for Moses, and one for Elias.

Mk 5:18 And when he was come into the ship, he that had been possessed with the devil prayed him that he might be with him.

Lu 22:30 That ye may eat and drink at my table in my kingdom, and sit on thrones judging the twelve tribes of Israel.

Lu 23:43 And Jesus said unto him, Verily I say unto thee, To day shalt thou be with me in paradise.

Jn 11:32 Then when Mary was come where Jesus was, and saw him, she fell down at his feet, saying unto him, Lord, if thou hadst been here, my brother had not died.

Jn 12:26 If any man serve me, let him follow me; and where I am, there shall also my servant be: if any man serve me, him will *my* Father honour.

Jn 14:3 And if I go and prepare a place for you, I will come again, and receive you unto myself; that where I am, *there* ye may be also.

Jn 17:24 Father, I will that they also, whom thou hast given me, be with me where I am; that they may behold my glory, which thou hast given me: for thou lovedst me before the foundation of the world.

2 Co 5:8 We are confident, *I say*, and willing rather to be absent from the body, and to be present with the Lord.

Ph 1:23 For I am in a strait betwixt two, having a desire to depart, and to be with Christ; which is far better:

1 Th 2:19 For what *is* our hope, or joy, or crown of rejoicing? *Are* not even ye in the presence of our Lord Jesus Christ at his coming?

1 Th 4:17 Then we which are alive *and* remain shall be caught up together with them in the clouds, to meet the Lord in the air: and so shall we ever be with the Lord.

1 Th 5:10 Who died for us, that, whether we wake or sleep, we should live together with him.

Re 7:15 Therefore are they before the throne of God, and serve him day and night in his temple: and he that sitteth on the throne shall dwell among them.

See **CROWNS, HEAVEN, HELL, PARADISE**

G

GAASH, *a hill of Mount Ephraim*
Jos 24:30; Jud 2:9; 2 S 23:30
See **MOUNTAINS AND HILLS**

GABRIEL, *an angelic messenger*
Da 8:16; 9:21; Lu 1:19, 26

GAD, *fortune*

1. Son of Jacob
Ge 30:11; 35:26; 46:16; 49:19; Ex 1:4;
Nu 1:14, 24; 2:14; 10:20; 13:15; 26:15;
32:1, 25, 33; 34:14; De 3:12; 33:20; Jos
13:8, 24; 21:7, 38; 22:9; 1 Chr 5:11;
6:63; Eze 48:28, 34; Re 7:5

2. David's Seer
1 S 22:5; 2 S 24:11; 1 Chr 29:29; 2 Chr
29:25

GADARENES, *or Gergesenes, a people
who lived east of the Sea of Galilee*
Mt 8:28; Mk 5:1; Lu 8:26

GAIN

THROUGH LOSS OF EARTHLY TREASURES
Mt 19:21 Jesus said unto him, If thou
wilt be perfect, go *and* sell that thou
hast, and give to the poor, and thou
shalt have treasure in heaven: and
come *and* follow me.

SELF-SACRIFICE, A PAYING INVESTMENT
Mt 19:29 And every one that hath
forsaken houses, or brethren, or sisters, or father, or mother, or wife, or
children, or lands, for my name's sake,
shall receive an hundredfold, and
shall inherit everlasting life.

A SPIRITUAL PARADOX
Mk 8:35 For whosoever will save his
life shall lose it; but whosoever shall
lose his life for my sake and the
gospel's, the same shall save it.

HUMILITY LEADS TO EXALTATION
Mk 9:35 And he sat down, and called
the twelve, and saith unto them, If
any man desire to be first, *the same*
shall be last of all, and servant of all.

LIFE COMES OUT OF DEATH
Jn 12:24 Verily, verily, I say unto you,
Except a corn of wheat fall into the
ground and die, it abideth alone: but
if it die, it bringeth forth much fruit.

PAUL LOST ALL AND WON THE GREAT PRIZE
Ph 3:8 Yea doubtless, and I count all
things *but* loss for the excellency of
the knowledge of Christ Jesus my
Lord: for whom I have suffered the
loss of all things, and do count them
but dung, that I may win Christ,
See **BUSINESS, LIFE**

GAIUS, *Paul's companion*
Ac 19:29; 20:4; Ro 16:23; 1 Co 1:14;
3 Jn 1

GALATIA, *a province of Asia Minor*
Ac 16:6; 18:23; 1 Co 16:1; Ga 1:2; 1 Pe
1:1

GALATIANS
Author: The apostle Paul.
Date Written: Probably between
A.D. 55 and 60.
Purpose: To defend the doctrine of
justification by faith, warn against a
reversion to Judaism, and vindicate
Paul's own apostolic authority.
To Whom Written: Addressed to
the churches in Galatia, a district in
Asia Minor, the exact boundaries of
which are uncertain.
Main Themes: This epistle has been
called the magna charta of the church.
The main argument is in favor of
Christian liberty in opposition to the

teachings of the Judaizers. These false teachers insisted that the observance of the ceremonial law was an essential part of the plan of salvation.

Key Words: Faith, Grace, Liberty, Cross.

Key Verses: 1:6; 2:11–16; 3:1–11; 4:9–11; 5:1–7; 6:15 (especially 5:1).

GALILEANS, *inhabitants of Galilee*

Mk 14:70; Lu 13:1; 22:58; 23:6; Jn 4:45; Ac 1:11; 2:7

GALILEE, *northern area of Israel*

1. A Province

Jos 20:7; 1 K 9:11; Is 9:1–2; Mt 2:22; 4:12, 25; 17:22; 19:1; 21:11; 26:32; 27:55; 28:7; Mk 1:28; 16:7; Lu 2:4, 39; 3:1; 4:14; 5:17; 8:26; 17:11; 23:6; Jn 4:3, 43, 54; 7:1, 9, 41; 12:21; Ac 1:11; 9:31

2. Sea of, *also Sea of Chinnereth, Sea of Gennesaret, Sea of Tiberias*

Nu 34:11; De 3:17; Jos 12:3; 13:27; Mt 4:15, 18; 8:24; 13:1; 14:25, 34; 15:29; 17:27; Mk 1:16; 2:13; 3:7; 4:1; 5:1, 21; 7:31; Lu 5:1; 8:22, 33; Jn 6:1, 16; 21:1

GALL, *poison, anything bitter*

De 29:18; Jb 20:14; Ps 69:21; Lam 3:19; Am 6:12; Mt 27:34; Ac 8:23

GALLOWS, *structure used to hang criminals*

Jos 8:29; 10:26; Est 5:14; 7:10; 9:13; Ga 3:13

GAMALIEL, *a celebrated doctor of the Jewish law*

Ac 5:34; 22:3

GARDENERS See **ARTS AND CRAFTS**

GARDENS See **AGRICULTURE**

GARMENTS See **DRESS**

GARRISONS, *fortresses manned by soldiers*

1 S 13:3, 23; 14:1; 2 S 8:6, 14; 23:14; 1 Chr 11:16; 18:13; 2 Chr 17:2

GATES, *an entrance and exit*

1. Of Cities and Towns

Ge 19:1; 23:10, 18; 34:20; De 16:18; 21:19; 22:15; 25:7; Jos 2:5; 20:4; Jud 5:11; 9:35, 44; 18:16; Ru 4:1, 11; 2 S 15:2; 18:24; 19:8; 1 K 22:10; 2 K 7:17; 10:8; 23:8; 1 Chr 19:9; 2 Chr 18:9; 26:9; Ne 1:3; 11:19; Jb 29:7; Ps 69:12; 127:5; Pr 1:21; 8:3; 22:22; 24:7; 31:23; Je 14:2; 17:19; Lam 5:14; Eze 48:31; Da 2:49; Zec 8:16; Lu 7:12

2. Criminals Punished

De 17:5; Ne 13:19; Is 45:2; Je 20:2; 22:19; He 13:12

3. Of Jerusalem

2 K 14:13; 2 Chr 25:23; Ne 2:13; 3:1, 13, 26; 7:3; 8:1, 16; 12:39; Je 17:19; 19:2; 31:40; 38:7; Lam 2:9

4. Of the Temple

2 K 15:35; Je 26:10; 36:10; Eze 11:1; 40:23; 43:4; 44:11; 46:1, 12; 47:2; Ac 3:2

5. Of Death, *figurative*

Jb 38:17; Ps 9:13; Is 38:10; Mt 16:18

See **CITIES**

GATH, *a city*

Jos 11:22; 1 S 5:8; 6:17; 7:14; 17:52; 21:10; 27:2; 2 S 1:20; 15:18; 21:22; 1 K 2:39; 2 K 12:17; 1 Chr 7:21; 18:1; 2 Chr 26:6; Am 6:2; Mi 1:10

See **CITIES**

GAZA, *or Azzah, a city of the Philistines*

Gaza, the most southern as well as the most famous of the five federated cities of the Philistines, was located two and a half miles from the Mediterranean Sea on a well-rounded hill 60 feet above the surrounding plain. Situated on the great coastal highway between Egypt and Mesopotamia, Gaza was at the junction of the trade route from south and central Arabia. It was an important commercial and military center from Canaanite times (Ge 10:19). Joshua and the Israelites conquered it (Jos 10:41) only to lose it again (Jos 13:3). Samson removed its large city gates (Jud 16:1–3) and ultimately returned there as a captive and wrought his final vengeance on the Philistines (Jud 16:21–31).

Ge 10:19; De 2:23; Jos 11:22; 15:44; Jud 1:18; 6:4; 16:1, 21; 1 S 6:17; 1 K 4:24; 2 K 18:8; Je 47:1, 5; Am 1:6; Zep 2:4; Zec 9:5; Ac 8:26

See **CITIES**

GEDALIAH, *a Jewish governor of Mizpeh*

2 K 25:22; Je 39:14; 40:8; 41:1, 18; 43:6

GEHAZI, *the servant of Elisha*

2 K 4:12, 31; 5:20; 8:4

GEHENNA   See **HELL**

GENEALOGIES, *history of one's ancestry*

1. Of Christ

Mt 1:1–14; Lu 3:23–28

2. Of David

1 Chr 3

See **CHRIST, DAVID**

GENERATION, *EVIL*

De 1:35; 2:14; 32:5, 20; Jud 2:10; 1 S 8:8; Ps 78:8; 95:10; Pr 30:12; Je 7:29; Ho 2:4; Mt 3:7; 11:16; 12:34, 39, 45; 16:4; Mk 8:12, 38; Lu 3:7; 7:31; 9:41; 11:29, 50; 17:25; Ac 2:40; Ph 2:15; He 3:10

See **WICKED**

GENESIS

Author: Moses (commonly accepted).

Date Written: 1450–1410 B.C.

Purpose: The Book of Origins.

A record of the origin of our universe, the human race, sin, redemption, family life, corruption of society, the nations, the different languages, and the Hebrew race. The early chapters of the book have been continually under the fire of modern criticism. But the facts they present, when rightly interpreted

and understood, have never been disproved. It is not the purpose of the author of Genesis to give an elaborate account of the creation. Only a single chapter is devoted to the subject, just a bare outline containing a few fundamental facts, while thirty-eight chapters are given to an account of the history of the chosen family.

To Whom Written: The people of Israel.

Main Theme: Sin and the initial steps taken for redemption by a divine covenant made with a chosen race whose early history is here portrayed.

Key Word: Beginning.

Key Verse: First Messianic Promise (3:15).

GENTILE BELIEVERS

Mt 8:10 When Jesus heard *it*, he marvelled, and said to them that followed, Verily I say unto you, I have not found so great faith, no, not in Israel.

Lu 7:2–3 And a certain centurion's servant, who was dear unto him, was sick, and ready to die.

And when he heard of Jesus, he sent unto him the elders of the Jews, beseeching him that he would come and heal his servant.

Lu 7:9 When Jesus heard these things, he marvelled at him, and turned him about, and said unto the people that followed him, I say unto you, I have not found so great faith, no, not in Israel.

Lu 23:47 Now when the centurion saw what was done, he glorified God, saying, Certainly this was a righteous man.

Jn 10:16 And other sheep I have, which are not of this fold: them also I must bring, and they shall hear my voice; and there shall be one fold, *and* one shepherd.

Ac 8:12 But when they believed Philip preaching the things concerning the kingdom of God, and the name of Jesus Christ, they were baptized, both men and women.

Ac 10:1–2 There was a certain man in Caesarea called Cornelius, a centurion of the band called the Italian *band,*

A devout *man,* and one that feared God with all his house, which gave much alms to the people, and prayed to God alway.

Ac 10:7 And when the angel which spake unto Cornelius was departed, he called two of his household servants, and a devout soldier of them that waited on him continually;

Ac 18:7 And he departed thence, and entered into a certain *man's* house, named Justus, *one* that worshipped God, whose house joined hard to the synagogue.

Ro 9:30 What shall we say then? That the Gentiles, which followed not after righteousness, have attained to righteousness, even the righteousness which is of faith.

Ro 15:12 And again, Esaias saith, There shall be a root of Jesse, and he that shall rise to reign over the Gentiles; in him shall the Gentiles trust.

See **FAITH, SALVATION, TRUST**

GENTILES *See* **MISSIONS**

GENTLENESS

1. Divine

2 S 22:36; Ps 18:35; Is 40:11; 42:3; Mt 12:20; Mk 10:16; 2 Co 10:1; 1 Th 2:7

2. Human

1 Th 2:7 But we were gentle among you, even as a nurse cherisheth her children:

1 Ti 3:3 Not given to wine, no striker, not greedy of filthy lucre; but patient, not a brawler, not covetous;

2 Ti 2:24 And the servant of the Lord must not strive; but be gentle unto all *men,* apt to teach, patient,

Tit 3:2 To speak evil of no man, to be no brawlers, *but* gentle, shewing all meekness unto all men.

Ja 3:17 But the wisdom that is from above is first pure, then peaceable, gentle, *and* easy to be intreated, full of mercy and good fruits, without partiality, and without hypocrisy.

See **GOODNESS**

GERAH, *a denomination of money*

Ex 30:13; Le 27:25

See **WEIGHTS AND MEASURES**

GERAR, *a city south of Gaza*

Gerar was the place where both Abraham and Isaac sojourned for a time, dug wells, and prospered under the generous treatment of "Abimelech King of Gerar" (Ge 20 and 26).

Ge 10:19; 20:1; 26:6; 2 Chr 14:13

See **CITIES**

GERIZIM *See* **MOUNTAINS AND HILLS**

GERSHON, *son of Levi*

Ge 46:11; Ex 6:16; Nu 3:17; 4:28; 26:57; Jos 21:6, 27; 1 Chr 6:1, 17; 15:7; 23:6

GERSHONITES, *descendants of Gershon*

Nu 3:25; 4:24, 38; 7:7; 10:17; Jos 21:33; 1 Chr 6:62, 71; 23:7; 2 Chr 29:12

GESHUR, *in Bashan*

De 3:14; Jos 13:2; 1 S 27:8; 2 S 3:3; 13:37; 14:23; 15:8; 1 Chr 3:2

GETHSEMANE, *a garden near Jerusalem*

The Garden of Gethsemane was an olive orchard across the brook Kidron from Jerusalem on the western slope of the Mount of Olives. It was a secluded retreat where Jesus often went with his disciples, and where he agonized in prayer before his betrayal by Judas (Lu 22:39–44).

Mt 26:36; Mk 14:32; Lu 22:39; Jn 18:1

GEZER, *a hilltop overlooking the Maritime Plain*

Eighteen miles west of Jerusalem, it guarded the pass from Joppa to Jerusalem and the highway from Egypt to Syria. This made it one of the most strategically located cities of Palestine. It switched hands between Egypt and Palestine a number of times and played an important role in the history of these two countries (e.g., Jos 10:33; Jud 1:29; 2 S 5:25). On the occasion of King Solomon's marriage to an Egyptian princess, it was given to her as a present from her father (1 K 9:16).

See **CITIES**

GIANTS, *abnormally tall and powerful human beings of ancient times*

Ge 6:4; 14:5; Nu 13:33; De 2:11, 20; 3:11; 9:2; Jos 12:4; 13:12; 17:15; 18:16; 1 S 17:4; 2 S 21:16, 20; 1 Chr 11:23; 20:4; Am 2:9

1. Anakim

Nu 13:22, 28, 33; De 1:28; 2:10, 21; 9:2; Jos 11:21; 14:12, 15; 15:14; 21:11; Jud 1:20

2. Emim

Ge 14:5; De 2:11

GIBEAH, *a city of Benjamin*

Jud 19:12; 20:4, 13, 19, 31, 43; 1 S 10:26; 11:4; 13:15; 14:2; 15:34; 22:6; 23:19; 26:1; 2 S 21:6; 23:29; 1 Chr 11:31; Is 10:29; Ho 5:8; 9:9; 10:9

See **CITIES**

GIBEON, *a city of the Hivites*

Gibeon lies seven miles northwest of Jerusalem. It was the home of the Gibeonites who traveled to Gilgal and tricked Joshua into making a treaty with them as servants (Jos 9:3–27); the place where the soldiers of Abner and Joab held a contest "by the pool of Gibeon" (2 S 2:12–17); and the location of the tabernacle after it was moved from Nob until Solomon's temple was completed. Here Solomon prepared a great feast, had a wonderful dream, and chose God and wisdom rather than riches and honor (2 Chr 1:3–13).

Jos 9:3, 17; 10:1, 12; 11:19; 18:25; 21:17; 2 S 2:12; 21:2; 1 K 3:4; 1 Chr 14:16; 16:39; 21:29; 2 Chr 1:3; Ne 3:7; 7:25; Is 28:21; Je 28:1

See **CITIES**

GIDEON, *or Jerubbaal, a judge of Israel*

He was the son of Joash, of the tribe of Manasseh (Jud 6:11). In his day Israel had forsaken God and was being terrorized by the Midianite robbers who desolated the country and made life intolerable (6:1–5). As usual in times of distress Israel repented and "cried unto the Lord" (6:6). A prophet was sent to rebuke the sinful people (6:7–10). Then an angel appeared and summoned Gideon to leadership (6:11–12). The outstanding event in Gideon's life was the battle with Midianites that he waged with only three hundred men (7:2–8). He conquered them and was offered the crown of Israel (8:22–23). He later made a golden ephod that became a snare to Israel (8:24–27). He died in a good old age (8:32). How to face severe tests with faith is the great lesson of his life.

HUMILITY

Jud 6:15 And he said unto him, Oh my Lord, wherewith shall I save Israel? behold, my family is poor in Manasseh, and I *am* the least in my father's house.

CAUTION

Jud 6:17 And he said unto him, If now I have found grace in thy sight, then shew me a sign that thou talkest with me.

SPIRITUALITY

Jud 6:24 Then Gideon built an altar there unto the LORD, and called it Jehovah-shalom: unto this day it is yet in Ophrah of the Abi-ezrites.

OBEDIENCE

Jud 6:27 Then Gideon took ten men of his servants, and did as the LORD had said unto him: and *so* it was, because he feared his father's household, and the men of the city, that he could not do *it* by day, that he did *it* by night.

DIVINE INSPIRATION

Jud 6:34 But the Spirit of the LORD came upon Gideon, and he blew a trumpet; and Abi-ezer was gathered after him.

DIVINE FELLOWSHIP

Jud 6:36 And Gideon said unto God, If thou wilt save Israel by mine hand, as thou hast said,

Jud 7:4 And the LORD said unto Gideon, The people *are* yet *too* many; bring them down unto the water, and I will try them for thee there: and it shall be, *that* of whom I say unto thee, This shall go with thee, the same shall go with thee; and of whomsoever I say unto thee, This shall not go with thee, the same shall not go.

Jud 7:7 And the LORD said unto Gideon, By the three hundred men that lapped will I save you, and deliver the Midianites into thine hand: and let all the *other* people go every man unto his place.

Jud 7:9 And it came to pass the same night, that the LORD said unto him, Arise, get thee down unto the host; for I have delivered it into thine hand.

STRATEGY

Jud 7:16–18 And he divided the three hundred men *into* three companies, and he put a trumpet in every man's hand, with empty pitchers, and lamps within the pitchers.

And he said unto them, Look on me, and do likewise: and, behold, when I come to the outside of the camp, it shall be *that,* as I do, so shall ye do.

When I blow with a trumpet, I and all that *are* with me, then blow ye the trumpets also on every side of all the camp, and say, *The sword* of the LORD, and of Gideon.

TACT

Jud 8:1–3 And the men of Ephraim said unto him, Why hast thou served us thus, that thou calledst us not, when thou wentest to fight with the Midianites? And they did chide with him sharply.

And he said unto them, What have I done now in comparison of you? *Is* not the gleaning of the grapes of Ephraim better than the vintage of Abi-ezer?

God hath delivered into your hands the princes of Midian, Oreb and Zeeb: and what was I able to do in comparison of you? Then their anger was abated toward him, when he had said that.

LOYALTY TO GOD

Jud 8:22–23 Then the men of Israel said unto Gideon, Rule thou over us, both thou, and thy son, and thy son's son also: for thou hast delivered us from the hand of Midian.

And Gideon said unto them, I will not rule over you, neither shall my son rule over you: the LORD shall rule over you.

WEAKENED BY PROSPERITY

Jud 8:27 And Gideon made an ephod thereof, and put it in his city, *even* in Ophrah: and all Israel went thither a whoring after it: which thing became a snare unto Gideon, and to his house.

See **ISRAEL**

GIFTS, *DIVINE*

1. Their Diversity

Da 1:17 As for these four children, God gave them knowledge and skill in all learning and wisdom: and Daniel had understanding in all visions and dreams.

Mt 25:15 And unto one he gave five talents, to another two, and to another one; to every man according to his several ability; and straightway took his journey.

Ro 12:6 Having then gifts differing according to the grace that is given to us, whether prophecy, *let us prophesy* according to the proportion of faith;

1 Co 4:7 For who maketh thee to differ *from another?* and what hast thou that thou didst not receive? now if thou didst receive *it,* why dost thou glory, as if thou hadst not received *it?*

1 Co 12:1 Now concerning spiritual *gifts,* brethren, I would not have you ignorant.

1 Co 12:4 Now there are diversities of gifts, but the same Spirit.

1 Co 14:26 How is it then, brethren? when ye come together, every one of you hath a psalm, hath a doctrine, hath a tongue, hath a revelation, hath an interpretation. Let all things be done unto edifying.

Ep 4:11 And he gave some, apostles; and some, prophets; and some, evangelists; and some, pastors and teachers;

2. Spiritual

AN EVERLASTING NAME

Is 56:4 For thus saith the LORD unto the eunuchs that keep my sabbaths, and choose *the things* that please me, and take hold of my covenant;

Is 56:5 Even unto them will I give in mine house and within my walls a place and a name better than of sons and of daughters: I will give them an everlasting name, that shall not be cut off.

SPIRITUAL KNOWLEDGE

Je 24:7 And I will give them an heart to know me, that I *am* the LORD: and they shall be my people, and I will be their God: for they shall return unto me with their whole heart.

A NEW HEART

Eze 11:19 And I will give them one heart, and I will put a new spirit within you; and I will take the stony heart out of their flesh, and will give them an heart of flesh:

SPIRITUAL REST

Mt 11:28 Come unto me, all *ye* that labour and are heavy laden, and I will give you rest.

THE HOLY SPIRIT

Lu 11:13 If ye then, being evil, know how to give good gifts unto your children: how much more shall *your* heavenly Father give the Holy Spirit to them that ask him?

ETERNAL LIFE

Jn 10:28 And I give unto them eternal life; and they shall never perish, neither shall any *man* pluck them out of my hand.

Ja 1:17 Every good gift and every perfect gift is from above, and cometh down from the Father of lights, with whom is no variableness, neither shadow of turning.

Re 2:10 Fear none of those things which thou shalt suffer: behold, the devil shall cast *some* of you into prison, that ye may be tried; and ye shall have tribulation ten days: be thou faithful unto death, and I will give thee a crown of life.

Re 2:17 He that hath an ear, let him hear what the Spirit saith unto the churches; To him that overcometh will I give to eat of the hidden manna, and will give him a white stone, and in the stone a new name written, which no man knoweth saving he that receiveth *it*.

3. Temporal

Ge 1:29 And God said, Behold, I have given you every herb bearing seed, which *is* upon the face of all the earth, and every tree, in the which *is* the fruit of a tree yielding seed; to you it shall be for meat.

Ge 9:3 Every moving thing that liveth shall be meat for you; even as the green herb have I given you all things.

De 8:18 But thou shalt remember the LORD thy God: for *it is* he that giveth thee power to get wealth, that he may establish his covenant which he sware unto thy fathers, as *it is* this day.

De 11:14 That I will give *you* the rain of your land in his due season, the first rain and the latter rain, that thou mayest gather in thy corn, and thy wine, and thine oil.

Ru 1:6 Then she arose with her daughters in law, that she might return from the country of Moab: for she had heard in the country of Moab how that the LORD had visited his people in giving them bread.

Jb 5:10 Who giveth rain upon the earth, and sendeth waters upon the fields:

Ps 127:2 *It is* vain for you to rise up early, to sit up late, to eat the bread of sorrows: *for* so he giveth his beloved sleep.

Ps 136:25 Who giveth food to all flesh: for his mercy *endureth* for ever.

Ps 145:15 The eyes of all wait upon thee; and thou givest them their meat in due season.

Ec 5:19 Every man also to whom God hath given riches and wealth, and hath given him power to eat thereof, and to take his portion, and to rejoice in his labour; this *is* the gift of God.

Jl 2:23 Be glad then, ye children of Zion, and rejoice in the LORD your God: for he hath given you the former rain moderately, and he will cause to come down for you the rain, the former rain, and the latter rain in the first *month.*

Mt 7:11 If ye then, being evil, know how to give good gifts unto your children, how much more shall your Father which is in heaven give good things to them that ask him?

4. Seven Given to Believers

REST

Mt 11:28 Come unto me, all *ye* that labour and are heavy laden, and I will give you rest.

KEYS OF THE KINGDOM

Mt 16:19 And I will give unto thee the keys of the kingdom of heaven: and whatsoever thou shalt bind on earth shall be bound in heaven: and whatsoever thou shalt loose on earth shall be loosed in heaven.

POWER OVER EVIL SPIRITS

Lu 10:19 Behold, I give unto you power to tread on serpents and scorpions, and over all the power of the enemy: and nothing shall by any means hurt you.

LIVING WATER

Jn 4:14 But whosoever drinketh of the water that I shall give him shall never thirst; but the water that I shall give him shall be in him a well of water springing up into everlasting life.

BREAD OF HEAVEN

Jn 6:51 I am the living bread which came down from heaven: if any man eat of this bread, he shall live for ever: and the bread that I will give is my flesh, which I will give for the life of the world.

ETERNAL LIFE

Jn 10:28 And I give unto them eternal life; and they shall never perish, neither shall any *man* pluck them out of my hand.

PEACE

Jn 14:27 Peace I leave with you, my peace I give unto you: not as the world giveth, give I unto you. Let not your heart be troubled neither let it be afraid.

Re 2:26 And he that overcometh, and keepeth my works unto the end, to him will I give power over the nations:

Re 2:28 And I will give him the morning star.

Re 21:6 And he said unto me, It is done. I am Alpha and Omega, the beginning and the end. I will give unto him that is athirst of the fountain of the water of life freely.

5. Distribution

THROUGH UNDERSTANDING

Jb 32:8 But *there is* a spirit in man: and the inspiration of the Almighty giveth them understanding.

ACCORDING TO CHARACTER

Ec 2:26 For *God* giveth to a man that *is* good in his sight wisdom, and knowledge, and joy: but to the sinner he giveth travail, to gather and to heap up, that he may give to *him that is* good before God. This also *is* vanity and vexation of spirit.

FOR COMFORT

Is 50:4 The Lord GOD hath given me the tongue of the learned, that I should know how to speak a word in season to *him that is* weary: he wakeneth morning by morning, ear to hear as the learned.

Mt 9:8 But when the multitudes saw *it,* they marvelled, and glorified God, which had given such power unto men.

ACCORDING TO ABILITY

Mt 25:15 And unto one he gave five talents, to another two, and to another one; to every man according to his several ability; and straightway took his journey.

TO THOSE WHO ASK

Lu 11:9 And I say unto you, Ask, and it shall be given you; seek, and ye shall find; knock, and it shall be opened unto you.

FROM HEAVEN

Jn 3:27 John answered and said, A man can receive nothing, except it be given him from heaven.

WITHOUT REASON FOR PRIDE

1 Co 4:7 For who maketh thee to differ *from another?* and what hast thou that thou didst not receive? now if thou didst receive *it,* why dost thou glory, as if thou hadst not received *it?*

WITH WISDOM

Ja 1:5 If any of you lack wisdom, let him ask of God, that giveth to all *men* liberally, and upbraideth not; and it shall be given him.

6. Cultivation

Mt 25:20 And so he that had received five talents came and brought other five talents, saying, Lord, thou deliveredst unto me five talents: behold, I have gained beside them five talents more.

1 Ti 4:7 But refuse profane and old wives' fables, and exercise thyself *rather* unto godliness.

1 Ti 4:14 Neglect not the gift that is in thee, which was given thee by prophecy, with the laying on of the hands of the presbytery.

2 Ti 1:6 Wherefore I put thee in remembrance that thou stir up the gift of God, which is in thee by the putting on of my hands.

See **PRESENTS**

GIHON, *a gushing fountain*

The Jebusite inhabitants of Jerusalem dug a deep underground channel or tunnel westward from the fountain, under the walls, and into the city so that they might draw water without having to go outside the walls. It also enabled them to obtain all the water they needed in time of siege without being exposed to the enemy. This tunnel from the spring is supposed to have been the water shaft by which Joab led his warriors into the city, took the garrison by surprise, and became David's general (2 S 5:6–10; 1 Chr 11:4–7).

After the conquest of Jerusalem by David, this underground tunnel was needed less and less, for David seems to have constructed upper and lower reservoirs (pools) for collecting the water for domestic use and for the irrigation of the gardens in the "Kings Valley" below.

Solomon was anointed king at the spring of Gihon and rode David's royal mule back into the city (1 K 1:33, 38), thus signifying to the people that he was their king, as his father had been before him. Hezekiah cut a conduit to take water from the spring to the pool of Siloam (2 Chr 32:30).

1. A River

Ge 2:13

2. A Pool

1 K 1:33, 45; 2 K 18:17; 20:20; 2 Chr 32:30; 33:14; Ne 2:14; Is 7:3

GILBOA *See* **MOUNTAINS AND HILLS**

GILEAD, *to be rough*

1. Land of, *east of the Jordan*

Nu 32:1, 29, 40; De 3:10; Jos 17:6; 22:9; Jud 10:4, 8, 18; 11:5; 12:4; 20:1; 1 S 13:7; 2 S 17:26; 24:6; 1 K 4:13; 17:1; 2 K 10:33; 1 Chr 5:9; Ps 108:8; Je 22:6; 46:11; Eze 47:18; Ho 12:11; Am 1:3; Obad 19; Zec 10:10

2. Grandson of Manasseh

Nu 26:29; 27:1

GILEAD See **MOUNTAINS AND HILLS**

GILGAL, *rolling*

Gilgal was Israel's first camping place after crossing the Jordan. Here they erected twelve memorial stones from the bed of the Jordan, circumcised the males, and kept the Passover (Jos 4–5). Israel encamped here while taking the city of Jericho, while making a treaty with the Gibeonites, and while launching the campaign against the five Amorite kings (Jos 6–10). Gilgal remained a rallying point for Israel for many generations to come. The city is described in the Bible as located "on the eastern edge of Jericho" (Jos 4:19).

De 11:30; Jos 4:19; 5:9; 9:6; 10:6, 15, 43; 15:7; Jud 3:19; 1 S 7:16; 10:8; 11:14; 13:4, 7; 15:12; 2 S 19:15, 40; 2 K 2:1; 4:38; Ho 4:15; 9:15; Am 4:4

GIRDLE, *referring to a number of different garments*

1. An Article of Dress

Ex 28:4, 8, 27, 39; 29:5, 9; 39:5, 21, 29; Le 8:7, 13; 16:4; 1 S 18:4; 2 K 1:8; Pr 31:24; Is 5:27; Eze 23:15; Da 10:5; Mt 3:4; Mk 1:6; Ac 21:11

2. Figurative

Pr 31:17; Is 11:5; 22:21; Je 13:1; Lu 12:35; Ep 6:14; Re 1:13; 15:6

See **APPAREL**

GIRGASHITES, *a Canaanite nation*

Ge 10:16; De 7:1; Jos 3:10; 24:11; Ne 9:8

See **NATION**

GIVING, *a privilege and requirement*

1. To God

Ex 23:15 Thou shalt keep the feast of unleavened bread: (thou shalt eat unleavened bread seven days, as I commanded thee, in the time appointed of the month Abib; for in it thou camest out from Egypt: and none shall appear before me empty:)

Ex 23:19 The first of the firstfruits of thy land thou shalt bring into the house of the LORD thy God. Thou shalt not seethe a kid in his mother's milk.

Ex 25:2 Speak unto the children of Israel, that they bring me an offering: of every man that giveth it willingly with his heart ye shall take my offering.

Ex 27:20 And thou shalt command the children of Israel, that they bring thee pure oil olive beaten for the light, to cause the lamp to burn always.

Ex 30:12 When thou takest the sum of the children of Israel after their number, then shall they give every man a ransom for his soul unto the LORD, when thou numberest them; that there be no plague among them, when *thou* numberest them.

Ex 34:20 But the firstling of an ass thou shalt redeem with a lamb: and if thou redeem *him* not, then shalt thou break his neck. All the firstborn of thy sons thou shalt redeem. And none shall appear before me empty.

Ex 35:5 Take ye from among you an offering unto the LORD: whosoever *is* of a willing heart, let him bring it, an offering of the LORD; gold, and silver, and brass,

Ex 35:21 And they came, every one whose heart stirred him up, and every one whom his spirit made willing, *and* they brought the LORD's offering to the work of the tabernacle of the congregation, and for all his service, and for the holy garments.

Le 7:30 His own hands shall bring the offerings of the LORD made by fire, the fat with the breast, it shall he bring, that the breast may be waved *for* a wave offering before the LORD.

Le 27:28 Notwithstanding no devoted thing, that a man shall devote unto the LORD of all that he hath, *both* of man and beast, and of the field of his possession, shall be sold or redeemed: every devoted thing *is* most holy unto the LORD.

Nu 7:2 That the princes of Israel, heads of the house of their fathers, who *were* the princes of the tribes, and were over them that were numbered, offered:

Nu 7:13 And his offering *was* one silver charger, the weight thereof *was* an hundred and thirty *shekels,* one silver bowl of seventy shekels, after the shekel of the sanctuary; both of them *were* full of fine flour mingled with oil for a meat offering:

Nu 7:25 His offering *was* one silver charger, the weight whereof *was* an hundred and thirty *shekels,* one silver bowl of seventy shekels, after the shekel of the sanctuary; both of them full of fine flour mingled with oil for a meat offering:

Nu 7:49 His offering *was* one silver charger, the weight whereof *was* an hundred and thirty *shekels,* one silver bowl of seventy shekels, after the shekel of the sanctuary; both of them full of fine flour mingled with oil for a meat offering:

Nu 7:79 His offering *was* one silver charger, the weight whereof *was* an hundred and thirty *shekels,* one silver bowl of seventy shekels, after the shekel of the sanctuary; both of them full of fine flour mingled with oil for a meat offering:

Nu 15:21 Of the first of your dough ye shall give unto the LORD an heave offering in your generations.

Nu 18:13 *And* whatsoever is first ripe in the land, which they shall bring unto the LORD, shall be thine; every one that is clean in thine house shall eat *of* it.

Nu 18:29 Out of all your gifts ye shall offer every heave offering of the LORD, of all the best thereof, *even* the hallowed part thereof out of it.

Nu 28:2 Command the children of Israel, and say unto them, My offering, *and* my bread for my sacrifices made by fire, *for* a sweet savour unto me, shall ye observe to offer unto me in their due season.

Nu 31:50 We have therefore brought an oblation for the LORD, what every man hath gotten, of jewels of gold, chains, and bracelets, rings, earrings, and tablets, to make an atonement for our souls before the LORD.

De 26:2 That thou shalt take of the first of all the fruit of the earth, which thou shalt bring of thy land that the LORD thy God giveth thee, and shalt put *it* in a basket, and shalt go unto the place which the LORD thy God shall choose to place his name there.

2 S 8:10–11 Then Toi sent Joram his son unto king David, to salute him, and to bless him, because he had fought against Hadadezer, and smitten him: for Hadadezer had wars with Toi. And *Joram* brought with him vessels of silver, and vessels of gold, and vessels of brass:

Which also king David did dedicate unto the LORD, with the silver and gold that he had dedicated of all nations which he subdued;

1 K 15:15 And he brought in the things which his father had dedicated, and the things which himself had dedicated, into the house of the LORD, silver, and gold, and vessels.

2 K 12:4 And Jehoash said to the priests, All the money of the dedicated things that is brought into the house of the LORD, *even* the money of every one that passeth *the account,* the money that every man is set at, *and* all the money that cometh into any man's heart to bring into the house of the LORD,

1 Chr 18:11 Them also king David dedicated unto the LORD, with the silver and the gold that he brought from all *these* nations; from Edom, and from Moab, and from the children of Ammon, and from the Philistines, and from Amalek.

1 Chr 26:27 Out of the spoils won in battles did they dedicate to maintain the house of the LORD.

1 Chr 29:7 And gave for the service of the house of God of gold five thousand talents and ten thousand drams, and of silver ten thousand talents, and of brass eighteen thousand talents, and one hundred thousand talents of iron.

1 Chr 29:9 Then the people rejoiced, for that they offered willingly, because with perfect heart they offered willingly to the LORD: and David the king also rejoiced with great joy.

1 Chr 29:17 I know also, my God, that thou triest the heart, and hast pleasure in uprightness. As for me, in the uprightness of mine heart I have willingly offered all these things: and now have I seen with joy thy people, which are present here, to offer willingly unto thee.

2 Chr 15:18 And he brought into the house of God the things that his father had dedicated, and that he himself had dedicated, silver, and gold, and vessels.

2 Chr 29:31 Then Hezekiah answered and said, Now ye have consecrated yourselves unto the LORD, come near and bring sacrifices and thank offerings into the house of the LORD. And the congregation brought in sacrifices and thank offerings; and as many as were of a free heart burnt offerings.

2 Chr 31:6 And *concerning* the children of Israel and Judah, that dwelt in the cities of Judah, they also brought in the tithe of oxen and sheep, and the tithe of holy things which were consecrated unto the LORD their God, and laid *them* by heaps.

2 Chr 32:23 And many brought gifts unto the LORD to Jerusalem, and presents to Hezekiah king of Judah: so that he was magnified in the sight of all nations from thenceforth.

2 Chr 35:8 And his princes gave willingly unto the people, to the priests, and to the Levites: Hilkiah and Zechariah and Jehiel, rulers of the house of God, gave unto the priests for the passover offerings two thousand and six hundred *small cattle,* and three hundred oxen.

Ezr 2:68 And *some* of the chief of the fathers, when they came to the house of the LORD which *is* at Jerusalem, offered freely for the house of God to set it up in his place:

Ezr 6:4 *With* three rows of great stones, and a row of new timber: and let the expences be given out of the king's house:

Ezr 7:16 And all the silver and gold that thou canst find in all the province of Babylon, with the freewill offering of the people, and of the priests, offering willingly for the house of their God which *is* in Jerusalem:

Ezr 8:28 And I said unto them, Ye *are* holy unto the LORD; the vessels *are* holy also; and the silver and the gold *are* a freewill offering unto the LORD God of your fathers.

Ne 10:32 Also we made ordinances for us, to charge ourselves yearly with the third part of a shekel for the service of the house of our God;

Ne 12:44 And at that time were some appointed over the chambers for the treasures, for the offerings, for the firstfruits, and for the tithes, to gather into them out of the fields of the cities the portions of the law for the priests and Levites: for Judah rejoiced for the priests and for the Levites that waited.

Ps 66:15 I will offer unto thee burnt sacrifices of fatlings, with the incense of rams; I will offer bullocks with goats. Selah.

Ps 76:11 Vow, and pay unto the LORD your God: let all that be round about him bring presents unto him that ought to be feared.

Ps 96:8 Give unto the LORD the glory *due unto* his name: bring an offering, and come into his courts.

Pr 3:9 Honour the LORD with thy substance, and with the firstfruits of all thine increase:

Is 60:9 Surely the isles shall wait for me, and the ships of Tarshish first, to bring thy sons from far, their silver and their gold with them, unto the name of the LORD thy God, and to the Holy One of Israel, because he hath glorified thee.

Je 17:26 And they shall come from the cities of Judah, and from the places about Jerusalem, and from the land of Benjamin, and from the plain, and from the mountains, and from the south, bringing burnt offerings, and sacrifices, and meat offerings, and incense, and bringing sacrifices of praise, unto the house of the LORD.

Je 41:5 That there came certain from Shechem, from Shiloh, and from Samaria, *even* fourscore men, having their beards shaven, and their clothes rent, and having cut themselves, with offerings and incense in their hand, to bring *them* to the house of the LORD.

Eze 20:40 For in mine holy mountain, in the mountain of the height of Israel, saith the Lord GOD, there shall all the house of Israel, all of them in the land, serve me: there will I accept them, and there will I require your offerings, and the firstfruits of your oblations, with all your holy things.

Eze 45:17 And it shall be the prince's part *to give* burnt offerings, and meat offerings, and drink offerings, in the feasts, and in the new moons, and in the sabbaths, in all solemnities of the house of Israel: he shall prepare the sin offering, and the meat offering, and the burnt offering, and the peace offerings, to make reconciliation for the house of Israel.

Mi 4:13 Arise and thresh, O daughter of Zion: for I will make thine horn iron, and I will make thy hoofs brass: and thou shalt beat in pieces many people: and I will consecrate their gain unto the LORD, and their substance unto the Lord of the whole earth.

Mk 12:41 And Jesus sat over against the treasury, and beheld how the people cast money into the treasury: and many that were rich cast in much.

Lu 21:4 For all these have of their abundance cast in unto the offerings of God: but she of her penury hath cast in all the living that she had.

Ac 4:37 Having land, sold *it,* and brought the money, and laid *it* at the apostles' feet.

Ac 24:17 Now after many years I came to bring alms to my nation, and offerings.

Ph 4:15 Now ye Philippians know also, that in the beginning of the gospel, when I departed from Macedonia, no church communicated with me as concerning giving and receiving, but ye only.

a. Scriptural Rules

ACCORDING TO INCOME

De 16:17 Every man *shall give* as he is able, according to the blessing of the LORD thy God which he hath given thee.

Mt 5:42 Give to him that asketh thee, and from him that would borrow of thee turn not thou away.

WITHOUT OSTENTATION

Mt 6:3 But when thou doest alms, let not thy left hand know what thy right hand doeth:

FREELY

Mt 10:8 Heal the sick, cleanse the lepers, raise the dead, cast out devils: freely ye have received, freely give.

Lu 6:38 Give, and it shall be given unto you; good measure, pressed down, and shaken together, and running over, shall men give into your bosom. For with the same measure that ye mete withal it shall be measured to you again.

Lu 12:33 Sell that ye have, and give alms; provide yourselves bags which wax not old, a treasure in the heavens that faileth not, where no thief approacheth, neither moth corrupteth.

WITH SIMPLICITY

Ro 12:8 Or he that exhorteth, on exhortation: he that giveth, *let him do it* with simplicity; he that ruleth, with diligence; he that sheweth mercy, with cheerfulness.

REGULARLY

1 Co 16:2 Upon the first *day* of the week let every one of you lay by him in store, as *God* hath prospered him, that there be no gatherings when I come.

CHEERFULLY

2 Co 9:7 Every man according as he purposeth in his heart, *so let him give;* not grudgingly, or of necessity: for God loveth a cheerful giver.

b. According to Ability

Le 14:30 And he shall offer the one of the turtledoves, or of the young pigeons, such as he can get;

Le 27:8 But if he be poorer than thy estimation, then he shall present himself before the priest, and the priest shall value him; according to his ability that vowed shall the priest value him.

De 16:17 Every man *shall give* as he is able, according to the blessing of the LORD thy God which he hath given thee.

Ezr 2:69 They gave after their ability unto the treasure of the work threescore and one thousand drams of gold, and five thousand pound of silver, and one hundred priests' garments.

Ne 5:8 And I said unto them, We after our ability have redeemed our brethren the Jews, which were sold unto the heathen; and will ye even sell your brethren? or shall they be sold unto us? Then held they their peace, and found nothing *to answer.*

Ac 11:29 Then the disciples, every man according to his ability, determined to send relief unto the brethren which dwelt in Judaea:

2 Co 8:12 For if there be first a willing mind, *it is* accepted according to that a man hath, *and* not according to that he hath not.

c. Tithes

Ge 14:20 And blessed be the most high God, which hath delivered thine enemies into thy hand. And he gave him tithes of all.

Ge 28:22 And this stone, which I have set *for* a pillar, shall be God's house: and of all that thou shalt give me I will surely give the tenth unto thee.

Nu 18:21 And, behold, I have given the children of Levi all the tenth in Israel for an inheritance, for their service which they serve, *even* the service of the tabernacle of the congregation.

Le 27:30 And all the tithe of the land, *whether* of the seed of the land, or of the fruit of the tree, *is* the LORD's: *it is* holy unto the LORD.

Nu 18:21 And, behold, I have given the children of Levi all the tenth in Israel for an inheritance, for their service which they serve, *even* the service of the tabernacle of the congregation.

Nu 18:24 But the tithes of the children of Israel, which they offer *as* an heave offering unto the LORD, I have given to the Levites to inherit: therefore I have said unto them, Among the children of Israel they shall have no inheritance.

De 12:6 And thither ye shall bring your burnt offerings, and your sacrifices, and your tithes, and heave offerings of your hand, and your vows, and your freewill offerings, and the firstlings of your herds and of your flocks:

De 12:11 Then there shall be a place which the LORD your God shall choose to cause his name to dwell there; thither shall ye bring all that I command you; your burnt offerings, and your sacrifices, your tithes, and the heave offering of your hand, and all your choice vows which ye vow unto the LORD:

De 12:17 Thou mayest not eat within thy gates the tithe of thy corn, or of thy wine, or of thy oil, or the firstlings of thy herds or of thy flock, nor any of thy vows which thou vowest, nor thy freewill offerings, or heave offering of thine hand:

De 14:22 Thou shalt truly tithe all the increase of thy seed, that the field bringeth forth year by year.

De 14:28 At the end of three years thou shalt bring forth all the tithe of thine increase the same year, and shalt lay *it* up within thy gates:

De 26:12 When thou hast made an end of tithing all the tithes of thine increase the third year, *which is* the year of tithing, and hast given *it* unto the Levite, the stranger, the fatherless, and the widow, that they may eat within thy gates, and be filled;

2 Chr 31:5 And as soon as the commandment came abroad, the children of Israel brought in abundance the firstfruits of corn, wine, and oil, and honey, and of all the increase of the field; and the tithe of all *things* brought they in abundantly.

2 Chr 31:12 And brought in the offerings and the tithes and the dedicated *things* faithfully: over which Cononiah the Levite *was* ruler, and Shimei his brother *was* the next.

Ne 10:37–38 And *that* we should bring the firstfruits of our dough, and our offerings, and the fruit of all manner of trees, of wine and of oil, unto the priests, to the chambers of the house of our God; and the tithes of our ground unto the Levites, that the same Levites might have the tithes in all the cities of our tillage.

And the priest the son of Aaron shall be with the Levites, when the Levites take tithes: and the Levites shall bring up the tithe of the tithes unto the house of our God, to the chambers, into the treasure house.

Ne 12:44 And at that time were some appointed over the chambers for the treasures, for the offerings, for the firstfruits, and for the tithes, to gather into them out of the fields of the cities the portions of the law for the priests and Levites: for Judah rejoiced for the priests and for the Levites that waited.

Ne 13:12 Then brought all Judah the tithe of the corn and the new wine and the oil unto the treasuries.

Am 4:4 Come to Bethel, and transgress; at Gilgal multiply transgression; and bring your sacrifices every morning, *and* your tithes after three years:

Mal 3:10 Bring ye all the tithes into the storehouse, that there may be meat in mine house, and prove me now herewith, saith the LORD of hosts, if I will not open you the windows of heaven, and pour you out a blessing, that *there shall* not *be room* enough *to receive it.*

Mt 23:23 Woe unto you, scribes and Pharisees, hypocrites! for ye pay tithe of mint and anise and cummin, and have omitted the weightier *matters* of the law, judgment, mercy, and faith: these ought ye to have done, and not to leave the other undone.

Lu 18:12 I fast twice in the week, I give tithes of all that I possess.

He 7:2 To whom also Abraham gave a tenth part of all; first being by interpretation King of righteousness, and after that also King of Salem, which is, King of peace;

He 7:5 And verily they that are of the sons of Levi, who receive the office of the priesthood, have a commandment to take tithes of the people according to the law, that is, of their brethren, though they come out of the loins of Abraham:

He 7:9 And as I may so say, Levi also, who receiveth tithes, payed tithes in Abraham.

2. Out of Generosity

Ex 36:5; 38:24; Nu 7:13, 43, 85; 1 K 3:4; 8:63; 10:10; 2 K 5:5; 8:9; 1 Chr 28:14; 29:3, 7, 21; 2 Chr 1:6; 5:6; 7:5; 9:9; 15:11; 29:32; 30:24; 35:7; Ezr 6:9, 17; 7:22; Ne 7:72; Mk 12:43; 14:3; Lu 21:3; Jn 12:3; 2 Co 8:3

3. Of Presents

Ge 20:14; 24:22, 53; 32:13, 18; 33:10; 43:11, 26; 45:22; Jud 3:17; Ru 3:17; 1 S 9:8; 16:20; 25:27; 30:26; 2 S 8:10; 16:1; 17:28; 1 K 9:16; 10:10, 13, 25; 14:3; 2 K 8:9; 16:8; 20:12; 1 Chr 18:10; 2 Chr 9:9, 12; 17:11; 32:23; Est 9:22; Jb 42:11; Pr 19:6; Eze 46:16; Da 2:48; Mt 2:11

4. Sacrificial

ISRAEL

Ex 36:5 And they spake unto Moses, saying, The people bring much more than enough for the service of the work, which the LORD commanded to make.

THE WIDOW OF ZAREPHATH

1 K 17:13 And Elijah said unto her, Fear not; go *and* do as thou hast said: but make me thereof a little cake first, and bring *it* unto me, and after make for thee and for thy son.

1 K 17:15 And she went and did according to the saying of Elijah: and she, and he, and her house, did eat *many* days.

MARY OF BETHANY

Mt 26:7 There came unto him a woman having an alabaster box of very precious ointment, and poured it on his head, as he sat *at meat.*

THE POOR WIDOW

Lu 21:4 For all these have of their abundance cast in unto the offerings of God: but she of her penury hath cast in all the living that she had.

MEMBERS OF THE EARLY CHURCH

Ac 4:34 Neither was there any among them that lacked: for as many as were possessors of lands or houses sold them, and brought the prices of the things that were sold,

THE CHURCHES OF MACEDONIA

2 Co 8:3–4 For to *their* power, I bear record, yea, and beyond *their* power *they were* willing of themselves;

Praying us with much intreaty that we would receive the gift, and *take upon us* the fellowship of the ministering to the saints.

See **COLLECTION, GREED, KINDNESS, POOR**

GLEANING *See* **AGRICULTURE**

GLORY, *manifestation of the divine attributes and perfections of God*

1. Of God

Ex 16:7 And in the morning, then ye shall see the glory of the LORD; for that he heareth your murmurings against the LORD: and what *are* we, that ye murmur against us?

Ex 16:10 And it came to pass, as Aaron spake unto the whole congregation of the children of Israel, that they looked toward the wilderness, and, behold, the glory of the LORD appeared in the cloud.

Ex 24:17 And the sight of the glory of the LORD *was* like devouring fire on the top of the mount in the eyes of the children of Israel.

Ex 40:34 Then a cloud covered the tent of the congregation, and the glory of the LORD filled the tabernacle.

1 K 8:11 So that the priests could not stand to minister because of the cloud: for the glory of the LORD had filled the house of the LORD.

Ps 8:1 O LORD our Lord, how excellent *is* thy name in all the earth! who hast set thy glory above the heavens.

Ps 19:1 The heavens declare the glory of God; and the firmament sheweth his handywork.

Lu 2:9 And, lo, the angel of the Lord came upon them, and the glory of the Lord shone round about them: and they were sore afraid.

Ac 7:55 But he, being full of the Holy Ghost, looked up stedfastly into heaven, and saw the glory of God, and Jesus standing on the right hand of God,

2 Co 3:18 But we all, with open face beholding as in a glass the glory of the Lord, are changed into the same image from glory to glory, *even* as by the Spirit of the Lord.

See **GOD**

2. Of Man, *transient*

Ps 39:6; 49:12, 17; Pr 27:24; Is 5:14; 14:18; 16:14; 17:4; 21:16; 22:24; Je 9:23; 22:18; Eze 24:25; 27:25; 31:18; 32:30; Da 2:37; 4:22, 30; 5:18; 7:9; 11:39; Ho 4:7; 9:11; Hab 2:16; Zec 11:3; Mt 6:29; 1 Pe 1:24

GNATS *See* **INSECTS**

GO, *some commands of Christ*

Mt 9:13 But go ye and learn what *that* meaneth, I will have mercy, and not sacrifice: for I am not come to call the righteous, but sinners to repentance.

Mt 21:28 But what think ye? A *certain* man had two sons; and he came to the first, and said, Son, go work to day in my vineyard.

Mt 28:7 And go quickly, and tell his disciples that he is risen from the dead; and, behold, he goeth before you into Galilee; there shall ye see him: lo, I have told you.

Lu 10:37 And he said, He that shewed mercy on him. Then said Jesus unto him, Go, and do thou likewise.

Jn 8:11 She said, No man, Lord. And Jesus said unto her, Neither do I condemn thee: go, and sin no more.

Jn 15:16 Ye have not chosen me, but I have chosen you, and ordained you, that ye should go and bring forth fruit, and *that* your fruit should remain: that whatsoever ye shall ask of the Father in my name, he may give it you.

Ac 9:6 And he trembling and astonished said, Lord, what wilt thou have me to do? And the Lord *said* unto him, Arise, and go into the city, and it shall be told thee what thou must do.

See **INVITATIONS**

GOADS, *tools for prodding animals*

Jud 3:31; 1 S 13:21; Ec 12:11; Ac 9:5

GOATS *See* **ANIMALS**

GOATS' HAIR, *useful for offerings, clothing, tabernacle curtains*

Ex 25:4; 26:7; 35:6; 36:14; Nu 31:20; 1 S 19:13

GOD

1. Is Unchanging

Ex 13:22 He took not away the pillar of the cloud by day, nor the pillar of fire by night, *from* before the people.

De 4:31 (For the LORD thy God *is* a merciful God;) he will not forsake thee, neither destroy thee, nor forget the covenant of thy fathers which he sware unto them.

De 31:6 Be strong and of a good courage, fear not, nor be afraid of them: for the LORD thy God, he *it is* that doth go with thee; he will not fail thee, nor forsake thee.

Jos 1:5 There shall not any man be able to stand before thee all the days of thy life: as I was with Moses, *so* I will be with thee: I will not fail thee, nor forsake thee.

1 S 12:22 For the LORD will not forsake his people for his great name's sake: because it hath pleased the LORD to make you his people.

2 S 15:21 And Ittai answered the king, and said, As the LORD liveth, and *as* my lord the king liveth, surely in

what place my lord the king shall be, whether in death or life, even there also will thy servant be.

1 K 6:13 And I will dwell among the children of Israel, and will not forsake my people Israel.

1 K 8:57 The LORD our God be with us, as he was with our fathers: let him not leave us, nor forsake us:

1 K 15:4 Nevertheless for David's sake did the LORD his God give him a lamp in Jerusalem, to set up his son after him, and to establish Jerusalem:

2 K 2:2 And Elijah said unto Elisha, Tarry here, I pray thee; for the LORD hath sent me to Bethel. And Elisha said *unto him,* As the LORD liveth, and as thy soul liveth, I will not leave thee. So they went down to Bethel.

2 K 2:6 And Elijah said unto him, Tarry, I pray thee, here; for the LORD hath sent me to Jordan. And he said, As the LORD liveth, and *as* thy soul liveth, I will not leave thee. And they two went on.

Ne 9:19 Yet thou in thy manifold mercies forsookest them not in the wilderness: the pillar of the cloud departed not from them by day, to lead them in the way; neither the pillar of fire by night, to shew them light, and the way wherein they should go.

Ps 27:9 Hide not thy face *far* from me; put not thy servant away in anger: thou hast been my help; leave me not, neither forsake me, O God of my salvation.

Ps 37:33 The LORD will not leave him in his hand, nor condemn him when he is judged.

Ps 38:21 Forsake me not, O LORD: O my God, be not far from me.

Ps 91:15 He shall call upon me, and I will answer him: I *will be* with him in trouble; I will deliver him, and honour him.

Ps 94:14 For the LORD will not cast off his people, neither will he forsake his inheritance.

Ps 121:8 The LORD shall preserve thy going out and thy coming in from this time forth, and even for evermore.

Ps 125:2 As the mountains *are* round about Jerusalem, so the LORD *is* round about his people from henceforth even for ever.

Is 41:17 *When* the poor and needy seek water, and *there is* none, *and* their tongue faileth for thirst, I the LORD will hear them, *I* the God of Israel will not forsake them.

Is 42:16 And I will bring the blind by a way *that* they knew not; I will lead them in paths *that* they have not known: I will make darkness light before them, and crooked things straight. These things will I do unto them, and not forsake them.

Is 43:2 When thou passest through the waters, I *will be* with thee; and through the rivers, they shall not overflow thee: when thou walkest through the fire, thou shalt not be burned; neither shall the flame kindle upon thee.

Is 44:21 Remember these, O Jacob and Israel; for thou *art* my servant: I have formed thee; thou *art* my servant: O Israel, thou shalt not be forgotten of me.

Is 46:4 And *even* to *your* old age I *am* he; and *even* to hoar hairs will I carry *you:* I have made, and I will bear; even I will carry, and will deliver *you.*

Is 49:15 Can a woman forget her sucking child, that she should not have compassion on the son of her womb? yea, they may forget, yet will I not forget thee.

Is 54:10 For the mountains shall depart, and the hills be removed; but my kindness shall not depart from thee, neither shall the covenant of my peace be removed, saith the LORD that hath mercy on thee.

Is 62:12 And they shall call them, The holy people, The redeemed of the LORD: and thou shalt be called, Sought out, A city not forsaken.

Is 63:11 Then he remembered the days of old, Moses, *and* his people, *saying,* Where *is* he that brought them up out of the sea with the shepherd of his flock? where *is* he that put his holy Spirit within him?

Je 31:3 The LORD hath appeared of old unto me, *saying,* Yea, I have loved thee with an everlasting love: therefore with lovingkindness have I drawn thee.

Je 32:40 And I will make an everlasting covenant with them, that I will not turn away from them, to do them good; but I will put my fear in their hearts, that they shall not depart from me.

Je 51:5 For Israel *hath* not *been* forsaken, nor Judah of his God, of the LORD of hosts; though their land was filled with sin against the Holy One of Israel.

Mal 3:6 For I *am* the LORD, I change not; therefore ye sons of Jacob are not consumed.

Jn 13:1 Now before the feast of the passover, when Jesus knew that his hour was come that he should depart out of this world unto the Father, having loved his own which were in the world, he loved them unto the end.

Jn 14:18 I will not leave you comfortless: I will come to you.

2 Co 4:9 Persecuted, but not forsaken; cast down, but not destroyed;

2 Ti 4:17 Notwithstanding the Lord stood with me, and strengthened me; that by me the preaching might be fully known, and *that* all the Gentiles might hear: and I was delivered out of the mouth of the lion.

He 13:5 *Let your* conversation *be* without covetousness; *and be* content with such things as ye have: for he hath said, I will never leave thee, nor forsake thee.

2. Is Light

Ex 13:21 And the LORD went before them by day in a pillar of a cloud, to lead them the way; and by night in a pillar of fire, to give them light; to go by day and night:

Ex 14:20 And it came between the camp of the Egyptians and the camp of Israel; and it was a cloud and darkness *to them,* but it gave light by night *to these:* so that the one came not near the other all the night.

De 33:2 And he said, The LORD came from Sinai, and rose up from Seir unto them; he shined forth from mount Paran, and he came with ten thousands of saints: from his right hand *went* a fiery law for them.

2 S 22:29 For thou *art* my lamp, O LORD: and the LORD will lighten my darkness.

Jb 29:3 When his candle shined upon my head, *and when* by his light I walked *through* darkness;

Jb 32:8 But *there is* a spirit in man: and the inspiration of the Almighty giveth them understanding.

Ps 27:1 The LORD *is* my light and my salvation; whom shall I fear? the LORD *is* the strength of my life; of whom shall I be afraid?

Ps 36:9 For with thee *is* the fountain of life: in thy light shall we see light.

Ps 43:3 O send out thy light and thy truth: let them lead me; let them bring me unto thy holy hill, and to thy tabernacles.

Ps 50:2 Out of Zion, the perfection of beauty, God hath shined.

Ps 84:11 For the LORD God *is* a sun and shield: the LORD will give grace and glory: no good *thing* will he withhold from them that walk uprightly.

Ps 104:2 Who coverest *thyself* with light as *with* a garment: who stretchest out the heavens like a curtain:

Ps 118:27 God *is* the LORD, which hath shewed us light: bind the sacrifice with cords, *even* unto the horns of the altar.

Is 2:5 O house of Jacob, come ye, and let us walk in the light of the LORD.

Is 10:17 And the light of Israel shall be for a fire, and his Holy One for a flame: and it shall burn and devour his thorns and his briers in one day;

Is 60:2 For, behold, the darkness shall cover the earth, and gross darkness the people: but the LORD shall arise upon thee and his glory shall be seen upon thee.

Is 60:20 Thy sun shall no more go down; neither shall thy moon withdraw itself: for the LORD shall be thine everlasting light, and the days of thy mourning shall be ended.

Da 2:22 He revealeth the deep and secret things: he knoweth what *is* in the darkness, and the light dwelleth with him.

Mi 7:8 Rejoice not against me, O mine enemy: when I fall, I shall arise; when I sit in darkness, the LORD *shall be* a light unto me.

Hab 3:4 And *his* brightness was as the light; he had horns *coming* out of his hand: and there *was* the hiding of his power.

Ja 1:17 Every good gift and every perfect gift is from above, and cometh down from the Father of lights, with whom is no variableness, neither shadow of turning.

1 Jn 1:5 This then is the message which we have heard of him, and declare unto you, that God is light, and in him is no darkness at all.

Re 21:23 And the city had no need of the sun, neither of the moon, to shine in it: for the glory of God did lighten it, and the Lamb *is* the light thereof.

Re 22:5 And there shall be no night there; and they need no candle, neither light of the sun; for the Lord God giveth them light: and they shall reign for ever and ever.

3. Is Living

Nu 14:28 Say unto them, *As truly as* I live, saith the LORD, as ye have spoken in mine ears, so will I do to you:

De 5:26 For who *is there of* all flesh, that hath heard the voice of the living God speaking out of the midst of the fire, as we *have,* and lived?

Jos 3:10 And Joshua said, Hereby ye shall know that the living God *is* among you, and *that* he will without fail drive out from before you the Canaanites, and the Hittites, and the Hivites, and the Perizzites, and the Girgashites, and the Amorites, and the Jebusites.

1 S 17:26 And David spake to the men that stood by him, saying, What shall be done to the man that killeth this Philistine, and taketh away the reproach from Israel? for who *is* this uncircumcised Philistine, that he should defy the armies of the living God?

1 S 17:36 Thy servant slew both the lion and the bear: and this uncircumcised Philistine shall be as one of them, seeing he hath defied the armies of the living God.

2 S 22:47 The LORD liveth; and blessed *be* my rock; and exalted be the God of the rock of my salvation.

1 K 1:29 And the king sware, and said, *As* the LORD liveth, that hath redeemed my soul out of all distress,

2 K 19:4 It may be the LORD thy God will hear all the words of Rab-shakeh, whom the king of Assyria his master hath sent to reproach the living God; and will reprove the words which the LORD thy God hath heard: wherefore lift up *thy* prayer for the remnant that are left.

2 K 19:16 LORD, bow down thine ear, and hear: open, LORD, thine eyes, and see: and hear the words of Sennacherib, which hath sent him to reproach the living God.

Ps 18:46 The LORD liveth; and blessed *be* my rock; and let the God of my salvation be exalted.

Ps 42:2 My soul thirsteth for God, for the living God: when shall I come and appear before God?

Ps 84:2 My soul longeth, yea, even fainteth for the courts of the LORD: my heart and my flesh crieth out for the living God.

Is 37:17 Incline thine ear, O LORD, and hear; open thine eyes, O LORD, and see: and hear all the words of Sennacherib, which hath sent to reproach the living God.

Je 10:10 But the LORD *is* the true God, he *is* the living God, and an everlasting king: at his wrath the earth shall tremble, and the nations shall not be able to abide his indignation.

Je 23:36 And the burden of the LORD shall ye mention no more: for every man's word shall be his burden; for ye have perverted the words of the living God, of the LORD of hosts our God.

Da 6:20 And when he came to the den, he cried with a lamentable voice unto Daniel: *and* the king spake and said to Daniel, O Daniel, servant of the living God, is thy God, whom thou servest continually, able to deliver thee from the lions?

Da 6:26 I make a decree, That in every dominion of my kingdom men tremble and fear before the God of Daniel: for he is the living God, and stedfast for ever, and his kingdom *that* which shall not be destroyed, and his dominion *shall be even* unto the end.

Mt 26:63 But Jesus held his peace. And the high priest answered and said unto him, I adjure thee by the living God, that thou tell us whether thou be the Christ the Son of God.

Jn 6:57 As the living Father hath sent me, and I live by the Father: so he that eateth me, even he shall live by me.

Ac 14:15 And saying, Sirs, why do ye these things? We also are men of like passions with you, and preach unto you that ye should turn from these vanities unto the living God, which made heaven, and earth, and the sea, and all things that are therein:

2 Co 3:3 *Forasmuch as ye are* manifestly declared to be the epistle of Christ ministered by us, written not with ink, but with the Spirit of the living God; not in tables of stone, but in fleshy tables of the heart.

1 Th 1:9 For they themselves shew of us what manner of entering in we had unto you, and how ye turned to God from idols to serve the living and true God;

1 Ti 3:15 But if I tarry long, that thou mayest know how thou oughtest to behave thyself in the house of God, which is the church of the living God, the pillar and ground of the truth.

1 Ti 4:10 For therefore we both labour and suffer reproach, because we trust in the living God, who is the Saviour of all men, specially of those that believe.

1 Ti 6:17 Charge them that are rich in this world, that they be not highminded, nor trust in uncertain riches, but in the living God, who giveth us richly all things to enjoy;

He 3:12 Take heed, brethren, lest there be in any of you an evil heart of unbelief, in departing from the living God.

He 9:14 How much more shall the blood of Christ, who through the eternal Spirit offered himself without spot to God, purge your conscience from dead works to serve the living God?

He 10:31 *It is* a fearful thing to fall into the hands of the living God.

He 12:22 But ye are come unto mount Sion, and unto the city of the living God, the heavenly Jerusalem, and to an innumerable company of angels,

Re 7:2 And I saw another angel ascending from the east, having the seal of the living God: and he cried with a loud voice to the four angels, to whom it was given to hurt the earth and the sea,

4. Is Unique, *an expression of testimony, praise, worship*

Ex 8:10 And he said, To morrow. And he said, *Be it* according to thy word: that thou mayest know that *there is* none like unto the LORD our God.

Ex 9:14 For I will at this time send all my plagues upon thine heart, and upon thy servants, and upon thy people; that thou mayest know that there is none like me in all the earth.

Ex 15:11 Who *is* like unto thee, O LORD, among the gods? who *is* like thee, glorious in holiness, fearful *in* praises, doing wonders?

Ex 18:11 Now I know that the LORD *is* greater than all gods: for in the thing wherein they dealt proudly *he was* above them.

De 3:24 O Lord GOD, thou hast begun to shew thy servant thy greatness, and thy mighty hand: for what God *is there* in heaven or in earth, that can do according to thy works, and according to thy might?

De 32:31 For their rock *is* not as our Rock, even our enemies themselves *being* judges.

De 33:26 *There is* none like unto the God of Jeshurun, *who* rideth upon the heaven in thy help, and in his excellency on the sky.

Jos 2:11 And as soon as we had heard *these things,* our hearts did melt, neither did there remain any more courage in any man, because of you: for the LORD your God, he *is* God in heaven above, and in earth beneath.

1 S 2:2 *There is* none holy as the LORD: for *there is* none beside thee: neither *is there* any rock like our God.

2 S 7:22 Wherefore thou art great, O LORD God: for *there is* none like thee, neither *is there any* God beside thee, according to all that we have heard with our ears.

2 S 22:32 For who *is* God, save the LORD? and who *is* a rock, save our God?

1 K 8:23 And he said, LORD God of Israel, *there is* no God like thee, in heaven above, or on earth beneath, who keepest covenant and mercy with thy servants that walk before thee with all their heart:

1 K 8:60 That all the people of the earth may know that the LORD *is* God, *and that there is* none else.

2 K 5:15 And he returned to the man of God, he and all his company, and came, and stood before him: and he said, Behold, now I know that *there is* no God in all earth, but in Israel: now therefore, I pray thee, take a blessing of thy servant.

2 K 19:15 And Hezekiah prayed before the LORD, and said, O LORD God of Israel, which dwellest *between* the cherubims, thou art the God, *even* thou alone, of all the kingdoms of the earth: thou hast made heaven and earth.

1 Chr 17:20 O LORD, *there is* none like thee, neither *is there any* God beside thee, according to all that we have heard with our ears.

2 Chr 2:5 And the house which I build *is* great: for great *is* our God above all gods.

2 Chr 6:14 And said, O LORD God of Israel, *there is* no God like thee in the heaven, nor in the earth; which keepest covenant, and *shewest* mercy unto thy servants, that walk before thee with all their hearts:

Ps 18:31 For who *is* God save the LORD? or who *is* a rock save our God?

Ps 35:10 All my bones shall say, LORD, who *is* like unto thee, which deliverest the poor from him that is too strong for him, yea, the poor and the needy from him that spoileth him?

Ps 71:19 Thy righteousness also, O God, *is* very high, who hast done great things: O God, who *is* like unto thee!

Ps 77:13 Thy way, O God, *is* in the sanctuary: who *is so* great a God as *our* God?

Ps 86:8 Among the gods *there is* none like unto thee, O Lord; neither *are there any works* like unto thy works.

Ps 89:6 For who in the heaven can be compared unto the Lord? *who* among the sons of the mighty can be likened unto the Lord?

Ps 113:5 Who *is* like unto the Lord our God, who dwelleth on high,

Ps 135:5 For I know that the Lord *is* great, and *that* our Lord *is* above all gods.

Is 37:16 O Lord of hosts, God of Israel, that dwellest *between* the cherubims, thou *art* the God, *even* thou alone, of all the kingdoms of the earth: thou hast made heaven and earth.

Is 40:18 To whom then will ye liken God? or what likeness will ye compare unto him?

Is 40:25 To whom then will ye liken me, or shall I be equal? saith the Holy One.

Is 43:11 I, *even* I, *am* the Lord; and beside me *there is* no saviour.

Is 44:8 Fear ye not, neither be afraid: have not I told thee from that time, and have declared *it?* ye *are* even my witnesses. Is there a God beside me? yea, *there is* no God; I know not *any.*

Is 45:5 I *am* the Lord, and *there is* none else, *there is* no God beside me: I girded thee, though thou hast not known me:

Is 45:22 Look unto me, and be ye saved, all the ends of the earth: for I *am* God, and *there is* none else.

Is 46:5 To whom will ye liken me, and make *me* equal, and compare me, that we may be like?

Is 64:4 For since the beginning of the world *men* have not heard, nor perceived by the ear, neither hath the eye seen, O God, beside thee, *what* he hath prepared for him that waiteth for him.

Je 10:6 Forasmuch as *there is* none like unto thee, O Lord; thou *art* great, and thy name is great in might.

Je 49:19 Behold, he shall come up like a lion from the swelling of Jordan against the habitation of the strong: but I will suddenly make him run away from her: and who *is* a chosen *man, that* I may appoint over her? for who *is* like me? and who will appoint me the time? and who *is* that shepherd that will stand before me?

Je 50:44 Behold, he shall come up like a lion from the swelling of Jordan unto the habitation of the strong: but I will make them suddenly run away from her: and who *is* a chosen *man that* I may appoint over her? for who *is* like me? and who will appoint me the time? and who *is* that shepherd that will stand before me?

Je 51:19 The portion of Jacob *is* not like them; for he *is* the former of all things: and *Israel is* the rod of his inheritance: the Lord of hosts is his name.

Da 3:29 Therefore I make a decree, That every people, nation, and language, which speak any thing amiss against the God of Shadrach, Meshach, and Abed-nego, shall be cut in pieces, and their houses shall be made a dunghill: because there is no other God that can deliver after this sort.

Mi 7:18 Who *is* a God like unto thee, that pardoneth iniquity, and passeth by the transgression of the remnant of his heritage? he retaineth not his anger for ever, because he delighteth *in* mercy.

Mk 12:32 And the scribe said unto him, Well, Master, thou hast said the truth: for there is one God; and there is none other but he:

Jn 17:3 And this is life eternal, that they might know thee the only true God, and Jesus Christ, whom thou hast sent.

1 Co 8:4 As concerning therefore the eating of those things that are offered in sacrifice unto idols, we know that an idol *is* nothing in the world, and that *there is* none other God but one.

1 Ti 1:17 Now unto the King eternal, immortal, invisible, the only wise God, *be* honour and glory for ever and ever. Amen.

5. Is One, *the only true one, above all that are false*

Ex 20:3 Thou shalt have no other gods before me.

De 4:35 Unto thee it was shewed, that thou mightest know that the Lord he *is* God; *there is* none else beside him.

De 4:39 Know therefore this day, and consider *it* in thine heart, that the Lord he *is* God in heaven above, and upon the earth beneath: *there is* none else.

De 5:7 Thou shalt have none other gods before me.

De 6:4 Hear, O Israel: The Lord our God *is* one Lord:

De 32:39 See now that I, *even* I, *am* he, and *there is* no god with me: I kill, and I make alive; I wound, and I heal: neither *is there any* that can deliver out of my hand.

2 S 7:22 Wherefore thou art great, O Lord God: for *there is* none like thee, neither *is there any* God beside thee, according to all that we have heard with our ears.

2 K 17:35 With whom the Lord had made a covenant, and charged them saying, Ye shall not fear other gods, nor bow yourselves to them, nor serve them, nor sacrifice to them:

2 K 19:19 Now therefore, O Lord our God, I beseech thee, save thou us out of his hand, that all the kingdoms of the earth may know that thou *art* the Lord God, *even* thou only.

1 Chr 17:20 O Lord, *there is* none like thee, neither *is there any* God beside thee, according to all that we have heard with our ears.

Ne 9:6 Thou, *even* thou, *art* Lord alone; thou hast made heaven, the heaven of heavens, with all their host, the earth, and all *things* that *are* therein, the seas, and all that *is* therein, and thou preservest them all; and the host of heaven worshippeth thee.

Ps 83:18 That *men* may know that thou, whose name alone *is* Jehovah, *art* the most high over all the earth.

Ps 86:10 For thou *art* great, and doest wondrous things: thou *art* God alone.

Is 26:13 O Lord our God, *other* lords besides thee have had dominion over us: *but* by thee only will we make mention of thy name.

Is 37:21 Then Isaiah the son of Amoz sent unto Hezekiah, saying, Thus saith the Lord God of Israel, Whereas thou hast prayed to me against Sennacherib king of Assyria:

Is 43:10 Ye *are* my witnesses, saith the Lord, and my servant whom I have chosen: that ye may know and believe me, and understand that I *am* he: before me there was no God formed, neither shall there be after me.

Is 44:6 Thus saith the Lord the King of Israel, and his redeemer the Lord of hosts; I *am* the first, and I *am* the last; and beside me *there is* no God.

Is 45:6 That they may know from the rising of the sun, and from the west, that *there is* none beside me. I *am* the Lord, and *there is* none else.

Is 45:14 Thus saith the Lord, The labour of Egypt, and merchandise of Ethiopia and of the Sabeans, men of stature, shall come over unto thee, and they shall be thine: they shall come after thee; in chains they shall come over, and they shall fall down unto thee, they shall make supplication unto thee, *saying*, Surely God *is* in thee; and *there is* none else, *there is* no God.

Is 45:18 For thus saith the Lord that created the heavens; God himself that formed the earth and made it; he hath established it, he created it not in vain, he formed it to be inhabited: I *am* the Lord; and *there is* none else.

Is 45:21 Tell ye, and bring *them* near; yea, let them take counsel together: who hath declared this from ancient time? *who* hath told it from that time? *have* not I the Lord? and *there is* no God else beside me; a just God and a Saviour; *there is* none beside me.

Is 46:9 Remember the former things of old: for I *am* God, and *there is* none else; *I am* God, and *there is* none like me,

Da 3:28 *Then* Nebuchadnezzar spake, and said, Blessed be the God of Shadrach, Meshach, and Abed-nego, who hath sent his angel, and delivered his servants that trusted in him, and have changed the king's word, and yielded their bodies, that they might not serve nor worship any god, except their own God.

Ho 13:4 Yet I *am* the Lord thy God from the land of Egypt, and thou shalt know no god but me: for *there is* no saviour beside me.

Jl 2:27 And ye shall know that I *am* in the midst of Israel, and *that* I *am* the Lord your God, and none else: and my people shall never be ashamed.

Zec 14:9 And the Lord shall be king over all the earth: in that day shall there be one Lord, and his name one.

Mk 12:29 And Jesus answered him, The first of all the commandments *is*, Hear, O Israel; The Lord our God is one Lord:

Mk 12:32 And the scribe said unto him, Well, Master, thou hast said the truth: for there is one God; and there is none other but he:

Ac 19:26 Moreover ye see and hear, that not alone at Ephesus, but almost throughout all Asia, this Paul hath persuaded and turned away much people, saying that they be no gods, which are made with hands:

Ro 3:30 Seeing *it is* one God, which shall justify the circumcision by faith, and uncircumcision through faith.

1 Co 8:4 As concerning therefore the eating of those things that are offered in sacrifice unto idols, we know that an idol *is* nothing in the world, and that *there is* none other God but one.

Ga 3:20 Now a mediator is not *a mediator* of one, but God is one.

Ep 4:6 One God and Father of all, who *is* above all, and through all, and in you all.

1 Ti 2:5 For *there is* one God, and one mediator between God and men, the man Christ Jesus;

Ja 2:19 Thou believest that there is one God; thou doest well: the devils also believe, and tremble.

1 Jn 5:7 For there are three that bear record in heaven, the Father, the Word, and the Holy Ghost: and these three are one.

See **CHRIST, HOLY SPIRIT, SATAN**

GODLESSNESS, *devoid of God and His ways*

De 25:18 How he met thee by the way, and smote the hindmost of thee, *even* all *that were* feeble behind thee, when thou *wast* faint and weary; and he feared not God.

2 K 17:25 And *so* it was at the beginning of their dwelling there, *that* they feared not the Lord: therefore the Lord sent lions among them, which slew *some* of them.

2 K 17:34 Unto this day they do after the former manners: they fear not the Lord, neither do they after their statutes, or after their ordinances, or after the law and commandment which the Lord commanded the children of Jacob, whom he named Israel;

2 Chr 15:3 Now for a long season Israel *hath been* without the true God, and without a teaching priest, and without law.

2 Chr 32:19 And they spake against the God of Jerusalem, as against the gods of the people of the earth, *which were* the work of the hands of man.

Jb 21:15 What *is* the Almighty, that we should serve him? and what profit should we have, if we pray unto him?

Jb 22:17 Which said unto God, Depart from us: and what can the Almighty do for them?

Jb 34:9 For he hath said, It profiteth a man nothing that he should delight himself with God.

Jb 35:10 But none saith, Where *is* God my maker, who giveth songs in the night;

Ps 10:4 The wicked, through the pride of his countenance, will not seek *after God:* God *is* not in all his thoughts.

Ps 28:5 Because they regard not the works of the Lord, nor the operation of his hands, he shall destroy them, and not build them up.

Ps 36:1 The transgression of the wicked saith within my heart, *that there is* no fear of God before his eyes.

Ps 52:7 Lo, *this is* the man *that* made not God his strength; but trusted in the abundance of his riches, *and* strengthened himself in his wickedness.

Ps 54:3 For strangers are risen up against me, and oppressors seek after my soul: they have not set God before them. Selah.

Ps 55:19 God shall hear, and afflict them, even he that abideth of old. Selah. Because they have no changes, therefore they fear not God.

Ps 86:14 O God, the proud are risen against me, and the assemblies of violent *men* have sought after my soul; and have not set thee before them.

Ec 8:13 But it shall not be well with the wicked, neither shall he prolong *his* days, *which are* as a shadow; because he feareth not before God.

Is 5:12 And the harp, and the viol, the tabret, and pipe, and wine, are in their feasts: but they regard not the work of the LORD, neither consider the operation of his hands.

Is 30:11 Get you out of the way, turn aside out of the path, cause the Holy One of Israel to cease from before us.

Is 57:11 And of whom hast thou been afraid or feared, that thou hast lied, and hast not remembered me, nor laid *it* to thy heart? have not I held my peace even of old, and thou fearest me not?

Je 2:19 Thine own wickedness shall correct thee, and thy backslidings shall reprove thee: know therefore and see that *it is* an evil *thing* and bitter, that thou hast forsaken the LORD thy God, and that my fear *is* not in thee, saith the Lord GOD of hosts.

Je 5:24 Neither say they in their heart, Let us now fear the LORD our God, that giveth rain, both the former and the latter, in his season: he reserveth unto us the appointed weeks of the harvest.

Je 44:10 They are not humbled *even* unto this day, neither have they feared, nor walked in my law, nor in my statutes, that I set before you and before your fathers.

Da 11:37 Neither shall he regard the God of his fathers, nor the desire of women, nor regard any god: for he shall magnify himself above all.

Ho 10:3 For now they shall say, We have no king, because we feared not the LORD; what then should a king do to us?

Mal 3:5 And I will come near to you to judgment; and I will be a swift witness against the sorcerers, and against the adulterers, and against false swearers, and against those that oppress the hireling in *his* wages, the widow, and the fatherless, and that turn aside the stranger *from his right,* and fear not me, saith the LORD of hosts.

Mal 3:14 Ye have said, It *is* vain to serve God: and what profit *is it* that we have kept his ordinance, and that we have walked mournfully before the LORD of hosts?

Lu 18:2 Saying, There was in a city a judge, which feared not God, neither regarded man:

Ro 1:30 Backbiters, haters of God, despiteful, proud, boasters, inventors of evil things, disobedient to parents,

Ro 3:11 There is none that understandeth, there is none that seeketh after God.

Ro 3:18 There is no fear of God before their eyes.

Ep 2:12 That at that time ye were without Christ, being aliens from the commonwealth of Israel, and strangers from the covenants of promise, having no hope, and without God in the world:

1 Ti 1:9 Knowing this, that the law is not made for a righteous man, but for the lawless and disobedient, for the ungodly and for sinners, for unholy and profane, for murderers of fathers and murderers of mothers, for manslayers,

See **WICKED**

GODLINESS

1. Exhortations

Ac 24:16 And herein do I exercise myself, to have always a conscience void of offence toward God, and *toward* men.

1 Ti 2:1–2 I exhort therefore, that, first of all, supplications, prayers, intercessions, *and* giving of thanks, be made for all men;

For kings, and *for* all that are in authority; that we may lead a quiet and peaceable life in all godliness and honesty.

1 Ti 4:7 But refuse profane and old wives' fables, and exercise thyself *rather* unto godliness.

1 Ti 6:3 If any man teach otherwise, and consent not to wholesome words, *even* the words of our Lord Jesus Christ, and to the doctrine which is according to godliness;

1 Ti 6:11 But thou, O man of God, flee these things; and follow after righteousness, godliness, faith, love, patience, meekness.

2 Ti 3:12 Yea, and all that will live godly in Christ Jesus shall suffer persecution.

Tit 1:1 Paul, a servant of God, and an apostle of Jesus Christ, according to the faith of God's elect, and the acknowledging of the truth which is after godliness;

Tit 2:12 Teaching us that, denying ungodliness and worldly lusts, we should live soberly, righteously, and godly, in this present world;

2 Pe 1:3 According as his divine power hath given unto us all things that *pertain* unto life and godliness, through the knowledge of him that hath called us to glory and virtue:

2 Pe 1:6 And to knowledge temperance; and to temperance patience; and to patience godliness;

2 Pe 3:11 *Seeing* then *that* all these things shall be dissolved, what manner *of persons* ought ye to be in *all* holy conversation and godliness,

2. Boasting in God's Glorious Acts

Ps 34:2; 44:8; 62:7; Is 41:16; 45:25; Je 4:2; 9:24; Ro 2:17; 15:17; 1 Co 1:31; 2 Co 10:17

3. Glorifying God

a. The Means

PRAISE

Ps 22:23 Ye that fear the LORD, praise him; all ye the seed of Jacob, glorify

him; and fear him, all ye the seed of Israel.

GOOD WORKS

Mt 5:16 Let your light so shine before men, that they may see your good works, and glorify your Father which is in heaven.

FRUIT-BEARING

Jn 15:8 Herein is my Father glorified, that ye bear much fruit; so shall ye be my disciples.

SPIRITUAL UNITY

Ro 15:6 That ye may with one mind *and* one mouth glorify God, even the Father of our Lord Jesus Christ.

CONSECRATION

1 Co 6:20 For ye are bought with a price: therefore glorify God in your body, and in your spirit, which are God's.

2 Th 1:12 That the name of our Lord Jesus Christ may be glorified in you, and ye in him, according to the grace of our God and the Lord Jesus Christ.

b. Examples

1 Chr 29:11 Thine, O LORD, *is* the greatness, and the power, and the glory, and the victory, and the majesty: for all *that is* in the heaven and in the earth *is thine;* thine *is* the kingdom, O LORD, and thou art exalted as head above all.

Is 6:3 And one cried unto another, and said, Holy, holy, holy, *is* the LORD of hosts: the whole earth *is* full of his glory.

Mt 15:31 Insomuch that the multitude wondered, when they saw the dumb to speak, the maimed to be whole, the lame to walk, and the blind to see: and they glorified the God of Israel.

Ac 4:21 So when they had further threatened them, they let them go, finding nothing how they might punish them, because of the people: for all *men* glorified God for that which was done.

Re 4:11 Thou art worthy, O Lord, to receive glory and honour and power:

for thou hast created all things, and for thy pleasure they are and were created.

Re 7:10 And cried with a loud voice, saying, Salvation to our God which sitteth upon the throne, and unto the Lamb.

Re 15:4 Who shall not fear thee, O Lord, and glorify thy name? for *thou* only *art* holy: for all nations shall come and worship before thee; for thy judgments are made manifest.

Re 19:1 And after these things I heard a great voice of much people in heaven, saying, Alleluia; Salvation, and glory, and honour, and power, unto the Lord our God:

c. God Glorified in Christ

Is 49:3 And said unto me, Thou *art* my servant, O Israel, in whom I will be glorified.

Jn 13:31 Therefore, when he was gone out, Jesus said, Now is the Son of man glorified, and God is glorified in him.

Jn 14:13 And whatsoever ye shall ask in my name, that will I do, that the Father may be glorified in the Son.

Jn 17:4 I have glorified thee on the earth: I have finished the work which thou gavest me to do.

1 Pe 4:11 If any man speak, *let him speak* as the oracles of God; if any man minister, *let him do it* as of the ability which God giveth: that God in all things may be glorified through Jesus Christ, to whom be praise and dominion for ever and ever. Amen.

See **CONSECRATION, DEVOTIONAL LIFE, DISCIPLESHIP**

GODS

Ge 31:19 And Laban went to shear his sheep: and Rachel had stolen the images that *were* her father's.

Ge 35:4 And they gave unto Jacob all the strange gods which *were* in their hand, and *all their* earrings which *were* in their ears; and Jacob hid them under the oak which *was* by Shechem.

Ex 23:33 They shall not dwell in thy land, lest they make thee sin against me: for if thou serve their gods, it will surely be a snare unto thee.

Nu 33:4 For the Egyptians buried all *their* firstborn, which the Lord had smitten among them: upon their gods also the Lord executed judgments.

De 4:28 And there ye shall serve gods, the work of men's hands, wood and stone, which neither see, nor hear, nor eat, nor smell.

De 6:14 Ye shall not go after other gods, of the gods of the people which *are* round about you;

De 11:28 And a curse, if ye will not obey the commandments of the Lord your God, but turn aside out of the way which I command you this day, to go after other gods, which ye have not known.

De 12:3 And ye shall overthrow their altars, and break their pillars, and burn their groves with fire; and ye shall hew down the graven images of their gods, and destroy the names of them out of that place.

De 12:30 Take heed to thyself that thou be not snared by following them, after that they be destroyed from before thee; and that thou enquire not after their gods, saying, How did these nations serve their gods? even so will I do likewise.

De 13:7 *Namely,* of the gods of the people which *are* round about you, nigh unto thee, or far off from thee, from the *one* end of the earth even unto the *other* end of the earth;

De 18:20 But the prophet, which shall presume to speak a word in my name, which I have not commanded him to speak, or that shall speak in the name of other gods, even that prophet shall die.

De 28:36 The Lord shall bring thee, and thy king which thou shalt set over thee, unto a nation which neither thou nor thy fathers have known; and there shalt thou serve other gods, wood and stone.

De 28:64 And the Lord shall scatter thee among all people, from the one end of the earth even unto the other; and there thou shalt serve other gods, which neither thou nor thy fathers have known, *even* wood and stone.

De 29:17 And ye have seen their abominations, and their idols, wood and stone, silver and gold, which *were* among them:)

De 29:26 For they went and served other gods, and worshipped them, gods whom they knew not, and *whom* he had not given unto them:

De 32:12 *So* the Lord alone did lead him, and *there was* no strange god with him.

De 32:17 They sacrificed unto devils, not to God; to gods whom they knew not, to new *gods that* came newly up, whom your fathers feared not.

De 32:37 And he shall say, Where *are* their gods, *their* rock in whom they trusted,

Jos 24:2 And Joshua said unto all the people, Thus saith the Lord God of Israel, Your fathers dwelt on the other side of the flood in old time, *even* Terah, the father of Abraham, and the father of Nachor: and they served other gods.

Jos 24:15 And if it seem evil unto you to serve the Lord, choose you this day whom ye will serve; whether the gods which your fathers served that *were* on the other side of the flood, or the gods of the Amorites, in whose land ye dwell: but as for me and my house, we will serve the Lord.

Jud 2:3 Wherefore I also said, I will not drive them out from before you; but they shall be *as thorns* in your sides, and their gods shall be a snare unto you.

Jud 2:13 And they forsook the Lord, and served Baal and Ashtaroth.

Jud 2:17 And yet they would not hearken unto their judges, but they went a whoring after other gods, and bowed themselves unto them: they turned quickly out of the way which their fathers walked in, obeying the commandments of the Lord; *but* they did not so.

Jud 6:31 And Joash said unto all that stood against him, Will ye plead for Baal? will ye save him? he that will plead for him, let him be put to death whilst *it is yet* morning: if he *be* a god, let him plead for himself, because *one* hath cast down his altar.

Jud 9:27 And they went out into the fields, and gathered their vineyards, and trode *the grapes,* and made merry, and went into the house of their god, and did eat and drink, and cursed Abimelech.

Jud 9:46 And when all the men of the tower of Shechem heard *that,* they entered into an hold of the house of the god Berith.

Jud 10:6 And the children of Israel did evil again in the sight of the Lord, and served Baalim, and Ashtaroth, and the gods of Syria, and the gods of Zidon, and the gods of Moab, and the gods of the children of Ammon, and the gods of the Philistines, and forsook the Lord, and served not him.

Jud 10:13 Yet ye have forsaken me, and served other gods: wherefore I will deliver you no more.

Jud 16:24 And when the people saw him, they praised their god: for they said, Our god hath delivered into our hands our enemy, and the destroyer of our country, which slew many of us.

Jud 17:5 And the man Micah had an house of gods, and made an ephod, and teraphim, and consecrated one of his sons, who became his priest.

Ru 1:15 And she said, Behold, thy sister in law is gone back unto her people, and unto her gods: return thou after thy sister in law.

1 S 5:4 And when they arose early on the morrow morning, behold, Dagon *was* fallen upon his face to the ground before the ark of the Lord; and the head of Dagon and both the palms of his hands *were* cut off upon the threshold; only *the stump of* Dagon was left to him.

1 S 17:43 And the Philistine said unto David, *Am* I a dog, that thou comest to me with staves? And the Philistine cursed David by his gods.

1 K 9:6 *But* if ye shall at all turn from following me, ye or your children, and will not keep my commandments *and* my statutes which I have set before you, but go and serve other gods, and worship them:

1 K 11:33 Because that they have forsaken me, and have worshipped Ashtoreth the goddess of the Zidonians, Chemosh the god of the Moabites, and Milcom the god of the children of Ammon, and have not walked in my ways, to do *that which is* right in mine eyes, and *to keep* my statutes and my judgments, as *did* David his father.

1 K 18:24 And call ye on the name of your gods, and I will call on the name of the Lord: and the God that answereth by fire, let him be God. And all the people answered and said, It is well spoken.

2 K 1:2 And Ahaziah fell down through a lattice in his upper chamber that *was* in Samaria, and was sick: and he sent messengers, and said unto them, Go, enquire of Baal-zebub the god of Ekron whether I shall recover of this disease.

2 K 17:31 And the Avites made Nibhaz and Tartak, and the Sepharvites burnt their children in fire to Adrammelech and Anammelech, the gods of Sepharvaim.

2 K 18:34 Where *are* the gods of Hamath, and of Arpad? where *are* the gods of Sepharvaim, Hena, and Ivah? have they delivered Samaria out of mine hand?

2 K 19:18 And have cast their gods into the fire: for they *were* no gods, but the work of men's hands, wood and stone: therefore they have destroyed them.

2 K 19:37 And it came to pass, as he was worshipping in the house of Nisroch his god, that Adrammelech and Sharezer his sons smote him with the sword: and they escaped into the land of Armenia. And Esar-haddon his son reigned in his stead.

1 Chr 14:12 And when they had left their gods there, David gave a commandment, and they were burned with fire.

1 Chr 16:26 For all the gods of the people *are* idols: but the Lord made the heavens.

2 Chr 7:19 But if ye turn away, and forsake my statutes and my commandments, which I have set before you, and shall go and serve other gods, and worship them;

2 Chr 13:9 Have ye not cast out the priests of the Lord, the sons of Aaron, and the Levites, and have made you priests after the manner of the nations of *other* lands? so that whosoever cometh to consecrate himself with a young bullock and seven rams, *the same* may be a priest of *them that are* no gods.

2 Chr 25:14 Now it came to pass, after that Amaziah was come from the slaughter of the Edomites, that he brought the gods of the children of Seir, and set them up *to be* his gods, and bowed down himself before them, and burned incense unto them.

2 Chr 28:23 For he sacrificed unto the gods of Damascus, which smote him: and he said, Because the gods of the kings of Syria help them, *therefore* will I sacrifice to them, that they may help me. But they were the ruin of him, and of all Israel.

2 Chr 28:25 And in every several city of Judah he made high places to burn incense unto other gods, and provoked to anger the Lord God of his fathers.

2 Chr 34:25 Because they have forsaken me, and have burned incense unto other gods, that they might provoke me to anger with all the works of their hands; therefore my wrath shall be poured out upon this place, and shall not be quenched.

Ps 44:20 If we have forgotten the name of our God, or stretched out our hands to a strange god;

Ps 81:9 There shall no strange god be in thee; neither shalt thou worship any strange god.

Ps 96:5 For all the gods of the nations *are* idols: but the Lord made the heavens.

Ps 97:9 For thou, Lord, *art* high above all the earth: thou art exalted far above all gods.

Ps 115:5 They have mouths, but they speak not: eyes have they, but they see not:

Ps 135:16 They have mouths, but they speak not; eyes have they, but they see not;

Is 2:8 Their land also is full of idols; they worship the work of their own hands, that which their own fingers have made:

Is 19:3 And the spirit of Egypt shall fail in the midst thereof; and I will destroy the counsel thereof: and they shall seek to the idols, and to the charmers, and to them that have familiar spirits, and to the wizards.

Is 21:9 And, behold, here cometh a chariot of men, *with* a couple of horsemen. And he answered and said, Babylon is fallen, is fallen; and all the graven images of her gods he hath broken unto the ground.

Is 36:20 Who *are they* among all the gods of these lands, that have delivered their land out of my hand, that the Lord should deliver Jerusalem out of my hand?

Is 37:19 And have cast their gods into the fire: for they *were* no gods, but the work of men's hands, wood and stone: therefore they have destroyed them.

Is 37:38 And it came to pass, as he was worshipping in the house of Nisroch his god, that Adrammelech and Sharezer his sons smote him with the sword; and they escaped into the land of Armenia: and Esar-haddon his son reigned in his stead.

Is 41:23 Shew the things that are to come hereafter, that we may know that ye *are* gods: yea, do good, or do evil, that we may be dismayed, and behold *it* together.

Is 42:17 They shall be turned back, they shall be greatly ashamed, that trust in graven images, that say to the molten images, Ye *are* our gods.

Is 44:9 They that make a graven image *are* all of them vanity; and their delectable things shall not profit; and they *are* their own witnesses; they see not, nor know; that they may be ashamed.

Is 45:20 Assemble yourselves and come; draw near together, ye *that are* escaped of the nations: they have no knowledge that set up the wood of their graven image, and pray unto a god *that* cannot save.

Is 46:6 They lavish gold out of the bag, and weigh silver in the balance, *and* hire a goldsmith; and he maketh it a god: they fall down, yea, they worship.

Je 2:11 Hath a nation changed *their* gods, which *are* yet no gods? but my people have changed their glory for *that which* doth not profit.

Je 2:28 But where *are* thy gods that thou hast made thee? let them arise, if they can save thee in the time of thy trouble: for *according to* the number of thy cities are thy gods, O Judah.

Je 5:7 How shall I pardon thee for this? thy children have forsaken me, and sworn by *them that are* no gods: when I had fed them to the full, they then committed adultery, and assembled themselves by troops in the harlots' houses.

Je 7:18 The children gather wood, and the fathers kindle the fire, and the women knead *their* dough, to make cakes to the queen of heaven, and to pour out drink offerings unto other gods, that they may provoke me to anger.

Je 10:5 They *are* upright as the palm tree, but speak not: they must needs be borne, because they cannot go. Be not afraid of them; for they cannot do evil, neither also *is it* in them to do good.

Je 10:11 Thus shall ye say unto them, The gods that have not made the heavens and the earth, *even* they shall perish from the earth, and from under these heavens.

Je 11:12 Then shall the cities of Judah and inhabitants of Jerusalem go, and cry unto the gods unto whom they offer incense: but they shall not save them at all in the time of their trouble.

Je 16:11 Then shalt thou say unto them, Because your fathers have forsaken me, saith the Lord, and have walked after other gods, and have served them, and have worshipped them, and have forsaken me, and have not kept my law;

Je 16:20 Shall a man make gods unto himself, and they *are* no gods?

Je 19:4 Because they have forsaken me, and have estranged this place, and have burned incense in it unto other gods, whom neither they nor their fathers have known, nor the kings of Judah, and have filled this place with the blood of innocents;

Je 19:13 And the houses of Jerusalem, and the houses of the kings of Judah, shall be defiled as the place of Tophet, because of all the houses upon whose roofs they have burned incense unto all the host of heaven, and have poured out drink offerings unto other gods.

Je 25:6 And go not after other gods to serve them, and to worship them, and provoke me not to anger with the works of your hands; and I will do you no hurt.

Je 43:12 And I will kindle a fire in the houses of the gods of Egypt; and he shall burn them, and carry them away captives: and he shall array himself with the land of Egypt, as a shepherd putteth on his garment; and he shall go forth from thence in peace.

Je 44:3 Because of their wickedness which they have committed to provoke me to anger, in that they went to burn incense, *and* to serve other gods, whom they knew not, *neither* they, ye, nor your fathers.

Je 46:25 The Lord of hosts, the God of Israel, saith; Behold, I will punish the multitude of No, and Pharaoh, and Egypt, with their gods, and their kings; even Pharaoh, and *all* them that trust in him:

Je 48:35 Moreover I will cause to cease in Moab, saith the Lord, him that offereth in the high places, and him that burneth incense to his gods.

Je 51:17 Every man is brutish by *his* knowledge; every founder is confounded by the graven image: for his molten image *is* falsehood, and *there is* no breath in them.

Eze 21:21 For the king of Babylon stood at the parting of the way, at the head of the two ways, to use divination: he made *his* arrows bright, he consulted with images, he looked in the liver.

Da 3:14 Nebuchadnezzar spake and said unto them, *Is it* true, O Shadrach, Meshach, and Abed-nego, do not ye serve my gods, nor worship the golden image which I have set up?

Da 5:4 They drank wine, and praised the gods of gold, and of silver, of brass, of iron, of wood, and of stone.

Da 11:8 And shall also carry captives into Egypt their gods, with their princes, *and* with their precious vessels of silver and of gold; and he shall continue *more* years than the king of the north.

Da 11:38 But in his estate shall he honour the God of forces: and a god whom his fathers knew not shall he honour with gold, and silver, and with precious stones, and pleasant things.

Ho 3:1 Then said the Lord unto me, Go yet, love a woman beloved of *her* friend, yet an adulteress, according to the love of the Lord toward the children of Israel, who look to other gods, and love flagons of wine.

Jona 1:5 Then the mariners were afraid, and cried every man unto his god, and cast forth the wares that *were* in the ship into the sea, to lighten *it* of them. But Jonah was gone down into the sides of the ship; and he lay, and was fast asleep.

Mi 4:5 For all people will walk every one in the name of his god, and we will walk in the name of the Lord our God for ever and ever.

Hab 1:11 Then shall *his* mind change, and he shall pass over, and offend, *imputing* this his power unto his god.

Hab 2:18 What profiteth the graven image that the maker thereof hath graven it; the molten image, and a teacher of lies, that the maker of his work trusteth therein, to make dumb idols?

Zep 2:11 The Lord *will be* terrible unto them: for he will famish all the gods of the earth; and *men* shall worship him, every one from his place, *even* all the isles of the heathen.

Ac 14:13 Then the priest of Jupiter, which was before their city, brought oxen and garlands unto the gates, and would have done sacrifice with the people.

Ac 19:26 Moreover ye see and hear, that not alone at Ephesus, but almost throughout all Asia, this Paul hath persuaded and turned away much people, saying that they be no gods, which are made with hands:

1 Co 8:5 For though there be that are called gods, whether in heaven or in earth, (as there be gods many, and lords many,)

1 Co 12:2 Ye know that ye were Gentiles, carried away unto these dumb idols, even as ye were led.

Ga 4:8 Howbeit then, when ye knew not God, ye did service unto them which by nature are no gods.

1. Names

a. Ashtoreth, or Ashtareth, a goddess of the Phoenicians

Jud 2:13 And they forsook the Lord, and served Baal and Ashtaroth.

Jud 10:6 And the children of Israel did evil again in the sight of the Lord, and served Baalim, and Ashtaroth, and the gods of Syria, and the gods of Zidon, and the gods of Moab, and the gods of the children of Ammon, and the gods of the Philistines, and forsook the Lord, and served not him.

1 S 7:3 And Samuel spake unto all the house of Israel, saying, If ye do return unto the Lord with all your hearts, then put away the strange gods and Ashtaroth from among you, and prepare your hearts unto the Lord, and serve him only: and he will deliver you out of the hand of the Philistines.

1 S 12:10 And they cried unto the Lord, and said, We have sinned, because we have forsaken the Lord, and have served Baalim and Ashtaroth: but now deliver us out of the hand of our enemies, and we will serve thee.

1 S 31:10 And they put his armour in the house of Ashtaroth: and they fastened his body to the wall of Bethshan.

1 K 11:5 For Solomon went after Ashtoreth the goddess of the Zidonians, and after Milcom the abomination of the Ammonites.

1 K 11:33 Because that they have forsaken me, and have worshipped Ashtoreth the goddess of the Zidonians, Chemosh the god of the Moabites, and Milcom the god of the

children of Ammon, and have not walked in my ways, to do that which is right in mine eyes, and to keep my statutes and my judgments, as did David his father.

2 K 23:13 And the high places that were before Jerusalem, which were on the right hand of the mount of corruption, which Solomon the king of Israel had builded for Ashtoreth the abomination of the Zidonians, and for Chemosh the abomination of the Moabites, and for Milcom the abomination of the children of Ammon, did the king defile.

b. Baal, a god of Phoenicia and the Canaanitish Tribes

Nu 22:41 And it came to pass on the morrow, that Balak took Balaam, and brought him up into the high places of Baal, that thence he might see the utmost part of the people.

Jud 2:11 And the children of Israel did evil in the sight of the Lord, and served Baalim:

Jud 3:7 And the children of Israel did evil in the sight of the Lord, and forgat the Lord their God, and served Baalim and the groves.

Jud 6:25 And it came to pass the same night, that the Lord said unto him, Take thy father's young bullock, even the second bullock of seven years old, and throw down the altar of Baal that thy father hath, and cut down the grove that is by it:

Jud 6:31 And Joash said unto all that stood against him, Will ye plead for Baal? will ye save him? he that will plead for him, let him be put to death whilst it is yet morning: if he be a god, let him plead for himself, because one hath cast down his altar.

Jud 8:33 And it came to pass, as soon as Gideon was dead, that the children of Israel turned again, and went a whoring after Baalim, and made Baalberith their god.

Jud 10:6 And the children of Israel did evil again in the sight of the Lord, and served Baalim, and Ashtaroth, and the gods of Syria, and the gods of Zidon, and the gods of Moab, and the gods of the children of Ammon, and the gods of the Philistines, and forsook the Lord, and served not him.

Jud 10:10 And the children of Israel cried unto the Lord, saying, We have sinned against thee, both because we have forsaken our God, and also served Baalim.

1 S 7:4 Then the children of Israel did put away Baalim and Ashtaroth, and served the Lord only.

1 K 16:32 And he reared up an altar for Baal in the house of Baal, which he had built in Samaria.

1 K 18:19 Now therefore send, *and* gather to me all Israel unto mount Carmel, and the prophets of Baal four hundred and fifty, and the prophets of the groves four hundred, which eat at Jezebel's table.

1 K 18:26 And they took the bullock which was given them, and they dressed *it,* and called on the name of Baal from morning even until noon, saying, O Baal, hear us. But *there was* no voice, nor any that answered. And they leaped upon the altar which was made.

1 K 19:18 Yet I have left *me* seven thousand in Israel, all the knees which have not bowed unto Baal, and every mouth which hath not kissed him.

1 K 22:53 For he served Baal, and worshipped him, and provoked to anger the Lord God of Israel, according to all that his father had done.

2 K 10:18–19 And Jehu gathered all the people together, and said unto them, Ahab served Baal a little; *but* Jehu shall serve him much.

Now therefore call unto me all the prophets of Baal, all his servants, and all his priests; let none be wanting: for I have a great sacrifice *to do* to Baal; whosoever shall be wanting, he shall not live. But Jehu did *it* in subtilty, to the intent that he might destroy the worshippers of Baal.

2 K 10:28 Thus Jehu destroyed Baal out of Israel.

2 K 17:16 And they left all the commandments of the Lord their God, and made them molten images, *even* two calves, and made a grove, and worshipped all the host of heaven, and served Baal.

2 K 21:3 For he built up again the high places which Hezekiah his father had destroyed; and he reared up altars for Baal, and made a grove, as did Ahab king of Israel; and worshipped all the host of heaven, and served them.

2 K 23:4 And the king commanded Hilkiah the high priest, and the priests of the second order, and the keepers of the door, to bring forth out of the temple of the Lord all the vessels that were made for Baal, and for the grove, and for all the host of heaven: and he burned them without Jerusalem in the fields of Kidron, and carried the ashes of them unto Bethel.

2 Chr 17:3 And the Lord was with Jehoshaphat, because he walked in the first ways of his father David, and sought not unto Baalim;

2 Chr 23:17 Then all the people went to the house of Baal, and brake it down, and brake his altars and his images in pieces, and slew Mattan the priest of Baal before the altars.

2 Chr 24:7 For the sons of Athaliah, that wicked woman, had broken up the house of God; and also all the dedicated things of the house of the Lord did they bestow upon Baalim.

2 Chr 28:2 For he walked in the ways of the kings of Israel, and made also molten images for Baalim.

2 Chr 33:3 For he built again the high places which Hezekiah his father had broken down, and he reared up altars for Baalim, and made groves, and worshipped all the host of heaven, and served them.

2 Chr 34:4 And they brake down the altars of Baalim in his presence; and the images, that *were* on high above them, he cut down; and the groves, and the carved images, and the molten images, he brake in pieces, and made dust *of them,* and strowed *it* upon the graves of them that had sacrificed unto them.

Je 2:8 The priests said not, Where *is* the Lord? and they that handle the law knew me not: the pastors also transgressed against me, and the prophets prophesied by Baal, and walked after *things that* do not profit.

Je 2:23 How canst thou say, I am not polluted, I have not gone after Baalim? see thy way in the valley, know what thou hast done: *thou art* a swift dromedary traversing her ways;

Je 7:9 Will ye steal, murder, and commit adultery, and swear falsely, and burn incense unto Baal, and walk after other gods whom ye know not;

Je 9:14 But have walked after the imagination of their own heart, and after Baalim, which their fathers taught them:

Je 11:13 For *according to* the number of thy cities were thy gods, O Judah; and *according to* the number of the streets of Jerusalem have ye set up altars to *that* shameful thing, *even* altars to burn incense unto Baal.

Je 11:17 For the Lord of hosts, that planted thee, hath pronounced evil against thee, for the evil of the house of Israel and of the house of Judah, which they have done against themselves to provoke me to anger in offering incense unto Baal.

Je 12:16 And it shall come to pass, if they will diligently learn the ways of my people, to swear by my name, The Lord liveth; as they taught my people to swear by Baal; then shall they be built in the midst of my people.

Je 19:5 They have built also the high places of Baal, to burn their sons with fire *for* burnt offerings unto Baal, which I commanded not, nor spake *it,* neither came *it* into my mind:

Je 23:13 And I have seen folly in the prophets of Samaria; they prophesied in Baal, and caused my people Israel to err.

Je 23:27 Which think to cause my people to forget my name by their dreams which they tell every man to his neighbour, as their fathers have forgotten my name for Baal.

Je 32:29 And the Chaldeans, that fight against this city, shall come and set fire on this city, and burn it with the houses, upon whose roofs they have offered incense unto Baal, and poured out drink offerings unto other gods, to provoke me to anger.

Je 32:35 And they built the high places of Baal, which *are* in the valley

of the son of Hinnom, to cause their sons and their daughters to pass through *the fire* unto Molech; which I commanded them not, neither came it into my mind, that they should do this abomination, to cause Judah to sin.

Ho 2:8 For she did not know that I gave her corn, and wine, and oil, and multiplied her silver and gold, *which* they prepared for Baal.

Ho 2:17 For I will take away the names of Baalim out of her mouth, and they shall no more be remembered by their name.

Ho 11:2 *As* they called them, so they went from them: they sacrificed unto Baalim, and burned incense to graven images.

Ho 13:1 When Ephraim spake trembling, he exalted himself in Israel; but when he offended in Baal, he died.

Zep 1:4 I will also stretch out mine hand upon Judah, and upon all the inhabitants of Jerusalem; and I will cut off the remnant of Baal from this place, *and* the name of the Chemarims with the priests;

Ro 11:4 But what saith the answer of God unto him? I have reserved to myself seven thousand men, who have not bowed the knee to *the image of* Baal.

c. Baal Peor, a god of the Moabites

Nu 25:3 And Israel joined himself unto Baal-peor: and the anger of the Lord was kindled against Israel.

De 4:3 Your eyes have seen what the Lord did because of Baal-peor: for all the men that followed Baal-peor, the Lord thy God hath destroyed them from among you.

Jos 22:17 *Is* the iniquity of Peor too little for us, from which we are not cleansed until this day, although there was a plague in the congregation of the Lord,

Ps 106:28 They joined themselves also unto Baal-peor, and ate the sacrifices of the dead.

Ho 9:10 I found Israel like grapes in the wilderness; I saw your fathers as the firstripe in the fig tree at her first time: *but* they went to Baal-peor, and separated themselves unto *that* shame; and *their* abominations were according as they loved.

d. Chemosh, a god of the Moabites

Nu 21:29 Woe to thee, Moab! thou art undone, O people of Chemosh: he hath given his sons that escaped, and his daughters, into captivity unto Sihon king of the Amorites.

Jud 11:24 Wilt not thou possess that which Chemosh thy god giveth thee to possess? So whomsoever the Lord our God shall drive out from before us, them will we possess.

2 K 23:13 And the high places that *were* before Jerusalem, which *were* on the right hand of the mount of corruption, which Solomon the king of Israel had builded for Ashtoreth the abomination of the Zidonians, and for Chemosh the abomination of the Moabites, and for Milcom the abomination of the children of Ammon, did the king defile.

Je 48:7 For because thou hast trusted in thy works and in thy treasures, thou shalt also be taken: and Chemosh shall go forth into captivity *with* his priests and his princes together.

Je 48:13 And Moab shall be ashamed of Chemosh, as the house of Israel was ashamed of Bethel their confidence.

Je 48:46 Woe be unto thee, O Moab! the people of Chemosh perisheth: for thy sons are taken captives, and thy daughters captives.

e. Dagon, a god of the Philistines

Jud 16:23 Then the lords of the Philistines gathered them together for to offer a great sacrifice unto Dagon their god, and to rejoice: for they said, Our god hath delivered Samson our enemy into our hand.

1 S 5:2 When the Philistines took the ark of God, they brought it into the house of Dagon, and set it by Dagon.

1 Chr 10:10 And they put his armour in the house of their gods, and fastened his head in the temple of Dagon.

f. Diana, a goddess of the Ephesians

Ac 19:24 For a certain *man* named Demetrius, a silversmith, which made silver shrines for Diana, brought no small gain unto the craftsmen;

Ac 19:28 And when they heard *these sayings,* they were full of wrath, and cried out, saying, Great *is* Diana of the Ephesians.

Ac 19:35 And when the townclerk had appeased the people, he said, Ye men of Ephesus, what man is there that knoweth not how that the city of the Ephesians is a worshipper of the great goddess Diana, and of the *image* which fell down from Jupiter?

g. Molech, Moloch, or Milcom, a god of the Ammonites

Le 18:21 And thou shalt not let any of thy seed pass through *the fire* to Molech, neither shalt thou profane the name of thy God: I *am* the Lord.

Le 20:3 And I will set my face against that man, and will cut him off from among his people; because he hath given of his seed unto Molech, to defile my sanctuary, and to profane my holy name.

1 K 11:7 Then did Solomon build an high place for Chemosh, the abomination of Moab, in the hill that *is* before Jerusalem, and for Molech, the abomination of the children of Ammon.

2 K 23:10 And he defiled Topheth, which *is* in the valley of the children of Hinnom, that no man might make his son or his daughter to pass through the fire to Molech.

Je 32:35 And they built the high places of Baal, which *are* in the valley of the son of Hinnom, to cause their sons and their daughters to pass through *the fire* unto Molech; which I commanded them not, neither came it into my mind, that they should do this abomination, to cause Judah to sin.

Ac 7:43 Yea, ye took up the tabernacle of Moloch, and the star of your god Remphan, figures which ye made to worship them: and I will carry you away beyond Babylon.

2. Other Objects of Worship

a. The Golden Calf Made by Aaron

Ex 32:4 And he received *them* at their hand, and fashioned it with a graving tool, after he had made it a molten calf: and they said, These *be* thy gods, O Israel, which brought thee up out of the land of Egypt.

Ex 32:19 And it came to pass, as soon as he came nigh unto the camp, that he saw the calf, and the dancing: and Moses' anger waxed hot, and he cast the tables out of his hands, and brake them beneath the mount.

Ex 32:35 And the Lord plagued the people, because they made the calf, which Aaron made.

De 9:16 And I looked, and, behold, ye had sinned against the Lord your God, *and* had made you a molten calf: ye had turned aside quickly out of the way which the Lord had commanded you.

De 9:21 And I took your sin, the calf which ye had made, and burnt it with fire, and stamped it, *and* ground *it* very small, *even* until it was as small as dust: and I cast the dust thereof into the brook that descended out of the mount.

Ne 9:18 Yea, when they had made them a molten calf, and said, This *is* thy God that brought thee up out of Egypt, and had wrought great provocations;

Ps 106:19 They made a calf in Horeb, and worshipped the molten image.

Ac 7:41 And they made a calf in those days, and offered sacrifice unto the idol, and rejoiced in the works of their own hands.

b. The Golden Calves of Jeroboam

1 K 12:28 Whereupon the king took counsel, and made two calves *of* gold, and said unto them, It is too much for you to go up to Jerusalem: behold thy gods, O Israel, which brought thee up out of the land of Egypt.

2 K 10:29 Howbeit *from* the sins of Jeroboam the son of Nebat, who made Israel to sin, Jehu departed not from after them, *to wit,* the golden calves

that *were* in Bethel, and that *were* in Dan.

2 K 17:16 And they left all the commandments of the Lord their God, and made them molten images, *even* two calves, and made a grove, and worshipped all the host of heaven, and served Baal.

2 K 17:21 For he rent Israel from the house of David; and they made Jeroboam the son of Nebat king: and Jeroboam drave Israel from following the Lord, and made them sin a great sin.

2 Chr 11:15 And he ordained him priests for the high places, and for the devils, and for the calves which he had made.

2 Chr 13:8 And now ye think to withstand the kingdom of the Lord in the hand of the sons of David; and ye *be* a great multitude, and *there are* with you golden calves, which Jeroboam made you for gods.

Ho 8:5 Thy calf, O Samaria, hath cast *thee* off; mine anger is kindled against them: how long *will it be* ere they attain to innocency?

Ho 10:5 The inhabitants of Samaria shall fear because of the calves of Beth-aven: for the people thereof shall mourn over it, and the priests thereof *that* rejoiced on it, for the glory thereof, because it is departed from it.

Ho 13:2 And now they sin more and more, and have made them molten images of their silver, *and* idols according to their own understanding, all of it the work of the craftsmen: they say of them, Let the men that sacrifice kiss the calves.

Am 8:14 They that swear by the sin of Samaria, and say, Thy god, O Dan, liveth; and, The manner of Beer-sheba liveth; even they shall fall, and never rise up again.

c. Heavenly Bodies

De 4:19 And lest thou lift up thine eyes unto heaven, and when thou seest the sun, and the moon, and the stars, *even* all the host of heaven, shouldest be driven to worship them, and serve them, which the Lord thy

God hath divided unto all nations under the whole heaven.

De 17:3 And hath gone and served other gods, and worshipped them, either the sun, or moon, or any of the host of heaven, which I have not commanded;

2 K 17:16 And they left all the commandments of the Lord their God, and made them molten images, *even* two calves, and made a grove, and worshipped all the host of heaven, and served Baal.

2 K 21:3 For he built up again the high places which Hezekiah his father had destroyed; and he reared up altars for Baal, and made a grove, as did Ahab king of Israel; and worshipped all the host of heaven, and served them.

2 K 23:5 And he put down the idolatrous priests, whom the kings of Judah had ordained to burn incense in the high places in the cities of Judah, and in the places round about Jerusalem; them also that burned incense unto Baal, to the sun, and to the moon, and to the planets, and to all the host of heaven.

2 K 23:11 And he took away the horses that the kings of Judah had given to the sun, at the entering in of the house of the Lord, by the chamber of Nathan-melech the chamberlain, which *was* in the suburbs, and burned the chariots of the sun with fire.

2 K 23:11 And he took away the horses that the kings of Judah had given to the sun, at the entering in of the house of the Lord, by the chamber of Nathan-melech the chamberlain, which *was* in the suburbs, and burned the chariots of the sun with fire.

2 Chr 33:3 For he built again the high places which Hezekiah his father had broken down, and he reared up altars for Baalim, and made groves, and worshipped all the host of heaven, and served them.

Jb 31:27 And my heart hath been secretly enticed, or my mouth hath kissed my hand:

Je 8:2 And they shall spread them before the sun, and the moon, and all the host of heaven, whom they have loved, and whom they have served, and after whom they have walked, and whom they have sought, and whom they have worshipped: they shall not be gathered, nor be buried; they shall be for dung upon the face of the earth.

Je 19:13 And the houses of Jerusalem, and the houses of the kings of Judah, shall be defiled as the place of Tophet, because of all the houses upon whose roofs they have burned incense unto all the host of heaven, and have poured out drink offerings unto other gods.

Je 44:17 But we will certainly do whatsoever thing goeth forth out of our own mouth, to burn incense unto the queen of heaven, and to pour out drink offerings unto her, as we have done, we, and our fathers, our kings, and our princes, in the cities of Judah, and in the streets of Jerusalem: for *then* had we plenty of victuals, and were well, and saw no evil.

Eze 8:16 And he brought me into the inner court of the Lord's house, and, behold, at the door of the temple of the Lord, between the porch and the altar, *were* about five and twenty men, with their backs toward the temple of the Lord, and their faces toward the east; and they worshipped the sun toward the east.

Zep 1:5 And them that worship the host of heaven upon the housetops; and them that worship *and* that swear by the Lord, and that swear by Malcham;

Ac 7:42 Then God turned, and gave them up to worship the host of heaven; as it is written in the book of the prophets, O ye house of Israel, have ye offered to me slain beasts and sacrifices *by the space of* forty years in the wilderness?

d. Teraphim Images, Household Gods

Ge 31:19 And Laban went to shear his sheep: and Rachel had stolen the images that *were* her father's.

Ge 31:34 Now Rachel had taken the images, and put them in the camel's furniture, and sat upon them. And

Laban searched all the tent, but found *them* not.

Jud 17:5 And the man Micah had an house of gods, and made an ephod, and teraphim, and consecrated one of his sons, who became his priest.

Jud 18:14 Then answered the five men that went to spy out the country of Laish, and said unto their brethren, Do ye know that there is in these houses an ephod, and teraphim, and a graven image, and a molten image? now therefore consider what ye have to do.

1 S 19:13 And Michal took an image, and laid *it* in the bed, and put a pillow of goats' *hair* for his bolster, and covered *it* with a cloth.

Ho 3:4 For the children of Israel shall abide many days without a king, and without a prince, and without a sacrifice, and without an image, and without an ephod, and *without* teraphim:

e. Humans Deified and Worshipped

Jb 32:22 For I know not to give flattering titles; *in so doing* my maker would soon take me away.

Da 2:46 Then the king Nebuchadnezzar fell upon his face, and worshipped Daniel, and commanded that they should offer an oblation and sweet odours unto him.

Ac 8:10 To whom they all gave heed, from the least to the greatest, saying, This man is the great power of God.

Ac 12:22 And the people gave a shout, *saying, It is* the voice of a god, and not of a man.

Ac 14:11 And when the people saw what Paul had done, they lifted up their voices, saying in the speech of Lycaonia, The gods are come down to us in the likeness of men.

Ac 14:13 Then the priest of Jupiter, which was before their city, brought oxen and garlands unto the gates, and would have done sacrifice with the people.

Ac 28:6 Howbeit they looked when he should have swollen, or fallen down dead suddenly: but after they had looked a great while, and saw no harm come to him, they changed

their minds, and said that he was a god.

1 Co 3:21 Therefore let no man glory in men. For all things are yours;

f. Devils Worshipped

Le 17:7 And they shall no more offer their sacrifices unto devils, after whom they have gone a whoring. This shall be a statute for ever unto them throughout their generations.

De 32:17 They sacrificed unto devils, not to God; to gods whom they knew not, to new *gods that* came newly up, whom your fathers feared not.

2 Chr 11:15 And he ordained him priests for the high places, and for the devils, and for the calves which he had made.

Ps 106:37 Yea, they sacrificed their sons and their daughters unto devils,

Mt 4:9 And saith unto him, All these things will I give thee, if thou wilt fall down and worship me.

Lu 4:7 If thou therefore wilt worship me, all shall be thine.

1 Co 10:20 But *I say,* that the things which the Gentiles sacrifice, they sacrifice to devils, and not to God: and I would not that ye should have fellowship with devils.

Re 9:20 And the rest of the men which were not killed by these plagues yet repented not of the works of their hands, that they should not worship devils, and idols of gold, and silver, and brass, and stone, and of wood: which neither can see, nor hear, nor walk:

Re 13:4 And they worshipped the dragon which gave power unto the beast: and they worshipped the beast, saying, Who *is* like unto the beast? who is able to make war with him?

Re 14:9 And the third angel followed them, saying with a loud voice, If any man worship the beast and his image, and receive *his* mark in his forehead, or in his hand,

Re 19:20 And the beast was taken, and with him the false prophet that wrought miracles before him, with which he deceived them that had received the mark of the beast, and them that worshipped his image.

These both were cast alive into a lake of fire burning with brimstone.

GOLAN, *a town of Bashan*

De 4:43; Jos 20:8; 21:27; 1 Chr 6:71

See **CITIES**

GOLD, *a precious metal*

Ge 2:12; Ex 12:35; 25:3, 11, 13, 28, 36; 26:6, 29, 32, 37; 28:6, 14, 20; 30:3; 31:4; 35:22; 36:13, 34; 37:2, 6, 11, 17, 22, 26; 38:24; 39:2, 13, 15; Nu 7:20, 50, 62, 80, 86; 8:4; 31:22, 51; Jos 6:19, 24; 7:24; Jud 8:26; 1 S 6:11; 2 S 8:7; 1 K 6:20, 28, 35; 9:11, 28; 10:10, 14, 18; 15:15; 22:48; 2 K 20:13; 23:33; 25:15; 1 Chr 22:16; 28:17; 29:2, 4; 2 Chr 1:15; 3:4; 4:7, 21; 5:1; 8:18; 9:10, 13, 24; 15:18; Ezr 1:9; 7:16; 8:25; Ne 7:71; Est 1:7; Jb 22:24; 28:1; Ps 45:9; 105:37; Ec 2:8; Is 60:6; Eze 28:4; 38:13; Da 2:32; Jl 3:5; Zep 1:18; Hag 2:8; Zec 6:11; Mt 2:11; 10:9; 23:16; Ac 3:6; 20:33; Ja 5:3; 1 Pe 1:18; Re 18:12

Things More Precious

Jb 28:15 It cannot be gotten for gold, neither shall silver be weighed *for* the price thereof.

Ps 19:10 More to be desired are they than gold, yea, than much fine gold: sweeter also than honey and the honeycomb.

Ps 119:127 Therefore I love thy commandments above gold; yea, above fine gold.

Pr 3:14 For the merchandise of it *is* better than the merchandise of silver, and the gain thereof than fine gold.

Pr 8:19 My fruit *is* better than gold, yea, than fine gold; and my revenue than choice silver.

Is 13:12 I will make a man more precious than fine gold; even a man than the golden wedge of Ophir.

GOLDEN RULE, *"whatsoever ye would that men should do to you, do ye even so to them"*

Mt 7:12 Therefore all things whatsoever ye would that men should do to you, do ye even so to them: for this is the law and the prophets.

Lu 6:31 And as ye would that men should do to you, do ye also to them likewise.

2 Co 8:14 But by an equality, *that* now at this time your abundance *may be a supply* for their want, that their abundance also may be *a supply* for your want: that there may be equality:

Ga 6:1 Brethren, if a man be overtaken in a fault, ye which are spiritual, restore such an one in the spirit of meekness; considering thyself, lest thou also be tempted.

Ja 2:8 If ye fulfil the royal law according to the scripture, Thou shalt love thy neighbour as thyself, ye do well:

See **COMMANDS**

GOLDSMITHS　See **ARTS AND CRAFTS**

GOLGOTHA, *place of a skull, the site of the crucifixion*

Mt 27:33; Mk 15:22; Jn 19:17

See **CHRIST, SUFFERING**

GOLIATH, *a giant slain by David*

1 S 17:4, 23; 21:9; 2 S 21:19; 1 Chr 20:5

GOOD AND EVIL

IN SOCIETY

Mt 9:10 And it came to pass, as Jesus sat at meat in the house, behold, many publicans and sinners came and sat down with him and his disciples.

IN CHRISTIAN WORK

Mt 10:16 Behold, I send you forth as sheep in the midst of wolves: be ye therefore wise as serpents, and harmless as doves.

IN THE CHURCH

Mt 13:29 But he said, Nay; lest while ye gather up the tares, ye root up also the wheat with them.

THE GOOD IN CONTACT WITH EVIL
AS A SAVING INFLUENCE

Mt 5:13 Ye are the salt of the earth: but if the salt have lost his savour, wherewith shall it be salted? it is thenceforth good for nothing, but to be cast out, and to be trodden under foot of men.

Jn 17:15 I pray not that thou shouldest take them out of the world, but that thou shouldest keep them from the evil.

A DAY OF SEPARATION

Lu 17:34 I tell you, in that night there shall be two *men* in one bed; the one shall be taken, and the other shall be left.

GOOD FOR EVIL, *response of kindness when mistreated*

1. Examples

JOSEPH

Ge 45:15 Moreover he kissed all his brethren, and wept upon them: and after that his brethren talked with him.

MOSES

Nu 12:13 And Moses cried unto the LORD, saying, Heal her now, O God, I beseech thee.

DAVID

1 S 24:17 And he said to David, Thou *art* more righteous than I: for thou hast rewarded me good, whereas I have rewarded thee evil.

1 S 26:11 The LORD forbid that I should stretch forth mine hand against the LORD's anointed: but, I pray thee, take thou now the spear that *is* at his bolster, and the cruse of water, and let us go.

ELISHA

Ps 35:13 But as for me, when they were sick, my clothing *was* sackcloth: I humbled my soul with fasting; and my prayer returned into mine own bosom.

JESUS

Lu 22:51 And Jesus answered and said, Suffer ye thus far. And he touched his ear, and healed him.

Lu 23:34 Then said Jesus, Father, forgive them; for they know not what they do. And they parted his raiment, and cast lots.

STEPHEN

Ac 7:60 And he kneeled down, and cried with a loud voice, Lord, lay not this sin to their charge. And when he had said this, he fell asleep.

1 Co 4:12 And labour, working with our own hands: being reviled, we bless; being persecuted, we suffer it:

2. Prescribed

Ex 23:5 If thou see the ass of him that hateth thee lying under his burden, and wouldest forbear to help him, thou shalt surely help with him.

Pr 24:29 Say not, I will do so to him as he hath done to me: I will render to the man according to his work.

Pr 25:21 If thine enemy be hungry, give him bread to eat; and if he be thirsty, give him water to drink:

Mt 5:44 But I say unto you, Love your enemies, bless them that curse you, do good to them that hate you, and pray for them which despitefully use you, and persecute you;

Lu 6:27 But I say unto you which hear, Love your enemies, do good to them which hate you,

Lu 6:35 But love ye your enemies, and do good, and lend, hoping for nothing again; and your reward shall be great, and ye shall be the children of the Highest: for he is kind unto the unthankful and *to* the evil.

Ro 12:20 Therefore if thine enemy hunger, feed him; if he thirst, give him drink: for in so doing thou shalt heap coals of fire on his head.

1 Th 5:15 See that none render evil for evil unto any *man;* but ever follow that which is good, both among yourselves, and to all *men.*

See **RETALIATION, REVENGE**

GOODNESS, OF GOD

Ex 18:9 And Jethro rejoiced for all the goodness which the LORD had done to Israel, whom he had delivered out of the hand of the Egyptians.

Ex 33:19 And he said, I will make all my goodness pass before thee, and I

will proclaim the name of the LORD before thee; and will be gracious to whom I will be gracious, and will shew mercy on whom I will shew mercy.

Ex 34:6 And the LORD passed by before him, and proclaimed, The LORD, The LORD God, merciful and gracious, longsuffering, and abundant in goodness and truth,

1 K 8:66 On the eighth day he sent the people away: and they blessed the king, and went unto their tents joyful and glad of heart for all the goodness that the LORD had done for David his servant, and for Israel his people.

1 Chr 16:34 O give thanks unto the LORD; for *he is* good; for his mercy *endureth* for ever.

2 Chr 5:13 It came even to pass, as the trumpeters and singers *were* as one, to make one sound to be heard in praising and thanking the LORD; and when they lifted up *their* voice with the trumpets and cymbals and instruments of musick, and praised the LORD, *saying,* For *he is* good; for his mercy *endureth* for ever: that *then* the house was filled with a cloud, *even* the house of the LORD;

2 Chr 7:3 And when all the children of Israel saw how the fire came down, and the glory of the LORD upon the house, they bowed themselves with their faces to the ground upon the pavement, and worshipped, and praised the LORD, *saying,* For *he is* good; for his mercy *endureth* for ever.

2 Chr 7:10 And on the three and twentieth day of the seventh month he sent the people away into their tents, glad and merry in heart for the goodness that the LORD had shewed unto David, and to Solomon, and to Israel his people.

Ezr 3:11 And they sang together by course in praising and giving thanks unto the LORD; because *he is* good, for his mercy *endureth* for ever toward Israel. And all the people shouted with a great shout, when they praised the LORD, because the foundation of the house of the LORD was laid.

Ne 9:25 And they took strong cities, and a fat land, and possessed houses full of all goods, wells digged, vine-

yards, and oliveyards, and fruit trees in abundance: so they did eat, and were filled, and became fat, and delighted themselves in thy great goodness.

Ne 9:35 For they have not served thee in their kingdom, and in thy great goodness that thou gavest them, and in the large and fat land which thou gavest before them, neither turned they from their wicked works.

Ps 23:6 Surely goodness and mercy shall follow me all the days of my life: and I will dwell in the house of the LORD for ever.

Ps 25:8 Good and upright *is* the LORD: therefore will he teach sinners in the way.

Ps 27:13 *I had fainted,* unless I had believed to see the goodness of the LORD in the land of the living.

Ps 31:19 *Oh* how great *is* thy goodness, which thou hast laid up for them that fear thee; *which* thou hast wrought for them that trust in thee before the sons of men!

Ps 33:5 He loveth righteousness and judgment: the earth is full of the goodness of the LORD.

Ps 34:8 O taste and see that the LORD *is* good: blessed *is* the man *that* trusteth in him.

Ps 52:1 Why boastest thou thyself in mischief, O mighty man? the goodness of God *endureth* continually.

Ps 65:11 Thou crownest the year with thy goodness; and thy paths drop fatness.

Ps 73:1 Truly God *is* good to Israel, *even* to such as are of a clean heart.

Ps 86:5 For thou, Lord, *art* good, and ready to forgive; and plenteous in mercy unto all them that call upon thee.

Ps 100:5 For the LORD *is* good; his mercy *is* everlasting; and his truth *endureth* to all generations.

Ps 106:1 Praise ye the LORD. O give thanks unto the LORD; for *he is* good: for his mercy *endureth* for ever.

Ps 107:1 O give thanks unto the LORD, for *he is* good: for his mercy *endureth* for ever.

Ps 107:8 Oh that *men* would praise the LORD *for* his goodness, and *for* his

wonderful works to the children of men!

Ps 107:15 Oh that *men* would praise the LORD *for* his goodness, and *for* his wonderful works to the children of men!

Ps 107:21 Oh that *men* would praise the LORD *for* his goodness, and *for* his wonderful works to the children of men!

Ps 107:31 Oh that *men* would praise the LORD *for* his goodness, and *for* his wonderful works to the children of men!

Ps 118:1 O give thanks unto the LORD; for *he is* good: because his mercy *endureth* for ever.

Ps 118:29 O give thanks unto the LORD; for *he is* good: for his mercy *endureth* for ever.

Ps 119:68 Thou *art* good, and doest good; teach me thy statutes.

Ps 125:4 Do good, O LORD, unto *those that be* good, and *to them that are* upright in their hearts.

Ps 135:3 Praise the LORD; for the LORD *is* good: sing praises unto his name; for *it is* pleasant.

Ps 136:1 O give thanks unto the LORD; for *he is* good: for his mercy *endureth* for ever.

Ps 145:7 They shall abundantly utter the memory of thy great goodness, and shall sing of thy righteousness.

Is 63:7 I will mention the lovingkindnesses of the LORD, *and* the praises of the LORD, according to all that the LORD hath bestowed on us, and the great goodness toward the house of Israel, which he hath bestowed on them according to his mercies, and according to the multitude of his lovingkindnesses.

Je 31:14 And I will satiate the soul of the priests with fatness, and my people shall be satisfied with my goodness, saith the LORD.

Je 32:40 And I will make an everlasting covenant with them, that I will not turn away from them, to do them good; but I will put my fear in their hearts, that they shall not depart from me.

Je 33:11 The voice of joy, and the voice of gladness, the voice of the bridegroom, and the voice of the bride, the voice of them that shall say, Praise the LORD of hosts: for the LORD *is* good; for his mercy *endureth* for ever: *and* of them that shall bring the sacrifice of praise into the house of the LORD. For I will cause to return the captivity of the land, as at the first, saith the LORD.

Lam 3:25 The LORD *is* good unto them that wait for him, to the soul *that* seeketh him.

Ho 3:5 Afterward shall the children of Israel return, and seek the LORD their God, and David their king; and shall fear the LORD and his goodness in the latter days.

Na 1:7 The LORD *is* good, a strong hold in the day of trouble; and he knoweth them that trust in him.

Zec 9:17 For how great *is* his goodness, and how great *is* his beauty! corn shall make the young men cheerful, and new wine the maids.

Mt 5:45 That ye may be the children of your Father which is in heaven: for he maketh his sun to rise on the evil and on the good, and sendeth rain on the just and on the unjust.

Mt 18:14 Even so it is not the will of your Father which is in heaven, that one of these little ones should perish.

Mt 19:17 And he said unto him, Why callest thou me good? *there is* none good but one, *that is,* God: but if thou wilt enter into life, keep the commandments.

Mt 20:15 Is it not lawful for me to do what I will with mine own? Is thine eye evil, because I am good?

Mk 10:18 And Jesus said unto him, Why callest thou me good? *there is* none good but one, *that is,* God.

Lu 6:35 But love ye your enemies, and do good, and lend, hoping for nothing again; and your reward shall be great, and ye shall be the children of the Highest: for he is kind unto the unthankful and *to* the evil.

Lu 15:12 And the younger of them said to *his* father, Father, give me the portion of goods that falleth *to me.* And he divided unto them *his* living.

Lu 15:31 And he said unto him, Son, thou art ever with me, and all that I have is thine.

Lu 18:19 And Jesus said unto him, Why callest thou me good? none *is* good, save one, *that is*, God.

Ro 2:4 Or despisest thou the riches of his goodness and forbearance and long-suffering; not knowing that the goodness of God leadeth thee to repentance?

Ro 11:22 Behold therefore the goodness and severity of God: on them which fell, severity; but toward thee, goodness, if thou continue in his goodness: otherwise thou also shalt be cut off.

2 Th 1:11 Wherefore also we pray always for you, that our God would count you worthy of *this* calling, and fulfil all the good pleasure of *his* goodness, and the work of faith with power:

See **EVIL**

GOOD SAMARITAN *See* KINDSNESS

GOSHEN, *a district of Egypt occupied by the Israelites*

Ge 45:10; 46:34; 47:4, 27; 50:8; Ex 8:22

GOSPEL, *GOOD NEWS*

Mt 4:23 And Jesus went about all Galilee, teaching in their synagogues, and preaching the gospel of the kingdom, and healing all manner of sickness and all manner of disease among the people.

Ac 20:24 But none of these things move me, neither count I my life dear unto myself, so that I might finish my course with joy, and the ministry, which I have received of the Lord Jesus, to testify the gospel of the grace of God.

1 Co 9:12 If others be partakers of *this* power over you, *are* not we rather? Nevertheless we have not used this power; but suffer all things, lest we should hinder the gospel of Christ.

2 Co 4:3 But if our gospel be hid, it is hid to them that are lost:

Ep 6:19 And for me, that utterance may be given unto me, that I may open my mouth boldly, to make known the mystery of the gospel,

Ph 1:27 Only let your conversation be as it becometh the gospel of Christ: that whether I come and see you, or else be absent, I may hear of your affairs, that ye stand fast in one spirit, with one mind striving together for the faith of the gospel;

1 Th 1:5 For our gospel came not unto you in word only, but also in power, and in the Holy Ghost, and in much assurance; as ye know what manner of men we were among you for your sake.

2 Th 1:8 In flaming fire taking vengeance on them that know not God, and that obey not the gospel of our Lord Jesus Christ:

1. Prophecies

Is 2:3 And many people shall go and say, Come ye, and let us go up to the mountain of the LORD, to the house of the God of Jacob; and he will teach us of his ways, and we will walk in his paths: for out of Zion shall go forth the law, and the word of the LORD from Jerusalem.

Is 29:18 And in that day shall the deaf hear the words of the book, and the eyes of the blind shall see out of obscurity, and out of darkness.

Is 40:9 O Zion, that bringest good tidings, get thee up into the high mountain; O Jerusalem, that bringest good tidings, lift up thy voice with strength; lift *it* up, be not afraid; say unto the cities of Judah, Behold your God!

Is 52:7 How beautiful upon the mountains are the feet of him that bringeth good tidings, that publisheth peace; that bringeth good tidings of good, that publisheth salvation; that saith unto Zion, Thy God reigneth!

Is 61:1 The Spirit of the Lord GOD *is* upon me; because the LORD hath anointed me to preach good tidings unto the meek; he hath sent me to bind up the brokenhearted, to proclaim liberty to the captives, and the opening of the prison to *them that are* bound;

Eze 47:5 Afterward he measured a thousand; *and it was* a river that I could not pass over: for the waters were risen, waters to swim in, a river that could not be passed over.

Mi 4:2 And many nations shall come, and say, Come, and let us go up to the mountain of the LORD, and to the house of the God of Jacob; and he will teach us of his ways, and we will walk in his paths: for the law shall go forth of Zion, and the word of the LORD from Jerusalem.

Mt 24:14 And this gospel of the kingdom shall be preached in all the world for a witness unto all nations; and then shall the end come.

2. *Universal*, to be preached throughout the world

Ps 22:27 All the ends of the world shall remember and turn unto the LORD: and all the kindreds of the nations shall worship before thee.

Is 11:9 They shall not hurt nor destroy in all my holy mountain: for the earth shall be full of the knowledge of the LORD, as the waters cover the sea.

Is 24:16 From the uttermost part of the earth have we heard songs, *even* glory to the righteous. But I said, My leanness, my leanness, woe unto me! the treacherous dealers have dealt treacherously; yea, the treacherous dealers have dealt very treacherously.

Is 42:4 He shall not fail nor be discouraged, till he have set judgment in the earth: and the isles shall wait for his law.

Is 49:6 And he said, It is a light thing that thou shouldest be my servant to raise up the tribes of Jacob, and to restore the preserved of Israel: I will also give thee for a light to the Gentiles, that thou mayest be my salvation unto the end of the earth.

Is 56:3 Neither let the son of the stranger, that hath joined himself to the LORD, speak, saying, The LORD hath utterly separated me from his people: neither let the eunuch say, Behold, I *am* a dry tree.

Is 66:19 And I will set a sign among them, and I will send those that escape of them unto the nations, *to* Tarshish, Pul, and Lud, that draw the bow, *to* Tubal, and Javan, *to* the isles afar off,

that have not heard my fame, neither have seen my glory; and they shall declare my glory among the Gentiles.

Hab 2:14 For the earth shall be filled with the knowledge of the glory of the LORD, as the waters cover the sea.

Zec 14:8 And it shall be in that day, *that* living waters shall go out from Jerusalem; half of them toward the former sea, and half of them toward the hinder sea: in summer and in winter shall it be.

Mal 1:11 For from the rising of the sun even unto the going down of the same my name *shall be* great among the Gentiles; and in every place incense *shall be* offered unto my name, and a pure offering: for my name *shall be* great among the heathen, saith the LORD of hosts.

Mt 13:33 Another parable spake he unto them; The kingdom of heaven is like unto leaven, which a woman took, and hid in three measures of meal, till the whole was leavened.

Mt 13:38 The field is the world; the good seed are the children of the kingdom; but the tares are the children of the wicked *one;*

Mt 22:10 So those servants went out into the highways, and gathered together all as many as they found, both bad and good: and the wedding was furnished with guests.

Mt 24:14 And this gospel of the kingdom shall be preached in all the world for a witness unto all nations; and then shall the end come.

Mt 26:13 Verily I say unto you, Wheresoever this gospel shall be preached in the whole world, *there* shall also this, that this woman hath done, be told for a memorial of her.

Mt 28:19 Go ye therefore, and teach all nations, baptizing them in the name of the Father, and of the Son, and of the Holy Ghost:

Mk 1:38 And he said unto them, Let us go into the next towns, that I may preach there also: for therefore came I forth.

Mk 13:10 And the gospel must first be published among all nations.

Mk 14:9 Verily I say unto you, Wheresoever this gospel shall be preached throughout the whole world, *this* also that she hath done shall be spoken of for a memorial of her.

Mk 16:15 And he said unto them, Go ye into all the world, and preach the gospel to every creature.

Lu 2:31 Which thou hast prepared before the face of all people;

Lu 13:21 It is like leaven, which a woman took and hid in three measures of meal, till the whole was leavened.

Lu 14:23 And the lord said unto the servant, Go out into the highways and hedges, and compel *them* to come in, that my house may be filled.

Lu 24:47 And that repentance and remission of sins should be preached in his name among all nations, beginning at Jerusalem.

Ac 1:8 But ye shall receive power, after that the Holy Ghost is come upon you: and ye shall be witnesses unto me both in Jerusalem, and in all Judaea, and in Samaria, and unto the uttermost part of the earth.

Ac 8:40 But Philip was found at Azotus: and passing through he preached in all the cities, till he came to Caesarea.

Ac 11:1 And the apostles and brethren that were in Judaea heard that the Gentiles had also received the word of God.

Ac 11:14 Who shall tell thee words, whereby thou and all thy house shall be saved.

Ac 13:32 And we declare unto you glad tidings, how that the promise which was made unto the fathers,

Ac 13:47 For so hath the Lord commanded us, *saying,* I have set thee to be a light of the Gentiles, that thou shouldest be for salvation unto the ends of the earth.

Ac 15:7 And when there had been much disputing, Peter rose up, and said unto them, Men *and* brethren, ye know how that a good while ago God made choice among us, that the Gentiles by my mouth should hear the word of the gospel, and believe.

Ac 26:20 But shewed first unto them of Damascus, and at Jerusalem, and

throughout all the coasts of Judaea, and *then* to the Gentiles, that they should repent and turn to God, and do works meet for repentance.

Ro 1:16 For I am not ashamed of the gospel of Christ: for it is the power of God unto salvation to every one that believeth; to the Jew first, and also to the Greek.

Ro 10:18 But I say, Have they not heard? Yes verily, their sound went into all the earth, and their words unto the ends of the world.

Ro 16:26 But now is made manifest, and by the scriptures of the prophets, according to the commandment of the everlasting God, made known to all nations for the obedience of faith:

Ep 3:6 That the Gentiles should be fellowheirs, and of the same body, and partakers of his promise in Christ by the gospel:

Col 1:6 Which is come unto you, as *it is* in all the world; and bringeth forth fruit, as *it doth* also in you, since the day ye heard *of it,* and knew the grace of God in truth:

Col 1:23 If ye continue in the faith grounded and settled, and *be* not moved away from the hope of the gospel, which ye have heard, *and* which was preached to every creature which is under heaven; whereof I Paul am made a minister;

2 Ti 4:17 Notwithstanding the Lord stood with me, and strengthened me; that by me the preaching might be fully known, and *that* all the Gentiles might hear: and I was delivered out of the mouth of the lion.

He 4:2 For unto us was the gospel preached, as well as unto them: but the word preached did not profit them, not being mixed with faith in them that heard *it.*

He 8:11 And they shall not teach every man his neighbour, and every man his brother, saying, Know the Lord: for all shall know me, from the least to the greatest.

Re 14:6 And I saw another angel fly in the midst of heaven, having the everlasting gospel to preach unto them that dwell on the earth, and to every nation, and kindred, and tongue, and people,

3. Stewardship, entrusted with the Good News of Jesus Christ

Eze 33:8 When I say unto the wicked, O wicked *man*, thou shalt surely die; if thou dost not speak to warn the wicked from his way, that wicked *man* shall die in his iniquity; but his blood will I require at thine hand.

1 Co 9:17 For if I do this thing willingly, I have a reward: but if against my will, a dispensation *of the gospel* is committed unto me.

Ga 2:7 But contrariwise, when they saw that the gospel of the uncircumcision was committed unto me, as *the gospel* of the circumcision *was* unto Peter;

Col 1:25 Whereof I am made a minister, according to the dispensation of God which is given to me for you, to fulfil the word of God;

1 Th 2:4 But as we were allowed of God to be put in trust with the gospel, even so we speak; not as pleasing men, but God, which trieth our hearts.

1 Ti 1:11 According to the glorious gospel of the blessed God, which was committed to my trust.

Tit 1:3 But hath in due times manifested his word through preaching, which is committed unto me according to the commandment of God our Saviour;

See **MISSIONS**

GOSSIPS *See* **ACTIVITY**

GOURDS, *swift growing plants, sometimes attaining a height of ten feet*
2 K 4:39

GOVERNMENT *See* **CHURCH, GOD, NATION**

GOZAN, *a river of Mesopotamia*
Ps 22:27; Is 11:9; 24:16; 42:4; 49:6; 56:3; 66:19; Hab 2:14; Zec 14:8; Mal 1:11; Mt 13:33, 38; 22:10; 24:14; 26:13; 28:19; Mk 1:38; 13:10; 14:9; 16:15; Lu 2:31; 13:21; 14:23; 24:47; Ac 1:8; 8:40; 11:1, 14; 13:32, 47; 15:7; 26:20; Ro 1:16;

10:18; 16:26; Ep 3:6; Col 1:6, 23; 2 Ti 4:17; He 4:2; 8:11; Re 14:6

See **RIVERS**

GRACE, *divine, unmerited favor, available to the sinner for salvation and the redeemed for victorious living*

1. Of God

FREELY GIVEN

Ps 84:11 For the LORD God *is* a sun and shield: the LORD will give grace and glory: no good *thing* will he withhold from them that walk uprightly.

Ac 11:23 Who, when he came, and had seen the grace of God, was glad, and exhorted them all, that with purpose of heart they would cleave unto the Lord.

Ac 13:43 Now when the congregation was broken up, many of the Jews and religious proselytes followed Paul and Barnabas: who, speaking to them, persuaded them to continue in the grace of God.

EMPOWERS MEN FOR SERVICE

1 Co 3:10 According to the grace of God which is given unto me, as a wise masterbuilder, I have laid the foundation, and another buildeth thereon. But let every man take heed how he buildeth thereupon.

1 Co 15:10 But by the grace of God I am what I am: and his grace *which was bestowed* upon me was not in vain; but I laboured more abundantly than they all: yet not I, but the grace of God which was with me.

ENABLES MEN TO LEAD THE SIMPLE LIFE

2 Co 1:12 For our rejoicing is this, the testimony of our conscience, that in simplicity and godly sincerity, not with fleshly wisdom, but by the grace of God, we have had our conversation in the world, and more abundantly to you-ward.

MAY BE RENDERED INEFFECTUAL

2 Co 6:1 We then, *as* workers together *with him*, beseech *you* also that ye receive not the grace of God in vain.

Ga 2:21 I do not frustrate the grace of God: for if righteousness *come* by the law, then Christ is dead in vain.

Ep 3:7 Whereof I was made a minister, according to the gift of the grace of God given unto me by the effectual working of his power.

He 2:9 But we see Jesus, who was made a little lower than the angels for the suffering of death, crowned with glory and honour; that he by the grace of God should taste death for every man.

Ja 4:6 But he giveth more grace. Wherefore he saith, God resisteth the proud, but giveth grace unto the humble.

PROMISED TO THE HUMBLE

1 Pe 5:5 Likewise, ye younger, submit yourselves unto the elder. Yea, all *of you* be subject one to another, and be clothed with humility: for God resisteth the proud, and giveth grace to the humble.

2. Of Christ

NOT GIVEN FOR SELFISH USE

1 Pe 4:10 As every man hath received the gift, *even so* minister the same one to another, as good stewards of the manifold grace of God.

EXHIBITED IN CHILDHOOD

Lu 2:40; Jn 1:17

MANIFESTED IN SELF-SACRIFICE

2 Co 8:9

SUFFICIENT FOR ALL HUMAN NEEDS

2 Co 12:9; Ep 4:7

BESTOWED UPON SINFUL MEN

1 Ti 1:12–13

THE SOURCE OF POWER

2 Ti 2:1; Re 22:21

3. Necessary for Salvation

Ac 15:11 But we believe that through the grace of the Lord Jesus Christ we shall be saved, even as they.

Ro 3:24 Being justified freely by his grace through the redemption that is in Christ Jesus:

Ro 4:16 Therefore *it is* of faith, that *it might be* by grace; to the end the promise might be sure to all the seed; not to that only which is of the law, but to that also which is of the faith of Abraham; who is the father of us all,

Ro 5:15 But not as the offence, so also *is* the free gift. For if through the offence of one many be dead, much more the grace of God, and the gift by grace, *which is* by one man, Jesus Christ, hath abounded unto many.

Ro 11:6 And if by grace, then *is it* no more of works: otherwise grace is no more grace. But if *it be* of works, then is it no more grace: otherwise work is no more work.

Ga 2:16 Knowing that a man is not justified by the works of the law, but by the faith of Jesus Christ, even we have believed in Jesus Christ, that we might be justified by the faith of Christ, and not by the works of the law: for by the works of the law shall no flesh be justified.

Ep 2:5 Even when we were dead in sins, hath quickened us together with Christ, (by grace ye are saved;)

Ep 2:8 For by grace are ye saved through faith; and that not of yourselves: *it is* the gift of God:

2 Ti 1:9 Who hath saved us, and called *us* with an holy calling, not according to our works, but according to his own purpose and grace, which was given us in Christ Jesus before the world began,

Tit 2:11 For the grace of God that bringeth salvation hath appeared to all men,

Tit 3:7 That being justified by his grace, we should be made heirs according to the hope of eternal life.

He 13:9 Be not carried about with divers and strange doctrines. For *it is* a good thing that the heart be established with grace; not with meats, which have not profited them that have been occupied therein.

4. Spiritual Riches

Is 55:7 Let the wicked forsake his way, and the unrighteous man his thoughts: and let him return unto the LORD, and he will have mercy upon him; and to our God, for he will abundantly pardon.

Lu 7:47 Wherefore I say unto thee, Her sins, which are many, are forgiven; for she loved much: but to whom little is forgiven, *the same* loveth little.

Lu 14:22 And the servant said, Lord, it is done as thou hast commanded, and yet there is room.

Lu 15:22 But the father said to his servants, Bring forth the best robe, and put *it* on him; and put a ring on his hand, and shoes on *his* feet:

Ro 2:4 Or despisest thou the riches of his goodness and forbearance and longsuffering; not knowing that the goodness of God leadeth thee to repentance?

Ro 5:20 Moreover the law entered, that the offence might abound. But where sin abounded, grace did much more abound:

Ro 8:32 He that spared not his own Son, but delivered him up for us all, how shall he not with him also freely give us all things?

Ro 9:23 And that he might make known the riches of his glory on the vessels of mercy, which he had afore prepared unto glory,

Ro 10:12 For there is no difference between the Jew and the Greek: for the same Lord over all is rich unto all that call upon him.

Ep 1:7 In whom we have redemption through his blood, the forgiveness of sins, according to the riches of his grace;

Ep 2:7 That in the ages to come he might shew the exceeding riches of his grace in *his* kindness toward us through Christ Jesus.

Ep 3:8 Unto me, who am less than the least of all saints, is this grace given, that I should preach among the Gentiles the unsearchable riches of Christ;

Ep 3:16 That he would grant you, according to the riches of his glory, to be strengthened with might by his Spirit in the inner man;

Ph 4:19 But my God shall supply all your need according to his riches in glory by Christ Jesus.

2 Th 2:16 Now our Lord Jesus Christ himself, and God, even our Father, which hath loved us, and hath given *us* everlasting consolation and good hope through grace,

1 Ti 1:14 And the grace of our Lord was exceeding abundant with faith and love which is in Christ Jesus.

Tit 3:6 Which he shed on us abundantly through Jesus Christ our Saviour;

1 Pe 1:3 Blessed *be* the God and Father of our Lord Jesus Christ, which according to his abundant mercy hath begotten us again unto a lively hope by the resurrection of Jesus Christ from the dead,

5. Is Unmerited

De 9:5 Not for thy righteousness, or for the uprightness of thine heart, dost thou go to possess their land: but for the wickedness of these nations the LORD thy God doth drive them out from before thee, and that he may perform the word which the LORD sware unto thy fathers, Abraham, Isaac, and Jacob.

Ps 103:10 He hath not dealt with us after our sins; nor rewarded us according to our iniquities.

Eze 20:44 And ye shall know that I *am* the LORD, when I have wrought with you for my name's sake, not according to your wicked ways, nor according to your corrupt doings, O ye house of Israel, saith the Lord GOD.

Eze 36:22 Therefore say unto the house of Israel, Thus saith the Lord GOD; I do not *this* for your sakes, O house of Israel, but for mine holy name's sake, which ye have profaned among the heathen, whither ye went.

Eze 36:32 Not for your sakes do I *this,* saith the Lord GOD, be it known unto you: be ashamed and confounded for your own ways, O house of Israel.

Da 9:18 O my God, incline thine ear, and hear; open thine eyes, and behold our desolations, and the city which is called by thy name: for we do not present our supplications before thee for our righteousnesses, but for thy great mercies.

Ro 4:16 Therefore *it is* of faith, that *it might be* by grace; to the end the promise might be sure to all the seed; not to that only which is of the law, but to that also which is of the faith of Abraham; who is the father of us all,

Ro 9:16 So then *it is* not of him that willeth, nor of him that runneth, but of God that sheweth mercy.

Tit 3:5 Not by works of righteousness which we have done, but according to his mercy he saved us, by the washing of regeneration, and renewing of the Holy Ghost;

6. Is Empowering

Lu 10:19 Behold, I give unto you power to tread on serpents and scorpions, and over all the power of the enemy: and nothing shall by any means hurt you.

Ro 14:4 Who art thou that judgest another man's servant? to his own master he standeth or falleth. Yea, he shall be holden up: for God is able to make him stand.

2 Co 3:6 Who also hath made us able ministers of the new testament; not of the letter, but of the spirit: for the letter killeth, but the spirit giveth life.

2 Co 9:8 And God *is* able to make all grace abound toward you; that ye, always having all sufficiency in all *things*, may abound to every good work:

Ph 4:13 I can do all things through Christ which strengtheneth me.

1 Ti 1:12 And I thank Christ Jesus our Lord, who hath enabled me, for that he counted me faithful, putting me into the ministry;

GRACE BEFORE MEALS *See* **FOOD**

GRAIN *See* **AGRICULTURE**

GRAPES *See* **AGRICULTURE**

GRASSHOPPERS *See* **INSECTS**

GRATITUDE

Ru 2:10 Then she fell on her face, and bowed herself to the ground, and said unto him, Why have I found grace in thine eyes, that thou shouldest take knowledge of me, seeing I *am* a stranger?

1 S 14:45 And the people said unto Saul, Shall Jonathan die, who hath wrought this great salvation in Israel? God forbid: *as* the LORD liveth, there shall not one hair of his head fall to the ground; for he hath wrought with God this day. So the people rescued Jonathan, that he died not.

1 S 15:6 And Saul said unto the Kenites, Go, depart, get you down from among the Amalekites, lest I destroy you with them: for ye shewed kindness to all the children of Israel, when they came up out of Egypt. So the Kenites departed from among the Amalekites.

2 S 9:1 And David said, Is there yet any that is left of the house of Saul, that I may shew him kindness for Jonathan's sake?

2 S 10:2 Then said David, I will shew kindness unto Hanun the son of Nahash, as his father shewed kindness unto me. And David sent to comfort him by the hand of his servants for his father. And David's servants came into the land of the children of Ammon.

1 K 2:7 But shew kindness unto the sons of Barzillai the Gileadite, and let them be of those that eat at thy table: for so they came to me when I fled because of Absalom thy brother.

2 K 4:13 And he said unto him, Say now unto her, Behold, thou hast been careful for us with all this care; what *is* to be done for thee? wouldest thou be spoken for to the king, or to the captain of the host? And she answered, I dwell among mine own people.

Ac 28:10 Who also honoured us with many honours; and when we departed, they laded *us* with such things as were necessary.

See **INGRATITUDE, THANKFULNESS, THANKLESSNESS**

GRAVE, *place of burial*

Ge 42:38; Jb 7:9; 10:22; 17:1, 13; 21:13, 32; 30:23; Ps 6:5; 49:14, 15; 141:7; Pr 30:16; Ec 9:10; 12:5; Is 5:14; 38:10; Eze 32:23; Ho 13:14; Jn 5:28; 11:17; 1 Co 15:55

See **DEATH**

GRAVE CLOTHES *See* **DEAD**

GREATNESS

1. Human

Ex 11:3; 2 Chr 17:12; Jb 1:3; 32:9; Pr 18:16; 25:6; Ec 2:9; Je 5:5; He 7:4

See **MAN**

2. God's

De 3:24 O Lord GOD, thou hast begun to shew thy servant thy greatness, and thy mighty hand: for what God *is there* in heaven or in earth, that can do according to thy works, and according to thy might?

De 5:24 And ye said, Behold, the LORD our God hath shewed us his glory and his greatness, and we have heard his voice out of the midst of the fire: we have seen this day that God doth talk with man, and he liveth.

De 9:26 I prayed therefore unto the LORD, and said, O Lord GOD, destroy not thy people and thine inheritance, which thou hast redeemed through thy greatness, which thou hast brought forth out of Egypt with a mighty hand.

De 10:17 For the LORD your God *is* God of gods, and Lord of lords, a great God, a mighty, and a terrible, which regardeth not persons, nor taketh reward:

De 11:2 And know ye this day: for *I speak* not with your children which have not known, and which have not seen the chastisement of the LORD your God, his greatness, his mighty hand, and his stretched out arm,

De 32:3 Because I will publish the name of the LORD: ascribe ye greatness unto our God.

2 S 7:22 Wherefore thou art great, O LORD God: for *there is* none like thee, neither *is there any* God beside thee, according to all that we have heard with our ears.

1 Chr 16:25 For great *is* the LORD, and greatly to be praised: he also *is* to be feared above all gods.

1 Chr 29:11 Thine, O LORD, *is* the greatness, and the power, and the glory, and the victory, and the majesty: for all *that is* in the heaven and in the earth *is thine*; thine *is* the kingdom, O LORD, and thou art exalted as head above all.

2 Chr 2:5 And the house which I build *is* great: for great *is* our God above all gods.

Ne 1:5 And said, I beseech thee, O LORD God of heaven, the great and terrible God, that keepeth covenant and mercy for them that love him and observe his commandments:

Ne 4:14 And I looked, and rose up, and said unto the nobles, and to the rulers, and to the rest of the people, Be not ye afraid of them: remember the Lord, *which is* great and terrible, and fight for your brethren, your sons, and your daughters, your wives, and your houses.

Ne 8:6 And Ezra blessed the LORD, the great God. And all the people answered, Amen, Amen, with lifting up their hands: and they bowed their heads, and worshipped the LORD with *their* faces to the ground.

Ne 9:32 Now therefore, our God, the great, the mighty, and the terrible God, who keepest covenant and mercy, let not all the trouble seem little before thee, that hath come upon us, on our kings, on our princes, and on our priests, and on our prophets, and on our fathers, and on all thy people, since the time of the kings of Assyria unto this day.

Jb 33:12 Behold, *in* this thou art not just: I will answer thee, that God is greater than man.

Jb 36:26 Behold, God *is* great, and we know *him* not, neither can the number of his years be searched out.

Ps 48:1 Great *is* the LORD, and greatly to be praised in the city of our God, *in* the mountain of his holiness.

Ps 77:13 Thy way, O God, *is* in the sanctuary: who *is* so great a God as *our* God?

Ps 86:10 For thou *art* great, and doest wondrous things: thou *art* God alone.

Ps 95:3 For the LORD *is* a great God, and a great King above all gods.

Ps 96:4 For the LORD *is* great, and greatly to be praised: he *is* to be feared above all gods.

Ps 99:2 The LORD *is* great in Zion; and he *is* high above all the people.

Ps 104:1 Bless the LORD, O my soul. O LORD my God, thou art very great; thou art clothed with honour and majesty.

Ps 135:5 For I know that the LORD *is* great, and *that* our Lord *is* above all gods.

Ps 145:3 Great *is* the LORD, and greatly to be praised; and his greatness *is* unsearchable.

Ps 145:6 And *men* shall speak of the might of thy terrible acts: and I will declare thy greatness.

Ps 147:5 Great *is* our Lord, and of great power: his understanding *is* infinite.

Ps 150:2 Praise him for his mighty acts: praise him according to his excellent greatness.

Is 12:6 Cry out and shout, thou inhabitant of Zion: for great *is* the Holy One of Israel in the midst of thee.

Is 40:12 Who hath measured the waters in the hollow of his hand, and meted out heaven with the span, and comprehended the dust of the earth in a measure, and weighed the mountains in scales, and the hills in a balance?

Je 10:6 Forasmuch as *there is* none like unto thee, O LORD; thou *art* great, and thy name is great in might.

Je 32:18 Thou shewest lovingkindness unto thousands, and recompensest the iniquity of the fathers into the bosom of their children after them: the Great, the Mighty God, the LORD of hosts, *is* his name,

Mal 1:11 For from the rising of the sun even unto the going down of the same my name *shall be* great among the Gentiles; and in every place incense *shall be* offered unto my name, and a pure offering: for my name *shall be* great among the heathen, saith the LORD of hosts.

Jn 10:29 My Father, which gave *them* me, is greater than all; and no *man* is able to pluck *them* out of my Father's hand.

Jn 14:28 Ye have heard how I said unto you, I go away, and come *again* unto you. If ye loved me, ye would rejoice, because I said, I go unto the Father: for my Father is greater than I.

He 6:13 For when God made promise to Abraham, because he could swear by no greater, he sware by himself,

See **GOD**

3. Christ's

Is 53:12 Therefore will I divide him *a portion* with the great, and he shall divide the spoil with the strong; because he hath poured out his soul unto death: and he was numbered with the transgressors; and he bare the sin of many, and made intercession for the transgressors.

Is 63:1 Who *is* this that cometh from Edom, with dyed garments from Bozrah? this *that is* glorious in his apparel, travelling in the greatness of his strength? I that speak in righteousness, mighty to save.

Mi 5:4 And he shall stand and feed in the strength of the LORD, in the majesty of the name of the LORD his God; and they shall abide: for now shall he be great unto the ends of the earth.

Mt 12:6 But I say unto you, That in this place is *one* greater than the temple.

Mt 12:41 The men of Nineveh shall rise in judgment with this generation, and shall condemn it: because they repented at the preaching of Jonas; and, behold, a greater than Jonas *is* here.

Lu 11:31 The queen of the south shall rise up in the judgment with the men of this generation, and condemn them: for she came from the utmost parts of the earth to hear the wisdom of Solomon; and, behold, a greater than Solomon is here.

Jn 3:31 He that cometh from above is above all: he that is of the earth is earthly, and speaketh of the earth: he that cometh from heaven is above all.

Jn 18:6 As soon then as he had said unto them, I am *he,* they went backward, and fell to the ground.

Ph 2:9–10 Wherefore God also hath highly exalted him, and given him a name which is above every name:

Ph 2:10 That at the name of Jesus every knee should bow, of *things* in heaven, and *things* in earth, and *things* under the earth;

See **CHRIST**

GREED, *an all-consuming desire for more than one needs or deserves*

1. Its Desire

1 S 8:3 And his sons walked not in his ways, but turned aside after lucre, and took bribes, and perverted judgment.

Pr 1:13 We shall find all precious substance, we shall fill our houses with spoil:

Pr 1:19 So *are* the ways of every one that is greedy of gain; *which* taketh away the life of the owners thereof.

Pr 15:27 He that is greedy of gain troubleth his own house; but he that hateth gifts shall live.

Pr 21:26 He coveteth greedily all the day long: but the righteous giveth and spareth not.

Is 56:11 Yea, *they are* greedy dogs *which* can never have enough, and they *are* shepherds *that* cannot understand: they all look to their own way, every one for his gain, from his quarter.

Mi 3:11 The heads thereof judge for reward, and the priests thereof teach for hire, and the prophets thereof divine for money: yet will they lean upon the LORD, and say, *Is* not the LORD among us? none evil can come upon us.

1 Ti 6:10 For the love of money is the root of all evil: which while some coveted after, they have erred from the faith, and pierced themselves through with many sorrows.

2. Its Misery

Pr 1:19 So *are* the ways of every one that is greedy of gain; *which* taketh away the life of the owners thereof.

Mt 27:5 And he cast down the pieces of silver in the temple, and departed, and went and hanged himself.

1 Ti 6:9 But they that will be rich fall into temptation and a snare, and *into* many foolish and hurtful lusts, which drown men in destruction and perdition.

Ja 5:3 Your gold and silver is cankered; and the rust of them shall be a witness against you, and shall eat your flesh as it were fire. Ye have heaped treasure together for the last days.

See **GIVING, MONEY**

GREEKS, *inhabitants of Greece*

Jn 12:20; Ac 6:1; 11:20; 14:1; 17:4, 12; 18:4; 19:10; 20:21; 21:28; Ro 1:14; 1 Co 1:22; Ga 2:3

GREYHOUND *See* **ANIMALS**

GROWTH, *development, progress toward maturity*

1. Prescribed

IN FRUITFULNESS

2 Co 9:10 Now he that ministereth seed to the sower both minister bread for *your* food, and multiply your seed sown, and increase the fruits of your righteousness;)

INTO CHRIST

Ep 4:15 But speaking the truth in love, may grow up into him in all things, which is the head, *even* Christ:

Col 1:10 That ye might walk worthy of the Lord unto all pleasing, being fruitful in every good work, and increasing in the knowledge of God;

IN LOVE

1 Th 3:12 And the Lord make you to increase and abound in love one toward another, and toward all *men,* even as we *do* toward you:

1 Th 4:10 And indeed ye do it toward all the brethren which are in all Macedonia: but we beseech you, brethren, that ye increase more and more;

UNTO PERFECTION

He 6:1 Therefore leaving the principles of the doctrine of Christ, let us go on unto perfection; not laying again the foundation of repentance from dead works, and of faith toward God,

2. Examples

THE BOY SAMUEL

1 S 2:26 And the child Samuel grew on, and was in favour both with the LORD, and also with men.

JOHN THE BAPTIST

Lu 1:80 And the child grew, and waxed strong in spirit, and was in the deserts till the day of his shewing unto Israel.

THE BOY CHRIST

Lu 2:40 And the child grew, and waxed strong in spirit, filled with wisdom: and the grace of God was upon him.

Lu 2:52 And Jesus increased in wisdom and stature, and in favour with God and man.

PAUL

Ac 9:22 But Saul increased the more in strength, and confounded the Jews which dwelt at Damascus, proving that this is very Christ.

THE THESSALONIANS

2 Th 1:3 We are bound to thank God always for you, brethren, as it is meet, because that your faith groweth exceedingly, and the charity of every one of you all toward each other aboundeth;

1 Pe 2:2 As newborn babes, desire the sincere milk of the word, that ye may grow thereby:

BY ACCRETION

2 Pe 1:5–6 And beside this, giving all diligence, add to your faith virtue; and to virtue knowledge;

And to knowledge temperance; and to temperance patience; and to patience godliness;

IN GRACE AND KNOWLEDGE

1 Pe 3:18 For Christ also hath once suffered for sins, the just for the unjust, that he might bring us to God, being put to death in the flesh, but quickened by the Spirit:

3. Pruning

Pr 10:31 The mouth of the just bringeth forth wisdom: but the froward tongue shall be cut out.

Mt 5:30 And if thy right hand offend thee, cut if off, and cast it from thee: for it is profitable for thee that one of thy members should perish, and not *that* thy whole body should be cast into hell.

Mt 18:8 Wherefore if thy hand or thy foot offend thee, cut them off, and cast *them* from thee: it is better for thee to enter into life halt or maimed, rather than having two hands or two feet to be cast into everlasting fire.

Mk 9:43 And if thy hand offend thee, cut it off: it is better for thee to enter into life maimed, than having two hands to go into hell, into the fire that never shall be quenched:

Jn 15:2 Every branch in me that beareth not fruit he taketh away: and every *branch* that beareth fruit, he purgeth it, that it may bring forth more fruit.

Ro 6:6 Knowing this, that our old man is crucified with *him*, that the body of sin might be destroyed, that henceforth we should not serve sin.

Ro 8:13 For if ye live after the flesh, ye shall die: but if ye through the Spirit do mortify the deeds of the body, ye shall live.

Ga 5:12 I would they were even cut off which trouble you.

Col 2:11 In whom also ye are circumcised with the circumcision made without hands, in putting off the body of the sins of the flesh by the circumcision of Christ:

Col 3:5 Mortify therefore your members which are upon the earth; fornication, uncleanness, inordinate affection, evil concupiscence, and covetousness, which is idolatry:

See **ABIDING IN CHRIST, DISCIPLESHIP**

GUESTS, *recipients of hospitality*

1. Advice

NOT TO PROLONG VISITS

Pr 25:17 Withdraw thy foot from thy neighbour's house; lest he be weary of thee, and *so* hate thee.

NOT TO SEEK SOCIAL PREEMINENCE

Lu 14:8–9 When thou art bidden of any *man* to a wedding, sit not down in the highest room; lest a more honourable man than thou be bidden of him;

And he that bade thee and him come and say to thee, Give this man place; and thou begin with shame to take the lowest room.

NOT TO BE CRITICAL OF FOOD

1 Co 10:27 If any of them that believe not bid you *to a feast,* and ye be disposed to go; whatsoever is set before you, eat, asking no question for conscience sake.

2. Anointing

2 Chr 28:15; Mt 26:7; Mk 14:3; Lu 7:38, 46; Jn 11:2; 12:3

3. Washing Their Feet

Ge 18:4; 19:2; 24:32; 43:24; Ex 30:19; Jud 19:21; 1 S 25:41; 2 S 11:8; Lu 7:44; Jn 13:5, 10; 1 Ti 5:10

See **HOSPITALITY**

GUIDANCE, *divine direction, leadership, instruction*

1. Promised to the Obedient

INTO PLEASANT PATHS

Ps 23:2 He maketh me to lie down in green pastures: he leadeth me beside the still waters.

IN MAKING DECISIONS

Ps 25:9 The meek will he guide in judgment: and the meek will he teach his way.

Ps 32:8 I will instruct thee and teach thee in the way which thou shalt go: I will guide thee with mine eye.

UNTO THE END OF LIFE

Ps 48:14 For this God *is* our God for ever and ever: he will be our guide *even* unto death.

BY WISE COUNSEL

Ps 73:24 Thou shalt guide me with thy counsel, and afterward receive me *to* glory.

BY THE STILL SMALL VOICE

Is 30:21 And thine ears shall hear a word behind thee, saying, This *is* the way, walk ye in it, when ye turn to the right hand, and when ye turn to the left.

IN THE MIDST OF UNCERTAINTIES

Is 42:16 And I will bring the blind by a way *that* they knew not; I will lead them in paths *that* they have not known: I will make darkness light before them, and crooked things straight. These things will I do unto them, and not forsake them.

Is 48:17 Thus saith the LORD, thy Redeemer, the Holy One of Israel; I *am* the LORD thy God which teacheth thee to profit, which leadeth thee by the way *that* thou shouldest go.

BY DIVINE ILLUMINATION

Lu 1:79 To give light to them that sit in darkness and *in* the shadow of death, to guide our feet into the way of peace.

Jn 10:4 And when he putteth forth his own sheep, he goeth before them, and the sheep follow him: for they know his voice.

INTO ALL TRUTH

Jn 16:13 Howbeit when he, the Spirit of truth, is come, he will guide you into all truth: for he shall not speak of himself; but whatsoever he shall hear, *that* shall he speak: and he will shew you things to come.

2. Sought

Ge 24:12; De 18:21; Jud 1:1; 13:8, 12; 1 S 23:4; 30:8; 2 S 2:1; 5:19, 23; 21:1; 1 K 22:5; 1 Chr 14:10; Ps 5:8; 25:5; 27:11; 31:3; 43:3; 61:2; 139:24; 143:10; Ac 1:24; 1 Th 3:11

3. Examples

Ge 24:27, 42; Ex 13:21; Nu 9:22; 1 S 16:12; 2 Chr 32:22; Ne 9:12, 19; Ps 78:14, 52; 107:30; Is 63:13; Eze 40:1; Mt 2:9; Ac 8:26

4. Directions Given

AS TO LEAVING OLD ASSOCIATIONS
Ge 12:1

RETURNING HOME
Ge 31:3

ASSUMING LEADERSHIP
Ex 3:10

FORWARD MOVEMENTS
Jos 1:2

WAGING WARFARE
Jud 6:14; 2 S 5:19

FINDING SUPPLIES
1 K 17:3–4, 9

COMING OUT FROM RETIREMENT
1 K 18:1

ANOINTING LEADERS
1 K 19:15

PRONOUNCING JUDGMENTS
1 K 21:18–19; 2 K 1:3

5. Inquiring of God

ABOUT BUSINESS AFFAIRS
1 S 9:8–9 And the servant answered Saul again, and said, Behold, I have here at hand the fourth part of a shekel of silver: *that* will I give to the man of God, to tell us our way.

(Beforetime in Israel, when a man went to enquire of God, thus he spake, Come, and let us go to the seer: for *he that is* now *called* a Prophet was beforetime called a Seer.)

ABOUT GREAT EMERGENCIES
2 K 3:11 But Jehoshaphat said, *Is there* not here a prophet of the LORD, that we may enquire of the LORD by him? And one of the king of Israel's servants answered and said, Here *is* Elisha the son of Shaphat, which poured water on the hands of Elijah.

ABOUT SICKNESS
2 K 8:8 And the king said unto Hazael, Take a present in thine hand, and go, meet the man of God, and enquire of the LORD by him, saying, Shall I recover of this disease?

ABOUT TEACHINGS OF THE SCRIPTURES
2 K 22:13 Go ye, enquire of the LORD for me, and for the people, and for all Judah, concerning the words of this book that is found: for great is the wrath of the LORD that is kindled against us, because our fathers have not hearkened unto the words of this book, to do according unto all that which is written concerning us.

ABOUT ISSUES OF WAR
1 S 23:2 Therefore David enquired of the LORD, saying, Shall I go and smite these Philistines? And the LORD said unto David, Go, and smite the Philistines, and save Keilah.
1 K 22:7 And Jehoshaphat said, *Is there* not here a prophet of the LORD besides, that we might enquire of him?
Je 21:2 Enquire, I pray thee, of the LORD for us; for Nebuchadrezzar king of Babylon maketh war against us; if so be that the LORD will deal with us according to all his wondrous works, that he may go up from us.
Je 37:7 Thus saith the LORD, the God of Israel; Thus shall ye say to the king of Judah, that sent you unto me to enquire of me; Behold, Pharaoh's army, which is come forth to help you, shall return to Egypt into their own land.

BY HYPOCRITES

Eze 14:7 For every one of the house of Israel, or of the stranger that sojourneth in Israel, which separateth himself from me, and setteth up his idols in his heart, and putteth the stumblingblock of his iniquity before his face, and cometh to a prophet to enquire of him concerning me; I the LORD will answer him by myself:

Eze 20:1 And it came to pass in the seventh year, in the fifth *month,* the tenth *day* of the month, *that* certain of the elders of Israel came to enquire of the LORD, and sat before me.

See **GOD, PRAYER, SEEKING**

GUILELESSNESS, *without deceit*

Ps 32:2; Je 50:20; Zep 3:13; Jn 1:47; 1 Pe 2:22; 3:10; Re 14:5

See **DECEPTION**

GUILT

JOSEPH'S BRETHREN

Ge 42:21 And they said one to another, We *are* verily guilty concerning our brother, in that we saw the anguish of his soul, when he besought us, and we would not hear; therefore is this distress come upon us.

Ex 9:27 And Pharaoh sent, and called for Moses and Aaron, and said unto them, I have sinned this time: the LORD is righteous, and I and my people *are* wicked.

ISRAEL IN THE WILDERNESS

Nu 21:7 Therefore the people came to Moses, and said, We have sinned, for we have spoken against the LORD, and against thee; pray unto the LORD, that he take away the serpents from us. And Moses prayed for the people.

THE JEWS OF EZRA'S TIME

Ezr 9:6 And said, O my God, I am ashamed and blush to lift up my face to thee, my God: for our iniquities are increased over *our* head, and our trespass is grown up unto the heavens.

THE PSALMIST

Ps 40:12 For innumerable evils have compassed me about: mine iniquities have taken hold upon me, so that I am not able to look up; they are more than the hairs of mine head: therefore my heart faileth me.

Da 5:6 Then the king's countenance was changed, and his thoughts troubled him, so that the joints of his loins were loosed, and his knees smote one against another.

THE SCRIBES AND PHARISEES

Jn 8:9 And they which heard *it,* being convicted by *their own* conscience, went beginning at the eldest, *even* unto the last: and Jesus was left alone, and the woman standing in the midst.

See **INNOCENCE, PRAYER, SELF-CONDEMNATION**

GUILTINESS, *deserving punishment*

Le 5:1; 7:18; 17:16; 19:8; 20:17, 19; Nu 5:6, 31; 14:34; 15:31; 30:15; 32:23; De 19:10; Ezr 10:19; Eze 39:26; 44:10, 12

See **SALVATION, SIN**

H

HABAKKUK, *a prophet of Judah*

1. Person
Hab 1:1; 3:1

2. Book
Author: Uncertain. Probably Habakkuk. Some have inferred from his psalm (3:1) and the direction to the chief musician (3:19) that he was a chorister in the temple, but this is purely conjectural.

Date Written: Uncertain. The prophet evidently lived in the Babylonian period. Many scholars fix the time of the prophecy during the reign of Jehoiakim (609 B.C.–597 B.C.)

Purpose: To remind the prophet himself and his listeners that the God of Israel is the true God, the one in control of everything and every event. He can be trusted, even in the face of the mysterious circumstances of life, which often appear to contradict his sovereign control.

To Whom Written: Judah, and God's people of all times who may be asking the "difficult" questions of life.

Main Theme: The mysteries of providence.

Key Word: Faith (2:4).

Key Verse: 1:3.

HABIT, *inclination, tendency, routine, bent*
Je 13:23; 22:21; Mi 2:1

HADES *See* **HELL**

HAGAR, *handmaid of Sarah*

BORE ABRAHAM A SON, ISHMAEL
Ge 16:15 And Hagar bare Abram a son: and Abram called his son's name, which Hagar bare, Ishmael.

CAST OUT OF THE HOME
Ge 21:9–14 And Sarah saw the son of Hagar the Egyptian, which she had born unto Abraham, mocking.

Wherefore she said unto Abraham, Cast out this bondwoman and her son: for the son of this bondwoman shall not be heir with my son, *even* with Isaac.

And the thing was very grievous in Abraham's sight because of his son.

And God said unto Abraham, Let it not be grievous in thy sight because of the lad, and because of thy bondwoman; in all that Sarah hath said unto thee, hearken unto her voice; for in Isaac shall thy seed be called.

And also of the son of the bondwoman will I make a nation, because he *is* thy seed.

And Abraham rose up early in the morning, and took bread, and a bottle of water, and gave *it* unto Hagar, putting *it* on her shoulder, and the child, and sent her away: and she departed, and wandered in the wilderness of Beer-sheba.

AN ANGEL APPEARS
Ge 21:17–19 And God heard the voice of the lad; and the angel of God called Hagar out of heaven, and said unto her, What aileth thee, Hagar? fear not; for God hath heard the voice of the lad where he *is*.

Arise, lift up the lad, and hold him in thine hand; for I will make him a great nation.

And God opened her eyes, and she saw a well of water; and she went, and filled the bottle with water, and gave the lad drink.

Ga 4:25 For this Agar is mount Sinai in Arabia, and answereth to Jerusalem which now is, and is in bondage with her children.

See **WOMEN**

HAGGAI

1. Person, *a prophet*

Ezr 5:1; 6:14; Hag 1:1; 2:1, 20

2. Book

Author: Haggai, "the prophet of the temple," who was reputed to have been born during the seventy years' captivity in Babylon and to have returned to Jerusalem with Zerubbabel. He was a colleague of Zechariah (Ezr 5:1; 6:14).

Date Written: 520 B.C. The remnant that had returned from captivity was selfishly preoccupied with their own affairs and were more concerned in beautifying their own dwellings than in rebuilding the Lord's house. The work had ceased for years (1:4).

Purpose: To motivate God's people to reorder their priorities, complete the temple, and restore proper worship. They could then expect the blessing of God.

To Whom Written: The remnant, especially the returnees from Babylon.

Main Theme: Sharp rebukes for the neglect to rebuild the temple coupled with cheering exhortations and promises to those undertaking the work.

Key Words: Build the temple (1:7–8).

Key Verses: 2:4–9.

HAIL See MIRACLES

HAILSTORMS See WEATHER

HAIR, *Hebrews bestowed special care on the hair and beard, regarding thick, abundant hair as an ornament*

Le 14:9; Nu 6:5, 18; 2 S 14:26; Jud 13:5; 16:17, 22; Jb 4:15; Mt 5:36; 10:30; Jn 11:2; 1 Co 11:14; 1 Ti 2:9; 1 Pe 3:3

HALFHEARTEDNESS

JEHU

2 K 10:31 But Jehu took no heed to walk in the law of the LORD God of Israel with all his heart: for he departed not from the sins of Jeroboam, which made Israel to sin.

JOASH

2 K 13:18–19 And he said, Take the arrows. And he took *them*. And he said unto the king of Israel, Smite upon the ground. And he smote thrice, and stayed.

And the man of God was wroth with him, and said, Thou shouldest have smitten five or six times; then hadst thou smitten Syria till thou hadst consumed *it*: whereas now thou shalt smite Syria *but* thrice.

JEHOSHAPHAT'S SUBJECTS

2 Chr 20:33 Howbeit the high places were not taken away: for as yet the people had not prepared their hearts unto the God of their fathers.

AMAZIAH

2 Chr 25:2 And he did *that which was* right in the sight of the LORD, but not with a perfect heart.

JUDAH

Je 3:10 And yet for all this her treacherous sister Judah hath not turned unto me with her whole heart, but feignedly, saith the LORD.

ISRAEL

Ho 10:2 Their heart is divided; now shall they be found faulty: he shall break down their altars, he shall spoil their images.

See **INDIFFERENCE**

HAM, *son of Noah*

Ge 5:32; 7:13; 9:18; 10:6; 1 Chr 1:8; 4:40; Ps 78:51

HAMAN, *an Agagite*

Est 3:1–9:24

HAMATH, *a city and kingdom north of Damascus*

Hamath, once the royal city of the Hittites, lies north of Baalbek on the Orontes River. Its king sent presents to David when he defeated the king of Zobah (2 S 8:3, 9–11), and it was frequently mentioned in the Bible as Israel's ideal northern border (e.g., 2 K 14:25). But it was only at brief intervals, under Solomon (2 Chr 8:4) and Jeroboam II (2 K 14:28), that Hamath was subject to Israel.

Nu 13:21; 34:8; Jos 13:5; 2 S 8:9; 2 K 14:28; 17:24, 30; 18:34; 19:13; 23:33; 1 Chr 18:3; 2 Chr 7:8; 8:4; Is 10:9; 11:11; 36:19; 37:13; Je 39:5; 49:23; 52:27; Eze 47:17; 48:1; Am 6:2; Zec 9:2

See **CITIES**

HAMMERS, *tools*

Jud 4:21; 5:26; 1 K 6:7; Is 41:7; Je 10:4; 23:29; 50:23

HAMOR, *the father of Shechem*

Ge 33:19; 34:6, 20, 26; 49:6; Jos 24:32; Jud 9:28; Ac 7:16

HANANI, *a prophet*

2 Chr 16:7

See **PROPHETS**

HANANIAH, *ruler of the palace*

Ne 7:2

HAND, *symbol of God's active and personal involvement in human affairs*

1. For Blessing

De 33:3 Yea, he loved the people; all his saints *are* in thy hand: and they sat down at thy feet; *every one* shall receive of thy words.

Jos 4:24 That all the people of the earth might know the hand of the LORD, that it *is* mighty: that ye might fear the LORD your God for ever.

2 Chr 30:12 Also in Judah the hand of God was to give them one heart to do the commandment of the king and of the princes, by the word of the LORD.

Ezr 7:9 For upon the first *day* of the first month began he to go up from Babylon, and on the first *day* of the fifth month came he to Jerusalem, according to the good hand of his God upon him.

Ezr 8:18 And by the good hand of our God upon us they brought us a man of understanding, of the sons of Mahli, the son of Levi, the son of Israel; and Shere-

biah, with his sons and his brethren, eighteen;

Ne 2:18 Then I told them of the hand of my God which was good upon me; as also the king's words that he had spoken unto me. And they said, Let us rise up and build. So they strengthened their hands for *this* good *work*.

Ps 37:24 Though he fall, he shall not be utterly cast down: for the LORD upholdeth *him with* his hand.

Ps 104:28 *That* thou givest them they gather: thou openest thine hand, they are filled with good.

Eze 37:1 The hand of the LORD was upon me, and carried me out in the spirit of the LORD, and set me down in the midst of the valley which *was* full of bones,

Jn 10:28 And I give unto them eternal life; and they shall never perish, neither shall any *man* pluck them out of my hand.

Ac 11:21 And the hand of the Lord was with them: and a great number believed, and turned unto the Lord.

See **BLESSINGS, FAVOR**

2. For Chastisement and Punishment

Ex 7:5 And the Egyptians shall know that I *am* the LORD, when I stretch forth mine hand upon Egypt, and bring out the children of Israel from among them.

De 2:15 For indeed the hand of the LORD was against them, to destroy them from among the host, until they were consumed.

Ru 1:13 Would ye tarry for them till they were grown? would ye stay for them from having husbands? nay, my daughters; for it grieveth me much for your sakes that the hand of the LORD is gone out against me.

1 S 5:6 But the hand of the LORD was heavy upon them of Ashdod, and he destroyed them, and smote them with emerods, *even* Ashdod and the coasts thereof.

Jb 1:11 But put forth thine hand now, and touch all that he hath, and he will curse thee to thy face.

Jb 2:10 But he said unto her, Thou speakest as one of the foolish women speaketh. What? shall we receive good at the hand of God, and shall we not receive evil? In all this did not Job sin with his lips.

Jb 19:21 Have pity upon me, have pity upon me, O ye my friends; for the hand of God hath touched me.

Ps 21:8 Thine hand shall find out all thine enemies: thy right hand shall find out those that hate thee.

Ps 32:4 For day and night thy hand was heavy upon me: my moisture is turned into the drought of summer. Selah.

Ps 74:11 Why withdrawest thou thy hand, even thy right hand? pluck *it* out of thy bosom.

Is 14:26 This *is* the purpose that is purposed upon the whole earth: and this *is* the hand that is stretched out upon all the nations.

Is 26:11 LORD, *when* thy hand is lifted up, they will not see: *but* they shall see, and be ashamed for *their* envy at the people; yea, the fire of thine enemies shall devour them.

Ac 13:11 And now, behold, the hand of the Lord *is* upon thee, and thou shalt be blind, not seeing the sun for a season. And immediately there fell on him a mist and a darkness; and he went about seeking some to lead him by the hand.

See **JUDGMENTS, PUNISHMENT**

3. Mighty

De 5:15 And remember that thou wast a servant in the land of Egypt, and *that* the LORD thy God brought thee out thence through a mighty hand and by a stretched out arm: therefore the LORD thy God commanded thee to keep the sabbath day.

Jos 4:24 That all the people of the earth might know the hand of the LORD, that it *is* mighty: that ye might fear the LORD your God for ever.

Ps 89:13 Thou hast a mighty arm: strong is thy hand, *and* high is thy right hand.

Ps 98:1 O sing unto the LORD a new song; for he hath done marvellous things: his right hand, and his holy arm, hath gotten him the victory.

Ps 118:15 The voice of rejoicing and salvation *is* in the tabernacles of the righteous: the right hand of the LORD doeth valiantly.

Is 59:1 Behold, the LORD's hand is not shortened, that it cannot save; neither his ear heavy, that it cannot hear:

Jn 10:29 My Father, which gave *them* me, is greater than all; and no *man* is able to pluck *them* out of my Father's hand.

1 Pe 5:6 Humble yourselves therefore under the mighty hand of God, that he may exalt you in due time:

See **GOD, POWER**

HANDBREADTH, *a measure*

Ex 25:25; 1 K 7:26; 2 Chr 4:5; Eze 40:5; 43:13

See **WEIGHTS AND MEASURES**

HANDKERCHIEFS, *used for wrapping money, for burial, and for protecting the head*

Lu 19:20; Jn 20:7; Ac 19:12

HANDS, *LAYING ON OF, a sign of identification*

1. In Consecration of Offerings

Ex 29:10, 15, 19; Le 1:4; 3:2, 8, 13; 4:4, 15, 29, 33; 8:14, 18, 22; 16:21; Nu 8:12; 2 Chr 29:23

See **CONSECRATION**

2. In Ordination or Consecration for Service

Nu 8:10 And thou shalt bring the Levites before the LORD: and the children of Israel shall put their hands upon the Levites:

Nu 27:18 And the LORD said unto Moses, Take thee Joshua the son of Nun, a man in whom *is* the spirit, and lay thine hand upon him;

De 34:9 And Joshua the son of Nun was full of the spirit of wisdom; for Moses had laid his hands upon him: and the children of Israel hearkened unto him, and did as the LORD commanded Moses.

Ac 6:6 Whom they set before the apostles: and when they had prayed, they laid *their* hands on them.

Ac 19:6 And when Paul had laid *his* hands upon them, the Holy Ghost came on them; and they spake with tongues, and prophesied.

1 Ti 4:14 Neglect not the gift that is in thee, which was given thee by prophecy, with the laying on of the hands of the presbytery.

1 Ti 5:22 Lay hands suddenly on no man, neither be partaker of other men's sins: keep thyself pure.

2 Ti 1:6 Wherefore I put thee in remembrance that thou stir up the gift of God, which is in thee by the putting on of my hands.

See **CONSECRATION**

3. In Blessing

Ge 48:14 And Israel stretched out his right hand, and laid it upon Ephraim's head, who *was* the younger, and his left hand upon Manasseh's head, guiding his hands wittingly; for Manasseh *was* the firstborn.

Mt 19:15 And he laid *his* hands on them, and departed thence.

Mk 10:16 And he took them up in his arms, put *his* hands upon them, and blessed them.

See **BLESSINGS**

4. In Healing

Mk 6:5 And he could there do no mighty work, save that he laid his hands upon a few sick folk, and healed *them.*

Mk 7:32 And they bring unto him one that was deaf, and had an impediment in his speech; and they beseech him to put his hand upon him.

Mk 16:18 They shall take up serpents; and if they drink any deadly thing, it shall not hurt them; they shall lay hands on the sick, and they shall recover.

Lu 4:40 Now when the sun was setting, all they that had any sick with divers diseases brought them unto him; and he laid his hands on every one of them, and healed them.

Lu 13:13 And he laid *his* hands on her: and immediately she was made straight, and glorified God.

Ac 28:8 And it came to pass, that the father of Publius lay sick of a fever and of a bloody flux: to whom Paul entered in, and prayed, and laid his hands on him, and healed him.

See **CHRIST, HEALING**

5. In Prayer Lifted Up

Ps 28:2 Hear the voice of my supplications, when I cry unto thee, when I lift up my hands toward thy holy oracle.

Ps 63:4 Thus will I bless thee while I live: I will lift up my hands in thy name.

Ps 134:2 Lift up your hands *in* the sanctuary, and bless the LORD.

Ps 141:2 Let my prayer be set forth before thee *as* incense; *and* the lifting up of my hands *as* the evening sacrifice.

Ps 143:6 I stretch forth my hands unto thee: my soul *thirsteth* after thee, as a thirsty land. Selah.

Is 1:15 And when ye spread forth your hands, I will hide mine eyes from you: yea, when ye make many prayers, I will not hear: your hands are full of blood.

Lam 2:19 Arise, cry out in the night: in the beginning of the watches pour out thine heart like water before the face of the Lord: lift up thy hands toward him for the life of thy young children, that faint for hunger in the top of every street.

1 Ti 2:8 I will therefore that men pray every where, lifting up holy hands, without wrath and doubting.

See **PRAYER**

6. Washed, *a symbol of innocence*

De 21:6; Jb 9:30; Ps 26:6; 73:13; Mt 27:24

See **INNOCENCE**

HANGING *See* **NATION**

HANNAH, *wife of Elkanah, mother of Samuel*

PRAYERFUL

1 S 1:10–11 And she *was* in bitterness of soul, and prayed unto the LORD, and wept sore.

And she vowed a vow, and said, O LORD of hosts, if thou wilt indeed look on the affliction of thine handmaid, and remember me, and not forget thine handmaid, but wilt give unto thine handmaid a man child, then I will give him unto the LORD all the days of his life, and there shall no razor come upon his head.

SELF-DENYING

1 S 1:27–28 For this child I prayed; and the LORD hath given me my petition which I asked of him:

Therefore also I have lent him to the LORD; as long as he liveth he shall be lent to the LORD. And he worshipped the LORD there.

THANKFUL

1 S 2:1–10 And Hannah prayed, and said, My heart rejoiceth in the LORD, mine horn is exalted in the LORD: my mouth is enlarged over mine enemies; because I rejoice in thy salvation.

There is none holy as the LORD: for *there is* none beside thee: neither *is there* any rock like our God.

Talk no more so exceeding proudly; let *not* arrogancy come out of your mouth: for the LORD is a God of knowledge, and by him actions are weighed.

The bows of the mighty men *are* broken, and they that stumbled are girded with strength.

They that were full have hired out themselves for bread; and *they that were* hungry ceased: so that the barren hath born seven; and she that hath many children is waxed feeble.

The LORD killeth, and maketh alive: he bringeth down to the grave, and bringeth up.

The LORD maketh poor, and maketh rich: he bringeth low, and lifteth up.

He raiseth up the poor out of the dust, *and* lifteth up the beggar from the dunghill, to set *them* among princes, and to make them inherit the throne of glory: for the pillars of the earth *are* the LORD's, and he hath set the world upon them.

He will keep the feet of his saints, and the wicked shall be silent in darkness; for by strength shall no man prevail.

The adversaries of the LORD shall be broken to pieces; out of heaven shall he thunder upon them: the LORD shall judge the ends of the earth; and he shall give strength unto his king, and exalt the horn of his anointed.

INDUSTRIOUS AND LOVING

1 S 2:19 Moreover his mother made him a little coat, and brought *it* to him from year to year, when she came up with her husband to offer the yearly sacrifice.

See **WOMEN**

HARAN

Haran, Abraham's first stopping place on the way to Canaan (Ge 11:31), was an important junction and trading center. It was located on the Balikh River about fifty miles east of Carchemish on the great highway along which caravans and armies frequently marched. It was six hundred miles northwest of Ur of the Chaldees, and about four hundred miles northeast of Canaan. Haran rebelled against the Assyrians in the eighth century B.C. and was used as a lesson to other cities of the consequences of rebellion against iron-clad Assyrian rule (2 K 19:11–12, Is 37:11–12).

See **CITIES**

1. Land of Charran

Ge 11:31; 12:5; 27:43; 28:10; 29:4; 2 K 19:12; Is 37:12; Eze 27:23; Ac 7:4

2. Father of Lot

Ge 11:26

HARD LABOR *See* **NATION**

HARLOTS, *prostitutes*

Ge 34:31 And they said, Should he deal with our sister as with an harlot?

Ge 38:15 When Judah saw her, he thought her *to be* an harlot; because she had covered her face.

Ge 38:21 Then he asked the men of that place, saying, Where *is* the harlot, that *was* openly by the way side? And they said, There was no harlot in this *place.*

Le 19:29 Do not prostitute thy daughter, to cause her to be a whore; lest the land fall to whoredom, and the land become full of wickedness.

Le 21:7 They shall not take a wife *that is* a whore, or profane; neither shall they take a woman put away from her husband: for he *is* holy unto his God.

Le 21:14 A widow, or a divorced woman, or profane, *or* an harlot, these shall he not take: but he shall take a virgin of his own people to wife.

De 23:18 Thou shalt not bring the hire of a whore, or the price of a dog, into the house of the Lord thy God for any vow: for even both these *are* abomination unto the Lord thy God.

1 K 3:16 Then came there two women, *that were* harlots, unto the king, and stood before him.

Pr 2:16 To deliver thee from the strange woman, *even* from the stranger *which* flattereth with her words;

Pr 9:13 A foolish woman *is* clamorous: *she is* simple, and knoweth nothing.

Is 23:15 And it shall come to pass in that day, that Tyre shall be forgotten seventy years, according to the days of one king: after the end of seventy years shall Tyre sing as an harlot.

Eze 23:44 Yet they went in unto her, as they go in unto a woman that playeth the harlot: so went they in unto Aholah and unto Aholibah, the lewd women.

Warnings

Pr 2:18 For her house inclineth unto death, and her paths unto the dead.

Pr 5:3 For the lips of a strange woman drop *as* an honeycomb, and her mouth *is* smoother than oil:

Pr 6:24 To keep thee from the evil woman, from the flattery of the tongue of a strange woman.

Pr 7:10 And, behold, there met him a woman *with* the attire of an harlot, and subtil of heart.

Pr 29:3 Whoso loveth wisdom rejoiceth his father: but he that keepeth company with harlots spendeth *his* substance.

Pr 30:20 Such *is* the way of an adulterous woman; she eateth, and wipeth her mouth, and saith, I have done no wickedness.

Ec 7:26 And I find more bitter than death the woman, whose heart *is* snares and nets, *and* her hands *as* bands: whoso pleaseth God shall escape from her; but the sinner shall be taken by her.

Ho 4:14 I will not punish your daughters when they commit whoredom, nor your spouses when they commit adultery: for themselves are separated with whores, and they sacrifice with harlots: therefore the people *that* doth not understand shall fall.

Lu 15:30 But as soon as this thy son was come, which hath devoured thy living with harlots, thou hast killed for him the fatted calf.

1 Co 6:16 What? know ye not that he which is joined to an harlot is one body? for two, saith he, shall be one flesh.

See **SIN**

HARPS *See* **MUSIC**

HARROWING

See **AGRICULTURE**

HARVEST *See* **AGRICULTURE**

HASTE, *rapidity, quickness*

1. In Duty

THE KING'S BUSINESS REQUIRES

1 S 21:8 And David said unto Ahimelech, And is there not here under thine hand spear or sword? for I have neither brought my sword nor my weapons with me, because the king's business required haste.

SALUTATIONS HINDER

2 K 4:29 Then he said to Gehazi, Gird up thy loins, and take my staff in thine hand, and go thy way: if thou meet any man, salute him not; and if any salute thee, answer him not again: and lay my staff upon the face of the child.

THE URGENCY OF THE WORK DEMANDS

2 Chr 24:5 And he gathered together the priests and the Levites, and said to them, Go out unto the cities of Judah, and gather of all Israel money to repair the house of your God from year to year, and see that ye hasten the matter. Howbeit the Levites hastened it not.

THE RASHNESS OF DELAYING
GOD'S MESSENGERS

2 Chr 35:21 But he sent ambassadors to him, saying, What have I to do with thee, thou king of Judah? *I come* not against thee this day, but against the house wherewith I have war: for God commanded me to make haste: forbear thee from *meddling with* God, who *is* with me, that he destroy thee not.

Ps 119:60 I made haste, and delayed not to keep thy commandments.

HASTENING TO THE PLACE OF PRAYER

Zec 8:21 And the inhabitants of one *city* shall go to another, saying, Let us go speedily to pray before the LORD, and to seek the LORD of hosts: I will go also.

HASTE IN DELIVERING THE MESSAGE

Mt 28:7 And go quickly, and tell his disciples that he is risen from the dead; and, behold, he goeth before you into Galilee; there shall ye see him: lo, I have told you.

Lu 10:4 Carry neither purse, nor scrip, nor shoes: and salute no man by the way.

HASTE IN GIVING THE INVITATION

Lu 14:21 So that servant came, and shewed his lord these things. Then the master of the house being angry said to his servant, Go out quickly into the streets and lanes of the city, and bring in hither the poor, and the maimed, and the halt, and the blind.

2. In Making Escape

Ge 19:15, 22; Ex 12:11, 34, 39; Jos 4:10; 1 S 20:38; 23:26; 2 S 15:14; 2 K 7:7; Ps 55:8; Zec 14:5; Mt 24:17; Mk 13:14; 14:52; Lu 17:31; 21:21; Ac 12:7

See **DELAY, PROCRASTINATION**

HATRED

1. Condemned

Le 19:17 Thou shalt not hate thy brother in thine heart: thou shalt in any wise rebuke thy neighbour, and not suffer sin upon him.

Pr 10:12 Hatred stirreth up strifes: but love covereth all sins.

Pr 15:17 Better *is* a dinner of herbs where love is, than a stalled ox and hatred therewith.

1 Jn 2:9 He that saith he is in the light, and hateth his brother, is in darkness even until now.

1 Jn 3:15 Whosoever hateth his brother is a murderer: and ye know that no murderer hath eternal life abiding in him.

1 Jn 4:20 If a man say, I love God, and hateth his brother, he is a liar: for he that loveth not his brother whom he hath seen, how can he love God whom he hath not seen?

2. Examples

ESAU

Ge 27:41 And Esau hated Jacob because of the blessing wherewith his father blessed him: and Esau said in his heart, The days of mourning for my father are at hand; then will I slay my brother Jacob.

JOSEPH'S BRETHREN

Ge 37:4 And when his brethren saw that their father loved him more than all his brethren, they hated him, and could not speak peaceably unto him.

Jud 11:7 And Jephthah said unto the elders of Gilead, Did not ye hate me, and expel me out of my father's house? and why are ye come unto me now when ye are in distress?

AHAB

1 K 22:8 And the king of Israel said unto Jehoshaphat, *There is* yet one man, Micaiah the son of Imlah, by whom we may enquire of the LORD: but I hate him; for he doth not prophesy good concerning me, but evil. And Jehoshaphat said, Let not the king say so.

HAMAN

Est 3:5–6 And when Haman saw that Mordecai bowed not, nor did him reverence, then was Haman full of wrath.

And he thought scorn to lay hands on Mordecai alone; for they had shewed him the people of Mordecai: wherefore Haman sought to destroy all the Jews that *were* throughout the whole kingdom of Ahasuerus, *even* the people of Mordecai.

Est 9:1 Now in the twelfth month, that *is,* the month Adar, on the thirteenth day of the same, when the king's commandment and his decree drew near to be put in execution, in the day that the enemies of the Jews hoped to have power over them, (though it was turned to the contrary, that the Jews had rule over them that hated them;)

HERODIAS

Mk 6:18–19 For John had said unto Herod, It is not lawful for thee to have thy brother's wife.

Therefore Herodias had a quarrel against him, and would have killed him; but she could not:

THE JEWS

Ac 23:12 And when it was day, certain of the Jews banded together, and bound themselves under a curse, saying that they would neither eat nor drink till they had killed Paul.

Tit 3:3 For we ourselves also were sometimes foolish, disobedient, deceived, serving divers lusts and pleasures, living in malice and envy, hateful, *and* hating one another.

3. Of Christ

Zec 11:9; Mt 2:13; 12:10; 21:38; 26:4, 59; 27:1, 23; Mk 11:18; 12:12; 14:55; 15:13; Lu 4:29; 6:11; 19:14, 47; 20:14, 19; 22:2; 23:21; Jn 5:18; 7:7, 25; 8:40, 59; 11:57; 15:18, 23, 25; 19:6, 15; Ac 13:28; 1 Co 16:22

See **CHRIST**

4. Of the Saints

1 K 22:8; 2 K 6:31; 2 Chr 18:7; Ps 11:2; 25:19; 34:21; 35:19; 37:14; 41:5; 44:7; 55:3; 69:14; 86:17; 109:3; Pr 29:27; Is 66:5; Je 11:19; 38:4; Am 5:10; Mt 24:9; Mk 6:25; 13:13; Lu 1:71; 6:22; 21:17; Jn 15:19; 17:14; Ac 9:1, 13, 24; 22:22; 25:3, 24; 26:21; 1 Jn 3:13

See **LOVE**

HAUGHTINESS, *great pride in oneself and disdain, contempt, or scorn for others*

2 S 22:28; Pr 18:12; 21:4; Is 2:11; 3:16; 16:6; 24:4; Je 48:29; Eze 16:50; Mi 2:3; Zep 3:11

See **PRIDE**

HAWKS *See* **BIRDS**

HAZAEL, *king of Syria*

1 K 19:15; 2 K 8:8, 28; 9:14; 10:32; 12:17; 13:22

HAZEROTH, *one of the resting places of the Israelites on their journey from Egypt to Canaan*

Nu 11:35; 12:16; 33:17; De 1:1

HAZOR, *a town captured by Joshua*

Hazor, the home of Jabin "King of Hazor" who organized opposition to Joshua, was located four miles southwest of the "waters of Merom," on a magnificent mound of about two hundred acres. Situated at the crossroads of two international trade routes, its position was commanding enough for it to be styled "the head of all" the northern kingdoms of the Canaanites (Jos 11:10). Joshua destroyed the place, but it was rebuilt by Solomon, along with Megiddo and Gezer (1 K 9:15). Tiglath-pileser III of Assyria destroyed it in 733 B.C. and carried its inhabitants to Assyria (2 K 15:29; Je 49:30).

See **CITIES**

HEALING, *to be made sound, well, whole, healthy*

1. A Gift

Mt 10:1 And when he had called unto *him* his twelve disciples, he gave them power *against* unclean spirits, to cast them out, and to heal all manner of sickness and all manner of disease.

Mk 3:15 And to have power to heal sicknesses, and to cast out devils:

Mk 16:18 They shall take up serpents; and if they drink any deadly thing, it shall not hurt them; they shall lay hands on the sick, and they shall recover.

1 Co 12:9 To another faith by the same Spirit; to another the gifts of healing by the same Spirit;

2. Practiced by Christ

Jb 5:18 For he maketh sore, and bindeth up: he woundeth, and his hands make whole.

Ps 103:3 Who forgiveth all thine iniquities; who healeth all thy diseases;

Mt 4:23 And Jesus went about all Galilee, teaching in their synagogues, and preaching the gospel of the kingdom, and healing all manner of sickness and all manner of disease among the people.

Mt 8:3 And Jesus put forth *his* hand, and touched him, saying, I will; be thou clean. And immediately his leprosy was cleansed.

Mt 8:16 When the even was come, they brought unto him many that were possessed with devils: and he cast out the spirits with *his* word, and healed all that were sick:

Mt 9:35 And Jesus went about all the cities and villages, teaching in their synagogues, and preaching the gospel of the kingdom, and healing every sickness and every disease among the people.

Mt 12:13 Then saith he to the man, Stretch forth thine hand. And he stretched *it* forth; and it was restored whole, like as the other.

Mt 12:22 Then was brought unto him one possessed with a devil, blind, and dumb: and he healed him, insomuch that the blind and dumb both spake and saw.

Mt 14:36 And besought him that they might only touch the hem of his garment: and as many as touched were made perfectly whole.

Mt 15:30 And great multitudes came unto him, having with them *those that were* lame, blind, dumb, maimed, and many others, and cast them down at Jesus' feet; and he healed them:

Mt 17:18 And Jesus rebuked the devil; and he departed out of him: and the child was cured from that very hour.

Mt 19:2 And great multitudes followed him; and he healed them there.

Mt 21:14 And the blind and the lame came to him in the temple; and he healed them.

Mk 1:31 And he came and took her by the hand, and lifted her up; and immediately the fever left her, and she ministered unto them.

Mk 10:52 And Jesus said unto him, Go thy way; thy faith hath made thee whole. And immediately he received his sight, and followed Jesus in the way.

Lu 7:21 And in that same hour he cured many of *their* infirmities and plagues, and of evil spirits; and unto many *that were* blind he gave sight.

Lu 13:13 And he laid *his* hands on her: and immediately she was made straight, and glorified God.

Lu 17:14 And when he saw *them,* he said unto them, Go shew yourselves unto the priests. And it came to pass, that, as they went, they were cleansed.

Lu 22:51 And Jesus answered and said, Suffer ye thus far. And he touched his ear, and healed him.

Jn 4:50 Jesus saith unto him, Go thy way; thy son liveth. And the man believed the word that Jesus had spoken unto him, and he went his way.

Jn 5:9 And immediately the man was made whole, and took up his bed, and walked: and on the same day was the sabbath.

Jn 9:6 When he had thus spoken, he spat on the ground, and made clay of the spittle, and he anointed the eyes of the blind man with the clay,

3. Preached by the Apostles

Ac 3:7 And he took him by the right hand, and lifted *him* up: and immediately his feet and ancle bones received strength.

Ac 5:16 There came also a multitude *out* of the cities round about unto Jerusalem, bringing sick folks, and them which were vexed with unclean spirits: and they were healed every one.

Ac 9:34 And Peter said unto him, Aeneas, Jesus Christ maketh thee whole: arise, and make thy bed. And he arose immediately.

Ac 14:10 Said with a loud voice, Stand upright on thy feet. And he leaped and walked.

Ac 16:18 And this did she many days. But Paul, being grieved, turned and said to the spirit, I command thee in the name of Jesus Christ to come out of her. And he came out the same hour.

Ac 19:12 So that from his body were brought unto the sick handkerchiefs or aprons, and the diseases departed from them, and the evil spirits went out of them.

Ac 28:8 And it came to pass, that the father of Publius lay sick of a fever and of a bloody flux: to whom Paul entered in, and prayed, and laid his hands on him, and healed him.

4. Of the Dumb

Is 35:6 Then shall the lame *man* leap as an hart, and the tongue of the dumb sing: for in the wilderness shall waters break out, and streams in the desert.

Mt 9:33 And when the devil was cast out, the dumb spake: and the multi-tudes marvelled, saying, It was never so seen in Israel.

Mt 12:22 Then was brought unto him one possessed with a devil, blind, and dumb: and he healed him, insomuch that the blind and dumb both spake and saw.

Mk 9:25 When Jesus saw that the people came running together, he rebuked the foul spirit, saying unto him, *Thou* dumb and deaf spirit, I charge thee, come out of him, and enter no more into him.

5. Its Power

Mk 6:56 And whithersoever he entered, into villages, or cities, or country, they laid the sick in the streets, and besought him that they might touch if it were but the border of his garment: and as many as touched him were made whole.

Lu 6:19 And the whole multitude sought to touch him: for there went virtue out of him, and healed *them* all.

Lu 8:46 And Jesus said, Somebody hath touched me: for I perceive that virtue is gone out of me.

Ac 5:15 Insomuch that they brought forth the sick into the streets, and laid *them* on beds and couches, that at the least the shadow of Peter passing by might overshadow some of them.

Ac 19:11–12 And God wrought special miracles by the hands of Paul:

So that from his body were brought unto the sick handkerchiefs or aprons, and the diseases departed from them, and the evil spirits went out of them.

See **MIRACLES**

HEALTH

Ex 15:26 And said, If thou wilt diligently hearken to the voice of the LORD thy God, and wilt do that which is right in his sight, and wilt give ear to his commandments, and keep all his statutes, I will put none of these diseases upon thee, which I have brought upon the Egyptians: for I *am* the LORD that healeth thee.

De 7:15 And the LORD will take away from thee all sickness, and will put none of the evil diseases of Egypt, which thou knowest, upon thee; but will lay them upon all *them* that hate thee.

2 K 20:7 And Isaiah said, Take a lump of figs. And they took and laid *it* on the boil, and he recovered.

Jb 33:25 His flesh shall be fresher than a child's: he shall return to the days of his youth:

Ps 30:2 O Lord my God, I cried unto thee, and thou hast healed me.

Ps 105:37 He brought them forth also with silver and gold: and *there was* not one feeble *person* among their tribes.

Pr 4:22 For they *are* life unto those that find them, and health to all their flesh.

Is 38:16 O Lord, by these *things men* live, and in all these *things is* the life of my spirit: so wilt thou recover me, and make me to live.

Je 30:17 For I will restore health unto thee, and I will heal thee of thy wounds, saith the Lord; because they called thee an Outcast, *saying,* This *is* Zion, whom no man seeketh after.

Da 1:15 And at the end of ten days their countenances appeared fairer and fatter in flesh than all the children which did eat the portion of the king's meat.

Ja 5:15 And the prayer of faith shall save the sick, and the Lord shall raise him up; and if he have committed sins, they shall be forgiven him.

3 Jn 2 Beloved, I wish above all things that thou mayest prosper and be in health, even as thy soul prospereth.

See **DISEASE, SICKNESS**

HEARING, *ability to perceive sounds, understanding*

1. *Spiritual*

De 6:3 Hear therefore, O Israel, and observe to do *it;* that it may be well with thee, and that ye may increase mightily, as the Lord God of thy fathers hath promised thee, in the land that floweth with milk and honey.

Pr 8:34 Blessed *is* the man that heareth me, watching daily at my gates, waiting at the posts of my doors.

Pr 15:31 The ear that heareth the reproof of life abideth among the wise.

Ec 5:1 Keep thy foot when thou goest to the house of God, and be more ready to hear, than to give the sacrifice of fools: for they consider not that they do evil.

Ec 9:17 The words of wise *men are* heard in quiet more than the cry of him that ruleth among fools.

Hab 3:2 O Lord, I have heard thy speech, *and* was afraid: O Lord, revive thy work in the midst of the years, in the midst of the years make known; in wrath remember mercy.

Lu 8:15 But that on the good ground are they, which in an honest and good heart, having heard the word, keep *it,* and bring forth fruit with patience.

Ja 1:19 Wherefore, my beloved brethren, let every man be swift to hear, slow to speak, slow to wrath:

Re 2:11 He that hath an ear, let him hear what the Spirit saith unto the churches; He that overcometh shall not be hurt of the second death.

2. *Careless*

SENTIMENTALITY

Eze 33:32 And, lo, thou *art* unto them as a very lovely song of one that hath a pleasant voice, and can play well on an instrument: for they hear thy words, but they do them not.

DISOBEDIENCE

Mt 7:26 And every one that heareth these sayings of mine, and doeth them not, shall be likened unto a foolish man, which built his house upon the sand:

SHALLOWNESS

Mt 13:19 When any one heareth the word of the kingdom, and understandeth *it* not, then cometh the wicked *one,* and catcheth away that which was sown in his heart. This is he which received seed by the way side.

HARDNESS

Lu 16:31 And he said unto him, If they hear not Moses and the prophets, neither will they be persuaded, though one rose from the dead.

FORGETFULNESS

Ja 1:23–24 For if any be a hearer of the word, and not a doer, he is like unto a man beholding his natural face in a glass:

For he beholdeth himself, and goeth his way, and straightway forgetteth what manner of man he was.

3. Divine

Ex 16:7 And in the morning, then ye shall see the glory of the LORD; for that he heareth your murmurings against the LORD: and what *are* we, that ye murmur against us?

2 S 22:7 In my distress I called upon the LORD, and cried to my God: and he did hear my voice out of his temple, and my cry *did enter* into his ears.

2 Chr 7:14 If my people, which are called by my name, shall humble themselves, and pray, and seek my face, and turn from their wicked ways; then will I hear from heaven, and will forgive their sin, and will heal their land.

Ps 34:15 The eyes of the LORD *are* upon the righteous, and his ears *are* open unto their cry.

Ps 84:8 O LORD God of hosts, hear my prayer: give ear, O God of Jacob. Selah.

Ps 94:9 He that planted the ear, shall he not hear? he that formed the eye, shall he not see?

Ps 130:2 LORD, hear my voice: let thine ears be attentive to the voice of my supplications.

Is 59:1 Behold, the LORD's hand is not shortened, that it cannot save; neither his ear heavy, that it cannot hear:

Is 65:24 And it shall come to pass, that before they call, I will answer; and while they are yet speaking, I will hear.

Ja 5:4 Behold, the hire of the labourers who have reaped down your fields, which is of you kept back by fraud, crieth: and the cries of them which have reaped are entered into the ears of the Lord of sabaoth.

1 Pe 3:12 For the eyes of the Lord *are* over the righteous, and his ears *are* open unto their prayers: but the face of the Lord *is* against them that do evil.

4. Emotional

Mt 8:19 And a certain scribe came, and said unto him, Master, I will follow thee whithersoever thou goest.

Mt 13:5 Some fell upon stony places, where they had not much earth: and forthwith they sprung up, because they had no deepness of earth:

Mt 13:20 But he that received the seed into stony places, the same is he that heareth the word, and anon with joy receiveth it;

Mk 4:5 And some fell on stony ground, where it had not much earth; and immediately it sprang up, because it had no depth of earth:

Mk 4:16 And these are they likewise which are sown on stony ground; who, when they have heard the word, immediately receive it with gladness;

Lu 8:6 And some fell upon a rock; and as soon as it was sprung up, it withered away, because it lacked moisture.

Lu 8:13 They on the rock *are they,* which, when they hear, receive the word with joy; and these have no root, which for a while believe, and in time of temptation fall away.

Lu 9:57 And it came to pass, that, as they went in the way, a certain *man* said unto him, Lord, I will follow thee whithersoever thou goest.

Lu 11:27 And it came to pass, as he spake these things, a certain woman of the company lifted up her voice, and said unto him, Blessed is the womb that bare thee, and the paps which thou hast sucked.

Ga 4:15 Where is then the blessedness ye spake of? for I bear you record, that, if *it had been* possible, ye would have plucked out your own eyes, and have given them to me.

See **DEAFNESS, INDIFFERENCE, PRAYER**

HEART, *the physical and spiritual center of humans*

1. Renewed

De 5:29 O that there were such an heart in them, that they would fear me, and keep all my commandments always, that it might be well with them, and with their children for ever!

2 K 10:15 And when he was departed thence, he lighted on Jehonadab the son of Rechab *coming* to meet him: and he saluted him, and said to him, Is thine heart right, as my heart *is* with thy heart? And Jehonadab answered, It is. If it be, give *me* thine hand. And he gave *him* his hand; and he took him up to him into the chariot.

2 Chr 11:16 And after them out of all the tribes of Israel such as set their hearts to seek the LORD God of Israel came to Jerusalem, to sacrifice unto the LORD God of their fathers.

Ne 9:8 And foundest his heart faithful before thee, and madest a covenant with him to give the land of the Canaanites, the Hittites, the Amorites, and the Perizzites, and the Jebusites, and the Girgashites, to give *it, I say,* to his seed, and hast performed thy words; for thou *art* righteous:

Ps 57:7 My heart is fixed, O God, my heart is fixed: I will sing and give praise.

Ps 84:5 Blessed *is* the man whose strength *is* in thee; in whose heart *are* the ways *of them.*

Ps 119:80 Let my heart be sound in thy statutes; that I be not ashamed.

Pr 14:30 A sound heart *is* the life of the flesh: but envy the rottenness of the bones.

Je 24:7 And I will give them an heart to know me, that I *am* the LORD: and they shall be my people, and I will be their God: for they shall return unto me with their whole heart.

Eze 11:19 And I will give them one heart, and I will put a new spirit within you; and I will take the stony heart out of their flesh, and will give them an heart of flesh:

Eze 36:26 A new heart also will I give you, and a new spirit will I put within you: and I will take away the stony heart out of your flesh, and I will give you an heart of flesh.

Lu 8:15 But that on the good ground are they, which in an honest and good heart, having heard the word, keep *it,* and bring forth fruit with patience.

1 Pe 3:4 But *let it be* the hidden man of the heart, in that which is not corruptible, *even the ornament* of a meek and quiet spirit, which is in the sight of God of great price.

2. Evil

STUBBORNNESS

Ec 8:11 Because sentence against an evil work is not executed speedily, therefore the heart of the sons of men is fully set in them to do evil.

MADNESS

Ec 9:3 This *is* an evil among all *things* that are done under the sun, that *there is* one event unto all: yea, also the heart of the sons of men is full of evil, and madness is in their heart while they live, and after that *they go to the* dead.

DEPRAVITY

Je 17:9 The heart *is* deceitful above all *things,* and desperately wicked: who can know it?

EXTORTION AND EXCESS

Mt 23:25 Woe unto you, scribes and Pharisees, hypocrites! for ye make clean the outside of the cup and of the platter, but within they are full of extortion and excess.

BEGINS IN THE HEART

Mk 7:21 For from within, out of the heart of men, proceed evil thoughts, adulteries, fornications, murders,

SOURCE OF UNBELIEF AND COVETOUSNESS

He 3:12 Take heed, brethren, lest there be in any of you an evil heart of unbelief, in departing from the living God.

2 Pe 2:14 Having eyes full of adultery, and that cannot cease from sin; beguiling unstable souls: an heart they have exercised with covetous practices; cursed children:

3. Center of Life

SHOULD BE CAREFULLY GUARDED

Pr 4:23 Keep thy heart with all diligence; for out of it *are* the issues of life.

DETERMINES CHARACTER

Pr 23:7 For as he thinketh in his heart, so *is* he: Eat and drink, saith he to thee; but his heart *is* not with thee.

Mt 6:18 That thou appear not unto men to fast, but unto thy Father which is in secret: and thy Father, which seeth in secret, shall reward thee openly.

SOURCE OF DEFILEMENT

Mt 15:18 But those things which proceed out of the mouth come forth from the heart; and they defile the man.

CONTROLS SPEECH

Lu 6:45 A good man out of the good treasure of his heart bringeth forth that which is good; and an evil man out of the evil treasure of his heart bringeth forth that which is evil: for of the abundance of the heart his mouth speaketh.

SOURCE OF FAITH

Ro 10:10 For with the heart man believeth unto righteousness; and with the mouth confession is made unto salvation.

HEARTLESSNESS

DISCIPLES

Mt 15:23 But he answered her not a word. And his disciples came and besought him, saying, Send her away; for she crieth after us.

PRIEST AND LEVITE

Lu 10:31–32 And by chance there came down a certain priest that way: and when he saw him, he passed by on the other side.

And likewise a Levite, when he was at the place, came and looked *on him*, and passed by on the other side.

UNJUST JUDGE

Lu 18:4 And he would not for a while: but afterward he said within himself, Though I fear not God, nor regard man;

PEOPLE WHO REBUKED THE BLIND MAN

Lu 18:39 And they which went before rebuked him, that he should hold his peace: but he cried so much the more, *Thou* Son of David, have mercy on me.

SPECTATORS AT THE CROSS

Mt 27:42 He saved others; himself he cannot save. If he be the King of Israel, let him now come down from the cross, and we will believe him.

THOSE WHO FAIL TO HELP THE POOR

Ja 2:16 And one of you say unto them, Depart in peace, be ye warmed and filled; notwithstanding ye give them not those things which are needful to the body; what *doth it* profit?

See **MIND, THOUGHTS**

HEAT *See* WEATHER

HEATHEN, *initially denoted all the nations of the world; later designated those outside the covenant relationship with God*

2 K 16:3; 17:8; Ezr 6:21; Ps 2:1; 9:15; 126:2; 125:15; Eze 39:21; Mt 6:7

HEAVE OFFERINGS

See **OFFERINGS**

HEAVEN

1. Its Inhabitants

a. A Great Host

Ge 32:2 And when Jacob saw them, he said, This *is* God's host: and he called the name of that place Mahanaim.

De 33:2 And he said, The LORD came from Sinai, and rose up from Seir unto them; he shined forth from mount Paran, and he came with ten thousands of saints: from his right hand *went* a fiery law for them.

1 K 22:19 And he said, Hear thou therefore the word of the LORD: I saw the LORD sitting on his throne, and all the host of heaven standing by him on his right hand and on his left.

1 Chr 12:22 For at *that* time day by day there came to David to help him, until *it was* a great host, like the host of God.

2 Chr 18:18 Again he said, Therefore hear the word of the LORD; I saw the LORD sitting upon his throne, and all the host of heaven standing on his right hand and *on* his left.

Ne 9:6 Thou, *even* thou, *art* LORD alone; thou hast made heaven, the heaven of heavens, with all their host, the earth, and all *things* that *are* therein, the seas, and all that *is* therein, and thou preservest them all; and the host of heaven worshippeth thee.

Ps 103:21 Bless ye the LORD, all *ye* his hosts; *ye* ministers of his, that do his pleasure.

Ps 148:2 Praise ye him, all his angels: praise ye him, all his hosts.

Da 7:10 A fiery stream issued and came forth from before him: thousand thousands ministered unto him, and ten thousand times ten thousand stood before him: the judgment was set, and the books were opened.

Da 8:10 And it waxed great, *even* to the host of heaven; and it cast down *some* of the host and of the stars to the ground, and stamped upon them.

Lu 2:13 And suddenly there was with the angel a multitude of the heavenly host praising God, and saying,

Lu 13:29 And they shall come from the east, and *from* the west, and from the north, and *from* the south, and shall sit down in the kingdom of God.

He 12:22 But ye are come unto mount Sion, and unto the city of the living God, the heavenly Jerusalem, and to an innumerable company of angels,

Re 5:11 And I beheld, and I heard the voice of many angels round about the throne and the beasts and the elders: and the number of them was ten thousand times ten thousand, and thousands of thousands;

Re 7:9 After this I beheld, and, lo, a great multitude, which no man could number, and kindreds, and people, and tongues, stood before the throne, and before the Lamb, clothed with white robes, and palms in their hands;

Re 14:1 And I looked, and, lo, a Lamb stood on the mount Sion, and with him an hundred forty *and* four thousand, having his Father's name written in their foreheads.

Re 19:6 And I heard as it were the voice of a great multitude, and as the voice of many waters, and as the voice of mighty thunderings, saying, Alleluia: for the Lord God omnipotent reigneth.

b. Description of the Saved

Lu 13:29 And they shall come from the east, and *from* the west, and from the north, and *from* the south, and shall sit down in the kingdom of God.

Lu 20:35–36 But they which shall be accounted worthy to obtain that world, and the resurrection from the dead, neither marry, nor are given in marriage:

Neither can they die any more: for they are equal unto the angels; and are the children of God, being the children of the resurrection.

Lu 21:36 Watch ye therefore, and pray always, that ye may be accounted worthy to escape all these things that shall come to pass, and to stand before the Son of man.

Ac 2:47 Praising God, and having favour with all the people. And the Lord added to the church daily such as should be saved.

1 Co 1:18 For the preaching of the cross is to them that perish foolishness; but unto us which are saved it is the power of God.

Re 3:4 Thou hast a few names even in Sardis which have not defiled their garments; and they shall walk with me in white: for they are worthy.

Re 7:13–17 And one of the elders answered, saying unto me, What are these which are arrayed in white robes? and whence came they?

And I said unto him, Sir, thou knowest. And he said to me, These are they which came out of great tribulation, and have washed their robes, and made them white in the blood of the Lamb.

Therefore are they before the throne of God, and serve him day and night in his temple: and he that sitteth on the throne shall dwell among them.

They shall hunger no more, neither thirst any more; neither shall the sun light on them, nor any heat.

For the Lamb which is in the midst of the throne shall feed them, and shall lead them unto living fountains of waters: and God shall wipe away all tears from their eyes.

Re 21:24 And the nations of them which are saved shall walk in the light of it: and the kings of the earth do bring their glory and honour into it.

Re 22:14 Blessed *are* they that do his commandments, that they may have right to the tree of life, and may enter in through the gates into the city.

2. The Dwelling Place of God

De 26:15 Look down from thy holy habitation, from heaven, and bless thy people Israel, and the land which thou hast given us, as thou swarest unto our fathers, a land that floweth with milk and honey.

1 K 8:30 And hearken thou to the supplication of thy servant, and of thy people Israel, when they shall pray toward this place: and hear thou in heaven thy dwelling place: and when thou hearest, forgive.

1 K 8:39 Then hear thou in heaven thy dwelling place, and forgive, and do, and give to every man according to his ways, whose heart thou knowest; (for thou, *even* thou only, knowest the hearts of all the children of men;)

1 K 8:43 Hear thou in heaven thy dwelling place, and do according to all that the stranger calleth to thee for:

that all people of the earth may know thy name, to fear thee, as do thy people Israel; and that they may know that this house, which I have builded, is called by thy name.

1 K 8:49 Then hear thou their prayer and their supplication in heaven thy dwelling place, and maintain their cause,

2 Chr 6:21 Hearken therefore unto the supplications of thy servant, and of thy people Israel, which they shall make toward this place: hear thou from thy dwelling place, *even* from heaven; and when thou hearest, forgive.

2 Chr 6:30 Then hear thou from heaven thy dwelling place, and forgive, and render unto every man according unto all his ways, whose heart thou knowest; (for thou only knowest the hearts of the children of men:)

2 Chr 6:33 Then hear thou from the heavens, *even* from thy dwelling place, and do according to all that the stranger calleth to thee for; that all people of the earth may know thy name, and fear thee, as doth thy people Israel, and may know that this house which I have built is called by thy name.

2 Chr 6:39 Then hear thou from the heavens, *even* from thy dwelling place, their prayer and their supplications, and maintain their cause, and forgive thy people which have sinned against thee.

2 Chr 20:6 And said, O Lord God of our fathers, *art* not thou God in heaven? and rulest *not* thou over all the kingdoms of the heathen? and in thine hand *is there not* power and might, so that none is able to withstand thee?

2 Chr 30:27 Then the priests the Levites arose and blessed the people: and their voice was heard, and their prayer came *up* to his holy dwelling place, *even* unto heaven.

Jb 22:12 *Is* not God in the height of heaven? and behold the height of the stars, how high they are!

Ps 14:2 The Lord looked down from heaven upon the children of men, to see if there were any that did understand, *and* seek God.

Ps 20:6 Now know I that the LORD saveth his anointed; he will hear him from his holy heaven with the saving strength of his right hand.

Ps 33:13 The LORD looketh from heaven; he beholdeth all the sons of men.

Ps 57:3 He shall send from heaven, and save *from* the reproach of him that would swallow me up. Selah. God shall send forth his mercy and his truth.

Ps 73:25 Whom have I in heaven *but thee?* and *there is* none upon earth *that* I desire beside thee.

Ps 102:19 For he hath looked down from the height of his sanctuary; from heaven did the LORD behold the earth;

Ps 103:19 The LORD hath prepared his throne in the heavens; and his kingdom ruleth over all.

Ps 113:5 Who *is* like unto the LORD our God, who dwelleth on high,

Ps 115:3 But our God *is* in the heavens: he hath done whatsoever he hath pleased.

Ps 123:1 Unto thee lift I up mine eyes, O thou that dwellest in the heavens.

Ps 139:8 If I ascend up into heaven, thou *art* there: if I make my bed in hell, behold, thou *art there.*

Pr 30:4 Who hath ascended up into heaven, or descended? who hath gathered the wind in his fists? who hath bound the waters in a garment? who hath established all the ends of the earth? what *is* his name, and what *is* his son's name, if thou canst tell?

Ec 5:2 Be not rash with thy mouth, and let not thine heart be hasty to utter *any* thing before God: for God *is* in heaven, and thou upon earth: therefore let thy words be few.

Is 33:5 The LORD is exalted; for he dwelleth on high: he hath filled Zion with judgment and righteousness.

Is 57:15 For thus saith the high and lofty One that inhabiteth eternity, whose name *is* Holy; I dwell in the high and holy place, with him also *that is* of a contrite and humble spirit, to revive the spirit of the humble, and to revive the heart of the contrite ones.

Is 63:15 Look down from heaven, and behold from the habitation of thy holiness and of thy glory: where *is* thy zeal and thy strength, the sounding of thy bowels and of thy mercies toward me? are they restrained?

Is 66:1 Thus saith the LORD, The heaven *is* my throne, and the earth *is* my footstool: where *is* the house that ye build unto me? and where *is* the place of my rest?

Je 10:12 He hath made the earth by his power, he hath established the world by his wisdom, and hath stretched out the heavens by his discretion.

Je 51:15 He hath made the earth by his power, he hath established the world by his wisdom, and hath stretched out the heaven by his understanding.

Lam 3:50 Till the LORD look down, and behold from heaven.

Mt 5:16 Let your light so shine before men, that they may see your good works, and glorify your Father which is in heaven.

Mt 5:34 But I say unto you, Swear not at all; neither by heaven; for it is God's throne:

Mt 10:32 Whosoever therefore shall confess me before men, him will I confess also before my Father which is in heaven.

Mt 18:14 Even so it is not the will of your Father which is in heaven, that one of these little ones should perish.

Mt 23:9 And call no *man* your father upon the earth: for one is your Father, which is in heaven.

Lu 11:2 And he said unto them, When ye pray, say, Our Father which art in heaven, Hallowed be thy name. Thy kingdom come. Thy will be done, as in heaven, so in earth.

Lu 24:51 And it came to pass, while he blessed them, he was parted from them, and carried up into heaven.

Ac 7:49 Heaven *is* my throne, and earth *is* my footstool: what house will ye build me? saith the Lord: or what *is* the place of my rest?

2 Co 12:2 I knew a man in Christ above fourteen years ago, (whether in the body, I cannot tell; or whether out of the body, I cannot tell: God knoweth;) such an one caught up to the third heaven.

Ep 1:20 Which he wrought in Christ, when he raised him from the dead, and set *him* at his own right hand in the heavenly *places,*

Col 4:1 Masters, give unto *your* servants that which is just and equal; knowing that ye also have a Master in heaven.

1 Th 4:16 For the Lord himself shall descend from heaven with a shout, with the voice of the archangel, and with the trump of God: and the dead in Christ shall rise first:

He 12:25 See that ye refuse not him that speaketh. For if they escaped not who refused him that spake on earth, much more *shall not* we *escape,* if we turn away from him that *speaketh* from heaven:

2 Pe 1:18 And this voice which came from heaven we heard, when we were with him in the holy mount.

1 Jn 5:7 For there are three that bear record in heaven, the Father, the Word, and the Holy Ghost: and these three are one.

Re 3:12 Him that overcometh will I make a pillar in the temple of my God, and he shall go no more out: and I will write upon him the name of my God, and the name of the city of my God, *which is* new Jerusalem, which cometh down out of heaven from my God: and *I will write upon him* my new name.

3. The Hope of Believers

A SAFE DEPOSIT FOR TREASURES

Mt 6:20 But lay up for yourselves treasures in heaven, where neither moth nor rust doth corrupt, and where thieves do not break through nor steal:

A SOURCE OF REAL JOY AND
A REGISTER OF THE SAINTS

Lu 10:20 Notwithstanding in this rejoice not, that the spirits are subject unto you; but rather rejoice, because your names are written in heaven.

Re 21:27 And there shall in no wise enter into it any thing that defileth, neither *whatsoever* worketh abomination, or *maketh* a lie: but they which are written in the Lamb's book of life.

A PLACE OF FUTURE EXALTATION

Lu 22:30 That ye may eat and drink at my table in my kingdom, and sit on thrones judging the twelve tribes of Israel.

A RESIDENCE OF BELIEVERS

Jn 14:2 In my Father's house are many mansions: if *it were* not *so,* I would have told you. I go to prepare a place for you.

Re 7:9 After this I beheld, and, lo, a great multitude, which no man could number, of all nations, and kindreds, and people, and tongues, stood before the throne, and before the Lamb, clothed with white robes, and palms in their hands;

A RESIDENCE OF THE GLORIFIED CHRIST

Ac 7:55–56 But he, being full of the Holy Ghost, looked up stedfastly into heaven, and saw the glory of God, and Jesus standing on the right hand of God,

And said, Behold, I see the heavens opened, and the Son of man standing on the right hand of God.

A WORK OF GOD'S HANDS

2 Co 5:1 For we know that if our earthly house of *this* tabernacle were dissolved, we have a building of God, an house not made with hands, eternal in the heavens.

He 11:10 For he looked for a city which hath foundations, whose builder and maker *is* God.

A BASIS FOR UNDYING HOPE

Ph 3:20 For our conversation is in heaven; from whence also we look for the Saviour, the Lord Jesus Christ:

Col 1:5 For the hope which is laid up for you in heaven, whereof ye heard before in the word of the truth of the gospel;

A PLACE OF GLORIOUS INHERITANCE

1 Pe 1:4 To an inheritance incorruptible, and undefiled, and that fadeth not away, reserved in heaven for you,

A PLACE ENTERED BY OBEDIENCE

Re 22:14 Blessed *are* they that do his commandments, that they may have right to the tree of life, and may enter in through the gates into the city.

4. The Origin of Christ

Jn 3:13 And no man hath ascended up to heaven, but he that came down from heaven, *even* the Son of man which is in heaven.

Jn 3:31 He that cometh from above is above all: he that is of the earth is earthly, and speaketh of the earth: he that cometh from heaven is above all.

Jn 6:33 For the bread of God is he which cometh down from heaven, and giveth life unto the world.

Jn 6:38 For I came down from heaven, not to do mine own will, but the will of him that sent me.

Jn 6:51 I am the living bread which came down from heaven: if any man eat of this bread, he shall live for ever: and the bread that I will give is my flesh, which I will give for the life of the world.

Jn 6:58 This is that bread which came down from heaven: not as your fathers did eat manna, and are dead: he that eateth of this bread shall live for ever.

Jn 6:62 *What* and if ye shall see the Son of man ascend up where he was before?

Jn 8:23 And he said unto them, Ye are from beneath; I am from above: ye are of this world; I am not of this world.

Jn 8:42 Jesus said unto them, If God were your Father, ye would love me: for I proceeded forth and came from God; neither came I of myself, but he sent me.

Jn 13:3 Jesus knowing that the Father had given all things into his hands, and that he was come from God, and went to God;

Jn 16:30 Now we are sure that thou knowest all things, and needest not that any man should ask thee: by this we believe that thou camest forth from God.

1 Co 15:47 The first man *is* of the earth, earthy: the second man *is* the Lord from heaven.

5. A Place of Blessing Now

Ep 1:3 Blessed *be* the God and Father of our Lord Jesus Christ, who hath blessed us with all spiritual blessings in heavenly *places* in Christ:

Ep 1:20 Which he wrought in Christ, when he raised him from the dead, and set *him* at his own right hand in the heavenly *places,*

Ep 2:6 And hath raised *us* up together, and made *us* sit together in heavenly *places* in Christ Jesus:

Ep 3:10 To the intent that now unto the principalities and powers in heavenly *places* might be known by the church the manifold wisdom of God,

6. A Place of Future Glory

BECOME RADIANT AS STARS

Da 12:3 And they that be wise shall shine as the brightness of the firmament; and they that turn many to righteousness as the stars for ever and ever.

RECEIVE A ROYAL WELCOME IN HEAVEN

Mt 25:34 Then shall the King say unto them on his right hand, Come, ye blessed of my Father, inherit the kingdom prepared for you from the foundation of the world:

2 Pe 1:11 For so an entrance shall be ministered unto you abundantly into the everlasting kingdom of our Lord and Saviour Jesus Christ.

AFFLICTIONS ADD TO THE FINAL GLORY

2 Co 4:17 For our light affliction, which is but for a moment, worketh for us a far more exceeding *and* eternal weight of glory;

A PLACE NEAR THE THRONE FOR SOME

Re 7:14–15 And I said unto him, Sir, thou knowest. And he said to me, These are they which came out of great tribulation, and have washed their robes, and made them white in the blood of the Lamb.

Therefore are they before the throne of God, and serve him day and night in his temple: and he that sitteth on the throne shall dwell among them.

See **FUTURE LIFE**

HEAVENS, *celestial expanse*

1. Created by God

Ge 1:1; 1 Chr 16:26; Ps 8:3; 96:5; 102:25; Pr 8:27; Is 40:22; 42:5; 45:12; 48:13; Je 32:17; Jl 2:30; Zec 12:1; 2 Pe 3:7; Re 10:6; 14:7

See **CREATOR**

2. Will Be Destroyed

Ps 102:26; Is 34:4; 51:6; Mt 5:18; 24:35; Lu 16:17; 21:33; 2 Pe 3:10; Re 6:14; 21:1

2. Will Be Recreated

Is 65:17 For, behold, I create new heavens and a new earth: and the former shall not be remembered, nor come into mind.

Is 66:22 For as the new heavens and the new earth, which I will make, shall remain before me, saith the LORD, so shall your seed and your name remain.

2 Pe 3:13 Nevertheless we, according to his promise, look for new heavens and a new earth, wherein dwelleth righteousness.

Re 21:1 And I saw a new heaven and a new earth: for the first heaven and the first earth were passed away; and there was no more sea.

See **MUTABILITY**

3. Will Be Opened

Eze 1:1; Mt 3:16; Mk 1:10; Lu 3:21; Ac 7:56; 10:11; Re 4:1; 19:11

HEBREW, *language spoken by the Israelites*

2 K 18:26; Ne 13:24; Est 8:9; Is 19:18; 36:11; Lu 23:38; Jn 5:2; 19:13, 20; Ac 1:19; 21:40; 22:2; 26:14; Re 9:11

See **LANGUAGES**

HEBREWS

1. Jewish People

Ge 14:13; 40:15; 41:12; 43:32; Ex 1:19; 2:6, 13; 5:3; 7:16; De 15:12; 1 S 4:6; 13:3, 19; 14:11; 29:3; Jona 1:9; Ac 6:1; 2 Co 11:22; Ph 3:5

2. Book

Author: Uncertain. The epistle has been ascribed to Paul, Barnabas, Luke, Apollos, and various other persons. The most that can be said is that the weight of opinion seems to favor the Pauline authorship.

Date Written: Uncertain, but probably before A.D. 70 when Jerusalem's temple was destroyed. The book highlights the sacrificial ceremonies of the temple and there is no mention of its demise.

Purpose: The chief doctrinal purpose of the writer was to show the transcendent glory of the Christian dispensation as compared with that of the Old Testament.

To Whom Written: Hebrew Christians. These converts were in constant danger of relapsing into Judaism, or at least of attaching too much importance to ceremonial observances.

Main Theme: The superiority of Christ and his work.

Key Word: Better.

Key Verses: 1:3, 4:14–16, 12:1–2.

HEBRON, *a city given to Caleb, Kirjath Arba*

Ge 13:18; 23:2, 19; 35:27; 37:14; Nu 13:22; Jos 10:3, 23, 36; 11:21; 12:10; 14:14; 15:13, 54; 19:28; 20:7; 21:11; Jud 1:10; 16:3; 1 S 30:31; 2 S 2:1; 3:2, 20; 4:8; 5:1, 13; 15:7; 1 K 2:11; 1 Chr 3:4; 6:55; 11:1; 12:38; 29:27; 2 Chr 11:10; Ne 11:25

See **CITIES**

HEDGES, *protective fences for vineyards, often thorny; figuratively used of God's protection*

Jb 1:10; Pr 15:19; Is 5:5; Eze 13:5; Lu 14:23

HEIFERS *See* **ANIMALS**

HEIRS

Ge 15:3; 21:10; 24:36; 25:5; Nu 27:8; 36:9; De 21:16; 2 S 14:7; Ec 2:18; Eze 46:18; Ga 4:30

HELL, *a place of separation from God*

1. Gehenna(Greek), *the place of punishment*

Mt 5:22 But I say unto you, That whosoever is angry with his brother without a cause shall be in danger of the judgment: and whosoever shall say to his brother, Raca, shall be in danger of the council: but whosoever shall say, Thou fool, shall be in danger of hell fire.

Mt 5:29 And if thy right eye offend thee, pluck it out, and cast *it* from thee: for it is profitable for thee that one of thy members should perish, and not *that* thy whole body should be cast into hell.

Mt 10:28 And fear not them which kill the body, but are not able to kill the soul: but rather fear him which is able to destroy both soul and body in hell.

Mt 18:9 And if thine eye offend thee, pluck it out, and cast *it* from thee: it is better for thee to enter into life with one eye, rather than having two eyes to be cast into hell fire.

Mt 23:15 Woe unto you, scribes and Pharisees, hypocrites! for ye compass sea and land to make one proselyte, and when he is made, ye make him twofold more the child of hell than yourselves.

Mt 23:33 *Ye* serpents, *ye* generation of vipers, how can ye escape the damnation of hell?

Mk 9:43 And if thy hand offend thee, cut it off: it is better for thee to enter into life maimed, than having two hands to go into hell, into the fire that never shall be quenched:

Lu 12:5 But I will forewarn you whom ye shall fear: Fear him, which after he hath killed hath power to cast into hell; yea, I say unto you, Fear him.

2. Hades(Greek), *the abode of the dead*

Mt 11:23 And thou, Capernaum, which art exalted unto heaven, shalt be brought down to hell: for if the mighty works, which have been done in thee, had been done in Sodom, it would have remained until this day.

Mt 16:18 And I say also unto thee, That thou art Peter, and upon this rock I will build my church; and the gates of hell shall not prevail against it.

Lu 10:15 And thou, Capernaum, which art exalted to heaven, shalt be thrust down to hell.

Lu 16:23 And in hell he lift up his eyes, being in torments, and seeth Abraham afar off, and Lazarus in his bosom.

Ac 2:27 Because thou wilt not leave my soul in hell, neither wilt thou suffer thine Holy One to see corruption.

Re 1:18 I *am* he that liveth, and was dead; and, behold, I am alive for evermore, Amen; and have the keys of hell and of death.

Re 6:8 And I looked, and behold a pale horse: and his name that sat on him was Death, and Hell followed with him. And power was given unto them over the fourth part of the earth, to kill with sword, and with hunger, and with death, and with the beasts of the earth.

Re 20:13 And the sea gave up the dead which were in it; and death and hell delivered up the dead which were in them: and they were judged every man according to their works.

See **GRAVE**

3. Sheol(Greek), *the grave or unseen state*

De 32:22 For a fire is kindled in mine anger, and shall burn unto the lowest hell, and shall consume the earth with her increase, and set on fire the foundations of the mountains.

2 S 22:6 The sorrows of hell compassed me about; the snares of death prevented me;

Jb 11:8 *It is* as high as heaven; what canst thou do? deeper than hell; what canst thou know?

Jb 17:16 They shall go down to the bars of the pit, when *our* rest together *is* in the dust.

Jb 26:6 Hell *is* naked before him, and destruction hath no covering.

Ps 9:17 The wicked shall be turned into hell, *and* all the nations that forget God.

Ps 16:10 For thou wilt not leave my soul in hell; neither wilt thou suffer thine Holy One to see corruption.

Ps 18:5 The sorrows of hell compassed me about: the snares of death prevented me.

Ps 55:15 Let death seize upon them, *and* let them go down quick into hell: for wickedness is in their dwellings, *and* among them.

Ps 86:13 For great *is* thy mercy toward me: and thou hast delivered my soul from the lowest hell.

Ps 116:3 The sorrows of death compassed me, and the pains of hell gat hold upon me: I found trouble and sorrow.

Ps 139:8 If I ascend up into heaven, thou *art* there: if I make my bed in hell, behold, thou *art there*.

Pr 5:5 Her feet go down to death; her steps take hold on hell.

Pr 7:27 Her house *is* the way to hell, going down to the chambers of death.

Pr 9:18 But he knoweth not that the dead *are* there; *and that* her guests *are* in the depths of hell.

Pr 15:11 Hell and destruction *are* before the LORD: how much more then the hearts of the children of men?

Pr 15:24 The way of life *is* above to the wise, that he may depart from hell beneath.

Pr 23:14 Thou shalt beat him with the rod, and shalt deliver his soul from hell.

Pr 27:20 Hell and destruction are never full; so the eyes of man are never satisfied.

Is 5:14 Therefore hell hath enlarged herself, and opened her mouth without measure: and their glory, and their multitude, and their pomp, and he that rejoiceth, shall descend into it.

Is 14:9 Hell from beneath is moved for thee to meet *thee* at thy coming: it stirreth up the dead for thee, *even* all the chief ones of the earth; it hath raised up from their thrones all the kings of the nations.

Is 14:15 Yet thou shalt be brought down to hell, to the sides of the pit.

Is 28:15 Because ye have said, We have made a covenant with death, and with hell are we at agreement; when the overflowing scourge shall pass through, it shall not come unto us: for we have made lies our refuge, and under falsehood have we hid ourselves:

Is 28:18 And your covenant with death shall be disannulled, and your agreement with hell shall not stand; when the overflowing scourge shall pass through, then ye shall be trodden down by it.

Is 57:9 And thou wentest to the king with ointment, and didst increase thy perfumes, and didst send thy messengers far off, and didst debase *thyself even* unto hell.

Eze 31:16 I made the nations to shake at the sound of his fall, when I cast him down to hell with them that descend into the pit: and all the trees of Eden, the choice and best of Lebanon, all that drink water, shall be comforted in the nether parts of the earth.

Eze 32:21 The strong among the mighty shall speak to him out of the midst of hell with them that help him: they are gone down, they lie uncircumcised, slain by the sword.

Eze 32:27 And they shall not lie with the mighty *that are* fallen of the uncircumcised, which are gone down to hell with their weapons of war: and they have laid their swords under their heads, but their iniquities shall be upon their bones, though *they were* the terror of the mighty in the land of the living.

Am 9:2 Though they dig into hell, thence shall mine hand take them; though they climb up to heaven, thence will I bring them down:

Jona 2:2 And said, I cried by reason of mine affliction unto the LORD, and he heard me; out of the belly of hell cried I, *and* thou heardest my voice.

Hab 2:5 Yea also, because he transgresseth by wine, *he is* a proud man, neither keepeth at home, who enlargeth his desire as hell, and *is* as death, and cannot be satisfied, but gathereth unto him all nations, and heapeth unto him all people:

4. Tartarus*(Greek), the place of punishment*

2 Pe 2:4 For if God spared not the angels that sinned, but cast *them* down to hell, and delivered *them* into chains of darkness, to be reserved unto judgment;

HELPER

1. God Helps His People
Ge 49:25 *Even* by the God of thy father, who shall help thee; and by the Almighty, who shall bless thee with blessings of heaven above, blessings of the deep that lieth under, blessings of the breasts, and of the womb:

Ex 18:4 And the name of the other *was* Eliezer; for the God of my father, *said he, was* mine help, and delivered me from the sword of Pharaoh:

De 33:7 And this *is the blessing* of Judah: and he said, Hear, LORD, the voice of Judah, and bring him unto his people: let his hands be sufficient for him; and be thou an help *to him* from his enemies.

De 33:26 *There is* none like unto the God of Jeshurun, *who* rideth upon the heaven in thy help, and in his excellency on the sky.

De 33:29 Happy *art* thou, O Israel: who *is* like unto thee, O people saved by the LORD, the shield of thy help, and who *is* the sword of thy excellency! and thine enemies shall be found liars unto thee; and thou shalt tread upon their high places.

Jos 8:18 And the LORD said unto Joshua, Stretch out the spear that *is* in thy hand toward Ai; for I will give it into thine hand. And Joshua stretched out the spear that *he had* in his hand toward the city.

1 S 7:12 Then Samuel took a stone, and set *it* between Mizpeh and Shen, and called the name of it Eben-ezer, saying, Hitherto hath the LORD helped us.

2 S 5:19 And David enquired of the LORD, saying, Shall I go up to the Philistines? wilt thou deliver them into mine hand? And the LORD said unto David, Go up: for I will doubtless deliver the Philistines into thine hand.

2 K 6:27 And he said, If the LORD do not help thee, whence shall I help thee? out of the barnfloor, or out of the winepress?

1 Chr 5:20 And they were helped against them, and the Hagarites were delivered into their hand, and all that *were* with them: for they cried to God in the battle, and he was intreated of them; because they put their trust in him.

1 Chr 12:18 Then the spirit came upon Amasai, *who was* chief of the captains, *and he said,* Thine *are* we, David, and on thy side, thou son of Jesse: peace, peace *be* unto thee, and peace *be* to thine helpers; for thy God helpeth thee. Then David received them, and made them captains of the band.

1 Chr 15:26 And it came to pass, when God helped the Levites that bare the ark of the covenant of the LORD, that they offered seven bullocks and seven rams.

2 Chr 14:11 And Asa cried unto the LORD his God, and said, LORD, *it is* nothing with thee to help, whether with many, or with them that have no power: help us, O LORD our God; for we rest on thee, and in thy name we go against this multitude. O LORD, thou *art* our God; let not man prevail against thee.

2 Chr 18:31 And it came to pass, when the captains of the chariots saw Jehoshaphat, that they said, It *is* the king of Israel. Therefore they compassed about him to fight: but Jehoshaphat cried out, and the LORD helped him; and God moved them *to depart* from him.

2 Chr 20:4 And Judah gathered themselves together, to ask *help* of the LORD: even out of all the cities of Judah they came to seek the LORD.

2 Chr 25:8 But if thou wilt go, do *it,* be strong for the battle: God shall make thee fall before the enemy: for

God hath power to help, and to cast down.

2 Chr 26:7 And God helped him against the Philistines, and against the Arabians that dwelt in Gur-baal, and the Mehunims.

2 Chr 32:8 With him *is* an arm of flesh; but with us *is* the LORD our God to help us, and to fight our battles. And the people rested themselves upon the words of Hezekiah king of Judah.

Ezr 8:22 For I was ashamed to require of the king a band of soldiers and horsemen to help us against the enemy in the way: because we had spoken unto the king, saying, The hand of our God *is* upon all them for good that seek him; but his power and his wrath *is* against all them that forsake him.

Ps 7:7 So shall the congregation of the people compass thee about: for their sakes therefore return thou on high.

Ps 10:14 Thou hast seen *it;* for thou beholdest mischief and spite, to requite *it* with thy hand: the poor committeth himself unto thee; thou art the helper of the fatherless.

Ps 18:16 He sent from above, he took me, he drew me out of many waters.

Ps 18:48 He delivereth me from mine enemies: yea, thou liftest me up above those that rise up against me: thou hast delivered me from the violent man.

Ps 20:2 Send thee help from the sanctuary, and strengthen thee out of Zion;

Ps 22:19 But be not thou far from me, O LORD: O my strength, haste thee to help me.

Ps 27:9 Hide not thy face *far* from me; put not thy servant away in anger: thou hast been my help; leave me not, neither forsake me, O God of my salvation.

Ps 28:7 The LORD *is* my strength and my shield; my heart trusted in him, and I am helped: therefore my heart greatly rejoiceth; and with my song will I praise him.

Ps 30:10 Hear, O LORD, and have mercy upon me: LORD, be thou my helper.

Ps 33:20 Our soul waiteth for the LORD: he *is* our help and our shield.

Ps 34:17 *The righteous* cry, and the LORD heareth, and delivereth them out of all their troubles.

Ps 35:2 Take hold of shield and buckler, and stand up for mine help.

Ps 37:40 And the LORD shall help them and deliver them: he shall deliver them from the wicked, and save them, because they trust in him.

Ps 38:22 Make haste to help me, O Lord my salvation.

Ps 40:13 Be pleased, O LORD, to deliver me: O LORD, make haste to help me.

Ps 40:17 But I *am* poor and needy; *yet* the Lord thinketh upon me: thou *art* my help and my deliverer; make no tarrying, O my God.

Ps 42:5 Why art thou cast down, O my soul? and why *art* thou disquieted in me? hope thou in God: for I shall yet praise him *for* the help of his countenance.

Ps 42:11 Why art thou cast down, O my soul? and why art thou disquieted within me? hope thou in God: for I shall yet praise him, *who is* the health of my countenance, and my God.

Ps 44:26 Arise for our help, and redeem us for thy mercies' sake.

Ps 46:1 God *is* our refuge and strength, a very present help in trouble.

Ps 46:5 God *is* in the midst of her; she shall not be moved: God shall help her, *and that* right early.

Ps 54:4 Behold, God *is* mine helper: the Lord *is* with them that uphold my soul.

Ps 56:9 When I cry *unto thee,* then shall mine enemies turn back: this I know; for God *is* for me.

Ps 59:4 They run and prepare themselves without *my* fault: awake to help me, and behold.

Ps 60:11 Give us help from trouble: for vain *is* the help of man.

Ps 63:7 Because thou hast been my help, therefore in the shadow of thy wings will I rejoice.

Ps 70:1 *Make haste,* O God, to deliver me; make haste to help me, O LORD.

Ps 70:5 But I *am* poor and needy: make haste unto me, O God: thou *art* my help and my deliverer; O LORD, make no tarrying.

Ps 71:12 O God, be not far from me: O my God, make haste for my help.

Ps 86:17 Shew me a token for good; that they which hate me may see *it,* and be ashamed: because thou, LORD, hast holpen me, and comforted me.

Ps 94:17 Unless the LORD *had been* my help, my soul had almost dwelt in silence.

Ps 107:14 He brought them out of darkness and the shadow of death, and brake their bands in sunder.

Ps 108:12 Give us help from trouble: for vain *is* the help of man.

Ps 115:10 O house of Aaron, trust in the LORD: he *is* their help and their shield.

Ps 116:6 The LORD preserveth the simple: I was brought low, and he helped me.

Ps 118:7 The LORD taketh my part with them that help me: therefore shall I see *my desire* upon them that hate me.

Ps 118:13 Thou hast thrust sore at me that I might fall: but the LORD helped me.

Ps 119:86 All thy commandments *are* faithful: they persecute me wrongfully; help thou me.

Ps 119:173 Let thine hand help me; for I have chosen thy precepts.

Ps 121:2 My help cometh from the LORD, which made heaven and earth.

Ps 124:8 Our help *is* in the name of the LORD, who made heaven and earth.

Ps 138:7 Though I walk in the midst of trouble, thou wilt revive me: thou shalt stretch forth thine hand against the wrath of mine enemies, and thy right hand shall save me.

Ps 144:2 My goodness, and my fortress; my high tower, and my deliverer; my shield, and *he* in whom I trust; who subdueth my people under me.

Ps 146:5 Happy *is he* that *hath* the God of Jacob for his help, whose hope *is* in the LORD his God:

Pr 22:23 For the LORD will plead their cause, and spoil the soul of those that spoiled them.

Is 41:10 Fear thou not; for I *am* with thee: be not dismayed; for I *am* thy God: I will strengthen thee; yea, I will help thee; yea, I will uphold thee with the right hand of my righteousness.

Is 41:14 Fear not, thou worm Jacob, *and* ye men of Israel; I will help thee, saith the LORD, and thy redeemer, the Holy One of Israel.

Is 44:2 Thus saith the LORD that made thee, and formed thee from the womb, *which* will help thee; Fear not, O Jacob, my servant; and thou, Jesurun, whom I have chosen.

Is 49:8 Thus saith the LORD, In an acceptable time have I heard thee, and in a day of salvation have I helped thee: and I will preserve thee, and give thee for a covenant of the people, to establish the earth, to cause to inherit the desolate heritages;

Is 50:9 Behold, the Lord GOD will help me; who *is* he *that* shall condemn me? lo, they all shall wax old as a garment; the moth shall eat them up.

Ho 13:9 O Israel, thou hast destroyed thyself; but in me *is* thine help.

Mt 15:25 Then came she and worshipped him, saying, Lord, help me.

Mk 1:31 And he came and took her by the hand, and lifted her up; and immediately the fever left her, and she ministered unto took him by the hand, and lifted him up; and he arose.

Mk 9:27 But Jesus took him by the hand, and lifted him up; and he arose.

Mk 13:11 But when they shall lead *you,* and deliver you up, take no thought beforehand what ye shall speak, neither do ye premeditate: but whatsoever shall be given you in that hour, that speak ye: for it is not ye that speak, but the Holy Ghost.

Mk 16:4 And when they looked, they saw that the stone was rolled away: for it was very great.

Lu 1:54 He hath holpen his servant Israel, in remembrance of *his* mercy;

Ac 12:11 And when Peter was come to himself, he said, Now I know of a surety, that the Lord hath sent his angel, and hath delivered me out of the hand of Herod, and *from* all the expectation of the people of the Jews.

Ac 26:22 Having therefore obtained help of God, I continue unto this day, witnessing both to small and great, saying none other things than those which the prophets and Moses did say should come:

Ro 8:26 Likewise the Spirit also helpeth our infirmities: for we know not what we should pray for as we ought: but the Spirit itself maketh intercession for us with groanings which cannot be uttered.

2 Co 6:2 (For he saith, I have heard thee in a time accepted, and in the day of salvation have I succoured thee: behold, now *is* the accepted time; behold, now *is* the day of salvation.)

He 4:16 Let us therefore come boldly unto the throne of grace, that we may obtain mercy, and find grace to help in time of need.

He 13:6 So that we may boldly say, The Lord *is* my helper, and I will not fear what man shall do unto me.

a. Difficulties Overcome

Ex 13:17 And it came to pass, when Pharaoh had let the people go, that God led them not *through* the way of the land of the Philistines, although that *was* near; for God said, Lest peradventure the people repent when they see war, and they return to Egypt:

Ex 14:16 But lift thou up thy rod, and stretch out thine hand over the sea, and divide it: and the children of Israel shall go on dry *ground* through the midst of the sea.

Ex 14:22 And the children of Israel went into the midst of the sea upon the dry *ground:* and the waters *were* a wall unto them on their right hand, and on their left.

Ex 15:19 For the horse of Pharaoh went in with his chariots and with his horsemen into the sea, and the LORD brought again the waters of the sea upon them; but the children of Israel went on dry *land* in the midst of the sea.

Jos 2:10 For we have heard how the LORD dried up the water of the Red sea for you, when ye came out of Egypt; and what ye did unto the two kings of the Amorites, that *were* on the other side Jordan, Sihon and Og, whom ye utterly destroyed.

Jos 3:4 Yet there shall be a space between you and it, about two thousand cubits by measure: come not near unto it, that ye may know the way by which ye must go: for ye have not passed this *way* heretofore.

Jos 3:17 And the priests that bare the ark of the covenant of the LORD stood firm on dry ground in the midst of Jordan, and all the Israelites passed over on dry ground, until all the people were passed clean over Jordan.

Jos 4:23 For the LORD your God dried up the waters of Jordan from before you, until ye were passed over, as the LORD your God did to the Red sea, which he dried up from before us, until we were gone over:

Jos 6:20 So the people shouted when *the priests* blew with the trumpets: and it came to pass, when the people heard the sound of the trumpet, and the people shouted with a great shout, that the wall fell down flat, so that the people went up into the city, every man straight before him, and they took the city.

2 S 22:16 And the channels of the sea appeared, the foundations of the world were discovered, at the rebuking of the LORD, at the blast of the breath of his nostrils.

2 K 2:8 And Elijah took his mantle, and wrapped *it* together, and smote the waters, and they were divided hither and thither, so that they two went over on dry ground.

2 K 2:14 And he took the mantle of Elijah that fell from him, and smote the waters, and said, Where *is* the LORD God of Elijah? and when he also had smitten the waters, they parted hither and thither: and Elisha went over.

Ne 9:11 And thou didst divide the sea before them, so that they went through the midst of the sea on the dry land; and their persecutors thou threwest into the deeps, as a stone into the mighty waters.

Ps 5:8 Lead me, O LORD, in thy righteousness because of mine enemies; make thy way straight before my face.

Ps 18:15 Then the channels of waters were seen, and the foundations of the world were discovered at thy rebuke, O LORD, at the blast of the breath of thy nostrils.

Ps 66:6 He turned the sea into dry *land:* they went through the flood on foot: there did we rejoice in him.

Ps 74:15 Thou didst cleave the fountain and the flood: thou driedst up mighty rivers.

Ps 77:16 The waters saw thee, O God, the waters saw thee; they were afraid: the depths also were troubled.

Ps 78:13 He divided the sea, and caused them to pass through; and he made the waters to stand as an heap.

Ps 106:9 He rebuked the Red sea also, and it was dried up: so he led them through the depths, as through the wilderness.

Ps 114:3 The sea saw *it,* and fled: Jordan was driven back.

Ps 136:14 And made Israel to pass through the midst of it: for his mercy *endureth* for ever:

Pr 15:19 The way of the slothful *man is* as an hedge of thorns: but the way of the righteous *is* made plain.

Is 11:16 And there shall be an highway for the remnant of his people, which shall be left, from Assyria; like as it was to Israel in the day that he came up out of the land of Egypt.

Is 30:21 And thine ears shall hear a word behind thee, saying, This *is* the way, walk ye in it, when ye turn to the right hand, and when ye turn to the left.

Is 40:4 Every valley shall be exalted, and every mountain and hill shall be made low: and the crooked shall be made straight, and the rough places plain:

Is 42:16 And I will bring the blind by a way *that* they knew not; I will lead them in paths *that* they have not known: I will make darkness light before them, and crooked things straight. These things will I do unto them, and not forsake them.

Is 43:16 Thus saith the LORD, which maketh a way in the sea, and a path in the mighty waters;

Is 44:27 That saith to the deep, Be dry, and I will dry up thy rivers:

Is 45:2 I will go before thee, and make the crooked places straight: I will break in pieces the gates of brass, and cut in sunder the bars of iron:

Is 49:11 And I will make all my mountains a way, and my highways shall be exalted.

Is 50:2 Wherefore, when I came, *was there* no man? when I called, *was there* none to answer? Is my hand shortened at all, that it cannot redeem? or have I no power to deliver? behold, at my rebuke I dry up the sea, I make the rivers a wilderness: their fish stinketh, because *there is* no water, and dieth for thirst.

Is 63:12 That led *them* by the right hand of Moses with his glorious arm, dividing the water before them, to make himself an everlasting name?

Mi 2:13 The breaker is come up before them: they have broken up, and have passed through the gate, and are gone out by it: and their king shall pass before them, and the LORD on the head of them.

Zec 4:7 Who *art* thou, O great mountain? before Zerubbabel *thou shalt become* a plain: and he shall bring forth the headstone *thereof with* shoutings, *crying,* Grace, grace unto it.

Zec 10:11 And he shall pass through the sea with affliction, and shall smite the waves in the sea, and all the deeps of the river shall dry up: and the pride of Assyria shall be brought down, and the sceptre of Egypt shall depart away.

Lu 3:5 Every valley shall be filled, and every mountain and hill shall be brought low; and the crooked shall be made straight, and the rough ways *shall be* made smooth;

Lu 23:46 And when Jesus had cried with a loud voice, he said, Father, into thy hands I commend my spirit: and having said thus, he gave up the ghost.

1 Co 10:1 Moreover, brethren, I would not that ye should be ignorant, how that all our fathers were under the cloud, and all passed through the sea;

1 Co 10:13 There hath no temptation taken you but such as is common to man: but God *is* faithful, who will not suffer you to be tempted above that ye are able; but will with the temptation also make a way to escape, that ye may be able to bear *it.*

He 11:29 By faith they passed through the Red sea as by dry *land:* which the Egyptians assaying to do were drowned.

b. Obstacles Removed

Is 40:4 Every valley shall be exalted, and every mountain and hill shall be made low: and the crooked shall be made straight, and the rough places plain:

Is 45:2 I will go before thee, and make the crooked places straight: I will break in pieces the gates of brass, and cut in sunder the bars of iron:

Is 49:11 And I will make all my mountains a way, and my highways shall be exalted.

Is 57:14 And shall say, Cast ye up, cast ye up, prepare the way, take up the stumblingblock out of the way of my people.

Is 62:10 Go through, go through the gates; prepare ye the way of the people; cast up, cast up the highways; gather out the stones; lift up a standard for the people.

Zec 4:7 Who *art* thou, O great mountain? before Zerubbabel *thou shalt become* a plain: and he shall bring forth the headstone *thereof with* shoutings, *crying,* Grace, grace unto it.

Zec 10:11 And he shall pass through the sea with affliction, and shall smite the waves in the sea, and all the deeps of the river shall dry up: and the pride of Assyria shall be brought down, and the sceptre of Egypt shall depart away.

Mt 21:21 Jesus answered and said unto them, Verily I say unto you, If ye have faith, and doubt not, ye shall not only do this *which is done* to the fig tree, but also if ye shall say unto this mountain, Be thou removed, and be thou cast into the sea; it shall be done.

Jn 11:41 Then they took away the stone *from the place* where the dead was laid. And Jesus lifted up *his* eyes, and said, Father, I thank thee that thou hast heard me.

c. The Right Way Shown

Pr 15:19 The way of the slothful *man* is as an hedge of thorns: but the way of the righteous *is* made plain.

Pr 16:17 The highway of the upright *is* to depart from evil: he that keepeth his way preserveth his soul.

Is 35:8 And an highway shall be there, and a way, and it shall be called The way of holiness; the unclean shall not pass over it; but it *shall be* for those: the wayfaring men, though fools, shall not err *therein.*

Is 43:19 Behold, I will do a new thing; now it shall spring forth; shall ye not know it? I will even make a way in the wilderness, *and* rivers in the desert.

Is 62:10 Go through, go through the gates; prepare ye the way of the people; cast up, cast up the highways; gather out the stones; lift up a standard for the people.

Je 18:15 Because my people hath forgotten me, they have burned incense to vanity, and they have caused them to stumble in their ways *from* the ancient paths, to walk in paths, *in* a way not cast up;

Je 31:21 Set thee up waymarks, make thee high heaps: set thine heart toward the highway, *even* the way *which* thou wentest: turn again, O virgin of Israel, turn again to these thy cities.

Jn 1:23 He said, I *am* the voice of one crying in the wilderness, Make straight the way of the Lord, as said the prophet Esaias.

2. God Cares about Kindness

CARRIES THE WEAK IN HIS BOSOM

Is 40:11 He shall feed his flock like a shepherd: he shall gather the lambs with his arm, and carry *them* in his bosom, *and* shall gently lead those that are with young.

REWARDS THOSE WHO CARE FOR THE WEAK

Mt 10:42 And whosoever shall give to drink unto one of these little ones a cup of cold *water* only in the name of a disciple, verily I say unto you, he shall in no wise lose his reward.

CONSIDERS THE WEAK

Mt 18:14 Even so it is not the will of your Father which is in heaven, that one of these little ones should perish.

IS PATIENT WITH THE WEAK

Jn 21:15 So when they had dined, Jesus saith to Simon Peter, Simon, *son of* Jonas, lovest thou me more than these? He saith unto him, Yea, Lord; thou knowest that I love thee. He saith unto him, Feed my lambs.

3. To Be without a Helper

2 K 14:26; Jb 5:1, 4; 9:33; 26:2; 29:12; Ps 7:2; 22:11; 69:20; 72:12; 107:12; 142:4; Ec 4:1; Is 5:29; 41:28; 42:22; 59:16; 63:5; Je 30:13; 47:4; Lam 1:7; 5:8; Eze 16:5; 22:30; 34:5; Am 5:2; Zec 10:2; Mt 9:36

See **HINDRANCES, KINDNESS**

HELPLESSNESS, *physical and spiritual*

Lu 13:11 And, behold, there was a woman which had a spirit of infirmity eighteen years, and was bowed together, and could in no wise lift up *herself*.

Jn 5:7 The impotent man answered him, Sir, I have no man, when the water is troubled, to put me into the pool: but while I am coming, another steppeth down before me.

Jn 6:44 No man can come to me, except the Father which hath sent me draw him: and I will raise him up at the last day.

Jn 15:5 I am the vine, ye *are* the branches: He that abideth in me, and I in him, the same bringeth forth much fruit: for without me ye can do nothing.

Ac 3:2 And a certain man lame from his mother's womb was carried, whom they laid daily at the gate of the temple which is called Beautiful, to ask alms of them that entered into the temple;

Ro 5:6 For when we were yet without strength, in due time Christ died for the ungodly.

Ro 7:18–19 For I know that in me (that is, in my flesh,) dwelleth no good thing: for to will is present with me; but *how* to perform that which is good I find not.

For the good that I would I do not: but the evil which I would not, that I do.

See **CHRIST, GOD**

HEMAN, *faithful*

1. The Wise Man

1 K 4:31; 1 Chr 2:6

2. The Singer

1 Chr 6:33; 15:17; 16:41; 25:1, 5; 2 Chr 5:12

HEN *See* **ANIMALS**

HERDS, *evidence of wealth*

Ge 18:7; 26:14; 46:32; 47:1, 18; Ex 10:9; Le 27:32; Nu 15:3; De 16:2; 1 S 11:5; 2 S 12:4; Is 65:10

HERDSMEN, *hired to watch the flock, keep it from straying, and lead it to suitable pasture*

Ge 13:7; 26:20; 1 S 21:7

HERESY

Mt 15:9; Ac 15:24; 1 Co 11:19; 1 Ti 4:1; Tit 3:10; 2 Pe 2:1; 3:17

See **APOSTASY**

HEREDITY, *transmission of family characteristics from parents to children*

Ex 34:7; Le 26:39; Ps 51:5; 58:3; Is 14:20; Je 3:25; Lam 5:7; Eze 18:2

1. Evil Influence of the Wicked

De 28:59; 1 K 21:29; 2 K 6:32; 10:1, 11; Est 9:10; Jb 5:4; 18:19; 20:10; 21:8; 27:14; 30:8; Ps 17:14; 21:10; 37:28; 109:10; Is 1:4; 14:20; 47:9; 51:20; 57:3; Je 15:7; 16:3; 22:30; 29:32; 49:10; Lam 2:22; Eze 23:25; Ho 9:12, 16; Jl 3:8; Am

4:2; 7:17; Na 3:10; Mt 12:34; 23:31; Lu 11:48

2. Good Influence of the Righteous

Ge 5:29; 9:9; 13:16; 15:4, 13; 17:2; 21:12; 22:17; 24:60; 26:4; 32:12; 46:6; 48:4; Ex 32:13; 33:1; Nu 14:24; 23:10; 25:13; De 1:10; 4:37; 7:13; 10:15; Jos 24:3; 2 S 7:12; 22:51; 1 K 3:6; 5:7; 1 Chr 17:11; Ne 9:8; Est 10:3; Jb 5:25; Ps 18:50; 22:30; 25:13; 37:25; 69:36; 89:4, 29; 102:28; 112:2; 147:13; Pr 11:21; 14:26; 20:7; Is 41:8; 44:3; 48:19; 59:21; 61:9; 65:23; 66:22; Je 46:27; Zec 10:7; Mal 2:15; Lu 1:55; Ac 3:25; 7:5, 17; He 11:12, 18

See **PARENTS, SIN**

HERITAGE, *expectations of the godly*

1. Earthly

Ex 6:8; Ps 25:13; 37:9, 11, 22, 29, 34; 69:36; 106:5; 111:6; 115:16; Pr 2:22; 13:22; Is 57:13; 60:21; 65:9; Je 3:19; 7:7; Eze 36:12; Mt 5:5; Ro 4:13

2. Spiritual

Ps 16:6 The lines are fallen unto me in pleasant *places;* yea, I have a goodly heritage.

Ps 37:18 The LORD knoweth the days of the upright: and their inheritance shall be for ever.

Ps 61:5 For thou, O God, hast heard my vows: thou hast given *me* the heritage of those that fear thy name.

Ps 119:111 Thy testimonies have I taken as an heritage for ever: for they *are* the rejoicing of my heart.

Pr 3:35 The wise shall inherit glory: but shame shall be the promotion of fools.

Pr 8:21 That I may cause those that love me to inherit substance; and I will fill their treasures.

Is 54:17 No weapon that is formed against thee shall prosper; and every tongue *that* shall rise against thee in judgment thou shalt condemn. This *is* the heritage of the servants of the LORD, and their righteousness *is* of me, saith the LORD.

Mt 25:34 Then shall the King say unto them on his right hand, Come, ye blessed of my Father, inherit the kingdom prepared for you from the foundation of the world:

Ac 20:32 And now, brethren, I commend you to God, and to the word of his grace, which is able to build you up, and to give you an inheritance among all them which are sanctified.

Ac 26:18 To open their eyes, *and* to turn *them* from darkness to light, and *from* the power of Satan unto God, that they may receive forgiveness of sins, and inheritance among them which are sanctified by faith that is in me.

2 Co 6:10 As sorrowful, yet alway rejoicing; as poor, yet making many rich; as having nothing, and *yet* possessing all things.

Ga 3:18 For if the inheritance *be* of the law, *it is* no more of promise: but God gave *it* to Abraham by promise.

Ep 1:11 In whom also we have obtained an inheritance, being predestinated according to the purpose of him who worketh all things after the counsel of his own will:

Ep 1:14 Which is the earnest of our inheritance until the redemption of the purchased possession, unto the praise of his glory.

Ep 1:18 The eyes of your understanding being enlightened; that ye may know what is the hope of his calling, and what the riches of the glory of his inheritance in the saints,

Col 1:12 Giving thanks unto the Father, which hath made us meet to be partakers of the inheritance of the saints in light:

Col 3:24 Knowing that of the Lord ye shall receive the reward of the inheritance: for ye serve the Lord Christ.

He 1:14 Are they not all ministering spirits, sent forth to minister for them who shall be heirs of salvation?

He 6:12 That ye be not slothful, but followers of them who through faith and patience inherit the promises.

He 9:15 And for this cause he is the mediator of the new testament, that by means of death, for the redemption of the transgressions *that were* under the first testament, they which are called might receive the promise of eternal inheritance.

He 10:34 For ye had compassion of me in my bonds, and took joyfully the spoiling of your goods, knowing in yourselves that ye have in heaven a better and an enduring substance.

1 Pe 1:4 To an inheritance incorruptible, and undefiled, and that fadeth not away, reserved in heaven for you,

1 Pe 3:9 Not rendering evil for evil, or railing for railing: but contrariwise blessing; knowing that ye are thereunto called, that ye should inherit a blessing.

HERMON See **MOUNTAINS AND HILLS**

HEROD AGRIPPA I(A. D. 37–44),a
zealous Jewish ruler who persecuted early Christians

Ac 12:1, 6, 11, 19, 20; 23:35

HEROD AGRIPPA II(A. D. 53–70),
known as Agrippa or King Agrippa, he heard Paul's defense at Caesarea

Ac 25:13, 22, 26; 26:1, 27, 31

HEROD ANTIPAS(4 B.C. –A.D. 39),
Herod the Tetrarch, imprisoned and executed John the Baptist

Mt 14:1, 3; Mk 6:14, 21; 8:15; Lu 3:1, 19; 8:3; 9:7; 13:31; 23:7, 11, 15; Ac 4:27; 13:1

HERODIANS See **SECTS AND PARTIES**

HERODIAS, *wife of Philip, instigated the death of John the Baptist*

Mt 14:3; Mk 6:17; Lu 3:19

See **WOMEN**

HEROD THE GREAT(40–4 B. C.)

Herod, enterprising, keen of intellect, builder of the temple, was also bloodthirsty and cruel. Son of Antipater, he was appointed governor of Coele-Syria and advanced from one position to another until made king of an extensive territory. The kingdom of Herod the Great was divided between his sons. Archelaus succeeded to Judea

and Samaria. Herod Antipas was made Tetrarch of Galilee and Perea. Herod Philip II received Ituraea, Gaulonitis, Trachonitis, etc.

HEROES, *ancient people whose confidence was in God*

1. Those Engaged in Battles

JOSHUA

Jos 11:23 So Joshua took the whole land, according to all that the LORD said unto Moses; and Joshua gave it for an inheritance unto Israel according to their divisions by their tribes. And the land rested from war.

GIDEON

Jud 7:14 And his fellow answered and said, This *is* nothing else save the sword of Gideon the son of Joash, a man of Israel: *for* into his hand hath God delivered Midian, and all the host.

JONATHAN

1 S 14:6 And Jonathan said to the young man that bare his armour, Come, and let us go over unto the garrison of these uncircumcised: it may be that the LORD will work for us: for *there is* no restraint to the LORD to save by many or by few.

DAVID

1 S 17:45 Then said David to the Philistine, Thou comest to me with a sword, and with a spear, and with a shield: but I come to thee in the name of the LORD of hosts, the God of the armies of Israel, whom thou hast defied.

ELISHA

2 K 6:17 And Elisha prayed, and said, LORD, I pray thee, open his eyes, that he may see. And the LORD opened the eyes of the young man; and he saw: and, behold, the mountain *was* full of horses and chariots of fire round about Elisha.

JEHOSHAPHAT

2 Chr 20:20 And they rose early in the morning, and went forth into the wilderness of Tekoa: and as they went forth, Jehoshaphat stood and said, Hear me, O Judah, and ye inhabitants of Jerusalem; Believe in the LORD your God, so shall ye be established; believe his prophets, so shall ye prosper.

2. Invincible When Obedient

Ex 23:27 I will send my fear before thee, and will destroy all the people to whom thou shalt come, and I will make all thine enemies turn their backs unto thee.

Le 26:7 And ye shall chase your enemies, and they shall fall before you by the sword.

Nu 14:9 Only rebel not ye against the LORD, neither fear ye the people of the land; for they *are* bread for us: their defence is departed from them, and the LORD *is* with us: fear them not.

Nu 22:3 And Moab was sore afraid of the people, because they *were* many: and Moab was distressed because of the children of Israel.

Nu 23:24 Behold, the people shall rise up as a great lion, and lift up himself as a young lion: he shall not lie down until he eat *of* the prey, and drink the blood of the slain.

Nu 24:8 God brought him forth out of Egypt; he hath as it were the strength of an unicorn: he shall eat up the nations his enemies, and shall break their bones, and pierce *them* through with his arrows.

De 2:25 This day will I begin to put the dread of thee and the fear of thee upon the nations *that are* under the whole heaven, who shall hear report of thee, and shall tremble, and be in anguish because of thee.

De 2:36 From Aroer, which *is* by the brink of the river of Arnon, and *from* the city that *is* by the river, even unto Gilead, there was not one city too strong for us: the LORD our God delivered all unto us:

De 7:24 And he shall deliver their kings into thine hand, and thou shalt destroy their name from under heaven: there shall no man be able to stand before thee, until thou have destroyed them.

De 11:25 There shall no man be able to stand before you: *for* the LORD your God shall lay the fear of you and the dread of you upon all the land that ye shall tread upon, as he hath said unto you.

De 28:7 The LORD shall cause thine enemies that rise up against thee to be smitten before thy face: they shall come out against thee one way, and flee before thee seven ways.

De 32:30 How should one chase a thousand, and two put ten thousand to flight, except their Rock had sold them, and the LORD had shut them up?

De 33:17 His glory *is like* the firstling of his bullock, and his horns *are like* the horns of unicorns: with them he shall push the people together to the ends of the earth: and they *are* the ten thousands of Ephraim, and they *are* the thousands of Manasseh.

De 33:29 Happy *art* thou, O Israel: who *is* like unto thee, O people saved by the LORD, the shield of thy help, and who *is* the sword of thy excellency! and thine enemies shall be found liars unto thee; and thou shalt tread upon their high places.

Jos 1:5 There shall not any man be able to stand before thee all the days of thy life: as I was with Moses, *so* I will be with thee: I will not fail thee, nor forsake thee.

Jos 2:24 And they said unto Joshua, Truly the LORD hath delivered into our hands all the land; for even all the inhabitants of the country do faint because of us.

Jos 10:8 And the LORD said unto Joshua, Fear them not: for I have delivered them into thine hand; there shall not a man of them stand before thee.

Jos 12:1 Now these *are* the kings of the land, which the children of Israel smote, and possessed their land on the other side Jordan toward the rising of the sun, from the river Arnon unto mount Hermon, and all the plain on the east:

Jos 21:44 And the LORD gave them rest round about, according to all that he sware unto their fathers: and there stood not a man of all their enemies before them; the LORD delivered all their enemies into their hand.

Jos 23:9 For the LORD hath driven out from before you great nations and strong: but *as for* you, no man hath been able to stand before you unto this day.

Jud 4:23 So God subdued on that day Jabin the king of Canaan before the children of Israel.

Jud 6:16 And the LORD said unto him, Surely I will be with thee, and thou shalt smite the Midianites as one man.

Jud 8:11 And Gideon went up by the way of them that dwelt in tents on the east of Nobah and Jogbehah, and smote the host: for the host was secure.

Jud 15:15 And he found a new jawbone of an ass, and put forth his hand, and took it, and slew a thousand men therewith.

1 S 14:14 And that first slaughter, which Jonathan and his armourbearer made, was about twenty men, within as it were an half acre of land, *which* a yoke *of oxen might plow.*

2 S 22:30 For by thee I have run through a troop: by my God have I leaped over a wall.

2 S 22:38 I have pursued mine enemies, and destroyed them; and turned not again until I had consumed them.

1 Chr 11:18 And the three brake through the host of the Philistines, and drew water out of the well of Bethlehem, that *was* by the gate, and took *it,* and brought *it* to David: but David would not drink *of* it, but poured it out to the LORD,

1 Chr 12:15 These *are* they that went over Jordan in the first month, when it had overflown all his banks; and they put to flight all *them* of the valleys, *both* toward the east, and toward the west.

1 Chr 14:17 And the fame of David went out into all lands; and the LORD brought the fear of him upon all nations.

Ne 9:25 And they took strong cities, and a fat land, and possessed houses full of all goods, wells digged, vineyards, and oliveyards, and fruit trees in abundance: so they did eat, and were filled, and became fat, and delighted themselves in thy great goodness.

Est 9:2 The Jews gathered themselves together in their cities throughout all the provinces of the king Ahasuerus, to lay hand on such as sought their hurt: and no man could withstand them; for the fear of them fell upon all people.

Ps 18:29 For by thee I have run through a troop; and by my God have I leaped over a wall.

Ps 18:37 I have pursued mine enemies, and overtaken them: neither did I turn again till they were consumed.

Ps 41:11 By this I know that thou favourest me, because mine enemy doth not triumph over me.

Ps 44:5 Through thee will we push down our enemies: through thy name will we tread them under that rise up against us.

Ps 60:12 Through God we shall do valiantly: for he *it is that* shall tread down our enemies.

Ps 89:23 And I will beat down his foes before his face, and plague them that hate him.

Ps 129:2 Many a time have they afflicted me from my youth: yet they have not prevailed against me.

Pr 21:22 A wise *man* scaleth the city of the mighty, and casteth down the strength of the confidence thereof.

Song 6:10 Who *is* she *that* looketh forth as the morning, fair as the moon, clear as the sun, *and* terrible as *an army* with banners?

Is 11:14 But they shall fly upon the shoulders of the Philistines toward the west; they shall spoil them of the east together: they shall lay their hand upon Edom and Moab; and the children of Ammon shall obey them.

Is 19:17 And the land of Judah shall be a terror unto Egypt, every one that maketh mention thereof shall be afraid in himself, because of the counsel of the LORD of hosts, which he hath determined against it.

Is 41:15 Behold, I will make thee a new sharp threshing instrument having teeth: thou shalt thresh the mountains, and beat *them* small, and shalt make the hills as chaff.

Is 54:17 No weapon that is formed against thee shall prosper; and every tongue *that* shall rise against thee in judgment thou shalt condemn. This *is* the heritage of the servants of the LORD, and their righteousness *is* of me, saith the LORD.

Je 15:20 And I will make thee unto this people a fenced brasen wall: and they shall fight against thee, but they shall not prevail against thee: for I *am* with thee to save thee and to deliver thee, saith the LORD.

Eze 39:20 Thus ye shall be filled at my table with horses and chariots, with mighty men, and with all men of war, saith the Lord GOD.

Da 11:16 But he that cometh against him shall do according to his own will, and none shall stand before him: and he shall stand in the glorious land, which by his hand shall be consumed.

Mi 4:13 Arise and thresh, O daughter of Zion: for I will make thine horn iron, and I will make thy hoofs brass: and thou shalt beat in pieces many people: and I will consecrate their gain unto the LORD, and their substance unto the Lord of the whole earth.

Mi 5:8 And the remnant of Jacob shall be among the Gentiles in the midst of many people as a lion among the beasts of the forest, as a young lion among the flocks of sheep: who, if he go through, both treadeth down, and teareth in pieces, and none can deliver.

Zec 9:13 When I have bent Judah for me, filled the bow with Ephraim, and raised up thy sons, O Zion, against thy sons, O Greece, and made thee as the sword of a mighty man.

Zec 10:5 And they shall be as mighty *men,* which tread down *their enemies* in the mire of the streets in the battle: and they shall fight, because the LORD

is with them, and the riders on horses shall be confounded.

Zec 12:6 In that day will I make the governors of Judah like an hearth of fire among the wood, and like a torch of fire in a sheaf; and they shall devour all the people round about, on the right hand and on the left: and Jerusalem shall be inhabited again in her own place, *even* in Jerusalem.

Mt 16:18 And I say also unto thee, That thou art Peter, and upon this rock I will build my church; and the gates of hell shall not prevail against it.

Lu 10:17 And the seventy returned again with joy, saying, Lord, even the devils are subject unto us through thy name.

Ep 6:16 Above all, taking the shield of faith, wherewith ye shall be able to quench all the fiery darts of the wicked.

See **COURAGE, FAITH**

HESHBON*, a city of the Amorites*

Nu 21:26, 34; De 2:24; 4:46; Jos 13:10, 17, 26; 21:39; Jud 11:19; 1 Chr 6:81; Ne 9:22; Is 15:4; 16:8; Je 49:3

HETH*, son of Canaan, father of the Hittites*

Ge 10:15; 23:3, 20; 27:46; 49:32; 1 Chr 1:13

HEZEKIAH*, king of Judah, son of Ahaz*

2 K 16:20; 18:1, 4, 9, 13; 19:3; 20:1, 10, 21; 1 Chr 3:13; 4:41; 2 Chr 28:24–25, 27; 31:20; 32:1–21, 24, 32; Pr 25:1; Is 1:1; 36:1; 38:1–5; 39:1–8; Je 26:19; Ho 1:1; Mi 1:1; Mt 1:10

See **ISRAEL**

HIGH PLACES*, places of worship, especially used for idol worship by the Canaanites*

1. Idolatry

See **WORSHIP**

2. Condemned

Le 26:30; Nu 33:52; De 12:2; 1 K 13:2, 32; 14:23; 2 K 23:8, 13; 2 Chr 14:3; 21:11; 28:4; 31:1; Ps 78:58; Is 16:12;

65:7; Je 2:20; 3:2, 6, 23; 7:31; 13:27; 17:3; 19:5; 32:35; 48:35; Eze 6:3, 13; 16:16, 24, 31, 39; 18:11; 20:28; 22:9; 43:7; Ho 4:13; 10:8; Am 7:9; Mi 1:5

3. Used for True Worship

Ge 22:2; 31:54; Jud 6:26; 1 S 9:12, 19; 10:5, 13; 1 K 3:4; 18:19; 1 Chr 21:29

HIDDEKEL   *See* RIVERS

HILKIAH, *the high priest*

2 K 22:4; 23:4, 24; 1 Chr 6:13; 9:11; 2 Chr 34:9; 35:8; Ezr 7:1; Je 29:3

See SACRIFICES

HIN, *a measure*

Ex 29:40; Le 19:36; 23:13; Nu 15:5; 28:7; Eze 4:11; 46:5, 11

See WEIGHTS AND MEASURES

HINDRANCES

WORLDLY ALLUREMENTS

Ge 19:26 But his wife looked back from behind him, and she became a pillar of salt.

IMPROPER EQUIPMENT

1 S 17:39 And David girded his sword upon his armour, and he assayed to go; for he had not proved *it*. And David said unto Saul, I cannot go with these; for I have not proved *them*. And David put them off him.

DISCOURAGEMENT

Ne 4:10 And Judah said, The strength of the bearers of burdens is decayed, and *there is* much rubbish; so that we are not able to build the wall.

UNBELIEF

Mt 13:58 And he did not many mighty works there because of their unbelief.

WORLDLY POSSESSIONS

Mt 19:22 But when the young man heard that saying, he went away sorrowful: for he had great possessions.

IMAGINARY HINDRANCES

Mk 16:3–4 And they said among themselves, Who shall roll us away the stone from the door of the sepulchre?

And when they looked, they saw that the stone was rolled away: for it was very great.

FAMILY TIES

Lu 9:59 And he said unto another, Follow me. But he said, Lord, suffer me first to go and bury my father.

WEIGHTS AS WELL AS SINS

He 12:1 Wherefore seeing we also are compassed about with so great a cloud of witnesses, let us lay aside every weight, and the sin which doth so easily beset us, and let us run with patience the race that is set before us,

See HELPER, INFLUENCE, PERSECUTION

HINNOM, *valley of*

Jos 15:8; 18:16; 2 K 23:10; 2 Chr 28:3; 33:6; Ne 11:30; Je 7:32; 19:2, 6; 31:40; 32:35

HIRAM, *exalted brother*

1. King of Tyre, or Huram

2 S 5:11; 1 K 5:1; 9:11, 27; 10:11, 22; 1 Chr 14:1; 2 Chr 2:3; 9:10

2. The Artificer

1 K 7:13; 2 Chr 2:13

HIRELING, *a temporary laborer*

Jb 7:1; 14:6; Is 16:14; Mal 3:5; Jn 10:13

HITTITES, *descendants of Heth*

Ge 36:2; Ex 13:5; 23:28; 33:2; Nu 13:29; De 7:1; 20:17; Jos 12:8; 24:11; Jud 1:26; 3:5; 1 K 10:29; 11:1; 2 K 7:6; 2 Chr 1:17; 8:7; Ezr 9:1; Eze 16:3, 45

HIVITES, *one of the nations of Canaan*

Ge 10:17; 36:2; Ex 23:28; 34:11; De 7:1; Jos 9:1; 11:3, 19; 12:8; Jud 3:3; 2 S 24:7; 1 K 9:20; 1 Chr 1:15; 2 Chr 8:7

See NATION

HOLINESS, *separation, a divine attribute*

Ex 39:30 And they made the plate of the holy crown *of* pure gold, and wrote upon it a writing, *like to* the engravings of a signet, HOLINESS TO THE LORD.

Ps 29:2 Give unto the LORD the glory due unto his name; worship the LORD in the beauty of holiness.

Is 35:8 And an highway shall be there, and a way, and it shall be called The way of holiness; the unclean shall not pass over it; but it *shall be* for those: the wayfaring men, though fools, shall not err *therein*.

Zec 14:20 In that day shall there be upon the bells of the horses, HOLINESS UNTO THE LORD; and the pots in the LORD's house shall be like the bowls before the altar.

1 Th 3:13 To the end he may stablish your hearts unblameable in holiness before God, even our Father, at the coming of our Lord Jesus Christ with all his saints.

He 12:10 For they verily for a few days chastened *us* after their own pleasure; but he for *our* profit, that *we* might be partakers of his holiness.

1 Pe 2:9 But ye *are* a chosen generation, a royal priesthood, an holy nation, a peculiar people; that ye should shew forth the praises of him who hath called you out of darkness into his marvellous light:

1. Of God

Ex 15:11 Who *is* like unto thee, O LORD, among the gods? who *is* like thee, glorious in holiness, fearful *in* praises, doing wonders?

Le 19:2 Speak unto all the congregation of the children of Israel, and say unto them, Ye shall be holy: for I the LORD your God *am* holy.

Le 20:26 And ye shall be holy unto me: for I the LORD *am* holy, and have severed you from *other* people, that ye should be mine.

Le 21:8 Thou shalt sanctify him therefore; for he offereth the bread of thy God: he shall be holy unto thee: for I the LORD, which sanctify you, *am* holy.

Jos 24:19 And Joshua said unto the people, Ye cannot serve the LORD: for he *is* an holy God; he *is* a jealous God; he will not forgive your transgressions nor your sins.

1 S 2:2 *There is* none holy as the LORD: for *there is* none beside thee: neither *is there* any rock like our God.

1 S 6:20 And the men of Beth-she-mesh said, Who is able to stand before this holy LORD God? and to whom shall he go up from us?

Jb 6:10 Then should I yet have comfort; yea, I would harden myself in sorrow: let him not spare; for I have not concealed the words of the Holy One.

Ps 22:3 But thou *art* holy, O *thou* that inhabitest the praises of Israel.

Ps 30:4 Sing unto the LORD, O ye saints of his, and give thanks at the remembrance of his holiness.

Ps 60:6 God hath spoken in his holiness; I will rejoice, I will divide Shechem, and mete out the valley of Succoth.

Ps 71:22 I will also praise thee with the psaltery, *even* thy truth, O my God: unto thee will I sing with the harp, O thou Holy One of Israel.

Ps 99:5 Exalt ye the LORD our God, and worship at his footstool; *for* he *is* holy.

Ps 99:9 Exalt the LORD our God, and worship at his holy hill; for the LORD our God *is* holy.

Ps 108:7 God hath spoken in his holiness; I will rejoice, I will divide Shechem, and mete out the valley of Succoth.

Is 5:16 But the LORD of hosts shall be exalted in judgment, and God that is holy shall be sanctified in righteousness.

Is 6:3 And one cried unto another, and said, Holy, holy, holy, *is* the LORD of hosts: the whole earth *is* full of his glory.

Is 63:15 Look down from heaven, and behold from the habitation of thy holiness and of thy glory: where *is* thy zeal and thy strength, the sounding of thy bowels and of thy mercies toward me? are they restrained?

Eze 39:7 So will I make my holy name known in the midst of my people Israel; and I will not *let them* pollute my holy name any more: and the heathen shall know that I *am* the LORD, the Holy One in Israel.

Ho 11:9 I will not execute the fierceness of mine anger, I will not return to destroy Ephraim: for I *am* God, and not man; the Holy One in the midst of thee: and I will not enter into the city.

Am 4:2 The Lord GOD hath sworn by his holiness, that, lo, the days shall come upon you, that he will take you away with hooks, and your posterity with fishhooks.

Hab 1:13 *Thou art* of purer eyes than to behold evil, and canst not look on iniquity: wherefore lookest thou upon them that deal treacherously, *and* holdest thy tongue when the wicked devoureth *the man that is* more righteous than he?

Zep 3:5 The just LORD *is* in the midst thereof; he will not do iniquity: every morning doth he bring his judgment to light, he faileth not; but the unjust knoweth no shame.

Mal 2:11 Judah hath dealt treacherously, and an abomination is committed in Israel and in Jerusalem; for Judah hath profaned the holiness of the LORD which he loved, and hath married the daughter of a strange god.

Jn 17:11 And now I am no more in the world, but these are in the world, and I come to thee. Holy Father, keep through thine own name those whom thou hast given me, that they may be one, as we *are.*

He 12:10 For they verily for a few days chastened *us* after their own pleasure; but he for *our* profit, that *we* might be partakers of his holiness.

Ja 1:13 Let no man say when he is tempted, I am tempted of God: for God cannot be tempted with evil, neither tempteth he any man:

1 Pe 1:15 But as he which hath called you is holy, so be ye holy in all manner of conversation.

Re 4:8 And the four beasts had each of them six wings about *him;* and *they were* full of eyes within: and they rest not day and night, saying, Holy, holy, holy, Lord God Almighty, which was, and is, and is to come.

Re 6:10 And they cried with a loud voice, saying, How long, O Lord, holy and true, dost thou not judge and avenge our blood on them that dwell on the earth?

Re 15:4 Who shall not fear thee, O Lord, and glorify thy name? for *thou* only *art* holy: for all nations shall come and worship before thee; for thy judgments are made manifest.

2. Prescribed

Ex 19:6 And ye shall be unto me a kingdom of priests, and an holy nation. These *are* the words which thou shalt speak unto the children of Israel.

Ex 22:31 And ye shall be holy men unto me: neither shall ye eat *any* flesh *that is* torn of beasts in the field; ye shall cast it to the dogs.

Le 11:45 For I *am* the LORD that bringeth you up out of the land of Egypt, to be your God: ye shall therefore be holy, for I *am* holy.

Le 19:2 Speak unto all the congregation of the children of Israel, and say unto them, Ye shall be holy: for I the LORD your God *am* holy.

Le 20:7 Sanctify yourselves therefore, and be ye holy: for I *am* the LORD your God.

Nu 6:5 All the days of the vow of his separation there shall no razor come upon his head: until the days be fulfilled, in the which he separateth *himself* unto the LORD, he shall be holy, *and* shall let the locks of the hair of his head grow.

Nu 15:40 That ye may remember, and do all my commandments, and be holy unto your God.

De 26:19 And to make thee high above all nations which he hath made, in praise, and in name, and in honour; and that thou mayest be an holy people unto the LORD thy God, as he hath spoken.

1 Chr 16:29 Give unto the LORD the glory *due* unto his name: bring an offering, and come before him: worship the LORD in the beauty of holiness.

Ps 93:5 Thy testimonies are very sure: holiness becometh thine house, O LORD, for ever.

Ps 96:9 O worship the LORD in the beauty of holiness: fear before him, all the earth.

Lu 1:74–75 That he would grant unto us, that we being delivered out of the hand of our enemies might serve him without fear,

In holiness and righteousness before him, all the days of our life.

Ro 6:19 I speak after the manner of men because of the infirmity of your flesh: for as ye have yielded your members servants to uncleanness and to iniquity unto iniquity; even so now yield your members servants to righteousness unto holiness.

Ro 12:1 I beseech you therefore, brethren, by the mercies of God, that ye present your bodies a living sacrifice, holy, acceptable unto God, *which is* your reasonable service.

2 Co 7:1 Having therefore these promises, dearly beloved, let us cleanse ourselves from all filthiness of the flesh and spirit, perfecting holiness in the fear of God.

Ep 1:4 According as he hath chosen us in him before the foundation of the world, that we should be holy and without blame before him in love:

Ep 4:24 And that ye put on the new man, which after God is created in righteousness and true holiness.

Ep 5:27 That he might present it to himself a glorious church, not having spot, or wrinkle, or any such thing; but that it should be holy and without blemish.

1 Th 4:7 For God hath not called us unto uncleanness, but unto holiness.

1 Ti 2:15 Notwithstanding she shall be saved in childbearing, if they continue in faith and charity and holiness with sobriety.

Tit 1:8 But a lover of hospitality, a lover of good men, sober, just, holy, temperate;

Tit 2:3 The aged women likewise, that *they be* in behaviour as becometh holiness, not false accusers, not given to much wine, teachers of good things;

He 12:14 Follow peace with all *men,* and holiness, without which no man shall see the Lord:

1 Pe 1:16 Because it is written, Be ye holy; for I am holy.

2 Pe 3:11 *Seeing* then *that* all these things shall be dissolved, what manner *of persons* ought ye to be in *all* holy conversation and godliness,

1 Jn 3:9 Whosoever is born of God doth not commit sin; for his seed remaineth in him: and he cannot sin, because he is born of God.

See **PERFECTION, PURITY, RIGHTEOUSNESS**

HOLY OF HOLIES, *the most sacred place in the tabernacle and in the temple*

Ex 26:33; Le 16:2, 16; Nu 18:7; 1 K 6:19; 8:6; 1 Chr 6:49; 2 Chr 3:8; 4:22; 5:7; 29:16; Ps 28:2; Eze 41:4; 44:13; He 9:3, 7; 10:19

See **TABERNACLE**

HOLY PLACE, *the interior portion of the tabernacle and temple, immediately outside the Holy of Holies*

Ex 26:33; 28:29, 35; 31:11; 35:19; 38:24; Le 6:16, 26; 10:17; 14:13; 16:20, 24; 21:23; 24:3, 9; Nu 28:7; 1 Chr 23:32; 2 Chr 5:11; 29:5; Eze 42:14; He 9:2, 6, 25

See **TABERNACLE**

HOLY SPIRIT, *the third person in the Trinity*

Zec 4:6 Then he answered and spake unto me, saying, This *is* the word of the LORD unto Zerubbabel, saying, Not by might, nor by power, but by my spirit, saith the LORD of hosts.

Mt 12:28 But if I cast out devils by the Spirit of God, then the kingdom of God is come unto you.

Jn 15:26 But when the Comforter is come, whom I will send unto you from the Father, *even* the Spirit of truth, which proceedeth from the Father, he shall testify of me:

Ro 8:11 But if the Spirit of him that raised up Jesus from the dead dwell in you, he that raised up Christ from the dead shall also quicken your mortal bodies by his Spirit that dwelleth in you.

Ro 8:26 Likewise the Spirit also helpeth our infirmities: for we know not what we should pray for as we ought: but the Spirit itself maketh intercession for us with groanings which cannot be uttered.

2 Co 3:6 Who also hath made us able ministers of the new testament; not of the letter, but of the spirit: for the letter killeth, but the spirit giveth life.

1 Pe 3:18 For Christ also hath once suffered for sins, the just for the unjust, that he might bring us to God, being put to death in the flesh, but quickened by the Spirit:

2 Pe 1:21 For the prophecy came not in old time by the will of man: but holy men of God spake *as they were* moved by the Holy Ghost.

Re 22:17 And the Spirit and the bride say, Come. And let him that heareth say, Come. And let him that is athirst come. And whosoever will, let him take the water of life freely.

1. Dwelling in Believers

Ge 41:38 And Pharaoh said unto his servants, Can we find *such a one* as this *is,* a man in whom the Spirit of God is?

Nu 27:18 And the LORD said unto Moses, Take thee Joshua the son of Nun, a man in whom *is* the spirit, and lay thine hand upon him;

Is 63:11 Then he remembered the days of old, Moses, *and* his people, *saying,* Where *is* he that brought them up out of the sea with the shepherd of his flock? where *is* he that put his holy Spirit within him?

Eze 36:27 And I will put my spirit within you, and cause you to walk in my statutes, and ye shall keep my judgments, and do *them.*

Eze 37:14 And shall put my spirit in you, and ye shall live, and I shall place you in your own land: then shall ye know that I the LORD have spoken *it,* and performed *it,* saith the LORD.

Da 4:8 But at the last Daniel came in before me, whose name *was* Belteshazzar, according to the name of my god, and in whom is the spirit of the holy

gods: and before him I told the dream, *saying,*

Jn 14:17 *Even* the Spirit of truth; whom the world cannot receive, because it seeth him not, neither knoweth him: but ye know him; for you, and shall be in you.

Jn 14:23 Jesus answered and said unto him, If a man love me, he will keep my words: and my Father will love him, and we will come unto him, and make our abode with him.

Ro 5:5 And hope maketh not ashamed; because the love of God is shed abroad in our hearts by the Holy Ghost which is given unto us.

Ro 8:9 But ye are not in the flesh, but in the Spirit, if so be that the Spirit of God dwell in you. Now if any man have not the Spirit of Christ, he is none of his.

1 Co 2:12 Now we have received, not the spirit of the world, but the spirit which is of God; that we might know the things that are freely given to us of God.

1 Co 3:16 Know ye not that ye are the temple of God, and *that* the Spirit of God dwelleth in you?

1 Co 6:19 What? know ye not that your body is the temple of the Holy Ghost *which is* in you, which ye have of God, and ye are not your own?

1 Co 12:7 But the manifestation of the Spirit is given to every man to profit withal.

1 Co 14:25 And thus are the secrets of his heart made manifest; and so falling down on *his* face he will worship God, and report that God is in you of a truth.

2 Co 6:16 And what agreement hath the temple of God with idols? for ye are the temple of the living God; as God hath said, I will dwell in them, and walk in *them;* and I will be their God, and they shall be my people.

Ga 4:6 And because ye are sons, God hath sent forth the Spirit of his Son into your hearts, crying, Abba, Father.

Ep 2:22 In whom ye also are builded together for an habitation of God through the Spirit.

Ep 4:6 One God and Father of all, who *is* above all, and through all, and in you all.

Ph 2:13 For it is God which worketh in you both to will and to do of *his* good pleasure.

2 Ti 1:14 That good thing which was committed unto thee keep by the Holy Ghost which dwelleth in us.

1 Pe 1:11 Searching what, or what manner of time the Spirit of Christ which was in them did signify, when it testified beforehand the sufferings of Christ, and the glory that should follow.

1 Jn 2:27 But the anointing which ye have received of him abideth in you, and ye need not that any man teach you: but as the same anointing teacheth you of all things, and is truth, and is no lie, and even as it hath taught you, ye shall abide in him.

1 Jn 4:12 No man hath seen God at any time. If we love one another, God dwelleth in us, and his love is perfected in us.

2. Outpouring Promised

UPON YOUNG AND OLD

Jl 2:28 And it shall come to pass afterward, *that* I will pour out my spirit upon all flesh; and your sons and your daughters shall prophesy, your old men shall dream dreams, your young men shall see visions:

Zec 12:10 And I will pour upon the house of David, and upon the inhabitants of Jerusalem, the spirit of grace and of supplications: and they shall look upon me whom they have pierced, and they shall mourn for him, as one mourneth for *his* only *son,* and shall be in bitterness for him, as one that is in bitterness for *his* firstborn.

GIVEN BY CHRIST

Mt 3:11 I indeed baptize you with water unto repentance: but he that cometh after me is mightier than I, whose shoes I am not worthy to bear: he shall baptize you with the Holy Ghost, and *with* fire:

BESTOWED IN ANSWER TO PRAYER

Lu 11:13 If ye then, being evil, know how to give good gifts unto your children: how much more shall *your* heavenly Father give the Holy Spirit to them that ask him?

THROUGH WAITING UPON GOD

Lu 24:49 And, behold, I send the promise of my Father upon you: but tarry ye in the city of Jerusalem, until ye be endued with power from on high.

Jn 7:39 (But this spake he of the Spirit, which they that believe on him should receive: for the Holy Ghost was not yet *given;* because that Jesus was not yet glorified.)

Jn 14:16 And I will pray the Father, and he shall give you another Comforter, that he may abide with you for ever;

Jn 16:7 Nevertheless I tell you the truth; It is expedient for you that I go away: for if I go not away, the Comforter will not come unto you; but if I depart, I will send him unto you.

EMPOWERS FOR SERVICE

Ac 1:8 But ye shall receive power, after that the Holy Ghost is come upon you: and ye shall be witnesses unto me both in Jerusalem, and in all Judaea, and in Samaria, and unto the uttermost part of the earth.

PERSONAL CLEANSING PRECEDES

Ac 2:38 Then Peter said unto them, Repent, and be baptized every one of you in the name of Jesus Christ for the remission of sins, and ye shall receive the gift of the Holy Ghost.

3. In the Old Testament

THE SEVENTY ELDERS

Nu 11:25 And the LORD came down in a cloud, and spake unto him, and took of the spirit that *was* upon him, and gave *it* unto the seventy elders: and it came to pass, *that,* when the spirit rested upon them, they prophesied, and did not cease.

BALAAM

Nu 24:2 And Balaam lifted up his eyes, and he saw Israel abiding *in his tents* according to their tribes; and the spirit of God came upon him.

OTHNIEL

Jud 3:10 And the Spirit of the LORD came upon him, and he judged Israel, and went out to war: and the LORD delivered Chushan-rishathaim king of Mesopotamia into his hand; and his hand prevailed against Chushan-rishathaim.

GIDEON

Jud 6:34 But the Spirit of the LORD came upon Gideon, and he blew a trumpet; and Abi-ezer was gathered after him.

SAMSON

Jud 14:6 And the Spirit of the LORD came mightily upon him, and he rent him as he would have rent a kid, and *he had* nothing in his hand: but he told not his father or his mother what he had done.

Jud 14:19 And the Spirit of the LORD came upon him, and he went down to Ashkelon, and slew thirty men of them, and took their spoil, and gave change of garments unto them which expounded the riddle. And his anger was kindled, and he went up to his father's house.

SAUL

1 S 10:10 And when they came thither to the hill, behold, a company of prophets met him; and the Spirit of God came upon him, and he prophesied among them.

DAVID

1 S 16:13 Then Samuel took the horn of oil, and anointed him in the midst of his brethren: and the Spirit of the LORD came upon David from that day forward. So Samuel rose up, and went to Ramah.

SAUL'S MESSENGERS

1 S 19:20 And Saul sent messengers to take David: and when they saw the company of the prophets prophesying, and Samuel standing *as* appointed over them, the Spirit of God was upon the messengers of Saul, and they also prophesied.

2 Chr 15:1 And the Spirit of God came upon Azariah the son of Oded:

Lu 2:25 And, behold, there was a man in Jerusalem, whose name *was* Simeon; and the same man *was* just and devout, waiting for the consolation of Israel: and the Holy Ghost was upon him.

4. In the New Testament

SIMEON

Lu 2:25 And, behold, there was a man in Jerusalem, whose name *was* Simeon; and the same man *was* just and devout, waiting for the consolation of Israel: and the Holy Ghost was upon him.

AT PENTECOST

Ac 2:3 And there appeared unto them cloven tongues like as of fire, and it sat upon each of them.

THE SAMARITAN CHRISTIANS

Ac 8:17 Then laid they *their* hands on them, and they received the Holy Ghost.

CORNELIUS AND HIS COMPANY

Ac 10:44 While Peter yet spake these words, the Holy Ghost fell on all them which heard the word.

THE EPHESIAN BELIEVERS

Ac 19:6 And when Paul had laid *his* hands upon them, the Holy Ghost came on them; and they spake with tongues, and prophesied.

Ac 19:7 And all the men were about twelve.

1 Co 12:13 For by one Spirit are we all baptized into one body, whether *we be* Jews or Gentiles, whether *we be* bond or free; and have been all made to drink into one Spirit.

1 Jn 2:20 But ye have an unction from the Holy One, and ye know all things.

5. Filling Believers

Ex 31:3 And I have filled him with the spirit of God, in wisdom, and in understanding, and in knowledge, and in all manner of workmanship,

Ex 35:31 And he hath filled him with the spirit of God, in wisdom, in understanding, and in knowledge, and in all manner of workmanship;

Lu 1:15 For he shall be great in the sight of the Lord, and shall drink neither wine nor strong drink; and he shall be filled with the Holy Ghost, even from his mother's womb.

Lu 1:41 And it came to pass, that, when Elisabeth heard the salutation of Mary, the babe leaped in her womb; and Elisabeth was filled with the Holy Ghost:

Lu 1:67 And his father Zacharias was filled with the Holy Ghost, and prophesied, saying,

Lu 4:1 And Jesus being full of the Holy Ghost returned from Jordan, and was led by the Spirit into the wilderness,

Ac 2:4 And they were all filled with the Holy Ghost, and began to speak with other tongues, as the Spirit gave them utterance.

Ac 4:8 Then Peter, filled with the Holy Ghost, said unto them, Ye rulers of the people, and elders of Israel,

Ac 4:31 And when they had prayed, the place was shaken where they were assembled together; and they were all filled with the Holy Ghost, and they spake the word of God with boldness.

Ac 6:5 And the saying pleased the whole multitude: and they chose Stephen, a man full of faith and of the Holy Ghost, and Philip, and Prochorus, and Nicanor, and Timon, and Parmenas, and Nicolas a proselyte of Antioch:

Ac 7:55 But he, being full of the Holy Ghost, looked up stedfastly into heaven, and saw the glory of God, and Jesus standing on the right hand of God,

Ac 9:17 And Ananias went his way, and entered into the house; and putting his hands on him said, Brother Saul, the Lord, *even* Jesus, that appeared unto thee in the way as thou camest, hath sent me, that thou mightest receive thy sight, and be filled with the Holy Ghost.

Ac 11:24 For he was a good man, and full of the Holy Ghost and of faith: and much people was added unto the Lord.

Ac 13:9 Then Saul, (who also *is called* Paul,) filled with the Holy Ghost, set his eyes on him,

Ac 13:52 And the disciples were filled with joy, and with the Holy Ghost.

6. As Witness

Ro 8:16 The Spirit itself beareth witness with our spirit, that we are the children of God:

Ga 4:6 And because ye are sons, God hath sent forth the Spirit of his Son into your hearts, crying, Abba, Father.

1 Jn 3:24 And he that keepeth his commandments dwelleth in him, and he in him. And hereby we know that he abideth in us, by the Spirit which he hath given us.

1 Jn 4:13 Hereby know we that we dwell in him, and he in us, because he hath given us of his Spirit.

1 Jn 5:6 This is he that came by water and blood, *even* Jesus Christ; not by water only, but by water and blood. And it is the Spirit that beareth witness, because the Spirit is truth.

7. As Teacher

Ne 9:20 Thou gavest also thy good spirit to instruct them, and withheldest not thy manna from their mouth, and gavest them water for their thirst.

Mt 10:20 For it is not ye that speak, but the Spirit of your Father which speaketh in you.

Mt 16:17 And Jesus answered and said unto him, Blessed art thou, Simon Barjona: for flesh and blood hath not revealed *it* unto thee, but my Father which is in heaven:

Mk 13:11 But when they shall lead *you*, and deliver you up, take no thought beforehand what ye shall speak, neither do ye premeditate: but whatsoever shall be given you in that hour, that speak ye: for it is not ye that speak, but the Holy Ghost.

Lu 2:26 And it was revealed unto him by the Holy Ghost, that he should not see death, before he had seen the Lord's Christ.

Lu 12:12 For the Holy Ghost shall teach you in the same hour what ye ought to say.

Jn 14:26 But the Comforter, *which is* the Holy Ghost, whom the Father will send in my name, he shall teach you all things, and bring all things to your remembrance, whatsoever I have said unto you.

Jn 16:13 Howbeit when he, the Spirit of truth, is come, he will guide you into all truth: for he shall not speak of himself; but whatsoever he shall hear, *that* shall he speak: and he will shew you things to come.

Ac 1:2 Until the day in which he was taken up, after that he through the Holy Ghost had given commandments unto the apostles whom he had chosen:

1 Co 2:10 But God hath revealed *them* unto us by his Spirit: for the Spirit searcheth all things, yea, the deep things of God.

1 Co 2:13 Which things also we speak, not in the words which man's wisdom teacheth, but which the Holy Ghost teacheth; comparing spiritual things with spiritual.

1 Co 7:40 But she is happier if she so abide, after my judgment: and I think also that I have the Spirit of God.

1 Co 12:3 Wherefore I give you to understand, that no man speaking by the Spirit of God calleth Jesus accursed: and *that* no man can say that Jesus is the Lord, but by the Holy Ghost.

Ep 3:5 Which in other ages was not made known unto the sons of men, as it is now revealed unto his holy apostles and prophets by the Spirit;

Ph 3:15 Let us therefore, as many as be perfect, be thus minded: and if in any thing ye be otherwise minded, God shall reveal even this unto you.

Ph 4:12 I know both how to be abased, and I know how to abound: every where and in all things I am instructed both to be full and to be hungry, both to abound and to suffer need.

1 Ti 4:1 Now the Spirit speaketh expressly, that in the latter times some shall depart from the faith, giving heed to seducing spirits, and doctrines of devils;

He 9:8 The Holy Ghost this signifying, that the way into the holiest of all was not yet made manifest, while as the first tabernacle was yet standing:

1 Jn 2:20 But ye have an unction from the Holy One, and ye know all things.

1 Jn 2:27 But the anointing which ye have received of him abideth in you, and ye need not that any man teach you: but as the same anointing teacheth you of all things, and is truth, and is no lie, and even as it hath taught you, ye shall abide in him.

Re 2:7 He that hath an ear, let him hear what the Spirit saith unto the churches; To him that overcometh will I give to eat of the tree of life, which is in the midst of the paradise of God.

Re 2:11 He that hath an ear, let him hear what the Spirit saith unto the churches; He that overcometh shall not be hurt of the second death.

Re 2:17 He that hath an ear, let him hear what the Spirit saith unto the churches; To him that overcometh will I give to eat of the hidden manna, and will give him a white stone, and in the stone a new name written, which no man knoweth saving he that receiveth *it*.

Re 2:29 He that hath an ear, let him hear what the Spirit saith unto the churches.

Re 3:6 He that hath an ear, let him hear what the Spirit saith unto the churches.

Re 3:13 He that hath an ear, let him hear what the Spirit saith unto the churches.

Re 3:22 He that hath an ear, let him hear what the Spirit saith unto the churches.

8. Sin Against

1 S 3:14 And therefore I have sworn unto the house of Eli, that the iniquity of Eli's house shall not be purged with sacrifice nor offering for ever.

Ps 109:14 Let the iniquity of his fathers be remembered with the LORD; and let not the sin of his mother be blotted out.

Is 22:14 And it was revealed in mine ears by the LORD of hosts, Surely this iniquity shall not be purged from you till ye die, saith the Lord GOD of hosts.

Is 63:10 But they rebelled, and vexed his holy Spirit: therefore he was turned to be their enemy, *and* he fought against them.

Mt 12:31 Wherefore I say unto you, All manner of sin and blasphemy shall be forgiven unto men: but the blasphemy *against* the *Holy* Ghost shall not be forgiven unto men.

Mk 3:29 But he that shall blaspheme against the Holy Ghost hath never forgiveness, but is in danger of eternal damnation:

Ac 5:3 But Peter said, Ananias, why hath Satan filled thine heart to lie to the Holy Ghost, and to keep back *part* of the price of the land?

Ac 7:51 Ye stiffnecked and uncircumcised in heart and ears, ye do always resist the Holy Ghost: as your fathers *did,* so *do* ye.

Ep 4:30 And grieve not the holy Spirit of God, whereby ye are sealed unto the day of redemption.

1 Th 5:19 Quench not the Spirit.

He 10:29 Of how much sorer punishment, suppose ye, shall he be thought worthy, who hath trodden under foot the Son of God, and hath counted the blood of the covenant, wherewith he was sanctified, an unholy thing, and hath done despite unto the Spirit of grace?

1 Jn 5:16 If any man see his brother sin a sin *which is* not unto death, he shall ask, and he shall give him life for them that sin not unto death. There is a sin unto death: I do not say that he shall pray for it.

9. His Withdrawal

Ge 6:3 And the LORD said, My spirit shall not always strive with man, for that he also *is* flesh: yet his days shall be an hundred and twenty years.

1 S 16:14 But the Spirit of the LORD departed from Saul, and an evil spirit from the LORD troubled him.

Ps 51:11 Cast me not away from thy presence; and take not thy holy spirit from me.

Song 5:6 I opened to my beloved; but my beloved had withdrawn himself, *and* was gone: my soul failed when he spake: I sought him, but I could not find him; I called him, but he gave me no answer.

10. His Baptism

Is 11:2 And the spirit of the LORD shall rest upon him, the spirit of wisdom and understanding, the spirit of counsel and might, the spirit of knowledge and of the fear of the LORD;

Is 42:1 Behold my servant, whom I uphold; mine elect, *in whom* my soul delighteth; I have put my spirit upon him: he shall bring forth judgment to the Gentiles.

Is 61:1 The Spirit of the Lord GOD *is* upon me; because the LORD hath anointed me to preach good tidings unto the meek; he hath sent me to bind up the brokenhearted, to proclaim liberty to the captives, and the opening of the prison to *them that are* bound;

Mt 3:16 And Jesus, when he was baptized, went up straightway out of the water: and, lo, the heavens were opened unto him, and he saw the Spirit of God descending like a dove, and lighting upon him:

Jn 1:32 And John bare record, saying, I saw the Spirit descending from heaven like a dove, and it abode upon him.

Ac 10:38 How God anointed Jesus of Nazareth with the Holy Ghost and with power: who went about doing good, and healing all that were oppressed of the devil; for God was with him.

11. His Leadership

GUIDES INTO ALL TRUTH

Jn 16:13 Howbeit when he, the Spirit of truth, is come, he will guide you into all truth: for he shall not speak of himself; but whatsoever he shall hear, *that* shall he speak: and he will shew you things to come.

Ac 8:39 And when they were come up out of the water, the Spirit of the Lord caught away Philip, that the eunuch saw him no more: and he went on his way rejoicing.

CONTROLS THE MOVEMENTS OF BELIEVERS

Ac 10:19–20 While Peter thought on the vision, the Spirit said unto him, Behold, three men seek thee.

Arise therefore, and get thee down, and go with them, doubting nothing: for I have sent them.

DIRECTS IN THE SELECTION OF LEADERS

Ac 13:2 As they ministered to the Lord, and fasted, the Holy Ghost said, Separate me Barnabas and Saul for the work whereunto I have called them.

CHOOSES THE FIELDS OF OPERATION

Ac 16:6 Now when they had gone throughout Phrygia and the region of Galatia, and were forbidden of the Holy Ghost to preach the word in Asia,

OBEDIENCE TO, A MARK OF SONSHIP

Ro 8:14 For as many as are led by the Spirit of God, they are the sons of God.
Ga 5:18 But if ye be led of the Spirit, ye are not under the law.

12. His Life

Lu 1:35 And the angel answered and said unto her, The Holy Ghost shall come upon thee, and the power of the Highest shall overshadow thee: therefore also that holy thing which shall be born of thee shall be called the Son of God.

Jn 6:63 It is the spirit that quickeneth; the flesh profiteth nothing: the words that I speak unto you, *they* are spirit, and *they* are life.

Ro 8:11 But if the Spirit of him that raised up Jesus from the dead dwell in you, he that raised up Christ from the dead shall also quicken your mortal bodies by his Spirit that dwelleth in you.

2 Co 3:6 Who also hath made us able ministers of the new testament; not of the letter, but of the spirit: for the letter killeth, but the spirit giveth life.

1 Pe 3:18 For Christ also hath once suffered for sins, the just for the unjust, that he might bring us to God, being put to death in the flesh, but quickened by the Spirit:

Re 11:11 And after three days and an half the Spirit of life from God entered into them, and they stood upon their feet; and great fear fell upon them which saw them.

13. Called Spirit of Truth

Jn 14:17 *Even* the Spirit of truth; whom the world cannot receive, because it seeth him not, neither knoweth him: but ye know him; for he dwelleth with you, and shall be in you.

Jn 15:26 But when the Comforter is come, whom I will send unto you from the Father, *even* the Spirit of truth, which proceedeth from the Father, he shall testify of me:

Jn 16:13 Howbeit when he, the Spirit of truth, is come, he will guide you into all truth: for he shall not speak of himself; but whatsoever he shall hear, *that* shall he speak: and he will shew you things to come.

1 Jn 2:27 But the anointing which ye have received of him abideth in you, and ye need not that any man teach you: but as the same anointing teacheth you of all things, and is truth, and is no lie, and even as it hath taught you, ye shall abide in him.

1 Jn 4:6 We are of God: he that knoweth God heareth us; he that is not of God heareth not us. Hereby know we the spirit of truth, and the spirit of error.

1 Jn 5:6 This is he that came by water and blood, *even* Jesus Christ; not by water only, but by water and blood.

And it is the Spirit that beareth witness, because the Spirit is truth.

14. Called the Comforter, helper
(parakletos—Greek)

ABIDES FOREVER

Jn 14:16 And I will pray the Father, and he shall give you another Comforter, that he may abide with you for ever;

BRINGS TO REMEMBRANCE CHRIST'S WORDS

Jn 14:26 But the Comforter, *which is* the Holy Ghost, whom the Father will send in my name, he shall teach you all things, and bring all things to your remembrance, whatsoever I have said unto you.

TESTIFIES CONCERNING CHRIST

Jn 15:26 But when the Comforter is come, whom I will send unto you from the Father, *even* the Spirit of truth, which proceedeth from the Father, he shall testify of me:

CONVICTS THE WORLD OF SIN

Jn 16:7–8 Nevertheless I tell you the truth; It is expedient for you that I go away: for if I go not away, the Comforter will not come unto you; but if I depart, I will send him unto you.

And when he is come, he will reprove the world of sin, and of righteousness, and of judgment:

GUIDES INTO ALL TRUTH

Jn 16:13 Howbeit when he, the Spirit of truth, is come, he will guide you into all truth: for he shall not speak of himself; but whatsoever he shall hear, *that* shall he speak: and he will shew you things to come.

15. His Work

TO COMFORT

Jn 16:7 Nevertheless I tell you the truth; It is expedient for you that I go away: for if I go not away, the Comforter will not come unto you; but if I depart, I will send him unto you.

TO REPROVE

Jn 16:8 And when he is come, he will reprove the world of sin, and of righteousness, and of judgment:

TO GUIDE

Jn 16:13 Howbeit when he, the Spirit of truth, is come, he will guide you into all truth: for he shall not speak of himself; but whatsoever he shall hear, *that* shall he speak: and he will shew you things to come.

TO GLORIFY JESUS

Jn 16:14 He shall glorify me: for he shall receive of mine, and shall shew *it* unto you.

TO EXHIBIT JESUS

Jn 16:15 All things that the Father hath are mine: therefore said I, that he shall take of mine, and shall shew *it* unto you.

TO EMPOWER

Ac 1:8 But ye shall receive power, after that the Holy Ghost is come upon you: and ye shall be witnesses unto me both in Jerusalem, and in all Judaea, and in Samaria, and unto the uttermost part of the earth.

TO WITNESS

Ro 8:1 *There is* therefore now no condemnation to them which are in Christ Jesus, who walk not after the flesh, but after the Spirit.

Ro 8:16 The Spirit itself beareth witness with our spirit, that we are the children of God.

TO HELP

Ro 8:5 For they that are after the flesh do mind the things of the flesh; but they that are after the Spirit the things of the Spirit.

Ro 8:26 Likewise the Spirit also helpeth our infirmities: for we know not what we should pray for as we ought: but the Spirit itself maketh intercession for us with groanings which cannot be uttered.

TO SOLICIT

Re 22:1 And he shewed me a pure river of water of life, clear as crystal, proceeding out of the throne of God and of the Lamb.

Re 22:17 And the Spirit and the bride say, Come. And let him that heareth say, Come. And let him that is athirst come. And whosoever will, let him take the water of life freely.

See **CHRIST, GOD, GUIDANCE, POWER, TEACHER**

HOME, *dwelling place*

De 21:12 Then thou shalt bring her home to thine house; and she shall shave her head, and pare her nails;

De 24:5 When a man hath taken a new wife, he shall not go out to war, neither shall he be charged with any business: *but* he shall be free at home one year, and shall cheer up his wife which he hath taken.

Jud 19:9 And when the man rose up to depart, he, and his concubine, and his servant, his father in law, the damsel's father, said unto him, Behold, now the day draweth toward evening, I pray you tarry all night: behold, the day groweth to an end, lodge here, that thine heart may be merry; and to morrow get you early on your way, that thou mayest go home.

Ru 1:21 I went out full, and the LORD hath brought me home again empty: why *then* call ye me Naomi, seeing the LORD hath testified against me, and the Almighty hath afflicted me?

Mark 5:19 Howbeit Jesus suffered him not, but saith unto him, Go home to thy friends, and tell them how great things the Lord hath done for thee, and hath had compassion on thee.

Jn 19:27 Then saith he to the disciple, Behold thy mother! And from that hour that disciple took her unto his own *home.*

1 Co 11:34 And if any man hunger, let him eat at home; that ye come not together unto condemnation. And the rest will I set in order when I come.

1 Ti 5:4 But if any widow have children or nephews, let them learn first

to shew piety at home, and to requite their parents: for that is good and acceptable before God.

Tit 2:5 *To be* discreet, chaste, keepers at home, good, obedient to their own husbands, that the word of God be not blasphemed.

1. Heavenly

Lu 16:9 And I say unto you, Make to yourselves friends of the mammon of unrighteousness; that, when ye fail, they may receive you into everlasting habitations.

Jn 14:2 In my Father's house are many mansions: if *it were* not so, I would have told you. I go to prepare a place for you.

2. Admonitions

Pr 25:17 Withdraw thy foot from thy neighbour's house; lest he be weary of thee, and *so* hate thee.

Hab 2:5 Yea also, because he transgresseth by wine, *he is* a proud man, neither keepeth at home, who enlargeth his desire as hell, and *is* as death, and cannot be satisfied, but gathereth unto him all nations, and heapeth unto him all people:

1 Ti 5:13 And withal they learn *to be* idle, wandering about from house to house; and not only idle, but tattlers also and busybodies, speaking things which they ought not.

Tit 2:5 *To be* discreet, chaste, keepers at home, good, obedient to their own husbands, that the word of God be not blasphemed.

3. Love of

JACOB

Ge 31:30 And now, *though* thou wouldest needs be gone, because thou sore longedst after thy father's house, *yet* wherefore hast thou stolen my gods?

HOBAB

Nu 10:30 And he said unto him, I will not go; but I will depart to mine own land, and to my kindred.

Ru 18:6 Then she arose with her daughters in law, that she might return from the country of Moab: for she had heard in the country of Moab how that the LORD had visited his people in giving them bread.

BARZILLAI

2 S 19:37 Let thy servant, I pray thee, turn back again, that I may die in mine own city, *and be buried* by the grave of my father and of my mother. But behold thy servant Chimham; let him go over with my lord the king; and do to him what shall seem good unto thee.

DAVID

2 S 23:15 And David longed, and said, Oh that one would give me drink of the water of the well of Bethlehem, which *is* by the gate!

THE JEWS IN EXILE

Ps 137:1–6 By the rivers of Babylon, there we sat down, yea, we wept, when we remembered Zion.

We hanged our harps upon the willows in the midst thereof.

For there they that carried us away captive required of us a song; and they that wasted us *required of us* mirth, *saying*, Sing us *one* of the songs of Zion.

How shall we sing the LORD's song in a strange land?

If I forget thee, O Jerusalem, let my right hand forget *her cunning.*

If I do not remember thee, let my tongue cleave to the roof of my mouth; if I prefer not Jerusalem above my chief joy.

4. Spiritual Life Manifested

a. Examples

MARY, *sits at Jesus' feet in her home*

Lu 10:39 And she had a sister called Mary, which also sat at Jesus' feet, and heard his word.

ANDREW, *leads his brother to Christ*

Jn 1:41 He first findeth his own brother Simon, and saith unto him, We have found the Messias, which is, being interpreted, the Christ.

NOBLEMAN, *entire family accepts Christ*

Jn 4:53 So the father knew that *it was* at the same hour, in the which Jesus said unto him, Thy son liveth: and himself believed, and his whole house.

LYDIA, *her household is converted*

Ac 16:15 And when she was baptized, and her household, she besought *us*, saying, If ye have judged me to be faithful to the Lord, come into my house, and abide *there.* And she constrained us.

PHILIPPIAN JAILER, *his family is baptized*

Ac 16:33 And he took them the same hour of the night, and washed *their* stripes; and was baptized, he and all his, straightway.

CHILDREN OR NEPHEWS OF WIDOWS, *showing piety*

1 Ti 5:4 But if any widow have children or nephews, let them learn first to shew piety at home, and to requite their parents: for that is good and acceptable before God.

b. Devout Fathers

ABRAHAM, *exerts a spiritual influence on his family*

Ge 18:19 For I know him, that he will command his children and his household after him, and they shall keep the way of the LORD, to do justice and judgment; that the LORD may bring upon Abraham that which he hath spoken of him.

ISAAC, *blesses his son*

Ge 27:26–27 And his father Isaac said unto him, Come near now, and kiss me, and my son.

And he came near, and kissed him: and he smelled the smell of his raiment, and blessed him, and said, See, the smell of my son *is* as the smell of a field which the LORD hath blessed:

JACOB, *commands his household to put away idols*

Ge 35:2 Then Jacob said unto his household, and to all that *were* with him, Put away the strange gods that *are* among you, and be clean, and change your garments:

MANOAH, *prays for instruction in regard to his coming child*

Jud 13:8 Then Manoah intreated the LORD, and said, O my Lord, let the man of God which thou didst send come again unto us, and teach us what we shall do unto the child that shall be born.

DAVID, *gives godly advice to his son Solomon*

1 K 2:1–4 Now the days of David drew nigh that he should die; and he charged Solomon his son, saying,

I go the way of all the earth: be thou strong therefore, and shew thyself a man;

And keep the charge of the LORD thy God, to walk in his ways, to keep his statutes, and his commandments, and his judgments, and his testimonies, as it is written in the law of Moses, that thou mayest prosper in all that thou doest, and whithersoever thou turnest thyself:

That the LORD may continue his word which he spake concerning me, saying, If thy children take heed to their way, to walk before me in truth with all their heart and with all their soul, there shall not fail thee (said he) a man on the throne of Israel.

ZECHARIAS, *the godly father of John the Baptist*

Lu 1:67 And his father Zacharias was filled with the Holy Ghost, and prophesied, saying,

CORNELIUS, *the head of a religious household*

Ac 10:2 A devout *man,* and one that feared God with all his house, which gave much alms to the people, and prayed to God alway.

c. Devout Mothers

EVE, *mother of all living*

Ge 3:20 And Adam called his wife's name Eve; because she was the mother of all living.

SARAH, *mother of the promised son*

Ge 21:6 And Sarah said, God hath made me to laugh, *so that* all that hear will laugh with me.

HANNAH, *dedicates her son, Samuel, to the Lord*

1 S 1:22 But Hannah went not up; for she said unto her husband, *I will not go up* until the child be weaned, and *then* I will bring him, that he may appear before the LORD, and there abide for ever.

ELIZABETH, *godly mother of John the Baptist*

Lu 1:41 And it came to pass, that, when Elisabeth heard the salutation of Mary, the babe leaped in her womb; and Elisabeth was filled with the Holy Ghost:

MARY, *mother of Jesus*

Lu 1:46 And Mary said, My soul doth magnify the Lord,

EUNICE, *faithful mother of Timothy*

2 Ti 1:5 When I call to remembrance the unfeigned faith that is in thee, which dwelt first in thy grandmother Lois, and thy mother Eunice; and I am persuaded that in thee also.

d. Parental Prayers

ABRAHAM
Ge 17:8

DAVID
2 S 12:16; 1 Chr 29:19

JOB
Jb 1:5

FATHER
Mt 17:15

SYROPHENICIAN MOTHER

Mk 7:26

See **PRAYER**

e. Bible Stories for Children

Ge 1:1–25; 3:1–6; 6:14–22; 7:1–24; 21:9–20; 22:1–13; 25:29–34; 37:1–34, 13–36; 39:20–23; 41:1–44; Ex 2:1–10; Nu 20:10–12; 21:4–9; De 3:23–26; Jos 2:1–24; 6:1–20, 22–24; Jud 6:36–40; Jos 7:20–26; Jud 7:15–22; 9:7–15; 16:1–31; 1 S 3:1–21; 6:19; 9:1–27; 10:1; 16:1–14; 17:1–58; 18:1–4; 20:21–40; 2 S 4:4; 9:1–13; 12:1–6; 18:9; 1 K 17:1–6, 10–16; 2 K 2:9–11, 13–14; 4:1–7, 18–36; 5:2–15; 6:1–7; 11:1–12; 2 Chr 20:20–24; Ec 12:2–7; Da 1:3–15; 3:1–30; 6:1–22; Jona 1:1–17; 2:1–10; Mt 2:1–11; 9:20–22; 25:1–13; Lu 2:40–52; 5:4–8; 10:30–37; 14:16–24; 15:11–24; 17:12–19; Jn 5:1–9; 6:5–13; 21:4–11; Ac 5:1–10; 16:16–28; 28:1–6

5. Duties, obligations to those in the family

Mk 5:19 Howbeit Jesus suffered him not, but saith unto him, Go home to thy friends, and tell them how great things the Lord hath done for thee, and hath had compassion on thee.
1 Ti 5:4 But if any widow have children or nephews, let them learn first to shew piety at home, and to requite their parents: for that is good and acceptable before God.
1 Ti 5:8 But if any provide not for his own, and specially for those of his own house, he hath denied the faith, and is worse than an infidel.

HOMELESS

Jb 24:8; Lam 4:5; Lu 9:58; 1 Co 4:11

See **POOR, RICHES**

HOMER, *the largest dry measure*

Le 27:16; Nu 11:32; Is 5:10; Eze 45:11; Ho 3:2

HOMICIDE *See* **MURDER**

HOMOSEXUALITY

Ge 19:4–5; Le 18:22; 20:13; Ro 1:26; 1 Co 6:9–11; Jude 7

HONESTY *See* **BUSINESS, RIGHTEOUSNESS**

HONEY

Ge 43:11; Ex 16:31; Le 2:11; Nu 13:27; De 8:8; 32:13; Jos 5:6; 1 S 14:27; 2 S 17:29; Jb 20:17; Ps 19:10; 81:16; Pr 24:13; 25:16, 27; 27:7; Song 5:1; Is 7:22; Je 41:8; Eze 27:17; Mt 3:4; Mk 1:6; Lu 24:42; Re 10:9

HONOR, *high regard or great respect*

1. Due to God

Jud 15:18 And he was sore athirst, and called on the LORD, and said, Thou hast given this great deliverance into the hand of thy servant: and now shall I die for thirst, and fall into the hand of the uncircumcised?
Ps 29:2 Give unto the LORD the glory due unto his name; worship the LORD in the beauty of holiness.
Ps 34:3 O magnify the LORD with me, and let us exalt his name together.
Ps 57:5 Be thou exalted, O God, above the heavens; *let* thy glory *be* above all the earth.
Ps 71:8 Let my mouth be filled *with* thy praise *and with* thy honour all the day.
Ps 107:32 Let them exalt him also in the congregation of the people, and praise him in the assembly of the elders.
Ps 145:5 I will speak of the glorious honour of thy majesty, and of thy wondrous works.
Is 25:1 O LORD, thou *art* my God; I will exalt thee, I will praise thy name; for thou hast done wonderful *things; thy* counsels of old *are* faithfulness *and* truth.
Jn 8:49 Jesus answered, I have not a devil; but I honour my Father, and ye do dishonour me.
1 Ti 1:17 Now unto the King eternal, immortal, invisible, the only wise God, *be* honour and glory for ever and ever. Amen.
Re 19:7 Let us be glad and rejoice, and give honour to him: for the marriage of the Lamb is come, and his wife hath made herself ready.

2. Given to Christ

Mk 11:8 And many spread their garments in the way: and others cut down branches off the trees, and strawed *them* in the way.

Lu 4:15 And he taught in their synagogues, being glorified of all.

Lu 19:35 And they brought him to Jesus: and they cast their garments upon the colt, and they set Jesus thereon.

Jn 12:13 Took branches of palm trees, and went forth to meet him, and cried, Hosanna: Blessed *is* the King of Israel that cometh in the name of the Lord.

Re 5:13 And every creature which is in heaven, and on the earth, and under the earth, and such as are in the sea, and all that are in them, heard I saying, Blessing, and honour, and glory, and power, *be* unto him that sitteth upon the throne, and unto the Lamb for ever and ever.

See **CHRIST, GLORY**

3. Prescribed

Ge 27:8, 43; 50:5; Ex 20:12; 21:17; Le 19:3; 20:9; 21:2; Nu 30:5; De 5:16; 27:16; 1 K 13:13; Pr 1:8; 6:20; 15:20; 17:6; 20:20; 23:22; 30:17; Is 45:10; Mal 1:6; Mt 15:4; 19:19; Mk 7:10; 10:19; Lu 18:20; Ep 6:2; 1 Ti 5:4

4. Examples

Ge 9:23; 28:7; 37:13; 44:34; 45:10, 23; 46:29; 47:12, 30; 48:12; Ex 4:18; 18:7, 24; Jos 2:13; Jud 11:34; Ru 2:18; 3:5; 1 S 17:20; 22:3; 2 S 14:33; 1 K 2:19; 13:27; 19:20; Est 2:10, 20; 4:4; Pr 31:28; Je 35:8, 16; Lu 2:51; Jn 19:25, 25–26; Ac 7:14; He 12:9

5. Obedience Prescribed

Ge 50:12; 1 S 9:4; Pr 1:8; 4:3; 6:20; 7:1; 23:22; Je 35:18; Ep 6:1; Col 3:20; 1 Ti 3:4

See **OBEDIENCE**

6. Due to Religious Leaders

Mt 10:41; 21:26; 2 Co 7:15; Ga 4:14; Ph 2:29; 1 Th 5:13; 1 Ti 5:17; He 13:7; 3 Jn 8

7. Comes from God

Nu 24:11 Therefore now flee thou to thy place: I thought to promote thee unto great honour; but, lo, the LORD hath kept thee back from honour.

1 K 3:13 And I have also given thee that which thou hast not asked, both riches, and honour: so that there shall not be any among the kings like unto thee all thy days.

Ps 91:15 He shall call upon me, and I will answer him: I *will be* with him in trouble; I will deliver him, and honour him.

Ec 6:2 A man to whom God hath given riches, wealth, and honour, so that he wanteth nothing for his soul of all that he desireth, yet God giveth him not power to eat thereof, but a stranger eateth it: this *is* vanity, and it *is* an evil disease.

Da 2:37 Thou, O king, *art* a king of kings: for the God of heaven hath given thee a kingdom, power, and strength, and glory.

Da 4:36 At the same time my reason returned unto me; and for the glory of my kingdom, mine honour and brightness returned unto me; and my counsellors and my lords sought unto me; and I was established in my kingdom, and excellent majesty was added unto me.

Da 5:18 O thou king, the most high God gave Nebuchadnezzar thy father a kingdom, and majesty, and glory, and honour:

Jn 12:26 If any man serve me, let him follow me; and where I am, there shall also my servant be: if any man serve me, him will *my* Father honour.

8. Earthly

Nu 22:17 For I will promote thee unto very great honour, and I will do whatsoever thou sayest unto me: come therefore, I pray thee, curse me this people.

1 Chr 29:28 And he died in a good old age, full of days, riches, and honour: and Solomon his son reigned in his stead.

2 Chr 17:5 Therefore the LORD established the kingdom in his hand; and all Judah brought to Jehoshaphat presents; and he had riches and honour in abundance.

2 Chr 32:27 And Hezekiah had exceeding much riches and honour: and he made himself treasuries for silver, and for gold, and for precious stones, and for spices, and for shields, and for all manner of pleasant jewels;

Est 1:4 When he shewed the riches of his glorious kingdom and the honour of his excellent majesty many days, *even* an hundred and fourscore days.

Jb 29:8 The young men saw me, and hid themselves: and the aged arose, *and* stood up.

Ps 49:12 Nevertheless man *being* in honour abideth not: he is like the beasts *that* perish.

Da 2:6 But if ye shew the dream, and the interpretation thereof, ye shall receive of me gifts and rewards and great honour: therefore shew me the dream, and the interpretation thereof.

Jn 5:44 How can ye believe, which receive honour one of another, and seek not the honour that *cometh* from God only?

1 Th 2:6 Nor of men sought we glory, neither of you, nor *yet* of others, when we might have been burdensome, as the apostles of Christ.

9. Requires Wisdom and Virtue

Pr 3:16 Length of days *is* in her right hand; *and* in her left hand riches and honour.

Pr 4:8 Exalt her, and she shall promote thee: she shall bring thee to honour, when thou dost embrace her.

Pr 8:18 Riches and honour *are* with me; *yea,* durable riches and righteousness.

Pr 13:18 Poverty and shame *shall be to* him that refuseth instruction: but he that regardeth reproof shall be honoured.

Pr 21:21 He that followeth after righteousness and mercy findeth life, righteousness, and honour.

Pr 22:4 By humility *and* the fear of the LORD *are* riches, and honour, and life.

Da 4:36 At the same time my reason returned unto me; and for the glory of my kingdom, mine honour and brightness returned unto me; and my counsellors and my lords sought unto me; and I was established in my kingdom, and excellent majesty was added unto me.

Ro 2:10 But glory, honour, and peace, to every man that worketh good, to the Jew first, and also to the Gentile:

See **DISHONOR**

HOPE, *a confident expectation in things beyond this world*

1. Spiritual

FATHER OF THE FAITHFUL

Ro 4:18 Who against hope believed in hope, that he might become the father of many nations; according to that which was spoken, So shall thy seed be.

Ro 5:5 And hope maketh not ashamed; because the love of God is shed abroad in our hearts by the Holy Ghost which is given unto us.

THE SAVING ELEMENT IN LIFE

Ro 8:24 For we are saved by hope: but hope that is seen is not hope: for what a man seeth, why doth he yet hope for?

THE SOURCE IS SCRIPTURE

Ro 15:4 For whatsoever things were written aforetime were written for our learning, that we through patience and comfort of the scriptures might have hope.

ABIDES FOREVER

1 Co 13:13 And now abideth faith, hope, charity, these three; but the greatest of these *is* charity.

Col 1:23 If ye continue in the faith grounded and settled, and *be* not moved away from the hope of the gospel, which ye have heard, *and* which was preached to every creature which is under heaven; whereof I Paul am made a minister;

2 Th 2:16 Now our Lord Jesus Christ himself, and God, even our Father, which hath loved us, and hath given us everlasting consolation and good hope through grace,

BELIEVERS CALLED TO TESTIFY

1 Pe 3:15 But sanctify the Lord God in your hearts: and *be* ready always to *give* an answer to every man that asketh you a reason of the hope that is in you with meekness and fear:

INSPIRES TO CLEAN LIVING

1 Jn 3:3 And every man that hath this hope in him purifieth himself, even as he is pure.

2. *Eternal*, a confident expectation of everlasting life

CHEERS THE DYING HOUR OF THE SAINTS

Pr 14:32 The wicked is driven away in his wickedness: but the righteous hath hope in his death.

ASSURES OF IMMORTALITY

Ac 24:15 And have hope toward God, which they themselves also allow, that there shall be a resurrection of the dead, both of the just and unjust.

A HEAVENLY TREASURE

Col 1:5 For the hope which is laid up for you in heaven, whereof ye heard before in the word of the truth of the gospel;

ANTICIPATES CHRIST'S COMING

Tit 2:13 Looking for that blessed hope, and the glorious appearing of the great God and our Saviour Jesus Christ;

THE SOUL'S SURE ANCHOR

He 6:18 That by two immutable things, in which *it was* impossible for God to lie, we might have a strong consolation, who have fled for refuge to lay hold upon the hope set before us:

He 6:19 Which *hope* we have as an anchor of the soul, both sure and stedfast, and which entereth into that within the veil;

GROUNDED IN THE RESURRECTION OF CHRIST

1 Pe 1:3 Blessed *be* the God and Father of our Lord Jesus Christ, which according to his abundant mercy hath begotten us again unto a lively hope by the resurrection of Jesus Christ from the dead,

See **FUTURE LIFE, RESURRECTION**

3. *Founded in God*, a steadfast confidence

Jb 11:18 And thou shalt be secure, because there is hope; yea, thou shalt dig *about thee, and* thou shalt take thy rest in safety.

Ps 31:24 Be of good courage, and he shall strengthen your heart, all ye that hope in the LORD.

Ps 33:18 Behold, the eye of the LORD *is* upon them that fear him, upon them that hope in his mercy;

Ps 39:7 And now, Lord, what wait I for? my hope *is* in thee.

Ps 42:11 Why art thou cast down, O my soul? and why art thou disquieted within me? hope thou in God: for I shall yet praise him, *who is* the health of my countenance, and my God.

Ps 71:5 For thou *art* my hope, O Lord God: *thou art* my trust from my youth.

Ps 119:81 My soul fainteth for thy salvation: *but* I hope in thy word.

Ps 119:147 I prevented the dawning of the morning, and cried: I hoped in thy word.

Ps 146:5 Happy *is* he that *hath* the God of Jacob for his help, whose hope *is* in the LORD his God:

Je 17:7 Blessed *is* the man that trusteth in the LORD, and whose hope the LORD is.

Je 17:13 O LORD, the hope of Israel, all that forsake thee shall be ashamed, *and* they that depart from me shall be written in the earth, because they have forsaken the LORD, the fountain of living waters.

Je 17:17 Be not a terror unto me: thou *art* my hope in the day of evil.

Jl 3:16 The LORD also shall roar out of Zion, and utter his voice from Jerusalem; and the heavens and the earth shall shake: but the LORD *will be* the hope of his people, and the strength of the children of Israel.

1 Pe 1:21 Who by him do believe in God, that raised him up from the dead, and gave him glory; that your faith and hope might be in God.

See **ASSURANCE, DESPAIR, SECURITY**

4. False, *empty or unrealized expectations*

1 S 15:32; Jb 6:20; 8:13; 11:20; 14:19; 27:8; 31:24; Ps 10:6; Pr 10:28; 11:7; Je 8:11; 13:25; 28:15; Lam 4:17; Eze 13:6; Ho 12:1; Mt 25:3, 8; Lu 13:26

HOPELESSNESS, *state of despair, having no expectation of a favorable outcome*

Jb 15:22 He believeth not that he shall return out of darkness, and he is waited for of the sword.

Jb 17:15 And where *is* now my hope? as for my hope, who shall see it?

Is 49:14 But Zion said, The LORD hath forsaken me, and my Lord hath forgotten me.

Je 2:25 Withhold thy foot from being unshod, and thy throat from thirst: but thou saidst, There is no hope: no; for I have loved strangers, and after them will I go.

Je 18:12 And they said, There is no hope: but we will walk after our own devices, and we will every one do the imagination of his evil heart.

Jona 4:8 And it came to pass, when the sun did arise, that God prepared a vehement east wind; and the sun beat upon the head of Jonah, that he fainted, and wished in himself to die, and said, *It is* better for me to die than to live.

Ep 2:12 That at that time ye were without Christ, being aliens from the commonwealth of Israel, and strangers from the covenants of promise, having no hope, and without God in the world:

1 Th 4:13 But I would not have you to be ignorant, brethren, concerning them which are asleep, that ye sorrow not, even as others which have no hope.

See **FUTURE LIFE**

HOPHNI *and Phinehas, sons of Eli*

1 S 1:3; 2:17, 34; 3:13; 4:4, 11

HOR See **MOUNTAINS AND HILLS**

HOREB See **MOUNTAINS AND HILLS**

HORMAH, *a town in the south of Judah*

Nu 14:45; 21:3; De 1:44; Jos 12:14; Jud 1:17; 1 S 30:30

HORN, *figurative*

2 S 22:3; 1 K 22:11; Ps 89:24; 92:10; 132:17

See **MUSIC**

HORNETS See **INSECTS**

HORSES See **ANIMALS**

HOSANNAH, *save now, or we pray*

Mt 21:9

HOSEA

1. Person, *a prophet*

Ho 1:1

2. Book

Author: Hosea, the son of Beeri (1:1). A contemporary of Isaiah and Micah, he was especially fit for his task.

Date Written: Approximately 715 B.C. recording the events of his ministry which stretched from about 755 B.C. to 710 B.C.

Purpose: To reveal God's unconditional love, especially illustrated in contrast to the sinful harlotry of his people.

To Whom Written: The Northern Kingdom (Israel).

Main Theme: A spiritual message. Apostasy from God is spiritual adultery.

(1) God, the husband (2:20; Is 54:5).

(2) Israel, the unchaste wife (2:2).

Key Words: Unconditional love.

Key Verse: 3:1.

See **LOVE**

HOSHEA, *a king of Israel, son of Elah*

2 K 15:30; 17:1; 18:1, 9

See **ISRAEL**

HOSPITALITY, *act of entertaining guests with warmth and generosity*

1. Our Duty

Ro 12:13 Distributing to the necessity of saints; given to hospitality.

1 Ti 3:2 A bishop then must be blameless, the husband of one wife, vigilant, sober, of good behaviour, given to hospitality, apt to teach;

1 Ti 5:10 Well reported of for good works; if she have brought up children, if she have lodged strangers, if she have washed the saints' feet, if she have relieved the afflicted, if she have diligently followed every good work.

Tit 1:8 But a lover of hospitality, a lover of good men, sober, just, holy, temperate;

He 13:2 Be not forgetful to entertain strangers: for thereby some have entertained angels unawares.

1 Pe 4:9 Use hospitality one to another without grudging.

2. Examples

Ge 18:4 Let a little water, I pray you, be fetched, and wash your feet, and rest yourselves under the tree:

Ge 19:2 And he said, Behold now, my lords, turn in, I pray you, into your servant's house, and tarry all night, and wash your feet, and ye shall rise up early, and go on your ways. And they said, Nay; but we will abide in the street all night.

Ge 24:31 And he said, Come in, thou blessed of the LORD; wherefore standest thou without? for I have prepared the house, and room for the camels.

Ex 2:20 And he said unto his daughters, And where *is* he? why *is* it *that* ye have left the man? call him, that he may eat bread.

Jud 13:15 And Manoah said unto the angel of the LORD, I pray thee, let us detain thee, until we shall have made ready a kid for thee.

Jud 19:4 And his father in law, the damsel's father, retained him; and he

abode with him three days: so they did eat and drink, and lodged there.

Jud 19:20 And the old man said, Peace *be* with thee; howsoever *let* all thy wants lie upon me; only lodge not in the street.

1 S 9:19 And Samuel answered Saul, and said, I *am* the seer: go up before me unto the high place; for ye shall eat with me to day, and to morrow I will let thee go, and will tell thee all that *is* in thine heart.

1 K 17:15 And she went and did according to the saying of Elijah: and she, and he, and her house, did eat *many* days.

2 K 4:8 And it fell on a day, that Elisha passed to Shunem, where *was* a great woman; and she constrained him to eat bread. And so it was, *that* as oft as he passed by, he turned in thither to eat bread.

Ne 5:17 Moreover *there were* at my table an hundred and fifty of the Jews and rulers, beside those that came unto us from among the heathen that *are* about us.

Jb 31:32 The stranger did not lodge in the street: *but* I opened my doors to the traveller.

Jb 42:11 Then came there unto him all his brethren, and all his sisters, and all they that had been of his acquaintance before, and did eat bread with him in his house: and they bemoaned him, and comforted him over all the evil that the LORD had brought upon him: every man also gave him a piece of money, and every one an earring of gold.

Ac 16:15 And when she was baptized, and her household, she besought *us*, saying, If ye have judged me to be faithful to the Lord, come into my house, and abide *there*. And she constrained us.

Ac 16:34 And when he had brought them into his house, he set meat before them, and rejoiced, believing in God with all his house.

Ac 21:8 And the next *day* we that were of Paul's company departed, and came unto Caesarea: and we entered into the house of Philip the evangelist, which was *one* of the seven; and abode with him.

Ac 28:2 And the barbarous people shewed us no little kindness: for they kindled a fire, and received us every one, because of the present rain, and because of the cold.

Ac 28:7 In the same quarters were possessions of the chief man of the island, whose name was Publius; who received us, and lodged us three days courteously.

He 6:10 For God *is* not unrighteous to forget your work and labour of love, which ye have shewed toward his name, in that ye have ministered to the saints, and do minister.

3. Those Who Entertained Christ in Their Homes

MATTHEW

Mt 9:10 And it came to pass, as Jesus sat at meat in the house, behold, many publicans and sinners came and sat down with him and his disciples.

SIMON THE LEPER

Mk 14:3 And being in Bethany in the house of Simon the leper, as he sat at meat, there came a woman having an alabaster box of ointment of spikenard very precious; and she brake the box, and poured *it* on his head.

A PHARISEE

Lu 7:36 And one of the Pharisees desired him that he would eat with him. And he went into the Pharisee's house, and sat down to meat.

MARTHA

Lu 10:38 Now it came to pass, as they went, that he entered into a certain village: and a certain woman named Martha received him into her house.

ONE OF THE CHIEF PHARISEES

Lu 14:1 And it came to pass, as he went into the house of one of the chief Pharisees to eat bread on the sabbath day, that they watched him.

ZACCHAEUS

Lu 19:7 And when they saw *it,* they all murmured, saying, That he was gone to be guest with a man that is a sinner.

TWO AT EMMAUS

Lu 24:29 But they constrained him, saying, Abide with us: for it is toward evening, and the day is far spent. And he went in to tarry with them.

PEOPLE IN CANA OF GALILEE

Jn 2:2 And both Jesus was called, and his disciples, to the marriage.

See **INHOSPITALITY**

HOUR

1. Christ's, the time at which he gave his life for the world

Mt 26:18, 45; Mk 14:35, 41; Lu 9:51; Jn 2:4; 7:6, 30; 8:20; 12:23, 27; 13:1; 16:32; 17:1

2. Of the Day

a. Third Hour

Mt 20:3; Mk 15:25; Ac 2:15; 23:23

b. Sixth Hour

Mt 20:5; 27:45; Lu 23:44; Jn 4:6; 19:14; Ac 10:9

c. Ninth Hour

Mt 20:5; 27:46; Mk 15:33; Ac 3:1; 10:3

d. Tenth Hour

Jn 1:39

e. Eleventh Hour

Mt 20:6

See **TIME**

HOUSE OF GOD, place of worship

2 S 7:5 Go and tell my servant David, Thus saith the LORD, Shalt thou build me an house for me to dwell in?

Ps 134:1 Behold, bless ye the LORD, all *ye* servants of the LORD, which by night stand in the house of the LORD.

Ec 5:1 Keep thy foot when thou goest to the house of God, and be more ready to hear, than to give the sacrifice of fools: for they consider not that they do evil.

Is 2:3 And many people shall go and say, Come ye, and let us go up to the mountain of the LORD, to the house of the God of Jacob; and he will teach us of his ways, and we will walk in his paths: for out of Zion shall go forth the law, and the word of the LORD from Jerusalem.

Is 56:7 Even them will I bring to my holy mountain, and make them joyful in my house of prayer: their burnt offerings and their sacrifices *shall be* accepted upon mine altar; for mine house shall be called an house of prayer for all people.

Is 60:7 All the flocks of Kedar shall be gathered together unto thee, the rams of Nebaioth shall minister unto thee: they shall come up with acceptance on mine altar, and I will glorify the house of my glory.

Lu 19:46 Saying unto them, It is written, My house is the house of prayer: but ye have made it a den of thieves.

Jn 2:16 And said unto them that sold doves, Take these things hence; make not my Father's house an house of merchandise.

1. Love for

1 Chr 29:3 Moreover, because I have set my affection to the house of my God, I have of mine own proper good, of gold and silver, *which* I have given to the house of my God, over and above all that I have prepared for the holy house,

2 Chr 24:4 And it came to pass after this, *that* Joash was minded to repair the house of the LORD.

Ne 10:39 For the children of Israel and the children of Levi shall bring the offering of the corn, of the new wine, and the oil, unto the chambers, where *are* the vessels of the sanctuary, and the priests that minister, and the porters, and the singers: and we will not forsake the house of our God.

Ps 5:7 But as for me, I will come *into* thy house in the multitude of thy mercy: *and* in thy fear will I worship toward thy holy temple.

Ps 23:6 Surely goodness and mercy shall follow me all the days of my life: and I will dwell in the house of the LORD for ever.

Ps 26:8 LORD, I have loved the habitation of thy house, and the place where thine honour dwelleth.

Ps 27:4 One *thing* have I desired of the LORD, that will I seek after; that I may dwell in the house of the LORD all the days of my life, to behold the beauty of the LORD, and to enquire in his temple.

Ps 42:4 When I remember these *things,* I pour out my soul in me: for I had gone with the multitude, I went with them to the house of God, with the voice of joy and praise, with a multitude that kept holyday.

Ps 43:3 O send out thy light and thy truth: let them lead me; let them bring me unto thy holy hill, and to thy tabernacles.

Ps 61:4 I will abide in thy tabernacle for ever: I will trust in the covert of thy wings. Selah.

Ps 65:4 Blessed *is the man whom* thou choosest, and causest to approach *unto thee, that* he may dwell in thy courts: we shall be satisfied with the goodness of thy house, *even* of thy holy temple.

Ps 84:2 My soul longeth, yea, even fainteth f the LORD: my heart and my flesh crieth out for the living God.

Ps 84:10 For a day in thy courts *is* better than a thousand. I had rather be a doorkeeper in the house of my God, than to dwell in the tents of wickedness.

Ps 102:14 For thy servants take pleasure in her stones, and favour the dust thereof.

Ps 122:1 I was glad when they said unto me, Let us go into the house of the LORD.

Ps 132:7 We will go into his tabernacles: we will worship at his footstool.

Is 2:3 And many people shall go and say, Come ye, and let us go up to the mountain of the LORD, to the house of the God of Jacob; and he will teach us of his ways, and we will walk in his paths: for out of Zion shall go forth the law, and the word of the LORD from Jerusalem.

Zep 3:18 I will gather *them that are* sorrowful for the solemn assembly, *who* are of thee, *to whom* the reproach of it *was* a burden.

2. Reasons for Attending

THE DIVINE COMMAND

De 12:5 But unto the place which the LORD your God shall choose out of all your tribes to put his name there, *even* unto his habitation shall ye seek, and thither thou shalt come:

De 16:16 Three times in a year shall all thy males appear before the LORD thy God in the place which he shall choose; in the feast of unleavened bread, and in the feast of weeks, and in the feast of tabernacles: and they shall not appear before the LORD empty:

BLESSINGS PRONOUNCED

Ps 84:4 Blessed *are* they that dwell in thy house: they will be still praising thee. Selah.

Ps 122:4 Whither the tribes go up, the tribes of the LORD, unto the testimony of Israel, to give thanks unto the name of the LORD.

A REFUGE IN TIMES OF TROUBLE

Is 37:1 And it came to pass, when king Hezekiah heard *it*, that he rent his clothes, and covered himself with sackcloth, and went into the house of the LORD.

Is 37:14 And Hezekiah received the letter from the hand of the messengers, and read it: and Hezekiah went up unto the house of the LORD, and spread it before the LORD.

A PLACE OF INSTRUCTION

Mi 4:2 And many nations shall come, and say, Come, and let us go up to the mountain of the LORD, and to the house of the God of Jacob; and he will teach us of his ways, and we will walk in his paths: for the law shall go forth of Zion, and the word of the LORD from Jerusalem.

A COMFORT IN OLD AGE

Lu 2:36–37 And there was one Anna, a prophetess, the daughter of Phanuel, of the tribe of Aser: she was of a great age, and had lived with an husband seven years from her virginity;

And she *was* a widow of about fourscore and four years, which departed not from the temple, but served *God* with fastings and prayers night and day.

THE EXAMPLE OF CHRIST

Lu 4:16 And he came to Nazareth, where he had been brought up: and, as his custom was, he went into the synagogue on the sabbath day, and stood up for to read.

Lu 18:10 Two men went up into the temple to pray; the one a Pharisee, and the other a publican.

THE EXAMPLE OF THE APOSTLES

Lu 24:52–53 And they worshipped him, and returned to Jerusalem with great joy:

And were continually in the temple, praising and blessing God.

Ac 2:46 And they, continuing daily with one accord in the temple, and breaking bread from house to house, did eat their meat with gladness and singleness of heart,

Ac 3:1 Now Peter and John went up together into the temple at the hour of prayer, *being* the ninth *hour.*

See **CHURCH, SYNAGOGUES**

HOUSETOPS, *places of resort*

Jos 2:6; Jud 16:27; 1 S 9:25; Ne 8:16; Pr 21:9; Is 15:3; 22:1; Je 19:13; Zep 1:5; Mt 10:27; 24:17; Mk 13:15; Lu 5:19; 12:3; 17:31; Ac 10:9

HULDAH, *a prophetess*

2 K 22:14; 2 Chr 34:22

See **PROPHETS, WOMEN**

HUMANENESS, *kind treatment of animals and other creatures*

Ex 23:5 If thou see the ass of him that hateth thee lying under his burden, and wouldest forbear to help him, thou shalt surely help with him.

De 22:6 If a bird's nest chance to be before thee in the way in any tree, or on the ground, *whether they be* young ones, or eggs, and the dam sitting upon the young, or upon the eggs, thou shalt not take the dam with the young:

Mt 12:11 And he said unto them, What man shall there be among you, that shall have one sheep, and if it fall into a pit on the sabbath day, will he not lay hold on it, and lift *it* out?

Lu 13:15 The Lord then answered him, and said, *Thou* hypocrite, doth not each one of you on the sabbath loose his ox or *his* ass from the stall, and lead *him* away to watering?

Lu 14:5 And answered them, saying, Which of you shall have an ass or an ox fallen into a pit, and will not straightway pull him out on the sabbath day?

See **ANIMALS, CREATOR**

HUMILIATION

1. Threatened

Ex 11:8; 1 S 2:36; 1 K 11:11; 16:4; 21:24; 2 K 19:28; Est 6:12; Ps 35:26; 76:5; Is 2:12; 5:15; 10:12–13; 13:11; 14:19; 16:14; 20:4; 22:19; 25:11; 26:5; 47:2; 63:6; Je 23:40; 48:26; 49:16; 51:53; Lam 4:21; Eze 28:8, 17; 31:18; Am 3:11; 4:2; 9:2; Obad 2; Mi 1:14; 6:14; 7:10; Hab 2:16

2. Examples

Ex 10:17; 32:20; Nu 12:15; Jos 9:21; Jud 6:6; 1 S 28:8; 2 S 15:30; 1 Chr 10:9; 2 Chr 28:19; 32:21; Est 7:10; Pr 14:19; Je 48:39; Lam 1:15; 2:3

HUMILITY, *gentleness, affliction, lowliness of mind*

1. Promises

Pr 16:19 Better *it is to be* of an humble spirit with the lowly, than to divide the spoil with the proud.

Pr 18:12 Before destruction the heart of man is haughty, and before honour *is* humility.

Pr 22:4 By humility *and* the fear of the LORD *are* riches, and honour, and life.

Pr 29:23 A man's pride shall bring him low: but honour shall uphold the humble in spirit.

Is 57:15 For thus saith the high and lofty One that inhabiteth eternity, whose name *is* Holy; I dwell in the high and holy *place,* with him also *that is* of a contrite and humble spirit, to revive the spirit of the humble, and to revive the heart of the contrite ones.

Mt 18:4 Whosoever therefore shall humble himself as this little child, the same is greatest in the kingdom of heaven.

Lu 18:14 I tell you, this man went down to his house justified *rather* than the other: for every one that exalteth himself shall be abased; and he that humbleth himself shall be exalted.

2. Prescribed

2 Chr 30:11 Nevertheless divers of Asher and Manasseh and of Zebulun humbled themselves, and came to Jerusalem.

Mi 6:8 He hath shewed thee, O man, what *is* good; and what doth the LORD require of thee, but to do justly, and to love mercy, and to walk humbly with thy God?

Lu 14:10 But when thou art bidden, go and sit down in the lowest room; that when he that bade thee cometh, he may say unto thee, Friend, go up higher: then shalt thou have worship in the presence of them that sit at meat with thee.

Lu 22:26 But ye *shall* not *be* so: but he that is greatest among you, let him be as the younger; and he that is chief, as he that doth serve.

Ro 11:20 Well; because of unbelief they were broken off, and thou standest by faith. Be not highminded, but fear:

Ro 12:3 For I say, through the grace given unto me, to every man that is among you, not to think *of himself* more highly than he ought to think; but to think soberly, according as God hath dealt to every man the measure of faith.

Ro 12:10 *Be* kindly affectioned one to another with brotherly love; in honour preferring one another;

Ph 2:5 Let this mind be in you, which was also in Christ Jesus:

Ja 4:10 Humble yourselves in the sight of the Lord, and he shall lift you up.

3. Examples

JACOB

Ge 32:10 I am not worthy of the least of all the mercies, and of all the truth, which thou hast shewed unto thy servant; for with my staff I passed over this Jordan; and now I am become two bands.

KING SAUL

1 S 9:21 And Saul answered and said, *Am* not I a Benjamite, of the smallest of the tribes of Israel? and my family the least of all the families of the tribe of Benjamin? wherefore then speakest thou so to me?

KING DAVID

2 S 7:18 Then went king David in, and sat before the LORD, and he said, Who *am* I, O Lord GOD? and what *is* my house, that thou hast brought me hitherto?

KING SOLOMON

1 K 3:7 And now, O LORD my God, thou hast made thy servant king instead of David my father: and I *am but* a little child: I know not *how* to go out or come in.

Ps 131:1 LORD, my heart is not haughty, nor mine eyes lofty: neither do I exercise myself in great matters, or in things too high for me.

JOHN THE BAPTIST

Mt 3:14 But John forbad him, saying, I have need to be baptized of thee, and comest thou to me?

THE CENTURION

Mt 8:8 The centurion answered and said, Lord, I am not worthy that thou shouldest come under my roof: but speak the word only, and my servant shall be healed.

THE SYROPHENICIAN WOMAN

Mt 15:27 And she said, Truth, Lord: yet the dogs eat of the crumbs which fall from their masters' table.

Jn 1:27 He it is, who coming after me is preferred before me, whose shoe's latchet I am not worthy to unloose.

PAUL

1 Ti 1:15 This *is* a faithful saying, and worthy of all acceptation, that Christ Jesus came into the world to save sinners; of whom I am chief.

4. Before Others

Ge 41:16 And Joseph answered Pharaoh, saying, *It is* not in me: God shall give Pharaoh an answer of peace.

1 S 18:18 And David said unto Saul, Who *am* I? and what *is* my life, *or* my father's family in Israel, that I should be son in law to the king?

1 S 24:14 After whom is the king of Israel come out? after whom dost thou pursue? after a dead dog, after a flea.

2 S 9:8 And he bowed himself, and said, What is thy servant, that thou shouldest look upon such a dead dog as I *am?*

Da 2:30 But as for me, this secret is not revealed to me for *any* wisdom that I have more than any living, but for *their* sakes that shall make known the interpretation to the king, and that thou mightest know the thoughts of thy heart.

5. Christ's Humility

Zec 9:9 Rejoice greatly, O daughter of Zion; shout, O daughter of Jerusalem: behold, thy King cometh unto thee: he *is* just, and having salvation; lowly, and riding upon an ass, and upon a colt the foal of an ass.

Mt 11:29 Take my yoke upon you, and learn of me; for I am meek and lowly in heart: and ye shall find rest unto your souls.

Jn 13:5 After that he poureth water into a bason, and began to wash the disciples' feet, and to wipe *them* with the towel wherewith he was girded.

2 Co 8:9 For ye know the grace of our Lord Jesus Christ, that, though he was rich, yet for your sakes he became poor, that ye through his poverty might be rich.

Ph 2:8 And being found in fashion as a man, he humbled himself, and became obedient unto death, even the death of the cross.

OF APPEARANCE

Is 53:2 For he shall grow up before him as a tender plant, and as a root out of a dry ground: he hath no form nor comeliness; and when we shall see him, *there is* no beauty that we should desire him.

OF WORLDLY SUCCESS

Is 53:3 He is despised and rejected of men; a man of sorrows, and acquainted with grief: and we hid as it were *our* faces from him; he was despised, and we esteemed him not.

OF REPUTATION

Mt 2:23 And he came and dwelt in a city called Nazareth: that it might be fulfilled which was spoken by the prophets, He shall be called a Nazarene.

OF RICHES

Mt 8:20 And Jesus saith unto him, The foxes have holes, and the birds of the air *have* nests; but the Son of man hath not where to lay *his* head.

OF RANK

Mt 13:55 Is not this the carpenter's son? is not his mother called Mary? and his brethren, James, and Joses, and Simon, and Judas?

OF KINGSHIP

Jn 13:5 After that he poureth water into a bason, and began to wash the disciples' feet, and to wipe *them* with the towel wherewith he was girded.

6. Sinners Humbling Themselves

AHAB

1 K 21:29 Seest thou how Ahab humbleth himself before me? because he humbleth himself before me, I will not bring the evil in his days: *but* in his son's days will I bring the evil upon his house.

REHOBOAM AND THE PRINCES

2 Chr 12:6 Whereupon the princes of Israel and the king humbled themselves; and they said, The LORD *is* righteous.

MANASSEH

2 Chr 33:12 And when he was in affliction, he besought the LORD his God, and humbled himself greatly before the God of his fathers,

JOSIAH

2 Chr 34:27 Because thine heart was tender, and thou didst humble thyself before God, when thou heardest his words against this place, and against the inhabitants thereof, and humbledst thyself before me, and didst rend thy clothes, and weep before me; I have even heard *thee* also, saith the LORD.

THE PRODIGAL SON

Lu 15:18 I will arise and go to my father, and will say unto him, Father, I have sinned against heaven, and before thee,

THE PUBLICAN

Lu 18:13 And the publican, standing afar off, would not lift up so much as *his* eyes unto heaven, but smote upon his breast, saying, God be merciful to me a sinner.

7. Persons at Christ's Feet

UNFORTUNATE SUFFERERS

Mt 15:30 And great multitudes came unto him, having with them *those that were* lame, blind, dumb, maimed, and many others, and cast them down at Jesus' feet; and he healed them:

AN AFFLICTED FATHER

Mk 5:22–23 And, behold, there cometh one of the rulers of the synagogue, Jairus by name; and when he saw him, he fell at his feet,

And besought him greatly, saying, My little daughter lieth at the point of death: *I pray thee,* come and lay thy hands on her, that she may be healed; and she shall live.

A SORROWING MOTHER

Mk 7:25 For a *certain* woman, whose young daughter had an unclean spirit, heard of him, and came and fell at his feet:

A SINFUL WOMAN

Lu 7:37–38 And, behold, a woman in the city, which was a sinner, when she knew that *Jesus* sat at meat in the Pharisee's house, brought an alabaster box of ointment,

And stood at his feet behind *him* weeping, and began to wash his feet with tears, and did wipe *them* with the hairs of her head, and kissed his feet, and anointed *them* with the ointment. **Lu 8:35** Then they went out to see what was done; and came to Jesus, and found the man, out of whom the devils were departed, sitting at the feet of Jesus, clothed, and in his right mind: and they were afraid.

A SEEKER AFTER TRUTH

Lu 10:39 And she had a sister called Mary, which also sat at Jesus' feet, and heard his word.

A BEREAVED SISTER

Jn 11:32 Then when Mary was come where Jesus was, and saw him, she fell down at his feet, saying unto him, Lord, if thou hadst been here, my brother had not died.

A REVERENT WORSHIPPER

Re 1:17 And when I saw him, I fell at his feet as dead. And he laid his right hand upon me, saying unto me, Fear not; I am the first and the last:

See **PRIDE**

HUNGER, *physical*

Ge 25:29; 41:55; Ex 16:3; De 8:3; Jud 8:5; 1 S 14:28; 2 S 17:29; 1 K 17:11; Pr 6:30; 27:7; Je 38:9; Lam 4:4; Mt 4:2; 12:1; 15:32; Mk 2:25; 8:1, 3; 11:12; Lu

4:2; 16:21; Jn 4:31; Ac 10:10; 1 Co 11:34; 2 Co 11:27

See **DESIRE**

HUNTERS, *those who lie in wait, those who run after*

Ge 10:9; 21:20; 25:27; 27:3; Le 17:13; Pr 12:27

See **BLOOD**

HUR, *coworker with Moses and Aaron*

Ex 17:12; 24:14

HUSBANDS

Ge 2:23–24 And Adam said, This *is* now bone of my bones, and flesh of my flesh: she shall be called Woman, because she was taken out of Man.

Therefore shall a man leave his father and his mother, and shall cleave unto his wife: and they shall be one flesh.

Ge 29:32 And Leah conceived, and bare a son, and she called his name Reuben: for she said, Surely the LORD hath looked upon my affliction; now therefore my husband will love me.

Nu 30:8 But if her husband disallowed her on the day that he heard *it;* then he shall make her vow which she vowed, and that which she uttered with her lips, wherewith she bound her soul, of none effect: and the LORD shall forgive her.

De 24:5 When a man hath taken a new wife, he shall not go out to war, neither shall he be charged with any business: *but* he shall be free at home one year, and shall cheer up his wife which he hath taken.

Pr 5:18 Let thy fountain be blessed: and rejoice with the wife of thy youth.

Pr 31:28 Her children arise up, and call her blessed; her husband *also,* and he praiseth her.

Ec 9:9 Live joyfully with the wife whom thou lovest all the days of the life of thy vanity, which he hath given thee under the sun, all the days of thy vanity: for that *is* thy portion in *this* life, and in thy labour which thou takest under the sun.

Mal 2:15 And did not he make one? Yet had he the residue of the spirit. And wherefore one? That he might seek a godly seed. Therefore take heed to your spirit, and let none deal treacherously against the wife of his youth.

Mt 5:32 But I say unto you, That whosoever shall put away his wife, saving for the cause of fornication, causeth her to commit adultery: and whosoever shall marry her that is divorced committeth adultery.

Mk 10:7 For this cause shall a man leave his father and mother, and cleave to his wife;

1 Co 7:3 Let the husband render unto the wife due benevolence: and likewise also the wife unto the husband.

1 Co 7:11 But and if she depart, let her remain unmarried, or be reconciled to *her* husband: and let not the husband put away *his* wife.

Ep 5:25 Husbands, love your wives, even as Christ also loved the church, and gave himself for it;

Ep 5:33 Nevertheless let every one of you in particular so love his wife even as himself; and the wife *see* that she reverence *her* husband.

Col 3:19 Husbands, love *your* wives, and be not bitter against them.

1 Pe 3:7 Likewise, ye husbands, dwell with *them* according to knowledge, giving honour unto the wife, as unto the weaker vessel, and as being heirs together of the grace of life; that your prayers be not hindered.

See **HOME, FAMILY**

HUSHAI, *David's companion*

2 S 15:37; 16:17; 17:6; 1 K 4:16

HUSKS, *also pods*

Lu 15:16

HYPROCRISY   *See* **RELIGION**

HYSSOP, *branch used in sprinkling blood*

Ex 12:22; Le 14:6, 49; Nu 19:6, 18; 1 K 4:33; Ps 51:7; Jn 19:29; He 9:19

I

I AM'S

1. Of God

Ex 3:14 And God said unto Moses, I AM THAT I AM: and he said, Thus shalt thou say unto the children of Israel, I AM hath sent me unto you.

2. Of Christ

THE MESSIAH

Jn 4:26 Jesus saith unto her, I that speak unto thee am *he.*

THE BREAD OF LIFE

Jn 6:35 And Jesus said unto them, I am the bread of life: he that cometh to me shall never hunger; and he that believeth on me shall never thirst.

FROM ABOVE

Jn 8:23 And he said unto them, Ye are from beneath; I am from above: ye are of this world; I am not of this world.

THE ETERNAL ONE

Jn 8:58 Jesus said unto them, Verily, verily, I say unto you, Before Abraham was, I am.

THE LIGHT OF THE WORLD

Jn 9:5 As long as I am in the world, I am the light of the world.

THE DOOR

Jn 10:7 Then said Jesus unto them again, Verily, verily, I say unto you, I am the door of the sheep.

THE GOOD SHEPHERD

Jn 10:11 I am the good shepherd: the good shepherd giveth his life for the sheep.

Jn 10:14 I am the good shepherd, and know my *sheep,* and am known of mine.

THE SON OF GOD

Jn 10:36 Say ye of him, whom the Father hath sanctified, and sent into the world, Thou blasphemest; because I said, I am the Son of God?

THE RESURRECTION AND LIFE

Jn 11:25 Jesus said unto her, I am the resurrection, and the life: he that believeth in me, though he were dead, yet shall he live:

THE LORD AND MASTER

Jn 13:13 Ye call me Master and Lord: and ye say well; for so I am.

THE WAY, TRUTH, AND LIFE

Jn 14:6 Jesus saith unto him, I am the way, the truth, and the life: no man cometh unto the Father, but by me.

THE TRUE VINE

Jn 15:1 I am the true vine, and my Father is the husbandman.

ALPHA AND OMEGA

Re 1:8 I am Alpha and Omega, the beginning and the ending, saith the Lord, which is, and which was, and which is to come, the Almighty.

THE FIRST AND THE LAST

Re 1:17–18 And when I saw him, I fell at his feet as dead. And he laid his right hand upon me, saying unto me, Fear not; I am the first and the last:

I *am* he that liveth, and was dead; and, behold, I am alive for evermore, Amen; and have the keys of hell and of death.

IBEX *See* ANIMALS

IBZAN *See* ISRAEL

ICE

Jb 6:16; 37:10; 38:29; Ps 147:17

ICONIUM, *a town of Lycaonia*

Ac 13:51; 14:19; 16:2; 2 Ti 3:11

IDENTIFICATION, *of Christ with believers*

Mt 10:40 He that receiveth you receiveth me, and he that receiveth me receiveth him that sent me.

Mt 18:5 And whoso shall receive one such little child in my name receiveth me.

Mt 25:40–41 And the King shall answer and say unto them, Verily I say unto you, Inasmuch as ye have done *it* unto one of the least of these my brethren, ye have done *it* unto me.

Then shall he say also unto them on the left hand, Depart from me, ye cursed, into everlasting fire, prepared for the devil and his angels:

Lu 10:16 He that heareth you heareth me; and he that despiseth you despiseth me; and he that despiseth me despiseth him that sent me.

Ac 9:4 And he fell to the earth, and heard a voice saying unto him, Saul, Saul, why persecutest thou me?

Ac 22:8 And I answered, Who art thou, Lord? And he said unto me, I am Jesus of Nazareth, whom thou persecutest.

Ac 26:16 But rise, and stand upon thy feet: for I have appeared unto thee for this purpose, to make thee a minister and a witness both of these things which thou hast seen, and of those things in the which I will appear unto thee;

1 Co 8:12 But when ye sin so against the brethren, and wound their weak conscience, ye sin against Christ.

See **CHRIST**

IDLENESS *See* **BUSINESS**

IDOLATRY, *worship of anything other than the true God*

1. Forbidden

Ge 35:2 Then Jacob said unto his household, and to all that *were* with him, Put away the strange gods that *are* among you, and be clean, and change your garments:

Ex 20:4 Thou shalt not make unto thee any graven image, or any likeness *of any thing* that *is* in heaven above, or that *is* in the earth beneath, or that *is* in the water under the earth:

Ex 34:17 Thou shalt make thee no molten gods.

Le 26:1 Ye shall make you no idols nor graven image, neither rear you up a standing image, neither shall ye set up *any* image of stone in your land, to bow down unto it: for I *am* the LORD your God.

De 7:25 The graven images of their gods shall ye burn with fire: thou shalt not desire the silver or gold *that is* on them, nor take *it* unto thee, lest thou be snared therein: for it *is* an abomination to the LORD thy God.

De 11:16 Take heed to yourselves, that your heart be not deceived, and ye turn aside, and serve other gods, and worship them;

De 16:22 Neither shalt thou set thee up *any* image; which the LORD thy God hateth.

Jud 17:3 And when he had restored the eleven hundred *shekels* of silver to his mother, his mother said, I had wholly dedicated the silver unto the LORD from my hand for my son, to make a graven image and a molten image: now therefore I will restore it unto thee.

Ps 81:9 There shall no strange god be in thee; neither shalt thou worship any strange god.

Is 42:8 I *am* the LORD: that *is* my name: and my glory will I not give to another, neither my praise to graven images.

1 Jn 5:21 Little children, keep yourselves from idols. Amen.

2. Prophecies

Is 2:20 In that day a man shall cast his idols of silver, and his idols of gold, which they made *each one* for himself to worship, to the moles and to the bats;

Is 17:8 And he shall not look to the altars, the work of his hands, neither shall respect *that* which his fingers have made, either the groves, or the images.

Is 27:9 By this therefore shall the iniquity of Jacob be purged; and this is all the fruit to take away his sin; when he maketh all the stones of the altar as chalkstones that are beaten in sunder, the groves and images shall not stand up.

Je 43:13 He shall break also the images of Beth-shemesh, that *is* in the land of Egypt; and the houses of the gods of the Egyptians shall he burn with fire.

Je 51:47 Therefore, behold, the days come, that I will do judgment upon the graven images of Babylon: and her whole land shall be confounded, and all her slain shall fall in the midst of her.

Eze 37:23 Neither shall they defile themselves any more with their idols, nor with their detestable things, nor with any of their transgressions: but I will save them out of all their dwellingplaces, wherein they have sinned, and will cleanse them: so shall they be my people, and I will be their God.

Ho 2:17 For I will take away the names of Baalim out of her mouth, and they shall no more be remembered by their name.

Mi 5:13 Thy graven images also will I cut off, and thy standing images out of the midst of thee; and thou shalt no more worship the work of thine hands.

Zep 1:4 I will also stretch out mine hand upon Judah, and upon all the inhabitants of Jerusalem; and I will cut off the remnant of Baal from this place, *and* the name of the Chemarims with the priests;

Zec 13:2 And it shall come to pass in that day, saith the LORD of hosts, *that* I will cut off the names of the idols out of the land, and they shall no more be remembered: and also I will cause the prophets and the unclean spirit to pass out of the land.

3. Characterizations

INSENTIENT

De 4:28 And there ye shall serve gods, the work of men's hands, wood and stone, which neither see, nor hear, nor eat, nor smell.

Ps 115:4 Their idols *are* silver and gold, the work of men's hands.

PERISHABLE

Is 40:20 He that *is* so impoverished that he hath no oblation chooseth a tree *that* will not rot; he seeketh unto him a cunning workman to prepare a graven image, *that* shall not be moved.

HELPLESS

Is 45:20 Assemble yourselves and come; draw near together, ye *that are* escaped of the nations: they have no knowledge that set up the wood of their graven image, and pray unto a god *that* cannot save.

Je 10:5 They *are* upright as the palm tree, but speak not: they must needs be borne, because they cannot go. Be not afraid of them; for they cannot do evil, neither also *is it* in them to do good.

Ac 14:18 And with these sayings scarce restrained they the people, that they had not done sacrifice unto them.

UNWORTHY OF WORSHIP

Ac 17:29 Forasmuch then as we are the offspring of God, we ought not to think that the Godhead is like unto gold, or silver, or stone, graven by art and man's device.

DEGRADING

Ro 1:22–23 Professing themselves to be wise, they became fools,

And changed the glory of the uncorruptible God into an image made like to corruptible man, and to birds, and fourfooted beasts, and creeping things.

1 Co 8:4 As concerning therefore the eating of those things that are offered in sacrifice unto idols, we know that an idol *is* nothing in the world, and that *there is* none other God but one.

1 Co 12:2 Ye know that ye were Gentiles, carried away unto these dumb idols, even as ye were led.

4. Examples

Ex 32:4 And he received *them* at their hand, and fashioned it with a graving tool, after he had made it a molten calf: and they said, These *be* thy gods, O Israel, which brought thee up out of the land of Egypt.

Ex 32:23 For they said unto me, Make us gods, which shall go before us: for *as for* this Moses, the man that brought us up out of the land of Egypt, we wot not what is become of him.

Ex 32:31 And Moses returned unto the Lord, and said, Oh, this people have sinned a great sin, and have made them gods of gold.

Nu 25:2 And they called the people unto the sacrifices of their gods: and the people did eat, and bowed down to their gods.

De 9:12 And the Lord said unto me, Arise, get thee down quickly from hence; for thy people which thou hast brought forth out of Egypt have corrupted *themselves;* they are quickly turned aside out of the way which I commanded them; they have made them a molten image.

De 9:16 And I looked, and, behold, ye had sinned against the Lord your God, *and* had made you a molten calf: ye had turned aside quickly out of the way which the Lord had commanded you.

De 17:3 And hath gone and served other gods, and worshipped them, either the sun, or moon, or any of the host of heaven, which I have not commanded;

De 28:64 And the Lord shall scatter thee among all people, from the one end of the earth even unto the other; and there thou shalt serve other gods, which neither thou nor thy fathers have known, *even* wood and stone.

De 29:26 For they went and served other gods, and worshipped them, gods whom they knew not, and *whom* he had not given unto them:

De 31:18 And I will surely hide my face in that day for all the evils which they shall have wrought, in that they are turned unto other gods.

De 32:17 They sacrificed unto devils, not to God; to gods whom they knew not, to new *gods that* came newly up, whom your fathers feared not.

Jos 23:16 When ye have transgressed the covenant of the Lord your God, which he commanded you, and have gone and served other gods, and bowed yourselves to them; then shall the anger of the Lord be kindled against you, and ye shall perish quickly from off the good land which he hath given unto you.

Jos 24:2 And Joshua said unto all the people, Thus saith the Lord God of Israel, Your fathers dwelt on the other side of the flood in old time, *even* Terah, the father of Abraham, and the father of Nachor: and they served other gods.

Jud 2:12 And they forsook the Lord God of their fathers, which brought them out of the land of Egypt, and followed other gods, of the gods of the people that *were* round about them, and bowed themselves unto them, and provoked the Lord to anger.

Jud 2:19 And it came to pass, when the judge was dead, *that* they returned, and corrupted *themselves* more than their fathers, in following other gods to serve them, and to bow down unto them; they ceased not from their own doings, nor from their stubborn way.

Jud 3:7 And the children of Israel did evil in the sight of the Lord, and forgat the Lord their God, and served Baalim and the groves.

Jud 10:6 And the children of Israel did evil again in the sight of the Lord, and served Baalim, and Ashtaroth, and the gods of Syria, and the gods of Zidon, and the gods of Moab, and the gods of the children of Ammon, and the gods of the Philistines, and forsook the Lord, and served not him.

Jud 16:23 Then the lords of the Philistines gathered them together for to offer a great sacrifice unto Dagon their god, and to rejoice: for they said, Our god hath delivered Samson our enemy into our hand.

Jud 17:4 Yet he restored the money unto his mother; and his mother took two hundred *shekels* of silver, and gave them to the founder, who made thereof a graven image and a molten image: and they were in the house of Micah.

Jud 18:30 And the children of Dan set up the graven image: and Jonathan, the son of Gershom, the son of Manasseh, he and his sons were priests to the tribe of Dan until the day of the captivity of the land.

1 S 8:8 According to all the works which they have done since the day that I brought them up out of Egypt even unto this day, wherewith they have forsaken me, and served other gods, so do they also unto thee.

1 K 9:9 And they shall answer, Because they forsook the Lord their God, who brought forth their fathers out of the land of Egypt, and have taken hold upon other gods, and have worshipped them, and served them: therefore hath the Lord brought upon them all this evil.

1 K 11:5 For Solomon went after Ashtoreth the goddess of the Zidonians, and after Milcom the abomination of the Ammonites.

1 K 11:8 And likewise did he for all his strange wives, which burnt incense and sacrificed unto their gods.

1 K 11:33 Because that they have forsaken me, and have worshipped Ashtoreth the goddess of the Zidonians, Chemosh the god of the Moabites, and Milcom the god of the children of Ammon, and have not walked in my ways, to do *that which is* right in mine eyes, and *to keep* my statutes and my judgments, as *did* David his father.

1 K 12:32 And Jeroboam ordained a feast in the eighth month, on the fifteenth day of the month, like unto the feast that *is* in Judah, and he offered upon the altar. So did he in Bethel, sacrificing unto the calves that he had made: and he placed in Bethel the priests of the high places which he had made.

1 K 14:9 But hast done evil above all that were before thee: for thou hast gone and made thee other gods, and molten images, to provoke me to anger, and hast cast me behind thy back:

1 K 14:23 For they also built them high places, and images, and groves, on every high hill, and under every green tree.

1 K 16:31 And it came to pass, as if it had been a light thing for him to walk in the sins of Jeroboam the son of Nebat, that he took to wife Jezebel the daughter of Ethbaal king of the Zidonians, and went and served Baal, and worshipped him.

1 K 18:18 And he answered, I have not troubled Israel; but thou, and thy father's house, in that ye have forsaken the commandments of the Lord, and thou hast followed Baalim.

1 K 18:26 And they took the bullock which was given them, and they dressed *it,* and called on the name of Baal from morning even until noon, saying, O Baal, hear us. But *there was* no voice, nor any that answered. And they leaped upon the altar which was made.

1 K 22:53 For he served Baal, and worshipped him, and provoked to anger the Lord God of Israel, according to all that his father had done.

2 K 1:2 And Ahaziah fell down through a lattice in his upper chamber that *was* in Samaria, and was sick: and he sent messengers, and said unto them, Go, enquire of Baal-zebub the god of Ekron whether I shall recover of this disease.

2 K 16:4 And he sacrificed and burnt incense in the high places, and on the hills, and under every green tree.

2 K 17:7 For *so* it was, that the children of Israel had sinned against the Lord their God, which had brought them up out of the land of Egypt, from under the hand of Pharaoh king of Egypt, and had feared other gods,

2 K 17:12 For they served idols, whereof the Lord had said unto them, Ye shall not do this thing.

2 K 17:16 And they left all the commandments of the Lord their God, and made them molten images, *even* two calves, and made a grove, and worshipped all the host of heaven, and served Baal.

2 K 17:29 Howbeit every nation made gods of their own, and put *them* in the houses of the high places which the Samaritans had made, every nation in their cities wherein they dwelt.

2 K 17:41 So these nations feared the Lord, and served their graven images, both their children, and their children's children: as did their fathers, so do they unto this day.

2 K 19:37 And it came to pass, as he was worshipping in the house of Nisroch his god, that Adrammelech and Sharezer his sons smote him with the sword: and they escaped into the land of Armenia. And Esar-haddon his son reigned in his stead.

2 K 21:3 For he built up again the high places which Hezekiah his father had destroyed; and he reared up altars for Baal, and made a grove, as did Ahab king of Israel; and worshipped all the host of heaven, and served them.

2 K 21:7 And he set a graven image of the grove that he had made in the house, of which the Lord said to David, and to Solomon his son, In this house, and in Jerusalem, which I have chosen out of all tribes of Israel, will I put my name for ever:

2 K 21:21 And he walked in all the way that his father walked in, and served the idols that his father served, and worshipped them:

1 Chr 5:25 And they transgressed against the God of their fathers, and went a whoring after the gods of the people of the land, whom God destroyed before them.

2 Chr 7:22 And it shall be answered, Because they forsook the Lord God of their fathers, which brought them forth out of the land of Egypt, and laid hold on other gods, and worshipped them, and served them: therefore hath he brought all this evil upon them.

2 Chr 13:8 And now ye think to withstand the kingdom of the Lord in the hand of the sons of David; and ye *be* a great multitude, and *there are* with you golden calves, which Jeroboam made you for gods.

2 Chr 24:18 And they left the house of the Lord God of their fathers, and served groves and idols: and wrath came upon Judah and Jerusalem for this their trespass.

2 Chr 25:14 Now it came to pass, after that Amaziah was come from the slaughter of the Edomites, that he brought the gods of the children of Seir, and set them up *to be* his gods, and bowed down himself before them, and burned incense unto them.

2 Chr 28:2 For he walked in the ways of the kings of Israel, and made also molten images for Baalim.

2 Chr 28:23 For he sacrificed unto the gods of Damascus, which smote him: and he said, Because the gods of the kings of Syria help them, *therefore* will I sacrifice to them, that they may help me. But they were the ruin of him, and of all Israel.

2 Chr 33:7 And he set a carved image, the idol which he had made, in the house of God, of which God had said to David and to Solomon his son, In this house, and in Jerusalem, which I have chosen before all the tribes of Israel, will I put my name for ever:

2 Chr 33:22 But he did *that which was* evil in the sight of the Lord, as did Manasseh his father: for Amon sacrificed unto all the carved images which Manasseh his father had made, and served them;

2 Chr 34:25 Because they have forsaken me, and have burned incense unto other gods, that they might provoke me to anger with all the works of their hands; therefore my wrath shall be poured out upon this place, and shall not be quenched.

Ne 9:18 Yea, when they had made them a molten calf, and said, This *is* thy God that brought thee up out of Egypt, and had wrought great provocations;

Ps 44:20 If we have forgotten the name of our God, or stretched out our hands to a strange god;

Ps 78:58 For they provoked him to anger with their high places, and moved him to jealousy with their graven images.

Ps 106:19 They made a calf in Horeb, and worshipped the molten image.

Ps 106:36 And they served their idols: which were a snare unto them.

Is 2:8 Their land also is full of idols; they worship the work of their own hands, that which their own fingers have made:

Is 37:38 And it came to pass, as he was worshipping in the house of Nisroch his god, that Adrammelech and Sharezer his sons smote him with the sword; and they escaped into the land of Armenia: and Esar-haddon his son reigned in his stead.

Is 44:17 And the residue thereof he maketh a god, *even* his graven image: he falleth down unto it, and worshippeth *it*, and prayeth unto it, and saith, Deliver me; for thou *art* my god.

Is 57:7 Upon a lofty and high mountain hast thou set thy bed: even thither wentest thou up to offer sacrifice.

Is 65:3 A people that provoketh me to anger continually to my face; that sacrificeth in gardens, and burneth incense upon altars of brick;

Je 1:16 And I will utter my judgments against them touching all their wickedness, who have forsaken me, and have burned incense unto other gods, and worshipped the works of their own hands.

Je 3:8 And I saw, when for all the causes whereby backsliding Israel committed adultery I had put her away, and given her a bill of divorce; yet her treacherous sister Judah feared not, but went and played the harlot also.

Je 5:19 And it shall come to pass, when ye shall say, Wherefore doeth the Lord our God all these *things* unto us? then shalt thou answer them, Like as ye have forsaken me, and served strange gods in your land, so shall ye serve strangers in a land *that is* not yours.

Je 7:18 The children gather wood, and the fathers kindle the fire, and the women knead *their* dough, to make cakes to the queen of heaven, and to pour out drink offerings unto other gods, that they may provoke me to anger.

Je 8:2 And they shall spread them before the sun, and the moon, and all the host of heaven, whom they have loved, and whom they have served, and after whom they have walked, and whom they have sought, and whom they have worshipped: they shall not be gathered, nor be buried; they shall be for dung upon the face of the earth.

Je 8:19 Behold the voice of the cry of the daughter of my people because of them that dwell in a far country: *Is* not the Lord in Zion? *is* not her king in her? Why have they provoked me to anger with their graven images, *and* with strange vanities?

Je 11:10 They are turned back to the iniquities of their forefathers, which refused to hear my words; and they went after other gods to serve them: the house of Israel and the house of Judah have broken my covenant which I made with their fathers.

Je 13:10 This evil people, which refuse to hear my words, which walk in the imagination of their heart, and walk after other gods, to serve them, and to worship them, shall even be as this girdle, which is good for nothing.

Je 16:11 Then shalt thou say unto them, Because your fathers have forsaken me, saith the Lord, and have walked after other gods, and have served them, and have worshipped them, and have forsaken me, and have not kept my law;

Je 19:4 Because they have forsaken me, and have estranged this place, and have burned incense in it unto other gods, whom neither they nor their fathers have known, nor the kings of Judah, and have filled this place with the blood of innocents;

Je 44:3 Because of their wickedness which they have committed to provoke me to anger, in that they went to burn incense, *and* to serve other gods, whom they knew not, *neither* they, ye, nor your fathers.

Je 44:8 In that ye provoke me unto wrath with the works of your hands, burning incense unto other gods in the land of Egypt, whither ye be gone to dwell, that ye might cut yourselves off, and that ye might be a curse and a reproach among all the nations of the earth?

Je 44:15 Then all the men which knew that their wives had burned incense unto other gods, and all the women that stood by, a great multitude, even all the people that dwelt in the land of Egypt, in Pathros, answered Jeremiah, saying,

Eze 6:13 Then shall ye know that I *am* the Lord, when their slain *men* shall be among their idols round about their altars, upon every high hill, in all the tops of the mountains, and under every green tree, and under every thick oak, the place where they did offer sweet savour to all their idols.

Eze 8:3 And he put forth the form of an hand, and took me by a lock of mine head; and the spirit lifted me up between the earth and the heaven, and brought me in the visions of God to Jerusalem, to the door of the inner gate that looketh toward the north; where *was* the seat of the image of jealousy, which provoketh to jealousy.

Eze 14:4–5 Therefore speak unto them, and say unto them, Thus saith the Lord God; Every man of the house of Israel that setteth up his idols in his heart, and putteth the stumblingblock of his iniquity before his face, and cometh to the prophet; I the Lord will answer him that cometh according to the multitude of his idols;

That I may take the house of Israel in their own heart, because they are all estranged from me through their idols.

Eze 16:17 Thou hast also taken thy fair jewels of my gold and of my silver, which I had given thee, and madest to thyself images of men, and didst commit whoredom with them,

Eze 16:36 Thus saith the Lord God; Because thy filthiness was poured out, and thy nakedness discovered through thy whoredoms with thy lovers, and with all the idols of thy abominations, and by the blood of thy children, which thou didst give unto them;

Eze 20:16 Because they despised my judgments, and walked not in my statutes, but polluted my sabbaths: for their heart went after their idols.

Eze 20:24 Because they had not executed my judgments, but had despised my statutes, and had polluted my sabbaths, and their eyes were after their fathers' idols.

Eze 20:31 For when ye offer your gifts, when ye make your sons to pass through the fire, ye pollute yourselves with all your idols, even unto this day: and shall I be enquired of by you, O house of Israel? *As* I live, saith the Lord God, I will not be enquired of by you.

Eze 20:39 As for you, O house of Israel, thus saith the Lord God; Go ye, serve ye every one his idols, and hereafter *also,* if ye will not hearken unto me: but pollute ye my holy name no more with your gifts, and with your idols.

Eze 22:4 Thou art become guilty in thy blood that thou hast shed; and hast defiled thyself in thine idols which thou hast made; and thou hast caused thy days to draw near, and art come *even* unto thy years: therefore have I made thee a reproach unto the heathen, and a mocking to all countries.

Eze 23:7 Thus she committed her whoredoms with them, with all them *that were* the chosen men of Assyria, and with all on whom she doted: with all their idols she defiled herself.

Eze 23:30 I will do these *things* unto thee, because thou hast gone a whoring after the heathen, *and* because thou art polluted with their idols.

Eze 23:37 That they have committed adultery, and blood is in their hands, and with their idols have they committed adultery, and have also caused their sons, whom they bare unto me, to pass for them through *the fire,* to devour *them.*

Eze 33:25 Wherefore say unto them, Thus saith the Lord God; Ye eat with the blood, and lift up your eyes toward your idols, and shed blood: and shall ye possess the land?

Eze 36:18 Wherefore I poured my fury upon them for the blood that they had shed upon the land, and for their idols *wherewith* they had polluted it:

Eze 44:10 And the Levites that are gone away far from me, when Israel went astray, which went astray away from me after their idols; they shall even bear their iniquity.

Da 3:7 Therefore at that time, when all the people heard the sound of the cornet, flute, harp, sackbut, psaltery, and all kinds of musick, all the people, the nations, and the languages, fell down *and* worshipped the golden image that Nebuchadnezzar the king had set up.

Da 5:4 They drank wine, and praised the gods of gold, and of silver, of brass, of iron, of wood, and of stone.

Da 5:23 But hast lifted up thyself against the Lord of heaven; and they have brought the vessels of his house before thee, and thou, and thy lords, thy wives, and thy concubines, have drunk wine in them; and thou hast praised the gods of silver, and gold, of brass, iron, wood, and stone, which see not, nor hear, nor know: and the God in whose hand thy breath *is,* and whose *are* all thy ways, hast thou not glorified:

Da 11:38 But in his estate shall he honour the God of forces: and a god whom his fathers knew not shall he honour with gold, and silver, and with precious stones, and pleasant things.

Ho 2:13 And I will visit upon her the days of Baalim, wherein she burned incense to them, and she decked herself with her earrings and her jewels, and she went after her lovers, and forgat me, saith the Lord.

Ho 3:1 Then said the Lord unto me, Go yet, love a woman beloved of *her* friend, yet an adulteress, according to the love of the Lord toward the children of Israel, who look to other gods, and love flagons of wine.

Ho 4:17 Ephraim *is* joined to idols: let him alone.

Ho 9:10 I found Israel like grapes in the wilderness; I saw your fathers as the firstripe in the fig tree at her first time: *but* they went to Baal-peor, and separated themselves unto *that*

shame; and *their* abominations were according as they loved.

Ho 11:2 *As* they called them, so they went from them: they sacrificed unto Baalim, and burned incense to graven images.

Am 5:26 But ye have borne the tabernacle of your Moloch and Chiun your images, the star of your god, which ye made to yourselves.

Am 8:14 They that swear by the sin of Samaria, and say, Thy god, O Dan, liveth; and, The manner of Beer-sheba liveth; even they shall fall, and never rise up again.

Jona 1:5 Then the mariners were afraid, and cried every man unto his god, and cast forth the wares that *were* in the ship into the sea, to lighten *it* of them. But Jonah was gone down into the sides of the ship; and he lay, and was fast asleep.

Hab 1:16 Therefore they sacrifice unto their net, and burn incense unto their drag; because by them their portion *is* fat, and their meat plenteous.

Ac 7:41 And they made a calf in those days, and offered sacrifice unto the idol, and rejoiced in the works of their own hands.

Ac 17:16 Now while Paul waited for them at Athens, his spirit was stirred in him, when he saw the city wholly given to idolatry.

Ac 19:27 So that not only this our craft is in danger to be set at nought; but also that the temple of the great goddess Diana should be despised, and her magnificence should be destroyed, whom all Asia and the world worshippeth.

Ro 1:25 Who changed the truth of God into a lie, and worshipped and served the creature more than the Creator, who is blessed for ever. Amen.

1 Co 5:11 But now I have written unto you not to keep company, if any man that is called a brother be a fornicator, or covetous, or an idolater, or a railer, or a drunkard, or an extortioner; with such an one no not to eat.

1 Co 10:7 Neither be ye idolaters, as *were* some of them; as it is written, The people sat down to eat and drink, and rose up to play.

Ga 4:8 Howbeit then, when ye knew not God, ye did service unto them which by nature are no gods.

1 Pe 4:3 For the time past of *our* life may suffice us to have wrought the will of the Gentiles, when we walked in lasciviousness, lusts, excess of wine, revellings, banquetings, and abominable idolatries:

Re 13:4 And they worshipped the dragon which gave power unto the beast: and they worshipped the beast, saying, Who *is* like unto the beast? who is able to make war with him?

Re 16:2 And the first went, and poured out his vial upon the earth; and there fell a noisome and grievous sore upon the men which had the mark of the beast, and *upon* them which worshipped his image.

5. Making of Idols

Is 31:7 For in that day every man shall cast away his idols of silver, and his idols of gold, which your own hands have made unto you *for* a sin.

Is 40:19 The workman melteth a graven image, and the goldsmith spreadeth it over with gold, and casteth silver chains.

Is 41:7 So the carpenter encouraged the goldsmith, *and* he that smootheth *with* the hammer him that smote the anvil, saying, It is ready for the sodering: and he fastened it with nails, *that* it should not be moved.

Is 44:10 Who hath formed a god, or molten a graven image *that* is profitable for nothing?

Is 44:15 Then shall it be for a man to burn: for he will take thereof, and warm himself; yea, he kindleth *it,* and baketh bread; yea, he maketh a god, and worshippeth *it;* he maketh it a graven image, and falleth down thereto.

Is 45:16 They shall be ashamed, and also confounded, all of them: they shall go to confusion together *that are* makers of idols.

Is 46:6 They lavish gold out of the bag, and weigh silver in the balance, *and* hire a goldsmith; and he maketh it a god: they fall down, yea, they worship.

Je 1:16 And I will utter my judgments against them touching all their wickedness, who have forsaken me, and have burned incense unto other gods, and worshipped the works of their own hands.

Je 2:11 Hath a nation changed *their* gods, which *are* yet no gods? but my people have changed their glory for *that which* doth not profit.

Je 2:27 Saying to a stock, Thou *art* my father; and to a stone, Thou hast brought me forth: for they have turned *their* back unto me, and not *their* face: but in the time of their trouble they will say, Arise, and save us.

Je 3:9 And it came to pass through the lightness of her whoredom, that she defiled the land, and committed adultery with stones and with stocks.

Je 10:3 For the customs of the people *are* vain: for *one* cutteth a tree out of the forest, the work of the hands of the workman, with the axe.

Je 16:20 Shall a man make gods unto himself, and they *are* no gods?

Je 44:8 In that ye provoke me unto wrath with the works of your hands, burning incense unto other gods in the land of Egypt, whither ye be gone to dwell, that ye might cut yourselves off, and that ye might be a curse and a reproach among all the nations of the earth?

Eze 7:20 As for the beauty of his ornament, he set it in majesty: but they made the images of their abominations *and* of their detestable things therein: therefore have I set it far from them.

Eze 16:17 Thou hast also taken thy fair jewels of my gold and of my silver, which I had given thee, and madest to thyself images of men, and didst commit whoredom with them,

Eze 22:3 Then say thou, Thus saith the Lord God, The city sheddeth blood in the midst of it, that her time may come, and maketh idols against herself to defile herself.

Da 3:1 Nebuchadnezzar the king made an image of gold, whose height *was* threescore cubits, *and* the breadth thereof six cubits: he set it up in the plain of Dura, in the province of Babylon.

Ho 8:4 They have set up kings, but not by me: they have made princes, and I knew *it* not: of their silver and their gold have they made them idols, that they may be cut off.

Ho 10:1 Israel *is* an empty vine, he bringeth forth fruit unto himself: according to the multitude of his fruit he hath increased the altars; according to the goodness of his land they have made goodly images.

Ho 13:2 And now they sin more and more, and have made them molten images of their silver, *and* idols according to their own understanding, all of it the work of the craftsmen: they say of them, Let the men that sacrifice kiss the calves.

Ho 14:3 Asshur shall not save us; we will not ride upon horses: neither will we say any more to the work of our hands, *Ye are* our gods: for in thee the fatherless findeth mercy.

Am 5:26 But ye have borne the tabernacle of your Moloch and Chiun your images, the star of your god, which ye made to yourselves.

Mi 5:13 Thy graven images also will I cut off, and thy standing images out of the midst of thee; and thou shalt no more worship the work of thine hands.

Hab 2:18 What profiteth the graven image that the maker thereof hath graven it; the molten image, and a teacher of lies, that the maker of his work trusteth therein, to make dumb idols?

Ac 7:43 Yea, ye took up the tabernacle of Moloch, and the star of your god Remphan, figures which ye made to worship them: and I will carry you away beyond Babylon.

Ac 17:29 Forasmuch then as we are the offspring of God, we ought not to think that the Godhead is like unto gold, or silver, or stone, graven by art and man's device.

Ac 19:24 For a certain *man* named Demetrius, a silversmith, which made silver shrines for Diana, brought no small gain unto the craftsmen;

Ro 1:23 And changed the glory of the uncorruptible God into an image made like to corruptible man, and to birds, and fourfooted beasts, and creeping things.

Re 9:20 And the rest of the men which were not killed by these plagues yet repented not of the works of their hands, that they should not worship devils, and idols of gold, and silver, and brass, and stone, and of wood: which neither can see, nor hear, nor walk:

Re 13:14 And deceiveth them that dwell on the earth by *the means of* those miracles which he had power to do in the sight of the beast; saying to them that dwell on the earth, that they should make an image to the beast, which had the wound by a sword, and did live.

6. Uselessness of Idols

Je 10:5 They *are* upright as the palm tree, but speak not: they must needs be borne, because they cannot go. Be not afraid of them; for they cannot do evil, neither also *is it* in them to do good.

Je 10:15 They *are* vanity, *and* the work of errors: in the time of their visitation they shall perish.

Je 14:22 Are there *any* among the vanities of the Gentiles that can cause rain? or can the heavens give showers? *art* not thou he, O Lord our God? therefore we will wait upon thee: for thou hast made all these *things*.

Je 50:38 A drought *is* upon her waters; and they shall be dried up: for it *is* the land of graven images, and they are mad upon *their* idols.

Je 51:17 Every man is brutish by *his* knowledge; every founder is confounded by the graven image: for his molten image *is* falsehood, and *there is* no breath in them.

Da 5:23 But hast lifted up thyself against the Lord of heaven; and they have brought the vessels of his house before thee, and thou, and thy lords, thy wives, and thy concubines, have drunk wine in them; and thou hast praised the gods of silver, and gold, of brass, iron, wood, and stone, which see not, nor hear, nor know: and the God in whose hand thy breath *is*, and whose *are* all thy ways, hast thou not glorified:

Ho 4:12 My people ask counsel at their stocks, and their staff declareth unto them: for the spirit of whoredoms hath caused *them* to err, and they have gone a whoring from under their God.

Ho 8:6 For from Israel *was* it also: the workman made it; therefore it *is* not God: but the calf of Samaria shall be broken in pieces.

Ho 13:2 And now they sin more and more, and have made them molten images of their silver, *and* idols according to their own understanding, all of it the work of the craftsmen: they say of them, Let the men that sacrifice kiss the calves.

Hab 2:18 What profiteth the graven image that the maker thereof hath graven it; the molten image, and a teacher of lies, that the maker of his work trusteth therein, to make dumb idols?

Zec 10:2 For the idols have spoken vanity, and the diviners have seen a lie, and have told false dreams; they comfort in vain: therefore they went their way as a flock, they were troubled, because *there was* no shepherd.

Ac 17:29 Forasmuch then as we are the offspring of God, we ought not to think that the Godhead is like unto gold, or silver, or stone, graven by art and man's device.

1 Co 8:4 As concerning therefore the eating of those things that are offered in sacrifice unto idols, we know that an idol *is* nothing in the world, and that *there is* none other God but one.

1 Co 10:19 What say I then? that the idol is any thing, or that which is offered in sacrifice to idols is any thing?

7. Places

a. Altars

Ex 32:5; De 12:3; 1 K 16:32; 18:26; 2 K 16:10; 21:4; 23:12; 2 Chr 23:17; 28:24; 30:14; 31:1; 33:5, 15; 34:4; Is 17:8; 27:9; 65:3; Je 11:13; 17:2; Eze 6:4, 13; Ho

8:11; 10:1, 8; 12:11; Am 2:8; 3:14; Ac 17:23

b. Temples

1 S 5:2; 1 K 12:31; 2 K 5:18; 10:21; 1 Chr 10:10; 2 Chr 36:7; Ezr 1:7; 5:14; Da 1:2; Jl 3:5; Ac 19:27; 1 Co 8:10

c. High Places

Nu 22:41; 1 K 11:7; 12:31; 15:14; 22:43; 2 K 12:3; 14:4; 15:4, 35; 16:4; 17:9, 29; 18:4; 21:3; 23:5; 2 Chr 11:15; 15:17; 17:6; 20:33; 28:25; 32:12; 33:3, 17; 34:3; Is 57:7; Eze 36:2

d. Groves, Asherah, Asherim, places where shrines were located

Ex 34:13; De 12:2; 16:21; Jud 6:25; 1 K 14:15, 23; 16:33; 2 K 13:6; 16:4; 17:10; 18:4; 21:3; 23:4, 14; 2 Chr 14:3; 15:16; 17:6; 24:18; 31:1; 33:3; 34:4; Is 1:29; 17:8; 57:5; Je 3:6, 13; 17:2; Eze 6:13; Ho 4:13; Mi 5:14

See **GODS, WORSHIP**

IGNORANCE, *lack of knowledge*

1. Human

BREVITY OF LIFE LIMITS KNOWLEDGE

Jb 8:9 (For we *are but of* yesterday, and know nothing, because our days upon earth *are* a shadow:)

Ps 73:22 So foolish *was* I, and ignorant: I was *as* a beast before thee.

THE FUTURE HIDDEN

Ec 8:7 For he knoweth not that which shall be: for who can tell him when it shall be?

Ec 9:12 For man also knoweth not his time: as the fishes that are taken in an evil net, and as the birds that are caught in the snare; so *are* the sons of men snared in an evil time, when it falleth suddenly upon them.

LIFE MYSTERIOUS

Ec 11:5 As thou knowest not what *is* the way of the spirit, *nor* how the bones *do grow* in the womb of her that is with child: even so thou knowest not the works of God who maketh all.

NATURE AND GRACE MYSTERIOUS

Jn 3:8 The wind bloweth where it listeth, and thou hearest the sound thereof, but canst not tell whence it cometh, and whither it goeth: so is every one that is born of the Spirit.

2. Spiritual

Is 1:3 The ox knoweth his owner, and the ass his master's crib: *but* Israel doth not know, my people doth not consider.

Is 59:8 The way of peace they know not; and *there is* no judgment in their goings: they have made them crooked paths: whosoever goeth therein shall not know peace.

Je 5:4 Therefore I said, Surely these *are* poor; they are foolish: for they know not the way of the LORD, *nor* the judgment of their God.

Je 49:7 Concerning Edom, thus saith the LORD of hosts; *Is* wisdom no more in Teman? is counsel perished from the prudent? is their wisdom vanished?

Am 3:10 For they know not to do right, saith the LORD, who store up violence and robbery in their palaces.

Mi 4:12 But they know not the thoughts of the LORD, neither understand they his counsel: for he shall gather them as the sheaves into the floor.

Ro 10:3 For they being ignorant of God's righteousness, and going about to establish their own righteousness, have not submitted themselves unto the righteousness of God.

Ep 4:18 Having the understanding darkened, being alienated from the life of God through the ignorance that is in them, because of the blindness of their heart:

1 Pe 1:14 As obedient children, not fashioning yourselves according to the former lusts in your ignorance:

3. Concerning God

Ex 5:2; Jud 2:10; 1 S 2:11–12; 3:7; 1 K 20:23; 2 K 17:26; 19:25; Jb 4:21; 18:21; 36:12, 26; Ps 14:4; 53:4; 79:6; 95:10; 147:20; Pr 5:23; 30:3; Is 1:3; 5:13; 40:28; 45:4–5; 56:10; Je 2:8; 4:22; 8:7; 9:3;

10:25; Ho 4:1; 5:4; 11:3; Mt 11:27; Lu 10:22; Jn 4:10, 22; 7:28; 8:19, 55; 15:21; 16:3; 17:25; Ac 13:27; 17:23; 1 Co 1:21; 15:35; Ga 4:8; 1 Th 4:5; 2 Th 1:8; 2 Ti 3:7; He 3:10; 1 Jn 4:8

4. Concerning Christ

Is 53:3; Mt 11:27; 14:1; Mk 6:2, 15; 8:28; Lu 5:21; 9:9, 19; 10:22; 24:16; Jn 1:10, 26, 31; 4:10, 25; 5:13; 6:42; 7:41; 8:19, 25; 9:21, 30; 12:34; 14:9; 16:3; 20:14; 21:4; Ac 13:27; 26:9; 1 Co 2:8; 1 Jn 3:1, 6

5. Willful

Jb 21:14; Zec 7:11, 12; Mt 13:15; Ro 1:28; 2 Pe 3:5

See **KNOWLEDGE**

IMAGE OF GOD, Christ

2 Co 4:4 In whom the god of this world hath blinded the minds of them which believe not, lest the light of the glorious gospel of Christ, who is the image of God, should shine unto them.

Ph 2:6 Who, being in the form of God, thought it not robbery to be equal with God:

Col 1:15 Who is the image of the invisible God, the firstborn of every creature:

He 1:3 Who being the brightness of *his* glory, and the express image of his person, and upholding all things by the word of his power, when he had by himself purged our sins, sat down on the right hand of the Majesty on high;

See **CHRIST**

IMAGINATION See **MIND**

IMITATION, SPIRITUAL

1 Co 4:16 Wherefore I beseech you, be ye followers of me.

Ph 4:9 Those things, which ye have both learned, and received, and heard, and seen in me, do: and the God of peace shall be with you.

1 Th 1:6 And ye became followers of us, and of the Lord, having received the word in much affliction, with joy of the Holy Ghost:

2 Th 3:9 Not because we have not power, but to make ourselves an ensample unto you to follow us.

He 6:12 That ye be not slothful, but followers of them who through faith and patience inherit the promises.

He 13:7 Remember them which have the rule over you, who have spoken unto you the word of God: whose faith follow, considering the end of *their* conversation.

He 13:17 Obey them that have the rule over you, and submit yourselves: for they watch for your souls, as they that must give account, that they may do it with joy, and not with grief: for that *is* unprofitable for you.

IMMANUEL, *God with us*

Is 7:14 Therefore the Lord himself shall give you a sign; Behold, a virgin shall conceive, and bear a son, and shall call his name Immanuel.

Is 8:8 And he shall pass through Judah; he shall overflow and go over, he shall reach *even* to the neck; and the stretching out of his wings shall fill the breadth of thy land, O Immanuel.

Mt 1:23 Behold, a virgin shall be with child, and shall bring forth a son, and they shall call his name Emmanuel, which being interpreted is, God with us.

See **TITLES AND NAMES**

IMMATURITY, *carnal, young in faith*

INABILITY TO RECEIVE STRONG DOCTRINE

1 Co 3:1–2 And I, brethren, could not speak unto you as unto spiritual, but as unto carnal, *even* as unto babes in Christ.

I have fed you with milk, and not with meat: for hitherto ye were not able *to bear it*, neither yet now are ye able.

1 Co 14:20 Brethren, be not children in understanding: howbeit in malice be ye children, but in understanding be men.

NECESSITY OF TUTORING

Ga 4:1–3 Now I say, *That* the heir, as long as he is a child, differeth nothing from a servant, though he be lord of all;

But is under tutors and governors until the time appointed of the father.

Even so we, when we were children, were in bondage under the elements of the world:

INSTABILITY OF FAITH

Ep 4:14 That we *henceforth* be no more children, tossed to and fro, and carried about with every wind of doctrine, by the sleight of men, *and* cunning craftiness, whereby they lie in wait to deceive;

CONTINUANCE IN THE PRIMARY DEPARTMENT

He 5:12 For when for the time ye ought to be teachers, ye have need that one teach you again which *be* the first principles of the oracles of God; and are become such as have need of milk, and not of strong meat.

1 Pe 2:2 As newborn babes, desire the sincere milk of the word, that ye may grow thereby:

See **DISCIPLESHIP, MATURITY**

IMMINENCE, *of death and judgment*

Je 48:16; Eze 11:3; 12:25; 30:3; Jl 1:15; 2:1; 3:14; Am 8:2; Obad 15; Zep 1:7, 14; Mt 25:6; Lu 3:8; 12:20, 40; Ph 4:5; He 10:37; Ja 5:9; 1 Pe 4:7; Re 22:10, 20

See **READINESS, SECOND COMING**

IMMORTALITY, *endless life*

Jb 19:26 And *though* after my skin worms destroy this *body*, yet in my flesh shall I see God:

Ps 49:15 But God will redeem my soul from the power of the grave: for he shall receive me. Selah.

Lu 20:36 Neither can they die any more: for they are equal unto the angels; and are the children of God, being the children of the resurrection.

Jn 6:50 This is the bread which cometh down from heaven, that a man may eat thereof, and not die.

Jn 8:51 Verily, verily, I say unto you, If a man keep my saying, he shall never see death.

Jn 11:26 And whosoever liveth and believeth in me shall never die. Believest thou this?

Ro 2:7 To them who by patient continuance in well doing seek for glory and honour and immortality, eternal life:

1 Co 15:53 For this corruptible must put on incorruption, and this mortal *must* put on immortality.

2 Co 5:1 For we know that if our earthly house of *this* tabernacle were dissolved, we have a building of God, an house not made with hands, eternal in the heavens.

1 Th 4:17 Then we which are alive *and* remain shall be caught up together with them in the clouds, to meet the Lord in the air: and so shall we ever be with the Lord.

2 Ti 1:10 But is now made manifest by the appearing of our Saviour Jesus Christ, who hath abolished death, and hath brought life and immortality to light through the gospel:

Of the Soul

Ec 12:7 Then shall the dust return to the earth as it was: and the spirit shall return unto God who gave it.

Mt 10:28 And fear not them which kill the body, but are not able to kill the soul: but rather fear him which is able to destroy both soul and body in hell.

Lu 12:20 But God said unto him, *Thou* fool, this night thy soul shall be required of thee: then whose shall those things be, which thou hast provided?

Re 20:4 And I saw thrones, and they sat upon them, and judgment was given unto them: and *I saw* the souls of them that were beheaded for the witness of Jesus, and for the word of God, and which had not worshipped the beast, neither his image, neither had received *his* mark upon their foreheads, or in their hands; and they lived and reigned with Christ a thousand years.

See **FUTURE LIFE, MORTALITY**

IMMUTABILITY, *unchangeable*

1. Divine

Nu 23:19 God *is* not a man, that he should lie; neither the son of man, that he should repent: hath he said, and shall he not do *it?* or hath he spoken, and shall he not make it good?

Nu 23:27 And Balak said unto Balaam, Come, I pray thee, I will bring thee unto another place; peradventure it will please God that thou mayest curse me them from thence.

De 7:9 Know therefore that the LORD thy God, he *is* God, the faithful God, which keepeth covenant and mercy with them that love him and keep his commandments to a thousand generations;

1 S 15:29 And also the Strength of Israel will not lie nor repent: for he *is* not a man, that he should repent.

Jb 23:13 But he *is* in one *mind,* and who can turn him? and *what* his soul desireth, even *that* he doeth.

Ps 33:11 The counsel of the LORD standeth for ever, the thoughts of his heart to all generations.

Ps 90:2 Before the mountains were brought forth, or ever thou hadst formed the earth and the world, even from everlasting to everlasting, thou *art* God.

Ps 102:12 But thou, O LORD, shalt endure for ever; and thy remembrance unto all generations.

Ps 102:27 But thou *art* the same, and thy years shall have no end.

Ps 103:17 But the mercy of the LORD *is* from everlasting to everlasting upon them that fear him, and his righteousness unto children's children;

Ec 3:14 I know that, whatsoever God doeth, it shall be for ever: nothing can be put to it, nor any thing taken from it: and God doeth *it,* that *men* should fear before him.

Is 14:24 The LORD of hosts hath sworn, saying, Surely as I have thought, so shall it come to pass; and as I have purposed, *so* shall it stand:

Eze 24:14 I the LORD have spoken *it:* it shall come to pass, and I will do *it;* I will not go back, neither will I spare, neither will I repent; according to thy ways, and according to thy doings, shall they judge thee, saith the Lord GOD.

Da 7:14 And there was given him dominion, and glory, and a kingdom, that all people, nations, and languages, should serve him: his dominion *is* an everlasting dominion, which shall not pass away, and his kingdom *that* which shall not be destroyed.

Mal 3:6 I *am* the LORD, I change not; therefore ye sons of Jacob are not consumed.

Ro 11:29 For the gifts and calling of God *are* without repentance.

2 Ti 2:19 Nevertheless the foundation of God standeth sure, having this seal, The Lord knoweth them that are his. And, Let every one that nameth the name of Christ depart from iniquity.

He 1:12 And as a vesture shalt thou fold them up, and they shall be changed: but thou art the same, and thy years shall not fail.

He 6:17 Wherein God, willing more abundantly to shew unto the heirs of promise the immutability of his counsel, confirmed *it* by an oath:

He 7:21 (For those priests were made without an oath; but this with an oath by him that said unto him, The Lord sware and will not repent, Thou *art* a priest for ever after the order of Melchisedec:)

He 13:8 Jesus Christ the same yesterday, and to day, and for ever.

Ja 1:17 Every good gift and every perfect gift is from above, and cometh down from the Father of lights, with whom is no variableness, neither shadow of turning.

2. God Eternal

Ge 21:33 And *Abraham* planted a grove in Beer-sheba, and called there on the name of the LORD, the everlasting God.

Ex 3:15 And God said moreover unto Moses, Thus shalt thou say unto the children of Israel, The LORD God of your fathers, the God of Abraham, the God of Isaac, and the God of Jacob, hath sent me unto you: this *is* my name for ever, and this *is* my memorial unto all generations.

Ex 15:18 The LORD shall reign for ever and ever.

De 32:40 For I lift up my hand to heaven, and say, I live for ever.

De 33:27 The eternal God *is* thy refuge, and underneath *are* the everlasting arms: and he shall thrust out the enemy from before thee; and shall say, Destroy *them.*

Jb 10:5 *Are* thy days as the days of man? *are* thy years as man's days,

Jb 36:26 Behold, God *is* great, and we know *him* not, neither can the number of his years be searched out.

Ps 9:7 But the LORD shall endure for ever: he hath prepared his throne for judgment.

Ps 41:13 Blessed *be* the LORD God of Israel from everlasting, and to everlasting. Amen, and Amen.

Ps 45:6 Thy throne, O God, *is* for ever and ever: the sceptre of thy kingdom *is* a right sceptre.

Ps 55:19 God shall hear, and afflict them, even he that abideth of old. Selah. Because they have no changes, therefore they fear not God.

Ps 90:2 Before the mountains were brought forth, or ever thou hadst formed the earth and the world, even from everlasting to everlasting, thou *art* God.

Ps 92:8 But thou, LORD, *art most* high for evermore.

Ps 93:2 Thy throne *is* established of old: thou *art* from everlasting.

Ps 102:12 But thou, O LORD, shalt endure for ever; and thy remembrance unto all generations.

Ps 102:24 I said, O my God, take me not away in the midst of my days: thy years *are* throughout all generations.

Ps 111:3 His work *is* honourable and glorious: and his righteousness endureth for ever.

Ps 135:13 Thy name, O LORD, *endureth* for ever; *and* thy memorial, O LORD, throughout all generations.

Ps 145:13 Thy kingdom *is* an everlasting kingdom, and thy dominion *endureth* throughout all generations.

Ps 146:10 The LORD shall reign for ever, *even* thy God, O Zion, unto all generations. Praise ye the LORD.

Is 40:28 Hast thou not known? hast thou not heard, *that* the everlasting God, the LORD, the Creator of the ends of the earth, fainteth not, neither is weary? *there is* no searching of his understanding.

Is 41:4 Who hath wrought and done *it,* calling the generations from the beginning? I the LORD, the first, and with the last; I *am* he.

Is 43:13 Yea, before the day *was* I *am* he; and *there is* none that can deliver out of my hand: I will work, and who shall let it?

Is 44:6 Thus saith the LORD the King of Israel, and his redeemer the LORD of hosts; I *am* the first, and I *am* the last; and beside me *there is* no God.

Is 48:12 Hearken unto me, O Jacob and Israel, my called; I *am* he; I *am* the first, I also *am* the last.

Is 57:15 For thus saith the high and lofty One that inhabiteth eternity, whose name *is* Holy; I dwell in the high and holy *place,* with him also *that is* of a contrite and humble spirit, to revive the spirit of the humble, and to revive the heart of the contrite ones.

Is 63:16 Doubtless thou *art* our father, though Abraham be ignorant of us, and Israel acknowledge us not: thou, O LORD, *art* our father, our redeemer; thy name *is* from everlasting.

Lam 5:19 Thou, O LORD, remainest for ever; thy throne from generation to generation.

Da 4:34 And at the end of the days I Nebuchadnezzar lifted up mine eyes unto heaven, and mine understanding returned unto me, and I blessed the most High, and I praised and honoured him that liveth for ever, whose dominion *is* an everlasting dominion, and his kingdom *is* from generation to generation:

Da 7:9 I beheld till the thrones were cast down, and the Ancient of days did sit, whose garment *was* white as snow, and the hair of his head like the pure

wool: his throne *was like* the fiery flame, *and* his wheels *as* burning fire.

Da 7:22 Until the Ancient of days came, and judgment was given to the saints of the most High; and the time came that the saints possessed the kingdom.

Da 12:7 And I heard the man clothed in linen, which *was* upon the waters of the river, when he held up his right hand and his left hand unto heaven, and sware by him that liveth for ever that *it shall be* for a time, times, and an half; and when he shall have accomplished to scatter the power of the holy people, all these *things* shall be finished.

Hab 1:12 *Art* thou not from everlasting, O LORD my God, mine Holy One? we shall not die. O LORD, thou hast ordained them for judgment; and, O mighty God, thou hast established them for correction.

Ro 16:26 But now is made manifest, and by the scriptures of the prophets, according to the commandment of the everlasting God, made known to all nations for the obedience of faith:

1 Ti 1:17 Now unto the King eternal, immortal, invisible, the only wise God, *be* honour and glory for ever and ever. Amen.

He 1:11 They shall perish; but thou remainest; and they all shall wax old as doth a garment;

2 Pe 3:8 But, beloved, be not ignorant of this one thing, that one day *is* with the Lord as a thousand years, and a thousand years as one day.

Jude 25 To the only wise God our Saviour, *be* glory and majesty, dominion and power, both now and ever. Amen.

Re 1:4 John to the seven churches which are in Asia: Grace *be* unto you, and peace, from him which is, and which was, and which is to come; and from the seven Spirits which are before his throne;

Re 1:8 I am Alpha and Omega, the beginning and the ending, saith the Lord, which is, and which was, and which is to come, the Almighty.

Re 4:8 And the four beasts had each of them six wings about *him;* and *they* *were* full of eyes within: and they rest not day and night, saying, Holy, holy, holy, Lord God Almighty, which was, and is, and is to come.

Re 5:14 And the four beasts said, Amen. And the four *and* twenty elders fell down and worshipped him that liveth for ever and ever.

Re 7:12 Saying, Amen: Blessing, and glory, and wisdom, and thanksgiving, and honour, and power, and might, *be* unto our God for ever and ever. Amen.

Re 10:6 And sware by him that liveth for ever and ever, who created heaven, and the things that therein are, and the earth, and the things that therein are, and the sea, and the things which are therein, that there should be time no longer:

Re 11:17 Saying, We give thee thanks, O Lord God Almighty, which art, and wast, and art to come; because thou hast taken to thee thy great power, and hast reigned.

Re 15:7 And one of the four beasts gave unto the seven angels seven golden vials full of the wrath of God, who liveth for ever and ever.

Re 16:5 And I heard the angel of the waters say, Thou art righteous, O Lord, which art, and wast, and shalt be, because thou hast judged thus.

Re 21:6 And he said unto me, It is done. I am Alpha and Omega, the beginning and the end. I will give unto him that is athirst of the fountain of the water of life freely.

3. Divine Counsels

Ps 33:11; Pr 19:21; Is 14:27; 25:1; 46:10; Je 4:28; Da 4:35; Ac 5:39; Ep 1:11; He 6:17

4. Eternal Kingdom of God and Christ

2 S 7:16 And thine house and thy kingdom shall be established for ever before thee: thy throne shall be established for ever.

1 Chr 17:12 He shall build me an house, and I will stablish his throne for ever.

Ps 72:5 They shall fear thee as long as the sun and moon endure, throughout all generations.

Ps 89:29 His seed also will I make *to endure* for ever, and his throne as the days of heaven.

Ps 89:36 His seed shall endure for ever, and his throne as the sun before me.

Ps 145:13 Thy kingdom *is* an everlasting kingdom, and thy dominion *endureth* throughout all generations.

Ps 146:10 The LORD shall reign for ever, *even* thy God, O Zion, unto all generations. Praise ye the LORD.

Is 9:7 Of the increase of *his* government and peace *there shall be* no end, upon the throne of David, and upon his kingdom, to order it, and to establish it with judgment and with justice from henceforth even for ever. The zeal of the LORD of hosts will perform this.

Eze 37:25 And they shall dwell in the land that I have given unto Jacob my servant, wherein your fathers have dwelt; and they shall dwell therein, *even* they, and their children, and their children's children for ever: and my servant David *shall be* their prince for ever.

Da 2:44 And in the days of these kings shall the God of heaven set up a kingdom, which shall never be destroyed: and the kingdom shall not be left to other people, *but* it shall break in pieces and consume all these kingdoms, and it shall stand for ever.

Da 4:3 How great *are* his signs! and how mighty *are* his wonders! his kingdom *is* an everlasting kingdom, and his dominion *is* from generation to generation.

Da 4:34 And at the end of the days I Nebuchadnezzar lifted up mine eyes unto heaven, and mine understanding returned unto d the most High, and I praised and honoured him that liveth for ever, whose dominion *is* an everlasting dominion, and his kingdom *is* from generation to generation:

Da 6:26 I make a decree, That in every dominion of my kingdom men tremble and fear before the God of

Daniel: for he is the living God, and stedfast for ever, and his kingdom *that* which shall not be destroyed, and his dominion *shall be even* unto the end.

Da 7:13–14 I saw in the night visions, and, behold, *one* like the Son of man came with the clouds of heaven, and came to the Ancient of days, and they brought him near before him.

Da 7:27 And the kingdom and dominion, and the greatness of the kingdom under the whole heaven, shall be given to the people of the saints of the most High, whose kingdom *is* an everlasting kingdom, and all dominions shall serve and obey him.

Mi 4:7 And I will make her that halted a remnant, and her that was cast far off a strong nation: and the LORD shall reign over them in mount Zion from henceforth, even for ever.

Lu 1:32–33 He shall be great, and shall be called the Son of the Highest: and the Lord God shall give unto him the throne of his father David:

And he shall reign over the house of Jacob for ever; and of his kingdom there shall be no end.

He 12:28 Wherefore we receiving a kingdom which cannot be moved, let us have grace, whereby we may serve God acceptably with reverence and godly fear:

2 Pe 1:11 For so an entrance shall be ministered unto you abundantly into the everlasting kingdom of our Lord and Saviour Jesus Christ.

Re 11:15 And the seventh angel sounded; and there were great voices in heaven, saying, The kingdoms of this world are become *the kingdoms* of our Lord, and of his Christ; and he shall reign for ever and ever.

See **KINGDOM, MUTABILITY**

IMPARTIALITY

1. In Favors Bestowed

Ex 30:15 The rich shall not give more, and the poor shall not give less than half a shekel, when *they* give an offering unto the LORD, to make an atonement for your souls.

Jb 34:18–19 *Is it fit* to say to a king, *Thou art* wicked? *and* to princes, *Ye are* ungodly?

How much less to him that accepteth not the persons of princes, nor regardeth the rich more than the poor? for they all *are* the work of his hands.

Is 56:4 For thus saith the LORD unto the eunuchs that keep my sabbaths, and choose *the things* that please me, and take hold of my covenant;

Eze 47:22 And it shall come to pass, *that* ye shall divide it by lot for an inheritance unto you, and to the strangers that sojourn among you, which shall beget children among you: and they shall be unto you as born in the country among the children of Israel; they shall have inheritance with you among the tribes of Israel.

Mt 5:45 That ye may be the children of your Father which is in heaven: for he maketh his sun to rise on the evil and on the good, and sendeth rain on the just and on the unjust.

Mt 20:14 Take *that* thine *is,* and go thy way: I will give unto this last, even as unto thee.

Ac 10:34–35 Then Peter opened *his* mouth, and said, Of a truth I perceive that God is no respecter of persons:

But in every nation he that feareth him, and worketh righteousness, is accepted with him.

Ac 15:9 And put no difference between us and them, purifying their hearts by faith.

Ro 2:11 For there is no respect of persons with God.

Ro 10:12 For there is no difference between the Jew and the Greek: for the same Lord over all is rich unto all that call upon him.

Ga 2:6 But of these who seemed to be somewhat, (whatsoever they were, it maketh no matter to me: God accepteth no man's person:) for they who seemed *to be somewhat* in conference added nothing to me:

Ep 6:9 And, ye masters, do the same things unto them, forbearing threatening: knowing that your Master also is in heaven; neither is there respect of persons with him.

2. In Judgment

Ex 12:29 And it came to pass, that at midnight the LORD smote all the first-born in the land of Egypt, from the firstborn of Pharaoh that sat on his throne unto the firstborn of the captive that *was* in the dungeon; and all the firstborn of cattle.

De 10:17 For the LORD your God *is* God of gods, and Lord of lords, a great God, a mighty, and a terrible, which regardeth not persons, nor taketh reward:

2 Chr 19:7 Wherefore now let the fear of the LORD be upon you; take heed and do *it:* for *there is* no iniquity with the LORD our God, nor respect of persons, nor taking of gifts.

Je 9:25 Behold, the days come, saith the LORD, that I will punish all *them which are* circumcised with the uncircumcised;

Ho 4:5 Therefore shalt thou fall in the day, and the prophet also shall fall with thee in the night, and I will destroy thy mother.

Am 2:3 And I will cut off the judge from the midst thereof, and will slay all the princes thereof with him, saith the LORD.

Ro 2:9 Tribulation and anguish, upon every soul of man that doeth evil, of the Jew first, and also of the Gentile;

Col 3:25 But he that doeth wrong shall receive for the wrong which he hath done: and there is no respect of persons.

1 Pe 1:17 And if ye call on the Father, who without respect of persons judgeth according to every man's work, pass the time of your sojourning *here* in fear:

See **JUDGMENTS, PARTIALITY, TOLERANCE**

IMPATIENCE

MOSES AT THE MURMURING OF ISRAEL

Nu 20:10 And Moses and Aaron gathered the congregation together before the rock, and he said unto them, Hear now, ye rebels; must we fetch you water out of this rock?

NAAMAN AT THE CONDITIONS IMPOSED BY THE PROPHET

2 K 5:11–12 But Naaman was wroth, and went away, and said, Behold, I thought, He will surely come out to me, and stand, and call on the name of the LORD his God, and strike his hand over the place, and recover the leper.

Are not Abana and Pharpar, rivers of Damascus, better than all the waters of Israel? may I not wash in them, and be clean? So he turned and went away in a rage.

JONAH AT THE BLASTING OF THE GOURD

Jona 4:8–9 And it came to pass, when the sun did arise, that God prepared a vehement east wind; and the sun beat upon the head of Jonah, that he fainted, and wished in himself to die, and said, *It is* better for me to die than to live.

And God said to Jonah, Doest thou well to be angry for the gourd? And he said, I do well to be angry, *even* unto death.

THE DISCIPLES AT THE OUTCRY OF THE SYROPHENICIAN WOMAN

Mt 15:23 But he answered her not a word. And his disciples came and besought him, saying, Send her away; for she crieth after us.

JAMES AND JOHN AT THE INHOSPITALITY OF THE SAMARITANS

Lu 9:54 And when his disciples James and John saw *this,* they said, Lord, wilt thou that we command fire to come down from heaven, and consume them, even as Elias did?

MARTHA WITH HER SISTER MARY

Lu 10:40 But Martha was cumbered about much serving, and came to him, and said, Lord, dost thou not care that my sister hath left me to serve alone? bid her therefore that she help me.

See **PATIENCE**

IMPENITENCE, *not showing remorse or contrition*

1. Warnings

Pr 1:24 Because I have called, and ye refused; I have stretched out my hand, and no man regarded;

Ec 8:11 Because sentence against an evil work is not executed speedily, therefore the heart of the sons of men is fully set in them to do evil.

Je 7:13 And now, because ye have done all these works, saith the LORD, and I spake unto you, rising up early and speaking, but ye heard not; and I called you, but ye answered not;

Ho 7:10 And the pride of Israel testifieth to his face: and they do not return to the LORD their God, nor seek him for all this.

Am 4:6 And I also have given you cleanness of teeth in all your cities, and want of bread in all your places: yet have ye not returned unto me, saith the LORD.

Hag 2:17 I smote you with blasting and with mildew and with hail in all the labours of your hands; yet ye *turned* not to me, saith the LORD.

Mt 11:20 Then began he to upbraid the cities wherein most of his mighty works were done, because they repented not:

Re 16:9 And men were scorched with great heat, and blasphemed the name of God, which hath power over these plagues: and they repented not to give him glory.

2. Examples

2 K 17:14 Notwithstanding they would not hear, but hardened their necks, like to the neck of their fathers, that did not believe in the LORD their God.

2 Chr 24:19 Yet he sent prophets to them, to bring them again unto the LORD; and they testified against them: but they would not give ear.

2 Chr 28:22 And in the time of his distress did he trespass yet more against the LORD: this *is that* king Ahaz.

2 Chr 33:23 And humbled not himself before the LORD, as Manasseh his father had humbled himself; but Amon trespassed more and more.

2 Chr 36:13 And he also rebelled against king Nebuchadnezzar, who had made him swear by God: but he stiffened his neck, and hardened his heart from turning unto the LORD God of Israel.

Ne 9:29 And testifiedst against them, that thou mightest bring them again unto thy law: yet they dealt proudly, and hearkened not unto thy commandments, but sinned against thy judgments, (which if a man do, he shall live in them;) and withdrew the shoulder, and hardened their neck, and would not hear.

Ne 9:35 For they have not served thee in their kingdom, and in thy great goodness that thou gavest them, and in the large and fat land which thou gavest before them, neither turned they from their wicked works.

Is 9:13 For the people turneth not unto him that smiteth them, neither do they seek the LORD of hosts.

Je 3:7 And I said after she had done all these *things,* Turn thou unto me. But she returned not. And her treacherous sister Judah saw *it.*

Je 5:3 O LORD, *are* not thine eyes upon the truth? thou hast stricken them, but they have not grieved; thou hast consumed them, *but* they have refused to receive correction: they have made their faces harder than a rock; they have refused to return.

Je 6:15 Were they ashamed when they had committed abomination? nay, they were not at all ashamed, neither could they blush: therefore they shall fall among them that fall: at the time *that* I visit them they shall be cast down, saith the LORD.

Je 8:6 I hearkened and heard, *but* they spake not aright: no man repented him of his wickedness, saying, What have I done? every one turned to his course, as the horse rusheth into the battle.

Je 15:7 And I will fan them with a fan in the gates of the land; I will bereave *them* of children, I will destroy my people, *since* they return not from their ways.

Je 35:15 I have sent also unto you all my servants the prophets, rising up early and sending *them,* saying, Return ye now every man from his evil way, and amend your doings, and go not after other gods to serve them, and ye shall dwell in the land which I have given to you and to your fathers: but ye have not inclined your ear, nor hearkened unto me.

Je 36:24 Yet they were not afraid, nor rent their garments, *neither* the king, nor any of his servants that heard all these words.

Je 44:5 But they hearkened not, nor inclined their ear to turn from their wickedness, to burn no incense unto other gods.

Je 44:10 They are not humbled *even* unto this day, neither have they feared, nor walked in my law, nor in my statutes, that I set before you and before your fathers.

Eze 3:19 Yet if thou warn the wicked, and he turn not from his wickedness, nor from his wicked way, he shall die in his iniquity; but thou hast delivered thy soul.

Eze 33:9 Nevertheless, if thou warn the wicked of his way to turn from it; if he do not turn from his way, he shall die in his iniquity; but thou hast delivered thy soul.

Da 9:13 As *it is* written in the law of Moses, all this evil is come upon us: yet made we not our prayer before the LORD our God, that we might turn from our iniquities, and understand thy truth.

Ho 7:16 They return, *but* not to the most High: they are like a deceitful bow: their princes shall fall by the sword for the rage of their tongue: this *shall be* their derision in the land of Egypt.

Ho 11:5 He shall not return into the land of Egypt, but the Assyrian shall be his king, because they refused to return.

Mal 3:14 Ye have said, It *is* vain to serve God: and what profit *is it* that we have kept his ordinance, and that we have walked mournfully before the LORD of hosts?

Mt 13:15 For this people's heart is waxed gross, and *their* ears are dull of hearing, and their eyes they have closed; lest at any time they should see with *their* eyes, and hear with *their* ears, and should understand with *their* heart, and should be converted, and I should heal them.

Lu 7:31 And the Lord said, Whereunto then shall I liken the men of this generation? and to what are they like?

Lu 10:13 Woe unto thee, Chorazin! woe unto thee, Bethsaida! for if the mighty works had been done in Tyre and Sidon, which have been done in you, they had a great while ago repented, sitting in sackcloth and ashes.

Lu 13:34 O Jerusalem, Jerusalem, which killest the prophets, and stonest them that are sent unto thee; how often would I have gathered thy children together, as a hen *doth gather* her brood under *her* wings, and ye would not!

Lu 16:31 And he said unto him, If they hear not Moses and the prophets, neither will they be persuaded, though one rose from the dead.

Re 2:21 And I gave her space to repent of her fornication; and she repented not.

Re 9:21 Neither repented they of their murders, nor of their sorceries, nor of their fornication, nor of their thefts.

3. Correction Despised

Is 1:5 Why should ye be stricken any more? ye will revolt more and more: the whole head is sick, and the whole heart faint.

Is 9:13 For the people turneth not unto him that smiteth them, neither do they seek the LORD of hosts.

Is 42:25 Therefore he hath poured upon him the fury of his anger, and the strength of battle: and it hath set him on fire round about, yet he knew not; and it burned him, yet he laid *it* not to heart.

Je 2:30 In vain have I smitten your children; they received no correction: your own sword hath devoured your prophets, like a destroying lion.

Je 5:3 O LORD, *are* not thine eyes upon the truth? thou hast stricken them, but they have not grieved; thou hast consumed them, *but* they have refused to receive correction: they have made their faces harder than a rock; they have refused to return.

Am 4:9 I have smitten you with blasting and mildew: when your gardens and your vineyards and your fig trees and your olive trees increased, the palmerworm devoured *them:* yet have ye not returned unto me, saith the LORD.

Zep 3:7 I said, Surely thou wilt fear me, thou wilt receive instruction; so their dwelling should not be cut off, howsoever I punished them: but they rose early, *and* corrupted all their doings.

He 12:5 And ye have forgotten the exhortation which speaketh unto you as unto children, My son, despise not thou the chastening of the Lord, nor faint when thou art rebuked of him:

Re 16:11 And blasphemed the God of heaven because of their pains and their sores, and repented not of their deeds.

4. Hardness of Heart

a. Condemned

Ps 95:8 Harden not your heart, as in the provocation, *and as in* the day of temptation in the wilderness:

Pr 28:14 Happy *is* the man that feareth alway: but he that hardeneth his heart shall fall into mischief.

Pr 29:1 He, that being often reproved hardeneth *his* neck, shall suddenly be destroyed, and that without remedy.

Is 42:25 Therefore he hath poured upon him the fury of his anger, and the strength of battle: and it hath set him on fire round about, yet he knew not; and it burned him, yet he laid *it* not to heart.

Is 63:17 O LORD, why hast thou made us to err from thy ways, *and* hardened our heart from thy fear? Return for thy servants' sake, the tribes of thine inheritance.

Am 6:12 Shall horses run upon the rock? will *one* plow *there* with oxen?

for ye have turned judgment into gall, and the fruit of righteousness into hemlock:

Mt 19:8 He saith unto them, Moses because of the hardness of your hearts suffered you to put away your wives: but from the beginning it was not so.

Ro 2:5 But after thy hardness and impenitent heart treasurest up unto thyself wrath against the day of wrath and revelation of the righteous judgment of God;

He 3:13 But exhort one another daily, while it is called To day; lest any of you be hardened through the deceitfulness of sin.

b. Examples

Ex 8:15 But when Pharaoh saw that there was respite, he hardened his heart, and hearkened not unto them; as the LORD had said.

Ex 9:35 And the heart of Pharaoh was hardened, neither would he let the children of Israel go; as the LORD had spoken by Moses.

2 Chr 36:13 And he also rebelled against king Nebuchadnezzar, who had made him swear by God: but he stiffened his neck, and hardened his heart from turning unto the LORD God of Israel.

Ne 9:17 And refused to obey, neither were mindful of thy wonders that thou didst among them; but hardened their necks, and in their rebellion appointed a captain to return to their bondage: but thou *art* a God ready to pardon, gracious and merciful, slow to anger, and of great kindness, and forsookest them not.

Jb 9:4 *He is* wise in heart, and mighty in strength: who hath hardened *himself* against him, and hath prospered?

Ps 78:32 For all this they sinned still, and believed not for his wondrous works.

Pr 27:22 Though thou shouldest bray a fool in a mortar among wheat with a pestle, *yet* will not his foolishness depart from him.

Je 5:3 O LORD, *are* not thine eyes upon the truth? thou hast stricken them, but they have not grieved; thou hast consumed them, *but* they have refused to receive correction: they have made their faces harder than a rock; they have refused to return.

Je 36:24 Yet they were not afraid, nor rent their garments, *neither* the king, nor any of his servants that heard all these words.

Da 5:20 But when his heart was lifted up, and his mind hardened in pride, he was deposed from his kingly throne, and they took his glory from him:

Zec 7:12 Yea, they made their hearts *as* an adamant stone, lest they should hear the law, and the words which the LORD of hosts hath sent in his spirit by the former prophets: therefore came a great wrath from the LORD of hosts.

Mk 3:5 And when he had looked round about on them with anger, being grieved for the hardness of their hearts, he saith unto the man, Stretch forth thine hand. And he stretched *it* out: and his hand was restored whole as the other.

Mk 8:17 And when Jesus knew *it*, he saith unto them, Why reason ye, because ye have no bread? perceive ye not yet, neither understand? have ye your heart yet hardened?

Mk 16:14 Afterward he appeared unto the eleven as they sat at meat, and upbraided them with their unbelief and hardness of heart, because they believed not them which had seen him after he was risen.

Ac 19:9 But when divers were hardened, and believed not, but spake evil of that way before the multitude, he departed from them, and separated the disciples, disputing daily in the school of one Tyrannus.

5. Insensibility

Pr 23:35 They have stricken me, *shalt thou say, and* I was not sick; they have beaten me, *and* I felt *it* not: when shall I awake? I will seek it yet again.

Is 42:25 Therefore he hath poured upon him the fury of his anger, and the strength of battle: and it hath set him on fire round about, yet he knew not; and it burned him, yet he laid *it* not to heart.

Ho 7:9 Strangers have devoured his strength, and he knoweth *it* not: yea, gray hairs are here and there upon him, yet he knoweth not.

Ac 28:27 For the heart of this people is waxed gross, and their ears are dull of hearing, and their eyes have they closed; lest they should see with *their* eyes, and hear with *their* ears, and understand with *their* heart, and should be converted, and I should heal them.

Ep 4:19 Who being past feeling have given themselves over unto lasciviousness, to work all uncleanness with greediness.

1 Ti 4:2 Speaking lies in hypocrisy; having their conscience seared with a hot iron;

See **HUMILITY, PRIDE, REPENTANCE**

IMPERFECTION, *the flawed condition of humanity*

Jb 9:20 If I justify myself, mine own mouth shall condemn me: *if I say, I am* perfect, it shall also prove me perverse.

Ec 7:20 For *there is* not a just man upon earth, that doeth good, and sinneth not.

Ph 3:12 Not as though I had already attained, either were already perfect: but I follow after, if that I may apprehend that for which also I am apprehended of Christ Jesus.

Ja 3:2 For in many things we offend all. If any man offend not in word, the same *is* a perfect man, *and* able also to bridle the whole body.

Re 3:2 Be watchful, and strengthen the things which remain, that are ready to die: for I have not found thy works perfect before God.

See **PERFECTION**

IMPIETY, *lacking reverence for God and that which He considers important*

Ex 5:2 And Pharaoh said, Who *is* the LORD, that I should obey his voice to let Israel go? I know not the LORD, neither will I let Israel go.

2 Chr 32:17 He wrote also letters to rail on the LORD God of Israel, and to speak against him, saying, As the gods of the nations of *other* lands have not delivered their people out of mine hand, so shall not the God of Hezekiah deliver his people out of mine hand.

Jb 21:14 Therefore they say unto God, Depart from us; for we desire not the knowledge of thy ways.

Jb 22:17 Which said unto God, Depart from us: and what can the Almighty do for them?

Pr 1:30 They would none of my counsel: they despised all my reproof.

Eze 28:9 Wilt thou yet say before him that slayeth thee, I *am* God? but thou *shalt be* a man, and no God, in the hand of him that slayeth thee.

Da 3:15 Now if ye be ready that at what time ye hear the sound of the cornet, flute, harp, sackbut, psaltery, and dulcimer, and all kinds of musick, ye fall down and worship the image which I have made; *well:* but if ye worship not, ye shall be cast the same hour into the midst of a burning fiery furnace; and who *is* that God that shall deliver you out of my hands?

Da 6:7 All the presidents of the kingdom, the governors, and the princes, the counsellors, and the captains, have consulted together to establish a royal statute, and to make a firm decree, that whosoever shall ask a petition of any God or man for thirty days, save of thee, O king, he shall be cast into the den of lions.

Da 11:36 And the king shall do according to his will; and he shall exalt himself, and magnify himself above every god, and shall speak marvellous things against the God of gods, and shall prosper till the indignation be accomplished: for that that is determined shall be done.

Ho 7:5 In the day of our king the princes have made him sick with bottles of wine; he stretched out his hand with scorners.

Zep 1:12 And it shall come to pass at that time, *that* I will search Jerusalem with candles, and punish the men that are settled on their lees: that say in their heart, The LORD will not do good, neither will he do evil.

Mal 1:6 A son honoureth *his* father, and a servant his master: if then I *be* a father, where *is* mine honour? and if I *be* a master, where *is* my fear? saith the LORD of hosts unto you, O priests, that despise my name. And ye say, Wherein have we despised thy name?

Mal 3:14 Ye have said, It *is* vain to serve God: and what profit *is it* that we have kept his ordinance, and that we have walked mournfully before the LORD of hosts?

Ro 1:28 And even as they did not like to retain God in *their* knowledge, God gave them over to a reprobate mind, to do those things which are not convenient;

Ro 3:18 There is no fear of God before their eyes.

See **DEVOTIONAL LIFE, RIGHTEOUSNESS, UNRIGHTEOUSNESS**

IMPRECATIONS, *prayers for evil toward another, curses*

Nu 5:21; Jos 6:26; 9:23; Jud 9:20, 57; 1 S 3:17; 14:24, 28; 26:19; 2 S 3:29; 2 K 1:10; 2:24; 6:31; Ne 4:5; 5:13; 6:14; Ps 5:10; 6:10; 10:15; 28:4; 35:8; 40:14; 55:15; 56:7; 58:6; 59:13; 68:2; 69:22; 70:2; 71:13; 79:6; 83:11; 104:35; 109:6, 17; 129:5; 137:7; 140:9; 143:12; Je 10:25; 11:20; 12:3; 17:18; 18:21; 20:12; 51:35; Lam 1:22; 3:65; Ho 9:14; Ac 23:3; Ro 11:9; 1 Co 16:22; Ga 1:9

See **PRAYER**

IMPRESSIONS, *temporary thoughts*

MADE BY THE MESSAGE

Eze 33:31 And they come unto thee as the people cometh, and they sit before thee as my people, and they hear thy words, but they will not do them: for with their mouth they shew much love, *but* their heart goeth after their covetousness.

SEED IN SHALLOW HEARTS

Mt 13:20–21 But he that received the seed into stony places, the same is he that heareth the word, and anon with joy receiveth it;

Yet hath he not root in himself, but dureth for a while: for when tribulation or persecution ariseth because of the word, by and by he is offended.

MIRACLES SOON FORGOTTEN

Mk 8:18–19 Having eyes, see ye not? and having ears, hear ye not? and do ye not remember?

When I brake the five loaves among five thousand, how many baskets full of fragments took ye up? They say unto him, Twelve.

THE TRUTH FAILS TO GRIP

2 Ti 3:7 Ever learning, and never able to come to the knowledge of the truth.

HEARERS WITH A SHORT MEMORY

Ja 1:24 For he beholdeth himself, and goeth his way, and straightway forgetteth what manner of man he was.

See **MIND, THOUGHTS**

IMPROVIDENCE, *waste*

Pr 12:27; 18:9; 21:20; 29:3; Lu 15:13; 16:1

IMPURITY

1. Fornication

Mt 5:32 But I say unto you, That whosoever shall put away his wife, saving for the cause of fornication, causeth her to commit adultery: and whosoever shall marry her that is divorced committeth adultery.

Ac 15:29 That ye abstain from meats offered to idols, and from blood, and from things strangled, and from fornication: from which if ye keep yourselves, ye shall do well. Fare ye well.

1 Co 5:1 It is reported commonly *that there is* fornication among you, and such fornication as is not so much as named among the Gentiles, that one should have his father's wife.

1 Co 6:18 Flee fornication. Every sin that a man doeth is without the body; but he that committeth fornication sinneth against his own body

1 Co 7:2 Nevertheless, *to avoid* fornication, let every man have his own wife, and let every woman have her own husband.

1 Co 10:8 Neither let us commit fornication, as some of them committed, and fell in one day three and twenty thousand.

Ep 5:3 But fornication, and all uncleanness, or covetousness, let it not be once named among you, as becometh saints;

Col 3:5 Mortify therefore your members which are upon the earth; fornication, uncleanness, inordinate affection, evil concupiscence, and covetousness, which is idolatry:

1 Th 4:3 For this is the will of God, *even* your sanctification, that ye should abstain from fornication:

Re 9:21 Neither repented they of their murders, nor of their sorceries, nor of their fornication, nor of their thefts.

2. Lasciviousness

Ge 19:5 And they called unto Lot, and said unto him, Where *are* the men which came in to thee this night? bring them out unto us, that we may know them.

Nu 25:6 And, behold, one of the children of Israel came and brought unto his brethren a Midianitish woman in the sight of Moses, and in the sight of all the congregation of the children of Israel, who *were* weeping *before* the door of the tabernacle of the congregation.

Jud 20:6 And I took my concubine, and cut her in pieces, and sent her throughout all the country of the inheritance of Israel: for they have committed lewdness and folly in Israel.

Jn 8:3 And the scribes and Pharisees brought unto him a woman taken in adultery; and when they had set her in the midst,

Ro 1:27 And likewise also the men, leaving the natural use of the woman, burned in their lust one toward another; men with men working that which is unseemly, and receiving in themselves that recompence of their error which was meet.

1 Co 5:1 It is reported commonly *that there is* fornication among you, and such fornication as is not so much as named among the Gentiles, that one should have his father's wife.

2 Co 12:21 *And* lest, when I come again, my God will humble me among you, and *that* I shall bewail many which have sinned already, and have not repented of the uncleanness and fornication and lasciviousness which they have committed.

Ep 4:19 Who being past feeling have given themselves over unto lasciviousness, to work all uncleanness with greediness.

Jude 7 Even as Sodom and Gomorrha, and the cities about them in like manner, giving themselves over to fornication, and going after strange flesh, are set forth for an example, suffering the vengeance of eternal fire.

3. Lust

De 27:20 Cursed *be* he that lieth with his father's wife; because he uncovereth his father's skirt. And all the people shall say, Amen.

1 K 11:1 But king Solomon loved many strange women, together with the daughter of Pharaoh, women of the Moabites, Ammonites, Edomites, Zidonians, *and* Hittites;

Pr 6:25 Lust not after her beauty in thine heart; neither let her take thee with her eyelids.

Ho 4:11 Whoredom and wine and new wine take away the heart.

Mt 5:28 But I say unto you, That whosoever looketh on a woman to lust after her hath committed adultery with her already in his heart.

Ro 13:14 But put ye on the Lord Jesus Christ, and make not provision for the flesh, to *fulfil* the lusts *thereof.*

Ga 5:16 *This* I say then, Walk in the Spirit, and ye shall not fulfil the lust of the flesh.

Col 3:5 Mortify therefore your members which are upon the earth; fornication, uncleanness, inordinate affection, evil concupiscence, and covetousness, which is idolatry:

1 Th 4:5 Not in the lust of concupiscence, even as the Gentiles which know not God:

2 Ti 2:22 Flee also youthful lusts: but follow righteousness, faith, charity, peace, with them that call on the Lord out of a pure heart.

Ja 1:15 Then when lust hath conceived, it bringeth forth sin: and sin, when it is finished, bringeth forth death.

1 Pe 2:11 Dearly beloved, I beseech *you* as strangers and pilgrims, abstain from fleshly lusts, which war against the soul;

See **PURITY**

INCENSE, *fragrant substance burned in worship*

Ex 25:6; 30:1, 7; 31:11; 35:8, 15, 28; 37:29; 39:38; 40:27; Le 10:1; 16:13; Nu 4:16; 7:14, 26, 38, 44, 68, 86; 16:7, 18, 35, 46; De 33:10; 1 S 2:28; 1 K 9:25; 12:33; 2 K 15:35; 1 Chr 9:29; 2 Chr 2:4; 13:11; 25:14; Ps 141:2; Is 1:13; 43:23; 60:6; Je 41:5; Eze 8:11; 23:41; Mal 1:11; Lu 1:9, 10; Re 5:8; 8:3

See **SACRIFICES, WORSHIP**

INCONSTANCY

Jud 14:20; 2 S 15:13, 31; 1 K 1:49; Jb 6:15; 16:20; 19:14, 19; Ps 38:11; 41:9; 55:13; Pr 25:19; Lam 1:2; Mi 7:5; Mt 26:15, 23, 56; Mk 14:20, 27, 50; Lu 21:16; Jn 16:32; 2 Ti 1:15; 4:10, 16

See **FAITHFULNESS, FRIENDSHIP**

INDECISION

1 K 18:21 And Elijah came unto all the people, and said, How long halt ye between two opinions? if the LORD *be* God, follow him: but if Baal, *then* follow him. And the people answered him not a word.

2 K 17:41 So these nations feared the LORD, and served their graven images, both their children, and their children's children: as did their fathers, so do they unto this day.

Ho 10:2 Their heart is divided; now shall they be found faulty: he shall break down their altars, he shall spoil their images.

Mt 6:24 No man can serve two masters: for either he will hate the one, and love the other; or else he will hold to the one, and despise the other. Ye cannot serve God and mammon.

Lu 9:62 And Jesus said unto him, No man, having put his hand to the plough, and looking back, is fit for the kingdom of God.

Ja 1:8 A double minded man *is* unstable in all his ways.

Ja 4:8 Draw nigh to God, and he will draw nigh to you. Cleanse *your* hands, *ye* sinners; and purify *your* hearts, *ye* double minded.

See **INSTABILITY, MIND**

INDIFFERENCE

1. In Spirit

2 S 11:1 And it came to pass, after the year was expired, at the time when kings go forth *to battle,* that David sent Joab, and his servants with him, and all Israel; and they destroyed the children of Ammon, and besieged Rabbah. But David tarried still at Jerusalem.

2 K 12:6 But it was *so, that* in the three and twentieth year of king Jehoash the priests had not repaired the breaches of the house.

2 Chr 29:34 But the priests were too few, so that they could not flay all the burnt offerings: wherefore their brethren the Levites did help them, till the work was ended, and until the *other* priests had sanctified themselves: for the Levites *were* more upright in heart to sanctify themselves than the priests.

2 Chr 30:3 For they could not keep it at that time, because the priests had not sanctified themselves sufficiently, neither had the people gathered themselves together to Jerusalem.

Ps 123:4 Our soul is exceedingly filled with the scorning of those that are at ease, *and* with the contempt of the proud.

Song 5:3 I have put off my coat; how shall I put it on? I have washed my feet; how shall I defile them?

Is 32:9 Rise up, ye women that are at ease; hear my voice, ye careless daughters; give ear unto my speech.

Is 47:8 Therefore hear now this, *thou that art* given to pleasures, that dwellest carelessly, that sayest in thine heart, I *am,* and none else beside me;

I shall not sit *as* a widow, neither shall I know the loss of children:

Is 64:7 And *there is* none that calleth upon thy name, that stirreth up himself to take hold of thee: for thou hast hid thy face from us, and hast consumed us, because of our iniquities.

Je 12:11 They have made it desolate, *and being* desolate it mourneth unto me; the whole land is made desolate, because no man layeth *it* to heart.

Am 6:1 Woe to them *that are* at ease in Zion, and trust in the mountain of Samaria, *which are* named chief of the nations, to whom the house of Israel came!

Am 6:6 That drink wine in bowls, and anoint themselves with the chief ointments: but they are not grieved for the affliction of Joseph.

Zep 1:12 And it shall come to pass at that time, *that* I will search Jerusalem with candles, and punish the men that are settled on their lees: that say in their heart, The LORD will not do good, neither will he do evil.

Zec 1:15 And I am very sore displeased with the heathen *that are* at ease: for I was but a little displeased, and they helped forward the affliction.

Mt 22:5 But they made light of *it,* and went their ways, one to his farm, another to his merchandise:

Mt 24:12 And because iniquity shall abound, the love of many shall wax cold.

Mark 4:15 And these are they by the way side, where the word is sown; but when they have heard, Satan cometh immediately, and taketh away the word that was sown in their hearts.

Lu 8:12 Those by the way side are they that hear; then cometh the devil, and taketh away the word out of their hearts, lest they should believe and be saved.

Lu 11:7 And he from within shall answer and say, Trouble me not: the door is now shut, and my children are with me in bed; I cannot rise and give thee.

Lu 14:20 And another said, I have married a wife, and therefore I cannot come.

Ph 2:20 For I have no man likeminded, who will naturally care for your state.

He 2:3 How shall we escape, if we neglect so great salvation; which at the first began to be spoken by the Lord, and was confirmed unto us by them that heard *him;*

Ja 1:23 For if any be a hearer of the word, and not a doer, he is like unto a man beholding his natural face in a glass:

Re 2:4 Nevertheless I have *somewhat* against thee, because thou hast left thy first love.

Re 3:16 So then because thou art lukewarm, and neither cold nor hot, I will spue thee out of my mouth.

2. In Service

Nu 32:6 And Moses said unto the children of Gad and to the children of Reuben, Shall your brethren go to war, and shall ye sit here?

Jos 18:3 And Joshua said unto the children of Israel, How long *are* ye slack to go to possess the land, which the LORD God of your fathers hath given you?

Jud 5:17 Gilead abode beyond Jordan: and why did Dan remain in ships? Asher continued on the sea shore, and abode in his breaches.

Jud 5:23 Curse ye Meroz, said the angel of the LORD, curse ye bitterly the inhabitants thereof; because they came not to the help of the LORD, to the help of the LORD against the mighty.

2 Chr 24:5 And he gathered together the priests and the Levites, and said to them, Go out unto the cities of Judah, and gather of all Israel money to repair the house of your God from year to year, and see that ye hasten the matter. Howbeit the Levites hastened it not.

Ne 3:5 And next unto them the Tekoites repaired; but their nobles put not their necks to the work of their Lord.

Je 48:10 Cursed *be* he that doeth the work of the LORD deceitfully, and cursed *be* he that keepeth back his sword from blood.

Eze 33:31 And they come unto thee as the people cometh, and they sit before thee as my people, and they hear thy words, but they will not do them: for with their mouth they shew much love, *but* their heart goeth after their covetousness.

Hag 1:2 Thus speaketh the LORD of hosts, saying, This people say, The time is not come, the time that the LORD's house should be built.

Lu 10:2 Therefore said he unto them, The harvest truly *is* great, but the labourers *are* few: pray ye therefore the Lord of the harvest, that he would send forth labourers into his harvest.

See **DULLNESS, EARNESTNESS, PROCRASTINATION, UNFAITHFULNESS**

INDIGNATION, *anger aroused by something unjust or unworthy*

1. Of God

Ps 69:24 Pour out thine indignation upon them, and let thy wrathful anger take hold of them.

Ps 78:49 He cast upon them the fierceness of his anger, wrath, and indignation, and trouble, by sending evil angels *among them.*

Ps 102:10 Because of thine indignation and thy wrath: for thou hast lifted me up, and cast me down.

Is 10:5 O Assyrian, the rod of mine anger, and the staff in their hand is mine indignation.

Is 10:25 For yet a very little while, and the indignation shall cease, and mine anger in their destruction.

Is 13:5 They come from a far country, from the end of heaven, *even* the LORD, and the weapons of his indignation, to destroy the whole land.

Is 26:20 Come, my people, enter thou into thy chambers, and shut thy doors about thee: hide thyself as it were for a little moment, until the indignation be overpast.

Is 30:27 Behold, the name of the LORD cometh from far, burning *with* his anger, and the burden *thereof is* heavy: his lips are full of indignation, and his tongue as a devouring fire:

Je 10:10 But the Lord *is* the true God, he *is* the living God, and an everlasting king: at his wrath the earth shall tremble, and the nations shall not be able to abide his indignation.

Da 11:36 And the king shall do according to his will; and he shall exalt himself, and magnify himself above every god, and shall speak marvellous things against the God of gods, and shall prosper till the indignation be accomplished: for that that is determined shall be done.

Na 1:6 Who can stand before his indignation? and who can abide in the fierceness of his anger? his fury is poured out like fire, and the rocks are thrown down by him.

He 10:27 But a certain fearful looking for of judgment and fiery indignation, which shall devour the adversaries.

Re 14:10 The same shall drink of the wine of the wrath of God, which is poured out without mixture into the cup of his indignation; and he shall be tormented with fire and brimstone in the presence of the holy angels, and in the presence of the Lamb:

2. Of Humans

Ex 32:19 And it came to pass, as soon as he came nigh unto the camp, that he saw the calf, and the dancing: and Moses' anger waxed hot, and he cast the tables out of his hands, and brake them beneath the mount.

Le 10:16 And Moses diligently sought the goat of the sin offering, and, behold, it was burnt: and he was angry with Eleazar and Ithamar, the sons of Aaron *which were* left *alive,* saying,

Nu 16:15 And Moses was very wroth, and said unto the Lord, Respect not thou their offering: I have not taken one ass from them, neither have I hurt one of them.

Jud 14:19 And the Spirit of the Lord came upon him, and he went down to Ashkelon, and slew thirty men of them, and took their spoil, and gave change of garments unto them which expounded the riddle. And his anger was kindled, and he went up to se.

1 S 11:6 And the Spirit of God came upon Saul when he heard those tidings, and his anger was kindled greatly.

Ne 5:6 And I was very angry when I heard their cry and these words.

Ac 23:3 Then said Paul unto him, God shall smite thee, *thou* whited wall: for sittest thou to judge me after the law, and commandest me to be smitten contrary to the law?

Ep 4:26 Be ye angry, and sin not: let not the sun go down upon your wrath:

See **ANGER, WRATH**

INDIGNITIES

Mt 9:24 He said unto them, Give place: for the maid is not dead, but sleepeth. And they laughed him to scorn.

Mt 26:55 In that same hour said Jesus to the multitudes, Are ye come out as against a thief with swords and staves for to take me? I sat daily with you teaching in the temple, and ye laid no hold on me.

Mt 26:67 Then did they spit in his face, and buffeted him; and others smote *him* with the palms of their hands,

Mt 27:29 And when they had platted a crown of thorns, they put *it* upon his head, and a reed in his right hand: and they bowed the knee before him, and mocked him, saying, Hail, King of the Jews!

Mt 27:31 And after that they had mocked him, they took the robe off from him, and put his own raiment on him, and led him away to crucify *him.*

Mk 14:48 And Jesus answered and said unto them, Are ye come out, as against a thief, with swords and *with* staves to take me?

Mk 14:65 And some began to spit on him, and to cover his face, and to buffet him, and to say unto him, Prophesy: and the servants did strike him with the palms of their hands.

Mk 15:19 And they smote him on the head with a reed, and did spit upon him, and bowing *their* knees worshipped him.

Mk 15:29 And they that passed by railed on him, wagging their heads, and saying, Ah, thou that destroyest the temple, and buildest *it* in three days,

Lu 22:64 And when they had blindfolded him, they struck him on the face, and asked him, saying, Prophesy, who is it that smote thee?

Jn 7:20 The people answered and said, Thou hast a devil: who goeth about to kill thee?

Jn 18:12 Then the band and the captain and officers of the Jews took Jesus, and bound him,

Jn 18:22 And when he had thus spoken, one of the officers which stood by struck Jesus with the palm of his hand, saying, Answerest thou the high priest so?

Jn 19:1 Then Pilate therefore took Jesus, and scourged *him*.

Jn 19:5 Then came Jesus forth, wearing the crown of thorns, and the purple robe. And *Pilate* saith unto them, Behold the man!

Jn 19:23 Then the soldiers, when they had crucified Jesus, took his garments, and made four parts, to every soldier a part; and also *his* coat: now the coat was without seam, woven from the top throughout.

See **CHRIST, SUFFERING**

INFANTICIDE *See* **MURDER**

INFATUATION

Jud 14:3 Then his father and his mother said unto him, *Is there* never a woman among the daughters of thy brethren, or among all my people, that thou goest to take a wife of the uncircumcised Philistines? And Samson said unto his father, Get her for me; for she pleaseth me well.

2 S 11:3 And David sent and enquired after the woman. And *one* said, *Is* not this Bath-sheba, the daughter of Eliam, the wife of Uriah the Hittite?

2 S 13:2 And Amnon was so vexed, that he fell sick for his sister Tamar; for she *was* a virgin; and Amnon thought it hard for him to do any thing to her.

1 K 2:17 And he said, Speak, I pray thee, unto Solomon the king, (for he will not say thee nay,) that he give me Abishag the Shunammite to wife.

Mk 6:23 And he sware unto her, Whatsoever thou shalt ask of me, I will give *it* thee, unto the half of my kingdom.

INFIDELITY *See* **UNBELIEF**

INFIRMITIES, *physical weaknesses*

Mt 4:24; 8:17; 12:10; Mk 3:1; Lu 5:15; 8:2; 13:11; Jn 5:5; Ac 3:2; 2 Co 5:4; 11:30; 12:5, 10; Ga 4:13; 1 Ti 5:23; He 4:15; 7:28

See **SICKNESS**

INFLUENCE

1. Of Unfaithful Christians

Ex 34:16; Nu 14:36; De 13:6; 20:18; 1 S 2:24; 1 K 14:16; 16:13; 2 K 17:21; 2 Chr 18:2; Je 2:33; 23:13; Mt 14:9; 18:6; Ro 14:13, 15; 1 Co 5:6; 8:10; Ga 2:13; 5:9; 2 Ti 2:14

2. Of the Ungodly

1 K 11:4; 21:25; 2 Chr 21:6; Pr 16:29; Ec 9:18; Is 3:12; Je 23:15; Mt 23:15; 27:20; Mk 15:11; Ac 8:11; 13:8; 14:19; Ro 2:24

3. Of the Upright and Godly

PRESERVING

Mt 5:13 Ye are the salt of the earth: but if the salt have lost his savour, wherewith shall it be salted? it is thenceforth good for nothing, but to be cast out, and to be trodden under foot of men.

Mk 9:50 Salt *is* good: but if the salt have lost his saltness, wherewith will ye season it? Have salt in yourselves, and have peace one with another.

SAVING

1 Co 7:16 For what knowest thou, O wife, whether thou shalt save *thy* husband? or how knowest thou, O man, whether thou shalt save *thy* wife?

INSPIRING

2 Co 9:2 For I know the forwardness of your mind, for which I boast of you to them of Macedonia, that Achaia was ready a year ago; and your zeal hath provoked very many.

EVANGELIZING

1 Th 1:8 For from you sounded out the word of the Lord not only in Macedonia and Achaia, but also in every place your faith to God-ward is spread abroad; so that we need not to speak any thing.

4. After Death

2 K 13:21 And it came to pass, as they were burying a man, that, behold, they spied a band *of men;* and they cast the man into the sepulchre of Elisha: and when the man was let down, and touched the bones of Elisha, he revived, and stood up on his feet.

Mt 26:13 Verily I say unto you, Wheresoever this gospel shall be preached in the whole world, *there* shall also this, that this woman hath done, be told for a memorial of her.

He 11:4 By faith Abel offered unto God a more excellent sacrifice than Cain, by which he obtained witness that he was righteous, God testifying of his gifts: and by it he being dead yet speaketh.

2 Pe 1:15 Moreover I will endeavour that ye may be able after my decease to have these things always in remembrance.

Re 14:13 And I heard a voice from heaven saying unto me, Write, Blessed *are* the dead which die in the Lord from henceforth: Yea, saith the Spirit, that they may rest from their labours; and their works do follow them.

See **ASSOCIATIONS, PARENTS**

INGRATITUDE, *unthankfulness*

1. To God

De 32:6 Do ye thus requite the LORD, O foolish people and unwise? *is* not he thy father *that* hath bought thee? hath he not made thee, and established thee?

Ezr 9:14 Should we again break thy commandments, and join in affinity with the people of these abominations? wouldest not thou be angry with us till thou hadst consumed *us,* so that *there should be* no remnant nor escaping?

Ne 9:26 Nevertheless they were disobedient, and rebelled against thee, and cast thy law behind their backs, and slew thy prophets which testified against them to turn them to thee, and they wrought great provocations.

Eze 16:17–18 Thou hast also taken thy fair jewels of my gold and of my silver, which I had given thee, and madest to thyself images of men, and didst commit whoredom with them,

And tookest thy broidered garments, and coveredst them: and thou hast set mine oil and mine incense before them.

Lu 17:17–18 And Jesus answering said, Were there not ten cleansed? but where *are* the nine?

There are not found that returned to give glory to God, save this stranger.

Ro 1:21 Because that, when they knew God, they glorified *him* not as God, neither were thankful; but became vain in their imaginations, and their foolish heart was darkened.

2. To Humans

Ge 40:23; Ex 14:12; 17:4; Nu 14:10; 16:13; 20:5; Jud 8:35; 9:18; 1 S 25:10, 21; 2 S 10:4; 2 Chr 24:22; Est 6:3; Ps 35:12; 38:19; 109:5; Pr 17:13; Ec 9:15; Je 18:20; Ac 7:27; 2 Co 12:16

3. Returning Evil for Good

1 S 25:21; 2 Chr 20:11; Ps 7:4; 35:12; 38:20; 109:5; Pr 17:13; Is 33:1; Je 18:20; Mt 14:8; Jn 10:32; 15:25

See **GRATITUDE, THANKFULNESS**

INHERITANCE

Ge 48:6; Le 25:10, 41; 27:24; Nu 26:53; 27:7; 32:18, 32; 34:15; 35:8; 36:2; De 19:14; Jos 12:7; 14:14; 16:4; 17:4; 18:20, 28; 19:1, 31, 39, 49; Jud 2:6; 21:17, 23; Ru 4:6; 1 K 21:3; Ne 11:20; Jb 42:15; Je 32:8; Eze 46:18; Lu 15:12

1. Laws of

See **REAL ESTATE**

2. Of Israel

Le 20:24; De 1:38; 4:21, 38, 47; 11:24; 12:9; 15:4; 19:8; 26:1; 29:8; 32:49; Jos 1:3, 6, 15; 11:23; 12:6; 13:6, 32; 14:2; 15:20; 18:10; 19:51; 23:4; 24:28; Jud 18:1; 2 Chr 6:27; Ne 9:15, 22; Ps 78:55; 105:11, 44; 135:12; 136:22; Is 58:14; Je 12:14; 49:2; Lam 5:2; Eze 33:24; 36:12; 37:25; 45:6; 47:13, 22; 48:29; Ac 7:5; 13:19

See **ISRAEL**

INHOSPITALITY, *unfriendly*

Nu 20:18; 21:23; De 2:30; 23:4; Jud 8:6; 11:17, 20; 19:15; 1 S 25:10; Ne 13:2; Mt 25:43; Mk 6:11; Lu 9:5, 53; 10:10; 3 Jn 10

See **HOSPITALITY**

INIQUITY

1. Lack of Righteousness

Jb 15:16; Ps 14:4; 41:6; 53:1; 64:6; 65:3; Pr 19:28; Is 5:18; 13:11; 30:13; 32:6; 43:24; 59:6; 65:7; Je 5:25; 30:14; 33:8; Lam 4:6, 22; Eze 3:19; 4:5; 7:13; 9:9; 14:4; 16:49; 18:24, 30; 21:24; 28:18; 32:27; 33:6, 9, 13; 44:12; Da 9:5; Ho 4:8; 7:1; 8:13; 9:7; 12:11; 14:1; Mi 2:1; Hab 2:12; Mt 13:41; 23:28; 24:12; Ac 3:26; Ro 6:19; He 8:12

2. Human

Ezr 9:7; Jb 14:17; Ps 31:10; 38:4; 40:12; 51:2; 90:8; 106:6; 130:3; Is 59:2, 12; 64:6; Je 2:22; 14:7; Eze 24:23; 36:31; Da 9:16; Mi 7:19

See **SIN, WICKED**

INJUSTICE, *unfairness, inequity*

1. Attributed to God

Ex 5:23; Jb 9:24; 10:3; 12:6; 21:7; 24:12; 30:21; 34:5; 40:8; Ps 73:5, 14; Ec 7:15; 8:14; 9:2; Je 12:1; Eze 18:25; Am 4:7; Hab 1:2, 13; Mt 20:12; 25:28; Lu 15:29; Ro 9:14

2. Condemned

De 16:19 Thou shalt not wrest judgment; thou shalt not respect persons, neither take a gift: for a gift doth blind the eyes of the wise, and pervert the words of the righteous.

De 24:17 Thou shalt not pervert the judgment of the stranger, *nor* of the fatherless; nor take a widow's raiment to pledge:

Ps 82:2 How long will ye judge unjustly, and accept the persons of the wicked? Selah.

Pr 24:23 These *things* also *belong* to the wise. *It is* not good to have respect of persons in judgment.

Pr 29:27 An unjust man *is* an abomination to the just: and *he that is* upright in the way *is* abomination to the wicked.

Pr 31:4–5 *It is* not for kings, O Lemuel, *it is* not for kings to drink wine; nor for princes strong drink:

Lest they drink, and forget the law, and pervert the judgment of any of the afflicted.

Ec 3:16 And moreover I saw under the sun the place of judgment, *that* wickedness *was* there; and the place of righteousness, *that* iniquity *was* there.

Am 5:7 Ye who turn judgment to wormwood, and leave off righteousness in the earth,

Mi 3:9 Hear this, I pray you, ye heads of the house of Jacob, and princes of the house of Israel, that abhor judgment, and pervert all equity.

Lu 16:10 He that is faithful in that which is least is faithful also in much: and he that is unjust in the least is unjust also in much.

3. Examples

Ge 39:20; 40:15; Ex 5:7, 18; 1 S 8:3; 20:31; 22:16; 1 K 21:13; Ne 5:5; Is 59:14; Je 26:21; Da 2:5, 12; Mt 26:66; 27:26; Mk 14:64; 15:15; Lu 18:4; 22:71; 23:18, 22, 25; Jn 19:1; Ac 5:40; 12:19; 16:37; 23:2; 24:27; 25:27

See **JUDGMENTS, JUSTICE**

INK, *colored liquid used for writing and drawing*

Je 36:18; 2 Co 3:3; 2 Jn 12; 3 Jn 13

See **BOOKS, WRITING**

INNOCENCE, *without guilt or guile*

Ge 2:25; 20:5; 40:15; Nu 32:22; 35:27; De 22:26; Jos 2:19; 1 S 22:15; 24:11; 2 S 3:28; Jb 22:30; Ps 19:13; 26:6; 73:13; Eze 18:6; Da 6:22; Ho 8:5; Lu 23:15, 22; Jn 18:38; 19:6; Ac 23:9; 25:25; 26:31; 28:18; Re 14:5

See **GUILT**

INSANITY *See* **DISEASE**

INSECTS

1. Ants

Pr 6:6; 30:25

2. Bees

De 1:44; Jud 14:8; Ps 118:12; Is 7:18

3. Cankerworms, locust

Jl 1:4; 2:25; Na 3:15

4. Caterpillars(caterpillers)

1 K 8:37; 2 Chr 6:28; Ps 78:46; Is 33:4; Je 51:27; Jl 1:4; 2 :25

5. Fleas

1 S 24:14; 26:20

6. Flies

Ex 8:21; Ps 78:45; 105:31; Ec 10:1

7. Gnats

Mt 23:24

8. Grasshoppers

Nu 13:33; Jud 6:5; 7:12; Is 40:22; Je 46:23; Am 7:1; Na 3:17

9. Hornets

Ex 23:28; De 7:20; Jos 24:12

10. Locusts

Ex 10:4, 12; Le 11:22; De 28:38, 42; 1 K 8:37; 2 Chr 6:28; 7:13; Ps 105:34; Pr 30:27; Is 33:4; Jl 1:4; 2:25; Na 3:15; Mt 3:4; Mk 1:6; Re 9:3

11. Moths

Jb 4:19; 13:28; 27:18; Is 50:9; Ho 5:12; Mt 6:19; Ja 5:2

12. Palmerworms

Jl 1:4; 2:25; Am 4:9

13. Scorpions, *of the spider species, having a poisonous sting*

De 8:15; Eze 2:6; Lu 11:12

14. Spiders

Jb 8:14; Pr 30:28; Is 59:5

INSECURITY

Jud 8:11 And Gideon went up by the way of them that dwelt in tents on the east of Nobah and Jogbehah, and smote the host: for the host was secure.

Ps 1:4 The ungodly *are* not so: but *are* like the chaff which the wind driveth away.

Ps 73:18 Surely thou didst set them in slippery places: thou castedst them down into destruction.

Pr 12:3 A man shall not be established by wickedness: but the root of the righteous shall not be moved.

Pr 21:12 The righteous *man* wisely considereth the house of the wicked: *but God* overthroweth the wicked for *their* wickedness.

Pr 23:34 Yea, thou shalt be as he that lieth down in the midst of the sea, or as he that lieth upon the top of a mast.

Is 22:25 In that day, saith the LORD of hosts, shall the nail that is fastened in the sure place be removed, and be cut down, and fall; and the burden that *was* upon it shall be cut off: for the LORD hath spoken *it*.

Is 28:18 And your covenant with death shall be disannulled, and your agreement with hell shall not stand; when the overflowing scourge shall pass through, then ye shall be trodden down by it.

Is 30:13 Therefore this iniquity shall be to you as a breach ready to fall, swelling out in a high wall, whose breaking cometh suddenly at an instant.

Is 40:24 Yea, they shall not be planted; yea, they shall not be sown: yea, their stock shall not take root in the earth: and he shall also blow upon them, and they shall wither, and the whirlwind shall take them away as stubble.

Je 13:16 Give glory to the Lord your God, before he cause darkness, and before your feet stumble upon the dark mountains, and, while ye look for light, he turn it into the shadow of death, *and* make *it* gross darkness.

Je 22:15 Shalt thou reign, because thou closest *thyself* in cedar? did not thy father eat and drink, and do judgment and justice, *and* then *it was* well with him?

Je 23:12 Wherefore their way shall be unto them as slippery *ways* in the darkness: they shall be driven on, and fall therein: for I will bring evil upon them, *even* the year of their visitation, saith the Lord.

Eze 13:10–11 Because, even because they have seduced my people, saying, Peace; and *there was* no peace; and one built up a wall, and, lo, others daubed it with untempered *morter:*

Say unto them which daub it with untempered *morter,* that it shall fall: there shall be an overflowing shower; and ye, O great hailstones, shall fall; and a stormy wind shall rend *it.*

Eze 30:4 And the sword shall come upon Egypt, and great pain shall be in Ethiopia, when the slain shall fall in Egypt, and they shall take away her multitude, and her foundations shall be broken down.

Am 5:11 Forasmuch therefore as your treading *is* upon the poor, and ye take from him burdens of wheat: ye have built houses of hewn stone, but ye shall not dwell in them; ye have planted pleasant vineyards, but ye shall not drink wine of them.

Na 3:12 All thy strong holds *shall be like* fig trees with the firstripe figs: if they be shaken, they shall even fall into the mouth of the eater.

Mt 7:26–27 And every one that heareth these sayings of mine, and doeth them not, shall be likened unto a foolish man, which built his house upon the sand:

And the rain descended, and the floods came, and the winds blew, and beat upon that house; and it fell: and great was the fall of it.

1 Th 5:3 For when they shall say, Peace and safety; then sudden destruction cometh upon them, as travail upon a woman with child; and they shall not escape.

1. Fall of the Wicked Foretold

1 S 2:10 The adversaries of the Lord shall be broken to pieces; out of heaven shall he thunder upon them: the Lord shall judge the ends of the earth; and he shall give strength unto his king, and exalt the horn of his anointed.

Est 6:13 And Haman told Zeresh his wife and all his friends every *thing* that had befallen him. Then said his wise men and Zeresh his wife unto him, If Mordecai *be* of the seed of the Jews, before whom thou hast begun to fall, thou shalt not prevail against him, but shalt surely fall before him.

Ps 18:38 I have wounded them that they were not able to rise: they are fallen under my feet.

Ps 94:13 That thou mayest give him rest from the days of adversity, until the pit be digged for the wicked.

Ps 140:11 Let not an evil speaker be established in the earth: evil shall hunt the violent man to overthrow *him.*

Pr 11:5 The righteousness of the perfect shall direct his way: but the wicked shall fall by his own wickedness.

Pr 12:3 A man shall not be established by wickedness: but the root of the righteous shall not be moved.

Pr 22:14 The mouth of strange women *is* a deep pit: he that is abhorred of the Lord shall fall therein.

Ec 10:8 He that diggeth a pit shall fall into it; and whoso breaketh an hedge, a serpent shall bite him.

Is 22:17 Behold, the Lord will carry thee away with a mighty captivity, and will surely cover thee.

Is 31:3 Now the Egyptians *are* men, and not God; and their horses flesh, and not spirit. When the LORD shall stretch out his hand, both he that helpeth shall fall, and he that is holpen shall fall down, and they all shall fail together.

Is 37:7 Behold, I will send a blast upon him, and he shall hear a rumour, and return to his own land; and I will cause him to fall by the sword in his own land.

Je 6:15 Were they ashamed when they had committed abomination? nay, they were not at all ashamed, neither could they blush: therefore they shall fall among them that fall: at the time *that* I visit them they shall be cast down, saith the LORD.

Je 8:4 Moreover thou shalt say unto them, Thus saith the LORD; Shall they fall, and not arise? shall he turn away, and not return?

Je 18:23 Yet, LORD, thou knowest all their counsel against me to slay *me:* forgive not their iniquity, neither blot out their sin from thy sight, but let them be overthrown before thee; deal *thus* with them in the time of thine anger.

Je 51:4 Thus the slain shall fall in the land of the Chaldeans, and *they that are* thrust through in her streets.

Je 51:49 As Babylon *hath caused* the slain of Israel to fall, so at Babylon shall fall the slain of all the earth.

Eze 26:15 Thus saith the Lord God to Tyrus; Shall not the isles shake at the sound of thy fall, when the wounded cry, when the slaughter is made in the midst of thee?

Eze 30:5 Ethiopia, and Libya, and Lydia, and all the mingled people, and Chub, and the men of the land that is in league, shall fall with them by the sword.

Da 8:25 And through his policy also he shall cause craft to prosper in his hand; and he shall magnify *himself* in his heart, and by peace shall destroy many: he shall also stand up against the Prince of princes; but he shall be broken without hand.

Ho 4:14 I will not punish your daughters when they commit whoredom, nor your spouses when they commit adultery: for themselves are separated with whores, and they sacrifice with harlots: therefore the people *that* doth not understand shall fall.

Am 8:14 They that swear by the sin of Samaria, and say, Thy god, O Dan, liveth; and, The manner of Beer-sheba liveth; even they shall fall, and never rise up again.

Hab 3:14 Thou didst strike through with his staves the head of his villages: they came out as a whirlwind to scatter me: their rejoicing *was* as to devour the poor secretly.

Lu 6:49 But he that heareth, and doeth not, is like a man that without a foundation built an house upon the earth; against which the stream did beat vehemently, and immediately it fell; and the ruin of that house was great.

2. Of Sinners

Ge 19:24 Then the LORD rained upon Sodom and upon Gomorrah brimstone and fire from the LORD out of heaven;

Ge 19:28 And he looked toward Sodom and Gomorrah, and toward all the land of the plain, and beheld, and, lo, the smoke of the country went up as the smoke of a furnace.

Nu 16:33 They, and all that *appertained* to them, went down alive into the pit, and the earth closed upon them: and they perished from among the congregation.

De 32:35 To me *belongeth* vengeance, and recompence; their foot shall slide in *due* time: for the day of their calamity *is* at hand, and the things that shall come upon them make haste.

Jos 11:7 So Joshua came, and all the people of war with him, against them by the waters of Merom suddenly; and they fell upon them.

Jb 18:12 His strength shall be hungerbitten, and destruction *shall be* ready at his side.

Ps 35:8 Let destruction come upon him at unawares; and let his net that he hath hid catch himself: into that very destruction let him fall.

Ps 64:7 But God shall shoot at them *with* an arrow; suddenly shall they be wounded.

Pr 6:15 Therefore shall his calamity come suddenly; suddenly shall he be broken without remedy.

Pr 24:22 For their calamity shall rise suddenly; and who knoweth the ruin of them both?

Pr 29:1 He, that being often reproved hardeneth *his* neck, shall suddenly be destroyed, and that without remedy.

Ec 9:12 For man also knoweth not his time: as the fishes that are taken in an evil net, and as the birds that are caught in the snare; so *are* the sons of men snared in an evil time, when it falleth suddenly upon them.

Is 30:13 Therefore this iniquity shall be to you as a breach ready to fall, swelling out in a high wall, whose breaking cometh suddenly at an instant.

Is 47:9 But these two *things* shall come to thee in a moment in one day, the loss of children, and widowhood: they shall come upon thee in their perfection for the multitude of thy sorceries, *and* for the great abundance of thine enchantments.

Is 47:11 Therefore shall evil come upon thee; thou shalt not know from whence it riseth: and mischief shall fall upon thee; thou shalt not be able to put if off: and desolation shall come upon thee suddenly, *which* thou shalt not know.

Je 8:16 The snorting of his horses was heard from Dan: the whole land trembled at the sound of the neighing of his strong ones; for they are come, and have devoured the land, and all that is in it; the city, and those that dwell therein.

Je 15:8 Their widows are increased to me above the sand of the seas: I have brought upon them against the mother of the young men a spoiler at noonday: I have caused *him* to fall upon it suddenly, and terrors upon the city.

Da 5:30 In that night was Belshazzar the king of the Chaldeans slain.

Na 1:9 What do ye imagine against the LORD? he will make an utter end:

affliction shall not rise up the second time.

Hab 2:7 Shall they not rise up suddenly that shall bite thee, and awake that shall vex thee, and thou shalt be for booties unto them?

Lu 10:18 And he said unto them, I beheld Satan as lightning fall from heaven.

Lu 17:27 They did eat, they drank, they married wives, they were given in marriage, until the day that Noe entered into the ark, and the flood came, and destroyed them all.

1 Th 5:3 For when they shall say, Peace and safety; then sudden destruction cometh upon them, as travail upon a woman with child; and they shall not escape.

2 Pe 2:1 But there were false prophets also among the people, even as there shall be false teachers among you, who privily shall bring in damnable heresies, even denying the Lord that bought them, and bring upon themselves swift destruction.

Re 18:10 Standing afar off for the fear of her torment, saying, Alas, alas, that great city Babylon, that mighty city! for in one hour is thy judgment come.

Re 18:19 And they cast dust on their heads, and cried, weeping and wailing, saying, Alas, alas, that great city, wherein were made rich all that had ships in the sea by reason of her costliness! for in one hour is she made desolate.

3. Because of False Confidence

De 32:37 And he shall say, Where *are* their gods, *their* rock in whom they trusted,

2 Chr 28:23 For he sacrificed unto the gods of Damascus, which smote him: and he said, Because the gods of the kings of Syria help them, *therefore* will I sacrifice to them, that they may help me. But they were the ruin of him, and of all Israel.

Jb 8:14 Whose hope shall be cut off, and whose trust *shall be* a spider's web.

Jb 15:31 Let not him that is deceived trust in vanity: for vanity shall be his recompence.

Ps 20:7 Some *trust* in chariots, and some in horses: but we will remember the name of the LORD our God.

Ps 49:6 They that trust in their wealth, and boast themselves in the multitude of their riches;

Ps 52:7 Lo, *this is* the man *that* made not God his strength; but trusted in the abundance of his riches, *and* strengthened himself in his wickedness.

Ps 115:8 They that make them are like unto them; *so is* every one that trusteth in them.

Ps 135:18 They that make them are like unto them: *so is* every one that trusteth in them.

Ps 146:3 Put not your trust in princes, nor in the son of man, in whom there is no help.

Pr 11:28 He that trusteth in his riches shall fall: but the righteous shall flourish as a branch.

Pr 18:11 The rich man's wealth *is* his strong city, and as an high wall in his own conceit.

Pr 28:26 He that trusteth in his own heart is a fool: but whoso walketh wisely, he shall be delivered.

Is 30:12 Wherefore thus saith the Holy One of Israel, Because ye despise this word, and trust in oppression and perverseness, and stay thereon:

Is 31:1 Woe to them that go down to Egypt for help; and stay on horses, and trust in chariots, because *they are* many; and in horsemen, because they are very strong; but they look not unto the Holy One of Israel, neither seek the LORD!

Is 47:10 For thou hast trusted in thy wickedness: thou hast said, None seeth me. Thy wisdom and thy knowledge, it hath perverted thee; and thou hast said in thine heart, I *am,* and none else beside me.

Is 59:4 None calleth for justice, nor *any* pleadeth for truth: they trust in vanity, and speak lies; they conceive mischief, and bring forth iniquity.

Je 2:13 For my people have committed two evils; they have forsaken me the fountain of living waters, *and* hewed them out cisterns, broken cisterns, that can hold no water.

Je 7:8 Behold, ye trust in lying words, that cannot profit.

Je 13:25 This *is* thy lot, the portion of thy measures from me, saith the LORD; because thou hast forgotten me, and trusted in falsehood.

Je 17:5 Thus saith the LORD; Cursed be the man that trusteth in man, and maketh flesh his arm, and whose heart departeth from the LORD.

Je 49:4 Wherefore gloriest thou in the valleys, thy flowing valley, O backsliding daughter? that trusted in her treasures, *saying,* Who shall come unto me?

Eze 13:11 Say unto them which daub it with untempered *morter,* that it shall fall: there shall be an overflowing shower; and ye, O great hailstones, shall fall; and a stormy wind shall rend *it.*

Eze 16:15 But thou didst trust in thine own beauty, and playedst the harlot because of thy renown, and pouredst out thy fornications on every one that passed by; his it was.

Am 6:1 Woe to them *that are* at ease in Zion, and trust in the mountain of Samaria, *which are* named chief of the nations, to whom the house of Israel came!

Am 6:13 Ye which rejoice in a thing of nought, which say, Have we not taken to us horns by our own strength?

Mi 5:10 And it shall come to pass in that day, saith the LORD, that I will cut off thy horses out of the midst of thee, and I will destroy thy chariots:

Mt 7:27 And the rain descended, and the floods came, and the winds blew, and beat upon that house; and it fell: and great was the fall of it.

Mk 10:24 And the disciples were astonished at his words. But Jesus answereth again, and saith unto them, Children, how hard is it for them that trust in riches to enter into the kingdom of God!

Lu 3:8 Bring forth therefore fruits worthy of repentance, and begin not to say within yourselves, We have Abraham to *our* father: for I say unto you, That God is able of these stones to raise up children unto Abraham.

Lu 6:49 But he that heareth, and doeth not, is like a man that without a foundation built an house upon the earth; against which the stream did beat vehemently, and immediately it fell; and the ruin of that house was great.

Ph 3:4 Though I might also have confidence in the flesh. If any other man thinketh that he hath whereof he might trust in the flesh, I more:

1 Ti 6:17 Charge them that are rich in this world, that they be not high-minded, nor trust in uncertain riches, but in the living God, who giveth us richly all things to enjoy;

See **GOD**

a. In Humans

2 Chr 16:2 Then Asa brought out silver and gold out of the treasures of the house of the LORD and of the king's house, and sent to Ben-hadad king of Syria, that dwelt at Damascus, saying,

2 Chr 16:12 And Asa in the thirty and ninth year of his reign was diseased in his feet, until his disease *was* exceeding *great:* yet in his disease he sought not to the LORD, but to the physicians.

Ps 33:16 There is no king saved by the multitude of an host: a mighty man is not delivered by much strength.

Ps 60:11 Give us help from trouble: for vain *is* the help of man.

Ps 108:12 Give us help from trouble: for vain *is* the help of man.

Ps 118:9 *It is* better to trust in the LORD than to put confidence in princes.

Ps 146:3 Put not your trust in princes, *nor* in the son of man, in whom *there is* no help.

Pr 25:19 Confidence in an unfaithful man in time of trouble *is like* a broken tooth, and a foot out of joint.

Is 2:22 Cease ye from man, whose breath *is* in his nostrils: for wherein is he to be accounted of?

Is 8:12 Say ye not, A confederacy, to all *them to* whom this people shall say, A confederacy; neither fear ye their fear, nor be afraid.

Is 10:20 And it shall come to pass in that day, *that* the remnant of Israel,

and such as are escaped of the house of Jacob, shall no more again stay upon him that smote them; but shall stay upon the LORD, the Holy One of Israel, in truth.

Is 20:5 And they shall be afraid and ashamed of Ethiopia their expectation, and of Egypt their glory.

Is 30:2 That walk to go down into Egypt, and have not asked at my mouth; to strengthen themselves in the strength of Pharaoh, and to trust in the shadow of Egypt!

Is 30:7 For the Egyptians shall help in vain, and to no purpose: therefore have I cried concerning this, Their strength *is* to sit still.

Is 31:3 Now the Egyptians *are* men, and not God; and their horses flesh, and not spirit. When the LORD shall stretch out his hand, both he that helpeth shall fall, and he that is holpen shall fall down, and they all shall fail together.

Is 36:6 Lo, thou trustest in the staff of this broken reed, on Egypt; whereon if a man lean, it will go into his hand, and pierce it: so *is* Pharaoh king of Egypt to all that trust in him.

Je 2:18 And now what hast thou to do in the way of Egypt, to drink the waters of Sihor? or what hast thou to do in the way of Assyria, to drink the waters of the river?

Je 2:37 Yea, thou shalt go forth from him, and thine hands upon thine head: for the LORD hath rejected thy confidences, and thou shalt not prosper in them.

Je 17:5 Thus saith the LORD; Cursed be the man that trusteth in man, and maketh flesh his arm, and whose heart departeth from the LORD.

Eze 17:15 But he rebelled against him in sending his ambassadors into Egypt, that they might give him horses and much people. Shall he prosper? shall he escape that doeth such *things?* or shall he break the covenant, and be delivered?

Eze 29:16 And it shall be no more the confidence of the house of Israel, which bringeth *their* iniquity to remembrance, when they shall look after them: but they shall know that I *am* the Lord GOD.

Ho 5:13 When Ephraim saw his sickness, and Judah *saw* his wound, then went Ephraim to the Assyrian, and sent to king Jareb: yet could he not heal you, nor cure you of your wound.

Ho 14:3 Asshur shall not save us; we will not ride upon horses: neither will we say any more to the work of our hands, *Ye are* our gods: for in thee the fatherless findeth mercy.

Obad 7 All the men of thy confederacy have brought thee *even* to the border: the men that were at peace with thee have deceived thee, *and* prevailed against thee; *they that eat* thy bread have laid a wound under thee: *there is* none understanding in him.

Na 3:9 Ethiopia and Egypt *were* her strength, and *it was* infinite; Put and Lubim were thy helpers.

Jn 5:45 Do not think that I will accuse you to the Father: there is *one* that accuseth you, *even* Moses, in whom ye trust.

See **TRUST**

b. In Riches

Jb 31:24–25 If I have made gold my hope, or have said to the fine gold, *Thou art* my confidence;

If I rejoiced because my wealth *was* great, and because mine hand had gotten much;

Jb 31:28 This also *were* an iniquity *to be punished by* the judge: for I should have denied the God *that is* above.

Ps 52:7 Lo, *this is* the man *that* made not God his strength; but trusted in the abundance of his riches, *and* strengthened himself in his wickedness.

Ps 62:10 Trust not in oppression, and become not vain in robbery: if riches increase, set not your heart *upon them.*

Pr 10:15 The rich man's wealth *is* his strong city: the destruction of the poor *is* their poverty.

Pr 11:28 He that trusteth in his riches shall fall: but the righteous shall flourish as a branch.

Pr 18:11 The rich man's wealth *is* his strong city, and as an high wall in his own conceit.

Ho 12:8 And Ephraim said, Yet I am become rich, I have found me out substance: *in* all my labours they shall find none iniquity in me that *were* sin.

Mk 10:24 And the disciples were astonished at his words. But Jesus answereth again, and saith unto them, Children, how hard is it for them that trust in riches to enter into the kingdom of God!

Lu 12:19 And I will say to my soul, Soul, thou hast much goods laid up for many years; take thine ease, eat, drink, *and* be merry.

1 Ti 6:17 Charge them that are rich in this world, that they be not highminded, nor trust in uncertain riches, but in the living God, who giveth us richly all things to enjoy;

See **RICHES**

c. In Weapons

1 S 17:39, 45, 50; 2 S 1:27; Ps 44:3, 6; Eze 32:27; 39:9; Ho 1:7; Am 2:15; Hag 2:22; Zec 4:6

4. Due to Self-Deception

DEATH

Is 28:15 Because ye have said, We have made a covenant with death, and with hell are we at agreement; when the overflowing scourge shall pass through, it shall not come unto us: for we have made lies our refuge, and under falsehood have we hid ourselves:

GRIEF

Is 47:8 Therefore hear now this, *thou that art* given to pleasures, that dwellest carelessly, that sayest in thine heart, I *am,* and none else beside me; I shall not sit *as* a widow, neither shall I know the loss of children:

WAR AND FAMINE

Je 5:12 They have belied the LORD, and said, *It is* not he; neither shall evil come upon us; neither shall we see sword nor famine:

Je 21:13 Behold, I *am* against thee, O inhabitant of the valley, *and* rock of the plain, saith the LORD; which say, Who shall come down against us? or who shall enter into our habitations?

Je 49:4 Wherefore gloriest thou in the valleys, thy flowing valley, O backsliding daughter? that trusted in her treasures, *saying,* Who shall come unto me?

Am 9:10 All the sinners of my people shall die by the sword, which say, The evil shall not overtake nor prevent us.

HUMILIATION

Obad 3 The pride of thine heart hath deceived thee, thou that dwellest in the clefts of the rock, whose habitation *is* high; that saith in his heart, Who shall bring me down to the ground?

POVERTY

Lu 12:19 And I will say to my soul, Soul, thou hast much goods laid up for many years; take thine ease, eat, drink, *and* be merry.

See **DECEPTION**

5. Due to Self-confidence

a. The Danger

Pr 28:26 He that trusteth in his own heart is a fool: but whoso walketh wisely, he shall be delivered.

Is 47:8 Therefore hear now this, *thou that art* given to pleasures, that dwellest carelessly, that sayest in thine heart, I *am,* and none else beside me; I shall not sit *as* a widow, neither shall I know the loss of children:

Ho 10:13 Ye have plowed wickedness, ye have reaped iniquity; ye have eaten the fruit of lies: because thou didst trust in thy way, in the multitude of thy mighty men.

Obad 3 The pride of thine heart hath deceived thee, thou that dwellest in the clefts of the rock, whose habitation *is* high; that saith in his heart, Who shall bring me down to the ground?

Mt 26:33 Peter answered and said unto him, Though all *men* shall be offended because of thee, *yet* will I never be offended.

Lu 18:9 And he spake this parable unto certain which trusted in themselves that they were righteous, and despised others:

1 Co 10:12 Wherefore let him that thinketh he standeth take heed lest he fall.

b. Miscellaneous References

De 29:19 And it come to pass, when he heareth the words of this curse, that he bless himself in his heart, saying, I shall have peace, though I walk in the imagination of mine heart, to add drunkenness to thirst:

Jud 7:2 And the LORD said unto Gideon, The people that *are* with thee *are* too many for me to give the Midianites into their hands, lest Israel vaunt themselves against me, saying, Mine own hand hath saved me.

Est 5:12 Haman said moreover, Yea, Esther the queen did let no man come in with the king unto the banquet that she had prepared but myself; and to morrow am I invited unto her also with the king.

Ps 10:5 His ways are always grievous; thy judgments *are* far above out of his sight: *as for* all his enemies, he puffeth at them.

Pr 14:16 A wise *man* feareth, and departeth from evil: but the fool rageth, and is confident.

Je 48:7 For because thou hast trusted in thy works and in thy treasures, thou shalt also be taken: and Chemosh shall go forth into captivity *with* his priests and his princes together.

Zep 2:15 This *is* the rejoicing city that dwelt carelessly, that said in her heart, I *am,* and *there is* none beside me: how is she become a desolation, a place for beasts to lie down in! every one that passeth by her shall hiss, *and* wag his hand.

Mt 20:22 But Jesus answered and said, Ye know not what ye ask. Are ye able to drink of the cup that I shall drink of, and to be baptized with the baptism that I am baptized with? They say unto him, We are able.

Mk 14:31 But he spake the more vehemently, If I should die with thee, I will not deny thee in any wise. Likewise also said they all.

Lu 22:33 And he said unto him, Lord, I am ready to go with thee, both into prison, and to death.

See **ASSURANCE, SECURITY**

INSEPARABLENESS, *of Christ and* *believers*

ACCOMPANIED BY HIS PRESENCE

Mt 28:20 Teaching them to observe all things whatsoever I have commanded you: and, lo, I am with you alway, *even* unto the end of the world. Amen.

HELD CLOSE BY HIS HAND

Jn 10:28 And I give unto them eternal life; and they shall never perish, neither shall any *man* pluck them out of my hand.

LIKE BRANCHES IN THE VINE

Jn 15:4 Abide in me, and I in you. As the branch cannot bear fruit of itself, except it abide in the vine; no more can ye, except ye abide in me.

IN PERPETUAL FELLOWSHIP

Jn 17:23 I in them, and thou in me, that they may be made perfect in one; and that the world may know that thou hast sent me, and hast loved them, as thou hast loved me.

NO POWER CAN SEVER

Ro 8:38–39 For I am persuaded, that neither death, nor life, nor angels, nor principalities, nor powers, nor things present, nor things to come,

Nor height, nor depth, nor any other creature, shall be able to separate us from the love of God, which is in Christ Jesus our Lord.

See **ABIDING IN CHRIST**

INSIGHT, *lack of, inability to perceive* *spiritual truths*

Mt 16:11 How is it that ye do not understand that I spake *it* not to you concerning bread, that ye should beware of the leaven of the Pharisees and of the Sadducees?

Mt 16:22 Then Peter took him, and began to rebuke him, saying, Be it far from thee, Lord: this shall not be unto thee.

Mk 9:32 But they understood not that saying, and were afraid to ask him.

Lu 24:21 But we trusted that it had been he which should have redeemed Israel: and beside all this, to day is the third day since these things were done.

Jn 3:4 Nicodemus saith unto him, How can a man be born when he is old? can he enter the second time into his mother's womb, and be born?

Jn 6:60 Many therefore of his disciples, when they had heard *this*, said, This is an hard saying; who can hear it?

Jn 20:2 Then she runneth, and cometh to Simon Peter, and to the other disciple, whom Jesus loved, and saith unto them, They have taken away the Lord out of the sepulchre, and we know not where they have laid him.

Jn 20:8 Then went in also that other disciple, which came first to the sepulchre, and he saw, and believed.

Jn 20:25 The other disciples therefore said unto him, We have seen the Lord. But he said unto them, Except I shall see in his hands the print of the nails, and put my finger into the print of the nails, and thrust my hand into his side, I will not believe.

Jn 21:4 But when the morning was now come, Jesus stood on the shore: but the disciples knew not that it was Jesus.

Ac 12:15 And they said unto her, Thou art mad. But she constantly affirmed that it was even so. Then said they, It is his angel.

1 Co 2:9 But as it is written, Eye hath not seen, nor ear heard, neither have entered into the heart of man, the things which God hath prepared for them that love him.

1 Co 3:1 And I, brethren, could not speak unto you as unto spiritual, but as unto carnal, *even* as unto babes in Christ.

2 Co 3:15 But even unto this day, when Moses is read, the vail is upon their heart.

See **PERCEPTION**

INSPIRATION, DIVINE, God breathed; supernatural means by which God communicated his Word

1. Of Prophets and Teachers

2 K 17:13 Yet the LORD testified against Israel, and against Judah, by all the prophets, *and by* all the seers, saying, Turn ye from your evil ways, and keep my commandments *and* my statutes, according to all the law which I commanded your fathers, and which I sent to you by my servants the prophets.

2 Chr 18:13 And Micaiah said, *As* the LORD liveth, even what my God saith, that will I speak.

Ne 9:30 Yet many years didst thou forbear them, and testifiedst against them by thy spirit in thy prophets: yet would they not give ear: therefore gavest thou them into the hand of the people of the lands.

Jb 32:8 But *there is* a spirit in man: and the inspiration of the Almighty giveth them understanding.

He 1:1 God, who at sundry times and in divers manners spake in time past unto the fathers by the prophets,

1 Pe 1:11 Searching what, or what manner of time the Spirit of Christ which was in them did signify, when it testified beforehand the sufferings of Christ, and the glory that should follow.

2 Pe 1:20–21 Knowing this first, that no prophecy of the scripture is of any private interpretation.

For the prophecy came not in old time by the will of man: but holy men of God spake *as they were* moved by the Holy Ghost.

2 Pe 3:2 That ye may be mindful of the words which were spoken before by the holy prophets, and of the commandment of us the apostles of the Lord and Saviour:

2. Promises of Special

Ex 4:12 Now therefore go, and I will be with thy mouth, and teach thee what thou shalt say.

2 K 7:1 Then Elisha said, Hear ye the word of the LORD; Thus saith the LORD, To morrow about this time *shall* a measure of fine flour *be sold* for a shekel, and two measures of barley for a shekel, in the gate of Samaria.

Ps 119:43 And take not the word of truth utterly out of my mouth; for I have hoped in thy judgments.

Pr 16:2 All the ways of a man *are* clean in his own eyes; but the LORD weigheth the spirits.

Is 50:4 The Lord GOD hath given me the tongue of the learned, that I should know how to speak a word in season to *him that is* weary: he wakeneth morning by morning, he wakeneth mine ear to hear as the learned.

Is 51:16 And I have put my words in thy mouth, and I have covered thee in the shadow of mine hand, that I may plant the heavens, and lay the foundations of the earth, and say unto Zion, Thou *art* my people.

Je 5:14 Wherefore thus saith the LORD God of hosts, Because ye speak this word, behold, I will make my words in thy mouth fire, and this people wood, and it shall devour them.

Mt 10:19 But when they deliver you up, take no thought how or what ye shall speak: for it shall be given you in that same hour what ye shall speak.

Lu 21:15 For I will give you a mouth and wisdom, which all your adversaries shall not be able to gainsay nor resist.

1 Co 2:13 Which things also we speak, not in the words which man's wisdom teacheth, but which the Holy Ghost teacheth; comparing spiritual things with spiritual.

3. Examples

THE SEVENTY ELDERS

Nu 11:25 And the LORD came down in a cloud, and spake unto him, and took of the spirit that *was* upon him, and gave *it* unto the seventy elders: and it came to pass, *that,* when the spirit rested upon them, they prophesied, and did not cease.

BALAAM
Nu 23:5 And the LORD put a word in Balaam's mouth, and said, Return unto Balak, and thus thou shalt speak.

DAVID
2 S 23:2 The Spirit of the LORD spake by me, and his word *was* in my tongue.

MICAIAH
1 K 22:14 And Micaiah said, As the LORD liveth, what the LORD saith unto me, that will I speak.
2 Chr 20:14 Then upon Jahaziel the son of Zechariah, the son of Benaiah, the son of Jeiel, the son of Mattaniah, a Levite of the sons of Asaph, came the Spirit of the LORD in the midst of the congregation;

ZECHARIAH
2 Chr 24:20 And the Spirit of God came upon Zechariah the son of Jehoiada the priest, which stood above the people, and said unto them, Thus saith God, Why transgress ye the commandments of the LORD, that ye cannot prosper? because ye have forsaken the LORD, he hath also forsaken you.

JEREMIAH
Je 1:9–10 Then the LORD put forth his hand, and touched my mouth. And the LORD said unto me, Behold, I have put my words in thy mouth.
    See, I have this day set thee over the nations and over the kingdoms, to root out, and to pull down, and to destroy, and to throw down, to build, and to plant.
Je 20:9 Then I said, I will not make mention of him, nor speak any more in his name. But *his word* was in mine heart as a burning fire shut up in my bones, and I was weary with forbearing, and I could not *stay.*

EZEKIEL
Eze 3:17 Son of man, I have made thee a watchman unto the house of Israel: therefore hear the word at my mouth, and give them warning from me.
Eze 11:5 And the Spirit of the LORD fell upon me, and said unto me, Speak; Thus saith the LORD; Thus have ye said, O house of Israel: for I know the things that come into your mind, *every one of* them.
Mi 3:8 But truly I am full of power by the spirit of the LORD, and of judgment, and of might, to declare unto Jacob his transgression, and to Israel his sin.
Ac 11:28 And there stood up one of them named Agabus, and signified by the spirit that there should be great dearth throughout all the world: which came to pass in the days of Claudius Caesar.
Ac 21:11 And when he was come unto us, he took Paul's girdle, and bound his own hands and feet, and said, Thus saith the Holy Ghost, So shall the Jews at Jerusalem bind the man that owneth this girdle, and shall deliver *him* into the hands of the Gentiles.

See **MIND, THOUGHTS**

INSTABILITY, *lack of steadfastness*

1. Warnings
Pr 5:6 Lest thou shouldest ponder the path of life, her ways are moveable, *that* thou canst not know *them.*
Pr 24:21 My son, fear thou the LORD and the king: *and* meddle not with them that are given to change:
Je 2:36 Why gaddest thou about so much to change thy way? thou also shalt be ashamed of Egypt, as thou wast ashamed of Assyria.
Ho 6:4 O Ephraim, what shall I do unto thee? O Judah, what shall I do unto thee? for your goodness *is* as a morning cloud, and as the early dew it goeth away.
Ep 4:14 That we *henceforth* be no more children, tossed to and fro, and carried about with every wind of doctrine, by the sleight of men, *and* cunning craftiness, whereby they lie in wait to deceive;
He 13:9 Be not carried about with divers and strange doctrines. For *it is a*

good thing that the heart be established with grace; not with meats, which have not profited them that have been occupied therein.

Ja 1:6 But let him ask in faith, nothing wavering. For he that wavereth is like a wave of the sea driven with the wind and tossed.

2. Examples

Ge 49:4; Ex 32:1 Ps 78:8; 106:13; Mt 11:7; 13:6; Mk 4:6, 17; Lu 8:6, 13; Ac 7:40; 13:13; Ga 1:6; 2:12; Jude 12

See **STEADFASTNESS**

INSTINCT, *an innate unlearned aptitude or ability*

Pr 1:17; 6:6–7; 30:24; Is 1:3; Je 8:7

See **MANKIND**

INSTRUCTION, *teaching, guidance*

1. Its Value

Ex 18:20 And thou shalt teach them ordinances and laws, and shalt shew them the way wherein they must walk, and the work that they must do.

Ps 2:10 Be wise now therefore, O ye kings: be instructed, ye judges of the earth.

Ps 78:1 Maschil of Asaph. Give ear, O my people, *to* my law: incline your ears to the words of my mouth.

Ps 105:22 To bind his princes at his pleasure; and teach his senators wisdom.

Pr 1:8 My son, hear the instruction of thy father, and forsake not the law of thy mother:

Pr 4:1 Hear, ye children, the instruction of a father, and attend to know understanding.

Pr 6:23 For the commandment *is* a lamp; and the law *is* light; and reproofs of instruction *are* the way of life:

Pr 8:10 Receive my instruction, and not silver; and knowledge rather than choice gold.

Pr 8:33 Hear instruction, and be wise, and refuse it not.

Pr 10:17 He *is in* the way of life that keepeth instruction: but he that refuseth reproof erreth.

Pr 12:1 Whoso loveth instruction loveth knowledge: but he that hateth reproof *is* brutish.

Pr 13:1 A wise son *heareth* his father's instruction: but a scorner heareth not rebuke.

Pr 19:20 Hear counsel, and receive instruction, that thou mayest be wise in thy latter end.

Pr 22:19 That thy trust may be in the LORD, I have made known to thee this day, even to thee.

Pr 23:12 Apply thine heart unto instruction, and thine ears to the words of knowledge.

Pr 23:19 Hear thou, my son, and be wise, and guide thine heart in the way.

Ec 12:11 The words of the wise *are* as goads, and as nails fastened by the masters of assemblies, *which* are given from one shepherd.

Je 6:8 Be thou instructed, O Jerusalem, lest my soul depart from thee; lest I make thee desolate, a land not inhabited.

Je 35:13 Thus saith the LORD of hosts, the God of Israel; Go and tell the men of Judah and the inhabitants of Jerusalem, Will ye not receive instruction to hearken to my words? saith the LORD.

1 Co 12:1 Now concerning spiritual *gifts*, brethren, I would not have you ignorant.

Col 3:16 Let the word of Christ dwell in you richly in all wisdom; teaching and admonishing one another in psalms and hymns and spiritual songs, singing with grace in your hearts to the Lord.

2. Examples

Ex 18:16 When they have a matter, they come unto me; and I judge between one and another, and I do make *them* know the statutes of God, and his laws.

Ex 19:7 And Moses came and called for the elders of the people, and laid before their faces all these words which the LORD commanded him.

Ex 24:3 And Moses came and told the people all the words of the LORD, and all the judgments: and all the people answered with one voice, and said, All the words which the LORD hath said will we do.

Ex 34:32 And afterward all the children of Israel came nigh: and he gave them in commandment all that the LORD had spoken with him in mount Sinai.

De 4:44 And this is the law which Moses set before the children of Israel:

De 31:28 Gather unto me all the elders of your tribes, and your officers, that I may speak these words in their ears, and call heaven and earth to record against them.

De 33:10 They shall teach Jacob thy judgments, and Israel thy law: they shall put incense before thee, and whole burnt sacrifice upon thine altar.

1 S 9:27 *And* as they were going down to the end of the city, Samuel said to Saul, Bid the servant pass on before us, (and he passed on,) but stand thou still a while, that I may shew thee the word of God.

1 S 10:8 And thou shalt go down before me to Gilgal; and, behold, I will come down unto thee, to offer burnt offerings, *and* to sacrifice sacrifices of peace offerings: seven days shalt thou tarry, till I come to thee, and shew thee what thou shalt do.

1 S 12:7 Now therefore stand still, that I may reason with you before the LORD of all the righteous acts of the LORD, which he did to you and to your fathers.

1 S 12:23 Moreover as for me, God forbid that I should sin against the LORD in ceasing to pray for you: but I will teach you the good and the right way:

1 S 15:1 Samuel also said unto Saul, The LORD sent me to anoint thee *to be* king over his people, over Israel: now therefore hearken thou unto the voice of the words of the LORD.

2 K 17:28 Then one of the priests whom they had carried away from Samaria came and dwelt in Bethel, and taught them how they should fear the LORD.

2 Chr 17:7 Also in the third year of his reign he sent to his princes, *even* to Ben-hail, and to Obadiah, and to Zechariah, and to Nethaneel, and to Michaiah, to teach in the cities of Judah.

2 Chr 30:22 And Hezekiah spake comfortably unto all the Levites that taught the good knowledge of the LORD: and they did eat throughout the feast seven days, offering peace offerings, and making confession to the LORD God of their fathers.

Ezr 7:10 For Ezra had prepared his heart to seek the law of the LORD, and to do *it,* and to teach in Israel statutes and judgments.

Ezr 7:25 And thou, Ezra, after the wisdom of thy God, that *is* in thine hand, set magistrates and judges, which may judge all the people that *are* beyond the river, all such as know the laws of thy God; and teach ye them that know *them* not.

Ne 8:2 And Ezra the priest brought the law before the congregation both of men and women, and all that could hear with understanding, upon the first day of the seventh month.

Ne 8:7 Also Jeshua, and Bani, and Sherebiah, Jamin, Akkub, Shabbethai, Hodijah, Maaseiah, Kelita, Azariah, Jozabad, Hanan, Pelaiah, and the Levites, caused the people to understand the law: and the people *stood* in their place.

Jb 4:3 Behold, thou hast instructed many, and thou hast strengthened the weak hands.

Pr 1:3 To receive the instruction of wisdom, justice, and judgment, and equity;

Pr 1:23 Turn you at my reproof: behold, I will pour out my spirit unto you, I will make known my words unto you.

Pr 10:21 The lips of the righteous feed many: but fools die for want of wisdom.

Eze 20:4 Wilt thou judge them, son of man, wilt thou judge *them?* cause them to know the abominations of their fathers:

Mal 2:7 For the priest's lips should keep knowledge, and they should seek the law at his mouth: for he *is* the messenger of the LORD of hosts.

Mt 5:2 And he opened his mouth, and taught them, saying,

Mt 13:52 Then said he unto them, Therefore every scribe *which is* instructed unto the kingdom of heaven is like unto a man *that is* an householder, which bringeth forth out of his treasure *things* new and old.

Mk 2:13 And he went forth again by the sea side; and all the multitude resorted unto him, and he taught them.

Lu 1:4 That thou mightest know the certainty of those things, wherein thou hast been instructed.

Lu 24:27 And beginning at Moses and all the prophets, he expounded unto them in all the scriptures the things concerning himself.

Lu 24:45 Then opened he their understanding, that they might understand the scriptures,

Ac 8:35 Then Philip opened his mouth, and began at the same scripture, and preached unto him Jesus.

Ac 11:26 And when he had found him, he brought him unto Antioch. And it came to pass, that a whole year they assembled themselves with the church, and taught much people. And the disciples were called Christians first in Antioch.

Ac 15:35 Paul also and Barnabas continued in Antioch, teaching and preaching the word of the Lord, with many others also.

Ac 16:32 And they spake unto him the word of the Lord, and to all that were in his house.

Ac 18:11 And he continued *there* a year and six months, teaching the word of God among them.

Ac 18:26 And he began to speak boldly in the synagogue: whom when Aquila and Priscilla had heard, they took him unto *them,* and expounded unto him the way of God more perfectly.

Ac 20:20 *And* how I kept back nothing that was profitable *unto you,* but have shewed you, and have taught you publickly, and from house to house,

Ac 28:23 And when they had appointed him a day, there came many to him into *his* lodging; to whom he expounded and testified the kingdom of God, persuading them concerning Jesus, both out of the law of Moses, and *out of* the prophets, from morning till evening.

Ro 11:25 For I would not, brethren, that ye should be ignorant of this mystery, lest ye should be wise in your own conceits; that blindness in part is happened to Israel, until the fulness of the Gentiles be come in.

1 Co 4:17 For this cause have I sent unto you Timotheus, who is my beloved son, and faithful in the Lord, who shall bring you into remembrance of my ways which be in Christ, as I teach every where in every church.

1 Co 7:35 And this I speak for your own profit; not that I may cast a snare upon you, but for that which is comely, and that ye may attend upon the Lord without distraction.

1 Co 10:1 Moreover, brethren, I would not that ye should be ignorant, how that all our fathers were under the cloud, and all passed through the sea;

1 Co 12:3 Wherefore I give you to understand, that no man speaking by the Spirit of God calleth Jesus accursed: and *that* no man can say that Jesus is the Lord, but by the Holy Ghost.

1 Co 12:31 But covet earnestly the best gifts: and yet shew I unto you a more excellent way.

1 Co 14:19 Yet in the church I had rather speak five words with my understanding, that *by my voice* I might teach others also, than ten thousand words in an *unknown* tongue.

Col 1:28 Whom we preach, warning every man, and teaching every man in all wisdom; that we may present every man perfect in Christ Jesus:

1 Ti 3:15 But if I tarry long, that thou mayest know how thou oughtest to behave thyself in the house of God, which is the church of the living God, the pillar and ground of the truth.

2 Ti 2:25 In meekness instructing those that oppose themselves; if God peradventure will give them repentance to the acknowledging of the truth;

He 8:11 And they shall not teach every man his neighbour, and every man his brother, saying, Know the Lord: for all shall know me, from the least to the greatest.

2 Pe 1:12 Wherefore I will not be negligent to put you always in remembrance of these things, though ye know *them,* and be established in the present truth.

3. Of Children

Jos 8:35 There was not a word of all that Moses commanded, which Joshua read not before all the congregation of Israel, with the women, and the little ones, and the strangers that were conversant among them.

2 K 12:2 And Jehoash did *that which was* right in the sight of the LORD all his days wherein Jehoiada the priest instructed him.

Ps 34:11 Come, ye children, hearken unto me: I will teach you the fear of the LORD.

Pr 3:1 My son, forget not my law; but let thine heart keep my commandments:

2 Ti 3:15 And that from a child thou hast known the holy scriptures, which are able to make thee wise unto salvation through faith which is in Christ Jesus.

See **PARENTS**

4. Divine

FOR THE YOUNG

Ps 71:17 O God, thou hast taught me from my youth: and hitherto have I declared thy wondrous works.

Is 8:11 For the LORD spake thus to me with a strong hand, and instructed me that I should not walk in the way of this people, saying,

Is 28:26 For his God doth instruct him to discretion, *and* doth teach him.

GIVEN WITH INFINITE PAINS

Je 32:3 For Zedekiah king of Judah had shut him up, saying, Wherefore

dost thou prophesy, and say, Thus saith the LORD, Behold, I will give this city into the hand of the king of Babylon, and he shall take it;

FORETOLD

Jn 6:45 It is written in the prophets, And they shall be all taught of God. Every man therefore that hath heard, and hath learned of the Father, cometh unto me.

1 Co 2:12 Now we have received, not the spirit of the world, but the spirit which is of God; that we might know the things that are freely given to us of God.

CHRIST, THE GREAT TEACHER

Ep 4:2 With all lowliness and meekness, with longsuffering, forbearing one another in love;

LOVE'S GREAT LESSON

1 Th 4:9 But as touching brotherly love ye need not that I write unto you: for ye yourselves are taught of God to love one another.

1 Jn 2:27 But the anointing which ye have received of him abideth in you, and ye need not that any man teach you: but as the same anointing teacheth you of all things, and is truth, and is no lie, and even as it hath taught you, ye shall abide in him.

5. Commanded

Le 10:11 And that ye may teach the children of Israel all the statutes which the LORD hath spoken unto them by the hand of Moses.

De 6:7 And thou shalt teach them diligently unto thy children, and shalt talk of them when thou sittest in thine house, and when thou walkest by the way, and when thou liest down, and when thou risest up.

2 Chr 35:3 And said unto the Levites that taught all Israel, which were holy unto the LORD, Put the holy ark in the house which Solomon the son of David king of Israel did build; *it shall* not *be* a burden upon *your* shoulders: serve now the LORD your God, and his people Israel,

Ne 8:7 Also Jeshua, and Bani, and Sherebiah, Jamin, Akkub, Shabbethai, Hodijah, Maaseiah, Kelita, Azariah, Jozabad, Hanan, Pelaiah, and the Levites, caused the people to understand the law: and the people *stood* in their place.

Ps 78:6 That the generation to come might know *them, even* the children *which* should be born; *who* should arise and declare *them* to their children:

Eze 44:23 And they shall teach my people *the difference* between the holy and profane, and cause them to discern between the unclean and the clean.

Col 3:16 Let the word of Christ dwell in you richly in all wisdom; teaching and admonishing one another in psalms and hymns and spiritual songs, singing with grace in your hearts to the Lord.

1 Ti 4:11 These things command and teach.

2 Ti 2:24 And the servant of the Lord must not strive; but be gentle unto all *men,* apt to teach, patient,

See **TEACHER, UNDERSTANDING**

INTEGRITY *See* **BUSINESS**

INTERCESSION, *pleading or praying on behalf of another*

1. Of Christ

FOR WEAK BELIEVERS
Lu 22:32 But I have prayed for thee, that thy faith fail not: and when thou art converted, strengthen thy brethren.

FOR ENEMIES
Lu 23:34 Then said Jesus, Father, forgive them; for they know not what they do. And they parted his raiment, and cast lots.

FOR SENDING OF THE COMFORTER
Jn 14:16 And I will pray the Father, and he shall give you another Comforter, that he may abide with you for ever;

SPECIAL FOR THE CHURCH
Jn 17:9 I pray for them: I pray not for the world, but for them which thou hast given me; for they are thine.

OUR ACCEPTANCE DEPENDS UPON
Ro 8:34 Who *is* he that condemneth? *It is* Christ that died, yea rather, that is risen again, who is even at the right hand of God, who also maketh intercession for us.

SALVATION THROUGH
He 7:25 Wherefore he is able also to save them to the uttermost that come unto God by him, seeing he ever liveth to make intercession for them.

2. Between Humans
Ge 37:21, 26; 44:33; 1 S 19:4; 25:24; 1 K 20:32; Est 4:8; 8:3; Je 38:9; Philemon 10

3. Examples

MOSES FOR ISRAEL
Ex 32:32 Yet now, if thou wilt forgive their sin—; and if not, blot me, I pray thee, out of thy book which thou hast written.

MOSES FOR MIRIAM
Nu 12:13 And Moses cried unto the LORD, saying, Heal her now, O God, I beseech thee.

MOSES FOR ISRAEL
Nu 14:17 And now, I beseech thee, let the power of my Lord be great, according as thou hast spoken, saying,

De 9:26 I prayed therefore unto the LORD, and said, O Lord GOD, destroy not thy people and thine inheritance, which thou hast redeemed through thy greatness, which thou hast brought forth out of Egypt with a mighty hand.

SAMUEL FOR ISRAEL
1 S 7:5 And Samuel said, Gather all Israel to Mizpeh, and I will pray for you unto the LORD.

A MAN OF GOD FOR JEROBOAM
1 K 13:6 And the king answered and said unto the man of God, Intreat now

the face of the LORD thy God, and pray for me, that my hand may be restored me again. And the man of God besought the LORD, and the king's hand was restored him again, and became as *it was* before.

DAVID FOR ISRAEL

1 Chr 21:17 And David said unto God, *Is it* not I *that* commanded the people to be numbered? even I it is that have sinned and done evil indeed; but *as for* these sheep, what have they done? let thine hand, I pray thee, O LORD my God, be on me, and on my father's house; but not on thy people, that they should be plagued.

HEZEKIAH FOR THE PEOPLE

2 Chr 30:18 For a multitude of the people, *even* many of Ephraim, and Manasseh, Issachar, and Zebulun, had not cleansed themselves, yet did they eat the passover otherwise than it was written. But Hezekiah prayed for them, saying, The good LORD pardon every one

OTHER INSTANCES

Jb 42:10 And the LORD turned the captivity of Job, when he prayed for his friends: also the LORD gave Job twice as much as he had before.

Ps 106:23 Therefore he said that he would destroy them, had not Moses his chosen stood before him in the breach, to turn away his wrath, lest he should destroy *them.*

Ep 1:16 Cease not to give thanks for you, making mention of you in my prayers;

4. With Christ

Mt 8:6; Mk 7:32; Lu 4:38; 7:4; 9:38; Jn 4:47

See **PRAYER**

INTOLERANCE *See* **BIGOTRY, TOLERANCE**

INTRUSION, *UPON CHRIST*

Mk 1:36 And Simon and they that were with him followed after him.

Mk 3:20 And the multitude cometh together again, so that they could not so much as eat bread.

Mk 6:33 And the people saw them departing, and many knew him, and ran afoot thither out of all cities, and outwent them, and came together unto him.

Mk 7:24 And from thence he arose, and went into the borders of Tyre and Sidon, and entered into an house, and would have no man know *it:* but he could not be hid.

Lu 4:42 And when it was day, he departed and went into a desert place: and the people sought him, and came unto him, and stayed him, that he should not depart from them.

Lu 9:11 And the people, when they knew *it,* followed him: and he received them, and spake unto them of the kingdom of God, and healed them that had need of healing.

INVINCIBILITY *See* **HEROES**

INVITATIONS

1. Come

INTO A PLACE OF SAFETY
Ge 7:1

TO A GOODLY FELLOWSHIP
Nu 10:29

FOR PERSONAL CLEANSING
Is 1:18

FOR A SATISFYING PORTION
Is 55:1

FOR REST OF SOUL
Mt 11:28

AT THE KING'S URGENT INVITATION
Mt 22:4

TO THE GOSPEL FEAST
Lu 14:17

AT THE THREEFOLD CALL
Re 22:17

2. Let Us . . .

FEAR

He 4:1 Let us therefore fear, lest, a promise being left *us* of entering into his rest, any of you should seem to come short of it.

LABOR

He 4:11 Let us labour therefore to enter into that rest, lest any man fall after the same example of unbelief.

COME BOLDLY

He 4:16 Let us therefore come boldly unto the throne of grace, that we may obtain mercy, and find grace to help in time of need.

GO ON

He 6:1 Therefore leaving the principles of the doctrine of Christ, let us go on unto perfection; not laying again the foundation of repentance from dead works, and of faith toward God,

DRAW NEAR

He 10:22 Let us draw near with a true heart in full assurance of faith, having our hearts sprinkled from an evil conscience, and our bodies washed with pure water.

HOLD FAST

He 10:23 Let us hold fast the profession of *our* faith without wavering; (for he is faithful that promised;)

CONSIDER ONE ANOTHER

He 10:24 And let us consider one another to provoke unto love and to good works:

See **WARNINGS**

IRRIGATION *See* AGRICULTURE

IRON, *a metal*

Ge 4:22; Nu 31:22; De 3:11; 8:9; Jos 8:31; 17:16; 1 K 22:11; 1 Chr 22:3, 14; 29:2, 7; Jb 19:24; 28:2; 41:27; Eze 22:18; 27:12; Da 2:34; Ac 12:10; Re 18:12

IRONY

2 S 6:20; 1 K 18:27; 22:15; Jb 12:2; Mt 22:16; 27:29; Mk 2:17; 15:9

ISAAC, *laughter, son of Abraham and Sarah*

Ge 17:19 And God said, Sarah thy wife shall bear thee a son indeed; and thou shalt call his name Isaac: and I will establish my covenant with him for an everlasting covenant, *and* with his seed after him.

Ge 21:3 And Abraham called the name of his son that was born unto him, whom Sarah bare to him, Isaac.

Ge 21:12 And God said unto Abraham, Let it not be grievous in thy sight because of the lad, and because of thy bondwoman; in all that Sarah hath said unto thee, hearken unto her voice; for in Isaac shall thy seed be called.

Ge 22:2 And he said, Take now thy son, thine only *son* Isaac, whom thou lovest, and get thee into the land of Moriah; and offer him there for a burnt offering upon one of the mountains which I will tell thee of.

Ge 22:6–9 And Abraham took the wood of the burnt offering, and laid *it* upon Isaac his son; and he took the fire in his hand, and a knife; and they went both of them together.

And Isaac spake unto Abraham his father, and said, My father: and he said, Here *am* I, my son. And he said, Behold the fire and the wood: but where *is* the lamb for a burnt offering?

And Abraham said, My son, God will provide himself a lamb for a burnt offering: so they went both of them together.

And they came to the place which God had told him of; and Abraham built an altar there, and laid the wood in order, and bound Isaac his son, and laid him on the altar upon the wood.

Ge 24:4 But thou shalt go unto my country, and to my kindred, and take a wife unto my son Isaac.

Ge 24:63 And Isaac went out to meditate in the field at the eventide: and he lifted up his eyes, and saw, and, behold, the camels *were* coming.

Ge 24:67 And Isaac brought her into his mother Sarah's tent, and took Rebekah, and she became his wife; and he loved her: and Isaac was comforted after his mother's *death.*

Ge 26:7 And the men of the place asked *him* of his wife; and he said, She *is* my sister: for he feared to say, *She is* my wife; lest, *said he,* the men of the place should kill me for Rebekah; because she *was* fair to look upon.

Ge 26:12 Then Isaac sowed in that land, and received in the same year an hundredfold: and the LORD blessed him.

Ge 26:20–22 And the herdmen of Gerar did strive with Isaac's herdmen, saying, The water *is* ours: and he called the name of the well Esek; because they strove with him.

And they digged another well, and strove for that also: and he called the name of it Sitnah.

And he removed from thence, and digged another well; and for that they strove not: and he called the name of it Rehoboth; and he said, For now the LORD hath made room for us, and we shall be fruitful in the land.

Ge 26:25 And he builded an altar there, and called upon the name of the LORD and pitched his tent there: and there Isaac's servants digged a well.

Ge 28:1 And Isaac called Jacob, and blessed him, and charged him, and said unto him, Thou shalt not take a wife of the daughters of Canaan.

Ge 35:29 And Isaac gave up the ghost, and died, and was gathered unto his people, *being* old and full of days: and his sons Esau and Jacob buried him.

Ge 49:31 There they buried Abraham and Sarah his wife; there they buried Isaac and Rebekah his wife; and there I buried Leah.

Ro 9:7 Neither, because they are the seed of Abraham, *are they* all children: but, In Isaac shall thy seed be called.

He 11:17 By faith Abraham, when he was tried, offered up Isaac: and he that had received the promises offered up his only begotten *son,*

He 11:20 By faith Isaac blessed Jacob and Esau concerning things to come.

Ja 2:21 Was not Abraham our father justified by works, when he had offered Isaac his son upon the altar?

ISAIAH, *or Esaias, son of Amoz, one of the greater prophets*

1. Person

2 K 19:2, 20; 20:1, 14; 2 Chr 26:22; 32:20; Is 1:1; 2:1; 6:1; 7:3; 13:1; 20:2; 37:2; 38:1; 39:3; Mt 3:3; 4:14; 8:17; 12:17; 13:14; 15:7; Jn 1:23; 12:39; Ac 28:25; Ro 9:27; 15:12

2. Book

Author: Isaiah, the prophet, the son of Amoz.

(1) Prophesied during the reigns of Uzziah, Jotham, Ahaz, and Hezekiah (1:1).

(2) His call and anointing (6:1–8).

(3) His family (7:3; 8:3–4).

(4) Generally regarded as the greatest of the Old Testament prophets.

Date Written: Isaiah's ministry extended about 60 years (c. 740–680 B.C.). Chapters 1–39 were probably recorded around 700 B.C.; chapters 40–66, toward the end of Isaiah's ministry (c. 681 B.C.).

Purpose: To reveal that salvation, physical and spiritual, is of the Lord.

To Whom Written: The nation of Judah.

Main Themes: Seven everlastings.

(1) Strength (26:4).

(2) Judgments (33:14).

(3) Joy (35:10).

(4) Salvation (45:17).

(5) Kindness (54:8).

(6) Covenant (55:3).

(7) Light (60:19).

Key Word: Salvation. Isaiah means "Salvation of Jehovah."

Key Verses: 9:6–7; 53:5–6.

ISHBOSHETH, *son of Saul*
2 S 2:8; 3:8; 4:1, 5, 8, 12

ISHMAEL, *God shall hear, son of Abraham and Hagar*

Ge 16:2–4, 11, 15; 17:18, 20; 21:1–7, 9, 10–14, 14, 18, 21; 25:9, 9, 12–16; 28:9; 36:3; Jud 8:24; 1 Chr 1:29; Ps 83:6; Ga 4:22

ISLANDS, *mentioned in the Scriptures*

Ac 28:1

ISRAEL, *God strives*

1. Name Given to Jacob

Ge 32:28; 35:10; 2 K 17:34; Is 48:1

2. Name Given to God's Chosen People

Ex 4:22; 6:7; 7:4; 12:41; 18:8; 29:45; Nu 10:29; 23:9, 21; 24:1; De 4:37; 10:15; 21:8; 26:15; 32:9; 2 S 5:12; 7:8, 23; 1 K 8:33, 41; 10:9; 1 Chr 17:9, 21, 24; 2 Chr 6:21, 32; 7:10; 9:8; 31:8; Ps 25:22; 33:12; 50:7; 78:71; 98:3; 135:4; 147:19; 148:14; Is 1:2; 5:7; 10:22; 19:25; 41:8; 43:1; 44:1, 21; 45:4; 46:13; 48:12; 49:3; 63:7; Je 10:16; 11:15; 12:14; 13:11; 31:36; 46:27; 51:5; Eze 3:5; 20:5; 21:12; 23:4; 25:14; 34:30; 38:14; Ho 11:1; Jl 3:2; Mt 15:24; 21:33; Lu 1:54; Ro 9:4, 27; 11:1; Ga 6:16; Ph 3:5

3. A Type of the True Church

a. Called to Separation

See **SEPARATION**

b. Exalted to a High Position

De 26:19 And to make thee high above all nations which he hath made, in praise, and in name, and in honour; and that thou mayest be an holy people unto the LORD thy God, as he hath spoken.

De 28:1 And it shall come to pass, if thou shalt hearken diligently unto the voice of the LORD thy God, to observe *and* to do all his commandments which I command thee this day, that the LORD thy God will set thee on high above all nations of the earth:

De 28:13 And the LORD shall make thee the head, and not the tail; and thou shalt be above only, and thou shalt not be beneath; if that thou hearken unto the commandments of the LORD thy God, which I command thee this day, to observe and to do *them:*

De 32:13 He made him ride on the high places of the earth, that he might eat the increase of the fields; and he made him to suck honey out of the rock, and oil out of the flinty rock;

De 33:29 Happy *art* thou, O Israel: who *is* like unto thee, O people saved by the LORD, the shield of thy help, and who *is* the sword of thy excellency! and thine enemies shall be found liars unto thee; and thou shalt tread upon their high places.

1 Chr 14:2 And David perceived that the LORD had confirmed him king over Israel, for his kingdom was lifted up on high, because of his people Israel.

Pr 14:34 Righteousness exalteth a nation: but sin *is* a reproach to any people.

Is 14:2 And the people shall take them, and bring them to their place: and the house of Israel shall possess them in the land of the LORD for servants and handmaids: and they shall take them captives, whose captives they were; and they shall rule over their oppressors.

Is 45:14 Thus saith the LORD, The labour of Egypt, and merchandise of Ethiopia and of the Sabeans, men of stature, shall come over unto thee, and they shall be thine: they shall come after thee; in chains they shall come over, and they shall fall down unto thee, they shall make supplication unto thee, *saying,* Surely God *is* in thee; and *there is* none else, *there is* no God.

Is 49:23 And kings shall be thy nursing fathers, and their queens thy nursing mothers: they shall bow down to thee with *their* face toward the earth, and lick up the dust of thy feet; and thou shalt know that I *am* the LORD: for they shall not be ashamed that wait for me.

Is 58:14 Then shalt thou delight thyself in the LORD; and I will cause thee to ride upon the high places of the earth, and feed thee with the heritage of Jacob thy father: for the mouth of the LORD hath spoken *it.*

Is 60:14 The sons also of them that afflicted thee shall come bending unto thee; and all they that despised thee shall bow themselves down at the soles of thy feet; and they shall call thee, The city of the LORD, The Zion of the Holy One of Israel.

Is 61:6 But ye shall be named the Priests of the LORD: *men* shall call you the Ministers of our God: ye shall eat the riches of the Gentiles, and in their glory shall ye boast yourselves.

Eze 16:12 And I put a jewel on thy forehead, and earrings in thine ears, and a beautiful crown upon thine head.

Eze 17:23 In the mountain of the height of Israel will I plant it: and it shall bring forth boughs, and bear fruit, and be a goodly cedar: and under it shall dwell all fowl of every wing; in the shadow of the branches thereof shall they dwell.

Eze 19:11 And she had strong rods for the sceptres of them that bare rule, and her stature was exalted among the thick branches, and she appeared in her height with the multitude of her branches.

Eze 29:21 In that day will I cause the horn of the house of Israel to bud forth, and I will give thee the opening of the mouth in the midst of them; and they shall know that I *am* the LORD.

Zep 3:19 Behold, at that time I will undo all that afflict thee: and I will save her that halteth, and gather her that was driven out; and I will get them praise and fame in every land where they have been put to shame.

Ac 13:17 The God of this people of Israel chose our fathers, and exalted the people when they dwelt as strangers in the land of Egypt, and with an high arm brought he them out of it.

c. Under the Special Protection of Jehovah

See **PROTECTION**

d. Victorious in Battle

Ge 14:15 And he divided himself against them, he and his servants, by night, and smote them, and pursued them unto Hobah, which *is* on the left hand of Damascus.

Ex 14:30 Thus the LORD saved Israel that day out of the hand of the Egyptians; and Israel saw the Egyptians dead upon the sea shore.

Jos 6:20 So the people shouted when *the priests* blew with the trumpets: and it came to pass, when the people heard the sound of the trumpet, and the people shouted with a great shout, that the wall fell down flat, so that the people went up into the city, every man straight before him, and they took the city.

Jos 10:11 And it came to pass, as they fled from before Israel, *and* were in the going down to Beth-horon, that the LORD cast down great stones from heaven upon them unto Azekah, and they died: *they were* more which died with hailstones than they whom the children of Israel slew with the sword.

Jud 7:21 And they stood every man in his place round about the camp: and all the host ran, and cried, and fled.

1 S 7:10 And as Samuel was offering up the burnt offering, the Philistines drew near to battle against Israel: but the LORD thundered with a great thunder on that day upon the Philistines, and discomfited them; and they were smitten before Israel.

1 S 11:11 And it was *so* on the morrow, that Saul put the people in three companies; and they came into the midst of the host in the morning watch, and slew the Ammonites until the heat of the day: and it came to pass, that they which remained were scattered, so that two of them were not left together.

1 S 17:51 Therefore David ran, and stood upon the Philistine, and took his sword, and drew it out of the sheath thereof, and slew him, and cut off his head therewith. And when the Philistines saw their champion was dead, they fled.

2 S 10:18 And the Syrians fled before Israel; and David slew *the men of* seven hundred chariots of the Syrians, and forty thousand horsemen, and smote Shobach the captain of their host, who died there.

2 S 23:10 He arose, and smote the Philistines until his hand was weary, and his hand clave unto the sword: and the LORD wrought a great victory that day; and the people returned after him only to spoil.

2 Chr 20:27 Then they returned, every man of Judah and Jerusalem, and Jehoshaphat in the forefront of them, to go again to Jerusalem with joy; for the LORD had made them to rejoice over their enemies.

Pr 20:26 A wise king scattereth the wicked, and bringeth the wheel over them.

Zec 9:13 When I have bent Judah for me, filled the bow with Ephraim, and raised up thy sons, O Zion, against thy sons, O Greece, and made thee as the sword of a mighty man.

He 11:30 By faith the walls of Jericho fell down, after they were compassed about seven days.

e. Promised Immunity from Calamities

Ex 8:22 And I will sever in that day the land of Goshen, in which my people dwell, that no swarms of *flies* shall be there; to the end thou mayest know that I *am* the LORD in the midst of the earth.

Ex 9:6 And the LORD did that thing on the morrow, and all the cattle of Egypt died: but of the cattle of the children of Israel died not one.

Ex 9:26 Only in the land of Goshen, where the children of Israel *were,* was there no hail.

Ex 11:7 But against any of the children of Israel shall not a dog move his tongue, against man or beast: that ye may know how that the LORD doth put a difference between the Egyptians and Israel.

Ex 12:13 And the blood shall be to you for a token upon the houses where ye *are:* and when I see the blood, I will pass over you, and the plague shall not be upon you to de-stroy *you,* when I smite the land of Egypt.

Ex 15:26 And said, If thou wilt diligently hearken to the voice of the LORD thy God, and wilt do that which is right in his sight, and wilt give ear to his commandments, and keep all his statutes, I will put none of these diseases upon thee, which I have brought upon the Egyptians: for I *am* the LORD that healeth thee.

Ex 30:12 When thou takest the sum of the children of Israel after their number, then shall they give every man a ransom for his soul unto the LORD, when thou numberest them; that there be no plague among them, when *thou* numberest them.

Nu 8:19 And I have given the Levites *as* a gift to Aaron and to his sons from among the children of Israel, to do the service of the children of Israel in the tabernacle of the congregation, and to make an atonement for the children of Israel: that there be no plague among the children of Israel, when the children of Israel come nigh unto the sanctuary.

Ps 91:7 A thousand shall fall at thy side, and ten thousand at thy right hand; *but* it shall not come nigh thee.

Mal 3:11 And I will rebuke the devourer for your sakes, and he shall not destroy the fruits of your ground; neither shall your vine cast her fruit before the time in the field, saith the LORD of hosts.

Mk 16:18 They shall take up serpents; and if they drink any deadly thing, it shall not hurt them; they shall lay hands on the sick, and they shall recover.

4. A Picture of Apostasy

a. Lost the Joy of Divine Favor

Jb 30:31 My harp also is *turned* to mourning, and my organ into the voice of them that weep.

Ps 137:2 We hanged our harps upon the willows in the midst thereof.

Is 16:10 And gladness is taken away, and joy out of the plentiful field; and in the vineyards there shall be no singing, neither shall there be shouting:

the treaders shall tread out no wine in *their* presses; I have made *their* vintage shouting to cease.

Is 23:12 And he said, Thou shalt no more rejoice, O thou oppressed virgin, daughter of Zidon: arise, pass over to Chittim; there also shalt thou have no rest.

Is 24:11 *There is* a crying for wine in the streets; all joy is darkened, the mirth of the land is gone.

Yet I will distress Ariel, and there shall be heaviness and sorrow: and it shall be unto me as Ariel.

Is 29:2 Yet I will distress Ariel, and there shall be heaviness and sorrow: and it shall be unto me as Ariel.

Is 32:13 Upon the land of my people shall come up thorns *and* briers; yea, upon all the houses of joy *in* the joyous city:

Je 7:34 Then will I cause to cease from the cities of Judah, and from the streets of Jerusalem, the voice of mirth, and the voice of gladness, the voice of the bridegroom, and the voice of the bride: for the land shall be desolate.

Je 16:9 For thus saith the LORD of hosts, the God of Israel; Behold, I will cause to cease out of this place in your eyes, and in your days, the voice of mirth, and the voice of gladness, the voice of the bridegroom, and the voice of the bride.

Je 25:10 Moreover I will take from them the voice of mirth, and the voice of gladness, the voice of the bridegroom, and the voice of the bride, the sound of the millstones, and the light of the candle.

Je 48:33 And joy and gladness is taken from the plentiful field, and from the land of Moab; and I have caused wine to fail from the winepresses: none shall tread with shouting; *their* shouting *shall be* no shouting.

Lam 5:15 The joy of our heart is ceased; our dance is turned into mourning.

Eze 7:16 But they that escape of them shall escape, and shall be on the mountains like doves of the valleys, all of them mourning, every one for his iniquity.

Eze 24:25 Also, thou son of man, *shall it* not *be* in the day when I take from them their strength, the joy of their glory, the desire of their eyes, and that whereupon they set their minds, their sons and their daughters,

Eze 26:13 And I will cause the noise of thy songs to cease; and the sound of thy harps shall be no more heard.

Ho 2:11 I will also cause all her mirth to cease, her feast days, her new moons, and her sabbaths, and all her solemn feasts.

Ho 9:1 Rejoice not, O Israel, for joy, as *other* people: for thou hast gone a whoring from thy God, thou hast loved a reward upon every cornfloor.

Jl 1:12 The vine is dried up, and the fig tree languisheth; the pomegranate tree, the palm tree also, and the apple tree, *even* all the trees of the field, are withered: because joy is withered away from the sons of men.

Jl 1:16 Is not the meat cut off before our eyes, *yea,* joy and gladness from the house of our God?

Am 5:16 Therefore the LORD, the God of hosts, the Lord, saith thus; Wailing *shall be* in all streets; and they shall say in all the highways, Alas! alas! and they shall call the husbandman to mourning, and such as are skilful of lamentation to wailing.

Am 8:3 And the songs of the temple shall be howlings in that day, saith the Lord GOD: *there shall be* many dead bodies in every place; they shall cast *them* forth with silence.

Am 8:10 And I will turn your feasts into mourning, and all your songs into lamentation; and I will bring up sackcloth upon all loins, and baldness upon every head; and I will make it as the mourning of an only *son,* and the end thereof as a bitter day.

Re 18:14 And the fruits that thy soul lusted after are departed from thee, and all things which were dainty and goodly are departed from thee, and thou shalt find them no more at all.

Re 18:23 And the light of a candle shall shine no more at all in thee; and the voice of the bridegroom and of the bride shall be heard no more at all in thee: for thy merchants were the great men of the earth; for by thy sorceries were all nations deceived.

b. Compared to an Unfruitful Vine

Ps 44:2 *How* thou didst drive out the heathen with thy hand, and plantedst them; *how* thou didst afflict the people, and cast them out.

Ps 80:8 Thou hast brought a vine out of Egypt: thou hast cast out the heathen, and planted it.

Ps 92:13 Those that be planted in the house of the LORD shall flourish in the courts of our God.

Song 6:11 I went down into the garden of nuts to see the fruits of the valley, *and* to see whether the vine flourished, *and* the pomegranates budded.

Song 8:11 Solomon had a vineyard at Baal-hamon; he let out the vineyard unto keepers; every one for the fruit thereof was to bring a thousand *pieces* of silver.

Is 5:2 And he fenced it, and gathered out the stones thereof, and planted it with the choicest vine, and built a tower in the midst of it, and also made a winepress therein: and he looked that it should bring forth grapes, and it brought forth wild grapes.

Is 37:31 And the remnant that is escaped of the house of Judah shall again take root downward, and bear fruit upward:

Is 60:21 Thy people also *shall be* all righteous: they shall inherit the land for ever, the branch of my planting, the work of my hands, that I may be glorified.

Je 2:21 Yet I had planted thee a noble vine, wholly a right seed: how then art thou turned into the degenerate plant of a strange vine unto me?

Je 18:9 And *at what* instant I shall speak concerning a nation, and concerning a kingdom, to build and to plant *it;*

Eze 15:2 Son of man, What is the vine tree more than any tree, *or than a* branch which is among the trees of the forest?

Eze 15:6 Therefore thus saith the Lord GOD; As the vine tree among the trees of the forest, which I have given to the fire for fuel, so will I give the inhabitants of Jerusalem.

Eze 17:6 And it grew, and became a spreading vine of low stature, whose branches turned toward him, and the roots thereof were under him: so it became a vine, and brought forth branches, and shot forth sprigs.

Eze 19:10 Thy mother *is* like a vine in thy blood, planted by the waters: she was fruitful and full of branches by reason of many waters.

Ho 10:1 Israel *is* an empty vine, he bringeth forth fruit unto himself: according to the multitude of his fruit he hath increased the altars; according to the goodness of his land they have made goodly images.

Jl 1:7 He hath laid my vine waste, and barked my fig tree: he hath made it clean bare, and cast *it* away; the branches thereof are made white.

c. Characterized as an Adulteress

Ex 34:15 Lest thou make a covenant with the inhabitants of the land, and they go a whoring after their gods, and do sacrifice unto their gods, and *one* call thee, and thou eat of his sacrifice;

Le 17:7 And they shall no more offer their sacrifices unto devils, after whom they have gone a whoring. This shall be a statute for ever unto them throughout their generations.

Le 20:6 And the soul that turneth after such as have familiar spirits, and after wizards, to go a whoring after them, I will even set my face against that soul, and will cut him off from among his people.

Nu 14:33 And your children shall wander in the wilderness forty years, and bear your whoredoms, until your carcases be wasted in the wilderness.

Nu 15:39 And it shall be unto you for a fringe, that ye may look upon it, and remember all the commandments of the LORD, and do them; and that ye seek not after your own heart and your own eyes, after which ye use to go a whoring:

De 31:16 And the LORD said unto Moses, Behold, thou shalt sleep with thy fathers; and this people will rise up, and go a whoring after the gods of the strangers of the land, whither they go *to be* among them, and will forsake me, and break my covenant which I have made with them.

Jud 2:17 And yet they would not hearken unto their judges, but they went a whoring after other gods, and bowed themselves unto them: they turned quickly out of the way which their fathers walked in, obeying the commandments of the LORD; *but* they did not so.

Jud 8:27 And Gideon made an ephod thereof, and put it in his city, *even* in Ophrah: and all Israel went thither a whoring after it: which thing became a snare unto Gideon, and to his house.

Jud 8:33 And it came to pass, as soon as Gideon was dead, that the children of Israel turned again, and went a whoring after Baalim, and made Baal-berith their god.

1 Chr 5:25 And they transgressed against the God of their fathers, and went a whoring after the gods of the people of the land, whom God destroyed before them.

2 Chr 21:11 Moreover he made high places in the mountains of Judah, and caused the inhabitants of Jerusalem to commit fornication, and compelled Judah *thereto.*

Ps 73:27 For, lo, they that are far from thee shall perish: thou hast destroyed all them that go a whoring from thee.

Ps 106:39 Thus were they defiled with their own works, and went a whoring with their own inventions.

Is 1:21 How is the faithful city become an harlot! it was full of judgment; righteousness lodged in it; but now murderers.

Is 57:8 Behind the doors also and the posts hast thou set up thy remembrance: for thou hast discovered *thyself to another* than me, and art gone up; thou hast enlarged thy bed, and made thee *a covenant* with them; thou lovedst their bed where thou sawest *it.*

Je 2:20 For of old time I have broken thy yoke, *and* burst thy bands; and thou saidst, I will not transgress; when upon every high hill and under every green tree thou wanderest, playing the harlot.

Je 2:33 Why trimmest thou thy way to seek love? therefore hast thou also taught the wicked ones thy ways.

Je 3:1 They say, If a man put away his wife, and she go from him, and become another man's, shall he return unto her again? shall not that land be greatly polluted? but thou hast played the harlot with many lovers; yet return again to me, saith the LORD.

Je 3:8 And I saw, when for all the causes whereby backsliding Israel committed adultery I had put her away, and given her a bill of divorce; yet her treacherous sister Judah feared not, but went and played the harlot also.

Je 3:20 Surely *as* a wife treacherously departeth from her husband, so have ye dealt treacherously with me, O house of Israel, saith the LORD.

Je 11:15 What hath my beloved to do in mine house, *seeing* she hath wrought lewdness with many, and the holy flesh is passed from thee? when thou doest evil, then thou rejoicest.

Je 13:27 I have seen thine adulteries, and thy neighings, the lewdness of thy whoredom, *and* thine abominations on the hills in the fields. Woe unto thee, O Jerusalem! wilt thou not be made clean? when *shall it* once *be?*

Eze 6:9 And they that escape of you shall remember me among the nations whither they shall be carried captives, because I am broken with their whorish heart, which hath departed from me, and with their eyes, which go a whoring after their idols: and they shall lothe themselves for the evils which they have committed in all their abominations.

Eze 16:15 But thou didst trust in thine own beauty, and playedst the harlot because of thy renown, and pouredst out thy fornications on every one that passed by; his it was.

Eze 16:25 Thou hast built thy high place at every head of the way, and hast made thy beauty to be abhorred, and hast opened thy feet to every one that passed by, and multiplied thy whoredoms.

Eze 20:30 Wherefore say unto the house of Israel, Thus saith the Lord

GOD; Are ye polluted after the manner of your fathers? and commit ye whoredom after their abominations?

Eze 23:3 And they committed whoredoms in Egypt; they committed whoredoms in their youth: there were their breasts pressed, and there they bruised the teats of their virginity.

Eze 23:11 And when her sister Aholibah saw *this,* she was more corrupt in her inordinate love than she, and in her whoredoms more than her sister in *her* whoredoms.

Eze 23:17 And the Babylonians came to her into the bed of love, and they defiled her with their whoredom, and she was polluted with them, and her mind was alienated from them.

Eze 23:30 I will do these *things* unto thee, because thou hast gone a whoring after the heathen, *and* because thou art polluted with their idols.

Eze 23:35 Therefore thus saith the Lord GOD; Because thou hast forgotten me, and cast me behind thy back, therefore bear thou also thy lewdness and thy whoredoms.

Eze 43:7 And he said unto me, Son of man, the place of my throne, and the place of the soles of my feet, where I will dwell in the midst of the children of Israel for ever, and my holy name, shall the house of Israel no more defile, *neither* they, nor their kings, by their whoredom, nor by the carcases of their kings in their high places.

Ho 1:2 The beginning of the word of the LORD by Hosea. And the LORD said to Hosea, Go, take unto thee a wife of whoredoms and children of whoredoms: for the land hath committed great whoredom, *departing* from the LORD.

Ho 2:2 Plead with your mother, plead: for she *is* not my wife, neither *am* I her husband: let her therefore put away her whoredoms out of her sight, and her adulteries from between her breasts;

Ho 3:1 Then said the LORD unto me, Go yet, love a woman beloved of *her* friend, yet an adulteress, according to the love of the LORD toward the children of Israel, who look to other gods, and love flagons of wine.

Ho 4:12 My people ask counsel at their stocks, and their staff declareth unto them: for the spirit of whoredoms hath caused *them* to err, and they have gone a whoring from under their God.

Ho 5:4 They will not frame their doings to turn unto their God: for the spirit of whoredoms *is* in the midst of them, and they have not known the LORD.

Ho 6:10 I have seen an horrible thing in the house of Israel: there *is* the whoredom of Ephraim, Israel is defiled.

Ho 9:1 Rejoice not, O Israel, for joy, as *other* people: for thou hast gone a whoring from thy God, thou hast loved a reward upon every cornfloor.

Mal 2:11 Judah hath dealt treacherously, and an abomination is committed in Israel and in Jerusalem; for Judah hath profaned the holiness of the LORD which he loved, and hath married the daughter of a strange god.

Mt 12:39 But he answered and said unto them, An evil and adulterous generation seeketh after a sign; and there shall no sign be given to it, but the sign of the prophet Jonas:

Ja 4:4 Ye adulterers and adulteresses, know ye not that the friendship of the world is enmity with God? whosoever therefore will be a friend of the world is the enemy of God.

Re 2:22 Behold, I will cast her into a bed, and them that commit adultery with her into great tribulation, except they repent of their deeds.

Re 14:8 And there followed another angel, saying, Babylon is fallen, is fallen, that great city, because she made all nations drink of the wine of the wrath of her fornication.

Re 17:2 With whom the kings of the earth have committed fornication, and the inhabitants of the earth have been made drunk with the wine of her fornication.

Re 18:3 For all nations have drunk of the wine of the wrath of her fornication, and the kings of the earth have committed fornication with her, and the merchants of the earth are waxed rich through the abundance of her delicacies.

d. Threatened with Reprobation

Le 26:17 And I will set my face against you, and ye shall be slain before your enemies: they that hate you shall reign over you; and ye shall flee when none pursueth you.

Le 26:30 And I will destroy your high places, and cut down your images, and cast your carcases upon the carcases of your idols, and my soul shall abhor you.

Nu 14:12 I will smite them with the pestilence, and disinherit them, and will make of thee a greater nation and mightier than they.

De 28:15 But it shall come to pass, if thou wilt not hearken unto the voice of the LORD thy God, to observe to do all his commandments and his statutes which I command thee this day; that all these curses shall come upon thee, and overtake thee:

De 28:63 And it shall come to pass, *that* as the LORD rejoiced over you to do you good, and to multiply you; so the LORD will rejoice over you to destroy you, and to bring you to nought; and ye shall be plucked from off the land whither thou goest to possess it.

De 31:17 Then my anger shall be kindled against them in that day, and I will forsake them, and I will hide my face from them, and they shall be devoured, and many evils and troubles shall befall them; so that they will say in that day, Are not these evils come upon us, because our God *is* not among us?

Jud 2:14 And the anger of the LORD was hot against Israel, and he delivered them into the hands of spoilers that spoiled them, and he sold them into the hands of their enemies round about, so that they could not any longer stand before their enemies.

Jud 10:13 Yet ye have forsaken me, and served other gods: wherefore I will deliver you no more.

1 S 2:32 And thou shalt see an enemy *in my* habitation, in all *the wealth* which *God* shall give Israel: and there shall not be an old man in thine house for ever.

1 S 15:28 And Samuel said unto him, The LORD hath rent the kingdom of Israel from thee this day, and hath given it to a neighbour of thine, *that is* better than thou.

1 K 9:7 Then will I cut off Israel out of the land which I have given them; and this house, which I have hallowed for my name, will I cast out of my sight; and Israel shall be a proverb and a byword among all people:

1 K 14:16 And he shall give Israel up because of the sins of Jeroboam, who did sin, and who made Israel to sin.

2 K 17:23 Until the LORD removed Israel out of his sight, as he had said by all his servants the prophets. So was Israel carried away out of their own land to Assyria unto this day.

2 K 21:14 And I will forsake the remnant of mine inheritance, and deliver them into the hand of their enemies; and they shall become a prey and a spoil to all their enemies;

2 K 24:20 For through the anger of the LORD it came to pass in Jerusalem and Judah, until he had cast them out from his presence, that Zedekiah rebelled against the king of Babylon.

Ps 60:1 O God, thou hast cast us off, thou hast scattered us, thou hast been displeased; O turn thyself to us again.

Ps 60:10 *Wilt* not thou, O God, *which* hadst cast us off? and *thou,* O God, *which* didst not go out with our armies?

Ps 106:41 And he gave them into the hand of the heathen; and they that hated them ruled over them.

Ps 108:11 *Wilt* not *thou,* O God, *who* hast cast us off? and wilt not thou, O God, go forth with our hosts?

Is 65:15 And ye shall leave your name for a curse unto my chosen: for the Lord GOD shall slay thee, and call his servants by another name:

Je 7:15 And I will cast you out of my sight, as I have cast out all your brethren, *even* the whole seed of Ephraim.

Je 12:7 I have forsaken mine house, I have left mine heritage; I have given the dearly beloved of my soul into the hand of her enemies.

Je 15:1 Then said the LORD unto me, Though Moses and Samuel stood before me, *yet* my mind *could* not *be* toward this people: cast *them* out of my sight, and let them go forth.

Je 22:26 And I will cast thee out, and thy mother that bare thee, into another country, where ye were not born; and there shall ye die.

Je 23:39 Therefore, behold, I, even I, will utterly forget you, and I will forsake you, and the city that I gave you and your fathers, *and cast you* out of my presence:

Je 31:28 And it shall come to pass, *that* like as I have watched over them, to pluck up, and to break down, and to throw down, and to destroy, and to afflict; so will I watch over them, to build, and to plant, saith the LORD.

Je 52:3 For through the anger of the LORD it came to pass in Jerusalem and Judah, till he had cast them out from his presence, that Zedekiah rebelled against the king of Babylon.

Lam 4:16 The anger of the LORD hath divided them; he will no more regard them: they respected not the persons of the priests, they favoured not the elders.

Eze 28:16 By the multitude of thy merchandise they have filled the midst of thee with violence, and thou hast sinned: therefore I will cast thee as profane out of the mountain of God: and I will destroy thee, O covering cherub, from the midst of the stones of fire.

Eze 31:11 I have therefore delivered him into the hand of the mighty one of the heathen; he shall surely deal with him: I have driven him out for his wickedness.

Eze 32:4 Then will I leave thee upon the land, I will cast thee forth upon the open field, and will cause all the fowls of the heaven to remain upon thee, and I will fill the beasts of the whole earth with thee.

Ho 1:6 And she conceived again, and bare a daughter. And *God* said unto him, Call her name Lo-ruhamah: for I will no more have mercy upon the house of Israel; but I will utterly take them away.

Ho 4:17 Ephraim *is* joined to idols: let him alone.

Ho 9:15 All their wickedness *is* in Gilgal: for there I hated them: for the wickedness of their doings I will drive them out of mine house, I will love them no more: all their princes *are* revolters.

Ho 9:17 My God will cast them away, because they did not hearken unto him: and they shall be wanderers among the nations.

Am 6:8 The Lord GOD hath sworn by himself, saith the LORD the God of hosts, I abhor the excellency of Jacob, and hate his palaces: therefore will I deliver up the city with all that is therein.

Am 9:4 And though they go into captivity before their enemies, thence will I command the sword, and it shall slay them: and I will set mine eyes upon them for evil, and not for good.

Zec 9:4 Behold, the Lord will cast her out, and he will smite her power in the sea; and she shall be devoured with fire.

Zec 11:9 Then said I, I will not feed you: that that dieth, let it die; and that that is to be cut off, let it be cut off; and let the rest eat every one the flesh of another.

Mal 1:3 And I hated Esau, and laid his mountains and his heritage waste for the dragons of the wilderness.

Mt 15:13 But he answered and said, Every plant, which my heavenly Father hath not planted, shall be rooted up.

Mk 12:9 What shall therefore the lord of the vineyard do? he will come and destroy the husbandmen, and will give the vineyard unto others.

Lu 13:27 But he shall say, I tell you, I know you not whence ye are; depart from me, all *ye* workers of iniquity.

Ro 11:22 Behold therefore the goodness and severity of God: on them which fell, severity; but toward thee, goodness, if thou continue in *his* goodness: otherwise thou also shalt be cut off.

2 Th 2:12 That they all might be damned who believed not the truth, but had pleasure in unrighteousness.

Jude 5 I will therefore put you in remembrance, though ye once knew this, how that the Lord, having saved the people out of the land of Egypt, afterward destroyed them that believed not.

Re 2:5 Remember therefore from whence thou art fallen, and repent, and do the first works; or else I will come unto thee quickly, and will remove thy candlestick out of his place, except thou repent.

Re 3:16 So then because thou art lukewarm, and neither cold nor hot, I will spue thee out of my mouth.

Re 22:19 And if any man shall take away from the words of the book of this prophecy, God shall take away his part out of the book of life, and out of the holy city, and *from* the things which are written in this book.

e. A Byword to Neighboring Nations

De 28:37 And thou shalt become an astonishment, a proverb, and a byword, among all nations whither the Lord shall lead thee.

1 K 9:7 Then will I cut off Israel out of the land which I have given them; and this house, which I have hallowed for my name, will I cast out of my sight; and Israel shall be a proverb and a byword among all people:

2 K 22:19 Because thine heart was tender, and thou hast humbled thyself before the Lord, when thou heardest what I spake against this place, and against the inhabitants thereof, that they should become a desolation and a curse, and hast rent thy clothes, and wept before me; I also have heard *thee,* saith the Lord.

2 Chr 7:20 Then will I pluck them up by the roots out of my land which I have given them; and this house, which I have sanctified for my name, will I cast out of my sight, and will make it *to be* a proverb and a byword among all nations.

2 Chr 29:8 Wherefore the wrath of the Lord was upon Judah and Jerusalem, and he hath delivered them to trouble, to astonishment, and to hissing, as ye see with your eyes.

Ps 44:14 Thou makest us a byword among the heathen, a shaking of the head among the people.

Ps 69:11 I made sackcloth also my garment; and I became a proverb to them.

Ps 79:4 We are become a reproach to our neighbours, a scorn and derision to them that are round about us.

Ps 80:6 Thou makest us a strife unto our neighbours: and our enemies laugh among themselves.

Ps 89:41 All that pass by the way spoil him: he is a reproach to his neighbours.

Is 43:28 Therefore I have profaned the princes of the sanctuary, and have given Jacob to the curse, and Israel to reproaches.

Je 18:16 To make their land desolate, *and* a perpetual hissing; every one that passeth thereby shall be astonished, and wag his head.

Je 19:8 And I will make this city desolate, and an hissing; every one that passeth thereby shall be astonished and hiss because of all the plagues thereof.

Je 24:9 And I will deliver them to be removed into all the kingdoms of the earth for *their* hurt, *to be* a reproach and a proverb, a taunt and a curse, in all places whither I shall drive them.

Je 25:9 Behold, I will send and take all the families of the north, saith the Lord, and Nebuchadrezzar the king of Babylon, my servant, and will bring them against this land, and against the inhabitants thereof, and against all these nations round about, and will utterly destroy them, and make them an astonishment, and an hissing, and perpetual desolations.

Je 25:18 *To wit,* Jerusalem, and the cities of Judah, and the kings thereof, and the princes thereof, to make them a desolation, an astonishment, an hissing, and a curse; as *it is* this day;

Je 29:18 And I will persecute them with the sword, with the famine, and with the pestilence, and will deliver them to be removed to all the kingdoms of the earth, to be a curse, and an astonishment, and an hissing, and a reproach, among all the nations whither I have driven them:

Je 42:18 For thus saith the Lord of hosts, the God of Israel; As mine anger and my fury hath been poured forth upon the inhabitants of Jerusalem; so shall my fury be poured forth upon you, when ye shall enter into Egypt: and ye shall be an execration, and an astonishment, and a curse, and a reproach; and ye shall see this place no more.

Je 44:8 In that ye provoke me unto wrath with the works of your hands, burning incense unto other gods in the land of Egypt, whither ye be gone to dwell, that ye might cut yourselves off, and that ye might be a curse and a reproach among all the nations of the earth?

Je 44:12 And I will take the remnant of Judah, that have set their faces to go into the land of Egypt to sojourn there, and they shall all be consumed, *and* fall in the land of Egypt; they shall *even* be consumed by the sword and by the famine: they shall die, from the least even unto the greatest, by the sword *and* by the famine: and they shall be an execration, *and* an astonishment, and a curse, and a reproach.

Lam 2:15 All that pass by clap *their* hands at thee; they hiss and wag their head at the daughter of Jerusalem, *saying, Is* this the city that *men* call The perfection of beauty, The joy of the whole earth?

Lam 3:45 Thou hast made us *as* the offscouring and refuse in the midst of the people.

Eze 5:14 Moreover I will make thee waste, and a reproach among the nations that *are* round about thee, in the sight of all that pass by.

Eze 22:4 Thou art become guilty in thy blood that thou hast shed; and hast defiled thyself in thine idols which thou hast made; and thou hast caused thy days to draw near, and art come *even* unto thy years: therefore have I made thee a reproach unto the heathen, and a mocking to all countries.

Eze 23:32 Thus saith the Lord God; Thou shalt drink of thy sister's cup deep and large: thou shalt be laughed to scorn and had in derision; it containeth much.

Eze 36:4 Therefore, ye mountains of Israel, hear the word of the Lord God; Thus saith the Lord God to the mountains, and to the hills, to the rivers, and to the valleys, to the desolate wastes, and to the cities that are forsaken, which became a prey and derision to the residue of the heathen that *are* round about;

Da 9:16 O Lord, according to all thy righteousness, I beseech thee, let thine anger and thy fury be turned away from thy city Jerusalem, thy holy mountain: because for our sins, and for the iniquities of our fathers, Jerusalem and thy people *are become* a reproach to all *that are* about us.

Ho 7:16 They return, *but* not to the most High: they are like a deceitful bow: their princes shall fall by the sword for the rage of their tongue: this *shall be* their derision in the land of Egypt.

Ho 8:8 Israel is swallowed up: now shall they be among the Gentiles as a vessel wherein *is* no pleasure.

Ho 12:14 Ephraim provoked *him* to anger most bitterly: therefore shall he leave his blood upon him, and his reproach shall his Lord return unto him.

Jl 2:19 Yea, the Lord will answer and say unto his people, Behold, I will send you corn, and wine, and oil, and ye shall be satisfied therewith: and I will no more make you a reproach among the heathen:

Mi 6:16 For the statutes of Omri are kept, and all the works of the house of Ahab, and ye walk in their counsels; that I should make thee a desolation, and the inhabitants thereof an hissing: therefore ye shall bear the reproach of my people.

Zec 8:13 And it shall come to pass, *that* as ye were a curse among the heathen, O house of Judah, and house of Israel; so will I save you, and ye shall be a blessing: fear not, *but* let your hands be strong.

f. Defeated in Battle

Le 26:25 And I will bring a sword upon you, that shall avenge the quarrel of *my* covenant: and when ye are gathered together within your cities, I will send the pestilence among you; and ye shall be delivered into the hand of the enemy.

Nu 14:45 Then the Amalekites came down, and the Canaanites which dwelt in that hill, and smote them, and discomfited them, *even* unto Hormah.

De 1:44 And the Amorites, which dwelt in that mountain, came out against you, and chased you, as bees do, and destroyed you in Seir, *even* unto Hormah.

De 28:25 The LORD shall cause thee to be smitten before thine enemies: thou shalt go out one way against them, and flee seven ways before them: and shalt be removed into all the kingdoms of the earth.

Jos 7:4 So there went up thither of the people about three thousand men: and they fled before the men of Ai.

Jos 7:12 Therefore the children of Israel could not stand before their enemies, *but* turned *their* backs before their enemies, because they were accursed: neither will I be with you any more, except ye destroy the accursed from among you.

Jud 3:13 And he gathered unto him the children of Ammon and Amalek, and went and smote Israel, and possessed the city of palm trees.

Jud 20:25 And Benjamin went forth against them out of Gibeah the second day, and destroyed down to the ground of the children of Israel again eighteen thousand men; all these drew the sword.

1 S 4:2 And the Philistines put themselves in array against Israel: and when they joined battle, Israel was smitten before the Philistines: and they slew of the army in the field about four thousand men.

1 S 4:10 And the Philistines fought, and Israel was smitten, and they fled every man into his tent: and there was a very great slaughter; for there fell of Israel thirty thousand footmen.

1 S 4:17 And the messenger answered and said, Israel is fled before the Philistines, and there hath been also a great slaughter among the people, and thy two sons also, Hophni and Phinehas, are dead, and the ark of God is taken.

1 S 31:3 And the battle went sore against Saul, and the archers hit him; and he was sore wounded of the archers.

2 S 1:4 And David said unto him, How went the matter? I pray thee, tell me. And he answered, That the people are fled from the battle, and many of the people also are fallen and dead; and Saul and Jonathan his son are dead also.

1 K 8:33 When thy people Israel be smitten down before the enemy, because they have sinned against thee, and shall turn again to thee, and confess thy name, and pray, and make supplication unto thee in this house:

2 K 14:12 And Judah was put to the worse before Israel; and they fled every man to their tents.

1 Chr 10:1 Now the Philistines fought against Israel; and the men of Israel fled from before the Philistines, and fell down slain in mount Gilboa.

2 Chr 6:24 And if thy people Israel be put to the worse before the enemy, because they have sinned against thee; and shall return and confess thy name, and pray and make supplication before thee in this house;

2 Chr 25:22 And Judah was put to the worse before Israel, and they fled every man to his tent.

2 Chr 28:5 Wherefore the LORD his God delivered him into the hand of the king of Syria; and they smote him, and carried away a great multitude of them captives, and brought *them* to Damascus. And he was also delivered into the hand of the king of Israel, who smote him with a great slaughter.

Ps 44:10 Thou makest us to turn back from the enemy: and they which hate us spoil for themselves.

Ps 89:43 Thou hast also turned the edge of his sword, and hast not made him to stand in the battle.

Is 3:25 Thy men shall fall by the sword, and thy mighty in the war.

Ho 1:5 And it shall come to pass at that day, that I will break the bow of Israel in the valley of Jezreel.

Am 5:3 For thus saith the Lord GOD; The city that went out *by* a thousand shall leave an hundred, and that which went forth *by* an hundred shall leave ten, to the house of Israel.

g. Humbled into the Dust

Ex 1:11 Therefore they did set over them taskmasters to afflict them with their burdens. And they built for Pharaoh treasure cities, Pithom and Raamses.

Ex 1:13 And the Egyptians made the children of Israel to serve with rigour:

Le 26:17 And I will set my face against you, and ye shall be slain before your enemies: they that hate you shall reign over you; and ye shall flee when none pursueth you.

De 28:43 The stranger that *is* within thee shall get up above thee very high; and thou shalt come down very low.

De 28:48 Therefore shalt thou serve thine enemies which the LORD shall send against thee, in hunger, and in thirst, and in nakedness, and in want of all *things:* and he shall put a yoke of iron upon thy neck, until he have destroyed thee.

Jud 3:14 So the children of Israel served Eglon the king of Moab eighteen years.

Jud 6:2 And the hand of Midian prevailed against Israel: *and* because of the Midianites the children of Israel made them the dens which *are* in the mountains, and caves, and strong holds.

Jud 10:8 And that year they vexed and oppressed the children of Israel: eighteen years, all the children of Israel that *were* on the other side Jordan in the land of the Amorites, which *is* in Gilead.

Jud 14:4 But his father and his mother knew not that it *was* of the LORD, that he sought an occasion against the Philistines: for at that time the Philistines had dominion over Israel.

Jud 15:11 Then three thousand men of Judah went to the top of the rock Etam, and said to Samson, Knowest thou not that the Philistines *are* rulers over us? what *is* this *that* thou hast done unto us? And he said unto them, As they did unto me, so have I done unto them.

1 S 4:22 And she said, The glory is departed from Israel: for the ark of God is taken.

1 S 12:9 And when they forgat the LORD their God, he sold them into the hand of Sisera, captain of the host of Hazor, and into the hand of the Philistines, and into the hand of the king of Moab, and they fought against them.

1 S 13:6 When the men of Israel saw that they were in a strait, (for the people were distressed,) then the people did hide themselves in caves, and in thickets, and in rocks, and in high places, and in pits.

1 S 13:20 But all the Israelites went down to the Philistines, to sharpen every man his share, and his coulter, and his axe, and his mattock.

1 S 17:11 When Saul and all Israel heard those words of the Philistine, they were dismayed, and greatly afraid.

1 S 31:7 And when the men of Israel that *were* on the other side of the valley, and *they* that *were* on the other side Jordan, saw that the men of Israel fled, and that Saul and his sons were dead, they forsook the cities, and fled; and the Philistines came and dwelt in them.

2 K 13:7 Neither did he leave of the people to Jehoahaz but fifty horsemen, and ten chariots, and ten thousand footmen; for the king of Syria had destroyed them, and had made them like the dust by threshing.

2 K 17:20 And the LORD rejected all the seed of Israel, and afflicted them, and delivered them into the hand of spoilers, until he had cast them out of his sight.

2 K 18:14 And Hezekiah king of Judah sent to the king of Assyria to Lachish, saying, I have offended; return from me: that which thou puttest on me will I bear. And the king of Assyria appointed unto Hezekiah king of Judah three hundred talents of silver and thirty talents of gold.

2 K 18:26 Then said Eliakim the son of Hilkiah, and Shebna, and Joah, unto Rab-shakeh, Speak, I pray thee, to thy servants in the Syrian language; for we understand *it:* and talk not with us in the Jews' language in the ears of the people that *are* on the wall.

2 K 21:14 And I will forsake the remnant of mine inheritance, and deliver them into the hand of their enemies; and they shall become a prey and a spoil to all their enemies;

1 Chr 10:7 And when all the men of Israel that *were* in the valley saw that they fled, and that Saul and his sons were dead, then they forsook their cities, and fled: and the Philistines came and dwelt in them.

2 Chr 24:24 For the army of the Syrians came with a small company of men, and the LORD delivered a very great host into their hand, because they had forsaken the LORD God of their fathers. So they executed judgment against Joash.

2 Chr 28:19 For the LORD brought Judah low because of Ahaz king of Israel; for he made Judah naked, and transgressed sore against the LORD.

Ezr 9:7 Since the days of our fathers *have* we *been* in a great trespass unto this day; and for our iniquities have we, our kings, and *our* priests, been delivered into the hand of the kings of the lands, to the sword, to captivity, and to a spoil, and to confusion of face, as *it is* this day.

Ne 9:28 But after they had rest, they did evil again before thee: therefore leftest thou them in the hand of their enemies, so that they had the dominion over them: yet when they returned, and cried unto thee, thou heardest *them* from heaven; and many times didst thou deliver them according to thy mercies;

Ne 9:36 Behold, we *are* servants this day, and *for* the land that thou gavest unto our fathers to eat the fruit thereof and the good thereof, behold, we *are* servants in it:

Ps 44:25 For our soul is bowed down to the dust: our belly cleaveth unto the earth.

Ps 79:8 O remember not against us former iniquities: let thy tender mercies speedily prevent us: for we are brought very low.

Ps 106:41 And he gave them into the hand of the heathen; and they that hated them ruled over them.

Is 3:4 And I will give children *to be* their princes, and babes shall rule over them.

Is 17:4 And in that day it shall come to pass, *that* the glory of Jacob shall be made thin, and the fatness of his flesh shall wax lean.

Is 26:13 O LORD our God, *other* lords besides thee have had dominion over us: *but* by thee only will we make mention of thy name.

Is 29:4 And thou shalt be brought down, *and* shalt speak out of the ground, and thy speech shall be low out of the dust, and thy voice shall be, as of one that hath a familiar spirit, out of the ground, and thy speech shall whisper out of the dust.

Is 36:1 Now it came to pass in the fourteenth year of king Hezekiah, *that* Sennacherib king of Assyria came up against all the defenced cities of Judah, and took them.

Is 42:24 Who gave Jacob for a spoil, and Israel to the robbers? did not the LORD, he against whom we have sinned? for they would not walk in his ways, neither were they obedient unto his law.

Is 47:6 I was wroth with my people, I have polluted mine inheritance, and given them into thine hand: thou didst shew them no mercy; upon the ancient hast thou very heavily laid thy yoke.

Is 51:23 But I will put it into the hand of them that afflict thee; which have said to thy soul, Bow down, that we may go over: and thou hast laid thy body as the ground, and as the street, to them that went over.

Je 2:14 *Is* Israel a servant? *is* he a homeborn *slave?* why is he spoiled?

Je 13:9 Thus saith the LORD, After this manner will I mar the pride of Judah, and the great pride of Jerusalem.

Je 14:17 Therefore thou shalt say this word unto them; Let mine eyes run down with tears night and day, and let them not cease: for the virgin daughter of my people is broken with a great breach, with a very grievous blow.

Je 17:4 And thou, even thyself, shalt discontinue from thine heritage that I gave thee; and I will cause thee to serve thine enemies in the land which thou knowest not: for ye have kindled a fire in mine anger, *which* shall burn for ever.

Je 25:11 And this whole land shall be a desolation, *and* an astonishment; and these nations shall serve the king of Babylon seventy years.

Lam 1:6 And from the daughter of Zion all her beauty is departed: her princes are become like harts *that* find no pasture, and they are gone without strength before the pursuer.

Lam 1:8 Jerusalem hath grievously sinned; therefore she is removed: all that honoured her despise her, because they have seen her nakedness: yea, she sigheth, and turneth backward.

Lam 2:1 How hath the Lord covered the daughter of Zion with a cloud in his anger, *and* cast down from heaven unto the earth the beauty of Israel, and remembered not his footstool in the day of his anger!

Lam 4:5 They that did feed delicately are desolate in the streets: they that were brought up in scarlet embrace dunghills.

Lam 5:8 Servants have ruled over us: *there is* none that doth deliver *us* out of their hand.

Lam 5:13 They took the young men to grind, and the children fell under the wood.

Eze 17:14 That the kingdom might be base, that it might not lift itself up, *but* that by keeping of his covenant it might stand.

Eze 19:12 But she was plucked up in fury, she was cast down to the ground, and the east wind dried up her fruit: her strong rods were broken and withered; the fire consumed them.

Eze 33:28 For I will lay the land most desolate, and the pomp of her strength shall cease; and the mountains of Israel shall be desolate, that none shall pass through.

Eze 36:3 Therefore prophesy and say, Thus saith the Lord GOD; Because they have made *you* desolate, and swallowed you up on every side, that ye might be a possession unto the residue of the heathen, and ye are taken up in the lips of talkers, and *are* an infamy of the people:

Eze 36:6 Prophesy therefore concerning the land of Israel, and say unto the mountains, and to the hills, to the rivers, and to the valleys, Thus saith the Lord GOD; Behold, I have spoken in my jealousy and in my fury, because ye have borne the shame of the heathen:

Am 5:2 The virgin of Israel is fallen; she shall no more rise: she is forsaken upon her land; *there is* none to raise her up.

h. Utterly Cut Off

2 K 10:32 In those days the LORD began to cut Israel short: and Hazael smote them in all the coasts of Israel;

Ps 89:45 The days of his youth hast thou shortened: thou hast covered him with shame. Selah.

Is 9:14 Therefore the LORD will cut off from Israel head and tail, branch and rush, in one day.

Je 44:11 Therefore thus saith the LORD of hosts, the God of Israel; Behold, I will set my face against you for evil, and to cut off all Judah.

Eze 17:9 Say thou, Thus saith the Lord GOD; Shall it prosper? shall he not pull up the roots thereof, and cut off the fruit thereof, that it wither? it shall wither in all the leaves of her spring, even without great power or many people to pluck it up by the roots thereof.

Eze 37:11 Then he said unto me, Son of man, these bones are the whole house of Israel: behold, they say, Our bones are dried, and our hope is lost: we are cut off for our parts.

Ho 9:17 My God will cast them away, because they did not hearken unto him: and they shall be wanderers among the nations.

Mt 8:12 But the children of the kingdom shall be cast out into outer darkness: there shall be weeping and gnashing of teeth.

Mt 21:43 Therefore say I unto you, The kingdom of God shall be taken from you, and given to a nation bringing forth the fruits thereof.

Mk 12:9 What shall therefore the lord of the vineyard do? he will come and destroy the husbandmen, and will give the vineyard unto others.

Lu 13:7 Then said he unto the dresser of his vineyard, Behold, these three years I come seeking fruit on this fig tree, and find none: cut it down; why cumbereth it the ground?

Lu 14:24 For I say unto you, That none of those men which were bidden shall taste of my supper.

Lu 20:16 He shall come and destroy these husbandmen, and shall give the vineyard to others. And when they heard *it,* they said, God forbid.

Ro 11:17 And if some of the branches be broken off, and thou, being a wild olive tree, wert graffed in among them, and with them partakest of the root and fatness of the olive tree;

Ro 11:19 Thou wilt say then, The branches were broken off, that I might be graffed in.

i. Carried into Bondage

Ge 15:13 And he said unto Abram, Know of a surety that thy seed shall be a stranger in a land *that is* not theirs, and shall serve them; and they shall afflict them four hundred years;

Ex 1:11 Therefore they did set over them taskmasters to afflict them with their burdens. And they built for Pharaoh treasure cities, Pithom and Raamses.

Ex 2:11 And it came to pass in those days, when Moses was grown, that he went out unto his brethren, and looked on their burdens: and he spied an Egyptian smiting an Hebrew, one of his brethren.

Ex 2:23 And it came to pass in process of time, that the king of Egypt died: and the children of Israel sighed by reason of the bondage, and they cried, and their cry came up unto God by reason of the bondage.

Ex 5:4 And the king of Egypt said unto them, Wherefore do ye, Moses and Aaron, let the people from their works? get you unto your burdens.

Ex 6:5 And I have also heard the groaning of the children of Israel, whom the Egyptians keep in bondage; and I have remembered my covenant.

Ex 13:3 And Moses said unto the people, Remember this day, in which ye came out from Egypt, out of the house of bondage; for by strength of hand the LORD brought you out from this *place:* there shall no leavened bread be eaten.

Ex 13:14 And it shall be when thy son asketh thee in time to come, saying, What *is* this? that thou shalt say unto him, By strength of hand the LORD brought us out from Egypt, from the house of bondage:

Ex 14:12 *Is* not this the word that we did tell thee in Egypt, saying, Let us alone, that we may serve the Egyptians? For *it had been* better for us to serve the Egyptians, than that we should die in the wilderness.

Ex 20:2 I *am* the LORD thy God, which have brought thee out of the land of Egypt, out of the house of bondage.

Nu 20:15 How our fathers went down into Egypt, and we have dwelt in Egypt a long time; and the Egyptians vexed us, and our fathers:

De 5:15 And remember that thou wast a servant in the land of Egypt, and *that* the LORD thy God brought thee out thence through a mighty hand and by a stretched out arm: therefore the LORD thy God commanded thee to keep the sabbath day.

De 6:12 *Then* beware lest thou forget the LORD, which brought thee forth out of the land of Egypt, from the house of bondage.

De 6:21 Then thou shalt say unto thy son, We were Pharaoh's bondmen in

Egypt; and the LORD brought us out of Egypt with a mighty hand:

De 8:14 Then thine heart be lifted up, and thou forget the LORD thy God, which brought thee forth out of the land of Egypt, from the house of bondage;

De 13:10 And thou shalt stone him with stones, that he die; because he hath sought to thrust thee away from the LORD thy God, which brought thee out of the land of Egypt, from the house of bondage.

De 15:15 And thou shalt remember that thou wast a bondman in the land of Egypt, and the LORD thy God redeemed thee: therefore I command thee this thing to day.

De 16:12 And thou shalt remember that thou wast a bondman in Egypt: and thou shalt observe and do these statutes.

De 24:18 But thou shalt remember that thou wast a bondman in Egypt, and the LORD thy God redeemed thee thence: therefore I command thee to do this thing.

De 24:22 And thou shalt remember that thou wast a bondman in the land of Egypt: therefore I command thee to do this thing.

De 26:6 And the Egyptians evil entreated us, and afflicted us, and laid upon us hard bondage:

De 28:48 Therefore shalt thou serve thine enemies which the LORD shall send against thee, in hunger, and in thirst, and in nakedness, and in want of all *things:* and he shall put a yoke of iron upon thy neck, until he have destroyed thee.

De 28:68 And the LORD shall bring thee into Egypt again with ships, by the way whereof I spake unto thee, Thou shalt see it no more again: and there ye shall be sold unto your enemies for bondmen and bondwomen, and no man shall buy *you.*

Jos 24:17 For the LORD our God, he *it is* that brought us up and our fathers out of the land of Egypt, from the house of bondage, and which did those great signs in our sight, and preserved us in all the way wherein we went, and among all the people through whom we passed:

Jud 3:14 So the children of Israel served Eglon the king of Moab eighteen years.

Jud 6:8 That the LORD sent a prophet unto the children of Israel, which said unto them, Thus saith the LORD God of Israel, I brought you up from Egypt, and brought you forth out of the house of bondage;

2 Chr 29:9 For, lo, our fathers have fallen by the sword, and our sons and our daughters and our wives are in captivity for this.

Ezr 9:8 And now for a little space grace hath been *shewed* from the LORD our God, to leave us a remnant to escape, and to give us a nail in his holy place, that our God may lighten our eyes, and give us a little reviving in our bondage.

Ne 9:36 Behold, we *are* servants this day, and *for* the land that thou gavest unto our fathers to eat the fruit thereof and the good thereof, behold, we *are* servants in it:

Ps 81:6 I removed his shoulder from the burden: his hands were delivered from the pots.

Ps 105:25 He turned their heart to hate his people, to deal subtilly with his servants.

Ps 106:42 Their enemies also oppressed them, and they were brought into subjection under their hand.

Eze 23:21 Thus thou calledst to remembrance the lewdness of thy youth, in bruising thy teats by the Egyptians for the paps of thy youth.

Jl 3:6 The children also of Judah and the children of Jerusalem have ye sold unto the Grecians, that ye might remove them far from their border.

Ac 7:6 And God spake on this wise, That his seed should sojourn in a strange land; and that they should bring them into bondage, and entreat *them* evil four hundred years.

See **CAPTIVES**

5. Her Judges, *leaders over the Hebrews from the time of Joshua to the accession of Saul*

OTHNIEL

Jud 3:9 And when the children of Israel cried unto the LORD, the LORD raised up a deliverer to the children of Israel, who delivered them, *even* Othniel the son of Kenaz, Caleb's younger brother.

EHUD

Jud 3:15 But when the children of Israel cried unto the LORD, the LORD raised them up a deliverer, Ehud the son of Gera, a Benjamite, a man lefthanded: and by him the children of Israel sent a present unto Eglon the king of Moab.

SHAMGAR

Jud 3:31 And after him was Shamgar the son of Anath, which slew of the Philistines six hundred men with an ox goad: and he also delivered Israel.

DEBORAH

Jud 4:5 And she dwelt under the palm tree of Deborah between Ramah and Bethel in mount Ephraim: and the children of Israel came up to her for judgment.

GIDEON

Jud 6:36 And Gideon said unto God, If thou wilt save Israel by mine hand, as thou hast said,

ABIMELECH

Jud 9:1 And Abimelech the son of Jerubbaal went to Shechem unto his mother's brethren, and communed with them, and with all the family of the house of his mother's father, saying,

TOLA

Jud 10:1 And after Abimelech there arose to defend Israel Tola the son of Puah, the son of Dodo, a man of Issachar; and he dwelt in Shamir in mount Ephraim.

JAIR

Jud 10:3 And after him arose Jair, a Gileadite, and judged Israel twenty and two years.

JEPHTHAH

Jud 11:11 Then Jephthah went with the elders of Gilead, and the people made him head and captain over them: and Jephthah uttered all his words before the LORD in Mizpeh.

IBZAN

Jud 12:8 And after him Ibzan of Bethlehem judged Israel.

ELON

Jud 12:11 And after him Elon, a Zebulonite, judged Israel; and he judged Israel ten years.

ABDON

Jud 12:13 And after him Abdon the son of Hillel, a Pirathonite, judged Israel.

SAMSON

Jud 16:30 And Samson said, Let me die with the Philistines. And he bowed himself with *all his* might; and the house fell upon the lords, and upon all the people that *were* therein. So the dead which he slew at his death were more than *they* which he slew in his life.

ELI

1 S 4:18 And it came to pass, when he made mention of the ark of God, that he fell from off the seat backward by the side of the gate, and his neck brake, and he died: for he was an old man, and heavy. And he had judged Israel forty years.

SAMUEL

1 S 7:15 And Samuel judged Israel all the days of his life.

6. Her Kings of Israel, *the Northern Kingdom*

JEROBOAM I

1 K 11:28 And the man Jeroboam *was* a mighty man of valour: and Solomon seeing the young man that he was industrious, he made him ruler over all the charge of the house of Joseph.

NADAB
1 K 14:20 And the days which Jeroboam reigned *were* two and twenty years: and he slept with his fathers, and Nadab his son reigned in his stead.

BAASHA
1 K 15:16 And there was war between Asa and Baasha king of Israel all their days.

ELAH
1 K 16:8 In the twenty and sixth year of Asa king of Judah began Elah the son of Baasha to reign over Israel in Tirzah, two years.

ZIMRI
1 K 16:15 In the twenty and seventh year of Asa king of Judah did Zimri reign seven days in Tirzah. And the people *were* encamped against Gibbethon, which *belonged* to the Philistines.

OMRI
1 K 16:16 And the people *that were* encamped heard say, Zimri hath conspired, and hath also slain the king: wherefore all Israel made Omri, the captain of the host, king over Israel that day in the camp.

AHAB
1 K 16:29 And in the thirty and eighth year of Asa king of Judah began Ahab the son of Omri to reign over Israel: and Ahab the son of Omri reigned over Israel in Samaria twenty and two years.

AHAZIAH
1 K 22:40 So Ahab slept with his fathers; and Ahaziah his son reigned in his stead.

JEHORAM, OR JORAM
2 K 1:17 So he died according to the word of the LORD which Elijah had

spoken. And Jehoram reigned in his stead in the second year of Jehoram the son of Jehoshaphat king of Judah; because he had no son.

JEHU
1 K 19:16 And Jehu the son of Nimshi shalt thou anoint *to be* king over Israel: and Elisha the son of Shaphat of Abel-meholah shalt thou anoint *to be* prophet in thy room.

JEHOAHAZ
2 K 10:35 And Jehu slept with his fathers: and they buried him in Samaria. And Jehoahaz his son reigned in his stead.

JEHOASH
2 K 13:10 In the thirty and seventh year of Joash king of Judah began Jehoash the son of Jehoahaz to reign over Israel in Samaria, *and reigned* sixteen years.

JEROBOAM II
2 K 14:23 In the fifteenth year of Amaziah the son of Joash king of Judah Jeroboam the son of Joash king of Israel began to reign in Samaria, *and reigned* forty and one years.

ZECHARIAH
2 K 14:29 And Jeroboam slept with his fathers, *even* with the kings of Israel; and Zechariah his son reigned in his stead.

SHALLUM
2 K 15:10 And Shallum the son of Jabesh conspired against him, and smote him before the people, and slew him, and reigned in his stead.

MENAHEM
2 K 15:14 For Menahem the son of Gadi went up from Tirzah, and came to Samaria, and smote Shallum the son of Jabesh in Samaria, and slew him, and reigned in his stead.

PEKAHIAH
2 K 15:23 In the fiftieth year of Azariah king of Judah Pekahiah the son

of Menahem began to reign over Israel in Samaria, *and reigned* two years.

PEKAH

2 K 15:25 But Pekah the son of Remaliah, a captain of his, conspired against him, and smote him in Samaria, in the palace of the king's house, with Argob and Arieh, and with him fifty men of the Gileadites: and he killed him, and reigned in his room.

HOSHEA

2 K 15:30 And Hoshea the son of Elah made a conspiracy against Pekah the son of Remaliah, and smote him, and slew him, and reigned in his stead, in the twentieth year of Jotham the son of Uzziah.

See **SAUL, DAVID, SOLOMON**

7. Her Kings of Judah, *the Southern Kingdom*

REHOBOAM

1 K 11:43 And Solomon slept with his fathers, and was buried in the city of David his father: and Rehoboam his son reigned in his stead.

ABIJAM, OR ABIJAH

1 K 14:31 And Rehoboam slept with his fathers, and was buried with his fathers in the city of David. And his mother's name *was* Naamah an Ammonitess. And Abijam his son reigned in his stead.

ASA

1 K 15:8 And Abijam slept with his fathers; and they buried him in the city of David: and Asa his son reigned in his stead.

JEHOSHAPHAT

1 K 15:24 And Asa slept with his fathers, and was buried with his fathers in the city of David his father: and Jehoshaphat his son reigned in his stead.

JEHORAM

1 Chr 21:1 And Satan stood up against Israel, and provoked David to number Israel.

AHAZIAH

2 K 8:25 In the twelfth year of Joram the son of Ahab king of Israel did Ahaziah the son of Jehoram king of Judah begin to reign.

ATHALIAH (QUEEN)

2 K 8:26 Two and twenty years old *was* Ahaziah when he began to reign; and he reigned one year in Jerusalem. And his mother's name *was* Athaliah, the daughter of Omri king of Israel.

JOASH, OR JEHOASH

2 K 11:2 But Jehosheba, the daughter of king Joram, sister of Ahaziah, took Joash the son of Ahaziah and stole him from among the king's sons *which were* slain; and they hid him, *even* him and his nurse, in the bedchamber from Athaliah, so that he was not slain.

AMAZIAH

2 K 14:1 In the second year of Joash son of Jehoahaz king of Israel reigned Amaziah the son of Joash king of Judah.

UZZIAH, OR AZARIAH

2 K 14:21 And all the people of Judah took Azariah, which *was* sixteen years old, and made him king instead of his father Amaziah.

JOTHAM

2 K 15:5 And the LORD smote the king, so that he was a leper unto the day of his death, and dwelt in a several house. And Jotham the king's son *was* over the house, judging the people of the land.

AHAZ

2 K 15:38 And Jotham slept with his fathers, and was buried with his fathers in the city of David his father: and Ahaz his son reigned in his stead.

HEZEKIAH

2 K 16:20 And Ahaz slept with his fathers, and was buried with his fathers in the city of David: and Hezekiah his son reigned in his stead.

MANASSEH

2 K 21:1 Manasseh *was* twelve years old when he began to reign, and reigned fifty and five years in Jerusalem. And his mother's name *was* Hephzi-bah.

AMON

2 K 21:19 Amon *was* twenty and two years old when he began to reign, and he reigned two years in Jerusalem. And his mother's name *was* Meshullemeth, the daughter of Haruz of Jotbah.

JOSIAH

1 K 13:2 And he cried against the altar in the word of the LORD, and said, O altar, altar, thus saith the LORD; Behold, a child shall be born unto the house of David, Josiah by name; and upon thee shall he offer the priest of the high places that burn incense upon thee, and men's bones shall be burnt upon thee.

JEHOAHAZ, OR SHALLUM

2 K 23:30 And his servants carried him in a chariot dead from Megiddo, and brought him to Jerusalem, and buried him in his own sepulchre. And the people of the land took Jehoahaz the son of Josiah, and anointed him, and made him king in his father's stead.

JEHOIAKIM

2 K 23:34 And Pharaoh-nechoh made Eliakim the son of Josiah king in the room of Josiah his father, and turned his name to Jehoiakim, and took Jehoahaz away: and he came to Egypt, and died there.

JEHOIACHIN, OR JECONIAH

2 K 24:1 In his days Nebuchadnezzar king of Babylon came up, and Jehoiakim became his servant three years: then he turned and rebelled against him.

ZEDEKIAH, OR MATTANIAH

2 K 24:17 And the king of Babylon made Mattaniah his father's brother king in his stead, and changed his name to Zedekiah.

See **SAUL, DAVID, SOLOMON**

8. Babylonian Captivity (587/6 B.C.)

a. Foretold

De 28:36 The LORD shall bring thee, and thy king which thou shalt set over thee, unto a nation which neither thou nor thy fathers have known; and there shalt thou serve other gods, wood and stone.

De 28:41 Thou shalt beget sons and daughters, but thou shalt not enjoy them; for they shall go into captivity.

De 28:68 And the LORD shall bring thee into Egypt again with ships, by the way whereof I spake unto thee, Thou shalt see it no more again: and there ye shall be sold unto your enemies for bondmen and bondwomen, and no man shall buy *you.*

De 29:28 And the LORD rooted them out of their land in anger, and in wrath, and in great indignation, and cast them into another land, as *it is* this day.

1 K 14:15 For the LORD shall smite Israel, as a reed is shaken in the water, and he shall root up Israel out of this good land, which he gave to their fathers, and shall scatter them beyond the river, because they have made their groves, provoking the LORD to anger.

2 K 20:18 And of thy sons that shall issue from thee, which thou shalt beget, shall they take away; and they shall be eunuchs in the palace of the king of Babylon.

2 Chr 6:36 If they sin against thee, (for *there is* no man which sinneth not,) and thou be angry with them, and deliver them over before *their* enemies, and they carry them away captives unto a land far off or near;

Is 6:12 And the LORD have removed men far away, and *there be* a great forsaking in the midst of the land.

Is 7:16 For before the child shall know to refuse the evil, and choose the good, the land that thou abhorrest shall be forsaken of both her kings.

Is 39:7 And of thy sons that shall issue from thee, which thou shalt beget, shall they take away; and they shall be eunuchs in the palace of the king of Babylon.

Je 5:19 And it shall come to pass, when ye shall say, Wherefore doeth the LORD our God all these *things* unto us? then shalt thou answer them, Like as ye have forsaken me, and served strange gods in your land, so shall ye serve strangers in a land *that is* not yours.

Je 7:15 And I will cast you out of my sight, as I have cast out all your brethren, *even* the whole seed of Ephraim.

Je 13:19 The cities of the south shall be shut up, and none shall open *them:* Judah shall be carried away captive all of it, it shall be wholly carried away captive.

Je 15:2 And it shall come to pass, if they say unto thee, Whither shall we go forth? then thou shalt tell them, Thus saith the LORD; Such as *are* for death, to death; and such as *are* for the sword, to the sword; and such as *are* for the famine, to the famine; and such as *are* for the captivity, to the captivity.

Je 15:14 And I will make *thee* to pass with thine enemies into a land *which* thou knowest not: for a fire is kindled in mine anger, *which* shall burn upon you.

Je 20:5 Moreover I will deliver all the strength of this city, and all the labours thereof, and all the precious things thereof, and all the treasures of the kings of Judah will I give into the hand of their enemies, which shall spoil them, and take them, and carry them to Babylon.

Je 22:12 But he shall die in the place whither they have led him captive, and shall see this land no more.

Je 22:22 The wind shall eat up all thy pastors, and thy lovers shall go into captivity: surely then shalt thou be ashamed and confounded for all thy wickedness.

Je 22:26 And I will cast thee out, and thy mother that bare thee, into another country, where ye were not born; and there shall ye die.

Je 24:1 The LORD shewed me, and, behold, two baskets of figs *were* set before the temple of the LORD, after that Nebuchadrezzar king of Babylon had carried away captive Jeconiah the son of Jehoiakim king of Judah, and the princes of Judah, with the carpenters and smiths, from Jerusalem, and had brought them to Babylon.

Je 25:9 Behold, I will send and take all the families of the north, saith the LORD, and Nebuchadrezzar the king of Babylon, my servant, and will bring them against this land, and against the inhabitants thereof, and against all these nations round about, and will utterly destroy them, and make them an astonishment, and an hissing, and perpetual desolations.

Je 25:11 And this whole land shall be a desolation, *and* an astonishment; and these nations shall serve the king of Babylon seventy years.

Eze 4:13 And the LORD said, Even thus shall the children of Israel eat their defiled bread among the Gentiles, whither I will drive them.

Eze 11:9 And I will bring you out of the midst thereof, and deliver you into the hands of strangers, and will execute judgments among you.

Eze 12:11 Say, I *am* your sign: like as I have done, so shall it be done unto them: they shall remove *and* go into captivity.

Eze 23:46 For thus saith the Lord GOD; I will bring up a company upon them, and will give them to be removed and spoiled.

Da 9:2 In the first year of his reign I Daniel understood by books the number of the years, whereof the word of the LORD came to Jeremiah the prophet, that he would accomplish seventy years in the desolations of Jerusalem.

Ho 1:4 And the LORD said unto him, Call his name Jezreel; for yet a little *while,* and I will avenge the blood of Jezreel upon the house of Jehu, and will cause to cease the kingdom of the house of Israel.

Ho 11:5 He shall not return into the land of Egypt, but the Assyrian shall be his king, because they refused to return.

Am 5:5 But seek not Bethel, nor enter into Gilgal, and pass not to Beersheba: for Gilgal shall surely go into captivity, and Bethel shall come to nought.

Am 5:27 Therefore will I cause you to go into captivity beyond Damascus, saith the LORD, whose name *is* The God of hosts.

Am 6:7 Therefore now shall they go captive with the first that go captive, and the banquet of them that stretched themselves shall be removed.

Am 7:11 For thus Amos saith, Jeroboam shall die by the sword, and Israel shall surely be led away captive out of their own land.

Am 7:17 Therefore thus saith the LORD; Thy wife shall be an harlot in the city, and thy sons and thy daughters shall fall by the sword, and thy land shall be divided by line; and thou shalt die in a polluted land: and Israel shall surely go into captivity forth of his land.

Mi 1:16 Make thee bald, and poll thee for thy delicate children; enlarge thy baldness as the eagle; for they are gone into captivity from thee.

Mi 4:10 Be in pain, and labour to bring forth, O daughter of Zion, like a woman in travail: for now shalt thou go forth out of the city, and thou shalt dwell in the field, and thou shalt go *even* to Babylon; there shalt thou be delivered; there the LORD shall redeem thee from the hand of thine enemies.

Zec 14:2 For I will gather all nations against Jerusalem to battle; and the city shall be taken, and the houses rifled, and the women ravished; and half of the city shall go forth into captivity, and the residue of the people shall not be cut off from the city.

Lu 21:24 And they shall fall by the edge of the sword, and shall be led away captive into all nations: and Jerusalem shall be trodden down of the Gentiles, until the times of the Gentiles be fulfilled.

Ac 7:43 Yea, ye took up the tabernacle of Moloch, and the star of your god Remphan, figures which ye made to worship them: and I will carry you away beyond Babylon.

b. Fulfillment of Prophecies

Jud 18:30 And the children of Dan set up the graven image: and Jonathan, the son of Gershom, the son of Manasseh, he and his sons were priests to the tribe of Dan until the day of the captivity of the land.

1 K 8:46 If they sin against thee, (for *there is* no man that sinneth not,) and thou be angry with them, and deliver them to the enemy, so that they carry them away captives unto the land of the enemy, far or near;

2 K 15:29 In the days of Pekah king of Israel came Tiglath-pileser king of Assyria, and took Ijon, and Abel-beth-maachah, and Janoah, and Kedesh, and Hazor, and Gilead, and Galilee, all the land of Naphtali, and carried them captive to Assyria.

2 K 17:6 In the ninth year of Hoshea the king of Assyria took Samaria, and carried Israel away into Assyria, and placed them in Halah and in Habor *by* the river of Gozan, and in the cities of the Medes.

2 K 17:18 Therefore the LORD was very angry with Israel, and removed them out of his sight: there was none left but the tribe of Judah only.

2 K 17:23 Until the LORD removed Israel out of his sight, as he had said by all his servants the prophets. So was Israel carried away out of their own land to Assyria unto this day.

2 K 18:11 And the king of Assyria did carry away Israel unto Assyria, and put them in Halah and in Habor *by* the river of Gozan, and in the cities of the Medes:

2 K 23:27 And the LORD said, I will remove Judah also out of my sight, as I have removed Israel, and will cast off this city Jerusalem which I have chosen, and the house of which I said, My name shall be there.

2 K 24:14 And he carried away all Jerusalem, and all the princes, and all the mighty men of valour, *even* ten thousand captives, and all the craftsmen and smiths: none remained, save the poorest sort of the people of the land.

2 K 25:11 Now the rest of the people *that were* left in the city, and the fugitives that fell away to the king of Babylon, with the remnant of the multitude, did Nebuzar-adan the captain of the guard carry away.

2 K 25:21 And the king of Babylon smote them, and slew them at Riblah in the land of Hamath. So Judah was carried away out of their land.

1 Chr 5:22 For there fell down many slain, because the war *was* of God. And they dwelt in their steads until the captivity.

1 Chr 5:26 And the God of Israel stirred up the spirit of Pul king of Assyria, and the spirit of Tilgath-pilneser king of Assyria, and he carried them away, even the Reubenites, and the Gadites, and the half tribe of Manasseh, and brought them unto Halah, and Habor, and Hara, and to the river Gozan, unto this day.

1 Chr 6:15 And Jehozadak went *into captivity,* when the LORD carried away Judah and Jerusalem by the hand of Nebuchadnezzar.

1 Chr 9:1 So all Israel were reckoned by genealogies; and, behold, they *were* written in the book of the kings of Israel and Judah, *who* were carried away to Babylon for their transgression.

2 Chr 21:17 And they came up into Judah, and brake into it, and carried away all the substance that was found in the king's house, and his sons also, and his wives; so that there was never a son left him, save Jehoahaz, the youngest of his sons.

2 Chr 28:5 Wherefore the LORD his God delivered him into the hand of the king of Syria; and they smote him, and carried away a great multitude of them captives, and brought *them* to Damascus. And he was also delivered

into the hand of the king of Israel, who smote him with a great slaughter.

2 Chr 29:9 For, lo, our fathers have fallen by the sword, and our sons and our daughters and our wives are in captivity for this.

2 Chr 36:4 And the king of Egypt made Eliakim his brother king over Judah and Jerusalem, and turned his name to Jehoiakim. And Necho took Jehoahaz his brother, and carried him to Egypt.

2 Chr 36:10 And when the year was expired, king Nebuchadnezzar sent, and brought him to Babylon, with the goodly vessels of the house of the LORD, and made Zedekiah his brother king over Judah and Jerusalem.

2 Chr 36:20 And them that had escaped from the sword carried he away to Babylon; where they were servants to him and his sons until the reign of the kingdom of Persia:

Ezr 2:1 Now these *are* the children of the province that went up out of the captivity, of those which had been carried away, whom Nebuchadnezzar the king of Babylon had carried away unto Babylon, and came again unto Jerusalem and Judah, every one unto his city;

Ezr 5:12 But after that our fathers had provoked the God of heaven unto wrath, he gave them into the hand of Nebuchadnezzar the king of Babylon, the Chaldean, who destroyed this house, and carried the people away into Babylon.

Ne 7:6 These *are* the children of the province, that went up out of the captivity, of those that had been carried away, whom Nebuchadnezzar the king of Babylon had carried away, and came again to Jerusalem and to Judah, every one unto his city;

Est 2:6 Who had been carried away from Jerusalem with the captivity which had been carried away with Jeconiah king of Judah, whom Nebuchadnezzar the king of Babylon had carried away.

Ps 78:61 And delivered his strength into captivity, and his glory into the enemy's hand.

Ps 137:1 By the rivers of Babylon, there we sat down, yea, we wept, when we remembered Zion.

Is 49:21 Then shalt thou say in thine heart, Who hath begotten me these, seeing I have lost my children, and am desolate, a captive, and removing to and fro? and who hath brought up these? Behold, I was left alone; these, where *had* they *been?*

Is 52:5 Now therefore, what have I here, saith the LORD, that my people is taken away for nought? they that rule over them make them to howl, saith the LORD; and my name continually every day is blasphemed.

Je 1:3 It came also in the days of Jehoiakim the son of Josiah king of Judah, unto the end of the eleventh year of Zedekiah the son of Josiah king of Judah, unto the carrying away of Jerusalem captive in the fifth month.

Je 27:20 Which Nebuchadnezzar king of Babylon took not, when he carried away captive Jeconiah the son of Jehoiakim king of Judah from Jerusalem to Babylon, and all the nobles of Judah and Jerusalem;

Je 29:1 Now these *are* the words of the letter that Jeremiah the prophet sent from Jerusalem unto the residue of the elders which were carried away captives, and to the priests, and to the prophets, and to all the people whom Nebuchadnezzar had carried away captive from Jerusalem to Babylon;

Je 29:14 And I will be found of you, saith the LORD: and I will turn away your captivity, and I will gather you from all the nations, and from all the places whither I have driven you, saith the LORD; and I will bring you again into the place whence I caused you to be carried away captive.

Je 34:3 And thou shalt not escape out of his hand, but shalt surely be taken, and delivered into his hand; and thine eyes shall behold the eyes of the king of Babylon, and he shall speak with thee mouth to mouth, and thou shalt go to Babylon.

Je 34:21 And Zedekiah king of Judah and his princes will I give into the hand of their enemies, and into the hand of them that seek their life, and

into the hand of the king of Babylon's army, which are gone up from you.

Je 39:9 Then Nebuzar-adan the captain of the guard carried away captive into Babylon the remnant of the people that remained in the city, and those that fell away, that fell to him, with the rest of the people that remained.

Je 52:15 Then Nebuzar-adan the captain of the guard carried away captive *certain* of the poor of the people, and the residue of the people that remained in the city, and those that fell away, that fell to the king of Babylon, and the rest of the multitude.

Je 52:27 And the king of Babylon smote them, and put them to death in Riblah in the land of Hamath. Thus Judah was carried away captive out of his own land.

Lam 1:3 Judah is gone into captivity because of affliction, and because of great servitude: she dwelleth among the heathen, she findeth no rest: all her persecutors overtook her between the straits.

Lam 1:18 The LORD is righteous; for I have rebelled against his commandment: hear, I pray you, all people, and behold my sorrow: my virgins and my young men are gone into captivity.

Eze 1:1 Now it came to pass in the thirtieth year, in the fourth *month,* in the fifth *day* of the month, as I *was* among the captives by the river of Chebar, *that* the heavens were opened, and I saw visions of God.

Eze 3:11 And go, get thee to them of the captivity, unto the children of thy people, and speak unto them, and tell them, Thus saith the Lord GOD; whether they will hear, or whether they will forbear.

Eze 11:24 Afterwards the spirit took me up, and brought me in a vision by the Spirit of God into Chaldea, to them of the captivity. So the vision that I had seen went up from me.

Eze 17:12 Say now to the rebellious house, Know ye not what these *things mean?* tell *them,* Behold, the king of Babylon is come to Jerusalem, and hath taken the king thereof, and the princes thereof, and led them with him to Babylon;

Eze 25:3 And say unto the Ammonites, Hear the word of the Lord GOD; Thus saith the Lord GOD; Because thou saidst, Aha, against my sanctuary, when it was profaned; and against the land of Israel, when it was desolate; and against the house of Judah, when they went into captivity;

Eze 33:21 And it came to pass in the twelfth year of our captivity, in the tenth *month*, in the fifth *day* of the month, *that* one that had escaped out of Jerusalem came unto me, saying, The city is smitten.

Eze 36:22 Therefore say unto the house of Israel, Thus saith the Lord GOD; I do not *this* for your sakes, O house of Israel, but for mine holy name's sake, which ye have profaned among the heathen, whither ye went.

Eze 39:23 And the heathen shall know that the house of Israel went into captivity for their iniquity: because they trespassed against me, therefore hid I my face from them, and gave them into the hand of their enemies: so fell they all by the sword.

Eze 39:28 Then shall they know that I *am* the LORD their God, which caused them to be led into captivity among the heathen: but I have gathered them unto their own land, and have left none of them any more there.

Eze 40:1 In the five and twentieth year of our captivity, in the beginning of the year, in the tenth *day* of the month, in the fourteenth year after that the city was smitten, in the selfsame day the hand of the LORD was upon me, and brought me thither.

Da 1:2 And the Lord gave Jehoiakim king of Judah into his hand, with part of the vessels of the house of God: which he carried into the land of Shinar to the house of his god; and he brought the vessels into the treasure house of his god.

Da 5:13 Then was Daniel brought in before the king. *And* the king spake and said unto Daniel, *Art* thou that Daniel, which *art* of the children of the captivity of Judah, whom the king my father brought out of Jewry?

Am 9:4 And though they go into captivity before their enemies, thence will I command the sword, and it shall slay them: and I will set mine eyes upon them for evil, and not for good.

Zec 2:7 Deliver thyself, O Zion, that dwellest *with* the daughter of Babylon.

Zec 6:10 Take of *them of* the captivity, *even* of Heldai, of Tobijah, and of Jedaiah, which are come from Babylon, and come thou the same day, and go into the house of Josiah the son of Zephaniah;

c. Return from Captivity

De 30:3 That then the LORD thy God will turn thy captivity, and have compassion upon thee, and will return and gather thee from all the nations, whither the LORD thy God hath scattered thee.

1 K 8:34 Then hear thou in heaven, and forgive the sin of thy people Israel, and bring them again unto the land which thou gavest unto their fathers.

Ezr 2:1 Now these *are* the children of the province that went up out of the captivity, of those which had been carried away, whom Nebuchadnezzar the king of Babylon had carried away unto Babylon, and came again unto Jerusalem and Judah, every one unto his city;

Ezr 6:21 And the children of Israel, which were come again out of captivity, and all such as had separated themselves unto them from the filthiness of the heathen of the land, to seek the LORD God of Israel, did eat,

Ezr 7:9 For upon the first *day* of the first month began he to go up from Babylon, and on the first *day* of the fifth month came he to Jerusalem, according to the good hand of his God upon him.

Ezr 8:1 These *are* now the chief of their fathers, and *this is* the genealogy of them that went up with me from Babylon, in the reign of Artaxerxes the king.

Ezr 8:31 Then we departed from the river of Ahava on the twelfth *day* of the first month, to go unto Jerusalem: and the hand of our God was upon us, and he delivered us from the hand of the enemy, and of such as lay in wait by the way.

Ezr 8:35 *Also* the children of those that had been carried away, which were come out of the captivity, offered burnt offerings unto the God of Israel, twelve bullocks for all Israel, ninety and six rams, seventy and seven lambs, twelve he goats *for* a sin offering: all *this was* a burnt offering unto the LORD.

Ne 1:9 But *if* ye turn unto me, and keep my commandments, and do them; though there were of you cast out unto the uttermost part of the heaven, *yet* will I gather them from thence, and will bring them unto the place that I have chosen to set my name there.

Ne 7:6 These *are* the children of the province, that went up out of the captivity, of those that had been carried away, whom Nebuchadnezzar the king of Babylon had carried away, and came again to Jerusalem and to Judah, every one unto his city;

Ne 8:17 And all the congregation of them that were come again out of the captivity made booths, and sat under the booths: for since the days of Jeshua the son of Nun unto that day had not the children of Israel done so. And there was very great gladness.

Ps 53:6 Oh that the salvation of Israel *were come* out of Zion! When God bringeth back the captivity of his people, Jacob shall rejoice, *and* Israel shall be glad.

Ps 85:1 LORD, thou hast been favourable unto thy land: thou hast brought back the captivity of Jacob.

Ps 106:47 Save us, O LORD our God, and gather us from among the heathen, to give thanks unto thy holy name, *and* to triumph in thy praise.

Ps 107:3 And gathered them out of the lands, from the east, and from the west, from the north, and from the south.

Ps 126:1 When the LORD turned again the captivity of Zion, we were like them that dream.

Ps 147:2 The LORD doth build up Jerusalem: he gathereth together the outcasts of Israel.

Is 11:11 And it shall come to pass in that day, *that* the Lord shall set his hand again the second time to recover the remnant of his people, which shall be left, from Assyria, and from Egypt, and from Pathros, and from Cush, and from Elam, and from Shinar, and from Hamath, and from the islands of the sea.

Is 14:1 For the LORD will have mercy on Jacob, and will yet choose Israel, and set them in their own land: and the strangers shall be joined with them, and they shall cleave to the house of Jacob.

Is 27:13 And it shall come to pass in that day, *that* the great trumpet shall be blown, and they shall come which were ready to perish in the land of Assyria, and the outcasts in the land of Egypt, and shall worship the LORD in the holy mount at Jerusalem.

Is 35:10 And the ransomed of the LORD shall return, and come to Zion with songs and everlasting joy upon their heads: they shall obtain joy and gladness, and sorrow and sighing shall flee away.

Is 43:5 Fear not: for I *am* with thee: I will bring thy seed from the east, and gather thee from the west;

Is 45:13 I have raised him up in righteousness, and I will direct all his ways: he shall build my city, and he shall let go my captives, not for price nor reward, saith the LORD of hosts.

Is 52:8 Thy watchmen shall lift up the voice; with the voice together shall they sing: for they shall see eye to eye, when the LORD shall bring again Zion.

Is 55:12 For ye shall go out with joy, and be led forth with peace: the mountains and the hills shall break forth before you into singing, and all the trees of the field shall clap *their* hands.

Is 56:8 The Lord GOD which gathereth the outcasts of Israel saith, Yet will I gather *others* to him, beside those that are gathered unto him.

Is 60:4 Lift up thine eyes round about, and see: all they gather themselves together, they come to thee: thy sons shall come from far, and thy daughters shall be nursed at *thy* side.

Je 3:14 Turn, O backsliding children, saith the LORD; for I am married unto you: and I will take you one of a city, and two of a family, and I will bring you to Zion:

Je 12:14 Thus saith the LORD against all mine evil neighbours, that touch the inheritance which I have caused my people Israel to inherit; Behold, I will pluck them out of their land, and pluck out the house of Judah from among them.

Je 16:15 But, The LORD liveth, that brought up the children of Israel from the land of the north, and from all the lands whither he had driven them: and I will bring them again into their land that I gave unto their fathers.

Je 23:3 And I will gather the remnant of my flock out of all countries whither I have driven them, and will bring them again to their folds; and they shall be fruitful and increase.

Je 23:8 But, The LORD liveth, which brought up and which led the seed of the house of Israel out of the north country, and from all countries whither I had driven them; and they shall dwell in their own land.

Je 24:6 For I will set mine eyes upon them for good, and I will bring them again to this land: and I will build them, and not pull *them* down; and I will plant them, and not pluck *them* up.

Je 27:22 They shall be carried to Babylon, and there shall they be until the day that I visit them, saith the LORD; then will I bring them up, and restore them to this place.

Je 29:10 For thus saith the LORD, That after seventy years be accomplished at Babylon I will visit you, and perform my good word toward you, in causing you to return to this place.

Je 30:3 For, lo, the days come, saith the LORD, that I will bring again the captivity of my people Israel and Judah, saith the LORD: and I will cause them to return to the land that I gave to their fathers, and they shall possess it.

Je 30:18 Thus saith the LORD; Behold, I will bring again the captivity of Ja-cob's tents, and have mercy on his dwellingplaces; and the city shall be builded upon her own heap, and the palace shall remain after the manner thereof.

Je 31:8 Behold, I will bring them from the north country, and gather them from the coasts of the earth, *and* with them the blind and the lame, the woman with child and her that tra-vaileth with child together: a great company shall return thither.

Je 31:16 Thus saith the LORD; Refrain thy voice from weeping, and thine eyes from tears: for thy work shall be rewarded, saith the LORD; and they shall come again from the land of the enemy.

Je 32:37 Behold, I will gather them out of all countries, whither I have driven them in mine anger, and in my fury, and in great wrath; and I will bring them again unto this place, and I will cause them to dwell safely:

Je 32:44 Men shall buy fields for money, and subscribe evidences, and seal *them*, and take witnesses in the land of Benjamin, and in the places about Jerusalem, and in the cities of Judah, and in the cities of the mountains, and in the cities of the valley, and in the cities of the south: for I will cause their captivity to return, saith the LORD.

Je 33:7 And I will cause the captivity of Judah and the captivity of Israel to return, and will build them, as at the first.

Je 33:11 The voice of joy, and the voice of gladness, the voice of the bridegroom, and the voice of the bride, the voice of them that shall say, Praise the LORD of hosts: for the LORD *is* good; for his mercy *endureth* for ever: *and* of them that shall bring the sacrifice of praise into the house of the LORD. For I will cause to return the captivity of the land, as at the first, saith the LORD.

Je 33:26 Then will I cast away the seed of Jacob, and David my servant, so that I will not take *any* of his seed *to be* rulers over the seed of Abraham, Isaac, and Jacob: for I will cause their captivity to return, and have mercy on them.

Je 40:12 Even all the Jews returned out of all places whither they were driven, and came to the land of Judah, to Gedaliah, unto Mizpah, and gathered wine and summer fruits very much.

Je 42:13 But if ye say, We will not dwell in this land, neither obey the voice of the LORD your God,

Je 46:27 But fear not thou, O my servant Jacob, and be not dismayed, O Israel: for, behold, I will save thee from afar off, and thy seed from the land of their captivity; and Jacob shall return, and be in rest and at ease, and none shall make *him* afraid.

Je 50:19 And I will bring Israel again to his habitation, and he shall feed on Carmel and Bashan, and his soul shall be satisfied upon mount Ephraim and Gilead.

Eze 11:17 Therefore say, Thus saith the Lord GOD; I will even gather you from the people, and assemble you out of the countries where ye have been scattered, and I will give you the land of Israel.

Eze 20:34 And I will bring you out from the people, and will gather you out of the countries wherein ye are scattered, with a mighty hand, and with a stretched out arm, and with fury poured out.

Eze 20:38 And I will purge out from among you the rebels, and them that transgress against me: I will bring them forth out of the country where they sojourn, and they shall not enter into the land of Israel: and ye shall know that I *am* the LORD.

Eze 20:42 And ye shall know that I *am* the LORD, when I shall bring you into the land of Israel, into the country *for* the which I lifted up mine hand to give it to your fathers.

Eze 28:25 Thus saith the Lord GOD; When I shall have gathered the house of Israel from the people among whom they are scattered, and shall be sanctified in them in the sight of the heathen, then shall they dwell in their land that I have given to my servant Jacob.

Eze 34:13 And I will bring them out from the people, and gather them from the countries, and will bring them to their own land, and feed them upon the mountains of Israel by the rivers, and in all the inhabited places of the country.

Eze 36:24 For I will take you from among the heathen, and gather you out of all countries, and will bring you into your own land.

Eze 36:35 And they shall say, This land that was desolate is become like the garden of Eden; and the waste and desolate and ruined cities *are become* fenced, *and* are inhabited.

Eze 37:14 And shall put my spirit in you, and ye shall live, and I shall place you in your own land: then shall ye know that I the LORD have spoken *it,* and performed *it,* saith the LORD.

Eze 37:21 And say unto them, Thus saith the Lord GOD; Behold, I will take the children of Israel from among the heathen, whither they be gone, and will gather them on every side, and bring them into their own land:

Eze 39:27 When I have brought them again from the people, and gathered them out of their enemies' lands, and am sanctified in them in the sight of many nations;

Jl 3:1 For, behold, in those days, and in that time, when I shall bring again the captivity of Judah and Jerusalem,

Am 9:14 And I will bring again the captivity of my people of Israel, and they shall build the waste cities, and inhabit *them;* and they shall plant vineyards, and drink the wine thereof; they shall also make gardens, and eat the fruit of them.

Obad 20 And the captivity of this host of the children of Israel *shall possess* that of the Canaanites, *even* unto Zarephath; and the captivity of Jerusalem, which *is* in Sepharad, shall possess the cities of the south.

Mi 2:12 I will surely assemble, O Jacob, all of thee; I will surely gather the remnant of Israel; I will put them together as the sheep of Bozrah, as the flock in the midst of their fold: they shall make great noise by reason of *the multitude of* men.

Mi 4:10 Be in pain, and labour to bring forth, O daughter of Zion, like a woman in travail: for now shalt thou go forth out of the city, and thou shalt dwell in the field, and thou shalt go *even* to Babylon; there shalt thou be delivered; there the LORD shall redeem thee from the hand of thine enemies.

Mi 7:12 *In* that day *also* he shall come even to thee from Assyria, and *from* the fortified cities, and from the fortress even to the river, and from sea to sea, and *from* mountain to mountain.

Zep 2:7 And the coast shall be for the remnant of the house of Judah; they shall feed thereupon: in the houses of Ashkelon shall they lie down in the evening: for the LORD their God shall visit them, and turn away their captivity.

Zep 3:20 At that time will I bring you *again,* even in the time that I gather you: for I will make you a name and a praise among all people of the earth, when I turn back your captivity before your eyes, saith the LORD.

Zec 6:15 And they *that are* far off shall come and build in the temple of the LORD, and ye shall know that the LORD of hosts hath sent me unto you. And *this* shall come to pass, if ye will diligently obey the voice of the LORD your God.

Zec 8:8 And I will bring them, and they shall dwell in the midst of Jerusalem: and they shall be my people, and I will be their God, in truth and in righteousness.

Zec 10:10 I will bring them again also out of the land of Egypt, and gather them out of Assyria; and I will bring them into the land of Gilead and Lebanon; and *place* shall not be found for them.

9. Remnant Will Remain

Le 26:44 And yet for all that, when they be in the land of their enemies, I will not cast them away, neither will I abhor them, to destroy them utterly, and to break my covenant with them: for I *am* the LORD their God.

1 K 19:18 Yet I have left *me* seven thousand in Israel, all the knees which have not bowed unto Baal, and every mouth which hath not kissed him.

2 K 19:31 For out of Jerusalem shall go forth a remnant, and they that escape out of mount Zion: the zeal of the LORD *of hosts* shall do this.

2 Chr 30:6 So the posts went with the letters from the king and his princes throughout all Israel and Judah, and according to the commandment of the king, saying, Ye children of Israel, turn again unto the LORD God of Abraham, Isaac, and Israel, and he will return to the remnant of you, that are escaped out of the hand of the kings of Assyria.

Ezr 2:64 The whole congregation together *was* forty and two thousand three hundred *and* threescore,

Ezr 9:8 And now for a little space grace hath been *shewed* from the LORD our God, to leave us a remnant to escape, and to give us a nail in his holy place, that our God may lighten our eyes, and give us a little reviving in our bondage.

Ezr 9:15 O LORD God of Israel, thou *art* righteous: for we remain yet escaped, as *it is* this day: behold, we *are* before thee in our trespasses: for we cannot stand before thee because of this.

Ne 1:3 And they said unto me, The remnant that are left of the captivity there in the province *are* in great affliction and reproach: the wall of Jerusalem also *is* broken down, and the gates thereof are burned with fire.

Ne 9:31 Nevertheless for thy great mercies' sake thou didst not utterly consume them, nor forsake them; for thou *art* a gracious and merciful God.

Is 1:9 Except the LORD of hosts had left unto us a very small remnant, we should have been as Sodom, *and* we should have been like unto Gomorrah.

Is 4:3 And it shall come to pass, *that* he that is left in Zion, and *he that* remaineth in Jerusalem, shall be called holy, *even* every one that is written among the living in Jerusalem:

Is 6:13 But yet in it *shall be* a tenth, and *it* shall return, and shall be eaten: as a teil tree, and as an oak, whose substance is in them, when they cast *their leaves: so* the holy seed *shall be* the substance thereof.

Is 10:20 And it shall come to pass in that day, *that* the remnant of Israel, and such as are escaped of the house of Jacob, shall no more again stay upon him that smote them; but shall stay upon the LORD, the Holy One of Israel, in truth.

Is 11:11 And it shall come to pass in that day, *that* the Lord shall set his hand again the second time to recover the remnant of his people, which shall be left, from Assyria, and from Egypt, and from Pathros, and from Cush, and from Elam, and from Shinar, and from Hamath, and from the islands of the sea.

Is 11:16 And there shall be an high-way for the remnant of his people, which shall be left, from Assyria; like as it was to Israel in the day that he came up out of the land of Egypt.

Is 17:6 Yet gleaning grapes shall be left in it, as the shaking of an olive tree, two *or* three berries in the top of the uppermost bough, four *or* five in the outmost fruitful branches thereof, saith the LORD God of Israel.

Is 37:4 It may be the LORD thy God will hear the words of Rabshakeh, whom the king of Assyria his master hath sent to reproach the living God, and will reprove the words which the LORD thy God hath heard: wherefore lift up *thy* prayer for the remnant that is left.

Is 37:32 For out of Jerusalem shall go forth a remnant, and they that escape out of mount Zion: the zeal of the LORD of hosts shall do this.

Is 45:20 Assemble yourselves and come; draw near together, ye *that are* escaped of the nations: they have no knowledge that set up the wood of their graven image, and pray unto a god *that* cannot save.

Is 46:3 Hearken unto me, O house of Jacob, and all the remnant of the house of Israel, which are borne *by me* from the belly, which are carried from the womb:

Is 65:8 Thus saith the LORD, As the new wine is found in the cluster, and

one saith, Destroy it not; for a blessing *is* in it: so will I do for my servants' sakes, that I may not destroy them all.

Je 3:14 Turn, O backsliding children, saith the LORD; for I am married unto you: and I will take you one of a city, and two of a family, and I will bring you to Zion:

Je 5:18 Nevertheless in those days, saith the LORD, I will not make a full end with you.

Je 6:9 Thus saith the LORD of hosts, They shall throughly glean the remnant of Israel as a vine: turn back thine hand as a grapegatherer into the baskets.

Je 23:3 And I will gather the remnant of my flock out of all countries whither I have driven them, and will bring them again to their folds; and they shall be fruitful and increase.

Je 30:11 For I *am* with thee, saith the LORD, to save thee: though I make a full end of all nations whither I have scattered thee, yet will I not make a full end of thee: but I will correct thee in measure, and will not leave thee altogether unpunished.

Je 31:7 For thus saith the LORD; Sing with gladness for Jacob, and shout among the chief of the nations: publish ye, praise ye, and say, O LORD, save thy people, the remnant of Israel.

Je 40:11 Likewise when all the Jews that *were* in Moab, and among the Ammonites, and in Edom, and that *were* in all the countries, heard that the king of Babylon had left a remnant of Judah, and that he had set over them Gedaliah the son of Ahikam the son of Shaphan;

Je 40:15 Then Johanan the son of Kareah spake to Gedaliah in Mizpah secretly, saying, Let me go, I pray thee, and I will slay Ishmael the son of Nethaniah, and no man shall know *it:* wherefore should he slay thee, that all the Jews which are gathered unto thee should be scattered, and the remnant in Judah perish?

Je 41:16 Then took Johanan the son of Kareah, and all the captains of the forces that *were* with him, all the remnant of the people whom he had recovered from Ishmael the son of

Nethaniah, from Mizpah, after *that* he had slain Gedaliah the son of Ahikam, *even* mighty men of war, and the women, and the children, and the eunuchs, whom he had brought again from Gibeon:

Je 42:2 And said unto Jeremiah the prophet, Let, we beseech thee, our supplication be accepted before thee, and pray for us unto the LORD thy God, *even* for all this remnant; (for we are left *but* a few of many, as thine eyes do behold us:)

Je 42:15 And now therefore hear the word of the LORD, ye remnant of Judah; Thus saith the LORD of hosts, the God of Israel; If ye wholly set your faces to enter into Egypt, and go to sojourn there;

Je 42:19 The LORD hath said concerning you, O ye remnant of Judah; Go ye not into Egypt: know certainly that I have admonished you this day.

Je 43:5 But Johanan the son of Kareah, and all the captains of the forces, took all the remnant of Judah, that were returned from all nations, whither they had been driven, to dwell in the land of Judah;

Je 44:12 And I will take the remnant of Judah, that have set their faces to go into the land of Egypt to sojourn there, and they shall all be consumed, *and* fall in the land of Egypt; they shall *even* be consumed by the sword and by the famine: they shall die, from the least even unto the greatest, by the sword *and* by the famine: and they shall be an execration, *and* an astonishment, and a curse, and a reproach.

Je 44:14 So that none of the remnant of Judah, which are gone into the land of Egypt to sojourn there, shall escape or remain, that they should return into the land of Judah, to the which they have a desire to return to dwell there: for none shall return but such as shall escape.

Je 46:28 Fear thou not, O Jacob my servant, saith the LORD: for I *am* with thee; for I will make a full end of all the nations whither I have driven thee: but I will not make a full end of thee, but correct thee in measure; yet will I not leave thee wholly unpunished.

Je 50:20 In those days, and in that time, saith the LORD, the iniquity of Israel shall be sought for, and *there shall be* none; and the sins of Judah, and they shall not be found: for I will pardon them whom I reserve.

Eze 6:8 Yet will I leave a remnant, that ye may have *some* that shall escape the sword among the nations, when ye shall be scattered through the countries.

Eze 11:13 And it came to pass, when I prophesied, that Pelatiah the son of Benaiah died. Then fell I down upon my face, and cried with a loud voice, and said, Ah Lord GOD! wilt thou make a full end of the remnant of Israel?

Eze 12:16 But I will leave a few men of them from the sword, from the famine, and from the pestilence; that they may declare all their abominations among the heathen whither they come; and they shall know that I *am* the LORD.

Eze 14:22 Yet, behold, therein shall be left a remnant that shall be brought forth, *both* sons and daughters: behold, they shall come forth unto you, and ye shall see their way and their doings: and ye shall be comforted concerning the evil that I have brought upon Jerusalem, *even* concerning all that I have brought upon it.

Jl 2:32 And it shall come to pass, *that* whosoever shall call on the name of the LORD shall be delivered: for in mount Zion and in Jerusalem shall be deliverance, as the LORD hath said, and in the remnant whom the LORD shall call.

Am 3:12 Thus saith the LORD; As the shepherd taketh out of the mouth of the lion two legs, or a piece of an ear; so shall the children of Israel be taken out that dwell in Samaria in the corner of a bed, and in Damascus *in* a couch.

Am 5:3 For thus saith the Lord GOD; The city that went out *by* a thousand shall leave an hundred, and that which went forth *by* an hundred shall leave ten, to the house of Israel.

Am 5:15 Hate the evil, and love the good, and establish judgment in the gate: it may be that the LORD God of hosts will be gracious unto the remnant of Joseph.

Am 9:8 Behold, the eyes of the Lord GOD *are* upon the sinful kingdom, and I will destroy it from off the face of the earth; saving that I will not utterly destroy the house of Jacob, saith the LORD.

Mi 2:12 I will surely assemble, O Jacob, all of thee; I will surely gather the remnant of Israel; I will put them together as the sheep of Bozrah, as the flock in the midst of their fold: they shall make great noise by reason of *the multitude of* men.

Mi 4:7 And I will make her that halted a remnant, and her that was cast far off a strong nation: and the LORD shall reign over them in mount Zion from henceforth, even for ever.

Mi 5:3 Therefore will he give them up, until the time *that* she which travaileth hath brought forth: then the remnant of his brethren shall return unto the children of Israel.

Mi 5:8 And the remnant of Jacob shall be among the Gentiles in the midst of many people as a lion among the beasts of the forest, as a young lion among the flocks of sheep: who, if he go through, both treadeth down, and teareth in pieces, and none can deliver.

Mi 7:18 Who *is* a God like unto thee, that pardoneth iniquity, and passeth by the transgression of the remnant of his heritage? he retaineth not his anger for ever, because he delighteth *in* mercy.

Zep 2:7 And the coast shall be for the remnant of the house of Judah; they shall feed thereupon: in the houses of Ashkelon shall they lie down in the evening: for the LORD their God shall visit them, and turn away their captivity.

Zep 2:9 Therefore *as* I live, saith the LORD of hosts, the God of Israel, Surely Moab shall be as Sodom, and the children of Ammon as Gomorrah, *even* the breeding of nettles, and saltpits, and a perpetual desolation: the residue of my people shall spoil them, and the remnant of my people shall possess them.

Zep 3:13 The remnant of Israel shall not do iniquity, nor speak lies; neither shall a deceitful tongue be found in their mouth: for they shall feed and lie down, and none shall make *them* afraid.

Zec 8:6 Thus saith the LORD of hosts; If it be marvellous in the eyes of the remnant of this people in these days, should it also be marvellous in mine eyes? saith the LORD of hosts.

Zec 8:12 For the seed *shall be* prosperous; the vine shall give her fruit, and the ground shall give her increase, and the heavens shall give their dew; and I will cause the remnant of this people to possess all these *things*.

Zec 13:8 And it shall come to pass, *that* in all the land, saith the LORD, two parts therein shall be cut off *and* die; but the third shall be left therein.

Ro 9:27 Esaias also crieth concerning Israel, Though the number of the children of Israel be as the sand of the sea, a remnant shall be saved:

Ro 9:29 And as Esaias said before, Except the Lord of Sabaoth had left us a seed, we had been as Sodoma, and been made like unto Gomorrha.

Ro 11:5 Even so then at this present time also there is a remnant according to the election of grace.

10. Her Persecution

2 K 16:6 At that time Rezin king of Syria recovered Elath to Syria, and drave the Jews from Elath: and the Syrians came to Elath, and dwelt there unto this day.

Est 3:13 And the letters were sent by posts into all the king's provinces, to destroy, to kill, and to cause to perish, all Jews, both young and old, little children and women, in one day, *even* upon the thirteenth *day* of the twelfth month, which *is* the month Adar, and *to take* the spoil of them for a prey.

Est 4:7 And Mordecai told him of all that had happened unto him, and of the sum of the money that Haman had promised to pay to the king's treasuries for the Jews, to destroy them.

Est 7:4 For we are sold, I and my people, to be destroyed, to be slain, and to perish. But if we had been sold for bondmen and bondwomen, I had held my tongue, although the enemy could not countervail the king's damage.

Ps 74:8 They said in their hearts, Let us destroy them together: they have burned up all the synagogues of God in the land.

Ps 83:4 They have said, Come, and let us cut them off from *being* a nation; that the name of Israel may be no more in remembrance.

Je 50:7 All that found them have devoured them: and their adversaries said, We offend not, because they have sinned against the LORD, the habitation of justice, even the LORD, the hope of their fathers.

Je 50:17 Israel *is* a scattered sheep; the lions have driven *him* away: first the king of Assyria hath devoured him; and last this Nebuchadrezzar king of Babylon hath broken his bones.

Lam 4:18 They hunt our steps, that we cannot go in our streets: our end is near, our days are fulfilled; for our end is come.

Eze 25:12 Thus saith the Lord GOD; Because that Edom hath dealt against the house of Judah by taking vengeance, and hath greatly offended, and revenged himself upon them;

Eze 36:3 Therefore prophesy and say, Thus saith the Lord GOD; Because they have made *you* desolate, and swallowed you up on every side, that ye might be a possession unto the residue of the heathen, and ye are taken up in the lips of talkers, and *are* an infamy of the people:

Da 3:8 Wherefore at that time certain Chaldeans came near, and accused the Jews.

Da 8:24 And his power shall be mighty, but not by his own power: and he shall destroy wonderfully, and shall prosper, and practise, and shall destroy the mighty and the holy people.

Ac 16:20 And brought them to the magistrates, saying, These men, being Jews, do exceedingly trouble our city,

Ac 18:2 And found a certain Jew named Aquila, born in Pontus, lately come from Italy, with his wife Priscilla; (because that Claudius had commanded all Jews to depart from Rome:) and came unto them.

Ac 19:34 But when they knew that he was a Jew, all with one voice about the space of two hours cried out, Great *is* Diana of the Ephesians.

See **NATION, GENTILE BELIEVERS**

ISSACHAR, *son of Jacob and Leah*

Ge 30:18; 35:23; 46:13; 49:14; Ex 1:3; Nu 1:8, 28; 2:5; 10:15; 13:7; 26:23; 34:26; De 33:18; Jos 17:10; 19:17, 23; 21:6, 28; Jud 5:15; 1 Chr 6:62, 72; 7:1; Eze 48:26, 33; Re 7:7

ITALY

Ac 18:2; 27:6; He 13:24

ITCH *See* **DISEASE**

ITHAMAR, *son of Aaron*

Ex 6:23; Nu 3:4; 4:28; Ezr 8:2

ITTAI, *the Gittite, one of David's captains*

2 S 15:19; 18:2; 23:29

IVORY, *elephants tusks, used in ornament making*

1 K 10:18; 22:39; 2 Chr 9:17; Ps 45:8; Song 7:4; Eze 27:6, 15; Am 3:15; 6:4; Re 18:12

I WILL'S, *OF CHRIST*

NOT AS I WILL

Mt 26:39 And he went a little farther, and fell on his face, and prayed, saying, O my Father, if it be possible, let this cup pass from me: nevertheless not as I will, but as thou *wilt*.

I WILL: BE THOU CLEAN

Lu 5:13 And he put forth *his* hand, and touched him, saying, I will: be thou clean. And immediately the leprosy departed from him.

I WILL RAISE HIM

Jn 6:40 And this is the will of him that sent me, that every one which seeth the Son, and believeth on him, may have everlasting life: and I will raise him up at the last day.

I WILL DRAW ALL MEN

Jn 12:32 And I, if I be lifted up from the earth, will draw all *men* unto me.

I WILL COME AGAIN

Jn 14:3 And if I go and prepare a place for you, I will come again, and receive you unto myself; that where I am, *there* ye may be also.

I WILL THAT THEY BE WITH ME

Jn 17:24 Father, I will that they also, whom thou hast given me, be with me where I am; that they may behold my glory, which thou hast given me: for thou lovedst me before the foundation of the world.

IF I WILL THAT HE TARRY

Jn 21:22 Jesus saith unto him, If I will that he tarry till I come, what *is that* to thee? follow thou me.

J

JABBOK, *one of the eastern tributaries of the Jordan*

Ge 32:22; Nu 21:24; De 2:37; 3:16; Jos 12:2; Jud 11:13

See **RIVERS**

JABESH GILEAD, *a town east of the Jordan*

Jud 21:8; 1 S 11:1; 31:11; 2 S 2:4; 21:12; 1 Chr 10:11

See **CITIES**

JACINTH *See* **STONES**

JACOB, *supplanter, son of Isaac*

No other Bible character represents more fully the conflict between the lower and higher nature than does Jacob. Yet no reader who studies the history of this man's career can doubt that he was a chosen instrument of God in spite of all his weaknesses. Two thoughts are key to understanding Jacob: (1) his unhappiness produced by family trouble and polygamy and (2) the transforming power of fellowship with God.

HIS BIRTH

Ge 25:26 And after that came his brother out, and his hand took hold on Esau's heel; and his name was called Jacob: and Isaac *was* threescore years old when she bare them.

BUYING OF BIRTHRIGHT

Ge 25:31–34 And Jacob said, Sell me this day thy birthright.

And Esau said, Behold, I *am* at the point to die: and what profit shall this birthright do to me?

And Jacob said, Swear to me this day; and he sware unto him: and he sold his birthright unto Jacob.

Then Jacob gave Esau bread and pottage of lentiles; and he did eat and drink, and rose up, and went his way: thus Esau despised *his* birthright.

DECEPTION OF FATHER

Ge 27:18–30 And he came unto his father, and said, My father: and he said, Here *am* I; who *art* thou, my son?

And Jacob said unto his father, I *am* Esau thy firstborn; I have done according as thou badest me: arise, I pray thee, sit and eat of my venison, that thy soul may bless me.

And Isaac said unto his son, How *is* it that thou hast found *it* so quickly, my son? And he said, Because the LORD thy God brought *it* to me.

And Isaac said unto Jacob, Come near, I pray thee, that I may feel thee, my son, whether thou *be* my very son Esau or not.

And Jacob went near unto Isaac his father; and he felt him, and said, The voice *is* Jacob's voice, but the hands *are* the hands of Esau.

And he discerned him not, because his hands were hairy, as his brother Esau's hands: so he blessed him.

And he said, *Art* thou my very son Esau? And he said, I *am.*

And he said, Bring *it* near to me, and I will eat of my son's venison, that my soul may bless thee. And he brought *it* near to him, and he did eat: and he brought him wine, and he drank.

And his father Isaac said unto him, Come near now, and kiss me, my son.

And he came near, and kissed him: and he smelled the smell of his raiment, and blessed him, and said, See, the smell of my son *is* as the smell of a field which the LORD hath blessed:

Therefore God give thee of the dew of heaven, and the fatness of the earth, and plenty of corn and wine:

Let people serve thee, and nations bow down to thee: be lord over thy brethren, and let thy mother's sons bow down to thee: cursed *be* every one that curseth thee, and blessed *be* he that blesseth thee.

And it came to pass, as soon as Isaac had made an end of blessing Jacob, and Jacob was yet scarce gone out from the presence of Isaac his father, that Esau his brother came in from his hunting.

WARNING OF MOTHER

Ge 27:42–43 And these words of Esau her elder son were told to Rebekah: and she sent and called Jacob her younger son, and said unto him, Behold, thy brother Esau, as touching thee, doth comfort himself, *purposing* to kill thee.

Now therefore, my son, obey my voice; and arise, flee thou to Laban my brother to Haran;

BLESSING OF FATHER

Ge 28:1 And Isaac called Jacob, and blessed him, and charged him, and said unto him, Thou shalt not take a wife of the daughters of Canaan.

JOURNEY TO HARAN

Ge 28:10 And Jacob went out from Beer-sheba, and went toward Haran.

JACOB'S VOW

Ge 28:20–21 And Jacob vowed a vow, saying, If God will be with me, and will keep me in this way that I go, and will give me bread to eat, and raiment to put on,

So that I come again to my father's house in peace; then shall the LORD be my God:

LOVE FOR RACHEL

Ge 29:18 And Jacob loved Rachel; and said, I will serve thee seven years for Rachel thy younger daughter.

DESIRE TO RETURN HOME

Ge 30:25 And it came to pass, when Rachel had born Joseph, that Jacob said unto Laban, Send me away, that I may go unto mine own place, and to my country.

WORD FROM GOD

Ge 31:3 And the LORD said unto Jacob, Return unto the land of thy fathers, and to thy kindred; and I will be with thee.

PRAYER TO GOD

Ge 32:9–12 And Jacob said, O God of my father Abraham, and God of my father Isaac, the LORD which saidst unto me, Return unto thy country, and to thy kindred, and I will deal well with thee:

I am not worthy of the least of all the mercies, and of all the truth, which thou hast shewed unto thy servant; for with my staff I passed over this Jordan; and now I am become two bands.

Deliver me, I pray thee, from the hand of my brother, from the hand of Esau: for I fear him, lest he will come and smite me, *and* the mother with the children.

And thou saidst, I will surely do thee good, and make thy seed as the sand of the sea, which cannot be numbered for multitude.

WRESTLING WITH GOD

Ge 32:24–30 And Jacob was left alone; and there wrestled a man with him until the breaking of the day.

And when he saw that he prevailed not against him, he touched the hollow of his thigh; and the hollow of Jacob's thigh was out of joint, as he wrestled with him.

And he said, Let me go, for the day breaketh. And he said, I will not let thee go, except thou bless me.

And he said unto him, What *is* thy name? And he said, Jacob.

And he said, Thy name shall be called no more Jacob, but Israel: for as a prince hast thou power with God and with men, and hast prevailed.

And Jacob asked *him*, and said, Tell *me*, I pray thee, thy name. And he said, Wherefore *is* it *that* thou dost ask after my name? And he blessed him there.

And Jacob called the name of the place Peniel: for I have seen God face to face, and my life is preserved.

MEETING WITH ESAU

Ge 33:10 And Jacob said, Nay, I pray thee, if now I have found grace in thy sight, then receive my present at my hand: for therefore I have seen thy face, as though I had seen the face of God, and thou wast pleased with me.

DWELLING IN SUCCOTH AND BETHEL

Ge 33:17 And Jacob journeyed to Succoth, and built him an house, and made booths for his cattle: therefore the name of the place is called Succoth.

Ge 35:1 And God said unto Jacob, Arise, go up to Bethel, and dwell there: and make there an altar unto God, that appeared unto thee when thou fleddest from the face of Esau thy brother.

LOVE FOR JOSEPH

Ge 37:3 Now Israel loved Joseph more than all his children, because he *was* the son of his old age: and he made him a coat of *many* colours.

SELLING OF JOSEPH

Ge 37:28 Then there passed by Midianites merchantmen; and they drew and lifted up Joseph out of the pit, and sold Joseph to the Ishmeelites for twenty *pieces* of silver: and they brought Joseph into Egypt.

SENDING OF SONS TO EGYPT

Ge 42:1 Now when Jacob saw that there was corn in Egypt, Jacob said unto his sons, Why do ye look one upon another?

SENDING OF BENJAMIN AND GIFTS TO EGYPT

Ge 42:36 And Jacob their father said unto them, Me have ye bereaved *of my children:* Joseph *is* not, and Simeon *is* not, and ye will take Benjamin *away:* all these things are against me.

Ge 43:11 And their father Israel said unto them, If *it must be* so now, do this; take of the best fruits in the land in your vessels, and carry down the man a present, a little balm, and a little honey, spices, and myrrh, nuts, and almonds:

REPORT THAT JOSEPH LIVES

Ge 45:26 And told him, saying, Joseph *is* yet alive, and he *is* governor over all the land of Egypt. And Jacob's heart fainted, for he believed them not.

JACOB GOES TO EGYPT

Ge 46:5 And Jacob rose up from Beersheba: and the sons of Israel carried Jacob their father, and their little ones, and their wives, in the wagons which Pharaoh had sent to carry him.

MEETING WITH JOSEPH

Ge 48:2 And *one* told Jacob, and said, Behold, thy son Joseph cometh unto thee: and Israel strengthened himself, and sat upon the bed.

DEATH OF JACOB

Ge 49:33 And when Jacob had made an end of commanding his sons, he gathered up his feet into the bed, and yielded up the ghost, and was gathered unto his people.

BURIAL IN CANAAN

Ge 50:13 For his sons carried him into the land of Canaan, and buried him in the cave of the field of Machpelah, which Abraham bought with the field for a possession of a burying-place of Ephron the Hittite, before Mamre.

RECOGNIZED AS MAN OF FAITH

He 11:20–21 By faith Isaac blessed Jacob and Esau concerning things to come.

By faith Jacob, when he was a dying, blessed both the sons of Joseph; and worshipped, *leaning* upon the top of his staff.

JAEL, *wife of Heber*

Jud 4:17; 5:6, 24

JAIR, *he enlightens*

1. Son of Manasseh

Nu 32:41; De 3:14

2. A Judge
Jud 10:3

See **ISRAEL**

JAIRUS, *ruler of a synagogue, whose child Christ raised to life*
Mt 9:18; Mk 5:22; Lu 8:41

JAMES, *supplanter*

1. An Apostle, *son of Zebedee, brother of John*
Mt 4:21; 10:2; 17:1; 26:37; Mk 1:19; 3:17; 5:37; 9:2; 10:35; 14:33; Lu 5:10; 6:14; 8:51; 9:28; Jn 21:2; Ac 1:13; 12:2

2. An Apostle, *son of Alphaeus*
Mt 10:3; Mk 3:18; Lu 6:15; Ac 1:13; 1 Co 15:7; Ga 2:9

3. The Lord's Brother, *authorities differ as to the existence and identity of this individual*

SLOW TO ACCEPT CHRIST
Jn 7:5 For neither did his brethren believe in him.

AFTER THE RESURRECTION JOINED THE DISCIPLES
Ac 1:14 These all continued with one accord in prayer and supplication, with the women, and Mary the mother of Jesus, and with his brethren.

POSSIBLY WAS WON BY THE APPEARANCE OF THE LORD AFTER THE RESURRECTION
1 Co 15:7 After that, he was seen of James; then of all the apostles.

POSSIBLY WAS ONE OF THE LEADERS OF THE CHURCH AT JERUSALEM
Ac 15:13 And after they had held their peace, James answered, saying, Men *and* brethren, hearken unto me:
Ac 21:18 And the *day* following Paul went in with us unto James; and all the elders were present.

POSSIBLY WAS AUTHOR OF THE EPISTLE OF JAMES (?)
Ja 1:1 James, a servant of God and of the Lord Jesus Christ, to the twelve tribes which are scattered abroad, greeting.

4. Book
Author: Uncertain. There are three prominent persons named James in the New Testament. It is generally agreed that James, called by Paul "the Lord's brother" (Ga 1:19), was the writer of the epistle.

Date Written: Possibly the earliest New Testament book written. Many feel it should be dated before A.D. 49 since the issues of the famous Council in Jerusalem of that year are not mentioned.

Purpose: To challenge believers to possess an active faith, one which will produce changes in a person's conduct and character.

To Whom Written: Apparently addressed to the Jewish converts who lived outside Israel; possibly also to the devout Jews of the dispersion (1:1).

Main Theme: Practical religion, manifesting itself in good works, contrasted with mere profession of faith.

Key Words: Faith and works (2:17).

Key Verses: 1:27; 2:26.

JAPHETH, *son of Noah*
Ge 5:32; 6:10; 7:13; 9:18; 10:2, 21; 1 Chr 1:5

JASHER, *book of*
Jos 10:13; 2 S 1:18

JASON, *disciple of Paul*
Ac 17:5; Ro 16:21

JASPER   *See* **STONES**

JAVELIN, *dart or spear*
Nu 25:7; 1 S 17:6; 18:10

JAZER, *a city of Gilead*
Nu 21:32; 32:1; Jos 13:25; 21:39; 2 S 24:5

JEALOUSY

1. Divine

Ex 20:5 Thou shalt not bow down thyself to them, nor serve them: for I the LORD thy God *am* a jealous God, visiting the iniquity of the fathers upon the children unto the third and fourth *generation* of them that hate me;

Ex 22:20 He that sacrificeth unto *any* god, save unto the LORD only, he shall be utterly destroyed.

Ex 23:13 And in all *things* that I have said unto you be circumspect: and make no mention of the name of other gods, neither let it be heard out of thy mouth.

Ex 34:14 For thou shalt worship no other god: for the LORD, whose name *is* Jealous, *is* a jealous God:

Le 26:1 Ye shall make you no idols nor graven image, neither rear you up a standing image, neither shall ye set up *any* image of stone in your land, to bow down unto it: for I *am* the LORD your God.

Nu 25:11 Phinehas, the son of Eleazar, the son of Aaron the priest, hath turned my wrath away from the children of Israel, while he was zealous for my sake among them, that I consumed not the children of Israel in my jealousy.

De 4:24 For the LORD thy God *is* a consuming fire, *even* a jealous God.

De 5:9 Thou shalt not bow down thyself unto them, nor serve them: for I the LORD thy God *am* a jealous God, visiting the iniquity of the fathers upon the children unto the third and fourth *generation* of them that hate me,

De 6:15 (For the LORD thy God *is* a jealous God among you) lest the anger of the LORD thy God be kindled against thee, and destroy thee from off the face of the earth.

De 29:20 The LORD will not spare him, but then the anger of the LORD and his jealousy shall smoke against that man, and all the curses that are written in this book shall lie upon him, and the LORD shall blot out his name from under heaven.

De 32:21 They have moved me to jealousy with *that which is* not God; they have provoked me to anger with their vanities: and I will move them to jealousy with *those which are* not a people; I will provoke them to anger with a foolish nation.

Jos 24:19 And Joshua said unto the people, Ye cannot serve the LORD: for he *is* an holy God; he *is* a jealous God; he will not forgive your transgressions nor your sins.

1 K 14:22 And Judah did evil in the sight of the LORD, and they provoked him to jealousy with their sins which they had committed, above all that their fathers had done.

Ps 78:58 For they provoked him to anger with their high places, and moved him to jealousy with their graven images.

Ps 79:5 How long, LORD? wilt thou be angry for ever? shall thy jealousy burn like fire?

Is 42:8 I *am* the LORD: that *is* my name: and my glory will I not give to another, neither my praise to graven images.

Is 48:11 For mine own sake, *even* for mine own sake, will I do *it*: for how should *my name* be polluted? and I will not give my glory unto another.

Eze 8:3 And he put forth the form of an hand, and took me by a lock of mine head; and the spirit lifted me up between the earth and the heaven, and brought me in the visions of God to Jerusalem, to the door of the inner gate that looketh toward the north; where *was* the seat of the image of jealousy, which provoketh to jealousy.

Eze 16:38 And I will judge thee, as women that break wedlock and shed blood are judged; and I will give thee blood in fury and jealousy.

Eze 16:42 So will I make my fury toward thee to rest, and my jealousy shall depart from thee, and I will be quiet, and will be no more angry.

Eze 23:25 And I will set my jealousy against thee, and they shall deal furiously with thee: they shall take away thy nose and thine ears; and thy remnant shall fall by the sword: they shall take thy sons and thy daughters; and thy residue shall be devoured by the fire.

Eze 36:5 Therefore thus saith the Lord GOD; Surely in the fire of my jealousy have I spoken against the residue of the heathen, and against all Idumea, which have appointed my land into their possession with the joy of all *their* heart, with despiteful minds, to cast it out for a prey.

Eze 38:19 For in my jealousy *and* in the fire of my wrath have I spoken, Surely in that day there shall be a great shaking in the land of Israel;

Eze 39:25 Therefore thus saith the Lord GOD; Now will I bring again the captivity of Jacob, and have mercy upon the whole house of Israel, and will be jealous for my holy name;

Ho 13:4 Yet I *am* the LORD thy God from the land of Egypt, and thou shalt know no god but me: for *there is* no saviour beside me.

Na 1:2 God *is* jealous, and the LORD revengeth; the LORD revengeth, and *is* furious; the LORD will take vengeance on his adversaries, and he reserveth *wrath* for his enemies.

Zep 1:18 Neither their silver nor their gold shall be able to deliver them in the day of the LORD's wrath; but the whole land shall be devoured by the fire of his jealousy: for he shall make even a speedy riddance of all them that dwell in the land.

Zep 3:8 Therefore wait ye upon me, saith the LORD, until the day that I rise up to the prey: for my determination *is* to gather the nations, that I may assemble the kingdoms, to pour upon them mine indignation, *even* all my fierce anger: for all the earth shall be devoured with the fire of my jealousy.

Zec 8:2 Thus saith the LORD of hosts; I was jealous for Zion with great jealousy, and I was jealous for her with great fury.

1 Co 10:22 Do we provoke the Lord to jealousy? are we stronger than he?

2. Human

JOSEPH'S BRETHREN

Ge 37:4 And when his brethren saw that their father loved him more than all his brethren, they hated him, and could not speak peaceably unto him.

THE MEN OF EPHRAIM

Jud 8:1 And the men of Ephraim said unto him, Why hast thou served us thus, that thou calledst us not, when thou wentest to fight with the Midianites? And they did chide with him sharply.

KING SAUL

1 S 18:8 And Saul was very wroth, and the saying displeased him; and he said, They have ascribed unto David ten thousands, and to me they have ascribed *but* thousands: and *what* can he have more but the kingdom?

2 S 19:41 And, behold, all the men of Israel came to the king, and said unto the king, Why have our brethren the men of Judah stolen thee away, and have brought the king, and his household, and all David's men with him, over Jordan?

Pr 6:34 For jealousy *is* the rage of a man: therefore he will not spare in the day of vengeance.

THE LABORERS IN THE VINEYARD

Mt 20:12 Saying, These last have wrought *but* one hour, and thou hast made them equal unto us, which have borne the burden and heat of the day.

THE ELDER BROTHER

Lu 15:28 And he was angry, and would not go in: therefore came his father out, and intreated him.

3. Jewish

Ac 13:45 But when the Jews saw the multitudes, they were filled with envy, and spake against those things which were spoken by Paul, contradicting and blaspheming.

Ac 17:5 But the Jews which believed not, moved with envy, took unto them certain lewd fellows of the baser sort, and gathered a company, and set all the city on an uproar, and assaulted the house of Jason, and sought to bring them out to the people.

Ac 17:13 But when the Jews of Thessalonica had knowledge that the word of God was preached of Paul at Berea, they came thither also, and stirred up the people.

Ac 22:22 And they gave him audience unto this word, and *then* lifted up their voices, and said, Away with such a *fellow* from the earth: for it is not fit that he should live.

Ro 10:19 But I say, Did not Israel know? First Moses saith, I will provoke you to jealousy by *them that are* no people, *and* by a foolish nation I will anger you.

Ro 11:11 I say then, Have they stumbled that they should fall? God forbid: but *rather* through their fall salvation *is come* unto the Gentiles, for to provoke them to jealousy.

JEBUSITES, *one of the Canaanite nations*

Ex 3:17; 13:5; 23:23; 33:2; 34:11; Nu 13:29; De 7:1; Jos 3:10; 9:1; 11:3; 12:8; 15:63; 24:11; Jud 1:21; 3:5; 19:11; 2 S 5:6, 8; 1 K 9:20; 1 Chr 1:14; 11:4; 21:28; 2 Chr 8:7

JECONIAH *See* **ISRAEL**

JEDUTHUN, *a musician*

1 Chr 16:41; 25:6

JEHOAHAZ, *Jehovah seized*

1. Son of Jehu, *king of Israel*

2 K 10:35; 13:1, 9; 14:1, 8

2. Son of Jehoram, *king of Judah*

See **AHAZIAH**

3. Or Shallum, *son of Josiah, king of Judah*

2 K 23:30, 34; 1 Chr 3:15; 2 Chr 36:1; Je 22:11

See **ISRAEL**

JEHOASH, *Jehovah is strong*

1. Or Joash, *king of Judah*

See **ISRAEL**

2. Or Joash, *king of Israel, son of Jehoahaz*

2 K 13:10, 14, 25; 14:8, 16; 2 Chr 18:25; 25:17, 23

See **ISRAEL**

JEHOIADA, *Jehovah knows*

1. Officer of David

2 S 8:18

2. High Priest

2 K 11:4, 17; 12:9; 2 Chr 22:11; 23:9, 16; 24:2, 15

JEHOIACHIN, *Coniah, or Jeconiah, king of Judah, son of Jehoiakim*

2 K 24:6, 8, 15; 25:27; 2 Chr 36:9; Est 2:6; Je 22:24; 24:1; 28:4; 29:2; 37:1; 52:31; Eze 1:2; Mt 1:11

See **ISRAEL**

JEHOIAKIM, *or Eliakim, king of Judah, son of Josiah*

2 K 23:34; 24:1, 5; 1 Chr 3:15; 2 Chr 36:8; Je 1:3; 22:18; 25:1; 26:1; 27:1; 35:1; 36:1; 46:2; 52:2; Da 1:1

See **ISRAEL**

JEHORAM, *Jehovah is high*

1. King of Judah, *son of Jehoshaphat*

1 K 22:50; 2 K 1:17; 8:16, 21, 28; 1 Chr 3:11; 2 Chr 21:1, 5, 9, 16, 20; Mt 1:8

2. Or Joram, *king of Israel, son of Ahab*

2 K 1:17; 3:1; 5:6; 6:21, 30; 7:17; 8:16; 9:14, 21, 24; 2 Chr 22:5

See **ISRAEL**

JEHOSHAPHAT, *Jehovah judged*

1. David's Recorder

2 S 8:16; 20:24; 1 K 4:3; 22:29; 1 Chr 3:10; 18:15; 2 Chr 22:9

2. King of Judah, *son of Asa*

HAD A GODLY FATHER

2 Chr 14:2

INAUGURATED A SYSTEM OF RELIGIOUS INSTRUCTION FOR THE PEOPLE

2 Chr 17:7–9

COMMANDED THE JUDGES TO BE JUST

2 Chr 19:6–9

WHEN SURROUNDING NATIONS ATTACKED HIM HE TRUSTED IN THE LORD AND GAINED A GREAT VICTORY

2 Chr 20:1–37

MANIFESTED WEAKNESS IN FORMING ALLIANCES WITH WICKED KINGS

1 K 22:1–36; 2 K 3:4–27

See **ISRAEL**

JEHOVAH-JIREH, *the Lord will provide*

Ge 22:14

JEHOVAH-NISSI, *the Lord my banner*

Ex 17:15

JEHOVAH-TSIDKENU, *the Lord our righteousness*

Je 23:6; 33:16

JEHOVAH-SHALOM, *the Lord send peace*

Jud 6:24

JEHOVAH-SHAMMAH, *the Lord is there*

Eze 48:35

JEHOZADAK, *Josedech, or Jozadak, high priest*

1 Chr 6:15; Ezr 3:2; 5:2; 10:18; Ne 12:26; Hag 1:1; Zec 6:11

JEHU, *Jehovah is he*

1. King of Israel, *son of Nimshi*

1 K 19:16; 2 K 9:2, 24; 10:1, 29, 35; 2 Chr 22:7; Ho 1:4

2. A prophet, *son of Hanani*

1 K 16:1; 2 Chr 19:2; 20:34

See **ISRAEL**

JEPHTHAH, *son of Gilead, a deliverer of Israel, one of the judges*

AN OUTCAST

Jud 11:1–2 Now Jephthah the Gileadite was a mighty man of valour, and he *was* the son of an harlot: and Gilead begat Jephthah.

And Gilead's wife bare him sons; and his wife's sons grew up, and they thrust out Jephthah, and said unto him, Thou shalt not inherit in our father's house; for thou *art* the son of a strange woman.

RISES TO LEADERSHIP

Jud 11:4–10 And it came to pass in process of time, that the children of Ammon made war against Israel.

And it was so, that when the children of Ammon made war against Israel, the elders of Gilead went to fetch Jephthah out of the land of Tob:

And they said unto Jephthah, Come, and be our captain, that we may fight with the children of Ammon.

And Jephthah said unto the elders of Gilead, Did not ye hate me, and expel me out of my father's house? and why are ye come unto me now when ye are in distress?

And the elders of Gilead said unto Jephthah, Therefore we turn again to thee now, that thou mayest go with us, and fight against the children of Ammon, and be our head over all the inhabitants of Gilead.

And Jephthah said unto the elders of Gilead, If ye bring me home again to fight against the children of Ammon, and the LORD deliver them before me, shall I be your head?

And the elders of Gilead said unto Jephthah, The LORD be witness between us, if we do not so according to thy words.

MOVED AT TIMES BY GOD'S SPIRIT

Jud 11:29 Then the Spirit of the LORD came upon Jephthah, and he passed over Gilead, and Manasseh, and passed over Mizpeh of Gilead, and from Mizpeh of Gilead he passed over *unto* the children of Ammon.

JEPHTHAH

MADE A RASH VOW

Jud 11:30–31 And Jephthah vowed a vow unto the LORD, and said, If thou shalt without fail deliver the children of Ammon into mine hands,

Then it shall be, that whatsoever cometh forth of the doors of my house to meet me, when I return in peace from the children of Ammon, shall surely be the LORD's, and I will offer it up for a burnt offering.

DELIVERED ISRAEL FROM THEIR ENEMIES

Jud 11:33 And he smote them from Aroer, even till thou come to Minnith, *even* twenty cities, and unto the plain of the vineyards, with a very great slaughter. Thus the children of Ammon were subdued before the children of Israel.

Jud 11:39 And it came to pass at the end of two months, that she returned unto her father, who did with her *according* to his vow which he had vowed: and she knew no man. And it was a custom in Israel,

JEPHTHAH *See* **ISRAEL**

JEPHTHAH'S DAUGHTER *See* **YOUNG PEOPLE**

JEREBOAM, *struggler for the people*

1. First King of Israel, *son of Nebat*

1 K 11:28; 12:2, 12, 20, 26, 32; 13:1; 14:7, 19; 15:1, 9, 25; 16:31; 21:22; 2 K 9:9; 10:29; 17:21; 23:15; 1 Chr 5:17; 2 Chr 10:2; 11:14; 13:4, 13, 20

2. King of Israel, *son and successor of Jehoash*

2 K 13:13; 14:16, 23, 27; 15:1; Ho 1:1; Am 1:1; 7:10

See **ISRAEL, YOUNG PEOPLE**

JEREMIAH

1. Person, *son of Hilkiah, one of the greater prophets*

2 Chr 36:12, 21; Ezr 1:1; Je 1:1; 3:6; 20:2; 21:3; 24:3; 25:2; 28:5; 36:4, 27; 37:13, 21; 38:6, 13, 27; 39:15; 40:1;

42:2, 7; 43:8; 44:1; 45:1; 46:1; 47:1; 49:34; 51:60; Lam 1:1; Mt 16:14

2. Book

Author: Jeremiah, "the weeping prophet." The book documents his life and message.

Date Written: During the ministry of Jeremiah (c. 627–580 B.C.). These were dark days in the kingdom of Judah (from the thirteenth year of Josiah, the last good king, until some years beyond the captivity).

Purpose: To declare God's judgment upon his people and call them to repentance and spiritual restoration.

To Whom Written: The nation of Judah.

Main Themes: The backsliding, bondage, and restoration of the Jews. **Key Word:** Heart. It is wicked and deceitful (17:9); but when broken it is the place upon which God writes his New Covenant (31:33).

Key Verses: 2:19; 31:33.

JERICHO, *a city west of the Jordan, near Jerusalem*

Jericho is best known to Bible students as the first city conquered by the invading Israelites, who employed an unorthodox strategy conveyed by the Lord to Joshua (Jos 5:13–6:27). After being destroyed by Joshua, the city was burned and the site apparently was abandoned for some time (Jos 6:26, 1 K 16:34), although its spring and nearby oasis were still used (e.g., 2 S 10:5, 1 Chr 19:5). Jericho was also a New Testament city. Jericho in the New Testament was home to the blind beggar Bartimaeus (Mk 10:46) and the wealthy Zacchaeus (Lu 19:1–2).

Nu 22:1; 26:3, 63; 31:12; 33:48; 34:15; 35:1; 36:13; De 34:3; Jos 2:1; 5:13; 6:1, 20; 7:2; 8:2; 9:3; 12:9; 13:32; 16:1, 7; 18:12, 21; 20:8; 24:11; Jud 3:13; 1 K 16:34; 2 K 2:4, 18; 25:5; 1 Chr 19:5; 2 Chr 28:15; Ezr 2:34; Ne 3:2; 7:36; Je 39:5; Mt 20:29; Mk 10:46; Lu 10:30; 18:35; 19:1; He 11:30

See **CITIES, JOSHUA**

JERUSALEM, *city of peace*

Jerusalem, a city of central importance to three of the world's major religions, was called by Pliny the Elder "by far the most renowned city of the ancient East." The city has been besieged, captured, or destroyed in whole or in part more than forty times over the past six thousand years. Archaeological evidence for the total destruction of Jerusalem by the Babylonians has been extensively documented (cf. 2 Ki 25:8–10; Je 39:8; 2 Chr 36:18–19). The Bible records that the temple and the walls of ancient Jerusalem were rebuilt during the time of the Persians under the direction of Ezra and Nehemiah. New Testament Jerusalem occupied the two hills on either side of the shallow Tyropean Valley. The majority of the remains of the temple from Herod's time were destroyed by the Roman general Titus in A.D. 70. Only the lower portions of the retaining wall foundation remain. A modern visitor to Jerusalem can view these portions of Herodian construction at the southeast corner of the temple mount area, the west side of the Wailing Wall, and south of the Wailing Wall.

Jos 10:1 Now it came to pass, when Adoni-zedek king of Jerusalem had heard how Joshua had taken Ai, and had utterly destroyed it; as he had done to Jericho and her king, so he had done to Ai and her king; and how the inhabitants of Gibeon had made peace with Israel, and were among them;

Jud 19:10 But the man would not tarry that night, but he rose up and departed, and came over against Jebus, which is Jerusalem; and *there were* with him two asses saddled, his concubine also *was* with him.

2 S 5:6 And the king and his men went to Jerusalem unto the Jebusites, the inhabitants of the land: which spake unto David, saying, Except thou take away the blind and the lame, thou shalt not come in hither: thinking, David cannot come in hither.

2 S 11:1 And it came to pass, after the year was expired, at the time when kings go forth *to battle*, that David sent Joab, and his servants with him, and all Israel; and they destroyed the children of Ammon, and besieged Rabbah. But David tarried still at Jerusalem.

2 S 15:14 And David said unto all his servants that *were* with him at Jerusalem, Arise, and let us flee; for we shall not *else* escape from Absalom: make speed to depart, lest he overtake us suddenly, and bring evil upon us, and smite the city with the edge of the sword.

2 S 20:3 And David came to his house at Jerusalem; and the king took the ten women *his* concubines, whom he had left to keep the house, and put them in ward, and fed them, but went not in unto them. So they were shut up unto the day of their death, living in widowhood.

1 K 2:11 And the days that David reigned over Israel *were* forty years: seven years reigned he in Hebron, and thirty and three years reigned he in Jerusalem.

1 K 8:1 Then Solomon assembled the elders of Israel, and all the heads of the tribes, the chief of the fathers of the children of Israel, unto king Solomon in Jerusalem, that they might bring up the ark of the covenant of the LORD out of the city of David, which *is* Zion.

1 K 10:2 And she came to Jerusalem with a very great train, with camels that bare spices, and very much gold, and precious stones: and when she was come to Solomon, she communed with him of all that was in her heart.

Mt 2:1 Now when Jesus was born in Bethlehem of Judaea in the days of Herod the king, behold, there came wise men from the east to Jerusalem,

Ac 1:4 And, being assembled together with *them*, commanded them that they should not depart from Jerusalem, but wait for the promise of the Father, which, *saith he*, ye have heard of me.

Ga 2:1 Then fourteen years after I went up again to Jerusalem with Barnabas, and took Titus with *me* also.

Re 11:8 And their dead bodies *shall lie* in the street of the great city, which spiritually is called Sodom and Egypt, where also our Lord was crucified.

1. Calamities

1 K 14:25 And it came to pass in the fifth year of king Rehoboam, *that* Shishak king of Egypt came up against Jerusalem:

2 K 14:13 And Jehoash king of Israel took Amaziah king of Judah, the son of Jehoash the son of Ahaziah, at Beth-shemesh, and came to Jerusalem, and brake down the wall of Jerusalem from the gate of Ephraim unto the corner gate, four hundred cubits.

2 K 16:5 Then Rezin king of Syria and Pekah son of Remaliah king of Israel came up to Jerusalem to war: and they besieged Ahaz, but could not overcome *him.*

2 K 18:35 Who *are* they among all the gods of the countries, that have delivered their country out of mine hand, that the LORD should deliver Jerusalem out of mine hand?

2 K 24:10 At that time the servants of Nebuchadnezzar king of Babylon came up against Jerusalem, and the city was besieged.

2 K 25:1 And it came to pass in the ninth year of his reign, in the tenth month, in the tenth *day* of the month, *that* Nebuchadnezzar king of Babylon came, he, and all his host, against Jerusalem, and pitched against it; and they built forts against it round about.

2 K 25:10 And all the army of the Chaldees, that *were with* the captain of the guard, brake down the walls of Jerusalem round about.

2 Chr 24:23 And it came to pass at the end of the year, *that* the host of Syria came up against him: and they came to Judah and Jerusalem, and destroyed all the princes of the people from among the people, and sent all the spoil of them unto the king of Damascus.

2 Chr 25:23 And Joash the king of Israel took Amaziah king of Judah, the son of Joash, the son of Jehoahaz, at Beth-shemesh, and brought him to Jerusalem, and brake down the wall of Jerusalem from the gate of Ephraim to the corner gate, four hundred cubits.

2 Chr 36:19 And they burnt the house of God, and brake down the wall of Jerusalem, and burnt all the palaces thereof with fire, and destroyed all the goodly vessels thereof.

Ne 1:3 And they said unto me, The remnant that are left of the captivity there in the province *are* in great affliction and reproach: the wall of Jerusalem also *is* broken down, and the gates thereof are burned with fire.

Ne 2:13 And I went out by night by the gate of the valley, even before the dragon well, and to the dung port, and viewed the walls of Jerusalem, which were broken down, and the gates thereof were consumed with fire.

Ps 79:1 O God, the heathen are come into thine inheritance; thy holy temple have they defiled; they have laid Jerusalem on heaps.

Ps 80:13 The boar out of the wood doth waste it, and the wild beast of the field doth devour it.

Is 1:7 Your country *is* desolate, your cities *are* burned with fire: your land, strangers devour it in your presence, and *it is* desolate, as overthrown by strangers.

Is 3:8 For Jerusalem is ruined, and Judah is fallen: because their tongue and their doings *are* against the LORD, to provoke the eyes of his glory.

Is 22:10 And ye have numbered the houses of Jerusalem, and the houses have ye broken down to fortify the wall.

Is 27:10 Yet the defenced city *shall be* desolate, *and* the habitation forsaken, and left like a wilderness: there shall the calf feed, and there shall he lie down, and consume the branches thereof.

Is 29:1 Woe to Ariel, to Ariel, the city *where* David dwelt! add ye year to year; let them kill sacrifices.

Is 64:10 Thy holy cities are a wilderness, Zion is a wilderness, Jerusalem a desolation.

Je 6:1 O ye children of Benjamin, gather yourselves to flee out of the midst of Jerusalem, and blow the trumpet in Tekoa, and set up a sign of fire in Beth-haccerem: for evil appeareth out of the north, and great destruction.

Je 6:6 For thus hath the LORD of hosts said, Hew ye down trees, and cast a mount against Jerusalem: this *is* the city to be visited; she *is* wholly oppression in the midst of her.

Je 32:29 And the Chaldeans, that fight against this city, shall come and set fire on this city, and burn it with the houses, upon whose roofs they have offered incense unto Baal, and poured out drink offerings unto other gods, to provoke me to anger.

Je 34:22 Behold, I will command, saith the LORD, and cause them to return to this city; and they shall fight against it, and take it, and burn it with fire: and I will make the cities of Judah a desolation without an inhabitant.

Je 39:2 *And* in the eleventh year of Zedekiah, in the fourth month, the ninth *day* of the month, the city was broken up.

Je 39:8 And the Chaldeans burned the king's house, and the houses of the people, with fire, and brake down the walls of Jerusalem.

Je 44:6 Wherefore my fury and mine anger was poured forth, and was kindled in the cities of Judah and in the streets of Jerusalem; and they are wasted *and* desolate, as at this day.

Je 44:13 For I will punish them that dwell in the land of Egypt, as I have punished Jerusalem, by the sword, by the famine, and by the pestilence:

Je 52:7 Then the city was broken up, and all the men of war fled, and went forth out of the city by night by the way of the gate between the two walls, which *was* by the king's garden; (now the Chaldeans *were* by the city round about:) and they went by the way of the plain.

Lam 1:1 How doth the city sit solitary, *that was* full of people *how* is she become as a widow she *that was* great among the nations, *and* princess among the provinces, *how* is she become tributary

Eze 4:1 Thou also, son of man, take thee a tile, and lay it before thee, and pourtray upon it the city, *even* Jerusalem:

Eze 33:21 And it came to pass in the twelfth year of our captivity, in the tenth *month*, in the fifth *day* of the month, *that* one that had escaped out of Jerusalem came unto me, saying, The city is smitten.

Da 1:1 In the third year of the reign of Jehoiakim king of Judah came Nebuchadnezzar king of Babylon unto Jerusalem, and besieged it.

Da 9:2 In the first year of his reign I Daniel understood by books the number of the years, whereof the word of the LORD came to Jeremiah the prophet, that he would accomplish seventy years in the desolations of Jerusalem.

Da 9:12 And he hath confirmed his words, which he spake against us, and against our judges that judged us, by bringing upon us a great evil: for under the whole heaven hath not been done as hath been done upon Jerusalem.

Da 9:26 And after threescore and two weeks shall Messiah be cut off, but not for himself: and the people of the prince that shall come shall destroy the city and the sanctuary; and the end thereof *shall be* with a flood, and unto the end of the war desolations are determined.

Mt 22:7 But when the king heard *thereof*, he was wroth: and he sent forth his armies, and destroyed those murderers, and burned up their city.

Lu 21:20 And when ye shall see Jerusalem compassed with armies, then know that the desolation thereof is nigh.

2. Prophecies

2 K 21:13 And I will stretch over Jerusalem the line of Samaria, and the plummet of the house of Ahab: and I will wipe Jerusalem as *a man* wipeth a dish, wiping *it*, and turning *it* upside down.

2 K 23:27 And the LORD said, I will remove Judah also out of my sight, as I have removed Israel, and will cast off this city Jerusalem which I have chosen, and the house of which I said, My name shall be there.

Is 3:1 For, behold, the Lord, the LORD of hosts, doth take away from Jerusalem and from Judah the stay and the staff, the whole stay of bread, and the whole stay of water,

Je 1:15 For, lo, I will call all the families of the kingdoms of the north, saith the LORD; and they shall come, and they shall set every one his throne at the entering of the gates of Jerusalem, and against all the walls thereof round about, and against all the cities of Judah.

Je 8:1 At that time, saith the LORD, they shall bring out the bones of the kings of Judah, and the bones of his princes, and the bones of the priests, and the bones of the prophets, and the bones of the inhabitants of Jerusalem, out of their graves:

Je 9:11 And I will make Jerusalem heaps, *and* a den of dragons; and I will make the cities of Judah desolate, without an inhabitant.

Je 19:8 And I will make this city desolate, and an hissing; every one that passeth thereby shall be astonished and hiss because of all the plagues thereof.

Je 21:10 For I have set my face against this city for evil, and not for good, saith the LORD: it shall be given into the hand of the king of Babylon, and he shall burn it with fire.

Je 23:39 Therefore, behold, I, even I, will utterly forget you, and I will forsake you, and the city that I gave you and your fathers, *and cast you* out of my presence:

Je 25:18 *To wit,* Jerusalem, and the cities of Judah, and the kings thereof, and the princes thereof, to make them a desolation, an astonishment, an hissing, and a curse; as *it is* this day;

Je 25:29 For, lo, I begin to bring evil on the city which is called by my name, and should ye be utterly unpunished? Ye shall not be unpunished: for I will call for a sword upon all the inhabitants of the earth, saith the LORD of hosts.

Je 26:6 Then will I make this house like Shiloh, and will make this city a curse to all the nations of the earth.

Je 34:2 Thus saith the LORD, the God of Israel; Go and speak to Zedekiah king of Judah, and tell him, Thus saith the LORD; Behold, I will give this city into the hand of the king of Babylon, and he shall burn it with fire:

Je 35:17 Therefore thus saith the LORD God of hosts, the God of Israel; Behold, I will bring upon Judah and upon all the inhabitants of Jerusalem all the evil that I have pronounced against them: because I have spoken unto them, but they have not heard; and I have called unto them, but they have not answered.

Je 37:10 For though ye had smitten the whole army of the Chaldeans that fight against you, and there remained *but* wounded men among them, *yet* should they rise up every man in his tent, and burn this city with fire.

Je 38:23 So they shall bring out all thy wives and thy children to the Chaldeans: and thou shalt not escape out of their hand, but shalt be taken by the hand of the king of Babylon: and thou shalt cause this city to be burned with fire.

Eze 4:7 Therefore thou shalt set thy face toward the siege of Jerusalem, and thine arm *shall be* uncovered, and thou shalt prophesy against it.

Eze 5:5 Thus saith the Lord GOD; This *is* Jerusalem: I have set it in the midst of the nations and countries *that are* round about her.

Eze 15:6 Therefore thus saith the Lord GOD; As the vine tree among the trees of the forest, which I have given to the fire for fuel, so will I give the inhabitants of Jerusalem.

Eze 21:2 Son of man, set thy face toward Jerusalem, and drop *thy word* toward the holy places, and prophesy against the land of Israel,

Eze 24:6 Wherefore thus saith the Lord GOD; Woe to the bloody city, to the pot whose scum is therein, and whose scum *is* not gone out of it! bring it out piece by piece; let no lot fall upon it.

Am 2:5 But I will send a fire upon Judah, and it shall devour the palaces of Jerusalem.

Mi 3:12 Therefore shall Zion for your sake be plowed *as* a field, and Jerusalem shall become heaps, and the mountain of the house as the high places of the forest.

Zec 14:2 For I will gather all nations against Jerusalem to battle; and the city shall be taken, and the houses rifled, and the women ravished; and half of the city shall go forth into captivity, and the residue of the people shall not be cut off from the city.

Mt 23:37 O Jerusalem, Jerusalem, *thou* that killest the prophets, and stonest them which are sent unto thee, how often would I have gathered thy children together, even as a hen gathereth her chickens under *her* wings, and ye would not!

Lu 19:43 For the days shall come upon thee, that thine enemies shall cast a trench about thee, and compass thee round, and keep thee in on every side,

Lu 21:24 And they shall fall by the edge of the sword, and shall be led away captive into all nations: and Jerusalem shall be trodden down of the Gentiles, until the times of the Gentiles be fulfilled.

Jn 4:21 Jesus saith unto her, Woman, believe me, the hour cometh, when ye shall neither in this mountain, nor yet at Jerusalem, worship the Father.

3. Other Names

ARIEL

Is 29:1 Woe to Ariel, to Ariel, the city *where* David dwelt! add ye year to year; let them kill sacrifices.

CITY OF DAVID

2 S 5:7 Nevertheless David took the strong hold of Zion: the same *is* the city of David.

Is 22:9 Ye have seen also the breaches of the city of David, that they are many: and ye gathered together the waters of the lower pool.

CITY OF GOD

Ps 46:4 *There is* a river, the streams whereof shall make glad the city of God, the holy *place* of the tabernacles of the most High.

Ps 87:3 Glorious things are spoken of thee, O city of God. Selah.

CITY OF THE GREAT KING

Ps 48:2 Beautiful for situation, the joy of the whole earth, *is* mount Zion, *on* the sides of the north, the city of the great King.

CITY OF JUDAH

2 Chr 25:28 And they brought him upon horses, and buried him with his fathers in the city of Judah.

CITY OF TRUTH

Zec 8:3 Thus saith the LORD; I am returned unto Zion, and will dwell in the midst of Jerusalem: and Jerusalem shall be called a city of truth; and the mountain of the LORD of hosts the holy mountain.

HOLY CITY

Ne 11:1 And the rulers of the people dwelt at Jerusalem: the rest of the people also cast lots, to bring one of ten to dwell in Jerusalem the holy city, and nine parts *to dwell* in *other* cities.

HOLY MOUNT

Da 9:16 O Lord, according to all thy righteousness, I beseech thee, let thine anger and thy fury be turned away from thy city Jerusalem, thy holy mountain: because for our sins, and for the iniquities of our fathers, Jerusalem and thy people *are become* a reproach to all *that are* about us.

JEBUS

Jos 18:28 And Zelah, Eleph, and Jebusi, which *is* Jerusalem, Gibeath, *and* Kirjath; fourteen cities with their villages. This *is* the inheritance of the children of Benjamin according to their families.

Jud 19:10 But the man would not tarry that night, but he rose up and departed, and came over against Jebus, which is Jerusalem; and *there were* with him two asses saddled, his concubine also *was* with him.

PERFECTION OF BEAUTY

Lam 2:15 All that pass by clap *their* hands at thee; they hiss and wag their head at the daughter of Jerusalem, *saying, Is* this the city that *men* call The perfection of beauty, The joy of the whole earth?

SALEM

Ge 14:18 And Melchizedek king of Salem brought forth bread and wine: and he *was* the priest of the most high God.

Ps 76:2 In Salem also is his tabernacle, and his dwelling place in Zion.

THRONE OF THE LORD

Je 3:17 At that time they shall call Jerusalem the throne of the LORD; and all the nations shall be gathered unto it, to the name of the LORD, to Jerusalem: neither shall they walk any more after the imagination of their evil heart.

ZION

1 K 8:1 Then Solomon assembled the elders of Israel, and all the heads of the tribes, the chief of the fathers of the children of Israel, unto king Solomon in Jerusalem, that they might bring up the ark of the covenant of the LORD out of the city of David, which *is* Zion.

Zec 9:13 When I have bent Judah for me, filled the bow with Ephraim, and raised up thy sons, O Zion, against thy sons, O Greece, and made thee as the sword of a mighty man.

4. Called the Holy City

He 11:10, 16; 12:22; 13:14; Re 21:2, 10; 22:19

5. New Jerusalem

Ps 107:7 And he led them forth by the right way, that they might go to a city of habitation.

Is 65:18 But be ye glad and rejoice for ever *in that* which I create: for, behold, I create Jerusalem a rejoicing, and her people a joy.

Je 17:25 Then shall there enter into the gates of this city kings and princes sitting upon the throne of David, riding in chariots and on horses, they, and their princes, the men of Judah, and the inhabitants of Jerusalem: and this city shall remain for ever.

Jl 3:20 But Judah shall dwell for ever, and Jerusalem from generation to generation.

Ga 4:26 But Jerusalem which is above is free, which is the mother of us all.

He 11:10 For he looked for a city which hath foundations, whose builder and maker *is* God.

He 11:16 But now they desire a better *country,* that is, an heavenly: wherefore God is not ashamed to be called their God: for he hath prepared for them a city.

He 12:22 But ye are come unto mount Sion, and unto the city of the living God, the heavenly Jerusalem, and to an innumerable company of angels,

He 13:14 For here have we no continuing city, but we seek one to come.

Re 3:12 Him that overcometh will I make a pillar in the temple of my God, and he shall go no more out: and I will write upon him the name of my God, and the name of the city of my God, *which is* new Jerusalem, which cometh down out of heaven from my God: and *I will write upon him* my new name.

Re 21:2 And I John saw the holy city, new Jerusalem, coming down from God out of heaven, prepared as a bride adorned for her husband.

Re 21:10 And he carried me away in the spirit to a great and high mountain, and shewed me that great city, the holy Jerusalem, descending out of heaven from God,

Re 22:19 And if any man shall take away from the words of the book of this prophecy, God shall take away his part out of the book of life, and out of the holy city, and *from* the things which are written in this book.

See **CITIES**

JESHURUN, *a name given to the Israelites*

De 32:15; 33:5; Is 44:2

JESHUA, *or Joshua, the priest*

Ezr 2:2; 3:2, 9; 4:3; 5:2; 8:33; 10:18; Ne 7:7, 39; 12:1, 10, 26

JESSE, *father of David*

1 S 16:1, 18; 17:13, 58; 20:27; 22:3; 1 Chr 2:13; Is 11:1, 10; Mt 1:5; Lu 3:32

JESTING, *forbidden*

Pr 10:23; 26:19; Ep 5:4

JESUS OF NAZARETH

Mt 2:23 And he came and dwelt in a city called Nazareth: that it might be fulfilled which was spoken by the prophets, He shall be called a Nazarene.

Mt 21:11 And the multitude said, This is Jesus the prophet of Nazareth of Galilee.

Mt 26:71 And when he was gone out into the porch, another *maid* saw him, and said unto them that were there, This *fellow* was also with Jesus of Nazareth.

Mk 1:24 Saying, Let *us* alone; what have we to do with thee, thou Jesus of Nazareth? art thou come to destroy us? I know thee who thou art, the Holy One of God.

Mk 10:47 And when he heard that it was Jesus of Nazareth, he began to cry out, and say, Jesus, *thou* Son of David, have mercy on me.

Mk 14:67 And when she saw Peter warming himself, she looked upon him, and said, And thou also wast with Jesus of Nazareth.

Mk 16:6 And he saith unto them, Be not affrighted: Ye seek Jesus of Nazareth, which was crucified: he is risen; he is not here: behold the place where they laid him.

Lu 4:34 Saying, Let *us* alone; what have we to do with thee, *thou* Jesus of Nazareth? art thou come to destroy us? I know thee who thou art; the Holy One of God.

Lu 18:37 And they told him, that Jesus of Nazareth passeth by.

Lu 24:19 And he said unto them, What things? And they said unto him, Concerning Jesus of Nazareth, which was a prophet mighty in deed and word before God and all the people.

Jn 1:45 Philip findeth Nathanael, and saith unto him, We have found him, of whom Moses in the law, and the prophets, did write, Jesus of Nazareth, the son of Joseph.

Jn 18:5 They answered him, Jesus of Nazareth. Jesus saith unto them, I am *he*. And Judas also, which betrayed him, stood with them.

Jn 19:19 And Pilate wrote a title, and put *it* on the cross. And the writing was, JESUS OF NAZARETH THE KING OF THE JEWS.

Ac 2:22 Ye men of Israel, hear these words; Jesus of Nazareth, a man approved of God among you by miracles and wonders and signs, which God did by him in the midst of you, as ye yourselves also know:

Ac 3:6 Then Peter said, Silver and gold have I none; but such as I have give I thee: In the name of Jesus Christ of Nazareth rise up and walk.

Ac 4:10 Be it known unto you all, and to all the people of Israel, that by the name of Jesus Christ of Nazareth, whom ye crucified, whom God raised from the dead, *even* by him doth this man stand here before you whole.

Ac 6:14 For we have heard him say, that this Jesus of Nazareth shall destroy this place, and shall change the customs which Moses delivered us.

Ac 10:38 How God anointed Jesus of Nazareth with the Holy Ghost and with power: who went about doing good, and healing all that were oppressed of the devil; for God was with him.

Ac 22:8 And I answered, Who art thou, Lord? And he said unto me, I am Jesus of Nazareth, whom thou persecutest.

Ac 26:9 I verily thought with myself, that I ought to do many things contrary to the name of Jesus of Nazareth.

See **CHRIST**

JETHRO, *Raguel or Reuel (?), a priest of Midian*

Ex 2:18; 3:1; 4:18; 18:1, 12; Nu 10:29

JEZEBEL, *the wicked queen, wife of Ahab*

1 K 16:31; 18:4, 19, 13; 19:1–2; 21:5–13, 23, 25; 2 K 9:10, 30, 33–36; Re 2:20

JEZREEL, *God sows*

Jezreel, the city after which the Valley of Jezreel was named, is perched on the spur of a prominent hill at the foot of Mount Gilboa. The city itself, as well as the striking view across the Valley of Jezreel and the Plain of Armageddon, presents a panoramic view of where many of the most stirring and tragic events of the ages took place. The royal palace of Ahab and Jezebel stood out boldly on this promontory, and many of the perverse and wicked events of their lives took place here. Elijah "girded up his loins" and outran Ahab's chariot from Mount Carmel to Jezreel, where Queen Jezebel vowed to take his life (1 K 18:46, 19:2). When Ahab coveted Naboth the Jezreelite's vineyard, Jezebel plotted to bring about Naboth's death and secure his vineyard (1 K 21). Elijah later appeared in this same vineyard and announced that dogs would lick Jezebel's blood (1 K 21:23). When Jehu came to Jezreel, the wicked Jezebel reaped the consequences of her sinful deeds. Some officials threw her into the street, Jehu's chariot horses trampled her underfoot, and dogs ate her flesh (2 K 9:30–36).

1. A City in the South of Judea

Jos 15:56

2. A City of Issachar

Jos 19:18

3. A Valley

Jos 17:16

JEWELS See **APPAREL**

JEZEBEL See **WOMEN**

JOAB, *son of Zeruiah, commander of David's army*

2 S 2:14, 18; 3:22, 27; 8:16; 10:13; 12:27; 14:2, 19; 18:14; 20:10; 23:37; 24:3; 1 K 1:7; 2:22, 29, 33–34; 11:15; 1 Chr 2:16; 11:6, 39; 18:15; 19:8; 20:1; 21:2; 26:28; 27:24, 34

JOASH, *or Jehoash, king of Judah, son of Ahaziah*

Jud 6:29; 2 K 11:2, 21; 12:1, 7, 18; 1 Chr 3:11; 2 Chr 22:11; 24:2, 17, 22, 24

See **ISRAEL, YOUNG PEOPLE**

JOB

1. Person, *of the land of Uz*

NEVER LOSES PATIENCE

Ja 5:11

LOSES PROPERTY

Jb 1:13–17

LOSES CHILDREN

Jb 1:18–19

LOSES HEALTH

Jb 2:7–9

RECEIVES NO SYMPATHY

Jb 16:1–3

LOSES FRIENDS

Jb 30:1–10

IS VICTORIOUS IN TRIAL

Jb 19:1–27

RECEIVES DELIVERANCE

Jb 42:10

BLESSINGS RESTORED

Jb 42:11, 13

2. Book

Author: Unknown.

Date Written: Subject of much discussion. Regarded by many scholars as the oldest book in the Bible; others place it as late as the exile.

Place: The land of Uz.

Purpose: To illustrate God's absolute sovereignty over the affairs of the world and, consequentially, to elicit trust in his ultimate goodness, especially from those in the midst of suffering.

To Whom Written: People everywhere, especially those who suffer.

Main Theme: The problem of Job's affliction.

Key Word: Sovereignty.

Key Verse: 2:3; 19:25–26.

JOB'S WIFE See WOMEN

JOEL

1. Person, *a prophet, son of Pethuel*
Jl 1:1

2. Book

Author: Joel, a prophet of Judah. Very little is known about him (1:1). His name means "Jehovah is God."

Date Written: Uncertain.

Purpose: To warn Judah of God's imminent judgment upon their sins and to call them to repentance.

To Whom Written: The Southern Kingdom (Judah). The occasion for the book was the visitation of a plague of locusts and a severe drought regarded as punishments for the sins of the people. The former was prophetic of coming invasions of the armies of Judah's enemies.

Main Theme: National repentance and its blessings.

Key Words: "The Day of the Lord" (1:15; 2:1, 11, 31; 3:14).

Key Verses: 2:12–13.

JOHANAN, *a Jewish captain*
2 K 25:23; Je 40:8; 41:11; 42:1; 43:2

JOHN, *the beloved disciple, son of Zebedee*

1. Person

FULL OF ENERGY

Mt 3:17 And lo a voice from heaven, saying, This is my beloved Son, in whom I am well pleased.

INTOLERANT

Mk 9:38 And John answered him, saying, Master, we saw one casting out devils in thy name, and he followeth not us: and we forbad him, because he followeth not us.

VINDICTIVE

Lu 9:54 And when his disciples James and John saw *this*, they said, Lord, wilt thou that we command fire to come down from heaven, and consume them, even as Elias did?

AMBITIOUS

Mk 10:36–37 And he said unto them, What would ye that I should do for you?
They said unto him, Grant unto us that we may sit, one on thy right hand, and the other on thy left hand, in thy glory.

LEARNED THE LESSON OF LOVE

Jn 13:23 Now there was leaning on Jesus' bosom one of his disciples, whom Jesus loved.

ENTRUSTED WITH THE CARE OF CHRIST'S MOTHER

Jn 19:26 When Jesus therefore saw his mother, and the disciple standing by, whom he loved, he saith unto his mother, Woman, behold thy son!

2. Books

a. THE GOSPEL

Author: The apostle John.

Date Written: Uncertain. Probably late in the first century.

Purpose: To inspire faith in Jesus Christ as the Son of God.

To Whom Written: Seekers who want to examine the life of Jesus Christ and believers who would be strengthened in their faith.

Main Theme: An encounter with Jesus Christ demands a response. Those who believe have eternal life but those who reject him are under the condemnation of God (3:36; 5:24-29; 10:27-29).

Key Word: Believe.

Key Verse: 20:31.

b. FIRST

Author: The apostle John.

Date Written: Uncertain. Probably written from Ephesus near the end of the first century.

Purposes: The writer mentions four reasons for writing this epistle to believers:

(1) To add to their joy (1:4).

(2) To guard them against sin (2:1).

(3) To warn them against false teachers (2:26).

(4) To strengthen their faith in Christ and assure them of eternal life (5:13).

To Whom Written: Apparently addressed to the church at large, as it has no greetings, farewells, or other personal allusions; hence it belongs to the "general epistles." It calls believers by affectionate titles: "little children" (2:1, 18, 28; 3:7, 18; 4:4; 5:21) and "beloved" (3:2, 21; 4:1, 7, 11).

Main Theme: God is life, light, and righteous love. His character calls for holy living and brotherly love on the part of believers.

Key Words: Fellowship, Know, Love. Knowing, with certainty, is of special interest to John. This book may be entitled "The Epistle of Certainties."

c. SECOND

Author: The apostle John.

Date Written: Uncertain. Probably written from Ephesus near the end of the first century.

Purpose: The epistle was apparently written to warn friends against heresy and association with false teachers (7–11).

To Whom Written: Addressed to the "elect lady and her children." Some think this refers to a Christian matron and her family living in Ephesus, others that a church and its members are personified. If the first supposition is correct, this is the only book in the New Testament addressed to a woman.

Main Theme: A discourse on truth and error.

Key Words: Love and truth.

Key Verses: 9–10.

d. THIRD

Author: The apostle John

Date Written: Uncertain. Probably written from Ephesus near the end of the first century.

Purposes:

(1) To commend Gaius for his loyalty to the truth and for his care of traveling teachers and missionaries.

(2) To rebuke Diotrephes for his pride.

(3) To recommend Demetrius to Gaius.

(4) To inform the readers of his (John's) imminent visit.

To Whom Written: Gaius (v. 1).

Main Theme: Christian hospitality.

Key Word: Truth (v. 4).

Key Verse: v. 8.

JOHN THE BAPTIST, *son of Zacharias and Elizabeth*

1. His Life

SELF-DENIAL

Mt 3:4 And the same John had his raiment of camel's hair, and a leathern girdle about his loins; and his meat was locusts and wild honey.

COURAGE

Mt 3:7 But when he saw many of the Pharisees and Sadducees come to his baptism, he said unto them, O generation of vipers, who hath warned you to flee from the wrath to come?

Mt 14:4 For John said unto him, It is not lawful for thee to have her.

OBEDIENCE

Mt 3:15 And Jesus answering said unto him, Suffer *it to be so* now: for thus it becometh us to fulfil all righteousness. Then he suffered him.

POWERFUL PREACHER

Mk 1:5 And there went out unto him all the land of Judaea, and they of Jerusalem, and were all baptized of him in the river of Jordan, confessing their sins.

HUMILITY

Mk 1:7 And preached, saying, There cometh one mightier than I after me, the latchet of whose shoes I am not worthy to stoop down and unloose.

Jn 1:19–23 And this is the record of John, when the Jews sent priests and Levites from Jerusalem to ask him, Who art thou?

And he confessed, and denied not; but confessed, I am not the Christ.

And they asked him, What then? Art thou Elias? And he saith, I am not. Art thou that prophet? And he answered, No.

Then said they unto him, Who art thou? that we may give an answer to them that sent us. What sayest thou of thyself?

He said, I *am* the voice of one crying in the wilderness, Make straight the way of the Lord, as said the prophet Esaias.

HOLINESS

Mk 6:20 For Herod feared John, knowing that he was a just man and an holy, and observed him; and when he heard him, he did many things, and heard him gladly.

BURNING ZEAL

Jn 5:35 He was a burning and a shining light: and ye were willing for a season to rejoice in his light.

HONORED BY CHRIST

Mt 11:11 Verily I say unto you, Among them that are born of women there hath not risen a greater than John the Baptist: notwithstanding he that is least in the kingdom of heaven is greater than he.

Lu 7:24–27 And when the messengers of John were departed, he began to speak unto the people concerning John, What went ye out into the wilderness for to see? A reed shaken with the wind?

But what went ye out for to see? A man clothed in soft raiment? Behold, they which are gorgeously apparelled, and live delicately, are in kings' courts.

But what went ye out for to see? A prophet? Yea, I say unto you, and much more than a prophet.

This is *he,* of whom it is written, Behold, I send my messenger before thy face, which shall prepare thy way before thee.

DID NO MIRACLE

Jn 10:41 And many resorted unto him, and said, John did no miracle: but all things that John spake of this man were true.

SUFFERED MARTYRDOM

Mt 14:10 And he sent, and beheaded John in the prison.

2. His Work as Forerunner

Is 40:3; Mal 3:1; Mt 3:3; 11:10; 17:11; Mk 1:3; Lu 1:17, 76; 3:4; 7:27; Jn 1:8, 23, 31; 3:28; Ac 19:4

3. His Baptism See **CHURCH**

4. His Disciples

Mt 9:14; 11:2; 14:12; Mk 2:18; 6:29; Lu 5:33; 7:18; 11:1; Jn 1:35; 3:25

5. His Testimony concerning Christ

Jn 1:18, 29, 30, 36; 3:26, 28–36, 33; 5:33; 10:41

JONADAB, *Jehovah gives*

1. David's Nephew

2 S 13:3, 32

2. Or Jehonadab, son of Rechab

2 K 10:15; Je 35:6, 19

JONAH

1. Person, or Jonas, son of Amittai, a prophet

SENT TO A FOREIGN FIELD

Jona 1:2

FLED AN UNWELCOME DUTY

Jona 1:3

OVERTAKEN IN HIS FLIGHT

Jona 1:4–17

FINDS GOD'S PRESENCE IN THE DEPTHS OF THE SEA

Ps 139:10; Jona 2:1–10

PROCEEDS UPON HIS MISSION

Jona 3:1–3

DISAPPOINTED AT HIS SUCCESS

Jona 3:5–10; Jona 4:1

REVEALS HIS BIGOTRY

Jona 4:1–3

TAUGHT A LESSON REGARDING DIVINE LOVE

Jona 4:4–11

2. Book

Author: Uncertain. Probably Jonah, a native of Galilee, one of the earlier prophets (2 K 14:25). Called to go as a missionary to Nineveh and warn the enemies of his country, he went with great reluctance.

Date Written: Sometime during the reign of Jeroboam II, 783 B.C. to 753 B.C.

Purpose: To reveal that salvation is of the Lord and that salvation extends to any who will repent and turn to him, even the Gentiles.

To Whom Written: Israel and people everywhere of all times.

Main Theme: Repentance reverses God's judgments.

Key Words: Salvation is of the Lord (2:9).

Key Verse: 2:9.

JONATHAN, *God is gracious*

1. A Levite, son of Gershom

Jud 17:7; 18:30

2. Son of Saul

HEROIC FAITH

1 S 14:6

UNDAUNTED COURAGE

1 S 14:7–13

SELF-SACRIFICING FRIEND

1 S 18:4; 1 S 19:2

3. Son of Abiathar

2 S 15:27; 17:17; 1 K 1:42

4. One of David's Warriors

2 S 21:21; 1 Chr 20:7

JOPPA, *or Japho, modern Jaffa, a seaport*

Joppa, the gateway of ancient Palestine, is built on a rocky knoll 116 feet high that projects sufficiently to form a small but beautiful cape. Its harbor, or breakwater, is formed by a circle of great rocks. It was the port to which the cedars of Lebanon were sent for the construction of Solomon's temple (2 Chr 2:16) and the port where the prophet Jonah boarded a ship bound for Tarshish (Jona 1:3). Peter engaged in missionary activity here (Ac 9:36).

Jos 19:46; 2 Chr 2:16; Ezr 3:7; Jona 1:3; Ac 9:36, 38; 10:5; 11:5, 13

JORAM *See* **ISRAEL**

JORDAN, *the descender*

1. River

Ge 32:10; Nu 32:5, 19, 32; 33:48; 34:12, 15; 35:14; De 1:1; 3:17, 25; 4:22, 46; 9:1; 11:31; 12:10; 27:2; Jos 1:11; 2:7; 3:13, 15; 4:3, 18; 12:1; 13:8; 14:3; 17:5; 18:12, 19; 19:22, 34; 20:8; 22:25; 24:11; Jud 7:24; 8:4; 12:5; 1 S 31:7; 2 S 17:22; 24:5;

2 K 2:8; 5:10; 6:4; 1 Chr 6:78; 12:15; Je 12:5; Eze 47:18; Zec 11:3; Mt 3:6; Mk 1:5, 10; Jn 10:40

See **RIVERS**

2. Plain

Ge 13:10; Nu 22:1; 26:3; 1 K 7:46; 2 Chr 4:17

JOSEPH, *he adds*

1. Son of Jacob

A YOUTHFUL DREAMER

Ge 37:5–9

DREAMS FULFILLED

Ge 41:42–44

FAITHFUL IN HARD PLACES

Ge 39:1–6, 20–23

RESISTED TEMPTATION

Ge 39:7–13

UNSPOILED BY SUDDEN PROSPERITY

Ge 41:14–46

MANIFESTED BROTHERLY LOVE

Ge 43:30; 45:14

FILIAL DEVOTION

Ge 45:23; 47:7

DEPENDED UPON GOD

Ge 41:16; 45:8

RETURNED GOOD FOR EVIL

Ge 50:16–21

2. Husband of Mary

CHARITABLE

Mt 1:19

FAITHFUL

Mt 1:24

OBEDIENT

Mt 2:14

FAITHFUL TO RELIGIOUS DUTY

Lu 2:41

3. Of Arimathea

Mt 27:57; Mk 15:43, 45; Lu 23:50; Jn 19:38

4. Or Barsabas

Ac 1:23

See **KINDNESS, YOUNG PEOPLE**

JOSES, *one of Christ's brothers*

Mt 13:55; 27:56

JOSHUA

1. Person, *Jehoshua, or Hoshea, successor of Moses*

FAITH

Nu 14:6–8 And Joshua the son of Nun, and Caleb the son of Jephunneh, *which were* of them that searched the land, rent their clothes:

And they spake unto all the company of the children of Israel, saying, The land, which we passed through to search it, *is* an exceeding good land.

If the LORD delight in us, then he will bring us into this land, and give it us; a land which floweth with milk and honey.

ENTIRE CONSECRATION

Nu 32:12 Save Caleb the son of Jephunneh the Kenezite, and Joshua the son of Nun: for they have wholly followed the LORD.

SPIRITUAL MINDEDNESS

Jos 3:5 And Joshua said unto the people, Sanctify yourselves: for to morrow the LORD will do wonders among you.

Jos 8:30 Then Joshua built an altar unto the LORD God of Israel in mount Ebal,

GODLY REVERENCE

Jos 5:14 And he said, Nay; but *as* captain of the host of the LORD am I now come. And Joshua fell on his face to the earth, and did worship, and said unto him, What saith my lord unto his servant?

COURAGE

Jos 10:25 And Joshua said unto them, Fear not, nor be dismayed, be strong and of good courage: for thus shall the Lord do to all your enemies against whom ye fight.

OBEDIENCE

Jos 11:15 As the Lord commanded Moses his servant, so did Moses command Joshua, and so did Joshua; he left nothing undone of all that the Lord commanded Moses.

DECISION

Jos 24:15 And if it seem evil unto you to serve the Lord, choose you this day whom ye will serve; whether the gods which your fathers served that *were* on the other side of the flood, or the gods of the Amorites, in whose land ye dwell: but as for me and my house, we will serve the Lord.

2. Book

Author: Uncertain, probably Joshua.

Date Written: 1407–1383 B.C.(?)

Purpose: To review the history of Israel's conquest of the Promised Land.

To Whom Written: The nation of Israel.

Main Theme: The conquest and division of the Land of Canaan.

Key Word: Possession.

Key Verses: 1:8–11.

JOSIAH, *king of Judah, son of Amon*

1 K 13:2; 2 K 21:24; 22:3, 9; 23:29; 1 Chr 3:14; 2 Chr 34:1, 16, 26; 35:1, 23; Je 1:2; 3:6; 25:1; Zep 1:1; Mt 1:10

See **HUMILITY, ISRAEL**

JOTHAM, *Jehovah is upright*

1. Son of Gideon

Jud 9:5; 1 Chr 5:17

2. King of Judah, son of Uzziah

2 K 15:5, 32, 38; 1 Chr 3:12; 2 Chr 26:21; 27:1, 6, 9; Is 1:1; Ho 1:1; Mi 1:1; Mt 1:9

See **ISRAEL, YOUNG PEOPLE**

JOY, *genuine happiness*

1. Christ's Joy

IN THE DIVINE METHOD OF REVELATION

Lu 10:21 In that hour Jesus rejoiced in spirit, and said, I thank thee, O Father, Lord of heaven and earth, that thou hast hid these things from the wise and prudent, and hast revealed them unto babes: even so, Father; for so it seemed good in thy sight.

IN FINDING THE LOST SHEEP

Lu 15:5 And when he hath found *it,* he layeth *it* on his shoulders, rejoicing.

ABIDES IN BELIEVERS

Jn 15:11 These things have I spoken unto you, that my joy might remain in you, and *that* your joy might be full.

BESTOWED THROUGH HIS WORDS

Jn 17:13 And now come I to thee; and these things I speak in the world, that they might have my joy fulfilled in themselves.

SUSTAINED HIM AT THE CROSS

He 12:2 Looking unto Jesus the author and finisher of *our* faith; who for the joy that was set before him endured the cross, despising the shame, and is set down at the right hand of the throne of God.

2. Occasions of Great Joy

LAYING THE FOUNDATION OF THE TEMPLE

Ezr 3:12 But many of the priests and Levites and chief of the fathers, *who were* ancient men, that had seen the first house, when the foundation of this house was laid before their eyes, wept with a loud voice; and many shouted aloud for joy:

THE CREATION

Jb 38:7 When the morning stars sang together, and all the sons of God shouted for joy?

THE COMING OF CHRIST

Mt 2:10 When they saw the star, they rejoiced with exceeding great joy.

THE RESURRECTION OF CHRIST

Mt 28:8 And they departed quickly from the sepulchre with fear and great joy; and did run to bring his disciples word.

THE ASCENSION OF CHRIST

Lu 24:52 And they worshipped him, and returned to Jerusalem with great joy:

THE CONVERSION OF THE GENTILES

Ac 15:3 And being brought on their way by the church, they passed through Phenice and Samaria, declaring the conversion of the Gentiles: and they caused great joy unto all the brethren.

3. Promised to Believers

Ne 8:10 Then he said unto them, Go your way, eat the fat, and drink the sweet, and send portions unto them for whom nothing is prepared: for *this* day *is* holy unto our Lord: neither be ye sorry; for the joy of the LORD is your strength.

Ps 16:11 Thou wilt shew me the path of life: in thy presence *is* fulness of joy; at thy right hand *there are* pleasures for evermore.

Ps 30:5 For his anger *endureth but* a moment; in his favour is life: weeping may endure for a night, but joy *cometh* in the morning.

Ps 89:16 In thy name shall they rejoice all the day: and in thy righteousness shall they be exalted.

Ps 126:5 They that sow in tears shall reap in joy.

Ps 132:16 I will also clothe her priests with salvation: and her saints shall shout aloud for joy.

Ec 2:26 For *God* giveth to a man that *is* good in his sight wisdom, and knowledge, and joy: but to the sinner he giveth travail, to gather and to heap up, that he may give to good before God. This also *is* vanity and vexation of spirit.

Is 12:3 Therefore with joy shall ye draw water out of the wells of salvation.

Is 35:10 And the ransomed of the LORD shall return, and come to Zion with songs and everlasting joy upon their heads: they shall obtain joy and gladness, and sorrow and sighing shall flee away.

Is 51:3 For the LORD shall comfort Zion: he will comfort all her waste places; and he will make her wilderness like Eden, and her desert like the garden of the LORD; joy and gladness shall be found therein, thanksgiving, and the voice of melody.

Is 61:7 For your shame *ye shall have* double; and *for* confusion they shall rejoice in their portion: therefore in their land they shall possess the double: everlasting joy shall be unto them.

Is 65:13 Therefore thus saith the Lord GOD, Behold, my servants shall eat, but ye shall be hungry: behold, my servants shall drink, but ye shall be thirsty: behold, my servants shall rejoice, but ye shall be ashamed:

Is 65:18 But be ye glad and rejoice for ever *in that* which I create: for, behold, I create Jerusalem a rejoicing, and her people a joy.

Mt 25:21 His lord said unto him, Well done, *thou* good and faithful servant: thou hast been faithful over a few things, I will make thee ruler over many things: enter thou into the joy of thy lord.

Lu 1:14 And thou shalt have joy and gladness; and many shall rejoice at his birth.

Lu 2:10 And the angel said unto them, Fear not: for, behold, I bring you good tidings of great joy, which shall be to all people.

Jn 15:11 These things have I spoken unto you, that my joy might remain in you, and *that* your joy might be full.

Jn 16:24 Hitherto have ye asked nothing in my name: ask, and ye shall receive, that your joy may be full.

Jn 17:13 And now come I to thee; and these things I speak in the world, that they might have my joy fulfilled in themselves.

Ro 14:17 For the kingdom of God is not meat and drink; but righteousness, and peace, and joy in the Holy Ghost.

4. Restored

AT THE RETURN OF DIVINE FAVOR

Ps 30:11 Thou hast turned for me my mourning into dancing: thou hast put off my sackcloth, and girded me with gladness;

TO THOSE WHO MOURN

Is 61:3 To appoint unto them that mourn in Zion, to give unto them beauty for ashes, the oil of joy for mourning, the garment of praise for the spirit of heaviness; that they might be called trees of righteousness, the planting of the LORD, that he might be glorified.

AT THE DELIVERANCE OF THE NATION

Je 30:19 And out of them shall proceed thanksgiving and the voice of them that make merry: and I will multiply them, and they shall not be few; I will also glorify them, and they shall not be small.

Je 31:13 Then shall the virgin rejoice in the dance, both young men and old together: for I will turn their mourning into joy, and will comfort them, and make them rejoice from their sorrow.

AT THE OPENING OF THE DOOR OF HOPE

Ho 2:15 And I will give her her vineyards from thence, and the valley of Achor for a door of hope: and she shall sing there, as in the days of her youth, and as in the day when she came up out of the land of Egypt.

AT THE VISION OF THE RISEN SAVIOR

Jn 16:20 Verily, verily, I say unto you, That ye shall weep and lament, but the world shall rejoice: and ye shall be sorrowful, but your sorrow shall be turned into joy.

5. Spiritual

THE DEDICATION OF GOD'S HOUSE

Ezr 6:22 And kept the feast of unleavened bread seven days with joy: for the LORD had made them joyful, and turned the heart of the king of Assyria unto them, to strengthen their hands in the work of the house of God, the God of Israel.

THE RETURN FROM CAPTIVITY

Ps 126:2 Then was our mouth filled with laughter, and our tongue with singing: then said they among the heathen, The LORD hath done great things for them.

THE BLESSINGS OF A SPIRITUAL LIFE

Is 61:10 I will greatly rejoice in the LORD, my soul shall be joyful in my God; for he hath clothed me with the garments of salvation, he hath covered me with the robe of righteousness, as a bridegroom decketh *himself* with ornaments, and as a bride adorneth *herself* with her jewels.

THE DELIGHTS OF GOD'S WORD

Je 15:16 Thy words were found, and I did eat them; and thy word was unto me the joy and rejoicing of mine heart: for I am called by thy name, O LORD God of hosts.

TIMES OF SPIRITUAL REFRESHING

Ac 8:5 Then Philip went down to the city of Samaria, and preached Christ unto them.

Ac 8:6 And the people with one accord gave heed unto those things which Philip spake, hearing and seeing the miracles which he did.

Ac 8:8 And there was great joy in that city.

Ac 8:39 And when they were come up out of the water, the Spirit of the Lord caught away Philip, that the eunuch saw him no more: and he went on his way rejoicing.

Ro 5:11 And not only *so*, but we also joy in God through our Lord Jesus Christ, by whom we have now received the atonement.

2 Co 7:4 Great *is* my boldness of speech toward you, great *is* my glorying of you: I am filled with comfort, I am exceeding joyful in all our tribulation.

THE LOVE OF CHRIST

1 Pe 1:8 Whom having not seen, ye love; in whom, though now ye see *him* not, yet believing, ye rejoice with joy unspeakable and full of glory:

6. Restored

Is 25:8; 35:10; 51:11; 60:20; 65:19; Je 31:12; Re 7:17; 21:4

7. Rejoicing

Est 8:16 The Jews had light, and gladness, and joy, and honour.

Est 9:22 As the days wherein the Jews rested from their enemies, and the month which was turned unto them from sorrow to joy, and from mourning into a good day: that they should make them days of feasting and joy, and of sending portions one to another, and gifts to the poor.

Jb 11:16 Because thou shalt forget *thy* misery, *and* remember *it* as waters *that* pass away:

Is 25:8 He will swallow up death in victory; and the Lord GOD will wipe away tears from off all faces; and the rebuke of his people shall he take away from off all the earth: for the LORD hath spoken *it*.

Is 30:19 For the people shall dwell in Zion at Jerusalem: thou shalt weep no more: he will be very gracious unto thee at the voice of thy cry; when he shall hear it, he will answer thee.

Is 35:10 And the ransomed of the LORD shall return, and come to Zion with songs and everlasting joy upon their heads: they shall obtain joy and gladness, and sorrow and sighing shall flee away.

Is 60:20 Thy sun shall no more go down; neither shall thy moon withdraw itself: for the LORD shall be thine everlasting light, and the days of thy mourning shall be ended.

Is 65:19 And I will rejoice in Jerusalem, and joy in my people: and the voice of weeping shall be no more heard in her, nor the voice of crying.

Je 31:12 Therefore they shall come and sing in the height of Zion, and shall flow together to the goodness of the LORD, for wheat, and for wine, and for oil, and for the young of the flock and of the herd: and their soul shall be as a watered garden; and they shall not sorrow any more at all.

Je 31:16 Thus saith the LORD; Refrain thy voice from weeping, and thine eyes from tears: for thy work shall be rewarded, saith the LORD; and they shall come again from the land of the enemy.

Lu 7:13 And when the Lord saw her, he had compassion on her, and said unto her, Weep not.

Re 7:17 For the Lamb which is in the midst of the throne shall feed them, and shall lead them unto living fountains of waters: and God shall wipe away all tears from their eyes.

Re 21:4 And God shall wipe away all tears from their eyes; and there shall be no more death, neither sorrow, nor crying, neither shall there be any more pain: for the former things are passed away.

a. The Duty

De 12:7 And there ye shall eat before the LORD your God, and ye shall rejoice in all that ye put your hand unto, ye and your households, wherein the LORD thy God hath blessed thee.

De 16:11 And thou shalt rejoice before the LORD thy God, thou, and thy son, and thy daughter, and thy manservant, and thy maidservant, and the Levite that *is* within thy gates, and the stranger, and the fatherless, and the widow, that *are* among you, in the place which the LORD thy God hath chosen to place his name there.

Ps 5:11 But let all those that put their trust in thee rejoice: let them ever shout for joy, because thou defendest them: let them also that love thy name be joyful in thee.

Ps 32:11 Be glad in the LORD, and rejoice, ye righteous: and shout for joy, all *ye that are* upright in heart.

Zep 3:14 Sing, O daughter of Zion; shout, O Israel; be glad and rejoice with all the heart, O daughter of Jerusalem.

Zec 9:9 Rejoice greatly, O daughter of Zion; shout, O daughter of Jerusalem: behold, thy King cometh unto thee: he *is* just, and having salvation; lowly, and riding upon an ass, and upon a colt the foal of an ass.

Lu 10:20 Notwithstanding in this rejoice not, that the spirits are subject unto you; but rather rejoice, because your names are written in heaven.

Ro 12:15 Rejoice with them that do rejoice, and weep with them that weep.

Ph 4:4 Rejoice in the Lord alway: *and* again I say, Rejoice.

1 Th 5:16 Rejoice evermore.

b. Instances

1 S 2:1 And Hannah prayed, and said, My heart rejoiceth in the LORD, mine horn is exalted in the LORD: my mouth is enlarged over mine enemies; because I rejoice in thy salvation.

1 S 11:15 And all the people went to Gilgal; and there they made Saul king before the LORD in Gilgal; and there they sacrificed sacrifices of peace offerings before the LORD; and there Saul and all the men of Israel rejoiced greatly.

Je 31:12 Therefore they shall come and sing in the height of Zion, and shall flow together to the goodness of the LORD, for wheat, and for wine, and for oil, and for the young of the flock and of the herd: and their soul shall be as a watered garden; and they shall not sorrow any more at all.

Mt 2:10 When they saw the star, they rejoiced with exceeding great joy.

Lu 1:47 And my spirit hath rejoiced in God my Saviour.

Ac 2:26 Therefore did my heart rejoice, and my tongue was glad; moreover also my flesh shall rest in hope:

Ac 8:39 And when they were come up out of the water, the Spirit of the Lord caught away Philip, that the eunuch saw him no more: and he went on his way rejoicing.

Ac 16:34 And when he had brought them into his house, he set meat before them, and rejoiced, believing in God with all his house.

Ro 5:2 By whom also we have access by faith into this grace wherein we stand, and rejoice in hope of the glory of God.

c. In Tribulation

FAMINE

Hab 3:17 Although the fig tree shall not blossom, neither *shall* fruit *be* in the vines; the labour of the olive shall fail, and the fields shall yield no meat; the flock shall be cut off from the fold, and *there shall be* no herd in the stalls:

Hab 3:18 Yet I will rejoice in the LORD, I will joy in the God of my salvation.

Mt 5:12 Rejoice, and be exceeding glad: for great *is* your reward in heaven: for so persecuted they the prophets which.

Lu 6:23 Rejoice ye in that day, and leap for joy: for, behold, your reward *is* great in heaven: for in the like manner did their fathers unto the prophets.

PERSECUTION

Ac 5:41 And they departed from the presence of the council, rejoicing that they were counted worthy to suffer shame for his name.

IMPRISONMENT

Ac 16:23 And when they had laid many stripes upon them, they cast *them* into prison, charging the jailer to keep them safely:

Ac 16:25 And at midnight Paul and Silas prayed, and sang praises unto God: and the prisoners heard them.

POVERTY

2 Co 6:10 As sorrowful, yet alway rejoicing; as poor, yet making many rich; as having nothing, and *yet* possessing all things.

Col 1:24 Who now rejoice in my sufferings for you, and fill up that which is behind of the afflictions of Christ in my flesh for his body's sake, which is the church:

LOSS OF PROPERTY

He 10:34 For ye had compassion of me in my bonds, and took joyfully the spoiling of your goods, knowing in yourselves that ye have in heaven a better and an enduring substance.

FIERY TRIALS

1 Pe 4:12 Beloved, think it not strange concerning the fiery trial which is to try you, as though some strange thing happened unto you:
1 Pe 4:13 But rejoice, inasmuch as ye are partakers of Christ's sufferings; that, when his glory shall be revealed, ye may be glad also with exceeding joy.

d. In Evil Forbidden

2 S 1:20 Tell it not in Gath, publish it not in the streets of Askelon; lest the daughters of the Philistines rejoice, lest the daughters of the uncircumcised triumph.
Jb 31:29 If I rejoiced at the destruction of him that hated me, or lifted up myself when evil found him:
Ps 13:4 Lest mine enemy say, I have prevailed against him; and those that trouble me rejoice when I am moved.
Ps 35:15 But in mine adversity they rejoiced, and gathered themselves together: yea, the abjects gathered themselves together against me, and I knew it not; they did tear me, and ceased not:
Ps 35:19 Let not them that are mine enemies wrongfully rejoice over me: neither let them wink with the eye that hate me without a cause.
Ps 35:26 Let them be ashamed and brought to confusion together that rejoice at mine hurt: let them be clothed with shame and dishonour that magnify themselves against me.
Ps 38:16 For I said, Hear me, lest otherwise they should rejoice over me: when my foot slippeth, they magnify themselves against me.
Pr 17:5 Whoso mocketh the poor reproacheth his Maker: and he that is glad at calamities shall not be unpunished.
Pr 24:17 Rejoice not when thine enemy falleth, and let not thine heart be glad when he stumbleth:
Je 48:27 For was not Israel a derision unto thee? was he found among thieves? for since thou spakest of him, thou skippedst for joy.
Je 50:11 Because ye were glad, because ye rejoiced, O ye destroyers of mine heritage, because ye are grown fat as the heifer at grass, and bellow as bulls;
Lam 1:21 They have heard that I sigh: there is none to comfort me: all mine enemies have heard of my trouble; they are glad that thou hast done it: thou wilt bring the day that thou hast called, and they shall be like unto me.
Lam 2:16 All thine enemies have opened their mouth against thee: they hiss and gnash the teeth: they say, We have swallowed her up: certainly this is the day that we looked for; we have found, we have seen it.
Lam 4:21 Rejoice and be glad, O daughter of Edom, that dwellest in the land of Uz; the cup also shall pass through unto thee: thou shalt be drunken, and shalt make thyself naked.
Eze 25:6 For thus saith the Lord GOD; Because thou hast clapped thine hands, and stamped with the feet, and rejoiced in heart with all thy despite against the land of Israel;
Eze 35:15 As thou didst rejoice at the inheritance of the house of Israel, because it was desolate, so will I do unto thee: thou shalt be desolate, O mount Seir, and all Idumea, even all of it: and they shall know that I am the LORD.
Eze 36:5 Therefore thus saith the Lord GOD; Surely in the fire of my jealousy have I spoken against the residue of the heathen, and against all Idumea, which have appointed my land into their possession with the joy of all their heart, with despiteful minds, to cast it out for a prey.
Obad 12 But thou shouldest not have looked on the day of thy brother in the day that he became a stranger;

neither shouldest thou have rejoiced over the children of Judah in the day of their destruction; neither shouldest thou have spoken proudly in the day of distress.

Mi 7:8 Rejoice not against me, O mine enemy: when I fall, I shall arise; when I sit in darkness, the LORD *shall be* a light unto me.

Hab 1:15 They take up all of them with the angle, they catch them in their net, and gather them in their drag: therefore they rejoice and are glad.

Hab 3:14 Thou didst strike through with his staves the head of his villages: they came out as a whirlwind to scatter me: their rejoicing *was* as to devour the poor secretly.

Lu 22:5 And they were glad, and covenanted to give him money.

1 Co 13:6 Rejoiceth not in iniquity, but rejoiceth in the truth;

8. Gladness

1 S 11:9 And they said unto the messengers that came, Thus shall ye say unto the men of Jabesh-gilead, To morrow, by *that time* the sun be hot, ye shall have help. And the messengers came and shewed *it* to the men of Jabesh; and they were glad.

2 S 6:12 And it was told king David, saying, The LORD hath blessed the house of Obed-edom, and all that *pertaineth* unto him, because of the ark of God. So David went and brought up the ark of God from the house of Obed-edom into the city of David with gladness.

1 Chr 15:28 Thus all Israel brought up the ark of the covenant of the LORD with shouting, and with sound of the cornet, and with trumpets, and with cymbals, making a noise with psalteries and harps.

1 Chr 29:22 And did eat and drink before the LORD on that day with great gladness. And they made Solomon the son of David king the second time, and anointed *him* unto the LORD *to be* the chief governor, and Zadok *to be* priest.

2 Chr 7:10 And on the three and twentieth day of the seventh month

he sent the people away into their tents, glad and merry in heart for the goodness that the LORD had shewed unto David, and to Solomon, and to Israel his people.

2 Chr 29:30 Moreover Hezekiah the king and the princes commanded the Levites to sing praise unto the LORD with the words of David, and of Asaph the seer. And they sang praises with gladness, and they bowed their heads and worshipped.

2 Chr 30:21 And the children of Israel that were present at Jerusalem kept the feast of unleavened bread seven days with great gladness: and the Levites and the priests praised the LORD day by day, *singing* with loud instruments unto the LORD.

Ne 8:17 And all the congregation of them that were come again out of the captivity made booths, and sat under the booths: for since the days of Jeshua the son of Nun unto that day had not the children of Israel done so. And there was very great gladness.

Ne 12:27 And at the dedication of the wall of Jerusalem they sought the Levites out of all their places, to bring them to Jerusalem, to keep the dedication with gladness, both with thanksgivings, and with singing, *with* cymbals, psalteries, and with harps.

Est 8:17 And in every province, and in every city, whithersoever the king's commandment and his decree came, the Jews had joy and gladness, a feast and a good day. And many of the people of the land became Jews; for the fear of the Jews fell upon them.

Est 9:19 Therefore the Jews of the villages, that dwelt in the unwalled towns, made the fourteenth day of the month Adar *a day of* gladness and feasting, and a good day, and of sending portions one to another.

Ps 4:7 Thou hast put gladness in my heart, more than in the time *that* their corn and their wine increased.

Ps 9:2 I will be glad and rejoice in thee: I will sing praise to thy name, O thou most High.

Ps 16:9 Therefore my heart is glad, and my glory rejoiceth: my flesh also shall rest in hope.

Ps 30:11 Thou hast turned for me my mourning into dancing: thou hast put off my sackcloth, and girded me with gladness;

Ps 45:15 With gladness and rejoicing shall they be brought: they shall enter into the king's palace.

Ps 64:10 The righteous shall be glad in the LORD, and shall trust in him; and all the upright in heart shall glory.

Ps 68:3 But let the righteous be glad; let them rejoice before God: yea, let them exceedingly rejoice.

Ps 69:32 The humble shall see *this, and* be glad: and your heart shall live that seek God.

Ps 70:4 Let all those that seek thee rejoice and be glad in thee: and let such as love thy salvation say continually, Let God be magnified.

Ps 90:15 Make us glad according to the days *wherein* thou hast afflicted us, *and* the years *wherein* we have seen evil.

Ps 92:4 For thou, LORD, hast made me glad through thy work: I will triumph in the works of thy hands.

Ps 97:8 Zion heard, and was glad; and the daughters of Judah rejoiced because of thy judgments, O LORD.

Ps 97:11 Light is sown for the righteous, and gladness for the upright in heart.

Ps 100:2 Serve the LORD with gladness: come before his presence with singing.

Ps 104:34 My meditation of him shall be sweet: I will be glad in the LORD.

Ps 119:74 They that fear thee will be glad when they see me; because I have hoped in thy word.

Ps 122:1 I was glad when they said unto me, Let us go into the house of the LORD.

Ps 126:3 The LORD hath done great things for us; *whereof* we are glad.

Song 3:11 Go forth, O ye daughters of Zion, and behold king Solomon with the crown wherewith his mother crowned him in the day of his espousals, and in the day of the gladness of his heart.

Is 25:9 And it shall be said in that day, Lo, this *is* our God; we have waited for him, and he will save us: this *is* the LORD; we have waited for him, we will be glad and rejoice in his salvation.

Is 30:29 Ye shall have a song, as in the night *when* a holy solemnity is kept; and gladness of heart, as when one goeth with a pipe to come into the mountain of the LORD, to the mighty One of Israel.

Is 35:10 And the ransomed of the LORD shall return, and come to Zion with songs and everlasting joy upon their heads: they shall obtain joy and gladness, and sorrow and sighing shall flee away.

Je 33:11 The voice of joy, and the voice of gladness, the voice of the bridegroom, and the voice of the bride, the voice of them that shall say, Praise the LORD of hosts: for the LORD *is* good; for his mercy *endureth* for ever: *and* of them that shall bring the sacrifice of praise into the house of the LORD. For I will cause to return the captivity of the land, as at the first, saith the LORD.

Je 41:13 Now it came to pass, *that* when all the people which *were* with Ishmael saw Johanan the son of Kareah, and all the captains of the forces that *were* with him, then they were glad.

Da 6:23 Then was the king exceeding glad for him, and commanded that they should take Daniel up out of the den. So Daniel was taken up out of the den, and no manner of hurt was found upon him, because he believed in his God.

Jl 2:23 Be glad then, ye children of Zion, and rejoice in the LORD your God: for he hath given you the former rain moderately, and he will cause to come down for you the rain, the former rain, and the latter rain in the first *month.*

Zec 4:10 For who hath despised the day of small things? for they shall rejoice, and shall see the plummet in the hand of Zerubbabel *with* those seven; they *are* the eyes of the LORD, which run to and fro through the whole earth.

Zec 8:19 Thus saith the LORD of hosts; The fast of the fourth *month,* and the fast of the fifth, and the fast of the seventh, and the fast of the tenth, shall be to the house of Judah joy and gladness, and cheerful feasts; therefore love the truth and peace.

Ac 2:46 And they, continuing daily with one accord in the temple, and breaking bread from house to house, did eat their meat with gladness and singleness of heart,

Ac 11:23 Who, when he came, and had seen the grace of God, was glad, and exhorted them all, that with purpose of heart they would cleave unto the Lord.

Ac 14:17 Nevertheless he left not himself without witness, in that he did good, and gave us rain from heaven, and fruitful seasons, filling our hearts with food and gladness.

9. Happiness

Ge 30:13 And Leah said, Happy am I, for the daughters will call me blessed: and she called his name Asher.

Ne 8:12 And all the people went their way to eat, and to drink, and to send portions, and to make great mirth, because they had understood the words that were declared unto them.

Jb 5:17 Behold, happy *is* the man whom God correcteth: therefore despise not thou the chastening of the Almighty:

Jb 36:11 If they obey and serve *him,* they shall spend their days in prosperity, and their years in pleasures.

Ps 94:12 Blessed *is* the man whom thou chastenest, O LORD, and teachest him out of thy law;

Ps 127:5 Happy *is* the man that hath his quiver full of them: they shall not be ashamed, but they shall speak with the enemies in the gate.

Ps 128:2 For thou shalt eat the labour of thine hands: happy *shalt* thou *be,* and *it shall be* well with thee.

Ps 144:15 Happy *is that* people, that is in such a case: *yea,* happy *is that* people, whose God *is* the LORD.

Ps 146:5 Happy *is he* that *hath* the God of Jacob for his help, whose hope *is* in the LORD his God:

Pr 3:13 Happy *is* the man *that* findeth wisdom, and the man *that* getteth understanding.

Pr 3:18 She *is* a tree of life to them that lay hold upon her: and happy *is every one* that retaineth her.

Pr 14:21 He that despiseth his neighbour sinneth: but he that hath mercy on the poor, happy *is* he.

Pr 16:20 He that handleth a matter wisely shall find good: and whoso trusteth in the LORD, happy *is* he.

Pr 28:14 Happy *is* the man that feareth alway: but he that hardeneth his heart shall fall into mischief.

Pr 29:18 Where *there is* no vision, the people perish: but he that keepeth the law, happy *is* he.

Jn 13:17 If ye know these things, happy are ye if ye do them.

2 Co 7:4 Great *is* my boldness of speech toward you, great *is* my glorying of you: I am filled with comfort, I am exceeding joyful in all our tribulation.

Ja 5:11 Behold, we count them happy which endure. Ye have heard of the patience of Job, and have seen the end of the Lord; that the Lord is very pitiful, and of tender mercy.

1 Pe 3:14 But and if ye suffer for righteousness' sake, happy *are ye:* and be not afraid of their terror, neither be troubled;

1 Pe 4:14 If ye be reproached for the name of Christ, happy *are ye;* for the spirit of glory and of God resteth upon you: on their part he is evil spoken of, but on your part he is glorified.

10. Shouting for Joy

Le 9:24 And there came a fire out from before the LORD, and consumed upon the altar the burnt offering and the fat: *which* when all the people saw, they shouted, and fell on their faces.

Nu 23:21 He hath not beheld iniquity in Jacob, neither hath he seen perverseness in Israel: the LORD his God *is* with him, and the shout of a king *is* among them.

Jos 6:5 And it shall come to pass, that when they make a long *blast* with the ram's horn, *and* when ye hear the sound of the trumpet, all the people shall shout with a great shout; and the wall of the city shall fall down flat, and the people shall ascend up every man straight before him.

Jos 6:20 So the people shouted when *the priests* blew with the trumpets: and it came to pass, when the people heard the sound of the trumpet, and the people shouted with a great shout, that the wall fell down flat, so that the people went up into the city, every man straight before him, and they took the city.

1 S 4:5 And when the ark of the covenant of the Lord came into the camp, all Israel shouted with a great shout, so that the earth rang again.

1 S 17:20 And David rose up early in the morning, and left the sheep with a keeper, and took, and went, as Jesse had commanded him; and he came to the trench, as the host was going forth to the fight, and shouted for the battle.

1 S 17:52 And the men of Israel and of Judah arose, and shouted, and pursued the Philistines, until thou come to the valley, and to the gates of Ekron. And the wounded of the Philistines fell down by the way to Shaaraim, even unto Gath, and unto Ekron.

2 S 6:15 So David and all the house of Israel brought up the ark of the Lord with shouting, and with the sound of the trumpet.

1 Chr 15:28 Thus all Israel brought up the ark of the covenant of the Lord with shouting, and with sound of the cornet, and with trumpets, and with cymbals, making a noise with psalteries and harps.

2 Chr 13:15 Then the men of Judah gave a shout: and as the men of Judah shouted, it came to pass, that God smote Jeroboam and all Israel before Abijah and Judah.

2 Chr 15:14 And they sware unto the Lord with a loud voice, and with shouting, and with trumpets, and with cornets.

Ezr 3:11 And they sang together by course in praising and giving thanks unto the Lord; because *he is* good, for his mercy *endureth* for ever toward Israel. And all the people shouted with a great shout, when they praised the Lord, because the foundation of the house of the Lord was laid.

Ps 5:11 But let all those that put their trust in thee rejoice: let them ever shout for joy, because thou defendest them: let them also that love thy name be joyful in thee.

Ps 32:11 Be glad in the Lord, and rejoice, ye righteous: and shout for joy, all *ye that are* upright in heart.

Ps 35:27 Let them shout for joy, and be glad, that favour my righteous cause: yea, let them say continually, Let the Lord be magnified, which hath pleasure in the prosperity of his servant.

Ps 47:1 O clap your hands, all ye people; shout unto God with the voice of triumph.

Ps 98:4 Make a joyful noise unto the Lord, all the earth: make a loud noise, and rejoice, and sing praise.

Ps 132:9 Let thy priests be clothed with righteousness; and let thy saints shout for joy.

Is 12:6 Cry out and shout, thou inhabitant of Zion: for great *is* the Holy One of Israel in the midst of thee.

Is 42:11 Let the wilderness and the cities thereof lift up *their voice,* the villages *that* Kedar doth inhabit: let the inhabitants of the rock sing, let them shout from the top of the mountains.

Is 44:23 Sing, O ye heavens; for the Lord hath done *it:* shout, ye lower parts of the earth: break forth into singing, ye mountains, O forest, and every tree therein: for the Lord hath redeemed Jacob, and glorified himself in Israel.

Je 31:7 For thus saith the Lord; Sing with gladness for Jacob, and shout among the chief of the nations: publish ye, praise ye, and say, O Lord, save thy people, the remnant of Israel.

Zep 3:14 Sing, O daughter of Zion; shout, O Israel; be glad and rejoice with all the heart, O daughter of Jerusalem.

Zec 4:7 Who *art* thou, O great mountain? before Zerubbabel *thou shalt become* a plain: and he shall bring forth the headstone *thereof with* shoutings, *crying,* Grace, grace unto it.

Zec 9:9 Rejoice greatly, O daughter of Zion; shout, O daughter of Jerusalem: behold, thy King cometh unto thee: he *is* just, and having salvation; lowly, and riding upon an ass, and upon a colt the foal of an ass.

1 Th 4:16 For the Lord himself shall descend from heaven with a shout, with the voice of the archangel, and with the trump of God: and the dead in Christ shall rise first:

11. Earthly

Jb 20:5 That the triumphing of the wicked *is* short, and the joy of the hypocrite *but* for a moment?

Pr 14:13 Even in laughter the heart is sorrowful; and the end of that mirth *is* heaviness.

Ec 2:10 And whatsoever mine eyes desired I kept not from them, I withheld not my heart from any joy; for my heart rejoiced in all my labour: and this was my portion of all my labour.

Ec 7:6 For as the crackling of thorns under a pot, so *is* the laughter of the fool: this also *is* vanity.

Is 16:10 And gladness is taken away, and joy out of the plentiful field; and in the vineyards there shall be no singing, neither shall there be shouting: the treaders shall tread out no wine in *their* presses; I have made *their vintage* shouting to cease.

Is 22:2 Thou that art full of stirs, a tumultuous city, a joyous city: thy slain *men are* not slain with the sword, nor dead in battle.

Mal 3:15 And now we call the proud happy; yea, they that work wickedness are set up; yea, *they that* tempt God are even delivered.

Lu 6:25 Woe unto you that are full! for ye shall hunger. Woe unto you that laugh now! for ye shall mourn and weep.

Ja 4:9 Be afflicted, and mourn, and weep: let your laughter be turned to mourning, and *your* joy to heaviness.

a. Innocent Mirth

Ge 31:27 Wherefore didst thou flee away secretly, and steal away from me; and didst not tell me, that I might

have sent thee away with mirth, and with songs, with tabret, and with harp?

Ge 43:34 And he took *and sent* messes unto them from before him: but Benjamin's mess was five times so much as any of theirs. And they drank, and were merry with him.

1 K 4:20 Judah and Israel *were* many, as the sand which *is* by the sea in multitude, eating and drinking, and making merry.

Ne 8:12 And all the people went their way to eat, and to drink, and to send portions, and to make great mirth, because they had understood the words that were declared unto them.

Pr 15:15 All the days of the afflicted *are* evil: but he that is of a merry heart *hath* a continual feast.

Pr 17:22 A merry heart doeth good *like* a medicine: but a broken spirit drieth the bones.

Ec 2:2 I said of laughter, *It is* mad: and of mirth, What doeth it?

Ec 7:4 The heart of the wise *is* in the house of mourning; but the heart of fools *is* in the house of mirth.

Ec 9:7 Go thy way, eat thy bread with joy, and drink thy wine with a merry heart; for God now accepteth thy works.

Je 30:19 And out of them shall proceed thanksgiving and the voice of them that make merry: and I will multiply them, and they shall not be few; I will also glorify them, and they shall not be small.

Je 31:4 Again I will build thee, and thou shalt be built, O virgin of Israel: thou shalt again be adorned with thy tabrets, and shalt go forth in the dances of them that make merry.

Lu 15:9 And when she hath found *it,* she calleth *her* friends and *her* neighbours together, saying, Rejoice with me; for I have found the piece which I had lost.

Lu 15:24 For this my son was dead, and is alive again; he was lost, and is found. And they began to be merry.

b. Manifested in Laughter

Ge 17:17 Then Abraham fell upon his face, and laughed, and said in his heart, Shall *a child* be born unto him that is an hundred years old? and shall Sarah, that is ninety years old, bear?

Ge 18:12 Therefore Sarah laughed within herself, saying, After I am waxed old shall I have pleasure, my lord being old also?

Pr 14:13 Even in laughter the heart is sorrowful; and the end of that mirth *is* heaviness.

Ec 2:2 I said of laughter, *It is* mad: and of mirth, What doeth it?

Ec 3:4 A time to weep, and a time to laugh; a time to mourn, and a time to dance;

Ec 7:3 Sorrow *is* better than laughter: for by the sadness of the countenance the heart is made better.

Ec 7:6 For as the crackling of thorns under a pot, so *is* the laughter of the fool: this also *is* vanity.

Ec 10:19 A feast is made for laughter, and wine maketh merry: but money answereth all *things*.

Lu 6:25 Woe unto you that are full! for ye shall hunger. Woe unto you that laugh now! for ye shall mourn and weep.

Ja 4:9 Be afflicted, and mourn, and weep: let your laughter be turned to mourning, and *your* joy to heaviness.

c. Enjoyment Sought

De 12:12 And ye shall rejoice before the LORD your God, ye, and your sons, and your daughters, and your menservants, and your maidservants, and the Levite that *is* within your gates; forasmuch as he hath no part nor inheritance with you.

De 14:26 And thou shalt bestow that money for whatsoever thy soul lusteth after, for oxen, or for sheep, or for wine, or for strong drink, or for whatsoever thy soul desireth: and thou shalt eat there before the LORD thy God, and thou shalt rejoice, thou, and thine household,

Jud 19:6 And they sat down, and did eat and drink both of them together: for the damsel's father had said unto the man, Be content, I pray thee, and tarry all night, and let thine heart be merry.

Ru 3:7 And when Boaz had eaten and drunk, and his heart was merry, he went to lie down at the end of the heap of corn: and she came softly, and uncovered his feet, and laid her down.

1 K 4:20 Judah and Israel *were* many, as the sand which *is* by the sea in multitude, eating and drinking, and making merry.

Ne 8:10 Then he said unto them, Go your way, eat the fat, and drink the sweet, and send portions unto them for whom nothing is prepared: for *this* day *is* holy unto our Lord: neither be ye sorry; for the joy of the LORD is your strength.

Jb 1:4 And his sons went and feasted *in their* houses, every one his day; and sent and called for their three sisters to eat and to drink with them.

Ec 2:10 And whatsoever mine eyes desired I kept not from them, I withheld not my heart from any joy; for my heart rejoiced in all my labour: and this was my portion of all my labour.

Ec 2:24 *There is* nothing better for a man, *than* that he should eat and drink, and *that* he should make his soul enjoy good in his labour. This also I saw, that it *was* from the hand of God.

Ec 3:13 And also that every man should eat and drink, and enjoy the good of all his labour, it *is* the gift of God.

Ec 3:22 Wherefore I perceive that *there is* nothing better, than that a man should rejoice in his own works; for that *is* his portion: for who shall bring him to see what shall be after him?

Ec 5:18 Behold *that* which I have seen: *it is* good and comely *for one* to eat and to drink, and to enjoy the good of all his labour that he taketh under the sun all the days of his life, which God giveth him: for it *is* his portion.

Ec 8:15 Then I commended mirth, because a man hath no better thing under the sun, than to eat, and to drink, and to be merry: for that shall abide with him of his labour the days of his life, which God giveth him under the sun.

Ec 9:9 Live joyfully with the wife whom thou lovest all the days of the life of thy vanity, which he hath given thee under the sun, all the days of thy vanity: for that *is* thy portion in *this* life, and in thy labour which thou takest under the sun.

Is 9:3 Thou hast multiplied the nation, *and* not increased the joy: they joy before thee according to the joy in harvest, *and* as *men* rejoice when they divide the spoil.

Is 65:22 They shall not build, and another inhabit; they shall not plant, and another eat: for as the days of a tree *are* the days of my people, and mine elect shall long enjoy the work of their hands.

12. Heavenly

Lu 2:13–14 And suddenly there was with the angel a multitude of the heavenly host praising God, and saying,

Glory to God in the highest, and on earth peace, good will toward men.

THE RETURN OF THE PENITENT SINNER

Lu 15:7 I say unto you, that likewise joy shall be in heaven over one sinner that repenteth, more than over ninety and nine just persons, which need no repentance.

THE EXALTATION OF THE LAMB

Re 5:9–10 And they sung a new song, saying, Thou art worthy to take the book, and to open the seals thereof: for thou wast slain, and hast redeemed us to God by thy blood out of every kindred, and tongue, and people, and nation;

And hast made us unto our God kings and priests: and we shall reign on the earth.

Re 12:12 Therefore rejoice, *ye* heavens, and ye that dwell in them. Woe to the inhabiters of the earth and of the sea! for the devil is come down unto you, having great wrath, because he knoweth that he hath but a short time.

THE GATHERING HOME OF THE SAINTS

Re 14:2–3 And I heard a voice from heaven, as the voice of many waters, and as the voice of a great thunder: and I heard the voice of harpers harping with their harps:

And they sung as it were a new song before the throne, and before the four beasts, and the elders: and no man could learn that song but the hundred *and* forty *and* four thousand, which were redeemed from the earth.

THE TRIUMPH OF RIGHTEOUSNESS

Re 19:6 And I heard as it were the voice of a great multitude, and as the voice of many waters, and as the voice of mighty thunderings, saying, Alleluia: for the Lord God omnipotent reigneth.

See **AFFLICTIONS, PERSECUTION, SORROW, SUFFERING**

JUBILEE, *YEAR OF, called year of liberty*

Le 25:10, 28, 33, 40, 50; 27:17, 24; Nu 36:4; Is 63:4; Eze 46:17; Lu 4:19

JUDAH, *praise*

1. Son of Jacob

Ge 29:35; 35:23; 37:26; 38:1; 43:3; 44:14; 46:12, 28; 49:8; Ex 1:2; Nu 1:7; 26:19; Jos 14:6; 15:1, 13; 1 Chr 2:1; 4:1, 21; 5:2; 9:3; Ps 60:7; Eze 48:31; Lu 3:33

2. Tribe of

Nu 1:27; 2:3; 10:14; 13:6; De 33:7; Jos 7:16; 15:21; 19:1, 9; 21:4; Jud 1:3; 2 S 2:10; 19:11; 1 K 12:21; 1 Chr 6:65; 12:24; 27:18; Ps 68:27; Eze 48:8, 22; He 7:14; 8:8; Re 5:5; 7:5

See **ISRAEL**

JUDAISM, *the culture and religion of the Jews*

1. Superseded by Christianity

Mk 2:22; Lu 5:36; Ga 5:6; Col 2:16; He 7:18; Lu 8:13

2. Its Doctrines, *introduced into the Christian church*

Mt 23:15; Ac 11:3; 15:1, 24; Ro 14:5; Ga 1:7; 2:4, 14; 5:13; 6:12; Ph 3:2; Tit 1:10, 14

See **CHRISTIANITY**

JUDAS, *praise*

1. Iscariot, *the betrayer of Jesus*

AVARICIOUSNESS

Mt 26:14–15 Then one of the twelve, called Judas Iscariot, went unto the chief priests,

And said *unto them*, What will ye give me, and I will deliver him unto you? And they covenanted with him for thirty pieces of silver.

HYPOCRISY

Jn 12:5–6 Why was not this ointment sold for three hundred pence, and given to the poor?

This he said, not that he cared for the poor; but because he was a thief, and had the bag, and bare what was put therein.

TREACHERY

Mk 14:10 And Judas Iscariot, one of the twelve, went unto the chief priests, to betray him unto them.

Lu 22:47–48 And while he yet spake, behold a multitude, and he that was called Judas, one of the twelve, went before them, and drew near unto Jesus to kiss him.

But Jesus said unto him, Judas, betrayest thou the Son of man with a kiss?

DISHONESTY

Jn 12:6 This he said, not that he cared for the poor; but because he was a thief, and had the bag, and bare what was put therein.

REMORSE

Mt 27:3–4 Then Judas, which had betrayeth him, when he saw that he was condemned, repented himself, and brought again the thirty pieces of silver to the chief priests and elders,

Saying, I have sinned in that I have betrayed the innocent blood. And they said, What *is that* to us? see thou *to that*.

Ac 1:18 Now this man purchased a field with the reward of iniquity; and falling headlong, he burst asunder in the midst, and all his bowels gushed out.

2. One of the Brothers of Christ

Mt 13:55; Mk 6:3

3. Jude, or Lebbaeus, *surnamed Thaddaeus, brother of the apostle James*

Mt 10:3; Mk 3:18; Lu 6:16; Jn 14:22; Ac 1:13

4. Of Galilee

Ac 5:37

5. A Disciple

Ac 9:11; 15:22

JUDE

1. Person, *author of the epistle, possibly the brother of the apostle James*

Jude 1

2. Book

Author: Probably Jude, the brother of James. If this is true, he may have been a brother of our Lord (Mk 6:3; Ga 1:19). The Lord's brothers did not believe in him at first (Jn 7:5); but after his resurrection they became his followers (Ac 1:14). It is possible that Jude, because of his early unbelief, felt that he was not worthy to sign himself as brother of Jesus, so in writing the epistle he called himself a servant (1).

Date Written: Uncertain.

Purpose: The epistle was evidently written to warn the church against immoral teachers and alarming heresies that were endangering the faith of believers.

To Whom Written: Christians who were threatened by apostates and heretics.

Main Theme: Heretical teachers in the church and the believer's godly response to that divisive threat.

Key Words: Contend earnestly for the faith (3).

Key Verses: 3–4.

JUDEA, or *Juda, Judah, the southern division of Palestine*

Mt 2:6; 4:25; 19:1; Mk 1:5; 3:7; 13:14; Lu 1:5, 39; 5:17; 7:17; Jn 3:22; 4:3, 47; 7:1, 3; 11:7; Ac 8:1; 9:31; 12:19

JUDGE, *at the Great Day*

1. God

Ge 16:5 And Sarai said unto Abram, My wrong *be* upon thee: I have given my maid into thy bosom; and when she saw that she had conceived, I was despised in her eyes: the LORD judge between me and thee.

Ge 18:25 That be far from thee to do after this manner, to slay the righteous with the wicked: and that the righteous should be as the wicked, that be far from thee: Shall not the Judge of all the earth do right?

Jud 11:27 Wherefore I have not sinned against thee, but thou doest me wrong to war against me: the LORD the Judge be judge this day between the children of Israel and the children of Ammon.

2 Chr 20:12 O our God, wilt thou not judge them? for we have no might against this great company that cometh against us; neither know we what to do: but our eyes *are* upon thee.

Ps 58:11 So that a man shall say, Verily *there is* a reward for the righteous: verily he is a God that judgeth in the earth.

Ps 75:7 But God *is* the judge: he putteth down one, and setteth up another.

Ps 76:9 When God arose to judgment, to save all the meek of the earth. Selah.

Ps 96:13 Before the LORD: for he cometh, for he cometh to judge the earth: he shall judge the world with righteousness, and the people with his truth.

Ec 3:17 I said in mine heart, God shall judge the righteous and the wicked: for *there is* a time there for every purpose and for every work.

He 12:23 To the general assembly and church of the firstborn, which are written in heaven, and to God the Judge of all, and to the spirits of just men made perfect,

Re 18:8 Therefore shall her plagues come in one day, death, and mourning, and famine; and she shall be utterly burned with fire: for strong *is* the Lord God who judgeth her.

Re 20:12 And I saw the dead, small and great, stand before God; and the books were opened: and another book was opened, which is *the book* of life: and the dead were judged out of those things which were written in the books, according to their works.

2. Christ

Is 11:4 But with righteousness shall he judge the poor, and reprove with equity for the meek of the earth: and he shall smite the earth with the rod of his mouth, and with the breath of his lips shall he slay the wicked.

Mt 25:32 And before him shall be gathered all nations: and he shall separate them one from another, as a shepherd divideth *his* sheep from the goats:

Jn 5:22 For the Father judgeth no man, but hath committed all judgment unto the Son:

Ac 10:42 And he commanded us to preach unto the people, and to testify that it is he which was ordained of God *to be* the Judge of quick and dead.

Ac 17:31 Because he hath appointed a day, in the which he will judge the world in righteousness by *that* man whom he hath ordained; *whereof* he hath given assurance unto all *men*, in that he hath raised him from the dead.

Ro 2:16 In the day when God shall judge the secrets of men by Jesus Christ according to my gospel.

Ro 14:10 But why dost thou judge thy brother? or why dost thou set at nought thy brother? for we shall all stand before the judgment seat of Christ.

1 Co 4:4 For I know nothing by myself; yet am I not hereby justified: but he that judgeth me is the Lord.

1 Co 4:5 Therefore judge nothing before the time, until the Lord come, who both will bring to light the hidden things of darkness, and will make manifest the counsels of the hearts: and then shall every man have praise of God.

2 Ti 4:1 I charge *thee* therefore before God, and the Lord Jesus Christ, who shall judge the quick and the dead at his appearing and his kingdom;

1 Pe 4:5 Who shall give account to him that is ready to judge the quick and the dead.

JUDGES

Author: Unknown; tradition attributes the authorship to Samuel.

Date Written: 1086–1035 B.C.(?)

Purpose: To review Israel's history following the conquest and prior to the monarchy; and to demonstrate the consequence of sinful rebellion, in spite of God's repeated gracious provision of political and spiritual leaders.

To Whom Written: The nation of Israel.

Main Theme: The history of Israel during the times of the fifteen judges.

Key Word: Apostasy.

Key Verse: 17:6.

JUDGMENTS, *emanating from God's holy character*

Ge 15:14 And also that nation, whom they shall serve, will I judge: and afterward shall they come out with great substance.

And I will stretch out my hand, and smite Egypt with all my wonders which I will do in the midst thereof: and after that he will let you go.

Ex 3:20 And I will stretch out my hand, and smite Egypt with all my wonders which I will do in the midst thereof: and after that he will let you go.

Ex 6:6 Wherefore say unto the children of Israel, I *am* the LORD, and I will bring you out from under the burdens of the Egyptians, and I will rid you out of their bondage, and I will redeem you with a stretched out arm, and with great judgments:

Ex 9:22 And the LORD said unto Moses, Stretch forth thine hand toward heaven, that there may be hail in all the land of Egypt, upon man, and upon beast, and upon every herb of the field, throughout the land of Egypt.

Ex 12:12 For I will pass through the land of Egypt this night, and will smite all the firstborn in the land of Egypt, both man and beast; and against all the gods of Egypt I will execute judgment: I *am* the LORD.

Nu 3:13 Because all the firstborn *are* mine; *for* on the day that I smote all the firstborn in the land of Egypt I hallowed unto me all the firstborn in Israel, both man and beast: mine shall they be: I *am* the LORD.

De 32:41 If I whet my glittering sword, and mine hand take hold on judgment; I will render vengeance to mine enemies, and will reward them that hate me.

2 K 6:18 And when they came down to him, Elisha prayed unto the LORD, and said, Smite this people, I pray thee, with blindness. And he smote them with blindness according to the word of Elisha.

Ps 7:12 If he turn not, he will whet his sword; he hath bent his bow, and made it ready.

Ps 9:16 The LORD is known *by* the judgment *which* he executeth: the wicked is snared in the work of his own hands. Higgaion. Selah.

Ps 36:6 Thy righteousness *is* like the great mountains; thy judgments *are* a great deep: O LORD, thou preservest man and beast.

Ps 136:10 To him that smote Egypt in their firstborn: for his mercy *endureth* for ever:

Is 25:2 For thou hast made of a city an heap; *of* a defenced city a ruin: a palace of strangers to be no city; it shall never be built.

Is 28:2 Behold, the Lord hath a mighty and strong one, *which* as a tempest of hail *and* a destroying storm, as a flood of mighty waters overflowing, shall cast down to the earth with the hand.

Is 30:30 And the LORD shall cause his glorious voice to be heard, and shall shew the lighting down of his arm, with the indignation of *his* anger, and *with* the flame of a devouring fire, *with* scattering, and tempest, and hailstones.

Je 4:12 *Even* a full wind from those *places* shall come unto me: now also will I give sentence against them.

Eze 25:11 And I will execute judgments upon Moab; and they shall know that I *am* the LORD.

Eze 30:14 And I will make Pathros desolate, and will set fire in Zoan, and will execute judgments in No.

Eze 38:22 And I will plead against him with pestilence and with blood; and I will rain upon him, and upon his bands, and upon the many people that *are* with him, an overflowing rain, and great hailstones, fire, and brimstone.

Eze 39:21 And I will set my glory among the heathen, and all the heathen shall see my judgment that I have executed, and my hand that I have laid upon them.

Mal 3:5 And I will come near to you to judgment; and I will be a swift witness against the sorcerers, and against the adulterers, and against false swearers, and against those that oppress the hireling in *his* wages, the widow, and the fatherless, and that turn aside the stranger *from his right,* and fear not me, saith the LORD of hosts.

Ac 5:9 Then Peter said unto her, How is it that ye have agreed together to tempt the Spirit of the Lord? behold, the feet of them which have buried thy husband *are* at the door, and shall carry thee out.

2 Pe 2:4 For if God spared not the angels that sinned, but cast *them* down to hell, and delivered *them* into chains of darkness, to be reserved unto judgment;

Re 17:1 And there came one of the seven angels which had the seven vials, and talked with me, saying unto me, Come hither; I will shew unto thee the judgment of the great whore that sitteth upon many waters:

1. Those Smitten

Nu 11:33; 1 S 25:38; 2 S 6:7; 12:15; 1 K 14:15; 2 K 6:18; 15:5; 19:35; 1 Chr 2:3; 13:10; 21:7; 2 Chr 13:15; 14:12; 20:22; 26:20; Jb 34:26; Ps 3:7; 78:31; Is 5:25; 37:36; Je 14:19; 21:6; Eze 7:9; 32:15; 39:3; Ho 9:16; Zec 12:4; Ac 5:5, 10; 12:23

2. Special Judgments Inflicted

a. Bones Scattered

2 K 23:14; Ps 53:5; Je 8:1; Eze 6:5

b. Disease Sent

Ex 9:10; Nu 12:10; 16:47; De 7:15; 28:22, 27, 35, 59; 1 S 5:6, 12; 2 S 12:15; 1 K 13:4; 2 K 5:27; 15:5; 2 Chr 13:20; 21:15, 18; 26:19; Ps 38:7; Zec 14:12; Ac 12:23

3. Drought

2 S 1:21; 1 K 17:1; 18:5; Ps 107:33; Je 3:3; 14:4; 50:38; Ho 13:15; Jl 1:19; Am 4:7; Hag 1:11; Lu 4:25; Ja 5:17

4. Pestilence

a. Threatened

Ex 9:15; Le 26:25; Nu 14:12; De 28:21; 2 S 24:13; 2 Chr 7:13; 21:14; Je 14:12; 21:6; 24:10; 27:13; 29:17; 32:36; 38:2; 42:17; 44:13; Eze 5:12, 17; 6:11; 7:15; 14:19; 28:23; 33:27; 38:22; Mt 24:7; Lu 21:11

b. Sent

2 S 24:15; 1 Chr 21:12, 14; 2 Chr 6:28; Ps 78:50; Am 4:10; Hab 3:5

5. Plagues

Ge 12:17; Le 13:29, 46, 50; 14:34, 43, 54; 26:21; Nu 8:19; 11:33; 14:37; 16:46; 25:9; 31:16; De 28:27, 59; 29:22; Jos 22:17; 1 S 5:6, 11; 6:4, 19; 2 S 24:21, 25; 1 K 8:37; 1 Chr 21:22; Ps 106:29; Zec 14:12, 15, 18; Re 15:1; 16:21; 18:8; 21:9; 22:18

Of Egypt

Ex 7:20; 8:6, 17, 24; 9:6, 10, 23; 10:13, 22; 12:29; De 4:34; Jos 24:5; 1 S 4:8; Ps 78:43; 105:29; Re 11:6

6. Divine View

2 K 21:13; Is 28:17; 34:11; Lam 2:8; Am 7:8

7. Judgment Forbidden

CHRIST'S COMMAND

Mt 7:1–2 Judge not, that ye be not judged.

For with what judgment ye judge, ye shall be judged: and with what measure ye mete, it shall be measured to you again.

INEXCUSABLE

Ro 2:1 Therefore thou art inexcusable, O man, whosoever thou art that judgest: for wherein thou judgest another, thou condemnest thyself; for thou that judgest doest the same things.

NOT OUR PREROGATIVE

Ro 14:4 Who art thou that judgest another man's servant? to his own master he standeth or falleth. Yea, he shall be holden up: for God is able to make him stand.

JUDGE OUR OWN LIVES

Ro 14:13 Let us not therefore judge one another any more: but judge this rather, that no man put a stumbling-block or an occasion to fall in *his* brother's way.

BECAUSE NOT ACQUAINTED WITH ALL FACTS

1 Co 4:5 Therefore judge nothing before the time, until the Lord come, who both will bring to light the hidden things of darkness, and will make manifest the counsels of the hearts: and then shall every man have praise of God.

IT IS ASSUMING TOO MUCH

Ja 4:12 There is one lawgiver, who is able to save and to destroy: who art thou that judgest another?

JUDGMENT SEAT, *Roman*

Mt 27:19; Ac 18:12; 25:10

JUNIPER *See* TREES

JUSTICE, *fairness, equity*

1. Divine

Ge 18:25 That be far from thee to do after this manner, to slay the righteous with the wicked: and that the righteous should be as the wicked, that be far from thee: Shall not the Judge of all the earth do right?

Ge 20:4 But Abimelech had not come near her: and he said, Lord, wilt thou slay also a righteous nation?

Ex 23:7 Keep thee far from a false matter; and the innocent and righteous slay thou not: for I will not justify the wicked.

Ex 34:7 Keeping mercy for thousands, forgiving iniquity and transgression and sin, and that will by no means clear *the guilty;* visiting the iniquity of the fathers upon the children, and upon the children's children, unto the third and to the fourth *generation.*

Nu 14:18 The LORD *is* longsuffering, and of great mercy, forgiving iniquity and transgression, and by no means clearing *the guilty,* visiting the iniquity of the fathers upon the children unto the third and fourth *generation.*

Nu 26:54 To many thou shalt give the more inheritance, and to few thou shalt give the less inheritance: to every one shall his inheritance be given according to those that were numbered of him.

De 10:18 He doth execute the judgment of the fatherless and widow, and loveth the stranger, in giving him food and raiment.

De 32:4 *He is* the Rock, his work *is* perfect: for all his ways *are* judgment: a God of truth and without iniquity, just and right *is* he.

De 33:21 And he provided the first part for himself, because there, *in* a portion of the lawgiver, *was he* seated; and he came with the heads of the people, he executed the justice of the LORD, and his judgments with Israel.

1 K 8:32 Then hear thou in heaven, and do, and judge thy servants, condemning the wicked, to bring his way upon his head; and justifying the righteous, to give him according to his righteousness.

1 K 8:39 Then hear thou in heaven thy dwelling place, and forgive, and do, and give to every man according to his ways, whose heart thou knowest; (for thou, *even* thou only, knowest the hearts of all the children of men;)

Ne 9:33 Howbeit thou *art* just in all that is brought upon us; for thou hast done right, but we have done wickedly:

Jb 4:7 Remember, I pray thee, who *ever* perished, being innocent? or where were the righteous cut off?

Jb 8:3 Doth God pervert judgment? or doth the Almighty pervert justice?

Jb 8:20 Behold, God will not cast away a perfect *man,* neither will he help the evil doers:

Jb 11:6 And that he would shew thee the secrets of wisdom, that *they are* double to that which is! Know therefore that God exacteth of thee *less* than thine iniquity *deserveth.*

Jb 34:12 Yea, surely God will not do wickedly, neither will the Almighty pervert judgment.

Jb 37:23 *Touching* the Almighty, we cannot find him out: *he is* excellent in power, and in judgment, and in plenty of justice: he will not afflict.

Ps 7:11 God judgeth the righteous, and God is angry *with the wicked* every day.

Ps 9:4 For thou hast maintained my right and my cause; thou satest in the throne judging right.

Ps 9:8 And he shall judge the world in righteousness, he shall minister judgment to the people in uprightness.

Ps 17:2 Let my sentence come forth from thy presence; let thine eyes behold the things that are equal.

Ps 18:25 With the merciful thou wilt shew thyself merciful; with an upright man thou wilt shew thyself upright;

Ps 33:5 He loveth righteousness and judgment: the earth is full of the goodness of the LORD.

Ps 35:23 Stir up thyself, and awake to my judgment, *even* unto my cause, my God and my Lord.

Ps 37:28 For the LORD loveth judgment, and forsaketh not his saints; they are preserved for ever: but the seed of the wicked shall be cut off.

Ps 37:33 The LORD will not leave him in his hand, nor condemn him when he is judged.

Ps 62:12 Also unto thee, O Lord, *belongeth* mercy: for thou renderest to every man according to his work.

Ps 67:4 O let the nations be glad and sing for joy: for thou shalt judge the people righteously, and govern the nations upon earth. Selah.

Ps 75:2 When I shall receive the congregation I will judge uprightly.

Ps 89:14 Justice and judgment *are* the habitation of thy throne: mercy and truth shall go before thy face.

Ps 94:15 But judgment shall return unto righteousness: and all the upright in heart shall follow it.

Ps 96:10 Say among the heathen *that* the LORD reigneth: the world also shall be established that it shall not be moved: he shall judge the people righteously.

Ps 97:2 Clouds and darkness *are* round about him: righteousness and judgment *are* the habitation of his throne.

Ps 98:9 Before the LORD; for he cometh to judge the earth: with righteousness shall he judge the world, and the people with equity.

Ps 99:4 The king's strength also loveth judgment; thou dost establish equity, thou executest judgment and righteousness in Jacob.

Ps 101:1 I will sing of mercy and judgment: unto thee, O LORD, will I sing.

Ps 103:6 The LORD executeth righteousness and judgment for all that are oppressed.

Ps 111:8 They stand fast for ever and ever, *and are* done in truth and uprightness.

Ps 119:137 Righteous *art* thou, O LORD, and upright *are* thy judgments.

Ps 146:7 Which executeth judgment for the oppressed: which giveth food to the hungry. The LORD looseth the prisoners:

Pr 16:11 A just weight and balance *are* the LORD's: all the weights of the bag *are* his work.

Is 11:4 But with righteousness shall he judge the poor, and reprove with equity for the meek of the earth: and he shall smite the earth with the rod of his mouth, and with the breath of his lips shall he slay the wicked.

Is 28:17 Judgment also will I lay to the line, and righteousness to the plummet: and the hail shall sweep away the refuge of lies, and the waters shall overflow the hiding place.

Is 30:18 And therefore will the LORD wait, that he may be gracious unto you, and therefore will he be exalted, that he may have mercy upon you: for the LORD *is* a God of judgment: blessed *are* all they that wait for him.

Is 42:3 A bruised reed shall he not break, and the smoking flax shall he not quench: he shall bring forth judgment unto truth.

Is 45:21 Tell ye, and bring *them* near; yea, let them take counsel together: who hath declared this from ancient time? *who* hath told it from that time I the LORD? and *there is* no God else beside me; a just God and a Saviour; *there is* none beside me.

Is 51:4 Hearken unto me, my people; and give ear unto me, O my nation: for a law shall proceed from me, and I will make my judgment to rest for a light of the people.

Is 61:8 For I the LORD love judgment, I hate robbery for burnt offering; and I will direct their work in truth, and I will make an everlasting covenant with them.

Je 11:20 But, O LORD of hosts, that judgest righteously, that triest the reins and the heart, let me see thy vengeance on them: for unto thee have I revealed my cause.

Je 23:5 Behold, the days come, saith the LORD, that I will raise unto David a righteous Branch, and a King shall reign and prosper, and shall execute judgment and justice in the earth.

Je 33:15 In those days, and at that time, will I cause the Branch of righteousness to grow up unto David; and he shall execute judgment and righteousness in the land.

Eze 14:23 And they shall comfort you, when ye see their ways and their doings: and ye shall know that I have not done without cause all that I have done in it, saith the Lord GOD.

Eze 18:20 The soul that sinneth, it shall die. The son shall not bear the iniquity of the father, neither shall the father bear the iniquity of the son: the righteousness of the righteous shall be upon him, and the wickedness of the wicked shall be upon him.

Eze 18:25 Yet ye say, The way of the Lord is not equal. Hear now, O house of Israel; Is not my way equal? are not your ways unequal?

Eze 33:12 Therefore, thou son of man, say unto the children of thy people, The righteousness of the righteous shall not deliver him in the day of his transgression: as for the wickedness of the wicked, he shall not fall thereby in the day that he turneth from his wickedness; neither shall the righteous be able to live for his *righteousness* in the day that he sinneth.

Da 4:37 Now I Nebuchadnezzar praise and extol and honour the King of heaven, all whose works *are* truth, and his ways judgment: and those that walk in pride he is able to abase.

Da 9:14 Therefore hath the LORD watched upon the evil, and brought it upon us: for the LORD our God *is* righteous in all his works which he doeth: for we obeyed not his voice.

Mi 7:9 I will bear the indignation of the LORD, because I have sinned against him, until he plead my cause, and execute judgment for me: he will bring me forth to the light, *and* I shall behold his righteousness.

Na 1:3 The LORD *is* slow to anger, and great in power, and will not at all acquit *the wicked:* the LORD hath his way in the whirlwind and in the storm, and the clouds *are* the dust of his feet.

Zep 3:5 The just LORD *is* in the midst thereof; he will not do iniquity: every morning doth he bring his judgment to light, he faileth not; but the unjust knoweth no shame.

Jn 5:30 I can of mine own self do nothing: as I hear, I judge: and my judgment is just; because I seek not mine own will, but the will of the Father which hath sent me.

Ro 2:2 But we are sure that the judgment of God is according to truth against them which commit such things.

Ro 3:26 To declare, *I say,* at this time his righteousness: that he might be just, and the justifier of him which believeth in Jesus.

2 Th 1:5 *Which is* a manifest token of the righteous judgment of God, that ye may be counted worthy of the kingdom of God, for which ye also suffer:

1 Pe 2:23 Who, when he was reviled, reviled not again; when he suffered, he threatened not; but committed *himself* to him that judgeth righteously:

1 Jn 1:9 If we confess our sins, he is faithful and just to forgive us *our* sins, and to cleanse us from all unrighteousness.

Re 15:3 And they sing the song of Moses the servant of God, and the song of the Lamb, saying, Great and marvellous *are* thy works, Lord God Almighty; just and true *are* thy ways, thou King of saints.

Re 16:5 And I heard the angel of the waters say, Thou art righteous, O Lord, which art, and wast, and shalt be, because thou hast judged thus.

Re 19:2 For true and righteous *are* his judgments: for he hath judged the great whore, which did corrupt the earth with her fornication, and hath avenged the blood of his servants at her hand.

2. Prescribed

Ex 21:10 If he take him another *wife;* her food, her raiment, and her duty of marriage, shall he not diminish.

Ex 21:22 If men strive, and hurt a woman with child, so that her fruit depart *from her,* and yet no mischief

follow: he shall be surely punished, according as the woman's husband will lay upon him; and he shall pay as the judges *determine.*

Ex 21:36 Or if it be known that the ox hath used to push in time past, and his owner hath not kept him in; he shall surely pay ox for ox; and the dead shall be his own.

Ex 23:3 Neither shalt thou countenance a poor man in his cause.

Le 19:15 Ye shall do no unrighteousness in judgment: thou shalt not respect the person of the poor, nor honour the person of the mighty: *but* in righteousness shalt thou judge thy neighbour.

Le 25:14 And if thou sell *ought* unto thy neighbour, or buyest ought of thy neighbour's hand, ye shall not oppress one another:

Nu 27:4 Why should the name of our father be done away from among his family, because he hath no son? Give unto us *therefore* a possession among the brethren of our father.

Nu 27:7 The daughters of Zelophehad speak right: thou shalt surely give them a possession of an inheritance among their father's brethren; and thou shalt cause the inheritance of their father to pass unto them.

Nu 33:54 And ye shall divide the land by lot for an inheritance among your families: *and* to the more ye shall give the more inheritance, and to the fewer ye shall give the less inheritance: every man's *inheritance* shall be in the place where his lot falleth; according to the tribes of your fathers ye shall inherit.

Nu 35:12 And they shall be unto you cities for refuge from the avenger; that the manslayer die not, until he stand before the congregation in judgment.

Nu 35:24 Then the congregation shall judge between the slayer and the revenger of blood according to these judgments:

De 1:16 And I charged your judges at that time, saying, Hear *the causes* between your brethren, and judge righteously between *every* man and his brother, and the stranger *that is* with him.

De 16:20 That which is altogether just shalt thou follow, that thou mayest live, and inherit the land which the LORD thy God giveth thee.

De 19:19 Then shall ye do unto him, as he had thought to have done unto his brother: so shalt thou put the evil away from among you.

De 25:1 If there be a controversy between men, and they come unto judgment, that *the judges* may judge them; then they shall justify the righteous, and condemn the wicked.

Jos 20:5 And if the avenger of blood pursue after him, then they shall not deliver the slayer up into his hand; because he smote his neighbour unwittingly, and hated him not beforetime.

2 S 23:3 The God of Israel said, the Rock of Israel spake to me, He that ruleth over men *must be* just, ruling in the fear of God.

1 K 10:9 Blessed be the LORD thy God, which delighted in thee, to set thee on the throne of Israel: because the LORD loved Israel for ever, therefore made he thee king, to do judgment and justice.

2 Chr 9:8 Blessed be the LORD thy God, which delighted in thee to set thee on his throne, *to be* king for the LORD thy God: because thy God loved Israel, to establish them for ever, therefore made he thee king over them, to do judgment and justice.

Ps 58:1 Do ye indeed speak righteousness, O congregation? do ye judge uprightly, O ye sons of men?

Ps 82:3 Defend the poor and fatherless: do justice to the afflicted and needy.

Ps 106:3 Blessed *are* they that keep judgment, *and* he that doeth righteousness at all times.

Ps 119:121 I have done judgment and justice: leave me not to mine oppressors.

Pr 3:27 Withhold not good from them to whom it is due, when it is in the power of thine hand to do *it.*

Pr 21:3 To do justice and judgment *is* more acceptable to the LORD than sacrifice.

Pr 31:9 Open thy mouth, judge righteously, and plead the cause of the poor and needy.

Is 1:17 Learn to do well; seek judgment, relieve the oppressed, judge the fatherless, plead for the widow.

Is 16:3 Take counsel, execute judgment; make thy shadow as the night in the midst of the noonday; hide the outcasts; bewray not him that wandereth.

Is 56:1 Thus saith the LORD, Keep ye judgment, and do justice: for my salvation *is* near to come, and my righteousness to be revealed.

Je 5:1 Run ye to and fro through the streets of Jerusalem, and see now, and know, and seek in the broad places thereof, if ye can find a man, if there be *any* that executeth judgment, that seeketh the truth; and I will pardon it.

Je 7:5 For if ye throughly amend your ways and ye throughly execute judgment between a man and his neighbour;

Je 21:12 O house of David, thus saith the LORD; Execute judgment in the morning, and deliver *him that is* spoiled out of the hand of the oppressor, lest my fury go out like fire, and burn that none can quench *it,* because of the evil of your doings.

Je 22:3 Thus saith the LORD; Execute ye judgment and righteousness, and deliver the spoiled out of the hand of the oppressor: and do no wrong, do no violence to the stranger, the fatherless, nor the widow, neither shed innocent blood in this place.

Lam 3:36 To subvert a man in his cause, the Lord approveth not.

Eze 18:5 But if a man be just, and do that which is lawful and right,

Eze 18:17 *That* hath taken off his hand from the poor, *that* hath not received usury nor increase, hath executed my judgments, hath walked in my statutes; he shall not die for the iniquity of his father, he shall surely live.

Eze 44:24 And in controversy they shall stand in judgment; *and* they shall judge it according to my judgments: and they shall keep my laws and my statutes in all mine assemblies; and they shall hallow my sab-baths.

Eze 45:9 Thus saith the Lord God; Let it suffice you, O princes of Israel: re-move violence and spoil, and execute judgment and justice, take away your exactions from my people, saith the Lord GOD.

Eze 46:18 Moreover the prince shall not take of the people's inheritance by oppression, to thrust them out of their possession; *but* he shall give his sons inheritance out of his own possession: that my people be not scattered every man from his possession.

Am 5:15 Hate the evil, and love the good, and establish judgment in the gate: it may be that the LORD God of hosts will be gracious unto the rem-nant of Joseph.

Am 5:24 But let judgment run down as waters, and righteousness as a mighty stream.

Mi 3:1 And I said, Hear, I pray you, O heads of Jacob, and ye princes of the house of Israel; *Is it* not for you to know judgment?

Mi 6:8 He hath shewed thee, O man, what *is* good; and what doth the LORD require of thee, but to do justly, and to love mercy, and to walk humbly with thy God?

Zec 7:9 Thus speaketh the LORD of hosts, saying, Execute true judgment, and shew mercy and compassions every man to his brother:

Zec 8:16 These *are* the things that ye shall do; Speak ye every man the truth to his neighbour; execute the judg-ment of truth and peace in your gates:

Lu 11:42 But woe unto you, Phari-sees! for ye tithe mint and rue and all manner of herbs, and pass over judg-ment and the love of God: these ought ye to have done, and not to leave the other undone.

Jn 7:24 Judge not according to the appearance, but judge righteous judg-ment.

Jn 7:51 Doth our law judge *any* man, before it hear him, and know what he doeth?

Ro 13:7 Render therefore to all their dues: tribute to whom tribute *is due;*

custom to whom custom; fear to whom fear; honour to whom honour.

Ph 4:8 Finally, brethren, whatsoever things are true, whatsoever things *are* honest, whatsoever things *are* just, whatsoever things *are* pure, whatso-ever things *are* lovely, whatsoever things *are* of good report; if *there be* any virtue, and if *there be* any praise, think on these things.

Col 4:1 Masters, give unto *your* ser-vants that which is just and equal; knowing that ye also have a Master in heaven.

Tit 1:8 But a lover of hospitality, a lover of good men, sober, just, holy, temperate;

3. Human

1 S 30:24 For who will hearken unto you in this matter? but as his part *is* that goeth down to the battle, so *shall* his part *be* that tarrieth by the stuff: they shall part alike.

2 S 8:15 And David reigned over all Israel; and David executed judgment and justice unto all his people.

1 K 1:52 And Solomon said, If he will shew himself a worthy man, there shall not an hair of him fall to the earth: but if wickedness shall be found in him, he shall die.

1 K 3:28 And all Israel heard of the judgment which the king had judged; and they feared the king: for they saw that the wisdom of God *was* in him, to do judgment.

2 K 14:6 But the children of the mur-derers he slew not: according unto that which is written in the book of the law of Moses, wherein the LORD commanded, saying, The fathers shall not be put to death for the children, nor the children be put to death for the fathers; but every man shall be put to death for his own sin.

Je 22:15 Shalt thou reign, because thou closest *thyself* in cedar? did not thy father eat and drink, and do judg-ment and justice, *and* then *it was* well with him?

Ac 25:16 To whom I answered, It is not the manner of the Romans to deliver any man to die, before that he which is accused have the accusers face to face, and have licence to answer for himself concerning the crime laid against him.

4. Unsparing

THE ANGELS THAT SINNED
2 Pe 2:4 For if God spared not the angels that sinned, but cast *them* down to hell, and delivered *them* into chains of darkness, to be reserved unto judgment;

THE ANTEDILUVIANS
2 Pe 2:5–6 And spared not the old world, but saved Noah the eighth *person,* a preacher of righteousness, bringing in the flood upon the world of the ungodly;

And turning the cities of Sodom and Gomorrah into ashes condemned *them* with an overthrow, making *them* an ensample unto those that after should live ungodly;

THE EGYPTIANS
Ex 12:29 And it came to pass, that at midnight the LORD smote all the firstborn in the land of Egypt, from the firstborn of Pharaoh that sat on his throne unto the firstborn of the captive that *was* in the dungeon; and all the firstborn of cattle.

THE CANAANITES
De 7:23 But the LORD thy God shall deliver them unto thee, and shall destroy them with a mighty destruction, until they be destroyed.

THE AMALEKITES
1 S 15:18 And the LORD sent thee on a journey, and said, Go and utterly destroy the sinners the Amalekites, and fight against them until they be consumed.

THE NATURAL BRANCHES (THE JEWS)
Ro 11:21 For if God spared not the natural branches, *take heed* lest he also spare not thee.

GOD'S OWN SON
Ro 8:32 He that spared not his own Son, but delivered him up for us all,

how shall he not with him also freely give us all things?

See **INJUSTICE**

JUSTIFICATION, *God's declaration that the believing sinner is righteous and acceptable before him*

1. By Faith
Ge 15:6 And he believed in the LORD; and he counted it to him for righteousness.

Is 45:25 In the LORD shall all the seed of Israel be justified, and shall glory.

Lu 18:14 I tell you, this man went down to his house justified *rather* than the other: for every one that exalteth himself shall be abased; and he that humbleth himself shall be exalted.

Ac 13:39 And by him all that believe are justified from all things, from which ye could not be justified by the law of Moses.

Ro 3:22 Even the righteousness of God *which is* by faith of Jesus Christ unto all and upon all them that believe: for there is no difference:

Ro 3:28 Therefore we conclude that a man is justified by faith without the deeds of the law.

Ro 4:5 But to him that worketh not, but believeth on him that justifieth the ungodly, his faith is counted for righteousness.

Ro 4:11 And he received the sign of circumcision, a seal of the righteousness of the faith which *he had yet* being uncircumcised: that he might be the father of all them that believe, though they be not circumcised; that righteousness might be imputed unto them also:

Ro 5:1 Therefore being justified by faith, we have peace with God through our Lord Jesus Christ:

Ro 5:9 Much more then, being now justified by his blood, we shall be saved from wrath through him.

Ro 5:18 Therefore as by the offence of one *judgment came* upon all men to condemnation; even so by the righteousness of one *the free gift came* upon all men unto justification of life.

Ro 8:30 Moreover whom he did predestinate, them he also called: and whom he called, them he also justified: and whom he justified, them he also glorified.

Ro 8:33 Who shall lay any thing to the charge of God's elect? *It is* God that justifieth.

Ro 9:30 What shall we say then? That the Gentiles, which followed not after righteousness, have attained to righteousness, even the righteousness which is of faith.

Ro 10:4 For Christ *is* the end of the law for righteousness to every one that believeth.

1 Co 4:4 For I know nothing by myself; yet am I not hereby justified: but he that judgeth me is the Lord.

1 Co 6:11 And such were some of you: but ye are washed, but ye are sanctified, but ye are justified in the name of the Lord Jesus, and by the Spirit of our God.

2 Co 5:21 For he hath made him *to be* sin for us, who knew no sin; that we might be made the righteousness of God in him.

Ga 2:16 Knowing that a man is not justified by the works of the law, but by the faith of Jesus Christ, even we have believed in Jesus Christ, that we might be justified by the faith of Christ, and not by the works of the law: for by the works of the law shall no flesh be justified.

Ga 2:21 I do not frustrate the grace of God: for if righteousness *come* by the law, then Christ is dead in vain.

Ga 3:6 Even as Abraham believed God, and it was accounted to him for righteousness.

Ga 3:11 But that no man is justified by the law in the sight of God, *it is* evident: for, The just shall live by faith.

Ga 3:24 Wherefore the law was our schoolmaster *to bring us* unto Christ, that we might be justified by faith.

Ga 5:5 For we through the Spirit wait for the hope of righteousness by faith.

Ph 3:9 And be found in him, not having mine own righteousness, which is of the law, but that which is through the faith of Christ, the righteousness which is of God by faith:

Tit 3:7 That being justified by his grace, we should be made heirs according to the hope of eternal life.

He 11:7 By faith Noah, being warned of God of things not seen as yet, moved with fear, prepared an ark to the saving of his house; by the which he condemned the world, and became heir of the righteousness which is by faith.

Ja 2:23 And the scripture was fulfilled which saith, Abraham believed God, and it was imputed unto him for righteousness: and he was called the Friend of God.

2. Of Self Impossible

Jb 9:2 I know *it is* so of a truth: but how should man be just with God?

Jb 9:31 Yet shalt thou plunge me in the ditch, and mine own clothes shall abhor me.

Jb 25:4 How then can man be justified with God? or how can he be clean *that is* born of a woman?

Jb 32:2 Then was kindled the wrath of Elihu the son of Barachel the Buzite, of the kindred of Ram: against Job was his wrath kindled, because he justified himself rather than God.

Ps 143:2 And enter not into judgment with thy servant: for in thy sight shall no man living be justified.

Je 2:22 For though thou wash thee with nitre, and take thee much sope, *yet* thine iniquity is marked before me, saith the Lord GOD.

Eze 14:14 Though these three men, Noah, Daniel, and Job, were in it, they should deliver *but* their own souls by their righteousness, saith the Lord GOD.

Lu 10:29 But he, willing to justify himself, said unto Jesus, And who is my neighbour?

Ro 3:20 Therefore by the deeds of the law there shall no flesh be justified in his sight: for by the law *is* the knowledge of sin.

Ga 5:4 Christ is become of no effect unto you, whosoever of you are justified by the law; ye are fallen from grace.

See **FAITH, GRACE, SALVATION**

K

KADESH-BARNEA, *a town on the southern frontier of Canaan*

Kadesh-Barnea was the well-known camping place of the children of Israel (Nu 13:26), a stopping place for Abraham (Ge 20:1), and the southernmost part of Israel's territory (Nu 34:4; Jos 10:41).

Nu 13:26; 32:8; 33:37; 34:4; De 1:2, 19; 2:14; 9:23; Jos 10:41; 14:6; 15:3; Jud 11:16

KANAH *See* **RIVERS**

KEDAR, *a clan of Ishmaelites*

Ps 120:5; Is 21:16; 42:11; 60:7; Je 2:10; 49:28

KEDESH, *a city of refuge*

Kedesh, or Kedesh-Naphtali, was a former Canaanite royal city. Captured by Joshua (Jos 12:22), it afterward became one of the six cities of refuge (Jos 20:7). It was the home of Barak, where he and Deborah gathered the forces from Naphtali and Zebulun for war against Sisera (Jud 4:6–11). Naphtali, Barak, Deborah, and Jael were buried here. Tiglath-pileser III captured the city in 734 B.C. and exiled its inhabitants to Assyria (2 K 15:29).

Jos 20:7; 21:32; Jud 4:6, 11; 2 K 15:29; 1 Chr 6:76

KEEPERS, *of the prison*

Ge 39:22; Ac 5:23; 12:6; 16:27, 36

KEILAH, *a city of Judah*

Jos 15:44; 1 S 23:1; Ne 3:17

KENITES, *pertaining to coppersmiths*

1. A Canaanitish Tribe or Nation

Ge 15:19; Nu 24:21; 1 S 15:6

2. Descendants of Jethro or Hobab

Jud 1:16; 4:11

KEYS, *symbols of authority*

Is 22:22; Mt 16:19; Re 1:18; 3:7; 9:1; 20:1

KIBROTH HATTAAVAH, *quails sent to the Israelites*

Nu 11:34; 33:16; De 9:22

KIDNAPPING, *abducting a person, often for ransom*

Ex 21:16; De 24:7; Jud 21:21

KIDRON, *or Cedron, a brook or valley on the east of Jerusalem*

The Valley of the Kidron rises north of Jerusalem in an insignificant depression known as Wadi el Joz. After angling in an easterly direction for a half mile, it turns southward, passing between the eastern wall of Jerusalem and the Mount of Olives. It passes through the King's Vale and the King's Garden (2 K 21:18), to finally join with the Valley of Hinnom at the En-rogel Spring. The valley was likely the site of many royal burials (e.g., 1 K 2:10, 15:8; 2 K 8:24). It became a favored spot for idol worship throughout Israel's history (2 K 23:12–13). Reformers of Israel often had pagan idols and temples demolished and dumped into the valley (2 Chr 29:16; 2 K 23:4–6).

2 S 15:23; 1 K 2:37; 15:13; 2 K 23:6; 2 Chr 15:16; 29:16; Ne 2:15; Je 31:40; Jn 18:1

KINDNESS, *warmheartedness, goodness, generosity, helpfulness*

1. Prescribed

Ge 40:14 But think on me when it shall be well with thee, and shew kindness, I pray thee, unto me, and make mention of me unto Pharaoh, and bring me out of this house:

Ex 23:5 If thou see the ass of him that hateth thee lying under his burden, and wouldest forbear to help him, thou shalt surely help with him.

Jos 2:12 Now therefore, I pray you, swear unto me by the LORD, since I have shewed you kindness, that ye will also shew kindness unto my father's house, and give me a true token:

1 S 20:15 But *also* thou shalt not cut off thy kindness from my house for ever: no, not when the LORD hath cut off the enemies of David every one from the face of the earth.

2 S 2:5 And David sent messengers unto the men of Jabesh-gilead, and said unto them, Blessed *be* ye of the LORD, that ye have shewed this kindness unto your lord, *even* unto Saul, and have buried him.

Ps 112:4 Unto the upright there ariseth light in the darkness: *he is* gracious, and full of compassion, and righteous.

Pr 19:22 The desire of a man *is* his kindness: and a poor man *is* better than a liar.

Is 16:3 Take counsel, execute judgment; make thy shadow as the night in the midst of the noonday; hide the outcasts; bewray not him that wandereth.

Is 58:7 *Is it* not to deal thy bread to the hungry, and that thou bring the poor that are cast out to thy house? when thou seest the naked, that thou cover him; and that thou hide not thyself from thine own flesh?

Mt 1:19 Then Joseph her husband, being a just *man,* and not willing to make her a publick example, was minded to put her away privily.

Ro 12:10 *Be* kindly affectioned one to another with brotherly love; in honour preferring one another;

1 Co 13:4 Charity suffereth long, *and* is kind; charity envieth not; charity vaunteth not itself, is not puffed up,

2 Co 6:6 By pureness, by knowledge, by longsuffering, by kindness, by the Holy Ghost, by love unfeigned,

Ep 4:32 And be ye kind one to another, tenderhearted, forgiving one another, even as God for Christ's sake hath forgiven you.

Col 3:12 Put on therefore, as the elect of God, holy and beloved, bowels of mercies, kindness, humbleness of mind, meekness, longsuffering;

2 Pe 1:5–7 And beside this, giving all diligence, add to your faith virtue; and to virtue knowledge;

And to knowledge temperance; and to temperance patience; and to patience godliness;

And to godliness brotherly kindness; and to brotherly kindness charity.

2. Examples

JOSEPH

Ge 50:21

MOSES

Ex 2:17

BOAZ

Ru 2:16

DAVID

2 S 9:1; Pr 31:26

THE GOOD SAMARITAN

Lu 10:34

THE PHILIPPIAN JAILER

Ac 16:33

THE BARBARIANS

Ac 28:2

See **CRUELTY**

KINGDOM, *SPIRITUAL, God's present and eternal sphere of authority*

1. Conditions of Entrance

SYMPATHETIC SERVICE

Mt 25:34; Mt 25:35; Lu 6:20

PERSEVERANCE

Lu 9:62

NEW BIRTH

Jn 3:3

Ac 14:22; 2 Th 1:5

Ja 2:5

2. Comes with Power

Da 2:44 And in the days of these kings shall the God of heaven set up a kingdom, which shall never be destroyed: and the kingdom shall not be left to other people, *but* it shall break in pieces and consume all these kingdoms, and it shall stand for ever.

Mk 9:1 And he said unto them, Verily I say unto you, That there be some of them that stand here, which shall not taste of death, till they have seen the kingdom of God come with power.

1 Co 4:20 For the kingdom of God *is* not in word, but in power.

Re 11:17 Saying, We give thee thanks, O Lord God Almighty, which art, and wast, and art to come; because thou hast taken to thee thy great power, and hast reigned.

Re 12:10 And I heard a loud voice saying in heaven, Now is come salvation, and strength, and the kingdom of our God, and the power of his Christ: for the accuser of our brethren is cast down, which accused them before our God day and night.

Re 19:6 And I heard as it were the voice of a great multitude, and as the voice of many waters, and as the voice of mighty thunderings, saying, Alleluia: for the Lord God omnipotent reigneth.

3. Eternal Kingdom of God and Christ

2 S 7:16 And thine house and thy kingdom shall be established for ever before thee: thy throne shall be established for ever.

1 Chr 17:12 He shall build me an house, and I will stablish his throne for ever.

Ps 72:5 They shall fear thee as long as the sun and moon endure, throughout all generations.

Ps 89:29 His seed also will I make *to* endure for ever, and his throne as the days of heaven.

Ps 89:36 His seed shall endure for ever, and his throne as the sun before me.

Ps 145:13 Thy kingdom *is* an everlasting kingdom, and thy dominion endureth throughout all generations.

Ps 146:10 The LORD shall reign for ever, *even* thy God, O Zion, unto all generations. Praise ye the LORD.

Is 9:7 Of the increase of *his* government and peace *there shall be* no end, upon the throne of David, and upon his kingdom, to order it, and to establish it with judgment and with justice from henceforth even for ever. The zeal of the LORD of hosts will perform this.

Eze 37:25 And they shall dwell in the land that I have given unto Jacob my servant, wherein your fathers have dwelt; and they shall dwell therein, *even* they, and their children, and their children's children for ever: and my servant David *shall be* their prince for ever.

Da 2:44 And in the days of these kings shall the God of heaven set up a kingdom, which shall never be destroyed: and the kingdom shall not be left to other people, *but* it shall break in pieces and consume all these kingdoms, and it shall stand for ever.

Da 4:3 How great *are* his signs! and how mighty *are* his wonders! his kingdom *is* an everlasting kingdom, and his dominion *is* from generation to generation.

Da 4:34 And at the end of the days I Nebuchadnezzar lifted up mine eyes unto heaven, and mine understanding returned unto me, and I blessed the most High, and I praised and honoured him that liveth for ever, whose dominion *is* an everlasting dominion, and his kingdom *is* from generation to generation:

Da 6:26 I make a decry dominion of my kingdom men tremble and fear before the God of Daniel: for he is the living God, and stedfast for ever, and his kingdom *that* which shall not be destroyed, and his dominion *shall be even* unto the end.

Da 7:13–14 I saw in the night visions, and, behold, *one* like the Son of man came with the clouds of heaven, and came to the Ancient of days, and they brought him near before him.

Da 7:27 And the kingdom and dominion, and the greatness of the kingdom under the whole heaven, shall be given to the people of the saints of the most High, whose kingdom *is* an everlasting kingdom, and all dominions shall serve and obey him.

Mi 4:7 And I will make her that halted a remnant, and her that was cast far off a strong nation: and the LORD shall reign over them in mount Zion from henceforth, even for ever.

Lu 1:32–33 He shall be great, and shall be called the Son of the Highest: and the Lord God shall give unto him the throne of his father David:

And he shall reign over the house of Jacob for ever; and of his kingdom there shall be no end.

He 12:28 Wherefore we receiving a kingdom which cannot be moved, let us have grace, whereby we may serve God acceptably with reverence and godly fear:

2 Pe 1:11 For so an entrance shall be ministered unto you abundantly into the everlasting kingdom of our Lord and Saviour Jesus Christ.

Re 11:15 And the seventh angel sounded; and there were great voices in heaven, saying, The kingdoms of this world are become *the kingdoms* of our Lord, and of his Christ; and he shall reign for ever and ever.

4. Its Growth

See **MISSIONS**

5. Near at Hand

Is 56:1 Thus saith the LORD, Keep ye judgment, and do justice: for my salvation *is* near to come, and my righteousness to be revealed.

Mt 3:2 And saying, Repent ye: for the kingdom of heaven is at hand.

Mt 4:17 From that time Jesus began to preach, and to say, Repent: for the kingdom of heaven is at hand.

Mt 10:7 And as ye go, preach, saying, The kingdom of heaven is at hand.

Lu 21:31 So likewise ye, when ye see these things come to pass, know ye that the kingdom of God is nigh at hand.

6. Preached

Mk 1:14 Now after that John was put in prison, Jesus came into Galilee, preaching the gospel of the kingdom of God,

Lu 4:43 And he said unto them, I must preach the kingdom of God to other cities also: for therefore am I sent.

Lu 8:1 And it came to pass afterward, that he went throughout every city and village, preaching and shewing the glad tidings of the kingdom of God: and the twelve *were* with him,

Lu 9:2 And he sent them to preach the kingdom of God, and to heal the sick.

Lu 16:16 The law and the prophets *were* until John: since that time the kingdom of God is preached, and every man presseth into it.

Ac 1:3 To whom also he shewed himself alive after his passion by many infallible proofs, being seen of them forty days, and speaking of the things pertaining to the kingdom of God:

Ac 8:12 But when they believed Philip preaching the things concerning the kingdom of God, and the name of Jesus Christ, they were baptized, both men and women.

Ac 20:25 And now, behold, I know that ye all, among whom I have gone preaching the kingdom of God, shall see my face no more.

Ac 28:23 And when they had appointed him a day, there came many to him into *his* lodging; to whom he expounded and testified the kingdom of God, persuading them concerning Jesus, both out of the law of Moses, and *out of* the prophets, from morning till evening.

7. *Of Christ*, realm of Christ's rule

Mt 13:41 The Son of man shall send forth his angels, and they shall gather out of his kingdom all things that offend, and them which do iniquity;

Mt 16:28 Verily I say unto you, There be some standing here, which shall not taste of death, till they see the Son of man coming in his kingdom.

Lu 1:33 And he shall reign over the house of Jacob for ever; and of his kingdom there shall be no end.

Lu 22:30 That ye may eat and drink at my table in my kingdom, and sit on thrones judging the twelve tribes of Israel.

Lu 23:42 And he said unto Jesus, Lord, remember me when thou comest into thy kingdom.

Jn 18:36 Jesus answered, My kingdom is not of this world: if my kingdom were of this world, then would my servants fight, that I should not be delivered to the Jews: but now is my kingdom not from hence.

1 Co 15:24 Then *cometh* the end, when he shall have delivered up the kingdom to God, even the Father; when he shall have put down all rule and all authority and power.

Ph 2:10 That at the name of Jesus every knee should bow, of *things* in heaven, and *things* in earth, and *things* under the earth;

Col 1:13 Who hath delivered us from the power of darkness, and hath translated *us* into the kingdom of his dear Son:

2 Ti 4:1 I charge *thee* therefore before God, and the Lord Jesus Christ, who shall judge the quick and the dead at his appearing and his kingdom;

2 Ti 4:18 And the Lord shall deliver me from every evil work, and will preserve *me* unto his heavenly kingdom: to whom *be* glory for ever and ever. Amen.

He 1:8 But unto the Son *he saith,* Thy throne, O God, *is* for ever and ever: a sceptre of righteousness *is* the sceptre of thy kingdom.

2 Pe 1:11 For so an entrance shall be ministered unto you abundantly into the everlasting kingdom of our Lord and Saviour Jesus Christ.

Re 1:9 I John, who also am your brother, and companion in tribulation, and in the kingdom and patience of Jesus Christ, was in the isle that is called Patmos, for the word of God, and for the testimony of Jesus Christ.

Re 11:15 And the seventh angel sounded; and there were great voices in heaven, saying, The kingdoms of this world are become *the kingdoms* of our Lord, and of his Christ; and he shall reign for ever and ever.

Re 17:14 These shall make war with the Lamb, and the Lamb shall overcome them: for he is Lord of lords, and King of kings: and they that are with him *are* called, and chosen, and faithful.

8. *Parables and Comparisons*

Mt 13:24 Another parable put he forth unto them, saying, The kingdom of heaven is likened unto a man which sowed good seed in his field:

Mt 13:31 Another parable put he forth unto them, saying, The kingdom of heaven is like to a grain of mustard seed, which a man took, and sowed in his field:

Mt 13:33 Another parable spake he unto them; The kingdom of heaven is like unto leaven, which a woman took, and hid in three measures of meal, till the whole was leavened.

Mt 13:44 Again, the kingdom of heaven is like unto treasure hid in a field; the which when a man hath found, he hideth, and for joy thereof goeth and selleth all that he hath, and buyeth that field.

Mt 13:47 Again, the kingdom of heaven is like unto a net, that was cast into the sea, and gathered of every kind:

Mt 13:52 Then said he unto them, Therefore every scribe *which is* instructed unto the kingdom of heaven is like unto a man *that is* an householder, which bringeth forth out of his treasure *things* new and old.

Mt 18:23 Therefore is the kingdom of heaven likened unto a certain king, which would take account of his servants.

Mt 20:1 For the kingdom of heaven is like unto a man *that is* an householder, which went out early in the morning to hire labourers into his vineyard.

Mt 22:2 The kingdom of heaven is like unto a certain king, which made a marriage for his son,

Mt 25:1 Then shall the kingdom of heaven be likened unto ten virgins, which took their lamps, and went forth to meet the bridegroom.

Mk 4:26 And he said, So is the kingdom of God, as if a man should cast seed into the ground;

Mk 4:30 And he said, Whereunto shall we liken the kingdom of God? or with what comparison shall we compare it?

Lu 13:18 Then said he, Unto what is the kingdom of God like? and whereunto shall I resemble it?

Lu 13:20 And again he said, Whereunto shall I liken the kingdom of God?

Lu 18:24 And when Jesus saw that he was very sorrowful, he said, How hardly shall they that have riches enter into the kingdom of God!

1 Co 4:20 For the kingdom of God *is* not in word, but in power

See **CHURCH, NATION**

KINGS

1. FIRST

Author: Unknown.

Date Written: Shortly before 587 B.C.

Purpose: To give an account of the reigns of the kings from Solomon to Jehoshaphat (Judah) and Ahaziah (Israel), contrasting those who obeyed God and those who did not.

To Whom Written: The nation of Israel.

Main Theme: The disruption and division of the kingdom because of the moral and spiritual decline of the Israelite community and its kings.

Key Words: Divided kingdom.

Key Verses: 9:4–5, 11:11.

2. SECOND

Author: Unknown.

Date Written: Shortly before 587 B.C. except for chapters 24–25 which were written about 550 B.C.

Purpose: To give an account of the reigns of the kings from Ahaziah (North) and Jehoram (South) until the fall of each kingdom; and to demonstrate God's pursuit of his people through the message of his prophets.

To Whom Written: The nation of Israel.

Main Theme: The history of the kingdoms of Israel and Judah, from the latter part of the reign of Ahaziah in Israel, and Jehoram in Judah, up to the time of the captivities. The book depicts the powerful influence of rulers upon a nation.

Key Words: Captured kingdoms.

Key Verses: 17:13–14.

KINGSHIP, *DIVINE*

Ex 15:18 The LORD shall reign for ever and ever.

1 Chr 16:31 Let the heavens be glad, and let the earth rejoice: and let *men* say among the nations, The LORD reigneth.

2 Chr 13:8 And now ye think to withstand the kingdom of the LORD in the hand of the sons of David; and ye *be* a great multitude, and *there are* with you golden calves, which Jeroboam made you for gods.

2 Chr 20:6 And said, O LORD God of our fathers, *art* not thou God in heaven? and rulest *not* thou over all the kingdoms of the heathen? and in thine hand *is there not* power and might, so that none is able to withstand thee?

Jb 25:2 Dominion and fear *are* with him, he maketh peace in his high places.

Ps 5:2 Hearken unto the voice of my cry, my King, and my God: for unto thee will I pray.

Ps 10:16 The LORD *is* King for ever and ever: the heathen are perished out of his land.

Ps 22:28 For the kingdom *is* the LORD's: and he *is* the governor among the nations.

Ps 24:10 Who is this King of glory? The LORD of hosts, he *is* the King of glory. Selah.

Ps 29:10 The LORD sitteth upon the flood; yea, the LORD sitteth King for ever.

Ps 44:4 Thou art my King, O God: command deliverances for Jacob.

Ps 47:7 For God *is* the King of all the earth: sing ye praises with understanding.

Ps 66:7 He ruleth by his power for ever; his eyes behold the nations: let not the rebellious exalt themselves. Selah.

Ps 67:4 O let the nations be glad and sing for joy: for thou shalt judge the people righteously, and govern the nations upon earth. Selah.

Ps 68:24 They have seen thy goings, O God; *even* the goings of my God, my King, in the sanctuary.

Ps 74:12 For God *is* my King of old, working salvation in the midst of the earth.

Ps 84:3 Yea, the sparrow hath found an house, and the swallow a nest for herself, where she may lay her young, *even* thine altars, hosts, my King, and my God.

Ps 89:18 For the LORD *is* our defence; and the Holy One of Israel *is* our king.

Ps 93:1 The LORD reigneth, he is clothed with majesty; the LORD is clothed with strength, *wherewith* he hath girded himself: the world also is stablished, that it cannot be moved.

Ps 95:3 For the LORD *is* a great God, and a great King above all gods.

Ps 96:10 Say among the heathen *that* the LORD reigneth: the world also shall be established that it shall not be moved: he shall judge the people righteously.

Ps 97:1 The LORD reigneth; let the earth rejoice; let the multitude of isles be glad *thereof.*

Ps 98:6 With trumpets and sound of cornet make a joyful noise before the LORD, the King.

Ps 99:1 The LORD reigneth; let the people tremble: he sitteth *between* the cherubims; let the earth be moved.

Ps 145:1 I will extol thee, my God, O king; and I will bless thy name for ever and ever.

Ps 146:10 The LORD shall reign for ever, *even* thy God, O Zion, unto all generations. Praise ye the LORD.

Ps 149:2 Let Israel rejoice in him that made him: let the children of Zion be joyful in their King.

Is 6:5 Then said I, Woe *is* me! for I am undone; because I *am* a man of unclean lips, and I dwell in the midst of a people of unclean lips: for mine eyes have seen the King, the LORD of hosts.

Is 24:23 Then the moon shall be confounded, and the sun ashamed, when the LORD of hosts shall reign in mount Zion, a and before his ancients gloriously.

Is 33:22 For the LORD *is* our judge, the LORD *is* our lawgiver, the LORD *is* our king; he will save us.

Is 43:15 I *am* the LORD, your Holy One, the creator of Israel, your King.

Is 44:6 Thus saith the LORD the King of Israel, and his redeemer the LORD of hosts; I *am* the first, and I *am* the last; and beside me *there is* no God.

Is 52:7 How beautiful upon the mountains are the feet of him that bringeth good tidings, that publisheth peace; that bringeth good tidings of good, that publisheth salvation; that saith unto Zion, Thy God reigneth!

Je 10:7 Who would not fear thee, O King of nations? for to thee doth it appertain: forasmuch as among all the wise *men* of the nations, and in all their kingdoms, *there is* none like unto thee.

Je 10:10 But the LORD *is* the true God, he *is* the living God, and an everlasting king: at his wrath the earth shall tremble, and the nations shall not be able to abide his indignation.

Je 46:18 *As* I live, saith the King, whose name *is* the LORD of hosts, Surely as Tabor *is* among the mountains, and as Carmel by the sea, *so* shall he come.

Je 48:15 Moab is spoiled, and gone up *out of* her cities, and his chosen young men are gone down to the slaughter, saith the King, whose name *is* the LORD of hosts.

Je 51:57 And I will make drunk her princes, and her wise *men,* her captains, and her rulers, and her mighty men: and they shall sleep a perpetual sleep, and not wake, saith the King, whose name *is* the LORD of hosts.

Da 2:47 The king answered unto Daniel, and said, Of a truth *it is,* that your God *is* a God of gods, and a Lord of kings, and a revealer of secrets, seeing thou couldst reveal this secret.

Da 4:17 This matter *is* by the decree of the watchers, and the demand by the word of the holy ones: to the intent that the living may know that the most High ruleth in the kingdom of men, and giveth it to whomsoever he will, and setteth up over it the basest of men.

Da 4:25 That they shall drive thee from men, and thy dwelling shall be with the beasts of the field, and they shall make thee to eat grass as oxen, and they shall wet thee with the dew of heaven, and seven times shall pass over thee, till thou know that the most High ruleth in the kingdom of men, and giveth it to whomsoever he will.

Da 4:37 Now I Nebuchadnezzar praise and extol and honour the King of heaven, all whose works *are* truth, and his ways judgment: and those that walk in pride he is able to abase.

Da 5:21 And he was driven from the sons of men; and his heart was made like the beasts, and his dwelling *was* with the wild asses: they fed him with grass like oxen, and his body was wet with the dew of heaven; till he knew that the most high God ruled in the kingdom of men, and *that* he appointeth over it whomsoever he will.

Mi 2:13 The breaker is come up before them: they have broken up, and have passed through the gate, and are gone out by it: and their king shall pass before them, and the LORD on the head of them.

Mi 4:7 And I will make her that halted a remnant, and her that was cast far off a strong nation: and the LORD shall reign over them in mount Zion from henceforth, even for ever.

Zep 3:15 The LORD hath taken away thy judgments, he hath cast out thine enemy: the king of Israel, *even* the LORD, *is* in the midst of thee: thou shalt not see evil any more.

Zec 14:16 And it shall come to pass, *that* every one that is left of all the nations which came against Jerusalem shall even go up from year to year to worship the King, the LORD of hosts, and to keep the feast of tabernacles.

Mal 1:14 But cursed *be* the deceiver, which hath in his flock a male, and voweth, and sacrificeth unto the LORD a corrupt thing: for I *am* a great King, saith the LORD of hosts, and my name *is* dreadful among the heathen.

Ro 14:11 For it is written, *As* I live, saith the Lord, every knee shall bow to me, and every tongue shall confess to God.

1 Ti 1:17 Now unto the King eternal, immortal, invisible, the only wise God, *be* honour and glory for ever and ever. Amen.

Re 11:17 Saying, We give thee thanks, O Lord God Almighty, which art, and wast, and art to come; because thou hast taken to thee thy great power, and hast reigned.

Re 15:3 And they sing the song of Moses the servant of God, and the song of the Lamb, saying, Great and marvellous *are* thy works, Lord God Almighty; just and true *are* thy ways, thou King of saints.

Re 19:6 And I heard as it were the voice of a great multitude, and as the voice of many waters, and as the voice of mighty thunderings, saying, Alleluia: for the Lord God omnipotent reigneth.

1. Of God

Nu 14:21 But *as* truly *as* I live, all the earth shall be filled with the glory of the LORD.

Ps 47:7 For God *is* the King of all the earth: sing ye praises with understanding.

Ps 59:13 Consume *them* in wrath, consume *them,* that they *may* not *be:* and let them know that God ruleth in Jacob unto the ends of the earth. Selah.

Ps 65:5 By terrible things in righteousness wilt thou answer us, O God of our salvation; *who art* the confidence of all the ends of the earth, and of them that are afar off *upon* the sea:

Ps 67:7 God shall bless us; and all the ends of the earth shall fear him.

Ps 68:31 Princes shall come out of Egypt; Ethiopia shall soon stretch out her hands unto God.

Ps 72:8 He shall have dominion also from sea to sea, and from the river unto the ends of the earth.

Ps 72:11 Yea, all kings shall fall down before him: all nations shall serve him.

Ps 82:8 Arise, O God, judge the earth: for thou shalt inherit all nations.

Ps 102:22 When the people are gathered together, and the kingdoms, to serve the LORD.

Ps 103:19 The LORD hath prepared his throne in the heavens; and his kingdom ruleth over all.

Ps 108:9 Moab *is* my washpot; over Edom will I cast out my shoe; over Philistia will I triumph.

Is 54:5 For thy Maker *is* thine husband; the LORD of hosts *is* his name; and thy Redeemer the Holy One of Israel; The God of the whole earth shall he be called.

Je 3:17 At that time they shall call Jerusalem the throne of the LORD; and all the nations shall be gathered unto it, to the name of the LORD, to Jerusalem: neither shall they walk any more after the imagination of their evil heart.

Da 7:27 And the kingdom and dominion, and the greatness of the kingdom under the whole heaven, shall be given to the people of the saints of the most High, whose kingdom *is* an everlasting kingdom, and all dominions shall serve and obey him.

Mi 5:4 And he shall stand and feed in the strength of the LORD, in the majesty of the name of the LORD his God;

and they shall abide: for now shall he be great unto the ends of the earth.

Zec 9:10 And I will cut off the chariot from Ephraim, and the horse from Jerusalem, and the battle bow shall be cut off: and he shall speak peace unto the heathen: and his dominion *shall be* from sea *even* to sea, and from river *even* to the ends of the earth.

Zec 14:9 And the LORD shall be king over all the earth: in that day shall there be one LORD, and his name one.

See **GOD**

2. Of Christ

Ps 2:6 Yet have I set my king upon my holy hill of Zion.

Ps 45:1 My heart is inditing a good matter: I speak of the things which I have made touching the king: my tongue *is* the pen of a ready writer.

Is 9:7 Of the increase of *his* government and peace *there shall be* no end, upon the throne of David, and upon his kingdom, to order it, and to establish it with judgment and with justice from henceforth even for ever. The zeal of the LORD of hosts will perform this.

Is 32:1 Behold, a king shall reign in righteousness, and princes shall rule in judgment.

Je 23:5 Behold, the days come, saith the LORD, that I will raise unto David a righteous Branch, and a King shall reign and prosper, and shall execute judgment and justice in the earth.

Eze 21:27 I will overturn, overturn, overturn, it: and it shall be no *more,* until he come whose right it is; and I will give it *him.*

Eze 37:25 And they shall dwell in the land that I have given unto Jacob my servant, wherein your fathers have dwelt; and they shall dwell therein, *even* they, and their children, and their children's children for ever: and my servant David *shall be* their prince for ever.

Da 7:14 And there was given him dominion, and glory, and a kingdom, that all people, nations, and languages, should serve him: his dominion *is* an everlasting dominion, which shall not pass away, and his kingdom *that* which shall not be destroyed.

Mi 5:2 But thou, Bethlehem Ephratah, *though* thou be little among the thousands of Judah, *yet* out of thee shall he come forth unto me *that is* to be ruler in Israel; whose goings forth *have been* from of old, from everlasting.

Zec 6:13 Even he shall build the temple of the LORD; and he shall bear the glory, and shall sit and rule upon his throne; and he shall be a priest upon his throne: and the counsel of peace shall be between them both.

Zec 9:9 Rejoice greatly, O daughter of Zion; shout, O daughter of Jerusalem: behold, thy King cometh unto thee: he *is* just, and having salvation; lowly, and riding upon an ass, and upon a colt the foal of an ass.

Mt 2:2 Saying, Where is he that is born King of the Jews? for we have seen his star in the east, and are come to worship him.

Mt 2:6 And thou Bethlehem, in the land of Juda, art not the least among the princes of Juda: for out of thee shall come a Governor, that shall rule my people Israel.

Mt 16:28 Verily I say unto you, There be some standing here, which shall not taste of death, till they see the Son of man coming in his kingdom.

Mt 21:5 Tell ye the daughter of Sion, Behold, thy King cometh unto thee, meek, and sitting upon an ass, and a colt the foal of an ass.

Mt 25:34 Then shall the King say unto them on his right hand, Come, ye blessed of my Father, inherit the kingdom prepared for you from the foundation of the world:

Mt 25:40 And the King shall answer and say unto them, Verily I say unto you, Inasmuch as ye have done *it* unto one of the least of these my brethren, ye have done *it* unto me.

Mt 27:11 And Jesus stood before the governor: and the governor asked him, saying, Art thou the King of the Jews? And Jesus said unto him, Thou sayest.

Mt 27:37 And set up over his head his accusation written, THIS IS JESUS THE KING OF THE JEWS.

Mk 11:10 Blessed *be* the kingdom of our father David, that cometh in the name of the Lord: Hosanna in the highest.

Mk 15:2 And Pilate asked him, Art thou the King of the Jews? And he answering said unto him, Thou sayest it.

Mk 15:26 And the superscription of his accusation was written over, THE KING OF THE JEWS.

Lu 1:33 And he shall reign over the house of Jacob for ever; and of his kingdom there shall be no end.

Lu 19:12 He said therefore, A certain nobleman went into a far country to receive for himself a kingdom, and to return.

Lu 19:38 Saying, Blessed *be* the King that cometh in the name of the Lord: peace in heaven, and glory in the highest.

Lu 23:3 And Pilate asked him, saying, Art thou the King of the Jews? And he answered him and said, Thou sayest *it*.

Jn 1:49 Nathanael answered and saith unto him, Rabbi, thou art the Son of God; thou art the King of Israel.

Jn 12:13 Took branches of palm trees, and went forth to meet him, and cried, Hosanna: Blessed *is* the King of Israel that cometh in the name of the Lord.

Jn 18:33 Then Pilate entered into the judgment hall again, and called Jesus, and said unto him, Art thou the King of the Jews?

Jn 18:37 Pilate therefore said unto him, Art thou a king then? Jesus answered, Thou sayest that I am a king. To this end was I born, and for this cause came I into the world, that I should bear witness unto the truth. Every one that is of the truth heareth my voice.

Jn 19:14 And it was the preparation of the passover, and about the sixth hour: and he saith unto the Jews, Behold your King!

Jn 19:19 And Pilate wrote a title, and put *it* on the cross. And the writing was, JESUS OF NAZARETH THE KING OF THE JEWS.

Ac 2:30 Therefore being a prophet, and knowing that God had sworn with an oath to him, that of the fruit of his loins, according to the flesh, he would raise up Christ to sit on this throne.

Ac 17:7 Whom Jason hath received: and these all do contrary to the decrees of Caesar, saying that there is another king, *one* Jesus.

Ro 15:12 And again, Esaias saith, There shall be a root of Jesse, and he that shall rise to reign over the Gentiles; in him shall the Gentiles trust.

1 Co 15:25 For he must reign, till he hath put all enemies under his feet.

Ep 1:22 And hath put all *things* under his feet, and gave him *to be* the head over all *things* to the church,

1 Ti 6:15 Which in his times he shall shew, *who is* the blessed and only Potentate, the King of kings, and Lord of lords;

Re 3:7 And to the angel of the church in Philadelphia write; These things saith he that is holy, he that is true, he that hath the key of David, he that openeth, and no man shutteth; and shutteth, and no man openeth;

Re 14:14 And I looked, and behold a white cloud, and upon the cloud *one* sat like unto the Son of man, having on his head a golden crown, and in his hand a sharp sickle.

Re 19:15 And out of his mouth goeth a sharp sword, that with it he should smite the nations: and he shall rule them with a rod of iron: and he treadeth the winepress of the fierceness and wrath of Almighty God.

See **CHRIST**

KIRJATH JEARIM, *or Baalah, a city of the Gibeonites*

It was here that the ark of the covenant remained for twenty years from the time that the Philistines sent it back to Israel until the reign of David, when David brought it to Jerusalem (1 Chr 13:5-8).

Jos 9:17; 15:9, 60; 18:14; Jud 18:12; 1 S 6:21; 7:2; 1 Chr 13:5; 2 Chr 1:4; Ezr 2:25; Ne 7:29; Je 26:20

KISH, *father of Saul*

1 S 9:1; 10:21; 14:51; 2 S 21:14; 1 Chr 8:33; 9:39; Ac 13:21

KISHON, *a river north of Mt Carmel*

Jud 4:7, 13; 5:21; 1 K 18:40; Ps 83:9

See **RIVERS**

KISS, *customary as an affectionate salutation*

1. Of Affection

Ge 27:27; 29:11; 31:28, 55; 45:15; 48:10; 50:1; Ex 4:27; 18:7; Ru 1:9; 1 S 10:1; 20:41; 2 S 14:33; 19:39; 1 K 19:20; Lu 7:38, 45; Ac 20:37

2. Of Charity

Ac 20:37; Ro 16:16; 1 Co 16:20; 2 Co 13:12; 1 Th 5:26; 1 Pe 5:14

See **BETRAYAL**

KNIVES, *instruments of hard stone or iron used for cutting*

1 K 18:28; Ezr 1:9; Pr 23:2; Je 36:23

KNOWLEDGE, *understanding gained through experience or study*

1. A Hindrance

A SOURCE OF TEMPTATION

Ge 3:5-6 For God doth know that in the day ye eat thereof, then your eyes shall be opened, and ye shall be as gods, knowing good and evil.

And when the woman saw that the tree *was* good for food, and that it *was* pleasant to the eyes, and a tree to be desired to make *one* wise, she took of the fruit thereof, and did eat, and gave also unto her husband with her; and he did eat.

TENDS TO PRESUMPTION

Ge 3:22-23 And the LORD God said, Behold, the man is become as one of us, to know good and evil: and now, lest he put forth his hand, and take also of the tree of life, and eat, and live for ever:

Therefore the LORD God sent him forth from the garden of Eden, to till the ground from whence he was taken.

ADDS TO THE BURDEN OF LIFE

Ec 1:18 For in much wisdom *is* much grief: and he that increaseth knowledge increaseth sorrow.

EXHAUSTING TO PURSUE

Ec 12:12

BEGETS PRIDE

1 Co 8:1 Now as touching things offered unto idols, we know that we all have knowledge. Knowledge puffeth up, but charity edifieth.

2. A Vain Endeavor

Ec 1:17; Is 44:25; 1 Co 1:20; 3:19; 8:2; 13:2, 8

3. A Help

Pr 2:3–5 Yea, if thou criest after knowledge, *and* liftest up thy voice for understanding;

If thou seekest her as silver, and searchest for her as *for* hid treasures;

Then shalt thou understand the fear of the LORD, and find the knowledge of God.

Pr 3:13 Happy *is* the man *that* findeth wisdom, and the man *that* getteth understanding.

Pr 4:1 Hear, ye children, the instruction of a father, and attend to know understanding.

Pr 4:5 Get wisdom, get understanding: forget *it* not; neither decline from the words of my mouth.

Pr 8:5 O ye simple, understand wisdom: and, ye fools, be ye of an understanding heart.

Pr 15:14 The heart of him that hath understanding seeketh knowledge: but the mouth of fools feedeth on foolishness.

Pr 19:2 Also, *that* the soul *be* without knowledge, *it is* not good; and he that hasteth with *his* feet sinneth.

Pr 23:23 Buy the truth, and sell *it* not; *also* wisdom, and instruction, and understanding.

2 Pe 1:5 And beside this, giving all diligence, add to your faith virtue; and to virtue knowledge;

4. Spiritual

A CAUSE FOR EXULTATION

Je 9:24 But let him that glorieth glory in this, that he understandeth and knoweth me, that I *am* the LORD which exercise lovingkindness, judgment, and righteousness, in the earth: for in these *things* I delight, saith the LORD.

Je 31:34 And they shall teach no more every man his neighbour, and every man his brother, saying, Know the LORD: for they shall all know me, from the least of them unto the greatest of them, saith the LORD; for I will forgive their iniquity, and I will remember their sin no more.

OBTAINED BY ACQUAINTANCE WITH GOD

Ho 6:3 Then shall we know, *if* we follow on to know the LORD: his going forth is prepared as the morning; and he shall come unto us as the rain, as the latter *and* former rain unto the earth.

OBEDIENCE, THE CONDITION OF RECEIVING

Jn 7:16 Jesus answered them, and said, My doctrine is not mine, but his that sent me.

Jn 7:17 If any man will do his will, he shall know of the doctrine, whether it be of God, or *whether* I speak of myself.

LIBERATES THE SOUL FROM ALL ERROR

Jn 8:31 Then said Jesus to those Jews which believed on him, If ye continue in my word, *then* are ye my disciples indeed;

Jn 8:32 And ye shall know the truth, and the truth shall make you free.

LEADS TO ETERNAL LIFE

Jn 17:3 And this is life eternal, that they might know thee the only true God, and Jesus Christ, whom thou hast sent.

Ph 3:10 That I may know him, and the power of his resurrection, and the fellowship of his sufferings, being made conformable unto his death;

Col 1:10 That ye might walk worthy of the Lord unto all pleasing, being fruitful in every good work, and increasing in the knowledge of God;

5. God Makes Himself Known

Ex 6:7; 7:5, 17; 8:10, 22; 9:14, 29; 10:2; 14:4, 18; 16:6, 12; Le 23:43; Nu 16:28; De 4:35; 29:6; Jos 3:10; 4:24; 1 S 17:46; 1 K 8:43, 60; 17:24; 18:37; 20:28; 2 K 5:8; 19:19; 2 Chr 6:33; 12:8; Ne 6:16; Jb 37:7; Ps 9:16; 59:13; 79:10; 83:18; 106:8; 109:27; Is 9:9; 26:9; 41:20; 45:3, 5; 49:23, 26; Eze 5:13; 6:7, 10, 14; 7:4, 9, 27; 11:10; 12:15, 20; 13:9, 14, 21; 14:8, 23; 15:7; 16:62; 17:21; 20:26, 38; 21:5; 22:16, 22; 23:49; 24:24; 25:5, 11, 17; 26:6; 28:22; 29:9, 16; 30:8, 19, 25; 32:15; 33:29; 34:27; 35:4, 9, 15; 36:36; 37:6, 28; 38:16, 23; 39:6; Da 4:17, 25; Jl 2:27; Zec 2:9; 4:9; Mal 2:4; Mt 9:6; Mk 2:10; Lu 5:24; Jn 10:38; 14:31; 17:23

6. Great Truths that May Be Known by Believers

Jb 19:25 For I know *that* my redeemer liveth, and *that* he shall stand at the latter *day* upon the earth:

Is 50:7 For the Lord GOD will help me; therefore shall I not be confounded: therefore have I set my face like a flint, and I know that I shall not be ashamed.

Jn 4:41–42 And many more believed because of his own word;

And said unto the woman, Now we believe, not because of thy saying: for we have heard *him* ourselves, and know that this is indeed the Christ, the Saviour of the world.

Ro 8:28 And we know that all things work together for good to them that love God, to them who are the called according to *his* purpose.

2 Co 5:1 For we know that if our earthly house of *this* tabernacle were dissolved, we have a building of God, an house not made with hands, eternal in the heavens.

2 Ti 1:12 For the which cause I also suffer these things: nevertheless I am not ashamed: for I know whom I have believed, and am persuaded that he is able to keep that which I have committed unto him against that day.

1 Jn 3:2 Beloved, now are we the sons of God, and it doth not yet appear what we shall be: but we know that, when he shall appear, we shall be like him; for we shall see him as he is.

1 Jn 3:14 We know that we have passed from death unto life, because we love the brethren. He that loveth not *his* brother abideth in death.

1 Jn 3:24 And he that keepeth his commandments dwelleth in him, and he in him. And hereby we know that he abideth in us, by the Spirit which he hath given us.

7. Intellectual

Ex 31:3; Jb 34:2; Ps 119:66; Pr 1:4; 2:10; 8:9; 14:6; 15:7; 18:15; 22:20; 24:4; Ec 12:9; Da 1:4, 17; 2:21; 5:12; 12:4; 2 Co 8:7

8. Withheld

a. Reasons for Withholding

Ge 2:17; Ex 33:12; De 29:29; Jud 13:18; Da 8:26; 12:4, 9; Mt 13:11, 17; 24:42; Mk 4:11; 9:10; 13:32; Lu 10:24; Jn 13:7; 16:4, 12; Ac 1:7; 1 Co 13:9, 12; 2 Co 5:7; Ep 3:5; 1 Pe 1:11; 1 Jn 3:2; Re 5:1–2; 10:4

b. Ignorance in Reference to the Future

Ge 27:2; Ps 74:9; Pr 27:1; Ec 3:22; 6:12; 8:7; 9:12; 10:14; 11:2, 6; Is 41:23; Mt 24:43; 25:13; Mk 13:35; Ac 20:22; Ro 15:28; 1 Co 13:12; Ph 2:23; Ja 4:14; Re 3:3

c. Secret Things Belong to God

De 29:29; 34:6; Jud 13:18; 2 K 4:27; Jb 9:10; 10:13; 11:6; 15:8; 42:3; Ps 25:14; Pr 25:2; Ec 7:24; 8:17; Is 52:15; Da 2:18, 29, 47; 8:27; 12:4, 9; Am 3:7; Mt 11:25; 13:11, 35; 24:36, 42; 25:13; Mk 4:11; 13:4, 32; Lu 10:21; 18:34; Jn 3:4, 12; Ac 1:7; Ro 16:25; 1 Co 2:9; 4:1; 13:2, 9; 2 Co 12:4; Ep 3:9; Col 1:26; 1 Pe 1:12; 2 Pe 3:16; Re 5:3; 10:4; 19:12

9. Christ's Knowledge of the Father

Is 11:2 And the spirit of the LORD shall rest upon him, the spirit of wisdom and understanding, the spirit of counsel and might, the spirit of knowledge and of the fear of the LORD;

Mt 11:27 All things are delivered unto me of my Father: and no man knoweth the Son, but the Father; neither knoweth any man the Father, save the Son, and *he* to whomsoever the Son will reveal *him.*

Lu 10:22 All things are delivered to me of my Father: and no man knoweth who the Son is, but the Father; and who the Father is, but the Son, and *he* to whom the Son will reveal *him.*

Jn 5:20 For the Father loveth the Son, and sheweth him all things that himself doeth: and he will shew him greater works than these, that ye may marvel.

Jn 7:29 But I know him: for I am from him, and he hath sent me.

Jn 8:55 Yet ye have not known him; but I know him: and if I should say, I know him not, I shall be a liar like unto you: but I know him, and keep his saying.

Jn 10:15 As the Father knoweth me, even so know I the Father: and I lay down my life for the sheep.

Jn 17:25 O righteous Father, the world hath not known thee: but I have known thee, and these have known that thou hast sent me.

Re 3:8 I know thy works: behold, I have set before thee an open door, and no man can shut it: for thou hast a little strength, and hast kept my word, and hast not denied my name.

10. Examples

Pr 1:5; 9:9; Da 1:4, 17; Ac 7:22; 22:3

11. Experimental

Ge 30:27; Jb 12:12; 32:7; Ps 37:25; Ec 1:14, 16; 7:15; Jn 3:11; 4:42; 9:25; Ph 4:11; 1 Ti 3:10

FITTED ISRAEL TO SYMPATHIZE WITH STRANGERS

Ex 23:9 Also thou shalt not oppress a stranger: for ye know the heart of a stranger, seeing ye were strangers in the land of Egypt.

PREPARED THE DEMONIAC TO WITNESS

Mk 5:19 Howbeit Jesus suffered him not, but saith unto him, Go home to thy friends, and tell them how great things the Lord hath done for thee, and hath had compassion on thee.

CHRIST'S MESSAGE GROUNDED IN EXPERIENCE

Jn 3:10–11 Jesus answered and said unto him, Art thou a master of Israel, and knowest not these things?

Verily, verily, I say unto thee, We speak that we do know, and testify that we have seen; and ye receive not our witness.

QUALIFIED THE BLIND MAN TO TESTIFY

Jn 9:25 He answered and said, Whether he be a sinner *or no,* I know not: one thing I know, that, whereas I was blind, now I see.

FITTED PAUL FOR A MINISTRY OF COMFORT

2 Co 1:4 Who comforteth us in all our tribulation, that we may be able to comfort them which are in any trouble, by the comfort wherewith we ourselves are comforted of God.

ENABLED THE APOSTLES TO SPEAK WITH AUTHORITY

2 Pe 1:16 For we have not followed cunningly devised fables, when we made known unto you the power and coming of our Lord Jesus Christ, but were eyewitnesses of his majesty.

12. Divine

Ge 6:13 And God said unto Noah, The end of all flesh is come before me; for the earth is filled with violence through them; and, behold, I will destroy them with the earth.

Ge 18:19 For I know him, that he will command his children and his household after him, and they shall keep the way of the LORD, to do justice and judgment; that the LORD may bring upon Abraham that which he hath spoken of him.

Ge 29:33 And she conceived again, and bare a son; and said, Because the LORD hath heard that I *was* hated, he hath therefore given me this *son* also: and she called his name Simeon.

Ge 31:12 And he said, Lift up now thine eyes, and see, all the rams which leap upon the cattle *are* ringstraked, speckled, and grisled: for I have seen all that Laban doeth unto thee.

Ex 3:9 Now therefore, behold, the cry of the children of Israel is come unto me: and I have also seen the oppression wherewith the Egyptians oppress them.

Ex 4:14 And the anger of the LORD was kindled against Moses, and he said, *Is* not Aaron the Levite thy brother? I know that he can speak well. And also, behold, he cometh forth to meet thee: and when he seeth thee, he will be glad in his heart.

Ex 33:17 And the LORD said unto Moses, I will do this thing also that thou hast spoken: for thou hast found grace in my sight, and I know thee by name.

De 2:7 For the LORD thy God hath blessed thee in all the works of thy hand: he knoweth thy walking through this great wilderness: these forty years the LORD thy God *hath been* with thee; thou hast lacked nothing.

1 S 2:3 Talk no more so exceeding proudly; let *not* arrogancy come out of your mouth: for the LORD is a God of knowledge, and by him actions are weighed.

2 S 7:20 And what can David say more unto thee? for thou, Lord God, knowest thy servant.

1 K 8:39 Then hear thou in heaven thy dwelling place, and forgive, and do, and give to every man according to his ways, whose heart thou knowest; (for thou, *even* thou only, knowest the hearts of all the children of men;)

1 K 21:18 Arise, go down to meet Ahab king of Israel, which *is* in Samaria: behold, *he is* in the vineyard of Naboth, whither he is gone down to possess it.

2 K 19:27 But I know thy abode, and thy going out, and thy coming in, and thy rage against me.

1 Chr 17:18 What can David *speak* more to thee for the honour of thy servant? for thou knowest thy servant.

Jb 11:11 For he knoweth vain men: he seeth wickedness also; will he not then consider *it?*

Jb 21:22 Shall *any* teach God knowledge? seeing he judgeth those that are high.

Jb 22:13 And thou sayest, How doth God know? can he judge through the dark cloud?

Jb 24:1 Why, seeing times are not hidden from the Almighty, do they that know him not see his days?

Jb 34:25 Therefore he knoweth their works, and he overturneth *them* in the night, so that they are destroyed.

Jb 36:4 For truly my words *shall* not *be* false: he that is perfect in knowledge *is* with thee.

Jb 37:16 Dost thou know the balancings of the clouds, the wondrous works of him which is perfect in knowledge?

Ps 33:15 He fashioneth their hearts alike; he considereth all their works.

Ps 40:10 I have not hid thy righteousness within my heart; I have declared thy faithfulness and thy salvation: I have not concealed thy lovingkindness and thy truth from the great congregation.

Ps 44:21 Shall not God search this out? for he knoweth the secrets of the heart.

Ps 69:5 O God, thou knowest my foolishness; and my sins are not hid from thee.

Ps 69:19 Thou hast known my reproach, and my shame, and my dishonour: mine adversaries *are* all before thee.

Ps 73:11 And they say, How doth God know? and is there knowledge in the most High?

Ps 94:11 The LORD knoweth the thoughts of man, that they *are* vanity.

Ps 103:14 For he knoweth our frame; he remembereth that we *are* dust.

Ps 119:168 I have kept thy precepts and thy testimonies: for all my ways *are* before thee.

Ps 139:2 Thou knowest my downsitting and mine uprising, thou understandest my thought afar off.

Pr 3:20 By his knowledge the depths are broken up, and down the dew.

Pr 24:12 If thou sayest, Behold, we knew it not; doth not he that pondereth the heart consider *it?* and he that keepeth thy soul, doth *not* he know *it?* and shall *not* he render to *every* man according to his works?

Ec 5:8 If thou seest the oppression of the poor, and violent perverting of judgment and justice in a province, marvel not at the matter: for *he that is* higher than the highest regardeth; and *there be* higher than they.

Is 29:15 Woe unto them that seek deep to hide their counsel from the LORD, and their works are in the dark, and they say, Who seeth us? and who knoweth us?

Is 37:4 It may be the LORD thy God will hear the words of Rabshakeh, whom the king of Assyria his master hath sent to reproach the living God, and will reprove the words which the LORD thy God hath heard: wherefore lift up *thy* prayer for the remnant that is left.

Is 37:28 But I know thy abode, and thy going out, and thy coming in, and thy rage against me.

Is 40:14 With whom took he counsel, and *who* instructed him, and taught him in the path of judgment, and taught him knowledge, and shewed to him the way of understanding?

Is 40:28 Hast thou not known? hast thou not heard, *that* the everlasting God, the LORD, the Creator of the ends of the earth, fainteth not, neither is weary? *there is* no searching of his understanding.

Is 66:18 For I *know* their works and their thoughts: it shall come, that I will gather all nations and tongues; and they shall come, and see my glory.

Je 18:23 Yet, LORD, thou knowest all their counsel against me to slay *me:* forgive not their iniquity, neither blot out their sin from thy sight, but let them be overthrown before thee; deal *thus* with them in the time of thine anger.

Je 29:23 Because they have committed villany in Israel, and have committed adultery with their neighbours' wives, and have spoken lying words in my name, which I have not commanded them; even I know, and *am* a witness, saith the LORD.

Lam 3:59 O LORD, thou hast seen my wrong: judge thou my cause.

Da 2:22 He revealeth the deep and secret things: he knoweth what *is* in the darkness, and the light dwelleth with him.

Ho 5:3 I know Ephraim, and Israel is not hid from me: for now, O Ephraim, thou committest whoredom, *and* Israel is defiled.

Jona 3:10 And God saw their works, that they turned from their evil way; and God repented of the evil, that he had said that he would do unto them; and he did *it* not.

Zep 2:8 I have heard the reproach of Moab, and the revilings of the children of Ammon, whereby they have reproached my people, and magnified *themselves* against their border.

Mt 6:4 That thine alms may be in secret: and thy Father which seeth in secret himself shall reward thee openly.

Mt 6:8 Be not ye therefore like unto them: for your Father knoweth what things ye have need of, before ye ask him.

Mt 10:26 Fear them not therefore: for there is nothing covered, that shall not be revealed; and hid, that shall not be known.

Lu 12:7 But even the very hairs of your head are all numbered. Fear not therefore: ye are of more value than many sparrows.

Lu 12:30 For all these things do the nations of the world seek after: and your Father knoweth that ye have need of these things.

Ro 11:4 But what saith the answer of God unto him? I have reserved to myself seven thousand men, who have not bowed the knee to *the image of* Baal.

Ro 11:33 O the depth of the riches both of the wisdom and knowledge of God! how unsearchable *are* his judgments, and his ways past finding out!

1 Co 3:20 And again, The Lord knoweth the thoughts of the wise, that they are vain.

2 Co 11:31 The God and Father of our Lord Jesus Christ, which is blessed for evermore, knoweth that I lie not.

He 4:13 Neither is there any creature that is not manifest in his sight: but all things *are* naked and opened unto the eyes of him with whom we have to do.

1 Jn 3:20 For if our heart condemn us, God is greater than our heart, and knoweth all things.

Re 2:2 I know thy works, and thy labour, and thy patience, and how thou canst not bear them which are evil: and thou hast tried them which say they are apostles, and are not, and hast found them liars:

Re 2:13 I know thy works, and where thou dwellest, *even* where Satan's seat *is:* and thou holdest fast my name, and hast not denied my faith, even in those days wherein Antipas *was* my faithful martyr, who was slain among you, where Satan dwelleth.

Re 2:19 I know thy works, and charity, and service, and faith, and thy patience, and thy works; and the last *to be* more than the first.

a. Hearts Searched by Jehovah

Ge 3:9 And the Lord God called unto Adam, and said unto him, Where *art* thou?

Jud 5:16 Why abodest thou among the sheepfolds, to hear the bleatings of the flocks? For the divisions of Reuben *there were* great searchings of heart.

2 K 6:12 And one of his servants said, None, my lord, O king: but Elisha, the prophet that *is* in Israel, telleth the king of Israel the words that thou speakest in thy bedchamber.

1 Chr 28:9 And thou, Solomon my son, know thou the God of thy father, and serve him with a perfect heart and

with a willing mind: for the Lord searcheth all hearts, and understandeth all the imaginations of the thoughts: if thou seek him, he will be found of thee; but if thou forsake him, he will cast thee off for ever.

Jb 22:13 And thou sayest, How doth God know? can he judge through the dark cloud?

Ps 10:15 Break thou the arm of the wicked and the evil *man:* seek out his wickedness *till* thou find none.

Ps 33:14 From the place of his habitation he looketh upon all the inhabitants of the earth.

Ps 44:21 Shall not God search this out? for he knoweth the secrets of the heart.

Pr 15:3 The eyes of the Lord *are* in every place, beholding the evil and the good.

Pr 16:2 All the ways of a man *are* clean in his own eyes; but the Lord weigheth the spirits.

Is 37:28 But I know thy abode, and thy going out, and thy coming in, and thy rage against me.

Je 17:10 I the Lord search the heart, *I* try the reins, even to give every man according to his ways, *and* according to the fruit of his doings.

Je 23:24 Can any hide himself in secret places that I shall not see him? saith the Lord. Do not I fill heaven and earth? saith the Lord.

Da 5:26 This *is* the interpretation of the thing: Mene; God hath numbered thy kingdom, and finished it.

Am 9:3 And though they hide themselves in the top of Carmel, I will search and take them out thence; and though they be hid from my sight in the bottom of the sea, thence will I command the serpent, and he shall bite them:

Zep 1:12 And it shall come to pass at that time, *that* I will search Jerusalem with candles, and punish the men that are settled on their lees: that say in their heart, The Lord will not do good, neither will he do evil.

Mt 3:12 Whose fan *is* in his hand, and he will throughly purge his floor, and gather his wheat into the garner;

but he will burn up the chaff with unquenchable fire.

Lu 11:13 If ye then, being evil, know how to give good gifts unto your children: how much more shall *your* heavenly Father give the Holy Spirit to them that ask him?

Ro 8:27 And he that searcheth the hearts knoweth what *is* the mind of the Spirit, because he maketh intercession for the saints according to *the will of* God.

b. Human Hearts Known by God

Ge 7:1 And the LORD said unto Noah, Come thou and all thy house into the ark; for thee have I seen righteous before me in this generation.

1 S 9:19 And Samuel answered Saul, and said, I *am* the seer: go up before me unto the high place; for ye shall eat with me to day, and to morrow I will let thee go, and will tell thee all that *is* in thine heart.

2 K 5:26 And he said unto him, Went not mine heart *with thee,* when the man turned again from his chariot to meet thee? *Is it* a time to receive money, and to receive garments, and oliveyards, and vineyards, and sheep, and oxen, and menservants, and maidservants?

2 K 6:32 But Elisha sat in his house, and the elders sat with him; and *the king* sent a man from before him: but ere the messenger came to him, he said to the elders, See ye how this son of a murderer hath sent to take away mine head? look, when the messenger cometh, shut the door, and hold him fast at the door: *is* not the sound of his master's feet behind him?

Ps 51:6 Behold, thou desirest truth in the inward parts: and in the hidden *part* thou shalt make me to know wisdom.

Ps 139:23 Search me, O God, and know my heart: try me, and know my thoughts:

Pr 15:11 Hell and destruction *are* before the LORD: how much more then the hearts of the children of men?

Je 20:12 But, O LORD of hosts, that triest the righteous, *and* seest the reins and the heart, let me see thy vengeance on them: for unto thee have I opened my cause.

Mt 12:25 And Jesus knew their thoughts, and said unto them, Every kingdom divided against itself is brought to desolation; and every city or house divided against itself shall not stand:

Mt 22:18 But Jesus perceived their wickedness, and said, Why tempt ye me, *ye* hypocrites?

Mk 2:8 And immediately when Jesus perceived in his spirit that they so reasoned within themselves, he said unto them, Why reason ye these things in your hearts?

Lu 6:8 But he knew their thoughts, and said to the man which had the withered hand, Rise up, and stand forth in the midst. And he arose and stood forth.

Lu 11:17 But he, knowing their thoughts, said unto them, Every kingdom divided against itself is brought to desolation; and a house *divided* against a house falleth.

Lu 16:15 And he said unto them, Ye are they which justify yourselves before men; but God knoweth your hearts: for that which is highly esteemed among men is abomination in the sight of God.

Jn 2:25 And needed not that any should testify of man: for he knew what was in man.

Ac 15:8 And God, which knoweth the hearts, bare them witness, giving them the Holy Ghost, even as *he did* unto us;

c. Human Ways Known by God

De 2:7 For the LORD thy God hath blessed thee in all the works of thy hand: he knoweth thy walking through this great wilderness: these forty years the LORD thy God *hath been* with thee; thou hast lacked nothing.

2 K 6:9 And the man of God sent unto the king of Israel, saying, Beware that thou pass not such a place; for thither the Syrians are come down.

2 K 19:27 But I know thy abode, and thy going out, and thy coming in, and thy rage against me.

Jb 33:11 He putteth my feet in the stocks, he marketh all my paths.

Jb 34:21 For his eyes *are* upon the ways of man, and he seeth all his goings.

Ps 1:6 For the LORD knoweth the way of the righteous: but the way of the ungodly shall perish.

Ps 119:168 I have kept thy precepts and thy testimonies: for all my ways *are* before thee.

Ps 139:3 Thou compassest my path and my lying down, and art acquainted *with* all my ways.

Ps 142:3 When my spirit was overwhelmed within me, then thou knewest my path. In the way wherein I walked have they privily laid a snare for me.

Pr 5:21 For the ways of man *are* before the eyes of the LORD, and he pondereth all his goings.

Is 57:18 I have seen his ways, and will heal him: I will lead him also, and restore comforts unto him and to his mourners.

Je 16:17 For mine eyes *are* upon all their ways: they are not hid from my face, neither is their iniquity hid from mine eyes.

Je 32:19 Great in counsel, and mighty in work: for thine eyes *are* open upon all the ways of the sons of men: to give every one according to his ways, and according to the fruit of his doings:

Eze 36:17 Son of man, when the house of Israel dwelt in their own land, they defiled it by their own way and by their doings: their way was before me as the uncleanness of a removed woman.

Da 5:23 But hast lifted up thyself against the Lord of heaven; and they have brought the vessels of his house before thee, and thou, and thy lords, thy wives, and thy concubines, have drunk wine in them; and thou hast praised the gods of silver, and gold, of brass, iron, wood, and stone, which see not, nor hear, nor know: and the God in whose hand thy breath *is*, and whose *are* all thy ways, hast thou not glorified:

d. Saints Known by God

IN TIME OF TROUBLE
Na 1:7

AT EVERY DAY TASK
Jn 1:48

THEIR INDIVIDUAL NAMES
Jn 10:3

INTIMATE ACQUAINTANCESHIP
Jn 10:14

TRUE LOVE RECOGNIZED
1 Co 8:3; Ga 4:9

THE SURE FOUNDATION OF CHRISTIAN HOPE
2 Ti 2:19

See **IGNORANCE, OMNISCIENCE, VISION**

KOHATH, *son of Levi*

Ge 46:11; Ex 6:16; Nu 3:19; 4:15; 10:21; Jos 21:20; 1 Chr 6:2, 18; 23:6

KOHATHITES, *descendants of Kohath*

Nu 3:30; 4:4, 15, 18, 34; 7:9; 10:21; 26:57; Jos 21:4; 1 Chr 6:33, 54, 61, 66; 9:32; 15:5; 23:12; 2 Chr 20:19; 34:12

KORAH, *grandson of Kohath*

Nu 16:1, 19, 32, 40; 26:9; Jude 11

L

LABAN, *brother of Rebekah*

Ge 24:29; 25:20; 28:2; 29:5, 16; 30:40; 31:1, 26, 51

LABOR *See* **WORK**

LABORERS, *SPIRITUAL, workers in the kingdom of God*

PRAYER FOR THEIR INCREASE

Mt 9:37–38 Then saith he unto his disciples, The harvest truly *is* plenteous, but the labourers *are* few;

Pray ye therefore the Lord of the harvest, that he will send forth labourers into his harvest.

Mt 20:8 So when even was come, the lord of the vineyard saith unto his steward, Call the labourers, and give them *their* hire, beginning from the last unto the first.

GREAT OPPORTUNITY AFFORDED TO THEM

Jn 4:35 Say not ye, There are yet four months, and *then* cometh harvest? behold, I say unto you, Lift up your eyes, and look on the fields; for they are white already to harvest.

Jn 4:36 And he that reapeth receiveth wages, and gathereth fruit unto life eternal: that both he that soweth and he that reapeth may rejoice together.

1 Co 3:9 For we are labourers together with God: ye are God's husbandry, *ye are* God's building.

WORTHY OF REWARD

1 Ti 5:17–18 Let the elders that rule well be counted worthy of double honour, especially they who labour in the word and doctrine.

For the scripture saith, Thou shalt not muzzle the ox that treadeth out the corn. And, The labourer *is* worthy of his reward.

LABOR TROUBLES, *difficulties with employees*

Mt 20:11–12; 21:33–35; Mk 12:1–9; Ac 19:28, 38

See **WORK**

LABOR UNIONS, *an association of workers formed to protect their general welfare, interests, and rights*

Ac 19:25–28

LACHISH, *a town of Judah*

Jos 10:3, 31; 12:11; 15:39; 2 K 14:19; 18:14, 17; 19:8; 2 Chr 32:9; Ne 11:30; Is 36:2; Je 34:7; Mi 1:13

LADDER, *JACOB'S, name given to the staircase leading to heaven, seen in his vision near Bethel*

Ge 28:12

LAMBS *See* **ANIMALS**

LAMECH, *son of Methuselah*

Ge 5:25; 1 Chr 1:3; Lu 3:36

LAMENESS, *crippled, especially in a leg or foot, impairing one's ability to walk*

Le 21:18; 2 S 4:4; 5:8; 9:3, 13; Is 35:6; Mt 11:5; 15:31; 21:14; Lu 7:22; Ac 3:2; 8:7; 14:8

See **SICKNESS**

LAMENTATIONS, *expressions of grief*

1. Examples

FOR JACOB

Ge 50:10 And they came to the threshingfloor of Atad, which *is* beyond Jordan, and there they mourned with a great and very sore lamentation: and he made a mourning for his father seven days.

FOR JEPHTHAH'S DAUGHTER

Jud 11:40 *That* the daughters of Israel went yearly to lament the daughter of Jephthah the Gileadite four days in a year.

FOR KING SAUL

2 S 1:17 And David lamented with this lamentation over Saul and over Jonathan his son:

FOR JOSIAH

2 Chr 35:25 And Jeremiah lamented for Josiah: and all the singing men and the singing women spake of Josiah in their lamentations to this day, and made them an ordinance in Israel: and, behold, they *are* written in the lamentations.

FOR THE JEWS

Est 4:1 When Mordecai perceived all that was done, Mordecai rent his clothes, and put on sackcloth with ashes, and went out into the midst of the city, and cried with a loud and a bitter cry;

FOR THE SLAUGHTERED INNOCENTS

Mt 2:18 In Rama was there a voice heard, lamentation, and weeping, and great mourning, Rachel weeping *for* her children, and would not be comforted, because they are not.

FOR CHRIST

Lu 23:27 And there followed him a great company of people, and of women, which also bewailed and lamented him.

FOR STEPHEN

Ac 8:2 And devout men carried Stephen *to his burial,* and made great lamentation over him.

2. Book

Author: Jeremiah.

Date Written: Soon after Jerusalem's fall (586 B.C.).

Purpose: To document that disobedience always results in divine judgment. In the midst of judgment,

however, God's mercies prevail. He will not forget his covenant promises.

To Whom Written: The survivors of Jerusalem's destruction.

Main Themes: Lament and restoration. The book is a sequel to the book of Jeremiah. It contains a series of dirges in the form of an acrostic, written as if for a national funeral, portraying the capture and destruction of Jerusalem.

Key Words: Lamentation and Mercies.

Key Verses: 1:12; 3:22–23.

LAND LEASED *See* **REAL ESTATE**

LANDMARKS, *not to be removed*

De 19:14; 27:17; Jb 24:2; Pr 22:28; 23:10; Ho 5:10

See **REAL ESTATE**

LAND PURCHASED *See* **REAL ESTATE**

LAND SOLD *See* **REAL ESTATE**

LANGUAGES, *CONFOUNDED, at the Tower of Babel*

Ge 11:9

LAODICEA, *town in Phrygia*

Laodicea was located on the ancient highway leading up from Ephesus through the Maeander and Lycus valleys to the east and on to Syria. Colosse lies ten miles farther east, while Hierapolis is six miles northeast of Laodicea. Laodicea was the home of one of the seven churches addressed in the Revelation to John (3:14–22). In the last part of the first century, when the Revelation was written, the Laodicean church was apparently taken with the atmosphere of affluence so prominent in the place and was reproached because it was rich in material things but lukewarm in things of the spirit. In Christ's counsel for the Laodicean church to buy from Him gold refined by fire, white garments, and salve to put on their eyes (Re 3:18), Sir William Ramsey saw references to Laodicea's wealth, its famous garments, and perhaps to the "Phrygian powder" for diseases of the eyes, which may have been compounded here.

LASCIVIOUSNESS See CHASTITY

LAST DAY

Jn 6:39 And this is the Father's will which hath sent me, that of all which he hath given me I should lose nothing, but should raise it up again at the last day.

Jn 11:24 Martha saith unto him, I know that he shall rise again in the resurrection at the last day.

Jn 12:48 He that rejecteth me, and receiveth not my words, hath one that judgeth him: the word that I have spoken, the same shall judge him in the last day.

See **FUTURE LIFE, JUDGMENTS, RESURRECTION**

LAST JUDGMENT, *man's final encounter with God*

Ps 1:5 Therefore the ungodly shall not stand in the judgment, nor sinners in the congregation of the righteous.

Da 7:10 A fiery stream issued and came forth from before him: thousand thousands ministered unto him, and ten thousand times ten thousand stood before him: the judgment was set, and the books were opened.

Da 7:26 But the judgment shall sit, and they shall take away his dominion, to consume and to destroy *it* unto the end.

Mt 7:2 For with what judgment ye judge, ye shall be judged: and with what measure ye mete, it shall be measured to you again.

Mt 11:22 But I say unto you, It shall be more tolerable for Tyre and Sidon at the day of judgment, than for you.

Mt 11:24 But I say unto you, That it shall be more tolerable for the land of Sodom in the day of judgment, than for thee.

Mt 12:36 But I say unto you, That every idle word that men shall speak,

they shall give account thereof in the day of judgment.

Mt 13:30 Let both grow together until the harvest: and in the time of harvest I will say to the reapers, Gather ye together first the tares, and bind them in bundles to burn them: but gather the wheat into my barn.

Mt 13:39 The enemy that sowed them is the devil; the harvest is the end of the world; and the reapers are the angels.

Mt 21:40 When the lord therefore of the vineyard cometh, what will he do unto those husbandmen?

Mt 25:31-32 When the Son of man shall come in his glory, and all the holy angels with him, then shall he sit upon the throne of his glory:

And before him shall be gathered all nations: and he shall separate them one from another, as a shepherd divideth *his* sheep from the goats:

Lu 10:14 But it shall be more tolerable for Tyre and Sidon at the judgment, than for you.

Ac 24:25 And as he reasoned of righteousness, temperance, and judgment to come Felix trembled, and answered, Go thy way for this time; when I have a convenient season, I will call for thee.

Ro 2:5 But after thy hardness and impenitent heart treasurest up unto thyself wrath against the day of wrath and revelation of the righteous judgment of God;

Ro 2:16 In the day when God shall judge the secrets of men by Jesus Christ according to my gospel.

Ro 14:10 But why dost thou judge thy brother? or why dost thou set at nought thy brother? for we shall all stand before the judgment seat of Christ.

2 Co 5:10 For we must all appear before the judgment seat of Christ; that every one may receive the things *done* in *his* body, according to that he hath done, whether *it be* good or bad.

He 6:2 Of the doctrine of baptisms, and of laying on of hands, and of resurrection of the dead, and of eternal judgment.

He 9:27 And as it is appointed unto men once to die, but after this the judgment:

1 Pe 4:6 For for this cause was the gospel preached also to them that are dead, that they might be judged according to men in the flesh, but live according to God in the spirit.

2 Pe 2:4 For if God spared not the angels that sinned, but cast *them* down to hell, and delivered *them* into chains of darkness, to be reserved unto judgment;

2 Pe 2:9 The Lord knoweth how to deliver the godly out of temptations, and to reserve the unjust unto the day of judgment to be punished:

2 Pe 3:7 But the heavens and the earth, which are now, by the same word are kept in store, reserved unto fire against the day of judgment and perdition of ungodly men.

1 Jn 4:17 Herein is our love made perfect, that we may have boldness in the day of judgment: because as he is, so are we in this world.

Jude 6 And the angels which kept not their first estate, but left their own habitation, he hath reserved in everlasting chains under darkness unto the judgment of the great day.

Jude 14–15 And Enoch also, the seventh from Adam, prophesied of these, saying, Behold, the Lord cometh with ten thousands of his saints,

To execute judgment upon all, and to convince all that are ungodly among them of all their ungodly deeds which they have ungodly committed, and of all their hard *speeches* which ungodly sinners have spoken against him.

Re 11:18 And the nations were angry, and thy wrath is come, and the time of the dead, that they should be judged, and that thou shouldest give reward unto thy servants the prophets, and to the saints, and them that fear thy name, small and great; and shouldest destroy them which destroy the earth.

Re 14:7 Saying with a loud voice, Fear God, and give glory to him; for the hour of his judgment is come: and worship him that made heaven, and earth, and the sea, and the fountains of waters.

Re 20:12 And I saw the dead, small and great, stand before God; and the books were opened: and another book was opened, which is *the book* of life: and the dead were judged out of those things which were written in the books, according to their works.

1. Judgment According to Privilege

Mt 10:15 Verily I say unto you, It shall be more tolerable for the land of Sodom and Gomorrha in the day of judgment, than for that city.

Mt 11:22 But I say unto you, It shall be more tolerable for Tyre and Sidon at the day of judgment, than for you.

Mk 6:11 And whosoever shall not receive you, nor hear you, when ye depart thence, shake off the dust under your feet for a testimony against them. Verily I say unto you, It shall be more tolerable for Sodom and Gomorrha in the day of judgment, than for that city.

Lu 12:48 But he that knew not, and did commit things worthy of stripes, shall be beaten with few *stripes*. For unto whomsoever much is given, of him shall be much required: and to whom men have committed much, of him they will ask the more.

Jn 3:19 And this is the condemnation, that light is come into the world, and men loved darkness rather than light, because their deeds were evil.

Jn 9:41 Jesus said unto them, If ye were blind, ye should have no sin: but now ye say, We see; therefore your sin remaineth.

Jn 15:22 If I had not come and spoken unto them, they had not had sin: but now they have no cloke for their sin.

Ro 2:12 For as many as have sinned without law shall also perish without law: and as many as have sinned in the law shall be judged by the law;

2. Judgment According to Works

1 K 20:40 And as thy servant was busy here and there, he was gone. And the king of Israel said unto him, So *shall* thy judgment *be;* thyself hast decided *it.*

Jb 14:3 And dost thou open thine eyes upon such an one, and bringest me into judgment with thee?

Jb 22:4 Will he reprove thee for fear of thee? will he enter with thee into judgment?

Ps 18:24 Therefore hath the LORD recompensed me according to my righteousness, according to the cleanness of my hands in his eyesight.

Ps 28:4 Give them according to their deeds, and according to the wickedness of their endeavours: give them after the work of their hands; render to them their desert.

Ps 62:12 Also unto thee, O Lord, *belongeth* mercy: for thou renderest to every man according to his work.

Pr 11:31 Behold, the righteous shall be recompensed in the earth: much more the wicked and the sinner.

Pr 12:14 A man shall be satisfied with good by the fruit of *his* mouth: and the recompense of a man's hands shall be rendered unto him.

Pr 24:12 If thou sayest, Behold, we knew it not; doth not he that pondereth the heart consider *it?* and he that keepeth thy soul, doth *not* he know *it?* and shall *not* he render to *every* man according to his works?

Is 40:27 Why sayest thou, O Jacob, and speakest, O Israel, My way is hid from the LORD, and my judgment is passed over from my God?

Je 17:10 I the LORD search the heart, *I* try the reins, even to give every man according to his ways, *and* according to the fruit of his doings.

Je 32:19 Great in counsel, and mighty in work: for thine eyes *are* open upon all the ways of the sons of men: to give every one according to his ways, and according to the fruit of his doings:

Je 34:17 Therefore thus saith the LORD; Ye have not hearkened unto me, in proclaiming liberty, every one to his brother, and every man to his neighbour: behold, I proclaim a liberty for you, saith the LORD, to the sword, to the pestilence, and to the famine; and I will make you to be

removed into all the kingdoms of the earth.

Lam 3:64 Render unto them a recompence, O LORD, according to the work of their hands.

Eze 16:59 For thus saith the Lord GOD; I will even deal with thee as thou hast done, which hast despised the oath in breaking the covenant.

Eze 18:20 The soul that sinneth, it shall die. The son shall not bear the iniquity of the father, neither shall the father bear the iniquity of the son: the righteousness of the righteous shall be upon him, and the wickedness of the wicked shall be upon him.

Eze 18:30 Therefore I will judge you, O house of Israel, every one according to his ways, saith the Lord GOD. Repent, and turn *yourselves* from all your transgressions; so iniquity shall not be your ruin.

Am 8:7 The LORD hath sworn by the excellency of Jacob, Surely I will never forget any of their works.

Mt 16:27 For the Son of man shall come in the glory of his Father with his angels; and then he shall reward every man according to his works.

Ro 2:6 Who will render to every man according to his deeds:

2 Co 5:10 For we must all appear before the judgment seat of Christ; that every one may receive the things *done* in *his* body, according to that he hath done, whether *it be* good or bad.

1 Pe 1:17 And if ye call on the Father, who without respect of persons judgeth according to every man's work, pass the time of your sojourning *here* in fear:

Re 2:23 And I will kill her children with death; and all the churches shall know that I am he which searcheth the reins and hearts: and I will give unto every one of you according to your works.

Re 20:12 And I saw the dead, small and great, stand before God; and the books were opened: and another book was opened, which is *the book* of life: and the dead were judged out of those things which were written in the books, according to their works.

Re 22:12 And, behold, I come quickly; and my reward *is* with me, to give every man according as his work shall be.

See **FUTURE LIFE, JUDGMENTS**

LAVER, *basin*

Ex 30:18, 28; 31:9; 35:16; 38:8; 39:39; 40:7, 11, 30; Le 8:11; 1 K 7:38; 2 Chr 4:6, 14

LAW

1. Insufficient to Save

Ro 3:19–20 Now we know that what things soever the law saith, it saith to them who are under the law: that every mouth may be stopped, and all the world may become guilty before God.

Therefore by the deeds of the law there shall no flesh be justified in his sight: for by the law *is* the knowledge of sin.

Ro 8:3 For what the law could not do, in that it was weak through the flesh, God sending his own Son in the likeness of sinful flesh, and for sin, condemned sin in the flesh:

Ga 2:19 For I through the law am dead to the law, that I might live unto God.

Ep 2:15 Having abolished in his flesh the enmity, *even* the law of commandments *contained* in ordinances; for to make in himself of twain one new man, *so* making peace;

He 7:19 For the law made nothing perfect, but the bringing in of a better hope *did;* by the which we draw nigh unto God.

2. Purpose, *to demonstrate human inability to fulfill God's standard of righteousness*

Ro 3:20 Therefore by the deeds of the law there shall no flesh be justified in his sight: for by the law *is* the knowledge of sin.

Ro 5:20 Moreover the law entered, that the offence might abound. But where sin abounded, grace did much more abound:

Ro 7:7 What shall we say then? *Is* the law sin? God forbid. Nay, I had not known sin, but by the law: for I had not known lust, except the law had said, Thou shalt not covet.

Ga 3:19 Wherefore then *serveth* the law? It was added because of transgressions, till the seed should come to whom the promise was made; *and it was* ordained by angels in the hand of a mediator.

Ga 3:24 Wherefore the law was our schoolmaster *to bring us* unto Christ, that we might be justified by faith.

1 Ti 1:9 Knowing this, that the law is not made for a righteous man, but for the lawless and disobedient, for the ungodly and for sinners, for unholy and profane, for murderers of fathers and murderers of mothers, for manslayers,

See **GRACE**

LAWGIVER

1. God

Ezr 7:6; Ne 9:14; Is 33:22; 51:4; Je 44:10; Ja 4:12

See **GOD**

2. Moses

Ex 18:16; 34:32; 35:1; Le 10:11; Nu 21:18; 36:13; De 1:3, 18; 4:2, 8, 44; 5:1; 6:2; 11:32; 30:2; 31:1, 9; 33:4; Jos 1:7; 8:33; 11:15; 22:9; 2 Chr 30:16; 35:6; Ne 1:7; 8:14; 10:29; Da 9:11; Mal 4:4; Mt 22:24; 23:2; Mk 7:10; 10:3; 12:19, 26; Lu 5:14; 16:29; 20:28; Jn 1:17; 7:19; 8:5; Ac 7:38; 15:21; He 10:28; 12:25

See **MOSES**

LAWS OF INHERITANCE

See **REAL ESTATE**

LAWYERS, *those versed in the Law of Moses*

Mt 22:35; Lu 10:25; 11:45–46; 14:3; Tit 3:13

LAZARUS, *help of God*

1. The Beggar
Lu 16:20

2. The Brother of Martha and Mary
Jn 11:1, 14, 43; 12:2, 10, 17

See **RESURRECTION**

LAZINESS *See* **BUSINESS**

LEAD, *a mineral*

Ex 15:10; Nu 31:22; Jb 19:24; Je 6:29; Eze 22:18; 27:12; Zec 5:8

LEADER

1. Divine

IN DIFFICULT PLACES
De 8:2 And thou shalt remember all the way which the LORD thy God led thee these forty years in the wilderness, to humble thee, *and* to prove thee, to know what *was* in thine heart, whether thou wouldest keep his commandments, or no.

LIKE A MOTHER BIRD
De 32:11 As an eagle stirreth up her nest, fluttereth over her young, spreadeth abroad her wings, taketh them, beareth them on her wings:
De 32:12 *So* the LORD alone did lead him, and *there was* no strange god with him.

IN A PLAIN PATH
Ps 27:11 Teach me thy way, O LORD, and lead me in a plain path, because of mine enemies.
Ps 60:9 Who will bring me *into* the strong city? who will lead me into Edom?

LIKE A SHEPHERD
Ps 77:20 Thou leddest thy people like a flock by the hand of Moses and Aaron.

NO PLACE BEYOND HIS REACH
Ps 139:9–10 *If* I take the wings of the morning, *and* dwell in the uttermost parts of the sea;

Even there shall thy hand lead me, and thy right hand shall hold me.
Pr 20:24 Man's goings *are* of the LORD; how can a man then understand his own way?
Is 63:14 As a beast goeth down into the valley, the Spirit of the LORD caused him to rest: so didst thou lead thy people, to make thyself a glorious name.

STEADILY TOWARD THE CROSS
Mk 10:32 And they were in the way going up to Jerusalem; and Jesus went before them: and they were amazed; and as they followed, they were afraid. And he took again the twelve, and began to tell them what things should happen unto him,

TO THE BORDER OF THE UNSEEN
Lu 24:50–51 And he led them out as far as to Bethany, and he lifted up his hands, and blessed them.
    And it came to pass, while he blessed them, he was parted from them, and carried up into heaven.

2. Human

MOSES
Ex 3:11

GIDEON
Jud 6:15

KING SAUL
1 S 9:21

KING DAVID
1 S 18:18

KING SOLOMON
1 K 3:7

ISAIAH
Is 6:5

JEREMIAH
Je 1:6

JOHN THE BAPTIST
Mt 3:14

See **GUIDANCE, TEACHER**

LEAH, *daughter of Laban, married to Jacob*

Ge 29:25; 30:14, 17; 31:4; 33:2; 35:23; 46:15; 49:31

LEAVEN, *a substance added to dough to cause it to rise*

Ex 12:15, 19; 13:3; 23:18; 34:25; Le 2:11; 6:17; 23:17; De 16:4; Mt 13:33; 16:6; Lu 13:21; 1 Co 5:6; Ga 5:9

LEBANON *See* **MOUNTAINS AND HILLS**

LEEK, *a kind of onion*

Nu 11:5

LEES, *dregs of wine*

Ps 75:8; Is 25:6; Je 48:11

LEGION, *a main division of the Roman army; from 3,000 to 6,000 men at the time of Christ*

1. Of Angels

Mt 26:53

2. Of Devils

Mk 5:9; Lu 8:30

LENTILS, *a cereal*

Ge 25:34; 2 S 17:28; 23:11; Eze 4:9

LEOPARDS *See* **ANIMALS**

LEPERS, *those having leprosy, a disfiguring disease marked by whiteness*

Le 13:45; 14:3; 22:4; Nu 5:2; 12:10; 2 K 5:1, 27; 7:3; 2 Chr 26:21; Mt 8:2; 11:5; 26:6; Mk 1:40; Lu 4:27; 5:12; 7:22; 17:12

See **HEALING, MIRACLES**

LEPROSY *See* **DISEASE**

LETTERS, *writings*

2 S 11:14; 1 K 21:8; 2 K 5:5; 10:1; 19:14; 20:12; 2 Chr 30:1; 32:17; Ezr 4:11; 5:5; 7:11; Ne 2:7; 6:5, 17; Est 1:22; 3:13; 8:10; 9:20; Is 37:14; 39:1; Je 29:1, 29; Ac 9:2; 15:23, 30; 18:27; 23:25; 2 Co 10:9; Ga 6:11; 1 Ti 3:14; He 13:22

See **BOOKS, INK, WRITING**

LEVI, *son of Jacob*

Ge 29:34; 34:25; 35:23; 46:11; 49:5; Ex 2:1; 6:16; 1 Chr 6:16; Ezr 8:18; Eze 40:46; 48:31; Re 7:7

LEVIATHAN, *sea monster*

Jb 41:1; Ps 74:13; 104:26; Is 27:1

LEVITES, *descendants of Levi, had charge of the tabernacle*

Ex 32:26; 38:21; Le 25:32; Nu 1:47, 50; 2:17, 33; 3:6, 15, 39, 45; 4:46; 7:5; 8:6, 11, 14, 18, 24; 16:10; 17:3; 18:3, 6, 23; 26:57; 35:2, 7; De 10:8; 12:19; 14:27; 16:11; 18:1; 21:5; 26:11; 27:14; 31:25; 33:8; Jos 3:3; 8:33; 13:33; 14:4; 18:7; 21:1, 41; Jud 17:7; 18:15; 19:1; 20:4; 1 S 6:15; 2 S 15:24; 1 K 8:4; 1 Chr 6:1, 48, 64; 9:14, 31; 12:26; 13:2; 15:2, 11; 16:4; 23:2, 27; 24:20; 27:17; 28:21; 2 Chr 5:4, 12; 7:6; 8:14; 11:13; 13:10; 17:8; 19:8; 20:19; 23:2; 24:5; 29:4, 12, 16, 25, 34; 30:16; 31:2, 17; 34:9, 13, 30; 35:9; Ezr 1:5; 2:40, 70; 3:8; 6:16, 18; 7:7, 24; 8:29; 10:5, 23; Ne 3:17; 7:43; 8:11, 13; 9:38; 10:39; 11:18; 12:8, 22; 13:22; Eze 44:10, 15; 45:5; 48:13, 22; Zec 12:13; Lu 10:32; Jn 1:19; Ac 4:36; He 7:5, 9

LEVITICUS

Name: Derived from the tribe of Levi.

Author: Moses, (commonly accepted).

Date Written: 1446–1410 B.C.

Purpose: To present a digest of divine laws.

To Whom Written: The children of Israel.

Main Theme: How can sinful man approach a holy God?

Key Words: Access and Holiness.

Key Verse: 19:2.

LIBERTY, *freedom, independence*

1. Civil

Ex 21:2; Le 25:10, 54; De 15:12; Is 9:4; 10:27; 14:25; Je 30:8; 34:8; Na 1:13; Ac 22:28; 1 Co 7:21

2. *Spiritual*

THE MISSION OF CHRIST TO PROCLAIM

Is 61:1 The Spirit of the Lord God *is* upon me; because the LORD hath anointed me to preach good tidings unto the meek; he hath sent me to bind up the brokenhearted, to proclaim liberty to the captives, and the opening of the prison to *them that are* bound;

Lu 4:18 The Spirit of the Lord is upon me, because he hath anointed me to preach the gospel to the poor; he hath sent me to heal the brokenhearted, to preach deliverance to the captives, and recovering of sight to the blind, to set at liberty them that are bruised,

FOUND IN TRUTH

Jn 8:32 And ye shall know the truth, and the truth shall make you free.

Ro 6:18 Being then made free from sin, ye became the servants of righteousness.

FOUND IN A NEW LAW OF LIFE

Ro 8:2 For the law of the Spirit of life in Christ Jesus hath made me free from the law of sin and death.

THE BONDAGE OF SIN BROKEN

Ro 8:21 Because the creature itself also shall be delivered from the bondage of corruption into the glorious liberty of the children of God.

SECURED BY GOD

2 Co 3:17 Now the Lord is that Spirit: and where the Spirit of the Lord *is*, there *is* liberty.

Ga 2:4 And that because of false brethren unawares brought in, who came in privily to spy out our liberty which we have in Christ Jesus, that they might bring us into bondage:

3. *Abuse*

1 Co 8:9; Ga 5:13; 1 Pe 2:16; 2 Pe 2:19

4. *Limitations*

1 Co 6:12 All things are lawful unto me, but all things are not expedient: all things are lawful for me, but I will

not be brought under the power of any.

1 Co 9:19 For though I be free from all *men,* yet have I made myself servant unto all, that I might gain the more.

1 Co 10:23 All things are lawful for me, but all things are not expedient: all things are lawful for me, but all things edify not.

1 Pe 2:16 As free, and not using *your* liberty for a cloke of maliciousness, but as the servants of God.

See **BONDAGE, JUBILEE, PRISONS, SALVATION**

LIBNAH, *a city of Canaan*

Jos 10:29; 21:13; 2 K 8:22; 19:8; Is 37:8

LIBYA, *a country west of Egypt*

Eze 30:5; 38:5; Ac 2:10

LICE *See* **MIRACLES**

LIFE, *physical*

1. *Its Origin*

Ge 2:7 And the LORD God formed man *of* the dust of the ground, and breathed into his nostrils the breath of life; and man became a living soul.

1 S 2:6 The LORD killeth, and maketh alive: he bringeth down to the grave, and bringeth up.

Jb 27:3 All the while my breath *is* in me, and the spirit of God *is* in my nostrils;

Ps 104:30 Thou sendest forth thy spirit, they are created: and thou renewest the face of the earth.

Ac 17:25 Neither is worshipped with men's hands, as though he needed any thing, seeing he giveth to all life, and breath, and all things;

2. *Its Brevity*

LIKE A SHADOW

1 Chr 29:15 For we *are* strangers before thee, and sojourners, as *were* all our fathers: our days on the earth *are* as a shadow, and *there is* none abiding.

Jb 8:9 (For we *are but of* yesterday, and know nothing, because our days upon earth *are* a shadow:)

Jb 14:2 He cometh forth like a flower, and is cut down: he fleeth also as a shadow, and continueth not.

Ps 102:11 My days *are* like a shadow that declineth; and I am withered like grass.

Ec 6:12 For who knoweth what *is* good for man in *this* life, all the days of his vain life which he spendeth as a shadow? for who can tell a man what shall be after him under the sun?

LIKE A FLYING SHUTTLE

Jb 7:6 My days are swifter than a weaver's shuttle, and are spent without hope.

Jb 8:9 (For we *are but of* yesterday, and know nothing, because our days upon earth *are* a shadow:)

LIKE HURRYING MESSENGERS

Jb 9:25 Now my days are swifter than a post: they flee away, they see no good.

Jb 14:2 He cometh forth like a flower, and is cut down: he fleeth also as a shadow, and continueth not.

ONLY A HANDBREADTH IN EXTENT

Ps 39:5 Behold, thou hast made my days *as* an handbreadth; and mine age *is* as nothing before thee: verily every man at his best state *is* altogether vanity. Selah.

Ps 89:47 Remember how short my time is: wherefore hast thou made all men in vain?

Ps 90:9 For all our days are passed away in thy wrath: we spend our years as a tale *that is told.*

Ps 102:11 My days *are* like a shadow that declineth; and I am withered like grass.

Ec 6:12 For who knoweth what *is* good for man in *this* life, his vain life which he spendeth as a shadow? for who can tell a man what shall be after him under the sun?

LIKE A WEAVER'S WEB

Is 38:12 Mine age is departed, and is removed from me as a shepherd's tent: I have cut off like a weaver my life: he will cut me off with pining sickness: from day *even* to night wilt thou make an end of me.

LIKE A VANISHING VAPOR

Ja 4:14 Whereas ye know not what *shall be* on the morrow. For what *is* your life? It is even a vapour, that appeareth for a little time, and then vanisheth away.

3. Of the Righteous

De 32:47 For it *is* not a vain thing for you; because it *is* your life: and through this thing ye shall prolong *your* days in the land, whither ye go over Jordan to possess it.

Ne 9:29 And testifiedst against them, that thou mightest bring them again unto thy law: yet they dealt proudly, and hearkened not unto thy commandments, but sinned against thy judgments, (which if a man do, he shall live in them;) and withdrew the shoulder, and hardened their neck, and would not hear.

Ps 37:27 Depart from evil, and do good; and dwell for evermore.

Pr 4:22 For they *are* life unto those that find them, and health to all their flesh.

Pr 8:35 For whoso findeth me findeth life, and shall obtain favour of the LORD.

Pr 11:4 Riches profit not in the day of wrath: but righteousness delivereth from death.

Pr 11:19 As righteousness *tendeth* to life: so he that pursueth evil *pursueth it* to his own death.

Pr 12:28 In the way of righteousness *is* life; and *in* the pathway *thereof there is* no death.

Pr 19:23 The fear of the LORD *tendeth* to life: and *he that hath it* shall abide satisfied; he shall not be visited with evil.

Is 38:16 O Lord, by these *things men* live, and in all these *things is* the life of my spirit: so wilt thou recover me, and make me to live.

Je 21:9 He that abideth in this city shall die by the sword, and by the famine, and by the pestilence: but he that goeth out, and falleth to the Chaldeans that besiege you, he shall live, and his life shall be unto him for a prey.

Je 39:18 For I will surely deliver thee, and thou shalt not fall by the sword, but thy life shall be for a prey unto thee: because thou hast put thy trust in me, saith the LORD.

Eze 3:21 Nevertheless if thou warn the righteous *man,* that the righteous sin not, and he doth not sin, he shall surely live, because he is warned; also thou hast delivered thy soul.

Eze 20:11 And I gave them my statutes, and shewed them my judgments, which *if* a man do, he shall even live in them.

Eze 33:13 When I shall say to the righteous, *that* he shall surely live; if he trust to his own righteousness, and commit iniquity, all his righteousnesses shall not be remembered; but for his iniquity that he hath committed, he shall die for it.

Eze 33:19 But if the wicked turn from his wickedness, and do that which is lawful and right, he shall live thereby.

Mal 2:5 My covenant was with him of life and peace; and I gave them to him *for* the fear wherewith he feared me, and was afraid before my name.

Lu 10:27–28 And he answering said, Thou shalt love the Lord thy God with all thy heart, and with all thy soul, and with all thy strength, and with all thy mind; and thy neighbour as thyself.

And he said unto him, Thou hast answered right: this do, and thou shalt live.

Ro 10:5 For Moses describeth the righteousness which is of the law, That the man which doeth those things shall live by them.

Ga 3:12 And the law is not of faith: but, The man that doeth them shall live in them.

4. From Christ

RADIANT

Jn 1:4 In him was life; and the life was the light of men.

Jn 5:26 For as the Father hath life in himself; so hath he given to the Son to have life in himself;

ABUNDANT

Jn 10:10 The thief cometh not, but for to steal, and to kill, and to destroy: I am come that they might have life, and that they might have *it* more abundantly.

FOR THE DEAD

Jn 11:25 Jesus said unto her, I am the resurrection, and the life: he that believeth in me, though he were dead, yet shall he live:

THE WAY, THE TRUTH, THE LIFE

Jn 14:6 Jesus saith unto him, I am the way, the truth, and the life: no man cometh unto the Father, but by me.

EVERLASTING

Ro 5:21 That as sin hath reigned unto death, even so might grace reign through righteousness unto eternal life by Jesus Christ our Lord.

1 Jn 1:2 (For the life was manifested, and we have seen *it,* and bear witness, and shew unto you that eternal life, which was with the Father, and was manifested unto us;)

DEATH ABOLISHED

2 Ti 1:10 But is now made manifest by the appearing of our Saviour Jesus Christ, who hath abolished death, and hath brought life and immortality to light through the gospel:

1 Jn 1:2 (For the life was manifested, and we have seen *it,* and bear witness, and shew unto you that eternal life, which was with the Father, and was manifested unto us;)

THE ONLY SOURCE OF LIFE

1 Jn 5:12 He that hath the Son hath life; *and* he that hath not the Son of God hath not life.

5. Divine

SUSTAINED BY THE WORD OF GOD

De 8:3; Is 55:3

SECURED THROUGH FAITH

Jn 5:24; Jn 20:31;Ro 6:11; 8:10

NECESSITATES DEATH TO SIN AND SELF

2 Co 4:11;Ga 2:20

THE SUPREME OBJECTIVE

Ph 1:21;1 Pe 4:6

THE DEMONSTRATION

1 Jn 3:14

6. Consistent, *characterizes spiritual maturity*

2 Co 6:3 Giving no offence in any thing, that the ministry be not blamed:

Ph 1:27 Only let your conversation be as it becometh the gospel of Christ: that whether I come and see you, or else be absent, I may hear of your affairs, that ye stand fast in one spirit, with one mind striving together for the faith of the gospel;

1 Ti 3:7 Moreover he must have a good report of them which are without; lest he fall into reproach and the snare of the devil.

1 Th 4:12 That ye may walk honestly toward them that are without, and *that* ye may have lack of nothing.

Ja 3:13 Who *is* a wise man and endued with knowledge among you? let him shew out of a good conversation his works with meekness of wisdom.

2 Pe 3:11 *Seeing* then *that* all these things shall be dissolved, what manner *of persons* ought ye to be in *all* holy conversation and godliness,

7. Conspicuous, *aim of the true disciple*

Mt 5:14; Lu 11:33; 1 Co 4:9

8. Risen

A NEW POWER

Ro 8:11 But if the Spirit of him that raised up Jesus from the dead dwell in you, he that raised up Christ from the dead shall also quicken your mortal bodies by his Spirit that dwelleth in you.

CHRISTLIKENESS

2 Co 4:10 Always bearing about in the body the dying of the Lord Jesus, that the life also of Jesus might be made manifest in our body.

DEVOTION TO A NEW MASTER

2 Co 5:15 And *that* he died for all, that they which live should not henceforth live unto themselves, but unto him which died for them, and rose again.

HEAVENLY AMBITION

Col 3:1 If ye then be risen with Christ, seek those things which are above, where Christ sitteth on the right hand of God.

HEAVENLY AFFECTIONS

Col 3:2 Set your affection on things above, not on things on the earth.

EXALTATION TO HEAVENLY PLACES

Ep 2:5–6 Even when we were dead in sins, hath quickened us together with Christ, (by grace ye are saved;)

And hath raised *us* up together, and made *us* sit together in heavenly *places* in Christ Jesus:

9. Hated

Jb 7:16; Ec 2:17

10. Lessons

LEARNED IN THE SCHOOL OF AFFLICTION

Ps 119:71 *It is* good for me that I have been afflicted; that I might learn thy statutes.

PRACTICAL

Is 1:16–17 Wash you, make you clean; put away the evil of your doings from before mine eyes; cease to do evil;

Learn to do well; seek judgment, relieve the oppressed, judge the fatherless, plead for the widow.

Is 1:17 Learn to do well; seek judgment, relieve the oppressed, judge the fatherless, plead for the widow.

OF THE GREAT TEACHER

Mt 11:29 Take my yoke upon you, and learn of me; for I am meek and lowly in heart: and ye shall find rest unto your souls.

ALL LEAD TO CHRIST

Jn 6:45 It is written in the prophets, And they shall be all taught of God. Every man therefore that hath heard, and hath learned of the Father, cometh unto me.

PURIFY THE SOUL

Ep 4:20–23 But ye have not so learned Christ;

If so be that ye have heard him, and have been taught by him, as the truth is in Jesus:

That ye put off concerning the former conversation the old man, which is corrupt according to the deceitful lusts;

And be renewed in the spirit of your mind;

RESULT IN PERFECT CONTENTMENT

Ph 4:11 Not that I speak in respect of want: for I have learned, in whatsoever state I am, *therewith* to be content.

1 Ti 5:4 But if any widow have children or nephews, let them learn first to shew piety at home, and to requite their parents: for that is good and acceptable before God.

11. *Manifested*

Mt 7:19–20 Every tree that bringeth not forth good fruit is hewn down, and cast into the fire.

Wherefore by their fruits ye shall know them.

Lu 8:17 For nothing is secret, that shall not be made manifest; neither *any thing* hid, that shall not be known and come abroad.

Lu 12:3 Therefore whatsoever ye have spoken in darkness shall be heard in the light; and that which ye have spoken in the ear in closets shall be proclaimed upon the housetops.

Jn 2:11 This beginning of miracles did Jesus in Cana of Galilee, and mani-fested forth his glory; and his disciples believed on him.

2 Co 11:6 But though *I be* rude in speech, yet not in knowledge; but we have been throughly made manifest among you in all things.

1 Ti 5:25 Likewise also the good works *of some* are manifest beforehand; and they that are otherwise cannot be hid.

2 Ti 3:9 But they shall proceed no further: for their folly shall be manifest unto all *men,* as theirs also was.

1 Jn 2:19 They went out from us, but they were not of us; for if they had been of us, they would *no doubt* have continued with us: but *they went out,* that they might be made manifest that they were not all of us.

1 Jn 3:10 In this the children of God are manifest, and the children of the devil: whosoever doeth not righteousness is not of God, neither he that loveth not his brother.

12. *Of Sin*

2 K 17:40 Howbeit they did not hearken, but they did after their former manner.

Ro 6:6 Knowing this, that our old man is crucified with *him,* that the body of sin might be destroyed, that henceforth we should not serve sin.

Ep 4:22 That ye put off concerning the former conversation the old man, which is corrupt according to the deceitful lusts;

Col 3:9 Lie not one to another, seeing that ye have put off the old man with his deeds;

1 Pe 4:3 For the time past of *our* life may suffice us to have wrought the will of the Gentiles, when we walked in lasciviousness, lusts, excess of wine, revellings, banquetings, and abominable idolatries:

2 Pe 1:9 But he that lacketh these things is blind, and cannot see afar off, and hath forgotten that he was purged from his old sins.

13. Its Purpose

TO SERVE OF GOD

Jos 24:15 And if it seem evil unto you to serve the LORD, choose you this day whom ye will serve; whether the gods which your fathers served that *were* on the other side of the flood, or the gods of the Amorites, in whose land ye dwell: but as for me and my house, we will serve the LORD.

TO SEEK GOD'S KINGDOM

Mt 6:33 But seek ye first the kingdom of God, and his righteousness; and all these things shall be added unto you.

TO DO THE FATHER'S WILL

Jn 4:34 Jesus saith unto them, My meat is to do the will of him that sent me, and to finish his work.

TO FINISH THE DIVINE TASK

Jn 17:4 I have glorified thee on the earth: I have finished the work which thou gavest me to do.

TO COMPLETE THE COURSE JOYFULLY

Ac 20:24 But none of these things move me, neither count I my life dear unto myself, so that I might finish my course with joy, and the ministry, which If the Lord Jesus, to testify the gospel of the grace of God.

TO ATTAIN CHRISTLIKENESS

Ph 3:13–14 Brethren, I count not myself to have apprehended: but *this* one thing *I do,* forgetting those things which are behind, and reaching forth unto those things which are before,

I press toward the mark for the prize of the high calling of God in Christ Jesus.

14. Its Testings

THE INWARD LIFE TRIED

Ps 17:3 Thou hast proved mine heart; thou hast visited *me* in the night; thou hast tried me, *and* shalt find nothing; I am purposed *that* my mouth shall not transgress.

Da 12:10 Many shall be purified, and made white, and tried; but the wicked shall do wickedly: and none of the wicked shall understand; but the wise shall understand.

THE REFINING PROCESS

Zec 13:9 And I will bring the third part through the fire, and will refine them as silver is refined, and will try them as gold is tried: they shall call on my name, and I will hear them: I will say, It *is* my people: and they shall say, The LORD *is* my God.

Mal 3:3 And he shall sit *as* a refiner and purifier of silver: and he shall purify the sons of Levi, and purge them as gold and silver, that they may offer unto the LORD an offering in righteousness.

THE TEST OF THE STORM

Lu 6:48 He is like a man which built an house, and digged deep, and laid the foundation on a rock: and when the flood arose, the stream beat vehemently upon that house, and could not shake it: for it was founded upon a rock.

THE FINAL TEST

1 Co 3:13 Every man's work shall be made manifest: for the day shall declare it, because it shall be revealed by fire; and the fire shall try every man's work of what sort it is.

15. Its Salvation Is Death

Lu 9:24 For whosoever will save his life shall lose it: but whosoever will lose his life for my sake, the same shall save it.

Jn 6:51 I am the living bread which came down from heaven: if any man eat of this bread, he shall live for ever: and the bread that I will give is my flesh, which I will give for the life of the world.

Jn 12:24 Verily, verily, I say unto you, Except a corn of wheat fall into the ground and die, it abideth alone: but if it die, it bringeth forth much fruit.

Ro 6:4 Therefore we are buried with him by baptism into death: that like as Christ was raised up from the dead by the glory of the Father, even so we also should walk in newness of life.

1 Co 15:36 *Thou* fool, that which thou sowest is not quickened, except it die:

2 Co 4:11–12 For we which live are alway delivered unto death for Jesus' sake, that the life also of Jesus might be made manifest in our mortal flesh.

So then death worketh in us, but life in you.

Gal 2:20 I am crucified with Christ: nevertheless I live; yet not I, but Christ liveth in me: and the life which I now live in the flesh I live by the faith of the Son of God, who loved me, and gave himself for me.

Col 3:3–4 For ye are dead, and your life is hid with Christ in God.

When Christ, *who is* our life, shall appear, then shall ye also appear with him in glory.

Re 1:18 I *am* he that liveth, and was dead; and, behold, I am alive for evermore, Amen; and have the keys of hell and of death.

16. Its Value

Jb 2:4 And Satan answered the LORD, and said, Skin for skin, yea, all that a man hath will he give for his life.

Ps 72:14 He shall redeem their soul from deceit and violence: and precious shall their blood be in his sight.

Mt 6:25 Therefore I say unto you, Take no thought for your life, what ye shall eat, or what ye shall drink; nor yet for your body, what ye shall put on. Is not the life more than meat, and the body than raiment?

Mt 10:31 Fear ye not therefore, ye are of more value than many sparrows.

Mt 16:26 For what is a man profited, if he shall gain the whole world, and lose his own soul? or what shall a man give in exchange for his soul?

Lu 9:25 For what is a man advantaged, if he gain the whole world, and lose himself, or be cast away?

17. Its Longevity

a. Promised to the Obedient

De 5:33 Ye shall walk in all the ways which the LORD your God hath commanded you, that ye may live, and *that it may be* well with you, and *that* ye may prolong *your* days in the land which ye shall possess.

De 11:21 That your days may be multiplied, and the days of your children, in the land which the LORD sware unto your fathers to give them, as the days of heaven upon the earth.

1 K 3:14 And if thou wilt walk in my ways, to keep my statutes and my commandments, as thy father David did walk, then I will lengthen thy days.

Jb 5:26 Thou shalt come to *thy* grave in a full age, like as a shock of corn cometh in in his season.

Ps 41:2 The LORD will preserve him, and keep him alive; *and* he shall be blessed upon the earth: and thou wilt not deliver him unto the will of his enemies.

Ps 90:10 The days of our years *are* threescore years and ten; and if by reason of strength *they be* fourscore years, yet *is* their strength labour and sorrow; for it is soon cut off, and we fly away.

Ps 91:16 With long life will I satisfy him, and shew him my salvation.

Ps 118:17 I shall not die, but live, and declare the works of the LORD.

Pr 3:2 For length of days, and long life, and peace, shall they add to thee.

Pr 9:11 For by me thy days shall be multiplied, and the years of thy life shall be increased.

Pr 10:27 The fear of the LORD prolongeth days: but the years of the wicked shall be shortened.

Is 38:5 Go, and say to Hezekiah, Thus saith the LORD, the God of David thy father, I have heard thy prayer, I have seen thy tears: behold, I will add unto thy days fifteen years.

Is 65:22 They shall not build, and another inhabit; they shall not plant, and another eat: for as the days of a tree *are* the days of my people, and mine elect shall long enjoy the work of their hands.

Zec 8:4 Thus saith the LORD of hosts; There shall yet old men and old women dwell in the streets of Jerusalem, and every man with his staff in his hand for very age.

1 Pe 3:10 For he that will love life, and see good days, let him refrain his tongue from evil, and his lips that they speak no guile:

b. Examples

Ge 5:4, 8, 11, 14, 17, 20, 27, 31; 7:6; 9:29; 11:11; 21:5; 23:1; 25:7, 17; 35:28; 47:9, 28; 50:22; Ex 6:16, 20; Nu 33:39; De 31:2; 34:7; Jos 14:10; 24:29; Jud 8:32; 1 S 4:15; 12:2; 2 S 19:35; 1 Chr 29:28; Jb 42:17; Ps 21:4; Ec 6:3, 6; 11:8; Lu 2:36

18. Its Eternality

Conditions of Receiving

RENUNCIATION OF THE WORLD

Lu 18:28–30 Then Peter said, Lo, we have left all, and followed thee.

And he said unto them, Verily I say unto you, There is no man that hath left house, or parents, or brethren, or wife, or children, for the kingdom of God's sake,

Who shall not receive manifold more in this present time, and in the world to come life everlasting.

FAITH IN CHRIST

Jn 3:14 And as Moses lifted up the serpent in the wilderness, even so must the Son of man be lifted up:

Jn 3:36 He that believeth on the Son hath everlasting life: and he that believeth not the Son shall not see life; but the wrath of God abideth on him.

Jn 4:14 But whosoever drinketh of the water that I shall give him shall never thirst; but the water that I shall give him shall be in him a well of water springing up into everlasting life.

SPIRITUAL SERVICE

Jn 4:35 Say not ye, There are yet four months, and *then* cometh harvest? behold, I say unto you, Lift up your eyes, and look on the fields; for they are white already to harvest.

Jn 5:24 Verily, verily, I say unto you, He that heareth my word, and believeth on him that sent me, hath everlasting life, and shall not come into condemnation; but is passed from death unto life.

Jn 6:40 And this is the will of him that sent me, that every one which seeth the Son, and believeth on him, may have everlasting life: and I will raise him up at the last day.

SELF-SACRIFICE

Jn 12:25 He that loveth his life shall lose it; and he that hateth his life in this world shall keep it unto life eternal.

KNOWLEDGE OF GOD

Jn 17:3 And this is life eternal, that they might know thee the only true God, and Jesus Christ, whom thou hast sent.

SOWING TO THE SPIRIT

Ga 6:8 For he that soweth to his flesh shall of the flesh reap corruption; but he that soweth to the Spirit shall of the Spirit reap life everlasting.

See **DEATH, FRAILITY, FUTURE LIFE, MORTALITY, JUDGMENTS, SALVATION, SIN**

LIGHT

1. Physical

Ge 1:3, 17; Ex 10:23; Jb 36:30; 38:19; Ps 74:16; Is 45:7; 2 Co 4:6

2. Spiritual

2 S 22:29 For thou *art* my lamp, O LORD: and the LORD will lighten my darkness.

Ps 36:9 For with thee *is* the fountain of life: in thy light shall we see light.

Is 58:10 And *if* thou draw out thy soul to the hungry, and satisfy the afflicted soul; then shall thy light rise in obscurity, and thy darkness *be* as the noonday:

Ac 26:18 To open their eyes, *and* to turn *them* from darkness to light, and *from* the power of Satan unto God, that they may receive forgiveness of sins, and inheritance among them which are sanctified by faith that is in me.

1 Pe 2:9 But ye *are* a chosen generation, a royal priesthood, an holy nation, a peculiar people; that ye should shew forth the praises of him who hath called you out of darkness into his marvellous light:

a. Reflected from Believers

Jud 5:31 So let all thine enemies perish, O LORD: but *let* them that love him *be* as the sun when he goeth forth in his might. And the land had rest forty years.

Is 60:3 And the Gentiles shall come to thy light, and kings to the brightness of thy rising.

Is 62:1 For Zion's sake will I not hold my peace, and for Jerusalem's sake I will not rest, until the righteousness thereof go forth as brightness, and the salvation thereof as a lamp *that* burneth.

Zec 4:2 And said unto me, What seest thou? And I said, I have looked, and behold a candlestick all *of* gold, with a bowl upon the top of it, and his seven lamps thereon, and seven pipes to the seven lamps, which *are* upon the top thereof:

Zec 14:7 But it shall be one day which shall be known to the LORD, not day, nor night: but it shall come to pass, *that* at evening time it shall be light.

Mt 5:14 Ye are the light of the world. A city that is set on an hill cannot be hid.

Ac 13:47 For so hath the Lord commanded us, *saying,* I have set thee to be a light of the Gentiles, that thou shouldest be for salvation unto the ends of the earth.

Ep 5:8 For ye were sometimes darkness, but now *are ye* light in the Lord: walk as children of light:

Ph 2:15 That ye may be blameless and harmless, the sons of God, without rebuke, in the midst of a crooked and perverse nation, among whom ye shine as lights in the world;

1 Th 5:5 Ye are all the children of light, and the children of the day: we are not of the night, nor of darkness.

b. Used by Believers

IN WORSHIP

2 Chr 5:13–14 It came even to pass, as the trumpeters and singers *were* as one, to make one sound to be heard in praising and thanking the LORD; and when they lifted up *their* voice with the trumpets and cymbals and instruments of musick, and praised the LORD, *saying,* For *he is* good; for his mercy *endureth* for ever: that *then* the house was filled with a cloud, *even* the house of the LORD;

So that the priests could not stand to minister by reason of the cloud: for the glory of the LORD had filled the house of God.

IN WORK

Jn 9:4 I must work the works of him that sent me, while it is day: the night cometh, when no man can work.

IN WAR

Ro 13:12 The night is far spent, the day is at hand: let us therefore cast off the works of darkness, and let us put on the armour of light.

IN WALKING

Ep 5:8 For ye were sometimes darkness, but now *are ye* light in the Lord: walk as children of light:

IN WITNESSING

Ph 2:15 That ye may be blameless and harmless, the sons of God, without rebuke, in the midst of a crooked and perverse nation, among whom ye shine as lights in the world;

IN WATCHING

1 Th 5:5–6 Ye are all the children of light, and the children of the day: we are not of the night, nor of darkness.

Therefore let us not sleep, as *do* others; but let us watch and be sober.

3. Promised

TO THE OBEDIENT

Jb 22:28 Thou shalt also decree a thing, and it shall be established unto thee: and the light shall shine upon thy ways.

Ps 97:11 Light is sown for the righteous, and gladness for the upright in heart.

TO THE UPRIGHT

Ps 112:4 Unto the upright there ariseth light in the darkness: *he is* gracious, and full of compassion, and righteous.

TO THE JUST

Pr 4:18 But the path of the just *is* as the shining light, that shineth more and more unto the perfect day.

TO THE BENEVOLENT

Is 58:8 Then shall thy light break forth as the morning, and thine health shall spring forth speedily: and thy righteousness shall go before thee; the glory of the LORD shall be thy rereward.

TO THE CHURCH OF THE FUTURE

Is 60:20 Thy sun shall no more go down; neither shall thy moon withdraw itself: for the LORD shall be thine everlasting light, and the days of thy mourning shall be ended.

TO THE FOLLOWERS OF CHRIST

Jn 8:12 Then spake Jesus again unto them, saying, I am the light of the world: he that followeth me shall not walk in darkness, but shall have the light of life.

1 Jn 2:10 He that loveth his brother abideth in the light, and there is none occasion of stumbling in him.

4. Universal

Jn 1:9 *That* was the true Light, which lighteth every man that cometh into the world.

Jn 3:19 And this is the condemnation, that light is come into the world, and men loved darkness rather than light, because their deeds were evil.

Ro 1:20 For the invisible things of him from the creation of the world are clearly seen, being understood by the things that are made, *even* his eternal power and Godhead; so that they are without excuse:

Ro 2:15 Which shew the work of the law written in their hearts, their conscience also bearing witness, and *their* thoughts the mean while accusing or else excusing one another;)

See **BLINDNESS, DARKNESS, GUIDANCE**

LIGHTNING *See* WEATHER

LILY

Song 2:1, 2; Ho 14:5; Mt 6:28; Lu 12:27

LIMITATIONS

1. Human

WAY HEDGED UP

Jb 3:23 *Why is light given* to a man whose way is hid, and whom God hath hedged in?

FEET IN THE STOCKS

Jb 13:27 Thou puttest my feet also in the stocks, and lookest narrowly unto all my paths; thou settest a print upon the heels of my feet.

Jb 19:8 He hath fenced up my way that I cannot pass, and he hath set darkness in my paths.

TIME LIMITED

Ps 90:10 The days of our years *are* threescore years and ten; and if by reason of strength *they be* fourscore years, yet *is* their strength labour and sorrow; for it is soon cut off, and we fly away.

Ec 8:8 *There is* no man that hath power over the spirit to retain the spirit; neither *hath he* power in the day of death: and *there is* no discharge in *that* war; neither shall wickedness deliver those that are given to it.

BOUNDARIES OF LIFE

Ps 139:5 Thou hast beset me behind and before, and laid thine hand upon me.

Lam 3:7 He hath hedged me about, that I cannot get out: he hath made my chain heavy.

NO POWER TO CHANGE A HAIR

Mt 5:36 Neither shalt thou swear by thy head, because thou canst not make one hair white or black.

NO POWER TO ADD TO STATURE

Mt 6:27 Which of you by taking thought can add one cubit unto his stature?

2. Resources

A LITTLE BREAD AND A BOTTLE OF WATER

Ge 21:14

A HANDFUL OF MEAL AND A CRUSE OF OIL

1 K 7:12

A POT OF OIL

2 K 4:2

FIVE BARLEY LOAVES AND TWO SMALL FISHES

Mt 15:33–34

AN EMPTY LARDER

Lu 11:6

SMALL OFFERINGS ACCEPTED FROM THE POOR

Le 14:21–22

TWO MITES FROM THE WIDOW

Mk 12:42–44

A CUP OF COLD WATER NOT DESPISED

Mt 10:42

FAITH THE SIZE OF MUSTARD SEED

Mt 17:20

TWO OR THREE ASSEMBLED IN CHRIST'S NAME

Mt 18:20

See **FAITH, GIVING, MAN**

LINEN, *fine cloth woven from fibers of flax*

Ge 41:42; Ex 26:1, 31, 36; 27:9, 16; 28:6, 8, 15, 39; 35:6, 23, 35; 36:8, 35; 38:9, 16, 18; 39:2, 5, 27; Le 16:23; 19:19; 2 S 6:14; 1 Chr 4:21; 15:27; 2 Chr 2:14; 3:14; 5:12; Est 1:6; Pr 7:16; 31:24; Is 3:23; Eze 9:2; 16:13; 27:7, 16; 44:18; Da 10:5;

12:6; Ho 2:5; Mt 27:59; Lu 16:19; Re 19:8

LIONS *See* **ANIMALS**

LITIGATION *See* **COURTS**

LIVING

1. Unto God

Lu 20:38 For he is not a God of the dead, but of the living: for all live unto him.

Ro 6:2 God forbid. How shall we, that are dead to sin, live any longer therein?

Ro 6:11 Likewise reckon ye also yourselves to be dead indeed unto sin, but alive unto God through Jesus Christ our Lord.

Ro 14:8 For whether we live, we live unto the Lord; and whether we die, we die unto the Lord: whether we live therefore, or die, we are the Lord's.

2 Co 1:12 For our rejoicing is this, the testimony of our conscience, that in simplicity and godly sincerity, not with fleshly wisdom, but by the grace of God, we have had our conversation in the world, and more abundantly to you-ward.

2 Co 5:15 And *that* he died for all, that they which live should not henceforth live unto themselves, but unto him which died for them, and rose again.

Ga 2:19 For I through the law am dead to the law, that I might live unto God.

Col 3:23 And whatsoever ye do, do *it* heartily, as to the Lord, and not unto men;

1 Pe 4:2 That he no longer should live the rest of *his* time in the flesh to the lusts of men, but to the will of God.

2. In Luxury

1 K 4:22–23 And Solomon's provision for one day was thirty measures of fine flour, and threescore measures of meal,

Ten fat oxen, and twenty oxen out of the pastures, and an hundred sheep, beside harts, and roebucks, and fallowdeer, and fatted fowl.

1 K 10:5 And the meat of his table, and the sitting of his servants, and the attendance of his ministers, and their apparel, and his cupbearers, and his ascent by which he went up unto the house of the LORD; there was no more spirit in her.

1 K 10:21–22 And all king Solomon's drinking vessels *were of* gold, and all the vessels of the house of the forest of Lebanon *were of* pure gold; none *were of* silver: it was nothing accounted of in the days of Solomon.

For the king had at sea a navy of Tharshish with the navy of Hiram: once in three years came the navy of Tharshish, bringing gold, and silver, ivory, and apes, and peacocks.

Est 1:5–7 And when these days were expired, the king made a feast unto all the people that were present in Shushan the palace, both unto great and small, seven days, in the court of the garden of the king's palace;

Where were white, green, and blue, *hangings,* fastened with cords of fine linen and purple to silver rings and pillars of marble: the beds *were of* gold and silver, upon a pavement of red, and blue, and white, and black, marble.

And they gave *them* drink in vessels of gold, (the vessels being diverse one from another,) and royal wine in abundance, according to the state of the king.

Eze 27:7 Fine linen with broidered work from Egypt was that which thou spreadest forth to be thy sail; blue and purple from the isles of Elishah was that which covered thee.

Am 6:4 That lie upon beds of ivory, and stretch themselves upon their couches, and eat the lambs out of the flock, and the calves out of the midst of the stall;

Lu 16:19 There was a certain rich man, which was clothed in purple and fine linen, and fared sumptuously every day:

3. In Worldliness

a. Results of Seeking Pleasure

POVERTY

Pr 21:17 He that loveth pleasure *shall be* a poor man: he that loveth wine and oil shall not be rich.

Is 22:13 And behold joy and gladness, slaying oxen, and killing sheep, eating flesh, and drinking wine: let us eat and drink; for to morrow we shall die.

FALSE SECURITY

Is 47:8–9 Therefore hear now this, *thou that art* given to pleasures, that dwellest carelessly, that sayest in thine heart, I *am,* and none else beside me; I shall not sit *as a* widow, neither shall I know the loss of children:

But these two *things* shall come to thee in a moment in one day, the loss of children, and widowhood: they shall come upon thee in their perfection for the multitude of thy sorceries, *and* for the great abundance of thine enchantments.

SPIRITUAL BARRENNESS

Lu 8:14 And that which fell among thorns are they, which, when they have heard, go forth, and are choked with cares and riches and pleasures of *this* life, and bring no fruit to perfection.

PRESUMPTION

Lu 12:19 And I will say to my soul, Soul, thou hast much goods laid up for many years; take thine ease, eat, drink, *and* be merry.

SPIRITUAL DEATH

1 Ti 5:6 But she that liveth in pleasure is dead while she liveth.

2 Ti 3:4 Traitors, heady, highminded, lovers of pleasures more than lovers of God;

Tit 3:3 For we ourselves also were sometimes foolish, disobedient, deceived, serving divers lusts and pleasures, living in malice and envy, hateful, *and* hating one another.

Ja 5:5 Ye have lived in pleasure on the earth, and been wanton; ye have nourished your hearts, as in a day of slaughter.

DESIRE FOR INCESSANT REVELRY

2 Pe 2:13 And shall receive the reward of unrighteousness, *as* they that count it pleasure to riot in the daytime. Spots *they are* and blemishes, sporting themselves with their own deceivings while they feast with you;

b. Pleasure Sought by the Epicureans

Ec 2:1, 24; 3:13; 5:18; 8:15; 9:7; Is 22:13; 56:12; Am 6:4; Lu 12:19, 45; 16:19; 17:28; Ac 17:18; 1 Co 15:32

See **LIFE**

LIZARDS *See* **ANIMALS, REPTILES**

LOAVES, *MIRACLES OF*

2 K 4:43; Mt 14:17; 15:34; Mk 6:38, 52; Lu 9:16; Jn 6:11

LOCUSTS *See* **MIRACLES, INSECTS**

LONELINESS, *sense of aloneness, isolation, lonesomeness*

1 K 19:10; Ps 38:11; 88:18; 102:7; 142:4; Is 63:5; Jn 16:32; 2 Ti 4:9–10, 16

See **COMFORT**

LONGEVITY *See* **AGE, LIFE**

LONGSUFFERING, *extreme patience*

1. Of God

Nu 14:18 The LORD *is* longsuffering, and of great mercy, forgiving iniquity and transgression, and by no means clearing *the guilty,* visiting the iniquity of the fathers upon the children unto the third and fourth *generation.*

Ps 78:38 But he, *being* full of compassion, forgave *their* iniquity, and destroyed *them* not: yea, many a time turned he his anger away, and did not stir up all his wrath.

Ps 89:33 Nevertheless my lovingkindness will I not utterly take from him, nor suffer my faithfulness to fail.

Ps 99:8 Thou answeredst them, O LORD our God: thou wast a God that forgavest them, though thou tookest vengeance of their inventions.

Is 48:9 For my name's sake will I defer mine anger, and for my praise will I refrain for thee, that I cut thee not off.

Eze 20:17 Nevertheless mine eye spared them from destroying them, neither did I make an end of them in the wilderness.

Eze 20:44 And ye shall know that I *am* the LORD, when I have wrought with you for my name's sake, not according to your wicked ways, nor according to your corrupt doings, O ye house of Israel, saith the Lord GOD.

Eze 33:10 Therefore, O thou son of man, speak unto the house of Israel; Thus ye speak, saying, If our transgressions and our sins *be* upon us, and we pine away in them, how should we then live?

Ro 9:22 *What* if God, willing to shew *his* wrath, and to make his power known, endured with much longsuffering the vessels of wrath fitted to destruction:

1 Pe 3:20 Which sometime were disobedient, when once the longsuffering of God waited in the days of Noah, while the ark was a preparing, wherein few, that is, eight souls were saved by water.

2 Pe 3:9 The Lord is not slack concerning his promise, as some men count slackness; but is longsuffering to us-ward, not willing that any should perish, but that all should come to repentance.

2. Prescribed

1 Co 13:4 Charity suffereth long, *and* is kind; charity envieth not; charity vaunteth not itself, is not puffed up,

2 Co 6:6 By pureness, by knowledge, by longsuffering, by kindness, by the Holy Ghost, by love unfeigned,

Ga 5:22 But the fruit of the Spirit is love, joy, peace, longsuffering, gentleness, goodness, faith,

Col 1:11 Strengthened with all might, according to his glorious power, unto all patience and longsuffering with joyfulness;

2 Ti 4:2 Preach the word; be instant in season, out of season; reprove, rebuke, exhort with all longsuffering and doctrine.

See **GOD, PATIENCE**

LOOKING BACKWARD, *yearning for the old life*

Ge 19:17, 26; Nu 11:5; 14:4; Lu 9:62; Ac 7:39

See **AGE, LIFE**

LORD'S PRAYER, *Jesus tells his disciples how to pray*

Mt 6:9–13; Lu 11:2

See **PRAYER**

LOSS, *SPIRITUAL*

1. Its Causes

SIN

Je 5:25 Your iniquities have turned away these *things,* and your sins have withholden good *things* from you.
Mt 16:26 For what is a man profited, if he shall gain the whole world, and lose his own soul? or what shall a man give in exchange for his soul?

BREACH OF TRUST

Mt 25:27–29 Thou oughtest therefore to have put my money to the exchangers, and *then* at my coming I should have received mine own with usury.

Take therefore the talent from him, and give *it* unto him which hath ten talents.

For unto every one that hath shall be given, and he shall have abundance: but from him that hath not shall be taken away even that which he hath.

WORLDLINESS

Mk 8:36 For what shall it profit a man, if he shall gain the whole world, and lose his own soul?

FALSE FOUNDATIONS

Lu 6:49 But he that heareth, and doeth not, is like a man that without a foundation built an house upon the earth; against which the stream did beat vehemently, and immediately it fell; and the ruin of that house was great.

PRODIGALITY

Lu 15:13 And not many days after the younger son gathered all together, and took his journey into a far country, and there wasted his substance with riotous living.

IMPERFECT SERVICE

1 Co 3:13 Every man's work shall be made manifest: for the day shall declare it, because it shall be revealed by fire; and the fire shall try every man's work of what sort it is.
1 Co 3:15 If any man's work shall be burned, he shall suffer loss: but he himself shall be saved; yet so as by fire.

2. Its Condition

Ps 36:12 There are the workers of iniquity fallen: they are cast down, and shall not be able to rise.
Pr 6:15 Therefore shall his calamity come suddenly; suddenly shall he be broken without remedy.
Je 25:27 Therefore thou shalt say unto them, Thus saith the LORD of hosts, the God of Israel; Drink ye, and be drunken, and spue, and fall, and rise no more, because of the sword which I will send among you.
Na 3:19 *There is* no healing of thy bruise; thy wound is grievous: all that hear the bruit of thee shall clap the hands over thee: for upon whom hath not thy wickedness passed continually?
Mk 3:29 But he that shall blaspheme against the Holy Ghost hath never forgiveness, but is in danger of eternal damnation:
Mk 9:48 Where their worm dieth not, and the fire is not quenched.
Lu 16:26 And beside all this, between us and you there is a great gulf fixed: so that they which would pass from hence to you cannot; neither can they pass to us, that *would come* from thence.
He 6:6 If they shall fall away, to renew them again unto repentance; seeing they crucify to themselves the Son

of God afresh, and put *him* to an open shame.

He 10:26 For if we sin wilfully after that we have received the knowledge of the truth, there remaineth no more sacrifice for sins,

He 12:17 For ye know how that afterward, when he would have inherited the blessing, he was rejected: for he found no place of repentance, though he sought it cars.

Re 14:11 And the smoke of their torment ascendeth up for ever and ever: and they have no rest day nor night, who worship the beast and his image, and whosoever receiveth the mark of his name.

See **GAIN**

LOT, *son of Haran*

A RELIGIOUS MAN

2 Pe 2:7–8 And delivered just Lot, vexed with the filthy conversation of the wicked:

(For that righteous man dwelling among them, in seeing and hearing, vexed *his* righteous soul from day to day with *their* unlawful deeds;)

MADE A WORLDLY CHOICE

Ge 13:10–11 And Lot lifted up his eyes, and beheld all the plain of Jordan, that it *was* well watered every where, before the LORD destroyed Sodom and Gomorrah, *even* as the garden of the LORD, like the land of Egypt, as thou comest unto Zoar.

Then Lot chose him all the plain of Jordan; and Lot journeyed east: and they separated themselves the one from the other.

ASSOCIATED WITH EVIL MEN

Ge 13:12–13 Abram dwelled in the land of Canaan, and Lot dwelled in the cities of the plain, and pitched *his* tent toward Sodom.

But the men of Sodom *were* wicked and sinners before the LORD exceedingly.

Ge 19:1 And there came two angels to Sodom at even; and Lot sat in the gate of Sodom: and Lot seeing *them*

rose up to meet them; and he bowed himself with his face toward the ground;

NARROW ESCAPE FROM DESTRUCTION

Ge 19:17

LOST PROPERTY, WIFE, AND REPUTATION

Ge 19:24–38

See **ABRAHAM**

LOTS, *CASTING, a form of decision-making and of discerning the will of God*

Le 16:8 And Aaron shall cast lots upon the two goats; one lot for the LORD, and the other lot for the scapegoat.

Nu 26:55 Notwithstanding the land shall be divided by lot: according to the names of the tribes of their fathers they shall inherit.

Jos 18:10 And Joshua cast lots for them in Shiloh before the LORD: and there Joshua divided the land unto the children of Israel according to their divisions.

1 S 14:41 Therefore Saul said unto the LORD God of Israel, Give a perfect *lot*. And Saul and Jonathan were taken: but the people escaped.

Est 3:7 In the first month, that *is*, the month Nisan, in the twelfth year of king Ahasuerus, they cast Pur, that *is*, the lot, before Haman from day to day, and from month to month, *to* the twelfth *month*, that *is*, the month Adar.

Est 9:24 Because Haman the son of Hammedatha, the Agagite, the enemy of all the Jews, had devised against the Jews to destroy them, and had cast Pur, that *is*, the lot, to consume them, and to destroy them;

Ps 22:18 They part my garments among them, and cast lots upon my vesture.

Pr 16:33 The lot is cast into the lap; but the whole disposing thereof *is* of the LORD.

Pr 18:18 The lot causeth contentions to cease, and parteth between the mighty.

Jona 1:7 And they said every one to his fellow, Come, and let us cast lots, that we may know for whose cause this evil *is* upon us. So they cast lots, and the lot fell upon Jonah.

Mt 27:35 And they crucified him, and parted his garments, casting lots: that it might be fulfilled which was spoken by the prophet, They parted my garments among them, and upon my vesture did they cast lots.

Lu 23:34 Then said Jesus, Father, forgive them; for they know not what they do. And they parted his raiment, and cast lots.

Ac 1:26 And they gave forth their lots; and the lot fell upon Matthias; and he was numbered with the eleven apostles.

LOVE

1. Family

a. Husbands and Wives

Ge 24:67 And Isaac brought her into his mother Sarah's tent, and took Rebekah, and she became his wife; and he loved her: and Isaac was comforted after his mother's *death.*

Ge 29:20 And Jacob served seven years for Rachel; and they seemed unto him *but* a few days, for the love he had to her.

Ge 29:30 And he went in also unto Rachel, and he loved also Rachel more than Leah, and served with him yet seven other years.

Ge 32:11 Deliver me, I pray thee, from the hand of my brother, from the hand of Esau: for I fear him, lest he will come and smite me, *and* the mother with the children.

Est 2:17 And the king loved Esther above all the women, and she obtained grace and favour in his sight more than all the virgins; so that he set the royal crown upon her head, and made her queen instead of Vashti.

Pr 5:19 *Let her be as* the loving hind and pleasant roe; let her breasts satisfy thee at all times; and be thou ravished always with her love.

Pr 31:11 The heart of her husband doth safely trust in her, so that he shall have no need of spoil.

Pr 31:28 Her children arise up, and call her blessed; her husband *also,* and he praiseth her.

Song 8:7 Many waters cannot quench love, neither can the floods drown it: if *a* man would give all the substance of his house for love, it would utterly be contemned.

Ep 5:28 So ought men to love their wives as their own bodies. He that loveth his wife loveth himself.

Ep 5:33 Nevertheless let every one of you in particular so love his wife even as himself; and the wife *see* that she reverence *her* husband.

Col 3:19 Husbands, love *your* wives, and be not bitter against them.

b. Mothers

HAGAR'S LOVE FOR HER CHILD

Ge 21:16 And she went, and sat her down over against *him* a good way off, as it were a bowshot: for she said, Let me not see the death of the child. And she sat over against *him,* and lift up her voice, and wept.

THE MOTHER OF MOSES

Ex 2:3 And when she could not longer hide him, she took for him an ark of bulrushes, and daubed it with slime and with pitch, and put the child therein; and she laid *it* in the flags by the river's brink.

THE MOTHER OF SAMUEL

1 S 2:19 Moreover his mother made him a little coat, and brought *it* to him from year to year, when she came up with her husband to offer the yearly sacrifice.

RIZPAH'S LOVE FOR HER SONS

2 S 21:9 And he delivered them into the hands of the Gibeonites, and they hanged them in the hill before the LORD: and they fell *all* seven together, and were put to death in the days of harvest, in the first *days,* in the beginning of barley harvest.

2 S 21:10 And Rizpah the daughter of Aiah took sackcloth, and spread it for her upon the rock, from the beginning of harvest until water dropped upon them out of heaven, and suffered neither the birds of the air to rest on them by day, nor the beasts of the field by night.

THE MOTHER IN SOLOMON'S KINGDOM

1 K 3:26 Then spake the woman whose the living child *was* unto the king, for her bowels yearned upon her son, and she said, O my lord, give her the living child, and in no wise slay it. But the other said, Let it be neither mine nor thine, *but* divide *it.*

THE SHUNAMMITE MOTHER

2 K 4:20 And when he had taken him, and brought him to his mother, he sat on her knees till noon, and *then* died.

THE MOTHER'S UNFORGETABLE LOVE

Is 49:15 Can a woman forget her sucking child, that she should not have compassion on the son of her womb? yea, they may forget, yet will I not forget thee.

THE CANAANITE MOTHER

Mt 15:22 And, behold, a woman of Canaan came out of the same coasts, and cried unto him, saying, Have mercy on me, O Lord, *thou* Son of David; my daughter is grievously vexed with a devil.

THE MOTHER OF JESUS

Jn 19:25 Now there stood by the cross of Jesus his mother, and his mother's sister, Mary the *wife* of Cleophas, and Mary Magdalene.

c. Fathers

LABAN

Ge 31:28 And hast not suffered me to kiss my sons and my daughters? thou hast now done foolishly in so doing.

JACOB

Ge 37:35 And all his sons and all his daughters rose up to comfort him; but he refused to be comforted; and he said, For I will go down into the grave unto my son mourning. Thus his father wept for him.

Ge 42:38 And he said, My son shall not go down with you; for his brother is dead, and he is left alone: if mischief befall him by the way in the which ye go, then shall ye bring down my gray hairs with sorrow to the grave.

Ge 46:30 And Israel said unto Joseph, Now let me die, since I have seen thy face, because thou *art* yet alive.

DAVID

2 S 12:16 David therefore besought God for the child; and David fasted, and went in, and lay all night upon the earth.

2 S 13:39 And *the soul of* king David longed to go forth unto Absalom: for he was comforted concerning Amnon, seeing he was dead.

2 S 18:5 And the king commanded Joab and Abishai and Ittai, saying, *Deal* gently for my sake with the young man, *even* with Absalom. And all the people heard when the king gave all the captains charge concerning Absalom.

JAIRUS

Mk 5:23 And besought him greatly, saying, My little daughter lieth at the point of death: *I pray thee,* come and lay thy hands on her, that she may be healed; and she shall live.

FATHER OF THE PRODIGAL

Lu 15:20 And he arose, and came to his father. But when he was yet a great way off, his father saw him, and had compassion, and ran, and fell on his neck, and kissed him.

2. Brotherly

1 Co 13:1 Though I speak with the tongues of men and of angels, and have not charity, I am become *as* sounding brass, or a tinkling cymbal.

Ga 5:13 For, brethren, ye have been called unto liberty; only *use* not liberty for an occasion to the flesh, but by love serve one another.

Ph 1:9 And this I pray, that your love may abound yet more and more in knowledge and *in* all judgment;

1 Th 4:9 But as touching brotherly love ye need not that I write unto you: for ye yourselves are taught of God to love one another.

1 Pe 4:8 And above all things have fervent charity among yourselves: for charity shall cover the multitude of sins.

1 Jn 2:10 He that loveth his brother abideth in the light, and there is none occasion of stumbling in him.

1 Jn 4:21 And this commandment have we from him, That he who loveth God love his brother also.

a. Special Teachings

IMPARTIAL

De 10:19 Love ye therefore the stranger: for ye were strangers in the land of Egypt.

UNSELFISH

Mt 22:39 And the second *is* like unto it, Thou shalt love thy neighbour as thyself.

PROOF OF DISCIPLESHIP

Jn 13:35 By this shall all *men* know that ye are my disciples, if ye have love one to another.

CHRIST'S STANDARD

Jn 15:12 This is my commandment, That ye love one another, as I have loved you.

SINCERE

Ro 12:9 *Let* love be without dissimulation. Abhor that which is evil; cleave to that which is good.

Ro 13:9 For this, Thou shalt not commit adultery, Thou shalt not kill, Thou shalt not steal, Thou shalt not bear false witness, Thou shalt not covet; and if *there be* any other commandment, it is briefly comprehended in this saying, namely, Thou shalt love thy neighbour as thyself.

ABOUNDING

1 Th 3:12 And the Lord make you to increase and abound in love one toward another, and toward all *men,* even as we *do* toward you:

He 13:1 Let brotherly love continue.

Ja 2:8 If ye fulfil the royal law according to the scripture, Thou shalt love thy neighbour as thyself, ye do well:

FERVENT

1 Pe 1:22 Seeing ye have purified your souls in obeying the truth through the Spirit unto unfeigned love of the brethren, *see that ye* love one another with a pure heart fervently:

b. Examples

Ge 29:13 And it came to pass, when Laban heard the tidings of Jacob his sister's son, that he ran to meet him, and embraced him, and kissed him, and brought him to his house. And he told Laban all these things.

1 S 18:3 Then Jonathan and David made a covenant, because he loved him as his own soul.

Ac 20:38 Sorrowing most of all for the words which he spake, that they should see his face no more. And they accompanied him unto the ship.

Ro 16:4 Who have for my life laid down their own necks: unto whom not only I give thanks, but also all the churches of the Gentiles.

2 Co 6:11 O *ye* Corinthians, our mouth is open unto you, our heart is enlarged.

2 Co 7:3 I speak not *this* to condemn *you:* for I have said before, that ye are in our hearts to die and live with *you.*

2 Co 12:15 And I will very gladly spend and be spent for you; though the more abundantly I love you, the less I be loved.

Ph 1:8 For God is my record, how greatly I long after you all in the bowels of Jesus Christ.

Ph 4:1 Therefore, my brethren dearly beloved and longed for, my joy and crown, so stand fast in the Lord, *my* dearly beloved.

2 Ti 1:17 But, when he was in Rome, he sought me out very diligently, and found *me*.

3. Spiritual

a. Of Christ

UNCHANGEABLE

Jn 13:1 Now before the feast of the passover, when Jesus knew that his hour was come that he should depart out of this world unto the Father, having loved his own which were in the world, he loved them unto the end.

DIVINE

Jn 15:9 As the Father hath loved me, so have I loved you: continue ye in my love.

SELF-SACRIFICING

Jn 15:13 Greater love hath no man than this, that a man lay down his life for his friends.

INSEPARABLE

Ro 8:35 Who shall separate us from the love of Christ? *shall* tribulation, or distress, or persecution, or famine, or nakedness, or peril, or sword?

CONSTRAINING

2 Co 5:14 For the love of Christ constraineth us; because we thus judge, that if one died for all, then were all dead:

SACRIFICIAL

Ga 2:20 I am crucified with Christ: nevertheless I live; yet not I, but Christ liveth in me: and the life which I now live in the flesh I live by the faith of the Son of God, who loved me, and gave himself for me.

Ep 5:2 And walk in love, as Christ also hath loved us, and hath given himself for us an offering and a sacrifice to God for a sweetsmelling savour.

MANIFESTED BY HIS DEATH

1 Jn 3:16 Hereby perceive we the love *of God*, because he laid down his life for us: and we ought to lay down *our* lives for the brethren.

b. For Christ

Mt 10:37 He that loveth father or mother more than me is not worthy of me: and he that loveth son or daughter more than me is not worthy of me.

Mt 28:1 In the end of the sabbath, as it began to dawn toward the first *day* of the week, came Mary Magdalene and the other Mary to see the sepulchre.

Mk 15:41 (Who also, when he was in Galilee, followed him, and ministered unto him;) and many other women which came up with him unto Jerusalem.

Jn 8:42 Jesus said unto them, If God were your Father, ye would love me: for I proceeded forth and came from God; neither came I of myself, but he sent me.

Jn 14:15–16 If ye love me, keep my commandments.

And I will pray the Father, and he shall give you another Comforter, that he may abide with you for ever;

Jn 14:22–23 Judas saith unto him, not Iscariot, Lord, how is it that thou wilt manifest thyself unto us, and not unto the world?

Jesus answered and said unto him, If a man love me, he will keep my words: and my Father will love him, and we will come unto him, and make our abode with him.

Jn 16:27 For the Father himself loveth you, because ye have loved me, and have believed that I came out from God.

Jn 19:25 Now there stood by the cross of Jesus his mother, and his mother's sister, Mary the *wife* of Cleophas, and Mary Magdalene.

Jn 20:14 And when she had thus said, she turned herself back, and saw Jesus standing, and knew not that it was Jesus.

Ep 6:24 Grace *be* with all them that love our Lord Jesus Christ in sincerity. Amen.

2 Ti 1:13 Hold fast the form of sound words, which thou hast heard of me, in faith and love which is in Christ Jesus.

Phm 5 Hearing of thy love and faith, which thou hast toward the Lord Jesus, and toward all saints;

1 Pe 1:8 Whom having not seen, ye love; in whom, though now ye see *him* not, yet believing, ye rejoice with joy unspeakable and full of glory:

c. Examples

THE SINFUL WOMAN

Lu 7:47 Wherefore I say unto thee, Her sins, which are many, are forgiven; for she loved much: but to whom little is forgiven, *the same* loveth little.

THOMAS

Jn 11:16 Then said Thomas, which is called Didymus, unto his fellow disciples, Let us also go, that we may die with him.

MARY OF BETHANY

Jn 12:3 Then took Mary a pound of ointment of spikenard, very costly, and anointed the feet of Jesus, and wiped his feet with her hair: and the house was filled with the odour of the ointment.

MARY MAGDALENE

Jn 20:11 But Mary stood without at the sepulchre weeping: and as she wept, she stooped down, *and looked* into the sepulchre,

PETER

Jn 21:16 He saith to him again the second time, Simon, *son* of Jonas, lovest thou me? He saith unto him, Yea, Lord; thou knowest that I love thee. He saith unto him, Feed my sheep.

PAUL

Ac 21:13 Then Paul answered, What mean ye to weep and to break mine heart? for I am ready not to be bound only, but also to die at Jerusalem for the name of the Lord Jesus.

d. Of God

De 7:8 But because the LORD loved you, and because he would keep the oath which he had sworn unto your fathers, hath the LORD brought you out with a mighty hand, and redeemed you out of the house of bondmen, from the hand of Pharaoh king of Egypt.

De 7:13 And he will love thee, and bless thee, and multiply thee: he will also bless the fruit of thy womb, and the fruit of thy land, thy corn, and thy wine, and thine oil, the increase of thy kine, and the flocks of thy sheep, in the land which he sware unto thy fathers to give thee.

De 23:5 Nevertheless the LORD thy God would not hearken unto Balaam; but the LORD thy God turned the curse into a blessing unto thee, because the LORD thy God loved thee.

De 33:3 Yea, he loved the people; all his saints *are* in thy hand: and they sat down at thy feet; *every one* shall receive of thy words.

2 S 12:24 And David comforted Bath-sheba his wife, and went in unto her, and lay with her: and she bare a son, and he called his name Solomon: and the LORD loved him.

2 Chr 2:11 Then Huram the king of Tyre answered in writing, which he sent to Solomon, Because the LORD hath loved his people, he hath made thee king over them.

Jb 14:15 Thou shalt call, and I will answer thee: thou wilt have a desire to the work of thine hands.

Ps 47:4 He shall choose our inheritance for us, the excellency of Jacob whom he loved. Selah.

Ps 146:8 The LORD openeth *the eyes of* the blind: the LORD raiseth them that are bowed down: the LORD loveth the righteous:

Pr 15:9 The way of the wicked *is* an abomination unto the LORD: but he loveth him that followeth after righteousness.

Is 38:17 Behold, for peace I had great bitterness: but thou hast in love to my soul *delivered it* from the pit of corruption: for thou hast cast all my sins behind thy back.

Is 43:4 Since thou wast precious in my sight, thou hast been honourable, and I have loved thee: therefore will I give men for thee, and people for thy life.

Is 48:14 All ye, assemble yourselves, and hear; which among them hath declared these *things?* The LORD hath loved him: he will do his pleasure on Babylon, and his arm *shall be on* the Chaldeans.

Is 49:15 Can a woman forget her sucking child, that she should not have compassion on the son of her womb? yea, they may forget, yet will I not forget thee.

Is 63:9 In all their affliction he was afflicted, and the angel of his presence saved them: in his love and in his pity he redeemed them; and he bare them, and carried them all the days of old.

Je 31:3 The LORD hath appeared of old unto me, *saying,* Yea, I have loved thee with an everlasting love: therefore with lovingkindness have I drawn thee.

Ho 2:14 Therefore, behold, I will allure her, and bring her into the wilderness, and speak comfortably unto her.

Ho 3:1 Then said the LORD unto me, Go yet, love a woman beloved of *her* friend, yet an adulteress, according to the love of the LORD toward the children of Israel, who look to other gods, and love flagons of wine.

Ho 11:1 as a child, then I loved him, and called my son out of Egypt.

Ho 11:8 How shall I give thee up, Ephraim? *how* shall I deliver thee, Israel? how shall I make thee as Admah? *how* shall I set thee as Zeboim? mine heart is turned within me, my repentings are kindled together.

Ho 14:4 I will heal their backsliding, I will love them freely: for mine anger is turned away from him.

Zep 3:17 The LORD thy God in the midst of thee *is* mighty; he will save, he will rejoice over thee with joy; he will rest in his love, he will joy over thee with singing.

Mal 1:2 I have loved you, saith the LORD. Yet ye say, Wherein hast thou loved us? *Was* not Esau Jacob's brother? saith the LORD: yet I loved Jacob,

Mt 18:14 Even so it is not the will of your Father which is in heaven, that one of these little ones should perish.

Mt 21:37 But last of all he sent unto them his son, saying, They will reverence my son.

Mk 12:6 Having yet therefore one son, his wellbeloved, he sent him also last unto them, saying, They will reverence my son.

Jn 3:16 For God so loved the world, that he gave his only begotten Son, that whosoever believeth in him should not perish, but have everlasting life.

Jn 14:21 He that hath my commandments, and keepeth them, he it is that loveth me: and he that loveth me shall be loved of my Father, and I will love him, and will manifest myself to him.

Jn 16:27 For the Father himself loveth you, because ye have loved me, and have believed that I came out from God.

Jn 17:23 I in them, and thou in me, that they may be made perfect in one; and that the world may know that thou hast sent me, and hast loved them, as thou hast loved me.

Ro 5:5 And hope maketh not ashamed; because the love of God is shed abroad in our hearts by the Holy Ghost which is given unto us.

Ro 5:8 But God commendeth his love toward us, in that, while we were yet sinners, Christ died for us.

Ro 8:32 He that spared not his own Son, but delivered him up for us all, how shall he not with him also freely give us all things?

Ro 8:39 Nor height, nor depth, nor any other creature, shall be able to separate us from the love of God, which is in Christ Jesus our Lord.

2 Co 13:14 The grace of the Lord Jesus Christ, and the love of God, and the communion of the Holy Ghost, *be* with you all. Amen.

Ep 2:4–5 But God, who is rich in mercy, for his great love wherewith he loved us,

Even when we were dead in sins, hath quickened us together with Christ, (by grace ye are saved;)

2 Th 2:16 Now our Lord Jesus Christ himself, and God, even our Father, which hath loved us, and hath given *us* everlasting consolation and good hope through grace,

Tit 3:4 But after that the kindness and love of God our Saviour toward man appeared,

He 12:6 For whom the Lord loveth he chasteneth, and scourgeth every son whom he receiveth.

1 Jn 3:1 Behold, what manner of love the Father hath bestowed upon us, that we should be called the sons of God: therefore the world knoweth us not, because it knew him not.

1 Jn 4:9 In this was manifested the love of God toward us, because that God sent his only begotten Son into the world, that we might live through him.

1 Jn 4:16 And we have known and believed the love that God hath to us. God is love; and he that dwelleth in love dwelleth in God, and God in him.

1 Jn 4:19 We love him, because he first loved us.

e. For God

De 6:5 And thou shalt love the LORD thy God with all thine heart, and with all thy soul, and with all thy might.

De 10:12 And now, Israel, what doth the LORD thy God require of thee, but to fear the LORD thy God, to walk in all his ways, and to love him, and to serve the LORD thy God with all thy heart and with all thy soul,

De 11:1 Therefore thou shalt love the LORD thy God, and keep his charge, and his statutes, and his judgments, and his commandments, alway.

De 11:13 And it shall come to pass, if ye shall hearken diligently unto my commandments which I command you this day, to love the LORD your God, and to serve him with all your heart and with all your soul,

De 11:22 For if ye shall diligently keep all these commandments which I command you, to do them, to love the LORD your God, to walk in all his ways, and to cleave unto him;

De 19:9 If thou shalt keep all these commandments to do them, which I

command thee this day, to love the LORD thy God, and to walk ever in his ways; then shalt thou add three cities more for thee, beside these three:

De 30:16 In that I command thee this day to love the LORD thy God, to walk in his ways, and to keep his commandments and his statutes and his judgments, that thou mayest live and multiply: and the LORD thy God shall bless thee in the land whither thou goest to possess it.

De 30:20 That thou mayest love the LORD thy God, *and* that thou mayest obey his voice, and that thou mayest cleave unto him: for he *is* thy life, and the length of thy days: that thou mayest dwell in the land which the LORD sware unto thy fathers, to Abraham, to Isaac, and to Jacob, to give them.

Jos 22:5 But take diligent heed to do the commandment and the law, which Moses the servant of the LORD charged you, to love the LORD your God, and to walk in all his ways, and to keep his commandments, and to cleave unto him, and to serve him with all your heart and with all your soul.

Jos 23:11 Take good heed therefore unto yourselves, that ye love the LORD your God.

Ps 31:23 O love the LORD, all ye his saints: *for* the LORD preserveth the faithful, and plentifully rewardeth the proud doer.

Mt 22:37 Jesus said unto him, Thou shalt love the Lord thy God with all thy heart, and with all thy soul, and with all thy mind.

Mk 12:30 And thou shalt love the Lord thy God with all thy heart, and with all thy soul, and with all thy mind, and with all thy strength: this is the first commandment.

Lu 10:27 And he answering said, Thou shalt love the Lord thy God with all thy heart, and with all thy soul, and with all thy strength, and with all thy mind; and thy neighbour as thyself.

Lu 11:42 But woe unto you, Pharisees! for ye tithe mint and rue and all manner of herbs, and pass over judgment and the love of God: these ought ye to have done, and not to leave the other undone.

Jn 13:34 A new commandment I give unto you, That ye love one another; as I have loved you, that ye also love one another.

Ro 8:28 And we know that all things work together for good to them that love God, to them who are the called according to *his* purpose.

Ep 1:4 According as he hath chosen us in him before the foundation of the world, that we should be holy and without blame before him in love:

2 Th 3:5 And the Lord direct your hearts into the love of God, and into the patient waiting for Christ.

Jude 21 Keep yourselves in the love of God, looking for the mercy of our Lord Jesus Christ unto eternal life.

f. Examples

Ps 18:1 And he said, I will love thee, O LORD, my strength.

Ps 37:4 Delight thyself also in the LORD; and he shall give thee the desires of thine heart.

Ps 42:1 As the hart panteth after the water brooks, so panteth my soul after thee, O God.

Ps 43:4 Then will I go unto the altar of God, unto God my exceeding joy: yea, upon the harp will I praise thee, O God my God.

Ps 73:25 Whom have I in heaven *but thee?* and *there is* none upon earth *that* I desire beside thee.

Ps 84:2 My soul longeth, yea, even fainteth for the courts of the LORD: my heart and my flesh crieth out for the living God.

Ps 116:1 I love the LORD, because he hath heard my voice *and* my supplications.

Ps 119:132 Look thou upon me, and be merciful unto me, as thou usest to do unto those that love thy name.

Is 58:14 Then shalt thou delight thyself in the LORD; and I will cause thee to ride upon the high places of the earth, and feed thee with the heritage of Jacob thy father: for the mouth of the LORD hath spoken *it.*

Mt 22:37 Jesus said unto him, Thou shalt love the Lord thy God with all

thy heart, and with all thy soul, and with all thy mind.

Jn 17:26 And I have declared unto them thy name, and will declare *it:* that the love wherewith thou hast loved me may be in them, and I in them.

1 Co 13:2 And though I have *the gift of* prophecy, and understand all mysteries, and all knowledge; and though I have all faith, so that I could remove mountains, and have not charity, I am nothing.

1 Co 13:13 And now abideth faith, hope, charity, these three; but the greatest of these *is* charity.

1 Co 16:24 My love *be* with you all in Christ Jesus. Amen.

Ga 5:6 For in Jesus Christ neither circumcision availeth any thing, nor uncircumcision; but faith which worketh by love.

Ga 5:22 But the fruit of the Spirit is love, joy, peace, longsuffering, gentleness, goodness, faith,

Ep 3:17–18 That Christ may dwell in your hearts by faith; that ye, being rooted and grounded in love,

May be able to comprehend with all saints what *is* the breadth, and length, and depth, and height;

Ep 4:16 From whom the whole body fitly joined together and compacted by that which every joint supplieth, according to the effectual working in the measure of every part, maketh increase of the body unto the edifying of itself in love.

Ep 5:2 And walk in love, as Christ also hath loved us, and hath given himself for us an offering and a sacrifice to God for a sweetsmelling savour.

Col 1:8 Who also declared unto us your love in the Spirit.

Col 3:14 And above all these things *put on* charity, which is the bond of perfectness.

1 Th 3:6 But now when Timotheus came from you unto us, and brought us good tidings of your faith and charity, and that ye have good remembrance of us always, desiring greatly to see us, as we also *to see* you:

1 Th 5:8 But let us, who are of the day, be sober, putting on the breastplate of faith and love; and for an helmet, the hope of salvation.

2 Th 1:3 We are bound to thank God always for you, brethren, as it is meet, because that your faith groweth exceedingly, and the charity of every one of you all toward each other aboundeth;

1 Ti 2:15 Notwithstanding she shall be saved in childbearing, if they continue in faith and charity and holiness with sobriety.

1 Ti 4:12 Let no man despise thy youth; but be thou an example of the believers, in word, in conversation, in charity, in spirit, in faith, in purity.

1 Ti 6:11 But thou, O man of God, flee these things; and follow after righteousness, godliness, faith, love, patience, meekness.

2 Ti 1:7 For God hath not given us the spirit of fear; but of power, and of love, and of a sound mind.

2 Ti 2:22 Flee also youthful lusts: but follow righteousness, faith, charity, peace, with them that call on the Lord out of a pure heart.

2 Ti 3:10 But thou hast fully known my doctrine, manner of life, purpose, faith, longsuffering, charity, patience,

Tit 2:2 That the aged men be sober, grave, temperate, sound in faith, in charity, in patience.

He 6:10 For God is not unrighteous to forget your work and labour of love, which ye have shewed toward his name, in that ye have ministered to the saints, and do minister.

2 Pe 1:7 And to godliness brotherly kindness; and to brotherly kindness charity.

1 Jn 4:16 And we have known and believed the love that God hath to us. God is love; and he that dwelleth in love dwelleth in God, and God in him.

1 Jn 4:19 We love him, because he first loved us.

1 Jn 5:1 Whosoever believeth that Jesus is the Christ is born of God: and every one that loveth him that begat loveth him also that is begotten of him.

2 Jn 1 The elder unto the elect lady and her children, whom I love in the truth; and not I only, but also all they that have known the truth;

3 Jn 6 Which have borne witness of thy charity before the church: whom if thou bring forward on their journey after a godly sort, thou shalt do well:

4. Preeminent

THE GREATEST COMMANDMENT

Mk 12:30–31 And thou shalt love the Lord thy God with all thy heart, and with all thy soul, and with all thy mind, and with all thy strength: this is the first commandment.

And the second is like, *namely* this, Thou shalt love thy neighbour as thyself. There is none other commandment greater than these.

THE FULFILLING OF THE LAW

Ro 13:10 Love worketh no ill to his neighbour: therefore love *is* the fulfilling of the law.

ABOVE THE GIFT OF TONGUES

1 Co 13:1 Though I speak with the tongues of men and of angels, and have not charity, I am become *as* sounding brass, or a tinkling cymbal.

ABOVE THE GIFTS OF PROPHECY, KNOWLEDGE, AND FAITH

1 Co 13:2 And though I have *the gift of* prophecy, and understand all mysteries, and all knowledge; and though I have all faith, so that I could remove mountains, and have not charity, I am nothing.

ABOVE SELF-SACRIFICE

1 Co 13:3 And though I bestow all my goods to feed *the poor,* and though I give my body to be burned, and have not charity, it profiteth me nothing.

THE GREATEST OF ALL

1 Co 13:13 And now abideth faith, hope, charity, these three; but the greatest of these *is* charity.

5. Its Evidence

TRUE DISCIPLESHIP
Jn 13:35 By this shall all *men* know that ye are my disciples, if ye have love one to another.

GENUINE SERVICE
Jn 21:16 He saith to him again the second time, Simon, *son* of Jonas, lovest thou me? He saith unto him, Yea, Lord; thou knowest that I love thee. He saith unto him, Feed my sheep.

LOVE FOR OTHERS
1 Jn 3:14 We know that we have passed from death unto life, because we love the brethren. He that loveth not *his* brother abideth in death.

LOVE FOR GOD
1 Jn 4:20 If a man say, I love God, and hateth his brother, he is a liar: for he that loveth not his brother whom he hath seen, how can he love God whom he hath not seen?

6. For Everyone

Lu 2:10 And the angel said unto them, Fear not: for, behold, I bring you good tidings of great joy, which shall be to all people.

Jn 3:16 For God so loved the world, that he gave his only begotten Son, that whosoever believeth in him should not perish, but have everlasting life.

Jn 10:16 And other sheep I have, which are not of this fold: them also I must bring, and they shall hear my voice; and there shall be one fold, *and* one shepherd.

Ro 10:12 For there is no difference between the Jew and the Greek: for the same Lord over all is rich unto all that call upon him.

1 Ti 2:4 Who will have all men to be saved, and to come unto the knowledge of the truth.

7. Grown Cold

Je 2:2 Go and cry in the ears of Jerusalem, saying, Thus saith the LORD; I remember thee, the kindness of thy youth, the love of thine espousals, when thou wentest after me in the wilderness, in a land *that was* not sown.

Ho 10:2 Their heart is divided; now shall they be found faulty: he shall break down their altars, he shall spoil their images.

Mt 24:12 And because iniquity shall abound, the love of many shall wax cold.

1 Ti 5:12 Having damnation, because they have cast off their first faith.

Re 2:4 Nevertheless I have *somewhat* against thee, because thou hast left thy first love.

See **CHRIST, COMPANIONSHIP, FAMILY, HATRED, HELPER, PARENTS, POOR, RETALIATION, REVENGE**

LOVINGKINDNESS

Ge 48:11 And Israel said unto Joseph, I had not thought to see thy face: and, lo, God hath shewed me also thy seed.

Ex 15:13 Thou in thy mercy hast led forth the people *which* thou hast redeemed: thou hast guided *them* in thy strength unto thy holy habitation.

De 8:16 Who fed thee in the wilderness with manna, which thy fathers knew not, that he might humble thee, and that he might prove thee, to do thee good at thy latter end;

2 S 22:51 *He is* the tower of salvation for his king: and sheweth mercy to his anointed, unto David, and to his seed for evermore.

Ps 5:7 But as for me, I will come *into* thy house in the multitude of thy mercy: *and* in thy fear will I worship toward thy holy temple.

Ps 17:7 Shew thy marvellous lovingkindness, O thou that savest by thy right hand them which put their trust *in thee* from those that rise up *against them.*

Ps 25:6 Remember, O LORD, thy tender mercies and thy lovingkindnesses; for they *have been* ever of old.

Ps 26:3 For thy lovingkindness *is* before mine eyes: and I have walked in thy truth.

Ps 31:21 Blessed *be* the LORD: for he hath shewed me his marvellous kindness in a strong city.

Ps 36:7 How excellent *is* thy lovingkindness, O God! therefore the children of men put their trust under the shadow of thy wings.

Ps 36:10 O continue thy lovingkindness unto them that know thee; and thy righteousness to the upright in heart.

Ps 40:10 I have not hid thy righteousness within my heart; I have declared thy faithfulness and thy salvation: I have not concealed thy lovingkindness and thy truth from the great congregation.

Ps 42:8 *Yet* the LORD will command his lovingkindness in the daytime, and in the night his song *shall be* with me, *and* my prayer unto the God of my life.

Ps 48:9 We have thought of thy lovingkindness, O God, in the midst of thy temple.

Ps 51:1 Have mercy upon me, O God, according to thy lovingkindness: according unto the multitude of thy tender mercies blot out my transgressions.

Ps 63:3 Because thy lovingkindness *is* better than life, my lips shall praise thee.

Ps 69:16 Hear me, O LORD; for thy lovingkindness *is* good: turn unto me according to the multitude of thy tender mercies.

Ps 88:11 Shall thy lovingkindness be declared in the grave? *or* thy faithfulness in destruction?

Ps 89:33 Nevertheless my lovingkindness will I not utterly take from him, nor suffer my faithfulness to fail.

Ps 89:49 Lord, where *are* thy former lovingkindnesses, *which* thou swarest unto David in thy truth?

Ps 92:2 To shew forth thy lovingkindness in the morning, and thy faithfulness every night,

Ps 101:1 I will sing of mercy and judgment: unto thee, O LORD, will I sing.

Ps 103:4 Who redeemeth thy life from destruction; who crowneth thee with lovingkindness and tender mercies;

Ps 107:43 Whoso *is* wise, and will observe these *things*, even they shall understand the lovingkindness of the LORD.

Ps 117:2 For his merciful kindness is great toward us: and the truth of the LORD *endureth* for ever. Praise ye the LORD.

Ps 119:76 Let, I pray thee, thy merciful kindness be for my comfort, according to thy word unto thy servant.

Ps 119:88 Quicken me after thy lovingkindness; so shall I keep the testimony of thy mouth.

Ps 119:149 Hear my voice according unto thy lovingkindness: O LORD, quicken me according to thy judgment.

Ps 119:159 Consider how I love thy precepts: quicken me, O LORD, according to thy lovingkindness.

Ps 138:2 I will worship toward thy holy temple, and praise thy name for thy lovingkindness and for thy truth: for thou hast magnified thy word above all thy name.

Ps 143:8 Cause me to hear thy lovingkindness in the morning; for in thee do I trust: cause me to know the way wherein I should walk; for I lift up my soul unto thee.

Is 54:8 In a little wrath I hid my face from thee for a moment; but with everlasting kindness will I have mercy on thee, saith the LORD thy Redeemer.

Is 63:7 I will mention the lovingkindnesses of the LORD, *and* the praises of the LORD, according to all that the LORD hath bestowed on us, and the great goodness toward the house of Israel, which he hath bestowed on them according to his mercies, and according to the multitude of his lovingkindnesses.

Je 9:24 But let him that glorieth glory in this, that he understandeth and knoweth me, that I *am* the LORD which exercise lovingkindness, judgment, and righteousness, in the earth: for in these *things* I delight, saith the LORD.

Je 16:5 For thus saith the LORD, Enter not into the house of mourning, neither go to lament nor bemoan them: for I have taken away my peace from this people, saith the L‍ORD, *even* lovingkindness and mercies.

Je 31:3 The L‍ORD hath appeared of old unto me, *saying,* Yea, I have loved thee with an everlasting love: therefore with lovingkindness have I drawn thee.

Je 32:18 Thou shewest lovingkindness unto thousands, and recompensest the iniquity of the fathers into the bosom of their children after them: the Great, the Mighty God, the L‍ORD of hosts, *is* his name,

Ho 2:19 And I will betroth thee unto me for ever; yea, I will betroth thee unto me in righteousness, and in judgment, and in lovingkindness, and in mercies.

Jl 2:13 And rend your heart, and not your garments, and turn unto the L‍ORD your God: for he *is* gracious and merciful, slow to anger, and of great kindness, and repenteth him of the evil.

Ep 2:7 That in the ages to come he might shew the exceeding riches of his grace in *his* kindness toward us through Christ Jesus.

Tit 3:4 But after that the kindness and love of God our Saviour toward man appeared,

See **HATRED, KINDNESS**

LUCRE, *money*

1 Ti 3:8; Tit 1:7; 1 Pe 5:2

See **MONEY**

LUKE

1. Person, *author of the gospel and Acts*

Lu 1:1, 3; Ac 1:1, 1; Col 4:14; 2 Ti 4:11; Phm 24

2. Book

Author: Luke, the beloved physician (Col 4:14). Reputed author of Acts; both books being addressed to the same person. Luke was a close friend and traveling companion of Paul, as is shown in his personal allusions recording the journeys of the apostle. See in the book of Acts where the author changes the pronouns to "we"

and "us," indicating that he himself was present at these times (Ac 16:10; 20:6; 27:1; 28:16). Many students see something of the stamp of Paul's doctrine in Luke's gospel.

Date Written: Most likely before A.D. 70.

Purpose: To give a connected and orderly narrative of the life of Christ as seen by eyewitnesses (1:1–4).

To Whom Written: Addressed to Theophilus, an unknown person. Internal evidence indicates that the book was written especially for the Gentiles. This is inferred from the fact that the writer takes pains to explain Jewish customs and sometimes substitutes Greek names for Hebrew.

Main Theme: Jesus of Nazareth is the perfect Son of Man who came "to seek and to save that which was lost" (19:10).

Key Words: Jesus the Son of Man.

Key Verse: 1:4

LUKEWARMNESS

See **INDIFFERENCE**

LUNCH   *See* **FOOD**

LUST

2 S 11:2–4; Jb 31:1; Mt 5:28; 1 Jn 2:16

See **DESIRE**

LYCAONIA, *a province of Asia Minor*

Ac 14:6, 11

LYDDA, *or Lod, a town southwest of Joppa*

It is a town of considerable importance that lies eleven miles southeast of Joppa. In Old Testament times it was known as Lod (1 Chr 8:12), and in New Testament times as the place where Peter healed the paralytic named Aeneas (Ac 9:32–38).

1 Chr 8:12; Ezr 2:33; Ne 11:35; Ac 9:32

See **CITIES**

LYDIA, *one of Paul's converts*

Ac 16:14, 40

See **WOMEN**

LYING *See* **FALSEHOOD**

LYSTRA, *a city of Lycaonia*

This was the place where Paul healed the crippled man. As a result of this, the people regarded Paul and Barnabas as gods—calling Barnabas "Zeus" and Paul "Hermes" (Ac 14:8–18). Yet later, at the instigation of Jews from Antioch, they stoned Paul and left him for dead (Ac 14:19–20).

See **CITIES**

M

MACEDONIA, *a district of Greece*

Ac 16:9; 19:21; 20:3; Ro 15:26; 1 Co 16:5; 2 Co 1:16; 2:13; 7:5; 8:1; 9:4; 11:9; Ph 4:15; 1 Th 1:8; 4:10; 1 Ti 1:3

MACHIR, *son of Manasseh*

Ge 50:22–23; Nu 26:29; 32:39; 36:1; De 3:15; Jos 17:1; 1 Chr 7:15

MACHPELAH, *a cave near Hebron*

Ge 23:19; 25:9; 49:30; 50:13

MADNESS, *charge against the righteous*

2 K 9:11; Je 29:26; Ho 9:7; Mk 3:21; Jn 10:20; Ac 26:24; 1 Co 14:23; 2 Co 5:13

MAGICIANS, *workers of wonders beyond human powers*

Ge 41:8, 24; Ex 7:11, 22; 8:7, 19; 9:11; Is 47:13; Da 1:20; 2:2, 10, 27; 4:7; 5:7

MAHANAIM, *a place east of the Jordan, where Jacob met the angels*

Ge 32:2

MAJESTY, *God's glory, excellence, and greatness*

Ex 19:18 And mount Sinai was altogether on a smoke, because the LORD descended upon it in fire: and the smoke thereof ascended as the smoke of a furnace, and the whole mount quaked greatly.

De 4:11 And ye came near and stood under the mountain; and the mountain burned with fire unto the midst of heaven, with darkness, clouds, and thick darkness.

De 18:16 According to all that thou desiredst of the LORD thy God in Horeb in the day of the assembly, saying, Let me not hear again the voice of the LORD my God, neither let me see this great fire any more, that I die not.

Jud 5:5 The mountains melted from before the LORD, *even* that Sinai from before the LORD God of Israel.

2 S 22:9 There went up a smoke out of his nostrils, and fire out of his mouth devoured: coals were kindled by it.

1 Chr 17:21 And what one nation in the earth *is* like thy people Israel, whom God went to redeem *to be* his own people, to make thee a name of greatness and terribleness, by driving out nations from before thy people, whom thou hast redeemed out of Egypt?

1 Chr 29:11 Thine, O LORD, *is* the greatness, and the power, and the glory, and the victory, and the majesty: for all *that is* in the heaven and in the earth *is thine;* thine *is* the kingdom, O LORD, and thou art exalted as head above all.

2 Chr 2:5 And the house which I build *is* great: for great *is* our God above all gods.

Ne 1:5 And said, I beseech thee, O LORD God of heaven, the great and terrible God, that keepeth covenant and mercy for them that love him and observe his commandments:

Ne 4:14 And I looked, and rose up, and said unto the nobles, and to the rulers, and to the rest of the people, Be not ye afraid of them: remember the Lord, *which is* great and terrible, and fight for your brethren, your sons, and your daughters, your wives, and your houses.

Ne 9:32 Now therefore, our God, the great, the mighty, and the terrible God, who keepest covenant and mercy, let not all the trouble seem little before thee, that hath come upon us, on our kings, on our princes, and on our priests, and on our prophets, and on our fathers, and on all thy people, since the time of the kings of Assyria unto this day.

Jb 13:11 Shall not his excellency make you afraid? and his dread fall upon you?

Jb 31:23 For destruction *from* God *was* a terror to me, and by reason of his highness I could not endure.

Jb 37:22 Fair weather cometh out of the north: with God is terrible majesty.

Jb 40:10 Deck thyself now *with* majesty and excellency; and array thyself with glory and beauty.

Ps 29:4 The voice of the LORD *is* powerful; the voice of the LORD *is* full of majesty.

Ps 45:3 Gird thy sword upon *thy* thigh, O *most* mighty, with thy glory and thy majesty.

Ps 47:2 For the LORD most high *is* terrible; *he is* a great King over all the earth.

Ps 66:3 Say unto God, How terrible *art thou in* thy works! through the greatness of thy power shall thine enemies submit themselves unto thee.

Ps 68:8 The earth shook, the heavens also dropped at the presence of God: *even* Sinai itself *was moved* at the presence of God, the God of Israel.

Ps 68:33 To him that rideth upon the heavens of heavens, *which were* of old; lo, he doth send out his voice, *and that* a mighty voice.

Ps 89:7 God is greatly to be feared in the assembly of the saints, and to be had in reverence of all *them that are* about him.

Ps 93:1 The LORD reigneth, he is clothed with majesty; the LORD is clothed with strength, *wherewith* he hath girded himself: the world also is stablished, that it cannot be moved.

Ps 96:6 Honour and majesty *are* before him: strength and beauty *are* in his sanctuary.

Ps 97:5 The hills melted like wax at the presence of the LORD, at the presence of the Lord of the whole earth.

Ps 104:1 Bless the LORD, O my soul. O LORD my God, thou art very great; thou art clothed with honour and majesty.

Ps 114:7 Tremble, thou earth, at the presence of the Lord, at the presence of the God of Jacob;

Ps 145:12 To make known to the sons of men his mighty acts, and the glorious majesty of his kingdom.

Is 2:10 Enter into the rock, and hide thee in the dust, for fear of the LORD, and for the glory of his majesty.

Is 2:19 And they shall go into the holes of the rocks, and into the caves of the earth, for fear of the LORD, and for the glory of his majesty, when he ariseth to shake terribly the earth.

Is 24:14 They shall lift up their voice, they shall sing for the majesty of the LORD, they shall cry aloud from the sea.

Is 26:10 Let favour be shewed to the wicked, *yet* will he not learn righteousness: in the land of uprightness will he deal unjustly, and will not behold the majesty of the LORD.

Is 40:22 *It is* he that sitteth upon the circle of the earth, and the inhabitants thereof *are* as grasshoppers; that stretcheth out the heavens as a curtain, and spreadeth them out as a tent to dwell in:

Is 57:15 For thus saith the high and lofty One that inhabiteth eternity, whose name *is* Holy; I dwell in the high and holy *place,* with him also *that is* of a contrite and humble spirit, to revive the spirit of the humble, and to revive the heart of the contrite ones.

Is 64:1 Oh that thou wouldest rend the heavens, that thou wouldest come down, that the mountains might flow down at thy presence,

Eze 38:20 So that the fishes of the sea, and the fowls of the heaven, and the beasts of the field, and all creeping things that creep upon the earth, and all the men that *are* upon the face of the earth, shall shake at my presence, and the mountains shall be thrown down, and the steep places shall fall, and every wall shall fall to the ground.

Eze 43:2 And, behold, the glory of the God of Israel came from the way of the east: and his voice *was* like a noise of many waters: and the earth shined with his glory.

Da 9:4 And I prayed unto the LORD my God, and made my confession, and said, O Lord, the great and dreadful God, keeping the covenant and mercy to them that love him, and to them that keep his commandments;

Am 4:13 For, lo, he that formeth the mountains, and createth the wind, and declareth unto man what *is* his thought, that maketh the morning darkness, and treadeth upon the high places of the earth, The LORD, The God of hosts, *is* his name.

Mi 5:4 And he shall stand and feed in the strength of the LORD, in the majesty of the name of the LORD his God; and they shall abide: for now shall he be great unto the ends of the earth.

Hab 3:3 God came from Teman, and the Holy One from mount Paran. Selah. His glory covered the heavens, and the earth was full of his praise.

He 1:3 Who being the brightness of *his* glory, and the express image of his person, and upholding all things by the word of his power, when he had by himself purged our sins, sat down on the right hand of the Majesty on high;

He 12:19 And the sound of a trumpet, and the voice of words; *which* voice they that heard intreated that the word should not be spoken to them any more:

Jude 25 To the only wise God our Saviour, *be* glory and majesty, dominion and power, both now and ever. Amen.

Re 15:8 And the temple was filled with smoke from the glory of God, and from his power; and no man was able to enter into the temple, till the seven plagues of the seven angels were fulfilled.

Re 20:11 And I saw a great white throne, and him that sat on it, from whose face the earth and the heaven fled away; and there was found no place for them.

See **GLORY**

MAKKEDAH, *a city of the Canaanites*

Jos 10:10, 28; 12:16; 15:41

See **CITIES**

MALACHI

Author: Malachi. Nothing is known of the prophet's life except what is found in his book. He was probably a contemporary of Nehemiah; the conditions described in the prophecy best answer to that time. His style is forceful and particular. Jehovah is represented as having a dialogue with his people. "You say" is contrasted with "thus says the LORD of hosts" through the first three chapters.

Date Written: Around 430 B.C.

Purpose: To confront God's people and their leaders with their sins and plead with them to return to holiness. God will someday judge the righteous and the wicked.

To Whom Written: The inhabitants of Jerusalem and their sinful leaders.

Main Theme: A graphic picture of the closing period of Old Testament history showing that great reforms were needed to prepare the way for the coming Messiah.

Key Word: Return (3:7).

Key Verse: 3:8.

MALICE, *ill will, spite*

1. Condemned

Ex 21:14; Nu 35:20; De 32:33; 1 S 18:11; 23:23; Ps 7:2; Pr 4:17; Ro 1:29; 1 Co 5:8; 14:20; Ga 5:15; Ep 4:31; Col 3:8; Tit 3:3; 1 Pe 2:1

2. Examples

Ge 26:15; 27:41; 37:20; De 19:11; 1 S 19:10, 10; 20:31; 22:19; 23:10; 1 K 21:7; Est 3:6, 13; 6:4; 8:5; Jb 2:3; Ps 10:8; 11:2; 37:14, 32; 69:4; 102:8; 119:95; 140:3; Pr 30:14; Is 59:5; Eze 25:6, 15; 35:5; 36:5; Da 6:15; Mt 14:8; 26:59; 27:18, 23; Mk 3:2, 6; 6:19, 24; 14:1; Lu 6:11; 20:19; 22:2; 23:18, 21; Jn 5:16; 7:1; 12:10; 15:25; Ac 7:54; 23:14; 25:3; Ro 3:13; Ph 1:16

See **EVIL, KINDNESS, LOVE, WICKED**

MAMRE, *plains of*

Ge 13:18; 14:13; 18:1

MANKIND

1. Insignificance

A TENANT IN A HOUSE OF CLAY

Jb 4:19 How much less *in* them that dwell in houses of clay, whose foundation *is* in the dust, *which* are crushed before the moth?

Jb 7:17 What *is* man, that thou shouldest magnify him? and that thou shouldest set thine heart upon him?

A WORM

Jb 25:6 How much less man, *that is* a worm? and the son of man, *which is* a worm?

AN ATOM IN THE NATURAL UNIVERSE

Ps 8:4 What is man, that thou art mindful of him? and the son of man, that thou visitest him?

A GRASSHOPPER WHEN COMPARED TO GOD

Is 40:22 *It is* he that sitteth upon the circle of the earth, and the inhabitants thereof *are* as grasshoppers; that stretcheth out the heavens as a curtain, and spreadeth them out as a tent to dwell in:

YET UNDER THE WATCHFUL CARE OF THE ALMIGHTY

Is 41:14 Fear not, thou worm Jacob, *and* ye men of Israel; I will help thee, saith the LORD, and thy redeemer, the Holy One of Israel.

2. Equality

Mt 23:8 But be not ye called Rabbi: for one is your Master, *even* Christ; and all ye are brethren.

Ac 10:28 And he said unto them, Ye know how that it is an unlawful thing for a man that is a Jew to keep company, or come unto one of another nation; but God hath shewed me that I should not call any man common or unclean.

Ro 10:12 For there is no difference between the Jew and the Greek: for the same Lord over all is rich unto all that call upon him.

Ga 3:28 There is neither Jew nor Greek, there is neither bond nor free, there is neither male nor female: for ye are all one in Christ Jesus.

Phm 1:16 Not now as a servant, but above a servant, a brother beloved, specially to me, but how much more unto thee, both in the flesh, and in the Lord?

Ja 2:5 Hearken, my beloved brethren, Hath not God chosen the poor of this world rich in faith, and heirs of the kingdom which he hath promised to them that love him?

3. Made in the Divine Image

Ge 9:6 Whoso sheddeth man's blood, by man shall his blood be shed: for in the image of God made he man.

Ac 17:28 For in him we live, and move, and have our being; as certain also of your own poets have said, For we are also his offspring.

1 Co 11:7 For a man indeed ought not to cover *his* head, forasmuch as he is the image and glory of God: but the woman is the glory of the man.

1 Co 15:45 And so it is written, The first man Adam *was made* a living soul; the last Adam was made a quickening spirit.

1 Co 15:49 And as we have borne the image of the earthy, we shall also bear the image of the heavenly.

Ja 3:9 Therewith bless we God, even the Father; and therewith curse we men, which are made after the similitude of God.

4. Preeminence over Other Creatures

Ge 1:28; 2:20; Ps 8:6; 82:6; Mt 6:26; 10:31; 12:12; Lu 12:7, 24; 13:15; Jn 10:34; 1 Co 15:39; He 2:7

5. Given Dominion over the Natural World

Ge 1:26; 2:19; 9:2; Jb 5:22; Ps 8:6; 91:13; Je 27:6; 28:14; Da 2:38; Ho 2:18; He 2:8, 8; Ja 3:7

6. A Spiritual Being

Ge 2:7 And the LORD God formed man of the dust of the ground, and breathed into his nostrils the breath of life; and man became a living soul.

Jb 32:8 But *there is* a spirit in man: and the inspiration of the Almighty giveth them understanding.

Pr 20:27 The spirit of man *is* the candle of the LORD, searching all the inward parts of the belly.

Ecc 3:21 Who knoweth the spirit of man that goeth upward, and the spirit of the beast that goeth downward to the earth?

Ec 12:7 Then shall the dust return to the earth as it was: and the spirit shall return unto God who gave it.

Ac 7:59 And they stoned Stephen, calling upon *God*, and saying, Lord Jesus, receive my spirit.

Ac 17:29 Forasmuch then as we are the offspring of God, we ought not to think that the Godhead is like unto gold, or silver, or stone, graven by art and man's device.

1 Co 2:11 For what man knoweth the things of a man, save the spirit of man which is in him? even so the things of God knoweth no man, but the Spirit of God.

1 Co 6:20 For ye are bought with a price: therefore glorify God in your body, and in your spirit, which are God's.

2 Co 4:16 For which cause we faint not; but though our outward man perish, yet the inward *man* is renewed day by day.

1 Th 5:23 And the very God of peace sanctify you wholly; and *I pray* God your whole spirit and soul and body be preserved blameless unto the coming of our Lord Jesus Christ.

He 12:23 To the general assembly and church of the firstborn, which are written in heaven, and to God the Judge of all, and to the spirits of just men made perfect,

Ja 2:26 For as the body without the spirit is dead, so faith without works is dead also.

7. Of Infinite Value

Jn 3:16 For God so loved the world, that he gave his only begotten Son, that whosoever believeth in him should not perish, but have everlasting life.

1 Co 6:20 For ye are bought with a price: therefore glorify God in your body, and in your spirit, which are God's.

1 Pe 1:18–19 Forasmuch as ye know that ye were not redeemed with corruptible things, *as* silver and gold, from your vain conversation *received* by tradition from your fathers;

But with the precious blood of Christ, as of a lamb without blemish and without spot:

Re 1:5 And from Jesus Christ, *who is* the faithful witness, *and* the first begotten of the dead, and the prince of the kings of the earth. Unto him that loved us, and washed us from our sins in his own blood,

See **CREATOR, FRAILTY, GLORY, IGNORANCE, IMMORTALITY, JEALOUSY, MORTALITY, REDEMPTION, TRUST**

MANASSEH, *causing to forget*

1. Son of Joseph

Ge 41:51; 46:20; 48:5, 14, 17; Nu 1:10; 2:20; 10:23; 13:11; 26:29; 32:33; 34:14, 23; 36:1, 12; De 3:13; 33:17; Jos 13:7, 29; 14:4; 16:4; 17:1, 2, 5; 21:5; 22:9; Jud 1:27; 6:35; 1 Chr 6:62; 7:14, 29; 9:3; 12:19; 27:21; Eze 48:5; Re 7:6

2. King of Judah, *son of Hezekiah*

Nu 1:34; 2 K 21:1, 9, 16; 23:12; 24:3; 1 Chr 3:13; 2 Chr 33:1, 11, 20; Je 15:4; Mt 1:10

See **HUMILITY, ISRAEL, YOUNG PEOPLE**

MANEH, *or Mina, rendered "pound" elsewhere*

Eze 45:12

See **WEIGHTS AND MEASURES**

MANGER, *stall or trough from which animals were fed*

Lu 2:7

MANLINESS, *strong in the Lord, fearless*

2 S 10:12 Be of good courage, and let us play the men for our people, and for the cities of our God: and the LORD do that which seemeth him good.

1 K 1:52 And Solomon said, If he will shew himself a worthy man, there shall not an hair of him fall to the earth: but if wickedness shall be found in him, he shall die.

1 K 2:2 I go the way of all the earth: be thou strong therefore, and shew thyself a man;

Jb 38:3 Gird up now thy loins like a man; for I will demand of thee, and answer thou me.

Jb 40:7 Gird up thy loins now like a man: I will demand of thee, and declare thou unto me.

Is 46:8 Remember this, and shew yourselves men: bring it again to mind, O ye transgressors.

Je 5:1 Run ye to and fro through the streets of Jerusalem, and see now, and know, and seek in the broad places thereof, if ye can find a man, if there be *any* that executeth judgment, that seeketh the truth; and I will pardon it.

Eze 22:30 And I sought for a man among them, that should make up the hedge, and stand in the gap before me for the land, that I should not destroy it: but I found none.

Ac 16:37 But Paul said unto them, They have beaten us openly uncondemned, being Romans, and have cast *us* into prison; and now do they thrust us out privily? nay verily; but let them come themselves and fetch us out.

1 Co 16:13 Watch ye, stand fast in the faith, quit you like men, be strong.

MANNA, *the food of the Israelites in the wilderness*

Ex 16:4, 15, 31, 33; Nu 11:6; 21:5; De 8:3, 16; Jos 5:12; Ne 9:15, 20; Ps 78:24; 105:40; Jn 6:31, 49; 1 Co 10:3; 2 Co 8:15; He 9:4; Re 2:17

MANTLES See **DRESS**

MARAH, *bitter*

Ex 15:23

MARBLE, *an irregularly colored stone, often used for ornamental purposes*

1 Chr 29:2; Est 1:6; Re 18:12

MARESHAH, *a city of Judah*

This was the home of the prophet Micah and of Eliezer son of Dodavahu. Eliezer prophesied about the breaking up of Jehoshaphat's ships so that they could not go to Tarshish (2 Chr 20:37). Rehoboam fortified Mareshah, and Asa not only strengthened these fortifications but used them to defeat the Ethiopian forces under Zerah (2 Chr 14:9–12).

See **CITIES**

MARINERS, *seafarers*

1 K 9:27; 22:49; Ps 107:23; Is 42:10; Eze 27:8, 29; Jona 1:5; Re 18:17

MARK, *JOHN*

1. Person, *Marcus, son of Mary, author of the Gospel*

HAD GODLY MOTHER

Ac 12:12 And when he had considered *the thing*, he came to the house of Mary the mother of John, whose surname was Mark; where many were gathered together praying.

RELATED TO BARNABAS

Col 4:10 Aristarchus my fellowprisoner saluteth you, and Marcus, sister's son to Barnabas, (touching whom ye received commandments: if he come unto you, receive him;)

HELPER OF PAUL AND BARNABAS

Ac 12:25 And Barnabas and Saul returned from Jerusalem, when they had fulfilled *their* ministry, and took with them John, whose surname was Mark.

UNCERTAIN DURING EARLY YEARS

Ac 13:13 Now when Paul and his company loosed from Paphos, they came to Perga in Pamphylia: and John departing from them returned to Jerusalem.

Ac 15:38 But Paul thought not good to take him with them, who departed from them from Pamphylia, and went not with them to the work.

BECAME A FAITHFUL COWORKER WITH PAUL

Col 4:10 Aristarchus my fellowprisoner saluteth you, and Marcus, sister's son to Barnabas, (touching whom ye received commandments: if he come unto you, receive him;)

2 Ti 4:11 Only Luke is with me. Take Mark, and bring him with thee: for he is profitable to me for the ministry.

COMPANION OF PETER

1 Pe 5:13 The *church that is* at Babylon, elected together with *you,* saluteth you; and *so doth* Marcus my son.

2. Book

Author: Mark, the son of Mary of Jerusalem (Ac 12:12). Referred to as John Mark (Ac 12:25). A relative of Barnabas (Col 4:10). Associated with Paul and Barnabas on their first missionary journey (Ac 12:25;13:5). Temporarily alienated from Paul (Ac 13:13; 15:37-39). Afterwards restored to his friendship (1 Ti 4:11). Ancient tradition certifies that Mark was a companion of Peter. The book is called Peter's Gospel by some very ancient writers. It is generally conceded that Peter may have furnished, or suggested, much of the material found in the book.

Date Written: Most likely the earliest of the gospels, about 58 B.C.

Purpose: To present Jesus of Nazareth as God's suffering servant, the redeemer of the world.

To Whom Written: Addressed primarily to Roman or Gentile Christians. That it was not especially adapted to Jewish readers seems clear from the fact that it contains few references to Old Testament prophecy. Furthermore, the explanation of Jewish words and customs would indicate that the author had foreigners in mind when he wrote. See 3:17; 5:41; 7:1-4, 11, 34.

Main Theme: Christ is the tireless servant of God and humanity. His life is portrayed as crowded with benevolent deeds.

Key Word: Immediately.
Key Verse: 10:45.

MARKETPLACE, *near the city gate where trials were held, citizens assembled, and commodities were sold*

Mt 20:3; 23:7; Mk 7:4; 12:38; Lu 7:32; 11:43; Ac 16:19; 17:17

MARRIAGE, *a God-ordained and God-originated institution*

1. Commended

Ge 24:67 And Isaac brought her into his mother Sarah's tent, and took Rebekah, and she became his wife; and he loved her: and Isaac was comforted after his mother's *death.*

Ex 2:21 And Moses was content to dwell with the man: and he gave Moses Zipporah his daughter.

Ru 1:4 And they took them wives of the women of Moab; the name of the one *was* Orpah, and the name of the other Ruth: and they dwelled there about ten years.

Pr 18:22 *Whoso* findeth a wife findeth a good *thing,* and obtaineth favour of the Lord.

Je 29:6 Take ye wives, and beget sons and daughters; and take wives for your sons, and give your daughters to husbands, that they may bear sons and daughters; that ye may be increased there, and not diminished.

1 Ti 3:12 Let the deacons be the husbands of one wife, ruling their children and their own houses well.

1 Ti 5:14 I will therefore that the younger women marry, bear children, guide the house, give none occasion to the adversary to speak reproachfully.

He 13:4 Marriage *is* honourable in all, and the bed undefiled: but whoremongers and adulterers God will judge.

2. Solemn Obligations

Ge 2:24 Therefore shall a man leave his father and his mother, and shall cleave unto his wife: and they shall be one flesh.

Pr 2:17 Which forsaketh the guide of her youth, and forgetteth the covenant of her God.

Mal 2:14 Yet ye say, Wherefore? Because the LORD hath been witness between thee and the wife of thy youth, against whom thou hast dealt treacherously: yet *is* she thy companion, and the wife of thy covenant.

Mt 5:32 But I say unto you, That whosoever shall put away his wife, saving for the cause of fornication, causeth her to commit adultery: and whosoever shall marry her that is divorced committeth adultery.

Mk 10:7 For this cause shall a man leave his father and mother, and cleave to his wife;

Ro 7:2 For the woman which hath an husband is bound by the law to *her* husband so long as he liveth; but if the husband be dead, she is loosed from the law of *her* husband.

1 Co 7:10 And unto the married I command, *yet* not I, but the Lord, Let not the wife depart from *her* husband:

1 Co 7:11 But and if she depart, let her remain unmarried, or be reconciled to *her* husband: and let not the husband put away *his* wife.

3. Forbidden with Heathen

Ge 24:3, 37; 28:1; 34:9, 14; 38:2; 46:10; Ex 6:15; 34:16; Le 24:10; De 7:3; Jos 23:12; Jud 3:6; 14:3; 1 K 3:1; 11:2; 16:31; 2 Chr 8:11; Ezr 9:2, 12; 10:14, 44; Ne 10:30; 13:23, 25

4. Figurative

Is 54:5; 62:5; Je 2:2; 3:14; 31:32; 50:5; Eze 16:8; Ho 2:19; Mt 22:2, 4, 8; 25:10; Ro 7:4; 1 Co 6:17; 2 Co 11:2; Ga 4:27; Re 19:7

5. Of the Kinsman's Widow

Ge 38:8; De 25:5; Ru 3:9; 4:5, 10; Mt 22:24; Mk 12:19; Lu 20:28

See **HOME**

MARTHA, *of Bethany, sister of Lazarus and Mary*

HOSPITALITY
Lu 10:38

ENERGY
Lu 10:40; Jn 11:20

ANXIOUS CARE
Lu 10:40

SPIRITUAL KNOWLEDGE
Jn 11:24

FAITH
Jn 11:27

See **YOUNG PEOPLE, HOSPITALITY, WOMEN**

MARTYRDOM, *dying for a cause*

Mt 10:21 And the brother shall deliver up the brother to death, and the father the child: and the children shall rise up against *their* parents, and cause them to be put to death.

Ac 21:13 Then Paul answered, What mean ye to weep and to break mine heart? for I am ready not to be bound only, but also to die at Jerusalem for the name of the Lord Jesus.

1 Co 13:3 And though I bestow all my goods to feed *the poor,* and though I give my body to be burned, and have not charity, it profiteth me nothing.

Re 6:9 And when he had opened the fifth seal, I saw under the altar the souls of them that were slain for the word of God, and for the testimony which they held:

Re 20:4 And I saw thrones, and they sat upon them, and judgment was given unto them: and *I saw* the souls of them that were beheaded for the witness of Jesus, and for the word of God, and which had not worshipped the beast, neither his image, neither had received *his* mark upon their foreheads, or in their hands; and they lived and reigned with Christ a thousand years.

Examples

ZECHARIAH

2 Chr 24:21 And they conspired against him, and stoned him with stones at the commandment of the king in the court of the house of the LORD.

JOHN THE BAPTIST

Mk 6:27 And immediately the king sent an executioner, and commanded his head to be brought: and he went and beheaded him in the prison,

ABEL

Lu 11:51 From the blood of Abel unto the blood of Zacharias, which perished between the altar and the temple: verily I say unto you, It shall be required of this generation.

STEPHEN

Ac 7:58 And cast *him* out of the city, and stoned *him:* and the witnesses laid down their clothes at a young man's feet, whose name was Saul.

JAMES

Ac 12:2 And he killed James the brother of John with the sword.

He 11:37 They were stoned, they were sawn asunder, were tempted, were slain with the sword: they wandered about in sheepskins and goatskins; being destitute, afflicted, tormented;

Re 6:9 And when he had opened the fifth seal, I saw under the altar the souls of them that were slain for the word of God, and for the testimony which they held:

See **SUFFERING**

MARY, *bitter*

1. Mother of Jesus

SUBMISSION

Lu 1:38 And Mary said, Behold the handmaid of the Lord; be it unto me according to thy word. And the angel departed from her.

FAITH AND PIETY

Lu 1:46–55 And Mary said, My soul doth magnify the Lord,

And my spirit hath rejoiced in God my Saviour.

For he hath regarded the low estate of his handmaiden: for, behold, from henceforth all generations shall call me blessed.

For he that is mighty hath done to me great things; and holy *is* his name.

And his mercy *is* on them that fear him from generation to generation.

He hath shewed strength with his arm; he hath scattered the proud in the imagination of their hearts.

He hath put down the mighty from *their* seats, and exalted them of low degree.

He hath filled the hungry with good things; and the rich he hath sent empty away.

He hath holpen his servant Israel, in remembrance of *his* mercy;

As he spake to our fathers, to Abraham, and to his seed for ever.

SPIRITUAL MINDEDNESS

Lu 2:51 And he went down with them, and came to Nazareth, and was subject unto them: but his mother kept all these sayings in her heart.

MATERNAL CONFIDENCE

Jn 2:3–5 And when they wanted wine, the mother of Jesus saith unto him, They have no wine.

Jesus saith unto her, Woman, what have I to do with thee? mine hour is not yet come.

His mother saith unto the servants, Whatsoever he saith unto you, do *it.*

MATERNAL LOVE

Jn 19:25 Now there stood by the cross of Jesus his mother, and his mother's sister, Mary the *wife* of Cleophas, and Mary Magdalene.

2. Magdalene

RECEIVED A GREAT SALVATION

Lu 8:32 And there was there an herd of many swine feeding on the mountain: and they besought him that he would suffer them to enter into them. And he suffered them.

MINISTERED TO CHRIST

Mk 15:40–41 There were also women looking on afar off: among whom was Mary Magdalene, and Mary the mother of James the less and of Joses, and Salome;

(Who also, when he was in Galilee, followed him, and ministered unto him;) and many other women which came up with him unto Jerusalem.

STOOD AT THE CROSS

Jn 19:25 Now there stood by the cross of Jesus his mother, and his mother's sister, Mary the *wife* of Cleophas, and Mary Magdalene.

VISITED THE SEPULCHER

Mt 27:61 And there was Mary Magdalene, and the other Mary, sitting over against the sepulchre.

Mt 28:1 In the end of the sabbath, as it began to dawn toward the first *day* of the week, came Mary Magdalene and the other Mary to see the sepulchre.

SAW CHRIST AFTER HIS RESURRECTION

Mk 16:9 Now when *Jesus* was risen early the first *day* of the week, he appeared first to Mary Magdalene, out of whom he had cast seven devils.

Jn 20:11–18 But Mary stood without at the sepulchre weeping: and as she wept, she stooped down, *and looked* into the sepulchre,

And seeth two angels in white sitting, the one at the head, and the other at the feet, where the body of Jesus had lain.

And they say unto her, Woman, why weepest thou? She saith unto them, Because they have taken away my Lord, and I know not where they have laid him.

And when she had thus said, she turned herself back, and saw Jesus standing, and knew not that it was Jesus.

Jesus saith unto her, Woman, why weepest thou? whom seekest thou? She, supposing him to be the gardener, saith unto him, Sir, if thou have

borne him hence, tell me where thou hast laid him, and I will take him away.

Jesus saith unto her, Mary. She turned herself, and saith unto him, Rabboni; which is to say, Master.

Jesus saith unto her, Touch me not; for I am not yet ascended to my Father: but go to my brethren, and say unto them, I ascend unto my Father, and your Father; and *to* my God, and your God.

Mary Magdalene came and told the disciples that she had seen the Lord, and *that* he had spoken these things unto her.

3. Of Bethany

SPIRITUAL RECEPTIVITY

Lu 10:39 And she had a sister called Mary, which also sat at Jesus' feet, and heard his word.

SPIRITUAL INSIGHT

Lu 10:42 But one thing is needful: and Mary hath chosen that good part, which shall not be taken away from her.

QUIET RESIGNATION

Jn 11:20 Then Martha, as soon as she heard that Jesus was coming, went and met him: but Mary sat *still* in the house.

AT CHRIST'S FEET FOR INSTRUCTION

Lu 10:39 And she had a sister called Mary, which also sat at Jesus' feet, and heard his word.

AT CHRIST'S FEET FOR COMFORT

Jn 11:32 Then when Mary was come where Jesus was, and saw him, she fell down at his feet, saying unto him, Lord, if thou hadst been here, my brother had not died.

AT CHRIST'S FEET FOR SERVICE

Jn 12:3 Then took Mary a pound of ointment of spikenard, very costly, and anointed the feet of Jesus, and wiped his feet with her hair: and the house was filled with the odour of the ointment.

4. Mother of James
Mt 27:56; Mk 15:40, 47; 16:1; Lu 24:10

5. Mother of Mark
Ac 12:12; Col 4:10

6. Disciple in the Church at Rome
Ro 16:6

MASONS *See* ARTS AND CRAFTS

MASTER *See* CHRIST, EMPLOYERS

MASTER-WORKMEN *See* ARTS AND CRAFTS

MATERIALISM, *the philosophical opinion that physical matter is all that exists*

Ps 6:5; Mt 22:23; Mk 12:18; Lu 20:27; Ac 17:18, 32; 23:8; 1 Co 15:12, 35; 1 Th 4:13

See FUTURE LIFE

MATTHEW

1. Person, *or Levi, a publican who became an apostle of Christ, author of the Gospel*
Mt 1:1; 9:9; 10:3; Mk 2:14; 3:18; Lu 5:29; 6:15; Ac 1:13

2. Book
Author: Matthew (also called Levi), one of the twelve apostles (Mk 2:14). Undoubtedly a Jew who was a Roman tax-gatherer (10:3). When called by Jesus he left all and followed him (Lu 5:27–28). He made a great feast for Christ, who attended it despite the fact that the tax-gatherers belonged to a despised class (Lu 5:29).

Date Written: About A.D. 60.

Purpose: To show that Jesus of Nazareth was the kingly Messiah of Jewish prophecy.

To Whom Written: Addressed primarily to the Jews. This view is confirmed by the fact that there are about sixty references to the Jewish prophecies and about forty quotations from the Old Testament. Christ's mission to the Jews is especially emphasized (10:5–6; 15:24).

Main Theme: Jesus is God's promised anointed Messiah, the King of the Jews.

Key Words: Fulfilled, which is repeated frequently to indicate that the Old Testament prophecies were fulfilled in Christ. Kingdom, which appears fifty times. Kingdom of Heaven, thirty times. The King, Jesus as (2:2; 21:5; 22:11; 25:34; 27:11,37,42).

Key Verses: 16:16–19.

MATTHIAS, *the apostle chosen in place of Judas Iscariot*
Ac 1:26

MATURITY, SPIRITUAL, *how to gain*

BY PUTTING AWAY CHILDISH THINGS
1 Co 13:11 When I was a child, I spake as a child, I understood as a child, I thought as a child: but when I became a man, I put away childish things.

BY CULTIVATING UNDERSTANDING
1 Co 14:20 Brethren, be not children in understanding: howbeit in malice be ye children, but in understanding be men.

BY FOLLOWING THE EXAMPLE OF CHRIST
Ep 4:13 Till we all come in the unity of the faith, and of the knowledge of the Son of God, unto a perfect man, unto the measure of the stature of the fulness of Christ:
Ep 4:15 But speaking the truth in love, may grow up into him in all things, which is the head, *even* Christ:

BY PARTAKING OF THE DEEPER TRUTHS OF THE GOSPEL
He 5:14 But strong meat belongeth to them that are of full age, *even* those who by reason of use have their senses exercised to discern both good and evil.

BY OVERCOMING TEMPTATION
1 Jn 2:14 I have written unto you, fathers, because ye have known him

that is from the beginning. I have written unto you, young men, because ye are strong, and the word of God abideth in you, and ye have overcome the wicked one.

See **GROWTH, IMMATURITY**

MEAL OFFERINGS See **OFFERINGS**

MEASURING ROD

Je 31:39; Eze 40:3; 42:16; Zec 2:1

MEDIA, *an ancient Asiatic country*

2 K 17:6; 18:11

MEDIATOR, *intermediary, middleman*

1. Christ

See **CHRIST**

2. Man

Ex 18:19; 20:19; Nu 14:13; 16:48; De 5:5, 27; 9:18; Jb 9:33; 20:19; Ga 3:19

MEDITATION See **MIND**

MEEKNESS, *to be bowed down, gentleness*

1. Principles

TO BE SOUGHT

Zep 2:3 Seek ye the LORD, all ye meek of the earth, which have wrought his judgment; seek righteousness, seek meekness: it may be ye shall be hid in the day of the LORD's anger.

NONRESISTANT

Lu 6:29 And unto him that smiteth thee on the *one* cheek offer also the other; and him that taketh away thy cloke forbid not *to take thy* coat also.

A FRUIT OF THE SPIRIT

Ga 5:22–23 But the fruit of the Spirit is love, joy, peace, longsuffering, gentleness, goodness, faith,

Meekness, temperance: against such there is no law.

Ga 6:1 Brethren, if a man be overtaken in a fault, ye which are spiritual, restore such an one in the spirit of

meekness; considering thyself, lest thou also be tempted.

Ep 4:2 With all lowliness and meekness, with longsuffering, forbearing one another in love;

ESSENTIAL IN TEACHING

2 Ti 2:25 In meekness instructing those that oppose themselves; if God peradventure will give them repentance to the acknowledging of the truth;

Tit 3:2 To speak evil of no man, to be no brawlers, *but* gentle, shewing all meekness unto all men.

ESSENTIAL IN HEARING

Ja 1:21 Wherefore lay apart all filthiness and superfluity of naughtiness, and receive with meekness the engrafted word, which is able to save your souls.

Ja 3:13 Who *is* a wise man and endued with knowledge among you? let him shew out of a good conversation his works with meekness of wisdom.

PRECIOUS IN GOD'S SIGHT

1 Pe 3:4 But *let it be* the hidden man of the heart, in that which is not corruptible, *even the ornament* of a meek and quiet spirit, which is in the sight of God of great price.

2. Promises to the Meek

Ps 22:26 The meek shall eat and be satisfied: they shall praise the LORD that seek him: your heart shall live for ever.

Ps 37:11 But the meek shall inherit the earth; and shall delight themselves in the abundance of peace.

Ps 147:6 The LORD lifteth up the meek: he casteth the wicked down to the ground.

Ps 149:4 For the LORD taketh pleasure in his people: he will beautify the meek with salvation.

Is 11:4 But with righteousness shall he judge the poor, and reprove with equity for the meek of the earth: and he shall smite the earth with the rod of his mouth, and with the breath of his lips shall he slay the wicked.

Is 29:19 The meek also shall increase *their* joy in the LORD, and the poor among men shall rejoice in the Holy One of Israel.

Mt 5:5 Blessed *are* the meek: for they shall inherit the earth.

3. Examples

MOSES

Nu 12:3 (Now the man Moses *was* very meek, above all the men which *were* upon the face of the earth.)

DAVID

2 S 16:11 And David said to Abishai, and to all his servants, Behold, my son, which came forth of my bowels, seeketh my life: how much more now *may this* Benjamite *do it?* let him alone, and let him curse; for the LORD hath bidden him.

JEREMIAH

Je 26:14 As for me, behold, I *am* in your hand: do with me as seemeth good and meet unto you.

STEPHEN

Ac 7:60 And he kneeled down, and cried with a loud voice, Lord, lay not this sin to their charge. And when he had said this, he fell asleep.

PAUL

2 Ti 4:16 At my first answer no man stood with me, but all *men* forsook me: *I pray God* that it may not be laid to their charge.

4. Christ's

Is 53:7 He was oppressed, and he was afflicted, yet he opened not his mouth: he is brought as a lamb to the slaughter, and as a sheep before her shearers is dumb, so he openeth not his mouth.

Mt 11:29 Take my yoke upon you, and learn of me; for I am meek and lowly in heart: and ye shall find rest unto your souls.

Mt 12:19 He shall not strive, nor cry; neither shall any man hear his voice in the streets.

Mt 21:5 Tell ye the daughter of Sion, Behold, thy King cometh unto thee, meek, and sitting upon an ass, and a colt the foal of an ass.

Mt 26:52 Then said Jesus unto him, Put up again thy sword into his place: for all they that take the sword shall perish with the sword.

Mt 27:31 And after that they had mocked him, they took the robe off from him, and put his own raiment on him, and led him away to crucify *him.*

Jn 18:23 Jesus answered him, If I have spoken evil, bear witness of the evil: but if well, why smitest thou me?

Ac 8:32 The place of the scripture which he read was this, He was led as a sheep to the slaughter; and like a lamb dumb before his shearer, so opened he not his mouth:

2 Co 10:1 Now I Paul myself beseech you by the meekness and gentleness of Christ, who in presence *am* base among you, but being absent am bold toward you:

Ja 5:6 Ye have condemned *and* killed the just; *and* he doth not resist you.

1 Pe 2:23 Who, when he was reviled, reviled not again; when he suffered, he threatened not; but committed *himself* to him that judgeth righteously:

See **KINDNESS, MERCY, FORGIVENESS, RETALIATION**

MEGIDDO, *a town and valley*

Megiddo was a leading city in the valley of Jezreel that figured prominently in the Old Testament. The Canaanite king of Megiddo was slain by the invading Israelites (Jos 12:21). Although the city was given to the tribe of Manasseh (Jos 17:11), they did not succeed in holding it (Jud 1:27). Eventually subjugated, Megiddo became a lead city under Solomon (1 K 4:12), who placed a deputy administrator there and later fortified it (1 K 9:15). Megiddo was also the site of the death of Ahaziah at the hand of Jehu (2 K 9:27) and of Josiah at the hand of Pharaoh Neco (2 K 23:29; cf. Zec 12:11).

MELCHIZEDEK, *king of Salem*

Ge 14:18; Ps 110:4; He 5:6, 10; 6:20; 7:1, 17, 21

MEMORIES

1. Painful

Ge 41:19 And, behold, seven other kine came up after them, poor and very ill favoured and leanfleshed, such as I never saw in all the land of Egypt for badness:

De 9:7 Remember, *and* forget not, how thou provokedst the Lord thy God to wrath in the wilderness: from the day that thou didst depart out of the land of Egypt, until ye came unto this place, ye have been rebellious against the Lord.

Ps 51:3 For I acknowledge my transgressions: and my sin *is* ever before me.

Ps 137:1 By the rivers of Babylon, there we sat down, yea, we wept, when we remembered Zion.

Mt 26:75 And Peter remembered the word of Jesus, which said unto him, Before the cock crow, thou shalt deny me thrice. And he went out, and wept bitterly.

Mk 14:72 And the second time the cock crew. And Peter called to mind the word that Jesus said unto him, Before the cock crow twice, thou shalt deny me thrice. And when he thought thereon, he wept.

Lu 16:25 But Abraham said, Son, remember that thou in thy lifetime receivedst thy good things, and likewise Lazarus evil things: but now he is comforted, and thou art tormented.

Lu 22:61 And the Lord turned, and looked upon Peter. And Peter remembered the word of the Lord, how he had said unto him, Before the cock crow, thou shalt deny me thrice.

1 Co 15:9 For I am the least of the apostles, that am not meet to be called an apostle, because I persecuted the church of God.

2. Of the Just

2 Chr 32:33 And Hezekiah slept with his fathers, and they buried him in the chiefest of the sepulchres of the sons of David: and all Judah and the inhabitants of Jerusalem did him honour at his death. And Manasseh his son reigned in his stead.

2 Chr 35:24 His servants therefore took him out of that chariot, and put him in the second chariot that he had; and they brought him to Jerusalem, and he died, and was buried in *one of* the sepulchres of his fathers. And all Judah and Jerusalem mourned for Josiah.

Ps 72:17 His name shall endure for ever: his name shall be continued as long as the sun: and *men* shall be blessed in him: all nations shall call him blessed.

Ps 112:6 Surely he shall not be moved for ever: the righteous shall be in everlasting remembrance.

Pr 10:7 The memory of the just is blessed: but the name of the wicked shall rot.

Is 48:19 Thy seed also had been as the sand, and the offspring of thy bowels like the gravel thereof; his name should not have been cut off nor destroyed from before me.

Is 56:5 Even unto them will I give in mine house and within my walls a place and a name better than of sons and of daughters: I will give them an everlasting name, that shall not be cut off.

Mt 26:13 Verily I say unto you, Wheresoever this gospel shall be preached in the whole world, *there* shall also this, that this woman hath done, be told for a memorial of her.

2 Ti 1:5 When I call to remembrance the unfeigned faith that is in thee, which dwelt first in thy grandmother Lois, and thy mother Eunice; and I am persuaded that in thee also.

3. Spiritual

PAST MERCIES

De 32:7 Remember the days of old, consider the years of many generations: ask thy father, and he will shew thee; thy elders, and they will tell thee.

THE WONDERFUL WORKS OF GOD

Ps 77:11 I will remember the works of the LORD: surely I will remember thy wonders of old.

THE LORD AS A DELIVERER

Jona 2:7 When my soul fainted within me I remembered the LORD: and my prayer came in unto thee, into thine holy temple.

WORDS OF CHRIST CONCERNING BENEVOLENCE

Ac 20:35 I have shewed you all things, how that so labouring ye ought to support the weak, and to remember the words of the Lord Jesus, how he said, It is more blessed to give than to receive.

THE DEATH OF CHRIST

1 Co 11:25–26 After the same manner also *he took* the cup, when he had supped, saying, This cup is the new testament in my blood: this do ye, as oft as ye drink *it*, in remembrance of me.

For as often as ye eat this bread, and drink *this* cup, ye do shew the Lord's death till he come.

ALL THE TEACHINGS OF THE GOSPEL

2 Pe 3:2 That ye may be mindful of the words which were spoken before by the holy prophets, and of the commandment of us the apostles of the Lord and Saviour:

BRINGS JOY IN THE NIGHT SEASON

Ps 63:5–6 My soul shall be satisfied as *with* marrow and fatness; and my mouth shall praise *thee* with joyful lips:

When I remember thee upon my bed, *and* meditate on thee in the *night* watches.

IS QUICKENED BY THE HOLY SPIRIT

Jn 14:26 But the Comforter, *which is* the Holy Ghost, whom the Father will send in my name, he shall teach you all things, and bring all things to your remembrance, whatsoever I have said unto you.

See **OBLIVION, REMEMBRANCE**

MEMPHIS, *the capital of Egypt in earliest times*

It was the greatest of all commercial cities of Egypt and was situated on the west bank of the Nile thirteen miles south of where Cairo is today. It was founded by Menes, the first ruler of united Egypt, who built the "White Fortress" here. Abraham and Sarah and their nephew Lot came almost four thousand years ago to "sojourn there" (Ge 12:10). Here Joseph was sold as a slave, and was later made a high ruler (second only to Pharaoh) and the federal food administrator of Egypt (Ge 37:36; 39:1; 41:40). It was here that Moses was brought up and became learned in all the wisdom of Egypt; and it was here that he and his brother Aaron stood before Pharaoh and demanded that the king let the people of Israel go (Ex 2:10; 10:3). Over this place the death angel passed Ex 12:30).

See **NOPH**

MENAHEM, *king of Israel*

2 K 15:14, 17, 21

See **ISRAEL**

MEN OF GOD

1. Prophets and Other Spiritual People

De 33:1; Jud 13:6; 1 S 2:27; 9:6; 1 K 12:22; 13:1, 4, 14, 29; 17:18, 24; 20:28; 2 K 1:9; 4:7, 9, 22, 40; 5:8, 14; 6:10; 7:2; 8:7; 13:19; 1 Chr 23:14; 2 Chr 8:14; 11:2; 25:7; Ne 12:36; Je 35:4; Da 5:11; Mt 10:41; 1 Ti 6:11; 2 Ti 2:24; 3:17

2. Deliverers of Israel

Jud 2:16; 3:9, 15, 31; 9:17; 13:5; 1 S 9:16; 11:9; 12:11; 14:48; 2 S 3:18; 19:9; 2 K 13:5; Ne 9:27; Ps 105:26; Ec 9:15; Is 10:26; 19:20; Obad 21; Mi 5:5; Ac 7:34–35

3. Chosen to Accomplish God's Purposes

Ex 3:10; 4:16; 7:2; Nu 3:12; 4:47; 8:19; 17:5; 18:6; 27:18; De 18:5; 1 S 9:17; 10:24; 16:12; 2 S 6:21; 1 K 8:16; 1 Chr 28:4; 2 Chr 29:11; Ps 78:70; 89:19; Is 41:2; 44:28; 49:2; Je 1:7; Hag 2:23; Jn 15:16; Ac 7:25, 34; 9:15; 10:6, 32; 15:7; 22:14, 21; Ro 6:13; 9:13; 1 Co 1:27–29; 2 Ti 2:4; 1 Pe 2:14; Re 1:16

4. Sent as Divine Messengers

Ge 19:13; 45:5; Ex 3:10; 4:28; Nu 16:28; Jos 24:5; Jud 6:8, 14; 13:8; 1 S 25:32; 2 S 7:5; 12:1; 1 Chr 21:18; Is 6:9; 7:3; 44:26; 48:16; 52:7; Je 1:7; 7:25; 19:14; 25:4, 17; 26:12; 43:1; Eze 2:3; 3:4; Da 10:11; Am 7:15; Jona 3:2; Hag 1:13; Zec 2:8; 4:9; Mal 2:7; Mt 9:38; 10:5; 21:34; 22:3; 28:6, 8; Mk 3:14; 12:5; 16:15; Lu 1:19, 26; 9:52; 10:1; 11:49; 14:17; 20:10; Jn 1:6, 33; 13:20; 17:18; 20:21; Ac 7:35; 9:17; 10:20; 13:3; 22:21; 26:17; Ro 10:15; 1 Co 1:17; 2 Co 5:20; Ep 6:20; He 1:14; Re 22:6

5. Mighty Men, strong, loyal, faithful

Ge 6:4; 10:8; Jud 6:12; 11:1; 18:2; 1 S 9:1; 14:52; 16:18; 2 S 1:23; 3:38; 10:7; 16:6; 17:8; 20:7; 23:8, 16, 22; 1 K 1:8; 11:28; 2 K 5:1; 24:16; 1 Chr 5:24; 7:5, 40; 11:10, 19, 26; 12:1; 19:8; 26:7, 31; 28:1; 29:24; 2 Chr 13:3; 17:17; 26:12; 28:7; Ne 11:14; Is 3:2; 21:17; Je 5:16; 41:16; 46:5; 50:36; 51:57; Eze 32:27; Jl 3:9; Am 2:16; Obad 9; Zep 1:14

MEPHIBOSHETH, son of Jonathan

2 S 4:4; 9:6; 16:4; 19:24; 21:7

A Type of the Redeemed Sinner

1 S 20:14–15; 2 S 4:4; 9:3–4, 5–7, 9; 16:3; 19:24, 27, 30

MERAIOTH, son of Zerahiah

1 Chr 6:6; Ezr 7:3

MERARI, son of Levi

Ge 46:11; Ex 6:16; Nu 3:17, 35; 1 Chr 6:1, 19

MERARITES, descendants of Merari

Nu 3:36; 4:29, 42; 7:8; 10:17; 26:57; Jos 21:7, 34; 1 Chr 6:19, 44, 63, 77; 15:6; 23:21; 24:26; 26:10; 2 Chr 34:12; Ezr 8:19

MERCHANDISE See BUSINESS

MERCHANTS See BUSINESS

MERCY, a form of love, especially directed toward the needy or unworthy

1. Divine

ETERNAL

Ps 103:17 But the mercy of the LORD *is* from everlasting to everlasting upon them that fear him, and his righteousness unto children's children;

Ps 106:1 Praise ye the LORD. O give thanks unto the LORD; for *he is* good: for his mercy *endureth* for ever.

BOUNDLESS

Ps 108:4 For thy mercy *is* great above the heavens: and thy truth *reacheth* unto the clouds.

Ps 119:64 The earth, O LORD, is full of thy mercy: teach me thy statutes.

PROLONGS LIFE

Lam 3:22–23 It is of the LORD's mercies that we are not consumed, because his compassions fail not.

They are new every morning: great *is* thy faithfulness.

ENCOURAGES TO PENITENCE

Jl 2:13 And rend your heart, and not your garments, and turn unto the LORD your God: for he *is* gracious and merciful, slow to anger, and of great kindness, and repenteth him of the evil.

FORGIVES SIN

Mi 7:18 Who *is* a God like unto thee, that pardoneth iniquity, and passeth by the transgression of the remnant of his heritage? he retaineth not his anger for ever, because he delighteth *in* mercy.

Lu 1:50 And his mercy *is* on them that fear him from generation to generation.

Ep 2:4 But God, who is rich in mercy, for his great love wherewith he loved us,

MAKES SALVATION POSSIBLE

Tit 3:5 Not by works of righteousness which we have done, but according to his mercy he saved us, by the washing of regeneration, and renewing of the Holy Ghost;

2. Commanded

2 S 19:22 And David said, What have I to do with you, ye sons of Zeruiah, that ye should this day be adversaries unto me? shall there any man be put to death this day in Israel? for do not I know that I *am* this day king over Israel?

2 S 21:7 But the king spared Mephibosheth, the son of Jonathan the son of Saul, because of the LORD's oath that *was* between them, between David and Jonathan the son of Saul.

1 K 2:26 And unto Abiathar the priest said the king, Get thee to Anathoth, unto thine own fields; for thou *art* worthy of death: but I will not at this time put thee to death, because thou barest the ark of the Lord GOD before David my father, and because thou hast been afflicted in all wherein my father was afflicted.

Pr 3:3 Let not mercy and truth forsake thee: bind them about thy neck; write them upon the table of thine heart:

Pr 11:17 The merciful man doeth good to his own soul: but *he that is* cruel troubleth his own flesh.

Is 16:5 And in mercy shall the throne be established: and he shall sit upon it in truth in the tabernacle of David, judging, and seeking judgment, and hasting righteousness.

Je 38:9 My lord the king, these men have done evil in all that they have done to Jeremiah the prophet, whom they have cast into the dungeon; and he is like to die for hunger in the place where he is: for *there is* no more bread in the city.

Ho 12:6 Therefore turn thou to thy God: keep mercy and judgment, and wait on thy God continually.

Mi 6:8 He hath shewed thee, O man, what *is* good; and what doth the LORD require of thee, but to do justly, and to love mercy, and to walk humbly with thy God?

Mt 5:7 Blessed *are* the merciful: for they shall obtain mercy.

Lu 6:36 Be ye therefore merciful, as your Father also is merciful.

Ja 2:13 For he shall have judgment without mercy, that hath shewed no mercy; and mercy rejoiceth against judgment.

3. Divine Promises

Ex 20:6 And shewing mercy unto thousands of them that love me, and keep my commandments.

Ex 33:19 And he said, I will make all my goodness pass before thee, and I will proclaim the name of the LORD before thee; and will be gracious to whom I will be gracious, and will shew mercy on whom I will shew mercy.

Ex 34:7 Keeping mercy for thousands, forgiving iniquity and transgression and sin, and that will by no means clear *the guilty;* visiting the iniquity of the fathers upon the children, and upon the children's children, unto the third and to the fourth *generation.*

Nu 21:8 And the LORD said unto Moses, Make thee a fiery serpent, and set it upon a pole: and it shall come to pass, that every one that is bitten, when he looketh upon it, shall live.

De 5:10 And shewing mercy unto thousands of them that love me and keep my commandments.

De 13:17 And there shall cleave nought of the cursed thing to thine hand: that the LORD may turn from the fierceness of his anger, and shew thee mercy, and have compassion upon thee, and multiply thee, as he hath sworn unto thy fathers;

2 S 22:26 With the merciful thou wilt shew thyself merciful, *and* with the upright man thou wilt shew thyself upright.

2 Chr 30:9 For if ye turn again unto the LORD, your brethren and your children *shall find* compassion before them that lead them captive, so that they shall come again into this land: for the LORD your God *is* gracious and merciful, and will not turn away *his* face from you, if ye return unto him.

Ps 18:25 With the merciful thou wilt shew thyself merciful; with an upright man thou wilt shew thyself upright;

Ps 23:6 Surely goodness and mercy shall follow me all the days of my life: and I will dwell in the house of the LORD for ever.

Ps 32:10 Many sorrows *shall be* to the wicked: but he that trusteth in the LORD, mercy shall compass him about.

Ps 52:8 But I *am* like a green olive tree in the house of God: I trust in the mercy of God for ever and ever.

Ps 57:3 He shall send from heaven, and save *from* the reproach of him that would swallow me up. Selah. God shall send forth his mercy and his truth.

Ps 89:28 My mercy will I keep for him for evermore, and my covenant shall stand fast with him.

Ps 103:8 The LORD *is* merciful and gracious, slow to anger, and plenteous in mercy.

Ps 130:7 Let Israel hope in the LORD: for with the LORD *there is* mercy, and with him *is* plenteous redemption.

Pr 14:22 Do they not err that devise evil? but mercy and truth *shall be* to them that devise good.

Pr 28:13 He that covereth his sins shall not prosper: but whoso confesseth and forsaketh *them* shall have mercy.

Is 43:25 I, *even* I, *am* he that blotteth out thy transgressions for mine own sake, and will not remember thy sins.

Is 49:13 Sing, O heavens; and be joyful, O earth; and break forth into singing, O mountains: for the LORD hath comforted his people, and will have mercy upon his afflicted.

Is 54:7 For a small moment have I forsaken thee; but with great mercies will I gather thee.

Is 55:7 Let the wicked forsake his way, and the unrighteous man his

thoughts: and let him return unto the LORD, and he will have mercy upon him; and to our God, for he will abundantly pardon.

Is 65:8 Thus saith the LORD, As the new wine is found in the cluster, and *one* saith, Destroy it not; for a blessing *is* in it: so will I do for my servants' sakes, that I may not destroy them all.

Je 3:12 Go and proclaim these words toward the north, and say, Return, thou backsliding Israel, saith the LORD; *and* I will not cause mine anger to fall upon you: for I *am* merciful, saith the LORD, *and* I will not keep *anger* for ever.

Je 18:8 If that nation, against whom I have pronounced, turn from their evil, I will repent of the evil that I thought to do unto them.

Je 33:26 Then will I cast away the seed of Jacob, and David my servant, so that I will not take *any* of his seed *to be* rulers over the seed of Abraham, Isaac, and Jacob: for I will cause their captivity to return, and have mercy on them.

Je 42:12 And I will shew mercies unto you, that he may have mercy upon you, and cause you to return to your own land.

Ho 1:7 But I will have mercy upon the house of Judah, and will save them by the LORD their God, and will not save them by bow, nor by sword, nor by battle, by horses, nor by horsemen.

Ho 2:23 And I will sow her unto me in the earth; and I will have mercy upon her that had not obtained mercy; and I will say to *them which were* not my people, Thou *art* my people; and they shall say, Thou *art* my God.

Zep 3:15 The LORD hath taken away thy judgments, he hath cast out thine enemy: the king of Israel, *even* the LORD, *is* in the midst of thee: thou shalt not see evil any more.

Zec 1:16 Therefore thus saith the LORD; I am returned to Jerusalem with mercies: my house shall be built in it, saith the LORD of hosts, and a line shall be stretched forth upon Jerusalem.

Zec 10:6 And I will strengthen the house of Judah, and I will save the house of Joseph, and I will bring them again to place them; for I have mercy upon them: and they shall be as though I had not cast them off: for I *am* the LORD their God, and will hear them.

Mal 3:17 And they shall be mine, saith the LORD of hosts, in that day when I make up my jewels; and I will spare them, as a man spareth his own son that serveth him.

Mt 5:7 Blessed *are* the merciful: for they shall obtain mercy.

Mt 6:15 But if ye forgive not men their trespasses, neither will your Father forgive your trespasses.

He 8:12 For I will be merciful to their unrighteousness, and their sins and their iniquities will I remember no more.

4. Divine Examples

Ge 18:26 And the LORD said, If I find in Sodom fifty righteous within the city, then I will spare all the place for their sakes.

Ge 19:16 And while he lingered, the men laid hold upon his hand, and upon the hand of his wife, and upon the hand of his two daughters; the LORD being merciful unto him: and they brought him forth, and set him without the city.

Ge 19:19 Behold now, thy servant hath found grace in thy sight, and thou hast magnified thy mercy, which thou hast shewed unto me in saving my life; and I cannot escape to the mountain, lest some evil take me, and I die:

Ex 22:27 For that *is* his covering only, it *is* his raiment for his skin: wherein shall he sleep? and it shall come to pass, when he crieth unto me, that I will hear; for I *am* gracious.

Ex 34:6 And the LORD passed by before him, and proclaimed, The LORD, The LORD God, merciful and gracious, longsuffering, and abundant in goodness and truth,

Nu 14:18 The LORD *is* longsuffering, and of great mercy, forgiving iniquity and transgression, and by no means clearing *the guilty,* visiting the iniquity of the fathers upon the children unto the third and fourth *generation.*

Nu 26:11 Notwithstanding the children of Korah died not.

De 32:43 Rejoice, O ye nations, *with* his people: for he will avenge the blood of his servants, and will render vengeance to his adversaries, and will be merciful unto his land, *and* to his people.

2 S 7:15 But my mercy shall not depart away from him, as I took *it* from Saul, whom I put away before thee.

2 S 24:16 And when the angel stretched out his hand upon Jerusalem to destroy it, the LORD repented him of the evil, and said to the angel that destroyed the people, It is enough: stay now thine hand. And the angel of the LORD was by the threshingplace of Araunah the Jebusite.

2 S 24:25 And David built there an altar unto the LORD, and offered burnt offerings and peace offerings. So the LORD was intreated for the land, and the plague was stayed from Israel.

1 K 3:6 And Solomon said, Thou hast shewed unto thy servant David my father great mercy, according as he walked before thee in truth, and in righteousness, and in uprightness of heart with thee; and thou hast kept for him this great kindness, that thou hast given him a son to sit on his throne, as *it is* this day.

1 K 21:29 Seest thou how Ahab humbleth himself before me? because he humbleth himself before me, I will not bring the evil in his days: *but* in his son's days will I bring the evil upon his house.

1 Chr 21:27 And the LORD commanded the angel; and he put up his sword again into the sheath thereof.

2 Chr 1:8 And Solomon said unto God, Thou hast shewed great mercy unto David my father, and hast made me to reign in his stead.

2 Chr 12:7 And when the LORD saw that they humbled themselves, the word of the LORD came to Shemaiah, saying, They have humbled themselves; *therefore* I will not destroy them, but I will grant them some deliverance; and my wrath shall not be poured out upon Jerusalem by the hand of Shishak.

2 Chr 33:13 And prayed unto him: and he was intreated of him, and heard his supplication, and brought him again to Jerusalem into his kingdom. Then Manasseh knew that the LORD he *was* God.

Ezr 9:13 And after all that is come upon us for our evil deeds, and for our great trespass, seeing that thou our God hast punished us less than our iniquities *deserve,* and hast given us *such* deliverance as this;

Ne 1:9 But *if* ye turn unto me, and keep my commandments, and do them; though there were of you cast out unto the uttermost part of the heaven, *yet* will I gather them from thence, and will bring them unto the place that I have chosen to set my name there.

Ne 9:17 And refused to obey, neither were mindful of thy wonders that thou didst among them; but hardened their necks, and in their rebellion appointed a captain to return to their bondage: but thou *art* a God ready to pardon, gracious and merciful, slow to anger, and of great kindness, and forsookest them not.

Ne 9:28 But after they had rest, they did evil again before thee: therefore leftest thou them in the hand of their enemies, so that they had the dominion over them: yet when they returned, and cried unto thee, thou heardest *them* from heaven; and many times didst thou deliver them according to thy mercies;

Ne 9:31 Nevertheless for thy great mercies' sake thou didst not utterly consume them, nor forsake them; for thou *art* a gracious and merciful God.

Ps 18:50 Great deliverance giveth he to his king; and sheweth mercy to his anointed, to David, and to his seed for evermore.

Ps 25:6 Remember, O LORD, thy tender mercies and thy lovingkindnesses; for they *have been* ever of old.

Ps 85:3 Thou hast taken away all thy wrath: thou hast turned *thyself* from the fierceness of thine anger.

Ps 103:11 For as the heaven is high above the earth, *so* great is his mercy toward them that fear him.

Ps 106:8 Nevertheless he saved them for his name's sake, that he might make his mighty power to be known.

Je 3:5 Will he reserve *his anger* for ever? will he keep *it* to the end? Behold, thou hast spoken and done evil things as thou couldest.

Je 51:5 For Israel *hath* not *been* forsaken, nor Judah of his God, of the LORD of hosts; though their land was filled with sin against the Holy One of Israel.

Eze 18:23 Have I any pleasure at all that the wicked should die? saith the Lord God: *and* not that he should return from his ways, and live?

Ho 11:9 I will not execute the fierceness of mine anger, I will not return to destroy Ephraim: for I *am* God, and not man; the Holy One in the midst of thee: and I will not enter into the city.

Jona 3:10 And God saw their works, that they turned from their evil way; and God repented of the evil, that he had said that he would do unto them; and he did *it* not.

Lu 1:54 He hath holpen his servant Israel, in remembrance of *his* mercy;

Lu 1:78 Through the tender mercy of our God; whereby the dayspring from on high hath visited us,

Lu 7:42 And when they had nothing to pay, he frankly forgave them both. Tell me therefore, which of them will love him most?

Ro 9:15 For he saith to Moses, I will have mercy on whom I will have mercy, and I will have compassion on whom I will have compassion.

Ro 9:18 Therefore hath he mercy on whom he will *have mercy,* and whom he will he hardeneth.

Ro 11:31 Even so have these also now not believed, that through your mercy they also may obtain mercy.

2 Co 1:3 Blessed *be* God, even the Father of our Lord Jesus Christ, the Father of mercies, and the God of all comfort;

1 Ti 1:16 Howbeit for this cause I obtained mercy, that in me first Jesus

Christ might shew forth all longsuffering, for a pattern to them which should hereafter believe on him to life everlasting.

Tit 1:4 To Titus, *mine* own son after the common faith: Grace, mercy, *and* peace, from God the Father and the Lord Jesus Christ our Saviour.

5. Supplications

De 9:27; 21:8; 1 K 8:30; Ps 4:1; 6:2; 9:13; 25:7, 16; 26:11; 27:7; 30:10; 31:9; 33:22; 40:11; 41:4, 10; 51:1; 56:1; 57:1; 67:1; 79:8; 85:7; 86:3, 16; 90:14; 119:41, 58, 77, 124, 132; 123:3; Is 63:15; 64:9; Je 14:21; Da 2:18; 9:16; Am 7:2; Hab 3:2; Mt 9:27; 17:15; 18:26, 29; 20:31; Mk 10:47; Lu 17:13; 18:13, 38

6. Human Examples

SAUL

1 S 11:13 And Saul said, There shall not a man be put to death this day: for to day the LORD hath wrought salvation in Israel.

DAVID

1 S 26:9 And David said to Abishai, Destroy him not: for who can stretch forth his hand against the LORD'S anointed, and be guiltless?

2 S 19:22 And David said, What have I to do with you, ye sons of Zeruiah, that ye should this day be adversaries unto me? shall there any man be put to death this day in Israel? for do not I know that I *am* this day king over Israel?

SOLOMON

1 K 1:52 And Solomon said, If he will shew himself a worthy man, there shall not an hair of him fall to the earth: but if wickedness shall be found in him, he shall die.

ELISHA

2 K 6:22 And he answered, Thou shalt not smite *them:* wouldest thou smite those whom thou hast taken captive with thy sword and with thy bow? set bread and water before them,

that they may eat and drink, and go to their master.

CHRIST

Lu 9:55 But he turned, and rebuked them, and said, Ye know not what manner of spirit ye are of.

Jn 8:7 So when they continued asking him, he lifted up himself, and said unto them, He that is without sin among you, let him first cast a stone at her.

See **FORGIVENESS, RETALIATION, UNMERCIFULNESS**

MERCY SEAT, *the lid of the ark of the covenant, over which hovered the cloud in which Jehovah himself appeared*

Ex 25:17 And thou shalt make a mercy seat *of* pure gold: two cubits and a half *shall be* the length thereof, and a cubit and a half the breadth thereof.

Ex 25:22 And there I will meet with thee, and I will commune with thee from above the mercy seat, from between the two cherubims which *are* upon the ark of the testimony, of all *things* which I will give thee in commandment unto the children of Israel.

Ex 26:34 And thou shalt put the mercy seat upon the ark of the testimony in the most holy *place.*

Ex 30:6 And thou shalt put it before the vail that *is* by the ark of the testimony, before the mercy seat that *is* over the testimony, where I will meet with thee.

Le 16:2 And the LORD said unto Moses, Speak unto Aaron thy brother, that he come not at all times into the holy *place* within the vail before the mercy seat, which *is* upon the ark; that he die not: for I will appear in the cloud upon the mercy seat.

Nu 7:89 And when Moses was gone into the tabernacle of the congregation to speak with him, then he heard the voice of one speaking unto him from off the mercy seat that *was* upon the ark of testimony, from between the two cherubims: and he spake unto him.

He 9:5 And over it the cherubims of glory shadowing the mercyseat; of which we cannot now speak particularly.

See **HOLY OF HOLIES, TABERNACLE**

MEROZ, *a place in the north of Palestine*
Jud 5:23

MESHACH, *one of the Hebrew captives*
Da 1:7; 2:49; 3:12, 23, 30

MESOPOTAMIA, *between the rivers, a country between the Tigris and Euphrates Rivers*
Ge 24:10; De 23:4; 1 Chr 19:6; Ac 2:9; 7:2

MESSIAH *See* **CHRIST**

MESSIANIC HOPE

JOSEPH OF ARIMATHAEA
Mk 15:43 Joseph of Arimathaea, an honourable counsellor, which also waited for the kingdom of God, came, and went in boldly unto Pilate, and craved the body of Jesus.

SIMEON
Lu 2:26 And it was revealed unto him by the Holy Ghost, that he should not see death, before he had seen the Lord's Christ.

ANNA
Lu 2:38 And she coming in that instant gave thanks likewise unto the Lord, and spake of him to all them that looked for redemption in Jerusalem.

THE JEWISH PEOPLE
Lu 3:15 And as the people were in expectation, and all men mused in their hearts of John, whether he were the Christ, or not;

JOHN THE BAPTIST
Jn 1:31 And I knew him not: but that he should be made manifest to Israel, therefore am I come baptizing with water.

THE WOMAN OF SAMARIA
Jn 4:25 The woman saith unto him, I know that Messias cometh, which is called Christ: when he is come, he will tell us all things.

ABRAHAM
Jn 8:56 Your father Abraham rejoiced to see my day: and he saw *it,* and was glad.

THE TWELVE TRIBES
Ac 26:7 Unto which *promise* our twelve tribes, instantly serving *God* day and night, hope to come. For which hope's sake, king Agrippa, I am accused of the Jews.

See **CHRIST**

METHODS, *the way God works*

FOOLISH THINGS, WEAK THINGS
1 Co 1:27 But God hath chosen the foolish things of the world to confound the wise; and God hath chosen the weak things of the world to confound the things which are mighty;

BASE THINGS, DESPISED THINGS
1 Co 1:28–29 And base things of the world, and things which are despised, hath God chosen, *yea,* and things which are not, to bring to nought things that are:
That no flesh should glory in his presence.

See **GOD**

METHUSELAH, *son of Enoch*
Ge 5:21, 27; 1 Chr 1:3; Lu 3:37

MICAH

1. Person, *the Morasthite, a prophet*
Mi 1:1

2. Book

Author: Micah, a native of Moresheth in Judah. He prophesied during the reigns of Jotham, Ahaz, and Hezekiah (his anointing mentioned, 3:8); a contemporary of Isaiah (1:1). Micah means "who is like Jehovah."

He belonged to the territory of Judah but spoke to both Judah and Israel.

Date Written: Sometime between 739 B.C. and 686 B.C. (the reigns of Jotham, Ahaz, and Hezekiah).

Purpose: To warn God's people of coming judgment for sin and to offer hope, based upon the mercy of God.

To Whom Written: Both Kingdoms, North (Israel) and South (Judah).

Main Themes: Sin is exposed, God's justice is required, but mercy is offered to those of humble and repentant hearts.

Key Words: Judgment and mercy.

Key Verses:

(1) The definition of true religion (6:8).

(2) The birthplace of Christ announced (5:2).

(3) God's disposal of the sins of believers (7:18–19).

MICAIAH, *a prophet*
1 K 22:8; 2 Chr 18:7

MICE See **ANIMALS**

MICHAEL, *the archangel*
Da 10:13, 21; 12:1; Jude 9; Re 12:7

MICHAL, *Saul's daughter, married to David*
1 S 14:49; 18:20, 27; 19:12; 25:44; 2 S 3:13; 6:16, 23; 21:8; 1 Chr 15:29

MICHMASH, *a town of Benjamin*
1 S 13:5; Ezr 2:27; Ne 11:31

MIDIAN, *strife*

1. Son of Abraham and Keturah
Ge 25:2; 36:35; Ex 18:1; Nu 22:4; 31:3; Jud 6:1; 7:8; 8:28; 1 Chr 1:32, 46

2. Land of
Ex 2:15; Nu 25:15; 1 K 11:18; Is 60:6; Hab 3:7; Ac 7:29

MIDIANITES, *descendants of Midian*
Ge 37:28, 36; Nu 25:14; 31:2; Jud 6:3, 7, 13, 33; 7:1, 12, 25; Ps 83:9

See **NATION**

MIDNIGHT, *scenes at*
Ex 11:4; 12:29; Jb 34:20; 36:20; Mt 25:6; Mk 13:35; Lu 11:5; Ac 16:25; 20:7

MIGDOL, *a town near the Red Sea*
Ex 14:2; Nu 33:7; Je 44:1; 46:14

MILDEW, *fungal or parasitic plant generated by moisture*
De 28:22; 1 K 8:37; Am 4:9; Hag 2:17

MILE, *a Roman measure*
Mt 5:41

See **WEIGHTS AND MEASURES**

MILETUS, *a seaport town near Ephesus*
Ac 20:15; 2 Ti 4:20

MILK, *from cows, sheep, camels, and goats*
Ge 18:8; Nu 13:27; De 32:14; Jud 4:19; Pr 27:27; 30:33; Is 7:22; 1 Co 9:7

MILLENNIUM See **SECOND COMING**

MILLO, *a fortification, a rampart consisting of two walls with a space between them filled in*
2 S 5:9; 1 K 9:15, 24; 11:27; 2 K 12:20; 1 Chr 11:8; 2 Chr 32:5

MILLS, *made of two stones*
Ex 11:5; Nu 11:8; Jb 31:10; Lam 5:13; Mt 24:41; Lu 17:35; Re 18:22

MILLSTONES, *cylindrical stones used in a mill for grinding grain*
De 24:6; Jud 9:53; Is 47:2; Je 25:10; Mt 18:6; Mk 9:42; Lu 17:2; Re 18:21

MIND

1. Human, carnal, earthly, natural; governed by mere human nature
Ps 49:11 Their inward thought *is, that* their houses *shall continue* for ever, *and* their dwelling places to all

generations; they call *their* lands after their own names.

Mt 16:23 But he turned, and said unto Peter, Get thee behind me, Satan: thou art an offence unto me: for thou savourest not the things that be of God, but those that be of men.

Mt 22:28 Therefore in the resurrection whose wife shall she be of the seven? for they all had her.

Mk 8:33 But when he had turned about and looked on his disciples, he rebuked Peter, saying, Get thee behind me, Satan: for thou savourest not the things that be of God, but the things that be of men.

Lu 9:55 But he turned, and rebuked them, and said, Ye know not what manner of spirit ye are of.

Ac 8:18 And when Simon saw that through laying on of the apostles' hands the Holy Ghost was given, he offered them money,

Ro 1:28 And even as they did not like to retain God in *their* knowledge, God gave them over to a reprobate mind, to do those things which are not convenient;

Ro 8:7 Because the carnal mind *is* enmity against God: for it is not subject to the law of God, neither indeed can be.

1 Co 3:3 For ye are yet carnal: for whereas *there is* among you envying, and strife, and divisions, are ye not carnal, and walk as men?

Ga 5:17 For the flesh lusteth against the Spirit, and the Spirit against the flesh: and these are contrary the one to the other: so that ye cannot do the things that ye would.

Ep 2:3 Among whom also we all had our conversation in times past in the lusts of our flesh, fulfilling the desires of the flesh and of the mind; and were by nature the children of wrath, even as others.

Ep 4:17 This I say therefore, and testify in the Lord, that ye henceforth walk not as other Gentiles walk, in the vanity of their mind,

Ph 3:19 Whose end *is* destruction, whose God *is their* belly, and *whose* glory *is* in their shame, who mind earthly things.)

Col 1:21 And you, that were sometime alienated and enemies in *your* mind by wicked works, yet now hath he reconciled

Col 2:18 Let no man beguile you of your reward in a voluntary humility and worshipping of angels, intruding into those things which he hath not seen, vainly puffed up by his fleshly mind,

1 Ti 6:5 Perverse disputings of men of corrupt minds, and destitute of the truth, supposing that gain is godliness: from such withdraw thyself.

2 Ti 3:8 Now as Jannes and Jambres withstood Moses, so do these also resist the truth: men of corrupt minds, reprobate concerning the faith.

Tit 1:15 Unto the pure all things *are* pure: but unto them that are defiled and unbelieving *is* nothing pure; but even their mind and conscience is defiled.

2. Evil Thoughts

De 15:9 Beware that there be not a thought in thy wicked heart, saying, The seventh year, the year of release, is at hand; and thine eye be evil against thy poor brother, and thou givest him nought; and he cry unto the LORD against thee, and it be sin unto thee.

Ps 56:5 Every day they wrest my words: all their thoughts *are* against me for evil.

Ps 64:6 They search out iniquities; they accomplish a diligent search: both the inward *thought* of every one *of them,* and the heart, *is* deep.

Ps 94:11 The LORD knoweth the thoughts of man, that they *are* vanity.

Pr 15:26 The thoughts of the wicked *are* an abomination to the LORD: but *the words* of the pure *are* pleasant words.

Pr 23:7 For as he thinketh in his heart, so *is* he: Eat and drink, saith he to thee; but his heart *is* not with thee.

Is 66:18 For I *know* their works and their thoughts: it shall come, that I will gather all nations and tongues; and they shall come, and see my glory.

Je 4:14 O Jerusalem, wash thine heart from wickedness, that thou mayest be saved. How long shall thy vain thoughts lodge within thee.

Je 6:19 Hear, O earth: behold, I will bring evil upon this people, *even* the fruit of their thoughts, because they have not hearkened unto my words, nor to my law, but rejected it.

Mt 9:4 And Jesus knowing their thoughts said, Wherefore think ye evil in your hearts?

Mt 15:19 For out of the heart proceed evil thoughts, murders, adulteries, fornications, thefts, false witness, blasphemies:

1 Co 3:20 And again, The Lord knoweth the thoughts of the wise, that they are vain.

3. Evil Imagination

Ge 6:5 And GOD saw that the wickedness of man *was* great in the earth, and *that* every imagination of the thoughts of his heart *was* only evil continually.

Ge 8:21 And the LORD smelled a sweet savour; and the LORD said in his heart, I will not again curse the ground any more for man's sake; for the imagination of man's heart *is* evil from his youth; neither will I again smite any more every thing living, as I have done.

Ge 11:6 And the LORD said, Behold, the people *is* one, and they have all one language; and this they begin to do: and now nothing will be restrained from them, which they have imagined to do.

De 31:21 And it shall come to pass, when many evils and troubles are befallen them, that this song shall testify against them as a witness; for it shall not be forgotten out of the mouths of their seed: for I know their imagination which they go about, even now, before I have brought them into the land which I sware.

Ps 38:12 They also that seek after my life lay snares *for me:* and they that seek my hurt speak mischievous things, and imagine deceits all the day long.

Pr 6:18 An heart that deviseth wicked imaginations, feet that be swift in running to mischief,

Ec 7:29 Lo, this only have I found, that God hath made man upright; but they have sought out many inventions.

Is 55:8 For my thoughts *are* not your thoughts, neither *are* your ways my ways, saith the LORD.

Je 23:17 They say still unto them that despise me, The LORD hath said, Ye shall have peace; and they say unto every one that walketh after the imagination of his own heart, No evil shall come upon you.

Eze 8:12 Then said he unto me, Son of man, hast thou seen what the ancients of the house of Israel do in the dark, every man in the chambers of his imagery? for they say, The LORD seeth us not; the LORD hath forsaken the earth.

Ro 1:21 Because that, when they knew God, they glorified *him* not as God, neither were thankful; but became vain in their imaginations, and their foolish heart was darkened.

4. Grossness

Ps 32:9; 49:20; 73:22; 92:6; 94:8; Pr 12:1; Ec 3:18; Is 19:11; Je 4:22; 10:8; 51:17; Eze 23:20; Da 4:16; Mt 7:6; 12:39; 13:15; 16:4; Mk 12:23; Ac 28:27; Ro 1:27; Tit 1:12; 2 Pe 2:12; Jude 10

5. Christ's

Ro 8:5 For they that are after the flesh do mind the things of the flesh; but they that are after the Spirit the things of the Spirit.

1 Co 2:16 For who hath known the mind of the Lord, that he may instruct him? But we have the mind of Christ.

Ph 2:5 Let this mind be in you, which was also in Christ Jesus:

1 Pe 4:1 Forasmuch then as Christ hath suffered for us in the flesh, arm yourselves likewise with the same mind: for he that hath suffered in the flesh hath ceased from sin;

6. Spiritual

a. Wise Thoughts

Jos 1:8 This book of the law shall not depart out of thy mouth; but thou shalt meditate therein day and night, that thou mayest observe to do according to all that is written therein: for then thou shalt make thy way prosperous, and then thou shalt have good success.

Jud 5:15 And the princes of Issachar *were* with Deborah; even Issachar, and also Barak: he was sent on foot into the valley. For the divisions of Reuben *there were* great thoughts of heart.

Ps 19:14 Let the words of my mouth, and the meditation of my heart, be acceptable in thy sight, O LORD, my strength, and my redeemer.

Ps 48:9 We have thought of thy lovingkindness, O God, in the midst of thy temple.

Ps 119:59 I thought on my ways, and turned my feet unto thy testimonies.

Ps 119:99 I have more understanding than all my teachers: for thy testimonies *are* my meditation.

Pr 12:5 The thoughts of the righteous *are* right: *but* the counsels of the wicked *are* deceit.

Pr 21:5 The thoughts of the diligent *tend* only to plenteousness; but of every one *that is* hasty only to want.

Lu 14:15 And when one of them that sat at meat with him heard these things, he said unto him, Blessed *is* he that shall eat bread in the kingdom of God.

Lu 16:3 Then the steward said within himself, What shall I do? for my lord taketh away from me the stewardship: I cannot dig; to beg I am ashamed.

Ro 12:3 For I say, through the grace given unto me, to every man that is among you, not to think *of himself* more highly than he ought to think; but to think soberly, according as God hath dealt to every man the measure of faith.

Ph 4:8 Finally, brethren, whatsoever things are true, whatsoever things *are* honest, whatsoever things *are* just, whatsoever things *are* pure, whatsoever things *are* lovely, whatsoever things *are* of good report; if *there be* any virtue, and if *there be* any praise, think on these things.

b. Think on These Things

THE PURPOSE OF CHASTISEMENT

De 8:5 Thou shalt also consider in thine heart, that, as a man chasteneth his son, *so* the LORD thy God chasteneth thee.

THE PAST

De 32:7 Remember the days of old, consider the years of many generations: ask thy father, and he will shew thee; thy elders, and they will tell thee.

THE END OF LIFE

De 32:29 O that they were wise, *that* they understood this, *that* they would consider their latter end!

GOD'S BLESSINGS

1 S 12:24 Only fear the LORD, and serve him in truth with all your heart: for consider how great *things* he hath done for you.

GOD'S WONDERFUL WORKS

Jb 37:14 Hearken unto this, O Job: stand still, and consider the wondrous works of God.

GOD'S INTEREST IN HUMANITY

Ps 8:3–4 When I consider thy heavens, the work of thy fingers, the moon and the stars, which thou hast ordained;

What is man, that thou art mindful of him? and the son of man, that thou visitest him?

Pr 6:6 Go to the ant, thou sluggard; consider her ways, and be wise:

Ec 7:13 Consider the work of God: for who can make *that* straight, which he hath made crooked?

THE DISAPPOINTMENT OF THE WORLDLY LIFE

Hag 1:5–6 Now therefore thus saith the LORD of hosts; Consider your ways.

Ye have sown much, and bring in little; ye eat, but ye have not enough; ye drink, but ye are not filled with drink; ye clothe you, but there is none warm; and he that earneth wages earneth wages *to put it* into a bag with holes.

THE LESSONS OF NATURE

Mt 6:28–29 And why take ye thought for raiment? Consider the lilies of the field, how they grow; they toil not, neither do they spin:

And yet I say unto you, That even Solomon in all his glory was not arrayed like one of these.

He 3:1 Wherefore, holy brethren, partakers of the heavenly calling, consider the Apostle and High Priest of our profession, Christ Jesus;

THE MATCHLESS LIFE OF CHRIST

He 12:3 For consider him that endured such contradiction of sinners against himself, lest ye be wearied and faint in your minds.

c. Meditation, Its Delight

Ge 24:63 And Isaac went out to meditate in the field at the eventide: and he lifted up his eyes, and saw, and, behold, the camels *were* coming.

Jos 1:8 This book of the law shall not depart out of thy mouth; but thou shalt meditate therein day and night, that thou mayest observe to do according to all that is written therein: for then thou shalt make thy way prosperous, and then thou shalt have good success.

Jb 4:13 In thoughts from the visions of the night, when deep sleep falleth on men,

Ps 1:2 But his delight *is* in the law of the LORD; and in his law doth he meditate day and night.

Ps 4:4 Stand in awe, and sin not: commune with your own heart upon your bed, and be still. Selah.

Ps 16:7 I will bless the LORD, who hath given me counsel: my reins also instruct me in the night seasons.

Ps 19:14 Let the words of my mouth, and the meditation of my heart, be acceptable in thy sight, O LORD, my strength, and my redeemer.

Ps 39:3 My heart was hot within me, while I was musing the fire burned: *then* spake I with my tongue,

Ps 48:9 We have thought of thy lovingkindness, O God, in the midst of thy temple.

Ps 49:3 My mouth shall speak of wisdom; and the meditation of my heart *shall be* of understanding.

Ps 63:6 When I remember thee upon my bed, *and* meditate on thee in the *night* watches.

Ps 77:6 I call to remembrance my song in the night: I commune with mine own heart: and my spirit made diligent search.

Ps 77:12 I will meditate also of all thy work, and talk of thy doings.

Ps 94:19 In the multitude of my thoughts within me thy comforts delight my soul.

Ps 104:34 My meditation of him shall be sweet: I will be glad in the LORD.

Ps 119:15 I will meditate in thy precepts, and have respect unto thy ways.

Ps 119:23 Princes also did sit *and* speak against me: *but* thy servant did meditate in thy statutes.

Ps 119:48 My hands also will I lift up unto thy commandments, which I have loved; and I will meditate in thy statutes.

Ps 119:78 Let the proud be ashamed; for they dealt perversely with me without a cause: *but* I will meditate in thy precepts.

Ps 119:99 I have more understanding than all my teachers: for thy testimonies *are* my meditation.

Ps 119:148 Mine eyes prevent the *night* watches, that I might meditate in thy word.

Ps 143:5 I remember the days of old; I meditate on all thy works; I muse on the work of thy hands.

Ec 1:16 I communed with mine own heart, saying, Lo, I am come to great estate, and have gotten more wisdom than all *they* that have been before me in Jerusalem: yea, my heart had great experience of wisdom and knowledge.

Mal 3:16 Then they that feared the LORD spake often one to another: and the LORD hearkened, and heard *it,* and a book of remembrance was written before him for them that feared the LORD, and that thought upon his name.

Mt 1:20 But while he thought on these things, behold, the angel of the

Lord appeared unto him in a dream, saying, Joseph, thou son of David, fear not to take unto thee Mary thy wife: for that which is conceived in her is of the Holy Ghost.

Mk 14:72 And the second time the cock crew. And Peter called to mind the word that Jesus said unto him, Before the cock crow twice, thou shalt deny me thrice. And when he thought thereon, he wept.

Lu 2:19 But Mary kept all these things, and pondered *them* in her heart.

Ac 10:19 While Peter thought on the vision, the Spirit said unto him, Behold, three men seek thee.

Ph 4:8 Finally, brethren, whatsoever things are true, whatsoever things *are* honest, whatsoever things *are* just, whatsoever things *are* pure, whatsoever things *are* lovely, whatsoever things *are* of good report; if *there be* any virtue, and if *there be* any praise, think on these things.

1 Ti 4:15 Meditate upon these things; give thyself wholly to them; that thy profiting may appear to all.

d. Way of Thinking

Ro 14:14 I know, and am persuaded by the Lord Jesus, that *there is* nothing unclean of itself: but to him that esteemeth any thing to be unclean, to him *it is* unclean.

Tit 1:15 Unto the pure all things *are* pure: but unto them that are defiled and unbelieving *is* nothing pure; but even their mind and conscience is defiled.

See **CARNALITY, HEART, EVIL, THOUGHTS**

MINISTERS, *those chosen by God to serve him and his people in a variety of ways*

1. Their Appointment

Am 2:11 And I raised up of your sons for prophets, and of your young men for Nazarites. *Is it* not even thus, O ye children of Israel? saith the LORD.

1 Co 3:5 Who then is Paul, and who *is* Apollos, but ministers by whom ye believed, even as the Lord gave to every man?

2 Co 3:6 Who also hath made us able ministers of the new testament; not of the letter, but of the spirit: for the letter killeth, but the spirit giveth life.

2 Co 4:1 Therefore seeing we have this ministry, as we have received mercy, we faint not;

2 Co 5:18 And all things *are* of God, who hath reconciled us to himself by Jesus Christ, and hath given to us the ministry of reconciliation;

2 Co 6:4 But in all *things* approving ourselves as the ministers of God, in much patience, in afflictions, in necessities, in distresses,

Ep 3:7 Whereof I was made a minister, according to the gift of the grace of God given unto me by the effectual working of his power.

Col 1:23 If ye continue in the faith grounded and settled, and *be* not moved away from the hope of the gospel, which ye have heard, *and* which was preached to every creature which is under heaven; whereof I Paul am made a minister;

1 Ti 1:12 And I thank Christ Jesus our Lord, who hath enabled me, for that he counted me faithful, putting me into the ministry;

2 Ti 1:11 Whereunto I am appointed a preacher, and an apostle, and a teacher of the Gentiles.

2. Their Attitude

Mt 20:26 But it shall not be so among you: but whosoever will be great among you, let him be your minister;

Lu 22:26 But ye *shall* not *be* so: but he that is greatest among you, let him be as the younger; and he that is chief, as he that doth serve.

Ac 20:24 But none of these things move me, neither count I my life dear unto myself, so that I might finish my course with joy, and the ministry, which I have received of the Lord Jesus, to testify the gospel of the grace of God.

1 Co 3:5 Who then is Paul, and who *is* Apollos, but ministers by whom ye believed, even as the Lord gave to every man?

1 Ti 6:11 But thou, O man of God, flee these things; and follow after righteousness, godliness, faith, love, patience, meekness.

2 Ti 2:24 And the servant of the Lord must not strive; but be gentle unto all *men,* apt to teach, patient,

3. Their Characteristics

Mt 20:26 But it shall not be so among you: but whosoever will be great among you, let him be your minister;

2 Co 4:2 But have renounced the hidden things of dishonesty, not walking in craftiness, nor handling the word of God deceitfully; but by manifestation of the truth commending ourselves to every man's conscience in the sight of God.

2 Co 6:4 But in all *things* approving ourselves as the ministers of God, in much patience, in afflictions, in necessities, in distresses,

1 Th 2:4 But as we were allowed of God to be put in trust with the gospel, even so we speak; not as pleasing men, but God, which trieth our hearts.

1 Th 5:14 Now we exhort you, brethren, warn them that are unruly, comfort the feebleminded, support the weak, be patient toward all *men.*

2 Th 3:9 Not because we have not power, but to make ourselves an ensample unto you to follow us.

1 Ti 3:2 A bishop then must be blameless, the husband of one wife, vigilant, sober, of good behaviour, given to hospitality, apt to teach;

1 Ti 4:12 Let no man despise thy youth; but be thou an example of the believers, in word, in conversation, in charity, in spirit, in faith, in purity.

2 Ti 2:1 Thou therefore, my son, be strong in the grace that is in Christ Jesus.

2 Ti 3:17 That the man of God may be perfect, throughly furnished unto all good works.

Tit 1:7 For a bishop must be blameless, as the steward of God; not selfwilled, not soon angry, not given to wine, no striker, not given to filthy lucre;

4. Their Position

Mt 10:10 Nor scrip for *your* journey, neither two coats, neither shoes, nor yet staves: for the workman is worthy of his meat.

Ro 10:15 And how shall they preach, except they be sent? as it is written, How beautiful are the feet of them that preach the gospel of peace, and bring glad tidings of good things!

Ro 15:30 Now I beseech you, brethren, for the Lord Jesus Christ's sake, and for the love of the Spirit, that ye strive together with me in *your* prayers to God for me;

1 Co 16:16 That ye submit yourselves unto such, and to every one that helpeth with *us,* and laboureth.

Ga 4:14 And my temptation which was in my flesh ye despised not, nor rejected; but received me as an angel of God, *even* as Christ Jesus.

Ph 2:29 Receive him therefore in the Lord with all gladness; and hold such in reputation:

1 Th 5:12–13 And we beseech you, brethren, to know them which labour among you, and are over you in the Lord, and admonish you;

And to esteem them very highly in love for their work's sake. *And* be at peace among yourselves.

1 Ti 5:17 Let the elders that rule well be counted worthy of double honour, especially they who labour in the word and doctrine.

He 13:7 Remember them which have the rule over you, who have spoken unto you the word of God: whose faith follow, considering the end of *their* conversation.

5. Their Unfaithfulness

2 Chr 30:3; Is 28:7; 56:10; Je 2:8; 6:13; 8:10; 12:10; 23:1, 4, 11; Lam 2:14; Eze 3:18; 13:4; 33:6; 34:2-3; Ho 9:8; Mi 3:11; Mt 25:42; Jn 10:8; Ph 1:15

6. Their Duty to Peach

a. Examples

Ps 40:9 I have preached righteousness in the great congregation: lo, I have not refrained my lips, O LORD, thou knowest.

Je 26:8 Now it came to pass, when Jeremiah had made an end of speaking all that the LORD had commanded *him* to speak unto all the people, that the priests and the prophets and all the people took him, saying, Thou shalt surely die.

Mt 3:1 In those days came John the Baptist, preaching in the wilderness of Judaea,

Mt 9:35 And Jesus went about all the cities and villages, teaching in their synagogues, and preaching the gospel of the kingdom, and healing every sickness and every disease among the people.

Mk 16:20 And they went forth, and preached every where, the Lord working with *them,* and confirming the word with signs following. Amen.

Lu 9:6 And they departed, and went through the towns, preaching the gospel, and healing every where.

Ac 28:31 Preaching the kingdom of God, and teaching those things which concern the Lord Jesus Christ, with all confidence, no man forbidding him.

Ep 2:17 And came and preached peace to you which were afar off, and to them that were nigh.

1 Pe 3:19 By which also he went and preached unto the spirits in prison;

1 Pe 4:6 For for this cause was the gospel preached also to them that are dead, that they might be judged according to men in the flesh, but live according to God in the spirit.

Re 14:6 And I saw another angel fly in the midst of heaven, having the everlasting gospel to preach unto them that dwell on the earth, and to every nation, and kindred, and tongue, and people,

b. Commanded

Is 66:19 And I will set a sign among them, and I will send those that escape of them unto the nations, *to* Tarshish, Pul, and Lud, that draw the bow, *to* Tubal, and Javan, *to* the isles afar off, that have not heard my fame, neither have seen my glory; and they shall declare my glory among the Gentiles.

Je 1:7 But the LORD said unto me, Say not, I *am* a child: for thou shalt go to all that I shall send thee, and whatsoever I command thee thou shalt speak.

Je 7:2 Stand in the gate of the LORD's house, and proclaim there this word, and say, Hear the word of the LORD, all *ye of* Judah, that enter in at these gates to worship the LORD.

Je 11:6 Then the LORD said unto me, Proclaim all these words in the cities of Judah, and in the streets of Jerusalem, saying, Hear ye the words of this covenant, and do them.

Je 23:28 The prophet that hath a dream, let him tell a dream; and he that hath my word, let him speak my word faithfully. What *is* the chaff to the wheat? saith the LORD.

Eze 3:1 Moreover he said unto me, Son of man, eat that thou findest; eat this roll, and go speak unto the house of Israel.

Am 7:15 And the LORD took me as I followed the flock, and the LORD said unto me, Go, prophesy unto my people Israel.

Zec 1:14 So the angel that communed with me said unto me, Cry thou, saying, Thus saith the LORD of hosts; I am jealous for Jerusalem and for Zion with a great jealousy.

Mt 10:7 And as ye go, preach, saying, The kingdom of heaven is at hand.

Mt 10:27 What I tell you in darkness, *that* speak ye in light: and what ye hear in the ear, *that* preach ye upon the housetops.

Mk 16:15 And he said unto them, Go ye into all the world, and preach the gospel to every creature.

Lu 9:2 And he sent them to preach the kingdom of God, and to heal the sick.

Lu 9:60 Jesus said unto him, Let the dead bury their dead: but go thou and preach the kingdom of God.

Ac 5:20 Go, stand and speak in the temple to the people all the words of this life.

Ac 16:10 And after he had seen the vision, immediately we endeavoured to go into Macedonia, assuredly gathering that the Lord had called us for to preach the gospel unto them.

Ac 26:16 But rise, and stand upon thy feet: for I have appeared unto thee for this purpose, to make thee a minister and a witness both of these things which thou hast seen, and of those things in the which I will appear unto thee;

c. Christ the Theme

Mt 24:14 And this gospel of the kingdom shall be preached in all the world for a witness unto all nations; and then shall the end come.

Lu 8:39 Return to thine own house, and shew how great things God hath done unto thee. And he went his way, and published throughout the whole city how great things Jesus had done unto him.

Ac 3:20 And he shall send Jesus Christ, which before was preached unto you:

Ac 4:2 Being grieved that they taught the people, and preached through Jesus the resurrection from the dead.

Ac 5:42 And daily in the temple, and in every house, they ceased not to teach and preach Jesus Christ.

Ac 8:5 Then Philip went down to the city of Samaria, and preached Christ unto them.

Ac 8:35 Then Philip opened his mouth, and began at the same scripture, and preached unto him Jesus.

Ac 9:20 And straightway he preached Christ in the synagogues, that he is the Son of God.

Ac 10:36 The word which *God* sent unto the children of Israel, preaching peace by Jesus Christ: (he is Lord of all:)

Ac 11:20 And some of them were men of Cyprus and Cyrene, which, when they were come to Antioch, spake unto the Grecians, preaching the Lord Jesus.

Ac 13:38 Be it known unto you therefore, men *and* brethren, that through this man is preached unto you the forgiveness of sins:

Ac 16:32 And they spake unto him the word of the Lord, and to all that were in his house.

Ac 17:3 Opening and alleging, that Christ must needs have suffered, and risen again from the dead; and that this Jesus, whom I preach unto you, is Christ.

Ac 17:7 When Jason hath received: and these all do contrary to the decrees of Caesar, saying that there is another king, *one* Jesus.

Ac 17:18 Then certain philosophers of the Epicureans, and of the Stoicks, encountered him. And some said, What will this babbler say? other some, He seemeth to be a setter forth of strange gods: because he preached unto them Jesus, and the resurrection.

Ac 18:28 For he mightily convinced the Jews, *and that* publickly, shewing by the scriptures that Jesus was Christ.

Ac 19:10 And this continued by the space of two years; so that all they which dwelt in Asia heard the word of the Lord Jesus, both Jews and Greeks.

Ac 28:23 And when they had appointed him a day, there came many to him into *his* lodging; to whom he expounded and testified the kingdom of God, persuading them concerning Jesus, both out of the law of Moses, and *out of* the prophets, from morning till evening.

Ac 28:31 Preaching the kingdom of God, and teaching those things which concern the Lord Jesus Christ, with all confidence, no man forbidding him.

Ro 10:15 And how shall they preach, except they be sent? as it is written, How beautiful are the feet of them that preach the gospel of peace, and bring glad tidings of good things!

Ro 15:19 Through mighty signs and wonders, by the power of the Spirit of God; so that from Jerusalem, and round about unto Illyricum, I have fully preached the gospel of Christ.

1 Co 1:23 But we preach Christ crucified, unto the Jews a stumblingblock, and unto the Greeks foolishness;

1 Co 2:2 For I determined not to know any thing among you, save Jesus Christ, and him crucified.

1 Co 14:24 But if all prophesy, and there come in one that believeth not, or *one* unlearned, he is convinced of all, he is judged of all:

1 Co 15:12 Now if Christ be preached that he rose from the dead, how say some among you that there is no resurrection of the dead?

2 Co 1:19 For the Son of God, Jesus Christ, who was preached among you by us, *even* by me and Silvanus and Timotheus, was not yea and nay, but in him was yea.

2 Co 2:17 For we are not as many, which corrupt the word of God: but as of sincerity, but as of God, in the sight of God speak we in Christ.

2 Co 4:5 For we preach not ourselves, but Christ Jesus the Lord; and ourselves your servants for Jesus' sake.

2 Co 10:14 For we stretch not ourselves beyond *our measure,* as though we reached not unto you: for we are come as far as to you also in *preaching* the gospel of Christ:

Ga 1:11 But I certify you, brethren, that the gospel which was preached of me is not after man.

Ga 1:16 To reveal his Son in me, that I might preach him among the heathen; immediately I conferred not with flesh and blood:

Ga 1:23 But they had heard only, That he which persecuted us in times past now preacheth the faith which once he destroyed.

Ga 3:1 O foolish Galatians, who hath bewitched you, that ye should not obey the truth, before whose eyes Jesus Christ hath been evidently set forth, crucified among you?

Ep 3:8 Unto me, who am less than the least of all saints, is this grace given, that I should preach among the Gentiles the unsearchable riches of Christ;

Ph 1:18 What then? notwithstanding, every way, whether in pretence, or in truth, Christ is preached; and I therein do rejoice, yea, and will rejoice.

Col 1:28 Whom we preach, warning every man, and teaching every man in all wisdom; that we may present every man perfect in Christ Jesus:

1 Ti 3:16 And without controversy great is the mystery of godliness: God was manifest in the flesh, justified in the Spirit, seen of angels, preached unto the Gentiles, believed on in the world, received up into glory.

7. Their Responsibility to Feed the Flock

2 S 5:2 Also in time past, when Saul was king over us, thou wast he that leddest out and broughtest in Israel: and the LORD said to thee, Thou shalt feed my people Israel, and thou shalt be a captain over Israel.

Ps 78:72 So he fed them according to the integrity of his heart; and guided them by the skilfulness of his hands.

Je 3:15 And I will give you pastors according to mine heart, which shall feed you with knowledge and understanding.

Je 23:4 And I will set up shepherds over them which shall feed them: and they shall fear no more, nor be dismayed, neither shall they be lacking, saith the LORD.

Eze 34:2 Son of man, prophesy against the shepherds of Israel, prophesy, and say unto them, Thus saith the Lord God unto the shepherds; Woe *be* to the shepherds of Israel that do feed themselves! should not the shepherds feed the flocks?

Eze 34:23 And I will set up one shepherd over them, and he shall feed them, *even* my servant David; he shall feed them, and he shall be their shepherd.

Mi 5:4 And he shall stand and feed in the strength of the LORD, in the majesty of the name of the LORD his God; and they shall abide: for now shall he be great unto the ends of the earth.

Zec 11:7 And I will feed the flock of slaughter, *even* you, O poor of the flock. And I took unto me two staves; the one I called Beauty, and the other I called Bands; and I fed the flock.

Jn 21:17 He saith unto him the third time, Simon, *son* of Jonas, lovest thou me? Peter was grieved because he said unto him the third time, Lovest thou me? And he said unto him, Lord, thou knowest all things; thou knowest that I love thee. Jesus saith unto him, Feed my sheep.

Ac 20:28 Take heed therefore unto yourselves, and to all the flock, over the which the Holy Ghost hath made you overseers, to feed the church of

God, which he hath purchased with his own blood.

1 Pe 5:2 Feed the flock of God which is among you, taking the oversight *thereof,* not by constraint, but willingly; not for filthy lucre, but of a ready mind;

8. Their Job as Spiritual Guardians

Is 21:11 The burden of Dumah. He calleth to me out of Seir, Watchman, what of the night? Watchman, what of the night?

Is 52:8 Thy watchmen shall lift up the voice; with the voice together shall they sing: for they shall see eye to eye, when the LORD shall bring again Zion.

Is 62:6 I have set watchmen upon thy walls, O Jerusalem, *which* shall never hold their peace day nor night: ye that make mention of the LORD, keep not silence,

Je 6:17 Also I set watchmen over you, *saying,* Hearken to the sound of the trumpet. But they said, We will not hearken.

Je 31:6 For there shall be a day, *that* the watchmen upon the mount Ephraim shall cry, Arise ye, and let us go up to Zion unto the LORD our God.

Eze 3:17 Son of man, I have made thee a watchman unto the house of Israel: therefore hear the word at my mouth, and give them warning from me.

He 13:17 Obey them that have the rule over you, and submit yourselves: for they watch for your souls, as they that must give account, that they may do it with joy, and not with grief: for that *is* unprofitable for you.

9. Their Call to Teach the Word

Mt 28:20 Teaching them to observe all things whatsoever I have commanded you: and, lo, I am with you alway, *even* unto the end of the world. Amen.

1 Ti 3:2 A bishop then must be blameless, the husband of one wife, vigilant, sober, of good behaviour, given to hospitality, apt to teach;

1 Ti 4:11 These things command and teach.

1 Ti 6:2 And they that have believing masters, let them not despise *them,* because they are brethren; but rather do *them* service, because they are faithful and beloved, partakers of the benefit. These things teach and exhort.

2 Ti 2:25 In meekness instructing those that oppose themselves; if God peradventure will give them repentance to the acknowledging of the truth;

10. Their Solemn Charges

MOSES TO JOSHUA

Nu 27:23 And he laid his hands upon him, and gave him a charge, as the LORD commanded by the hand of Moses.

De 31:23 And he gave Joshua the son of Nun a charge, and said, Be strong and of a good courage: for thou shalt bring the children of Israel into the land which I sware unto them: and I will be with thee.

DAVID TO SOLOMON

1 K 2:1 Now the days of David drew nigh that he should die; and he charged Solomon his son, saying,

JEHOSHAPHAT TO LEADERS OF JUDAH

2 Chr 19:9 And he charged them, saying, Thus shall ye do in the fear of the LORD, faithfully, and with a perfect heart.

CHRIST TO THE DISCIPLES

Mt 10:5 These twelve Jesus sent forth, and commanded them, saying, Go not into the way of the Gentiles, and into *any* city of the Samaritans enter ye not:

PAUL TO THE EPHESIAN ELDERS

Ac 20:28 Take heed therefore unto yourselves, and to all the flock, over the which the Holy Ghost hath made you overseers, to feed the church of God, which he hath purchased with his own blood.

PAUL TO TIMOTHY

1 Ti 5:21 I charge *thee* before God, and the Lord Jesus Christ, and the elect angels, that thou observe these things without preferring one before another, doing nothing by partiality.

1 Ti 6:13 I give thee charge in the sight of God, who quickeneth all things, and *before* Christ Jesus, who before Pontius Pilate witnessed a good confession;

2 Ti 4:1 I charge *thee* therefore before God, and the Lord Jesus Christ, who shall judge the quick and the dead at his appearing and his kingdom;

11. Their Mission

Eze 33:6 But if the watchman see the sword come, and blow not the trumpet, and the people be not warned; if the sword come, and take *any* person from among them, he is taken away in his iniquity; but his blood will I require at the watchman's hand.

2 Co 2:16 To the one *we are* the savour of death unto death; and to the other the savour of life unto life. And who *is* sufficient for these things?

12. Their Support

a. Of Priests under the Mosaic Law

See **PRIESTS**

Ex 29:28; Le 2:3, 10; 5:13; 6:17; 7:8, 10, 14, 34; 10:13; 14:13; 23:20; 27:21; Nu 3:48; 5:9; 6:20; 18:9, 12, 18, 21, 24, 31; 31:30; De 18:3; 1 S 2:14, 28; 2 K 4:42; 12:16; 2 Chr 31:4, 19; Ezr 7:24; Ne 10:37; 12:44; 13:10; Eze 44:29; 1 Co 9:6, 13; He 7:5

b. In the Christian Church

2 K 4:42; Mt 6:10; Mk 6:10; Lu 10:7; 1 Co 9:6; 14; Ga 6:6; Ph 4:4; 1 Ti 5:18

c. Self-support Practiced by Paul

Ne 5:14, 18; Ac 18:3; 20:34; 28:30; 1 Co 4:12; 9:12, 15, 18; 2 Co 11:8; 12:13; 1 Th 2:9; 2 Th 3:8

13. Their Duty to Be Good

Ph 1:17 But the other of love, knowing that I am set for the defence of the gospel.

1 Ti 4:6 If thou put the brethren in remembrance of these things, thou shalt be a good minister of Jesus Christ, nourished up in the words of faith and of good doctrine, whereunto thou hast attained.

14. Their Affection for Believers

2 Co 7:3 I speak not *this* to condemn *you:* for I have said before, that ye are in our hearts to die and live with *you.*

Ph 4:1 Therefore, my brethren dearly beloved and longed for, my joy and crown, so stand fast in the Lord, *my* dearly beloved.

1 Th 2:19 For what *is* our hope, or joy, or crown of rejoicing? *Are* not even ye in the presence of our Lord Jesus Christ at his coming?

2 Jn 4 I rejoiced greatly that I found of thy children walking in truth, as we have received a commandment from the Father.

See **CHURCH, GOODNESS, LEADERS, TEACHER**

MIRACLES, *acts that defy the laws of nature*

1. Spurious   See **MAGICIAN**

2. Of Moses and Aaron

ROD MADE SERPENT

Ex 4:3 And he said, Cast it on the ground. And he cast it on the ground, and it became a serpent; and Moses fled from before it.

Ex 7:10 And Moses and Aaron went in unto Pharaoh, and they did so as the LORD had commanded: and Aaron cast down his rod before Pharaoh, and before his servants, and it became a serpent.

ROD RESTORED

Ex 4:4 And the LORD said unto Moses, Put forth thine hand, and take it by the tail. And he put forth his hand, and caught it, and it became a rod in his hand:

HAND MADE LEPROUS

Ex 4:6 And the LORD said furthermore unto him, Put now thine hand into thy bosom. And he put his hand into his bosom: and when he took it out, behold, his hand *was* leprous as snow.

Ex 4:7 And he said, Put thine hand into thy bosom again. And he put his hand into his bosom again; and plucked it out of his bosom, and, behold, it was turned again as his *other* flesh.

Ex 4:9 And it shall come to pass, if they will not believe also these two signs, neither hearken unto thy voice, that thou shalt take of the water of the river, and pour *it* upon the dry *land:* and the water which thou takest out of the river shall become blood upon the dry *land.*

Ex 4:30 And Aaron spake all the words which the LORD had spoken unto Moses, and did the signs in the sight of the people.

RIVER INTO BLOOD

Ex 7:20 And Moses and Aaron did so, as the LORD commanded; and he lifted up the rod, and smote the waters that *were* in the river, in the sight of Pharaoh, and in the sight of his servants; and all the waters that *were* in the river were turned to blood.

FROGS

Ex 8:6 And Aaron stretched out his hand over the waters of Egypt; and the frogs came up, and covered the land of Egypt.

Ex 8:13 And the LORD did according to the word of Moses; and the frogs died out of the houses, out of the villages, and out of the fields.

LICE

Ex 8:17 And they did so; for Aaron stretched out his hand with his rod, and smote the dust of the earth, and it became lice in man, and in beast; all the dust of the land became lice throughout all the land of Egypt.

FLIES

Ex 8:21 Else, if thou wilt not let my people go, behold, I will send swarms *of flies* upon thee, and upon thy servants, and upon thy people, and into thy houses: and the houses of the Egyptians shall be full of swarms *of flies,* and also the ground whereon they *are.*

Ex 8:31 And the LORD did according to the word of Moses; and he removed the swarms *of flies* from Pharaoh, from his servants, and from his people; there remained not one.

MURRAIN

Ex 9:3 Behold, the hand of the LORD is upon thy cattle which *is* in the field, upon the horses, upon the asses, upon the camels, upon the oxen, and upon the sheep: *there shall be* a very grievous murrain.

BOILS

Ex 9:10 And they took ashes of the furnace, and stood before Pharaoh; and Moses sprinkled it up toward heaven; and it became a boil breaking forth with blains upon man, and upon beast.

HAIL

Ex 9:23 And Moses stretched forth his rod toward heaven: and the LORD sent thunder and hail, and the fire ran along upon the ground; and the LORD rained hail upon the land of Egypt.

LOCUSTS

Ex 10:13 And Moses stretched forth his rod over the land of Egypt, and the LORD brought an east wind upon the land all that day, and all *that* night; *and* when it was morning, the east wind brought the locusts.

Ex 10:19 And the LORD turned a mighty strong west wind, which took away the locusts, and cast them into the Red sea; there remained not one locust in all the coasts of Egypt.

DARKNESS

Ex 10:22 And Moses stretched forth his hand toward heaven; and there was a thick darkness in all the land of Egypt three days:

FIRST-BORN DESTROYED

Ex 12:29 And it came to pass, that at midnight the LORD smote all the first-born in the land of Egypt, from the firstborn of Pharaoh that sat on his throne unto the firstborn of the captive that *was* in the dungeon; and all the firstborn of cattle.

SEA DIVIDED

Ex 14:21 And Moses stretched out his hand over the sea; and the LORD caused the sea to go *back* by a strong east wind all that night, and made the sea dry *land,* and the waters were divided.

EGYPTIANS OVERWHELMED

Ex 14:26–28 And the LORD said unto Moses, Stretch out thine hand over the sea, that the waters may come again upon the Egyptians, upon their chariots, and upon their horsemen.

And Moses stretched forth his hand over the sea, and the sea returned to his strength when the morning appeared; and the Egyptians fled against it; and the LORD overthrew the Egyptians in the midst of the sea.

And the waters returned, and covered the chariots, and the horsemen, *and* all the host of Pharaoh that came into the sea after them; there remained not so much as one of them.

Ex 15:25 And he cried unto the LORD; and the LORD shewed him a tree, *which* when he had cast into the waters, the waters were made sweet: there he made for them a statute and an ordinance, and there he proved them,

WATER FROM ROCK

Ex 17:6 Behold, I will stand before thee there upon the rock in Horeb; and thou shalt smite the rock, and there shall come water out of it, that the people may drink. And Moses did so in the sight of the elders of Israel.

AMALEK VANQUISHED

Ex 17:11 And it came to pass, when Moses held up his hand, that Israel prevailed: and when he let down his hand, Amalek prevailed.

DESTRUCTION OF KORAH

Nu 16:32 And the earth opened her mouth, and swallowed them up, and their houses, and all the men that *appertained* unto Korah, and all *their* goods.

WATER FROM ROCK IN KADESH

Nu 20:11 And Moses lifted up his hand, and with his rod he smote the rock twice: and the water came out abundantly, and the congregation drank, and their beasts *also.*

BRAZEN SERPENT

Nu 21:8 And the LORD said unto Moses, Make thee a fiery serpent, and set it upon a pole: and it shall come to pass, that every one that is bitten, when he looketh upon it, shall live.

AARON'S ROD BLOSSOMS

Nu 17:8 And it came to pass, that on the morrow Moses went into the tabernacle of witness; and, behold, the rod of Aaron for the house of Levi was budded, and brought forth buds, and bloomed blossoms, and yielded almonds.

3. Of Joshua

JORDAN DIVIDED

Jos 3:17 And the priests that bare the ark of the covenant of the LORD stood firm on dry ground in the midst of Jordan, and all the Israelites passed over on dry ground, until all the people were passed clean over Jordan.

JERICHO TAKEN

Jos 6:20 So the people shouted when the priests blew with the trumpets: and it came to pass, when the people heard the sound of the trumpet, and the people shouted with a great shout, that the wall fell down flat, so that the people went up into the city, every man straight before him, and they took the city.

SUN AND MOON STAYED

Jos 10:12 So the people shouted when the priests blew with the trumpets: and it came to pass, when the people heard the sound of the trumpet, and the people shouted with a great shout, that the wall fell down flat, so that the people went up into the city, every man straight before him, and they took the city.

4. Of Samson

LION SLAIN

Jud 14:6 And the Spirit of the LORD came mightily upon him, and he rent him as he would have rent a kid, and *he had* nothing in his hand: but he told not his father or his mother what he had done.

PHILISTINES KILLED

Jud 14:19 And the Spirit of the LORD came upon him, and he went down to Ashkelon, and slew thirty men of them, and took their spoil, and gave change of garments unto them which expounded the riddle. And his anger was kindled, and he went up to his father's house.

GATES CARRIED AWAY

Jud 16:3 And Samson lay till midnight, and arose at midnight, and took the doors of the gate of the city, and the two posts, and went away with them, bar and all, and put *them* upon his shoulders, and carried them up to the top of an hill that is before Hebron.

Jud 16:30 And Samson said, Let me die with the Philistines. And he bowed himself with *all his* might; and the house fell upon the lords, and upon all the people that *were* therein. So the dead which he slew at his death were more than *they* which he slew in his life.

5. Of Samuel

THUNDER AND RAIN

1 S 12:18 So Samuel called unto the LORD; and the LORD sent thunder and rain that day: and all the people greatly feared the LORD and Samuel.

6. Of the Prophet of Judah

JEROBOAM'S HAND RESTORED

1 K 13:4–6 And it came to pass, when king Jeroboam heard the saying of the man of God, which had cried against the altar in Bethel, that he put forth his hand from the altar, saying, Lay hold on him. And his hand, which he put forth against him, dried up, so that he could not pull it in again to him.

The altar also was rent, and the ashes poured out from the altar, according to the sign which the man of God had given by the word of the LORD.

And the king answered and said unto the man of God, Intreat now the face of the LORD thy God, and pray for me, that my hand may be restored me again. And the man of God besought the LORD, and the king's hand was restored him again, and became as it was before.

7. Of Elijah

DROUGHT

1 K 17:1 And Elijah the Tishbite, *who was* of the inhabitants of Gilead, said unto Ahab, As the LORD God of Israel liveth, before whom I stand, there shall not be dew nor rain these years, but according to my word.

Ja 5:17 Elias was a man subject to like passions as we are, and he prayed earnestly that it might not rain: and it rained not on the earth by the space of three years and six months.

MEAL AND OIL MULTIPLIED

1 K 17:14 For thus saith the LORD God of Israel, The barrel of meal shall not waste, neither shall the cruse of oil fail, until the day *that* the LORD sendeth rain upon the earth.

CHILD RESTORED TO LIFE

1 K 17:22 And the LORD heard the voice of Elijah; and the soul of the child came into him again, and he revived.

SACRIFICE CONSUMED BY FIRE
1 K 18:38 Then the fire of the LORD fell, and consumed the burnt sacrifice, and the wood, and the stones, and the dust, and licked up the water that *was* in the trench.

CAPTAIN AND SOLDIERS SLAIN BY FIRE
2 K 1:10 And Elijah answered and said to the captain of fifty, If I *be* a man of God, then let fire come down from heaven, and consume thee and thy fifty. And there came down fire from heaven, and consumed him and his fifty.

RAIN BROUGHT
1 K 18:41 And Elijah said unto Ahab, Get thee up, eat and drink; for *there is* a sound of abundance of rain.

JORDAN DIVIDED
2 K 2:8 And Elijah took his mantle, and wrapped *it* together, and smote the waters, and they were divided hither and thither, so that they two went over on dry ground. 2 Kings 2:8

8. Of Elisha

JORDAN DIVIDED
2 K 2:14 And he took the mantle of Elijah that fell from him, and smote the waters, and said, Where *is* the LORD God of Elijah? and when he also had smitten the waters, they parted hither and thither: and Elisha went over.

WATERS HEALED
2 K 2:21 And he went forth unto the spring of the waters, and cast the salt in there, and said, Thus saith the LORD, I have healed these waters; there shall not be from thence any more death or barren *land.*

MOCKING CHILDREN TORN BY BEARS
2 K 2:24 And he turned back, and looked on them, and cursed them in the name of the LORD. And there came forth two she bears out of the wood, and tare forty and two children of them.

WATER SUPPLIED
2 K 3:16 And he said, Thus saith the LORD, Make this valley full of ditches.

WIDOW'S OIL MULTIPLIED
2 K 4:5 So she went from him, and shut the door upon her and upon her sons, who brought *the vessels* to her; and she poured out.

POTTAGE RENDERED HARMLESS
2 K 4:41 But he said, Then bring meal. And he cast *it* into the pot; and he said, Pour out for the people, that they may eat. And there was no harm in the pot.

LOAVES MULTIPLIED
2 K 4:43 And his servitor said, What, should I set this before an hundred men? He said again, Give the people, that they may eat: for thus saith the LORD, They shall eat, and shall leave *thereof.*

CHILD RAISED TO LIFE
2 K 4:35 Then he returned, and walked in the house to and fro; and went up, and stretched himself upon him: and the child sneezed seven times, and the child opened his eyes.

NAAMAN HEALED
2 K 5:10 And Elisha sent a messenger unto him, saying, Go and wash in the Jordan seven times, and thy flesh shall come again to thee, and thou shalt be clean.

GEHAZI STRUCK WITH LEPROSY
2 K 5:27 The leprosy therefore of Naaman shall cleave unto thee, and unto thy seed for ever. And he went out from his presence a leper *as white* as snow.

IRON CAUSED TO SWIM
2 K 6:6 And the man of God said, Where fell it? And he shewed him the place. And he cut down a stick, and cast *it* in thither; and the iron did swim.

SYRIANS SMITTEN

2 K 6:18 And when they came down to him, Elisha prayed unto the LORD, and said, Smite this people, I pray thee, with blindness. And he smote them with blindness according to the word of Elisha.

RESURRECTION OF A MAN

2 K 13:21 And it came to pass, as they were burying a man, that, behold, they spied a band *of men;* and they cast the man into the sepulchre of Elisha: and when the man was let down, and touched the bones of Elisha, he revived, and stood up on his feet.

9. Of Isaiah

HEZEKIAH HEALED

2 K 20:7 And Isaiah said, Take a lump of figs. And they took and laid *it* on the boil, and he recovered.

TIME TURNED BACK

2 K 20:11 And Isaiah the prophet cried unto the LORD: and he brought the shadow ten degrees backward, by which it had gone down in the dial of Ahaz.

10. Of Christ

WATER CHANGED TO WINE

Jn 2:9 When the ruler of the feast had tasted the water that was made wine, and knew not whence it was: (but the servants which drew the water knew;) the governor of the feast called the bridegroom,

NOBLEMAN'S SON HEALED

Jn 4:46 So Jesus came again into Cana of Galilee, where he made the water wine. And there was a certain nobleman, whose son was sick at Capernaum.

DRAUGHT OF FISHES

Lu 5:6 And when they had this done, they inclosed a great multitude of fishes: and their net brake.

DEMONIAC FREED

Mk 1:26 And when the unclean spirit had torn him, and cried with a loud voice, he came out of him.

Lu 4:35 And Jesus rebuked him, saying, Hold thy peace, and come out of him. And when the devil had thrown him in the midst, he came out of him, and hurt him not.

PETER'S MOTHER-IN-LAW HEALED

Mt 8:14 And when Jesus was come into Peter's house, he saw his wife's mother laid, and sick of a fever.

Mk 1:31 And he came and took her by the hand, and lifted her up; and immediately the fever left her, and she ministered unto them.

Lu 4:38 And he arose out of the synagogue, and entered into Simon's house. And Simon's wife's mother was taken with a great fever; and they besought him for her.

LEPER CLEANSED

Mt 8:3 And Jesus put forth *his* hand, and touched him, saying, I will; be thou clean. And immediately his leprosy was cleansed.

Mk 1:41 And Jesus, moved with compassion, put forth *his* hand, and touched him, and saith unto him, I will; be thou clean.

Lu 5:13 And he put forth *his* hand, and touched him, saying, I will: be thou clean. And immediately the leprosy departed from him.

PARALYTIC WALKS

Mt 9:2 And, behold, they brought to him a man sick of the palsy, lying on a bed: and Jesus seeing their faith said unto the sick of the palsy; Son, be of good cheer; thy sins be forgiven thee.

Mk 2:3 And they come unto him, bringing one sick of the palsy, which was borne of four.

Lu 5:18 And, behold, men brought in a bed a man which was taken with a palsy: and they sought *means* to bring him in, and to lay *him* before him.

IMPOTENT MAN HEALED

Jn 5:5 And a certain man was there, which had an infirmity thirty and eight years.

WITHERED HAND RESTORED

Mt 12:10 And, behold, there was a man which had *his* hand withered. And they asked him, saying, Is it lawful to heal on the sabbath days? that they might accuse him.

Mk 3:1 And he entered again into the synagogue; and there was a man there which had a withered hand.

Lu 6:6 And it came to pass also on another sabbath, that he entered into the synagogue and taught: and there was a man whose right hand was withered.

CENTURION'S SERVANT HEALED

Mt 8:5 And when Jesus was entered into Capernaum, there came unto him a centurion, beseeching him,

Lu 7:2 And a certain centurion's servant, who was dear unto him, was sick, and ready to die.

WIDOW'S SON RAISED TO LIFE

Lu 7:11 And it came to pass the day after, that he went into a city called Nain; and many of his disciples went with him, and much people.

DEMONIAC HEALED

Mt 12:22 Then was brought unto him one possessed with a devil, blind, and dumb:and he healed him, insomuch that the blind and dumb both spake and saw.

Lu 11:14 And he was casting out a devil, and it was dumb. And it came to pass, when the devil was gone out, the dumb spake; and the people wondered.

TEMPEST STILLED

Mt 8:26 And he saith unto them, Why are ye fearful, O ye of little faith? Then he arose, and rebuked the winds and the sea; and there was a great calm.

Mk 4:39 And he arose, and rebuked the wind, and said unto the sea, Peace, be still. And the wind ceased, and there was a great calm.

Lu 8:24 And they came to him, and awoke him, saying, Master, master, we perish. Then he arose, and rebuked the wind and the raging of the water: and they ceased, and there was a calm.

DEMONIACS OF GADARA HEALED

Mt 8:28 And when he was come to the other side into the country of the Gergesenes, there met him two possessed with devils, coming out of the tombs, exceeding fierce, so that no man might pass by that way.

Mk 5:1 And they came over unto the other side of the sea, into the country of the Gadarenes.

Lu 8:26 And they arrived at the country of the Gadarenes, which is over against Galilee.

JAIRUS' DAUGHTER RAISED TO LIFE

Mt 9:18 While he spake these things unto them, behold, there came a certain ruler, and worshipped him, saying, My daughter is even now dead: but come and lay thy hand upon her, and she shall live.

Mk 5:42 And straightway the damsel arose, and walked; for she was *of the age* of twelve years. And they were astonished with a great astonishment.

Lu 8:41 And, behold, there came a man named Jairus, and he was a ruler of the synagogue: and he fell down at Jesus' feet, and besought him that he would come into his house:

ISSUE OF BLOOD STOPPED

Mt 9:20 And, behold, a diseased with an issue of blood twelve years, came behind *him,* and touched the hem of his garment:

Mk 5:25 And a certain woman, which had an issue of blood twelve years,

Lu 8:43 And a woman having an issue of blood twelve years, which had spent all her living upon physicians, neither could be healed of any,

BLIND MEN GIVEN SIGHT

Mt 9:27 And when Jesus departed thence, two blind men followed him, crying, and saying, *Thou* Son of David, have mercy on us.

DEMONIAC HEALED

Mt 9:32 As they went out, behold, they brought to him a dumb man possessed with a devil.

FIVE THOUSAND FED

Mt 14:15 And when it was evening, his disciples came to him, saying, This is a desert place, and the time is now past; send the multitude away, that they may go into the villages, and buy themselves victuals.

Mk 6:41 And when he had taken the five loaves and the two fishes, he looked up to heaven, and blessed, and brake the loaves, and gave *them* to his disciples to set before them; and the two fishes divided he among them all.

Lu 9:12 And when the day began to wear away, then came the twelve, and said unto him, Send the multitude away, that they may go into the towns and country round about, and lodge, and get victuals: for we are here in a desert place.

Jn 6:5 When Jesus then lifted up *his* eyes, and saw a great company come unto him, he saith unto Philip, Whence shall we buy bread, that these may eat?

WALKING ON THE SEA

Mt 14:25 And in the fourth watch of the night Jesus went unto them, walking on the sea.

Mk 6:49 But when they saw him walking upon the sea, they supposed it had been a spirit, and cried out:

Jn 6:19 So when they had rowed about five and twenty or thirty furlongs, they see Jesus walking on the sea, and drawing nigh unto the ship: and they were afraid.

DAUGHTER OF SYROPHENICIAN HEALED

Mt 15:22 And, behold, a woman of Canaan came out of the same coasts, and cried unto him, saying, Have mercy on me, O Lord, *thou* Son of David; my daughter is grievously vexed with a devil.

Mk 7:25 For a *certain* woman, whose young daughter had an unclean spirit, heard of him, and came and fell at his feet:

FOUR THOUSAND FED

Mt 15:32 Then Jesus called his disciples *unto him,* and said, I have compassion on the multitude, because they continue with me now three days, and have nothing to eat: and I will not send them away fasting, lest they faint in the way.

Mk 8:8 So they did eat, and were filled: and they took up of the broken *meat* that was left seven baskets.

DEAF AND DUMB HEALED

Mk 7:33 And he took him aside from the multitude, and put his fingers into his ears, and he spit, and touched his tongue;

BLIND MAN GIVEN SIGHT

Mk 8:23 And he took the blind man by the hand, and led him out of the town; and when he had spit on his eyes, and put his hands upon him, he asked him if he saw ought.

LUNATIC CHILD HEALED

Mt 17:14 And when they were come to the multitude, there came to him a *certain* man, kneeling down to him, and saying,

Mk 9:26 And *the spirit* cried, and rent him sore, and came out of him: and he was as one dead; insomuch that many said, He is dead.

Lu 9:37 And it came to pass, that on the next day, when they were come down from the hill, much people met him.

TRIBUTE MONEY PROVIDED BY FISH

Mt 17:24 And when they were come to Capernaum, they that received tribute *money* came to Peter, and said, Doth not your master pay tribute?

TEN LEPERS HEALED

Lu 17:12 And as he entered into a certain village, there met him ten men that were lepers, which stood afar off:

BLIND MAN GIVEN SIGHT

Jn 9:1 And as *Jesus* passed by, he saw a man which was blind from *his* birth.

LAZARUS RAISED TO LIFE

Jn 11:43–44 And when he thus had spoken, he cried with a loud voice, Lazarus, come forth.

And he that was dead came forth, bound with graveclothes: and his face was bound about with a napkin. Jesus saith unto them, Loose him, and let him go.

WOMAN WITH INFIRMITY HEALED

Lu 13:11 And, behold, there was a woman which had a spirit of infirmity eighteen years, and was bowed together, and could in no wise lift up *herself.*

MAN WITH DROPSY HEALED

Lu 14:2 And, behold, there was a certain man before him which had the dropsy.

BLIND MEN GIVEN SIGHT

Mt 20:30 And, behold, two blind men sitting by the way side, when they heard that Jesus passed by, cried out, saying, Have mercy on us, O Lord, *thou* Son of David.

Mk 10:46 And they came to Jericho: and as he went out of Jericho with his disciples and a great number of people, blind Bartimaeus, the son of Timaeus, sat by the highway side begging.

THE FIG TREE CURSED

Mt 21:19 And when he saw a fig tree in the way, he came to it, and found nothing thereon, but leaves only, and said unto it, Let no fruit grow on thee henceforward for ever. And presently the fig tree withered away.

MALCHUS HEALED

Lu 22:51 And Jesus answered and said, Suffer ye thus far. And he touched his ear, and healed him.

SECOND DRAUGHT OF FISHES

Jn 21:6 And he said unto them, Cast the net on the right side of the ship, and ye shall find. They cast therefore, and now they were not able to draw it for the multitude of fishes.

HIS RESURRECTION

Lu 24:6 He is not here, but is risen: remember how he spake unto you when he was yet in Galilee,

Jn 10:18 No man taketh it from me, but I lay it down of myself. I have power to lay it down, and I have power to take it again. This commandment have I received of my Father.

11. Of Peter

LAME MAN CURED

Ac 3:7 And he took him by the right hand, and lifted *him* up: and immediately his feet and ancle bones received strength.

ANANIAS AND SAPPHIRA EXPOSED

Ac 5:5 And Ananias hearing these words fell down, and gave up the ghost: and great fear came on all them that heard these things.

Ac 5:10 Then fell she down straightway at his feet, and yielded up the ghost: and the young men came in, and found her dead, and, carrying *her* forth, buried *her* by her husband.

SICK HEALED

Ac 5:15 Insomuch that they brought forth the sick into the streets, and laid *them* on beds and couches, that at the least the shadow of Peter passing by might overshadow some of them.

AENEAS HEALED

Ac 9:34 And Peter said unto him, Aeneas, Jesus Christ maketh thee whole: arise, and make thy bed. And he arose immediately.

DORCAS RAISED TO LIFE

Ac 9:40 Peter put them all forth, and kneeled down, and prayed; and turning *him* to the body said, Tabitha, arise. And she opened her eyes: and when she saw Peter, she sat up.

12. Of Paul

ELYMAS BLINDED

Ac 13:11 And now, behold, the hand of the Lord *is* upon thee, and thou shalt be blind, not seeing the sun for a season. And immediately there fell on him a mist and a darkness; and he went about seeking some to lead him by the hand.

LAME MAN CURED

Ac 14:10 Said with a loud voice, Stand upright on thy feet. And he leaped and walked.

DAMSEL WITH THE SPIRIT
OF DIVINATION HEALED

Ac 16:18 And this did she many days. But Paul, being grieved, turned and said to the spirit, I command thee in the name of Jesus Christ to come out of her. And he came out the same hour.
Ac 19:11 And God wrought special miracles by the hands of Paul:

EUTYCHUS RESTORED TO LIFE

Ac 20:10 And Paul went down, and fell on him, and embracing *him* said, Trouble not yourselves; for his life is in him.

VIPER'S BITE HARMLESS

Ac 28:5 And he shook off the beast into the fire, and felt no harm.

FATHER OF PUBLIUS HEALED

Ac 28:8 And it came to pass, that the father of Publius lay sick of a fever and of a bloody flux: to whom Paul entered in, and prayed, and laid his hands on him, and healed him.

OTHER SPECIAL MIRACLES BY PAUL

Ac 14:3 Long time therefore abode they speaking boldly in the Lord, which gave testimony unto the word of his grace, and granted signs and wonders to be done by their hands.
Ac 19:11 And God wrought special miracles by the hands of Paul:

13. Of the Disciples and Apostles
See **HEALING**

14. Of the Seventy

Lu 10:17 And the seventy returned again with joy, saying, Lord, even the devils are subject unto us through thy name.

15. Of Stephen

Ac 6:8 And Stephen, full of faith and power, did great wonders and miracles among the people.

16. Of Philip

Ac 8:13 Then Simon himself believed also: and when he was baptized, he continued with Philip, and wondered, beholding the miracles and signs which were done.

17. As Testimonies

Mt 11:4 Jesus answered and said unto them, Go and shew John again those things which ye do hear and see:
Jn 2:11 This beginning of miracles did Jesus in Cana of Galilee, and manifested forth his glory; and his disciples believed on him.
Jn 3:2 The same came to Jesus by night, and said unto him, Rabbi, we know that thou art a teacher come from God: for no man can do these miracles that thou doest, except God be with him.
Jn 7:31 And many of the people believed on him, and said, When Christ cometh, will he do more miracles than these which this *man* hath done?
Jn 10:25 Jesus answered them, I told you, and ye believed not: the works that I do in my Father's name, they bear witness of me.
Jn 10:37-38 If I do not the works of my Father, believe me not.
But if I do, though ye believe not me, believe the works: that ye may know, and believe, that the Father is in me, and I in him.
Jn 20:30 And many other signs truly did Jesus in the presence of his disciples, which are not written in this book:
Ac 8:6 And the people with one accord gave heed unto those things which Philip spake, hearing and seeing the miracles which he did.

See **HEALING, MAGICIANS, POWER, WONDERS**

MIRIAM, *sister of Moses*

HELPFUL IN YOUTH

Ex 2:7 Then said his sister to Pharaoh's daughter, Shall I go and call to thee a nurse of the Hebrew women, that she may nurse the child for thee?

MUSICAL

Ex 15:21 And Miriam answered them, Sing ye to the LORD, for he hath triumphed gloriously; the horse and his rider hath he thrown into the sea.

AMBITIOUS

Nu 12:1–2 And Miriam and Aaron spake against Moses because of the Ethiopian woman whom he had married: for he had married an Ethiopian woman.

And they said, Hath the LORD indeed spoken only by Moses? hath he not spoken also by us? And the LORD heard *it.*

A LEADER IN ISRAEL

Mi 6:4 For I brought thee up out of the land of Egypt, and redeemed thee out of the house of servants; and I sent before thee Moses, Aaron, and Miriam.

See **WOMEN**

MIRRORS, *glasses*

Ex 38:8; Jb 37:18; Is 3:23; 1 Co 13:12; 2 Co 3:18; Ja 1:23

MISCHIEF, *causing harm*

1 S 23:9; 1 K 20:7; Ne 6:2; Jb 15:34–35; Ps 7:14; 10:7; 26:10; 28:3; 36:4; 52:1; 55:10; 62:3; 119:150; 140:2; Pr 4:16; 6:14; 10:23; 16:27; 24:2; 28:14; Eze 7:26; Da 11:27; Ac 13:10

See **WICKED**

MISERY, *result of sin and suffering*

Ge 42:21 And they said one to another, We *are* verily guilty concerning our brother, in that we saw the anguish of his soul, when he besought us, and we would not hear; therefore is this distress come upon us.

Ex 32:35 And the LORD plagued the people, because they made the calf, which Aaron made.

Le 26:16 I also will do this unto you; I will even appoint over you terror, consumption, and the burning ague, that shall consume the eyes, and cause sorrow of heart: and ye shall sow your seed in vain, for your enemies shall eat it.

Nu 5:27 And when he hath made her to drink the water, then it shall come to pass, *that,* if she be defiled, and have done trespass against her husband, that the water that causeth the curse shall enter into her, *and become* bitter, and her belly shall swell, and her thigh shall rot: and the woman shall be a curse among her people.

De 28:20 The LORD shall send upon thee cursing, vexation, and rebuke, in all that thou settest thine hand unto for to do, until thou be destroyed, and until thou perish quickly; because of the wickedness of thy doings, whereby thou hast forsaken me.

De 28:67 In the morning thou shalt say, Would God it were even! and at even thou shalt say, Would God it were morning! for the fear of thine heart wherewith thou shalt fear, and for the sight of thine eyes which thou shalt see.

De 31:21 And it shall come to pass, when many evils and troubles are befallen them, that this song shall testify against them as a witness; for it shall not be forgotten out of the mouths of their seed: for I know their imagination which they go about, even now, before I have brought them into the land which I sware.

De 31:29 For I know that after my death ye will utterly corrupt *yourselves,* and turn aside from the way which I have commanded you; and evil will befall you in the latter days; because ye will do evil in the sight of the LORD, to provoke him to anger through the work of your hands.

Jud 2:15 Whithersoever they went out, the hand of the LORD was against them for evil, as the LORD had said, and as the LORD had sworn unto them: and they were greatly distressed.

Jud 10:9 Moreover the children of Ammon passed over Jordan to fight also against Judah, and against Benjamin, and against the house of Ephraim; so that Israel was sore distressed.

1 S 28:15 And Samuel said to Saul, Why hast thou disquieted me, to bring me up? And Saul answered, I am sore distressed; for the Philistines make war against me, and God is departed from me, and answereth me no more, neither by prophets, nor by dreams: therefore I have called thee, that thou mayest make known unto me what I shall do.

1 K 9:9 And they shall answer, Because they forsook the LORD their God, who brought forth their fathers out of the land of Egypt, and have taken hold upon other gods, and have worshipped them, and served them: therefore hath the LORD brought upon them all this evil.

2 K 6:29 So we boiled my son, and did eat him: and I said unto her on the next day, Give thy son, that we may eat him: and she hath hid her son.

2 Chr 15:5 And in those times *there was* no peace to him that went out, nor to him that came in, but great vexations *were* upon all the inhabitants of the countries.

2 Chr 28:22 And in the time of his distress did he trespass yet more against the LORD: this *is that* king Ahaz.

2 Chr 29:9 For, lo, our fathers have fallen by the sword, and our sons and our daughters and our wives are in captivity for this.

Ne 9:37 And it yieldeth much increase unto the kings whom thou hast set over us because of our sins: also they have dominion over our bodies, and over our cattle, at their pleasure, and we *are* in great distress.

Jb 10:15 If I be wicked, woe unto me; and *if* I be righteous, *yet* will I not lift up my head. *I am* full of confusion; therefore see thou mine affliction;

Jb 15:20 The wicked man travaileth with pain all *his* days, and the number of years is hidden to the oppressor.

Jb 20:14 *Yet* his meat in his bowels is turned, *it is* the gall of asps within him.

Jb 31:3 *Is* not destruction to the wicked? and a strange *punishment* to the workers of iniquity?

Ps 16:4 Their sorrows shall be multiplied *that* hasten *after* another *god:* their drink offerings of blood will I not offer, nor take up their names into my lips.

Ps 38:5 My wounds stink *and* are corrupt because of my foolishness.

Ps 75:8 For in the hand of the LORD *there is* a cup, and the wine is red; it is full of mixture; and he poureth out of the same: but the dregs thereof, all the wicked of the earth shall wring *them* out, *and* drink *them.*

Ps 78:33 Therefore their days did he consume in vanity, and their years in trouble.

Ps 107:17 Fools because of their transgression, and because of their iniquities, are afflicted.

Pr 1:28 Then shall they call upon me, but I will not answer; they shall seek me early, but they shall not find me:

Pr 13:15 Good understanding giveth favour: but the way of transgressors *is* hard.

Pr 22:5 Thorns *and* snares *are* in the way of the froward: he that doth keep his soul shall be far from them.

Pr 23:32 At the last it biteth like a serpent, and stingeth like an adder.

Ec 8:13 But it shall not be well with the wicked, neither shall he prolong *his* days, *which are* as a shadow; because he feareth not before God.

Is 3:11 Woe unto the wicked! *it shall be* ill *with him:* for the reward of his hands shall be given him.

Is 5:13 Therefore my people are gone into captivity, because *they have* no knowledge: and their honourable men *are* famished, and their multitude dried up with thirst.

Is 8:22 And they shall look unto the earth; and behold trouble and darkness, dimness of anguish; and *they shall be* driven to darkness.

Is 17:14 And behold at eveningtide trouble; *and* before the morning he *is* not. This *is* the portion of them that spoil us, and the lot of them that rob us.

Is 24:17 Fear, and the pit, and the snare, *are* upon thee, O inhabitant of the earth.

Is 57:20 But the wicked *are* like the troubled sea, when it cannot rest, whose waters cast up mire and dirt.

Je 2:19 Thine own wickedness shall correct thee, and thy backslidings shall reprove thee: know therefore and see that *it is* an evil *thing* and bitter, that thou hast forsaken the LORD thy God, and that my fear *is* not in thee, saith the Lord GOD of hosts.

Je 4:31 For I have heard a voice as of a woman in travail, *and* the anguish as of her that bringeth forth her first child, the voice of the daughter of Zion, *that* bewaileth herself, *that* spreadeth her hands, *saying,* Woe *is* me now! for my soul is wearied because of murderers.

Je 8:17 For, behold, I will send serpents, cockatrices, among you, which *will* not *be* charmed, and they shall bite you, saith the LORD.

Je 13:21 What wilt thou say when he shall punish thee? for thou hast taught them *to be* captains, *and* as chief over thee: shall not sorrows take thee, as a woman in travail?

Je 14:18 If I go forth into the field, then behold the slain with the sword! and if I enter into the city, then behold them that are sick with famine! yea, both the prophet and the priest go about into a land that they know not.

Je 32:23 And they came in, and possessed it; but they obeyed not thy voice, neither walked in thy law; they have done nothing of all that thou commandedst them to do: therefore thou hast caused all this evil to come upon them:

Je 44:2 Thus saith the LORD of hosts, the God of Israel; Ye have seen all the evil that I have brought upon Jerusalem, and upon all the cities of Judah; and, behold, this day they *are* a desolation, and no man dwelleth therein,

Lam 1:7 Jerusalem remembered in the days of her affliction and of her miseries all her pleasant things that she had in the days of old, when her people fell into the hand of the enemy, and none did help her: the adversaries saw her, *and* did mock at her sabbaths.

Lam 1:20 Behold, O LORD; for I *am* in distress: my bowels are troubled; mine heart is turned within me; for I have grievously rebelled: abroad the sword bereaveth, at home *there is* as death.

Lam 2:10 The elders of the daughter of Zion sit upon the ground, *and* keep silence: they have cast up dust upon their heads; they have girded themselves with sackcloth: the virgins of Jerusalem hang down their heads to the ground.

Lam 4:8 Their visage is blacker than a coal; they are not known in the streets: their skin cleaveth to their bones; it is withered, it is become like a stick.

Lam 5:16 The crown is fallen *from* our head: woe unto us, that we have sinned!

Eze 5:17 So will I send upon you famine and evil beasts, and they shall bereave thee; and pestilence and blood shall pass through thee; and I will bring the sword upon thee. I the LORD have spoken *it*.

Eze 7:15 The sword *is* without, and the pestilence and the famine within: he that *is* in the field shall die with the sword; and he that *is* in the city, famine and pestilence shall devour him.

Eze 23:29 And they shall deal with thee hatefully, and shall take away all thy labour, and shall leave thee naked and bare: and the nakedness of thy whoredoms shall be discovered, both thy lewdness and thy whoredoms.

Eze 23:34 Thou shalt even drink it and suck *it* out, and thou shalt break the sherds thereof, and pluck off thine own breasts: for I have spoken *it,* saith the Lord GOD.

Eze 24:23 And your tires *shall be* upon your heads, and your shoes upon your feet: ye shall not mourn nor weep; but ye shall pine away for your iniquities, and mourn one toward another.

Eze 30:16 And I will set fire in Egypt: Sin shall have great pain, and No shall be rent asunder, and Noph *shall have* distresses daily.

Ho 4:3 Therefore shall the land mourn, and every one that dwelleth therein shall languish, with the beasts of the field, and with the fowls of heaven; yea, the fishes of the sea also shall be taken away.

Ho 5:11 Ephraim *is* oppressed *and* broken in judgment, because he willingly walked after the commandment.

Ho 13:13 The sorrows of a travailing woman shall come upon him: he *is* an unwise son; for he should not stay long in *the place of* the breaking forth of children.

Am 8:10 And I will turn your feasts into mourning, and all your songs into lamentation; and I will bring up sackcloth upon all loins, and baldness upon every head; and I will make it as the mourning of an only *son,* and the end thereof as a bitter day.

Mt 27:5 And he cast down the pieces of silver in the temple, and departed, and went and hanged himself.

Mk 6:26 And the king was exceeding sorry; *yet* for his oath's sake, and for their sakes which sat with him, he would not reject her.

Lu 15:16 And he would fain have filled his belly with the husks that the swine did eat: and no man gave unto him.

Ac 9:5 And he said, Who art thou, Lord? And the Lord said, I am Jesus whom thou persecutest: *it is* hard for thee to kick against the pricks.

Ac 26:14 And when we were all fallen to the earth, I heard a voice speaking unto me, and saying in the Hebrew tongue, Saul, Saul, why persecutest thou me? *it is* hard for thee to kick against the pricks.

Ro 2:9 Tribulation and anguish, upon every soul of man that doeth evil, of the Jew first, and also of the Gentile;

Ro 3:16 Destruction and misery *are* in their ways:

Ro 7:24 O wretched man that I am! who shall deliver me from the body of this death?

1 Co 15:56 The sting of death *is* sin; and the strength of sin *is* the law.

Ja 5:1 Go to now, *ye* rich men, weep and howl for your miseries that shall come upon *you.*

See **ADVERSITY, AFFLICTIONS, COMFORT, DESPAIR, SIN**

MISSION, *various tasks assigned to individuals*

JOSEPH SENT TO EGYPT TO PRESERVE THE CHOSEN FAMILY

Ge 45:5 Now therefore be not grieved, nor angry with yourselves, that ye sold me hither: for God did send me before you to preserve life.

ESTHER CALLED TO PRESERVE THE JEWS

Est 4:14 For if thou altogether holdest thy peace at this time, *then* shall there enlargement and deliverance arise to the Jews from another place; but thou and thy father's house shall be destroyed: and who knoweth whether thou art come to the kingdom for *such* a time as this?

THE DISCIPLES SENT FORTH

Mt 10:16 Behold, I send you forth as sheep in the midst of wolves: be ye therefore wise as serpents, and harmless as doves.

Jn 20:21 Then said Jesus to them again, Peace *be* unto you: as *my* Father hath sent me, even so send I you.

THE HEALED DEMONIAC SENT WITH A MESSAGE

Mk 5:19 Howbeit Jesus suffered him not, but saith unto him, Go home to thy friends, and tell them how great things the Lord hath done for thee, and hath had compassion on thee.

A SPECIAL WORK FOR EACH PERSON

Mk 13:34 For *the Son of man is* as a man taking a far journey, who left his house, and gave authority to his servants, and to every man his work, and commanded the porter to watch.

See CALL

MISSIONS, *fulfilling the Great Commission of Christ*

1. Triumph

Ps 2:8; 22:27; 68:31; 96:3; Is 2:2; 11:9; 24:16; 42:4; 60:9; Da 2:44-45; Zec 8:23; Mal 1:11; Mt 13:38; 22:10; 24:14; 28:19; Mk 13:10; 16:15; Lu 24:47; Ac 13:3, 47; 16:9; 26:17–18; 28:28; Ro 10:15; 15:21; 2 Co 10:16; Re 14:6

2. Growth of Christ's Kingdom Prophesied

Ps 72:16; Is 2:2; 9:7; 27:6; 35:1; 42:4; 49:19; 54:3; 55:5, 13; 56:8; 60:5, 10, 22; 61:11; 66:12; Eze 17:23; 36:37; 47:5; Da 2:35; Mi 4:1; Hab 2:14; Zec 2:4; 8:22; 9:7; 10:8; Mal 1:11; Mt 12:21; 13:31; Mk 2:15; 4:31-32; Lu 13:19; Jn 3:30; Ac 4:4; 5:14; 6:1, 7; 12:24; 19:20; 21:20; Ro 10:20; He 8:11; Re 11:15

3. Examples of Missionaries

NOAH

2 Pe 2:5 And spared not the old world, but saved Noah the eighth *person,* a preacher of righteousness, bringing in the flood upon the world of the ungodly;

MESSENGERS OF HEZEKIAH

2 Chr 30:6 So the posts went with the letters from the king and his princes throughout all Israel and Judah, and according to the commandment of the king, saying, Ye children of Israel, turn again unto the LORD God of Abraham, Isaac, and Israel, and he will return to the remnant of you, that are escaped out of the hand of the kings of Assyria.

JONAH

Jona 3:2 Arise, go unto Nineveh, that great city, and preach unto it the preaching that I bid thee.

CHRIST

Lu 19:10 For the Son of man is come to seek and to save that which was lost.

MEMBERS OF THE EARLY CHURCH

Ac 8:4 Therefore they that were scattered abroad went every where preaching the word.

PHILIP

Ac 8:5 Then Philip went down to the city of Samaria, and preached Christ unto them.

PETER

Ac 15:7 And when there had been much disputing, Peter rose up, and said unto them, Men *and* brethren, ye know how that a good while ago God made choice among us, that the Gentiles by my mouth should hear the word of the gospel, and believe.

APOLLOS

Ac 18:24 And a certain Jew named Apollos, born at Alexandria, an eloquent man, *and* mighty in the scriptures, came to Ephesus.

4. Paul's Journeys

FIRST WITH BARNABAS AND JOHN MARK

Ac 13–14

SECOND WITH SILAS

Ac 15:36–21:15

THIRD WITH TIMOTHY AND OTHERS

Ac 18–21

VOYAGE TO ROME WITH LUKE, ARISTARCHUS, AND OTHERS

Ac 27–28

5. Conversion of the Gentiles

a. Foretold

Ge 18:18 Seeing that Abraham shall surely become a great and mighty nation, and all the nations of the earth shall be blessed in him?
Ge 22:18 And in thy seed shall all the nations of the earth be blessed; because thou hast obeyed my voice.
Ge 28:14 And thy seed shall be as the dust of the earth, and thou shalt spread abroad to the west, and to the east, and to the north, and to the

south: and in thee and in thy seed shall all the families of the earth be blessed.

Ps 2:8 Ask of me, and I shall give *thee* the heathen *for* thine inheritance, and the uttermost parts of the earth *for* thy possession.

Ps 22:27 All the ends of the world shall remember and turn unto the LORD: and all the kindreds of the nations shall worship before thee.

Ps 68:31 Princes shall come out of Egypt; Ethiopia shall soon stretch out her hands unto God.

Ps 86:9 All nations whom thou hast made shall come and worship before thee, O Lord; and shall glorify thy name.

Ps 98:3 He hath remembered his mercy and his truth toward the house of Israel: all the ends of the earth have seen the salvation of our God.

Is 9:2 The people that walked in darkness have seen a great light: they that dwell in the land of the shadow of death, upon them hath the light shined.

Is 18:7 In that time shall the present be brought unto the LORD of hosts of a people scattered and peeled, and from a people terrible from their beginning hitherto; a nation meted out and trodden under foot, whose land the rivers have spoiled, to the place of the name of the LORD of hosts, the mount Zion.

Is 19:18 In that day shall five cities in the land of Egypt speak the language of Canaan, and swear to the LORD of hosts; one shall be called, The city of destruction.

Is 19:21 And the LORD shall be known to Egypt, and the Egyptians shall know the LORD in that day, and shall do sacrifice and oblation; yea, they shall vow a vow unto the LORD, and perform *it*.

Is 19:24 In that day shall Israel be the third with Egypt and with Assyria, *even* a blessing in the midst of the land:

Is 27:6 He shall cause them that come of Jacob to take root: Israel shall blossom and bud, and fill the face of the world with fruit.

Is 42:1 Behold my servant, whom I uphold; mine elect, *in whom* my soul delighteth; I have put my spirit upon him: he shall bring forth judgment to the Gentiles.

Is 44:5 One shall say, I *am* the LORD's; and another shall call *himself* by the name of Jacob; and another shall subscribe *with* his hand unto the LORD, and surname *himself* by the name of Israel.

Is 45:14 Thus saith the LORD, The labour of Egypt, and merchandise of Ethiopia and of the Sabeans, men of stature, shall come over unto thee, and they shall be thine: they shall come after thee; in chains they shall come over, and they shall fall down unto thee, they shall make supplication unto thee, *saying,* Surely God *is* in thee; and *there is* none else, *there is* no God.

Is 49:6 And he said, It is a light thing that thou shouldest be my servant to raise up the tribes of Jacob, and to restore Israel: I will also give thee for a light to the Gentiles, that thou mayest be my salvation unto the end of the earth.

Is 53:10 Yet it pleased the LORD to bruise him; he hath put *him* to grief: when thou shalt make his soul an offering for sin, he shall see *his* seed, he shall prolong *his* days, and the pleasure of the LORD shall prosper in his hand.

Is 55:5 Behold, thou shalt call a nation *that* thou knowest not, and nations *that* knew not thee shall run unto thee because of the LORD thy God, and for the Holy One of Israel; for he hath glorified thee.

Is 56:7 Even them will I bring to my holy mountain, and make them joyful in my house of prayer: their burnt offerings and their sacrifices *shall be* accepted upon mine altar; for mine house shall be called an house of prayer for all people.

Is 57:19 I create the fruit of the lips; Peace, peace to *him that is* far off, and to *him that is* near, saith the LORD; and I will heal him.

Is 59:19 So shall they fear the name of the LORD from the west, and his glory from the rising of the sun. When the enemy shall come in like a flood, the Spirit of the LORD shall lift up a standard against him.

Is 60:3 And the Gentiles shall come to thy light, and kings to the brightness of thy rising.

Je 3:17 At that time they shall call Jerusalem the throne of the LORD; and all the nations shall be gathered unto it, to the name of the LORD, to Jerusalem: neither shall they walk any more after the imagination of their evil heart.

Je 31:8 Behold, I will bring them from the north country, and gather them from the coasts of the earth, *and* with them the blind and the lame, the woman with child and her that travaileth with child together: a great company shall return thither.

Je 49:39 But it shall come to pass in the latter days, *that* I will bring again the captivity of Elam, saith the LORD.

Eze 47:22 And it shall come to pass, *that* ye shall divide it by lot for an inheritance unto you, and to the strangers that sojourn among you, which shall beget children among you: and they shall be unto you as born in the country among the children of Israel; they shall have inheritance with you among the tribes of Israel.

Da 7:14 And there was given him dominion, and glory, and a kingdom, that all people, nations, and languages, should serve him: his dominion *is* an everlasting dominion, which shall not pass away, and his kingdom *that* which shall not be destroyed.

Ho 2:23 And I will sow her unto me in the earth; and I will have mercy on her that had not obtained mercy; and I will say to *them which were* not my people, Thou *art* my people; and they shall say, *Thou art* my God.

Zec 8:20 Thus saith the LORD of hosts; *It shall* yet *come to pass,* that there shall come people, and the inhabitants of many cities:

Zec 9:7 And I will take away his blood out of his mouth, and his abominations from between his teeth: but he that remaineth, even he, *shall be* for our God, and he shall be as a governor in Judah, and Ekron as a Jebusite.

Zec 14:16 And it shall come to pass, *that* every one that is left of all the nations which came against Jerusalem shall even go up from year to year to worship the King, the LORD of hosts, and to keep the feast of tabernacles.

Mal 1:11 For from the rising of the sun even unto the going down of the same my name *shall be* great among the Gentiles; and in every place incense *shall be* offered unto my name, and a pure offering: for my name *shall be* great among the heathen, saith the LORD of hosts.

Mt 8:11 And I say unto you, That many shall come from the east and west, and shall sit down with Abraham, and Isaac, and Jacob, in the kingdom of heaven.

Ac 13:46 Then Paul and Barnabas waxed bold, and said, It was necessary that the word of God should first have been spoken to you: but seeing ye put it from you, and judge yourselves unworthy of everlasting life, lo, we turn to the Gentiles.

Ep 3:6 That the Gentiles should be fellowheirs, and of the same body, and partakers of his promise in Christ by the gospel:

b. Examples

Ge 12:3 And I will bless them that bless thee, and curse him that curseth thee: and in thee shall all families of the earth be blessed.

Is 14:1 For the LORD will have mercy on Jacob, and will yet choose Israel, and set them in their own land: and the strangers shall be joined with them, and they shall cleave to the house of Jacob.

Is 49:18 Lift up thine eyes round about, and behold: all these gather themselves together, *and* come to thee. *As* I live, saith the LORD, thou shalt surely clothe thee with them all, as with an ornament, and bind them *on thee,* as a bride *doeth.*

Is 65:1 I am sought of *them that* asked not *for me;* I am found of *them that* sought me not: I said, Behold me, behold me, unto a nation *that* was not called by my name.

Eze 3:6 Not to many people of a strange speech and of an hard language, whose words thou canst not understand. Surely, had I sent thee to them, they would have hearkened unto thee.

Eze 16:61 Then thou shalt remember thy ways, and be ashamed, when thou shalt receive thy sisters, thine elder and thy younger: and I will give them unto thee for daughters, but not by thy covenant.

Zec 2:11 And many nations shall be joined to the LORD in that day, and shall be my people: and I will dwell in the midst of thee, and thou shalt know that the LORD of hosts hath sent me unto thee.

Zec 6:15 And they *that are* far off shall come and build in the temple of the LORD, and ye shall know that the LORD of hosts hath sent me unto you. And *this* shall come to pass, if ye will diligently obey the voice of the LORD your God.

Zec 8:23 Thus saith the LORD of hosts; In those days *it shall come to pass,* that ten men shall take hold out of all languages of the nations, even shall take hold of the skirt of him that is a Jew, saying, We will go with you: for we have heard *that* God *is* with you.

Ac 10:45 And they of the circumcision which believed were astonished, as many as came with Peter, because that on the Gentiles also was poured out the gift of the Holy Ghost.

Ac 11:1 And the apostles and brethren that were in Judaea heard that the Gentiles had also received the word of God.

Ac 13:48 And when the Gentiles heard this, they were glad, and glorified the word of the Lord: and as many as were ordained to eternal life believed.

Ac 15:7 And when there had been much disputing, Peter rose up, and said unto them, Men *and* brethren, ye know how that a good while ago God made choice among us, that the Gen-

tiles by my mouth should hear the word of the gospel, and believe.

Ac 18:6 And when they opposed themselves, and blasphemed, he shook *his* raiment, and said unto them, Your blood *be* upon your own heads; I *am* clean: from henceforth I will go unto the Gentiles.

Ac 28:28 Be it known therefore unto you, that the salvation of God is sent unto the Gentiles, and *that* they will hear it.

Ro 9:24 Even us, whom he hath called, not of the Jews only, but also of the Gentiles?

Ro 15:9 And that the Gentiles might glorify God for *his* mercy; as it is written, For this cause I will confess to thee among the Gentiles, and sing unto thy name.

Ga 3:14 That the blessing of Abraham might come on the Gentiles through Jesus Christ; that we might receive the promise of the Spirit through faith.

Re 11:15 And the seventh angel sounded; and there were great voices in heaven, saying, The kingdoms of this world are become *the kingdoms* of our Lord, and of his Christ; and he shall reign for ever and ever.

Re 15:4 Who shall not fear thee, O Lord, and glorify thy name? for *thou* only *art* holy: for all nations shall come and worship before thee; for thy judgments are made manifest.

6. Culminating in Universal Worship

Ex 10:9 And Moses said, We will go with our young and with our old, with our sons and with our daughters, with our flocks and with our herds will we go; for we *must hold* a feast unto the LORD.

De 16:11 And thou shalt rejoice before the LORD thy God, thou, and thy son, and thy daughter, and thy manservant, and thy maidservant, and the Levite that *is* within thy gates, and the stranger, and the fatherless, and the widow, that *are* among you, in the place which the LORD thy God hath chosen to place his name there.

1 K 8:43 Hear thou in heaven thy dwelling place, and do according to all that the stranger calleth to thee for: that all people of the earth may know thy name, to fear thee, as *do* thy people Israel; and that they may know that this house, which I have builded, is called by thy name.

Ps 22:27–28 All the ends of the world shall remember and turn unto the LORD: and all the kindreds of the nations shall worship before thee.

For the kingdom *is* the LORD's: and he *is* the governor among the nations.

Ps 65:2 O thou that hearest prayer, unto thee shall all flesh come.

Ps 66:4 All the earth shall worship thee, and shall sing unto thee; they shall sing *to* thy name. Selah.

Ps 67:3 Let the people praise thee, O God; let all the people praise thee.

Ps 86:9 All nations whom thou hast made shall come and worship before thee, O Lord; and shall glorify thy name.

Ps 113:3 From the rising of the sun unto the going down of the same the LORD's name *is* to be praised.

Ps 148:11 Kings of the earth, and all people; princes, and all judges of the earth:

Is 19:19 In that day shall there be an altar to the LORD in the midst of the land of Egypt, and a pillar at the border thereof to the LORD.

Is 45:22–23 Look unto me, and be ye saved, all the ends of the earth: for I *am* God, and *there is* none else.

I have sworn by myself, the word is gone out of my mouth *in* righteousness, and shall not return, That unto me every knee shall bow, every tongue shall swear.

Is 49:7 Thus saith the LORD, the Redeemer of Israel, *and* his Holy One, to him whom man despiseth, to him whom the nation abhorreth, to a servant of rulers, Kings shall see and arise, princes also shall worship, because of the LORD that is faithful, *and* the Holy One of Israel, and he shall choose thee.

Is 56:7 Even them will I bring to my holy mountain, and make them joyful in my house of prayer: their burnt offerings and their sacrifices *shall be* accepted upon mine altar; for mine

house shall be called an house of prayer for all people.

Is 66:23 And it shall come to pass, *that* from one new moon to another, and from one sabbath to another, shall all flesh come to worship before me, saith the LORD.

Da 7:14 And there was given him dominion, and glory, and a kingdom, that all people, nations, and languages, should serve him: his dominion *is* an everlasting dominion, which shall not pass away, and his kingdom *that* which shall not be destroyed.

Zep 2:11 The LORD *will be* terrible unto them: for he will famish all the gods of the earth; and *men* shall worship him, every one from his place, *even* all the isles of the heathen.

Zec 8:22 Yea, many people and strong nations shall come to seek the LORD of hosts in Jerusalem, and to pray before the LORD.

Zec 14:16 And it shall come to pass, *that* every one that is left of all the nations which came against Jerusalem shall even go up from year to year to worship the King, the LORD of hosts, and to keep the feast of tabernacles.

Mal 1:11 For from the rising of the sun even unto the going down of the same my name *shall be* great among the Gentiles; and in every place incense *shall be* offered unto my name, and a pure offering: for my name *shall be* great among the heathen, saith the LORD of hosts.

Jn 4:21 Jesus saith unto her, Woman, believe me, the hour cometh, when ye shall neither in this mountain, nor yet at Jerusalem, worship the Father.

Ro 14:11 For it is written, *As* I live, saith the Lord, every knee shall bow to me, and every tongue shall confess to God.

Ph 2:9–11 Wherefore God also hath highly exalted him, and given him a name which is above every name:

That at the name of Jesus every knee should bow, of *things* in heaven, and *things* in earth, and *things* under the earth;

And *that* every tongue should confess that Jesus Christ *is* Lord, to the glory of God the Father.

Re 3:9 Behold, I will make them of the synagogue of Satan, which say they are Jews, and are not, but do lie; behold, I will make them to come and worship before thy feet, and to know that I have loved thee.

Re 5:13 And every creature which is in heaven, and on the earth, and under the earth, and such as are in the sea, and all that are in them, heard I saying, Blessing, and honour, and glory, and power, *be* unto him that sitteth upon the throne, and unto the Lamb for ever and ever.

Re 15:4 Who shall not fear thee, O Lord, and glorify thy name? for *thou* only *art* holy: for all nations shall come and worship before thee; for thy judgments are made manifest.

See **CALL, CONVERSION, GOSPEL, SALVATION**

MIST *See* **WEATHER**

MITE, *widow's*
Mk 12:42; Lu 21:2

MITRE, *crown or headdress worn by the priests*
Ex 28:4, 37; 29:6; 39:28, 31; Le 8:9; 16:4; Zec 3:5

See **PRIESTHOOD, PRIESTS**

MIZAR *See* **MOUNTAINS AND HILLS**

MIZPAH, *watch tower*

1. In Gilead
Ge 31:49; Jud 10:17; 11:11, 34; Ne 3:7

2. In Benjamin
Jos 18:26; Jud 20:1; 21:1; 1 S 7:5, 16; 10:17; 1 K 15:22; 2 K 25:23, 25; 2 Chr 16:6; Ne 3:19; Je 40:6

MOAB, *PLAINS OF*
Nu 21:11, 15; 22:1, 36; 26:3, 63; 31:12; 33:44, 48; 35:1; 36:13; De 1:5; 2:18; 29:1; 32:49; 34:1; Jos 13:32; Jud 3:28; 10:6; 11:18; Ru 1:1; 2:6; 1 S 12:9; 14:47; 22:3; 2 S 8:2, 12; 2 K 1:1; 1 Chr 8:8; 11:22; 18:2, 11; Ne 13:23; Ps 60:8; 108:9; Is 11:14; 15:1; 16:7; 25:10; Je

25:21; 27:3; 40:11; 48:1, 13; Eze 25:9; Da 11:41; Am 2:1; Zep 2:9

MOABITES, *descendants of Moab*
Ge 19:37; Nu 25:1; De 2:9, 29; 23:3; 1 K 11:1; 2 K 3:21; 24:2; 2 Chr 20:1, 23; Ezr 9:1; Ne 13:1, 23; Ps 83:6

MOCKING, *treating with scorn, ridiculing, scoffing*
Ge 21:9; Jud 16:10; Jb 16:4; Pr 14:9; 17:5; 30:17; Is 28:22; 57:4; Lam 1:7; 2:15; 3:46; Lu 14:29; Jude 18

1. Of Christ
See **SUFFERING**

2. Of the Righteous
2 K 2:23; 2 Chr 30:10; 36:16; Ne 4:1; Jb 12:4; 21:3; 30:1; Ps 22:7; 31:18; 35:16; 40:15; Je 20:7; Zep 2:8; Ac 2:13; 17:32; He 11:36

See **PERSECUTION**

MODERATION, *restraint*
Ec 7:16; 1 Co 7:31

MOLDING *See* **ARTS AND CRAFTS**

MONEY, *medium of exchange*
Ge 42:35 And it came to pass as they emptied their sacks, that, behold, every man's bundle of money *was* in his sack: and when *both* they and their father saw the bundles of money, they were afraid.

Ge 43:12 And take double money in your hand; and the money that was brought again in the mouth of your sacks, carry *it* again in your hand; peradventure it *was* an oversight:

Ge 43:21 And it came to pass, when we came to the inn, that we opened our sacks, and, behold, *every* man's money *was* in the mouth of his sack, our money in full weight: and we have brought it again in our hand.

Ge 44:1 And he commanded the steward of his house, saying, Fill the men's sacks *with* food, as much as they can carry, and put every man's money in his sack's mouth.

Ge 47:14 And Joseph gathered up all the money that was found in the land of Egypt, and in the land of Canaan, for the corn which they bought: and Joseph brought the money into Pharaoh's house.

Ge 47:18 When that year was ended, they came unto him the second year, and said unto him, We will not hide *it* from my lord, how that our money is spent; my lord also hath our herds of cattle; there is not ought left in the sight of my lord, but our bodies, and our lands:

Le 27:15 And if he that sanctified it will redeem his house, then he shall add the fifth *part* of the money of thy estimation unto it, and it shall be his.

Le 27:18 But if he sanctify his field after the jubile, then the priest shall reckon unto him the money according to the years that remain, even unto the year of the jubile, and it shall be abated from thy estimation.

De 2:6 Ye shall buy meat of them for money, that ye may eat; and ye shall also buy water of them for money, that ye may drink.

De 2:28 Thou shalt sell me meat for money, that I may eat; and give me water for money, that I may drink: only I will pass through on my feet;

De 14:25 Then shalt thou turn *it* into money, and bind up the money in thine hand, and shalt go unto the place which the Lord thy God shall choose:

1 K 21:2 And Ahab spake unto Naboth, saying, Give me thy vineyard, that I may have it for a garden of herbs, because it *is* near unto my house: and I will give thee for it a better vineyard than it; *or,* if it seem good to thee, I will give thee the worth of it in money.

2 K 12:10 And it was *so,* when they saw that *there was* much money in the chest, that the king's scribe and the high priest came up, and they put up in bags, and told the money that was found in the house of the Lord.

2 Chr 24:11 Now it came to pass, that at what time the chest was brought unto the king's office by the hand of the Levites, and when they saw that *there was* much money, the king's scribe and the high priest's officer came and emptied the chest, and took it, and carried it to his place again. Thus they did day by day, and gathered money in abundance.

2 Chr 34:9 And when they came to Hilkiah the high priest, they delivered the money that was brought into the house of God, which the Levites that kept the doors had gathered of the hand of Manasseh and Ephraim, and of all the remnant of Israel, and of all Judah and Benjamin; and they returned to Jerusalem.

2 Chr 34:17 And they have gathered together the money that was found in the house of the Lord, and have delivered it into the hand of the overseers, and to the hand of the workmen.

Ne 5:11 Restore, I pray you, to them, even this day, their lands, their vineyards, their oliveyards, and their houses, also the the hundredth *part* of the money, and of the corn, the wine, and the oil, that ye exact of them.

Ne 5:15 But the former governors that *had been* before me were chargeable unto the people, and had taken of them bread and wine, beside forty shekels of silver; yea, even their servants bare rule over the people: but so did not I, because of the fear of God.

Ec 7:12 For wisdom *is* a defence, *and* money *is* a defence: but the excellency of knowledge *is, that* wisdom giveth life to them that have it.

Ec 10:19 A feast is made for laughter, and wine maketh merry: but money answereth all *things.*

Je 32:10 And I subscribed the evidence, and sealed *it,* and took witnesses, and weighed *him* the money in the balances.

Mt 22:19 Shew me the tribute money. And they brought unto him a penny.

Mk 12:41 And Jesus sat over against the treasury, and beheld how the people cast money into the treasury: and many that were rich cast in much.

Mk 14:11 And when they heard *it,* they were glad, and promised to give him money. And he sought how he might conveniently betray him.

1 Ti 6:10 For the love of money is the root of all evil: which while some coveted after, they have erred from the faith, and pierced themselves through with many sorrows.

See **AVARICE, COVETOUSNESS, RICHES**

MONEY CHANGERS, *bankers sitting in the Temple exchanging foreign coins in local currency for a fee*

Mt 21:12; Mk 11:15; Jn 2:15

MONOGAMY, *marriage of one man and one woman*

Mt 19:5 And said, For this cause shall a man leave father and mother, and shall cleave to his wife: and they twain shall be one flesh?

1 Ti 3:2 A bishop then must be blameless, the husband of one wife, vigilant, sober, of good behaviour, given to hospitality, apt to teach;

1 Ti 3:12 Let the deacons be the husbands of one wife, ruling their children and their own houses well.

1 Ti 5:9 Let not a widow be taken into the number under threescore years old, having been the wife of one man,

See **MARRIAGE**

MONTHS

1—ABIB, OR NISAN, APRIL

Ex 13:4 This day came ye out in the month Abib.

2—ZIF, MAY

1 K 6:1 And it came to pass in the four hundred and eightieth year after the children of Israel were come out of the land of Egypt, in the fourth year of Solomon's reign over Israel, in the month Zif, which *is* the second month, that he began to build the house of the LORD.

3—SIVAN, JUNE

Est 8:9 Then were the king's scribes called at that time in the third month, that *is*, the month Sivan, on the three and twentieth *day* thereof; and it was written according to all that Mordecai commanded unto the Jews, and to the lieutenants, and the deputies and rul-

ers of the provinces which *are* from India unto Ethiopia, an hundred twenty and seven provinces, unto every province according to the writing thereof, and unto every people after their language, and to the Jews according to their writing, and according to their language.

4—TAMMUZ, JULY

Je 39:2 *And* in the eleventh year of Zedekiah, in the fourth month, the ninth *day* of the month, the city was broken up.

Zec 8:19 Thus saith the LORD of hosts; The fast of the fourth *month*, and the fast of the fifth, and the fast of the seventh, and the fast of the tenth, shall be to the house of Judah joy and gladness, and cheerful feasts; therefore love the truth and peace.

5—AB, AUGUST

Nu 33:38 And Aaron the priest went up into mount Hor at the commandment of the LORD, and died there, in the fortieth year after the children of Israel were come out of the land of Egypt, in the first *day* of the fifth month.

Zec 7:3 *And* to speak unto the priests which *were* in the house of the LORD of hosts, and to the prophets, saying, Should I weep in the fifth month, separating myself, as I have done these so many years?

6—ELUL, SEPTEMBER

Ne 6:15 So the wall was finished in the twenty and fifth *day* of *the month* Elul, in fifty and two days.

7—ETHANIM, OR TISRI, OCTOBER

1 K 8:2 And all the men of Israel assembled themselves unto king Solomon at the feast in the month Ethanim, which *is* the seventh month.

8—BUL, NOVEMBER

1 K 6:38 And in the eleventh year, in the month Bul, which *is* the eighth month, was the house finished throughout all the parts thereof, and according to all the fashion of it. So was he seven years in building it.

9—CHISLEU, DECEMBER

Ezr 10:9 Then all the men of Judah and Benjamin gathered themselves together unto Jerusalem within three days. It *was* the ninth month, on the twentieth *day* of the month; and all the people sat in the street of the house of God, trembling because of *this* matter, and for the great rain.

10—TEBETH, JANUARY

Est 2:16 So Esther was taken unto king Ahasuerus into his house royal in the tenth month, which *is* the month Tebeth, in the seventh year of his reign.

11—SEBAT, FEBRUARY

Zec 1:7 Upon the four and twentieth day of the eleventh month, which *is* the month Sebat, in the second year of Darius, came the word of the LORD unto Zechariah, the son of Berechiah, the son of Iddo the prophet, saying,

12—ADAR, MARCH

Est 3:7 In the first month, that *is*, the month Nisan, in the twelfth year of king Ahasuerus, they cast Pur, that *is*, the lot, before Haman from day to day, and from month to month, *to* the twelfth *month*, that *is*, the month Adar.

MOON, *created on the fourth day, called the lesser light*

Ge 1:16; De 17:3; Jos 10:13; Ps 104:19; 136:9; 148:3; Is 24:23; Je 31:35; Eze 32:7; Jl 2:31; 1 Co 15:41; Re 8:12

Feast of New Moon

Nu 10:10; 28:11; 1 S 20:5, 18, 24; 2 K 4:23; 1 Chr 23:31; 2 Chr 2:4; 8:13; 31:3; Ezr 3:5; Ne 10:33; Ps 81:3; Is 1:14; 66:23; Eze 45:17; 46:1, 6; Ho 2:11; Am 8:5; Ga 4:10; Col 2:16

MORDECAI, *a captive Jew*

Est 2:5, 15, 21; 3:2; 4:1; 5:14; 6:3, 10; 7:9; 8:15; 9:20; 10:3

MOREH, *near Shechem*

Ge 12:6; De 11:30; Jud 7:1

MORIAH *See* **MOUNTAINS AND HILLS**

MORNING STAR, *precedes the brightness of the sun's light*

Nu 24:17 I shall see him, but not now: I shall behold him, but not nigh: there shall come a Star out of Jacob, and a Sceptre shall rise out of Israel, and shall smite the corners of Moab, and destroy all the children of Sheth.

2 Pe 1:19 We have also a more sure word of prophecy; whereunto ye do well that ye take heed, as unto a light that shineth in a dark place, until the day dawn, and the day star arise in your hearts:

Re 2:28 And I will give him the morning star.

Re 22:16 I Jesus have sent mine angel to testify unto you these things in the churches. I am the root and the off-spring of David, *and* the bright and morning star.

See **CHRIST**

MORTALITY

Ge 27:2 And he said, Behold now, I am old, I know not the day of my death:

Jb 4:19 How much less *in* them that dwell in houses of clay, whose foundation *is* in the dust, *which* are crushed before the moth?

Jb 10:9 Remember, I beseech thee, that thou hast made me as the clay; and wilt thou bring me into dust again?

Ps 89:48 What man *is* he *that* liveth, and shall not see death? shall he deliver his soul from the hand of the grave? Selah.

Ps 103:16 For the wind passeth over it, and it is gone; and the place thereof shall know it no more.

Ec 3:20 All go unto one place; all are of the dust, and all turn to dust again.

Eze 32:25 They have set her a bed in the midst of the slain with all her multitude: her graves *are* round about him: all of them uncircumcised, slain by the sword: though their terror was caused in the land of the living, yet have they borne their shame with them that go down to the pit: he is put in the midst of *them that be* slain.

1 Co 15:53 For this corruptible must put on incorruption, and this mortal *must* put on immortality.

2 Co 4:7 But we have this treasure in earthen vessels, that the excellency of the power may be of God, and not of us.

2 Co 4:16 For which cause we faint not; but though our outward man perish, yet the inward *man* is renewed day by day.

2 Co 5:1 For we know that if our earthly house of *this* tabernacle were dissolved, we have a building of God, an house not made with hands, eternal in the heavens.

2 Co 5:4 For we that are in *this* tabernacle do groan, being burdened: not for that we would be unclothed, but clothed upon, that mortality might be swallowed up of life.

He 9:27 And as it is appointed unto men once to die, but after this the judgment:

Humans Are like Withering Grass

Ps 39:5 Behold, thou hast made my days *as* an handbreadth; and mine age *is* as nothing before thee: verily every man at his best state *is* altogether vanity. Selah.

Ps 90:5–6 Thou carriest them away as with a flood; they are *as* a sleep: in the morning *they are* like grass *which* groweth up.

In the morning it flourisheth, and groweth up; in the evening it is cut down, and withereth.

Ps 103:15–16 *As for* man, his days *are* as grass: as a flower of the field, so he flourisheth.

For the wind passeth over it, and it is gone; and the place thereof shall know it no more.

Ps 129:6 Let them be as the grass *upon* the housetops, which withereth afore it groweth up:

Is 37:27 Therefore their inhabitants *were* of small power, they were dismayed and confounded: they were *as*

the grass of the field, and *as* the green herb, *as* the grass on the housetops, and *as corn* blasted before it be grown up.

Is 40:6–7 The voice said, Cry. And he said, What shall I cry? All flesh *is* grass, and all the goodliness thereof *is* as the flower of the field:

The grass withereth, the flower fadeth: because the spirit of the LORD bloweth upon it: surely the people *is* grass.

Ja 1:10 But the rich, in that he is made low: because as the flower of the grass he shall pass away.

1 Pe 1:24 For all flesh *is* as grass, and all the glory of man as the flower of grass. The grass withereth, and the flower thereof falleth away:

See **IMMORTALITY**

MORTAR

1. Cement, or mud slime

Ex 1:14; Le 14:42; Eze 13:10; Na 3:14

2. A Vessel Used for Pulverizing

Nu 11:8 *And* the people went about, and gathered *it*, and ground *it* in mills, or beat *it* in a mortar, and baked *it* in pans, and made cakes of it: and the taste of it was as the taste of fresh oil.

Pr 27:22 Though thou shouldest bray a fool in a mortar among wheat with a pestle, *yet* will not his foolishness depart from him.

MORTGAGE, *a lien upon real estate for debt*

Ne 5:3

See **BUSINESS**

MOSES, *drawn out, son of Amram, of the tribe of Levi, the leader and lawgiver of Israel*

Ge 1:1 In the beginning God created the heaven and the earth.

Ex 1:1 Now these *are* the names of the children of Israel, which came into Egypt; every man and his household came with Jacob.

Ex 2:2 And the woman conceived, and bare a son: and when she saw him that he *was a* goodly *child,* she hid him three months.

Ex 2:10 And the child grew, and she brought him unto Pharaoh's daughter, and he became her son. And she called his name Moses: and she said, Because I drew him out of the water.

Ex 2:14 And he said, Who made thee a prince and a judge over us? intendest thou to kill me, as thou killedst the Egyptian? And Moses feared, and said, Surely this thing is known.

Ex 3:3 And Moses said, I will now turn aside, and see this great sight, why the bush is not burnt.

Ex 3:11 And Moses said unto God, Who *am* I, that I should go unto Pharaoh, and that I should bring forth the children of Israel out of Egypt?

Ex 6:20 And Amram took him Jochebed his father's sister to wife; and she bare him Aaron and Moses: and the years of the life of Amram *were* an hundred and thirty and seven years.

Ex 7:7 And Moses *was* fourscore years old, and Aaron fourscore and three years old, when they spake unto Pharaoh.

Ex 11:3 And the LORD gave the people favour in the sight of the Egyptians. Moreover the man Moses *was* very great in the land of Egypt, in the sight of Pharaoh's servants, and in the sight of the people.

Ex 12:21 Then Moses called for all the elders of Israel, and said unto them, Draw out and take you a lamb according to your families, and kill the passover.

Ex 14:21 And Moses stretched out his hand over the sea; and the LORD caused the sea to go *back* by a strong east wind all that night, and made the sea dry *land,* and the waters were divided.

Ex 19:20 And the LORD came down upon mount Sinai, on the top of the mount: and the LORD called Moses *up* to the top of the mount; and Moses went up.

Ex 33:11 And the LORD spake unto Moses face to face, as a man speaketh unto his friend. And he turned again into the camp: but his servant Joshua,

the son of Nun, a young man, departed not out of the tabernacle.

Ex 34:29 And it came to pass, when Moses came down from mount Sinai with the two tables of testimony in Moses' hand, when he came down from the mount, that Moses wist not that the skin of his face shone while he talked with him.

Le 1:1 And the LORD called unto Moses, and spake unto him out of the tabernacle of the congregation, saying,

Nu 1:1 And the LORD spake unto Moses in the wilderness of Sinai, in the tabernacle of the congregation, on the first *day* of the second month, in the second year after they were come out of the land of Egypt, saying,

Nu 10:29 And Moses said unto Hobab, the son of Raguel the Midianite, Moses' father in law, We are journeying unto the place of which the LORD said, I will give it you: come thou with us, and we will do thee good: for the LORD hath spoken good concerning Israel.

Nu 12:3 (Now the man Moses *was* very meek, above all the men which *were* upon the face of the earth.)

Nu 20:10 And Moses and Aaron gathered the congregation together before the rock, and he said unto them, Hear now, ye rebels; must we fetch you water out of this rock?

Nu 26:59 And the name of Amram's wife *was* Jochebed, the daughter of Levi, whom *her mother* bare to Levi in Egypt: and she bare unto Amram Aaron and Moses, and Miriam their sister.

Nu 31:3 And Moses spake unto the people, saying, Arm some of yourselves unto the war, and let them go against the Midianites, and avenge the LORD of Midian.

Nu 33:2 And Moses wrote their goings out according to their journeys by the commandment of the LORD: and these *are* their journeys according to their goings out.

De 1:1 These *be* the words which Moses spake unto all Israel on this side Jordan in the wilderness, in the plain over against the Red *sea,* between

Paran, and Tophel, and Laban, and Hazeroth, and Dizahab.

De 1:1 These *be* the words which Moses spake unto all Israel on this side Jordan in the wilderness, in the plain over against the Red *sea*, between Paran, and Tophel, and Laban, and Hazeroth, and Dizahab.

De 33:1 And this *is* the blessing, wherewith Moses the man of God blessed the children of Israel before his death.

De 34:1 And Moses went up from the plains of Moab unto the mountain of Nebo, to the top of Pisgah, that *is* over against Jericho. And the LORD shewed him all the land of Gilead, unto Dan,

De 34:5 So Moses the servant of the LORD died there in the land of Moab, according to the word of the LORD.

1 Chr 6:3 And the children of Amram; Aaron, and Moses, and Miriam. The sons also of Aaron; Nadab, and Abihu, Eleazar, and Ithamar.

1 Chr 23:14 Now *concerning* Moses the man of God, his sons were named of the tribe of Levi.

Ps 77:20 Thou leddest thy people like a flock by the hand of Moses and Aaron.

Ps 99:6 Moses and Aaron among his priests, and Samuel among them that call upon his name; they called upon the LORD, and he answered them.

Ps 105:26 He sent Moses his servant; *and* Aaron whom he had chosen.

Mi 6:4 For I brought thee up out of the land of Egypt, and redeemed thee out of the house of servants; and I sent before thee Moses, Aaron, and Miriam.

Mt 17:3 And, behold, there appeared unto them Moses and Elias talking with him.

Mt 19:7 They say unto him, Why did Moses then command to give a writing of divorcement, and to put her away?

Mk 9:4 And there appeared unto them Elias with Moses: and they were talking with Jesus.

Lu 9:30 And, behold, there talked with him two men, which were Moses and Elias:

Lu 9:33 And it came to pass, as they departed from him, Peter said unto Jesus, Master, it is good for us to be here: and let us make three tabernacles; one for thee, and one for Moses, and one for Elias: not knowing what he said.

Jn 5:45 Do not think that I will accuse you to the Father: there is *one* that accuseth you, *even* Moses, in whom ye trust.

Jn 9:28 Then they reviled him, and said, Thou art his disciple; but we are Moses' disciples.

Ac 7:20 In which time Moses was born, and was exceeding fair, and nourished up in his father's house three months:

Ac 7:22 And Moses was learned in all the wisdom of the Egyptians, and was mighty in words and in deeds.

He 11:23–24 By faith Moses, when he was born, was hid three months of his parents, because they saw *he was* a proper child; and they were not afraid of the king's commandment.

By faith Moses, when he was come to years, refused to be called the son of Pharaoh's daughter;

1. His Life in Parallel with Christ's

PRESERVED IN CHILDHOOD

Ex 2:2–10 And the woman conceived, and bare a son: and when she saw him that he *was a* goodly *child,* she hid him three months.

And when she could not longer hide him, she took for him an ark of bulrushes, and daubed it with slime and with pitch, and put the child therein; and she laid *it* in the flags by the river's brink.

And his sister stood afar off, to wit what would be done to him.

And the daughter of Pharaoh came down to wash *herself* at the river; and her maidens walked along by the river's side; and when she saw the ark among the flags, she sent her maid to fetch it.

And when she had opened *it,* she saw the child: and, behold, the babe wept. And she had compassion on him, and said, This *is one* of the Hebrews' children.

Then said his sister to Pharaoh's daughter, Shall I go and call to thee a nurse of the Hebrew women, that she may nurse the child for thee?

And Pharaoh's daughter said to her, Go. And the maid went and called the child's mother.

And Pharaoh's daughter said unto her, Take this child away, and nurse it for me, and I will give *thee* thy wages. And the woman took the child, and nursed it.

And the child grew, and she brought him unto Pharaoh's daughter, and he became her son. And she called his name Moses: and she said, Because I drew him out of the water.

Mt 2:14–15 When he arose, he took the young child and his mother by night, and departed into Egypt:

And was there until the death of Herod: that it might be fulfilled which was spoken of the Lord by the prophet, saying, Out of Egypt have I called my son.

CONTENDED WITH MASTERS OF EVIL

Ex 7:11 Then Pharaoh also called the wise men and the sorcerers: now the magicians of Egypt, they also did in like manner with their enchantments.

Mt 4:1 Then was Jesus led up of the Spirit into the wilderness to be tempted of the devil.

FASTED FORTY DAYS

Ex 34:28 And he was there with the LORD forty days and forty nights; he did neither eat bread, nor drink water. And he wrote upon the tables the words of the covenant, the ten commandments.

Mt 4:2 And when he had fasted forty days and forty nights, he was afterward an hungred.

CONTROLLED THE SEA

Ex 14:2 Moses stretched out his hand over the sea; and the LORD caused the sea to go *back* by a strong east wind all that night, and made the sea dry *land,* and the waters were divided.

Mt 8:26 And he saith unto them, Why are ye fearful, O ye of little faith? Then he arose, and rebuked the winds and the sea; and there was a great calm.

FED A MULTITUDE

Ex 16:15 And when the children of Israel saw *it,* they said one to another, It *is* manna: for they wist not what it *was.* And Moses said unto them, This *is* the bread which the LORD hath given you to eat.

Mt 14:20–21 And they did all eat, and were filled: and they took up of the fragments that remained twelve baskets full.

HAD RADIANT FACES

Ex 34:35 And the children of Israel saw the face of Moses, that the skin of Moses' face shone: and Moses put the vail upon his face again, until he went in to speak with him.

Mt 17:2 And was transfigured before them: and his face did shine as the sun, and his raiment was white as the light.

ENDURED MURMURINGS

Ex 15:24 And the people murmured against Moses, saying, What shall we drink?

Mk 7:2 And when they saw some of his disciples eat bread with defiled, that is to say, with unwashen, hands, they found fault.

DISCREDITED IN THE HOME

Nu 12:1 And Miriam and Aaron spake against Moses because of the Ethiopian woman whom he had married: for he had married an Ethiopian woman.

Jn 7:5 For neither did his brethren believe in him.

MADE INTERCESSORY PRAYERS

Ex 32:32 Yet now, if thou wilt forgive their sin—; and if not, blot me, I pray thee, out of thy book which thou hast written.

Jn 17:9 I pray for them: I pray not for the world, but for them which thou hast given me; for they are thine.

SPOKE AS ORACLES

De 18:18 I will raise them up a Prophet from among their brethren, like unto thee, and will put my words in his mouth; and he shall speak unto them all that I shall command him.

HAD SEVENTY HELPERS

Nu 11:16–17 And the LORD said unto Moses, Gather unto me seventy men of the elders of Israel, whom thou knowest to be the elders of the people, and officers over them; and bring them unto the tabernacle of the congregation, that they may stand there with thee.

Lu 10:1 After these things the Lord appointed other seventy also, and sent them two and two before his face into every city and place, whither he himself would come.

ESTABLISHED MEMORIALS

Ex 12:14 And this day shall be unto you for a memorial; and ye shall keep it a feast to the LORD throughout your generations; ye shall keep it a feast by an ordinance for ever.

Lu 22:19 And he took bread, and gave thanks, and brake *it,* and gave unto them, saying, This is my body which is given for you: this do in remembrance of me.

REAPPEARED AFTER DEATH

Mt 17:3 And, behold, there appeared unto them Moses and Elias talking with him.

Ac 1:3 To whom also he shewed himself alive after his passion by many infallible proofs, being seen of them forty days, and speaking of the things pertaining to the kingdom of God:

2. His Rod

Ex 4:2, 17, 20; 7:9, 19; 8:16; 9:23; 10:13; 14:16; 17:5, 9

See **ISRAEL, NATION**

MOST HIGH, *a title given to Jehovah*

Ge 14:22 And Abram said to the king of Sodom, I have lift up mine hand unto the LORD, the most high God, the possessor of heaven and earth,

De 32:8 When the most High divided to the nations their inheritance, when he separated the sons of Adam, he set the bounds of the people according to the number of the children of Israel.

2 S 22:14 The LORD thundered from heaven, and the most High uttered his voice.

Ps 7:17 I will praise the LORD according to his righteousness: and will sing praise to the name of the LORD most high.

Ps 9:2 I will be glad and rejoice in thee: I will sing praise to thy name, O thou most High.

Ps 47:2 For the LORD most high *is* terrible; *he is* a great King over all the earth.

Ps 56:2 Mine enemies would daily swallow *me* up: for *they be* many that fight against me, O thou most High.

Ps 57:2 I will cry unto God most high; unto God that performeth *all things* for me.

Ps 73:11 And they say, How doth God know? and is there knowledge in the most High?

Ps 83:18 That *men* may know that thou, whose name alone *is* JEHOVAH, *art* the most high over all the earth.

Ps 91:9 Because thou hast made the LORD, *which is* my refuge, *even* the most High, thy habitation;

Da 3:26 Then Nebuchadnezzar came near to the mouth of the burning fiery furnace, *and* spake, and said, Shadrach, Meshach, and Abed-nego, ye servants of the most high God, come forth, and come *hither.* Then Shadrach, Meshach, and Abed-nego, came forth of the midst of the fire.

Da 4:17 This matter *is* by the decree of the watchers, and the demand by the word of the holy ones: to the intent that the living may know that the most High ruleth in the kingdom of men, and giveth it to whomsoever he will, and setteth up over it the basest of men.

Da 4:24 This *is* the interpretation, O king, and this *is* the decree of the most High, which is come upon my lord the king:

Da 4:32 And they shall drive thee from men, and thy dwelling *shall be* with the beasts of the field: they shall make thee to eat grass as oxen, and seven times shall pass over thee, until thou know that the most High ruleth in the kingdom of men, and giveth it to whomsoever he will.

Da 5:18 O thou king, the most high God gave Nebuchadnezzar thy father a kingdom, and majesty, and glory, and honour:

Da 7:27 And the kingdom and dominion, and the greatness of the kingdom under the whole heaven, shall be given to the people of the saints of the most High, whose kingdom *is* an everlasting kingdom, and all dominions shall serve and obey him.

Mt 2:14 When he arose, he took the young child and his mother by night, and departed into Egypt:

Ac 7:48 Howbeit the most High dwelleth not in temples made with hands; as saith the prophet,

MOTHERHOOD, *cares of*

Ge 3:16 Unto the woman he said, I will greatly multiply thy sorrow and thy conception; in sorrow thou shalt bring forth children; and thy desire *shall be* to thy husband, and he shall rule over thee.

Ge 21:16 And she went, and sat her down over against *him* a good way off, as it were a bowshot: for she said, Let me not see the death of the child. And she sat over against *him,* and lift up her voice, and wept.

Ex 2:3 And when she could not longer hide him, she took for him an ark of bulrushes, and daubed it with slime and with pitch, and put the child therein; and she laid *it* in the flags by the river's brink.

2 S 21:10 And Rizpah the daughter of Aiah took sackcloth, and spread it for her upon the rock, from the beginning of harvest until water dropped upon them out of heaven, and suffered neither the birds of the air to rest on them by day, nor the beasts of the field by night.

1 K 3:26 Then spake the woman whose the living child *was* unto the king, for her bowels yearned upon her son, and she said, O my lord, give her the living child, and in no wise slay it. But the other said, Let it be neither mine nor thine, *but* divide *it.*

2 K 4:19–20 And he said unto his father, My head, my head. And he said to a lad, Carry him to his mother.

And when he had taken him, and brought him to his mother, he sat on her knees till noon, and *then* died.

Je 31:15 Thus saith the Lord; A voice was heard in Ramah, lamentation, *and* bitter weeping; Rahel weeping for her children refused to be comforted for her children, because they *were* not.

Is 49:15 Can a woman forget her sucking child, that she should not have compassion on the son of her womb? yea, they may forget, yet will I not forget thee.

Mt 15:22 And, behold, a woman of Canaan came out of the same coasts, and cried unto him, saying, Have mercy on me, O Lord, *thou* Son of David; my daughter is grievously vexed with a devil.

Mt 24:19 And woe unto them that are with child, and to them that give suck in those days!

See **FAMILY, HOME, WOMEN**

MOTHERS-IN-LAW

Ru 1:14; Mt 8:14; 10:35; Mk 1:30

See **FAMILY**

MOTHS　*See* **INSECTS**

MOUNTAINS AND HILLS

1. Names

a. Abarim, east of Jordan

Nu 27:12; Nu 33:48; De 32:49

b. Ararat, in Armenia

Je 51:27

c. Bashan

Ps 68:15

d. Bethel

1 S 13:2

e. Carmel, on the seacoast of Palestine

Jos 19:26; 1 K 18:19; 2 K 2:25; 4:25; Is 33:9; 35:2; Je 46:18; 50:19; Am 1:2; 9:3; Mi 7:14; Na 1:4

f. Ebal, in Samaria

De 11:29; 27:4, 13; Jos 8:30, 33

g. Ephraim, in central Palestine

Jos 17:15; 19:50; 20:7; 21:21; 24:30, 33; Jud 2:9; 3:27; 4:5; 7:24; 10:1; 17:1, 8; 18:2, 13; 19:1, 16; 1 S 1:1; 9:4; 14:22; 2 S 2:9; 1 K 12:25; 2 K 5:22; 1 Chr 6:67; 2 Chr 13:4; 15:8; 19:4

h. Gerizim, in Samaria

Mount Gerizim and Mount Ebal are twin mountains located in central Palestine. Ebal is 3,077 feet above sea level, and Gerizim is 2,849 feet. These mountains played an important role in Israel's early history and in the history of the Samaritans from 700 B.C. to the present. Little wonder, for between the two lies the fertile half-mile-wide Vale of Shechem, the best watered valley in central Palestine. Mount Gerizim has usually been called the "Mount of Blessing," because after crossing the Jordan River Joshua placed half the people over against Mount Gerizim and half of them over against Mount Ebal.

The blessings on those who kept the law were pronounced from Gerizim, and the curses on breakers of the law came from Ebal (Jos 8:30–35; De 27–28). Jotham's parable of the trees was later spoken to the men of Shechem from Mount Gerizim (Jud 9:7–20). A prominent ledge halfway up the slope is now popularly called "Jotham's pulpit." On returning from Babylonian captivity, the Jews refused the Samaritan offer of help in rebuilding the temple at Jerusalem (Ezr 4:1–3). The Samaritans set up their own priesthood and built their own temple on Mount Gerizim, the mountain they believe is Mount Moriah (Ge 22:2; De 12:5; 2 Chr 3:1; Jn 4:20).

i. Gilboa, on which Saul died

1 S 28:4; 31:1, 8; 2 S 1:6, 21; 21:12; 1 Chr 10:1, 8

j. Gilead

Ge 31:21, 25; Jud 7:3; Song 4:1; Je 50:19

k. Hermon, also Sirion

The "Chief of the Mountains" of Palestine, it is five miles wide and twenty miles long. It has three peaks, the tallest of which is 9,166 feet above the Mediterranean Sea. For centuries before Abraham's time the mountain had been venerated in connection with Baal. The mountain marked the northern border of the tribe of Manasseh (1 Chr 5:23) and is praised in Scripture for its dew (Ps 133:3), its lions and leopards (Song 4:8), and its cypresses (Eze 27:5). The psalmist mentions the mountain crying with joy to the Lord as part of the creation (Ps 89:12), but the mountain and the surrounding area was the site of extensive Baal worship over many centuries (e.g., Jos 11:17; 1 Chr 5:23).

l. Hor, Aaron's burial place

Nu 20:22, 27; 21:4; 33:37; De 32:50

m. Horeb, Sinai or Mount of God

Ex 3:1; 17:6; 18:5; 33:6; De 1:2, 19; 4:10; 5:2–3, 3; 9:8; 1 K 8:9; 19:8; 2 Chr 5:10; Ps 106:19; Mal 4:4

n. Lebanon

De 3:25; Jud 3:3; 1 K 5:14; Ps 72:16; Song 4:8; Is 29:17; 33:9; 35:2; 40:16; 60:13; Je 22:6; Eze 17:3; Na 1:4; Zec 10:10; 11:1

o. Mizar

Ps 42:6

p. Moriah, in Jerusalem, where the temple was built and where it is supposed Abraham offered up Isaac

Ge 22:2; 2 S 24:18; 1 Chr 21:18; 22:1; 2 Chr 3:1

q. Nebo

Mount Nebo is the mountain from which Moses viewed the Promised

Land and where he was buried (De 32:49-52; 34:1-8; Is 15:2; Je 48:1).

r. Olives

The Mount of Olives is "the mountain which is east of the city" of Jerusalem (Eze 11:23). Only the half-mile-wide Kidron Valley separates the Holy City from the mountain. In reality there are three distinctly marked, rounded summits on the two-mile ridge: Mount Scopus on the north, the "Mount of Offense" on the south, and the Mount of Olives in the center. The central mountain stands 2,680 feet above sea level, which means that it is about 100 feet higher than the temple area in Jerusalem.

2 S 15:30; Zec 14:4; Mt 21:1; 24:3; 26:30; Mk 11:1; 13:3; 14:26; Lu 19:29, 37; 21:37; 22:39; Jn 8:1; Ac 1:12

s. Pisgah, in Moab, from whence Moses viewed the Promised Land

Nu 21:20; 23:14; De 3:27; 4:49; 34:1; Jos 12:3

t. Seir

Ge 14:6; 36:8; De 1:2; 2:5; Eze 25:8; 35:2

u. Sinai, upon which Moses received the Decalogue

Ex 16:1; 19:2, 11; 24:13, 16; 31:18; 34:2; Le 7:38; 25:1; 26:46; 27:34; Nu 3:1; 10:33; 28:6; De 10:3; 33:2; Ne 9:13; Ps 68:8, 17; Ac 7:30, 38; Ga 4:24; He 12:18

v. Tabor

Jud 4:6, 14; 8:18; Ps 89:12; Je 46:18; Ho 5:1

w. Zion, or Sion

1 S 5:7; 1 K 8:1; Ps 78:68; 87:2; Is 37:32; Rom 11:26; He 12:22; Re 14:1

2. Scenes of Great Events

ON ARARAT THE ARK RESTED

Ge 8:4 And the ark rested in the seventh month, on the seventeenth day of the month, upon the mountains of Ararat.

ON MORIAH ABRAHAM SACRIFICED ISAAC

Ge 22:2 And he said, Take now thy son, thine only *son* Isaac, whom thou lovest, and get thee into the land of Moriah; and offer him there for a burnt offering upon one of the mountains which I will tell thee of.

ON HOREB MOSES SAW THE BURNING BUSH

Ex 3:1 Now Moses kept the flock of Jethro his father in law, the priest of Midian: and he led the flock to the backside of the desert, and came to the mountain of God, *even* to Horeb.

ON SINAI THE LAW WAS GIVEN

Ex 19:11–20 And be ready against the third day: for the third day the LORD will come down in the sight of all the people upon mount Sinai.

ON EBAL AND GERIZIM WERE READ THE BLESSINGS AND CURSES

De 11:29 And it shall come to pass, when the LORD thy God hath brought thee in unto the land whither thou goest to possess it, that thou shalt put the blessing upon mount Gerizim, and the curse upon mount Ebal.

De 27:11–13 And Moses charged the people the same day, saying,

These shall stand upon mount Gerizim to bless the people, when ye are come over Jordan; Simeon, and Levi, and Judah, and Issachar, and Joseph, and Benjamin:

And these shall stand upon mount Ebal to curse; Reuben, Gad, and Asher, and Zebulun, Dan, and Naphtali.

ON CARMEL OCCURRED ELIJAH'S SACRIFICE

1 K 18:19 Now therefore send, *and* gather to me all Israel unto mount Carmel, and the prophets of Baal four hundred and fifty, and the prophets of the groves four hundred, which eat at Jezebel's table.

ON HERMON, OR TABOR, CHRIST WAS TRANSFIGURED

Mk 9:2 And after six days Jesus taketh *with him* Peter, and James, and John, and leadeth them up into an high mountain apart by themselves: and he was transfigured before them.

ON OLIVET OCCURRED CHRIST'S ASCENSION

Ac 1:12 Then returned they unto Jerusalem from the mount called Olivet, which is from Jerusalem a sabbath day's journey.

MOURNING, *accompanied burial ceremonies*

Ge 37:34; 50:3, 10; Le 10:6; Nu 20:29; De 21:13; 34:8; 2 S 1:12; 3:31; 11:26; 13:36; 19:2; 1 K 14:18; 1 Chr 7:22; 2 Chr 35:24; Ps 35:14; Ec 3:4; 7:4; Je 6:26; Mk 16:10; Jn 11:31

1. Grief

Ge 23:2; 37:35; 42:38; 44:29; 50:1; Ex 11:6; Jud 21:2; Ru 1:9, 20; 1 S 30:4; 2 S 13:31; 18:33; Est 4:4; Jb 1:20; Je 31:15; Jn 11:31, 33; 20:11; Ac 9:39; 1 Th 4:13

2. Hired Mourners

2 Chr 35:25; Ec 12:5; Je 9:17; 16:7; 34:5; Am 5:16; Mt 9:23; 11:17; Mk 5:38; Lu 7:12; 8:52

3. Sackcloth, *a coarse garment, or cloth, worn as a symbol of grief or penitence*

Ge 37:34; 2 S 3:31; 21:10; 1 K 20:32; 21:27; 2 K 6:30; 19:1; 1 Chr 21:16; Ne 9:1; Est 4:1; Jb 16:15; Ps 30:11; 35:13; 69:11; Is 3:24; 15:3; 20:2; 22:12; 37:1; 58:5; Je 4:8; 6:26; 48:37; 49:3; Lam 2:10; Eze 7:18; 27:31; Da 9:3; Jl 1:8, 13; Am 8:10; Jona 3:5, 8; Mt 11:21; Lu 10:13; Re 11:3

4. Clothes Torn

Ge 37:29, 34; 44:13; Le 13:45; 21:10; Nu 14:6; Jos 7:6; Jud 11:35; 1 S 4:12; 2 S 1:2, 11; 3:31; 13:19, 31; 15:32; 1 K 21:27; 2 K 2:12; 5:8; 6:30; 18:37; 22:11; 2 Chr 23:13; 34:19; Ezr 9:3, 5; Est 4:1; Jb 1:20; 2:12; Ec 3:7; Is 36:22; Je 41:5; Mt 26:65; Mk 14:63; Ac 14:14

See **DEATH**

MOWING *See* **AGRICULTURE**

MULBERRY *See* **TREES**

MULES *See* **ANIMALS**

MULTITUDE

1. The Rabble

Ex 12:38; Nu 11:4; Mt 13:30, 47; 22:10

2. Fed

Ex 16:13; Nu 11:13, 31; 2 S 6:19; 17:29; 2 K 4:43; 1 Chr 16:3; Mt 14:21; 15:38; 16:9; Mk 6:42; 8:9, 19; Lu 9:17; Jn 6:11

MURDER, *premeditated or malicious killing of another human being*

1. Forbidden

Ex 1:16 And he said, When ye do the office of a midwife to the Hebrew women, and see *them* upon the stools; if it *be* a son, then ye shall kill him: but if it *be* a daughter, then she shall live.

Ex 20:13 Thou shalt not kill.

De 5:17 Thou shalt not kill.

De 27:25 Cursed *be* he that taketh reward to slay an innocent person. And all the people shall say, Amen.

1 S 19:1 And Saul spake to Jonathan his son, and to all his servants, that they should kill David.

Jb 24:14 The murderer rising with the light killeth the poor and needy, and in the night is as a thief.

Ps 10:8 He sitteth in the lurking places of the villages: in the secret places doth he murder the innocent: his eyes are privily set against the poor.

Ps 94:6 They slay the widow and the stranger, and murder the fatherless.

Je 7:9 Will ye steal, murder, and commit adultery, and swear falsely, and burn incense unto Baal, and walk after other gods whom ye know not;

Ho 4:2 By swearing, and lying, and killing, and stealing, and committing adultery, they break out, and blood toucheth blood.

Mt 5:21 Ye have heard that it was said by them of old time, Thou shalt not kill; and whosoever shall kill shall be in danger of the judgment:

Mt 19:18 He saith unto him, Which? Jesus said, Thou shalt do no murder, Thou shalt not commit adultery, Thou shalt not steal, Thou shalt not bear false witness,

Mt 22:6 And the remnant took his servants, and entreated *them* spitefully, and slew *them.*

Mt 23:35 That upon you may come all the righteous blood shed upon the earth, from the blood of righteous Abel unto the blood of Zacharias son of Barachias, whom ye slew between the temple and the altar.

Mk 7:21 For from within, out of the heart of men, proceed evil thoughts, adulteries, fornications, murders,

Mk 10:19 Thou knowest the commandments, Do not commit adultery, Do not kill, Do not steal, Do not bear false witness, Defraud not, Honour thy father and mother.

Lu 18:20 Thou knowest the commandments, Do not commit adultery, Do not kill, Do not steal, Do not bear false witness, Honour thy father and thy mother.

Ac 23:14 And they came to the chief priests and elders, and said, We have bound ourselves under a great curse, that we will eat nothing until we have slain Paul.

Ro 13:9 For this, Thou shalt not commit adultery, Thou shalt not kill, Thou shalt not steal, Thou shalt not bear false witness, Thou shalt not covet; and if *there be* any other commandment, it is briefly comprehended in this saying, namely, Thou shalt love thy neighbour as thyself.

1 Ti 1:9 Knowing this, that the law is not made for a righteous man, but for the lawless and disobedient, for the ungodly and for sinners, for unholy and profane, for murderers of fathers and murderers of mothers, for manslayers,

Ja 2:11 For he that said, Do not commit adultery, said also, Do not kill. Now if thou commit no adultery, yet if thou kill, thou art become a transgressor of the law.

1 Pe 4:15 But let none of you suffer as a murderer, or *as* a thief, or *as* an evildoer, or as a busybody in other men's matters.

1 Jn 3:15 Whosoever hateth his brother is a murderer: and ye know that no murderer hath eternal life abiding in him.

Re 21:8 But the fearful, and unbelieving, and the abominable, and murderers, and whoremongers, and sorcerers, and idolaters, and all liars, shall have their part in the lake which burneth with fire and brimstone: which is the second death.

Re 22:15 For without *are* dogs, and sorcerers, and whoremongers, and murderers, and idolaters, and whosoever loveth and maketh a lie.

2. Examples

Ge 4:8, 23; 49:6; Ex 2:12; Jud 9:5, 18, 56; 19:28; 20:5; 1 S 22:18; 2 S 4:7; 11:15; 12:9; 13:28; 20:10; 1 K 21:13; 2 K 11:1; 2 Chr 21:4, 13; 22:10; 24:21; Jb 1:15; Is 1:21; Je 41:3, 7; Eze 23:39; Mt 2:16; 21:35; Mk 12:8; 15:7; Lu 23:19, 25; Ac 7:58; Ro 3:15; Ga 5:21; 1 Jn 3:12; Re 9:21

3. Punishment of Willful

Ge 9:6; Ex 21:12; Le 24:17; Nu 35:16, 31; De 19:11; 1 K 2:32; 2 K 14:5; Pr 28:17; Eze 11:6; Eze 18:10

4. Of Children

Ex 1:16, 22; 1 S 22:19; Mt 2:16; Ac 7:19

See **SIN, WICKED**

MURMURING, *complaining*

1. Condemned

Jb 33:12 Behold, *in* this thou art not just: I will answer thee, that God is greater than man.

Pr 19:3 The foolishness of man perverteth his way: and his heart fretteth against the LORD.

Is 29:24 They also that erred in spirit shall come to understanding, and they that murmured shall learn doctrine.

Lam 3:39 Wherefore doth a living man complain, a man for the punishment of his sins?

Eze 18:29 Yet saith the house of Israel, The way of the LORD is not equal. O house of Israel, are not my ways equal? are not your ways unequal?

Eze 33:17 Yet the children of thy people say, The way of the LORD is not equal: but as for them, their way is not equal.

Jona 4:2 And he prayed unto the LORD, and said, LORD, wherefore hast thou *so* evil entreated this people? why *is* it *that* thou hast sent me?

Mt 20:11 And when they had received it, they murmured against the goodman of the house,

Mt 21:16 And said unto him, Hearest thou what these say? And Jesus saith unto them, Yea; have ye never read, Out of the mouth of babes and sucklings thou hast perfected praise?

Mt 25:24 Then he which had received the one talent came and said, Lord, I knew thee that thou art an hard man, reaping where thou hast not sown, and gathering where thou hast not strawed:

Mt 26:8 But when his disciples saw *it,* they had indignation, saying, To what purpose *is* this waste?

Mk 7:5 Then the Pharisees and scribes asked him, Why walk not thy disciples according to the tradition of the elders, but eat bread with unwashen hands?

Lu 10:40 But Martha was cumbered about much serving, and came to him, and said, LORD, dost thou not care that my sister hath left me to serve alone? bid her therefore that she help me.

Lu 15:29 And he answering said to *his* father, Lo, these many years do I serve thee, neither transgressed I at any time thy commandment: and yet thou never gavest me a kid, that I might make merry with my friends:

Jn 6:43 Jesus therefore answered and said unto them, Murmur not among yourselves.

Jn 6:61 When Jesus knew in himself that his disciples murmured at it, he said unto them, Doth this offend you?

1 Co 10:10 Neither murmur ye, as some of them also murmured, and were destroyed of the destroyer.

Ph 2:14 Do all things without murmurings and disputings:

2. Examples

Ex 5:22 And Moses returned unto the LORD, and said, LORD, wherefore hast thou *so* evil entreated this people? why *is* it *that* thou hast sent me?

Ex 14:11 And they said unto Moses, Because *there were* no graves in Egypt, hast thou taken us away to die in the wilderness? wherefore hast thou dealt thus with us, to carry us forth out of Egypt?

Ex 15:24 And the people murmured against Moses, saying, What shall we drink?

Ex 16:2 And the whole congregation of the children of Israel murmured against Moses and Aaron in the wilderness:

Ex 16:8 And Moses said, *This shall be,* when the LORD shall give you in the evening flesh to eat, and in the morning bread to the full; for that the LORD heareth your murmurings which ye murmur against him: and what *are* we? your murmurings *are* not against us, but against the LORD.

Ex 17:3 And the people thirsted there for water; and the people murmured against Moses, and said, Wherefore *is* this *that* thou hast brought us up out of Egypt, to kill us and our children and our cattle with thirst?

Nu 11:1 And *when* the people complained, it displeased the LORD: and the LORD heard *it;* and his anger was kindled; and the fire of the LORD burnt among them, and consumed *them that were* in the uttermost parts of the camp

Nu 11:18 And say thou unto the people, Sanctify yourselves against to morrow, and ye shall eat flesh: for ye have wept in the ears of the LORD, saying, Who shall give us flesh to eat? for *it was* well with us in Egypt: therefore the LORD will give you flesh, and ye shall eat.

Nu 14:2 And all the children of Israel murmured against Moses and against Aaron: and the whole congregation said unto them, Would God that we had died in the land of Egypt! or would God we had died in this wilderness!

Nu 14:27 How long *shall I bear with* this evil congregation, which murmur against me? I have heard the murmurings of the children of Israel, which they murmur against me.

Nu 14:29 Your carcases shall fall in this wilderness; and all that were numbered of you, according to your whole number, from twenty years old and upward, which have murmured against me,

Nu 16:41 But on the morrow all the congregation of the children of Israel murmured against Moses and against Aaron, saying, Ye have killed the people of the LORD.

Nu 17:5 And it shall come to pass, *that* the man's rod, whom I shall choose, shall blossom: and I will make to cease from me the murmurings of the children of Israel, whereby they murmur against you.

Nu 17:10 And the LORD said unto Moses, Bring Aaron's rod again before the testimony, to be kept for a token against the rebels; and thou shalt quite take away their murmurings from me, that they die not.

Nu 20:3 And the people chode with Moses, and spake, saying, Would God that we had died when our brethren died before the LORD!

Nu 21:5 And the people spake against God, and against Moses, Wherefore have ye brought us up out of Egypt to die in the wilderness? for *there is* no bread, neither *is there any* water; and our soul loatheth this light bread.

De 1:27 And ye murmured in your tents, and said, Because the LORD hated us, he hath brought us forth out of the land of Egypt, to deliver us into the hand of the Amorites, to destroy us.

Jos 7:7 And Joshua said, Alas, O LORD God, wherefore hast thou at all brought this people over Jordan, to deliver us into the hand of the Amorites, to destroy us? would to God we had been content, and dwelt on the other side Jordan!

1 K 17:18 And she said unto Elijah, What have I to do with thee, O thou man of God? art thou come unto me to call my sin to remembrance, and to slay my son?

2 K 3:10 And the king of Israel said, Alas! that the LORD hath called these three kings together, to deliver them into the hand of Moab!

Ps 77:3 I remembered God, and was troubled: I complained, and my spirit was overwhelmed. Selah.

Ps 106:25 But murmured in their tents, *and* hearkened not unto the voice of the LORD.

Ac 13:18 And about the time of forty years suffered he their manners in the wilderness.

1 Co 10:10 Neither murmur ye, as some of them also murmured, and were destroyed of the destroyer.

Jude 16 These are murmurers, complainers, walking after their own lusts; and their mouth speaketh great swelling *words,* having men's persons in admiration because of advantage.

See **DISCONTENTMENT**

MURRAIN, *or pestilence, the plague of*
Ex 9:3; Ps 78:50

See **MIRACLES, JUDGMENTS**

MUSIC, *the art of combining notes to make melody, harmony and rhythm*

1. Musical Instruments

Ge 4:21; 31:27; 1 S 10:5; 18:6; 2 S 6:5; 1 K 10:12; 1 Chr 16:42; 23:5; 2 Chr 5:12; 7:6; 30:21; Ne 12:36; Jb 21:12; Ps 150:4; Ec 2:8; Is 5:12; Da 3:7; 6:18; Am 6:5; 1 Co 14:7

2. Names

a. Cornet, or Horn
Ps 98:6; Ho 5:8

b. Cymbals
2 S 6:5; 1 Chr 15:16; 16:5; 2 Chr 29:25; Ezr 3:10; Ps 150:5; 1 Co 13:1

c. Dulcimer
Da 3:5

d. Flute
Da 3:5

e. Harps

Ge 4:21; 1 S 16:16, 23; 2 S 6:5; 1 K 10:12; 1 Chr 13:8; 15:21; 16:5; 25:3; 2 Chr 9:11; Ne 12:27; Jb 21:12; Ps 33:2; 43:4; 49:4; 57:8; 81:2; 92:3; 98:5; 108:2; 137:2; 147:7; 149:3; 150:3; Is 5:12; 23:16; Eze 26:13; Da 3:5, 15; Re 5:8; 14:2; 15:2

f. Organs

Ge 4:21

g. Pipes, or Flutes

Ge 4:21; Jb 21:12; 30:31; Ps 150:4; Mt 11:17; Lu 7:32

h. Psalteries, Stringed Instruments

1 S 10:5; 2 S 6:5; 1 Chr 13:8; 15:20; 16:5; 25:1; 2 Chr 5:12; 9:11; Ps 33:2; 71:22; 81:2; 92:3; 108:2; 144:9; 150:3; Da 3:5, 15

i. Sackbut

Da 3:5

j. Tabrets

Ge 31:27; 1 S 10:5; 1 S 18:6; Is 5:12; 24:8; 30:32; Eze 28:13

k. Timbrels, or Tambourines

Ex 15:20; Jud 11:34; 2 S 6:5; Jb 21:12; Ps 68:25; 81:2; 149:3; 150:4

l. Trumpets

1). Used in War

Nu 10:9; 31:6; Jos 6:4, 13, 20; Jud 3:27; 6:34; 7:8, 16; 1 S 13:3; 2 S 2:28; 15:10; 18:16; 20:1, 22; 2 Chr 13:12; Ne 4:20; Jb 39:24; Is 18:3; Je 4:19; 6:1; 42:14; 51:27; Eze 7:14; 33:3; Ho 5:8; Jl 2:1; Am 3:6; Zep 1:16; 1 Co 14:8

2). Used in Worship and Celebrations

Le 25:9; Nu 10:2, 10; 2 S 6:15; 1 K 1:34, 39; 2 K 9:13; 11:14; 1 Chr 15:24; 16:6; 2 Chr 5:12; 7:6; 15:14; 20:28; 23:13; 29:26–27; Ezr 3:10; Ne 12:35; Ps 47:5; 81:3; 98:6; 150:3; Is 27:13; Ho 8:1; Jl 2:15; 1 Co 15:52; 1 Th 4:16

m. Viols, or Stringed Instruments

Is 14:11; Am 5:23

3. Full Orchestra

2 S 6:5; 1 Chr 13:8; 15:28; 16:42; 23:5; 25:1, 6; 2 Chr 5:12; 20:28; 29:25, 27; Ezr 3:10; Ne 12:27; Ps 68:25; 98:6; Da 3:5, 10

4. Musicians

Ge 4:21 And his brother's name *was* Jubal: he was the father of all such as handle the harp and organ.

1 S 16:16 Let our lord now command thy servants, *which are* before thee, to seek out a man, *who is* a cunning player on an harp: and it shall come to pass, when the evil spirit from God is upon thee, that he shall play with his hand, and thou shalt be well.

1 Chr 25:7 So the number of them, with their brethren that were instructed in the songs of the LORD, *even* all that were cunning, was two hundred fourscore and eight.

2 Chr 34:12 And the men did the work faithfully: and the overseers of them *were* Jahath and Obadiah, the Levites, of the sons of Merari; and Zechariah and Meshullam, of the sons of the Kohathites, to set *it* forward; and *other of* the Levites, all that could skill of instruments of musick.

Mt 9:23 And when Jesus came into the ruler's house, and saw the minstrels and the people making a noise,

Re 18:22 And the voice of harpers, and musicians, and of pipers, and trumpeters, shall be heard no more at all in thee; and no craftsman, of whatsoever craft *he be,* shall be found any more in thee; and the sound of a millstone shall be heard no more at all in thee;

Players on Instruments

1 S 16:16 Let our lord now command thy servants, *which are* before thee, to seek out a man, *who is* a cunning player on an harp: and it shall come to pass, when the evil spirit from God is upon thee, that he shall play with his hand, and thou shalt be well.

1 S 18:10 And it came to pass on the morrow, that the evil spirit from God came upon Saul, and he prophesied in the midst of the house: and David played with his hand, as at other times: and *there was* a javelin in Saul's hand.

2 K 3:15 But now bring me a minstrel. And it came to pass, when the minstrel played, that the hand of the LORD came upon him.

Ps 68:25 The singers went before, the players on instruments *followed* after; among *them were* the damsels playing with timbrels.

Eze 33:32 And, lo, thou *art* unto them as a very lovely song of one that hath a pleasant voice, and can play well on an instrument: for they hear thy words, but they do them not.

5. Singing

a. A Religious Duty

Ps 13:6 I will sing unto the LORD, because he hath dealt bountifully with me.

Ps 27:6 And now shall mine head be lifted up above mine enemies round about me: therefore will I offer in his tabernacle sacrifices of joy; I will sing, yea, I will sing praises unto the LORD.

Ps 81:1 Sing aloud unto God our strength: make a joyful noise unto the God of Jacob.

Ps 95:1 O come, let us sing unto the LORD: let us make a joyful noise to the rock of our salvation.

Ps 126:2 Then was our mouth filled with laughter, and our tongue with singing: then said they among the heathen, The LORD hath done great things for them.

Is 30:29 Ye shall have a song, as in the night *when* a holy solemnity is kept; and gladness of heart, as when one goeth with a pipe to come into the mountain of the LORD, to the mighty One of Israel.

1 Co 14:15 What is it then? I will pray with the spirit, and I will pray with the understanding also: I will sing with the spirit, and I will sing with the understanding also.

Ep 5:19 Speaking to yourselves in psalms and hymns and spiritual songs, singing and making melody in your heart to the Lord;

Col 3:16 Let the word of Christ dwell in you richly in all wisdom; teaching and admonishing one another in psalms and hymns and spiritual songs, singing with grace in your hearts to the Lord.

Ja 5:13 Is any among you afflicted? let him pray. Is any merry? let him sing psalms.

b. Examples

Nu 21:17 Then Israel sang this song, Spring up, O well; sing ye unto it:

2 Chr 20:22 And when they began to sing and to praise, the LORD set ambushments against the children of Ammon, Moab, and mount Seir, which were come against Judah; and they were smitten.

Ezr 3:11 And they sang together by course in praising and giving thanks unto the LORD; because *he is* good, for his mercy *endureth* for ever toward Israel. And all the people shouted with a great shout, when they praised the LORD, because the foundation of the house of the LORD was laid.

Is 65:14 Behold, my servants shall sing for joy of heart, but ye shall cry for sorrow of heart, and shall howl for vexation of spirit.

Mk 14:26 And when they had sung an hymn, they went out into the mount of Olives.

Ac 16:25 And at midnight Paul and Silas prayed, and sang praises unto God: and the prisoners heard them.

Re 5:9 And they sung a new song, saying, Thou art worthy to take the book, and to open the seals thereof: for thou wast slain, and hast redeemed us to God by thy blood out of every kindred, and tongue, and people, and nation;

6. Ancient Choirs

REGULARLY EMPLOYED

1 Chr 9:33 And these *are* the singers, chief of the fathers of the Levites, *who remaining* in the chambers *were* free: for they were employed in that work day and night.

ASSISTED BY AN ORCHESTRA

1 Chr 15:16 And David spake to the chief of the Levites to appoint their brethren *to be* the singers with instruments of musick, psalteries and harps and cymbals, sounding, by lifting up the voice with joy.

VESTED CHOIR

1 Chr 15:27 And David *was* clothed with a robe of fine linen, and all the Levites that bare the ark, and the singers, and Chenaniah the master of the song with the singers: David also *had* upon him an ephod of linen.

GREAT CHORUS CHOIR

1 Chr 25:5–7 All these *were* the sons of Heman the king's seer in the words of God, to lift up the horn. And God gave to Heman fourteen sons and three daughters.

All these *were* under the hands of their father for song *in* the house of the Lord, with cymbals, psalteries, and harps, for the service of the house of God, according to the king's order to Asaph, Jeduthun, and Heman.

So the number of them, with their brethren that were instructed in the songs of the Lord, *even* all that were cunning, was two hundred fourscore and eight.

MILITANT CHOIR

2 Chr 20:21 And when he had consulted with the people, he appointed singers unto the Lord, and that should praise the beauty of holiness, as they went out before the army, and to say, Praise the Lord; for his mercy *endureth* for ever.

2 Chr 23:13 And she looked, and, behold, the king stood at his pillar at the entering in, and the princes and the trumpets by the king: and all the people of the land rejoiced, and sounded with trumpets, also the singers with instruments of musick, and such as taught to sing praise. Then Athaliah rent her clothes, and said, Treason, Treason.

2 Chr 35:15 And the singers the sons of Asaph *were* in their place, according to the commandment of David, and Asaph, and Heman, and Jeduthun the king's seer; and the porters *waited* at every gate; they might not depart from their service; for their brethren the Levites prepared for them.

Ezr 2:65 Beside their servants and their maids, of whom *there were* seven thousand three hundred thirty and seven: and *there were* among them two hundred singing men and singing women.

Ne 12:42 And Maaseiah, and Shemaiah, and Eleazar, and Uzzi, and Jehohanan, and Malchijah, and Elam, and Ezer. And the singers sang loud, with Jezrahiah *their* overseer.

Ec 2:8 I gathered me also silver and gold, and the peculiar treasure of kings and of the provinces: I gat me men singers and women singers, and the delights of the sons of men, *as* musical instruments, and that of all sorts.

7. Songs

a. Idle

Jb 30:9; Ps 69:12; Ec 7:5; Lam 3:14, 63; Am 5:23; 6:5; 8:10

b. In the Night

Jb 35:10; Ps 42:8; 77:6; 149:5; Is 30:29; Ac 16:25

c. Of Victory

Ex 15:1, 21; Jud 5:1, 12; 1 S 18:7; 2 S 22:1; Ps 32:7; 105:43; 106:12; Is 14:7; 26:1; Je 51:48; Ho 2:15; Re 14:3; 15:3

See **PRAISE TO GOD, WORSHIP**

MUSTARD SEED, *minute seeds, from a common plant*

Mt 13:31; 17:20; Mk 4:31; Lu 13:19; 17:6

MUTABILITY, *of material things*

Jb 14:18 And surely the mountain falling cometh to nought, and the rock is removed out of his place.

Ps 102:25–26 Of old hast thou laid the foundation of the earth: and the heavens *are* the work of thy hands.

They shall perish, but thou shalt endure: yea, all of them shall wax old like a garment; as a vesture shalt thou change them, and they shall be changed:

Is 24:4 The earth mourneth *and* fadeth away, the world languisheth *and* fadeth away, the haughty people of the earth do languish.

Is 34:4 And all the host of heaven shall be dissolved, and the heavens shall be rolled together as a scroll: and all their host shall fall down, as the leaf falleth off from the vine, and as a falling *fig* from the fig tree.

Is 50:9 Behold, the Lord GOD will help me; who *is* he *that* shall condemn me? lo, they all shall wax old as a garment; the moth shall eat them up.

Is 51:6 Lift up your eyes to the heavens, and look upon the earth beneath: for the heavens shall vanish away like smoke, and the earth shall wax old like a garment, and they that dwell therein shall die in like manner: but my salvation shall be for ever, and my righteousness shall not be abolished.

Is 54:10 For the mountains shall depart, and the hills be removed; but my kindness shall not depart from thee, neither shall the covenant of my peace be removed, saith the LORD that hath mercy on thee.

Jona 4:7 But God prepared a worm when the morning rose the next day, and it smote the gourd that it withered.

Mt 6:30 Wherefore, if God so clothe the grass of the field, which to day is, and to morrow is cast into the oven, *shall he* not much more *clothe* you, O ye of little faith?

Mt 24:2 And Jesus said unto them, See ye not all these things? verily I say unto you, There shall not be left here one stone upon another, that shall not be thrown down.

Mt 24:35 Heaven and earth shall pass away, but my words shall not pass away.

Mk 13:2 And Jesus answering said unto him, Seest thou these great buildings? there shall not be left one stone upon another, that shall not be thrown down.

Mk 13:31 Heaven and earth shall pass away: but my words shall not pass away.

Lu 21:6 *As for* these things which ye behold, the days will come, in the which there shall not be left one stone upon another, that shall not be thrown down.

Lu 21:33 Heaven and earth shall pass away: but my words shall not pass away.

Jn 4:21 Jesus saith unto her, Woman, believe me, the hour cometh, when ye shall neither in this mountain, nor yet at Jerusalem, worship the Father.

1 Co 7:31 And they that use this world, as not abusing *it:* for the fashion of this world passeth away.

2 Co 4:18 While we look not at the things which are seen, but at the things which are not seen: for the things which are seen *are* temporal; but the things which are not seen *are* eternal.

He 1:11 They shall perish; but thou remainest; and they all shall wax old as doth a garment;

He 12:27 And this *word,* Yet once more, signifieth the removing of those things that are shaken, as of things that are made, that those things which cannot be shaken may remain.

2 Pe 3:10 But the day of the Lord will come as a thief in the night; in the which the heavens shall pass away with a great noise, and the elements shall melt with fervent heat, the earth also and the works that are therein shall be burned up.

1 Jn 2:17 And the world passeth away, and the lust thereof: but he that doeth the will of God abideth for ever.

Re 6:14 And the heaven departed as a scroll when it is rolled together; and every mountain and island were moved out of their places.

Re 18:19 And they cast dust on their heads, and cried, weeping and wailing, saying, Alas, alas, that great city, wherein were made rich all that had ships in the sea by reason of her costliness! for in one hour is she made desolate.

Re 20:11 And I saw a great white throne, and him that sat on it, from whose face the earth and the heaven fled away; and there was found no place for them.

Re 21:1 And I saw a new heaven and a new earth: for the first heaven and the first earth were passed away; and there was no more sea.

See **IMMUTABILITY**

MUTILATION, *OF THE BODY*

Le 19:28; 21:5; De 14:1; Jud 1:6; 16:21; 2 S 4:12; 1 K 18:28; Je 41:5; 47:5; 48:37; Eze 23:25; Mk 5:5

See **BEAUTY, BODY**

MUTINY, *open rebellion*

Nu 14:4

See **REBELLION**

MUZZLING, *OF OXEN*

De 25:4; 1 Co 9:9; 1 Ti 5:18

See **MONEY**

MYRRH, *an odorous gum*

Ge 37:25; 43:11; Ex 30:23; Est 2:12; Ps 45:8; Song 1:13; 4:6, 14; Mt 2:11; Mk 15:23; Jn 19:39

MYRTLE   *See* **TREES**

MYSTERIES

1. Concerning Faith

OF THE PROSPERITY OF THE WICKED

Je 12:1 Righteous *art* thou, O LORD, when I plead with thee: yet let me talk with thee of *thy* judgments: Wherefore doth the way of the wicked prosper? *wherefore* are all they happy that deal very treacherously?

OF THE NEW BIRTH

Jn 3:8 The wind bloweth where it listeth, and thou hearest the sound thereof, but canst not tell whence it cometh, and whither it goeth: so is every one that is born of the Spirit.

OF PROVIDENCE

Ro 11:33 O the depth of the riches both of the wisdom and knowledge of

God! how unsearchable *are* his judgments, and his ways past finding out!

OF THE FUTURE LIFE

1 Co 15:51 Behold, I shew you a mystery; We shall not all sleep, but we shall all be changed,

OF THE UNION OF CHRIST WITH THE CHURCH

Ep 5:32 This is a great mystery: but I speak concerning Christ and the church.

OF THE INCARNATION

1 Ti 3:16 And without controversy great is the mystery of godliness: God was manifest in the flesh, justified in the Spirit, seen of angels, preached unto the Gentiles, believed on in the world, received up into glory.

OF SUFFERING

He 12:11 Now no chastening for the present seemeth to be joyous, but grievous: nevertheless afterward it yieldeth the peaceable fruit of righteousness unto them which are exercised thereby.

2. Concerning Christ and Redemption

Is 52:15 So shall he sprinkle many nations; the kings shall shut their mouths at him: for *that* which had not been told them shall they see; and *that* which they had not heard shall they consider.

Ro 16:25 Now to him that is of power to stablish you according to my gospel, and the preaching of Jesus Christ, according to the revelation of the mystery, which was kept secret since the world began,

1 Co 2:7 But we speak the wisdom of God in a mystery, *even* the hidden *wisdom*, which God ordained before the world unto our glory:

Ep 1:9 Having made known unto us the mystery of his will, according to his good pleasure which he hath purposed in himself:

Ep 3:4 Whereby, when ye read, ye may understand my knowledge in the mystery of Christ)

Ep 3:9 And to make all *men* see what *is* the fellowship of the mystery, which from the beginning of the world hath been hid in God, who created all things by Jesus Christ:

Col 1:26–27 *Even* the mystery which hath been hid from ages and from generations, but now is made manifest to his saints:

To whom God would make known what *is* the riches of the glory of this mystery among the Gentiles; which is Christ in you, the hope of glory:

Col 2:2 That their hearts might be comforted, being knit together in love, and unto all riches of the full assurance of understanding, to the acknowledgement of the mystery of God, and of the Father, and of Christ;

Col 4:3 Withal praying also for us, that God would open unto us a door of utterance, to speak the mystery of Christ, for which I am also in bonds:

1 Ti 3:16 And without controversy great is the mystery of godliness: God was manifest in the flesh, justified in the Spirit, seen of angels, preached unto the Gentiles, believed on in the world, received up into glory.

3. Concerning God

Jb 5:9 Which doeth great things and unsearchable; marvellous things without number:

Jb 11:7 Canst thou by searching find out God? canst thou find out the Almighty unto perfection?

Jb 33:13 Why dost thou strive against him? for he giveth not account of any of his matters.

Jb 37:23 *Touching* the Almighty, we cannot find him out: *he is* excellent in power, and in judgment, and in plenty of justice: he will not afflict.

Ec 3:11 He hath made every *thing* beautiful in his time: also he hath set the world in their heart, so that no man can find out the work that God maketh from the beginning to the end.

Ec 8:17 Then I beheld all the work of God, that a man cannot find out the work that is done under the sun: because though a man labour to seek *it* out, yet he shall not find *it;* yea fur-

ther; though a wise *man* think to know *it,* yet shall he not be able to find *it.*

Is 40:28 Hast thou not known? hast thou not heard, *that* the everlasting God, the Lord, the Creator of the ends of the earth, fainteth not, neither is weary? *there is* no searching of his understanding.

Je 23:18 For who hath stood in the counsel of the Lord, and hath perceived and heard his word? who hath marked his word, and heard *it?*

Ro 11:34 For who hath known the mind of the Lord? or who hath been his counsellor?

1 Co 2:16 For who hath known the mind of the Lord, that he may instruct him? But we have the mind of Christ.

4. Deity Veiled, God spoken of as hiding himself

Ex 19:9 And the Lord said unto Moses, Lo, I come unto thee in a thick cloud, that the people may hear when I speak with thee, and believe thee for ever. And Moses told the words of the people unto the Lord.

1 K 8:12 Then spake Solomon, The Lord said that he would dwell in thick darkness.

2 Chr 6:1 Then said Solomon, The Lord hath said that he would dwell in the thick darkness.

Jb 23:9 On the left hand, where he doth work, but I cannot behold *him:* he hideth himself on the right hand, that I cannot see *him:*

Ps 10:1 Why standest thou afar off, O Lord? *why* hidest thou *thyself* in times of trouble?

Ps 13:1 How long wilt thou forget me, O Lord? for ever? how long wilt thou hide thy face from me?

Ps 89:46 How long, Lord? wilt thou hide thyself for ever? shall thy wrath burn like fire?

Is 45:15 Verily thou *art* a God that hidest thyself, O God of Israel, the Saviour.

Ac 17:27 That they should seek the Lord, if haply they might feel after him, and find him, though he be not far from every one of us:

5. Concerning Invisibility

Ex 3:6 Moreover he said, I *am* the God of thy father, the God of Abraham, the God of Isaac, and the God of Jacob. And Moses hid his face; for he was afraid to look upon God.

Ex 33:20 And he said, Thou canst not see my face: for there shall no man see me, and live.

Jb 9:11 Lo, he goeth by me, and I see *him* not: he passeth on also, but I perceive him not.

Jb 23:8 Behold, I go forward, but he *is* not *there;* and backward, but I cannot perceive him:

Jn 1:18 No man hath seen God at any time; the only begotten Son, which is in the bosom of the Father, he hath declared *him.*

Jn 5:37 And the Father himself, which hath sent me, hath borne witness of me. Ye have neither heard his voice at any time, nor seen his shape.

Col 1:15 Who is the image of the invisible God, the firstborn of every creature:

1 Ti 1:17 Now unto the King eternal, immortal, invisible, the only wise God, *be* honour and glory for ever and ever. Amen.

1 Ti 6:16 Who only hath immortality, dwelling in the light which no man can approach unto; whom no man hath seen, nor can see: to whom *be* honour and power everlasting. Amen.

1 Jn 4:12 No man hath seen God at any time. If we love one another, God dwelleth in us, and his love is perfected in us.

6. Concerning Knowledge

a. Reasons for Withholding

BECAUSE PERILOUS

Ge 2:17 But of the tree of the knowledge of good and evil, thou shalt not eat of it: for in the day that thou eatest thereof thou shalt surely die.

De 29:29 The secret *things belong* unto the LORD our God: but *those things which* are revealed *belong* unto us and to our children for ever, that *we* may do all the words of this law.

INABILITY TO APPREHEND TRUTH

Jn 13:7 Jesus answered and said unto him, What I do thou knowest not now; but thou shalt know hereafter.

HUMAN WEAKNESS NECESSITATES

Jn 16:12 I have yet many things to say unto you, but ye cannot bear them now.

EARTHLY LIMITATIONS FETTER

1 Co 13:12 For now we see through a glass, darkly; but then face to face: now I know in part; but then shall I know even as also I am known.

GRADUAL REVELATION, THE DIVINE PLAN

Ep 3:5 Which in other ages was not made known unto the sons of men, as it is now revealed unto his holy apostles and prophets by the Spirit;

TO GIVE OPPORTUNITY FOR FAITH

1 Jn 3:2 Beloved, now are we the sons of God, and it doth not yet appear what we shall be: but we know that, when he shall appear, we shall be like him; for we shall see him as he is.

b. Ignorance of the Future

Ge 27:2 And he said, Behold now, I am old, I know not the day of my death:

Ps 74:9 We see not our signs: *there is* no more any prophet: neither *is there* among us any that knoweth how long.

Pr 27:1 Boast not thyself of to morrow; for thou knowest not what a day may bring forth.

Ec 3:22 Wherefore I perceive that *there is* nothing better, than that a man should rejoice in his own works; for that *is* his portion: for who shall bring him to see what shall be after him?

Ec 6:12 For who knoweth what *is* good for man in *this* life, all the days of his vain life which he spendeth as a shadow? for who can tell a man what shall be after him under the sun?

Ec 8:7 For he knoweth not that which shall be: for who can tell him when it shall be?

Ec 9:12 For man also knoweth not his time: as the fishes that are taken in an evil net, and as the birds that are caught in the snare; so *are* the sons of men snared in an evil time, when it falleth suddenly upon them.

Ec 10:14 A fool also is full of words: a man cannot tell what shall be; and what shall be after him, who can tell him?

Ec 11:2 Give a portion to seven, and also to eight; for thou knowest not what evil shall be upon the earth.

Ec 11:6 In the morning sow thy seed, and in the evening withhold not thine hand: for thou knowest not whether shall prosper, either this or that, or whether they both *shall be* alike good.

Is 41:23 Shew the things that are to come hereafter, that we may know that ye *are* gods: yea, do good, or do evil, that we may be dismayed, and behold *it* together.

Mt 24:43 But know this, that if the goodman of the house had known in what watch the thief would come, he would have watched, and would not have suffered his house to be broken up.

Mt 25:13 Watch therefore, for ye know neither the day nor the hour wherein the Son of man cometh.

Mk 13:35 Watch ye therefore: for ye know not when the master of the house cometh, at even, or at midnight, or at the cockcrowing, or in the morning:

Ac 20:22 And now, behold, I go bound in the spirit unto Jerusalem, not knowing the things that shall befall me there:

Ro 15:28 When therefore I have performed this, and have sealed to them this fruit, I will come by you into Spain.

1 Co 13:12 For now we see through a glass, darkly; but then face to face: now I know in part; but then shall I know even as also I am known.

Ph 2:23 Him therefore I hope to send presently, so soon as I shall see how it will go with me.

Ja 4:14 Whereas ye know not what *shall be* on the morrow. For what *is* your life? It is even a vapour, that appeareth for a little time, and then vanisheth away.

Re 3:3 Remember therefore how thou hast received and heard, and hold fast, and repent. If therefore thou shalt not watch, I will come on thee as a thief, and thou shalt not know what hour I will come upon thee.

c. Secret Things Belong to God

De 29:29 The secret *things belong* unto the LORD our God: but *those things which* are revealed *belong* unto us and to our children for ever, that *we* may do all the words of this law.

Jb 9:10 Which doeth great things past finding out; yea, and wonders without number.

Jb 10:13 And these *things* hast thou hid in thine heart: I know that this *is* with thee.

Ps 25:14 The secret of the LORD *is* with them that fear him; and he will shew them his covenant.

Pr 25:2 *It is* the glory of God to conceal a thing: but the honour of kings *is* to search out a matter.

Is 52:15 So shall he sprinkle many nations; the kings shall shut their mouths at him: for *that* which had not been told them shall they see; and *that* which they had not heard shall they consider.

Da 2:29 As for thee, O king, thy thoughts came *into thy mind* upon thy bed, what should come to pass hereafter: and he that revealeth secrets maketh known to thee what shall come to pass.

Da 2:47 The king answered unto Daniel, and said, Of a truth *it is,* that your God is a God of gods, and a Lord of kings, and a revealer of secrets, seeing thou couldst reveal this secret.

Da 8:27 And I Daniel fainted, and was sick *certain* days; afterward I rose up, and did the king's business; and I was astonished at the vision, but none understood *it.*

Da 12:9 And he said, Go thy way, Daniel: for the words *are* closed up and sealed till the time of the end.

Mk 13:32 But of that day and *that* hour knoweth no man, no, not the angels which are in heaven, neither the Son, but the Father.

Re 5:3 And no man in heaven, nor in earth, neither under the earth, was able to open the book, neither to look thereon.

Re 10:4 And when the seven thunders had uttered their voices, I was about to write: and I heard a voice from heaven saying unto me, Seal up those things which the seven thunders uttered, and write them not.

See **IGNORANCE, KNOWLEDGE, LIMITATIONS, REVELATIONS, SECRETS**

N

NAAMAN, *chief captain of Benhadad, healed of leprosy by Elisha*

2 K 5:1; Lu 4:27

NABAL, *refuses food for David and his soldiers*

1 S 25:10

NABOTH, *the Jezreelite, murdered by Jezebel*

1 K 21:1; 2 K 9:21

NADAB, *king of Israel, son of Jeroboam II*

Nu 3:2; 1 K 14:20; 15:25

See **ISRAEL**

NAHASH, *oracle*

1 S 11:1-2; 12:12; 10:2; 17:25; 17:27; 1 Chr 4:12; 19:1-2

NAHOR

1. Grandfather of Abraham

Ge 11:22, 25; 1 Chr 1:26

2. Brother of Abraham

Ge 11:27; 22:20; 24:10, 15; 31:53

NAHUM

Author: Uncertain. Probably Nahum. The name Nahum means "compassionate" or "full of comfort."

Date Written: Sometime before the fall of Nineveh (612 B.C.) and after the fall of Thebes (664 B.C.) (3:8–10). This book is regarded by some scholars as a sequel to Jonah. It would appear that the Assyrians, after their repentance at the preaching of Jonah, soon relapsed into gross idolatry. They plundered other nations, and their capital became like a lions' den full of prey (2:11–12).

Purpose: To pronounce divine vengeance upon the bloody city and to console Judah with promises of future deliverance (3:1; 1:13–15).

To Whom Written: God's people in Judah and the inhabitants of Nineveh.

Main Theme: The destruction of Nineveh.

Key Word: Judgment.

Key Verses: 1:7–9.

NAILS

1 Chr 22:3; 2 Chr 3:9; Is 22:23

NAME, *reflection of one's character*

1. Good

Ru 2:11 And Boaz answered and said unto her, It hath fully been shewed me, all that thou hast done unto thy mother in law since the death of thine husband: and *how* thou hast left thy father and thy mother, and the land of thy nativity, and art come unto a people which thou knewest not heretofore.

Ru 3:11 And now, my daughter, fear not; I will do to thee all that thou requirest: for all the city of my people doth know that thou *art* a virtuous woman.

1 S 3:20 And all Israel from Dan even to Beer-sheba knew that Samuel *was* established *to be* a prophet of the LORD.

1 S 16:18 Then answered one of the servants, and said, Behold, I have seen a son of Jesse the Bethlehemite, *that is* cunning in playing, and a mighty valiant man, and a man of war, and prudent in matters, and a comely person, and the LORD *is* with him.

1 S 18:30 Then the princes of the Philistines went forth: and it came to pass, after they went forth, *that* David behaved himself more wisely than all the servants of Saul; so that his name was much set by.

1 S 22:14 Then Ahimelech answered the king, and said, And who *is so* faithful among all thy servants as David, which is the king's son in law, and goeth at thy bidding, and is honourable in thine house?

Pr 11:26 He that withholdeth corn, the people shall curse him: but blessing *shall be* upon the head of him that selleth *it.*

Pr 12:8 A man shall be commended according to his wisdom: but he that is of a perverse heart shall be despised.

Pr 22:1 A *good* name *is* rather to be chosen than great riches, *and* loving favour rather than silver and gold.

Ec 7:1 A good name *is* better than precious ointment; and the day of death than the day of one's birth.

Da 5:12 Forasmuch as an excellent spirit, and knowledge, and understanding, interpreting of dreams, and shewing of hard sentences, and dissolving of doubts, were found in the same Daniel, whom the king named Belteshazzar: now let Daniel be called, and he will shew the interpretation.

Lu 7:4 And when they came to Jesus, they besought him instantly, saying, That he was worthy for whom he should do this:

Ac 5:34 Then stood there up one in the council, a Pharisee, named Gamaliel, a doctor of the law, had in reputation among all the people, and commanded to put the apostles forth a little space;

Ac 6:3 Wherefore, brethren, look ye out among you seven men of honest report, full of the Holy Ghost and wisdom, whom we may appoint over this business.

Ac 10:22 And they said, Cornelius the centurion, a just man, and one that feareth God, and of good report among all the nation of the Jews, was warned from God by an holy angel to send for thee into his house, and to hear words of thee.

Ac 16:2 Which was well reported of by the brethren that were at Lystra and Iconium.

Ac 22:12 And one Ananias, a devout man according to the law, having a good report of all the Jews which dwelt *there,*

Ro 14:18 For he that in these things serveth Christ *is* acceptable to God, and approved of men.

Ro 16:7 Salute Andronicus and Junia, my kinsmen, and my fellowprisoners, who are of note among the apostles, who also were in Christ before me.

Ro 16:19 For your obedience is come abroad unto all *men.* I am glad therefore on your behalf: but yet I would have you wise unto that which is good, and simple concerning evil.

2 Co 8:18 And we have sent with him the brother, whose praise is in the gospel throughout all the churches;

1 Ti 3:7 Moreover he must have a good report of them which are without; lest he fall into reproach and the snare of the devil.

1 Ti 5:10 Well reported of for good works; if she have brought up children, if she have lodged strangers, if she have washed the saints' feet, if she have relieved the afflicted, if she have diligently followed every good work.

He 11:39 And these all, having obtained a good report through faith, received not the promise:

3 Jn 3 For I rejoiced greatly, when the brethren came and testified of the truth that is in thee, even as thou walkest in the truth.

3 Jn 12 Demetrius hath good report of all *men,* and of the truth itself: yea, and we *also* bear record; and ye know that our record is true.

2. Mighty

Ex 23:21 Beware of him, and obey his voice, provoke him not; for he will not pardon your transgressions: for my name *is* in him.

Ex 33:19 And he said, I will make all my goodness pass before thee, and I will proclaim the name of the LORD before thee; and will be gracious to whom I will be gracious, and will shew mercy on whom I will shew mercy.

Ex 34:5 And the LORD descended in the cloud, and stood with him there, and proclaimed the name of the LORD.

De 32:3 Because I will publish the name of the LORD: ascribe ye greatness unto our God.

Jos 9:9 And they said unto him, From a very far country thy servants are come because of the name of the LORD thy God: for we have heard the fame of him, and all that he did in Egypt,

1 S 17:45 Then said David to the Philistine, Thou comest to me with a sword, and with a spear, and with a shield: but I come to thee in the name of the LORD of hosts, the God of the armies of Israel, whom thou hast defied.

2 S 7:23 And what one nation in the earth *is* like thy people, *even* like Israel, whom God went to redeem for a people to himself, and to make him a name, and to do for you great things and terrible, for thy land, before thy people, which thou redeemedst to thee from Egypt, *from* the nations and their gods?

1 K 8:29 That thine eyes may be open toward this house night and day, *even* toward the place of which thou hast said, My name shall be there: that thou mayest hearken unto the prayer which thy servant shall make toward this place.

1 K 9:3 And the LORD said unto him, I have heard thy prayer and thy supplication, that thou hast made before me: I have hallowed this house, which thou hast built, to put my name there for ever; and mine eyes and mine heart shall be there perpetually.

1 K 10:1 And when the queen of Sheba heard of the fame of Solomon concerning the name of the LORD, she came to prove him with hard questions.

1 Chr 16:10 Glory ye in his holy name: let the heart of them rejoice that seek the LORD.

1 Chr 17:21 And what one nation in the earth *is* like thy people Israel, whom God went to redeem *to be* his own people, to make thee a name of greatness and terribleness, by driving out nations from before thy people, whom thou hast redeemed out of Egypt?

1 Chr 22:19 Now set your heart and your soul to seek the LORD your God; arise therefore, and build ye the sanctuary of the LORD God, to bring the ark of the covenant of the LORD, and the holy vessels of God, into the house that is to be built to the name of the LORD.

1 Chr 29:13 Now therefore, our God, we thank thee, and praise thy glorious name.

2 Chr 6:7 Now it was in the heart of David my father to build an house for the name of the LORD God of Israel.

2 Chr 14:11 And Asa cried unto the LORD his God, and said, LORD, *it is* nothing with thee to help, whether with many, or with them that have no power: help us, O LORD our God; for we rest on thee, and in thy name we go against this multitude. O LORD, thou *art* our God; let not man prevail against thee.

Ezr 6:12 And the God that hath caused his name to dwell there destroy all kings and people, that shall put to their hand to alter *and* to destroy this house of God which is at Jerusalem. I Darius have made a decree; let it be done with speed.

Ne 9:5 Then the Levites, Jeshua, and Kadmiel, Bani, Hashabniah, Sherebiah, Hodijah, Shebaniah, *and* Pethahiah, said, Stand up *and* bless the LORD your God for ever and ever: and blessed be thy glorious name, which is exalted above all blessing and praise.

Ps 8:9 O LORD our Lord, how excellent is thy name in all the earth!

Ps 20:1 The LORD hear thee in the day of trouble; the name of the God of Jacob defend thee;

Ps 20:5 We will rejoice in thy salvation, and in the name of our God we will set up *our* banners: the LORD fulfil all thy petitions.

Ps 33:21 For our heart shall rejoice in him, because we have trusted in his holy name.

Ps 48:10 According to thy name, O God, so *is* thy praise unto the ends of the earth: thy right hand is full of righteousness.

Ps 52:9 I will praise thee for ever, because thou hast done *it:* and I will wait on thy name; for *it is* good before thy saints.

Ps 54:1 Save me, O God, by thy name, and judge me by thy strength.

Ps 72:19 And blessed *be* his glorious name for ever: and let the whole earth be filled *with* his glory; Amen, and Amen.

Ps 76:1 In Judah *is* God known: his name *is* great in Israel.

Ps 102:21 To declare the name of the LORD in Zion, and his praise in Jerusalem;

Ps 113:3 From the rising of the sun unto the going down of the same the LORD's name *is* to be praised.

Ps 118:12 They compassed me about like bees; they are quenched as the fire of thorns: for in the name of the LORD I will destroy them.

Ps 118:26 Blessed *be* he that cometh in the name of the LORD: we have blessed you out of the house of the LORD.

Ps 135:1 Praise ye the LORD. Praise ye the name of the LORD; praise *him,* O ye servants of the LORD.

Ps 135:13 Thy name, O LORD, *endureth* for ever; *and* thy memorial, O LORD, throughout all generations.

Ps 148:13 Let them praise the name of the LORD: for his name alone is excellent; his glory *is* above the earth and heaven.

Pr 18:10 The name of the LORD *is* a strong tower: the righteous runneth into it, and is safe.

Is 12:4 And in that day shall ye say, Praise the LORD, call upon his name, declare his doings among the people, make mention that his name is exalted.

Is 24:15 Wherefore glorify ye the LORD in the fires, *even* the LORD God of Israel in the isles of the sea.

Is 26:8 Yea, in the way of thy judgments, O LORD, have we waited for thee; the desire of *our* soul *is* to thy name, and to the remembrance of thee.

Is 30:27 Behold, the name of the LORD cometh from far, burning *with* his anger, and the burden *thereof is* heavy: his lips are full of indignation, and his tongue as a devouring fire:

Is 42:8 I *am* the LORD: that *is* my name: and my glory will I not give to another, neither my praise to graven images.

Is 48:1 Hear ye this, O house of Jacob, which are called by the name of Israel, and are come forth out of the waters of Judah, which swear by the name of the LORD, and make mention of the God of Israel, *but* not in truth, nor in righteousness.

Is 50:10 Who *is* among you that feareth the LORD, that obeyeth the voice of his servant, that walketh *in* darkness, and hath no light? let him trust in the name of the LORD, and stay upon his God.

Is 56:6 Also the sons of the stranger, that join themselves to the LORD, to serve him, and to love the name of the LORD, to be his servants, every one that keepeth the sabbath from polluting it, and taketh hold of my covenant;

Is 60:9 Surely the isles shall wait for me, and the ships of Tarshish first, to bring thy sons from far, their silver and their gold with them, unto the name of the LORD thy God, and to the Holy One of Israel, because he hath glorified thee.

Is 63:12 That led *them* by the right hand of Moses with his glorious arm, dividing the water before them, to make himself an everlasting name?

Is 64:2 As *when* the melting fire burneth, the fire causeth the waters to boil, to make thy name known to thine adversaries, *that* the nations may tremble at thy presence!

Je 10:6 Forasmuch as *there is* none like unto thee, O LORD; thou *art* great, and thy name is great in might.

Je 32:20 Which hast set signs and wonders in the land of Egypt, *even* unto this day, and in Israel, and among *other* men; and hast made thee a name, as at this day;

Am 4:13 For, lo, he that formeth the mountains, and createth the wind, and declareth unto man what *is* his thought, that maketh the morning darkness, and treadeth upon the high places of the earth, The LORD, The God of hosts, *is* his name.

Mi 5:4 And he shall stand and feed in the strength of the LORD, in the majesty of the name of the LORD his God; and they shall abide: for now shall he be great unto the ends of the earth.

Zep 3:12 I will also leave in the midst of thee an afflicted and poor people, and they shall trust in the name of the LORD.

Mal 1:11 For from the rising of the sun even unto the going down of the same my name *shall be* great among the Gentiles; and in every place incense *shall be* offered unto my name, and a pure offering: for my name *shall be* great among the heathen, saith the LORD of hosts.

Mal 1:14 But cursed *be* the deceiver, which hath in his flock a male, and voweth, and sacrificeth unto the LORD a corrupt thing: for I *am* a great King, saith the LORD of hosts, and my name *is* dreadful among the heathen.

Mt 23:39 For I say unto you, Ye shall not see me henceforth, till ye shall say, Blessed *is* he that cometh in the name of the Lord.

3. To Be Reverenced

Ex 3:14 And God said unto Moses, I AM THAT I AM: and he said, Thus shalt thou say unto the children of Israel, I AM hath sent me unto you.

Ex 9:16 And in very deed for this *cause* have I raised thee up, for to shew *in* thee my power; and that my name may be declared throughout all the earth.

Ex 20:7 Thou shalt not take the name of the LORD thy God in vain; for the LORD will not hold him guiltless that taketh his name in vain.

Le 22:2 Speak unto Aaron and to his sons, that they separate themselves from the holy things of the children of Israel, and that they profane not my holy name *in those things* which they hallow unto me: I *am* the LORD.

Le 22:32 Neither shall ye profane my holy name; but I will be hallowed among the children of Israel: I *am* the LORD which hallow you,

De 5:11 Thou shalt not take the name of the LORD thy God in vain: for

the LORD will not hold *him* guiltless that taketh his name in vain.

De 28:58 If thou wilt not observe to do all the words of this law that are written in this book, that thou mayest fear this glorious and fearful name, THE LORD THY GOD;

2 S 7:26 And let thy name be magnified for ever, saying, The LORD of hosts *is* the God over Israel: and let the house of thy servant David be established before thee.

1 K 8:42 (For they shall hear of thy great name, and of thy strong hand, and of thy stretched out arm;) when he shall come and pray toward this house;

1 Chr 17:24 Let it even be established, that thy name may be magnified for ever, saying, The LORD of hosts *is* the God of Israel, *even* a God to Israel: and *let* the house of David thy servant *be* established before thee.

2 Chr 33:7 And he set a carved image, the idol which he had made, in the house of God, of which God had said to David and to Solomon his son, In this house, and in Jerusalem, which I have chosen before all the tribes of Israel, will I put my name for ever:

Ne 9:10 And shewedst signs and wonders upon Pharaoh, and on all his servants, and on all the people of his land: for thou knewest that they dealt proudly against them. So didst thou get thee a name, as *it is* this day.

Ps 8:1 O LORD our Lord, how excellent *is* thy name in all the earth! who hast set thy glory above the heavens.

Ps 34:3 O magnify the LORD with me, and let us exalt his name together.

Ps 54:6 I will freely sacrifice unto thee: I will praise thy name, O LORD; for *it is* good.

Ps 61:8 So will I sing praise unto thy name for ever, that I may daily perform my vows.

Ps 74:10 O God, how long shall the adversary reproach? shall the enemy blaspheme thy name for ever?

Ps 99:3 Let them praise thy great and terrible name; *for it is* holy.

Ps 111:9 He sent redemption unto his people: he hath commanded his covenant for ever: holy and reverend *is* his name.

Ps 113:2 Blessed be the name of the LORD from this time forth and for evermore.

Is 29:23 But when he seeth his children, the work of mine hands, in the midst of him, they shall sanctify my name, and sanctify the Holy One of Jacob, and shall fear the God of Israel.

Is 48:11 For mine own sake, *even* for mine own sake, will I do *it:* for how should *my name* I will not give my glory unto another.

Is 57:15 For thus saith the high and lofty One that inhabiteth eternity, whose name *is* Holy; I dwell in the high and holy *place,* with him also *that is* of a contrite and humble spirit, to revive the spirit of the humble, and to revive the heart of the contrite ones.

Je 12:16 And it shall come to pass, if they will diligently learn the ways of my people, to swear by my name, The LORD liveth; as they taught my people to swear by Baal; then shall they be built in the midst of my people.

Je 16:21 Therefore, behold, I will this once cause them to know, I will cause them to know mine hand and my might; and they shall know that my name *is* The LORD.

Je 34:16 But ye turned and polluted my name, and caused every man his servant, and every man his handmaid, whom ye had set at liberty at their pleasure, to return, and brought them into subjection, to be unto you for servants and for handmaids.

Eze 20:9 But I wrought for my name's sake, that it should not be polluted before the heathen, among whom they *were,* in whose sight I made myself known unto them, in bringing them forth out of the land of Egypt.

Eze 20:22 Nevertheless I withdrew mine hand, and wrought for my name's sake, that it should not be polluted in the sight of the heathen, in whose sight I brought them forth.

Eze 20:39 As for you, O house of Israel, thus saith the Lord GOD; Go ye, serve ye every one his idols, and hereafter *also,* if ye will not hearken unto me: but pollute ye my holy name no more with your gifts, and with your idols.

Eze 36:20 And when they entered unto the heathen, whither they went, they profaned my holy name, when they said to them, These *are* the people of the LORD, and are gone land.

Eze 36:23 And I will sanctify my great name, which was profaned among the heathen, which ye have profaned in the midst of them; and the heathen shall know that I *am* the LORD, saith the Lord GOD, when I shall be sanctified in you before their eyes.

Eze 39:7 So will I make my holy name known in the midst of my people Israel; and I will not *let them* pollute my holy name any more: and the heathen shall know that I *am* the LORD, the Holy One in Israel.

Eze 43:7 And he said unto me, Son of man, the place of my throne, and the place of the soles of my feet, where I will dwell in the midst of the children of Israel for ever, and my holy name, shall the house of Israel no more defile, *neither* they, nor their kings, by their whoredom, nor by the carcases of their kings in their high places.

Da 2:20 Daniel answered and said, Blessed be the name of God for ever and ever: for wisdom and might are his:

Am 2:7 That pant after the dust of the earth on the head of the poor, and turn aside the way of the meek: and a man and his father will go in unto the *same* maid, to profane my holy name:

Mt 6:9 After this manner therefore pray ye: Our Father which art in heaven, Hallowed be thy name.

Lu 1:49 For he that is mighty hath done to me great things; and holy *is* his name.

Lu 11:2 And he said unto them, When ye pray, say, Our Father which art in heaven, Hallowed be thy name. Thy kingdom come. Thy will be done, as in heaven, so in earth.

Jn 17:26 And I have declared unto them thy name, and will declare *it:* that the love wherewith thou hast loved me may be in them, and I in them.

Ro 9:17 For the scripture saith unto Pharaoh, Even for this same purpose have I raised thee up, that I might shew my power in thee, and that my name might be declared throughout all the earth.

1 Ti 6:1 Let as many servants as are under the yoke count their own masters worthy of all honour, that the name of God and *his* doctrine be not blasphemed.

Re 16:9 And men were scorched with great heat, and blasphemed the name of God, which hath power over these plagues: and they repented not to give him glory.

4. Christ's

a. Wonderful

Ps 72:17 His name shall endure for ever: his name shall be continued as long as the sun: and *men* shall be blessed in him: all nations shall call him blessed.

Song 1:3 Because of the savour of thy good ointments thy name *is as* ointment poured forth, therefore do the virgins love thee.

Is 9:6 For unto us a child is born, unto us a son is given: and the government shall be upon his shoulder: and his name shall be called Wonderful, Counsellor, The mighty God, The everlasting Father, The Prince of Peace.

Mt 1:21 And she shall bring forth a son, and thou shalt call his name JESUS: for he shall save his people from their sins.

Mt 1:25 And knew her not till she had brought forth her firstborn son: and he called his name JESUS.

Mt 12:21 And in his name shall the Gentiles trust.

Lu 1:31 And, behold, thou shalt conceive in thy womb, and bring forth a son, and shalt call his name JESUS.

Lu 2:21 And when eight days were accomplished for the circumcising of the child, his name was called JESUS, which was so named of the angel before he was conceived in the womb.

Ac 2:38 Then Peter said unto them, Repent, and be baptized every one of you in the name of Jesus Christ for the remission of sins, and ye shall receive the gift of the Holy Ghost.

Ac 3:16 And his name through faith in his name hath made this man strong, whom ye see and know: yea, the faith which is by him hath given him this perfect soundness in the presence of you all.

Ac 4:12 Neither is there salvation in any other: for there is none other name under heaven given among men, whereby we must be saved.

Ac 4:17 But that it spread no further among the people, let us straitly threaten them, that they speak henceforth to no man in this name.

Ac 19:17 And this was known to all the Jews and Greeks also dwelling at Ephesus; and fear fell on them all, and the name of the Lord Jesus was magnified.

1 Co 1:10 Now I beseech you, brethren, by the name of our Lord Jesus Christ, that ye all speak the same thing, and *that* there be no divisions among you; but *that* ye be perfectly joined together in the same mind and in the same judgment.

Ep 1:21 Far above all principality, and power, and might, and dominion, and every name that is named, not only in this world, but also in that which is to come:

Ph 2:9–11 Wherefore God also hath highly exalted him, and given him a name which is above every name:

That at the name of Jesus every knee should bow, of *things* in heaven, and *things* in earth, and *things* under the earth;

And *that* every tongue should confess that Jesus Christ *is* Lord, to the glory of God the Father.

2 Th 1:12 That the name of our Lord Jesus Christ may be glorified in you, and ye in him, according to the grace of our God and the Lord Jesus Christ.

He 1:4 Being made so much better than the angels, as he hath by inheritance obtained a more excellent name than they.

Ja 2:7 Do not they blaspheme that worthy name by the which ye are called?

Re 19:12 His eyes *were* as a flame of fire, and on his head *were* many crowns; and he had a name written, that no man knew, but he himself.

Re 19:16 And he hath on *his* vesture and on his thigh a name written, KING OF KINGS, AND LORD OF LORDS.

b. Used in Prayer and Service

Mt 18:5 And whoso shall receive one such little child in my name receiveth me.

Mk 9:39 But Jesus said, Forbid him not: for there is no man which shall do a miracle in my name, that can lightly speak evil of me.

Mk 16:17 And these signs shall follow them that believe; In my name shall they cast out devils; they shall speak with new tongues;

Lu 10:17 And the seventy returned again with joy, saying, Lord, even the devils are subject unto us through thy name.

Lu 24:47 And that repentance and remission of sins should be preached in his name among all nations, beginning at Jerusalem.

Jn 14:13 And whatsoever ye shall ask in my name, that will I do, that the Father may be glorified in the Son.

Jn 15:16 Ye have not chosen me, but I have chosen you, and ordained you, that ye should go and bring forth fruit, and *that* your fruit should remain: that whatsoever ye shall ask of the Father in my name, he may give it you.

Jn 16:23 And in that day ye shall ask me nothing. Verily, verily, I say unto you, Whatsoever ye shall ask the Father in my name, he will give *it* you.

Jn 16:26 At that day ye shall ask in my name: and I say not unto you, that I will pray the Father for you:

Jn 20:31 But these are written, that ye might believe that Jesus is the Christ, the Son of God; and that believing ye might have life through his name.

Ac 3:6 Then Peter said, Silver and gold have I none; but such as I have give I thee: In the name of Jesus Christ of Nazareth rise up and walk.

Ac 3:16 And his name through faith in his name hath made this man

strong, whom ye see and know: yea, the faith which is by him hath given him this perfect soundness of you all.

Ac 4:10 Be it known unto you all, and to all the people of Israel, that by the name of Jesus Christ of Nazareth, whom ye crucified, whom God raised from the dead, *even* by him doth this man stand here before you whole.

Ac 4:30 By stretching forth thine hand to heal; and that signs and wonders may be done by the name of thy holy child Jesus.

Ac 8:16 (For as yet he was fallen upon none of them: only they were baptized in the name of the Lord Jesus.)

Ac 9:29 And he spake boldly in the name of the Lord Jesus, and disputed against the Grecians: but they went about to slay him.

Ac 10:43 To him give all the prophets witness, that through his name whosoever believeth in him shall receive remission of sins.

Ac 10:48 And he commanded them to be baptized in the name of the Lord. Then prayed they him to tarry certain days.

Ac 16:18 And this did she many days. But Paul, being grieved, turned and said to the spirit, I command thee in the name of Jesus Christ to come out of her. And he came out the same hour.

Ac 19:5 When they heard *this,* they were baptized in the name of the Lord Jesus.

1 Co 1:15 Lest any should say that I had baptized in mine own name.

1 Co 5:4 In the name of our Lord Jesus Christ, when ye are gathered together, and my spirit, with the power of our Lord Jesus Christ,

Ep 5:20 Giving thanks always for all things unto God and the Father in the name of our Lord Jesus Christ;

Col 3:17 And whatsoever ye do in word or deed, *do* all in the name of the Lord Jesus, giving thanks to God and the Father by him.

2 Th 3:6 Now we command you, brethren, in the name of our Lord Jesus Christ, that ye withdraw yourselves from every brother that walketh disorderly, and not after the tradition which he received of us.

Ja 5:14 Is any sick among you? let him call for the elders of the church; and let them pray over him, anointing him with oil in the name of the Lord:

1 Jn 2:12 I write unto you, little children, because your sins are forgiven you for his name's sake.

5. Changed

Ge 17:5, 15; 32:28; 35:10; 41:45; Jud 6:32; 2 S 12:25; 1 K 18:31; 2 K 24:17; 2 Chr 36:4; Ne 9:7; Da 1:7; 5:12; Jn 1:42; Ac 4:36; 13:9

See **TITLES AND NAMES**

NAOMI, *mother-in-law of Ruth*

Ru 1:20

NAPHTALI, *my wrestling*

1. Son of Jacob

Ge 30:8; 35:25; 46:24; 49:21; Nu 1:15; 26:48; 1 K 7:14; 1 Chr 2:2; 7:13; Eze 48:34

2. Tribe of

Nu 1:43; 2:29; 10:27; 13:14; 34:28; De 33:23; Jos 19:32, 39; 21:32; Jud 1:33; 4:6; 6:35; 2 K 15:29; 1 Chr 6:62; 12:34; Ps 68:27; Eze 48:4; Re 7:6

NAPKIN, *a small cloth*

Jn 11:44

NATHAN, *God has given*

1. The Prophet

2 S 7:2; 12:1, 7, 25; 1 K 1:8, 10, 22, 32; 1 Chr 17:1; 29:29; 2 Chr 9:29; 29:25; Zec 12:12

2. Son of David

2 S 5:14; Lu 3:31

NATHANAEL, *an apostle*

NATION, *miscellaneous topics*

1. Civic Duties

a. Citizen's Duties

De 17:10 And thou shalt do according to the sentence, which they of that place which the LORD shall choose shall shew thee; and thou shalt observe to do according to all that they inform thee:

2 S 18:12 And the man said unto Joab, Though I should receive a thousand *shekels* of silver in mine hand, yet would I not put forth mine hand against the king's son: for in our hearing the king charged thee and Abishai and Ittai, saying, Beware that none *touch* the young man Absalom.

2 Chr 8:15 And they departed not from the commandment of the king unto the priests and Levites concerning any matter, or concerning the treasures.

Ezr 7:26 And whosoever will not do the law of thy God, and the law of the king, let judgment be executed speedily upon him, whether *it be* unto death, or to banishment, or to confiscation of goods, or to imprisonment.

Ne 5:12 Then said they, We will restore *them,* and will require nothing of them; so will we do as thou sayest. Then I called the priests, and took an oath of them, that they should do according to this promise.

Pr 24:21 My son, fear thou the LORD and the king: *and* meddle not with them that are given to change:

Ec 8:2 I *counsel thee* to keep the king's commandment, and *that* in regard of the oath of God.

Je 34:10 Now when all the princes, and all the people, which had entered into the covenant, heard that every one should let his manservant, and every one his maidservant, go free, that none should serve themselves of them any more, then they obeyed, and let *them* go.

Je 40:9 And Gedaliah the son of Ahikam the son of Shaphan sware unto them and to their men, saying, Fear not to serve the Chaldeans: dwell in the land, and serve the king of Babylon, and it shall be well with you.

Mt 17:27 Notwithstanding, lest we should offend them, go thou to the sea, and cast an hook, and take up the fish that first cometh up; and when thou hast opened his mouth, thou shalt find a piece of money: that take, and give unto them for me and thee.

Mt 22:21 They say unto him, Caesar's. Then saith he unto them, Render therefore unto Caesar the things which are Caesar's; and unto God the things that are God's.

Ro 13:1 Let every soul be subject unto the higher powers. For there is no power but of God: the powers that be are ordained of God.

Tit 3:1 Put them in mind to be subject to principalities and powers, to obey magistrates, to be ready to every good work,

1 Pe 2:13–14 Submit yourselves to every ordinance of man for the Lord's sake: whether it be to the king, as supreme;

Or unto governors, as unto them that are sent by him for the punishment of evildoers, and for the praise of them that do well.

b. To Honor Rulers

Ex 22:28 Thou shalt not revile the gods, nor curse the ruler of thy people.

1 S 24:6 And he said unto his men, The LORD forbid that I should do this thing unto my master, the LORD's anointed, to stretch forth mine hand against him, seeing he is the anointed of the LORD.

2 S 16:6 And he cast stones at David, and at all the servants of king David: and all the people and all the mighty men *were* on his right hand and on his left.

1 K 2:8 And, behold, *thou hast* with thee Shimei the son of Gera, a Benjamite of Bahurim, which cursed me with a grievous curse in the day when I went to Mahanaim: but he came down to meet me at Jordan, and I sware to him by the LORD, saying, I will not put thee to death with the sword.

2 K 9:34 And when he was come in, he did eat and drink, and said, Go, see now this cursed *woman,* and bury her: for she *is* a king's daughter.

Jb 34:18 *Is it fit* to say to a king, *Thou art* wicked? *and* to princes, *Ye are* ungodly?

Pr 17:26 Also to punish the just *is* not good, *nor* to strike princes for equity.

Pr 24:21 My son, fear thou the LORD and the king: *and* meddle not with them that are given to change:

Ec 10:20 Curse not the king, no not in thy thought; and curse not the rich in thy bedchamber: for a bird of the air shall carry the voice, and that which hath wings shall tell the matter.

Da 6:21 Then said Daniel unto the king, O king, live for ever.

Ac 23:5 Then said Paul, I wist not, brethren, that he was the high priest: for it is written, Thou shalt not speak evil of the ruler of thy people.

Ro 13:1 Let every soul be subject unto the higher powers. For there is no power but of God: the powers that be are ordained of God.

1 Pe 2:14 Or unto governors, as unto them that are sent by him for the punishment of evildoers, and for the praise of them that do well.

1 Pe 2:17 Honour all *men.* Love the brotherhood. Fear God. Honour the king.

Jude 8 Likewise also these *filthy* dreamers defile the flesh, despise dominion, and speak evil of dignities.

2. Civic Righteousness

De 4:6 Keep therefore and do *them;* for this *is* your wisdom and your understanding in the sight of the nations, which shall hear all these statutes, and say, Surely this great nation *is* a wise and understanding people.

Pr 11:11 By the blessing of the upright the city is exalted: but it is overthrown by the mouth of the wicked.

Pr 14:34 Righteousness exalteth a nation: but sin *is* a reproach to any people.

Pr 16:12 *It is* an abomination to kings to commit wickedness: for the throne is established by righteousness.

Pr 25:5 Take away the wicked *from* before the king, and his throne shall be established in righteousness.

Pr 28:2 For the transgression of a land many *are* the princes thereof: but by a man of understanding *and* knowledge the state *thereof* shall be prolonged.

Pr 29:4 The king by judgment establisheth the land: but he that receiveth gifts overthroweth it.

Pr 29:14 The king that faithfully judgeth the poor, his throne shall be established for ever.

Is 16:5 And in mercy shall the throne be established: and he shall sit upon it in truth in the tabernacle of David, judging, and seeking judgment, and hasting righteousness.

Is 32:16 Then judgment shall dwell in the wilderness, and righteousness remain in the fruitful field.

Is 33:5 The LORD is exalted; for he dwelleth on high: he hath filled Zion with judgment and righteousness.

Is 54:14 In righteousness shalt thou be established: thou shalt be far from oppression; for thou shalt not fear: and from terror; for it shall not come near thee.

Is 60:17 For brass I will bring gold, and for iron I will bring silver, and for wood brass, and for stones iron: I will also make thy officers peace, and thine exactors righteousness.

3. Patriotism

2 S 10:12 Be of good courage, and let us play the men for our people, and for the cities of our God: and the LORD do that which seemeth him good.

2 S 20:2 So every man of Israel went up from after David, *and* followed Sheba the son of Bichri: but the men of Judah clave unto their king, from Jordan even to Jerusalem.

1 K 11:21 And when Hadad heard in Egypt that David slept with his fathers, and that Joab the captain of the host was dead, Hadad said to Pharaoh, Let me depart, that I may go to mine own country.

1 Chr 19:13 Be of good courage, and let us behave ourselves valiantly for our people, and for the cities of our God: and let the LORD do *that which is* good in his sight.

Ne 1:4 And it came to pass, when I heard these words, that I sat down and wept, and mourned *certain* days, and fasted, and prayed before the God of heaven,

Ne 2:3 And said unto the king, Let the king live for ever: why should not my countenance be sad, when the city, the place of my fathers' sepulchres, *lieth* waste, and the gates thereof are consumed with fire?

Ps 122:6 Pray for the peace of Jerusalem: they shall prosper that love thee.

Ps 137:1 By the rivers of Babylon, there we sat down, yea, we wept, when we remembered Zion.

Is 66:10 Rejoice ye with Jerusalem, and be glad with her, all ye that love her: rejoice for joy with her, all ye that mourn for her:

4. Payment of Taxes

Ge 41:34 Let Pharaoh do *this,* and let him appoint officers over the land, and take up the fifth part of the land of Egypt in the seven plenteous years.

Ge 47:26 And Joseph made it a law over the land of Egypt unto this day, *that* Pharaoh should have the fifth *part;* except the land of the priests only, *which* became not Pharaoh's.

1 S 8:15 And he will take the tenth of your seed, and of your vineyards, and give to his officers, and to his servants.

2 K 23:35 And Jehoiakim gave the silver and the gold to Pharaoh; but he taxed the land to give the money according to the commandment of Pharaoh: he exacted the silver and the gold of the people of the land, of every one according to his taxation, to give *it* unto Pharaoh-nechoh.

1 Chr 18:2 And he smote Moab; and the Moabites became David's servants, *and* brought gifts.

2 Chr 17:11 Also *some* of the Philistines brought Jehoshaphat presents, and tribute silver; and the Arabians brought him flocks, seven thousand and seven hundred rams, and seven thousand and seven hundred he goats.

Ne 5:4 There were also that said, We have borrowed money for the king's tribute, *and that upon* our lands and vineyards.

Est 10:1 And the king Ahasuerus laid a tribute upon the land, and *upon* the isles of the sea.

Is 16:1 Send ye the lamb to the ruler of the land from Sela to the wilderness, unto the mount of the daughter of Zion.

Mt 17:24 And when they were come to Capernaum, they that received tribute *money* came to Peter, and said, Doth not your master pay tribute?

Mt 22:17 Tell us therefore, What thinkest thou? Is it lawful to give tribute unto Caesar, or not?

Ro 13:6 For for this cause pay ye tribute also: for they are God's ministers, attending continually upon this very thing.

5. Civil Liberty

Le 25:10 And ye shall hallow the fiftieth year, and proclaim liberty throughout *all* the land unto all the inhabitants thereof: it shall be a jubile unto you; and ye shall return every man unto his possession, and ye shall return every man unto his family.

Is 9:4 For thou hast broken the yoke of his burden, and the staff of his shoulder, the rod of his oppressor, as in the day of Midian.

Is 10:27 And it shall come to pass in that day, *that* his burden shall be taken away from off thy shoulder, and his yoke from off thy neck, and the yoke shall be destroyed because of the anointing.

Is 14:25 That I will break the Assyrian in my land, and upon my mountains tread him under foot: then shall his yoke depart from off them, and his burden depart from off their shoulders.

Je 34:8 *This is* the word that came unto Jeremiah from the Lord, after that the king Zedekiah had made a covenant with all the people which *were* at Jerusalem, to proclaim liberty unto them;

1 Co 7:21 Art thou called *being* a servant? care not for it: but if thou mayest be made free, use *it* rather.

6. Civil Strife

2 Chr 15:6; Ps 55:9; Is 9:21; 19:2; Je 51:46; Eze 38:21; Ho 10:14; Hag 2:22; Zec 8:10; 11:6; 14:13; Mk 13:7; Lu 11:17; 21:10–11

7. Kings

a. Coronations

Jud 9:6; 1 S 11:15; 2 S 5:3; 1 K 12:1, 20; 2 K 11:12; 23:30; 1 Chr 11:3; 2 Chr 23:11

b. Decrees

Ezr 5:13; 6:1; 7:21; Est 1:20; 2:1, 8; 3:15; 4:8; 8:14; 9:1; Da 2:13; 3:4, 10, 22, 29; 6:9, 26; Jona 3:7; Lu 2:1

c. Favor

Ge 41:41; 45:16; 47:6; 1 S 17:25; 2 S 9:7; 19:33, 39; 1 K 4:5; 11:19; 2 K 25:28; Ne 2:5; Est 1:14; 2:17; 3:1, 10; 5:2, 8; 6:7, 11; 7:3; 8:5; Pr 14:35; 16:15; 19:6, 12; 22:11; 29:26; Je 37:21; 38:9; 39:11; 52:33; Da 1:19; 2:48; 6:3, 14, 23; Mt 24:45; Mk 6:20; Ro 13:4

d. Promises

1 K 1:30; Est 5:6; 7:2; 9:12; Da 5:7; Mt 14:7; Mk 6:22

e. Scepters

Ge 49:10; Nu 24:17; Est 4:11; 5:2; 8:4; Is 14:5; Eze 19:11; He 1:8

f. Thrones

1 K 7:7; 10:18; 22:10; 2 K 11:19; 2 Chr 9:17; Ne 3:7; Est 5:1; Jona 3:6; Ac 12:21

g. Wrath

Ge 40:2; 41:10; Ex 5:4; 10:11, 28; 1 S 20:30; 23:26; 2 S 11:20; 12:5; 13:21; 1 K 1:50; 2:23; 21:4; Est 1:12; 2:1; Pr 14:35; 16:14; 19:12; 20:2; Ec 10:4; Da 1:10; 2:12; 3:13, 19; 11:11, 44; Ac 12:20; Ro 13:4; He 11:27

8. Rulers

a. Wisdom and Integrity Are Essential

Ge 41:33 Now therefore let Pharaoh look out a man discreet and wise, and set him over the land of Egypt.

Ex 18:21 Moreover thou shalt provide out of all the people able men, such as fear God, men of truth, hating covetousness; and place *such* over them, *to be* rulers of thousands, *and* rulers of hundreds, rulers of fifties, and rulers of tens:

De 1:13 Take you wise men, and understanding, and known among your tribes, and I will make them rulers over you.

De 16:18 Judges and officers shalt thou make thee in all thy gates, which the LORD thy God giveth thee, throughout thy tribes: and they shall judge the people with just judgment.

Pr 24:23 These *things* also *belong* to the wise. *It is* not good to have respect of persons in judgment.

Pr 25:2 *It is* the glory of God to conceal a thing: but the honour of kings *is* to search out a matter.

Pr 31:4 *It is* not for kings, O Lemuel, *it is* not for kings to drink wine; nor for princes strong drink:

b. Duties

De 17:16 But he shall not multiply horses to himself, nor cause the people to return to Egypt, to the end that he should multiply horses: forasmuch as the LORD hath said unto you, Ye shall henceforth return no more that way.

2 S 23:3 The God of Israel said, the Rock of Israel spake to me, He that ruleth over men *must be* just, ruling in the fear of God.

1 K 12:7 And they spake unto him, saying, If thou wilt be a servant unto this people this day, and wilt serve them, and answer them, and speak good words to them, then they will be thy servants for ever.

2 Chr 19:6 And said to the judges, Take heed what ye do: for ye judge not for man, but for the LORD, who is with you in the judgment.

Ps 2:10–11 Be wise now therefore, O ye kings: be instructed, ye judges of the earth.

Serve the LORD with fear, and rejoice with trembling.

Ps 72:2 He shall judge thy people with righteousness, and thy poor with judgment.

Pr 16:12 *It is* an abomination to kings to commit wickedness: for the throne is established by righteousness.

Pr 20:28 Mercy and truth preserve the king: and his throne is upholden by mercy.

Pr 29:4 The king by judgment establisheth the land: but he that receiveth gifts overthroweth it.

Pr 29:14 The king that faithfully judgeth the poor, his throne shall be established for ever.

Jn 18:31 Then said Pilate unto them, Take ye him, and judge him according to your law. The Jews therefore said unto him, It is not lawful for us to put any man to death:

c. Warnings

De 27:19 Cursed *be* he that perverteth the judgment of the stranger, fatherless, and widow. And all the people shall say, Amen.

1 S 15:26 And Samuel said unto Saul, I will not return with thee: for thou hast rejected the word of the LORD, and the LORD hath rejected thee from being king over Israel.

Ne 5:7 Then I consulted with myself, and I rebuked the nobles, and the rulers, and said unto them, Ye exact usury, every one of his brother. And I set a great assembly against them.

Ps 110:5 The Lord at thy right hand shall strike through kings in the day of his wrath.

Pr 16:12 *It is* an abomination to kings to commit wickedness: for the throne is established by righteousness.

Pr 28:15 *As* a roaring lion, and a ranging bear; *so is* a wicked ruler over the poor people.

Ec 4:13 Better *is* a poor and a wise child than an old and foolish king, who will no more be admonished.

Is 1:23 Thy princes *are* rebellious, and companions of thieves: every one loveth gifts, and followeth after rewards: they judge not the fatherless, neither doth the cause of the widow come unto them.

Is 3:14 The LORD will enter into judgment with the ancients of his people, and the princes thereof: for ye have eaten up the vineyard; the spoil of the poor *is* in your houses.

Is 10:1 Woe unto them that decree unrighteous decrees, and that write grievousness *which* they have prescribed;

Is 28:14 Wherefore hear the word of the LORD, ye scornful men, that rule this people which *is* in Jerusalem.

Eze 22:27 Her princes in the midst thereof *are* like wolves ravening the prey, to shed blood, *and* to destroy souls, to get dishonest gain.

Eze 28:2 Son of man, say unto the prince of Tyrus, Thus saith the Lord God; Because thine heart *is* lifted up, ad, I *am* a God, I sit *in* the seat of God, in the midst of the seas; yet thou *art* a man, and not God, though thou set thine heart as the heart of God:

Eze 45:9 Thus saith the Lord GOD; Let it suffice you, O princes of Israel: remove violence and spoil, and execute judgment and justice, take away your exactions from my people, saith the Lord God.

Ho 5:10 The princes of Judah were like them that remove the bound: *therefore* I will pour out my wrath upon them like water.

Mi 3:1 And I said, Hear, I pray you, O heads of Jacob, and ye princes of the house of Israel; *Is it* not for you to know judgment?

Mi 7:3 That they may do evil with both hands earnestly, the prince asketh, and the judge *asketh* for a reward; and the great *man,* he uttereth his mischievous desire: so they wrap it up.

d. Examples

Ge 41:43 And he made him to ride in the second chariot which he had; and they cried before him, Bow the knee: and he made him *ruler* over all the land of Egypt.

1 S 10:24 And Samuel said to all the people, See ye him whom the LORD hath chosen, that *there is* none like him among all the people? And all the people shouted, and said, God save the king.

1 S 15:30 Then he said, I have sinned: *yet* honour me now, I pray thee, before the elders of my people, and before Israel, and turn again with me, that I may worship the LORD thy God.

1 S 24:8 David also arose afterward, and went out of the cave, and cried after Saul, saying, My lord the king. And when Saul looked behind him, David stooped with his face to the earth, and bowed himself.

2 S 9:11 Then said Ziba unto the king, According to all that my lord the king hath commanded his servant, so shall thy servant do. As for Mephibosheth, *said the king,* he shall eat at my table, as one of the king's sons.

2 S 14:4 And when the woman of Tekoah spake to the king, she fell on her face to the ground, and did obeisance, and said, Help, O king.

2 S 18:3 But the people answered, Thou shalt not go forth: for if we flee away, they will not care for us; neither if half of us die, will they care for us: but now *thou art* worth ten thousand of us: therefore now *it is* better that thou succour us out of the city.

2 S 19:15 So the king returned, and came to Jordan. And Judah came to Gilgal, to go to meet the king, to conduct the king over Jordan.

2 S 19:31 And Barzillai the Gileadite came down from Rogelim, and went over Jordan with the king, to conduct him over Jordan.

2 S 19:40 Then the king went on to Gilgal, and Chimham went on with him: and all the people of Judah conducted the king, and also half the people of Israel.

2 S 21:17 But Abishai the son of Zeruiah succoured him, and smote the Philistine, and killed him. Then the men of David sware unto him, saying, Thou shalt go no more out with us to battle, that thou quench not the light of Israel.

2 S 24:20 And Araunah looked, and saw the king and his servants coming on toward him: and Araunah went out, and bowed himself before the king on his face upon the ground.

1 K 1:16 And Bath-sheba bowed, and did obeisance unto the king. And the king said, What wouldest thou?

1 K 1:31 Then Bath-sheba bowed with *her* face to the earth, and did reverence to the king, and said, Let my lord king David live for ever.

1 K 1:39 And Zadok the priest took an horn of oil out of the tabernacle, and anointed Solomon. And they blew the trumpet; and all the people said, God save king Solomon.

1 K 8:66 On the eighth day he sent the people away: and they blessed the king, and went unto their tents joyful and glad of heart for all the goodness that the LORD had done for David his servant, and for Israel his people.

2 K 11:12 And he brought forth the king's son, and put the crown upon him, and *gave him* the testimony; and they made him king, and anointed him; and they clapped their hands, and said, God save the king.

1 Chr 21:21 And as David came to Ornan, Ornan looked and saw David, and went out of the threshingfloor, and bowed himself to David with *his* face to the ground.

Da 3:9 They spake and said to the king Nebuchadnezzar, O king, live for ever.

Mt 21:9 And the multitudes that went before, and that followed, cried, saying, Hosanna to the Son of David: Blessed *is* he that cometh in the name of the Lord; Hosanna in the highest.

Ac 24:3 We accept *it* always, and in all places, most noble Felix, with all thankfulness.

Ac 26:2 I think myself happy, king Agrippa, because I shall answer for myself this day before thee touching all the things whereof I am accused of the Jews:

See **REBELLION**

e. Rebuked

1 S 15:23 For rebellion *is as* the sin of witchcraft, and stubbornness *is as* iniquity and idolatry. Because thou hast rejected the word of the LORD, he hath also rejected thee from *being* king.

2 S 12:7 And Nathan said to David, Thou *art* the man. Thus saith the LORD God of Israel, I anointed thee king over Israel, and I delivered thee out of the hand of Saul;

1 K 14:7 Go, tell Jeroboam, Thus saith the LORD God of Israel, Forasmuch as I exalted thee from among the people, and made thee prince over my people Israel,

1 K 16:1 Then the word of the LORD came to Jehu the son of Hanani against Baasha, saying,

1 K 18:18 And he answered, I have not troubled Israel; but thou, and thy father's house, in that ye have forsaken the commandments of the LORD, and thou hast followed Baalim.

1 K 21:20 And Ahab said to Elijah, Hast thou found me, O mine enemy? And he answered, I have found *thee:* because thou hast sold thyself to work evil in the sight of the LORD.

2 K 3:13 And Elisha said unto the king of Israel, What have I to do with thee? get thee to the prophets of thy father, and to the prophets of thy mother. And the king of Israel said unto him, Nay: for the LORD hath called these three kings together, to deliver them into the hand of Moab.

2 Chr 12:5 Then came Shemaiah the prophet to Rehoboam, and *to* the princes of Judah, that were gathered together to Jerusalem because of Shishak, and said unto them, Thus saith the LORD, Ye have forsaken me, and therefore have I also left you in the hand of Shishak.

2 Chr 16:9 For the eyes of the LORD run to and fro throughout the whole earth, to shew himself strong in the behalf of *them* whose heart *is* perfect toward him. Herein thou hast done foolishly: therefore from henceforth thou shalt have wars.

2 Chr 19:2 And Jehu the son of Hanani the seer went out to meet him, and said to king Jehoshaphat, Shouldest thou help the ungodly, and love them that hate the LORD? therefore is wrath upon thee from before the LORD.

2 Chr 20:37 Then Eliezer the son of Dodavah of Mareshah prophesied against Jehoshaphat, saying, Because thou hast joined thyself with Ahaziah, the LORD hath broken thy works. And the ships were broken, that they were not able to go to Tarshish.

2 Chr 21:12 And there came a writing to him from Elijah the prophet, saying, Thus saith the LORD God of David thy father, Because thou hast not walked in the ways of Jehoshaphat thy father, nor in the ways of Asa king of Judah,

2 Chr 26:18 And they withstood Uzziah the king, and said unto him, *It appertaineth* not unto thee, Uzziah, to burn incense unto the LORD, but to the priests the sons of Aaron, that are consecrated to burn incense: go out of the sanctuary; for thou hast trespassed; neither *shall it be* for thine honour from the LORD God.

Is 39:5 Then said Isaiah to Hezekiah, Hear the word of the LORD of hosts:

Je 22:17 But thine eyes and thine heart *are* not but for thy covetousness, and for to shed innocent blood, and for oppression, and for violence, to do *it.*

Je 36:30 Therefore thus saith the LORD of Jehoiakim king of Judah; He shall have none to sit upon the throne of David: and his dead body shall be cast out in the day to the heat, and in the night to the frost.

Da 4:27 Wherefore, O king, let my counsel be acceptable unto thee, and break off thy sins by righteousness, and thine iniquities by shewing mercy to the poor; if it may be a lengthening of thy tranquility.

Da 5:23 But hast lifted up thyself against the Lord of heaven; and they have brought the vessels of his house before thee, and thou, and thy lords, thy wives, and thy concubines, have drunk wine in them; and thou hast praised the gods of silver, and gold, of brass, iron, wood, and stone, which see not, nor hear, nor know: and the God in whose hand thy breath *is,* and whose *are* all thy ways, hast thou not glorified:

Mal 2:1 And now, O ye priests, this commandment *is* for you.

Mk 6:18 For John had said unto Herod, It is not lawful for thee to have thy brother's wife.

Ac 23:3 Then said Paul unto him, God shall smite thee, *thou* whited wall: for sittest thou to judge me after the law, and commandest me to be smitten contrary to the law?

9. Social and Political Corruption

Ge 6:5 And GOD saw that the wickedness of man *was* great in the earth, and *that* every imagination of the thoughts of his heart *was* only evil continually.

Ge 6:11 The earth also was corrupt before God, and the earth was filled with violence.

Ge 13:13 But the men of Sodom *were* wicked and sinners before the LORD exceedingly.

Ge 18:20 And the LORD said, Because the cry of Sodom and Gomorrah is great, and because their sin is very grievous;

Ge 19:5 And they called unto Lot, and said unto him, Where *are* the men which came in to thee this night? bring them out unto us, that we may know them.

Ge 19:9 And they said, Stand back. And they said *again,* This one *fellow* came in to sojourn, and he will needs be a judge: now will we deal worse with thee, than with them. And they pressed sore upon the man, *even* Lot, and came near to break the door.

Ge 19:32 Come, let us make our father drink wine, and we will lie with him, that we may preserve seed of our father.

Ge 38:7 And Er, Judah's firstborn, was wicked in the sight of the LORD; and the LORD slew him.

Ex 32:7 And the LORD said unto Moses, Go, get thee down; for thy people, which thou broughtest out of the land of Egypt, have corrupted *themselves:*

Le 18:25 And the land is defiled: therefore I do visit the iniquity thereof upon it, and the land itself vomiteth out her inhabitants.

De 4:25 When thou shalt beget children, and children's children, and ye shall have remained long in the land, and shall corrupt *yourselves,* and make a graven image, *or* the likeness of any *thing,* and shall do evil in the sight of the LORD thy God, to provoke him to anger:

De 9:5 Not for thy righteousness, or for the uprightness of thine heart, dost thou go to possess their land: but for the wickedness of these nations the LORD thy God doth drive them out from before thee, and that he may perform the word which the LORD sware unto thy fathers, Abraham, Isaac, and Jacob.

De 9:12 And the LORD said unto me, Arise, get thee down quickly from hence; for thy people which thou hast brought forth out of Egypt have corrupted *themselves;* they are quickly turned aside out of the way which I commanded them; they have made them a molten image.

De 27:21 Cursed *be* he that lieth with any manner of beast. And all the people shall say, Amen.

De 32:5 They have corrupted themselves, their spot *is* not *the spot* of his children: *they are* a perverse and crooked generation.

Jud 19:25 But the men would not hearken to him: so the man took his concubine, and brought her forth unto them; and they knew her, and abused her all the night until the morning: and when the day began to spring, they let her go.

1 K 16:25 But Omri wrought evil in the eyes of the LORD, and did worse than all that *were* before him.

1 K 21:25 But there was none like unto Ahab, which did sell himself to work wickedness in the sight of the LORD, whom Jezebel his wife stirred up.

2 K 21:11 Because Manasseh king of Judah hath done these abominations, *and* hath done wickedly above all that the Amorites did, which *were* before him, and hath made Judah also to sin with his idols:

2 Chr 27:2 And he did *that which was* right in the sight of the LORD, according to all that his father Uzziah did: howbeit he entered not into the temple of the LORD. And the people did yet corruptly.

2 Chr 33:9 So Manasseh made Judah and the inhabitants of Jerusalem to err, *and* to do worse than the heathen, whom the LORD had destroyed before the children of Israel.

2 Chr 33:23 And humbled not himself before the LORD, as Manasseh his father had humbled himself; but Amon trespassed more and more.

Jb 14:4 Who can bring a clean *thing* out of an unclean? not one.

Jb 15:16 How much more abominable and filthy *is* man, which drinketh iniquity like water?

Ps 7:14 Behold, he travaileth with iniquity, and hath conceived mischief, and brought forth falsehood.

Ps 14:3 They are all gone aside, they are *all* together become filthy: *there is* none that doeth good, no, not one.

Ps 51:5 Behold, I was shapen in iniquity; and in sin did my mother conceive me.

Ps 53:3 Every one of them is gone back: they are altogether become filthy; *there is* none that doeth good, no, not one.

Ps 55:15 Let death seize upon them, *and* let them go down quick into hell: for wickedness is in their dwellings, *and* among them.

Ps 73:8 They are corrupt, and speak wickedly *concerning* oppression: they speak loftily.

Pr 5:14 I was almost in all evil in the midst of the congregation and assembly.

Ec 3:16 And moreover I saw under the sun the place of judgment, *that* wickedness *was* there; and the place of righteousness, *that* iniquity *was* there.

Ec 9:3 This *is* an evil among all *things* that are done under the sun, that *there is* one event unto all: yea, also the heart of the sons of men is full of evil, and madness is in their heart while they live, and after that *they go* to the dead.

Is 1:6 From the sole of the foot even unto the head *there is* no soundness in it; *but* wounds, and bruises, and putrifying sores: they have not been closed, neither bound up, neither mollified with ointment.

Is 24:5 The earth also is defiled under the inhabitants thereof; because they have transgressed the laws, changed the ordinance, broken the everlasting covenant.

Is 48:8 Yea, thou heardest not; yea, thou knewest not; yea, from that time *that* thine ear was not opened: for I knew that thou wouldest deal very treacherously, and wast called a transgressor from the womb.

Is 59:3 For your hands are defiled with blood, and your fingers with iniquity; your lips have spoken lies, your tongue hath muttered perverseness.

Is 59:7 Their feet run to evil, and they make haste to shed innocent blood: their thoughts *are* thoughts of iniquity; wasting and destruction *are* in their paths.

Is 64:6 But we are all as an unclean *thing,* and all our righteousnesses *are* as filthy rags; and we all do fade as a leaf; and our iniquities, like the wind, have taken us away.

Je 5:27 As a cage is full of birds, so *are* their houses full of deceit: therefore they are become great, and waxen rich.

Je 16:12 And ye have done worse than your fathers; for, behold, ye walk every one after the imagination of his evil heart, that they may not hearken unto me:

Je 18:13 Therefore thus saith the LORD; Ask ye now among the heathen, who hath heard such things: the virgin of Israel hath done a very horrible thing.

Je 23:14 I have seen also in the prophets of Jerusalem an horrible thing: they commit adultery, and walk in lies: they strengthen also the hands of evildoers, that none doth return from his wickedness: they are all of

them unto me as Sodom, and the inhabitants thereof as Gomorrah.

Eze 16:47 Yet hast thou not walked after their ways, nor done after their abominations: but, as *if that were* a very little *thing,* thou wast corrupted more than they in all thy ways.

Eze 22:11 And one hath committed abomination with his neighbour's wife; and another hath lewdly defiled his daughter in law; and another in thee hath humbled his sister, his father's daughter.

Eze 23:11 And when her sister Aholibah saw *this,* she was more corrupt in her inordinate love than she, and in her whoredoms more than her sister in *her* whoredoms.

Ho 6:10 I have seen an horrible thing in the house of Israel: there *is* the whoredom of Ephraim, Israel is defiled.

Ho 9:9 They have deeply corrupted *themselves,* as in the days of Gibeah: *therefore* he will remember their iniquity, he will visit their sins.

Jl 3:13 Put ye in the sickle, for the harvest is ripe: come, get you down; for the press is full, the fats overflow; for their wickedness *is* great.

Mi 7:3 That they may do evil with both hands earnestly, the prince asketh, and the judge *asketh* for a reward; and the great *man,* he uttereth his mischievous desire: so they wrap it up.

Mt 23:27 Woe unto you, scribes and Pharisees, hypocrites! for ye are like unto whited sepulchres, which indeed appear beautiful outward, but are within full of dead *men's* bones, and of all uncleanness.

Mt 27:44 The thieves also, which were crucified with him, cast the same in his teeth.

Mk 7:21 For from within, out of the heart of men, proceed evil thoughts, adulteries, fornications, murders,

Lu 11:44 Woe unto you, scribes and Pharisees, hypocrites! for ye are as graves which appear not, and the men that walk over *them* are not aware *of them.*

Ro 1:24 Wherefore God also gave them up to uncleanness through the lusts of their own hearts, to dishonour their own bodies between themselves:

Ro 3:12 They are all gone out of the way, they are together become unprofitable; there is none that doeth good, no, not one.

Tit 1:12 One of themselves, *even* a prophet of their own, said, The Cretians *are* alway liars, evil beasts, slow bellies.

2 Pe 2:12 But these, as natural brute beasts, made to be taken and destroyed, speak evil of the things that they understand not; and shall utterly perish in their own corruption;

Jude 10 But these speak evil of those things which they know not: but what they know naturally, as brute beasts, in those things they corrupt themselves.

a. Evil Times

Ge 6:12 And God looked upon the earth, and, behold, it was corrupt; for all flesh had corrupted his way upon the earth.

1 K 19:10 And he said, I have been very jealous for the LORD God of hosts: for the children of Israel have forsaken thy covenant, thrown down thine altars, and slain thy prophets with the sword; and I, *even* I only, am left; and they seek my life, to take it away.

Ps 12:1 Help, LORD; for the godly man ceaseth; for the faithful fail from among the children of men.

Ps 14:1 The fool hath said in his heart, *There is* no God. They are corrupt, they have done abominable works, *there is* none that doeth good.

Is 57:1 The righteous perisheth, and no man layeth *it* to heart: and merciful men *are* taken away, none considering that the righteous is taken away from the evil *to come.*

Is 59:14 And judgment is turned away backward, and justice standeth afar off: for truth is fallen in the street, and equity cannot enter.

Je 5:1 Run ye to and fro through the streets of Jerusalem, and see now, and know, and seek in the broad places thereof, if ye can find a man, if there be *any* that executeth judgment, that seeketh the truth; and I will pardon it.

Ho 4:1 Hear the word of the LORD, ye children of Israel: for the LORD hath a controversy with the inhabitants of the land, because *there is* no truth, nor mercy, nor knowledge of God in the land.

Am 5:13 Therefore the prudent shall keep silence in that time; for it *is* an evil time.

Mi 7:2 The good *man* is perished out of the earth: and *there is* none upright among men: they all lie in wait for blood; they hunt every man his brother with a net.

Hab 1:3 Why dost thou shew me iniquity, and cause *me* to behold grievance? for spoiling and violence *are* before me: and there are *that* raise up strife and contention.

Zec 8:10 For before these days there was no hire for man, nor any hire for beast; neither *was there any* peace to him that went out or came in because of the affliction: for I set all men every one against his neighbour.

Ep 5:16 Redeeming the time, because the days are evil.

2 Ti 3:1–2 This know also, that in the last days perilous times shall come.

For men shall be lovers of their own selves, covetous, boasters, proud, blasphemers, disobedient to parents, unthankful, unholy,

2 Ti 4:3 For the time will come when they will not endure sound doctrine; but after their own lusts shall they heap to themselves teachers, having itching ears;

b. The Prevalence of Violence

Ge 6:11 The earth also was corrupt before God, and the earth was filled with violence.

Ge 6:13 And God said unto Noah, The end of all flesh is come before me; for the earth is filled with violence through them; and, behold, I will destroy them with the earth.

Ge 19:9 And they said, Stand back. And they said *again*, This one *fellow* came in to sojourn, and he will needs be a judge: now will we deal worse with thee, than with them. And they pressed sore upon the man, *even* Lot, and came near to break the door.

Ge 21:25 And Abraham reproved Abimelech because of a well of water, which Abimelech's servants had violently taken away.

Jb 20:19 Because he hath oppressed *and* hath forsaken the poor; *because* he hath violently taken away an house which he builded not;

Jb 24:2 *Some* remove the landmarks; they violently take away flocks, and feed *thereof.*

Ps 7:16 His mischief shall return upon his own head, and his violent dealing shall come down upon his own pate.

Ps 11:5 The LORD trieth the righteous: but the wicked and him that loveth violence his soul hateth.

Ps 55:9 Destroy, O Lord, *and* divide their tongues: for I have seen violence and strife in the city.

Ps 58:2 Yea, in heart ye work wickedness; ye weigh the violence of your hands in the earth.

Ps 73:6 Therefore pride compasseth them about as a chain; violence covereth them *as* a garment.

Ps 74:20 Have respect unto the covenant: for the dark places of the earth are full of the habitations of cruelty.

Ps 86:14 O God, the proud are risen against me, and the assemblies of violent *men* have sought after my soul; and have not set thee before them.

Ps 140:1 Deliver me, O LORD, from the evil man: preserve me from the violent man;

Pr 4:17 For they eat the bread of wickedness, and drink the wine of violence.

Pr 10:6 Blessings *are* upon the head of the just: but violence covereth the mouth of the wicked.

Pr 10:11 The mouth of a righteous *man is* a well of life: but violence covereth the mouth of the wicked.

Pr 21:7 The robbery of the wicked shall destroy them; because they refuse to do judgment.

Is 1:21 How is the faithful city become an harlot! it was full of judgment; righteousness lodged in it; but now murderers.

Is 59:6 Their webs shall not become garments, neither shall they cover themselves with their works: their works *are* works of iniquity, and the act of violence *is* in their hands.

Is 60:18 Violence shall no more be heard in thy land, wasting nor destruction within thy borders; but thou shalt call thy walls Salvation, and thy gates Praise.

Je 6:7 As a fountain casteth out her waters, so she casteth out her wickedness: violence and spoil is heard in her; before me continually is grief and wounds.

Je 22:17 But thine eyes and thine heart *are* not but for thy covetousness, and for to shed innocent blood, and for oppression, and for violence, to do *it.*

Je 51:46 And lest your heart faint, and ye fear for the rumour that shall be heard in the land; a rumour shall both come *one* year, and after that in *another* year *shall come* a rumour, and violence in the land, ruler against ruler.

Eze 7:11 Violence is risen up into a rod of wickedness: none of them *shall remain,* nor of their multitude, nor of any of theirs: neither *shall there be* wailing for them.

Eze 7:23 Make a chain: for the land is full of bloody crimes, and the city is full of violence.

Eze 8:17 Then he said unto me, Hast thou seen *this,* O son of man? Is it a light thing to the house of Judah that they commit the abominations which they commit here? for they have filled the land with violence, and have returned to provoke me to anger: and, lo, they put the branch to their nose.

Eze 12:19 And say unto the people of the land, Thus saith the Lord GOD of the inhabitants of Jerusalem, *and* of the land of Israel; They shall eat their bread with carefulness, and drink their water with astonishment, that her land may be desolate from all that is therein, because of the violence of all them that dwell therein.

Eze 18:12 Hath oppressed the poor and needy, hath spoiled by violence, hath not restored the pledge, and hath lifted up his eyes to the idols, hath committed abomination,

Eze 18:18 *As for* his father, because he cruelly oppressed, spoiled his brother by violence, and did *that* which *is* not good among his people, lo, even he shall die in his iniquity.

Eze 28:16 By the multitude of thy merchandise they have filled the midst of thee with violence, and thou hast sinned: therefore I will cast thee as profane out of the mountain of God: and I will destroy thee, O covering cherub, from the midst of the stones of fire.

Eze 45:9 Thus saith the Lord GOD; Let it suffice you, O princes of Israel: remove violence and spoil, and execute judgment and justice, take away your exactions from my people, saith the Lord GOD.

Jl 3:19 Egypt shall be a desolation, and Edom shall be a desolate wilderness, for the violence *against* the children of Judah, because they have shed innocent blood in their land.

Am 3:10 For they know not to do right, saith the LORD, who store up violence and robbery in their palaces.

Am 6:3 Ye that put far away the evil day, and cause the seat of violence to come near;

Obad 10 For *thy* violence against thy brother Jacob shame shall cover thee, and thou shalt be cut off for ever.

Jona 3:8 But let man and beast be covered with sackcloth, and cry mightily unto God: yea, let them turn every one from his evil way, and from the violence that *is* in their hands.

Mi 2:2 And they covet fields, and take *them* by violence; and houses, and take *them* away: so they oppress a man and his house, even a man and his heritage.

Mi 2:8 Even of late my people is risen up as an enemy: ye pull off the robe with the garment from them that pass by securely as men averse from war.

Mi 6:12 For the rich men thereof are full of violence, and the inhabitants thereof have spoken lies, and their tongue *is* deceitful in their mouth.

Na 3:1 Woe to the bloody city! it is all full of lies *and* robbery; the prey departeth not;

Hab 1:3 Why dost thou shew me iniquity, and cause *me* to behold grievance? for spoiling and violence *are* before me: and there are *that* raise up strife and contention.

Hab 1:9 They shall come all for violence: their faces shall sup up *as* the east wind, and they shall gather the captivity as the sand.

Hab 2:8 Because thou hast spoiled many nations, all the remnant of the people shall spoil thee; because of men's blood, and *for* the violence of the land, of the city, and of all that dwell therein.

Hab 2:17 For the violence of Lebanon shall cover thee, and the spoil of beasts, *which* made them afraid, because of men's blood, and for the violence of the land, of the city, and of all that dwell therein.

Zep 1:9 In the same day also will I punish all those that leap on the threshold, which fill their masters' houses with violence and deceit.

Mal 2:16 For the LORD, the God of Israel, saith that he hateth putting away: for *one* covereth violence with his garment, saith the LORD of hosts: therefore take heed to your spirit, that ye deal not treacherously.

Mt 18:28 But the same servant went out, and found one of his fellowservants, which owed him an hundred pence: and he laid hands on him, and took *him* by the throat, saying, Pay me that thou owest.

Mt 24:49 And shall begin to smite *his* fellowservants, and to eat and drink with the drunken;

Mk 5:4 Because that he had been often bound with fetters and chains, and the chains had been plucked asunder by him, and the fetters broken in pieces: neither could any *man* tame him.

Lu 23:23 And they were instant with loud voices, requiring that he might be crucified. And the voices of them and of the chief priests prevailed.

Ac 21:35 And when he came upon the stairs, so it was, that he was borne of the soldiers for the violence of the people.

10. Bribery

a. Condemned

Ex 23:8 And thou shalt take no gift: for the gift blindeth the wise, and perverteth the words of the righteous.

De 16:19 Thou shalt not wrest judgment; thou shalt not respect persons, neither take a gift: for a gift doth blind the eyes of the wise, and pervert the words of the righteous.

De 27:25 Cursed *be* he that taketh reward to slay an innocent person. And all the people shall say, Amen.

Jb 15:34 For the congregation of hypocrites *shall be* desolate, and fire shall consume the tabernacles of bribery.

Ps 15:5 *He that* putteth not out his money to usury, nor taketh reward against the innocent. He that doeth these *things* shall never be moved.

Ps 26:10 In whose hands *is* mischief, and their right hand is full of bribes.

Pr 15:27 He that is greedy of gain troubleth his own house; but he that hateth gifts shall live.

Pr 17:23 A wicked *man* taketh a gift out of the bosom to pervert the ways of judgment.

Pr 29:4 The king by judgment establisheth the land: but he that receiveth gifts overthroweth it.

Ec 7:7 Surely oppression maketh a wise man mad; and a gift destroyeth the heart.

Is 1:23 Thy princes *are* rebellious, and companions of thieves: every one loveth gifts, and followeth after rewards: they judge not the fatherless, neither doth the cause of the widow come unto them.

Is 5:23 Which justify the wicked for reward, and take away the righteousness of the righteous from him!

Is 33:15 He that walketh righteously, and speaketh uprightly; he that despiseth the gain of oppressions, that shaketh his hands from holding of bribes, that stoppeth his ears from hearing of blood, and shutteth his eyes from seeing evil;

Eze 13:19 And will ye pollute me among my people for handfuls of barley and for pieces of bread, to slay the souls that should not die, and to save the souls alive that should not live, by your lying to my people that hear *your* lies?

Eze 22:12 In thee have they taken gifts to shed blood; thou hast taken usury and increase, and thou hast greedily gained of thy neighbours by extortion, and hast forgotten me, saith the Lord GOD.

Am 5:12 For I know your manifold transgressions and your mighty sins: they afflict the just, they take a bribe, and they turn aside the poor in the gate *from their right.*

Ac 24:26 He hoped also that money should have been given him of Paul, that he might loose him: wherefore he sent for him the oftener, and communed with him.

b. Examples

Nu 22:17 For I will promote thee unto very great honour, and I will do whatsoever thou sayest unto me: come therefore, I pray thee, curse me this people.

Jud 16:5 And the lords of the Philistines came up unto her, and said unto her, Entice him, and see wherein his great strength *lieth,* and by what *means* we may prevail against him, that we may bind him to afflict him: and we will give thee every one of us eleven hundred *pieces* of silver.

Jud 16:18 And when Delilah saw that he had told her all his heart, she sent and called for the lords of the Philistines, saying, Come up this once, for he hath shewed me all his heart. Then the lords of the Philistines came up unto her, and brought money in their hand.

1 S 8:3 And his sons walked not in his ways, but turned aside after lucre, and took bribes, and perverted judgment.

1 S 12:3 Behold, here I *am:* witness against me before the LORD, and before his anointed: whose ox have I taken? or whose ass have I taken? or whom have I defrauded? whom have I oppressed? or of whose hand have I received *any* bribe to blind mine eyes therewith? and I will restore it you.

1 K 15:19 *There is* a league between me and thee, *and* between my father and thy father: behold, I have sent unto thee a present of silver and gold; come and break thy league with Baasha king of Israel, that he may depart from me.

2 K 15:19 *And* Pul the king of Assyria came against the land: and Menahem gave Pul a thousand talents of silver, that his hand might be with him to confirm the kingdom in his hand.

Ne 6:12 And, lo, I perceived that God had not sent him; but that he pronounced this prophecy against me: for Tobiah and Sanballat had hired him.

Ne 13:2 Because they met not the children of Israel with bread and with water, but hired Balaam against them, that he should curse them: howbeit our God turned the curse into a blessing.

Est 3:9 If it please the king, let it be written that they may be destroyed: and I will pay ten thousand talents of silver to the hands of those that have the charge of the business, to bring *it* into the king's treasuries.

Est 4:7 And Mordecai told him of all that had happened unto him, and of the sum of the money that Haman had promised to pay to the king's treasuries for the Jews, to destroy them.

Mi 7:3 That they may do evil with both hands earnestly, the prince asketh, and the judge *asketh* for a reward; and the great *man,* he uttereth his mischievous desire: so they wrap it up.

Mt 28:12 And when they were assembled with the elders, and had taken counsel, they gave large money unto the soldiers,

Mk 14:11 And when they heard *it,* they were glad, and promised to give him money. And he sought how he might conveniently betray him.

Lu 22:5 And they were glad, and covenanted to give him money.

Ac 8:18 And when Simon saw that through laying on of the apostles' hands the Holy Ghost was given, he offered them money,

11. *Crimes against the Nation*

a. Assassination

Ge 4:8 And Cain talked with Abel his brother: and it came to pass, when they were in the field, that Cain rose up against Abel his brother, and slew him.

Ge 4:23 And Lamech said unto his wives, Adah and Zillah, Hear my voice; ye wives of Lamech, hearken unto my speech: for I have slain a man to my wounding, and a young man to my hurt.

Ge 49:6 O my soul, come not thou into their secret; unto their assembly, mine honour, be not thou united: for in their anger they slew a man, and in their selfwill they digged down a wall.

Ex 2:12 And he looked this way and that way, and when he saw that *there was* no man, he slew the Egyptian, and hid him in the sand.

Jud 9:5 And he went unto his father's house at Ophrah, and slew his brethren the sons of Jerubbaal, *being* threescore and ten persons, upon one stone: notwithstanding yet Jotham the youngest son of Jerubbaal was left; for he hid himself.

Jud 9:18 And ye are risen up against my father's house this day, and have slain his sons, threescore and ten persons, upon one stone, and have made Abimelech, the son of his maidservant, king over the men of Shechem, because he *is* your brother;)

Jud 9:56 Thus God rendered the wickedness of Abimelech, which he did unto his father, in slaying his seventy brethren:

Jud 19:28 And he said unto her, Up, and let us be going. But none answered. Then the man took her *up* upon an ass, and the man rose up, and gat him unto his place.

Jud 20:5 And the men of Gibeah rose against me, and beset the house round about upon me by night, *and* thought to have slain me: and my concubine have they forced, that she is dead.

1 S 22:18 And the king said to Doeg, Turn thou, and fall upon the priests. And Doeg the Edomite turned, and he fell upon the priests, and slew on that day fourscore and five persons that did wear a linen ephod.

2 S 4:7 For when they came into the house, he lay on his bed in his bedchamber, and they smote him, and slew him, and beheaded him, and took his head, and gat them away through the plain all night.

2 S 11:15 And he wrote in the letter, saying, Set ye Uriah in the forefront of the hottest battle, and retire ye from him, that he may be smitten, and die.

2 S 12:9 Wherefore hast thou despised the commandment of the LORD, to do evil in his sight? thou hast killed Uriah the Hittite with the sword, and hast taken his wife *to be* thy wife, and hast slain him with the sword of the children of Ammon.

2 S 13:28 Now Absalom had commanded his servants, saying, Mark ye now when Amnon's heart is merry with wine, and when I say unto you, Smite Amnon; then kill him, fear not: have not I commanded you? be courageous and be valiant.

2 S 20:10 But Amasa took no heed to the sword that *was* in Joab's hand: so he smote him therewith in the fifth *rib,* and shed out his bowels to the ground, and struck him not again; and he died. So Joab and Abishai his brother pursued after Sheba the son of Bichri.

1 K 21:13 And there came in two men, children of Belial, and sat before him: and the men of Belial witnessed against him, *even* against Naboth, in the presence of the people, saying, Naboth did blaspheme God and the king. Then they carried him forth out of the city, and stoned him with stones, that he died.

2 K 11:1 And when Athaliah the mother of Ahaziah saw that her son was dead, she arose and destroyed all the seed royal.

2 Chr 21:4 Now when Jehoram was risen up to the kingdom of his father, he strengthened himself, and slew all his brethren with the sword, and *divers* also of the princes of Israel.

2 Chr 21:13 But hast walked in the way of the kings of Israel, and hast made Judah and the inhabitants of Jerusalem to go a whoring, like to the whoredoms of the house of Ahab, and also hast slain thy brethren of thy father's house, *which were* better than thyself:

2 Chr 22:10 But when Athaliah the mother of Ahaziah saw that her son was dead, she arose and destroyed all the seed royal of the house of Judah.

2 Chr 24:21 And they conspired against him, and stoned him with stones at the commandment of the king in the court of the house of the LORD.

Jb 1:15 And the Sabeans fell *upon them,* and took them away; yea, they have slain the servants with the edge of the sword; and I only am escaped alone to tell thee.

Is 1:21 How is the faithful city become an harlot! it was full of judgment; righteousness lodged in it; but now murderers.

Je 41:3 Ishmael also slew all the Jews that were with him, *even* with Gedaliah, at Mizpah, and the Chaldeans that were found there, *and* the men of war.

Je 41:7 And it was *so,* when they came into the midst of the city, that Ishmael the son of Nethaniah slew them, *and cast them* into the midst of the pit, he, and the men that *were* with him.

Eze 23:39 For when they had slain their children to their idols, then they came the same day into my sanctuary to profane it; and, lo, thus have they done in the midst of mine house.

Mt 2:16 Then Herod, when he saw that he was mocked of the wise men, was exceeding wroth, and sent forth, and slew all the children that were in Bethlehem, and in all the coasts thereof, from two years old and under, according to the time which he had diligently enquired of the wise men.

Mt 21:35 And the husbandmen took his servants, and beat one, and killed another, and stoned another.

Mk 12:8 And they took him, and killed *him,* and cast *him* out of the vineyard.

Mk 15:7 And there was *one* named Barabbas, *which lay* bound with them that had made insurrection with him, who had committed murder in the insurrection.

Lu 23:19 (Who for a certain sedition made in the city, and for murder, was cast into prison.)

Lu 23:25 And he released unto them him that for sedition and murder was cast into prison, whom they had desired; but he delivered Jesus to their will.

Ac 7:58 And cast *him* out of the city, and stoned *him:* and the witnesses laid down their clothes at a young man's feet, whose name was Saul.

Ro 3:15 Their feet *are* swift to shed blood:

Ga 5:21 Envyings, murders, drunkenness, revellings, and such like: of the which I tell you before, as I have also told *you* in time past, that they which do such things shall not inherit the kingdom of God.

1 Jn 3:12 Not as Cain, *who* was of that wicked one, and slew his brother. And wherefore slew he him? Because his own works were evil, and his brother's righteous.

Re 9:21 Neither repented they of their murders, nor of their sorceries, nor of their fornication, nor of their thefts.

b. Rebellion

Ge 9:6 Whoso sheddeth man's blood, by man shall his blood be shed: for in the image of God made he man.

Ex 21:12 He that smiteth a man, so that he die, shall be surely put to death.

Le 24:17 And he that killeth any man shall surely be put to death.

Nu 35:16 And if he smite him with an instrument of iron, so that he die, he *is* a murderer: the murderer shall surely be put to death.

Nu 35:31 Moreover ye shall take no satisfaction for the life of a murderer, which *is* guilty of death: but he shall be surely put to death.

De 19:11 But if any man hate his neighbour, and lie in wait for him, and rise up against him, and smite him mortally that he die, and fleeth into one of these cities:

1 K 2:32 And the LORD shall return his blood upon his own head, who fell upon two men more righteous and better than he, and slew them with the sword, my father David not knowing *thereof, to wit,* Abner the son of Ner, captain of the host of Israel, and Amasa the son of Jether, captain of the host of Judah.

2 K 14:5 And it came to pass, as soon as the kingdom was confirmed in his hand, that he slew his servants which had slain the king his father.

Pr 28:17 A man that doeth violence to the blood of *any* person shall flee to the pit; let no man stay him.

Eze 18:10 If he beget a son *that is* a robber, a shedder of blood, and *that* doeth the like to *any* one of these *things,*

c. Treason

Ex 1:16 And he said, When ye do the office of a midwife to the Hebrew women, and see *them* upon the stools; if it *be* a son, then ye shall kill him: but if it *be* a daughter, then she shall live.

Ex 1:22 And Pharaoh charged all his people, saying, Every son that is born ye shall cast into the river, and every daughter ye shall save alive.

1 S 22:19 And Nob, the city of the priests, smote he with the edge of the sword, both men and women, children and sucklings, and oxen, and asses, and sheep, with the edge of the sword.

Ac 7:19 The same dealt subtilly with our kindred, and evil entreated our fathers, so that they cast out their young children, to the end they might not live.

12. Punishments

a. Banishment

2 S 14:13 And the woman said, Wherefore then hast thou thought such a thing against the people of God? for the king doth speak this thing as one which is faulty, in that the king doth not fetch home again his banished.

Ezr 7:26 And whosoever will not do the law of thy God, and the law of the king, let judgment be executed speedily upon him, whether *it be* unto death, or to banishment, or to confiscation of goods, or to imprisonment.

Ac 18:2 And found a certain Jew named Aquila, born in Pontus, lately come from Italy, with his wife Priscilla; (because that Claudius had commanded all Jews to depart from Rome:) and came unto them.

b. Beatings

Ex 5:14 And the officers of the children of Israel, which Pharaoh's taskmasters had set over them, were beaten, *and* demanded, Wherefore have ye not fulfilled your task in making brick both yesterday and to day, as heretofore?

De 25:3 Forty stripes he may give him, *and* not exceed: lest, *if* he should exceed, and beat him above these with many stripes, then thy brother should seem vile unto thee.

Mt 21:35 And the husbandmen took his servants, and beat one, and killed another, and stoned another.

Mk 12:3 And they caught *him,* and beat him, and sent *him* away empty.

Mk 13:9 But take heed to yourselves: for they shall deliver you up to councils; and in the synagogues ye shall be beaten: and ye shall be brought before rulers and kings for my sake, for a testimony against them.

Lu 20:10 And at the season he sent a servant to the husbandmen, that they should give him of the fruit of the vineyard: but the husbandmen beat him, and sent *him* away empty.

Ac 5:40 And to him they agreed: and when they had called the apostles, and beaten *them,* they commanded that they should not speak in the name of Jesus, and let them go.

Ac 16:22 And the multitude rose up together against them: and the magistrates rent off their clothes, and commanded to beat *them.*

Ac 18:17 Then all the Greeks took Sosthenes, the chief ruler of the synagogue, and beat *him* before the judgment seat. And Gallio cared for none of those things.

Ac 21:32 Who immediately took soldiers and centurions, and ran down unto them: and when they saw the chief captain and the soldiers, they left beating of Paul.

2 Co 11:25 Thrice was I beaten with rods, once was I stoned, thrice I suffered shipwreck, a night and a day I have been in the deep;

He 11:35 Women received their dead raised to life again: and others were tortured, not accepting deliverance; that they might obtain a better resurrection:

c. Beheading

2 S 20:22 Then the woman went unto all the people in her wisdom. And they cut off the head of Sheba the son of Bichri, and cast *it* out to Joab. And he blew a trumpet, and they retired from the city, every man to his tent. And Joab returned to Jerusalem unto the king.

Mt 14:10 And he sent, and beheaded John in the prison.

Mk 6:16 But when Herod heard *thereof,* he said, It is John, whom I beheaded: he is risen from the dead.

Mk 6:27 And immediately the king sent an executioner, and commanded his head to be brought: and he went and beheaded him in the prison,

Lu 9:9 And Herod said, John have I beheaded: but who is this, of whom I hear such things? And he desired to see him.

Ac 12:2 And he killed James the brother of John with the sword.

Re 20:4 And I saw thrones, and they sat upon them, and judgment was given unto them: and *I saw* the souls of them that were beheaded for the witness of Jesus, and for the word of God, and which had not worshipped the beast, neither his image, neither had received *his* mark upon their foreheads, or in their hands; and they lived and reigned with Christ a thousand years.

d. Burning

Ge 38:24 And it came to pass about three months after, that it was told Judah, saying, Tamar thy daughter in law hath played the harlot; and also, behold, she *is* with child by whoredom. And Judah said, Bring her forth, and let her be burnt.

Le 20:14 And if a man take a wife and her mother, it *is* wickedness: they shall be burnt with fire, both he and they; that there be no wickedness among you.

Le 21:9 And the daughter of any priest, if she profane herself by playing the whore, she profaneth her father: she shall be burnt with fire.

Da 3:6 And whoso falleth not down and worshippeth shall the same hour be cast into the midst of a burning fiery furnace.

Da 3:21 Then these men were bound in their coats, their hosen, and their hats, and their *other* garments, and were cast into the midst of the burning fiery furnace.

e. Confiscation of Property

2 S 16:4 Then said the king to Ziba, Behold, thine *are* all that *pertained* unto Mephibosheth. And Ziba said, I humbly beseech thee *that* I may find grace in thy sight, my lord, O king.

1 K 21:16 And it came to pass, when Ahab heard that Naboth was dead, that Ahab rose up to go down to the vineyard of Naboth the Jezreelite, to take possession of it.

Ezr 7:26 And whosoever will not do the law of thy God, and the law of the king, let judgment be executed speedily upon him, whether *it be* unto death, or to banishment, or to confiscation of goods, or to imprisonment.

Ezr 10:8 And that whosoever would not come within three days, according to the counsel of the princes and the elders, all his substance should be forfeited, and himself separated from the congregation of those that had been carried away.

Est 8:1 On that day did the king Ahasuerus give the house of Haman the Jews' enemy unto Esther the queen. And Mordecai came before the king; for Esther had told what he *was* unto her.

f. Exposure to Wild Beasts

Da 6:16 Then the king commanded, and they brought Daniel, and cast *him* into the den of lions. *Now* the king spake and said unto Daniel, Thy God whom thou servest continually, he will deliver thee.

1 Co 15:32 If after the manner of men I have fought with beasts at Ephesus, what advantageth it me, if the dead rise not? let us eat and drink; for to morrow we die.

g. Hanging

Ge 40:22 But he hanged the chief baker: as Joseph had interpreted to them.

De 21:23 His body shall not remain all night upon the tree, but thou shalt in any wise bury him that day; (for he that is hanged *is* accursed of God;) that thy land be not defiled, which the LORD thy God giveth thee *for* an inheritance.

Jos 8:29 And the king of Ai he hanged on a tree until eventide: and as soon as the sun was down, Joshua commanded that they should take his carcase down from the tree, and cast it at the entering of the gate of the city, and raise thereon a great heap of stones, *that remaineth* unto this day.

Jos 10:26 And afterward Joshua smote them, and slew them, and hanged them on five trees: and they were hanging upon the trees until the evening.

2 S 21:9 And he delivered them into the hands of the Gibeonites, and they hanged them in the hill before the LORD: and they fell *all* seven together, and were put to death in the days of harvest, in the first *days,* in the beginning of barley harvest.

Ezr 6:11 Also I have made a decree, that whosoever shall alter this word, let timber be pulled down from his house, and being set up, let him be hanged thereon; and let his house be made a dunghill for this.

Est 2:23 And when inquisition was made of the matter, it was found out; therefore they were both hanged on a tree: and it was written in the book of the chronicles before the king.

Est 7:9 And Harbonah, one of the chamberlains, said before the king, Behold also, the gallows fifty cubits high, which Haman had made for Mordecai, who had spoken good for the king, standeth in the house of Haman. Then the king said, Hang him thereon.

Est 9:14 And the king commanded it so to be done: and the decree was given at Shushan; and they hanged Haman's ten sons.

Lam 5:12 Princes are hanged up by their hand: the faces of elders were not honoured.

Ga 3:13 Christ hath redeemed us from the curse of the law, being made a curse for us: for it is written, Cursed *is* every one that hangeth on a tree:

h. Hard Labor

Ex 1:11–14 Therefore they did set over them taskmasters to afflict them with their burdens. And they built for Pharaoh treasure cities, Pithom and Raamses.

But the more they afflicted them, the more they multiplied and grew. And they were grieved because of the children of Israel.

And the Egyptians made the children of Israel to serve with rigour:

And they made their lives bitter with hard bondage, in morter, and in brick, and in all manner of service in the field: all their service, wherein they made them serve, *was* with rigour.

Jos 9:27 And Joshua made them that day hewers of wood and drawers of water for the congregation, and for the altar of the LORD, even unto this day, in the place which he should choose.

Jud 16:21 But the Philistines took him, and put out his eyes, and brought him down to Gaza, and bound him with fetters of brass; and he did grind in the prison house.

i. Scourging

Jud 8:16 And he took the elders of the city, and thorns of the wilderness and briers, and with them he taught the men of Succoth.

Is 53:8 He was taken from prison and from judgment: and who shall declare his generation? for he was cut off out of the land of the living: for the transgression of my people was he stricken.

Mt 10:17 But beware of men: for they will deliver you up to the councils, and they will scourge you in their synagogues;

Mt 20:19 And shall deliver him to the Gentiles to mock, and to scourge, and to crucify *him:* and the third day he shall rise again.

Mt 23:34 Wherefore, behold, I send unto you prophets, and wise men, and scribes: and *some* of them ye shall kill and crucify; and *some* of them shall ye scourge in your synagogues, and persecute *them* from city to city:

Mt 27:26 Then released he Barabbas unto them: and when he had scourged Jesus, he delivered *him* to be crucified.

Mk 10:34 And they shall mock him, and shall scourge him, and shall spit upon him, and shall kill him: and the third day he shall rise again.

Mk 15:15 And *so* Pilate, willing to content the people, released Barabbas unto them, and delivered Jesus, when he had scourged *him,* to be crucified.

Lu 18:32 For he shall be delivered unto the Gentiles, and shall be mocked, and spitefully entreated, and spitted on:

Lu 23:16 I will therefore chastise him, and release *him.*

Jn 19:1 Then Pilate therefore took Jesus, and scourged *him.*

Ac 22:24 The chief captain commanded him to be brought into the castle, and bade that he should be examined by scourging; that he might know wherefore they cried so against him.

He 11:36 And others had trial of *cruel* mockings and scourgings, yea, moreover of bonds and imprisonment:

j. Stoning

1). Laws Concerning

Ex 19:13 There shall not an hand touch it, but he shall surely be stoned, or shot through; whether *it be* beast or man, it shall not live: when the trumpet soundeth long, they shall come up to the mount.

Le 20:2 Again, thou shalt say to the children of Israel, Whosoever *he be* of the children of Israel, or of the strangers that sojourn in Israel, that giveth *any* of his seed unto Molech; he shall surely be put to death: the people of the land shall stone him with stones.

Le 20:27 A man also or woman that hath a familiar spirit, or that is a wizard, shall surely be put to death: they shall stone them with stones: their blood *shall be* upon them.

Le 24:14 Bring forth him that hath cursed without the camp; and let all that heard *him* lay their hands upon his head, and let all the congregation stone him.

Nu 15:35 And the LORD said unto Moses, The man shall be surely put to death: all the congregation shall stone him with stones without the camp.

De 13:10 And thou shalt stone him with stones, that he die; because he hath sought to thrust thee away from the LORD thy God, which brought thee out of the land of Egypt, from the house of bondage.

De 17:5 Then shalt thou bring forth that man or that woman, which have committed that wicked thing, unto thy gates, *even* that man or that woman, and shalt stone them with stones, till they die.

De 22:21 Then they shall bring out the damsel to the door of her father's house, and the men of her city shall stone her with stones that she die: because she hath wrought folly in Israel, to play the whore in her father's house: so shalt thou put evil away from among you.

De 22:24 Then ye shall bring them both out unto the gate of that city, and ye shall stone them with stones that they die; the damsel, because she cried not, *being* in the city; and the man, because he hath humbled his neighbour's wife: so thou shalt put away evil from among you.

Eze 16:40 They shall also bring up a company against thee, and they shall stone thee with stones, and thrust thee through with their swords.

Eze 23:47 And the company shall stone them with stones, and dispatch them with their swords; they shall slay their sons and their daughters, and burn up their houses with fire.

He 12:20 (For they could not endure that which was commanded, And if so much as a beast touch the mountain, it shall be stoned, or thrust through with a dart:

2). Examples

Le 24:23 And Moses spake to the children of Israel, that they should bring forth him that had cursed out of the camp, and stone him with stones. And the children of Israel did as the LORD commanded Moses.

Nu 14:10 But all the congregation bade stone them with stones. And the glory of the LORD appeared in the tabernacle of the congregation before all the children of Israel.

Jos 7:25 And Joshua said, Why hast thou troubled us? the LORD shall trouble thee this day. And all Israel stoned him with stones, and burned them with fire, after they had stoned them with stones.

1 K 12:18 Then king Rehoboam sent Adoram, who *was* over the tribute; and all Israel stoned him with stones, that he died. Therefore king Rehoboam made speed to get him up to his chariot, to flee to Jerusalem.

1 K 21:13 And there came in two men, children of Belial, and sat before him: and the men of Belial witnessed against him, *even* against Naboth, in the presence of the people, saying, Naboth did blaspheme God and the king. Then they carried him forth out of the city, and stoned him with stones, that he died.

2 Chr 10:18 Then king Rehoboam sent Hadoram that *was* over the tribute; and the children of Israel stoned him with stones, that he died. But king Rehoboam made speed to get him up to *his* chariot, to flee to Jerusalem.

2 Chr 24:21 And they conspired against him, and stoned him with stones at the commandment of the king in the court of the house of the LORD.

Mt 21:35 And the husbandmen took his servants, and beat one, and killed another, and stoned another.

Mk 12:4 And again he sent unto them another servant; and at him they cast stones, and wounded *him* in the head, and sent *him* away shamefully handled.

Lu 20:6 But and if we say, Of men; all the people will stone us: for they be persuaded that John was a prophet.

Jn 8:59 Then took they up stones to cast at him: but Jesus hid himself, and went out of the temple, going through the midst of them, and so passed by.

Jn 10:31 Then the Jews took up stones again to stone him.

Jn 11:8 *His* disciples say unto him, Master, the Jews of late sought to stone thee; and goest thou thither again?

Ac 7:59 And they stoned Stephen, calling upon *God*, and saying, Lord Jesus, receive my spirit.

Ac 14:5 And when there was an assault made both of the Gentiles, and also of the Jews with their rulers, to use *them* despitefully, and to stone them,

Ac 14:19 And there came thither *certain* Jews from Antioch and Iconium, who persuaded the people, and, having stoned Paul, drew *him* out of the city, supposing he had been dead.

2 Co 11:25 Thrice was I beaten with rods, once was I stoned, thrice I suffered shipwreck, a night and a day I have been in the deep;

He 11:37 They were stoned, they were sawn asunder, were tempted, were slain with the sword: they wandered about in sheepskins and goatskins; being destitute, afflicted, tormented;

k. Stripes

1). Number Limited by Mosaic Law

De 25:3 Forty stripes he may give him, *and* not exceed: lest, *if* he should exceed, and beat him above these with many stripes, then thy brother should seem vile unto thee.

2 Co 11:24 Of the Jews five times received I forty *stripes* save one.

2). Examples

Is 53:5 But he *was* wounded for our transgressions, *he was* bruised for our iniquities: the chastisement of our peace *was* upon him; and with his stripes we are healed.

Ac 16:23 And when they had laid many stripes upon them, they cast *them* into prison, charging the jailer to keep them safely:

2 Co 6:5 In stripes, in imprisonments, in tumults, in labours, in watchings, in fastings;

2 Co 11:24 Of the Jews five times received I forty *stripes* save one.

1 Pe 2:24 Who his own self bare our sins in his own body on the tree, that we, being dead to sins, should live unto righteousness: by whose stripes ye were healed.

See **MUTILATION**

13. Nations Used to Judge Other Nations

Nu 14:45 Then the Amalekites came down, and the Canaanites which dwelt in that hill, and smote them, and discomfited them, *even* unto Hormah.

De 28:50 A nation of fierce countenance, which shall not regard the person of the old, nor shew favour to the young:

De 32:21 They have moved me to jealousy with *that which is* not God; they have provoked me to anger with their vanities: and I will move them to jealousy with *those which are* not a people; I will provoke them to anger with a foolish nation.

Jud 3:12 And the children of Israel did evil again in the sight of the LORD: and the LORD strengthened Eglon the king of Moab against Israel, because they had done evil in the sight of the LORD.

2 S 7:14 I will be his father, and he shall be my son. If he commit iniquity, I will chasten him with the rod of men, and with the stripes of the children of men:

1 K 11:14 And the LORD stirred up an adversary unto Solomon, Hadad the Edomite: he *was* of the king's seed in Edom.

1 K 11:23 And God stirred him up *another* adversary, Rezon the son of Eliadah, which fled from his lord Hadadezer king of Zobah:

1 K 14:25 And it came to pass in the fifth year of king Rehoboam, *that* Shishak king of Egypt came up against Jerusalem:

1 K 19:17 And it shall come to pass, *that* him that escapeth the sword of Hazael shall Jehu slay: and him that escapeth from the sword of Jehu shall Elisha slay.

2 K 15:37 In those days the LORD began to send against Judah Rezin the king of Syria, and Pekah the son of Remaliah.

2 K 19:25 Hast thou not heard long ago *how* I have done it, *and* of ancient times that I have formed it? now have I brought it to pass, that thou shouldest be to lay waste fenced cities *into* ruinous heaps.

2 K 24:2 And the LORD sent against him bands of the Chaldees, and bands of the Syrians, and bands of the Moabites, and bands of the children of Ammon, and sent them against Judah to destroy it, according to the word of the LORD, which he spake by his servants the prophets.

1 Chr 5:26 And the God of Israel stirred up the spirit of Pul king of Assyria, and the spirit of Tilgath-pilneser king of Assyria, and he carried them away, even the Reubenites, and the Gadites, and the half tribe of Manasseh, and brought them unto Halah, and Habor, and Hara, and to the river Gozan, unto this day.

2 Chr 21:16 Moreover the LORD stirred up against Jehoram the spirit of the Philistines, and of the Arabians, that *were* near the Ethiopians:

2 Chr 22:7 And the destruction of Ahaziah was of God by coming to Joram: for when he was come, he went out with Jehoram against Jehu the son of Nimshi, whom the LORD had anointed to cut off the house of Ahab.

2 Chr 24:23 And it came to pass at the end of the year, *that* the host of Syria came up against him: and they came to Judah and Jerusalem, and destroyed all the princes of the people from among the people, and sent all the spoil of them unto the king of Damascus.

2 Chr 33:11 Wherefore the LORD brought upon them the captains of the host of the king of Assyria, which took Manasseh among the thorns, and bound him with fetters, and carried him to Babylon.

2 Chr 36:17 Therefore he brought upon them the king of the Chaldees, who slew their young men with the sword in the house of their sanctuary, and had no compassion upon young man or maiden, old man, or him that stooped for age: he gave *them* all into his hand.

Ps 89:42 Thou hast set up the right hand of his adversaries; thou hast made all his enemies to rejoice.

Is 5:26 And he will lift up an ensign to the nations from far, and will hiss unto them from the end of the earth: and, behold, they shall come with speed swiftly:

Is 7:18 And it shall come to pass in that day, *that* the LORD shall hiss for the fly that *is* in the uttermost part of the rivers of Egypt, and for the bee that *is* in the land of Assyria.

Is 8:7 Now therefore, behold, the Lord bringeth up upon them the waters of the river, strong and many, *even* the king of Assyria, and all his glory: and he shall come up over all his channels, and go over all his banks:

Is 9:12 The Syrians before, and the Philistines behind; and they shall devour Israel with open mouth. For all this his anger is not turned away, but his hand *is* stretched out still.

Is 10:5 O Assyrian, the rod of mine anger, and the staff in their hand is mine indignation.

Is 13:3 I have commanded my sanctified ones, I have also called my mighty ones for mine anger, *even* them that rejoice in my highness.

Is 13:17 Behold, I will stir up the Medes against them, which shall not regard silver; and *as for* gold, they shall not delight in it.

Is 29:3 And I will camp against thee round about, and will lay siege against thee with a mount, and I will raise forts against thee.

Is 37:26 Hast thou not heard long ago, *how* I have done it; *and* of ancient times, that I have formed it? now have I brought it to pass, that thou shouldest be to lay waste defenced cities *into* ruinous heaps.

Is 41:25 I have raised up *one* from the north, and he shall come: from the rising of the sun shall he call upon my name: and he shall come upon princes as *upon* morter, and as the potter treadeth clay.

Is 46:11 Calling a ravenous bird from the east, the man that executeth my counsel from a far country: yea, I have spoken *it,* I will also bring it to pass; I have purposed *it,* I will also do it.

Is 54:16 Behold, I have created the smith that bloweth the coals in the fire, and that bringeth forth an instrument for his work; and I have created the waster to destroy.

Je 5:15 Lo, I will bring a nation upon you from far, O house of Israel, saith the LORD: it *is* a mighty nation, it *is* an ancient nation, a nation whose language thou knowest not, neither understandest what they say.

Je 6:22 Thus saith the LORD, Behold, a people cometh from the north country, and a great nation shall be raised from the sides of the earth.

Je 8:16 The snorting of his horses was heard from Dan: the whole land trembled at the sound of the neighing of his strong ones; for they are come, and have devoured the land, and all that is in it; the city, and those that dwell therein.

Je 12:9 Mine heritage *is* unto me *as* a speckled bird, the birds round about *are* against her; come ye, assemble all the beasts of the field, come to devour.

Je 18:22 Let a cry be heard from their houses, when thou shalt bring a troop suddenly upon them: for they have digged a pit to take me, and hid snares for my feet.

Je 21:4 Thus saith the LORD God of Israel; Behold, I will turn back the weapons of war that *are* in your hands, wherewith ye fight *against* the king of Babylon, and against the Chaldeans, which besiege you without the walls, and I will assemble them into the midst of this city.

Je 22:7 And I will prepare destroyers against thee, every one with his weapons: and they shall cut down thy choice cedars, and cast *them* into the fire.

Je 25:9 Behold, I will send and take all the families of the north, saith the LORD, and Nebuchadrezzar the king of Babylon, my servant, and will bring them against this land, and against the inhabitants thereof, and against all these nations round about, and will utterly destroy them, and make them an astonishment, and an hissing, and perpetual desolations.

Je 34:22 Behold, I will command, saith the LORD, and cause them to return to this city; and they shall fight against it, and take it, and burn it with fire: and I will make the cities of Judah a desolation without an inhabitant.

Je 37:8 And the Chaldeans shall come again, and fight against this city, and take it, and burn it with fire.

Je 43:11 And when he cometh, he shall smite the land of Egypt, *and deliver* such *as are* for death to death; and such *as are* for captivity to captivity; and such *as are* for the sword to the sword.

Je 46:22 The voice thereof shall go like a serpent; for they shall march with an army, and come against her with axes, as hewers of wood.

Je 49:14 I have heard a rumour from the LORD, and an ambassador is sent unto the heathen, *saying,* Gather ye together, and come against her, and rise up to the battle.

Je 50:9 For, lo, I will raise and cause to come up against Babylon an assembly of great nations from the north country: and they shall set themselves in array against her; from thence she shall be taken: their arrows *shall be* as of a mighty expert man; none shall return in vain.

Je 50:21 Go up against the land of Merathaim, *even* against it, and against the inhabitants of Pekod: waste and utterly destroy after them, saith the LORD, and do according to all that I have commanded thee.

Je 50:29 Call together the archers against Babylon: all ye that bend the bow, camp against it round about; let none thereof escape: recompense her according to her work; according to all that she hath done, do unto her: for she hath been proud against the LORD, against the Holy One of Israel.

Je 51:11 Make bright the arrows; gather the shields: the LORD hath raised up the spirit of the kings of the Medes: for his device *is* against Babylon, to destroy it; because it *is* the vengeance of the LORD, the vengeance of his temple.

Je 51:20 Thou *art* my battle axe *and* weapons of war: for with thee will I break in pieces the nations, and with thee will I destroy kingdoms;

Lam 1:17 Zion spreadeth forth her hands, *and there is* none to comfort her: the LORD hath commanded concerning Jacob, *that* his adversaries *should be* round about him: Jerusalem is as a menstruous woman among them.

Lam 2:17 The LORD hath done *that* which he had devised; he hath fulfilled his word that he had commanded in the days of old: he hath thrown down, and hath not pitied: and he hath caused *thine* enemy to rejoice over thee, he hath set up the horn of thine adversaries.

Eze 21:11 And he hath given it to be furbished, that it may be handled: this sword is sharpened, and it is furbished, to give it into the hand of the slayer.

Eze 23:10 These discovered her nakedness: they took her sons and her daughters, and slew her with the sword: and she became famous among women; for they had executed judgment upon her.

Eze 23:22 Therefore, O Aholibah, thus saith the Lord GOD; Behold, I will raise up thy lovers against thee, from whom thy mind is alienated, and I will bring them against thee on every side;

Eze 23:46 For thus saith the Lord GOD; I will bring up a company upon them, and will give them to be removed and spoiled.

Eze 26:7 For thus saith the Lord GOD; Behold, I will bring upon Tyrus Nebuchadrezzar king of Babylon, a king of kings, from the north, with horses, and with chariots, and with horsemen, and companies, and much people.

Eze 28:7 Behold, therefore I will bring strangers upon thee, the terrible of the nations: and they shall draw their swords against the beauty of thy wisdom, and they shall defile thy brightness.

Eze 28:10 Thou shalt die the deaths of the uncircumcised by the hand of strangers: for I have spoken *it,* saith the Lord GOD.

Eze 29:18 Son of man, Nebuchadrezzar king of Babylon caused his army to serve a great service against Tyrus: every head *was* made bald, and every shoulder *was* peeled: yet had he no wages, nor his army, for Tyrus, for the service that he had served against it:

Eze 30:11 He and his people with him, the terrible of the nations, shall be brought to destroy the land: and they shall draw their swords against Egypt, and fill the land with the slain.

Eze 30:25 But I will strengthen the arms of the king of Babylon, and the arms of Pharaoh shall fall down; and they shall know that I *am* the LORD, when I shall put my sword into the hand of the king of Babylon, and he shall stretch it out upon the land of Egypt.

Eze 32:11 For thus saith the Lord GOD; The sword of the king of Babylon shall come upon thee.

Ho 10:10 *It is* in my desire that I should chastise them; and the people shall be gathered against them, when they shall bind themselves in their two furrows.

Ho 13:15 Though he be fruitful among *his* brethren, an east wind shall come, the wind of the LORD shall come up from the wilderness, and his spring shall become dry, and his fountain shall be dried up: he shall spoil the treasure of all pleasant vessels.

Jl 1:6 For a nation is come up upon my land, strong, and without number, whose teeth *are* the teeth of a lion, and he hath the cheek teeth of a great lion.

Jl 2:2 A day of darkness and of gloominess, a day of clouds and of thick darkness, as the morning spread upon the mountains: a great people and a strong; there hath not been ever the like, neither shall be any more after it, *even* to the years of many generations.

Am 3:11 Therefore thus saith the Lord GOD; An adversary *there shall be* even round about the land; and he shall bring down thy strength from thee, and thy palaces shall be spoiled.

Am 6:14 But, behold, I will raise up against you a nation, O house of Israel, saith the LORD the God of hosts; and they shall afflict you from the entering in of Hemath unto the river of the wilderness.

Hab 1:7 They *are* terrible and dreadful: their judgment and their dignity shall proceed of themselves.

Mt 22:7 But when the king heard *thereof,* he was wroth: and he sent forth his armies, and destroyed those murderers, and burned up their city.

Lu 19:43 For the days shall come upon thee, that thine enemies shall cast a trench about thee, and compass thee round, and keep thee in on every side,

Re 17:16 And the ten horns which thou sawest upon the beast, these shall hate the whore, and shall make her desolate and naked, and shall eat her flesh, and burn her with fire.

14. Ambassadors

Nu 20:14 And Moses sent messengers from Kadesh unto the king of Edom, Thus saith thy brother Israel, Thou knowest all the travail that hath befallen us:

Nu 21:21 And Israel sent messengers unto Sihon king of the Amorites, saying,

De 2:26 And I sent messengers out of the wilderness of Kedemoth unto Sihon king of Heshbon with words of peace, saying,

Jos 9:4 They did work wilily, and went and made as if they had been ambassadors, and took old sacks upon their asses, and wine bottles, old, and rent, and bound up;

Jos 22:14 And with him ten princes, of each chief house a prince throughout all the tribes of Israel; and each one *was* an head of the house of their fathers among the thousands of Israel.

Jud 11:14 And Jephthah sent messengers again unto the king of the children of Ammon:

Jud 11:19 And Israel sent messengers unto Sihon king of the Amorites, the king of Heshbon; and Israel said unto him, Let us pass, we pray thee, through thy land into my place.

2 S 5:11 And Hiram king of Tyre sent messengers to David, and cedar trees, and carpenters, and masons: and they built David an house.

1 K 5:1 And Hiram king of Tyre sent his servants unto Solomon; for he had heard that they had anointed him king in the room of his father: for Hiram was ever a lover of David.

1 K 20:2 And he sent messengers to Ahab king of Israel into the city, and said unto him, Thus saith Ben-hadad,

2 K 14:8 Then Amaziah sent messengers to Jehoash, the son of Jehoahaz son of Jehu, king of Israel, saying, Come, let us look one another in the face.

2 K 16:7 So Ahaz sent messengers to Tiglath-pileser king of Assyria, saying, I *am* thy servant and thy son: come up, and save me out of the hand of the king of Syria, and out of the hand of the king of Israel, which rise up against me.

1 Chr 18:10 He sent Hadoram his son to king David, to enquire of his welfare, and to congratulate him, because he had fought against Hadarezer, and smitten him; (for Hadarezer had war with Tou;) and *with him* all manner of vessels of gold and silver and brass.

1 Chr 19:2 And David said, I will shew kindness unto Hanun the son of Nahash, because his father shewed kindness to me. And David sent messengers to comfort him concerning his father. So the servants of David came into the land of the children of Ammon to Hanun, to comfort him.

2 Chr 35:21 But he sent ambassadors to him, saying, What have I to do with thee, thou king of Judah? *I come* not against thee this day, but against the house wherewith I have war: for God commanded me to make haste: forbear thee from *meddling with* God, who *is* with me, that he destroy thee not.

Is 18:2 That sendeth ambassadors by the sea, even in vessels of bulrushes upon the waters, *saying,* Go, ye swift messengers, to a nation scattered and peeled, to a people terrible from their beginning hitherto; a nation meted out and trodden down, whose land the rivers have spoiled!

Eze 17:15 But he rebelled against him in sending his ambassadors into Egypt, that they might give him horses and much people. Shall he prosper? shall he escape that doeth such *things?* or shall he break the covenant, and be delivered?

Obad 1 The vision of Obadiah. Thus saith the Lord GOD concerning Edom; We have heard a rumour from the LORD, and an ambassador is sent among the heathen, Arise ye, and let us rise up against her in battle.

Lu 14:32 Or else, while the other is yet a great way off, he sendeth an ambassage, and desireth conditions of peace.

15. Census Taken of the Israelites

Ex 30:12 When thou takest the sum of the children of Israel after their number, then shall they give every man a ransom for his soul unto the LORD, when thou numberest them; that there be no plague among them, when *thou* numberest them.

Nu 1:2 Take ye the sum of all the congregation of the children of Israel, after their families, by the house of their fathers, with the number of *their* names, every male by their polls;

Nu 3:15 Number the children of Levi after the house of their fathers, by their families: every male from a

month old and upward shalt thou number them.

Nu 4:2 Take the sum of the sons of Kohath from among the sons of Levi, after their families, by the house of their fathers,

Nu 4:22 Take also the sum of the sons of Gershon, throughout the houses of their fathers, by their families;

Nu 4:36 And those that were numbered of them by their families were two thousand seven hundred and fifty.

Nu 26:2 Take the sum of all the congregation of the children of Israel, from twenty years old and upward, throughout their fathers' house, all that are able to go to war in Israel.

Nu 26:63–64 These *are* they that were numbered by Moses and Eleazar the priest, who numbered the children of Israel in the plains of Moab by Jordan *near* Jericho.

But among these there was not a man of them whom Moses and Aaron the priest numbered, when they numbered the children of Israel in the wilderness of Sinai.

Nu 31:49 And they said unto Moses, Thy servants have taken the sum of the men of war which *are* under our charge, and there lacketh not one man of us.

2 S 24:2 For the king said to Joab the captain of the host, which *was* with him, Go now through all the tribes of Israel, from Dan even to Beer-sheba, and number ye the people, that I may know the number of the people.

2 K 3:6 And king Jehoram went out of Samaria the same time, and numbered all Israel.

1 Chr 21:1 And Satan stood up against Israel, and provoked David to number Israel.

1 Chr 27:24 Joab the son of Zeruiah began to number, but he finished not, because there fell wrath for it against Israel; neither was the number put in the account of the chronicles of king David.

Lu 2:1 And it came to pass in those days, that there went out a decree from Caesar Augustus, that all the world should be taxed.

See **ISRAEL, JUDGMENTS, JUSTICE**

NATURE

1. Its Beauty, *reflects God's glory*

Song 2:12 The flowers appear on the earth; the time of the singing *of birds* is come, and the voice of the turtle is heard in our land;

Is 35:1 The wilderness and the solitary place shall be glad for them; and the desert shall rejoice, and blossom as the rose.

Mt 6:29 And yet I say unto you, That even Solomon in all his glory was not arrayed like one of these.

2. Its Lessons, *reveal God's careful design*

Ps 8:3–4 When I consider thy heavens, the work of thy fingers, the moon and the stars, which thou hast ordained;

What is man, that thou art mindful of him? and the son of man, that thou visitest him?

Mt 6:28 And why take ye thought for raiment? Consider the lilies of the field, how they grow; they toil not, neither do they spin:

Mt 13:31 Another parable put he forth unto them, saying, The kingdom of heaven is like to a grain of mustard seed, which a man took, and sowed in his field:

Mk 4:28 For the earth bringeth forth fruit of herself; first the blade, then the ear, after that the full corn in the ear.

Mk 13:28 Now learn a parable of the fig tree; When her branch is yet tender, and putteth forth leaves, ye know that summer is near:

3. Its Mysteries

Ps 139:15 My substance was not hid from thee, when I was made in secret, *and* curiously wrought in the lowest parts of the earth.

Ec 11:5 As thou knowest not what *is* the way of the spirit, *nor* how the bones *do grow* in the womb of her that is with child: even so thou knowest not the works of God who maketh all.

Mk 4:27–28 And should sleep, and rise night and day, and the seed should spring and grow up, he knoweth not how.

For the earth bringeth forth fruit of herself; first the blade, then the ear, after that the full corn in the ear.

Jn 3:8 The wind bloweth where it listeth, and thou hearest the sound thereof, but canst not tell whence it cometh, and whither it goeth: so is every one that is born of the Spirit.

See **CREATOR, MYSTERIES, REVELATIONS**

NAZARENE, *an inhabitant or native of the town of Nazareth*

Mt 2:23; Ac 24:5

NAZARETH, *a town of Galilee, early home of Christ*

It is the village where Joseph and Mary lived and was the home of Jesus until He began His public ministry. The Mediterranean Sea is twenty miles to the west, and fifteen miles to the east is the Sea of Galilee. The town lies near one of the main highways between Egypt and Mesopotamia. The village covered no more than sixty acres in Jesus' time, with a population estimated at about five hundred.

Mt 2:23; 4:13; 13:54; Mk 1:9; 6:1; Lu 1:26; 2:4, 39, 51; 4:16, 29; Jn 1:46

See **CHRIST**

NEARNESS, *TO GOD*

1. Available to All Who Seek

De 4:7 For what nation *is there so* great, who *hath* God so nigh unto them, as the LORD our God *is* in all *things that* we call upon him *for?*

Ps 16:8 I have set the LORD always before me: because *he is* at my right hand, I shall not be moved.

Ps 35:22 *This* thou hast seen, O LORD: keep not silence: O Lord, be not far from me.

Ps 38:21 Forsake me not, O LORD: O my God, be not far from me.

Ps 71:12 O God, be not far from me: O my God, make haste for my help.

Ps 75:1 Unto thee, O God, do we give thanks, *unto thee* do we give thanks:

for *that* thy name is near thy wondrous works declare.

Ps 119:151 Thou *art* near, O Lord; and all thy commandments *are* truth.

Ps 145:18 The Lord *is* nigh unto all them that call upon him, to all that call upon him in truth.

Is 50:8 *He is* near that justifieth me; who will contend with me? let us stand together: who *is* mine adversary? let him come near to me.

Is 55:6 Seek ye the Lord while he may be found, call ye upon him while he is near:

Je 23:23 *Am* I a God at hand, saith the Lord, and not a God afar off?

Lam 3:57 Thou drewest near in the day *that* I called upon thee: thou saidst, Fear not.

Mt 20:30 And, behold, two blind men sitting by the way side, when they heard that Jesus passed by, cried out, saying, Have mercy on us, O Lord, *thou* Son of David.

Ac 2:25 For David speaketh concerning him, I foresaw the Lord always before my face, for he is on my right hand, that I should not be moved:

Ac 17:27 That they should seek the Lord, if haply they might feel after him, and find him, though he be not far from every one of us:

Ro 10:6 But the righteousness which is of faith speaketh on this wise, Say not in thine heart, Who shall ascend into heaven? (that is, to bring Christ down *from above:*)

Re 3:20 Behold, I stand at the door, and knock: if any man hear my voice, and open the door, I will come in to him, and will sup with him, and he with me.

2. Prayer and Fellowship

Ex 16:9 And Moses spake unto Aaron, Say unto all the congregation of the children of Israel, Come near before the Lord: for he hath heard your murmurings.

Ex 19:17 And Moses brought forth the people out of the camp to meet with God; and they stood at the nether part of the mount.

Ex 24:1 And he said unto Moses, Come up unto the Lord, thou, and

Aaron, Nadab, and Abihu, and seventy of the elders of Israel; and worship ye afar off.

Ex 24:12 And the Lord said unto Moses, Come up to me into the mount, and be there: and I will give thee tables of stone, and a law, and commandments which I have written; that thou mayest teach them.

Le 9:5 And they brought *that* which Moses commanded before the tabernacle of the congregation: and all the congregation drew near and stood before the Lord.

De 5:27 Go thou near, and hear all that the Lord our God shall say: and speak thou unto us all that the Lord our God shall speak unto thee; and we will hear *it,* and do *it.*

1 S 14:36 And Saul said, Let us go down after the Philistines by night, and spoil them until the morning light, and let us not leave a man of them. And they said, Do whatsoever seemeth good unto thee. Then said the priest, Let us draw near hither unto God.

Ps 73:28 But *it is* good for me to draw near to God: I have put my trust in the Lord God, that I may declare all thy works.

Zep 3:2 She obeyed not the voice; she received not correction; she trusted not in the Lord; she drew not near to her God.

He 7:19 For the law made nothing perfect, but the bringing in of a better hope *did;* by the which we draw nigh unto God.

He 10:22 Let us draw near with a true heart in full assurance of faith, having our hearts sprinkled from an evil conscience, and our bodies washed with pure water.

Ja 4:8 Draw nigh to God, and he will draw nigh to you. Cleanse *your* hands, *ye* sinners; and purify *your* hearts, *ye* double minded.

3. Abiding in Christ

Jn 8:31 Then said Jesus to those Jews which believed on him, If ye continue in my word, *then* are ye my disciples indeed;

Jn 15:4–5 Abide in me, and I in you. As the branch cannot bear fruit of itself, except it abide in the vine; no more can ye, except ye abide in me.

I am the vine, ye *are* the branches: He that abideth in me, and I in him, the same bringeth forth much fruit: for without me ye can do nothing.

Jn 15:7 If ye abide in me, and my words abide in you, ye shall ask what ye will, and it shall be done unto you.

Jn 15:10 If ye keep my commandments, ye shall abide in my love even as I have kept my Father's commandments, and abide in his love.

1 Jn 2:6 He that saith he abideth in him ought himself also so to walk, even as he walked.

1 Jn 2:10 He that loveth his brother abideth in the light, and there is none occasion of stumbling in him.

1 Jn 2:28 And now, little children, abide in him; that, when he shall appear, we may have confidence, and not be ashamed before him at his coming.

1 Jn 3:6 Whosoever abideth in him sinneth not: whosoever sinneth hath not seen him, neither known him.

1 Jn 5:20 *And* we know that the Son of God is come, and hath given us an understanding, that we may know him that is true, and we are in him that is true, *even* in his Son Jesus Christ. This is the true God, and eternal life.

2 Jn 9 Whosoever transgresseth, and abideth not in the doctrine of Christ, hath not God. He that abideth in the doctrine of Christ, he hath both the Father and the Son.

See **CONSECRATION, DEEPER LIFE, DEVOTIONAL LIFE, PRAYER**

NEBO, *to be high; may refer to a Babylonian deity*

1. Mount

See **MOUNTAINS AND HILLS**

2. An Idol

Is 46:1

3. Town and District

Nu 32:3; 1 Chr 5:8; Is 15:2; 46:1; Je 48:1

NEBUCHADNEZZAR, *Babylonian ruler during Israel's captivity*

2 K 24:1, 11; 25:1, 22; 1 Chr 6:15; 2 Chr 36:6; Ezr 2:1; 5:12; Ne 7:6; Je 21:2, 7; 22:25; 25:1; 27:6, 20; 32:1, 28; 34:1; 35:11; 39:1, 11; 43:10; 49:30; 50:17; 51:34; 52:4; Eze 26:7; Da 1:1, 18; 2:1, 46; 3:1; 4:1, 28, 37

Prophecies

Je 21:1–14; 25:1–38; 27:1–22; 28:1–17; 32:1–44; 34:1–22

NEBUZARADAN, *a Babylonian general*

2 K 25:8, 20; Je 39:9, 11; 40:1; 43:6; 52:12

NECROMANCY, *consulting the dead*

De 18:11; 1 S 28:11; Is 8:19; 65:4

See **MAGICIANS**

NEEDLES, *used by Jesus in explaining about salvation*

Mt 19:24; Mk 10:25

NEEDLEWORK See **ARTS AND CRAFTS**

NEGLECT, *negligence*

1. Of Duty

Ex 4:13; Nu 9:13; De 28:47; Jud 5:16, 23; 21:8; 1 S 26:16; 2 K 12:6; 23:9; Ne 3:5; 9:35; Est 4:14; Je 20:9; 23:2; 48:10; Eze 3:20; 33:8; 34:6; Jona 1:3; Hag 1:2; Mt 7:26; 20:6; 25:18, 27; Lu 11:46; 12:47; 19:20; Ro 16:18; He 10:25; Ja 2:14; 4:17

2. Of Mercy and Help

1 S 30:13; Jb 16:7; 22:7; 24:21; Ps 109:16; Pr 21:13; 24:11; 29:7; Is 58:7; Eze 16:49; 34:4; Obad 13; Zec 11:16; Mt 23:23; 25:43; Lu 10:31; 16:20–21; Ja 4:17; 1 Jn 3:17

3. Of Salvation

IMPENITENCE

Eze 33:9 Nevertheless, if thou warn the wicked of his way to turn from it; if he do not turn from his way, he shall die in his iniquity; but thou hast delivered thy soul.

ABSORPTION IN BUSINESS

Lu 14:18 And they all with one *consent* began to make excuse. The first said unto him, I have bought a piece of ground, and I must needs go and see it: I pray thee have me excused.

PROCRASTINATION

Ac 24:25 And as he reasoned of righteousness, temperance, and judgment to come, Felix trembled, and answered, Go thy way for this time; when I have a convenient season, I will call for thee.

INSENSIBILITY

Ac 28:27 For the heart of this people is waxed gross, and their ears are dull of hearing, and their eyes have they closed; lest they should see with *their* eyes, and hear with *their* ears, and understand with *their* heart, and should be converted, and I should heal them.

ITS PERILOUSNESS

He 2:3 How shall we escape, if we neglect so great salvation; which at the first began to be spoken by the Lord, and was confirmed unto us by them that heard *him;*

He 12:25 See that ye refuse not him that speaketh. For if they escaped not who refused him that spake on earth, much more *shall not* we *escape,* if we turn away from him that *speaketh* from heaven:

See **HELPER, MERCY, SALVATION**

NEHEMIAH

1. Person, *Jehovah consoles; appointed governor and rebuilder of Jerusalem*

PATRIOTISM
Ne 1:1–4

PRAYERFULNESS
Ne 1:5–11; 4:4–5, 9

FAITH
Ne 2:20; 4:14

COURAGE
Ne 4:20; 6:10–11

DILIGENCE
Ne 4:21–23; 6:3

EXECUTIVE ABILITY
Ne 4:13–20

FIRMNESS IN THE RIGHT
Ne 13:11, 17, 25

EARNESTNESS IN REFORM
Ne 5; 13:15–31

2. Book

Author: Uncertain. A large portion of the book is regarded by many students as an autobiography of Nehemiah.

Date Written: Around 445 B.C. to 430 B.C.

Purpose: To document the political restoration of Judah under Nehemiah's leadership.

To Whom Written: The restored remnant in Jerusalem and future generations.

Main Themes: The rebuilding of the walls of Jerusalem, the rehearsal of certain divine laws, and the restoration of ancient ordinances.

Key Word: Wall.

Key Verses: 6:3, 15–16.

NEIGHBORS *See* **SOCIAL DUTIES**

NEW BIRTH *See* **SALVATION**

NET, *meshed strings used by fishermen and hunters*

1. For Fish

Eze 26:5; Mi 7:2; Hab 1:15; Mt 4:18; Mk 1:19; Lu 5:2; Jn 21:6, 8

2. A Snare for Men

Ps 9:15; 10:9; 25:15; 31:4; 35:7; 57:6; 140:5; Pr 1:17; 29:5; Je 5:26; Eze 12:13; Mi 7:2

NETHINIM, *servants of the Levites*

1 Chr 9:2; Ezr 2:43; 7:7; 8:20; Ne 3:26; 7:46, 60, 73; 10:28; 11:3, 21

NETTLES, *thorns, scrubs, brush*

Jb 30:7; Pr 24:31; Is 34:13; Ho 9:6; Zep 2:9

NEUTRALITY, *not possible in relation to spiritual things*

Jos 24:19; Mt 6:24; 12:30; Mk 9:40; Lu 9:50; 11:23; 12:52; 16:13

See **HALFHEARTEDNESS, INDECISION**

NEW PERSON

1. Believers

Ps 40:3 And he hath put a new song in my mouth, *even* praise unto our God: many shall see *it,* and fear, and shall trust in the LORD.

Eze 11:19 And I will give them one heart, and I will put a new spirit within you; and I will take the stony heart out of their flesh, and will give them an heart of flesh:

Mt 20:26 But it shall not be so among you: but whosoever will be great among you, let him be your minister;

Mk 5:15 And they come to Jesus, and see him that was possessed with the devil, and had the legion, sitting, and clothed, and in his right mind: and they were afraid.

Lu 8:35 Then they went out to see what was done; and came to Jesus, and found the man, out of whom the devils were departed, sitting at the feet of Jesus, clothed, and in his right mind: and they were afraid.

Jn 1:13 Which were born, not of blood, nor of the will of the flesh, nor of the will of man, but of God.

Jn 3:7 Marvel not that I said unto thee, Ye must be born again.

Jn 9:8 The neighbours therefore, and they which before had seen him that he was blind, said, Is not this he that sat and begged?

Ro 6:4 Therefore we are buried with him by baptism into death: that like as Christ was raised up from the dead by the glory of the Father, even so we also should walk in newness of life.

Ro 6:19 I speak after the manner of men because of the infirmity of your flesh: for as ye have yielded your members servants to uncleanness and to iniquity unto iniquity; even so now yield your members servants to righteousness unto holiness.

Ro 7:6 But now we are delivered from the law, that being dead wherein we were held; that we should serve in newness of spirit, and not *in* the oldness of the letter.

Ro 8:9 But ye are not in the flesh, but in the Spirit, if so be that the Spirit of God dwell in you. Now if any man have not the Spirit of Christ, he is none of his.

1 Co 5:7 Purge out therefore the old leaven, that ye may be a new lump, as ye are unleavened. For even Christ our passover is sacrificed for us:

2 Co 5:17 Therefore if any man *be* in Christ, *he is* a new creature: old things are passed away; behold, all things are become new.

Ga 6:15 For in Christ Jesus neither circumcision availeth any thing, nor uncircumcision, but a new creature.

Ep 2:10 For we are his workmanship, created in Christ Jesus unto good works, which God hath before ordained that we should walk in them.

Ep 2:15 Having abolished in his flesh the enmity, *even* the law of commandments *contained* in ordinances; for to make in himself of twain one new man, *so* making peace;

Ep 4:24 And that ye put on the new man, which after God is created in righteousness and true holiness.

Col 3:10 And have put on the new *man,* which is renewed in knowledge after the image of him that created him:

1 Pe 4:2 That he no longer should live the rest of *his* time in the flesh to the lusts of men, but to the will of God.

2. Raised from Spiritual Death

Is 26:19 Thy dead *men* shall live, *together with* my dead body shall they arise. Awake and sing, ye that dwell in dust: for thy dew *is as* the dew of herbs, and the earth shall cast out the dead.

Eze 37:10 So I prophesied as he commanded me, and the breath came into them, and they lived, and stood up upon their feet, an exceeding great army.

Ho 6:2 After two days will he revive us: in the third day he will raise us up, and we shall live in his sight.

Lu 15:24 For this my son was dead, and is alive again; he was lost, and is found. And they began to be merry.

Jn 5:25 Verily, verily, I say unto you, The hour is coming, and now is, when the dead shall hear the voice of the Son of God: and they that hear shall live.

Ro 6:5 For if we have been planted together in the likeness of his death, we shall be also *in the likeness of his* resurrection:

Ro 6:13 Neither yield ye your members *as* instruments of unrighteousness unto sin: but yield yourselves unto God, as those that are alive from the dead, and your members *as* instruments of righteousness unto God.

Ro 8:11 But if the Spirit of him that raised up Jesus from the dead dwell in you, he that raised up Christ from the dead shall also quicken your mortal bodies by his Spirit that dwelleth in you.

Ro 11:15 For if the casting away of them *be* the reconciling of the world, what *shall* the receiving *of them be,* but life from the dead?

Ep 2:1 And you *hath he quickened,* who were dead in trespasses and sins;

Ep 2:6 And hath raised *us* up together, and made *us* sit together in heavenly *places* in Christ Jesus:

Ph 3:10 That I may know him, and the power of his resurrection, and the fellowship of his sufferings, being made conformable unto his death;

Col 2:12–13 Buried with him in baptism, wherein also ye are risen with *him* through the faith of the operation of God, who hath raised him from the dead.

And you, being dead in your sins and the uncircumcision of your flesh, hath he quickened together with him, having forgiven you all trespasses;

Col 3:1 If ye then be risen with Christ, seek those things which are above, where Christ sitteth on the right hand of God.

3. Strengthened and Renewed by the Holy Spirit

1 S 10:6 And the Spirit of the LORD will come upon thee, and thou shalt prophesy with them, and shalt be turned into another man.

Ps 51:10 Create in me a clean heart, O God; and renew a right spirit within me.

Is 40:31 But they that wait upon the LORD shall renew *their* strength; they shall mount up with wings as eagles; they shall run, and not be weary; *and* they shall walk, and not faint.

Is 41:1 Keep silence before me, O islands; and let the people renew *their* strength: let them come near; then let them speak: let us come near together to judgment.

Eze 18:31 Cast away from you all your transgressions, whereby ye have transgressed; and make you a new heart and a new spirit: for why will ye die, O house of Israel?

Ro 12:2 And be not conformed to this world: but be ye transformed by the renewing of your mind, that ye may prove what is that good, and acceptable, and perfect, will of God.

2 Co 4:16 For which cause we faint not; but though our outward man perish, yet the inward *man* is renewed day by day.

2 Co 5:17 Therefore if any man *be* in Christ, *he is* a new creature: old things are passed away; behold, all things are become new.

Ep 4:23 And be renewed in the spirit of your mind;

Ph 1:6 Being confident of this very thing, that he which hath begun a good work in you will perform *it* until the day of Jesus Christ:

Ph 2:13 For it is God which worketh in you both to will and to do of *his* good pleasure.

Col 2:11 In whom also ye are circumcised with the circumcision made without hands, in putting off the body of the sins of the flesh by the circumcision of Christ:

Col 3:10 And have put on the new *man,* which is renewed in knowledge after the image of him that created him:

Tit 3:5 Not by works of righteousness which we have done, but according to his mercy he saved us, by the washing of regeneration, and renewing of the Holy Ghost;

1 Pe 1:14 As obedient children, not fashioning yourselves according to the former lusts in your ignorance:

4. Called by a New Name

Is 56:5 Even unto them will I give in mine house and within my walls a place and a name better than of sons and of daughters: I will give them an everlasting name, that shall not be cut off.

Is 62:2 And the Gentiles shall see thy righteousness, and all kings thy glory: and thou shalt be called by a new name, which the mouth of the LORD shall name.

Is 65:15 And ye shall leave your name for a curse unto my chosen: for the Lord God shall slay thee, and call his servants by another name:

Is 66:22 For as the new heavens and the new earth, which I will make, shall remain before me, saith the LORD, so shall your seed and your name remain.

Mk 3:17 And James the *son* of Zebedee, and John the brother of James; and he surnamed them Boanerges, which is, The sons of thunder:

Ac 11:26 And when he had found him, he brought him unto Antioch. And it came to pass, that a whole year they assembled themselves with the church, and taught much people. And the disciples were called Christians first in Antioch.

Re 2:17 He that hath an ear, let him hear what the Spirit saith unto the churches; To him that overcometh will I give to eat of the hidden manna, and will give him a white stone, and in the stone a new name written, which no man knoweth saving he that receiveth *it.*

Re 3:12 Him that overcometh will I make a pillar in the temple of my God, and he shall go no more out: and I will write upon him the name of my God, and the name of the city of my God, *which is* new Jerusalem, which cometh down out of heaven from my God: and *I will write upon him* my new name.

5. Given a New Song

Ps 33:3 Sing unto him a new song; play skilfully with a loud noise.

Ps 40:3 And he hath put a new song in my mouth, *even* praise unto our God: many shall see *it,* and fear, and shall trust in the LORD.

Ps 96:1 O sing unto the LORD a new song: sing unto the LORD, all the earth.

Ps 98:1 O sing unto the LORD a new song; for he hath done marvellous things: his right hand, and his holy arm, hath gotten him the victory.

Ps 144:9 I will sing a new song unto thee, O God: upon a psaltery *and* an instrument of ten strings will I sing praises unto thee.

Ps 149:1 Praise ye the LORD. Sing unto the LORD a new song, *and* his praise in the congregation of saints.

Is 42:10 Sing unto the LORD a new song, *and* his praise from the end of the earth, ye that go down to the sea, and all that is therein; the isles, and the inhabitants thereof.

Ep 5:19 Speaking to yourselves in psalms and hymns and spiritual songs, singing and making melody in your heart to the Lord;

Re 5:9 And they sung a new song, saying, Thou art worthy to take the book, and to open the seals thereof: for thou wast slain, and hast redeemed us to God by thy blood out of every kindred, and tongue, and people, and nation;

Re 14:3 And they sung as it were a new song before the throne, and before the four beasts, and the elders: and no man could learn that song but the hundred *and* forty *and* four thousand, which were redeemed from the earth.

Re 15:3 And they sing the song of Moses the servant of God, and the song of the Lamb, saying, Great and marvellous *are* thy works, Lord God Almighty; just and true *are* thy ways, thou King of saints.

NEW THINGS

Is 42:9 Behold, the former things are come to pass, and new things do I declare: before they spring forth I tell you of them.

Is 43:19 Behold, I will do a new thing; now it shall spring forth; shall ye not know it? I will even make a way in the wilderness, *and* rivers in the desert.

Is 48:6 Thou hast heard, see all this; and will not ye declare *it?* I have shewed thee new things from this time, even hidden things, and thou didst not know them.

Is 65:17 For, behold, I create new heavens and a new earth: and the former shall not be remembered, nor come into mind.

2 Co 5:17 Therefore if any man *be* in Christ, *he is* a new creature: old things are passed away; behold, all things are become new.

Re 21:5 And he that sat upon the throne said, Behold, I make all things new. And he said unto me, Write: for these words are true and faithful.

See **CLEANSING, CONVERSION, REGENERATION**

NICODEMUS, *Jewish religious leader who came to Jesus at night*

A RULER OF THE JEWS

Jn 3:1 There was a man of the Pharisees, named Nicodemus, a ruler of the Jews:

A CAUTIOUS INQUIRER, BUT A MAN OF SPIRITUAL PERCEPTION

Jn 3:2 The same came to Jesus by night, and said unto him, Rabbi, we know that thou art a teacher come from God: for no man can do these miracles that thou doest, except God be with him.

IMMATURE

Jn 3:10 Jesus answered and said unto him, Art thou a master of Israel, and knowest not these things?

FAIR-MINDED

Jn 7:50–51 Nicodemus saith unto them, (he that came to Jesus by night, being one of them,)

Doth our law judge *any* man, before it hear him, and know what he doeth?

RENDERED A LOVING, THOUGH BELATED, SERVICE TO CHRIST

Jn 19:39–40 And there came also Nicodemus, which at the first came to Jesus by night, and brought a mixture of myrrh and aloes, about an hundred pound *weight*.

Then took they the body of Jesus, and wound it in linen clothes with the spices, as the manner of the Jews is to bury.

NIGHT, *literal and figurative*

1. Type of Ignorance and Sin

Ro 13:12; 1 Th 5:5; Re 21:25; 22:5

2. References to the Natural

Ge 1:5; Ps 19:2; 134:1; 139:11

NILE, *called The River*

Ex 1:22; 4:9; 7:17; Is 11:15; Je 2:18; Eze 29:4

See **RIVERS**

NIMROD, *son of Cush*

Ge 10:8; 1 Chr 1:10; Mi 5:6

NINEVEH, *the capital of Assyria*

Nineveh, the famous capital of the Assyrian Empire in its later years, was located 280 miles north of Babylon on the eastern bank of the Tigris. It was called a "bloody city, completely full of lies and pillage" by Nahum (3:1) because it overran and robbed other countries to enrich itself. It had a colorful yet tragic history, especially from the ninth century B.C. to the time of its final destruction in 612 B.C. by a coalition of forces led by the Medes and the Babylonians (cf. Zep 2:13).

Ge 10:11; 2 K 19:36; Is 37:37; Jona 1:2; 3:3; 4:11; Na 1:1; 2:8; Zep 2:13; Mt 12:41; Lu 11:32

See **ASSYRIA, CITIES**

NISROCH, *an Assyrian idol*

2 K 19:37; Is 37:38

NISAN *See* **MONTHS**

NOADIAH *See* **WOMEN**

NOAH, *son of Lamech*

His Origin And Early Life: Nothing is known of his early days. He first appeared upon the scene when he was five hundred years old.

His great-grandfather Enoch was a man who walked with God. He escaped death because God took him up (Ge 5:22–24; He 11:5).

Noah's grandfather Methuselah was the longest-living man, according to Genesis 5:25–27.

Noah's father, Lamech, was apparently a religious man and gave his child a name that is thought to mean "rest" (Ge 5:29).

The Condition Of Society: He lived in an extremely corrupt age when men had become so universally depraved that the Lord had determined to destroy the race (Ge 6:1–7). In the midst of this moral darkness Noah's life was radiant with righteousness (Ge 6:8–9).

His Divine Commission: It was divinely revealed to Noah that there was going to be a great flood that would destroy mankind from the face of the earth because the earth was filled with violence.

Noah was given a strange and, from a human standpoint, apparently impossible task to perform: to build an immense boat to preserve the lives of his own family as well as certain numbers of the animal kingdom.

It must be remembered that he was surrounded by a mass of godless unbelievers, who, attracted by curiosity, would come to see his work and remain to mock him. He became a laughingstock.

Year after year he had to maintain his faith and continue his work on a task that made him look as if he had gone mad.

Considering his surroundings, the magnitude of the work he was called on to perform, and the many years spent in hard labor, Noah stands among all the workers of the Bible unsurpassed, if not unequaled, in persistent faith.

WALKED WITH GOD AMIDST EVIL SURROUNDINGS

Ge 6:8–12 But Noah found grace in the eyes of the LORD.

These *are* the generations of Noah: Noah was a just man *and* perfect in his generations, *and* Noah walked with God.

And Noah begat three sons, Shem, Ham, and Japheth.

The earth also was corrupt before God, and the earth was filled with violence.

And God looked upon the earth, and, behold, it was corrupt; for all flesh had corrupted his way upon the earth.

OBEDIENT WHEN GIVEN A HARD TASK

Ge 6:14 Make thee an ark of gopher wood; rooms shalt thou make in the ark, and shalt pitch it within and without with pitch.

Ge 6:22 Thus did Noah; according to all that God commanded him, so did he.

Ge 7:5 And Noah did according unto all that the LORD commanded him.

REMEMBERED BY THE LORD AND DELIVERED FROM DEATH

Ge 8:1 And God remembered Noah, and every living thing, and all the cattle that *was* with him in the ark: and God made a wind to pass over the earth, and the waters asswaged;

BY FAITH WORKED OUT HIS OWN SALVATION

He 11:7 By faith Noah, being warned of God of things not seen as yet, moved with fear, prepared an ark to the saving of his house; by the which he condemned the world, and became heir of the righteousness which is by faith.

WARNED HIS NEIGHBORS OF IMPENDING JUDGMENT

2 Pe 2:5 And spared not the old world, but saved Noah the eighth *person,* a preacher of righteousness, bringing in the flood upon the world of the ungodly;

BUILT THE FIRST ALTAR RECORDED

Ge 8:20 And Noah builded an altar unto the LORD; and took of every clean beast, and of every clean fowl, and offered burnt offerings on the altar.

HONORED BY GOD WITH AN EVERLASTING COVENANT

Ge 9:12–17 And God said, This *is* the token of the covenant which I make between me and you and every living creature that *is* with you, for perpetual generations:

I do set my bow in the cloud, and it shall be for a token of a covenant between me and the earth.

And it shall come to pass, when I bring a cloud over the earth, that the bow shall be seen in the cloud:

And I will remember my covenant, which *is* between me and you and every living creature of all flesh; and the waters shall no more become a flood to destroy all flesh.

And the bow shall be in the cloud; and I will look upon it, that I may remember the everlasting covenant between God and every living creature of all flesh that *is* upon the earth.

And God said unto Noah, This *is* the token of the covenant, which I have established between me and all flesh that *is* upon the earth.

NOB, *a city of the priests*

It was a town just north of Jerusalem. After the capture of the ark and the destruction of Shiloh, the Jewish priests fled here with the ephod and set up quarters dedicated to carrying out the sacred functions of the tabernacle. After David had escaped from Saul, he came to Nob to see Abimelech the priest and ask him for bread. Abimelech gave him holy bread (showbread) and the sword of Goliath and sent him on his way. Doeg the Edomite, who was "the chief of Saul's shepherds," informed the king of the incident and, at Saul's command, exterminated Abimelech's family and eighty-five men who wore the linen ephod (1 S 22:18). Nob was Sennacherib's last stop in his advance on Jerusalem (Is 10:32).

See **CITIES**

NOBLE   *See* **GOODNESS**

NOBLES, *princes*

1 K 21:8; 2 Chr 23:20; Ezr 8:25; Ne 2:16; 3:5; 4:14, 19; 5:7; 6:17; 7:5; Est 1:3; Je 30:21; Mk 6:21

NOON, *midday*

De 28:29; Jb 11:17; Ps 55:17; 91:6; Is 58:10; Ac 22:6

NONRESISTANCE

See **ENEMIES, SOCIAL DUTIES**

NOPH, *a city of Egypt (Memphis)*

Is 19:13; Je 2:16; 44:1; 46:14; Eze 30:13; Ho 9:6

See **MEMPHIS**

NORTH, *to the Hebrews the reference point was east; thus, north was to the left, going up*

Jb 26:7; 37:9, 22; Is 43:6; Lu 13:29

NOSE

Le 21:18; 2 K 19:28; Ps 115:6

See **BODY**

NOSTRILS, *openings of the nose*

Ge 2:7; Ex 15:8; Jb 27:3; 41:20; Is 2:22

NUMBERS

Name: Derived from the numberings of Israel.

Author: Moses (commonly accepted).

Date Written: 1446–1410 B.C.

Purpose: To relate the discipline of the wilderness generation, delivered from Egypt, and its purging, in order to prepare its children for a victorious entrance into the Promised Land.

To Whom Written: The children of Israel.

Main Theme: Unbelief bars the entrance to abundant life (He 3:7–19).

Key Word: Wilderness.

Key Verses: 14:20–23.

NURSES, *positions of honor and importance, from words meaning to give milk, support, nurture*

Ge 24:59; 35:8; Ex 2:7; Ru 4:16; 2 S 4:4; 2 K 11:2; 1 Th 2:7

O

OAK *See* **TREES**

OATHS, *solemn and binding promises*

1. Permitted in Bearing Witness

Ex 22:11 *Then* shall an oath of the LORD be between them both, that he hath not put his hand unto his neighbour's goods; and the owner of it shall accept *thereof,* and he shall not make *it* good.

Nu 5:19 And the priest shall charge her by an oath, and say unto the woman, If no man have lain with thee, and if thou hast not gone aside to uncleanness *with another* instead of thy husband, be thou free from this bitter water that causeth the curse:

Nu 5:21 Then the priest shall charge the woman with an oath of cursing, and the priest shall say unto the woman, The LORD make thee a curse and an oath among thy people, when the LORD doth make thy thigh to rot, and thy belly to swell;

De 6:13 Thou shalt fear the LORD thy God, and serve him, and shalt swear by his name.

1 K 1:17 And she said unto him, My lord, thou swarest by the LORD thy God unto thine handmaid, *saying,* Assuredly Solomon thy son shall reign after me, and he shall sit upon my throne.

1 K 1:30 Even as I sware unto thee by the LORD God of Israel, saying, Assuredly Solomon thy son shall reign after me, and he shall sit upon my throne in my stead; even so will I certainly do this day.

1 K 8:31 If any man trespass against his neighbour, and an oath be laid upon him to cause him to swear, and the oath come before thine altar in this house:

Ne 13:25 And I contended with them, and cursed them, and smote certain of them, and plucked off their hair, and made them swear by God, *saying,* Ye shall not give your daughters unto their sons, nor take their daughters unto your sons, or for yourselves.

Ps 63:11 But the king shall rejoice in God; every one that sweareth by him shall glory: but the mouth of them that speak lies shall be stopped.

Je 12:16 And it shall come to pass, if they will diligently learn the ways of my people, to swear by my name, The LORD liveth; as they taught my people to swear by Baal; then shall they be built in the midst of my people.

He 6:16 For men verily swear by the greater: and an oath for confirmation *is* to them an end of all strife.

Ja 5:12 But above all things, my brethren, swear not, neither by heaven, neither by the earth, neither by any other oath: but let your yea be yea; and *your* nay, nay; lest ye fall into condemnation.

Re 10:6 And sware by him that liveth for ever and ever, who created heaven, and the things that therein are, and the earth, and the things that therein are, and the sea, and the things which are therein, that there should be time no longer:

2. Of Allegiance

2 K 11:4 And the seventh year Jehoiada sent and fetched the rulers over hundreds, with the captains and the guard, and brought them to him into the house of the LORD, and made a covenant with them, and took an oath of them in the house of the LORD, and shewed them the king's son.

Ec 8:2 I *counsel thee* to keep the king's commandment, and *that* in regard of the oath of God.

Eze 17:13 And hath taken of the king's seed, and made a covenant with him, and hath taken an oath of him:

he hath also taken the mighty of the land:

3. In Covenants

Ge 21:24 And Abraham said, I will swear.

Ge 24:3 And I will make thee swear by the LORD, the God of heaven, and the God of the earth, that thou shalt not take a wife unto my son of the daughters of the Canaanites, among whom I dwell:

Ge 26:31 And they rose up betimes in the morning, and sware one to another: and Isaac sent them away, and they departed from him in peace.

Ge 31:53 The God of Abraham, and the God of Nahor, the God of their father, judge betwixt us. And Jacob sware by the fear of his father Isaac.

Ge 47:31 And he said, Swear unto me. And he sware unto him. And Israel bowed himself upon the bed's head.

Ge 50:25 And Joseph took an oath of the children of Israel, saying, God will surely visit you, and ye shall carry up my bones from hence.

Jos 9:15 And Joshua made peace with them, and made a league with them, to let them live: and the princes of the congregation sware unto them.

1 S 24:22 And David sware unto Saul. And Saul went home; but David and his men gat them up unto the hold.

2 S 21:2 And the king called the Gibeonites, and said unto them; (now the Gibeonites *were* not of the children of Israel, but of the remnant of the Amorites; and the children of Israel had sworn unto them: and Saul sought to slay them in his zeal to the children of Israel and Judah.)

1 K 2:8 And, behold, *thou hast* with thee Shimei the son of Gera, a Benjamite of Bahurim, which cursed me with a grievous curse in the day when I went to Mahanaim: but he came down to meet me at Jordan, and I sware to him by the LORD, saying, I will not put thee to death with the sword.

1 K 2:23 Then king Solomon sware by the LORD, saying, God do so to me,

and more also, if Adonijah have not spoken this word against his own life.

Ezr 10:5 Then arose Ezra, and made the chief priests, the Levites, and all Israel, to swear that they should do according to this word. And they sware.

Ne 5:12 Then said they, We will restore *them,* and will require nothing of them; so will we do as thou sayest. Then I called the priests, and took an oath of them, that they should do according to this promise.

Je 38:16 So Zedekiah the king sware secretly unto Jeremiah, saying, *As* the LORD liveth, that made us this soul, I will not put thee to death, neither will I give thee into the hand of these men that seek thy life.

Mt 5:33 Again, ye have heard that it hath been said by them of old time, Thou shalt not forswear thyself, but shalt perform unto the Lord thine oaths:

Mt 23:16 Woe unto you, *ye* blind guides, which say, Whosoever shall swear by the temple, it is nothing; but whosoever shall swear by the gold of the temple, he is a debtor!

4. Examples of Rash

Ge 25:33 And Jacob said, Swear to me this day; and he sware unto him: and he sold his birthright unto Jacob.

Le 5:4 Or if a soul swear, pronouncing with *his* lips to do evil, or to do good, whatsoever *it be* that a man shall pronounce with an oath, and it be hid from him; when he knoweth *of it,* then he shall be guilty in one of these.

Jos 9:19 But all the princes said unto all the congregation, We have sworn unto them by the LORD God of Israel: now therefore we may not touch them.

Jud 21:5 And the children of Israel said, Who *is there* among all the tribes of Israel that came not up with the congregation unto the LORD? For they had made a great oath concerning him that came not up to the LORD to Mizpeh, saying, He shall surely be put to death.

1 S 14:39 For, *as* the LORD liveth, which saveth Israel, though it be in

Jonathan my son, he shall surely die. But *there was* not a man among all the people *that* answered him.

Mt 14:7 Whereupon he promised with an oath to give her whatsoever she would ask.

Mk 6:23 And he sware unto her, Whatsoever thou shalt ask of me, I will give *it* thee, unto the half of my kingdom.

Ac 23:14 And they came to the chief priests and elders, and said, We have bound ourselves under a great curse, that we will eat nothing until we have slain Paul.

Ac 23:21 But do not thou yield unto them: for there lie in wait for him of them more than forty men, which have bound themselves with an oath, that they will neither eat nor drink till they have killed him: and now are they ready, looking for a promise from thee.

5. Divine

Ge 22:16 And said, By myself have I sworn, saith the LORD, for because thou hast done this thing, and hast not withheld thy son, thine only *son:*

Ge 24:7 The LORD God of heaven, which took me from my father's house, and from the land of my kindred, and which spake unto me, and that sware unto me, saying, Unto thy seed will I give this land; he shall send his angel before thee, and thou shalt take a wife unto my son from thence.

Ge 26:3 Sojourn in this land, and I will be with thee, and will bless thee; for unto thee, and unto thy seed, I will give all these countries, and I will perform the oath which I sware unto Abraham thy father;

Ex 6:8 And I will bring you in unto the land, concerning the which I did swear to give it to Abraham, to Isaac, and to Jacob; and I will give it you for an heritage: I *am* the LORD.

Ex 13:11 And it shall be when the LORD shall bring thee into the land of the Canaanites, as he sware unto thee and to thy fathers, and shall give it thee,

Ex 17:16 For he said, Because the LORD hath sworn *that* the LORD *will*

have war with Amalek from generation to generation.

Ex 32:13 Remember Abraham, Isaac, and Israel, thy servants, to whom thou swarest by thine own self, and saidst unto them, I will multiply your seed as the stars of heaven, and all this land that I have spoken of will I give unto your seed, and they shall inherit *it* for ever.

Ex 33:1 And the LORD said unto Moses, Depart, *and* go up hence, thou and the people which thou hast brought up out of the land of Egypt, unto the land which I sware unto Abraham, to Isaac, and to Jacob, saying, Unto thy seed will I give it:

Nu 32:10 And the LORD's anger was kindled the same time, and he sware, saying,

De 1:8 Behold, I have set the land before you: go in and possess the land which the LORD sware unto your fathers, Abraham, Isaac, and Jacob, to give unto them and to their seed after them.

De 1:34 And the LORD heard the voice of your words, and was wroth, and sware, saying,

De 7:8 But because the LORD loved you, and because he would keep the oath which he had sworn unto your fathers, hath the LORD brought you out with a mighty hand, and redeemed you out of the house of bondmen, from the hand of Pharaoh king of Egypt.

De 10:11 And the LORD said unto me, Arise, take *thy* journey before the people, that they may go in and possess the land, which I sware unto their fathers to give unto them.

De 19:8 And if the LORD thy God enlarge thy coast, as he hath sworn unto thy fathers, and give thee all the land which he promised to give unto thy fathers;

De 26:3 And thou shalt go unto the priest that shall be in those days, and say unto him, I profess this day unto the LORD thy God, that I am come unto the country which the LORD sware unto our fathers for to give us.

De 29:14 Neither with you only do I make this covenant and this oath;

Jud 2:15 Whithersoever they went out, the hand of the LORD was against them for evil, as the LORD had said, and as the LORD had sworn unto them: and they were greatly distressed.

1 S 3:14 And therefore I have sworn unto the house of Eli, that the iniquity of Eli's house shall not be purged with sacrifice nor offering for ever.

1 Chr 16:16 *Even of the covenant* which he made with Abraham, and of his oath unto Isaac;

Ne 9:15 And gavest them bread from heaven for their hunger, and broughtest forth water for them out of the rock for their thirst, and promisedst them that they should go in to possess the land which thou hadst sworn to give them.

Ps 89:3 I have made a covenant with my chosen, I have sworn unto David my servant,

Ps 89:35 Once have I sworn by my holiness that I will not lie unto David.

Ps 95:11 Unto whom I sware in my wrath that they should not enter into my rest.

Ps 110:4 The LORD hath sworn, and will not repent, Thou *art* a priest for ever after the order of Melchizedek.

Ps 132:11 The LORD hath sworn *in* truth unto David; he will not turn from it; Of the fruit of thy body will I set upon thy throne.

Is 14:24 The LORD of hosts hath sworn, saying, Surely as I have thought, so shall it come to pass; and as I have purposed, *so* shall it stand:

Is 45:23 I have sworn by myself, the word is gone out of my mouth *in* righteousness, and shall not return, That unto me every knee shall bow, every tongue shall swear.

Is 54:9 For this *is as* the waters of Noah unto me: for *as* I have sworn that the waters of Noah should no more go over the earth; so have I sworn that I would not be wroth with thee, nor rebuke thee.

Is 62:8 The LORD hath sworn by his right hand, and by the arm of his strength, Surely I will no more give thy corn *to be* meat for thine enemies; and the sons of the stranger shall not

drink thy wine, for the which thou hast laboured:

Je 11:5 That I may perform the oath which I have sworn unto your fathers, to give them a land flowing with milk and honey, as *it is* this day. Then answered I, and said, So be it, O LORD.

Je 22:5 But if ye will not hear these words, I swear by myself, saith the LORD, that this house shall become a desolation.

Je 49:13 For I have sworn by myself, saith the LORD, that Bozrah shall become a desolation, a reproach, a waste, and a curse; and all the cities thereof shall be perpetual wastes.

Je 51:14 The LORD of hosts hath sworn by himself, *saying,* Surely I will fill thee with men, as with caterpillers; and they shall lift up a shout against thee.

Eze 17:19 Therefore thus saith the Lord GOD; *As* I live, surely mine oath that he hath despised, and my covenant that he hath broken, even it will I recompense upon his own head.

Am 4:2 The Lord GOD hath sworn by his holiness, that, lo, the days shall come upon you, that he will take you away with hooks, and your posterity with fishhooks.

Am 6:8 The Lord GOD hath sworn by himself, saith the LORD the God of hosts, I abhor the excellency of Jacob, and hate his palaces: therefore will I deliver up the city with all that is therein.

Am 8:7 The LORD hath sworn by the excellency of Jacob, Surely I will never forget any of their works.

Mi 7:20 Thou wilt perform the truth to Jacob, *and* the mercy to Abraham, which thou hast sworn unto our fathers from the days of old.

Lu 1:73 The oath which he sware to our father Abraham,

He 3:11 So I sware in my wrath, They shall not enter into my rest.)

He 4:3 For we which have believed do enter into rest, as he said, As I have sworn in my wrath, if they shall enter into my rest: although the works were finished from the foundation of the world.

He 6:13 For when God made promise to Abraham, because he could swear by no greater, he sware by himself,

He 6:17 Wherein God, willing more abundantly to shew unto the heirs of promise the immutability of his counsel, confirmed *it* by an oath:

See **PROFANITY**

OBADIAH

1. Person, *the prophet*
Obad 1

2. Book
Author: Uncertain. Probably Obadiah.

Date Written: Uncertain.

Purpose: To declare Edom's coming doom because of its cruelty to Judah and to reveal God's faithfulness to his own people and to his covenant promises.

To Whom Written: The Edomites and God's people. The prophecy centers on an ancient feud between Edom and Israel. The Edomites were descendants of Esau, and had a grudge against Israel because Jacob had cheated their ancestor out of his birthright (Ge 25:12-34; 27:41). They had later refused Israel passage through their country (Nu 20:14–21). They also rejoiced over the capture of Jerusalem (Ps 137:7).

Main Theme: A spiritual message. God's special providential care over the Jews and the certainty of punishment upon those who persecute them.

Key Words: Edom's Judgment.

Key Verse: 10

OBED, *son of Boaz and Ruth*
Ru 4:17; 1 Chr 2:12; Lu 3:32

OBED-EDOM, *the Gittite, blessed while keeping the ark*
2 S 6:10; 1 Chr 13:13; 15:18; 16:38; 26:4

OBEDIENCE, *submitting to a request or command*

1. To God

WHOLE-HEARTED REQUIRED
De 26:16 This day the LORD thy God hath commanded thee to do these statutes and judgments: thou shalt therefore keep and do them with all thine heart, and with all thy soul.

De 32:46 And he said unto them, Set your hearts unto all the words which I testify among you this day, which ye shall command your children to observe to do, all the words of this law.

THE PRICE OF SUCCESS
Jos 1:8 This book of the law shall not depart out of thy mouth; but thou shalt meditate therein day and night, that thou mayest observe to do according to all that is written therein: for then thou shalt make thy way prosperous, and then thou shalt have good success.

BETTER THAN SACRIFICE
1 S 15:22 And Samuel said, Hath the LORD *as great* delight in burnt offerings and sacrifices, as in obeying the voice of the LORD? Behold, to obey *is* better than sacrifice, *and* to hearken than the fat of rams.

Je 7:23 But this thing commanded I them, saying, Obey my voice, and I will be your God, and ye shall be my people: and walk ye in all the ways that I have commanded you, that it may be well unto you.

2. Examples

NOAH
Ge 6:22; 12:4

ABRAHAM
Ge 22:2–3

BEZALEEL
Ex 36:1; Nu 9:23

JOSHUA
Jos 11:15

HEZEKIAH

2 K 18:6; Ezr 7:23; Ps 27:8

JOSEPH AND MARY

Lu 2:39; Ac 16:10

PAUL

Ac 26:19; Ro 16:19

CHRIST

He 5:8

3. Results in Blessings

Ex 1:21 And it came to pass, because the midwives feared God, that he made them houses.

Ex 15:26 And said, If thou wilt diligently hearken to the voice of the LORD thy God, and wilt do that which is right in his sight, and wilt give ear to his commandments, and keep all his statutes, I will put none of these diseases upon thee, which I have brought upon the Egyptians: for I *am* the LORD that healeth thee.

Ex 19:5 Now therefore, if ye will obey my voice indeed, and keep my covenant, then ye shall be a peculiar treasure unto me above all people: for all the earth *is* mine:

De 4:30 When thou art in tribulation, and all these things are come upon thee, *even* in the latter days, if thou turn to the LORD thy God, and shalt be obedient unto his voice;

De 5:10 And shewing mercy unto thousands of them that love me and keep my commandments.

De 5:29 O that there were such an heart in them, that they would fear me, and keep all my commandments always, that it might be well with them, and with their children for ever!

De 6:18 And thou shalt do *that which is* right and good in the sight of the LORD: that it may be well with thee, and that thou mayest go in and possess the good land which the LORD sware unto thy fathers,

De 6:24 And the LORD commanded us to do all these statutes, to fear the LORD our God, for our good always, that he might preserve us alive, as *it is* at this day.

De 7:12 Wherefore it shall come to pass, if ye hearken to these judgments, and keep, and do them, that the LORD thy God shall keep unto thee the covenant and the mercy which he sware unto thy fathers:

De 11:13 And it shall come to pass, if ye shall hearken diligently unto my commandments which I command you this day, to love the LORD your God, and to serve him with all your heart and with all your soul,

De 11:22 For if ye shall diligently keep all these commandments which I command you, to do them, to love the LORD your God, to walk in all his ways, and to cleave unto him;

De 15:5 Only if thou carefully hearken unto the voice of the LORD thy God, to observe to do all these commandments which I command thee this day.

De 28:1 And it shall come to pass, if thou shalt hearken diligently unto the voice of the LORD thy God, to observe *and* to do all his commandments which I command thee this day, that the LORD thy God will set thee on high above all nations of the earth:

De 28:13 And the LORD shall make thee the head, and not the tail; and thou shalt be above only, and thou shalt not be beneath; if that thou hearken unto the commandments of the LORD thy God, which I command thee this day, to observe and to do *them:*

De 30:2 And shalt return unto the LORD thy God, and shalt obey his voice according to all that I command thee this day, thou and thy children, with all thine heart, and with all thy soul;

Jos 14:9 And Moses sware on that day, saying, Surely the land whereon thy feet have trodden shall be thine inheritance, and thy children's for ever, because thou hast wholly followed the LORD my God.

1 S 12:14 If ye will fear the LORD, and serve him, and obey his voice, and not rebel against the commandment of the LORD, then shall both ye and also the king that reigneth over you continue following the LORD your God:

1 K 3:14 And if thou wilt walk in my ways, to keep my statutes and my commandments, as thy father David did walk, then I will lengthen thy days.

1 K 6:12 *Concerning* this house which thou art in building, if thou wilt walk in my statutes, and execute my judgments, and keep all my commandments to walk in them; then will I perform my word with thee, which I spake unto David thy father:

2 K 5:14 Then went he down, and dipped himself seven times in Jordan, according to the saying of the man of God: and his flesh came again like unto the flesh of a little child, and he was clean.

2 K 10:30 And the Lᴏʀᴅ said unto Jehu, Because thou hast done well in executing *that which is* right in mine eyes, *and* hast done unto the house of Ahab according to all that *was* in mine heart, thy children of the fourth *generation* shall sit on the throne of Israel.

1 Chr 28:7 Moreover I will establish his kingdom for ever, if he be constant to do my commandments and my judgments, as at this day.

2 Chr 6:16 Now therefore, O Lᴏʀᴅ God of Israel, keep with thy servant David my father that which thou hast promised him, saying, There shall not fail thee a man in my sight to sit upon the throne of Israel; yet so that thy children take heed to their way to walk in my law, as thou hast walked before me.

2 Chr 7:17 And as for thee, if thou wilt walk before me, as David thy father walked, and do according to all that I have commanded thee, and shalt observe my statutes and my judgments;

Ne 1:9 But *if* ye turn unto me, and keep my commandments, and do them; though there were of you cast out unto the uttermost part of the heaven, *yet* will I gather them from thence, and will bring them unto the place that I have chosen to set my name there.

Jb 36:11 If they obey and serve *him,* they shall spend their days in prosperity, and their years in pleasures.

Ps 81:13 Oh that my people had hearkened unto me, *and* Israel had walked in my ways!

Ps 119:2 Blessed *are* they that keep his testimonies, *and that* seek him with the whole heart.

Ps 119:56 This I had, because I kept thy precepts.

Ps 128:4 Behold, that thus shall the man be blessed that feareth the Lᴏʀᴅ.

Pr 8:32 Now therefore hearken unto me, O ye children: for blessed *are they that* keep my ways.

Pr 29:18 Where *there is* no vision, the people perish: but he that keepeth the law, happy *is* he.

Ec 8:5 Whoso keepeth the commandment shall feel no evil thing: and a wise man's heart discerneth both time and judgment.

Je 17:24 And it shall come to pass, if ye diligently hearken unto me, saith the Lᴏʀᴅ, to bring in no burden through the gates of this city on the sabbath day, but hallow the sabbath day, to do no work therein;

Eze 18:19 Yet say ye, Why? doth not the son bear the iniquity of the father? When the son hath done that which is lawful and right, *and* hath kept all my statutes, and hath done them, he shall surely live.

Eze 18:21 But if the wicked will turn from all his sins that he hath committed, and keep all my statutes, and do that which is lawful and right, he shall surely live, he shall not die.

Eze 33:15 *If* the wicked restore the pledge, give again that he had robbed, walk in the statutes of life, without committing iniquity; he shall surely live, he shall not die.

Eze 36:27 And I will put my spirit within you, and cause you to walk in my statutes, and ye shall keep my judgments, and do *them.*

Eze 37:24 And David my servant *shall be* king over them; and they all shall have one shepherd: they shall also walk in my judgments, and observe my statutes, and do them.

Da 9:4 And I prayed unto the Lᴏʀᴅ my God, and made my confession, and said, O Lord, the great and dreadful God, keeping the covenant and mercy to them that love him, and to them that keep his commandments;

Zec 3:7 Thus saith the LORD of hosts; If thou wilt walk in my ways, and if thou wilt keep my charge, then thou shalt also judge my house, and shalt also keep my courts, and I will give thee places to walk among these that stand by.

Mt 28:9 And as they went to tell his disciples, behold, Jesus met them, saying, All hail. And they came and held him by the feet, and worshipped him.

Lu 12:43 Blessed *is* that servant, whom his lord when he cometh shall find so doing.

Jn 9:31 Now we know that God heareth not sinners: but if any man be a worshipper of God, and doeth his will, him he heareth.

Jn 14:15 If ye love me, keep my commandments.

Ro 2:13 (For not the hearers of the law *are* just before God, but the doers of the law shall be justified.

Ro 6:16 Know ye not, that to whom ye yield yourselves servants to obey, his servants ye are to whom ye obey; whether of sin unto death, or of obedience unto righteousness?

Ja 1:25 But whoso looketh into the perfect law of liberty, and continueth *therein,* he being not a forgetful hearer, but a doer of the work, this man shall be blessed in his deed.

1 Pe 1:22 Seeing ye have purified your souls in obeying the truth through the Spirit unto unfeigned love of the brethren, *see that ye* love one another with a pure heart fervently:

1 Jn 2:5 But whoso keepeth his word, in him verily is the love of God perfected: hereby know we that we are in him.

1 Jn 3:22 And whatsoever we ask, we receive of him, because we keep his commandments, and do those things that are pleasing in his sight.

1 Jn 3:24 And he that keepeth his commandments dwelleth in him, and he in him. And hereby we know that he abideth in us, by the Spirit which he hath given us.

Re 22:7 Behold, I come quickly: blessed is he that keepeth the sayings of the prophecy of this book.

Re 22:14 Blessed *are* they that do his commandments, that they may have right to the tree of life, and may enter in through the gates into the city.

4. Christ's

De 18:18 I will raise them up a Prophet from among their brethren, like unto thee, and will put my words in his mouth; and he shall speak unto them all that I shall command him.

Is 50:5 The Lord God hath opened mine ear, and I was not rebellious, neither turned away back.

Jn 4:34 Jesus saith unto them, My meat is to do the will of him that sent me, and to finish his work.

Jn 6:38 For I came down from heaven, not to do mine own will, but the will of him that sent me.

Jn 8:55 Yet ye have not known him; but I know him: and if I should say, I know him not, I shall be a liar like unto you: but I know him, and keep his saying.

Jn 10:18 No man taketh it from me, but I lay it down of myself. I have power to lay it down, and I have power to take it again. This commandment have I received of my Father.

Jn 14:31 But that the world may know that I love the Father; and as the Father gave me commandment, even so I do. Arise, let us go hence.

Jn 15:10 If ye keep my commandments, ye shall abide in my love; even as I have kept my Father's commandments, and abide in his love.

Ro 5:19 For as by on man's disobedience many were made sinners, so by the obedience of one shall many be made righteous.

1 Co 15:28 And when all things shall be subdued unto him, then shall the Son also himself be subject unto him that put all things under him, that God may be all in all.

He 5:8 Though he were a Son, yet learned he obedience by the things which he suffered;

He 10:9 Then said he, Lo, I come to do thy will, O God. He taketh away the first, that he may establish the second.

5. Christ's Teaching

THE BASE ROCK OF CHARACTER

Mt 7:24 Therefore whosoever heareth these sayings of mine, and doeth them, I will liken him unto a wise man, which built his house upon a rock:

ESSENTIAL TO MEMBERSHIP
IN GOD'S FAMILY

Mt 12:50 For whosoever shall do the will of my Father which is in heaven, the same is my brother, and sister, and mother.

THE KEY TO SPIRITUAL KNOWLEDGE

Jn 7:17 If any man will do his will, he shall know of the doctrine, whether it be of God, or *whether* I speak of myself.

SECURES THE BLESSING OF
DIVINE FELLOWSHIP

Jn 14:23 Jesus answered and said unto him, If a man love me, he will keep my words: and my Father will love him, and we will come unto him, and make our abode with him.

1 Jn 2:17 And the world passeth away, and the lust thereof: but he that doeth the will of God abideth for ever.

6. To Christ

Mt 4:20; 7:24; 9:9; 21:6; 26:19; Lu 5:5; 6:47; Jn 2:7; 11:29; 14:21; 21:6

See **APOSTASY, BACKSLIDING, DISOBEDIENCE**

OBEISANCE, *homage, respect, reverence*

Ge 18:2; 19:1; 23:7; 33:3, 7; 37:7; 42:6; 43:28; 44:14; 50:18; Ex 18:7; Ru 2:10; 1 S 20:41; 24:8; 25:23; 28:14; 2 S 1:2; 9:6; 14:4, 22, 33; 15:5; 18:28; 24:20; 1 K 1:16, 23, 31, 53; 2 K 2:15; 1 Chr 21:21; 2 Chr 24:17; Est 8:3; Is 49:23; Mt 2:11; 18:26; Lu 8:41

See **SALUTATIONS**

OBLIVION, *the condition of being completely forgotten*

1. Doom of the Wicked

Ex 17:14 And the LORD said unto Moses, Write this *for* a memorial in a book, and rehearse *it* in the ears of Joshua: for I will utterly put out the remembrance of Amalek from under heaven.

De 32:26 I said, I would scatter them into corners, I would make the remembrance of them to cease from among men:

Jb 8:18 If he destroy him from his place, then *it* shall deny him, *saying,* I have not seen thee.

Jb 18:17 His remembrance shall perish from the earth, and he shall have no name in the street.

Ps 34:16 The face of the LORD *is* against them that do evil, to cut off the remembrance of them from the earth.

Ps 69:28 Let them be blotted out of the book of the living, and not be written with the righteous.

Ps 109:15 Let them be before the LORD continually, that he may cut off the memory of them from the earth.

Ec 2:16 For *there is* no remembrance of the wise more than of the fool for ever; seeing that which now *is* in the days to come shall all be forgotten. And how dieth the wise *man?* as the fool.

Ec 6:4 For he cometh in with vanity, and departeth in darkness, and his name shall be covered with darkness.

Ec 8:10 And so I saw the wicked buried, who had come and gone from the place of the holy, and they were forgotten in the city where they had so done: this *is* also vanity.

Ec 9:5 For the living know that they shall die: but the dead know not any thing, neither have they any more a reward; for the memory of them is forgotten.

Is 14:20 Thou shalt not be joined with them in burial, because thou hast destroyed thy land, *and* slain thy people: the seed of evildoers shall never be renowned.

2. The Name of the Wicked to Be Blotted Out

De 9:14 Let me alone, that I may destroy them, and blot out their name from under heaven: and I will make of thee a nation mightier and greater than they.

De 29:20 The LORD will not spare him, but then the anger of the LORD and his jealousy shall smoke against that man, and all the curses that are written in this book shall lie upon him, and the LORD shall blot out his name from under heaven.

Ps 9:5 Thou hast rebuked the heathen, thou hast destroyed the wicked, thou hast put out their name for ever and ever.

Ps 109:13 Let his posterity be cut off; *and* in the generation following let their name be blotted out.

Pr 10:7 The memory of the just is blessed: but the name of the wicked shall rot.

Is 14:22 For I will rise up against them, saith the LORD of hosts, and cut off from Babylon the name, and remnant, and son, and nephew, saith the LORD.

See **FORGETFULNESS, MEMORIES, REMEMBRANCE**

ODED, *a prophet*

2 Chr 28:9

ODORS, *sweet, pleasant scents or smells*

2 Chr 16:14; Ps 45:8; Pr 27:9; Song 3:6; 4:10–11; 5:5; Da 2:46; Jn 12:3; Re 5:8

OFFENSES, *causes of stumbling*

Pr 18:19; Mt 5:29; 18:7; Mk 9:42; Lu 17:1; Ro 14:21; 16:17; 1 Co 8:9; 10:32; 2 Co 6:3; 2 Ti 2:18; 1 Jn 2:10

1. Examples

Ex 17:8; Nu 20:20; 21:1, 23, 33; De 2:30; 3:1; Ezr 4:1, 4; Ne 2:19; 4:1, 8; Da 9:25; Zec 3:1; Mt 23:13; Ac 13:8, 45; 14:2; 17:13; 18:6; 19:9; Ro 11:28; 1 Co 16:9; Ga 5:8; 1 Th 2:2, 16; 2 Th 3:2; 2 Ti 2:25; 3:8; 4:15; 3 Jn 10

2. Seek to Silence the Prophets and Religious Leaders

1 K 13:4; 2 Chr 25:16; Is 29:21; 30:10; Je 11:21; 20:10; 29:27; Eze 3:25; Am 2:12; 7:13, 16; Mi 2:6; Lu 11:52; Ac 4:1, 18, 26; 5:28, 40; 6:9; 9:1

See **EVIL, INFLUENCE, SIN, WICKED**

OFFERINGS, *Old Testament's means for man to approach God in worship, praise, and acts of reconciliation*

1. Acceptable

Le 1:4; Ps 20:3; 51:19; Is 56:7; 60:7; Mal 3:4; Ro 12:1; 15:16; Ph 4:18; He 13:16; 1 Pe 2:5

2. Burnt

Ge 8:20; 22:2, 13; Ex 18:12; 20:24; 24:5; 29:18, 25, 42; 40:29; Le 1:3, 6, 9, 13, 17; 5:10; 6:9; 7:2, 37; 8:18; 9:2, 3, 7, 12, 16; 10:19; 12:6; 14:13, 19, 22, 31; 15:15, 30; 16:3, 24; 22:18; 23:8, 12, 18, 25, 36–37; Nu 6:11, 16; 7:15, 21, 27, 39, 45, 63, 81, 87; 8:12; 10:10; 15:3, 5, 13, 24; 23:15; 28:3, 11, 19, 27; 29:2, 6, 8, 13, 19, 22, 28, 36, 39; De 12:6, 11, 27; 27:6; 33:10; Jos 8:31; 22:27; Jud 6:26; 11:31; 13:16; 20:26; 21:4; 1 S 6:14, 15; 7:9; 10:8; 13:10; 2 S 6:17; 24:25; 1 K 3:4, 15; 8:64; 2 K 16:13; 1 Chr 16:1, 40; 21:26; 23:31; 29:21; 2 Chr 1:6; 2:4; 7:1, 7; 8:12; 13:11; 23:18; 24:14; 29:24, 27, 32, 35; 30:15; 31:2; 35:12; Ezr 3:2, 3; 8:35; Ne 10:33; Jb 1:5; 42:8; Ps 51:19; 66:13; Is 40:16; Je 17:26; 33:18; Eze 40:38, 42; 43:18, 27; 44:11; 45:15, 23; 46:12; Am 5:22; He 5:1; 8:3; 9:9; 10:1, 6

3. Drink

Ge 35:14; Ex 29:40; Le 23:13, 18, 37; Nu 6:15; 15:5, 10, 24; 28:7, 14, 31; 29:6, 18, 22, 27, 30, 37, 39; 2 S 23:16; 2 K 16:13; 1 Chr 29:21; 2 Chr 29:35; Ezr 7:17; Eze 20:28; 45:17; Jl 1:9, 13; 2:14

4. Freewill

Ex 25:2; 35:5, 29; 36:3; Le 1:3; 7:16; 19:5; 22:18, 23; 23:38; Nu 15:3; 29:39; De 12:6, 17; 16:10; 23:23; 2 Chr 15:11; 29:31; 31:14; 35:7; Ezr 1:4; 3:5; 7:16; 8:28; Ps 119:108; Eze 46:12; Am 4:5

5. Heave

Ex 29:27; Le 7:14, 32; Nu 15:19; 18:8, 11, 19, 24, 29; 31:29, 41, 52; De 12:6, 11, 17

6. Meal, or Meat, or Grain

Ex 29:40; 40:29; Le 2:1, 9, 15; 6:14, 20; 7:9, 37; 9:4, 17; 10:12; 14:10, 20; 23:13, 16, 18, 37; Nu 4:16; 6:15; 7:13, 31, 49, 61, 79, 87; 8:8; 15:4, 9, 24; 18:9; 28:5, 9, 13, 20, 28; 29:3, 14, 18, 27, 28, 30, 37, 39; Jos 22:29; Jud 13:19; 1 K 8:64; 2 K 16:13; 1 Chr 21:23; Ezr 7:17; Ne 10:33; 13:5, 9; Je 17:26; 33:18; Eze 42:13; 44:29; 45:17, 24; 46:5, 11, 14, 20; Jl 1:9, 13; 2:14; Am 5:22

7. Peace

Ex 20:24; 24:5; 29:28; Le 3:1, 6, 9; 4:26; 6:12; 7:11, 21, 29, 37; 9:4, 18, 22; 10:14; 17:5; 19:5; 22:21; 23:19; Nu 6:14, 18; 7:17, 23, 29, 35, 41, 47, 65, 83, 88; 10:10; 15:8; 29:39; De 27:7; Jos 8:31; 22:27; Jud 20:26; 21:4; 1 S 10:8; 11:15; 2 S 6:17; 24:25; 1 K 3:15; 8:63; 9:25; 2 K 16:13; 1 Chr 16:1; 21:26; 2 Chr 7:7; 29:35; 30:22; 31:2; 33:16; Pr 7:14; Eze 43:27; 45:15; 46:2, 12; Am 5:22

8. Sin

Ex 29:14, 36; 30:10; Le 4:3, 21, 33; 5:8, 11; 6:17, 25, 30; 7:7, 37; 8:2, 14; 9:2, 7, 15, 22; 10:17; 12:6; 14:13, 19, 22, 31; 15:15, 30; 16:3, 9, 11, 25; 23:19; Nu 6:11, 16; 7:16, 22, 28, 40, 46, 64, 82, 87; 8:8, 12; 15:24, 27; 18:9; 28:15, 22; 29:5, 16, 19, 22, 31, 38; 2 Chr 29:21; Ezr 6:17; 8:35; Ne 10:33; Is 53:10; Eze 40:39; 42:13; 43:19; 44:29; 45:17, 22; 46:20; He 5:3; 7:27; 9:13; 10:6, 11; 13:11

9. Thank

Le 7:12; 22:29; 2 Chr 29:31; 33:16; Ps 116:17; Je 33:11

10. Trespass

Le 5:6, 15, 19; 6:6, 17; 7:1, 37; 14:12, 21, 25; 19:21; Nu 6:12; 18:9; 1 S 6:3, 8, 17; 2 K 12:16; Ezr 10:19; Eze 40:39; 42:13; 46:20

11. Unacceptable

Ge 4:5; Le 7:18; 10:19; 19:7; 22:20, 25; 26:31; 1 S 13:9; Ps 50:9; Pr 15:8; 21:27; Is 1:11; 66:3; Je 6:20; 7:21; 14:12; Eze 20:28, 39; Ho 8:13; 9:4; Am 5:22; Hag 2:14; Mal 1:8, 10, 13; 2:13; He 10:6

12. Wave

Ex 29:24; Le 7:30; 8:27; 9:21; 10:14; 14:12, 24; 23:11, 20; Nu 5:25; 6:20; 18:11

13. Generous

GIFTS OF ISRAEL FOR THE TABERNACLE

Ex 35:22 And they came, both men and women, as many as were willing hearted, *and* brought bracelets, and earrings, and rings, and tablets, all jewels of gold: and every man that offered *offered* an offering of gold unto the LORD.

ABUNDANT GIVING

Ex 36:5 And they spake unto Moses, saying, The people bring much more than enough for the service of the work, which the LORD commanded to make.

OFFERINGS AT THE DEDICATION

Nu 7:3 And they brought their offering before the LORD, six covered wagons, and twelve oxen; a wagon for two of the princes, and for each one an ox: and they brought them before the tabernacle.

DAVID'S GIFTS FOR THE TEMPLE

1 Chr 29:3–4 Moreover, because I have set my affection to the house of my God, I have of mine own proper good, of gold and silver, *which* I have given to the house of my God, over and above all that I have prepared for the holy house,

Even three thousand talents of gold, of the gold of Ophir, and seven thousand talents of refined silver, to overlay the walls of the houses *withal:*

GIFTS FOR THE REPAIRING OF GOD'S HOUSE

2 Chr 24:10 And all the princes and all the people rejoiced, and brought in, and cast into the chest, until they had made an end.

OFFERINGS FOR THE REBUILDING OF THE TEMPLE

Ezr 1:6 And all they that *were* about them strengthened their hands with vessels of silver, with gold, with goods, and with beasts, and with precious things, beside all *that* was willingly offered.

Ezr 2:69 They gave after their ability unto the treasure of the work threescore and one thousand drams of gold, and five thousand pound of silver, and one hundred priests' garments.

Ezr 8:25 And weighed unto them the silver, and the gold, and the vessels, *even* the offering of the house of our God, which the king, and his counsellors, and his lords, and all Israel *there* present, had offered:

Ne 7:70 And some of the chief of the fathers gave unto the work. The Tirshatha gave to the treasure a thousand drams of gold, fifty basons, five hundred and thirty priests' garments.

Lu 19:8 And Zacchaeus stood, and said unto the Lord; Behold, Lord, the half of my goods I give to the poor; and if I have taken any thing from any man by false accusation, I restore *him* fourfold.

THE POOR WIDOW'S OFFERING

Lu 21:1–4 And he looked up, and saw the rich men casting their gifts into the treasury.

And he saw also a certain poor widow casting in thither two mites.

And he said, Of a truth I say unto you, that this poor widow hath cast in more than they all:

For all these have of their abundance cast in unto the offerings of God: but she of her penury hath cast in all the living that she had.

LIBERALITY IN THE EARLY CHURCH

Ac 4:34–35 Neither was there any among them that lacked: for as many as were possessors of lands or houses sold them, and brought the prices of the things that were sold,

And laid at the apostles' feet: and distribution was made unto every man according as he had need.

Ac 11:29 Then the disciples, every man according to his ability, determined to send relief unto the brethren which dwelt in Judaea:

2 Co 8:2 How that in a great trial of affliction the abundance of their joy and their deep poverty abounded unto the riches of their liberality.

Ph 4:16 For even in Thessalonica ye sent once and again unto my necessity.

See **GIVING, SACRIFICES, WORSHIP**

OG, *king of Bashan*

Nu 21:33; De 3:1, 11; 4:47; Jos 13:12; Ne 9:22; Ps 135:11; 136:20

OIL, *most often from the olive*

1. For Lamps

Ex 25:6; 27:20; 35:8, 14, 28; 39:37; Le 24:2; Nu 4:16; Mt 25:3

2. For Food

Ex 29:2, 40; Le 2:1, 15; 6:15, 21; 7:10, 12; 14:10; 23:13; Nu 7:25, 37, 43, 79; 8:8; 11:8; 15:4; 28:5, 13, 20, 28; 29:3, 14; De 12:17; 14:23; 28:51; 1 K 5:11; 17:12; 2 K 4:2; 1 Chr 9:29; 2 Chr 2:10, 15; 31:5; 32:28; Ezr 6:9; Ne 5:11; 10:37; 13:5, 12; Pr 21:17; Eze 16:13; 45:14, 25; 46:5, 15; Jl 1:10; Hag 1:11; Lu 16:6; Re 6:6; 18:13

3. Used Figuratively

Ps 23:5; 45:7; 141:5; Is 61:3; Zec 4:12

4. For Anointing

Ex 25:6; 29:7, 21; 30:25, 31; 31:11; 35:8, 15, 28; 37:29; 39:38; 40:9; Le 8:2, 10; 10:7; 21:10; Nu 4:16; 1 S 10:1; 2 K 9:1; 1 Chr 9:30; Ps 133:2; Ec 7:1; Lu 7:37

See **ANOINTING, TREES**

OMEGA, *last letter of the Greek alphabet, a name applied to Christ*

Re 1:8; 21:6; 22:13

OLIVE *See* **TREES**

OLIVES, *MOUNT OF*

See **MOUNTAINS AND HILLS**

OLIVEYARDS *See* **AGRICULTURE**

OMER, *one-tenth of an ephah*
Ex 16:16, 32, 36

OMNIPOTENCE *See* **GOD**

OMNIPRESENCE

Ge 28:16 And Jacob awaked out of his sleep, and he said, Surely the LORD is in this place; and I knew *it* not.

De 4:39 Know therefore this day, and consider *it* in thine heart, that the LORD he *is* God in heaven above, and upon the earth beneath: *there is* none else.

1 K 8:27 But will God indeed dwell on the earth? behold, the heaven and heaven of heavens cannot contain thee; how much less this house that I have builded?

1 K 19:9 And he came thither unto a cave, and lodged there; and, behold, the word of the LORD *came* to him, and he said unto him, What doest thou here, Elijah?

2 Chr 2:6 But who is able to build him an house, seeing the heaven and heaven of heavens cannot contain him? who *am* I then, that I should build him an house, save only to burn sacrifice before him?

2 Chr 6:18 But will God in very deed dwell with men on the earth? behold, heaven and the heaven of heavens cannot contain thee; how much less this house which I have built!

Ps 139:8 If I ascend up into heaven, thou *art* there: if I make my bed in hell, behold, thou *art there*.

Pr 15:3 The eyes of the LORD *are* in every place, beholding the evil and the good.

Is 66:1 Thus saith the LORD, The heaven *is* my throne, and the earth *is* my footstool: where *is* the house that ye build unto me? and where *is* the place of my rest?

Je 23:24 Can any hide himself in secret places that I shall not see him? saith the LORD. Do not I fill heaven and earth? saith the LORD.

Ac 17:27 That they should seek the Lord, if haply they might feel after him, and find him, though he be not far from every one of us:

OMNISCIENCE, *God's all-knowing ability*

1. Of Christ

Mt 12:25 And Jesus knew their thoughts, and said unto them, Every kingdom divided against itself is brought to desolation; and every city or house divided against itself shall not stand:

Mt 22:18 But Jesus perceived their wickedness, and said, Why tempt ye me, *ye* hypocrites?

Mk 2:8 And immediately when Jesus perceived in his spirit that they so reasoned within themselves, he said unto them, Why reason ye these things in your hearts?

Mk 5:30 And Jesus, immediately knowing in himself that virtue had gone out of him, turned him about in the press, and said, Who touched my clothes?

Mk 11:2 And saith unto them, Go your way into the village over against you: and as soon as ye be entered into it, ye shall find a colt tied, whereon never man sat; loose him, and bring *him*.

Lu 5:6 And when they had this done, they inclosed a great multitude of fishes: and their net brake.

Lu 8:46 And Jesus said, Somebody hath touched me: for I perceive that virtue is gone out of me.

Lu 19:30 Saying, Go ye into the village over against *you;* in the which at your entering ye shall find a colt tied, whereon yet never man sat: loose him, and bring *him hither*.

Lu 22:10 And he said unto them, Behold, when ye are entered into the city, there shall a man meet you, bearing a pitcher of water; follow him into the house where he entereth in.

Jn 2:24 But Jesus did not commit himself unto them, because he knew all *men*,

Jn 6:6 And this he said to prove him: for he himself knew what he would do.

Jn 13:3 Jesus knowing that the Father had given all things into his hands, and that he was come from God, and went to God;

Jn 16:30 Now are we sure that thou knowest all things, and needest not that any man should ask thee: by this we believe that thou camest forth from God.

Jn 19:28 After this, Jesus knowing that all things were now accomplished, that the scripture might be fulfilled, saith, I thirst.

Jn 21:17 He saith unto him the third time, Simon, *son* of Jonas, lovest thou me? Peter was grieved because he said unto him the third time, Lovest thou me? And he said unto him, Lord, thou knowest all things; thou knowest that I love thee. Jesus saith unto him, Feed my sheep.

Ac 1:24 And they prayed, and said, Thou, Lord, which knowest the hearts of all *men,* shew whether of these two thou hast chosen,

Re 3:1 And unto the angel of the church in Sardis write; These things saith he that hath the seven Spirits of God, and the seven stars; I know thy works, that thou hast a name that thou livest, and art dead.

Re 3:8 I know thy works: behold, I have set before thee an open door, and no man can shut it: for thou hast a little strength, and hast kept my word, and hast not denied my name.

Re 3:14 And unto the angel of the church of the Laodiceans write; These things saith the Amen, the faithful and true witness, the beginning of the creation of God;

2. Of God

Jos 22:22 The LORD God of gods, the LORD God of gods, he knoweth, and Israel he shall know; if *it be* in rebellion, or if in transgression against the LORD, (save us not this day,)

Jb 26:6 Hell *is* naked before him, and destruction hath no covering.

Jb 28:23 God understandeth the way thereof, and he knoweth the place thereof.

Jb 31:4 Doth not he see my ways, and count all my steps?

Jb 34:21 For his eyes *are* upon the ways of man, and he seeth all his goings.

Ps 139:4 For *there is* not a word in my tongue, *but,* lo, O LORD, thou knowest it altogether.

Ps 147:5 Great *is* our Lord, and of great power: his understanding *is* infinite.

Pr 15:11 Hell and destruction *are* before the LORD: how much more then the hearts of the children of men?

Is 40:26 Lift up your eyes on high, and behold who hath created these *things,* that bringeth out their host by number: he calleth them all by names by the greatness of his might, for that *he is* strong in power; not one faileth.

Eze 37:3 And he said unto me, Son of man, can these bones live? And I answered, O Lord GOD, thou knowest.

Am 4:13 For, lo, he that formeth the mountains, and createth the wind, and declareth unto man what *is* his thought, that maketh the morning darkness, and treadeth upon the high places of the earth, The LORD, The God of hosts, *is* his name.

2 Co 12:2 I knew a man in Christ above fourteen years ago, (whether in the body, I cannot tell; or whether out of the body, I cannot tell: God knoweth;) such an one caught up to the third heaven.

He 4:13 Neither is there any creature that is not manifest in his sight: but all things *are* naked and opened unto the eyes of him with whom we have to do.

1 Jn 3:20 For if our heart condemn us, God is greater than our heart, and knoweth all things.

See **FOREKNOWLEDGE, GOD, KNOWLEDGE, PREDESTINATION**

OMRI, *king of Israel, succeeds Elah*

1 K 16:16, 22, 28; 2 K 8:26; Mi 6:16

See **ISRAEL**

ON, *Heliopolis (?)*

Ge 41:45; 46:20

ONAN, *son of Judah*

Ge 38:4; 46:12; Nu 26:19; 1 Chr 2:3

ONESIMUS, *a slave for whom Paul intercedes*

Col 4:9; Phm 10

ONESIPHORUS, *a friend of Paul*

2 Ti 1:16; 4:19

ONE THING

DESIRED

Ps 27:4 One *thing* have I desired of the LORD, that will I seek after; that I may dwell in the house of the LORD all the days of my life, to behold the beauty of the LORD, and to enquire in his temple.

HAPPENS TO ALL

Ec 3:19 For that which befalleth the sons of men befalleth beasts; even one thing befalleth them: as the one dieth, so dieth the other; yea, they have all one breath; so that a man hath no preeminence above a beast: for all *is* vanity.

LACKING

Mk 10:21 Then Jesus beholding him loved him, and said unto him, One thing thou lackest: go thy way, sell whatsoever thou hast, and give to the poor, and thou shalt have treasure in heaven: and come, take up the cross, and follow me.

NEEDFUL

Lu 10:42 But one thing is needful: and Mary hath chosen that good part, which shall not be taken away from her.

KNOWN

Jn 9:25 He answered and said, Whether he be a sinner *or no*, I know not: one thing I know, that, whereas I was blind, now I see.

TO DO

Ph 3:13 Brethren, I count not myself to have apprehended: but *this* one thing *I do*, forgetting those things which are behind, and reaching forth unto those things which are before,

ABOUT TIME

2 Pe 3:8 But, beloved, be not ignorant of this one thing, that one day *is* with the Lord as a thousand years, and a thousand years as one day.

See **DESIRE**

ONIONS, *a vegetable desired by the Israelites while in the desert*

Nu 11:5

ONYX   *See* **STONES**

OPHEL, *a part of Jerusalem*

2 Chr 27:3; 33:14; Ne 3:26; 11:21

OPHIR, *a country rich in gold*

Ge 10:29; 1 K 9:28; 10:11; 22:48; 1 Chr 29:4; 2 Chr 8:18; 9:10; Jb 22:24; 28:16; Ps 45:9; Is 13:12

OPHRAH, *a town*

Jos 18:23; Jud 6:11; 8:32; 1 S 13:17

See **CITIES**

OPINION, *PUBLIC, the prevailing or common feeling of the people*

1. Its Power

SAVED JONATHAN'S LIFE

1 S 14:45 And the people said unto Saul, Shall Jonathan die, who hath wrought this great salvation in Israel? God forbid: *as* the LORD liveth, there shall not one hair of his head fall to the ground; for he hath wrought with God this day. So the people rescued Jonathan, that he died not.

COST SAUL HIS KINGDOM

1 S 15:24 And Saul said unto Samuel, I have sinned: for I have transgressed the commandment of the LORD, and thy words: because I feared the people, and obeyed their voice.

SAVED THE LIFE OF JOHN THE BAPTIST

Mt 14:5 And when he would have put him to death, he feared the multitude, because they counted him as a prophet.

PREVENTED MEN
FROM CONFESSING CHRIST

Jn 7:13 Howbeit no man spake openly of him for fear of the Jews.

SECURED THE IMPRISONMENT OF PETER

Ac 12:3 And because he saw it pleased the Jews, he proceeded further to take Peter also. (Then were the days of unleavened bread.)

2. *Divided*, concerning Christ and his work

Mt 10:35 For I am come to set a man at variance against his father, and the daughter against her mother, and the daughter in law against her mother in law.

Mt 22:42 Saying, What think ye of Christ? whose son is he? They say unto him, *The Son* of David.

Lu 9:8 And of some, that Elias had appeared; and of others, that one of the old prophets was risen again.

Lu 12:51 Suppose ye that I am come to give peace on earth? I tell you, Nay; but rather division:

Jn 7:12 And there was much murmuring among the people concerning him: for some said, He is a good man: others said, Nay; but he deceiveth the people.

Jn 7:43 So there was a division among the people because of him.

Jn 9:16 Therefore said some of the Pharisees, This man is not of God, because he keepeth not the sabbath day. Others said, How can a man that is a sinner do such miracles? And there was a division among them.

Jn 10:19 There was a division therefore again among the Jews for these sayings.

Ac 14:4 But the multitude of the city was divided: and part held with the Jews, and part with the apostles.

Ac 28:25 And when they agreed not among themselves, they departed, after that Paul had spoken one word, Well spake the Holy Ghost by Esaias the prophet unto our fathers,

See **POPULARITY**

OPPORTUNITY

1. *Lost by Indifference or Neglect*

FOR A COMPLETE VICTORY—BY A
HALF-HEARTED KING

2 K 13:19 And the man of God was wroth with him, and said, Thou shouldest have smitten five or six times; then hadst thou smitten Syria till thou hadst consumed *it:* whereas now thou shalt smite Syria *but* thrice.

FOR REPENTANCE—BY ISRAEL

Je 8:20 The harvest is past, the summer is ended, and we are not saved.

FOR PROVIDING OIL—BY THE FOOLISH
VIRGINS

Mt 25:10 And while they went to buy, the bridegroom came; and they that were ready went in with him to the marriage: and the door was shut.

FOR INVESTMENT—BY THE ONE-TALENTED
MAN

Mt 25:26–27 His lord answered and said unto him, *Thou* wicked and slothful servant, thou knewest that I reap where I sowed not, and gather where I have not strawed:

Thou oughtest therefore to have put my money to the exchangers, and *then* at my coming I should have received mine own with usury.

FOR SYMPATHETIC SERVICE—BY THE
CASTAWAYS

Mt 25:44–45 Then shall they also answer him, saying, Lord, when saw we thee an hungred, or athirst, or a stranger, or naked, or sick, or in prison, and did not minister unto thee?

Then shall he answer them, saying, Verily I say unto you, Inasmuch as ye did *it* not to one of the least of these, ye did *it* not to me.

FOR SYMPATHY WITH THE MASTER—BY THE DISCIPLES

Mt 26:40–41 And he cometh unto the disciples, and findeth them asleep, and saith unto Peter, What, could ye not watch with me one hour?

Watch and pray, that ye enter not into temptation: the spirit indeed *is* willing, but the flesh *is* weak.

FOR ACCEPTING CHRIST—BY JERUSALEM

Lu 19:41–42 And when he was come near, he beheld the city, and wept over it,

Saying, If thou hadst known, even thou, at least in this thy day, the things *which belong* unto thy peace! but now they are hid from thine eyes.

FOR MEETING THE RISEN LORD—BY THOMAS

Jn 20:24 But Thomas, one of the twelve, called Didymus, was not with them when Jesus came.

2. Requires Responsibility

Pr 1:24; Eze 3:19; Mt 10:14; 11:20; Lu 12:47

3. For Great Service

Mt 9:37 Then saith he unto his disciples, The harvest truly *is* plenteous, but the labourers *are* few;

Mt 25:15 And unto one he gave five talents, to another two, and to another one; to every man according to his several ability; and straightway took his journey.

Lu 19:13 And he called his ten servants, and delivered them ten pounds, and said unto them, Occupy till I come.

Jn 4:35 Say not ye, There are yet four months, and *then* cometh harvest? behold, I say unto you, Lift up your eyes, and look on the fields; for they are white already to harvest.

Ac 16:9 And a vision appeared to Paul in the night; There stood a man of Macedonia, and prayed him, saying, Come over into Macedonia, and help us.

4. An Open Door

Ac 10:24 And the morrow after they entered into Caesarea. And Cornelius waited for them, and had called together his kinsmen and near friends.

Ac 13:15 And after the reading of the law and the prophets the rulers of the synagogue sent unto them, saying, *Ye* men *and* brethren, if ye have any word of exhortation for the people, say on.

Ac 14:27 And when they were come, and had gathered the church together, they rehearsed all that God had done with them, and how he had opened the door of faith unto the Gentiles.

1 Co 16:9 For a great door and effectual is opened unto me, and *there are* many adversaries.

2 Co 2:12 Furthermore, when I came to Troas to *preach* Christ's gospel, and a door was opened unto me of the Lord,

Re 3:8 I know thy works: behold, I have set before thee an open door, and no man can shut it: for thou hast a little strength, and hast kept my word, and hast not denied my name.

5. Examples of Seizing

Jn 9:4 I must work the works of him that sent me, while it is day: the night cometh, when no man can work.

Ac 3:12 And when Peter saw *it,* he answered unto the people, Ye men of Israel, why marvel ye at this? or why look ye so earnestly on us, as though by our own power or holiness we had made this man to walk?

Ac 21:40 And when he had given him licence, Paul stood on the stairs, and beckoned with the hand unto the people. And when there was made a great silence, he spake unto *them* in the Hebrew tongue, saying,

6. Universal

FOR THE SINFUL

Mk 16:15 And he said unto them, Go ye into all the world, and preach the gospel to every creature.

FOR PRAYER

Lu 11:10 For every one that asketh receiveth; and he that seeketh findeth; and to him that knocketh it shall be opened.

PETER DISCOVERED

Ac 10:34 Then Peter opened *his* mouth, and said, Of a truth I perceive that God is no respecter of persons:

PAUL DECLARED

Ro 10:12 For there is no difference between the Jew and the Greek: for the same Lord over all is rich unto all that call upon him.

THE SPIRIT INVITES ALL

Re 22:17 And the Spirit and the bride say, Come. And let him that heareth say, Come. And let him that is athirst come. And whosoever will, let him take the water of life freely.

See **INDIFFERENCE, GOSPEL, MISSIONS, NEGLECT**

OPPRESSION, *harsh and rigorous imposition of power*

1. Forbidden

Ge 16:6; Ex 22:21; 23:9; Le 19:13, 33; 25:14, 17, 43, 46, 53; De 23:16; 24:14; 1 K 12:4, 14; 2 Chr 10:11; 16:10; Jb 3:18; 20:19; 22:9; 24:4, 9; Ps 12:5; 42:9; 62:10; Pr 3:31; 14:31; 22:16, 22; 28:3, 16; 30:14; 31:5; Ec 5:8; Is 10:2; 16:4; 30:12; 47:6; 49:26; 58:6, 9; Je 6:6; 7:6; 22:13, 17; Eze 18:7, 12, 18; 22:7; 45:8; 46:18; Am 2:7; 3:9; 4:1; Mi 2:2; Zep 3:1; Zec 7:10; Mal 3:5; Lu 12:45

2. Examples

Ex 1:14; 3:9; 5:4, 8; 6:9; Nu 20:15; De 26:6; 28:33; Jud 2:18; 4:3; 6:9; 10:8, 12; 1 S 10:18; 13:20; 2 K 4:1; 13:4, 22; 15:20; 2 Chr 10:4; Ne 5:1; Jb 35:9; Ps 17:9; 55:3; 56:1; 74:21; 103:6; 106:42; 107:39; Pr 28:15; Ec 4:1; 7:7; 8:9; Is 3:15; 5:7; 14:17; 19:20; 51:23; 52:4; Je 34:11; 50:33; Eze 22:29; 34:4, 27; Da 7:23; Am 8:4; Mt 18:25, 30; 24:49; Ac 7:19; Ja 2:6

See **INJUSTICE, POOR**

ORACLES, *the Scriptures*

Ac 7:38; Ro 3:2; He 5:12; 1 Pe 4:11

See **WORD OF GOD**

ORATOR, *a person skilled in speech*

Is 3:3; Ac 24:1

See **SPEECH**

ORDINANCES, OF GOD

Ex 13:10; 18:20; Le 18:4; 22:9; Nu 9:14; 19:2; 31:21; 2 S 22:23; 1 K 8:58; 2 K 17:37; 1 Chr 15:13; 2 Chr 2:4; Ps 18:22; 19:9; 147:20; Eze 11:20; 43:11; 44:5; Mal 3:7; Lu 1:6; Ro 13:2; He 9:1

See **LAW**

ORGANS *See* **MUSIC**

ORNAMENTS *See* **APPAREL**

ORION, *a heavenly constellation*

Jb 9:9; 38:31; Am 5:8

ORPHAN *See* **WIDOWS AND ORPHANS**

OSTRICHES *See* **BIRDS**

OTHNIEL, *son of Kenaz, the first judge of Israel*

Jos 15:17; Jud 1:13; 3:9

See **ISRAEL**

OUTCASTS

1. Israel

Jud 11:2; Is 11:12; 16:3; 27:13; Je 30:17

2. Received

THE LEPERS

Mt 8:3 And Jesus put forth *his* hand, and touched him, saying, I will; be thou clean. And immediately his leprosy was cleansed.

THE PUBLICANS AND HARLOTS

Mt 21:31 Whether of them twain did the will of *his* father? They say unto him, The first. Jesus saith unto them, Verily I say unto you, That the publicans and the harlots go into the kingdom of God before you.

Lu 7:29 And all the people that heard *him,* and the publicans, justified God, being baptized with the baptism of John.

THE SINFUL WOMEN

Lu 7:47 Wherefore I say unto thee, Her sins, which are many, are forgiven; for she loved much: but to whom little is forgiven, *the same* loveth little.

Jn 8:11 She said, No man, Lord. And Jesus said unto her, Neither do I condemn thee: go, and sin no more.

DESPISED SINNERS

Lu 15:2 And the Pharisees and scribes murmured, saying, This man receiveth sinners, and eateth with them.

THE DYING THIEF

Lu 23:43 And Jesus said unto him, Verily I say unto thee, To day shalt thou be with me in paradise.

THE EXCOMMUNICATED BLIND MAN

Jn 9:35 Jesus heard that they had cast him out; and when he had found him, he said unto him, Dost thou believe on the Son of God?

See **KINDNESS, LOVE**

OVENS

Le 2:4; 26:26; Lam 5:10; Mal 4:1; Mt 6:30

OVERSEERS *See* **TITLES AND NAMES**

OWLS *See* **BIRDS**

OWNERSHIP

1. Of the Natural World

Ge 13:17 Arise, walk through the land in the length of it and in the breadth of it; for I will give it unto thee.

Ge 14:19 And he blessed him, and said, Blessed *be* Abram of the most high God, possessor of heaven and earth:

Ge 31:9 Thus God hath taken away the cattle of your father, and given *them* to me.

Ex 9:29 And Moses said unto him, As soon as I am gone out of the city, I will spread abroad my hands unto the LORD; *and* the thunder shall cease, neither shall there be any more hail; that

thou mayest know how that the earth *is* the LORD's.

Ex 13:2 Sanctify unto me all the firstborn, whatsoever openeth the womb among the children of Israel, *both* of man and of beast: it *is* mine.

Ex 13:12 That thou shalt set apart unto the LORD all that openeth the matrix, and every firstling that cometh of a beast which thou hast; the males *shall be* the LORD's.

Ex 19:5 Now therefore, if ye will obey my voice indeed, and keep my covenant, then ye shall be a peculiar treasure unto me above all people: for all the earth *is* mine:

Ex 22:30 Likewise shalt thou do with thine oxen, *and* with thy sheep: seven days it shall be with his dam; on the eighth day thou shalt give it me.

Ex 34:19 All that openeth the matrix *is* mine; and every firstling among thy cattle, *whether* ox or sheep, *that is male.*

Le 25:23 The land shall not be sold for ever: for the land *is* mine; for ye *are* strangers and sojourners with me.

Le 27:26 Only the firstling of the beasts, which should be the LORD's firstling, no man shall sanctify it; whether *it be* ox, or sheep: it *is* the LORD's.

Nu 18:6 And I, behold, I have taken your brethren the Levites from among the children of Israel: to you *they are* given *as* a gift for the LORD, to do the service of the tabernacle of the congregation.

Nu 18:12 All the best of the oil, and all the best of the wine, and of the wheat, the firstfruits of them which they shall offer unto the LORD, them have I given thee.

Nu 33:53 And ye shall dispossess *the inhabitants* of the land, and dwell therein: for I have given you the land to possess it.

De 10:14 Behold, the heaven and the heaven of heavens *is* the LORD's thy God, the earth *also*, with all that therein *is*.

Jos 6:2 And the LORD said unto Joshua, See, I have given into thine hand Jericho, and the king thereof, *and* the mighty men of valour.

Jos 6:19 But all the silver, and gold, and vessels of brass and iron, *are* consecrated unto the LORD: they shall come into the treasury of the LORD.

Jos 6:24 And they burnt the city with fire, and all that *was* therein: only the silver, and the gold, and the vessels of brass and of iron, they put into the treasury of the house of the LORD.

1 Chr 29:11 Thine, O LORD, *is* the greatness, and the power, and the glory, and the victory, and the majesty: for all *that is* in the heaven and in the earth *is thine*; thine *is* the kingdom, O LORD, and thou art exalted as head above all.

1 Chr 29:14 But who *am* I, and what *is* my people, that we should be able to offer so willingly after this sort? for all things *come* of thee, and of thine own have we given thee.

Jb 41:11 Who hath prevented me, that I should repay *him? whatsoever is* under the whole heaven is mine.

Ps 24:1 The earth *is* the LORD's, and the fulness thereof; the world, and they that dwell therein.

Ps 50:10 For every beast of the forest *is* mine, *and* the cattle upon a thousand hills.

Ps 60:7 Gilead *is* mine, and Manasseh *is* mine; Ephraim also *is* the strength of mine head; Judah *is* my lawgiver;

Ps 74:16 The day *is* thine, the night also *is* thine: thou hast prepared the light and the sun.

Ps 89:11 The heavens *are* thine, the earth also *is* thine: *as for* the world and the fulness thereof, thou hast founded them.

Ps 95:5 The sea *is* his, and he made it: and his hands formed the dry *land*.

Ps 104:24 O LORD, how manifold are thy works! in wisdom hast thou made them all: the earth is full of thy riches.

Ps 108:8 Gilead *is* mine; Manasseh *is* mine; Ephraim also *is* the strength of mine head; Judah *is* my lawgiver;

Ps 115:16 The heaven, *even* the heavens, *are* the LORD's: but the earth hath he given to the children of men.

Je 27:5 I have made the earth, the man and the beast that *are* upon the ground, by my great power and by my outstretched arm, and have given it unto whom it seemed meet unto me.

Eze 29:3 Speak, and say, Thus saith the Lord GOD; Behold, I *am* against thee, Pharaoh king of Egypt, the great dragon that lieth in the midst of his rivers, which hath said, My river *is* mine own, and I have made *it* for myself.

Eze 29:9 And the land of Egypt shall be desolate and waste; and they shall know that I *am* the LORD: because he hath said, The river *is* mine, and I have made *it*.

Eze 29:20 I have given him the land of Egypt *for* his labour wherewith he served against it, because they wrought for me, saith the Lord GOD.

Eze 36:5 Therefore thus saith the Lord GOD; Surely in the fire of my jealousy have I spoken against the residue of the heathen, and against all Idumea, which have appointed my land into their possession with the joy of all *their* heart, with despiteful minds, to cast it out for a prey.

Da 4:17 This matter *is* by the decree of the watchers, and the demand by the word of the holy ones: to the intent that the living may know that the most High ruleth in the kingdom of men, and giveth it to whomsoever he will, and setteth up over it the basest of men.

Jl 3:5 Because ye have taken my silver and my gold, and have carried into your temples my goodly pleasant things:

Hag 2:8 The silver *is* mine, and the gold *is* mine, saith the LORD of hosts.

Mt 5:35 Nor by the earth; for it is his footstool: neither by Jerusalem; for it is the city of the great King.

Mt 20:15 Is it not lawful for me to do what I will with mine own? Is thine eye evil, because I am good?

Mt 21:3 And if any *man* say ought unto you, ye shall say, The Lord hath need of them; and straightway he will send them.

Mt 25:14 For *the kingdom of heaven is* as a man travelling into a far country, *who* called his own servants, and delivered unto them his goods.

Lu 19:23 Wherefore then gavest not thou my money into the bank, that at my coming I might have required mine own with usury?

Lu 19:31 And if any man ask you, Why do ye loose *him?* thus shall ye say unto him, Because the Lord hath need of him.

Ac 17:25 Neither is worshipped with men's hands, as though he needed any thing, seeing he giveth to all life, and breath, and all things;

1 Co 10:26 For the earth *is* the Lord's, and the fulness thereof.

1 Co 10:28 But if any man say unto you, This is offered in sacrifice unto idols, eat not for his sake that shewed it, and for conscience sake: for the earth *is* the Lord's, and the fulness thereof:

2. Of the Souls of Men

Ex 15:16 Fear and dread shall fall upon them; by the greatness of thine arm they shall be *as* still as a stone; till thy people pass over, O LORD, till the people pass over, *which* thou hast purchased.

Nu 3:12 And I, behold, I have taken the Levites from among the children of Israel instead of all the firstborn that openeth the matrix among the children of Israel: therefore the Levites shall be mine;

Nu 3:45 Take the Levites instead of all the firstborn among the children of Israel, and the cattle of the Levites instead of their cattle; and the Levites shall be mine: I *am* the LORD.

Nu 8:14 Thus shalt thou separate the Levites from among the children of Israel: and the Levites shall be mine.

Nu 8:17 For all the firstborn of the children of Israel *are* mine, *both* man and beast: on the day that I smote every firstborn in the land of Egypt I sanctified them for myself.

De 32:6 Do ye thus requite the LORD, O foolish people and unwise? *is* not he thy father *that* hath bought thee? hath he not made thee, and established thee?

Ps 24:1 The earth *is* the LORD's, and the fulness thereof; the world, and they that dwell therein.

Song 2:16 My beloved *is* mine, and I *am* his: he feedeth among the lilies.

Eze 18:4 Behold, all souls are mine; as the soul of the father, so also the soul of the son is mine: the soul that sinneth, it shall die.

Mt 21:40 When the lord therefore of the vineyard cometh, what will he do unto those husbandmen?

Mt 25:27 Thou oughtest therefore to have put my money to the exchangers, and *then* at my coming I should have received mine own with usury.

Jn 17:6 I have manifested thy name unto the men which thou gavest me out of the world: thine they were, and thou gavest them me; and they have kept thy word.

Ro 14:8 For whether we live, we live unto the Lord; and whether we die, we die unto the Lord: whether we live therefore, or die, we are the Lord's.

1 Co 3:23 And ye are Christ's; and Christ *is* God's.

1 Co 6:19 What? know ye not that your body is the temple of the Holy Ghost *which is* in you, which ye have of God, and ye are not your own?

2 Co 10:7 Do ye look on things after the outward appearance? If any man trust to himself that he is Christ's, let him of himself think this again, that, as he *is* Christ's, even so *are* we Christ's.

Ga 3:29 And if ye *be* Christ's, then are ye Abraham's seed, and heirs according to the promise.

3. Gives God Priority

a. Upon All Human Possessions

Ex 13:2 Sanctify unto me all the firstborn, whatsoever openeth the womb among the children of Israel, *both* of man and of beast: it *is* mine.

Nu 3:13 Because all the firstborn *are* mine; *for* on the day that I smote all the firstborn in the land of Egypt I hallowed unto me all the firstborn in Israel, both man and beast: mine shall they be: I *am* the LORD.

De 15:19 All the firstling males that come of thy herd and of thy flock thou shalt sanctify unto the LORD thy God: thou shalt do no work with the firstling of thy bullock, nor shear the firstling of thy sheep.

De 26:2 That thou shalt take of the first of all the fruit of the earth, which thou shalt bring of thy land that the LORD thy God giveth thee, and shalt put *it* in a basket, and shalt go unto the place which the LORD thy God shall choose to place his name there.

1 K 17:13 And Elijah said unto her, Fear not; go *and* do as thou hast said: but make me thereof a little cake first, and bring *it* unto me, and after make for thee and for thy son.

Mt 4:22 And they immediately left the ship and their father, and followed him.

Mt 6:33 But seek ye first the kingdom of God, and his righteousness; and all these things shall be added unto you.

Mt 8:21 And another of his disciples said unto him, Lord, suffer me first to go and bury my father.

Mt 10:37 He that loveth father or mother more than me is not worthy of me: and he that loveth son or daughter more than me is not worthy of me.

Mt 22:21 They say unto him, Caesar's. Then saith he unto them, Render therefore unto Caesar the things which are Caesar's; and unto God the things that are God's.

Mk 1:20 And straightway he called them: and they left their father Zebedee in the ship with the hired servants, and went after him.

Mk 11:3 And if any man say unto you, Why do ye this? say ye that the Lord hath need of him; and straightway he will send him hither.

Lu 2:23 (As it is written in the law of the Lord, Every male that openeth the womb shall be called holy to the Lord;)

Lu 9:62 And Jesus said unto him, No man, having put his hand to the plough, and looking back, is fit for the kingdom of God.

Lu 14:26 If any *man* come to me, and hate not his father, and mother, and wife, and children, and brethren, and sisters, yea, and his own life also, he cannot be my disciple.

Lu 17:8 And will not rather say unto him, Make ready wherewith I may sup, and gird thyself, and serve me, till I have eaten and drunken; and afterward thou shalt eat and drink?

Lu 20:25 And he said unto them, Render therefore unto Caesar the things which be Caesar's, and unto God the things which be God's.

See **DISCIPLESHIP**

b. Upon Firstborn Son

Ge 4:4; 27:32; 48:18; 49:3; Ex 4:23; 11:5; 12:12, 29; 13:2, 12; 22:29; 34:19; Le 27:26; Nu 3:13, 43; 8:17; 18:15; De 15:19; 21:17; Ne 10:36; Mi 6:7; Mt 1:25; Lu 2:7, 23, 27; He 11:28; 12:23

See **FAMILY**

c. Upon First-fruits of Labor

Ex 22:29 Thou shalt not delay *to offer* the first of thy ripe fruits, and of thy liquors: the firstborn of thy sons shalt thou give unto me.

Le 2:12 As for the oblation of the firstfruits, ye shall offer them unto the LORD: but they shall not be burnt on the altar for a sweet savour.

Nu 18:12 All the best of the oil, and all the best of the wine, and of the wheat, the firstfruits of them which they shall offer unto the LORD, them have I given thee.

De 18:4 The firstfruit *also* of thy corn, of thy wine, and of thine oil, and the first of the fleece of thy sheep, shalt thou give him.

De 26:2 That thou shalt take of the first of all the fruit of the earth, which thou shalt bring of thy land that the LORD thy God giveth thee, and shalt put *it* in a basket, and shalt go unto the place which the LORD thy God shall choose to place his name there.

Ne 10:35 And to bring the firstfruits of our ground, and the firstfruits of all fruit of all trees, year by year, unto the house of the LORD:

Pr 3:9 Honour the LORD with thy substance, and with the firstfruits of all thine increase:

Je 2:3 Israel *was* holiness unto the LORD, *and* the firstfruits of his increase:

all that devour him shall offend; evil shall come upon them, saith the LORD.

Ro 11:16 For if the firstfruit *be* holy, the lump *is* also *holy:* and if the root *be* holy, so *are* the branches.

Ro 16:5 Likewise *greet* the church that is in their house. Salute my well-beloved Epaenetus, who is the firstfruits of Achaia unto Christ.

1 Co 15:20 But now is Christ risen from the dead, *and* become the firstfruits of them that slept.

Ja 1:18 Of his own will begat he us with the word of truth, that we should be a kind of firstfruits of his creatures.

See **GIVING, OPPORTUNITY, REWARD, RICHES, STEWARDSHIP**

OXEN *See* **ANIMALS**

P

PAIN, *suffering or distress*

Jb 2:13; 14:22; 30:17; 33:19; Ps 25:18; Is 21:3; 26:18; Ro 8:22; Re 16:10; 21:4

See **SUFFERING**

PAINTING, *THE FACE*

2 K 9:30; Je 4:30; Eze 23:40

See **ARTS AND CRAFTS**

PALACES, *residences of royalty*

2 S 5:11; 7:2; 1 K 3:1; 7:1, 8; 9:1, 10; 10:4; 16:18; 21:1; 22:39; 2 K 25:9; 1 Chr 15:1; 17:1; 2 Chr 7:11; 8:11; 9:11; Ezr 6:2; Ne 1:1; 2:8; Est 1:2, 9; 2:16; 3:15; 5:1; 9:11; Ps 45:15; 48:3, 13; 122:7; 144:12; Pr 30:28; Ec 2:4; Song 8:9; Is 23:13; 32:14; Je 6:5; 17:27; 22:14; 30:18; 39:8; Lam 2:5; Da 1:4; 4:4, 29; 5:5; 6:18; 8:2; Am 1:7; 2:5; 3:9, 15; Mt 11:8; Mk 14:54; Jn 18:15

PALM *See* **TREES**

PALM BRANCHES, *symbols of victory*

Le 23:40; Ne 8:15; Jn 12:13

PALMERWORM *See* **INSECTS**

PAMPHYLIA, *a province of Asia Minor*

Ac 2:10; 13:13; 14:24; 15:38; 27:5

PANIC, *situations of overpowering terror, often affecting many people at one time*

Ex 12:30; 14:25; De 20:8; Jud 7:22; 20:42; 1 S 4:10; 14:16; 17:51; 1 K 20:20; 2 K 7:7, 15; 1 Chr 10:7; 2 Chr 14:12; 20:23; Je 46:16; 48:6; Na 2:8

See **COWARDICE, FEAR**

PAPER, *papyrus reeds*

Is 19:7; 2 Jn 12

PAPHOS, *capital city of Cyprus*

Ac 13:6

PARABLES, *stories or sayings illustrating a lesson*

1. Of the Old Testament

OF JOTHAM

Jud 9:7 And when they told *it* to Jotham, he went and stood in the top of mount Gerizim, and lifted up his voice, and cried, and said unto them, Hearken unto me, ye men of Shechem, that God may hearken unto you.

OF NATHAN

2 S 12:1 And the LORD sent Nathan unto David. And he came unto him, and said unto him, There were two men in one city; the one rich, and the other poor.

OF WOMAN OF TEKOA

2 S 14:5 And the king said unto her, What aileth thee? And she answered, I *am* indeed a widow woman, and mine husband is dead.

OF A PROPHET

1 K 20:39 And as the king passed by, he cried unto the king: and he said, Thy servant went out into the midst of the battle; and, behold, a man turned aside, and brought a man unto me, and said, Keep this man: if by any means he be missing, then shall thy life be for his life, or else thou shalt pay a talent of silver.

OF JOASH

2 K 14:9 And Jehoash the king of Israel sent to Amaziah king of Judah, saying, The thistle that *was* in Lebanon sent to the cedar that *was* in Lebanon, saying, Give thy daughter to my son to wife: and there passed by a wild beast that *was* in Lebanon, and trode down the thistle.

2 Chr 25:18 And Joash king of Israel sent to Amaziah king of Judah, saying, The thistle that *was* in Lebanon sent to the cedar that *was* in Lebanon, saying, Give thy daughter to my son to wife: and there passed by a wild beast that *was* in Lebanon, and trode down the thistle.

OF THE PROPHETS

Is 5:1 Now will I sing to my wellbeloved a song of my beloved touching his vineyard. My wellbeloved hath a vineyard in a very fruitful hill:

Je 13:1 Thus saith the LORD unto me, Go and get thee a linen girdle, and put it upon thy loins, and put it not in water.

Eze 17:3 And say, Thus saith the Lord GOD; A great eagle with great wings, longwinged, full of feathers, which had divers colours, came unto Lebanon, and took the highest branch of the cedar:

Eze 19:2–3 And say, What *is* thy mother? A lioness: she lay down among lions, she nourished her whelps among young lions.

And she brought up one of her whelps: it became a young lion, and it learned to catch the prey; it devoured men.

Eze 24:3 And utter a parable unto the rebellious house, and say unto them, Thus saith the Lord GOD; Set on a pot, set *it* on, and also pour water into it:

2. Of Christ

See chart on the following page.

PARACLETE *See* HOLY SPIRIT

PARADISE, *abode of believers*

Lu 23:43 And Jesus said unto him, Verily I say unto thee, To day shalt thou be with me in paradise.

2 Co 12:4 How that he was caught up into paradise, and heard unspeakable words, which it is not lawful for a man to utter.

Re 2:7 He that hath an ear, let him hear what the Spirit saith unto the churches; To him that overcometh will I give to eat of the tree of life, which is in the midst of the paradise of God.

See HEAVEN, HELL

PARADOXES, *scriptural*

Mt 10:39; 16:25; Mk 8:35; Lu 6:24; 2 Co 4:18; 6:8–10; 12:10; Ep 3:19; He 11:12

PARAN, *wilderness of*

Nu 10:12; 12:16; 13:26; De 1:1; 33:2

PARDON

1. Promised

Nu 14:20 And the LORD said, I have pardoned according to thy word:

Ps 103:12 As far as the east is from the west, *so* far hath he removed our transgressions from us.

Is 27:9 By this therefore shall the iniquity of Jacob be purged; and this is all the fruit to take away his sin; when he maketh all the stones of the altar as chalkstones that are beaten in sunder, the groves and images shall not stand up.

Is 33:24 And the inhabitant shall not say, I am sick: the people that dwell therein *shall be* forgiven *their* iniquity.

Is 40:2 Speak ye comfortably to Jerusalem, and cry unto her, that her warfare is accomplished, that her iniquity is pardoned: for she hath received of the LORD's hand double for all her sins.

Is 43:25 I, *even I, am* he that blotteth out thy transgressions for mine own sake, and will not remember thy sins.

Is 44:22 I have blotted out, as a thick cloud, thy transgressions, and, as a cloud, thy sins: return unto me; for I have redeemed thee.

Is 55:7 Let the wicked forsake his way, and the unrighteous man his thoughts: and let him return unto the LORD, and he will have mercy upon him; and to our God, for he will abundantly pardon.

Je 5:1 Run ye to and fro through the streets of Jerusalem, and see now, and know, and seek in the broad places thereof, if ye can find a man, if there be *any* that executeth judgment, that seeketh the truth; and I will pardon it.

PARABLES OF CHRIST

Parables	Matthew	Mark	Luke	John
In One Gospel Only				
The Barren Fig Tree			13	
The Dragnet	13			
The Friend at Midnight			11	
The Good Samaritan			10	
The Good Shepherd				10
The Fine Pearl	13			
The Great Supper			14	
The Hidden Treasure	13			
The Householder		13		
The Laborers in the Vineyard	20			
The Marriage Feast for King's Son	22			
The Pharisee and Tax-gatherer			18	
The Pieces of Money			15	
The Pounds			19	
The Prodigal Son			15	
The Rich Fool			12	
The Rich Man and Lazarus			16	
The Seed Growing in Secret		4		
The Sheep and Goats	25			
The Tares	13			
The Ten Talents	25			
The Ten Virgins	25			
The Two Debtors			7	
The Two Sons	21			
The Unjust Judge			18	
The Unjust Steward			16	
The Unmerciful Servant	18			
The Unprofitable Servants			17	
The Wedding Feast			12	
The Wise Steward			12	
In Two Gospels Only				
The House on the Rock	7		6	
The Yeast	13		13	
The Lost Sheep	18		15	
In Three Gospels				
New Cloth	9	2	5	
New Wine in Old Wineskins	9	2	5	
The Fig Tree	24	13	21	
The Mustard Seed	13	4	13	
The Sower	13	4	8	
The Wicked Farmer	21	12	20	

Je 31:34 And they shall teach no more every man his neighbour, and every man his brother, saying, Know the LORD: for they shall all know me, from the least of them unto the greatest of them, saith the LORD; for I will forgive their iniquity, and I will remember their sin no more.

Je 33:8 And I will cleanse them from all their iniquity, whereby they have sinned against me; and I will pardon all their iniquities, whereby they have sinned, and whereby they have transgressed against me.

Je 50:20 In those days, and in that time, saith the LORD, the iniquity of Israel shall be sought for, and *there shall be* none; and the sins of Judah, and they shall not be found: for I will pardon them whom I reserve.

Eze 16:63 That thou mayest remember, and be confounded, and never open thy mouth any more because of thy shame, when I am pacified toward thee for all that thou hast done, saith the Lord GOD.

Eze 18:21 But if the wicked will turn from all his sins that he hath committed, and keep all my statutes, and do that which is lawful and right, he shall surely live, he shall not die.

Eze 33:12 Therefore, thou son of man, say unto the children of thy people, The righteousness of the righteous shall not deliver him in the day of his transgression: as for the wickedness of the wicked, he shall not fall thereby in the day that he turneth from his wickedness; neither shall the righteous be able to live for his *righteousness* in the day that he sinneth.

Eze 36:25 Then will I sprinkle clean water upon you, and ye shall be clean: from all your filthiness, and from all your idols, will I cleanse you.

Mi 7:18 Who *is* a God like unto thee, that pardoneth iniquity, and passeth by the transgression of the remnant of his heritage? he retaineth not his anger for ever, because he delighteth *in* mercy.

Zec 3:9 For behold the stone that I have laid before Joshua; upon one stone *shall be* seven eyes: behold, I will engrave the graving thereof, saith the

LORD of hosts, and I will remove the iniquity of that land in one day.

Mk 11:25 And when ye stand praying, forgive, if ye have ought against any: that your Father also which is in heaven may forgive you your trespasses.

Lu 6:37 Judge not, and ye shall not be judged: condemn not, and ye shall not be condemned: forgive, and ye shall be forgiven:

He 8:12 For I will be merciful to their unrighteousness, and their sins and their iniquities will I remember no more.

He 10:17 And their sins and iniquities will I remember no more.

Ja 5:15 And the prayer of faith shall save the sick, and the Lord shall raise him up; and if he have committed sins, they shall be forgiven him.

1 Jn 1:9 If we confess our sins, he is faithful and just to forgive us *our* sins, and to cleanse us from all unrighteousness.

1 Jn 5:16 If any man see his brother sin a sin *which is* not unto death, he shall ask, and he shall give him life for them that sin not unto death. There is a sin unto death: I do not say that he shall pray for it.

2. Sought

Ex 32:32 Yet now, if thou wilt forgive their sin–; and if not, blot me, I pray thee, out of thy book which thou hast written.

Ex 34:9 And he said, If now I have found grace in thy sight, O Lord, let my Lord, I pray thee, go among us; for it *is* a stiffnecked people; and pardon our iniquity and our sin, and take us for thine inheritance.

Nu 14:19 Pardon, I beseech thee, the iniquity of this people according unto the greatness of thy mercy, and as thou hast forgiven this people, from Egypt even until now.

1 S 15:25 Now therefore, I pray thee, pardon my sin, and turn again with me, that I may worship the LORD.

2 S 24:10 And David's heart smote him after that he had numbered the people. And David said unto the LORD, I have sinned greatly in that I have done: and now, I beseech thee, O LORD, take away the iniquity of thy servant; for I have done very foolishly.

Ps 25:11 For thy name's sake, O LORD, pardon mine iniquity; for it *is* great.

Ps 39:8 Deliver me from all my transgressions: make me not the reproach of the foolish.

Ps 51:1 Have mercy upon me, O God, according to thy lovingkindness: according unto the multitude of thy tender mercies blot out my transgressions.

Da 9:19 O Lord, hear; O Lord, forgive; O Lord, hearken and do; defer not, for thine own sake, O my God: for thy city and thy people are called by thy name.

Mt 6:12 And forgive us our debts, as we forgive our debtors.

See **FORGIVENESS, MERCY, RESTORATION**

PARENTS

1. Evil Influence

Nu 32:14 And, behold, ye are risen up in your fathers' stead, an increase of sinful men, to augment yet the fierce anger of the LORD toward Israel.

1 K 22:52 And he did evil in the sight of the LORD, and walked in the way of his father, and in the way of his mother, and in the way of Jeroboam the son of Nebat, who made Israel to sin:

2 Chr 22:3 He also walked in the ways of the house of Ahab: for his mother was his counsellor to do wickedly.

2 Chr 30:7 And be not ye like your fathers, and like your brethren, which trespassed against the LORD God of their fathers, *who* therefore gave them up to desolation, as ye see.

Ps 78:8 And might not be as their fathers, a stubborn and rebellious generation; a generation *that* set not their heart aright, and whose spirit was not stedfast with God.

Ps 78:57 But turned back, and dealt unfaithfully like their fathers: they were turned aside like a deceitful bow.

Je 9:14 But have walked after the imagination of their own heart, and

after Baalim, which their fathers taught them:

Je 11:10 They are turned back to the iniquities of their forefathers, which refused to hear my words; and they went after other gods to serve them: the house of Israel and the house of Judah have broken my covenant which I made with their fathers.

Eze 20:18 But I said unto their children in the wilderness, Walk ye not in the statutes of your fathers, neither observe their judgments, nor defile yourselves with their idols:

Am 2:4 Thus saith the LORD; For three transgressions of Judah, and for four, I will not turn away *the punishment* thereof; because they have despised the law of the LORD, and have not kept his commandments, and their lies caused them to err, after the which their fathers have walked:

Zec 1:4 Be ye not as your fathers, unto whom the former prophets have cried, saying, Thus saith the LORD of hosts; Turn ye now from your evil ways, and *from* your evil doings: but they did not hear, nor hearken unto me, saith the LORD.

Mt 14:8 And she, being before instructed of her mother, said, Give me here John Baptist's head in a charger.

Ac 7:51 Ye stiffnecked and uncircumcised in heart and ears, ye do always resist the Holy Ghost: as your fathers *did,* so *do* ye.

2. Good Influence

1 K 9:4 And if thou wilt walk before me, as David thy father walked, in integrity of heart, and in uprightness, to do according to all that I have commanded thee, *and* wilt keep my statutes and my judgments:

2 Chr 17:3 And the LORD was with Jehoshaphat, because he walked in the first ways of his father David, and sought not unto Baalim;

2 Chr 20:32 And he walked in the way of Asa his father, and departed not from it, doing *that which was* right in the sight of the LORD.

2 Chr 26:4 And he did *that which was* right in the sight of the LORD, according to all that his father Amaziah did.

2 Chr 27:2 And he did *that which was* right in the sight of the Lord, according to all that his father Uzziah did: howbeit he entered not into the temple of the Lord. And the people did yet corruptly.

2 Ti 1:5 When I call to remembrance the unfeigned faith that is in thee, which dwelt first in thy grandmother Lois, and thy mother Eunice; and I am persuaded that in thee also.

3. Parental Love

Ge 24:36 And Sarah my master's wife bare a son to my master when she was old: and unto him hath he given all that he hath.

Ge 37:3 Now Israel loved Joseph more than all his children, because he *was* the son of his old age: and he made him a coat of *many* colours.

Jos 15:19 Who answered, Give me a blessing; for thou hast given me a south land; give me also springs of water. And he gave her the upper springs, and the nether springs.

1 S 2:19 Moreover his mother made him a little coat, and brought *it* to him from year to year, when she came up with her husband to offer the yearly sacrifice.

Lu 11:13 If ye then, being evil, know how to give good gifts unto your children: how much more shall *your* heavenly Father give the Holy Spirit to them that ask him?

4. Joy

Pr 15:20 A wise son maketh a glad father: but a foolish man despiseth his mother.

Pr 23:15 My son, if thine heart be wise, my heart shall rejoice, even mine.

Pr 23:24 The father of the righteous shall greatly rejoice: and he that begetteth a wise *child* shall have joy of him.

Pr 27:11 My son, be wise, and make my heart glad, that I may answer him that reproacheth me.

Pr 29:3 Whoso loveth wisdom rejoiceth his father: but he that keepeth company with harlots spendeth *his* substance.

Lu 15:23–24 And bring hither the fatted calf, and kill *it*; and let us eat, and be merry:

For this my son was dead, and is alive again; he was lost, and is found. And they began to be merry.

5. Sorrow

2 S 15:30 And David went up by the ascent of *mount* Olivet, and wept as he went up, and had his head covered, and he went barefoot: and all the people that *was* with him covered every man his head, and they went up, weeping as they went up.

2 S 18:33 And the king was much moved, and went up to the chamber over the gate, and wept: and as he went, thus he said, O my son Absalom, my son, my son Absalom! would God I had died for thee, O Absalom, my son, my son!

Pr 10:1 The proverbs of Solomon. A wise son maketh a glad father: but a foolish son *is* the heaviness of his mother.

Pr 17:21 He that begetteth a fool *doeth it* to his sorrow: and the father of a fool hath no joy.

Pr 17:25 A foolish son *is* a grief to his father, and bitterness to her that bare him.

Pr 19:13 A foolish son *is* the calamity of his father: and the contentions of a wife *are* a continual dropping.

Pr 19:26 He that wasteth *his* father, *and* chaseth away *his* mother, *is* a son that causeth shame, and bringeth reproach.

Pr 28:7 Whoso keepeth the law *is* a wise son: but he that is a companion of riotous *men* shameth his father.

Pr 29:15 The rod and reproof give wisdom: but a child left *to himself* bringeth his mother to shame.

1 Co 7:28 But and if thou marry, thou hast not sinned; and if a virgin marry, she hath not sinned. Nevertheless such shall have trouble in the flesh: but I spare you.

6. Solicitude

Ge 37:14 And he said to him, Go, I pray thee, see whether it be well with thy brethren, and well with the flocks;

and bring me word again. So he sent him out of the vale of Hebron, and he came to Shechem.

De 28:32 Thy sons and thy daughters *shall be* given unto another people, and thine eyes shall look, and fail *with longing* for them all the day long: and *there shall be* no might in thine hand.

1 S 9:5 *And* when they were come to the land of Zuph, Saul said to his servant that *was* with him, Come, and let us return; lest my father leave *caring* for the asses, and take thought for us.

1 S 10:2 When thou art departed from me to day, then thou shalt find two men by Rachel's sepulchre in the border of Benjamin at Zelzah; and they will say unto thee, The asses which thou wentest to seek are found: and, lo, thy father hath left the care of the asses, and sorroweth for you, saying, What shall I do for my son?

2 S 18:29 And the king said, Is the young man Absalom safe? And Ahimaaz answered, When Joab sent the king's servant, and *me* thy servant, I saw a great tumult, but I knew not what *it was*.

Est 2:11 And Mordecai walked every day before the court of the women's house, to know how Esther did, and what should become of her.

Lu 2:45 And when they found him not, they turned back again to Jerusalem, seeking him.

7. Special Duties

TO TEACH

De 6:7 And thou shalt teach them diligently unto thy children, and shalt talk of them when thou sittest in thine house, and when thou walkest by the way, and when thou liest down, and when thou risest up.

De 6:20 *And* when thy son asketh thee in time to come, saying, What *mean* the testimonies, and the statutes, and the judgments, which the LORD our God hath commanded you?

De 21:19 Then shall his father and his mother lay hold on him, and bring him out unto the elders of his city, and unto the gate of his place;

TO TRAIN

Pr 22:6 Train up a child in the way he should go: and when he is old, he will not depart from it.

Is 38:19 The living, the living, he shall praise thee, as I *do* this day: the father to the children shall make known thy truth.

Lam 2:19 Arise, cry out in the night: in the beginning of the watches pour out thine heart like water before the face of the Lord: lift up thy hands toward him for the life of thy young children, that faint for hunger in the top of every street.

TO PROVIDE FOR

2 Co 12:14 Behold, the third time I am ready to come to you; and I will not be burdensome to you: for I seek not yours, but you: for the children ought not to lay up for the parents, but the parents for the children.

TO NURTURE

Ep 6:4 And, ye fathers, provoke not your children to wrath: but bring them up in the nurture and admonition of the Lord.

Col 3:21 Fathers, provoke not your children *to anger,* lest they be discouraged.

TO CONTROL

1 Ti 3:4 One that ruleth well his own house, having his children in subjection with all gravity;

1 Ti 3:12 Let the deacons be the husbands of one wife, ruling their children and their own houses well.

TO LOVE

Tit 2:4 That they may teach the young women to be sober, to love their husbands, to love their children,

8. Correction of Children

Pr 3:12 For whom the LORD loveth he correcteth; even as a father the son *in whom* he delighteth.

Pr 13:24 He that spareth his rod hateth his son: but he that loveth him chasteneth him betimes.

Pr 19:18 Chasten thy son while there is hope, and let not thy soul spare for his crying.

Pr 22:15 Foolishness *is* bound in the heart of a child; *but* the rod of correction shall drive it far from him.

Pr 23:13 Withhold not correction from the child: for *if* thou beatest him with the rod, he shall not die.

Ep 6:4 And, ye fathers, provoke not your children to wrath: but bring them up in the nurture and admonition of the Lord.

9. Instruction of Children

De 4:9 Only take heed to thyself, and keep thy soul diligently, lest thou forget the things which thine eyes have seen, and lest they depart from thy heart all the days of thy life: but teach them thy sons, and thy sons' sons;

De 6:7 And thou shalt teach them diligently unto thy children, and shalt talk of them when thou sittest in thine house, and when thou walkest by the way, and when thou liest down, and when thou risest up.

De 11:19 And ye shall teach them your children, speaking of them when thou sittest in thine house, when thou walkest by the way, when thou liest down, and when thou risest up.

De 31:13 And *that* their children, which have not known *any thing,* may hear, and learn to fear the LORD your God, as long as ye live in the land whither ye go over Jordan to possess it.

Jud 13:12 And Manoah said, Now let thy words come to pass. How shall we order the child, and *how* shall we do unto him?

2 K 12:2 And Jehoash did *that which was* right in the sight of the LORD all his days wherein Jehoiada the priest instructed him.

Ps 78:3 Which we have heard and known, and our fathers have told us.

Ps 78:5 For he established a testimony in Jacob, and appointed a law in Israel, which he commanded our fathers, that they should make them known to their children:

Pr 22:6 Train up a child in the way he should go: and when he is old, he will not depart from it.

Is 28:9 Whom shall he teach knowledge? and whom shall he make to understand doctrine? *them that are* weaned from the milk, *and* drawn from the breasts.

Jn 21:15 So when they had dined, Jesus saith to Simon Peter, Simon, *son* of Jonas, lovest thou me more than these? He saith unto him, Yea, Lord; thou knowest that I love thee. He saith unto him, Feed my lambs.

1 Th 2:11 As ye know how we exhorted and comforted and charged every one of you, as a father *doth* his children,

10. The Heritage of God-fearing Parents

Ex 3:13; De 1:11; 4:1; Jos 18:3; 2 Chr 28:9; 29:5

See **HOME, FAMILY**

PARRICIDE, *murder of a close relative*

2 K 19:37; 2 Chr 32:21; Is 37:38

See **MURDER**

PARSIMONY, *excessive frugality*

De 15:10; Ne 13:10; Jb 31:16; Pr 11:24; 13:7; 21:13; 28:27; Ec 5:13; Is 43:23; Hag 1:4; Mal 1:8; 3:8; Mt 26:8; Mk 14:4; Jn 12:5; Ac 5:2; 2 Co 9:7; Ph 4:15; Ja 2:16; 1 Jn 3:17

In Withholding Offerings

2 Chr 29:7 Also they have shut up the doors of the porch, and put out the lamps, and have not burned incense nor offered burnt offerings in the holy *place* unto the God of Israel.

Ne 13:10 And I perceived that the portions of the Levites had not been given *them:* for the Levites and the singers, that did the work, were fled every one to his field.

Pr 11:24 There is that scattereth, and yet increaseth; and *there is* that withholdeth more than is meet, but *it tendeth* to poverty.

Is 43:24 Thou hast bought me no sweet cane with money, neither hast thou filled me with the fat of thy sacrifices: but thou hast made me to serve with thy sins, thou hast wearied me with thine iniquities.

Mal 3:8 Will a man rob God? Yet ye have robbed me. But ye say, Wherein have we robbed thee? In tithes and offerings.

Ac 5:2 And kept back *part* of the price, his wife also being privy *to it,* and brought a certain part, and laid *it* at the apostles' feet.

See **GIVING, GREED, MONEY**

PARTAKERS

1 Co 10:17 For we *being* many are one bread, *and* one body: for we are all partakers of that one bread.

2 Co 1:7 And our hope of you *is* stedfast, knowing, that as ye are partakers of the sufferings, so *shall ye be* also of the consolation.

Ph 1:7 Even as it is meet for me to think this of you all, because I have you in my heart; inasmuch as both in my bonds, and in the defence and confirmation of the gospel, ye all are partakers of my grace.

Col 1:2 To the saints and faithful brethren in Christ which are at Colosse: Grace *be* unto you, and peace, from God our Father and the Lord Jesus Christ.

1 Ti 6:2 And they that have believing masters, let them not despise *them,* because they are brethren; but rather do *them* service, because they are faithful and beloved, partakers of the benefit. These things teach and exhort.

He 3:1 Wherefore, holy brethren, partakers of the heavenly calling, consider the Apostle and High Priest of our profession, Christ Jesus;

He 3:14 For we are made partakers of Christ, if we hold the beginning of our confidence stedfast unto the end;

He 6:4 For *it is* impossible for those who were once enlightened, and have tasted of the heavenly gift, and were made partakers of the Holy Ghost,

He 12:10 For they verily for a few days chastened *us* after their own

pleasure; but he for *our* profit, that *we* might be partakers of his holiness.

1 Pe 4:13 But rejoice, inasmuch as ye are partakers of Christ's sufferings; that, when his glory shall be revealed, ye may be glad also with exceeding joy.

1 Pe 5:1 The elders which are among you I exhort, who am also an elder, and a witness of the sufferings of Christ, and also a partaker of the glory that shall be revealed:

2 Pe 1:4 Whereby are given unto us exceeding great and precious promises: that by these ye might be partakers of the divine nature, having escaped the corruption that is in the world through lust.

See **DEEPER LIFE, DEVOTIONAL LIFE**

PARTIALITY, *bias, favoritism*

Le 19:15 Ye shall do no unrighteousness in judgment: thou shalt not respect the person of the poor, nor honour the person of the mighty: *but* in righteousness shalt thou judge thy neighbour.

De 1:17 Ye shall not respect persons in judgment; *but* ye shall hear the small as well as the great; ye shall not be afraid of the face of man; for the judgment *is* God's: and the cause that is too hard for you, bring *it* unto me, and I will hear it.

1 K 1:10 But Nathan the prophet, and Benaiah, and the mighty men, and Solomon his brother, he called not.

Jb 13:10 He will surely reprove you, if ye do secretly accept persons.

Jb 32:21 Let me not, I pray you, accept any man's person, neither let me give flattering titles unto man.

Pr 18:5 *It is* not good to accept the person of the wicked, to overthrow the righteous in judgment.

Pr 24:23 These *things* also *belong* to the wise. *It is* not good to have respect of persons in judgment.

Mal 2:9 Therefore have I also made you contemptible and base before all the people, according as ye have not kept my ways, but have been partial in the law.

1 Ti 5:21 I charge *thee* before God, and the Lord Jesus Christ, and the elect angels, that thou observe these things without preferring one before another, doing nothing by partiality.

Ja 2:4 Are ye not then partial in yourselves, and are become judges of evil thoughts?

Jude 16 These are murmurers, complainers, walking after their own lusts; and their mouth speaketh great swelling *words,* having men's persons in admiration because of advantage.

See **IMPARTIALITY**

PASSIONS, *evil, powerful undesirable emotions or appetites*

Ge 49:4; Ho 7:6; Ro 1:26; 7:5; 1 Co 7:9; Ga 5:24; Col 3:5; 1 Th 4:5; 2 Ti 3:6; 1 Pe 2:11; Jude 18

See **DESIRE, LUST**

PASSOVER, *most important feast of Israel*

Ex 12:11 And thus shall ye eat it; *with* your loins girded, your shoes on your feet, and your staff in your hand; and ye shall eat it in haste: it *is* the LORD's passover.

Ex 12:27 That ye shall say, It *is* the sacrifice of the LORD's passover, who passed over the houses of the children of Israel in Egypt, when he smote the Egyptians, and delivered our houses. And the people bowed the head and worshipped.

Ex 12:43 And the LORD said unto Moses and Aaron, This *is* the ordinance of the passover: There shall no stranger eat thereof:

Nu 9:2 Let the children of Israel also keep the passover at his appointed season.

Nu 33:3 And they departed from Rameses in the first month, on the fifteenth day of the first month; on the morrow after the passover the children of Israel went out with an high hand in the sight of all the Egyptians.

De 16:1 Observe the month of Abib, and keep the passover unto the LORD thy God: for in the month of Abib the LORD thy God brought thee forth out of Egypt by night.

De 16:5 Thou mayest not sacrifice the passover within any of thy gates, which the LORD thy God giveth thee:

2 Chr 30:15 Then they killed the passover on the fourteenth *day* of the second month: and the priests and the Levites were ashamed, and sanctified themselves, and brought in the burnt offerings into the house of the LORD.

2 Chr 35:11 And they killed the passover, and the priests sprinkled *the blood* from their hands, and the Levites flayed *them.*

2 Chr 35:16 So all the service of the LORD was prepared the same day, to keep the passover, and to offer burnt offerings upon the altar of the LORD, according to the commandment of king Josiah.

Ezr 6:20 For the priests and the Levites were purified together, all of them *were* pure, and killed the passover for all the children of the captivity, and for their brethren the priests, and for themselves.

Mk 14:12 And the first day of unleavened bread, when they killed the passover, his disciples said unto him, Where wilt thou that we go and prepare that thou mayest eat the passover?

Lu 22:8 And he sent Peter and John, saying, Go and prepare us the passover, that we may eat.

1 Co 5:7–8 Purge out therefore the old leaven, that ye may be a new lump, as ye are unleavened. For even Christ our passover is sacrificed for us:

Therefore let us keep the feast, not with old leaven, neither with the leaven of malice and wickedness; but with the unleavened *bread* of sincerity and truth.

See **FESTIVALS**

PATHROS, *upper Egypt*

Is 11:11; Je 44:1; Eze 29:14; 30:14

PATHS

Ps 16:11 Thou wilt shew me the path of life: in thy presence *is* fulness of joy;

at thy right hand *there are* pleasures for evermore.

Ps 23:3 He restoreth my soul: he leadeth me in the paths of righteousness for his name's sake.

Ps 25:10 All the paths of the LORD *are* mercy and truth unto such as keep his covenant and his testimonies.

Ps 119:35 Make me to go in the path of thy commandments; for therein do I delight.

Pr 2:9 Then shalt thou understand righteousness, and judgment, and equity; *yea,* every good path.

Pr 2:19 None that go unto her return again, neither take they hold of the paths of life.

Pr 3:17 Her ways *are* ways of pleasantness, and all her paths *are* peace.

Pr 4:11 I have taught thee in the way of wisdom; I have led thee in right paths.

Pr 4:18 But the path of the just *is* as the shining light, that shineth more and more unto the perfect day.

Pr 8:20 I lead in the way of righteousness, in the midst of the paths of judgment:

Pr 12:28 In the way of righteousness *is* life; and *in* the pathway *thereof there is* no death.

Is 2:3 And many people shall go and say, Come ye, and let us go up to the mountain of the LORD, to the house of the God of Jacob; and he will teach us of his ways, and we will walk in his paths: for out of Zion shall go forth the law, and the word of the LORD from Jerusalem.

Is 26:7 The way of the just *is* uprightness: thou, most upright, dost weigh the path of the just.

Je 6:16 Thus saith the LORD, Stand ye in the ways, and see, and ask for the old paths, where is the good way, and walk therein, and ye shall find rest for your souls. But they said, We will not walk *therein.*

Je 31:21 Set thee up waymarks, make thee high heaps: set thine heart toward the highway, *even* the way *which* thou wentest: turn again, O virgin of Israel, turn again to these thy cities.

He 12:13 And make straight paths for your feet, lest that which is lame be turned out of the way; but let it rather be healed.

See **WAY**

PATIENCE, *endurance, forbearance*

1. Prescribed

Ec 7:8 Better *is* the end of a thing than the beginning thereof: *and* the patient in spirit *is* better than the proud in spirit.

Lu 21:19 In your patience possess ye your souls.

Ro 12:12 Rejoicing in hope; patient in tribulation; continuing instant in prayer;

1 Th 5:14 Now we exhort you, brethren, warn them that are unruly, comfort the feebleminded, support the weak, be patient toward all *men.*

2 Ti 2:24 And the servant of the Lord must not strive; but be gentle unto all *men,* apt to teach, patient,

Tit 2:2 That the aged men be sober, grave, temperate, sound in faith, in charity, in patience.

He 10:36 For ye have need of patience, that, after ye have done the will of God, ye might receive the promise.

Ja 1:4 But let patience have *her* perfect work, that ye may be perfect and entire, wanting nothing.

Ja 5:7 Be patient therefore, brethren, unto the coming of the Lord. Behold, the husbandman waiteth for the precious fruit of the earth, and hath long patience for it, until he receive the early and latter rain.

2 Pe 1:6 And to knowledge temperance; and to temperance patience; and to patience godliness;

2. Examples

Jb 14:14; Lu 8:15; Ro 8:25; 2 Co 6:4; 12:12; 2 Th 1:4; 2 Ti 3:10; He 6:15; Ja 5:11; 1 Pe 2:23; Re 1:9; 2:2, 19; 13:10; 14:12

3. In Waiting for God

Ge 49:18 I have waited for thy salvation, O LORD.

1 K 18:43 And said to his servant, Go up now, look toward the sea. And he went up, and looked, and said, *There is* nothing. And he said, Go again seven times.

2 K 6:33 And while he yet talked with them, behold, the messenger came down unto him: and he said, Behold, this evil *is* of the LORD; what should I wait for the LORD any longer?

Ps 33:20 Our soul waiteth for the LORD: he *is* our help and our shield.

Ps 37:7 Rest in the LORD, and wait patiently for him: fret not thyself because of him who prospereth in his way, because of the man who bringeth wicked devices to pass.

Ps 40:1 I waited patiently for the LORD; and he inclined unto me, and heard my cry.

Ps 130:6 My soul *waiteth* for the Lord more than they that watch for the morning: *I say, more than* they that watch for the morning.

Is 25:9 And it shall be said in that day, Lo, this *is* our God; we have waited for him, and he will save us: this *is* the LORD; we have waited for him, we will be glad and rejoice in his salvation.

Is 26:8 Yea, in the way of thy judgments, O LORD, have we waited for thee; the desire of *our* soul *is* to thy name, and to the remembrance of thee.

Is 33:2 O LORD, be gracious unto us; we have waited for thee: be thou their arm every morning, our salvation also in the time of trouble.

Lam 3:25 The LORD *is* good unto them that wait for him, to the soul *that* seeketh him.

Da 12:12 Blessed *is* he that waiteth, and cometh to the thousand three hundred and five and thirty days.

Lu 2:25 And, behold, there was a man in Jerusalem, whose name *was* Simeon; and the same man *was* just and devout, waiting for the consolation of Israel: and the Holy Ghost was upon him.

Ac 1:4 And, being assembled them, commanded them that they should not depart from Jerusalem, but wait for the promise of the Father, which, *saith he,* ye have heard of me.

See **IMPATIENCE, STEADFASTNESS**

PATMOS, *an island in the Mediterranean Sea*

Re 1:9

PATRIARCHS, *fathers; specifically applied to those recorded in Scripture prior to the time of Moses*

Ac 2:29; He 7:4; 7:8

See **ABRAHAM**

PATRIOTISM *See* **NATION**

PAUL, *the apostle, previously called Saul*

1. A Man of Vision

THE VISION OF CHRIST

Ac 9:3–6 And as he journeyed, he came near Damascus: and suddenly there shined round about him a light from heaven.

And he fell to the earth, and heard a voice saying unto him, Saul, Saul, why persecutest thou me?

And he said, Who art thou, Lord? And the Lord said, I am Jesus whom thou persecutest: *it is* hard for thee to kick against the pricks.

And he trembling and astonished said, Lord, what wilt thou have me to do? And the Lord *said* unto him, Arise, and go into the city, and it shall be told thee what thou must do.

Ac 26:13–15 At midday, O king, I saw in the way a light from heaven, above the brightness of the sun, shining round about me and them which journeyed with me.

And when we were all fallen to the earth, I heard a voice speaking unto me, and saying in the Hebrew tongue, Saul, Saul, why persecutest thou me? *it is* hard for thee to kick against the pricks.

And I said, Who art thou, Lord? And he said, I am Jesus whom thou persecutest.

THE MISSIONARY VISION

Ac 16:9 And a vision appeared to Paul in the night; There stood a man of Macedonia, and prayed him, saying, Come over into Macedonia, and help us.

THE VISION OF TESTIMONY

Ac 18:9 Then spake the Lord to Paul in the night by a vision, Be not afraid, but speak, and hold not thy peace:

THE VISION OF WARNING

Ac 22:18 And saw him saying unto me, Make haste, and get thee quickly out of Jerusalem: for they will not receive thy testimony concerning me.

THE VISION OF WORK

Ac 23:11 And the night following the Lord stood by him, and said, Be of good cheer, Paul: for as thou hast testified of me in Jerusalem, so must thou bear witness also at Rome.

THE VISION OF ENCOURAGEMENT

Ac 27:23 For there stood by me this night the angel of God, whose I am, and whom I serve,

THE VISION OF PARADISE

2 Co 12:1–4 It is not expedient for me doubtless to glory. I will come to visions and revelations of the Lord.

I knew a man in Christ above fourteen years ago, (whether in the body, I cannot tell; or whether out of the body, I cannot tell: God knoweth;) such an one caught up to the third heaven.

And I knew such a man, (whether in the body, or out of the body, I cannot tell: God knoweth;)

How that he was caught up into paradise, and heard unspeakable words, which it is not lawful for a man to utter.

OBEDIENCE TO THESE VISIONS

Ac 26:19 Whereupon, O king Agrippa, I was not disobedient unto the heavenly vision:

2. His Characteristics

JOY

Ac 16:25 And at midnight Paul and Silas prayed, and sang praises unto God: and the prisoners heard them.

2 Co 6:10 As sorrowful, yet alway rejoicing; as poor, yet making many rich; as having nothing, and *yet* possessing all things.

2 Co 7:4 Great *is* my boldness of speech toward you, great *is* my glorying of you: I am filled with comfort, I am exceeding joyful in all our tribulation.

Ph 4:4 Rejoice in the Lord alway: *and* again I say, Rejoice.

COURAGE

Ac 16:36–37 And the keeper of the prison told this saying to Paul, The magistrates have sent to let you go: now therefore depart, and go in peace.

But Paul said unto them, They have beaten us openly uncondemned, being Romans, and have cast *us* into prison; and now do they thrust us out privily? nay verily; but let them come themselves and fetch us out.

Ac 22:25 And as they bound him with thongs, Paul said unto the centurion that stood by, Is it lawful for you to scourge a man that is a Roman, and uncondemned?

Ac 24:25 And as he reasoned of righteousness, temperance, and judgment to come, Felix trembled, and answered, Go thy way for this time; when I have a convenient season, I will call for thee.

STEADFASTNESS

Ac 20:24 But none of these things move me, neither count I my life dear unto myself, so that I might finish my course with joy, and the ministry, which I have received of the Lord Jesus, to testify the gospel of the grace of God.

EARNESTNESS

Ac 20:31 Therefore watch, and remember, that by the space of three years I ceased not to warn every one night and day with tears.

Ro 9:3 For I could wish that myself were accursed from Christ for my brethren, my kinsmen according to the flesh:

Ph 3:18 (For many walk, of whom I have told you often, and now tell you even weeping, *that they are* the enemies of the cross of Christ:

INDUSTRY

Ac 20:34 Yea, ye yourselves know, that these hands have ministered unto my necessities, and to them that were with me.

1 Th 2:9 For ye remember, brethren, our labour and travail: for labouring night and day, because we would not be chargeable unto any of you, we preached unto you the gospel of God.

ENTIRE CONSECRATION

Ac 21:13 Then Paul answered, What mean ye to weep and to break mine heart? for I am ready not to be bound only, but also to die at Jerusalem for the name of the Lord Jesus.

Ph 3:7–14 But what things were gain to me, those I counted loss for Christ.

Yea doubtless, and I count all things *but* loss for the excellency of the knowledge of Christ Jesus my Lord: for whom I have suffered the loss of all things, and do count them *but* dung, that I may win Christ,

And be found in him, not having mine own righteousness, which is of the law, but that which is through the faith of Christ, the righteousness which is of God by faith:

That I may know him, and the power of his resurrection, and the fellowship of his sufferings, being made conformable unto his death;

If by any means I might attain unto the resurrection of the dead.

Not as though I had already attained, either were already perfect: but I follow after, if that I may apprehend that for which also I am apprehended of Christ Jesus.

Brethren, I count not myself to have apprehended: but *this* one thing *I do,* forgetting those things which are behind, and reaching forth unto those things which are before,

I press toward the mark for the prize of the high calling of God in Christ Jesus.

TACT

1 Co 9:19–22 For though I be free from all *men,* yet have I made myself servant unto all, that I might gain the more.

And unto the Jews I became as a Jew, that I might gain the Jews; to them that are under the law, as under the law, that I might gain them that are under the law;

To them that are without law, as without law, (being not without law to God, but under the law to Christ,) that I might gain them that are without law.

To the weak became I as weak, that I might gain the weak: I am made all things to all *men,* that I might by all means save some.

SELF-SACRIFICE

2 Co 11:24–33 Of the Jews five times received I forty *stripes* save one.

Thrice was I beaten with rods, once was I stoned, thrice I suffered shipwreck, a night and a day I have been in the deep;

In journeyings often, *in* perils of waters, *in* perils of robbers, *in* perils by *mine own* countrymen, *in* perils by the heathen, *in* perils in the city, *in* perils in the wilderness, *in* perils in the sea, *in* perils among false brethren;

In weariness and painfulness, in watchings often, in hunger and thirst, in fastings often, in cold and nakedness.

Beside those things that are without, that which cometh upon me daily, the care of all the churches.

Who is weak, and I am not weak? who is offended, and I burn not?

If I must needs glory, I will glory of the things which concern mine infirmities.

The God and Father of our Lord Jesus Christ, which is blessed for evermore, knoweth that I lie not.

In Damascus the governor under Aretas the king kept the city of the Damascenes with a garrison, desirous to apprehend me:

And through a window in a basket was I let down by the wall, and escaped his hands.

PATIENCE

2 Co 12:12 Truly the signs of an apostle were wrought among you in all patience, in signs, and wonders, and mighty deeds.

LOVE

1 Co 16:24 My love *be* with you all in Christ Jesus. Amen.

2 Co 2:4 For out of much affliction and anguish of heart I wrote unto you with many tears; not that ye should be grieved, but that ye might know the love which I have more abundantly unto you.

FAITHFULNESS

2 Ti 4:7–8 I have fought a good fight, I have finished *my* course, I have kept the faith:

Henceforth there is laid up for me a crown of righteousness, which the Lord, the righteous judge, shall give me at that day: and not to me only, but unto all them also that love his appearing.

ENDURANCE

2 Ti 2:10 Therefore I endure all things for the elect's sakes, that they may also obtain the salvation which is in Christ Jesus with eternal glory.

3. His Apostleship

Ac 9:15; 20:24; Ro 1:1, 5; 11:13; 15:16; 1 Co 1:1; 9:1; 14:37; 15:9; 2 Co 1:1; 10:8; 11:5; 12:11; Ga 1:1; Ep 1:1; 3:7; Col 1:1; 1 Th 2:7; 1 Ti 1:1, 12; 2:7; 2 Ti 1:1, 11; Tit 1:1

PAVILION, *symbolic of God's protection*

2 S 22:12; Ps 27:5; 31:20

See **PROTECTION**

PEACE

1. Spiritual

Ps 4:8 I will both lay me down in peace, and sleep: for thou, LORD, only makest me dwell in safety.

Lu 1:78–79 Through the tender mercy of our God; whereby the dayspring from on high hath visited us,

To give light to them that sit in darkness and *in* the shadow of death, to guide our feet into the way of peace.

Lu 2:13–14 And suddenly there was with the angel a multitude of the heavenly host praising God, and saying,

Glory to God in the highest, and on earth peace, good will toward men.

Jn 20:19 Then the same day at evening, being the first *day* of the week, when the doors were shut where the disciples were assembled for fear of the Jews, came Jesus and stood in the midst, and saith unto them, Peace *be* unto you.

Ro 8:6 For to be carnally minded *is* death; but to be spiritually minded *is* life and peace.

Ro 14:17 For the kingdom of God is not meat and drink; but righteousness, and peace, and joy in the Holy Ghost.

Ga 1:3 Grace *be* to you and peace from God the Father, and *from* our Lord Jesus Christ,

Ga 5:22–23 But the fruit of the Spirit is love, joy, peace, longsuffering, gentleness, goodness, faith,

Meekness, temperance: against such there is no law.

2 Th 3:16 Now the Lord of peace himself give you peace always by all means. The Lord *be* with you all.

2. Promised to Believers

THE GIFT OF GOD

Ps 29:11 The LORD will give strength unto his people; the LORD will bless his people with peace.

ABUNDANT

Ps 119:165 Great peace have they which love thy law: and nothing shall offend them.

Pr 3:17 Her ways *are* ways of pleasantness, and all her paths *are* peace.

PERFECT

Is 26:3 Thou wilt keep *him* in perfect peace, *whose* mind *is* stayed *on thee:* because he trusteth in thee.

LIKE A RIVER

Is 48:18 O that thou hadst hearkened to my commandments! then had thy peace been as a river, and thy right-eousness as the waves of the sea:

Is 54:13 And all thy children *shall be* taught of the LORD; and great *shall be* the peace of thy children.

Eze 34:25 And I will make with them a covenant of peace, and will cause the evil beasts to cease out of the land: and they shall dwell safely in the wilder-ness, and sleep in the woods.

LEGACY OF CHRIST

Jn 14:27 Peace I leave with you, my peace I give unto you: not as the world giveth, give I unto you. Let not your heart be troubled, neither let it be afraid.

Jn 16:33 These things I have spoken unto you, that in me ye might have peace. In the world ye shall have tribu-lation: but be of good cheer; I have overcome the world.

PASSETH UNDERSTANDING

Ph 4:7 And the peace of God, which passeth all understanding, shall keep your hearts and minds through Christ Jesus.

3. Bestowed through Christ

Is 9:6 For unto us a child is born, unto us a son is given: and the government shall be upon his shoulder: and his name shall be called Wonderful, Counsellor, The mighty God, The ev-erlasting Father, The Prince of Peace.

Is 53:5 But he *was* wounded for our transgressions, *he was* bruised for our iniquities: the chastisement of our peace *was* upon him; and with his stripes we are healed.

Mi 5:5 And this *man* shall be the peace, when the Assyrian shall come into our land: and when he shall tread in our palaces, then shall we raise against him seven shepherds, and eight principal men.

Zec 6:13 Even he shall build the tem-ple of the LORD; and he shall bear the glory, and shall sit and rule upon his throne; and he shall be a priest upon his throne: and the counsel of peace shall be between them both.

Lu 7:50 And he said to the woman, Thy faith hath saved thee; go in peace.

Ac 10:36 The word which *God* sent unto the children of Israel, preaching peace by Jesus Christ: (he is Lord of all:)

Ro 5:1 Therefore being justified by faith, we have peace with God through our Lord Jesus Christ:

Ep 2:14 For he is our peace, who hath made both one, and hath broken down the middle wall of partition *be-tween us;*

Ep 2:17 And came and preached peace to you which were afar off, and to them that were nigh.

Col 1:20 And, having made peace through the blood of his cross, by him to reconcile all things unto himself; by him, *I say,* whether *they be* things in earth, or things in heaven.

4. Duty of Seeking

Jb 22:21 Acquaint now thyself with him, and be at peace: thereby good shall come unto thee.

Ps 34:14 Depart from evil, and do good; seek peace, and pursue it.

Is 27:5 Or let him take hold of my strength, *that* he may make peace with me; *and* he shall make peace with me.

Col 3:15 And let the peace of God rule in your hearts, to the which also ye are called in one body; and be ye thankful.

1 Pe 3:11 Let him eschew evil, and do good; let him seek peace, and ensue it.

5. God of

Ro 15:33 Now the God of peace *be* with you all. Amen.

Ro 16:20 And the God of peace shall bruise Satan under your feet shortly. The grace of our Lord Jesus Christ *be* with you. Amen.

2 Co 13:11 Finally, brethren, fare-well. Be perfect, be of good comfort, be of one mind, live in peace; and the God of love and peace shall be with you.

Ph 4:9 Those things, which ye have both learned, and received, and heard, and seen in me, do: and the God of peace shall be with you.

1 Th 5:23 And the very God of peace sanctify you wholly; and *I pray God* your whole spirit and soul and body be preserved blameless unto the coming of our Lord Jesus Christ.

2 Th 3:16 Now the Lord of peace himself give you peace always by all means. The Lord *be* with you all.

Tit 1:4 To Titus, *mine* own son after the common faith: Grace, mercy, *and* peace, from God the Father and the Lord Jesus Christ our Saviour.

He 13:20 Now the God of peace, that brought again from the dead our Lord Jesus, that great shepherd of the sheep, through the blood of the everlasting covenant,

6. To be Cultivated in the Church

Ps 122:8 For my brethren and companions' sakes, I will now say, Peace *be* within thee.

1 Co 14:33 For God is not *the author* of confusion, but of peace, as in all churches of the saints.

2 Co 13:11 Finally, brethren, farewell. Be perfect, be of good comfort, be of one mind, live in peace; and the God of love and peace shall be with you.

Ep 4:3 Endeavouring to keep the unity of the Spirit in the bond of peace.

Ph 4:2 I beseech Euodias, and beseech Syntyche, that they be of the same mind in the Lord.

1 Th 5:13 And to esteem them very highly in love for their work's sake. *And* be at peace among yourselves.

2 Ti 2:22 Flee also youthful lusts: but follow righteousness, faith, charity, peace, with them that call on the Lord out of a pure heart.

7. Social

a. The Obligation to Preserve Peace

Ge 26:31; Ps 120:7; Pr 3:30; 25:8; Je 29:7; Zec 8:19; Mk 9:50; Lu 14:32; Ac 12:20; Ro 12:18; 14:19; 1 Co 1:10; 7:15; He 12:14

b. Foretold by the Prophets

Le 26:6; De 12:10; Ps 46:9; 72:3, 7; 85:10; 128:6; 147:14; Is 2:4; 9:7; 11:6, 9; 14:3, 7; 32:17; 33:20; 60:18; 65:25; Je

46:27; 50:34; Ho 2:18; Mi 4:4; Zec 9:10; 1 Ti 2:2

c. Periods of Peace in the History of Israel

De 25:19; Jos 11:23; 14:15; 21:44; 22:4; 23:1; Jud 3:11, 30; 5:31; 8:28; 1 S 7:14; 2 S 7:1, 11; 10:19; 1 K 2:33; 4:24; 5:4; 22:1, 44; 1 Chr 4:40; 19:19; 22:9, 18; 23:25; 2 Chr 14:1, 6; 15:15, 19; 17:10; 20:30; 23:21; Is 39:8; Zec 1:11

8. Invoked

Ge 43:23; Jud 6:23; 18:6; 19:20; 1 S 1:17; 25:6, 35; 2 K 5:19; 1 Chr 12:18; Da 4:1; 6:25; 10:19; Mt 10:13; Lu 8:48; 10:5; 24:36; Jn 20:21, 26; Ac 16:36; Ro 1:7; Ga 6:16; Ep 6:23; Col 1:2; 1 Th 1:1; 2 Th 1:2; 3:16; 1 Ti 1:2; 2 Ti 1:2; Phm 3; 1 Pe 5:14; 2 Pe 1:2; 2 Jn 3; 3 Jn 14; Jude 2; Re 1:4

9. False, *a temporary absence of war or hostilities*

Ps 123:4 Our soul is exceedingly filled with the scorning of those that are at ease, *and* with the contempt of the proud.

Je 6:14 They have healed also the hurt *of the daughter* of my people slightly, saying, Peace, peace; when *there is* no peace.

Eze 13:10 Because, even because they have seduced my people, saying, Peace; and *there was* no peace; and one built up a wall, and, lo, others daubed it with untempered *morter:*

Eze 23:42 And a voice of a multitude being at ease *was* with her: and with the men of the common sort *were* brought Sabeans from the wilderness, which put bracelets upon their hands, and beautiful crowns upon their heads.

Am 6:1 Woe to them *that are* at ease in Zion, and trust in the mountain of Samaria, *which are* named chief of the nations, to whom the house of Israel came!

See **CONTENTMENT, DISCONTENTMENT, WAR**

PEACEABLENESS, *promoting the cessation of conflict*

1. Cultivated by the Righteous
Ge 13:8 And Abram said unto Lot, Let there be no strife, I pray thee, between me and thee, and between my herdmen and thy herdmen; for we *be* brethren.

Jud 8:3 God hath delivered into your hands the princes of Midian, Oreb and Zeeb: and what was I able to do in comparison of you? Then their anger was abated toward him, when he had said that.

Jud 21:13 And the whole congregation sent *some* to speak to the children of Benjamin that *were* in the rock Rimmon, and to call peaceably unto them.

2 S 20:19 I *am one of them that are* peaceable *and* faithful in Israel: thou seekest to destroy a city and a mother in Israel: why wilt thou swallow up the inheritance of the LORD?

Pr 15:18 A wrathful man stirreth up strife: but *he that is* slow to anger appeaseth strife.

Pr 16:14 The wrath of a king *is as* messengers of death: but a wise man will pacify it.

Pr 25:8 Go not forth hastily to strive, lest *thou know not* what to do in the end thereof, when thy neighbour hath put thee to shame.

Ec 10:4 If the spirit of the ruler rise up against thee, leave not thy place; for yielding pacifieth great offences.

Mt 5:24 Leave there thy gift before the altar, and go thy way; first be reconciled to thy brother, and then come and offer thy gift.

Ro 12:18 If it be possible, as much as lieth in you, live peaceably with all men.

Tit 1:6 If any be blameless, the husband of one wife, having faithful children not accused of riot or unruly.

He 12:14 Follow peace with all *men,* and holiness, without which no man shall see the Lord:

Ja 3:17 But the wisdom that is from above is first pure, then peaceable, gentle, *and* easy to be intreated, full of mercy and good fruits, without partiality, and without hypocrisy.

2. Peacemakers
Pr 12:20 Deceit *is* in the heart of them that imagine evil: but to the counsellors of peace *is* joy.

Pr 29:8 Scornful men bring a city into a snare: but wise *men* turn away wrath.

Mt 5:9 Blessed *are* the peacemakers: for they shall be called the children of God.

Ro 14:19 Let us therefore follow after the things which make for peace, and things wherewith one may edify another.

See **FORBEARANCE, WAR**

PEACE OFFERINGS
See **OFFERINGS**

PEACOCKS *See* **BIRDS**

PEARLS

1. Examples
Mt 13:45; 1 Ti 2:9; Re 17:4; 18:12; 21:21

2. Cast before Swine, *teaching offered which surpasses the spiritual receptivity level of the listeners*
Pr 9:7; 16:22; 23:9; 26:4; Eze 3:26; Mt 7:6

PEKAH, *king of Israel, son of Remaliah*

See **ISRAEL**

2 K 15:25, 30, 37; 16:5; 2 Chr 28:6; Is 7:1, 9

PEKAHIAH, *king of Israel, son of Menahem*

2 K 15:23, 26

See **ISRAEL**

PELETHITES, *part of David's guard*

2 S 8:18; 15:18; 20:7, 23; 1 K 1:38; 1 Chr 18:17

PELICANS *See* **BIRDS**

PENALTY, *punishment*

1. Physical and Spiritual Death
Ge 2:17 But of the tree of the knowledge of good and evil, thou shalt not

eat of it: for in the day that thou eatest thereof thou shalt surely die.

Ge 3:19 In the sweat of thy face shalt thou eat bread, till thou return unto the ground; for out of it wast thou taken: for dust thou *art,* and unto dust shalt thou return.

Ge 4:11 And now *art* thou cursed from the earth, which hath opened her mouth to receive thy brother's blood from thy hand;

Ge 6:17 And, behold, I, even I, do bring a flood of waters upon the earth, to destroy all flesh, wherein *is* the breath of life, from under heaven; *and* every thing that *is* in the earth shall die.

Ge 7:22 All in whose nostrils *was* the breath of life, of all that *was* in the dry *land,* died.

Ge 20:7 Now therefore restore the man *his* wife; for he *is* a prophet, and he shall pray for thee, and thou shalt live: and if thou restore *her* not, know thou that thou shalt surely die, thou, and all that *are* thine.

Ge 26:11 And Abimelech charged all *his* people, saying, He that toucheth this man or his wife shall surely be put to death.

Ex 19:12 And thou shalt set bounds unto the people round about, saying, Take heed to yourselves, *that ye* go *not* up into the mount, or touch the border of it: whosoever toucheth the mount shall be surely put to death:

Ex 31:15 Six days may work be done; but in the seventh is the sabbath of rest, holy to the LORD: whosoever doeth *any* work in the sabbath day, he shall surely be put to death.

Ex 32:33 And the LORD said unto Moses, Whosoever hath sinned against me, him will I blot out of my book.

Le 20:12 And if a man lie with his daughter in law, both of them shall surely be put to death: they have wrought confusion; their blood *shall be* upon them.

Le 23:30 And whatsoever soul *it be* that doeth any work in that same day, the same soul will I destroy from among his people.

Nu 11:34 And he called the name of that place Kibroth-hattaavah: because there they buried the people that lusted.

Nu 14:29 Your carcases shall fall in this wilderness; and all that were numbered of you, according to your whole number, from twenty years old and upward, which have murmured against me,

Nu 15:35 And the LORD said unto Moses, The man shall be surely put to death: all the congregation shall stone him with stones without the camp.

Nu 20:26 And strip Aaron of his garments, and put them upon Eleazar his son: and Aaron shall be gathered *unto his people,* and shall die there.

Nu 26:65 For the LORD had said of them, They shall surely die in the wilderness. And there was not left a man of them, save Caleb the son of Jephunneh, and Joshua the son of Nun.

Nu 27:3 Our father died in the wilderness, and he was not in the company of them that gathered themselves together against the LORD in the company of Korah; but died in his own sin, and had no sons.

De 2:16 So it came to pass, when all the men of war were consumed and dead from among the people,

De 4:22 But I must die in this land, I must not go over Jordan: but ye shall go over, and possess that good land.

De 8:19 And it shall be, if thou do at all forget the LORD thy God, and walk after other gods, and serve them, and worship them, I testify against you this day that ye shall surely perish.

De 13:5 And that prophet, or that dreamer of dreams, shall be put to death; because he hath spoken to turn *you* away from the LORD your God, which brought you out of the land of Egypt, and redeemed you out of the house of bondage, to thrust thee out of the way which the LORD thy God commanded thee to walk in. So shalt thou put the evil away from the midst of thee.

De 18:20 But the prophet, which shall presume to speak a word in my name, which I have not commanded him to speak, or that shall speak in the name of other gods, even that prophet shall die.

De 22:22 If a man be found lying with a woman married to an husband, then they shall both of them die, *both* the man that lay with the woman, and the woman: so shalt thou put away evil from Israel.

De 30:15 See, I have set before thee this day life and good, and death and evil;

De 32:51 Because ye trespassed against me among the children of Israel at the waters of Meribah-Kadesh, in the wilderness of Zin; because ye sanctified me not in the midst of the children of Israel.

Jos 1:18 Whosoever *he be* that doth rebel against thy commandment, and will not hearken unto thy words in all that thou commandest him, he shall be put to death: only be strong and of a good courage.

Jos 5:4 And this *is* the cause why Joshua did circumcise: All the people that came out of Egypt, *that were* males, *even* all the men of war, died in the wilderness by the way, after they came out of Egypt.

Jos 5:6 For the children of Israel walked forty years in the wilderness, till all the people *that were* men of war, which came out of Egypt, were consumed, because they obeyed not the voice of the LORD: unto whom the LORD sware that he would not shew them the land, which the LORD sware unto their fathers that he would give us, a land that floweth with milk and honey.

Jos 7:15 And it shall be, *that* he that is taken with the accursed thing shall be burnt with fire, he and all that he hath: because he hath transgressed the covenant of the LORD, and because he hath wrought folly in Israel.

Jos 22:20 Did not Achan the son of Zerah commit a trespass in the accursed thing, and wrath fell on all the congregation of Israel? and that man perished not alone in his iniquity.

Jos 23:15 Therefore it shall come to pass, *that* as all good things are come upon you, which the LORD your God promised you; so shall the LORD bring upon you all evil things, until he have destroyed you from off this good land which the LORD your God hath given you.

1 S 2:33 And the man of thine, *whom* I shall not cut off from mine altar, *shall be* to consume thine eyes, and to grieve thine heart: and all the increase of thine house shall die in the flower of their age.

1 S 12:25 But if ye shall still do wickedly, ye shall be consumed, both ye and your king.

2 S 6:7 And the anger of the LORD was kindled against Uzzah; and God smote him there for *his* error; and there he died by the ark of God.

2 S 18:15 And ten young men that bare Joab's armour compassed about and smote Absalom, and slew him.

1 K 1:52 And Solomon said, If he will shew himself a worthy man, there shall not an hair of him fall to the earth: but if wickedness shall be found in him, he shall die.

1 K 2:34 So Benaiah the son of Jehoiada went up, and fell upon him, and slew him: and he was buried in his own house in the wilderness.

1 K 2:46 So the king commanded Benaiah the son of Jehoiada; which went out, and fell upon him, that he died. And the kingdom was established in the hand of Solomon.

1 K 13:25 And, behold, men passed by, and saw the carcase cast in the way, and the lion standing by the carcase: and they came and told it in the city where the old prophet dwelt.

1 K 15:29 And it came to pass, when he reigned, *that* he smote all the house of Jeroboam; he left not to Jeroboam any that breathed, until he had destroyed him, according unto the saying of the LORD, which he spake by his servant Ahijah the Shilonite:

1 K 16:12 Thus did Zimri destroy all the house of Baasha, according to the word of the LORD, which he spake against Baasha by Jehu the prophet,

1 K 16:19 For his sins which he sinned in doing evil in the sight of the LORD, in walking in the way of Jeroboam, and in his sin which he did, to make Israel to sin.

1 K 20:36 Then said he unto him, Because thou hast not obeyed the voice of the LORD, behold, as soon as thou art departed from me, a lion shall slay thee. And as soon as he was departed from him, a lion found him, and slew him.

2 K 1:4 Now therefore thus saith the LORD, Thou shalt not come down from that bed on which thou art gone up, but shalt surely die. And Elijah departed.

2 K 1:16 And he said unto him, Thus saith the LORD, Forasmuch as thou hast sent messengers to enquire of Baal-zebub the god of Ekron, *is it* not because *there is* no God in Israel to enquire of his word? therefore thou shalt not come down off that bed on which thou art gone up, but shalt surely die.

2 K 7:17 And the king appointed the lord on whose hand he leaned to have the charge of the gate: and the people trode upon him in the gate, and he died, as the man of God had said, who spake when the king came down to him.

2 K 10:25 And it came to pass, as soon as he had made an end of offering the burnt offering, that Jehu said to the guard and to the captains, Go in, *and* slay them; let none come forth. And they smote them with the edge of the sword; and the guard and the captains cast *them* out, and went to the city of the house of Baal.

2 K 11:16 And they laid hands on her; and she went by the way by the which the horses came into the king's house: and there was she slain.

2 K 14:6 But the children of the murderers he slew not: according unto that which is written in the book of the law of Moses, wherein the LORD commanded, saying, The fathers shall not be put to death for the children, nor the children be put to death for the fathers; but every man shall be put to death for his own sin.

1 Chr 10:13 So Saul died for his transgression which he committed against the LORD, *even* against the word of the LORD, which he kept not, and also for

asking *counsel* of *one that had* a familiar spirit, to enquire *of it;*

1 Chr 13:10 And the anger of the LORD was kindled against Uzza, and he smote him, because he put his hand to the ark: and there he died before God.

1 Chr 24:2 But Nadab and Abihu died before their father, and had no children: therefore Eleazar and Ithamar executed the priest's office.

2 Chr 13:17 And Abijah and his people slew them with a great slaughter: so there fell down slain of Israel five hundred thousand chosen men.

2 Chr 15:13 That whosoever would not seek the LORD God of Israel should be put to death, whether small or great, whether man or woman.

2 Chr 21:19 And it came to pass, that in process of time, after the end of two years, his bowels fell out by reason of his sickness: so he died of sore diseases. And his people made no burning for him, like the burning of his fathers.

2 Chr 25:4 But he slew not their children, but *did* as *it is* written in the law in the book of Moses, where the LORD commanded, saying, The fathers shall not die for the children, neither shall the children die for the fathers, but every man shall die for his own sin.

2 Chr 28:6 For Pekah the son of Remaliah slew in Judah an hundred and twenty thousand in one day, *which were* all valiant men; because they had forsaken the LORD God of their fathers.

Est 8:7 Then the king Ahasuerus said unto Esther the queen and to Mordecai the Jew, Behold, I have given Esther the house of Haman, and him they have hanged upon the gallows, because he laid his hand upon the Jews.

Jb 8:4 If thy children have sinned against him, and he have cast them away for their transgression;

Jb 24:19 Drought and heat consume the snow waters: *so doth* the grave *those which* have sinned.

Ps 37:38 But the transgressors shall be destroyed together: the end of the wicked shall be cut off.

Ps 55:23 But thou, O God, shalt bring them down into the pit of destruction: bloody and deceitful men shall not live out half their days; but I will trust in thee.

Ps 76:6 At thy rebuke, O God of Jacob, both the chariot and horse are cast into a dead sleep.

Ps 78:31 The wrath of God came upon them, and slew the fattest of them, and smote down the chosen *men* of Israel.

Ps 106:18 And a fire was kindled in their company; the flame burned up the wicked.

Pr 1:32 For the turning away of the simple shall slay them, and the prosperity of fools shall destroy them.

Pr 8:36 But he that sinneth against me wrongeth his own soul: all they that hate me love death.

Pr 11:19 As righteousness *tendeth* to life: so he that pursueth evil *pursueth it* to his own death.

Is 24:6 Therefore hath the curse devoured the earth, and they that dwell therein are desolate: therefore the inhabitants of the earth are burned, and few men left.

Je 5:6 Wherefore a lion out of the forest shall slay them, *and* a wolf of the evenings shall spoil them, a leopard shall watch over their cities: every one that goeth out thence shall be torn in pieces: because their transgressions are many, *and* their backslidings are increased.

Je 10:18 For thus saith the LORD, Behold, I will sling out the inhabitants of the land at this once, and will distress them, that they may find *it* so.

Je 15:2 And it shall come to pass, if they say unto thee, Whither shall we go forth? then thou shalt tell them, Thus saith the LORD; Such as *are* for death, to death; and such as *are* for the sword, to the sword; and such as *are* for the famine, to the famine; and such as *are* for the captivity, to the captivity.

Je 16:6 Both the great and the small shall die in this land: they shall not be buried, neither shall *men* lament for them, nor cut themselves, nor make themselves bald for them:

Je 29:21 Thus saith the LORD of hosts, the God of Israel, of Ahab the son of Kolaiah, and of Zedekiah the son of Maaseiah, which prophesy a lie unto you in my name; Behold, I will deliver them into the hand of Nebuchadrezzar king of Babylon; and he shall slay them before your eyes;

Je 31:30 But every one shall die for his own iniquity: every man that eateth the sour grape, his teeth shall be set on edge.

Je 33:5 They come to fight with the Chaldeans, but *it is* to fill them with the dead bodies of men, whom I have slain in mine anger and in my fury, and for all whose wickedness I have hid my face from this city.

Je 42:17 So shall it be with all the men that set their faces to go into Egypt to sojourn there; they shall die by the sword, by the famine, and by the pestilence: and none of them shall remain or escape from the evil that I will bring upon them.

Je 42:22 Now therefore know certainly that ye shall die by the sword, by the famine, and by the pestilence, in the place whither ye desire to go *and* to sojourn.

Lam 2:21 The young and the old lie on the ground in the streets: my virgins and my young men are fallen by the sword; thou hast slain *them* in the day of thine anger; thou hast killed, *and* not pitied.

Eze 3:20 Again, When a righteous *man* doth turn from his righteousness, and commit iniquity, and I lay a stumblingblock before him, he shall die: because thou hast not given him warning, he shall die in his sin, and his righteousness which he hath done shall not be remembered; but his blood will I require at thine hand.

Eze 14:9 And if the prophet be deceived when he hath spoken a thing, I the LORD have deceived that prophet, and I will stretch out my hand upon him, and will destroy him from the midst of my people Israel.

Eze 18:4 Behold, all souls are mine; as the soul of the father, so also the soul of the son is mine: the soul that sinneth, it shall die.

Eze 18:13 Hath given forth upon usury, and hath taken increase: shall he then live? he shall not live: he hath done all these abominations; he shall surely die; his blood shall be upon him.

Eze 18:20 The soul that sinneth, it shall die. The son shall not bear the iniquity of the father, neither shall the father bear the iniquity of the son: the righteousness of the righteous shall be upon him, and the wickedness of the wicked shall be upon him.

Eze 18:26 When a righteous *man* turneth away from his righteousness, and committeth iniquity, and dieth in them; for his iniquity that he hath done shall he die.

Eze 23:47 And the company shall stone them with stones, and dispatch them with their swords; they shall slay their sons and their daughters, and burn up their houses with fire.

Eze 28:10 Thou shalt die the deaths of the uncircumcised by the hand of strangers: for I have spoken *it,* saith the Lord God.

Eze 33:8 When I say unto the wicked, O wicked *man,* thou shalt surely die; if thou dost not speak to warn the wicked from his way, that wicked *man* shall die in his iniquity; but his blood will I require at thine hand.

Eze 33:13 When I shall say to the righteous, *that* he shall surely live; if he trust to his own righteousness, and commit iniquity, all his righteousnesses shall not be remembered; but for his iniquity that he hath committed, he shall die for it.

Eze 33:18 When the righteous turneth from his righteousness, and committeth iniquity, he shall even die thereby.

Da 5:30 In that night was Belshazzar the king of the Chaldeans slain.

Ho 13:1 When Ephraim spake trembling, he exalted himself in Israel; but when he offended in Baal, he died.

Am 6:9 And it shall come to pass, if there remain ten men in one house, that they shall die.

Am 9:10 All the sinners of my people shall die by the sword, which say, The evil shall not overtake nor prevent us.

Zec 13:3 And it shall come to pass, *that* when any shall yet prophesy, then his father and his mother that begat him shall say unto him, Thou shalt not live; for thou speakest lies in the name of the LORD: and his father and his mother that begat him shall thrust him through when he prophesieth.

Mt 5:30 And if thy right hand offend thee, cut if off, and cast it from thee: for it is profitable for thee that one of thy members should perish, and not *that* thy whole body should be cast into hell.

Mt 22:7 But when the king heard *thereof,* he was wroth: and he sent forth his armies, and destroyed those murderers, and burned up their city.

Lu 17:27 They did eat, they drank, they married wives, they were given in marriage, until the day that Noe entered into the ark, and the flood came, and destroyed them all.

Ac 12:23 And immediately the angel of the Lord smote him, because he gave not God the glory: and he was eaten of worms, and gave up the ghost.

Ro 1:32 Who knowing the judgment of God, that they which commit such things are worthy of death, not only do the same, but have pleasure in them that do them.

Ro 5:12 Wherefore, as by one man sin entered into the world, and death by sin; and so death passed upon all men, for that all have sinned:

Ro 5:21 That as sin hath reigned unto death, even so might grace reign through righteousness unto eternal life by Jesus Christ our Lord.

Ro 6:16 Know ye not, that to whom ye yield yourselves servants to obey, his servants ye are to whom ye obey; whether of sin unto death, or of obedience unto righteousness?

Ro 6:23 For the wages of sin *is* death; but the gift of God *is* eternal life through Jesus Christ our Lord.

1 Co 10:8 Neither let us commit fornication, as some of them committed, and fell in one day three and twenty thousand.

1 Co 15:21 For since by man *came* death, by man *came* also the resurrection of the dead.

He 3:17 But with whom was he grieved forty years? *was it* not with them that had sinned, whose carcases fell in the wilderness?

He 10:28 He that despised Moses' law died without mercy under two or three witnesses:

Ja 1:15 Then when lust hath conceived, it bringeth forth sin: and sin, when it is finished, bringeth forth death.

2. Separation from God

Ge 3:24 So he drove out the man; and he placed at the east of the garden of Eden Cherubims, and a flaming sword which turned every way, to keep the way of the tree of life.

Ge 4:16 And Cain went out from the presence of the LORD, and dwelt in the land of Nod, on the east of Eden.

Ex 19:24 And the LORD said unto him, Away, get thee down, and thou shalt come up, thou, and Aaron with thee: but let not the priests and the people break through to come up unto the LORD, lest he break forth upon them.

Ex 33:3 Unto a land flowing with milk and honey: for I will not go up in the midst of thee; for thou *art* a stiffnecked people: lest I consume thee in the way.

Nu 14:42 Go not up, for the LORD *is* not among you; that ye be not smitten before your enemies.

De 1:42 And the LORD said unto me, Say unto them, Go not up, neither fight; for I *am* not among you; lest ye be smitten before your enemies.

De 31:17 Then my anger shall be kindled against them in that day, and I will forsake them, and I will hide my face from them, and they shall be devoured, and many evils and troubles shall befall them; so that they will say in that day, Are not these evils come upon us, because our God *is* not among us?

Jos 7:11–12 Israel hath sinned, and they have also transgressed my covenant which I commanded them: for they have even taken of the accursed thing, and have also stolen, and dissembled also, and they have put *it* even among their own stuff.

Therefore the children of Israel could not stand before their enemies, *but* turned *their* backs before their enemies, because they were accursed: neither will I be with you any more, except ye destroy the accursed from among you.

1 S 14:38 And Saul said, Draw ye near hither, all the chief of the people: and know and see wherein this sin hath been this day.

2 K 24:3 Surely at the commandment of the LORD came *this* upon Judah, to remove *them* out of his sight, for the sins of Manasseh, according to all that he did;

2 K 24:20 For through the anger of the LORD it came to pass in Jerusalem and Judah, until he had cast them out from his presence, that Zedekiah rebelled against the king of Babylon.

2 Chr 25:7 But there came a man of God to him, saying, O king, let not the army of Israel go with thee; for the LORD *is* not with Israel, *to wit, with* all the children of Ephraim.

2 Chr 26:21 And Uzziah the king was a leper unto the day of his death, and dwelt in a several house, *being* a leper; for he was cut off from the house of the LORD: and Jotham his son *was* over the king's house, judging the people of the land.

Jb 13:16 He also *shall be* my salvation: for an hypocrite shall not come before him.

Ps 5:4 For thou *art* not a God that hath pleasure in wickedness: neither shall evil dwell with thee.

Ps 51:11 Cast me not away from thy presence; and take not thy holy spirit from me.

Ps 66:18 If I regard iniquity in my heart, the Lord will not hear *me:*

Ps 78:60 So that he forsook the tabernacle of Shiloh, the tent *which* he placed among men;

Ps 94:20 Shall the throne of iniquity have fellowship with thee, which frameth mischief by a law?

Pr 15:29 The LORD *is* far from the wicked: but he heareth the prayer of the righteous.

Is 50:1 Thus saith the LORD, Where *is* the bill of your mother's divorcement, whom I have put away? or which of my creditors *is it* to whom I have sold you? Behold, for your iniquities have ye sold yourselves, and for your transgressions is your mother put away.

Is 59:2 But your iniquities have separated between you and your God, and your sins have hid *his* face from you, that he will not hear.

Is 64:7 And *there is* none that calleth upon thy name, that stirreth up himself to take hold of thee: for thou hast hid thy face from us, and hast consumed us, because of our iniquities.

Je 7:15 And I will cast you out of my sight, as I have cast out all your brethren, *even* the whole seed of Ephraim.

Je 14:12 When they fast, I will not hear their cry; and when they offer burnt offering and an oblation, I will not accept them: but I will consume them by the sword, and by the famine, and by the pestilence.

Eze 8:6 He said furthermore unto me, Son of man, seest thou what they do? *even* the great abominations that the house of Israel committeth here, that I should go far off from my sanctuary? but turn thee yet again, *and* thou shalt see greater abominations.

Eze 8:18 Therefore will I also deal in fury: mine eye shall not spare, neither will I have pity: and though they cry in mine ears with a loud voice, *yet* will I not hear them.

Eze 39:24 According to their uncleanness and according to their transgressions have I done unto them, and hid my face from them.

Eze 44:13 And they shall not come near unto me, to do the office of a priest unto me, nor to come near to any of my holy things, in the most holy *place:* but they shall bear their shame, and their abominations which they have committed.

Ho 5:6 They shall go with their flocks and with their herds to seek the LORD; but they shall not find *him;* he hath withdrawn himself from them.

Ho 5:15 I will go *and* return to my place, till they acknowledge their offence, and seek my face: in their affliction they will seek me early.

Ho 9:15 All their wickedness *is* in Gilgal: for there I hated them: for the wickedness of their doings I will drive them out of mine house, I will love them no more: all their princes *are* revolters.

Jona 2:4 Then I said, I am cast out of thy sight; yet I will look again toward thy holy temple.

Mal 2:13 And this have ye done again, covering the altar of the LORD with tears, with weeping, and with crying out, insomuch that he regardeth not the offering any more, or receiveth *it* with good will at your hand.

Mt 7:23 And then will I profess unto them, I never knew you: depart from me, ye that work iniquity.

Mt 8:29 And, behold, they cried out, saying, What have we to do with thee, Jesus, thou Son of God? art thou come hither to torment us before the time?

Mt 25:41 Then shall he say also unto them on the left hand, Depart from me, ye cursed, into everlasting fire, prepared for the devil and his angels:

Mk 1:24 Saying, Let *us* alone; what have we to do with thee, thou Jesus of Nazareth? art thou come to destroy us? I know thee who thou art, the Holy One of God.

Mk 5:7 And cried with a loud voice, and said, What have I to do with thee, Jesus, *thou* Son of the most high God? I adjure thee by God, that thou torment me not.

Lu 4:34 Saying, Let *us* alone; what have we to do with thee, *thou* Jesus of Nazareth? art thou come to destroy us? I know thee who thou art; the Holy One of God.

Lu 8:28 When he saw Jesus, he cried out, and fell down before him, and with a loud voice said, What have I to do with thee, Jesus, *thou* Son of God most high? I beseech thee, torment me not.

Lu 13:27 But he shall say, I tell you, I know you not whence ye are; depart from me, all *ye* workers of iniquity.

Lu 16:26 And beside all this, between us and you there is a great gulf fixed: so that they which would pass from hence to you cannot; neither can they pass to us, that *would come* from thence.

He 12:14 Follow peace with all *men,* and holiness, without which no man shall see the Lord:

3. Abandonment by God

Ex 10:29 And Moses said, Thou hast spoken well, I will see thy face again no more.

Jud 16:20 And she said, The Philistines *be* upon thee, Samson. And he awoke out of his sleep, and said, I will go out as at other times before, and shake myself. And he wist not that the LORD was departed from him.

1 S 16:14 But the Spirit of the LORD departed from Saul, and an evil spirit from the LORD troubled him.

1 S 28:6 And when Saul enquired of the LORD, the LORD answered him not, neither by dreams nor by Urim, nor by prophets.

2 Chr 30:7 And be not ye like your fathers, and like your brethren, which trespassed against the LORD God of their fathers, *who* therefore gave them up to desolation, as ye see.

Ps 44:9 But thou hast cast off, and put us to shame; and goest not forth with our armies.

Ps 81:12 So I gave them up unto their own hearts' lust: *and* they walked in their own counsels.

Pr 1:28 Then shall they call upon me, but I will not answer; they shall seek me early, but they shall not find me:

Is 59:11 We roar all like bears, and mourn sore like doves: we look for judgment, but *there is* none; for salvation, *but* it is far off from us.

Je 22:25 And I will give thee into the hand of them that seek thy life, and into the hand *of them* whose face thou fearest, even into the hand of Nebuchadrezzar king of Babylon, and into the hand of the Chaldeans.

Je 34:2 Thus saith the LORD, the God of Israel; Go and speak to Zedekiah king of Judah, and tell him, Thus saith the LORD; Behold, I will give this city into the hand of the king of Babylon, and he shall burn it with fire:

Je 34:20 I will even give them into the hand of their enemies, and into the hand of them that seek their life: and their dead bodies shall be for meat unto the fowls of the heaven, and to the beasts of the earth.

Lam 2:1 How hath the Lord covered the daughter of Zion with a cloud in his anger, *and* cast down from heaven unto the earth the beauty of Israel, and remembered not his footstool in the day of his anger!

Eze 32:20 They shall fall in the midst of *them that are* slain by the sword: she is delivered to the sword: draw her and all her multitudes.

Mt 23:38 Behold, your house is left unto you

Ac 7:42 Then God turned, and gave them up to worship the host of heaven; as it is written in the book of the prophets, O ye house of Israel, have ye offered to me slain beasts and sacrifices *by the space of* forty years in the wilderness?

Ro 1:24 Wherefore God also gave them up to uncleanness through the lusts of their own hearts, to dishonour their own bodies between themselves:

4. Sometimes Delayed

Ge 15:16 But in the fourth generation they shall come hither again: for the iniquity of the Amorites *is* not yet full.

1 K 11:12 Notwithstanding in thy days I will not do it for David thy father's sake: *but* I will rend it out of the hand of thy son.

1 K 21:29 Seest thou how Ahab humbleth himself before me? because he humbleth himself before me, I will not bring the evil in his days: *but* in his son's days will I bring the evil upon his house.

2 K 13:23 And the LORD was gracious unto them, and had compassion on them, and had respect unto them, because of his covenant with Abraham, Isaac, and Jacob, and would not destroy them, neither cast he them from his presence as yet.

2 Chr 12:7 And when the LORD saw that they humbled themselves, the word of the LORD came to Shemaiah, saying, They have humbled themselves; *therefore* I will not destroy them, but I will grant them some deliverance; and my wrath shall not be poured out upon Jerusalem by the hand of Shishak.

2 Chr 34:28 Behold, I will gather thee to thy fathers, and thou shalt be gathered to thy grave in peace, neither shall thine eyes see all the evil that I will bring upon this place, and upon the inhabitants of the same. So they brought the king word again.

Ec 8:11 Because sentence against an evil work is not executed speedily, therefore the heart of the sons of men is fully set in them to do evil.

Is 48:9 For my name's sake will I defer mine anger, and for my praise will I refrain for thee, that I cut thee not off.

Da 7:12 As concerning the rest of the beasts, they had their dominion taken away: yet their lives were prolonged for a season and time.

Da 8:23 And in the latter time of their kingdom, when the transgressors are come to the full, a king of fierce countenance, and understanding dark sentences, shall stand up.

Hab 1:13 *Thou art* of purer eyes than to behold evil, and canst not look on iniquity: wherefore lookest thou upon them that deal treacherously, *and* holdest thy tongue when the wicked devoureth *the man that is* more righteous than he?

Lu 13:7–9 Then said he unto the dresser of his vineyard, Behold, these three years I come seeking fruit on this fig tree, and find none: cut it down; why cumbereth it the ground?

And he answering said unto him, Lord, let it alone this year also, till I shall dig about it, and dung *it:*

And if it bear fruit, *well:* and if not, *then* after that thou shalt cut it down.

1 Pe 3:20 Which sometime were disobedient, when once the longsuffering of God waited in the days of Noah, while the ark was a preparing, wherein few, that is, eight souls were saved by water.

5. Inevitable

De 32:39 See now that I, *even I, am* he, and *there is* no god with me: I kill, and I make alive; I wound, and I heal: neither *is there any* that can deliver out of my hand.

1 K 19:17 And it shall come to pass, *that* him that escapeth the sword of Hazael shall Jehu slay: and him that escapeth from the sword of Jehu shall Elisha slay.

1 K 22:34 And a *certain* man drew a bow at a venture, and smote the king of Israel between the joints of the harness: wherefore he said unto the driver of his chariot, Turn thine hand, and carry me out of the host; for I am wounded.

2 K 10:24 And when they went in to offer sacrifices and burnt offerings, Jehu appointed fourscore men without, and said, If any of the men whom I have brought into your hands escape, *he that letteth him go,* his life *shall be* for the life of him.

2 Chr 18:33 And a *certain* man drew a bow at a venture, and smote the king of Israel between the joints of the harness: therefore he said to his chariot man, Turn thine hand, that thou mayest carry me out of the host; for I am wounded.

2 Chr 20:24 And when Judah came toward the watch tower in the wilderness, they looked unto the multitude, and, behold, they *were* dead bodies fallen to the earth, and none escaped.

Ezr 9:14 Should we again break thy commandments, and join in affinity with the people of these abominations? wouldest not thou be angry with us till thou hadst consumed *us,* so that *there should be* no remnant nor escaping?

Jb 11:20 But the eyes of the wicked shall fail, and they shall not escape, and their hope *shall be as* the giving up of the ghost.

Jb 20:24 He shall flee from the iron weapon, *and* the bow of steel shall strike him through.

Jb 27:22 For *God* shall cast upon him, and not spare: he would fain flee out of his hand.

Jb 36:18 Because *there is* wrath, *beware* lest he take thee away with *his* stroke: then a great ransom cannot deliver thee.

Ps 56:7 Shall they escape by iniquity? in *thine* anger cast down the people, O God.

Pr 11:21 *Though* hand *join* in hand, the wicked shall not be unpunished: but the seed of the righteous shall be delivered.

Pr 16:5 Every one *that is* proud in heart *is* an abomination to the LORD: *though* hand *join* in hand, he shall not be unpunished.

Pr 19:5 A false witness shall not be unpunished, and *he that* speaketh lies shall not escape.

Ec 8:8 *There is* no man that hath power over the spirit to retain the spirit; neither *hath he* power in the day of death: and *there is* no discharge in *that* war; neither shall wickedness deliver those that are given to it.

Is 10:3 And what will ye do in the day of visitation, and in the desolation *which* shall come from far? to whom will ye flee for help? and where will ye leave your glory?

Is 20:6 And the inhabitant of this isle shall say in that day, Behold, such *is* our expectation, whither we flee for help to be delivered from the king of Assyria: and how shall we escape?

Is 24:18 And it shall come to pass, *that* he who fleeth from the noise of the fear shall fall into the pit; and he that cometh up out of the midst of the pit shall be taken in the snare: for the windows from on high are open, and the foundations of the earth do shake.

Is 30:16 But ye said, No; for we will flee upon horses; therefore shall ye flee: and, We will ride upon the swift; therefore shall they that pursue you be swift.

Is 47:11 Therefore shall evil come upon thee; thou shalt not know from whence it riseth: and mischief shall fall upon thee; thou shalt not be able to put if off: and desolation shall come upon thee suddenly, *which* thou shalt not know.

Is 47:15 Thus shall they be unto thee with whom thou hast laboured, *even* thy merchants, from thy youth: they shall wander every one to his quarter; none shall save thee.

Je 11:11 Therefore thus saith the LORD, Behold, I will bring evil upon them, which they shall not be able to escape; and though they shall cry unto me, I will not hearken unto them.

Je 25:28 And it shall be, if they refuse to take the cup at thine hand to drink, then shalt thou say unto them, Thus saith the LORD of hosts; Ye shall certainly drink.

Je 25:35 And the shepherds shall have no way to flee, nor the principal of the flock to escape.

Je 34:3 And thou shalt not escape out of his hand, but shalt surely be taken, and delivered into his hand; and thine eyes shall behold the eyes of the king of Babylon, and he shall speak with thee mouth to mouth, and thou shalt go to Babylon.

Je 38:23 So they shall bring out all thy wives and thy children to the Chaldeans: and thou shalt not escape out of their hand, but shalt be taken by the hand of the king of Babylon: and thou shalt cause this city to be burned with fire.

Je 42:17 So shall it be with all the men that set their faces to go into Egypt to sojourn there; they shall die by the sword, by the famine, and by the pestilence: and none of them shall remain or escape from the evil that I will bring upon them.

Je 44:14 So that none of the remnant of Judah, which are gone into the land of Egypt to sojourn there, shall escape or remain, that they should return into the land of Judah, to the which they have a desire to return to dwell there: for none shall return but such as shall escape.

Je 46:6 Let not the swift flee away, nor the mighty man escape; they shall stumble, and fall toward the north by the river Euphrates.

Je 48:8 And the spoiler shall come upon every city, and no city shall escape: the valley also shall perish, and the plain shall be destroyed, as the LORD hath spoken.

Je 48:44 He that fleeth from the fear shall fall into the pit; and he that getteth up out of the pit shall be taken in the snare: for I will bring upon it, *even* upon Moab, the year of their visitation, saith the LORD.

Je 50:29 Call together the archers against Babylon: all ye that bend the bow, camp against it round about; let none thereof escape: recompense her according to her work; according to all that she hath done, do unto her: for she hath been proud against the LORD, against the Holy One of Israel.

Lam 2:22 Thou hast called as in a solemn day my terrors round about, so that in the day of the LORD's anger none escaped nor remained: those that I have swaddled and brought up hath mine enemy consumed.

Eze 15:7 And I will set my face against them; they shall go out from *one* fire, and *another* fire shall devour them; and ye shall know that I *am* the LORD, when I set my face against them.

Eze 17:15 But he rebelled against him in sending his ambassadors into Egypt, that they might give him horses and much people. Shall he prosper? shall he escape that doeth such *things?* or shall he break the covenant, and be delivered?

Ho 2:10 And now will I discover her lewdness in the sight of her lovers, and none shall deliver her out of mine hand.

Ho 5:14 For I will *be* unto Ephraim as a lion, and as a young lion to the house of Judah: I, *even* I, will tear and go away; I will take away, and none shall rescue *him.*

Am 2:14 Therefore the flight shall perish from the swift, and the strong shall not strengthen his force, neither shall the mighty deliver himself:

Am 5:18–19 Woe unto you that desire the day of the LORD! to what end *is* it for you? the day of the LORD *is* darkness, and not light.

As if a man did flee from a lion, and a bear met him; or went into the house, and leaned his hand on the wall, and a serpent bit him.

Am 9:2 Though they dig into hell, thence shall mine hand take them; though they climb up to heaven, thence will I bring them down:

Mi 2:3 Therefore thus saith the LORD; Behold, against this family do I devise an evil, from which ye shall not remove your necks; neither shall ye go haughtily: for this time *is* evil.

Zep 1:18 Neither their silver nor their gold shall be able to deliver them in the day of the LORD's wrath; but the whole land shall be devoured by the fire of his jealousy: for he shall make even a speedy riddance of all them that dwell in the land.

Mt 5:26 Verily I say unto thee, Thou shalt by no means come out thence, till thou hast paid the uttermost farthing.

Mt 23:33 *Ye* serpents, *ye* generation of vipers, how can ye escape the damnation of hell?

Lu 12:59 I tell thee, thou shalt not depart thence, till thou hast paid the very last mite.

Ro 2:3 And thinkest thou this, O man, that judgest them which do such things, and doest the same, that thou shalt escape the judgment of God?

1 Th 5:3 For when they shall say, Peace and safety; then sudden destruction cometh upon them, as travail upon a woman with child; and they shall not escape.

He 2:3 How shall we escape, if we neglect so great salvation; which at the first began to be spoken by the Lord, and was confirmed unto us by them that heard *him;*

He 12:25 See that ye refuse not him that speaketh. For if they escaped not who refused him that spake on earth, much more *shall not* we *escape,* if we turn away from him that *speaketh* from heaven:

2 Pe 2:3 And through covetousness shall they with feigned words make merchandise of you: whose judgment now of a long time lingereth not, and their damnation slumbereth not.

See **JUDGMENTS, JUSTICE, PUNISHMENT**

PENITENCE *See* **REPENTANCE**

PENNY, *denarius, a Roman coin*

Mt 22:19; Mk 12:16; Lu 7:41; 20:24; Jn 6:7

See **WEIGHTS AND MEASURES**

PENS, *for writing*

Jb 19:24; Ps 45:1; Is 8:1; Je 8:8; 17:1

PENTECOST, *day of firstfruits, coming fifty days after Passover*

Ac 2:1; 20:16; 1 Co 16:8

See **FESTIVALS**

PEOPLE

1. Those Belonging to God

A PECULIAR TREASURE

Ex 19:5 Now therefore, if ye will obey my voice indeed, and keep my covenant, then ye shall be a peculiar treasure unto me above all people: for all the earth *is* mine:

CHOSEN BY JEHOVAH

De 14:2 for thou *art* an holy people unto the LORD thy God, and the LORD hath chosen thee to be a peculiar people unto himself, above all the nations that *are* upon the earth.

EXALTED ABOVE ALL NATIONS

De 26:19 And to make thee high above all nations which he hath made, in praise, and in name, and in honour; and that thou mayest be an holy people unto the LORD thy God, as he hath spoken.

1 S 12:22 For the LORD will not forsake his people for his great name's sake: because it hath pleased the LORD to make you his people.

Ps 29:11 The LORD will give strength unto his people; the LORD will bless his people with peace.

GUIDED LIKE A FLOCK

Ps 78:52 But made his own people to go forth like sheep, and guided them in the wilderness like a flock.

Ps 100:3 Know ye that the LORD he *is* God: *it is* he *that* hath made us, and not we ourselves; *we are* his people, and the sheep of his pasture.

PREPARED FOR SERVICE

Lu 1:17 And he shall go before him in the spirit and power of Elias, to turn the hearts of the fathers to the children, and the disobedient to the wisdom of the just; to make ready a people prepared for the Lord.

Ac 15:14 Simeon hath declared how God at the first did visit the Gentiles, to take out of them a people for his name.

CHARACTERIZED BY ZEAL

Tit 2:14 Who gave himself for us, that he might redeem us from all iniquity, and purify unto himself a peculiar people, zealous of good works.

THE LAW WRITTEN UPON THEIR HEARTS

He 8:10 For this *is* the covenant that I will make with the house of Israel after those days, saith the Lord; I will put my laws into their mind, and write them in their hearts: and I will be to them a God, and they shall be to me a people:

1 Pe 2:9 But ye *are* a chosen generation, a royal priesthood, an holy nation, a peculiar people; that ye should shew forth the praises of him who hath called you out of darkness into his marvellous light:

Re 21:3 And I heard a great voice out of heaven saying, Behold, the tabernacle of God *is* with men, and he will dwell with them, and they shall be his people, and God himself shall be with them, *and be* their God.

2. Called as the Elect

Is 65:9 And I will bring forth a seed out of Jacob, and out of Judah an inheritor of my mountains: and mine elect shall inherit it, and my servants shall dwell there.

Mt 24:22 And except those days should be shortened, there should no flesh be saved: but for the elect's sake those days shall be shortened.

Mt 24:31 And he shall send his angels with a great sound of a trumpet, and they shall gather together his elect from the four winds, from one end of heaven to the other.

Lu 18:7 And shall not God avenge his own elect, which cry day and night unto him, though he bear long with them?

Ro 8:33 Who shall lay any thing to the charge of God's elect? *It is* God that justifieth.

2 Ti 2:10 Therefore I endure all things for the elect's sakes, that they may also obtain the salvation which is in Christ Jesus with eternal glory.

1 Pe 1:2 Elect according to the foreknowledge of God the Father, through sanctification of the Spirit, unto obedience and sprinkling of the blood of Jesus Christ: Grace unto you, and peace, be multiplied.

3. Called the Chosen Ones

De 4:7 For what nation *is there so* great, who *hath* God *so* nigh unto them, as the LORD our God *is* in all *things that* we call upon him *for?*

De 7:6 For thou *art* an holy people unto the LORD thy God: the LORD thy God hath chosen thee to be a special people unto himself, above all people that *are* upon the face of the earth.

1 K 11:13 Howbeit I will not rend away all the kingdom; *but* will give one tribe to thy son for David my servant's sake, and for Jerusalem's sake which I have chosen.

2 K 23:27 And the LORD said, I will remove Judah also out of my sight, as I have removed Israel, and will cast off this city Jerusalem which I have chosen, and the house of which I said, My name shall be there.

1 Chr 16:22 *Saying,* Touch not mine anointed, and do my prophets no harm.

Ezr 9:2 For they have taken of their daughters for themselves, and for their sons: so that the holy seed have mingled themselves with the people

of *those* lands: yea, the hand of the princes and rulers hath been chief in this trespass.

Ps 4:3 But know that the LORD hath set apart him that is godly for himself: the LORD will hear when I call unto him.

Ps 60:5 That thy beloved may be delivered; save *with* thy right hand, and hear me.

Ps 74:2 Remember thy congregation, *which* thou hast purchased of old; the rod of thine inheritance, *which* thou hast redeemed; this mount Zion, wherein thou hast dwelt.

Da 8:25 And through his policy also he shall cause craft to prosper in his hand; and he shall magnify *himself* in his heart, and by peace shall destroy many: he shall also stand up against the Prince of princes; but he shall be broken without hand.

Jl 2:17 Let the priests, the ministers of the LORD, weep between the porch and the altar, and let them say, Spare thy people, O LORD, and give not thine heritage to reproach, that the heathen should rule over them: wherefore should they say among the people, Where *is* their God?

Mal 1:2 I have loved you, saith the LORD. Yet ye say, Wherein hast thou loved us? *Was* not Esau Jacob's brother? saith the LORD: yet I loved Jacob,

1 Co 1:26 For ye see your calling, brethren, how that not many wise men after the flesh, not many mighty, not many noble, *are called:*

Ep 1:4 According as he hath chosen us in him before the foundation of the world, that we should be holy and without blame before him in love:

Ja 2:5 Hearken, my beloved brethren, Hath not God chosen the poor of this world rich in faith, and heirs of the kingdom which he hath promised to them that love him?

1 Pe 2:10 Which in time past *were* not a people, but *are* now the people of God: which had not obtained mercy, but now have obtained mercy.

See **CHURCH, ISRAEL**

PEOR, *a mountain in Moab*

Nu 23:28; 25:18; Jos 22:17

PERCEPTION, *SPIRITUAL*

DAVID

2 S 5:12 And David perceived that the LORD had established him king over Israel, and that he had exalted his kingdom for his people Israel's sake.

THE SHUNAMMITE WOMAN

2 K 4:9 And she said unto her husband, Behold now, I perceive that this *is* an holy man of God, which passeth by us continually.

NEHEMIAH

Ne 6:12 And, lo, I perceived that God had not sent him; but that he pronounced this prophecy against me: for Tobiah and Sanballat had hired him.

THE WISE MAN

Ec 2:14 The wise man's eyes *are* in his head; but the fool walketh in darkness: and I myself perceived also that one event happeneth to them all.

JESUS

Lu 5:22 But when Jesus perceived their thoughts, he answering said unto them, What reason ye in your hearts?

THE SAMARITAN WOMAN

Jn 4:19 The woman saith unto him, Sir, I perceive that thou art a prophet.

PETER

Ac 10:34 Then Peter opened *his* mouth, and said, Of a truth I perceive that God is no respecter of persons:

See **INSIGHT, THOUGHTS, WISDOM**

PERDITION, *the loss of eternal life*

Jn 17:12 While I was with them in the world, I kept them in thy name: those that thou gavest me I have kept, and none of them is lost, but the son of perdition; that the scripture might be fulfilled.

Ph 1:28 And in nothing terrified by your adversaries: which is to them an evident token of perdition, but to you of salvation, and that of God.

2 Th 2:3 Let no man deceive you by any means: for *that day shall not come,* except there come a falling away first, and that man of sin be revealed, the son of perdition;

1 Ti 6:9 But they that will be rich fall into temptation and a snare, and *into* many foolish and hurtful lusts, which drown men in destruction and perdition.

He 10:39 But we are not of them who draw back unto perdition; but of them that believe to the saving of the soul.

2 Pe 3:7 But the heavens and the earth, which are now, by the same word are kept in store, reserved unto fire against the day of judgment and perdition of ungodly men.

Re 17:8 The beast that thou sawest was, and is not; and shall ascend out of the bottomless pit, and go into perdition: and they that dwell on the earth shall wonder, whose names were not written in the book of life from the foundation of the world, when they behold the beast that was, and is not, and yet is.

See **PUNISHMENT**

PERFECTION, *complete or whole*

1. Essential Elements

BENEVOLENCE

Mt 19:21 Jesus said unto him, If thou wilt be perfect, go *and* sell that thou hast, and give to the poor, and thou shalt have treasure in heaven: and come *and* follow me.

LOVE

Col 3:14 And above all these things *put on* charity, which is the bond of perfectness.

GOOD WORKS

Ja 2:22 Seest thou how faith wrought with his works, and by works was faith made perfect?

CONTROL OF THE TONGUE

Ja 3:2 For in many things we offend all. If any man offend not in word, the same *is* a perfect man, *and* able also to bridle the whole body.

OBEDIENCE

1 Jn 2:5 But whoso keepeth his word, in him verily is the love of God perfected: hereby know we that we are in him.

1 Jn 4:12 No man hath seen God at any time. If we love one another, God dwelleth in us, and his love is perfected in us.

2. Striving after

Ge 17:1 And when Abram was ninety years old and nine, the LORD appeared to Abram, and said unto him, I *am* the Almighty God; walk before me, and be thou perfect.

De 18:13 Thou shalt be perfect with the LORD thy God.

2 S 22:26 With the merciful thou wilt shew thyself merciful, *and* with the upright man thou wilt shew thyself upright.

1 K 8:61 Let your heart therefore be perfect with the LORD our God, to walk in his statutes, and to keep his commandments, as at this day.

2 Chr 15:17 But the high places were not taken away out of Israel: nevertheless the heart of Asa was perfect all his days.

2 Chr 16:9 For the eyes of the LORD run to and fro throughout the whole earth, to shew himself strong in the behalf of *them* whose heart *is* perfect toward him. Herein thou hast done foolishly: therefore from henceforth thou shalt have wars.

Ps 18:32 *It is* God that girdeth me with strength, and maketh my way perfect.

Ps 101:2 I will behave myself wisely in a perfect way. O when wilt thou come unto me? I will walk within my house with a perfect heart.

Mt 5:48 Be ye therefore perfect, even as your Father which is in heaven is perfect.

2 Co 13:11 Finally, brethren, farewell. Be perfect, be of good comfort, be of one mind, live in peace; and the God of love and peace shall be with you.

Ep 4:13 Till we all come in the unity of the faith, and of the knowledge of the Son of God, unto a perfect man, unto the measure of the stature of the fulness of Christ:

Ph 3:15 Let us therefore, as many as be perfect, be thus minded: and if in any thing ye be otherwise minded, God shall reveal even this unto you.

Col 1:28 Whom we preach, warning every man, and teaching every man in all wisdom; that we may present every man perfect in Christ Jesus:

2 Ti 3:17 That the man of God may be perfect, throughly furnished unto all good works.

He 6:1 Therefore leaving the principles of the doctrine of Christ, let us go on unto perfection; not laying again the foundation of repentance from dead works, and of faith toward God,

He 13:21 Make you perfect in every good work to do his will, working in you that which is wellpleasing in his sight, through Jesus Christ; to whom *be* glory for ever and ever. Amen.

Ja 1:4 But let patience have *her* perfect work, that ye may be perfect and entire, wanting nothing.

1 Pe 5:10 But the God of all grace, who hath called us unto his eternal glory by Christ Jesus, after that ye have suffered a while, make you perfect, stablish, strengthen, settle *you.*

3. Divine

De 32:4 *He is* the Rock, his work *is* perfect: for all his ways *are* judgment: a God of truth and without iniquity, just and right *is* he.

2 S 22:31 *As for* God, his way *is* perfect; the word of the LORD *is* tried: he *is* a buckler to all them that trust in him.

2 Chr 19:7 Wherefore now let the fear of the LORD be upon you; take heed and do *it:* for *there is* no iniquity with the LORD our God, nor respect of persons, nor taking of gifts.

Jb 34:10 Therefore hearken unto me, ye men of understanding: far be it from God, *that he should do* wickedness; and *from* the Almighty, *that he should commit* iniquity.

Ps 18:30 *As for* God, his way *is* perfect: the word of the LORD is tried: he *is* a buckler to all those that trust in him.

Ec 3:14 I know that, whatsoever God doeth, it shall be for ever: nothing can be put to it, nor any thing taken from it: and God doeth *it,* that *men* should fear before him.

Zec 9:17 For how great *is* his goodness, and how great *is* his beauty! corn shall make the young men cheerful, and new wine the maids.

Mt 5:48 Be ye therefore perfect, even as your Father which is in heaven is perfect.

4. Pictured in Christ

Ps 45:2 Thou art fairer than the children of men: grace is poured into thy lips: therefore God hath blessed thee for ever.

Song 2:1 I *am* the rose of Sharon, *and* the lily of the valleys.

Song 5:10 My beloved *is* white and ruddy, the chiefest among ten thousand.

Is 11:6 The wolf also shall dwell with the lamb, and the leopard shall lie down with the kid; and the calf and the young lion and the fatling together; and a little child shall lead them.

Mt 3:15 And Jesus answering said unto him, Suffer *it to be so* now: for thus it becometh us to fulfil all righteousness. Then he suffered him.

Mt 26:60 But found none: yea, though many false witnesses came, *yet* found they none. At the last came two false witnesses,

Lu 6:40 The disciple is not above his master: but every one that is perfect shall be as his master.

Jn 1:14 And the Word was made flesh, and dwelt among us, (and we beheld his glory, the glory as of the only begotten of the Father,) full of grace and truth.

Jn 8:29 And he that sent me is with me: the Father hath not left me alone; for I do always those things that please him.

Jn 19:4 Pilate therefore went forth again, and saith unto them, Behold, I bring him forth to you, that ye may know that I find no fault in him.

He 2:10 For it became him, for whom *are* all things, and by whom *are* all things, in bringing many sons unto glory, to make the salvation perfect through sufferings.

He 5:9 And being made perfect, he became the author of eternal salvation unto all them that obey him;

He 7:28 For the law maketh men high priests which have infirmity; but the word of the oath, which was since the law, *maketh* the Son, who is consecrated for evermore.

Re 3:7 And to the angel of the church in Philadelphia write; These things saith he that is holy, he that is true, he that hath the key of David, he that openeth, and no man shutteth; and shutteth, and no man openeth;

5. Sinlessness of Christ

Is 53:9 And he made his grave with the wicked, and with the rich in his death; because he had done no violence, neither *was any* deceit in his mouth.

Mt 27:4 Saying, I have sinned in that I have betrayed the innocent blood. And they said, What *is that* to us? see thou *to that.*

Mt 27:19 When he was set down on the judgment seat, his wife sent unto him, saying, Have thou nothing to do with that just man: for I have suffered many things this day in a dream because of him.

Mt 27:23 And the governor said, Why, what evil hath he done? But they cried out the more, saying, Let him be crucified.

Mk 1:24 Saying, Let *us* alone; what have we to do with thee, thou Jesus of Nazareth? art thou come to destroy us? I know thee who thou art, the Holy One of God.

Mk 15:14 Then Pilate said unto them, Why, what evil hath he done?

And they cried out the more exceedingly, Crucify him.

Lu 1:35 And the angel answered and said unto her, The Holy Ghost shall come upon thee, and the power of the Highest shall overshadow thee: therefore also that holy thing which shall be born of thee shall be called the Son of God.

Lu 23:14 Said unto them, Ye have brought this man unto me, as one that perverteth the people: and, behold, I, having examined *him* before you, have found no fault in this man touching those things whereof ye accuse him:

Lu 23:22 And he said unto them the third time, Why, what evil hath he done? I have found no cause of death in him: I will therefore chastise him, and let *him* go.

Lu 23:41 And we indeed justly; for we receive the due reward of our deeds: but this man hath done nothing amiss.

Lu 23:47 Now when the centurion saw what was done, he glorified God, saying, Certainly this was a righteous man.

Jn 7:18 He that speaketh of himself seeketh his own glory: but he that seeketh his glory that sent him, the same is true, and no unrighteousness is in him.

Jn 8:46 Which of you convinceth me of sin? And if I say the truth, why do ye not believe me?

Jn 14:30 Hereafter I will not talk much with you: for the prince of this world cometh, and hath nothing in me.

Jn 18:38 Pilate saith unto him, What is truth? And when he had said this, he went out again unto the Jews, and saith unto them, I find in him no fault *at all.*

Jn 19:4 Pilate therefore went forth again, and saith unto them, Behold, I bring him forth to you, that ye may know that I find no fault in him.

Ac 3:14 But ye denied the Holy One and the Just, and desired a murderer to be granted unto you;

Ac 4:27 For of a truth against thy holy child Jesus, whom thou hast anointed, both Herod, and Pontius Pilate, with the Gentiles, and the people of Israel, were gathered together,

Ac 7:52 Which of the prophets have not your fathers persecuted? and they have slain them which shewed before of the coming of the Just One; of whom ye have been now the betrayers and murderers:

Ac 13:28 And though they found no cause of death *in him,* yet desired they Pilate that he should be slain.

Ac 22:14 And he said, The God of our fathers hath chosen thee, that thou shouldest know his will, and see that Just One, and shouldest hear the voice of his mouth.

2 Co 5:21 For he hath made him *to be* sin for us, who knew no sin; that we might be made the righteousness of God in him.

He 1:9 Thou hast loved righteousness, and hated iniquity; therefore God, *even* thy God, hath anointed thee with the oil of gladness above thy fellows.

He 4:15 For we have not an high priest which cannot be touched with the feeling of our infirmities; but was in all points tempted like as *we are, yet* without sin.

He 7:26 For such an high priest became us, *who is* holy, harmless, undefiled, separate from sinners, and made higher than the heavens;

He 9:14 How much more shall the blood of Christ, who through the eternal Spirit offered himself without spot to God, purge your conscience from dead works to serve the living God?

He 9:28 So Christ was once offered to bear the sins of many; and unto them that look for him shall he appear the second time without sin unto salvation.

Ja 5:6 Ye have condemned *and* killed the just; *and* he doth not resist you.

1 Pe 1:19 But with the precious blood of Christ, as of a lamb without blemish and without spot:

1 Pe 2:22 Who did no sin, neither was guile found in his mouth:

1 Jn 3:3 And every man that hath this hope in him purifieth himself, even as he is pure.

1 Jn 3:5 And ye know that he was manifested to take away our sins; and in him is no sin.

See **HOLINESS, IMPERFECTION, RIGHTEOUSNESS**

PERGA, *a town of Pamphylia*
Ac 13:13; 14:25

PERGAMOS, *a town of Mysia*
It was the home of one of the seven churches addressed in the Revelation to John (Re 2:12–17) and is located about fifteen miles from the Aegean Sea, sixty miles north of Smyrna.

Re 1:11; 2:12

See **CITIES**

PERIODS OF TIME, *and numbers, significant ones mentioned*

1. Forty Days

THE GREAT FLOOD

Ge 7:17 And the flood was forty days upon the earth; and the waters increased, and bare up the ark, and it was lift up above the earth.

Ge 8:6 And it came to pass at the end of forty days, that Noah opened the window of the ark which he had made:

THE EMBALMING OF JACOB

Ge 50:3 And forty days were fulfilled for him; for so are fulfilled the days of those which are embalmed: and the Egyptians mourned for him threescore and ten days.

MOSES FASTED ON THE MOUNT

Ex 24:18 And Moses went into the midst of the cloud, and gat him up into the mount: and Moses was in the mount forty days and forty nights.

Ex 34:28 And he was there with the LORD forty days and forty nights; he did neither eat bread, nor drink water. And he wrote upon the tables the words of the covenant, the ten commandments.

SPIES IN THE LAND OF CANAAN

Nu 13:25 And they returned from searching of the land after forty days.

MOSES PRAYED FOR ISRAEL

De 9:25 Thus I fell down before the LORD forty days and forty nights, as I fell down *at the first;* because the LORD had said he would destroy you.

GOLIATH'S DEFIANCE

1 S 17:16 And the Philistine drew near morning and evening, and presented himself forty days.

ELIJAH'S MEAL

1 K 19:8 And he arose, and did eat and drink, and went in the strength of that meat forty days and forty nights unto Horeb the mount of God.

EZEKIEL'S TYPICAL PERIOD

Eze 4:6 And when thou hast accomplished them, lie again on thy right side, and thou shalt bear the iniquity of the house of Judah forty days: I have appointed thee each day for a year.

JONAH'S WARNING CONCERNING THE DESTRUCTION OF NINEVEH

Jona 3:4 And Jonah began to enter into the city a day's journey, and he cried, and said, Yet forty days, and Nineveh shall be overthrown.

CHRIST'S TEMPTATION

Lu 4:2 Being forty days tempted of the devil. And in those days he did eat nothing: and when they were ended, he afterward hungered.

CHRIST'S APPEARANCE AFTER THE RESURRECTION

Ac 1:3 To whom also he shewed himself alive after his passion by many infallible proofs, being seen of them forty days, and speaking of the things pertaining to the kingdom of God:

See **DAYS**

2. Forty Years
Ex 16:35 And the children of Israel did eat manna forty years, until they

came to a land inhabited; they did eat manna, until they came unto the borders of the land of Canaan.

Nu 14:33 And your children shall wander in the wilderness forty years, and bear your whoredoms, until your carcases be wasted in the wilderness.

Nu 32:13 And the LORD's anger was kindled against Israel, and he made them wander in the wilderness forty years, until all the generation, that had done evil in the sight of the LORD, was consumed.

De 2:7 For the LORD thy God hath blessed thee in all the works of thy hand: he knoweth thy walking through this great wilderness: these forty years the LORD thy God *hath been* with thee; thou hast lacked nothing.

De 8:4 Thy raiment waxed not old upon thee, neither did thy foot swell, these forty years.

Jos 5:6 For the children of Israel walked forty years in the wilderness, till all the people *that were* men of war, which came out of Egypt, were consumed, because they obeyed not the voice of the LORD: unto whom the LORD sware that he would not shew them the land, which the LORD sware unto their fathers that he would give us, a land that floweth with milk and honey.

Jud 3:11 And the land had rest forty years. And Othniel the son of Kenaz died.

Jud 13:1 And the children of Israel did evil again in the sight of the LORD; and the LORD delivered them into the hand of the Philistines forty years.

1 K 2:11 And the days that David reigned over Israel *were* forty years: seven years reigned he in Hebron, and thirty and three years reigned he in Jerusalem.

Ne 9:21 Yea, forty years didst thou sustain them in the wilderness, *so that* they lacked nothing; their clothes waxed not old, and their feet swelled not.

Ps 95:10 Forty years long was I grieved with *this* generation, and said, It *is* a people that do err in their heart, and they have not known my ways:

Eze 29:11 No foot of man shall pass through it, nor foot of beast shall pass through it, neither shall it be inhabited forty years.

Am 2:10 Also I brought you up from the land of Egypt, and led you forty years through the wilderness, to possess the land of the Amorite.

Am 5:25 Have ye offered unto me sacrifices and offerings in the wilderness forty years, O house of Israel?

Ac 7:23 And when he was full forty years old, it came into his heart to visit his brethren the children of Israel.

Ac 7:30 And when forty years were expired, there appeared to him in the wilderness of mount Sina an angel of the Lord in a flame of fire in a bush.

Ac 7:36 He brought them out, after that he had shewed wonders and signs in the land of Egypt, and in the Red sea, and in the wilderness forty years.

Ac 7:42 Then God turned, and gave them up to worship the host of heaven; as it is written in the book of the prophets, O ye house of Israel, have ye offered to me slain beasts and sacrifices *by the space of* forty years in the wilderness?

Ac 13:18 And about the time of forty years suffered he their manners in the wilderness.

He 3:9 When your fathers tempted me, proved me, and saw my works forty years.

He 3:17 But with whom was he grieved forty years? *was it* not with them that had sinned, whose carcases fell in the wilderness?

3. Seven Days

Ge 2:3 And God blessed the seventh day, and sanctified it: because that in it he had rested from all his work which God created and made.

Ge 7:4 For yet seven days, and I will cause it to rain upon the earth forty days and forty nights; and every living substance that I have made will I destroy from off the face of the earth.

Ge 8:10 And he stayed yet other seven days; and again he sent forth the dove out of the ark;

Ge 50:10 And they came to the threshingfloor of Atad, which *is* beyond Jordan, and there they mourned with a great and very sore lamentation: and he made a mourning for his father seven days.

Ex 7:25 And seven days were fulfilled, after that the LORD had smitten the river.

Ex 12:15 Seven days shall ye eat unleavened bread; even the first day ye shall put away leaven out of your houses: for whosoever eateth leavened bread from the first day until the seventh day, that soul shall be cut off from Israel.

Ex 12:19 Seven days shall there be no leaven found in your houses: for whosoever eateth that which is leavened, even that soul shall be cut off from the congregation of Israel, whether he be a stranger, or born in the land.

Ex 13:6 Seven days thou shalt eat unleavened bread, and in the seventh day *shall be* a feast to the LORD.

Ex 20:11 For *in* six days the LORD made heaven and earth, the sea, and all that in them *is,* and rested the seventh day: wherefore the LORD blessed the sabbath day, and hallowed it.

Ex 24:16 And the glory of the LORD abode upon mount Sinai, and the cloud covered it six days: and the seventh day he called unto Moses out of the midst of the cloud.

Ex 29:30 *And* that son that is priest in his stead shall put them on seven days, when he cometh into the tabernacle of the congregation to minister in the holy *place.*

Ex 29:35 And thus shalt thou do unto Aaron, and to his sons, according to all *things* which I have commanded thee: seven days shalt thou consecrate them.

Ex 34:18 The feast of unleavened bread shalt thou keep. Seven days thou shalt eat unleavened bread, as I commanded thee, in the time of the month Abib: for in the month Abib thou camest out from Egypt.

Le 8:33 And ye shall not go out of the door of the tabernacle of the congregation *in* seven days, until the days of your consecration be at an end: for seven days shall he consecrate you.

Le 13:4 If the bright spot *be* white in the skin of his flesh, and in sight *be* not deeper than the skin, and the hair thereof be not turned white; then the priest shall shut up *him that hath* the plague seven days:

Le 13:27 And the priest shall look upon him the seventh day: *and* if it be spread much abroad in the skin, then the priest shall pronounce him unclean: it *is* the plague of leprosy.

Le 15:13 And when he that hath an issue is cleansed of his issue; then he shall number to himself seven days for his cleansing, and wash his clothes, and bathe his flesh in running water, and shall be clean.

Le 15:28 But if she be cleansed of her issue, then she shall number to herself seven days, and after that she shall be clean.

Le 22:27 When a bullock, or a sheep, or a goat, is brought forth, then it shall be seven days under the dam; and from the eighth day and thenceforth it shall be accepted for an offering made by fire unto the LORD.

Le 23:40 And ye shall take you on the first day the boughs of goodly trees, branches of palm trees, and the boughs of thick trees, and willows of the brook; and ye shall rejoice before the LORD your God seven days.

Nu 19:11 He that toucheth the dead body of any man shall be unclean seven days.

Nu 28:24 After this manner ye shall offer daily, throughout the seven days, the meat of the sacrifice made by fire, of a sweet savour unto the LORD: it shall be offered beside the continual burnt offering, and his drink offering.

Nu 29:12 And on the fifteenth day of the seventh month ye shall have an holy convocation; ye shall do no servile work, and ye shall keep a feast unto the LORD seven days:

Nu 31:19 And do ye abide without the camp seven days: whosoever hath killed any person, and whosoever hath touched any slain, purify *both* yourselves and your captives on the third day, and on the seventh day.

Nu 31:24 And ye shall wash your clothes on the seventh day, and ye shall be clean, and afterward ye shall come into the camp.

De 16:3 Thou shalt eat no leavened bread with it; seven days shalt thou eat unleavened bread therewith, *even* the bread of affliction; for thou camest forth out of the land of Egypt in haste: that thou mayest remember the day when thou camest forth out of the land of Egypt all the days of thy life.

De 16:13 Thou shalt observe the feast of tabernacles seven days, after that thou hast gathered in thy corn and thy wine:

Jos 6:15 And it came to pass on the seventh day, that they rose early about the dawning of the day, and compassed the city after the same manner seven times: only on that day they compassed the city seven times.

1 S 10:8 And thou shalt go down before me to Gilgal; and, behold, I will come down unto thee, to offer burnt offerings, *and* to sacrifice sacrifices of peace offerings: seven days shalt thou tarry, till I come to thee, and shew thee what thou shalt do.

1 S 11:3 And the elders of Jabesh said unto him, Give us seven days' respite, that we may send messengers unto all the coasts of Israel: and then, if *there be* no man to save us, we will come out to thee.

1 S 13:8 And he tarried seven days, according to the set time that Samuel *had appointed:* but Samuel came not to Gilgal; and the people were scattered from him.

1 Chr 9:25 And their brethren, *which were* in their villages, *were* to come after seven days from time to time with them.

2 Chr 7:8 Also at the same time Solomon kept the feast seven days, and all Israel with him, a very great congregation, from the entering in of Hamath unto the river of Egypt.

2 Chr 30:21 And the children of Israel that were present at Jerusalem kept the feast of unleavened bread seven days with great gladness: and the Levites and the priests praised the LORD day by day, *singing* with loud instruments unto the LORD.

2 Chr 30:23 And the whole assembly took counsel to keep other seven days: and they kept *other* seven days with gladness.

Jb 2:13 So they sat down with him upon the ground seven days and seven nights, and none spake a word unto him: for they saw that *his* grief was very great.

Eze 3:15 Then I came to them of the captivity at Tel-abib, that dwelt by the river of Chebar, and I sat where they sat, and remained there astonished among them seven days.

Eze 43:25 Seven days shalt thou prepare every day a goat *for* a sin offering: they shall also prepare a young bullock, and a ram out of the flock, without blemish.

Eze 45:23 And seven days of the feast he shall prepare a burnt offering to the LORD, seven bullocks and seven rams without blemish daily the seven days; and a kid of the goats daily *for* a sin offering.

Ac 20:6 And we sailed away from Philippi after the days of unleavened bread, and came unto them to Troas in five days; where we abode seven days.

Ac 21:4 And finding disciples, we tarried there seven days: who said to Paul through the Spirit, that he should not go up to Jerusalem.

Ac 21:27 And when the seven days were almost ended, the Jews which were of Asia, when they saw him in the temple, stirred up all the people, and laid hands on him,

Ac 28:14 Where we found brethren, and were desired to tarry with them seven days: and so we went toward Rome.

He 11:30 By faith the walls of Jericho fell down, after they were compassed about seven days.

See **DAYS**

4. Seven Years

Ge 29:18 And Jacob loved Rachel; and said, I will serve thee seven years for Rachel thy younger daughter.

Ge 41:29 Behold, there come seven years of great plenty throughout all the land of Egypt:

Ge 41:54 And the seven years of dearth began to come, according as Joseph had said: and the dearth was in all the land of Egypt there was bread.

De 15:1 At the end of *every* seven years thou shalt make a release.

2 K 8:1 Then spake Elisha unto the woman, whose son he had restored to life, saying, Arise, and go thou and thine household, and sojourn wheresoever thou canst sojourn: for the LORD hath called for a famine; and it shall also come upon the land seven years.

Eze 39:9 And they that dwell in the cities of Israel shall go forth, and shall set on fire and burn the weapons, both the shields and the bucklers, the bows and the arrows, and the handstaves, and the spears, and they shall burn them with fire seven years:

Da 4:23 And whereas the king saw a watcher and an holy one coming down from heaven, and saying, Hew the tree down, and destroy it; yet leave the stump of the roots thereof in the earth, even with a band of iron and brass, in the tender grass of the field; and let it be wet with the dew of heaven, and *let* his portion *be* with the beasts of the field, till seven times pass over him;

5. Seventy, weeks, years, persons, and things

SEVENTY ELDERS APPOINTED

Nu 11:16 And the LORD said unto Moses, Gather unto me seventy men of the elders of Israel, whom thou knowest to be the elders of the people, and officers over them; and bring them unto the tabernacle of the congregation, that they may stand there with thee.

SEVENTY YEARS OF CAPTIVITY

Je 25:11 And this whole land shall be a desolation, *and* an astonishment; and these nations shall serve the king of Babylon seventy years.

SEVENTY WEEKS REFERRED TO BY DANIEL

Da 9:24 Seventy weeks are determined upon thy people and upon thy holy city, to finish the transgression, and to make an end of sins, and to make reconciliation for iniquity, and to bring in everlasting righteousness, and to seal up the vision and prophecy, and to anoint the most Holy.

SEVENTY TIMES OF FORGIVENESS

Mt 18:22 Jesus saith unto him, I say not unto thee, Until seven times: but, Until seventy times seven.

SEVENTY DISCIPLES SENT FORTH

Lu 10:1 After these things the Lord appointed other seventy also, and sent them two and two before his face into every city and place, whither he himself would come.

PERIZZITES, *one of the Canaanitish nations*

Ge 13:7; 15:20; Ex 3:17; 23:23; De 20:17; Jos 3:10; 11:3; 17:15; 24:11; Jud 1:4; 3:5; 2 Chr 8:7; Ezr 9:1; Ne 9:8

PERJURY *See* **COURTS**

PERSECUTION *See* **SUFFERING**

PERSIA, *a world empire which flourished from 539–331 B.C.*

2 Chr 36:20; Ezr 1:1; Est 1:3, 14, 18; 10:2; Eze 38:5; Da 8:20; 10:1; 11:2

PERSEVERANCE

See **STEADFASTNESS**

PERSPECTIVE

1. God's View of Doing Evil

Ge 13:13; 38:7; De 4:25; 9:18; 31:29; Jud 2:11; 3:12; 4:1; 6:1; 10:6; 13:1; 1 S 12:17; 2 S 12:9; 1 K 14:22; 15:26; 16:7, 25; 21:20; 2 K 8:27; 13:2, 11; 14:24; 15:9, 18, 24, 28; 17:2; 21:2, 15; 23:32, 37; 24:9, 19; 1 Chr 2:3; 2 Chr 21:6; 22:4; 29:6; 33:2; 36:5, 9; Ps 9:19; Is 66:4; Je 32:30; Lu 15:21

2. God's View of Doing Good

De 6:18; 12:25; 21:9; 2 S 22:25; 1 K
15:5, 11; 22:43; 2 K 3:2; 12:2; 14:3;
15:34; 18:3; 22:2; 2 Chr 20:32; 25:2;
26:4; 27:2; 29:2; 34:2; Ps 18:24; 51:4; Is
38:3; Ac 4:19; 10:31; 2 Co 2:17; 4:2;
8:21; 1 Th 1:3; 1 Ti 2:3; He 13:21; Ja
1:27; 1 Jn 3:22

See **GOD, JUSTICE**

PERSUASION, *SPIRITUAL*

OF THE DIVINE ABILITY

Ro 4:21 And being fully persuaded
that, what he had promised, he was
able also to perform.

OF THE INSEPARABLE LOVE OF GOD

Ro 8:38–39 For I am persuaded, that
neither death, nor life, nor angels, nor
principalities, nor powers, nor things
present, nor things to come,
    Nor height, nor depth, nor any
other creature, shall be able to separate us from the love of God, which is
in Christ Jesus our Lord.

OF THE DIVINE KEEPING POWER

2 Ti 1:12 For the which cause I also
suffer these things: nevertheless I am
not ashamed: for I know whom I have
believed, and am persuaded that he is
able to keep that which I have committed unto him against that day.

OF THE CERTAINTY OF THE DIVINE PROMISES

He 11:13 These all died in faith, not
having received the promises, but
having seen them afar off, and were
persuaded of *them,* and embraced
them, and confessed that they were
strangers and pilgrims on the earth.

See **ASSURANCE, CERTAINTIES**

PERVERSENESS, *perversion, away*
from that which is right

Le 26:15 And if ye shall despise my
statutes, or if your soul abhor my judgments, so that ye will not do all my
commandments, *but* that ye break my
covenant:
Nu 22:32 And the angel of the LORD
said unto him, Wherefore hast thou

smitten thine ass these three times?
behold, I went out to withstand thee,
because *thy* way is perverse before me:
De 32:20 And he said, I will hide my
face from them, I will see what their
end *shall be:* for they *are* a very froward
generation, children in whom *is* no
faith.
2 S 22:27 With the pure thou wilt
shew thyself pure; and with the
froward thou wilt shew thyself unsavoury.
Ps 18:26 With the pure thou wilt
shew thyself pure; and with the
froward thou wilt shew thyself
froward.
Ps 78:17 And they sinned yet more
against him by provoking the most
High in the wilderness.
Ps 78:32 For all this they sinned still,
and believed not for his wondrous
works.
Pr 2:14 Who rejoice to do evil, *and*
delight in the frowardness of the
wicked;
Pr 6:14 Frowardness *is* in his heart,
he deviseth mischief continually; he
soweth discord.
Pr 11:3 The integrity of the upright
shall guide them: but the perverseness
of transgressors shall destroy them.
Pr 12:8 A man shall be commended
according to his wisdom: but he that
is of a perverse heart shall be despised.
Pr 14:2 He that walketh in his uprightness feareth the LORD: but *he that*
is perverse in his ways despiseth him.
Pr 15:4 A wholesome tongue *is* a tree
of life: but perverseness therein *is* a
breach in the spirit.
Pr 17:20 He that hath a froward heart
findeth no good: and he that hath a
perverse tongue falleth into mischief.
Pr 19:1 Better *is* the poor that
walketh in his integrity, than *he that is*
perverse in his lips, and is a fool.
Pr 28:6 Better *is* the poor that
walketh in his uprightness, than *he*
that is perverse *in his* ways, though he
be rich.
Pr 28:18 Whoso walketh uprightly
shall be saved: but *he that is* perverse
in his ways shall fall at once.
Is 30:12 Wherefore thus saith the
Holy One of Israel, Because ye despise

this word, and trust in oppression and perverseness, and stay thereon:

Eze 9:9 Then said he unto me, The iniquity of the house of Israel and Judah *is* exceeding great, and the land is full of blood, and the city full of perverseness: for they say, The LORD hath forsaken the earth, and the LORD seeth not.

Mt 12:39 But he answered and said unto them, An evil and adulterous generation seeketh after a sign; and there shall no sign be given to it, but the sign of the prophet Jonas:

Mt 17:17 Then Jesus answered and said, O faithless and perverse generation, how long shall I be with you? how long shall I suffer you? bring him hither to me.

Lu 9:41 And Jesus answering said, O faithless and perverse generation, how long shall I be with you, and suffer you? Bring thy son hither.

1 Ti 6:5 Perverse disputings of men of corrupt minds, and destitute of the truth, supposing that gain is godliness: from such withdraw thyself.

See **STUBBORNNESS**

PESTILENCE *See* **JUDGMENTS**

PETER

1. Person, *an apostle and author of two Bible books*

a. From Reed to Rock

NATURALLY IMPULSIVE

Mt 14:28 And Peter answered him and said, Lord, if it be thou, bid me come unto thee on the water.

Mt 17:4 Then answered Peter, and said unto Jesus, Lord, it is good for us to be here: if thou wilt, let us make here three tabernacles; one for thee, and one for Moses, and one for Elias.

Jn 21:7 Therefore that disciple whom Jesus loved saith unto Peter, It is the Lord. Now when Simon Peter heard that it was the Lord, he girt *his* fisher's coat *unto him,* (for he was naked,) and did cast himself into the sea.

TENDERHEARTED AND AFFECTIONATE

Mt 26:75 And Peter remembered the word of Jesus, which said unto him, Before the cock crow, thou shalt deny me thrice. And he went out, and wept bitterly.

Jn 13:9 Simon Peter saith unto him, Lord, not my feet only, but also *my* hands and *my* head.

Jn 21:15–17 So when they had dined, Jesus saith to Simon Peter, Simon, *son* of Jonas, lovest thou me more than these? He saith unto him, Yea, Lord; thou knowest that I love thee. He saith unto him, Feed my lambs.

He saith to him again the second time, Simon, *son* of Jonas, lovest thou me? He saith unto him, Yea, Lord; thou knowest that I love thee. He saith unto him, Feed my sheep.

He saith unto him the third time, Simon, *son* of Jonas, lovest thou me? Peter was grieved because he said unto him the third time, Lovest thou me? And he said unto him, Lord, thou knowest all things; thou knowest that I love thee. Jesus saith unto him, Feed my sheep.

FULL OF STRANGE CONTRADICTIONS:
AT TIMES PRESUMPTUOUS

Mt 16:22 Then Peter took him, and began to rebuke him, saying, Be it far from thee, Lord: this shall not be unto thee.

Jn 13:8 Peter saith unto him, Thou shalt never wash my feet. Jesus answered him, If I wash thee not, thou hast no part with me.

Jn 18:10 Then Simon Peter having a sword drew it, and smote the high priest's servant, and cut off his right ear. The servant's name was Malchus.

AT TIMES TIMID AND COWARDLY

Mt 14:30 But when he saw the wind boisterous, he was afraid; and beginning to sink, he cried, saying, Lord, save me.

Mt 26:69–72 Now Peter sat without in the palace: and a damsel came unto him, saying, Thou also wast with Jesus of Galilee.

But he denied before *them* all, saying, I know not what thou sayest.

And when he was gone out into the porch, another *maid* saw him, and said unto them that were there, This *fellow* was also with Jesus of Nazareth.

And again he denied with an oath, I do not know the man.

SELF-SACRIFICING

Mk 1:18 And straightway they forsook their nets, and followed him.

YET INCLINED TO BE SELF-SEEKING

Mt 19:27 Then answered Peter and said unto him, Behold, we have forsaken all, and followed thee; what shall we have therefore?

GIFTED WITH SPIRITUAL INSIGHT

Jn 6:68 Then Simon Peter answered him, Lord, to whom shall we go? thou hast the words of eternal life.

YET SLOW TO APPREHEND
THE DEEPER TRUTHS

Mt 15:15 Then answered Peter and said unto him, Declare unto us this parable.
Mt 15:16 And Jesus said, Are ye also yet without understanding?

MADE TWO GREAT CONFESSIONS
OF FAITH IN CHRIST

Mt 16:16 And Simon Peter answered and said, Thou art the Christ, the Son of the living God.
Jn 6:69 And we believe and are sure that thou art that Christ, the Son of the living God.

YET GUILTY OF THE MOST COWARDLY DENIAL

Mk 14:67–71 And when she saw Peter warming himself, she looked upon him, and said, And thou also wast with Jesus of Nazareth.

But he denied, saying, I know not, neither understand I what thou sayest. And he went out into the porch; and the cock crew.

And a maid saw him again, and began to say to them that stood by, This is *one* of them.

And he denied it again. And a little after, they that stood by said again to Peter, Surely thou art *one* of them: for thou art a Galilaean, and thy speech agreeth *thereto*.

But he began to curse and to swear, *saying,* I know not this man of whom ye speak.

b. Seven Steps in His Fall

CONCEIT

Mt 26:33 Peter answered and said unto him, Though all *men* shall be offended because of thee, *yet* will I never be offended.

EASE

Mt 26:40 And he cometh unto the disciples, and findeth them asleep, and saith unto Peter, What, could ye not watch with me one hour?

RASHNESS

Jn 18:10–11 Then Simon Peter having a sword drew it, and smote the high priest's servant, and cut off his right ear. The servant's name was Malchus.

Then said Jesus unto Peter, Put up thy sword into the sheath: the cup which my Father hath given me, shall I not drink it?

FOLLOWING AFAR OFF

Mt 26:58 But Peter followed him afar off unto the high priest's palace, and went in, and sat with the servants, to see the end.

EVIL ASSOCIATIONS

Jn 18:18 And the servants and officers stood there, who had made a fire of coals; for it was cold: and they warmed themselves: and Peter stood with them, and warmed himself.

OPEN DENIAL

Jn 18:25 And Simon Peter stood and warmed himself. They said therefore unto him, Art not thou also *one* of his disciples? He denied *it,* and said, I am not.

BLASPHEMY

Mk 14:71 But he began to curse and to swear, *saying*, I know not this man of whom ye speak.

c. After Pentecost

Mt 16:18 And I say also unto thee, That thou art Peter, and upon this rock I will build my church; and the gates of hell shall not prevail against it.

Jn 1:42 And he brought him to Jesus. And when Jesus beheld him, he said, Thou art Simon the son of Jona: thou shalt be called Cephas, which is by interpretation, A stone.

Ac 1:8 But ye shall receive power, after that the Holy Ghost is come upon you: and ye shall be witnesses unto me both in Jerusalem, and in all Judaea, and in Samaria, and unto the uttermost part of the earth.

WAS COURAGEOUS AND IMMOVABLE

Ac 4:19–20 But Peter and John answered and said unto them, Whether it be right in the sight of God to hearken unto you more than unto God, judge ye.

For we cannot but speak the things which we have seen and heard.

Ac 5:28–29 Saying, Did not we straitly command you that ye should not teach in this name? and, behold, ye have filled Jerusalem with your doctrine, and intend to bring this man's blood upon us.

Then Peter and the *other* apostles answered and said, We ought to obey God rather than men.

Ac 5:40 And to him they agreed: and when they had called the apostles, and beaten *them,* they commanded that they should not speak in the name of Jesus, and let them go.

Ac 5:42 And daily in the temple, and in every house, they ceased not to teach and preach Jesus Christ.

d. Empowered by the Holy Spirit

WITH BOLDNESS AND COURAGE

Ac 2:14 But Peter, standing up with the eleven, lifted up his voice, and said unto them, Ye men of Judaea, and all *ye* that dwell at Jerusalem, be this

known unto you, and hearken to my words:

Ac 4:13 Now when they saw the boldness of Peter and John, and perceived that they were unlearned and ignorant men, they marvelled; and they took knowledge of them, that they had been with Jesus.

Ac 4:19–20 But Peter and John answered and said unto them, Whether it be right in the sight of God to hearken unto you more than unto God, judge ye.

For we cannot but speak the things which we have seen and heard.

TO BE A CHANNEL
OF BLESSING TO THE SICK

Ac 5:15 Insomuch that they brought forth the sick into the streets, and laid *them* on beds and couches, that at the least the shadow of Peter passing by might overshadow some of them.

TO RAISE TABITHA FROM DEATH

Ac 9:40 But Peter put them all forth, and kneeled down, and prayed; and turning *him* to the body said, Tabitha, arise. And she opened her eyes: and when she saw Peter, she sat up.

TO TAKE THE SPIRIT TO THE GENTILES

Ac 10:44 While Peter yet spake these words, the Holy Ghost fell on all them which heard the word.

2. Books

a. FIRST

Author: The apostle Peter. The author was not the original Simon Peter, impulsive and full of weaknesses, whom Christ called "Simon" (Mk 14:37; Lu 22:31; Jn 21:15–17). It was the Peter Christ prophesied should become a rock (Jn 1:42), the same man, chastened by years of suffering and trial and strengthened by the baptism of the Holy Spirit.

Date Written: Uncertain. The Babylon referred to in 5:13 may or may not have been the city on the Euphrates River. Many think it was Rome, figuratively called Babylon.

Purpose: In writing this epistle, Peter obeyed two specific commands that Jesus had given him.

(1) To encourage and strengthen the brethren (Lu 22:32).

(2) To feed the flock of God (Jn 21:15–17).

To Whom Written: Addressed to the elect scattered throughout Asia Minor. Probably to the whole body of Christians in that region, both Jew and Gentile converts. To the churches largely founded by Paul, Peter sends this spiritual message of encouragement, instruction, and admonition.

Main Theme: Victory over suffering as exemplified in the life of Christ.

Key Word: Suffering.

Key Verse: 4:1.

b. SECOND

Author: The apostle Peter.

Date Written: Probably between A.D. 64 and 70.

Purpose: To warn believers of the dangerous and seductive work of false teachers, and to encourage them to "grow in the grace, *and* in the knowledge of our Lord and Saviour Jesus Christ" (3:18).

To Whom Written: Christians everywhere (1:1).

Main Theme: A warning against corrupt teachers and scoffers. In order to counteract the influence of false doctrine, great emphasis is laid upon the Word of God and the certainty of the fulfillment of the divine promises.

Key Words: False Teachers (2:1).

Key Verses: 1:20–21; 3:1–2.

PHARAOH, *the common title of kings of Egypt*

1. King of Egypt in Abraham's Time

Ge 12:15

2. Of the Time of the Exodus

Ex 1:8; Ac 7:18

PHAREZ, *Perez, or Phares, son of Judah*

Ge 38:29; 46:12; Nu 26:20; 1 Chr 2:4; 4:1; Ne 11:4; Mt 1:3; Lu 3:33

PHARISAISM, *separated ones; likeness to the teachings of the Pharisees, one of many Jewish sects at the time of Christ*

Is 65:5 Which say, Stand by thyself, come not near to me; for I am holier than thou. *These* are a smoke in my nose, a fire that burneth all the day.

Mt 6:2 Therefore when thou doest *thine* alms, do not sound a trumpet before thee, as the hypocrites do in the synagogues and in the streets, that they may have glory of men. Verily I say unto you, They have their reward.

Mt 6:16 Moreover when ye fast, be not, as the hypocrites, of a sad countenance: for they disfigure their faces, that they may appear unto men to fast. Verily I say unto you, They have their reward.

Mt 9:11 And when the Pharisees saw *it,* they said unto his disciples, Why eateth your Master with publicans and sinners?

Mt 12:2 But when the Pharisees saw *it,* they said unto him, Behold, thy disciples do that which is not lawful to do upon the sabbath day.

Mt 15:2 Why do thy disciples transgress the tradition of the elders? for they wash not their hands when they eat bread.

Mt 23:4 For they bind heavy burdens and grievous to be borne, and lay *them* on men's shoulders; but they *themselves* will not move them with one of their fingers.

Mt 23:13 But woe unto you, scribes and Pharisees, hypocrites! for ye shut up the kingdom of heaven against men: for ye neither go in *yourselves,* neither suffer ye them that are entering to go in.

Mt 23:23 Woe unto you, scribes and Pharisees, hypocrites! for ye pay tithe of mint and anise and cummin, and have omitted the weightier *matters* of the law, judgment, mercy, and faith: these ought ye to have done, and not to leave the other undone.

Mt 23:27 Woe unto you, scribes and Pharisees, hypocrites! for ye are like unto whited sepulchres, which indeed appear beautiful outward, but are within full of dead *men's* bones, and of all uncleanness.

Mk 2:16 And when the scribes and Pharisees saw him eat with publicans and sinners, they said unto his disciples, How is it that he eateth and drinketh with publicans and sinners?

Mk 2:18 And the disciples of John and of the Pharisees used to fast: and they come and say unto him, Why do the disciples of John and of the Pharisees fast, but thy disciples fast not?

Mk 2:24 And the Pharisees said unto him, Behold, why do they on the sabbath day that which is not lawful?

Mk 7:2 And when they saw some of his disciples eat bread with defiled, that is to say, with unwashen, hands, they found fault.

Lu 6:2 And certain of the Pharisees said unto them, Why do ye that which is not lawful to do on the sabbath days?

Lu 7:39 Now when the Pharisee which had bidden him saw *it,* he spake within himself, saying, This man, if he were a prophet, would have known who and what manner of woman *this is* that toucheth him: for she is a sinner.

Lu 11:38 And when the Pharisee saw *it,* he marvelled that he had not first washed before dinner.

Lu 11:42 But woe unto you, Pharisees! for ye tithe mint and rue and all manner of herbs, and pass over judgment and the love of God: these ought ye to have done, and not to leave the other undone.

Lu 12:1 In the mean time, when there were gathered together an innumerable multitude of people, insomuch that they trode one upon another, he began to say unto his disciples first of all, Beware ye of the leaven of the Pharisees, which is hypocrisy.

Jn 7:47 Then answered them the Pharisees, Are ye also deceived?

Ac 15:5 But there rose up certain of the sect of the Pharisees which be-

lieved, saying, That it was needful to circumcise them, and to command *them* to keep the law of Moses.

Ja 1:26 If any man among you seem to be religious, and bridleth not his tongue, but deceiveth his own heart, this man's religion *is* vain.

See **SECTS AND PARTIES**

PHARPAR *See* **RIVERS**

PHILADELPHIA, *a city of Asia Minor*
Re 1:11; 3:7

PHILEMON

Author: The apostle Paul.

Date Written: About A.D. 60. This is a private letter of intercession, probably written from Rome during Paul's first imprisonment and sent to Philemon at Colosse (Col 4:7–9).

Purpose: To appeal to Philemon to receive, forgive, and restore Onesimus, even as he (Philemon) would receive Paul.

To Whom Written: Philemon. He was apparently a member of the church at Colosse, which seems to have held its assemblies in his house (2). His benevolence (5–7) and Paul's request for him to prepare a lodging (22) indicate that he was a man of some means. As Paul had never been in Colosse (Col 2:1), Philemon must have met him elsewhere, possibly in Ephesus, which was not far away. It would seem that he owed his conversion to the apostle.

Main Theme: A personal plea with Philemon to forgive and restore Onesimus, his runaway slave, now converted through the ministry of Paul. It is inferred that Onesimus robbed his master and fled to Rome. There he came under the influence of Paul and was converted. He became a devoted disciple of Christ (Col 4:9). Paul would have chosen to have detained him in Rome as a helper (13), but not having the consent of Philemon (14), the apostle felt it his duty to send the slave back to his master. So the apostle writes this beautiful letter of intercession, pleading with Philemon to receive Onesimus as though he were receiving the apostle himself.

Key Word: Receive (forgive and restore) (12, 17).

Key Verses: 16–17.

PHEBE *See* WOMEN

PHILIP, *lover of horses*

1. The Apostle

A PERSONAL WORKER

Jn 1:45 Philip findeth Nathanael, and saith unto him, We have found him, of whom Moses in the law, and the prophets, did write, Jesus of Nazareth, the son of Joseph.

Jn 12:21–22 The same came therefore to Philip, which was of Bethsaida of Galilee, and desired him, saying, Sir, we would see Jesus.

Philip cometh and telleth Andrew: and again Andrew and Philip tell Jesus.

TESTED BY CHRIST

Jn 6:5 When Jesus then lifted up *his* eyes, and saw a great company come unto him, he saith unto Philip, Whence shall we buy bread, that these may eat?

SLOW TO APPREHEND TRUTH

Jn 14:8 Philip saith unto him, Lord, shew us the Father, and it sufficeth us.

2. The Evangelistic Deacon

BROADMINDED

Ac 8:5 Then Philip went down to the city of Samaria, and preached Christ unto them.

LED OF THE SPIRIT

Ac 8:26 And the angel of the Lord spake unto Philip, saying, Arise, and go toward the south unto the way that goeth down from Jerusalem unto Gaza, which is desert.

PREACHER OF THE WORD

Ac 8:34 And the eunuch answered Philip, and said, I pray thee, of whom

speaketh the prophet this? of himself, or of some other man?

HAD A GODLY HOUSEHOLD

Ac 21:8 And the next *day* we that were of Paul's company departed, and came unto Caesarea: and we entered into the house of Philip the evangelist, which was *one* of the seven; and abode with him.

3. The Brother of Herod

Mt 14:3; Mk 6:17; Lu 3:1, 19

PHILIPPI, *a city of Macedonia*

It owes its name to Philip of Macedon (father of Alexander the Great), who took it from the Thracians in the fourth century B.C. and named it after himself. It was strategically located on the east-west Egnatian Highway between Rome and Asia and served as a starting point for Alexander the Great when he began his military campaigns to conquer the world. Paul came directly to Philippi after his vision of a man saying, "Come over to Macedonia and help us" (Ac 16:9–12). Here he preached the gospel by "a riverside," was placed in prison, and established his first church on the European continent (Ac 16:13–40; cf. 20:6; Ph 1:1; 1 Th 2:2).

PHILIPPIAN JAILER

See KINDNESS

PHILIPPIANS

Author: The apostle Paul.

Date Written: Uncertain. Probably written from Rome between A.D. 60 and 64.

Purpose: To express Paul's affection for the believers in Philippi, thank them for their gift, and encourage them to a lifestyle of unity, holiness, and joy.

To Whom Written: The church in Philippi. This church was ideal in many respects. It was very appreciative and generous (4:15–16, 2 Co 8:2). It was founded by Paul on his second missionary journey in the midst of a storm of persecution. The beginnings of the work were small, among a few women at the riverside. Lydia, a seller of purple, was the first convert, and she was soon joined by the Philippian jailer and his family. These, and perhaps a few others, became the nucleus of the church (Ac 16:12–40).

Main Theme: Jesus Christ.

Key Word: Joy.

(1) In prayer (1:4).

(2) In the Gospel (1:18).

(3) In Christian fellowship (2:1–2).

(4) In sacrifices for the cause (2:17–18).

(5) In the Lord (3:1).

(6) For the loving care of the church (4:10).

Key Verse: 4:4.

PHILISTIA, *the country of the Philistines*

Ge 21:34; Ex 13:17; Jos 13:2; 1 K 4:21; 2 K 8:2; Ps 60:8; 87:4; 108:9

PHILISTINES, *a powerful sea people that settled in the coastal strip of southwest Palestine*

Ge 21:32; 26:18; Jos 13:3; Jud 3:3, 31; 10:7; 13:5; 14:1, 4; 15:3, 9; 16:14, 27; 1 S 4:1; 5:2; 6:1; 7:8; 10:5; 12:9; 13:5, 19; 14:1, 46; 17:1; 23:1, 28; 27:1; 28:1, 4; 31:1; 2 S 5:17; 21:15; 23:16; 2 K 18:8; 1 Chr 1:12; 10:1; 11:13; 14:8; 18:1, 11; 20:4; 2 Chr 17:11; 26:6; 28:18; Ps 83:7; Is 2:6; 11:14; Je 25:20; 47:1; Eze 25:15; Am 1:8; 6:2; 9:7; Obad 19; Zep 2:5

PHILOSOPHY

Ac 17:18; 1 Co 1:19–20; 2:6; 3:18; Col 2:8

PHINEHAS, *the high priest, son of Eleazar*

Ex 6:25; Nu 25:7; 31:6; Jos 22:13, 30; 24:33; Jud 20:28; 1 S 14:3; 1 Chr 6:4, 50; 9:20; Ezr 7:5; 8:2; Ps 106:30

PHOEBE, *a servant of the church at Cenchrea*

Ro 16:

PHOENICIA, *country northwest of Palestine*

Ac 11:19; 15:3; 21:2

PHRYGIA, *an inland province of Asia Minor*

Ac 16:6; 18:23

PHYLACTERIES

See **REMEMBRANCE**

PIGEONS *See* **BIRDS**

PIGS *See* **ANIMALS**

PILATE, *PONTIUS, Roman governor of Judea, the ruler who shirked responsibility*

BY TURNING CHRIST OVER TO JEWISH AUTHORITIES

Jn 18:31 Then said Pilate unto them, Take ye him, and judge him according to your law. The Jews therefore said unto him, It is not lawful for us to put any man to death:

BY SENDING HIM TO HEROD

Lu 23:7 And as soon as he knew that he belonged unto Herod's jurisdiction, he sent him to Herod, who himself also was at Jerusalem at that time.

BY PROPOSING TO INFLICT A MINOR PENALTY

Lu 23:22 And he said unto them the third time, Why, what evil hath he done? I have found no cause of death in him: I will therefore chastise him, and let *him* go.

BY DIRECTING ATTENTION TO BARABBAS

Mt 27:17 Therefore when they were gathered together, Pilate said unto them, Whom will ye that I release unto you? Barabbas, or Jesus which is called Christ?

BY A HYPOCRITICAL CEREMONY

Mt 27:24 When Pilate saw that he could prevail nothing, but *that* rather a tumult was made, he took water, and washed *his* hands before the multitude, saying, I am innocent of the blood of this just person: see ye *to it.*

PILGRIMS, *wayfarers, strangers*

OBEYED THE CALL

He 11:8 By faith Abraham, when he was called to go out into a place which he should after receive for an inheritance, obeyed; and he went out, not knowing whither he went.

NEVER SETTLED DOWN

He 11:9–10 By faith he sojourned in the land of promise, as *in* a strange country, dwelling in tabernacles with Isaac and Jacob, the heirs with him of the same promise.

For he looked for a city which hath foundations, whose builder and maker *is* God.

HAD TELESCOPIC VISION

He 11:13 These all died in faith, not having received the promises, but having seen them afar off, and were persuaded of *them,* and embraced *them,* and confessed that they were strangers and pilgrims on the earth.

NEVER TURNED BACK

He 11:15 And truly, if they had been mindful of that *country* from whence they came out, they might have had opportunity to have returned.

LONGED FOR A BETTER LAND

He 11:16 But now they desire a better *country,* that is, an heavenly: wherefore God is not ashamed to be called their God: for he hath prepared for them a city.

DIED IN THE FAITH

He 11:13 These all died in faith, not having received the promises, but having seen them afar off, and were persuaded of *them,* and embraced *them,* and confessed that they were strangers and pilgrims on the earth.

See **LIFE**

PILLARS

1. Memorial

Ge 28:18; 31:13, 45; 35:14, 20; Ex 24:4; De 27:2; Jos 4:9, 20; 22:28; 24:26; 1 S

7:12; 14:33; 15:12; 2 S 18:18; 1 K 7:21; Is 19:19

2. Saints

Je 1:18; Ga 2:9; Re 3:12

PILLOWS, *or bolsters*

1 S 19:13; Eze 13:18; Mk 4:38

PINE *See* **TREES**

PINING AWAY, *to wither or waste away from longing or grief*

Le 26:39; Is 24:16; Lam 4:9; Eze 4:17; 24:23; 33:10

PIPES *See* **MUSIC**

PISIDIA, *a district of Asia Minor*

Ac 13:14; 14:24

PISGAH *See* **MOUNTAINS AND HILLS**

PISON *See* **RIVERS**

PIT, *a hole dug as a well or cistern; used as a place of burial, a prison, or place of destruction*

Jb 33:18, 22; Ps 28:1; 30:3, 9; 55:23; 69:15; 88:4; 143:7; Is 14:15; 38:17; Eze 26:20; 32:18, 24, 29

PITCH, *tar*

Ge 6:14; Ex 2:3; Is 34:9

PITCHERS, *jars for temple or personal use*

Ge 24:14; Jud 7:16; Ec 12:6; Mk 14:13

PITILESSNESS, *condemned*

Ge 42:22; 2 S 11:25; 12:6; 2 Chr 36:17; Est 3:15; Jb 6:27; 24:9; Ps 35:15; 69:21; 109:16; Pr 24:11; 25:20; 28:3; Is 3:14; 9:19; 32:6; Je 6:23; 21:7; Eze 34:21; Am 1:11; Mt 18:25, 30; 20:31; Mk 15:24; Lu 10:32; Ja 2:16

See **MERCY, SYMPATHY**

PITY *See* **COMPASSION**

PLAGUES *See* **JUDGMENTS**

PLAN

1. Divine, *of the ark, tabernacle, and temple*

Ge 24:14; Jud 7:16; Ec 12:6; Mk 14:13

2. Human Schemes

a. Presumptuous

THE MEN AFTER THE FLOOD

Ge 11:4 And they said, Go to, let us build us a city and a tower, whose top *may reach* unto heaven; and let us make us a name, lest we be scattered abroad upon the face of the whole earth.

THE NATURAL MAN

Pr 19:21 *There are* many devices in a man's heart; nevertheless the counsel of the LORD, that shall stand.

THE LUXURIOUS KING

Je 22:13 Woe unto him that buildeth his house by unrighteousness, and his chambers by wrong; *that* useth his neighbour's service without wages, and giveth him not for his work;

Je 22:14 That saith, I will build me a wide house and large chambers, and cutteth him out windows; and *it is* cieled with cedar, and painted with vermilion.

THE RICH FOOL

Lu 12:18 And he said, This will I do: I will pull down my barns, and build greater; and there will I bestow all my fruits and my goods.

THE VENTURESOME BUSINESSMAN

Ja 4:13 Go to now, ye that say, To day or to morrow we will go into such a city, and continue there a year, and buy and sell, and get gain:

b. Evil

Ex 1:10 Come on, let us deal wisely with them; lest they multiply, and it come to pass, that, when there falleth out any war, they join also unto our enemies, and fight against us, and *so* get them up out of the land.

2 S 11:13 And when David had called him, he did eat and drink before him; and he made him drunk: and at even he went out to lie on his bed with the servants of his lord, but went not down to his house.

1 K 12:33 So he offered upon the altar which he had made in Bethel the fifteenth day of the eighth month, *even* in the month which he had devised of his own heart; and ordained a feast unto the children of Israel: and he offered upon the altar, and burnt incense.

1 K 21:10 And set two men, sons of Belial, before him, to bear witness against him, saying, Thou didst blaspheme God and the king. And *then* carry him out, and stone him, that he may die.

Ne 6:2 That Sanballat and Geshem sent unto me, saying, Come, let us meet together in *some one of* the villages in the plain of Ono. But they thought to do me mischief.

Est 8:3 And Esther spake yet again before the king, and fell down at his feet, and besought him with tears to put away the mischief of Haman the Agagite, and his device that he had devised against the Jews.

Est 9:24 Because Haman the son of Hammedatha, the Agagite, the enemy of all the Jews, had devised against the Jews to destroy them, and had cast Pur, that *is,* the lot, to consume them, and to destroy them;

Jb 15:35 They conceive mischief, and bring forth vanity, and their belly prepareth deceit.

Jb 21:27 Behold, I know your thoughts, and the devices *which* ye wrongfully imagine against me.

Ps 7:15 He made a pit, and digged it, and is fallen into the ditch *which* he made.

Ps 31:13 For I have heard the slander of many: fear *was* on every side: while they took counsel together against me, they devised to take away my life.

Ps 35:4 Let them be confounded and put to shame that seek after my soul: let them be turned back and brought to confusion that devise my hurt.

Ps 35:20 For they speak not peace: but they devise deceitful matters against *them that are* quiet in the land.

Ps 36:4 He deviseth mischief upon his bed; he setteth himself in a way *that is* not good; he abhorreth not evil.

Ps 37:7 Rest in the LORD, and wait patiently for him: fret not thyself because of him who prospereth in his way, because of the man who bringeth wicked devices to pass.

Ps 41:7 All that hate me whisper together against me: against me do they devise my hurt.

Ps 64:5 They encourage themselves *in* an evil matter: they commune of laying snares privily; they say, Who shall see them?

Ps 74:8 They said in their hearts, Let us destroy them together: they have burned up all the synagogues of God in the land.

Ps 140:4 Keep me, O LORD, from the hands of the wicked; preserve me from the violent man; who have purposed to overthrow my goings.

Ps 140:8 Grant not, O LORD, the desires of the wicked: further not his wicked device; *lest* they exalt themselves. Selah.

Pr 1:11 If they say, Come with us, let us lay wait for blood, let us lurk privily for the innocent without cause:

Pr 3:29 Devise not evil against thy neighbour, seeing he dwelleth securely by thee.

Pr 4:16 For they sleep not, except they have done mischief; and their sleep is taken away, unless they cause *some* to fall.

Pr 6:14 Frowardness *is* in his heart, he deviseth mischief continually; he soweth discord.

Pr 14:17 *He that is* soon angry dealeth foolishly: and a man of wicked devices is hated.

Pr 14:22 Do they not err that devise evil? but mercy and truth *shall be* to them that devise good.

Pr 16:30 He shutteth his eyes to devise froward things: moving his lips he bringeth evil to pass.

Pr 24:2 For their heart studieth destruction, and their lips talk of mischief.

Pr 24:8 He that deviseth to do evil shall be called a mischievous person.

Is 32:7 The instruments also of the churl *are* evil: he deviseth wicked devices to destroy the poor with lying words, even when the needy speaketh right.

Is 59:4 None calleth for justice, nor *any* pleadeth for truth: they trust in vanity, and speak lies; they conceive mischief, and bring forth iniquity.

Je 11:19 But I *was* like a lamb *or* an ox *that* is brought to the slaughter; and I knew not that they had devised devices against me, *saying,* Let us destroy the tree with the fruit thereof, and let us cut him off from the land of the living, that his name may be no more remembered.

Je 18:12 And they said, There is no hope: but we will walk after our own devices, and we will every one do the imagination of his evil heart.

Je 18:18 Then said they, Come, and let us devise devices against Jeremiah; for the law shall not perish from the priest, nor counsel from the wise, nor the word from the prophet. Come, and let us smite him with the tongue, and let us not give heed to any of his words.

Lam 3:62 The lips of those that rose up against me, and their device against me all the day.

Eze 11:2 Then said he unto me, Son of man, these *are* the men that devise mischief, and give wicked counsel in this city:

Eze 38:10 Thus saith the Lord GOD; It shall also come to pass, *that* at the same time shall things come into thy mind, and thou shalt think an evil thought:

Da 11:24 He shall enter peaceably even upon the fattest places of the province; and he shall do *that* which his fathers have not done, nor his fathers' fathers; he shall scatter among them the prey, and spoil, and riches: *yea,* and he shall forecast his devices against the strong holds, even for a time.

Ho 5:2 And the revolters are profound to make slaughter, though I *have been* a rebuker of them all.

Mi 2:1 Woe to them that devise iniquity, and work evil upon their beds! when the morning is light, they practise it, because it is in the power of their hand.

Na 1:8 But with an overrunning flood he will make an utter end of the place thereof, and darkness shall pursue his enemies.

Zec 7:10 And oppress not the widow, nor the fatherless, the stranger, nor the poor; and let none of you imagine evil against his brother in your heart.

Zec 8:17 And let none of you imagine evil in your hearts against his neighbour; and love no false oath: for all these *are things* that I hate, saith the Lord.

Mt 26:16 And from that time he sought opportunity to betray him.

Mt 27:64 Command therefore that the sepulchre be made sure until the third day, lest his disciples come by night, and steal him away, and say unto the people, He is risen from the dead: so the last error shall be worse than the first.

Mt 28:13 Saying, Say ye, His disciples came by night, and stole him *away* while we slept.

Mk 12:12 And they sought to lay hold on him, but feared the people: for they knew that he had spoken the parable against them: and they left him, and went their way.

Mk 14:11 And when they heard *it*, they were glad, and promised to give him money. And he sought how he might conveniently betray him.

Lu 22:6 And he promised, and sought opportunity to betray him unto them in the absence of the multitude.

Ac 5:4 Whiles it remained, was it not thine own? and after it was sold, was it not in thine own power? why hast thou conceived this thing in thine heart? thou hast not lied unto men, but unto God.

2 Ti 4:18 And the Lord shall deliver me from every evil work, and will preserve *me* unto his heavenly kingdom: to whom *be* glory for ever and ever. Amen.

c. Doomed

Est 9:1 Now in the twelfth month, that *is*, the month Adar, on the thirteenth day of the same, when the king's commandment and his decree drew near to be put in execution, in the day that the enemies of the Jews hoped to have power over them, (though it was turned to the contrary, that the Jews had rule over them that hated them;)

Est 9:25 But when *Esther* came before the king, he commanded by letters that his wicked device, which he devised against the Jews, should return upon his own head, and that he and his sons should be hanged on the gallows.

Jb 5:12 He disappointeth the devices of the crafty, so that their hands cannot perform *their* enterprise.

Ps 10:2 The wicked in *his* pride doth persecute the poor: let them be taken in the devices that they have imagined.

Ps 33:10 The Lord bringeth the counsel of the heathen to nought: he maketh the devices of the people of none effect.

Pr 6:18 An heart that deviseth wicked imaginations, feet that be swift in running to mischief,

Pr 12:2 A good *man* obtaineth favour of the Lord: but a man of wicked devices will he condemn.

Ac 5:9 Then Peter said unto her, How is it that ye have agreed together to tempt the Spirit of the Lord? behold, the feet of them which have buried thy husband *are* at the door, and shall carry thee out.

See **GOD, WICKED**

PLANTING *See* **AGRICULTURE**

PLANTS *See* **AGRICULTURE**

PLEADINGS, DIVINE, *earnest appeals of God*

Ps 81:13; Pr 1:24; Is 1:18; 3:13; 55:1; 65:2; Je 2:5, 9; 3:14; 7:25; 27:13; 31:22; 44:4; Eze 17:20; 18:23, 31; 20:36; 33:11; Ho 2:14; 14:1; Jl 3:2; Mi 6:3; Mt 22:4; 23:37; Ro 10:21; 2 Co 5:20

PLEIADES, *a group of stars*

Jb 9:9; 38:31; Am 5:8; Est 3:9; 5:14; Ps 36:4; 37:12; 59:3; 62:4; 64:2; 83:5; 94:21; Pr 6:14; 24:15; Is 32:7; Je 5:26; 18:20; Mi 2:1; Jn 12:10; Ac 23:30

PLEDGES *See* **CREDIT SYSTEM**

PLENTY, *promised to the obedient*

Ge 27:28 Therefore God give thee of the dew of heaven, and the fatness of the earth, and plenty of corn and wine:

Ge 41:29 Behold, there come seven years of great plenty throughout all the land of Egypt:

Ge 49:11 Binding his foal unto the vine, and his ass's colt unto the choice vine; he washed his garments in wine, and his clothes in the blood of grapes:

Ex 3:8 And I am come down to deliver them out of the hand of the Egyptians, and to bring them up out of that land unto a good land and a large, unto a land flowing with milk and honey; unto the place of the Canaanites, and the Hittites, and the Amorites, and the Perizzites, and the Hivites, and the Jebusites.

Ex 16:8 And Moses said, *This shall be,* when the LORD shall give you in the evening flesh to eat, and in the morning bread to the full; for that the LORD heareth your murmurings which ye murmur against him: and what *are* we? your murmurings *are* not against us, but against the LORD.

Le 25:19 And the land shall yield her fruit, and ye shall eat your fill, and dwell therein in safety.

Le 26:5 And your threshing shall reach unto the vintage, and the vintage shall reach unto the sowing time: and ye shall eat your bread to the full, and dwell in your land safely.

De 6:11 And houses full of all good *things,* which thou filledst not, and wells digged, which thou diggedst not, vineyards and olive trees, which thou plantedst not; when thou shalt have eaten and be full;

De 8:9 A land wherein thou shalt eat bread without scarceness, thou shalt not lack any *thing* in it; a land whose

stones are iron, and out of whose hills thou mayest dig brass.

De 11:15 And I will send grass in thy fields for thy cattle, that thou mayest eat and be full.

De 28:5 Blessed *shall be* thy basket and thy store.

De 28:11 And the LORD shall make thee plenteous in goods, in the fruit of thy body, and in the fruit of thy cattle, and in the fruit of thy ground, in the land which the LORD sware unto thy fathers to give thee.

De 30:9 And the LORD thy God will make thee plenteous in every work of thine hand, in the fruit of thy body, and in the fruit of thy cattle, and in the fruit of thy land, for good: for the LORD will again rejoice over thee for good, as he rejoiced over thy fathers:

De 33:19 They shall call the people unto the mountain; there they shall offer sacrifices of righteousness: for they shall suck *of* the abundance of the seas, and *of* treasures hid in the sand.

Ru 2:14 And Boaz said unto her, At mealtime come thou hither, and eat of the bread, and dip thy morsel in the vinegar. And she sat beside the reapers: and he reached her parched *corn,* and she did eat, and was sufficed, and left.

1 K 17:14 For thus saith the LORD God of Israel, The barrel of meal shall not waste, neither shall the cruse of oil fail, until the day *that* the LORD sendeth rain upon the earth.

2 K 4:44 So he set *it* before them, and they did eat, and left *thereof,* according to the word of the LORD.

2 K 19:29 And this *shall be* a sign unto thee, Ye shall eat this year such things as grow of themselves, and in the second year that which springeth of the same; and in the third year sow ye, and reap, and plant vineyards, and eat the fruits thereof.

Job 36:16 Even so would he have removed thee out of the strait *into* a broad place, where *there is* no straitness; and that which *should be* set on thy table should be full of fatness.

Ps 34:9 O fear the LORD, ye his saints: for *there is* no want to them that fear him.

Ps 78:27 He rained flesh also upon them as dust, and feathered fowls like as the sand of the sea:

Ps 81:16 He should have fed them also with the finest of the wheat: and with honey out of the rock should I have satisfied thee.

Ps 85:12 Yea, the LORD shall give *that which is* good; and our land shall yield her increase.

Ps 132:15 I will abundantly bless her provision: I will satisfy her poor with bread.

Ps 144:13 *That* our garners *may be* full, affording all manner of store: *that* our sheep may bring forth thousands and ten thousands in our streets:

Ps 147:14 He maketh peace *in* thy borders, *and* filleth thee with the finest of the wheat.

Pr 3:10 So shall thy barns be filled with plenty, and thy presses shall burst out with new wine.

Pr 10:3 The LORD will not suffer the soul of the righteous to famish: but he casteth away the substance of the wicked.

Pr 13:25 The righteous eateth to the satisfying of his soul: but the belly of the wicked shall want.

Pr 27:27 And *thou shalt have* goats' milk enough for thy food, for the food of thy household, and *for* the maintenance for thy maidens.

Pr 28:19 He that tilleth his land shall have plenty of bread: but he that followeth after vain *persons* shall have poverty enough.

Is 1:19 If ye be willing and obedient, ye shall eat the good of the land:

Is 4:2 In that day shall the branch of the LORD be beautiful and glorious, and the fruit of the earth *shall be* excellent and comely for them that are escaped of Israel.

Is 30:23 Then shall he give the rain of thy seed, that thou shalt sow the ground withal; and bread of the increase of the earth, and it shall be fat and plenteous: in that day shall thy cattle feed in large pastures.

Is 33:16 He shall dwell on high: his place of defence *shall be* the munitions of rocks: bread shall be given him; his waters *shall be* sure.

Is 37:30 And this *shall be* a sign unto thee, Ye shall eat *this* year such as groweth of itself; and the second year that which springeth of the same: and in the third year sow ye, and reap, and plant vineyards, and eat the fruit thereof.

Is 62:9 But they that have gathered it shall eat it, and praise the LORD; and they that have brought it together shall drink it in the courts of my holiness.

Je 31:12 Therefore they shall come and sing in the height of Zion, and shall flow together to the goodness of the LORD, for wheat, and for wine, and for oil, and for the young of the flock and of the herd: and their soul shall be as a watered garden; and they shall not sorrow any more at all.

Eze 34:27 And the tree of the field shall yield her fruit, and the earth shall yield her increase, and they shall be safe in their land, and shall know that I *am* the LORD, when I have broken the bands of their yoke, and delivered them out of the hand of those that served themselves of them.

Eze 34:29 And I will raise up for them a plant of renown, and they shall be no more consumed with hunger in the land, neither bear the shame of the heathen any more.

Eze 36:30 And I will multiply the fruit of the tree, and the increase of the field, that ye shall receive no more reproach of famine among the heathen.

Joel 2:24 And the floors shall be full of wheat, and the fats shall overflow with wine and oil.

Joel 3:18 And it shall come to pass in that day, *that* the mountains shall drop down new wine, and the hills shall flow with milk, and all the rivers of Judah shall flow with waters, and a fountain shall come forth of the house of the LORD, and shall water the valley of Shittim.

Am 9:13 Behold, the days come, saith the LORD, that the plowman shall overtake the reaper, and the treader of grapes him that soweth seed; and the mountains shall drop sweet wine, and all the hills shall melt.

Zec 8:12 For the seed *shall be* prosperous; the vine shall give her fruit, and the ground shall give her increase, and the heavens shall give their dew; and I will cause the remnant of this people to possess all these *things*.

Zec 9:17 For how great *is* his goodness, and how great *is* his beauty! corn shall make the young men cheerful, and new wine the maids.

Mal 3:10 Bring ye all the tithes into the storehouse, that there may be meat in mine house, and prove me now herewith, saith the LORD of hosts, if I will not open you the windows of heaven, and pour you out a blessing, that *there shall* not *be room* enough *to receive it.*

Mt 6:32 (For after all these things do the Gentiles seek:) for your heavenly Father knoweth that ye have need of all these things.

Mk 6:42 And they did all eat, and were filled.

Lu 12:31 But rather seek ye the kingdom of God; and all these things shall be added unto you.

See **ABUNDANCE, POOR, RICHES,**

PLOTTING, *prearranging secretly or deviously*

Est 3:9; 5:14; Ps 36:4; 37:12; 59:3; 62:4; 64:2; 83:5; 94:21; Pr 6:14; 24:15; Is 32:7; Je 5:26; 18:20; Mi 2:1; Jn 12:10; Ac 23:30

1. Against Christ

Ps 64:4 That they may shoot in secret at the perfect: suddenly do they shoot at him, and fear not.

Mt 12:14 Then the Pharisees went out, and held a council against him, how they might destroy him.

Mt 21:38 But when the husbandmen saw the son, they said among themselves, This is the heir; come, let us kill him, and let us seize on his inheritance.

Mt 21:46 But when they sought to lay hands on him, they feared the multitude, because they took him for a prophet.

Mt 22:15 Then went the Pharisees, and took counsel how they might entangle him in *his* talk.

Mt 22:17 Tell us therefore, What thinkest thou? Is it lawful to give tribute unto Caesar, or not?

Mt 26:4 And consulted that they might take Jesus by subtilty, and kill *him.*

Mt 26:16 And from that time he sought opportunity to betray him.

Mt 27:1 When the morning was come, all the chief priests and elders of the people took counsel against Jesus to put him to death:

Mt 28:12 And when they were assembled with the elders, and had taken counsel, they gave large money unto the soldiers,

Mk 3:6 And the Pharisees went forth, and straightway took counsel with the Herodians against him, how they might destroy him.

Mk 11:18 And the scribes and chief priests heard *it,* and sought how they might destroy him: for they feared him, because all the people was astonished at his doctrine.

Mk 12:7 But those husbandmen said among themselves, This is the heir; come, let us kill him, and the inheritance shall be ours.

Mk 12:15 Shall we give, or shall we not give? But he, knowing their hypocrisy, said unto them, Why tempt ye me? bring me a penny, that I may see *it.*

Mk 14:1 After two days was *the feast of* the passover, and of unleavened bread: and the chief priests and the scribes sought how they might take him by craft, and put *him* to death.

Mk 14:55 And the chief priests and all the council sought for witness against Jesus to put him to death; and found none.

Lu 6:11 And they were filled with madness; and communed one with another what they might do to Jesus.

Lu 19:47 And he taught daily in the temple. But the chief priests and the scribes and the chief of the people sought to destroy him,

Lu 20:14 But when the husbandmen saw him, they reasoned among themselves, saying, This is the heir: come, let us kill him, that the inheritance may be ours.

Lu 22:4 And he went his way, and communed with the chief priests and captains, how he might betray him unto them.

Jn 5:16 And therefore did the Jews persecute Jesus, and sought to slay him, because he had done these things on the sabbath day.

Jn 7:19 Did not Moses give you the law, and *yet* none of you keepeth the law? Why go ye about to kill me?

Jn 7:30 Then they sought to take him: but no man laid hands on him, because his hour was not yet come.

Jn 8:37 I know that ye are Abraham's seed; but ye seek to kill me, because my word hath no place in you.

Jn 11:47 Then gathered the chief priests and the Pharisees a council, and said, What do we? for this man doeth many miracles.

Jn 11:53 Then from that day forth they took counsel together for to put him to death.

Ac 9:23 And after that many days were fulfilled, the Jews took counsel to kill him:

Ac 23:15 Now therefore ye with the council signify to the chief captain that he bring him down unto you to morrow, as though ye would enquire something more perfectly concerning him: and we, or ever he come near, are ready to kill him.

2. Examples

Ge 37:18; Nu 16:3; Jud 9:1; 2 S 15:12; 1 K 1:7; 15:27; 16:9; 21:10; 2 K 9:14; 12:20; 14:19; 15:10, 15, 25, 30; 17:4; 21:23; 2 Chr 24:21, 25; 25:27; 33:24; Est 2:21; 6:2; Ps 31:13; 56:6; 59:3; Pr 11:21; 16:5; Is 7:5; Je 40:14; Da 6:4; Mt 12:14; 27:1; Mk 3:6; Ac 23:12, 15

See **BETRAYAL, TREACHERY**

PLOWING *See* AGRICULTURE

PLUMMET, *plumb line*

Am 7:7; Zec 4:10

POISON, *burning venom of poisonous snakes*

De 32:24; Jb 20:16; Ps 58:4; 140:3; Ja 3:8

POLITICAL CORRUPTION

See **NATION**

POLLUTIONS, *contaminations*

1. Ceremonial, *under the Mosaic Law*

Le 7:21; 11:24, 27, 31, 35, 39; 15:11, 21, 27; 21:1; 22:5; Nu 9:6; 19:14, 22; 35:33; De 21:23 Eze 4:14

2. Of the Heathen

Le 18:24; 20:23; De 18:12; Eze 14:11; 23:30; 2 Pe 2:7, 20

3. Of God's House

Nu 19:13, 20; 2 K 16:18; 21:4, 7; 2 Chr 29:5; 33:7; 36:14; Ne 13:7; Ps 74:3; 79:1; Is 63:18; Je 7:11, 30; 23:11; 32:34; 51:51; Lam 1:10; Eze 5:11; 7:22; 8:6, 16; 23:38; 25:3; 44:7; Da 8:13; 11:31; Zep 3:4; Mt 21:13; Mk 11:15; Lu 19:46; Jn 2:14

See **CLEANSING**

POLYGAMY

See **FAMILY, MARRIAGE**

POMEGRANATES

See **AGRICULTURE, TREES**

PONTUS, *a province of Asia Minor*

Ac 2:9; 1 Pe 1:1

POOLS, *a gathering of water*

2 S 2:13; 1 K 22:38; 2 K 20:20; Ne 3:15; Ec 2:6; Is 14:23; 35:7

POOR, *those who need help*

Ps 9:18 For the needy shall not alway be forgotten: the expectation of the poor shall *not* perish for ever.

Ps 35:10 All my bones shall say, Lord, who *is* like unto thee, which deliverest the poor from him that is too strong for him, yea, the poor and the needy from him that spoileth him?

Ps 40:17 But I *am* poor and needy; *yet* the Lord thinketh upon me: thou *art* my help and my deliverer; make no tarrying, O my God.

Ps 69:29 But I *am* poor and sorrowful: let thy salvation, O God, set me up on high.

Ps 70:5 But I *am* poor and needy: make haste unto me, O God: thou *art* my help and my deliverer; O LORD, make no tarrying.

Ps 72:12 For he shall deliver the needy when he crieth; the poor also, and *him* that hath no helper.

Ps 74:21 O let not the oppressed return ashamed: let the poor and needy praise thy name.

Ps 82:4 Deliver the poor and needy: rid *them* out of the hand of the wicked.

Ps 86:1 Bow down thine ear, O LORD, hear me: for I *am* poor and needy.

Ps 109:22 For I *am* poor and needy, and my heart is wounded within me.

Eze 22:29 The people of the land have used oppression, and exercised robbery, and have vexed the poor and needy: yea, they have oppressed the stranger wrongfully.

Lu 6:20 And he lifted up his eyes on his disciples, and said, Blessed *be ye* poor: for yours is the kingdom of God.

See **GIVING, HELP, KINDNESS, MONEY, OPPRESSION**

POPULARITY, *state of being widely acclaimed*

1. Of Christ

a. The Multitudes Follow Him

2 Chr 30:13 And there assembled at Jerusalem much people to keep the feast of unleavened bread in the second month, a very great congregation.

Is 60:8 Who *are* these *that* fly as a cloud, and as the doves to their windows?

Mt 4:25 And there followed him great multitudes of people from Galilee, and *from* Decapolis, and *from* Jerusalem, and *from* Judaea, and *from* beyond Jordan.

Mt 13:2 And great multitudes were gathered together unto him, so that he went into a ship, and sat; and the whole multitude stood on the shore.

Mt 15:30 And great multitudes came unto him, having with them *those that were* lame, blind, dumb, maimed, and many others, and cast them down at Jesus' feet; and he healed them:

Mt 19:2 And great multitudes followed him; and he healed them there.

Mk 1:33 And all the city was gathered together at the door.

Mk 2:13 And he went forth again by the sea side; and all the multitude resorted unto him, and he taught them.

Mk 3:20 And the multitude cometh together again, so that they could not so much as eat bread.

Lu 12:1 In the mean time, when there were gathered together an innumerable multitude of people, insomuch that they trode one upon another, he began to say unto his disciples first of all, Beware ye of the leaven of the Pharisees, which is hypocrisy.

b. The Crowds Press upon Him

Mk 2:2 And straightway many were gathered together, insomuch that there was no room to receive *them*, no, not so much as about the door: and he preached the word unto them.

Mk 3:10 For he had healed many; insomuch that they pressed upon him for to touch him, as many as had plagues.

Mk 5:24 And *Jesus* went with him; and much people followed him, and thronged him.

Lu 5:1 And it came to pass, that, as the people pressed upon him to hear the word of God, he stood by the lake of Gennesaret,

Lu 8:19 Then came to him *his* mother and his brethren, and could not come at him for the press.

Lu 8:45 And Jesus said, Who touched me? When all denied,, Peter and they that were with him said, Master, the multitude throng thee and press *thee*, and sayest thou, Who touched me?

Jn 12:19 The Pharisees therefore said among themselves, Perceive ye how ye prevail nothing? behold, the world is gone after him.

c. The Common People Heard Him Gladly

Mt 4:25; Mk 12:12, 37; 14:2; Lu 19:48; Jn 12:9

2. Sought by Men

Je 38:5; Mt 26:5; 27:15; Mk 15:15; Jn 12:43; 19:16; Ac 12:1–3; 24:27; 25:9; Ga 1:10; Ep 6:6; Col 3:22; 1 Th 2:4

See **HATE, PARADOXES, PERSPECTIVE, WORLDLINESS**

PORCHES, *vestibules, porticos*

Jud 3:23; 1 K 6:3; 7:6; 1 Chr 28:11; 2 Chr 3:4; Eze 40:7, 39, 49; 41:15, 26; 46:8; Jn 10:23; Ac 3:11

PORTERS *See* **ARTS AND CRAFTS**

POSTERITY

Ge 13:16 And I will make thy seed as the dust of the earth: so that if a man can number the dust of the earth, *then* shall thy seed also be numbered.

Ge 15:5 And he brought him forth abroad, and said, Look now toward heaven, and tell the stars, if thou be able to number them: and he said unto him, So shall thy seed be.

Ge 15:18 In the same day the LORD made a covenant with Abram, saying, Unto thy seed have I given this land, from the river of Egypt unto the great river, the river Euphrates:

Ge 16:10 And the angel of the LORD said unto her, I will multiply thy seed exceedingly, that it shall not be numbered for multitude.

Ge 17:6 And I will make thee exceeding fruitful, and I will make nations of thee, and kings shall come out of thee.

Ge 17:20 And as for Ishmael, I have heard thee: Behold, I have blessed him, and will make him fruitful, and will multiply him exceedingly; twelve princes shall he beget, and I will make him a great nation.

Ge 22:17 That in blessing I will bless thee, and in multiplying I will multiply thy seed as the stars of the heaven, and as the sand which *is* upon the sea shore; and thy seed shall possess the gate of his enemies;

Ge 26:4 And I will make thy seed to multiply as the stars of heaven, and will give unto thy seed all these countries; and in thy seed shall all the nations of the earth be blessed;

Ge 26:24 And the LORD appeared unto him the same night, and said, I *am* the God of Abraham thy father: fear not, for I *am* with thee, and will bless thee, and multiply thy seed for my servant Abraham's sake.

Ge 28:14 And thy seed shall be as the dust of the earth, and thou shalt spread abroad to the west, and to the east, and to the north, and to the south: and in thee and in thy seed shall all the families of the earth be blessed.

Ge 35:11 And God said unto him, I *am* God Almighty: be fruitful and multiply; a nation and a company of nations shall be of thee, and kings shall come out of thy loins;

Ge 46:3 And he said, I *am* God, the God of thy father: fear not to go down into Egypt; for I will there make of thee a great nation:

Ge 48:4 And said unto me, Behold, I will make thee fruitful, and multiply thee, and I will make of thee a multitude of people; and will give this land to thy seed after thee *for* an everlasting possession.

Ge 48:19 And his father refused, and said, I know *it*, my son, I know *it:* he also shall become a people, and he also shall be great: but truly his younger brother shall be greater than he, and his seed shall become a multitude of nations.

Ex 1:7 And the children of Israel were fruitful, and increased abundantly, and multiplied, and waxed exceeding mighty; and the land was filled with them.

Ex 12:37 And the children of Israel journeyed from Rameses to Succoth, about six hundred thousand on foot *that were* men, beside children.

Ex 32:13 Remember Abraham, Isaac, and Israel, thy servants, to whom thou swarest by thine own self, and saidst unto them, I will multiply your seed as the stars of heaven, and all this land that I have spoken of will I give unto your seed, and they shall inherit *it* for ever.

Le 26:9 For I will have respect unto you, and make you fruitful, and multiply you, and establish my covenant with you.

Nu 23:10 Who can count the dust of Jacob, and the number of the fourth *part* of Israel? Let me die the death of the righteous, and let my last end be like his!

De 1:11 (The LORD God of your fathers make you a thousand times so many more as ye *are,* and bless you, as he hath promised you!)

De 6:3 Hear therefore, O Israel, and observe to do *it;* that it may be well with thee, and that ye may increase mightily, as the LORD God of thy fathers hath promised thee, in the land that floweth with milk and honey.

De 7:13 And he will love thee, and bless thee, and multiply thee: he will also bless the fruit of thy womb, and the fruit of thy land, thy corn, and thy wine, and thine oil, the increase of thy kine, and the flocks of thy sheep, in the land which he sware unto thy fathers to give thee.

De 10:22 Thy fathers went down into Egypt with threescore and ten persons; and now the LORD thy God hath made thee as the stars of heaven for multitude.

De 13:17 And there shall cleave nought of the cursed thing to thine hand: that the LORD may turn from the fierceness of his anger, and shew thee mercy, and have compassion upon thee, and multiply thee, as he hath sworn unto thy fathers;

De 26:5 And thou shalt speak and say before the LORD thy God, A Syrian ready to perish *was* my father, and he went down into Egypt, and sojourned there with a few, and became there a nation, great, mighty, and populous:

De 28:11 And the LORD shall make thee plenteous in goods, in the fruit of thy body, and in the fruit of thy cattle, and in the fruit of thy ground, in the

land which the LORD sware unto thy fathers to give thee.

De 30:5 And the LORD thy God will bring thee into the land which thy fathers possessed, and thou shalt possess it; and he will do thee good, and multiply thee above thy fathers.

De 30:16 In that I command thee this day to love the LORD thy God, to walk in his ways, and to keep his commandments and his statutes and his judgments, that thou mayest live and multiply: and the LORD thy God shall bless thee in the land whither thou goest to possess it.

De 33:24 And of Asher he said, *Let* Asher *be* blessed with children; let him be acceptable to his brethren, and let him dip his foot in oil.

2 S 7:12 And when thy days be fulfilled, and thou shalt sleep with thy fathers, I will set up thy seed after thee, which shall proceed out of thy bowels, and I will establish his kingdom.

1 K 4:20 Judah and Israel *were* many, as the sand which *is* by the sea in multitude, eating and drinking, and making merry.

1 Chr 17:11 And it shall come to pass, when thy days be expired that thou must go *to be* with thy fathers, that I will raise up thy seed after thee, which shall be of thy sons; and I will establish his kingdom.

1 Chr 27:23 But David took not the number of them from twenty years old and under: because the LORD had said he would increase Israel like to the stars of the heavens.

Ne 9:23 Their children also multipliedst thou as the stars of heaven, and broughtest them into the land, concerning which thou hadst promised to their fathers, that they should go in to possess *it.*

Jb 5:25 Thou shalt know also that thy seed *shall be* great, and thine offspring as the grass of the earth.

Ps 107:38 He blesseth them also, so that they are multiplied greatly; and suffereth not their cattle to decrease.

Ps 113:9 He maketh the barren woman to keep house, *and to be* a joyful mother of children. Praise ye the LORD.

Ps 115:14 The LORD shall increase you more and more, you and your children.

Ps 128:3 Thy wife *shall be* as a fruitful vine by the sides of thine house: thy children like olive plants round about thy table.

Is 48:19 Thy seed also had been as the sand, and the offspring of thy bowels like the gravel thereof; his name should not have been cut off nor destroyed from before me.

Is 51:2 Look unto Abraham your father, and unto Sarah *that* bare you: for I called him alone, and blessed him, and increased him.

Je 30:19 And out of them shall proceed thanksgiving and the voice of them that make merry: and I will multiply them, and they shall not be few; I will also glorify them, and they shall not be small.

Je 33:22 As the host of heaven cannot be numbered, neither the sand of the sea measured: so will I multiply the seed of David my servant, and the Levites that minister unto me.

Je 35:19 Therefore thus saith the LORD of hosts, the God of Israel; Jonadab the son of Rechab shall not want a man to stand before me for ever.

Eze 16:7 I have caused thee to multiply as the bud of the field, and thou hast increased and waxen great, and thou art come to excellent ornaments: *thy* breasts are fashioned, and thine hair is grown, whereas thou *wast* naked and bare.

Eze 37:26 Moreover I will make a covenant of peace with them; it shall be an everlasting covenant with them: and I will place them, and multiply them, and will set my sanctuary in the midst of them for evermore.

Ho 1:10 Yet the number of the children of Israel shall be as the sand of the sea, which cannot be measured nor numbered; and it shall come to pass, *that* in the place where it was said unto them, Ye *are* not my people, *there* it shall be said unto them, *Ye are* the sons of the living God.

Zec 10:8 I will hiss for them, and gather them; for I have redeemed them: and they shall increase as they have increased.

Ac 7:17 But when the time of the promise drew nigh, which God had sworn to Abraham, the people grew and multiplied in Egypt,

Ro 4:18 Who against hope believed in hope, that he might become the father of many nations; according to that which was spoken, So shall thy seed be.

He 6:14 Saying, Surely blessing I will bless thee, and multiplying I will multiply thee.

He 11:11 Through faith also Sara herself received strength to conceive seed, and was delivered of a child when she was past age, because she judged him faithful who had promised.

See **CHILDREN, FAMILY**

POSTS, *runners*

2 Chr 30:6; Est 3:13; 8:10; Jb 9:25; Je 51:31

POTTAGE, *a thick vegetable soup, stew*

Ge 25:29; 2 K 4:38; Hag 2:12

POTTERS *See* **ARTS AND CRAFTS**

POVERTY, *state of being poor*

Ne 5:5 Yet now our flesh *is* as the flesh of our brethren, our children as their children: and, lo, we bring into bondage our sons and our daughters to be servants, and *some* of our daughters are brought unto bondage *already:* neither *is it* in our power *to redeem them;* for other men have our lands and vineyards.

Jb 24:7 They cause the naked to lodge without clothing, that *they have* no covering in the cold.

Pr 10:15 The rich man's wealth *is* his strong city: the destruction of the poor *is* their poverty.

Pr 30:8 Remove far from me vanity and lies: give me neither poverty nor riches; feed me with food convenient for me:

Is 3:7 In that day shall he swear, saying, I will not be an healer; for in my house *is* neither bread nor clothing: make me not a ruler of the people.

Mk 5:26 And had suffered many things of many physicians, and had spent all that she had, and was nothing bettered, but rather grew worse,

1. Of the Righteous

GIDEON

Jud 6:15 And he said unto him, Oh my Lord, wherewith shall I save Israel? behold, my family is poor in Manasseh, and I *am* the least in my father's house.

THE WIDOW OF ZAREPHATH

1 K 17:12 And she said, *As* the LORD thy God liveth, I have not a cake, but an handful of meal in a barrel, and a little oil in a cruse: and, behold, I *am* gathering two sticks, that I may go in and dress it for me and my son, that we may eat it, and die.

THE PROPHET'S WIDOW

2 K 4:1 Now there cried a certain woman of the wives of the sons of the prophets unto Elisha, saying, Thy servant my husband is dead; and thou knowest that thy servant did fear the LORD: and the creditor is come to take unto him my two sons to be bondmen.

CHRIST

Mt 8:20 And Jesus saith unto him, The foxes have holes, and the birds of the air *have* nests; but the Son of man hath not where to lay *his* head.

THE WIDOW WHO GAVE TWO MITES

Mk 12:42 And there came a certain poor widow, and she threw in two mites, which make a farthing.

PAUL

2 Co 6:10 As sorrowful, yet alway rejoicing; as poor, yet making many rich; as having nothing, and *yet* possessing all things.

2 Co 8:9 For ye know the grace of our Lord Jesus Christ, that, though he was rich, yet for your sakes he became poor, that ye through his poverty might be rich.

THE CHURCH AT SMYRNA

Re 2:9 I know thy works, and tribulation, and poverty, (but thou art rich) and *I know* the blasphemy of them which say they are Jews, and are not, but *are* the synagogue of Satan.

2. Contributing Causes

INDOLENCE

Pr 6:10 *Yet* a little sleep, a little slumber, a little folding of the hands to sleep:

Pr 6:11 So shall thy poverty come as one that travelleth, and thy want as an armed man.

PARSIMONY

Pr 11:24 There is that scattereth, and yet increaseth; and *there is* that withholdeth more than is meet, but *it tendeth* to poverty.

Pr 20:13 Love not sleep, lest thou come to poverty; open thine eyes, *and* thou shalt be satisfied with bread.

LOVE OF PLEASURE

Pr 21:17 He that loveth pleasure *shall be* a poor man: he that loveth wine and oil shall not be rich.

DRUNKENNESS AND GLUTTONY

Pr 23:21 For the drunkard and the glutton shall come to poverty: and drowsiness shall clothe *a man* with rags.

Pr 24:34 So shall thy poverty come as one that travelleth; and thy want as an armed man.

EVIL ASSOCIATIONS

Pr 28:19 He that tilleth his land shall have plenty of bread: but he that followeth after vain *persons* shall have poverty enough.

3. Spiritual

a. Destitution of the Truth

1 S 3:1 And the child Samuel ministered unto the LORD before Eli. And the word of the LORD was precious in those days; *there was* no open vision.

2 Chr 15:3 Now for a long season Israel *hath been* without the true God, and without a teaching priest, and without law.

Ps 74:9 We see not our signs: *there is* no more any prophet: neither *is there* among us any that knoweth how long.

Is 30:20 And *though* the Lord give you the bread of adversity, and the water of affliction, yet shall not thy teachers be removed into a corner any more, but thine eyes shall see thy teachers:

Is 51:18 *There is* none to guide her among all the sons *whom* she hath brought forth; neither *is there any* that taketh her by the hand of all the sons *that* she hath brought up.

Lam 2:9 Her gates are sunk into the ground; he hath destroyed and broken her bars: her king and her princes *are* among the Gentiles: the law *is* no *more;* her prophets also find no vision from the LORD.

Eze 7:26 Mischief shall come upon mischief, and rumour shall be upon rumour; then shall they seek a vision of the prophet; but the law shall perish from the priest, and counsel from the ancients.

Am 8:11 Behold, the days come, saith the Lord God, that I will send a famine in the land, not a famine of bread, nor a thirst for water, but of hearing the words of the LORD:

Lu 15:14 And when he had spent all, there arose a mighty famine in that land; and he began to be in want.

Ep 2:12 That at that time ye were without Christ, being aliens from the commonwealth of Israel, and strangers from the covenants of promise, having no hope, and without God in the world:

1 Ti 6:5 Perverse disputings of men of corrupt minds, and destitute of the truth, supposing that gain is godliness: from such withdraw thyself.

Re 3:17 Because thou sayest, I am rich, and increased with goods, and have need of nothing; and knowest not that thou art wretched, and miserable, and poor, and blind, and naked:

b. Examples of Moral and Spiritual Bankruptcy

INHABITANTS OF JERUSALEM

Je 5:4 Therefore I said, Surely these *are* poor; they are foolish: for they know not the way of the LORD, *nor* the judgment of their God.

THE BANKRUPT SERVANT

Mt 18:23–25 Therefore is the kingdom of heaven likened unto a certain king, which would take account of his servants.

And when he had begun to reckon, one was brought unto him, which owed him ten thousand talents.

But forasmuch as he had not to pay, his lord commanded him to be sold, and his wife, and children, and all that he had, and payment to be made.

THE PRODIGAL SON

Lu 15:14 And when he had spent all, there arose a mighty famine in that land; and he began to be in want.

THE GENTILES

Ep 2:12 That at that time ye were without Christ, being aliens from the commonwealth of Israel, and strangers from the covenants of promise, having no hope, and without God in the world:

THE LAODICEAN CHURCH

Re 3:17 Because thou sayest, I am rich, and increased with goods, and have need of nothing; and knowest not that thou art wretched, and miserable, and poor, and blind, and naked:

4. The Poor

De 15:11 For the poor shall never cease out of the land: therefore I command thee, saying, Thou shalt open thine hand wide unto thy brother, to thy poor, and to thy needy, in thy land.

Is 7:21 And it shall come to pass, in that day, *that* a man shall nourish a young cow, and two sheep;

Zep 3:12 I will also leave in the midst of thee an afflicted and poor people, and they shall trust in the name of the LORD.

Mt 26:11 For ye have the poor always with you; but me ye have not always.

Ep 4:28 Let him that stole steal no more: but rather let him labour, working with *his* hands the thing which is good, that he may have to give to him that needeth.

a. Divine Care

Le 14:21 And if he *be* poor, and cannot get so much; then he shall take one lamb *for* a trespass offering to be waved, to make an atonement for him, and one tenth deal of fine flour mingled with oil for a meat offering, and a log of oil;

De 15:4 Save when there shall be no poor among you; for the LORD shall greatly bless thee in the land which the LORD thy God giveth thee *for* an inheritance to possess it:

1 S 2:8 He raiseth up the poor out of the dust, *and* lifteth up the beggar from the dunghill, to set *them* among princes, and to make them inherit the throne of glory: for the pillars of the earth *are* the LORD's, and he hath set the world upon them.

Jb 36:6 He preserveth not the life of the wicked: but giveth right to the poor.

Jb 36:15 He delivereth the poor in his affliction, and openeth their ears in oppression.

Ps 9:18 For the needy shall not alway be forgotten: the expectation of the poor shall *not* perish for ever.

Ps 10:14 Thou hast seen *it;* for thou beholdest mischief and spite, to requite *it* with thy hand: the poor committeth himself unto thee; thou art the helper of the fatherless.

Ps 10:18 To judge the fatherless and the oppressed, that the man of the earth may no more oppress.

Ps 35:10 All my bones shall say, LORD, who *is* like unto thee, which deliverest the poor from him that is

too strong for him, yea, the poor and the needy from him that spoileth him?

Ps 74:19 O deliver not the soul of thy turtledove unto the multitude *of the wicked:* forget not the congregation of thy poor for ever.

Pr 22:23 For the LORD will plead their cause, and spoil the soul of those that spoiled them.

Pr 23:11 For their redeemer *is* mighty; he shall plead their cause with thee.

Ec 5:8 If thou seest the oppression of the poor, and violent perverting of judgment and justice in a province, marvel not at the matter: for *he that is* higher than the highest regardeth; and *there be* higher than they.

Je 20:13 Sing unto the LORD, praise ye the LORD: for he hath delivered the soul of the poor from the hand of evildoers.

Je 39:10 But Nebuzar-adan the captain of the guard left of the poor of the people, which had nothing, in the land of Judah, and gave them vineyards and fields at the same time.

Lu 16:22 And it came to pass, that the beggar died, and was carried by the angels into Abraham's bosom: the rich man also died, and was buried;

Jn 13:29 For some *of them* thought, because Judas had the bag, that Jesus had said unto him, Buy *those things* that we have need of against the feast; or, that he should give something to the poor.

b. Human Justice Commanded

Ps 82:3 Defend the poor and fatherless: do justice to the afflicted and needy.

Pr 21:13 Whoso stoppeth his ears at the cry of the poor, he also shall cry himself, but shall not be heard.

Pr 29:14 The king that faithfully judgeth the poor, his throne shall be established for ever.

Je 22:16 He judged the cause of the poor and needy; then *it was* well *with him: was* not this to know me? saith the LORD.

Ja 2:2 For if there come unto your assembly a man with a gold ring, in goodly apparel, and there come in also a poor man in vile raiment;

c. Human Kindness Prescribed

Ex 23:11 But the seventh *year* thou shalt let it rest and lie still; that the poor of thy people may eat: and what they leave the beasts of the field shall eat. In like manner thou shalt deal with thy vineyard, *and* with thy oliveyard.

Le 25:25 If thy brother be waxen poor, and hath sold away *some* of his possession, and if any of his kin come to redeem it, then shall he redeem that which his brother sold.

De 15:7 If there be among you a poor man of one of thy brethren within any of thy gates in thy land which the LORD thy God giveth thee, thou shalt not harden thine heart, nor shut thine hand from thy poor brother:

De 24:12 And if the man *be* poor, thou shalt not sleep with his pledge:

Ps 41:1 Blessed *is* he that considereth the poor: the LORD will deliver him in time of trouble.

Pr 14:21 He that despiseth his neighbour sinneth: but he that hath mercy on the poor, happy *is* he.

Pr 19:17 He that hath pity upon the poor lendeth unto the LORD; and that which he hath given will he pay him again.

Pr 28:8 He that by usury and unjust gain increaseth his substance, he shall gather it for him that will pity the poor.

Pr 28:27 He that giveth unto the poor shall not lack: but he that hideth his eyes shall have many a curse.

Mt 19:21 Jesus said unto him, If thou wilt be perfect, go *and* sell that thou hast, and give to the poor, and thou shalt have treasure in heaven: and come *and* follow me.

Ga 2:10 Only *they would* that we should remember the poor; the same which I also was forward to do.

d. Neglect and Oppression

2 S 12:4; Jb 24:4; 31:16; 34:28; Ps 10:2, 9; 37:14; 109:16; Pr 14:31; 17:5; 28:3; 30:14; Ec 5:8; Is 3:15; 10:2; 32:7; Eze 16:49; 18:12; Am 2:6; 4:1; 5:11; 8:4; Hab 3:14; Zec 7:10; Mt 25:42

e. Despised

Pr 14:20; 19:4, 7; Ec 9:16; Ja 2:3, 6

See **AVARICE, COVETOUSNESS, GREED, JUSTICE, KINDNESS, OPPRESSION, PARTIALITY, POOR, RICHES**

POWER

1. Spiritual

GIVES MEN COURAGE TO REBUKE SIN

Mi 3:8 But truly I am full of power by the spirit of the LORD, and of judgment, and of might, to declare unto Jacob his transgression, and to Israel his sin.

IS MIGHTIER THAN PHYSICAL FORCES

Zec 4:6 Then he answered and spake unto me, saying, This *is* the word of the LORD unto Zerubbabel, saying, Not by might, nor by power, but by my spirit, saith the LORD of hosts.

REVEALED IN CHRIST

Lu 4:14 And Jesus returned in the power of the Spirit into Galilee: and there went out a fame of him through all the region round about.

ACCOMPANIES THE BAPTISM OF THE HOLY SPIRIT

Ac 1:8 But ye shall receive power, after that the Holy Ghost is come upon you: and ye shall be witnesses unto me both in Jerusalem, and in all Judaea, and in Samaria, and unto the uttermost part of the earth.

Ac 2:2 And suddenly there came a sound from heaven as of a rushing mighty wind, and it filled all the house where they were sitting.

ENABLES MEN TO SPEAK WITH AUTHORITY

Ac 4:33 And with great power gave the apostles witness of the resurrection of the Lord Jesus: and great grace was upon them all.

Ac 6:8 And Stephen, full of faith and power, did great wonders and miracles among the people.

IS ABLE TO HEAL

Ac 19:11–12 And God wrought special miracles by the hands of Paul:

So that from his body were brought unto the sick handkerchiefs or aprons, and the diseases departed from them, and the evil spirits went out of them.

1 Co 2:4 And my speech and my preaching *was* not with enticing words of man's wisdom, but in demonstration of the Spirit and of power:

Ep 3:16 That he would grant you, according to the riches of his glory, to be strengthened with might by his Spirit in the inner man;

1 Th 1:5 For our gospel came not unto you in word only, but also in power, and in the Holy Ghost, and in much assurance; as ye know what manner of men we were among you for your sake.

2 Ti 1:7 For God hath not given us the spirit of fear; but of power, and of love, and of a sound mind.

2. Belongs to God

Ge 11:7 Go to, let us go down, and there confound their language, that they may not understand one another's speech.

Ex 4:11 And the LORD said unto him, Who hath made man's mouth? or who maketh the dumb, or deaf, or the seeing, or the blind? have not I the LORD?

Ex 9:16 And in very deed for this *cause* have I raised thee up, for to shew *in* thee my power; and that my name may be declared throughout all the earth.

Ex 10:19 And the LORD turned a mighty strong west wind, which took away the locusts, and cast them into the Red sea; there remained not one locust in all the coasts of Egypt.

Ex 14:21 And Moses stretched out his hand over the sea; and the LORD caused the sea to go *back* by a strong east wind all that night, and made the sea dry *land,* and the waters were divided.

Ex 14:31 And Israel saw that great work which the LORD did upon the Egyptians: and the people feared the LORD, and believed the LORD, and his servant Moses.

Ex 15:6 Thy right hand, O LORD, is become glorious in power: thy right hand, O LORD, hath dashed in pieces the enemy.

Nu 11:23 And the LORD said unto Moses, Is the LORD's hand waxed short? thou shalt see now whether my word shall come to pass unto thee or not.

Nu 14:17 And now, I beseech thee, let the power of my Lord be great, according as thou hast spoken, saying,

De 3:24 O Lord GOD, thou hast begun to shew thy servant thy greatness, and thy mighty hand: for what God *is there* in heaven or in earth, that can do according to thy works, and according to thy might?

De 4:37 And because he loved thy fathers, therefore he chose their seed after them, and brought thee out in his sight with his mighty power out of Egypt;

De 7:21 Thou shalt not be affrighted at them: for the LORD thy God *is* among you, a mighty God and terrible.

De 9:29 Yet they *are* thy people and thine inheritance, which thou broughtest out by thy mighty power and by thy stretched out arm.

De 10:17 For the LORD your God *is* God of gods, and Lord of lords, a great God, a mighty, and a terrible, which regardeth not persons, nor taketh reward:

Jos 3:16 That the waters which came down from above stood *and* rose up upon an heap very far from the city Adam, that *is* beside Zaretan: and those that came down toward the sea of the plain, *even* the salt sea, failed, *and* were cut off: and the people passed over right against Jericho.

Jos 5:1 And it came to pass, when all the kings of the Amorites, which *were* on the side of Jordan westward, and all the kings of the Canaanites, which *were* by the sea, heard that the LORD had dried up the waters of Jordan from before the children of Israel, until we were passed over, that their heart melted, neither was there spirit in them any more, because of the children of Israel.

Jos 6:20 So the people shouted when *the priests* blew with the trumpets: and it came to pass, when the people heard the sound of the trumpet, and the people shouted with a great shout, that the wall fell down flat, so that the people went up into the city, every man straight before him, and they took the city.

Jud 5:4 LORD, when thou wentest out of Seir, when thou marchedst out of the field of Edom, the earth trembled, and the heavens dropped, the clouds also dropped water.

1 S 2:6 The LORD killeth, and maketh alive: he bringeth down to the grave, and bringeth up.

1 S 4:8 Woe unto us! who shall deliver us out of the hand of these mighty Gods? these *are* the Gods that smote the Egyptians with all the plagues in the wilderness.

2 K 17:36 But the LORD, who brought you up out of the land of Egypt with great power and a stretched out arm, him shall ye fear, and him shall ye worship, and to him shall ye do sacrifice.

1 Chr 29:12 Both riches and honour *come* of thee, and thou reignest over all; and in thine hand *is* power and might; and in thine hand *it is* to make great, and to give strength unto all.

2 Chr 14:11 And Asa cried unto the LORD his God, and said, LORD, *it is* nothing with thee to help, whether with many, or with them that have no power: help us, O LORD our God; for we rest on thee, and in thy name we go against this multitude. O LORD, thou *art* our God; let not man prevail against thee.

2 Chr 16:9 For the eyes of the LORD run to and fro throughout the whole earth, to shew himself strong in the behalf of *them* whose heart *is* perfect toward him. Herein thou hast done foolishly: therefore from henceforth thou shalt have wars.

2 Chr 20:6 And said, O LORD God of our fathers, *art* not thou God in heaven? and rulest *not* thou over all the kingdoms of the heathen? and in

thine hand *is there not* power and might, so that none is able to withstand thee?

2 Chr 25:8 But if thou wilt go, do *it,* be strong for the battle: God shall make thee fall before the enemy: for God hath power to help, and to cast down.

Ne 1:10 Now these *are* thy servants and thy people, whom thou hast redeemed by thy great power, and by thy strong hand.

Jb 9:4 *He is* wise in heart, and mighty in strength: who hath hardened *himself* against him, and hath prospered?

Jb 9:19 If *I speak* of strength, lo, *he is* strong: and if of judgment, who shall set me a time *to plead?*

Jb 12:16 With him *is* strength and wisdom: the deceived and the deceiver *are* his.

Jb 23:6 Will he plead against me with *his* great power? No; but he would put *strength* in me.

Jb 26:12 He divideth the sea with his power, and by his understanding he smiteth through the proud.

Jb 34:14 If he set his heart upon man, *if* he gather unto himself his spirit and his breath;

Jb 36:5 Behold, God *is* mighty, and despiseth not *any: he is* mighty in strength *and* wisdom.

Jb 37:12 And it is turned round about by his counsels: that they may do whatsoever he commandeth them upon the face of the world in the earth.

Jb 37:23 *Touching* the Almighty, we cannot find him out: *he is* excellent in power, and in judgment, and in plenty of justice: he will not afflict.

Jb 38:11 And said, Hitherto shalt thou come, but no further: and here shall thy proud waves be stayed?

Ps 18:7 Then the earth shook and trembled; the foundations also of the hills moved and were shaken, because he was wroth.

Ps 21:13 Be thou exalted, LORD, in thine own strength: *so* praise thy power.

Ps 24:8 Who *is* this King of glory? The LORD strong and mighty, the LORD mighty in battle.

Ps 29:4 The voice of the Lord *is* powerful; the voice of the Lord *is* full of majesty.

Ps 33:6 By the word of the Lord were the heavens made; and all the host of them by the breath of his mouth.

Ps 33:9 For he spake, and it was *done;* he commanded, and it stood fast.

Ps 47:3 He shall subdue the people under us, and the nations under our feet.

Ps 50:1 The mighty God, *even* the Lord, hath spoken, and called the earth from the rising of the sun unto the going down thereof.

Ps 54:1 Save me, O God, by thy name, and judge me by thy strength.

Ps 59:16 But I will sing of thy power; yea, I will sing aloud of thy mercy in the morning: for thou hast been my defence and refuge in the day of my trouble.

Ps 62:11 God hath spoken once; twice have I heard this; that power *belongeth* unto God.

Ps 63:2 To see thy power and thy glory, so *as* I have seen thee in the sanctuary.

Ps 65:6 Which by his strength setteth fast the mountains; *being* girded with power:

Ps 66:3 Say unto God, How terrible *art thou in* thy works! through the greatness of thy power shall thine enemies submit themselves unto thee.

Ps 68:34 Ascribe ye strength unto God: his excellency *is* over Israel, and his strength *is* in the clouds.

Ps 77:14 Thou *art* the God that doest wonders: thou hast declared thy strength among the people.

Ps 78:4 We will not hide *them* from their children, shewing to the generation to come the praises of the Lord, and his strength, and his wonderful works that he hath done.

Ps 78:26 He caused an east wind to blow in the heaven: and by his power he brought in the south wind.

Ps 79:11 Let the sighing of the prisoner come before thee; according to the greatness of thy power preserve thou those that are appointed to die;

Ps 89:8 O Lord God of hosts, who *is* a strong Lord like unto thee? or to thy faithfulness round about thee?

Ps 93:4 The Lord on high *is* mightier than the noise of many waters, *yea, than* the mighty waves of the sea.

Ps 104:7 At thy rebuke they fled; at the voice of thy thunder they hasted away.

Ps 104:32 He looketh on the earth, and it trembleth: he toucheth the hills, and they smoke.

Ps 106:8 Nevertheless he saved them for his name's sake, that he might make his mighty power to be known.

Ps 111:6 He hath shewed his people the power of his works, that he may give them the heritage of the heathen.

Ps 114:4 The mountains skipped like rams, *and* the little hills like lambs.

Ps 144:5 Bow thy heavens, O Lord, and come down: touch the mountains, and they shall smoke.

Ps 145:6 And *men* shall speak of the might of thy terrible acts: and I will declare thy greatness.

Ps 145:11 They shall speak of the glory of thy kingdom, and talk of thy power;

Ps 147:5 Great *is* our Lord, and of great power: his understanding *is* infinite.

Ps 150:2 Praise him for his mighty acts: praise him according to his excellent greatness.

Is 1:24 Therefore saith the Lord, the Lord of hosts, the mighty One of Israel, Ah, I will ease me of mine adversaries, and avenge me of mine enemies:

Is 28:2 Behold, the Lord hath a mighty and strong one, *which* as a tempest of hail *and* a destroying storm, as a flood of mighty waters overflowing, shall cast down to the earth with the hand.

Is 33:13 Hear, ye *that are* far off, what I have done; and, ye *that are* near, acknowledge my might.

Is 38:8 Behold, I will bring again the shadow of the degrees, which is gone down in the sun dial of Ahaz, ten degrees backward. So the sun returned ten degrees, by which degrees it was gone down.

Is 40:10 Behold, the Lord GOD will come with strong *hand,* and his arm shall rule for him: behold, his reward *is* with him, and his work before him.

Is 40:12 Who hath measured the waters in the hollow of his hand, and meted out heaven with the span, and comprehended the dust of the earth in a measure, and weighed the mountains in scales, and the hills in a balance?

Is 40:26 Lift up your eyes on high, and behold who hath created these *things,* that bringeth out their host by number: he calleth them all by names by the greatness of his might, for that *he is* strong in power; not one faileth.

Is 42:13 The LORD shall go forth as a mighty man, he shall stir up jealousy like a man of war: he shall cry, yea, roar; he shall prevail against his enemies.

Is 49:26 And I will feed them that oppress thee with their own flesh; and they shall be drunken with their own blood, as with sweet wine: and all flesh shall know that I the LORD *am* thy Saviour and thy Redeemer, the mighty One of Jacob.

Is 50:2 Wherefore, when I came, *was there* no man? when I called, *was there* none to answer? Is my hand shortened at all, that it cannot redeem? or have I no power to deliver? behold, at my rebuke I dry up the sea, I make the rivers a wilderness: their fish stinketh, because *there is* no water, and dieth for thirst.

Is 60:16 Thou shalt also suck the milk of the Gentiles, and shalt suck the breast of kings: and thou shalt know that I the LORD *am* thy Saviour and thy Redeemer, the mighty One of Jacob.

Je 10:12 He hath made the earth by his power, he hath established the world by his wisdom, and hath stretched by his discretion.

Je 16:21 Therefore, behold, I will this once cause them to know, I will cause them to know mine hand and my might; and they shall know that my name *is* The LORD.

Je 27:5 I have made the earth, the man and the beast that *are* upon the ground, by my great power and by my outstretched arm, and have given it unto whom it seemed meet unto me.

Je 32:17 Ah Lord God! behold, thou hast made the heaven and the earth by thy great power and stretched out arm, *and* there is nothing too hard for thee:

Lam 3:37 Who *is* he *that* saith, and it cometh to pass, *when* the Lord commandeth *it* not?

Eze 20:33 *As* I live, saith the Lord GOD, surely with a mighty hand, and with a stretched out arm, and with fury poured out, will I rule over you:

Da 2:20 Daniel answered and said, Blessed be the name of God for ever and ever: for wisdom and might are his:

Da 4:35 And all the inhabitants of the earth *are* reputed as nothing: and he doeth according to his will in the army of heaven, and *among* the inhabitants of the earth: and none can stay his hand, or say unto him, What doest thou?

Jl 2:11 And the LORD shall utter his voice before his army: for his camp *is* very great: for *he is* strong that executeth his word: for the day of the LORD *is* great and very terrible; and who can abide it?

Am 5:8 *Seek him* that maketh the seven stars and Orion, and turneth the shadow of death into the morning, and maketh the day dark with night: that calleth for the waters of the sea, and poureth them out upon the face of the earth: The LORD *is* his name:

Am 9:5 And the Lord GOD of hosts *is* he that to and it shall melt, and all that dwell therein shall mourn: and it shall rise up wholly like a flood; and shall be drowned, as *by* the flood of Egypt.

Jona 1:14 Wherefore they cried unto the LORD, and said, We beseech thee, O LORD, we beseech thee, let us not perish for this man's life, and lay not upon us innocent blood: for thou, O LORD, hast done as it pleased thee.

Mi 1:4 And the mountains shall be molten under him, and the valleys shall be cleft, as wax before the fire, *and* as the waters *that are* poured down a steep place.

Na 1:3 The LORD *is* slow to anger, and great in power, and will not at all acquit *the wicked:* the LORD hath his way in the whirlwind and in the storm, and the clouds *are* the dust of his feet.

Hab 3:4 And *his* brightness was as the light; he had horns *coming* out of his hand: and there *was* the hiding of his power.

Zep 3:17 The LORD thy God in the midst of thee *is* mighty; he will save, he will rejoice over thee with joy; he will rest in his love, he will joy over thee with singing.

Mt 3:9 And think not to say within yourselves, We have Abraham to *our* father: for I say unto you, that God is able of these stones to raise up children unto Abraham.

Mt 6:13 And lead us not into temptation, but deliver us from evil: For thine is the kingdom, and the power, and the glory, for ever. Amen.

Mt 22:29 Jesus answered and said unto them, Ye do err, not knowing the scriptures, nor the power of God.

Mt 28:2 And, behold, there was a great earthquake: for the angel of the Lord descended from heaven, and came and rolled back the stone from the door, and sat upon it.

Mk 10:27 And Jesus looking upon them saith, With men *it is* impossible, but not with God: for with God all things are possible.

Mk 12:24 And Jesus answering said unto them, Do ye not therefore err, because ye know not the scriptures, neither the power of God?

Lu 1:49 For he that is mighty hath done to me great things; and holy *is* his name.

Lu 12:5 But I will forewarn you whom ye shall fear: Fear him, which after he hath killed hath power to cast into hell; yea, I say unto you, Fear him.

Jn 10:29 My Father, which gave *them* me, is greater than all; and no *man* is able to pluck *them* out of my Father's hand.

Jn 19:11 Jesus answered, Thou couldest have no power *at all* against me, except it were given thee from above: therefore he that delivered me unto thee hath the greater sin.

Ac 12:10 When they were past the first and the second ward, they came unto the iron gate that leadeth unto the city; which opened to them of his own accord: and they went out, and passed on through one street; and forthwith the angel departed from him.

Ro 1:20 For the invisible things of him from the creation of the world are clearly seen, being understood by the things that are made, *even* his eternal power and Godhead; so that they are without excuse:

Ro 9:17 For the scripture saith unto Pharaoh, Even for this same purpose have I raised thee up, that I might shew my power in thee, and that my name might be declared throughout all the earth.

Ro 9:22 *What* if God, willing to shew *his* wrath, and to make his power known, endured with much longsuffering the vessels of wrath fitted to destruction:

Ro 16:25 Now to him that is of power to stablish you according to my gospel, and the preaching of Jesus Christ, according to the revelation of the mystery, which was kept secret since the world began,

Ro 16:27 To God only wise, *be* glory through Jesus Christ for ever. Amen.

1 Co 1:25 Because the foolishness of God is wiser than men; and the weakness of God is stronger than men.

1 Co 2:5 That your faith should not stand in the wisdom of men, but in the power of God.

1 Co 6:14 And God hath both raised up the Lord, and will also raise up us by his own power.

2 Co 4:7 But we have this treasure in earthen vessels, that the excellency of the power may be of God, and not of us.

2 Co 13:4 For though he was crucified through weakness, yet he liveth by the power of God. For we also are weak in him, but we shall live with him by the power of God toward you.

Ep 1:19 And what *is* the exceeding greatness of his power to us-ward who believe, according to the working of his mighty power,

Ep 3:7 Whereof I was made a minister, according to the gift of the grace of God given unto me by the effectual working of his power.

Col 1:11 Strengthened with all might, according to his glorious power, unto all patience and longsuffering with joyfulness;

1 Ti 6:16 Who only hath immortality, dwelling in the light which no man can approach unto; whom no man hath seen, nor can see: to whom *be* honour and power everlasting. Amen.

1 Pe 1:5 Who are kept by the power of God through faith unto salvation ready to be revealed in the last time.

2 Pe 1:3 According as his divine power hath given unto us all things that *pertain* unto life and godliness, through the knowledge of him that hath called us to glory and virtue:

Jude 25 To the only wise God our Saviour, *be* glory and majesty, dominion and power, both now and ever. Amen.

Re 7:12 Saying, Amen: Blessing, and glory, and wisdom, and thanksgiving, and honour, and power, and might, *be* unto our God for ever and ever. Amen.

Re 11:17 Saying, We give thee thanks, O Lord God Almighty, which art, and wast, and art to come; because thou hast taken to thee thy great power, and hast reigned.

Re 16:9 And men were scorched with great heat, and blasphemed the name of God, which hath power over these plagues: and they repented not to give him glory.

Re 19:1 And after these things I heard a great voice of much people in heaven, saying, Alleluia; Salvation, and glory, and honour, and power, unto the Lord our God:

a. Is Infinite

Ge 1:3 And God said, Let there be light: and there was light.

Ge 17:1 And when Abram was ninety years old and nine, the LORD appeared to Abram, and said unto him, I *am* the Almighty God; walk before me, and be thou perfect.

Ge 18:14 Is any thing too hard for the LORD? At the time appointed I will return unto thee, according to the time of life, and Sarah shall have a son.

De 32:39 See now that I, *even I, am* he, and *there is* no god with me: I kill, and I make alive; I wound, and I heal: neither *is there any* that can deliver out of my hand.

1 S 14:6 And Jonathan said to the young man that bare his armour, Come, and let us go over unto the garrison of these uncircumcised: it may be that the LORD will work for us: for *there is* no restraint to the LORD to save by many or by few.

1 K 19:11 And he said, Go forth, and stand upon the mount before the LORD. And, behold, the LORD passed by, and a great and strong wind rent the mountains, and brake in pieces the rocks before the LORD; *but* the LORD *was* not in the wind: and after the wind an earthquake; *but* the LORD *was* not in the earthquake:

2 K 3:18 And this is *but* a light thing in the sight of the LORD: he will deliver the Moabites also into your hand.

2 K 7:2 Then a lord on whose hand the king leaned answered the man of God, and said, Behold, *if* the LORD would make windows in heaven, might this thing be? And he said, Behold, thou shalt see *it* with thine eyes, but shalt not eat thereof.

2 K 20:11 And Isaiah the prophet cried unto the LORD: and he brought the shadow ten degrees backward, by which it had gone down in the dial of Ahaz.

2 Chr 20:6 And said, O LORD God of our fathers, *art* not thou God in heaven? and rulest *not* thou over all the kingdoms of the heathen? and in thine hand *is there not* power and might, so that none is able to withstand thee?

Jb 9:5 Which removeth the mountains, and they know not: which overturneth them in his anger.

Jb 9:12 Behold, he taketh away, who can hinder him? who will say unto him, What doest thou?

Jb 12:14 Behold, he breaketh down, and it cannot be built again: he shutteth up a man, and there can be no opening.

Jb 12:23 He increaseth the nations, and destroyeth them: he enlargeth the nations, and straiteneth them *again.*

Jb 23:13 But he *is* in one *mind,* and who can turn him? and *what* his soul desireth, even *that* he doeth.

Jb 26:7 He stretcheth out the north over the empty place, *and* hangeth the earth upon nothing.

Jb 42:2 I know that thou canst do every *thing,* and *that* no thought can be withholden from thee.

Ps 21:13 Be thou exalted, LORD, in thine own strength: *so* will we sing and praise thy power.

Ps 93:1 The LORD reigneth, he is clothed with majesty; the LORD is clothed with strength, *wherewith* he hath girded himself: the world also is stablished, that it cannot be moved.

Ps 115:3 But our God *is* in the heavens: he hath done whatsoever he hath pleased.

Ps 135:6 Whatsoever the LORD pleased, *that* did he in heaven, and in earth, in the seas, and all deep places.

Is 14:27 For the LORD of hosts hath purposed, and who shall disannul *it?* and his hand *is* stretched out, and who shall turn it back?

Is 40:15 Behold, the nations *are* as a drop of a bucket, and are counted as the small dust of the balance: behold, he taketh up the isles as a very little thing.

Is 43:13 Yea, before the day *was* I *am* he; and *there is* none that can deliver out of my hand: I will work, and who shall let it?

Is 45:7 I form the light, and create darkness: I make peace, and create evil: I the LORD do all these *things.*

Is 46:10 Declaring the end from the beginning, and from ancient times *the things* that are not *yet* done, saying, My counsel shall stand, and I will do all my pleasure:

Je 32:17 Ah Lord GOD! behold, thou hast made the heaven and the earth by thy great power and stretched out arm, *and* there is nothing too hard for thee:

Je 32:27 Behold I *am* the LORD, the God of all flesh: is there any thing too hard for me?

Da 4:35 And all the inhabitants of the earth *are* reputed as nothing: and he doeth according to his will in the army of heaven, and *among* the inhabitants of the earth: and none can stay his hand, or say unto him, What doest thou?

Hab 3:6 He stood, and measured the earth: he beheld, and drove asunder the nations; and the everlasting mountains were scattered, the perpetual hills did bow: his ways *are* everlasting.

Mt 19:26 But Jesus beheld *them,* and said unto them, With men this is impossible; but with God all things are possible.

Mk 10:27 And Jesus looking upon them saith, With men *it is* impossible, but not with God: for with God all things are possible.

Mk 14:36 And he said, Abba, Father, all things *are* possible unto thee; take away this cup from me: nevertheless not what I will, but what thou wilt.

Lu 1:37 For with God nothing shall be impossible.

Lu 18:27 And he said, The things which are impossible with men are possible with God.

Re 1:8 I am Alpha and Omega, the beginning and the ending, saith the Lord, which is, and which was, and which is to come, the Almighty.

Re 4:8 And the four beasts had each of them six wings about *him;* and *they were* full of eyes within: and they rest not day and night, saying, Holy, holy, holy, Lord God Almighty, which was, and is, and is to come.

Re 19:6 And I heard as it were the voice of a great multitude, and as the voice of many waters, and as the voice of mighty thunderings, saying, Alleluia: for the Lord God omnipotent reigneth.

Re 21:22 And I saw no temple therein: for the Lord God Almighty and the Lamb are the temple of it.

b. Is Useful

TO DELIVER
Da 3:17 If it be *so,* our God whom we serve is able to deliver us from the burning fiery furnace, and he will deliver *us* out of thine hand, O king.

TO RAISE UP CHILDREN FROM STONES
Lu 3:8 Bring forth therefore fruits worthy of repentance, and begin not to say within yourselves, We have Abraham to *our* father: for I say unto you, That God is able of these stones to raise up children unto Abraham.

TO FULFILL PROMISES
Ro 4:21 And being fully persuaded that, what he had promised, he was able also to perform.

TO MAKE GRACE ABOUND
2 Co 9:8 And God *is* able to make all grace abound toward you; that ye, always having all sufficiency in all *things,* may abound to every good work:

TO DO EXCEEDING ABUNDANTLY
Ep 3:20 Now unto him that is able to do exceeding abundantly above all that we ask or think, according to the power that worketh in us,

TO SUBDUE ALL THINGS
Ph 3:21 Who shall change our vile body, that it may be fashioned like unto his glorious body, according to the working whereby he is able even to subdue all things unto himself.

TO GUARD THE SOUL'S TREASURE
2 Ti 1:12 For the which cause I also suffer these things: nevertheless I am not ashamed: for I know whom I have believed, and am persuaded that he is able to keep that which I have committed unto him against that day.

TO PARDON
Mt 9:6 But that ye may know that the Son of man hath power on earth to forgive sins, (then saith he to the sick of the palsy,) Arise, take up thy bed, and go unto thine house.

TO SAVE TO THE UTTERMOST
He 7:25 Wherefore he is able also to save them to the uttermost that come unto God by him, seeing he ever liveth to make intercession for them.

TO KEEP FROM FALLING
Jude 24 Now unto him that is able to keep you from falling, and to present *you* faultless before the presence of his glory with exceeding joy,

c. Is Shown in Surprising Things

A ROD
Ex 4:2 And the LORD said unto him, What *is* that in thine hand? And he said, A rod.

A JAW-BONE
Jud 15:15 And he found a new jawbone of an ass, and put forth his hand, and took it, and slew a thousand men therewith.

FIVE SMOOTH STONES
1 S 17:40 And he took his staff in his hand, and chose him five smooth stones out of the brook, and put them in a shepherd's bag which he had, even in a scrip; and his sling *was* in his hand: and he drew near to the Philistine.

A HANDFUL OF FLOUR AND A LITTLE OIL
1 K 17:12 And she said, *As* the LORD thy God liveth, I have not a cake, but an handful of meal in a barrel, and a little oil in a cruse: and, behold, I *am* gathering two sticks, that I may go in and dress it for me and my son, that we may eat it, and die.

A CLOUD THE SIZE OF A MAN'S HAND
1 K 18:44 And it came to pass at the seventh time, that he said, Behold, there ariseth a little cloud out of the sea, like a man's hand. And he said, Go up, say unto Ahab, Prepare *thy chariot,* and get thee down, that the rain stop thee not.

SMALL THINGS
Zec 4:10 For who hath despised the day of small things? for they shall

rejoice, and shall see the plummet in the hand of Zerubbabel *with* those seven; they *are* the eyes of the LORD, which run to and fro through the whole earth.

THE MUSTARD SEED

Mt 13:32 Which indeed is the least of all seeds: but when it is grown, it is the greatest among herbs, and becometh a tree, so that the birds of the air come and lodge in the branches thereof.

FIVE BARLEY LOAVES

Jn 6:9 There is a lad here, which hath five barley loaves, and two small fishes: but what are they among so many?

GOD'S INSTRUMENT CASE

1 Co 1:27–29 But God hath chosen the foolish things of the world to confound the wise; and God hath chosen the weak things of the world to confound the things which are mighty;

And base things of the world, and things which are despised, hath God chosen, *yea,* and things which are not, to bring to nought things that are:

That no flesh should glory in his presence.

3. Over Nature

a. Sea

Ex 14:21 And Moses stretched out his hand over the sea; and the LORD caused the sea to go *back* by a strong east wind all that night, and made the sea dry *land,* and the waters were divided.

Jos 3:16 That the waters which came down from above stood *and* rose up upon an heap very far from the city Adam, that *is* beside Zaretan: and those that came down toward the sea of the plain, *even* the salt sea, failed, *and* were cut off: and the people passed over right against Jericho.

Jb 9:8 Which alone spreadeth out the heavens, and treadeth upon the waves of the sea.

Jb 26:10 He hath compassed the waters with bounds, until the day and night come to an end.

Jb 38:8 Or *who* shut up the sea with doors, when it brake forth, *as if* it had issued out of the womb?

Jb 38:11 And said, Hitherto shalt thou come, but no further: and here shall thy proud waves be stayed?

Ps 33:7 He gathereth the waters of the sea together as an heap: he layeth up the depth in storehouses.

Ps 77:16 The waters saw thee, O God, the waters saw thee; they were afraid: the depths also were troubled.

Ps 93:4 The LORD on high *is* mightier than the noise of many waters, *yea, than* the mighty waves of the sea.

Ps 104:9 Thou hast set a bound that they may not pass over; that they turn not again to cover the earth.

Ps 106:9 He rebuked the Red sea also, and it was dried up: so he led them through the depths, as through the wilderness.

Pr 8:29 When he gave to the sea his decree, that the waters should not pass his commandment: when he appointed the foundations of the earth:

Is 50:2 Wherefore, when I came, *was there* no man? when I called, *was there* none to answer? Is my hand shortened at all, that it cannot redeem? or have I no power to deliver? behold, at my rebuke I dry up the sea, I make the rivers a wilderness: their fish stinketh, because *there is* no water, and dieth for thirst.

Je 5:22 Fear ye not me? saith the LORD: will ye not tremble at my presence, which have placed the sand *for* the bound of the sea by a perpetual decree, that it cannot pass it: and though the waves thereof toss themselves, yet can they not prevail; though they roar, yet can they not pass over it?

Hab 3:8 Was the LORD displeased against the rivers? *was* thine anger against the rivers? *was* thy wrath against the sea, that thou didst ride upon thine horses *and* thy chariots of salvation?

Lu 8:24 And they came to him, and awoke him, saying, Master, master, we perish. Then he arose, and rebuked the wind and the raging of the water: and they ceased, and there was a calm.

b. Tempest

Ps 65:7 Which stilleth the noise of the seas, the noise of their waves, and the tumult of the people.

Ps 89:9 Thou rulest the raging of the sea: when the waves thereof arise, thou stillest them.

Ps 93:4 The LORD on high *is* mightier than the noise of many waters, *yea, than* the mighty waves of the sea.

Ps 107:29 He maketh the storm a calm, so that the waves thereof are still.

Jona 1:15 So they took up Jonah, and cast him forth into the sea: and the sea ceased from her raging.

Mt 8:26 And he saith unto them, Why are ye fearful, O ye of little faith? Then he arose, and rebuked the winds and the sea; and there was a great ca

Mt 14:32 And when they were come into the ship, the wind ceased.

c. Wind

Ps 48:7 Thou breakest the ships of Tarshish with an east wind.

Ps 135:7 He causeth the vapours to ascend from the ends of the earth; he maketh lightnings for the rain; he bringeth the wind out of his treasuries.

Ps 148:8 Fire, and hail; snow, and vapours; stormy wind fulfilling his word:

Pr 30:4 Who hath ascended up into heaven, or descended? who hath gathered the wind in his fists? who hath bound the waters in a garment? who hath established all the ends of the earth? what *is* his name, and what *is* his son's name, if thou canst tell?

Mk 4:39 And he arose, and rebuked the wind, and said unto the sea, Peace, be still. And the wind ceased, and there was a great calm.

Re 7:1 And after these things I saw four angels standing on the four corners of the earth, holding the four winds of the earth, that the wind should not blow on the earth, nor on the sea, nor on any tree.

d. Elements

Ge 7:4 For yet seven days, and I will cause it to rain upon the earth forty days and forty nights; and every living substance that I have made will I destroy from off the face of the earth.

Ex 9:33 And Moses went out of the city from Pharaoh, and spread abroad his hands unto the LORD: and the thunders and hail ceased, and the rain was not poured upon the earth.

De 11:17 And *then* the LORD'S wrath be kindled against you, and he shut up the heaven, that there be no rain, and that the land yield not her fruit; and *lest* ye perish quickly from off the good land which the LORD giveth you.

Jb 37:6 For he saith to the snow, Be thou *on* the earth; likewise to the small rain, and to the great rain of his strength.

Ps 148:8 Fire, and hail; snow, and vapours; stormy wind fulfilling his word:

Je 10:13 When he uttereth his voice, *there is* a multitude of waters in the heavens, and he causeth the vapors to ascend from the ends of the earth; he maketh lightnings with rain, and bringeth forth the wind out of his treasures.

4. Realized

ABILITY TO HEAL LEPERS

Mt 8:2 And, behold, there came a leper and worshipped him, saying, Lord, if thou wilt, thou canst make me clean.

ABILITY TO GIVE ABSENT HEALING

Lu 7:7 Wherefore neither thought I myself worthy to come unto thee: but say in a word, and my servant shall be healed.

ABILITY TO CONTROL DEMONS

Lu 8:31–32 And they besought him that he would not command them to go out into the deep.

And there was there an herd of many swine feeding on the mountain: and they besought him that he would suffer them to enter into them. And he suffered them.

ABILITY TO RAISE THE DEAD
Jn 11:22 But I know, that even now, whatsoever thou wilt ask of God, God will give *it* thee.

ABILITY TO HOLD FAST TO THE BELIEVER
Ro 8:39 Nor height, nor depth, nor any other creature, shall be able to separate us from the love of God, which is in Christ Jesus our Lord.

ABILITY TO KEEP SPIRITUAL TREASURES
2 Ti 1:12 For the which cause I also suffer these things: nevertheless I am not ashamed: for I know whom I have believed, and am persuaded that he is able to keep that which I have committed unto him against that day.

ABILITY TO SAVE TO THE UTTERMOST
He 7:25 Wherefore he is able also to save them to the uttermost that come unto God by him, seeing he ever liveth to make intercession for them.

5. Comes from God
Is 40:31 But they that wait upon the LORD shall renew *their* strength; they shall mount up with wings as eagles; they shall run, and not be weary; *and* they shall walk, and not faint.
Mk 9:29 And he said unto them, This kind can come forth by nothing, but by prayer and fasting.
Ac 1:8 But ye shall receive power, after that the Holy Ghost is come upon you: and ye shall be witnesses unto me both in Jerusalem, and in all Judaea, and in Samaria, and unto the uttermost part of the earth.

6. Unrealized

TO STILL THE TEMPEST
Mt 8:27 But the men marvelled, saying, What manner of man is this, that even the winds and the sea obey him!

TO FORGIVE SINS
Mk 2:7 Why doth this *man* thus speak blasphemies? who can forgive sins but God only?

TO HEAL THE SICK
Mk 2:12 And immediately he arose, took up the bed, and went forth before them all; insomuch that they were all amazed, and glorified God, saying, We never saw it on this fashion.

TO PROVIDE FOR THE MULTITUDE
Mk 8:4 And his disciples answered him, From whence can a man satisfy these *men* with bread here in the wilderness?

TO CAST OUT DEMONS
Mk 9:22 And ofttimes it hath cast him into the fire, and into the waters, to destroy him: but if thou canst do any thing, have compassion on us, and help us.

TO CONTROL THE FORCES OF NATURE
Mk 11:21 And Peter calling to remembrance saith unto him, Master, behold, the fig tree which thou cursedst is withered away.

TO COME DOWN FROM THE CROSS
Mk 15:31 Likewise also the chief priests mocking said among themselves with the scribes, He saved others; himself he cannot save.

TO RAISE THE DEAD
Jn 11:37 And some of them said, Could not this man, which opened the eyes of the blind, have caused that even this man should not have died?

TO CONQUER DEATH
Jn 20:25 The other disciples therefore said unto him, We have seen the Lord. But he said unto them, Except I shall see in his hands the print of the nails, and put my finger into the print of the nails, and thrust my hand into his side, I will not believe.

See **CHRIST, CREATOR, GOD, HOLY SPIRIT, POWERLESSNESS, WEAKNESS**

POWERLESSNESS

ISRAEL BEFORE THEIR ENEMIES
Le 26:37 And they shall fall one upon another, as it were before a sword,

when none pursueth: and ye shall have no power to stand before your enemies.

De 28:32 Thy sons and thy daughters *shall be* given unto another people, and thine eyes shall look, and fail *with longing* for them all the day long: and *there shall be* no might in thine hand.

Jos 7:12 Therefore the children of Israel could not stand before their enemies, *but* turned *their* backs before their enemies, because they were accursed: neither will I be with you any more, except ye destroy the accursed from among you.

Jud 1:21 And the children of Benjamin did not drive out the Jebusites that inhabited Jerusalem; but the Jebusites dwell with the children of Benjamin in Jerusalem unto this day.

Jud 2:14 And the anger of the LORD was hot against Israel, and he delivered them into the hands of spoilers that spoiled them, and he sold them into the hands of their enemies round about, so that they could not any longer stand before their enemies.

SAMSON BY BREAKING COVENANT

Jud 16:17 That he told her all his heart, and said unto her. There hath not come a razor upon mine head; for I *have been* a Nazarite unto God from my mother's womb: if I be shaven, then my strength will go from me, and I shall become weak, and be like any *other* man.

COWARDS IN ISRAEL

1 S 17:24 And all the men of Israel, when they saw the man, fled from him, and were sore afraid.

BABYLON ENERVATED BY IDOLATRY

Je 51:30 The mighty men of Babylon have forborn to fight, they have remained in *their* holds: their might hath failed; they became as women: they have burned her dwellingplaces; her bars are broken.

APOSTLES HELPLESS
AGAINST SATANIC FORCES

Mk 9:18 And wheresoever he taketh him, he teareth him: and he foameth, and gnasheth with his teeth, and pineth away: and I spake to thy disciples that they should cast him out; and they could not.

Jn 15:5 I am the vine, ye *are* the branches: He that abideth in me, and I in him, the same bringeth forth much fruit: for without me ye can do nothing.

See **CHRIST, CREATOR, GOD, HOLY SPIRIT, POWER, SIN, UNBELIEF, WEAKNESS**

PRAISE TO GOD

1 Chr 16:31 Let the heavens be glad, and let the earth rejoice: and let *men* say among the nations, The LORD reigneth.

Ps 65:13 The pastures are clothed with flocks; the valleys also are covered over with corn; they shout for joy, they also sing.

Ps 69:34 Let the heaven and earth praise him, the seas, and every thing that moveth therein.

Ps 96:12 Let the field be joyful, and all that *is* therein: then shall all the trees of the wood rejoice

Ps 98:8 Let the floods clap *their* hands: let the hills be joyful together

Ps 145:10 All thy works shall praise thee, O LORD; and thy saints shall bless thee.

Ps 148:3 Praise ye him, sun and moon: praise him, all ye stars of light.

Is 42:11 Let the wilderness and the cities thereof lift up *their voice,* the villages *that* Kedar doth inhabit: let the inhabitants of the rock sing, let them shout from the top of the mountains.

Is 44:23 Sing, O ye heavens; for the LORD hath done *it:* shout, ye lower parts of the earth: break forth into singing, ye mountains, O forest, and every tree therein: for the LORD hath redeemed Jacob, and glorified himself in Israel.

Is 49:13 Sing, O heavens; and be joyful, O earth; and break forth into singing, O mountains: for the LORD hath comforted his people, and will have mercy upon his afflicted.

Is 55:12 For ye shall go out with joy, and be led forth with peace: the mountains and the hills shall break forth before you into singing, and all the trees of the field sir hands.

Hab 3:3 God came from Teman, and the Holy One from mount Paran. Selah. His glory covered the heavens, and the earth was full of his praise.

Lu 19:40 And he answered and said unto them, I tell you that, if these should hold their peace, the stones would immediately cry out.

1. Prescribed

IN SONG

Ps 9:11 Sing praises to the LORD, which dwelleth in Zion: declare among the people his doings.

WITH MUSICAL INSTRUMENTS

Ps 33:2 Praise the LORD with harp: sing unto him with the psaltery *and* an instrument of ten strings.

UNIVERSAL

Ps 67:3 Let the people praise thee, O God; let all the people praise thee.

Is 42:12 Let them give glory unto the LORD, and declare his praise in the islands.

PERPETUAL

He 13:15 By him therefore let us offer the sacrifice of praise to God continually, that is, the fruit of *our* lips giving thanks to his name.

FOUR REASONS

1 Pe 2:9 But ye *are* a chosen generation, a royal priesthood, an holy nation, a peculiar people; that ye should shew forth the praises of him who hath called you out of darkness into his marvellous light:

2. Examples

2 Chr 5:13 It came even to pass, as the trumpeters and singers *were* as one, to make one sound to be heard in praising and thanking the LORD; and when they lifted up *their* voice with the trumpets and cymbals and instruments of musick, and praised the LORD, *saying,* For *he is* good; for his mercy *endureth* for ever: that *then* the house was filled with a cloud, *even* the house of the LORD;

2 Chr 20:22 And when they began to sing and to praise, the LORD set ambushments against the children of Ammon, Moab, and mount Seir, which were come against Judah; and they were smitten.

2 Chr 31:2 And Hezekiah appointed the courses of the priests and the Levites after their courses, every man according to his service, the priests and Levites for burnt offerings and for peace offerings, to minister, and to give thanks, and to praise in the gates of the tents of the LORD.

Ps 35:28 And my tongue shall speak of thy righteousness *and* of thy praise all the day long.

Ps 51:15 O Lord, open thou my lips; and my mouth shall shew forth thy praise.

Ps 119:164 Seven times a day do I praise thee because of thy righteous judgments.

Is 12:1 And in that day thou shalt say, O LORD, I will praise thee: though thou wast angry with me, thine anger is turned away, and thou comfortedst me.

Is 61:3 To appoint unto them that mourn in Zion, to give unto them beauty for ashes, the oil of joy for mourning, the garment of praise for the spirit of heaviness; that they might be called trees of righteousness, the planting of the LORD, that he might be glorified.

Je 33:11 The voice of joy, and the voice of gladness, the voice of the bridegroom, and the voice of the bride, the voice of them that shall say, Praise the LORD of hosts: for the LORD *is* good; for his mercy *endureth* for ever: *and* of them that shall bring the sacrifice of praise into the house of the LORD. For I will cause to return the captivity of the land, as at the first, saith the LORD.

Lu 2:20 And the shepherds returned, glorifying and praising God for all the things that they had heard and seen, as it was told unto them.

Lu 19:37 And when he was come nigh, even now at the descent of the mount of Olives, the whole multitude of the disciples began to rejoice and praise God with a loud voice for all the mighty works that they had seen;

Lu 24:53 And were continually in the temple, praising and blessing God. Amen.

Ac 2:47 Praising God, and having favour with all the people. And the Lord added to the church daily such as should be saved.

Ac 16:25 And at midnight Paul and Silas prayed, and sang praises unto God: and the prisoners heard them.

Ro 15:9 And that the Gentiles might glorify God for *his* mercy; as it is written, For this cause I will confess to thee among the Gentiles, and sing unto thy name.

3. Heavenly

Ps 148:2 Praise ye him, all his angels: praise ye him, all his hosts.

Lu 2:13-14 And suddenly there was with the angel a multitude of the heavenly host praising God, and saying,

Glory to God in the highest, and on earth peace, good will toward men.

Re 4:8 And the four beasts had each of them six wings about *him;* and *they were* full of eyes within: and they rest not day and night, saying, Holy, holy, holy, Lord God Almighty, which was, and is, and is to come.

Re 5:11-12 And I beheld, and I heard the voice of many angels round about the throne and the beasts and the elders: and the number of them was ten thousand times ten thousand, and thousands of thousands;

Saying with a loud voice, Worthy is the Lamb that was slain to receive power, and riches, and wisdom, and strength, and honour, and glory, and blessing.

Re 7:11-12 And all the angels stood round about the throne, and *about* the elders and the four beasts, and fell before the throne on their faces, and worshipped God,

Saying, Amen: Blessing, and glory, and wisdom, and thanksgiving, and honour, and power, and might, *be* unto our God for ever and ever. Amen.

Re 11:17 Saying, We give thee thanks, O Lord God Almighty, which art, and wast, and art to come; because thou hast taken to thee thy great power, and hast reigned.

Re 14:3 And they sung as it were a new song before the throne, and before the four beasts, and the elders: and no man could learn that song but the hundred *and* forty *and* four thousand, which were redeemed from the earth.

Re 19:5 And a voice came out of the throne, saying, Praise our God, all ye his servants, and ye that fear him, both small and great.

4. Nature's

Nu 1:2 Take ye the sum of all the congregation of the children of Israel, after their families, by the house of their fathers, with the number of *their* names, every male by their polls;

Nu 26:2 Take the sum of all the congregation of the children of Israel, from twenty years old and upward, throughout their fathers' house, all that are able to go to war in Israel.

Nu 26:63-64 These *are* they that were numbered by Moses and Eleazar the priest, who numbered the children of Israel in the plains of Moab by Jordan *near* Jericho.

But among these there was not a man of them whom Moses and Aaron the priest numbered, when they numbered the children of Israel in the wilderness of Sinai.

2 S 24:2 For the king said to Joab the captain of the host, which *was* with him, Go now through all the tribes of Israel, from Dan even to Beer-sheba, and number ye the people, that I may know the number of the people.

1 Chr 21:1 And Satan stood up against Israel, and provoked David to number Israel.

Lu 2:1 And it came to pass in those days, that there went out a decree from Caesar Augustus, that all the world should be taxed.

5. Unceasing

Ps 35:28 And my tongue shall speak of thy righteousness *and* of thy praise all the day long.

Ps 71:6 By thee have I been holden up from the womb: thou art he that took me out of my mother's bowels: my praise *shall be* continually of thee.

Ps 71:14 But I will hope continually, and will yet praise thee more and more.

Ps 104:33 I will sing unto the LORD as long as I live: I will sing praise to my God while I have my being.

Ps 145:1 I will extol thee, my God, O king; and I will bless thy name for ever and ever.

Re 4:8 And the four beasts had each of them six wings about *him;* and *they were* full of eyes within: and they rest not day and night, saying, Holy, holy, holy, Lord God Almighty, which was, and is, and is to come.

Re 5:13 And every creature which is in heaven, and on the earth, and under the earth, and such as are in the sea, and all that are in them, heard I saying, Blessing, and honour, and glory, and power, *be* unto him that sitteth upon the throne, and unto the Lamb for ever and ever.

See **THANKFULNESS, WORSHIP**

PRAYER, *communication with God*

FIRST MENTIONED
Ge 4:26

UNIVERSAL NEED
Ps 65:2; Is 56:7; Lu 11:2

OF THE SAINTS
Re 5:8

ASCENDS TO GOD AS INCENSE
Re 8:3–4

1. Prescribed

1 Chr 16:8 Give thanks unto the LORD, call upon his name, make known his deeds among the people.

1 Chr 16:11 Seek the LORD and his strength, seek his face continually.

Jb 8:5 If thou wouldest seek unto God betimes, and make thy supplication to the Almighty;

Ps 32:6 For this shall every one that is godly pray unto thee in a time when thou mayest be found: surely in the floods of great waters they shall not come nigh unto him.

Ps 62:8 Trust in him at all times; *ye* people, pour out your heart before him: God *is* a refuge for us. Selah.

Ps 105:1 O give thanks unto the LORD; call upon his name: make known his deeds among the people.

Is 12:4 And in that day shall ye say, Praise the LORD, call upon his name, declare his doings among the people, make mention that his name is exalted.

Is 55:6 Seek ye the LORD while he may be found, call ye upon him while he is near:

Je 3:4 Wilt thou not from this time cry unto me, My father, thou art the guide of my youth?

Je 29:7 And seek the peace of the city whither I have caused you to be carried away captives, and pray unto the LORD for it: for in the peace thereof shall ye have peace.

Lam 2:19 Arise, cry out in the night: in the beginning of the watches pour out thine heart like water before the face of the Lord: lift up thy hands toward him for the life of thy young children, that faint for hunger in the top of every street.

Lam 3:41 Let us lift up our heart with *our* hands unto God in the heavens.

Eze 36:37 Thus saith the Lord God; I will yet *for* this be enquired of by the house of Israel, to do *it* for them; I will increase them with men like a flock.

Ho 14:2 Take with you words, and turn to the LORD: say unto him, Take away all iniquity, and receive *us* graciously: so will we render the calves of our lips.

Jl 1:14 Sanctify ye a fast, call a solemn assembly, gather the elders *and* all the inhabitants of the land *into* the house of the LORD your God, and cry unto the LORD,

Jl 2:17 Let the priests, the ministers of the LORD, weep between the porch and the altar, and let them say, Spare thy people, O LORD, and give not thine heritage to reproach, that the heathen should rule over them: wherefore should they say among the people, Where *is* their God?

Jona 3:8 But let man and beast be covered with sackcloth, and cry mightily unto God: yea, let them turn every one from his evil way, and from the violence that *is* in their hands.

Zep 3:9 For then will I turn to the people a pure language, that they may all call upon the name of the LORD, to serve him with one consent.

Zec 10:1 Ask ye of the LORD rain in the time of the latter rain; *so* the LORD shall make bright clouds, and give them showers of rain, to every one grass in the field.

Mt 7:7 Ask, and it shall be given you; seek, and ye shall find; knock, and it shall be opened unto you:

Mt 9:38 Pray ye therefore the Lord of the harvest, that he will send forth labourers into his harvest.

Mt 24:20 But pray ye that your flight be not in the winter, neither on the sabbath day:

Mt 26:41 Watch and pray, that ye enter not into temptation: the spirit indeed *is* willing, but the flesh *is* weak.

Mk 9:29 And he said unto them, This kind can come forth by nothing, but by prayer and fasting.

Mk 13:33 Take ye heed, watch and pray: for ye know not when the time is.

Mk 14:38 Watch ye and pray, lest ye enter into temptation. The spirit truly *is* ready, but the flesh *is* weak.

Lu 6:28 Bless them that curse you, and pray for them which despitefully use you.

Lu 10:2 Therefore said the harvest truly *is* great, but the labourers *are* few: pray ye therefore the Lord of the harvest, that he would send forth labourers into his harvest.

Lu 11:10 For every one that asketh receiveth; and he that seeketh findeth; and to him that knocketh it shall be opened.

Lu 18:1 And he spake a parable unto them *to this end,* that men ought always to pray, and not to faint;

Lu 21:36 Watch ye therefore, and pray always, that ye may be accounted worthy to escape all these things that shall come to pass, and to stand before the Son of man.

Lu 22:40 And when he was at the place, he said unto them, Pray that ye enter not into temptation.

Lu 22:46 And said unto them, Why sleep ye? rise and pray, lest ye enter into temptation.

Jn 16:24 Hitherto have ye asked nothing in my name: ask, and ye shall receive, that your joy may be full.

Ac 8:22 Repent therefore of this thy wickedness, and pray God, if perhaps the thought of thine heart may be forgiven thee.

Ac 22:16 And now why tarriest thou? arise, and be baptized, and wash away thy sins, calling on the name of the Lord.

Ro 10:13 For whosoever shall call upon the name of the Lord shall be saved.

Ro 12:12 Rejoicing in hope; patient in tribulation; continuing instant in prayer;

1 Co 7:5 Defraud ye not one the other, except *it be* with consent for a time, that ye may give yourselves to fasting and prayer; and come together again, that Satan tempt you not for your incontinency.

1 Co 14:13 Wherefore let him that speaketh in an *unknown* tongue pray that he may interpret.

Ep 6:18 Praying always with all prayer and supplication in the Spirit, and watching thereunto with all perseverance and supplication for all saints;

Ph 4:6 Be careful for nothing; but in every thing by prayer and supplication with thanksgiving let your requests be made known unto God.

Col 4:2 Continue in prayer, and watch in the same with thanksgiving;

1 Th 5:17 Pray without ceasing.

1 Ti 2:1 I exhort therefore, that, first of all, supplications, prayers, intercessions, *and* giving of thanks, be made for all men;

1 Ti 2:8 I will therefore that men pray every where, lifting up holy hands, without wrath and doubting.

He 4:16 Let us therefore come boldly unto the throne of grace, that we may obtain mercy, and find grace to help in time of need.

Ja 5:13 Is any among you afflicted? let him pray. Is any merry? let him sing psalms.

1 Pe 4:7 But the end of all things is at hand: be ye therefore sober, and watch unto prayer.

Jude 20 But ye, beloved, building up yourselves on your most holy faith, praying in the Holy Ghost,

2. Answered

MOSES

Ex 15:24–25 And the people murmured against Moses, saying, What shall we drink?

And he cried unto the LORD; and the LORD shewed him a tree, *which* when he had cast into the waters, the waters were made sweet: there he made for them a statute and an ordinance, and there he proved them,

GIDEON

Jud 6:39–40 And Gideon said unto God, Let not thine anger be hot against me, and I will speak but this once: let me prove, I pray thee, but this once with the fleece; let it now be dry only upon the fleece, and upon all the ground let there be dew.

And God did so that night: for it was dry upon the fleece only, and there was dew on all the ground.

Jud 13:9 And God hearkened to the voice of Manoah; and the angel of God came again unto the woman as she sat in the field: but Manoah her husband *was* not with her.

HANNAH

1 S 1:27 For this child I prayed; and the LORD hath given me my petition which I asked of him:

SAMUEL

1 S 7:9–10 And Samuel took a sucking lamb, and offered *it for* a burnt offering wholly unto the LORD: and Samuel cried unto the LORD for Israel; and the LORD heard him.

And as Samuel was offering up the burnt offering, the Philistines drew near to battle against Israel: but the LORD thundered with a great thunder on that day upon the Philistines, and discomfited them; and they were smitten before Israel.

1 K 3:12 Behold, I have done according to thy words: lo, I have given thee a wise and an understanding heart; so that there was none like thee before thee, neither after thee shall any arise like unto thee.

SOLOMON

1 K 9:3 And the LORD said unto him, I have heard thy prayer and thy supplication, that thou hast made before me: I have hallowed this house, which thou hast built, to put my name there for ever; and mine eyes and mine heart shall be there perpetually.

ELIJAH

1 K 18:37–38 Hear me, O LORD, hear me, that this people may know that thou *art* the LORD God, and *that* thou hast turned their heart back again.

Then the fire of the LORD fell, and consumed the burnt sacrifice, and the wood, and the stones, and the dust, and licked up the water that *was* in the trench.

2 K 6:18 And when they came down to him, Elisha prayed unto the LORD, and said, Smite this people, I pray thee, with blindness. And he smote them with blindness according to the word of Elisha.

2 K 13:4 And Jehoahaz besought the LORD, and the LORD hearkened unto him: for he saw the oppression of Israel, because the king of Syria oppressed them.

HEZEKIAH

2 K 19:19–20 Now therefore, O LORD our God, I beseech thee, save thou us out of his hand, that all the kingdoms of the earth may know that thou *art* the LORD God, *even* thou only.

Then Isaiah the son of Amoz sent to Hezekiah, saying, Thus saith the LORD God of Israel, *That* which thou hast prayed to me against Sennacherib king of Assyria I have heard.

1 Chr 5:20 And they were helped against them, and the Hagarites were delivered into their hand, and all that *were* with them: for they cried to God in the battle, and he was intreated of them; because they put their trust in him.

JEHOSHAPHAT

2 Chr 18:31 And it came to pass, when the captains of the chariots saw Jehoshaphat, that they said, It *is* the king of Israel. Therefore they compassed about him to fight: but Jehoshaphat cried out, and the LORD helped him; and God moved them *to depart* from him.

2 Chr 32:21 And the LORD sent an angel, which cut off all the mighty men of valour, and the leaders and captains in the camp of the king of Assyria. So he returned with shame of face to his own land. And when he was come into the house of his god, they that came forth of his own bowels slew him there with the sword.

2 Chr 33:13 And prayed unto him: and he was intreated of him, and heard his supplication, and brought him again to Jerusalem into his kingdom. Then Manasseh knew that the LORD he *was* God.

EZRA

Ezr 8:23 So we fasted and besought our God for this: and he was intreated of us.

Ne 9:27 Therefore thou deliveredst them into the hand of their enemies, who vexed them: and in the time of their trouble, when they cried unto thee, thou heardest *them* from heaven; and according to thy manifold mercies thou gavest them saviours, who saved them out of the hand of their enemies.

Da 2:19 Then was the secret revealed unto Daniel in a night vision. Then Daniel blessed the God of heaven.

Da 9:22 And he informed *me,* and talked with me, and said, O Daniel, I am now come forth to give thee skill and understanding.

Da 10:12 Then said he unto me, Fear not, Daniel: for from the first day that thou didst set thine heart to understand, and to chasten thyself before thy God, thy words were heard, and I am come for thy words.

ZACHARIAS

Lu 1:13 But the angel said unto him, Fear not, Zacharias: for thy prayer is heard; and thy wife Elisabeth shall bear thee a son, and thou shalt call his name John.

THE EARLY CHURCH

Ac 4:31 And when they had prayed, the place was shaken where they were assembled together; and they were all filled with the Holy Ghost, and they spake the word of God with boldness.

3. Answers Promised

Ps 20:1 The LORD hear thee in the day of trouble; the name of the God of Jacob defend thee;

Ps 37:4 Delight thyself also in the LORD; and he shall give thee the desires

Ps 91:15 He shall call upon me, and I will answer him: I *will be* with him in trouble; I will deliver him, and honour him.

Ps 102:17 He will regard the prayer of the destitute, and not despise their prayer.

Pr 10:24 The fear of the wicked, it shall come upon him: but the desire of the righteous shall be granted.

Pr 15:8 The sacrifice of the wicked *is* an abomination to the LORD: but the prayer of the upright *is* his delight.

Is 41:17 *When* the poor and needy seek water, and *there is* none, *and* their tongue faileth for thirst, I the LORD will hear them, *I* the God of Israel will not forsake them.

Is 58:9 Then shalt thou call, and the LORD shall answer; thou shalt cry, and he shall say, Here I *am*. If thou take away from the midst of thee the yoke, the putting forth of the finger, and speaking vanity;

Is 65:24 And it shall come to pass, that before they call, I will answer; and while they are yet speaking, I will hear.

Je 33:3 Call unto me, and I will answer thee, and shew thee great and mighty things, which thou knowest not.

Zec 13:9 And I will bring the third part through the fire, and will refine them as silver is refined, and will try them as gold is tried: they shall call on my name, and I will hear them: I will say, It *is* my people: and they shall say, The LORD *is* my God.

Lu 11:9 And I say unto you, Ask, and it shall be given you; seek, and ye shall find; knock, and it shall be opened unto you.

Jn 14:14 If ye shall ask any thing in my name, I will do *it*.

Jn 15:7 If ye abide in me, and my words abide in you, ye will ask what ye will, and it shall be done unto you.

1 Jn 3:22 And whatsoever we ask, we receive of him, because we keep his commandments, and do those things that are pleasing in his sight.

4. Answers Denied

TO THE DISOBEDIENT

De 1:45 And ye returned and wept before the LORD; but the LORD would not hearken to your voice, nor give ear unto you.

1 S 14:37 And Saul asked counsel of God, Shall I go down after the Philistines? wilt thou deliver them into the hand of Israel? But he answered him not that day.

1 S 28:6 And when Saul enquired of the LORD, the LORD answered him not, neither by dreams, nor by Urim, nor by prophets.

TO THOSE WHO HOLD ONTO SIN

Ps 66:18 If I regard iniquity in my heart, the Lord will not hear *me*:

TO THE INDIFFERENT

Pr 1:28 Then shall they call upon me, but I will not answer; they shall seek me early, but they shall not find me:

TO THOSE WHO NEGLECT MERCY

Pr 21:13 Whoso stoppeth his ears at the cry of the poor, he also shall cry himself, but shall not be heard.

TO THOSE WHO DESPISE THE LAW

Pr 28:9 He that turneth away his ear from hearing the law, even his prayer *shall be* abomination.

TO THOSE WHO SHED BLOOD

Is 1:15 And when ye spread forth your hands, I will hide mine eyes from you: yea, when ye make many prayers, I will not hear: your hands are full of blood.

TO THOSE LIVING IN SIN

Is 59:2 But your iniquities have separated between you and your God, and your sins have hid *his* face from you, that he will not hear.

Mi 3:4 Then shall they cry unto the LORD, but he will not hear them: he will even hide his face from them at that time, as they have behaved themselves ill in their doings.

TO THE STUBBORN

Zec 7:13 Therefore it is come to pass, *that* as he cried, and they would not hear; so they cried, and I would not hear, saith the LORD of hosts:

TO THOSE WHO WAVER

Ja 1:6–7 But let him ask in faith, nothing wavering. For he that wavereth is like a wave of the sea driven with the wind and tossed.

For let not that man think that he shall receive any thing of the Lord.

TO THE SELF-INDULGENT

Ja 4:3 Ye ask, and receive not, because ye ask amiss, that ye may consume *it* upon your lusts.

5. Requests Heard

Ex 2:24 And God heard their groaning, and God remembered his covenant with Abraham, with Isaac, and with Jacob.

Ex 6:5 And I have also heard the groaning of the children of Israel, whom the Egyptians keep in bondage; and I have remembered my covenant.

De 4:7 For what nation *is there so* great, who *hath* God *so* nigh unto them, as the LORD our God *is* in all *things that* we call upon him *for?*

2 Chr 6:19 Have respect therefore to the prayer of thy servant, and to his supplication, O LORD my God, to hearken unto the cry and the prayer which thy servant prayeth before thee:

2 Chr 6:39 Then hear thou from the heavens, *even* from thy dwelling place, their prayer and their supplications, and maintain their cause, and forgive thy people which have sinned against thee.

2 Chr 30:27 Then the priests the Levites arose and blessed the people: and their voice was heard, and their prayer came *up* to his holy dwelling place, *even* unto heaven.

Jb 34:28 So that they cause the cry of the poor to come unto him, and he heareth the cry of the afflicted.

Ps 4:3 But know that the LORD hath set apart him that is godly for himself: the LORD will hear when I call unto him.

Ps 18:6 In my distress I called upon the LORD, and cried unto my God: he heard my voice out of his temple, and my cry came before him, *even* into his ears.

Ps 34:17 *The righteous* cry, and the LORD heareth, and delivereth them out of all their troubles.

Ps 38:15 For in thee, O LORD, do I hope: thou wilt hear, O Lord my God.

Ps 55:17 Evening, and morning, and at noon, will I pray, and cry aloud: and he shall hear my voice.

Pr 15:29 The LORD *is* far from the wicked: but he heareth the prayer of the righteous.

Is 30:19 For the people shall dwell in Zion at Jerusalem: thou shalt weep no more: he will be very gracious unto thee at the voice of thy cry; when he shall hear it, he will answer thee.

Is 65:24 And it shall come to pass, that before they call, I will answer; and while they are yet speaking, I will hear.

Mi 7:7 Therefore I will look unto the LORD; I will wait for the God of my salvation: my God will hear me.

Zec 10:6 And I will strengthen the house of Judah, and I will save the house of Joseph, and I will bring them again to place them; for I have mercy upon them: and they shall be as though I had not cast them off: for I *am* the LORD their God, and will hear them.

Jn 9:31 Now we know that God heareth not sinners: but if any man be a worshipper of God, and doeth his will, him he heareth.

Ac 10:31 And said, Cornelius, thy prayer is heard, and thine alms are had in remembrance in the sight of God.

1 Jn 5:14 And this is the confidence that we have in him, that, if we ask any thing according to his will, he heareth us:

6. Requests Refused

Ex 33:20 And he said, Thou canst not see my face: for there shall no man see me, and live.

De 3:26 But the LORD was wroth with me for your sakes, and would not hear me: and the LORD said unto me, Let it suffice thee; speak no more unto me of this matter.

2 S 12:16 David therefore besought God for the child; and David fasted, and went in, and lay all night upon the earth.

Eze 20:3 Son of man, speak unto the elders of Israel, and say unto them, Thus saith the Lord GOD; Are ye come to enquire of me? *As* I live, saith the Lord GOD, I will not be enquired of by you.

2 Co 12:8 For this thing I besought the Lord thrice, that it might depart from me.

7. Social and Family

Zec 8:21 And the inhabitants of one *city* shall go to another, saying, Let us go speedily to pray before the LORD, and to seek the LORD of hosts: I will go also.

Mt 18:19 Again I say unto you, That if two of you shall agree on earth as touching any thing that they shall ask, it shall be done for them of my Father which is in heaven.

Lu 1:10 And the whole multitude of the people were praying without at the time of incense.

Ac 1:14 These all continued with one accord in prayer and supplication, with the women, and Mary the mother of Jesus, and with his brethren.

Ac 4:24 And when they heard that, they lifted up their voice to God with one accord, and said, Lord, thou *art* God, which hast made heaven, and earth, and the sea, and all that in them is:

Ac 12:12 And when he had considered *the thing*, he came to the house of Mary the mother of John, whose surname was Mark; where many were gathered together praying.

Ac 21:5 And when we had accomplished those days, we departed and went our way; and they all brought us on our way, with wives and children, till *we were* out of the city: and we kneeled down on the shore, and prayed.

8. Necessary Attitudes

CONTRITION

2 Chr 7:14 If my people, which are called by my name, shall humble themselves, and pray, and seek my face, and turn from their wicked ways; then will I hear from heaven, and will forgive their sin, and will heal their land.

Is 58:9 Then shalt thou call, and the LORD shall answer; thou shalt cry, and he shall say, Here I *am*. If thou take away from the midst of thee the yoke, the putting forth of the finger, and speaking vanity;

WHOLE-HEARTEDNESS

Je 29:13 And ye shall seek me, and find *me*, when ye shall search for me with all your heart.

FAITH

Mk 11:24 Therefore I say unto you, What things soever ye desire, when ye pray, believe that ye receive *them*, and ye shall have *them*.

RIGHTEOUSNESS

Ja 5:16 Confess *your* faults one to another, and pray one for another, that ye may be healed. The effectual fervent prayer of a righteous man availeth much.

OBEDIENCE

1 Jn 3:22 And whatsoever we ask, we receive of him, because we keep his commandments, and do those things that are pleasing in his sight.

1 Jn 5:14 And this is the confidence that we have in him, that, if we ask any thing according to his will, he heareth us:

9. Notable Prayers

ABRAHAM FOR SODOM

Ge 18:23 And Abraham drew near, and said, Wilt thou also destroy the righteous with the wicked?

JACOB AT PENIEL

Ge 32:24 And Jacob was left alone; and there wrestled a man with him until the breaking of the day.

DAVID WHEN DENIED THE PRIVILEGE OF BUILDING THE TEMPLE

2 S 7:18 Then went king David in, and sat before the LORD, and he said, Who *am* I, O Lord GOD? and what *is* my house, that thou hast brought me hitherto?

SOLOMON AT GIBEON

1 K 3:6 And Solomon said, Thou hast shewed unto thy servant David my father great mercy, according as he walked before thee in truth, and in righteousness, and in uprightness of heart with thee; and thou hast kept for him this great kindness, that thou hast given him a son to sit on his throne, as *it is* this day.

SOLOMON AT THE DEDICATION
OF THE TEMPLE

1 K 8:22 And Solomon stood before the altar of the LORD in the presence of all the congregation of Israel, and spread forth his hands toward heaven:

HEZEKIAH AT THE INVASION OF SENNACHERIB

2 K 19:15 And Hezekiah prayed before the LORD, and said, O LORD God of Israel, which dwellest *between* the cherubims, thou art the God, *even* thou alone, of all the kingdoms of the earth: thou hast made heaven and earth.
1 Chr 17:16 And David the king came and sat before the LORD, and said, Who *am* I, O LORD God, and what *is* mine house, that thou hast brought me hitherto?

EZRA FOR THE SINS OF THE PEOPLE

Ezr 9:6 And said, O my God, I am ashamed and blush to lift up my face to thee, my God: for our iniquities are increased over *our* head, and our trespass is grown up unto the heavens.

DANIEL FOR THE CAPTIVE JEWS

Da 9:4 And I prayed unto the LORD my God, and made my confession, and said, O Lord, the great and dreadful God, keeping the covenant and mercy to them that love him, and to them that keep his commandments;

HABAKKUK'S PRAYER

Hab 3:1 A prayer of Habakkuk the prophet upon Shigionoth.

THE LORD'S PRAYER

Mt 6:9 After this manner therefore pray ye: Our Father which art in heaven, Hallowed be thy name.

CHRIST'S INTERCESSORY PRAYER

Jn 17:1 These words spake Jesus, and lifted up his eyes to heaven, and said, Father, the hour is come; glorify thy Son, that thy Son also may glorify thee:

PAUL FOR THE EPHESIANS

Ep 3:14 For this cause I bow my knees unto the Father of our Lord Jesus Christ,

10. Brevity

a. Examples

ELIJAH AT CARMEL

1 K 18:36–37 And it came to pass at *the time of* the offering of the *evening* sacrifice, that Elijah the prophet came near, and said, LORD God of Abraham, Isaac, and of Israel, let it be known this day that thou art God in Israel, and *that* I *am* thy servant, and *that* I have done all these things at thy word.

Hear me, O LORD, hear me, that this people may know that thou *art* the LORD God, and *that* thou hast turned their heart back again.

JABEZ

1 Chr 4:10 And Jabez called on the God of Israel, saying, Oh that thou wouldest bless me indeed, and enlarge my coast, and that thine hand might be with me, and that thou wouldest keep *me* from evil, that it may not grieve me! And God granted him that which he requested.

HEZEKIAH WHEN SICK

Is 38:2–3 Then Hezekiah turned his face toward the wall, and prayed unto the LORD,

And said, Remember now, O LORD, I beseech thee, how I have walked before thee in truth and with a perfect heart, and have done *that which is* good in thy sight. And Hezekiah wept sore.

THE PUBLICAN

Lu 18:13 And the publican, standing afar off, would not lift up so much as *his* eyes unto heaven, but smote upon his breast, saying, God be merciful to me a sinner.

JESUS ON THE CROSS

Lu 23:34 Then said Jesus, Father, forgive them; for they know not what they do. And they parted his raiment, and cast lots.

THE DYING THIEF

Lu 23:42 And he said unto Jesus, Lord, remember me when thou comest into thy kingdom.

STEPHEN

Ac 7:60 And he kneeled down, and cried with a loud voice, Lord, lay not this sin to their charge. And when he had said this, he fell asleep.

b. Prescribed

Ec 5:2 Be not rash with thy mouth, and let not thine heart be hasty to utter *any* thing before God: for God *is* in heaven, and thou upon earth: therefore let thy words be few.

Mt 6:7 But when ye pray, use not vain repetitions, as the heathen *do:* for they think that they shall be heard for their much speaking.

Mt 23:14 Woe unto you, scribes and Pharisees, hypocrites! for ye devour widows' houses, and for a pretence make long prayer: therefore ye shall receive the greater damnation.

11. Special Pleas

Ge 18:32 And he said, Oh let not the Lord be angry, and I will speak yet but this once: Peradventure ten shall be found there. And he said, I will not destroy *it* for ten's sake.

Ge 32:9 And Jacob said, O God of my father Abraham, and God of my father Isaac, the LORD which saidst unto me, Return unto thy country, and to thy kindred, and I will deal well with thee:

Nu 14:13 And Moses said unto the LORD, Then the Egyptians shall hear *it,* (for thou broughtest up this people in thy might from among them;)

2 K 20:3 I beseech thee, O LORD, remember now how I have walked before thee in truth and with a perfect heart, and have done *that which is* good in thy sight. And Hezekiah wept sore.

Ps 71:18 Now also when I am old and greyheaded, O God, forsake me not; until I have shewed thy strength unto

this generation, *and* thy power to every one *that* is to come.

Je 14:20 We acknowledge, O LORD, our wickedness, *and* the iniquity of our fathers: for we have sinned against thee.

Da 9:18 O my God, incline thine ear, and hear; open thine eyes, and behold our desolations, and the city which is called by thy name: for we do not present our supplications before thee for our righteousnesses, but for thy great mercies.

12. Postures

a. Bowing

Ge 24:26 And the man bowed down his head, and worshipped the LORD.

Ex 4:31 And the people believed: and when they heard that the LORD had visited the children of Israel, and that he had looked upon their affliction, then they bowed their heads and worshipped.

Ex 12:27 That ye shall say, It *is* the sacrifice of the LORD'S passover, who passed over the houses of the children of Israel in Egypt, when he smote the Egyptians, and delivered our houses. And the people bowed the head and worshipped.

Ex 34:8 And Moses made haste, and bowed his head toward the earth, and worshipped.

b. Kneeling

1 K 8:54 And it was *so,* that when Solomon had made an end of praying all this prayer and supplication unto the LORD, he arose from before the altar of the LORD, from kneeling on his knees with his hands spread up to heaven.

2 Chr 6:13 For Solomon had made a brasen scaffold, of five cubits long, and five cubits broad, and three cubits high, and had set it in the midst of the court: and upon it he stood, and kneeled down upon his knees before all the congregation of Israel, and spread forth his hands toward heaven,

Ezr 9:5 And at the evening sacrifice I arose up from my heaviness; and having rent my garment and my mantle,

I fell upon my knees, and spread out my hands unto the LORD my God.

Ps 95:6 O come, let us worship and bow down: let us kneel before the LORD our maker.

Is 45:23 I have sworn by myself, the word is gone out of my mouth *in* righteousness, and shall not return, That unto me every knee shall bow, every tongue shall swear.

Da 6:10 Now when Daniel knew that the writing was signed, he went into his house; and his windows being open in his chamber toward Jerusalem, he kneeled upon his knees three times a day, and prayed, and gave thanks before his God, as he did aforetime.

Lu 22:41 And he was withdrawn from them about a stone's cast, and kneeled down, and prayed,

Ac 7:60 And he kneeled down, and cried with a loud voice, Lord, lay not this sin to their charge. And when he had said this, he fell asleep.

Ac 9:40 But Peter put them all forth, and kneeled down, and prayed; and turning *him* to the body said, Tabitha, arise. And she opened her eyes: and when she saw Peter, she sat up.

Ac 20:36 And when he had thus spoken, he kneeled down, and prayed with them all.

Ac 21:5 And when we had accomplished those days, we departed and went our way; and they all brought us on our way, with wives and children, till *we were* out of the city: and we kneeled down on the shore, and prayed.

Ep 3:14 For this cause I bow my knees unto the Father of our Lord Jesus Christ,

c. On the Face before God

Nu 20:6 And Moses and Aaron went from the presence of the assembly unto the door of the tabernacle of the congregation, and they fell upon their faces: and the glory of the LORD appeared unto them.

Jos 5:14 And he said, Nay; but *as* captain of the host of the LORD am I now come. And Joshua fell on his face to the earth, and did worship, and said

unto him, What saith my lord unto his servant?

Jos 7:6 And Joshua rent his clothes, and fell to the earth upon his face before the ark of the LORD until the eventide, he and the elders of Israel, and put dust upon their heads.

1 K 18:42 So Ahab went up to eat and to drink. And Elijah went up to the top of Carmel; and he cast himself down upon the earth, and put his face between his knees,

2 Chr 20:18 And Jehoshaphat bowed his head with *his* face to the ground: and all Judah and the inhabitants of Jerusalem fell before the LORD, worshipping the LORD.

Ne 8:6 And Ezra blessed the LORD, the great God. And all the people answered, Amen, Amen, with lifting up their hands: and they bowed their heads, and worshipped the LORD with *their* faces to the ground.

Mt 26:39 And he went a little farther, and fell on his face, and prayed, saying, O my Father, if it be possible, let this cup pass from me: nevertheless not as I will, but as thou *wilt*.

d. Standing

1 K 8:22 And Solomon stood before the altar of the LORD in the presence of all the congregation of Israel, and spread forth his hands toward heaven:

Mk 11:25 And when ye stand praying, forgive, if ye have ought against any: that your Father also which is in heaven may forgive you your trespasses.

Lu 18:11 The Pharisee stood and prayed thus with himself, God, I thank thee, that I am not as other men *are*, extortioners, unjust, adulterers, or even as this publican.

13. Secret

MOSES

De 9:25 Thus I fell down before the LORD forty days and forty nights, as I fell down *at the first*; because the LORD had said he would destroy you.

SAMUEL

1 S 15:11 It repenteth me that I have set up Saul *to be* king: for he is turned back from following me, and hath not performed my commandments. And it grieved Samuel; and he cried unto the LORD all night.

ELIJAH

1 K 17:19–20 And he said unto her, Give me thy son. And he took him out of her bosom, and carried him up into a loft, where he abode, and laid him upon his own bed.

And he cried unto the LORD, and said, O LORD my God, hast thou also brought evil upon the widow with whom I sojourn, by slaying her son?

DANIEL

Da 6:10 Now when Daniel knew that the writing was signed, he went into his house; and his windows being open in his chamber toward Jerusalem, he kneeled upon his knees three times a day, and prayed, and gave thanks before his God, as he did aforetime.

CHRIST'S COMMAND

Mt 6:6 But thou, when thou prayest, enter into thy closet, and when thou hast shut thy door, pray to thy Father which is in secret; and thy Father which seeth in secret shall reward thee openly.

PETER

Ac 10:9 On the morrow, as they went on their journey, and drew nigh unto the city, Peter went up upon the housetop to pray about the sixth hour:

CORNELIUS

Ac 10:30 And Cornelius said, Four days ago I was fasting until this hour; and at the ninth hour I prayed in my house, and, behold, a man stood before me in bright clothing,

14. Private Devotions of Christ

MORNING DEVOTIONS

Mk 1:35 And in the morning, rising up a great while before day, he went out, and departed into a solitary place, and there prayed.

EVENING PRAYER

Mk 6:46–47 And when he had sent them away, he departed into a mountain to pray.

And when even was come, the ship was in the midst of the sea, and he alone on the land.

SOLITARY COMMUNION

Lu 5:15–16 But so much the more went there a fame abroad of him: and great multitudes came together to hear, and to be healed by him of their infirmities.

And he withdrew himself into the wilderness, and prayed.

ALL-NIGHT PRAYER

Lu 6:12 And it came to pass in those days, that he went out into a mountain to pray, and continued all night in prayer to God.

ONLY THE DISCIPLES NEAR

Lu 9:18 And it came to pass, as he was alone praying, his disciples were with him: and he asked them, saying, Whom say the people that I am?

IN THE GARDEN OF GETHSEMANE

Lu 22:41–42 And he was withdrawn from them about a stone's cast, and kneeled down, and prayed,

Saying, Father, if thou be willing, remove this cup from me: nevertheless not my will, but thine, be done.

15. Public Prayers of Christ

Mt 11:25 At that time Jesus answered and said, I thank thee, O Father, Lord of heaven and earth, because thou hast hid these things from the wise and prudent, and hast revealed them unto babes.

Lu 3:21 Now when all the people were baptized, it came to pass, that

Jesus also being baptized, and praying, the heaven was opened,

Jn 11:41 Then they took away the stone *from the place* where the dead was laid. And Jesus lifted up *his* eyes, and said, Father, I thank thee that thou hast heard me.

Jn 17:1 These words spake Jesus, and lifted up his eyes to heaven, and said, Father, the hour is come; glorify thy Son, that thy Son also may glorify thee:

16. Requests for Prayer

1 S 7:8 And the children of Israel said to Samuel, Cease not to cry unto the LORD our God for us, that he will save us out of the hand of the Philistines.

1 S 12:19 And all the people said unto Samuel, Pray for thy servants unto the LORD thy God, that we die not: for we have added unto all our sins *this* evil, to ask us a king.

1 K 13:6 And the king answered and said unto the man of God, Intreat now the face of the LORD thy God, and pray for me, that my hand may be restored me again. And the man of God besought the LORD, and the king's hand was restored him again, and became as *it was* before.

Ac 8:24 Then answered Simon, and said, Pray ye to the Lord for me, that none of these things which ye have spoken come upon me.

Ro 15:30 Now I beseech you, brethren, for the Lord Jesus Christ's sake, and for the love of the Spirit, that ye strive together with me in *your* prayers to God for me;

Ep 6:19 And for me, that utterance may be given unto me, that I may open my mouth boldly, to make known the mystery of the gospel,

1 Th 5:25 Brethren, pray for us.

2 Th 3:1 Finally, brethren, pray for us, that the word of the Lord may have *free* course, and be glorified, even as *it is* with you:

He 13:18 Pray for us: for we trust we have a good conscience, in all things willing to live honestly.

17. Unwise Prayers

Nu 11:15 And if thou deal thus with me, kill me, I pray thee, out of hand, if I have found favour in thy sight; and let me not see my wretchedness.

1 K 19:4 But he himself went a day's journey into the wilderness, and came and sat down under a juniper tree: and he requested for himself that he might die; and said, It is enough; now, O LORD, take away my life; for I *am* not better than my fathers.

Jona 4:3 Therefore now, O LORD, take, I beseech thee, my life from me; for *it is* better for me to die than to live.

Mt 20:21 And he said unto her, What wilt thou? She saith unto him, Grant that these my two sons may sit, the one on thy right hand, and the other on the left, in thy kingdom.

Ja 4:3 Ye ask, and receive not, because ye ask amiss, that ye may consume *it* upon your lusts.

18. For Food

Ge 28:20 And Jacob vowed a vow, saying, If God will be with me, and will keep me in this way that I go, and will give me bread to eat, and raiment to put on,

Pr 30:8 Remove far from me vanity and lies: give me neither poverty nor riches; feed me with food convenient for me:

Mt 6:11 Give us this day our daily bread.

19. For the Church

1 S 12:23 Moreover as for me, God forbid that I should sin against the LORD in ceasing to pray for you: but I will teach you the good and the right way:

Ps 122:6 Pray for the peace of Jerusalem: they shall prosper that love thee.

Is 63:15 Look down from heaven, and behold from the habitation of thy holiness and of thy glory: where *is* thy zeal and thy strength, the sounding of thy bowels and of thy mercies toward me? are they restrained?

Jn 17:20 Neither pray I for these alone, but for them also which shall believe on me through their word;

Ro 1:9 For God is my witness, whom I serve with my spirit in the gospel of his Son, that without ceasing I make mention of you always in my prayers;

Ep 1:16 Cease not to give thanks for you, making mention of you in my prayers;

Ep 3:14 For this cause I bow my knees unto the Father of our Lord Jesus Christ,

Ph 1:4 Always in every prayer of mine for you all making request with joy,

Col 1:3 We give thanks to God and the Father of our Lord Jesus Christ, praying always for you,

20. Importunity

ABRAHAM

Ge 18:32 And he said, Oh let not the Lord be angry, and I will speak yet but this once: Peradventure ten shall be found there. And he said, I will not destroy *it* for ten's sake.

JACOB

Ge 32:26 And he said, Let me go, for the day breaketh. And he said, I will not let thee go, except thou bless me.

MOSES

De 9:18 And I fell down before the LORD, as at the first, forty days and forty nights: I did neither eat bread, nor drink water, because of all your sins which ye sinned, in doing wickedly in the sight of the LORD, to provoke him to anger.

THE SYROPHOENICIAN

Mt 15:27 And she said, Truth, Lord: yet the dogs eat of the crumbs which fall from their masters' table.

Lu 11:8 I say unto you, Though he will not rise and give him, because he is his friend, yet because of his importunity he will rise and give him as many as he needeth.

Lu 18:5 Yet because this widow troubleth me, I will avenge her, lest by her continual coming she weary me.

JESUS

Lu 22:44 And being in an agony he prayed more earnestly: and his sweat was as it were great drops of blood falling down to the ground.

THE NOBLEMAN FROM CAPERNAUM

Jn 4:49 The nobleman saith unto him, Sir, come down ere my child die.

THE EARLY CHURCH

Ac 12:5 Peter therefore was kept in prison: but prayer was made without ceasing of the church unto God for him.

Ja 5:16 Confess *your* faults one to another, and pray one for another, that ye may be healed. The effectual fervent prayer of a righteous man availeth much.

ELIJAH

Ja 5:17 Elias was a man subject to like passions as we are, and he prayed earnestly that it might not rain: and it rained not on the earth by the space of three years and six months.

21. Special Exhortations

1 K 3:5 In Gibeon the LORD appeared to Solomon in a dream by night: and God said, Ask what I shall give thee.

Is 65:24 And it shall come to pass, that before they call, I will answer; and while they are yet speaking, I will hear.

Zec 10:1 Ask ye of the LORD rain in the time of the latter rain; *so* the LORD shall make bright clouds, and give them showers of rain, to every one grass in the field.

Mt 7:8 For every one that asketh receiveth; and he that seeketh findeth; and to him that knocketh it shall be opened.

Mt 21:22 And all things, whatsoever ye shall ask in prayer, believing, ye shall receive.

Lu 11:9 And I say unto you, Ask, and it shall be given you; seek, and ye shall find; knock, and it shall be opened unto you.

Jn 14:13 And whatsoever ye shall ask in my name, that will I do, that the Father may be glorified in the Son.

Jn 15:7 If ye abide in me, and my words abide in you, ye shall ask what ye will, and it shall be done unto you.

Jn 16:24 Hitherto have ye asked nothing in my name: ask, and ye shall receive, that your joy may be full.

Ja 1:5 If any of you lack wisdom, let him ask of God, that giveth to all *men* liberally, and upbraideth not; and it shall be given him.

1 Jn 5:14 And this is the confidence that we have in him, that, if we ask any thing according to his will, he heareth us:

22. For Enemies

Mt 5:44 But I say unto you, Love your enemies, bless them that curse you, do good to them that hate you, and pray for them which despitefully use you, and persecute you;

Lu 23:34 Then said Jesus, Father, forgive them; for they know not what they do. And they parted his raiment, and cast lots.

Ac 7:60 And he kneeled down, and cried with a loud voice, Lord, lay not this sin to their charge. And when he had said this, he fell asleep.

See **DEEPER LIFE, DEVOTIONAL LIFE, NEARNESS, SEEKING GOD**

PRAYERLESSNESS

1 Chr 13:3 And let us bring again the ark of our God to us: for we enquired not at it in the days of Saul.

2 Chr 12:14 And he did evil, because he prepared not his heart to seek the LORD.

2 Chr 15:13 That whosoever would not seek the LORD God of Israel should be put to death, whether small or great, whether man or woman.

Job 15:4 Yea, thou castest off fear, and restrainest prayer before God.

Job 21:15 What *is* the Almighty, that we should serve him? and what profit should we have, if we pray unto him?

Job 36:13 But the hypocrites in heart heap up wrath: they cry not when he bindeth them.

Ps 14:5 There were they in great fear: for God *is* in the generation of the righteous.

Ps 53:4 Have the workers of iniquity no knowledge? who eat up my people *as* they eat bread: they have not called upon God.

Ps 79:6 Pour out thy wrath upon the heathen that have not known thee, and upon the kingdoms that have not called upon thy name.

Is 9:13 For the people turneth not unto him that smiteth them, neither do they seek the LORD of hosts.

Is 30:2 That walk to go down into Egypt, and have not asked at my mouth; to strengthen themselves in the strength of Pharaoh, and to trust in the shadow of Egypt!

Is 31:1 Woe to them that go down to Egypt for help; and stay on horses, and trust in chariots, because *they are* many; and in horsemen, because they are very strong; but they look not unto the Holy One of Israel, neither seek the LORD!

Is 43:22 But thou hast not called upon me, O Jacob; but thou hast been weary of me, O Israel.

Is 64:7 And *there is* none that calleth upon thy name, that stirreth up himself to take hold of thee: for thou hast hid thy face from us, and hast consumed us, because of our iniquities.

Je 2:8 The priests said not, Where *is* the LORD? and they that handle the law knew me not: the pastors also transgressed against me, and the prophets prophesied by Baal, and walked after *things that* do not profit.

Je 10:21 For the pastors are become brutish, and have not sought the LORD: therefore they shall not prosper, and all their flocks shall be scattered.

Je 10:25 Pour out thy fury upon the heathen that know thee not, and upon the families that call not on thy name: for they have eaten up Jacob, and devoured him, and consumed him, and have made his habitation desolate.

Da 6:7 All the presidents of the kingdom, the governors, and the princes, the counsellors, and the captains, have consulted together to establish a royal statute, and to make a firm decree, that whosoever shall ask a petition of any God or man for thirty days, save of thee, O king, he shall be cast into the den of lions.

Da 9:13 As *it is* written in the law of Moses, all this evil is come upon us: yet made we not our prayer before the LORD our God, that we might turn from our iniquities, and understand thy truth.

Ho 7:7 They are all hot as an oven, and have devoured their judges; all their kings are fallen: *there is* none among them that calleth unto me.

Ho 7:14 And they have not cried unto me with their heart, when they howled upon their beds: they assemble themselves for corn and wine, *and* they rebel against me.

Zep 1:6 And them that are turned back from the LORD; and *those* that have not sought the LORD, nor enquired for him.

Ro 3:11 There is none that understandeth, there is none that seeketh after God.

Ja 4:2 Ye lust, and have not: ye kill, and desire to have, and cannot obtain: ye fight and war, yet ye have not, because ye ask not.

See **INDIFFERENCE, NEGLECT, PRAYER**

PRECEPTS, *human commandments and laws*

2 K 17:19 Also Judah kept not the commandments of the LORD their God, but walked in the statutes of Israel which they made.

Is 29:13 Wherefore the Lord said, Forasmuch as this people draw near *me* with their mouth, and with their lips do honour me, but have removed their heart far from me, and their fear toward me is taught by the precept of men:

Je 23:16 Thus saith the LORD of hosts, Hearken not unto the words of the prophets that prophesy unto you: they make you vain: they speak a vision of their own heart, *and* not out of the mouth of the LORD.

Ho 5:11 Ephraim *is* oppressed *and* broken in judgment, because he willingly walked after the commandment.

Mt 15:9 But in vain they do worship me, teaching *for* doctrines the commandments of men.

Mk 7:7 Howbeit in vain do they worship me, teaching *for* doctrines the commandments of men.

Mk 7:13 Making the word of God of none effect through your tradition, which ye have delivered: and many such like things do ye.

2 Co 3:6 Who also hath made us able ministers of the new testament; not of the letter, but of the spirit: for the letter killeth, but the spirit giveth life.

Col 2:8 Beware lest any man spoil you through philosophy and vain deceit, after the tradition of men, after the rudiments of the world, and not after Christ.

Col 2:22 Which all are to perish with the using;) after the commandments and doctrines of men?

1 Ti 4:3 Forbidding to marry, *and commanding* to abstain from meats, which God hath created to be received with thanksgiving of them which believe and know the truth.

Tit 1:14 Not giving heed to Jewish fables, and commandments of men, that turn from the truth.

See **LAW, WORD OF GOD**

PREDESTINATION, *the act whereby God is believed to have foreordained all things, including the salvation of individual souls*

Pr 16:4 The LORD hath made all *things* for himself: yea, even the wicked for the day of evil.

Ac 4:28 For to do whatsoever thy hand and thy counsel determined before to be done.

Ro 8:29 For whom he did foreknow, he also did predestinate *to be* conformed to the image of his Son, that he might be the firstborn among many brethren.

Ro 9:11 (For *the children* being not yet born, neither having done any good or evil, that the purpose of God according to election might stand, not of works, but of him that calleth;)

Ep 1:4 According as he hath chosen us in him before the foundation of the world, that we should be holy and without blame before him in love:

Ep 3:11 According to the eternal purpose which he purposed in Christ Jesus our Lord:

1 Pe 1:20 Who verily was foreordained before the foundation of the world, but was manifest in these last times for you,

See **KNOWLEDGE, FOREKNOWLEDGE**

PREJUDICE

Lu 9:53 And they did not receive him, because his face was as though he would go to Jerusalem.

Jn 4:9 Then saith the woman of Samaria unto him, How is it that thou, being a Jew, askest drink of me, which am a woman of Samaria? for the Jews have no dealings with the Samaritans.

Jn 4:27 And upon this came his disciples, and marvelled that he talked with the woman: yet no man said, What seekest thou? or, Why talkest thou with her?

Jn 8:48 Then answered the Jews, and said unto him, Say we not well that thou art a Samaritan, and hast a devil?

Ac 10:28 And he said unto them, Ye know how that it is an unlawful thing for a man that is a Jew to keep company, or come unto one of another nation; but God hath shewed me that I should not call any man common or unclean.

Ac 11:3 Saying, Thou wentest in to men uncircumcised, and didst eat with them.

Ac 19:34 But when they knew that he was a Jew, all with one voice about the space of two hours cried out, Great is Diana of the Ephesians.

Ga 2:12 For before that certain came from James, he did eat with the Gentiles: but when they were come, he withdrew and separated himself, fearing them which were of the circumcision

See **IMPARTIALITY, PARTIALITY**

PRESENCE, DIVINE

1. A Comfort to Saints

IN THE PILGRIMAGE OF LIFE

Ge 28:15 And, behold, I *am* with thee, and will keep thee in all *places* whither thou goest, and will bring thee again into this land; for I will not leave thee, until I have done *that* which I have spoken to thee of.

Ge 31:3 And the LORD said unto Jacob, Return unto the land of thy fathers, and to thy kindred; and I will be with thee.

Ex 3:12 And he said, Certainly I will be with thee; and this *shall be* a token unto thee, that I have sent thee: When thou hast brought forth the people out of Egypt, ye shall serve God upon this mountain.

Ex 29:45 And I will dwell among the children of Israel, and will be their God.

AFFORDS REST

Ex 33:14 And he said, My presence shall go *with thee,* and I will give thee rest.

Le 26:12 And I will walk among you, and will be your God, and ye shall be my people.

GIVES COURAGE IN LIFE'S BATTLES

De 20:1 When thou goest out to battle against thine enemies, and seest horses, and chariots, *and* a people more than thou, be not afraid of them: for the LORD thy God *is* with thee, which brought thee up out of the land of Egypt.

PROVIDES COMFORT IN TRIALS

Is 43:2 When thou passest through the waters, I *will be* with thee; and through the rivers, they shall not overflow thee: when thou walkest through the fire, thou shalt not be burned; neither shall the flame kindle upon thee.

Zec 2:10 Sing and rejoice, O daughter of Zion: for, lo, I come, and I will dwell in the midst of thee, saith the LORD.

ASSURED TO THE SMALLEST ASSEMBLY OF BELIEVERS

Mt 18:20 For where two or three are gathered together in my name, there am I in the midst of them.

LASTS FOREVER

Mt 28:20 Teaching them to observe all things whatsoever I have commanded you: and, lo, I am with you alway, *even* unto the end of the world. Amen.

2. A Terror to Evildoers

Ge 3:8 And they heard the voice of the LORD God walking in the garden in the cool of the day: and Adam and his wife hid themselves from the presence of the LORD God amongst the trees of the garden.

Ex 14:24 And it came to pass, that in the morning watch the LORD looked unto the host of the Egyptians through the pillar of fire and of the cloud, and troubled the host of the Egyptians,

Jb 23:15 Therefore am I troubled at his presence: when I consider, I am afraid of him.

Ps 9:3 When mine enemies are turned back, they shall fall and perish at thy presence.

Ps 68:2 As smoke is driven away, *so* drive *them* away: as wax melteth before the fire, *so* let the wicked perish at the presence of God.

Ps 139:7 Whither shall I go from thy spirit? or whither shall I flee from thy presence?

Is 64:2 As *when* the melting fire burneth, the fire causeth the waters to boil, to make thy name known to thine adversaries, *that* the nations may tremble at thy presence!

Je 4:26 I beheld, and, lo, the fruitful place *was* a wilderness, and all the cities thereof were broken down at the presence of the LORD, *and* by his fierce anger.

Je 5:22 Fear ye not me? saith the LORD: will ye not tremble at my presence, which have placed the sand *for* the bound of the sea by a perpetual decree, that it cannot pass it: and

though the waves thereof toss themselves, yet can they not prevail; though they roar, yet can they not pass over it.

Eze 35:10 Because thou hast said, These two nations and these two countries shall be mine, and we will possess it; whereas the LORD was there:

Jona 1:3 But Jonah rose up to flee unto Tarshish from the presence of the LORD, and went down to Joppa; and he found a ship going to Tarshish: so he paid the fare thereof, and went down into it, to go with them unto Tarshish from the presence of the LORD.

Jona 1:10 Then were the men exceedingly afraid, and said unto him, Why hast thou done this? For the men knew that he fled from the presence of the LORD, because he had told them.

3. Overpowering Presence of Christ

Jn 18:6 As soon then as he had said unto them, I am *he*, they went backward, and fell to the ground.

Ac 9:3–4 And as he journeyed, he came near Damascus: and suddenly there shined round about him a light from heaven:

And he fell to the earth, and heard a voice saying unto him, Saul, Saul, why persecutest thou me?

Ac 22:7 And I fell unto the ground, and heard a voice saying unto me, Saul, Saul, why persecutest thou me?

Ac 26:14 And when we were all fallen to the earth, I heard a voice speaking unto me, and saying in the Hebrew tongue, Saul, Saul, why persecutest thou me? *it is* hard for thee to kick against the pricks.

2 Th 2:8 And then shall that Wicked be revealed, whom the Lord shall consume with the spirit of his mouth, and shall destroy with the brightness of his coming:

He 12:19 And the sound of a trumpet, and the voice of words; *which* voice they that heard intreated that the word should not be spoken to them any more:

Re 1:7 Behold, he cometh with clouds; and every eye shall see him, and they *also* which pierced him: and all kindreds of the earth shall wail because of him. Even so, Amen.

Re 1:17 And when I saw him, I fell at his feet as dead. And he laid his right hand upon me, saying unto me, Fear not; I am the first and the last:

See **COMFORT, FEAR, GUIDANCE**

PRESENTS *See* **GIFTS**

PRESUMPTION, *behavior or language that is arrogant or offensive; assuming something to be true*

1. Warnings

Ex 17:2 Wherefore the people did chide with Moses, and said, Give us water that we may drink. And Moses said unto them, Why chide ye with me? wherefore do ye tempt the LORD?

Nu 15:30 But the soul that doeth *ought* presumptuously, *whether he be* born in the land, or a stranger, the same reproacheth the LORD; and that soul shall be cut off from among his people.

De 1:43 So I spake unto you; and ye would not hear, but rebelled against the commandment of the LORD, and went presumptuously up into the hill.

De 6:16 Ye shall not tempt the LORD your God, as ye tempted *him* in Massah.

De 18:20 But the prophet, which shall presume to speak a word in my name, which I have not commanded him to speak, or that shall speak in the name of other gods, even that prophet shall die.

1 K 22:29 So the king of Israel and Jehoshaphat the king of Judah went up to Ramoth-gilead.

Ps 19:13 Keep back thy servant also from presumptuous *sins;* let them not have dominion over me: then shall I be upright, and I shall be innocent from the great transgression.

Ps 95:9 When your fathers tempted me, proved me, and saw my work.

Ps 106:14 But lusted exceedingly in the wilderness, and tempted God in the desert.

Is 5:18 Woe unto them that draw iniquity with cords of vanity, and sin as it were with a cart rope:

Is 45:9 Woe unto him that striveth with his Maker! *Let* the potsherd *strive* with the potsherds of the earth. Shall the clay say to him that fashioneth it, What makest thou? or thy work, He hath no hands?

Mt 4:6 And saith unto him, If thou be the Son of God, cast thyself down: for it is written, He shall give his angels charge concerning thee: and in *their* hands they shall bear thee up, lest at any time thou dash thy foot against a stone.

Ro 1:32 Who knowing the judgment of God, that they which commit such things are worthy of death, not only do the same, but have pleasure in them that do them.

Ro 6:1 What shall we say then? Shall we continue in sin, that grace may abound?

1 Co 10:9 Neither let us tempt Christ, as some of them also tempted, and were destroyed of serpents.

He 10:31 *It is* a fearful thing to fall into the hands of the living God.

Ja 4:13 Go to now, ye that say, To day or to morrow we will go into such a city, and continue there a year, and buy and sell, and get gain:

2 Pe 2:10 But chiefly them that walk after the flesh in the lust of uncleanness, and despise government. Presumptuous *are they,* selfwilled, they are not afraid to speak evil of dignities.

2. Examples

Ge 11:4 And they said, Go to, let us build us a city and a tower, whose top *may reach* unto heaven; and let us make us a name, lest we be scattered abroad upon the face of the whole earth.

Nu 14:44 But they presumed to go up unto the hill top: nevertheless the ark of the covenant of the LORD, and Moses, departed not out of the camp.

Nu 20:11 And Moses lifted up his hand, and with his rod he smote the rock twice: and the water came out abundantly, and the congregation drank, and their beasts *also.*

1 K 16:34 In his days did Hiel the Bethelite build Jericho: he laid the foundation thereof in Abiram his firstborn, and set up the gates thereof in his youngest *son* Segub, according to the word of the LORD, which he spake by Joshua the son of Nun.

2 Chr 26:16 But when he was strong, his heart was lifted up to *his* destruction: for he transgressed against the LORD his God, and went into the temple of the LORD to burn incense upon the altar of incense.

Mt 20:22 But Jesus answered and said, Ye know not what ye ask. Are ye able to drink of the cup that I shall drink of, and to be baptized with the baptism that I am baptized with? They say unto him, We are able.

Mk 8:32 And he spake that saying openly. And Peter took him, and began to rebuke him.

Lu 12:19 And I will say to my soul, Soul, thou hast much goods laid up for many years; take thine ease, eat, drink, *and* be merry.

Ac 5:9 Then Peter said unto her, How is it that ye have agreed together to tempt the Spirit of the Lord? behold, the feet of them which have buried thy husband *are* at the door, and shall carry thee out.

3. Of Time and Opportunity

BOASTING OF THE FUTURE

Pr 27:1 Boast not thyself of to morrow; for thou knowest not what a day may bring forth.

PLANNING FOR TOMORROW'S
SELF-INDULGENCE

Is 56:12 Come ye, *say they,* I will fetch wine, and we will fill ourselves with strong drink; and to morrow shall be as this day, *and* much more abundant.

THINKING THE DAY OF TRIAL IS REMOTE

Am 6:3 Ye that put far away the evil day, and cause the seat of violence to come near;

PREPARING FOR MANY YEARS OF ENJOYMENT

Lu 12:19 And I will say to my soul, Soul, thou hast much goods laid up for many years; take thine ease, eat, drink, *and* be merry.

RECKONING ON FUTURE
OPPORTUNITIES FOR REFORM

Ac 24:25 And as he reasoned of righteousness, temperance, and judgment to come, Felix trembled, and answered, Go thy way for this time; when I have a convenient season, I will call for thee.

INDULGING IN DREAMS OF FUTURE GAIN

Ja 4:13–14 Go to now, ye that say, To day or to morrow we will go into such a city, and continue there a year, and buy and sell, and get gain:

Whereas ye know not what *shall be* on the morrow. For what *is* your life? It is even a vapour, that appeareth for a little time, and then vanisheth away.

See **PLAN**

PRIDE, *conceit, self-love, haughtiness, arrogance*

1. Warnings

Est 5:11 And Haman told them of the glory of his riches, and the multitude of his children, and all *the things* wherein the king had promoted him, and how he had advanced him above the princes and servants of the king.

Ps 10:2 The wicked in *his* pride doth persecute the poor: let them be taken in the devices that they have imagined.

Ps 73:6 Therefore pride compasseth them about as a chain; violence covereth them *as* a garment.

Ps 75:4 I said unto the fools, Deal not foolishly: and to the wicked, Lift not up the horn:

Ps 119:21 Thou hast rebuked the proud *that are* cursed, which do err from thy commandments.

Pr 6:17 A proud look, a lying tongue, and hands that shed innocent blood,

Pr 11:2 *When* pride cometh, then cometh shame: but with the lowly *is* wisdom.

Pr 13:10 Only by pride cometh contention: but with the well advised *is* wisdom.

Pr 16:18 Pride *goeth* before destruction, and an haughty spirit before a fall.

Pr 21:4 An high look, and a proud heart, *and* the plowing of the wicked, *is* sin.

Pr 28:25 He that is of a proud heart stirreth up strife: but he that putteth his trust in the LORD shall be made fat.

Ho 7:10 And the pride of Israel testifieth to his face: and they do not return to the LORD their God, nor seek him for all this.

Hab 2:4 Behold, his soul *which* is lifted up is not upright in him: but the just shall live by his faith.

Mk 7:22 Thefts, covetousness, wickedness, deceit, lasciviousness, an evil eye, blasphemy, pride, foolishness:

1 Jn 2:16 For all that *is* in the world, the lust of the flesh, and the lust of the eyes, and the pride of life, is not of the Father, but is of the world.

2. Examples

PHARAOH

Ex 5:2

NAAMAN

2 K 5:11

UZZIAH

2 Chr 26:16

HEZEKIAH

2 Chr 32:25

HAMAN

Est 3:5

NEBUCHADNEZZAR

Da 4:30

BELSHAZZAR

Da 5:23

3. Spiritual

Jb 33:9 I am clean without transgression, I *am* innocent; neither *is there* iniquity in me.

Zep 3:11 In that day shalt thou not be ashamed for all thy doings,

wherein thou hast transgressed against me: for then I will take away out of the midst of thee them that rejoice in thy pride, and thou shalt no more be haughty because of my holy mountain.

Lu 18:11 The Pharisee stood and prayed thus with himself, God, I thank thee, that I am not as other men *are*, extortioners, unjust, adulterers, or even as this publican.

Jn 9:41 Jesus said unto them, If ye were blind, ye should have no sin: but now ye say, We see; therefore your sin remaineth.

1 Co 4:18 Now some are puffed up, as though I would not come to you.

Re 3:17 Because thou sayest, I am rich, and increased with goods, and have need of nothing; and knowest not that thou art wretched, and miserable, and poor, and blind, and naked:

4. Jewish

Mt 3:9; 24:1; Mk 13:1; Lu 3:8; Jn 8:33, 39; 9:28; 19:21; Ro 2:19

5. Proud Humbled

2 Chr 36:12; Ne 9:16; Jb 40:11; Ps 40:4; 86:14; 119:51, 78, 85; 123:4; 138:6; Is 9:9; Je 43:2; 50:31; Hab 1:10; Mal 3:15; 4:1; 1 Ti 6:4; 2 Ti 3:2; Ja 4:6; 1 Pe 5:5

See **HUMILITY**

PRIESTHOOD, *the office of man's representatives before God*

1. Of Christ

HUMAN AS WELL AS DIVINE

He 2:17 Wherefore in all things it behoved him to be made like unto *his* brethren, that he might be a merciful and faithful high priest in things *pertaining* to God, to make reconciliation for the sins of the people.

He 3:1 Wherefore, holy brethren, partakers of the heavenly calling, consider the Apostle and High Priest of our profession, Christ Jesus;

SYMPATHETIC

He 4:14–15 Seeing then that we have a great high priest, that is passed into the heavens, Jesus the Son of God, let us hold fast *our* profession.

For we have not an high priest which cannot be touched with the feeling of our infirmities; but was in all points tempted like as *we are, yet* without sin.

DIVINELY APPOINTED

He 5:5 So also Christ glorified not himself to be made an high priest; but he that said unto him, Thou art my Son, to day have I begotten thee.

ETERNAL

He 6:20 Whither the forerunner is for us entered, *even* Jesus, made an high priest for ever after the order of Melchisedec.

SINLESS

He 7:26 For such a high priest became us, *who is* holy, harmless, undefiled, separate from sinners, and made higher than the heavens;

EXALTED

He 8:1 Now of the things which we have spoken *this is* the sum: We have such an high priest, who is set on the right hand of the throne of the Majesty in the heavens;

He 9:11 But Christ being come an high priest of good things to come, by a greater and more perfect tabernacle, not made with hands, that is to say, not of this building;

He 10:21 And *having* an high priest over the house of God;

2. Of Believers

Ex 19:6 And ye shall be unto me a kingdom of priests, and an holy nation. These *are* the words which thou shalt speak unto the children of Israel.

Is 61:6 But ye shall be named the Priests of the LORD: *men* shall call you the Ministers of our God: ye shall eat the riches of the Gentiles, and in their glory shall ye boast yourselves.

Is 66:21 And I will also take of them for priests *and* for Levites, saith the LORD.

1 Pe 2:5 Ye also, as lively stones, are built up a spiritual house, an holy priesthood, to offer up spiritual sacrifices, acceptable to God by Jesus Christ.

1 Pe 2:9 But ye *are* a chosen generation, a royal priesthood, an holy nation, a peculiar people; that ye should shew forth the praises of him who hath called you out of darkness into his marvellous light:

Re 1:6 And hath made us kings and priests unto God and his Father; to him *be* glory and dominion for ever and ever. Amen.

Re 5:10 And hast made us unto our God kings and priests: and we shall reign on the earth.

Re 20:6 Blessed and holy *is* he that hath part in the first resurrection: on such the second death hath no power, but they shall be priests of God and of Christ, and shall reign with him a thousand years.

See **INTERCESSION**

PRIESTS, *representatives of man before God*

Ge 14:18; Ex 18:1; 24:5; Nu 3:4; 10:8; Jos 3:6; 4:16; Jud 17:12; 18:4; 1 Chr 9:2; 2 Chr 11:13; 17:8; 26:17; 29:4; 31:2; 34:30; Ezr 1:5; 2:36, 61, 70; 6:18; 8:15, 24; 9:1; 10:5; Ne 3:22, 28; 5:12; 7:63, 73; 8:13; 9:38; 10:39; 11:10; 12:22, 41; 13:30; Eze 42:13; 43:19; Zec 7:3; Mt 12:5; Mk 14:1; Lu 1:8; 5:14; 22:2, 52; Jn 1:19; Ac 4:1

1. Laws that Apply

Ex 29:1; 40:15; Le 10:9; 21:1; Ezr 7:24; Ne 7:65

2. Holiness Recognized

Ex 19:22; Le 10:3, 7; 21:6; 22:9; 2 Chr 6:41; 23:6; 35:3; Ezr 8:28; Ne 13:29; Is 52:11; Mal 2:7

3. Their Corruption

Je 2:8; 5:31; 6:13; Lam 1:19; 4:13; Eze 22:26; Ho 5:1; 6:9; Mi 3:11; Zep 3:4; Mal

1:6; 2:1, 8; Mt 26:47, 59; 27:6, 20, 41; Mk 15:11, 31; Lu 19:47; 24:20; Jn 11:49; 19:6; Ac 23:4

4. Their Idolatry

Jud 17:5; 1 S 5:5; 1 K 12:31; 13:2, 33; 2 K 10:11; 11:18; 23:5, 20; 2 Chr 11:15; 13:9; 23:17; Je 48:7

5. Their Support

Ex 29:28; Le 2:3, 10; 5:13; 6:17; 7:8, 10, 14, 34; 10:13; 14:13; 23:20; 27:21; Nu 3:48; 5:9; 6:20; 18:9, 12, 18, 21, 24, 31; 31:30; De 18:3; 1 S 2:14, 28; 2 K 4:42; 12:16; 2 Chr 31:4, 19; Ezr 7:24; Ne 10:37; 12:44; 13:10; Eze 44:29; 1 Co 9:6, 13; He 7:5

6. Their Food

Ex 29:32; Le 6:16, 26, 29; 7:6, 15, 31; 8:31; 10:12, 17; 21:22; 22:7; 24:9; Nu 18:12, 31; De 18:1; Eze 44:31; Lu 6:4

7. Their Inheritance

Le 25:33; Nu 18:20; 26:62; 35:2, 8; De 10:9; 12:12; 14:27; 18:2; Jos 13:14, 33; 14:3; 18:7; 21:4, 8; Eze 44:28; 45:4; 48:10, 22

8. High Priests

Ex 28:1; Le 21:10; Nu 35:25; Jos 20:6; 1 S 2:28; 1 Chr 27:5; 2 Chr 19:11; 26:20; 31:10; 34:9; Ezr 8:29; Ne 3:1, 20; 13:28; Je 52:24; Hag 1:12; 2:2; Zec 3:1; Mt 26:3; Mk 14:10, 53, 55; 15:1; Lu 22:54; 23:4; Jn 11:49, 57; 18:13; Ac 4:6; 5:17; 7:1; 9:1, 14; 19:14; 22:5; He 5:1, 5; 8:3; 9:7; 13:11

See **LEADERS, SACRIFICES**

PRINCE OF PEACE, *Messianic title*

Is 9:6 For unto us a child is born, unto us a son is given: and the government shall be upon his shoulder: and his name shall be called Wonderful, Counsellor, The mighty God, The everlasting Father, The Prince of Peace.

See **TITLES AND NAMES**

PRINCES, *leaders of tribes, regions, or nations*

Nu 1:16; 7:2, 10, 78, 84; 10:4; 16:2; 17:2, 6; 21:18; 25:14; 27:2; 31:13; 32:2; 34:18; 36:1; Jos 9:15; 22:14, 30; Jud 5:3, 15; 1 K 4:2; 9:22; 20:14; 1 Chr 4:38; 7:40; 19:3; 22:17; 23:2; 27:22–23; 28:1, 21; 29:6, 24; 2 Chr 12:5; 17:7; 21:4, 9; 22:8; 23:13; 24:10, 17, 23; 28:14; 29:30; 30:6, 24; Ezr 1:8; 8:20; 9:1; 10:8; Ne 9:34; 12:31; Est 1:3, 14; 2:18; 6:9; Ps 68:27; Je 24:1; 29:2; 34:10; 36:21; 37:14; 38:27; 52:10–11; Eze 21:12; 22:6; 45:8; 46:8; Da 1:3; Ho 5:10; Mt 20:25

See **NATION**

PRINCIPALITIES

Ep 1:21; 3:10; Col 1:16; 2:10, 15

PRISCILLA *See* **WOMEN**

PRISONS

1. Places for Confining Criminals

Ge 40:3; 42:16; Nu 15:34; Jud 16:21; 2 K 17:4; Ne 3:25; Is 42:22; Je 37:15, 21; 38:11, 28; 39:14; 52:11; Mt 5:25; Lu 12:59; Ac 16:26

2. Opened

JOSEPH'S

Ge 41:14 Then Pharaoh sent and called Joseph, and they brought him hastily out of the dungeon: and he shaved *himself,* and changed his raiment, and came in unto Pharaoh.

THE APOSTLES'

Ac 5:19 But the angel of the Lord by night opened the prison doors, and brought them forth, and said,

PETER'S

Ac 12:10 When they were past the first and the second ward, they came unto the iron gate that leadeth unto the city; which opened to them of his own accord: and they went out, and passed on through one street; and forthwith the angel departed from him.

Ac 16:26 And suddenly there was a great earthquake, so that the foundations of the prison were shaken: and immediately all the doors were opened, and every one's bands were loosed.

PRIVILEGES

1. Special

Mt 13:11 He answered and said unto them, Because it is given unto you to know the mysteries of the kingdom of heaven, but to them it is not given.

Mt 13:17 For verily I say unto you, That many prophets and righteous *men* have desired to see *those things* which ye see, and have not seen *them;* and to hear *those things* which ye hear, and have not heard *them.*

Mk 4:11 And he said unto them, Unto you it is given to know the mystery of the kingdom of God: but unto them that are without, all these *things* are done in parables:

Mk 4:34 But without a parable spake he not unto them: and when they were alone, he expounded all things to his disciples.

Lu 8:10 And he said, Unto you it is given to know the mysteries of the kingdom of God: but to others in parables; that seeing they might not see, and hearing they might not understand.

Lu 10:23 And he turned him unto *his* disciples, and said privately, Blessed *are* the eyes which see the things that ye see:

Lu 15:31 And he said unto him, Son, thou art ever with me, and all that I have is thine.

Ac 10:41 Not to all the people, but unto witnesses chosen before of God, *even* to us, who did eat and drink with him after he rose from the dead.

Ro 5:2 By whom also we have access by faith into this grace wherein we stand, and rejoice in hope of the glory of God.

Ro 9:3 For I could wish that myself were accursed from Christ for my brethren, my kinsmen according to the flesh:

1 Co 2:10 But God hath revealed *them* unto us by his Spirit: for the Spirit searcheth all things, yea, the deep things of God.

Col 1:26–27 *Even* the mystery which hath been hid from ages and from generations, but now is made manifest to his saints:

To whom God would make known what *is* the riches of the glory of this mystery among the Gentiles; which is Christ in you, the hope of glory:

1 Jn 2:20 But ye have an unction from the Holy One, and ye know all things.

Re 3:3 Remember therefore how thou hast received and heard, and hold fast, and repent. If therefore thou shalt not watch, I will come on thee as a thief, and thou shalt not know what hour I will come upon thee.

2. Withdrawn

Mt 21:43 Therefore say I unto you, The kingdom of God shall be taken from you, and given to a nation bringing forth the fruits thereof.

Mt 25:28 Take therefore the talent from him, and give *it* unto him which hath ten talents.

Mk 6:11 And whosoever shall not receive you, nor hear you, when ye depart thence, shake off the dust under your feet for a testimony against them. Verily I say unto you, It shall be more tolerable for Sodom and Gomorrha in the day of judgment, than for that city.

Lu 16:2 And he called him, and said unto him, How is it that I hear this of thee? give an account of thy stewardship; for thou mayest be no longer steward.

Lu 19:24 And he said unto them that stood by, Take from him the pound, and give *it* to him that hath ten pounds.

Lu 20:16 He shall come and destroy these husbandmen, and shall give the vineyard to others. And when they heard *it,* they said, God forbid.

Re 2:5 Remember therefore from whence thou art fallen, and repent, and do the first works; or else I will come unto thee quickly, and will remove thy candlestick out of his place, except thou repent.

3. Misuses

BY THE GADARENES

Mk 5:17 And they began to pray him to depart out of their coasts.

BY THE NAZARENES

Mk 6:4–5 But Jesus said unto them, A prophet is not without honour, but in his own country, and among his own kin, and in his own house.

And he could there do no mighty work, save that he laid his hands upon a few sick folk, and healed *them*.

BY THE PEOPLE OF NORTHERN GALILEE

Lu 10:14 But it shall be more tolerable for Tyre and Sidon at the judgment, than for you.

BY THE PEOPLE OF JERUSALEM

Lu 19:42 Saying, If thou hadst known, even thou, at least in this thy day, the things *which belong* unto thy peace! but now they are hid from thine eyes.

BY ISRAEL IN DIFFERENT PERIODS

Jn 15:22 If I had not come and spoken unto them, they had not had sin: but now they have no cloke for their sin.

He 3:17 But with whom was he grieved forty years? *was it* not with them that had sinned, whose carcases fell in the wilderness?

See **INGRATITUDE**

PROBATION

Ge 2:17; 15:16; De 8:2; Jud 3:1; 1 K 3:14; Lu 13:8; 19:13; Jn 6:6; 1 Ti 3:10

See **FUTURE LIFE**

PROCLAMATIONS

Ex 32:5; 1 K 15:22; 21:9; 22:36; 2 K 10:20; 2 Chr 24:9; 30:5; 36:22; Ezr 1:1; 5:17; 10:7; Ne 8:15; Jona 3:7

See **GOSPEL, MISSIONS**

PROCONSULS, *Roman official who served as deputy consul in a Roman province*

Ac 13:7; 18:12; 19:38

PROCRASTINATION

BECAUSE OF WORLDLY ENTANGLEMENTS

Ge 19:16 And while he lingered, the men laid hold upon his hand, and upon the hand of his wife, and upon the hand of his two daughters; the LORD being merciful unto him: and they brought him forth, and set him without the city.

BECAUSE OF FAMILY CARES

Mt 8:21 And another of his disciples said unto him, Lord, suffer me first to go and bury my father.

Lu 9:61 And another also said, Lord, I will follow thee; but let me first go bid them farewell, which are at home at my house.

BECAUSE OF UNBELIEF

Ac 17:32 And when they heard of the resurrection of the dead, some mocked: and others said, We will hear thee again of this *matter*.

BECAUSE OF PERSONAL CONVENIENCE

Ac 24:25 And as he reasoned of righteousness, temperance, and judgment to come, Felix trembled, and answered, Go thy way for this time; when I have a convenient season, I will call for thee.

See **DELAY, OPPORTUNITY, TIME**

PRODIGAL SON

Lu 15:11–32

See **HUMILITY, YOUNG PEOPLE**

PROFANITY

Ge 27:20; Ex 20:7; Le 18:21; 19:12; 22:32; 24:15; De 5:11; 2 K 19:10; Ps 139:20; Pr 30:9; Is 32:6; 37:24; Je 23:11; Eze 36:21; Ho 4:2; Mt 5:34; 26:72, 74; Mk 14:71; 1 Ti 1:9; Ja 5:12

See **BLASPHEMY**

PROFITABLENESS

1. Benefits of Holy Living

Ex 1:21 And it came to pass, because the midwives feared God, that he made them houses.

De 4:40 Thou shalt keep therefore his statutes, and his commandments, which I command thee this day, that it may go well with thee, and with thy children after thee, and that thou mayest prolong *thy* days upon the earth, which the LORD thy God giveth thee, for ever.

De 5:29 O that there were such an heart in them, that they would fear me, and keep all my commandments always, that it might be well with them, and with their children for ever!

2 Chr 27:6 So Jotham became mighty, because he prepared his ways before the LORD his God.

2 Chr 32:29 Moreover he provided him cities, and possessions of flocks and herds in abundance: for God had given him substance very much.

Jb 1:10 Hast not thou made an hedge about him, and about his house, and about all that he hath on every side? thou hast blessed the work of his hands, and his substance is increased in the land.

Jb 35:8 Thy wickedness *may hurt* a man as thou *art;* and thy righteousness *may profit* the son of man.

Ps 128:2 For thou shalt eat the labour of thine hands: happy *shalt* thou *be,* and *it shall be* well with thee.

Pr 11:6 The righteousness of the upright shall deliver them: but transgressors shall be taken in *their own* naughtiness.

Ec 8:12 Though a sinner do evil an hundred times, and his *days* be prolonged, yet surely I know that it shall be well with them that fear God, which fear before him:

Is 3:10 Say ye to the righteous, that *it shall be* well *with him:* for they shall eat the fruit of their doings.

Is 39:8 Then said Hezekiah to Isaiah, Good *is* the word of the LORD which thou hast spoken. He said moreover, For there shall be peace and truth in my days.

Is 65:22 They shall not build, and another inhabit; they shall not plant, and another eat: for as the days of a tree *are* the days of my people, and mine elect shall long enjoy the work of their hands.

Je 7:23 But this thing commanded I them, saying, Obey my voice, and I will be your God, and ye shall be my people: and walk ye in all the ways that I have commanded you, that it may be well unto you.

Je 22:15 Shalt thou reign, because thou closest *thyself* in cedar? did not thy father eat and drink, and do judgment and justice, *and* then it was well with him?

Je 32:39 And I will give them one heart, and one way, that they may fear me for ever, for the good of them, and of their children after them:

Da 6:28 So this Daniel prospered in the reign of Darius, and in the reign of Cyrus the Persian.

Ho 2:7 And she shall follow after her lovers, but she shall not overtake them; and she shall seek them, but shall not find *them:* then shall she say, I will go and return to my first husband; for then *was it* better with me than now.

Mal 3:11 And I will rebuke the devourer for your sakes, and he shall not destroy the fruits of your ground; neither shall your vine cast her fruit before the time in the field, saith the LORD of hosts.

Mt 13:12 For whosoever hath, to him shall be given, and he shall have more abundance: but whosoever hath not, from him shall be taken away even that he hath.

Mt 19:29 And every one that hath forsaken houses, or brethren, or sisters, or father, or mother, or wife, or children, or lands, for my name's sake, shall receive an hundredfold, and shall inherit everlasting life.

Mt 25:22 He also that had received two talents came and said, Lord, thou deliveredst unto me two talents: behold, I have gained two other talents beside them.

Mk 4:25 For he that hath, to him shall be given: and he that hath not, from him shall be taken even that which he hath.

Mk 10:30 But he shall receive an hundredfold now in this time, houses, and brethren, and sisters, and mothers, and children, and lands, with persecutions; and in the world to come eternal life.

Lu 6:38 Give, and it shall be given unto you; good measure, pressed down, and shaken together, and running over, shall men give into your bosom. For with the same measure that ye mete withal it shall be measured to you again.

Lu 18:30 Who shall not receive manifold more in this present time, and in the world to come life everlasting.

1 Ti 4:8 For bodily exercise profiteth little: but godliness is profitable unto all things, having promise of the life that now is, and of that which is to come.

1 Ti 6:6 But godliness with contentment is great gain.

Tit 3:8 *This is* a faithful saying, and these things I will that thou affirm constantly, that they which have believed in God might be careful to maintain good works. These things are good and profitable unto men.

2. Loss Because of Sinful Living

a. Transgression Is without Gain

1 S 12:21 And turn ye not aside: for *then should ye go* after vain *things,* which cannot profit nor deliver; for they *are* vain.

1 K 14:26 And he took away the treasures of the house of the LORD, and the treasures of the king's house; he even took away all: and he took away all the shields of gold which Solomon had made.

2 Chr 12:10 Instead of which king Rehoboam made shields of brass, and committed *them* to the hands of the chief of the guard, that kept the entrance of the king's house.

2 Chr 28:20 And Tilgath-pilneser king of Assyria came unto him, and distressed him, but strengthened him not.

Ne 9:37 And it yieldeth much increase unto the kings whom thou hast set over us because of our sins: also they have dominion over our bodies, and over our cattle, at their pleasure, and we *are* in great distress.

Jb 27:8 For what *is* the hope of the hypocrite, though he hath gained, when God taketh away his soul?

Jb 33:27 He looketh upon men, and *if any* say, I have sinned, and perverted *that which was* right, and it profited me not;

Pr 5:10 Lest strangers be filled with thy wealth; and thy labours *be* in the house of a stranger;

Pr 10:2 Treasures of wickedness profit nothing: but righteousness delivereth from death.

Pr 17:20 He that hath a froward heart findeth no good: and he that hath a perverse tongue falleth into mischief.

Pr 24:20 For there shall be no reward to the evil *man;* the candle of the wicked shall be put out.

Ec 7:25 I applied mine heart to know, and to search, and to seek out wisdom, and the reason *of things,* and to know the wickedness of folly, even of foolishness *and* madness:

Ec 8:13 But it shall not be well with the wicked, neither shall he prolong *his* days, *which are* as a shadow; because he feareth not before God.

Is 44:9 They that make a graven image *are* all of them vanity; and their delectable things shall not profit; and they *are* their own witnesses; they see not, nor know; that they may be ashamed.

Is 52:3 For thus saith the LORD, Ye have sold yourselves for nought; and ye shall be redeemed without money.

Is 55:2 Wherefore do ye spend money for *that which is* not bread? and your labour for *that which* satisfieth not? hearken diligently unto me, and eat ye *that which is* good, and let your soul delight itself in fatness.

Is 57:12 I will declare thy righteousness, and thy works; for they shall not profit thee.

Je 2:8 The priests said not, Where *is* the LORD? and they that handle the law knew me not: the pastors also transgressed against me, and the prophets prophesied by Baal, and walked after *things that* do not profit.

Je 5:25 Your iniquities have turned away these *things,* and your sins have withholden good *things* from you.

Je 7:8 Behold, ye trust in lying words, that cannot profit.

Je 7:19 Do they provoke me to anger? saith the LORD: *do they* not *provoke* themselves to the confusion of their own faces?

Je 12:13 They have sown wheat, but shall reap thorns: they have put themselves to pain, *but* shall not profit: and they shall be ashamed of your revenues because of the fierce anger of the LORD.

Je 16:19 O LORD, my strength, and my fortress, and my refuge in the day of affliction, the Gentiles shall come unto thee from the ends of the earth, and shall say, Surely our fathers have inherited lies, vanity, and *things* wherein *there is* no profit.

Je 44:2 Thus saith the LORD of hosts, the God of Israel; Ye have seen all the evil that I have brought upon Jerusalem, and upon all the cities of Judah; and, behold, this day they *are* a desolation, and no man dwelleth therein,

Mt 16:26 For what is a man profited, if he shall gain the whole world, and lose his own soul? or what shall a man give in exchange for his soul?

Lu 9:25 For what is a man advantaged, if he gain the whole world, and lose himself, or be cast away?

Ro 3:12 They are all gone out of the way, they are together become unprofitable; there is none that doeth good, no, not one.

b. Sin Does Not Profit

Jb 15:31 Let not him that is deceived trust in vanity: for vanity shall be his recompence.

Jb 20:29 This *is* the portion of a wicked man from God, and the heritage appointed unto him by God.

Jb 27:13 This *is* the portion of a wicked man with God, and the heritage of oppressors, *which* they shall receive of the Almighty.

Ps 34:21 Evil shall slay the wicked: and they that hate the righteous shall be desolate.

Ps 107:17 Fools because of their transgression, and because of their iniquities, are afflicted.

Pr 12:21 There shall no evil happen to the just: but the wicked shall be filled with mischief.

Pr 15:6 In the house of the righteous *is* much treasure: but in the revenues of the wicked is trouble.

Ec 2:26 For *God* giveth to a man that *is* good in his sight wisdom, and knowledge, and joy: but to the sinner he giveth travail, to gather and to heap up, that he may give to *him that is* good before God. This also *is* vanity and vexation of spirit.

Is 3:9 The shew of their countenance doth witness against them; and they declare their sin as Sodom, they hide *it* not. Woe unto their soul! for they have rewarded evil unto themselves.

Is 40:2 Speak ye comfortably to Jerusalem, and cry unto her, that her warfare is accomplished, that her iniquity is pardoned for she hath received of the LORD's hand double for all her sins.

Is 59:18 According to *their* deeds, accordingly he will repay, fury to his adversaries, recompence to his enemies; to the islands he will repay recompence.

Is 65:7 Your iniquities, and the iniquities of your fathers together, saith the LORD, which have burned incense upon the mountains, and blasphemed me upon the hills: therefore will I measure their former work into their bosom.

Je 4:18 Thy way and thy doings have procured these *things* unto thee; this *is* thy wickedness, because it is bitter, because it reacheth unto thine heart.

Je 8:14 Why do we sit still? assemble yourselves, and let us enter into the defenced cities, and let us be silent there: for the LORD our God hath put us to silence, and given us water of gall to drink, because we have sinned against the LORD.

Je 12:13 They have sown wheat, but shall reap thorns: they have put themselves to pain, *but* shall not profit: and they shall be ashamed of your revenues because of the fierce anger of the LORD.

Je 13:22 And if thou say in thine heart, Wherefore come these things upon me? For the greatness of thine iniquity are thy skirts discovered, *and* thy heels made bare.

Je 30:14 All thy lovers have forgotten thee; they seek thee not; for I have wounded thee with the wound of an enemy, with the chastisement of a cruel one, for the multitude of thine iniquity; *because* thy sins were increased.

Je 50:7 All that found them have devoured them: and their adversaries said, We offend not, because they have sinned against the LORD, the habitation of justice, even the LORD, the hope of their fathers.

Lam 1:8 Jerusalem hath grievously sinned; therefore she is removed: all that honoured her despise her, because they have seen her nakedness: yea, she sigheth, and turneth backward.

Ro 6:23 For the wages of sin *is* death; but the gift of God *is* eternal life through Jesus Christ our Lord.

He 2:2 For if the word spoken by angels was stedfast, and every transgression and disobedience received a just recompence of reward;

2 Pe 2:13 And shall receive the reward of unrighteousness, *as* they that count it pleasure to riot in the daytime. Spots *they are* and blemishes, sporting themselves with their own deceivings while they feast with you;

3. God's Scale of Values

Mt 5:29 And if thy right eye offend thee, pluck it out, and cast *it* from thee: for it is profitable for thee that one of thy members should perish, and not *that* thy whole body should be cast into hell.

1 Ti 4:8 For bodily exercise profiteth little: but godliness is profitable unto all things, having promise of the life that now is, and of that which is to come.

2 Ti 3:16 All scripture *is* given by inspiration of God, and *is* profitable for doctrine, for reproof, for correction, for instruction in righteousness:

Tit 3:8 *This is* a faithful saying, and these things I will that thou affirm constantly, that they which have believed in God might be careful to maintain good works. These things are good and profitable unto men.

See **HOLINESS, MISERY, RETRIBUTION, REWARD, RIGHTEOUSNESS**

PROGRESS, *growth and development toward maturity*

1. A Characteristic of the Righteous

Ex 14:15 And the LORD said unto Moses, Wherefore criest thou unto me? speak unto the children of Israel, that they go forward:

Jos 1:2 Moses my servant is dead; now therefore arise, go over this Jordan, thou, and all this people, unto the land which I do give to them, *even* to the children of Israel.

Jb 8:7 Though thy beginning was small, yet thy latter end should greatly increase.

Jb 17:9 The righteous also shall hold on his way, and he that hath clean hands shall be stronger and stronger.

Ps 84:7 They go from strength to strength, *every one of them* in Zion appeareth before God.

Ps 92:12 The righteous shall flourish like the palm tree: he shall grow like a cedar in Lebanon.

Pr 4:18 But the path of the just *is* as the shining light, that shineth more and more unto the perfect day.

Pr 9:9 Give *instruction* to a wise *man,* and he will be yet wiser: teach a just *man,* and he will increase in learning.

Is 40:31 But they that wait upon the LORD shall renew *their* strength; they shall mount up with wings as eagles; they shall run, and not be weary; *and* they shall walk, and not faint.

Eze 47:5 Afterward he measured a thousand; *and it was* a river that I could not pass over: for the waters were risen, waters to swim in, a river that could not be passed over.

Ho 14:5 I will be as the dew unto Israel: he shall grow as the lily, and cast forth his roots as Lebanon.

Mt 25:20 And so he that had received five talents came and brought other five talents, saying, Lord, thou deliveredst unto me five talents: behold, I have gained beside them five talents more.

Lu 19:15 And it came to pass, that when he was returned, having received the kingdom, then he commanded these servants to be called unto him, to whom he had given the money, that he might know how much every man had gained by trading.

1 Co 13:11 When I was a child, I spake as a child, I understood as a child, I thought as a child: but when I became a man, I put away childish things.

2 Co 3:18 But we all, with open face beholding as in a glass the glory of the Lord, are changed into the same image from glory to glory, *even* as by the Spirit of the Lord.

Ep 4:16 From whom the whole body fitly joined together and compacted by that which every joint supplieth, according to the effectual working in the measure of every part, maketh increase of the body unto the edifying of itself in love.

Ph 1:25 And having this confidence, I know that I shall abide and continue with you all for your furtherance and joy of faith;

Ph 3:13 Brethren, I count not myself to have apprehended: but *this* one thing *I do,* forgetting those things which are behind, and reaching forth unto those things which are before,

1 Th 4:1 Furthermore then we beseech you, brethren, and exhort *you* by the Lord Jesus, that as ye have received of us how ye ought to walk and to please God, *so* ye would abound more and more.

1 Ti 4:15 Meditate upon these things; give thyself wholly to them; that thy profiting may appear to all.

He 6:1 Therefore leaving the principles of the doctrine of Christ, let us go on unto perfection; not laying again the foundation of repentance from dead works, and of faith toward God,

He 12:1 Wherefore seeing we also are compassed about with so great a cloud of witnesses, let us lay aside every weight, and the sin which doth so easily beset us, and let us run with patience the race that is set before us,

2. The Life Enlarged and Enhanced

1 S 2:1 And Hannah prayed, and said, My heart rejoiceth in the Lord, mine horn is exalted in the Lord: my mouth is enlarged over mine enemies; because I rejoice in thy salvation.

2 S 22:20 He brought me forth also into a large place: he delivered me, because he delighted in me.

2 S 22:37 Thou hast enlarged my steps under me; so that my feet did not slip.

1 K 4:29 And God gave Solomon wisdom and understanding exceeding much, and largeness of heart, even as the sand that *is* on the sea shore.

1 Chr 4:10 And Jabez called on the God of Israel, saying, Oh that thou wouldest bless me indeed, and enlarge my coast, and that thine hand might be with me, and that thou wouldest keep *me* from evil, that it may not grieve me! And God granted him that which he requested.

Jb 8:7 Though thy beginning was small, yet thy latter end should greatly increase.

Jb 36:16 Even so would he have removed thee out of the strait *into* a broad place, where *there is* no straitness; and that which *should be* set on thy table should be full of fatness.

Ps 4:1 Hear me when I call, O God of my righteousness: thou hast enlarged me *when I was* in distress; have mercy upon me, and hear my prayer.

Ps 18:19 He brought me forth also into a large place; he delivered me, because he delighted in me.

Ps 18:36 Thou hast enlarged my steps under me, that my feet did not slip.

Ps 31:8 And hast not shut me up into the hand of the enemy: thou hast set my feet in a large room.

Ps 66:12 Thou hast caused men to ride over our heads; we went through fire and through water: but thou broughtest us out into a wealthy *place.*

Ps 118:5 I called upon the LORD in distress: the LORD answered me, *and set me* in a large place.

Ps 119:32 I will run the way of thy commandments, when thou shalt enlarge my heart.

Is 54:2 Enlarge the place of thy tent, and let them stretch forth the curtains of thine habitations: spare not, lengthen thy cords, and strengthen thy stakes;

Lu 12:15 And he said unto them, Take heed, and beware of covetousness: for a man's life consisteth not in the abundance of the things which he possesseth.

Jn 10:10 The thief cometh not, but for to steal, and to kill, and to destroy: I am come that they might have life, and that they might have *it* more abundantly.

2 Co 6:11 O *ye* Corinthians, our mouth is open unto you, our heart is enlarged.

Ep 3:17–19 That Christ may dwell in your hearts by faith; that ye, being rooted and grounded in love,

May be able to comprehend with all saints what *is* the breadth, and length, and depth, and height;

And to know the love of Christ, which passeth knowledge, that ye might be filled with all the fulness of God.

See **DEEPER LIFE, GROWTH, JOY**

PROMISES, *God's pledges or assurances*

1. Characteristics

UNFAILING

1 K 8:56 Blessed *be* the LORD, that hath given rest unto his people Israel, according to all that he promised: there hath not failed one word of all his good promise, which he promised by the hand of Moses his servant.

ASSURED BY DIVINE ABILITY

Ro 4:21 And being fully persuaded that, what he had promised, he was able also to perform.

GROUNDED IN CHRIST

2 Co 1:20 For all the promises of God in him *are* yea, and in him Amen, unto the glory of God by us.

2 Co 7:1 Having therefore these promises, dearly beloved, let us cleanse ourselves from all filthiness of the flesh and spirit, perfecting holiness in the fear of God.

OF INFINITE VALUE

2 Pe 1:4 Whereby are given unto us exceeding great and precious promises: that by these ye might be partakers of the divine nature, having escaped the corruption that is in the world through lust.

CULMINATE IN EVERLASTING LIFE

1 Jn 2:25 And this is the promise that he hath promised us, *even* eternal life.

2. To the Afflicted

BRIGHTER DAYS

Ps 30:5 For his anger *endureth but* a moment; in his favour is life: weeping may endure for a night, but joy *cometh* in the morning.

DELIVERANCE

Ps 34:19–20 Many *are* the afflictions of the righteous: but the LORD delivereth him out of them all.

DIVINE CARE IN SICKNESS

Ps 41:3 The LORD will strengthen him upon the bed of languishing: thou wilt make all his bed in his sickness.

Ps 94:12 Blessed *is* the man whom thou chastenest, O LORD, and teachest him out of thy law;

Ps 138:7 Though I walk in the midst of trouble, thou wilt revive me: thou shalt stretch forth thine hand against the wrath of mine enemies, and thy right hand shall save me.

COMFORT OF GOD'S PRESENCE

Is 43:2 When thou passest through the waters, I *will be* with thee; and through the rivers, they shall not overflow thee: when thou walkest through the fire, thou shalt not be burned; neither shall the flame kindle upon thee.

AN ETERNAL HOME

Jn 14:1–2 Let not your heart be troubled: ye believe in God, believe also in me.

In my Father's house are many mansions: if *it were* not so, I would have told you. I go to prepare a place for you.

ALL THINGS WORK FOR THE BELIEVER'S GOOD

Ro 8:28 And we know that all things work together for good to them that love God, to them who are the called according to *his* purpose.

2 Co 4:17 For our light affliction, which is but for a moment, worketh for us a far more exceeding *and* eternal weight of glory;

SUFFICIENCY OF DIVINE GRACE

2 Co 12:9 And he said unto me, My grace is sufficient for thee: for my strength is made perfect in weakness. Most gladly therefore will I rather glory in my infirmities, that the power of Christ may rest upon me.

FELLOWSHIP IN CHRIST'S SUFFERINGS

1 Pe 4:12–13 Beloved, think it not strange concerning the fiery trial which is to try you, as though some strange thing happened unto you:

But rejoice, inasmuch as ye are partakers of Christ's sufferings; that, when his glory shall be revealed, ye may be glad also with exceeding joy.

MEMBERSHIP IN THE COMPANY OF THE REDEEMED

Re 7:13–14 And one of the elders answered, saying unto me, What are these which are arrayed in white robes? and whence came they?

And I said unto him, Sir, thou knowest. And he said to me, These are they which came out of great tribulation, and have washed their robes, and made them white in the blood of the Lamb.

FINAL DELIVERANCE FROM SORROW AND PAIN

Re 21:4 And God shall wipe away all tears from their eyes; and there shall be no more death, neither sorrow, nor crying, neither shall there be any more pain: for the former things are passed away.

3. To Believers

FOOD
Ps 37:3

UNLIMITED BLESSINGS
Mk 9:23

ANSWERS TO PRAYER
Mk 11:24

REMOVAL OF OBSTACLES
Lu 17:6

DIVINE SONSHIP
Jn 1:12

ETERNAL LIFE
Jn 3:14–15; 5:24

SPIRITUAL FULLNESS
Jn 6:35; 11:26

SPIRITUAL LIGHT
Jn 12:46

POWER FOR SERVICE
Jn 14:12

SALVATION
Ro 1:16;1 Pe 2:6

4. To the Humble

Jb 22:29 When *men* are cast down, then thou shalt say, *There is* lifting up; and he shall save the humble person.

Ps 138:6 Though the LORD *be* high, yet hath he respect unto the lowly: but the proud he knoweth afar off.

Is 66:2 For all those *things* hath mine hand made, and all those *things* have been, saith the LORD: but to this *man* will I look, *even* to *him that is* poor and of a contrite spirit, and trembleth at my word.

Ho 13:1 When Ephraim spake trembling, he exalted himself in Israel; but when he offended in Baal, he died.

Mk 10:40 But to sit on my right hand and on my left hand is not mine to give; but *it shall be given to them* for whom it is prepared.

Lu 9:48 And said unto them, Whosoever shall receive this child in my name receiveth me: and whosoever shall receive me receiveth him that sent me: for he that is least among you all, the same shall be great.

Lu 14:11 For whosoever exalteth himself shall be abased; and he that humbleth himself shall be exalted.

Lu 18:14 I tell you, this man went down to his house justified *rather* than the other: for every one that exalteth himself shall be abased; and he that humbleth himself shall be exalted.

Ja 4:6 But he giveth more grace. Wherefore he saith, God resisteth the proud, but giveth grace unto the humble.

Ja 4:10 Humble yourselves in the sight of the Lord, and he shall lift you up.

1 Pe 5:5 Likewise, ye younger, submit yourselves unto the elder. Yea, all *of you* be subject one to another, and be clothed with humility: for God resisteth the proud, and giveth grace to the humble.

5. To the Liberal

Ps 41:1 Blessed *is* he that considereth the poor: the LORD will deliver him in time of trouble.

Ps 112:9 He hath dispersed, he hath given to the poor; his righteousness endureth for ever; his horn shall be exalted with honour.

Pr 3:9–10 Honour the LORD with thy substance, and with the firstfruits of all thine increase:

So shall thy barns be filled with plenty, and thy presses shall burst out with new wine.

Pr 11:25 The liberal soul shall be made fat: and he that watereth shall be watered also himself.

Pr 22:9 He that hath a bountiful eye shall be blessed; for he giveth of his bread to the poor.

Pr 25:22 For thou shalt heap coals of fire upon his head, and the LORD shall reward thee.

Pr 28:27 He that giveth unto the poor shall not lack: but he that hideth his eyes shall have many a curse.

Ec 11:1 Cast thy bread upon the waters: for thou shalt find it after many days.

Is 32:8 But the liberal deviseth liberal things; and by liberal things shall he stand.

Is 58:10 And *if* thou draw out thy soul to the hungry, and satisfy the afflicted soul; then shall thy light rise in obscurity, and thy darkness *be* as the noonday:

Mal 3:10 Bring ye all the tithes into the storehouse, that there may be meat in mine house, and prove me now herewith, saith the LORD of hosts, if I will not open you the windows of heaven, and pour you out a blessing, that *there shall* not *be room* enough *to receive it.*

Lu 6:38 Give, and it shall be given unto you; good measure, pressed down, and shaken together, and running over, shall men give into your bosom. For with the same measure that ye mete withal it shall be measured to you again.

Lu 14:14 And thou shalt be blessed; for they cannot recompense thee: for thou shalt be recompensed at the resurrection of the just.

2 Co 9:7 Every man according as he purposeth in his heart, *so let him give;* not grudgingly, or of necessity: for God loveth a cheerful giver.

Ph 4:16 For even in Thessalonica ye sent once and again unto my necessity.

6. To the Obedient

Ge 22:18 And in thy seed shall all the nations of the earth be blessed; because thou hast obeyed my voice.

Ex 20:6 And shewing mercy unto thousands of them that love me, and keep my commandments.

Ex 23:22 But if thou shalt indeed obey his voice, and do all that I speak; then I will be an enemy unto thine enemies, and an adversary unto thine adversaries.

Le 18:5 Ye shall therefore keep my statutes, and my judgments: which if a man do, he shall live in them: I *am* the LORD.

Le 25:18 Wherefore ye shall do my statutes, and keep my judgments, and do them; and ye shall dwell in the land in safety.

Le 26:3 If ye walk in my statutes, and keep my commandments, and do them;

De 4:40 Thou shalt keep therefore his statutes, and his commandments, which I command thee this day, that it may go well with thee, and with thy children after thee, and that thou mayest prolong *thy* days upon the earth, which the LORD thy God giveth thee, for ever.

De 5:10 And shewing mercy unto thousands of them that love me and keep my commandments.

De 5:29 O that there were such an heart in them, that they would fear me, and keep all my commandments always, that it might be well with them, and with their children for ever!

De 7:9 Know therefore that the LORD thy God, he *is* God, the faithful God, which keepeth covenant and mercy with them that love him and keep his commandments to a thousand generations;

De 11:14 That I will give *you* the rain of your land in his due season, the first rain and the latter rain, that thou mayest gather in thy corn, and thy wine, and thine oil.

De 11:27 A blessing, if ye obey the commandments of the LORD your God, which I command you this day:

De 12:25 Thou shalt not eat it; that it may go well with thee, and with thy children after thee, when thou shalt do *that which is* right in the sight of the LORD.

De 12:28 Observe and hear all these words which I command thee, that it may go well with thee, and with thy children after thee for ever, when thou doest *that which is* good and right in the sight of the LORD thy God.

De 15:10 Thou shalt surely give him, and thine heart shall not be grieved when thou givest unto him: because that for this thing the LORD thy God shall bless thee in all thy works, and in all that thou puttest thine hand unto.

De 19:9 If thou shalt keep all these commandments to do them, which I command thee this day, to love the LORD thy God, and to walk ever in his ways; then shalt thou add three cities more for thee, beside these three:

Jos 14:9 And Moses sware on that day, saying, Surely the land whereon thy feet have trodden shall be thine inheritance, and thy children's for ever, because thou hast wholly followed the LORD my God.

1 S 12:14 If ye will fear the LORD, and serve him, and obey his voice, and not rebel against the commandment of the LORD, then shall both ye and also the king that reigneth over you continue following the LORD your God:

1 K 2:3 And keep the charge of the LORD thy God, to walk in his ways, to keep his statutes, and his commandments, and his judgments, and his testimonies, as it is written in the law of Moses, that thou mayest prosper in all that thou doest, and whithersoever thou turnest thyself:

1 K 6:12 *Concerning* this house which thou art in building, if thou wilt walk in my statutes, and execute my judgments, and keep all my commandments to walk in them; then will I perform my word with thee, which I spake unto David thy father:

1 K 8:25 Therefore now, LORD God of Israel, keep with thy servant David my father that thou promisedst him, saying, There shall not fail thee a man in my sight to sit on the throne of Israel; so that thy children take heed to their way, that they walk before me as thou hast walked before me.

1 K 9:4 And if thou wilt walk before me, as David thy father walked, in integrity of heart, and in uprightness, to do according to all that I have commanded thee, *and* wilt keep my statutes and my judgments:

1 K 11:38 And it shall be, if thou wilt hearken unto all that I command thee, and wilt walk in my ways, and do *that is* right in my sight, to keep my statutes and my commandments, as David my servant did; that I will be with thee, and build thee a sure house, as I built for David, and will give Israel unto thee.

2 K 21:8 Neither will I make the feet of Israel move any more out of the land which I gave their fathers; only if they will observe to do according to all that I have commanded them, and according to all the law that my servant Moses commanded them.

1 Chr 22:13 Then shalt thou prosper, if thou takest heed to fulfil the statutes and judgments which the LORD charged Moses with concerning Israel: be strong, and of good courage; dread not, nor be dismayed.

2 Chr 6:16 Now therefore, O LORD God of Israel, keep with thy servant David my father that which thou hast promised him, saying, There shall not fail thee a man in my sight to sit upon the throne of Israel; yet so that thy children take heed to their way to walk in my law, as thou hast walked before me.

2 Chr 33:8 Neither will I any more remove the foot of Israel from out of the land which I have appointed for your fathers; so that they will take heed to do all that I have commanded them, according to the whole law and the statutes and the ordinances by the hand of Moses.

Ne 1:5 And said, I beseech thee, O LORD God of heaven, the great and terrible God, that keepeth covenant and mercy for them that love him and observe his commandments:

Ps 50:23 Whoso offereth praise glorifieth me: and to him that ordereth *his* conversation *aright* will I shew the salvation of God.

Ps 51:18 Do good in thy good pleasure unto Zion: build thou the walls of Jerusalem.

Ps 103:11 For as the heaven is high above the earth, *so* great is his mercy toward them that fear him.

Ps 103:18 To such as keep his covenant, and to those that remember his commandments to do them.

Ps 132:12 If thy children will keep my covenant and my testimony that I shall teach them, their children shall also sit upon thy throne for evermore.

Ps 145:20 The LORD preserveth all them that love him: but all the wicked will he destroy.

Ec 2:26 For *God* giveth to a man that *is* good in his sight wisdom, and knowledge, and joy: but to the sinner he giveth travail, to gather and to heap up, that he may give to *him that is* good before God. This also *is* vanity and vexation of spirit.

Ec 7:18 *It is* good that thou shouldest take hold of this; yea, also from this withdraw not thine hand: for he that feareth God shall come forth of them all.

Is 1:19 If ye be willing and obedient, ye shall eat the good of the land:

Is 48:18 O that thou hadst hearkened to my commandments! then had thy peace been as a river, and thy righteousness as the waves of the sea:

Is 64:5 Thou meetest him that rejoiceth and worketh righteousness, *those that* remember thee in thy ways: behold, thou art wroth; for we have sinned: in those is continuance, and we shall be saved.

Is 65:23 They shall not labour in vain, nor bring forth for trouble; for they *are* the seed of the blessed of the LORD, and their offspring with them.

Je 7:23 But this thing commanded I them, saying, Obey my voice, and I will be your God, and ye shall be my people: and walk ye in all the ways that I have commanded you, that it may be well unto you.

Je 11:4 Which I commanded your fathers in the day *that* I brought them forth out of the land of Egypt, from the iron furnace, saying, Obey my voice, and do them, according to all which I command you: so shall ye be my people, and I will be your God:

Je 17:25 Then shall there enter into the gates of this city kings and princes sitting upon the throne of David, riding in chariots and on horses, they, and their princes, the men of Judah, and the inhabitants of Jerusalem: and this city shall remain for ever.

Je 22:4 For if ye do this thing indeed, then shall there enter in by the gates of this house kings sitting upon the throne of David, riding in chariots and on horses, he, and his servants, and his people.

Je 38:2 Thus saith the LORD, He that remaineth in this city shall die by the sword, by the famine, and by the pestilence: but he that goeth forth to the Chaldeans shall live; for he shall have his life for a prey, and shall live.

Je 38:20 But Jeremiah said, They shall not deliver *thee*. Obey, I beseech thee, the voice of the LORD, which I speak unto thee: so it shall be well unto thee, and thy soul shall live.

Je 42:6 Whether *it be* good, or whether *it be* evil, we will obey the voice of the LORD our God, to whom we send thee; that it may be well with us, when we obey the voice of the LORD our God.

Eze 18:9 Hath walked in my statutes, and hath kept my judgments, to deal truly; he *is* just, he shall surely live, saith the Lord GOD.

Eze 18:17 *That* hath taken off his hand from the poor, *that* hath not received usury nor increase, hath executed my judgments, hath walked in my statutes; he shall not die for the iniquity of his father, he shall surely live.

Eze 33:15 *If* the wicked restored the pledge, give again that he had robbed, walk in the statutes of life, without committing iniquity; he shall surely live, he shall not die.

Da 9:4 And I prayed unto the LORD my God, and made my confession, and said, O Lord, the great and dreadful God, keeping the covenant and mercy to them that love him, and to them that keep his commandments;

Zec 3:7 Thus saith the LORD of hosts; If thou wilt walk in my ways, and if thou wilt keep my charge, then thou shalt also judge my house, and shalt also keep my courts, and I will give thee places to walk among these that stand by.

Zec 6:15 And they *that are* far off shall come and build in the temple of the LORD, and ye shall know that the LORD of hosts hath sent me unto you. And *this* shall come to pass, if ye will diligently obey the voice of the LORD your God.

Mk 3:35 For whosoever shall do the will of God, the same is my brother, and my sister, and mother.

Lu 1:50 And his mercy *is* on them that fear him from generation to generation.

Lu 11:28 But he said, Yea rather, blessed *are* they that hear the word of God, and keep it.

Jn 7:17 If any man will do his will, he shall know of the doctrine, whether it be of God, or *whether* I speak of myself.

Jn 14:23 Jesus answered and said unto him, If a man love me, he will keep my words: and my Father will love him, and we will come unto him, and make our abode with him.

Ac 10:35 But in every nation he that feareth him, and worketh righteousness, is accepted with him.

1 Ti 4:8 For bodily exercise profiteth little: but godliness is profitable unto all things, having promise of the life that now is, and of that which is to come.

He 4:1 Let us therefore fear, lest, a promise being left *us* of entering into his rest, any of you should seem to come short of it.

He 5:9 And being made perfect, he became the author of eternal salvation unto all them that obey him;

He 10:36 For ye have need of patience, that, after ye have done the will of God, ye might receive the promise.

Re 22:7 Behold, I come quickly: blessed is he that keepeth the sayings of the prophecy of this book.

7. To the Penitent

2 K 22:18 But to the king of Judah which sent you to enquire of the LORD, thus shall ye say to him, Thus saith the LORD God of Israel, *As touching* the words which thou hast heard;

2 Chr 30:6 So the posts went with the letters from the king and his princes throughout all Israel and Judah, and according to the commandment of the king, saying, Ye children of Israel, turn again unto the LORD God of Abraham, Isaac, and Israel, and he will return to the remnant of you, that are escaped out of the hand of the kings of Assyria.

2 Chr 30:9 For if ye turn again unto the LORD, your brethren and your children *shall find* compassion before them that lead them captive, so that they shall come again into this land: for the LORD your God *is* gracious and merciful, and will not turn away *his* face from you, if ye return unto him.

Ps 34:18 The LORD *is* nigh unto them that are of a broken heart; and saveth such as be of a contrite spirit.

Is 57:18 I have seen his ways, and will heal him: I will lead him also, and restore comforts unto him and to his mourners.

Is 61:1 The Spirit of the Lord GOD *is* upon me; because the LORD hath anointed me to preach good tidings unto the meek; he hath sent me to bind up the brokenhearted, to proclaim liberty to the captives, and the opening of the prison to *them that are* bound;

Je 3:12 Go and proclaim these words toward the north, and say, Return, thou backsliding Israel, saith the LORD; *and* I will not cause mine anger to fall upon you: for I *am* merciful, saith the LORD, *and* I will not keep *anger* for ever.

Je 3:22 Return, ye backsliding children, *and* I will heal your backslidings. Behold, we come unto thee; for thou *art* the LORD our God.

Je 7:3 Thus saith the LORD of hosts, the God of Israel, Amend your ways and your doings, and I will cause you to dwell in this place.

Je 12:16 And it shall come to pass, if they will diligently learn the ways of my people, to swear by my name, The LORD liveth; as they taught my people to swear by Baal; then shall they be built in the midst of my people.

Je 25:6 And go not after other gods to serve them, and to worship them, and provoke me not to anger with the works of your hands; and I will

Je 26:3 If so be they will hearken, and turn every man from his evil way, that I may repent me of the evil, which I purpose to do unto them because of the evil of their doings.

Je 26:13 Therefore now amend your ways and your doings, and obey the voice of the LORD your God; and the LORD will repent him of the evil that he hath pronounced against you.

Je 31:20 *Is* Ephraim my dear son? *is he* a pleasant child? for since I spake against him, I do earnestly remember him still: therefore my bowels are troubled for him; I will surely have mercy upon him, saith the LORD.

Eze 18:22 All his transgressions that he hath committed, they shall not be mentioned unto him: in his righteousness that he hath done he shall live.

Eze 18:27 Again, when the wicked *man* turneth away from his wickedness that he hath committed, and doeth that which is lawful and right, he shall save his soul alive.

Da 4:27 Wherefore, O king, let my counsel be acceptable unto thee, and break off thy sins by righteousness, and thine iniquities by shewing mercy to the poor; if it may be a lengthening of thy tranquility.

Ho 14:4 I will heal their backsliding, I will love them freely: for mine anger is turned away from him.

Jl 2:13 And rend your heart, and not your garments, and turn unto the LORD your God: for he *is* gracious and merciful, slow to anger, and of great kindness, and repenteth him of the evil.

Mi 7:18 Who *is* a God like unto thee, that pardoneth iniquity, and passeth by the transgression of the remnant of his heritage? he retaineth not his anger for ever, because he delighteth *in* mercy.

Zec 1:3 Therefore say thou unto them, Thus saith the Lord of hosts; Turn ye unto me, saith the Lord of hosts, and I will turn unto you, saith the Lord of hosts.

Mal 3:7 Even from the days of your fathers ye are gone away from mine ordinances, and have not kept *them.* Return unto me, and I will return unto you, saith the Lord of hosts. But ye said, Wherein shall we return?

Lu 6:21 Blessed *are* ye that hunger now: for ye shall be filled. Blessed *are ye* that weep now: for ye shall laugh.

Lu 15:7 I say unto you, that likewise joy shall be in heaven over one sinner that repenteth, more than over ninety and nine just persons, which need no repentance.

Ac 2:38 Then Peter said unto them, Repent, and be baptized every one of you in the name of Jesus Christ for the remission of sins, and ye shall receive the gift of the Holy Ghost.

Ac 3:19 Repent ye therefore, and be converted, that your sins may be blotted out, when the times of refreshing shall come from the presence of the Lord;

Ro 11:23 And they also, if they abide not still in unbelief, shall be graffed in: for God is able to graff them in again.

2 Co 7:10 For godly sorrow worketh repentance to salvation not to be repented of: but the sorrow of the world worketh death.

8. To the Poor

DIVINE PROTECTION

Ps 12:5 For the oppression of the poor, for the sighing of the needy, now will I arise, saith the Lord; I will set *him* in safety *from him that* puffeth at him.

Ps 14:6 Ye have shamed the counsel of the poor, because the Lord *is* his refuge.

Ps 68:10 Thy congregation hath dwelt therein: thou, O God, hast prepared of thy goodness for the poor.

Ps 69:33 For the Lord heareth the poor, and despiseth not his prisoners.

Ps 109:31 For he shall stand at the right hand of the poor, to save *him* from those that condemn his soul.

Ps 140:12 I know that the Lord will maintain the cause of the afflicted, *and* the right of the poor.

Is 11:4 But with righteousness shall he judge the poor, and reprove with equity for the meek of the earth: and he shall smite the earth with the rod of his mouth, and with the breath of his lips shall he slay the wicked.

AN OVERSHADOWING PROVIDENCE

Is 25:4 For thou hast been a strength to the poor, a strength to the needy in his distress, a refuge from the storm, a shadow from the heat, when the blast of the terrible ones *is* as a storm *against* the wall.

ANSWER TO PRAYER

Is 41:17 *When* the poor and needy seek water, and *there is* none, *and* their tongue faileth for thirst, I the Lord will hear them, *I* the God of Israel will not forsake them.

HEAVENLY INHERITANCE

Ja 2:5 Hearken, my beloved brethren, Hath not God chosen the poor of this world rich in faith, and heirs of the kingdom which he hath promised to them that love him?

9. To Seekers

De 4:29 But if from thence thou shalt seek the Lord thy God, thou shalt find *him,* if thou seek him with all thy heart and with all thy soul.

1 Chr 28:9 And thou, Solomon my son, know thou the God of thy father, and serve him with a perfect heart and with a willing mind: for the Lord searcheth all hearts, and understandeth all the imaginations of the thoughts: if thou seek him, he will be found of thee; but if thou forsake him, he will cast thee off for ever.

2 Chr 7:14 If my people, which are called by my name, shall humble themselves, and pray, and seek my face, and turn from their wicked ways; then will I hear from heaven, and will forgive their sin, and will heal their land.

2 Chr 15:2 And he went out to meet Asa, and said unto him, Hear ye me, Asa, and all Judah and Benjamin; The LORD *is* with you, while ye be with him; and if ye seek him, he will be found of you; but if ye forsake him, he will forsake you.

Jb 33:26 He shall pray unto God, and he will be favourable unto him: and he shall see his face with joy: for he will render unto man his righteousness.

Ps 9:10 And they that know thy name will put their trust in thee: for thou, LORD, hast not forsaken them that seek thee.

Ps 22:26 The meek shall eat and be satisfied: they shall praise the LORD that seek him: your heart shall live for ever.

Ps 34:10 The young lions do lack, and suffer hunger: but they that seek the LORD shall not want any good *thing.*

Ps 119:2 Blessed *are* they that keep his testimonies, *and that* seek him with the whole heart.

Pr 2:4 If thou seekest her as silver, and searchest for her as *for* hid treasures;

Pr 8:17 I love them that love me; and those that seek me early shall find me.

Is 45:19 I have not spoken in secret, in a dark place of the earth: I said not unto the seed of Jacob, Seek ye me in vain: I the LORD speak righteousness, I declare things that are right.

Is 65:10 And Sharon shall be a fold of flocks, and the valley of Achor a place for the herds to lie down in, for my people that have sought me.

Je 29:13 And ye shall seek me, and find *me,* when ye shall search for me with all your heart.

Da 10:12 Then said he unto me, Fear not, Daniel: for from the first day that thou didst set thine heart to understand, and to chasten thyself before thy God, thy words were heard, and I am come for thy words.

Jl 2:32 And it shall come to pass, *that* whosoever shall call on the name of the LORD shall be delivered: for in mount Zion and in Jerusalem shall be deliverance, as the LORD hath said, and in the remnant whom the LORD shall call.

Am 5:4 For thus saith the LORD unto the house of Israel, Seek ye me, and ye shall live:

Mt 7:8 For every one that asketh receiveth; and he that seeketh findeth; and to him that knocketh it shall be opened.

Lu 11:9 And I say unto you, Ask, and it shall be given you; seek, and ye shall find; knock, and it shall be opened unto you.

Lu 18:7 And shall not God avenge his own elect, which cry day and night unto him, though he bear long with them?

Jn 6:37 All that the Father giveth me shall come to me; and him that cometh to me I will in no wise cast out.

Jn 14:14 If ye shall ask any thing in my name, I will do *it.*

Ac 2:21 And it shall come to pass, *that* whosoever shall call on the name of the Lord shall be saved.

He 11:6 But without faith *it is* impossible to please *him:* for he that cometh to God must believe that he is, and *that* he is a rewarder of them that diligently seek him.

Ja 4:8 Draw nigh to God, and he will draw nigh to you. Cleanse *your* hands, *ye* sinners; and purify *your* hearts, *ye* double minded.

10. To the Tempted

POWER TO TREAD ON EVIL FORCES

Lu 10:19 Behold, I give unto you power to tread on serpents and scorpions, and over all the power of the enemy: and nothing shall by any means hurt you.

SAFETY THROUGH CHRIST'S INTERCESSION

Lu 22:31–32 And the Lord said, Simon, Simon, behold, Satan hath desired *to have* you, that he may sift *you* as wheat:

But I have prayed for thee, that thy faith fail not: and when thou art converted, strengthen thy brethren.

THE BRUISING OF THE SERPENT'S HEAD

Ro 16:20 And the God of peace shall bruise Satan under your feet shortly. The grace of our Lord Jesus Christ *be* with you. Amen.

PROVISION OF A WAY OF ESCAPE

1 Co 10:13 There hath no temptation taken you but such as is common to man: but God *is* faithful, who will not suffer you to be tempted above that ye are able; but will with the temptation also make a way to escape, that ye may be able to bear *it.*

SUCCOR IN THE TRYING HOUR

He 2:18 For in that he himself hath suffered being tempted, he is able to succour them that are tempted.

FINAL VICTORY

Ja 4:7 Submit yourselves therefore to God. Resist the devil, and he will flee from you.

1 Jn 4:4 Ye are of God, little children, and have overcome them: because greater is he that is in you, than he that is in the world.

Re 3:10 Because thou hast kept the word of my patience, I also will keep thee from the hour of temptation, which shall come upon all the world, to try them that dwell upon the earth.

ENTHRONEMENT WITH CHRIST

Re 3:21 To him that overcometh will I grant to sit with me in my throne, even as I also overcame, and am set down with my Father in his throne.

11. To Religious Workers

Da 12:3 And they that be wise shall shine as the brightness of the firmament; and they that turn many to righteousness as the stars for ever and ever.

Mt 24:46 Blessed *is* that servant, whom his lord when he cometh shall find so doing.

Mk 9:41 For whosoever shall give you a cup of water to drink in my name, because ye belong to Christ, verily I say unto you, he shall not lose his reward.

Jn 4:36 And he that reapeth receiveth wages, and gathereth fruit unto life eternal: that both he that soweth and he that reapeth may rejoice together.

Ro 2:10 But glory, honour, and peace, to every man that worketh good, to the Jew first, and also to the Gentile:

1 Co 3:8 Now he that planteth and he that watereth are one: and every man shall receive his own reward according to his own labour.

1 Co 3:14 If any man's work abide which he hath built thereupon, he shall receive a reward.

1 Co 15:58 Therefore, my beloved brethren, be ye stedfast, unmovable, always abounding in the work of the Lord, forasmuch as ye know that your labour is not in vain in the Lord.

Ep 6:8 Knowing that whatsoever good thing any man doeth, the same shall he receive of the Lord, whether *he be* bond or free.

He 6:10 For God *is* not unrighteous to forget your work and labour of love, which ye have shewed toward his name, in that ye have ministered to the saints, and do minister.

Ja 1:25 But whoso looketh into the perfect law of liberty, and continueth *therein,* he being not a forgetful hearer, but a doer of the work, this man shall be blessed in his deed.

12. To the Merciful and Benevolent

Ps 41:3 The LORD will strengthen him upon the bed of languishing: thou wilt make all his bed in his sickness.

Ps 112:9 He hath dispersed, he hath given to the poor; his righteousness endureth for ever; his horn shall be exalted with honour.

Pr 11:17 The merciful man doeth good to his own soul: but *he that is* cruel troubleth his own flesh.

Pr 14:31 He that oppresseth the poor reproacheth his Maker: but he that honoureth him hath mercy on the poor.

Is 58:10 And *if* thou draw out thy soul to the hungry, and satisfy the afflicted soul; then shall thy light rise in obscurity, and thy darkness *be* as the noonday:

Da 4:27 Wherefore, O king, let my counsel be acceptable unto thee, and break off thy sins by righteousness, and thine iniquities by shewing mercy to the poor; if it may be a lengthening of thy tranquility.

Mt 5:7 Blessed *are* the merciful: for they shall obtain mercy.

Mt 6:14 For if ye forgive men their trespasses, your heavenly Father will also forgive you:

Mt 25:40 And the King shall answer and say unto them, Verily I say unto you, Inasmuch as ye have done *it* unto one of the least of these my brethren, ye have done *it* unto me.

Lu 6:38 Give, and it shall be given unto you; good measure, pressed down, and shaken together, and running over, shall men give into your bosom. For with the same measure that ye mete withal it shall be measured to you again.

See **DELIVERANCE, FAITH, PLENTY, PRAYER, SEEKING GOD, REWARD, TRUTH**

PROMOTION, *advancement, graduation*

1. Examples

Ge 39:5, 22; 40:13; 41:40; 45:13; 47:6; Ex 18:25; Nu 22:37; 27:22; De 1:15; Jud 8:22; 11:6; 1 S 9:22; 11:15; 15:17; 18:5; 2 S 9:10; 19:28; 1 K 1:38; 2:35; 11:28; 2 K 24:17; 1 Chr 11:6, 25; Est 2:17; 6:11; 8:2, 15; 9:4; 10:2; Ps 105:21; Pr 22:11, 29; Is 22:21; Je 40:7; 52:32; Da 2:48–49; 3:30; 5:29; 6:2; Lu 14:10; Ac 7:10

2. Of the Unworthy

Jud 9:6; Est 3:1; 5:11; Ps 12:8; Pr 3:35; 19:10; 26:1, 8; 28:12, 28; 29:2; 30:22; Ec 10:7; Da 11:21

See **REWARD**

PROOF

1. In the Light of God's Word

Je 6:27 I have set thee *for* a tower *and* a fortress among my people, that thou mayest know and try their way.

Ep 5:10 Proving what is acceptable unto the Lord.

1 Th 5:21 Prove all things; hold fast that which is good.

1 Jn 4:1 Beloved, believe not every spirit, but try the spirits whether they are of God: because many false prophets are gone out into the world.

2. By Actions

Mt 4:16 The people which sat in darkness saw great light; and to them which sat in the region and shadow of death light is sprung up.

Mt 5:16 Let your light so shine before men, that they may see your good works, and glorify your Father which is in heaven.

Lu 6:43 For a good tree bringeth not forth corrupt fruit; neither doth a corrupt tree bring forth good fruit.

Lu 10:36–37 Which now of these three, thinkest thou, was neighbour unto him that fell among the thieves?

And he said, He that shewed mercy on him. Then said Jesus unto him, Go, and do thou likewise.

Jn 5:36 But I have greater witness than *that* of John: for the works which the Father hath given me to finish, the same works that I do, bear witness of me, that the Father hath sent me.

Jn 14:11 Believe me that I *am* in the Father, and the Father in me: or else believe me for the very works' sake.

2 Co 8:24 Wherefore shew ye to them, and before the churches, the proof of your love, and of our boasting on your behalf.

2 Co 12:12 Truly the signs of an apostle were wrought among you in all patience, in signs, and wonders, and mighty deeds.

2 Ti 4:5 But watch thou in all things, endure afflictions, do the work of an evangelist, make full proof of thy ministry.

Ja 2:18 Yea, a man may say, Thou hast faith, and I have works: shew me thy faith without thy works, and I will shew thee my faith by my works.

1 Pe 2:12 Having your conversation honest among the Gentiles: that, whereas they speak against you as evildoers, they may by *your* good works, which they shall behold, glorify God in the day of visitation.

See **DISCIPLESHIP, WORKS**

PROPHECY, *revelation of God's will or message, often of future events*

1. General Prophecies

OF THE CAPTIVITY OF THE JEWS

See **ISRAEL**

OF THE CONVERSION OF THE GENTILES

See **MISSIONS**

OF THE DESTRUCTION OF BABYLON

See **BABYLON**

OF THE DESTRUCTION OF JERUSALEM

See **JERUSALEM**

OF THE SPREAD OF THE GOSPEL

See **GOSPEL**

OF THE LAST DAYS

See **LAST DAY**

OF THE LAST JUDGMENT

See **JUDGMENTS**

OF THE OUTPOURING OF THE HOLY SPIRIT

See **HOLY SPIRIT**

OF THE PERSECUTION OF THE CHURCH

See **SUFFERING**

OF THE RETURN OF THE JEWS

See **ISRAEL**

2. Relating to Christ

a. Messianic

Ge 3:15 And I will put enmity between thee and the woman, and between thy seed and her seed; it shall bruise thy head, and thou shalt bruise his heel.

Ge 12:3 And I will bless them that bless thee, and curse him that curseth thee: and in thee shall all families of the earth be blessed.

Ge 49:10 The sceptre shall not depart from Judah, nor a lawgiver from between his feet, until Shiloh come; and

unto him *shall* the gathering of the people *be*.

De 18:15 The LORD thy God will raise up unto thee a Prophet from the midst of thee, of thy brethren, like unto me; unto him ye shall hearken;

Ps 2:2 The kings of the earth set themselves, and the rulers take counsel together, against the LORD, and against his anointed, *saying,*

Ps 45:2 Thou art fairer than the children of men: grace is poured into thy lips: therefore God hath blessed thee for ever.

Ps 68:18 Thou hast ascended on high, thou hast led captivity captive: thou hast received gifts for men; yea, *for* the rebellious also, that the LORD God might dwell *among them.*

Ps 69:21 They gave me also gall for my meat; and in my thirst they gave me vinegar to drink.

Ps 110:1 The LORD said unto my Lord, Sit thou at my right hand, until I make thine enemies thy footstool.

Ps 118:22 The stone *which* the builders refused is become the head *stone* of the corner.

Ps 132:11 The LORD hath sworn *in* truth unto David; he will not turn from it; Of the fruit of thy body will I set upon thy throne.

Is 2:4 And he shall judge among the nations, and shall rebuke many people: and they shall beat their swords into plowshares, and their spears into pruninghooks: nation shall not lift up sword against nation, neither shall they learn war any more.

Is 7:14 Therefore the Lord himself shall give you a sign; Behold, a virgin shall conceive, and bear a son, and shall call his name Immanuel.

Is 9:2 The people that walked in darkness have seen a great light: they that dwell in the land of the shadow of death, upon them hath the light shined.

Is 9:7 Of the increase of *his* government and peace there shall be no end, upon the throne of David, and upon his kingdom, to order it, and to establish it with judgment and with justice from henceforth even for ever. The zeal of the LORD of hosts will perform this.

Is 11:10 And in that day there shall be a root of Jesse, which shall stand for an ensign of the people; to it shall the Gentiles seek: and his rest shall be glorious.

Is 25:8 He will swallow up death in victory; and the Lord God will wipe away tears from off all faces; and the rebuke of his people shall he take away from off all the earth: for the LORD hath spoken *it*.

Is 28:16 Therefore thus saith the Lord GOD, Behold, I lay in Zion for a foundation a stone, a tried stone, a precious corner *stone*, a sure foundation: he that believeth shall not make haste.

Is 42:1 Behold my servant, whom I uphold; mine elect, *in whom* my soul delighteth; I have put my spirit upon him: he shall bring forth judgment to the Gentiles.

Is 49:6 And he said, It is a light thing that thou shouldest be my servant to raise up the tribes of Jacob, and to restore the preserved of Israel: I will also give thee for a light to the Gentiles, that thou mayest be my salvation unto the end of the earth.

Is 52:14 As many were astonied at thee; his visage was so marred more than any man, and his form more than the sons of men:

Is 53:2 For he shall grow up before him as a tender plant, and as a root out of a dry ground: he hath no form nor comeliness; and when we shall see him, *there is* no beauty that we should desire him.

Is 55:4 Behold, I have given him *for* a witness to the people, a leader and commander to the people.

Is 59:16 And he saw that *there was* no man, and wondered that *there was* no intercessor: therefore his arm brought salvation unto him; and his righteousness, it sustained him.

Is 61:1 The Spirit of the Lord GOD *is* upon me; because the LORD hath anointed me to preach good tidings unto the meek; he hath sent me to bind up the brokenhearted, to proclaim liberty to the captives, and the opening of the prison to *them that are* bound;

Is 62:11 Behold, the LORD hath proclaimed unto the end of the world, Say ye to the daughter of Zion, Behold, thy salvation cometh; behold, his reward *is* with him, and his work before him.

Is 63:1 Who *is* this that cometh from Edom, with dyed garments from Bozrah? this *that is* glorious in his apparel, travelling in the greatness of his strength? I that speak in righteousness, mighty to save.

Je 23:5 Behold, the days come, saith the LORD, that I will raise unto David a righteous Branch, and a King shall reign and prosper, and shall execute judgment and justice in the earth.

Eze 17:22 Thus saith the Lord GOD; I will also take of the highest branch of the high cedar, and will set *it*; I will crop off from the top of his young twigs a tender one, and will plant *it* upon an high mountain and eminent:

Da 2:34 Thou sawest till that a stone was cut out without hands, which smote the image upon his feet *that were* of iron and clay, and brake them to pieces.

Da 2:44 And in the days of these kings shall the God of heaven set up a kingdom, which shall never be destroyed: and the kingdom shall not be left to other people, *but* it shall break in pieces and consume all these kingdoms, and it shall stand for ever.

Da 7:13 I saw in the night visions, and, behold, *one* like the Son of man came with the clouds of heaven, and came to the Ancient of days, and they brought him near before him.

Da 9:25 Know therefore and understand, *that* from the going forth of the commandment to restore and to build Jerusalem unto the Messiah the Prince *shall be* seven weeks, and threescore and two weeks: the street shall be built again, and the wall, even in troublous times.

Mi 5:2 But thou, Bethlehem Ephratah, *though* thou be little among the thousands of Judah, *yet* out of thee shall he come forth unto me *that is* to be ruler in Israel; whose goings forth *have been* from of old, from everlasting.

Hag 2:7 And I will shake all nations, and the desire of all nations shall come: and I will fill this house with glory, saith the Lord of hosts.

Zec 3:8 Hear now, O Joshua the high priest, thou, and thy fellows that sit before thee: for they *are* men wondered at: for, behold, I will bring forth my servant the BRANCH.

Zec 6:12 And speak unto him, saying, Thus speaketh the Lord of hosts, saying, Behold the man whose name *is* The BRANCH; and he shall grow up out of his place, and he shall build the temple of the Lord:

Zec 9:9 Rejoice greatly, O daughter of Zion; shout, O daughter of Jerusalem: behold, thy thee: he *is* just, and having salvation; lowly, and riding upon an ass, and upon a colt the foal of an ass.

Zec 11:12 And I said unto them, If ye think good, give *me* my price; and if not, forbear. So they weighed for my price thirty *pieces* of silver.

Zec 12:10 And I will pour upon the house of David, and upon the inhabitants of Jerusalem, the spirit of grace and of supplications: and they shall look upon me whom they have pierced, and they shall mourn for him, as one mourneth for *his* only *son,* and shall be in bitterness for him, as one that is in bitterness for *his* firstborn.

Zec 13:7 Awake, O sword, against my shepherd, and against the man *that is* my fellow, saith the Lord of hosts: smite the shepherd, and the sheep shall be scattered: and I will turn mine hand upon the little ones.

Mal 3:1 Behold, I will send my messenger, and he shall prepare the way before me: and the Lord, whom ye seek, shall suddenly come to his temple, even the messenger of the covenant, whom ye delight in: behold, he shall come, saith the Lord of hosts.

Mt 1:22 Now all this was done, that it might be fulfilled which was spoken of the Lord by the prophet, saying,

Mt 2:4 And when he had gathered all the chief priests and scribes of the people together, he demanded of them where Christ should be born.

Mt 2:15 And was there until the death of Herod: that it might be fulfilled which was spoken of the Lord by the prophet, saying, Out of Egypt have I called my son.

Mt 8:17 That it might be fulfilled which was spoken by Esaias the prophet, saying, Himself took our infirmities, and bare *our* sicknesses.

Mk 1:2 As it is written in the prophets, Behold, I send my messenger before thy face, which shall prepare thy way before thee.

Mk 15:28 And the scripture was fulfilled, which saith, And he was numbered with the transgressors.

Lu 1:70 As he spake by the mouth of his holy prophets, which have been since the world began:

Lu 4:17 And there was delivered unto him the book of the prophet Esaias. And when he had opened the book, he found the place where it was written,

Lu 18:31 Then he took *unto him* the twelve, and said unto them, Behold, we go up to Jerusalem, and all things that are written by the prophets concerning the Son of man shall be accomplished.

Lu 24:27 And beginning at Moses and all the prophets, he expounded unto them in all the scriptures the things concerning himself.

Lu 24:44 And he said unto them, These *are* the words which I spake unto you, while I was yet with you, that all things must be fulfilled, which were written in the law of Moses, and *in* the prophets, and *in* the psalms, concerning me.

Jn 1:45 Philip findeth Nathanael, and saith unto him, We have found him, of whom Moses in the law, and the prophets, did write, Jesus of Nazareth, the son of Joseph.

Jn 4:25 The woman saith unto him, I know that Messias cometh, which is called Christ: when he is come, he will tell us all things.

Jn 5:39 Search the scriptures; for in them ye think ye have eternal life: and they are they which testify of me.

Jn 5:46 For had ye believed Moses, ye would have believed me: for he wrote of me.

Jn 8:18 I am one that bear witness of myself, and the Father that sent me beareth witness of me.

Jn 19:28 After this, Jesus knowing that all things were now accomplished, that the scripture might be fulfilled, saith, I thirst.

Ac 2:30 Therefore being a prophet, and knowing that God had sworn with an oath to him, that of the fruit of his loins, according to the flesh, he would raise up Christ to sit on his throne;

Ac 3:18 But those things, which God before had shewed by the mouth of all his prophets, that Christ should suffer, he hath so fulfilled.

Ac 3:24 Yea, and all the prophets from Samuel and those that follow after, as many as have spoken, have likewise foretold of these days.

Ac 7:37 This is that Moses, which said unto the children of Israel, A prophet shall the Lord your God raise up unto you of your brethren, like unto me; him shall ye hear.

Ac 8:32 The place of the scripture which he read was this, He was led as a sheep to the slaughter; and like a lamb dumb before his shearer, so opened he not his mouth:

Ac 10:43 To him give all the prophets witness, that through his name whosoever believeth in him shall receive remission of sins.

Ac 13:27 For they that dwell at Jerusalem, and their rulers, because they knew him not, nor yet the voices of the prophets which are read every sabbath day, they have fulfilled *them* in condemning *him*.

Ac 13:32 And we declare unto you glad tidings, how that the promise which was made unto the fathers,

Ac 17:3 Opening and alleging, that Christ must needs have suffered, and risen again from the dead; and that this Jesus, whom I preach unto you, is Christ.

Ac 18:28 For he mightily convinced the Jews, *and that* publickly, shewing by the scriptures that Jesus was Christ.

Ac 26:6 And now I stand and am judged for the hope of the promise made of God unto our fathers:

Ac 26:22 Having therefore obtained help of God, I continue unto this day, witnessing both to small and great, saying none other things than those which the prophets and Moses did say should come:

Ro 1:2 (Which he had promised afore by his prophets in the holy scriptures),

Ro 9:4 Who are Israelites; to whom *pertaineth* the adoption, and the glory, and the covenants, and the giving of the law, and the service *of God,* and the promises;

Ro 15:8 Now I say that Jesus Christ was a minister of the circumcision for the truth of God, to confirm the promises *made* unto the fathers:

Ro 16:26 But now is made manifest, and by the scriptures of the prophets, according to the commandment of the everlasting God, made known to all nations for the obedience of faith:

Ga 3:23 But before faith came, we were kept under the law, shut up unto the faith which should afterwards be revealed.

1 Pe 1:11 Searching what, or what manner of time the Spirit of Christ which was in them did signify, when it testified beforehand the sufferings of Christ, and the glory that should follow.

b. General Prophecies concerning Christ

HIS DEATH

See **CHRIST**

HIS DOMINION

See **CHRIST**

HIS INCARNATION

See **CHRIST**

HIS KINGDOM

See **KINGDOM**

HIS MEEKNESS

See **SPEECH**

HIS PRIESTHOOD

See **PRIESTHOOD**

HIS PROPHETIC OFFICE

See **CHRIST**

HIS REJECTION

See **CHRIST**

HIS RESURRECTION

See **IMMORTALITY**

HIS RIGHTEOUS GOVERNMENT

See **RIGHTEOUSNESS**

HIS SUFFERINGS

See **CHRIST**

HIS TRIUMPH

See **EXALTATION**

DEPARTURE FORETOLD

See **CHRIST**

SUFFERINGS PREDICTED

See **CHRIST**

3. Fulfillment

a. By Christ

Mt 1:22 Now all this was done, that it might be fulfilled which was spoken of the Lord by the prophet, saying,

Mt 2:15 And was there until the death of Herod: that it might be fulfilled which was spoken of the Lord by the prophet, saying, Out of Egypt have I called my son.

Mt 2:23 And he came and dwelt in a city called Nazareth: that it might be fulfilled which was spoken by the prophets, He shall be called a Nazarene.

Mt 3:3 For this is he that was spoken of by the prophet Esaias, saying, The voice of one crying in the wilderness, Prepare ye the way of the Lord, make his paths straight.

Mt 4:14 That it might be fulfilled which was spoken by Esaias the prophet, saying,

Mt 5:17 Think not that I am come to destroy the law, or the prophets: I am not come to destroy, but to fulfil.

Mt 8:17 That it might be fulfilled which was spoken by Esaias the prophet, saying, Himself took our infirmities, and bare *our* sicknesses.

Mt 12:17 That it might be fulfilled which was spoken by Esaias the prophet, saying,

Mt 13:14 And in them is fulfilled the prophecy of Esaias, which saith, By hearing ye shall hear, and shall not understand; and seeing ye shall see, and shall not perceive:

Mt 13:35 That it might be fulfilled which was spoken by the prophet, saying, I will open my mouth in parables; I will utter things which have been kept secret from the foundation of the world.

Mt 21:4 All this was done, that it might be fulfilled which was spoken by the prophet, saying,

Mt 26:24 The Son of man goeth as it is written of him: but woe unto that man by whom the Son of man is betrayed! it had been good for that man if he had not been born.

Mt 26:54 But how then shall the scriptures be fulfilled, that thus it must be?

Mt 26:56 But all this was done, that the scriptures of the prophets might be fulfilled. Then all the disciples forsook him, and fled.

Mt 27:9 Then was fulfilled that which was spoken by Jeremy the prophet, saying, And they took the thirty pieces of silver, the price of him that was valued, whom they of the children of Israel did value;

Mt 27:35 And they crucified him, and parted his garments, casting lots: that it might be fulfilled which was spoken by the prophet, They parted my garments among them, and upon my vesture did they cast lots.

Mt 27:60 And laid it in his own new tomb, which he had hewn out in the rock: and he rolled a great stone to the door of the sepulchre, and departed.

Mk 11:7 And they brought the colt to Jesus, and cast their garments on him; and he sat upon him.

Mk 14:21 The Son of man indeed goeth, as it is written of him: but woe to that man by whom the Son of man is betrayed! good were it for that man if he had never been born.

Mk 14:49 I was daily with you in the temple teaching, and ye took me not: but the scriptures must be fulfilled.

Mk 15:28 And the scripture was fulfilled, which saith, And he was numbered with the transgressors.

Lu 4:21 And he began to say unto them, This day is this scripture fulfilled in your ears.

Lu 18:31 Then he took *unto him* the twelve, and said unto them, Behold, we go up to Jerusalem, and all things that are written by the prophets concerning the Son of man shall be accomplished.

Lu 20:16 He shall come and destroy these husbandmen, and shall give the vineyard to others. And when they heard *it,* they said, God forbid.

Lu 21:22 For these be the days of vengeance, that all things which are written may be fulfilled.

Lu 24:44 And he said unto them, These *are* the words which I spake unto you, while I was yet with you, that all things must be fulfilled, which were written in the law of Moses, and *in* the prophets, and *in* the psalms, concerning me.

Jn 12:14 And Jesus, when he had found a young ass, sat thereon; as it is written,

Jn 12:16 These things understood not his disciples at the first: but when Jesus was glorified, then remembered they that these things were written of him, and *that* they had done these things unto him.

Jn 12:38 That the saying of Esaias the prophet might be fulfilled, which he spake, Lord, who hath believed our report? and to whom hath the arm of the Lord been revealed?

Jn 15:25 But *this cometh to pass,* that the word might be fulfilled that is written in their law, They hated me without a cause.

Jn 17:12 While I was with them in the world, I kept them in thy name: those that thou gavest me I have kept, and none of them is lost, but the son of perdition; that the scripture might be fulfilled.

Jn 18:9 That the saying might be fulfilled, which he spake, Of them which thou gavest me have I lost none.

Jn 18:32 That the saying of Jesus might be fulfilled, which he spake, signifying what death he should die.

Jn 19:24 They said therefore among themselves, Let us not rend it, but cast lots for it, whose it shall be: that the scripture might be fulfilled, which saith, They parted my raiment among them, and for my vesture they did cast lots. These things therefore the soldiers did.

Jn 19:28 After this, Jesus knowing that all things were now accomplished, that the scripture might be fulfilled, saith, I thirst.

Jn 19:36 For these things were done, that the scripture should be fulfilled, A bone of him shall not be broken.

Ac 3:18 But those things, which God before had shewed by the mouth of all his prophets, that Christ should suffer, he hath so fulfilled.

Ac 13:29 And when they had fulfilled all that was written of him, they took *him* down from the tree, and laid *him* in a sepulchre.

Ac 13:33 God hath fulfilled the same unto us their children, in that he hath raised up Jesus again; as it is also written in the second psalm, Thou art my Son, this day have I begotten thee.

b. Examples

1 K 2:27 So Solomon thrust out Abiathar from being priest unto the Lord; that he might fulfil the word of the Lord, which he spake concerning the house of Eli in Shiloh.

1 K 13:5 The altar also was rent, and the ashes poured out from the altar, according to the sign which the man of God had given by the word of the Lord.

1 K 14:17 And Jeroboam's wife arose, and departed, and came to Tirzah: *and* when she came to the threshold of the door, the child died;

1 K 15:29 And it came to pass, when he reigned, *that* he smote all the house of Jeroboam; he left not to Jeroboam any that breathed, until he had destroyed him, according unto the saying of the LORD, which he spake by his servant Ahijah the Shilonite:

1 K 16:12 Thus did Zimri destroy all the house of Baasha, according to the word of the LORD, which he spake against Baasha by Jehu the prophet,

1 K 16:34 In his days did Hiel the Bethelite build Jericho: he laid the foundation thereof in Abiram his firstborn, and set up the gates thereof in his youngest *son* Segub, according to the word of the LORD, which he spake by Joshua the son of Nun.

1 K 18:45 And it came to pass in the mean while, that the heaven was black with clouds and wind, and there was a great rain. And Ahab rode, and went to Jezreel.

1 K 20:21 And the king of Israel went out, and smote the horses and chariots, and slew the Syrians with a great slaughter.

1 K 20:26 And it came to pass at the return of the year, that Ben-hadad numbered the Syrians, and went up to Aphek, to fight against Israel.

1 K 22:38 And *one* washed the chariot in the pool of Samaria; and the dogs licked up his blood; and they washed his armour; according unto the word of the LORD which he spake.

2 K 1:17 So he died according to the word of the LORD which Elijah had spoken. And Jehoram reigned in his stead in the second year of Jehoram the son of Jehoshaphat king of Judah; because he had no son.

2 K 2:22 So the waters were healed unto this day, according to the saying of Elisha which he spake.

2 K 3:20 And it came to pass in the morning, when the meat offering was offered, that, behold, there came water by the way of Edom, and the country was filled with water.

2 K 4:17 And the woman conceived, and bare a son at that season that Elisha had said unto her, according to the time of life.

2 K 4:44 So he set *it* before them, and they did eat, and left *thereof,* according to the word of the LORD.

2 K 7:17 And the king appointed the lord on whose hand he leaned to have the charge of the gate: and the people trode upon him in the gate, and he died, as the man of God had said, who spake when the king came down to him.

2 K 10:10 Know now that there shall fall unto the earth nothing of the word of the LORD, which the LORD spake concerning the house of Ahab: for the LORD hath done *that* which he spake by his servant Elijah.

2 K 15:12 This *was* the word of the LORD which he spake unto Jehu, saying, Thy sons shall sit on the throne of Israel unto the fourth *generation.* And so it came to pass.

2 K 19:37 And it came to pass, as he was worshipping in the house of Nisroch his god, that Adrammelech and Sharezer his sons smote him with the sword: and they escaped into the land of Armenia. And Esar-haddon his son reigned in his stead.

2 K 24:13 And he carried out thence all the treasures of the house of the LORD, and the treasures of the king's house, and cut in pieces all the vessels of gold which Solomon king of Israel had made in the temple of the LORD, as the LORD had said.

2 Chr 20:37 Then Eliezer the son of Dodavah of Mareshah prophesied against Jehoshaphat, saying, Because thou hast joined thyself with Ahaziah, the LORD hath broken thy works. And the ships were broken, that they were not able to go to Tarshish.

2 Chr 36:22 Now in the first year of Cyrus king of Persia, that the word of the LORD *spoken* by the mouth of Jeremiah might be accomplished, the LORD stirred up the spirit of Cyrus king of Persia, that he made a proclamation throughout all his kingdom, and *put it* also in writing, saying,

Je 28:17 So Hananiah the prophet died the same year in the seventh month.

Jn 1:23 He said, I *am* the voice of one crying in the wilderness, Make straight the way of the Lord, as said the prophet Esaias.

Ac 1:16 Men *and* brethren, this scripture must needs have been fulfilled, which the Holy Ghost by the mouth of David spake before concerning Judas, which was guide to them that took Jesus.

4. Prophesying

Nu 11:25 And the LORD came down in a cloud, and spake unto him, and took of the spirit that *was* upon him, and gave *it* unto the seventy elders: and it came to pass, *that,* when the spirit rested upon them, they prophesied, and did not cease.

Nu 24:14 And now, behold, I go unto my people: come *therefore, and* I will advertise thee what this people shall do to thy people in the latter days.

De 31:29 For I know that after my death ye will utterly corrupt *yourselves,* and turn aside from the way which I have commanded you; and evil will befall you in the latter days; because ye will do evil in the sight of the LORD, to provoke him to anger through the work of your hands.

1 S 10:2 When thou art departed from me to day, then thou shalt find two men by Rachel's sepulchre in the border of Benjamin at Zelzah; and they will say unto thee, The asses which thou wentest to seek are found: and, lo, thy father hath left the care of the asses, and sorroweth for you, saying, What shall I do for my son?

1 K 11:31 And he said to Jeroboam, Take thee ten pieces: for thus saith the LORD, the God of Israel, Behold, I will rend the kingdom out of the hand of Solomon, and will give ten tribes to thee:

1 K 13:3 And he gave a sign the same day, saying, This *is* the sign which the LORD hath spoken; Behold, the altar shall be rent, and the ashes that *are* upon it shall be poured out.

1 K 14:12 Arise thou therefore, get thee to thine own house: *and* when thy feet enter into the city, the child shall die.

1 K 18:41 And Elijah said unto Ahab, Get thee up, eat and drink; for *there is* a sound of abundance of rain.

1 K 18:44 And it came to pass at the seventh time, that he said, Behold, there ariseth a little cloud out of the sea, like a man's hand. And he said, Go up, say unto Ahab, Prepare *thy chariot,* and get thee down, that the rain stop thee not.

1 K 20:13 And, behold, there came a prophet unto Ahab king of Israel, saying, Thus saith the LORD, Hast thou seen all this great multitude? behold, I will deliver it into thine hand this day; and thou shalt know that I *am* the LORD.

1 K 20:22 And the prophet came to the king of Israel, and said unto him, Go, strengthen thyself, and mark, and see what thou doest: for at the return of the year the king of Syria will come up against thee.

1 K 22:18 And the king of Israel said unto Jehoshaphat, Did I not tell thee that he would prophesy no good concerning me, but evil?

1 K 22:25 And Micaiah said, Behold, thou shalt see in that day, when thou shalt go into an inner chamber to hide thyself.

2 K 1:4 Now therefore thus saith the LORD, Thou shalt not come down from that bed on which thou art gone up, but shalt surely die. And Elijah departed.

2 K 3:17 For thus saith the LORD, Ye shall not see wind, neither shall ye see rain; yet that valley shall be filled with water, that ye may drink, both ye, and your cattle, and your beasts.

2 K 7:1 Then Elisha said, Hear ye the word of the LORD; Thus saith the LORD, To morrow about this time *shall* a measure of fine flour *be sold* for a shekel, and two measures of barley for a shekel, in the gate of Samaria.

2 K 8:12 And Hazael said, Why weepeth my lord? And he answered, Because I know the evil that thou wilt do unto the children of Israel: their strong holds wilt thou set on fire, and their young men wilt thou slay with the sword, and wilt dash their children, and rip up their women with child.

2 K 19:6 And Isaiah said unto them, Thus shall ye say to your master, Thus saith the LORD, Be not afraid of the words which thou hast heard, with which the servants of the king of Assyria have blasphemed me.

2 K 20:17 Behold, the days come, that all that *is* in thine house,and that which thy fathers have laid up in store unto this day, shall be carried into Babylon: nothing shall be left, saith the LORD.

2 Chr 20:37 Then Eliezer the son of Dodavah of Mareshah prophesied against Jehoshaphat, saying, Because thou hast joined thyself with Ahaziah, the LORD hath broken thy works. And the ships were broken, that they were not able to go to Tarshish.

Ezr 5:1 Then the prophets, Haggai the prophet, and Zechariah the son of Iddo, prophesied unto the Jews that *were* in Judah and Jerusalem in the name of the God of Israel, *even* unto them.

Is 2:2 And it shall come to pass in the last days, *that* the mountain of the LORD's house shall be established in the top of the mountains, and shall be exalted above the hills; and all nations shall flow unto it.

Is 7:8 For the head of Syria *is* Damascus, and the head of Damascus *is* Rezin; and within threescore and five years shall Ephraim be broken, that it be not a people.

Is 39:5 Then said Isaiah to Hezekiah, Hear the word of the LORD of hosts:

Je 19:15 Thus saith the LORD of hosts, the God of Israel; Behold, I will bring upon this city and upon all her towns all the evil that I have pronounced against it, because they have hardened their necks, that they might not hear my words.

Je 21:11 And touching the house of the king of Judah, say, Hear ye the word of the LORD;

Je 26:18 Micah the Morasthite prophesied in the days of Hezekiah king of Judah, and spake to all the people of Judah, saying, Thus saith the LORD of hosts; Zion shall be plowed *like* a field, and Jerusalem shall become heaps, and the mountain of the house as the high places of a forest.

Je 28:8 The prophets that have been before me and before thee of old prophesied both against many countries, and against great kingdoms, of war, and of evil, and of pestilence.

Je 38:3 Thus saith the LORD, This city shall surely be given into the hand of the king of Babylon's army, which shall take it.

Eze 4:7 Therefore thou shalt set thy face toward the siege of Jerusalem, and thine arm *shall be* uncovered, and thou shalt prophesy against it.

Eze 6:2 Son of man, set thy face toward the mountains of Israel, and prophesy against them,

Eze 20:46 Son of man, set thy face toward the south, and drop *thy word* toward the south, and prophesy against the forest of the south field;

Eze 21:2 Son of man, set thy face toward Jerusalem, and drop *thy word* toward the holy places, and prophesy against the land of Israel,

Eze 21:9 Son of man, prophesy, and say, Thus saith the LORD; Say, A sword, a sword is sharpened, and also furbished:

Eze 21:14 Thou therefore, son of man, prophesy, and smite *thine* hands together, and let the sword be doubled the third time, the sword of the slain: it *is* the sword of the great *men that are* slain, which entereth into their privy chambers.

Eze 21:28 And thou, son of man, prophesy and say, Thus saith the Lord GOD concerning the Ammonites, and concerning their reproach; even say thou, The sword, the sword *is* drawn: for the slaughter *it is* furbished, to consume because of the glittering:

Eze 30:9 In that day shall messengers go forth from me in ships to make the careless Ethiopians afraid, and great pain shall come upon them, as in the day of Egypt: for, lo, it cometh.

Eze 36:1 Also, thou son of man, prophesy unto the mountains of Israel, and say, Ye mountains of Israel, hear the word of the LORD:

Eze 37:7 So I prophesied as I was commanded: and as I prophesied, there was a noise, and behold a shaking, and the bones came together, bone to his bone.

Eze 38:17 Thus saith the Lord GOD; *Art* thou he of whom I have spoken in old time by my servants the prophets of Israel, which prophesied in those days *many* years that I would bring thee against them?

Jl 2:28 And it shall come to pass afterward, *that* I will pour out my spirit upon all flesh; and your sons and your daughters shall prophesy, your old men shall dream dreams, your young men shall see visions:

Mi 4:1 But in the last days it shall come to pass, *that* the mountain of the house of the LORD shall be established in the top of the mountains, and it shall be exalted above the hills; and people shall flow unto it.

Lu 1:67 And his father Zacharias was filled with the Holy Ghost, and prophesied, saying,

Ac 2:18 And on my servants and on my handmaidens I will pour out in those days of my Spirit; and they shall prophesy:

Jude 14 And Enoch also, the seventh from Adam, prophesied of these, saying, Behold, the Lord cometh with ten thousands of his saints,

PROPHETS, *those divinely inspired to communicate God's message to his people, sometimes disclosing future events*

Nu 12:6; 1 S 3:20; 10:5, 10–11; 19:20, 23; 1 K 18:4; 19:16; 20:13, 41; 2 Chr 18:6; 20:20; 24:19; 28:9; 36:16; Ezr 5:2; 9:11; Ps 74:9; 105:15; Je 1:5; 28:8; Eze 33:33; Ho 6:5; 12:10; Am 2:11; 3:7; Hag 2:1; Zec 8:9; Mt 11:9; 13:57; 23:37; Mk 11:32; Lu 1:70, 76; 7:26; 20:6, 10; Jn 4:44; 7:52; Ac 26:27; Ep 2:20; 1 Pe 1:10

1. Persons Spoken of as Prophets

AARON

Ex 7:1 And the LORD said unto Moses, See, I have made thee a god to Pharaoh: and Aaron thy brother shall be thy prophet.

ABRAHAM

Ge 20:7 Now therefore restore the man *his* wife; for he *is* a prophet, and

he shall pray for thee, and thou shalt live: and if thou restore *her* not, know thou that thou shalt surely die, thou, and all that *are* thine.

AGABUS

Ac 21:10 And as we tarried *there* many days, there came down from Judaea a certain prophet, named Agabus.

AHIJAH

1 K 11:29 And it came to pass at that time when Jeroboam went out of Jerusalem, that the prophet Ahijah the Shilonite found him in the way; and he had clad himself with a new garment; and they two *were* alone in the field:

AMOS

Am 1:1 The words of Amos, who was among the herdmen of Tekoa, which he saw concerning Israel in the days of Uzziah king of Judah, and in the days of Jeroboam the son of Joash king of Israel, two years before the earthquake.

BALAAM

Nu 22:5 He sent messengers therefore unto Balaam the son of Beor to Pethor, which *is* by the river of the land of the children of his people, to call him, saying, Behold, there is a people come out from Egypt: behold, they cover the face of the earth, and they abide over against me:

DANIEL

Mt 24:15 When ye therefore shall see the abomination of desolation, spoken of by Daniel the prophet, stand in the holy place, (whoso readeth, let him understand:)

DAVID

Mt 13:35 That it might be fulfilled which was spoken by the prophet, saying, I will open my mouth in parables; I will utter things which have been kept secret from the foundation of the world.

ELDAD

Nu 11:26 But there remained two *of the* men in the camp, the name of the one *was* Eldad, and the name of the other Medad: and the spirit rested upon them; and they *were* of them that were written, but went not out unto the tabernacle: and they prophesied in the camp.

ELIJAH

1 K 18:36 And it came to pass at *the time of* the offering of the *evening* sacrifice, that Elijah the prophet came near, and said, LORD God of Abraham, Isaac, and of Israel, let it be known this day that thou art God in Israel, and *that* I *am* thy servant, and *that* I have done all these things at thy word.

ELISHA

1 K 19:16 And Jehu the son of Nimshi shalt thou anoint *to be* king over Israel: and Elisha the son of Shaphat of Abel-meholah shalt thou anoint *to be* prophet in thy room.

EZEKIEL

Eze 1:3 The word of the LORD came expressly unto Ezekiel the priest, the son of Buzi, in the land of the Chaldeans by the river Chebar; and the hand of the LORD was there upon him.

GAD

1 S 22:5 And the prophet Gad said unto David, Abide not in the hold; depart, and get thee into the land of Judah. Then David departed, and came into the forest of Hareth.

HABAKKUK

Hab 1:1 The burden which Habakkuk the prophet did see.

HAGGAI

Ezr 5:1 Then the prophets, Haggai the prophet, and Zechariah the son of Iddo, prophesied unto the Jews that *were* in Judah and Jerusalem, *even* unto them.

HANANIAH

Je 28:17 So Hananiah the prophet died the same year in the seventh month.

HOSEA

Ho 1:1 The word of the LORD that came unto Hosea, the son of Beeri, in the days of Uzziah, Jotham, Ahaz, *and* Hezekiah, kings of Judah, and in the days of Jeroboam the son of Joash, king of Israel.

IDDO

2 Chr 13:22 And the rest of the acts of Abijah, and his ways, and his sayings, *are* written in the story of the prophet Iddo.

ISAIAH

2 K 19:2 And he sent Eliakim, which *was* over the household, and Shebna the scribe, and the elders of the priests, covered with sackcloth, to Isaiah the prophet the son of Amoz.

JEHU

1 K 16:7 And also by the hand of the prophet Jehu the son of Hanani came the word of the LORD against Baasha, and against his house, even for all the evil that he did in the sight of the LORD, in provoking him to anger with the work of his hands, in being like the house of Jeroboam; and because he killed him.

JEREMIAH

Je 1:5 Before I formed thee in the belly I knew thee; and before thou camest forth out of the womb I sanctified thee, *and* I ordained thee a prophet unto the nations.

JOEL

Jl 1:1 The word of the LORD that came to Joel the son of Pethuel.

JOHN THE BAPTIST

Lu 7:28 For I say unto you, Among those that are born of women there is not a greater prophet than John the Baptist: but he that is least in the kingdom of God is greater than he.

JOSHUA

1 K 16:34 In his days did Hiel the Bethelite build Jericho: he laid the foundation thereof in Abiram his firstborn, and set up the gates thereof in his youngest *son* Segub, according to the word of the LORD, which he spake by Joshua the son of Nun.

JONAH

2 K 14:25 He restored the coast of Israel from the entering of Hamath unto the sea of the plain, according to the word of the LORD God of Israel, which he spake by the hand of his servant Jonah, the son of Amittai, the prophet, which *was* of Gath-hepher.

MALACHI

Mal 1:1 The burden of the word of the LORD to Israel by Malachi.

MEDAD

Nu 11:26 But there remained two *of the* men in the camp, the name of the one *was* Eldad, and the name of the other Medad: and the spirit rested upon them; and they *were* of them that were written, but went not out unto the tabernacle: and they prophesied in the camp.

MICAH

Je 26:18 Micah the Morasthite prophesied in the days of Hezekiah king of Judah, and spake to all the people of Judah, saying, Thus saith the LORD of hosts; Zion shall be plowed *like* a field, and Jerusalem shall become heaps, and the mountain of the house as the high places of a forest.

MICAIAH

1 K 22:8 And the king of Israel said unto Jehoshaphat, *There is* yet one man, Micaiah the son of Imlah, by whom we may enquire of the LORD: but I hate him; for he doth not prophesy good concerning me, but evil. And Jehoshaphat said, Let not the king say so.

MOSES

De 34:10 And there arose not a prophet since in Israel like unto Moses, whom the LORD knew face to face,

NAHUM

Na 1:1 The burden of Nineveh. The book of the vision of Nahum the Elkoshite.

NATHAN

2 S 7:2 That the king said unto Nathan the prophet, See now, I dwell in an house of cedar, but the ark of God dwelleth within curtains.

OBADIAH

Obad 1 The vision of Obadiah. Thus saith the Lord God concerning Edom; We have heard a rumour from the LORD, and an ambassador is sent among the heathen, Arise ye, and let us rise up against her in battle.

ODED

2 Chr 28:9 But a prophet of the LORD was there, whose name *was* Oded: and he went out before the host that came to Samaria, and said unto them, Behold, because the LORD God of your fathers was wroth with Judah, he hath delivered them into your hand, and ye have slain them in a rage *that* reacheth up unto heaven.

SAMUEL

1 S 3:20 And all Israel from Dan even to Beer-sheba knew that Samuel *was* established *to be* a prophet of the LORD.

SHEMAIAH

2 Chr 12:5 Then came Shemaiah the prophet to Rehoboam, and *to* the princes of Judah, that were gathered together to Jerusalem because of Shishak, and said unto them, Thus saith the LORD, Ye have forsaken me, and therefore have I also left you in the hand of Shishak.

ZACHARIAS

Lu 1:67 And his father Zacharias was filled with the Holy Ghost, and prophesied, saying,

ZECHARIAH

Zec 1:1 In the eighth month, in the second year of Darius, came the word of the LORD unto Zechariah, the son of Berechiah, the son of Iddo the prophet, saying,

ZEPHANIAH

Zep 1:1 The word of the LORD which came unto Zephaniah the son of Cushi, the son of Gedaliah, the son of Amariah, the son of Hizkiah, in the days of Josiah the son of Amon, king of Judah.

2. Warnings against False Prophets

De 13:1, 5; 18:20, 22; 1 K 18:19, 29; 22:6, 12, 22; 2 K 3:13; 2 Chr 18:5, 21; Ne 6:14; Is 9:15; Je 2:8; 5:31; 14:14; 20:6; 23:13, 16, 26, 32; 26:11; 27:10; 28:1, 15; 29:9, 21; 37:19; Lam 2:14; 4:13; Eze 12:24; 13:2, 16; 21:29; 22:25, 28; Ho 9:7; Mi 2:11; 3:5, 11; Zep 3:4; Zec 13:3; Mt 7:15, 22; 24:11, 24; Mk 13:22; Lu 6:26; 21:8; Ac 13:6; 2 Co 11:13; 2 Pe 2:1; 1 Jn 4:1

3. Unnamed

Jud 6:8; 1 S 2:27; 1 K 13:11; 20:35; 2 Chr 25:15

4. In the Church

Ac 11:27; 13:1; 15:32; 21:10; Ro 12:6; 1 Co 12:10, 28; 13:2; 14:1, 22, 29; Ep 4:11

5. Called Seers

1 S 9:9, 18; 2 S 15:27; 24:11; 1 Chr 25:5; 26:28; 29:29; 2 Chr 16:7; 19:2; 33:18; 35:15; Is 30:10; Am 7:12; Mi 3:7

6. In Training

2 K 2:5; 4:38; 6:1; 2 Chr 17:9; Da 1:4

7. God's Mouthpiece to His People

Mt 13:35 That it might be fulfilled which was spoken by the prophet, saying, I will open my mouth in parables; I will utter things which have been kept secret from the foundation of the world.

Mt 21:4 All this was done, that it might be fulfilled which was spoken by the prophet, saying,

Mt 27:35 And they crucified him, and parted his garments, casting lots: that it might be fulfilled which was spoken by the prophet, They parted my garments among them, and upon my vesture did they cast lots.

Lu 1:70 As he spake by the mouth of his holy prophets, which have been since the world began:

Jn 19:24 They said therefore among themselves, Let us not rend it, but cast lots for it, whose it shall be: that the scripture might be fulfilled, which saith, They parted my raiment among them, and for my vesture they did cast lots. These things therefore the soldiers did.

Ac 3:21 Whom the heaven must receive until the times of restitution of all things, which God hath spoken by the mouth of all his holy prophets since the world began.

Ro 1:2 (Which he had promised afore by his prophets in the holy scriptures,)

Ro 3:21 But now the righteousness of God without the law is manifested, being witnessed by the law and the prophets;

He 1:1 God, who at sundry times and in divers manners spake in time past unto the fathers by the prophets,

Ja 5:10 Take, my brethren, the prophets, who have spoken in the name of the Lord, for an example of suffering affliction, and of patience.

2 Pe 3:2 That ye may be mindful of the words which were spoken before by the holy prophets, and of the commandment of us the apostles of the Lord and Saviour:

Re 10:7 But in the days of the voice of the seventh angel, when he shall begin to sound, the mystery of God should be finished, as he hath declared to his servants the prophets.

See **LEADER**

PROPITIATION, *God's covering for sin*

Ro 3:25 Whom God hath set forth *to be* a propitiation through faith in his blood, to declare his righteousness for the remission of sins that are past, through the forbearance of God;

1 Jn 2:2 And he is the propitiation for our sins: and not for ours only, but also for *the sins of* the whole world.

1 Jn 4:10 Herein is love, not that we loved God, but that he loved us, and sent his Son *to be* the propitiation for our sins.

See **ATONEMENT**

PROSELYTES, *converts*

1. In Jewish Law

Ex 12:48; Ezr 6:21; Est 9:27; Ac 2:10

2. Examples

Est 8:17; Jn 12:20; Ac 6:5; 13:43; 17:4

See **GOSPEL, MISSIONS**

PROSPERITY, *wealth*

1. Of the Wicked

1 S 25:2; Jb 9:24; 12:6; 21:7; 22:18; Ps 17:14; 37:7, 35; 49:16; 73:3, 12; 92:7; Ec 9:11; Je 5:28; 12:1; 48:11; Lam 1:5; Eze 31:5; Da 8:12; 11:36; Mal 3:15; Lu 16:25

2. Its Perils

FORGETFULNESS OF GOD

De 6:10–12 And it shall be, when the LORD thy God shall have brought thee into the land which he sware unto thy fathers, to Abraham, to Isaac, and to Jacob, to give thee great and goodly cities, which thou buildedst not,

And houses full of all good *things*, which thou filledst not, and wells digged, which thou diggedst not, vineyards and olive trees, which thou plantedst not; when thou shalt have eaten and be full;

Then beware lest thou forget the LORD, which brought thee forth out of the land of Egypt, from the house of bondage.

REBELLION

De 32:15 But Jeshurun waxed fat, and kicked: thou art waxen fat, thou art grown thick, thou art covered *with fatness;* then he forsook God *which* made him, and lightly esteemed the Rock of his salvation.

DESTRUCTION

Pr 1:32 For the turning away of the simple shall slay them, and the prosperity of fools shall destroy them.

DENIAL OF GOD

Pr 30:9 Lest I be full, and deny *thee*, and say, Who *is* the LORD? or lest I be poor, and steal, and take the name of my God *in vain*.

3. Its Evil Effects

De 32:15; 1 K 11:4; Da 4:22, 30; 5:20; 8:24; Ho 13:6; Lu 12:16–19

4. Of the Righteous

Ge 9:27 God shall enlarge Japheth, and he shall dwell in the tents of Shem; and Canaan shall be his servant.

Ge 33:11 Take, I pray thee, my blessing that is brought to thee; because God hath dealt graciously with me, and because I have enough. And he urged him, and he took *it*.

Ge 39:3 And his master saw that the LORD *was* with him, and that the LORD made all *that* he did to prosper in his hand.

De 29:9 Keep therefore the words of this covenant, and do them, that ye may prosper in all that ye do.

Jos 1:7–8 Only be thou strong and very courageous, that thou mayest observe to do according to all the law, which Moses my servant commanded thee: turn not from it *to* the right hand or *to* the left, that thou mayest prosper whithersoever thou goest.

This book of the law shall not depart out of thy mouth; but thou shalt meditate therein day and night, that thou mayest observe to do according to all that is written therein: for then thou shalt make thy way prosperous, and then thou shalt have good success.

1 Chr 22:13 Then shalt thou prosper, if thou takest heed to fulfil the statutes and judgments which the LORD charged Moses with concerning Israel: be strong, and of good courage; dread not, nor be dismayed.

2 Chr 20:20 And they rose early in the morning, and went forth into the wilderness of Tekoa: and as they went forth, Jehoshaphat stood and said, Hear me, O Judah, and ye inhabitants of Jerusalem; Believe in the LORD your God, so shall ye be established; believe his prophets, so shall ye prosper.

2 Chr 26:5 And he sought God in the days of Zechariah, who had understanding in the visions of God: and as long as he sought the LORD, God made him to prosper.

2 Chr 31:21 And in every work that he began in the service of the house of God, and in the law, and in the commandments, to seek his God, he did *it* with all his heart, and prospered.

2 Chr 32:30 This same Hezekiah also stopped the upper watercourse of Gihon, and brought it straight down to the west side of the city of David. And Hezekiah prospered in all his works.

Ne 2:20 Then answered I them, and said unto them, The God of heaven, he will prosper us; therefore we his servants will arise and build: but ye have no portion, nor right, nor memorial, in Jerusalem.

Jb 8:7 Though thy beginning was small, yet thy latter end should greatly increase.

Ps 1:3 And he shall be like a tree planted by the rivers of water, that bringeth forth his fruit in his season; his leaf also shall not wither; and whatsoever he doeth shall prosper.

Ps 112:3 Wealth and riches *shall be* in his house: and his righteousness endureth for ever.

Ps 122:6 Pray for the peace of Jerusalem: they shall prosper that love thee.

Pr 3:16 Length of days *is* in her right hand; *and* in her left hand riches and honour.

Pr 8:21 That I may cause those that love me to inherit substance; and I will fill their treasures.

Pr 21:20 *There is* treasure to be desired and oil in the dwelling of the wise; but a foolish man spendeth it up.

Pr 28:10 Whoso causeth the righteous to go astray in an evil way, he shall fall himself into his own pit: but the upright shall have good *things* in possession.

Ec 2:7 I got *me* servants and maidens, and had servants born in my house; also I had great possessions of great and small cattle above all that were in Jerusalem before me:

Is 65:21 And they shall build houses, and inhabit *them;* and they shall plant vineyards, and eat the fruit of them.

3 Jn 2 Beloved, I wish above all things that thou mayest prosper and be in health, even as thy soul prospereth.

5. Warnings

De 32:15 But Jeshurun waxed fat, and kicked: thou art waxen fat, thou art grown thick, thou art covered *with fatness;* then he forsook God *which* made him, and lightly esteemed the Rock of his salvation.

1 S 2:5 *They that were* full have hired out themselves for bread; and *they that were* hungry ceased: so that the barren hath born seven; and she that hath many children is waxed feeble.

Ps 17:10 They are inclosed in their own fat: with their mouth they speak proudly.

Ps 22:29 All *they that be* fat upon earth shall eat and worship: all they that go down to the dust shall bow before him: and none can keep alive his own soul.

Pr 14:14 The backslider in heart shall be filled with his own ways: and a good man *shall be satisfied* from himself.

Is 6:10 Make the heart of this people fat, and make their ears heavy, and shut their eyes; lest they see with their eyes, and hear with their ears, and understand with their heart, and convert, and be healed.

Is 10:16 Therefore shall the Lord, the Lord of hosts, send among his fat ones leanness; and under his glory he shall kindle a burning like the burning of a fire.

Je 5:7 How shall I pardon thee for this? thy children have forsaken me, and sworn by *them that are* no gods: when I had fed them to the full, they then committed adultery, and assembled themselves by troops in the harlots' houses.

Je 5:28 They are waxen fat, they shine: yea, they overpass the deeds of the wicked: they judge not the cause, the cause of the fatherless, yet they prosper; and the right of the needy do they not judge.

Je 48:11 Moab hath been at ease from his youth, and he hath settled on his lees, and hath not been emptied from vessel to vessel, neither hath he gone into captivity: therefore his taste remained in him, and his scent is not changed.

Je 50:11 Because ye were glad, because ye rejoiced, O ye destroyers of mine heritage, because ye are grown fat as the heifer at grass, and bellow as bulls;

Eze 16:49 Behold, this was the iniquity of thy sister Sodom, pride, fulness of bread, and abundance of idleness was in her and in her daughters, neither did she strengthen the hand of the poor and needy.

Eze 34:16 I will seek that which was lost, and bring again that which was driven away, and will bind up *that which was* broken, and will strengthen that which was sick: but I will destroy the fat and the strong; I will feed them with judgment.

Lu 6:25 Woe unto you that are full! for ye shall hunger. Woe unto you that laugh now! for ye shall mourn and weep.

Re 3:17 Because thou sayest, I am rich, and increased with goods, and have need of nothing; and knowest not that thou art wretched, and miserable, and poor, and blind, and naked:

See **ADVERSITY, BLESSINGS, MISERY, FAMINE, PESTILENCE, RICHES, WANT**

PROTECTION

1. Promised to Believers

Ge 19:10 But the men put forth their hand, and pulled Lot into the house to them, and shut to the door.

1 S 26:24 And, behold, as thy life was much set by this day in mine eyes, so let my life be much set by in the eyes of the Lord, and let him deliver me out of all tribulation.

2 Chr 16:9 For the eyes of the Lord run to and fro throughout the whole earth, to shew himself strong in the behalf of *them* whose heart *is* perfect toward him. Herein thou hast done foolishly: therefore from henceforth thou shalt have wars.

Jb 11:19 Also thou shalt lie down, and none shall make *thee* afraid; yea, many shall make suit unto thee.

Ps 7:6 Arise, O Lord, in thine anger, lift up thyself because of the rage of mine enemies: and awake for me *to* the judgment *that* thou hast commanded.

Ps 34:7 The angel of the Lord encampeth round about them that fear him, and delivereth them.

Ps 41:2 The Lord will preserve him, and keep him alive; *and* he shall be blessed upon the earth: and thou wilt not deliver him unto the will of his enemies.

Ps 91:4 He shall cover thee with his feathers, and under his wings shalt thou trust: his truth *shall be thy* shield and buckler.

Ps 125:2 As the mountains *are* round about Jerusalem, so the Lord *is* round about his people from henceforth even for ever.

Is 49:17 Thy children shall make haste; thy destroyers and they that made thee waste shall go forth of thee.

Is 58:8 Then shall thy light break forth as the morning, and thine health shall spring forth speedily: and thy righteousness shall go before thee; the glory of the Lord shall be thy rereward.

Je 15:20 And I will make thee unto this people a fenced brasen wall: and they shall fight against thee, but they shall not prevail against thee: for I *am* with thee to save thee and to deliver thee, saith the LORD.

Zec 2:5 For I, saith the LORD, will be unto her a wall of fire round about and will be the glory in the midst of her.

Lu 21:18 But there shall not an hair of your head perish.

Re 20:9 And they went up on the breadth of the earth, and compassed the camp of the saints about, and the beloved city: and fire came down from God out of heaven, and devoured them.

2. Examples

Ge 35:5 And they journeyed: and the terror of God was upon the cities that *were* round about them, and they did not pursue after the sons of Jacob.

Ex 14:20 And it came between the camp of the Egyptians and the camp of Israel; and it was a cloud and darkness *to them,* but it gave light by night *to these:* so that the one came not near the other all the night.

2 K 6:17 And Elisha prayed, and said, LORD, I pray thee, open his eyes, that he may see. And the LORD opened the eyes of the young man; and he saw: and, behold, the mountain *was* full of horses and chariots of fire round about Elisha.

Ezr 8:31 Then we departed from the river of Ahava on the twelfth *day* of the first month, to go unto Jerusalem: and the hand of our God was upon us, and he delivered us from the hand of the enemy, and of such as lay in wait by the way.

Da 6:22 My God hath sent his angel, and hath shut the lions' mouths, that they have not hurt me: forasmuch as before him innocency was found in me; and also before thee, O king, have I done no hurt.

Re 7:3 Saying, Hurt not the earth, neither the sea, nor the trees, till we have sealed the servants of our God in their foreheads.

3. Given by God

a. Our Warrior

Ge 14:20 And blessed be the most high God, which hath delivered thine enemies into thy hand. And he gave him tithes of all.

Ex 14:14 The LORD shall fight for you, and ye shall hold your peace.

Ex 15:3 The LORD *is* a man of war: the LORD *is* his name.

Ex 23:27 I will send my fear before thee, and will destroy all the people to whom thou shalt come, and I will make all thine enemies turn their backs unto thee.

De 1:30 The LORD your God which goeth before you, he shall fight for you, according to all that he did for you in Egypt before your eyes;

De 3:22 Ye shall not fear them: for the LORD your God he shall fight for you.

Jos 6:16 And it came to pass at the seventh time, when the priests blew with the trumpets, Joshua said unto the people, Shout; for the LORD hath given you the city.

1 S 30:23 Then said David, Ye shall not do so, my brethren, with that which the LORD hath given us, who hath preserved us, and delivered the company that came against us into our hand.

2 S 5:24 And let it be, when thou hearest the sound of a going in the tops of the mulberry trees, that then thou shalt bestir thyself: for then shall the LORD go out before thee, to smite the host of the Philistines.

1 K 8:45 Then hear thou in heaven their prayer and their supplication, and maintain their cause.

1 K 20:28 And there came a man of God, and spake unto the king of Israel, and said, Thus saith the LORD, Because the Syrians have said, The LORD *is* God of the hills, but he *is* not God of the valleys, therefore will I deliver all this great multitude into thine hand, and ye shall know that I *am* the LORD.

2 K 5:1 Now Naaman, captain of the host of the king of Syria, was a great man with his master, and honourable, because by him the LORD had given deliverance unto Syria: he was also a mighty man in valour, *but he was* a leper.

2 K 6:16 And he answered, Fear not: for they that *be* with us *are* more than they that *be* with them.

2 K 7:6 For the LORD had made the host of the Syrians to hear a noise of chariots, and a noise of horses, *even* the noise of a great host: and they said one to another, Lo, the king of Israel hath hired against us the kings of the Hittites, and the kings of the Egyptians, to come upon us.

1 Chr 5:22 For there fell down many slain, because the war *was* of God. And they dwelt in their steads until the captivity.

1 Chr 14:11 So they came up to Baal-perazim; and David smote them there. Then David said, God hath broken in upon mine enemies by mine hand like the breaking forth of waters: therefore they called the name of that place Baal-perazim.

2 Chr 6:35 Then hear thou from the heavens their prayer and their supplication, and maintain their cause.

2 Chr 20:22 And when they began to sing and to praise, the LORD set ambushments against the children of Ammon, Moab, and mount Seir, which were come against Judah; and they were smitten.

2 Chr 20:29 And the fear of God was on all the kingdoms of *those* countries, when they had heard that the LORD fought against the enemies of Israel.

2 Chr 32:8 With him *is* an arm of flesh; but with us *is* the LORD our God to help us, and to fight our battles. And the people rested themselves upon the words of Hezekiah king of Judah.

Ne 4:20 In what place *therefore* ye hear the sound of the trumpet, resort ye thither unto us: our God shall fight for us.

Ne 9:24 So the children went in and possessed the land, and thou subduedst before them the inhabitants of the land, the Canaanites, and gavest them into their hands, with their kings, and the people of the land, that they might do with them as they would.

Jb 38:23 Which I have reserved against the time of trouble, against the day of battle and war?

Ps 9:3 When mine enemies are turned back, they shall fall and perish at thy presence.

Ps 18:17 He delivered me from my strong enemy, and from them which hated me: for they were too strong for me.

Ps 24:8 Who *is* this King of glory? The LORD strong and mighty, the LORD mighty in battle.

Ps 44:3 For they got not the land in possession by their own sword, neither did their own arm save them: but thy right hand, and thine arm, and the light of thy countenance, because thou hadst a favour unto them.

Ps 47:3 He shall subdue the people under us, and the nations under our feet.

Ps 108:11 *Wilt* not *thou,* O God, *who* hast cast us off? and wilt not thou, O God, go forth with our hosts?

Ps 124:1 If *it had not been* the LORD who was on our side, now may Israel say;

Ec 9:11 I returned, and saw under the sun, that the race *is* not to the swift, nor the battle to the strong, neither yet bread to the wise, nor yet riches to men of understanding, nor yet favour to men of skill; but time and chance happeneth to them all.

Is 28:6 And for a spirit of judgment to him that sitteth in judgment, and for strength to them that turn the battle to the gate.

Is 30:32 And *in* every place where the grounded staff shall pass, which the LORD shall lay upon him, *it* shall be with tabrets and harps: and in battles of shaking will he fight with it.

Je 50:25 The LORD hath opened his armoury, and hath brought forth the weapons of his indignation: for this *is* the work of the Lord GOD of hosts in the land of the Chaldeans.

Da 10:20 Then said he, Knowest thou wherefore I come unto thee? and now will I return to fight with the prince of Persia: and when I am gone forth, lo, the prince of Grecia shall come.

Zec 12:4 In that day, saith the LORD, I will smite every horse with astonishment, and his rider with madness: and I will open mine eyes upon the house of Judah, and will smite every horse go forth, and fight against those nations, as when he fought in the day of battle.

b. Our Defense

2 K 6:10 And the king of Israel sent to the place which the man of God told him and warned him of, and saved himself there, not once nor twice.

Ps 5:11 But let all those that put their trust in thee rejoice: let them ever shout for joy, because thou defendest them: let them also that love thy name be joyful in thee.

Ps 31:2 Bow down thine ear to me; deliver me speedily: be thou my strong rock, for an house of defence to save me.

Ps 36:11 Let not the foot of pride come against me, and let not the hand of the wicked remove me.

Is 31:5 As birds flying, so will the LORD of hosts defend Jerusalem; defending also he will deliver it; and passing over he will preserve it.

Is 37:35 For I will defend this city to save it for mine own sake, and for my servant David's sake.

Is 54:15 Behold, they shall surely gather together, but not by me: whosoever shall gather together against thee shall fall for thy sake.

Je 1:18 For, behold, I have made thee this day a defenced city, and an iron pillar, and brasen walls against the whole land, against the kings of Judah, against the princes thereof, against the priests thereof, and against the people of the land.

Zec 9:15 The LORD of hosts shall defend them; and they shall devour, and subdue with sling stones; and they shall drink, and make a noise as through wine; and they shall be filled like bowls, and as the corners of the altar.

Zec 12:8 In that day shall the LORD defend the inhabitants of Jerusalem;

and he that is feeble among them at that day shall be as David; and the house of David shall be as God, as the angel of the LORD before them.

Mk 14:6 And Jesus said, Let her alone; why trouble ye her? she hath wrought a good work on me.

c. Our Fortress

2 S 22:2 And he said, The LORD is my rock, and my fortress, and my deliverer;

Ps 18:2 The LORD is my rock, and my fortress, and my deliverer; my God, my strength, in whom I will trust; my buckler, and the horn of my salvation, and my high tower.

Ps 91:2 I will say of the LORD, He is my refuge and my fortress: my God; in him will I trust.

Ps 144:2 My goodness, and my fortress; my high tower, and my deliverer; my shield, and he in whom I trust; who subdueth my people under me.

Na 1:7 The LORD is good, a strong hold in the day of trouble; and he knoweth them that trust in him.

d. Our Hiding Place

Ps 17:8 Keep me as the apple of the eye, hide me under the shadow of thy wings,

Ps 27:5 For in the time of trouble he shall hide me in his pavilion: in the secret of his tabernacle shall he hide me; he shall set me up upon a rock.

Ps 31:20 Thou shalt hide them in the secret of thy presence from the pride of man: thou shalt keep them secretly in a pavilion from the strife of tongues.

Ps 32:7 Thou art my hiding place; thou shalt preserve me from trouble; thou shalt compass me about with songs of deliverance. Selah.

Ps 64:2 Hide me from the secret counsel of the wicked; from the insurrection of the workers of iniquity:

Ps 91:1 He that dwelleth in the secret place of the most High shall abide under the shadow of the Almighty.

Ps 119:114 Thou art my hiding place and my shield: I hope in thy word.

Ps 143:9 Deliver me, O LORD, from mine enemies: I flee unto thee to hide me.

Is 26:20 Come, my people, enter thou into thy chambers, and shut thy doors about thee: hide thyself as it were for a little moment, until the indignation be overpast.

Is 32:2 And a man shall be as an hiding place from the wind, and a covert from the tempest; as rivers of water in a dry place, as the shadow of a great rock in a weary land.

Mt 2:15 And was there until the death of Herod: that it might be fulfilled which was spoken of the LORD by the prophet, saying, Out of Egypt have I called my son.

e. Our Refuge

Ex 33:22 And it shall come to pass, while my glory passeth by, that I will put thee in a clift of the rock, and will cover thee with my hand while I pass by:

De 33:27 The eternal God *is thy* refuge, and underneath *are* the everlasting arms: and he shall thrust out the enemy from before thee; and shall say, Destroy *them.*

Ps 27:5 For in the time of trouble he shall hide me in his pavilion: in the secret of his tabernacle shall he hide me; he shall set me up upon a rock.

Ps 31:20 Thou shalt hide them in the secret of thy presence from the pride of man: thou shalt keep them secretly in a pavilion from the strife of tongues.

Ps 46:1 God is our refuge and strength, a very present help in trouble.

Ps 71:3 Be thou my strong habitation, whereunto I may continually resort: thou hast given commandment to save me; for thou *art* my rock and my fortress.

Pr 14:26 In the fear of the LORD *is* strong confidence: and his children shall have a place of refuge.

Pr 18:10 The name of the LORD *is* a strong tower: the righteous runneth into it, and is safe.

Is 4:6 And there shall be a tabernacle for a shadow in the daytime from the heat, and for a place of refuge, and for a covert from storm and from rain.

Is 14:32 What shall *one* then answer the messengers of the nation? That the LORD hath founded Zion, and the poor of his people shall trust in it.

Is 25:4 For thou hast been a strength to the poor, a strength to the needy in his distress, a refuge from the storm, a shadow from the heat, when the blast of the terrible ones *is* as a storm *against* the wall.

Eze 11:16 Therefore say, Thus saith the Lord GOD; Although I have cast them far off among the heathen, and although I have scattered them among the countries, yet will I be to them as a little sanctuary in the countries where they shall come.

Zec 9:12 Turn you to the strong hold, ye prisoners of hope: even to day do I declare *that* I will render double unto thee;

Lu 8:24 And they came to him, and awoke him, saying, Master, master, we perish. Then he arose, and rebuked the wind and the raging of the water: and they ceased, and there was a calm.

f. Our Shield

Ge 15:1 After these things the word of the LORD came unto Abram in a vision, saying, Fear not, Abram: I *am* thy shield, *and* thy exceeding great reward.

De 33:29 Happy *art* thou, O Israel: who *is* like unto thee, O people saved by the LORD, the shield of thy help, and who *is* the sword of thy excellency! and thine enemies shall be found liars unto thee; and thou shalt tread upon their high places.

2 K 6:16 And he answered, Fear not: for they that *be* with us *are* more than they that *be* with them.

Ps 33:20 Our soul waiteth for the LORD: he *is* our help and our shield.

Ps 84:11 For the LORD God *is* a sun and shield: the LORD will give grace and glory: no good *thing* will he withhold from them that walk uprightly.

Ps 115:9 O Israel, trust thou in the LORD: he *is* their help and their shield.

Pr 30:5 Every word of God *is* pure: he *is* a shield unto them that put their trust in him.

Da 6:23 Then was the king exceeding glad for him, and commanded that they should take Daniel up out of the den. So Daniel was taken up out of the den, and no manner of hurt was found upon him, because he believed in his God.

See **GUIDANCE, SECURITY**

PROVENDER, *food for livestock*

Ge 24:25; 42:27; Jud 19:19; 1 K 4:28; Is 11:7

PROVERBS, *short and pithy sayings*

1. General

1 K 4:32; Pr 1:1; 10:1; 25:1; Ec 12:9; Eze 12:22; 16:44; Jn 16:25

2. Book

Authors: Solomon is generally credited with the authorship of a large portion of the Proverbs. It is quite probable that all were not original with him. In chapters 30 and 31 are found the words of Agur and Lemuel.

Date Written: Solomon's proverbs were probably written, collected, and edited before his moral decline (c. 931 B.C.). King Hezekiah (715–686 B.C.) and others later collected them.

Purpose: To give moral instruction.

To Whom Written: Especially for young people. "My son," used frequently, demonstrates Solomon's personal concern for his children. It also applies to the pupil of any wise sage who would wish to give guidance to his young learner.

Main Theme: The fear of the Lord.

Key Words: Wisdom, Understanding.

Key Verse: 1:4.

PROVIDENCE, *God's care and control*

1. God's Provision

Ge 1:30 And to every beast of the earth, and to every fowl of the air, and to every thing that creepeth upon the earth, wherein *there is* life, *I have given* every green herb for meat: and it was so.

Jb 38:41 Who provideth for the raven his food? when his young ones cry unto God, they wander for lack of meat.

Ps 104:21 The young lions roar after their prey, and seek their meat from God.

Ps 121:3 He will not suffer thy foot to be moved: he that keepeth thee will not slumber.

Ps 145:9 The LORD *is* good to all: and his tender mercies *are* over all his works.

Mt 5:45 That ye may be the children of your Father which is in heaven: for he maketh his sun to rise on the evil and on the good, and sendeth rain on the just and on the unjust.

Mt 6:26 Behold the fowls of the air: for they sow not, neither do they reap, nor gather into barns; yet your heavenly Father feedeth them. Are ye not much better than they?

Mt 10:29 Are not two sparrows sold for a farthing? and one of them shall not fall on the ground without your Father.

Ac 14:17 Nevertheless he left not himself without witness, in that he did good, and gave us rain from heaven, and fruitful seasons, filling our hearts with food and gladness.

a. Plentiful Supplies

FOR ISRAEL IN THE WILDERNESS

De 2:7 For the LORD thy God hath blessed thee in all the works of thy hand: he knoweth thy walking through this great wilderness: these forty years the LORD thy God *hath been* with thee; thou hast lacked nothing.

1 K 17:6 And the ravens brought him bread and flesh in the morning, and bread and flesh in the evening; and he drank of the brook.

1 K 17:16 *And* the barrel of meal wasted not, neither did the cruse of oil fail, according to the word of the LORD, which he spake by Elijah.

FOR ELIJAH IN THE WILDERNESS

1 K 19:6 And he looked, and, behold, *there was* a cake baken on the coals, and a cruse of water at his head. And he did eat and drink, and laid him down again.

FOR THE ARMY OF THE THREE KINGS

2 K 3:20 And it came to pass in the morning, when the meat offering was offered, that, behold, there came water by the way of Edom, and the country was filled with water.

FOR THE PROPHET'S WIDOW

2 K 4:6 And it came to pass, when the vessels were full, that she said unto her son, Bring me yet a vessel. And he said unto her, *There is* not a vessel more. And the oil stayed.

FOR SAMARIA IN TIME OF FAMINE

2 K 7:8 And when these lepers came to the uttermost part of the camp, they went into one tent, and did eat and drink, and carried thence silver, and gold, and raiment, and went and hid *it;* and came again, and entered into another tent, and carried thence *also,* and went and hid *it.*

FOR THE MULTITUDE THAT FOLLOWED CHRIST

Mt 14:20 And they did all eat, and were filled: and they took up of the fragments that remained twelve baskets full.

FOR THE SAINTS

Ph 4:19 But my God shall supply all your need according to his riches in glory by Christ Jesus.

b. Preparation Ongoing

OVERFLOWING BLESSINGS

Ps 23:5 Thou preparest a table before me in the presence of mine enemies: thou anointest my head with oil; my cup runneth over.

TREASURES OF GOODNESS

Ps 31:19 *Oh* how great *is* thy goodness, which thou hast laid up for them that fear thee; *which* thou hast

wrought for them that trust in thee before the sons of men!

Ps 68:10 Thy congregation hath dwelt therein: thou, O God, hast prepared of thy goodness for the poor.

Is 64:4 For since the beginning of the world *men* have not heard, nor perceived by the ear, neither hath the eye seen, O God, beside thee, *what* he hath prepared for him that waiteth for him.

Jona 4:6 And the LORD God prepared a gourd, and made *it* to come up over Jonah, that it might be a shadow over his head, to deliver him from his grief. So Jonah was exceeding glad of the gourd.

A SPIRITUAL FEAST

Mt 22:4 Again, he sent forth other servants, saying, Tell them which are bidden, Behold, I have prepared my dinner: my oxen and *my* fatlings *are* killed, and all things *are* ready: come unto the marriage.

A GLORIOUS INHERITANCE

Mt 25:34 Then shall the King say unto them on his right hand, Come, ye blessed of my Father, inherit the kingdom prepared for you from the foundation of the world:

Lu 2:31 Which thou hast prepared before the face of all people;

Lu 14:17 And sent his servant at supper time to say to them that were bidden, Come; for all things are now ready.

A HEAVENLY HOME

Jn 14:2 In my Father's house are many mansions: if *it were* not so, I would have told you. I go to prepare a place for you.

1 Co 2:9 But as it is written, Eye hath not seen, nor ear heard, neither have entered into the heart of man, the things which God hath prepared for them that love him.

He 11:16 But now they desire a better *country,* that is, an heavenly: wherefore God is not ashamed to be called their God: for he hath prepared for them a city.

c. Abundant Giving

De 32:13 He made him ride on the high places of the earth, that he might eat the increase of the fields; and he made him to suck honey out of the rock, and oil out of the flinty rock;

Jb 42:10 And the LORD turned the captivity of Job, when he prayed for his friends: also the LORD gave Job twice as much as he had before.

Ps 13:6 I will sing unto the LORD, because he hath dealt bountifully with me.

Ps 23:5 Thou preparest a table before me in the presence of mine enemies: thou anointest my head with oil; my cup runneth over.

Jl 2:24 And the floors shall be full of wheat, and the fats shall overflow with wine and oil.

Mal 3:10 Bring ye all the tithes into the storehouse, that there may be meat in mine house, and prove me now herewith, saith the LORD of hosts, if I will not open you the windows of heaven, and pour you out a blessing, that *there shall* not *be room* enough *to receive it.*

Mt 14:20 And they did all eat, and were filled: and they took up of the fragments that remained twelve baskets full.

Lu 6:38 Give, and it shall be given unto you; good measure, pressed down, and shaken together, and running over, shall men give into your bosom. For with the same measure that ye mete withal it shall be measured to you again.

2. God's Protection

a. Shelters His People

IN THE ROCK OF AGES

Ex 33:22 And it shall come to pass, while my glory passeth by, that I will put thee in a clift of the rock, and will cover thee with my hand while I pass by:

IN TIME OF TROUBLE

Ps 57:1 Be merciful unto me, O God, be merciful unto me: for my soul trusteth in thee: yea, in the shadow of thy wings will I make my refuge, until *these* calamities be overpast.

Ps 63:7 Because thou hast been my help, therefore in the shadow of thy wings will I rejoice.

Ps 91:1 He that dwelleth in the secret place of the most High shall abide under the shadow of the Almighty.

Ps 121:5 The LORD *is* thy keeper: the LORD *is* thy shade upon thy right hand.

Song 2:3 As the apple tree among the trees of the wood, so *is* my beloved among the sons. I sat down under his shadow with great delight, and his fruit *was* sweet to my taste.

A REFUGE FROM THE STORM

Is 25:4 For thou hast been a strength to the poor, a strength to the needy in his distress, a refuge from the storm, a shadow from the heat, when the blast of the terrible ones *is* as a storm *against* the wall.

Is 32:2 And a man shall be as an hiding place from the wind, and a covert from the tempest; as rivers of water is the shadow of a great rock in a weary land.

IN THE SHADOW OF HIS HAND

Is 51:16 And I have put my words in thy mouth, and I have covered thee in the shadow of mine hand, that I may plant the heavens, and lay the foundations of the earth, and say unto Zion, Thou *art* my people.

UNDER THE SHADOW OF HIS WINGS

Mt 23:37 O Jerusalem, Jerusalem, *thou* that killest the prophets, and stonest them which are sent unto thee, how often would I have gathered thy children together, even as a hen gathereth her chickens under *her* wings, and ye would not!

b. Keeps the Saints

THE PILGRIM'S COMPANION

Ge 28:15 And, behold, I *am* with thee, and will keep thee in all *places* whither thou goest, and will bring thee again into this land; for I will not leave thee, until I have done *that* which I have spoken to thee of.

Ps 34:20 He keepeth all his bones: not one of them is broken.

THE SLEEPLESS WATCHMAN

Ps 121:4 Behold, he that keepeth Israel shall neither slumber nor sleep.

THE PROTECTING FATHER

Jn 17:11 And now I am no more in the world, but these are in the world, and I come to thee. Holy Father, keep through thine own name those whom thou hast given me, that they may be one, as we *are*.

Ph 4:7 And the peace of God, which passeth all understanding, shall keep your hearts and minds through Christ Jesus.

2 Th 3:3 But the Lord is faithful, who shall stablish you, and keep *you* from evil.

THE ALMIGHTY GUARDIAN

2 Ti 1:12 For the which cause I also suffer these things: nevertheless I am not ashamed: for I know whom I have believed, and am persuaded that he is able to keep that which I have committed unto him against that day.

1 Pe 1:5 Who are kept by the power of God through faith unto salvation ready to be revealed in the last time.

Jude 24 Now unto him that is able to keep you from falling, and to present *you* faultless before the presence of his glory with exceeding joy,

Re 3:10 Because thou hast kept the word of my patience, I also will keep thee from the hour of temptation, which shall come upon all the world, to try them that dwell upon the earth.

c. Watches over His People

Ge 3:21 Unto Adam also and to his wife did the LORD God make coats of skins, and clothed them.

Ge 7:16 And they that went in, went in male and female of all flesh, as God had commanded him: and the LORD shut him in.

Ge 16:7 And the angel of the LORD found her by a fountain of water in the wilderness, by the fountain in the way to Shur.

Ge 26:22 And he removed from thence, and digged another well; and for that they strove not: and he called the name of it Rehoboth; and he said, For now the LORD hath made room for us, and we shall be fruitful in the land.

Ge 29:31 And when the LORD saw that Leah *was* hated, he opened her womb: but Rachel *was* barren.

Ge 31:7 And your father hath deceived me, and changed my wages ten times; but God suffered him not to hurt me.

Ge 31:29 It is in the power of my hand to do you hurt: but the God of your father spake unto me yesternight, saying, Take thou heed that thou speak not to Jacob either good or bad.

Ge 45:7 And God sent me before you to preserve you a posterity in the earth, and to save your lives by a great deliverance.

Ex 2:25 And God looked upon the children of Israel, and God had respect unto *them*.

De 7:22 And the LORD thy God will put out those nations before thee by little and little: thou mayest not consume them at once, lest the beasts of the field increase upon thee.

De 29:5 And I have led you forty years in the wilderness: your clothes are not waxen old upon you, and thy shoe is not waxen old upon thy foot.

De 32:10 He found him in a desert land, and in the waste howling wilderness; he led him about, he instructed him, he kept him as the apple of his eye.

1 K 8:29 That thine eyes may be open toward this house night and day, *even* toward the place of which thou hast said, My name shall be there: that thou mayest hearken unto the prayer which thy servant shall make toward this place.

1 K 17:6 And the ravens brought him bread and flesh in the morning, and bread and flesh in the evening; and he drank of the brook.

1 K 19:7 And the angel of the LORD came again the second time, and touched him, and said, Arise *and* eat; because the journey *is* too great for thee.

Ps 40:17 But I *am* poor and needy; *yet* the Lord thinketh upon me: thou *art* my help and my deliverer; make no tarrying, O my God.

Ps 56:8 Thou tellest my wanderings: put thou my tears into thy bottle: *are they* not in thy book?

Ps 115:12 The LORD hath been mindful of us: he will bless *us;* he will bless the house of Israel; he will bless the house of Aaron.

Ps 121:4 Behold, he that keepeth Israel shall neither slumber nor sleep.

Is 63:14 As a beast goeth down into the valley, the Spirit of the LORD caused him to rest: so didst thou lead thy people, to make thyself a glorious name.

Eze 16:8 Now when I passed by thee, and looked upon thee, behold, thy time *was* the time of love; and I spread my skirt over thee, and covered thy nakedness: yea, I sware unto thee, and entered into a covenant with thee, saith the Lord God, and thou becamest mine.

Eze 34:12 As a shepherd seeketh out his flock in the day that he is among his sheep *that are* scattered; so will I seek out my sheep, and will deliver them out of all places where they have been scattered in the cloudy and dark day.

Da 1:9 Now God had brought Daniel into favour and tender love with the prince of the eunuchs.

Ho 13:5 I did know thee in the wilderness, in the land of great drought.

Jona 1:17 Now the LORD had prepared a great fish to swallow up Jonah. And Jonah was in the belly of the fish three days and three nights.

Jona 4:6 And the LORD God prepared a gourd, and made *it* to come up over Jonah, that it might be a shadow over his head, to deliver him from his grief. So Jonah was exceeding glad of the gourd.

Mi 4:6 In that day, saith the LORD, will I assemble her that halteth, and I will gather her that is driven out, and her that I have afflicted;

Mt 2:20 Saying, Arise, and take the young child and his mother, and go into the land of Israel: for they are dead which sought the young child's life.

Mt 6:32 (For after all these things do the Gentiles seek:) for your heavenly Father knoweth that ye have need of all these things.

Mt 10:30 But the very hairs of your head are all numbered.

Mt 13:30 Let both grow together until the harvest: and in the time of harvest I will say to the reapers, Gather ye together first the tares, and bind them in bundles to burn them: but gather the wheat into my barn.

Mt 14:16 But Jesus said unto them, They need not depart; give ye them to eat.

Mt 15:32 Then Jesus called his disciples *unto him,* and said, I have compassion on the multitude, because they continue with me now three days, and have nothing to eat: and I will not send them away fasting, lest they faint in the way.

Mk 5:43 And he charged them straitly that no man should know it; and commanded that something should be given her to eat.

Mk 6:37 He answered and said unto them, Give ye them to eat. And they say unto him, Shall we go and buy two hundred pennyworth of bread, and give them to eat?

Mk 6:48 And he saw them toiling in rowing; for the wind was contrary unto them: and about the fourth watch of the night he cometh unto them, walking upon the sea, and would have passed by them.

Mk 8:2 I have compassion on the multitude, because they have now been with me three days, and have nothing to eat:

Lu 8:55 And her spirit came again, and she arose straightway: and he commanded to give her meat.

Lu 12:7 But even the very hairs of your head are all numbered. Fear not therefore: ye are of more value than many sparrows.

Lu 12:30 For all these things do the nations of the world seek after: and your Father knoweth that ye have need of these things.

Jn 6:5 When Jesus then lifted up *his* eyes, and saw a great company come unto him, he saith unto Philip, Whence shall we buy bread, that these may eat?

Jn 15:1 I am the true vine, and my Father is the husbandman.

Jn 16:1 These things have I spoken unto you, that ye should not be offended.

Jn 18:8 Jesus answered, I have told you that I am *he:* if therefore ye seek me, let these go their way:

Ac 7:10 And delivered him out of all his afflictions, and gave him favour and wisdom in the sight of Pharaoh king of Egypt; and he made him governor over Egypt and all his house.

1 Pe 5:7 Casting all your care upon him; for he careth for you.

Re 12:6 And the woman fled into the wilderness, where she hath a place prepared of God, that they should feed her there a thousand two hundred *and* threescore days.

Re 12:14 And to the woman were given two wings of a great eagle, that she might fly into the wilderness, into her place, where she is nourished for a time, and times, and half a time, from the face of the serpent.

3. God's Sustenance

a. Supports the Weak

Ex 19:4 Ye have seen what I did unto the Egyptians, and *how* I bare you on eagles' wings, and brought you unto myself.

De 1:31 And in the wilderness, where thou hast seen how that the LORD thy God bare thee, as a man doth bear his son, in all the way that ye went, until ye came into this place.

De 32:11 As an eagle stirreth up her nest, fluttereth over her young, spreadeth abroad her wings, taketh them, beareth them on her wings:

De 33:27 The eternal God *is thy* refuge, and underneath *are* the everlasting arms: and he shall thrust out the enemy from before thee; and shall say, Destroy *them.*

1 S 2:8 He raiseth up the poor out of the dust, *and* lifteth up the beggar from the dunghill, to set *them* among princes, and to make them inherit the throne of glory: for the pillars of the earth *are* the LORD's, and he hath set the world upon them.

Ps 3:5 I laid me down and slept; I awaked; for the LORD sustained me.

Ps 17:5 Hold up my goings in thy paths, *that* my footsteps slip not.

Ps 18:35 Thou hast also given me the shield of thy salvation: and thy right hand hath holden me up, and thy gentleness hath made me great.

Ps 28:9 Save thy people, and bless thine inheritance: feed them also, and lift them up for ever.

Ps 37:17 For the arms of the wicked shall be broken: but the LORD upholdeth the righteous.

Ps 37:24 Though he fall, he shall not be utterly cast down: for the LORD upholdeth *him with* his hand.

Ps 41:12 And as for me, thou upholdest me in mine integrity, and settest me before thy face for ever.

Ps 51:12 Restore unto me the joy of thy salvation; and uphold me *with thy* free spirit.

Ps 54:4 Behold, God *is* mine helper: the Lord *is* with them that uphold my soul.

Ps 55:22 Cast thy burden upon the LORD, and he shall sustain thee: he shall never suffer the righteous to be moved.

Ps 63:8 My soul followeth hard after thee: thy right hand upholdeth me.

Ps 73:23 Nevertheless I *am* continually with thee: thou hast holden *me* by my right hand.

Ps 91:12 They shall bear thee up in *their* hands, lest thou dash thy foot against a stone.

Ps 94:18 When I said, My foot slippeth; thy mercy, O LORD, held me up.

Ps 119:116 Uphold me according unto thy word, that I may live: and let me not be ashamed of my hope.

Ps 145:14 The LORD upholdeth all that fall, and raiseth up all *those that be* bowed down.

Song 8:5 Who *is* this that cometh up from the wilderness, leaning upon her beloved? I raised thee up under the apple tree: there thy mother brought thee forth: there she brought thee forth *that* bare thee.

Is 41:10 Fear thou not; for I *am* with thee: be not dismayed; for I *am* thy God: I will strengthen thee; yea, I will help thee; yea, I will uphold thee with the right hand of my righteousness.

Is 46:4 And *even* to *your* old age I *am* he; and *even* to hoar hairs will I carry *you:* I have made, and I will bear; even I will carry, and will deliver *you.*

Is 63:9 In all their affliction he was afflicted, and the angel of his presence saved them: in his love and in his pity he redeemed them; and he bare them, and carried them all the days of old.

Ho 11:3 I taught Ephraim also to go, taking them by their arms; but they knew not that I healed them.

Mt 14:29 And he said, Come. And when Peter was come down out of the ship, he walked on the water, to go to Jesus.

Lu 4:11 And in *their* hands they shall bear thee up, lest at any time thou dash thy foot against a stone.

Lu 15:4 What man of you, having an hundred sheep, if he lose one of them, doth not leave the ninety and nine in the wilderness, and go after that which is lost, until he find it?

Ac 17:28 For in him we live, and move, and have our being; as certain also of your own poets have said, For we are also his offspring.

Ro 14:4 Who art thou that judgest another man's servant? to his own master he standeth or falleth. Yea, he shall be holden up: for God is able to make him stand.

2 Ti 4:17 Notwithstanding the Lord stood with me, and strengthened me; that by me the preaching might be fully known, and *that* all the Gentiles might hear: and I was delivered out of the mouth of the lion.

He 1:3 Who being the brightness of *his* glory, and the express image of his person, and upholding all things by the word of his power, when he had by himself purged our sins, sat down on the right hand of the Majesty on high;

Re 2:1 Unto the angel of the church of Ephesus write; These things saith he that holdeth the seven stars in his right hand, who walketh in the midst of the seven golden candlesticks;

b. Preserves the Faithful

Ge 7:23 And every living substance was destroyed which was upon the face of the ground, both man, and cattle, and the creeping things, and the fowl of the heaven; and they were destroyed from the earth: and Noah only remained *alive,* and they that *were* with him in the ark.

Ge 19:19 Behold now, thy servant hath found grace in thy sight, and thou hast magnified thy mercy, which thou hast shewed unto me in saving my life; and I cannot escape to the mountain, lest some evil take me, and I die:

Ge 45:7 And God sent me before you to preserve you a posterity in the earth, and to save your lives by a great deliverance.

De 4:4 But ye that did cleave unto the LORD your God *are* alive every one of you this day.

De 6:24 And the LORD commanded us to do all these statutes, to fear the LORD our God, for our good always, that he might preserve us alive, as *it is* at this day.

De 8:4 Thy raiment waxed not old upon thee, neither did thy foot swell, these forty years.

De 32:11 As an eagle stirreth up her nest, fluttereth over her young, spreadeth abroad her wings, taketh them, beareth them on her wings:

De 34:7 And Moses *was* an hundred and twenty years old when he died: his eye was not dim, nor his natural force abated.

Jos 14:10 And now, behold, the LORD hath kept me alive, as he said, these forty and five years, even since the LORD spake this word unto Moses, while *the children of* Israel wandered in the wilderness: and now, lo, I *am* this day fourscore and five years old.

Jos 24:17 For the LORD our God, he *it is* that brought us up and our fathers out of the land of Egypt, from the house of bondage, and which did those great signs in our sight, and preserved us in all the way wherein we went, and among all the people through whom we passed:

1 S 30:23 Then said David, Ye shall not do so, my brethren, with that which the LORD hath given us, who hath preserved us, and delivered the company that came against us into our hand.

2 S 8:6 Then David put garrisons in Syria of Damascus: and the Syrians became servants to David, *and* brought gifts. And the LORD preserved David whithersoever he went.

2 S 8:14 And he put garrisons in Edom; throughout all Edom put he garrisons, and all they of Edom became David's servants. And the LORD preserved David whithersoever he went.

2 K 11:2 But Jehosheba, the daughter of king Joram, sister of Ahaziah, took Joash the son of Ahaziah and stole him from among the king's sons *which were* slain; and they hid him, *even* him and his nurse, in the bedchamber from Athaliah, so that he was not slain.

1 Chr 18:6 Then David put *garrisons* in Syria-damascus; and the Syrians became David's servants, *and* brought gifts. Thus the LORD preserved David whithersoever he went.

1 Chr 18:13 And he put garrisons in Edom; and all the Edomites became David's servants. Thus the LORD preserved David whithersoever he went.

Ne 9:6 Thou, *even* thou, *art* LORD alone; thou hast made heaven, the heaven of heavens, with all their host, the earth, and all *things* that *are* therein, the seas, and all that *is* therein, and thou preservest them all; and the host of heaven worshippeth thee.

Ne 9:21 Yea, forty years didst thou sustain them in the wilderness, *so that* they lacked nothing; their clothes waxed not old, and their feet swelled not.

Jb 5:20 In famine he shall redeem thee from death: and in war from the power of the sword.

Jb 10:12 Thou hast granted me life and favour, and thy visitation hath preserved my spirit.

Jb 29:2 Oh that I were as *in* months past, as *in* the days *when* God preserved me;

Jb 33:18 He keepeth back his soul from the pit, and his life from perishing by the sword.

Ps 3:5 I laid me down and slept; I awaked; for the LORD sustained me.

Ps 12:7 Thou shalt keep them, O LORD, thou shalt preserve them from this generation for ever.

Ps 16:1 Preserve me, O God: for in thee do I put my trust.

Ps 17:8 Keep me as the apple of the eye, hide me under the shadow of thy wings,

Ps 30:3 O LORD, thou hast brought up my soul from the grave: thou hast kept me alive, that I should not go down to the pit.

Ps 31:23 O love the LORD, all ye his saints: *for* the LORD preserveth the faithful, and plentifully rewardeth the proud doer.

Ps 32:7 Thou *art* my hiding place; thou shalt preserve me from trouble; thou shalt compass me about with songs of deliverance. Selah.

Ps 33:19 To deliver their soul from death, and to keep them alive in famine.

Ps 34:20 He keepeth all his bones: not one of them is broken.

Ps 36:6 Thy righteousness *is* like the great mountains; thy judgments *are* a great deep: O LORD, thou preservest man and beast.

Ps 37:28 For the LORD loveth judgment, and forsaketh not his saints; they are preserved for ever: but the seed of the wicked shall be cut off.

Ps 40:11 Withhold not thou thy tender mercies from me, O LORD: let thy lovingkindness and thy truth continually preserve me.

Ps 41:2 The LORD will preserve him, and keep him alive; *and* he shall be blessed upon the earth: and thou wilt not deliver him unto the will of his enemies.

Ps 61:7 He shall abide before God for ever: O prepare mercy and truth, *which* may preserve him.

Ps 64:1 Hear my voice, O God, in my prayer: preserve my life from fear of the enemy.

Ps 66:9 Which holdeth our soul in life, and suffereth not our feet to be moved.

Ps 71:6 By thee have I been holden up from the womb: thou art he that took me out of my mother's bowels: my praise *shall be* continually of thee.

Ps 79:11 Let the sighing of the prisoner come before thee; according to the greatness of thy power preserve thou those that are appointed to die;

Ps 86:2 Preserve my soul; for I *am* holy: O thou my God, save thy servant that trusteth in thee.

Ps 91:3 Surely he shall deliver thee from the snare of the fowler, *and* from the noisome pestilence.

Ps 97:10 Ye that love the LORD, hate evil: he preserveth the souls of his saints; he delivereth them out of the hand of the wicked.

Ps 103:4 Who redeemeth thy life from destruction; who crowneth thee with lovingkindness and tender mercies;

Ps 116:6 The LORD preserveth the simple: I was brought low, and he helped me.

Ps 118:17 I shall not die, but live, and declare the works of the LORD.

Ps 121:7 The LORD shall preserve thee from all evil: he shall preserve thy soul.

Ps 140:1 Deliver me, O LORD, from the evil man: preserve me from the violent man;

Ps 145:20 The LORD preserveth all them that love him: but all the wicked will he destroy.

Ps 146:9 The LORD preserveth the strangers; he relieveth the fatherless and widow: but the way of the wicked he turneth upside down.

Pr 2:8 He keepeth the paths of judgment, and preserveth the way of his saints.

Pr 22:12 The eyes of the LORD preserve knowledge, and he overthroweth the words of the transgressor.

Is 27:3 I the LORD do keep it; I will water it every moment: lest *any* hurt it, I will keep it night and day.

Is 31:5 As birds flying, so will the LORD of hosts defend Jerusalem; defending also he will deliver *it; and* passing over he will preserve *it.*

Is 43:2 When thou passest through the waters, I *will be* with thee; and through the rivers, they shall not overflow thee: when thou walkest through the fire, thou shalt not be burned; neither shall the flame kindle upon thee.

Is 48:19 Thy seed also had been as the sand, and the offspring of thy bowels like the gravel thereof; his name should not have been cut off nor destroyed from before me.

Is 49:8 Thus saith the LORD, In an acceptable time have I heard thee, and in a day of salvation have I helped thee: and I will preserve thee, and give thee for a covenant of the people, to establish the earth, to cause to inherit the desolate heritages;

Je 39:18 For I will surely deliver thee, and thou shalt not fall by the sword, but thy life shall be for a prey unto thee: because thou hast put thy trust in me, saith the LORD.

Je 44:17 But we will certainly do whatsoever thing goeth forth out of our own mouth, to burn incense unto the queen of heaven, and to pour out drink offerings unto her, as we have done, we, and our fathers, our kings, and our princes, in the cities of Judah, and in the streets of Jerusalem: for *then* had we plenty of victuals, and were well, and saw no evil.

Je 49:11 Leave thy fatherless children, I will preserve *them* alive; and let thy widows trust in me.

Eze 9:6 Slay utterly old *and* young, both maids, and little children, and women: but come not near any man upon whom *is* the mark; and begin at my sanctuary. Then they began at the ancient men which *were* before the house.

Da 3:25 He answered and said, Lo, I see four men loose, walking in the midst of the fire, and they have no hurt; and the form of the fourth is like the Son of God.

Da 6:23 Then was the king exceeding glad for him, and commanded that they should take Daniel up out of the den. So Daniel was taken up out of the den, and no manner of hurt was found upon him, because he believed in his God.

Ho 12:13 And by a prophet the LORD brought Israel out of Egypt, and by a prophet was he preserved.

Jona 1:17 Now the LORD had prepared a great fish to swallow up Jonah. And Jonah was in the belly of the fish three days and three nights.

Jona 2:6 I went down to the bottoms of the mountains; the earth with her bars *was* about me for ever: yet hast thou brought up my life from corruption, O LORD my God.

Hab 1:12 *Art* thou not from everlasting, O LORD my God, mine Holy One? we shall not die. O LORD, thou hast ordained them for judgment; and, O mighty God, thou hast established them for correction.

Mal 3:6 For I *am* the LORD, I change not; therefore ye sons of Jacob are not consumed.

Mt 2:13 And when they were departed, behold, the angel of the Lord appeareth to Joseph in a dream, saying, Arise, and take the young child and his mother, and flee into Egypt, and be thou there until I bring thee word: for Herod will seek the young child to destroy him.

Jn 19:36 For these things were done, that the scripture should be fulfilled, A bone of him shall not be broken.

Ac 17:28 For in him we live, and move, and have our being; as certain also of your own poets have said, For we are also his offspring.

Ac 27:34 Wherefore I pray you to take *some* meat: for this is for your health: for there shall not an hair fall from the head of any of you.

2 Co 4:9 Persecuted, but not forsaken; cast down, but not destroyed;

2 Ti 4:18 And the Lord shall deliver me from every evil work, and will preserve *me* unto his heavenly king-dom: to whom *be* glory for ever and ever. Amen.

He 11:34 Quenched the violence of fire, escaped the edge of the sword, out of weakness were made strong, waxed valiant in fight, turned to flight the armies of the aliens.

Jude 1 Jude, the servant of Jesus Christ, and brother of James, to them that are sanctified by God the Father, and preserved in Jesus Christ, *and* called:

See **ABUNDANCE, BLESSINGS, GUIDANCE, HELPER, PLENTY, PROTECTION**

PROVIDENCES, *strange, perplexing events*

Is 55:8; Mt 14:24; Lu 2:7, 12, 18; Ac 7:6; 16:23; Ro 11:33

PROVOCATION, *inciting anger*

Nu 14:11 And the LORD said unto Moses, How long will this people provoke me? and how long will it be ere they believe me, for all the signs which I have shewed among them?

Nu 14:23 Surely they shall not see the land which I sware unto their fathers, neither shall any of them that provoked me see it:

Nu 16:30 But if the LORD make a new thing, and the earth open her mouth, and swallow them up, with all that *appertain* unto them, and they go down quick into the pit; then ye shall understand that these men have provoked the LORD.

De 4:25 When thou shalt beget children, and children's children, and ye shall have remained long in the land, and shall corrupt *yourselves,* and make a graven image, *or* the likeness of any *thing,* and shall do evil in the sight of the LORD thy God, to provoke him to anger:

De 9:7 Remember, *and* forget not, how thou provokedst the LORD thy God to wrath in the wilderness: from the day that thou didst depart out of the land of Egypt, until ye came unto this place, ye have been rebellious against the LORD.

De 9:18 And I fell down before the LORD, as at the first, forty days and forty nights: I did neither eat bread, nor drink water, because of all your sins which ye sinned, in doing wickedly in the sight of the LORD, to provoke him to anger.

De 9:22 And at Taberah, and at Massah, and at Kibroth-hattaavah, ye provoked the LORD to wrath.

De 31:20 For when I shall have brought them into the land which I sware unto their fathers, that floweth with milk and honey; and they shall have eaten and filled themselves, and waxen fat; then will they turn unto other gods, and serve them, and provoke me, and break my covenant.

De 31:29 For I know that after my death ye will utterly corrupt *yourselves,* and turn aside from the way which I have commanded you; and evil will befall you in the latter days; because ye will do evil in the sight of the LORD, to provoke him to anger through the work of your hands.

De 32:16 They provoked him to jealousy with strange *gods,* with abominations provoked they him to anger.

Jud 2:12 And they forsook the LORD God of their fathers, which brought them out of the land of Egypt, and followed other gods, of the gods of the people that *were* round about them, and bowed themselves unto them, and provoked the LORD to anger.

1 K 14:9 But hast done evil above all that were before thee: for thou hast gone and made thee other gods, and molten images, to provoke me to anger, and hast cast me behind thy back:

1 K 15:30 Because of the sins of Jeroboam which he sinned, and which he made Israel sin, by his provocation wherewith he provoked the LORD God of Israel to anger.

1 K 16:2 Forasmuch as I exalted thee out of the dust, and made thee prince over my people Israel; and thou hast walked in the way of Jeroboam, and hast made my people Israel to sin, to provoke me to anger with their sins;

1 K 16:7 And also by the hand of the prophet Jehu the son of Hanani came the word of the LORD against Baasha, and against his house, even for all the evil that he did in the sight of the LORD, in provoking him to anger with the work of his hands, in being like the house of Jeroboam; and because he killed him.

1 K 16:13 For all the sins of Baasha, and the sins of Elah his son, by which they sinned, and by which they made Israel to sin, in provoking the LORD God of Israel to anger with their vanities.

1 K 16:26 For he walked in all the way of Jeroboam the son of Nebat, and in his sin wherewith he made Israel to sin, to provoke the LORD God of Israel to anger with their vanities.

1 K 16:33 And Ahab made a grove; and Ahab did more to provoke the LORD God of Israel to anger than all the kings of Israel that were before him.

1 K 21:22 And will make thine house like the house of Jeroboam the son of Nebat, and like the house of Baasha the son of Ahijah, for the provocation wherewith thou hast provoked *me* to anger, and made Israel to sin.

2 K 17:17 And they caused their sons and their daughters to pass through the fire, and used divination and enchantments, and sold themselves to do evil in the sight of the LORD, to provoke him to anger.

2 K 21:6 And he made his son pass through the fire, and observed times, and used enchantments, and dealt with familiar spirits and wizards: he wrought much wickedness in the sight of the LORD, to provoke *him* to anger.

2 K 21:15 Because they have done *that which was* evil in my sight, and have provoked me to anger, since the day their fathers came forth out of Egypt, even unto this day.

2 K 22:17 Because they have forsaken me, and have burned incense unto other gods, that they might provoke me to anger with all the works of their hands; therefore my wrath shall be kindled against this place, and shall not be quenched.

2 K 23:19 And all the houses also of the high places that *were* in the cities of Samaria, which the kings of Israel had made to provoke *the* LORD to anger, Josiah took away, and did to them according to all the acts that he had done in Bethel.

2 K 23:26 Notwithstanding the LORD turned not from the fierceness of his great wrath, wherewith his anger was kindled against Judah, because of all the provocations that Manasseh had provoked him withal.

2 Chr 28:25 And in every several city of Judah he made high places to burn incense unto other gods, and provoked to anger the LORD God of his fathers.

2 Chr 34:25 Because they have forsaken me, and have burned incense unto other gods, that they might provoke me to anger with all the works of their hands; therefore my wrath shall be poured out upon this place, and shall not be quenched.

Ezr 5:12 But after that our fathers had provoked the God of heaven unto wrath, he gave them into the hand of Nebuchadnezzar the king of Babylon, the Chaldean, who destroyed this house, and carried the people away into Babylon.

Ne 4:5 And cover not their iniquity, and let not their sin be blotted out from before thee: for they have provoked *thee* to anger before the builders.

Ne 9:18 Yea, when they had made them a molten calf, and said, This *is* thy God that brought thee up out of Egypt, and had wrought great provocations;

Ne 9:26 Nevertheless they were disobedient, and rebelled against thee, and cast thy law behind their backs, and slew thy prophets which testified against them to turn them to thee, and they wrought great provocations.

Ps 78:17 And they sinned yet more against him by provoking the most High in the wilderness.

Ps 78:40 How oft did they provoke him in the wilderness, *and* grieve him in the desert!

Ps 78:56 Yet they tempted and provoked the most high God, and kept not his testimonies:

Ps 106:7 Our fathers understood not thy wonders in Egypt; they remembered not the multitude of thy mercies; but provoked *him* at the sea, *even* at the Red sea.

Ps 106:29 Thus they provoked *him* to anger with their inventions: and the plague brake in upon them.

Ps 106:43 Many times did he deliver them; but they provoked *him* with their counsel, and were brought low for their iniquity.

Is 1:4 Ah sinful nation, a people laden with iniquity, a seed of evildoers, children that are corrupters: they have forsaken the LORD, they have provoked the Holy One of Israel unto anger, they are gone away backward.

Is 3:8 For Jerusalem is ruined, and Judah is fallen: because their tongue and their doings *are* against the LORD, to provoke the eyes of his glory.

Is 65:3 A people that provoketh me to anger continually to my face; that sacrificeth in gardens, and burneth incense upon altars of brick;

Je 7:18 The children gather wood, and the fathers kindle the fire, and the women knead *their* dough, to make cakes to the queen of heaven, and to pour out drink offerings unto other gods, that they may provoke me to anger.

Je 8:19 Behold the voice of the cry of the daughter of my people because of them that dwell in a far country: *Is* not the LORD in Zion? *is* not her king in her? Why have they provoked me to anger with their graven images, *and* with strange vanities?

Je 11:17 For the LORD of hosts, that planted thee, hath pronounced evil against thee, for the evil of the house of Israel and of the house of Judah, which they have done against themselves to provoke me to anger in offering incense unto Baal.

Je 25:7 Yet ye have not hearkened unto me, saith the LORD; that ye might provoke me to anger with the works of your hands to your own hurt.

Je 32:31 For this city hath been to me *as* a provocation of mine anger and of my fury from the day that they built it even unto this day; that I should remove it from before my face,

Je 44:3 Because of their wickedness which they have committed to provoke me to anger, in that they went to burn incense, *and* to serve other gods, whom they knew not, *neither* they, ye, nor your fathers.

Je 44:8 In that ye provoke me unto wrath with the works of your hands, burning incense unto other gods in the land of Egypt, whither ye be gone to dwell, that ye might cut yourselves off, and that ye might be a curse and a reproach among all the nations of the earth?

Eze 8:3 And he put forth the form of an hand, and took me by a lock of mine head; and the spirit lifted me up between the earth and the heaven, and brought me in the visions of God to Jerusalem, to the door of the inner gate that looketh toward the north; where *was* the seat of the image of jealousy, which provoketh to jealousy.

Eze 8:17 Then he said unto me, Hast thou seen *this*, O son of man? Is it a light thing to the house of Judah that they commit the abominations which they commit here? for they have filled the land with violence, and have returned to provoke me to anger: and, lo, they put the branch to their nose.

Eze 16:26 Thou hast also committed fornication with the Egyptians thy neighbours, great of flesh; and hast increased thy whoredoms, to provoke me to anger.

Eze 20:28 *For* when I had brought them into the land, *for* the which I lifted up mine hand to give it to them, then they saw every high hill, and all the thick trees, and they offered there their sacrifices, and there they presented the provocation of their offering: there also they made their sweet savour, and poured out there their drink offerings.

Ho 12:14 Ephraim provoked *him* to anger most bitterly: therefore shall he leave his blood upon him, and his reproach shall his Lord return unto him.

Zec 8:14 For thus saith the LORD of hosts; As I thought to punish you,

when your fathers provoked me to wrath, saith the LORD of hosts, and I repented not:

He 3:16 For some, when they had heard, did provoke: howbeit not all that came out of Egypt by Moses.

See **ANGER, PEACE, WRATH**

PRUDENCE

RESERVE

Pr 12:23 A prudent man concealeth knowledge: but the heart of fools proclaimeth foolishness.

Pr 13:16 Every prudent *man* dealeth with knowledge: but a fool layeth open *his* folly.

CAUTION

Pr 14:15 The simple believeth every word: but the prudent *man* looketh well to his going.

TEACHABLENESS

Pr 15:5 A fool despiseth his father's instruction: but he that regardeth reproof is prudent.

Pr 18:15 The heart of the prudent getteth knowledge; and the ear of the wise seeketh knowledge.

FORESIGHT

Pr 22:3 A prudent *man* foreseeth the evil, and hideth himself: but the simple pass on, and are punished.

SPIRITUAL INSIGHT

Ho 14:9 Who *is* wise, and he shall understand these *things?* prudent, and he shall know them? for the ways of the LORD *are* right, and the just shall walk in them: but the transgressors shall fall therein.

SILENCE

Am 5:13 Therefore the prudent shall keep silence in that time; for it *is* an evil time.

See **RASHNESS**

PRUNING See **AGRICULTURE**

PRUNING HOOK See **AGRICULTURE**

PSALMS

Authors: The authorship of many is uncertain. It is probable that in some cases the name affixed to certain psalms may refer to the collector rather than the author. The following is a possible list of authors along with the number of psalms attributed to them: David, 73; to Sons of Korah, 11; to Asaph, 12; to Heman, 1; to Ethan, 1; to Solomon, 2; to Moses, 1; to Haggai, 1; to Zechariah, 1; to Hezekiah, number doubtful; to Ezra, 1; the remainder, anonymous.

Date Written: From the time of Moses (c. 1440 B.C.) to Ezra (c. 450 B.C.)

Purpose: One hundred and fifty spiritual songs and poems used by God's people in all ages in worship and devotional exercises (private and public). It was used as the hymnbook of the second temple.

To Whom Written: Sometimes to God, sometimes for the author himself, often to the chief musician for worship and devotional use with God's people.

Main Themes: The predominant themes are prayer and praise, but the psalms cover a great variety of religious experiences. They are quoted more frequently in the New Testament than any other book except Isaiah. They are often called the Psalms of David because he was the author of a large number of them.

Key Words: Worship, Praise.

Key Verse: 150:6.

PSALTERIES *See* MUSIC

PUBLICANS, *collectors of Roman revenues*

Mt 5:46 For if ye love them which love you, what reward have ye? do not even the publicans the same?

Mt 9:10 And it came to pass, as Jesus sat at meat in the house, behold, many publicans and sinners came and sat down with him and his disciples.

Mt 17:24 And when they were come to Capernaum, they that received tribute *money* came to Peter, and said, Doth not your master pay tribute?

Mt 18:17 And if he shall neglect to hear them, tell *it* unto the church: but if he neglect to hear the church, let him be unto thee as an heathen man and a publican.

Mt 21:31 Whether of them twain did the will of *his* father? They say unto him, The first. Jesus saith unto them, Verily I say unto you, That the publicans and the harlots go into the kingdom of God before you.

Mk 2:15 And it came to pass, that, as Jesus sat at meat in his house, many publicans and sinners sat also together with Jesus and his disciples: for there were many, and they followed him.

Lu 3:12 Then came also publicans to be baptized, and said unto him, Master, what shall we do?

Lu 5:27 And after these things he went forth, and saw a publican, named Levi, sitting at the receipt of custom: and he said unto him, Follow me.

Lu 5:29 And Levi made him a great feast in his own house: and there was a great company of publicans and of others that sat down with them.

Lu 7:29 And all the people that heard *him,* and the publicans, justified God, being baptized with the baptism of John.

Lu 7:34 The Son of man is come eating and drinking; and ye say, Behold a gluttonous man, and a winebibber, a friend of publicans and sinners!

Lu 15:1 Then drew near unto him all the publicans and sinners for to hear him.

Lu 18:10 Two men went up into the temple to pray; the one a Pharisee, and the other a publican.

Lu 19:2 And, behold, *there was* a man named Zacchaeus, which was the chief among the publicans, and he was rich.

See HUMILITY

PUL, *king of Assyria*

2 K 15:19; 1 Chr 5:26

PUNISHMENT, *penalty imposed for wrongdoing*

1. Of the Wicked

Ge 4:13 And Cain said unto the LORD, My punishment *is* greater than I can bear.

Ps 149:7 To execute vengeance upon the heathen, *and* punishments upon the people;

Is 13:11 And I will punish the world for *their* evil, and the wicked for their iniquity; and I will cause the arrogancy of the proud to cease, and will lay low the haughtiness of the terrible.

Is 24:21 And it shall come to pass in that day, *that* the LORD shall punish the host of the high ones *that are* on high, and the kings of the earth upon the earth.

Is 26:21 For, behold, the LORD cometh out of his place to punish the inhabitants of the earth for their iniquity: the earth also shall disclose her blood, and shall no more cover her slain.

Is 59:18 According to *their* deeds, accordingly he will repay, fury to his adversaries, recompence to his enemies; to the islands he will repay recompence.

Je 21:14 But I will punish you according to the fruit of your doings, saith the LORD: and I will kindle a fire in the forest thereof, and it shall devour all things round about it.

Zep 1:12 And it shall come to pass at that time, *that* I will search Jerusalem with candles, and punish the men that are settled on their lees: that say in their heart, The LORD will not do good, neither will he do evil.

Lu 12:47 And that servant, which knew his lord's will, and prepared not *himself,* neither did according to his will, shall be beaten with many *stripes.*

Ro 2:8 But unto them that are contentious, and do not obey the truth, but obey unrighteousness, indignation and wrath,

He 10:29 Of how much sorer punishment, suppose ye, shall he be thought worthy, who hath trodden under foot the Son of God, and hath counted the blood of the covenant, wherewith he was sanctified, an unholy thing, and hath done despite unto the Spirit of grace?

2. In the Future

Ps 11:6 Upon the wicked he shall rain snares, fire and brimstone, and an horrible tempest: *this shall be* the portion of their cup.

Mal 4:1 For, behold, the day cometh, that shall burn as an oven; and all the proud, yea, and all that do wickedly, shall be stubble: and the day that cometh shall burn them up, saith the LORD of hosts, that it shall leave them neither root nor branch.

Mt 18:9 And if thine eye offend thee, pluck it out, and cast *it* from thee: it is better for thee to enter into life with one eye, rather than having two eyes to be cast into hell fire.

Mt 25:46 And these shall go away into everlasting punishment: but the righteous into life eternal.

Mk 3:29 But he that shall blaspheme against the Holy Ghost hath never forgiveness, but is in danger of eternal damnation:

Lu 3:17 Whose fan *is* in his hand, and he will throughly purge his floor, and will gather the wheat into his garner; but the chaff he will burn with fire unquenchable.

2 Th 1:9 Who shall be punished with everlasting destruction from the presence of the Lord, and from the glory of his power;

2 Pe 2:9 The Lord knoweth how to deliver the godly out of temptations, and to reserve the unjust unto the day of judgment to be punished:

Re 14:11 And the smoke of their torment ascendeth up for ever and ever: and they have no rest day nor night, who worship the beast and his image, and whosoever receiveth the mark of his name.

Re 20:15 And whosoever was not found written in the book of life was cast into the lake of fire.

See **JUDGMENTS, REWARD**

PURIFICATION, *ceremonial*

Le 12:4; Nu 8:21; 31:20; 2 Chr 30:19; Ne 12:30; Lu 2:22; Jn 11:55; Ac 21:26; 24:18

PURITY

Ge 39:8 But he refused, and said unto his master's wife, Behold, my master wotteth not what *is* with me in the house, and he hath committed all that he hath to my hand;

Ex 19:15 And he said unto the people, Be ready against the third day: come not at *your* wives.

Le 18:11 The nakedness of thy father's wife's daughter, begotten of thy father, she *is* thy sister, thou shalt not uncover her nakedness.

2 S 13:12 And she answered him, Nay, my brother, do not force me; for no such thing ought to be done in Israel: do not thou this folly.

2 S 22:27 With the pure thou wilt shew thyself pure; and with the froward thou wilt shew thyself unsavoury.

Jb 22:30 He shall deliver the island of the innocent: and it is delivered by the pureness of thine hands.

Ps 18:26 With the pure thou wilt shew thyself pure; and with the froward thou wilt shew thyself froward.

Ps 24:3–4 Who shall ascend into the hill of the LORD? or who shall stand in his holy place?

He that hath clean hands, and a pure heart; who hath not lifted up his soul unto vanity, nor sworn deceitfully.

Ps 51:7 Purge me with hyssop, and I shall be clean: wash me, and I shall be whiter than snow.

Ps 73:1 Truly God *is* good to Israel, *even* to such as are of a clean heart.

Ps 119:3 They also do no iniquity: they walk in his ways.

Pr 22:11 He that loveth pureness of heart, *for* the grace of his lips the king shall *be* his friend.

Eze 18:8 He *that* hath not given forth upon usury, neither hath taken any increase, *that* hath withdrawn his hand from iniquity, hath executed true judgment between man and man,

Mt 5:8 Blessed *are* the pure in heart: for they shall see God.

Mt 23:26 *Thou* blind Pharisee, cleanse first that *which is* within the cup and platter, that the outside of them may be clean also.

1 Co 6:13 Meats for the belly, and the belly for meats: but God shall destroy both it and them. Now the body *is* not for fornication, but for the Lord; and the Lord for the body.

2 Co 6:6 By pureness, by knowledge, by longsuffering, by kindness, by the Holy Ghost, by love unfeigned,

Ep 5:3 But fornication, and all uncleanness, or covetousness, let it not be once named among you, as becometh saints;

Ph 4:8 Finally, brethren, whatsoever things are true, whatsoever things *are* honest, whatsoever things *are* just, whatsoever things *are* pure, whatsoever things *are* lovely, whatsoever things *are* of good report; if *there be* any virtue, and if *there be* any praise, think on these things.

1 Th 4:6 That no *man* go beyond and defraud his brother in *any* matter: because that the Lord *is* the avenger of all such, as we also have forewarned you and testified.

1 Ti 1:5 Now the end of the commandment is charity out of a pure heart, and *of* a good conscience, and *of* faith unfeigned:

1 Ti 4:12 Let no man despise thy youth; but be thou an example of the believers, in word, in conversation, in charity, in spirit, in faith, in purity.

1 Ti 5:2 The elder women as mothers; the younger as sisters, with all purity.

1 Ti 5:22 Lay hands suddenly on no man, neither be partaker of other men's sins: keep thyself pure.

2 Ti 2:22 Flee also youthful lusts: but follow righteousness, faith, charity, peace, with them that call on the Lord out of a pure heart.

Tit 1:15 Unto the pure all things *are* pure: but unto them that are defiled and unbelieving *is* nothing pure; but even their mind and conscience is defiled.

Ja 1:27 Pure religion and undefiled before God and the Father is this, To visit the fatherless and widows in their affliction, *and* to keep himself unspotted from the world.

Ja 3:17 But the wisdom that is from above is first pure, then peaceable, gentle, *and* easy to be intreated, full of mercy and good fruits, without partiality, and without hypocrisy.

Ja 4:8 Draw nigh to God, and he will draw nigh to you. Cleanse *your* hands, *ye* sinners; and purify *your* hearts, *ye* double minded.

1 Pe 1:22 Seeing ye have purified your souls in obeying the truth through the Spirit unto unfeigned love of the brethren, *see that ye* love one another with a pure heart fervently:

2 Pe 3:14 Wherefore, beloved, seeing that ye look for such things, be diligent that ye may be found of him in peace, without spot, and blameless.

Re 14:4 These are they which were not defiled with women; for they are virgins. These are they which follow the Lamb whithersoever he goeth. These were redeemed from among men, *being* the firstfruits unto God and to the Lamb.

See **IMPURITY**

PURPLE, *a brilliant red-blue color prized by the ancients*

1. Used in the Tabernacle

Ex 25:4; 26:31, 36; 27:16; 28:5, 8, 15; 35:6, 23, 35; 36:8, 35; 38:18; 39:1, 5; Nu 4:13; 2 Chr 3:14; Est 1:6

2. Rich Clothing

Est 8:15; Pr 31:22; Je 10:9; Eze 23:6; 27:7, 16; Da 5:7, 29; Mk 15:17; Lu 16:19; Re 18:12, 16

PURPOSES, DIVINE

IRRESISTIBLE

Is 14:27 For the LORD of hosts hath purposed, and who shall disannul *it*?

and his hand *is* stretched out, and who shall turn it back?

SURE OF FULFILLMENT

Je 51:29 And the land shall tremble and sorrow: for every purpose of the LORD shall be performed against Babylon, to make the land of Babylon a desolation without an inhabitant.

SEEN IN HIS CHOICE OF INSTRUMENTS

Ac 26:16 But rise, and stand upon thy feet: for I have appeared unto thee for this purpose, to make thee a minister and a witness both of these things which thou hast seen, and of those things in the which I will appear unto thee;

REVEALED IN THE GOSPEL

Ep 1:9 Having made known unto us the mystery of his will, according to his good pleasure which he hath purposed in himself:

ETERNAL IN CHRIST

Ep 3:11 According to the eternal purpose which he purposed in Christ Jesus our Lord:

INVOLVES THE OVERTHROW OF SATAN

1 Jn 3:8 He that committeth sin is of the devil; for the devil sinneth from the beginning. For this purpose the Son of God was manifested, that he might destroy the works of the devil.

See **PROVIDENCE**

PURSES, *bags in which money was carried*

Pr 1:14; 7:20; Is 46:6; Mt 10:9; Mk 6:8; Lu 10:4; 22:35; Jn 12:6; 13:29

PYGARG *See* **ANIMALS**

Q

QUAILS See BIRDS

QUEEN OF SHEBA See SHEBA

QUESTIONS, inquiries that call for a reply

1. Asked of Christ

Mt 9:11, 14; 11:3, 7; 18:1; 19:3, 16, 27; 21:23; 22:17, 24, 36; 24:3; Mk 2:18; 8:11; Lu 20:22; Jn 6:28

2. To Be Avoided

Mt 19:3; 22:28; Mk 12:23; Lu 20:33; 1 Ti 1:4; 6:4; 2 Ti 2:14, 23; Tit 3:9

3. Inescapable

DIVERSE OPINIONS OF MEN

Mt 16:13–15 When Jesus came into the coasts of Caesarea Philippi, he asked his disciples, saying, Whom do men say that I the Son of man am?

And they said, Some *say that thou art* John the Baptist: some, Elias; and others, Jeremias, or one of the prophets.

He saith unto them, But whom say ye that I am?

PETER'S OPINION

Mt 16:16 And Simon Peter answered and said, Thou art the Christ, the Son of the living God.

QUESTION OF THE MULTITUDE

Mt 21:10 And when he was come into Jerusalem, all the city was moved, saying, Who is this?

THE PHARISEES' OPINION SOUGHT

Mt 22:41–43 While the Pharisees were gathered together, Jesus asked them,

Saying, What think ye of Christ? whose son is he? They say unto him, *The Son* of David.

He saith unto them, How then doth David in spirit call him Lord, saying,

PILATE'S DILEMMA

Mt 27:22 Pilate saith unto them, What shall I do then with Jesus which is called Christ? *They* all say unto him, Let him be crucified.

See **INSIGHT, MIND, PERCEPTION, THOUGHTS**

QUICKENING See AWAKENING

QUIETNESS

Jb 34:29 When he giveth quietness, who then can make trouble? and when he hideth *his* face, who then can behold him? whether *it be done* against a nation, or against a man only:

Ps 131:2 Surely I have behaved and quieted myself, as a child that is weaned of his mother: my soul *is* even as a weaned child.

Pr 1:33 But whoso hearkeneth unto me shall dwell safely, and shall be quiet from fear of evil.

Is 32:17 And the work of righteousness shall be peace; and the effect of righteousness quietness and assurance for ever.

Lam 3:26 *It is* good that *a man* should both hope and quietly wait for the salvation of the LORD.

Mk 4:39 And he arose, and rebuked the wind, and said unto the sea, Peace, be still. And the wind ceased, and there was a great calm.

Jn 11:20 Then Martha, as soon as she heard that Jesus was coming, went and met him: but Mary sat *still* in the house.

Ac 19:36 Seeing then that these things cannot be spoken against, ye ought to be quiet, and to do nothing rashly.

1. Prescribed

Pr 17:1 Better *is* a dry morsel, and quietness therewith, than an house full of sacrifices *with* strife.

Ec 4:6 Better *is* an handful *with* quietness, than both the hands full *with* travail and vexation of spirit.

1 Th 4:11 And that ye study to be quiet, and to do your own business, and to work with your own hands, as we commanded you;

2 Th 3:12 Now them that are such we command and exhort by our Lord Jesus Christ, that with quietness they work, and eat their own bread.

1 Ti 2:2 For kings, and *for* all that are in authority; that we may lead a quiet and peaceable life in all godliness and honesty.

1 Pe 3:4 But *let it be* the hidden man of the heart, in that which is not corruptible, *even the ornament* of a meek and quiet spirit, which is in the sight of God of great price.

2. Essential for Instruction

Ex 14:13 And Moses said unto the people, Fear ye not, stand still, and see the salvation of the LORD, which he will shew to you to day: for the Egyptians whom ye have seen to day, ye shall see them again no more for ever.

Nu 9:8 And Moses said unto them, Stand still, and I will hear what the LORD will command concerning you.

Jud 7:21 And they stood every man in his place round about the camp: and all the host ran, and cried, and fled.

1 S 9:27 *And* as they were going down to the end of the city, Samuel said to Saul, Bid the servant pass on before us, (and he passed on,) but stand thou still a while, that I may shew thee the word of God.

1 S 12:7 Now therefore stand still, that I may reason with you before the LORD of all the righteous acts of the LORD, which he did to you and to your fathers.

Jb 37:14 Hearken unto this, O Job: stand still, and consider the wondrous works of God.

Ps 4:4 Stand in awe, and sin not: commune with your own heart upon your bed, and be still. Selah.

Ps 37:7 Rest in the LORD, and wait patiently for him: fret not thyself because of him who prospereth in his way, because of the man who bringeth wicked devices to pass.

Ps 46:10 Be still, and know that I *am* God: I will be exalted among the heathen, I will be exalted in the earth.

Ps 62:1 Truly my soul waiteth upon God: from him *cometh* my salvation.

Is 23:2 Be still, ye inhabitants of the isle; thou whom the merchants of Zidon, that pass over the sea, have replenished.

Is 30:15 For thus saith the Lord GOD, the Holy One of Israel; In returning and rest shall ye be saved; in quietness and in confidence shall be your strength: and ye would not.

See **PEACE, REST, STRIFE, TUMULTS**

QUIVERS, *a portable case for arrows*
Ge 27:3; Jb 39:23; Ps 127:5; Is 49:2

R

RABBAH, *or Rabbath, captured by Joab*
It was capital of the ancient kingdom of the Ammonites and the present capital (Amman) of Jordan is thought to have been built by the sons of Ammon (Lot's son) who gave it the name of their father (De 3:11). It was besieged by Joab for two years before it was taken, and in front of its walls Uriah the Hittite was killed unjustly at King David's indirect command (2 S 11:16–17).

RACHEL, *daughter of Laban, married to Jacob*

Ge 29:6, 18; 30:1, 22; 31:4; 33:2; 35:19; 46:22; 48:7; Ru 4:11; 1 S 10:2; Je 31:15; Mt 2:18

RADIANCE

Jb 11:17 And *thine* age shall be clearer than the noonday; thou shalt shine forth, thou shalt be as the morning.

Ps 34:5 They looked unto him, and were lightened: and their faces were not ashamed.

Ec 8:1 Who *is* as the wise *man?* and who knoweth the interpretation of a thing? a man's wisdom maketh his face to shine, and the boldness of his face shall be changed.

Is 58:10 And *if* thou draw out thy soul to the hungry, and satisfy the afflicted soul; then shall thy light rise in obscurity, and thy darkness *be* as the noonday:

Is 62:1 For Zion's sake will I not hold my peace, and for Jerusalem's sake I will not rest, until the righteousness thereof go forth as brightness, and the salvation thereof as a lamp *that* burneth.

Da 12:3 And they that be wise shall shine as the brightness of the firmament; and they that turn many to righteousness as the stars for ever and ever.

Jn 5:35 He was a burning and a shining light: and ye were willing for a season to rejoice in his light.

Ac 6:15 And all that sat in the council, looking stedfastly on him, saw his face as it had been the face of an angel.

2 Co 3:18 But we all, with open face beholding as in a glass the glory of the Lord, are changed into the same image from glory to glory, *even* as by the Spirit of the Lord.

Ph 2:15 That ye may be blameless and harmless, the sons of God, without rebuke, in the midst of a crooked and perverse nation, among whom ye shine as lights in the world;

Re 21:11 Having the glory of God: and her light *was* like unto a stone most precious, even like a jasper stone, clear as crystal;

See **LIGHT**

RAHAB, *of Jericho, receives the spies*

Jos 2:1; 6:17, 25; Ps 87:4; He 11:31; Ja 2:25

RAIMENT *See* **APPAREL**

RAIN *See* **WEATHER**

RAINBOW, *arc of spectral colors*
Ge 9:13; Eze 1:28; Re 4:3; 10:1

RAISINS
1 S 25:18; 30:12; 2 S 16:1; 1 Chr 12:40

RAMAH, *a height; thus many towns situated on hilltops were given that name*
Jos 18:25; Jud 19:13; 1 S 8:4; 15:34; 16:13; 19:18; 22:6; 25:1; 28:3; 1 K 15:17; Ezr 2:26; Mt 2:18

RAMESES, *or Raamses, a city and district in Egypt*
Ge 47:11; Ex 1:11; 12:37; Nu 33:3

RAMOTH GILEAD, *a city of refuge*

De 4:43; Jos 20:8; 21:38; 1 K 22:3, 29; 2 K 8:28; 9:1; 1 Chr 6:80; 2 Chr 18:2; 22:5

See **CITIES**

RAMS *See* **ANIMALS**

RANSOM, *payment made to have someone released from captivity*

Mt 20:28; 1 Ti 2:6

RAPACITY, *living on prey*

Mt 23:14; Mk 12:7, 40; Lu 11:39; 20:14, 47; Jn 10:8, 12; Ac 20:29; 2 Co 11:20; Ga 5:15; Ja 4:2; 1 Pe 5:8

RASHNESS, *acting without forethought or due caution*

1. Warnings

Pr 14:29; 19:2; 21:5; 29:20; Ec 5:2; 7:9; Je 8:6; Ac 19:36

2. Examples

Jud 11:31; 1 S 14:24; 2 S 6:6; 2 Chr 35:22; Mt 26:51

See **PRUDENCE**

RAVENS *See* **BIRDS**

RAZORS, *sharp-edged cutting instruments*

Nu 6:5; Ps 52:2; Is 7:20; Eze 5:1

READINESS, *state of being prepared*

1. For the Future

2 K 20:1 In those days was Hezekiah sick unto death. And the prophet Isaiah the son of Amoz came to him, and said unto him, Thus saith the LORD, Set thine house in order; for thou shalt die, and not live.

Is 38:1 In those days was Hezekiah sick unto death. And Isaiah the prophet the son of Amoz came unto him, and said unto him, Thus saith the LORD, Set thine house in order: for thou shalt die, and not live.

Am 4:12 Therefore thus will I do unto thee, O Israel: *and* because I will

do this unto thee, prepare to meet thy God, O Israel.

Mt 24:44 Therefore be ye also ready: for in such an hour as ye think not the Son of man cometh.

Mt 25:4 But the wise took oil in their vessels with their lamps.

Mt 25:10 And while they went to buy, the bridegroom came; and they that were ready went in with him to the marriage: and the door was shut.

Mk 13:35 Watch ye therefore: for ye know not when the master of the house cometh, at even, or at midnight, or at the cockcrowing, or in the morning:

Lu 12:35–36 Let your loins be girded about, and *your* lights burning;

And ye yourselves like unto men that wait for their lord, when he will return from the wedding; that when he cometh and knocketh, they may open unto him immediately.

Lu 12:40 Be ye therefore ready also: for the Son of man cometh at an hour when ye think not.

Ph 1:23 For I am in a strait betwixt two, having a desire to depart, and to be with Christ; which is far better:

1 Th 5:4 But ye, brethren, are not in darkness, that that day should overtake you as a thief.

2 Pe 3:14 Wherefore, beloved, seeing that ye look for such things, be diligent that ye may be found of him in peace, without spot, and blameless.

Re 19:7 Let us be glad and rejoice, and give honour to him: for the marriage of the Lamb is come, and his wife hath made herself ready.

2. For Spiritual Service

Ex 12:11 And thus shall ye eat it; *with* your loins girded, your shoes on your feet, and your staff in your hand; and ye shall eat it in haste: it *is* the LORD's passover.

Ex 34:2 And be ready in the morning, and come up in the morning unto mount Sinai, and present thyself there to me in the top of the mount.

2 Co 8:19 And not *that* only, but who was also chosen of the churches to travel with us with this grace, which is administered by us to the glory of the same Lord, and *declaration of* your ready mind:

2 Co 9:2 For I know the forwardness of your mind, for which I boast of you to them of Macedonia, that Achaia was ready a year ago; and your zeal hath provoked very many.

2 Ti 2:21 If a man therefore purge himself from these, he shall be a vessel unto honour, sanctified, and meet for the master's use, *and* prepared unto every good work.

Tit 3:1 Put them in mind to be subject to principalities and powers, to obey magistrates, to be ready to every good work,

1 Pe 3:15 But sanctify the Lord God in your hearts: and *be* ready always to *give* an answer to every man that asketh you a reason of the hope that is in you with meekness and fear:

1 Pe 5:2 Feed the flock of God which is among you, taking the oversight *thereof,* not by constraint, but willingly; not for filthy lucre, but of a ready mind;

3. Spiritual Steps Required

ABANDONMENT OF IDOLS

1 S 7:3 And Samuel spake unto all the house of Israel, saying, If ye do return unto the LORD with all your hearts, *then* put away the strange gods and Ashtaroth from among you, and prepare your hearts unto the LORD, and serve him only: and he will deliver you out of the hand of the Philistines.

2 Chr 19:3 Nevertheless there are good things found in thee, in that thou hast taken away the groves out of the land, and hast prepared thine heart to seek God.

CLEANSING OF GOD'S TEMPLE

2 Chr 29:15 And they gathered their brethren, and sanctified themselves, and came, according to the commandment of the king, by the words of the LORD, to cleanse the house of the LORD.

RETURNING UNTO THE LORD

Lu 1:17 And he shall go before him in the spirit and power of Elias, to turn the hearts of the fathers to the children, and the disobedient to the wisdom of the just; to make ready a people prepared for the Lord.

PERSONAL PURIFICATION

2 Ti 2:21 If a man therefore purge himself from these, he shall be a vessel unto honour, sanctified, and meet for the master's use, *and* prepared unto every good work.

4. Precedes Blessings

NO WATER FOR THE ARMY UNTIL DITCHES WERE DUG

2 K 3:16–17 And he said, Thus saith the LORD, Make this valley full of ditches.

For thus saith the LORD, Ye shall not see wind, neither shall ye see rain; yet that valley shall be filled with water, that ye may drink, both ye, and your cattle, and your beasts.

NO OIL UNTIL THE VESSELS WERE GATHERED

2 K 4:3–4 Then he said, Go, borrow thee vessels abroad of all thy neighbours, *even* empty vessels; borrow not a few.

And when thou art come in, thou shalt shut the door upon thee and upon thy sons, and shalt pour out into all those vessels, and thou shalt set aside that which is full.

NO HEALING UNTIL THE LEPER HAD DIPPED SEVEN TIMES

2 K 5:10 And Elisha sent a messenger unto him, saying, Go and wash in the Jordan seven times, and thy flesh shall come again to thee, and thou shalt be clean.

NO MESSIAH UNTIL THE WAY HAD BEEN PREPARED

Is 40:3 The voice of him that crieth in the wilderness, Prepare ye the way of the LORD, make straight in the desert a highway for our God.

NO HARVEST UNTIL THE GROUND HAD BEEN BROKEN UP

Ho 10:12 Sow to yourselves in righteousness, reap in mercy; break up your fallow ground: for *it is* time to seek the LORD, till he come and rain righteousness upon you.

NO RECONCILIATION WITHOUT REPENTANCE

Jl 2:12–13 Therefore also now, saith the LORD, turn ye *even* to me with all your heart, and with fasting, and with weeping, and with mourning:

And rend your heart, and not your garments, and turn unto the LORD your God: for he *is* gracious and merciful, slow to anger, and of great kindness, and repenteth him of the evil.

NO VISION WITHOUT OBEDIENCE

Jn 9:7 And said unto him, Go, wash in the pool of Siloam, (which is by interpretation, Sent.) He went his way therefore, and washed, and came seeing.

NO RESURRECTION UNTIL THE STONE IS REMOVED

Jn 11:39 Jesus said, Take ye away the stone. Martha, the sister of him that was dead, saith unto him, Lord, by this time he stinketh: for he hath been *dead* four days.

NO ENTRANCE INTO HEAVEN WITHOUT CLEANSING

Re 7:13–14 And one of the elders answered, saying unto me, What are these which are arrayed in white robes? and whence came they?

And I said unto him, Sir, thou knowest. And he said to me, These are they which came out of great tribulation, and have washed their robes, and made them white in the blood of the Lamb.

See **SECOND COMING, UNREADINESS, WATCHING**

READING

Ec 12:12; Da 5:17; Jn 19:20

REAL ESTATE, *land, including its natural resources, and any buildings or other improvements made*

1. Land Leased
Mt 21:33–41; Mk 12:1–9

2. Land Purchased
Lu 14:18

3. Record and Witnesses
Je 32:11–12

4. Land Sold
Ge 23:15; 47:20; Ru 4:3; 2 S 24:24

5. Laws of Inheritance
Nu 27:8; 33:54; 36:7; De 21:16; Jos 17:4; Eze 46:16; Lu 12:13

6. In the Year of Jubilee
Le 25:23, 33

7. Landmarks
De 19:14; 27:17

REASON

1. Appeals
Is 1:18; Eze 14:14; Ro 12:1

2. Human
Mt 16:7 And they reasoned among themselves, saying, *It is* because we have taken no bread.

Mt 21:25 The baptism of John, whence was it? from heaven, or of men? And they reasoned with themselves, saying, If we shall say, From heaven; he will say unto us, Why did ye not then believe him?

Mk 2:6 But there were certain of the scribes sitting there, and reasoning in their hearts,

Mk 2:8 And immediately when Jesus perceived in his spirit that they so reasoned within themselves, he said unto them, Why reason ye these things in your hearts?

Mk 8:16 And they reasoned among themselves, saying, *It is* because we have no bread.

Mk 11:31 And they reasoned with themselves, saying, If we shall say, From heaven; he will say, Why then did ye not believe him?

Mk 12:28 And one of the scribes came, and having heard them reasoning together, and perceiving that he had answered them well, asked him, Which is the first commandment of all?

Lu 5:21 And the scribes and the Pharisees began to reason, saying, Who is this which speaketh blasphemies? Who can forgive sins, but God alone?

Lu 7:49 And they that sat at meat with him began to say within themselves, Who is this that forgiveth sins also?

Lu 9:46 Then there arose a reasoning among them, which of them should be greatest.

Lu 20:5 And they reasoned with themselves, saying, If we shall say, From heaven; he will say, Why then believed ye him not?

Lu 20:14 But when the husbandmen saw him, they reasoned among themselves, saying, This is the heir: come, let us kill him, that the inheritance may be ours.

Jn 6:52 The Jews therefore strove among themselves, saying, How can this man give us *his* flesh to eat?

Ac 28:29 And when he had said these words, the Jews departed, and had great reasoning among themselves.

1 Co 1:20 Where *is* the wise? where *is* the scribe? where *is* the disputer of this world? hath not God made foolish the wisdom of this world?

3. Dethroned by God's Wisdom

Da 4:33 The same hour was the thing fulfilled upon Nebuchadnezzar: and he was driven from men, and did eat grass as oxen, and his body was wet with the dew of heaven, till his hairs were grown like eagles' *feathers*, and his nails like birds' *claws*.

Mt 8:28 And when he was come to the other side into the country of the Gergesenes, there met him two possessed with devils, coming out of the tombs, exceeding fierce, so that no man might pass by that way.

Mt 17:15 Lord, have mercy on my son: for he is lunatick, and sore vexed: for ofttimes he falleth into the fire, and oft into the water.

2 Pe 2:12 But these, as natural brute beasts, made to be taken and destroyed, speak evil of the things that they understand not; and shall utterly perish in their own corruption;

See **UNDERSTANDING**

REBEKAH, *or Rebecca, daughter of Bethuel, married to Isaac*

BEAUTIFUL

Ge 24:16 And the damsel *was* very fair to look upon, a virgin, neither had any man known her: and she went down to the well, and filled her pitcher, and came up.

INDUSTRIOUS

Ge 24:19 And when she had done giving him drink, she said, I will draw *water* for thy camels also, until they have done drinking.

HOSPITABLE

Ge 24:25 She said moreover unto him, We have both straw and provender enough, and room to lodge in.

A WOMAN OF DECISION

Ge 24:57–58 And they said, We will call the damsel, and enquire at her mouth.

And they called Rebekah, and said unto her, Wilt thou go with this man? And she said, I will go.

MODEST

Ge 24:65 For she *had* said unto the servant, What man *is* this that walketh in the field to meet us? And the servant *had* said, It *is* my master: therefore she took a vail, and covered herself.

BROUGHT TROUBLE INTO THE HOME BY TEACHING HER SON DECEPTION

Ge 27:15–17 And Rebekah took goodly raiment of her eldest son Esau, which *were* with her in the house, and put them upon Jacob her younger son:

And she put the skins of the kids of the goats upon his hands, and upon the smooth of his neck:

And she gave the savoury meat and the bread, which she had prepared, into the hand of her son Jacob.

REBELLION, *defiance toward authority*

1. Against God

Nu 14:9 Only rebel not ye against the LORD, neither fear ye the people of the land; for they *are* bread for us: their defence is departed from them, and the LORD *is* with us: fear them not.

Nu 16:11 For which cause *both* thou and all thy company *are* gathered together against the LORD: and what *is* Aaron, that ye murmur against him?

De 1:43 So I spake unto you; and ye would not hear, but rebelled against the commandment of the LORD, and went presumptuously up into the hill.

De 9:7 Remember, *and* forget not, how thou provokedst the LORD thy God to wrath in the wilderness: from the day that thou didst depart out of the land of Egypt, until ye came unto this place, ye have been rebellious against the LORD.

De 9:24 Ye have been rebellious against the LORD from the day that I knew you.

De 31:27 For I know thy rebellion, and thy stiff neck: behold, while I am yet alive with you this day, ye have been rebellious against the LORD; and how much more after my death?

De 32:15 But Jeshurun waxed fat, and kicked: thou art waxen fat, thou art grown thick, thou art covered *with fatness;* then he forsook God *which* made him, and lightly esteemed the Rock of his salvation.

Jos 22:29 God forbid that we should rebel against the LORD, and turn this day from following the LORD, to build an altar for burnt offerings, for meat offerings, or for sacrifices, beside the altar of the LORD our God that *is* before his tabernacle.

1 S 12:15 But if ye will not obey the voice of the LORD, but rebel against the commandment of the LORD, then shall the hand of the LORD be against you, as *it was* against your fathers.

1 S 15:23 For rebellion *is as* the sin of witchcraft, and stubbornness *is as* iniquity and idolatry. Because thou hast rejected the word of the LORD, he hath also rejected thee from *being* king.

Ne 9:17 And refused to obey, neither were mindful of thy wonders that thou didst among them; but hardened their necks, and in their rebellion appointed a captain to return to their bondage: but thou *art* a God ready to pardon, gracious and merciful, slow to anger, and of great kindness, and forsookest them not.

Jb 15:13 That thou turnest thy spirit against God, and lettest *such* words go out of thy mouth?

Jb 15:25 For he stretcheth out his hand against God, and strengtheneth himself against the Almighty.

Jb 34:37 For he addeth rebellion unto his sin, he clappeth *his hands* among us, and multiplieth his words against God.

Ps 2:3 Let us break their bands asunder, and cast away their cords from us.

Ps 5:10 Destroy thou them, O God; let them fall by their own counsels; cast them out in the multitude of their transgressions; for they have rebelled against thee.

Ps 21:11 For they intended evil against thee: they imagined a mischievous device, *which* they are not able *to perform.*

Ps 68:6 God setteth the solitary in families: he bringeth out those which are bound with chains: but the rebellious dwell in a dry *land.*

Ps 107:11 Because they rebelled against the words of God, and contemned the counsel of the most High:

Pr 17:11 An evil *man* seeketh only rebellion: therefore a cruel messenger shall be sent against him.

Is 1:23 Thy princes *are* rebellious, and companions of thieves: every one loveth gifts, and followeth after rewards: they judge not the fatherless, neither doth the cause of the widow come unto them.

Is 30:1 Woe to the rebellious children, saith the LORD, that take counsel, but not of me; and that cover with a covering, but not of my spirit, that they may add sin to sin:

Is 30:9 That this *is* a rebellious people, lying children, children *that* will not hear the law of the LORD:

Is 31:6 Turn ye unto *him from* whom the children of Israel have deeply revolted.

Is 63:10 But they rebelled, and vexed his holy Spirit: therefore he was turned to be their enemy, *and* he fought against them.

Is 65:2 I have spread out my hands all the day unto a rebellious people, which walketh in a way *that was* not good, after their own thoughts;

Je 2:31 O generation, see ye the word of the LORD. Have I been a wilderness unto Israel? a land of darkness? wherefore say my people, We are lords; we will come no more unto thee?

Je 4:17 As keepers of a field, are they against her round about; because she hath been rebellious against me, saith the LORD.

Je 5:5 I will get me unto the great men, and will speak unto them; for they have known the way of the LORD, *and* the judgment of their God: but these have altogether broken the yoke, *and* burst the bonds.

Je 5:23 But this people hath a revolting and a rebellious heart; they are revolted and gone.

Je 11:9 And the LORD said unto me, A conspiracy is found among the men of Judah, and among the inhabitants of Jerusalem.

Je 28:16 Therefore thus saith the LORD; Behold, I will cast thee from off the face of the earth: this year thou shalt die, because thou hast taught rebellion against the LORD.

Je 50:24 I have laid a snare for thee, and thou art also taken, O Babylon, and thou wast not aware: thou art found, and also caught, because thou hast striven against the LORD.

Lam 1:18 The LORD is righteous; for I have rebelled against his commandment: hear, I pray you, all people, and

behold my sorrow: my virgins and my young men are gone into captivity.

Eze 2:3 And he said unto me, Son of man, I send thee to the children of Israel, to a rebellious nation that hath rebelled against me: they and their fathers have transgressed against me, *even* unto this very day.

Eze 2:7 And thou shalt speak my words unto them, whether they will hear, or whether they will forbear: for they *are* most rebellious.

Eze 3:9 As an adamant harder than flint have I made thy forehead: fear them not, neither be dismayed at their looks, though they *be* a rebellious house.

Eze 12:2 Son of man, thou dwellest in the midst of a rebellious house, which have eyes to see, and see not; they have ears to hear, and hear not: for they *are* a rebellious house.

Eze 12:9 Son of man, hath not the house of Israel, the rebellious house, said unto thee, What doest thou?

Eze 12:25 For I *am* the LORD: I will speak, and the word that I shall speak shall come to pass; it shall be no more prolonged: for in your days, O rebellious house, will I say the word, and will perform it, saith the Lord GOD.

Eze 17:12 Say now to the rebellious house, Know ye not what these *things mean?* tell *them*, Behold, the king of Babylon is come to Jerusalem, and hath taken the king thereof, and the princes thereof, and led them with him to Babylon;

Eze 20:8 But they rebelled against me, and would not hearken unto me: they did not every man cast away the abominations of their eyes, neither did they forsake the idols of Egypt: then I said, I will pour out my fury upon them to accomplish my anger against them in the midst of the land of Egypt.

Eze 20:13 But the house of Israel rebelled against me in the wilderness: they walked not in my statutes, and they despised my judgments, which *if* a man do, he shall even live in them; and my sabbaths they greatly polluted: then I said, I would pour out my fury upon them in the wilderness, to consume them.

Eze 20:21 Notwithstanding the children rebelled against me: they walked not in my statutes, neither kept my judgments to do them, which *if* a man do, he shall even live in them; they polluted my sabbaths: then I said, I would pour out my fury upon them, to accomplish my anger against them in the wilderness.

Eze 24:3 And utter a parable unto the rebellious house, and say unto them, Thus saith the Lord GOD; Set on a pot, set *it* on, and also pour water into it:

Eze 44:6 And thou shalt say to the rebellious, *even* to the house of Israel, Thus saith the Lord GOD; O ye house of Israel, let it suffice you of all your abominations,

Ho 9:15 All their wickedness *is* in Gilgal: for there I hated them: for the wickedness of their doings I will drive them out of mine house, I will love them no more: all their princes *are* revolters.

Ho 13:16 Samaria shall become desolate; for she hath rebelled against her God: they shall fall by the sword: their infants shall be dashed in pieces, and their women with child shall be ripped up.

Mal 1:6 A son honoureth *his* father, and a servant his master: if then I *be* a father, where *is* mine honour? and if I *be* a master, where *is* my fear? saith the LORD of hosts unto you, O priests, that despise my name. And ye say, Wherein have we despised thy name?

Jn 13:18 I speak not of you all: I know whom I have chosen: but that the scripture may be fulfilled, He that eateth bread with me hath lifted up his heel against me.

Ro 8:7 Because the carnal mind *is* enmity against God: for it is not subject to the law of God, neither indeed can be.

Ro 10:21 But to Israel he saith, All day long I have stretched forth my hands unto a disobedient and gainsaying people.

1 Ti 1:9 Knowing this, that the law is not made for a righteous man, but for the lawless and disobedient, for the ungodly and for sinners, for unholy and profane, for murderers of fathers and murderers of mothers, for manslayers,

2. Examples

Nu 14:4 And they said one to another, Let us make a captain, and let us return into Egypt.

Nu 14:35 I the LORD have said, I will surely do it unto all this evil congregation, that are gathered together against me: in this wilderness they shall be consumed, and there they shall die.

Nu 17:10 And the LORD said unto Moses, Bring Aaron's rod again before the testimony, to be kept for a token against the rebels; and thou shalt quite take away their murmurings from me, that they die not.

Nu 20:24 Aaron shall be gathered unto his people: for he shall not enter into the land which I have given unto the children of Israel, because ye rebelled against my word at the water of Meribah.

Nu 26:9 And the sons of Eliab; Nemuel, and Dathan, and Abiram. This *is that* Dathan and Abiram, *which were* famous in the congregation, who strove against Moses and against Aaron in the company of Korah, when they strove against the LORD:

De 1:26 Notwithstanding ye would not go up, but rebelled against the commandment of the LORD your God:

1 S 8:7 And the LORD said unto Samuel, Hearken unto the voice of the people in all that they say unto thee: for they have not rejected thee, but they have rejected me, that I should not reign over them.

Ne 9:26 Nevertheless they were disobedient, and rebelled against thee, and cast thy law behind their backs, and slew thy prophets which testified against them to turn them to thee, and they wrought great provocations.

Ps 78:8 And might not be as their fathers, a stubborn and rebellious generation; a generation *that* set not their heart aright, and whose spirit was not stedfast with God.

Is 1:2 Hear, O heavens, and give ear, O earth: for the Lord hath spoken, I have nourished and brought up children, and they have rebelled against me.

Is 1:5 Why should ye be stricken any more? ye will revolt more and more: the whole head is sick, and the whole heart faint.

Is 59:13 In transgressing and lying against the Lord, and departing away from our God, speaking oppression and revolt, conceiving and uttering from the heart words of falsehood.

Je 6:28 They *are* all grievous revolters, walking with slanders: *they are* brass and iron; they *are* all corrupters.

Lam 3:42 We have transgressed and have rebelled: thou hast not pardoned.

Eze 3:27 But when I speak with thee, I will open thy mouth, and thou shalt say unto them, Thus saith the Lord God; He that heareth, let him hear; and he that forbeareth, let him forbear: for they *are* a rebellious house.

Da 9:5 We have sinned, and have committed iniquity, and have done wickedly, and have rebelled, even by departing from thy precepts and from thy judgments:

Da 9:9 To the Lord our God *belong* mercies and forgivenesses, though we have rebelled against him;

Ho 7:14 And they have not cried unto me with their heart, when they howled upon their beds: they assemble themselves for corn and wine, *and* they rebel against me.

See **NATION, WICKED**

RECEPTION, *acceptance of God and divine truth*

1. Spiritual Receptivity

1 S 3:10 And the Lord came, and stood, and called as at other times, Samuel, Samuel. Then Samuel answered, Speak; for thy servant heareth.

Ne 8:3 And he read therein before the street that *was* before the water gate from the morning until midday, before the men and the women, and those that could understand; and the ears of all the people *were attentive* unto the book of the law.

Ne 8:12 And all the people went their way to eat, and to drink, and to send portions, and to make great mirth, because they had understood the words that were declared unto them.

Jb 22:22 Receive, I pray thee, the law from his mouth, and lay up his words in thine heart.

Ps 85:8 I will hear what God the Lord will speak: for he will speak peace unto his people, and to his saints: but let them not turn again to folly.

Pr 1:3 To receive the instruction of wisdom, justice, and judgment, and equity;

Pr 2:1 My son, if thou wilt receive my words, and hide my commandments with thee;

Pr 4:20 My son, attend to my words; incline thine ear unto my sayings.

Pr 8:10 Receive my instruction, and not silver; and knowledge rather than choice gold.

Pr 9:9 Give *instruction* to a wise *man,* and he will be yet wiser: teach a just *man,* and he will increase in learning.

Pr 10:8 The wise in heart will receive commandments: but a prating fool shall fall.

Pr 15:32 He that refuseth instruction despiseth his own soul: but he that heareth reproof getteth understanding.

Pr 21:11 When the scorner is punished, the simple is made wise: and when the wise is instructed, he receiveth knowledge.

Pr 24:32 Then I saw, *and* considered *it* well: I looked upon *it, and* received instruction.

Is 29:24 They also that erred in spirit shall come to understanding, and they that murmured shall learn doctrine.

Is 50:5 The Lord God hath opened mine ear, and I was not rebellious, neither turned away back.

Je 9:20 Yet hear the word of the Lord, O ye women, and let your ear receive the word of his mouth, and teach your daughters wailing, and every one her neighbour lamentation.

Je 12:16 And it shall come to pass, if they will diligently learn the ways of my people, to swear by my name, The LORD liveth; as they taught my people to swear by Baal; then shall they be built in the midst of my people.

Eze 2:8 But thou, son of man, hear what I say unto thee; Be not thou rebellious like that rebellious house: open thy mouth, and eat that I give thee.

Eze 3:2 So I opened my mouth, and he caused me to eat that roll.

Eze 3:10 Moreover he said unto me, Son of man, all my words that I shall speak unto thee receive in thine heart, and hear with thine ears.

Eze 44:5 And the LORD said unto me, Son of man, mark well, and behold with thine eyes, and hear with thine ears all that I say unto thee concerning all the ordinances of the house of the LORD, and all the laws thereof; and mark well the entering in of the house, with every going forth of the sanctuary.

Da 10:19 And said, O man greatly beloved, fear not: peace *be* unto thee, be strong, yea, be strong. And when he had spoken unto me, I was strengthened, and said, Let my lord speak; for thou hast strengthened me.

Mt 10:41 He that receiveth a prophet in the name of a prophet shall receive a prophet's reward; and he that receiveth a righteous man in the name of a righteous man shall receive a righteous man's reward.

Mt 11:15 He that hath ears to hear, let him hear.

Mt 13:8 But other fell into good ground, and brought forth fruit, some an hundredfold, some sixtyfold, some thirtyfold.

Mt 13:23 But he that to the good ground is he that heareth the word, and understandeth *it;* which also beareth fruit, and bringeth forth, some an hundredfold, some sixty, some thirty.

Mt 19:12 For there are some eunuchs, which were so born from *their* mother's womb: and there are some eunuchs, which were made eunuchs of men: and there be eunuchs, which have made themselves eunuchs for the kingdom of heaven's sake. He that is able to receive *it,* let him receive *it.*

Mk 4:8–9 And other fell on good ground, and did yield fruit that sprang up and increased; and brought forth, some thirty, and some sixty, and some an hundred.

And he said unto them, He that hath ears to hear, let him hear.

Mk 4:20 And these are they which are sown on good ground; such as hear the word, and receive *it,* and bring forth fruit, some thirtyfold, some sixty, and some an hundred.

Mk 4:23 If any man have ears to hear, let him hear.

Mk 7:16 If any man have ears to hear, let him hear.

Mk 10:15 Verily I say unto you, Whosoever shall not receive the kingdom of God as a little child, he shall not enter therein.

Mk 15:39 And when the centurion, which stood over against him, saw that he so cried out, and gave up the ghost, he said, Truly this man was the Son of God.

Lu 8:8 And other fell on good ground, and sprang up, and bare fruit an hundredfold. And when he had said these things, he cried, He that hath ears to hear, let him hear.

Lu 10:8 And into whatsoever city ye enter, and they receive you, eat such things as are set before you:

Lu 10:38–39 Now it came to pass, as they went, that he entered into a certain village: and a certain woman named Martha received him into her house.

And she had a sister called Mary, which also sat at Jesus' feet, and heard his word.

Lu 11:34 The light of the body is the eye: therefore when thine eye is single, thy whole body also is full of light; but when *thine eye* is evil, thy body also *is* full of darkness.

Lu 18:17 Verily I say unto you, Whosoever shall not receive the kingdom of God as a little child shall in no wise enter therein.

Jn 8:47 He that is of God heareth God's words: ye therefore hear *them* not, because ye are not of God.

Jn 9:36 He answered and said, Who is he, Lord, that I might believe on him?

Jn 17:8 For I have given unto them the words which thou gavest me; and they have received *them,* and have known surely that I came out from thee, and they have believed that thou didst send me.

Jn 18:37 Pilate therefore said unto him, Art thou a king then? Jesus answered, Thou sayest that I am a king. To this end was I born, and for this cause came I into the world, that I should bear witness unto the truth. Every one that is of the truth heareth my voice.

Ac 2:41 Then they that gladly received his word were baptized: and the same day there were added *unto them* about three thousand souls.

Ac 4:4 Howbeit many of them which heard the word believed; and the number of the men was about five thousand.

Ac 6:7 And the word of God increased; and the number of the disciples multiplied in Jerusalem greatly; and a great company of the priests were obedient to the faith.

Ac 8:6 And the people with one accord gave heed unto those things which Philip spake, hearing and seeing the miracles which he did.

Ac 8:31 And he said, How can I, except some man should guide me? And he desired Philip that he would come up and sit with him.

Ac 8:36 And as they went on *their* way, they came unto a certain water: and the eunuch said, See, *here is* water; what doth hinder me to be baptized?

Ac 10:33 Immediately therefore I sent to thee; and thou hast well done that thou art come. Now therefore are we all here present before God, to hear all things that are commanded thee of God.

Ac 13:7 Which was with the deputy of the country, Sergius Paulus, a prudent man; who called for Barnabas and Saul, and desired to hear the word of God.

Ac 13:42 And when the Jews were gone out of the synagogue, the Gentiles besought that these words might be preached to them the next sabbath.

Ac 13:48 And when the Gentiles heard this, they were glad, and glorified the word of the Lord: and as many as were ordained to eternal life believed.

Ac 16:14 And a certain woman named Lydia, a seller of purple, of the city of Thyatira, which worshipped God, heard *us:* whose heart the Lord opened, that she attended unto the things which were spoken of Paul.

Ac 17:11 These were more noble than those in Thessalonica, in that they received the word with all readiness of mind, and searched the scriptures daily, whether those things were so.

Ac 17:34 Howbeit certain men clave unto him, and believed: among the which *was* Dionysius the Areopagite, and a woman named Damaris, and others with them.

1 Co 15:1 Moreover, brethren, I declare unto you the gospel which I preached unto you, which also ye have received, and wherein ye stand;

1 Th 2:13 For this cause also thank we God without ceasing, because, when ye received the word of God which ye heard of us, ye received *it* not *as* the word of men, but as it is in truth, the word of God, which effectually worketh also in you that believe.

2 Th 1:10 When he shall come to be glorified in his saints, and to be admired in all them that believe (because our testimony among you was believed) in that day.

He 2:1 Therefore we ought to give the more earnest heed to the things which we have heard, lest at any time we should let *them* slip.

Ja 1:21 Wherefore lay apart all filthiness and superfluity of naughtiness, and receive with meekness the engrafted word, which is able to save your souls.

Re 2:7 He that hath an ear, let him hear what the Spirit saith unto the churches; To him that overcometh will I give to eat of the tree of life, which is in the midst of the paradise of God.

Re 4:2 And immediately I was in the spirit: and, behold, a throne was set in heaven, and *one* sat on the throne.

Receiving Christ

Ps 116:13 I will take the cup of salvation, and call upon the name of the LORD.

Mt 10:40 He that receiveth you receiveth me, and he that receiveth me receiveth him that sent me.

Mt 18:5 And whoso shall receive one such little child in my name receiveth me.

Mk 2:2 And straightway many were gathered together, insomuch that there was no room to receive *them,* no, not so much as about the door: and he preached the word unto them.

Mk 9:37 Whosoever shall receive one of such children in my name, receiveth me: and whosoever shall receive me, receiveth not me, but him that sent me.

Lu 8:40 And it came to pass, that, when Jesus was returned, the people *gladly* received him: for they were all waiting for him.

Lu 9:48 And said unto them, Whosoever shall receive this child in my name receiveth me: and whosoever shall receive me receiveth him that sent me: for he that is all, the same shall be great.

Lu 19:6 And he made haste, and came down, and received him joyfully.

Jn 1:12 But as many as received him, to them gave he power to become the sons of God, *even* to them that believe on his name:

Jn 3:33 He that hath received his testimony hath set to his seal that God is true.

Jn 4:40–41 So when the Samaritans were come unto him, they besought him that he would tarry with them: and he abode there two days.

And many more believed because of his own word;

Jn 4:45 Then when he was come into Galilee, the Galilaeans received him, having seen all the things that he did

at Jerusalem at the feast: for they also went unto the feast.

Jn 6:21 Then they willingly received him into the ship: and immediately the ship was at the land whither they went.

Jn 8:30 As he spake these words, many believed on him.

Jn 13:20 Verily, verily, I say unto you, He that receiveth whomsoever I send receiveth me; and he that receiveth me receiveth him that sent me.

Ac 8:36 And as they went on *their* way, they came unto a certain water: and the eunuch said, See, *here is* water; what doth hinder me to be baptized?

Col 2:6 As ye have therefore received Christ Jesus the Lord, *so* walk ye in him:

1 Ti 3:16 And without controversy great is the mystery of godliness: God was manifest in the flesh, justified in the Spirit, seen of angels, preached unto the Gentiles, believed on in the world, received up into glory.

Re 3:20 Behold, I stand at the door, and knock: if any man hear my voice, and open the door, I will come in to him, and will sup with him, and he with me.

2. Teachableness

ILLUSTRATED IN THE LIFE OF EZRA

Ezr 8:21 Then I proclaimed a fast there, at the river of Ahava, that we might afflict ourselves before our God, to seek of him a right way for us, and for our little ones, and for all our substance.

ESSENTIAL TO ENTRANCE
INTO GOD'S KINGDOM

Mt 18:3 And said, Verily I say unto you, Except ye be converted, and become as little children, ye shall not enter into the kingdom of heaven.

EXHIBITED BY THE DISCIPLES

Lu 11:1 And it came to pass, that, as he was praying in a certain place, when he ceased, one of his disciples said unto him, Lord, teach us to pray, as John also taught his disciples.

MANIFESTED BY THE BLIND MAN

Jn 9:36 He answered and said, Who is he, Lord, that I might believe on him?

Ac 2:37 Now when they heard *this*, they were pricked in their heart, and said unto Peter and to the rest of the apostles, Men *and* brethren, what shall we do?

SEEN IN THE ETHIOPIAN EUNUCH

Ac 8:31 And he said, How can I, except some man should guide me? And he desired Philip that he would come up and sit with him.

THE SECRET OF PAUL'S SUCCESS

Ac 9:6 And he trembling and astonished said, Lord, what wilt thou have me to do? And the Lord *said* unto him, Arise, and go into the city, and it shall be told thee what thou must do.

RESULTS IN THE PHILIPPIAN JAILOR'S CONVERSION

Ac 16:30 And brought them out, and said, Sirs, what must I do to be saved?

a. Manifested by the Disciples

Eze 24:19 And the people said unto me, Wilt thou not tell us what these *things are* to us, that thou doest *so?*

Eze 37:18 And when the children of thy people shall speak unto thee, saying, Wilt thou not shew us what thou *meanest* by these?

Da 7:16 I came near unto one of them that stood by, and asked him the truth of all this. So he told me, and made me know the interpretation of the things.

Da 8:15 And it came to pass, when I, *even* I Daniel, had seen the vision, and sought for the meaning, then, behold, there stood before me as the appearance of a man.

Zec 1:9 Then said I, O my lord, what *are* these? And the angel that talked with me said unto me, I will shew thee what these *be.*

Zec 1:19 And I said unto the angel that talked with me, What *be* these? And he answered me, These *are* the horns which have scattered Judah, Israel, and Jerusalem.

Mt 13:36 Then Jesus sent the multitude away, and went into the house: and his disciples came unto him, saying, Declare unto us the parable of the tares of the field.

Mk 4:10 And when he was alone, they that were about him with the twelve asked of him the parable.

Mk 7:17 And when he was entered into the house from the people, his disciples asked him concerning the parable.

Mk 9:11 And they asked him, saying, Why say the scribes that Elias must first come?

Mk 9:28 And when he was come into the house, his disciples asked him privately, Why could not we cast him out?

Mk 10:10 And in the house his disciples asked him again otter.

Mk 13:4 Tell us, when shall these things be? and what *shall be* the sign when all these things shall be fulfilled?

Lu 3:12 Then came also publicans to be baptized, and said unto him, Master, what shall we do?

Lu 11:1 And it came to pass, that, as he was praying in a certain place, when he ceased, one of his disciples said unto him, Lord, teach us to pray, as John also taught his disciples.

Lu 18:18 And a certain ruler asked him, saying, Good Master, what shall I do to inherit eternal life?

Jn 6:28 Then said they unto him, What shall we do, that we might work the works of God?

b. A Characteristic of the Wise

Jb 42:5 I have heard of thee by the hearing of the ear: but now mine eye seeth thee.

Ps 40:6 Sacrifice and offering thou didst not desire; mine ears hast thou opened: burnt offering and sin offering hast thou not required.

Ps 78:1 Give ear, O my people, *to* my law: incline your ears to the words of my mouth.

Pr 18:15 The heart of the prudent getteth knowledge; and the ear of the wise seeketh knowledge.

Pr 20:12 The hearing ear, and the seeing eye, the LORD hath made even both of them.

Pr 25:12 *As* an earring of gold, and an ornament of fine gold, *so is* a wise reprover upon an obedient ear.

Mt 11:15 He that hath ears to hear, let him hear.

Mt 13:16 But blessed *are* your eyes, for they see: and your ears, for they hear.

Re 2:29 He that hath an ear, let him hear what the Spirit saith unto the churches.

Re 13:9 If any man have an ear, let him hear.

See **HEARING, REJECTION**

RECHABITES, *descendants of the Kenites*

1 Chr 2:55; Je 35:2, 6

RECIPROCATION, *mutual give and take*

Mt 18:33; Ro 15:27; 1 Co 9:11; 2 Co 8:14; Ga 6:6; Phm 19

RECOMPENSE, *reward*

1. Of Evil

Nu 14:23 Surely they shall not see the land which I sware unto their fathers, neither shall any of them that provoked me see it:

De 32:35 To me *belongeth* vengeance, and recompence; their foot shall slide in *due* time: for the day of their calamity *is* at hand, and the things that shall come upon them make haste.

De 32:43 Rejoice, O ye nations, *with* his people: for he will avenge the blood of his servants, and will render vengeance to his adversaries, and will be merciful unto his land, *and* to his people.

Jud 9:57 And all the evil of the men of Shechem did God render upon their heads: and upon them came the curse of Jotham the son of Jerubbaal.

2 S 3:39 And I *am* this day weak, though anointed king; and these men the sons of Zeruiah *be* too hard for me: the LORD shall reward the doer of evil according to his wickedness.

1 K 2:6 Do therefore according to thy wisdom, and let not his hoar head go down to the grave in peace.

2 Chr 6:23 Then hear thou from heaven, and do, and judge thy servants, by requiting the wicked, by recompensing his way upon his own head; and by justifying the righteous, by giving him according to his righteousness.

2 Chr 25:20 But Amaziah would not hear; for it *came* of God, that he might deliver them into the hand *of their enemies,* because they sought after the gods of Edom.

2 Chr 26:20 And Azariah the chief priest, and all the priests, looked upon him, and, behold, he *was* leprous in his forehead, and they thrust him out from thence; yea, himself hasted also to go out, because the LORD had smitten him.

2 Chr 33:11 Wherefore the LORD brought upon them the captains of the host of the king of Assyria, which took Manasseh among the thorns, and bound him with fetters, and carried him to Babylon.

Ezr 9:7 Since the days of our fathers *have* we *been* in a great trespass unto this day; and for our iniquities have we, our kings, and *our* priests, been delivered into the hand of the kings of the lands, to the sword, to captivity, and to a spoil, and to confusion of face, as *it is* this day.

Ne 4:4 Hear, O our God; for we are despised: and turn their reproach upon their own head, and give them for a prey in the land of captivity:

Jb 21:19 God layeth up his iniquity for his children: he rewardeth him, and he shall know *it.*

Jb 21:31 Who shall declare his way to his face? and who shall repay him *what* he hath done?

Jb 34:11 For the work of a man shall he render unto him, and cause every man to find according to *his* ways.

Ps 10:14 Thou hast seen *it;* for thou beholdest mischief and spite, to requite *it* with thy hand: the poor committeth himself unto thee; thou art the helper of the fatherless.

Ps 28:4 Give them according to their deeds, and according to the wickedness of their endeavours: give them after the work of their hands; render to them their desert.

Ps 31:23 O love the LORD, all ye his saints: *for* the LORD preserveth the faithful, and plentifully rewardeth the proud doer.

Ps 54:5 He shall reward evil unto mine enemies: cut them off in thy truth.

Ps 79:12 And render unto our neighbours sevenfold into their bosom their reproach, wherewith they have reproached thee, O Lord.

Ps 91:8 Only with thine eyes shalt thou behold and see the reward of the wicked.

Ps 94:2 Lift up thyself, thou judge of the earth: render a reward to the proud.

Ps 94:23 And he shall bring upon them their own iniquity, and shall cut them off in their own wickedness; *yea,* the LORD our God shall cut them off.

Ps 109:20 *Let* this *be* the reward of mine adversaries from the LORD, and of them that speak evil against my soul.

Ps 137:8 O daughter of Babylon, who art to be destroyed; happy *shall he be,* that rewardeth thee as thou hast served us.

Pr 11:31 Behold, the righteous shall be recompensed in the earth: much more the wicked and the sinner.

Pr 26:10 The great *God* that formed all *things* both rewardeth the fool, and rewardeth transgressors.

Is 3:11 Woe unto the wicked! *it shall be* ill *with him:* for the reward of his hands shall be given him.

Is 34:8 For *it is* the day of the LORD's vengeance, *and* the year of recompences for the controversy of Zion.

Is 40:2 Speak ye comfortably to Jerusalem, and cry unto her, that her warfare is accomplished, that her iniquity is pardoned: for she hath received of the LORD's hand double for all her sins.

Is 59:18 According to *their* deeds, accordingly he will repay, fury to his adversaries, recompence to his ene-

mies; to the islands he will repay recompence.

Is 65:7 Your iniquities, and the iniquities of your fathers together, saith the LORD, which have burned incense upon the mountains, and blasphemed me upon the hills: therefore will I measure their former work into their bosom.

Je 11:11 Therefore thus saith the LORD, Behold, I will bring evil upon them, which they shall not be able to escape; and though they shall cry unto me, I will not hearken unto them.

Je 16:18 And first I will recompense their iniquity and their sin double; because they have defiled my land, they have filled mine inheritance with the carcases of their detestable and abominable things.

Je 25:14 For many nations and great kings shall serve themselves of them also: and I will recompense them according to their deeds, and according to the works of their own hands.

Je 30:16 Therefore all they that devour thee shall be devoured; and all thine adversaries, every one of them, shall go into captivity; and they that spoil thee shall be a spoil, and all that prey upon thee will I give for a prey.

Je 32:18 Thou shewest lovingkindness unto thousands, and recompensest the iniquity of the fathers into the bosom of their children after them: the Great, the Mighty God, the LORD of hosts, *is* his name,

Je 32:23 And they came in, and possessed it; but they obeyed not thy voice, neither walked in thy law; they have done nothing of all that thou commandedst them to do: therefore thou hast caused all this evil to come upon them:

Je 35:17 Therefore thus saith the LORD God of hosts, the God of Israel; Behold, I will bring upon Judah and upon all the inhabitants of Jerusalem all the evil that I have pronounced against them: because I have spoken unto them, but they have not heard; and I have called unto them, but they have not answered.

Je 44:3 Because of their wickedness which they have committed to provoke me to anger, in that they went to burn incense, *and* to serve other gods, whom they knew not, *neither* they, ye, nor your fathers.

Je 50:14 Put yourselves in array against Babylon round about: all ye that bend the bow, shoot at her, spare no arrows: for she hath sinned against the Lord.

Je 50:29 Call together the archers against Babylon: all ye that bend the bow, camp against it round about; let none thereof escape: recompense her according to her work; according to all that she hath done, do unto her: for she hath been proud against the Lord, against the Holy One of Israel.

Je 51:6 Flee out of the midst of Babylon, and deliver every man his soul: be not cut off in her iniquity; for this *is* the time of the Lord's vengeance; he will render unto her a recompence.

Je 51:24 And I will render unto Babylon and to all the inhabitants of Chaldea all their evil that they have done in Zion in your sight, saith the Lord.

Je 51:49 As Babylon *hath caused* the slain of Israel to fall, so at Babylon shall fall the slain of all the earth.

Lam 3:64 Render unto them a recompence, O Lord, according to the work of their hands.

Eze 7:4 And mine eye shall not spare thee, neither will I have pity: but I will recompense thy ways upon thee, and thine abominations shall be in the midst of thee: and ye shall know that I *am* the Lord.

Eze 7:8 Now will I shortly pour out my fury upon thee, and accomplish mine anger upon thee: and I will judge thee according to thy ways, and will recompense thee for all thine abominations.

Eze 9:10 And as for me also, mine eye shall not spare, neither will I have pity, *but* I will recompense their way upon their head.

Eze 11:21 But *as for them* whose heart walketh after the heart of their detestable things and their abominations, I will recompense their way upon their own heads, saith the Lord God.

Eze 16:43 Because thou hast not remembered the days of thy youth, but hast fretted me in all these *things;* behold, therefore I also will recompense thy way upon *thine* head, saith the Lord God: and thou shalt not commit this lewdness above all thine abominations.

Eze 17:19 Therefore thus saith the Lord God; *As* I live, surely mine oath that he hath despised, and my covenant that he hath broken, even it will I recompense upon his own head.

Eze 22:31 Therefore have I poured out mine indignation upon them; I have consumed them with the fire of my wrath: their own way have I recompensed upon their heads, saith the Lord God.

Eze 23:49 And they shall recompense your lewdness upon you, and ye shall bear the sins of your idols: and ye shall know that I *am* the Lord God.

Ho 4:9 And there shall be, like people, like priest: and I will punish them for their ways, and reward them their doings.

Ho 5:11 Ephraim *is* oppressed *and* broken in judgment, because he willingly walked after the commandment.

Ho 9:7 The days of visitation are come, the days of recompence are come; Israel shall know *it:* the prophet *is* a fool, the spiritual man *is* mad, for the multitude of thine iniquity, and the great hatred.

Ho 12:2 The Lord hath also a controversy with Judah, and will punish Jacob according to his ways; according to his doings will he recompense him.

Jl 3:4 Yea, and what have ye to do with me, O Tyre, and Zidon, and all the coasts of Palestine? will ye render me a recompence? and if ye recompense me, swiftly *and* speedily will I return your recompence upon your own head;

Mt 7:2 For with what judgment ye judge, ye shall be judged: and with what measure ye mete, it shall be measured to you again.

Mt 18:34 And his lord was wroth, and delivered him to the tormentors, till he should pay all that was due unto him.

Mt 25:30 And cast ye the unprofitable servant into outer darkness: there shall be weeping and gnashing of teeth.

Ro 1:27 And likewise also the men, leaving the natural use of the woman, burned in their lust one toward another; men with men working that which is unseemly, and receiving in themselves that recompence of their error which was meet.

Ro 11:9 And David saith, Let their table be made a snare, and a trap, and a stumblingblock, and a recompence unto them:

Ro 12:19 Dearly beloved, avenge not yourselves, but *rather* give place unto wrath: for it is written, Vengeance *is* mine; I will repay, saith the Lord.

2 Th 1:6 Seeing *it is* a righteous thing with God to recompense tribulation to them that trouble you;

2 Ti 4:14 Alexander the coppersmith did me much evil: the Lord reward him according to his works:

He 2:2 For if the word spoken by angels was stedfast, and every transgression and disobedience received a just recompence of reward;

He 10:30 For we know him that hath said, Vengeance *belongeth* unto me, I will recompense, saith the Lord. And again, The Lord shall judge his people.

2 Pe 2:13 And shall receive the reward of unrighteousness, *as* they that count it pleasure to riot in the daytime. Spots *they are* and blemishes, sporting themselves with their own deceivings while they feast with you;

Re 16:6 For they have shed the blood of saints and prophets, and thou hast given them blood to drink; for they are worthy.

Re 18:6 Reward her even as she rewarded you, and double unto her double according to her works: in the cup which she hath filled fill to her double.

2. Of Righteousness

Ru 2:12 The LORD recompense thy work, and a full reward be given thee of the LORD God of Israel, under whose wings thou art come to trust.

2 S 22:25 Therefore the LORD hath recompensed me according to my righteousness; according to my cleanness in his eye sight.

Pr 11:31 Behold, the righteous shall be recompensed in the earth: much more the wicked and the sinner.

Pr 13:21 Evil pursueth sinners: but to the righteous good shall be repaid.

Is 35:4 Say to them *that are* of a fearful heart, Be strong, fear not: behold, your God will come *with* vengeance, *even* God *with* a recompence; he will come and save you.

Lu 14:14 And thou shalt be blessed; for they cannot recompense thee: for thou shalt be recompensed at the resurrection of the just.

He 10:35 Cast not away therefore your confidence, which hath great recompence of reward.

See **JUDGMENTS, JUSTICE, REWARD**

RECONCILIATION, *to reestablish a fractured relationship*

1. With God through Christ

Mt 18:33 Shouldest not thou also have had compassion on thy fellowservant, even as I had pity on thee?

Ro 15:27 It hath pleased them verily; and their debtors they are. For if the Gentiles have been made partakers of their spiritual things, their duty is also to minister unto them in carnal things.

1 Co 9:11 If we have sown unto you spiritual things, *is it* a great thing if we shall reap your carnal things?

2 Co 8:14 But by an equality, *that* now at this time your abundance *may be a supply* for their want, that their abundance also may be *a supply* for your want: that there may be equality:

Ga 6:6 Let him that is taught in the word communicate unto him that teacheth in all good things.

Phm 9 I Paul have written *it* with mine own hand, I will repay *it:* albeit I do not say to thee how thou owest unto me even thine own self besides.

2. With Men

Ge 33:4 And Esau ran to meet him, and embraced him, and fell on his neck, and kissed him: and they wept.

Ge 45:15 Moreover he kissed all his brethren, and wept upon them: and after that his brethren talked with him.

Jos 22:33 And the thing pleased the children of Israel; and the children of Israel blessed God, and did not intend to go up against them in battle, to destroy the land wherein the children of Reuben and Gad dwelt.

Jb 42:8 Therefore take unto you now seven bullocks and seven rams, and go to my servant Job, and offer up for yourselves a burnt offering; and my servant Job shall pray for you: for him will I accept: lest I deal with you *after your* folly, in that ye have not spoken of me *the thing which is* right, like my servant Job.

Mt 5:24 Leave there thy gift before the altar, and go thy way; first be reconciled to thy brother, and then come and offer thy gift.

Mt 18:15 Moreover if thy brother shall trespass against thee, go and tell him his fault between thee and him alone: if he shall hear thee, thou hast gained thy brother.

See **ATONEMENT, REDEMPTION, SALVATION**

RECORDER, *a state officer of high rank among the Jews*

2 S 8:16; 20:24; 1 K 4:3; 2 K 18:18; 2 Chr 34:8

RED

Ex 35:23; Nu 19:2; Is 1:18; 63:2

REDEEMED, *those delivered, by being purchased, from the bondage of sin and its consequences*

Is 35:9 No lion shall be there, nor *any* ravenous beast shall go up thereon, it shall not be found there; but the redeemed shall walk *there:*

Is 51:11 Therefore the redeemed of the LORD shall return, and come with singing unto Zion; and everlasting joy *shall be* upon their head: they shall obtain gladness and joy; *and* sorrow and mourning shall flee away.

Is 62:12 And they shall call them, The holy people, The redeemed of the LORD: and thou shalt be called, Sought out, A city not forsaken.

Mt 8:11 And I say unto you, That many shall come from the east and west, and shall sit down with Abraham, and Isaac, and Jacob, in the kingdom of heaven.

He 12:23 To the general assembly and church of the firstborn, which are written in heaven, and to God the Judge of all, and to the spirits of just men made perfect,

Re 5:9 And they sung a new song, saying, Thou art worthy to take the book, and to open the seals thereof: for thou wast slain, and hast redeemed us to God by thy blood out of every kindred, and tongue, and people, and nation;

Re 7:9 After this I beheld, and, lo, a great multitude, which no man could number, of all nations, and kindreds, and people, and tongues, stood before the throne, and before the Lamb, clothed with white robes, and palms in their hands;

Re 14:1 And I looked, and, lo, a Lamb stood on the mount Sion, and with him an hundred forty *and* four thousand, having his Father's name written in their foreheads.

Re 14:4 These are they which were not defiled with women; for they are virgins. These are they which follow the Lamb whithersoever he goeth. These were redeemed from among men, *being* the firstfruits unto God and to the Lamb.

Re 15:2 And I saw as it were a sea of glass mingled with fire: and them that had gotten the victory over the beast, and over his image, and over his mark, *and* over the number of his name, stand on the sea of glass, having the harps of God.

Re 19:6 And I heard as it were the voice of a great multitude, and as the voice of many waters, and as the voice of mighty thunderings, saying, Alleluia: for the Lord God omnipotent reigneth.

See **ATONEMENT, CHRIST**

REDEEMER

De 7:8 But because the LORD loved you, and because he would keep the oath which he had sworn unto your fathers, hath the LORD brought you out with a mighty hand, and redeemed you out of the house of bondmen, from the hand of Pharaoh king of Egypt.

2 S 4:9 And David answered Rechab and Baanah his brother, the sons of Rimmon the Beerothite, and said unto them, As the LORD liveth, who hath redeemed my soul out of all adversity,

1 K 1:29 And the king sware, and said, As the LORD liveth, that hath redeemed my soul out of all distress,

Jb 19:25 For I know *that* my redeemer liveth, and *that* he shall stand at the latter *day* upon the earth:

Ps 19:14 Let the words of my mouth, and the meditation of my heart, be acceptable in thy sight, O LORD, my strength, and my redeemer.

Ps 25:22 Redeem Israel, O God, out of all his troubles.

Ps 78:35 And they remembered that God *was* their rock, and the high God their redeemer.

Ps 130:8 And he shall redeem Israel from all his iniquities.

Pr 23:11 For their redeemer is mighty; he shall plead their cause with thee.

Is 41:14 Fear not, thou worm Jacob, *and* ye men of Israel; I will help thee, saith the LORD, and thy redeemer, the Holy One of Israel.

Is 43:14 Thus saith the LORD, your redeemer, the Holy One of Israel; For your sake I have sent to Babylon, and have brought down all their nobles, and the Chaldeans, whose cry *is* in the ships.

Is 44:6 Thus saith the LORD the King of Israel, and his redeemer the LORD of hosts; I *am* the first, and I *am* the last; and beside me *there is* no God.

Is 44:24 Thus saith the LORD, thy redeemer, and he that formed thee from the womb, I *am* the LORD that maketh all *things;* that stretcheth forth the heavens alone; that spreadeth abroad the earth by myself;

Is 47:4 *As for* our redeemer, the LORD of hosts *is* his name, the Holy One of Israel.

Is 48:17 Thus saith the LORD, thy Redeemer, the Holy One of Israel; I *am* the LORD thy God which teacheth thee to profit, which leadeth thee by the way *that* thou shouldest go.

Is 49:7 Thus saith the LORD, the Redeemer of Israel, *and* his Holy One, to him whom man despiseth, to him whom the nation abhorreth, to a servant of rulers, Kings shall see and arise, princes also shall worship, because of the LORD that is faithful, *and* the Holy One of Israel, and he shall choose thee.

Is 49:26 And I will feed them that oppress thee with their own flesh; and they shall be drunken with their own blood, as with sweet wine: and all flesh shall know that I the LORD *am* thy Saviour and thy Redeemer, the mighty One of Jacob.

Is 54:5 For thy Maker *is* thine husband; the LORD of hosts *is* his name; and thy Redeemer the Holy One of Israel; The God of the whole earth shall he be called.

Is 59:20 And the Redeemer shall come to Zion, and unto them that turn from transgressith the LORD.

Is 60:16 Thou shalt also suck the milk of the Gentiles, and shalt suck the breast of kings: and thou shalt know that I the LORD *am* thy Saviour and thy Redeemer, the mighty One of Jacob.

Is 63:16 Doubtless thou *art* our father, though Abraham be ignorant of us, and Israel acknowledge us not: thou, O LORD, *art* our father, our redeemer; thy name *is* from everlasting.

Je 15:21 And I will deliver thee out of the hand of the wicked, and I will redeem thee out of the hand of the terrible.

Je 50:34 Their Redeemer *is* strong; the LORD of hosts *is* his name: he shall throughly plead their cause, that he may give rest to the land, and disquiet the inhabitants of Babylon.

Lam 3:58 O Lord, thou hast pleaded the causes of my soul; thou hast redeemed my life.

Ho 7:13 Woe unto them! for they have fled from me: destruction unto them! because they have transgressed against me: though I have redeemed them, yet they have spoken lies against me.

Ho 13:14 I will ransom them from the power of the grave; I will redeem them from death: O death, I will be thy plagues; O grave, I will be thy destruction: repentance shall be hid from mine eyes.

Ro 11:26 And so all Israel shall be saved: as it is written, There shall come out of Sion the Deliverer, and shall turn away ungodliness from Jacob:

See **CHRIST**

REDEMPTION, *the process of buying back, ransoming, recovering something by paying a price; deliverance from the enslavement of sin and release to a new freedom in Jesus Christ*

1. God Is the Author

Ge 48:16 The Angel which redeemed me from all evil, bless the lads; and let my name be named on them, and the name of my fathers Abraham and Isaac; and let them grow into a multitude in the midst of the earth.

Ex 6:6 Wherefore say unto the children of Israel, I *am* the LORD, and I will bring you out from under the burdens of the Egyptians, and I will rid you out of their bondage, and I will redeem you with a stretched out arm, and with great judgments:

Ex 15:13 Thou in thy mercy hast led forth the people *which* thou hast redeemed: thou hast guided *them* in thy strength unto thy holy habitation.

De 21:8 Be merciful, O LORD, unto thy people Israel, whom thou hast redeemed, and lay not innocent blood unto thy people of Israel's charge. And the blood shall be forgiven them.

De 24:18 But thou shalt remember that thou wast a bondman in Egypt, and the LORD thy God redeemed thee thence: therefore I command thee to do this thing.

2 S 7:23 And what one nation in the earth *is* like thy people, *even* like Israel, whom God went to redeem for a people to himself, and to make him a name, and to do for you great things and terrible, for thy land, before thy people, which thou redeemedst to thee from Egypt, *from* the nations and their gods?

1 Chr 17:21 And what one nation in the earth *is* like thy people Israel, whom God went to redeem *to be* his own people, to make thee a name of greatness and terribleness, by driving out nations from before thy people, whom thou hast redeemed out of Egypt?

Ne 1:10 Now these *are* thy servants and thy people, whom thou hast redeemed by thy great power, and by thy strong hand.

Jb 5:20 In famine he shall redeem thee from death: and in war from the power of the sword.

Ps 26:11 But as for me, I will walk in mine integrity: redeem me, and be merciful unto me.

Ps 31:5 Into thine hand I commit my spirit: thou hast redeemed me, O LORD God of truth.

Ps 34:22 The LORD redeemeth the soul of his servants: and none of them that trust in him shall be desolate.

Ps 44:26 Arise for our help, and redeem us for thy mercies' sake.

Ps 69:18 Draw nigh unto my soul, *and* redeem it: deliver me because of mine enemies.

Ps 71:23 My lips shall greatly rejoice when I sing unto thee; and my soul, which thou hast redeemed.

Ps 74:2 Remember thy congregation, *which* thou hast purchased of old; the rod of thine inheritance, *which* thou hast redeemed; this mount Zion, wherein thou hast dwelt.

Ps 77:15 Thou hast with *thine* arm redeemed thy people, the sons of Jacob and Joseph. Selah.

Ps 103:4 Who redeemeth thy life from destruction; who crowneth thee with lovingkindness and tender mercies;

Ps 107:2 Let the redeemed of the LORD say so, whom he hath redeemed from the hand of the enemy;

Ps 111:9 He sent redemption unto his people: he hath commanded his covenant for ever: holy and reverend *is* his name.

Ps 130:7 Let Israel hope in the LORD: for with the LORD *there is* mercy, and with him *is* plenteous redemption.

Ps 136:24 And hath redeemed us from our enemies: for his mercy *endureth* for ever.

Is 1:27 Zion shall be redeemed with judgment, and her converts with righteousness.

Is 29:22 Therefore thus saith the LORD, who redeemed Abraham, concerning the house of Jacob, Jacob shall not now be ashamed, neither shall his face now wax pale.

Is 43:1 But now thus saith the LORD that created thee, O Jacob, and he that formed thee, O Israel, Fear not: for I have redeemed thee, I have called *thee* by thy name; thou *art* mine.

Is 44:22 I have blotted out, as a thick cloud, thy transgressions, and, as a cloud, thy sins: return unto me; for I have redeemed thee.

Is 48:20 Go ye forth of Babylon, flee ye from the Chaldeans, with a voice of singing declare ye, tell this, utter it *even* to the end of the earth; say ye, The LORD hath redeemed his servant Jacob.

Is 52:9 Break forth into joy, sing together, ye waste places of Jerusalem: for the LORD hath comforted his people, he hath redeemed Jerusalem.

Is 63:9 In all their affliction he was afflicted, and the angel of his presence saved them: in his love and in his pity he redeemed them; and he bare them, and carried them all the days of old.

Je 31:11 For the LORD hath redeemed Jacob, and ransomed him from the hand of *him that was* stronger than he.

Mi 4:10 Be in pain, and labour to bring forth, O daughter of Zion, like a woman in travail: for now shalt thou go forth out of the city, and thou shalt dwell in the field, and thou shalt go *even* to Babylon; there shalt thou be delivered; there the LORD shall redeem thee from the hand of thine enemies.

Mi 6:4 For I brought thee up out of the land of Egypt, and redeemed thee

out of the house of servants; and I sent before thee Moses, Aaron, and Miriam.

Zec 10:8 I will hiss for them, and gather them; for I have redeemed them: and they shall increase as they have increased.

Lu 1:68 Blessed *be* the Lord God of Israel; for he hath visited and redeemed his people,

Lu 2:38 And she coming in that instant gave thanks likewise unto the Lord, and spake of him to all them that looked for redemption in Jerusalem.

Ep 4:30 And grieve not the holy Spirit of God, whereby ye are sealed unto the day of redemption.

2. Christ Is the Message

Is 53:10 Yet it pleased the LORD to bruise him; he hath put *him* to grief: when thou shalt make his soul an offering for sin, he shall see *his* seed, he shall prolong *his* days, and the pleasure of the LORD shall prosper in his hand.

Mk 10:45 For even the Son of man came not to be ministered unto, but to minister, and to give his life a ransom for many.

Lu 24:21 But we trusted that it had been he which should have redeemed Israel: and beside all this, to day is the third day since these things were done.

Ac 20:28 Take heed therefore unto yourselves, and to all the flock, over the which the Holy Ghost hath made you overseers, to feed the church of God, which he hath purchased with his own blood.

Ro 3:24 Being justified freely by his grace through the redemption that is in Christ Jesus:

1 Co 1:30 But of him are ye in Christ Jesus, who of God is made unto us wisdom, and righteousness, and sanctification, and redemption:

1 Co 6:20 For ye are bought with a price: therefore glorify God in your body, and in your spirit, which are God's.

1 Co 7:23 Ye are bought with a price; be not ye the servants of men.

Ga 3:13 Christ hath redeemed us from the curse of the law, being made a curse for us: for it is written, Cursed *is* every one that hangeth on a tree:

Ga 4:5 To redeem them that were under the law, that we might receive the adoption of sons.

Ep 1:7 In whom we have redemption through his blood, the forgiveness of sins, according to the riches of his grace;

Col 1:14 In whom we have redemption through his blood, *even* the forgiveness of sins:

1 Ti 2:6 Who gave himself a ransom for all, to be testified in due time.

Tit 2:14 Who gave himself for us, that he might redeem us from all iniquity, and purify unto himself a peculiar people, zealous of good works.

He 9:12 Neither by the blood of goats and calves, but by his own blood he entered in once into the holy place, having obtained eternal redemption *for us.*

He 9:15 And for this cause he is the mediator of the new testament, that by means of death, for the redemption of the transgressions *that were* under the first testament, they which are called might receive the promise of eternal inheritance.

1 Pe 1:18 Forasmuch as ye know that ye were not redeemed with corruptible things, *as* silver and gold, from your vain conversation *received* by tradition from your fathers;

2 Pe 2:1 But there were false prophets also among the people, even as there shall be false teachers among you, who privily shall bring in damnable heresies, even denying the Lord that bought them, and bring upon themselves swift destruction.

Re 5:9 And they sung a new song, saying, Thou art worthy to take the book, and to open the seals thereof: for thou wast slain, and hast redeemed us to God by thy blood out of every kindred, and tongue, and people, and nation;

Re 14:3 And they sung as it were a new song before the throne, and before the four beasts, and the elders: and no man could learn that song but

the hundred *and* forty *and* four thousand, which were redeemed from the earth.

3. Of Land and Persons

Le 25:27, 49; 27:19; Ne 5:8

See **CHRIST, SALVATION**

RED SEA, *Suph (Heb.), sea of reeds*

Ex 10:19; 14:2; 15:4, 22; 23:31; Nu 11:31; 14:25; 21:4; 33:8; De 1:1, 40; 2:1; Jos 4:23; 24:6; Jud 11:16; 1 K 9:26; Ps 106:22; 136:13; Is 11:15; Ac 7:36; He 11:29

REED

1. Swamp Grass, Bulrushes

1 K 14:15; Jb 41:2; Is 42:3; Mt 11:7; 27:29; Lu 7:24

2. A Measure

Eze 40:5

3. Descriptive of the Weak

2 K 18:21; Is 42:3; Eze 29:6

REFINERS *See* **ARTS AND CRAFTS**

REFORMERS, *those who rebuked sinful rulers*

1. Examples

NATHAN BEFORE KING DAVID

2 S 12:7 And Nathan said to David, Thou *art* the man. Thus saith the LORD God of Israel, I anointed thee king over Israel, and I delivered thee out of the hand of Saul;

ELIJAH BEFORE KING AHAB

1 K 21:20 And Ahab said to Elijah, Hast thou found me, O mine enemy? And he answered, I have found *thee:* because thou hast sold thyself to work evil in the sight of the LORD.

MICAIAH BEFORE KING AHAB

1 K 22:14 And Micaiah said, *As* the LORD liveth, what the LORD saith unto me, that will I speak.

ELISHA BEFORE KING JEHORAM

2 K 3:14 And Elisha said, *As* the LORD of hosts liveth, before whom I stand, surely, were it not that I regard the presence of Jehoshaphat the king of Judah, I would not look toward thee, nor see thee.

DANIEL BEFORE KING BELSHAZZAR

Da 5:22 And thou his son, O Belshazzar, hast not humbled thine heart, though thou knewest all this;

JOHN THE BAPTIST BEFORE HEROD

Mt 14:4 For John said unto him, It is not lawful for thee to have her.

PETER AND JOHN BEFORE THE SANHEDRIN

Ac 4:18–20 And they called them, and commanded them not to speak at all nor teach in the name of Jesus.

But Peter and John answered and said unto them, Whether it be right in the sight of God to hearken unto you more than unto God, judge ye.

For we cannot but speak the things which we have seen and heard.

STEPHEN BEFORE THE COUNCIL

Ac 7:51 Ye stiffnecked and uncircumcised in heart and ears, ye do always resist the Holy Ghost: as your fathers *did,* so *do* ye.

2. *Their Incorruptibility*

1 K 13:8; 2 K 5:15–16; Da 5:17

See **LEADERS**

REGENERATION

BIRTH OF A NEW SPIRIT

Eze 36:26 A new heart also will I give you, and a new spirit will I put within you: and I will take away the stony heart out of your flesh, and I will give you an heart of flesh.

OF DIVINE ORIGIN

Jn 1:13 Which were born, not of blood, nor of the will of the flesh, nor of the will of man, but of God.

ESSENTIAL TO SPIRITUAL VISION

Jn 3:3 Jesus answered and said unto him, Verily, verily, I say unto thee, Except a man be born again, he cannot see the kingdom of God.

2 Co 3:3 *Forasmuch as ye are* manifestly declared to be the epistle of Christ ministered by us, written not with ink, but with the Spirit of the living God; not in tables of stone, but in fleshy tables of the heart.

A NEW CREATION

2 Co 5:17 Therefore if any man *be* in Christ, *he is* a new creature: old things are passed away; behold, all things are become new.

NECESSARY TO SALVATION

Tit 3:5 Not by works of righteousness which we have done, but according to his mercy he saved us, by the washing of regeneration, and renewing of the Holy Ghost;

Ja 1:18 Of his own will begat he us with the word of truth, that we should be a kind of firstfruits of his creatures.

1 Pe 1:3 Blessed *be* the God and Father of our Lord Jesus Christ, which according to his abundant mercy hath begotten us again unto a lively hope by the resurrection of Jesus Christ from the dead,

BY THE WORD OF GOD

1 Pe 1:23 Being born again, not of corruptible seed, but of incorruptible, by the word of God, which liveth and abideth for ever.

1 Jn 2:29 If ye know that he is righteous, ye know that every one that doeth righteousness is born of him.

1 Jn 3:9 Whosoever is born of God doth not commit sin; for his seed remaineth in him: and he cannot sin, because he is born of God.

1 Jn 4:7 Beloved, let us love one another: for love is of God; and every one that loveth is born of God, and knoweth God.

OBTAINED BY FAITH

1 Jn 5:1 Whosoever believeth that Jesus is the Christ is born of God: and every one that loveth him that begat loveth him also that is begotten of him.

See **SALVATION**

REHOBOAM, *king of Judah, son and successor of Solomon*

1 K 11:43; 12:1; 14:21; 1 Chr 3:10; 2 Chr 10:1, 6; 11:5; 12:1, 16; 13:7; Mt 1:7

See **ISRAEL, HUMILITY, YOUNG PEOPLE**

REINS, *strength; figuratively, refers to loins or kidneys*

Ps 7:9; 26:2; 73:21; 139:13; Pr 23:16

REJECTION, *the act of denying*

1. Of Christ

THE GERGESENES

Mt 8:34 And, behold, the whole city came out to meet Jesus: and when they saw him, they besought *him* that he would depart out of their coasts.

Mt 21:42 Jesus saith unto them, Did ye never read in the scriptures, The stone which the builders rejected, the same is become the head of the corner: this is the Lord's doing, and it is marvellous in our eyes?

THE PEOPLE OF NAZARETH

Mk 6:3 Is not this the carpenter, the son of Mary, the brother of James, and Joses, and of Juda, and Simon? and are not his sisters here with us? And they were offended at him.

Lu 4:28–29 And all they in the synagogue, when they heard these things, were filled with wrath,

And rose up, and thrust him out of the city, and led him unto the brow of the hill whereon their city was built, that they might cast him down headlong.

Lu 17:25 But first must he suffer many things, and be rejected of this generation.

THE CHIEF PRIESTS AND RULERS

Lu 23:18 And they cried out all at once, saying, Away with this *man*, and release unto us Barabbas:

THE JEWISH NATION

Jn 1:11 He came unto his own, and his own received him not.

Jn 5:43 I am come in my Father's name, and ye receive me not: if another shall come in his own name, him ye will receive.

Jn 12:48 He that rejecteth me, and receiveth not my words, hath one that judgeth him: the word that I have spoken, the same shall judge him in the last day.

2. Of God

1 S 8:7 And the Lord said unto Samuel, Hearken unto the voice of the people in all that they say unto thee: for they have not rejected thee, but they have rejected me, that I should not reign over them.

Ps 81:11 But my people would not hearken to my voice; and Israel would none of me.

Pr 1:24 Because I have called, and ye refused; I have stretched out my hand, and no man regarded;

Je 9:6 Thine habitation *is* in the midst of deceit; through deceit they refuse to know me, saith the Lord.

Je 32:33 And they have turned unto me the back, and not the face: though I taught them, rising up early and teaching *them*, yet they have not hearkened to receive instruction.

Ho 8:4 They have set up kings, but not by me: they have made princes, and I knew *it* not: of their silver and their gold have they made them idols, that they may be cut off.

Lu 7:30 But the Pharisees and lawyers rejected the counsel of God against themselves, being not baptized of him.

1 Th 4:8 He therefore that despiseth, despiseth not man, but God, who hath also given unto us his holy Spirit.

3. Of Spiritual Instruction

2 Chr 30:10 So the posts passed from city to city through the country of Ephraim and Manasseh even unto Zebulun: but they laughed them to scorn, and mocked them.

2 Chr 36:16 But they mocked the messengers of God, and despised his words, and misused his prophets, until the wrath of the LORD arose against his people, till *there was* no remedy.

Ps 50:17 Seeing thou hatest instruction, and castest my words behind thee.

Pr 1:7 The fear of the LORD *is* the beginning of knowledge: *but* fools despise wisdom and instruction.

Pr 1:22 How long, ye simple ones, will ye love simplicity? and the scorners delight in their scorning, and fools hate knowledge?

Pr 5:12 And say, How have I hated instruction, and my heart despised reproof;

Pr 15:12 A scorner loveth not one that reproveth him: neither will he go unto the wise.

Pr 17:16 Wherefore *is there* a price in the hand of a fool to get wisdom, seeing *he hath* no heart *to it?*

Ho 4:6 My people are destroyed for lack of knowledge: because thou hast rejected knowledge, I will also reject thee, that thou shalt be no priest to me: seeing thou hast forgotten the law of thy God, I will also forget thy children.

Ac 22:18 And saw him saying unto me, Make haste, and get thee quickly out of Jerusalem: for they will not receive thy testimony concerning me.

4. Of the Word of God

Ex 9:21 And he that regarded not the word of the LORD left his servants and his cattle in the field.

2 Chr 30:10 So the posts passed from city to city through the country of Ephraim and Manasseh even unto Zebulun: but they laughed them to scorn, and mocked them.

Ps 50:17 Seeing thou hatest instruction, and castest my words behind thee.

Ps 119:155 Salvation *is* far from the wicked: for they seek not thy statutes.

Is 5:24 Therefore as the fire devoureth the stubble, and the flame consumeth the chaff, *so* their root shall be as rottenness, and their blossom shall go up as dust: because they have cast away the law of the LORD of hosts, and despised the word of the Holy One of Israel.

Is 30:12 Wherefore thus saith the Holy One of Israel, Because ye despise this word, and trust in oppression and perverseness, and stay thereon:

Je 6:10 To whom shall I speak, and give warning, that they may hear? behold, their ear *is* uncircumcised, and they cannot hearken: behold, the word of the LORD is unto them a reproach; they have no delight in it.

Je 8:9 The wise *men* are ashamed, they are dismayed and taken: lo, they have rejected the word of the LORD; and what wisdom *is* in them?

Je 18:18 Then said they, Come, and let us devise devices against Jeremiah; for the law shall not perish from the priest, nor counsel from the wise, nor the word from the prophet. Come, and let us smite him with the tongue, and let us not give heed to any of his words.

Je 20:8 For since I spake, I cried out, I cried violence and spoil; because the word of the LORD was made a reproach unto me, and a derision, daily.

Je 36:23 And it came to pass, *that* when Jehudi had read three or four leaves, he cut it with the penknife, and cast *it* into the fire that *was* on the hearth, until all the roll was fire that *was* on the hearth.

Zec 7:12 Yea, they made their hearts *as* an adamant stone, lest they should hear the law, and the words which the LORD of hosts hath sent in his spirit by the former prophets: therefore came a great wrath from the LORD of hosts.

Mal 2:2 If ye will not hear, and if ye will not lay *it* to heart, to give glory unto my name, saith the LORD of hosts, I will even send a curse upon you, and I will curse your blessings: yea, I have cursed them already, because ye do not lay *it* to heart.

Mk 7:13 Making the word of God of none effect through your tradition, which ye have delivered: and many such like things do ye.

1 Th 5:20 Despise not prophesyings.

2 Ti 4:3 For the time will come when they will not endure sound doctrine;

but after their own lusts shall they heap to themselves teachers, having itching ears;

See **RECEPTION**

RELIGION, *worship of God through word and deed*

1. Scriptural Definition

De 10:12 And now, Israel, what doth the LORD thy God require of thee, but to fear the LORD thy God, to walk in all his ways, and to love him, and to serve the LORD thy God with all thy heart and with all thy soul,

Ec 12:13 Let us hear the conclusion of the whole matter: Fear God, and keep his commandments: for this *is* the whole *duty* of man.

Is 58:6 *Is* not this the fast that I have chosen? to loose the bands of wickedness, to undo the heavy burdens, and to let the oppressed go free, and that ye break every yoke?

Eze 18:7 And hath not oppressed any, *but* hath restored to the debtor his pledge, hath spoiled none by violence, hath given his bread to the hungry, and hath covered the naked with a garment;

Ho 6:6 For I desired mercy, and not sacrifice; and the knowledge of God more than burnt offerings.

Mi 6:8 He hath shewed thee, O man, what *is* good; and what doth the LORD require of thee, but to do justly, and to love mercy, and to walk humbly with thy God?

Zec 8:15 So again have I thought in these days to do well unto Jerusalem and to the house of Judah: fear ye not.

Mt 7:12 Therefore all things whatsoever ye would that men should do to you, do ye even so to them: for this is the law and the prophets.

Mt 12:7 But if ye had known what *this* meaneth, I will have mercy, and not sacrifice, ye would not have condemned the guiltless.

Mt 22:40 On these two commandments hang all the law and the prophets.

Mt 23:23 Woe unto you, scribes and Pharisees, hypocrites! for ye pay tithe of mint and anise and cummin, and have omitted the weightier *matters* of the law, judgment, mercy, and faith: these ought ye to have done, and not to leave the other undone.

Mt 25:4 But the wise took oil in their vessels with their lamps.

Mk 12:33 And to love him with all the heart, and with all the understanding, and with all the soul, and with all the strength, and to love *his* neighbour as himself, is more than all whole burnt offerings and sacrifices.

Lu 6:33 And if ye do good to them which do good to you, what thank have ye? for sinners also do even the same.

Lu 10:33 But a certain Samaritan, as he journeyed, came where he was: and when he saw him, he had compassion *on him,*

Lu 11:42 But woe unto you, Pharisees! for ye tithe mint and rue and all manner of herbs, and pass over judgment and the love of God: these ought ye to have done, and not to leave the other undone.

Ro 2:29 But he *is* a Jew, which is one inwardly; and circumcision is *that* of the heart, in the spirit, *and* not in the letter; whose praise *is* not of men, but of God.

Ro 13:10 Love worketh no ill to his neighbour: therefore love *is* the fulfilling of the law.

1 Co 10:31 Whether therefore ye eat, or drink, or whatsoever ye do, do all to the glory of God.

Ja 1:27 Pure religion and undefiled before God and the Father is this, To visit the fatherless and widows in their affliction, *and* to keep himself unspotted from the world.

2. Examples of Piety

ENOCH

Ge 5:24 And Enoch walked with God: and he *was* not; for God took him.

NOAH

Ge 6:9 These *are* the generations of Noah: Noah was a just man *and* perfect in his generations, *and* Noah walked with God.

JABEZ

1 Chr 4:10 And Jabez called on the God of Israel, saying, Oh that thou wouldest bless me indeed, and enlarge my coast, and that thine hand might be with me, and that thou wouldest keep *me* from evil, that it may not grieve me! And God granted him that which he requested.

HEZEKIAH

2 Chr 31:20 And thus did Hezekiah throughout all Judah, and wrought *that which was* good and right and truth before the LORD his God.

JOB

Jb 1:1 There was a man in the land of Uz, whose name *was* Job; and that man was perfect and upright, and one that feared God, and eschewed evil.

DANIEL

Da 6:10 Now when Daniel knew that the writing was signed, he went into his house; and his windows being open in his chamber toward Jerusalem, he kneeled upon his knees three times a day, and prayed, and gave thanks before his God, as he did aforetime.

SIMEON

Lu 2:25 And, behold, there was a man in Jerusalem, whose name *was* Simeon; and the same man *was* just and devout, waiting for the consolation of Israel: and the Holy Ghost was upon him.

ANNA

Lu 2:37 And she *was* a widow of about fourscore and four years, which departed not from the temple, but served *God* with fastings and prayers night and day.

NATHANAEL

Jn 1:47 Jesus saw Nathanael coming to him, and saith of him, Behold an Israelite indeed, in whom is no guile!

CHRIST

Jn 8:29 And he that sent me is with me: the Father hath not left me alone; for I do always those things that please him.

CORNELIUS

Ac 10:2 A devout *man,* and one that feared God with all his house, which gave much alms to the people, and prayed to God alway.

BARNABAS

Ac 11:24 For he was a good man, and full of the Holy Ghost and of faith: and much people was added unto the Lord.

ANANIAS

Ac 22:12 And one Ananias, a devout man according to the law, having a good report of all the Jews which dwelt *there,*

TIMOTHY
2 Ti 1:5

3. Sincere

Jos 24:14 No the LORD, and serve him in sincerity and in truth: and put away the gods which your fathers served on the other side of the flood, and in Egypt; and serve ye the LORD.

Ps 145:18 The LORD *is* nigh unto all them that call upon him, to all that call upon him in truth.

1 Co 5:8 Therefore let us keep the feast, not with old leaven, neither with the leaven of malice and wickedness; but with the unleavened *bread* of sincerity and truth.

2 Co 1:12 For our rejoicing is this, the testimony of our conscience, that in simplicity and godly sincerity, not with fleshly wisdom, but by the grace of God, we have had our conversation in the world, and more abundantly to you-ward.

2 Co 2:17 For we are not as many, which corrupt the word of God: but as of sincerity, but as of God, in the sight of God speak we in Christ.

Ph 1:10 That ye may approve things that are excellent; that ye may be sincere and without offence till the day of Christ;

Tit 2:7 In all things shewing thyself a pattern of good works: in doctrine *shewing* uncorruptness, gravity, sincerity,

1 Jn 3:18 My little children, let us not love in word, neither in tongue; but in deed and in truth.

4. False

a. Ceremonialism

Mt 15:2; 23:4; Mk 7:4; Lu 11:38; Jn 3:25; 18:28; Ac 15:1, 10; Ga 1:14; 2:4; 4:9, 25; 5:1; Col 2:14, 17, 20; He 9:10

b. Empty Profession

Ps 78:36 Nevertheless they did flatter him with their mouth, and they lied unto him with their tongues.

Pr 26:23 Burning lips and a wicked heart *are like* a potsherd covered with silver dross.

Is 48:1 Hear ye this, O house of Jacob, which are called by the name of Israel, and are come forth out of the waters of Judah, which swear by the name of the LORD, and make mention of the God of Israel, *but* not in truth, nor in righteousness.

Is 58:4 Behold, ye fast for strife and debate, and to smite with the fist of wickedness: ye shall not fast as *ye do this* day, to make your voice to be heard on high.

Je 5:2 And though they say, The LORD liveth; surely they swear falsely.

Eze 33:31–32 And they come unto thee as the people cometh, and they sit before thee as my people, and they hear thy words, but they will not do them: for with their mouth they shew much love, *but* their heart goeth after their covetousness.

And, lo, thou *art* unto them as a very lovely song of one that hath a pleasant voice, and can play well on an instrument: for they hear thy words, but they do them not.

Ho 11:12 Ephraim compasseth me about with lies, and the house of Israel with deceit: but Judah yet ruleth with God, and is faithful with the saints.

Mt 7:21 Not every one that saith unto me, Lord, Lord, shall enter into the kingdom of heaven; but he that doeth the will of my Father which is in heaven.

Mk 7:6 He answered and said unto them, Well hath Esaias prophesied of you hypocrites, as it is written, This people honoureth me with *their* lips, but their heart is far from me.

Lu 6:46 And why call ye me, Lord, Lord, and do not the things which I say?

Tit 1:16 They profess that they know God; but in works they deny *him*, being abominable, and disobedient, and unto every good work reprobate.

Ja 3:14 But if ye have bitter envying and strife in your hearts, glory not, and lie not against the truth.

1 Jn 2:9 He that saith he is in the light, and hateth his brother, is in darkness even until now.

1 Jn 3:18 My little children, let us not love in word, neither in tongue; but in deed and in truth.

c. Legalism

Mk 2:24 And the Pharisees said unto him, Behold, why do they on the sabbath day that which is not lawful?

Lu 6:2 And certain of the Pharisees said unto them, Why do ye that which is not lawful to do on the sabbath days?

Lu 13:14 And the ruler of the synagogue answered with indignation, because that Jesus had healed on the sabbath day, and said unto the people, There are six days in which men ought to work: in them therefore come and be healed, and not on the sabbath day.

Jn 5:10 The Jews therefore said unto him that was cured, It is the sabbath day: it is not lawful for thee to carry *thy* bed.

Ac 15:5 But there rose up certain of the sect of the Pharisees which believed, saying, That it was needful to circumcise them, and to command *them* to keep the law of Moses.

Ac 16:3 Him would Paul have to go forth with him; and took and circumcised him because of the Jews which were in those quarters: for they knew all that his father was a Greek.

Ac 21:20 And when they heard *it,* they glorified the Lord, and said unto him, Thou seest, brother, how many thousands of Jews there are which believe; and they are all zealous of the law:

Ac 22:3 I am verily a man *which am* a Jew, born in Tarsus, a city in Cilicia, yet brought up in this city at the feet of Gamaliel, *and* taught according to the perfect manner of the law of the fathers, and was zealous toward God, as ye all are this day.

Ro 10:2 For I bear them record that they have a zeal of God, but not according to knowledge.

Ga 1:14 And profited in the Jews' religion above many my equals in mine own nation being more exceedingly zealous of the traditions of my fathers.

d. Sanctimony

AN OUTWARD SHOW OF RIGHTEOUSNESS

Is 58:2 Yet they seek me daily, and delight to know my ways, as a nation that did righteousness, and forsook not the ordinance of their God: they ask of me the ordinances of justice; they take delight in approaching to God.

PHARISAIC SEPARATION

Is 65:5 Which say, Stand by thyself, come not near to me; for I am holier than thou. *These* are a smoke in my nose, a fire that burneth all the day.

ASSUMED INNOCENCE

Je 2:35 Yet thou sayest, Because I am innocent, surely his anger shall turn from me. Behold, I will plead with thee, because thou sayest, I have not sinned.

RELIGIOUS DISPLAY

Mt 6:5 And when thou prayest, thou shalt not be as the hypocrites *are:* for they love to pray standing in the synagogues and in the corners of the streets, that they may be seen of men. Verily I say unto you, They have their reward.

Mt 23:14 Woe unto you, scribes and Pharisees, hypocrites! for ye devour widows' houses, and for a pretence make long prayer: therefore ye shall receive the greater damnation.

e. Formalism

1). Warnings

Ps 50:16 But unto the wicked God saith, What hast thou to do to declare my statutes, or *that* thou shouldest take my covenant in thy mouth?

Is 1:13 Bring no more vain oblations; incense is an abomination unto me; the new moons and sabbaths, the calling of assemblies, I cannot away with; *it is* iniquity, even the solemn meeting.

Is 29:1 Woe to Ariel, to Ariel, the city *where* David dwelt! add ye year to year; let them kill sacrifices.

Is 29:13 Wherefore the Lord said, Forasmuch as this people draw near *me* with their mouth, and with their lips do honour me, but have removed their heart far from me, and their fear toward me is taught by the precept of men:

Is 58:2 Yet they seek me daily, and delight to know my ways, as a nation that did righteousness, and forsook not the ordinance of their God: they ask of me the ordinances of justice; they take delight in approaching to God.

Eze 33:31 And they come unto thee as the people cometh, and they sit before thee as my people, and they hear thy words, but they will not do them: for with their mouth they shew much love, *but* their heart goeth after their covetousness.

Ho 8:13 They sacrifice flesh *for* the sacrifices of mine offerings, and *eat it;* but the LORD accepteth them not; now will he remember their iniquity, and visit their sins: they shall return to Egypt.

Am 5:21 I hate, I despise your feast days, and I will not smell in your solemn assemblies.

Zec 7:6 And when ye did eat, and when ye did drink, did not ye eat *for yourselves,* and drink *for yourselves?*

Mt 6:7 But when ye pray, use not vain repetitions, as the heathen *do:* for they think that they shall be heard for their much speaking.

Mt 15:8 This people draweth nigh unto me with their mouth, and honoureth me with *their* lips; but their heart is far from me.

Mt 23:23 Woe unto you, scribes and Pharisees, hypocrites! for ye pay tithe of mint and anise and cummin, and have omitted the weightier *matters* of the law, judgment, mercy, and faith: these ought ye to have done, and not to leave the other undone.

Mt 25:3 They that *were* foolish took their lamps, and took no oil with them:

Mk 7:4 And *when they come* from the market, except they wash, they eat not. And many other things there be, which they have received to hold, *as* the washing of cups, and pots, brasen vessels, and of tables.

Lu 5:33 And they said unto him, Why do the disciples of John fast often, and make prayers, and likewise *the disciples* of the Pharisees; but thine eat and drink?

Lu 14:34 Salt *is* good: but if the salt have lost his savour, wherewith shall it be seasoned?

Ro 2:20 An instructor of the foolish, a teacher of babes, which hast the form of knowledge and of the truth in the law.

Ro 2:28 For he is not a Jew, which is one outwardly; neither *is that* circumcision, which is outward in the flesh:

Ro 7:6 But now we are delivered from the law, that being dead wherein we were held; that we should serve in newness of spirit, and not *in* the oldness of the letter.

Ro 9:31 But Israel, which followed after the law of righteousness, hath not attained to the law of righteousness.

1 Co 13:1 Though I speak with the tongues of men and of angels, and have not charity, I am become *as* sounding brass, or a tinkling cymbal.

Ga 4:10–11 Ye observe days, and months, and times, and years.

I am afraid of you, lest I have bestowed upon you labour in vain.

Col 2:16 Let no man therefore judge you in meat, or in drink, or in respect of an holyday, or of the new moon, or of the sabbath *days:*

Col 2:20 Wherefore if ye be dead with Christ from the rudiments of the world, why, as though living in the world, are ye subject to ordinances,

1 Ti 4:8 For bodily exercise profiteth little: but godliness is profitable unto all things, having promise of the life that now is, and of that which is to come.

2 Ti 3:5 Having a form of godliness, but denying the power thereof: from such turn away.

He 13:9 Be not carried about with divers and strange doctrines. For *it is* a good thing that the heart be established with grace; not with meats, which have not profited them that have been occupied therein.

Jude 19 These be they who separate themselves, sensual, having not the Spirit.

Re 3:1 And unto the angel of the church in Sardis write; These things saith he that hath the seven Spirits of God, and the seven stars; I know thy works, that thou hast a name that thou livest, and art dead.

Re 3:16 So then because thou art lukewarm, and neither cold nor hot, I will spue thee out of my mouth.

2). Its Insufficiency

1 S 15:22 And Samuel said, Hath the LORD *as great* delight in burnt offerings and sacrifices, as in obeying the voice of the LORD? Behold, to obey *is* better than sacrifice, *and* to hearken than the fat of rams.

Ps 51:16 For thou desirest not sacrifice; else would I give *it:* thou delightest not in burnt offering.

Ec 5:1 Keep thy foot when thou goest to the house of God, and be more ready to hear, than to give the sacrifice of fools: for they consider not that they do evil.

Ho 6:6 For I desired mercy, and not sacrifice; and the knowledge of God more than burnt offerings.

Mi 6:7 Will the LORD be pleased with thousands of rams, *or* with ten thousands of rivers of oil? shall I give my firstborn *for* my transgression, the fruit of my body *for* the sin of my soul?

Ro 14:17 For the kingdom of God is not meat and drink; but righteousness, and peace, and joy in the Holy Ghost.

1 Co 7:19 Circumcision is nothing, and uncircumcision is nothing, but the keeping of the commandments of God.

1 Co 8:8 But meat commendeth us not to God: for neither, if we eat, are we the better; neither, if we eat not, are we the worse.

He 9:10 *Which stood* only in meats and drinks, and divers washings, and carnal ordinances, imposed *on them* until the time of reformation.

f. Hypocrisy

Pr 21:27 The sacrifice of the wicked *is* abomination: how much more, *when* he bringeth it with a wicked mind?

Pr 23:7 For as he thinketh in his heart, so *is* he: Eat and drink, saith he to thee; but his heart *is* not with thee.

Pr 26:25 When he speaketh fair, believe him not: for *there are* seven abominations in his heart.

Is 66:3 He that killeth an ox *is as if* he slew a man; he that sacrificeth a lamb, *as if* he cut off a dog's neck; he that offereth an oblation, *as if he offered* swine's blood; he that burneth incense, *as if* he blessed an idol. Yea, they have chosen their own ways, and their soul delighteth in their abominations.

Mt 15:7 *Ye* hypocrites, well did Esaias prophesy of you, saying,

Mt 22:18 But Jesus perceived their wickedness, and said, Why tempt ye me, *ye* hypocrites?

Mt 23:13 But woe unto you, scribes and Pharisees, hypocrites! for ye shut up the kingdom of heaven against men: for ye neither go in *yourselves,* neither suffer ye them that are entering to go in.

Mt 23:28 Even so ye also outwardly appear righteous unto men, but within ye are full of hypocrisy and iniquity.

Mt 24:51 And shall cut him asunder, and appoint *him* his portion with the hypocrites: there shall be weeping and gnashing of teeth.

Lu 6:42 Either how canst thou say to thy brother, Brother, let me pull out the mote that is in thine eye, when thou thyself beholdest not the beam that is in thine own eye? Thou hypocrite, cast out first the beam out of thine own eye, and then shalt thou see clearly to pull out the mote that is in thy brother's eye.

Lu 12:1 In the mean time, when there were gathered together an innumerable multitude of people, insomuch that they trode one upon another, he began to say unto his disciples first of all, Beware ye of the leaven of the Pharisees, which is hypocrisy.

Lu 12:56 *Ye* hypocrites, ye can discern the face of the sky and of the earth; but how is it that ye do not discern this time?

Lu 13:15 The Lord then answered him, and said, *Thou* hypocrite, doth not each one of you on the sabbath loose his ox or *his* ass from the stall, and lead *him* away to watering?

Jn 12:6 This he said, not that he cared for the poor; but because he was a thief, and had the bag, and bare what was put therein.

Ro 16:18 For they that are such serve not our Lord Jesus Christ, but their own belly; and by good words and fair speeches deceive the hearts of the simple.

1 Ti 4:2 Speaking lies in hypocrisy; having their conscience seared with a hot iron;

Tit 1:16 They profess that they know God; but in works they deny *him,* being abominable, and disobedient, and unto every good work reprobate.

g. Inconsistency

1). Characteristics

UNCHARITABLENESS

Mt 7:3 And why beholdest thou the mote that is in thy brother's eye, but considerest not the beam that is in thine own eye?

Mt 23:3 All therefore whatsoever they bid you observe, *that* observe and do; but do not ye after their works: for they say, and do not.

RELIGIOUS TALK

Lu 6:46 And why call ye me, Lord, Lord, and do not the things which I say?

LEGALISM

Jn 7:23 If a man on the sabbath day receive circumcision, that the law of Moses should not be broken; are ye angry at me, because I have made a man every whit whole on the sabbath day?

HARSH JUDGMENT

Ro 2:1 Therefore thou art inexcusable, O man, whosoever thou art that judgest: for wherein thou judgest another, thou condemnest thyself; for thou that judgest doest the same things.

PREACHING AND NOT PRACTICING

Ro 2:21 Thou therefore which teachest another, teachest thou not thyself? thou that preachest a man should not steal, dost thou steal?

Ga 2:14 But when I saw that they walked not uprightly according to the truth of the gospel, I said unto Peter before *them* all, If thou, being a Jew, livest after the manner of Gentiles, and not as do the Jews, why compellest thou the Gentiles to live as do the Jews?

FALSE PROFESSION

Tit 1:16 They profess that they know God; but in works they deny *him,* being abominable, and disobedient, and unto every good work repress to know God, but in works they deny Him, being abominable, disobedient, and disqualified for every good work.

SELFISHNESS

Ja 2:15–16 If a brother or sister be naked, and destitute of daily food,

And one of you say unto them, Depart in peace, be ye warmed and filled; notwithstanding ye give them not those things which are needful to the body; what *doth it* profit?

THE DOUBLE TONGUE

Ja 3:10 Out of the same mouth proceedeth blessing and cursing. My brethren, these things ought not so to be.

1 Jn 2:4 He that saith, I know him, and keepeth not his commandments, is a liar, and the truth is not in him.

2). Brings Reproach

1 S 11:2 And Nahash the Ammonite answered them, On this *condition* will I make *a covenant* with you, that I may thrust out all your right eyes, and lay it *for* a reproach upon all Israel.

2 S 12:14 Howbeit, because by this deed thou hast given great occasion to the enemies of the LORD to blaspheme, the child also *that is* born unto thee shall surely die.

Ne 4:4 Hear, O our God; for we are despised: and turn their reproach upon their own head, and give them for a prey in the land of captivity:

Ne 5:9 Also I said, It *is* not good that ye do: ought ye not to walk in the fear of our God because of the reproach of the heathen our enemies?

Ps 39:8 Deliver me from all my transgressions: make me not the reproach of the foolish.

Ps 55:12 For *it was* not an enemy *that* reproached me; then I could have borne *it:* neither *was it* he that hated me *that* did magnify *himself* against me; then I would have hid myself from him:

Is 25:8 He will swallow up death in victory; and the Lord God will wipe away tears from off all faces; and the rebuke of his people shall he take away from off all the earth: for the LORD hath spoken *it.*

Eze 36:20 And when they entered unto the heathen, whither they went, they profaned my holy name, when they said to them, These *are* the people of the LORD, and are gone forth out of his land.

Ro 2:23–24 Thou that makest thy boast of the law, through breaking the law dishonourest thou God?

For the name of God is blasphemed among the Gentiles through you, as it is written.

2 Pe 2:2 And many shall follow their pernicious ways; by reason of whom the way of truth shall be evil spoken of.

h. Superstitious

1 S 4:3; 1 K 20:23; Je 10:2; 44:18; Mt 14:2, 26; Mk 6:49; Lu 24:37; Ac 12:15; 14:11; 17:23; 19:35; 28:4

See **PRIDE, PHARISAISM, SELF-RIGHTEOUSNESS**

REMEMBRANCE

1. Prayer to Be Remembered by God

Ge 40:14; Jud 16:28; 1 S 1:11; 2 K 20:3; Ne 5:19; 13:14, 22, 31; Jb 14:13; Ps 25:7; 106:4; 132:1; Is 38:3; Je 15:15; Lu 23:42; Jn 15:20

2. Saints Remembered

Ge 8:1 And God remembered Noah, and every living thing, and all the cattle that *was* with him in the ark: and God made a wind to pass over the earth, and the waters asswaged;

Ge 19:29 And it came to pass, when God destroyed the cities of the plain, that God remembered Abraham, and sent Lot out of the midst of the overthrow, when he overthrew the cities in the which Lot dwelt.

Nu 10:9 And if ye go to war in your land against the enemy that oppresseth you, then ye shall blow an alarm with the trumpets; and ye shall be remembered before the LORD your God, and ye shall be saved from your enemies.

Ps 98:3 He hath remembered his mercy and his truth toward the house of Israel: all the ends of the earth have seen the salvation of our God.

Ps 136:23 Who remembered us in our low estate: for his mercy *endureth* for ever:

Is 49:14–16 But Zion said, The LORD hath forsaken me, and my Lord hath forgotten me.

Can a woman forget her sucking child, that she should not have compassion on the son of her womb? yea, they may forget, yet will I not forget thee.

Behold, I have graven thee upon the palms of *my* hands; thy walls *are* continually before me.

He 6:10 For God *is* not unrighteous to forget your work and labour of love, which ye have shewed toward his name, in that ye have ministered to the saints, and do minister.

3. Human Recollection

a. The Duty of Remembering God

IN THE BATTLES OF LIFE

Ne 4:14 And I looked, and rose up, and said unto the nobles, and to the rulers, and to the rest of the people, Be not ye afraid of them: remember the Lord, *which is* great and terrible, and fight for your brethren, your sons, and your daughters, your wives, and your houses.

IN THE NIGHT SEASON

Ps 63:6 When I remember thee upon my bed, *and* meditate on thee in the *night* watches.

IN EARLY LIFE

Ec 12:1 Remember now thy Creator in the days of thy youth, while the evil days come not, nor the years draw nigh, when thou shalt say, I have no pleasure in them;

IN TIME OF TROUBLE

Jona 2:7 When my soul fainted within me I remembered the LORD: and my prayer came in unto thee, into thine holy temple.

WHEN AWAY FROM HOME

Zec 10:9 And I will sow them among the people: and they shall remember me in far countries; and they shall live with their children, and turn again.

b. Fringes of Remembrance Used on Garments

Nu 15:38; De 22:12; Mt 23:5

c. Phylacteries, or Frontlets, Worn to Preserve the Law in Memory

Ex 13:9, 16; De 6:8; 11:18; Pr 7:3; Mt 23:5

d. The Duty of Believers to Act as Remembrancers

Is 26:14 *They are* dead, they shall not live; *they are* deceased, they shall not rise: therefore hast thou visited and destroyed them, and made all their memory to perish.

Is 62:6 I have set watchmen upon thy walls, O Jerusalem, *which* shall never hold their peace day nor night: ye that make mention of the LORD, keep not silence,

1 Co 4:17 For this cause have I sent unto you Timotheus, who is my beloved son, and faithful in the Lord, who shall bring you into remembrance of my ways which be in Christ, as I teach every where in every church.

1 Ti 4:6 If thou put the brethren in remembrance of these things, thou shalt be a good minister of Jesus Christ, nourished up in the words of faith and of good doctrine, whereunto thou hast attained.

2 Pe 1:12 Wherefore I will not be negligent to put you always in remembrance of these things, though ye know *them,* and be established in the present truth.

2 Pe 3:1 This second epistle, beloved, I now write unto you; in *both* which I stir up your pure minds by way of remembrance:

See **FORGETFULNESS, MEMORIES**

REMISSION, *release from the debt of sin*

Ps 32:2 Blessed *is* the man unto whom the LORD imputeth not iniquity, and in whose spirit *there is* no guile.

Ps 51:9 Hide thy face from my sins, and blot out all mine iniquities.

Mt 26:28 For this is my blood of the new testament, which is shed for many for the remission of sins.

Mk 1:4 John did baptize in the wilderness, and preach the baptism of repentance for the remission of sins.

Lu 1:77 To give knowledge of salvation unto his people by the remission of their sins,

Lu 3:3 And he came into all the country about Jordan, preaching the baptism of repentance for the remission of sins;

Lu 24:47 And that repentance and remission of sins should be preached in his name among all nations, beginning at Jerusalem.

Ac 2:38 Then Peter said unto them, Repent, and be baptized every one of you in the name of Jesus Christ for the remission of sins, and ye shall receive the gift of the Holy Ghost.

Ac 3:19 Repent ye therefore, and be converted, that your sins may be blotted out, when the times of refreshing shall come from the presence of the Lord;

Ac 5:31 Him hath God exalted with his right hand *to be* a Prince and a Saviour, for to give repentance to Israel, and forgiveness of sins.

Ac 10:43 To him give all the prophets witness, that through his name whosoever believeth in him shall receive remission of sins.

Ac 13:38 Be it known unto you therefore, men *and* brethren, that through this man is preached unto you the forgiveness of sins:

Ro 3:25 Whom God hath set forth *to be* a propitiation through faith in his blood, to declare his righteousness for the remission of sins that are past, through the forbearance of God;

Ro 11:27 For this *is* my covenant unto them, when I shall take away their sins.

2 Co 5:19 To wit, that God was in Christ, reconciling the world unto himself, not imputing their trespasses unto them; and hath committed unto us the word of reconciliation.

Ep 1:7 In whom we have redemption through his blood, the forgiveness of sins, according to the riches of his grace;

He 9:22 And almost all things are by the law purged with blood; and without shedding of blood is no remission.

He 10:18 Now where remission of these *is, there is* no more offering for sin.

See **ATONEMENT, REDEMPTION, SALVATION**

REMORSE

THE ISRAELITES

Nu 14:39 And Moses told these sayings unto all the children of Israel: and the people mourned greatly.

DAVID

1 Chr 21:17 And David said unto God, *Is it* not I *that* commanded the people to be numbered? even I it is that have sinned and done evil indeed; but *as for* these sheep, what have they done? let thine hand, I pray thee, O LORD my God, be on me, and on my father's house; but not on thy people, that they should be plagued.

PETER

Mt 26:75 And Peter remembered the word of Jesus, which said unto him, Before the cock crow, thou shalt deny me thrice. And he went out, and wept bitterly.

JUDAS

Mt 27:3 Then Judas, which had betrayeth him, when he saw that he was condemned, repented himself, and brought again the thirty pieces of silver to the chief priests and elders,

Mt 27:5 And he cast down the pieces of silver in the temple, and departed, and went and hanged himself.

ESAU

He 12:16–17 Lest there *be* any fornicator, or profane person, as Esau, who for one morsel of meat sold his birthright.

For ye know how that afterward, when he would have inherited the blessing, he was rejected: for he found no place of repentance, though he sought it carefully with tears.

See **GUILT**

RENUNCIATION See SPEECH

REPENTANCE, *a fundamental change of heart and mind from sin toward God*

1. Human Responsibility

Le 16:31 It *shall be* a sabbath of rest unto you, and ye shall afflict your souls, by a statute for ever.

Le 23:27 Also on the tenth *day* of this seventh month *there shall be* a day of atonement: it shall be an holy convocation unto you; and ye shall afflict your souls, and offer an offering made by fire unto the LORD.

Le 23:32 It *shall be* unto you a sabbath of rest, and ye shall afflict your souls: in the ninth *day* of the month at even, from even unto even, shall ye celebrate your sabbath.

1 K 8:33 When thy people Israel be smitten down before the enemy, because they have sinned against thee, and shall turn again to thee, and confess thy name, and pray, and make supplication unto thee in this house:

2 K 17:13 Yet the LORD testified against Israel, and against Judah, by all the prophets, *and by* all the seers, saying, Turn ye from your evil ways, and keep my commandments *and* my statutes, according to all the law which I commanded your fathers, and which I sent to you by my servants the prophets.

2 Chr 30:6 So the posts went with the letters from the king and his princes throughout all Israel and Judah, and according to the commandment of the king, saying, Ye children of Israel, turn again unto the LORD God of Abraham, Isaac, and Israel, and he will return to the remnant of you, that are escaped out of the hand of the kings of Assyria.

Jb 36:10 He openeth also their ear to discipline, and commandeth that they return from iniquity.

Jb 42:8 Therefore take unto you now seven bullocks and seven rams, and go to my servant Job, and offer up for yourselves a burnt offering; and my servant Job shall pray for you: for him will I accept: lest I deal with you *after your* folly, in that ye have not spoken of me *the thing which is* right, like my servant Job.

Ps 51:17 The sacrifices of God *are* a broken spirit: a broken and a contrite heart, O God, thou wilt not despise.

Pr 1:23 Turn you at my reproof: behold, I will pour out my spirit unto you, I will make known my words unto you.

Is 22:12 And in that day did the Lord God of hosts call to weeping, and to mourning, and to baldness, and to girding with sackcloth:

Is 31:6 Turn ye unto *him from* whom the children of Israel have deeply revolted.

Is 32:11 Tremble, ye women that are at ease; be troubled, ye careless ones: strip you, and make you bare, and gird *sackcloth* upon *your* loins.

Is 44:22 I have blotted out, as a thick cloud, thy transgressions, and, as a cloud, thy sins: return unto me; for I have redeemed thee.

Je 3:1 They say, If a man put away his wife, and she go from him, and become another man's, shall he return unto her again? shall not that land be greatly polluted? but thou hast played the harlot with many lovers; yet return again to me, saith the LORD.

Je 3:7 And I said after she had done all these *things,* Turn thou unto me. But she returned not. And her treacherous sister Judah saw *it.*

Je 3:13 Only acknowledge thine iniquity, that thou hast transgressed against the LORD thy God, and hast scattered thy ways to the strangers under every green tree, and ye have not obeyed my voice, saith the LORD.

Je 3:22 Return, ye backsliding children, *and* I will heal your backslidings. Behold, we come unto thee; for thou *art* the LORD our God.

Je 18:11 Now therefore go to, speak to the men of Judah, and to the inhabitants of Jerusalem, saying, Thus saith the LORD; Behold, I frame evil against you, and devise a device against you: return ye now every one from his evil way, and make your ways and your doings good.

Je 25:5 They said, Turn ye again now every one from his evil way, and from the evil of your doings, and dwell in the land that the LORD hath given

unto you and to your fathers for ever and ever:

Je 26:13 Therefore now amend your ways and your doings, and obey the voice of the LORD your God; and the LORD will repent him of the evil that he hath pronounced against you.

Je 35:15 I have sent also unto you all my servants the prophets, rising up early and sending *them,* saying, Return ye now every man from his evil way, and amend your doings, and go not after other gods to serve them, and ye shall dwell in the land which I have given to you and to your fathers: but ye have not inclined your ear, nor hearkened unto me.

Je 36:3 It may be that the house of Judah will hear all the evil which I purpose to do unto them; that they may return every man from his evil way; that I may forgive their iniquity and their sin.

Je 36:7 It may be they will present their supplication before the LORD, and will return every one from his evil way: for great *is* the anger and the fury that the LORD hath pronounced against this people.

Eze 14:6 Therefore say unto the house of Israel, Thus saith the Lord GOD; Repent, and turn *yourselves* from your idols; and turn away your faces from all your abominations.

Eze 18:31 Cast away from you all your transgressions, whereby ye have transgressed; and make you a new heart and a new spirit: for why will ye die, O house of Israel?

Eze 33:11 Say unto them, *As* I live, saith the Lord GOD, I have no pleasure in the death of the wicked; but that the wicked turn from his way and live: turn ye, turn ye from your evil ways; for why will ye die, O house of Israel?

Da 4:27 Wherefore, O king, let my cable unto thee, and break off thy sins by righteousness, and thine iniquities by shewing mercy to the poor; if it may be a lengthening of thy tranquility.

Ho 10:12 Sow to yourselves in righteousness, reap in mercy; break up your fallow ground: for *it is* time to seek the

LORD, till he come and rain righteousness upon you.

Ho 12:6 Therefore turn thou to thy God: keep mercy and judgment, and wait on thy God continually.

Ho 14:2 Take with you words, and turn to the LORD: say unto him, Take away all iniquity, and receive *us* graciously: so will we render the calves of our lips.

Jl 1:13 Gird yourselves, and lament, ye priests: howl, ye ministers of the altar: come, lie all night in sackcloth, ye ministers of my God: for the meat offering and the drink offering is withholden from the house of your God.

Jl 2:12 Therefore also now, saith the LORD, turn ye *even* to me with all your heart, and with fasting, and with weeping, and with mourning:

Mal 3:7 Even from the days of your fathers ye are gone away from mine ordinances, and have not kept *them*. Return unto me, and I will return unto you, saith the LORD of hosts. But ye said, Wherein shall we return?

Mt 3:2 And saying, Repent ye: for the kingdom of heaven is at hand.

Mt 3:11 I indeed baptize you with water unto repentance: but he that cometh after me is mightier than I, whose shoes I am not worthy to bear: he shall baptize you with the Holy Ghost, and *with* fire:

Mt 4:17 From that time Jesus began to preach, and to say, Repent: for the kingdom of heaven is at hand.

Mk 1:4 John did baptize in the wilderness, and preach the baptism of repentance for the remission of sins.

Mk 1:15 And saying, The time is fulfilled, and the kingdom of God is at hand: repent ye, and believe the gospel.

Mk 2:17 When Jesus heard *it,* he saith unto them, They that are whole have no need of the physician, but they that are sick: I came not to call the righteous, but sinners to repentance.

Mk 6:12 And they went out, and preached that men should repent.

Lu 3:3 And he came into all the country about Jordan, preaching the baptism of repentance for the remission of sins;

Lu 5:32 I came not to call the righteous, but sinners to repentance.

Lu 13:2–3 And Jesus answering said unto them, Suppose ye that these Galilaeans were sinners above all the Galilaeans, because they suffered such things?

I tell you, Nay: but, except ye repent, ye shall all likewise perish.

Lu 24:47 And that repentance and remission of sins should be preached in his name among all nations, beginning at Jerusalem.

Ac 3:19 Repent ye therefore, and be converted, that your sins may be blotted out, when the times of refreshing shall come from the presence of the Lord;

Ac 3:26 Unto you first God, having raised up his Son Jesus, sent him to bless you, in turning away every one of you from his iniquities.

Ac 8:22 Repent therefore of this thy wickedness, and pray God, if perhaps the thought of thine heart may be forgiven thee.

Ac 13:24 When John had first preached before his coming the baptism of repentance to all the people of Israel.

Ac 17:30 And the times of this ignorance God winked at; but now commandeth all men every where to repent:

Ac 20:21 Testifying both to the Jews, and also to the Greeks, repentance toward God, and faith toward our Lord Jesus Christ.

Ac 26:20 But shewed first unto them of Damascus, and at Jerusalem, and throughout all the coasts of Judaea, and *then* to the Gentiles, that they should repent and turn to God, and do works meet for repentance.

Ro 2:4 Or despisest thou the riches of his goodness and forbearance and longsuffering; not knowing that the goodness of God leadeth thee to repentance?

2 Ti 2:25 In meekness instructing those that oppose themselves; if God peradventure will give them repentance to the acknowledging of the truth;

Ja 4:9 Be afflicted, and mourn, and weep: let your laughter be turned to mourning, and *your* joy to heaviness.

Re 2:5 Remember therefore from whence thou art fallen, and repent, and do the first works; or else I will come unto thee quickly, and will remove thy candlestick out of his place, except thou repent.

Re 2:16 Repent; or else I will come unto thee quickly, and will fight against them with the sword of my mouth.

Re 2:22 Behold, I will cast her into a bed, and them that commit adultery with her into great tribulation, except they repent of their deeds.

Re 3:3 Remember therefore how thou hast received and heard, and hold fast, and repent. If therefore thou shalt not watch, I will come on thee as a thief, and thou shalt not know what hour I will come upon thee.

Re 3:19 As many as I love, I rebuke and chasten: be zealous therefore, and repent.

2. Promises to the Penitent

ANSWER TO PRAYER

2 Chr 7:14 If my people, which are called by my name, shall humble themselves, and pray, and seek my face, and turn from their wicked ways; then will I hear from heaven, and will forgive their sin, and will heal their land.

2 Chr 30:9 For if ye turn again unto the LORD, your brethren and your children *shall find* compassion before them that lead them captive, so that they shall come again into this land: for the LORD your God *is* gracious and merciful, and will not turn away *his* face from you, if ye return unto him.

Ne 1:9 But *if* ye turn unto me, and keep my commandments, and do them; though there were of you cast out unto the uttermost part of the heaven, *yet* will I gather them from thence, and will bring them unto the place that I have chosen to set my name there.

PARDON FOR SIN

Is 55:7 Let the wicked forsake his way, and the unrighteous man his thoughts: and let him return unto the LORD, and he will have mercy upon him; and to our God, for he will abundantly pardon.

Is 31:9 And he shall pass over to his strong hold for fear, and his princes shall be afraid of the ensign, saith the LORD, whose fire *is* in Zion, and his furnace in Jerusalem.

LIFE

Eze 18:21 But if the wicked will turn from all his sins that he hath committed, and keep all my statutes, and do that which is lawful and right, he shall surely live, he shall not die.

Zec 1:3 Therefore say thou unto them, Thus saith the LORD of hosts; Turn ye unto me, saith the LORD of hosts, and I will turn unto you, saith the LORD of hosts.

COMFORT

Mt 5:4 Blessed *are* they that mourn: for they shall be comforted.

Lu 15:7 I say unto you, that likewise joy shall be in heaven over one sinner that repenteth, more than over ninety and nine just persons, which need no repentance.

THE GIFT OF THE HOLY SPIRIT

Ac 2:38 Then Peter said unto them, Repent, and be baptized every one of of Jesus Christ for the remission of sins, and ye shall receive the gift of the Holy Ghost.

3. Examples

AHAB

1 K 21:27 And it came to pass, when Ahab heard those words, that he rent his clothes, and put sackcloth upon his flesh, and fasted, and lay in sackcloth, and went softly.

JOSIAH

2 K 22:19 Because thine heart was tender, and thou hast humbled thyself before the LORD, when thou heardest what I spake against this place, and against the inhabitants thereof, that they should become a desolation and a curse, and hast rent thy clothes, and wept before me; I also have heard *thee*, saith the LORD.

ISRAEL IN EZRA'S TIME

Ezr 10:1 Now when Ezra had prayed, and when he had confessed, weeping and casting himself down before the house of God, there assembled unto him out of Israel a very great congregation of men and women and children: for the people wept very sore.

JOB

Jb 42:1 Then Job answered the LORD, and said,

Jb 42:6 Wherefore I abhor *myself*, and repent in dust and ashes.

Ps 38:18 For I will declare mine iniquity; I will be sorry for my sin.

Je 3:21 A voice was heard upon the high places, weeping *and* supplications of the children of Israel: for they have perverted their way, *and* they have forgotten the LORD their God.

Ho 6:1 Come, and let us return unto the LORD: for he hath torn, and he will heal us; he hath smitten, and he will bind us up.

THE NINEVITES

Jona 3:6–9 For word came unto the king of Nineveh, and he arose from his throne, and he laid his robe from him, and covered *him* with sackcloth, and sat in ashes.

And he caused *it* to be proclaimed and published through Nineveh by the decree of the king and his nobles, saying, Let neither man nor beast, herd nor flock, taste any thing: let them not feed, nor drink water:

But let man and beast be covered with sackcloth, and cry mightily unto God: yea, let them turn every one from his evil way, and from the violence that *is* in their hands.

Who can tell *if* God will turn and repent, and turn away from his fierce anger, that we perish not?

PETER

Mk 14:72 And the second time the cock crew. And Peter called to mind the word that Jesus said unto him, Before the cock crow twice, thou shalt deny me thrice. And when he thought thereon, he wept.

THE PRODIGAL SON

Lu 15:21 And the son said unto him, Father, I have sinned against heaven, and in thy sight, and am no more worthy to be called thy son.

THE PUBLICAN

Lu 18:13 And the publican, standing afar off, would not lift up so much as *his* eyes unto heaven, but smote upon his breast, saying, God be merciful to me a sinner.

4. Ascribed to God

Ge 6:7 And the LORD said, I will destroy man whom I have created from the face of the earth; both man, and beast, and the creeping thing, and the fowls of the air; for it repenteth me that I have made them.

Ex 32:14 And the LORD repented of the evil which he thought to do unto his people.

1 S 15:11 It repenteth me that I have set up Saul *to be* king: for he is turned back from following me, and hath not performed my commandments. And it grieved Samuel; and he cried unto the LORD all night.

Ps 106:45 And he remembered for them his covenant, and repented according to the multitude of his mercies.

Ho 11:8 How shall I give thee up, Ephraim? *how* shall I deliver thee, Israel? how shall I make thee as Admah? *how* shall I set thee as Zeboim? mine heart is turned within me, my repentings are kindled together.

Jl 2:13 And rend your heart, and not your garments, and turn unto the LORD your God: for he *is* gracious and merciful, slow to anger, and of great kindness, and repenteth him of the evil.

Jona 3:9 Who can tell *if* God will turn and repent, and turn away from his fierce anger, that we perish not?

5. Associated with Fasting

1 K 21:9; 2 Chr 20:3; Ezr 8:21; Est 4:16; Je 36:9; Jl 2:15; Jona 3:5

6. Returning to God

De 4:30 When thou art in tribulation, and all these things are come upon thee, *even* in the latter days, if thou turn to the LORD thy God, and shalt be obedient unto his voice;

De 30:10 If thou shalt hearken unto the voice of the LORD thy God, to keep his commandments and his statutes which are written in this book of the law, *and* if thou turn unto the LORD thy God with all thine heart, and with all thy soul.

1 S 7:3 And Samuel spake unto all the house of Israel, saying, If ye do return unto the LORD with all your hearts, *then* put away the strange gods and Ashtaroth from among you, and prepare your hearts unto the LORD, and serve him only: and he will deliver you out of the hand of the Philistines.

1 K 8:33 When thy people Israel be smitten down before the enemy, because they have sinned against thee, and shall turn again to thee, and confess thy name, and pray, and make supplication unto thee in this house:

1 K 8:48 And *so* return unto thee with all their heart, and with all their soul, in the land of their enemies, which led them away captive, and pray unto thee toward their land, which thou gavest unto their fathers, the city which thou hast chosen, and the house which I have built for thy name:

1 K 18:37 Hear me, O LORD, hear me, that this people may know that thou *art* the LORD God, and *that* thou hast turned their heart back again.

2 K 13:4 And Jehoahaz besought the LORD, and the LORD hearkened unto him: for he saw the oppression of Israel, because the king of Syria oppressed them.

2 Chr 6:24 And if thy people Israel be put to the worse before the enemy, because they have sinned against thee; and shall return and confess thy name, and pray and make supplication before thee in this house;

2 Chr 6:38 If they return to thee with all their heart and with all their soul in the land of their captivity, whither they have carried them captives, and pray toward their land, which thou gavest unto their fathers, and *toward* the city which thou hast chosen, and toward the house which I have built for thy name:

2 Chr 15:4 But when they in their trouble did turn unto the LORD God of Israel, and sought him, he was found of them.

2 Chr 19:4 And Jehoshaphat dwelt at Jerusalem: and he went out again through the people from Beer-sheba to mount Ephraim, and brought them back unto the LORD God of their fathers.

2 Chr 30:9 For if ye turn again unto the LORD, your brethren and your children *shall find* compassion before them that lead them captive, so that they shall come again into this land: for the LORD your God *is* gracious and merciful, and will not turn away *his* face from you, if ye return unto him.

Jb 22:23 If thou return to the Almighty, thou shalt be built up, thou shalt put away iniquity far from thy tabernacles.

Ps 78:34 When he slew them, then they sought him: and they returned and enquired early after God.

Is 10:21 The remnant shall return, *even* the remnant of Jacob, unto the mighty God.

Is 19:22 And the LORD shall smite Egypt: he shall smite and heal *it:* and they shall return *even* to the LORD, and he shall be intreated of them, and shall heal them.

Is 30:15 For thus saith the Lord GOD, the Holy One of Israel; In returning and rest shall ye be saved; in quietness and in confidence shall be your strength: and ye would not.

Is 31:6 Turn ye unto *him from* whom the children of Israel have deeply revolted.

Is 55:7 Let the wicked forsake his way, and the unrighteous man his thoughts: and let him return unto the LORD, and he will have mercy upon him; and to our God, for he will abundantly pardon.

Je 3:22 Return, ye backsliding children, *and* I will heal your backslidings. Behold, we come unto thee; for thou *art* the LORD our God.

Je 15:19 Therefore thus saith the LORD, If thou return, then will I bring thee again, *and* thou shalt stand before me: and if thou take forth the precious from the vile, thou shalt be as my mouth: let them return unto thee; but return not thou unto them.

Je 24:7 And I will give them an heart to know me, that I *am* the LORD: and they shall be my people, and I will be their God: for they shall return unto me with their whole heart.

Je 31:18 I have surely heard Ephraim bemoaning himself *thus;* Thou hast chastised me, and I was chastised, as a bullock unaccustomed *to the yoke:* turn thou me, and I shall be turned; for thou *art* the LORD my God.

Je 36:7 It may be they will present their supplication before the LORD, and will return every one from his evil way: for great *is* the anger and the fury that the LORD hath pronounced against this people.

Je 50:5 They shall ask the way to Zion with their faces thitherward, *saying,* Come, and let us join ourselves to the LORD in a perpetual covenant *that* shall not be forgotten.

Lam 3:40 Let us search and try our ways, and turn again to the LORD.

Eze 18:21 But if the wicked will turn from all his sins that he hath committed, and keep all my statutes, and do that which is lawful and right, he shall surely live, he shall not die.

Ho 2:7 And she shall follow after her lovers, but she shall not overtake them; and she shall seek them, but shall not find *them:* then shall she say, I will go and return to my first hus-

band; for then *was it* better with me than now.

Ho 6:1 Come, and let us return unto the LORD: for he hath torn, and he will heal us; he hath smitten, and he will bind us up.

Ho 14:1 O Israel, return unto the LORD thy God; for thou hast fallen by thine iniquity.

Zep 3:11 In that day shalt thou not be ashamed for all thy doings, wherein thou hast transgressed against me: for then I will take away out of the midst of thee them that rejoice in thy pride, and thou shalt no more be haughty because of my holy mountain.

Zec 1:4 Be ye not as your fathers, unto whom the former prophets have cried, saying, Thus saith the LORD of hosts; Turn ye now from your evil ways, and *from* your evil doings: but they did not hear, nor hearken unto me, saith the LORD.

Mal 3:7 Even from the days of your fathers ye are gone away from mine ordinances, and have not kept *them.* Return unto me, and I will return unto you, saith the LORD of hosts. But ye said, Wherein shall we return?

Lu 1:16 And many of the children of Israel shall he turn to the Lord their God.

Lu 15:20 And he arose, and came to his father. But when he was yet a great way off, his father saw him, and had compassion, and ran, and fell on his neck, and kissed him.

Ac 14:15 And saying, Sirs, why do ye these things? We also are men of like passions with you, and preach unto you that ye should turn from these vanities unto the living God, which made heaven, and earth, and the sea, and all things that are therein:

Ro 6:17 But God be thanked, that ye were the servants of sin, but ye have obeyed from the heart that form of doctrine which was delivered you.

Ro 11:23 And they also, if they abide not still in unbelief, shall be graffed in: for God is able to graff them in again.

1 Th 1:9 For they themselves shew of us what manner of entering in we had unto you, and how ye turned to God from idols to serve the living and true God;

1 Pe 2:25 For ye were as sheep going astray; but are now returned unto the Shepherd and Bishop of your souls.

Re 2:5 Remember therefore from whence thou art fallen, and repent, and do the first works; or else I will come unto thee quickly, and will remove thy candlestick out of his place, except thou repent.

7. Promises to Those Who Are Contrite

Ex 33:4 And when the people heard these evil tidings, they mourned: and no man did put on him his ornaments.

2 K 22:19 Because thine heart was tender, and thou hast humbled thyself before the LORD, when thou heardest what I spake against this place, and against the inhabitants thereof, that they should become a desolation and a curse, and hast rent thy clothes, and wept before me; I also have heard *thee*, saith the LORD.

2 Chr 6:37 Yet *if* they bethink themselves in the land whither they are carried captive, and turn and pray unto thee in the land of their captivity, saying, We have sinned, we have done amiss, and have dealt wickedly;

2 Chr 7:14 If my people, which are called by my name, shall humble themselves, and pray, and seek my face, and turn from their wicked ways; then will I hear from heaven, and will forgive their sin, and will heal their land.

2 Chr 12:6 Whereupon the princes of Israel and the king humbled themselves; and they said, The LORD *is* righteous.

2 Chr 30:11 Nevertheless divers of Asher and Manasseh and of Zebulun humbled themselves, and came to Jerusalem.

2 Chr 32:26 Notwithstanding Hezekiah humbled himself for the pride of his heart, *both* he and the inhabitants of Jerusalem, so that the wrath of the LORD came not upon them in the days of Hezekiah.

2 Chr 33:12 And when he was in affliction, he besought the LORD his God, and humbled himself greatly before the God of his fathers,

2 Chr 34:19 And it came to pass, when the king had heard the words of the law, that he rent his clothes.

2 Chr 34:27 Because thine heart was tender, and thou didst humble thyself before God, when thou heardest his words against this place, and against the inhabitants thereof, and humbledst thyself before me, and didst rend thy clothes, and weep before me; I have even heard *thee* also, saith the LORD.

Ezr 8:21 Then I proclaimed a fast there, at the river of Ahava, that we might afflict ourselves before our God, to seek of him a right way for us, and for our little ones, and for all our substance.

Ezr 9:5 And at the evening sacrifice I arose up from my heaviness; and having rent my garment and my mantle, I fell upon my knees, and spread out my hands unto the LORD my God.

Ezr 10:1 Now when Ezra had prayed, and when he had confessed, weeping and casting himself down before the house of God, there assembled unto him out of Israel a very great congregation of men and women and children: for the people wept very sore.

Ezr 10:6 Then Ezra rose up from before the house of God, and went into the chamber of Johanan the son of Eliashib: and *when* he came thither, he did eat no bread, nor drink water: for he mourned because of the transgression of them that had been carried away.

Ps 34:18 The LORD *is* nigh unto them that are of a broken heart; and saveth such as be of a contrite spirit.

Ps 51:17 The sacrifices of God *are* a broken spirit: a broken and a contrite heart, O God, thou wilt not despise.

Is 57:15 For thus saith the high and lofty One that inhabiteth eternity, whose name *is* Holy; I dwell in the high and holy *place*, with him also *that is* of a contrite and humble spirit, to revive the spirit of the humble, and to revive the heart of the contrite ones.

Is 66:2 For all those *things* hath mine hand made, and all those *things* have been, saith the LORD: but to this *man* will I look, *even* to *him that is* poor and of a contrite spirit, and trembleth at my word.

Da 10:2 In those days I Daniel was mourning three full weeks.

Da 10:12 Then said he unto me, Fear not, Daniel: for from the first day that thou didst set thine heart to understand, and to chasten thyself before thy God, thy words were heard, and I am come for thy words.

Jl 2:13 And rend your heart, and not your garments, and turn unto the LORD your God: for he *is* gracious and merciful, slow to anger, and of great kindness, and repenteth him of the evil.

Jl 2:17 Let the priests, the ministers of the LORD, weep between the porch and the altar, and let them say, Spare thy people, O LORD, and give not thine heritage to reproach, that the heathen should rule over them: wherefore should they say among the people, Where *is* their God?

Jona 3:5 So the people of Nineveh believed God, and proclaimed a fast, and put on sackcloth, from the greatest of them even to the least of them.

Zec 12:10 And I will pour upon the house of David, and upon the inhabitants of Jerusalem, the spirit of grace and of supplications: and they shall look upon me whom they have pierced, and they shall mourn for him, as one mourneth for *his* only *son*, and shall be in bitterness for him, as one that is in bitterness for *his* firstborn.

Mt 5:4 Blessed *are* they that mourn: for they shall be comforted.

Lu 7:38 And stood at his feet behind *him* weeping, and began to wash his feet with tears, and did wipe *them* with the hairs of her head, and kissed his feet, and anointed *them* with the ointment.

Lu 15:7 I say unto you, that likewise joy shall be in heaven over one sinner that repenteth, more than over ninety and nine just persons, which need no repentance.

Lu 18:13 And the publican, standing afar off, would not lift up so much as *his* eyes unto heaven, but smote upon his breast, saying, God be merciful to me a sinner.

Ac 2:37 Now when they heard *this,* they were pricked in their heart, and said unto Peter and to the rest of the apostles, Men *and* brethren, what shall we do?

Ac 9:11 And the Lord *said* unto him, Arise, and go into the street which is called Straight, and enquire in the house of Judas for *one* called Saul, of Tarsus: for, behold, he prayeth,

2 Co 7:10 For godly sorrow worketh repentance to salvation not to be repented of: but the sorrow of the world worketh death.

Ja 4:9 Be afflicted, and mourn, and weep: let your laughter be turned to mourning, and *your* joy to heaviness.

See **CLEANSING, CONFESSING CHRIST, IMPENITENCE, PARDON**

REPHAIM, *a valley*

Ge 14:5; 15:20; 2 S 5:18; 23:13; 1 Chr 11:15; 14:9; Is 17:5

REPRESSION, *seven evils to be repressed*

1 S 6:19; Ps 39:1; Mt 6:19; Mk 10:44; 2 Co 10:5; Col 3:5; 1 Jn 2:15

REPROBATES

Ge 4:12; 1 S 3:13; 1 K 21:22; Ho 4:17; Ac 8:20; Ro 1:28; 2 Co 13:5

See **WICKED**

REPROOF, *to rebuke for a fault or wrong*

1. Its Place and Purpose

2 Chr 19:10 And what cause soever shall come to you of your brethren that dwell in their cities, between blood and blood, between law and commandment, statutes and judgments, ye shall even warn them that they trespass not against the LORD, and so wrath come upon you, and upon your brethren: this do, and ye shall not trespass.

Jb 11:3 Should thy lies make men hold their peace? and when thou mockest, shall no man make thee ashamed?

Pr 24:25 But to them that rebuke *him* shall be delight, and a good blessing shall come upon them.

Lu 17:3 Take heed to yourselves: If thy brother trespass against thee, rebuke him; and if he repent, forgive him.

Ep 5:11 And have no fellowship with the unfruitful works of darkness, but rather reprove *them*.

1 Ti 5:20 Them that sin rebuke before all, that others also may fear.

2 Ti 4:2 Preach the word; be instant in season, out of season; reprove, rebuke, exhort with all longsuffering and doctrine.

Tit 1:13 This witness is true. Wherefore rebuke them sharply, that they may be sound in the faith;

Tit 2:15 These things speak, and exhort, and rebuke with all authority. Let no man despise thee.

2. Its Value

Ge 12:18 And Pharaoh called Abram, and said, What *is* this *that* thou hast done unto me? why didst thou not tell me that she *was* thy wife?

Ge 20:16 And unto Sarah he said, Behold, I have given thy brother a thousand *pieces* of silver: behold, he *is* to thee a covering of the eyes, unto all that *are* with thee, and with all *other:* thus she was reproved.

Ps 141:5 Let the righteous smite me; *it shall be* a kindness: and let him reprove me; *it shall be* an excellent oil, *which* shall not break my head: for yet my prayer also *shall be* in their calamities.

Pr 15:5 A fool despiseth his father's instruction: but he that regardeth reproof is prudent.

Pr 17:10 A reproof entereth more into a wise man than an hundred stripes into a fool.

Pr 25:12 *As* an earring of gold, and an ornament of fine gold, *so is* a wise reprover upon an obedient ear.

Pr 27:5 Open rebuke *is* better than secret love.

Pr 29:15 The rod and reproof give wisdom: but a child left *to himself* bringeth his mother to shame.

Ec 7:5 *It is* better to hear the rebuke of the wise, than for a man to hear the song of fools.

He 12:5 And ye have forgotten the exhortation which speaketh unto you as unto children, My son, despise not thou the chastening of the Lord, nor faint when thou art rebuked of him:

3. Its Source

Jb 13:10 He will surely reprove you, if ye do secretly accept persons.

Ps 6:1 O LORD, rebuke me not in thine anger, neither chasten me in thy hot displeasure.

Ps 9:5 Thou hast rebuked the heathen, thou hast destroyed the wicked, thou hast put out their name for ever and ever.

Ps 18:15 Then the channels of waters were seen, and the foundations of the world were discovered at thy rebuke, O LORD, at the blast of the breath of thy nostrils.

Ps 38:1 O LORD, rebuke me not in thy wrath: neither chasten me in thy hot displeasure.

Ps 45:5 Thine arrows *are* sharp in the heart of the king's enemies; *whereby* the people fall under thee.

Ps 50:21 These *things* hast thou done, and I kept silence; thou thoughtest that I was altogether *such an one* as thyself: *but* I will reprove thee, and set *them* in order before thine eyes.

Ps 76:6 At thy rebuke, O God of Jacob, both the chariot and horse are cast into a dead sleep.

Ps 80:16 *It is* burned with fire, *it is* cut down: they perish at the rebuke of thy countenance.

Ps 105:14 He suffered no man to do them wrong: yea, he reproved kings for their sakes;

Ps 119:21 Thou hast rebuked the proud *that are* cursed, which do err from thy commandments.

Is 17:13 The nations shall rush like the rushing of many waters: but *God* shall rebuke them, and they shall flee far off, and shall be chased as the chaff of the mountains before the wind, and like a rolling thing before the whirlwind.

Is 37:4 It may be the he king of Assyria his master hath sent to reproach the living God, and will reprove the words which the LORD thy God hath heard: wherefore lift up *thy* prayer for the remnant that is left.

Is 66:15 For, behold, the LORD will come with fire, and with his chariots like a whirlwind, to render his anger with fury, and his rebuke with flames of fire.

Eze 25:17 And I will execute great vengeance upon them with furious rebukes; and they shall know that I *am* the LORD, when I shall lay my vengeance upon them.

Mi 4:3 And he shall judge among many people, and rebuke strong nations afar off; and they shall beat their swords into plowshares, and their spears into pruninghooks: nation shall not lift up a sword against nation, neither shall they learn war any more.

Zec 3:2 And the LORD said unto Satan, The LORD rebuke thee, O Satan; even the LORD that hath chosen Jerusalem rebuke thee: *is* not this a brand plucked out of the fire?

Lu 9:55 But he turned, and rebuked them, and said, Ye know not what manner of spirit ye are of.

2 Th 2:8 And then shall that Wicked be revealed, whom the Lord shall consume with the spirit of his mouth, and shall destroy with the brightness of his coming:

Re 2:16 Repent; or else I will come unto thee quickly, and will fight against them with the sword of my mouth.

Re 19:15 And out of his mouth goeth a sharp sword, that with it he should smite the nations: and he shall rule them with a rod of iron: and he treadeth the winepress of the fierceness and wrath of Almighty God.

4. Our Response

Pr 1:25 But ye have set at nought all my counsel, and would none of my reproof:

Pr 5:12 And say, How have I hated instruction, and my heart despised reproof;

Pr 9:7 He that reproveth a scorner getteth to himself shame: and he that rebuketh a wicked *man getteth* himself a blot.

Pr 10:17 He *is in* the way of life that keepeth instruction: but he that refuseth reproof erreth.

Pr 12:1 Whoso loveth instruction loveth knowledge: but he that hateth reproof *is* brutish.

Pr 15:10 Correction *is* grievous unto him that forsaketh the way: *and* he that hateth reproof shall die.

Pr 29:1 He, that being often reproved hardeneth *his* neck, shall suddenly be destroyed, and that without remedy.

Am 5:10 They hate him that rebuketh in the gate, and they abhor him that speaketh uprightly.

Jn 7:7 The world cannot hate you; but me it hateth, because I testify of it, that the works thereof are evil.

5. Christ's Example

TO PETER

Mk 8:33 But when he had turned about and looked on his disciples, he rebuked Peter, saying, Get thee behind me, Satan: for thou savourest not the things that be of God, but the things that be of men.

TO THE ELEVEN, *disbelieving in his resurrection*

Mk 16:14 Afterward he appeared unto the eleven as they sat at meat, and upbraided them with their unbelief and hardness of heart, because they believed not them which had seen him after he was risen.

Lu 24:25 Then he said unto them, O fools, and slow of heart to believe all that the prophets have spoken:

TO THE DISCIPLES, *powerless to heal the demoniac*

Lu 9:41 And Jesus answering said, O faithless and perverse generation, how long shall I be with you, and suffer you? Bring thy son hither.

TO THE SEEKERS, *after eating the loaves and fishes*

Jn 6:26 Jesus answered them and said, Verily, verily, I say unto you, Ye seek me, not because ye saw the miracles, but because ye did eat of the loaves, and were filled.

TO THOSE WHO CRITICISED MARY

Jn 12:7 Then said Jesus, Let her alone: against the day of my burying hath she kept this.

Re 3:19 As many as I love, I rebuke and chasten: be zealous therefore, and repent.

See **COMMENDATION**

REPTILES, *cold-blooded vertebrates*

1. Adders

Ge 49:17 Dan shall be a serpent by the way, an adder in the path, that biteth the horse heels, so that his rider shall fall backward.

De 32:33; Ps 58:4; 91:13; 140:3; Pr 23:32; Is 11:8

2. Asps

Is 11:8 And the sucking child shall play on the hole of the asp, and the weaned child shall put his hand on the cockatrice' den.

De 32:33; Jb 20:16; Is 11:8; Ro 3:13

3. Chameleons

Le 11:30 And the ferret, and the chameleon, and the lizard, and the snail, and the mole.

4. Dragons

Eze 29:3 Speak, and say, Thus saith the Lord GOD; Behold, I *am* against thee, Pharaoh king of Egypt, the great dragon that lieth in the midst of his rivers, which hath said, My river *is* mine own, and I have made *it* for myself.

5. Frogs

Ex 8:2 And if thou refuse to let *them* go, behold, I will smite all thy borders with frogs:

6. Lizards

Le 11:30 And the ferret, and the chameleon, and the lizard, and the snail, and the mole.

7. Serpents

Ex 7:10 And Moses and Aaron went in unto Pharaoh, and they did so as the LORD had commanded: and Aaron cast down his rod before Pharaoh, and before his servants, and it became a serpent.

Ex 4:3; Nu 21:6; De 8:15; Pr 23:32; 30:19; Ec 10:8; Is 30:6; 65:25; Am 5:19; Mt 7:10; 10:16; Lu 11:11; 1 Co 10:9

Evil Men Compared to

Ps 58:4; 140:3; Ec 10:11; Mt 12:34; 23:33; Lu 3:7

8. Tortoises

Le 11:29 These also shall be unclean unto you among the creeping things that creep upon the earth; the weasel, and the mouse, and the tortoise after his kind,

9. Vipers

Jb 20:16 He shall suck the poison of asps: the viper's tongue shall slay him.

Is 59:5 They hatch cockatrice' eggs, and weave the spider's web: he that eateth of their eggs dieth, and that which is crushed breaketh out into a viper.

REQUIREMENTS

De 10:12 And now, Israel, what doth the LORD thy God require of thee, but to fear the LORD thy God, to walk in all his ways, and to love him, and to serve the LORD thy God with all thy heart and with all thy soul,

Ps 15:1 LORD, who shall abide in thy tabernacle? who shall dwell in thy holy hill?

Ps 40:6 Sacrifice and offering thou didst not desire; mine ears hast thou opened: burnt offering and sin offering hast thou not required.

Ec 2:3 I sought in mine heart to give myself unto wine, yet acquainting mine heart with wisdom; and to lay hold on folly, till I might see what *was*

that good for the sons of men, which they should do under the heaven all the days of their life.

Ec 6:12 For who knoweth what *is* good for man in *this* life, all the days of his vain life which he spendeth as a shadow? for who can tell a man what shall be after him under the sun?

Is 58:6 *Is* not this the fast that I have chosen? to loose the bands of wickedness, to undo the heavy burdens, and to let the oppressed go free, and that ye break every yoke?

Je 22:3 Thus saith the LORD; Execute ye judgment and righteousness, and deliver the spoiled out of the hand of the oppressor: and do no wrong, do no violence to the stranger, the fatherless, nor the widow, neither shed innocent blood in this place.

Mi 6:8 He hath shewed thee, O man, what *is* good; and what doth the LORD require of thee, but to do justly, and to love mercy, and to walk humbly with thy God?

Zec 7:9 Thus speaketh the LORD of hosts, saying, Execute true judgment, and shew mercy and compassions every man to his brother:

Zec 8:16 These *are* the things that ye shall do; Speak ye every man the truth to his neighbour; execute the judgment of truth and peace in your gates:

Mt 19:17 And he said unto him, Why callest thou me good? *there is* none good but one, *that is,* God: but if thou wilt enter into life, keep the commandments.

Ja 2:12 So speak ye, and so do, as they that shall be judged by the law of liberty.

Spiritual Necessities, emphasized by Christ

INWARD RIGHTEOUSNESS

Mt 5:20

A CHILDLIKE SPIRIT

Mt 18:3

REPENTANCE

Lu 13:2–3

THE NEW BIRTH

Jn 3:5

SPIRITUAL WORSHIP

Jn 4:24

SPIRITUAL FOOD

Jn 6:53

PERSONAL FAITH

Jn 8:24; Ac 4:12; He 9:22; 11:6; 12:14

See **RELIGION, SALVATION**

REPUTATION

Ac 9:38 And forasmuch as Lydda was nigh to Joppa, and the disciples had heard that Peter was there, they sent unto him two men, desiring *him* that he would not delay to come to them.

Ac 16:2 Which was well reported of by the brethren that were at Lystra and Iconium.

Ro 1:8 First, I thank my God through Jesus Christ for you all, that your faith is spoken of throughout the whole world.

Ro 16:7 Salute Andronicus and Junia, my kinsmen, and my fellowprisoners, who are of note among the apostles, who also were in Christ before me.

Ro 16:19 For your obedience is come abroad unto all *men.* I am glad therefore on your behalf: but yet I would have you wise unto that which is good, and simple concerning evil.

2 Co 8:18 And we have sent with him the brother, whose praise is in the gospel throughout all the churches;

1 Ti 3:7 Moreover he must have a good report of them which are without; lest he fall into reproach and the snare of the devil.

Phm 5 Hearing of thy love and faith, which thou hast toward the Lord Jesus, and toward all saints;

He 11:2 For by it the elders obtained a good report.

He 11:4–39 By faith Abel offered unto God a more excellent sacrifice than Cain, by which he obtained witness that he was righteous, God testifying of his gifts: and by it he being dead yet speaketh.

By faith Enoch was translated that he should not see death; and was not found, because God had translated him: for before his translation he had this testimony, that he pleased God.

But without faith *it is* impossible to please *him:* for he that cometh to God must believe that he is, and *that* he is a rewarder of them that diligently seek him.

By faith Noah, being warned of God of things not seen as yet, moved with fear, prepared an ark to the saving of his house; by the which he condemned the world, and became heir of the righteousness which is by faith.

By faith Abraham, when he was called to go out into a place which he should after receive for an inheritance, obeyed; and he went out, not knowing whither he went.

By faith he sojourned in the land of promise, as *in* a strange country, dwelling in tabernacles with Isaac and Jacob, the heirs with him of the same promise:

For he looked for a city which hath foundations, whose builder and maker *is* God.

Through faith also Sara herself received strength to conceive seed, and was delivered of a child when she was past age, because she judged him faithful who had promised.

Therefore sprang there even of one, and him as good as dead, *so many* as the stars of the sky in multitude, and as the sand which is by the sea shore innumerable.

These all died in faith, not having received the promises, but having seen them afar off, and were persuaded of *them,* and embraced *them,* and confessed that they were strangers and pilgrims on the earth.

For they that say such things declare plainly that they seek a country.

And truly, if they had been mindful of that *country* from whence they came out, they might have had opportunity to have returned.

But now they desire a better *country,* that is, an heavenly: wherefore God is not ashamed to be called their God: for he hath prepared for them a city.

By faith Abraham, when he was tried, offered up Isaac: and he that had received the promises offered up his only begotten *son,*

Of whom it was said, That in Isaac shall thy seed be called:

Accounting that God *was* able to raise *him* up, even from the dead; from whence also he received him in a figure.

By faith Isaac blessed Jacob and Esau concerning things to come.

By faith Jacob, when he was a dying, blessed both the sons of Joseph; and worshipped, *leaning* upon the top of his staff.

By faith Joseph, when he died, made mention of the departing of the children of Israel; and gave commandment concerning his bones.

By faith Moses, when he was born, was hid three months of his parents, because they saw *he was* a proper child; and they were not afraid of the king's commandment.

By faith Moses, when he was come to years, refused to be called the son of Pharaoh's daughter;

Choosing rather to suffer affliction with the people of God, than to enjoy the pleasures of sin for a season;

Esteeming the reproach of Christ greater riches than the treasures in Egypt: for he had respect unto the recompence of the reward.

By faith he forsook Egypt, not fearing the wrath of the king: for he endured, as seeing him who is invisible.

Through faith he kept the passover, and the sprinkling of blood, lest he that destroyed the firstborn should touch them.

By faith they passed through the Red sea as by dry *land:* which the Egyptians assaying to do were drowned.

By faith the walls of Jericho fell down, after they were compassed about seven days.

By faith the harlot Rahab perished not with them that believed not, when she had received the spies with peace.

And what shall I more say? for the time would fail me to tell of Gedeon, and *of* Barak, and *of* Samson, and *of*

Jephthae; *of* David also, and Samuel, and *of* the prophets:

Who through faith subdued kingdoms, wrought righteousnessses, stopped the mouths of lions,

Quenched the violence of fire, escaped the edge of the sword, out of weakness were made strong, waxed valiant in fight, turned to flight the armies of the aliens.

Women received their dead raised to life again: and others were tortured, not accepting deliverance; that they might obtain a better resurrection:

And others had trial of *cruel* mockings and scourgings, yea, moreover of bonds and imprisonment:

They were stoned, they were sawn asunder, were tempted, were slain with the sword: they wandered about in sheepskins and goatskins; being destitute, afflicted, tormented;

(Of whom the world was not worthy:) they wandered in deserts, and *in* mountains, and *in* dens and caves of the earth.

And these all, having obtained a good report through faith, received not the promise:

3 Jn 6 Which have borne witness of thy charity before the church: whom if thou bring forward on their journey after a godly sort, thou shalt do well:

See **NAME**

RESIGNATION *See* **SURRENDER**

RESPONSIBILITY

See **STEWARDSHIP**

REST, *state of ceasing from work, activity, and motion*

1. Physical

Ge 2:2 And on the seventh day God ended his work which he had made; and he rested on the seventh day from all his work which he had made.

Ex 12:16 And in the first day *there shall be* an holy convocation, and in the seventh day there shall be an holy convocation to you; no manner of work shall be done in them, save *that*

which every man must eat, that only may be done of you.

Ex 16:23 And he said unto them, This *is that* which the LORD hath said, To morrow *is* the rest of the holy sabbath unto the LORD: bake *that* which ye will bake *to day,* and seethe that ye will seethe; and that which remaineth over lay up for you to be kept until the morning.

Ex 16:29 See, for that the LORD hath given you the sabbath, therefore he giveth you on the sixth day the bread of two days; abide ye every man in his place, let no man go out of his place on the seventh day.

Ex 20:10 But the seventh day *is* the sabbath of the LORD thy God: *in it* thou shalt not do any work, thou, nor thy son, nor thy daughter, thy manservant, nor thy maidservant, nor thy cattle, nor thy stranger that *is* within thy gates:

Ex 23:12 Six days thou shalt do thy work, and on the seventh day thou shalt rest: that thine ox and thine ass may rest, and the son of thy handmaid, and the stranger, may be refreshed.

Ex 31:15 Six days may work be done; but in the seventh is the sabbath of rest, holy to the LORD: whosoever doeth *any* work in the sabbath day, he shall surely be put to death.

Ex 34:21 Six days thou shalt work, but on the seventh day thou shalt rest: in earing time and in harvest thou shalt rest.

Ex 35:2 Six days shall work be done, but on the seventh day there shall be to you an holy day, a sabbath of rest to the LORD: whosoever doeth work therein shall be put to death.

Le 16:29 And *this* shall be a statute for ever unto you: *that* in the seventh month, on the tenth *day* of the month, ye shall afflict your souls, and do no work at all, *whether it be* one of your own country, or a stranger that sojourneth among you:

Le 23:3 Six days shall work be done: but the seventh day *is* the sabbath of rest, an holy convocation; ye shall do no work *therein:* it *is* the sabbath of the LORD in all your dwellings.

Le 23:7 In the first day ye shall have an holy convocation: ye shall do no servile work therein.

Le 23:21 And ye shall proclaim on the selfsame day, *that* it may be an holy convocation unto you: ye shall do no servile work *therein: it shall be* a statute for ever in all your dwellings throughout your generations.

Le 23:25 Ye shall do no servile work *therein:* but ye shall offer an offering made by fire unto the LORD.

Le 23:30 And whatsoever soul *it be* that doeth any work in that same day, the same soul will I destroy from among his people.

Le 23:35 On the first day *shall be* an holy convocation: ye shall do no servile work *therein.*

Nu 28:18 In the first day *shall be* an holy convocation; ye shall do no manner of servile work *therein:*

Nu 28:25 And on the seventh day ye shall have an holy convocation; ye shall do no servile work.

Nu 28:26 Also in the day of the firstfruits, when ye bring a new meat offering unto the LORD, after your weeks *be out,* ye shall have an holy convocation; ye shall do no servile work:

Nu 29:1 And in the seventh month, on the first *day* of the month, ye shall have an holy convocation; ye shall do no servile work: it is a day of blowing the trumpets unto you.

Nu 29:7 And ye shall have on the tenth *day* of this seventh month an holy convocation; and ye shall afflict your souls: ye shall not do any work *therein:*

Nu 29:12 And on the fifteenth day of the seventh month ye shall have an holy convocation; ye shall do no servile work, and ye shall keep a feast unto the LORD seven days:

Nu 29:35 On the eighth day ye shall have a solemn assembly: ye shall do no servile work *therein:*

De 5:14 But the seventh day *is* the sabbath of the LORD thy God: *in it* thou shalt not do any work, thou, nor thy son, nor thy daughter, nor thy manservant, nor thy maidservant, nor thine ox, nor thine ass, nor any of thy cattle, nor thy stranger that *is* within thy gates; that thy manservant and thy maidservant may rest as well as thou.

De 16:8 Six days thou shalt eat unleavened bread: and on the seventh day *shall be* a solemn assembly to the LORD thy God: thou shalt do no work *therein.*

Mk 6:31 And he said unto them, Come ye yourselves apart into a desert place, and rest a while: for there were many coming and going, and they had no leisure so much as to eat.

2. Spiritual

THE DIVINE PRESENCE GIVES

Ex 33:14 And he said, My presence shall go *with thee,* and I will give thee rest.

Ps 23:2 He maketh me to lie down in green pastures: he leadeth me beside the still waters.

VAINLY SOUGHT IN ESCAPE FROM TROUBLE

Ps 55:6 And I said, Oh that I had wings like a dove! *for then* would I fly away, and be at rest.

TRUE REPOSE FOUND IN GOD

Ps 116:7 Return unto thy rest, O my soul; for the LORD hath dealt bountifully with thee.

Is 14:3 And it shall come to pass in the day that the LORD shall give thee rest from thy sorrow, and from thy fear, and from the hard bondage wherein thou wast made to serve,

LOST BY STUBBORNNESS

Is 28:12 To whom he said, This *is* the rest wherewith ye may cause the weary to rest; and this *is* the refreshing: yet they would not hear.

Is 30:15 For thus saith the Lord GOD, the Holy One of Israel; In returning and rest shall ye be saved; in quietness and in confidence shall be your strength: and ye would not.

FOUND IN CHRIST'S SERVICE

Mt 11:29 Take my yoke upon you, and learn of me; for I am meek and lowly in heart: and ye shall find rest unto your souls.

APPROPRIATED BY FAITH

He 4:3 For we which have believed do enter into rest, as he said, As I have sworn in my wrath, if they shall enter into my rest: although the works were finished from the foundation of the world.

ETERNAL

Re 14:13 And I heard a voice from heaven saying unto me, Write, Blessed *are* the dead which die in the Lord from henceforth: Yea, saith the Spirit, that they may rest from their labours; and their works do follow them.

3. Future

Jb 3:17; 2 Th 1:7; He 4:9; Re 14:13

See **QUIETNESS, UNREST**

RESTITUTION, *the act of restoring*

1. Prescribed

Ex 22:3, 12; Le 5:16; 6:4; 24:18; Nu 5:7; 2 S 12:6; Ne 5:11; Jb 20:10; Pr 6:31; Eze 33:15

2. Examples

Jud 17:3; 1 K 20:34; 2 K 8:6; Ne 5:12; Lu 19:8

RESTORATION, *the state of being reinstated, made new, repaired*

1. Spiritual

1 K 18:37 Hear me, O LORD, hear me, that this people may know that thou *art* the LORD God, and *that* thou hast turned their heart back again.

2 Chr 19:4 And Jehoshaphat dwelt at Jerusalem: and he went out again through the people from Beer-sheba to mount Ephraim, and brought them back unto the LORD God of their fathers.

Jb 33:26 He shall pray unto God, and he will be favourable unto him: and he shall see his face with joy: for he will render unto man his righteousness.

Ps 23:3 He restoreth my soul: he leadeth me in the paths of righteousness for his name's sake.

Ps 51:12 Restore unto me the joy of thy salvation; and uphold me *with thy* free spirit.

Ps 85:4 Turn us, O God of our salvation, and cause thine anger toward us to cease.

Is 57:18 I have seen his ways, and will heal him: I will lead him also, and restore comforts unto him and to his mourners.

Je 3:22 Return, ye backsliding children, *and* I will heal your backslidings. Behold, we come unto thee; for thou *art* the LORD our God.

Je 30:17 For I will restore health unto thee, and I will heal thee of thy wounds, saith the LORD; because they called thee an Outcast, *saying,* This *is* Zion, whom no man seeketh after.

Ho 6:2 After two days will he revive us: in the third day he will raise us up, and we shall live in his sight.

Ho 14:4 I will heal their backsliding, I will love them freely: for mine anger is turned away from him.

Mi 7:19 He will turn again, he will have compassion upon us; he will subdue our iniquities; and thou wilt cast all their sins into the depths of the sea.

Lu 8:35 Then they went out to see what was done; and came to Jesus, and found the man, out of whom the devils were departed, sitting at the feet of Jesus, clothed, and in his right mind: and they were afraid.

Lu 15:22 But the father said to his servants, Bring forth the best robe, and put *it* on him; and put a ring on his hand, and shoes on *his* feet:

Lu 15:32 It was meet that we should make merry, and be glad: for this thy brother was dead, and is alive again; and was lost, and is found.

Ga 4:19 My little children, of whom I travail in birth again until Christ be formed in you,

Ga 6:1 Brethren, if a man be overtaken in a fault, ye which are spiritual, restore such an one in the spirit of meekness; considering thyself, lest thou also be tempted.

2. Of Israel

De 30:4 If *any* of thine be driven out unto the outmost *parts* of heaven, from thence will the LORD thy God gather thee, and from thence will he fetch thee:

2 Chr 30:9 For if ye turn again unto the LORD, your brethren and your children *shall find* compassion before them that lead them captive, so that they shall come again into this land: for the LORD your God *is* gracious and merciful, and will not turn away *his* face from you, if ye return unto him.

Ezr 9:8 And now for a little space grace hath been *shewed* from the LORD our God, to leave us a remnant to escape, and to give us a nail in his holy place, that our God may lighten our eyes, and give us a little reviving in our bondage.

Ps 14:7 Oh that the salvation of Israel *were come* out of Zion! when the LORD bringeth back the captivity of his people, Jacob shall rejoice, *and* Israel shall be glad.

Ps 53:6 Oh that the salvation of Israel *were come* out of Zion! When God bringeth back the captivity of his people, Jacob shall rejoice, *and* Israel shall be glad.

Ps 80:3 Turn us again, O God, and cause thy face to shine; and we shall be saved.

Ps 80:7 Turn us again, O God of hosts, and cause thy face to shine; and we shall be saved.

Ps 80:19 Turn us again, O LORD God of hosts, cause thy face to shine; and we shall be saved.

Ps 85:1 LORD, thou hast been favourable unto thy land: thou hast brought back the captivity of Jacob.

Ps 102:16 When the LORD shall build up Zion, he shall appear in his glory.

Ps 126:1 When the LORD turned again the captivity of Zion, we were like them that dream.

Is 1:26 And I will restore thy judges as at the first, and thy counsellors as at the beginning: afterward thou shalt be called, The city of righteousness, the faithful city.

Is 11:12 And he shall set up an ensign for the nations, and shall assemble the outcasts of Israel, and gather together the dispersed of Judah from the four corners of the earth.

Is 14:1 For the LORD will have mercy on Jacob, and will yet choose Israel, and set them in their own land: and the strangers shall be joined with them, and they shall cleave to the house of Jacob.

Is 27:13 And it shall come to pass in that day, *that* the great trumpet shall be blown, and they shall come which were ready to perish in the land of Assyria, and the outcasts in the land of Egypt, and shall worship the LORD in the holy mount at Jerusalem.

Is 29:17 *Is* it not yet a very little while, and Lebanon shall be turned into a fruitful field, and the fruitful field shall be esteemed as a forest?

Is 32:16 Then judgment shall dwell in the wilderness, and righteousness remain in the fruitful field.

Is 33:20 Look upon Zion, the city of our solemnities: thine eyes shall see Jerusalem a quiet habitation, a tabernacle *that* shall not be taken down; not one of the stakes thereof shall ever be removed, neither shall any of the cords thereof be broken.

Is 35:1 The wilderness and the solitary place shall be glad for them; and the desert shall rejoice, and blossom as the rose.

Is 40:2 Speak ye comfortably to Jerusalem, and cry unto her, that her warfare is accomplished, that her iniquity is pardoned: for she hath received of the LORD's hand double for all her sins.

Is 41:27 The first *shall say* to Zion, Behold, behold them: and I will give to Jerusalem one that bringeth good tidings.

Is 44:26 That confirmeth the word of his servant, and performeth the counsel of his messengers; that saith to Jerusalem, Thou shalt be inhabited; and to the cities of Judah, Ye shall be built, and I will raise up the decayed places thereof:

Is 49:6 And he said, It is a light thing that thou shouldest be my servant to raise up the tribes of Jacob, and to restore the preserved of Israel: I will also give thee for a light to the Gentiles, that thou mayest be my salvation unto the end of the earth.

Is 49:8 Thus saith the LORD, In an acceptable time have I heard thee, and in a day of salvation have I helped thee: and I will preserve thee, and give thee for a covenant of the people, to establish the earth, to cause to inherit the desolate heritages;

Is 49:22 Thus saith the Lord GOD, Behold, I will lift up mine hand to the Gentiles, and set up my standard to the people: and they shall bring thy sons in *their* arms, and thy daughters shall be carried upon *their* shoulders.

Is 51:3 For the LORD shall comfort Zion: he will comfort all her waste places; and he will make her wilderness like Eden, and her desert like the garden of the LORD; joy and gladness shall be found therein, thanksgiving, and the voice of melody.

Is 54:3 For thou shalt break forth on the right hand and on the left; and thy seed shall inherit the Gentiles, and make the desolate cities to be inhabited.

Is 58:12 And *they that shall be* of thee shall build the old waste places: thou shalt raise up the foundations of many generations; and thou shalt be called, The repairer of the breach, The restorer of paths to dwell in.

Is 60:10 And the sons of strangers shall build up thy walls, and their kings shall minister unto thee: for in my wrath I smote thee, but in my favour have I had mercy on thee.

Is 60:15 Whereas thou hast been forsaken and hated, so that no man went through *thee,* I will make thee an eternal excellency, a joy of many generations.

Is 62:4 Thou shalt no more be termed Forsaken; neither shall thy land any more be termed Desolate: but thou shalt be called Hephzi-bah, and thy land Beulah: for the LORD delighteth in thee, and thy land shall be married.

Je 3:18 In those days the house of Judah shall walk with the house of Israel, and they shall come together out of the land of the north to the land

that I have given for an inheritance unto your fathers.

Je 12:14 Thus saith the LORD against all mine evil neighbours, that touch the inheritance which I have caused my people Israel to inherit; Behold, I will pluck them out of their land, and pluck out the house of Judah from among them.

Je 29:14 And I will be found of you, saith the LORD: and I will turn away your captivity, and I will gather you from all the nations, and from all the places whither I have driven you, saith the LORD; and I will bring you again into the place whence I caused you to be carried away captive.

Je 30:10 Therefore fear thou not, O my servant Jacob, saith the LORD; neither be dismayed, O Israel: for, lo, I will save thee from afar, and thy seed from the land of their captivity; and Jacob shall return, and shall be in rest, and be quiet, and none shall make *him* afraid.

Je 31:4 Again I will build thee, and thou shalt be built, O virgin of Israel: thou shalt again be adorned with thy tabrets, and shalt go forth in the dances of them that make merry.

Je 31:10 Hear the word of the LORD, O ye nations, and declare *it* in the isles afar off, and say, He that scattered Israel will gather him, and keep him, as a shepherd *doth* his flock.

Je 31:23 Thus saith the LORD of hosts, the God of Israel; As yet they shall use this speech in the land of Judah and in the cities thereof, when I shall bring again their captivity; The LORD bless thee, O habitation of justice, *and* mountain of holiness.

Je 31:38 Behold, the days come, saith the LORD, that the city shall be built to the LORD from the tower of Hananeel unto the gate of the corner.

Je 32:15 For thus saith the LORD of hosts, the God of Israel; Houses and fields and vineyards shall be possessed again in this land.

Je 32:41 Yea, I will rejoice over them to do them good, and I will plant them in this land assuredly with my whole heart and with my whole soul.

Je 33:7 And I will cause the captivity of Judah and the captivity of Israel to return, and will build them, as at the first.

Je 33:12 Thus saith the LORD of hosts; Again in this place, which is desolate without man and without beast, and in all the cities thereof, shall be an habitation of shepherds causing *their* flocks to lie down.

Eze 14:22 Yet, behold, therein shall be left a remnant that shall be brought forth, *both* sons and daughters: behold, they shall come forth unto you, and ye shall see their way and their doings: and ye shall be comforted concerning the evil that I have brought upon Jerusalem, *even* concerning all that I have brought upon it.

Eze 20:40 For in mine holy mountain, in the mountain of the height of Israel, saith the Lord GOD, there shall all the house of Israel, all of them in the land, serve me: there will I accept them, and there will I require your offerings, and the firstfruits of your oblations, with all your holy things.

Eze 28:25 Thus saith the Lord GOD; When I shall have gathered the house of Israel from the people among whom they are scattered, and shall be sanctified in them in the sight of the heathen, then shall they dwell in their land that I have given to my servant Jacob.

Eze 29:21 In that day will I cause the horn of the house of Israel to bud forth, and I will give thee the opening of the mouth in the midst of them; and they shall know that I *am* the LORD.

Eze 34:13 And I will bring them out from the people, and gather them from the countries, and will bring them to their own land, and feed them upon the mountains of Israel by the rivers, and in all the inhabited places of the country.

Eze 36:8 But ye, O mountains of Israel, ye shall shoot forth your branches, and yield your fruit to my people of Israel; for they are at hand to come.

Eze 36:35 And they shall say, This land that was desolate is become like the garden of Eden; and the waste and desolate and ruined cities *are become* fenced, *and* are inhabited.

Eze 37:12 Therefore prophesy and say unto them, Thus saith the Lord GOD; Behold, O my people, I will open your graves, and cause you to come up out of your graves, and bring you into the land of Israel.

Eze 38:12 To take a spoil, and to take a prey; to turn thine hand upon the desolate places *that are now* inhabited, and upon the people *that are* gathered out of the nations, which have gotten cattle and goods, that dwell in the midst of the land.

Eze 39:25 Therefore thus saith the Lord GOD; Now will I bring again the captivity of Jacob, and have mercy upon the whole house of Israel, and will be jealous for my holy name;

Da 9:25 Know therefore and understand, *that* from the going forth of the commandment to restore and to build Jerusalem unto the Messiah the Prince *shall be* seven weeks, and threescore and two weeks: the street shall be built again, and the wall, even in troublous times.

Ho 2:15 And I will give her her vineyards from thence, and the valley of Achor for a door of hope: and she shall sing there, as in the days of her youth, and as in the day when she came up out of the land of Egypt.

Ho 11:11 They shall tremble as a bird out of Egypt, and as a dove out of the land of Assyria: and I will place them in their houses, saith the LORD.

Ho 13:14 I will ransom them from the power of the grave; I will redeem them from death: O death, I will be thy plagues; O grave, I will be thy destruction: repentance shall be hid from mine eyes.

Ho 14:7 They that dwell under his shadow shall return; they shall revive *as* the corn, and grow as the vine: the scent thereof *shall be* as the wine of Lebanon.

Jl 3:1 For, behold, in those days, and in that time, when I shall bring again the captivity of Judah and Jerusalem,

Jl 3:7 Behold, I will raise them out of the place whither ye have sold them, and will return your recompence upon your own head:

Am 9:11 In that day will I raise up the tabernacle of David that is fallen, and close up the breaches thereof; and I will raise up his ruins, and I will build it as in the days of old:

Am 9:14 And I will bring again the captivity of my people of Israel, and they shall build the waste cities, and inhabit *them;* and they shall plant vineyards, and drink the wine thereof; they shall also make gardens, and eat the fruit of them.

Obad 17 But upon mount Zion shall be deliverance, and there shall be holiness; and the house of Jacob shall possess their possessions.

Mi 2:12 I will surely assemble, O Jacob, all of thee; I will surely gather the remnant of Israel; I will put them together as the sheep of Bozrah, as the flock in the midst of their fold: they shall make great noise by reason of *the multitude of* men.

Mi 4:6 In that day, saith the LORD, will I assemble her that halteth, and I will gather her that is driven out, and her that I have afflicted;

Mi 7:11 *In* the day that thy walls are to be built, *in* that day shall the decree be far removed.

Zep 2:7 And the coast shall be for the remnant of the house of Judah; they shall feed thereupon: in the houses of Ashkelon shall they lie down in the evening: for the LORD their God shall visit them, and turn away their captivity.

Zep 3:15 The LORD hath taken away thy judgments, he hath cast out thine enemy: the king of Israel, *even* the LORD, *is* in the midst of thee: thou shalt not see evil any more.

Zep 3:20 At that time will I bring you *again,* even in the time that I gather you: for I will make you a name and a praise among all people of the earth, when I turn back your captivity before your eyes, saith the LORD.

Zec 1:17 Cry yet, saying, Thus saith the LORD of hosts; My cities through prosperity shall yet be spread abroad; and the LORD shall yet comfort Zion, and shall yet choose Jerusalem.

Zec 2:4 And said unto him, Run, speak to this young man, saying, Jerusalem shall be inhabited *as* towns without walls for the multitude of men and cattle therein:

Zec 8:7 Thus saith the LORD of hosts; Behold, I will save my people from the east country, and from the west country;

Zec 10:6 And I will strengthen the house of Judah, and I will save the house of Joseph, and I will bring them again to place them; for I have mercy upon them: and they shall be as though I had not cast them off: for I *am* the LORD their God, and will hear them.

Zec 12:6 In that day will I make the governors of Judah like an hearth of fire among the wood, and like a torch of fire in a sheaf; and they shall devour all the people round about, on the right hand and on the left: and Jerusalem shall be inhabited again in her own place, *even* in Jerusalem.

Zec 14:11 And *men* shall dwell in it, and there shall be no more utter destruction; but Jerusalem shall be safely inhabited.

Mal 3:4 Then shall the offering of Judah and Jerusalem be pleasant unto the LORD, as in the days of old, and as in former years.

Ac 3:21 Whom the heaven must receive until the times of restitution of all things, which God hath spoken by the mouth of all his holy prophets since the world began.

Ac 15:16 After this I will return, and will build again the tabernacle of David, which is fallen down; and I will build again the ruins thereof, and I will set it up:

Ro 11:24 For if thou wert cut out of the olive tree which is wild by nature, and wert graffed contrary to nature into a good olive tree: how much more shall these, which be the natural *branches,* be graffed into their own olive tree?

Ro 11:26 And so all Israel shall be saved: as it is written, There shall come out of Sion the Deliverer, and shall turn away ungodliness from Jacob:

See **ISRAEL, MERCY, PARDON, WASTE PLACES**

RESTRAINTS

1. Exercised over the Righteous

1 S 25:39 And when David heard that Nabal was dead, he said, Blessed *be* the LORD, that hath pleaded the cause of my reproach from the hand of Nabal, and hath kept his servant from evil: for the LORD hath returned the wickedness of Nabal upon his own head. And David sent and communed with Abigail, to take her to him to wife.

1 Chr 4:10 And Jabez called on the God of Israel, saying, Oh that thou wouldest bless me indeed, and enlarge my coast, and that thine hand might be with me, and that thou wouldest keep *me* from evil, that it may not grieve me! And God granted him that which he requested.

Ps 19:13 Keep back thy servant also from presumptuous *sins;* let them not have dominion over me: then shall I be upright, and I shall be innocent from the great transgression.

Ps 119:11 Thy word have I hid in mine heart, that I might not sin against thee.

Ps 141:3 Set a watch, O LORD, before my mouth; keep the door of my lips.

Pr 6:24 To keep thee from the evil woman, from the flattery of the tongue of a strange woman.

Lu 11:4 And forgive us our sins; for we also forgive every one that is indebted to us. And lead us not into temptation; but deliver us from evil.

Jn 17:15 I pray not that thou shouldest take them out of the world, but that thou shouldest keep them from the evil.

2. Exercised over the Wicked

2 K 19:28 Because thy rage against me and thy tumult is come up into mine ears, therefore I will put my hook in thy nose, and my bridle in thy lips, and I will turn thee back by the way by which thou camest.

Ps 32:9 Be ye not as the horse, *or* as the mule, *which* have no understanding: whose mouth must be held in with bit and bridle, lest they come near unto thee.

Ps 76:10 Surely the wrath of man shall praise thee: the remainder of wrath shalt thou restrain.

Jn 7:44 And some of them would have taken him; but no man laid hands on him.

2 Ti 3:9 But they shall proceed no further: for their folly shall be manifest unto all *men,* as theirs also was.

See **GOD, WICKED**

RESULTS

Mt 3:8 Bring forth therefore fruits meet for repentance:

Mt 5:16 Let your light so shine before men, that they may see your good works, and glorify your Father which is in heaven.

Mk 4:20 And these are they which are sown on good ground; such as hear the word, and receive *it,* and bring forth fruit, some thirtyfold, some sixty, and some an hundred.

Lu 13:9 And if it bear fruit, *well:* and if not, *then* after that thou shalt cut it down.

Jn 15:8 Herein is my Father glorified, that ye bear much fruit; so shall ye be my disciples.

Jn 15:16 Ye have not chosen me, but I have chosen you, and ordained you, that ye should go and bring forth fruit, and *that* your fruit should remain: that whatsoever ye shall ask of the Father in my name, he may give it you.

Lu 19:23 Wherefore then gavest not thou my money into the bank, that at my coming I might have required mine own with usury?

RESURRECTION, *restoration of bodily life*

1. Promises

Jb 14:14 If a man die, shall he live *again?* all the days of my appointed time will I wait, till my change come.

Ps 49:15 But God will redeem my soul from the power of the grave: for he shall receive me. Selah.

Ps 71:20 *Thou,* which hast shewed me great and sore troubles, shalt quicken me again, and shalt bring me up again from the depths of the earth.

Ec 3:21 Who knoweth the spirit of man that goeth upward, and the spirit of the beast that goeth downward to the earth.

Is 25:8 He will swallow up death in victory; and the Lord God will wipe away tears from off all faces; and the rebuke of his people shall he take away from off all the earth: for the LORD hath spoken *it*.

Da 12:2 And many of them that sleep in the dust of the earth shall awake, some to everlasting life, and some to shame *and* everlasting contempt.

Ho 13:14 I will ransom them from the power of the grave; I will redeem them from death: O death, I will be thy plagues; O grave, I will be thy destruction: repentance shall be hid from mine eyes.

Mt 22:31 But as touching the resurrection of the dead, have ye not read that which was spoken unto you by God, saying,

Mk 12:26 And as touching the dead, that they rise: have ye not read in the book of Moses, how in the bush God spake unto him, saying, I *am* the God of Abraham, and the God of Isaac, and the God of Jacob?

Mk 16:6 And he saith unto them, Be not affrighted: Ye seek Jesus of Nazareth, which was crucified: he is risen; he is not here: behold the place where they laid him.

Lu 14:14 And thou shalt be blessed; for they cannot recompense thee: for thou shalt be recompensed at the resurrection of the just.

Lu 20:37 Now that the dead are raised, even Moses shewed at the bush, when he calleth the Lord the God of Abraham, and the God of Isaac, and the God of Jacob.

Lu 24:6 He is not here, but is risen: remember how he spake unto you when he was yet in Galilee,

Lu 24:26 Ought not Christ to have suffered these things, and to enter into his glory?

Lu 24:46 And said unto them, Thus it is written, and thus it behoved Christ to suffer, and to rise from the dead the third day:

Jn 5:21 For as the Father raiseth up the dead, and quickeneth *them;* even so the Son quickeneth whom he will.

Jn 5:25 Verily, verily, I say unto you, The hour is coming, and now is, when the dead shall hear the voice of the Son of God: and they that hear shall live.

Jn 5:29 And shall come forth; they that have done good, unto the resurrection of life; and they that have done evil, unto the resurrection of damnation.

Jn 6:40 And this is the will of him that sent me, that every one which seeth the Son, and believeth on him, may have everlasting life: and I will raise him up at the last day.

Jn 6:45 It is written in the prophets, And they shall be all taught of God. Every man therefore that hath heard, and hath learned of the Father, cometh unto me.

Jn 6:54 Whoso eateth my flesh, and drinketh my blood, hath eternal life; and I will raise him up at the last day.

Jn 11:25–26 Jesus said unto her, I am the resurrection, and the life: he that believeth in me, though he were dead, yet shall he live:

And whosoever liveth and believeth in me shall never die. Believest thou this?

Ac 23:6 But when Paul perceived that the one part were Sadducees, and the other Pharisees, he cried out in the council, Men *and* brethren, I am a Pharisee, the son of a Pharisee: of the hope and resurrection of the dead I am called in question.

Ac 24:15 And have hope toward God, which they themselves also allow, that there shall be a resurrection of the dead, both of the just and unjust.

Ac 24:21 Except it be for this one voice, that I cried standing among them, Touching the resurrection of the dead I am called in question by you this day.

Ac 26:8 Why should it be thought a thing incredible with you, that God should raise the dead?

Ro 4:17 (As it is written, I have made thee a father of many nations,) before him whom he believed, *even* God, who quickeneth the dead, and calleth those things which be not as though they were.

1 Co 6:14 And God hath both raised up the Lord, and will also raise up us by his own power.

1 Co 15:22 For as in Adam all die, even so in Christ shall all be made alive.

1 Co 15:42 So also *is* the resurrection of the dead. It is sown in corruption; it is raised in incorruption:

1 Co 15:52 In a moment, in the twinkling of an eye, at the last trump: for the trumpet shall sound, and the dead shall be raised incorruptible, and we shall be changed.

1 Co 15:54 So when this corruptible shall have put on incorruption, and this mortal shall have put on immortality, then shall be brought to pass the saying that is written, Death is swallowed up in victory.

2 Co 1:9 But we had the sentence of death in ourselves, that we should not trust in ourselves, but in God which raiseth the dead:

2 Co 4:14 Knowing that he which raised up the Lord Jesus shall raise up us also by Jesus, and shall present *us* with you.

Ph 3:11 If by any means I might attain unto the resurrection of the dead.

1 Th 4:16 For the Lord himself shall descend from heaven with a shout, with the voice of the archangel, and with the trump of God: and the dead in Christ shall rise first:

He 6:2 Of the doctrine of baptisms, and of laying on of hands, and of resurrection of the dead, and of eternal judgment.

He 11:35 Women received their dead raised to life again: and others were tortured, not accepting deliverance; that they might obtain a better resurrection:

Re 20:13 And the sea gave up the dead which were in it; and death and hell delivered up the dead which were in them: and they were judged every man according to their works.

2. Doubts

Jb 14:12; Mt 22:23; Lu 20:27; Ac 17:18, 32; 1 Co 15:12; 2 Ti 2:18

3. Examples

SON OF THE WIDOW OF ZAREPHATH

1 K 17:22

SON OF THE SHUNAMMITE

2 K 4:35

DEAD MAN RESTORED TO LIFE AT TOUCH OF ELISHA'S BONES

2 K 13:21

JAIRUS' DAUGHTER

Mt 9:25; Mk 5:42

SAINTS AT THE TIME OF THE CRUCIFIXION

Mt 27:52

SON OF THE WIDOW OF NAIN

Lu 7:15

LAZARUS OF BETHANY

Jn 11:44

DORCAS

Ac 9:40

4. Of Christ

Ps 16:10 For thou wilt not leave my soul in hell; neither wilt thou suffer thine Holy One to see corruption.

Mt 16:21 From that time forth began Jesus to shew unto his disciples, how that he must go unto Jerusalem, and suffer many things of the elders and chief priests and scribes, and be killed, and be raised again the third day.

Mt 20:19 And shall deliver him to the Gentiles to mock, and to scourge, and to crucify *him:* and the third day he shall rise again.

Mt 26:32 But after I am risen again, I will go before you into Galilee.

Mk 9:9 And as they came down from the mountain, he charged them that they should tell no man what things they had seen, till the Son of man were risen from the dead.

Mk 14:28 But after that I am risen, I will go before you into Galilee.

Jn 2:19 Jesus answered and said unto them, Destroy this temple, and in three days I will raise it up.

Ac 2:31 He seeing this before spake of the resurrection of Christ, that his soul was not left in hell, neither his flesh did see corruption.

Ac 26:22–23 Having therefore obtained help of God, I continue unto this day, witnessing both to small and great, saying none other things than those which the prophets and Moses did say should come:

That Christ should suffer, *and* that he should be the first that should rise from the dead, and should shew light unto the people, and to the Gentiles.

5. Announced by Angels

Mt 28:6 He is not here: for he is risen, as he said. Come, see the place where the Lord lay.

6. Infallible Proofs

Mt 27:66 So they went, and made the sepulchre sure, sealing the stone, and setting a watch.

Lu 24:39–40 Behold my hands and my feet, that it is I myself: handle me, and see; for a spirit hath not flesh and bones, as ye see me have.

And when he had thus spoken, he shewed them *his* hands and *his* feet.

Jn 20:20 And when he had so said, he shewed unto them *his* hands and his side. Then were the disciples glad, when they saw the Lord.

Ac 1:3 To whom also he shewed himself alive after his passion by many infallible proofs, being seen of them forty days, and speaking of the things pertaining to the kingdom of God:

7. Central Truth of the Gospel

Lu 24:34 Saying, The Lord is risen indeed, and hath appeared to Simon.

Jn 2:22 When therefore he was risen from the dead, his disciples remembered that he had said this unto them; and they believed the scripture, and the word which Jesus had said.

Ac 1:22 Beginning from the baptism of John, unto that same day that he was taken up from us, must one be ordained to be a witness with us of his resurrection.

Ac 2:23–24 Him, being delivered by the determinate counsel and foreknowledge of God, ye have taken, and by wicked hands have crucified and slain:

Whom God hath raised up, having loosed the pains of death: because it was not possible that he should be holden of it.

Ac 2:32 This Jesus hath God raised up, whereof we all are witnesses.

Ac 3:14–15 But ye denied the Holy One and the Just, and desired a murderer to be granted unto you;

And killed the Prince of life, whom God hath raised from the dead; whereof we are witnesses.

Ac 3:26 Unto you first God, having raised up his Son Jesus, sent him to bless you, in turning away every one of you from his iniquities.

Ac 4:2 Being grieved that they taught the people, and preached through Jesus the resurrection from the dead.

Ac 4:10 Be it known unto you all, and to all the people of Israel, that by the name of Jesus Christ of Nazareth, whom ye crucified, whom God raised from the dead, *even* by him doth this man stand here before you whole.

Ac 4:33 And with great power gave the apostles witness of the resurrection of the Lord Jesus: and great grace was upon them all.

Ac 5:30 The God of our fathers raised up Jesus, whom ye slew and hanged on a tree.

Ac 10:39–41 And we are witnesses of all things which he did both in the land of the Jews, and in Jerusalem; whom they slew and hanged on a tree:

Him God raised up the third day, and shewed him openly;

Not to all the people, but unto witnesses chosen before of God, *even* to us, who did eat and drink with him after he rose from the dead.

Ac 13:30 But God raised him from the dead:

Ac 17:2–3 And Paul, as his manner was, went in unto them, and three sabbath days reasoned with them out of the scriptures,

Opening and alleging, that Christ must needs have suffered, and risen again from the dead; and that this Jesus, whom I preach unto you, is Christ.

Ac 17:31 Because he hath appointed a day, in the which he will judge the world in righteousness by *that* man whom he hath ordained; *whereof* he hath given assurance unto all *men,* in that he hath raised him from the dead.

Ro 1:4 And declared *to be* the Son of God with power, according to the spirit of holiness, by the resurrection from the dead:

Ro 6:4 Therefore we are buried with him by baptism into death: that like as Christ was raised up from the dead by the glory of the Father, even so we also should walk in newness of life.

1 Co 15:14 And if Christ be not risen, then *is* our preaching vain, and your faith *is* also vain.

Re 1:18 I *am* he that liveth, and was dead; and, behold, I am alive for evermore, Amen; and have the keys of hell and of death.

Re 2:8 And unto the angel of the church in Smyrna write; These things saith the first and the last, which was dead, and is alive;

8. Emphasized in the Epistles

Ro 1:4 And declared *to be* the Son of God with power, according to the spirit of holiness, by the resurrection from the dead:

Ro 4:25 Who was delivered for our offences, and was raised again for our justification.

Ro 6:9 Knowing that Christ being raised from the dead dieth no more; death hath no more dominion over him.

Ro 7:4 Wherefore, my brethren, ye also are become dead to the law by the body of Christ; that ye should be married to another, *even* to him who is raised from the dead, that we should bring forth fruit unto God.

Ro 8:11 But if the Spirit of him that raised up Jesus from the dead dwell in you, he that raised up Christ from the

dead shall also quicken your mortal bodies by his Spirit that dwelleth in you.

Ro 8:34 Who *is* he that condemneth? *It is* Christ that died, yea rather, that is risen again, who is even at the right hand of God, who also maketh intercession for us.

Ro 10:9 That if thou shalt confess with thy mouth the Lord Jesus, and shalt believe in thine heart that God hath raised him from the dead, thou shalt be saved.

Ro 14:9 For to this end Christ both died, and rose, and revived, that he might be Lord both of the dead and living.

1 Co 6:14 And God hath both raised up the Lord, and will also raise up us by his own power.

1 Co 15:4 And that he was buried, and that he rose again the third day according to the scriptures:

1 Co 15:17 And if Christ be not raised, your faith *is* vain; ye are yet in your sins.

2 Co 4:14 Knowing that he which raised up the Lord Jesus shall raise up us also by Jesus, and shall present *us* with you.

2 Co 5:15 And *that* he died for all, that they which live should not henceforth live unto themselves, but unto him which died for them, and rose again.

2 Co 13:4 For though he was crucified through weakness, yet he liveth by the power of God. For we also are weak in him, but we shall live with him by the power of God toward you.

Ga 1:1 Paul, an apostle, (not of men, neither by man, but by Jesus Christ, and God the Father, who raised him from the dead;)

Ep 1:20 Which he wrought in Christ, when he raised him from the dead, and set *him* at his own right hand in the heavenly *places,*

Col 1:18 And he is the head of the body, the church: who is the beginning, the firstborn from the dead; that in all *things* he might have the preeminence.

Col 2:13 And you, being dead in your sins and the uncircumcision of your flesh, hath he quickened together with him, having forgiven you all trespasses;

1 Th 1:10 And to wait for his Son from heaven, whom he raised from the dead, *even* Jesus, which delivered us from the wrath to come.

1 Th 4:14 For if we believe that Jesus died and rose again, even so them also which sleep in Jesus will God bring with him.

2 Ti 2:8 Remember that Jesus Christ of the seed of David was raised from the dead according to my gospel:

He 13:20 Now the God of peace, that brought again from the dead our Lord Jesus, that great shepherd of the sheep, through the blood of the everlasting covenant,

1 Pe 1:3 Blessed *be* the God and Father of our Lord Jesus Christ, which according to his abundant mercy hath begotten us again unto a lively hope by the resurrection of Jesus Christ from the dead,

1 Pe 1:21 Who by him do believe in God, that raised him up from the dead, and gave him glory; that your faith and hope might be in God.

1 Pe 3:18 For Christ also hath once suffered for sins, the just for the unjust, that he might bring us to God, being put to death in the flesh, but quickened by the Spirit:

1 Pe 3:21 The like figure whereunto *even* baptism doth also now save us (not the putting away of the filth of the flesh, but the answer of a good conscience toward God,) by the resurrection of Jesus Christ:

9. Appearances of Christ after His Resurrection

TO MARY MAGDALENE

Mk 16:9 Now when *Jesus* was risen early the first *day* of the week, he appeared first to Mary Magdalene, out of whom he had cast seven devils.

TO THE OTHER WOMEN

Mt 28:9 And as they went to tell his disciples, behold, Jesus met them, saying, All hail. And they came and held him by the feet, and worshipped him.

TO TWO DISCIPLES

Lu 24:15 And it came to pass, that, while they communed *together* and reasoned, Jesus himself drew near, and went with them.

TO THE ELEVEN DISCIPLES

Lu 24:36 And as they thus spake, Jesus himself stood in the midst of them, and saith unto them, Peace *be* unto you.

TO PETER

1 Co 15:5 And that he was seen of Cephas, then of the twelve:

TO THE TEN, THOMAS ABSENT

Jn 20:19 Then the same day at evening, being the first *day* of the week, when the doors were shut where the disciples were assembled for fear of the Jews, came Jesus and stood in the midst, and saith unto them, Peace *be* unto you.

TO THE ELEVEN DISCIPLES

Jn 20:26 And after eight days again his disciples were within, and Thomas with them: *then* came Jesus, the doors being shut, and stood in the midst, and said, Peace *be* unto you.

AT THE SEA OF GALILEE

Jn 21:1 After these things Jesus shewed himself again to the disciples at the sea of Tiberias; and on this wise shewed he *himself*.

TO FIVE HUNDRED BRETHREN

1 Co 15:6 After that, he was seen of above five hundred brethren at once; of whom the greater part remain unto this present, but some are fallen asleep.

TO ELEVEN DISCIPLES IN GALILEE

Mt 28:17 And when they saw him, they worshipped him: but some doubted.

TO JAMES

1 Co 15:7 After that, he was seen of James; then of all the apostles.

AT THE TIME OF HIS ASCENSION

Lu 24:50 And he led them out as far as to Bethany, and he lifted up his hands, and blessed them.

TO PAUL AT HIS CONVERSION

Ac 9:5 And he said, Who art thou, Lord? And the Lord said, I am Jesus whom thou persecutest: *it is* hard for thee to kick against the pricks.

1 Co 15:8 And last of all he was seen of me also, as of one born out of due time.

10. Of All People

Da 12:2 And many of them that sleep in the dust of the earth shall awake, some to everlasting life, and some to shame *and* everlasting contempt.

Lu 20:35 But they which shall be accounted worthy to obtain that world, and the resurrection from the dead, neither marry, nor are given in marriage:

Jn 5:28–29 Marvel not at this: for the hour is coming, in the which all that are in the graves shall hear his voice,

And shall come forth; they that have done good, unto the resurrection of life; and they that have done evil, unto the resurrection of damnation.

Jn 11:24 Martha saith unto him, I know that he shall rise again in the resurrection at the last day.

Ac 24:15 And have hope toward God, which they themselves also allow, that there shall be a resurrection of the dead, both of the just and unjust.

Re 20:13 And the sea gave up the dead which were in it; and death and hell delivered up the dead which were in them: and they were judged every man according to their works.

See **CHRIST, DEATH, FUTURE LIFE**

RETALIATION, *returning evil for evil*

1. Forbidden

Le 19:18 Thou shalt not avenge, nor bear any grudge against the children of thy people, but thou shalt love thy neighbour as thyself: I *am* the LORD.

Ps 41:10 But thou, O LORD, be merciful unto me, and raise me up, that I may requite them.

Pr 20:22 Say not thou, I will recompense evil; *but* wait on the LORD, and he shall save thee.

Pr 24:29 Say not, I will do so to him as he hath done to me: I will render to the man according to his work.

Mt 5:39 But I say unto you, That ye resist not evil: but whosoever shall smite thee on thy right cheek, turn to him the other also.

Ro 12:17 Recompense to no man evil for evil. Provide things honest in the sight of all men.

1 Th 5:15 See that none render evil for evil unto any *man*; but ever follow that which is good, both among yourselves, and to all *men*.

1 Pe 3:9 Not rendering evil for evil, or railing for railing: but contrariwise blessing; knowing that ye are thereunto called, that ye should inherit a blessing.

2. Examples

Ge 34:27; Jud 8:7; 15:5, 7; 16:28; 1 S 11:12; 25:22; 2 S 3:27; 14:30; 21:6; 1 K 2:9; Est 9:5, 16; Mt 26:51; Lu 9:54

See **FORGIVENESS, MEEKNESS, REVENGE**

RETRIBUTION, *punishment*

1. Threatened

Ex 20:5 Thou shalt not bow down thyself to them, nor serve them: for I the LORD thy God *am* a jealous God, visiting the iniquity of the fathers upon the children unto the third and fourth *generation* of them that hate me;

Ex 32:34 Therefore now go, lead the people unto *the place* of which I have spoken unto thee: behold, mine Angel shall go before thee: nevertheless in the day when I visit I will visit their sin upon them.

Le 18:25 And the land is defiled: therefore I do visit the iniquity thereof upon it, and the land itself vomiteth out her inhabitants.

De 5:9 Thou shalt not bow down thyself unto them, nor serve them: for

I the LORD thy God *am* a jealous God, visiting the iniquity of the fathers upon the children unto the third and fourth *generation* of them that hate me,

De 7:10 And repayeth them that hate him to their face, to destroy them: he will not be slack to him that hateth him, he will repay him to his face.

De 32:23 I will heap mischiefs upon them; I will spend mine arrows upon them.

De 32:42 I will make mine arrows drunk with blood, and my sword shall devour flesh; *and that* with the blood of the slain and of the captives, from the beginning of revenges upon the enemy.

Jud 20:41 And when the men of Israel turned again, the men of Benjamin were amazed: for they saw that evil was come upon them.

2 S 12:10 Now therefore the sword shall never depart from thine house; because thou hast despised me, and hast taken the wife of Uriah the Hittite to be thy wife.

2 S 15:30 And David went up by the ascent of *mount* Olivet, and wept as he went up, and had his head covered, and he went barefoot: and all the people that *was* with him covered every man his head, and they went up, weeping as they went up.

1 K 9:9 And they shall answer, Because they forsook the LORD their God, who brought forth their fathers out of the land of Egypt, and have taken hold upon other gods, and have worshipped them, and served them: therefore hath the LORD brought upon them all this evil.

1 K 13:24 And when he was gone, a lion met him by the way, and slew him: and his carcase was cast in the way, and the ass stood by it, the lion also stood by the carcase.

1 K 14:10 Therefore, behold, I will bring evil upon the house of Jeroboam, and will cut off from Jeroboam him that pisseth against the wall, *and* him that is shut up and left in Israel, and will take away the remnant of the house of Jeroboam, as a

man taketh away dung, till it be all gone.

1 K 15:30 Because of the sins of Jeroboam which he sinned, and which he made Israel sin, by his provocation wherewith he provoked the LORD God of Israel to anger.

1 K 21:19 And thou shalt speak unto him, saying, Thus saith the LORD, Hast thou killed, and also taken possession? And thou shalt speak unto him, saying, Thus saith the LORD, In the place where dogs licked the blood of Naboth shall dogs lick thy blood, even thine.

1 K 22:38 And *one* washed the chariot in the pool of Samaria; and the dogs licked up his blood; and they washed his armour; according unto the word of the LORD which he spake.

2 K 21:12 Therefore thus saith the LORD God of Israel, Behold, I *am* bringing *such* evil upon Jerusalem and Judah, that whosoever heareth of it, both his ears shall tingle.

2 Chr 6:23 Then hear thou from heaven, and do, and judge thy servants, by requiting the wicked, by recompensing his way upon his own head; and by justifying the righteous, by giving him according to his righteousness.

Ne 13:18 Did not your fathers thus, and did not our God bring all this evil upon us, and upon this city? yet ye bring more wrath upon Israel by profaning the sabbath.

Ps 7:16 His mischief shall return upon his own head, and his violent dealing shall come down upon his own pate.

Ps 37:15 Their sword shall enter into their own heart, and their bows shall be broken.

Pr 1:31 Therefore shall they eat of the fruit of their own way, and be filled with their own devices.

Pr 7:23 Till a dart strike through his liver; as a bird hasteth to the snare, and knoweth not that it *is* for his life.

Is 33:1 Woe to thee that spoilest, and thou *wast* not spoiled; and dealest not treacherously, and they dealt not treacherously with thee! when thou shalt cease to spoil, thou shalt be spoiled; *and* when thou shalt make an end to deal treacherously, they shall deal treacherously with thee.

Is 51:23 But I will put it into the hand of them that afflict thee; which have said to thy soul, Bow down, that we may go over: and thou hast laid thy body as the ground, and as the street, to them that went over.

Is 65:6 Behold, *it is* written before me: I will not keep silence, but will recompense, even recompense into their bosom,

Is 66:6 A voice of noise from the city, a voice from the temple, a voice of the LORD that rendereth recompence to his enemies.

Is 66:17 They that sanctify themselves, and purify themselves in the gardens behind one *tree* in the midst, eating swine's flesh, and the abomination, and the mouse, shall be consumed together, saith the LORD.

Je 23:2 Therefore thus saith the LORD God of Israel against the pastors that feed my people; Ye have scattered my flock, and driven them away, and have not visited them: behold, I will visit upon you the evil of your doings, saith the LORD.

Je 50:15 Shout against her round about: she hath given her hand: her foundations are fallen, her walls are thrown down: for it *is* the vengeance of the LORD: take vengeance upon her; as she hath done, do unto her.

Je 51:56 Because the spoiler is come upon her, *even* upon Babylon, and her mighty men are taken, every one of their bows is broken: for the LORD God of recompences shall surely requite.

Lam 4:13 For the sins of her prophets, *and* the iniquities of her priests, that have shed the blood of the just in the midst of her,

Eze 17:18 Seeing he despised the oath by breaking the covenant, when, lo, he had given his hand, and hath done all these *things,* he shall not escape.

Eze 35:6 Therefore, *as* I live, saith the Lord GOD, I will prepare thee unto blood, and blood shall pursue thee: sith thou hast not hated blood, even blood shall pursue thee.

Eze 39:10 So that they shall take no wood out of the field, neither cut down *any* out of the forests; for they shall burn the weapons with fire: and they shall spoil those that spoiled them, and rob those that robbed them, saith the Lord GOD.

Eze 39:23 And the heathen shall know that the house of Israel went into captivity for their iniquity: because they trespassed against me, therefore hid I my face from them, and gave them into the hand of their enemies: so fell they all by the sword.

Da 9:7 O Lord, righteousness *belongeth* unto thee, but unto us confusion of faces, as at this day; to the men of Judah, and to the inhabitants of Jerusalem, and unto all Israel, *that are* near, and *that are* far off, through all the countries whither thou hast driven them, because of their trespass that they have trespassed against thee.

Da 9:12 And he hath confirmed his words, which he spake against us, and against our judges that judged us, by bringing upon us a great evil: for under the whole heaven hath not been done as hath been done upon Jerusalem.

Ho 1:4 And the LORD said unto him, Call his name Jezreel; for yet a little *while,* and I will avenge the blood of Jezreel upon the house of Jehu, and will cause to cease the kingdom of the house of Israel.

Ho 6:11 Also, O Judah, he hath set an harvest for thee, when I returned the captivity of my people.

Ho 8:3 Israel hath cast off *the thing that is* good: the enemy shall pursue him.

Ho 10:15 So shall Bethel do unto you because of your great wickedness: in a morning shall the king of Israel utterly be cut off.

Jl 3:8 And I will sell your sons and your daughters into the hand of the children of Judah, and they shall sell them to the Sabeans, to a people far off: for the LORD hath spoken *it.*

Am 5:27 Therefore will I cause you to go into captivity beyond Damascus, saith the LORD, whose name *is* The God of hosts.

Obad 10 For *thy* violence against thy brother Jacob shame shall cover thee, and thou shalt be cut off for ever.

Obad 15 For the day of the LORD *is* near upon all the heathen: as thou hast done, it shall be done unto thee: thy reward shall return upon thine own head.

Mi 1:5 For the transgression of Jacob *is* all this, and for the sins of the house of Israel. What *is* the transgression of Jacob? *is it* not Samaria? and what *are* the high places of Judah? *are they* not Jerusalem?

Mi 1:12 For the inhabitant of Maroth waited carefully for good: but evil came down from the LORD unto the gate of Jerusalem.

Mi 2:3 Therefore thus saith the LORD; Behold, against this family do I devise an evil, from which ye shall not remove your necks; neither shall ye go haughtily: for this time *is* evil.

Hab 2:8 Because thou hast spoiled many nations, all the remnant of the people shall spoil thee; because of men's blood, and *for* the violence of the land, of the city, and of all that dwell therein.

Zep 1:17 And I will bring distress upon men, that they shall walk like blind men, because they have sinned against the LORD: and their blood shall be poured out as dust, and their flesh as the dung.

Zec 7:12 Yea, they made their hearts *as* an adamant stone, lest they should hear the law, and the words which the LORD of hosts hath sent in his spirit by the former prophets: therefore came a great wrath from the LORD of hosts.

Zec 8:14 For thus saith the LORD of hosts; As I thought to punish you, when your fathers provoked me to wrath, saith the LORD of hosts, and I repented not:

Mt 18:34 And his lord was wroth, and delivered him to the tormentors, till he should pay all that was due unto him.

Mt 23:35 That upon you may come all the righteous blood shed upon the earth, from the blood of righteous Abel unto the blood of Zacharias son

of Barachias, whom ye slew between the temple and the altar.

Ac 13:40 Beware therefore, lest that come upon you, which is spoken of in the prophets;

He 10:30 For we know him that hath said, Vengeance *belongeth* unto me, I will recompense, saith the Lord. And again, The Lord shall judge his people.

2. Examples

Ge 19:28 And he looked toward Sodom and Gomorrah, and toward all the land of the plain, and beheld, and, lo, the smoke of the country went up as the smoke of a furnace.

Ge 42:17 And he put them all together into ward three days.

Ge 42:28 And he said unto his brethren, My money is restored; and, lo, *it is* even in my sack: and their heart failed *them*, and they were afraid, saying one to another, What *is* this *that* God hath done unto us?

Ex 12:36 And the LORD gave the people favour in the sight of the Egyptians, so that they lent unto them *such things as they required*. And they spoiled the Egyptians.

Nu 31:2 Avenge the children of Israel of the Midianites: afterward shalt thou be gathered unto thy people.

De 19:19 Then shall ye do unto him, as he had thought to have done unto his brother: so shalt thou put the evil away from among you.

Jos 7:25 And Joshua said, Why hast thou troubled us? the LORD shall trouble thee this day. And all Israel stoned him with stones, and burned them with fire, after they had stoned them with stones.

Jud 1:7 And Adoni-bezek said, Threescore and ten kings, having their thumbs and their great toes cut off, gathered *their meat* under my table: as I have done, so God hath requited me. And they brought him to Jerusalem, and there he died.

Jud 8:19 And he said, They *were* my brethren, *even* the sons of my mother: *as* the LORD liveth, if ye had saved them alive, I would not slay you.

Jud 9:24 That the cruelty *done* to the threescore and ten sons of Jerubbaal might come, and their blood be laid upon Abimelech their brother, which slew them; and upon the men of Shechem, which aided him in the killing of his brethren.

Jud 9:56 Thus God rendered the wickedness of Abimelech, which he did unto his father, in slaying his seventy brethren:

Jud 15:6 Then the Philistines said, Who hath done this? And they answered, Samson, the son in law of the Timnite, because he had taken his wife, and given her to his companion. And the Philistines came up, and burnt her and her father with fire.

Jud 16:30 And Samson said, Let me die with the Philistines. And he bowed himself with *all his* might; and the house fell upon the lords, and upon all the people that *were* therein. So the dead which he slew at his death were more than *they* which he slew in his life.

1 S 15:33 And Samuel said, As thy sword hath made women childless, so shall thy mother be childless among women. And Samuel hewed Agag in pieces before the LORD in Gilgal.

1 S 25:39 And when David heard that Nabal was dead, he said, Blessed *be* the LORD, that hath pleaded the cause of my reproach from the hand of Nabal, and hath kept his servant from evil: for the LORD hath returned the wickedness of Nabal upon his own head. And David sent and communed with Abigail, to take her to him to wife.

2 S 1:15 And David called one of the young men, and said, Go near, *and* fall upon him. And he smote him that he died.

2 S 4:12 And David commanded his young men, and they slew them, and cut off their hands and their feet, and hanged *them* up over the pool in Hebron. But they took the head of Ishbosheth, and buried *it* in the sepulchre of Abner in Hebron.

2 S 17:14 And Absalom and all the men of Israel said, The counsel of Hushai the Archite *is* better than the counsel of Ahithophel. For the LORD had appointed to defeat the good counsel of Ahithophel, to the intent that the LORD might bring evil upon Absalom.

2 S 18:17 And they took Absalom, and cast him into a great pit in the wood, and laid a very great heap of stones upon him: and all Israel fled every one to his tent.

2 S 21:6 Let seven men of his sons be delivered unto us, and we will hang them up unto the LORD in Gibeah of Saul, *whom* the LORD did choose. And the king said, I will give *them*.

1 K 2:9 Now therefore hold him not guiltless: for thou *art* a wise man, and knowest what thou oughtest to do unto him; but his hoar head bring thou down to the grave with blood.

1 K 2:25 And king Solomon sent by the hand of Benaiah the son of Jehoiada; and he fell upon him that he died.

1 K 2:32 And the LORD shall return his blood upon his own head, who fell upon two men more righteous and better than he, and slew them with the sword, my father David not knowing *thereof, to wit*, Abner the son of Ner, captain of the host of Israel, and Amasa the son of Jether, captain of the host of Judah.

1 K 2:44 The king said moreover to Shimei, Thou knowest all the wickedness which thine heart is privy to, that thou didst to David my father: therefore the LORD shall return thy wickedness upon thine own head;

2 K 9:26 Surely I have seen yesterday the blood of Naboth, and the blood of his sons, saith the LORD; and I will requite thee in this plat, saith the LORD. Now therefore take *and* cast him into the plat *of ground*, according to the word of the LORD.

2 K 11:16 And they laid hands on her; and she went by the way by the which the horses came into the king's house: and there was she slain.

2 K 21:24 And the people of the land slew all them that had conspired against king Amon; and the people of the land made Josiah his son king in his stead.

2 Chr 22:7 And the destruction of Ahaziah was of God by coming to

Joram: for when he was come, he went out with Jehoram against Jehu the son of Nimshi, whom the LORD had anointed to cut off the house of Ahab.

2 Chr 25:3 Now it came to pass, when the kingdom was established to him, that he slew his servants that had killed the king his father.

2 Chr 33:25 But the people of the land slew all them that had conspired against king Amon; and the people of the land made Josiah his son king in his stead.

Est 7:10 So they hanged Haman on the gallows that he had prepared for Mordecai. Then was the king's wrath pacified.

Est 9:25 But when *Esther* came before the king, he commanded by letters that his wicked device, which he devised against the Jews, should return upon his own head, and that he and his sons should be hanged on the gallows.

Jb 4:8 Even as I have seen, they that plow iniquity, and sow wickedness, reap the same.

Ps 9:16 The LORD is known *by* the judgment *which* he executeth: the wicked is snared in the work of his own hands. Higgaion. Selah.

Ps 35:8 Let destruction come upon him at unawares; and let his net that he hath hid catch himself: into that very destruction let him fall.

Ps 109:18 As he clothed himself with cursing like as with his garment, so let it come into his bowels like water, and like oil into his bones.

Ps 141:10 Let the wicked fall into their own nets, whilst that I withal escape.

Pr 11:17 The merciful man doeth good to his own soul: but *he that is* cruel troubleth his own flesh.

Pr 11:27 He that diligently seeketh good procureth favour: but he that seeketh mischief, it shall come unto him.

Pr 26:27 Whoso diggeth a pit shall fall therein: and he that rolleth a stone, it will return upon him.

Ec 10:8 He that diggeth a pit shall fall into it; and whoso breaketh an hedge, a serpent shall bite him.

Je 2:17 Hast thou not procured this unto thyself, in that thou hast forsaken the LORD thy God, when he led thee by the way?

Je 13:22 And if thou say in thine heart, Wherefore come these things upon me? For the greatness of thine iniquity are thy skirts discovered, *and* thy heels made bare.

Je 40:3 Now the LORD hath brought *it,* and done according as he hath said: because ye have sinned against the LORD, and have not obeyed his voice, therefore this thing is come upon you.

Eze 31:11 I have therefore delivered him into the hand of the mighty one of the heathen; he shall surely deal with him: I have driven him out for his wickedness.

Eze 35:15 As thou didst rejoice at the inheritance of the house of Israel, because it was desolate, so will I do unto thee: thou shalt be desolate, O mount Seir, and all Idumea, *even* all of it: and they shall know that I *am* the LORD.

Da 6:24 And the king commanded, and they brought those men which had accused Daniel, and they cast *them* into the den of lions, them, their children, and their wives; and the lions had the mastery of them, and brake all their bones in pieces or ever they came at the bottom of the den.

Jona 1:15 So they took up Jonah, and cast him forth into the sea: and the sea ceased from her raging.

Ac 1:18 Now this man purchased a field with the reward of iniquity; and falling headlong, he burst asunder in the midst, and all his bowels gushed out.

See **JUDGMENTS, PUNISHMENT, WRATH**

REUBEN, *son of Jacob and Leah*

Ge 29:32; 30:14; 35:22; 37:21; 42:22, 37; 46:8; 49:3; Ex 1:2; 6:14; Nu 1:5, 20; 2:10; 10:18; 13:4; 26:5; 32:1, 25, 33; 34:14; De 3:12; 33:6; Jos 12:6; 13:8, 15, 23; 18:17; 21:7, 36; 22:9; 1 Chr 2:1; 5:1, 18; 6:63, 78; 12:37; Eze 48:7, 31; Re 7:5

REVELATION

Author: The apostle John.

Date Written: Uncertain; according to traditional opinion, about A.D. 96. The place was probably the Island of Patmos, off the western coast of Asia Minor, where John was banished because of the Word of God and of the testimony of Jesus (1:2).

Purpose: To give hope to Christians, especially those who suffer, by revealing Jesus Christ as the ultimate victorious King of Kings and Lord of Lords (19:16). The book manifests its own authority in declaring itself to be the revelation of Jesus Christ (1:1).

To Whom Written: The seven churches of Asia Minor.

Main Theme: Moral and spiritual conflict.

Key Words: Revelation of Jesus Christ (1:1).

Key Verses: 1:19; 19:11–16.

REVELATIONS, *God's means of communicating with humans*

1. Divine

Ge 18:17 And the LORD said, Shall I hide from Abraham that thing which I do;

Ge 40:8 And they said unto him, We have dreamed a dream, and *there is* no interpreter of it. And Joseph said unto them, *Do* not interpretations *belong* to God? tell me *them,* I pray you.

Ge 41:25 And Joseph said unto Pharaoh, The dream of Pharaoh *is* one: God hath shewed Pharaoh what he *is* about to do.

Ge 41:39 And Pharaoh said unto Joseph, Forasmuch as God hath shewed thee all this, *there is* none so discreet and wise as thou *art:*

Nu 12:6 And he said, Hear now my words: If there be a prophet among you, *I* the LORD will make myself known unto him in a vision, *and* will speak unto him in a dream.

De 29:29 The secret *things belong* unto the LORD our God: but *those things which* are revealed *belong* unto us and to our children for ever, that *we* may do all the words of this law.

Jud 13:23 But his wife said unto him, If the LORD were pleased to kill us, he would not have received a burnt offering and a meat offering at our hands, neither would he have shewed us all these *things,* nor would as at this time have told us *such things* as these.

1 S 3:7 Now Samuel did not yet know the LORD, neither was the word of the LORD yet revealed unto him.

1 S 3:21 And the LORD appeared again in Shiloh: for the LORD revealed himself to Samuel in Shiloh by the word of the LORD.

1 S 9:15 Now the LORD had told Samuel in his ear a day before Saul came, saying,

2 S 7:4 And it came to pass that night, that the word of the LORD came unto Nathan, saying,

2 S 7:21 For thy word's sake, and according to thine own heart, hast thou done all these great things, to make thy servant know *them.*

2 S 7:27 For thou, O LORD of hosts, God of Israel, hast revealed to thy servant, saying, I will build thee an house: therefore hath thy servant found in his heart to pray this prayer unto thee.

1 K 14:5 And the LORD said unto Ahijah, Behold, the wife of Jeroboam cometh to ask a thing of thee for her son; for he is sick: thus and thus shalt thou say unto her: for it shall be, when she cometh in, that she shall feign herself *to be* another *woman.*

1 K 18:1 And it came to pass *after* many days, that the word of the LORD came to Elijah in the third year, saying, Go, shew thyself unto Ahab; and I will send rain upon the earth.

2 K 2:3 And the sons of the prophets that *were* at Bethel came forth to Elisha, and said unto him, Knowest thou that the LORD will take away thy master from thy head to day? And he said, Yea, I know *it;* hold ye your peace.

2 K 8:13 And Hazael said, But what, *is* thy servant a dog, that he should do this great thing? And Elisha answered, The LORD hath shewed me that thou *shalt be* king over Syria.

1 Chr 17:19 O LORD, for thy servant's sake, and according to thine own heart, hast thou done all this greatness, in making known all these great things.

Ps 25:14 The secret of the LORD *is* with them that fear him; and he will shew them his covenant.

Ps 98:2 The LORD hath made known his salvation: his righteousness hath he openly shewed in the sight of the heathen.

Ps 103:7 He made known his ways unto Moses, his acts unto the children of Israel.

Ps 111:6 He hath shewed his people the power of his works, that he may give them the heritage of the heathen.

Ps 147:19 He sheweth his word unto Jacob, his statutes and his judgments unto Israel.

Pr 3:32 For the froward *is* abomination to the LORD: but his secret *is* with the righteous.

Is 22:14 And it was revealed in mine ears by the LORD of hosts, Surely this iniquity shall not be purged from you till ye die, saith the Lord GOD of hosts.

Is 48:6 Thou hast heard, see all this; and will not ye declare *it?* I have shewed thee new things from this time, even hidden things, and thou didst not know them.

Je 33:6 Behold, I will bring it health and cure, and I will cure them, and will reveal unto them the abundance of peace and truth.

Je 38:21 But if thou refuse to go forth, this *is* the word that the LORD hath shewed me:

Eze 11:25 Then I spake unto them of the captivity all the things that the LORD had shewed me.

Eze 40:4 And the man said unto me, Son of man, behold with thine eyes, and hear with thine ears, and set thine heart upon all that I shall shew thee; for to the intent that I might shew *them* unto thee *art* thou brought hither: declare all that thou seest to the house of Israel.

Da 2:19 Then was the secret revealed unto Daniel in a night vision. Then Daniel blessed the God of heaven.

Da 2:22 He revealeth the deep and secret things: he knoweth what *is* in the darkness, and the light dwelleth with him.

Da 2:28 But there is a God in heaven that revealeth secrets, and maketh known to the king Nebuchadnezzar what shall be in the latter days. Thy dream, and the visions of thy head upon thy bed, are these;

Da 2:45 Forasmuch as thou sawest that the stone was cut out of the mountain without hands, and that it brake in pieces the iron, the brass, the clay, the silver, and the gold; the great God hath made known to the king what shall come to pass hereafter: and the dream is certain, and the interpretation thereof sure.

Da 2:47 The king answered unto Daniel, and said, Of a truth *it is,* that your God is a God of gods, and a Lord of kings, and a revealer of secrets, seeing thou couldst reveal this secret.

Da 7:16 I came near unto one of them that stood by, and asked him the truth of all this. So he told me, and made me know the interpretation of the things.

Da 8:17 So he came near where I stood: and when he came, I was afraid, and fell upon my face: but he said unto me, Understand, O son of man: for at the time of the end *shall be* the vision.

Da 9:23 At the beginning of thy supplications the commandment came forth, and I am come to shew *thee;* for thou *art* greatly beloved: therefore understand the matter, and consider the vision.

Da 10:1 In the third year of Cyrus king of Persia a thing was revealed unto Daniel, whose name was call and the thing *was* true, but the time appointed *was* long: and he understood the thing, and had understanding of the vision.

Da 10:11 And he said unto me, O Daniel, a man greatly beloved, understand the words that I speak unto thee, and stand upright: for unto thee am I now sent. And when he had spoken this word unto me, I stood trembling.

Da 10:14 Now I am come to make thee understand what shall befall thy people in the latter days: for yet the vision *is* for *many* days.

Da 11:2 And now will I shew thee the truth. Behold, there shall stand up yet three kings in Persia; and the fourth shall be far richer than *they* all: and by his strength through his riches he shall stir up all against the realm of Grecia.

Am 3:7 Surely the Lord GOD will do nothing, but he revealeth his secret unto his servants the prophets.

Am 7:4 Thus hath the Lord GOD shewed unto me: and, behold, the Lord God called to contend by fire, and it devoured the great deep, and did eat up a part.

Hab 3:2 O LORD, I have heard thy speech, *and* was afraid: O LORD, revive thy work in the midst of the years, in the midst of the years make known; in wrath remember mercy.

Zec 1:9 Then said I, O my lord, what *are* these? And the angel that talked with me said unto me, I will shew thee what these *be*.

Mt 11:25 At that time Jesus answered and said, I thank thee, O Father, Lord of heaven and earth, because thou hast hid these things from the wise and prudent, and hast revealed them unto babes.

Mt 16:17 And Jesus answered and said unto him, Blessed art thou, Simon Barjona: for flesh and blood hath not revealed *it* unto thee, but my Father which is in heaven.

Mk 4:11 And he said unto them, Unto you it is given to know the mystery of the kingdom of God: but unto them that are without, all these *things* are done in parables:

Lu 2:15 And it came to pass, as the angels were gone away from them into heaven, the shepherds said one to another, Let us now go even unto Bethlehem, and see this thing which is come to pass, which the Lord hath made known unto us.

Lu 2:26 And it was revealed unto him by the Holy Ghost, that he should not see death, before he had seen the Lord's Christ.

Lu 10:21–22 In that hour Jesus rejoiced in spirit, and said, I thank thee, O Father, Lord of heaven and earth, that thou hast hid these things from the wise and prudent, and hast revealed them unto babes: even so, Father; for so it seemed good in thy sight.

All things are delivered to me of my Father: and no man knoweth who the Son is, but the Father; and who the Father is, but the Son, and *he* to whom the Son will reveal *him*.

Jn 4:26 Jesus saith unto her, I that speak unto thee am *he*.

Jn 9:37 And Jesus said unto him, Thou hast both seen him, and it is he that talketh with thee.

Jn 15:15 Henceforth I call you not servants; for the servant knoweth not what his lord doeth: but I have called you friends; for all things that I have heard of my Father I have made known unto you.

Jn 16:13 Howbeit when he, the Spirit of truth, is come, he will guide you into all truth: for he shall not speak of himself; but whatsoever he shall hear, *that* shall he speak: and he will shew you things to come.

Ac 21:11 And when he was come unto us, he took Paul's girdle, and bound his own hands and feet, and said, Thus saith the Holy Ghost, So shall the Jews at Jerusalem bind the man that owneth this girdle, and shall deliver *him* into the hands of the Gentiles.

Ac 22:14 And he said, The God of our fathers hath chosen thee, that thou shouldest know his will, and see that Just One, and shouldest hear the voice of his mouth.

Ro 16:26 But now is made manifest, and by the scriptures of the prophets, according to the commandment of the everlasting God, made known to all nations for the obedience of faith:

1 Co 2:9–10 But as it is written, Eye hath not seen, nor ear heard, neither have entered into the heart of man, the things which God hath prepared for them that love him.

But God hath revealed *them* unto us by his Spirit: for the Spirit searcheth all things, yea, the deep things of God.

1 Co 14:30 If *any thing* be revealed to another that sitteth by, let the first hold his peace.

2 Co 12:1 It is not expedient for me doubtless to glory. I will come to visions and revelations of the Lord.

2 Co 12:7 And lest I should be exalted above measure through the abundance of the revelations, there was given to me a thorn in the flesh, the messenger of Satan to buffet me, lest I should be exalted above measure.

Ga 1:16 To reveal his Son in me, that I might preach him among the heathen; immediately I conferred not with flesh and blood:

Ep 1:9–10 Having made known unto us the mystery of his will, according to his good pleasure which he hath purposed in himself:

That in the dispensation of the fulness of times he might gather together in one all things in Christ, both which are in heaven, and which are on earth; *even* in him:

Ep 3:3 How that by revelation he made known unto me the mystery; (as I wrote afore in few words,

Ep 3:5 Which in other ages was not made known unto the sons of men, as it is now revealed unto his holy apostles and prophets by the Spirit;

Col 1:26 *Even* the mystery which hath been hid from ages and from generations, but now is made manifest to his saints:

1 Pe 1:12 Unto whom it was revealed, that not unto themselves, but unto us they did minister the things, which are now reported unto you by them that have preached the gospel unto you with the Holy Ghost sent down from heaven; which things the angels desire to look into.

Re 1:1 The Revelation of Jesus Christ, which God gave unto him, to shew unto his servants things which must shortly come to pass; and he sent and signified *it* by his angel unto his servant John:

Re 4:1 After this I looked, and, behold, a door *was* opened in heaven: and the first voice which I heard *was* as it were of a trumpet talking with me; which said, Come up hither, and I will shew thee things which must be hereafter.

Re 17:7 And the angel said unto me, Wherefore didst thou marvel? I will tell thee the mystery of the woman, and of the beast that carrieth her, which hath the seven heads and ten horns.

Re 22:6 And he said unto me, These sayings *are* faithful and true: and the Lord God of the holy prophets sent his angel to shew unto his servants the things which must shortly be done.

Re 22:16 I Jesus have sent mine angel to testify unto you these things in the churches. I am the root and the offspring of David, *and* the bright and morning star.

2. Methods

a. Visions for the Present

Ge 15:1 After these things the word of the LORD came unto Abram in a vision, saying, Fear not, Abram: I *am* thy shield, *and* thy exceeding great reward.

Ge 26:24 And the LORD appeared unto him the same night, and said, I *am* the God of Abraham thy father: fear not, for I *am* with thee, and will bless thee, and multiply thy seed for my servant Abraham's sake.

Ge 46:2 And God spake unto Israel in the visions of the night, and said, Jacob, Jacob. And he said, Here *am* I.

Nu 12:6 And he said, Hear now my words: If there be a prophet among you, *I* the LORD will make myself known unto him in a vision, *and* will speak unto him in a dream.

Eze 37:1 The hand of the LORD was upon me, and carried me out in the spirit of the LORD, and set me down in the midst of the valley which *was* full of bones,

Da 4:5 I saw a dream which made me afraid, and the thoughts upon my bed and the visions of my head troubled me.

Ho 12:10 I have also spoken by the prophets, and I have multiplied visions, and used similitudes, by the ministry of the prophets.

Ac 9:10 And there was a certain disciple at Damascus, named Ananias; and to him said the Lord in a vision, Ananias. And he said, Behold, I *am here,* Lord.

Ac 10:3 He saw in a vision evidently about the ninth hour of the day an angel of God coming in to him, and saying unto him, Cornelius.

Ac 10:11 And saw heaven opened, and a certain vessel descending unto him, as it had been a great sheet knit at the four corners, and let down to the earth:

Ac 16:9 And a vision appeared to Paul in the night; There stood a man of Macedonia, and prayed him, saying, Come over into Macedonia, and help us.

Ac 18:9 Then spake the Lord to Paul in the night by a vision, Be not afraid, but speak, and hold not thy peace:

Ac 22:18 And saw him saying unto me, Make haste, and get thee quickly out of Jerusalem: for they will not receive thy testimony concerning me.

Ac 23:11 And the night following the Lord stood by him, and said, Be of good cheer, Paul: for as thou hast testified of me in Jerusalem, so must thou bear witness also at Rome.

1 Co 9:1 Am I not an apostle? am I not free? have I not seen Jesus Christ our Lord? are not ye my work in the Lord?

2 Co 12:1 It is not expedient for me doubtless to glory. I will come to visions and revelations of the Lord.

Re 1:12 And I turned to see the voice that spake with me. And being turned, I saw seven golden candlesticks;

b. Visions for the Future

Is 1:1 The vision of Isaiah the son of Amoz, which he saw concerning Judah and Jerusalem in the days of Uzziah, Jotham, Ahaz, *and* Hezekiah, kings of Judah.

Is 2:1 The word that Isaiah the son of Amoz saw concerning Judah and Jerusalem.

Is 13:1 The burden of Babylon, which Isaiah the son of Amoz did see.

Is 21:2 A grievous vision is declared unto me; the treacherous dealer dealeth treacherously, and the spoiler spoileth. Go up, O Elam: besiege, O Media; all the sighing thereof have I made to cease.

Is 22:1 The burden of the valley of vision. What aileth thee now, that thou art wholly gone up to the housetops?

Je 1:11 Moreover the word of the LORD came unto me, saying, Jeremiah, what seest thou? And I said, I see a rod of an almond tree.

Je 14:1 The word of the LORD that came to Jeremiah concerning the dearth.

Je 24:3 Then said the LORD unto me, What seest thou, Jeremiah? And I said, Figs; the good figs, very good; and the evil, very evil, that cannot be eaten, they are so evil.

Eze 1:1 Now it came to pass in the thirtieth year, in the fourth *month,* in the fifth *day* of the month, as I *was* among the captives by the river of Chebar, *that* the heavens were opened, and I saw visions of God.

Eze 8:2 Then I beheld, and lo a likeness as the appearance of fire: from the appearance of his loins even downward, fire; and from his loins even upward, as the appearance of brightness, as the colour of amber.

Eze 11:24 Afterwards the spirit took me up, and brought me in a vision by the Spirit of God into Chaldea, to them of the captivity. So the vision that I had seen went up from me.

Eze 12:27 Son of man, behold, *they of* the house of Israel say, The vision that he seeth *is* for many days *to come,* and he prophesieth of the times *that are* far off.

Eze 37:2 And caused me to pass by them round about: and, behold, *there were* very many in the open valley; and, lo, *they were* very dry.

Eze 40:2 In the visions of God brought he me into the land of Israel, and set me upon a very high mountain, by which *was* as the frame of a city on the south.

Eze 43:3 And *it was* according to the appearance of the vision which I saw, *even* according to the vision that I saw when I came to destroy the city: and the visions *were* like the vision that I saw by the river Chebar; and I fell upon my face.

Eze 47:1 Afterward he brought me again unto the door of the house; and, behold, waters issued out from under the threshold of the house eastward: for the forefront of the house *stood toward* the east, and the waters came down from under from the right side of the house, at the south *side* of the altar.

Da 7:1 In the first year of Belshazzar king of Babylon Daniel had a dream and visions of his head upon his bed: then he wrote the dream, *and* told the sum of the matters.

Da 7:7 After this I saw in the night visions, and behold a fourth beast, dreadful and terrible, and strong exceedingly; and it had great iron teeth: it devoured and brake in pieces, and stamped the residue with the feet of it: and it *was* diverse from all the beasts that *were* before it; and it had ten horns.

Da 8:1 In the third year of the reign of king Belshazzar a vision appeared unto me, *even unto* me Daniel, after that which appeared unto me at the first.

Da 8:15 And it came to pass, when I, *even* I Daniel, had seen the vision, and sought for the meaning, then, behold, there stood before me as the appearance of a man.

Am 1:1 The words of Amos, who was among the herdmen of Tekoa, which he saw concerning Israel in the days of Uzziah king of Judah, and in the days of Jeroboam the son of Joash king of Israel, two years before the earthquake.

Am 7:1 Thus hath the Lord GOD shewed unto me; and, behold, he formed grasshoppers in the beginning of the shooting up of the latter growth; and, lo, *it was* the latter growth after the king's mowings.

Am 8:1 Thus hath the Lord GOD shewed unto me: and behold a basket of summer fruit.

Am 9:1 I saw the LORD standing upon the altar: and he said, Smite the lintel of the door, that the posts may shake: and cut them in the head, all of them; and I will slay the last of them with the sword: he that fleeth of them shall not flee away, and he that escapeth of them shall not be delivered.

Obad 1 The vision of Obadiah. Thus saith the Lord GOD concerning Edom; We have heard a rumour from the LORD, and an ambassador is sent among the heathen, Arise ye, and let us rise up against her in battle.

Mi 1:1 The word of the LORD that came to Micah the Morasthite in the days of Jotham, Ahaz, *and* Hezekiah, kings of Judah, which he saw concerning Samaria and Jerusalem.

Na 1:1 The burden of Nineveh. The book of the vision of Nahum the Elkoshite.

Hab 1:1 The burden which Habakkuk the prophet did see.

Hab 2:2 And the LORD answered me, and said, Write the vision, and make *it* plain upon tables, that he may run that readeth it.

Zec 1:8 I saw by night, and behold a man riding upon a red horse, and he stood among the myrtle trees that *were* in the bottom; and behind him *were there* red horses, speckled, and white.

Zec 1:20 And the LORD shewed me four carpenters.

Zec 3:1 And he shewed me Joshua the high priest standing before the angel of the LORD, and Satan standing at his right hand to resist him.

Zec 5:1 Then I turned, and lifted up mine eyes, and looked, and behold a flying roll.

Zec 6:1 And I turned, and lifted up mine eyes, and looked, and, behold, there came four chariots out from between two mountains; and the mountains *were* mountains of brass.

c. Urim and Thummim

Ex 28:30 And thou shalt put in the breastplate of judgment the Urim and the Thummim; and they shall be upon Aaron's heart, when he goeth in before the LORD: and Aaron shall bear the judgment of the children of Israel upon his heart before the LORD continually.

Le 8:8 And he put the breastplate upon him: also he put in the breastplate the Urim and the Thummim.

Nu 27:21 And he shall stand before Eleazar the priest, who shall ask *counsel* for him after the judgment of Urim before the LORD: at his word shall they go out, and at his word they shall come in, *both* he, and all the children of Israel with him, even all the congregation.

De 33:8 And of Levi he said, *Let* thy Thummim and thy Urim *be* with thy holy one, whom thou didst prove at Massah, *and with* whom thou didst strive at the waters of Meribah;

Jud 1:1 Now after the death of Joshua it came to pass, that the children of Israel asked the LORD, saying, Who shall go up for us against the Canaanites first, to fight against them?

Jud 20:18 And the children of Israel arose, and went up to the house of God, and asked counsel of God, and said, Which of us shall go up first to the battle against the children of Benjamin? And the LORD said, Judah *shall go up* first.

1 S 23:9 And David knew that Saul secretly practised mischief against him; and he said to Abiathar the priest, Bring hither the ephod.

1 S 28:6 And when Saul enquired of the LORD, the LORD answered him not, neither by dreams nor by Urim, nor by prophets.

1 S 30:7 And David said to Abiathar the priest, Ahimelech's son, I pray thee, bring me hither the ephod. And Abiathar brought thither the ephod to David.

Ezr 2:63 And the Tirshatha said unto them, that they should not eat of the most holy things, till there stood up a priest with Urim and with Thummim.

Ne 7:65 And the Tirshatha said unto them, that they should not eat of the most holy things, till there stood *up* a priest with Urim and Thummim.

d. Nature

Jb 36:25 Every man may see it; man may behold *it* afar off.

Ps 19:1 The heavens declare the glory of God; and the firmament sheweth his handiwork.

Ps 50:6 And the heavens shall declare his righteousness: for God *is* judge himself. Selah.

Ps 97:6 The heavens declare his righteousness, and all the people see his glory.

Is 40:21 Have ye not known? have ye not heard? hath it not been told you from the beginning? have ye not understood from the foundations of the earth?

Ac 14:17 Nevertheless he left not himself without witness, in that he did good, and gave us rain from heaven, and fruitful seasons, filling our hearts with food and gladness.

Ro 1:20 For the invisible things of him from the creation of the world are clearly seen, being understood by the things that are made, *even* his eternal power and Godhead; so that they are without excuse:

e. The Holy Spirit

See **HOLY SPIRIT**

f. The Prophets

See **PROPHETS**

g. God's Word

See **WORD OF GOD**

h. Dreams

See **DREAMS**

i. The Incarnation

See **CHRIST**

3. Progressive

Jn 1:50 Jesus answered and said unto him, Because I said unto thee, I saw thee under the fig tree, believest thou? thou shalt see greater things than these.

Jn 13:7 Jesus answered and said unto him, What I do thou knowest not now; but thou shalt know hereafter.

Jn 16:13 Howbeit when he, the Spirit of truth, is come, he will guide you into all truth: for he shall not speak of himself; but whatsoever he shall hear, *that* shall he speak: and he will shew you things to come.

Ac 22:10 And I said, What shall I do, Lord? And the Lord said unto me, Arise, and go into Damascus; and there it shall be told thee of all things which are appointed for thee to do.

1 Co 13:12 For now we see through a glass, darkly; but then face to face: now I know in part; but then shall I know even as also I am known.

4. Christ as the Oracle of God

De 18:18 I will raise them up a Prophet from among their brethren, like unto thee, and will put my words in his mouth; and he shall speak unto them all that I shall command him.

Mt 11:27 All things are delivered unto me of my Father: and no man knoweth the Son, but the Father; neither knoweth any man the Father, save the Son, and *he* to whomsoever the Son will reveal *him*.

Mt 17:5 While he yet spake, behold, a bright cloud overshadowed them: and behold a voice out of the cloud, which said, This is my beloved Son, in whom I am well pleased; hear ye him.

Mk 9:7 And there was a cloud that overshadowed them: and a voice came out of the cloud, saying, This is my beloved Son: hear him.

Lu 9:35 And there came a voice out of the cloud, saying, This is my beloved Son: hear him.

Jn 3:34 For he whom God hath sent speaketh the words of God: for God giveth not the Spirit by measure *unto him.*

Jn 8:26 I have many things to say and to judge of you: but he that sent me is true; and I speak to the world those things which I have heard of him.

Jn 8:40 But now ye seek to kill me, a man that hath told you the truth, which I have heard of God: this did not Abraham.

Jn 12:49 For I have not spoken of myself; but the Father which sent me, he gave me a commandment, what I should say, and what I should speak.

Jn 14:10 Believest thou not that I am in the Father, and the Father in me? the words that I speak unto you I speak not of myself: but the Father that dwelleth in me, he doeth the works.

Jn 14:24 He that loveth me not keepeth not my sayings: and the word which ye hear is not mine, but the Father's which sent me.

Jn 15:15 Henceforth I call you not servants; for the servant knoweth not what his lord doeth: but I have called you friends; for all things that I have heard of my Father I have made known unto you.

Jn 17:8 For I have given unto them the words which thou gavest me; and they have received *them,* and have known surely that I came out from thee, and they have believed that thou didst send me.

Jn 17:14 I have given them thy word; and the world hath hated them, because they are not of the world, even as I am not of the world.

Ac 2:28 Thou hast made known to me the ways of life; thou shalt make me full of joy with thy countenance.

Ac 3:22 For Moses truly said unto the fathers, A prophet shall the Lord your God raise up unto you of your brethren, like unto me; him shall ye hear in all things whatsoever he shall say unto you.

Ac 7:37 This is that Moses, which said unto the children of Israel, A prophet shall the Lord your God raise up unto you of your brethren, like unto me; him shall ye hear.

2 Co 3:14 But their minds were blinded: for until this day remaineth the same vail untaken away in the reading of the old testament; which *vail* is done away in Christ.

Re 1:1 The Revelation of Jesus Christ, which God gave unto him, to shew unto his servants things which must shortly come to pass; and he sent and signified *it* by his angel unto his servant John:

5. Special Manifestations

a. Pillar of Cloud and Fire

Ex 13:21 And the LORD went before them by day in a pillar of a cloud, to lead them the way; and by night in a pillar of fire, to give them light; to go by day and night:

Ex 14:19 And the angel of God, which went before the camp of Israel, removed and went behind them; and the pillar of the cloud went from before their face, and stood behind them:

Ex 16:10 And it came to pass, as Aaron spake unto the whole congregation of the children of Israel, that they looked toward the wilderness, and, behold, the glory of the LORD appeared in the cloud.

Ex 33:9 And it came to pass, as Moses entered into the tabernacle, the cloudy pillar descended, and stood at the door of the tabernacle, and the LORD talked with Moses.

Ex 40:36 And when the cloud was taken up from over the tabernacle, the children of Israel went onward in all their journeys:

Nu 9:17 And when the cloud was taken up from the tabernacle, then after that the children of Israel journeyed: and in the place where the cloud abode, there the children of Israel pitched their tents.

Nu 10:11 And it came to pass on the twentieth day of the second month, in the second year, that the cloud was taken up from off the tabernacle of the testimony.

Nu 12:5 And the LORD came down in the pillar of the cloud, and stood in the door of the tabernacle, and called Aaron and Miriam: and they both came forth.

Nu 16:42 And it came to pass, when the congregation was gathered against Moses and against Aaron, that they looked toward the tabernacle of the congregation: and, behold, the cloud covered it, and the glory of the LORD appeared.

De 1:33 Who went in the way before you, to search you out a place to pitch your tents in, in fire by night, to shew you by what way ye should go, and in a cloud by day.

De 31:15 And the LORD appeared in the tabernacle in a pillar of a cloud: and the pillar of the cloud stood over the door of the tabernacle.

Ne 9:12 Moreover thou leddest them in the day by a cloudy pillar; and in the night by a pillar of fire, to give them light in the way wherein they should go.

Ps 78:14 In the daytime also he led them with a cloud, and all the night with a light of fire.

Ps 105:39 He spread a cloud for a covering; and fire to give light in the night.

Is 4:5 And the LORD will create upon every dwelling place of mount Zion, and upon her assemblies, a cloud and smoke by day, and the shining of a flaming fire by night: for upon all the glory shall be a defence.

Is 58:8 Then shall thy light break forth as the morning, and thine health shall spring forth speedily: and thy righteousness shall go before thee; the glory of the LORD shall be thy rereward.

1 Co 10:1 Moreover, brethren, I would not that ye should be ignorant, how that all our fathers were under the cloud, and all passed through the sea;

b. The Shekinah, the supernatural light or cloud, which appeared on the mercy seat

Ex 40:35 And Moses was not able to enter into the tent of the congregation, because the cloud abode thereon, and the glory of the LORD filled the tabernacle.

Le 16:2 And the LORD said unto Moses, Speak unto Aaron thy brother, that he come not at all times into the holy place within the vail before the mercy seat, which is upon the ark; that he die not: for I will appear in the cloud upon the mercy seat.

2 S 6:2 And David arose, and went with all the people that were with him from Baale of Judah, to bring up from thence the ark of God, whose name is called by the name of the LORD of hosts that dwelleth between the cherubims.

1 K 8:10 And it came to pass, when the priests were come out of the holy *place,* that the cloud filled the house of the LORD,

2 Chr 5:13 It came even to pass, as the trumpeters and singers *were* as one, to make one sound to be heard in praising and thanking the LORD; and when they lifted up *their* voice with the trumpets and cymbals and instruments of musick, and praised the LORD, *saying,* For *he is* good; for his mercy *endureth* for ever: that *then* the house was filled with a cloud, *even* the house of the LORD;

Ps 11:4 The LORD *is* in his holy temple, the LORD's throne *is* in heaven: his eyes behold, his eyelids try, the children of men.

Ps 80:1 Give ear, O Shepherd of Israel, thou that leadest Joseph like a flock; thou that dwellest *between* the cherubims, shine forth.

Ps 99:1 The LORD reigneth; let the people tremble: he sitteth *between* the cherubims; let the earth be moved.

Is 37:16 O LORD of hosts, God of Israel, that dwellest *between* the cherubims, thou *art* the God, *even* thou alone, of all the kingdoms of the earth: thou hast made heaven and earth.

Eze 9:3 And the glory of the God of Israel was gone up from the cherub, whereupon he was, to the threshold of the house. And he called to the man clothed with linen, which *had* the writer's inkhorn by his side;

Eze 11:22 Then did the cherubims lift up their wings, and the wheels beside them; and the glory of the God of Israel *was* over them above.

Eze 44:4 Then brought he me the way of the north gate before the house: and I looked, and, behold, the glory of the LORD filled the house of the LORD: and I fell upon my face.

Hab 2:20 But the LORD *is* in his holy temple: let all the earth keep silence before him.

Hag 2:7 And I will shake all nations, and the desire of all nations shall come: and I will fill this house with glory, saith the LORD of hosts.

Zec 2:5 For I, saith the LORD, will be unto her a wall of fire round about, and will be the glory in the midst of her.

Zec 2:10 Sing and rejoice, O daughter of Zion: for, lo, I come, and I will dwell in the midst of thee, saith the LORD.

Mt 23:21 And whoso shall swear by the temple, sweareth by it, and by him that dwelleth therein.

c. Signs

Ge 15:9 And he said unto him, Take me an heifer of three years old, and a she goat of three years old, and a ram of three years old, and a turtledove, and a young pigeon.

Jud 6:38 And it was so: for he rose up early on the morrow, and thrust the fleece together, and wringed the dew out of the fleece, a bowl full of water.

1 S 12:17 *Is it* not wheat harvest to day? I will call unto the LORD, and he shall send thunder and rain; that ye may perceive and see that your wickedness *is* great, which ye have done in the sight of the LORD, in asking you a king.

1 S 14:10 But if they say thus, Come up unto us; then we will go up: for the LORD hath delivered them into our hand: and this *shall be* a sign unto us.

1 K 13:3 And he gave a sign the same day, saying, This *is* the sign which the LORD hath spoken; Behold, the altar shall be rent, and the ashes that *are* upon it shall be poured out.

2 K 20:9 And Isaiah said, This sign shalt thou have of the LORD, that the LORD will do the thing that he hath spoken: shall the shadow go forward ten degrees, or go back ten degrees?

2 Chr 32:24 In those days Hezekiah was sick to the death, and prayed unto the LORD: and he spake unto him, and he gave him a sign.

Is 7:14 Therefore the Lord himself shall give you a sign; Behold, a virgin shall conceive, and bear a son, and shall call his name Immanuel.

Is 37:30 And this *shall be* a sign unto thee, Ye shall eat *this* year such as groweth of itself; and the second year that which springeth of the same: and in the third year sow ye, and reap, and plant vineyards, and eat the fruit thereof.

Is 55:13 Instead of the thorn shall come up the fir tree, and instead of the brier shall come up the myrtle tree: and it shall be to the LORD for a name, for an everlasting sign *that* shall not be cut off.

Lu 2:12 And this *shall be* a sign unto you; Ye shall find the babe wrapped in swaddling clothes, lying in a manger.

d. The Holy Spirit in the Form of a Dove
Mt 3:16; Jn 1:32

6. Necessary for Fuller Understanding

PERSEVERANCE

Ho 6:3 Then shall we know, *if* we follow on to know the LORD: his going forth is prepared as the morning; and he shall come unto us as the rain, as the latter *and* former rain unto the earth.

INTIMATE FELLOWSHIP WITH CHRIST

Mt 13:11 He answered and said unto them, Because it is given unto you to know the mysteries of the kingdom of heaven, but to them it is not given.

ABIDING IN CHRIST'S WORDS

Jn 8:31–32 Then said Jesus to those Jews which believed on him, If ye continue in my word, *then* are ye my disciples indeed;
And ye shall know the truth, and the truth shall make you free.

PATIENCE

Jn 13:7 Jesus answered and said unto him, What I do thou knowest not now; but thou shalt know hereafter.

GUIDANCE OF THE HOLY SPIRIT

Jn 16:13 Howbeit when he, the Spirit of truth, is come, he will guide you into all truth: for he shall not speak of himself; but whatsoever he shall hear, *that* shall he speak: and he will shew you things to come.

See **MYSTERIES**

REVENGE

JEZEBEL TOWARD ELIJAH

1 K 19:2 Then Jezebel sent a messenger unto Elijah, saying, So let the gods do *to me,* and more also, if I make not thy life as the life of one of them by to morrow about this time.

AHAB TOWARD MICAIAH

1 K 22:27 And say, Thus saith the king, Put this *fellow* in the prison, and feed him with bread of affliction and with water of affliction, until I come in peace.

HAMAN TOWARD THE JEWS

Est 3:6 And he thought scorn to lay hands on Mordecai alone; for they had shewed him the people of Mordecai: wherefore Haman sought to destroy all the Jews that *were* throughout the whole kingdom of Ahasuerus, *even* the people of Mordecai.

PHILISTINES TOWARD ISRAEL

Eze 25:15 Thus saith the Lord GOD; Because the Philistines have dealt by revenge, and have taken vengeance with a despiteful heart, to destroy *it* for the old hatred;

HERODIAS TOWARD JOHN THE BAPTIST

Mt 14:8 And she, being before instructed of her mother, said, Give me here John Baptist's head in a charger.

NAZARENES TOWARD CHRIST

Lu 4:29 And rose up, and thrust him out of the city, and led him unto the brow of the hill whereon their city was built, that they might cast him down headlong.

JEWS TOWARD THE APOSTLES

Ac 5:33 When they heard *that,* they were cut *to the heart,* and took counsel to slay them.

Ac 23:12 And when it was day, certain of the Jews banded together, and bound themselves under a curse, saying that they would neither eat nor drink till they had killed Paul.

See **FORGIVENESS, RETALIATION**

REVERENCE, *respect and awe*

1. For God and Sacred things

Ex 3:5 And he said, Draw not nigh hither: put off thy shoes from off thy feet, for the place whereon thou standest is holy ground.

Ex 19:12 And thou shalt set bounds unto the people round about, saying, Take heed to yourselves, *that ye* go *not* up into the mount, or touch the border of it: whosoever toucheth the mount shall be surely put to death:

Ex 20:18 And all the people saw the thunderings, and the lightnings, and the noise of the trumpet, and the mountain smoking: and when the people saw *it,* they removed, and stood afar off.

Ex 33:10 And all the people saw the cloudy pillar stand *at* the tabernacle door: and all the people rose up and worshipped, every man *in* his tent door.

Ex 34:8 And Moses made haste, and bowed his head toward the earth, and worshipped.

Le 9:5 And they brought *that* which Moses commanded before the tabernacle of the congregation: and all the congregation drew near and stood before the LORD.

Le 9:24 And there came a fire out from before the LORD, and consumed upon the altar the burnt offering and the fat: *which* when all the people saw, they shouted, and fell on their faces.

Le 10:3 Then Moses said unto Aaron, This *is it* that the LORD spake, saying, I will be sanctified in them that come nigh me, and before all the people I will be glorified. And Aaron held his peace.

De 5:5 (I stood between the LORD and you at that time, to shew you the word of the LORD: for ye were afraid by reason of the fire, and went not up into the mount;) saying,

Jos 3:4 Yet there shall be a space between you and it, about two thousand cubits by measure: come not near unto it, that ye may know the way by which ye must go: for ye have not passed this *way* heretofore.

Jos 5:15 And the captain of the LORD's host said unto Joshua, Loose thy shoe from off thy foot; for the place whereon thou standest *is* holy. And Joshua did so.

Jud 13:20 For it came to pass, when the flame went up toward heaven from off the altar, that the angel of the LORD ascended in the flame of the altar. And Manoah and his wife looked on *it,* and fell on their faces to the ground.

1 K 18:39 And when all the people saw *it,* they fell on their faces: and they said, The LORD, he *is* the God; the LORD, he *is* the God.

1 K 19:13 And it was *so,* when Elijah heard *it,* that he wrapped his face in his mantle, and went out, and stood in the entering in of the cave. And, behold, *there came* a voice unto him, and said, What doest thou here, Elijah?

1 Chr 21:16 And David lifted up his eyes, and saw the angel of the LORD stand between the earth and the heaven, having a drawn sword in his hand stretched out over Jerusalem. Then David and the elders *of Israel, who were* clothed in sackcloth, fell upon their faces.

2 Chr 6:3 And the king turned his face, and blessed the whole congregation of Israel: and all the congregation of Israel stood.

2 Chr 7:3 And when all the children of Israel saw how the fire came down, and the glory of the LORD upon the house, they bowed themselves with their faces to the ground upon the pavement, and worshipped, and praised the LORD, *saying,* For *he is* good; for his mercy *endureth* for ever.

2 Chr 20:18 And Jehoshaphat bowed his head with *his* face to the ground: and all Judah and the inhabitants of Jerusalem fell before the LORD, worshipping the LORD.

2 Chr 29:29 And when they had made an end of offering, the king and all that were present with him bowed themselves, and worshipped.

Ne 8:5 And Ezra opened the book in the sight of all the people; (for he was above all the people;) and when he opened it, all the people stood up:

Jb 40:4 Behold, I am vile; what shall I answer thee? I will lay mine hand upon my mouth.

Ps 4:4 Stand in awe, and sin not: commune with your own heart upon your bed, and be still. Selah.

Ps 33:8 Let all the earth fear the LORD: let all the inhabitants of the world stand in awe of him.

Ps 89:7 God is greatly to be feared in the assembly of the saints, and to be had in reverence of all *them that are* about him.

Ps 111:9 He sent redemption unto his people: he hath commanded his covenant for ever: holy and reverend *is* his name.

Is 6:2 Above it stood the seraphims: each one had six wings; with twain he covered his face, and with twain he covered his feet, and with twain he did fly.

Is 8:13 Sanctify the LORD of hosts himself; and *let* him *be* your fear, and *let* him *be* your dread.

Eze 1:28 As the appearance of the bow that is in the cloud in the day of rain, so *was* the appearance of the brightness round about. This *was* the appearance of the likeness of the glory of the LORD. And when I saw *it*, I fell upon my face, and I heard a voice of one that spake.

Eze 3:23 Then I arose, and went forth into the plain: and, behold, the glory of the LORD stood there, as the glory which I saw by the river of Chebar: and I fell on my face.

Eze 44:4 Then brought he me the way of the north gate before the house: and I looked, and, behold, the glory of the LORD filled the house of the LORD: and I fell upon my face.

Da 3:29 Therefore I make a decree, That every people, nation, and language, which speak any thing amiss against the God of Shadrach, Meshach, and Abed-nego, shall be cut in pieces, and their houses shall be made a dunghill: because there is no other God that can deliver after this sort.

Da 8:17 So he came near where I stood: and when he came, I was afraid, and fell upon my face: but he said unto me, Understand, O son of man: for at the time of the end *shall be* the vision.

Da 10:15 And when he had spoken such words unto me, I set my face toward the ground, and I became dumb.

Hab 2:20 But the LORD *is* in his holy temple: let all the earth keep silence before him.

Zec 2:13 Be silent, O all flesh, before the LORD: for he is raised up out of his holy habitation.

Lu 24:5 And as they were afraid, and bowed down *their* faces to the earth, they said unto them, Why seek ye the living among the dead?

Ac 7:33 Then said the Lord to him, Put off thy shoes from thy feet: for the place where thou standest is holy ground.

He 12:28 Wherefore we receiving a kingdom which cannot be moved, let us have grace, whereby we may serve God acceptably with reverence and godly fear:

Re 4:10 The four and twenty elders fall down before him that sat on the throne, and worship him that liveth for ever and ever, and cast their crowns before the throne, saying,

Re 7:11 And all the angels stood round about the throne, and *about* the elders and the four beasts, and fell before the throne on their faces, and worshipped God,

Re 11:16 And the four and twenty elders, which sat before God on their seats, fell upon their faces, and worshipped God,

2. For the Aged

See **YOUNG PEOPLE**

3. For the Sanctuary

Le 19:30 Ye shall keep my sabbaths, and reverence my sanctuary: I *am* the LORD.

Ec 5:1 Keep thy foot when thou goest to the house of God, and be more ready to hear, than to give the sacrifice of fools: for they consider not that they do evil.

Jn 2:16 And said unto them that sold doves, Take these things hence; make not my Father's house an house of merchandise.

4. For Men of God

Ex 33:8 And it came to pass, when Moses went out unto the tabernacle, *that* all the people rose up, and stood every man *at* his tent door, and looked after Moses, until he was gone into the tabernacle.

Nu 12:8 With him will I speak mouth to mouth, even apparently, and not in dark speeches; and the similitude of the LORD shall he behold: wherefore then were ye not afraid to speak against my servant Moses?

1 S 13:10 And it came to pass, that as soon as he had made an end of offering the burnt offering, behold, Samuel came; and Saul went out to meet him, that he might salute him.

Jb 29:8 The young men saw me, and hid themselves: and the aged arose, *and* stood up.

Ps 15:4 In whose eyes a vile person is contemned; but he honoureth them that fear the LORD. *He that* sweareth to *his own* hurt, and changeth not.

Ac 28:10 Who also honoured us with many honours; and when we departed, they laded *us* with such things as were necessary.

Ph 2:29 Receive him therefore in the Lord with all gladness; and hold such in reputation:

1 Th 5:12–13 And we beseech you, brethren, to know them which labour among you, and are over you in the Lord, and admonish you;

And to esteem them very highly in love for their work's sake. *And* be at peace among yourselves.

1 Ti 5:17 Let the elders that rule well be counted worthy of double honour, especially they who labour in the word and doctrine.

He 13:7 Remember them which have the rule over you, who have spoken unto you the word of God: whose faith follow, considering the end of *their* conversation.

5. For Christ

Mt 8:2 And, behold, there came a leper and worshipped him, saying, Lord, if thou wilt, thou canst make me clean.

Mt 9:18 While he spake these things unto them, behold, there came a certain ruler, and worshipped him, saying, My daughter is even now dead: but come and lay thy hand upon her, and she shall live.

Mt 15:25 Then came she and worshipped him, saying, Lord, help me.

Mt 17:14 And when they were come to the multitude, there came to him a *certain* man, kneeling down to him, and saying,

Mt 19:16 And, behold, one came and said unto him, Good Master, what good thing shall I do, that I may have eternal life?

Mt 20:20 Then came to him the mother of Zebedee's children with her sons, worshipping *him,* and desiring a certain thing of him.

Mt 21:37 But last of all he sent unto them his son, saying, They will reverence my son.

Mt 26:7 There came unto him a woman having an alabaster box of very precious ointment, and poured it on his head, as he sat *at meat.*

Mk 1:40 And there came a leper to him, beseeching him, and kneeling down to him, and saying unto him, If thou wilt, thou canst make me clean.

Mk 3:11 And unclean spirits, when they saw him, fell down before him, and cried, saying, Thou art the Son of God.

Mk 5:6 But when he saw Jesus afar off, he ran and worshipped him,

Mk 5:22 And, behold, there cometh one of the rulers of the synagogue, Jairus by name; and when he saw him, he fell at his feet,

Mk 7:25 For a *certain* woman, whose young daughter had an unclean spirit, heard of him, and came and fell at his feet:

Mk 9:15 And straightway all the people, when they beheld him, were greatly amazed, and running to *him* saluted him.

Mk 9:32 But they understood not that saying, and were afraid to ask him.

Mk 10:17 And when he was gone forth into the way, there came one running, and kneeled to him, and asked him, Good Master, what shall I do that I may inherit eternal life?

Lu 5:12 And it came to pass, when he was in a certain city, behold a man full of leprosy: who seeing Jesus fell on *his* face, and besought him, saying, Lord, if thou wilt, thou canst make me clean.

Lu 8:41 And, behold, there came a man named Jairus, and he was a ruler of the synagogue: and he fell down at Jesus' feet, and besought him that he would come into his house:

Lu 17:16 And fell down on *his* face at his feet, giving him thanks: and he was a Samaritan.

Jn 4:27 And upon this came his disciples, and marvelled that he talked with the woman: yet no man said, What seekest thou? or, Why talkest thou with her?

Jn 9:38 And he said, Lord, I believe. And he worshipped him.

Jn 21:12 Jesus saith unto them, Come *and* dine. And none of the disciples durst ask him, Who art thou? knowing that it was the Lord.

6. For God's Name

See **NAME**

7. For Parents

See **YOUNG PEOPLE**

8. For Religious Leaders

See **HONOR**

9. For Word of God

See **WORD OF GOD**

REVERSALS, *changes in position because of God's intervention*

Ps 75:7; 107:41; 147:6; Is 22:25; 26:5; 40:23; Eze 21:26; Da 4:31; Mt 19:30; 20:16; 25:29; Mk 10:31; Lu 1:52; 6:25; 13:30; 16:25

See **PROVIDENCE**

REVOLTS

Ge 14:4; Nu 16:19; 2 S 17:1; 20:2, 21; 1 K 12:16; 2 K 3:5; 8:20; 24:1, 20; 2 Chr 10:16; 13:6; 21:8; Je 52:3

See **REBELLION**

REWARD, *recompense*

Ge 15:1 After these things the word of the LORD came unto Abram in a vision, saying, Fear not, Abram: I *am* thy shield, *and* thy exceeding great reward.

Ex 1:20 Therefore God dealt well with the midwives: and the people multiplied, and waxed very mighty.

2 S 22:25 Therefore the LORD hath recompensed me according to my righteousness; according to my cleanness in his eye sight.

Ps 18:20 The LORD rewarded me according to my righteousness; according to the cleanness of my hands hath he recompensed me.

Ps 19:9 The fear of the LORD *is* clean, enduring for ever: the judgments of the LORD *are* true *and* righteous altogether.

Ps 19:11 Moreover by them is thy servant warned: *and* in keeping of them *there is* great reward.

Ps 58:11 So that a man shall say, Verily *there is* a reward for the righteous: verily he is a God that judgeth in the earth.

Pr 13:13 Whoso despiseth the word shall be destroyed: but he that feareth the commandment shall be rewarded.

Pr 24:14 So *shall* the knowledge of wisdom *be* unto thy soul: when thou hast found *it,* then there shall be a reward, and thy expectation shall not be cut off.

Pr 25:22 For thou shalt heap coals of fire upon his head, and the LORD shall reward thee.

Is 3:10 Say ye to the righteous, that *it* shall be* well *with him:* for they shall eat the fruit of their doings.

Is 40:10 Behold, the Lord GOD will come with strong *hand,* and his arm shall rule for him: behold, his reward *is* with him, and his work before him.

Is 49:4 Then I said, I have laboured in vain, I have spent my strength for nought, and in vain: *yet* surely my judgment *is* with the LORD, and my work with my God.

Is 62:11 Behold, the LORD hath proclaimed unto the end of the world, Say ye to the daughter of Zion, Behold, thy salvation cometh; behold, his reward *is* with him, and his work before him.

Je 31:16 Thus saith the LORD; Refrain thy voice from weeping, and thine eyes from tears: for thy work shall be rewarded, saith the LORD; and they shall come again from the land of the enemy.

Mt 6:1 Take heed that ye do not your alms before men, to be seen of them: otherwise ye have no reward of your Father which is in heaven.

Mt 6:4 That thine alms may be in secret: and thy Father which seeth in secret himself shall reward thee openly.

Mt 6:18 That thou appear not unto men to fast, but unto thy Father which is in secret: and thy Father, which seeth in secret, shall reward thee openly.

Mt 10:41 He that receiveth a prophet in the name of a prophet shall receive a prophet's reward; and he that receiveth a righteous man in the name of a righteous man shall receive a righteous man's reward.

Mt 24:47 Verily I say unto you, That he shall make him ruler over all his goods.

Mk 10:30 But he shall receive an hundredfold now in this time, houses, and brethren, and sisters, and mothers, and children, and lands, with persecutions; and in the world to come eternal life.

Ro 8:18 For I reckon that the sufferings of this present time *are* not worthy *to be compared* with the glory which shall be revealed in us.

1 Co 9:17 For if I do this thing willingly, I have a reward: but if against my will, a dispensation *of the gospel* is committed unto me.

Col 3:24 Knowing that of the Lord ye shall receive the reward of the inheritance: for ye serve the Lord Christ.

He 11:6 But without faith *it is* impossible to please *him:* for he that cometh to God must believe that he is, and *that* he is a rewarder of them that diligently seek him.

2 Jn 8 Look to yourselves, that we lose not those things which we have wrought, but that we receive a full reward.

Re 22:12 And, behold, I come quickly; and my reward is with me, to give every man according as his work shall be.

1. Earthly

Nu 22:7 And the elders of Moab and the elders of Midian departed with the rewards of divination in their hand; and they came unto Balaam, and spake unto him the words of Balak.

Nu 22:17 For I will promote thee unto very great honour, and I will do whatsoever thou sayest unto me: come therefore, I pray thee, curse me this people.

De 16:19 Thou shalt not wrest judgment; thou shalt not respect persons, neither take a gift: for a gift doth blind the eyes of the wise, and pervert the words of the righteous.

1 K 13:7 And the king said unto the man of God, Come home with me, and refresh thyself, and I will give thee a reward.

2 K 5:15 And he returned to the man of God, he and all his company, and came, and stood before him: and he said, Behold, now I know that *there is* no God in all earth, but in Israel: now therefore, I pray thee, take a blessing of thy servant.

Is 1:23 Thy princes *are* rebellious, and companions of thieves: every one loveth gifts, and followeth after rewards: they judge not the fatherless, neither doth the cause of the widow come unto them.

Da 2:6 But if ye shew the dream, and the interpretation thereof, ye shall receive of me gifts and rewards and great honour: therefore shew me the dream, and the interpretation thereof.

Da 5:7 The king cried aloud to bring in the astrologers, the Chaldeans, and the soothsayers. *And* the king spake, and said to the wise *men* of Babylon, Whosoever shall read this writing, and shew me the interpretation thereof, shall be clothed with scarlet, and *have* a chain of gold about his neck, and shall be the third ruler in the kingdom.

Da 5:17 Then Daniel answered and said before the king, Let thy gifts be to thyself, and give thy rewards to another; yet I will read the writing unto the king, and make known to him the interpretation.

Mi 3:11 The heads thereof judge for reward, and the priests thereof teach for hire, and the prophets thereof divine for money: yet will they lean upon the LORD, and say, *Is* not the LORD among us? none evil can come upon us.

Mi 7:3 That they may do evil with both hands earnestly, the prince asketh, and the judge *asketh* for a reward; and the great *man,* he uttereth his mischievous desire: so they wrap it up.

Mt 4:9 And saith unto him, All these things will I give thee, if thou wilt fall down and worship me.

Mt 6:2 Therefore when thou doest *thine* alms, do not sound a trumpet before thee, as the hypocrites do in the synagogues and in the streets, that they may have glory of men. Verily I say unto you, They have their reward.

Mt 6:5 And when thou prayest, thou shalt not be as the hypocrites *are:* for they love to pray standing in the synagogues and in the corners of the streets, that they may be seen of men. Verily I say unto you, They have their reward.

Mt 6:16 Moreover when ye fast, be not, as the hypocrites, of a sad countenance: for they disfigure their faces, that they may appear unto men to fast. Verily I say unto you, They have their reward.

2 Pe 2:15 Which have forsaken the right way, and are gone astray, following the way of Balaam *the son* of Bosor, who loved the wages of unrighteousness;

2. Proportionate

GREAT SOUL-WINNERS RADIANT
Da 12:3 And they that be wise shall shine as the brightness of the firmament; and they that turn many to righteousness as the stars for ever and ever.

AT THE COMING OF CHRIST
Mt 16:27 For the Son of man shall come in the glory of his Father with his angels; and then he shall reward every man according to his works.

EVEN IN THE PRESENT LIFE
Lu 18:30 Who shall not receive manifold more in this present time, and in the world to come life everlasting.

IN THE LORD'S VINEYARD
1 Co 3:8 Now he that planteth and he that watereth are one: and every man shall receive his own reward according to his own labour.

REAPING ACCORDING TO THE AMOUNT OF SEED SOWN
2 Co 9:6 But this *I say,* He which soweth sparingly shall reap also sparingly; and he which soweth bountifully shall reap also bountifully.

ASSIGNED BY THE LORD
Re 22:12 And, behold, I come quickly; and my reward *is* with me, to give every man according as his work shall be.

3. For Spiritual Service

THE SOUL-WINNERS
Da 12:3 And they that be wise shall shine as the brightness of the firmament; and they that turn many to righteousness as the stars for ever and ever.

HUMBLE SERVANTS
Mt 10:42 And whosoever shall give to drink unto one of these little ones

a cup of cold *water* only in the name of a disciple, verily I say unto you, he shall in no wise lose his reward.

THE FAITHFUL STEWARDS

Mt 25:23 His lord said unto him, Well done, good and faithful servant; thou hast been faithful over a few things, I will make thee ruler over many things: enter thou into the joy of thy lord.

Mt 25:34 Then shall the King say unto them on his right hand, Come, ye blessed of my Father, inherit the kingdom prepared for you from the foundation of the world:

Mk 9:41 For whosoever shall give you a cup of water to drink in my name, because ye belong to Christ, verily I say unto you, he shall not lose his reward.

THE BENEVOLENT

Lu 6:35 But love ye your enemies, and do good, and lend, hoping for nothing again; and your reward shall be great, and ye shall be the children of the Highest: for he is kind unto the unthankful and *to* the evil.

THE GOOD OF ALL NATIONS

Ro 2:10 But glory, honour, and peace, to every man that worketh good, to the Jew first, and also to the Gentile:

1 Co 3:8 Now he that planteth and he that watereth are one: and every man shall receive his own reward according to his own labour.

ALL RANKS AND STATIONS

Ep 6:8 Knowing that whatsoever good thing any man doeth, the same shall he receive of the Lord, whether *he be* bond or free.

Col 3:24 Knowing that of the Lord ye shall receive the reward of the inheritance: for ye serve the Lord Christ.

4. For Suffering Endured

Mt 5:11 Blessed are ye, when *men* shall revile you, and persecute *you,* and shall say all manner of evil against you falsely, for my sake.

Lu 6:23 Rejoice ye in that day, and leap for joy: for, behold, your reward *is* great in heaven: for in the like manner did their fathers unto the prophets.

Ro 8:17 And if children, then heirs; heirs of God, and joint-heirs with Christ; if so be that we suffer with *him,* that we may be also glorified together.

2 Ti 2:12 If we suffer, we shall also reign with *him:* if we deny *him,* he also will deny us:

He 10:34 For ye had compassion of me in my bonds, and took joyfully the spoiling of your goods, knowing in yourselves that ye have in heaven a better and an enduring substance.

He 11:26 Esteeming the reproach of Christ greater riches than the treasures in Egypt: for he had respect unto the recompence of the reward.

1 Pe 1:7 That the trial of your faith, being much more precious than of gold that perisheth, though it be tried with fire, might be found unto praise and honour and glory at the appearing of Jesus Christ:

Re 20:4 And I saw thrones, and they sat upon them, and judgment was given unto them: and *I saw* the souls of them that were beheaded for the witness of Jesus, and for the word of God, and which had not worshipped the beast, neither his image, neither had received *his* mark upon their foreheads, or in their hands; and they lived and reigned with Christ a thousand years.

5. Rest from Labor

Jb 3:17 There the wicked cease *from* troubling; and there the weary be at rest.

Is 57:2 He shall enter into peace: they shall rest in their beds, *each one* walking *in* his uprightness.

Da 12:13 But go thou thy way till the end *be:* for thou shalt rest, and stand in thy lot at the end of the days.

2 Th 1:7 And to you who are troubled rest with us, when the Lord Jesus shall be revealed from heaven with his mighty angels,

He 4:9 There remaineth therefore a rest to the people of God.

Re 6:11 And white robes were given unto every one of them; and it was said unto them, that they should rest yet for a little season, until their fellowservants also and their brethren, that should be killed as they *were,* should be fulfilled.

Re 14:13 And I heard a voice from heaven saying unto me, Write, Blessed *are* the dead which die in the Lord from henceforth: Yea, saith the Spirit, that they may rest from their labours; and their works do follow them.

6. Spiritual Crowns

THE INCORRUPTIBLE CROWN

1 Co 9:25

THE CROWN OF RIGHTEOUSNESS

2 Ti 4:8

THE CROWN OF LIFE

Ja 1:12

THE CROWN OF GLORY

1 Pe 5:4; Re 2:10

TO BE GUARDED

Re 3:11

CAST AT JESUS' FEET

Re 4:10

See **FUTURE LIFE, JUDGMENTS, PUNISHMENT, RECOMPENSE**

REZIN, *king of Syria*

2 K 15:37; 16:5, 9; Is 7:1; 9:11

RIBLAH, *a city in Syria (?)*

2 K 23:33; 25:6, 20; Je 39:5; 52:9, 26

RICHES, *abundance*

1. Earthly

a. The Gift of God

Ge 24:35 And the LORD hath blessed my master greatly; and he is become great: and he hath given him flocks, and herds, and silver, and gold, and menservants, and maidservants, and camels, and asses.

Ge 31:16 For all the riches which God hath taken from our father, that *is* ours, and our children's: now then, whatsoever God hath said unto thee, do.

De 8:18 But thou shalt remember the LORD thy God: for *it is* he that giveth thee power to get wealth, that he may establish his covenant which he sware unto thy fathers, as *it is* this day.

Jos 22:8 And he spake unto them, saying, Return with much riches unto your tents, and with very much cattle, with silver, and with gold, and with brass, and with iron, and with very much raiment: divide the spoil of your enemies with your brethren.

1 S 2:7 The LORD maketh poor, and maketh rich: he bringeth low, and lifteth up.

1 K 3:13 And I have also given thee that which thou hast not asked, both riches, and honour: so that there shall not be any among the kings like unto thee all thy days.

1 Chr 29:12 Both riches and honour *come* of thee, and thou reignest over all; and in thine hand *is* power and might; and in thine hand *it is* to make great, and to give strength unto all.

2 Chr 1:12 Wisdom and knowledge *is* granted unto thee; and I will give thee riches, and wealth, and honour, such as none of the kings have had that *have been* before thee, neither shall there any after thee have the like.

2 Chr 25:9 And Amaziah said to the man of God, But what shall we do for the hundred talents which I have given to the army of Israel? And the man of God answered, The LORD is able to give thee much more than this.

2 Chr 32:29 Moreover he provided him cities, and possessions of flocks and herds in abundance: for God had given him substance very much.

Est 1:4 When he shewed the riches of his glorious kingdom and the honour of his excellent majesty many days, *even* an hundred and fourscore days.

Jb 1:10 Hast not thou made an hedge about him, and about his house, and about all that he hath on every side? thou hast blessed the work of his hands, and his substance is increased in the land.

Jb 22:24 Then shalt thou lay up gold as dust, and the *gold* of Ophir as the stones of the brooks.

Pr 30:8 Remove far from me vanity and lies: give me neither poverty nor riches; feed me with food convenient for me:

Ec 5:19 Every man also to whom God hath given riches and wealth, and hath given him power to eat thereof, and to take his portion, and to rejoice in his labour; this *is* the gift of God.

Ec 6:2 A man to whom God hath given riches, wealth, and honour, so that he wanteth nothing for his soul of all that he desireth, yet God giveth him not power to eat thereof, but a stranger eateth it: this *is* vanity, and it *is* an evil disease.

Is 45:3 And I will give thee the treasures of darkness, and hidden riches of secret places, that thou mayest know that I, the LORD, which call *thee* by thy name, *am* the God of Israel.

Je 27:5 I have made the earth, the man and the beast that *are* upon the ground, by my great power and by my outstretched arm, and have given it unto whom it seemed meet unto me.

Ho 2:8 For she did gave her corn, and wine, and oil, and multiplied her silver and gold, *which* they prepared for Baal.

Lu 11:3 Give us day by day our daily bread.

Lu 11:13 If ye then, being evil, know how to give good gifts unto your children: how much more shall *your* heavenly Father give the Holy Spirit to them that ask him?

Lu 12:16–21 And he spake a parable unto them, saying, The ground of a certain rich man brought forth plentifully:

And he thought within himself, saying, What shall I do, because I have no room where to bestow my fruits?

And he said, This will I do: I will pull down my barns, and build greater; and there will I bestow all my fruits and my goods.

And I will say to my soul, Soul, thou hast much goods laid up for many

years; take thine ease, eat, drink, *and* be merry.

But God said unto him, *Thou* fool, this night thy soul shall be required of thee: then whose shall those things be, which thou hast provided?

So *is* he that layeth up treasure for himself, and is not rich toward God.

Lu 16:1 And he said also unto his disciples, There was a certain rich man, which had a steward; and the same was accused unto him that he had wasted his goods.

Lu 16:25 But Abraham said, Son, remember that thou in thy lifetime receivedst thy good things, and likewise Lazarus evil things: but now he is comforted, and thou art tormented.

b. The Perils of Having Too Much

INCLINES TO FORGETFULNESS OF GOD
De 8:13–14

BEGETS AVARICE
Ps 62:10

ENDANGERS INTEGRITY
Pr 28:20

HINDERS ENTRANCE INTO GOD'S KINGDOM
Mt 19:23

RESULTS IN BARRENNESS OF LIFE
Mk 4:19

SUBJECTS PEOPLE TO POWERFUL TEMPTATIONS
1 Ti 6:9

c. Of No Value in Time of Trial

Est 5:11; Ps 49:7; Pr 11:4; Ec 4:8; 5:11; 6:2; Je 9:23; 50:37; Eze 7:19; 27:27; Zep 1:18; Re 18:17

d. Not Necessarily Destructive

Ge 12:16 And he entreated Abram well for her sake: and he had sheep, and oxen, and he asses, and menservants, and maidservants, and she asses, and camels.

Ge 13:2 And Abram *was* very rich in cattle, in silver, and in gold.

Ge 26:14 For he had possession of flocks, and possession of herds, and great store of servants: and the Philistines envied him.

Ge 30:43 And the man increased exceedingly, and had much cattle, and maidservants, and menservants, and camels, and asses.

Ge 32:5 And I have oxen, and asses, flocks, and menservants, and womenservants: and I have sent to tell my lord, that I may find grace in thy sight.

Ge 36:7 For their riches were more than that they might dwell together; and the land wherein they were strangers could not bear them because of their cattle.

2 S 19:32 Now Barzillai was a very aged man, *even* fourscore years old: and he had provided the king of sustenance while he lay at Mahanaim; for he *was* a very great man.

1 Chr 29:28 And he died in a good old age, full of days, riches, and honour: and Solomon his son reigned in his stead.

2 Chr 1:15 And the king made silver and gold at Jerusalem *as plenteous* as stones, and cedar trees made he as the sycomore trees that *are* in the vale for abundance.

2 Chr 9:22 And king Solomon passed all the kings of the earth in riches and wisdom.

Jb 1:3 His substance also was seven thousand sheep, and three thousand camels, and five hundred yoke of oxen, and five hundred she asses, and a very great household; so that this man was the greatest of all the men of the east.

Pr 14:24 The crown of the wise is their riches: *but* the foolishness of fools *is* folly.

Pr 15:6 In the house of the righteous *is* much treasure: but in the revenues of the wicked is trouble.

Mt 27:57 When the even was come, there came a rich man of Arimathaea, named Joseph, who also himself was Jesus' disciple:

e. Fleeting and Uncertain

Jb 15:29 He shall not be rich, neither shall his substance continue, neither shall he prolong the perfection thereof upon the earth.

Jb 20:28 The increase of his house shall depart, *and his goods* shall flow away in the day of his wrath.

Jb 27:17 He may prepare *it,* but the just shall put *it* on, and the innocent shall divide the silver.

Ps 49:10 For he seeth *that* wise men die, likewise the fool and the brutish person perish, and leave their wealth to others.

Pr 23:5 Wilt thou set thine eyes upon that which is not? for *riches* certainly make themselves wings; they fly away as an eagle toward heaven.

Pr 27:24 For riches *are* not for ever: and doth the crown *endure* to every generation?

Pr 28:22 He that hasteth to be rich *hath* an evil eye, and considereth not that poverty shall come upon him.

Ec 2:18 Yea, I hated all my labour which I had taken under the sun: because I should leave it unto the man that shall be after me.

Ec 2:26 For *God* giveth to a man that *is* good in his sight wisdom, and knowledge, and joy: but to the sinner he giveth travail, to gather and to heap up, that he may give to *him that is* good before God. This also *is* vanity and vexation of spirit.

Is 15:7 Therefore the abundance they have gotten, and that which they have laid up, shall they carry away to the brook of the willows.

Is 39:6 Behold, the days come, that all that *is* in thine house, and *that* which thy fathers have laid up in store until this day, shall be carried to Babylon: nothing shall be left, saith the LORD.

Je 17:11 As the partridge sitteth *on eggs,* and hatcheth *them* not; *so* he that getteth riches, and not by right, shall leave them in the midst of his days, and at his end shall be a fool.

Eze 27:23 When thy wares went forth out of the seas, thou filledst many people; thou didst enrich the kings of the earth with the multitude of thy riches and of thy merchandise.

Obad 6 How are *the things* of Esau searched out! *how* are his hidden things sought up!

1 Ti 6:7 For we brought nothing into *this* world, *and it is* certain we can carry nothing out.

f. Are Deceptive Treasures

Hag 1:6 Ye have sown much, and bring in little; ye eat, but ye have not enough; ye drink, but ye are not filled with drink; ye clothe you, but there is none warm; and he that earneth wages earneth wages *to put it* into a bag with holes.

Lu 12:21 So *is* he that layeth up treasure for himself, and is not rich toward God.

1 Ti 6:7 For we brought nothing into *this* world, *and it is* certain we can carry nothing out.

He 11:26 Esteeming the reproach of Christ greater riches than the treasures in Egypt: for he had respect unto the recompence of the reward.

Re 3:17 Because thou sayest, I am rich, and increased with goods, and have need of nothing; and knowest not that thou art wretched, and miserable, and poor, and blind, and naked:

g. Accumulation Disappointing

Nu 11:32 And the people stood up all that day, and all *that* night, and all the next day, and they gathered the quails: he that gathered least gathered ten homers: and they spread *them* all abroad for themselves round about the camp.

2 Chr 32:27 And Hezekiah had exceeding much riches and honour: and he made himself treasuries for silver, and for gold, and for precious stones, and for spices, and for shields, and for all manner of pleasant jewels;

Jb 3:15 Or with princes that had gold, who filled their houses with silver:

Jb 27:16–17 Though he heap up silver as the dust, and prepare raiment as the clay;

He may prepare *it,* but the just shall put *it* on, and the innocent shall divide the silver.

Jb 31:25 If I rejoiced because my wealth *was* great, and because mine hand had gotten much;

Ps 39:6 Surely every man walketh in a vain shew: surely they are disquieted in vain: he heapeth up *riches,* and knoweth not who shall gather them.

Ps 73:12 Behold, these *are* the ungodly, who prosper in the world; they increase *in* riches.

Pr 20:21 An inheritance *may be* gotten hastily at the beginning; but the end thereof shall not be blessed.

Pr 28:8 He that by usury and unjust gain increaseth his substance, he shall gather it for him that will pity the poor.

Pr 28:22 He that hasteth to be rich *hath* an evil eye, and considereth not that poverty shall come upon him.

Ec 2:8 I gathered me also silver and gold, and the peculiar treasure of kings and of the provinces: I gat me men singers and women singers, and the delights of the sons of men, *as* musical instruments, and that of all sorts.

Ec 2:26 For *God* giveth to a man that *is* good in his sight wisdom, and knowledge, and joy: but to the sinner he giveth travail, to gather and to heap up, that he may give to *him that is* good before God. This also *is* vanity and vexation of spirit.

Ec 5:10 He that loveth silver shall not be satisfied with silver; nor he that loveth abundance with increase: this *is* also vanity.

Is 2:7 Their land also is full of silver and gold, neither *is there any* end of their treasures; their land is also full of horses, neither *is there any* end of their chariots:

Is 15:7 Therefore the abundance they have gotten, and that which they have laid up, shall they carry away to the brook of the willows.

Is 39:2 And Hezekiah was glad of them, and shewed them the house of his precious things, the silver, and the gold, and the spices, and the precious ointment, and all the house of his armour, and all that was found in his treasures: there was nothing in his house, nor in all his dominion, that Hezekiah shewed them not.

Eze 28:4 With thy wisdom and with thine understanding thou hast gotten thee riches, and hast gotten gold and silver into thy treasures:

Ho 12:8 And Ephraim said, Yet I am become rich, I have found me out substance: *in* all my labours they shall find none iniquity in me that *were* sin.

Zec 9:3 And Tyrus did build herself a strong hold, and heaped up silver as the dust, and fine gold as the mire of the streets.

Mt 6:19 Lay not up for yourselves treasures upon earth, where moth and rust doth corrupt, and where thieves break through and steal:

Lu 12:18 And he said, This will I do: I will pull down my barns, and build greater; and there will I bestow all my fruits and my goods.

Lu 12:21 So *is* he that layeth up treasure for himself, and is not rich toward God.

Ja 5:3 Your gold and silver is cankered; and the rust of them shall be a witness against you, and shall eat your flesh as it were fire. Ye have heaped treasure together for the last days.

2. Spiritual

ENDURING
Pr 8:18

GOD'S BLESSING
Pr 10:22

A PARADOX
Pr 13:7

DISCOVERED BY SPIRITUAL VISION
Ep 1:18

UNSEARCHABLE
Ep 3:8

PRECIOUS
He 11:26

THE INHERITANCE OF GOD'S ELECT
Ja 2:5

a. Examples

1 Co 1:5 That in every thing ye are enriched by him, in all utterance, and *in* all knowledge;

2 Co 6:10 As sorrowful, yet alway rejoicing; as poor, yet making many rich; as having nothing, and *yet* possessing all things.

2 Co 8:9 For ye know the grace of our Lord Jesus Christ, that, though he was rich, yet for your sakes he became poor, that ye through his poverty might be rich.

b. Spiritual Investments

Mt 6:20 But lay up for yourselves treasures in heaven, where neither moth nor rust doth corrupt, and where thieves do not break through nor steal:

Mt 13:44 Again, the kingdom of heaven is like unto treasure hid in a field; the which when a man hath found, he hideth, and for joy thereof goeth and selleth all that he hath, and buyeth that field.

Mt 13:46 Who, when he had found one pearl of great price, went and sold all that he had, and bought it.

Mt 19:21 Jesus said unto him, If thou wilt be perfect, go *and* sell that thou hast, and give to the poor, and thou shalt have treasure in heaven: and come *and* follow me.

Mt 25:17 And likewise he that *had* received two, he also gained other two.

Mt 25:22 He also that had received two talents came and said, Lord, thou deliveredst unto me two talents: behold, I have gained two other talents beside them.

Mk 10:21 Then Jesus beholding him loved him, and said unto him, One thing thou lackest: go thy way, sell whatsoever thou hast, and give to the poor, and thou shalt have treasure in heaven: and come, take up the cross, and follow me.

Mk 10:29 And Jesus answered and said, Verily I say unto you, There is no man that hath left house, or brethren, or sisters, or father, or mother, or wife, or children, or lands, for my sake, and the gospel's,

Lu 12:33 Sell that ye have, and give alms; provide yourselves bags which wax not old, a treasure in the heavens that faileth not, where no thief approacheth, neither moth corrupteth.

Lu 16:9 And I say unto you, Make to yourselves friends of the mammon of unrighteousness; that, when ye fail, they may receive you into everlasting habitations.

Lu 16:11 If therefore ye have not been faithful in the unrighteous mammon, who will commit to your trust the true *riches?*

Lu 18:22 Now when Jesus heard these things, he said unto him, Yet lackest thou one thing: sell all that thou hast, and distribute unto the poor, and thou shalt have treasure in heaven: and come, follow me.

Lu 19:15 And it came to pass, that when he was returned, having received the kingdom, then he commanded these servants to be called unto him, to whom he had given the money, that he might know how much every man had gained by trading.

Ph 3:8 Yea doubtless, and I count all things *but* loss for the excellency of the knowledge of Christ Jesus my Lord: for whom I have suffered the loss of all things, and do count them *but* dung, that I may win Christ,

1 Ti 6:19 Laying up in store for themselves a good foundation against the time to come, that they may lay hold on eternal life.

Re 3:18 I counsel thee to buy of me gold tried in the fire, that thou mayest be rich; and white raiment, that thou mayest be clothed, and *that* the shame of thy nakedness do not appear; and anoint thine eyes with eyesalve, that thou mayest see.

c. Spiritual Wealth

Pr 17:16 Wherefore *is there* a price in the hand of a fool to get wisdom, seeing *he hath* no heart *to it?*

Pr 23:23 Buy the truth, and sell *it* not; *also* wisdom, and instruction, and understanding.

Is 55:1 Ho, every one that thirsteth, come ye to the waters, and he that hath no money; come ye, buy, and eat; yea, come, buy wine and milk without money and without price.

Mt 13:44 Again, the kingdom of heaven is like unto treasure hid in a field; the which when a man hath found, he hideth, and for joy thereof goeth and selleth all that he hath, and buyeth that field.

Mt 25:9 But the wise answered, saying, *Not so;* lest there be not enough for us and you: but go ye rather to them that sell, and buy for yourselves.

Re 3:18 I counsel thee to buy of me gold tried in the fire, that thou mayest be rich; and white raiment, that thou mayest be clothed, and *that* the shame of thy nakedness do not appear; and anoint thine eyes with eyesalve, that thou mayest see.

See **AVARICE, GREED, MONEY, POOR, POVERTY**

RIDDLES, *hidden sayings*

Jud 14:12; Eze 17:2

RIGHTEOUS

1. Promises to

Ge 18:23 And Abraham drew near, and said, Wilt thou also destroy the righteous with the wicked?

2 S 22:22 For I have kept the ways of the LORD, and have not wickedly departed from my God.

1 K 8:32 Then hear thou in heaven, and do, and judge thy servants, condemning the wicked, to bring his way upon his head; and justifying the righteous, to give him according to his righteousness.

2 K 15:34 And he did *that which was* right in the sight of the LORD: he did according to all that his father Uzziah had done.

2 K 22:2 And he did *that which was* right in the sight of the LORD, and walked in all the way of David his father, and turned not aside to the right hand or to the left.

Jb 4:7 Remember, I pray thee, who *ever* perished, being innocent? or where were the righteous cut off?

Jb 8:20 Behold, God will not cast away a perfect *man,* neither will he help the evil doers:

Jb 17:9 The righteous also shall hold on his way, and he that hath clean hands shall be stronger and stronger.

Jb 36:7 He withdraweth not his eyes from the righteous: but with kings *are they* on the throne; yea, he doth establish them for ever, and they are exalted.

Ps 34:15 The eyes of the LORD *are* upon the righteous, and his ears *are open* unto their cry.

Ps 37:17 For the arms of the wicked shall be broken: but the LORD upholdeth the righteous.

Ps 37:25 I have been young, and *now* am old; yet have I not seen the righteous forsaken, nor his seed begging bread.

Ps 64:10 The righteous shall be glad in the LORD, and shall trust in him; and all the upright in heart shall glory.

Ps 68:3 But let the righteous be glad; let them rejoice before God: yea, let them exceedingly rejoice.

Ps 72:7 In his days shall the righteous flourish; and abundance of peace so long as the moon endureth.

Ps 92:12 The righteous shall flourish like the palm tree: he shall grow like a cedar in Lebanon.

Ps 107:42 The righteous shall see *it,* and rejoice: and all iniquity shall stop her mouth.

Ps 118:20 This gate of the LORD, into which the righteous shall enter.

Ps 119:1 Blessed *are* the undefiled in the way, who walk in the law of the LORD.

Ps 140:13 Surely the righteous shall give thanks unto thy name: the upright shall dwell in thy presence.

Ps 146:8 The LORD openeth *the eyes of* the blind: the LORD raiseth them that are bowed down: the LORD loveth the righteous:

Pr 2:7 He layeth up sound wisdom for the righteous: *he is* a buckler to them that walk uprightly.

Pr 3:32 For the froward *is* abomination to the LORD: but his secret *is* with the righteous.

Pr 4:18 But the path of the just *is* as the shining light, that shineth more and more unto the perfect day.

Pr 12:13 The wicked is snared by the transgression of *his* lips: but the just shall come out of trouble.

Pr 12:26 The righteous *is* more excellent than his neighbour: but the way of the wicked seduceth them.

Pr 13:25 The righteous eateth to the satisfying of his soul: but the belly of the wicked shall want.

Pr 14:9 Fools make a mock at sin: but among the righteous *there is* favour.

Pr 14:19 The evil bow before the good; and the wicked at the gates of the righteous.

Pr 20:7 The just *man* walketh in his integrity: his children *are* blessed after him.

Pr 29:6 In the transgression of an evil man *there is* a snare: but the righteous doth sing and rejoice.

Pr 29:16 When the wicked are multiplied, transgression increaseth: but the righteous shall see their fall.

Ec 9:1 For all this I considered even to declare all this, that the righteous, and the wise, and their works, are in the hand of God: no man knoweth either love or hatred *by* all *that is* before them.

Is 3:10 Say ye to the righteous, that *it shall be* well *with him:* for they shall eat the fruit of their doings.

Is 41:2 Who raised up the righteous *man* from the east, called him to his foot, gave the nations before him, and made *him* rule over kings? he gave *them* as the dust to his sword, *and* as driven stubble to his bow.

Eze 23:45 And the righteous men, they shall judge them after the manner of adulteresses, and after the manner of women that shed blood; because they *are* adulteresses, and blood *is* in their hands.

Mal 3:18 Then shall ye return, and discern between the righteous and the wicked, between him that serveth God and him that serveth him not.

Mt 13:43 Then shall the righteous shine forth as the sun in the kingdom of their Father. Who hath ears to hear, let him hear.

Mt 13:48 Which, when it was full, they drew to shore, and sat down, and gathered the good into vessels, but cast the bad away.

Mt 25:37 Then shall the righteous answer him, saying, Lord, when saw we thee an hungred, and fed *thee?* or thirsty, and gave *thee* drink?

Ep 1:1 Paul, an apostle of Jesus Christ by the will of God, to the saints which are at Ephesus, and to the faithful in Christ Jesus:

Ph 1:1 Paul and Timotheus, the servants of Jesus Christ, to all the saints in Christ Jesus which are at Philippi, with the bishops and deacons:

1 Th 3:13 To the end he may stablish your hearts unblameable in holiness before God, even our Father, at the coming of our Lord Jesus Christ with all his saints.

Ja 5:16 Confess *your* faults one to another, and pray one for another, that ye may be healed. The effectual fervent prayer of a righteous man availeth much.

1 Pe 3:12 For the eyes of the Lord *are* over the righteous, and his ears *are open* unto their prayers: but the face of the Lord *is* against them that do evil.

2 Pe 2:8 (For that righteous man dwelling among them, in seeing and hearing, vexed *his* righteous soul from day to day with *their* unlawful deeds;)

1 Jn 3:12 Not as Cain, who was of that wicked one, and slew his brother. And wherefore slew he him? Because his own works were evil, and his brother's righteous.

Re 3:4 Thou hast a few names even in Sardis which have not defiled their garments; and they shall walk with me in white: for they are worthy.

2. Mouth of

Ps 37:30 The mouth of the righteous speaketh wisdom, and his tongue talketh of judgment.

Ps 145:21 My mouth shall speak the praise of the LORD: and let all flesh bless his holy name for ever and ever.

Pr 10:11 The mouth of a righteous *man is* a well of life: but violence covereth the mouth of the wicked.

Pr 15:4 A wholesome tongue *is* a tree of life: but perverseness therein *is* a breach in the spirit.

Pr 23:16 Yea, my reins shall rejoice, when thy lips speak right things.

Pr 31:26 She openeth her mouth with wisdom; and in her tongue *is* the law of kindness.

Am 5:10 They hate him that rebuketh in the gate, and they abhor him that speaketh uprightly.

Mal 2:6 The law of truth was in his mouth, and iniquity was not found in his lips: he walked with me in peace and equity, and did turn many away from iniquity.

Ro 15:6 That ye may with one mind *and* one mouth glorify God, even r Lord Jesus Christ.

1 Pe 2:22 Who did no sin, neither was guile found in his mouth:

Re 14:5 And in their mouth was found no guile: for they are without fault before the throne of God.

See **WICKED**

RIGHTEOUSNESS, *purity of heart and rectitude of life*

1. Of God

Ge 18:25 That be far from thee to do after this manner, to slay the righteous with the wicked: and that the righteous should be as the wicked, that be far from thee: Shall not the Judge of all the earth do right?

Ex 9:27 And Pharaoh sent, and called for Moses and Aaron, and said unto them, I have sinned this time: the LORD *is* righteous, and I and my people *are* wicked.

De 32:5 They have corrupted themselves, their spot *is* not *the spot* of his children: *they are* a perverse and crooked generation.

Jud 5:11 *They that are delivered* from the noise of archers in the places of drawing water, there shall they rehearse the righteous acts of the LORD, *even* the righteous acts *toward the inhabitants* of his villages in Israel: then shall the people of the LORD go down to the gates.

1 S 12:7 Now therefore stand still, that I may reason with you before the LORD of all the righteous acts of the LORD, which he did to you and to your fathers.

2 Chr 12:6 Whereupon the princes of Israel and the king humbled themselves; and they said, The LORD *is* righteous.

2 Chr 19:7 Wherefore now let the fear of the LORD be upon you; take heed and do *it:* for *there is* no iniquity with the LORD our God, nor respect of persons, nor taking of gifts.

Ezr 9:15 O LORD God of Israel, thou *art* righteous: for we remain yet escaped, as *it is* this day: behold, we *are* before thee in our trespasses: for we cannot stand before thee because of this.

Ne 9:8 And foundest his heart faithful before thee, and madest a covenant with him to give the land of the Canaanites, the Hittites, the Amorites, and the Perizzites, and the Jebusites, and the Girgashites, to give *it, I say,* to his seed, and hast performed thy words; for thou *art* righteous:

Ne 9:33 Howbeit thou *art* just in all that is brought upon us; for thou hast done right, but we have done wickedly:

Jb 34:10 Therefore hearken unto me, ye men of understanding: far be it from God, *that he should do* wickedness; and *from* the Almighty, *that he should commit* iniquity.

Jb 36:3 I will fetch my knowledge from afar, and will ascribe righteousness to my Maker.

Jb 36:23 Who hath enjoined him his way? or who can say, Thou hast wrought iniquity?

Ps 5:8 Lead me, O LORD, in thy righteousness because of mine enemies; make thy way straight before my face.

Ps 7:9 Oh let the wickedness of the wicked come to an end; but establish the just: for the righteous God trieth the hearts and reins.

Ps 7:17 I will praise the LORD according to his righteousness: and will sing praise to the name of the LORD most high.

Ps 9:8 And he shall judge the world in righteousness, he shall minister judgment to the people in uprightness.

Ps 11:7 For the righteous LORD loveth righteousness; his countenance doth behold the upright.

Ps 22:31 They shall come, and shall declare his righteousness unto a people that shall be born, that he hath done *this.*

Ps 33:5 He loveth righteousness and judgment: the earth is full of the goodness of the LORD.

Ps 35:24 Judge me, O LORD my God, according to thy righteousness; and let them not rejoice over me.

Ps 36:6 Thy righteousness *is* like the great mountains; thy judgments *are* a great deep: O LORD, thou preservest man and beast.

Ps 40:10 I have not hid thy righteousness within my heart; I have declared thy faithfulness and thy salvation: I have not concealed thy lovingkindness and thy truth from the great congregation.

Ps 45:4 And in thy majesty ride prosperously because of truth and meekness *and* righteousness; and thy right hand shall teach thee terrible things.

Ps 48:10 According to thy name, O God, so *is* thy praise unto the ends of the earth: thy right hand is full of righteousness.

Ps 50:6 And the heavens shall declare his righteousness: for God *is* judge himself. Selah.

Ps 51:14 Deliver me from bloodguiltiness, O God, thou God of my salvation: *and* my tongue shall sing aloud of thy righteousness.

Ps 65:5 By terrible things in righteousness wilt thou answer us, O God of our salvation; *who art* the confidence of all the ends of the earth, and of them that are afar off *upon* the sea:

Ps 71:16 I will go in the strength of the Lord GOD: I will make mention of thy righteousness, *even* of thine only.

Ps 71:19 Thy righteousness also, O God, *is* very high, who hast done great things: O God, who *is* like unto thee!

Ps 85:13 Righteousness shall go before him; and shall set *us* in the way of his steps.

Ps 88:12 Shall thy wonders be known in the dark? and thy righteousness in the land of forgetfulness?

Ps 92:15 To shew that the LORD *is* upright: *he is* my rock, and *there is* no unrighteousness in him.

Ps 96:13 Before the LORD: for he cometh, for he cometh to judge the earth: he shall judge the world with righteousness, and the people with his truth.

Ps 97:2 Clouds and darkness *are* round about him: righteousness and judgment *are* the habitation of his throne.

Ps 98:2 The LORD hath made known his salvation: his righteousness hath he openly shewed in the sight of the heathen.

Ps 103:17 But the mercy of the LORD *is* from everlasting to everlasting upon them that fear him, and his righteousness unto children's children;

Ps 111:3 His work *is* honourable and glorious: and his righteousness endureth for ever.

Ps 116:5 Gracious *is* the LORD, and righteous; yea, our God *is* merciful.

Ps 119:137 Righteous *art* thou, O LORD, and upright *are* thy judgments.

Ps 119:142 Thy righteousness *is* an everlasting righteousness, and thy law *is* the truth.

Ps 129:4 The LORD *is* righteous: he hath cut asunder the cords of the wicked.

Ps 143:1 Hear my prayer, O LORD, give ear to my supplications: in thy faithfulness answer me, *and* in thy righteousness.

Ps 143:11 Quicken me, O LORD, for thy name's sake: for thy righteousness' sake bring my soul out of trouble.

Ps 145:7 They shall abundantly utter the memory of thy great goodness, and shall sing of thy righteousness.

Ps 145:17 The LORD *is* righteous in all his ways, and holy in all his works.

Is 5:16 But the LORD of hosts shall be exalted in judgment, and God that is holy shall be sanctified in righteousness.

Is 46:13 I bring near my righteousness; it shall not be far off, and my salvation shall not tarry: and I will place salvation in Zion for Israel my glory.

Is 56:1 Thus saith the LORD, Keep ye judgment, and do justice: for my salvation *is* near to come, and my righteousness to be revealed.

Je 9:24 But let him that glorieth glory in this, that he understandeth and knoweth me, that I *am* the LORD which exercise lovingkindness, judgment, and righteousness, in the earth: for in these *things* I delight, saith the LORD.

Je 12:1 Righteous *art* thou, O LORD, when I plead with thee: yet let me talk with thee of *thy* judgments: Wherefore doth the way of the wicked prosper? *wherefore* are all they happy that deal very treacherously?

Je 23:6 In his days Judah shall be saved, and Israel shall dwell safely: and this *is* his name whereby he shall be called, THE LORD OUR RIGHTEOUSNESS.

Lam 1:18 The LORD is righteous; for I have rebelled against his commandment: hear, I pray you, all people, and behold my sorrow: my virgins and my young men are gone into captivity.

Da 9:7 O Lord, righteousness *belongeth* unto thee, but unto us confusion of faces, as at this day; to the men of Judah, and to the inhabitants of Jerusalem, and unto all Israel, *that are* near, and *that are* far off, through all the countries whither thou hast driven them, because of their trespass that they have trespassed against thee.

Da 9:14 Therefore hath the LORD watched upon the evil, and brought it upon us: for the LORD our God *is* righteous in all his works which he doeth: for we obeyed not his voice.

Ho 2:19 And I will betroth thee unto me for ever; yea, I will betroth thee unto me in righteousness, and in judgment, and in lovingkindness, and in mercies.

Mi 6:5 O my people, remember now what Balak king of Moab consulted, and what Balaam the son of Beor answered him from Shittim unto Gilgal; that ye may know the righteousness of the LORD.

Mi 7:9 I will bear the indignation of the LORD, because I have sinned against him, until he plead my cause, and execute judgment for me: he will bring me forth to the light, *and* I shall behold his righteousness.

Mt 20:13 But he answered one of them, and said, Friend, I do thee no wrong: didst not thou agree with me for a penny?

Jn 17:25 O righteous Father, the world hath not known thee: but I have known thee, and these have known that thou hast sent me.

Ac 17:31 Because he hath appointed a day, in the which he will judge the world in righteousness by *that* man whom he hath ordained; *whereof* he hath given assurance unto all *men,* in that he hath raised him from the dead.

Ro 1:17 For therein is the righteousness of God revealed from faith to faith: as it is written, The just shall live by faith.

Ro 2:2 But we are sure that the judgment of God is according to truth against them which commit

Ro 3:5 But if our unrighteousness commend the righteousness of God, what shall we say? *Is* God unrighteous who taketh vengeance? (I speak as a man)

Ro 3:21 But now the righteousness of God without the law is manifested, being witnessed by the law and the prophets;

Ro 9:14 What shall we say then? *Is there* unrighteousness with God? God forbid.

Ro 10:3 For they being ignorant of God's righteousness, and going about to establish their own righteousness, have not submitted themselves unto the righteousness of God.

Ja 1:20 For the wrath of man worketh not the righteousness of God.

2 Pe 1:1 Simon Peter, a servant and an apostle of Jesus Christ, to them that have obtained like precious faith with

us through the righteousness of God and our Saviour Jesus Christ:

1 Jn 2:29 If ye know that he is righteous, ye know that every one that doeth righteousness is born of him.

Re 16:5 And I heard the angel of the waters say, Thou art righteous, O Lord, which art, and wast, and shalt be, because thou hast judged thus.

2. Of Christ

Ps 45:7 Thou lovest righteousness, and hatest wickedness: therefore God, thy God, hath anointed thee with the oil of gladness above thy fellows.

Is 11:5 And righteousness shall be the girdle of his loins, and faithfulness the girdle of his reins.

Is 32:1 Behold, a king shall reign in righteousness, and princes shall rule in judgment.

Is 42:6 I the LORD have called thee in righteousness, and will hold thine hand, and will keep thee, and give thee for a covenant of the people, for a light of the Gentiles;

Is 53:11 He shall see of the travail of his soul, *and* shall be satisfied: by his knowledge shall my righteous servant justify many; for he shall bear their iniquities.

Is 59:16 And he saw that *there was* no man, and wondered that *there was* no intercessor: therefore his arm brought salvation unto him; and his righteousness, it sustained him.

Je 23:5 Behold, the days come, saith the LORD, that I will raise unto David a righteous Branch, and a King shall reign and prosper, and shall execute judgment and justice in the earth.

Zec 9:9 Rejoice greatly, O daughter of Zion; shout, O daughter of Jerusalem: behold, thy King cometh unto thee: he *is* just, and having salvation; lowly, and riding upon an ass, and upon a colt the foal of an ass.

Mt 3:15 And Jesus answering said unto him, Suffer *it to be so* now: for thus it becometh us to fulfil all righteousness. Then he suffered him.

Mt 27:19 When he was set down on the judgment seat, his wife sent unto him, saying, Have thou nothing to do with that just man: for I have suffered many things this day in a dream because of him.

Mt 27:24 When Pilate saw that he could prevail nothing, but *that* rather a tumult was made, he took water, and washed *his* hands before the multitude, saying, I am innocent of the blood of this just person: see ye *to it.*

Lu 1:35 And the angel answered and said unto her, The Holy Ghost shall come upon thee, and the power of the Highest shall overshadow thee: therefore also that holy thing which shall be born of thee shall be called the Son of God.

Lu 23:47 Now when the centurion saw what was done, he glorified God, saying, Certainly this was a righteous man.

He 1:9 Thou hast loved righteousness, and hated iniquity; therefore God, *even* thy God, hath anointed thee with the oil of gladness above thy fellows.

He 7:26 For such an high priest became us, *who is* holy, harmless, undefiled, separate from sinners, and made higher than the heavens;

1 Jn 2:1 My little children, these things write I unto you, that ye sin not. And if any man sin, we have an advocate with the Father, Jesus Christ the righteous:

1 Jn 3:7 Little children, let no man deceive you: he that doeth righteousness is righteous, even as he is righteous.

Re 19:11 And I saw heaven opened, and behold a white horse; and he that sat upon him *was* called Faithful and True, and in righteousness he doth judge and make war.

3. Examples

Ge 7:1 And the LORD said unto Noah, Come thou and all thy house into the ark; for thee have I seen righteous before me in this generation.

1 K 15:14 But the high places were not removed: nevertheless Asa's heart was perfect with the LORD all his days.

2 Chr 14:2 And Asa did *that which was* good and right in the eyes of the LORD his God:

2 Chr 29:2 And he did *that which was* right in the sight of the LORD, according to all that David his father had done.

2 Chr 31:20 And thus did Hezekiah throughout all Judah, and wrought *that which was* good and right and truth before the LORD his God.

Jb 1:1 There was a man in the land of Uz, whose name *was* Job; and that man was perfect and upright, and one that feared God, and eschewed evil.

Ps 7:8 The LORD shall judge the people: judge me, O LORD, according to my righteousness, and according to mine integrity *that is* in me.

Zep 3:13 The remnant of Israel shall not do iniquity, nor speak lies; neither shall a deceitful tongue be found in their mouth: for they shall feed and lie down, and none shall make *them* afraid.

Lu 1:6 And they were both righteous before God, walking in all the commandments and ordinances of the Lord blameless.

Lu 2:37 And she *was* a widow of about fourscore and four years, which departed not from the temple, but served God with fastings and prayers night and day.

Ac 24:16 And herein do I exercise myself, to have always a conscience void of offence toward God, and *toward* men.

4. Prescribed

De 4:27 And the LORD shall scatter you among the nations, and ye shall be left few in number among the heathen, whither the LORD shall lead you.

De 6:18 And thou shalt do *that which is* right and good in the sight of the LORD: that it may be well with thee, and that thou mayest go in and possess the good land which the LORD sware unto thy fathers,

De 6:25 And it shall be our righteousness, if we observe to do all these commandments before the LORD our God, as he hath commanded us.

De 12:25 Thou shalt not eat it; that it may go well with thee, and with thy children after thee, when thou shalt do that which is right in the sight of the LORD.

De 13:18 When thou shalt hearken to the voice of the LORD thy God, to keep all his commandments which I command thee this day, to do *that which is* right in the eyes of the LORD thy God.

De 24:13 In any case thou shalt deliver him the pledge again when the sun goeth down, that he may sleep in his own raiment, and bless thee: and it shall be righteousness unto thee before the LORD thy God.

Ps 15:2 He that walketh uprightly, and worketh righteousness, and speaketh the truth in his heart.

Ps 24:4 He that hath clean hands, and a pure heart; who hath not lifted up his soul unto vanity, nor sworn deceitfully.

Ps 106:3 Blessed *are* they that keep judgment, *and* he that doeth righteousness at all times.

Pr 10:2 Treasures of wickedness profit nothing: but righteousness delivereth from death.

Pr 11:4 Riches profit not in the day of wrath: but righteousness delivereth from death.

Pr 15:9 The way of the wicked *is* an abomination unto the LORD: but he loveth him that followeth after righteousness.

Pr 16:6 By mercy and truth iniquity is purged: and by the fear of the LORD *men* depart from evil.

Pr 21:3 To do justice and judgment *is* more acceptable to the LORD than sacrifice.

Pr 21:21 He that followeth after righteousness and mercy findeth life, righteousness, and honour.

Is 51:1 Hearken to me, ye that follow after righteousness, ye that seek the LORD: look unto the rock *whence* ye are hewn, and to the hole of the pit *whence* ye are digged.

Is 56:2 Blessed *is* the man *that* doeth this, and the son of man *that* layeth hold on it; that keepeth the sabbath from polluting it, and keepeth his hand from doing any evil.

Je 22:3 Thus saith the LORD; Execute ye judgment and righteousness, and

deliver the spoiled out of the hand of the oppressor: and do no wrong, do no violence to the stranger, the fatherless, nor the widow, neither shed innocent blood in this place.

Eze 3:21 Nevertheless if thou warn the righteous *man*, that the righteous sin not, and he doth not sin, he shall surely live, because he is warned; also thou hast delivered thy soul.

Eze 18:5 But if a man be just, and do that which is lawful and right,

Da 4:27 Wherefore, O king, let my counsel be acceptable unto thee, and break off thy sins by righteousness, and thine iniquities by shewing mercy to the poor; if it may be a lengthening of thy tranquility.

Ho 10:12 Sow to yourselves in righteousness, reap in mercy; break up your fallow ground: for *it is* time to seek the LORD, till he come and rain righteousness upon you.

Am 5:14 Seek good, and not evil, that ye may live: and so the LORD, the God of hosts, shall be with you, as ye have spoken.

Am 5:24 But let judgment run down as waters, and righteousness as a mighty stream.

Zep 2:3 Seek ye the LORD, all ye meek of the earth, which have wrought his judgment; seek righteousness, seek meekness: it may be ye shall be hid in the day of the LORD's anger.

Zec 8:19 Thus saith the LORD of hosts; The fast of the fourth *month,* and the fast of the fifth, and the fast of the seventh, and the fast of the tenth, shall be to the house of Judah joy and gladness, and cheerful feasts; therefore love the truth and peace.

Mt 5:20 For I say unto you, That except your righteousness shall exceed *the righteousness* of the scribes and Pharisees, ye shall in no case enter into the kingdom of heaven.

Lu 1:75 In holiness and righteousness before him, all the days of our life.

Jn 16:10 Of righteousness, because I go to my Father, and ye see me no more;

Ac 24:25 And as he reasoned of righteousness, temperance, and judgment to come Felix trembled, and answered, Go thy way for this time; when I have a convenient season, I will call for thee.

Ro 6:16 Know ye not, that to whom ye yield yourselves servants to obey, his servants ye are to whom ye obey; whether of sin unto death, or of obedience unto righteousness?

Ro 6:19 I speak after the manner of men because of the infirmity of your flesh: for as ye have yielded your members servants to uncleanness and to iniquity unto iniquity; even so now yield your members servants to righteousness unto holiness.

Ro 14:17 For the kingdom of God is not meat and drink; but righteousness, and peace, and joy in the Holy Ghost.

1 Co 15:34 Awake to righteousness, and sin not; for some have not the knowledge of God: I speak *this* to your shame.

Ep 4:24 And that ye put on the new man, which after God is created in righteousness and true holiness.

Ep 5:9 (For the fruit of the Spirit is in all goodness and righteousness and truth;)

Ep 6:14 Stand therefore, having your loins girt about with truth, and having on the breastplate of righteousness;

Ph 1:11 Being filled with the fruits of righteousness, which are by Jesus Christ, unto the glory and praise of God.

1 Ti 6:11 But thou, O man of God, flee these things; and follow after righteousness, godliness, faith, love, patience, meekness.

2 Ti 2:22 Flee also youthful lusts: but follow righteousness, faith, charity, peace, with them that call on the Lord out of a pure heart.

Tit 2:12 Teaching us that, denying ungodliness and worldly lusts, we should live soberly, righteously, and godly, in this present world;

Ja 3:18 And the fruit of righteousness is sown in peace of them that make peace.

1 Jn 2:29 If ye know that he is righteous, ye know that every one that doeth righteousness is born of him.

1 Jn 3:7 Little children, let no man deceive you: he that doeth righteousness is righteous, even as he is righteous.

Re 22:11 He that is unjust, let him be unjust still: and he which is filthy, let him be filthy still: and he that is righteous, let him be righteous still: and he that is holy, let him be holy still.

See **UNRIGHTEOUSNESS**

RINGS *See* **APPAREL**

RIVERS

1. Names

ABANA

2 K 5:12 *Are* not Abana and Pharpar, rivers of Damascus, better than all the waters of Israel? may I not wash in them, and be clean? So he turned and went away in a rage.

ARNON

De 2:36 From Aroer, which *is* by the brink of the river of Arnon, and *from* the city that *is* by the river, even unto Gilead, there was not one city too strong for us: the LORD our God delivered all unto us:

CHEBAR

Eze 1:1 Now it came to pass in the thirtieth year, in the fourth *month,* in the fifth *day* of the month, as I *was* among the captives by the river of Chebar, *that* the heavens were opened, and I saw visions of God.

EUPHRATES

Ge 2:14 And the name of the third river *is* Hiddekel: that *is* it which goeth toward the east of Assyria. And the fourth river *is* Euphrates.

GOZAN

2 K 17:6 In the ninth year of Hoshea the king of Assyria took Samaria, and carried Israel away into Assyria, and placed them in Halah and in Habor *by* the river of Gozan, and in the cities of the Medes.

1 Chr 5:26 And the God of Israel stirred up the spirit of Pul king of

Assyria, and the spirit of Tilgath-pilne-ser king of Assyria, and he carried them away, even the Reubenites, and the Gadites, and the half tribe of Manasseh, and brought them unto Halah, and Habor, and Hara, and to the river Gozan, unto this day.

JORDAN

See **JORDAN**

KANAH

Jos 16:8 The border went out from Tappuah westward unto the river Kanah; and the goings out thereof were at the sea. This *is* the inheritance of the tribe of the children of Ephraim by their families.

KISHON

Jud 5:21 The river of Kishon swept them away, that ancient river, the river Kishon. O my soul, thou hast trodden down strength.

OF EGYPT (NILE)

Ex 1:22 And Pharaoh charged all his people, saying, Every son that is born ye shall cast into the river, and every daughter ye shall save alive.

PHARPAR

2 K 5:12 *Are* not Abana and Pharpar, rivers of Damascus, better than all the waters of Israel? may I not wash in them, and be clean? So he turned and went away in a rage.

PISON

Ge 2:11 The name of the first *is* Pison: that *is* it which compasseth the whole land of Havilah, where *there is* gold;

HIDDEKEL (OR TIGRIS)

Ge 2:14 And the name of the third river *is* Hiddekel: that *is* it which goeth toward the east of Assyria. And the fourth river *is* Euphrates.

ULAI

Da 8:16 And I heard a man's voice between *the banks of* Ulai, which called, and said, Gabriel, make this *man* to understand the vision.

2. Spiritual, *a symbol of divine blessings*

Ps 1:3 And he shall be like a tree planted by the rivers of water, that bringeth forth his fruit in his season; his leaf also shall not wither; and whatsoever he doeth shall prosper.

Ps 36:8 They shall be abundantly satisfied with the fatness of thy house; and thou shalt make them drink of the river of thy pleasures.

Ps 46:4 *There is* a river, the streams whereof shall make glad the city of God, the holy *place* of the tabernacles of the most High.

Is 41:18 I will open rivers in high places, and fountains in the midst of the valleys: I will make the wilderness a pool of water, and the dry land springs of water.

Is 48:18 O that thou hadst hearkened to my commandments! then had thy peace been as a river, and thy righteousness as the waves of the sea:

Eze 47:5 Afterward he measured a thousand; *and it was* a river that I could not pass over: for the waters were risen, waters to swim in, a river that could not be passed over.

Re 22:1 And he shewed me a pure river of water of life, clear as crystal, proceeding out of the throne of God and of the Lamb.

RIZPAH, *daughter of Aiah, displayed maternal love*

2 S 3:7; 21:8

ROBBERY

Le 6:2; Jud 6:4; 9:25; 1 K 20:6; Jb 1:17; 5:5; 24:2, 16; Pr 1:13; Eze 22:29; Ho 6:9; 7:1; Am 3:10; Mi 2:8; Na 3:1; Lu 10:30

See **NATION**

ROBE See **APPAREL**

ROCK, *water brought from*

Nu 20:11; De 8:15; Ps 78:15–16, 20

See **WATER**

ROD OF MOSES

Ex 4:2, 17, 20; 7:9, 19; 8:16; 9:23; 10:13; 14:16; 17:5, 9

See **MOSES**

ROD OF CORRECTION, *symbol or means of discipline*

Jb 9:34 Let him take his rod away from me, and let not his fear terrify me:

Ps 89:32 Then will I visit their transgression with the rod, and their iniquity with stripes.

Ps 94:10 He that chastiseth the heathen, shall not he correct? he that teacheth man knowledge, *shall not he know?*

Pr 10:13 In the lips of him that hath understanding wisdom is found: but a rod *is* for the back of him that is void of understanding.

Pr 13:24 He that spareth his rod hateth his son: but he that loveth him chasteneth him betimes.

Pr 15:10 Correction *is* grievous unto him that forsaketh the way: *and* he that hateth reproof shall die.

Pr 19:29 Judgments are prepared for scorners, and stripes for the back of fools.

Pr 22:15 Foolishness *is* bound in the heart of a child; *but* the rod of correction shall drive it far from him.

Pr 23:14 Thou shalt beat him with the rod, and shalt deliver his soul from hell.

Pr 26:3 A whip for the horse, a bridle for the ass, and a rod for the fool's back.

Pr 29:15 The rod and reproof give wisdom: but a child left *to himself* bringeth his mother to shame.

Is 30:32 And *in* every place where the grounded staff shall pass, which the LORD shall lay upon him, *it* shall be with tabrets and harps: and in battles of shaking will he fight with it.

Lam 3:1 I *am* the man *that* hath seen affliction by the rod of his wrath.

Mi 6:9 The LORD's voice crieth unto the city, and *the man of* wisdom shall see thy name: hear ye the rod, and who hath appointed it.

See **PUNISHMENT**

RODS, *branches, sticks, staffs used for various purposes*

Nu 17:8; 1 S 14:27

ROLLS, *scrolls*

Is 8:1; Je 36:2, 21, 27; Eze 2:9; 3:1; Hab 2:2; Zec 5:1

See **BOOKS**

ROMANS

Author: The apostle Paul.

Date Written: A.D. 57, near the end of his third missionary journey. Evidently written from Corinth.

Purpose: To prepare the believers of Rome for his long-awaited visit. He wanted to spiritually edify them and also establish his apostolic authority through a foundational theological treatise.

To Whom Written: Roman Christians (1:7).

Main Themes:

(1) Part I (1–11): The plan of salvation; justification by faith and sanctification through the Holy Spirit.

(2) Part II (12-16): Exhortations concerning Christian duties.

Key Word: Faith.

Key Verses: 1:16; 3:22-23, 28; 4:3; 5:1, 18; 9:31–32; 10:3-4, 6–9.

ROME, *capital of the Roman empire*

Here in the Mamertine Prison Paul (2 Ti 4:6–8) was probably imprisoned and Peter may have awaited martyrdom. It may have been the home of Clement (Ph 4:3) and Pudens (2 Ti 4:21).

See **CITIES**

ROSE, *a flower*

Song 2:1; Is 35:1

ROSE OF SHARON

See **TITLES AND NAMES**

RUBIES See **STONES**

RULER

See **NATION**

RUNNING, *the Christian life compared to a race*

STRIVING FOR THE PRIZE

1 Co 9:24 Know ye not that they which run in a race run all, but one receiveth the prize? So run, that ye may obtain.

Ga 2:2 And I went up by revelation, and communicated unto them that gospel which I preach among the Gentiles, but privately to them which were of reputation, lest by any means I should run, or had run, in vain.

HINDRANCES TO THE RUNNER

Ga 5:7 Ye did run well; who did hinder you that ye should not obey the truth?

PRESSING TOWARD THE GOAL

Ph 3:14 I press toward the mark for the prize of the high calling of God in Christ Jesus.

PREPARING FOR THE CONTEST

He 12:1 Wherefore seeing we also are compassed about with so great a cloud of witnesses, let us lay aside every weight, and the sin which doth so easily beset us, and let us run with patience the race that is set before us,

THE HOME STRETCH

2 Ti 4:7 I have fought a good fight, I have finished *my* course, I have kept the faith:

THE PRIZE WON

2 Ti 4:8 Henceforth there is laid up for me a crown of righteousness, which the Lord, the righteous judge, shall give me at that day: and not to me only, but unto all them also that love his appearing.

See **DISCIPLESHIP**

RUTH

1. Person, *a Moabite woman, daughter-in-law of Naomi*

FILIAL LOVE, CONSTANCY, PIETY

Ru 1:16 And Ruth said, Intreat me not to leave thee, *or* to return from following after thee: for whither thou goest, I will go; and where thou lodgest, I will lodge: thy people *shall be* my people, and thy God my God:

INDUSTRY

Ru 2:7 And she said, I pray you, let me glean and gather after the reapers among the sheaves: so she came, and hath continued even from the morning until now, that she tarried a little in the house.

Ru 2:23 So she kept fast by the maidens of Boaz to glean unto the end of barley harvest and of wheat harvest; and dwelt with her mother in law.

FILIAL OBEDIENCE

Ru 3:5 And she said unto her, All that thou sayest unto me I will do.

A SPOTLESS NAME

Ru 3:11 And now, my daughter, fear not; I will do to thee all that thou requirest: for all the city of my people doth know that thou *art* a virtuous woman.

2. Book

Author: Unknown; possibly Samuel.

Date Written: 1046–1035 B.C.(?)

Purpose: To show how a Gentile woman became one of the ancestors of Christ.

To Whom Written: The nation of Israel and possibly surrounding Gentile peoples.

Main Theme: The kinsman redeemer, a type of Christ, truly liberates, when he fulfills his divinely ordained function.

Key Word: Redeem.

Key Verses: 1:16, 4:4.

See **WOMEN, YOUNG PEOPLE**

S

SABBATH, *to cease, to desist, to rest*

Ge 2:3; Ex 16:23; 31:17; Le 24:8; 2 Chr 8:13; 23:8; 31:3; Ne 9:14; 13:22; Ps 118:24; Eze 20:12; 45:17; 46:1; Ho 2:11; Mt 12:1, 8; 28:1; Mk 2:23, 27; Lu 6:1; He 4:4

1. Its Restrictions

Ex 16:30 So the people rested on the seventh day.

Ex 20:8 Remember the sabbath day, to keep it holy.

Ex 31:15 Six days may work be done; but in the seventh is the sabbath of rest, holy to the LORD: whosoever doeth *any* work in the sabbath day, he shall surely be put to death.

Ex 34:21 Six days thou shalt work, but on the seventh day thou shalt rest: in earing time and in harvest thou shalt rest.

Ex 35:3 Ye shall kindle no fire throughout your habitations upon the sabbath day.

Le 26:2 Ye shall keep my sabbaths, and reverence my sanctuary: I *am* the LORD.

De 5:12 Keep the sabbath day to sanctify it, as the LORD thy God hath commanded thee.

Ne 10:31 And *if* the people of the land bring ware or any victuals on the sabbath day to sell, *that* we would not buy it of them on the sabbath, or on the holy day: and *that* we would leave the seventh year, and the exaction of every debt.

Ne 13:17 Then I contended with the nobles of Judah, and said unto them, What evil thing *is* this that ye do, and profane the sabbath day?

Is 56:2 Blessed *is* the man *that* doeth this, and the son of man *that* layeth hold on it; that keepeth the sabbath from polluting it, and keepeth his hand from doing any evil.

Is 58:13-14 If thou turn away thy foot from the sabbath, *from* doing thy pleasure on my holy day; and call the sabbath a delight, the holy of the LORD, honourable; and shalt honour him, not doing thine own ways, nor finding thine own pleasure, nor speaking *thine own* words:

Then shalt thou delight thyself in the LORD; and I will cause thee to ride upon the high places of the earth, and feed thee with the heritage of Jacob thy father: for the mouth of the LORD hath spoken *it*.

Je 17:21 Thus saith the LORD; Take heed to yourselves, and bear no burden on the sabbath day, nor bring *it* in by the gates of Jerusalem;

Eze 44:24 And in controversy they shall stand in judgment; *and* they shall judge it according to my judgments: and they shall keep my laws and my statutes in all mine assemblies; and they shall hallow my sabbaths.

Lu 4:16 And he came to Nazareth, where he had been brought up: and, as his custom was, he went into the synagogue on the sabbath day, and stood up for to read.

Jn 5:10 The Jews therefore said unto him that was cured, It is the sabbath day: it is not lawful for thee to carry *thy* bed.

Ac 13:14 But when they departed from Perga, they came to Antioch in Pisidia, and went into the synagogue on the sabbath day, and sat down.

2. Its Good Deeds

Mt 12:12 How much then is a man better than a sheep? Wherefore it is lawful to do well on the sabbath days.

Mk 6:2 And when the sabbath day was come, he began to teach in the synagogue: and many hearing *him* were astonished, saying, From whence hath this *man* these things?

and what wisdom *is* this which is given unto him, that even such mighty works are wrought by his hands?

Lu 6:6 And it came to pass also on another Sabbath, that he entered into the synagogue and taught: and there was a man whose right hand was withered.

Jn 5:9 And immediately the man was made whole, and took up his bed, and walked: and on the same day was the sabbath.

Jn 7:23 If a man on the sabbath day receive circumcision, that the law of Moses should not be broken; are ye angry at me, because I have made a man every whit whole on the sabbath day?

Jn 9:14 And it was the sabbath day when Jesus made the clay, and opened his eyes.

Ac 16:13 And on the sabbath we went out of the city by a river side, where prayer was wont to be made; and we sat down, and spake unto the women which resorted *thither.*

Ac 17:2 And Paul, as his manner was, went in unto them, and three sabbath days reasoned with them out of the scriptures,

Ac 18:4 And he reasoned in the synagogue every sabbath, and persuaded the Jews and the Greeks.

3. Its Desecration

DOING ORDINARY WORK

Ne 13:15 In those days saw I in Judah *some* treading winepresses on the sabbath, and bringing in sheaves, and lading asses; as also wine, grapes, and figs, and all *manner of* burdens, which they brought into Jerusalem on the sabbath day: and I testified *against them* in the day wherein they sold victuals.

BY GATHERING MANNA

Ex 16:27–28 And it came to pass, *that* there went out *some* of the people on the seventh day for to gather, and they found none

And the LORD said unto Moses, How long refuse ye to keep my commandments and my law?

WARNINGS

Je 17:27 But if ye will not hearken unto me to hallow the sabbath day, and not to bear a burden, even entering in at the gates of Jerusalem on the sabbath day; then will I kindle a fire in the gates thereof, and it shall devour the palaces of Jerusalem, and it shall not be quenched.

Eze 20:13 But the house of Israel rebelled against me in the wilderness: they walked not in my statutes, and they despised my judgments, which *if* a man do, he shall even live in them; and my sabbaths they greatly polluted: then I said, I would pour out my fury upon them in the wilderness, to consume them.

Eze 22:8 Thou hast despised mine holy things, and hast profaned my sabbaths.

Eze 22:15 And I will scatter thee among the heathen, and disperse thee in the countries, and will consume thy filthiness out of thee.

DEATH PENALTY

Ex 31:14 Ye shall keep the sabbath therefore; for it *is* holy unto you: every one that defileth it shall surely be put to death: for whosoever doeth *any* work therein, that soul shall be cut off from among his people.

Nu 15:32 And while the children of Israel were in the wilderness, they found a man that gathered sticks upon the sabbath day.

Nu 15:35 And the LORD said unto Moses, The man shall be surely put to death: all the congregation shall stone him with stones without the camp.

4. First Day of the Week, the day after Sabbath

CHRIST APPEARED TO MARY

Mk 16:9 Now when *Jesus* was risen early the first *day* of the week, he appeared first to Mary Magdalene, out of whom he had cast seven devils.

CHRIST APPEARED TO THE TWO ON THE WAY TO EMMAUS

Lu 24:13–15 And, behold, two of them went that same day to a village called Emmaus, which was from Jerusalem *about* threescore furlongs.

And they talked together of all these things which had happened.

And it came to pass, that, while they communed *together* and reasoned, Jesus himself drew near, and went with them.

CHRIST APPEARED TO THE DISCIPLES

Jn 20:19 Then the same day at evening, being the first *day* of the week, when the doors were shut where the disciples were assembled for fear of the Jews, came Jesus and stood in the midst, and saith unto them, Peace *be* unto you.

PAUL PREACHED AT TROAS

Ac 20:7 And upon the first *day* of the week, when the disciples came together to break bread, Paul preached unto them, ready to depart on the morrow; and continued his speech until midnight.

PUT ASIDE MONEY

1 Co 16:2 Upon the first *day* of the week let every one of you lay by him in store, as *God* hath prospered him, that there be no gatherings when I come.

RECEIVED HIS REVELATION

Re 1:10–11 I was in the Spirit on the Lord's day, and heard behind me a great voice, as of a trumpet,

Saying, I am Alpha and Omega, the first and the last: and, What thou seest, write in a book, and send *it* unto the seven churches which are in Asia; unto Ephesus, and unto Smyrna, and unto Pergamos, and unto Thyatira, and unto Sardis, and unto Philadelphia, and unto Laodicea.

See **CHURCH**

SABBATH DAY'S JOURNEY

Ac 1:12

See **WEIGHTS AND MEASURES**

SABBATIC YEAR, *one year in seven, year of release*

Ex 23:11; Le 25:4; De 15:1, 9; 31:10; 2 Chr 36:21; Ne 10:31; Je 34:14

SABEANS, *inhabitants of a kingdom in southwest Arabia*

Jb 1:15; Is 43:3; 45:14

SACKBUT *See* **MUSIC**

SACRED PLACES, *dedicated to or set apart for the worship of God*

Ex 15:17; 20:24; Le 17:5; De 12:5, 11, 14, 18, 21; 14:23; 15:20; 16:2, 6; 17:8; 26:2; 31:11; Jos 9:27; 18:1; 1 K 14:21; 1 Chr 17:9; 22:1; 2 Chr 3:1; 6:6, 20, 34, 38; 7:12, 15; 12:13; 29:6; 33:4, 7; Ezr 7:15; Ne 1:9; Ps 2:6; 3:4; 15:1; 24:3; 26:8; 43:3; 46:4; 78:68; 84:3; 87:2; 122:2; 132:13; Is 18:7; 27:13; 30:29; 60:13; 62:9; Je 7:12; 17:12; 26:2; Eze 20:40; 21:2; 43:12; 45:1, 4; Da 9:16; 11:45; Jn 4:20

See **WORSHIP**

SACRIFICES

1. Offering

Ge 4:4; 31:54; 46:1; Ex 3:18; 5:3; 8:27; 10:25; 18:12; Le 17:5; Nu 22:40; 23:3, 30; De 16:2; Jud 2:5; 1 S 1:3, 21, 25; 6:15; 9:12; 11:15; 2 S 6:13; 15:12; 1 K 3:4; 8:5, 63; 1 Chr 15:26; 21:28; 29:21; 2 Chr 2:6; 5:6; 7:4; 11:16; Ezr 6:10; Ne 12:43; Ps 50:5; 54:6; 66:15; Is 19:21; Je 17:26; Jona 1:16; He 5:1; 11:4

2. Insufficient to Secure Salvation

1 S 15:22 And Samuel said, Hath the LORD *as great* delight in burnt offerings and sacrifices, as in obeying the voice of the LORD? Behold, to obey *is* better than sacrifice, *and* to hearken than the fat of rams.

Ps 40:6 Sacrifice and offering thou didst not desire; mine ears hast thou opened: burnt offering and sin offering hast thou not required.

Ps 51:16–17 For thou desirest not sacrifice; else would I give *it:* thou delightest not in burnt offering.

The sacrifices of God *are* a broken spirit: a broken and a contrite heart, O God, thou wilt not despise.

Ps 69:31 *This* also shall please the LORD better than an ox *or* bullock that hath horns and hoofs.

Pr 21:3 To do justice and judgment *is* more acceptable to the LORD than sacrifice.

Ec 5:1 Keep thy foot when thou goest to the house of God, and be more ready to hear, than to give the sacrifice of fools: for they consider not that they do evil.

Is 1:11 To what purpose *is* the multitude of your sacrifices unto me? saith the LORD: I am full of the burnt offerings of rams, and the fat of fed beasts; and I delight not in the blood of bullocks, or of lambs, or of he goats.

Je 6:20 To what purpose cometh there to me incense from Sheba, and the sweet cane from a far country? your burnt offerings *are* not acceptable, nor your sacrifices sweet unto me.

Je 7:22 For I spake not unto your fathers, nor commanded them in the day that I brought them out of the land of Egypt, concerning burnt offerings or sacrifices:

Ho 6:6 For I desired mercy, and not sacrifice; and the knowledge of God more than burnt offerings.

Ho 8:13 They sacrifice flesh *for* the sacrifices of mine offerings, and *eat it;* but the LORD accepteth them not; now will he remember their iniquity, and visit their sins: they shall return to Egypt.

Am 5:22 Though ye offer me burnt offerings and your meat offerings, I will not accept *them:* neither will I regard the peace offerings of your fat beasts.

Mi 6:6 Wherewith shall I come before the LORD, *and* bow myself before the high God? shall I come before him with burnt offerings, with calves of a year old?

Mt 9:13 But go ye and learn what *that* meaneth, I will have mercy, and not sacrifice: for I am not come to call the righteous, but sinners to repentance.

Mt 12:7 But if ye had known what *this* meaneth, I will have mercy, and not sacrifice, ye would not have condemned the guiltless.

Mk 12:33 And to love him with all the heart, and with all the understanding, and with all the soul, and with all the strength, and to love *his* neighbour as himself, is more than all whole burnt offerings and sacrifices.

1 Co 13:3 And though I bestow all my goods to feed *the poor,* and though I give my body to be burned, and have not charity, it profiteth me nothing.

He 9:9 Which *was* a figure for the time then present, in which were offered both gifts and sacrifices, that could not make him that did the service perfect, as pertaining to the conscience;

He 10:1 For the law having a shadow of good things to come, *and* not the very image of the things, can never with those sacrifices which they offered year by year continually make the comers thereunto perfect.

He 10:5 Wherefore when he cometh into the world, he saith, Sacrifice and offering thou wouldest not, but a body hast thou prepared me:

He 10:11 And every priest standeth daily ministering and offering oftentimes the same sacrifices, which can never take away sins:

3. Of Human Beings

Ge 22:2, 9; Le 18:21; 20:2; De 12:31; 18:10; 2 K 3:27; 16:3; 17:17, 31; 21:6; 23:10; 2 Chr 28:3; 33:6; Ps 106:38; Is 57:5; Je 7:31; 19:5; 32:35; Eze 16:20, 36; 20:26, 31; 23:37; Mi 6:7; He 11:17

4. Of Praise

Ps 69:30 I will praise the name of God with a song, and will magnify him with thanksgiving.

Ps 107:22 And let them sacrifice the sacrifices of thanksgiving, and declare his works with rejoicing.

Ps 116:17 I will offer to thee the sacrifice of thanksgiving, and will call upon the name of the LORD.

Ps 119:108 Accept, I beseech thee, the freewill offerings of my mouth, O LORD, and teach me thy judgments.

Je 17:26 And they shall come from the cities of Judah, and from the places about Jerusalem, and from the land of Benjamin, and from the plain, and from the mountains, and from the south, bringing burnt offerings, and sacrifices, and meat offerings, and incense, and bringing sacrifices of praise, unto the house of the LORD.

Je 33:11 The voice of joy, and the voice of gladness, the voice of the bridegroom, and the voice of the bride, the voice of them that shall say, Praise the LORD of hosts: for the LORD *is* good; for his mercy *endureth* for ever: *and* of them that shall bring the sacrifice of praise into the house of the LORD. For I will cause to return the captivity of the land, as at the first, saith the LORD.

Jona 2:9 But I will sacrifice unto thee with the voice of thanksgiving; I will pay *that* that I have vowed. Salvation *is* of the LORD.

He 13:15 By him therefore let us offer the sacrifice of praise to God continually, that is, the fruit of *our* lips giving thanks to his name.

5. Of Righteousness

De 33:19 They shall call the people unto the mountain; there they shall offer sacrifices of righteousness: for they shall suck *of* the abundance of the seas, and *of* treasures hid in the sand.

Ps 4:5 Offer the sacrifices of righteousness, and put your trust in the LORD.

Ps 51:19 Then shalt thou be pleased with the sacrifices of righteousness, with burnt offering and whole burnt offering: then shall they offer bullocks upon thine altar.

Mal 3:3 And he shall sit *as* a refiner and purifier of silver: and he shall purify the sons of Levi, and purge them as gold and silver, that they may offer unto the LORD an offering in righteousness.

See **OFFERINGS, THANKSGIVING, WORSHIP**

SACRILEGE, *profaning something holy*

1. Condemned

Le 19:8; 20:3; Nu 18:32; 1 S 2:29; Pr 20:25; Eze 22:8; Mal 1:12; Mk 11:17; Jn 2:16; Ro 2:22; 1 Co 11:22

2. Examples

Ex 30:9; Le 10:1; Nu 3:4; 26:61; 1 S 2:17; 6:19; 13:9; 2 S 6:6; 1 K 19:10; 2 K 21:7; 25:13; 1 Chr 13:9; 2 Chr 24:7; 26:16; 28:24; 33:5; 36:7; Je 36:23; Eze 22:26; Da 5:2, 23; 8:11, 13; Mt 21:13; Ac 8:19

3. Despoiling the Temple

2 K 12:18; 16:8; 18:16; 2 Chr 12:9; 16:2; 25:24; 28:21, 24; 36:10; Ezr 5:14; Ps 74:6; Je 52:17; Eze 7:22; Jl 3:5

See **POLLUTIONS**

SADDUCEES

See **SECTS AND PARTIES**

SAFETY

Ex 11:7 But against any of the children of Israel shall not a dog move his tongue, against man or beast: that ye may know how that the LORD doth put a difference between the Egyptians and Israel.

1 S 24:3 And he came to the sheepcotes by the way, where *was* a cave; and Saul went in to cover his feet: and David and his men remained in the sides of the cave.

2 K 13:5 (And the LORD gave Israel a saviour, so that they went out from under the hand of the Syrians: and the children of Israel dwelt in their tents, as beforetime.

2 K 19:29 And this *shall be* a sign unto thee, Ye shall eat this year such things as grow of themselves, and in the second year that which springeth of the same; and in the third year sow ye, and reap, and plant vineyards, and eat the fruits thereof.

Jb 5:20 In famine he shall redeem thee from death: and in war from the power of the sword.

Jb 11:18 And thou shalt be secure, because there is hope; yea, thou shalt dig *about thee, and* thou shalt take thy rest in safety.

Ps 4:8 I will both lay me down in peace, and sleep: for thou, LORD, only makest me dwell in safety.

Ps 91:10 There shall no evil befall thee, neither shall any plague come nigh thy dwelling.

Ps 112:8 His heart *is* established, he shall not be afraid, until he see *his desire* upon his enemies.

Ps 121:3 He will not suffer thy foot to be moved: he that keepeth thee will not slumber.

Pr 1:33 But whoso hearkeneth unto me shall dwell safely, and shall be quiet from fear of evil.

Pr 3:23 Then shalt thou walk in thy way safely, and thy foot shall not stumble.

Pr 12:21 There shall no evil happen to the just: but the wicked shall be filled with mischief.

Pr 21:31 The horse is prepared against the day of battle: but safety is of the LORD.

Is 11:8 And the sucking child shall play on the hole of the asp, and the weaned child shall put his hand on the cockatrice' den.

Is 32:18 And my people shall dwell in a peaceable habitation, and in sure dwellings, and in quiet resting places;

Je 23:6 In his days Judah shall be saved, and Israel shall dwell safely: and this *is* his name whereby he shall be called, THE LORD OUR RIGHTEOUSNESS.

Je 32:37 Behold, I will gather them out of all countries, whither I have driven them in mine anger, and in my fury, and in great wrath; and I will bring them again unto this place, and I will cause them to dwell safely:

Je 33:16 In those days shall Judah be saved, and Jerusalem shall dwell safely: and this *is the name* wherewith she shall be called, The LORD our righteousness.

Je 38:20 But Jeremiah said, They shall not deliver *thee.* Obey, I beseech thee, the voice of the LORD, which I speak unto thee: so it shall be well unto thee, and thy soul shall live.

Je 39:12 Take him, and look well to him, and do him no harm; but do unto him even as he shall say unto thee.

Eze 28:26 And they shall dwell safely therein, and shall build houses, and plant vineyards; yea, they shall dwell with confidence, when I have executed judgments upon all those that despise them round about them; and they shall know that I *am* the LORD their God.

Eze 34:27 And the tree of the field shall yield her fruit, and the earth shall yield her increase, and they shall be safe in their land, and shall know that I *am* the LORD, when I have broken the bands of their yoke, and delivered them out of the hand of those that served themselves of them.

Da 3:27 And the princes, governors, and captains, and the king's counsellors, being gathered together, saw these men, upon whose bodies the fire had no power, nor was an hair of their head singed, neither were their coats changed, nor the smell of fire had passed on them.

Ho 2:18 And in that day will I make a covenant for them with the beasts of the field, and with the fowls of heaven, and *with* the creeping things of the ground: and I will break the bow and the sword and the battle out of the earth, and will make them to lie down safely.

Zep 2:3 Seek ye the LORD, all ye meek of the earth, which have wrought his judgment; seek righteousness, seek meekness: it may be ye shall be hid in the day of the LORD's anger.

Zec 2:4 And said unto him, Run, speak to this young man, saying, Jerusalem shall be inhabited *as* towns without walls for the multitude of men and cattle therein:

Zec 3:10 In that day, saith the LORD of hosts, shall ye call every man his neighbour under the vine and under the fig tree.

Lu 21:18 But there shall not an hair of your head perish.

Ac 27:22 And now I exhort you to be of good cheer: for there shall be no loss of *any man's* life among you, but of the ship.

Re 21:25 And the gates of it shall not be shut at all by day: for there shall be no night there.

See **PEACE, SECURITY**

SAINTS, *separated ones—to God and from the world, uniquely consecrated ones*

1. Contrasted with Sinners

Ps 18:26 With the pure thou wilt shew thyself pure; and with the froward thou wilt shew thyself froward.

Pr 10:6 Blessings *are* upon the head of the just: but violence covereth the mouth of the wicked.

Pr 10:16 The labour of the righteous *tendeth* to life: the fruit of the wicked to sin.

Pr 10:25 As the whirlwind passeth, so *is* the wicked no *more:* but the righteous *is* an everlasting foundation.

Pr 11:5 The righteousness of the perfect shall direct his way: but the wicked shall fall by his own wickedness.

Pr 12:7 The wicked are overthrown, and *are* not: but the house of the righteous shall stand.

Pr 13:21 Evil pursueth sinners: but to the righteous good shall be repaid.

Pr 14:32 The wicked is driven away in his wickedness: but the righteous hath hope in his death.

Pr 15:6 In the house of the righteous *is* much treasure: but in the revenues of the wicked is trouble.

Pr 21:15 *It is* joy to the just to do judgment: but destruction *shall be* to the workers of iniquity.

Ro 2:9–10 Tribulation and anguish, upon every soul of man that doeth evil, of the Jew first, and also of the Gentile;

But glory, honour, and peace, to every man that worketh good, to the Jew first, and also to the Gentile:

1 Pe 4:18 And if the righteous scarcely be saved, where shall the ungodly and the sinner appear?

2. Their Feet

1 S 2:9 He will keep the feet of his saints, and the wicked shall be silent in darkness; for by strength shall no man prevail.

2 S 22:34 He maketh my feet like hinds' *feet:* and setteth me upon my high places.

Ps 40:2 He brought me up also out of an horrible pit, out of the miry clay, and set my feet upon a rock, *and* established my goings.

Pr 24:16 For a just *man* falleth seven times, and riseth up again: but the wicked shall fall into mischief.

Is 52:7 How beautiful upon the mountains are the feet of him that bringeth good tidings, that publisheth peace; that bringeth good tidings of good, that publisheth salvation; that saith unto Zion, Thy God reigneth!

Is 63:13 That led them through the deep, as an horse in the wilderness, *that* they should not stumble?

Ep 6:15 And your feet shod with the preparation of the gospel of peace;

3. Their Portion

Nu 18:20 And the LORD spake unto Aaron, Thou shalt have no inheritance in their land, neither shalt thou have any part among them: I *am* thy part and thine inheritance among the children of Israel.

Jb 22:25 Yea, the Almighty shall be thy defence, and thou shalt have plenty of silver.

Ps 16:5 The LORD *is* the portion of mine inheritance and of my cup: thou maintainest my lot.

Ps 73:26 My flesh and my heart faileth: *but* God *is* the strength of my heart, and my portion for ever.

Ps 119:57 *Thou art* my portion, O LORD: I have said that I would keep thy words.

Ps 142:5 I cried unto thee, O LORD: I said, Thou *art* my refuge *and* my portion in the land of the living.

Je 51:19 The portion of Jacob *is* not like them; for he *is* the former of all things: and *Israel is* the rod of his inheritance: the LORD of hosts is his name.

Lam 3:24 The LORD *is* my portion therefore will I hope in him.

Mt 19:27 Then answered Peter and said unto him, Behold, we have forsaken all, and followed thee; what shall we have therefore?

Ac 3:6 Then Peter said, Silver and gold have I none; but such as I have give I thee: In the name of Jesus Christ of Nazareth rise up and walk.

4. Promises to Them

Ps 16:3 *But* to the saints that *are* in the earth, and *to* the excellent, in whom *is* all my delight.

Ps 37:28 For the LORD loveth judgment, and forsaketh not his saints; they are preserved for ever: but the seed of the wicked shall be cut off.

Ps 97:10 Ye that love the LORD, hate evil: he preserveth the souls of his saints; he delivereth them out of the hand of the wicked.

Ps 116:15 Precious in the sight of the LORD *is* the death of his saints.

Ps 125:4 Do good, O LORD, unto *those that be* good, and *to them that are* upright in their hearts.

Ps 132:16 I will also clothe her priests with salvation: and her saints shall shout aloud for joy.

Ps 149:9 To execute upon them the judgment written: this honour have all his saints. Praise ye the LORD.

Pr 2:21 For the upright shall dwell in the land, and the perfect shall remain in it.

Pr 14:22 Do they not err that devise evil? but mercy and truth *shall be* to them that devise good.

Da 7:27 And the kingdom and dominion, and the greatness of the kingdom under the whole heaven, shall be given to the people of the saints of the most High, whose kingdom *is* an everlasting kingdom, and all dominions shall serve and obey him.

1 Co 6:2 Do ye not know that the saints shall judge the world? and if the world shall be judged by you, are ye unworthy to judge the smallest matters?

Re 11:18 And the nations were angry, and thy wrath is come, and the time of the dead, that they should be judged, and that thou shouldest give reward unto thy servants the prophets, and to the saints, and them that fear thy name, small and great; and shouldest destroy them which destroy the earth.

5. Sealed by God

Eze 9:4 And the LORD said unto him, Go through the midst of the city, through the midst of Jerusalem, and set a mark upon the foreheads of the men that sigh and that cry for all the abominations that be done in the midst thereof.

2 Co 1:22 Who hath also sealed us, and given the earnest of the Spirit in our hearts.

Re 7:3 Saying, Hurt not the earth, neither the sea, nor the trees, till we have sealed the servants of our God in their foreheads.

Re 9:4 And it was commanded them that they should not hurt the grass of the earth, neither any green thing, neither any tree; but only those men which have not the seal of God in their foreheads.

Re 14:1 And I looked, and, lo, a Lamb stood on the mount Sion, and with him an hundred forty *and* four thousand, having his Father's name written in their foreheads.

Re 22:4 And they shall see his face; and his name *shall be* in their foreheads.

6. Their Steps

Jb 14:16 For now thou numberest my steps: dost thou not watch over my sin?

Jb 31:4 Doth not he see my ways, and count all my steps?

Jb 31:37 I would declare unto him the number of my steps; as a prince would I go near unto him.

Ps 18:36 Thou hast enlarged my steps under me, that my feet did not slip.

Ps 37:23 The steps of a *good* man are ordered by the LORD: and he delighteth in his way.

Ps 40:2 He brought me up also out of an horrible pit, out of the miry clay, and set my feet upon a rock, *and* established my goings.

Ps 91:12 They shall bear thee up in *their* hands, lest thou dash thy foot against a stone.

Ps 121:8 The LORD shall preserve thy going out and thy coming in from this time forth, and even for evermore.

Pr 4:12 When thou goest, thy steps shall not be straitened; and when thou runnest, thou shalt not stumble.

Pr 16:9 A man's heart deviseth his way: but the LORD directeth his steps.

2 Co 12:18 I desired Titus, and with *him* I sent a brother. Did Titus make a gain of you? walked we not in the same spirit? *walked we* not in the same steps?

7. Scattered

Mt 8:11 And I say unto you, That many shall come from the east and west, and shall sit down with Abraham, and Isaac, and Jacob, in the kingdom of heaven.

Mt 26:31 Then saith Jesus unto them, All ye shall be offended because of me this night: for it is written, I will smite the shepherd, and the sheep of the flock shall be scattered abroad.

Mk 13:27 And then shall he send his angels, and shall gather together his elect from the four winds, from the uttermost part of the earth to the uttermost part of heaven.

Lu 13:29 And they shall come from the east, and *from* the west, and from the north, and *from* the south, and shall sit down in the kingdom of God.

Jn 11:52 And not for that nation only, but that also he should gather together in one the children of God that were scattered abroad.

Ac 8:1 And Saul was consenting unto his death. And at that time there was a great persecution against the church which was at Jerusalem; and they were all scattered abroad throughout the regions of Judaea and Samaria, except the apostles.

Ja 1:1 James, a servant of God and of the Lord Jesus Christ, to the twelve tribes which are scattered abroad, greeting.

See **FUTURE LIFE**

SALOME, *mother of James and John*

Mk 15:40; 16:1

See **WOMEN**

SALT, *seasoning used for preservation and flavoring*

Ge 19:26; Le 2:12–13; Nu 18:19; Jud 9:45; 2 K 2:20; Ezr 6:9; 7:22; Eze 43:24; Col 4:6

Lot's Wife Becomes a Pillar of Salt

Ge 19:26; Lu 17:32

SALUTATIONS, *greetings*

1. Examples

Ge 43:29; Jud 18:15; 19:20; Ru 2:4; 1 S 10:4; 15:13; 17:22; 25:6; 2 K 4:26; 1 Chr 12:18; Ezr 5:7; Mt 5:47; 10:12; 23:7; 28:9; Mk 9:15; 12:38; Lu 1:28, 40; 10:5; Ro 16:22; 1 Co 16:19; 1 Th 1:1

2. Of Affection

Ge 33:4; 45:14; Lu 15:20; Ro 16:16

SALVATION, *deliverance from sin and death, available through the death of Jesus Christ*

1. Planned

FIRST RECORDED PROMISE

Ge 3:15 And I will put enmity between thee and the woman, and between thy seed and her seed; it shall bruise thy head, and thou shalt bruise his heel.

ANNOUNCED BY THE PROPHETS

Ac 2:16 But this is that which was spoken by the prophet Joel;

Ac 2:23 Him, being delivered by the determinate counsel and foreknowledge of God, ye have taken, and by wicked hands have crucified and slain:

BASED UPON THE FOREKNOWLEDGE OF GOD

Ro 8:29 For whom he did foreknow, he also did predestinate *to be* conformed to the image of his Son, that he might be the firstborn among many brethren.

Ep 1:5 Having predestinated us unto the adoption of children by Jesus Christ to himself, according to the good pleasure of his will,

HIDDEN WISDOM

1 Co 2:7 But we speak the wisdom of God in a mystery, *even* the hidden *wisdom,* which God ordained before the world unto our glory:

AN UNCHANGING PURPOSE

2 Ti 1:9 Who hath saved us, and called *us* with an holy calling, not according to our works, but according to his own purpose and grace, which was given us in Christ Jesus before the world began,

ANTECEDENT TO CREATION

Tit 1:2 In hope of eternal life, which God, that cannot lie, promised before the world began;

PROVIDED FOR THE
SANCTIFICATION OF BELIEVERS

1 Pe 1:2 Elect according to the foreknowledge of God the Father, through sanctification of the Spirit, unto obedience and sprinkling of the blood of Jesus Christ: Grace unto you, and peace, be multiplied.

CENTERED ON THE DEATH OF CHRIST

Re 13:8 And all that dwell upon the earth shall worship him, whose names are not written in the book of life of the Lamb slain from the foundation of the world.

2. Of God

Ex 14:13 And Moses said unto the people, Fear ye not, stand still, and see the salvation of the LORD, which he will shew to you to day: for the Egyptians whom ye have seen to day, ye shall see them again no more for ever.
1 S 2:1 And Hannah prayed, and said, My heart rejoiceth in the LORD, mine horn is exalted in the LORD: my mouth is enlarged over mine enemies; because I rejoice in thy salvation.
Ps 14:7 Oh that the salvation of Israel *were come* out of Zion! when the LORD bringeth back the captivity of his peo-

ple, Jacob shall rejoice, *and* Israel shall be glad.
Ps 27:1 The LORD *is* my light and my salvation; whom shall I fear? the LORD *is* the strength of my life; of whom shall I be afraid?
Ps 37:39 But the salvation of the righteous *is* of the LORD: he *is* their strength in the time of trouble.
Ps 62:2 He only *is* my rock and my salvation; *he is* my defence; I shall not be greatly moved.
Is 12:2 Behold, God *is* my salvation; I will trust, and not be afraid: for the LORD JEHOVAH *is* my strength and *my* song; he also is become my salvation.
Is 25:9 And it shall be said in that day, Lo, this *is* our God; we have waited for him, and he will save us: this *is* the LORD; we have waited for him, we will be glad and rejoice in his salvation.
Je 3:23 Truly in vain *is salvation hoped for* from the hills, *and from* the multitude of mountains: truly in the LORD our God *is* the salvation of Israel.
Zep 3:17 The LORD thy God in the midst of thee *is* mighty; he will save, he will rejoice over thee with joy; he will rest in his love, he will joy over thee with singing.
1 Ti 4:10 For therefore we both labour and suffer reproach, because we trust in the living God, who is the Saviour of all men, specially of those that believe.
Re 19:1 And after these things I heard a great voice of much people in heaven, saying, Alleluia; Salvation, and glory, and honour, and power, unto the Lord our God:

3. Available Only Through Christ

THE ONLY DOOR

Jn 10:9 I am the door: by me if any man enter in, he shall be saved, and shall go in and out, and find pasture.

THE ONLY SAVIOR

Ac 4:12 Neither is there salvation in any other: for there is none other name under heaven given among men, whereby we must be saved.

HIS GRACE SUFFICIENT

Ac 15:11 But we believe that through the grace of the Lord Jesus Christ we shall be saved, even as they.

HIS BLOOD AVAILS

Ro 5:9 Much more then, being now justified by his blood, we shall be saved from wrath through him.

1 Th 5:9 For God hath not appointed us to wrath, but to obtain salvation by our Lord Jesus Christ,

FOR THE OBEDIENT

He 5:9 And being made perfect, he became the author of eternal salvation unto all them that obey him;

AT HIS COMING

He 9:28 So Christ was once offered to bear the sins of many; and unto them that look for him shall he appear the second time without sin unto salvation.

4. Conditions Required

ENDURANCE

Mt 10:22 And ye shall be hated of all *men* for my name's sake: but he that endureth to the end shall be saved.

FAITH AND CONFESSION

Ro 10:9 That if thou shalt confess with thy mouth the Lord Jesus, and shalt believe in thine heart that God hath raised him from the dead, thou shalt be saved.

1 Co 1:21 For after that in the wisdom of God the world by wisdom knew not God, it pleased God by the foolishness of preaching to save them that believe.

1 Co 15:2 By which also ye are saved, if ye keep in memory what I preached unto you, unless ye have believed in vain.

2 Ti 3:15 And that from a child thou hast known the holy scriptures, which are able to make thee wise unto salvation through faith which is in Christ Jesus.

SPIRITUAL RECEPTIVITY

Ja 1:21 Wherefore lay apart all filthiness and superfluity of naughtiness, and receive with meekness the engrafted word, which is able to save your souls.

SPIRITUAL DILIGENCE

2 Pe 1:10–11 Wherefore the rather, brethren, give diligence to make your calling and election sure: for if ye do these things, ye shall never fall:

For so an entrance shall be ministered unto you abundantly into the everlasting kingdom of our Lord and Saviour Jesus Christ.

SPIRITUAL CLEANSING

Re 22:14 Blessed *are* they that do his commandments, that they may have right to the tree of life, and may enter in through the gates into the city.

5. Available to All

Ps 67:2 That thy way may be known upon earth, thy saving health among all nations.

Ps 98:3 He hath remembered his mercy and his truth toward the house of Israel: all the ends of the earth have seen the salvation of our God.

Is 25:6 And in this mountain shall the LORD of hosts make unto all people a feast of fat things, a feast of wines on the lees, of fat things full of marrow, of wines on the lees well refined.

Is 40:5 And the glory of the LORD shall be revealed, and all flesh shall see *it* together: for the mouth of the LORD hath spoken *it.*

Is 49:6 And he said, It is a light thing that thou shouldest be my servant to raise up the tribes of Jacob, and to restore the preserved of Israel: I will also give thee for a light to the Gentiles, that thou mayest be my salvation unto the end of the earth.

Is 52:10 The LORD hath made bare his holy arm in the eyes of all the nations; and all the ends of the earth shall see the salvation of our God.

Is 56:5–6 Even unto them will I give in mine house and within my walls a place and a name better than of sons and of daughters: I will give them an everlasting name, that shall not be cut off.

Also the sons of the stranger, that join themselves to the LORD, to serve him, and to love the name of the LORD, to be his servants, every one that keepeth the sabbath from polluting it, and taketh hold of my covenant;

Eze 33:11 Say unto them, *As* I live, saith the Lord GOD, I have no pleasure in the death of the wicked; but that the wicked turn from his way and live: turn ye, turn ye from your evil ways; for why will ye die, O house of Israel?

Jl 2:32 And it shall come to pass, *that* whosoever shall call on the name of the LORD shall be delivered: for in mount Zion and in Jerusalem shall be deliverance, as the LORD hath said, and in the remnant whom the LORD shall call.

Mt 8:11 And I say unto you, That many shall come from the east and west, and shall sit down with Abraham, and Isaac, and Jacob, in the kingdom of heaven.

Mt 18:14 Even so it is not the will of your Father which is in heaven, that one of these little ones should perish.

Mt 21:31 Whether of them twain did the will of *his* father? They say unto him, The first. Jesus saith unto them, Verily I say unto you, That the publicans and the harlots go into the kingdom of God before you.

Mt 22:10 So those servants went out into the highways, and gathered together all as many as they found, both bad and good: and the wedding was furnished with guests.

Mt 26:28 For this is my blood of the new testament, which is shed for many for the remission of sins.

Mk 10:27 And Jesus looking upon them saith, With men *it is* impossible, but not with God: for with God all things are possible.

Mk 11:17 And he taught, saying unto them, Is it not written, My house shall be called of all nations the house of prayer? but ye have made it a den of thieves.

Mk 14:24 And he said unto them, This is my blood of the new testament, which is shed for many.

Lu 2:10 And the angel said unto them, Fear not: for, behold, I bring you good tidings of great joy, which shall be to all people.

Lu 3:6 And all flesh shall see the salvation of God.

Lu 13:29 And they shall come from the east, and *from* the west, and from the north, and *from* the south, and shall sit down in the kingdom of God.

Lu 14:16 Then said he unto him, A certain man made a great supper, and bade many:

Lu 14:21 So that servant came, and shewed his lord these things. Then the master of the house being angry said to his servant, Go out quickly into the streets and lanes of the city, and bring in hither the poor, and the maimed, and the halt, and the blind.

Jn 6:40 And this is the will of him that sent me, that every one which seeth the Son, and believeth on him, may have everlasting life: and I will raise him up at the last day.

Jn 11:52 And not for that nation only, but that also he should gather together in one the children of God that were scattered abroad.

Ac 2:21 And it shall come to pass, *that* whosoever shall call on the name of the Lord shall be saved.

Ac 13:47 For so hath the Lord commanded us, *saying,* I have set thee to be a light of the Gentiles, that thou shouldest be for salvation unto the ends of the earth.

Ro 1:16 For I am not ashamed of the gospel of Christ: for it is the power of God unto salvation to every one that believeth; to the Jew first, and also to the Greek.

Ro 3:22 Even the righteousness of God *which is* by faith of Jesus Christ unto all and upon all them that believe: for there is no difference:

Ro 4:9 *Cometh* this blessedness then upon the circumcision *only,* or upon the uncircumcision also? for we say that faith was reckoned to Abraham for righteousness.

Ro 4:16 Therefore *it is* of faith, that *it might be* by grace; to the end the promise might be sure to all the seed; not to that only which is of the law, but to that also which is of the faith of Abraham; who is the father of us all,

Ro 5:15 But not as the offence, so also *is* the free gift. For if through the offence of one many be dead, much more the grace of God, and the gift by grace, *which is* by one man, Jesus Christ, hath abounded unto many.

Ro 5:18 Therefore as by the offence of one *judgment came* upon all men to condemnation; even so by the righteousness of one *the free gift came* upon all men unto justification of life.

Ro 10:13 For whosoever shall call upon the name of the Lord shall be saved.

Ro 11:11 I say then, Have they stumbled that they should fall? God forbid: but *rather* through their fall salvation *is come* unto the Gentiles, for to provoke them to jealousy.

Ro 11:15 For if the casting away of them *be* the reconciling of the world, what *shall* the receiving *of them be,* but life from the dead?

Ro 11:25 For I would not, brethren, that ye should be ignorant of this mystery, lest ye should be wise in your own conceits; that blindness in part is happened to Israel, until the fulness of the Gentiles be come in.

2 Co 1:6 And whether we be afflicted, *it is* for your consolation and salvation, which is effectual in the enduring of the same sufferings which we also suffer: or whether we be comforted, *it is* for your consolation and salvation.

1 Ti 2:4 Who will have all men to be saved, and to come unto the knowledge of the truth.

1 Ti 2:15 Notwithstanding she shall be saved in childbearing, if they continue in faith and charity and holiness with sobriety.

1 Ti 4:10 For therefore we both labour and suffer reproach, because we trust in the living God, who is the Saviour of all men, specially of those that believe.

Tit 2:11–12 For the grace of God that bringeth salvation hath appeared to all men,

Teaching us that, denying ungodliness and worldly lusts, we should live soberly, righteously, and godly, in this present world;

He 2:9 But we see Jesus, who was made a little lower than the angels for the suffering of death, crowned with glory and honour; that he by the grace of God should taste death for every man.

2 Pe 3:9 The Lord is not slack concerning his promise, as some men count slackness; but is longsuffering to us-ward, not willing that any should perish, but that all should come to repentance.

1 Jn 2:2 And he is the propitiation for our sins: and not for ours only, but also for *the sins of* the whole world.

Jude 3 Beloved, when I gave all diligence to write unto you of the common salvation, it was needful for me to write unto you, and exhort *you* that ye should earnestly contend for the faith which was once delivered unto the saints.

Re 5:9 And they sung a new song, saying, Thou art worthy to take the book, and to open the seals thereof: for thou wast slain, and hast redeemed us to God by thy blood out of every kindred, and tongue, and people, and nation;

Re 7:9 After this I beheld, and, lo, a great multitude, which no man could number, of all nations, and kindreds, and people, and tongues, stood before the throne, and before the Lamb, clothed with white robes, and palms in their hands;

6. Free

Is 55:1 Ho, every one that thirsteth, come ye to the waters, and he that hath no money; come ye, buy, and eat; yea, come, buy wine and milk without money and without price.

Ro 3:24 Being justified freely by his grace through the redemption that is in Christ Jesus:

Re 22:17 And the Spirit and the bride say, Come. And let him that heareth say, Come. And let him that is athirst come. And whosoever will, let him take the water of life freely.

7. Sought

1 Chr 16:35 And say ye, Save us, O God of our salvation, and gather us together, and deliver us from the heathen, that we may give thanks to thy holy name, *and* glory in thy praise.

Ps 31:16 Make thy face to shine upon thy servant: save me for thy mercies' sake.

Ps 54:1 Save me, O God, by thy name, and judge me by thy strength.

Ps 85:7 Shew us thy mercy, O LORD, and grant us thy salvation.

Ps 106:4 Remember me, O LORD, with the favour *that thou bearest unto* thy people: O visit me with thy salvation;

Ps 119:41 Let thy mercies come also unto me, O LORD, *even* thy salvation, according to thy word.

Ac 16:30 And brought them out, and said, Sirs, what must I do to be saved?

8. Promised

Ps 91:16 With long life will I satisfy him, and shew him my salvation.

Is 45:17 *But* Israel shall be saved in the LORD with an everlasting salvation: ye shall not be ashamed nor confounded world without end.

Is 64:5 Thou meetest him that rejoiceth and worketh righteousness, *those that* remember thee in thy ways: behold, thou art wroth; for we have sinned: in those is continuance, and we shall be saved.

Mk 16:16 He that believeth and is baptized shall be saved; but he that believeth not shall be damned.

Lu 19:9 And Jesus said unto him, This day is salvation come to this house, forsomuch as he also is a son of Abraham.

Ac 11:14 Who shall tell thee words, whereby thou and all thy house shall be saved.

Ac 16:31 And they said, Believe on the Lord Jesus Christ, and thou shalt be saved, and thy house.

9. The Gift of God

Mt 7:11 If ye then, being evil, know how to give good gifts unto your children, how much more shall your Father which is in heaven give good things to them that ask him?

Jn 3:16 For God so loved the world, that he gave his only begotten Son, that whosoever believeth in him should not perish, but have everlasting life.

Jn 4:10 Jesus answered and said unto her, If thou knewest the gift of God, and who it is that saith to thee, Give me to drink; thou wouldest have asked of him, and he would have given thee living water.

Jn 6:32 Then Jesus said unto them, Verily, verily, I say unto you, Moses gave you not that bread from heaven; but my Father giveth you the true bread from heaven.

Ac 15:11 But we believe that through the grace of the Lord Jesus Christ we shall be saved, even as they.

Ro 5:15 But not as the offence, so also *is* the free gift. For if through the offence of one many be dead, much more the grace of God, and the gift by grace, *which is* by one man, Jesus Christ, hath abounded unto many.

Ro 5:18 Therefore as by the offence of one *judgment came* upon all men to condemnation; even so by the righteousness of one *the free gift came* upon all men unto justification of life.

Ro 6:23 For the wages of sin *is* death; but the gift of God *is* eternal life through Jesus Christ our Lord.

Ro 8:32 He that spared not his own Son, but delivered him up for us all, how shall he not with him also freely give us all things?

2 Co 9:15 Thanks *be* unto God for his unspeakable gift.

Ep 2:8 For by grace are ye saved through faith; and that not of yourselves: *it is* the gift of God:

1 Jn 4:9 In this was manifested the love of God toward us, because that God sent his only begotten Son into the world, that we might live through him.

1 Jn 5:11 And this is the record, that God hath given to us eternal life, and this life is in his Son.

10. Few Saved

Mt 7:14; 19:25; 20:16; 22:14; Lu 13:24; 18:26; 1 Pe 3:20; Re 3:4–5

See **CONDEMNATION, FORGIVENESS, REDEMPTION, JUSTIFICATION, PARDON, RESTORATION**

SAMARIA, *important city in central Palestine, noted as the capital of the Northern Kingdom and giving its name to the surrounding region*

Samaria fell to Shalmaneser V in 722 B.C. after a three-year siege (2 K 17:6 and the Babylonian Chronicle). The following year the inhabitants refused to pay tribute and suffered the wrath of Sargon II, who brought in colonists from other conquered areas and settled them in Samaria (2 K 17:24). In his own annals, Sargon II records that over 27,000 Israelites were deported to places in Syria, Assyria, and Babylonia. The New Testament city of Samaria was known as Sebaste to honor Caesar Augustus. It was rebuilt in about 30 B.C. according to the grand designs of Herod the Great.

1. The City

1 K 16:24, 29; 20:1, 17; 22:37; 2 K 1:2; 6:19; 10:12, 36; 14:14, 23; 15:17, 23; 17:1, 5; 18:9; 2 Chr 22:9; 25:24; 28:8; Is 7:9; 8:4; 36:19; Je 41:5; Eze 16:46; Am 3:12; Mi 1:6; Ac 8:5, 9, 14

2. The Province

2 K 17:24, 26; 23:19; Ezr 4:10, 17; Obad 19; Lu 17:11; Jn 4:4; Ac 8:1; 9:31; 15:3

SAMARITANS, *a term of contempt among the Jews*

1. Facts concerning

a. Colonists whom the king of Assyria sent to inhabit the land of Israel
2 K 17:24–41; Jn 4:9

b. In the time of Zerubbabel sought to form an alliance with the returned captives but were rejected
Ezr 4:2–3

c. Had a temple on Mt. Gerizim
Jn 4:20

d. Treated with charity by Christ
Lu 10:30

e. Healing of the Ten Lepers
Lu 17:12–18

f. Instruction of the Samaritan woman
Jn 4:1–54

g. Two days' work in Samaria
Jn 4:40

h. Philip's successful work among them
Ac 8:5–8

2. Descriptive Texts

2 K 17:24; Ezr 4:2; Ne 4:2; Mt 10:5; Lu 9:52; 10:33; 17:16; Jn 4:9, 39; 8:48; Ac 8:25

SAMSON, *son of Manoah, one of the Judges*

SEPARATED AS A NAZARITE

Jud 13:5 For, lo, thou shalt conceive, and bear a son; and no razor shall come on his head: for the child shall be a Nazarite unto God from the womb: and he shall begin to deliver Israel out of the hand of the Philistines.

Jud 16:17 That he told her all his heart, and said unto her. There hath not come a razor upon mine head; for I *have been* a Nazarite unto God from my mother's womb: if I be shaven, then my strength will go from me, and I shall become weak, and be like any *other* man.

YET HAVING EVIL ASSOCIATIONS

Jud 14:1–3 And Samson went down to Timnath, and saw a woman in Timnath of the daughters of the Philistines.

And he came up, and told his father and his mother, and said, I have seen a woman in Timnath of the daughters of the Philistines: now therefore get her for me to wife.

Then his father and his mother said unto him, *Is there* never a woman among the daughters of thy brethren, or among all my people, that thou goest to take a wife of the uncircumcised Philistines? And Samson said unto his father, Get her for me; for she pleaseth me well.

SPIRITUAL AT TIMES

Jud 13:25 And the Spirit of the LORD began to move him at times in the camp of Dan between Zorah and Eshtaol.

Jud 15:14 *And* when he came unto Lehi, the Philistines shouted against him: and the Spirit of the LORD came mightily upon him, and the cords that *were* upon his arms became as flax that was burnt with fire, and his bands loosed from off his hands.

SUBJECT TO CARNAL APPETITES

Jud 16:1–4 Then went Samson to Gaza, and saw there an harlot, and went in unto her.

And it was told the Gazites, saying, Samson is come hither. And they compassed *him* in, and laid wait for him all night in the gate of the city, and were quiet all the night, saying, In the morning, when it is day, we shall kill him.

And Samson lay till midnight, and arose at midnight, and took the doors of the gate of the city, and the two posts, and went away with them, bar and all, and put *them* upon his shoulders, and carried them up to the top of an hill that is before Hebron.

And it came to pass afterward, that he loved a woman in the valley of Sorek, whose name *was* Delilah.

CHILDISH IN HIS PLANS

Jud 15:4 And Samson went and caught three hundred foxes, and took firebrands, and turned tail to tail, and put a firebrand in the midst between two tails.

YET COURAGEOUS IN BATTLE

Jud 15:11–14 Then three thousand men of Judah went to the top of the rock Etam, and said to Samson, Knowest thou not that the Philistines *are* rulers over us? what *is* this *that* thou hast done unto us? And he said unto them, As they did unto me, so have I done unto them.

And they said unto him, We are come down to bind thee, that we may deliver thee into the hand of the Philistines. And Samson said unto them, Swear unto me, that ye will not fall upon me yourselves.

And they spake unto him, saying, No; but we will bind thee fast, and deliver thee into their hand: but surely we will not kill thee. And they bound him with two new cords, and brought him up from the rock.

And when he came unto Lehi, the Philistines shouted against him: and the Spirit of the LORD came mightily upon him, and the cords that *were* upon his arms became as flax that was burnt with fire, and his bands loosed from off his hands.

MIGHTY IN PHYSICAL STRENGTH

Jud 16:3 And Samson lay till midnight, and arose at midnight, and took the doors of the gate of the city, and the two posts, and went away with them, bar and all, and put *them* upon his shoulders, and carried them up to the top of an hill that is before Hebron.

Jud 16:9 Now *there were* men lying in wait, abiding with her in the chamber. And she said unto him, The Philistines *be* upon thee, Samson. And he brake the withs, as a thread of tow is broken when it toucheth the fire. So his strength was not known.

Jud 16:12 Delilah therefore took new ropes, and bound him therewith, and said unto him, The Philistines be upon thee, Samson. And *there were* liers in wait abiding in the chamber. And he brake them from off his arms like a thread.

Jud 16:14 And she fastened *it* with the pin, and said unto him, The Philistines *be* upon thee, Samson. And he awaked out of his sleep, and went away with the pin of the beam, and with the web.

YET WEAK IN RESISTING TEMPTATION

Jud 16:15–17 And she said unto him, How canst thou say, I love thee, when thine heart *is* not with me? thou hast mocked me these three times, and hast not told me wherein thy great strength *lieth.*

And it came to pass, when she pressed him daily with her words, and urged him, *so* that his soul was vexed unto death;

That he told her all his heart, and said unto her. There hath not come a razor upon mine head; for I *have been* a Nazarite unto God from my mother's womb: if I be shaven, then my strength will go from me, and I shall become weak, and be like any *other* man.

HIS SAD END

Jud 16:30 And Samson said, Let me die with the Philistines. And he bowed himself with *all his* might; and the house fell upon the lords, and upon all the people that *were* therein. So the dead which he slew at his death were more than *they* which he slew in his life.

See **ISRAEL**

SAMUEL

*1. **Person**, son of Elkanah and Hannah, the last of the Judges*

CONSECRATED TO GOD BY HIS PARENTS

1 S 1:24–28

A WONDERFUL CHILDHOOD

1 S 2:18–21, 26

HEARD GOD'S VOICE IN BOYHOOD

1 S 3:10

COURAGEOUS

1 S 13:13; 15:16

A MAN OF PRAYER

1 S 7:5–8; 8:6; 12:17; 15:11

AN INSPIRED PROPHET

1 S 3:19, 21; 8:22

A CIRCUIT JUDGE

1 S 7:16

THE UPRIGHT JUDGE

1 S 12:3–4

See **ISRAEL, YOUNG PEOPLE**

2. Books

a. Samuel, First

Author: Unknown.

Date Written: After 1011 B.C. The period was one of transition during which the rule of the Judges ended and the Kingdom was established.

Purpose: To record the founding of the Hebrew monarchy.

To Whom Written: The nation of Israel.

Main Themes: The career of Samuel, the last of the Judges and God's appointed kingmaker; the career of Saul, the first king of Israel, who became a tyrant; and the anointing of David, Israel's second king.

Key Word: King.

Key Verses: 8:7–8; 15:22.

b. Samuel, Second

Author: Unknown.

Date Written: After 973 B.C.

Purpose: To record the history of David's reign, who foreshadowed Christ, the ideal leader of a new and perfect kingdom.

To Whom Written: The nation of Israel.

Main Theme: The reign of David.

Key Word: David.

Key Verses: 5:12; 7:12–13.

SANBALLAT, *opposes the rebuilding of Jerusalem*

Ne 2:10, 19; 4:1; 6:2; 13:28

SANCTIFICATION, *set apart, made holy*

1. How Secured

2 Chr 31:18 And to the genealogy of all their little ones, their wives, and their sons, and their daughters, through all the congregation: for in their set office they sanctified themselves in holiness:

Jn 17:17 Sanctify them through thy truth: thy word is truth.

Ro 15:16 That I should be the minister of Jesus Christ to the Gentiles, ministering the gospel of God, that the offering up of the Gentiles might be acceptable, being sanctified by the Holy Ghost.

1 Co 1:2 Unto the church of God which is at Corinth, to them that are sanctified in Christ Jesus, called *to be* saints, with all that in every place call upon the name of Jesus Christ our Lord, both theirs and ours:

1 Co 1:30 But of him are ye in Christ Jesus, who of God is made unto us wisdom, and righteousness, and sanctification, and redemption:

Ep 5:26 That he might sanctify and cleanse it with the washing of water by the word,

2 Th 2:13 But we are bound to give thanks alway to God for you, brethren beloved of the Lord, because God hath from the beginning chosen you to salvation through sanctification of the Spirit and belief of the truth:

2 Ti 2:21 If a man therefore purge himself from these, he shall be a vessel unto honour, sanctified, and meet for the master's use, *and* prepared unto every good work.

He 10:10 By the which will we are sanctified through the offering of the body of Jesus Christ once *for all*.

He 10:29 Of how much sorer punishment, suppose ye, shall he be thought worthy, who hath trodden under foot the Son of God, and hath counted the blood of the covenant, wherewith he was sanctified, an unholy thing, and hath done despite unto the Spirit of grace?

He 13:12 Wherefore Jesus also, that he might sanctify the people with his own blood, suffered without the gate.

1 Pe 1:2 Elect according to the foreknowledge of God the Father, through sanctification of the Spirit, unto obedience and sprinkling of the blood of Jesus Christ: Grace unto you, and peace, be multiplied.

2. Prescribed

Ex 19:14 And Moses went down from the mount unto the people, and sanctified the people; and they washed their clothes.

Ex 19:22 And let the priests also, which come near to the LORD, sanctify themselves, lest the LORD break forth upon them.

Le 20:26 And ye shall be holy unto me: for I the LORD *am* holy, and have severed you from *other* people, that ye should be mine.

Nu 11:18 And say thou unto the people, Sanctify yourselves against to morrow, and ye shall eat flesh: for ye have wept in the ears of the LORD, saying, Who shall give us flesh to eat? for *it was* well with us in Egypt: therefore the LORD will give you flesh, and ye shall eat.

Jos 3:5 And Joshua said unto the people, Sanctify yourselves: for to morrow the LORD will do wonders among you.

1 S 16:5 And he said, Peaceably: I am come to sacrifice unto the LORD: sanctify yourselves, and come with me to the sacrifice. And he sanctified Jesse and his sons, and called them to the sacrifice.

2 Chr 29:5 And said unto them, Hear me, ye Levites, sanctify now yourselves, and sanctify the house of the LORD God of your fathers, and carry forth the filthiness out of the holy *place*.

Jb 1:5 And it was so, when the days of *their* feasting were gone about, that Job sent and sanctified them, and rose up early in the morning, and offered burnt offerings *according* to the number of them all: for Job said, It may be that my sons have sinned, and cursed God in their hearts. Thus did Job continually.

1 Th 4:3 For this is the will of God, *even* your sanctification, that ye should abstain from fornication:

1 Th 5:23 And the very God of peace sanctify you wholly; and *I pray God* your whole spirit and soul and body be preserved blameless unto the coming of our Lord Jesus Christ.

3. Those Set Apart

2 Chr 29:34 But the priests were too few, so that they could not flay all the burnt offerings: wherefore their brethren the Levites did help them, till the work was ended, and until the *other* priests had sanctified themselves: for the Levites *were* more upright in heart to sanctify themselves than the priests.

Je 1:5 Before I formed thee in the belly I knew thee; and before thou camest forth out of the womb I sanctified thee, *and* I ordained thee a prophet unto the nations.

Jn 17:19 And for their sakes I sanctify myself, that they also might be sanctified through the truth.

Ac 20:32 And now, brethren, I commend you to God, and to the word of his grace, which is able to build you up, and to give you an inheritance among all them which are sanctified.

Ac 26:18 To open their eyes, *and* to turn *them* from darkness to light, and *from* the power of Satan unto God, that they may receive forgiveness of sins, and inheritance among them which are sanctified by faith that is in me.

1 Co 1:2 Unto the church of God which is at Corinth, to them that are sanctified in Christ Jesus, called *to be* saints, with all that in every place call upon the name of Jesus Christ our Lord, both theirs and ours:

1 Co 6:11 And such were some of you: but ye are washed, but ye are sanctified, but ye are justified in the name of the Lord Jesus, and by the Spirit of our God.

Ep 5:26 That he might sanctify and cleanse it with the washing of water by the word,

He 2:11 For both he that sanctifieth and they who are sanctified *are* all of one: for which cause he is not ashamed to call them brethren,

He 10:14 For by one offering he hath perfected for ever them that are sanctified.

Jude 1 Jude, the servant of Jesus Christ, and brother of James, to them that are sanctified by God the Father, and preserved in Jesus Christ, *and* called:

See **DEEPER LIFE, DEVOTIONAL LIFE, HOLY SPIRIT, PERFECTION**

SAND

Ge 22:17; 41:49; 1 S 13:5; Jb 6:3; Ho 1:10; He 11:12; Re 20:8

SANDALS *See* **DRESS**

SANHEDRIN *See* **COURTS**

SANITY, *spiritual, clear and godly thinking*

Pr 12:5 The thoughts of the righteous *are* right: *but* the counsels of the wicked *are* deceit.

Mk 5:15 And they come to Jesus, and see him that was possessed with the devil, and had the legion, sitting, and clothed, and in his right mind: and they were afraid.

Lu 8:35 Then they went out to see what was done; and came to Jesus, and found the man, out of whom the devils were departed, sitting at the feet of Jesus, clothed, and in his right mind: and they were afraid.

Lu 15:17 And when he came to himself, he said, How many hired servants of my father's have bread enough and to spare, and I perish with hunger!

2 Co 10:5 Casting down imaginations, and every high thing that exalteth itself against the knowledge of God, and bringing into captivity every thought to the obedience of Christ;

2 Ti 1:7 For God hath not given us the spirit of fear; but of power, and of love, and of a sound mind.

Tit 2:6 Young men likewise exhort to be sober minded.

See **INSIGHT, MIND, PERCEPTION, THOUGHTS**

SAPPHIRA, *wife of Ananias*

Ac 5:1

SAPPHIRE *See* **STONES**

SARAH, *or Sarai, wife of Abraham*

THE MOTHER OF NATIONS

Ge 17:15–16 And God said unto Abraham, As for Sarai thy wife, thou shalt not call her name Sarai, but Sarah *shall* her name *be*.

And I will bless her, and give thee a son also of her: yea, I will bless her, and she shall be *a mother* of nations; kings of people shall be of her.

BEAUTIFUL

Ge 12:11 And it came to pass, when he was come near to enter into Egypt, that he said unto Sarai his wife, Behold now, I know that thou *art* a fair woman to look upon:

IMPATIENT OF DIVINE DELAYS, ATTEMPTS TO ANTICIPATE THE PLANS OF PROVIDENCE

Ge 16:2 And Sarai said unto Abram, Behold now, the LORD hath restrained me from bearing: I pray thee, go in unto my maid; it may be that I may obtain children by her. And Abram hearkened to the voice of Sarai.

BRINGS FAMILY TROUBLE UPON HERSELF

Ge 16:5–6 And Sarai said unto Abram, My wrong be upon thee: I have given my maid into thy bosom; and when she saw that she had conceived, I was despised in her eyes: the LORD judge between me and thee.

But Abram said unto Sarai, Behold, thy maid *is* in thy hand; do to her as it pleaseth thee. And when Sarai dealt hardly with her, she fled from her face.

DISBELIEVES GOD'S PROMISE

Ge 18:12–15 Therefore Sarah laughed within herself, saying, After I am waxed old shall I have pleasure, my lord being old also?

And the LORD said unto Abraham, Wherefore did Sarah laugh, saying, Shall I of a surety bear a child, which am old?

Is any thing too hard for the LORD? At the time appointed I will return unto thee, according to the time of life, and Sarah shall have a son.

Then Sarah denied, saying, I laughed not; for she was afraid. And he said, Nay; but thou didst laugh.

THE RULING PERSONALITY IN THE HOME

Ge 21:10–12 Wherefore she said unto Abraham, Cast out this bondwoman and her son: for the son of this bondwoman shall not be heir with my son, *even* with Isaac.

And the thing was very grievous in Abraham's sight because of his son.

And God said unto Abraham, Let it not be grievous in thy sight because of the lad, and because of thy bondwoman; in all that Sarah hath said unto thee, hearken unto her voice; for in Isaac shall thy seed be called.

HONORED OF GOD

Ge 17:15 And God said unto Abraham, As for Sarai thy wife, thou shalt not call her name Sarai, but Sarah *shall* her name *be*.

MENTIONED IN THE ROLL OF BIBLE WORTHIES

He 11:11 Through faith also Sara herself received strength to conceive seed, and was delivered of a child when she was past age, because she judged him faithful who had promised.

See **ABRAHAM**

SARCASM, *mocking remarks*

Jud 9:7–15; 10:14; 1 S 11:10; 17:28; 1 K 18:27; 20:11; 2 K 14:9; Ne 4:2; Jn 19:3

See **SPEECH**

SARDIS, *the capital of Lydia*

It was the home of one of the seven churches addressed in the Revelation to John (Re 3:1–6). In Roman times

(63 B.C.–A.D. 70) it was a leading city within the province of Asia. It was located about sixty miles east of Smyrna on the south side of the fertile valley of the Hermus, just where the river Pactolus issued from the Tmolus Mountains.

See **CITIES**

SARDIUS See **STONES**

SATAN, *devil, accuser*

1. Facts

Ge 3:14 And the LORD God said unto the serpent, Because thou hast done this, thou *art* cursed above all cattle, and above every beast of the field; upon thy belly shalt thou go, and dust shalt thou eat all the days of thy life:

Jb 1:6 Now there was a day when the sons of God came to present themselves before the LORD, and Satan came also among them.

Jb 2:2 And the LORD said unto Satan, From whence comest thou? And Satan answered the LORD, and said, From going to and fro in the earth, and from walking up and down in it.

Mt 12:26 And if Satan cast out Satan, he is divided against himself; how shall then his kingdom stand?

Lu 11:18 If Satan also be divided against himself, how shall his kingdom stand? because ye say that I cast out devils through Beelzebub.

2 Co 11:14 And no marvel; for Satan himself is transformed into an angel of light.

1 Ti 5:15 For some are already turned aside after Satan.

Jude 9 Yet Michael the archangel, when contending with the devil he disputed about the body of Moses, durst not bring against him a railing accusation, but said, The Lord rebuke thee.

Re 9:11 And they had a king over them, *which is* the angel of the bottomless pit, whose name in the Hebrew tongue *is* Abaddon, but in the Greek tongue hath *his* name Apollyon.

Re 20:2 And he laid hold on the dragon, that old serpent, which is the Devil, and Satan, and bound him a thousand years,

Re 20:7 And when the thousand years are expired, Satan shall be loosed out of his prison,

2. His Defeat

Ge 3:15 And I will put enmity between thee and the woman, and between thy seed and her seed; it shall bruise thy head, and thou shalt bruise his heel.

Mt 2:12 And being warned of God in a dream that they should not return to Herod, they departed into their own country another way.

Mt 4:11 Then the devil leaveth him, and, behold, angels came and ministered unto him.

Mt 12:29 Or else how can one enter into a strong man's house, and spoil his goods, except he first bind the strong man? and then he will spoil his house.

Mk 3:27 No man can enter into a strong man's house, and spoil his goods, except he will first bind the strong man; and then he will spoil his house.

Lu 4:13 And when the devil had ended all the temptation, he departed from him for a season.

Lu 11:22 But when a stronger than he shall come upon him, and overcome him, he taketh from him all his armour wherein he trusted, and divideth his spoils.

Jn 12:30–31 Jesus answered and said, This voice came not because of me, but for your sakes.

Now is the judgment of this world: now shall the prince of this world be cast out.

Jn 14:30 Hereafter I will not talk much with you: for the prince of this world cometh, and hath nothing in me.

Ro 16:20 And the God of peace shall bruise Satan under your feet shortly. The grace of our Lord Jesus Christ *be* with you. Amen.

1 Co 15:26 The last enemy *that* shall be destroyed *is* death.

2 Th 2:8 And then shall that Wicked be revealed, whom the Lord shall consume with the spirit of his mouth, and shall destroy with the brightness of his coming:

He 2:14 Forasmuch then as the children are partakers of flesh and blood, he also himself likewise took part of the same; that through death he might destroy him that had the power of death, that is, the devil;

1 Jn 3:8 He that committeth sin is of the devil; for the devil sinneth from the beginning. For this purpose the Son of God was manifested, that he might destroy the works of the devil.

Re 20:10 And the devil that deceived them was cast into the lake of fire and brimstone, where the beast and the false prophet *are*, and shall be tormented day and night for ever and ever.

3. His Power

PERMITTED TO AFFLICT THE RIGHTEOUS

Jb 1:12 And the LORD said unto Satan, Behold, all that he hath *is* in thy power; only upon himself put not forth thine hand. So Satan went forth from the presence of the LORD.

CLAIMS AUTHORITY OVER THE WORLD

Lu 4:6 And the devil said unto him, All this power will I give thee, and the glory of them: for that is delivered unto me; and to whomsoever I will I give it.

SINNERS UNDER HIS DOMINION

Ac 26:18 To open their eyes, *and* to turn *them* from darkness to light, and *from* the power of Satan unto God, that they may receive forgiveness of sins, and inheritance among them which are sanctified by faith that is in me.

BLINDS THE MINDS OF UNBELIEVERS

2 Co 4:3–4 But if our gospel be hid, it is hid to them that are lost:

In whom the god of this world hath blinded the minds of them which believe not, lest the light of the glorious gospel of Christ, who is the image of God, should shine unto them.

CONTENDS WITH THE SAINTS

Ep 6:12 For we wrestle not against flesh and blood, but against principalities, against powers, against the rulers of the darkness of this world, against spiritual wickedness in high *places.*

INSPIRES LYING WONDERS

2 Th 2:9 *Even him,* whose coming is after the working of Satan with all power and signs and lying wonders,

He 2:14 Forasmuch then as the children are partakers of flesh and blood, he also himself likewise took part of the same; that through death he might destroy him that had the power of death, that is, the devil;

4. His Malignant Work

TEMPTING TO DISOBEDIENCE

Ge 3:4–5 And the serpent said unto the woman, Ye shall not surely die:

For God doth know that in the day ye eat thereof, then your eyes shall be opened, and ye shall be as gods, knowing good and evil.

1 Chr 21:1 And Satan stood up against Israel, and provoked David to number Israel.

SLANDERING SAINTS

Jb 1:9–11 Then Satan answered the LORD, and said, Doth Job fear God for nought?

Hast not thou made an hedge about him, and about his house, and about all that he hath on every side? thou hast blessed the work of his hands, and his substance is increased in the land.

But put forth thine hand now, and touch all that he hath, and he will curse thee to thy face.

INFLICTING DISEASE

Jb 2:7 So went Satan forth from the presence of the LORD, and smote Job with sore boils from the sole of his foot unto his crown.

OPPOSING THE RIGHTEOUS

Zec 3:1 And he shewed me Joshua the high priest standing before the angel of the LORD, and Satan standing at his right hand to resist him.

TEMPTING CHRIST

Mt 4:1 Then was Jesus led up of the Spirit into the wilderness to be tempted of the devil.

Mt 4:3 And when the tempter came to him, he said, If thou be the Son of God, command that these stones be made bread.

REMOVING THE GOOD SEED

Mt 13:19 When any one heareth the word of the kingdom, and understandeth *it* not, then cometh the wicked *one,* and catcheth away that which was sown in his heart. This is he which received seed by the way side.

SOWING THE TARES

Mt 13:38–39 The field is the world; the good seed are the children of the kingdom; but the tares are the children of the wicked *one;*

The enemy that sowed them is the devil; the harvest is the end of the world; and the reapers are the angels.

RUINING SOUL AND BODY

Lu 9:42 And as he was yet a coming, the devil threw him down, and tare *him.* And Jesus rebuked the unclean spirit, and healed the child, and delivered him again to his father.

Lu 13:16 And ought not this woman, being a daughter of Abraham, whom Satan hath bound, lo, these eighteen years, be loosed from this bond on the sabbath day?

LYING

Jn 8:44 Ye are of your father the devil, and the lusts of *your* father ye will do. He was a murderer from the beginning, and abode not in the truth, because there is no truth in him. When he speaketh a lie, he speaketh of his own: for he is a liar, and the father of it.

INSTIGATING SIN

Jn 13:2 And supper being ended, the devil having now put into the heart of Judas Iscariot, Simon's *son,* to betray him;

Ac 5:3 But Peter said, Ananias, why hath Satan filled thine heart to lie to the Holy Ghost, and to keep back *part* of the price of the land?

2 Co 12:7 And lest I should be exalted above measure through the abundance of the revelations, there was given to me a thorn in the flesh, the messenger of Satan to buffet me, lest I should be exalted above measure.

Ep 2:2 Wherein in time past ye walked according to the course of this world, according to the prince of the power of the air, the spirit that now worketh in the children of disobedience:

1 Th 2:18 Wherefore we would have come unto you, even I Paul, once and again; but Satan hindered us.

PREYING ON PEOPLE

1 Pe 5:8 Be sober, be vigilant; because your adversary the devil, as a roaring lion, walketh about, seeking whom he may devour:

Re 2:10 Fear none of those things which thou shalt suffer: behold, the devil shall cast *some* of you into prison, that ye may be tried; and ye shall have tribulation ten days: be thou faithful unto death, and I will give thee a crown of life.

5. Humbled

Ge 3:14; Zec 3:2; Mt 8:31; 12:29; Mk 3:11; 5:10; Lu 8:31; 10:18; Re 12:9; 20:3

6. Arch Deceiver

BY LYING PROMISES

Ge 3:5

WRESTING THE SCRIPTURES

Mt 4:6

CUNNING PLANS

2 Co 2:11

APPEARING AS AN ANGEL OF LIGHT

2 Co 11:14

7. Resisting

De 13:8 Thou shalt not consent unto him, nor hearken unto him; neither shall thine eye pity him, neither shalt thou spare, neither shalt thou conceal him:

Mt 4:10 Then saith Jesus unto him, Get thee hence, Satan: for it is written, Thou shalt worship the Lord thy God, and him only shalt thou serve.

Lu 4:8 And Jesus answered and said unto him, Get thee behind me, Satan: for it is written, Thou shalt worship the Lord thy God, and him only shalt thou serve.

Ep 4:26–27 Be ye angry, and sin not: let not the sun go down upon your wrath:

Neither give place to the devil.

Ep 6:11 Put on the whole armour of God, that ye may be able to stand against the wiles of the devil.

Ja 4:7 Submit yourselves therefore to God. Resist the devil, and he will flee from you.

1 Pe 5:8–9 Be sober, be vigilant; because your adversary the devil, as a roaring lion, walketh about, seeking whom he may devour:

Whom resist stedfast in the faith, knowing that the same afflictions are accomplished in your brethren that are in the world.

1 Jn 5:18 We know that whosoever is born of God sinneth not; but he that is begotten of God keepeth himself, and that wicked one toucheth him not.

8. Called the Prince of This World

Jn 12:31 Now is the judgment of this world: now shall the prince of this world be cast out.

Jn 14:30 Hereafter I will not talk much with you: for the prince of this world cometh, and hath nothing in me.

Jn 16:11 Of judgment, because the prince of this world is judged.

9. His Ambition

Ge 3:4 And the serpent said unto the woman, Ye shall not surely die:

Is 14:13–14 For thou hast said in thine heart, I will ascend into heaven, I will exalt my throne above the stars of God: I will sit also upon the mount of the congregation, in the sides of the north:

I will ascend above the heights of the clouds; I will be like the most High.

Eze 28:2 Son of man, say unto the prince of Tyrus, Thus saith the Lord God; Because thine heart *is* lifted up, and thou hast said, I *am* a God, I sit *in* the seat of God, in the midst of the seas; yet thou *art* a man, and not God, though thou set thine heart as the heart of God:

2 Th 2:4 Who opposeth and exalteth himself above all that is called God, or that is worshipped; so that he as God sitteth in the temple of God, shewing himself that he is God.

2 Th 2:7 For the mystery of iniquity doth already work: only he who now letteth *will let,* until he be taken out of the way.

10. His Discernment of Christ's Divinity

Mk 1:24 Saying, Let *us* alone; what have we to do with thee, thou Jesus of Nazareth? art thou come to destroy us? I know thee who thou art, the Holy One of God.

Mk 1:34 And he healed many that were sick of divers diseases, and cast out many devils; and suffered not the devils to speak, because they knew him.

Mk 5:7 And cried with a loud voice, and said, What have I to do with thee, Jesus, *thou* Son of the most high God? I adjure thee by God, that thou torment me not.

Lu 4:41 And devils also came out of many, crying out, and saying, Thou art Christ the Son of God. And he rebuking *them* suffered them not to speak: for they knew that he was Christ.

11. His Tricks

2 Co 2:11 Lest Satan should get an advantage of us: for we are not ignorant of his devices.

2 Co 11:3 But I fear, lest by any means, as the serpent beguiled Eve through his subtilty, so your minds should be corrupted from the simplicity that is in Christ.

Ep 6:11 Put on the whole armour of God, that ye may be able to stand against the wiles of the devil.

2 Th 2:9 *Even him,* whose coming is after the working of Satan with all power and signs and lying wonders,

Re 12:9 And the great dragon was cast out, that old serpent, called the Devil, and Satan, which deceiveth the whole world: he was cast out into the earth, and his angels were cast out with him.

Re 20:7–8 And when the thousand years are expired, Satan shall be loosed out of his prison,

And shall go out to deceive the nations which are in the four quarters of the earth, Gog and Magog, to gather them together to battle: the number of whom *is* as the sand of the sea.

12. His Princehood

Jn 12:31 Now is the judgment of this world: now shall the prince of this world be cast out.

Jn 14:30 Hereafter I will not talk much with you: for the prince of this world cometh, and hath nothing in me.

Jn 16:11 Of judgment, because the prince of this world is judged.

2 Co 4:4 In whom the god of this world hath blinded the minds of them which believe not, lest the light of the glorious gospel of Christ, who is the image of God, should shine unto them.

Ep 2:2 Wherein in time past ye walked according to the course of this world, according to the prince of the power of the air, the spirit that now worketh in the children of disobedience:

13. His Limited Power

Jb 1:12 And the LORD said unto Satan, Behold, all that he hath *is* in thy power; only upon himself put not forth thine hand. So Satan went forth from the presence of the LORD.

Lu 10:19 Behold, I give unto you power to tread on serpents and scorpions, and over all the power of the enemy: and nothing shall by any means hurt you.

Ro 16:20 And the God of peace shall bruise Satan under your feet shortly. The grace of our Lord Jesus Christ *be* with you. Amen.

1 Co 10:13 There hath no temptation taken you but such as is common to man: but God *is* faithful, who will not suffer you to be tempted above that ye are able; but will with the temptation also make a way to escape, that ye may be able to bear *it.*

Ja 4:7 Submit yourselves therefore to God. Resist the devil, and he will flee from you.

Re 12:12 Therefore rejoice, *ye* heavens, and ye that dwell in them. Woe to the inhabiters of the earth and of the sea! for the devil is come down unto you, having great wrath, because he knoweth that he hath but a short time.

Re 13:5 And there was given unto him a mouth speaking great things and blasphemies; and power was given unto him to continue forty *and* two months.

14. Satanic "If"

Mt 4:3 And when the tempter came to him, he said, If thou be the Son of God, command that these stones be made bread.

Mt 4:6 And saith unto him, If thou be the Son of God, cast thyself down: for it is written, He shall give his angels charge concerning thee: and in *their* hands they shall bear thee up, lest at any time thou dash thy foot against a stone.

Mt 27:40 And saying, Thou that destroyest the temple, and buildest *it* in three days, save thyself. If thou be the Son of God, come down from the cross.

Lu 23:37 And saying, If thou be the king of the Jews, save thyself.

Lu 23:39 And one of the malefactors which were hanged railed on him, saying, If thou be Christ, save thyself and us.

15. His Influence

OF MARY MAGDALENE

Lu 8:2 And certain women, which had been healed of evil spirits and infirmities, Mary called Magdalene, out of whom went seven devils,

OF THE MAN OF GADARA

Lu 8:30 And Jesus asked him, saying, What is thy name? And he said, Legion: because many devils were entered into him.

OF THE BACKSLIDER'S HEART

Lu 11:26 Then goeth he, and taketh *to him* seven other spirits more wicked than himself; and they enter in, and dwell there: and the last *state* of that man is worse than the first.

OF JUDAS ISCARIOT

Lu 22:3 Then entered Satan into Judas surnamed Iscariot, being of the number of the twelve.

OF ALL WHO WILL GIVE HIM ENTRANCE

1 Pe 5:8 Be sober, be vigilant; because your adversary the devil, as a roaring lion, walketh about, seeking whom he may devour:

See **CHRIST, GOD, JUDGMENTS, TEMPTATION**

SATISFACTION, *of the saints' desires*

1. Promised

Ps 17:15 As for me, I will behold thy face in righteousness: I shall be satisfied, when I awake, with thy likeness.

Ps 36:8 They shall be abundantly satisfied with the fatness of thy house; and thou shalt make them drink of the river of thy pleasures.

Ps 37:19 They shall not be ashamed in the evil time: and in the days of famine they shall be satisfied.

Ps 63:5 My soul shall be satisfied as *with* marrow and fatness; and my mouth shall praise *thee* with joyful lips:

Ps 65:4 Blessed *is the man whom* thou choosest, and causest to approach *unto thee, that* he may dwell in thy courts: we shall be satisfied with the goodness of thy house, *even* of thy holy temple.

Ps 81:16 He should have fed them also with the finest of the wheat: and with honey out of the rock should I have satisfied thee.

Ps 103:5 Who satisfieth thy mouth with good *things; so that* thy youth is renewed like the eagle's.

Ps 107:9 For he satisfieth the longing soul, and filleth the hungry soul with goodness.

Pr 14:14 The backslider in heart shall be filled with his own ways: and a good man *shall be satisfied* from himself.

Pr 19:23 The fear of the LORD *tendeth* to life: and *he that hath it* shall abide satisfied; he shall not be visited with evil.

Is 58:11 And the LORD shall guide thee continually, and satisfy thy soul in drought, and make fat thy bones: and thou shalt be like a watered garden, and like a spring of water, whose waters fail not.

Je 31:14 And I will satiate the soul of the priests with fatness, and my people shall be satisfied with my goodness, saith the LORD.

Je 31:25 For I have satiated the weary soul, and I have replenished every sorrowful soul.

Je 50:19 And I will bring Israel again to his habitation, and he shall feed on Carmel and Bashan, and his soul shall be satisfied upon mount Ephraim and Gilead.

Mk 8:8 So they did eat, and were filled: and they took up of the broken *meat* that was left seven baskets.

Jn 4:14 But whosoever drinketh of the water that I shall give him shall never thirst; but the water that I shall give him shall be in him a well of water springing up into everlasting life.

Jn 6:35 And Jesus said unto them, I am the bread of life: he that cometh to me shall never hunger; and he that believeth on me shall never thirst.

Jn 10:9 I am the door: by me if any man enter in, he shall be saved, and shall go in and out, and find pasture.

2. Spiritual Thirst Satisfied

Ps 36:8 They shall be abundantly satisfied with the fatness of thy house; and thou shalt make them drink of the river of thy pleasures.

Ps 145:19 He will fulfil the desire of them that fear him: he also will hear their cry, and will save them.

Pr 9:5 Come, eat of my bread, and drink of the wine *which* I have mingled.

Is 12:3 Therefore with joy shall ye draw water out of the wells of salvation.

Is 43:20 The beast of the field shall honour me, the dragons and the owls: because I give waters in the wilderness, *and* rivers in the desert, to give drink to my people, my chosen.

Is 44:3 For I will pour water upon him that is thirsty, and floods upon the dry ground: I will pour my spirit upon thy seed, and my blessing upon thine offspring:

Is 49:10 They shall not hunger nor thirst; neither shall the heat nor sun smite them: for he that hath mercy on them shall lead them, even by the springs of water shall he guide them.

Is 55:1 Ho, every one that thirsteth, come ye to the waters, and he that hath no money; come ye, buy, and eat; yea, come, buy wine and milk without money and without price.

Je 31:25 For I have satiated the weary soul, and I have replenished every sorrowful soul.

Mt 5:6 Blessed *are* they which do hunger and thirst after righteousness: for they shall be filled.

Jn 4:14 But whosoever drinketh of the water that I shall give him shall never thirst; but the water that I shall give him shall be in him a well of

water springing up into everlasting life.

Jn 6:35 And Jesus said unto them, I am the bread of life: he that cometh to me shall never hunger; and he that believeth on me shall never thirst.

Jn 7:37 In the last day, that great *day* of the feast, Jesus stood and cried, saying, If any man thirst, let him come unto me, and drink.

Re 7:16 They shall hunger no more, neither thirst any more; neither shall the sun light on them, nor any heat.

Re 21:6 And he said unto me, It is done. I am Alpha and Omega, the beginning and the end. I will give unto him that is athirst of the fountain of the water of life freely.

Re 22:17 And the Spirit and the bride say, Come. And let him that heareth say, Come. And let him that is athirst come. And whosoever will, let him take the water of life freely.

See **DISSATISFACTION, UNREST**

SAUL, *son of Kish, first king of Israel*

HANDSOME

1 S 9:2 And he had a son, whose name *was* Saul, a choice young man, and a goodly: and *there was* not among the children of Israel a goodlier person than he: from his shoulders and upward *he was* higher than any of the people.

1 S 10:24 And Samuel said to all the people, See ye him whom the LORD hath chosen, that *there is* none like him among all the people? And all the people shouted, and said, God save the king.

HUMBLE

1 S 10:22 Therefore they enquired of the LORD further, if the man should yet come thither. And the LORD answered, Behold, he hath hid himself among the stuff.

SELF-CONTROLLED

1 S 10:27 But the children of Belial said, How shall this man save us? And they despised him, and brought him no presents. But he held his peace.

1 S 11:13 And Saul said, There shall not a man be put to death this day: for to day the LORD hath wrought salvation in Israel.

SELF-WILLED

1 S 13:12–13 Therefore said I, The Philistines will come down now upon me to Gilgal, and I have not made supplication unto the LORD: I forced myself therefore, and offered a burnt offering.

And Samuel said to Saul, Thou hast done foolishly: thou hast not kept the commandment of the LORD thy God, which he commanded thee: for now would the LORD have established thy kingdom upon Israel for ever.

DISOBEDIENT

1 S 15:11 It repenteth me that I have set up Saul *to be* king: for he is turned back from following me, and hath not performed my commandments. And it grieved Samuel; and he cried unto the LORD all night.

JEALOUS AND HATE-FILLED

1 S 18:8 And Saul was very wroth, and the saying displeased him; and he said, They have ascribed unto David ten thousands, and to me they have ascribed *but* thousands: and *what* can he have more but the kingdom?

1 S 19:1 And Saul spake to Jonathan his son, and to all his servants, that they should kill David.

SUPERSTITIOUS

1 S 28:7 Then said Saul unto his servants, Seek me a woman that hath a familiar spirit, that I may go to her, and enquire of her. And his servants said to him, Behold, *there is* a woman that hath a familiar spirit at Endor.

SUICIDAL

1 S 31:4 Then said Saul unto his armourbearer, Draw thy sword, and thrust me through therewith; lest these uncircumcised come and thrust me through, and abuse me. But his armourbearer would not; for he was sore afraid. Therefore Saul took a sword, and fell upon it.

SAVIOR, *Jesus Christ*

THE GIFT OF LOVE

Jn 3:16 For God so loved the world, that he gave his only begotten Son, that whosoever believeth in him should not perish, but have everlasting life.

HE ALONE HAS THE SAVING MESSAGE

Jn 6:68 Then Simon Peter answered him, Lord, to whom shall we go? thou hast the words of eternal life.

REJECTION OF HIM MEANS DEATH

Jn 8:24 I said therefore unto you, that ye shall die in your sins: for if ye believe not that I am *he,* ye shall die in your sins.

HIS IS THE ONLY SAVING NAME

Ac 4:12 Neither is there salvation in any other: for there is none other name under heaven given among men, whereby we must be saved.

HIS SACRIFICIAL DEATH IS THE CENTRAL THEME OF PREACHING

1 Co 2:2 For I determined not to know any thing among you, save Jesus Christ, and him crucified.

ALL HOPE OF ETERNAL LIFE IS BUILT UPON HIM

1 Co 3:11 For other foundation can no man lay than that is laid, which is Jesus Christ.

See **CHRIST, SIN**

SAVOR, *sweet, taste or flavor*

Ge 8:21; Ex 29:18, 25; Le 1:9, 13, 17; 2:9; 3:5, 16; 4:31; 6:15, 21; 8:21, 28; 17:6; 23:13, 18; Nu 15:7, 13, 24; 18:17; 28:2, 6, 13, 24; 29:2, 8, 36; Ezr 6:10; Eze 20:28, 41; 2 Co 2:15; Ep 5:2

SAWS, *instruments for cutting*

2 S 12:31; 1 K 7:9; Is 10:15

SCAPEGOAT, *a live goat over whose head the high priest confessed all the sins of Israel and which then was sent into the*

wilderness, symbolically bearing their sin on the Day of Atonement

Le 16:8, 21; Is 53:6

SCARLET, *a bright crimson red*

Ex 25:4; 26:31, 36; 27:16; 28:8, 15; 35:23, 35; 36:8, 35; 38:18; 39:1, 5; Le 14:4, 49; Nu 4:8; 19:6; Jos 2:18; 2 S 1:24; Pr 31:21; Is 1:18; Lam 4:5; Mt 27:28; Re 17:3; 18:16

SCEPTERS *See* **NATION**

SCHISM, *division*

1 Co 1:13; 11:18; 12:25

SCOFFERS, *those who deride or mock*

2 K 18:30; 2 Chr 32:15; Ps 42:3; 73:11; 79:10; 123:4; Pr 9:7; 13:1; 14:6; 15:12; 19:25, 29; 21:11, 24; 22:10; 24:9; 29:8; Is 5:19; 36:15; 37:10; Je 17:15; Mal 2:17; 3:14; Mt 12:24; 27:29, 37; Ac 2:13; 17:18; 2 Pe 3:3; Jude 18

See **SPEECH**

SCORNERS

Ne 2:19; Ps 1:1; Pr 1:22; 3:34; Is 28:14; 29:20; 36:4; Ho 7:5; Mal 1:13; Mt 9:24; 27:39; Mk 5:40; 15:29; Lu 8:53; Jn 7:52; 18:38

See **SPEECH**

SCORPIONS

De 8:15; Eze 2:6; Lu 11:12

See **INSECTS**

SCOURGING *See* **NATION**

SCRIBES, *writers or secretaries, men who copied the scriptures*

2 S 8:17; 2 K 12:10; 18:18; 19:2; 22:3, 12; 1 Chr 18:16; 24:6; 2 Chr 24:11; 26:11; 34:13; Ezr 4:8, 17; 7:6, 11; Ne 8:1; 12:26; 13:13; Est 3:12; 8:9; Is 36:3; Je 8:8; 36:4, 21, 32; 52:25; Mt 5:20; 7:29; 8:19; 9:3; 12:38; 13:52; 15:1; 16:21; 17:10; 20:18; 23:2, 15; 26:3; 27:41; Mk 1:22; 2:6; 3:22; 7:1; 9:11; 11:27; 12:28, 38; 14:1, 43; Lu 5:21; 11:53; 20:1, 19, 39, 46; 23:10; Jn 8:3; Ac 4:5; 6:12; 23:9; 1 Co 1:20

See **BOOKS, WRITING**

SCRIPTURES

1. Writings

Mt 22:29; Lu 24:32; Ro 16:26; Ja 2:8

2. Misused

Mt 4:6 And saith unto him, If thou be the Son of God, cast thyself down: for it is written, He shall give his angels charge concerning thee: and in *their* hands they shall bear thee up, lest at any time thou dash thy foot against a stone.

Mt 22:29 Jesus answered and said unto them, Ye do err, not knowing the scriptures, nor the power of God.

2 Co 2:17 For we are not as many, which corrupt the word of God: but as of sincerity, but as of God, in the sight of God speak we in Christ.

2 Co 4:2 But have renounced the hidden things of dishonesty, not walking in craftiness, nor handling the word of God deceitfully; but by manifestation of the truth commending ourselves to every man's conscience in the sight of God.

2 Pe 3:16 As also in all *his* epistles, speaking in them of these things; in which are some things hard to be understood, which they that are unlearned and unstable wrest, as *they do* also the other scriptures, unto their own destruction.

See **WORD OF GOD**

SEA, *Great, Western Sea, or Mediterranean*

Nu 34:6; De 11:24; Jos 1:4; 9:1; 15:12, 47; 23:4; Eze 47:10, 15, 20; 48:28; Da 7:2; Jl 2:20; Re 8:8

SEAL, *a signet or stamp*

1 K 21:8; Est 8:8; Je 32:10; Da 6:17; Mt 27:66

SEARCH

Jb 23:3 Oh that I knew where I might find him! *that* I might come *even* to his seat!

Je 29:13 And ye shall seek me, and find *me,* when ye shall search for me with all your heart.

Ho 6:3 Then shall we know, *if* we follow on to know the LORD: his going forth is prepared as the morning; and he shall come unto us as the rain, as the latter *and* former rain unto the earth.

Ac 17:27 That they should seek the Lord, if haply they might feel after him, and find him, though he be not far from every one of us:

See **SEEKING GOD**

SEASONS, *the four main climatic divisions of the year*

Ge 1:14; 8:22; Ps 104:19; Da 2:21; Mt 21:41

SEBAT *See* **MONTHS**

SECLUSION, *sought by those about to perform miracles*

BY ELIJAH, *in raising the widow's son*

1 K 17:19 And he said unto her, Give me thy son. And he took him out of her bosom, and carried him up into a loft, where he abode, and laid him upon his own bed.

2 K 4:5 So she went from him, and shut the door upon her and upon her sons, who brought *the vessels* to her; and she poured out.

BY ELISHA, *in the resurrection of the Shunammite's son*

2 K 4:33 He went in therefore, and shut the door upon them twain, and prayed unto the LORD.

BY CHRIST, *in raising Jairus' daughter*

Mk 5:40 And they laughed him to scorn. But when he had put them all out, he taketh the father and the mother of the damsel, and them that were with him, and entereth in where the damsel was lying.

BY CHRIST, *in healing the deaf and dumb man*

Mk 7:33 And he took him aside from the multitude, and put his fingers into his ears, and he spit, and touched his tongue;

BY CHRIST, *in healing the blind man*

Mk 8:23 And he took the blind man by the hand, and led him out of the town; and when he had spit on his eyes, and put his hands upon him, he asked him if he saw ought.

BY PETER, *in the resurrection of Dorcas*

Ac 9:40 Peter put them all forth, and kneeled down, and prayed; and turning *him* to the body said, Tabitha, arise. And she opened her eyes: and when she saw Peter, she sat up.

See **QUIETNESS**

SECOND COMING, *the future reappearing of Christ, according to his promise*

1. Foretold

Ps 98:9 Before the LORD; for he cometh to judge the earth: with righteousness shall he judge the world, and the people with equity.

Da 7:13 I saw in the night visions, and, behold, *one* like the Son of man came with the clouds of heaven, and came to the Ancient of days, and they brought him near before him.

Zec 14:5 And ye shall flee *to* the valley of the mountains; for the valley of the mountains shall reach unto Azal: yea, ye shall flee, like as ye fled from before the earthquake in the days of Uzziah king of Judah: and the LORD my God shall come, *and* all the saints with thee.

Mt 10:23 But when they persecute you in this city, flee ye into another: for verily I say unto you, Ye shall not have gone over the cities of Israel, till the Son of man be come.

Mt 26:64 Jesus saith unto him, Thou hast said: nevertheless I say unto you, Hereafter shall ye see the Son of man sitting on the right hand of power, and coming in the clouds of heaven.

Mk 13:26 And then shall they see the Son of man coming in the clouds with great power and glory.

Mk 13:35 Watch ye therefore: for ye know not when the master of the house cometh, at even, or at midnight, or at the cockcrowing, or in the morning:

Mk 14:62 And Jesus said, I am: and ye shall see the Son of man sitting on the right hand of power, and coming in the clouds of heaven.

Lu 9:26 For whosoever shall be ashamed of me and of my words, of him shall the Son of man be ashamed, when he shall come in his own glory, and *in his* Father's, and of the holy angels.

Lu 19:15 And it came to pass, that when he was returned, having received the kingdom, then he commanded these servants to be called unto him, to whom he had given the money, that he might know how much every man had gained by trading.

Lu 21:27 And then shall they see the Son of man coming in a cloud with power and great glory.

Jn 21:22 Jesus saith unto him, If I will that he tarry till I come, what *is that* to thee? follow thou me.

Ac 1:11 Which also said, Ye men of Galilee, why stand ye gazing up into heaven? this same Jesus, which is taken up from you into heaven, shall so come in like manner as ye have seen him go into heaven.

1 Co 11:26 For as often as ye eat this bread, and drink *this* cup, ye do shew the Lord's death till he come.

1 Co 15:23 But every man in his own order: Christ the firstfruits; afterward they that are Christ's at his coming.

He 9:28 So Christ was once offered to bear the sins of many; and unto them that look for him shall he appear the second time without sin unto salvation.

2 Pe 3:10 But the day of the Lord will come as a thief in the night; in the which the heavens shall pass away with a great noise, and the elements shall melt with fervent heat, the earth also and the works that are therein shall be burned up.

2. Its Timing

Mt 24:3 And as he sat upon the mount of Olives, the disciples came unto him privately, saying, Tell us,

when shall these things be? and what *shall be* the sign of thy coming, and of the end of the world?

Mt 24:27 For as the lightning cometh out of the east, and shineth even unto the west; so shall also the coming of the Son of man be.

Mt 24:36 But of that day and hour knoweth no *man,* no, not the angels of heaven, but my Father only.

Mt 24:39 And knew not until the flood came, and took them all away; so shall also the coming of the Son of man be.

Mt 24:50 The lord of that servant shall come in a day when he looketh not for *him,* and in an hour that he is not aware of,

Mt 25:13 Watch therefore, for ye know neither the day nor the hour wherein the Son of man cometh.

Mk 13:32 But of that day and *that* hour knoweth no man, no, not the angels which are in heaven, neither the Son, but the Father.

Lu 12:38 And if he shall come in the second watch, or come in the third watch, and find *them* so, blessed are those servants.

Lu 12:40 Be ye therefore ready also: for the Son of man cometh at an hour when ye think not.

Lu 12:46 The lord of that servant will come in a day when he looketh not for *him,* and at an hour when he is not aware of, and will cut him in sunder, and will appoint him his portion with the unbelievers.

Lu 17:24 For as the lightning, that lighteneth out of the one *part* under heaven, shineth unto the other *part* under heaven; so shall also the Son of man be in his day.

1 Th 5:2 For yourselves know perfectly that the day of the Lord so cometh as a thief in the night.

2 Th 2:1 Now we beseech you, brethren, by the coming of our Lord Jesus Christ, and *by* our gathering together unto him,

2 Pe 3:4 And saying, Where is the promise of his coming? for since the fathers fell asleep, all things continue as *they were* from the beginning of the creation.

Re 3:3 Remember therefore how thou hast received and heard, and hold fast, and repent. If therefore thou shalt not watch, I will come on thee as a thief, and thou shalt not know what hour I will come upon thee.

Re 16:15 Behold, I come as a thief. Blessed *is* he that watcheth, and keepeth his garments, lest he walk naked, and they see his shame.

3. Its Nearness

Ph 4:5 Let your moderation be known unto all men. The Lord *is* at hand.

He 10:25 Not forsaking the assembling of ourselves together, as the manner of some *is;* but exhorting *one another:* and so much the more, as ye see the day approaching.

He 10:37 For yet a little while, and he that shall come will come, and will not tarry.

Ja 5:8 Be ye also patient; stablish your hearts: for the coming of the Lord draweth nigh.

Re 3:11 Behold, I come quickly: hold that fast which thou hast, that no man take thy crown.

Re 22:7 Behold, I come quickly: blessed is he that keepeth the sayings of the prophecy of this book.

Re 22:20 He which testifieth these things saith, Surely I come quickly. Amen. Even so, come, Lord Jesus.

4. Its Purpose

Mt 16:27 For the Son of man shall come in the glory of his Father with his angels; and then he shall reward every man according to his works.

Mt 25:31 When the Son of man shall come in his glory, and all the holy angels with him, then shall he sit upon the throne of his glory:

1 Co 4:5 Therefore judge nothing before the time, until the Lord come, who both will bring to light the hidden things of darkness, and will make manifest the counsels of the hearts: and then shall every man have praise of God.

2 Ti 4:1 I charge *thee* therefore before God, and the Lord Jesus Christ, who shall judge the quick and the dead at his appearing and his kingdom;

Jude 14–15 And Enoch also, the seventh from Adam, prophesied of these, saying, Behold, the Lord cometh with ten thousands of his saints,

To execute judgment upon all, and to convince all that are ungodly among them of all their ungodly deeds which they have ungodly committed, and of all their hard *speeches* which ungodly sinners have spoken against him.

5. Our Preparation

READINESS

Mt 24:44

STEWARDSHIP

Lu 19:13

PATIENT WAITING

1 Co 1:7

CHARITABLENESS

1 Co 4:5

BLAMELESS LIVING

1 Th 5:23

PERFECT OBEDIENCE

1 Ti 6:14

JOYFUL EXPECTATION

Tit 2:13

CONSTANT ABIDING

1 Jn 2:28

6. Rewards Bestowed

HONOR FROM THE KING

Lu 12:37 Blessed *are* those servants, whom the lord when he cometh shall find watching: verily I say unto you, that he shall gird himself, and make them to sit down to meat, and will come forth and serve them.

FELLOWSHIP WITH THE KING

Jn 14:3 And if I go and prepare a place for you, I will come again, and receive you unto myself; that where I am, *there* ye may be also.

LIKENESS TO THE KING

Ph 3:20–21 For our conversation is in heaven; from whence also we look for the Saviour, the Lord Jesus Christ:

Who shall change our vile body, that it may be fashioned like unto his glorious body, according to the working whereby he is able even to subdue all things unto himself.

GLORY WITH THE KING

Col 3:4 When Christ, *who is* our life, shall appear, then shall ye also appear with him in glory.

1 Th 3:13 To the end he may stablish your hearts unblameable in holiness before God, even our Father, at the coming of our Lord Jesus Christ with all his saints.

1 Th 4:16 For the Lord himself shall descend from heaven with a shout, with the voice of the archangel, and with the trump of God: and the dead in Christ shall rise first:

THE FADELESS CROWN

1 Pe 5:4 And when the chief Shepherd shall appear, ye shall receive a crown of glory that fadeth not away.

THE BEATIFIC VISION

1 Jn 3:2 Beloved, now are we the sons of God, and it doth not yet appear what we shall be: but we know that, when he shall appear, we shall be like him; for we shall see him as he is.

7. Warnings to the Wicked

Mt 24:30 And then shall appear the sign of the Son of man in heaven: and then shall all the tribes of the earth mourn, and they shall see the Son of man coming in the clouds of heaven with power and great glory.

Mk 8:38 Whosoever therefore shall be ashamed of me and of my words in this adulterous and sinful generation; of him also shall the Son of man be ashamed, when he cometh in the glory of his Father with the holy angels.

Lu 21:26 Men's hearts failing them for fear, and for looking after those things which are coming on the earth: for the powers of heaven shall be shaken.

2 Th 1:7–8 And to you who are troubled rest with us, when the Lord Jesus shall be revealed from heaven with his mighty angels,

In flaming fire taking vengeance on them that know not God, and that obey not the gospel of our Lord Jesus Christ:

Re 1:7 Behold, he cometh with clouds; and every eye shall see him, and they *also* which pierced him: and all kindreds of the earth shall wail because of him. Even so, Amen.

See **FUTURE LIFE, JUDGMENTS, REWARD**

SECRETS

Pr 11:13; 20:19; 25:9; Je 38:24; Mt 18:15

SECTS AND PARTIES, *divisions within the Jewish community at the time of Christ*

1. Pharisees

This party among the Jews laid great stress upon the observance of rites and ceremonies. They made a pretense of superior piety and separated themselves from the common people. They were believers in the immortality of the soul, the resurrection of the body, and the existence of angels and spirits.

Mt 3:7; 5:20; 12:14, 24, 38; 15:1, 12; 16:1, 11; 19:3; 21:45; 22:15, 34; 23:2; Mk 3:6; 7:1; 10:2; 12:13; Lu 5:17, 30; 7:30, 36; 11:37, 53; 13:31; 14:1, 3; 17:20; 18:10; 19:39; Jn 1:24; 3:1; 4:1; 7:32; 8:3; 9:13, 40; 11:47, 57; 12:19, 42; Ac 5:34; 23:6; 26:5; Ph 3:5

See **PHARISAISM**

2. Sadducees

This materialistic party among the Jews denied the resurrection and the existence of angels and spirits. They also rejected the traditions of the elders.

Mt 3:7; 16:1, 6, 11; 22:23, 34; Mk 12:18; Lu 20:27; Ac 4:1; 5:17; 23:8

3. Herodians

This party opposed Jesus and probably formed under Herod the Great. Apparently they believed it was right to pay homage to a sovereign who might be able to bring to them the friendship of Rome and provide other advantages for the people.

Mt 22:16; Mk 3:6; 12:13

SECURITY

1. Of the Saints

Ex 11:7 But against any of the children of Israel shall not a dog move his tongue, against man or beast: that ye may know how that the LORD doth put a difference between the Egyptians and Israel.

Ex 12:23 For the LORD will pass through to smite the Egyptians; and when he seeth the blood upon the lintel, and on the two side posts, the LORD will pass over the door, and will not suffer the destroyer to come in unto your houses to smite *you.*

Ex 14:29 But the children of Israel walked upon dry *land* in the midst of the sea; and the waters *were* a wall unto them on their right hand, and on their left.

Le 26:5 And your threshing shall reach unto the vintage, and the vintage shall reach unto the sowing time: and ye shall eat your bread to the full, and dwell in your land safely.

Nu 23:23 Surely *there is* no enchantment against Jacob, neither *is there* any divination against Israel: according to this time it shall be said of Jacob and of Israel, What hath God wrought!

De 12:10 But *when* ye go over Jordan, and dwell in the land which the LORD your God giveth you to inherit, and *when* he giveth you rest from all your enemies round about, so that ye dwell in safety;

De 33:12 *And* of Benjamin he said, The beloved of the LORD shall dwell in safety by him; *and the* Lord shall cover

him all the day long, and he shall dwell between his shoulders.

De 33:28 Israel then shall dwell in safety alone: the fountain of Jacob *shall be* upon a land of corn and wine; also his heavens shall drop down dew.

1 S 2:35 And I will raise me up a faithful priest, *that* shall do according to *that* which *is* in mine heart and in my mind: and I will build him a sure house; and he shall walk before mine anointed for ever.

1 S 25:29 Yet a man is risen to pursue thee, and to seek thy soul: but the soul of my lord shall be bound in the bundle of life with the LORD thy God; and the souls of thine enemies, them shall he sling out, *as out* of the middle of a sling.

2 S 22:37 Thou hast enlarged my steps under me; so that my feet did not slip.

1 K 4:25 And Judah and Israel dwelt safely, every man under his vine and under his fig tree, from Dan even to Beer-sheba, all the days of Solomon.

Jb 11:18 And thou shalt be secure, because there is hope; yea, thou shalt dig *about thee, and* thou shalt take thy rest in safety.

Ps 12:5 For the oppression of the poor, for the sighing of the needy, now will I arise, saith the LORD; I will set *him* in safety *from him that* puffeth at him.

Ps 18:36 Thou hast enlarged my steps under me, that my feet did not slip.

Ps 25:13 His soul shall dwell at ease; and his seed shall inherit the earth.

Ps 27:5 For in the time of trouble he shall hide me in his pavilion: in the secret of his tabernacle shall he hide me; he shall set me up upon a rock.

Ps 32:6 For this shall every one that is godly pray unto thee in a time when thou mayest be found: surely in the floods of great waters they shall not come nigh unto him.

Ps 37:31 The law of his God *is* in his heart; none of his steps shall slide.

Ps 91:5 Thou shalt not be afraid for the terror by night; *nor* for the arrow *that* flieth by day;

Ps 112:7 He shall not be afraid of evil tidings: his heart is fixed, trusting in the LORD.

Ps 119:117 Hold thou me up, and I shall be safe: and I will have respect unto thy statutes continually.

Ps 125:1 They that trust in the LORD *shall be* as mount Zion, *which* cannot be removed, *but* abideth for ever.

Ps 144:14 *That* our oxen *may be* strong to labour; *that there be* no breaking in, nor going out; that *there be* no complaining in our streets.

Pr 1:33 But whoso hearkeneth unto me shall dwell safely, and shall be quiet from fear of evil.

Pr 3:24 When thou liest down, thou shalt not be afraid: yea, thou shalt lie down, and thy sleep shall be sweet.

Pr 10:9 He that walketh uprightly walketh surely: but he that perverteth his ways shall be known.

Pr 12:7 The wicked are overthrown and *are* not: but the house of the righteous shall stand.

Pr 12:21 There shall no evil happen to the just: but the wicked shall be filled with mischief.

Pr 18:11 The rich man's wealth *is* his strong city, and as an high wall in his own conceit.

Pr 29:25 The fear of man bringeth a snare: but whoso putteth his trust in the LORD shall be safe.

Is 14:30 And the firstborn of the poor shall feed, and the needy shall lie down in safety: and I will kill thy root with famine, and he shall slay thy remnant.

Is 22:23 And I will fasten him as a nail in a sure place; and he shall be for a glorious throne to his father's house.

Is 26:1 In that day shall this song be sung in the land of Judah; We have a strong city; salvation will *God* appoint *for* walls and bulwarks.

Is 32:18 And my people shall dwell in a peaceable habitation, and in sure dwellings, and in quiet resting places;

Is 33:16 He shall dwell on high: his place of defence *shall be* the munitions of rocks: bread shall be given him; his waters *shall be* sure.

Is 35:9 No lion shall be there, nor *any* ravenous beast shall go up thereon, it shall not be found there; but the redeemed shall walk *there:*

Is 41:3 He pursued them, *and* passed safely; *even* by the way *that* he had not gone with his feet.

Is 43:2 When thou passest through the waters, I *will be* with thee; and through the rivers, they shall not overflow thee: when thou walkest through the fire, thou shalt not be burned; neither shall the flame kindle upon thee.

Is 54:14 In righteousness shalt thou be established: thou shalt be far from oppression; for thou shalt not fear: and from terror; for it shall not come near thee.

Is 54:17 No weapon that is formed against thee shall prosper; and every tongue *that* shall rise against thee in judgment thou shalt condemn. This *is* the heritage of the servants of the LORD, and their righteousness *is* of me, saith the LORD.

Je 23:4 And I will set up shepherds over them which shall fee shall fear no more, nor be dismayed, neither shall they be lacking, saith the LORD.

Je 30:10 Therefore fear thou not, O my servant Jacob, saith the LORD; neither be dismayed, O Israel: for, lo, I will save thee from afar, and thy seed from the land of their captivity; and Jacob shall return, and shall be in rest, and be quiet, and none shall make *him* afraid.

Je 46:27 But fear not thou, O my servant Jacob, and be not dismayed, O Israel: for, behold, I will save thee from afar off, and thy seed from the land of their captivity; and Jacob shall return, and be in rest and at ease, and none shall make *him* afraid.

Eze 9:6 Slay utterly old *and* young, both maids, and little children, and women: but come not near any man upon whom *is* the mark; and begin at my sanctuary. Then they began at the ancient men which *were* before the house.

Eze 28:26 And they shall dwell safely therein, and shall build houses, and plant vineyards; yea, they shall dwell with confidence, when I have executed judgments upon all those that despise them round about them; and they shall know that I *am* the LORD their God.

Eze 34:14 I will feed them in a good pasture, and upon the high mountains of Israel shall their fold be: there shall they lie in a good fold, and *in* a fat pasture shall they feed upon the mountains of Israel.

Eze 34:25 And I will make with them a covenant of peace, and will cause the evil beasts to cease out of the land: and they shall dwell safely in the wilderness, and sleep in the woods.

Eze 34:28 And they shall no more be a prey to the heathen, neither shall the beast of the land devour them; but they shall dwell safely, and none shall make *them* afraid.

Eze 38:8 After many days thou shalt be visited: in the latter years thou shalt come into the land *that is* brought back from the sword, *and is* gathered out of many people, against the mountains of Israel, which have been always waste: but it is brought forth out of the nations, and they shall dwell safely all of them.

Eze 39:26 After that they have borne their shame, and all their trespasses whereby they have trespassed against me, when they dwelt safely in their land, and none made *them* afraid.

Da 3:25 He answered and said, Lo, I see four men loose, walking in the midst of the fire, and they have no hurt; and the form of the fourth is like the Son of God.

Am 9:15 And I upon their land, and they shall no more be pulled up out of their land which I have given them, saith the LORD thy God.

Mi 4:4 But they shall sit every man under his vine and under his fig tree; and none shall make *them* afraid: for the mouth of the LORD of hosts hath spoken *it.*

Zep 3:13 The remnant of Israel shall not do iniquity, nor speak lies; neither shall a deceitful tongue be found in their mouth: for they shall feed and lie down, and none shall make *them* afraid.

Zec 9:8 And I will encamp about mine house because of the army, be-

cause of him that passeth by, and because of him that returneth: and no oppressor shall pass through them any more: for now have I seen with mine eyes.

Zec 14:11 And *men* shall dwell in it, and there shall be no more utter destruction; but Jerusalem shall be safely inhabited.

Mt 6:21 For where your treasure is, there will your heart be also.

Mt 7:25 And the rain descended, and the floods came, and the winds blew, and beat upon that house; and it fell not: for it was founded upon a rock.

Lu 1:74 That he would grant unto us, that we being delivered out of the hand of our enemies might serve him without fear,

Lu 6:48 He is like a man which built an house, and digged deep, and laid the foundation on a rock: and when the flood arose, the stream beat vehemently upon that house, and could not shake it: for it was founded upon a rock.

Lu 10:19 Behold, I give unto you power to tread on serpents and scorpions, and over all the power of the enemy: and nothing shall by any means hurt you.

Lu 13:33 Nevertheless I must walk to day, and to morrow, and the *day* following: for it cannot be that a prophet perish out of Jerusalem.

Jn 10:28 And I give unto them eternal life; and they shall never perish, neither shall any *man* pluck them out of my hand.

Ro 8:31 What shall we then say to these things? If God *be* for us, who *can be* against us?

Ro 8:33 Who shall lay any thing to the charge of God's elect? *It is* God that justifieth.

He 6:19 Which *hope* we have as an anchor of the soul, both sure and stedfast, and which entereth into that within the veil;

He 13:6 So that we may boldly say, The Lord *is* my helper, and I will not fear what man shall do unto me.

1 Pe 3:13 And who *is* he that will harm you, if ye be followers of that which is good?

2 Pe 1:10 Wherefore the rather, brethren, give diligence to make your calling and election sure: for if ye do these things, ye shall never fall:

2. Firmly Established

De 28:9 The LORD shall establish thee an holy people unto himself, as he hath sworn unto thee, if thou shalt keep the commandments of the LORD thy God, and walk in his ways.

De 29:13 That he may establish thee to day for a people unto himself, and *that* he may be unto thee a God, as he hath said unto thee, and as he hath sworn unto thy fathers, to Abraham, to Isaac, and to Jacob.

De 32:7 Remember the days of old, consider the years of many generations: ask thy father, and he will shew thee; thy elders, and they will tell thee.

1 S 2:35 And I will raise me up a faithful priest, *that* shall do according to *that* which *is* in mine heart and in my mind: and I will build him a sure house; and he shall walk before mine anointed for ever.

1 S 3:20 And all Israel from Dan even to Beer-sheba knew that Samuel *was* established *to be* a prophet of the LORD.

1 S 25:28 I pray thee, forgive the trespass of thine handmaid: for the LORD will certainly make my lord a sure house; because my lord fighteth the battles of the LORD, and evil hath not been found in thee *all* thy days.

2 S 5:12 And David perceived that the LORD had established him king over Israel, and that he had exalted his kingdom for his people Israel's sake.

2 S 7:13 He shall build an house for my name, and I will stablish the throne of his kingdom for ever.

2 S 7:26 And let thy name be magnified for ever, saying, The LORD of hosts *is* the God over Israel: and let the house of thy servant David be established before thee.

1 K 2:12 Then sat Solomon upon the throne of David his father; and his kingdom was established greatly.

1 K 2:45 And king Solomon *shall be* blessed, and the throne of David shall

be established before the LORD for ever.

1 K 9:5 Then I will establish the throne of thy kingdom upon Israel for ever, as I promised to David thy father, saying, There shall not fail thee a man upon the throne of Israel.

1 K 11:38 And it shall be, if thou wilt hearken unto all that I command thee, and wilt walk in my ways, and do *that is* right in my sight, to keep my statutes and my commandments, as David my servant did; that I will be with thee, and build thee a sure house, as I built for David, and will give Israel unto thee.

2 K 21:8 Neither will I make the feet of Israel move any more out of the land which I gave their fathers; only if they will observe to do according to all that I have commanded them, and according to all the law that my servant Moses commanded them.

1 Chr 17:9 Also I will ordain a place for my people Israel, and will plant them, and they shall dwell in their place, and shall be moved no more; neither shall the children of wickedness waste them any more, as at the beginning,

1 Chr 17:14 But I will settle him in mine house and in my kingdom for ever: and his throne shall be established for evermore.

1 Chr 17:24 Let it even be established, that thy name may be magnified for ever, saying, The LORD of hosts *is* the God of Israel, *even* a God to Israel: and *let* the house of David thy servant *be* established before thee.

1 Chr 22:10 He shall build an house for my name; and he shall be my son, and I *will be* his father; and I will establish the throne of his kingdom over Israel for ever.

2 Chr 7:18 Then will I stablish the throne of thy kingdom, according as I have covenanted with David thy father, saying, There shall not fail thee a man *to be* ruler in Israel.

2 Chr 9:8 Blessed be the LORD thy God, which delighted in thee to set thee on his throne, *to be* king for the LORD thy God: because thy God loved Israel, to establish them for ever, therefore made he thee king over them, to do judgment and justice.

2 Chr 17:5 Therefore the Lord established the kingdom in his hand; and all Judah brought to Jehoshaphat presents; and he had riches and honour in abundance.

2 Chr 20:20 And they rose early in the morning, and went forth into the wilderness of Tekoa: and as they went forth, Jehoshaphat stood and said, Hear me, O Judah, and ye inhabitants of Jerusalem; Believe in the Lord your God, so shall ye be established; believe his prophets, so shall ye prosper.

Jb 22:23 If thou return to the Almighty, thou shalt be built up, thou shalt put away iniquity far from thy tabernacles.

Jb 22:28 Thou shalt also decree a thing, and it shall be established unto thee: and the light shall shine upon thy ways.

Jb 36:7 He withdraweth not his eyes from the righteous: but with kings *are they* on the throne; yea, he doth establish them for ever, and they are exalted.

Ps 7:9 Oh let the wickedness of the wicked come to an end; but establish the just: for the righteous God trieth the hearts and reins.

Ps 20:8 They are brought down and fallen: but we are risen, and stand upright.

Ps 37:31 The law of his God *is* in his heart; none of his steps shall slide.

Ps 40:2 He brought me up also out of an horrible pit, out of the miry clay, and set my feet upon a rock, *and* established my goings.

Ps 48:8 As we have heard, so have we seen in the city of the Lord of hosts, in the city of our God: God will establish it for ever. Selah.

Ps 55:22 Cast thy burden upon the Lord, and he shall sustain thee: he shall never suffer the righteous to be moved.

Ps 87:5 And of Zion it shall be said, This and *that man* was born in her: and the highest himself shall establish her.

Ps 89:4 Thy seed will I establish for ever, and build up thy throne to all generations. Selah.

Ps 90:17 And let the beauty of the Lord our God be upon us: and establish thou the work of our hands upon us; yea, the work of our hands establish thou it.

Ps 102:28 The children of thy servants shall continue, and their seed shall be established before thee.

Ps 112:8 His heart *is* established, he shall not be afraid, until he see *his desire* upon his enemies.

Pr 12:19 The lip of truth shall be established for ever: but a lying tongue *is* but for a moment.

Pr 16:3 Commit thy works unto the Lord, and thy thoughts shall be established.

Pr 24:3 Through wisdom is an house builded; and by understanding it is established:

Is 27:6 He shall cause them that come of Jacob to take root: Israel shall blossom and bud, and fill the face of the world with fruit.

Is 32:18 And my people shall dwell in a peaceable habitation, and in sure dwellings, and in quiet resting places.

Is 33:20 Look upon Zion, the city of our solemnities: thine eyes shall see Jerusalem a quiet habitation, a tabernacle *that* shall not be taken down; not one of the stakes thereof shall ever be removed, neither shall any of the cords thereof be broken.

Is 54:14 In righteousness shalt thou be established: thou shalt be far from oppression; for thou shalt not fear: and from terror; for it shall not come near thee.

Je 24:6 For I will set mine eyes upon them for good, and I will bring them again to this land: and I will build them, and not pull *them* down; and I will plant them, and not pluck *them* up.

Je 30:20 Their children also shall be as aforetime, and their congregation shall be established before me, and I will punish all that oppress them.

Je 31:28 And it shall come to pass, *that* like as I have watched over them, to pluck up, and to break down, and to throw down, and to destroy, and to afflict; so will I watch over them, to build, and to plant, saith the Lord.

Je 42:10 If ye will still abide in this land, then will I build you, and not pull *you* down, and I will plant you, and not pluck *you* up: for I repent me of the evil that I have done unto you.

Eze 36:11 And I will multiply upon you man and beast; and they shall increase and bring fruit: and I will settle you after your old estates, and will do better *unto you* than at your beginnings: and ye shall know that I *am* the LORD.

Da 4:36 At the same time my reason returned unto me; and for the glory of my kingdom, mine honour and brightness returned unto me; and my counsellors and my lords sought unto me; and I was established in my kingdom, and excellent majesty was added unto me.

Am 9:15 And I will plant them upon their land, and they shall no more be pulled up out of their land which I have given them, saith the LORD thy God.

Ac 16:5 And so were the churches established in the faith, and increased in number daily.

Ro 1:11 For I long to see you, that I may impart unto you some spiritual gift, to the end ye may be established;

Ro 16:25 Now to him that is of power to stablish you according to my preaching of Jesus Christ, according to the revelation of the mystery, which was kept secret since the world began,

2 Co 1:21 Now he which stablisheth us with you in Christ, and hath anointed us, *is* God;

Ep 3:17 That Christ may dwell in your hearts by faith; that ye, being rooted and grounded in love,

Col 2:7 Rooted and built up in him, and stablished in the faith, as ye have been taught, abounding therein with thanksgiving.

1 Th 3:2 And sent Timotheus, our brother, and minister of God, and our fellowlabourer in the gospel of Christ, to establish you, and to comfort you concerning your faith:

1 Th 3:13 To the end he may stablish your hearts unblameable in holiness before God, even our Father, at the coming of our Lord Jesus Christ with all his saints.

2 Th 2:17 Comfort your hearts, and stablish you in every good word and work.

He 13:9 Be not carried about with divers and strange doctrines. For *it is* a good thing that the heart be established with grace; not with meats, which have not profited them that have been occupied therein.

1 Pe 5:10 But the God of all grace, who hath called us unto his eternal glory by Christ Jesus, after that ye have suffered a while, make you perfect, stablish, strengthen, settle *you*.

2 Pe 1:12 Wherefore I will not be negligent to put you always in remembrance of these things, though ye know *them*, and be established in the present truth.

3. Cannot Be Moved

2 S 7:10 Moreover I will appoint a place for my people Israel, and will plant them, that they may dwell in a place of their own, and move no more; neither shall the children of wickedness afflict them any more, as beforetime,

Ps 15:5 *He that* putteth not out his money to usury, nor taketh reward against the innocent. He that doeth these *things* shall never be moved.

Ps 16:8 I have set the LORD always before me: because *he is* at my right hand, I shall not be moved.

Ps 21:7 For the king trusteth in the LORD, and through the mercy of the most High he shall not be moved.

Ps 26:1 Judge me, O LORD; for I have walked in mine integrity: I have trusted also in the LORD; *therefore* I shall not slide.

Ps 30:7 LORD, by thy favour thou hast made my mountain to stand strong: thou didst hide thy face, *and* I was troubled.

Ps 36:11 Let not the foot of pride come against me, and let not the hand of the wicked remove me.

Ps 46:5 God *is* in the midst of her; she shall not be moved: God shall help her, *and that* right early.

Ps 55:22 Cast thy burden upon the LORD, and he shall sustain thee: he shall never suffer the righteous to be moved.

Ps 62:2 He only *is* my rock and my salvation; *he is* my defence; I shall not be greatly moved.

Ps 62:6 He only *is* my rock and my salvation: *he is* my defence; I shall not be moved.

Ps 66:9 Which holdeth our soul in life, and suffereth not our feet to be moved.

Ps 112:6 Surely he shall not be moved for ever: the righteous shall be in everlasting remembrance.

Ps 121:3 He will not suffer thy foot to be moved: he that keepeth thee will not slumber.

Ps 125:1 They that trust in the LORD *shall be* as mount Zion, *which* cannot be removed, *but* abideth for ever.

Pr 10:25 As the whirlwind passeth, so *is* the wicked no *more:* but the righteous *is* an everlasting foundation.

Pr 10:30 The righteous shall never be removed: but the wicked shall not inhabit the earth.

Pr 12:3 A man shall not be established by wickedness: but the root of the righteous shall not be moved.

Mt 7:25 And the rain descended, and the floods came, and the winds blew, and beat upon that house; and it fell not: for it was founded upon a rock.

Lu 6:48 He is like a man which built an house, and digged deep, and laid the foundation on a rock: and when the flood arose, the stream beat vehemently upon that house, and could not shake it: for it was founded upon a rock.

Ac 2:25 For David speaketh concerning him, I foresaw the Lord always before my face, for he is on my right hand, that I should not be moved:

Ep 6:13 Wherefore take unto you the whole armour of God, that ye may be able to withstand in the evil day, and having done all, to stand.

Col 1:23 If ye continue in the faith grounded and settled, and *be* not moved away from the hope of the gospel, which ye have heard, *and* which was preached to every creature

which is under heaven; whereof I Paul am made a minister;

1 Pe 5:10 But the God of all grace, who hath called us unto his eternal glory by Christ Jesus, after that ye have suffered a while, make you perfect, stablish, strengthen, settle *you.*

Re 3:12 Him that overcometh will I make a pillar in the temple of my God, and he shall go no more out: and I will write upon him the name of my God, and the name of the city of my God, *which is* new Jerusalem, which cometh down out of heaven from my God: and *I will write upon him* my new name.

4. *Spiritual Foundation*

Ps 27:5 For in the time of trouble he shall hide me in his pavilion: in the secret of his tabernacle shall he hide me; he shall set me up upon a rock.

Ps 40:2 He brought me up also out of an horrible pit, out of the miry clay, and set my feet upon a rock, *and* established my goings.

Ps 87:1 His foundation *is* in the holy mountains.

Pr 10:25 As the whirlwind passeth, so *is* the wicked no *more:* but the righteous *is* an everlasting foundation.

Is 28:16 Therefore thus saith the Lord GOD, Behold, I lay in Zion for a foundation a stone, a tried stone, a precious corner *stone,* a sure foundation: he that believeth shall not make haste.

Is 54:11 O thou afflicted, tossed with tempest, *and* not comforted, behold, I will lay thy stones with fair colors, and lay thy foundations with sapphires.

Mt 7:24 Therefore whosoever heareth these sayings of mine, and doeth them, I will liken him unto a wise man, which built his house upon a rock:

Mt 16:18 And I say also unto thee, That thou art Peter, and upon this rock I will build my church; and the gates of hell shall not prevail against it.

Lu 6:48 He is like a man which built an house, and digged deep, and laid the foundation on a rock: and when the flood arose, the stream beat vehemently upon that house, and could not shake it: for it was founded upon a rock.

1 Co 3:11 For other foundation can no man lay than that is laid, which is Jesus Christ.

Ep 2:20 And are built upon the foundation of the apostles and prophets, Jesus Christ himself being the chief corner *stone;*

Col 2:7 Rooted and built up in him, and stablished in the faith, as ye have been taught, abounding therein with thanksgiving.

1 Ti 6:19 Laying up in store for themselves a good foundation against the time to come, that they may lay hold on eternal life.

2 Ti 2:19 Nevertheless the foundation of God standeth sure, having this seal, The Lord knoweth them that are his. And, Let every one that nameth the name of Christ depart from iniquity.

1 Pe 2:6 Wherefore also it is contained in the scripture, Behold, I lay in Sion a chief corner stone, elect, precious: and he that believeth on him shall not be confounded.

Jude 20 But ye, beloved, building up yourselves on your most holy faith, praying in the Holy Ghost,

Re 21:14 And the wall of the city had twelve foundations, and in them the names of the twelve apostles of the Lamb.

5. God as Rock

De 32:4 *He is* the Rock, his work *is* perfect: for all his ways *are* judgment: a God of truth and without iniquity, just and right *is* he.

De 32:15 But Jeshurun waxed fat, and kicked: thou art waxen fat, thou art grown thick, thou art covered *with fatness;* then he forsook God *which* made him, and lightly esteemed the Rock of his salvation.

De 32:31 For their rock *is* not as our Rock, even our enemies themselves *being* judges.

1 S 2:2 *There is* none holy as the Lord: for *there is* none beside thee: neither *is there* any rock like our God.

2 S 22:2 And he said, The Lord *is* my rock, and my fortress, and my deliverer;

2 S 22:32 For who *is* God, save the Lord? and who *is* a rock, save our God?

2 S 22:47 The Lord liveth; and blessed *be* my rock; and exalted be the God of the rock of my salvation.

2 S 23:3 The God of Israel said, the Rock of Israel spake to me, He that ruleth over men *must be* just, ruling in the fear of God.

Ps 18:2 The Lord *is* my rock, and my fortress, and my deliverer; my God, my strength, in whom I will trust; my buckler, and the horn of my salvation, *and* my high tower.

Ps 18:31 For who *is* God save the Lord? or who *is* a rock save our God?

Ps 18:46 The Lord liveth; and blessed *be* my rock; and let the God of my salvation be exalted.

Ps 28:1 Unto thee will I cry, O Lord my rock; be not silent to me: lest, *if* thou be silent to me, I become like them that go down into the pit.

Ps 31:3 For thou *art* my rock and my fortress; therefore for thy name's sake lead me, and guide me.

Ps 42:9 I will say unto God my rock, Why hast thou forgotten me? why go I mourning because of the oppression of the enemy?

Ps 61:2 From the end of the earth will I cry unto thee, when my heart is overwhelmed: lead me to the rock *that* is higher than I.

Ps 62:2 He only *is* my rock and my salvation; *he is* my defence; I shall not be greatly moved.

Ps 62:6 He only *is* my rock and my salvation: *he is* my defence; I shall not be moved.

Ps 71:3 Be thou my strong habitation, whereunto I may continually resort: thou hast given commandment to save me; for thou *art* my rock and my fortress.

Ps 78:35 And they remembered that God *was* their rock, and the high God their redeemer.

Ps 89:26 He shall cry unto me, Thou *art* my father, my God, and the rock of my salvation.

Ps 92:15 To shew that the Lord *is* upright: *he is* my rock, and *there is* no unrighteousness in him.

Ps 94:22 But the LORD is my defence; and my God *is* the rock of my refuge.

Ps 95:1 O come, let us sing unto the LORD: let us make a joyful noise to the rock of our salvation.

Is 26:4 Trust ye in the LORD for ever: for in the LORD JEHOVAH *is* everlasting strength:

Is 32:2 And a man shall be as an hiding place from the wind, and a covert from the tempest; as rivers of water in a dry place, as the shadow of a great rock in a weary land.

Lu 6:48 He is like a man which built an house, and digged deep, and laid the foundation on a rock: and when the flood arose, the stream beat vehemently upon that house, and could not shake it: for it was founded upon a rock.

6. Christ the Cornerstone

Ps 118:22 The stone *which* the builders refused is become the head *stone* of the corner.

Mt 21:42 Jesus saith unto them, Did ye never read in the scriptures, The stone which the builders rejected, the same is become the head of the corner: this is the Lord's doing, and it is marvellous in our eyes?

Ac 4:11 This is the stone which was set at nought of you builders, which is become the head of the corner.

Ep 2:20 And are built upon the foundation of the apostles and prophets, Jesus Christ himself being the chief corner *stone;*

1 Pe 2:6 Wherefore also it is contained in the scripture, Behold, I lay in Sion a chief corner stone, elect, precious: and he that believeth on him shall not be confounded.

7. Ultimate

KEPT IN THE FATHER'S NAME

Jn 17:11 And now I am no more in the world, but these are in the world, and I come to thee. Holy Father, keep through thine own name those whom thou hast given me, that they may be one, as we *are.*

KEPT IN SAFETY

Jn 17:12 While I was with them in the world, I kept them in thy name: those that thou gavest me I have kept, and none of them is lost, but the son of perdition; that the scripture might be fulfilled.

KEPT IN JOYFULNESS

John 17:13 And now come I to thee; and these things I speak in the world, that they might have my joy fulfilled in themselves.

KEPT IN PURITY

Jn 17:15 I pray not that thou shouldest take them out of the world, but that thou shouldest keep them from the evil.

KEPT SEPARATED FROM THE WORLD

Jn 17:16 They are not of the world, even as I am not of the world.

KEPT IN PROCESS OF SANCTIFICATION

Jn 17:17 Sanctify them through thy truth: thy word is truth.

KEPT IN ACTIVE SERVICE

Jn 17:18 As thou hast sent me into the world, even so have I also sent them into the world.

KEPT IN PERFECT UNITY

Jn 17:20–21 Neither pray I for these alone, but for them also which shall believe on me through their word;

That they all may be one; as thou, Father, *art* in me, and I in thee, that they also may be one in us: that the world may believe that thou hast sent me.

KEPT FOR THE COMING GLORY

Jn 17:22–24 And the glory which thou gavest me I have given them; that they may be one, even as we are one:

I in them, and thou in me, that they may be made perfect in one; and that the world may know that thou hast sent me, and hast loved them, as thou hast loved me.

Father, I will that they also, whom thou hast given me, be with me where I am; that they may behold my glory, which thou hast given me: for thou lovedst me before the foundation of the world.

See **INSECURITY, PRIDE, PROTECTION, SAFETY**

SEEING GOD

Ge 16:13; 32:30; Ex 24:10; Nu 12:8; 14:14; Jud 6:22; 13:22; Jb 19:27; 42:5; Ps 27:4; 141:8; Is 6:5; 33:17; Mt 5:8; Jn 14:9

See **GOD**

SEEKING GOD

1. The Duty of All People

De 4:29 But if from thence thou shalt seek the LORD thy God, thou shalt find *him*, if thou seek him with all thy heart and with all thy soul.

De 12:5 But unto the place which the LORD your God shall choose out of all your tribes to put his name there, *even* unto his habitation shall ye seek, and thither thou shalt come:

1 Chr 16:11 Seek the LORD and his strength, seek his face continually.

1 Chr 22:19 Now set your heart and your soul to seek the LORD your God; arise therefore, and build ye the sanctuary of the LORD God, to bring the ark of the covenant of the LORD, and the holy vessels of God, into the house that is to be built to the name of the LORD.

1 Chr 28:9 And thou, Solomon my son, know thou the God of thy father, and serve him with a perfect heart and with a willing mind: for the LORD searcheth all hearts, and understandeth all the imaginations of the thoughts: if thou seek him, he will be found of thee; but if thou forsake him, he will cast thee off for ever.

2 Chr 7:14 If my people, which are called by my name, shall humble themselves, and pray, and seek my face, and turn from their wicked ways; then will I hear from heaven, and will forgive their sin, and will heal their land.

2 Chr 14:4 And commanded Judah to seek the LORD God of their fathers, and to do the law and the commandment.

2 Chr 15:2 And he went out to meet Asa, and said unto him, Hear ye me, Asa, and all Judah and Benjamin; The LORD *is* with you, while ye be with him; and if ye seek him, he will be found of you; but if ye forsake him, he will forsake you.

Jb 5:8 I would seek unto God, and unto God would I commit my cause:

Jb 8:5 If thou wouldest seek unto God betimes, and make thy supplication to the Almighty;

Jb 11:13 If thou prepare thine heart, and stretch out thine hands toward him;

Ps 27:8 *When thou saidst,* Seek ye my face; my heart said unto thee, Thy face, LORD, will I seek.

Ps 32:6 For this shall every one that is godly pray unto thee in a time when thou mayest be found: surely in the floods of great waters they shall not come nigh unto him.

Ps 83:16 Fill their faces with shame; that they may seek thy name, O LORD.

Ps 105:4 Seek the LORD, and his strength: seek his face evermore.

Is 8:19 And when they shall say unto you, Seek unto them that have familiar spirits, and unto wizards that peep, and that mutter: should not a people seek unto their God? for the living to the dead?

Is 55:6 Seek ye the LORD while he may be found, call ye upon him while he is near:

Je 29:13 And ye shall seek me, and find *me*, when ye shall search for me with all your heart.

Lam 2:19 Arise, cry out in the night: in the beginning of the watches pour out thine heart like water before the face of the Lord: lift up thy hands toward him for the life of thy young children, that faint for hunger in the top of every street.

Ho 10:12 Sow to yourselves in righteousness, reap in mercy; break up your fallow ground: for *it is* time to seek the LORD, till he come and rain righteousness upon you.

Am 5:4 For thus saith the LORD unto the house of Israel, Seek ye me, and ye shall live:

Zep 2:3 Seek ye the LORD, all ye meek of the earth, which have wrought his judgment; seek righteousness, seek meekness: it may be ye shall be hid in the day of the LORD's anger.

Mt 6:33 But seek ye first the kingdom of God, and his righteousness; and all these things shall be added unto you.

Mt 7:7 Ask, and it shall be given you; seek, and ye shall find; knock, and it shall be opened unto you:

Lu 11:10 For every one that asketh receiveth; and he that seeketh findeth; and to him that knocketh it shall be opened.

Lu 12:31 But rather seek ye the kingdom of God; and all these things shall be added unto you.

Ac 15:17 That the residue of men might seek after the Lord, and all the Gentiles, upon whom my name is called, saith the Lord, who doeth all these things.

Ac 17:27 That they should seek the Lord, if haply they might feel after him, and find him, though he be not far from every one of us:

2. Examples

2 K 19:1 And it came to pass, when king Hezekiah heard *it*, that he rent his clothes, and covered himself with sackcloth, and went into the house of the LORD.

2 Chr 11:16 And after them out of all the tribes of Israel such as set their hearts to seek the LORD God of Israel came to Jerusalem, to sacrifice unto the LORD God of their fathers.

2 Chr 14:7 Therefore he said unto Judah, Let us build these cities, and make about *them* walls, and towers, gates, and bars, *while* the land *is* yet before us; because we have sought the LORD our God, we have sought *him*, and he hath given us rest on every side. So they built and prospered.

2 Chr 17:4 But sought to the Lord God of his father, and walked in his commandments, and not after the doings of Israel.

2 Chr 26:5 And he sought God in the days of Zechariah, who had understanding in the visions of God: and as long as he sought the LORD, God made him to prosper.

Ezr 8:21 Then I proclaimed a fast there, at the river of Ahava, that we might afflict ourselves before our God, to seek of him a right way for us, and for our little ones, and for all our substance.

Ps 14:2 The LORD looked down from heaven upon the children of men, to see if there were any that did understand, *and* seek God.

Ps 24:6 This *is* the generation of them that seek him, that seek thy face, O Jacob. Selah.

Ps 27:8 *When thou saidst,* Seek ye my face; my heart said unto thee, Thy face, LORD, will I seek.

Ps 42:2 My soul thirsteth for God, for the living God: when shall I come and appear before God?

Ps 53:2 God looked down from heaven upon the children of men, to see if there were *any* that did understand, that did seek God.

Ps 119:10 With my whole heart have I sought thee: O let me not wander from thy commandments.

Da 9:3 And I set my face unto the Lord God, to seek by prayer and supplications, with fasting, and sackcloth, and ashes:

Jn 12:21 The same came therefore to Philip, which was of Bethsaida of Galilee, and desired him, saying, Sir, we would see Jesus.

3. Finding the Saviour

Mt 18:12 How think ye? if a man have an hundred sheep, and one of them be gone astray, doth he not leave the ninety and nine, and goeth into the mountains, and seeketh that which is gone astray?

Lu 15:4 What man of you, having an hundred sheep, if he lose one of them, doth not leave the ninety and nine in the wilderness, and go after that which is lost, until he find it?

Lu 19:10 For the Son of man is come to seek and to save that which was lost.

Jn 1:43 The day following Jesus would go forth into Galilee, and findeth Philip, and saith unto him, Follow me.

Jn 5:14 Afterward Jesus findeth him in the temple, and said unto him, Behold, thou art made whole: sin no more, lest a worse thing come unto thee.

Jn 9:35 Jesus heard that they had cast him out; and when he had found him, he said unto him, Dost thou believe on the Son of God?

See **DESIRE**

SEIR *See* **MOUNTAINS AND HILLS**

SELF-ABASEMENT

Ge 18:27 And Abraham answered and said, Behold now, I have taken upon me to speak unto the Lord, which *am but* dust and ashes:

Ex 3:11 And Moses said unto God, Who *am* I, that I should go unto Pharaoh, and that I should bring forth the children of Israel out of Egypt?

Ex 4:10 And Moses said unto the LORD, O my Lord, I *am* not eloquent, neither heretofore, nor since thou hast spoken unto thy servant: but I *am* slow of speech, and of a slow tongue.

1 S 9:21 And Saul answered and said, *Am* not I a Benjamite, of the smallest of the tribes of Israel? and my family the least of all the families of the tribe of Benjamin? wherefore then speakest thou so to me?

1 S 15:17 And Samuel said, When thou *wast* little in thine own sight, *wast* thou not *made* the head of the tribes of Israel, and the LORD anointed thee king over Israel?

1 S 18:23 And Saul's servants spake those words in the ears of David. And David said, Seemeth it to you *a* light *thing* to be a king's son in law, seeing that I *am* a poor man, and lightly esteemed?

1 S 24:14 After whom is the king of Israel come out? after whom dost thou pursue? after a dead dog, after a flea.

1 S 25:41 And she arose, and bowed herself on *her* face to the earth, and said, Behold, *let* thine handmaid *be* a servant to wash the feet of the servants of my lord.

1 S 26:20 Now therefore, let not my blood fall to the earth before the face of the LORD: for the king of Israel is come out to seek a flea, as when one doth hunt a partridge in the mountains.

2 S 6:22 And I will yet be more vile than thus, and will be base in mine own sight: and of the maidservants which thou hast spoken of, of them shall I be had in honour.

2 S 9:8 And he bowed himself, and said, What is thy servant, that thou shouldest look upon such a dead dog as I *am?*

1 K 3:7 And now, O LORD my God, thou hast made thy servant king instead of David my father: and I *am but* a little child: I know not *how* to go out or come in.

2 Chr 2:6 But who is able to build him an house, seeing the heaven and heaven of heavens cannot contain him? who *am* I then, that I should build him an house, save only to burn sacrifice before him?

Jb 9:21 *Though* I *were* perfect, *yet* would I not know my soul: I would despise my life.

Jb 10:15 If I be wicked, woe unto me; and *if* I be righteous, *yet* will I not lift up my head. *I am* full of confusion; therefore see thou mine affliction;

Ps 22:6 But I *am* a worm, and no man; a reproach of men, and despised of the people.

Pr 30:2 Surely I *am* more brutish than *any* man, and have not the understanding of a man.

Song 1:6 Look not upon me, because I *am* black, because the sun hath looked upon me: my mother's children were angry with me; they made me the keeper of the vineyards; *but* mine own vineyard have I not kept.

Is 6:5 Then said I, Woe *is* me! for I am undone; because I *am* a man of unclean lips, and I dwell in the midst of a people of unclean lips: for mine eyes have seen the King, the LORD of hosts.

Je 1:6 Then said I, Ah, Lord GOD! behold, I cannot speak: for I *am* a child.

Lam 1:11 All her people sigh, they seek bread; they have given their pleasant things for meat to relieve the soul: see, O LORD, and consider; for I am become vile.

Eze 43:3 And *it was* according to the appearance of the vision which I saw, *even* according to the vision that I saw when I came to destroy the city: and the visions *were* like the vision that I saw by the river Chebar; and I fell upon my face.

Da 10:15 And when he had spoken such words unto me, I set my face toward the ground, and I became dumb.

Jona 3:6 For word came unto the king of Nineveh, and he arose from his throne, and he laid his robe from him, and covered *him* with sackcloth, and sat in ashes.

Mt 3:14 But John forbad him, saying, I have need to be baptized of thee, and comest thou to me?

Mt 15:27 And she said, Truth, Lord: yet the dogs eat of the crumbs which fall from their masters' table.

Mk 1:7 And preached, saying, There cometh one mightier than I after me, the latchet of whose shoes I am not worthy to stoop down and unloose.

Mk 7:28 And she answered and said unto him, Yes, Lord: yet the dogs under the table eat of the children's crumbs.

Lu 3:16 John answered, saying unto *them* all, I indeed baptize you with water; but one mightier than I cometh, the latchet of whose shoes I am not worthy to unloose: he shall baptize you with the Holy Ghost and with fire:

Lu 7:7 Wherefore neither thought I myself worthy to come unto thee: but say in a word, and my servant shall be healed.

Jn 1:23 He said, I *am* the voice of one crying in the wilderness, Make straight the way of the Lord, as said the prophet Esaias.

Jn 1:27 He it is, who coming after me is preferred before me, whose shoe's latchet I am not worthy to unloose.

Jn 3:30 He must increase, but I *must* decrease.

1 Co 1:15 Lest any should say that I had baptized in mine own name.

1 Co 2:3 And I was with you in weakness, and in fear, and in much trembling.

1 Co 3:7 So then neither is he that planteth any thing, neither he that watereth; but God that giveth the increase.

1 Co 13:4 Charity suffereth long, *and* is kind; charity envieth not; charity vaunteth not itself, is not puffed up,

1 Co 15:9 For I am the least of the apostles, that am not meet to be called an apostle, because I persecuted the church of God.

2 Co 3:5 Not that we are sufficient of ourselves to think any thing as of ourselves; but our sufficiency *is* of God;

2 Co 11:7 Have I committed an offence in abasing myself that ye might be exalted, because I have preached to you the gospel of God freely?

Ep 3:8 Unto me, who am less than the least of all saints, is this grace given, that I should preach among the Gentiles the unsearchable riches of Christ;

See **SELF-EXALTATION**

SELF-CONDEMNATION

Jb 9:20 If I justify myself, mine own mouth shall condemn me: *if I say, I am* perfect, it shall also prove me perverse.

Jb 15:6 Thine own mouth condemneth thee, and not I: yea, thine own lips testify against thee.

Ps 64:8 So they shall make their own tongue to fall upon themselves: all that see them shall flee away.

Mt 23:31 Wherefore ye be witnesses unto yourselves, that ye are the children of them which killed the prophets.

Lu 19:22 And he saith unto him, Out of thine own mouth will I judge thee, *thou* wicked servant. Thou knewest that I was an austere man, taking up that I laid not down, and reaping that I did not sow:

Jn 8:9 And they which heard *it*, being convicted by *their own* conscience, went out one by one, beginning at the eldest, *even* unto the last: and Jesus was left alone, and the woman standing in the midst.

Ro 2:1 Therefore thou art inexcusable, O man, whosoever thou art that judgest: for wherein thou judgest another, thou condemnest thyself; for thou that judgest doest the same things.

1 Jn 3:20 For if our heart condemn us, God is greater than our heart, and knoweth all things.

See **CONDEMNATION, JUSTICE**

SELF-CONFIDENCE

See **CONFIDENCE**

SELF-CONTROL

1. The Duty of Believers

OVER THE LIFE

Ac 24:25 And as he reasoned of righteousness, temperance, and judgment to come, Felix trembled, and answered, Go thy way for this time; when I have a convenient season, I will call for thee.

OVER THE LUSTS OF THE FLESH

Ro 6:12 Let not sin therefore reign in your mortal body, that ye should obey it in the lusts thereof.

1 Co 6:12 All things are lawful unto me, but all things are not expedient: all things are lawful for me, but I will not be brought under the power of any.

OVER THE TONGUE

Ja 3:2 For in many things we offend all. If any man offend not in word, the same *is* a perfect man, *and* able also to bridle the whole body.

A CARDINAL VIRTUE

2 Pe 1:5–7 And beside this, giving all diligence, add to your faith virtue; and to virtue knowledge;

And to knowledge temperance; and to temperance patience; and to patience godliness;

And to godliness brotherly kindness; and to brotherly kindness charity.

2. Examples

2 S 11:11 And Uriah said unto David, The ark, and Israel, and Judah, abide in tents; and my lord Joab, and the servants of my lord, are encamped in the open fields; shall I then go into mine house, to eat and to drink, and to lie with my wife? *as* thou livest, and *as* thy soul liveth, I will not do this thing.

Est 5:10 Nevertheless Haman refrained himself: and when he came home, he sent and called for his friends, and Zeresh his wife.

Is 36:21 But they held their peace, and answered him not a word: for the king's commandment was, saying, Answer him not.

Je 35:6 But they said, We will drink no wine: for Jonadab the son of Rechab our father commanded us, saying, Ye shall drink no wine, *neither* ye, nor your sons for ever:

Da 1:8 But Daniel purposed in his heart that he would not defile himself with the portion of the king's meat, nor with the wine which he drank: therefore he requested of the prince of the eunuchs that he might not defile himself.

1 Co 9:27 But I keep under my body, and bring *it* into subjection: lest that by any means, when I have preached to others, I myself should be a castaway.

2 Co 12:6 For though I would desire to glory, I shall not be a fool; for I will say the truth: but *now* I forbear, lest any man should think of me above that which he seeth me *to be*, or *that* he heareth of me.

1 Th 4:4 That every one of you should know how to possess his vessel in sanctification and honour;

See **MEEKNESS**

SELF-DECEPTION

FLATTERY

Ps 36:2 For he flattereth himself in his own eyes, until his iniquity be found to be hateful.

SPIRITUAL BONDAGE

Is 44:20 He feedeth on ashes: a deceived heart hath turned him aside, that he cannot deliver his soul, nor say, *Is there* not a lie in my right hand?

CONCEIT

Ga 6:3 For if a man think himself to be something, when he is nothing, he deceiveth himself.

CARELESS HEARING

Ja 1:22 But be ye doers of the word, and not hearers only, deceiving your own selves.

AN UNBRIDLED TONGUE

Ja 1:26 If any man among you seem to be religious, and bridleth not his tongue, but deceiveth his own heart, this man's religion *is* vain.

SANCTIMONY

1 Jn 1:8 If we say that we have no sin, we deceive ourselves, and the truth is not in us.

SPIRITUAL POVERTY

Re 3:17 Because thou sayest, I am rich, and increased with goods, and have need of nothing; and knowest not that thou art wretched, and miserable, and poor, and blind, and naked:

See **DECEPTION, TRUST**

SELF-DENIAL

1. By Obeying

Ex 33:6 And the children of Israel stripped themselves of their ornaments by the mount Horeb.

Mt 16:24 Then said Jesus unto his disciples, If any *man* will come after me, let him deny himself, and take up his cross, and follow me.

Lu 14:26–27 If any *man* come to me, and hate not his father, and mother, and wife, and children, and brethren, and sisters, yea, and his own life also, he cannot be my disciple.

And whosoever doth not bear his cross, and come after me, cannot be my disciple.

Ro 8:13 For if ye live after the flesh, ye shall die: but if ye through the Spirit do mortify the deeds of the body, ye shall live.

Ro 15:1 We then that are strong ought to bear the infirmities of the weak, and not to please ourselves.

Ga 5:24 And they that are Christ's have crucified the flesh with the affections and lusts.

2. By Renouncing All Things for Christ

LEAVING HOME AND FRIENDS

Mk 10:28 Then Peter began to say unto him, Lo, we have left all, and have followed thee.

Lu 5:11 And when they had brought their ships to land, they forsook all, and followed him.

LEAVING BUSINESS

Lu 5:27–28 And after these things he went forth, and saw a publican, named Levi, sitting at the receipt of custom: and he said unto him, Follow me.

And he left all, rose up, and followed him.

A CONDITION OF DISCIPLESHIP

Lu 14:33 So likewise, whosoever he be of you that forsaketh not all that he hath, he cannot be my disciple.

REWARD PROMISED

Lu 18:29–30 And he said unto them, Verily I say unto you, There is no man that hath left house, or parents, or brethren, or wife, or children, for the kingdom of God's sake,

Who shall not receive manifold more in this present time, and in the world to come life everlasting.

PAUL'S RENUNCIATION

Ph 3:8 Yea doubtless, and I count all things *but* loss for the excellency of the knowledge of Christ Jesus my Lord: for whom I have suffered the loss of all things, and do count them *but* dung, that I may win Christ,

3. By Restraining the Appetites

Ps 141:5 Let the righteous smite me; *it shall be* a kindness: and let him reprove me; *it shall be* an excellent oil, *which* shall not break my head: for yet my prayer also *shall be* in their calamities.

Pr 23:1–2 When thou sittest to eat with a ruler, consider diligently what *is* before thee:

And put a knife to thy throat, if thou *be* a man given to appetite.

Pr 23:20 Be not among winebibbers; among riotous eaters of flesh:

Pr 25:16 Hast thou found honey? eat so much as is sufficient for thee, lest thou be filled therewith, and vomit it.

Lu 12:22 And he said unto his disciples, Therefore I say unto you, Take no thought for your life, what ye shall eat; neither for the body, what ye shall put on.

Lu 21:34 And take heed to yourselves, lest at any time your hearts be overcharged with surfeiting, and drunkenness, and cares of this life, and so that day come upon you unawares.

1 Co 9:27 But I keep under my body, and bring *it* into subjection: lest that by any means, when I have preached to others, I myself should be a castaway.

4. By Subduing Fleshly Lusts

Mt 5:29 And if thy right eye offend thee, pluck it out, and cast *it* from thee: for it is profitable for thee that one of thy members should perish, and not *that* thy whole body should be cast into hell.

Mt 18:8 Wherefore if thy hand or thy foot offend thee, cut them off, and cast *them* from thee: it is better for thee to enter into life halt or maimed,

rather than having two hands or two feet to be cast into everlasting fire.

Ro 6:6 Knowing this, that our old man is crucified with *him,* that the body of sin might be destroyed, that henceforth we should not serve sin.

Ro 8:13 For if ye live after the flesh, ye shall die: but if ye through the Spirit do mortify the deeds of the body, ye shall live.

Ro 13:14 But put ye on the Lord Jesus Christ, and make not provision for the flesh, to *fulfil* the lusts *thereof.*

Ga 5:16 *This* I say then, Walk in the Spirit, and ye shall not fulfil the lust of the flesh.

Ga 5:24 And they that are Christ's have crucified the flesh with the affections and lusts.

Col 3:5 Mortify therefore your members which are upon the earth; fornication, uncleanness, inordinate affection, evil concupiscence, and covetousness, which is idolatry:

1 Pe 2:11 Dearly beloved, I beseech *you* as strangers and pilgrims, abstain from fleshly lusts, which war against the soul;

1 Pe 4:2 That he no longer should live the rest of *his* time in the flesh to the lusts of men, but to the will of God.

See **SELF-INDULGENCE**

SELF-EXALTATION

Ex 9:17 As yet exaltest thou thyself against my people, that thou wilt not let them go?

Nu 12:2 And they said, Hath the Lord indeed spoken only by Moses? hath he not spoken also by us? And the Lord heard *it.*

Nu 16:7 And put fire therein, and put incense in them before the Lord to morrow: and it shall be *that* the man whom the Lord doth choose, he *shall be* holy: *ye take* too much upon you, ye sons of Levi.

Nu 20:10 And Moses and Aaron gathered the congregation together before the rock, and he said unto them, Hear now, ye rebels; must we fetch you water out of this rock?

De 8:14 Then thine heart be lifted up, and thou forget the LORD thy God, which brought thee forth out of the land of Egypt, from the house of bondage;

De 9:4 Speak not thou in thine heart, after that the LORD thy God hath cast them out from before thee, saying, For my righteousness the LORD hath brought me in to possess this land: but for the wickedness of these nations the LORD doth drive them out from before thee.

De 32:27 Were it not that I feared the wrath of the enemy, lest their adversaries should behave themselves strangely, *and* lest they should say, Our hand is high, and the LORD hath not done all this.

Jud 9:2 Speak, I pray you, in the ears of all the men of Shechem, Whether is better for you, either that all the sons of Jerubbaal, *which are* threescore and ten persons, reign over you, or that one reign over you? remember also that I *am* your bone and your flesh.

Jud 9:29 And would to God this people were under my hand! then would I remove Abimelech. And he said to Abimelech, Increase thine army, and come out.

2 S 15:1 And it came to pass after this, that Absalom prepared him chariots and horses, and fifty men to run before him.

1 K 1:5 Then Adonijah the son of Haggith exalted himself, saying, I will be king: and he prepared him chariots and horsemen, and fifty men to run before him.

2 K 19:22 Whom hast thou reproached and blasphemed? and against whom hast thou exalted *thy* voice, and lifted up thine eyes on high? *even* against the Holy *One* of Israel.

2 Chr 25:19 Thou sayest, Lo, thou hast smitten the Edomites; and thine heart lifteth thee up to boast: abide now at home; why shouldest thou meddle to *thine* hurt, that thou shouldest fall, *even* thou, and Judah with thee?

2 Chr 26:16 But when he was strong, his heart was lifted up to *his* destruction: for he transgressed against the LORD his God, and went into the temple of the LORD to burn incense upon the altar of incense.

2 Chr 32:25 But Hezekiah rendered not again according to the benefit *done* unto him; for his heart was lifted up: therefore there was wrath upon him, and upon Judah and Jerusalem.

Jb 31:29 If I rejoiced at the destruction of him that hated me, or lifted up myself when evil found him:

Ps 66:7 He ruleth by his power for ever; his eyes behold the nations: let not the rebellious exalt themselves. Selah.

Ps 83:2 For, lo, thine enemies make a tumult: and they that hate thee have lifted up the head.

Ps 140:8 Grant not, O LORD, the desires of the wicked: further not his wicked device; *lest* they exalt themselves. Selah.

Pr 12:9 *He that is* despised, and hath a servant, *is* better than he that honoureth himself, and lacketh bread.

Pr 17:19 He loveth transgression that loveth strife: *and* he that exalteth his gate seeketh destruction.

Pr 25:6–7 Put not forth thyself in the presence of the king, and stand not in the place of great *men:*

For better *it is* that it be said unto thee, Come up hither; than that thou shouldest be put lower in the presence of the prince whom thine eyes have seen.

Pr 25:27 *It is* not good to eat much honey: so *for men* to search their own glory *is not* glory.

Pr 27:2 Let another man praise thee, and not thine own mouth; a stranger, and not thine own lips.

Pr 30:13 *There is* a generation, O how lofty are their eyes! and their eyelids are lifted up.

Pr 30:32 If thou hast done foolishly in lifting up thyself, or if thou hast thought evil, *lay* thine hand upon thy mouth.

Is 10:8 For he saith, *Are* not my princes altogether kings?

Is 14:13–14 For thou hast said in thine heart, I will ascend into heaven, I will exalt my throne above the stars of God: I will sit also upon the mount of the congregation, in the sides of the north:

I will ascend above the heights of the clouds; I will be like the most High.

Is 37:23 Whom hast thou reproached and blasphemed? and against whom hast thou exalted *thy* voice, and lifted up thine eyes on high? *even* against the Holy One of Israel.

Is 47:10 For thou hast trusted in thy wickedness: thou hast said, None seeth me. Thy wisdom and thy knowledge, it hath perverted thee; and thou hast said in thine heart, I *am,* and none else beside me.

Je 48:26 Make ye him drunken: for he magnified *himself* against the LORD: Moab also shall wallow in his vomit, and he also shall be in derision.

Je 48:42 And Moab shall be destroyed from *being* a people, because he hath magnified *himself* against the LORD.

Eze 27:3 And say unto Tyrus, O thou that art situate at the entry of the sea, *which art* a merchant of the people for many isles, Thus saith the Lord GOD; O Tyrus, thou hast said, I *am* of perfect beauty.

Eze 28:2 Son of man, say unto the prince of Tyrus, Thus saith the Lord GOD; Because thine heart *is* lifted up, and thou hast said, I *am* a God, I sit *in* the seat of God, in the midst of the seas; yet thou *art* a man, and not God, though thou set thine heart as the heart of God:

Eze 28:6 Therefore thus saith the Lord GOD; Because thou hast set thine heart as the heart of God;

Eze 28:17 Thine heart was lifted up because of thy beauty, thou hast corrupted thy wisdom by reason of thy brightness: I will cast thee to the ground, I will lay thee before kings, that they may behold thee.

Eze 31:10 Therefore thus saith the Lord GOD; Because thou hast lifted up thyself in height, and he hath shot up his top among the thick boughs, and his heart is lifted up in his height;

Da 4:30 The king spake, and said, Is not this great Babylon, that I have built for the house of the kingdom by the might of my power, and for the honour of my majesty?

Da 5:20 But when his heart was lifted up, and his mind hardened in pride, he was deposed from his kingly throne, and they took his glory from him:

Da 8:11 Yea, he magnified *himself* even to the prince of the host, and by him the daily *sacrifice* was taken away, and the place of his sanctuary was cast down.

Da 8:25 And through his policy also he shall cause craft to prosper in his hand; and he shall magnify *himself* in his heart, and by peace shall destroy many: he shall also stand up against the Prince of princes; but he shall be broken without hand.

Da 11:12 *And* when he hath taken away the multitude, his heart shall be lifted up; and he shall cast down *many* ten thousands: but he shall not be strengthened *by it.*

Da 11:36 And the king shall do according to his will; and he shall exalt himself, and magnify himself above every god, and shall speak marvellous things against the God of gods, and shall prosper till the indignation be accomplished: for that that is determined shall be done.

Ho 13:6 According to their pasture, so were they filled; they were filled, and their heart was exalted; therefore have they forgotten me.

Obad 4 Though thou exalt *thyself* as the eagle, and though thou set thy nest among the stars, thence will I bring thee down, saith the LORD.

Hab 2:4 Behold, his soul *which* is lifted up is not upright in him: but the just shall live by his faith.

Zep 2:10 This shall they have for their pride, because they have reproached and magnified *themselves* against the people of the LORD of hosts.

Mt 18:1 At the same time came the disciples unto Jesus, saying, Who is the greatest in the kingdom of heaven?

Mt 20:21 And he said unto her, What wilt thou? She saith unto him, Grant that these my two sons may sit, the one on thy right hand, and the other on the left, in thy kingdom.

Mt 23:6 And love the uppermost rooms at feasts, and the chief seats in the synagogues,

Mt 23:12 And whosoever shall exalt himself shall be abased; and he that shall humble himself shall be exalted.

Mk 9:34 But they held their peace: for by the way they had disputed among themselves, who *should be* the greatest.

Mk 10:37 They said unto him, Grant unto us that we may sit, one on thy right hand, and the other on thy left hand, in thy glory.

Mk 12:39 And the chief seats in the synagogues, and the uppermost rooms at feasts:

Lu 9:46 Then there arose a reasoning among them, which of them should be greatest.

Lu 11:43 Woe unto you, Pharisees! for ye love the uppermost seats in the synagogues, and greetings in the markets.

Lu 14:7 And he put forth a parable to those which were bidden, when he marked how they chose out the chief rooms; saying unto them,

Lu 14:11 For whosoever exalteth himself shall be abased; and he that humbleth himself shall be exalted.

Lu 18:11 The Pharisee stood and prayed thus with himself, God, I thank thee, that I am not as other men *are,* extortioners, unjust, adulterers, or even as this publican.

Lu 18:14 I tell you, this man went down to his house justified *rather* than the other: for every one that exalteth himself shall be abased; and he that humbleth himself shall be exalted.

Lu 20:46 Beware of the scribes, which desire to walk in long robes, and love greetings in the markets, and the highest seats in the synagogues, and the chief rooms at feasts;

Lu 22:24 And there was also a strife among them, which of them should be accounted the greatest.

Jn 7:18 He that speaketh of himself seeketh his own glory: but he that seeketh his glory that sent him, the same is true, and no unrighteousness is in him.

Jn 8:54 Jesus answered, If I honour myself, my honour is nothing: it is my Father that honoureth me; of whom ye say, that he is your God:

Ac 8:9 But there was a certain man, called Simon, which beforetime in the same city used sorcery, and bewitched the people of Samaria, giving out that himself was some great one:

Ro 12:3 For I say, through the grace given unto me, to every man that is among you, not to think *of himself* more highly than he ought to think; but to think soberly, according as God hath dealt to every man the measure of faith.

1 Co 4:6 And these things, brethren, I have in a figure transferred to myself and *to* Apollos for your sakes; that ye might learn in us not to think *of men* above that which is written, that no one of you be puffed up for one against another.

2 Co 10:5 Casting down imaginations, and every high thing that exalteth itself against the knowledge of God, and bringing into captivity every thought to the obedience of Christ;

2 Co 10:18 For not he that commendeth himself is approved, but whom the Lord commendeth.

2 Co 11:20 For ye suffer, if a man bring you into bondage, if a man devour *you,* if a man take *of you,* if a man exalt himself, if a man smite you on the face.

Ph 2:3 *Let* nothing *be done* through strife or vainglory; but in lowliness of mind let each esteem other better than themselves.

2 Th 2:4 Who opposeth and exalteth himself above all that is called God, or that is worshipped; so that he as God sitteth in the temple of God, shewing himself that he is God.

1 Pe 5:3 Neither as being lords over *God's* heritage, but being ensamples to the flock.

3 Jn 9 I wrote unto the church: but Diotrephes, who loveth to have the preeminence among them, receiveth us not.

See **SELF-ABASEMENT**

SELF-EXAMINATION

Ps 77:6 I call to remembrance my song in the night: I commune with mine own heart: and my spirit made diligent search.

Ps 119:59 I thought on my ways, and turned my feet unto thy testimonies.

Lam 3:40 Let us search and try our ways, and turn again to the LORD.

Mt 7:5 Thou hypocrite, first cast out the beam out of thine own eye; and then shalt thou see clearly to cast out the mote out of thy brother's eye.

Mt 25:7 Then all those virgins arose, and trimmed their lamps.

Lu 6:42 Either how canst thou say to thy brother, Brother, let me pull out the mote that is in thine eye, when thou thyself beholdest not the beam that is in thine own eye? Thou hypocrite, cast out first the beam out of thine own eye, and then shalt thou see clearly to pull out the mote that is in thy brother's eye.

Lu 22:23 And they began to enquire among themselves, which of them it was that should do this thing.

Ac 20:28 Take heed therefore unto yourselves, and to all the flock, over the which the Holy Ghost hath made you overseers, to feed the church of God, which he hath purchased with his own blood.

1 Co 11:28 But let a man examine himself, and so let him eat of *that* bread, and drink of *that* cup.

2 Co 13:5 Examine yourselves, whether ye be in the faith; prove your own selves. Know ye not your own selves, how that Jesus Christ is in you, except ye be reprobates?

Ga 6:4 But let every man prove his own work, and then shall he have rejoicing in himself alone, and not in another.

SELF-IGNORANCE

MISLEADS AND DECEIVES

Is 44:20 He feedeth on ashes: a deceived heart hath turned him aside, that he cannot deliver his soul, nor say, *Is there* not a lie in my right hand?

RESULTS IN UNCONSCIOUS DETERIORATION

Ho 7:9 Strangers have devoured his strength, and he knoweth *it* not: yea, gray hairs are here and there upon him, yet he knoweth not.

MANIFESTS ITSELF IN SELF-CONFIDENCE

Mk 10:39 And they said unto him, We can. And Jesus said unto them, Ye shall indeed drink of the cup that I drink of; and with the baptism that I am baptized withal shall ye be baptized:

Jn 13:37 Peter said unto him, Lord, why cannot I follow thee now? I will lay down my life for thy sake.

RETAINS SIN IN THE HEART

Jn 9:41 Jesus said unto them, If ye were blind, ye should have no sin: but now ye say, We see; therefore your sin remaineth.

Ro 7:18 For I know that in me (that is, in my flesh,) dwelleth no good thing: for to will is present with me; but *how* to perform that which is good I find not.

ALIENATES FROM GOD

Ep 4:18 Having the understanding darkened, being alienated from the life of God through the ignorance that is in them, because of the blindness of their heart:

IS ASSOCIATED WITH SELF-RIGHTEOUSNESS

Re 3:17 Because thou sayest, I am rich, and increased with goods, and have need of nothing; and knowest not that thou art wretched, and miserable, and poor, and blind, and naked:

See **IGNORANCE**

SELF-INDULGENCE, *yielding to the whims and desires of oneself*

1. The Power of Appetite

Ge 25:30 And Esau said to Jacob, Feed me, I pray thee, with that same red *pottage;* for I *am* faint: therefore was his name called Edom.

Ex 16:3 And the children of Israel said unto them, Would to God we had died by the hand of the LORD in the land of Egypt, when we sat by the flesh pots, *and* when we did eat bread to the full; for ye have brought us forth into this wilderness, to kill this whole assembly with hunger.

Nu 11:5 We remember the fish, which we did eat in Egypt freely; the cucumbers, and the melons, and the leeks, and the onions, and the garlick:

Pr 16:26 He that laboureth laboureth for himself; for his mouth craveth it of him.

Pr 18:20 A man's belly shall be satisfied with the fruit of his mouth; *and* with the increase of his lips shall he be filled.

Pr 23:2 And put a knife to thy throat, if thou *be* a man given to appetite.

Pr 23:35 They have stricken me, *shalt thou say, and* I was not sick; they have beaten me, *and* I felt *it* not: when shall I awake? I will seek it yet again.

Ec 6:7 All the labour of man *is* for his mouth, and yet the appetite is not filled.

Is 29:8 It shall even be as when an hungry *man* dreameth, and, behold, he eateth; but he awaketh, and his soul is empty: or as when a thirsty man dreameth, and, behold, he drinketh; but he awaketh, and, behold, *he is* faint, and his soul hath appetite: so shall the multitude of all the nations be, that fight against mount Zion.

Is 56:12 Come ye, *say they,* I will fetch wine, and we will fill ourselves with strong drink; and to morrow shall be as this day, *and* much more abundant.

Lu 4:3 And the devil said unto him, If thou be the Son of God, command this stone that it be made bread.

1 Co 6:13 Meats for the belly, and the belly for meats: but God shall destroy both it and them. Now the body *is* not for fornication, but for the Lord; and the Lord for the body.

2. Gluttony

Nu 11:32 And the people stood up all that day, and all *that* night, and all the next day, and they gathered the quails: he that gathered least gathered ten homers: and they spread *them* all abroad for themselves round about the camp.

De 21:20 And they shall say unto the elders of his city, This our son *is* stubborn and rebellious, he will not obey our voice; *he is* a glutton, and a drunkard.

Ps 106:15 And he gave them their request; but sent leanness into their soul.

Pr 23:1–3 When thou sittest to eat with a ruler, consider diligently what *is* before thee:

And put a knife to thy throat, if thou *be* a man given to appetite.

Be not desirous of his dainties: for they *are* deceitful meat.

Pr 23:21 For the drunkard and the glutton shall come to poverty: and drowsiness shall clothe *a man* with rags.

Pr 25:16 Hast thou found honey? eat so much as is sufficient for thee, lest thou be filled therewith, and vomit it.

Pr 30:22 For a servant when he reigneth; and a fool when he is filled with meat;

Ph 3:19 Whose end *is* destruction, whose God *is their* belly, and *whose* glory *is* in their shame, who mind earthly things.)

See **APPAREL, EATING, SELF-DENIAL**

SELFISHNESS, *the state of being overly concerned with one's self, egotism*

1. Different Forms

HOARDING FOOD

Pr 11:26 He that withholdeth corn, the people shall curse him: but blessing *shall be* upon the head of him that selleth *it*.

Pr 24:11 If thou forbear to deliver *them that are* drawn unto death, and *those that are* ready to be slain;

GREED FOR REAL ESTATE

Is 5:8 Woe unto them that join house to house, *that* lay field to field, till *there be* no place, that they may be placed alone in the midst of the earth!

DISREGARD OF THE RIGHTS OF OTHERS

Eze 34:18 *Seemeth it* a small thing unto you to have eaten up the good pasture, but ye must tread down with your feet the residue of your pastures? and to have drunk of the deep waters, but ye must foul the residue with your feet?

Ho 10:1 Israel *is* an empty vine, he bringeth forth fruit unto himself: according to the multitude of his fruit he hath increased the altars; according to the goodness of his land they have made goodly images.

Hab 2:6 Shall not all these take up a parable against him, and a taunting proverb against him, and say, Woe to him that increaseth *that which is* not his! how long? and to him that ladeth himself with thick clay!

Zec 7:6 And when ye did eat, and when ye did drink, did not ye eat *for yourselves,* and drink *for yourselves?*

NEGLECT OF THE NEEDY AND SUFFERING

Mt 25:43 I was a stranger, and ye took me not in: naked, and ye clothed me not: sick, and in prison, and ye visited me not.

HEARTLESS INDIFFERENCE TOWARD SINNERS

Mt 27:3–4 Then Judas, which had betrayeth him, when he saw that he was condemned, repented himself, and brought again the thirty pieces of silver to the chief priests and elders,

Saying, I have sinned in that I have betrayed the innocent blood. And they said, What *is that* to us? see thou to that.

2 Ti 3:2 For men shall be lovers of their own selves, covetous, boasters, proud, blasphemers, disobedient to parents, unthankful, unholy,

1 Jn 3:17 But whoso hath this world's good, and seeth his brother have need, and shutteth up his bowels *of compassion* from him, how dwelleth the love of God in him?

2. Examples

CAIN'S COLD-BLOODED WORDS CONCERNING ABEL

Ge 4:9 And the LORD said unto Cain, Where *is* Abel thy brother? And he said, I know not: *Am* I my brother's keeper?

NABAL REFUSES FOOD TO DAVID

1 S 25:11 Shall I then take my bread, and my water, and my flesh that I have killed for my shearers, and give *it* unto men, whom I know not whence they *be?*

HAMAN'S SELFISH CONCEIT

Est 6:6 So Haman came in. And the king said unto him, What shall be done unto the man whom the king delighteth to honour? Now Haman thought in his heart, To whom would the king delight to do honour more than to myself?

JAMES AND JOHN SEEK THE BEST PLACES

Mk 10:37 They said unto him, Grant unto us that we may sit, one on thy right hand, and the other on thy left hand, in thy glory.

THE PRIEST AND LEVITE PASS BY THE WOUNDED MAN

Lu 10:31–32 And by chance there came down a certain priest that way: and when he saw him, he passed by on the other side.

And likewise a Levite, when he was at the place, came and looked *on him,* and passed by on the other side.

OTHER

Ex 2:17 And the shepherds came and drove them away: but Moses stood up and helped them, and watered their flock.

Nu 20:21 Thus Edom refused to give Israel passage through his border: wherefore Israel turned away from him.

Jud 8:6 And the princes of Succoth said, *Are* the hands of Zebah and Zalmunna now in thine hand, that we should give bread unto thine army?

2 K 7:8 And when these lepers came to the uttermost part of the camp, they went into one tent, and did eat and drink, and carried thence silver, and gold, and raiment, and went and hid *it;* and came again, and entered into another tent, and carried thence *also,* and went and hid *it.*

Is 56:11 Yea, *they are* greedy dogs *which* can never have enough, and they *are* shepherds *that* cannot understand: they all look to their own way, every one for his gain, from his quarter.

Mt 23:4 For they bind heavy burdens and grievous to be borne, and lay *them* on men's shoulders; but they *themselves* will not move them with one of their fingers.

Ph 2:21 For all seek their own, not the things which are Jesus Christ's.

Ja 2:16 And one of you say unto them, Depart in peace, be ye warmed and filled; notwithstanding ye give them not those things which are needful to the body; what *doth it* profit?

See **UNSELFISHNESS**

SELF-JUSTIFICATION, *a sinner's vain attempt to find restoration with God through personal merit*

1. Its Impossibility

Jb 14:4 Who can bring a clean *thing* out of an unclean? not one.

Ps 130:3 If thou, LORD, shouldest mark iniquities, O Lord, who shall stand?

Pr 20:9 Who can say, I have made my heart clean, I am pure from my sin?

Ec 7:20 For *there is* not a just man upon earth, that doeth good, and sinneth not.

Eze 14:14 Though these three men, Noah, Daniel, and Job, were in it, they should deliver *but* their own souls by their righteousness, saith the Lord GOD.

Mt 27:24 When Pilate saw that he could prevail nothing, but *that* rather a tumult was made, he took water, and washed *his* hands before the multitude, saying, I am innocent of the blood of this just person: see ye *to it.*

Ro 3:19 Now we know that what things soever the law saith, it saith to them who are under the law: that every mouth may be stopped, and all the world may become guilty before God.

2. Its Lack of Standing before God

1 S 6:20 And the men of Beth-she-mesh said, Who is able to stand before this holy LORD God? and to whom shall he go up from us?

2 Chr 5:14 So that the priests could not stand to minister by reason of the cloud: for the glory of the LORD had filled the house of God.

Ezr 9:15 O LORD God of Israel, thou *art* righteous: for we remain yet escaped, as *it is* this day: behold, we *are* before thee in our trespasses: for we cannot stand before thee because of this.

Jb 41:10 None *is* so fierce that dare stir him up: who then is able to stand before me?

Ps 5:5 The foolish shall not stand in thy sight: thou hatest all workers of iniquity.

Ps 76:7 Thou, *even* thou, *art* to be feared: and who may stand in thy sight when once thou art angry?

Ps 130:3 If thou, LORD, shouldest mark iniquities, O Lord, who shall stand?

Je 49:19 Behold, he shall come up like a lion from the swelling of Jordan against the habitation of the strong: but I will suddenly make him run away from her: and who *is* a chosen *man, that* I may appoint over her? for who *is* like me? and who will appoint me the time? and who *is* that shepherd that will stand before me?

Je 50:44 Behold, he shall come up like a lion from the swelling of Jordan unto the habitation of the strong: but I will make them suddenly run away from her: and who *is* a chosen *man, that* I may appoint over her? for who *is* like me? and who will appoint me the time? and who *is* that shepherd that will stand before me?

Eze 22:14 Can thine heart endure, or can thine hands be strong, in the days that I shall deal with thee? I the LORD have spoken *it,* and will do *it.*

Jl 2:11 And the LORD shall utter his voice before his army: for his camp *is* very great: for *he is* strong that executeth his word: for the day of the LORD *is* great and very terrible; and who can abide it?

Na 1:6 Who can stand before his indignation? and who can abide in the fierceness of his anger? his fury is poured out like fire, and the rocks are thrown down by him.

Mal 3:2 But who may abide the day of his coming? and who shall stand when he appeareth? for he *is* like a refiner's fire, and like fullers' soap:

Lu 21:36 Watch ye therefore, and pray always, that ye may be accounted worthy to escape all these things that shall come to pass, and to stand before the Son of man.

Re 6:17 For the great day of his wrath is come; and who shall be able to stand?

See **JUSTIFICATION**

SELF-RIGHTEOUSNESS, *the attempt to meet God's standards based upon one's own merits*

1. Its Folly

De 9:4 Speak not thou in thine heart, after that the LORD thy God hath cast them out from before thee, saying, For my righteousness the LORD hath brought me in to possess this land: but for the wickedness of these nations the LORD doth drive them out from before thee.

Jb 9:20 If I justify myself, mine own mouth shall condemn me: *if I say, I am* perfect, it shall also prove me perverse.

Jb 35:2 Thinkest thou this to be right, *that* thou saidst, My righteousness *is* more than God's?

Pr 12:15 The way of a fool *is* right in his own eyes: but he that hearkeneth unto counsel *is* wise.

Pr 16:2 All the ways of a man *are* clean in his own eyes; but the LORD weigheth the spirits.

Pr 20:6 Most men will proclaim every one his own goodness: but a faithful man who can find?

Pr 21:2 Every way of a man *is* right in his own eyes: but the LORD pondereth the hearts.

Pr 30:12 *There is* a generation *that are* pure in their own eyes, and *yet* is not washed from their filthiness.

Je 2:35 Yet thou sayest, Because I am innocent, surely his anger shall turn from me. Behold, I will plead with thee, because thou sayest, I have not sinned.

2 Co 10:12 For we dare not make ourselves of the number, or compare ourselves with some that commend themselves: but they measuring themselves by themselves, and comparing themselves among themselves, are not wise.

Re 3:17 Because thou sayest, I am rich, and increased with goods, and have need of nothing; and knowest not that thou art wretched, and miserable, and poor, and blind, and naked:

2. Examples

Jb 11:4 For thou hast said, My doctrine *is* pure, and I am clean in thine eyes.

Jb 32:1 So these three men ceased to answer Job, because he *was* righteous in his own eyes.

Jb 33:9 I am clean without transgression, I *am* innocent; neither *is there* iniquity in me.

Jb 34:5 For Job hath said, I am righteous: and God hath taken away my judgment.

Mt 23:30 And say, If we had been in the days of our fathers, we would not have been partakers with them in the blood of the prophets.

Lu 10:29 But he, willing to justify himself, said unto Jesus, And who is my neighbour?

Lu 16:15 And he said unto them, Ye are they which justify yourselves before men; but God knoweth your hearts: for that which is highly esteemed among men is abomination in the sight of God.

Lu 18:9 And he spake this parable unto certain which trusted in themselves that they were righteous, and despised others:

Ro 10:3 For they being ignorant of God's righteousness, and going about to establish their own righteousness, have not submitted themselves unto the righteousness of God.

See **RIGHTEOUSNESS**

SELF-SACRIFICE, *laying aside one's personal interests or well-being for the sake of another*

1. Its Duty

Mt 10:39 He that findeth his life shall lose it: and he that loseth his life for my sake shall find it.

Mt 16:25 For whosoever will save his life shall lose it: and whosoever will lose his life for my sake shall find it.

Mt 19:21 Jesus said unto him, If thou wilt be perfect, go *and* sell that thou hast, and give to the poor, and thou shalt have treasure in heaven: and come *and* follow me.

Mk 8:35 For whosoever will save his life shall lose it; but whosoever shall lose his life for my sake and the gospel's, the same shall save it.

Mk 10:29 And Jesus answered and said, Verily I say unto you, There is no man that hath left house, or brethren, or sisters, or father, or mother, or wife, or children, or lands, for my sake, and the gospel's,

Lu 9:24 For whosoever will save his life shall lose it: but whosoever will lose his life for my sake, the same shall save it.

Lu 10:34 And went to *him,* and bound up his wounds, pouring in oil and wine, and set him on his own beast, and brought him to an inn, and took care of him.

Lu 14:26 If any *man* come to me, and hate not his father, and mother, and wife, and children, and brethren, and sisters, yea, and his own life also, he cannot be my disciple.

Lu 17:33 Whosoever shall seek to save his life shall lose it; and whosoever shall lose his life shall preserve it.

Lu 18:29 And he said unto them, Verily I say unto you, There is no man that hath left house, or parents, or brethren, or wife, or children, for the kingdom of God's sake,

Jn 12:25 He that loveth his life shall lose it; and he that hateth his life in this world shall keep it unto life eternal.

Ro 12:1 I beseech you therefore, brethren, by the mercies of God, that ye present your bodies a living sacrifice, holy, acceptable unto God, *which is* your reasonable service.

Ro 14:21 *It is* good neither to eat flesh, nor to drink wine, nor *any thing* whereby thy brother stumbleth, or is offended, or is made weak.

1 Co 10:24 Let no man seek his own, but every man another's *wealth.*

1 Co 13:5 Doth not behave itself unseemly, seeketh not her own, is not easily provoked, thinketh no evil;

2 Co 5:15 And *that* he died for all, that they which live should not henceforth live unto themselves, but unto him which died for them, and rose again.

Ph 2:4 Look not every man on his own things, but every man also on the things of others.

Ph 2:30 Because for the work of Christ he was nigh unto death, not regarding his life, to supply your lack of service toward me.

1 Jn 3:16 Hereby perceive we the love *of God,* because he laid down his life for us: and we ought to lay down *our* lives for the brethren.

2. Examples

JUDAH

Ge 44:33 Now therefore, I pray thee, let thy servant abide instead of the lad a bondman to my lord; and let the lad go up with his brethren.

MOSES

Ex 32:32 Yet now, if thou wilt forgive their sin–; and if not, blot me, I pray thee, out of thy book which thou hast written.

JEPHTHAH'S DAUGHTER

Jud 11:36 And she said unto him, My father, *if* thou hast opened thy mouth unto the LORD, do to me according to that which hath proceeded out of thy mouth; forasmuch as the LORD hath taken vengeance for thee of thine enemies, *even* of the children of Ammon.

RUTH

Ru 2:11 And Boaz answered and said unto her, It hath fully been shewed me, all that thou hast done unto thy mother in law since the death of thine husband: and *how* thou hast left thy father and thy mother, and the land of thy nativity, and art come unto a people which thou knewest not heretofore.

ESTHER

Est 4:16 Go, gather together all the Jews that are present in Shushan, and fast ye for me, and neither eat nor drink three days, night or day: I also and my maidens will fast likewise; and so will I go in unto the king, which *is* not according to the law: and if I perish, I perish.

MOSES

He 11:25 Choosing rather to suffer affliction with the people of God, than to enjoy the pleasures of sin for a season;

3. Of Paul

Ac 20:24 But none of these things move me, neither count I my life dear unto myself, so that I might finish my course with joy, and the ministry, which I have received of the Lord Jesus, to testify the gospel of the grace of God.

Ac 21:13 Then Paul answered, What mean ye to weep and to break mine heart? for I am ready not to be bound only, but also to die at Jerusalem for the name of the Lord Jesus.

1 Co 8:13 Wherefore, if meat make my brother to offend, I will eat no

flesh while the world standeth, lest I make my brother to offend.

1 Co 9:23 And this I do for the gospel's sake, that I might be partaker thereof with *you.*

1 Co 10:33 Even as I please all *men* in all *things,* not seeking mine own profit, but the *profit* of many, that they may be saved.

2 Co 12:15 And I will very gladly spend and be spent for you; though the more abundantly I love you, the less I be loved.

Ph 1:20 According to my earnest expectation and *my* hope, that in nothing I shall be ashamed, but *that* with all boldness, as always, *so* now also Christ shall be magnified in my body, whether *it be* by life, or by death.

Ph 3:8 Yea doubtless, and I count all things *but* loss for the excellency of the knowledge of Christ Jesus my Lord: for whom I have suffered the loss of all things, and do count them *but* dung, that I may win Christ,

1 Th 2:8 So being affectionately desirous of you, we were willing to have imparted unto you, not the gospel of God only, but also our own souls, because ye were dear unto us.

2 Ti 2:10 Therefore I endure all things for the elect's sakes, that they may also obtain the salvation which is in Christ Jesus with eternal glory.

See **DISCIPLESHIP**

SELF-WILL, *stubbornness*

De 1:43 So I spake unto you; and ye would not hear, but rebelled against the commandment of the LORD, and went presumptuously up into the hill.

Is 28:12 To whom he said, This *is* the rest *wherewith* ye may cause the weary to rest; and this *is* the refreshing: yet they would not hear.

Is 30:15 For thus saith the Lord GOD, the Holy One of Israel; In returning and rest shall ye be saved; in quietness and in confidence shall be your strength: and ye would not.

Da 11:36 And the king shall do according to his will; and he shall exalt himself, and magnify himself above every god, and shall speak marvellous things against the God of gods, and shall prosper till the indignation be accomplished: for that that is determined shall be done.

Lu 19:14 But his citizens hated him, and sent a message after him, saying, We will not have this *man* to reign over us.

2 Pe 2:10 But chiefly them that walk after the flesh in the lust of uncleanness, and despise government. Presumptuous *are they*, selfwilled, they are not afraid to speak evil of dignities.

See **SUBMISSION**

SENNACHERIB, *king of Assyria*

2 K 18:13; 19:16, 36; 2 Chr 32:1, 10, 22; Is 36:1; 37:37

SENSUALITY *See* **LUST**

SEPARATION

1. From the Physically Unclean and Diseased

Le 12:2; 13:5, 21, 26, 31, 33, 46; 15:20, 26, 31; Nu 5:3; 6:21; 12:14; 19:14

2. From the Heathen

Ge 12:1 Now the LORD had said unto Abram, Get thee out of thy country, and from thy kindred, and from thy father's house, unto a land that I will shew thee:

Ge 21:10 Wherefore she said unto Abraham, Cast out this bondwoman and her son: for the son of this bondwoman shall not be heir with my son, *even* with Isaac.

Ex 23:32 Thou shalt make no covenant with them, nor with their gods.

Ex 33:16 For wherein shall it be known here that I and thy people have found grace in thy sight? *is it* not in that thou goest with us? so shall we be separated, I and thy people, from all the people that *are* upon the face of the earth.

Ex 34:12 Take heed to thyself, lest thou make a covenant with the inhabitants of the land whither thou goest, lest it be for a snare in the midst of thee:

Ex 34:16 And thou take of their daughters unto thy sons, and their daughters go a whoring after their gods, and make thy sons go a whoring after their gods.

Le 20:24 But I have said unto you, Ye shall inherit their land, and I will give it unto you to possess it, a land that floweth with milk and honey: I *am* the LORD your God, which have separated you from *other* people.

Le 20:26 And ye shall be holy unto me: for I the LORD *am* holy, and have severed you from *other* people, that ye should be mine.

1 K 8:53 For thou didst separate them from among all the people of the earth, *to be* thine inheritance, as thou spakest by the hand of Moses thy servant, when thou broughtest our fathers out of Egypt, O Lord God.

1 K 11:2 Of the nations *concerning* which the LORD said unto the children of Israel, Ye shall not go in to them, neither shall they come in unto you: *for* surely they will turn away your heart after their gods: Solomon clave unto these in love.

2 K 17:15 And they rejected his statutes, and his covenant that he made with their fathers, and his testimonies which he testified against them; and they followed vanity, and became vain, and went after the heathen that *were* round about them, *concerning* whom the LORD had charged them, that they should not do like them.

Ezr 9:1 Now when these things were done, the princes came to me, saying, The people of Israel, and the priests, and the Levites, have not separated themselves from the people of the lands, *doing* according to their abominations, *even* of the Canaanites, the Hittites, the Perizzites, the Jebusites, the Ammonites, the Moabites, the Egyptians, and the Amorites.

Ezr 9:12 Now therefore give not your daughters unto their sons, neither take their daughters unto your sons, nor seek their peace or their wealth for ever: that ye may be strong, and eat the good of the land, and leave *it* for an inheritance to your children for ever.

Ne 10:28 And the rest of the people, the priests, the Levites, the porters, the singers, the Nethinims, and all they that had separated themselves from the people of the lands unto the law of God, their wives, their sons, and their daughters, every one having knowledge, and having understanding;

Ne 13:30 Thus cleansed I them from all strangers, and appointed the wards of the priests and the Levites, every one in his business;

Is 52:1 Awake, awake; put on thy strength, O Zion; put on thy beautiful garments, O Jerusalem, the holy city: for henceforth there shall no more come into thee the uncircumcised and the unclean.

Je 15:19 Therefore thus saith the LORD, If thou return, then will I bring thee again, *and* thou shalt stand before me: and if thou take forth the precious from the vile, thou shalt be as my mouth: let them return unto thee; but return not thou unto them.

Je 51:45 My people, go ye out of the midst of her, and deliver ye every man his soul from the fierce anger of the LORD.

Eze 20:41 I will accept you with your sweet savour, when I bring you out from the people, and gather you out of the countries wherein ye have been scattered; and I will be sanctified in you before the heathen.

Ho 7:8 Ephraim, he hath mixed himself among the people; Ephraim is a cake not turned.

Ac 10:28 And he said unto them, Ye know how that it is an unlawful thing for a man that is a Jew to keep company, or come unto one of another nation; but God hath shewed me that I should not call any man common or unclean.

Ga 2:12 For before that certain came from James, he did eat with the Gentiles: but when they were come, he withdrew and separated himself, fearing them which were of the circumcision.

3. From Evil Associations

Ex 32:26 Then Moses stood in the gate of the camp, and said, Who *is* on the LORD's side? *let him come* unto me. And all the sons of Levi gathered themselves together unto him.

Ps 84:10 For a day in thy courts *is* better than a thousand. I had rather be a doorkeeper in the house of my God, than to dwell in the tents of wickedness.

Ps 141:4 Incline not my heart to *any* evil thing, to practise wicked works with men that work iniquity: and let me not eat of their dainties.

Is 52:11 Depart ye, depart ye, go ye out from thence, touch no unclean *thing;* go ye out of the midst of her; be ye clean, that bear the vessels of the LORD.

Je 6:29 The bellows are burned, the lead is consumed of the fire; the founder melteth in vain: for the wicked are not plucked away.

Je 9:2 Oh that I had in the wilderness a lodging place of wayfaring men; that I might leave my people, and go from them! for they *be* all adulterers, an assembly of treacherous men.

Je 16:8 Thou shalt not also go into the house of feasting, to sit with them to eat and to drink.

Jn 15:19 If ye were of the world, the world would love his own: but because ye are not of the world, but I have chosen you out of the world, therefore the world hateth you.

Jn 17:16 They are not of the world, even as I am not of the world.

Ac 2:40 And with many other words did he testify and exhort, saying, Save yourselves from this untoward generation.

2 Co 6:17 Wherefore come out from among them, and be ye separate, saith the Lord, and touch not the unclean *thing;* and I will receive you,

Ep 5:11 And have no fellowship with the unfruitful works of darkness, but rather reprove *them.*

2 Th 3:6 Now we command you, brethren, in the name of our Lord Jesus Christ, that ye withdraw yourselves from every brother that walketh disorderly, and not after the tradition which he received of us.

1 Jn 2:15 Love not the world, neither the things *that are* in the world. If any man love the world, the love of the Father is not in him.

4. From the Wicked in Last Day

Ps 5:5 The foolish shall not stand in thy sight: thou hatest all workers of iniquity.

Eze 20:38 And I will purge out from among you the rebels, and them that transgress against me: I will bring them forth out of the country where they sojourn, and they shall not enter into the land of Israel: and ye shall know that I *am* the LORD.

Mt 13:30 Let both grow together until the harvest: and in the time of harvest I will say to the reapers, Gather ye together first the tares, and bind them in bundles to burn them: but gather the wheat into my barn.

Mt 13:49 So shall it be at the end of the world: the angels shall come forth, and sever the wicked from among the just,

Mt 24:40 Then shall two be in the field; the one shall be taken, and the other left.

Mt 25:32 And before him shall be gathered all nations: and he shall separate them one from another, as a shepherd divideth *his* sheep from the goats:

Mt 25:46 And these shall go away into everlasting punishment: but the righteous into life eternal.

Lu 16:26 And beside all this, between us and you there is a great gulf fixed: so that they which would pass from hence to you cannot; neither can they pass to us, that *would come* from thence.

Lu 17:34 I tell you, in that night there shall be two *men* in one bed; the one shall be taken, and the other shall be left.

Re 22:15 For without *are* dogs, and sorcerers, and whoremongers, and murderers, and idolaters, and whosoever loveth and maketh a lie.

6. From False Professors

Eze 20:38 And I will purge out from among you the rebels, and them that transgress against me: I will bring them forth out of the country where they sojourn, and they shall not enter into the land of Israel: and ye shall know that I *am* the LORD.

Mt 18:17 And if he shall neglect to hear them, tell *it* unto the church: but if he neglect to hear the church, let him be unto thee as an heathen man and a publican.

Ac 19:9 But when divers were hardened, and believed not, but spake evil of that way before the multitude, he departed from them, and separated the disciples, disputing daily in the school of one Tyrannus.

Ro 16:17 Now I beseech you, brethren, mark them which cause divisions and offences contrary to the doctrine which ye have learned; and avoid them.

1 Co 5:11 But now I have written unto you not to keep company, if any man that is called a brother be a fornicator, or covetous, or an idolater, or a railer, or a drunkard, or an extortioner; with such an one no not to eat.

2 Th 3:6 Now we command you, brethren, in the name of our Lord Jesus Christ, that ye withdraw yourselves from every brother that walketh disorderly, and not after the tradition which he received of us.

2 Th 3:14 And if any man obey not our word by this epistle, note that man, and have no company with him, that he may be ashamed.

1 Ti 6:5 Perverse disputings of men of corrupt minds, and destitute of the truth, supposing that gain is godliness: from such withdraw thyself.

2 Ti 3:5 Having a form of godliness, but denying the power thereof: from such turn away.

1 Jn 2:19 They went out from us, but they were not of us; for if they had been of us, they would *no doubt* have continued with us: but *they went out*, that they might be made manifest that they were not all of us.

2 Jn 10 If there come any unto you, and bring not this doctrine, receive him not into *your* house, neither bid him God speed:

7. Under Mosaic Law

a. Of the Clean and Unclean Things

Le 7:21; 10:10; 11:47; 20:25; Eze 22:26; Ac 10:14; Ro 14:14

b. Removed from the camp

Ex 29:14; 33:7; Le 4:12, 21; 6:11; 8:17; 9:11; 10:4; 13:46; 14:3; 16:27; 24:14, 23; Nu 5:3; 12:14; 15:35; 19:3, 9; 31:19; De 23:12; Jos 6:23; 2 K 23:4; Eze 43:21; Jn 19:17; He 13:11; Re 14:20

See **ASSOCIATIONS**

SEPULCHRES *See* **DEAD**

SERAPHIM, *angelic beings*

Is 6:2, 6

SERMON ON THE MOUNT, *name usually given to a discourse delivered by Jesus to his disciples and a multitude on a mountain near Capernaum*

Mt 5–7; Lu 6:20–49

SERPENTS *See* **ANIMALS, REPTILES**

SERVANTS, *God's*

Le 25:42 For they *are* my servants, which I brought forth out of the land of Egypt: they shall not be sold as bondmen.

Le 25:55 For unto me the children of Israel *are* servants; they *are* my servants whom I brought forth out of the land of Egypt: I *am* the LORD your God.

Nu 12:8 With him will I speak mouth to mouth, even apparently, and not in dark speeches; and the similitude of the LORD shall he behold: wherefore then were ye not afraid to speak against my servant Moses?

Nu 16:28 And Moses said, Hereby ye shall know that the LORD hath sent me to do all these works; for *I have* not *done them* of mine own mind.

De 34:5 So Moses the servant of the LORD died there in the land of Moab, according to the word of the LORD.

Jos 1:1 Now after the death of Moses the servant of the LORD it came to pass, that the LORD spake unto Joshua the son of Nun, Moses' minister, saying,

Jos 8:31 As Moses the servant of the LORD commanded the children of Israel, as it is written in the book of the law of Moses, an altar of whole stones, over which no man hath lift up *any* iron: and they offered thereon burnt offerings unto the LORD, and sacrificed peace offerings.

Jud 2:7 And the people served the LORD all the days of Joshua, and all the days of the elders that outlived Joshua, who had seen all the great works of the LORD, that he did for Israel.

Jud 10:16 And they put away the strange gods from among them, and served the LORD: and his soul was grieved for the misery of Israel.

1 K 18:36 And it came to pass at *the time of* the offering of the *evening* sacrifice, that Elijah the prophet came near, and said, LORD God of Abraham, Isaac, and of Israel, let it be known this day that thou art God in Israel, and *that* I *am* thy servant, and *that* I have done all these things at thy word.

1 Chr 6:49 But Aaron and his sons offered upon the altar of the burnt offering, and on the altar of incense, *and were appointed* for all the work of the *place* most holy, and to make an atonement for Israel, according to all that Moses the servant of God had commanded.

2 Chr 24:6 And the king called for Jehoiada the chief, and said unto him, Why hast thou not required of the Levites to bring in out of Judah and out of Jerusalem the collection, *according to the commandment* of Moses the servant of the LORD, and of the congregation of Israel, for the tabernacle of witness?

Ezr 5:11 And thus they returned us answer, saying, We are the servants of the God of heaven and earth, and build the house that was builded these many years ago, which a great king of Israel builded and set up.

Ps 35:27 Let them shout for joy, and be glad, that favour my righteous cause: yea, let them say continually, Let the LORD be magnified, which hath pleasure in the prosperity of his servant.

Ps 113:1 Praise ye the LORD. Praise, O ye servants of the LORD, praise the name of the LORD.

Ps 116:16 O LORD, truly I *am* thy servant; I *am* thy servant, *and* the son of thine handmaid: thou hast loosed my bonds.

Ps 134:1 Behold, bless ye the LORD, all *ye* servants of the LORD, which by night stand in the house of the LORD.

Ps 143:12 And of thy mercy cut off mine enemies, and destroy all them that afflict my soul: for I *am* thy servant.

Da 3:26 Then Nebuchadnezzar came near to the mouth of the burning fiery furnace, *and* spake, and said, Shadrach, Meshach, and Abed-nego, ye servants of the most high God, come forth, and come *hither.* Then Shadrach, Meshach, and Abed-nego, came forth of the midst of the fire.

Da 6:20 And when he came to the den, he cried with a lamentable voice unto Daniel: *and* the king spake and said to Daniel, O Daniel, servant of the living God, is thy God, whom thou servest continually, able to deliver thee from the lions?

Mt 10:24 The disciple is not above *his* master, nor the servant above his lord.

Mt 25:14 For *the kingdom of heaven is* as a man travelling into a far country, *who* called his own servants, and delivered unto them his goods.

Mk 12:2 And at the season he sent to the husbandmen a servant, that he might receive from the husbandmen of the fruit of the vineyard.

Ac 16:17 The same followed Paul and us, and cried, saying, These men are the servants of the most high God, which shew unto us the way of salvation.

Ac 27:23 For there stood by me this night the angel of God, whose I am, and whom I serve,

Ro 1:1 Paul, a servant of Jesus Christ, called *to be* an apostle, separated unto the gospel of God,

Ro 1:9 For God is my witness, whom I serve with my spirit in the gospel of his Son, that without ceasing I make mention of you always in my prayers;

Ro 6:18 Being then made free from sin, ye became the servants of righteousness.

Ro 6:22 But now being made free from sin, and become servants to God, ye have your fruit unto holiness, and the end everlasting life.

2 Ti 1:3 I thank God, whom I serve from *my* forefathers with pure conscience, that without ceasing I have remembrance of thee in my prayers night and day;

Tit 1:1 Paul, a servant of God, and an apostle of Jesus Christ, according to the faith of God's elect, and the acknowledging of the truth which is after godliness;

He 3:5 And Moses verily *was* faithful in all his house, as a servant, for a testimony of those things which were to be spoken after;

Ja 1:1 James, a servant of God and of the Lord Jesus Christ, to the twelve tribes which are scattered abroad, greeting.

1 Pe 2:16 As free, and not using *your* liberty for a cloke of maliciousness, but as the servants of God.

Re 1:1 The Revelation of Jesus Christ, which God gave unto him, to shew unto his servants things which must shortly come to pass; and he sent and signified *it* by his angel unto his servant John:

Re 7:3 Saying, Hurt not the earth, neither the sea, nor the trees, till we have sealed the servants of our God in their foreheads.

Re 19:5 And a voice came out of the throne, saying, Praise our God, all ye his servants, and ye that fear him, both small and great.

See **LEADERS**

SERVICE, *spiritual, ministry done for God's glory*

1. For God

Ex 7:16 And thou shalt say unto him, The LORD God of the Hebrews hath sent me unto thee, saying, Let my people go, that they may serve me in the wilderness: and, behold, hitherto thou wouldest not hear.

Ex 8:1 And the LORD spake unto Moses, Go unto Pharaoh, and say unto him, Thus saith the LORD, Let my people go, that they may serve me.

Ex 9:1 Then the LORD said unto Moses, Go in unto Pharaoh, and tell him, Thus saith the LORD God of the Hebrews, Let my people go, that they may serve me.

Ex 9:13 And the LORD said unto Moses, Rise up early in the morning, and stand before Pharaoh, and say unto him, Thus saith the LORD God of the Hebrews, Let my people go, that they may serve me.

Ex 23:25 And ye shall serve the LORD your God, and he shall bless thy bread, and thy water; and I will take sickness away from the midst of thee.

Nu 18:7 Therefore thou and thy sons with thee shall keep your priest's office for every thing of the altar, and within the vail; and ye shall serve: I have given your priest's office *unto you as* a service of gift: and the stranger that cometh nigh shall be put to death.

De 6:13 Thou shalt fear the LORD thy God, and serve him, and shalt swear by his name.

De 10:12 And now, Israel, what doth the LORD thy God require of thee, but to fear the LORD thy God, to walk in all his ways, and to love him, and to serve the LORD thy God with all thy heart and with all thy soul,

De 10:20 Thou shalt fear the LORD thy God; him shalt thou serve, and to him shalt thou cleave, and swear by his name.

De 11:13 And it shall come to pass, if ye shall hearken diligently unto my commandments which I command you this day, to love the LORD your God, and to serve him with all your heart and with all your soul,

De 13:4 Ye shall walk after the LORD your God, and fear him, and keep his commandments, and obey his voice, and ye shall serve him, and cleave unto him.

Jos 24:14 Now therefore fear the LORD, and serve him in sincerity and in truth: and put away the gods which your fathers served on the other side of the flood, and in Egypt; and serve ye the LORD.

1 S 12:20 And Samuel said unto the people, Fear not: ye have done all this wickedness: yet turn not aside from following the LORD, but serve the LORD with all your heart;

1 S 12:24 Only fear the LORD, and serve him in truth with all your heart: for consider how great *things* he hath done for you.

1 Chr 28:9 And thou, Solomon my son, know thou the God of thy father, and serve him with a perfect heart and with a willing mind: for the LORD searcheth all hearts, and understandeth all the imaginations of the thoughts: if thou seek him, he will be found of thee; but if thou forsake him, he will cast thee off for ever.

2 Chr 12:8 Nevertheless they shall be his servants; that they may know my service, and the service of the kingdoms of the countries.

2 Chr 30:8 Now be ye not stiffnecked, as your fathers *were, but* yield yourselves unto the LORD, and enter into his sanctuary, which he hath sanctified for ever: and serve the LORD your God, that the fierceness of his wrath may turn away from you.

2 Chr 33:16 And he repaired the altar of the LORD, and sacrificed thereon peace offerings and thank offerings, and commanded Judah to serve the LORD God of Israel.

2 Chr 34:33 And Josiah took away all the abominations out of all the countries that *pertained* to the children of Israel, and made all that were present in Israel to serve, *even* to serve the LORD their God. *And* all his days they departed not from following the LORD, the God of their fathers.

2 Chr 35:3 And said unto the Levites that taught all Israel, which were holy unto the LORD, Put the holy ark in the house which Solomon the son of David king of Israel did build; *it shall* not *be* a burden upon *your* shoulders:

serve now the LORD your God, and his people Israel,

Ps 2:11 Serve the LORD with fear, and rejoice with trembling.

Ps 100:2 Serve the LORD with gladness: come before his presence with singing.

Ps 102:22 When the people are gathered together, and the kingdoms, to serve the LORD.

Is 56:6 Also the sons of the stranger, that join themselves to the LORD, to serve him, and to love the name of the LORD, to be his servants, every one that keepeth the sabbath from polluting it, and taketh hold of my covenant;

Eze 20:40 For in mine holy mountain, in the mountain of the height of Israel, saith the Lord GOD, there shall all the house of Israel, all of them in the land, serve me: there will I accept them, and there will I require your offerings, and the firstfruits of your oblations, with all your holy things.

Zep 3:9 For then will I turn to the people a pure language, that they may all call upon the name of the LORD, to serve him with one consent.

Lu 1:74 That he would grant unto us, that we being delivered out of the hand of our enemies might serve him without fear,

Lu 4:8 And Jesus answered and said unto him, Get thee behind me, Satan: for it is written, Thou shalt worship the Lord thy God, and him only shalt thou serve.

Lu 17:8 And will not rather say unto him, Make ready wherewith I may sup, and gird thyself, and serve me, till I have eaten and drunken; and afterward thou shalt eat and drink?

Ac 7:7 And the nation to whom they shall be in bondage will I judge, said God: and after that shall they come forth, and serve me in this place.

Ro 7:6 But now we are delivered from the law, that being dead wherein we were held; that we should serve in newness of spirit, and not *in* the oldness of the letter.

Ro 12:11 Not slothful in business; fervent in spirit; serving the Lord;

1 Co 15:58 Therefore, my beloved brethren, be ye stedfast, unmovable, always abounding in the work of the Lord, forasmuch as ye know that your labour is not in vain in the Lord.

Ep 6:7 With good will doing service, as to the Lord, and not to men:

Col 3:23 And whatsoever ye do, do *it* heartily, as to the Lord, and not unto men;

1 Th 1:9 For they themselves shew of us what manner of entering in we had unto you, and how ye turned to God from idols to serve the living and true God;

2 Ti 1:3 I thank God, whom I serve from *my* forefathers with pure conscience, that without ceasing I have remembrance of thee in my prayers night and day;

He 9:14 How much more shall the blood of Christ, who through the eternal Spirit offered himself without spot to God, purge your conscience from dead works to serve the living God?

He 12:28 Wherefore we receiving a kingdom which cannot be moved, let us have grace, whereby we may serve God acceptably with reverence and godly fear:

2. For Christ

Lu 17:8 And will not rather say unto him, Make ready wherewith I may sup, and gird thyself, and serve me, till I have eaten and drunken; and afterward thou shalt eat and drink?

Jn 12:26 If any man serve me, let him follow me; and where I am, there shall also my servant be: if any man serve me, him will *my* Father honour.

Ro 1:1 Paul, a servant of Jesus Christ, called *to be* an apostle, separated unto the gospel of God,

Ro 14:18 For he that in these things serveth Christ *is* acceptable to God, and approved of men.

1 Co 7:22 For he that is called in the Lord, *being* a servant, is the Lord's freeman: likewise also he that is called, *being* free, is Christ's servant.

Ga 1:10 For do I now persuade men, or God? or do I seek to please men? for if I yet pleased men, I should not be the servant of Christ.

Ep 6:6 Not with eyeservice, as men-pleasers; but as the servants of Christ, doing the will of God from the heart;

Ph 1:1 Paul and Timotheus, the servants of Jesus Christ, to all the saints in Christ Jesus which are at Philippi, with the bishops and deacons:

Col 3:24 Knowing that of the Lord ye shall receive the reward of the inheritance: for ye serve the Lord Christ.

Col 4:12 Epaphras, who is *one* of you, a servant of Christ, saluteth you, always labouring fervently for you in prayers, that ye may stand perfect and complete in all the will of God.

Tit 1:1 Paul, a servant of God, and an apostle of Jesus Christ, according to the faith of God's elect, and the acknowledging of the truth which is after godliness;

Ja 1:1 James, a servant of God and of the Lord Jesus Christ, to the twelve tribes which are scattered abroad, greeting.

2 Pe 1:1 Simon Peter, a servant and an apostle of Jesus Christ, to them that have obtained like precious faith with us through the righteousness of God and our Saviour Jesus Christ:

Re 7:15 Therefore are they before the throne of God, and serve him day and night in his temple: and he that sitteth on the throne shall dwell among them.

Re 22:3 And there shall be no more curse: but the throne of God and of the Lamb shall be in it; and his servants shall serve him:

3. For People

IT ENNOBLES LIFE

Mk 10:43–44 But so shall it not be among you: but whosoever will be great among you, shall be your minister:

And whosoever of you will be the chiefest, shall be servant of all.

IT EXEMPLIFIES NEIGHBORLINESS

Lu 10:36–37 Which now of these three, thinkest thou, was neighbour unto him that fell among the thieves?

And he said, He that shewed mercy on him. Then said Jesus unto him, Go, and do thou likewise.

IT IS CHRISTLIKE

Jn 13:14 If I then, *your* Lord and Master, have washed your feet; ye also ought to wash one another's feet.

IT DEMONSTRATES LOVE

Jn 21:16 He saith to him again the second time, Simon, *son* of Jonas, lovest thou me? He saith unto him, Yea, Lord; thou knowest that I love thee. He saith unto him, Feed my sheep.

Ga 5:13 For, brethren, ye have been called unto liberty; only *use* not liberty for an occasion to the flesh, but by love serve one another.

IT LIGHTENS LIFE'S BURDENS

Ga 6:2 Bear ye one another's burdens, and so fulfil the law of Christ.

Ga 6:10 As we have therefore opportunity, let us do good unto all *men,* especially unto them who are of the household of faith.

4. In Humility

Mt 10:42 And whosoever shall give to drink unto one of these little ones a cup of cold *water* only in the name of a disciple, verily I say unto you, he shall in no wise lose his reward.

Mt 25:23 His lord said unto him, Well done, good and faithful servant; thou hast been faithful over a few things, I will make thee ruler over many things: enter thou into the joy of thy lord.

Mt 25:37 Then shall the righteous answer him, saying, Lord, when saw we thee an hungred, and or thirsty, and gave *thee* drink?

Mt 25:40 And the King shall answer and say unto them, Verily I say unto you, Inasmuch as ye have done *it* unto one of the least of these my brethren, ye have done *it* unto me.

Mt 27:32 And as they came out, they found a man of Cyrene, Simon by name: him they compelled to bear his cross.

Mk 9:41 For whosoever shall give you a cup of water to drink in my name, because ye belong to Christ, verily I say unto you, he shall not lose his reward.

Lu 7:38 And stood at his feet behind *him* weeping, and began to wash his feet with tears, and did wipe *them* with the hairs of her head, and kissed his feet, and anointed *them* with the ointment.

Lu 10:34 And went to *him,* and bound up his wounds, pouring in oil and wine, and set him on his own beast, and brought him to an inn, and took care of him.

Jn 12:3 Then took Mary a pound of ointment of spikenard, very costly, and anointed the feet of Jesus, and wiped his feet with her hair: and the house was filled with the odour of the ointment.

Jn 13:14 If I then, *your* Lord and Master, have washed your feet; ye also ought to wash one another's feet.

Ac 20:18 And when they were come to him, he said unto them, Ye know, from the first day that I came into Asia, after what manner I have been with you at all seasons,

Ac 20:18–19 And when they were come to him, he said unto them, Ye know, from the first day that I came into Asia, after what manner I have been with you at all seasons,

Serving the Lord with all humility of mind, and with many tears, and temptations, which befell me by the lying in wait of the Jews:

1 Co 9:19 For though I be free from all *men,* yet have I made myself servant unto all, that I might gain the more.

2 Co 4:5 For we preach not ourselves, but Christ Jesus the Lord; and ourselves your servants for Jesus' sake.

5. With Undivided Attitude

Jos 22:5 But take diligent heed to do the commandment and the law, which Moses the servant of the LORD charged you, to love the LORD your God, and to walk in all his ways, and to keep his commandments, and to cleave unto him, and to serve him

with all your heart and with all your soul.

1 S 7:3 And Samuel spake unto all the house of Israel, saying, If ye do return unto the LORD with all your hearts, *then* put away the strange gods and Ashtaroth from among you, and prepare your hearts unto the LORD, and serve him only: and he will deliver you out of the hand of the Philistines.

1 S 12:20 And Samuel said unto the people, Fear not: ye have done all this wickedness: yet turn not aside from following the LORD, but serve the LORD with all your heart;

2 Chr 15:15 And all Judah rejoiced at the oath: for they had sworn with all their heart, and sought him with their whole desire; and he was found of them: and the LORD gave them rest round about.

2 Chr 34:31 And the king stood in his place, and made a covenant before the LORD, to walk after the LORD, and to keep his commandments, and his testimonies, and his statutes, with all his heart, and with all his soul, to perform the words of the covenant which are written in this book.

Zep 1:5 And them that worship the host of heaven upon the housetops; and them that worship *and* that swear by the LORD, and that swear by Malcham;

Mt 4:10 Then saith Jesus unto him, Get thee hence, Satan: for it is written, Thou shalt worship the Lord thy God, and him only shalt thou serve.

Mt 6:24 No man can serve two masters: for either he will hate the one, and love the other; or else he will hold to the one, and despise the other. Ye cannot serve God and mammon.

Lu 4:8 And Jesus answered and said unto him, Get thee behind me, Satan: for it is written, Thou shalt worship the Lord thy God, and him only shalt thou serve.

Lu 16:13 No servant can serve two masters: for either he will hate the one, and love the other; or else he will hold to the one, and despise the other. Ye cannot serve God and mammon.

6. With Promptness

ELISHA

1 K 19:20 And he left the oxen, and ran after Elijah, and said, Let me, I pray thee, kiss my father and my mother, and *then* I will follow thee. And he said unto him, Go back again: for what have I done to thee?

PETER AND ANDREW

Mk 1:18 And straightway they forsook their nets, and followed him.

PETER'S MOTHER-IN-LAW

Lu 4:39 And he stood over her, and rebuked the fever; and it left her: and immediately she arose and ministered unto them.

ZACCHEUS

Lu 19:6 And he made haste, and came down, and received him joyfully.

PAUL AFTER HIS CONVERSION

Ac 9:20 And straightway he preached Christ in the synagogues, that he is the Son of God.
Ac 10:29 Therefore came I *unto you* without gainsaying, as soon as I was sent for: I ask therefore for what intent ye have sent for me?

PAUL AND SILAS IN RESPONDING TO THE MACEDONIAN CALL

Ac 16:10 And after he had seen the vision, immediately we endeavoured to go into Macedonia, assuredly gathering that the Lord had called us for to preach the gospel unto them.
Ga 1:16 To reveal his Son in me, that I might preach him among the heathen; immediately I conferred not with flesh and blood:

7. With Joy

Ne 12:43 Also that day they offered great sacrifices, and rejoiced: for God had made them rejoice with great joy: the wives also and the children rejoiced: so that the joy of Jerusalem was heard even afar off.
Ps 40:8 I delight to do thy will, O my God: yea, thy law *is* within my heart.

Ps 100:2 Serve the LORD with gladness: come before his presence with singing.
Ps 126:5–6 They that sow in tears shall reap in joy.

He that goeth forth and weepeth, bearing precious seed, shall doubtless come again with rejoicing, bringing his sheaves *with him.*
Mt 18:13 And if so be that he find it, verily I say unto you, he rejoiceth more of that *sheep,* than of the ninety and nine which went not astray.
Mt 25:23 His lord said unto him, Well done, good and faithful servant; thou hast been faithful over a few things, I will make thee ruler over many things: enter thou into the joy of thy lord.
Mt 28:8 And they departed quickly from the sepulchre with fear and great joy; and did run to bring his disciples word.
Lu 10:17 And the seventy returned again with joy, saying, Lord, even the devils are subject unto us through thy name.
Lu 15:6 And when he cometh home, he calleth together *his* friends and neighbours, saying unto them, Rejoice with me; for I have found my sheep which was lost.
Jn 4:36 And he that reapeth receiveth wages, and gathereth fruit unto life eternal: that both he that soweth and he that reapeth may rejoice together.
Ac 11:23 Who, when he came, and had seen the grace of God, was glad, and exhorted them all, that with purpose of heart they would cleave unto the Lord.

8. Test of

IT WAS ESTABLISHED IN ISRAEL

De 10:12 And now, Israel, what doth the LORD thy God require of thee, but to fear the LORD thy God, to walk in all his ways, and to love him, and to serve the LORD thy God with all thy heart and with all thy soul,

KING SAUL WAS CONDEMNED BY IT

1 S 15:22 And Samuel said, Hath the LORD *as great* delight in burnt offerings and sacrifices, as in obeying the voice of the LORD? Behold, to obey is better than sacrifice, *and* to hearken than the fat of rams.

IT EXCLUDES MERE PROFESSORS OF RELIGION FROM THE KINGDOM

Mt 7:21 Not every one that saith unto me, Lord, Lord, shall enter into the kingdom of heaven; but he that doeth the will of my Father which is in heaven.

CHRIST APPLIES IT IN THE PARABLE OF THE GOOD SAMARITAN

Lu 10:37 And he said, He that shewed mercy on him. Then said Jesus unto him, Go, and do thou likewise.

IT REVEALS THE QUALITY OF LOVE

Jn 21:17 He saith unto him the third time, Simon, *son* of Jonas, lovest thou me? Peter was grieved because he said unto him the third time, Lovest thou me? And he said unto him, Lord, thou knowest all things; thou knowest that I love thee. Jesus saith unto him, Feed my sheep.

IT WILL BE APPLIED IN DETERMINING FINAL DESTINY OF HUMANITY

Mt 25:35–36 For I was an hungred, and ye gave me meat: I was thirsty, and ye gave me drink: I was a stranger, and ye took me in:

Naked, and ye clothed me: I was sick, and ye visited me: I was in prison, and ye came unto me.

9. Unrealized

OF THE RIGHTEOUS

Mt 25:38 When saw we thee a stranger, and took *thee* in? or naked, and clothed *thee?*

OF MARY

Mt 26:12 For in that she hath poured this ointment on my body, she did *it* for my burial.

OF THE POOR WIDOW

Mk 12:44 For all *they* did cast in of their abundance; but she of her want did cast in all that she had, *even* all her living.

OF ANDREW IN BRINGING PETER TO JESUS

Jn 1:42 And he brought him to Jesus. And when Jesus beheld him, he said, Thou art Simon the son of Jona: thou shalt be called Cephas, which is by interpretation, A stone.

OF BARNABAS IN GOING AFTER PAUL

Ac 11:25–26 Then departed Barnabas to Tarsus, for to seek Saul:

And when he had found him, he brought him unto Antioch. And it came to pass, that a whole year they assembled themselves with the church, and taught much people. And the disciples were called Christians first in Antioch.

10. Timely

Mt 8:15 And he touched her hand, and the fever left her: and she arose, and ministered unto them.

Mk 14:3 And being in Bethany in the house of Simon the leper, as he sat at meat, there came a woman having an alabaster box of ointment of spikenard very precious; and she brake the box, and poured *it* on his head.

Mk 14:8 She hath done what she could: she is come aforehand to anoint my body to the burying.

Mk 15:41 (Who also, when he was in Galilee, followed him, and ministered unto him;) and many other women which came up with him unto Jerusalem.

1 Co 16:17 I am glad of the coming of Stephanas and Fortunatus and Achaicus: for that which was lacking on your part they have supplied.

2 Co 11:9 And when I was present with you, and wanted, I was chargeable to no man: for that which was lacking to me the brethren which came from Macedonia supplied: and in all *things* I have kept myself from being burdensome unto you, and so will I keep *myself.*

Ph 2:25 Yet I supposed it necessary to send to you Epaphroditus, my brother, and companion in labour, and fellow soldier, but your messenger, and he that ministered to my wants.

2 Ti 1:18 The Lord grant unto him that he may find mercy of the Lord in that day: and in how many things he ministered unto me at Ephesus, thou knowest very well.

See **OBEDIENCE, SUBMISSION**

SERVILITY, *subjection to control, slavery*
Ex 14:12; Jud 6:2; 1 K 20:4

See **SLAVES**

SEVEN

1. The Number of Perfection

Ex 25:37 And thou shalt make the seven lamps thereof: and they shall light the lamps thereof, that they may give light over against it.

Nu 23:1 And Balaam said unto Balak, Build me here seven altars, and prepare me here seven oxen and seven rams.

De 28:25 The LORD shall cause thee to be smitten before thine enemies: thou shalt go out one way against them, and flee seven ways before them: and shalt be removed into all the kingdoms of the earth.

Jb 5:19 He shall deliver thee in six troubles: yea, in seven there shall no evil touch thee.

Pr 26:16 The sluggard *is* wiser in his own conceit than seven men that can render a reason.

Ec 11:2 Give a portion to seven, and also to eight; for thou knowest not what evil shall be upon the earth.

Is 4:1 And in that day seven women shall take hold of one man, saying, We will eat our own bread, and wear our own apparel: only let us be called by thy name, to take away our reproach.

Is 11:15 And the LORD shall utterly destroy the tongue of the Egyptian sea; and with his mighty wind shall he shake his hand over the river, and shall smite it in the seven streams, and make *men* go over dryshod.

Eze 40:22 And their windows, and their arches, and their palm trees, *were* after the measure of the gate that looketh toward the east; and they went up unto it by seven steps; and the arches thereof *were* before them.

Mt 22:25 Now there were with us seven brethren: and the first, when he had married a wife, deceased, and, having no issue, left his wife unto his brother:

Mk 8:5 And he asked them, How many loaves have ye? And they said, Seven.

Mk 12:20 Now there were seven brethren: and the first took a wife, and dying left no seed.

Mk 16:9 Now when *Jesus* was risen early the first *day* of the week, he appeared first to Mary Magdalene, out of whom he had cast seven devils.

Ac 6:3 Wherefore, brethren, look ye out among you seven men of honest report, full of the Holy Ghost and wisdom, whom we may appoint over this business.

Re 1:12 And I turned to see the voice that spake with me. And being turned, I saw seven golden candlesticks;

Re 4:5 And out of the throne proceeded lightnings and thunderings and voices: and *there were* seven lamps of fire burning before the throne, which are the seven Spirits of God.

Re 5:6 And I beheld, and, lo, in the midst of the throne and of the four beasts, and in the midst of the elders, stood a Lamb as it had been slain, having seven horns and seven eyes, which are the seven Spirits of God sent forth into all the earth.

Re 8:2 And I saw the seven angels which stood before God; and to them were given seven trumpets.

Re 10:3 And cried with a loud voice, as *when* a lion roareth: and when he had cried, seven thunders uttered their voices.

Re 15:1 And I saw another sign in heaven, great and marvellous, seven angels having the seven last plagues; for in them is filled up the wrath of God.

Re 17:1 And there came one of the seven angels which had the seven vials, and talked with me, saying unto me, Come hither; I will shew unto thee the judgment of the great whore that sitteth upon many waters:

2. Attitudes of the Spiritual Life

LYING DOWN FOR SPIRITUAL REST

Ps 23:2 He maketh me to lie down in green pastures: he leadeth me beside the still waters.

SITTING FOR INSTRUCTION

Lu 10:39 And she had a sister called Mary, which also sat at Jesus' feet, and heard his word.

STANDING FOR WARFARE

Ep 6:14 Stand therefore, having your loins girt about with truth, and having on the breastplate of righteousness;

WALKING FOR FELLOWSHIP

1 Jn 1:7 But if we walk in the light, as he is in the light, we have fellowship one with another, and the blood of Jesus Christ his Son cleanseth us from all sin.

RUNNING FOR PROGRESS

He 12:1 Wherefore seeing we also are compassed about with so great a cloud of witnesses, let us lay aside every weight, and the sin which doth so easily beset us, and let us run with patience the race that is set before us,

LEAPING FOR ECSTACY

Ac 3:8 And he leaping up stood, and walked, and entered with them into the temple, walking, and leaping, and praising God.

MOUNTING UP FOR EXALTATION

Is 40:31 But they that wait upon the LORD shall renew *their* strength; they shall mount up with wings as eagles; they shall run, and not be weary; *and* they shall walk, and not faint.

3. Things Opened

HANDS FOR BENEVOLENCE

De 15:8 But thou shalt open thine hand wide unto him, and shalt surely lend him sufficient for his need, *in that* which he wanteth.

EYES FOR VISION

2 K 6:17 And Elisha prayed, and said, LORD, I pray thee, open his eyes, that he may see. And the LORD opened the eyes of the young man; and he saw: and, behold, the mountain *was* full of horses and chariots of fire round about Elisha.

EARS FOR HEARING

Ps 40:6 Sacrifice and offering thou didst not desire; mine ears hast thou opened: burnt offering and sin offering hast thou not required.

LIPS FOR TESTIMONY

Ps 51:15 O Lord, open thou my lips; and my mouth shall shew forth thy praise.

WINDOWS FOR PRAYER

Da 6:10 Now when Daniel knew that the writing was signed, he went into his house; and his windows being open in his chamber toward Jerusalem, he kneeled upon his knees three times a day, and prayed, and gave thanks before his God, as he did aforetime.

HEART FOR GOD'S MESSAGE

Ac 16:14 And a certain woman named Lydia, a seller of purple, of the city of Thyatira, which worshipped God, heard *us:* whose heart the Lord opened, that she attended unto the things which were spoken of Paul.

DOORS FOR SERVICE

2 Co 2:12 Furthermore, when I came to Troas to *preach* Christ's gospel, and a door was opened unto me of the Lord,

4. Indications of Completion

BLOOD SPRINKLED

Le 4:6 And the priest shall dip his finger in the blood, and sprinkle of the blood seven times before the LORD, before the vail of the sanctuary.

Nu 19:4 And Eleazar the priest shall take of her blood with his finger, and sprinkle of her blood directly before the tabernacle of the congregation seven times:

THE LEPER SPRINKLED

Le 14:7 And he shall sprinkle upon him that is to be cleansed from the leprosy seven times, and shall pronounce him clean, and shall let the living bird loose into the open field.

PRIESTS ENCOMPASS JERICHO

Jos 6:4 And seven priests shall bear before the ark seven trumpets of rams' horns: and the seventh day ye shall compass the city seven times, and the priests shall blow with the trumpets.

ELIJAH'S SERVANT LOOKS FOR RAIN

1 K 18:43 And said to his servant, Go up now, look toward the sea. And he went up, and looked, and said, *There is* nothing. And he said, Go again seven times.

NAAMAN DIPS IN THE JORDAN

2 K 5:10 And Elisha sent a messenger unto him, saying, Go and wash in the Jordan seven times, and thy flesh shall come again to thee, and thou shalt be clean.

PRAISE SEVEN TIMES A DAY

Ps 119:164 Seven times a day do I praise thee because of thy righteous judgments.

THE JUST MAN RISETH AFTER FALLING

Pr 24:16 For a just *man* falleth seven times, and riseth up again: but the wicked shall fall into mischief.

5. Expressions of Responsibility

WITNESSES *(testifying)*

Is 43:10 Ye *are* my witnesses, saith the LORD, and my servant whom I have chosen: that ye may know and believe me, and understand that I *am* he: before me there was no God formed, neither shall there be after me.

SALT *(preserving)*

Mt 5:13 Ye are the salt of the earth: but if the salt have lost his savour, wherewith shall it be salted? it is thenceforth good for nothing, but to be cast out, and to be trodden under foot of men.

LIGHT *(illuminating)*

Mt 5:14 Ye are the light of the world. A city that is set on an hill cannot be hid.

BRANCHES *(bearing fruit)*

Jn 15:5 I am the vine, ye *are* the branches: He that abideth in me, and I in him, the same bringeth forth much fruit: for without me ye can do nothing.

EPISTLES *(instructing)*

2 Co 3:2 Ye are our epistle written in our hearts, known and read of all men:

AMBASSADORS *(representing)*

2 Co 5:20 Now then we are ambassadors for Christ, as though God did beseech *you* by us: we pray *you* in Christ's stead, be ye reconciled to God.

STEWARDS *(distributing)*

1 Pe 4:10 As every man hath received the gift, *even so* minister the same one to another, as good stewards of the manifold grace of God.

SEWING See **ARTS AND CRAFTS**

SEX, *proper use of*

Ge 12:19 Why saidst thou, She *is* my sister? so I might have taken her to me to wife: now therefore behold thy wife, take *her,* and go thy way.

De 5:18 Neither shalt thou commit adultery.

Jb 31:1 I made a covenant with mine eyes; why then should I think upon a maid?

Jb 31:9 If mine heart have been deceived by a woman, or *if* I have laid wait at my neighbour's door;

Pr 5:20 And why wilt thou, my son, be ravished with a strange woman, and embrace the bosom of a stranger?

Mt 5:28 But I say unto you, That whosoever looketh on a woman to lust after her hath committed adultery with her already in his heart.

1 Co 7:1 Now concerning the things whereof ye wrote unto me: *It is* good for a man not to touch a woman.

1 Th 4:3 For this is the will of God, *even* your sanctification, that ye should abstain from fornication:

Tit 2:5 *To be* discreet, chaste, keepers at home, good, obedient to their own husbands, that the word of God be not blasphemed.

Re 14:4 These are they which were not defiled with women; for they are virgins. These are they which follow the Lamb whithersoever he goeth. These were redeemed from among men, *being* the firstfruits unto God and to the Lamb.

See **MARRIAGE**

SHADOW OF DEATH, *emotional despair or grief*

Jb 3:5; 10:21; 12:22; 16:16; 24:17; 38:17; Ps 23:4; 44:19; 107:10; Je 13:16; Mt 4:16; Lu 1:79

See **DESPAIR, DESPONDENCY**

SHADRACH, *one of the Hebrew captives*

Da 1:7; 2:49; 3:12, 23, 30, 30

SHALLUM, *peace, well-being*

1. King of Israel, slain by Menahem

2 K 15:10, 15

See **ISRAEL**

2. King of Judah *See* **ISRAEL, JEHOAHAZ**

SHALMANESER, *king of Assyria*

2 K 17:3; 18:9

SHAME, *the painful emotion caused by guilt, embarrassment, unworthiness, or disgrace*

Pr 3:35; 10:5; 11:2; 13:5; 29:15

1. The Wicked Ashamed

Ps 6:10 Let all mine enemies be ashamed and sore vexed: let them return *and* be ashamed suddenly.

Ps 25:3 Yea, let none that wait on thee be ashamed: let them be ashamed which transgress without cause.

Ps 31:17 Let me not be ashamed, O LORD; for I have called upon thee: let the wicked be ashamed, *and* let them be silent in the grave.

Ps 35:26 Let them be ashamed and brought to confusion together that rejoice at mine hurt: let them be clothed with shame and dishonour that magnify *themselves* against me.

Ps 40:14 Let them be ashamed and confounded together that seek after my soul to destroy it; let them be driven backward and put to shame that wish me evil.

Ps 44:7 But thou hast saved us from our enemies, and hast put them to shame that hated us.

Ps 53:5 There were they in great fear, *where* no fear was: for God hath scattered the bones of him that encampeth *against* thee: thou hast put *them* to shame, because God hath despised them.

Ps 70:2 Let them be ashamed and confounded that seek after my soul: let them be turned backward, and put to confusion, that desire my hurt.

Ps 71:24 My tongue also shall talk of thy righteousness all the day long: for they are confounded, for they are brought unto shame, that seek my hurt.

Ps 83:17 Let them be confounded and troubled for ever; yea, let them be put to shame, and perish:

Ps 86:17 Shew me a token for good; that they which hate me may see *it*, and be ashamed: because thou, LORD, hast holpen me, and comforted me.

Ps 97:7 Confounded be all they that serve graven images, that boast themselves of idols: worship him, all *ye* gods.

Ps 109:28 Let them curse, but bless thou: when they arise, let them be ashamed; but let thy servant rejoice.

Ps 119:78 Let the proud be ashamed; for they dealt perversely with me without a cause: *but* I will meditate in thy precepts.

Ps 132:18 His enemies will I clothe with shame: but upon himself shall his crown flourish.

Is 1:29 For they shall be ashamed of the oaks which ye have desired, and ye shall be confounded for the gardens that ye have chosen.

Is 26:11 LORD, *when* thy hand is lifted up, they will not see: *but* they shall see, and be ashamed for *their* envy at the people; yea, the fire of thine enemies shall devour them.

Is 30:5 They were all ashamed of a people *that* could not profit them, nor be an help nor profit, but a shame, and also a reproach.

Is 41:11 Behold, all they that were incensed against thee shall be ashamed and confounded: they shall be as nothing; and they that strive with thee shall perish.

Is 42:17 They shall be turned back, they shall be greatly ashamed, that trust in graven images, that say to the molten images, Ye *are* our gods.

Is 44:11 Behold, all his fellows shall be ashamed: and the workmen, they *are* of men: let them all be gathered together, let them stand up; *yet* they shall fear, *and* they shall be ashamed together.

Is 45:16 They shall be ashamed, and also confounded, all of them: they shall go to confusion together *that are* makers of idols.

Is 45:24 Surely, shall *one* say, in the LORD have I righteousness and strength: *even* to him shall *men* come; and all that are incensed against him shall be ashamed.

Is 65:13 Therefore thus saith the Lord GOD, Behold, my servants shall eat, but ye shall be hungry: behold, my servants shall drink, but ye shall be thirsty: behold, my servants shall rejoice, but ye shall be ashamed:

Is 66:5 Hear the word of the LORD, ye that tremble at his word; your brethren that hated you, that cast you out for my name's sake, said, Let the LORD be glorified: but he shall appear to your joy, and they shall be ashamed.

Je 2:26 As the thief is ashamed when he is found, so is the house of Israel ashamed; they, their kings, their princes, and their priests, and their prophets,

Je 12:13 They have sown wheat, but shall reap thorns: they have put themselves to pain, *but* shall not profit: and they shall be ashamed of your revenues because of the fierce anger of the LORD.

Je 14:3 And their nobles have sent their little ones to the waters: they came to the pits, *and* found no water; they returned with their vessels empty; they were ashamed and confounded, and covered their heads.

Je 15:9 She that hath borne seven languisheth: she hath given up the ghost; her sun is gone down while *it was* yet day: she hath been ashamed and confounded: and the residue of them will I deliver to the sword before their enemies, saith the LORD.

Je 17:13 O LORD, the hope of Israel, all that forsake thee shall be ashamed, *and* they that depart from me shall be written in the earth, because they have forsaken the LORD, the fountain of living waters.

Je 20:11 But the LORD *is* with me as a mighty terrible one: therefore my persecutors shall stumble, and they shall not prevail: they shall be greatly ashamed; for they shall not prosper: *their* everlasting confusion shall never be forgotten.

Je 22:22 The wind shall eat up all thy pastors, and thy lovers shall go into captivity: surely then shalt thou be ashamed and confounded for all thy wickedness.

Je 48:13 And Moab shall be ashamed of Chemosh, as the house of Israel was ashamed of Bethel their confidence.

Je 48:39 They shall howl, *saying,* How is it broken down! how hath Moab turned the back with shame! so shall Moab be a derision and a dismaying to all them about him.

Eze 16:61 Then thou shalt remember thy ways, and be ashamed, when thou shalt receive thy sisters, thine elder and thy younger: and I will give them unto thee for daughters, but not by thy covenant.

Eze 36:32 Not for your sakes do I *this,* saith the Lord God, be it known unto you: be ashamed and confounded for your own ways, O house of Israel.

Eze 43:10 Thou son of man, shew the house to the house of Israel, that they may be ashamed of their iniquities: and let them measure the pattern.

Da 9:8 O Lord, to us *belongeth* confusion of face, to our kings, to our princes, and to our fathers, because we have sinned against thee.

Ho 4:19 The wind hath bound her up in her wings, and they shall be ashamed because of their sacrifices.

Ho 10:6 It shall be also carried unto Assyria *for* a present to king Jareb: Ephraim shall receive shame, and Israel shall be ashamed of his own counsel.

Mi 3:7 Then shall the seers be ashamed, and the diviners confounded: yea, they shall all cover their lips; for *there is* no answer of God.

Mi 7:10 Then *she that is* mine enemy shall see *it,* and shame shall cover her which said unto me, Where is the Lord thy God? mine eyes shall behold her: now shall she be trodden down as the mire of the streets.

Hab 2:10 Thou hast consulted shame to thy house by cutting off many people, and hast sinned *against* thy soul.

Zec 13:4 And it shall come to pass in that day, *that* the prophets shall be ashamed every one of his vision, when he hath prophesied; neither shall they wear a rough garment to deceive:

Lu 13:17 And when he had said these things, all his adversaries were ashamed: and all the people rejoiced for all the glorious things that were done by him.

Ro 6:21 What fruit had ye then in those things whereof ye are now ashamed? for the end of those things *is* death.

2 Th 3:14 And if any man obey not our word by this epistle, note that man, and have no company with him, that he may be ashamed.

2. Shame of Sin

Ge 3:7 And the eyes of them both were opened, and they knew that they *were* naked; and they sewed fig leaves together, and made themselves aprons.

Ge 3:10 And he said, I heard thy voice in the garden, and I was afraid, because I *was* naked; and I hid myself.

Ex 32:25 And when Moses saw that the people *were* naked; (for Aaron had made them naked unto *their* shame among their enemies:)

Ezr 9:6 And said, O my God, I am ashamed and blush to lift up my face to thee, my God: for our iniquities are increased over *our* head, and our trespass is grown up unto the heavens.

Jb 8:22 They that hate thee shall be clothed with shame; and the dwelling place of the wicked shall come to nought.

Ps 44:15 My confusion *is* continually before me, and the shame of my face hath covered me,

Je 23:40 And I will bring an everlasting reproach upon you, and a perpetual shame, which shall not be forgotten.

Eze 32:30 There *be* the princes of the north, all of them, and all the Zidonians, which are gone down with the slain; with their terror they are ashamed of their might; and they lie uncircumcised with *them that be* slain by the sword, and bear their shame with them that go down to the pit.

Eze 36:7 Therefore thus saith the Lord God; I have lifted up mine hand, Surely the heathen that *are* about you, they shall bear their shame.

Da 12:2 And many of them that sleep in the dust of the earth shall awake, some to everlasting life, and some to shame *and* everlasting contempt.

Lu 15:19 And am no more worthy to be called thy son: make me as one of thy hired servants.

Re 16:15 Behold, I come as a thief. Blessed *is* he that watcheth, and keepeth his garments, lest he walk naked, and they see his shame.

SHAME

3. The Righteous Not Ashamed

See **UNASHAMED**

SHAMELESSNESS, *without decency or modesty, brazen*

Ge 9:22; Je 3:3; 6:15; 8:12; Zep 3:5

SHAMGAR, *a judge of Israel*

Jud 3:31; 5:6

See **ISRAEL**

SHAPHAN, *a scribe*

2 K 22:3, 10; 2 Chr 34:8, 16

SHARON, *a district of the Holy Land*

1 Chr 5:16; 27:29; Song 2:1; Is 33:9; 35:2; 65:10; Ac 9:35

SHAVING, *removing hair with a razor*

Ge 41:14; Le 13:33; 14:9; Nu 6:9, 18; 8:7; De 21:12; Jud 16:19; 2 S 10:4; 1 Chr 19:4; Jb 1:20; Eze 44:20; Ac 21:24

SHEAVES, *bundles of grain*

Ge 37:7; De 24:19; Jb 24:10

SHEBA

1. Country

Jb 6:19; Ps 72:10; Is 60:6; Je 6:20; Eze 27:22; 38:13

2. Queen, *from southern Arabia; visited King Solomon*

1 K 10:1; 2 Chr 9:1; Mt 12:42; Lu 11:31

SHECHEM, *Sichem, Sychar, or Sychem*

1. Son of Hamor, *the Hivite prince*

Ge 33:19

2. A Man of Manasseh

Nu 26:31; Josh 17:2

3. A Son of Shemidah, *a Gileadite*

1 Chr 7:19

4. A City, *called by various names*

a. Shechem

This was the first place Abraham visited in Palestine (Ge 12:6–7). Jacob and his family came to Shechem and erected an altar (Ge 33:18–20). Joseph's brothers pastured their flocks there, and Joseph was buried there (Ge 37:12–13; Jos 24:32). It was also the site where Joshua gathered the tribes of Israel, where Rehoboam was crowned, where the united monarchy was divided, and where Jeroboam established his royal residence (Jos 24:1; 1 K 12).

b. Sichem

Ge 12:6

c. Sychar

Jn 4:5

d. Sychem

Acts 7:16

SHEEP See **ANIMALS**

SHEEPFOLDS, *enclosures, often made of thorny bushes, intended to protect sheep*

Nu 32:16, 36; Jud 5:16; Ps 78:70; Jn 10:1

SHEKELS, *ancient unit of weight and money*

Ex 30:13; 38:24, 26; Le 5:15; 27:4, 5, 25; Nu 3:47, 50; 7:13, 19, 25, 32, 43, 61, 79, 85; 18:16; 31:52; De 22:19; 1 S 9:8; 2 S 24:24; 1 K 10:29; Je 32:9; Eze 45:12

See **WEIGHTS AND MEASURES**

SHEM, *son of Noah*

Ge 5:32; 6:10; 7:13; 9:18; 10:21; 11:10; 1 Chr 1:17; Lu 3:36

SHEMAIAH, *a prophet*

1 K 12:22; 2 Chr 11:2; 12:5, 15

SHEOL See **HELL**

SHEPHERDS

1. Guardians of the Flock

Ge 4:2 And she again bare his brother Abel. And Abel was a keeper of sheep, but Cain was a tiller of the ground.

Ge 13:5 And Lot also, which went with Abram, had flocks, and herds, and tents.

Ge 29:9 And while he yet spake with them, Rachel came with her father's sheep: for she kept them.

Ge 30:31 And he said, What shall I give thee? And Jacob said, Thou shalt not give me any thing: if thou wilt do this thing for me, I will again feed *and* keep thy flock:

Ge 37:2 These *are* the generations of Jacob. Joseph, *being* seventeen years old, was feeding the flock with his brethren; and the lad *was* with the sons of Bilhah, and with the sons of Zilpah, his father's wives: and Joseph brought unto his father their evil report.

Ge 46:32 And the men *are* shepherds, for their trade hath been to feed cattle; and they have brought their flocks, and their herds, and all that they have.

Ge 46:34 That ye shall say, Thy servants' trade hath been about cattle from our youth even until now, both we, *and* also our fathers: that ye may dwell in the land of Goshen; for every shepherd *is* an abomination unto the Egyptians.

Ge 47:3 And Pharaoh said unto his brethren, What *is* your occupation? And they said unto Pharaoh, Thy servants *are* shepherds, both we, *and* also our fathers.

Ex 2:17 And the shepherds came and drove them away: but Moses stood up and helped them, and watered their flock.

Ex 3:1 Now Moses kept the flock of Jethro his father in law, the priest of Midian: and he led the flock to the backside of the desert, and came to the mountain of God, *even* to Horeb.

1 S 16:11 And Samuel said unto Jesse, Are here all *thy* children? And he said, There remaineth yet the youngest, and, behold, he keepeth the sheep. And Samuel said unto Jesse, Send and fetch him: for we will not sit down till he come hither.

1 S 17:15 But David went and returned from Saul to feed his father's sheep at Bethlehem.

1 S 17:20 And David rose up early in the morning, and left the sheep with a keeper, and took, and went, as Jesse

had commanded him; and he came to the trench, as the host was going forth to the fight, and shouted for the battle.

2 S 7:8 Now therefore so shalt thou say unto my servant David, Thus saith the Lord of hosts, I took thee from the sheepcote, from following the sheep, to be ruler over my people, over Israel:

1 Chr 4:39 And they went to the entrance of Gedor, *even* unto the east side of the valley, to seek pasture for their flocks.

1 Chr 27:29 And over the herds that fed in Sharon *was* Shitrai the Sharonite: and over the herds *that were* in the valleys *was* Shaphat the son of Adlai:

Pr 27:23 Be thou diligent to know the state of thy flocks, *and* look well to thy herds.

Je 25:36 A voice of the cry of the shepherds, and an howling of the principal of the flock, *shall be heard:* for the Lord hath spoiled their pasture.

Am 1:2 And he said, The Lord will roar from Zion, and utter his voice from Jerusalem; and the habitations of the shepherds shall mourn, and the top of Carmel shall wither.

Am 3:12 Thus saith the Lord; As the shepherd taketh out of the mouth of the lion two legs, or a piece of an ear; so shall the children of Israel be taken out that dwell in Samaria in the corner of a bed, and in Damascus *in* a couch.

Zep 2:6 And the sea coast shall be dwellings *and* cottages for shepherds, and folds for flocks.

Mt 25:32 And before him shall be gathered all nations: and he shall separate them one from another, as a shepherd divideth *his* sheep from the goats:

Lu 2:8 And there were in the same country shepherds abiding in the field, keeping watch over their flock by night.

Lu 2:15 And it came to pass, as the angels were gone away from them into heaven, the shepherds said one to another, Let us now go even unto Bethlehem, and see this thing which is come to pass, which the Lord hath made known unto us.

1 Co 9:7 Who goeth a warfare any time at his own charges? who planteth a vineyard, and eateth not of the fruit thereof? or who feedeth a flock, and eateth not of the milk of the flock?

2. False

INSENTIATE AND PLEASURE-LOVING

Is 56:10–12 His watchmen *are* blind: they are all ignorant, they *are* all dumb dogs, they cannot bark; sleeping, lying down, loving to slumber.

Yea, *they are* greedy dogs *which* can never have enough, and they *are* shepherds *that* cannot understand: they all look to their own way, every one for his gain, from his quarter.

Come ye, *say they,* I will fetch wine, and we will fill ourselves with strong drink; and to morrow shall be as this day, *and* much more abundant.

SCATTER THE FLOCK

Je 23:2 Therefore thus saith the LORD God of Israel against the pastors that feed my people; Ye have scattered my flock, and driven them away, and have not visited them: behold, I will visit upon you the evil of your doings, saith the LORD.

LEAD THE SHEEP ASTRAY

Je 50:6 My people hath been lost sheep: their shepherds have caused them to go astray, they have turned them away *on* the mountains: they have gone from mountain to hill, they have forgotten their restingplace.

PREY UPON THE FLOCK
INSTEAD OF FEEDING IT

Eze 34:2–3 Son of man, prophesy against the shepherds of Israel, prophesy, and say unto them, Thus saith the Lord GOD unto the shepherds; Woe *be* to the shepherds of Israel that do feed themselves! should not the shepherds feed the flocks?

Ye eat the fat, and ye clothe you with the wool, ye kill them that are fed: *but* ye feed not the flock.

Zec 11:17 Woe to the idol shepherd that leaveth the flock! the sword *shall be* upon his arm, and upon his right eye: his arm shall be clean dried up, and his right eye shall be utterly darkened.

HIRELINGS FORSAKE THE SHEEP

Jn 10:12 But he that is an hireling, and not the shepherd, whose own t, seeth the wolf coming, and leaveth the sheep, and fleeth: and the wolf catcheth them, and scattereth the sheep.

See **CHRIST, GOD, GUIDANCE**

SHEWBREAD, *hallowed bread placed in the tabernacle*

Ex 25:30; 35:13; 39:36; 40:23; Le 24:5; Nu 4:7; 1 S 21:4, 6; 22:10; 1 K 7:48; 1 Chr 9:32; 23:29; 2 Chr 2:4; 13:11; Ne 10:33; Ho 9:4; Mt 12:4; Mk 2:26; Lu 6:4; He 9:2

SHIBBOLETH

Jud 12:5–6

SHIELDS, *used in battle*

1 S 17:7; 2 S 1:21; 8:7; 1 K 10:16–17; 14:27; 2 K 11:10; 1 Chr 12:8; 18:7; 2 Chr 9:15–16; 11:12; 12:9; 17:17; 23:9; 26:14; 32:5; Ne 4:16; Je 46:3, 9; 51:11; Eze 23:24; 27:10; 38:4; 39:9; Na 2:3

SHILOH, *a city of Ephraim*

It was located ten miles north of Bethel on the east side of the highway that ran from Bethel to Shechem (Jud 21:19). It is the place where Israel set up the tabernacle soon after they entered Canaan (Jos 18:1). Here the boy Samuel ministered and became the first of a long line of Hebrew prophets. The Philistines defeated Israel about 1050 B.C., captured the ark of the covenant, and probably burned Shiloh (Je 7:12; 26:6; Ps 78:60). By the time of Jeroboam, the town was again inhabited (1 K 14:2).

See **CITIES**

SHINAR, *land where Babylon was located; the place of exile for the Jews*

Ge 10:10; 11:2; 14:1; Is 11:11; Da 1:2; Zec 5:11

SHIPS, *vessels for deep-water navigation*

Nu 24:24; 1 K 9:26; 22:48; 2 Chr 8:18; 9:21; 20:36; Ps 104:26; Pr 30:19; Is 60:9; Eze 27:9, 25, 29; Da 11:30, 40; Jona 1:3; Mk 8:10; Lu 5:2; Jn 6:17; Ac 20:13; 21:2; 27:2, 41; Ja 3:4; Re 8:9; 18:17

SHISHAK, *king of Egypt*

1 K 11:40; 2 Chr 12:2

SHITTAH See **TREES**

SHOES, *removed, used as a sign of respect; also done during the transaction of business*

Ex 3:5; De 25:9; Jos 5:15; Ru 4:8; 2 S 15:30; Is 20:2; Ac 7:33

SHOULDER, *or thigh, sacrificial*

Ex 29:22; Le 7:34; 10:14; Nu 6:19

SHOUTING See **JOY**

SHOVELS, *tabernacle utensils used to clear ashes off the altar of burnt sacrifices*

Ex 27:3; Is 30:24; Je 52:18

SHOWERS, *spiritual*

De 32:2; Ps 68:9; 72:6; Is 27:3; 44:3; Eze 34:26; Ho 6:3; 10:12; Mal 3:10; Ac 3:19

See **BLESSINGS, DROUGHT**

SHUNAMMITE, *an inhabitant of Shunem*

2 K 4:8, 12, 16, 20, 27, 36

SHUNEM, *a town of Issachar*

Jos 19:18; 1 S 28:4; 2 K 4:8

SHUSHAN, *Susa, capital of Persia*

It was the scene of many biblical events in the time of Daniel, Nehemiah, Queen Esther and King Ahasuerus (Xerxes).

Ne 1:1; Est 1:2; 2:5, 8; 3:15; 4:8; 8:14; 9:6, 11; Da 8:2

SICKLES See **AGRICULTURE**

SICKNESS, *disease, illness*

1. As Judgment for Sin

Le 26:15-16 And if ye shall despise my statutes, or if your soul abhor my judgments, so that ye will not do all my commandments, *but* that ye break my covenant:

I also will do this unto you; I will even appoint over you terror, consumption, and the burning ague, that shall consume the eyes, and cause sorrow of heart: and ye shall sow your seed in vain, for your enemies shall eat it.

De. 28:61 Also every sickness, and every plague, which *is* not written in the book of this law, them will the LORD bring upon thee, until thou be destroyed.

De 29:22 So that the generation to come of your children that shall rise up after you, and the stranger that shall come from a far land, shall say, when they see the plagues of that land, and the sicknesses which the LORD hath laid upon it;

1 K 14:1 At that time Abijah the son of Jeroboam fell sick.

2 Chr 6:21 Hearken therefore unto the supplications of thy servant, and of thy people Israel, which they shall make toward this place: hear thou from thy dwelling place, *even* from heaven; and when thou hearest, forgive.

2 Chr 21:15 And thou *shalt have* great sickness by disease of thy bowels, until thy bowels fall out by reason of the sickness day by day.

2 Chr 22:6 And he returned to be healed in Jezreel because of the wounds which were given him at Ramah, when he fought with Hazael king of Syria. And Azariah the son of Jehoram king of Judah went down to see Jehoram the son of Ahab at Jezreel, because he was sick.

2 Chr 24:25 And when they were departed from him, (for they left him in great diseases,) his own servants conspired against him for the blood of the sons of Jehoiada the priest, and slew him on his bed, and he died: and they buried him in the city of David, but they buried him not in the sepulchres of the kings.

Jb 33:21 His flesh is consumed away, that it cannot be seen; and his bones *that* were not seen stick out.

Ps 38:3 *There is* no soundness in my flesh because of thine anger; neither *is there any* rest in my bones because of my sin.

Ps 107:17-18 Fools because of their transgression, and because of their iniquities, are afflicted.

Their soul abhorreth all manner of meat; and they draw near unto the gates of death.

Pr 5:11 And thou mourn at the last, when thy flesh and thy body are consumed,

Ecc 5:17 All his days also he eateth in darkness, and *he hath* much sorrow and wrath with his sickness.

Mi 6:13 Therefore also will I make *thee* sick in smiting thee, in making *thee* desolate because of thy sins.

Jn 6:2 And a great multitude followed him, because they saw his miracles which he did on them that were diseased.

1 Co 11:30 For this cause many *are* weak and sickly among you, and many sleep.

2. Sometimes the Righteous Suffer

Ge 48:1 And it came to pass after these things, that *one* told Joseph, Behold, thy father *is* sick: and he took with him his two sons, Manasseh and Ephraim.

1 K 15:23 The rest of all the acts of Asa, and all his might, and all that he did, and the cities which he built, *are* they not written in the book of the chronicles of the kings of Judah? Nevertheless in the time of his old age he was diseased in his feet.

1 K 17:17 And it came to pass after these things, *that* the son of the woman, the mistress of the house, fell sick; and his sickness was so sore, that there was no breath left in him.

2 K 13:14 Now Elisha was fallen sick of his sickness whereof he died. And Joash the king of Israel came down unto him, and wept over his face, and said, O my father, my father, the char-

iot of Israel, and the horsemen thereof.

2 K 20:1 In those days was Hezekiah sick unto death. And the prophet Isaiah the son of Amoz came to him, and said unto him, Thus saith the LORD, Set thine house in order; for thou shalt die, and not live.

2 Chr 16:12 And Asa in the thirty and ninth year of his reign was diseased in his feet, until his disease *was* exceeding *great:* yet in his disease he sought not to the LORD, but to the physicians.

2 Chr 32:24 In those days Hezekiah was sick to the death, and prayed unto the LORD: and he spake unto him, and he gave him a sign.

Jb 2:7 So went Satan forth from the presence of the LORD, and smote Job with sore boils from the sole of his foot unto his crown.

Jb 7:5 My flesh is clothed with worms and clods of dust; my skin is broken, and become loathsome.

Jb 30:30 My skin is black upon me, and my bones are burned with heat.

Is 38:1 In those days was Hezekiah sick unto death. And Isaiah the prophet the son of Amoz came unto him, and said unto him, Thus saith the LORD, Set thine house in order: for thou shalt die, and not live.

Da 8:27 And I Daniel fainted, and was sick *certain* days; afterward I rose up, and did the king's business; and I was astonished at the vision, but none understood *it.*

Jn 5:3 In these lay a great multitude of impotent folk, of blind, halt, withered, waiting for the moving of the water.

Jn 11:1 Now a certain *man* was sick, *named* Lazarus, of Bethany, the town of Mary and her sister Martha.

Ac 9:37 And it came to pass in those days, that she was sick, and died: whom when they had washed, they laid *her* in an upper chamber.

Ph 2:27 For indeed he was sick nigh unto death: but God had mercy on him; and not on him only, but on me also, lest I should have sorrow upon sorrow.

2 Ti 4:20 Erastus abode at Corinth: but Trophimus have I left at Miletum sick.

Ja 5:14 Is any sick among you? let him call for the elders of the church; and let them pray over him, anointing him with oil in the name of the Lord:

3. *Spiritual*, rooted in sin and the rebellious nature of humanity

1 K 8:38 What prayer and supplication soever be *made* by any man, *or* by all thy people Israel, which shall know every man the plague of his own heart, and spread forth his hands toward this house:

Is 1:5 Why should ye be stricken any more? ye will revolt more and more: the whole head is sick, and the whole heart faint.

Je 8:22 *Is there* no balm in Gilead; *is there* no physician there? why then is not the health of the daughter of my people recovered?

Je 14:19 Hast thou utterly rejected Judah? hath thy soul lothed Zion? why hast thou smitten us, and *there is* no healing for us? we looked for peace, and *there is* no good; and for the time of healing, and behold trouble!

Je 30:12 For thus saith the LORD, Thy bruise *is* incurable, *and* thy wound *is* grievous.

Mi 1:9 For her wound *is* incurable; for it is come unto Judah; he is come unto the gate of my people, *even* to Jerusalem.

Mk 2:17 When Jesus heard *it,* he saith unto them, They that are whole have no need of the physician, but they that are sick: I came not to call the righteous, but sinners to repentance.

4. Healing

2 Chr 30:20 And the LORD hearkened to Hezekiah, and healed the people.

Ps 41:4 I said, LORD, be merciful unto me: heal my soul; for I have sinned against thee.

Ps 147:3 He healeth the broken in heart, and bindeth up their wounds.

Is 53:5 But he *was* wounded for our transgressions, *he was* bruised for our

iniquities: the chastisement of our peace *was* upon him; and with his stripes we are healed.

Is 57:18 I have seen his ways, and will heal him: I will lead him also, and restore comforts unto him and to his mourners.

Je 3:22 Return, ye backsliding children, *and* I will heal your backslidings. Behold, we come unto thee; for thou *art* the LORD our God.

Je 17:14 Heal me, O LORD, and I shall be healed; save me, and I shall be saved: for thou *art* my praise.

Je 51:9 We would have healed Babylon, but she is not healed: forsake her, and let us go every one into his own country: for her judgment reacheth unto heaven, and is lifted up *even* to the skies.

Lam 2:13 What thing shall I take to witness for thee? what thing shall I liken to thee, O daughter of Jerusalem? what shall I equal to thee, that I may comfort thee, O virgin daughter of Zion? for thy breach is great like the sea: who can heal thee?

Ho 6:1 Come, and let us return unto the LORD: for he hath torn, and he will heal us; he hath smitten, and he will bind us up.

Lu 4:18 The Spirit of the Lord is upon me, because he hath anointed me to preach the gospel to the poor; he hath sent me to heal the brokenhearted, to preach deliverance to the captives, and recovering of sight to the blind, to set at liberty them that are bruised,

Re 22:2 In the midst of the street of it, and on either side of the river, *was there* the tree of life, which bare twelve *manner* of fruits, *and* yielded her fruit every month: and the leaves of the tree *were* for the healing of the nations.

See **DISEASE, MIRACLES**

SIDON, *or Zidon, a city of Phoenicia*

Ge 10:19; 49:13; Jos 13:6; 19:28; Jud 1:31; 10:6; 18:28; 1 K 17:9; Ezr 3:7; Is 23:2, 4, 12; Je 25:22; 27:3; 47:4; Eze 27:8; 28:22; Jl 3:4; Zec 9:2; Mt 11:21; Mk 3:8; 7:24; Lu 6:17; Ac 27:3

SIEGES, *acts of surrounding and blockading a town*

De 20:12, 19; 28:52; Jos 6:1; 2 S 5:6; 20:15; 1 K 8:37; 15:27; 16:17; 20:1; 2 K 6:24; 17:5; 18:9; 24:10; 25:1; 1 Chr 20:1; 2 Chr 6:28; 32:10; Ec 9:14; Je 32:2; 39:1; 52:5; Eze 26:8; Da 1:1; Mi 5:1; Na 3:14

See **WAR**

SIGHING, *expressing sorrow or weariness*

Ex 2:23; Jb 3:24; Ps 31:10; Is 24:7; Je 45:3; Lam 1:4, 11, 22; Mk 7:34; 8:12

See **SORROW, WEARINESS**

SIGNETS, *official seals*

Ge 38:18; Ex 28:11, 21; 39:6; Je 22:24; Da 6:17; Hag 2:23

SIHON, *king of the Amorites*

Nu 21:21, 26, 34; 32:33; De 1:4; 2:24, 31; 3:2; 4:46; 29:7; 31:4; Jos 2:10; 9:10; 12:2, 5; 13:10, 21, 27; Jud 11:19, 21; 1 K 4:19; Ne 9:22; Ps 135:11; 136:19

SIHOR, *or Shihor, the Nile (?)*

Jos 13:3; 1 Chr 13:5; Is 23:3; Je 2:18

SILAS, *or Silvanus, accompanied Paul on his Second Missionary Journey*

Ac 15:22, 34, 40; 16:19; 17:4, 14; 18:5; 2 Co 1:19; 1 Th 1:1; 2 Th 1:1; 1 Pe 5:12

SILENCE, *the absence of any sound*

1 S 10:16 And Saul said unto his uncle, He told us plainly that the asses were found. But of the matter of the kingdom, whereof Samuel spake, he told him not.

1 S 10:27 But the children of Belial said, How shall this man save us? And they despised him, and brought him no presents. But he held his peace.

1 S 25:19 And she said unto her servants, Go on before me; behold, I come after you. But she told not her husband Nabal.

Jb 2:13 So they sat down with him upon the ground seven days and seven nights, and none spake a word unto him: for they saw that *his* grief was very great.

Jb 13:5 Oh that ye would altogether hold your peace! and it should be your wisdom.

Jb 21:5 Mark me, and be astonished, and lay *your* hand upon *your* mouth.

Jb 29:9 The princes refrained talking, and laid *their* hand on their mouth.

Jb 29:21 Unto me *men* gave ear, and waited, and kept silence at my counsel.

Jb 40:5 Once have I spoken; but I will not answer: yea, twice; but I will proceed no further.

Ps 38:13 But I, as a deaf *man*, heard not; and *I was* as a dumb man *that* openeth not his mouth.

Ps 39:2 I was dumb with silence, I held my peace, *even* from good; and my sorrow was stirred.

Ps 39:9 I was dumb, I opened not my mouth; because thou didst *it*.

Pr 10:19 In the multitude of words there wanteth not sin: but he that refraineth his lips *is* wise.

Pr 11:12 He that is void of wisdom despiseth his neighbour: but a man of understanding holdeth his peace.

Pr 13:3 He that keepeth his mouth keepeth his life: *but* he that openeth wide his lips shall have destruction.

Pr 17:28 Even a fool, when he holdeth his peace, is counted wise: *and* he that shutteth his lips *is esteemed* a man of understanding.

Pr 21:23 Whoso keepeth his mouth and his tongue keepeth his soul from troubles.

Pr 29:11 A fool uttereth all his mind: but a wise *man* keepeth it in till afterwards.

Pr 30:32 If thou hast done foolishly in lifting up thyself, or if thou hast thought evil, *lay* thine hand upon thy mouth.

Lam 3:28 He sitteth alone and keepeth silence, because he hath borne it upon him.

Eze 3:15 Then I came to them of the captivity at Tel-abib, that dwelt by the river of Chebar, and I sat where they sat, and remained there astonished among them seven days.

1 Co 14:28 But if there be no interpreter, let him keep silence in the church; and let him speak to himself, and to God.

1 Ti 2:11 Let the woman learn in silence with all subjection.

1. Time for Keeping

WHEN THE CIRCUMSTANCES DEMAND

Ec 3:7 A time to rend, and a time to sew; a time to keep silence, and a time to speak;

IN EVIL TIMES

Am 5:13 Therefore the prudent shall keep silence in that time; for it *is* an evil time.

IN GOD'S HOUSE

Hab 2:20 But the LORD *is* in his holy temple: let all the earth keep silence before him.

IN GOD'S PRESENCE

Zep 1:7 Hold thy peace at the presence of the Lord GOD: for the day of the LORD *is* at hand: for the LORD hath prepared a sacrifice, he hath bid his guests.

Zec 2:13 Be silent, O all flesh, before the LORD: for he is raised up out of his holy habitation.

2. Of Christ

FORETOLD

Is 42:2; Is 53:7

BEFORE THE HIGH PRIEST

Mt 26:62–63

BEFORE PILATE

Mt 27:14; Mk 15:3

BEFORE HEROD

Lu 23:9

IN THE PRESENCE OF
A WOMAN'S ACCUSERS

Jn 8:6

IN THE CLOSING DAYS OF HIS WORK

Jn 14:30

3. Commanded by Christ

Mt 8:4 And Jesus saith unto him, See thou tell no man; but go thy way, shew thyself to the priest, and offer the gift that Moses commanded, for a testimony unto them.

Mt 9:30 And their eyes were opened; and Jesus straitly charged them, saying, See *that* no man know *it*.

Mt 12:16 And charged them that they should not make him known:

Mt 16:20 Then charged he his disciples that they should tell no man that he was Jesus the Christ.

Mt 17:9 And as they came down from the mountain, Jesus charged them, saying, Tell the vision to no man, until the Son of man be risen again from the dead.

Mk 1:44 And saith unto him, See thou say nothing to any man: but go thy way, shew thyself to the priest, and offer for thy cleansing those things which Moses commanded, for a testimony unto them.

Mk 3:12 And he straitly charged them that they should not make him known.

Mk 5:43 And he charged them straitly that no man should know it; and commanded that something should be given her to eat.

Mk 7:36 And he charged them that they should tell no man: but the more he charged them, so much the more a great deal they published *it;*

Mk 8:26 And he sent him away to his house, saying, Neither go into the town, nor tell *it* to any in the town.

Mk 8:30 And he charged them that they should tell no man of him.

Mk 9:9 And as they came down from the mountain, he charged them that they should tell no man what things they had seen, till the Son of man were risen from the dead.

Lu 5:14 And he charged him to tell no man: but go, and shew thyself to the priest, and offer for thy cleansing, according as Moses commanded, for a testimony unto them.

Lu 8:56 And her parents were astonished: but he charged them that they should tell no man what was done.

Lu 9:21 And he straitly charged them, and commanded *them* to tell no man that thing;

4. Commanded by Other Scripture

Jos 6:10 And Joshua had commanded the people, saying, Ye shall not shout, nor make any noise with your voice, neither shall *any* word proceed out of your mouth, until the day I bid you shout; then shall ye shout.

Ex 14:14 The LORD shall fight for you, and ye shall hold your peace.

Jud 18:19 And they said unto him, Hold thy peace, lay thine hand upon thy mouth, and go with us, and be to us a father and a priest: *is it* better for thee to be a priest unto the house of one man, or that thou be a priest unto a tribe and a family in Israel?

2 K 2:3 And the sons of the prophets that *were* at Bethel came forth to Elisha, and said unto him, Knowest thou that the LORD will take away thy master from thy head to day? And he said, Yea, I know *it;* hold ye your peace.

2 K 2:5 And the sons of the prophets that *were* at Jericho came to Elisha, and said unto him, Knowest thou that the LORD will take away thy master from thy head to day? And he answered, Yea, I know *it;* hold ye your peace.

Ne 8:11 So the Levites stilled all the people, saying, Hold your peace, for the day *is* holy; neither be ye grieved.

Jb 13:13 Hold your peace, let me alone, that I may speak, and let come on me what *will.*

Jb 33:31 Mark well, O Job, hearken unto me: hold thy peace, and I will speak.

Ps 39:2 I was dumb with silence, I held my peace, *even* from good; and my sorrow was stirred.

Mk 1:25 And Jesus rebuked him, saying, Hold thy peace, and come out of him.

Mk 10:48 And many charged him that he should hold his peace: but he cried the more a great deal, *Thou* Son of David, have mercy on me.

Mk 14:61 But he held his peace, and answered nothing. Again the high priest asked him, and said unto him, Art thou the Christ, the Son of the Blessed?

Lu 4:35 And Jesus rebuked him, saying, Hold thy peace, and come out of him. And when the devil had thrown him in the midst, he came out of him, and hurt him not.

Ac 12:17 But he, beckoning unto them with the hand to hold their peace, declared unto them how the Lord had brought him out of the prison. And he said, Go shew these things unto James, and to the brethren. And he departed, and went into another place.

5. Evil Men Quieted

Jos 10:21 And all the people returned to the camp to Joshua at Makkedah in peace: none moved his tongue against any of the children of Israel.

1 S 2:9 He will keep the feet of his saints, and the wicked shall be silent in darkness; for by strength shall no man prevail.

1 K 18:21 And Elijah came unto all the people, and said, How long halt ye between two opinions? if the LORD *be* God, follow him: but if Baal, *then* follow him. And the people answered him not a word.

2 K 18:36 But the people held their peace, and answered him not a word: for the king's commandment was, saying, Answer him not.

Ne 5:8 And I said unto them, We after our ability have redeemed our brethren the Jews, which were sold unto the heathen; and will ye even sell your brethren? or shall they be sold unto us? Then held they their peace, and found nothing *to answer.*

Jb 5:16 So the poor hath hope, and iniquity stoppeth her mouth.

Jb 12:20 He removeth away the speech of the trusty, and taketh away the understanding of the aged.

Jb 32:15 They were amazed, they answered no more: they left off speaking.

Ps 8:2 Out of the mouth of babes and sucklings hast thou ordained strength because of thine enemies, that thou mightest still the enemy and the avenger.

Ps 31:18 Let the lying lips be put to silence; which speak grievous things proudly and contemptuously against the righteous.

Ps 63:11 But the king shall rejoice in God; every one that sweareth by him shall glory: but the mouth of them that speak lies shall be stopped.

Ps 107:42 The righteous shall see *it*, and rejoice: and all iniquity shall stop her mouth.

Is 52:15 So shall he sprinkle many nations; the kings shall shut their mouths at him: for *that* which had not been told them shall they see; and *that* which they had not heard shall they consider.

Is 54:17 No weapon that is formed against thee shall prosper; and every tongue *that* shall rise against thee in judgment thou shalt condemn. This *is* the heritage of the servants of the Lord, and their righteousness *is* of me, saith the Lord.

Je 8:14 Why do we sit still? assemble yourselves, and let us enter into the defenced cities, and let us be silent there: for the Lord our God hath put us to silence, and given us water of gall to drink, because we have sinned against the Lord.

Eze 16:63 That thou mayest remember, and be confounded, and never open thy mouth any more because of thy shame, when I am pacified toward thee for all that thou hast done, saith the Lord God.

Mi 7:16 The nations shall see and be confounded at all their might: they shall lay *their* hand upon *their* mouth, their ears shall be deaf.

Mt 21:27 And they answered Jesus, and said, We cannot tell. And he said unto them, Neither tell I you by what authority I do these things.

Mt 22:12 And he saith unto him, Friend, how camest thou in hither not having a wedding garment? And he was speechless.

Mt 22:22 When they had heard *these words*, they marvelled, and left him, and went their way.

Mt 22:34 But when the Pharisees had heard that he had put the Sadducees to silence, they were gathered together.

Mt 22:46 And no man was able to answer him a word, neither durst any *man* from that day forth ask him any more *questions*.

Mk 3:4 And he saith unto them, Is it lawful to do good on the sabbath days, or to do evil? to save life, or to kill? But they held their peace.

Mk 11:33 And they answered and said unto Jesus, We cannot tell. And Jesus answering saith unto them, Neither do I tell you by what authority I do these things.

Mk 12:34 And when Jesus saw that he answered discreetly, he said unto him, Thou art not far from the kingdom of God. And no man after that durst ask him *any question*.

Lu 13:17 And when he had said these things, all his adversaries were ashamed: and all the people rejoiced for all the glorious things that were done by him.

Lu 14:6 And they could not answer him again to these things.

Lu 20:7 And they answered, that they could not tell whence *it was*.

Lu 20:26 And they could not take hold of his words before the people: and they marvelled at his answer, and held their peace.

Lu 20:40 And after that they durst not ask him any *question at all*.

Ac 4:14 And beholding the man which was healed standing with them, they could say nothing against it.

Ac 9:7 And the men which journeyed with him stood speechless, hearing a voice, but seeing no man.

Ro 3:19 Now we know that what things soever the law saith, it saith to them who are under the law: that every mouth may be stopped, and all the world may become guilty before God.

Tit 1:11 Whose mouths must be stopped, who subvert whole houses, teaching things which they ought not, for filthy lucre's sake.

Tit 2:8 Sound speech, that cannot be condemned; that he that is of the contrary part may be ashamed, having no evil thing to say of you.

1 Pe 2:15 For so is the will of God, that with well doing ye may put to silence the ignorance of foolish men:

1 Pe 3:16 Having a good conscience; that, whereas they speak evil of you, as of evildoers, they may be ashamed that falsely accuse your good conversation in Christ.

See **QUIETNESS, PRAYER, SOLITUDE, SPEECH, WAITING**

SILOAM, or Siloah or Shelah, a fountain or pool near Jerusalem

The Pool of Siloam, where Jesus sent a blind man to be healed (Jn 9:7), was located in the Tyropoeon Valley at the lower end of Hezekiah's underground conduit (Siloam Tunnel) that brought water into Jerusalem from the Gihon Spring. The gently flowing waters of Shiloah (Is 8:6) referred to these waters that flowed through the 1,770–foot tunnel and into this pool, which was called Siloam because it was just across the Kidron Valley from the village of Siloam.

SILVER, valued metal

Ex 25:3; 26:19, 32; 27:11, 17; 31:4; 35:5, 24; 36:24; 38:11, 17, 19; Jos 6:19, 24; 1 K 7:51; 15:15; 1 Chr 28:14; 29:2; 2 Chr 2:14; 5:1; Ezr 7:16; 8:25; Ne 7:71; Ec 2:8; Je 10:9; Eze 27:12; 38:13; Zec 6:11

1. Money

Ge 20:16; 23:15; Ex 38:25; Le 27:3; Jos 7:22; 22:8; 24:32; Jud 17:2, 10; 2 S 18:11; 24:24; 2 K 5:22; 6:25; 20:13; 22:4; 2 Chr 1:17; Eze 7:19; Ho 3:2; Ja 5:3

2. Christ's Betrayal

Ge 37:28 Then there passed by Midianites merchantmen; and they drew and lifted up Joseph out of the pit, and sold Joseph to the Ishmeelites for twenty *pieces* of silver: and they brought Joseph into Egypt.

Am 2:6 Thus saith the LORD; For three transgressions of Israel, and for four, I will not turn away *the punishment*

thereof; because they sold the righteous for silver, and the poor for a pair of shoes;

Am 8:6 That we may buy the poor for silver, and the needy for a pair of shoes; *yea,* and sell the refuse of the wheat?

Zec 11:12 And I said unto them, If ye think good, give *me* my price; and if not, forbear. So they weighed for my price thirty *pieces* of silver.

Mt 26:15 And said *unto them,* What will ye give me, and I will deliver him unto you? And they covenanted with him for thirty pieces of silver.

Mt 27:3 Then Judas, which had betrayeth him, when he saw that he was condemned, repented himself, and brought again the thirty pieces of silver to the chief priests and elders,

Mt 27:9 Then was fulfilled that which was spoken by Jeremy the prophet, saying, And they took the thirty pieces of silver, the price of him that was valued, whom they of the children of Israel did value;

Ac 1:18 Now this man purchased a field with the reward of iniquity; and falling headlong, he burst asunder in the midst, and all his bowels gushed out.

3. Vessels

Ge 44:2; Nu 7:19, 31, 37, 61, 79, 84; 2 S 8:10; 2 K 12:13; 25:15; 2 Chr 9:24; 16:2; Ezr 1:6, 9; 5:14; 8:26; Da 11:8

4. Symbol

Ps 12:6 The words of the LORD *are* pure words: *as* silver tried in a furnace of earth, purified seven times.

Ps 66:10 For thou, O God, hast proved us: thou hast tried us, as silver is tried.

Pr 3:14 For the merchandise of it *is* better than the merchandise of silver, and the gain thereof than fine gold.

Pr 8:19 My fruit *is* better than gold, yea, than fine gold; and my revenue than choice silver.

Pr 10:20 The tongue of the just *is as* choice silver: the heart of the wicked *is* little worth.

Pr 16:16 How much better *is it* to get wisdom than gold! and to get understanding rather to be chosen than silver!

Je 6:30 Reprobate silver shall *men* call them, because the LORD hath rejected them.

Eze 22:18 Son of man, the house of Israel is to me become dross: all they *are* brass, and tin, and iron, and lead, in the midst of the furnace; they are *even* the dross of silver.

Eze 22:22 As silver is melted in the midst of the furnace, so shall ye be melted in the midst thereof; and ye shall know that I the LORD have poured out my fury upon you.

Da 2:32 This image's head *was* of fine gold, his breast and his arms of silver, his belly and his thighs of brass,

Zec 13:9 And I will bring the third part through the fire, and will refine them as silver is refined, and will try them as gold is tried: they shall call on my name, and I will hear them: I will say, It *is* my people: and they shall say, The LORD *is* my God.

SILVERSMITHS See ARTS AND CRAFTS

SIMEON, *he has heard, or obedient one*

1. Son of Jacob

Ge 29:33; 34:25; 42:24; 46:10; 49:5; Ex 6:15; Nu 1:6; 26:12; 1 Chr 4:24, 42; Eze 48:33

2. Tribe

Nu 1:22; 2:12; 10:19; 13:5; 25:14; 26:14; 34:20; Jos 19:1, 9; 21:4; Jud 1:3; 1 Chr 6:65; 12:25; 27:16; Eze 48:25; Re 7:7

3. Devout Man Who Blessed Christ

Lu 2:25

4. Niger

Ac 13:1

SIMON, *he has heard, or obedient one*

1. The Canaanite (Zelotes) an Apostle

Mt 10:4; Mk 3:18; Lu 6:15; Ac 1:13

2. Kinsman of Christ

Mt 13:55; Mk 6:3

3. The Leper

Mt 26:6; Mk 14:3

See **HOSPITALITY**

4. Of Cyrene

Mt 27:32; Mk 15:21; Lu 23:26

5. The Pharisee

Lu 7:36

6. Father of Judas (?)

Jn 6:71; 12:4; 13:2

7. The Sorcerer

Ac 8:9, 18

8. The Tanner

Ac 9:43; 10:6

SIMPLICITY, *sincerity*

Ps 116:6 The LORD preserveth the simple: I was brought low, and he helped me.

Ps 119:130 The entrance of thy words giveth light; it giveth understanding unto the simple.

Ps 131:1 LORD, my heart is not haughty, nor mine eyes lofty: neither do I exercise myself in great matters, or in things too high for me.

Mt 11:25 At that time Jesus answered and said, I thank thee, O Father, Lord of heaven and earth, because thou hast hid these things from the wise and prudent, and hast revealed them unto babes.

Lu 18:17 Verily I say unto you, Whosoever shall not receive the kingdom of God as a little child shall in no wise enter therein.

Ro 16:19 For your obedience is come abroad unto all *men*. I am glad therefore on your behalf: but yet I would have you wise unto that which is good, and simple concerning evil.

2 Co 1:12 For our rejoicing is this, the testimony of our conscience, that in simplicity and godly sincerity, not with fleshly wisdom, but by the grace of God, we have had our conversation in the world, and more abundantly to you-ward.

Singleness of Heart

1 Chr 12:33 Of Zebulun, such as went forth to battle, expert in war, with all instruments of war, fifty thousand, which could keep rank: *they were* not of double heart.

Lu 11:34 The light of the body is the eye: therefore when thine eye is single, thy whole body also is full of light; but when *thine eye* is evil, thy body also *is* full of darkness.

Ac 2:46 And they, continuing daily with one accord in the temple, and breaking bread from house to house, did eat their meat with gladness and singleness of heart,

Ep 6:5 Servants, be obedient to them that are *your* masters according to the flesh, with fear and trembling, in singleness of your heart, as unto Christ;

Col 3:22 Servants, obey in all things *your* masters according to the flesh; not with eyeservice, as menpleasers; but in singleness of heart, fearing God:

See **CONSECRATION, DEVOTIONAL LIFE, DUPLICITY**

SIN

1. Concealed

Ge 3:8 And they heard the voice of the LORD God walking in the garden in the cool of the day: and Adam and his wife hid themselves from the presence of the LORD God amongst the trees of the garden.

Jos 7:21 When I saw among the spoils a goodly Babylonish garment, and two hundred shekels of silver, and a wedge of gold of fifty shekels weight, then I coveted them, and took them; and, behold, they *are* hid in the earth in the midst of my tent, and the silver under it.

2 S 12:12 For thou didst *it* secretly: but I will do this thing before all Israel, and before the sun.

2 K 5:24 And when he came to the tower, he took *them* from their hand, and bestowed *them* in the house: and he let the men go, and they departed.

2 K 17:9 And the children of Israel did secretly *those* things that *were* not right against the LORD their God, and they built them high places in all their cities, from the tower of the watchmen to the fenced city.

Jb 24:16 In the dark they dig through houses, *which* they had marked for themselves in the daytime: they know not the light.

Jb 31:33 If I covered my transgressions as Adam, by hiding mine iniquity in my bosom:

Ps 19:12 Who can understand *his* errors? cleanse thou me from secret *faults*.

Ps 32:5 I acknowledged my sin unto thee, and mine iniquity have I not hid. I said, I will confess my transgressions unto the LORD; and thou forgavest the iniquity of my sin. Selah.

Ps 90:8 Thou hast set our iniquities before thee, our secret *sins* in the light of thy countenance.

Ps 139:11 If I say, Surely the darkness shall cover me; even the night shall be light about me.

Pr 9:17 Stolen waters are sweet, and bread *eaten* in secret is pleasant.

Pr 26:26 *Whose* hatred is covered by deceit, his wickedness shall be shewed before the *whole* congregation.

Pr 28:13 He that covereth his sins shall not prosper: but whoso confesseth and forsaketh *them* shall have mercy.

Is 28:15 Because ye have said, We have made a covenant with death, and with hell are we at agreement; when the overflowing scourge shall pass through, it shall not come unto us: for we have made lies our refuge, and under falsehood have we hid ourselves:

Is 29:15 Woe unto them that seek deep to hide their counsel from the LORD, and their works are in the dark, and they say, Who seeth us? and who knoweth us?

Is 30:1 Woe to the rebellious children, saith the LORD, that take counsel, but not of me; and that cover with a covering, but not of my spirit, that they may add sin to sin:

Is 40:27 Why sayest thou, O Jacob, and speakest, O Israel, My way is hid from the LORD, and my judgment is passed over from my God?

Is 47:10 For thou hast trusted in thy wickedness: thou hast said, None seeth me. Thy wisdom and thy knowledge, it hath perverted thee; and thou hast said in thine heart, *I am*, and none else beside me.

Eze 8:8 Then said he unto me, Son of man, dig now in the wall: and when I had digged in the wall, behold a door.

Eze 8:12 Then said he unto me, Son of man, hast thou seen what the ancients of the house of Israel do in the dark, every man in the chambers of his imagery? for they say, The LORD seeth us not; the LORD hath forsaken the earth.

Lu 11:44 Woe unto you, scribes and Pharisees, hypocrites! for ye are as graves which appear not, and the men that walk over *them* are not aware *of them.*

Lu 12:2 For there is nothing covered, that shall not be revealed; neither hid, that shall not be known.

Ep 5:12 For it is a shame even to speak of those things which are done of them in secret.

1 Ti 5:24 Some men's sins are open beforehand, going before to judgment; and some *men* they follow after.

2 Ti 3:6 For of this sort are they which creep into houses, and lead captive silly women laden with sins, led away with divers lusts,

Re 6:16 And said to the mountains and rocks, Fall on us, and hide us from the face of him that sitteth on the throne, and from the wrath of the Lamb:

2. Exposed

Ex 2:14 And he said, Who made thee a prince and a judge over us? intendest thou to kill me, as thou killedst the

Egyptian? And Moses feared, and said, Surely this thing is known.

Nu 32:23 But if ye will not do so, behold, ye have sinned against the LORD: and be sure your sin will find you out.

Jos 7:18 And he brought his household man by man; and Achan, the son of Carmi, the son of Zabdi, the son of Zerah, of the tribe of Judah, was taken.

1 S 15:14 And Samuel said, What *meaneth* then this bleating of the sheep in mine ears, and the lowing of the oxen which I hear?

2 S 12:12 For thou didst *it* secretly: but I will do this thing before all Israel, and before the sun.

1 K 21:19 And thou shalt speak unto him, saying, Thus saith the LORD, Hast thou killed, and also taken possession? And thou shalt speak unto him, saying, Thus saith the LORD, In the place where dogs licked the blood of Naboth shall dogs lick thy blood, even thine.

2 K 5:26 And he said unto him, Went not mine heart *with thee,* when the man turned again from his chariot to meet thee? *Is it* a time to receive money, and to receive garments, and oliveyards, and vineyards, and sheep, and oxen, and menservants, and maidservants?

Ezr 9:15 O LORD God of Israel, thou *art* righteous: for we remain yet escaped, as *it is* this day: behold, we *are* before thee in our trespasses: for we cannot stand before thee because of this.

Est 2:23 And when inquisition was made of the matter, it was found out; therefore they were both hanged on a tree: and it was written in the book of the chronicles before the king.

Est 7:6 And Esther said, The adversary and enemy *is* this wicked Haman. Then Haman was afraid before the king and the queen.

Jb 12:22 He discovereth deep things out of darkness, and bringeth out to light the shadow of death.

Jb 20:27 The heaven shall reveal his iniquity; and the earth shall rise up against him.

Jb 24:17 For the morning *is* to them even as the shadow of death: if *one* know *them, they are in* the terrors of the shadow of death.

Jb 34:22 *There is* no darkness, nor shadow of death, where the workers of iniquity may hide themselves.

Ps 139:12 Yea, the darkness hideth not from thee; but the night shineth as the day: the darkness and the light *are* both alike *to thee.*

Pr 10:9 He that walketh uprightly walketh surely: but he that perverteth his ways shall be known.

Pr 14:33 Wisdom resteth in the heart of him that hath understanding: but *that which is* in the midst of fools is made known.

Pr 26:26 *Whose* hatred is covered by deceit, his wickedness shall be shewed before the *whole* congregation.

Ec 12:14 For God shall bring every work into judgment, with every secret thing, whether *it be* good, or whether *it be* evil.

Is 26:21 For, behold, the Lord cometh out of his place to punish the inhabitants of the earth for their iniquity: the earth also shall disclose her blood, and shall no more cover her slain.

Is 28:17 Judgment also will I lay to the line, and righteousness to the plummet: and the hail shall sweep away the refuge of lies, and the waters shall overflow the hiding place.

Is 28:20 For the bed is shorter than that *a man* can stretch himself *on it:* and the covering narrower than that he can wrap himself *in it.*

Is 47:3 Thy nakedness shall be uncovered, yea, thy shame shall be seen: I will take vengeance, and I will not meet *thee as* a man.

Is 59:6 Their webs shall not become garments, neither shall they cover themselves with their works: their works *are* works of iniquity, and the act of violence *is* in their hands.

Je 2:34 Also in thy skirts is found the blood of the souls of the poor innocents: I have not found it by secret search, but upon all these.

Je 13:22 And if thou say in thine heart, Wherefore come these things

upon me? For the greatness of thine iniquity are thy skirts discovered, *and* thy heels made bare.

Je 29:23 Because they have committed villany in Israel, and have committed adultery with their neighbours' wives, and have spoken lying words in my name, which I have not commanded them; even I know, and *am* a witness, saith the Lord.

Lam 2:14 Thy prophets have seen vain and foolish things for thee: and they have not discovered thine iniquity, to turn away thy captivity, but have seen for thee false burdens and causes of banishment.

Lam 4:22 The punishment of thine iniquity is accomplished, O daughter of Zion; he will no more carry thee away into captivity: he will visit thine iniquity, O daughter of Edom; he will discover thy sins.

Eze 8:9 And he said unto me, Go in, and behold the wicked abominations that they do here.

Eze 16:37 Behold, therefore I will gather all thy lovers, with whom thou hast taken pleasure, and all *them* that thou hast loved, with all *them* that thou hast hated; I will even gather them round about against thee, and will discover thy nakedness unto them, that they may see all thy nakedness.

Eze 16:57 Before thy wickedness was discovered, as at the time of *thy* reproach of the daughters of Syria, and all *that are* round about her, the daughters of the Philistines, which despise thee round about.

Eze 21:24 Therefore thus saith the Lord God; Because ye have made your iniquity to be remembered, in that your transgressions are discovered, so that in all your doings your sins do appear; because, *I say,* that ye are come to remembrance, ye shall be taken with the hand.

Eze 22:2 Now, thou son of man, wilt thou judge, wilt thou judge the bloody city? yea, thou shalt shew her all her abominations.

Eze 23:29 And they shall deal with thee hatefully, and shall take away all thy labour, and shall leave thee naked and bare: and the nakedness of thy whoredoms shall be discovered, both thy lewdness and thy whoredoms.

Eze 24:8 That it might cause fury to come up to take vengeance; I have set her blood upon the top of a rock, that it should not be covered.

Eze 28:15 Thou *wast* perfect in thy ways from the day that thou wast created, till iniquity was found in thee.

Ho 2:3 Lest I strip her naked, and set her as in the day that she was born, and make her as a wilderness, and set her like a dry land, and slay her with will I discover her lewdness in the sight of her lovers, and none shall deliver her out of mine hand.

Ho 7:1 When I would have healed Israel, then the iniquity of Ephraim was discovered, and the wickedness of Samaria: for they commit falsehood; and the thief cometh in, *and* the troop of robbers spoileth without.

Am 9:3 And though they hide themselves in the top of Carmel, I will search and take them out thence; and though they be hid from my sight in the bottom of the sea, thence will I command the serpent, and he shall bite them:

Jona 1:7 And they said every one to his fellow, Come, and let us cast lots, that we may know for whose cause this evil *is* upon us. So they cast lots, and the lot fell upon Jonah.

Mi 1:13 O thou inhabitant of Lachish, bind the chariot to the swift beast: she *is* the beginning of the sin to the daughter of Zion: for the transgressions of Israel were found in thee.

Na 3:5 Behold, I *am* against thee, saith the LORD of hosts; and I will discover thy skirts upon thy face, and I will shew the nations thy nakedness, and the kingdoms thy shame.

Mt 26:73 And after a while came unto *him* they that stood by, and said to Peter, Surely thou also art *one* of them; for thy speech bewrayeth thee.

Lu 12:2 For there is nothing covered, that shall not be revealed; neither hid, that shall not be known.

Jn 4:18 For thou hast had five husbands; and he whom thou now hast is

not thy husband: in that saidst thou truly.

Ac 7:28 Wilt thou kill me, as thou diddest the Egyptian yesterday?

Ro 2:16 In the day when God shall judge the secrets of men by Jesus Christ according to my gospel.

1 Co 4:5 Therefore judge nothing before the time, until the Lord come, who both will bring to light the hidden things of darkness, and will make manifest the counsels of the hearts: and then shall every man have praise of God.

1 Co 14:25 And thus are the secrets of his heart made manifest; and so falling down on *his* face he will worship God, and report that God is in you of a truth.

Ep 5:13 But all things that are reproved are made manifest by the light: for whatsoever doth make manifest is light.

2 Ti 3:9 But they shall proceed no further: for their folly shall be manifest unto all *men,* as theirs also was.

He 4:12 For the word of God *is* quick, and powerful, and sharper than any twoedged sword, piercing even to the dividing asunder of soul and spirit, and of the joints and marrow, and *is* a discerner of the thoughts and intents of the heart.

Ja 1:24 For he beholdeth himself, and goeth his way, and straightway forgetteth what manner of man he was.

Jude 15 To execute judgment upon all, and to convince all that are ungodly among them of all their ungodly deeds which they have ungodly committed, and of all their hard *speeches* which ungodly sinners have spoken against him.

Re 2:2 I know thy works, and thy labour, and thy patience, and how thou canst not bear them which are evil: and thou hast tried them which say they are apostles, and are not, and hast found them liars:

a. By God's Infinite Knowledge

Ge 4:10 And he said, What hast thou done? the voice of thy brother's blood crieth unto me from the ground.

Ge 19:13 For we will destroy this place, because the cry of them is waxen great before the face of the LORD; and the LORD hath sent us to destroy it.

Ge 44:16 And Judah said, What shall we say unto my lord? what shall we speak? or how shall we clear ourselves? God hath found out the iniquity of thy servants: behold, we *are* my lord's servants, both we, and *he* also with whom the cup is found.

De 32:34 *Is* not this laid up in store with me, *and* sealed up among my treasures?

1 S 2:17 Wherefore the sin of the young men was very great before the LORD: for men abhorred the offering of the LORD.

Jb 10:6 That thou enquirest after mine iniquity, and searchest after my sin?

Jb 10:14 If I sin, then thou markest me, and thou wilt not acquit me from mine iniquity.

Jb 11:11 For he knoweth vain men: he seeth wickedness also; will he not then consider *it*?

Jb 14:16 For now thou numberest my steps: dost thou not watch over my sin?

Ps 10:14 Thou hast seen *it;* for thou beholdest mischief and spite, to requite *it* with thy hand: the poor committeth himself unto thee; thou art the helper of the fatherless.

Ps 51:4 Against thee, thee only, have I sinned, and done *this* evil in thy sight: that thou mightest be justified when thou speakest, *and* be clear when thou judgest.

Ps 69:5 O God, thou knowest my foolishness; and my sins are not hid from thee.

Ps 109:15 Let them be before the Lord continually, that he may cut off the memory of them from the earth.

Is 65:6 Behold, *it is* written before me: I will not keep silence, but will recompense, even recompense into their bosom,

Je 2:22 For though thou wash thee with nitre, and take thee much sope, *yet* thine iniquity is marked before me, saith the Lord GOD.

Je 14:10 Thus saith the LORD unto this people, Thus have they loved to wander, they have not refrained their feet, therefore the LORD doth not accept them; he will now remember their iniquity, and visit their sins.

Je 16:17 For mine eyes *are* upon all their ways: they are not hid from my face, neither is their iniquity hid from mine eyes.

Lam 1:22 Let all their wickedness come before thee; and do unto them, as thou hast done unto me for all

Lam 3:60 Thou hast seen all their vengeance *and* all their imaginations against me.

Lam 4:22 The punishment of thine iniquity is accomplished, O daughter of Zion; he will no more carry thee away into captivity: he will visit thine iniquity, O daughter of Edom; he will discover thy sins.

Eze 11:5 And the Spirit of the LORD fell upon me, and said unto me, Speak; Thus saith the LORD; Thus have ye said, O house of Israel: for I know the things that come into your mind, *every one of* them.

Eze 21:24 Therefore thus saith the Lord GOD; Because ye have made your iniquity to be remembered, in that your transgressions are discovered, so that in all your doings your sins do appear; because, *I say,* that ye are come to remembrance, ye shall be taken with the hand.

Ho 5:3 I know Ephraim, and Israel is not hid from me: for now, O Ephraim, thou committest whoredom, *and* Israel is defiled.

Ho 7:2 And they consider not in their hearts *that* I remember all their wickedness: now their own doings have beset them about; they are before my face.

Ho 13:12 The iniquity of Ephraim *is* bound up; his sin *is* hid.

Am 5:12 For I know your manifold transgressions and your mighty sins: they afflict the just, they take a bribe, and they turn aside the poor in the gate *from their right.*

Am 9:8 Behold, the eyes of the Lord God *are* upon the sinful kingdom, and I will destroy it from off the face of the earth; saving that I will not utterly destroy the house of Jacob, saith the LORD.

Jona 1:2 Arise, go to Nineveh, that great city, and cry against it; for their wickedness is come up before me.

Jn 4:18 For thou hast had five husbands; and he whom thou now hast is not thy husband: in that saidst thou truly.

Re 18:5 For her sins have reached unto heaven, and God hath remembered her iniquities.

b. Regardless of How Committed

LIKE THE SIN OF CAIN, *it may be done in secret*

Ge 4:8–10 And Cain talked with Abel his brother: and it came to pass, when they were in the field, that Cain rose up against Abel his brother, and slew him.

And the LORD said unto Cain, where is Abel thy brother? And he said, I know not: *Am* I my brother's keeper?

And he said, What hast thou done? the voice of thy brother's blood crieth unto me from the ground.

LIKE THE SIN OF ESAU, *it may be done under the impulse of the moment*

Ge 25:32, 33 And Esau said, Behold, I *am* at the point to die: and what profit shall this birthright do to me?

And Jacob said, Swear to me this day; and he sware unto him: and he sold his birthright unto Jacob.

He 12:16–17 Lest there *be* any fornicator, or profane person, as Esau, who for one morsel of meat sold his birthright.

For ye know how that afterward, when he would have inherited the blessing, he was rejected: for he found no place of repentance, though he sought it carefully with tears.

LIKE THE SIN OF JOSEPH'S BRETHREN, *it may be years before its discovery*

Ge 42:21 And they said one to another, We *are* verily guilty concerning our brother, in that we saw the an-

guish of his soul, when he besought us, and we would not hear; therefore is this distress come upon us.

LIKE THE SIN OF ACHAN, *it may be well covered up*

Jos 7:21 When I saw among the spoils a goodly Babylonish garment, and two hundred shekels of silver, and a wedge of gold of fifty shekels weight, then I coveted them, and took them; and, behold, they *are* hid in the earth in the midst of my tent, and the silver under it.

LIKE THE SIN OF SAMSON, *it may be done reluctantly*

Jud 16:16–17 And it came to pass, when she pressed him daily with her words, and urged him, *so* that his soul was vexed unto death;

That he told her all his heart, and said unto her. There hath not come a razor upon mine head; for I *have been* a Nazarite unto God from my mother's womb: if I be shaven, then my strength will go from me, and I shall become weak, and be like any *other* man.

LIKE THE SIN OF AHAB, *it may be prompted by others*

1 K 21:7 And Jezebel his wife said unto him, Dost thou now govern the kingdom of Israel? arise, *and* eat bread, and let thine heart be merry: I will give thee the vineyard of Naboth the Jezreelite.

1 K 21:20 And Ahab said to Elijah, Hast thou found me, O mine enemy? And he answered, I have found *thee:* because thou hast sold thyself to work evil in the sight of the LORD.

LIKE THE SIN OF BELSHAZZAR, *it may be done under the influence of strong drink*

Da 5:1–2, Belshazzar the king made a great feast to a thousand of his lords, and drank wine before the thousand.

Belshazzar, whiles he tasted the wine, commanded to bring the golden and silver vessels which his father Nebuchadnezzar had taken out of the temple which *was* in Jerusalem; that the king, and his princes, his wives, and his concubines, might drink therein.

Da 5:27 TEKEL; Thou art weighed in the balances, and art found wanting.

LIKE THE SIN OF HEROD, *it may be the result of a foolish promise*

Mt 14:6–10 But when Herod's birthday was kept, the daughter of Herodias danced before them, and pleased Herod.

Whereupon he promised with an oath to give her whatsoever she would ask.

And she, being before instructed of her mother, said, Give me here John Baptist's head in a charger.

And the king was sorry: nevertheless for the oath's sake, and them which sat with him at meat, he commanded *it* to be given *her.*

And he sent, and beheaded John in the prison.

LIKE THE SIN OF JUDAS, *it may have the approval of the authorities*

Mk 14:10–11 And Judas Iscariot, one of the twelve, went unto the chief priests, to betray him unto them.

And when they heard *it,* they were glad, and promised to give him money. And he sought how he might conveniently betray him.

LIKE THE SIN OF PILATE, *it may be done to gratify the public*

Mk 15:15 And *so* Pilate, willing to content the people released Barabbas unto them, and delivered Jesus, when he had scourged *him,* to be crucified.

LIKE THE SIN OF THE JEWS, *it may be done in ignorance*

Lu 23:34 Then said Jesus, Father, forgive them; for they know not what they do. And they parted his raiment, and cast lots.

3. A Falling Away

a. Palliation

Ex 32:24; Pr 17:15; 24:24; 28:4; Is 5:20; Je 6:14; 8:11; Lam 2:14; Eze 13:22; 16:51; Mal 2:17; Ro 1:32; 2 Jn 11

b. Denunciations

De 30:18; Is 30:1; Je 7:20; 11:17; Eze 16:37; Am 1:11; Mt 3:7; 11:20; 23:33; Lu 10:13; 11:47; 19:46; Ac 7:52; 13:10; 23:3

c. Examples

A MAN OF GOD REBUKES ELI

1 S 2:29 Wherefore kick ye at my sacrifice and at mine offering, which I have commanded *in my* habitation; and honourest thy sons above me, to make yourselves fat with the chiefest of all the offerings of Israel my people?

SAMUEL REBUKES SAUL

1 S 13:13 And Samuel said to Saul, Thou hast done foolishly: thou hast not kept the commandment of the Lord thy God, which he commanded thee: for now would the Lord have established thy kingdom upon Israel for ever.

NATHAN REBUKES DAVID

2 S 12:7 And Nathan said to David, Thou *art* the man. Thus saith the Lord God of Israel, I anointed thee king over Israel, and I delivered thee out of the hand of Saul;

2 S 12:9 Wherefore hast thou despised the commandment of the Lord, to do evil in his sight? thou hast killed Uriah the Hittite with the sword, and hast taken his wife *to be* thy wife, and hast slain him with the sword of the children of Ammon.

ELIJAH REBUKES AHAB

1 K 18:18 And he answered, I have not troubled Israel; but thou, and thy father's house, in that ye have forsaken the commandments of the Lord, and thou hast followed Baalim.

1 K 21:20 And Ahab said to Elijah, Hast thou found me, O mine enemy? And he answered, I have found *thee:*

because thou hast sold thyself to work evil in the sight of the LORD.

ZECHARIAH REBUKES JUDAH

2 Chr 24:20 And the Spirit of God came upon Zechariah the son of Jehoiada the priest, which stood above the people, and said unto them, Thus saith God, Why transgress ye the commandments of the LORD, that ye cannot prosper? because ye have forsaken the LORD, he hath also forsaken you.

EZRA REBUKES THE PEOPLE

Ezr 10:10–11 And Ezra the priest stood up, and said unto them, Ye have transgressed, and have taken strange wives, to increase the trespass of Israel.

Now therefore make confession unto the LORD God of your fathers, and do his pleasure: and separate yourselves from the people of the land, and from the strange wives.

DYING THIEF REBUKES HIS COMPANION

Lu 23:39–40 And one of the malefactors which were hanged railed on him, saying, If thou be Christ, save thyself and us.

But the other answering rebuked him, saying, Dost not thou fear God, seeing thou art in the same condemnation?

4. Its Pathway

Jb 8:13 So *are* the paths of all that forget God; and the hypocrite's hope shall perish:

Ps 139:24 And see if *there be any* wicked way in me, and lead me in the way everlasting.

Pr 2:15 Whose ways *are* crooked, and *they* froward in their paths:

Pr 12:15 The way of a fool *is* right in his own eyes: but he that hearkeneth unto counsel *is* wise.

Pr 13:15 Good understanding giveth favour: but the way of transgressors *is* hard.

Pr 14:12 There is a way which seemeth right unto a man, but the end thereof *are* the ways of death.

Pr 15:9 The way of the wicked *is* an abomination unto the LORD: but he loveth him that followeth after righteousness.

Is 59:8 The way of peace they know not; and *there is* no judgment in their goings: they have made them crooked paths: whosoever goeth therein shall not know peace.

Eze 11:21 But *as for them* whose heart walketh after the heart of their detestable things and their abominations, I will recompense their way upon their own heads, saith the Lord GOD.

Mt 7:13 Enter ye in at the strait gate: for wide *is* the gate, and broad *is* the way, that leadeth to destruction, and many there be which go in thereat:

Jude 11 Woe unto them! for they have gone in the way of Cain, and ran greedily after the error of Balaam for reward, and perished in the gainsaying of Core.

5. Its Manner of Life

De 29:19 And it come to pass, when he heareth the words of this curse, that he bless himself in his heart, saying, I shall have peace, though I walk in the imagination of mine heart, to add drunkenness to thirst:

Jb 31:5 If I have walked with vanity, or if my foot hath hasted to deceit;

Je 7:24 But they hearkened not, nor inclined their ear, but walked in the counsels *and* in the imagination of their evil heart, and went backward, and not forward.

Je 32:23 And they came in, and possessed it; but they obeyed not thy voice, neither walked in thy law; they have done nothing of all that thou commandedst them to do: therefore thou hast caused all this evil to come upon them:

Eze 11:12 And ye shall know that I *am* the LORD: For ye have not walked in my statutes, neither executed my judgments, but have done after the manners of the heathen that *are* round about you.

Ep 2:2 Wherein in time past ye walked according to the course of this world, according to the prince of the power of the air, the spirit that now worketh in the children of disobedience:

Ph 3:18 (For many walk, of whom I have told you often, and now tell you even weeping, *that they are* the enemies of the cross of Christ:

1 Pe 4:3 For the time past of *our* life may suffice us to have wrought the will of the Gentiles, when we walked in lasciviousness, lusts, excess of wine, revellings, banquetings, and abominable idolatries:

2 Pe 2:10 But chiefly them that walk after the flesh in the lust of uncleanness, and despise government. Presumptuous *are they,* selfwilled, they are not afraid to speak evil of dignities.

2 Pe 3:3 Knowing this first, that there shall come in the last days scoffers, walking after their own lusts,

Jude 18 How that they told you there should be mockers in the last time, who should walk after their own ungodly lusts.

6. Its Insanity

Ec 9:3 This *is* an evil among all *things* that are done under the sun, that *there is* one event unto all: yea, also the heart of the sons of men is full of evil, and madness is in their heart while they live, and after that *they go* to the dead.

NEBUCHADNEZZAR

Da 4:33–34 The same hour was the thing fulfilled upon Nebuchadnezzar: and he was driven from men, and did eat grass as oxen, and his body was wet with the dew of heaven, till his hairs were grown like eagles' *feathers,* and his nails like birds' *claws.*

And at the end of the days I Nebuchadnezzar lifted up mine eyes unto heaven, and mine understanding returned unto me, and I blessed the most High, and I praised and honoured him that liveth for ever, whose dominion *is* an everlasting dominion, and his kingdom *is* from generation to generation:

THE PRODIGAL SON

Lu 15:17 And when he came to himself, he said, How many hired servants of my father's have bread enough and to spare, and I perish with hunger!

THE JEWS

Ac 7:54 When they heard these things, they were cut to the heart, and they gnashed on him with *their* teeth.

THE RULERS OF ISRAEL

1 Co 2:8 Which none of the princes of this world knew: for had they known *it,* they would not have crucified the Lord of glory.

BALAAM

2 Pe 2:16 But was rebuked for his iniquity: the dumb ass speaking with man's voice forbad the madness of the prophet.

7. Its Increments

SEEN IN THE HISTORY OF ISRAEL

Ezr 9:6 And said, O my God, I am ashamed and blush to lift up my face to thee, my God: for our iniquities are increased over *our* head, and our trespass is grown up unto the heavens.

Je 5:28 They are waxen fat, they shine: yea, they overpass the deeds of the wicked: they judge not the cause, the cause of the fatherless, yet they prosper; and the right of the needy do they not judge.

ILLUSTRATED IN THE LIFE OF BACKSLIDERS

Mt 12:45 Then goeth he, and taketh with himself seven other spirits more wicked than himself, and they enter in and dwell there: and the last *state* of that man is worse than the first. Even so shall it be also unto this wicked generation.

2 Pe 2:20 For if after they have escaped the pollutions of the world through the knowledge of the Lord and Saviour Jesus Christ, they are again entangled therein, and overcome, the latter end is worse with them than the beginning.

SHOWN BY INCREASING
SPIRITUAL INSENSITIVITY

Mt 13:15 For this people's heart is waxed gross, and *their* ears are dull of hearing, and their eyes they have closed; lest at any time they should see with *their* eyes, and hear with *their*

ears, and should understand with *their* heart, and should be converted, and I should heal them.

THE STEPS IN PETER'S FALL

Mt 26:74 Then began he to curse and to swear, *saying,* I know not the man. And immediately the cock crew.

MORE EVIDENT IN THE LAST DAYS

2 Ti 3:13 But evil men and seducers shall wax worse and worse, deceiving, and being deceived.

8. Its Disfigurement

a. Wounds

Pr 6:33; 7:26; 23:29; Is 1:6; 30:26; Je 6:7; 16:6; 30:12; Ho 5:13; Mi 1:9; Na 3:19; Lu 4:18; 10:30

b. Degrading Marks

Pr 21:29; Is 3:9; Je 3:3; Re 13:16; 14:9; 16:2; 19:20

9. Its Confession

a. Prescribed

Le 5:5 And it shall be, when he shall be guilty in one of these *things,* that he shall confess that he hath sinned in that *thing:*

Le 16:21 And Aaron shall lay both his hands upon the head of the live goat, and confess over him all the iniquities of the children of Israel, and all their transgressions in all their sins, putting them upon the head of the goat, and shall send *him* away by the hand of a fit man into the wilderness:

Le 26:40 If they shall confess their iniquity, and the iniquity of their fathers, with their trespass which they trespassed against me, and that also they have walked contrary unto me;

Nu 5:7 Then they shall confess their sin which they have done: and he shall recompense his trespass with the principal thereof, and add unto it the fifth *part* thereof, and give *it* unto *him* against whom he hath trespassed.

Jos 7:19 And Joshua said unto Achan, My son, give, I pray thee, glory to the LORD God of Israel, and make confes-

sion unto him; and tell me now what thou

Ezr 10:11 Now therefore make confession unto the LORD God of your fathers, and do his pleasure: and separate yourselves from the people of the land, and from the strange wives.

Jb 33:27 He looketh upon men, and *if any* say, I have sinned, and perverted *that which was* right, and it profited me not;

Ps 5:10 Destroy thou them, O God; let them fall by their own counsels; cast them out in the multitude of their transgressions; for they have rebelled against thee.

Pr 28:13 He that covereth his sins shall not prosper: but whoso confesseth and forsaketh *them* shall have mercy.

Je 3:13 Only acknowledge thine iniquity, that thou hast transgressed against the LORD thy God, and hast scattered thy ways to the strangers under every green tree, and ye have not obeyed my voice, saith the LORD.

Ho 5:15 I will go *and* return to my place, till they acknowledge their offence, and seek my face: in their affliction they will seek me early.

Ho 14:2 Take with you words, and turn to the LORD: say unto him, Take away all iniquity, and receive *us* graciously: so will we render the calves of our lips.

1 Jn 1:9 If we confess our sins, he is faithful and just to forgive us *our* sins, and to cleanse us from all unrighteousness.

b. Examples of National

Ex 32:31 And Moses returned unto the LORD, and said, Oh, this people have sinned a great sin, and have made them gods of gold.

Nu 14:40 And they rose up early in the morning, and gat them up into the top of the mountain, saying, Lo, we *be here,* and will go up unto the place which the LORD hath promised: for we have sinned.

Nu 21:7 Therefore the people came to Moses, and said, We have sinned, for we have spoken against the LORD, and against thee; pray unto the LORD, that he take away the serpents from us. And Moses prayed for the people.

De 1:41 Then ye answered and said unto me, We have sinned against the LORD, we will go up and fight, according to all that the LORD our God commanded us. And when ye had girded on every man his weapons of war, ye were ready to go up into the hill.

Jud 10:10 And the children of Israel cried unto the LORD, saying, We have sinned against thee, both because we have forsaken our God, and also served Baalim.

1 S 7:6 And they gathered together to Mizpeh, and drew water, and poured *it* out before the LORD, and fasted on that day, and said there, We have sinned against the LORD. And Samuel judged the children of Israel in Mizpeh.

1 S 12:10 And they cried unto the LORD, and said, We have sinned, because we have forsaken the LORD, and have served Baalim and Ashtaroth: but now deliver us out of the hand of our enemies, and we will serve thee.

1 S 12:19 And all the people said unto Samuel, Pray for thy servants unto the LORD thy God, that we die not: for we have added unto all our sins *this* evil, to ask us a king.

1 K 8:33 When thy people Israel be smitten down before the enemy, because they have sinned against thee, and shall turn again to thee, and confess thy name, and pray, and make supplication unto thee in this house:

1 K 8:47 *Yet* if they shall bethink themselves in the land whither they were carried captives, and repent, and make supplication unto thee in the land of them that carried them captives, saying, We have sinned, and have done perversely, we have committed wickedness;

2 Chr 29:6 For our fathers have trespassed, and done *that which was* evil in the eyes of the LORD our God, and have forsaken him, and have turned away their faces from the habitation of the LORD, and turned *their* backs.

2 Chr 30:22 And Hezekiah spake comfortably unto all the Levites that taught the good knowledge of the LORD: and they did eat throughout the feast seven days, offering peace offerings, and making confession to the LORD God of their fathers.

Ezr 5:12 But after that our fathers had provoked the God of heaven unto wrath, he gave them into the hand of Nebuchadnezzar the king of Babylon, the Chaldean, who destroyed this house, and carried the people away into Babylon.

Ezr 9:6 And said, O my God, I am ashamed and blush to lift up my face to thee, my God: for our iniquities are increased over *our* head, and our trespass is grown up unto the heavens.

Ezr 10:1 Now when Ezra had prayed, and when he had confessed, weeping and casting himself down before the house of God, there assembled unto him out of Israel a very great congregation of men and women and children: for the people wept very sore.

Ne 1:6 Let thine ear now be attentive, and thine eyes open, that thou mayest hear the prayer of thy servant, which I pray before thee now, day and night, for the children of Israel thy servants, and confess the sins of the children of Israel, which we have sinned against thee: both I and my father's house have sinned.

Ne 9:2 And the seed of Israel separated themselves from all strangers, and stood and confessed their sins, and the iniquities of their fathers.

Ne 9:33 Howbeit thou *art* just in all that is brought upon us; for thou hast done right, but we have done wickedly:

Ps 106:6 We have sinned with our fathers, we have committed iniquity, we have done wickedly.

Is 42:24 Who gave Jacob for a spoil, and Israel to the robbers? did not the LORD, he against whom we have sinned? for they would not walk in his ways, neither were they obedient unto his law.

Is 59:12 For our transgressions are multiplied before thee, and our sins testify against us: for our transgressions *are* with us; and *as for* our iniquities, we know them;

Is 64:5 Thou meetest him that rejoiceth and worketh righteousness, *those that* remember thee in thy ways: behold, thou art wroth; for we have sinned: in those is continuance, and we shall be saved.

Je 3:25 We lie down in our shame, and our confusion covereth us: for we have sinned against the LORD our God, we and our fathers, from our youth even unto this day, and have not obeyed the voice of the LORD our God.

Je 8:14 Why do we sit still? assemble yourselves, and let us enter into the defenced cities, and let us be silent there: for the LORD our God hath put us to silence, and given us water of gall to drink, because we have sinned against the LORD.

Je 14:7 O LORD, though our iniquities testify against us, do thou *it* for thy name's sake: for our backslidings are many; we have sinned against thee.

Je 14:20 We acknowledge, O LORD, our wickedness, *and* the iniquity of our fathers: for we have sinned against thee.

Lam 1:18 The LORD is righteous; for I have rebelled against his commandment: hear, I pray you, all people, and behold my sorrow: my virgins and my young men are gone into captivity.

Lam 3:42 We have transgressed and have rebelled: thou hast not pardoned.

Lam 5:16 The crown is fallen *from* our head: woe unto us, that we have sinned!

Da 9:5 We have sinned, and have committed iniquity, and have done wickedly, and have rebelled, even by departing from thy precepts and from thy judgments:

Da 9:15 And now, O LORD our God, that hast brought thy people forth out of the land of Egypt with a mighty hand, and hast gotten thee renown, as at this day; we have sinned, we have done wickedly.

Da 9:20 And whiles I *was* speaking, and praying, and confessing my sin and the sin of my people Israel, and presenting my supplication before the LORD my God for the holy mountain of my God;

c. Examples of Personal

BALAAM

Nu 22:34 And Balaam said unto the angel of the LORD, I have sinned; for I knew not that thou stoodest in the way against me: now therefore, if it displease thee, I will get me back again.

ACHAN

Jos 7:20 And Achan answered Joshua, and said, Indeed I have sinned against the LORD God of Israel, and thus and thus have I done:

SAUL

1 S 15:24 And Saul said unto Samuel, I have sinned: for I have transgressed the commandment of the LORD, and thy words: because I feared the people, and obeyed their voice.

DAVID

2 S 12:13 And David said unto Nathan, I have sinned against the LORD. And Nathan said unto David, The LORD also hath put away thy sin; thou shalt not die.

2 S 24:10 And David's heart smote him after that he had numbered the people. And David said unto the LORD, I have sinned greatly in that I have done: and now, I beseech thee, O LORD, take away the iniquity of thy servant; for I have done very foolishly.

Jb 7:20 I have sinned; what shall I do unto thee, O thou preserver of men? why hast thou set me as a mark against thee, so that I am a burden to myself?

Ps 41:4 I said, LORD, be merciful unto me: heal my soul; for I have sinned against thee.

Ps 51:3 For I acknowledge my transgressions: and my sin *is* ever before me.

Mt 27:4 Saying, I have sinned in that I have betrayed the innocent blood. And they said, What *is that* to us? see thou *to that.*

CONVERTS OF JOHN THE BAPTIST

Mk 1:5 And there went out unto him all the land of Judaea, and they of Jerusalem, and were all baptized of him in the river of Jordan, confessing their sins.

PETER

Lu 5:8 When Simon Peter saw *it,* he fell down at Jesus' knees, saying, Depart from me; for I am a sinful man, O Lord.

PRODIGAL SON

Lu 15:18 I will arise and go to my father, and will say unto him, Father, I have sinned against heaven, and before thee,

10. Related Topics

a. Definition

VAIN TALK

Pr 10:19 In the multitude of words there wanteth not sin: but he that refraineth his lips *is* wise.

CONTEMPT FOR OTHERS

Pr 14:21 He that despiseth his neighbour sinneth: but he that hath mercy on the poor, happy *is* he.

FOOLISH THOUGHTS

Pr 24:9 The thought of foolishness *is* sin: and the scorner *is* an abomination to men.

UNBELIEF

Ro 14:23 And he that doubteth is damned if he eat, because *he eateth* not of faith: for whatsoever *is* not of faith is sin.

NEGLECT OF OPPORTUNITY

Ja 4:17 Therefore to him that knoweth to do good, and doeth *it* not, to him it is sin.

TRANSGRESSION OF THE LAW

1 Jn 3:4 Whosoever committeth sin transgresseth also the law: for sin is the transgression of the law.

ALL UNRIGHTEOUSNESS

1 Jn 5:17 All unrighteousness is sin: and there is a sin not unto death.

b. Origin

Ge 3:6 And when the woman saw that the tree *was* good for food, and that it *was* pleasant to the eyes, and a tree to be desired to make *one* wise, she took of the fruit thereof, and did eat, and gave also unto her husband with her; and he did eat.

Ps 51:5 Behold, I was shapen in iniquity; and in sin did my mother conceive me.

Mt 15:19 For out of the heart proceed evil thoughts, murders, adulteries, fornications, thefts, false witness, blasphemies:

Ja 1:15 Then when lust hath conceived, it bringeth forth sin: and sin, when it is finished, bringeth forth death.

Ja 4:1 From whence *come* wars and fightings among you? *come they* not hence, *even* of your lusts that war in your members?

c. Universality

Ge 6:5 And GOD saw that the wickedness of man *was* great in the earth, and *that* every imagination of the thoughts of his heart *was* only evil continually.

Nu 15:22 And if ye have erred, and not observed all these commandments, which the LORD hath spoken unto Moses,

1 K 8:46 If they sin against thee, (for *there is* no man that sinneth not,) and thou be angry with them, and deliver them to the enemy, so that they carry them away captives unto the land of the enemy, far or near;

Jb 4:17 Shall mortal man be more just than God? shall a man be more pure than his maker?

Ps 14:3 They are all gone aside, they are *all* together become filthy: *there is* none that doeth good, no, not one.

Ps 19:12 Who can understand *his* errors? cleanse thou me from secret *faults.*

Ps 53:3 Every one of them is gone back: they are altogether become filthy; *there is* none that doeth good, no, not one.

Ps 130:3 If thou, LORD, shouldest mark iniquities, O Lord, who shall stand?

Pr 20:9 Who can say, I have made my heart clean, I am pure from my sin?

Ec 3:16 And moreover I saw under the sun the place of judgment, *that* wickedness *was* there; and the place of righteousness, *that* iniquity *was* there.

Ec 7:20 For *there is* not a just man upon earth, that doeth good, and sinneth not.

Is 53:6 All we like sheep have gone astray; we have turned every one to his own way; and the LORD hath laid on him the iniquity of us all.

Is 64:6 But we are all as an unclean *thing,* and all our righteousnesses *are* as filthy rags; and we all do fade as a leaf; and our iniquities, like the wind, have taken us away.

Lam 3:39 Wherefore doth a living man complain, a man for the punishment of his sins?

Da 9:11 Yea, all Israel have transgressed thy law, even by departing, that they might not obey thy voice; therefore the curse is poured upon us, and the oath that *is* written in the law of Moses the servant of God, because we have sinned against him.

Mi 7:2 The good *man* is perished out of the earth: and *there is* none upright among men: they all lie in wait for blood; they hunt every man his brother with a net.

Ro 3:23 For all have sinned, and come short of the glory of God;

Ga 3:22 But the scripture hath concluded all under sin, that the promise by faith of Jesus Christ might be given to them that believe.

1 Jn 1:8 If we say that we have no sin, we deceive ourselves, and the truth is not in us.

1 Jn 5:19 And we know that we are of God, and the whole world lieth in wickedness.

d. Consequences—Parents' Sins upon Children

Ex 20:5 Thou shalt not bow down thyself to them, nor serve them: for I the LORD thy God *am* a jealous God, visiting the iniquity of the fathers upon the children unto the third and fourth *generation* of them that hate me;

Nu 14:33 And your children shall wander in the wilderness forty years, and bear your whoredoms, until your carcases be wasted in the wilderness.

Ps 37:28 For the LORD loveth judgment, and forsaketh not his saints; they are preserved for ever: but the seed of the wicked shall be cut off.

Pr 14:11 The house of the wicked shall be overthrown: but the tabernacle of the upright shall flourish.

Is 14:20 Thou shalt not be joined with them in burial, because thou hast destroyed thy land, *and* slain thy people: the seed of evildoers shall never be renowned.

Lam 5:7 Our fathers have sinned, *and are* not; and we have borne their iniquities.

e. Deception

Ge 3:13 And the LORD God said unto the woman, What *is* this *that* thou hast done? And the woman said, The serpent beguiled me, and I did eat.

Ro 7:11 For sin, taking occasion by the commandment, deceived me, and by it slew *me.*

Ep 4:22 That ye put off concerning the former conversation the old man, which is corrupt according to the deceitful lusts;

1 Ti 2:14 And Adam was not deceived, but the woman being deceived was in the transgression.

2 Ti 3:13 But evil men and seducers shall wax worse and worse, deceiving, and being deceived.

Tit 3:3 For we ourselves also were sometimes foolish, disobedient, deceived, serving divers lusts and pleasures, living in malice and envy, hateful, *and* hating one another.

He 3:13 But exhort one another daily, while it is called To day; lest any of you be hardened through the deceitfulness of sin.

Re 19:20 And the beast was taken, and with him the false prophet that wrought miracles before him, with which he deceived them that had received the mark of the beast, and them that worshipped his image. These both were cast alive into a lake of fire burning with brimstone.

f. Despised by Saints

Jb 1:8 And the LORD said unto Satan, Hast thou considered my servant Job, that *there is* none like him in the earth, a perfect and an upright man, one that feareth God, and escheweth evil?

Jb 34:32 *That which* I see not teach thou me: if I have done iniquity, I will do no more.

Ps 26:5 I have hated the congregation of evildoers; and will not sit with the wicked.

Ps 97:10 Ye that love the LORD, hate evil: he preserveth the souls of his saints; he delivereth them out of the hand of the wicked.

Ps 101:3 I will set no wicked thing before mine eyes: I hate the work of them that turn aside; *it* shall not cleave to me.

Ps 119:104 Through thy precepts I get understanding: therefore I hate every false way.

Ps 119:113 I hate *vain* thoughts: but thy law do I love.

Pr 8:7 For my mouth shall speak truth; and wickedness *is* an abomination to my lips.

Pr 8:13 The fear of the LORD *is* to hate evil: pride and the evil way, and the froward mouth, do I hate.

Pr 13:5 A righteous *man* hateth lying: but a wicked *man* is loathsome, and cometh to shame.

Am 5:15 Hate the evil, and love the good, and establish judgment in the gate: it may be that the LORD God of hosts will be gracious unto the remnant of Joseph.

Hab 1:3 Why dost thou shew me iniquity, and cause *me* to behold grievance? for spoiling and violence *are* before me: and there are *that* raise up strife and contention.

Ro 7:15 For that which I do I allow not: for what I would, that do I not; but what I hate, that do I.

2 Pe 2:7–8 And delivered just Lot, vexed with the filthy conversation of the wicked:

(For that righteous man dwelling among them, in seeing and hearing, vexed *his* righteous soul from day to day with *their* unlawful deeds;)

g. Forbidden

Ex 20:20 And Moses said unto the people, Fear not: for God is come to prove you, and that his fear may be before your faces, that ye sin not.

1 S 14:34 And Saul said, Disperse yourselves among the people, and say unto them, Bring me hither every man his ox, and every man his sheep, and slay *them* here, and eat; and sin not against the LORD in eating with the blood. And all the people brought every man his ox with him that night, and slew *them* there.

Jb 36:10 He openeth also their ear to discipline, and commandeth that they return from iniquity.

Ps 4:4 Stand in awe, and sin not: commune with your own heart upon your bed, and be still. Selah.

Ec 7:17 Be not over much wicked, neither be thou foolish: why shouldest thou die before thy time?

Is 1:16 Wash you, make you clean; put away the evil of your doings from before mine eyes; cease to do evil;

Je 22:3 Thus saith the LORD; Execute ye judgment and righteousness, and deliver the spoiled out of the hand of the oppressor: and do no wrong, do no violence to the stranger, the fatherless, nor the widow, neither shed innocent blood in this place.

Jn 5:14 Afterward Jesus findeth him in the temple, and said unto him, Behold, thou art made whole: sin no more, lest a worse thing come unto thee.

Jn 8:11 She said, No man, Lord. And Jesus said unto her, Neither do I condemn thee: go, and sin no more.

Ro 6:12 Let not sin therefore reign in your mortal body, that ye should obey it in the lusts thereof.

Ro 6:15 What then? shall we sin, because we are not under the law, but under grace? God forbid.

1 Co 15:34 Awake to righteousness, and sin not; for some have not the knowledge of God: I speak *this* to your shame.

1 Jn 2:1 My little children, these things write I unto you, that ye sin not. And if any man sin, we have an advocate with the Father, Jesus Christ the righteous:

1 Jn 3:8 He that committeth sin is of the devil; for the devil sinneth from the beginning. For this purpose the Son of God was manifested, that he might destroy the works of the devil.

h. Forgiven

2 S 12:13 And David said unto Nathan, I have sinned against the LORD. And Nathan said unto David, The LORD also hath put away thy sin; thou shalt not die.

Ps 32:5 I acknowledged my sin unto thee, and mine iniquity have I not hid. I said, I will confess my transgressions unto the LORD; and thou forgavest the iniquity of my sin. Selah.

Ps 78:38 But he, *being* full of compassion, forgave *their* iniquity, and destroyed *them* not: yea, many a time turned he his anger away, and did not stir up all his wrath.

Ps 85:2 Thou hast forgiven the iniquity of thy people, thou hast covered all their sin. Selah.

Ps 99:8 Thou answeredst them, O LORD our God: thou wast a God that forgavest them, though thou tookest vengeance of their inventions.

Ps 103:12 As far as the east is from the west, *so* far hath he removed our transgressions from us.

Is 38:17 Behold, for peace I had great bitterness: but thou hast in love to my soul *delivered it* from the pit of corruption: for thou hast cast all my sins behind thy back.

Is 43:25 I, *even* I, *am* he that blotteth out thy transgressions for mine own sake, and will not remember thy sins.

Is 44:22 I have blotted out, as a thick cloud, thy transgressions, and, as a cloud, thy sins: return unto me; for I have redeemed thee.

Mi 7:19 He will turn again, he will have compassion upon us; he will subdue our iniquities; and thou wilt cast all their sins into the depths of the sea.

Mt 9:2 And, behold, they brought to him a man sick of the palsy, lying on a bed: and Jesus seeing their faith said unto the sick of the palsy; Son, be of good cheer; thy sins be forgiven thee.

Mk 2:5 When Jesus, he said unto the sick of the palsy, Son, thy sins be forgiven thee.

Mk 4:12 That seeing they may see, and not perceive; and hearing they may hear, and not understand; lest at any time they should be converted, and *their* sins should be forgiven them.

Lu 5:20 And when he saw their faith, he said unto him, Man, thy sins are forgiven thee.

Lu 7:48 And he said unto her, Thy sins are forgiven.

Jn 8:11 She said, No man, Lord. And Jesus said unto her, Neither do I condemn thee: go, and sin no more.

Ep 4:32 And be ye kind one to another, tenderhearted, forgiving one another, even as God for Christ's sake hath forgiven you.

Col 2:13 And you, being dead in your sins and the uncircumcision of your flesh, hath he quickened together with him, having forgiven you all trespasses;

Col 3:13 Forbearing one another, and forgiving one another, if any man have a quarrel against any: even as Christ forgave you, so also *do* ye.

He 10:17 And their sins and iniquities will I remember no more.

1 Jn 2:12 I write unto you, little children, because your sins are forgiven you for his name's sake.

i. To Be Forsaken

Jb 11:14 If iniquity *be* in thine hand, put it far away, and let not wickedness dwell in thy tabernacles.

Jb 22:23 If thou return to the Almighty, thou shalt be built up, thou shalt put away iniquity far from thy tabernacles.

Pr 15:24 The way of life *is* above to the wise, that he may depart from hell beneath.

Pr 16:6 By mercy and truth iniquity is purged: and by the fear of the LORD *men* depart from evil.

Pr 28:13 He that covereth his sins shall not prosper: but whoso confesseth and forsaketh *them* shall have mercy.

Is 55:7 Let the wicked forsake his way, and the unrighteous man his thoughts: and let him return unto the LORD, and he will have mercy upon him; and to our God, for he will abundantly pardon.

Eze 18:27 Again, when the wicked *man* turneth away from his wickedness that he hath committed, and doeth that which is lawful and right, he shall save his soul alive.

Eze 18:31 Cast away from you all your transgressions, whereby ye have transgressed; and make you a new heart and a new spirit: for why will ye die, O house of Israel?

Eze 20:7 Then said I unto them, Cast ye away every man the abominations of his eyes, and defile not yourselves with the idols of Egypt: I *am* the LORD your God.

Eze 33:11 Say unto them, *As* I live, saith the Lord GOD, I have no pleasure in the death of the wicked; but that the wicked turn from his way and live: turn ye, turn ye from your evil ways; for why will ye die, O house of Israel?

Ho 2:2 Plead with your mother, plead: for she *is* not my wife, neither *am* I her husband: let her therefore put away her whoredoms out of her sight, and her adulteries from between her breasts;

Jona 3:8 But let man and beast be covered with sackcloth, and cry mightily unto God: yea, let them turn every one from his evil way, and from the violence that *is* in their hands.

Lu 15:19 And am no more worthy to be called thy son: make me as one of thy hired servants.

Ep 4:22 That ye put off concerning the former conversation the old man, which is corrupt according to the deceitful lusts;

Col 2:11 In whom also ye are circumcised with the circumcision made without hands, in putting off the body of the sins of the flesh by the circumcision of Christ:

2 Ti 2:19 Nevertheless the foundation of God standeth sure, having this seal, The Lord knoweth them that are his. And, Let every one that nameth the name of Christ depart from iniquity.

He 12:1 Wherefore seeing we also are compassed about with so great a cloud of witnesses, let us lay aside every weight, and the sin which doth so easily beset us, and let us run with patience the race that is set before us,

Ja 1:21 Wherefore lay apart all filthiness and superfluity of naughtiness, and receive with meekness the engrafted word, which is able to save your souls.

1 Pe 2:11 Dearly beloved, I beseech *you* as strangers and pilgrims, abstain from fleshly lusts, which war against the soul;

j. Inexcusable

Jn 15:22 If I had not come and spoken unto them, they had not had sin: but now they have no cloke for their sin.

Ro 1:20 For the invisible things of him from the creation of the world are clearly seen, being understood by the things that are made, *even* his eternal power and Godhead; so that they are without excuse:

Ro 2:1 Therefore thou art inexcusable, O man, whosoever thou art that judgest: for wherein thou judgest another, thou condemnest thyself; for thou that judgest doest the same things.

k. Loved by Humans

Jb 15:16 How much more abominable and filthy *is* man, which drinketh iniquity like water?

Jb 20:12 Though wickedness be sweet in his mouth, *though* he hide it under his tongue;

Ps 52:3 Thou lovest evil more than good; *and* lying rather than to speak righteousness. Selah.

Ps 62:4 They only consult to cast *him* down from his excellency: they delight in lies: they bless with their mouth, but they curse inwardly. Selah.

Pr 2:14 Who rejoice to do evil, *and* delight in the frowardness of the wicked;

Pr 5:14 I was almost in all evil in the midst of the congregation and assembly.

Is 5:18 Woe unto them that draw iniquity with cords of vanity, and sin as it were with a cart rope:

Je 5:31 The prophets prophesy falsely, and the priests bear rule by their means; and my people love *to have it* so: and what will ye do in the end thereof?

Je 14:10 Thus saith the LORD unto thee, thus have they loved to wander, they have not refrained their feet, therefore the LORD doth not accept them; he will now remember their iniquity, and visit their sins.

Mi 3:2 Who hate the good, and love the evil; who pluck off their skin from off them, and their flesh from off their bones;

2 Th 2:11–12 And for this cause God shall send them strong delusion, that they should believe a lie:

That they all might be damned who believed not the truth, but had pleasure in unrighteousness.

I. Hated by God

De 25:16 For all that do such things, *and* all that do unrighteously, *are* an abomination unto the LORD thy God.

2 S 11:27 And when the mourning was past, David sent and fetched her to his house, and she became his wife, and bare him a son. But the thing that David had done displeased the LORD.

Ps 5:4 For thou *art* not a God that hath pleasure in wickedness: neither shall evil dwell with thee.

Ps 11:5 The LORD trieth the righteous: but the wicked and him that loveth violence his soul hateth.

Ps 36:2 For he flattereth himself in his own eyes, until his iniquity be found to be hateful.

Ps 53:5 There were they in great fear, *where* no fear was: for God hath scattered the bones of him that encampeth *against* thee: thou hast put *them* to shame, because God hath despised them.

Ps 78:59 When God heard *this,* he was wroth, and greatly abhorred Israel:

Pr 6:16 These six *things* doth the LORD hate: yea, seven *are* an abomination unto him:

Pr 15:9 The way of the wicked *is* an abomination unto the LORD: but he loveth him that followeth after righteousness.

Pr 15:26 The thoughts of the wicked *are* an abomination to the LORD: but *the words* of the pure *are* pleasant words.

Is 1:14 Your new moons and your appointed feasts my soul hateth: they are a trouble unto me; I am weary to bear *them.*

Is 43:24 Thou hast bought me no sweet cane with money, neither hast thou filled me with the fat of thy sacrifices: but thou hast made me to serve with thy sins, thou hast wearied me with thine iniquities.

Is 61:8 For I the LORD love judgment, I hate robbery for burnt offering; and I will direct their work in truth, and I will make an everlasting covenant with them.

Eze 13:20 Wherefore thus saith the Lord GOD; Behold, I *am* against your pillows, wherewith ye there hunt the souls to make *them* fly, and I will tear them from your arms, and will let the souls go, *even* the souls that ye hunt to make *them* fly.

Hab 1:13 *Thou art* of purer eyes than to behold evil, and canst not look on iniquity: wherefore lookest thou upon them that deal treacherously, *and* holdest thy tongue when the wicked devoureth *the man that is* more righteous than he?

Zec 8:17 And let none of you imagine evil in your hearts against his neighbour; and love no false oath: for all these *are things* that I hate, saith the LORD.

Zec 11:8 Three shepherds also I cut off in one month; and my soul lothed them, and their soul also abhorred me.

Lu 16:15 And he said unto them, Ye are they which justify yourselves before men; but God knoweth your hearts: for that which is highly esteemed among men is abomination in the sight of God.

Re 2:6 But this thou hast, that thou hatest the deeds of the Nicolaitanes, which I also hate.

Re 2:15 So hast thou also them that hold the doctrine of the Nicolaitanes, which thing I hate.

Re 18:4 And I heard another voice from heaven, saying, Come out of her, my people, that ye be not partakers of her sins, and that ye receive not of her plagues.

m. Destructive

Nu 16:38 The censers of these sinners against their own souls, let them make them broad plates *for* a covering of the altar: for they offered them before the LORD, therefore they are hallowed: and they shall be a sign unto the children of Israel.

2 Chr 22:4 Wherefore he did evil in the sight of the LORD like the house of Ahab: for they were his counsellors after the death of his father to his destruction.

2 Chr 28:23 For he sacrificed unto the gods of Damascus, which smote him: and he said, Because the gods of the kings of Syria help them, *therefore* will I sacrifice to them, that they may help me. But they were the ruin of him, and of all Israel.

Jb 18:8 For he is cast into a net by his own feet, and he walketh upon a snare.

Jb 20:16 He shall suck the poison of asps: the viper's tongue shall slay him.

Jb 35:8 Thy wickedness *may hurt* a man as thou *art;* and thy righteousness *may profit* the son of man.

Ps 7:15 He made a pit, and digged it, and is fallen into the ditch *which* he made.

Ps 9:15 The heathen are sunk down in the pit *that* they made: in the net which they hid is their own foot taken.

Ps 34:21 Evil shall slay the wicked: and they that hate the righteous shall be desolate.

Ps 94:23 And he shall bring upon them their own iniquity, and shall cut them off in their own wickedness; *yea,* the LORD our God shall cut them off.

Ps 140:11 Let not an evil speaker be established in the earth: evil shall hunt the violent man to overthrow *him.*

Pr 1:18 And they lay wait for their *own* blood; they lurk privily for their *own* lives.

Pr 5:22 His own iniquities shall take the wicked himself, and he shall be holden with the cords of his sins.

Pr 6:27 Can a man take fire in his bosom, and his clothes not be burned?

Pr 7:23 Till a dart strike through his liver; as a bird hasteth to the snare, and knoweth not that it *is* for his life.

Pr 8:36 But he that sinneth against me wrongeth his own soul: all they that hate me love death.

Pr 11:3 The integrity of the upright shall guide them: but the perverseness of transgressors shall destroy them.

Pr 11:19 As righteousness *tendeth* to life: so he that pursueth evil *pursueth it* to his own death.

Pr 13:6 Righteousness keepeth *him that is* upright in the way: but wickedness overthroweth the sinner.

Pr 13:20 He that walketh with wise *men* shall be wise: but a companion of fools shall be destroyed.

Pr 18:7 A fool's mouth *is* his destruction, and his lips *are* the snare of his soul.

Pr 21:7 The robbery of the wicked shall destroy them; because they refuse to do judgment.

Pr 26:27 Whoso diggeth a pit shall fall therein: and he that rolleth a stone, it will return upon him.

Pr 29:24 Whoso is partner with a thief hateth his own soul: he heareth cursing, and bewrayeth *it* not.

Ec 7:25 I applied mine heart to know, and to search, and to seek out wisdom, and the reason *of things,* and to know the wickedness of folly, even of foolishness *and* madness:

Is 3:9 The shew of their countenance doth witness against them; and they declare their sin as Sodom, they hide *it* not. Woe unto their soul! for they have rewarded evil unto themselves.

Je 26:19 Did Hezekiah king of Judah and all Judah put him at all to death? did he not fear the LORD, and besought the LORD, and the LORD repented him of the evil which he had pronounced against them? Thus might we procure great evil against our souls.

Je 44:7 Therefore now thus saith the LORD, the God of hosts, the God of Israel; Wherefore commit ye *this* great evil against your souls, to cut off from you man and woman, child and suckling, out of Judah, to leave you none to remain;

Eze 7:5 Thus saith the Lord GOD; An evil, an only evil, behold, is come.

Eze 18:30 Therefore I will judge you, O house of Israel, every one according to his ways, saith the Lord GOD. Repent, and turn *yourselves* from all your transgressions; so iniquity shall not be your ruin.

Eze 31:13 Upon his ruin shall all the fowls of the heaven remain, and all the beasts of the field shall be upon his branches:

Eze 33:8 When I say unto the wicked, O wicked *man,* thou shalt surely die; if thou dost not speak to warn the wicked from his way, that wicked *man* shall die in his iniquity; but his blood will I require at thine hand.

Ho 4:6 My people are destroyed for lack of knowledge: because thou hast rejected knowledge, I will also reject thee, that thou shalt be no priest to me: seeing thou hast forgotten the law of thy God, I will also forget thy children.

Ho 13:9 O Israel, thou hast destroyed thyself; but in me *is* thine help.

Jona 2:8 They that observe lying vanities forsake their own mercy.

Hab 2:10 Thou hast consulted shame to thy house by cutting off many people, and hast sinned *against* thy soul.

Zec 5:4 I will bring it forth, saith the LORD of hosts, and it shall enter into the house of the thief, and into the house of him that sweareth falsely by my name: and it shall remain in the midst of his house, and shall consume it with the timber thereof and the stones thereof.

Mt 7:13 Enter ye in at the strait gate: for wide *is* the gate, and broad *is* the way, that leadeth to destruction, and many there be which go in thereat:

Mk 5:5 And always, night and day, he was in the mountains, and in the tombs, crying, and cutting himself with stones.

Ro 7:11 For sin, taking occasion by the commandment, deceived me, and by it slew *me.*

Ro 7:13 Was then that which is good made death unto me? God forbid. But sin, that it might appear sin, working death in me by that which is good; that sin by the commandment might become exceeding sinful.

Ph 3:19 Whose end *is* destruction, whose God *is their* belly, and *whose* glory *is* in their shame, who mind earthly things.)

1 Ti 6:9 But they that will be rich fall into temptation and a snare, and *into* many foolish and hurtful lusts, which drown men in destruction and perdition.

n. Allurements

Ge 3:6 And when the woman saw that the tree *was* good for food, and that it *was* pleasant to the eyes, and a tree to be desired to make *one* wise, she took of the fruit thereof, and did eat, and gave also unto her husband with her; and he did eat.

Jos 7:21 When I saw among the spoils a goodly Babylonish garment, and two hundred shekels of silver, and a wedge of gold of fifty shekels weight, then I coveted them, and took them; and, behold, they *are* hid in the earth in the midst of my tent, and the silver under it.

Jud 14:3 Then his father and his mother said unto him, *Is there* never a woman among the daughters of thy brethren, or among all my people, that thou goest to take a wife of the uncircumcised Philistines? And Samson said unto his father, Get her for me; for she pleaseth me well.

2 K 18:32 Until I come and take you away to a land like your own land, a land of corn and wine, a land of bread and vineyards, a land of oil olive and of honey, that ye may live, and not die: and hearken not unto Hezekiah, when he persuadeth you, saying, The LORD will deliver us.

Pr 9:17 Stolen waters are sweet, and bread *eaten* in secret is pleasant.

Pr 14:12 There is a way which seemeth right unto a man, but the end thereof *are* the ways of death.

Ja 1:14 But every man is tempted, when he is drawn away of his own lust, and enticed.

2 Pe 2:18 For when they speak great swelling *words* of vanity, they allure through the lusts of the flesh, *through much* wantonness, those that were clean escaped from them who live in error.

11. Called Works of Darkness

Jb 24:14 The murderer rising with the light killeth the poor and needy, and in the night is as a thief.

Pr 7:8–9 Passing through the street near her corner; and he went the way to her house,

In the twilight, in the evening, in the black and dark night:

Jn 3:20 For every one that doeth evil hateth the light, neither cometh to the light, lest his deeds should be reproved.

Ro 13:12 The night is far spent, the day is at hand: let us therefore cast off the works of darkness, and let us put on the armour of light.

1 Co 4:5 Therefore judge nothing before the time, until the Lord come, who both will bring to light the hidden things of darkness, and will make manifest the counsels of the hearts: and then shall every man have praise of God.

Ep 5:11 And have no fellowship with the unfruitful works of darkness, but rather reprove *them.*

1 Th 5:7 For they that sleep sleep in the night; and they that be drunken are drunken in the night.

12. Done in Ignorance

Le 4:2 Speak unto the children of Israel, saying, If a soul shall sin through ignorance against any of the commandments of the LORD *concerning*

things which ought not to be done, and shall do against any of them:

Le 5:17 And if a soul sin, and commit any of these things which are forbidden to be done by the commandments of the LORD; though he wist *it* not, yet is he guilty, and shall bear his iniquity.

De 19:4 And this *is* the case of the slayer, which shall flee thither, that he may live: Whoso killeth his neighbour ignorantly, whom he hated not in time past;

Lu 12:48 But he that knew not, and did commit things worthy of stripes, shall be beaten with few *stripes.* For unto whomsoever much is given, of him shall be much required: and to whom men have committed much, of him they will ask the more.

Ac 3:17 And now, brethren, I wot that through ignorance ye did *it*, as *did* also your rulers.

1 Ti 1:13 Who was before a blasphemer, and a persecutor, and injurious: but I obtained mercy, because I did *it* ignorantly in unbelief.

13. Done by Omission

Ps 36:3 The words of his mouth *are* iniquity and deceit: he hath left off to be wise, *and* to do good.

Mt 23:23 Woe unto you, scribes and Pharisees, hypocrites! for ye pay tithe of mint and anise and cummin, and have omitted the weightier *matters* of the law, judgment, mercy, and faith: these ought ye to have done, and not to leave the other undone.

Mt 25:45 Then shall he answer them, saying, Verily I say unto you, Inasmuch as ye did *it* not to one of the least of these, ye did *it* not to me.

Lu 11:42 But woe unto you, Pharisees! for ye tithe mint and rue and all manner of herbs, and pass over judgment and the love of God: these ought ye to have done, and not to leave the other undone.

Lu 12:47 And that servant, which knew his lord's will, and prepared not *himself,* neither did according to his will, shall be beaten with many *stripes.*

Ja 4:17 Therefore to him that knoweth to do good, and doeth *it* not, to him it is sin.

14. Deliverance through Christ

Ps 103:12 As far as the east is from the west, *so* far hath he removed our transgressions from us.

Eze 33:10 Therefore, O thou son of man, speak unto the house of Israel; Thus ye speak, saying, If our transgressions and our sins *be* upon us, and we pine away in them, how should we then live?

1 Co 15:3 For I delivered unto you first of all that which I also received, how that Christ died for our sins according to the scriptures;

Ga 1:4 Who gave himself for our sins, that he might deliver us from this present evil world, according to the will of God and our Father:

1 Pe 2:24 Who his own self bare our sins in his own body on the tree, that we, being dead to sins, should live unto righteousness: by whose stripes ye were healed.

1 Jn 2:2 And he is the propitiation for our sins: and not for ours only, but also for *the sins of* the whole world.

1 Jn 4:10 Herein is love, not that we loved God, but that he loved us, and sent his Son *to be* the propitiation for our sins.

Re 1:5 And from Jesus Christ, *who is* the faithful witness, *and* the first begotten of the dead, and the prince of the kings of the earth. Unto him that loved us, and washed us from our sins in his own blood,

a. By Coming to Earth

Ps 72:13 He shall spare the poor and needy, and shall save the souls of the needy.

Mt 1:21 And she shall bring forth a son, and thou shalt call his name JESUS: for he shall save his people from their sins.

Mt 18:11 For the Son of man is come to save that which was lost.

Lu 2:11 For unto you is born this day in the city of David a Saviour, which is Christ the Lord.

Lu 2:34 And Simeon blessed them, and said unto Mary his mother, Behold, this *child* is set for the fall and rising again of many in Israel; and for a sign which shall be spoken against;

Lu 5:20 And when he saw their faith, he said unto him, Man, thy sins are forgiven thee.

Lu 7:47 Wherefore I say unto thee, Her sins, which are many, are forgiven; for she loved much: but to whom little is forgiven, *the same* loveth little.

Lu 9:56 For the Son of man is not come to destroy men's lives, but to save *them.* And they went to another village.

Lu 19:10 For the Son of man is come to seek and to save that which was lost.

Jn 3:17 For God sent not his Son into the world to condemn the world; but that the world through him might be saved.

Jn 4:42 And said unto the woman, Now we believe, not because of thy saying: for we have heard *him* ourselves, and know that this is indeed the Christ, the Saviour of the world.

Jn 5:34 But I receive not testimony from man: but these things I say, that ye might be saved.

Jn 12:47 And if any man hear my words, and believe not, I judge him not: for I came not to judge the world, but to save the world.

Ac 3:26 Unto you first God, having raised up his Son Jesus, sent him to bless you, in turning away every one of you from his iniquities.

Ac 5:31 Him hath God exalted with his right hand *to be* a Prince and a Saviour, for to give repentance to Israel, and forgiveness of sins.

Ac 13:23 Of this man's seed hath God according to *his* promise raised unto Israel a Saviour, Jesus:

Ro 5:10 For if, when we were enemies, we were reconciled to God by the death of his Son, much more, being reconciled, we shall be saved by his life.

Ro 8:3 For what the law could not do, in that it was weak through the flesh, God sending his own Son in the likeness of sinful flesh, and for sin, condemned sin in the flesh:

Ro 11:26 And so all Israel shall be saved: as it is written, There shall come out of Sion the Deliverer, and shall turn away ungodliness from Jacob:

Ga 3:16 Now to Abraham and his seed were the promises made. He saith not, And to seeds, as of many; but as of one, And to thy seed, which is Christ.

Ep 5:23 For the husband is the head of the wife, even as Christ is the head of the church: and he is the saviour of the body.

Ph 3:20 For our conversation is in heaven; from whence also we look for the Saviour, the Lord Jesus Christ:

1 Th 5:9 For God hath not appointed us to wrath, but to obtain salvation by our Lord Jesus Christ,

1 Ti 1:15 This *is* a faithful saying, and worthy of all acceptation, that Christ Jesus came into the world to save sinners; of whom I am chief.

2 Ti 1:10 But is now made manifest by the appearing of our Saviour Jesus Christ, who hath abolished death, and hath brought life and immortality to light through the gospel:

Tit 1:4 To Titus, *mine* own son after the common faith: Grace, mercy, *and* peace, from God the Father and the Lord Jesus Christ our Saviour.

Tit 2:13 Looking for that blessed hope, and the glorious appearing of the great God and our Saviour Jesus Christ;

Tit 3:6 Which he shed on us abundantly through Jesus Christ our Saviour;

He 2:10 For it became him, for whom *are* all things, and by whom *are* all things, in bringing many sons unto glory, to make the captain of their salvation perfect through sufferings.

He 7:25 Wherefore he is able also to save them to the uttermost that come unto God by him, seeing he ever liveth to make intercession for them.

2 Pe 1:1 Simon Peter, a servant and an apostle of Jesus Christ, to them that have obtained like precious faith with us through the righteousness of God and our Saviour Jesus Christ:

2 Pe 3:18 But grow in grace, and *in* the knowledge of our Lord and Saviour Jesus Christ. To him *be* glory both now and for ever. Amen.

1 Jn 3:5 And ye know that he was manifested to take away our sins; and in him is no sin.

1 Jn 4:14 And we have seen and do testify that the Father sent the Son *to be* the Saviour of the world.

b. By Becoming Our Substitute

Ps 69:9 For the zeal of thine house hath eaten me up; and the reproaches of them that reproached thee are fallen upon me.

Is 53:5 But he *was* wounded for our transgressions, *he was* bruised for our iniquities: the chastisement of our peace *was* upon him; and with his stripes we are healed.

Is 53:11 He shall see of the travail of his soul, *and* shall be satisfied: by his knowledge shall my righteous servant justify many; for he shall bear their iniquities.

Jn 10:15 As the Father knoweth me, even so know I the Father: and I lay down my life for the sheep.

Ro 4:25 Who was delivered for our offences, and was raised again for our justification.

Ro 5:8 But God commendeth his love toward us, in that, while we were yet sinners, Christ died for us.

Ro 15:3 For even Christ pleased not himself; but, as it is written, The reproaches of them that reproached thee fell on me.

1 Co 15:3 For I delivered unto you first of all that which I also received, how that Christ died for our sins according to the scriptures;

2 Co 5:14 For the love of Christ constraineth us; because we thus judge, that if one died for all, then were all dead:

2 Co 5:21 For he hath made him *to be* sin for us, who knew no sin; that we might be made the righteousness of God in him.

Ga 3:13 Christ hath redeemed us from the curse of the law, being made a curse for us: for it is written, Cursed *is* every one that hangeth on a tree:

He 2:9 But we see Jesus, who was made a little lower than the angels for the suffering of death, crowned with glory and honour; that he by the grace of God should taste death for every man.

He 9:28 So Christ was once offered to bear the sins of many; and unto them that look for him shall he appear the second time without sin unto salvation.

1 Pe 2:24 Who his own self bare our sins in his own body on the tree, that we, being dead to sins, should live unto righteousness: by whose stripes ye were healed.

1 Pe 3:18 For Christ also hath once suffered for sins, the just for the unjust, that he might bring us to God, being put to death in the flesh, but quickened by the Spirit:

c. By Bearing the Sins of Many

Ex 28:38 And it shall be upon Aaron's forehead, that Aaron may bear the iniquity of the holy things, which the children of Israel shall hallow in all their holy gifts; and it shall be always upon his forehead, that they may be accepted before the LORD.

Le 10:17 Wherefore have ye not eaten the sin offering in the holy place, seeing it *is* most holy, and *God* hath given it you to bear the iniquity of the congregation, to make atonement for them before the LORD?

Le 16:22 And the goat shall bear upon him all their iniquities unto a land not inhabited: and he shall let go the goat in the wilderness.

Nu 18:1 And the LORD said unto Aaron, Thou and thy sons and thy father's house with thee shall bear the iniquity of the sanctuary: and thou and thy sons with thee shall bear the iniquity of your priesthood.

Is 53:6 All we like sheep have gone astray; we have turned every one to his own way; and the LORD hath laid on him the iniquity of us all.

Is 53:12 Therefore will I divide him *a portion* with the great, and he shall divide the spoil with the strong; because he hath poured out his soul unto death: and he was numbered with the transgressors; and he bare the sin of many, and made intercession for the transgressors.

Eze 4:5 For I have laid upon thee the years of their iniquity, according to the number of the days, three hundred and ninety days: so shalt thou bear the iniquity of the house of Israel.

Mt 27:46 And about the ninth hour Jesus cried with a loud voice, saying, Eli, Eli, lama sabachthani? that is to say, My God, my God, why hast thou forsaken me?

Mk 15:34 And at the ninth hour Jesus cried with a loud voice, saying, Eloi, Eloi, lama sabachthani? which is, being interpreted, My God, my God, why hast thou forsaken me?

Lu 22:37 For I say unto you, that this that is written must yet be accomplished in me, And he was reckoned among the transgressors: for the things concerning me have an end.

Jn 1:29 The next day John seeth Jesus coming unto him, and saith, Behold the Lamb of God, which taketh away the sin of the world.

2 Co 5:21 For he hath made him *to be* sin for us, who knew no sin; that we might be made the righteousness of God in him.

Ga 3:13 Christ hath redeemed us from the curse of the law, being made a curse for us: for it is written, Cursed *is* every one that hangeth on a tree:

He 9:28 So Christ was once offered to bear the sins of many; and unto them that look for him shall he appear the second time without sin unto salvation.

He 10:14 For by one offering he hath perfected for ever them that are sanctified.

1 Pe 2:24 Who his own self bare our sins in his own body on the tree, that we, being dead to sins, should live unto righteousness: by whose stripes ye were healed.

1 Jn 3:5 And ye know that he was manifested to take away our sins; and in him is no sin.

d. By Carrying the Burdens of Humanity

Ge 22:6 And Abraham took the wood of the burnt offering, and laid *it* upon

Isaac his son; and he took the fire in his hand, and a knife; and they went both of them together.

Ps 55:22 Cast thy burden upon the LORD, and he shall sustain thee: he shall never suffer the righteous to be moved.

Is 53:4 Surely he hath borne our griefs, and carried our sorrows: yet we did esteem him stricken, smitten of God, and afflicted.

Mt 4:24 And his fame went throughout all Syria: and they brought unto him all sick people that were taken with divers diseases and torments, and those which were possessed with devils, and those which were lunatick, and those that had the palsy; and he healed them.

Mt 8:17 That it might be fulfilled which was spoken by Esaias the prophet, saying, Himself took our infirmities, and bare *our* sicknesses.

Mt 11:28 Come unto me, all *ye* that labour and are heavy laden, and I will give you rest.

Mt 14:35 And when the men of that place had knowledge of him, they sent out into all that country round about, and brought unto him all that were diseased;

Mt 15:30 And great multitudes came unto him, having with them *those that were* lame, blind, dumb, maimed, and many others, and cast them down at Jesus' feet; and he healed them:

Mk 1:32 And at even, when the sun did set, they brought unto him all that were diseased, and them that were possessed with devils.

Mk 6:55 And ran through that whole region round about, and began to carry about in beds those that were sick, where they heard he was.

Mk 8:2 I have compassion on the multitude, because they have now been with me three days, and have nothing to eat:

Mk 9:19 He answereth him, and saith, O faithless generation, how long shall I be with you? how long shall I suffer you? bring him unto me.

Lu 4:40 Now when the sun was setting, all they that had any sick with divers diseases brought them unto him; and he laid his hands on every one of them, and healed them.

Lu 5:15 But so much the more went there a fame abroad of him: and great multitudes came together to hear, and to be healed by him of their infirmities.

Lu 6:17 And he came down with them, and stood in the plain, and the company of his disciples, and a great multitude of people out of all Judaea and Jerusalem, and from the sea coast of Tyre and Sidon, which came to hear him, and to be healed of their diseases;

Lu 7:21 And in that same hour he cured many of *their* infirmities and plagues, and of evil spirits; and unto many *that were* blind he gave sight.

Jn 11:38 Jesus therefore again groaning in himself cometh to the grave. It was a cave, and a stone lay upon it.

Jn 19:17 And he bearing his cross went forth into a place called *the place* of a skull, which is called in the Hebrew Golgotha:

e. By Becoming the Mediator

Je 18:20 Shall evil be recompensed for good? for they have digged a pit for my soul. Remember that I stood before thee to speak good for them, *and* to turn away thy wrath from them.

Jn 14:6 Jesus saith unto him, I am the way, the truth, and the life: no man cometh unto the Father, but by me.

Ep 2:18 For through him we both have access by one Spirit unto the Father.

1 Ti 2:5 For *there is* one God, and one mediator between God and men, the man Christ Jesus;

He 8:6 But now hath he obtained a more excellent ministry, by how much also he is the mediator of a better covenant, which was established upon better promises.

He 9:15 And for this cause he is the mediator of the new testament, that by means of death, for the redemption of the transgressions *that were* under the first testament, they which are called might receive the promise of eternal inheritance.

He 9:24 For Christ is not entered into the holy places made with hands, *which are* the figures of the true; but into heaven itself, now to appear in the presence of God for us:

He 12:24 And to Jesus the mediator of the new covenant, and to the blood of sprinkling, that speaketh better things than *that of* Abel.

1 Jn 2:1 My little children, these things write I unto you, that ye sin not. And if any man sin, we have an advocate with the Father, Jesus Christ the righteous:

f. By Being the Lamb

Is 53:7 He was oppressed, and he was afflicted, yet he opened not his mouth: he is brought as a lamb to the slaughter, and as a sheep before her shearers is dumb, so he openeth not his mouth.

Is 53:10 Yet it pleased the LORD to bruise him; he hath put *him* to grief: when thou shalt make his soul an offering for sin, he shall see *his* seed, he shall prolong *his* days, and the pleasure of the LORD shall prosper in his hand.

Jn 1:29 The next day John seeth Jesus coming unto him, and saith, Behold the Lamb of God, which taketh away the sin of the world.

Jn 1:36 And looking upon Jesus as he walked, he saith, Behold the Lamb of God!

Ac 8:32 The place of the scripture which he read was this, He was led as a sheep to the slaughter; and like a lamb dumb before his shearer, so opened he not his mouth:

1 Co 5:7 Purge out therefore the old leaven, that ye may be a new lump, as ye are unleavened. For even Christ our passover is sacrificed for us:

1 Pe 1:19 But with the precious blood of Christ, as of a lamb without blemish and without spot:

Re 5:6 And I beheld, and, lo, in the midst of the throne and of the four beasts, and in the midst of the elders, stood a Lamb as it had been slain, having seven horns and seven eyes, which are the seven Spirits of God sent forth into all the earth.

Re 5:12 Saying with a loud voice, Worthy is the Lamb that was slain to receive power, and riches, and wisdom, and strength, and honour, and glory, and blessing.

Re 6:1 And I saw when the Lamb opened one of the seals, and I heard, as it were the noise of thunder, one of the four beasts saying, Come and see.

Re 6:16 And said to the mountains and rocks, Fall on us, and hide us from the face of him that sitteth on the throne, and from the wrath of the Lamb:

Re 7:9 After this I beheld, and, lo, a great multitude, which no man could number, of all nations, and kindreds, and people, and tongues, stood before the throne, and before the Lamb, clothed with white robes, and palms in their hands;

Re 7:17 For the Lamb which is in the midst of the throne shall feed them, and shall lead them unto living fountains of waters: and God shall wipe away all tears from their eyes.

Re 12:11 And they overcame him by the blood of the Lamb, and by the word of their testimony; and they loved not their lives unto the death.

Re 13:8 And all that dwell upon the earth shall worship him, whose names are not written in the book of life of the Lamb slain from the foundation of the world.

Re 14:1 And I looked, and, lo, a Lamb stood on the mount Sion, and with him an hundred and forty *and* four thousand, having his Father's name written in their foreheads.

Re 14:10 The same shall drink of the wine of the wrath of God, which is poured out without mixture into the cup of his indignation; and he shall be tormented with fire and brimstone in the presence of the holy angels, and in the presence of the Lamb:

Re 15:3 And they sing the song of Moses the servant of God, and the song of the Lamb, saying, Great and marvellous *are* thy works, Lord God Almighty; just and true *are* thy ways, thou King of saints.

Re 17:14 These shall make war with the Lamb, and the Lamb shall overcome them: for he is Lord of lords, and King of kings: and they that are with him *are* called, and chosen, and faithful.

Re 19:7 Let us be glad and rejoice, and give honour to him: for the marriage of the Lamb is come, and his wife hath made herself ready.

Re 19:9 And he saith unto me, Write, Blessed *are* they which are called unto the marriage supper of the Lamb. And he saith unto me, These are the true sayings of God.

Re 21:9 And there came unto me one of the seven angels which had the seven vials full of the seven last plagues, and talked with me, saying, Come hither, I will shew thee the bride, the Lamb's wife.

Re 21:14 And the wall of the city had twelve foundations, and in them the names of the twelve apostles of the Lamb.

Re 21:22 And I saw no temple therein: for the Lord God Almighty and the Lamb are the temple of it.

Re 22:1 And he shewed me a pure river of water of life, clear as crystal, proceeding out of the throne of God and of the Lamb.

g. By Offering Himself as a Sacrifice

Is 53:4 Surely he hath borne our griefs, and carried our sorrows: yet we did esteem him stricken, smitten of God, and afflicted.

Mt 20:28 Even as the Son of man came not to be ministered unto, but to minister, and to give his life a ransom for many.

Mt 27:42 He saved others; himself he cannot save. If he be the King of Israel, let him now come down from the cross, and we will believe him.

Mk 10:45 For even the Son of man came not to be ministered unto, but to minister, and to give his life a ransom for many.

Lu 22:19 And he took bread, and gave thanks, and brake *it,* and gave unto them, saying, This is my body which is given for you: this do in remembrance of me.

Jn 1:29 The next day John seeth Jesus coming unto him, and saith, Behold the Lamb of God, which taketh away the sin of the world.

Jn 6:51 I am the living bread which came down from heaven: if any man eat of this bread, he shall live for ever: and the bread that I will give is my flesh, which I will give for the life of the world.

Jn 10:11 I am the good shepherd: the good shepherd giveth his life for the sheep.

Jn 10:15 As the Father knoweth me, even so know I the Father: and I lay down my life for the sheep.

Jn 10:17 Therefore doth my Father love me, because I lay down my life, that I might take it again.

Jn 11:50 Nor consider that it is expedient for us, that one man should die for the people, and that the whole nation perish not.

Jn 15:13 Greater love hath no man than this, that a man lay down his life for his friends.

Jn 18:14 Now Caiaphas was he, which gave counsel to the Jews, that it was expedient that one man should die for the people.

Ro 5:8 But God commendeth his love toward us, in that, while we were yet sinners, Christ died for us.

1 Co 5:7 Purge out therefore the old leaven, that ye may be a new lump, as ye are unleavened. For even Christ our passover is sacrificed for us:

1 Co 8:11 And through thy knowledge shall the weak brother perish, for whom Christ died?

2 Co 5:15 And *that* he died for all, that they which live should not henceforth live unto themselves, but unto him which died for them, and rose again.

2 Co 8:9 For ye know the grace of our Lord Jesus Christ, that, though he was rich, yet for your sakes he became poor, that ye through his poverty might be rich.

Ga 1:4 Who gave himself for our sins, that he might deliver us from this present evil world, according to the will of God and our Father:

Ga 2:20 I am crucified with Christ: nevertheless I live; yet not I, but Christ liveth in me: and the life which I now live in the flesh I live by the faith of the Son of God, who loved me, and gave himself for me.

He 9:26 For then must he often have suffered since the foundation of the world: but now once in the end of the world hath he appeared to put away sin by the sacrifice of himself.

Ep 5:2 And walk in love, as Christ also hath loved us, and hath given himself for us an offering and a sacrifice to God for a sweetsmelling savour.

Ep 5:25 Husbands, love your wives, even as Christ also loved the church, and gave himself for it;

1 Ti 2:6 Who gave himself a ransom for all, to be testified in due time.

Tit 2:14 Who gave himself for us, that he might redeem us from all iniquity, and purify unto himself a peculiar people, zealous of good works.

He 7:27 Who needeth not daily, as those high priests, to offer up sacrifice, first for his own sins, and then for the people's: for this he did once, when he offered up himself.

He 9:14 How much more shall the blood of Christ, who through the eternal Spirit offered himself without spot to God, purge your conscience from dead works to serve the living God?

He 9:26 For then must he often have suffered since the foundation of the world: but now once in the end of the world hath he appeared to put away sin by the sacrifice of himself.

He 10:12 But this man, after he had offered one sacrifice for sins for ever, sat down on the right hand of God;

1 Pe 3:18 For Christ also hath once suffered for sins, the just for the unjust, that he might bring us to God, being put to death in the flesh, but quickened by the Spirit:

1 Jn 3:16 Hereby perceive we the love *of God*, because he laid down his life for us: and we ought to lay down *our* lives for the brethren.

Re 1:5 And from Jesus Christ, *who is* the faithful witness, *and* the first begotten of the dead, and the prince of the kings of the earth. Unto him that loved us, and washed us from our sins in his own blood,

h. By Suffering and Dying to Redeem the Race

Is 53:8 He was taken from prison and from judgment: and who shall declare his generation? for he was cut off out of the land of the living: for the transgression of my people was he stricken.

Is 53:12 Therefore will I divide him *a portion* with the great, and he shall divide the spoil with the strong; because he hath poured out his soul unto death: and he was numbered with the transgressors; and he bare the sin of many, and made intercession for the transgressors.

Da 9:26 And after threescore and two weeks shall Messiah be cut off, but not for himself: and the people of the prince that shall come shall destroy the city and the sanctuary; and the end thereof *shall be* with a flood, and unto the end of the war desolations are determined.

Mt 16:21 From that time forth began Jesus to shew unto his disciples, how that he must go unto Jerusalem, and suffer many things of the elders and chief priests and scribes, and be killed, and be raised again the third day.

Mt 17:23 And they shall kill him, and the third day he shall be raised again. And they were exceeding sorry.

Mt 21:39 And they caught him, and cast *him* out of the vineyard, and slew *him.*

Mt 26:42 He went away again the second time, and prayed, saying, O my Father, if this cup may not pass away from me, except I drink it, thy will be done.

Mt 27:50 Jesus, when he had cried again with a loud voice, yielded up the ghost.

Mk 8:31 And he began to teach them, that the Son of man must suffer many things, and be rejected of the elders, and *of* the chief priests, and scribes, and be killed, and after three days rise again.

Mk 9:31 For he taught his disciples, and said unto them, The Son of man is delivered into the hands of men, and they shall kill him; and after that he is killed, he shall rise the third day.

Mk 10:45 For even the Son of man came not to be ministered unto, but to minister, and to give his life a ransom for many.

Mk 12:8 And they took him, and killed *him,* and cast *him* out of the vineyard.

Mk 14:1 After two days was *the feast of* the passover, and of unleavened bread: and the chief priests and the scribes sought how they might take him by craft, and put *him* to death.

Mk 15:37 And Jesus cried with a loud voice, and gave up the ghost.

Lu 9:22 Saying, The Son of man must suffer many things, and be rejected of the elders and chief priests and scribes, and be slain, and be raised the third day.

Lu 9:31 Who appeared in glory, and spake of his decease which he should accomplish at Jerusalem.

Lu 23:46 And when Jesus had cried with a loud voice, he said, Father, into thy hands I commend my spirit: and having said thus, he gave up the ghost.

Jn 10:11 I am the good shepherd: the good shepherd giveth his life for the sheep.

Jn 11:51 And this spake he not of himself: but being high priest that year, he prophesied that Jesus should die for that nation;

Jn 12:23-24 And Jesus answered them, saying, The hour is come, that the Son of man should be glorified.

Verily, verily, I say unto you, Except a corn of wheat fall into the ground and die, it abideth alone: but if it die, it bringeth forth much fruit.

Jn 12:33 This he said, signifying what death he should die.

Jn 19:30 When Jesus therefore had received the vinegar, he said, It is finished: and he bowed his head, and gave up the ghost.

Ac 8:33 In his humiliation his judgment was taken away: and who shall declare his generation? for his life is taken from the earth.

Ac 10:39 And we are witnesses of all things which he did both in the land of the Jews, and in Jerusalem; whom they slew and hanged on a tree:

Ro 4:25 Who was delivered for our offences, and was raised again for our justification.

Ro 5:6 For when we were yet without strength, in due time Christ died for the ungodly.

Ro 8:34 Who *is* he that condemneth? *It is* Christ that died, yea rather, that is risen again, who is even at the right hand of God, who also maketh intercession for us.

Ro 14:9 For to this end Christ both died, and rose, and revived, that he might be Lord both of the dead and living.

Ro 14:15 But if thy brother be grieved with *thy* meat, now walkest thou not charitably. Destroy not him with thy meat, for whom Christ died.

1 Co 11:26 For as often as ye eat this bread, and drink *this* cup, ye do shew the Lord's death till he come.

1 Co 15:3 For I delivered unto you first of all that which I also received, how that Christ died for our sins according to the scriptures;

2 Co 4:10 Always bearing about in the body the dying of the Lord Jesus, that the life also of Jesus might be made manifest in our body.

2 Co 5:15 And *that* he died for all, that they which live should not henceforth live unto themselves, but unto him which died for them, and rose again.

Ga 3:1 O foolish Galatians, who hath bewitched you, that ye should not obey the truth, before whose eyes Jesus Christ hath been evidently set forth, crucified among you?

Ph 2:8 And being found in fashion as a man, he humbled himself, and became obedient unto death, even the death of the cross.

Col 1:22 In the body of his flesh through death, to present you holy and unblameable and unreproveable in his sight:

1 Th 5:10 Who died for us, that, whether we wake or sleep, we should live together with him.

He 2:9 But we see Jesus, who was made a little lower than the angels for the suffering of death, crowned with glory and honour; that he by the grace of God should taste death for every man.

He 7:27 Who needeth not daily, as those high priests, to offer up sacrifice, first for his own sins, and then for the people's: for this he did once, when he offered up himself.

He 9:15 And for this cause he is the mediator of the new testament, that by means of death, for the redemption of the transgressions *that were* under the first testament, they which are called might receive the promise of eternal inheritance.

He 10:10 By the which will we are sanctified through the offering of the body of Jesus Christ once *for all.*

He 12:2 Looking unto Jesus the author and finisher of *our* faith; who for the joy that was set before him endured the cross, despising the shame, and is set down at the right hand of the throne of God.

1 Pe 3:18 For Christ also hath once suffered for sins, the just for the unjust, that he might bring us to God, being put to death in the flesh, but quickened by the Spirit:

1 Jn 3:16 Hereby perceive we the love *of God,* because he laid down his life for us: and we ought to lay down *our* lives for the brethren.

Re 2:8 And unto the angel of the church in Smyrna write; These things saith the first and the last, which was dead, and is alive;

Re 5:6 And I beheld, and, lo, in the midst of the throne and of the four beasts, and in the midst of the elders, stood a Lamb as it had been slain, having seven horns and seven eyes, which are the seven Spirits of God sent forth into all the earth.

Re 5:9 And they sung a new song, saying, Thou art worthy to take the book, and to open the seals thereof: for thou wast slain, and hast redeemed us to God by thy blood out of every kindred, and tongue, and people, and nation;

Re 5:12 Saying with a loud voice, Worthy is the Lamb that was slain to receive power, and riches, and wisdom, and strength, and honour, and glory, and blessing.

i. By Being Indispensable

THE ONLY INTERCESSOR

Is 59:16 And he saw that *there was* no man, and wondered that *there was* no intercessor: therefore his arm brought salvation unto him; and his righteousness, it sustained him.

THE ONLY REMEDY

Jn 3:14–15 And as Moses lifted up the serpent in the wilderness, even so must the Son of man be lifted up:

That whosoever believeth in him should not perish, but have eternal life.

THE ONLY NOURISHMENT

Jn 6:35 And Jesus said unto them, I am the bread of life: he that cometh to me shall never hunger; and he that believeth on me shall never thirst.

THE ONLY SOURCE OF TRUTH

Jn 6:67–68 Then said Jesus unto the twelve, Will ye also go away?

Then Simon Peter answered him, Lord, to whom shall we go? thou hast the words of eternal life.

THE ONLY SAVIOR

Ac 4:12 Neither is there salvation in any other: for there is none other name under heaven given among men, whereby we must be saved.

THE ONLY FOUNDATION

1 Co 3:11 For other foundation can no man lay than that is laid, which is Jesus Christ.

See **EVIL, REDEMPTION, SAVIOR, SALVATION, WICKED**

SINAI, *in the peninsula east of the Red Sea*

1. Mount

See **MOUNTAINS AND HILLS**

2. Wilderness

Nu 10:12; 26:64

SINCERITY

See **SIMPLICITY**

SINEWS, *tendons*

Ge 32:32; Is 48:4; Eze 37:6

SIN OFFERINGS

See **OFFERINGS**

SION See **MOUNTAINS AND HILLS**

SIRION See **MOUNTAINS AND HILLS**

SISERA, *a general of Jabin's army*

Jud 4:2, 9, 15, 22; 5:20; 1 S 12:9; Ps 83:9

SIVAN, *the third month of the Jewish year (June)*

Est 8:9

See **MONTHS**

SKILL

Ex 28:3 And thou shalt speak unto all *that are* wise hearted, whom I have filled with the spirit of wisdom, that they may make Aaron's garments to consecrate him, that he may minister unto me in the priest's office.

Ex 31:3 And I have filled him with the spirit of God, in wisdom, and in understanding, and in knowledge, and in all manner of workmanship,

Ex 35:10 And every wise hearted among you shall come, and make all that the Lord hath commanded;

Ex 35:25 And all the women that were wise hearted did spin with their hands, and brought that which they had spun, *both* of blue, and of purple, *and* of scarlet, and of fine linen.

Ex 35:35 Them hath he filled with wisdom of heart, to work all manner of work, of the engraver, and of the cunning workman, and of the embroiderer, in blue, and in purple, in scarlet, and in fine linen, and of the weaver, *even* of them that do any work, and of those that devise cunning work.

Ex 36:1 Then wrought Bezaleel and Aholiab, and every wise hearted man, in whom the Lord put wisdom and understanding to know how to work all manner of work for the service of the sanctuary, according to all that the Lord had commanded.

Ex 38:23 And with him *was* Aholiab, son of Ahisamach, of the tribe of Dan, an engraver, and a cunning workman, and an embroiderer in blue, and in purple, and in scarlet, and fine linen.

Ex 39:3 And they did beat the gold into thin plates, and cut *it into* wires, to work *it* in the blue, and in the purple, and in the scarlet, and in the fine linen, *with* cunning work.

1 K 5:6 Now therefore command thou that they hew me cedar trees out of Lebanon; and my servants shall be with thy servants: and unto thee will I give hire for thy servants according to all that thou shalt appoint: for thou knowest that *there is* not among us any that can skill to hew timber like unto the Sidonians.

1 K 7:14 He *was* a widow's son of the tribe of Naphtali, and his father *was* a man of Tyre, a worker in brass: and he was filled with wisdom, and understanding, and cunning to work all works in brass. And he came to king Solomon, and wrought all his work.

1 Chr 4:21 The sons of Shelah the son of Judah *were*, Er the father of Lecah, and Laadah the father of Mareshah, and the families of the house of them that wrought fine linen, of the house of Ashbea,

1 Chr 22:15 Moreover *there are* workmen with thee in abundance, hewers and workers of stone and timber, and all manner of cunning men for every manner of work.

1 Chr 28:21 And, behold, the courses of the priests and the Levites, *even they shall be with thee* for all the service of the house of God: and *there shall be* with thee for all manner of workmanship every willing skilful man, for any manner of service: also the princes and all the people *will be* wholly at thy commandment.

2 Chr 2:7 Send me now therefore a man cunning to work in gold, and in silver, and in brass, and in iron, and in purple, and crimson, and blue, and that can skill to grave with the cunning men that *are* with me in Judah and in Jerusalem, whom David my father did provide.

2 Chr 2:13 And now I have sent a cunning man, endued with understanding, of Huram my father's,

2 Chr 26:15 And he made in Jerusalem engines, invented by cunning men, to be on the towers and upon the bulwarks, to shoot arrows and great stones withal. And his name spread far abroad; for he was marvellously helped, till he was strong.

Is 3:3 The captain of fifty, and the honourable man, and the counsellor, and the cunning artificer, and the eloquent orator.

Da 1:4 Children in whom *was* no blemish, but well favoured, and skilful in all wisdom, and cunning in knowledge, and understanding science, and such as *had* ability in them to stand in the king's palace, and whom they might teach the learning and the tongue of the Chaldeans.

See **ARTS AND CRAFTS**

SKY, firmament, *expanse of the heavens*
De 33:26; 2 S 22:12; Jb 37:18; Mt 16:2

SLANDER *See* **SPEECH**

SLAVERY *See* **LIBERTY**

SLAVES

Ge 37:28 Then there passed by Midianites merchantmen; and they drew and lifted up Joseph out of the pit, and sold Joseph to the Ishmeelites for twenty *pieces* of silver: and they brought Joseph into Egypt.

Ge 37:36 And the Midianites sold him into Egypt unto Potiphar, an officer of Pharaoh's, *and* captain of the guard.

Ge 39:1 And Joseph was brought down to Egypt; and Potiphar, an officer of Pharaoh, captain of the guard, an Egyptian, bought him of the hands of the Ishmeelites, which had brought him down thither.

Ge 47:23 Then Joseph said unto the people, Behold, I have bought you this day and your land for Pharaoh: lo, *here*

is seed for you, and ye shall sow the land.

Ex 21:2 If thou buy an Hebrew servant, six years he shall serve: and in the seventh he shall go out free for nothing.

Ex 21:16 And he that stealeth a man, and selleth him, or if he be found in his hand, he shall surely be put to death.

Le 22:11 But if the priest buy *any* soul with his money, he shall eat of it, and he that is born in his house: they shall eat of his meat.

Le 25:44 Both thy bondmen, and thy bondmaids, which thou shalt have, *shall be* of the heathen that are round about you; of them shall ye buy bondmen and bondmaids.

De 15:12 *And* if thy brother, an Hebrew man, or an Hebrew woman, be sold unto thee, and serve thee six years; then in the seventh year thou shalt let him go free from thee.

De 24:7 If a man be found stealing any of his brethren of the children of Israel, and maketh merchandise of him, or selleth him; then that thief shall die; and thou shalt put evil away from among you.

Ne 5:8 And I said unto them, We after our ability have redeemed our brethren the Jews, which were sold unto the heathen; and will ye even sell your brethren? or shall they be sold unto us? Then held they their peace, and found nothing *to answer.*

Eze 27:13 Javan, Tubal, and Meshech, they *were* thy merchants: they traded the persons of men and vessels of brass in thy market.

Jl 3:3 And they have cast lots for my people; and have given a boy for an harlot, and sold a girl for wine, that they might drink.

Jl 3:6 The children also of Judah and the children of Jerusalem have ye sold unto the Grecians, that ye might remove them far from their border.

Am 2:6 Thus saith the Lord; For three transgressions of Israel, and for four, I will not turn away *the punishment* thereof; because they sold the righteous for silver, and the poor for a pair of shoes;

Am 8:6 That we may buy the poor for silver, and the needy for a pair of shoes; *yea,* and sell the refuse of the wheat?

Zec 11:12 And I said unto them, If ye think good, give *me* my price; and if not, forbear. So they weighed for my price thirty *pieces* of silver.

Mt 18:25 But forasmuch as he had not to pay, his lord commanded him to be sold, and his wife, and children, and all that he had, and payment to be made.

Mt 26:15 And said *unto them,* What will ye give me, and I will deliver him unto you? And they covenanted with him for thirty pieces of silver.

Ac 7:9 And the patriarchs, moved with envy, sold Joseph into Egypt: but God was with him,

1 Ti 1:10 For whoremongers, for them that defile themselves with mankind, for menstealers, for liars, for perjured persons, and if there be any other thing that is contrary to sound doctrine;

2 Pe 2:3 And through covetousness shall they with feigned words make merchandise of you: whose judgment now of a long time lingereth not, and their damnation slumbereth not.

Re 18:13 And cinnamon, and odours, and ointments, and frankincense, and wine, and oil, and fine flour, and wheat, and beasts, and sheep, and horses, and chariots, and slaves, and souls of men.

SLAYER, *unintentional murderer*

Nu 35:11; De 4:42; 19:3; Jos 20:3

SLEEP

1. Physical

a. Of the Righteous Is Sweet

Le 26:6 And I will give peace in the land, and ye shall lie down, and none shall make *you* afraid: and I will rid evil beasts out of the land, neither shall the sword go through your land.

Jb 11:18 And thou shalt be secure, because there is hope; yea, thou shalt dig *about thee, and* thou shalt take thy rest in safety.

Ps 3:5 I laid me down and slept; I awaked; for the LORD sustained me.

Ps 4:8 I will both lay me down in peace, and sleep: for thou, LORD, only makest me dwell in safety.

Ps 127:2 *It is* vain for you to rise up early, to sit up late, to eat the bread of sorrows: *for* so he giveth his beloved sleep.

Pr 3:24 When thou liest down, thou shalt not be afraid: yea, thou shalt lie down, and thy sleep shall be sweet.

Pr 6:22 When thou goest, it shall lead thee; when thou sleepest, it shall keep thee; and *when* thou awakest, it shall talk with thee.

Ec 5:12 The sleep of a labouring man *is* sweet, whether he eat little or much: but the abundance of the rich will not suffer him to sleep.

Je 31:26 Upon this I awaked, and beheld; and my sleep was sweet unto me.

Eze 34:25 And I will make with them a covenant of peace, and will cause the evil beasts to cease out of the land: and they shall dwell safely in the wilderness, and sleep in the woods.

Mk 4:38 And he was in the hinder part of the ship, asleep on a pillow: and they awake him, and say unto him, Master, carest thou not that we perish?

Ac 12:6 And when Herod would have brought him forth, the same night Peter was sleeping between two soldiers, bound with two chains: and the keepers before the door kept the prison.

b. Love of Is a Mark of Indolence

Pr 6:4 Give not sleep to thine eyes, nor slumber to thine eyelids.

Pr 6:9–10 How long wilt thou sleep, O sluggard? when wilt thou arise out of thy sleep?

Yet a little sleep, a little slumber, a little folding of the hands to sleep:

Pr 10:5 He that gathereth in summer *is* a wise son: *but* he that sleepeth in harvest *is* a son that causeth shame.

Pr 19:15 Slothfulness casteth into a deep sleep; and an idle soul shall suffer hunger.

Pr 20:13 Love not sleep, lest thou come to poverty; open thine eyes, *and* thou shalt be satisfied with bread.

Pr 23:21 For the drunkard and the glutton shall come to poverty: and drowsiness shall clothe *a man* with rags.

Pr 26:14 *As* the door turneth upon his hinges, so *doth* the slothful upon his bed.

c. Symbolizes Death

2 S 7:12 And when thy days be fulfilled, and thou shalt sleep with thy fathers, I will set up thy seed after thee, which shall proceed out of thy bowels, and I will establish his kingdom.

1 K 2:10 So David slept with his fathers, and was buried in the city of David.

1 K 11:43 And Solomon slept with his fathers, and was buried in the city of David his father: and Rehoboam his son reigned in his stead.

1 K 22:50 And Jehoshaphat slept with his fathers, and was buried with his fathers in the city of David his father: and Jehoram his son reigned in his stead.

Jb 14:12 So man lieth down, and riseth not: till the heavens *be* no more, they shall not awake, nor be raised out of their sleep.

Ps 13:3 Consider *and* hear me, O LORD my God: lighten mine eyes, lest I sleep the *sleep of* death;

Mt 9:24 He said unto them, Give place: for the maid is not dead, but sleepeth. And they laughed him to scorn.

Ac 7:60 And he kneeled down, and cried with a loud voice, Lord, lay not this sin to their charge. And when he had said this, he fell asleep.

1 Co 15:51 Behold, I shew you a mystery; We shall not all sleep, but we shall all be changed,

d. Natural

Ge 2:21; 15:12; 28:11; Jud 16:20; 1 S 26:12; 1 K 19:5; Jb 4:13; 33:15; Da 8:18; Jona 1:5; Mt 8:24; 26:40; Mk 14:40; Lu 9:32; Ac 20:9

2. Warnings against Spiritual Slumber

Is 56:10 His watchmen *are* blind: they are all ignorant, they *are* all dumb dogs, they cannot bark; sleeping, lying down, loving to slumber.

Mk 13:35–36 Watch ye therefore: for ye know not when the master of the house cometh, at even, or at midnight, or at the cockcrowing, or in the morning:

Lest coming suddenly he find you sleeping.

Ro 11:8 (According as it is written, God hath given them the spirit of slumber, eyes that they should not see, and ears that they should not hear;) unto this day.

Ro 13:11 And that, knowing the time, that now *it is* high time to awake out of sleep: for now *is* our salvation nearer than when we believed.

Ep 5:14 Wherefore he saith, Awake thou that sleepest, and arise from the dead, and Christ shall give thee light.

1 Th 5:6 Therefore let us not sleep, as *do* others; but let us watch and be sober.

3. Common Causes of Loss of Sleep

BURDENS OF STATE

Est 6:1 On that night could not the king sleep, and he commanded to bring the book of records of the chronicles; and they were read before the king.

SICKNESS

Jb 7:4–5 When I lie down, I say, When shall I arise, and the night be gone? and I am full of tossings to and fro unto the dawning of the day.

My flesh is clothed with worms and clods of dust; my skin is broken, and become loathsome.

Jb 30:17 My bones are pierced in me in the night season: and my sinews take no rest.

CARE OF WEALTH

Ec 5:12 The sleep of a labouring man *is* sweet, whether he eat little or much: but the abundance of the rich will not suffer him to sleep.

OLD AGE

Ec 12:4 And the doors shall be shut in the streets, when the sound of the grinding is low, and he shall rise up at the voice of the bird, and all the daughters of musick shall be brought low;

Da 2:1 And in the second year of the reign of Nebuchadnezzar Nebuchadnezzar dreamed dreams, wherewith his spirit was troubled, and his sleep brake from him.

GRIEF AND REMORSE

Da 6:18–19 Then the king went to his palace, and passed the night fasting: neither were instruments of musick brought before him: and his sleep went from him.

Then the king arose very early in the morning, and went in haste unto the den of lions.

4. Exhortations to Awake

Jud 5:12 Awake, awake, Deborah: awake, awake, utter a song: arise, Barak, and lead thy captivity captive, thou son of Abinoam.

Is 26:19 Thy dead *men* shall live, *together with* my dead body shall they arise. Awake and sing, ye that dwell in dust: for thy dew *is as* the dew of herbs, and the earth shall cast out the dead.

Is 32:9 Rise up, ye women that are at ease; hear my voice, ye careless daughters; give ear unto my speech.

Is 50:4 The Lord God hath given me the tongue of the learned, that I should know how to speak a word in season to *him that is* weary: he wakeneth morning by morning, he wakeneth mine ear to hear as the learned.

Is 51:17 Awake, awake, stand up, O Jerusalem, which hast drunk at the hand of the LORD the cup of his fury; thou hast drunken the dregs of the cup of trembling, *and* wrung *them* out.

Is 52:1 Awake, awake; put on thy strength, O Zion; put on thy beautiful garments, O Jerusalem, the holy city: for henceforth there shall no more come into thee the uncircumcised and the unclean.

Mt 25:6 And at midnight there was a cry made, Behold, the bridegroom cometh; go ye out to meet him.

Mk 14:42 Rise up, let us go; lo, he that betrayeth me is at hand.

Lu 22:46 And said unto them, Why sleep ye? rise and pray, lest ye enter into temptation.

Ro 13:11 And that, knowing the time, that now *it is* high time to awake out of sleep: for now *is* our salvation nearer than when we believed.

1 Co 15:34 Awake to righteousness, and sin not; for some have not the knowledge of God: I speak *this* to your shame.

Ep 5:14 Wherefore he saith, Awake thou that sleepest, and arise from the dead, and Christ shall give thee light.

1 Th 5:6 Therefore let us not sleep, as *do* others; but let us watch and be sober.

See **AWAKENINGS, DEATH, DREAMS**

SLINGS, *a weapon in which a stone is whirled and then let fly*

Jud 20:16; 1 S 17:40; 25:29; 2 K 3:25; Pr 26:8; Zec 9:15

SLOTHFULNESS *See* **BUSINESS**

SLUGGARD, *slothful person*

Pr 6:6; 10:26; 13:4; 15:19; 18:9; 19:24; 20:4; 21:25; 24:30; 26:16; 2 Th 3:10

SMELTERS *See* **ARTS AND CRAFTS**

SMITHS *See* **ARTS AND CRAFTS**

SMITING, *striking or assaulting the upright*

1 K 22:24 But Zedekiah the son of Chenaanah went near, and smote Micaiah on the cheek, and said, Which way went the Spirit of the LORD from me to speak unto thee?

Is 50:6 I gave my back to the smiters, and my cheeks to them that plucked off the hair: I hid not my face from shame and spitting.

Mt 27:30 And they spit upon him, and took the reed, and smote him on the head.

Jn 18:22 And when he had thus spoken, one of the officers which stood by struck Jesus with the palm of his hand, saying, Answerest thou the high priest so?

Ac 23:2 And the high priest Ananias commanded them that stood by him to smite him on the mouth.

Upon the Cheek

1 K 22:24; 2 Chr 18:23; Jb 16:10; Lu 6:29

See **STRIFE, SUFFERING**

SNAIL

Ps 58:8

See **ANIMALS**

SNAKES *See* **REPTILES**

SNARES, *laid by the wicked*

Jud 8:27 And Gideon made an ephod thereof, and put it in his city, *even in* Ophrah: and all Israel went thither a whoring after it: which thing became a snare unto Gideon, and to his house.

Jud 16:5 And the lords of the Philistines came up unto her, and said unto her, Entice him, and see wherein his great strength *lieth,* and by what *means* we may prevail against him, that we may bind him to afflict him: and we will give thee every one of us eleven hundred *pieces* of silver.

2 S 11:13 And when David had called him, he did eat and drink before him; and he made him drunk: and at even he went out to lie on his bed with the servants of his lord, but went not down to his house.

Ne 6:13 Therefore *was* he hired, that I should be afraid, and do so, and sin, and *that* they might have *matter* for an evil report, that they might reproach me.

Ps 10:8 He sitteth in the lurking places of the villages: in the secret places doth he murder the innocent: his eyes are privily set against the poor.

Ps 31:4 Pull me out of the net that they have laid privily for me: for thou *art* my strength.

Ps 35:7 For without cause have they hid for me their net *in* a pit, *which* without cause they have digged for my soul.

Ps 38:12 They also that seek after my life lay snares *for me:* and they that seek my hurt speak mischievous things, and imagine deceits all the day long.

Ps 56:6 They gather themselves together, they hide themselves, they mark my steps, when they wait for my soul.

Ps 57:6 They have prepared a net for my steps; my soul is bowed down: they have digged a pit before me, into the midst whereof they are fallen *themselves.* Selah.

Ps 64:5 They encourage themselves *in* an evil matter: they commune of laying snares privily; they say, Who shall see them?

Ps 71:10 For mine enemies speak against me; and they that lay wait for my soul take counsel together,

Ps 119:85 The proud have digged pits for me, which *are* not after thy law.

Ps 119:110 The wicked have laid a snare for me: yet I erred not from thy precepts.

Ps 124:7 Our soul is escaped as a bird out of the snare of the fowlers: the snare is broken, and we are escaped.

Ps 140:5 The proud have hid a snare for me, and cords; they have spread a net by the wayside; they have set gins for me. Selah.

Ps 141:9 Keep me from the snares *which* they have laid for me, and the gins of the workers of iniquity.

Ps 142:3 When my spirit was overwhelmed within me, then thou knewest my path. In the way wherein I walked have they privily laid a snare for me.

Pr 1:11 If they say, Come with us, let us lay wait for blood, let us lurk privily for the innocent without cause:

Pr 12:6 The words of the wicked *are* to lie in wait for blood: but the mouth of the upright shall deliver them.

Is 29:21 That make a man an offender for a word, and lay a snare for him that reproveth in the gate, and turn aside the just for a thing of nought.

Is 59:5 They hatch cockatrice' eggs, and weave the spider's web: he that eateth of their eggs dieth, and that which is crushed breaketh out into a viper.

Je 5:26 For among my people are found wicked *men:* they lay wait, as he that setteth snares; they set a trap, they catch men.

Je 18:22 Let a cry be heard from their houses, when thou shalt bring a troop suddenly upon them: for they have digged a pit to take me, and hid snares for my feet.

Lam 4:19 Our persecutors are swifter than the eagles of the heaven: they pursued us upon the mountains, they laid wait for us in the wilderness.

Da 6:7 All the presidents of the kingdom, the governors, and the princes, the counsellors, and the captains, have consulted together to establish a royal statute, and to make a firm decree, that whosoever shall ask a petition of any God or man for thirty days, save of thee, O king, he shall be cast into the den of lions.

Ho 5:1 Hear ye this, O priests; and hearken, ye house of Israel; and give ye ear, O house of the king; for judgment *is* toward you, because ye have been a snare on Mizpah, and a net spread upon Tabor.

Ac 20:3 And *there* abode three months. And when the Jews laid wait for him, as he was about to sail into Syria, he purposed to return through Macedonia.

For Christ

Mt 12:10 And, behold, there was a man which had *his* hand withered. And they asked him, saying, Is it lawful to heal on the sabbath days? that they might accuse him.

Mt 16:1 The Pharisees also with the Sadducees came, and tempting desired him that he would shew them a sign from heaven.

Mt 19:3 The Pharisees also came unto him, tempting him, and saying unto him, Is it lawful for a man to put away his wife for every cause?

Mt 22:15 Then went the Pharisees, and took counsel how they might entangle him in *his* talk.

Mk 3:2 And they watched him, whether he would heal him on the sabbath day; that they might accuse him.

Mk 8:11 And the Pharisees came forth, and began to question with him, seeking of him a sign from heaven, tempting him.

Mk 10:2 And the Pharisees came to him, and asked him, Is it lawful for a man to put away *his* wife? tempting him.

Mk 12:13 And they send unto him certain of the Pharisees and of the Herodians, to catch him in *his* words.

Lu 6:7 And the scribes and Pharisees watched him, whether he would heal on the sabbath day; that they might find an accusation against him.

Lu 11:54 Laying wait for him, and seeking to catch something out of his mouth, that they might accuse him.

Lu 20:20 And they watched *him,* and sent forth spies, which should feign themselves just men, that they might take hold of his words, that so they might deliver him unto the power and authority of the governor.

Jn 8:6 This they said, tempting him, that they might have to accuse him. But Jesus stooped down, and with *his* finger wrote on the ground, *as though he heard them not.*

SNOW, *white or translucent ice crystals*

2 S 23:20; Jb 6:16; 37:6; 38:22; Ps 147:16; 148:8; Pr 26:1; 31:21; Is 55:10; Je 18:14

A Symbol of Whiteness

Ps 51:7; 68:14; Pr 25:13; Is 1:18; Lam 4:7; Da 7:9

SNUFFERS, *used in the Tabernacle and the Temple to trim and adjust the wicks of the lamps*

Ex 25:38; 1 K 7:50; 2 K 12:13; 25:14; Je 52:18

SOAP, *cleansing agent*

Je 2:22; Mal 3:2

SOBERNESS

Ac 26:25 But he said, I am not mad, most noble Festus; but speak forth the words of truth and soberness.

Ro 12:3 For I say, through the grace given unto me, to every man that is among you, not to think *of himself* more highly than he ought to think; but to think soberly, according as God hath dealt to every man the measure of faith.

2 Co 5:13 For whether we be beside ourselves, *it is* to God: or whether we be sober, *it is* for your cause.

1 Th 5:6 Therefore let us not sleep, as *do* others; but let us watch and be sober.

1 Ti 2:9 In like manner also, that women adorn themselves in modest apparel, with shamefacedness and sobriety; not with broided hair, or gold, or pearls, or costly array;

1 Ti 2:15 Notwithstanding she shall be saved in childbearing, if they continue in faith and charity and holiness with sobriety.

1 Ti 3:2 A bishop then must be blameless, the husband of one wife, vigilant, sober, of good behaviour, given to hospitality, apt to teach;

1 Ti 3:8 Likewise *must* the deacons *be* grave, not doubletongued, not given to much wine, not greedy of filthy lucre;

1 Ti 3:11 Even so *must their* wives be grave, not slanderers, sober, faithful in all things.

Tit 1:8 But a lover of hospitality, a lover of good men, sober, just, holy, temperate;

Tit 2:2 That the aged men be sober, grave, temperate, sound in faith, in charity, in patience.

Tit 2:4 That they may teach the young women to be sober, to love their husbands, to love their children,

Tit 2:6 Young men likewise exhort to be sober minded.

Tit 2:12 Teaching us that, denying ungodliness and worldly lusts, we should live soberly, righteously, and godly, in this present world;

1 Pe 1:13 Wherefore gird up the loins of your mind, be sober, and hope to the end for the grace that is to be brought unto you at the revelation of Jesus Christ;

1 Pe 4:7 But the end of all things is at hand: be ye therefore sober, and watch unto prayer.

1 Pe 5:8 Be sober, be vigilant; because your adversary the devil, as a roaring lion, walketh about, seeking whom he may devour:

See **WATCHING, WATCHMAN**

SOCHOH, *or Socoh, a city of Judah*

Jos 15:35; 1 S 17:1; 2 Chr 11:7; 2 Chr 28:18

See **CITIES**

SOCIAL DUTIES, *obligations to the community*

1. To All People

A COMMON FATHER

Pr 22:2 The rich and poor meet together: the LORD *is* the maker of them all.

Mal 2:10 Have we not all one father? hath not one God created us? why do we deal treacherously every man against his brother, by profaning the covenant of our fathers?

A SPIRITUAL KINSHIP

Mk 3:34 And he looked round about on them which sat about him, and said, Behold my mother and my brethren!

A BLOOD RELATIONSHIP

Ac 17:26 And hath made of one blood all nations of men for to dwell on all the face of the earth, and hath determined the times before appointed, and the bounds of their habitation;

FORBIDS HARSH JUDGMENT

Ro 14:13 Let us not therefore judge one another any more: but judge this rather, that no man put a stumblingblock or an occasion to fall in *his* brother's way.

DEMANDS SELF-SACRIFICE

1 Co 8:13 Wherefore, if meat make my brother to offend, I will eat no flesh while the world standeth, lest I make my brother to offend.

2. To Neighbors

Ex 20:17 Thou shalt not covet thy neighbour's house, thou shalt not covet thy neighbour's wife, nor his manservant, nor his maidservant, nor his ox, nor his ass, nor any thing that *is* thy neighbour's.

Ex 22:8 If the thief be not found, then the master of the house shall be brought unto the judges, *to see* whether he have put his hand unto his neighbour's goods.

Le 19:18 Thou shalt not avenge, nor bear any grudge against the children of thy people, but thou shalt love thy neighbour as thyself: I *am* the LORD.

Mk 12:31 And the second *is* like, *namely* this, Thou shalt love thy neighbour as thyself. There is none other commandment greater than these.

Ro 13:10 Love worketh no ill to his neighbour: therefore love *is* the fulfilling of the law.

Ro 15:1–2 We then that are strong ought to bear the infirmities of the weak, and not to please ourselves.

Let every one of us please *his* neighbour for *his* good to edification.

Ga 5:14 For all the law is fulfilled in one word, *even* in this; Thou shalt love thy neighbour as thyself.

Ja 2:8 If ye fulfil the royal law according to the scripture, Thou shalt love thy neighbour as thyself, ye do well:

3. To Enemies

Ex 23:4 If thou meet thine enemy's ox or his ass going astray, thou shalt surely bring it back to him again.

2 K 6:22 And he answered, Thou shalt not smite *them:* wouldest thou smite those whom thou hast taken captive with thy sword and with thy bow? set bread and water before them, that they may eat and drink, and go to their master.

Jb 31:29 If I rejoiced at the destruction of him that hated me, or lifted up myself when evil found him:

Pr 24:17 Rejoice not when thine enemy falleth, and let not thine heart be glad when he stumbleth:

Pr 25:21–22 If thine enemy be hungry, give him bread to eat; and if he be thirsty, give him water to drink:

For thou shalt heap coals of fire upon his head, and the LORD shall reward thee.

Mt 5:44 But I say unto you, Love your enemies, bless them that curse you, do good to them that hate you, and pray for them which despitefully use you, and persecute you;

Ro 12:20 Therefore if thine enemy hunger, feed him; if he thirst, give him drink: for in so doing thou shalt heap coals of fire on his head.

4. To Strangers

Ex 22:21 Thou shalt neither vex a stranger, nor oppress him: for ye were strangers in the land of Egypt.

Ex 23:9 Also thou shalt not oppress a stranger: for ye know the heart of a stranger, seeing ye were strangers in the land of Egypt.

Le 19:34 *But* the stranger that dwelleth with you shall be unto you as one born among you, and thou shalt love him as thyself; for ye were strangers in the land of Egypt: I *am* the LORD your God.

Le 25:35 And if thy brother be waxen poor, and fallen in decay with thee; then thou shalt relieve him: *yea, though he be* a stranger, or a sojourner; that he may live with thee.

Nu 35:15 These six cities shall be a refuge, *both* for the children of Israel, and for the stranger, and for the sojourner among them: that every one that killeth any person unawares may flee thither.

De 10:19 Love ye therefore the stranger: for ye were strangers in the land of Egypt.

Mt 25:35 For I was an hungred, and ye gave me meat: I was thirsty, and ye gave me drink: I was a stranger, and ye took me in:

5. To Sick

2 K 8:29 And king Joram went back to be healed in Jezreel of the wounds which the Syrians had given him at Ramah, when he fought against Hazael king of Syria. And Ahaziah the son of Jehoram king of Judah went down to see Joram the son of Ahab in Jezreel, because he was sick.

2 K 13:14 Now Elisha was fallen sick of his sickness whereof he died. And Joash the king of Israel came down unto him, and wept over his face, and said, O my father, my father, the chariot of Israel, and the horsemen thereof.

Jb 2:11 Now when Job's three friends heard of all this evil that was come upon him, they came every one from his own place; Eliphaz the Temanite, and Bildad the Shuhite, and Zophar the Naamathite: for they had made an appointment together to come to mourn with him and to comfort him.

Mt 25:36 Naked, and ye clothed me: I was sick, and ye visited me: I was in prison, and ye came unto me.

Ja 5:14 Is any sick among you? let him call for the elders of the church; and let them pray over him, anointing him with oil in the name of the Lord:

See **BENEVOLENCE, HOSPITALITY, KINDNESS, LOVE, SELFISHNESS, RETALIATION**

SOCIAL FUNCTIONS, *community gatherings*

Ge 19:3; 21:8; 26:30; 29:22; 40:20; 43:16; Jud 14:10; 1 S 9:24; 25:36; 2 S 3:20; 1 K 1:9, 25; 3:15; 8:65; 19:21; 2 K 6:23; 1 Chr 12:39; 2 Chr 18:2; Est 1:3, 5, 9; 2:18; 5:5; 7:1; Jb 1:4, 18; Is 5:12; Je 16:8; Da 5:1; Am 6:7; Mk 6:21; Lu 5:29; Jn 2:8; 6:13; 12:2

1. Wedding Feasts

JACOB'S

Ge 29:22 And Laban gathered together all the men of the place, and made a feast.

SAMSON'S

Jud 14:12 And Samson said unto them, I will now put forth a riddle unto you: if ye can certainly declare it me within the seven days of the feast, and find *it* out, then I will give you thirty sheets and thirty change of garments:

ESTHER'S

Est 2:18 Then the king made a great feast unto all his princes and his servants, *even* Esther's feast; and he made a release to the provinces, and gave gifts, according to the state of the king.

THE KING'S SON

Mt 22:2–4 The kingdom of heaven is like unto a certain king, which made a marriage for his son,

And sent forth his servants to call them that were bidden to the wedding: and they would not come.

Again, he sent forth other servants, saying, Tell them which are bidden, Behold, I have prepared my dinner: my oxen and *my* fatlings *are* killed, and all things *are* ready: come unto the marriage.

AT CANA OF GALILEE

Jn 2:1 And the third day there was a marriage in Cana of Galilee; and the mother of Jesus was there:

2. Birthdays

Ge 40:20; Mt 14:6; Mk 6:21

3. Revelry

Ex 32:6, 18; Jud 9:27; 16:25; 1 S 25:36; 30:16; Ec 7:4; 10:19; Mt 24:49; Ro 13:13; 1 Co 10:7; Ga 5:21; 1 Pe 4:3; 2 Pe 2:13

SODOM, *a city of ancient Palestine*

1. Its Wickedness

Ge 10:19; 13:13; 14:2, 8, 11, 17; 18:20; 19:24, 28; De 29:23; Is 3:9; Je 20:16; 49:18; 50:40; Eze 16:46; Am 4:11; Mt 11:23; Mk 6:11; Lu 10:12; 17:29; Ro 9:29; 2 Pe 2:6; Jude 7

2. A Type of Gross Sin

De 32:32; Is 1:9; 13:19; Je 23:14; Lam 4:6; Zep 2:9; Mt 10:15; Re 11:8

SOJOURNERS, *travellers, those without permanent residence*

Ge 12:10 And there was a famine in the land: and Abram went down into Egypt to sojourn there; for the famine *was* grievous in the land.

Ge 20:1 And Abraham journeyed from thence toward the south country, and dwelled between Kadesh and Shur, and sojourned in Gerar.

Genesis 21:34 And Abraham sojourned in the Philistines' land many days.

Ge 23:4 I *am* a stranger and a sojourner with you: give me a possession of a buryingplace with you, that I may bury my dead out of my sight.

Ge 37:1 And Jacob dwelt in the land wherein his father was a stranger, in the land of Canaan.

Ge 47:4 They said moreover unto Pharaoh, For to sojourn in the land are we come; for thy servants have no pasture for their flocks; for the famine *is* sore in the land of Canaan: now therefore, we pray thee, let thy servants dwell in the land of Goshen.

Ex 2:22 And she bare *him* a son, and he called his name Gershom: for he said, I have been a stranger in a strange land.

Ex 6:4 And I have also established my covenant with them, to give them the land of Canaan, the land of their pilgrimage, wherein they were strangers.

Ex 12:40 Now the sojourning of the children of Israel, who dwelt in Egypt, *was* four hundred and thirty years.

Ex 18:3 And her two sons; of which the name of the one *was* Gershom; for he said, I have been an alien in a strange land:

Le 17:13 And whatsoever man *there be* of the children of Israel, or of the strangers that sojourn among you, which hunteth and catcheth any beast or fowl that may be eaten; he shall even pour out the blood thereof, and cover it with dust.

Le 18:26 Ye shall therefore keep my statutes and my judgments, and shall not commit any of these abominations; *neither* any of your own nation, nor any stranger that sojourneth among you:

Le 19:33-34 And if a stranger sojourn with thee in your land, ye shall not vex him. *But* the stranger that dwelleth with you shall be unto you as one born among you, and thou shalt love him as thyself; for ye were strangers in the land of Egypt: I *am* the Lord your God.

Le 20:2 Again, thou shalt say to the children of Israel, Whosoever *he be* of the children of Israel, or of the strangers that sojourn in Israel, that giveth *any* of his seed unto Molech; he shall surely be put to death: the people of the land shall stone him with stones.

Le 25:6 And the sabbath of the land shall be meat for you; for thee, and for thy servant, and for thy maid, and for thy hired servant, and for thy stranger that sojourneth with thee,

Le 25:23 The land shall not be sold for ever: for the land *is* mine; for ye *are* strangers and sojourners with me.

Le 25:40 But as an hired servant, *and* as a sojourner, he shall be with thee, *and* shall serve thee unto the year of jubile:

Nu 15:15 One ordinance *shall be both* for you of the congregation, and also for the stranger that sojourneth *with you*, an ordinance for ever in your generations: as ye *are*, so shall the stranger be before the Lord.

Nu 15:29 Ye shall have one law for him that sinneth through ignorance, *both for* him that is born among the children of Israel, and for the stranger that sojourneth among them.

Nu 35:15 These six cities shall be a refuge, *both* for the children of Israel, and for the stranger, and for the sojourner among them: that every one that killeth any person unawares may flee thither.

De 18:6 And if a Levite come from any of thy gates out of all Israel, where he sojourned, and come with all the desire of his mind unto the place which the Lord shall choose;

De 23:7 Thou shalt not abhor an Edomite; for he *is* thy brother: thou shalt not abhor an Egyptian; because thou wast a stranger in his land.

De 26:5 And thou shalt speak and say before the Lord thy God, A Syrian ready to perish *was* my father, and he went down into Egypt, and sojourned there with a few, and became there a nation, great, mighty, and populous:

De 29:22 So that the generation to come of your children that shall rise up after you, and the stranger that shall come from a far land, shall say, when they see the plagues of that land, and the sicknesses which the Lord hath laid upon it;

Jud 17:7 And there was a young man out of Beth-lehem-judah of the family of Judah, who was a Levite, and he sojourned there.

Ru 1:1 Now it came to pass in the days when the judges ruled, that there was a famine in the land. And a certain man of Beth-lehem-judah went to sojourn in the country of Moab, he, and his wife, and his two sons.

1 Chr 29:15 For we *are* strangers before thee, and sojourners, as *were* all our fathers: our days on the earth *are* as a shadow, and *there is* none abiding.

Ps 39:12 Hear my prayer, O Lord, and give ear unto my cry; hold not thy peace at my tears: for I *am* a stranger with thee, *and* a sojourner, as all my fathers were.

Ps 105:12 When they were *but* a few men in number; yea, very few, and strangers in it.

Ps 119:19 I *am* a stranger in the earth: hide not thy commandments from me.

He 11:9 By faith he sojourned in the land of promise, as *in* a strange country, dwelling in tabernacles with Isaac and Jacob, the heirs with him of the same promise:

He 11:13 These all died in faith, not having received the promises, but having seen them afar off, and were persuaded of *them*, and embraced *them*, and confessed that they were strangers and pilgrims on the earth.

1 Pe 2:11 Dearly beloved, I beseech *you* as strangers and pilgrims, abstain from fleshly lusts, which war against the soul;

SOLDIERS *See* **TITLES AND NAMES**

SOLICITUDE, *persistent pleading*

1. For the Wayward

1 S 15:35 And Samuel came no more to see Saul until the day of his death: nevertheless Samuel mourned for Saul: and the Lord repented that he had made Saul king over Israel.

Ps 119:53 Horror hath taken hold upon me because of the wicked that forsake thy law.

Ps 119:136 Rivers of waters run down mine eyes, because they keep not thy law.

Ps 119:158 I beheld the transgressors, and was grieved; because they kept not thy word.

Ps 139:21 Do not I hate them, O Lord, that hate thee? and am not I grieved with those that rise up against thee?

Is 15:5 My heart shall cry out for Moab; his fugitives *shall flee* unto Zoar, an heifer of three years old: for by the mounting up of Luhith with weeping shall they go it up; for in the way of Horonaim they shall raise up a cry of destruction.

Is 21:3 Therefore are my loins filled with pain: pangs have taken hold upon me, as the pangs of a woman that travaileth: I was bowed down at the hearing *of it;* I was dismayed at the seeing *of it.*

Je 13:17 But if ye will not hear it, my soul shall weep in secret places for *your* pride; and mine eye shall weep sore, and run down with tears, because the Lord's flock is carried away captive.

Je 14:17 Therefore thou shalt say this word unto them; Let mine eyes run down with tears night and day, and let them not cease: for the virgin daughter of my people is broken with a great breach, with a very grievous blow.

Je 23:9 Mine heart within me is broken because of the prophets; all my bones shake; I am like a drunken man, and like a man whom wine hath overcome, because of the LORD, and because of the words of his holiness.

Je 48:32 O vine of Sibmah, I will weep for thee with the weeping of Jazer: thy plants are gone over the sea, they reach *even* to the sea of Jazer: the spoiler is fallen upon thy summer fruits and upon thy vintage.

Eze 9:4 And the LORD said unto him, Go through the midst of the city, through the midst of Jerusalem, and set a mark upon the foreheads of the men that sigh and that cry for all the abominations that be done in the midst thereof.

Eze 19:1 Moreover take thou up a lamentation for the princes of Israel,

Eze 21:7 And it shall be, when they say unto thee, Wherefore sighest thou? that thou shalt answer, For the tidings; because it cometh: and every heart shall melt, and all hands shall be feeble, and every spirit shall faint, and all knees shall be weak *as* water: behold, it cometh, and shall be brought to pass, saith the Lord GOD.

Eze 32:18 Son of man, wail for the multitude of Egypt, and cast them down, *even* her, and the daughters of the famous nations, unto the nether parts of the earth, with them that go down into the pit.

Da 4:19 Then Daniel, whose name *was* Belteshazzar, was astonied for one hour, and his thoughts troubled him. The king spake, and said, Belteshazzar, let not the dream, or the interpretation thereof, trouble thee. Belteshazzar answered and said, My lord, the dream *be* to them that hate thee, and the interpretation thereof to thine enemies.

Mt 23:37 O Jerusalem, Jerusalem, *thou* that killest the prophets, and stonest them which are sent unto thee, how often would I have gathered thy children together, even as a hen gathereth her chickens under *her* wings, and ye would not!

Mk 3:5 And when he had looked round about on them with anger, being grieved for the hardness of their hearts, he saith unto the man, Stretch forth thine hand. And he stretched *it* out: and his hand was restored whole as the other.

Mk 8:12 And he sighed deeply in his spirit, and saith, Why doth this generation seek after a sign? verily I say unto you, There shall no sign be given unto this generation.

Ac 17:16 Now while Paul waited for them at Athens, his spirit was stirred in him, when he saw the city wholly given to idolatry.

Ac 20:31 Therefore watch, and remember, that by the space of three years I ceased not to warn every one night and day with tears.

2 Co 2:3 And I wrote this same unto you, lest, when I came, I should have sorrow from them of whom I ought to rejoice; having confidence in you all, that my joy is *the joy* of you all.

2 Co 12:20 For I fear, lest, when I come, I shall not find you such as I would, and *that* I shall be found unto you such as ye would not: lest *there be* debates, envyings, wraths, strifes, backbitings, whisperings, swellings, tumults:

Ph 3:18 (For many walk, of whom I have told you often, and now tell you even weeping, *that they are* the enemies of the cross of Christ:

2 Pe 2:8 (For that righteous man dwelling among them, in seeing and hearing, vexed *his* righteous soul from day to day with *their* unlawful deeds;)

2. For the Welfare of the Church

Ac 15:36 And some days after Paul said unto Barnabas, Let us go again and visit our brethren in every city where we have preached the word of the Lord, *and see* how they do.

Ro 1:11 For I long to see you, that I may impart unto you some spiritual gift, to the end ye may be established;

1 Co 7:32 But I would have you without carefulness. He that is unmarried careth for the things that belong to the Lord, how he may please the Lord:

2 Co 2:4 For out of much affliction and anguish of heart I wrote unto you with many tears; not that ye should be grieved, but that ye might know the love which I have more abundantly unto you.

2 Co 7:12 Wherefore, though I wrote unto you, *I did it* not for his cause that had done the wrong, nor for his cause that suffered wrong, but that our care for you in the sight of God might appear unto you.

2 Co 11:3 But I fear, lest by any means, as the serpent beguiled Eve through his subtilty, so your minds should be corrupted from the simplicity that is in Christ.

2 Co 11:29 Who is weak, and I am not weak? who is offended, and I burn not?

Ga 4:11 I am afraid of you, lest I have bestowed upon you labour in vain.

Ga 4:19 My little children, of whom I travail in birth again until Christ be formed in you,

Ph 1:7 Even as it is meet for me to think this of you all, because I have you in my heart; inasmuch as both in my bonds, and in the defence and confirmation of the gospel, ye all are partakers of my grace.

Ph 2:19 But I trust in the Lord Jesus to send Timotheus shortly unto you, that I also may be of good comfort, when I know your state.

Ph 2:26 For he longed after you all, and was full of heaviness, because that ye had heard that he had been sick.

Col 1:9 For this cause we also, since the day we heard *it,* do not cease to pray for you, and to desire that ye might be filled with the knowledge of his will in all wisdom and spiritual understanding;

Col 2:1 For I would that ye knew what great conflict I have for you, and *for* them at Laodicea, and *for* as many as have not seen my face in the flesh;

1 Th 2:8 So being affectionately desirous of you, we were willing to have imparted unto you, not the gospel of God only, but also our own souls, because ye were dear unto us.

1 Th 3:1 Wherefore when we could no longer forbear, we thought it good to be left at Athens alone;

1 Th 3:5 For this cause, when I could no longer forbear, I sent to know your faith, lest by some means the tempter have tempted you, and our labour be in vain.

3. For Israel

2 K 8:12 And Hazael said, Why weepeth my lord? And he answered, Because I know the evil that thou wilt do unto the children of Israel: their strong holds wilt thou set on fire, and their young men wilt thou slay with the sword, and wilt dash their children, and rip up their women with child.

Ezr 9:3 And when I heard this thing, I rent my garment and my mantle, and plucked off the hair of my head and of my beard, and sat down astonied.

Ne 1:4 And it came to pass, when I heard these words, that I sat down and wept, and mourned *certain* days, and fasted, and prayed before the God of heaven,

Ne 13:8 And it grieved me sore: therefore I cast forth all the household stuff of Tobiah out of the chamber.

Est 8:6 For how can I endure to see the evil that shall come unto my people? or how can I endure to see the destruction of my kindred?

Is 22:4 Therefore said I, Look away from me; I will weep bitterly, labour not to comfort me, because of the spoiling of the daughter of my people.

Is 62:1 For Zion's sake will I not hold my peace, and for Jerusalem's sake I will not rest, until the righteousness thereof go forth as brightness, and the salvation thereof as a lamp *that* burneth.

Je 4:19 My bowels, my bowels! I am pained at my very heart; my heart maketh a noise in me; I cannot hold my peace, because thou hast heard, O my soul, the sound of the trump, the alarm of war.

Je 8:21 For the hurt of the daughter of my people am I hurt; I am black; astonishment hath taken hold on me.

Je 9:1 Oh that my head were waters, and mine eyes a fountain of tears, that I might weep day and night for the slain of the daughter of my people!

Lam 1:16 For these *things* I weep; mine eye, mine eye runneth down with water, because the comforter that should relieve my soul is far from me:

my children are desolate, because the enemy prevailed.

Lam 2:11 Mine eyes do fail with tears, my bowels are troubled, my liver is poured upon the earth, for the destruction of the daughter of my people; because the children and the sucklings swoon in the streets of the city.

Lam 2:13 What thing shall I take to witness for thee? what thing shall I liken to thee, O daughter of Jerusalem? what shall I equal to thee, that I may comfort thee, O virgin daughter of Zion? for thy breach is great like the sea: who can heal thee?

Lam 3:48 Mine eye runneth down with rivers of water for the destruction of the daughter of my people.

Mi 1:8 Therefore I will wail and howl, I will go stripped and naked: I will make a wailing like the dragons, and mourning as the owls.

Mi 7:1 Woe is me! for I am as when they have gathered the summer fruits, as the grapegleanings of the vintage: *there is* no cluster to eat: my soul desired the firstripe fruit.

Lu 13:34 O Jerusalem, Jerusalem, which killest the prophets, and stonest them that are sent unto thee; how often would I have gathered thy children together, as a hen *doth gather* her brood under *her* wings, and ye would not!

Lu 19:41 And when he was come near, he beheld the city, and wept over it,

Ro 9:2 That I have great heaviness and continual sorrow in my heart.

Ro 10:1 Brethren, my heart's desire and prayer to God for Israel is, that they might be saved.

See **PRAYER**

SOLITUDE, *being alone, remote from others*

Ge 28:11 And he lighted upon a certain place, and tarried there all night, because the sun was set; and he took of the stones of that place, and *put* them for his pillows, and lay down in that place to sleep.

Ge 32:24 And Jacob was left alone; and there wrestled a man with him until the breaking of the day.

Ps 55:7 Lo, *then* would I wander far off, *and* remain in the wilderness. Selah.

Je 9:2 Oh that I had in the wilderness a lodging place of wayfaring men; that I might leave my people, and go from them! for they *be* all adulterers, an assembly of treacherous men.

Je 15:17 I sat not in the assembly of the mockers, nor rejoiced; I sat alone because of thy hand: for thou hast filled me with indignation.

Lu 5:16 And he withdrew himself into the wilderness, and prayed.

See **QUIETNESS, PRAYER, SILENCE, WAITING**

SOLOMON, *king of Israel, son of David and Bath-sheba*

1. Overview of Life

His Parentage: He was the son of David and Bathsheba (2 S 12:24–25). He was both fortunate and unfortunate in his parentage and home surroundings. He was fortunate in having a father like David, a great genius, who on the whole was eminently religious. He was unfortunate, in that there were some elements in his father's example that would inevitably have a bad effect on Solomon's life. He was reared in a home where polygamy was practiced and hence there was much jealousy.

Accession to the Throne: David, having many sons, had promised that Solomon should be his successor, and he was anointed king before his father's death (1 K 1:17–39).

Early Years of His Reign: Considering the age in which he lived, he began his reign well, but he made a fatal mistake in choosing a heathen king's daughter for his wife (1 K 3:1). This no doubt was an act of political expediency and was the first of his foreign alliances, which had much to do with his later moral downfall.

His Wisdom: Early in his reign he had a vision at Gibeon in which the

LORD appeared to him and told him to ask what he would have. He confessed his weakness and ignorance and asked for wisdom. Because of his wise choice his request was granted, and he was promised by the Lord that he should be the wisest of men and have great riches and honor. This promise was fulfilled, for he excelled in wisdom over all the great men of his times. He spoke three thousand proverbs, and his songs were one thousand and five. His fame spread abroad over the world (1 K 4:29–34).

His Policy and Enterprises: He carried out the plans of his father, David, consolidated the kingdom, and engaged in many commercial ventures, while his wealth and renown grew. His greatest enterprise was the construction of the temple at Jerusalem, in which he was occupied seven years, and it was most elaborately adorned (1 K 5–6). At the completion of the work Solomon offered a dedicatory prayer (2 Chr 6:12–7:3).

His Later Years: He was honored by the memorable visit of the Queen of Sheba (1 K 10:1–13). As he increased in wealth and honor his love of display grew, and he maintained a most luxurious and extravagant establishment beyond what the resources of his people would warrant (1 K 10:14–29). This led to social discontent and prepared the way for the later disruption of the kingdom (1 K 12:4–19).

His Moral Downfall and Idolatry: At last he plunged into sensuality and was influenced by his many wives to introduce the worship of false gods into Jerusalem (1 K 11:1–8). He was sharply rebuked by the Lord for his apostasy, and the disruption of the kingdom in his son's time was foretold (11:9–13).

The Question of His Repentance: Of his actual end nothing positive is known. Whether he finally repented and returned to God has been warmly debated by students of his history. Those who believe that he wrote the

substance of the book of Ecclesiastes see him there wandering in the labyrinth of human philosophy and seeming at last to emerge into the light of faith in divine providence.

His Life Furnishes a Great Warning: He is known as the wisest man, yet his wisdom did not teach him self-control. He taught well but failed to practice his own precepts. He describes the fool in the book of Proverbs and thus draws a vivid picture of his own failings.

2. His Wisdom Seen

IN HIS WISE CHOICE

1 Kings 3:5-9 In Gibeon the LORD appeared to Solomon in a dream by night: and God said, Ask what I shall give thee.

And Solomon said, Thou hast shewed unto thy servant David my father great mercy, according as he walked before thee in truth, and in righteousness, and in uprightness of heart with thee; and thou hast kept for him this great kindness, that thou hast given him a son to sit on his throne, as *it is* this day.

And now, O LORD my God, thou hast made thy servant king instead of David my father: and I *am but* a little child: I know not *how* to go out or come in.

And thy servant *is* in the midst of thy people which thou hast chosen, a great people, that cannot be numbered nor counted for multitude.

Give therefore thy servant an understanding heart to judge thy people, that I may discern between good and bad: for who is able to judge this thy so great a people?

IN JUDICIAL INSIGHT

1 Kings 3:16-28 Then came there two women, *that were* harlots, unto the king, and stood before him.

And the one woman said, O my lord, I and this woman dwell in one house; and I was delivered of a child with her in the house.

And it came to pass the third day after that I was delivered, that this woman was delivered also: and we *were* together; *there was* no stranger with us in the house, save we two in the house.

And this woman's child died in the night; because she overlaid it.

And she arose at midnight, and took my son from beside me, while thine handmaid slept, and laid it in her bosom, and laid her dead child in my bosom.

And when I rose in the morning to give my child suck, behold, it was dead: but when I had considered it in the morning, behold, it was not my son, which I did bear.

And the other woman said, Nay; but the living *is* my son, and the dead *is* thy son. And this said, No; but the dead *is* thy son, and the living *is* my son. Thus they spake before the king.

Then said the king, The one saith, This *is* my son that son *is* the dead: and the other saith, Nay; but thy son *is* the dead, and my son *is* the living.

And the king said, Bring me a sword. And they brought a sword before the king.

And the king said, Divide the living child in two, and give half to the one, and half to the other.

Then spake the woman whose the living child *was* unto the king, for her bowels yearned upon her son, and she said, O my lord, give her the living child, and in no wise slay it. But the other said, Let it be neither mine nor thine, *but* divide *it*.

Then the king answered and said, Give her the living child, and in no wise slay it: she *is* the mother thereof.

And all Israel heard of the judgment which the king had judged; and they feared the king: for they saw that the wisdom of God *was* in him, to do judgment.

IN SURPASSING OTHER WISE MEN
1 Kings 4:29-31

And God gave Solomon wisdom and understanding exceeding much, and largeness of heart, even as the sand that *is* on the sea shore.

And Solomon's wisdom excelled the wisdom of all the children of the east country, and all the wisdom of Egypt.

For he was wiser than all men; than Ethan the Ezrahite, and Heman, and Chalcol, and Darda, the sons of Mahol: and his fame was in all nations round about.

IN UTTERING PROVERBS AND DISCOURSES
1 K 32-34 And he spake three thousand proverbs: and his songs were a thousand and five.

And he spake of trees, from the cedar tree that *is* in Lebanon even unto the hyssop that springeth out of the wall: he spake also of beasts, and of fowl, and of creeping things, and of fishes.

And there came of all people to hear the wisdom of Solomon, from all kings of the earth, which had heard of his wisdom.

IN ERECTION OF THE TEMPLE
1 K 6:38 And in the eleventh year, in the month Bul, which *is* the eighth month, was the house finished throughout all the parts thereof, and according to all the fashion of it. So was he seven years in building it.

IN HIS PRAYER OF DEDICATION
1 Kings 8:22-28 And Solomon stood before the altar of the LORD in the presence of all the congregation of Israel, and spread forth his hands toward heaven:

And he said, LORD God of Israel, *there is* no God like thee, in heaven above, or on earth beneath, who keepest covenant and mercy with thy servants that walk before thee with all their heart:

Who hast kept with thy servant David my father that thou promisedst him: thou spakest also with thy mouth, and hast fulfilled *it* with thine hand, as *it is* this day.

Therefore now, LORD God of Israel, keep with thy servant David my father that thou promisedst him, saying, There shall not fail thee a man in my sight to sit on the throne of Israel; so that thy children take heed to their way, that they walk before me as thou hast walked before me.

And now, O God of Israel, let thy word, I pray thee, be verified, which thou spakest unto thy servant David my father.

But will God indeed dwell on the earth? behold, the heaven of heavens cannot contain thee; how much less this house that I have builded?

Yet have thou respect unto the prayer of thy servant, and to his supplication, O LORD my God, to hearken unto the cry and to the prayer, which thy servant prayeth before thee to day:

3. His Folly Shown

IN LUXURIOUS LIVING

1 Kings 4:22-23 And Solomon's provision for one day was thirty measures of fine flour, and threescore measures of meal,

Ten fat oxen, and twenty oxen out of the pastures, and an hundred sheep, beside harts, and roebucks, and fallowdeer, and fatted fowl.

IN MARRYING HEATHEN WOMEN

1 Kings 11:1 But king Solomon loved many strange women, together with the daughter of Pharaoh, women of the Moabites, Ammonites, Edomites, Zidonians, and Hittites;

Ne. 13:23–26 In those days also saw I Jews that had married wives of Ashdod, of Ammon, and of Moab:

And their children spake half in the speech of Ashdod, and could not speak in the Jews' language, but according to the language of each people.

And I contended with them, and cursed them, and smote certain of them, and plucked off their hair, and made them swear by God, saying, Ye shall not give your daughters unto their sons, nor take their daughters unto your sons, or for yourselves.

Did not Solomon king of Israel sin by these things? yet among many nations was there no king like him, who was beloved of his God, and God made him king over all Israel: nevertheless even him did outlandish women cause to sin.

IN EXCESSIVE SENSUALITY

1 Kings 11:3 And he had seven hundred wives, princesses, and three hundred concubines: and his wives turned away his heart.

IN OPPRESSING THE PEOPLE

1 Kings 12:4 Thy father made our yoke grievous: now therefore make thou the grievous service of thy father, and his heavy yoke which he put upon us, lighter, and we will serve thee.

IN SANCTIONING IDOLATRY

1 K 11:4-7 For it came to pass, when Solomon was old, that his wives turned away his heart after other gods: and his heart was not perfect with the LORD his God, as was the heart of David his father.

For Solomon went after Ashtoreth the goddess of the Zidonians, and after Milcom the abomination of the Ammonites.

And Solomon did evil in the sight of the LORD, and went not fully after the LORD, as did David his father.

Then did Solomon build an high place for Chemosh, the abomination of Moab, in the hill that is before Jerusalem, and for Molech, the abomination of the children of Ammon.

See **ISRAEL**

SONG OF SOLOMON

Author: Solomon, according to tradition.

Date Written: Early in Solomon's reign, probably around 965 B.C.

Purpose: To illustrate God's passionate love for his people through a love story, likely an actual romance of king Solomon.

To Whom Written: The lovers address each other throughout the book. Believers of all ages have benefited from this beautiful love story. They have been reminded of God's intense love for them and have been given God's ideal for true love within marriage.

Main Themes: Love between bride and bridegroom; may illustrate God's love for Israel or Christ's for the church.

Key Words: "My Beloved," the believer's title for Christ (2:16).

Key Verse: 6:3.

SONS OF ELI *See* **YOUNG PEOPLE**

SONS OF SAMUEL *See* **YOUNG PEOPLE**

SOOTHSAYERS, *pagan counterpart of the prophet, forecasters of future events*

Jos 13:22; Is 2:6; Da 2:27; 4:7; 5:7; Mi 5:12; Ac 16:16

SORCERY, *practice of the occult*

Le 19:26; De 18:10; 2 K 17:17; 21:6; 2 Chr 33:6; Is 47:9, 12; Je 27:9; Mal 3:5; Ac 8:11; 13:6; 19:19; Re 9:21; 18:23; 21:8

See **MAGICIANS**

SORROW, *grief, remorse, sadness*

Ge 3:16; Ps 102:4; 109:22; Pr 14:13; 15:13; Is 53:3; Eze 23:33; Mt 24:8; 26:22; Mk 14:19; Jn 16:6; Ac 20:38; 1 Co 7:30

See **SUFFERING, JOY**

SOUL

1. Its Distress

Ps 32:4 For day and night thy hand was heavy upon me: my moisture is turned into the drought of summer. Selah.

Ps 42:6 O my God, my soul is cast down within me: therefore will I remember thee from the land of Jordan, and of the Hermonites, from the hill Mizar.

Ps 119:28 My soul melteth for heaviness: strengthen thou me according unto thy word.

Ac 9:9 And he was three days without sight, and neither did eat nor drink.

2. Its Enemies, *unseen spiritual forces of evil*

1 S 25:29 Yet a man is risen to pursue thee, and to seek thy soul: but the soul of my lord shall be bound in the bundle of life with the LORD thy God; and the souls of thine enemies, them shall he sling out, *as out* of the middle of a sling.

2 S 22:4 I will call on the LORD, *who is* worthy to be praised: so shall I be saved from mine enemies.

Jb 19:2 How long will ye vex my soul, and break me in pieces with words?

Jb 30:14 They came *upon me* as a wide breaking in *of waters:* in the desolation they rolled themselves *upon me.*

Ps 3:2 Many *there be* which say of my soul, *There is* no help for him in God. Selah.

Ps 6:7 Mine eye is consumed because of grief; it waxeth old because of all mine enemies.

Ps 17:9 From the wicked that oppress me, *from* my deadly enemies, *who* compass me about.

Ps 18:18 They prevented me in the day of my calamity: but the LORD was my stay.

Ps 22:12 Many bulls have compassed me: strong *bulls* of Bashan have beset me round.

Ps 25:19 Consider mine enemies; for they are many; and they hate me with cruel hatred.

Ps 27:2 When the wicked, *even* mine enemies and my foes, came upon me to eat up my flesh, they stumbled and fell.

Ps 27:12 Deliver me not over unto the will of mine enemies: for false witnesses are risen up against me, and such as breathe out cruelty.

Ps 35:4 Let them be confounded and put to shame that seek after my soul: let them be turned back and brought to confusion that devise my hurt.

Ps 38:12 They also that seek after my life lay snares *for me:* and they that seek my hurt speak mischievous things, and imagine deceits all the day long.

Ps 38:19 But mine enemies *are* lively, *and* they are strong: and they that hate me wrongfully are multiplied.

Ps 40:14 Let them be ashamed and confounded together that seek after my soul to destroy it; let them be driven backward and put to shame that wish me evil.

Ps 54:3 For strangers are risen up against me, and oppressors seek after my soul: they have not set God before them. Selah.

Ps 56:2 Mine enemies would daily swallow *me* up: for *they be* many that fight against me, O thou most High.

Ps 59:3 For, lo, they lie in wait for my soul: the mighty are gathered against me; not *for* my transgression, nor *for* my sin, O LORD.

Ps 63:9 But those *that* seek my soul, to destroy *it,* shall go into the lower parts of the earth.

Ps 69:4 They that hate me without a cause are more than the hairs of mine head: they that would destroy me, *being* mine enemies wrongfully, are mighty: then I restored *that* which I took not away.

Ps 69:18 Draw nigh unto my soul, *and* redeem it: deliver me because of mine enemies.

Ps 70:2 Let them be ashamed and confounded that seek after my soul: let them be turned backward, and put to confusion, that desire my hurt.

Ps 71:10 For mine enemies speak against me; and they that lay wait for my soul take counsel together,

Ps 74:19 O deliver not the soul of thy turtledove unto the multitude *of the wicked:* forget not the congregation of thy poor for ever.

Ps 86:14 O God, the proud are risen against me, and the assemblies of violent *men* have sought after my soul; and have not set thee before them.

Ps 92:11 Mine eye also shall see *my desire* on mine enemies, *and* mine ears shall hear *my desire* of the wicked that rise up against me.

Ps 94:21 They gather themselves together against the soul of the righteous, and condemn the innocent blood.

Ps 102:8 Mine enemies reproach me all the day; *and* they that are mad against me are sworn against me.

Ps 109:3 They compassed me about also with words of hatred; and fought against me without a cause.

Ps 109:20 *Let* this *be* the reward of mine adversaries from the LORD, and of them that speak evil against my soul.

Ps 118:13 Thou hast thrust sore at me that I might fall: but the LORD helped me.

Ps 119:95 The wicked have waited for me to destroy me: *but* I will consider thy testimonies.

Ps 124:3 Then they had swallowed us up quick, when their wrath was kindled against us:

Ps 140:4 Keep me, O LORD, from the hands of the wicked; preserve me from the violent man; who have purposed to overthrow my goings.

Ps 143:3 For the enemy hath persecuted my soul; he hath smitten my life down to the ground; he hath made me to dwell in darkness, as those that have been long dead.

Je 2:34 Also in thy skirts is found the blood of the souls of the poor innocents: I have not found it by secret search, but upon all these.

Je 18:20 Shall evil be recompensed for good? for they have digged a pit for my soul. Remember that I stood before thee to speak good for them, *and* to turn away thy wrath from them.

Lam 3:52 Mine enemies chased me sore, like a bird, without cause.

Eze 13:18 And say, Thus saith the Lord GOD; Woe to the *women* that sew pillows to all armholes, and make kerchiefs upon the head of every stature to hunt souls! Will ye hunt the souls of my people, and will ye save the souls alive *that come* unto you?

Eze 22:25 *There is* a conspiracy of her prophets in the midst thereof, like a roaring lion ravening the prey; they have devoured souls; they have taken the treasure and precious things; they have made her many widows in the midst thereof.

Eze 22:27 Her princes in the midst thereof *are* like wolves ravening the prey, to shed blood, *and* to destroy souls, to get dishonest gain.

Mi 3:3 Who also eat the flesh of my people, and flay their skin from off them; and they break their bones, and chop them in pieces, as for the pot, and as flesh within the caldron.

Mk 14:70 And he denied it again. And a little after, they that stood by said again to Peter, Surely thou art *one* of them: for thou art a Galilaean, and thy speech agreeth *thereto*.

Lu 1:71 That we should be saved from our enemies, and from the hand of all that hate us;

Lu 22:31 And the Lord said, Simon, Simon, behold, Satan hath desired *to have* you, that he may sift *you* as wheat:

Ep 6:12 For we wrestle not against flesh and blood, but against principalities, against powers, against the rulers of the darkness of this world, against spiritual wickedness in high *places*.

1 Pe 5:8 Be sober, be vigilant; because your adversary the devil, as a roaring lion, walketh about, seeking whom he may devour:

See **MANKIND**

SOUL-WINNERS

1. Their Work

DISPLAY THE HIGHEST WISDOM

Pr 11:30 The fruit of the righteous *is* a tree of life; and he that winneth souls *is* wise.

WIN A RADIANT CROWN

Da 12:3 And they that be wise shall shine as the brightness of the firmament; and they that turn many to righteousness as the stars for ever and ever.

TRAINED BY CHRIST IN A NEW CALLING

Mt 4:19 And he saith unto them, Follow me, and I will make you fishers of men.

Lu 5:10 And so *was* also James, and John, the sons of Zebedee, which were partners with Simon. And Jesus said

unto Simon, Fear not; from henceforth thou shalt catch men.

SACRIFICE PERSONAL RIGHTS AND PRIVILEGES

1 Co 9:19–20 For though I be free from all *men,* yet have I made myself servant unto all, that I might gain the more.

And unto the Jews I became as a Jew, that I might gain the Jews; to them that are under the law, as under the law, that I might gain them that are under the law;

Ja 5:20 Let him know, that he which converteth the sinner from the error of his way shall save a soul from death, and shall hide a multitude of sins.

SNATCH PEOPLE FROM THE FIRE

Jude 23 And others save with fear, pulling *them* out of the fire; hating even the garment spotted by the flesh.

2. Their Joy

ESSENTIAL TO SUCCESS IN CHRISTIAN WORK

Ps 51:12–13 Restore unto me the joy of thy salvation; and uphold me *with* thy free spirit.

Then will I teach transgressors thy ways; and sinners shall be converted unto thee.

COMES FROM BRINGING IN THE SHEAVES

Ps 126:6 He that goeth forth and weepeth, bearing precious seed, shall doubtless come again with rejoicing, bringing his sheaves *with him.*

IN FINDING THE LOST SHEEP

Lu 15:6–7 And when he cometh home, he calleth together *his* friends and neighbours, saying unto them, Rejoice with me; for I have found my sheep which was lost.

I say unto you, that likewise joy shall be in heaven over one sinner that repenteth, more than over ninety and nine just persons, which need no repentance.

THE SOWER AND THE REAPER
REJOICE TOGETHER

Jn 4:36 And he that reapeth receiveth wages, and gathereth fruit unto life eternal: that both he that soweth and he that reapeth may rejoice together.

THRILLS THE CHURCH

Ac 15:3 And being brought on their way by the church, they passed through Phenice and Samaria, declaring the conversion of the Gentiles: and they caused great joy unto all the brethren.

Ph 2:16 Holding forth the word of life; that I may rejoice in the day of Christ, that I have not run in vain, neither laboured in vain.

SOULS WON ARE A CROWN OF REJOICING

1 Th 2:19–20 For what *is* our hope, or joy, or crown of rejoicing? *Are* not even ye in the presence of our Lord Jesus Christ at his coming?

For ye are our glory and joy.

IT SUSTAINED CHRIST IN HIS SUFFERING UPON THE CROSS

He 12:2 Looking unto Jesus the author and finisher of *our* faith; who for the joy that was set before him endured the cross, despising the shame, and is set down at the right hand of the throne of God.

SOVEREIGNTY, *God's supreme authority*

Ge 45:8 So now it *was* not you *that* sent me hither, but God: and he hath made me a father to Pharaoh, and lord of all his house, and a ruler throughout all the land of Egypt.

Ge 50:20 But as for you, ye thought evil against me; *but* God meant it unto good, to bring to pass, as *it is* this day, to save much people alive.

Nu 22:12 And God said unto Balaam, Thou shalt not go with them; thou shalt not curse the people: for they *are* blessed.

Nu 22:18 And Balaam answered and said unto the servants of Balak, If Balak would give me his house full of silver and gold, I cannot go beyond the word of the LORD my God, to do less or more.

Nu 23:26 But Balaam answered and said unto Balak, Told not I thee, saying, All that the LORD speaketh, that I must do?

Nu 24:13 If Balak would give me his house full of silver and gold, I cannot go beyond the commandment of the LORD, to do *either* good or bad of mine own mind; *but* what the LORD saith, that will I speak?

De 4:39 Know therefore this day, and consider *it* in thine heart, that the LORD he *is* God in heaven above, and upon the earth beneath: *there is* none else.

2 S 5:23 And when David enquired of the LORD, he said, Thou shalt not go up; *but* fetch a compass behind them, and come upon them over against the mulberry trees.

2 S 7:26 And let thy name be magnified for ever, saying, The LORD of hosts *is* the God over Israel: and let the house of thy servant David be established before thee.

2 S 12:11 Thus saith the LORD, Behold, I will raise up evil against thee out of thine own house, and I will take thy wives before thine eyes, and give *them* unto thy neighbour, and he shall lie with thy wives in the sight of this sun.

2 S 17:14 And Absalom and all the men of Israel said, The counsel of Hushai the Archite *is* better than the counsel of Ahithophel. For the LORD had appointed to defeat the good counsel of Ahithophel, to the intent that the LORD might bring evil upon Absalom.

1 K 11:35 But I will take the kingdom out of his son's hand, and will give it unto thee, *even* ten tribes.

1 K 12:15 Wherefore the king hearkened not unto the people; for the cause was from the LORD, that he might perform his saying, which the LORD spake by Ahijah the Shilonite unto Jeroboam the son of Nebat.

1 Chr 21:10 Go and tell David, saying, Thus saith the LORD, I offer thee three *things:* choose thee one of them, that I may do *it* unto thee.

1 Chr 28:3 But God said unto me, Thou shalt not build an house for my name, because thou *hast been* a man of war, and hast shed blood.

1 Chr 29:12 Both riches and honour *come* of thee, and thou reignest over all; and in thine hand *is* power and might; and in thine hand *it is* to make great, and to give strength unto all.

2 Chr 6:9 Notwithstanding thou shalt not build the house; but thy son which shall come forth out of thy loins, he shall build the house for my name.

2 Chr 10:15 So the king hearkened not unto the people: for the cause was of God, that the LORD might perform his word, which he spake by the hand of Ahijah the Shilonite to Jeroboam the son of Nebat.

2 Chr 35:21 But he sent ambassadors to him, saying, What have I to do with thee, thou king of Judah? *I come* not against thee this day, but against the house wherewith I have war: for God commanded me to make haste: forbear thee from *meddling with* God, who *is* with me, that he destroy thee not.

2 Chr 36:23 Thus saith Cyrus king of Persia, All the kingdoms of the earth hath the LORD God of heaven given me; and he hath charged me to build him an house in Jerusalem, which *is* in Judah. Who *is there* among you of all his people? The LORD his God *be* with him, and let him go up.

Ezr 6:22 And kept the feast of unleavened bread seven days with joy: for the LORD had made them joyful, and turned the heart of the king of Assyria unto them, to strengthen their hands in the work of the house of God, the God of Israel.

Jb 9:12 Behold, he taketh away, who can hinder him? who will say unto him, What doest thou?

Jb 12:14 Behold, he breaketh down, and it cannot be built again: he shutteth up a man, and there can be no opening.

Ps 22:28 For the kingdom *is* the LORD's: and he *is* the governor among the nations.

Ps 24:8 Who *is* this King of glory? The LORD strong and mighty, the LORD mighty in battle.

Ps 29:10 The LORD sitteth upon the flood; yea, the LORD sitteth King for ever.

Ps 47:2 For the LORD most high *is* terrible; *he is* a great King over all the earth.

Ps 47:8 God reigneth over the heathen: God sitteth upon the throne of his holiness.

Ps 83:18 That *men* may know that thou, whose name alone *is* JEHOVAH, *art* the most high over all the earth.

Ps 93:1 The LORD reigneth, he is clothed with majesty; the LORD is clothed with strength, *wherewith* he hath girded himself: the world also is stablished, that it cannot be moved.

Ps 135:6 Whatsoever the LORD pleased, *that* did he in heaven, and in earth, in the seas, and all deep places.

Pr 21:1 The king's heart *is* in the hand of the LORD, *as* the rivers of water: he turneth it whithersoever he will.

Is 7:7 Thus saith the Lord GOD, It shall not stand, neither shall it come to pass.

Is 10:12 Wherefore it shall come to pass, *that* when the Lord hath performed his whole work upon mount Zion and on Jerusalem, I will punish the fruit of the stout heart of the king of Assyria, and the glory of his high looks.

Is 37:16 O LORD of hosts, God of Israel, that dwellest *between* the cherubims, thou *art* the God, *even* thou alone, of all the kingdoms of the earth: thou hast made heaven and earth.

Is 41:2 Who raised up the righteous *man* from the east, called him to his foot, gave the nations before him, and made *him* rule over kings? he gave *them* as the dust to his sword, *and* as driven stubble to his bow.

Is 44:28 That saith of Cyrus, *He is* my shepherd, and shall perform all my pleasure: even saying to Jerusalem, Thou shalt be built; and to the temple, Thy foundation shall be laid.

Is 45:23 I have sworn by myself, the word is gone out of my mouth *in* righteousness, and shall not return, That unto me every knee shall bow, every tongue shall swear.

Je 18:6 O house of Israel, cannot I do with you as this potter? saith the LORD. Behold, as the clay *is* in the potter's hand, so *are* ye in mine hand, O house of Israel.

Je 28:14 For thus saith the LORD of hosts, the God of Israel; I have put a yoke of iron upon the neck of all these nations, that they may serve Nebuchadnezzar king of Babylon; and they shall serve him: and I have given him the beasts of the field also.

Eze 20:33 *As* I live, saith the Lord GOD, surely with a mighty hand, and with a stretched out arm, and with fury poured out, will I rule over you:

Eze 26:3 Therefore thus saith the Lord GOD; Behold, I *am* against thee, O Tyrus, and will cause many nations to come up against thee, as the sea causeth his waves to come up.

Eze 28:7 Behold, therefore I will bring strangers upon thee, the terrible of the nations: and they shall draw their swords against the beauty of thy wisdom, and they shall defile thy brightness.

Eze 29:19 Therefore thus saith the Lord GOD; Behold, I will give the land of Egypt unto Nebuchadrezzar king of Babylon; and he shall take her multitude, and take her spoil, and take her prey; and it shall be the wages for his army.

Da 2:20 Daniel answered and said, Blessed be the name of God for ever and ever: for wisdom and might are his:

Da 4:26 And whereas they commanded to leave the stump of the tree roots; thy kingdom shall be sure unto thee, after that thou shalt have known that the heavens do rule.

Da 4:32 And they shall drive thee from men, and thy dwelling *shall be* with the beasts of the field: they shall make thee to eat grass as oxen, and seven times shall pass over thee, until thou know that the most High ruleth in the kingdom of men, and giveth it to whomsoever he will.

Da 4:35 And all the inhabitants of the earth *are* reputed as nothing: and he doeth according to his will in the army of heaven, and *among* the in-habitants of the earth: and none can stay his hand, or say unto him, What doest thou?

Da 5:21 And he was driven from the sons of men; and his heart was made like the beasts, and his dwelling *was* with the wild asses: they fed him with grass like oxen, and his body was wet with the dew of heaven; till he knew that the most high God ruled in the kingdom of men, and *that* he appointeth over it whomsoever he will.

Da 5:26 This *is* the interpretation of the thing: MENE; God hath numbered thy kingdom, and finished it.

Mt 6:13 And lead us not into temptation, but deliver us from evil: For thine is the kingdom, and the power, and the glory, for ever. Amen.

Mt 20:15 Is it not lawful for me to do what I will with mine own? Is thine eye evil, because I am good?

Ac 17:24 God that made the world and all things therein, seeing that he is Lord of heaven and earth, dwelleth not in temples made with hands;

Ro 9:11 (For *the children* being not yet born, neither having done any good or evil, that the purpose of God according to election might stand, not of works, but of him that calleth;)

Ro 9:19 Thou wilt say then unto me, Why doth he yet find fault? For who hath resisted his will?

Ro 11:7 What then? Israel hath not obtained that which he seeketh for; but the election hath obtained it, and the rest were blinded

Ro 11:29 For the gifts and calling of God *are* without repentance.

1 Co 12:18 But now hath God set the members every one of them in the body, as it hath pleased him.

Ep 1:11 In whom also we have obtained an inheritance, being predestinated according to the purpose of him who worketh all things after the counsel of his own will:

Jude 25 To the only wise God our Saviour, *be* glory and majesty, dominion and power, both now and ever. Amen.

1. Manifested in the Control of Men

Ge 11:9 Therefore is the name of it called Babel; because the LORD did there confound the language of all the earth: and from thence did the LORD scatter them abroad upon the face of all the earth.

Ex 14:4 And I will harden Pharaoh's heart, that he shall follow after them; and I will be honoured upon Pharaoh, and upon all his host; that the Egyptians may know that I *am* the LORD. And they did so.

Ex 14:25 And took off their chariot wheels, that they drave them heavily: so that the Egyptians said, Let us flee from the face of Israel; for the LORD fighteth for them against the Egyptians.

Jud 7:22 And the three hundred blew the trumpets, and the LORD set every man's sword against his fellow, even throughout all the host: and the host fled to Beth-shittah in Zererath, *and* to the border of Abel-meholah, unto Tabbath.

1 S 19:24 And he stript off his clothes also, and prophesied before Samuel in like manner, and lay down naked all that day and all that night. Wherefore they say, *Is* Saul also among the prophets?

2 S 17:14 And Absalom and all the men of Israel said, The counsel of Hushai the Archite *is* better than the counsel of Ahithophel. For the LORD had appointed to defeat the good counsel of Ahithophel, to the intent that the LORD might bring evil upon Absalom.

2 K 7:6 For the Lord had made the host of the Syrians to hear a noise of chariots, and a noise of horses, *even* the noise of a great host: and they said one to another, Lo, the king of Israel hath hired against us the kings of the Hittites, and the kings of the Egyptians, to come upon us.

2 K 19:7 Behold, I will send a blast upon him, and he shall hear a rumour, and shall return to his own land; and I will cause him to fall by the sword in his own land.

2 K 19:28 Because thy rage against me and thy tumult is come up into mine ears, therefore I will put my hook in thy nose, and my bridle in thy lips, and I will turn thee back by the way by which thou camest.

2 Chr 11:4 Thus saith the LORD, Ye shall not go up, nor fight against your brethren: return every man to his house: for this thing is done of me. And they obeyed the words of the LORD, and returned from going against Jeroboam.

2 Chr 18:31 And it came to pass, when the captains of the chariots saw Jehoshaphat, that they said, It *is* the king of Israel. Therefore they compassed about him to fight: but Jehoshaphat cried out, and the LORD helped him; and God moved them *to depart* from him.

Jb 12:19 He leadeth princes away spoiled, and overthroweth the mighty.

Ps 21:12 Therefore shalt thou make them turn their back, *when* thou shalt make ready *thine arrows* upon thy strings against the face of them.

Ps 32:10 Many sorrows *shall be* to the wicked: but he that trusteth in the LORD, mercy shall compass him about.

Ps 35:4 Let them be confounded and put to shame that seek after my soul: let them be turned back and brought to confusion that devise my hurt.

Ps 76:10 Surely the wrath of man shall praise thee: the remainder of wrath shalt thou restrain.

Ps 125:5 As for such as turn aside unto their crooked ways, the LORD shall lead them forth with the workers of iniquity: *but* peace *shall be* upon Israel.

Pr 16:9 A man's heart deviseth his way: but the LORD directeth his steps.

Pr 21:1 The king's heart *is* in the hand of the LORD, *as* the rivers of water: he turneth it whithersoever he will.

Is 30:28 And his breath, as an overflowing stream, shall reach to the midst of the neck, to sift the nations with the sieve of vanity: and *there shall be* a bridle in the jaws of the people, causing *them* to err.

Is 37:7 Behold, I will send a blast upon him, and he shall hear a rumour, and return to his own land; and I will cause him to fall by the sword in his own land.

Is 37:29 Because thy rage against me, and thy tumult, mine ears, therefore will I put my hook in thy nose, and my bridle in thy lips, and I will turn thee back by the way by which thou camest.

Is 37:34 By the way that he came, by the same shall he return, and shall not come into this city, saith the LORD.

Is 40:23 That bringeth the princes to nothing; he maketh the judges of the earth as vanity.

Is 42:17 They shall be turned back, they shall be greatly ashamed, that trust in graven images, that say to the molten images, Ye *are* our gods.

Is 44:25 That frustrateth the tokens of the liars, and maketh diviners mad; that turneth wise *men* backward, and maketh their knowledge foolish;

Je 18:7 *At what* instant I shall speak concerning a nation, and concerning a kingdom, to pluck up, and to pull down, and to destroy *it;*

Lam 1:13 From above hath he sent fire into my bones, and it prevaileth against them: he hath spread a net for my feet, he hath turned me back: he hath made me desolate *and* faint all the day.

Eze 17:20 And I will spread my net upon him, and he shall be taken in my snare, and I will bring him to Babylon, and will plead with him there for his trespass that he hath trespassed against me.

Eze 29:4 But I will put hooks in thy jaws, and I will cause the fish of thy rivers to stick unto thy scales, and I will bring thee up out of the midst of thy rivers, and all the fish of thy rivers shall stick unto thy scales.

Eze 30:24 And I will strengthen the arms of the king of Babylon, and put my sword in his hand: but I will break Pharaoh's arms, and he shall groan before him with the groanings of a deadly wounded *man.*

Eze 32:3 Thus saith the Lord GOD; I will therefore spread out my net over thee with a company of many people; and they shall bring thee up in my net.

Eze 38:4 And I will turn thee back, and put hooks into thy jaws, and I will bring thee forth, and all thine army, horses and horsemen, all of them clothed with all sorts *of armour, even* a great company *with* bucklers and shields, all of them handling swords:

Eze 39:2 And I will turn thee back, and leave but the sixth part of thee, and will cause thee to come up from the north parts, and will bring thee upon the mountains of Israel:

Da 4:25 That they shall drive thee from men, and thy dwelling shall be with the beasts of the field, and they shall make thee to eat grass as oxen, and they shall wet thee with the dew of heaven, and seven times shall pass over thee, till thou know that the most High ruleth in the kingdom of men, and giveth it to whomsoever he will.

Am 4:2 The Lord GOD hath sworn by his holiness, that, lo, the days shall come upon you, that he will take you away with hooks, and your posterity with fishhooks.

Mk 1:34 And he healed many that were sick of divers diseases, and cast out many devils; and suffered not the devils to speak, because they knew him.

Jn 7:30 Then they sought to take him: but no man laid hands on him, because his hour was not yet come.

Jn 7:44 And some of them would have taken him; but no man laid hands on him.

Jn 8:20 These words spake Jesus in the treasury, as he taught in the temple: and no man laid hands on him; for his hour was not yet come.

Ac 5:25 Then came one and told them, saying, Behold, the men whom ye put in prison are standing in the temple, and teaching the people.

Ac 17:26 And hath made of one blood all nations of men for to dwell on all the face of the earth, and hath determined the times before appointed, and the bounds of their habitation;

Ac 23:23 And he called unto *him* two centurions, saying, Make ready two hundred soldiers to go to Caesarea, and horsemen threescore and ten, and spearmen two hundred, at the third hour of the night;

Re 17:17 For God hath put in their hearts to fulfil his will, and to agree, and give their kingdom unto the beast, until the words of God shall be fulfilled.

2. Over Israel

Ex 17:1 And all the congregation of the children of Israel journeyed from the wilderness of Sin, after their journeys, according to the commandment of the LORD, and pitched in Rephidim: and *there was* no water for the people to drink.

Ex 19:8 And all the people answered together, and said, All that the LORD hath spoken we will do. And Moses returned the words of the people unto the LORD.

Nu 9:18 At the commandment of the LORD the children of Israel journeyed, and at the commandment of the LORD they pitched: as long as the cloud abode upon the tabernacle they rested in their tents.

De 29:12 That thou shouldest enter into covenant with the LORD thy God, and into his oath, which the LORD thy God maketh with thee this day:

Jud 8:23 And Gideon said unto them, I will not rule over you, neither shall my son rule over you: the LORD shall rule over you.

1 S 8:7 And the LORD said unto Samuel, Hearken unto the voice of the people in all that they say unto thee: for they have not rejected thee, but they have rejected me, that I should not reign over them.

1 S 12:12 And when ye saw that Nahash the king of the children of Ammon came against you, ye said unto me, Nay; but a king shall reign over us: when the LORD your God *was* your king.

3. God's Throne as a Symbol

Ps 9:7 But the LORD shall endure for ever: he hath prepared his throne for judgment.

Ps 11:4 The LORD *is* in his holy temple, the LORD's throne *is* in heaven: his eyes behold, his eyelids try, the children of men.

Ps 45:6 Thy throne, O God, *is* for ever and ever: the sceptre of thy kingdom *is* a right sceptre.

Ps 47:8 God reigneth over the heathen: God sitteth upon the throne of his holiness.

Ps 93:2 Thy throne *is* established of old: thou *art* from everlasting.

Ps 97:2 Clouds and darkness *are* round about him: righteousness and judgment *are* the habitation of his throne.

Ps 103:19 The LORD hath prepared his throne in the heavens; and his kingdom ruleth over all.

Is 6:1 In the year that king Uzziah died I saw also the Lord sitting upon a throne, high and lifted up, and his train filled the temple.

Is 66:1 Thus saith the LORD, The heaven *is* my throne, and the earth *is* my footstool: where *is* the house that ye build unto me? and where *is* the place of my rest?

Je 49:38 And I will set my throne in Elam, and will destroy from thence the king and the princes, saith the LORD.

Lam 5:19 Thou, O LORD, remainest for ever; thy throne from generation to generation.

Eze 1:26 And above the firmament that *was* over their heads *was* the likeness of a throne, as the appearance of a sapphire stone: and upon the likeness of the throne *was* the likeness as the appearance of a man above upon it.

Eze 10:1 Then I looked, and, behold, in the firmament that was above the head of the cherubims there appeared over them as it were a sapphire stone, as the appearance of the likeness of a throne.

Eze 43:7 And he said unto me, Son of man, the place of my throne, and the place of the soles of my feet, where I will dwell in the midst of the children of Israel for ever, and my holy name, shall the house of Israel no more defile, *neither* they, nor their kings, by their whoredom, nor by the carcases of their kings in their high places.

Da 7:9 I beheld till the thrones were cast down, and the Ancient of days did sit, whose garment *was* white as snow, and the hair of his head like the pure wool: his throne *was like* the fiery flame, *and* his wheels *as* burning fire.

Mt 5:34 But I say unto you, Swear not at all; neither by heaven; for it is God's throne:

Mt 23:22 And he that shall swear by heaven, sweareth by the throne of God, and by him that sitteth thereon.

Ac 7:49 Heaven *is* my throne, and earth *is* my footstool: what house will ye build me? saith the Lord: or what *is* the place of my rest?

He 8:1 Now of the things which we have spoken *this is* the sum: We have such an high priest, who is set on the right hand of the throne of the Majesty in the heavens;

He 12:2 Looking unto Jesus the author and finisher of *our* faith; who for the joy that was set before him endured the cross, despising the shame, and is set down at the right hand of the throne of God.

Re 1:4 John to the seven churches which are in Asia: Grace *be* unto you, and peace, from him which is, and which was, and which is to come; and from the seven Spirits which are before his throne;

Re 4:2 And immediately I was in the spirit: and, behold, a throne was set in heaven, and *one* sat on the throne.

Re 4:6 And before the throne *there was* a sea of glass like unto crystal: and in the midst of the throne, and round about the throne, *were* four beasts full of eyes before and behind.

Re 5:11 And I beheld, and I heard the voice of many angels round about the throne and the beasts and the elders: and the number of them was ten thousand times ten thousand, and thousands of thousands;

Re 7:10 And cried with a loud voice, saying, Salvation to our God which sitteth upon the throne, and unto the Lamb.

Re 12:5 And she brought forth a man child, who was to rule all nations with a rod of iron: and her child was caught up unto God, and *to* his throne.

Re 14:3 And they sung as it were a new song before the throne, and before the four beasts, and the elders: and no man could learn that song but the hundred *and* forty *and* four thousand, which were redeemed from the earth.

Re 19:4 And the four and twenty elders and the four beasts fell down and worshipped God that sat on the throne, saying, Amen; Alleluia.

Re 20:11 And I saw a great white throne, and him that sat on it, from whose face the earth and the heaven fled away; and there was found no place for them.

Re 21:5 And he that sat upon the throne said, Behold, I make all things new. And he said unto me, Write: for these words are true and faithful.

Re 22:1 And he shewed me a pure river of water of life, clear as crystal, proceeding out of the throne of God and of the Lamb.

Re 22:3 And there shall be no more curse: but the throne of God and of the Lamb shall be in it; and his servants shall serve him:

See **FUTURE LIFE, GOD, GUIDANCE, POWER**

SOWING, *to scatter seed over the ground for growing*

1. Evil

Jb 4:8 Even as I have seen, they that plow iniquity, and sow wickedness, reap the same.

Pr 6:14 Frowardness *is* in his heart, he deviseth mischief continually; he soweth discord.

Pr 16:28 A froward man soweth strife: and a whisperer separateth chief friends.

Pr 22:8 He that soweth iniquity shall reap vanity: and the rod of his anger shall fail.

Pr 26:18 As a mad *man* who casteth firebrands, arrows, and death,

Ho 8:7 For they have sown the wind, and they shall reap the whirlwind: it hath no stalk: the bud shall yield no meal: if so be it yield, the strangers shall swallow it up.

Ga 6:8 For he that soweth to his flesh shall of the flesh reap corruption; but he that soweth to the Spirit shall of the Spirit reap life everlasting.

2. Spiritual

Ps 126:5–6 They that sow in tears shall reap in joy.

He that goeth forth and weepeth, bearing precious seed, shall doubtless come again with rejoicing, bringing his sheaves *with him.*

Pr 11:18 The wicked worketh a deceitful work: but to him that soweth righteousness *shall be* a sure reward.

Ec 11:1 Cast thy bread upon the waters: for thou shalt find it after many days.

Is 32:20 Blessed *are* ye that sow beside all waters, that send forth *thither* the feet of the ox and the ass.

Is 55:11 So shall my word be that goeth forth out of my mouth: it shall not return unto me void, but it shall accomplish that which I please, and it shall prosper *in the thing* whereto I sent it.

Je 1:10 See, I have this day set thee over the nations and over the kingdoms, to root out, and to pull down, and to destroy, and to throw down, to build, and to plant.

Ho 10:12 Sow to yourselves in righteousness, reap in mercy; break up your fallow ground: for *it is* time to seek the LORD, till he come and rain righteousness upon you.

Mt 13:3 And he spake many things unto them in parables, saying, Behold, a sower went forth to sow;

Mt 13:24 Another parable put he forth unto them, saying, The kingdom of heaven is likened unto a man which sowed good seed in his field:

Mt 13:37 He answered and said unto them, He that soweth the good seed is the Son of man;

Mk 4:3 Hearken; Behold, there went out a sower to sow:

Mk 4:14 The sower soweth the word.

Lu 8:5 A sower went out to sow his seed: and as he sowed, some fell by the way side; and it was trodden down, and the fowls of the air devoured it.

Jn 4:37 And herein is that saying true, One soweth, and another reapeth.

1 Co 9:11 If we have sown unto you spiritual things, *is it* a great thing if we shall reap your carnal things?

2 Co 9:6 But this *I say,* He which soweth sparingly shall reap also sparingly; and he which soweth bountifully shall reap also bountifully.

Ga 6:8 For he that soweth to his flesh shall of the flesh reap corruption; but he that soweth to the Spirit shall of the Spirit reap life everlasting.

Ja 3:18 And the fruit of righteousness is sown in peace of them that make peace.

3. Harvest

a. Of Sin

DISAPPOINTING

Is 17:11 In the day shalt thou make thy plant to grow, and in the morning shalt thou make thy seed to flourish: *but* the harvest *shall be* a heap in the day of grief and of desperate sorrow.

PROFITLESS

Je 12:13 They have sown wheat, but shall reap thorns: they have put themselves to pain, *but* shall not profit: and they shall be ashamed of your revenues because of the fierce anger of the LORD.

Je 51:33 For thus saith the LORD of hosts, the God of Israel; The daughter of Babylon *is* like a threshingfloor, *it is* time to thresh her: yet a little while, and the time of her harvest shall come.

Ho 6:11 Also, O Judah, he hath set an harvest for thee, when I returned the captivity of my people.

Ho 8:7 For they have sown the wind, and they shall reap the whirlwind: it hath no stalk: the bud shall yield no meal: if so be it yield, the strangers shall swallow it up.

REAPED AT THE JUDGMENT DAY

Jl 3:12–13 Let the heathen be wakened, and come up to the valley of Jehoshaphat: for there will I sit to judge all the heathen round about.

Put ye in the sickle, for the harvest is ripe: come, get you down; for the press is full, the fats overflow; for their wickedness *is* great.

ACCORDING TO THE SEED SOWN

Ga 6:7–8 Be not deceived; God is not mocked: for whatsoever a man soweth, that shall he also reap.

For he that soweth to his flesh shall of the flesh reap corruption; but he that soweth to the Spirit shall of the Spirit reap life everlasting.

SURE TO COME IN THE FULLNESS OF TIME

Re 14:15 And another angel came out of the temple, crying with a loud voice to him that sat on the cloud, Thrust in thy sickle, and reap: for the time is come for thee to reap; for the harvest of the earth is ripe.

b. Of Good

Ps 126:6 He that goeth forth and weepeth, bearing precious seed, shall doubtless come again with rejoicing, bringing his sheaves *with him*.

Ho 10:12 Sow to yourselves in righteousness, reap in mercy; break up your fallow ground: for *it is* time to seek the LORD, till he come and rain righteousness upon you.

Mt 9:37 Then saith he unto his disciples, The harvest truly *is* plenteous, but the labourers *are* few;

Mk 4:29 But when the fruit is brought forth, immediately he putteth in the sickle, because the harvest is come.

Lu 10:2 Therefore said he unto them, The harvest truly *is* great, but the labourers *are* few: pray ye therefore the Lord of the harvest, that he would send forth labourers into his harvest.

Jn 4:35–36 Say not ye, There are yet four months, and *then* cometh harvest? behold, I say unto you, Lift up your eyes, and look on the fields; for they are white already to harvest.

And he that reapeth receiveth wages, and gathereth fruit unto life eternal: that both he that soweth and he that reapeth may rejoice together.

Ro 1:13 Now I would not have you ignorant, brethren, that oftentimes I purposed to come unto you, (but was let hitherto,) that I might have some fruit among you also, even as among other Gentiles.

1 Co 3:7 So then neither is he that planteth any thing, neither he that watereth; but God that giveth the increase.

2 Co 9:6 But this *I say*, He which soweth sparingly shall reap also sparingly; and he which soweth bountifully shall reap also bountifully.

Ga 6:9 And let us not be weary in well doing: for in due season we shall reap, if we faint not.

See **AGRICULTURE, EVANGELISM, WITNESSES**

SPAN, *a measure*

Ex 28:16; 39:9; 1 S 17:4; Is 40:12; Eze 43:13

See **WEIGHTS AND MEASURES**

SPARROWS *See* **BIRDS**

SPEARS, *weapons of warfare*

Jos 8:18; 1 S 17:7; 22:6; 26:11, 22; 2 S 21:19; 23:21; 1 Chr 11:23; 12:34; 2 Chr 11:12; 26:14; Ne 4:16; Jb 39:23; 41:26; Ps 46:9; Is 2:4; Na 3:3; Jn 19:34

See **WAR, WEAPONS AND ARMOR**

SPECTACLES

Mt 27:39 And they that passed by reviled him, wagging their heads,

1 Co 4:9 For I think that God hath set forth us the apostles last, as it were appointed to death: for we are made a spectacle unto the world, and to angels, and to men.

He 10:33 Partly, whilst ye were made a gazingstock both by reproaches and afflictions; and partly, whilst ye became companions of them that were so used.

See **TESTIMONY**

SPEECH

1. Wise

Pr 17:27 He that hath knowledge spareth his words: *and* a man of understanding is of an excellent spirit.

Mt 5:37 But let your communication be, Yea, yea; Nay, nay: for whatsoever is more than these cometh of evil.

Col 4:6 Let your speech *be* alway with grace, seasoned with salt, that ye may know how ye ought to answer every man.

2 Ti 1:13 Hold fast the form of sound words, which thou hast heard of me, in faith and love which is in Christ Jesus.

Tit 2:8 Sound speech, that cannot be condemned; that he that is of the contrary part may be ashamed, having no evil thing to say of you.

Ja 3:2 For in many things we offend all. If any man offend not in word, the same *is* a perfect man, *and* able also to bridle the whole body.

2. Plain

Mt 3:7 But when he saw many of the Pharisees and Sadducees come to his baptism, he said unto them, O generation of vipers, who hath warned you to flee from the wrath to come?

Mt 23:33 *Ye* serpents, *ye* generation of vipers, how can ye escape the damnation of hell?

Lu 3:7 Then said he to the multitude that came forth to be baptized of him, O generation of vipers, who hath warned you to flee from the wrath to come?

Ac 7:52 Which of the prophets have not your fathers persecuted? and they have slain them which shewed before of the coming of the Just One; of whom ye have been now the betrayers and murderers:

2 Co 3:12 Seeing then that we have such hope, we use great plainness of speech:

Ga 4:16 Am I therefore become your enemy, because I tell you the truth?

3. Wicked

Ps 5:9 For *there is* no faithfulness in their mouth; their inward part *is* very wickedness; their throat *is* an open sepulchre; they flatter with their tongue.

Ps 10:7 His mouth is full of cursing and deceit and fraud: under his tongue *is* mischief and vanity.

Ps 12:2 They speak vanity every one with his neighbour: *with* flattering lips *and* with a double heart do they speak.

Ps 31:18 Let the lying lips be put to silence; which speak grievous things proudly and contemptuously against the righteous.

Ps 36:3 The words of his mouth *are* iniquity and deceit: he hath left off to be wise, *and* to do good.

Ps 38:12 They also that seek after my life lay snares *for me:* and they that seek my hurt speak mischievous things, and imagine deceits all the day long.

Ps 41:5 Mine enemies speak evil of me, When shall he die, and his name perish?

Ps 50:19 Thou givest thy mouth to evil, and thy tongue frameth deceit.

Ps 52:2 Thy tongue deviseth mischiefs; like a sharp rasor, working deceitfully.

Ps 55:21 *The words* of his mouth were smoother than butter, but war *was* in his heart: his words were softer than oil, yet *were* they drawn swords.

Ps 59:7 Behold, they belch out with their mouth: swords *are* in their lips: for who, *say they,* doth hear?

Ps 71:10 For mine enemies speak against me; and they that lay wait for my soul take counsel together,

Ps 73:8 They are corrupt, and speak wickedly *concerning* oppression: they speak loftily.

Ps 94:4 *How long* shall they utter *and* speak hard things? *and* all the workers of iniquity boast themselves?

Ps 109:2 For the mouth of the wicked and the mouth of the deceitful are opened against me: they have spoken against me with a lying tongue.

Ps 120:3 What shall be given unto thee? or what shall be done unto thee, thou false tongue?

Ps 139:20 For they speak against thee wickedly, *and* thine enemies take *thy name* in vain.

Ps 140:3 They have sharpened their tongues like a serpent; adders' poison *is* under their lips. Selah.

Ps 144:8 Whose mouth speaketh vanity, and their right hand *is* a right hand of falsehood.

Pr 2:12 To deliver thee from the way of the evil *man,* from the man that speaketh froward things;

Pr 8:13 The fear of the LORD *is* to hate evil: pride, and arrogancy, and the evil way, and the froward mouth, do I hate.

Pr 10:6 Blessings *are* upon the head of the just: but violence covereth the mouth of the wicked.

Pr 10:14 Wise *men* lay up knowledge: but the mouth of the foolish *is* near destruction.

Pr 11:11 By the blessing of the upright the city is exalted: but it is overthrown by the mouth of the wicked.

Pr 12:18 There is that speaketh like the piercings of a sword: but the tongue of the wise *is* health.

Pr 14:3 In the mouth of the foolish is a rod of pride: but the lips of the wise shall preserve them.

Pr 15:28 The heart of the righteous studieth to answer: but the mouth of the wicked poureth out evil things.

Pr 16:27 An ungodly man diggeth up evil: and in his lips *there is* as a burning fire.

Pr 24:2 For their heart studieth destruction, and their lips talk of mischief.

Is 9:17 Therefore the Lord shall have no joy in their young men, neither shall have mercy on their fatherless and widows: for every one is an hypocrite and an evildoer, and every mouth speaketh folly. For all this his anger is not turned away, but his hand *is* stretched out still.

Is 32:6 For the vile person will speak villany, and his heart will work iniquity, to practise hypocrisy, and to utter error against the LORD, to make empty the soul of the hungry, and he will cause the drink of the thirsty to fail.

Is 59:3 For your hands are defiled with blood, and your fingers with iniquity; your lips have spoken lies, your tongue hath muttered perverseness.

Je 9:3 And they bend their tongues *like* their bow *for* lies: but they are not valiant for the truth upon the earth; for they proceed from evil to evil, and they know not me, saith the LORD.

Ho 7:16 They return, *but* not to the most High: they are like a deceitful bow: their princes shall fall by the sword for the rage of their tongue: this *shall be* their derision in the land of Egypt.

Ho 10:4 They have spoken words, swearing falsely in making a covenant: thus judgment springeth up as hemlock in the furrows of the field.

Obad 12 But thou shouldest not have looked on the day of thy brother in the day that he became a stranger; neither shouldest thou have rejoiced over the children of Judah in the day of their destruction; neither shouldest thou have spoken proudly in the day of distress.

Mi 6:12 For the rich men thereof are full of violence, and the inhabitants thereof have spoken lies, and their tongue *is* deceitful in their mouth.

Mt 12:34 O generation of vipers, how can ye, being evil, speak good things? for out of the abundance of the heart the mouth speaketh.

Mt 15:11 Not that which goeth into the mouth defileth a man; but that which cometh out of the mouth, this defileth a man.

Lu 6:45 A good man out of the good treasure of his heart bringeth forth that which is good; and an evil man out of the evil treasure of his heart bringeth forth that which is evil: for of the abundance of the heart his mouth speaketh.

Ro 3:13-14 Their throat *is* an open sepulchre; with their tongues they have used deceit; the poison of asps *is* under their lips:

Whose mouth *is* full of cursing and bitterness:

Ja 3:6 And the tongue *is* a fire, a world of iniquity: so is the tongue among our members, that it defileth the whole body, and setteth on fire the course of nature; and it is set on fire of hell.

2 Pe 2:12 But these, as natural brute beasts, made to be taken and destroyed, speak evil of the things that they understand not; and shall utterly perish in their own corruption;

Jude 8 Likewise also these *filthy* dreamers defile the flesh, despise dominion, and speak evil of dignities.

Jude 15 To execute judgment upon all, and to convince all that are ungodly among them of all their ungodly deeds which they have ungodly committed, and of all their hard *speeches* which ungodly sinners have spoken against him.

Re 13:5 And there was given unto him a mouth speaking great things and blasphemies; and power was given unto him to continue forty *and* two months.

a. Warnings

Is 58:9 Then shalt thou call, and the LORD shall answer; thou shalt cry, and he shall say, Here I *am*. If thou take away from the midst of thee the yoke, the putting forth of the finger, and speaking vanity;

Ep 4:31 Let all bitterness, and wrath, and anger, and clamour, and evil speaking, be put away from you, with all malice:

Tit 3:1–2 Put them in mind to be subject to principalities and powers, to obey magistrates, to be ready to every good work,

To speak evil of no man, to be no brawlers, *but* gentle, shewing all meekness unto all men.

Ja 3:6 And the tongue *is* a fire, a world of iniquity: so is the tongue among our members, that it defileth the whole body, and setteth on fire the course of nature; and it is set on fire of hell.

Ja 4:11 Speak not evil one of another, brethren. He that speaketh evil of *his* brother, and judgeth his brother, speaketh evil of the law, and judgeth the law: but if thou judge the law, thou art not a doer of the law, but a judge.

1 Pe 2:1 Wherefore laying aside all malice, and all guile, and hypocrisies, and envies, and all evil speakings,

1 Pe 3:10 For he that will love life, and see good days, let him refrain his tongue from evil, and his lips that they speak no guile:

b. Backbiting

Ps 15:3 *He that* backbiteth not with his tongue, nor doeth evil to his neighbour, nor taketh up a reproach against his neighbour.

Ps 50:20 Thou sittest *and* speakest against thy brother; thou slanderest thine own mother's son.

Ps 101:5 Whoso privily slandereth his neighbour, him will I cut off: him that hath an high look and a proud heart will not I suffer.

Pr 25:23 The north wind driveth away rain: so *doth* an angry countenance a backbiting tongue.

Pr 29:12 If a ruler hearken to lies, all his servants *are* wicked.

Ec 10:11 Surely the serpent will bite without enchantment; and a babbler is no better.

Je 9:4 Take ye heed every one of his neighbour, and trust ye not in any brother: for every brother will utterly supplant, and every neighbour will walk with slanders.

Ro 1:30 Backbiters, haters of God, despiteful, proud, boasters, inventors of evil things, disobedient to parents,

2 Co 12:20 For I fear, lest, when I come, I shall not find you such as I would, and *that* I shall be found unto you such as ye would not: lest *there be* debates, envyings, wraths, strifes, backbitings, whisperings, swellings, tumults:

c. Vain

2 K 18:27 But Rab-shakeh said unto them, Hath my master sent me to thy master, and to thee, to speak these words? *hath he* not *sent me* to the men which sit on the wall, that they may eat their own dung, and drink their own piss with you.

Jb 8:2 How long wilt thou speak these *things?* and *how long shall* the words of thy mouth be like a strong wind?

Jb 11:2 Should not the multitude of words be answered? and should a man full of talk be justified?

Jb 15:3 Should he reason with unprofitable talk? or with speeches wherewith he can do no good?

Jb 16:3 Shall vain words have an end? or what emboldeneth thee that thou answerest?

Jb 34:35 Job hath spoken without knowledge, and his words *were* without wisdom.

Jb 35:16 Therefore doth Job open his mouth in vain; he multiplieth words without knowledge.

Jb 38:2 Who *is* this that darkeneth counsel by words without knowledge?

Ps 41:6 And if he come to see *me,* he speaketh vanity: his heart gathereth iniquity to itself; *when* he goeth abroad, he telleth *it.*

Pr 10:19 In the multitude of words there wanteth not sin: but he that refraineth his lips *is* wise.

Pr 12:13 The wicked is snared by the transgression of *his* lips: but the just shall come out of trouble.

Pr 13:3 He that keepeth his mouth keepeth his life: *but* he that openeth wide his lips shall have destruction.

Pr 14:23 In all labour there is profit: but the talk of the lips *tendeth* only to penury.

Pr 15:2 The tongue of the wise useth knowledge aright: but the mouth of fools poureth out foolishness.

Pr 23:33 Thine eyes shall behold strange women, and thine heart shall utter perverse things.

Pr 29:11 A fool uttereth all his mind: but a wise *man* keepeth it in till afterwards.

Ec 5:3 For a dream cometh through the multitude of business; and a fool's voice *is known* by multitude of words.

Ec 10:13 The beginning of the words of his mouth *is* foolishness: and the end of his talk *is* mischievous madness.

Is 58:13 If thou turn away thy foot from the sabbath, *from* doing thy pleasure on my holy day; and call the sabbath a delight, the holy of the

LORD, honourable; and shalt honour him, not doing thine own ways, nor finding thine own pleasure, nor speaking *thine own* words:

Eze 33:30 Also, thou son of man, the children of thy people still are talking against thee by the walls and in the doors of the houses, and speak one to another, every one to his brother, saying, Come, I pray you, and hear what is the word that cometh forth from the LORD.

Eze 35:13 Thus with your mouth ye have boasted against me, and have multiplied your words against me: I have heard *them.*

Eze 36:3 Therefore prophesy and say, Thus saith the Lord GOD; Because they have made *you* desolate, and swallowed you up on every side, that ye might be a possession unto the residue of the heathen, and ye are taken up in the lips of talkers, and *are* an infamy of the people:

Mt 12:35 A good man out of the good treasure of the heart bringeth forth good things: and an evil man out of the evil treasure bringeth forth evil things.

Ep 5:4 Neither filthiness, nor foolish talking, nor jesting, which are not convenient: but rather giving of thanks.

1 Ti 1:6 From which some having swerved have turned aside unto vain jangling;

1 Ti 5:13 And withal they learn *to be* idle, wandering about from house to house; and not only idle, but tattlers also and busybodies, speaking things which they ought not.

2 Ti 2:18 Who concerning the truth have erred, saying that the resurrection is past already; and overthrow the faith of some.

Tit 1:10 For there are many unruly and vain talkers and deceivers, specially they of the circumcision:

Ja 1:26 If any man among you seem to be religious, and bridleth not his tongue, but deceiveth his own heart, this man's religion *is* vain.

Ja 3:5 Even so the tongue is a little member, and boasteth great things.

Behold, how great a matter a little fire kindleth!

1 Jn 4:5 They are of the world: therefore speak they of the world, and the world heareth them.

d. Talebearing

Le 19:16 Thou shalt not go up and down *as* a talebearer among thy people: neither shalt thou stand against the blood of thy neighbour: I *am* the LORD.

Pr 11:13 A talebearer revealeth secrets: but he that is of a faithful spirit concealeth the matter.

Pr 17:9 He that covereth a transgression seeketh love; but he that repeateth a matter separateth *very* friends.

Pr 18:8 The words of a talebearer *are* as wounds, and they go down into the innermost parts of the belly.

Pr 20:19 He that goeth about *as* a talebearer revealeth secrets: therefore meddle not with him that flattereth with his lips.

Pr 26:20 Where no wood is, *there* the fire goeth out: so where *there is* no talebearer, the strife ceaseth.

e. Whispering

Ps 41:7 All that hate me whisper together against me: against me do they devise my hurt.

Pr 16:28 A froward man soweth strife: and a whisperer separateth chief friends.

Pr 26:22 The words of a talebearer *are* as wounds, and they go down into the innermost parts of the belly.

Ro 1:29 Being filled with all unrighteousness, fornication, wickedness, covetousness, maliciousness; full of envy, murder, debate, deceit, malignity; whisperers,

2 Co 12:20 For I fear, lest, when I come, I shall not find you such as I would, and *that* I shall be found unto you such as ye would not: lest *there be* debates, envyings, wraths, strifes, backbitings, whisperings, swellings, tumults:

f. Slander

Ge 39:14 That she called unto the men of her house, and spake unto them, saying, See, he hath brought in an Hebrew unto us to mock us; he came in unto me to lie with me, and I cried with a loud voice:

De 22:17 And, lo, he hath given occasions of speech *against her,* saying, I found not thy daughter a maid; and yet these *are the tokens of* my daughter's virginity. And they shall spread the cloth before the elders of the city.

Est 3:8 And Haman said unto king Ahasuerus, There is a certain people scattered abroad and dispersed among the people in all the provinces of thy kingdom; and their laws *are* diverse from all people; neither keep they the king's laws: therefore it *is* not for the king's profit to suffer them.

Ps 31:13 For I have heard the slander of many: fear *was* on every side: while they took counsel together against me, they devised to take away my life.

Ps 101:5 Whoso privily slandereth his neighbour, him will I cut off: him that hath an high look and a proud heart will not I suffer.

Pr 10:18 He that hideth hatred *with* lying lips, and he that uttereth a slander, *is* a fool.

Pr 11:9 An hypocrite with *his* mouth destroyeth his neighbour: but through knowledge shall the just be delivered.

Pr 30:10 Accuse not a servant unto his master, lest he curse thee, and thou be found guilty.

Mt 27:64 Command therefore that the sepulchre be made sure until the third day, lest his disciples come by night, and steal him away, and say unto the people, He is risen from the dead: so the last error shall be worse than the first.

Tit 2:3 The aged women likewise, that *they be* in behaviour as becometh holiness, not false accusers, not given to much wine, teachers of good things;

Ja 4:11 Speak not evil one of another, brethren. He that speaketh evil of *his* brother, and judgeth his brother, speaketh evil of the law, and judgeth the law: but if thou judge the law, thou art not a doer of the law, but a judge.

1). Examples

1 S 24:9 And David said to Saul, Wherefore hearest thou men's words, saying, Behold, David seeketh thy hurt?

2 S 3:25 Thou knowest Abner the son of Ner, that he came to deceive thee, and to know thy going out and thy coming in, and to know all that thou doest.

2 S 10:3 And the princes of the children of Ammon said unto Hanun their lord, Thinkest thou that David doth honour thy father, that he hath sent comforters unto thee? hath not David *rather* sent his servants unto thee, to search the city, and to spy it out, and to overthrow it?

2 S 16:3 And the king said, And where *is* thy master's son? And Ziba said unto the king, Behold, he abideth at Jerusalem: for he said, Today shall the house of Israel restore me the kingdom of my father.

1 Chr 19:3 But the princes of the children of Ammon said to Hanun, Thinkest thou that David doth honour thy father, that he hath sent comforters unto thee? are not his servants come unto thee for to search, and to overthrow, and to spy out the land?

Ezr 4:12 Be it known unto the king, that the Jews which came up from thee to us are come unto Jerusalem, building the rebellious and the bad city, and have set up the walls *thereof,* and joined the foundations.

Ne 6:6 Wherein *was* written, It is reported among the heathen, and Gashmu saith *it,* *that* thou and the Jews think to rebel: for which cause thou buildest the wall, that thou mayest be their king, according to these words.

Jb 1:11 But put forth thine hand now, and touch all that he hath, and he will curse thee to thy face.

Ps 50:20 Thou sittest *and* speakest against thy brother; thou slanderest thine own mother's son.

Je 18:18 Then said they, Come, and let us devise devices against Jeremiah; for the law shall not perish from the priest, nor counsel from the wise, nor the word from the prophet. Come, and let us smite him with the tongue, and let us not give heed to any of his words.

Da 6:13 Then answered they and said before the king, That Daniel, which *is* of the children of the captivity of Judah, regardeth not thee, O king, nor the decree that thou hast signed, but maketh his petition three times a day.

Am 7:10 Then Amaziah the priest of Bethel sent to Jeroboam king of Israel, saying, Amos hath conspired against thee in the midst of the house of Israel: the land is not able to bear all his words.

Lu 7:33 For John the Baptist came neither eating bread nor drinking wine; and ye say, He hath a devil.

Ac 16:20 And brought them to the magistrates, saying, These men, being Jews, do exceedingly trouble our city,

Ac 24:5 For we have found this man *a* pestilent *fellow,* and a mover of sedition among all the Jews throughout the world, and a ringleader of the sect of the Nazarenes:

Ro 3:8 And not *rather,* (as we be slanderously reported, and as some affirm that we say,) Let us do evil, that good may come? whose damnation is just.

2 Ti 3:3 Without natural affection, trucebreakers, false accusers, incontinent, fierce, despisers of those that are good,

1 Pe 4:4 Wherein they think it strange that ye run not with *them* to the same excess of riot, speaking evil of *you:*

3 Jn 10 Wherefore, if I come, I will remember his deeds which he doeth, prating against us with malicious words: and not content therewith, neither doth he himself receive the brethren, and forbiddeth them that would, and casteth *them* out of the church.

2). Of Christ and His Disciples

Mt 9:34 But the Pharisees said, He casteth out devils through the prince of the devils.

Mt 11:19 The Son of man came eating and drinking, and they say, Behold a man gluttonous, and a winebibber, a friend of publicans and sinners. But wisdom is justified of her children.

Mt 26:65 Then the high priest rent his clothes, saying, He hath spoken blasphemy; what further need have we of witnesses? behold, now ye have heard his blasphemy.

Mk 3:22 And the scribes which came down from Jerusalem said, He hath Beelzebub, and by the prince of the devils casteth he out devils.

Lu 23:2 And they began to accuse him, saying, We found this *fellow* perverting the nation, and forbidding to give tribute to Caesar, saying that he himself is Christ a King.

Ac 2:13 Others mocking said, These men are full of new wine.

Ac 6:13 And set up false witnesses, which said, This man ceaseth not to speak blasphemous words against this holy place, and the law:

Ac 24:5 For we have found this man *a* pestilent *fellow*, and a mover of sedition among all the Jews throughout the world, and a ringleader of the sect of the Nazarenes:

1 Pe 2:12 Having your conversation honest among the Gentiles: that, whereas they speak against you as evildoers, they may by *your* good works, which they shall behold, glorify God in the day of visitation.

1 Pe 3:16 Having a good conscience; that, whereas they speak evil of you, as of evildoers, they may be ashamed that falsely accuse your good conversation in Christ.

Re 12:15 And the serpent cast out of his mouth water as a flood after the woman, that he might cause her to be carried away of the flood.

3). False Accusations

Ge 31:1 And he heard the words of Laban's sons, saying, Jacob hath taken away all that *was* our father's; and of that which *was* our father's hath he gotten all this glory.

Ex 23:1 Thou shalt not raise a false report: put not thine hand with the wicked to be an unrighteous witness.

Nu 16:3 And they gathered themselves together against Moses and against Aaron, and said unto them, *Ye take* too much upon you, seeing all the congregation *are* holy, every one of them, and the LORD *is* among them: wherefore then lift ye up yourselves above the congregation of the LORD?

De 22:19 And they shall amerce him in an hundred *shekels* of silver, and give *them* unto the father of the damsel, because he hath brought up an evil name upon a virgin of Israel: and she shall be his wife; he may not put her away all his days.

1 S 1:14 And Eli said unto her, How long wilt thou be drunken? put away thy wine from thee.

1 S 17:28 And Eliab his eldest brother heard when he spake unto the men; and Eliab's anger was kindled against David, and he said, Why camest thou down hither? and with whom hast thou left those few sheep in the wilderness? I know thy pride, and the naughtiness of thine heart; for thou art come down that thou mightest see the battle.

1 S 22:13 And Saul said unto him, Why have ye conspired against me, thou and the son of Jesse, in that thou hast given him bread, and a sword, and hast enquired of God for him, that he should rise against me, to lie in wait, as at this day?

1 K 18:17 And it came to pass, when Ahab saw Elijah, that Ahab said unto him, *Art* thou he that troubleth Israel?

1 K 21:10 And set two men, sons of Belial, before him, to bear witness against him, saying, Thou didst blaspheme God and the king. And *then* carry him out, and stone him, that he may die.

2 K 18:22 But if ye say unto me, We trust in the LORD our God: *is* not that he, whose high places and whose altars Hezekiah hath taken away, and hath said to Judah and Jerusalem, Ye shall worship before this altar in Jerusalem?

Ezr 4:6 And in the reign of Ahasuerus, in the beginning of his reign, wrote they *unto him* an accusation against the inhabitants of Judah and Jerusalem.

Ne 6:7 And thou hast also appointed prophets to preach of thee at Jerusalem, saying, *There is* a king in Judah: and now shall it be reported to the king according to these words. Come now therefore, and let us take counsel together.

Jb 2:5 But put forth thine hand now, and touch his bone and his flesh, and he will curse thee to thy face.

Jb 22:6 For thou hast taken a pledge from thy brother for nought, and stripped the naked of their clothing.

Pr 17:15 He that justifieth the wicked, and he that condemneth the just, even they both *are* abomination to the LORD.

Je 37:13 And when he was in the gate of Benjamin, a captain of the ward *was* there, whose name *was* Irijah, the son of Shelemiah, the son of Hananiah; and he took Jeremiah the prophet, saying, Thou fallest away to the Chaldeans.

Mt 5:11 Blessed are ye, when *men* shall revile you, and persecute *you*, and shall say all manner of evil against you falsely, for my sake.

Mt 11:18 For John came neither eating nor drinking, and they say, He hath a devil.

Mt 26:66 What think ye? They answered and said, He is guilty of death.

Mt 27:12 And when he was accused of the chief priests and elders, he answered nothing.

Mt 27:64 Command therefore that the sepulchre be made sure until the third day, lest his disciples come by night, and steal him away, and say unto the people, He is risen from the dead: so the last error shall be worse than the first.

Mk 3:2 And they watched him, whether he would heal him on the sabbath day; that they might accuse him.

Mk 15:3 And the chief priests accused him of many things: but he answered nothing.

Lu 3:14 And the soldiers likewise demanded of him, saying, And what shall we do? And he said unto them, Do violence to no man, neither accuse *any* falsely; and be content with your wages.

Lu 6:7 And the scribes and Pharisees watched him, whether he would heal on the sabbath day; that they might find an accusation against him.

Lu 23:10 And the chief priests and scribes stood and vehemently accused him.

Ac 6:11 Then they suborned men, which said, We have heard him speak blasphemous words against Moses, and *against* God.

Ac 16:21 And teach customs, which are not lawful for us to receive, neither to observe, being Romans.

Ac 17:7 Whom Jason hath received: and these all do contrary to the decrees of Caesar, saying that there is another king, *one* Jesus.

Ac 18:13 Saying, This *fellow* persuadeth men to worship God contrary to the law.

Ac 21:21 And they are informed of thee, that thou teachest all the Jews which are among the Gentiles to forsake Moses, saying that they ought not to circumcise *their* children, neither to walk after the customs.

Ac 21:28 Crying out, Men of Israel, help: This is the man, that teacheth all *men* every where against the people, and the law, and this place: and further brought Greeks also into the temple, and hath polluted this holy place.

Ac 22:30 On the morrow, because he would have known the certainty wherefore he was accused of the Jews, he loosed him from *his* bands, and commanded the chief priests and all their council to appear, and brought Paul down, and set him before them.

Ac 23:29 Whom I perceived to be accused of questions of their law, but to have nothing laid to his charge worthy of death or of bonds.

Ac 24:5 For we have found this man *a* pestilent *fellow*, and a mover of sedition among all the Jews throughout the world, and a ringleader of the sect of the Nazarenes:

Ac 24:13 Neither can they prove the things whereof they now accuse me.

Ac 25:2 Then the high priest and the chief of the Jews informed him against Paul, and besought him,

Ac 26:2 I think myself happy, king Agrippa, because I shall answer for myself this day before thee touching all the things whereof I am accused of the Jews:

Ro 3:8 And not *rather,* (as we be slanderously reported, and as some affirm that we say,) Let us do evil, that good may come? whose damnation is just.

1 Pe 3:16 Having a good conscience; that, whereas they speak evil of you, as of evildoers, they may be ashamed that falsely accuse your good conversation in Christ.

4. Restrained

2 Chr 10:13 And the king answered them roughly; and king Rehoboam forsook the counsel of the old men,

Jb 2:10 But he said unto her, Thou speakest as one of the foolish women speaketh. What? shall we receive good at the hand of God, and shall we not receive evil? In all this did not Job sin with his lips.

Jb 27:4 My lips shall not speak wickedness, nor my tongue utter deceit.

Jb 31:30 Neither have I suffered my mouth to sin by wishing a curse to his soul.

Ps 17:3 Thou hast proved mine heart; thou hast visited *me* in the night; thou hast tried me, *and* shalt find nothing; I am purposed *that* my mouth shall not transgress.

Ps 34:13 Keep thy tongue from evil, and thy lips from speaking guile.

Ps 39:1 I said, I will take heed to my ways, that I sin not with my tongue: I will keep my mouth with a bridle, while the wicked is before me.

Ps 106:33 Because they provoked his spirit, so that he spake unadvisedly with his lips.

Ps 141:3 Set a watch, O LORD, before my mouth; keep the door of my lips.

Pr 10:19 In the multitude of words there wanteth not sin: but he that refraineth his lips *is* wise.

Pr 13:3 He that keepeth his mouth keepeth his life: *but* he that openeth wide his lips shall have destruction.

Pr 17:27 He that hath knowledge spareth his words: *and* a man of understanding is of an excellent spirit.

Pr 21:23 Whoso keepeth his mouth and his tongue keepeth his soul from troubles.

Pr 30:32 If thou hast done foolishly in lifting up thyself, or if thou hast thought evil, *lay* thine hand upon thy mouth.

Ec 5:6 Suffer not thy mouth to cause thy flesh to sin; neither say thou before the angel, that it *was* an error: wherefore should God be angry at thy voice, and destroy the work of thine hands?

Mt 5:37 But let your communication be, Yea, yea; Nay, nay: for whatsoever is more than these cometh of evil.

Mt 12:37 For by thy words thou shalt be justified, and by thy words thou shalt be condemned.

Ja 1:19 Wherefore, my beloved brethren, let every man be swift to hear, slow to speak, slow to wrath:

Ja 1:26 If any man among you seem to be religious, and bridleth not his tongue, but deceiveth his own heart, this man's religion *is* vain.

Ja 3:10 Out of the same mouth proceedeth blessing and cursing. My brethren, these things ought not so to be.

1 Pe 3:10 For he that will love life, and see good days, let him refrain his tongue from evil, and his lips that they speak no guile:

See **HEARING, SILENCE**

SPICES, *aromatic substances used as flavors or scents*

Ge 43:11; Ex 30:23, 34; 37:29; 1 K 10:2, 10; 2 K 20:13; 2 Chr 9:1, 9, 24; 16:14; 32:27; Song 5:1; Is 39:2; Eze 27:22; Mk 16:1; Jn 19:40

SPIDERS *See* **INSECTS**

SPIES

Ge 42:9, 30; Nu 13:2, 16; 14:36; 21:32; De 1:22; Jos 2:1; 6:23; 7:2; Jud 1:24; 18:2; 1 S 26:4; 2 S 15:10; 2 K 6:13; Lu 20:20

SPIKENARD, *a costly perfume*

Mk 14:3; Jn 12:3

SPINDLES, *implements used in spinning*

Pr 31:19

SPINNERS   See ARTS AND CRAFTS

SPIRIT, *God*

1 K 8:27 But will God indeed dwell on the earth? behold, the heaven and heaven of heavens cannot contain thee; how much less this house that I have builded?

Jn 4:24 God *is* a Spirit: and they that worship him must worship *him* in spirit and in truth.

Ac 7:48 Howbeit the most High dwelleth not in temples made with hands; as saith the prophet,

Ac 17:24 God that made the world and all things therein, seeing that he is Lord of heaven and earth, dwelleth not in temples made with hands;

Ac 17:29 Forasmuch then as we are the offspring of God, we ought not to think that the Godhead is like unto gold, or silver, or stone, graven by art and man's device.

2 Co 3:17 Now the Lord is that Spirit: and where the Spirit of the Lord *is,* there *is* liberty.

See **HOLY SPIRIT**

SPIRITS

1. Evil

Mk 16:9 Now when *Jesus* was risen early the first *day* of the week, he appeared first to Mary Magdalene, out of whom he had cast seven devils.

Lu 8:30 And Jesus asked him, saying, What is thy name? And he said, Legion: because many devils were entered into him.

Lu 11:26 Then goeth he, and taketh *to him* seven other spirits more wicked than himself; and they enter in, and

dwell there: and the last *state* of that man is worse than the first.

Ep 6:12 For we wrestle not against flesh and blood, but against principalities, against powers, against the rulers of the darkness of this world, against spiritual wickedness in high *places.*

2. Destiny

Mt 8:29 And, behold they cried out, saying, What have we to do with thee, Jesus, thou Son of God? art thou come hither to torment us before the time?

Mt 25:41 Then shall he say also unto them on the left hand, Depart from me, ye cursed, into everlasting fire, prepared for the devil and his angels:

2 Pe 2:4 For if God spared not the angels that sinned, but cast *them* down to hell, and delivered *them* into chains of darkness, to be reserved unto judgment;

Jude 6 And the angels which kept not their first estate, but left their own habitation, he hath reserved in everlasting chains under darkness unto the judgment of the great day.

Re 19:20 And the beast was taken, and with him the false prophet that wrought miracles before him, with which he deceived them that had received the mark of the beast, and them that worshipped his image. These both were cast alive into a lake of fire burning with brimstone.

Re 20:3 And cast him into the bottomless pit, and shut him up, and set a seal upon him, that he should deceive the nations no more, till the thousand years should be fulfilled: and after that he must be loosed a little season.

Re 20:10 And the devil that deceived them was cast into the lake of fire and brimstone, where the beast and the false prophet *are,* and shall be tormented day and night for ever and ever.

See **DEMONS, SATAN**

SPIT UPON

De 25:9; Jb 17:6; 30:10; Is 50:6; Mt 26:67; 27:30; Mk 10:34; 14:65; 15:19; Lu 18:32

SPOILS *See* WAR

SPOONS, *holy vessels*

2 Chr 24:14

SPOTLESSNESS, *spiritual purity*

Jb 11:15 For then shalt thou lift up thy face without spot; yea, thou shalt be stedfast, and shalt not fear:

Jb 31:7 If my step hath turned out of the way, and mine heart walked after mine eyes, and if any blot hath cleaved to mine hands;

Song 4:7 Thou *art* all fair, my love; *there is* no spot in thee.

Song 5:2 I sleep, but my heart waketh: *it is* the voice of my beloved that knocketh, *saying,* Open to me, my sister, my love, my dove, my undefiled: for my head is filled with dew, *and* my locks with the drops of the night.

Ep 5:27 That he might present it to himself a glorious church, not having spot, or wrinkle, or any such thing; but that it should be holy and without blemish.

2 Pe 3:14 Wherefore, beloved, seeing that ye look for such things, be diligent that ye may be found of him in peace, without spot, and blameless.

See PURITY, IMPURITY

SPRING, *the season*

Ge 8:22; Pr 27:25; Song 2:11

SPRINGS *See* WATER

STAFF, *a rod or stick carried for various purposes*

Ge 32:10; Ex 12:11; 1 S 17:40; 2 K 4:29; Mk 6:8; He 11:21

STARS, *celestial bodies*

Ge 1:16; 15:5; Jud 5:20; Jb 38:7; Ps 8:3; 136:9; 147:4; Je 33:22; Eze 32:8; Jl 2:10; Mt 2:7; Mk 13:25; 1 Co 15:41; Re 6:13; 8:12; 22:16

STEADFASTNESS, *loyalty, constancy*

1. Exhortations

De 5:32 Ye shall observe to do therefore as the LORD your God hath commanded you: ye shall not turn aside to the right hand or to the left.

De 10:20 Thou shalt fear the LORD thy God; him shalt thou serve, and to him shalt thou cleave, and swear by his name.

De 11:22 For if ye shall diligently keep all these commandments which I command you, to do them, to love the LORD your God, to walk in all his ways, and to cleave unto him;

De 13:4 Ye shall walk after the LORD your God, and fear him, and keep his commandments, and obey his voice, and ye shall serve him, and cleave unto him.

De 30:20 That thou mayest love the LORD thy God, *and* that thou mayest obey his voice, and that thou mayest cleave unto him: for he *is* thy life, and the length of thy days: that thou mayest dwell in the land which the LORD sware unto thy fathers, to Abraham, to Isaac, and to Jacob, to give them.

Jos 1:7 Only be thou strong and very courageous, that thou mayest observe to do according to all the law, which Moses my servant commanded thee: turn not from it *to* the right hand or *to* the left, that thou mayest prosper whithersoever thou goest.

Jos 22:5 But take diligent heed to do the commandment and the law, which Moses the servant of the LORD charged you, to love the LORD your God, and to walk in all his ways, and to keep his commandments, and to cleave unto him, and to serve him with all your heart and with all your soul.

Jos 23:7–8 That ye come not among these nations, these that remain among you; neither make mention of the names of their gods, nor cause to swear *by them,* neither serve them, nor bow yourselves unto them:

But cleave unto the LORD your God, as ye have done unto this day.

1 S 12:21 And turn ye not aside: for *then should ye go* after vain *things,* which cannot profit nor deliver; for they *are* vain.

1 Chr 28:7 Moreover I will establish his kingdom for ever, if he be constant to do my commandments and my judgments, as at this day.

2 Chr 34:33 And Josiah took away all the abominations out of all the countries that *pertained* to the children of Israel, and made all that were present in Israel to serve, *even* to serve the LORD their God. *And* all his days they departed not from following the LORD, the God of their fathers.

Jb 11:14–15 If iniquity *be* in thine hand, put it far away, and let not wickedness dwell in thy tabernacles.

For then shalt thou lift up thy face without spot; yea, thou shalt be stedfast, and shalt not fear:

Ps 108:1 O God, my heart is fixed; I will sing and give praise, even with my glory.

Ps 119:31 I have stuck unto thy testimonies: O LORD, put me not to shame.

Is 56:2 Blessed *is* the man *that* doeth this, and the son of man *that* layeth hold on it; that keepeth the sabbath from polluting it, and keepeth his hand from doing any evil.

Je 32:40 And I will make an everlasting covenant with them, that I will not turn away from them, to do them good; but I will put my fear in their hearts, that they shall not depart from me.

Mi 4:5 For all people will walk every one in the name of his god, and we will walk in the name of the LORD our God for ever and ever.

Lu 7:24 And when the messengers of John were departed, he began to speak unto the people concerning John, What went ye out into the wilderness for to see? A reed shaken with the wind?

Ac 11:23 Who, when he came, and had seen the grace of God, was glad, and exhorted them all, that with purpose of heart they would cleave unto the Lord.

Ac 14:22 Confirming the souls of the disciples, *and* exhorting them to continue in the faith, and that we must through much tribulation enter into the kingdom of God.

1 Co 15:2 By which also ye are saved, if ye keep in memory what I preached unto you, unless ye have believed in vain.

1 Co 15:58 Therefore, my beloved brethren, be ye stedfast, unmovable, always abounding in the work of the Lord, forasmuch as ye know that your labour is not in vain in the Lord.

1 Co 16:13 Watch ye, stand fast in the faith, quit you like men, be strong.

Ga 4:18 But *it is* good to be zealously affected always in *a* good *thing,* and not only when I am present with you.

Ga 5:1 Stand fast therefore in the liberty wherewith Christ hath made us free, and be not entangled again with the yoke of bondage.

Ep 4:14 That we *henceforth* be no more children, tossed to and fro, and carried about with every wind of doctrine, by the sleight of men, *and* cunning craftiness, whereby they lie in wait to deceive;

Ep 6:14 Stand therefore, having your loins girt about with truth, and having on the breastplate of righteousness;

Ph 1:27 Only let your conversation be as it becometh the gospel of Christ: that whether I come and see you, or else be absent, I may hear of your affairs, that ye stand fast in one spirit, with one mind striving together for the faith of the gospel;

Ph 4:1 Therefore, my brethren dearly beloved and longed for, my joy and crown, so stand fast in the Lord, *my* dearly beloved.

Col 1:23 If ye continue in the faith grounded and settled, and *be* not moved away from the hope of the gospel, which ye have heard, *and* which was preached to every creature which is under heaven; whereof I Paul am made a minister;

1 Th 3:3 That no man should be moved by these afflictions: for yourselves know that we are appointed thereunto.

1 Th 3:8 For now we live, if ye stand fast in the Lord.

2 Th 2:2 That ye be not soon shaken in mind, or be troubled, neither by spirit, nor by word, nor by letter as from us, as that the day of Christ is at hand.

2 Th 2:15 Therefore, brethren, stand fast, and hold the traditions which ye have been taught, whether by word, or our epistle.

He 3:14 For we are made partakers of Christ, if we hold the beginning of our confidence stedfast unto the end;

He 10:23 Let us hold fast the profession of *our* faith without wavering; (for he is faithful that promised;)

Ja 5:8 Be ye also patient; stablish your hearts: for the coming of the Lord draweth nigh.

1 Pe 5:9 Whom resist stedfast in the faith, knowing that the same afflictions are accomplished in your brethren that are in the world.

1 Pe 5:12 By Silvanus, a faithful brother unto you, as I suppose, I have written briefly, exhorting, and testifying that this is the true grace of God wherein ye stand.

2 Pe 3:17 Ye therefore, beloved, seeing ye know *these things* before, beware lest ye also, being led away with the error of the wicked, fall from your own stedfastness.

Re 2:13 I know thy works, and where thou dwellest, *even* where Satan's seat *is:* and thou holdest fast my name, and hast not denied my faith, even in those days wherein Antipas *was* my faithful martyr, who was slain among you, where Satan dwelleth.

Re 2:25 But that which ye have *already* hold fast till I come.

2. Notable Examples

A MAN OF GOD, *in refusing a reward*

1 K 13:8 And the man of God said unto the king, If thou wilt give me half thine house, I will not go in with thee, neither will I eat bread nor drink water in this place:

2 K 18:6 For he clave to the LORD, *and* departed not from following him, but kept his commandments, which the LORD commanded Moses.

JOSIAH, *in his duties as a king*

2 K 22:2 And he did *that which was* right in the sight of the LORD, and walked in all the way of David his father, and turned not aside to the right hand or to the left.

JOB, *in his religious life*

Jb 23:11 My foot hath held his steps, his way have I kept, and not declined.

Jb 27:6 My righteousness I hold fast, and will not let it go: my heart shall not reproach *me* so long as I live.

THE THREE HEBREW CAPTIVES

Da 3:18 But if not, be it known unto thee, O king, that we will not serve thy gods, nor worship the golden image which thou hast set up.

CHRIST, *in going to the cross*

Lu 9:51 And it came to pass, when the time was come that he should be received up, he stedfastly set his face to go to Jerusalem,

PETER AND JOHN

Ac 4:19–20 But Peter and John answered and said unto them, Whether it be right in the sight of God to hearken unto you more than unto God, judge ye.

For we cannot but speak the things which we have seen and heard.

PAUL, *in finishing his course*

Ac 20:24 But none of these things move me, neither count I my life dear unto myself, so that I might finish my course with joy, and the ministry, which I have received of the Lord Jesus, to testify the gospel of the grace of God.

3. Enduring Hardship

Mt 10:22 And ye shall be hated of all *men* for my name's sake: but he that endureth to the end shall be saved.

Mk 13:13 And ye shall be hated of all *men* for my name's sake: but he that shall endure unto the end, the same shall be saved.

He 12:7 If ye endure chastening, God dealeth with you as with sons; for what son is he whom the father chasteneth not?

Ja 1:12 Blessed *is* the man that endureth temptation: for when he is tried, he shall receive the crown of life, which the Lord hath promised to them that love him.

Ja 5:11 Behold, we count them happy which endure. Ye have heard of the patience of Job, and have seen the end of the Lord; that the Lord is very pitiful, and of tender mercy.

1 Pe 2:19 For this *is* thankworthy, if a man for conscience toward God endure grief, suffering wrongfully.

4. Persevering to the End

2 K 4:30 And the mother of the child said, *As* the LORD liveth, and *as* thy soul liveth, I will not leave thee. And he arose, and followed her.

2 K 13:19 And the man of God was wroth with him, and said, Thou shouldest have smitten five or six times; then hadst thou smitten Syria till thou hadst consumed *it:* whereas now thou shalt smite Syria *but* thrice.

Jb 17:9 The righteous also shall hold on his way, and he that hath clean hands shall be stronger and stronger.

Jn 15:9 As the Father hath loved me, so have I loved you: continue ye in my love.

Ac 13:43 Now when the congregation was broken up, many of the Jews and religious proselytes followed Paul and Barnabas: who, speaking to them, persuaded them to continue in the grace of God.

Ro 2:7 To them who by patient continuance in well doing seek for glory and honour and immortality, eternal life:

Ga 6:9 And let us not be weary in well doing: for in due season we shall reap, if we faint not.

2 Ti 3:14 But continue thou in the things which thou hast learned and hast been assured of, knowing of whom thou hast learned *them;*

He 12:1 Wherefore seeing we also are compassed about with so great a cloud of witnesses, let us lay aside every weight, and the sin which doth so easily beset us, and let us run with patience the race that is set before us,

1 Pe 1:13 Wherefore gird up the loins of your mind, be sober, and hope to the end for the grace that is to be brought unto you at the revelation of Jesus Christ;

Re 3:11 Behold, I come quickly: hold that fast which thou hast, that no man take thy crown.

5. Moving toward the Goal

Ge 19:17 And it came to pass, when they had brought them forth abroad, that he said, Escape for thy life; look not behind thee, neither stay thou in all the plain; escape to the mountain, lest thou be consumed.

De 5:32 Ye shall observe to do therefore as the LORD your God hath commanded you: ye shall not turn aside to the right hand or to the left.

Jos 1:7 Only be thou strong and very courageous, that thou mayest observe to do according to all the law, which Moses my servant commanded thee: turn not from it *to* the right hand or *to* the left, that thou mayest prosper whithersoever thou goest.

Pr 4:27 Turn not to the right hand nor to the left: remove thy foot from evil.

Eze 1:12 And they went every one straight forward: whither the spirit was to go, they went; *and* they turned not when they went.

Lu 9:62 And Jesus said unto him, No man, having put his hand to the plough, and looking back, is fit for the kingdom of God.

Ph 3:13 Brethren, I count not myself to have apprehended: but *this* one thing *I do,* forgetting those things which are behind, and reaching forth unto those things which are before,

See **BACKSLIDING, FAITHFULNESS, INSTABILTY**

STEALING

1. Forbidden

Ge 44:8 Behold, the money, which we found in our sacks' mouths, we brought again unto thee out of the land of Canaan: how then should we steal out of thy lord's house silver or gold?

Ex 20:15 Thou shalt not steal.

Ex 22:1 If a man shall steal an ox, or a sheep, and kill it, or sell it; he shall restore five oxen for an ox, and four sheep for a sheep.

Ex 22:7 If a man shall deliver unto his neighbour money or stuff to keep, and it be stolen out of the man's house; if the thief be found, let him pay double.

Le 19:11 Ye shall not steal, neither deal falsely, neither lie one to another.

De 5:19 Neither shalt thou steal.

De 23:24 When thou comest into thy neighbour's vineyard, then thou mayest eat grapes thy fill at thine own pleasure; but thou shalt not put *any* in thy vessel.

Jb 24:14 The murderer rising with the light killeth the poor and needy, and in the night is as a thief.

Pr 30:9 Lest I be full, and deny *thee,* and say, Who *is* the LORD? or lest I be poor, and steal, and take the name of my God *in vain.*

Je 7:9 Will ye steal, murder, and commit adultery, and swear falsely, and burn incense unto Baal, and walk after other gods whom ye know not;

Ho 7:1 When I would have healed Israel, then the iniquity of Ephraim was discovered, and the wickedness of Samaria: for they commit falsehood; and the thief cometh in, *and* the troop of robbers spoileth without.

Zec 5:3 Then said he unto me, This *is* the curse that goeth forth over the face of the whole earth: for every one that stealeth shall be cut off *as* on this side according to it; and every one that sweareth shall be cut off *as* on that side according to it.

Mt 19:18 He saith unto him, Which? Jesus said, Thou shalt do no murder, Thou shalt not commit adultery, Thou shalt not steal, Thou shalt not bear false witness,

Mk 10:19 Thou knowest the commandments, Do not commit adultery, Do not kill, Do not steal, Do not bear false witness, Defraud not, Honour thy father and mother.

Lu 18:20 Thou knowest the commandments, Do not commit adultery, Do not kill, Do not steal, Do not bear false witness, Honour thy father and thy mother.

Ro 13:9 For this, Thou shalt not commit adultery, Thou shalt not kill, Thou shalt not steal, Thou shalt not bear false witness, Thou shalt not covet; and if *there be* any other commandment, it is briefly comprehended in this saying, namely, Thou shalt love thy neighbour as thyself.

1 Co 6:10 Nor thieves, nor covetous, nor drunkards, nor revilers, nor extortioners, shall inherit the kingdom of God.

Ep 4:28 Let him that stole steal no more: but rather let him labour, working with *his* hands the thing which is good, that he may have to give to him that needeth.

Tit 2:10 Not purloining, but shewing all good fidelity; that they may adorn the doctrine of God our Saviour in all things.

1 Pe 4:15 But let none of you suffer as a murderer, or *as* a thief, or *as* an evildoer, or as a busybody in other men's matters.

Re 9:21 Neither repented they of their murders, nor of their sorceries, nor of their fornication, nor of their thefts.

2. Examples

Ge 31:19, 30; Jos 7:21; Ho 4:2

STEPHANAS, *one of Paul's converts*

1 Co 1:16; 16:15

STEPHEN, *one of the seven deacons in the early church*

ELECTED TO SUPERVISE BENEVOLENCES

Ac 6:5 And the saying pleased the whole multitude: and they chose Stephen, a man full of faith and of the Holy Ghost, and Philip, and Prochorus, and Nicanor, and Timon, and Parmenas, and Nicolas a proselyte of Antioch:

BECAME A POWERFUL PREACHER

Ac 7:2 And he said, Men, brethren, and fathers, hearken; The God of glory appeared unto our father Abraham, when he was in Mesopotamia, before he dwelt in Charran,

FULL OF FAITH AND THE HOLY SPIRIT

Ac 6:5 And the saying pleased the whole multitude: and they chose Stephen, a man full of faith and of the Holy Ghost, and Philip, and Prochorus, and Nicanor, and Timon, and Parmenas, and Nicolas a proselyte of Antioch:

FULL OF WISDOM

Ac 6:3 Wherefore, brethren, look ye out among you seven men of honest report, full of the Holy Ghost and wisdom, whom we may appoint over this business.

Ac 6:10 And they were not able to resist the wisdom and the spirit by which he spake.

FULL OF POWER

Ac 6:8 And Stephen, full of faith and power, did great wonders and miracles among the people.

FULL OF LIGHT

Ac 6:15 And all that sat in the council, looking stedfastly on him, saw his face as it had been the face of an angel.

FULLNESS OF VISION

Ac 7:55-56 But he, being full of the Holy Ghost, looked up stedfastly into heaven, and saw the glory of God, and Jesus standing on the right hand of God,

And said, Behold, I see the heavens opened, and the Son of man standing on the right hand of God.

FULLNESS OF LOVE

Ac 7:60 And he kneeled down, and cried with a loud voice, Lord, lay not this sin to their charge. And when he had said this, he fell asleep.

A MARTYR FOR THE FAITH

Ac 7:56 And said, Behold, I see the heavens opened, and the Son of man standing on the right hand of God.

STEWARDSHIP

1. Remembered Truths

THE DIVERSITY OF GIFTS

Mt 25:14-15 For *the kingdom of heaven is* as a man travelling into a far country, *who* called his own servants, and delivered unto them his goods.

And unto one he gave five talents, to another two, and to another one; to every man according to his several ability; and straightway took his journey.

STEWARDS, NOT OWNERS

Lu 19:13 And he called his ten servants, and delivered them ten pounds, and said unto them, Occupy till I come.

FAITHFULNESS REQUIRED

1 Co 4:2 Moreover it is required in stewards, that a man be found faithful.

LIFE PRECIOUS

1 Co 6:20 For ye are bought with a price: therefore glorify God in your body, and in your spirit, which are God's.

Ep 6:7 With good will doing service, as to the Lord, and not to men:

A SACRED TREASURE TO BE KEPT

1 Ti 6:20 O Timothy, keep that which is committed to thy trust, avoiding profane *and* vain babblings, and oppositions of science falsely so called:

2 Ti 1:14 That good thing which was committed unto thee keep by the Holy Ghost which dwelleth in us.

MINISTERING AS STEWARDS

1 Pe 4:10 As every man hath received the gift, *even so* minister the same one to another, as good stewards of the manifold grace of God.

2. Accountability

De 18:19 And it shall come to pass, *that* whosoever will not hearken unto my words which he shall speak in my name, I will require *it* of him.

Jb 31:14 What then shall I do when God riseth up? and when he visiteth, what shall I answer him?

Is 45:23 I have sworn by myself, the word is gone out of my mouth *in* righteousness, and shall not return, That unto me every knee shall bow, every tongue shall swear.

Mt 12:36 But I say unto you, That every idle word that men shall speak, they shall give account thereof in the day of judgment.

Mt 18:23 Therefore is the kingdom of heaven likened unto a certain king, which would take account of his servants.

Mt 21:34 And when the time of the fruit drew near, he sent his servants to the husbandmen, that they might receive the fruits of it.

Mt 25:19 After a long time the lord of those servants cometh, and reckoneth with them.

Mt 25:26 His lord answered and said unto him, *Thou* wicked and slothful servant, thou knewest that I reap where I sowed not, and gather where I have not strawed:

Mk 12:2 And at the season he sent to the husbandmen a servant, that he might receive from the husbandmen of the fruit of the vineyard.

Lu 11:50 That the blood of all the prophets, which was shed from the foundation of the world, may be required of this generation;

Lu 12:20 But God said unto him, *Thou* fool, this night thy soul shall be required of thee: then whose shall those things be, which thou hast provided?

Lu 12:48 But he that knew not, and did commit things worthy of stripes, shall be beaten with few *stripes*. For unto whomsoever much is given, of him shall be much required: and to whom men have committed much, of him they will ask the more.

Lu 16:2 And he called him, and said unto him, How is it that I hear this of thee? give an account of thy stewardship; for thou mayest be no longer steward.

Lu 19:15 And it came to pass, that when he was returned, having received the kingdom, then he commanded these servants to be called unto him, to whom he had given the money, that he might know how much every man had gained by trading.

Lu 19:23 Wherefore then gavest not thou my money into the bank, that at my coming I might have required mine own with usury?

Lu 20:10 And at the season he sent a servant to the husbandmen, that they should give him of the fruit of the vineyard: but the husbandmen beat him, and sent *him* away empty.

Ro 14:12 So then every one of us shall give account of himself to God.

2 Co 5:10 For we must all appear before the judgment seat of Christ; that every one may receive the things *done* in *his* body, according to that he hath done, whether *it be* good or bad.

He 13:17 Obey them that have the rule over you, and submit yourselves: for they watch for your souls, as they that must give account, that they may do it with joy, and not with grief: for that *is* unprofitable for you.

1 Pe 4:4–5 Wherein they think it strange that ye run not with *them* to the same excess of riot, speaking evil of *you:*

Who shall give account to him that is ready to judge the quick and the dead.

Re 20:12 And I saw the dead, small and great, stand before God; and the books were opened: and another book was opened, which is *the book* of life: and the dead were judged out of those things which were written in the books, according to their works.

3. Responsibility

a. Personal

Ex 32:33 And the LORD said unto Moses, Whosoever hath sinned against me, him will I blot out of my book.

Nu 32:15 For if ye turn away from after him, he will yet again leave them in the wilderness; and ye shall destroy all this people.

De 24:16 The fathers shall not be put to death for the children, neither shall the children be put to death for the fathers: every man shall be put to death for his own sin.

2 K 10:24 And when they went in to offer sacrifices and burnt offerings, Jehu appointed fourscore men without, and said, *If* any of the men whom I have brought into your hands escape, *he that letteth him go,* his life *shall be* for the life of him.

2 K 14:6 But the children of the murderers he slew not: according unto that which is written in the book of the law of Moses, wherein the Lord commanded, saying, The fathers shall not be put to death for the children, nor the children be put to death for the fathers; but every man shall be put to death for his own sin.

2 Chr 25:4 But he slew not their children, but *did* as *it is* written in the law in the book of Moses, where the Lord commanded, saying, The fathers shall not die for the children, neither shall the children die for the fathers, but every man shall die for his own sin.

Jb 19:4 And be it indeed *that* I have erred, mine error remaineth with myself.

Pr 9:12 If thou be wise, thou shalt be wise for thyself: but *if* thou scornest, thou alone shalt bear *it.*

Je 31:30 But every one shall die for his own iniquity: every man that eateth the sour grape, his teeth shall be set on edge.

Eze 14:16 *Though* these three men *were* in it, *as* I live, saith the Lord God, they shall deliver neither sons nor daughters; they only shall be delivered, but the land shall be desolate.

Eze 18:4 Behold, all souls are mine; as the soul of the father, so also the soul of the son is mine: the soul that sinneth, it shall die.

Eze 18:20 The soul that sinneth, it shall die. The son shall not bear the iniquity of the father, neither shall the father bear the iniquity of the son: the righteousness of the righteous shall be upon him, and the wickedness of the wicked shall be upon him.

Eze 33:4 Then whosoever heareth the sound of the trumpet, and taketh not warning; if the sword come, and take him away, his blood shall be upon his own head.

Mt 12:36 But I say unto you, That every idle word that men shall speak, they shall give account thereof in the day of judgment.

Mt 25:9 But the wise answered, saying, *Not so;* lest there be not enough for us and you: but go ye rather to them that sell, and buy for yourselves.

Ac 18:6 And when they opposed themselves, and blasphemed, he shook his raiment, and said unto them, Your blood *be* upon your own heads; I *am* clean: from henceforth I will go unto the Gentiles.

Ro 14:4 Who art thou that judgest another man's servant? to his own master he standeth or falleth. Yea, he shall be holden up: for God is able to make him stand.

Ro 14:12 So then every one of us shall give account of himself to God.

Ro 14:22 Hast thou faith? have *it* to thyself before God. Happy *is* he that condemneth not himself in that thing which he alloweth.

2 Co 2:5 But if any have caused grief, he hath not grieved me, but in part: that I may not overcharge you all.

Ga 6:5 For every man shall bear his own burden.

b. Evaded

Ge 3:13; 16:5; 27:36; Ex 32:22; 1 S 15:21; Mt 27:24; Jn 9:21

c. Of Ministers and Religious Leaders

See **MINISTERS, OWNERSHIP, RICHES**

STOCKS

Jb 13:27; 33:11; Pr 7:22; Je 20:3; 29:26; Ac 16:24

STOICS, *a school of Grecian philosophers*

Ac 17:18

STONES, *valuable jewels*

Ex 28:17; 35:27; 39:10; De 33: 15; 2 S 12:30; 1 K 10:2, 10; 1 Chr 20:2; 29:2, 8; 2 Chr 3:6; 9:1, 10; 32:27; Pr 17:8; Is 54:12; Eze 27:22; 28:13-14; Da 11:38; 1 Co 3:12; Re 17:4; 18:12, 16; 21:11, 19

Names

a. Agate

Ex 28:19; 39:12; Eze 27:16

b. Amethyst

Ex 28:19; 39:12; Re 21:20

c. Beryl

Ex 28:20; 39:13; Song 5:14; Eze 1:16; 10:9; 28:13; Da 10:6; Re 21:20

d. Carbuncle

Ex 28:17; 39:10; Eze 28:13

e. Chalcedony

Re 21:19

f. Chrysolite

Re 21:20

g. Chrysoprasus

Re 21:20

h. Crystal

Jb 28:17; Eze 1:22; Re 4:6; 21:11; 22:1

i. Diamonds

Ex 28:18; 39:11; Je 17:1; Eze 28:13

j. Emeralds

Ex 28:18; 39:11; Eze 27:16; 28:13; Re 4:3; 21:19

k. Jacinth

Re 9:17; 21:20

l. Jasper

Ex 28:20; 39:13; Eze 28:13; Re 4:3; 21:11, 18–19

m. Onyx

Ge 2:12; Ex 25:7; 28:9, 20; 35:9, 27; 39:6, 13; 1 Chr 29:2; Jb 28:16; Eze 28:13

n. Rubies

Jb 28:18; Pr 3:15; 8:11; 31:10; Lam 4:7

o. Sapphire

Ex 24:10; 28:18; 39:11; Jb 28:6, 16; Song 5:14; Is 54:11; Lam 4:7; Eze 1:26; 10:1; 28:13; Re 21:19

p. Sardius

Ex 28:17; 39:10; Eze 28:13; Re 21:20

q. Topaz

Ex 28:17; 39:10; Jb 28:19; Eze 28:13; Re 21:20

STONECUTTERS *See* **ARTS AND CRAFTS**

STONING *See* **NATION**

STOREHOUSES, *places for keeping treasures, supplies, and equipment*

Ge 41:48, 56; 1 Chr 27:25; 2 Chr 31:11; 32:28; Je 50:26; Lu 12:24

STORKS *See* **BIRDS**

STORMS *See* **WEATHER**

STRANGERS, *outsiders or foreigners*

1. Duty to

See **SOCIAL DUTIES, SOCIAL FUNCTIONS**

2. Jewish Prohibitions

Ex 12:43; 29:33; 30:33; Le 17:8; 22:10; 24:16; Nu 1:51; 3:10, 38; 16:40; De 5:14; 17:15; Lam 1:10; Eze 44:9

See **SEPARATION**

3. General Laws

Ex 12:19, 49; 20:10; Le 16:29; 17:10, 15; Nu 15:14, 26, 30; 18:4; 19:10; De 14:21, 29; 26:11; Jos 8:33; 20:9

See **PILGRIMS**

STREETS, *public ways or thoroughfares*

Pr 1:20; Na 2:4; Mk 6:56; Lu 14:21; Ac 9:11

STRENGTH

1. Physical

Jud 14:6; 16:3, 6, 12, 17, 30; 1 S 17:35; 2 S 22:35; 23:21; 1 Chr 11:23; Ps 18:34; Pr 20:29; 31:17; Mk 2:12; 5:3; Ac 3:8

2. Spiritual

Ge 49:24 But his bow abode in strength, and the arms of his hands were made strong by the hands of the mighty *God* of Jacob; (from thence *is* the shepherd, the stone of Israel:)

Ex 15:2 The LORD *is* my strength and song, and he is become my salvation: he *is* my God, and I will prepare him an habitation; my father's God, and I will exalt him.

1 S 15:29 And also the Strength of Israel will not lie nor repent: for he *is* not a man, that he should repent.

1 S 23:16 And Jonathan Saul's son arose, and went to David into the wood, and strengthened his hand in God.

1 S 30:6 And David was greatly distressed; for the people spake of stoning him, because the soul of all the people was grieved, every man for his sons and for his daughters: but David encouraged himself in the LORD his God.

2 S 5:20 And David came to Baal-perazim, and David smote them there, and said, The LORD hath broken forth upon mine enemies before me, as the breach of waters. Therefore he called the name of that place Baal-perazim.

2 S 22:30 For by thee I have run through a troop: by my God have I leaped over a wall.

2 S 22:33 God *is* my strength *and* power: and he maketh my way perfect.

2 S 22:40 For thou hast girded me with strength to battle: them that rose up against me hast thou subdued under me.

2 S 23:10 He arose, and smote the Philistines until his hand was weary, and his hand clave unto the sword: and the LORD wrought a great victory that day; and the people returned after him only to spoil.

1 K 18:46 And the hand of the LORD was on Elijah; and he girded up his loins, and ran before Ahab to the entrance of Jezreel.

1 K 19:8 And he arose, and did eat and drink, and went in the strength of that meat forty days and forty nights unto Horeb the mount of God.

1 Chr 29:12 Both riches and honour *come* of thee, and thou reignest over all; and in thine hand *is* power and might; and in thine hand *it is* to make great, and to give strength unto all.

2 Chr 16:9 For the eyes of the LORD run to and fro throughout the whole earth, to shew himself strong in the behalf of *them* whose heart *is* perfect toward him. Herein thou hast done foolishly: therefore from henceforth thou shalt have wars.

2 Chr 26:8 And the Ammonites gave gifts to Uzziah: and his name spread abroad *even* to the entering in of Egypt; for he strengthened *himself* exceedingly.

Ezr 7:28 And hath extended mercy unto me before the king, and his counsellors, and before all the king's mighty princes. And I was strengthened as the hand of the LORD my God *was* upon me, and I gathered together out of Israel chief men to go up with me.

Ne 6:9 For they all made us afraid, saying, Their hands shall be weakened from the work, that it be not done. Now therefore, *O God,* strengthen my hands.

Jb 12:13 With him *is* wisdom and strength, he hath counsel and understanding.

Ps 18:1 I will love thee, O LORD, my strength.

Ps 18:18 They prevented me in the day of my calamity: but the LORD was my stay.

Ps 18:29 For by thee I have run through a troop; and by my God have I leaped over a wall.

Ps 18:39 For thou hast girded me with strength unto the battle: thou hast subdued under me those that rose up against me.

Ps 19:14 Let the words of my mouth, and the meditation of my heart, be acceptable in thy sight, O Lord, my strength, and my redeemer.

Ps 20:2 Send thee help from the sanctuary, and strengthen thee out of Zion;

Ps 22:19 But be not thou far from me, O Lord: O my strength, haste thee to help me.

Ps 27:1 The Lord is my light and my salvation; whom shall I fear? the Lord is the strength of my life; of whom shall I be afraid?

Ps 28:7 The Lord is my strength and my shield; my heart trusted in him, and I am helped: therefore my heart greatly rejoiceth; and with my song will I praise him.

Ps 28:8 The Lord is their strength, and he is the saving strength of his anointed.

Ps 31:4 Pull me out of the net that they have laid privily for me: for thou art my strength.

Ps 31:24 Be of good courage, and he shall strengthen your heart, all ye that hope in the Lord.

Ps 37:39 But the salvation of the righteous is of the Lord: he is their strength in the time of trouble.

Ps 41:3 The Lord will strengthen him upon the bed of languishing: thou wilt make all his bed in his sickness.

Ps 43:2 For thou art the God of my strength: why dost thou cast me off? why go I mourning because of the oppression of the enemy?

Ps 46:1 God is our refuge and strength, a very present help in trouble.

Ps 59:17 Unto thee, O my strength, will I sing: for God is my defence, and the God of my mercy.

Ps 62:7 In God is my salvation and my glory: the rock of my strength, and my refuge, is in God.

Ps 68:28 Thy God hath commanded thy strength: strengthen, O God, that which thou hast wrought for us.

Ps 68:35 O God, thou art terrible out of thy holy places: the God of Israel is he that giveth strength and power unto his people. Blessed be God.

Ps 71:16 I will go in the strength of the Lord God: I will make mention of thy righteousness, even of thine only.

Ps 73:26 My flesh and my heart faileth: but God is the strength of my heart, and my portion for ever.

Ps 81:1 Sing aloud unto God our strength: make a joyful noise unto the God of Jacob.

Ps 84:5 Blessed is the man whose strength is in thee; in whose heart are the ways of them.

Ps 89:17 For thou art the glory of their strength: and in thy favour our horn shall be exalted.

Ps 89:21 With whom my hand shall be established: mine arm also shall strengthen him.

Ps 118:14 The Lord is my strength and song, and is become my salvation.

Ps 138:3 In the day when I cried thou answeredst me, and strengthenedst me with strength in my soul.

Ps 140:7 O God the Lord, the strength of my salvation, thou hast covered my head in the day of battle.

Ps 144:1 Blessed be the Lord my strength, which teacheth my hands to war, and my fingers to fight:

Ps 147:13 For he hath strengthened the bars of thy gates; he hath blessed thy children within thee.

Pr 14:26 In the fear of the Lord is strong confidence: and his children shall have a place of refuge.

Pr 21:31 The horse is prepared against the day of battle: but safety is of the Lord.

Is 12:2 Behold, God is my salvation; I will trust, and not be afraid: for the Lord JEHOVAH is my strength and my song; he also is become my salvation.

Is 17:10 Because thou hast forgotten the God of thy salvation, and hast not been mindful of the rock of thy strength, therefore shalt thou plant pleasant plants, and shalt set it with strange slips:

Is 25:4 For thou hast been a strength to the poor, a strength to the needy in his distress, a refuge from the storm, a shadow from the heat, when the blast of the terrible ones is as a storm against the wall.

Is 26:4 Trust ye in the Lord for ever: for in the Lord JEHOVAH is everlasting strength:

Is 27:5 Or let him take hold of my strength, *that* he may make peace with me; *and* he shall make peace with me.

Is 40:29 He giveth power to the faint; and to *them that have* no might he increaseth strength.

Is 45:24 Surely, shall *one* say, in the LORD have I righteousness and strength: *even* to him shall *men* come; and all that are incensed against him shall be ashamed.

Is 49:5 And now, saith the LORD that formed me from the womb *to be* his servant, to bring Jacob again to him, Though Israel be not gathered, yet shall I be glorious in the eyes of the LORD, and my God shall be my strength.

Je 16:19 O LORD, my strength, and my fortress, and my refuge in the day of affliction, the Gentiles shall come unto thee from the ends of the earth, and shall say, Surely our fathers have inherited lies, vanity, and *things* wherein *there is* no profit.

Je 50:34 Their Redeemer *is* strong; the LORD of hosts *is* his name: he shall throughly plead their cause, that he may give rest to the land, and disquiet the inhabitants of Babylon.

Eze 2:2 And the spirit entered into me when he spake unto me, and set me upon my feet, that I heard him that spake unto me.

Eze 3:14 So the spirit lifted me up, and took me away, and I went in bitterness, in the heat of my spirit; but the hand of the LORD was strong upon me.

Ho 7:15 Though I have bound *and* strengthened their arms, yet do they imagine mischief against me.

Jl 3:16 The LORD also shall roar out of Zion, and utter his voice from Jerusalem; and the heavens and the earth shall shake: but the LORD *will be* the hope of his people, and the strength of the children of Israel.

Am 5:9 That strengtheneth the spoiled against the strong, so that the spoiled shall come against the fortress.

Hab 3:19 The LORD God *is* my strength, and he will make my feet like hinds' *feet,* and he will make me to walk upon mine high places. To the

chief singer on my stringed instruments.

Zec 10:6 And I will strengthen the house of Judah, and I will save the house of Joseph, and I will bring them again to place them; for I have mercy upon them: and they shall be as though I had not cast them off: for I *am* the LORD their God, and will hear them.

Zec 10:12 And I will strengthen them in the LORD; and they shall walk up and down in his name, saith the LORD.

Zec 12:5 And the governors of Judah shall say in their heart, The inhabitants of Jerusalem *shall be* my strength in the LORD of hosts their God.

Ep 6:10 Finally, my brethren, be strong in the Lord, and in the power of his might.

1 Ti 1:12 And I thank Christ Jesus our Lord, who hath enabled me, for that he counted me faithful, putting me into the ministry;

3. Moral and Spiritual

De 33:25 Thy shoes *shall be* iron and brass; and as thy days, *so shall* thy strength *be.*

1 S 2:10 The adversaries of the LORD shall be broken to pieces; out of heaven shall he thunder upon them: the LORD shall judge the ends of the earth; and he shall give strength unto his king, and exalt the horn of his anointed.

2 S 22:40 For thou hast girded me with strength to battle: them that rose up against me hast thou subdued under me.

Ps 18:32 *It is* God that girdeth me with strength, and maketh my way perfect.

Ps 27:14 Wait on the LORD: be of good courage, and he shall strengthen thine heart: wait, I say, on the LORD.

Ps 29:11 The LORD will give strength unto his people; the LORD will bless his people with peace.

Ps 119:28 My soul melteth for heaviness: strengthen thou me according unto thy word.

Ps 138:3 In the day when I cried thou answeredst me, *and* strengthenedst me *with* strength in my soul.

Pr 10:29 The way of the Lord *is* strength to the upright: but destruction *shall be* to the workers of iniquity.

Is 28:5–6 In that day shall the Lord of hosts be for a crown of glory, and for a diadem of beauty, unto the residue of his people,

And for a spirit of judgment to him that sitteth in judgment, and for strength to them that turn the battle to the gate.

Is 40:31 But they that wait upon the Lord shall renew *their* strength; they shall mount up with wings as eagles; they shall run, and not be weary; *and* they shall walk, and not faint.

Is 41:10 Fear thou not; for I *am* with thee: be not dismayed; for I *am* thy God: I will strengthen thee; yea, I will help thee; yea, I will uphold thee with the right hand of my righteousness.

Je 1:18 For, behold, I have made thee this day a defenced city, and an iron pillar, and brasen walls against the whole land, against the kings of Judah, against the princes thereof, against the priests thereof, and against the people of the land.

Eze 3:8 Behold, I have made thy face strong against their faces, and thy forehead strong against their foreheads.

Da 11:32 And such as do wickedly against the covenant shall he corrupt by flatteries: but the people that do know their God shall be strong, and do *exploits*.

Zec 10:3 Mine anger was kindled against the shepherds, and I punished the goats: for the Lord of hosts hath visited his flock the house of Judah, and hath made them as his goodly horse in the battle.

Zec 12:8 In that day shall the Lord defend the inhabitants of Jerusalem; and he that is feeble among them at that day shall be as David; and the house of David *shall be* as God, as the angel of the Lord before them.

Lu 5:24 But that ye may know that the Son of man hath power upon earth to forgive sins, (he said unto the sick of the palsy,) I say unto thee, Arise, and take up thy couch, and go into thine house.

2 Co 12:9 And he said unto me, My grace is sufficient for thee: for my strength is made perfect in weakness. Most gladly therefore will I rather glory in my infirmities, that the power of Christ may rest upon me.

Ep 3:16 That he would grant you, according to the riches of his glory, to be strengthened with might by his Spirit in the inner man;

Ph 4:13 I can do all things through Christ which strengtheneth me.

Col 1:11 Strengthened with all might, according to his glorious power, unto all patience and longsuffering with joyfulness;

4. In Weakness

Ex 17:12 But Moses' hands *were* heavy; and they took a stone, and put *it* under him, and he sat thereon; and Aaron and Hur stayed up his hands, the one on the one side, and the other on the other side; and his hands were steady until the going down of the sun.

1 S 2:4 The bows of the mighty men *are* broken, and they that stumbled are girded with strength.

Ps 8:2 Out of the mouth of babes and sucklings hast thou ordained strength because of thine enemies, that thou mightest still the enemy and the avenger.

Da 10:18 Then there came again and touched me *one* like the appearance of a man, and he strengthened me,

1 Co 1:27 But God hath chosen the foolish things of the world to confound the wise; and God hath chosen the weak things of the world to confound the things which are mighty;

2 Co 12:9–10 And he said unto me, My grace is sufficient for thee: for my strength is made perfect in weakness. Most gladly therefore will I rather glory in my infirmities, that the power of Christ may rest upon me.

Therefore I take pleasure in infirmities, in reproaches, in necessities, in persecutions, in distresses for Christ's sake: for when I am weak, then am I strong.

2 Co 13:4 For though he was crucified through weakness, yet he liveth

by the power of God. For we also are weak in him, but we shall live with him by the power of God toward you.
He 11:33–34 Who through faith subdued kingdoms, wrought righteousness, obtained promises, stopped the mouths of lions,

Quenched the violence of fire, escaped the edge of the sword, out of weakness were made strong, waxed valiant in fight, turned to flight the armies of the aliens.

STRIFE, *contention, bitter conflict*

1. Causes

HATRED

Pr 10:12 Hatred stirreth up strifes: but love covereth all sins.

PRIDE

Pr 13:10 Only by pride cometh contention: but with the well advised *is* wisdom.

CONTENTIOUS SPIRIT

Pr 26:21 *As* coals *are* to burning coals, and wood to fire; so *is* a contentious man to kindle strife.

ANGER

Pr 29:22 An angry man stirreth up strife, and a furious man aboundeth in transgression.

FOOLISH QUESTIONS

1 Ti 6:4 He is proud, knowing nothing, but doting about questions and strifes of words, whereof cometh envy, strife, railings, evil surmisings,
Ja 3:16 For where envying and strife *is,* there *is* confusion and every evil work.

2. Forbidden

Ge 13:8 And Abram said unto Lot, Let there be no strife, I pray thee, between me and thee, and between my herdmen and thy herdmen; for we *be* brethren.
Ex 2:13 And when he went out the second day, behold, two men of the Hebrews strove together: and he said

to him that did the wrong, Wherefore smitest thou thy fellow?
Le 24:10 And the son of an Israelitish woman, whose father *was* an Egyptian, went out among the children of Israel: and this son of the Israelitish *woman* and a man of Israel strove together in the camp;
Pr 3:30 Strive not with a man without cause, if he have done thee no harm.
Pr 17:14 The beginning of strife *is as* when one letteth out water: therefore leave off contention, before it be meddled with.
Pr 20:3 *It is* an honour for a man to cease from strife: but every fool will be meddling.
Pr 25:8 Go not forth hastily to strive, lest *thou know not* what to do in the end thereof, when thy neighbour hath put thee to shame.
Pr 26:17 He that passeth by, *and* meddleth with strife *belonging* not to him, *is like* one that taketh a dog by the ears.
Ph 2:3 *Let* nothing *be done* through strife or vainglory; but in lowliness of mind let each esteem other better than themselves.
2 Ti 2:14 Of these things put *them* in remembrance, charging *them* before the Lord that they strive not about words to no profit, *but* to the subverting of the hearers.
2 Ti 2:24 And the servant of the Lord must not strive; but be gentle unto all *men,* apt to teach, patient,
Ja 3:14 But if ye have bitter envying and strife in your hearts, glory not, and lie not against the truth.

3. In the Church

See **CHURCH**

4. In the Family

Ge 21:10 Wherefore she said unto Abraham, Cast out this bondwoman and her son: for the son of this bondwoman shall not be heir with my son, *even* with Isaac.
Pr 18:19 A brother offended *is harder to be won* than a strong city: and *their*

contentions *are* like the bars of a castle.

Pr 19:13 A foolish son *is* the calamity of his father: and the contentions of a wife *are* a continual dropping.

Pr 21:9 *It is* better to dwell in a corner of the housetop, than with a brawling woman in a wide house.

Pr 21:19 *It is* better to dwell in the wilderness, than with a contentious and an angry woman.

Pr 27:15 A continual dropping in a very rainy day and a contentious woman are alike.

Mk 13:12 Now the brother shall betray the brother to death, and the father the son; and children shall rise up against *their* parents, and shall cause them to be put to death.

5. Examples

Ge 13:7 And there was a strife between the herdmen of Abram's cattle and the herdmen of Lot's cattle: and the Canaanite and the Perizzite dwelled then in the land.

Ge 26:20 And the herdmen of Gerar did strive with Isaac's herdmen, saying, The water *is* ours: and he called the name of the well Esek; because they strove with him.

Ex 17:7 And he called the name of the place Massah, and Meribah, because of the chiding of the children of Israel, and because they tempted the Lord, saying, Is the Lord among us, or not?

De 1:12 How can I myself alone bear your cumbrance, and your burden, and your strife?

2 S 19:43 And the men of Israel answered the men of Judah, and said, We have ten parts in the king, and we have also more *right* in David than ye: why then did ye despise us, that our advice should not be first had in bringing back our king? And the words of the men of Judah were fiercer than the words of the men of Israel.

Pr 26:20 Where no wood is, *there* the fire goeth out: so where *there* is no talebearer, the strife ceaseth.

Pr 29:9 *If* a wise man contendeth with a foolish man, whether he rage or laugh, *there is* no rest.

Ac 23:9 And there arose a great cry: and the scribes *that were* of the Pharisees' part arose, and strove, saying, We find no evil in this man: but if a spirit or an angel hath spoken to him, let us not fight against God.

6. Civil

See **NATION**

7. The Contentious Spirit

Ps 120:7 I *am for* peace: but when I speak, they *are* for war.

Ps 140:2 Which imagine mischiefs in *their* heart; continually are they gathered together *for* war.

Pr 15:18 A wrathful man stirreth up strife: but *he that is* slow to anger appeaseth strife.

Pr 17:19 He loveth transgression that loveth strife: *and* he that exalteth his gate seeketh destruction.

Pr 18:6 A fool's lips enter into contention, and his mouth calleth for strokes.

Pr 26:21 *As* coals *are* to burning coals, and wood to fire; so *is* a contentious man to kindle strife.

Eze 32:2 Son of man, take up a lamentation for Pharaoh king of Egypt, and say unto him, Thou art like a young lion of the nations, and thou *art* as a whale in the seas: and thou camest forth with thy rivers, and troubledst the waters with thy feet, and fouledst their rivers.

Hab 1:3 Why dost thou shew me iniquity, and cause *me* to behold grievance? for spoiling and violence *are* before me: and there are *that* raise up strife and contention.

Ac 13:50 But the Jews stirred up the devout and honourable women, and the chief men of the city, and raised persecution against Paul and Barnabas, and expelled them out of their coasts.

Ja 4:1 From whence *come* wars and fightings among you? *come they* not hence, *even* of your lusts that war in your members?

See **UNITY**

STRIPES *See* **MUTILATION**

STRIVING

1. Spiritual, *seeking earnestly those things which are of value to God*

Mt 7:13; 11:12; Lu 13:24; Ac 24:16; 1 Co 9:25; 2 Co 5:9; Ph 1:27; 3:14; Col 1:29; 2 Ti 2:5; He 4:11; 12:4

2. Selfish

Jb 9:3; 10:2; 33:13; 40:2; Ec 6:10; Is 45:9; Je 50:24; Mal 1:6; Ro 9:20; 1 Co 10:22

STUBBLE, *or straw*

Ex 15:7; Jb 21:18; Is 5:24; 33:11; 40:24; 47:14; Je 13:24; Jl 2:5; Obad 18; Na 1:10; Mal 4:1

STUBBORNNESS, *obstinacy*

1. Warnings

2 K 5:12 *Are* not Abana and Pharpar, rivers of Damascus, better than all the waters of Israel? may I not wash in them, and be clean? So he turned and went away in a rage.

2 Chr 25:16 And it came to pass, as he talked with him, that *the king* said unto him, Art thou made of the king's counsel? forbear; why shouldest thou be smitten? Then the prophet forbare, and said, I know that God hath determined to destroy thee, because thou hast done this, and hast not hearkened unto my counsel.

Ps 32:9 Be ye not as the horse, *or* as the mule, *which* have no understanding: whose mouth must be held in with bit and bridle, lest they come near unto thee.

Ps 78:8 And might not be as their fathers, a stubborn and rebellious generation; a generation *that* set not their heart aright, and whose spirit was not stedfast with God.

Pr 26:3 A whip for the horse, a bridle for the ass, and a rod for the fool's back.

Pr 29:19 A servant will not be corrected by words: for though he understand he will not answer.

Is 46:12 Hearken unto me, ye stouthearted, that *are* far from righteousness:

Is 48:4 Because I knew that thou *art* obstinate, and thy neck *is* an iron sinew, and thy brow brass;

Je 16:12 And ye have done worse than your fathers; for, behold, ye walk every one after the imagination of his evil heart, that they may not hearken unto me:

Eze 33:31 And they come unto thee as the people cometh, and they sit before thee as my people, and they hear thy words, but they will not do them: for with their mouth they shew much love, *but* their heart goeth after their covetousness.

Mal 2:2 If ye will not hear, and if ye will not lay *it* to heart, to give glory unto my name, saith the LORD of hosts, I will even send a curse upon you, and I will curse your blessings: yea, I have cursed them already, because ye do not lay *it* to heart.

Ro 10:3 For they being ignorant of God's righteousness, and going about to establish their own righteousness, have not submitted themselves unto the righteousness of God.

2. Examples

Ex 32:9 And the LORD said unto Moses, I have seen this people, and, behold, it *is* a stiffnecked people:

De 21:20 And they shall say unto the elders of his city, This our son *is* stubborn and rebellious, he will not obey our voice; *he is* a glutton, and a drunkard.

De 31:27 For I know thy rebellion, and thy stiff neck: behold, while I am yet alive with you this day, ye have been rebellious against the LORD; and how much more after my death?

1 S 8:19 Nevertheless the people refused to obey the voice of Samuel; and they said, Nay; but we will have a king over us;

1 Chr 21:4 Nevertheless the king's word prevailed against Joab. Wherefore Joab departed, and went throughout all Israel, and came to Jerusalem.

2 Chr 24:19 Yet he sent prophets to them, to bring them again unto the LORD; and they testified against them: but they would not give ear.

2 Chr 30:8 Now be ye not stiffnecked, as your fathers *were, but* yield yourselves unto the Lord, and enter into his sanctuary, which he hath sanctified for ever: and serve the Lord your God, that the fierceness of his wrath may turn away from you.

Ps 68:21 But God shall wound the head of his enemies, *and* the hairy scalp of such an one as goeth on still in his trespasses.

Ps 76:5 The stouthearted are spoiled, they have slept their sleep: and none of the men of might have found their hands.

Je 32:33 And they have turned unto me the back, and not the face: though I taught them, rising up early and teaching *them,* yet they have not hearkened to receive instruction.

Je 44:16 *As for* the word that thou hast spoken unto us in the name of the Lord, we will not hearken unto thee.

Zec 7:11 But they refused to hearken, and pulled away the shoulder, and stopped their ears, that they should not hear.

Ac 7:51 Ye stiffnecked and uncircumcised in heart and ears, ye do always resist the Holy Ghost: as your fathers *did,* so *do* ye.

Re 2:21 And I gave her space to repent of her fornication; and she repented not.

See **SUBMISSION**

STUMBLING BLOCKS

SHOULD BE REMOVED

Is 57:14 And shall say, Cast ye up, cast ye up, prepare the way, take up the stumblingblock out of the way of my people.

UNFAITHFUL LEADERS

Mal 2:7 For the priest's lips should keep knowledge, and they should seek the law at his mouth: for he *is* the messenger of the Lord of hosts.

Mal 2:8 But ye are departed out of the way; ye have caused many to stumble at the law; ye have corrupted the covenant of Levi, saith the Lord of hosts.

Mt 16:23 But he turned, and said unto Peter, Get thee behind me, Satan: thou art an offence unto me: for thou savourest not the things that be of God, but those that be of men.

HYPOCRITES IN THE CHURCH

Mt 23:13 But woe unto you, scribes and Pharisees, hypocrites! for ye shut up the kingdom of heaven against men: for ye neither go in *yourselves,* neither suffer ye them that are entering to go in.

Lu 11:52 Woe unto you, lawyers! for ye have taken away the key of knowledge: ye entered not in yourselves, and them that were entering in ye hindered.

GUARD AGAINST BECOMING

Ro 14:13 Let us not therefore judge one another any more: but judge this rather, that no man put a stumblingblock or an occasion to fall in *his* brother's way.

1 Co 8:9 But take heed lest by any means this liberty of yours become a stumblingblock to them that are weak.

PREVENTION

1 Jn 2:10 He that loveth his brother abideth in the light, and there is none occasion of stumbling in him.

See **INFLUENCE**

SUBJECTION

Jb 13:27; 33:11; Pr 7:22; Je 20:3; 29:26; Ac 16:24

SUBMISSION, *placing oneself under the authority of another*

1. To the Authority of the Church

1 Co 16:16 That ye submit yourselves unto such, and to every one that helpeth with *us,* and laboureth.

Ep 5:21 Submitting yourselves one to another in the fear of God.

He 13:17 Obey them that have the rule over you, and submit yourselves: for they watch for your souls, as they that must give account, that they may do it with joy, and not with grief: for that *is* unprofitable for you.

1 Pe 5:5 Likewise, ye younger, submit yourselves unto the elder. Yea, all *of you* be subject one to another, and be clothed with humility: for God resisteth the proud, and giveth grace to the humble.

2. To the Divine Will

Jb 40:5 Once have I spoken; but I will not answer: yea, twice; but I will proceed no further.

Ps 123:2 Behold, as the eyes of servants *look* unto the hand of their masters, *and* as the eyes of a maiden unto the hand of her mistress; so our eyes *wait* upon the LORD our God, until that he have mercy upon us.

Je 27:11 But the nations that bring their neck under the yoke of the king of Babylon, and serve him, those will I let remain still in their own land, saith the LORD; and they shall till it, and dwell therein.

Mt 6:10 Thy kingdom come. Thy will be done in earth, as *it is* in heaven.

Mt 26:39 And he went a little farther, and fell on his face, and prayed, saying, O my Father, if it be possible, let this cup pass from me: nevertheless not as I will, but as thou *wilt*.

Lu 1:38 And Mary said, Behold the handmaid of the Lord; be it unto me according to thy word. And the angel departed from her.

Ro 6:13 Neither yield ye your members *as* instruments of unrighteousness unto sin: but yield yourselves unto God, as those that are alive from the dead, and your members *as* instruments of righteousness unto God.

Ja 4:7 Submit yourselves therefore to God. Resist the devil, and he will flee from you.

See **STUBBORNNESS, SELFISHNESS, SELF-WILL**

SUCCOTH, *booth*

1. In Cannan, town where Jacob built booths for his cattle

Ge 33:17; Jos 13:27; 1 K 7:46; 2 Chr 4:17

2. In Egypt, first encampment of Israel after leaving Rameses

Ex 12:37; 13:20

SUFFERING

1. For Christ

Ps 44:22 Yea, for thy sake are we killed all the day long; we are counted as sheep for the slaughter.

Ps 69:7 Because for thy sake I have borne reproach; shame hath covered my face.

Je 15:15 O LORD, thou knowest: remember me, and visit me, and revenge me of my persecutors; take me not away in thy longsuffering: know that for thy sake I have suffered rebuke.

Da 3:23 And these three men, Shadrach, Meshach, and Abed-nego, fell down bound into the midst of the burning fiery furnace.

Mt 10:18 And ye shall be brought before governors and kings for my sake, for a testimony against them and the Gentiles.

Mt 20:23 And he saith unto them, Ye shall drink indeed of my cup, and be baptized with the baptism that I am baptized with: but to sit on my right hand, and on my left, is not mine to give, but *it shall be given to them* for whom it is prepared of my Father.

Mk 13:9 But take heed to yourselves: for they shall deliver you up to councils; and in the synagogues ye shall be beaten: and ye shall be brought before rulers and kings for my sake, for a testimony against them.

Lu 21:12 But before all these, they shall lay their hands on you, and persecute *you*, delivering *you* up to the synagogues, and into prisons, being brought before kings and rulers for my name's sake.

Jn 9:28 Then they reviled him, and said, Thou art his disciple; but we are Moses' disciples.

Jn 15:21 But all these things will they do unto you for my name's sake, because they know not him that sent me.

Jn 16:3 And these things will they do unto you, because they have not known the Father, nor me.

Ac 5:41 And they departed from the presence of the council, rejoicing that they were counted worthy to suffer shame for his name.

Ac 9:16 For I will shew him how great things he must suffer for my name's sake.

Ac 15:26 Men that have hazarded their lives for the name of our Lord Jesus Christ.

Ac 20:23 Save that the Holy Ghost witnesseth in every city, saying that bonds and afflictions abide me.

Ro 8:17 And if children, then heirs; heirs of God, and joint-heirs with Christ; if so be that we suffer with *him,* that we may be also glorified together.

Ro 8:36 As it is written, For thy sake we are killed all the day long; we are accounted as sheep for the slaughter.

1 Co 4:9 For I think that God hath set forth us the apostles last, as it were appointed to death: for we are made a spectacle unto the world, and to angels, and to men.

1 Co 4:11 Even unto this present hour we both hunger, and thirst, and are naked, and are buffeted, and have no certain dwellingplace;

1 Co 15:19 If in this life only we have hope in Christ, we are of all men most miserable.

1 Co 15:31 I protest by your rejoicing which I have in Christ Jesus our Lord, I die daily.

2 Co 1:5 For as the sufferings of Christ abound in us, so our consolation also aboundeth by Christ.

2 Co 1:7 And our hope of you *is* stedfast, knowing, that as ye are partakers of the sufferings, so *shall ye be* also of the consolation.

2 Co 4:8 We *are* troubled on every side, yet not distressed; *we are* perplexed, but not in despair;

2 Co 6:4 But in all *things* approving ourselves as the ministers of God, in much patience, in afflictions, in necessities, in distresses,

2 Co 11:23 Are they ministers of Christ? (I speak as a fool) I *am* more; in labours more abundant, in stripes above measure, in prisons more frequent, in deaths oft.

2 Co 11:27 In weariness and painfulness, in watchings often, in hunger and thirst, in fastings often, in cold and nakedness.

Ph 1:13 So that my bonds in Christ are manifest in all the palace, and in all other *places;*

Ph 1:29 For unto you it is given in the behalf of Christ, not only to believe on him, but also to suffer for his sake;

Ph 2:30 Because for the work of Christ he was nigh unto death, not regarding his life, to supply your lack of service toward me.

Ph 3:8 Yea doubtless, and I count all things *but* loss for the excellency of the knowledge of Christ Jesus my Lord: for whom I have suffered the loss of all things, and do count them *but* dung, that I may win Christ,

Ph 3:10 That I may know him, and the power of his resurrection, and the fellowship of his sufferings, being made conformable unto his death;

Col 1:24 Who now rejoice in my sufferings for you, and fill up that which is behind of the afflictions of Christ in my flesh for his body's sake, which is the church:

1 Th 2:2 But even after that we had suffered before, and were shamefully entreated, as ye know, at Philippi, we were bold in our God to speak unto you the gospel of God with much contention.

1 Th 2:14 For ye, brethren, became followers of the churches of God which in Judaea are in Christ Jesus: for ye also have suffered like things of your own countrymen, even as they *have* of the Jews:

2 Th 1:5 *Which is* a manifest token of the righteous judgment of God, that ye may be counted worthy of the kingdom of God, for which ye also suffer:

2 Ti 1:8 Be not thou therefore ashamed of the testimony of our Lord, nor of me his prisoner: but be thou partaker of the afflictions of the gospel according to the power of God;

2 Ti 2:12 If we suffer, we shall also reign with *him:* if we deny *him,* he also will deny us:

Phm 1 Paul, a prisoner of Jesus Christ, and Timothy our brother, unto Philemon our dearly beloved, and fellowlabourer,

He 10:33 Partly, whilst ye were made a gazingstock both by reproaches and afflictions; and partly, whilst ye became companions of them that were so used.

He 11:25 Choosing rather to suffer affliction with the people of God, than to enjoy the pleasures of sin for a season;

Ja 5:10 Take, my brethren, the prophets, who have spoken in the name of the Lord, for an example of suffering affliction, and of patience.

1 Pe 2:20 For what glory *is it,* if, when ye be buffeted for your faults, ye shall take it patiently? but if, when ye do well, and suffer *for it,* ye take it patiently, this *is* acceptable with God.

1 Pe 3:14 But and if ye suffer for righteousness' sake, happy *are ye:* and be not afraid of their terror, neither be troubled;

1 Pe 3:17 For *it is* better, if the will of God be so, that ye suffer for well doing, than for evil doing.

1 Pe 4:13 But rejoice, inasmuch as ye are partakers of Christ's sufferings; that, when his glory shall be revealed, ye may be glad also with exceeding joy.

1 Pe 4:16 Yet if *any man suffer* as a Christian, let him not be ashamed; but let him glorify God on this behalf.

1 Pe 5:10 But the God of all grace, who hath called us unto his eternal glory by Christ Jesus, after that ye have suffered a while, make you perfect, stablish, strengthen, settle *you.*

Re 1:9 I John, who also am your brother, and companion in tribulation, and in the kingdom and patience of Jesus Christ, was in the isle that is called Patmos, for the word of God, and for the testimony of Jesus Christ.

Re 2:10 Fear none of those things which thou shalt suffer: behold, the devil shall cast *some* of you into prison, that ye may be tried; and ye shall have tribulation ten days: be thou faithful unto death, and I will give thee a crown of life.

Re 6:9 And when he had opened the fifth seal, I saw under the altar the souls of them that were slain for the word of God, and for the testimony which they held:

2. Of Believers

PERSECUTION

Mt 5:11 Blessed are ye, when *men* shall revile you, and persecute *you,* and shall say all manner of evil against you falsely, for my sake.

HATRED

Mt 10:22 And ye shall be hated of all *men* for my name's sake: but he that endureth to the end shall be saved.

LOSS OF LIFE

Mt 10:39 He that findeth his life shall lose it: and he that loseth his life for my sake shall find it.

RENUNCIATION OF WORLDLY TREASURES

Mt 19:29 And every one that hath forsaken houses, or brethren, or sisters, or father, or mother, or wife, or children, or lands, for my name's sake, shall receive an hundredfold, and shall inherit everlasting life.

SUFFERING

Ac 9:16 For I will shew him how great things he must suffer for my name's sake.

LOSS OF REPUTATION

1 Co 4:10 We *are* fools for Christ's sake, but ye *are* wise in Christ; we *are* weak, but ye *are* strong; ye *are* honourable, but we *are* despised.

2 Co 4:5 For we preach not ourselves, but Christ Jesus the Lord; and ourselves your servants for Jesus' sake.

DEATH

2 Co 4:11 For we which live are alway delivered unto death for Jesus' sake, that the life also of Jesus might be made manifest in our mortal flesh.

2 Co 12:10 Therefore I take pleasure in infirmities, in reproaches, in necessities, in persecutions, in distresses for

Christ's sake: for when I am weak, then am I strong.

Ph 1:29 For unto you it is given in the behalf of Christ, not only to believe on him, but also to suffer for his sake;

3. Reproach Endured

Ps 57:3 He shall send from heaven, and save *from* the reproach of him that would swallow me up. Selah. God shall send forth his mercy and his truth.

Ps 119:39 Turn away my reproach which I fear: for thy judgments *are* good.

Lu 6:22 Blessed are ye, when men shall hate you, and when they shall separate you *from their company,* and shall reproach *you,* and cast out your name as evil, for the Son of man's sake.

1 Ti 4:10 For therefore we both labour and suffer reproach, because we trust in the living God, who is the Saviour of all men, specially of those that believe.

He 10:33 Partly, whilst ye were made a gazingstock both by reproaches and afflictions; and partly, whilst ye became companions of them that were so used.

He 11:26 Esteeming the reproach of Christ greater riches than the treasures in Egypt: for he had respect unto the recompence of the reward.

He 13:13 Let us go forth therefore unto him without the camp, bearing his reproach.

1 Pe 4:14 If ye be reproached for the name of Christ, happy *are ye;* for the spirit of glory and of God resteth upon you: on their part he is evil spoken of, but on your part he is glorified.

4. Saints Despised

1 S 17:42 And when the Philistine looked about, and saw David, he disdained him: for he was *but* a youth, and ruddy, and of a fair countenance.

2 S 6:16 And as the ark of the LORD came into the city of David, Michal Saul's daughter looked through a window, and saw king David leaping and dancing before the LORD; and she despised him in her heart.

Ne 2:19 But when Sanballat the Horonite, and Tobiah the servant, the Ammonite, and Geshem the Arabian, heard *it,* they laughed us to scorn, and despised us, and said, What *is* this thing that ye do? will ye rebel against the king?

Ne 4:2 And he spake before his brethren and the army of Samaria, and said, What do these feeble Jews? will they fortify themselves? will they sacrifice? will they make an end in a day? will they revive the stones out of the heaps of the rubbish which are burned?

Jb 12:4 I am *as* one mocked of his neighbour, who calleth upon God, and he answereth him: the just upright *man is* laughed to scorn.

Jb 30:10 They abhor me, they flee far from me, and spare not to spit in my face.

Ps 119:141 I *am* small and despised: *yet* do not I forget thy precepts.

1 Co 1:28 And base things of the world, and things which are despised, hath God chosen, *yea,* and things which are not, to bring to nought things that are:

1 Co 4:13 Being defamed, we intreat: we are made as the filth of the world, *and are* the offscouring of all things unto this day.

5. Imprisonment

a. Of People

Ge 39:20 And Joseph's master took him, and put him into the prison, a place where the king's prisoners *were* bound: and he was there in the prison.

1 K 22:27 And say, Thus saith the king, Put this *fellow* in the prison, and feed him with bread of affliction and with water of affliction, until I come in peace.

2 Chr 16:10 Then Asa was wroth with the seer, and put him in a prison house; for *he was* in a rage with him because of this *thing.* And Asa oppressed *some* of the people the same time.

2 Chr 18:26 And say, Thus saith the king, Put this *fellow* in the prison, and feed him with bread of affliction and with water of affliction, until I return in peace.

Ps 105:18 Whose feet they hurt with fetters: he was laid in iron:

Je 29:26 The Lord hath made thee priest in the stead of Jehoiada the priest, that ye should be officers in the house of the Lord, for every man *that is* mad, and maketh himself a prophet, that thou shouldest put him in prison, and in the stocks.

Je 32:2 For then the king of Babylon's army besieged Jerusalem: and Jeremiah the prophet was shut up in the court of the prison, which *was* in the king of Judah's house.

Je 33:1 Moreover the word of the Lord came unto Jeremiah the second time, while he was yet shut up in the court of the prison, saying,

Je 36:5 And Jeremiah commanded Baruch, saying, I *am* shut up; I cannot go into the house of the Lord:

Je 37:15 Wherefore the princes were wroth with Jeremiah, and smote him, and put him in prison in the house of Jonathan the scribe: for they had made that the prison.

Je 38:6 Then took they Jeremiah, and cast him into the dungeon of Malchiah the son of Hammelech, that *was* in the court of the prison: and they let down Jeremiah with cords. And in the dungeon *there was* no water, but mire: so Jeremiah sunk in the mire.

Lam 3:53 They have cut off my life in the dungeon, and cast a stone upon me.

Mt 4:12 Now when Jesus had heard that John was cast into prison, he departed into Galilee;

Mt 11:2 Now when John had heard in the prison the works of Christ, he sent two of his disciples,

Mt 14:3 For Herod had laid hold on John, and bound him, and put *him* in prison for Herodias' sake, his brother Philip's wife.

Mk 1:14 Now after that John was put in prison, Jesus came into Galilee, preaching the gospel of the kingdom of God,

Mk 6:17 For Herod himself had sent forth and laid hold upon John, and bound him in prison for Herodias'

sake, his brother Philip's wife: for he had married her.

Lu 3:20 Added yet this above all, that he shut up John in prison.

Lu 21:12 But before all these, they shall lay their hands on you, and persecute *you,* delivering *you* up to the synagogues, and into prisons, being brought before kings and rulers for my name's sake.

Jn 3:24 For John was not yet cast into prison.

Ac 4:3 And they laid hands on them, and put *them* in hold unto the next day: for it was now eventide.

Ac 5:18 And laid their hands on the apostles, and put them in the common prison.

Ac 8:3 As for Saul, he made havock of the church, entering into every house, and haling men and women committed *them* to prison.

Ac 12:4 And when he had apprehended him, he put *him* in prison, and delivered *him* to four quaternions of soldiers to keep him; intending after Easter to bring him forth to the people.

Ac 16:23 And when they had laid many stripes upon them, they cast *them* into prison, charging the jailer to keep them safely:

Ac 22:4 And I persecuted this way unto the death, binding and delivering into prisons both men and women.

Ac 22:19 And I said, Lord, they know that I imprisoned and beat in every synagogue them that believed on thee:

Ac 23:35 I will hear thee, said he, when thine accusers are also come. And he commanded him to be kept in Herod's judgment hall.

Ac 24:27 But after two years Porcius Festus came into Felix' room: and Felix, willing to shew the Jews a pleasure, left Paul bound.

Ac 26:10 Which thing I also did in Jerusalem: and many of the saints did I shut up in prison, having received authority from the chief priests; and when they were put to death, I gave my voice against *them.*

2 Co 6:5 In stripes, in imprisonments, in tumults, in labours, in watchings, in fastings;

2 Co 11:23 Are they ministers of Christ? (I speak as a fool) I *am* more; in labours more abundant, in stripes above measure, in prisons more frequent, in deaths oft.

Ep 3:1 For this cause I Paul, the prisoner of Jesus Christ for you Gentiles,

Phm 1 Paul, a prisoner of Jesus Christ, and Timothy our brother, unto Philemon our dearly beloved, and fellowlabourer,

Phm 23 There salute thee Epaphras, my fellowprisoner in Christ Jesus;

He 11:36 And others had trial of *cruel* mockings and scourgings, yea, moreover of bonds and imprisonment:

Re 2:10 Fear none of those things which thou shalt suffer: behold, the devil shall cast *some* of you into prison, that ye may be tried; and ye shall have tribulation ten days: be thou faithful unto death, and I will give thee a crown of life.

b. Of Paul

Ac 26:29 And Paul said, I would to God, that not only thou, but also all that hear me this day, were both almost, and altogether such as I am, except these bonds.

2 Co 11:23 Are they ministers of Christ? (I speak as a fool) I *am* more; in labours more abundant, in stripes above measure, in prisons more frequent, in deaths oft.

Ep 3:1 For this cause I Paul, the prisoner of Jesus Christ for you Gentiles,

Ep 4:1 I therefore, the prisoner of the Lord, beseech you that ye walk worthy of the vocation wherewith ye are called,

Ep 6:20 For which I am an ambassador in bonds: that therein I may speak boldly, as I ought to speak.

Ph 1:7 Even as it is meet for me to think this of you all, because I have you in my heart; inasmuch as both in my bonds, and in the defence and confirmation of the gospel, ye all are partakers of my grace.

Ph 1:13 So that my bonds in Christ are manifest in all the palace, and in all other *places;*

Col 4:3 Withal praying also for us, that God would open unto us a door of utterance, to speak the mystery of Christ, for which I am also in bonds:

Col 4:18 The salutation by the hand of me Paul. Remember my bonds. Grace *be* with you. Amen.

2 Ti 1:8 Be not thou therefore ashamed of the testimony of our Lord, nor of me his prisoner: but be thou partaker of the afflictions of the gospel according to the power of God;

2 Ti 1:16 The Lord give mercy unto the house of Onesiphorus; for he oft refreshed me, and was not ashamed of my chain:

2 Ti 2:9 Wherein I suffer trouble, as an evil doer, *even* unto bonds; but the word of God is not bound.

Phm 1 Paul, a prisoner of Jesus Christ, and Timothy our brother, unto Philemon our dearly beloved, and fellowlabourer,

Phm 9 Yet for love's sake I rather beseech *thee,* being such an one as Paul the aged, and now also a prisoner of Jesus Christ.

Phm 23 There salute thee Epaphras, my fellowprisoner in Christ Jesus;

6. Persecution

Jb 30:15 Terrors are turned upon me: they pursue my soul as the wind: and my welfare passeth away as a cloud.

Ps 7:1 O Lord my God, in thee do I put my trust: save me from all them that persecute me, and deliver me:

Ps 31:15 My times *are* in thy hand: deliver me from the hand of mine enemies, and from them that persecute me.

Ps 37:14 The wicked have drawn out the sword, and have bent their bow, to cast down the poor and needy, *and* to slay such as be of upright conversation.

Ps 57:4 My soul *is* among lions: *and* I lie *even among* them that are set on fire, *even* the sons of men, whose teeth *are* spears and arrows, and their tongue a sharp sword.

Ps 79:3 Their blood have they shed like water round about Jerusalem; and *there was* none to bury *them.*

Ps 102:8 Mine enemies reproach me all the day; *and* they that are mad against me are sworn against me.

Ps 119:86 All thy commandments *are* faithful: they persecute me wrongfully; help thou me.

Ps 119:157 Many *are* my persecutors and mine enemies; *yet* do I not decline from thy testimonies.

Ps 119:161 Princes have persecuted me without a cause: but my heart standeth in awe of thy word.

Ps 143:3 For the enemy hath persecuted my soul; he hath smitten my life down to the ground; he hath made me to dwell in darkness, as those that have been long dead.

Is 59:15 Yea, truth faileth; and he *that* departeth from evil maketh himself a prey: and the LORD saw *it,* and it displeased him that *there was* no judgment.

Je 11:19 But I *was* like a lamb *or* an ox *that* is brought to the slaughter; and I knew not that they had devised devices against me, *saying,* Let us destroy the tree with the fruit thereof, and let us cut him off from the land of the living, that his name may be no more remembered.

Je 15:15 O LORD, thou knowest: remember me, and visit me, and revenge me of my persecutors; take me not away in thy longsuffering: know that for thy sake I have suffered rebuke.

Lam 5:5 Our necks *are* under persecution: we labour, *and* have no rest.

2 Th 1:4 So that we ourselves glory in you in the churches of God for your patience and faith in all your persecutions and tribulations that ye endure:

1 Pe 3:17 For *it is* better, if the will of God be so, that ye suffer for well doing, than for evil doing.

a. Of God's Followers

Ex 10:11 Not so: go now ye *that are* men, and serve the LORD; for that ye did desire. And they were driven out from Pharaoh's presence.

1 K 19:2 Then Jezebel sent a messenger unto Elijah, saying, So let the gods do *to me,* and more also, if I make not thy life as the life of one of them by to morrow about this time.

1 K 22:27 And say, Thus saith the king, Put this *fellow* in the prison, and feed him with bread of affliction and with water of affliction, until I come in peace.

2 Chr 16:10 Then Asa was wroth with the seer, and put him in a prison house; for *he was* in a rage with him because of this *thing.* And Asa oppressed *some* of the people the same time.

2 Chr 24:21 And they conspired against him, and stoned him with stones at the commandment of the king in the court of the house of the LORD.

Ps 14:4 Have all the workers of iniquity no knowledge? who eat up my people *as* they eat bread, and call not upon the LORD.

Je 15:10 Woe is me, my mother, that thou hast borne me a man of strife and a man of contention to the whole earth! I have neither lent on usury, nor men have lent to me on usury; *yet* every one of them doth curse me.

Je 20:2 Then Pashur smote Jeremiah the prophet, and put him in the stocks that *were* in the high gate of Benjamin, which *was* by the house of the LORD.

Je 32:2 For then the king of Babylon's army besieged Jerusalem: and Jeremiah the prophet was shut up in the court of the prison, which *was* in the king of Judah's house.

Da 3:20 And he commanded the most mighty men that *were* in his army to bind Shadrach, Meshach, and Abed-nego, *and* to cast *them* into the burning fiery furnace.

Da 6:16 Then the king commanded, and they brought Daniel, and cast *him* into the den of lions. *Now* the king spake and said unto Daniel, Thy God whom thou servest continually, he will deliver thee.

Am 7:10 Then Amaziah the priest of Bethel sent to Jeroboam king of Israel, saying, Amos hath conspired against thee in the midst of the house of Israel: the land is not able to bear all his words.

Hab 1:4 Therefore the law is slacked, and judgment doth never go forth: for the wicked doth compass about the righteous; therefore wrong judgment proceedeth.

Ac 4:3 And they laid hands on them, and put *them* in hold unto the next day: for it was now eventide.

Ac 5:40 And to him they agreed: and when they had called the apostles, and beaten *them*, they commanded that they should not speak in the name of Jesus, and let them go.

Ac 8:1 And Saul was consenting unto his death. And at that time there was a great persecution against the church which was at Jerusalem; and they were all scattered abroad throughout the regions of Judaea and Samaria, except the apostles.

Ac 11:19 Now they which were scattered abroad upon the persecution that arose about Stephen travelled as far as Phenice, and Cyprus, and Antioch, preaching the word to none but unto the Jews only.

Ga 1:13 For ye have heard of my conversation in time past in the Jews' religion, how that beyond measure I persecuted the church of God, and wasted it:

Ph 3:6 Concerning zeal, persecuting the church; touching the righteousness which is in the law, blameless.

1 Ti 1:13 Who was before a blasphemer, and a persecutor, and injurious: but I obtained mercy, because I did *it* ignorantly in unbelief.

He 11:36 And others had trial of *cruel* mockings and scourgings, yea, moreover of bonds and imprisonment:

b. Of Christ

Ps 69:26 For they persecute *him* whom thou hast smitten; and they talk to the grief of those whom thou hast wounded.

Lu 4:29 And rose up, and thrust him out of the city, and led him unto the brow of the hill whereon their city was built, that they might cast him down headlong.

Lu 23:11 And Herod with his men of war set him at nought, and mocked *him,* and arrayed him in a gorgeous robe, and sent him again to Pilate.

Jn 5:16 And therefore did the Jews persecute Jesus, and sought to slay him, because he had done these things on the sabbath day.

Jn 7:1 After these things Jesus walked in Galilee: for he would not walk in Jewry, because the Jews sought to kill him.

Jn 8:37 I know that ye are Abraham's seed; but ye seek to kill me, because my word hath no place in you.

Jn 10:39 Therefore they sought again to take him: but he escaped out of their hand,

See **CHRIST**

c. Of Paul

Ac 9:23 And after that many days were fulfilled, the Jews took counsel to kill him:

Ac 9:29 And he spake boldly in the name of the Lord Jesus, and disputed against the Grecians: but they went about to slay him.

Ac 13:50 But the Jews stirred up the devout and honourable women, and the chief men of the city, and raised persecution against Paul and Barnabas, and expelled them out of their coasts.

Ac 14:5 And when there was an assault made both of the Gentiles, and also of the Jews with their rulers, to use *them* despitefully, and to stone them,

Ac 14:19 And there came thither *certain* Jews from Antioch and Iconium, who persuaded the people, and, having stoned Paul, drew *him* out of the city, supposing he had been dead.

Ac 16:22 And the multitude rose up together against them: and the magistrates rent off their clothes, and commanded to beat *them*.

Ac 17:6 And when they found them not, they drew Jason and certain brethren unto the rulers of the city, crying, These that have turned the world upside down are come hither also;

Ac 18:12 And when Gallio was the deputy of Achaia, the Jews made insurrection with one accord against Paul, and brought him to the judgment seat,

Ac 20:3 And *there* abode three months. And when the Jews laid wait for him, as he was about to sail into Syria, he purposed to return through Macedonia.

Ac 20:19 Serving the Lord with all humility of mind, and with many tears, and temptations, which befell me by the lying in wait of the Jews:

Ac 21:27 And when the seven days were almost ended, the Jews which were of Asia, when they saw him in the temple, stirred up all the people, and laid hands on him,

Ac 21:31 And as they went about to kill him, tidings came unto the chief captain of the band, that all Jerusalem was in an uproar.

Ac 21:36 For the multitude of the people followed after, crying, Away with him.

Ac 22:22 And they gave him audience unto this word, and *then* lifted up their voices, and said, Away with such a *fellow* from the earth: for it is not fit that he should live.

Ac 23:10 And when there arose a great dissension, the chief captain, fearing lest Paul should have been pulled in pieces of them, commanded the soldiers to go down, and to take him by force from among them, and to bring *him* into the castle.

Ac 23:14 And they came to the chief priests and elders, and said, We have bound ourselves under a great curse, that we will eat nothing until we have slain Paul.

Ac 24:5 For we have found this man *a* pestilent *fellow,* and a mover of sedition among all the Jews throughout the world, and a ringleader of the sect of the Nazarenes:

Ac 25:7 And when he was come, the Jews which came down from Jerusalem stood round about, and laid many and grievous complaints against Paul, which they could not prove.

Ac 26:21 For these causes the Jews caught me in the temple, and went about to kill *me.*

1 Co 4:9 For I think that God hath set forth us the apostles last, as it were appointed to death: for we are made a spectacle unto the world, and to angels, and to men.

1 Co 4:12 And labour, working with our own hands: being reviled, we bless; being persecuted, we suffer it:

1 Co 15:19 If in this life only we have hope in Christ, we are of all men most miserable.

1 Co 15:30 And why stand we in jeopardy every hour?

2 Co 1:5 For as the sufferings of Christ abound in us, so our consolation also aboundeth by Christ.

2 Co 1:8 For we would not, brethren, have you ignorant of our trouble which came to us in Asia, that we were pressed out of measure, above strength, insomuch that we despaired even of life:

2 Co 4:9 Persecuted, but not forsaken; cast down, but not destroyed;

2 Co 6:8 By honour and dishonour, by evil report and good report: as deceivers, and *yet* true;

2 Co 7:5 For, when we were come into Macedonia, our flesh had no rest, but we were troubled on every side; without *were* fightings, within *were* fears.

2 Co 11:24 Of the Jews five times received I forty *stripes* save one.

2 Co 11:32 In Damascus the governor under Aretas the king kept the city of the Damascenes with a garrison, desirous to apprehend me:

2 Co 12:10 Therefore I take pleasure in infirmities, in reproaches, in necessities, in persecutions, in distresses for Christ's sake: for when I am weak, then am I strong.

Ga 4:29 But as then he that was born after the flesh persecuted him *that was born* after the Spirit, even so *it is* now.

Ga 5:11 And I, brethren, if I yet preach circumcision, why do I yet suffer persecution? then is the offence of the cross ceased.

Ph 1:12 But I would ye should understand, brethren, that the things *which*

happened unto me have fallen out rather unto the furtherance of the gospel;

Ph 1:30 Having the same conflict which ye saw in me, and now hear *to be* in me.

1 Th 2:2 But even after that we had suffered before, and were shamefully entreated, as ye know, at Philippi, we were bold in our God to speak unto you the gospel of God with much contention.

1 Th 2:15 Who both killed the Lord Jesus, and their own prophets, and have persecuted us; and they please not God, and are contrary to all men:

2 Ti 1:12 For the which cause I also suffer these things: nevertheless I am not ashamed: for I know whom I have believed, and am persuaded that he is able to keep that which I have committed unto him against that day.

2 Ti 2:9 Wherein I suffer trouble, as an evil doer, *even* unto bonds; but the word of God is not bound.

2 Ti 3:11 Persecutions, afflictions, which came unto me at Antioch, at Iconium, at Lystra; what persecutions I endured: but out of *them* all the Lord delivered me.

d. Of the Church

Je 15:20 And I will make thee unto this people a fenced brasen wall: and they shall fight against thee, but they shall not prevail against thee: for I *am* with thee to save thee and to deliver thee, saith the LORD.

Mt 10:17 But beware of men: for they will deliver you up to the councils, and they will scourge you in their synagogues;

Mt 24:9 Then shall they deliver you up to be afflicted, and shall kill you: and ye shall be hated of all nations for my name's sake.

Lu 21:12 But before all these, they shall lay their hands on you, and persecute *you*, delivering *you* up to the synagogues, and into prisons, being brought before kings and rulers for my name's sake.

Jn 15:20 Remember the word that I said unto you, The servant is not greater than his lord. If they have per-

secuted me, they will also persecute you; if they have kept my saying, they will keep yours also.

Jn 16:2 They shall put you out of the synagogues: yea, the time cometh, that whosoever killeth you will think that he doeth God service.

Ga 3:4 Have ye suffered so many things in vain? if *it be* yet in vain.

2 Ti 3:12 Yea, and all that will live godly in Christ Jesus shall suffer persecution.

Re 2:10 Fear none of those things which thou shalt suffer: behold, the devil shall cast *some* of you into prison, that ye may be tried; and ye shall have tribulation ten days: be thou faithful unto death, and I will give thee a crown of life.

See **JOY, TEMPTATION, TESTS**

SUMMER, *the season*

Ge 8:22; Ps 74:17; Pr 6:8; 26:1; Zec 14:8; Mt 24:32; Mk 13:28; Lu 21:30

SUN, *created on the fourth day, called the greater light*

Ge 1:16; 37:9; De 17:3; 33:14; Jos 10:12; Ps 19:4; 104:19; 121:6; 136:8; 148:3; Ec 1:5; Is 38:8; Je 31:35; Jl 2:10, 31; Ac 26:13; 1 Co 15:41; Re 8:12

Figurative

Is 60:19; Am 8:9; Mal 4:2

SUN-DIAL, *an indicator of time*

Is 38:8

SUN-STROKE *See* **DISEASE**

SUPERSCRIPTION, *over the cross*

Mt 27:37

SUPREMACY, *granted to certain men*

Ge 25:23; 27:29, 37; 37:7; 48:19; 49:8; Jos 10:24; Jud 5:13; 2 S 3:1; 1 K 4:21; Je 27:7; Da 2:40; Mk 10:42; Lu 22:25

SURRENDER

1. Death to Sin

Ro 6:2 God forbid. How shall we, that are dead to sin, live any longer therein?

Ro 6:7 For he that is dead is freed from sin.

Ro 6:11 Likewise reckon ye also yourselves to be dead indeed unto sin, but alive unto God through Jesus Christ our Lord.

Ro 8:10 And if Christ *be* in you, the body *is* dead because of sin; but the Spirit *is* life because of righteousness.

Ga 2:20 I am crucified with Christ: nevertheless I live; yet not I, but Christ liveth in me: and the life which I now live in the flesh I live by the faith of the Son of God, who loved me, and gave himself for me.

Ga 5:24 And they that are Christ's have crucified the flesh with the affections and lusts.

Col 2:20 Wherefore if ye be dead with Christ from the rudiments of the world, why, as though living in the world, are ye subject to ordinances,

Col 3:3 For ye are dead, and your life is hid with Christ in God.

2 Ti 2:11 *It is* a faithful saying: For if we be dead with *him,* we shall also live with *him:*

1 Pe 2:24 Who his own self bare our sins in his own body on the tree, that we, being dead to sins, should live unto righteousness: by whose stripes ye were healed.

1 Pe 4:1 Forasmuch then as Christ hath suffered for us in the flesh, arm yourselves likewise with the same mind: for he that hath suffered in the flesh hath ceased from sin;

2. Fellowship with Christ's Death

Mk 8:34 And when he had called the people *unto him* with his disciples also, he said unto them, Whosoever will come after me, let him deny himself, and take up his cross, and follow me.

Ro 6:4 Therefore we are buried with him by baptism into death: that like as Christ was raised up from the dead by the glory of the Father, even so we also should walk in newness of life.

Ro 6:6 Knowing this, that our old man is crucified with *him,* that the body of sin might be destroyed, that henceforth we should not serve sin.

Ro 6:8 Now if we be dead with Christ, we believe that we shall also live with him:

Ro 8:36 As it is written, For thy sake we are killed all the day long; we are accounted as sheep for the slaughter.

2 Co 4:11 For we which live are alway delivered unto death for Jesus' sake, that the life also of Jesus might be made manifest in our mortal flesh.

2 Co 6:9 As unknown, and *yet* well known; as dying, and, behold, we live; as chastened, and not killed;

Ga 2:20 I am crucified with Christ: nevertheless I live; yet not I, but Christ liveth in me: and the life which I now live in the flesh I live by the faith of the Son of God, who loved me, and gave himself for me.

Ga 6:14 But God forbid that I should glory, save in the cross of our Lord Jesus Christ, by whom the world is crucified unto me, and I unto the world.

Ph 3:10 That I may know him, and the power of his resurrection, and the fellowship of his sufferings, being made conformable unto his death;

Col 2:20 Wherefore if ye be dead with Christ from the rudiments of the world, why, as though living in the world, are ye subject to ordinances,

Col 3:3 For ye are dead, and your life is hid with Christ in God.

2 Ti 2:11 *It is* a faithful saying: For if we be dead with *him,* we shall also live with *him:*

3. Rendering of Service

NOAH

Ge 6:22 Thus did Noah; according to all that God commanded him, so did he.

ELISHA

1 K 19:20 And he left the oxen, and ran after Elijah, and said, Let me, I pray thee, kiss my father and my mother, and *then* I will follow thee. And he said unto him, Go back again: for what have I done to thee?

DAVID

Ps 40:8 I delight to do thy will, O my God: yea, thy law *is* within my heart.

ISAIAH

Is 6:8 Also I heard the voice of the Lord, saying, Whom shall I send, and who will go for us? Then said I, Here *am* I; send me.

CHRIST

Jn 4:34 Jesus saith unto them, My meat is to do the will of him that sent me, and to finish his work.

PAUL

Ac 9:6 And he trembling and astonished said, Lord, what wilt thou have me to do? And the Lord *said* unto him, Arise, and go into the city, and it shall be told thee what thou must do.

4. Resignation in Trial

ELI

1 S 3:18 And Samuel told him every whit, and hid nothing from him. And he said, It *is* the LORD: let him do what seemeth him good.

DAVID

2 S 12:23 But now he is dead, wherefore should I fast? can I bring him back again? I shall go to him, but he shall not return to me.
2 S 15:26 But if he thus say, I have no delight in thee; behold, *here am* I, let him do to me as seemeth good unto him.
2 K 20:19 Then said Hezekiah unto Isaiah, Good is the word of the LORD which thou hast spoken. And he said, *Is it* not *good,* if peace and truth be in my days?

JOB

Jb 1:21 And said, Naked came I out of my mother's womb, and naked shall I return thither: the LORD gave, and the LORD hath taken away; blessed be the name of the LORD.

CHRIST

Mk 14:36 And he said, Abba, Father, all things *are* possible unto thee; take away this cup from me: nevertheless not what I will, but what thou wilt.

PAUL'S FRIENDS

Ac 21:14 And when he would not be persuaded, we ceased, saying, The will of the Lord be done.

5. Submission to the Divine Will

THE RESULT OF INWARD LAW

Ps 40:8 I delight to do thy will, O my God: yea, thy law *is* within my heart.

PRAYER IS ESSENTIAL

Ps 143:10 Teach me to do thy will; for thou *art* my God: thy spirit *is* good; lead me into the land of uprightness.
Mt 6:10 Thy kingdom come. Thy will be done in earth, as *it is* in heaven.

ESTABLISHES A DIVINE RELATIONSHIP

Mt 12:50 For whosoever shall do the will of my Father which is in heaven, the same is my brother, and sister, and mother.

CHRIST IS THE PERFECT EXAMPLE

Mt 26:42 He went away again the second time, and prayed, saying, O my Father, if this cup may not pass away from me, except I drink it, thy will be done.

Jn 5:30 I can of mine own self do nothing: as I hear, I judge: and my judgment is just; because I seek not mine own will, but the will of the Father which hath sent me.

TENDS TO SPIRITUAL KNOWLEDGE

Jn 7:17 If any man will do his will, he shall know of the doctrine, whether it be of God, or *whether* I speak of myself.
Ac 21:14 And when he would not be persuaded, we ceased, saying, The will of the Lord be done.
Ro 12:2 And be not conformed to this world: but be ye transformed by the renewing of your mind, that ye may prove what is that good, and acceptable, and perfect, will of God.

WHOLE-HEARTED

Ep 6:6 Not with eyeservice, as men-pleasers; but as the servants of Christ, doing the will of God from the heart; **He 13:21** Make you perfect in every good work to do his will, working in you that which is wellpleasing in his sight, through Jesus Christ; to whom *be* glory for ever and ever. Amen.

THE RULE OF EVERYDAY LIFE

Ja 4:15 For that ye *ought* to say, If the Lord will, we shall live, and do this, or that.

1 Jn 2:17 And the world passeth away, and the lust thereof: but he that doeth the will of God abideth for ever.

See **SUBMISSION**

SWINE *See* **ANIMALS**

SWORD OF THE LORD, *symbol for judgment and protection*

Ge 3:24 So he drove out the man; and he placed at the east of the garden of Eden Cherubims, and a flaming sword which turned every way, to keep the way of the tree of life.

Nu 22:23 And the ass saw the angel of the Lord standing in the way, and his sword drawn in his hand: and the ass turned aside out of the way, and went into the field: and Balaam smote the ass, to turn her into the way.

De 32:41 If I whet my glittering sword, and mine hand take hold on judgment; I will render vengeance to mine enemies, and will reward them that hate me.

Jos 5:13 And it came to pass, when Joshua was by Jericho, that he lifted up his eyes and looked, and, behold, there stood a man over against him with his sword drawn in his hand: and Joshua went unto him, and said unto him, *Art* thou for us, or for our adversaries?

Jud 7:20 And the three companies blew the trumpets, and brake the pitchers, and held the lamps in their left hands, and the trumpets in their right hands to blow *withal:* and they cried, The sword of the Lord, and of Gideon.

1 Chr 21:12 Either three years' famine; or three months to be destroyed before thy foes, while that the sword of thine enemies overtaketh *thee;* or else three days the sword of the Lord, even the pestilence, in the land, and the angel of the Lord destroying throughout all the coasts of Israel. Now therefore advise thyself what word I shall bring again to him that sent me.

1 Chr 21:16 And David lifted up his eyes, and saw the angel of the Lord stand between the earth and the heaven, having a drawn sword in his hand stretched out over Jerusalem. Then David and the elders *of Israel, who were* clothed in sackcloth, fell upon their faces.

Jb 19:29 Be ye afraid of the sword: for wrath *bringeth* the punishments of the sword, that ye may know *there is* a judgment.

Ps 7:12 If he turn not, he will whet his sword; he hath bent his bow, and made it ready.

Ps 17:13 Arise, O Lord, disappoint him, cast him down: deliver my soul from the wicked, *which is* thy sword:

Ps 45:3 Gird thy sword upon *thy* thigh, O *most* mighty, with thy glory and thy majesty.

Is 27:1 In that day the Lord with his sore and great and strong sword shall punish leviathan the piercing serpent, even leviathan that crooked serpent; and he shall slay the dragon that *is* in the sea.

Is 34:6 The sword of the Lord is filled with blood, it is made fat with fatness, *and* with the blood of lambs and goats, with the fat of the kidneys of rams: for the Lord hath a sacrifice in Bozrah, and a great slaughter in the land of Idumea.

Is 66:16 For by fire and by his sword will the Lord plead with all flesh: and the slain of the Lord shall be many.

Je 12:12 The spoilers are come upon all high places through the wilderness: for the sword of the Lord shall devour from the *one* end of the land even to the *other* end of the land: no flesh shall have peace.

Je 47:6 O thou sword of the Lord, how long *will it be* ere thou be quiet? put up thyself into thy scabbard, rest, and be still.

Je 50:35 A sword *is* upon the Chaldeans, saith the Lord, and upon the inhabitants of Babylon, and upon her princes, and upon her wise *men*.

Eze 5:12 A third part of thee shall die with the pestilence, and with famine shall they be consumed in the midst of thee: and a third part shall fall by the sword round about thee and I will scatter a third part into all the winds, and I will draw out a sword after them.

Eze 21:3 And say to the land of Israel, Thus saith the Lord; Behold, I *am* against thee, and will draw forth my sword out of his sheath, and will cut off from thee the righteous and the wicked.

Eze 30:24 And I will strengthen the arms of the king of Babylon, and put my sword in his hand: but I will break Pharaoh's arms, and he shall groan before him with the groanings of a deadly wounded *man*.

Eze 32:10 Yea, I will make many people amazed at thee, and their kings shall be horribly afraid for thee, when I shall brandish my sword before them; and they shall tremble at *every* moment, every man for his own life, in the day of thy fall.

Eze 38:21 And I will call for a sword against him throughout all my mountains, saith the Lord God: every man's sword shall be against his brother.

Am 7:9 And the high places of Isaac shall be desolate, and the sanctuaries of Israel shall be laid waste; and I will rise against the house of Jeroboam with the sword.

Zep 2:12 Ye Ethiopians also, ye *shall be* slain by my sword.

Re 19:15 And out of his mouth goeth a sharp sword, that with it he should smite the nations: and he shall rule them with a rod of iron: and he treadeth the winepress of the fierceness and wrath of Almighty God.

See **JUDGMENTS**

SYCOMORE See **TREES**

SYMPATHY

1. Divine

2 K 20:5 Turn again, and tell Hezekiah the captain of my people, Thus saith the LORD, the God of David thy father, I have heard thy prayer, I have seen thy tears: behold, I will heal thee: on the third day thou shalt go up unto the house of the LORD.

Ps 38:9 Lord, all my desire *is* before thee; and my groaning is not hid from thee.

Ps 78:39 For he remembered that they *were but* flesh; a wind that passeth away, and cometh not again.

Ps 103:13 Like as a father pitieth *his* children, *so* the LORD pitieth them that fear him.

Is 38:5 Go, and say to Hezekiah, Thus saith the LORD, the God of David thy father, I have heard thy prayer, I have seen thy tears: behold, I will add unto thy days fifteen years.

Is 57:16 For I will not contend for ever, neither will I be always wroth: for the spirit should fail before me, and the souls *which* I have made.

Is 63:9 In all their affliction he was afflicted, and the angel of his presence saved them: in his love and in his pity he redeemed them; and he bare them, and carried them all the days of old.

Mt 12:20 A bruised reed shall he not break, and smoking flax shall he not quench, till he send forth judgment unto victory.

Mt 26:41 Watch and pray, that ye enter not into temptation: the spirit indeed *is* willing, but the flesh *is* weak.

Mk 14:38 Watch ye and pray, lest ye enter into temptation. The spirit truly *is* ready, but the flesh *is* weak.

Jn 11:35–36 Jesus wept.
Then said the Jews, Behold how he loved him!

He 4:15 For we have not an high priest which cannot be touched with the feeling of our infirmities; but was in all points tempted like as *we are, yet* without sin.

2. Human

a. Characteristics

BENEVOLENCE

Is 58:7 *Is it* not to deal thy bread to the hungry, and that thou bring the poor that are cast out to thy house? when thou seest the naked, that thou cover him; and that thou hide not thyself from thine own flesh?

HELPFULNESS

Ac 20:35 I have shewed you all things, how that so labouring ye ought to support the weak, and to remember the words of the Lord Jesus, how he said, It is more blessed to give than to receive.

Ro 12:15 Rejoice with them that do rejoice, and weep with them that weep.

BURDEN-BEARING

Ro 15:1 We then that are strong ought to bear the infirmities of the weak, and not to please ourselves.

Ga 6:2 Bear ye one another's burdens, and so fulfil the law of Christ.

FEELING FOR THE UNFORTUNATE

He 13:3 Remember them that are in bonds, as bound with them; *and* them which suffer adversity, as being yourselves also in the body.

VISITATION OF THE NEEDY

Ja 1:27 Pure religion and undefiled before God and the Father is this, To visit the fatherless and widows in their affliction, *and* to keep himself unspotted from the world.

1 Pe 3:8 Finally, *be ye* all of one mind, having compassion one of another, love as brethren, *be* pitiful, *be* courteous:

b. Examples

Ge 23:6 Hear us, my lord: thou *art* a mighty prince among us: in the choice of our sepulchres bury thy dead; none of us shall withhold from thee his sepulchre, but that thou mayest bury thy dead.

2 S 15:23 And all the country wept with a loud voice, and all the people passed over: the king also himself passed over the brook Kidron, and all the people passed over, toward the way of the wilderness.

2 K 4:27 And when she came to the man of God to the hill, she caught him by the feet: but Gehazi came near to thrust her away. And the man of God said, Let her alone; for her soul *is* vexed within her: and the Lord hath hid *it* from me, and hath not told me.

2 K 8:29 And king Joram went back to be healed in Jezreel of the wounds which the Syrians had given him at Ramah, when he fought against Hazael king of Syria. And Ahaziah the son of Jehoram king of Judah went down to see Joram the son of Ahab in Jezreel, because he was sick.

2 K 20:12 At that time Berodach-baladan, the son of Baladan, king of Babylon, sent letters and a present unto Hezekiah: for he had heard that Hezekiah had been sick.

1 Chr 19:2 And David said, I will shew kindness unto Hanun the son of Nahash, because his father shewed kindness to me. And David sent messengers to comfort him concerning his father. So the servants of David came into the land of the children of Ammon to Hanun, to comfort him.

2 Chr 22:6 And he returned to be healed in Jezreel because of the wounds which were given him at Ramah, when he fought with Hazael king of Syria. And Azariah the son of Jehoram king of Judah went down to see Jehoram the son of Ahab at Jezreel, because he was sick.

Jb 2:11 Now when Job's three friends heard of all this evil that was come upon him, they came every one from his own place; Eliphaz the Temanite, and Bildad the Shuhite, and Zophar the Naamathite: for they had made an appointment together to come to mourn with him and to comfort him.

Jb 30:25 Did not I weep for him that was in trouble? was *not* my soul grieved for the poor?

Jb 42:11 Then came there unto him all his brethren, and all his sisters, and all they that had been of his acquaintance before, and did eat bread with him in his house: and they bemoaned him, and comforted him over all the evil that the Lord had brought upon him: every man also gave him a piece of money, and every one an earring of gold.

Ps 35:14 I behaved myself as though *he had been* my friend *or* brother: I bowed down heavily, as one that mourneth *for his* mother.

Pr 25:20 *As* he that taketh away a garment in cold weather, *and as* vinegar upon nitre, so *is* he that singeth songs to an heavy heart.

Is 16:11 Wherefore my bowels shall sound like an harp for Moab, and mine inward parts for Kir-haresh.

Is 39:1 At that time Merodachbaladan, the son of Baladan, king of Babylon, sent letters and a present to Hezekiah: for he had heard that he had been sick, and was recovered.

Mt 18:31 So when his fellowservants saw what was done, they were very sorry, and came and told unto their lord all that was done.

Lu 7:12 Now when he came nigh to the gate of the city, behold, there was a dead man carried out, the only son of his mother, and she was a widow: and much people of the city was with her.

Lu 10:35 And on the morrow when he departed, he took out two pence, and gave *them* to the host, and said unto him, Take care of him; and whatsoever thou spendest more, when I come again, I will repay thee.

Lu 23:27 And there followed him a great company of people, and of women, which also bewailed and lamented him.

Jn 11:19 And many of the Jews came to Martha and Mary, to comfort them concerning their brother.

Jn 11:31 The Jews then which were with her in the house, and comforted her, when they saw Mary, that she rose up hastily and went out, followed her, saying, She goeth unto the grave to weep there.

Ac 3:4 And Peter, fastening his eyes upon him with John, said, Look on us.

2 Co 11:29 Who is weak, and I am not weak? who is offended, and I burn not?

Ga 4:14 And my temptation which was in my flesh ye despised not, nor rejected; but received me as an angel of God, *even* as Christ Jesus.

See **HELPER, KINDNESS, PITILESSNESS**

SYNAGOGUES, *places of Jewish worship and religious teaching*

1. Teaching and Preaching

Mt 9:35 And Jesus went about all the cities and villages, teaching in their synagogues, and preaching the gospel of the kingdom, and healing every sickness and every disease among the people.

Mt 12:9 And when he was departed thence, he went into their synagogue:

Mt 13:54 And when he was come into his own country, he taught them in their synagogue, insomuch that they were astonished, and said, Whence hath this *man* this wisdom, and *these* mighty works?

Mt 23:34 Wherefore, behold, I send unto you prophets, and wise men, and scribes: and *some* of them ye shall kill and crucify; and *some* of them shall ye scourge in your synagogues, and persecute *them* from city to city:

Mk 1:21 And they went into Capernaum; and straightway on the sabbath day he entered into the synagogue, and taught.

Mk 1:29 And forthwith, when they were come out of the synagogue, they entered into the house of Simon and Andrew, with James and John.

Mk 1:39 And he preached in their synagogues throughout all Galilee, and cast out devils.

Mk 6:2 And when the sabbath day was come, he began to teach in the synagogue: and many hearing *him* were astonished, saying, From whence hath this *man* these things? and what wisdom *is* this which is given unto him, that even such mighty works are wrought by his hands?

Lu 4:44 And he preached in the synagogues of Galilee.

Lu 13:10 And he was teaching in one of the synagogues on the sabbath.

Jn 6:59 These things said he in the synagogue, as he taught in Capernaum.

Jn 18:20 Jesus answered him, I spake openly to the world; I ever taught in the synagogue, and in the temple, whither the Jews always resort; and in secret have I said nothing.

Ac 9:20 And straightway he preached Christ in the synagogues, that he is the Son of God.

Ac 13:5 And when they were at Salamis, they preached the word of God in the synagogues of the Jews: and they had also John to *their* minister.

Ac 14:1 And it came to pass in Iconium, that they went both together into the synagogue of the Jews, and so spake, that a great multitude both of the Jews and also of the Greeks believed.

Ac 15:21 For Moses of old time hath in every city them that preach him, being read in the synagogues every sabbath day.

Ac 17:1 Now when they had passed through Amphipolis and Apollonia, they came to Thessalonica, where was a synagogue of the Jews:

Ac 17:10 And the brethren immediately sent away Paul and Silas by night unto Berea: who coming *thither* went into the synagogue of the Jews.

Ac 18:19 And he came to Ephesus, and left them there: but he himself entered into the synagogue, and reasoned with the Jews.

Ac 19:8 And he went into the synagogue, and spake boldly for the space of three months, disputing and persuading the things concerning the kingdom of God.

Ja 2:2 For if there come unto your assembly a man with a gold ring, in goodly apparel, and there come in also a poor man in vile raiment;

2. Attendance

Mt 12:9 And when he was departed thence, he went into their synagogue:

Mk 1:21 And they went into Capernaum; and straightway on the sabbath day he entered into the synagogue, and taught.

Mk 3:1 And he entered again into the synagogue; and there was a man there which had a withered hand.

Lu 4:15–16 And he taught in their synagogues, being glorified of all.

And he came to Nazareth, where he had been brought up: and, as his custom was, he went into the synagogue on the sabbath day, and stood up for to read.

Lu 6:6 And it came to pass also on another sabbath, that he entered into the synagogue and taught: and there was a man whose right hand was withered.

Ac 13:14 But when they departed from Perga, they came to Antioch in Pisidia, and went into the synagogue on the sabbath day, and sat down.

Ac 17:2 And Paul, as his manner was, went in unto them, and three sabbath days reasoned with them out of the scriptures,

Ac 17:10 And the brethren immediately sent away Paul and Silas by night unto Berea: who coming *thither* went into the synagogue of the Jews.

He 10:25 Not forsaking the assembling of ourselves together, as the manner of some *is;* but exhorting *one another:* and so much the more, as ye see the day approaching.

See **CHURCH**

SYRIA, *northern neighbor of Israel*

Jud 10:6; 2 S 8:6; 2 K 6:23; 13:17; 2 Chr 18:10; 28:5; Is 7:8; Am 1:5; Mt 4:24; Lu 2:2; Ac 15:23, 41; 18:18; 20:3; 21:3; Ga 1:21

SYROPHENICIAN WOMAN,
Gentile woman whose daughter was healed by Jesus

Mk 7:26

See **WOMEN**

T

TAANACH, *a Canaanite city*

Jos 12:21; 17:11; 21:25; Jud 1:27; 5:19;
1 K 4:12

TABERAH, *campsite of Israel in the wilderness where God consumed complainers with fire*

Nu 11:3; De 9:22

TABERNACLE, *a portable sanctuary transported through the wilderness by the Hebrews*

Ex 25:8 And let them make me a sanctuary; that I may dwell among them.

Ex 26:1 Moreover thou shalt make the tabernacle *with* ten curtains *of* fine twined linen, and blue, and purple, and scarlet: *with* cherubims of cunning work shalt thou make them.

Ex 26:12 And the remnant that remaineth of the curtains of the tent, the half curtain that remaineth, shall hang over the backside of the tabernacle.

Ex 26:30 And thou shalt rear up the tabernacle according to the fashion thereof which was shewed thee in the mount.

Ex 27:9 And thou shalt make the court of the tabernacle: for the south side southward *there shall be* hangings for the court *of* fine twined linen of an hundred cubits long for one side:

Ex 27:21 In the tabernacle of the congregation without the vail, which *is* before the testimony, Aaron and his sons shall order it from evening to morning before the Lord: *it shall be* a statute for ever unto their generations on the behalf of the children of Israel.

Ex 28:43 And they shall be upon Aaron, and upon his sons, when they come in unto the tabernacle of the congregation, or when they come near unto the altar to minister in the holy *place;* that they bear not iniquity, and die: *it shall be* a statute for ever unto him and his seed after him.

Ex 29:32 And Aaron and his sons shall eat the flesh of the ram, and the bread that *is* in the basket, *by* the door of the tabernacle of the congregation.

Ex 30:18 Thou shalt also make a laver *of* brass, and his foot *also of* brass, to wash *withal:* and thou shalt put it between the tabernacle of the congregation and the altar, and thou shalt put water therein.

Ex 30:36 And thou shalt beat *some* of it very small, and put of it before the testimony in the tabernacle of the congregation, where I will meet with thee: it shall be unto you most holy.

Ex 31:7 The tabernacle of the congregation, and the ark of the testimony, and the mercy seat that *is* thereupon, and all the furniture of the tabernacle,

Ex 35:11 The tabernacle, his tent, and his covering, his taches, and his boards, his bars, his pillars, and his sockets,

Ex 36:13 And he made fifty taches of gold, and coupled the curtains one unto another with the taches: so it became one tabernacle.

Ex 38:21 This is the sum of the tabernacle, *even* of the tabernacle of testimony, as it was counted, according to the commandment of Moses, *for* the service of the Levites, by the hand of Ithamar, son to Aaron the priest.

Ex 39:32 Thus was all the work of the tabernacle of the tent of the congregation finished: and the children of Israel did according to all that the Lord commanded Moses, so did they.

Ex 39:40 The hangings of the court, his pillars, and his sockets, and the hanging for the court gate, his cords, and his pins, and all the vessels of the service of the tabernacle, for the tent of the congregation,

Ex 40:2 On the first day of the first month shalt thou set up the tabernacle of the tent of the congregation.

Ex 40:17 And it came to pass in the first month in the second year, on the first *day* of the month, *that* the tabernacle was reared up.

Ex 40:34 Then a cloud covered the tent of the congregation, and the glory of the Lord filled the tabernacle.

Le 4:7 And the priest shall put *some* of the blood upon the horns of the altar of sweet incense before the Lord, which *is* in the tabernacle of the congregation: and shall pour all the blood of the bullock at the bottom of the altar of the burnt offering, which *is at* the door of the tabernacle of the congregation.

Le 6:16 And the remainder thereof shall Aaron and his sons eat: with unleavened bread shall it be eaten in the holy place; in the court of the tabernacle of the congregation they shall eat it.

Le 6:26 The priest that offereth it for sin shall eat it: in the holy place shall it be eaten, in the court of the tabernacle of the congregation.

Le 8:3 And gather thou all the congregation together unto the door of the tabernacle of the congregation.

Le 8:10 And Moses took the anointing oil, and anointed the tabernacle and all that *was* therein, and sanctified them.

Le 8:31 And Moses said unto Aaron and to his sons, Boil the flesh at the door of the tabernacle of the congregation: and there eat it with the bread that *is* in the basket of consecrations, as I commanded, saying, Aaron and his sons shall eat it.

Le 9:5 And they brought *that* which Moses commanded before the tabernacle of the congregation: and all the congregation drew near and stood before the Lord.

Le 14:11 And the priest that maketh *him* clean shall present the man that is to be made clean, and those things, before the Lord, *at* the door of the tabernacle of the congregation:

Le 15:14 And on the eighth day he shall take to him two turtledoves, or two young pigeons, and come before the Lord unto the door of the tabernacle of the congregation, and give them unto the priest:

Le 15:29 And on the eighth day she shall take unto her two turtles, or two young pigeons, and bring them unto the priest, to the door of the tabernacle of the congregation.

Le 16:7 And he shall take the two goats, and present them before the Lord *at* the door of the tabernacle of the congregation.

Le 16:16 And he shall make an atonement for the holy *place,* because of the uncleanness of the children of Israel, and because of their transgressions in all their sins: and so shall he do for the tabernacle of the congregation, that remaineth among them in the midst of their uncleanness.

Le 16:20 And when he hath made an end of reconciling the holy *place,* and the tabernacle of the congregation, and the altar, he shall bring the live goat:

Le 16:33 And he shall make an atonement for the holy sanctuary, and he shall make an atonement for the tabernacle of the congregation, and for the altar, and he shall make an atonement for the priests, and for all the people of the congregation.

Le 17:5 To the end that the children of Israel may bring their sacrifices, which they offer in the open field, even that they may bring them unto the Lord, unto the door of the tabernacle of the congregation, unto the priest, and offer them *for* peace offerings unto the Lord.

Le 24:3 Without the vail of the testimony, in the tabernacle of the congregation, shall Aaron order it from the evening unto the morning before the Lord continually: *it shall be* a statute for ever in your generations.

Le 26:11 And I will set my tabernacle among you: and my soul shall not abhor you.

Nu 1:1 And the Lord spake unto Moses in the wilderness of Sinai, in the tabernacle of the congregation, on the first *day* of the second month, in the second year after they were come out of the land of Egypt, saying,

Nu 1:51 And when the tabernacle setteth forward, the Levites shall take it down: and when the tabernacle is to be pitched, the Levites shall set it up: and the stranger that cometh nigh shall be put to death.

Nu 2:17 Then the tabernacle of the congregation shall set forward with the camp of the Levites in the midst of the camp: as they encamp, so shall they set forward, every man in his place by their standards.

Nu 3:7 And they shall keep his charge, and the charge of the whole congregation before the tabernacle of the congregation, to do the service of the tabernacle.

Nu 3:25 And the charge of the sons of Gershon in the tabernacle of the congregation *shall be* the tabernacle, and the tent, the covering thereof, and the hanging for the door of the tabernacle of the congregation,

Nu 3:38 But those that encamp before the tabernacle toward the east, *even* before the tabernacle of the congregation eastward, *shall be* Moses, and Aaron and his sons, keeping the charge of the sanctuary for the charge of the children of Israel; and the stranger that cometh nigh shall be put to death.

Nu 4:4 This *shall be* the service of the sons of Kohath in the tabernacle of the congregation, *about* the most holy things:

Nu 4:16 And to the office of Eleazar the son of Aaron the priest *pertaineth* the oil for the light, and the sweet incense, and the daily meat offering, and the anointing oil, *and* the oversight of all the tabernacle, and of all that therein *is*, in the sanctuary, and in the vessels thereof.

Nu 4:25 And they shall bear the curtains of the tabernacle, and the tabernacle of the congregation, his covering, and the covering of the badgers' skins that *is* above upon it, and the hanging for the door of the tabernacle of the congregation,

Nu 4:31 And this *is* the charge of their burden, according to all their service in the tabernacle of the congregation; the boards of the tabernacle, and the bars thereof, and the pillars thereof, and sockets thereof,

Nu 4:41 These *are* they that were numbered of the families of the sons of Gershon, of all that might do service in the tabernacle of the congregation, whom Moses and Aaron did number according to the commandment of the Lord.

Nu 6:18 And the Nazarite shall shave the head of his separation *at* the door of the tabernacle of the congregation, and shall take the hair of the head of his separation, and put *it* in the fire which *is* under the sacrifice of the peace offerings.

Nu 7:1 And it came to pass on the day that Moses had fully set up the tabernacle, and had anointed it, and sanctified it, and all the instruments thereof, both the altar and all the vessels thereof, and had anointed them, and sanctified them;

Nu 7:89 And when Moses was gone into the tabernacle of the congregation to speak with him, then he heard the voice of one speaking unto him from off the mercy seat that *was* upon the ark of testimony, from between the two cherubims: and he spake unto him.

Nu 8:9 And thou shalt bring the Levites before the tabernacle of the congregation: and thou shalt gather the whole assembly of the children of Israel together:

Nu 8:22 And after that went the Levites in to do their service in the tabernacle of the congregation before Aaron, and before his sons: as the Lord had commanded Moses concerning the Levites, so did they unto them.

Nu 9:15 And on the day that the tabernacle was reared up the cloud covered the tabernacle, *namely,* the tent of the testimony: and at even there was upon the tabernacle as it were the appearance of fire, until the morning.

Nu 10:3 And when they shall blow with them, all the assembly shall assemble themselves to thee at the door of the tabernacle of the congregation.

Nu 10:21 And the Kohathites set forward, bearing the sanctuary: and *the other* did set up the tabernacle against they came.

Nu 11:16 And the Lord said unto Moses, Gather unto me seventy men of the elders of Israel, whom thou knowest to be the elders of the people, and officers over them; and bring them unto the tabernacle of the congregation, that they may stand there with thee.

Nu 11:24 And Moses went out, and told the people the words of the Lord, and gathered the seventy men of the elders of the people, and set them round about the tabernacle.

Nu 14:10 But all the congregation bade stone them with stones. And the glory of the Lord appeared in the tabernacle of the congregation before all the children of Israel.

Nu 16:9 *Seemeth it but* a small thing unto you, that the God of Israel hath separated you from the congregation of Israel, to bring you near to himself to do the service of the tabernacle of the Lord, and to stand before the congregation to minister unto them?

Nu 16:18 And they took every man his censer, and put fire in them, and laid incense thereon, and stood in the door of the tabernacle of the congregation with Moses and Aaron.

Nu 16:42 And it came to pass, when the congregation was gathered against Moses and against Aaron, that they looked toward the tabernacle of the congregation: and, behold, the cloud covered it, and the glory of the Lord appeared.

Nu 17:4 And thou shalt lay them up in the tabernacle of the congregation before the testimony, where I will meet with you.

Nu 17:7 And Moses laid up the rods before the Lord in the tabernacle of witness.

Nu 19:4 And Eleazar the priest shall take of her blood with his finger, and sprinkle of her blood directly before the tabernacle of the congregation seven times:

Nu 20:6 And Moses and Aaron went from the presence of the assembly unto the door of the tabernacle of the congregation, and they fell upon their faces: and the glory of the Lord appeared unto them.

Nu 25:6 And, behold, one of the children of Israel came and brought unto his brethren a Midianitish woman in the sight of Moses, and in the sight of all the congregation of the children of Israel, who *were* weeping *before* the door of the tabernacle of the congregation.

Nu 27:2 And they stood before Moses, and before Eleazar the priest, and before the princes and all the congregation, *by* the door of the tabernacle of the congregation, saying,

Nu 31:54 And Moses and Eleazar the priest took the gold of the captains of thousands and of hundreds, and brought it into the tabernacle of the congregation, *for* a memorial for the children of Israel before the Lord.

De 31:14 And the Lord said unto Moses, Behold, thy days approach that thou must die: call Joshua, and present yourselves in the tabernacle of the congregation, that I may give him a charge. And Moses and Joshua went, and presented themselves in the tabernacle of the congregation.

Jos 18:1 And the whole congregation of the children of Israel assembled together at Shiloh, and set up the tabernacle of the congregation there. And the land was subdued before them.

Jos 19:51 These *are* the inheritances which Eleazar the priest, and Joshua the son of Nun, and the heads of the fathers of the tribes of the children of Israel, divided for an inheritance by lot in Shiloh before the Lord, at the door of the tabernacle of the congregation. So they made an end of dividing the country.

Jos 22:19 Notwithstanding, if the land of your possession *be* unclean, *then* pass ye over unto the land of the possession of the Lord, wherein the Lord's tabernacle dwelleth, and take possession among us: but rebel not against the Lord, nor rebel against us, in building you an altar beside the altar of the Lord our God.

Jos 22:29 God forbid that we should rebel against the Lord, and turn this day from following the Lord, to build an altar for burnt offerings, for meat offerings, or for sacrifices, beside the altar of the Lord our God that *is* before his tabernacle.

1 S 1:7 And *as* he did so year by year, when she went up to the house of the Lord, so she provoked her; therefore she wept, and did not eat.

1 S 1:9 So Hannah rose up after they had eaten in Shiloh, and after they had drunk. Now Eli the priest sat upon a seat by a post of the temple of the Lord.

1 S 3:3 And ere the lamp of God went out in the temple of the Lord, where the ark of God *was,* and Samuel was laid down *to sleep;*

1 S 3:15 And Samuel lay until the morning, and opened the doors of the house of the Lord. And Samuel feared to shew Eli the vision.

2 S 7:6 Whereas I have not dwelt in *any* house since the time that I brought up the children of Israel out of Egypt, even to this day, but have walked in a tent and in a tabernacle.

1 K 2:28 Then tidings came to Joab: for Joab had turned after Adonijah, though he turned not after Absalom. And Joab fled unto the tabernacle of the Lord, and caught hold on the horns of the altar.

1 K 8:4 And they brought up the ark of the Lord, and the tabernacle of the congregation, and all the holy vessels that *were* in the tabernacle, even those did the priests and the Levites bring up.

1 Chr 6:48 Their brethren also the Levites *were* appointed unto all manner of service of the tabernacle of the house of God.

1 Chr 9:21 *And* Zechariah the son of Meshelemiah *was* porter of the door of the tabernacle of the congregation.

1 Chr 16:39 And Zadok the priest, and his brethren the priests, before the tabernacle of the Lord in the high place that *was* at Gibeon,

1 Chr 17:5 For I have not dwelt in an house since the day that I brought up Israel unto this day; but have gone from tent to tent, and from *one* tabernacle *to another.*

1 Chr 21:29 For the tabernacle of the Lord, which Moses made in the wilderness, and the altar of the burnt offering, *were* at that season in the high place at Gibeon.

1 Chr 23:32 And that they should keep the charge of the tabernacle of the congregation, and the charge of the holy *place,* and the charge of the sons of Aaron their brethren, in the service of the house of the Lord.

2 Chr 1:3 So Solomon, and all the congregation with him, went to the high place that *was* at Gibeon; for there was the tabernacle of the congregation of God, which Moses the servant of the Lord had made in the wilderness.

2 Chr 5:5 And they brought up the ark, and the tabernacle of the congregation, and all the holy vessels that *were* in the tabernacle, these did the priests and the Levites bring up.

2 Chr 24:6 And the king called for Jehoiada the chief, and said unto him, Why hast thou not required of the Levites to bring in out of Judah and out of Jerusalem the collection, *according to the commandment* of Moses the servant of the Lord, and of the congregation of Israel, for the tabernacle of witness?

Ps 78:60 So that he forsook the tabernacle of Shiloh, the tent *which* he placed among men;

Eze 41:1 Afterward he brought me to the temple, and measured the posts, six cubits broad on the one side, and six cubits broad on the other side, *which was* the breadth of the tabernacle.

Mt 12:4 How he entered into the house of God, and did eat the shewbread, which was not lawful for him to eat, neither for them which were with him, but only for the priests?

Ac 7:44 Our fathers had the tabernacle of witness in the wilderness, as he had appointed, speaking unto Moses, that he should make it according to the fashion that he had seen.

He 8:2 A minister of the sanctuary, and of the true tabernacle, which the Lord pitched, and not man.

He 9:2 For there was a tabernacle made; the first, wherein *was* the candlestick, and the table, and the shewbread; which is called the sanctuary.

He 9:8 The Holy Ghost this signifying, that the way into the holiest of all was not yet made manifest, while as the first tabernacle was yet standing:

He 9:11 But Christ being come an high priest of good things to come, by a greater and more perfect tabernacle, not made with hands, that is to say, not of this building;

See **TEMPLE**

TABLE

1. An Article of Furniture

Jud 1:7; 2 S 9:7; 1 K 2:7; 10:5; 18:19; 2 Chr 4:8; Ne 5:17; Eze 40:39, 42; Mt 15:27

2. Of Shewbread, used in the tabernacle

See **SHEWBREAD**

TABLETS, of stone, upon which the Decalogue was written

Ex 24:12 And the Lord said unto Moses, Come up to me into the mount, and be there: and I will give thee tables of stone, and a law, and commandments which I have written; that thou mayest teach them.

Ex 25:21 And thou shalt put the mercy seat above upon the ark; and in the ark thou shalt put the testimony that I shall give thee.

Ex 31:18 And he gave unto Moses, when he had made an end of communing with him upon mount Sinai, two tables of testimony, tables of stone, written with the finger of God.

Ex 32:15 And Moses turned, and went down from the mount, and the two tables of the testimony *were* in his hand: the tables *were* written on both their sides; on the one side and on the other *were* they written.

Ex 34:1 And the Lord said unto Moses, Hew thee two tables of stone like unto the first: and I will write upon *these* tables the words that were in the first tables, which thou brakest.

Ex 34:28 And he was there with the Lord forty days and forty nights; he did neither eat bread, nor drink water. And he wrote upon the tables the words of the covenant, the ten commandments.

Ex 40:20 And he took and put the testimony into the ark, and set the staves on the ark, and put the mercy seat above upon the ark:

De 4:13 And he declared unto you his covenant, which he commanded you to perform, *even* ten commandments; and he wrote them upon two tables of stone.

De 5:22 These words the Lord spake unto all your assembly in the mount out of the midst of the fire, of the cloud, and of the thick darkness, with a great voice: and he added no more. And he wrote them in two tables of stone, and delivered them unto me.

De 9:9 When I was gone up into the mount to receive the tables of stone, *even* the tables of the covenant which the Lord made with you, then I abode in the mount forty days and forty nights, I neither did eat bread nor drink water:

De 9:15 So I turned and came down from the mount, and the mount burned with fire: and the two tables of the covenant *were* in my two hands.

De 10:1 At that time the Lord said unto me, Hew thee two tables of stone like unto the first, and come up unto me into the mount, and make thee an ark of wood.

De 10:5 And I turned myself and came down from the mount, and put the tables in the ark which I had made; and there they be, as the Lord commanded me.

1 K 8:9 *There was* nothing in the ark save the two tables of stone, which Moses put there at Horeb, when the Lord made *a covenant* with the children of Israel, when they came out of the land of Egypt.

2 Chr 5:10 *There was* nothing in the ark save the two tables which Moses put *therein* at Horeb, when the Lord made *a covenant* with the children of Israel, when they came out of Egypt.

2 Co 3:3 *Forasmuch as ye are* manifestly declared to be the epistle of Christ ministered by us, written not with ink, but with the Spirit of the living God; not in tables of stone, but in fleshy tables of the heart.

2 Co 3:7 But if the ministration of death, written *and* engraven in stones, was glorious, so that the children of Israel could not stedfastly behold the face of Moses for the glory of his countenance; which *glory* was to be done away:

He 9:4 Which had the golden censer, and the ark of the covenant overlaid round about with gold, wherein *was* the golden pot that had manna, and Aaron's rod that budded, and the tables of the covenant;

See **LAW**

TABOR *See* **MOUNTAINS AND HILLS**

TABRETS *See* **MUSIC**

TACT *See* **PRUDENCE**

TADMOR, *or Palmyra (?)*
1 K 9:18; 2 Chr 8:4

TAILOR *See* **ARTS AND CRAFTS**

TALENT, *a weight*

1. Of Gold
Ex 25:39; 37:24; 38:24; 2 S 12:30; 1 K 9:14, 28; 10:14; 2 Chr 3:8; 9:13; Ezr 8:26; Mt 18:24

2. Of Silver
Ex 38:25; 1 K 16:24; 20:39; 2 K 5:5, 23; 15:19; 18:14; 23:33; 1 Chr 19:6; 22:14; 29:4, 7; 2 Chr 25:6; 27:5; 36:3; Ezr 7:22; 8:26; Est 3:9

3. A Parable
Mt 18:24; 25:15

See **WEIGHTS AND MEASURES**

TAMBOURINES *See* **MUSIC**

TAMMUZ *See* **MONTHS**

TANNERS *See* **ARTS AND CRAFTS**

TAPESTRY, *curtains, veil, significant for its use in the temple*
Pr 7:16; 31:22

TARGETS, *small shield*
1 S 17:6; 1 K 10:16; 2 Chr 9:15

TARSHISH, *or Tharshish*
2 Chr 9:21; 20:36; Ps 48:7; 72:10; Is 2:16; 23:6; 60:9; Je 10:9; Eze 27:12, 25; 38:13; Jona 1:3

TARSUS, *a city of Cilicia, Paul's birthplace*
Ac 9:11, 30; 11:25; 21:39; 22:3

TARTAK, *an idol*
2 K 17:31

TASKMASTERS, *overseers of slaves and laborers*
Ex 1:11; 5:6, 10

TATNAI, *a governor*
Ezr 5:3, 6; 6:6, 13

TAXES *See* **NATION**

TEACHER, *DIVINE*

1. God
Ex 4:15 And thou shalt speak unto him, and put words in his mouth: and I will be with thy mouth, and with his mouth, and will teach you what ye shall do.

De 4:36 Out of heaven he made thee to hear his voice, that he might instruct thee: and upon earth he shewed thee his great fire; and thou heardest his words out of the midst of the fire.

De 29:29 The secret *things belong* unto the LORD our God: but *those things which* are revealed *belong* unto us and to our children for ever, that *we* may do all the words of this law.

1 K 8:36 Then hear thou in heaven, and forgive the sin of thy servants, and of thy people Israel, that thou teach them the good way wherein they should walk, and give rain upon thy land, which thou hast given to thy people for an inheritance.

2 Chr 6:27 Then hear thou from heaven, and forgive the sin of thy servants, and of thy people Israel, when thou hast taught them the good way, wherein they should walk; and send rain upon thy land, which thou hast given unto thy people for an inheritance.

Jb 11:6 And that he would shew thee the secrets of wisdom, that *they are* double to that which is! Know therefore that God exacteth of thee *less* than thine iniquity *deserveth.*

Jb 33:16 Then he openeth the ears of men, and sealeth their instruction,

Jb 35:11 Who teacheth us more than the beasts of the earth, and maketh us wiser than the fowls of heaven?

Jb 36:22 Behold, God exalteth by his power: who teacheth like him?

Ps 25:12 What man *is* he that feareth the LORD? him shall he teach in the way *that* he shall choose.

Ps 32:8 I will instruct thee and teach thee in the way which thou shalt go: I will guide thee with mine eye.

Ps 71:17 O God, thou hast taught me from my youth: and hitherto have I declared thy wondrous works.

Ps 94:10 He that chastiseth the heathen, shall not he correct? he that teacheth man knowledge, *shall not he know?*

Ps 119:26 I have declared my ways, and thou heardest me: teach me thy statutes.

Ps 119:66 Teach me good judgment and knowledge: for I have believed thy commandments.

Ps 119:102 I have not departed from thy judgments: for thou hast taught me.

Ps 119:135 Make thy face to shine upon thy servant; and teach me thy statutes.

Ps 132:12 If thy children will keep my covenant and my testimony that I shall teach them, their children shall also sit upon thy throne for evermore.

Is 2:3 And many people shall go and say, Come ye, and let us go up to the mountain of the LORD, to the house of the God of Jacob; and he will teach us

of his ways, and we will walk in his paths: for out of Zion shall go forth the law, and the word of the LORD from Jerusalem.

Is 28:13 But the word of the LORD was unto them precept upon precept, precept upon precept; line upon line, line upon line; here a little, *and* there a little; that they might go, and fall backward, and be broken, and snared, and taken.

Is 28:26 For his God doth instruct him to discretion, *and* doth teach him.

Is 43:12 I have declared, and have saved, and I have shewed, when *there was* no strange *god* among you: therefore ye *are* my witnesses, saith the LORD, that I *am* God.

Is 48:17 Thus saith the LORD, thy Redeemer, the Holy One of Israel; I *am* the LORD thy God which teacheth thee to profit, which leadeth thee by the way *that* thou shouldest go.

Is 54:13 And all thy children *shall be* taught of the LORD; and great *shall be* the peace of thy children.

Je 11:18 And the LORD hath given me knowledge *of it,* and I know *it:* then thou shewedst me their doings.

Je 16:21 Therefore, behold, I will this once cause them to know, I will cause them to know mine hand and my might; and they shall know that my name *is* The LORD.

Je 18:2 Arise, and go down to the potter's house, and there I will cause thee to hear my words.

Je 32:33 And they have turned unto me the back, and not the face: though I taught them, rising up early and teaching *them,* yet they have not hearkened to receive instruction.

Je 42:3 That the LORD thy God may shew us the way wherein we may walk, and the thing that we may do.

Eze 2:1 And he said unto me, Son of man, stand upon thy feet, and I will speak unto thee.

Eze 20:11 And I gave them my statutes, and shewed them my judgments, which *if* a man do, he shall even live in them.

Eze 40:4 And the man said unto me, Son of man, behold with thine eyes, and hear with thine ears, and set thine heart upon all that I shall shew thee; for to the intent that I might shew *them* unto thee *art* thou brought hither: declare all that thou seest to the house of Israel.

Da 2:23 I thank thee, and praise thee, O thou God of my fathers, who hast given me wisdom and might, and hast made known unto me now what we desired of thee: for thou hast *now* made known unto us the king's matter.

Da 8:19 And he said, Behold, I will make thee know what shall be in the last end of the indignation: for at the time appointed the end *shall be.*

Da 9:22 And he informed *me,* and talked with me, and said, O Daniel, I am now come forth to give thee skill and understanding.

Ho 11:3 I taught Ephraim also to go, taking them by their arms; but they knew not that I healed them.

Mi 4:2 And many nations shall come, and say, Come, and let us go up to the mountain of the LORD, and to the house of the God of Jacob; and he will teach us of his ways, and we will walk in his paths: for the law shall go forth of Zion, and the word of the LORD from Jerusalem.

Mi 6:8 He hath shewed thee, O man, what *is* good; and what doth the LORD require of thee, but to do justly, and to love mercy, and to walk humbly with thy God?

Jn 6:45 It is written in the prophets, And they shall be all taught of God. Every man therefore that hath heard, and hath learned of the Father, cometh unto me.

1 Co 2:12 Now we have received, not the spirit of the world, but the spirit which is of God; that we might know the things that are freely given to us of God.

2. Christ

a. Examples

Mt 4:23 And Jesus went about all Galilee, teaching in their synagogues, and preaching the gospel of the kingdom, and healing all manner of sick-

ness and all manner of disease among the people.

Mt 5:2 And he opened his mouth, and taught them, saying,

Mt 7:29 For he taught them as *one* having authority, and not as the scribes.

Mt 9:35 And Jesus went about all the cities and villages, teaching in their synagogues, and preaching the gospel of the kingdom, and healing every sickness and every disease among the people.

Mt 11:1 And it came to pass, when Jesus had made an end of commanding his twelve disciples, he departed thence to teach and to preach in their cities.

Mt 11:29 Take my yoke upon you, and learn of me; for I am meek and lowly in heart: and ye shall find rest unto your souls.

Mt 13:3 And he spake many things unto them in parables, saying, Behold, a sower went forth to sow;

Mt 13:34 All these things spake Jesus unto the multitude in parables; and without a parable spake he not unto them:

Mt 13:54 And when he was come into his own country, he taught them in their synagogue, insomuch that they were astonished, and said, Whence hath this *man* this wisdom, and *these* mighty works?

Mt 19:16 And, behold, one came and said unto him, Good Master, what good thing shall I do, that I may have eternal life?

Mt 20:25 But Jesus called them *unto him,* and said, Ye know that the princes of the Gentiles exercise dominion over them, and they that are great exercise authority upon them.

Mt 21:23 And when he was come into the temple, the chief priests and the elders of the people came unto him as he was teaching, and said, By what authority doest thou these things? and who gave thee this authority?

Mt 22:16 And they sent out unto him their disciples with the Herodians, saying, Master, we know that thou art true, and teachest the way of

God in truth, neither carest thou for any *man:* for thou regardest not the person of men.

Mt 22:33 And when the multitude heard *this,* they were astonished at his doctrine.

Mt 22:36 Master, which *is* the great commandment in the law?

Mt 23:1 Then spake Jesus to the multitude, and to his disciples,

Mt 23:10 Neither be ye called masters: for one is your Master, *even* Christ.

Mt 26:55 In that same hour said Jesus to the multitudes, Are ye come out as against a thief with swords and staves for to take me? I sat daily with you teaching in the temple, and ye laid no hold on me.

Mk 2:13 And he went forth again by the sea side; and all the multitude resorted unto him, and he taught them.

Mk 4:1 And he began again to teach by the sea side: and there was gathered unto him a great multitude, so that he entered into a ship, and sat in the sea; and the whole multitude was by the sea on the land.

Mk 4:34 But without a parable spake he not unto them: and when they were alone, he expounded all things to his disciples.

Mk 6:2 And when the sabbath day was come, he began to teach in the synagogue: and many hearing *him* were astonished, saying, From whence hath this *man* these things? and what wisdom *is* this which is given unto him, that even such mighty works are wrought by his hands?

Mk 6:6 And he marvelled because of their unbelief. And he went round about the villages, teaching.

Mk 6:34 And Jesus, when he came out, saw much people, and was moved with compassion toward them, because they were as sheep not having a shepherd: and he began to teach them many things.

Mk 8:31 And he began to teach them, that the Son of man must suffer many things, and be rejected of the elders, and *of* the chief priests, and

scribes, and be killed, and after three days rise again.

Mk 9:12 And he answered and told them, Elias verily cometh first, and restoreth all things; and how it is written of the Son of man, that he must suffer many things, and be set at nought.

Mk 10:1 And he arose from thence, and cometh into the coasts of Judaea by the farther side of Jordan: and the people resort unto him again; and, as he was wont, he taught them again.

Mk 12:35 And Jesus answered and said, while he taught in the temple, How say the scribes that Christ is the Son of David?

Mk 14:49 I was daily with you in the temple teaching, and ye took me not: but the scriptures must be fulfilled.

Lu 4:15 And he taught in their synagogues, being glorified of all.

Lu 4:21 And he began to say unto them, This day is this scripture fulfilled in your ears.

Lu 4:31 And came down to Capernaum, a city of Galilee, and taught them on the sabbath days.

Lu 5:3 And he entered into one of the ships, which was Simon's, and prayed him that he would thrust out a little from the land. And he sat down, and taught the people out of the ship.

Lu 5:17 And it came to pass on a certain day, as he was teaching, that there were Pharisees and doctors of the law sitting by, which were come out of every town of Galilee, and Judaea, and Jerusalem: and the power of the Lord was *present* to heal them.

Lu 6:6 And it came to pass also on another sabbath, that he entered into the synagogue and taught: and there was a man whose right hand was withered.

Lu 9:11 And the people, when they knew *it,* followed him, and he received them, and spake unto them of the kingdom of God, and healed them that had need of healing.

Lu 13:10 And he was teaching in one of the synagogues on the sabbath.

Lu 13:22 And he went through the cities and villages, teaching, and journeying toward Jerusalem.

Lu 14:25 And there went great multitudes with him: and he turned, and said unto them,

Lu 19:47 And he taught daily in the temple. But the chief priests and the scribes and the chief of the people sought to destroy him,

Lu 20:21 And they asked him, saying, Master, we know that thou sayest and teachest rightly, neither acceptest thou the person *of any,* but teachest the way of God truly:

Lu 20:39 Then certain of the scribes answering said, Master, thou hast well said.

Lu 21:37 And in the day time he was teaching in the temple; and at night he went out, and abode in the mount that is called *the mount* of Olives.

Lu 22:11 And ye shall say unto the goodman of the house, The Master saith unto thee, Where is the guestchamber, where I shall eat the passover with my disciples?

Lu 23:5 And they were the more fierce, saying, He stirreth up the people, teaching throughout all Jewry, beginning from Galilee to this place.

Jn 3:2 The same came to Jesus by night, and said unto him, Rabbi, we know that thou art a teacher come from God: for no man can do these miracles that thou doest, except God be with him.

Jn 4:25 The woman saith unto him, I know that Messias cometh, which is called Christ: when he is come, he will tell us all things.

Jn 7:14 Now about the midst of the feast Jesus went up into the temple, and taught.

Jn 8:2 And early in the morning he came again into the temple, and all the people came unto him; and he sat down, and taught them.

Jn 8:20 These words spake Jesus in the treasury, as he taught in the temple: and no man laid hands on him; for his hour was not yet come.

Jn 8:26 I have many things to say and to judge of you: but he that sent me is true; and I speak to the world those things which I have heard of him.

Jn 11:28 And when she had so said, she went her way, and called Mary her sister secretly, saying, The Master is come, and calleth for thee.

Jn 18:20 Jesus answered him, I spake openly to the world; I ever taught in the synagogue, and in the temple, whither the Jews always resort; and in secret have I said nothing.

Jn 20:16 Jesus saith unto her, Mary. She turned herself, and saith unto him, Rabboni; which is to say, Master.

b. Exposition of Scriptures

Mt 13:37 He answered and said unto them, He that soweth the good seed is the Son of man;

Mt 24:33 So likewise ye, when ye shall see all these things, know that it is near, *even* at the doors.

Mk 4:34 But without a parable spake he not unto them: and when they were alone, he expounded all things to his disciples.

Lu 8:11 Now the parable is this: The seed is the word of God.

Lu 24:27 And beginning at Moses and all the prophets, he expounded unto them in all the scriptures the things concerning himself.

c. His Doctrine

Mt 7:28 And it came to pass, when Jesus had ended these sayings, the people were astonished at his doctrine:

Mt 22:33 And when the multitude heard *this,* they were astonished at his doctrine.

Mk 1:22 And they were astonished at his doctrine: for he taught them as one that had authority, and not as the scribes.

Mk 1:27 And they were all amazed, insomuch that they questioned among themselves, saying, What thing is this? what new doctrine *is* this? for with authority commandeth he even the unclean spirits, and they do obey him.

Mk 4:2 And he taught them many things by parables, and said unto them in his doctrine,

Mk 11:18 And the scribes and chief priests heard *it,* and sought how they might destroy him: for they feared him, because all the people was astonished at his doctrine.

Mk 12:38 And he said unto them in his doctrine, Beware of the scribes, which love to go in long clothing, and *love* salutations in the marketplaces,

Lu 4:32 And they were astonished at his doctrine: for his word was with power.

Lu 20:1 And it came to pass, *that* on one of those days, as he taught the people in the temple, and preached the gospel, the chief priests and the scribes came upon *him* with the elders,

Jn 7:16 Jesus answered them, and said, My doctrine is not mine, but his that sent me.

Jn 18:19 The high priest then asked Jesus of his disciples, and of his doctrine.

Ac 1:1 The former treatise have I made, O Theophilus, of all that Jesus began both to do and teach,

1 Ti 4:13 Till I come, give attendance to reading, to exhortation, to doctrine.

He 6:1 Therefore leaving the principles of the doctrine of Christ, let us go on unto perfection; not laying again the foundation of repentance from dead works, and of faith toward God,

2 Jn 9 Whosoever transgresseth, and abideth not in the doctrine of Christ, hath not God. He that abideth in the doctrine of Christ, he hath both the Father and the Son.

3. False

Is 5:20 Woe unto them that call evil good, and good evil; that put darkness for light, and light for darkness; that put bitter for sweet, and sweet for bitter!

Je 28:16 Therefore thus saith the LORD; Behold, I will cast thee from off the face of the earth: this year thou shalt die, because thou hast taught rebellion against the LORD.

Eze 13:7 Have ye not seen a vain vision, and have ye not spoken a lying divination, whereas ye say, The LORD saith *it;* albeit I have not spoken?

Mt 5:19 Whosoever therefore shall break one of these least commandments, and shall teach men so, he shall be called the least in the kingdom of heaven: but whosoever shall do and teach *them,* the same shall be called great in the kingdom of heaven.

Mt 15:9 But in vain they do worship me, teaching *for* doctrines the commandments of men.

2 Co 11:4 For if he that cometh preacheth another Jesus, whom we have not preached, or *if* ye receive another spirit, which ye have not received, or another gospel, which ye have not accepted, ye might well bear with *him.*

2 Co 11:13 For such *are* false apostles, deceitful workers, transforming themselves into the apostles of Christ.

1 Ti 1:7 Desiring to be teachers of the law; understanding neither what they say, nor whereof they affirm.

1 Ti 4:2 Speaking lies in hypocrisy; having their conscience seared with a hot iron;

1 Ti 6:3 If any man teach otherwise, and consent not to wholesome words, *even* the words of our Lord Jesus Christ, and to the doctrine which is according to godliness;

2 Ti 4:3 For the time will come when they will not endure sound doctrine; but after their own lusts shall they heap to themselves teachers, having itching ears;

Tit 1:11 Whose mouths must be stopped, who subvert whole houses, teaching things which they ought not, for filthy lucre's sake.

2 Pe 2:1 But there were false prophets also among the people, even as there shall be false teachers among you, who privily shall bring in damnable heresies, even denying the Lord that bought them, and bring upon themselves swift destruction.

4. Christian

Ps 51:13 *Then* will I teach transgressors thy ways; and sinners shall be converted unto thee.

Ac 11:26 And when he had found him, he brought him unto Antioch. And it came to pass, that a whole year they assembled themselves with the church, and taught much people. And the disciples were called Christians first in Antioch.

Ac 13:1 Now there were in the church that was at Antioch certain prophets and teachers; as Barnabas, and Simeon that was called Niger, and Lucius of Cyrene, and Manaen, which had been brought up with Herod the tetrarch, and Saul.

Ac 15:35 Paul also and Barnabas continued in Antioch, teaching and preaching the word of the Lord, with many others also.

Ac 18:11 And he continued *there* a year and six months, teaching the word of God among them.

Ac 18:25 This man was instructed in the way of the Lord; and being fervent in the spirit, he spake and taught diligently the things of the Lord, knowing only the baptism of John.

Ac 28:31 Preaching the kingdom of God, and teaching those things which concern the Lord Jesus Christ, with all confidence, no man forbidding him.

1 Co 12:28 And God hath set some in the church, first apostles, secondarily prophets, thirdly teachers, after that miracles, then gifts of healings, helps, governments, diversities of tongues.

Ep 4:11 And he gave some, apostles; and some, prophets; and some, evangelists; and some, pastors and teachers;

See **INSTRUCTION, LEADERS**

TEARS

1. Over Sinners

Ps 126:6 He that goeth forth and weepeth, bearing precious seed, shall doubtless come again with rejoicing, bringing his sheaves *with him.*

Is 22:4 Therefore said I, Look away from me; I will weep bitterly, labour not to comfort me, because of the spoiling of the daughter of my people.

Je 9:1 Oh that my head were waters, and mine eyes a fountain of tears, that I might weep day and night for the slain of the daughter of my people!

Je 9:18 And let them make haste, and take up a wailing for us, that our eyes may run down with tears, and our eyelids gush out with waters.

Je 13:17 But if ye will not hear it, my soul shall weep in secret places for *your* pride; and mine eye shall weep sore, and run down with tears, because the Lord's flock is carried away captive.

Je 14:17 Therefore thou shalt say this word unto them; Let mine eyes run down with tears night and day, and let them not cease: for the virgin daughter of my people is broken with a great breach, with a very grievous blow.

Lam 2:11 Mine eyes do fail with tears, my bowels are troubled, my liver is poured upon the earth, for the destruction of the daughter of my people; because the children and the sucklings swoon in the streets of the city.

Jl 2:17 Let the priests, the ministers of the Lord, weep between the porch and the altar, and let them say, Spare thy people, O Lord, and give not thine heritage to reproach, that the heathen should rule over them: wherefore should they say among the people, Where *is* their God?

Zec 7:3 *And* to speak unto the priests which *were* in the house of the Lord of hosts, and to the prophets, saying, Should I weep in the fifth month, separating myself, as I have done these so many years?

Mk 9:24 And straightway the father of the child cried out, and said with tears, Lord, I believe; help thou mine unbelief.

Lu 19:41 And when he was come near, he beheld the city, and wept over it,

Ac 20:19 Serving the Lord with all humility of mind, and with many tears, and temptations, which befell me by the lying in wait of the Jews:

Ac 20:31 Therefore watch, and remember, that by the space of three years I ceased not to warn every one night and day with tears.

2 Co 2:4 For out of much affliction and anguish of heart I wrote unto you with many tears; not that ye should be grieved, but that ye might know the love which I have more abundantly unto you.

Ph 3:18 (For many walk, of whom I have told you often, and now tell you even weeping, *that they are* the enemies of the cross of Christ:

2. Of Disappointment and Grief

Jb 16:16 My face is foul with weeping, and my eyelids is the shadow of death;

Jb 30:31 My harp also is *turned* to mourning, and my organ into the voice of them that weep.

Ps 6:6 I am weary with my groaning; all the night make I my bed to swim; I water my couch with my tears.

Ps 39:12 Hear my prayer, O Lord, and give ear unto my cry; hold not thy peace at my tears: for I *am* a stranger with thee, *and* a sojourner, as all my fathers *were*.

Ps 42:3 My tears have been my meat day and night, while they continually say unto me, Where *is* thy God?

Ps 56:8 Thou tellest my wanderings: put thou my tears into thy bottle: *are they* not in thy book?

Ps 69:3 I am weary of my crying: my throat is dried: mine eyes fail while I wait for my God.

Ps 80:5 Thou feedest them with the bread of tears; and givest them tears to drink in great measure.

Ps 102:9 For I have eaten ashes like bread, and mingled my drink with weeping,

Ec 4:1 So I returned, and considered all the oppressions that are done under the sun: and behold the tears of *such as were* oppressed, and they had no comforter; and on the side of their oppressors *there was* power; but they had no comforter.

Lam 3:49 Mine eye trickleth down, and ceaseth not, without any intermission,

Mk 9:24 And straightway the father of the child cried out, and said with tears, Lord, I believe; help thou mine unbelief.

See **SOLICITUDE, WEEPING**

TEBETH *See* **MONTHS**

TEETH

1. Gnashing

a. In Disappointment

Ps 112:10; Mt 8:12; 13:42, 50; 22:13; 24:51; 25:30; Lu 13:28

b. In Rage

Jb 16:9; Ps 35:16; 37:12; Lam 2:16; Ac 7:54

2. Broken

Jb 4:10; 29:17; Ps 3:7; 58:6–7; Lam 3:16

See **WICKED**

TEIL *See* **TREES**

TEKOAH, *city in Judah*

2 S 14:2; 2 Chr 11:6

TEMAN, *south, or right*

Ge 36:11; Is 5:1–30; Je 49:7; Eze 25:13; Da 1:1–21; Am 1:12; Hab 3:3

TEMPERANCE, *self-restraint*

Pr 21:17 He that loveth pleasure *shall be* a poor man: he that loveth wine and oil shall not be rich.

Pr 23:29–35 Who hath woe? who hath sorrow? who hath contentions? who hath babbling? who hath wounds without cause? who hath redness of eyes?

They that tarry long at the wine; they that go to seek mixed wine.

Look not thou upon the wine when it is red, when it giveth his colour in the cup, *when* it moveth itself aright.

At the last it biteth like a serpent, and stingeth like an adder.

Thine eyes shall behold strange women, and thine heart shall utter perverse things.

Yea, thou shalt be as he that lieth down in the midst of the sea, or as he that lieth upon the top of a mast.

They have stricken me, *shalt thou say, and* I was not sick; they have beaten me, *and* I felt *it* not: when shall I awake? I will seek it yet again.

Pr 25:16 Hast thou found honey? eat so much as is sufficient for thee, lest thou be filled therewith, and vomit it.

Ac 24:25 And as he reasoned of righteousness, temperance, and judgment to come, Felix trembled, and answered, Go thy way for this time; when I have a convenient season, I will call for thee.

1 Co 9:25 And every man that striveth for the mastery is temperate in all things. Now they *do it* to obtain a corruptible crown; but we an incorruptible.

Ga 5:23 Meekness, temperance: against such there is no law.

Tit 2:2 That the aged men be sober, grave, temperate, sound in faith, in charity, in patience.

2 Pe 1:6 And to knowledge temperance; and to temperance patience; and to patience godliness;

Abstinence from Strong Drink

ENJOINED UPON THE PRIESTS

Le 10:9 Do not drink wine nor strong drink, thou, nor thy sons with thee, when ye go into the tabernacle of the congregation, lest ye die: *it shall be* a statute for ever throughout your generations:

LAW FOR THE NAZARITES

Nu 6:3 He shall separate *himself* from wine and strong drink, and shall drink no vinegar of wine, or vinegar of strong drink, neither shall he drink any liquor of grapes, nor eat moist grapes, or dried.

De 29:6 Ye have not eaten bread, neither have ye drunk wine or strong drink: that ye might know that I *am* the LORD your God.

Jud 13:4 Now therefore beware, I pray thee, and drink not wine nor strong drink, and eat not any unclean *thing:*

THE WISE MAN'S INJUNCTION

Pr 23:31 Look not thou upon the wine when it is red, when it giveth his colour in the cup, *when* it moveth itself aright.

RULE FOR KINGS

Pr 31:4 *It is* not for kings, O Lemuel, *it is* not for kings to drink wine; nor for princes strong drink:

THE LAW OF THE RECHABITES

Je 35:6 But they said, We will drink no wine: for Jonadab the son of Rechab our father commanded us, saying, Ye shall drink no wine, *neither* ye, nor your sons for ever:

DANIEL'S TEMPERANCE PRINCIPLES

Da 1:8 But Daniel purposed in his heart that he would not defile himself with the portion of the king's meat, nor with the wine which he drank: therefore he requested of the prince of the eunuchs that he might not defile himself.

Da 10:3 I ate no pleasant bread, neither came flesh nor wine in my mouth, neither did I anoint myself at all, till three whole weeks were fulfilled.

JOHN THE BAPTIST A TOTAL ABSTAINER

Mt 11:18 For John came neither eating nor drinking, and they say, He hath a devil.

Lu 1:15 For he shall be great in the sight of the Lord, and shall drink neither wine nor strong drink; and he shall be filled with the Holy Ghost, even from his mother's womb.

BROTHERLY LOVE DEMANDS

Ro 14:21 *It is* good neither to eat flesh, nor to drink wine, nor *any thing* whereby thy brother stumbleth, or is offended, or is made weak.

1 Co 8:13 Wherefore, if meat make my brother to offend, I will eat no flesh while the world standeth, lest I make my brother to offend.

See **DRUNKENNESS, WINE, SELF-CONTROL**

TEMPESTS *See* **WEATHER**

TEMPLE, *central place of Israel's worship throughout her history; in the New Testament, used symbolically of*

Christ's place of dwelling within the life of the redeemed

1. Solomon's

2 S 7:13 He shall build an house for my name, and I will stablish the throne of his kingdom for ever.

1 K 3:1 And Solomon made affinity with Pharaoh king of Egypt, and took Pharaoh's daughter, and brought her into the city of David, until he had made an end of building his own house, and the house of the LORD, and the wall of Jerusalem round about.

1 K 5:5 And, behold, I purpose to build an house unto the name of the LORD my God, as the LORD spake unto David my father, saying, Thy son, whom I will set upon thy throne in thy room, he shall build an house unto my name.

1 K 6:1 And it came to pass in the four hundred and eightieth year after the children of Israel were come out of the land of Egypt, in the fourth year of Solomon's reign over Israel, in the month Zif, which *is* the second month, that he began to build the house of the Lord.

1 K 6:37 In the fourth year was the foundation of the house of the LORD laid, in the month Zif:

1 K 8:13 I have surely built thee an house to dwell in, a settled place for thee to abide in for ever.

1 K 8:20 And the LORD hath performed his word that he spake, and I am risen up in the room of David my father, and sit on the throne of Israel, as the Lord promised, and have built an house for the name of the LORD God of Israel.

1 K 8:38 What prayer and supplication soever be *made* by any man, *or* by all thy people Israel, which shall know every man the plague of his own heart, and spread forth his hands toward this house:

1 K 8:43 Hear thou in heaven thy dwelling place, and do according to all that the stranger calleth to thee for: that all people of the earth may know thy name, to fear thee, as *do* thy people Israel; and that they may know that this house, which I have builded, is called by thy name.

1 K 8:63 And Solomon offered a sacrifice of peace offerings, which he offered unto the LORD, two and twenty thousand oxen, and an hundred and twenty thousand sheep. So the king and all the children of Israel dedicated the house of the LORD.

1 K 9:1 And it came to pass, when Solomon had finished the building of the house of the LORD, and the king's house, and all Solomon's desire which he was pleased to do,

1 K 9:10 And it came to pass at the end of twenty years, when Solomon had built the two houses, the house of the LORD, and the king's house,

1 K 10:12 And the king made of the almug trees pillars for the house of the LORD, and for the king's house, harps also and psalteries for singers: there came no such almug trees, nor were seen unto this day.

2 K 11:10 And to the captains over hundreds did the priest give king David's spears and shields, that *were* in the temple of the LORD.

2 K 11:13 And when Athaliah heard the noise of the guard *and* of the people, she came to the people into the temple of the LORD.

2 K 12:5 Let the priests take *it* to them, every man of his acquaintance: and let them repair the breaches of the house, wheresoever any breach shall be found.

2 K 18:16 At that time did Hezekiah cut off *the gold from* the doors of the temple of the LORD, and *from* the pillars which Hezekiah king of Judah had overlaid, and gave it to the king of Assyria.

2 K 21:7 And he set a graven image of the grove that he had made in the house, of which the LORD said to David, and to Solomon his son, In this house, and in Jerusalem, which I have chosen out of all tribes of Israel, will I put my name for ever:

2 K 22:5 And let them deliver it into the hand of the doers of the work, that have the oversight of the house of the LORD: and let them give it to the doers of the work which *is* in the house of the LORD, to repair the breaches of the house,

2 K 24:13 And he carried out thence all the treasures of the house of the LORD, and the treasures of the king's house, and cut in pieces all the vessels of gold which Solomon king of Israel had made in the temple of the LORD, as the LORD had said.

2 K 25:9 And he burnt the house of the LORD, and the king's house, and all the houses of Jerusalem, and every great *man's* house burnt he with fire.

1 Chr 6:10 And Johanan begat Azariah, (he *it is* that executed the priest's office in the temple that Solomon built in Jerusalem:)

1 Chr 17:12 He shall build me an house, and I will stablish his throne for ever.

1 Chr 22:10 He shall build an house for my name; and he shall be my son, and I *will be* his father; and I will establish the throne of his kingdom over Israel for ever.

1 Chr 28:10 Take heed now; for the LORD hath chosen thee to build an house for the sanctuary: be strong, and do *it*.

1 Chr 29:19 And give unto Solomon my son a perfect heart, to keep thy commandments, thy testimonies, and thy statutes, and to do all *these things*, and to build the palace, for the which I have made provision.

2 Chr 2:1 And Solomon determined to build an house for the name of the LORD, and an house for his kingdom.

2 Chr 2:4 Behold, I build an house to the name of the LORD my God, to dedicate *it* to him, *and* to burn before him sweet incense, and for the continual shewbread, and for the burnt offerings morning and evening, on the sabbaths, and on the new moons, and on the solemn feasts of the LORD our God. This *is an ordinance* for ever to Israel.

2 Chr 3:1 Then Solomon began to build the house of the LORD at Jerusalem in mount Moriah, where *the LORD* appeared unto David his father, in the place that David had prepared in the threshingfloor of Ornan the Jebusite.

2 Chr 6:2 But I have built an house of habitation for thee, and a place for thy dwelling for ever.

2 Chr 6:29 *Then* what prayer *or* what supplication soever shall be made of any man, or of all thy people Israel, when every one shall know his own sore and his own grief, and shall spread forth his hands in this house:

2 Chr 6:38 If they return to thee with all their heart and with all their soul in the land of their captivity, whither they have carried them captives, and pray toward their land, which thou gavest unto their fathers, and *toward* the city which thou hast chosen, and toward the house which I have built for thy name:

2 Chr 7:11 Thus Solomon finished the house of the LORD, and the king's house: and all that came into Solomon's heart to make in the house of the LORD, and in his own house, he prosperously effected.

2 Chr 7:20 Then will I pluck them up by the roots out of my land which I have given them; and this house, which I have sanctified for my name, will I cast out of my sight, and will make it *to be* a proverb and a byword among all nations.

2 Chr 8:1 And it came to pass at the end of twenty years, wherein Solomon had built the house of the LORD, and his own house,

2 Chr 16:2 Then Asa brought out silver and gold out of the treasures of the house of the LORD and of the king's house, and sent to Ben-hadad king of Syria, that dwelt at Damascus, saying,

2 Chr 20:5 And Jehoshaphat stood in the congregation of Judah and Jerusalem, in the house of the LORD, before the new court,

2 Chr 20:8 And they dwelt therein, and have built thee a sanctuary therein for thy name, saying,

2 Chr 23:10 And he set all the people, every man having his weapon in his hand, from the right side of the temple to the left side of the temple, along by the altar and the temple, by the king round about.

2 Chr 24:4 And it came to pass after this, *that* Joash was minded to repair the house of the LORD.

2 Chr 24:13 So the workmen wrought, and the work was perfected by them, and they set the house of God in his state, and strengthened it.

2 Chr 29:3 He in the first year of his reign, in the first month, opened the doors of the house of the LORD, and repaired them.

2 Chr 33:5 And he built altars for all the host of heaven in the two courts of the house of the LORD.

2 Chr 34:8 Now in the eighteenth year of his reign, when he had purged the land, and the house, he sent Shaphan the son of Azaliah, and Maaseiah the governor of the city, and Joah the son of Joahaz the recorder, to repair the house of the LORD his God.

2 Chr 35:3 And said unto the Levites that taught all Israel, which were holy unto the LORD, Put the holy ark in the house which Solomon the son of David king of Israel did build; *it shall* not *be* a burden upon *your* shoulders: serve now the LORD your God, and his people Israel,

2 Chr 35:20 After all this, when Josiah had prepared the temple, Necho king of Egypt came up to fight against Charchemish by Euphrates: and Josiah went out against him.

2 Chr 36:19 And they burnt the house of God, and brake down the wall of Jerusalem, and burnt all the palaces thereof with fire, and destroyed all the goodly vessels thereof.

Ezr 3:12 But many of the priests and Levites and chief of the fathers, *who were* ancient men, that had seen the first house, when the foundation of this house was laid before their eyes, wept with a loud voice; and many shouted aloud for joy:

Ezr 5:11 And thus they returned us answer, saying, We are the servants of the God of heaven and earth, and build the house that was builded these many years ago, which a great king of Israel builded and set up.

Ezr 5:14 And the vessels also of gold and silver of the house of God, which Nebuchadnezzar took out of the tem-ple that *was* in Jerusalem, and brought them into the temple of Babylon, those did Cyrus the king take out of the temple of Babylon, and they were delivered unto *one,* whose name *was* Sheshbazzar, whom he had made governor;

Ezr 6:5 And also let the golden and silver vessels of the house of God, which Nebuchadnezzar took forth out of the temple which is at Jerusalem, and brought unto Babylon, be restored, and brought again unto the temple which is at Jerusalem, *every one* to his place, and place *them* in the house of God.

Ps 68:29 Because of thy temple at Jerusalem shall kings bring presents unto thee.

Ps 78:69 And he built his sanctuary like high *palaces,* like the earth which he hath established for ever.

Je 19:14 Then came Jeremiah from Tophet, whither the LORD had sent him to prophesy; and he stood in the court of the LORD's house; and said to all the people,

Je 26:2 Thus saith the LORD; Stand in the court of the LORD's house, and speak unto all the cities of Judah, which come to worship in the LORD's house, all the words that I command thee to speak unto them; diminish not a word:

Je 26:6 Then will I make this house like Shiloh, and will make this city a curse to all the nations of the earth.

Je 35:4 And I brought them into the house of the LORD, into the chamber of the sons of Hanan, the son of Igdaliah, a man of God, which *was* by the chamber of the princes, which *was* above the chamber of Maaseiah the son of Shallum, the keeper of the door:

Je 36:6 Therefore go thou, and read in the roll, which thou hast written from my mouth, the words of the LORD in the ears of the people in the LORD's house upon the fasting day: and also thou shalt read them in the ears of all Judah that come out of their cities.

Je 52:17 Also the pillars of brass that *were* in the house of the LORD, and the bases, and the brasen sea that *was* in the house of the LORD, the Chaldeans brake, and carried all the brass of them to Babylon.

Eze 8:16 And he brought me into the inner court of the LORD's house, and, behold, at the door of the temple of the LORD, between the porch and the altar, *were* about five and twenty men, with their backs toward the temple of the LORD, and their faces toward the east; and they worshipped the sun toward the east.

Da 5:3 Then they brought the golden vessels that were taken out of the temple of the house of God which *was* at Jerusalem; and the king, and his princes, his wives, and his concubines, drank in them.

Hag 2:3 Who *is* left among you that saw this house in her first glory? and how do ye see it now? *is it* not in your eyes in comparison of it as nothing?

Hag 2:9 The glory of this latter house shall be greater than of the former, saith the LORD of hosts: and in this place will I give peace, saith the LORD of hosts.

Ac 7:47 But Solomon built him an house.

See **SOLOMON**

2. The Second

2 Chr 36:23 Thus saith Cyrus king of Persia, All the kingdoms of the earth hath the LORD God of heaven given me; and he hath charged me to build him an house in Jerusalem, which *is* in Judah. Who *is there* among you of all his people? The LORD his God *be* with him, and let him go up.

Ezr 1:2 Thus saith Cyrus king of Persia, The LORD God of heaven hath given me all the kingdoms of the earth; and he hath charged me to build him an house at Jerusalem, which *is* in Judah.

Ezr 1:3 Who *is there* among you of all his people? his God be with him, and let him go up to Jerusalem, which is in Judah, and build the house of the LORD God of Israel, (he *is* the God,) which *is* in Jerusalem.

Ezr 2:68 And *some* of the chief of the fathers, when they came to the house

of the LORD which *is* at Jerusalem, offered freely for the house of God to set it up in his place:

Ezr 3:10 And when the builders laid the foundation of the temple of the LORD, they set the priests in their apparel with trumpets, and the Levites the sons of Asaph with cymbals, to praise the LORD, after the ordinance of David king of Israel.

Ezr 4:1 Now when the adversaries of Judah and Benjamin heard that the children of the captivity builded the temple unto the LORD God of Israel;

Ezr 4:24 Then ceased the work of the house of God which *is* at Jerusalem. So it ceased unto the second year of the reign of Darius king of Persia.

Ezr 5:2 Then rose up Zerubbabel the son of Shealtiel, and Jeshua the son of Jozadak, and began to build the house of God which *is* at Jerusalem: and with them *were* the prophets of God helping them.

Ezr 5:8 Be it known unto the king, that we went into the province of Judea, to the house of the great God, which is builded with great stones, and timber is laid in the walls, and this work goeth fast on, and prospereth in their hands.

Ezr 5:16 Then came the same Sheshbazzar, *and* laid the foundation of the house of God which *is* in Jerusalem: and since that time even until now hath it been in building, and *yet* it is not finished.

Ezr 6:8 Moreover I make a decree what ye shall do to the elders of these Jews for the building of this house of God: that of the king's goods, *even* of the tribute beyond the river, forthwith expences be given unto these men, that they be not hindered.

Ezr 6:14 And the elders of the Jews builded, and they prospered through the prophesying of Haggai the prophet and Zechariah the son of Iddo. And they builded, and finished *it*, according to the commandment of the God of Israel, and according to the commandment of Cyrus, and Darius, and Artaxerxes king of Persia.

Ezr 7:16 And all the silver and gold that thou canst find in all the province of Babylon, with the freewill offering of the people, and of the priests, offering willingly for the house of their God which *is* in Jerusalem:

Ezr 7:27 Blessed *be* the LORD God of our fathers, which hath put *such a thing* as this in the king's heart, to beautify the house of the LORD which *is* in Jerusalem:

Ezr 8:30 So took the priests and the Levites the weight of the silver, and the gold, and the vessels, to bring *them* to Jerusalem unto the house of our God.

Ezr 8:36 And they delivered the king's commissions unto the king's lieutenants, and to the governors on this side the river: and they furthered the people, and the house of God.

Ezr 9:9 For we *were* bondmen; yet our God hath not forsaken us in our bondage, but hath extended mercy unto us in the sight of the kings of Persia, to give us a reviving, to set up the house of our God, and to repair the desolations thereof, and to give us a wall in Judah and in Jerusalem.

Ezr 10:6 Then Ezra rose up from before the house of God, and went into the chamber of Johanan the son of Eliashib: and *when* he came thither, he did eat no bread, nor drink water: for he mourned because of the transgression of them that had been carried away.

Ne 6:10 Afterward I came unto the house of Shemaiah the son of Delaiah the son of Mehetabeel, who *was* shut up; and he said, Let us meet together in the house of God, within the temple, and let us shut the doors of the temple: for they will come to slay thee; yea, in the night will they come to slay thee.

Ne 8:16 So the people went forth, and brought *them,* and made themselves booths, every one upon the roof of his house, and in their courts, and in the courts of the house of God, and in the street of the water gate, and in the street of the gate of Ephraim.

Ne 10:38 And the priest the son of Aaron shall be with the Levites, when the Levites take tithes: and the Levites shall bring up the tithe of the tithes

unto the house of our God, to the chambers, into the treasure house.

Is 60:13 The glory of Lebanon shall come unto thee, the fir tree, the pine tree, and the box together, to beautify the place of my sanctuary; and I will make the place of my feet glorious.

Hag 1:2 Thus speaketh the LORD of hosts, saying, This people say, The time is not come, the time that the LORD's house should be built.

Hag 1:8 Go up to the mountain, and bring wood, and build the house; and I will take pleasure in it, and I will be glorified, saith the LORD.

Hag 2:9 The glory of this latter house shall be greater than of the former, saith the LORD of hosts: and in this place will I give peace, saith the LORD of hosts.

Hag 2:15 And now, I pray you, consider from this day and upward, from before a stone was laid upon a stone in the temple of the LORD:

Zec 1:16 Therefore thus saith the LORD; I am returned to Jerusalem with mercies: my house shall be built in it, saith the LORD of hosts, and a line shall be stretched forth upon Jerusalem.

Zec 8:9 Thus saith the LORD of hosts; Let your hands be strong, ye that hear in these days these words by the mouth of the prophets, which *were* in the day *that* the foundation of the house of the LORD of hosts was laid, that the temple might be built.

3. Herod's

Mal 3:1 Behold, I will send my messenger, and he shall prepare the way before me: and the LORD, whom ye seek, shall suddenly come to his temple, even the messenger of the covenant, whom ye delight in: behold, he shall come, saith the LORD of hosts.

Mt 21:23 And when he was come into the temple, the chief priests and the elders of the people came unto him as he was teaching, and said, By what authority doest thou these things? and who gave thee this authority?

Mt 23:16 Woe unto you, *ye* blind guides, which say, Whosoever shall swear by the temple, it is nothing; but whosoever shall swear by the gold of the temple, he is a debtor!

Mt 24:1 And Jesus went out, and departed from the temple: and his disciples came to *him* for to shew him the buildings of the temple.

Mt 27:51 And, behold, the veil of the temple was rent in twain from the top to the bottom; and the earth did quake, and the rocks rent;

Mk 11:11 And Jesus entered into Jerusalem, and into the temple: and when he had looked round about upon all things, and now the eventide was come, he went out unto Bethany with the twelve.

Mk 11:15 And they come to Jerusalem: and Jesus went into the temple, and began to cast out them that sold and bought in the temple, and overthrew the tables of the moneychangers, and the seats of them that sold doves;

Mk 11:27 And they come again to Jerusalem: and as he was walking in the temple, there come to him the chief priests, and the scribes, and the elders,

Mk 13:1 And as he went out of the temple, one of his disciples saith unto him, Master, see what manner of stones and what buildings *are here!*

Mk 14:58 We heard him say, I will destroy this temple that is made with hands, and within three days I will build another made without hands.

Lu 1:9 According to the custom of the priest's office, his lot was to burn incense when he went into the temple of the Lord.

Lu 1:22 And when he came out, he could not speak unto them: and they perceived that he had seen a vision in the temple: for he beckoned unto them, and remained speechless.

Lu 2:27 And he came by the Spirit into the temple: and when the parents brought in the child Jesus, to do for him after the custom of the law,

Lu 2:46 And it came to pass, that after three days they found him in the temple, sitting in the midst of the doctors, both hearing them, and asking them questions.

Lu 4:9 And he brought him to Jerusalem, and set him on a pinnacle of the temple, and said unto him, If thou be the Son of God, cast thyself down from hence:

Lu 21:5 And as some spake of the temple, how it was adorned with goodly stones and gifts, he said,

Lu 22:53 When I was daily with you in the temple, ye stretched forth no hands against me: but this is your hour, and the power of darkness.

Jn 2:20 Then said the Jews, Forty and six years was this temple in building, and wilt thou rear it up in three days?

Jn 7:14 Now about the midst of the feast Jesus went up into the temple, and taught.

Jn 8:2 And early in the morning he came again into the temple, and all the people came unto him; and he sat down, and taught them.

Jn 10:23 And Jesus walked in the temple in Solomon's porch.

Jn 18:20 Jesus answered him, I spake openly to the world; I ever taught in the synagogue, and in the temple, whither the Jews always resort; and in secret have I said nothing.

Ac 3:10 And they knew that it was he which sat for alms at the Beautiful gate of the temple: and they were filled with wonder and amazement at that which had happened unto him.

Ac 5:25 Then came one and told them, saying, Behold, the men whom ye put in prison are standing in the temple, and teaching the people.

Ac 21:29 (For they had seen before with him in the city Trophimus an Ephesian, whom they supposed that Paul had brought into the temple.)

Ac 22:17 And it came to pass, that, when I was come again to Jerusalem, even while I prayed in the temple, I was in a trance;

4. Cleansed

See **AWAKENINGS**

5. Destroyed

Le 26:31 And I will make your cities waste, and bring your sanctuaries unto desolation, and I will not smell the savour of your sweet odours.

1 K 9:7 Then will I cut off Israel out of the land which I have given them; and this house, which I have hallowed for my name, will I cast out of my sight; and Israel shall be a proverb and a byword among all people:

2 K 23:27 And the LORD said, I will remove Judah also out of my sight, as I have removed Israel, and will cast off this city Jerusalem which I have chosen, and the house of which I said, My name shall be there.

2 K 25:9 And he burnt the house of the LORD, and the king's house, and all the houses of Jerusalem, and every great *man's* house burnt he with fire.

2 Chr 7:21 And this house, which is high, shall be an astonishment to every one that passeth by it; so that he shall say, Why hath the LORD done thus unto this land, and unto this house?

2 Chr 36:19 And they burnt the house of God, and brake down the wall of Jerusalem, and burnt all the palaces thereof with fire, and destroyed all the goodly vessels thereof.

Ezr 5:12 But after that our fathers had provoked the God of heaven unto wrath, he gave them into the hand of Nebuchadnezzar the king of Babylon, the Chaldean, who destroyed this house, and carried the people away into Babylon.

Ps 74:7 They have cast fire into thy sanctuary, they have defiled *by casting down* the dwelling place of thy name to the ground.

Is 64:11 Our holy and our beautiful house, where our fathers praised thee, is burned up with fire: and all our pleasant things are laid waste.

Je 7:14 Therefore will I do unto *this* house, which is called by my name, wherein ye trust, and unto the place which I gave to you and to your fathers, as I have done to Shiloh.

Je 52:13 And burned the house of the LORD, and the king's house; and all the houses of Jerusalem, and all the houses of the great *men,* burned he with fire:

Lam 2:6 And he hath violently taken away his tabernacle, as *if it were of* a garden: he hath destroyed his places

of the assembly: the LORD hath caused the solemn feasts and sabbaths to be forgotten in Zion, and hath despised in the indignation of his anger the king and the priest.

Lam 4:1 How is the gold become dim! *how* is the most fine gold changed! the stones of the sanctuary are poured out in the top of every street.

Eze 24:21 Speak unto the house of Israel, Thus saith the Lord GOD; Behold, I will profane my sanctuary, the excellency of your strength, the desire of your eyes, and that which your soul pitieth; and your sons and your daughters whom ye have left shall fall by the sword.

Da 9:17 Now therefore, O our God, hear the prayer of thy servant, and his supplications, and cause thy face to shine upon thy sanctuary that is desolate, for the LORD's sake.

Da 9:26 And after threescore and two weeks shall Messiah be cut off, but not for himself: and the people of the prince that shall come shall destroy the city and the sanctuary; and the end thereof *shall be* with a flood, and unto the end of the war desolations are determined.

Ho 8:1 *Set* the trumpet to thy mouth. *He shall come* as an eagle against the house of the LORD, because they have transgressed my covenant, and trespassed against my law.

Mi 3:12 Therefore shall Zion for your sake be plowed *as* a field, and Jerusalem shall become heaps, and the mountain of the house as the high places of the forest.

Mt 24:2 And Jesus said unto them, See ye not all these things? verily I say unto you, There shall not be left here one stone upon another, that shall not be thrown down.

Mk 13:2 And Jesus answering said unto him, Seest thou these great buildings? there shall not be left one stone upon another, that shall not be thrown down.

Lu 13:35 Behold, your house is left unto you desolate: and verily I say unto you, Ye shall not see me, until *the time* come when ye shall say, Blessed *is* he that cometh in the name of the Lord.

Lu 21:6 *As for* these things which ye behold, the days will come, in the which there shall not be left one stone upon another, that shall not be thrown down.

6. Spiritual

a. The Building

Zec 6:13 Even he shall build the temple of the Lord; and he shall bear the glory, and shall sit and rule upon his throne; and he shall be a priest upon his throne: and the counsel of peace shall be between them both.

1 Co 3:16 Know ye not that ye are the temple of God, and *that* the Spirit of God dwelleth in you?

1 Co 6:19 What? know ye not that your body is the temple of the Holy Ghost *which is* in you, which ye have of God, and ye are not your own?

2 Co 6:16 And what agreement hath the temple of God with idols? for ye are the temple of the living God; as God hath said, I will dwell in them, and walk in *them;* and I will be their God, and they shall be my people.

Ep 2:20–22 And are built upon the foundation of the apostles and prophets, Jesus Christ himself being the chief corner *stone;*

In whom all the building fitly framed together groweth unto an holy temple in the Lord:

In whom ye also are builded together for an habitation of God through the Spirit.

1 Pe 2:5 Ye also, as lively stones, are built up a spiritual house, an holy priesthood, to offer up spiritual sacrifices, acceptable to God by Jesus Christ.

b. The Inhabitant

REVEALED IN THE COMING OF THE HOLY SPIRIT

Jn 14:20 At that day ye shall know that I *am* in my Father, and ye in me, and I in you.

DEMONSTRATES TO THE WORLD CHRIST'S MISSION

Jn 17:23 I in them, and thou in me, that they may be made perfect in one; and that the world may know that thou hast sent me, and hast loved them, as thou hast loved me.

Ro 8:10 And if Christ *be* in you, the body *is* dead because of sin; but the Spirit *is* life because of righteousness.

THE OLD LIFE DIES THAT THE NEW MAY LIVE

Ga 2:20 I am crucified with Christ: nevertheless I live; yet not I, but Christ liveth in me: and the life which I now live in the flesh I live by the faith of the Son of God, who loved me, and gave himself for me.

OBTAINED BY FAITH

Ep 3:17–19 That Christ may dwell in your hearts by faith; that ye, being rooted and grounded in love,

May be able to comprehend with all saints what *is* the breadth, and length, and depth, and height;

And to know the love of Christ, which passeth knowledge, that ye might be filled with all the fulness of God.

A GLORIOUS MYSTERY

Col 1:27 To whom God would make known what *is* the riches of the glory of this mystery among the Gentiles; which is Christ in you, the hope of glory:

OBEDIENCE ESSENTIAL

1 Jn 3:24 And he that keepeth his commandments dwelleth in him, and he in him. And hereby we know that he abideth in us, by the Spirit which he hath given us.

POSSIBLE TO ALL

Re 3:20 Behold, I stand at the door, and knock: if any man hear my voice, and open the door, I will come in to him, and will sup with him, and he with me.

See **HOLY SPIRIT**

TEMPTATION, *allurements toward sin, or trials and difficulties of believers*

1. Satan the Chief Agent

Ge 3:1 Now the serpent was more subtil than any beast of the field which the LORD God had made. And he said unto the woman, Yea, hath God said, Ye shall not eat of every tree of the garden?

1 Chr 21:1 And Satan stood up against Israel, and provoked David to number Israel.

Mt 4:3 And when the tempter came to him, he said, If thou be the Son of God, command that these stones be made bread.

2 Co 2:11 Lest Satan should get an advantage of us: for we are not ignorant of his devices.

2 Co 11:3 But I fear, lest by any means, as the serpent beguiled Eve through his subtilty, so your minds should be corrupted from the simplicity that is in Christ.

1 Th 3:5 For this cause, when I could no longer forbear, I sent to know your faith, lest by some means the tempter have tempted you, and our labour be in vain.

1 Ti 6:9 But they that will be rich fall into temptation and a snare, and *into* many foolish and hurtful lusts, which drown men in destruction and perdition.

Ja 1:14 But every man is tempted, when he is drawn away of his own lust, and enticed.

2 Pe 2:18 For when they speak great swelling *words* of vanity, they allure through the lusts of the flesh, *through much* wantonness, those that were clean escaped from them who live in error.

2. Yielding

Ge 3:6 And when the woman saw that the tree *was* good for food, and that it *was* pleasant to the eyes, and a tree to be desired to make *one* wise, she took of the fruit thereof, and did eat, and gave also unto her husband with her; and he did eat.

Ge 12:13 Say, I pray thee, thou *art* my sister: that it may be well with me for thy sake; and my soul shall live because of thee.

Ge 13:12 Abram dwelled in the land of Canaan, and Lot dwelled in the cities of the plain, and pitched *his* tent toward Sodom.

Ge 26:7 And the men of the place asked *him* of his wife; and he said, She *is* my sister: for he feared to say, *She is* my wife; lest, *said he,* the men of the place should kill me for Rebekah; because she *was* fair to look upon.

1 S 21:2–3 And David said unto Ahimelech the priest, The king hath commanded me a business, and hath said unto me, Let no man know any thing of the business whereabout I send thee, and what I have commanded thee: and I have appointed *my* servants to such and such a place.

Now therefore what is under thine hand? give *me* five *loaves of* bread in mine hand, or what there is present.

2 K 10:18 And Jehu gathered all the people together, and said unto them, Ahab served Baal a little; *but* Jehu shall serve him much.

Mt 26:41 Watch and pray, that ye enter not into temptation: the spirit indeed *is* willing, but the flesh *is* weak.

Mt 26:73–74 And after a while came unto *him* they that stood by, and said to Peter, Surely thou also art *one* of them; for thy speech bewrayeth thee.

Then began he to curse and to swear, *saying,* I know not the man. And immediately the cock crew.

Lu 22:40 And when he was at the place, he said unto them, Pray that ye enter not into temptation.

3. Encouragement

Lu 11:4 And forgive us our sins; for we also forgive every one that is indebted to us. And lead us not into temptation; but deliver us from evil.

1 Co 10:13 There hath no temptation taken you but such as is common to man: but God *is* faithful, who will not suffer you to be tempted above that ye are able; but will with the temptation also make a way to escape, that ye may be able to bear *it*.

He 2:18 For in that he himself hath suffered being tempted, he is able to succour them that are tempted.

Ja 1:2–3 My brethren, count it all joy when ye fall into divers temptations;

Knowing *this*, that the trying of your faith worketh patience.

Ja 1:12 Blessed *is* the man that endureth temptation: for when he is tried, he shall receive the crown of life, which the Lord hath promised to them that love him.

2 Pe 2:9 The Lord knoweth how to deliver the godly out of temptations, and to reserve the unjust unto the day of judgment to be punished:

Re 3:10 Because thou hast kept the word of my patience, I also will keep thee from the hour of temptation, which shall come upon all the world, to try them that dwell upon the earth.

4. Of Christ

Mt 4:1 Then was Jesus led up of the Spirit into the wilderness to be tempted of the devil.

Mt 4:5 Then the devil taketh him up into the holy city, and setteth him on a pinnacle of the temple,

Mt 16:23 But he turned, and said unto Peter, Get thee behind me, Satan: thou art an offence unto me: for thou savourest not the things that be of God, but those that be of men.

Mk 1:13 And he was there in the wilderness forty days, tempted of Satan; and was with the wild beasts; and the angels ministered unto him.

Lu 4:2 Being forty days tempted of the devil. And in those days he did eat nothing: and when they were ended, he afterward hungered.

Lu 22:28 Ye are they which have continued with me in my temptations.

Jn 14:30 Hereafter I will not talk much with you: for the prince of this world cometh, and hath nothing in me.

He 2:18 For in that he himself hath suffered being tempted, he is able to succour them that are tempted.

He 4:15 For we have not an high priest which cannot be touched with the feeling of our infirmities; but was in all points tempted like as *we are, yet* without sin.

5. Allurements

FORBIDDEN FRUIT

Ge 3:6

FERTILE FIELDS

Ge 13:10–11

APPETITE

Ge 25:29–30, 33

SILVER AND GOLD

Jos 7:21; 14:17; 16:17; 1 S 13:12

A WOMAN

1 K 11:1, 4

AMBITION

Mk 10:35–37; 2 Pe 2:20

6. Resistance

a. Examples

ABRAHAM, *by refusing a reward for service rendered*

Ge 14:23 That I will not *take* from a thread even to a shoelatchet, and that I will not take any thing that *is* thine, lest thou shouldest say, I have made Abram rich:

MAN OF GOD, *by rejecting the king's reward*

1 K 13:8 And the man of God said unto the king, If thou wilt give me half thine house, I will not go in with thee, neither will I eat bread nor drink water in this place:

ELISHA, *by refusing payment for healing*

2 K 5:16 But he said, As the Lord liveth, before whom I stand, I will receive none. And he urged him to take *it;* but he refused.

JOB, *by rejecting evil counsel*

Jb 2:9–10 Then said his wife unto him, Dost thou still retain thine integrity? curse God, and die.

But he said unto her, Thou speakest as one of the foolish women speaketh. What? shall we receive good at the hand of God, and shall we not receive evil? In all this did not Job sin with his lips.

THE RECHABITES AND DANIEL, *by refusing wine*

Je 35:5–6 And I set before the sons of the house of the Rechabites pots full of wine, and cups, and I said unto them, Drink ye wine.

But they said, We will drink no wine: for Jonadab the son of Rechab our father commanded us, saying, Ye shall drink no wine, *neither* ye, nor your sons for ever:

Da 1:8 But Daniel purposed in his heart that he would not defile himself with the portion of the king's meat, nor with the wine which he drank: therefore he requested of the prince of the eunuchs that he might not defile himself.

CHRIST, *by refusing worldly honor*

Lu 4:5–8 And the devil, taking him up into an high mountain, shewed unto him all the kingdoms of the world in a moment of time.

And the devil said unto him, All this power will I give thee, and the glory of them: for that is delivered unto me; and to whomsoever I will I give it.

If thou therefore wilt worship me, all shall be thine.

And Jesus answered and said unto him, Get thee behind me, Satan: for it is written, Thou shalt worship the Lord thy God, and him only shalt thou serve.

Jn 6:15 When Jesus therefore perceived that they would come and take him by force, to make him a king, he departed again into a mountain himself alone.

PETER, *by refusing a bribe*

Ac 8:20 But Peter said unto him, Thy money perish with thee, because thou hast thought that the gift of God may be purchased with money.

b. The Duty of Resisting

Pr 1:10 My son, if sinners entice thee, consent thou not.

Pr 4:14 Enter not into the path of the wicked, and go not in the way of evil *men.*

Lu 21:34 And take heed to yourselves, lest at any time your hearts be overcharged with surfeiting, and drunkenness, and cares of this life, and so that day come upon you unawares.

Lu 22:40 And when he was at the place, he said unto them, Pray that ye enter not into temptation.

Ro 6:13 Neither yield ye your members *as* instruments of unrighteousness unto sin: but yield yourselves unto God, as those that are alive from the dead, and your members *as* instruments of righteousness unto God.

Ep 6:13 Wherefore take unto you the whole armour of God, that ye may be able to withstand in the evil day, and having done all, to stand.

2 Pe 3:17 Ye therefore, beloved, seeing ye know *these things* before, beware lest ye also, being led away with the error of the wicked, fall from your own stedfastness.

7. Special Sources

a. Worldly Snares

FALSE GODS

Ex 23:33 They shall not dwell in thy land, lest they make thee sin against me: for if thou serve their gods, it will surely be a snare unto thee.

SINFUL COVENANTS

Ex 34:12 Take heed to thyself, lest thou make a covenant with the inhabitants of the land whither thou goest, lest it be for a snare in the midst of thee:

SILVER AND GOLD

De 7:25 The graven images of their gods shall ye burn with fire: thou shalt not desire the silver or gold *that is* on them, nor take *it* unto thee, lest thou be snared therein: for it *is* an abomination to the LORD thy God.

EVIL ASSOCIATIONS

Jos 23:13 Know for a certainty that the LORD your God will no more drive out *any of* these nations from before you; but they shall be snares and traps unto you, and scourges in your sides, and thorns in your eyes, until ye perish from off this good land which the LORD your God hath given you.

IDOLATRY

Ps 106:36 And they served their idols: which were a snare unto them.

BROKEN VOWS

Pr 20:25 *It is* a snare to the man *who* devoureth *that which is* holy, and after vows to make enquiry.

FRIENDSHIP WITH VIOLENT PEOPLE

Pr 22:25 Lest thou learn his ways, and get a snare to thy soul.

SCOFFING

Pr 29:8 Scornful men bring a city into a snare: but wise *men* turn away wrath.

AVARICE

1 Ti 6:9 But they that will be rich fall into temptation and a snare, and *into* many foolish and hurtful lusts, which drown men in destruction and perdition.

b. Enticers

Nu 25:18 For they vex you with their wiles, wherewith they have beguiled you in the matter of Peor, and in the matter of Cozbi, the daughter of a prince of Midian, their sister, which was slain in the day of the plague for Peor's sake.

De 7:4 For they will turn away thy son from following me, that they may serve other gods: so will the anger of the LORD be kindled against you, and destroy thee suddenly.

De 13:2 And the sign or the wonder come to pass, whereof he spake unto thee, saying, Let us go after other gods, which thou hast not known, and let us serve them;

De 13:6 If thy brother, the son of thy mother, or thy son, or thy daughter, or the wife of thy bosom, or thy friend, which *is* as thine own soul, entice thee secretly, saying, Let us go and serve other gods, which thou hast not known, thou, nor thy fathers;

De 20:18 That they teach you not to do after all their abominations, which they have done unto their gods; so should ye sin against the LORD your God.

De 29:18 Lest there should be among you man, or woman, or family, or tribe, whose heart turneth away this day from the LORD our God, to go *and* serve the gods of these nations; lest there should be among you a root that beareth gall and wormwood;

Jud 16:16 And it came to pass, when she pressed him daily with her words, and urged him, *so* that his soul was vexed unto death;

1 K 13:15 Then he said unto him, Come home with me, and eat bread.

1 K 22:13 And the messenger that was gone to call Micaiah spake unto him, saying, Behold now, the words of the prophets *declare* good unto the king with one mouth: let thy word, I pray thee, be like the word of one of them, and speak *that which is* good.

1 K 22:20 And the LORD said, Who shall persuade Ahab, that he may go up and fall at Ramoth-gilead? And one said on this manner, and another said on that manner.

2 K 21:11 Because Manasseh king of Judah hath done these abominations, *and* hath done wickedly above all that the Amorites did, which *were* before him, and hath made Judah also to sin with his idols:

Pr 1:10 My son, if sinners entice thee, consent thou not.

Pr 16:29 A violent man enticeth his neighbour, and leadeth him into the way *that is* not good.

Pr 28:10 Whoso causeth the righteous to go astray in an evil way, he shall fall himself into his own pit: but the upright shall have good *things* in possession.

Is 8:19 And when they shall say unto you, Seek unto them that have familiar spirits, and unto wizards that peep, and that mutter: should not a people seek unto their God? for the living to the dead?

Is 9:16 For the leaders of this people cause *them* to err; and *they that are* led of them *are* destroyed.

Is 30:11 Get you out of the way, turn aside out of the path, cause the Holy One of Israel to cease from before us.

Da 6:8 Now, O king, establish the decree, and sign the writing, that it be not changed, according to the law of the Medes and Persians, which altereth not.

Ho 5:1 Hear ye this, O priests; and hearken, ye house of Israel; and give ye ear, O house of the king; for judgment *is* toward you, because ye have been a snare on Mizpah, and a net spread upon Tabor.

Am 2:12 But ye gave the Nazarites wine to drink; and commanded the prophets, saying, Prophesy not.

Zec 13:3 And it shall come to pass, *that* when any shall yet prophesy, then his father and his mother that begat him shall say unto him, Thou shalt not live; for thou speakest lies in the name of the Lord: and his father and his mother that begat him shall thrust him through when he prophesieth.

Mt 4:6 And saith unto him, If thou be the Son of God, cast thyself down: for it is written, He shall give his angels charge concerning thee: and in *their* hands they shall bear thee up, lest at any time thou dash thy foot against a stone.

Mt 16:23 But he turned, and said unto Peter, Get thee behind me, Satan: thou art an offence unto me: for thou savourest not the things that be of God, but those that be of men.

Mt 24:26 Wherefore if they shall say unto you, Behold, *he is* in the desert; go not forth: behold, he is in the secret chambers; believe *it* not.

Mk 8:32 And he spake that saying openly. And Peter took him, and began to rebuke him.

Ac 13:8 But Elymas the sorcerer (for so is his name by interpretation) with-stood them, seeking to turn away the deputy from the faith.

2 Pe 2:14 Having eyes full of adultery, and that cannot cease from sin; beguiling unstable souls: an heart they have exercised with covetous practices; cursed children:

2 Pe 2:18 For when they speak great swelling *words* of vanity, they allure through the lusts of the flesh, *through much* wantonness, those that were clean escaped from them who live in error.

c. Seducers

De 13:5 And that prophet, or that dreamer of dreams, shall be put to death; because he hath spoken to turn *you* away from the LORD your God, which brought you out of the land of Egypt, and redeemed you out of the house of bondage, to thrust thee out of the way which the LORD thy God commanded thee to walk in. So shalt thou put the evil away from the midst of thee.

De 13:8 Thou shalt not consent unto him, nor hearken unto him; neither shall thine eye pity him, neither shalt thou spare, neither shalt thou conceal him:

De 13:13 *Certain* men, the children of Belial, are gone out from among you, and have withdrawn the inhabitants of their city, saying, Let us go and serve other gods, which ye have not known;

2 K 21:9 But they hearkened not: and Manasseh seduced them to do more evil than did the nations whom the LORD destroyed before the children of Israel.

2 Chr 33:9 So Manasseh made Judah and the inhabitants of Jerusalem to err, *and* to do worse than the heathen, whom the LORD had destroyed before the children of Israel.

Pr 12:26 The righteous *is* more excellent than his neighbour: but the way of the wicked seduceth them.

Is 19:13 The princes of Zoan are become fools, the princes of Noph are deceived; they have also seduced Egypt, *even they that are* the stay of the tribes thereof.

Je 23:27 Which think to cause my people to forget my name by their dreams which they tell every man to his neighbour, as their fathers have forgotten my name for Baal.

Eze 13:10 Because, even because they have seduced my people, saying, Peace; and *there was* no peace; and one built up a wall, and, lo, others daubed it with untempered *morter:*

Mi 3:5 Thus saith the LORD concerning the prophets that make my people err, that bite with their teeth, and cry, Peace; and he that putteth not into their mouths, they even prepare war against him.

Mal 2:8 But ye are departed out of the way; ye have caused many to stumble at the law; ye have corrupted the covenant of Levi, saith the LORD of hosts.

Mk 13:22 For false Christs and false prophets shall rise, and shall shew signs and wonders, to seduce, if *it were* possible, even the elect.

Ac 8:11 And to him they had regard, because that of long time he had bewitched them with sorceries.

Ac 20:30 Also of your own selves shall men arise, speaking perverse things, to draw away disciples after them.

Ga 5:10 I have confidence in you through the Lord, that ye will be none otherwise minded: but he that troubleth you shall bear his judgment, whosoever he be.

1 Ti 4:1 Now the Spirit speaketh expressly, that in the latter times some shall depart from the faith, giving heed to seducing spirits, and doctrines of devils;

2 Ti 3:13 But evil men and seducers shall wax worse and worse, deceiving, and being deceived.

2 Pe 2:18 For when they speak great swelling *words* of vanity, they allure through the lusts of the flesh, *through much* wantonness, those that were clean escaped from them who live in error.

1 Jn 2:26 These *things* have I written unto you concerning them that seduce you.

Jude 4 For there are certain men crept in unawares, who were before of old ordained to this condemnation, ungodly men, turning the grace of our God into lasciviousness, and denying the only Lord God, and our Lord Jesus Christ.

Re 2:20 Notwithstanding I have a few things against thee, because thou sufferest that woman Jezebel, which calleth herself a prophetess, to teach and to seduce my servants to commit fornication, and to eat things sacrificed unto idols.

d. Evil Companions

INJURED LOT

Ge 13:12–13 Abram dwelled in the land of Canaan, and Lot dwelled in the cities of the plain, and pitched *his* tent toward Sodom.

But the men of Sodom *were* wicked and sinners before the LORD exceedingly.

A DETRIMENT TO ISRAEL

Nu 11:4 And the mixt multitude that *was* among them fell a lusting: and the children of Israel also wept again, and said, Who shall give us flesh to eat?

A SNARE TO JEHOSHAPHAT

2 Chr 18:1 Now Jehoshaphat had riches and honour in abundance, and joined affinity with Ahab.

2 Chr 19:2 And Jehu the son of Hanani the seer went out to meet him, and said to king Jehoshaphat, Shouldest thou help the ungodly, and love them that hate the LORD? therefore is wrath upon thee from before the LORD.

DEVOURED THE STRENGTH OF EPHRAIM

Ho 7:9 Strangers have devoured his strength, and he knoweth *it* not: yea, gray hairs are here and there upon him, yet he knoweth not.

CORRUPT GOOD MORALS

1 Co 15:33 Be not deceived: evil communications corrupt good manners.

See **SATAN, TESTS**

TENTMAKING *See* **ARTS AND CRAFTS**

TENTS, *movable habitations used by nomadic and semi-nomadic peoples*

Ge 13:18; 26:17; 31:25; Jos 7:22; 2 K 13:5; Je 35:7; He 11:9

TERAH, *father of Abraham*

Ge 11:24, 31; Jos 24:2; 1 Chr 1:26; Ac 7:4

TERROR *See* **FEAR**

TESTIMONY, *religious, open declaration of one's personal experience with God*

1. What

Ps 26:7 That I may publish with the voice of thanksgiving, and tell of all thy wondrous works.

Ps 119:172 My tongue shall speak of thy word: for all thy commandments *are* righteousness.

Ps 145:4 One generation shall praise thy works to another, and shall declare thy mighty acts.

Ps 145:11 They shall speak of the glory of thy kingdom, and talk of thy power;

Is 32:4 The heart also of the rash shall understand knowledge, and the tongue of the stammerers shall be ready to speak plainly.

Is 43:10 Ye *are* my witnesses, saith the LORD, and my servant whom I have chosen: that ye may know and believe me, and understand that I *am* he: before me there was no God formed, neither shall there be after me.

Eze 24:27 In that day shall thy mouth be opened to him which is escaped, and thou shalt speak, and be no more dumb: and thou shalt be a sign unto them; and they shall know that I *am* the LORD.

Mt 10:20 For it is not ye that speak, but the Spirit of your Father which speaketh in you.

Lu 21:13 And it shall turn to you for a testimony.

2. When, Where, How

UNCEASINGLY

Is 62:6 I have set watchmen upon thy walls, O Jerusalem, *which* shall never hold their peace day nor night: ye that make mention of the LORD, keep not silence,

Je 51:10 The LORD hath brought forth our righteousness: come, and let us declare in Zion the work of the LORD our God.

IN THE HOME

Mk 5:18–19 And when he was come into the ship, he that had been possessed with the devil prayed him that he might be with him.

Howbeit Jesus suffered him not, but saith unto him, Go home to thy friends, and tell them how great things the Lord hath done for thee, and hath had compassion on thee.

EMPOWERED BY THE HOLY SPIRIT

Ac 1:8 But ye shall receive power, after that the Holy Ghost is come upon you: and ye shall be witnesses unto me both in Jerusalem, and in all Judaea, and in Samaria, and unto the uttermost part of the earth.

IN THE ASSEMBLY OF THE SAINTS

Ep 5:19 Speaking to yourselves in psalms and hymns and spiritual songs, singing and making melody in your heart to the Lord;

WITHOUT SHAME OR FEAR

2 Ti 1:8 Be not thou therefore ashamed of the testimony of our Lord, nor of me his prisoner: but be thou partaker of the afflictions of the gospel according to the power of God;

CONSTANTLY READY

1 Pe 3:15 But sanctify the Lord God in your hearts: and *be* ready always to *give* an answer to every man that asketh you a reason of the hope that is in you with meekness and fear:

3. Characteristics

RELATES TO PERSONAL EXPERIENCE

Ps 66:16 Come *and* hear, all ye that fear God, and I will declare what he hath done for my soul.

Ps 71:15 My mouth shall shew forth thy righteousness *and* thy salvation all the day; for I know not the numbers *thereof.*

Ps 119:13 With my lips have I declared all the judgments of thy mouth.

Ps 119:46 I will speak of thy testimonies also before kings, and will not be ashamed.

RECOUNTS GOD'S BLESSINGS

Is 63:7 I will mention the lovingkindnesses of the LORD, *and* the praises of the LORD, according to all that the LORD hath bestowed on us, and the great goodness toward the house of Israel, which he hath bestowed on them according to his mercies, and according to the multitude of his lovingkindnesses.

BURSTS FORTH FROM AN INWARD FIRE

Je 20:9 Then I said, I will not make mention of him, nor speak any more in his name. But *his word* was in mine heart as a burning fire shut up in my bones, and I was weary with forbearing, and I could not *stay.*

Da 4:2 I thought it good to shew the signs and wonders that the high God hath wrought toward me.

Jona 1:9 And he said unto them, I *am* an Hebrew; and I fear the LORD, the God of heaven, which hath made the sea and the dry *land.*

AN EVERYDAY DUTY

Mal 3:16 Then they that feared the LORD spake often one to another: and the LORD hearkened, and heard *it,* and a book of remembrance was written before him for them that feared the LORD, and that thought upon his name.

Mt 9:31 But they, when they were departed, spread abroad his fame in all that country.

INSPIRED BY THE SPIRIT

Ac 2:4 And they were all filled with the Holy Ghost, and began to speak with other tongues, as the Spirit gave them utterance.

BECOMES IRREPRESSIBLE

Ac 4:20 For we cannot but speak the things which we have seen and heard.

Ac 5:32 And we are his witnesses of these things; and *so is* also the Holy Ghost, whom God hath given to them that obey him.

Ac 26:22 Having therefore obtained help of God, I continue unto this day, witnessing both to small and great, saying none other things than those which the prophets and Moses did say should come:

THE OUTGROWTH OF FAITH

2 Co 4:13 We having the same spirit of faith, according as it is written, I believed, and therefore have I spoken; we also believe, and therefore speak;

1 Pe 5:12 By Silvanus, a faithful brother unto you, as I suppose, I have written briefly, exhorting, and testifying that this is the true grace of God wherein ye stand.

4. Special Utterances

Ex 4:11 And the LORD said unto him, Who hath made man's mouth? or who maketh the dumb, or deaf, or the seeing, or the blind? have not I the LORD?

Nu 11:25 And the LORD came down in a cloud, and spake unto him, and took of the spirit that *was* upon him, and gave *it* unto the seventy elders: and it came to pass, *that,* when the spirit rested upon them, they prophesied, and did not cease.

Ps 145:7 They shall abundantly utter the memory of thy great goodness, and shall sing of thy righteousness.

Is 32:4 The heart also of the rash shall understand knowledge, and the tongue of the stammerers shall be ready to speak plainly.

Is 35:6 Then shall the lame *man* leap as an hart, and the tongue of the dumb sing: for in the wilderness shall waters break out, and streams in the desert.

Je 15:19 Therefore thus saith the LORD, If thou return, then will I bring thee again, *and* thou shalt stand before me: and if thou take forth the precious from the vile, thou shalt be as my mouth: let them return unto thee; but return not thou unto them.

Eze 3:27 But when I speak with thee, I will open thy mouth, and thou shalt say unto them, Thus saith the Lord GOD; He that heareth, let him hear; and he that forbeareth, let him forbear: for they *are* a rebellious house.

Eze 24:27 In that day shall thy mouth be opened to him which is escaped, and thou shalt speak, and be no more dumb: and thou shalt be a sign unto them; and they shall know that I *am* the Lord.

Eze 29:21 In that day will I cause the horn of the house of Israel to bud forth, and I will give thee the opening of the mouth in the midst of them; and they shall know that I *am* the LORD.

Eze 33:22 Now the hand of the LORD was upon me in the evening, afore he that was escaped came; and had opened my mouth, until he came to me in the morning; and my mouth was opened, and I was no more dumb.

Da 10:16 And, behold, *one* like the similitude of the sons of men touched my lips: then I opened my mouth, and spake, and said unto him that stood before me, O my lord, by the vision my sorrows are turned upon me, and I have retained no strength.

Jl 2:28 And it shall come to pass afterward, *that* I will pour out my spirit upon all flesh; and your sons and your daughters shall prophesy, your old men shall dream dreams, your young men shall see visions:

Lu 1:42 And she spake out with a loud voice, and said, Blessed *art* thou among women, and blessed *is* the fruit of thy womb.

Lu 1:64 And his mouth was opened immediately, and his tongue *loosed,* and he spake, and praised God.

Lu 21:15 For I will give you a mouth and wisdom, which all your adversaries shall not be able to gainsay nor resist.

Ac 2:4 And they were all filled with the Holy Ghost, and began to speak with other tongues, as the Spirit gave them utterance.

Ac 2:17 And it shall come to pass in the last days, saith God, I will pour out of my Spirit upon all flesh: and your sons and your daughters shall prophesy, and your young men shall see visions, and your old men shall dream dreams:

Ac 4:31 And when they had prayed, the place was shaken where they were assembled together; and they were all filled with the Holy Ghost, and they spake the word of God with boldness.

Ac 10:34 Then Peter opened *his* mouth, and said, Of a truth I perceive that God is no respecter of persons:

1 Co 1:5 That in every thing ye are enriched by him, in all utterance, and *in* all knowledge;

1 Co 14:1 Follow after charity, and desire spiritual *gifts,* but rather that ye may prophesy.

2 Co 6:11 O *ye* Corinthians, our mouth is open unto you, our heart is enlarged.

2 Co 8:7 Therefore, as ye abound in every *thing, in* faith, and utterance, and knowledge, and *in* all diligence, and *in* your love to us, *see* that ye abound in this grace also.

Ep 6:19 And for me, that utterance may be given unto me, that I may open my mouth boldly, to make known the mystery of the gospel,

Col 4:3 Withal praying also for us, that God would open unto us a door of utterance, to speak the mystery of Christ, for which I am also in bonds:

a. Prescribed

1 S 8:10 And Samuel told all the words of the LORD unto the people that asked of him a king.

Ps 66:16 Come *and* hear, all ye that fear God, and I will declare what he hath done for my soul.

Ps 71:16 I will go in the strength of the Lord GOD: I will make mention of thy righteousness, *even* of thine only.

Ps 105:2 Sing unto him, sing psalms unto him: talk ye of all his wondrous works.

Ps 145:12 To make known to the sons of men his mighty acts, and the glorious majesty of his kingdom.

Pr 22:21 That I might make thee know the certainty of the words of truth; that thou mightest answer the words of truth to them that send unto thee?

Ec 3:7 A time to rend, and a time to sew; a time to keep silence, and a time to speak;

Is 43:10 Ye *are* my witnesses, saith the LORD, and my servant whom I have chosen: that ye may know and believe me, and understand that I *am* he: before me there was no God formed, neither shall there be after me.

Is 44:8 Fear ye not, neither be afraid: have not I told thee from that time, and have declared *it?* ye *are* even my witnesses. Is there a God beside me? yea, *there is* no God; I know not *any.*

Je 1:17 Thou therefore gird up thy loins, and arise, and speak unto them all that I command thee: be not dismayed at their faces, lest I confound thee before them.

Mt 10:18 And ye shall be brought before governors and kings for my sake, for a testimony against them and the Gentiles.

Mt 10:27 What I tell you in darkness, *that* speak ye in light: and what ye hear in the ear, *that* preach ye upon the housetops.

Mt 11:4 Jesus answered and said unto them, Go and shew John again those things which ye do hear and see:

Mt 28:7 And go quickly, and tell his disciples that he is risen from the dead; and, behold, he goeth before you into Galilee; there shall ye see him: lo, I have told you.

Mk 5:20 And he departed, and began to publish in Decapolis how great things Jesus had done for him: and all *men* did marvel.

Lu 21:13 And it shall turn to you for a testimony.

Jn 15:27 And ye also shall bear witness, because ye have been with me from the beginning.

Jn 20:17 Jesus saith unto her, Touch me not; for I am not yet ascended to my Father: but go to my brethren, and say unto them, I ascend unto my Father, and your Father; and *to* my God, and your God.

Ac 1:8 But ye shall receive power, after that the Holy Ghost is come upon you: and ye shall be witnesses unto me both in Jerusalem, and in all Judaea, and in Samaria, and unto the uttermost part of the earth.

Ac 5:20–21 Go, stand and speak in the temple to the people all the words of this life.

And when they heard *that,* they entered into the temple early in the morning, and taught. But the high priest came, and they that were with him, and called the council together, and all the senate of the children of Israel and sent to the prison to have them brought.

Ac 18:9–10 Then spake the Lord to Paul in the night by a vision, Be not afraid, but speak, and hold not thy peace:

For I am with thee, and no man shall set on thee to hurt thee: for I have much people in this city.

Ac 22:14–15 And he said, The God of our fathers hath chosen thee, that thou shouldest know his will, and see that Just One, and shouldest hear the voice of his mouth.

For thou shalt be his witness unto all men of what thou hast seen and heard.

Ac 23:11 And the night following the Lord stood by him, and said, Be of good cheer, Paul: for as thou hast testified of me in Jerusalem, so must thou bear witness also at Rome.

Tit 2:15 These things speak, and exhort, and rebuke with all authority. Let no man despise thee.

Re 20:4 And I saw thrones, and they sat upon them, and judgment was given unto them: and *I saw* the souls of them that were beheaded for the witness of Jesus, and for the word of God, and which had not worshipped the beast, neither his image, neither had received *his* mark upon their foreheads, or in their hands; and they lived and reigned with Christ a thousand years.

b. Examples

Ps 119:46 I will speak of thy testimonies also before kings, and will not be ashamed.

Jn 1:15 John bare witness of him, and cried, saying, This was he of whom I spake, He that cometh after me is preferred before me: for he was before me.

Ac 2:32 This Jesus hath God raised up, whereof we all are witnesses.

Ac 4:33 And with great power gave the apostles witness of the resurrection of the Lord Jesus: and great grace was upon them all.

Ac 16:32 And they spake unto him the word of the Lord, and to all that were in his house.

Ac 26:22 Having therefore obtained help of God, I continue unto this day, witnessing both to small and great, saying none other things than those which the prophets and Moses did say should come:

1 Co 15:15 Yea, and we are found false witnesses of God; because we have testified of God that he raised up Christ: whom he raised not up, if so be that the dead rise not.

c. Living Witnesses

Mk 2:12 And immediately he arose, took up the bed, and went forth before them all; insomuch that they were all amazed, and glorified God, saying, We never saw it on this fashion.

Mk 5:15–16 And they come to Jesus, and see him that was possessed with the devil, and had the legion, sitting, and clothed, and in his right mind: and they were afraid.

And they that saw *it* told them how it befell to him that was possessed with the devil, and *also* concerning the swine.

Jn 9:8–9 The neighbours therefore, and they which before had seen him that he was blind, said, Is not this he that sat and begged?

Some said, This is he: others *said,* He is like him: *but* he said, I am *he.*

Jn 12:9 Much people of the Jews therefore knew that he was there: and they came not for Jesus' sake only, but that they might see Lazarus also, whom he had raised from the dead.

Ac 4:14 And beholding the man which was healed standing with them, they could say nothing against it.

See **CONFESSING CHRIST, EVANGELISM, WITNESSES**

TESTS, *means used by God to conform believers to the image of Christ*

1. Divine Methods

BY DEMANDING GREAT SACRIFICES
Ge 22:1–2;Ex 20:20

BY LEADING IN A DIFFICULT WAY
De 8:2; De 13:3

BY GIVING OPPORTUNITIES FOR CHOICE
1 K 3:5;2 Chr 32:31; Ps 7:9; 11:5; 17:3

BY PROPOSING HARD TASKS
Jn 6:5–6; 11:6

BY PERMITTING PEOPLE TO SUFFER
Ac 16:23–24

BY PERMITTING TEMPTATION
Ja 1:2–3

2. Divine Delays

See **DELAY**

3. Faith Tested

BY A STRANGE PLAN OF CAMPAIGN
Jos 6:3 And ye shall compass the city, all *ye* men of war, *and* go round about the city once. Thus shalt thou do six days.

BY REDUCING A GENERAL'S ARMY
Jud 7:7 And the LORD said unto Gideon, By the three hundred men that lapped will I save you, and deliver the Midianites into thine hand: and

let all the *other* people go every man unto his place.

**BY REQUIRING DEPENDENCE
UPON A POOR WIDOW**
1 K 17:9 Arise, get thee to Zarephath, which *belongeth* to Zidon, and dwell there: behold, I have commanded a widow woman there to sustain thee.

BY DEMANDING THE LAST MORSEL OF BREAD
1 K 17:13 And Elijah said unto her, Fear not; go *and* do as thou hast said: but make me thereof a little cake first, and bring *it* unto me, and after make for thee and for thy son.

**BY REQUIRING WHAT APPEARED
TO BE USELESS WORK**
2 K 3:16 And he said, Thus saith the LORD, Make this valley full of ditches.

**BY REQUIRING EXTENSIVE PREPARATION
WITH NO BLESSING IN SIGHT**
2 K 4:3 Then he said, Go, borrow thee vessels abroad of all thy neighbours, *even* empty vessels; borrow not a few.

OTHER EXAMPLES
Mt 9:28 And when he was come into the house, the blind men came to him: and Jesus saith unto them, Believe ye that I am able to do this? They said unto him, Yea, Lord.
Mk 7:27 But Jesus said unto her, Let the children first be filled: for it is not meet to take the children's bread, and to cast *it* unto the dogs.
He 11:8 By faith Abraham, when he was called to go out into a place which he should after receive for an inheritance, obeyed; and he went out, not knowing whither he went.
He 11:17 By faith Abraham, when he was tried, offered up Isaac: and he that had received the promises offered up his only begotten *son,*
He 11:36 And others had trial of *cruel* mockings and scourgings, yea, moreover of bonds and imprisonment:
Ja 1:3 Knowing *this,* that the trying of your faith worketh patience.
1 Pe 1:7 That the trial of your faith, being much more precious than of

gold that perisheth, though it be tried with fire, might be found unto praise and honour and glory at the appearing of Jesus Christ:

See **TEMPTATION, WAITING**

THADDAEUS, *or Thaddeus, an apostle*
Mt 10:3; Mk 3:18

THANIM *See* **MONTHS**

THANKFULNESS, *gratitude*

1. Exhortations
De 8:10 When thou hast eaten and art full, then thou shalt bless the LORD thy God for the good land which he hath given thee.
1 Chr 16:8 Give thanks unto the LORD, call upon his name, make known his deeds among the people.
Ps 50:14 Offer unto God thanksgiving; and pay thy vows unto the most High:
Ps 92:1 It is a good *thing* to give thanks unto the LORD, and to sing praises unto thy name, O most High:
Ps 100:4 Enter into his gates with thanksgiving, *and* into his courts with praise: be thankful unto him, *and* bless his name.
Ps 107:22 And let them sacrifice the sacrifices of thanksgiving, and declare his works with rejoicing.
Ps 136:26 O give thanks unto the God of heaven: for his mercy *endureth* for ever.
Ep 5:20 Giving thanks always for all things unto God and the Father in the name of our Lord Jesus Christ;
Ph 4:6 Be careful for nothing; but in every thing by prayer and supplication with thanksgiving let your requests be made known unto God.
Col 1:12 Giving thanks unto the Father, which hath made us meet to be partakers of the inheritance of the saints in light:
Col 2:7 Rooted and built up in him, and stablished in the faith, as ye have been taught, abounding therein with thanksgiving.
Col 3:15 And let the peace of God rule in your hearts, to the which also

ye are called in one body; and be ye thankful.

1 Th 5:18 In every thing give thanks: for this is the will of God in Christ Jesus concerning you.

1 Ti 4:4 For every creature of God *is* good, and nothing to be refused, if it be received with thanksgiving:

2. Examples

Ps 68:19 Blessed *be* the Lord, *who* daily loadeth us *with benefits, even* the God of our salvation. Selah.

Ps 119:62 At midnight I will rise to give thanks unto thee because of thy righteous judgments.

Ps 122:4 Whither the tribes go up, the tribes of the LORD, unto the testimony of Israel, to give thanks unto the name of the LORD.

Da 2:23 I thank thee, and praise thee, O thou God of my fathers, who hast given me wisdom and might, and hast made known unto me now what we desired of thee: for thou hast *now* made known unto us the king's matter.

Lu 17:16 And fell down on *his* face at his feet, giving him thanks: and he was a Samaritan.

Ac 28:15 And from thence, when the brethren heard of us, they came to meet us as far as Appii forum, and The three taverns: whom when Paul saw, he thanked God, and took courage.

1 Co 15:57 But thanks *be* to God, which giveth us the victory through our Lord Jesus Christ.

2 Co 9:15 Thanks *be* unto God for his unspeakable gift.

1 Ti 1:12 And I thank Christ Jesus our Lord, who hath enabled me, for that he counted me faithful, putting me into the ministry;

See **PRAISE**

THANKLESSNESS, *ingratitude*

Is 43:24 Thou hast bought me no sweet cane with money, neither hast thou filled me with the fat of thy sacrifices: but thou hast made me to serve with thy sins, thou hast wearied me with thine iniquities.

Lu 17:18 There are not found that returned to give glory to God, save this stranger.

2 Ti 3:2 For men shall be lovers of their own selves, covetous, boasters, proud, blasphemers, disobedient to parents, unthankful, unholy,

THANK OFFERINGS *See* OFFERINGS

THESSALONIANS

1. FIRST

Author: The apostle Paul.

Date Written: Time and place are uncertain. It is generally thought that this was the earliest of Paul's epistles and was probably written from Corinth between A.D. 49 and 54. Paul had sent Timothy to encourage and strengthen the church. On his return, the report that he gave apparently inspired the apostle to write the epistle (3:6).

Purpose: To comfort believers and encourage them to a life of purity by expounding on the doctrine of Christ's imminent return.

To Whom Written: The church in Thessalonica. It had been founded by Paul on his second missionary journey. He met with violent opposition in his work, but he succeeded in winning some Jews and a multitude of Greeks. This enabled him to establish a faithful church (Ac 17:1–10).

Main Themes: This is one of the most personal of all of Paul's epistles. It is not so doctrinal or polemical as some of the others. The body of the epistle consists chiefly of commendations, personal reminiscences, counsels, and exhortations. The central truth that is emphasized is the future hope of the advent of Christ.

Key Word: Sanctification (4:3).

Key Verses: 3:12–13; 4:16–18.

2. SECOND

Author: The apostle Paul..

Date Written: Probably written from Corinth shortly after the first epistle, between A.D. 50 and 54.

Purpose: It is apparent that certain expressions in Paul's first epistle to this church had been misinterpreted. When he had referred to the uncertainty of the time of Christ's coming, his words had been understood as teaching that the day of the Lord had come (2:2). This resulted in undue excitement. They entertained wrong views about the nearness of the Lord's advent. Paul's purpose was to correct this perspective.

To Whom Written: The church in Thessalonica.

Main Theme: The Second Coming of Christ.

Key Words: Day of Christ (2:2); That Day (1:10, 2:3).

Key Verse: 3:5.

THESSALONICA, *a city of Macedonia*
This is the second city in Europe to hear the preaching voice of St. Paul and probably the first church to receive an epistle from him.
Ac 17:1, 11; 27:2; Ph 4:16; 2 Ti 4:10

THICKET, *dense growth of shrubs or underbrush*
1 S 13:6; Je 4:7

THIEF, *on the Cross*

REBUKED HIS SINFUL COMPANION
Lu 23:40 But the other answering rebuked him, saying, Dost not thou fear God, seeing thou art in the same condemnation?

CONFESSED HIS OWN SIN
Lu 23:41 And we indeed justly; for we receive the due reward of our deeds: but this man hath done nothing amiss.

DECLARED CHRIST TO BE SINLESS
Lu 23:41 And we indeed justly; for we receive the due reward of our deeds: but this man hath done nothing amiss.

EXHIBITED WONDERFUL FAITH
Lu 23:42 And he said unto Jesus, Lord, remember me when thou comest into thy kingdom.

CALLED CHRIST LORD
Lu 23:42 And he said unto Jesus, Lord, remember me when thou comest into thy kingdom.

PRAYED
Lu 23:42 And he said unto Jesus, Lord, remember me when thou comest into thy kingdom.

RECEIVED AN IMMEDIATE ANSWER
Lu 23:43 And Jesus said unto him, Verily I say unto thee, To day shalt thou be with me in paradise.

See **REPENTANCE**

THIRST
Ge 24:17; Ex 17:3; Jud 4:19; 15:18; 2 S 23:15; 1 K 17:10; 1 Chr 11:17; Ne 9:20; Is 41:17; Lam 4:4; Jn 4:7; 19:28; 1 Co 4:11

See **DESIRE, SATISFACTION**

THISTLES, *weedy plants with prickly leaves*
Ge 3:18; 2 K 14:9; Jb 31:40; Ho 10:8; Mt 7:16

THOMAS, *one of the twelve apostles*

DEVOTED TO CHRIST
Jn 11:16

SLOW TO APPREHEND THE MEANING OF CHRIST'S WORDS
Jn 14:5

ABSENT WHEN CHRIST APPEARED AFTER THE RESURRECTION
Jn 20:24

DOUBTED THE RESURRECTION
Jn 20:25–26

GIVEN INDUBITABLE EVIDENCE
Jn 20:27

CONFESSED HIS FAITH

Jn 20:28; 21:2

THORN

1. Sharp Woody Spines

Ge 3:18; Pr 24:31; Ho 9:6; Mi 7:4; Mt 13:7; 27:29; Mk 4:7, 18; Lu 6:44; He 6:8

2. Paul's, *likely denoting some painful disorder or mortifying infirmity*

2 Co 12:7; Ga 4:13

THOUGHTS, GOD'S

Ps 33:11 The counsel of the LORD standeth for ever, the thoughts of his heart to all generations.

Ps 40:5 Many, O LORD my God, *are* thy wonderful works *which* thou hast done, and thy thoughts *which are* to us-ward: they cannot be reckoned up in order unto thee: *if* I would declare and speak *of them,* they are more than can be numbered.

Ps 40:17 But I *am* poor and needy; *yet* the Lord thinketh upon me: thou *art* my help and my deliverer; make no tarrying, O my God.

Ps 92:5 O LORD, how great are thy works! *and* thy thoughts are very deep.

Ps 139:17 How precious also are thy thoughts unto me, O God! how great is the sum of them!

Is 14:24 The LORD of hosts hath sworn, saying, Surely as I have thought, so shall it come to pass; and as I have purposed, *so* shall it stand:

Is 55:9 For *as* the heavens are higher than the earth, so are my ways higher than your ways, and my thoughts than your thoughts.

Je 29:11 For I know the thoughts that I think toward you, saith the LORD, thoughts of peace, and not of evil, to give you an expected end.

See **MIND**

THREAD, *used in sewing*

Ge 14:23; Jud 16:12; Song 4:3

THREATENINGS, *of God against the wicked*

Ge 19:13 For we will destroy this place, because the cry of them is waxen great before the face of the LORD; and the LORD hath sent us to destroy it.

Ex 4:23 And I say unto thee, Let my son go, that he may serve me: and if thou refuse to let him go, behold, I will slay thy son, *even* thy firstborn.

Ex 8:2 And if thou refuse to let *them* go, behold, I will smite all thy borders with frogs:

Ex 8:21 Else, if thou wilt not let my people go, behold, I will send swarms *of flies* upon thee, and upon thy servants, and upon thy people, and into thy houses: and the houses of the Egyptians shall be full of swarms *of flies,* and also the ground whereon they *are.*

Ex 10:4 Else, if thou refuse to let my people go, behold, to morrow will I bring the locusts into thy coast:

Le 26:16 I also will do this unto you; I will even appoint over you terror, consumption, and the burning ague, that shall consume the eyes, and cause sorrow of heart: and ye shall sow your seed in vain, for your enemies shall eat it.

Nu 33:56 Moreover it shall come to pass, *that* I shall do unto you, as I thought to do unto them.

De 8:20 As the nations which the LORD destroyeth before your face, so shall ye perish; because ye would not be obedient unto the voice of the LORD your God.

De 28:45 Moreover all these curses shall come upon thee, and shall pursue thee, and overtake thee, till thou be destroyed; because thou hearkenedst not unto the voice of the LORD thy God, to keep his commandments and his statutes which he commanded thee:

De 30:18 I denounce unto you this day, that ye shall surely perish, *and that* ye shall not prolong *your* days upon the land, whither thou passest over Jordan to go to possess it.

De 32:23 I will heap mischiefs upon them; I will spend mine arrows upon them.

De 32:42 I will make mine arrows drunk with blood, and my sword shall devour flesh; *and that* with the blood of the slain and of the captives, from the beginning of revenges upon the enemy.

Jos 23:15 Therefore it shall come to pass, *that* as all good things are come upon you, which the LORD your God promised you; so shall the Lord bring upon you all evil things, until he have destroyed you from off this good land which the LORD your God hath given you.

1 S 2:31 Behold, the days come, that I will cut off thine arm, and the arm of thy father's house, that there shall not be an old man in thine house.

1 S 3:12 In that day I will perform against Eli all *things* which I have spoken concerning his house: when I begin, I will also make an end.

1 S 12:25 But if ye shall still do wickedly, ye shall be consumed, both ye and your king.

1 K 9:7 Then will I cut off Israel out of the land which I have given them; and this house, which I have hallowed for my name, will I cast out of my sight; and Israel shall be a proverb and a byword among all people:

1 K 21:21 Behold, I will bring evil upon thee, and will take away thy posterity, and will cut off from Ahab him that pisseth against the wall, and him that is shut up and left in Israel,

2 K 21:12 Therefore thus saith the LORD God of Israel, Behold, I *am* bringing *such* evil upon Jerusalem and Judah, that whosoever heareth of it, both his ears shall tingle.

2 K 22:16 Thus saith the LORD, Behold, I will bring evil upon this place, and upon the inhabitants thereof, *even* all the words of the book which the king of Judah hath read:

2 Chr 34:24 Thus saith the LORD, Behold, I will bring evil upon this place, and upon the inhabitants thereof, *even* all the curses that are written in the book which they have read before the king of Judah:

Ps 7:12 If he turn not, he will whet his sword; he hath bent his bow, and made it ready.

Ps 50:22 Now consider this, ye that forget God, lest I tear *you* in pieces, and *there be* none to deliver.

Ps 68:21 But God shall wound the head of his enemies, *and* the hairy scalp of such an one as goeth on still in his trespasses.

Is 9:11 Therefore the LORD shall set up the adversaries of Rezin against him, and join his enemies together;

Is 10:6 I will send him against an hypocritical nation, and against the people of my wrath will I give him a charge, to take the spoil, and to take the prey, and to tread them down like the mire of the streets.

Is 14:23 I will also make it a possession for the bittern, and pools of water: and I will sweep it with the besom of destruction, saith the Lord of hosts.

Is 14:31 Howl, O gate; cry, O city; thou, whole Palestina, *art* dissolved: for there shall come from the north a smoke, and none *shall be* alone in his appointed times.

Is 29:2 Yet I will distress Ariel, and there shall be heaviness and sorrow: and it shall be unto me as Ariel.

Is 34:3 Their slain also shall be cast out, and their stink shall come up out of their carcases, and the mountains shall be melted with their blood.

Is 42:14 I have long time holden my peace; I have been still, *and* refrained myself: *now* will I cry like a travailing woman; I will destroy and devour at once.

Is 65:12 Therefore will I number you to the sword, and ye shall all bow down to the slaughter: because when I called, ye did not answer; when I spake, ye did not hear; but did evil before mine eyes, and did choose *that* wherein I delighted not.

Is 66:4 I also will choose their delusions, and will bring their fears upon them; because when I called, none did answer; when I spake, they did not hear: but they did evil before mine eyes, and chose *that* in which I delighted not.

Je 4:6 Set up the standard toward Zion: retire, stay not: for I will bring evil from the north, and a great destruction.

Je 5:6 Wherefore a lion out of the forest shall slay them, *and* a wolf of the evenings shall spoil them, a leopard shall watch over their cities: every one that goeth out thence shall be torn in pieces: because their transgressions are many, *and* their backslidings are increased.

Je 6:19 Hear, O earth: behold, I will bring evil upon this people, *even* the fruit of their thoughts, because they have not hearkened unto my words, nor to my law, but rejected it.

Je 8:13 I will surely consume them, saith the LORD: *there shall be* no grapes on the vine, nor figs on the fig tree, and the leaf shall fade; and *the things that* I have given them shall pass away from them.

Je 11:23 And there shall be no remnant of them: for I will bring evil upon the men of Anathoth, *even* the year of their visitation.

Je 13:13 Then shalt thou say unto them, Thus saith the LORD, Behold, I will fill all the inhabitants of this land, even the kings that sit upon David's throne, and the priests, and the prophets, and all the inhabitants of Jerusalem, with drunkenness.

Je 15:3 And I will appoint over them four kinds, saith the LORD: the sword to slay, and the dogs to tear, and the fowls of the heaven, and the beasts of the earth, to devour and destroy.

Je 18:11 Now therefore go to, speak to the men of Judah, and to the inhabitants of Jerusalem, saying, Thus saith the LORD; Behold, I frame evil against you, and devise a device against you: return ye now every one from his evil way, and make your ways and your doings good.

Je 19:3 And say, Hear ye the word of the LORD, O kings of Judah, and inhabitants of Jerusalem; Thus saith the LORD of hosts, the God of Israel; Behold, I will bring evil upon this place, the which whosoever heareth, his ears shall tingle.

Je 19:11 And shalt say unto them, Thus saith the LORD of hosts; Even so will I break this people and this city, as *one* breaketh a potter's vessel, that cannot be made whole again: and they shall bury *them* in Tophet, till *there be* no place to bury.

Je 19:15 Thus saith the LORD of hosts, the God of Israel; Behold, I will bring upon this city and upon all her towns all the evil that I have pronounced against it, because they have hardened their necks, that they might not hear my words.

Je 22:5 But if ye will not hear these words, I swear by myself, saith the LORD, that this house shall become a desolation.

Je 25:29 For, lo, I begin to bring evil on the city which is called by my name, and should ye be utterly unpunished? Ye shall not be unpunished: for I will call for a sword upon all the inhabitants of the earth, saith the LORD of hosts.

Je 35:17 Therefore thus saith the LORD God of hosts, the God of Israel; Behold, I will bring upon Judah and upon all the inhabitants of Jerusalem all the evil that I have pronounced against them: because I have spoken unto them, but they have not heard; and I have called unto them, but they have not answered.

Je 36:31 And I will punish him and his seed and his servants for their iniquity; and I will bring upon them, and upon the inhabitants of Jerusalem, and upon the men of Judah, all the evil that I have pronounced against them; but they hearkened not.

Je 39:16 Go and speak to Ebed-melech the Ethiopian, saying, Thus saith the LORD of hosts, the God of Israel; Behold, I will bring my words upon this city for evil, and not for good; and they shall be *accomplished* in that day before thee.

Je 44:17 But we will certainly do whatsoever thing goeth forth out of our own mouth, to burn incense unto the queen of heaven, and to pour out drink offerings unto her, as we have done, we, and our fathers, our kings, and our princes, in the cities of Judah, and in the streets of Jerusalem: for *then* had we plenty of victuals, and were well, and saw no evil.

Eze 5:11 Wherefore, *as* I live, saith the Lord GOD; Surely, because thou hast defiled my sanctuary with all thy detestable things, and with all thine abominations, therefore will I also diminish *thee;* neither shall mine eye spare, neither will I have any pity.

Eze 14:13 Son of man, when the land sinneth against me by trespassing grievously, then will I stretch out mine hand upon it, and will break the staff of the bread thereof, and will send famine upon it, and will cut off man and beast from it:

Eze 15:7 And I will set my face against them; they shall go out from *one* fire, and *another* fire shall devour them; and ye shall know that I *am* the Lord, when I set my face against them.

Eze 21:15 I have set the point of the sword against all their gates, that *their* heart may faint, and *their* ruins be multiplied: ah! *it is* made bright, *it is* wrapped up for the slaughter.

Eze 33:27 Say thou thus unto them, Thus saith the Lord GOD; *As* I live, surely they that *are* in the wastes shall fall by the sword, and him that *is* in the open field will I give to the beasts to be devoured, and they that be in the forts and in the caves shall die of the pestilence.

Eze 35:3 And say unto it, Thus saith the Lord GOD; Behold, O mount Seir, I *am* against thee, and I will stretch out mine hand against thee, and I will make thee most desolate.

Ho 5:12 Therefore *will* I *be* unto Ephraim as a moth, and to the house of Judah as rottenness.

Ho 9:12 Though they bring up their children, yet will I bereave them, *that there shall* not *be* a man *left:* yea, woe also to them when I depart from them!

Ho 13:8 I will meet them as a bear *that is* bereaved *of her whelps,* and will rend the caul of their heart, and there will I devour them like a lion: the wild beast shall tear them.

Am 1:10 But I will send a fire on the wall of Tyrus, which shall devour the palaces thereof.

Am 3:1 Hear this word that the LORD hath spoken against you, O children of Israel, against the whole family which I brought up from the land of Egypt, saying,

Am 3:15 And I will smite the winter house with the summer house; and the houses of ivory shall perish, and the great houses shall have an end, saith the Lord.

Am 7:17 Therefore thus saith the LORD; Thy wife shall be an harlot in the city, and thy sons and thy daughters shall fall by the sword, and thy land shall be divided by line; and thou shalt die in a polluted land: and Israel shall surely go into captivity forth of his land.

Mal 3:5 And I will come near to you to judgment; and I will be a swift witness against the sorcerers, and against the adulterers, and against false swearers, and against those that oppress the hireling in *his* wages, the widow, and the fatherless, and that turn aside the stranger *from his right,* and fear not me, saith the LORD of hosts.

Re 2:22 Behold, I will cast her into a bed, and them that commit adultery with her into great tribulation, except they repent of their deeds.

See **RETRIBUTION, WICKED**

THRESHING *See* **AGRICULTURE**

THRONE, *symbol of the kingdom*

De 17:18 And it shall be, when he sitteth upon the throne of his kingdom, that he shall write him a copy of this law in a book out of *that which is* before the priests the Levites:

2 S 3:10 To translate the kingdom from the house of Saul, and to set up the throne of David over Israel and over Judah, from Dan even to Beersheba.

2 S 7:13 He shall build an house for my name, and I will stablish the throne of his kingdom for ever.

1 K 1:37 As the LORD hath been with my lord the king, even so be he with Solomon, and make his throne greater than the throne of my lord king David.

1 K 1:46 And also Solomon sitteth on the throne of the kingdom.

1 K 2:4 That the LORD may continue his word which he spake concerning me, saying, If thy children take heed to their way, to walk before me in truth with all their heart and with all their soul, there shall not fail thee (said he) a man on the throne of Israel.

1 K 2:12 Then sat Solomon upon the throne of David his father; and his kingdom was established greatly.

1 Chr 29:23 Then Solomon sat on the throne of the LORD as king instead of David his father, and prospered; and all Israel obeyed him.

Est 1:2 *That* in those days, when the king Ahasuerus sat on the throne of his kingdom, which *was* in Shushan the palace,

Ps 89:36 His seed shall endure for ever, and his throne as the sun before me.

Pr 25:5 Take away the wicked *from* before the king, and his throne shall be established in righteousness.

Je 22:4 For if ye do this thing indeed, then shall there enter in by the gates of this house kings sitting upon the throne of David, riding in chariots and on horses, he, and his servants, and his people.

Da 7:9 I beheld till the thrones were cast down, and the Ancient of days did sit, whose garment *was* white as snow, and the hair of his head like the pure wool: his throne *was like* the fiery flame, *and* his wheels *as* burning fire.

Lu 1:32 He shall be great, and shall be called the Son of the Highest: and the Lord God shall give unto him the throne of his father David:

See **KINGDOM, GOD**

THUMBS

Ex 29:20; Le 8:23; 14:17; Jud 1:7

THUNDER *See* WEATHER

THYATIRA, *a city of Asia Minor*

Ac 16:14; Re 1:11; 2:18

TIBERIAS, *sea of*

Jn 6:23

TIDINGS, *GOOD, positive news*

1. Spiritual

Is 40:9 O Zion, that bringest good tidings, get thee up into the high mountain; O Jerusalem, that bringest good tidings, lift up thy voice with strength; lift *it* up, be not afraid; say unto the cities of Judah, Behold your God!

Is 41:27 The first *shall say* to Zion, Behold, behold them: and I will give to Jerusalem one that bringeth good tidings.

Is 52:7 How beautiful upon the mountains are the feet of him that bringeth good tidings, that publisheth peace; that bringeth good tidings of good, that publisheth salvation; that saith unto Zion, Thy God reigneth!

Is 61:1 The Spirit of the Lord GOD *is* upon me; because the LORD hath anointed me to preach good tidings unto the meek; he hath sent me to bind up the brokenhearted, to proclaim liberty to the captives, and the opening of the prison to *them that are* bound;

Na 1:15 Behold upon the mountains the feet of him that bringeth good tidings, that publisheth peace! O Judah, keep thy solemn feasts, perform thy vows: for the wicked shall no more pass through thee; he is utterly cut off.

Mk 16:7 But go your way, tell his disciples and Peter that he goeth before you into Galilee: there shall ye see him, as he said unto you.

Mk 16:10 *And* she went and told them that had been with him, as they mourned and wept.

Lu 1:19 And the angel answering said unto him, I am Gabriel, that stand in the presence of God; and am sent to speak unto thee, and to shew thee these glad tidings.

Lu 2:10 And the angel said unto them, Fear not: for, behold, I bring you good tidings of great joy, which shall be to all people.

Lu 8:1 And it came to pass afterward, that he went throughout every city and village, preaching and shewing the glad tidings of the kingdom of God: and the twelve *were* with him,

Ac 13:32 And we declare unto you glad tidings, how that the promise which was made unto the fathers,

Ro 10:15 And how shall they preach, except they be sent? as it is written, How beautiful are the feet of them that preach the gospel of peace, and bring glad tidings of good things!

1 Th 3:6 But now when Timotheus came from you unto us, and brought us good tidings of your faith and charity, and that ye have good remembrance of us always, desiring greatly to see us, as we also *to see* you:

See **GOSPEL**

2. Of Human Affairs

2 S 18:19, 27; 2 K 7:9; Pr 15:30; 25:25

TIGLATH-PILESER, *or*

Tilgath-pilneser, king of Assyria

2 K 15:29; 16:7; 1 Chr 5:6, 26; 2 Chr 28:20

TIGRIS *See* **RIVERS**

TIMBRELS *See* **MUSIC**

TIME, *the right use of*

1. How Secured

BY REALIZING THE BREVITY OF LIFE

Ps 90:12 So teach *us* to number our days, that we may apply *our* hearts unto wisdom.

BY YOUTHFUL PIETY

Ec 12:1 Remember now thy Creator in the days of thy youth, while the evil days come not, nor the years draw nigh, when thou shalt say, I have no pleasure in them;

BY SUBORDINATING EARTHLY
DUTIES TO HEAVENLY

1 Co 7:29 But this I say, brethren, the time *is* short: it remaineth, that both they that have wives be as though they had none;

1 Co 7:31 And they that use this world, as not abusing *it:* for the fashion of this world passeth away.

BY SERIOUS LIVING

Ep 5:15–16 See then that ye walk circumspectly, not as fools, but as wise,

Redeeming the time, because the days are evil.

BY A CONSISTENT EXAMPLE
BEFORE THE WORLD

Col 4:5 Walk in wisdom toward them that are without, redeeming the time.

2. Bible Chronology

See the chart on the following page.

3. Accepted Period

Ex 28:38 And it shall be upon Aaron's forehead, that Aaron may bear the iniquity of the holy things, which the children of Israel shall hallow in all their holy gifts; and it shall be always upon his forehead, that they may be accepted before the LORD.

2 S 24:23 All *these* things did Araunah, *as* a king, give unto the king. And Araunah said unto the king, The LORD thy God accept thee.

Jb 42:9 So Eliphaz the Temanite and Bildad the Shuhite *and* Zophar the Naamathite went, and did according as the LORD commanded them: the LORD also accepted Job.

Ps 6:9 The LORD hath heard my supplication; the LORD will receive my prayer.

Eze 20:40 For in mine holy mountain, in the mountain of the height of Israel, saith the Lord GOD, there shall all the house of Israel, all of them in the land, serve me: there will I accept them, and there will I require your offerings, and the firstfruits of your oblations, with all your holy things.

Eze 43:27 And when these days are expired, it shall be, *that* upon the eighth day, and *so* forward, the priests shall make your burnt offerings upon the altar, and your peace offerings;

B.C.	Main Events
-2100	Fall, Flood, and Dispersion of Races
2092	Call of Abraham
1931	Jacob flees from Esau
1886	Joseph becomes Prime Minister of Egypt
1877	Jacob's family enters Egypt
1806	Death of Joseph
1527	Birth of Moses
1447	The Exodus
1408	Joshua appointed leader
1407	Crossing the Jordan
1407–1382	Conquest of Canaan
1376–1336	Othniel
1197–1157	Gideon
1115–1075	Eli
1075–1035	Samuel
1051–1011	Saul
1011–971	David
971–931	Solomon
960	Dedication of the Temple
931	Jeroboam (Israel) and Rehoboam (Judah)
722	Hoshea (Israel) and the captivity of Israel
587/6	Zedekiah (Judah) and the captivity of Judah
536	Jews return under Zerubbabel
516	Temple dedicated
458	Ezra leads back a caravan of Jews
445	Nehemiah returns to Jerusalem to repair city walls
320	Judea annexed to Egypt
193	Judea annexed to Syria
166–63	Jewish independence under the Maccabees
168	Antiochus pollutes the temple
167	Beginning of the Maccabaean revolt
165	Temple is rededicated
4	Birth of Christ
2	Birth of Paul

A. D.	
25–27	Baptism of Christ
29–30	Crucifixion
31–37	Conversion of Paul
45–58	Paul's Missionary Journeys
61–68	Paul's one or two imprisonments at Rome
70	End of the Jewish state. Jerusalem destroyed by Titus
90–100	Persecution of Christians by Domitian. Death of John and close of apostolic age.

and I will accept you, saith the Lord
GOD.

Ac 10:35 But in every nation he that
feareth him, and worketh righteousness, is accepted with him.

2 Co 5:9 Wherefore we labour, that,
whether present or absent, we may be
accepted of him.

Ep 1:6 To the praise of the glory of his
grace, wherein he hath made us accepted in the beloved.

4. Those Who Ask When

Mt 24:3 And as he sat upon the
mount of Olives, the disciples came
unto him privately, saying, Tell us,
when shall these things be? and what
shall be the sign of thy coming, and of
the end of the world?

Mk 13:4 Tell us, when shall these
things be? and what *shall be* the sign
when all these things shall be fulfilled?

Lu 17:20 And when he was demanded of the Pharisees, when the
kingdom of God should come, he answered them and said, The kingdom
of God cometh not with observation:

Lu 21:7 And they asked him, saying,
Master, but when shall these things
be? and what sign *will there be* when
these things shall come to pass?

Ac 1:6–7 When they therefore were
come together, they asked of him, saying, Lord, wilt thou at this time restore
again the kingdom to Israel?

And he said unto them, It is not for
you to know the times or the seasons,
which the Father hath put in his own
power.

See **FUTURE LIFE, SECOND COMING**

TIMOTHY, *or Timotheus, Paul's
colaborer*

1. Person

FATHER A GREEK

Ac 16:1 Then came he to Derbe and
Lystra: and, behold, a certain disciple
was there, named Timotheus, the son
of a certain woman, which was a
Jewess, and believed; but his father
was a Greek:

MOTHER A GODLY WOMAN

2 Ti 1:5 When I call to remembrance
the unfeigned faith that is in thee,
which dwelt first in thy grandmother
Lois, and thy mother Eunice; and I am
persuaded that in thee also.

TRAINED EARLY IN THE SCRIPTURES

2 Ti 3:15 And that from a child thou
hast known the holy scriptures, which
are able to make thee wise unto salvation through faith which is in Christ
Jesus.

CIRCUMCISED BY PAUL

Ac 16:3 Him would Paul have to go
forth with him; and took and circumcised him because of the Jews which
were in those quarters: for they knew
all that his father was a Greek.

BECAME PAUL'S ASSISTANT

Ac 16:3 Him would Paul have to go
forth with him; and took and circumcised him because of the Jews which
were in those quarters: for they knew
all that his father was a Greek.

See **YOUNG PEOPLE**

2. Books

a. FIRST

Author: The apostle Paul.

Date Written: Uncertain, but possibly about A.D. 64 after Paul's first imprisonment.

Purpose: To encourage Timothy,
Paul's young assistant, to be a godly
example (4:12), exercising his spiritual
gifts (4:14); and to give guidance in his
pastoral responsibilities during Paul's
absence (3:14–15).

To Whom Written: Timothy, Paul's
"own son in the faith" (1:2).

Main Themes: Advice and exhortation to a young pastor respecting his
personal conduct and ministerial
work.

Key Word: Conduct.

Key Verse: 3:15.

b. SECOND

Author: The apostle Paul.

Date Written: Probably written from Rome between A.D. 65 and 67. It is generally believed that Paul suffered two imprisonments at Rome and that it was during the second that this epistle was written. Formerly he had had a certain degree of liberty and had lived in his own hired house (Ac 28:30). At that time he had been accessible to his friends, but now he is in close confinement and Onesiphorus had difficulty in finding him (1:17). He had been deserted by many of his former associates (1:15) and was expecting very soon to be led out to execution (4:6). There is a pathetic strain of loneliness running through the epistle, and it is not surprising that he was anxious to see his beloved Timothy. The letter contains the last recorded words of the apostle.

Purpose:

(1) General, to encourage and instruct a young pastor in his ministerial work.

(2) Special, to request Timothy, his son in the Gospel, to hasten to Rome so that Paul might have the comfort of his companionship (1:4; 4:9, 21).

To Whom Written: Timothy. Both epistles to Timothy contain urgent exhortations.

Main Themes: Faithfulness and boldness in the ministry, especially in the face of opposition and suffering.

Key Words: Endure (2:3); Continue (3:14).

Key Verses: 2:1–4; 3:14–17.

TIN

Nu 31:22; Eze 22:18; 27:12

TIRZAH

1. A Canaanite city

Jos 12:24; 1 K 14:17; 15:21, 33; 16:6, 15, 23; 2 K 15:14

2. Daughter of Zelophehad

Nu 26:33; 36:11; Jos 17:3

TISRI *See* MONTHS

TITLES AND NAMES

1. Of Christ

ADAM

1 Co 15:45 And so it is written, The first man Adam was made a living soul; the last Adam *was made* a quickening spirit.

ADVOCATE

1 Jn 2:1 My little children, these things write I unto you, that ye sin not. And if any man sin, we have an advocate with the Father, Jesus Christ the righteous:

ALMIGHTY

Re 1:8 I am Alpha and Omega, the beginning and the ending, saith the Lord, which is, and which was, and which is to come, the Almighty.

ALPHA AND OMEGA

Re 1:8 I am Alpha and Omega, the beginning and the ending, saith the Lord, which is, and which was, and which is to come, the Almighty.

Re 22:13 I am Alpha and Omega, the beginning and the end, the first and the last.

AMEN

Re 3:14 And unto the angel of the church of the Laodiceans write; These things saith the Amen, the faithful and true witness, the beginning of the creation of God;

APOSTLE OF OUR PROFESSION

He 3:1 Wherefore, holy brethren, partakers of the heavenly calling, consider the Apostle and High Priest of our profession, Christ Jesus;

ARM OF THE LORD

Is 51:9 Awake, awake, put on strength, O arm of the LORD; awake, as in the ancient days, in the generations of old. *Art* thou not it that hath cut Rahab, *and* wounded the dragon?

Is 53:1 Who hath believed our report? and to whom is the arm of the LORD revealed?

AUTHOR AND FINISHER OF OUR FAITH

He 12:2 Looking unto Jesus the author and finisher of *our* faith; who for the joy that was set before him endured the cross, despising the shame, and is set down at the right hand of the throne of God.

AUTHOR OF ETERNAL SALVATION

He 5:9 And being made perfect, he became the author of eternal salvation unto all them that obey him;

BEGINNING OF THE CREATION OF GOD

Re 3:14 And unto the angel of the church of the Laodiceans write; These things saith the Amen, the faithful and true witness, the beginning of the creation of God;

BELOVED SON

Mt 12:18 Behold my servant, whom I have chosen; my beloved, in whom my soul is well pleased: I will put my spirit upon him, and he shall shew judgment to the Gentiles.

BLESSED AND ONLY POTENTATE

1 Ti 6:15 Which in his times he shall shew, *who is* the blessed and only Potentate, the King of kings, and Lord of lords;

BRANCH

Is 4:2 In that day shall the branch of the Lord be beautiful and glorious, and the fruit of the earth *shall be* excellent and comely for them that are escaped of Israel.

BREAD OF LIFE

Jn 6:32 Then Jesus said unto them, Verily, verily, I say unto you, Moses gave you not that bread from heaven; but my Father giveth you the true bread from heaven.

CAPTAIN OF SALVATION

He 2:10 For it became him, for whom *are* all things, and by whom *are* all things, in bringing many sons unto glory, to make the captain of their salvation perfect through sufferings.

CHIEF SHEPHERD

1 Pe 5:4 And when the chief Shepherd shall appear, ye shall receive a crown of glory that fadeth not away.

CHRIST OF GOD

Lu 9:20 He said unto them, But whom say ye that I am? Peter answering said, The Christ of God.

CONSOLATION OF ISRAEL

Lu 2:25 And, behold, there was a man in Jerusalem, whose name *was* Simeon; and the same man *was* just and devout, waiting for the consolation of Israel: and the Holy Ghost was upon him.

CORNERSTONE

Ps 118:22 The stone *which* the builders refused is become the head *stone* of the corner.

COUNSELLOR

Is 9:6 For unto us a child is born, unto us a son is given: and the government shall be upon his shoulder: and his name shall be called Wonderful, Counsellor, The mighty God, The everlasting Father, The Prince of Peace.

CREATOR

Jn 1:3 All things were made by him; and without him was not any thing made that was made.

DAYSPRING

Lu 1:78 Through the tender mercy of our God; whereby the dayspring from on high hath visited us,

DELIVERER

Ro 11:26 And so all Israel shall be saved: as it is written, There shall come out of Sion the Deliverer, and shall turn away ungodliness from Jacob:

DESIRED OF ALL NATIONS

Hag 2:7 And I will shake all nations, and the desire of all nations shall come: and I will fill this house with glory, saith the Lord of hosts.

DOOR

Jn 10:7 Then said Jesus unto them again, Verily, verily, I say unto you, I am the door of the sheep.

ELECT OF GOD

Is 42:1 Behold my servant, whom I uphold; mine elect, *in whom* my soul delighteth; I have put my spirit upon him: he shall bring forth judgment to the Gentiles.

EVERLASTING FATHER

Is 9:6 For unto us a child is born, unto us a son is given: and the government shall be upon his shoulder: and his name shall be called Wonderful, Counsellor, The mighty God, The everlasting Father, The Prince of Peace.

FAITHFUL WITNESS

Re 1:5 And from Jesus Christ, *who is* the faithful witness, *and* the first begotten of the dead, and the prince of the kings of the earth. Unto him that loved us, and washed us from our sins in his own blood,

FIRST AND LAST

Re 1:17 And when I saw him, I fell at his feet as dead. And he laid his right hand upon me, saying unto me, Fear not; I am the first and the last:

FIRST BEGOTTEN

Re 1:5 And from Jesus Christ, *who is* the faithful witness, *and* the first begotten of the dead, and the prince of the kings of the earth. Unto him that loved us, and washed us from our sins in his own blood,

FORERUNNER

He 6:20 Whither the forerunner is for us entered, *even* Jesus, made an high priest for ever after the order of Melchisedec.

GLORY OF THE LORD

Is 40:5 And the glory of the LORD shall be revealed, and all flesh shall see *it* together: for the mouth of the LORD hath spoken *it.*

GOD

Is 40:3 The voice of him that crieth in the wilderness, Prepare ye the way of the LORD, make straight in the desert a highway for our God.

Jn 20:28 And Thomas answered and said unto him, My Lord and my God.

GOD BLESSED

Ro 9:5 Whose *are* the fathers, and of whom as concerning the flesh Christ *came,* who is over all, God blessed for ever. Amen.

GOOD SHEPHERD

Jn 10:11 I am the good shepherd: the good shepherd giveth his life for the sheep.

GOVERNOR

Mt 2:6 And thou Bethlehem, in the land of Juda, art not the least among the princes of Juda: for out of thee shall come a Governor, that shall rule my people Israel.

GREAT HIGH PRIEST

He 4:14 Seeing then that we have a great high priest, that is passed into the heavens, Jesus the Son of God, let us hold fast *our* profession.

HEAD OF THE CHURCH

Ep 1:22 And hath put all *things* under his feet, and gave him *to be* the head over all *things* to the church,

HEIR OF ALL THINGS

He 1:2 Hath in these last days spoken unto us by *his* Son, whom he hath appointed heir of all things, by whom also he made the worlds;

HOLY CHILD

Ac 4:27 For of a truth against thy holy child Jesus, whom thou hast anointed, both Herod, and Pontius Pilate, with the Gentiles, and the people of Israel, were gathered together,

HOLY ONE

Ac 3:14 But ye denied the Holy One and the Just, and desired a murderer to be granted unto you;

HOLY ONE OF GOD

Mk 1:24 Saying, Let *us* alone; what have we to do with thee, thou Jesus of Nazareth? art thou come to destroy us? I know thee who thou art, the Holy One of God.

HOLY ONE OF ISRAEL

Is 41:14 Fear not, thou worm Jacob, *and* ye men of Israel; I will help thee, saith the LORD, and thy redeemer, the Holy One of Israel.

HORN OF SALVATION

Lu 1:69 And hath raised up an horn of salvation for us in the house of his servant David;

I AM

Jn 8:58 Jesus said unto them, Verily, verily, I say unto you, Before Abraham was, I am.

IMAGE OF GOD

2 Co 4:4 In whom the god of this world hath blinded the minds of them which believe not, lest the light of the glorious gospel of Christ, who is the image of God, should shine unto them.

IMMANUEL

Is 7:14 Therefore the Lord himself shall give you a sign; Behold, a virgin shall conceive, and bear a son, and shall call his name Immanuel.

JEHOVAH

Is 26:4 Trust ye in the LORD for ever: for in the LORD JEHOVAH *is* everlasting strength:

JESUS

Mt 1:21 And she shall bring forth a son, and thou shalt call his name JESUS: for he shall save his people from their sins.

JESUS OF NAZARETH

Mt 21:11 And the multitude said, This is Jesus the prophet of Nazareth of Galilee.

JUDGE OF ISRAEL

Mi 5:1 Now gather thyself in troops, O daughter of troops: he hath laid siege against us: they shall smite the judge of Israel with a rod upon the cheek.

JUST ONE

Ac 7:52 Which of the prophets have not your fathers persecuted? and they have slain them which shewed before of the coming of the Just One; of whom ye have been now the betrayers and murderers:

KING

Zec 9:9 Rejoice greatly, O daughter of Zion; shout, O daughter of Jerusalem: behold, thy King cometh unto thee: he *is* just, and having salvation; lowly, and riding upon an ass, and upon a colt the foal of an ass.

KING OF KINGS

1 Ti 6:15 Which in his times he shall shew, *who is* the blessed and only Potentate, the King of kings, and Lord of lords;

KING OF SAINTS

Re 15:3 And they sing the song of Moses the servant of God, and the song of the Lamb, saying, Great and marvellous *are* thy works, Lord God Almighty; just and true *are* thy ways, thou King of saints.

KING OF THE AGES

1 Ti 1:17 Now unto the King eternal, immortal, invisible, the only wise God, be honour and glory for ever and ever. Amen.

KING OF THE JEWS

Mt 2:2 Saying, Where is he that is born King of the Jews? for we have seen his star in the east, and are come to worship him.

LAWGIVER

Is 33:22 For the LORD *is* our judge, the LORD *is* our lawgiver, the LORD *is* our king; he will save us.

LAMB

Re 13:8 And all that dwell upon the earth shall worship him, whose names are not written in the book of life of the Lamb slain from the foundation of the world.

LAMB OF GOD

Jn 1:29 The next day John seeth Jesus coming unto him, and saith, Behold the Lamb of God, which taketh away the sin of the world.

LEADER

Is 55:4 Behold, I have given him *for* a witness to the people, a leader and commander to the people.

LIFE

Jn 14:6 Jesus saith unto him, I am the way, the truth, and the life: no man cometh unto the Father, but by me.

LIGHT OF THE WORLD

Jn 8:12 Then spake Jesus again unto them, saying, I am the light of the world: he that followeth me shall not walk in darkness, but shall have the light of life.

LION OF THE TRIBE OF JUDAH

Re 5:5 And one of the elders saith unto me, Weep not: behold, the Lion of the tribe of Juda, the Root of David, hath prevailed to open the book, and to loose the seven seals thereof.

LORD OF ALL

Ac 10:36 The word which *God* sent unto the children of Israel, preaching peace by Jesus Christ: (he is Lord of all:)

LORD OF GLORY

1 Co 2:8 Which none of the princes of this world knew: for had they known *it,* they would not have crucified the Lord of glory.

LORD OF LORDS

1 Ti 6:15 Which in his times he shall shew, *who is* the blessed and only Potentate, the King of kings, and Lord of lords;

LORD OUR RIGHTEOUSNESS

Je 23:6 In his days Judah shall be saved, and Israel shall dwell safely: and this *is* his name whereby he shall be called, THE LORD OUR RIGHTEOUSNESS.

MAN OF SORROWS

Is 53:3 He is despised and rejected of men; a man of sorrows, and acquainted with grief: and we hid as it were *our* faces from him; he was despised, and we esteemed him not.

MEDIATOR

1 Ti 2:5 For *there is* one God, and one mediator between God and men, the man Christ Jesus;

MESSENGER OF THE COVENANT

Mal 3:1 Behold, I will send my messenger, and he shall prepare the way before me: and the Lord, whom ye seek, shall suddenly come to his temple, even the messenger of the covenant, whom ye delight in: behold, he shall come, saith the LORD of hosts.

MESSIAH

Da 9:25 Know therefore and understand, *that* from the going forth of the commandment to restore and to build Jerusalem unto the Messiah the Prince *shall be* seven weeks, and threescore and two weeks: the street shall be built again, and the wall, even in troublous times.

Jn 1:41 He first findeth his own brother Simon, and saith unto him, We have found the Messias, which is, being interpreted, the Christ.

MIGHTY GOD

Is 9:6 For unto us a child is born, unto us a son is given: and the government shall be upon his shoulder: and his name shall be called Wonderful, Counsellor, The mighty God, The everlasting Father, The Prince of Peace.

MIGHTY ONE

Is 60:16 Thou shalt also suck the milk of the Gentiles, and shalt suck the breast of kings: and thou shalt know that I the LORD *am* thy Saviour and thy Redeemer, the mighty One of Jacob.

MORNING STAR

Re 22:16 I Jesus have sent mine angel to testify unto you these things in the churches. I am the root and the offspring of David, *and* the bright and morning star.

NAZARENE

Mt 2:23 And he came and dwelt in a city called Nazareth: that it might be fulfilled which was spoken by the prophets, He shall be called a Nazarene.

ONLY BEGOTTEN SON

Jn 1:18 No man hath seen God at any time; the only begotten Son, which is in the bosom of the Father, he hath declared *him.*

OUR PASSOVER

1 Co 5:7 Purge out therefore the old leaven, that ye may be a new lump, as ye are unleavened. For even Christ our passover is sacrificed for us:

PRINCE OF KINGS

Re 1:5 And from Jesus Christ, *who is* the faithful witness, *and* the first begotten of the dead, and the prince of the kings of the earth. Unto him that loved us, and washed us from our sins in his own blood,

PRINCE OF LIFE

Ac 3:15 And killed the Prince of life, whom God hath raised from the dead; whereof we are witnesses.

PRINCE OF PEACE

Is 9:6 For unto us a child is born, unto us a son is given: and the government shall be upon his shoulder: and his name shall be called Wonderful, Counsellor, The mighty God, The everlasting Father, The Prince of Peace.

PROPHET

Lu 24:19 And he said unto them, What things? And they said unto him, Concerning Jesus of Nazareth, which was a prophet mighty in deed and word before God and all the people:

Ac 3:22 For Moses truly said unto the fathers, A prophet shall the Lord your God raise up unto you of your brethren, like unto me; him shall ye hear in all things whatsoever he shall say unto you.

REDEEMER

Jb 19:25 For I know *that* my redeemer liveth, and *that* he shall stand at the latter *day* upon the earth:

RESURRECTION AND LIFE

Jn 11:25 Jesus said unto her, I am the resurrection, and the life: he that believeth in me, though he were dead, yet shall he live:

ROCK

1 Co 10:4 And did all drink the same spiritual drink: for they drank of that spiritual Rock that followed them: and that Rock was Christ.

ROOT OF DAVID

Re 22:16 I Jesus have sent mine angel to testify unto you these things in the churches. I am the root and the offspring of David, *and* the bright and morning star.

ROSE OF SHARON

Song 2:1 I *am* the rose of Sharon, *and* the lily of the valleys.

SAVIOR

Lu 2:11 For unto you is born this day in the city of David a Saviour, which is Christ the Lord.

SEED OF WOMAN

Ge 3:15 And I will put enmity between thee and the woman, and between thy seed and her seed; it shall bruise thy head, and thou shalt bruise his heel.

SHEPHERD AND BISHOP OF SOULS

1 Pe 2:25 For ye were as sheep going astray; but are now returned unto the Shepherd and Bishop of your souls.

SHILOH

Ge 49:10 The sceptre shall not depart from Judah, nor a lawgiver from between his feet, until Shiloh come; and unto him *shall* the gathering of the people *be.*

SON OF DAVID

Mt 1:1 The book of the generation of Jesus Christ, the son of David, the son of Abraham.

SON OF GOD

Mt 2:15 And was there until the death of Herod: that it might be fulfilled which was spoken of the Lord by the prophet, saying, Out of Egypt have I called my son.

SON OF MAN

Mt 8:20 And Jesus saith unto him, The foxes have holes, and the birds of the air *have* nests; but the Son of man hath not where to lay *his* head.

SON OF RIGHTEOUSNESS

Mal 4:2 But unto you that fear my name shall the Sun of righteousness arise with healing in his wings; and ye shall go forth, and grow up as calves of the stall.

SON OF THE BLESSED

Mk 14:61 But he held his peace, and answered nothing. Again the high priest asked him, and said unto him, Art thou the Christ, the Son of the Blessed?

SON OF THE HIGHEST

Lu 1:32 He shall be great, and shall be called the Son of the Highest: and the Lord God shall give unto him the throne of his father David:

TRUE LIGHT

Jn 1:9 *That* was the true Light, which lighteth every man that cometh into the world.

TRUE VINE

Jn 15:1 I am the true vine, and my Father is the husbandman.

TRUTH

Jn 1:14 And the Word was made flesh, and dwelt among us, (and we beheld his glory, the glory as of the only begotten of the Father,) full of grace and truth.

WITNESS

Is 55:4 Behold, I have given him *for* a witness to the people, a leader and commander to the people.

WORD

Jn 1:1 In the beginning was the Word, and the Word was with God, and the Word was God.

WORD OF GOD

Re 19:13 And he *was* clothed with a vesture dipped in blood: and his name is called The Word of God.

See **CHRIST**

2. Of God the Father

ALMIGHTY

Ge 17:1 And when Abram was ninety years old and nine, the LORD appeared to Abram, and said unto him, I *am* the Almighty God; walk before me, and be thou perfect.

ETERNAL GOD

De 33:27 The eternal God *is thy* refuge, and underneath *are* the everlasting arms: and he shall thrust out the enemy from before thee; and shall say, Destroy *them.*

FATHER OF LIGHTS

Ja 1:17 Every good gift and every perfect gift is from above, and cometh down from the Father of lights, with whom is no variableness, neither shadow of turning.

FORTRESS

2 S 22:2 And he said, The LORD *is* my rock, and my fortress, and my deliverer;

HEAVENLY FATHER

Mt 6:26 Behold the fowls of the air: for they sow not, neither do they reap, nor gather into barns; yet your heavenly Father feedeth them. Are ye not much better than they?

HOLY ONE OF ISRAEL

Ps 71:22 I will also praise thee with the psaltery, *even* thy truth, O my God: unto thee will I sing with the harp, O thou Holy One of Israel.

I AM

Ex 3:14 And God said unto Moses, I AM THAT I AM: and he said, Thus shalt thou say unto the children of Israel, I AM hath sent me unto you.

JEHOVAH

Ex 6:3 And I appeared unto Abraham, unto Isaac, and unto Jacob, by *the name of* God Almighty, but by my name JEHOVAH was I not known to them.

JUDGE

Ge 18:25 That be far from thee to do after this manner, to slay the righteous with the wicked: and that the righteous should be as the wicked, that be far from thee: Shall not the Judge of all the earth do right?

LIVING GOD

Jos 3:10 And Joshua said, Hereby ye shall know that the living God *is* among you, and *that* he will without fail drive out from before you the Canaanites, and the Hittites, and the Hivites, and the Perizzites, and the Girgashites, and the Amorites, and the Jebusites.

LORD OF HOSTS

1 S 1:11 And she vowed a vow, and said, O LORD of hosts, if thou wilt indeed look on the affliction of thine handmaid, and remember me, and not forget thine handmaid, but wilt give unto thine handmaid a man child, then I will give him unto the LORD all the days of his life, and there shall no razor come upon his head.

LORD OF LORDS

De 10:17 For the LORD your God *is* God of gods, and Lord of lords, a great

God, a mighty, and a terrible, which regardeth not persons, nor taketh reward:

LORD OF SABAOTH

Ja 5:4 Behold, the hire of the labourers who have reaped down your fields, which is of you kept back by fraud, crieth: and the cries of them which have reaped are entered into the ears of the Lord of sabaoth.

MOST HIGH

De 32:8 When the most High divided to the nations their inheritance, when he separated the sons of Adam, he set the bounds of the people according to the number of the children of Israel.

OUR FATHER

1 Chr 29:10 Wherefore David blessed the LORD before all the congregation: and David said, Blessed *be* thou, LORD God of Israel our father, for ever and ever.

Mt 6:9 After this manner therefore pray ye: Our Father which art in heaven, Hallowed be thy name.

OUR STRENGTH

Ex 15:2 The LORD *is* my strength and song, and he is become my salvation: he *is* my God, and I will prepare him an habitation; my father's God, and I will exalt him.

See **GOD**

3. Of the Holy Spirit

COMFORTER

Jn 14:16 And I will pray the Father, and he shall give you another Comforter, that he may abide with you for ever;

ETERNAL SPIRIT

He 9:14 How much more shall the blood of Christ, who through the eternal Spirit offered himself without spot to God, purge your conscience from dead works to serve the living God?

FREE SPIRIT

Ps 51:12 Restore unto me the joy of thy salvation; and uphold me *with thy* free spirit.

HOLY SPIRIT

Ps 51:11 Cast me not away from thy presence; and take not thy holy spirit from me.

Ep 1:13 In whom ye also *trusted,* after that ye heard the word of truth, the gospel of your salvation: in whom also after that ye believed, ye were sealed with that holy Spirit of promise,

Ep 4:30 And grieve not the holy Spirit of God, whereby ye are sealed unto the day of redemption.

POWER OF THE HIGHEST

Lu 1:35 And the angel answered and said unto her, The Holy Ghost shall come upon thee, and the power of the Highest shall overshadow thee: therefore also that holy thing which shall be born of thee shall be called the Son of God.

SPIRIT OF ADOPTION

Ro 8:15 For ye have not received the spirit of bondage again to fear; but ye have received the Spirit of adoption, whereby we cry, Abba, Father.

SPIRIT OF CHRIST

1 Pe 1:11 Searching what, or what manner of time the Spirit of Christ which was in them did signify, when it testified beforehand the sufferings of Christ, and the glory that should follow.

SPIRIT OF COUNSEL

Is 11:2 And the spirit of the LORD shall rest upon him, the spirit of wisdom and understanding, the spirit of counsel and might, the spirit of knowledge and of the fear of the LORD;

SPIRIT OF GLORY

1 Pe 4:14 If ye be reproached for the name of Christ, happy *are ye;* for the spirit of glory and of God resteth upon you: on their part he is evil spoken of, but on your part he is glorified.

SPIRIT OF GOD

Ge 1:2 And the earth was without form, and void; and darkness *was* upon the face of the deep. And the Spirit of God moved upon the face of the waters.

SPIRIT OF GRACE

Zec 12:10 And I will pour upon the house of David, and upon the inhabitants of Jerusalem, the spirit of grace and of supplications: and they shall look upon me whom they have pierced, and they shall mourn for him, as one mourneth for *his* only *son,* and shall be in bitterness for him, as one that is in bitterness for *his* first-born.

SPIRIT OF HOLINESS

Ro 1:4 And declared *to be* the Son of God with power, according to the spirit of holiness, by the resurrection from the dead:

SPIRIT OF JUDGMENT

Is 4:4 When the Lord shall have washed away the filth of the daughters of Zion, and shall have purged the blood of Jerusalem from the midst thereof by the spirit of judgment, and by the spirit of burning.

SPIRIT OF KNOWLEDGE

Is 11:2 And the spirit of the LORD shall rest upon him, the spirit of wisdom and understanding, the spirit of counsel and might, the spirit of knowledge and of the fear of the LORD;

SPIRIT OF LIFE

Ro 8:2 For the law of the Spirit of life in Christ Jesus hath made me free from the law of sin and death.

SPIRIT OF LORD GOD

Is 61:1 The Spirit of the Lord GOD *is* upon me; because the LORD hath anointed me to preach good tidings unto the meek; he hath sent me to bind up the brokenhearted, to proclaim liberty to the captives, and the opening of the prison to *them that are* bound;

SPIRIT OF MIGHT

Is 11:2 And the spirit of the LORD shall rest upon him, the spirit of wisdom and understanding, the spirit of counsel and might, the spirit of knowledge and of the fear of the LORD;

SPIRIT OF PROPHECY

Re 19:10 And I fell at his feet to worship him. And he said unto me, See *thou do it* not: I am thy fellowservant, and of thy brethren that have the testimony of Jesus: worship God: for the testimony of Jesus is the spirit of prophecy.

SPIRIT OF THE FATHER

Mt 10:20 For it is not ye that speak, but the Spirit of your Father which speaketh in you.

SPIRIT OF THE LORD

Is 11:2 And the spirit of the LORD shall rest upon him, the spirit of wisdom and understanding, the spirit of counsel and might, the spirit of knowledge and of the fear of the LORD;

SPIRIT OF THE SON

Ga 4:6 And because ye are sons, God hath sent forth the Spirit of his Son into your hearts, crying, Abba, Father.

SPIRIT OF UNDERSTANDING

Is 11:2 And the spirit of the LORD shall rest upon him, the spirit of wisdom and understanding, the spirit of counsel and might, the spirit of knowledge and of the fear of the LORD;

SPIRIT OF WISDOM

Is 11:2 And the spirit of the LORD shall rest upon him, the spirit of wisdom and understanding, the spirit of counsel and might, the spirit of knowledge and of the fear of the LORD;

See **HOLY SPIRIT**

4. Of the Church

ASSEMBLY OF THE SAINTS

Ps 89:7 God is greatly to be feared in the assembly of the saints, and to be had in reverence of all *them that are* about him.

ASSEMBLY OF THE UPRIGHT

Ps 111:1 Praise ye the LORD. I will praise the LORD with *my* whole heart, in the assembly of the upright, and *in* the congregation.

BODY OF CHRIST

Ro 12:5 So we, *being* many, are one body in Christ, and every one members one of another.

BRANCH

Is 60:21 Thy people also *shall be* all righteous: they shall inherit the land for ever, the branch of my planting, the work of my hands, that I may be glorified.

BRIDE

Re 21:9 And there came unto me one of the seven angels which had the seven vials full of the seven last plagues, and talked with me, saying, Come hither, I will shew thee the bride, the Lamb's wife.

FAMILY IN HEAVEN

Ep 3:15 Of whom the whole family in heaven and earth is named,

FLOCK

Is 40:11 He shall feed his flock like a shepherd: he shall gather the lambs with his arm, and carry *them* in his bosom, *and* shall gently lead those that are with young.

GENERAL ASSEMBLY

He 12:23 To the general assembly and church of the firstborn, which are written in heaven, and to God the Judge of all, and to the spirits of just men made perfect,

GOD'S BUILDING

1 Co 3:9 For we are labourers together with God: ye are God's husbandry, *ye are* God's building.

GOD'S HUSBANDRY

1 Co 3:9 For we are labourers together with God: ye are God's husbandry, *ye are* God's building.

HABITATION OF GOD

Ep 2:22 In whom ye also are builded together for an habitation of God through the Spirit.

HEAVENLY JERUSALEM

He 12:22 But ye are come unto mount Sion, and unto the city of the living God, the heavenly Jerusalem, and to an innumerable company of angels,

HOLY CITY

Re 21:2 And I John saw the holy city, new Jerusalem, coming down from God out of heaven, prepared as a bride adorned for her husband.

HOUSE OF GOD

1 Ti 3:15 But if I tarry long, that thou mayest know how thou oughtest to behave thyself in the house of God, which is the church of the living God, the pillar and ground of the truth.
He 10:21 And *having* an high priest over the house of God;

HOUSEHOLD OF GOD

Ep 2:19 Now therefore ye are no more strangers and foreigners, but fellowcitizens with the saints, and of the household of God;

ISRAEL OF GOD

Ga 6:16 And as many as walk according to this rule, peace *be* on them, and mercy, and upon the Israel of God.

LAMB'S WIFE

Re 19:7 Let us be glad and rejoice, and give honour to him: for the marriage of the Lamb is come, and his wife hath made herself ready.
Re 21:9 And there came unto me one of the seven angels which had the seven vials full of the seven last plagues, and talked with me, saying, Come hither, I will shew thee the bride, the Lamb's wife.

NEW JERUSALEM

Re 21:2 And I John saw the holy city, new Jerusalem, coming down from God out of heaven, prepared as a bride adorned for her husband.

PILLAR AND GROUND OF TRUTH

1 Ti 3:15 But if I tarry long, that thou mayest know how thou oughtest to behave thyself in the house of God, which is the church of the living God, the pillar and ground of the truth.

SPIRITUAL HOUSE

1 Pe 2:5 Ye also, as lively stones, are built up a spiritual house, an holy priesthood, to offer up spiritual sacrifices, acceptable to God by Jesus Christ.

SPOUSE OF CHRIST

Song 4:12 A garden inclosed *is* my sister, *my* spouse; a spring shut up, a fountain sealed.

TEMPLE OF GOD

1 Co 3:16 Know ye not that ye are the temple of God, and *that* the Spirit of God dwelleth in you?

See **CHURCH**

5. Of Ministers

AMBASSADORS

2 Co 5:20 Now then we are ambassadors for Christ, as though God did beseech *you* by us: we pray *you* in Christ's stead, be ye reconciled to God.

ANGELS OF THE CHURCH

Re 1:20 The mystery of the seven stars which thou sawest in my right hand, and the seven golden candlesticks. The seven stars are the angels of the seven churches: and the seven candlesticks which thou sawest are the seven churches.

ELDERS

1 Ti 5:17 Let the elders that rule well be counted worthy of double honour, especially they who labour in the word and doctrine.

EVANGELISTS

Ac 21:8 And the next *day* we that were of Paul's company departed, and came unto Caesarea: and we entered into the house of Philip the evangelist, which was *one* of the seven; and abode with him.

FISHERS OF MEN

Mt 4:19 And he saith unto them, Follow me, and I will make you fishers of men.

LABORERS

Mt 9:38 Pray ye therefore the Lord of the harvest, that he will send forth labourers into his harvest.

MEN OF GOD

De 33:1 And this *is* the blessing, wherewith Moses the man of God blessed the children of Israel before his death.

MESSENGERS

2 Co 8:23 Whether *any do enquire* of Titus, *he is* my partner and fellowhelper concerning you: or our brethren *be enquired of, they are* the messengers of the churches, *and* the glory of Christ.

MINISTERS

Col 1:25 Whereof I am made a minister, according to the dispensation of God which is given to me for you, to fulfil the word of God;

MINISTERS OF CHRIST

Ro 15:16 That I should be the minister of Jesus Christ to the Gentiles, ministering the gospel of God, that the offering up of the Gentiles might be acceptable, being sanctified by the Holy Ghost.

MINISTERS OF GOD

2 Co 6:4 But in all *things* approving ourselves as the ministers of God, in much patience, in afflictions, in necessities, in distresses,

MINISTERS OF THE GOSPEL

Ep 3:7 Whereof I was made a minister, according to the gift of the grace of God given unto me by the effectual working of his power.

MINISTERS OF THE LORD

Jl 2:17 Let the priests, the ministers of the LORD, weep between the porch and the altar, and let them say, Spare thy people, O LORD, and give not thine heritage to reproach, that the heathen should rule over them: wherefore should they say among the people, Where *is* their God?

MINISTERS OF THE WORD

Lu 1:2 Even as they delivered them unto us, which from the beginning were eyewitnesses, and ministers of the word;

OVERSEERS

Ac 20:28 Take heed therefore unto yourselves, and to all the flock, over the which the Holy Ghost hath made you overseers, to feed the church of God, which he hath purchased with his own blood.

PASTORS

Je 3:15 And I will give you pastors according to mine heart, which shall feed you with knowledge and understanding.

PREACHERS

Ro 10:14 How then shall they call on him in whom they have not believed? and how shall they believe in him of whom they have not heard? and how shall they hear without a preacher?

PREACHERS OF RIGHTEOUSNESS

2 Pe 2:5 And spared not the old world, but saved Noah the eighth *person,* a preacher of righteousness, bringing in the flood upon the world of the ungodly;

SERVANTS

2 Co 4:5 For we preach not ourselves, but Christ Jesus the Lord; and ourselves your servants for Jesus' sake.

SERVANTS OF CHRIST

Ph 1:1 Paul and Timotheus, the servants of Jesus Christ, to all the saints in Christ Jesus which are at Philippi, with the bishops and deacons:

SERVANTS OF GOD

Tit 1:1 Paul, a servant of God, and an apostle of Jesus Christ, according to the faith of God's elect, and the acknowledging of the truth which is after godliness;

SERVANTS OF THE LORD

2 Ti 2:24 And the servant of the Lord must not strive; but be gentle unto all *men,* apt to teach, patient,

SHEPHERDS

Je 23:4 And I will set up shepherds over them which shall feed them: and they shall fear no more, nor be dismayed, neither shall they be lacking, saith the LORD.

SOLDIERS

Ph 2:25 Yet I supposed it necessary to send to you Epaphroditus, my brother, and companion in labour, and fellow soldier, but your messenger, and he that ministered to my wants.

STARS

Re 1:20 The mystery of the seven stars which thou sawest in my right hand, and the seven golden candlesticks. The seven stars are the angels of the seven churches: and the seven candlesticks which thou sawest are the seven churches.

STEWARDS OF GOD

Tit 1:7 For a bishop must be blameless, as the steward of God; not selfwilled, not soon angry, not given to wine, no striker, not given to filthy lucre;

STEWARDS OF GRACE

1 Pe 4:10 As every man hath received the gift, *even so* minister the same one to another, as good stewards of the manifold grace of God.

STEWARDS OF MYSTERIES

1 Co 4:1 Let a man so account of us, as of the ministers of Christ, and stewards of the mysteries of God.

TEACHERS

Is 30:20 And *though* the Lord give you the bread of adversity, and the water of affliction, yet shall not thy teachers be removed into a corner any more, but thine eyes shall see thy teachers:

WATCHMEN

Is 62:6 I have set watchmen upon thy walls, O Jerusalem, *which* shall never hold their peace day nor night: ye that make mention of the LORD, keep not silence,

WITNESSES

Ac 1:8 But ye shall receive power, after that the Holy Ghost is come upon you: and ye shall be witnesses unto me both in Jerusalem, and in all Judaea, and in Samaria, and unto the uttermost part of the earth.

WORKERS

2 Co 6:1 We then, *as* workers together *with him,* beseech *you* also that ye receive not the grace of God in vain.

See **MINISTERS**

6. Of the Saints

BELIEVERS

Ac 5:14 And believers were the more added to the Lord, multitudes both of men and women.)

BELOVED BRETHREN

1 Co 15:58 Therefore, my beloved brethren, be ye stedfast, unmovable, always abounding in the work of the Lord, forasmuch as ye know that your labour is not in vain in the Lord.

BRETHREN SPIRITUAL

Mt 23:8 But be not ye called Rabbi: for one is your Master, *even* Christ; and all ye are brethren.

CHILDREN OF GOD

Mt 5:9 Blessed *are* the peacemakers: for they shall be called the children of God.

CHILDREN OF LIGHT

Lu 16:8 And the lord commended the unjust steward, because he had done wisely: for the children of this world are in their generation wiser than the children of light.

CHOSEN ONES

De 7:6 For thou *art* an holy people unto the LORD thy God: the LORD thy God hath chosen thee to be a special people unto himself, above all people that *are* upon the face of the earth.

CHRISTIANS

Ac 11:26 And when he had found him, he brought him unto Antioch. And it came to pass, that a whole year they assembled themselves with the church, and taught much people. And the disciples were called Christians first in Antioch.

DEAR CHILDREN

Ep 5:1 Be ye therefore followers of God, as dear children;

ELECT

Mt 24:22 And except those days should be shortened, there should no flesh be saved: but for the elect's sake those days shall be shortened.

HEIRS

Ro 4:13 For the promise, that he should be the heir of the world, *was* not to Abraham, or to his seed, through the law, but through the righteousness of faith.

LIGHTS

Mt 5:14 Ye are the light of the world. A city that is set on an hill cannot be hid.

RANSOMED OF THE LORD

Is 35:10 And the ransomed of the LORD shall return, and come to Zion with songs and everlasting joy upon their heads: they shall obtain joy and gladness, and sorrow and sighing shall flee away.

RIGHTEOUS

Jb 36:7 He withdraweth not his eyes from the righteous: but with kings *are they* on the throne; yea, he doth establish them for ever, and they are exalted.

SALT

Mt 5:13 Ye are the salt of the earth: but if the salt have lost his savour, wherewith shall it be salted? it is thenceforth good for nothing, but to be cast out, and to be trodden under foot of men.

SHEEP

Ps 74:1 O God, why hast thou cast us off for ever? *why* doth thine anger smoke against the sheep of thy pasture?

SONS OF GOD

Ho 1:10 Yet the number of the children of Israel shall be as the sand of the sea, which cannot be measured nor numbered; and it shall come to pass, *that* in the place where it was said unto them, Ye *are* not my people, *there* it shall be said unto them, *Ye are* the sons of the living God.

TREES OF RIGHTEOUSNESS

Is 61:3 To appoint unto them that mourn in Zion, to give unto them beauty for ashes, the oil of joy for mourning, the garment of praise for the spirit of heaviness; that they might be called trees of righteousness, the planting of the LORD, that he might be glorified.

VESSELS OF HONOR

2 Ti 2:21 If a man therefore purge himself from these, he shall be a vessel unto honour, sanctified, and meet for the master's use, *and* prepared unto every good work.

VESSELS OF MERCY

Ro 9:23 And that he might make known the riches of his glory on the vessels of mercy, which he had afore prepared unto glory,

See **SAINTS**

7. Of Satan

ABADDON

Re 9:11 And they had a king over them, *which is* the angel of the bottomless pit, whose name in the Hebrew tongue *is* Abaddon, but in the Greek tongue hath *his* name Apollyon.

ACCUSER

Re 12:10 And I heard a loud voice saying in heaven, Now is come salvation, and strength, and the kingdom of our God, and the power of his Christ: for the accuser of our brethren is cast down, which accused them before our God day and night.

ADVERSARY

1 Pe 5:8 Be sober, be vigilant; because your adversary the devil, as a roaring lion, walketh about, seeking whom he may devour:

ANGEL OF THE BOTTOMLESS PIT

Re 9:11 And they had a king over them, *which is* the angel of the bottomless pit, whose name in the Hebrew tongue *is* Abaddon, but in the Greek tongue hath *his* name Apollyon.

APOLLYON

Re 9:11 And they had a king over them, *which is* the angel of the bottomless pit, whose name in the Hebrew tongue *is* Abaddon, but in the Greek tongue hath *his* name Apollyon.

BELIAL

2 Co 6:15 And what concord hath Christ with Belial? or what part hath he that believeth with an infidel?

BEELZEBUB

Mt 12:24 But when the Pharisees heard *it,* they said, This *fellow* doth not cast out devils, but by Beelzebub the prince of the devils.

DEVIL

Mt 4:1 Then was Jesus led up of the Spirit into the wilderness to be tempted of the devil.

GOD OF THIS WORLD

2 Co 4:4 In whom the god of this world hath blinded the minds of them which believe not, lest the light of the glorious gospel of Christ, who is the image of God, should shine unto them.

MURDERER

Jn 8:44 Ye are of your father the devil, and the lusts of *your* father ye will do. He was a murderer from the beginning, and abode not in the truth, because there is no truth in him. When he speaketh a lie, he speaketh of his own: for he is a liar, and the father of it.

PRINCE OF DEVILS

Mt 12:24 But when the Pharisees heard *it,* they said, This *fellow* doth not cast out devils, but by Beelzebub the prince of the devils.

PRINCE OF THE POWER OF THE AIR

Ep 2:2 Wherein in time past ye walked according to the course of this world, according to the prince of the power of the air, the spirit that now worketh in the children of disobedience:

PRINCE OF THIS WORLD

Jn 14:30 Hereafter I will not talk much with you: for the prince of this world cometh, and hath nothing in me.

RULER OF DARKNESS

Ep 6:12 For we wrestle not against flesh and blood, but against principalities, against powers, against the rulers of the darkness of this world, against spiritual wickedness in high *places.*

SERPENT

Ge 3:4 And the serpent said unto the woman, Ye shall not surely die:

TEMPTER

Mt 4:3 And when the tempter came to him, he said, If thou be the Son of God, command that these stones be made bread.

UNCLEAN SPIRIT

Mt 12:43 When the unclean spirit is gone out of a man, he walketh through dry places, seeking rest, and findeth none.

WICKED ONE

Mt 13:19 When any one heareth the word of the kingdom, and understandeth *it* not, then cometh the wicked *one,* and catcheth away that which was sown in his heart. This is he which received seed by the way side.

See **SATAN**

8. Of the Wicked

ABOMINABLE BRANCHES

Is 14:19 But thou art cast out of thy grave like an abominable branch, *and as* the raiment of those that are slain, thrust through with a sword, that go down to the stones of the pit; as a carcase trodden under feet.

CHILDREN OF BELIAL

De 13:13 *Certain* men, the children of Belial, are gone out from among you, and have withdrawn the inhabitants of their city, saying, Let us go and serve other gods, which ye have not known;

CHILDREN OF DISOBEDIENCE

Ep 2:2 Wherein in time past ye walked according to the course of this world, according to the prince of the power of the air, the spirit that now worketh in the children of disobedience:

CHILDREN OF HELL

Mt 23:15 Woe unto you, scribes and Pharisees, hypocrites! for ye compass sea and land to make one proselyte, and when he is made, ye make him twofold more the child of hell than yourselves.

CHILDREN OF PRIDE

Jb 41:34 He beholdeth all high *things:* he *is* a king over all the children of pride.

CHILDREN OF THE BONDWOMAN

Ga 4:31 So then, brethren, we are not children of the bondwoman, but of the free.

CHILDREN OF THE DEVIL

1 Jn 3:10 In this the children of God are manifest, and the children of the devil: whosoever doeth not righteousness is not of God, neither he that loveth not his brother.

CHILDREN OF THE WICKED ONE

Mt 13:38 The field is the world; the good seed are the children of the kingdom; but the tares are the children of the wicked *one;*

CHILDREN OF THE WORLD

Lu 16:8 And the lord commended the unjust steward, because he had done wisely: for the children of this world are in their generation wiser than the children of light.

CHILDREN OF WRATH

Ep 2:3 Among whom also we all had our conversation in times past in the lusts of our flesh, fulfilling the desires of the flesh and of the mind; and were by nature the children of wrath, even as others.

CROOKED GENERATION

De 32:5 They have corrupted themselves, their spot *is* not *the spot* of his children: *they are* a perverse and crooked generation.

CURSED CHILDREN

2 Pe 2:14 Having eyes full of adultery, and that cannot cease from sin; beguiling unstable souls: an heart they have exercised with covetous practices; cursed children:

DOGS

Re 22:15 For without *are* dogs, and sorcerers, and whoremongers, and murderers, and idolaters, and whosoever loveth and maketh a lie.

ENEMIES OF GOD

Ex 15:6 Thy right hand, O LORD, is become glorious in power: thy right hand, O LORD, hath dashed in pieces the enemy.

ENEMIES OF THE CROSS

Ph 3:18 (For many walk, of whom I have told you often, and now tell you even weeping, *that they are* the enemies of the cross of Christ:

ENEMIES OF RIGHTEOUSNESS

Ac 13:10 And said, O full of all subtilty and all mischief, *thou* child of the devil, *thou* enemy of all righteousness, wilt thou not cease to pervert the right ways of the Lord?

EVILDOERS

Ps 37:9 For evildoers shall be cut off: but those that wait upon the LORD, they shall inherit the earth.

EVIL MEN

Pr 4:14 Enter not into the path of the wicked, and go not in the way of evil *men.*

FOOLS

Ps 53:1 The fool hath said in his heart, *There is* no God. Corrupt are they, and have done abominable iniquity: *there is* none that doeth good.

GOATS

Mt 25:32 And before him shall be gathered all nations: and he shall separate them one from another, as a shepherd divideth *his* sheep from the goats:

REBELLIOUS CHILDREN

Is 30:1 Woe to the rebellious children, saith the LORD, that take counsel, but not of me; and that cover with a covering, but not of my spirit, that they may add sin to sin:

REBELLIOUS NATION

Eze 2:3 And he said unto me, Son of man, I send thee to the children of Israel, to a rebellious nation that hath rebelled against me: they and their fathers have transgressed against me, *even* unto this very day.

REBELLIOUS PEOPLE

Is 30:9 That this *is* a rebellious people, lying children, children *that* will not hear the law of the LORD:

REPROBATES

2 Co 13:5 Examine yourselves, whether ye be in the faith; prove your own selves. Know ye not your own selves, how that Jesus Christ is in you, except ye be reprobates?

TARES

Mt 13:38 The field is the world; the good seed are the children of the kingdom; but the tares are the children of the wicked *one;*

TRANSGRESSORS

Ps 37:38 But the transgressors shall be destroyed together: the end of the wicked shall be cut off.

UNGODLY

Ro 1:18 For the wrath of God is revealed from heaven against all ungodliness and unrighteousness of men, who hold the truth in unrighteousness;

VESSELS OF WRATH

Ro 9:22 *What* if God, willing to shew *his* wrath, and to make his power known, endured with much longsuffering the vessels of wrath fitted to destruction:

WANDERING STARS

Jude 13 Raging waves of the sea, foaming out their own shame; wandering stars, to whom is reserved the blackness of darkness for ever.

WHITED SEPULCHRES

Mt 23:27 Woe unto you, scribes and Pharisees, hypocrites! for ye are like unto whited sepulchres, which indeed appear beautiful outward, but are within full of dead *men's* bones, and of all uncleanness.

WOLVES

Mt 7:15 Beware of false prophets, which come to you in sheep's clothing, but inwardly they are ravening wolves.

See **WICKED**

9. Of the Word of God

WORD

Lu 11:28 But he said, Yea rather, blessed *are* they that hear the word of God, and keep it.

Ph 2:16 Holding forth the word of life; that I may rejoice in the day of Christ, that I have not run in vain, neither laboured in vain.

Col 3:16 Let the word of Christ dwell in you richly in all wisdom; teaching and admonishing one another in psalms and hymns and spiritual songs, singing with grace in your hearts to the Lord.

2 Ti 2:15 Study to shew thyself approved unto God, a workman that needeth not to be ashamed, rightly dividing the word of truth.

Ja 1:21 Wherefore lay apart all filthiness and superfluity of naughtiness, and receive with meekness the engrafted word, which is able to save your souls.

1 Pe 2:2 As newborn babes, desire the sincere milk of the word, that ye may grow thereby:

BOOK

Ps 40:7 Then said I, Lo, I come: in the volume of the book *it is* written of me,

BOOK OF THE LAW

De 31:26 Take this book of the law, and put it in the side of the ark of the covenant of the LORD your God, that it may be there for a witness against thee.

HOLY SCRIPTURES

Ro 1:2 (Which he had promised afore by his prophets in the holy scriptures,)

ORACLES

Ac 7:38 This is he, that was in the church in the wilderness with the angel which spake to him in the mount Sina, and *with* our fathers: who received the lively oracles to give unto us:

SCRIPTURES

Jn 5:39 Search the scriptures; for in them ye think ye have eternal life: and they are they which testify of me.

SWORD OF THE SPIRIT

Ep 6:17 And take the helmet of salvation, and the sword of the Spirit, which is the word of God:

He 4:12 For the word of God *is* quick, and powerful, and sharper than any twoedged sword, piercing even to the dividing asunder of soul and spirit, and of the joints and marrow, and *is* a discerner of the thoughts and intents of the heart.

WORD OF GOD

He 6:5 And have tasted the good word of God, and the powers of the world to come,

See **WORD OF GOD**

TITUS, *a Grecian convert who became a co-worker with Paul and to whom the epistle of Titus was written*

1. Person

2 Co 2:13; 7:6, 13; 8:6, 16, 23; 12:18; Ga 2:1; Tit 1:4–5

2. Book

Author: The apostle Paul.

Date Written: About A.D. 64, shortly after 1 Timothy was written.

Purpose: To counsel and exhort Titus, a young pastor, relating to his ministerial duties and doctrines, with special emphasis on the maintenance of good works.

To Whom Written: Titus. He was a Gentile (Ga 2:3); a beloved friend and helper of Paul (2 Co 2:13; 7:6, 13; 8:23). A messenger of the church at Corinth (2 Co 8:16–18). He was thoroughly trustworthy and unselfish (2 Co 12:18). A companion of Paul and Barnabas on a journey to Jerusalem (Ga 2:1). He was left in Crete by Paul to superintend the churches (Tit 1:5).He was in Rome with Paul during the latter's imprisonment (2 Ti 4:10). He seems to have been a more sturdy man than Timothy and probably more mature.

Main Theme: Good works (1:16; 2:7, 14; 3:1, 8, 14). Some have claimed that there is a conflict of doctrine between Paul's epistles and that of James. But the character of the Cretans was such that Paul thought it necessary to advise their minister to insist upon consistent Christian living. Nevertheless this epistle does not teach salvation by works (3:5).

Key Words: Good works (3:8).

Key Verses: (1:5; 3:8).

TOBIAH, *the Ammonite, an enemy of the Jews*

Ne 4:3; 6:1; 13:4

TOKENS

Ge 9:12; 17:11; Ex 12:13; 13:9, 16; Nu 17:10; Ps 86:17; Mt 3:16; Jn 1:33

TOLA, *one of the judges*

Jud 10:1

See **ISRAEL**

TOLERANCE, *accepting others as they are*

Mt 9:10 And it came to pass, as Jesus sat at meat in the house, behold, many publicans and sinners came and sat down with him and his disciples.

Mk 9:38–39 And John answered him, saying, Master, we saw one casting out devils in thy name, and he followeth not us: and we forbad him, because he followeth not us.

But Jesus said, Forbid him not: for there is no man which shall do a miracle in my name, that can lightly speak evil of me.

Lu 9:49–50 And John answered and said, Master, we saw one casting out devils in thy name; and we forbad him, because he followeth not with us.

And Jesus said unto him, Forbid *him* not: for he that is not against us is for us.

Ph 1:17–18 But the other of love, knowing that I am set for the defence of the gospel.

What then? notwithstanding, every way, whether in pretence, or in truth, Christ is preached; and I therein do rejoice, yea, and will rejoice.

See **PREJUDICE**

TOMBSTONES *See* **DEAD**

TONGS, *instruments used to tend the temple lamps*

Ex 25:38

TONGUES, *languages*

1. Confusion

Ge 11:9

2. Gift

Mk 16:17 And these signs shall follow them that believe; In my name shall they cast out devils; they shall speak with new tongues;

Ac 2:4 And they were all filled with the Holy Ghost, and began to speak with other tongues, as the Spirit gave them utterance.

Ac 10:46 For they heard them speak with tongues, and magnify God. Then answered Peter,

Ac 19:6 And when Paul had laid *his* hands upon them, the Holy Ghost came on them; and they spake with tongues, and prophesied.

1 Co 12:10 To another the working of miracles; to another prophecy; to another discerning of spirits; to another *divers* kinds of tongues; to another the interpretation of tongues:

1 Co 12:28 And God hath set some in the church, first apostles, secondarily prophets, thirdly teachers, after that miracles, then gifts of healings, helps, governments, diversities of tongues.

1 Co 13:1 Though I speak with the tongues of men and of angels, and have not charity, I am become *as* sounding brass, or a tinkling cymbal.

1 Co 13:8 Charity never faileth: but whether *there be* prophecies, they shall fail; whether *there be* tongues, they shall cease; whether *there be* knowledge, it shall vanish away.

1 Co 14:5 I would that ye all spake with tongues, but rather that ye prophesied: for greater *is* he that prophesieth than he that speaketh with tongues, except he interpret, that the church may receive edifying.

1 Co 14:18 I thank my God, I speak with tongues more than ye all:

1 Co 14:26 How is it then, brethren? when ye come together, every one of you hath a psalm, hath a doctrine, hath a tongue, hath a revelation, hath an interpretation. Let all things be done unto edifying.

1 Co 14:39 Wherefore, brethren, covet to prophesy, and forbid not to speak with tongues.

See **LANGUAGES**

TOPAZ *See* **STONES**

TOPHETH, *high place in the valley of Hinnom outside Jerusalem where child sacrifices were made to the god Molech*

2 K 23:10; Is 30:33; Je 7:32; 19:6, 11; 32:35

TORCHES, *poles with rags soaked in oil wrapped around the top*

Jud 7:16; 15:4; Na 2:3; Jn 18:3

TORMENT, *of the wicked*

Lu 16:23 And in hell he lift up his eyes, being in torments, and seeth Abraham afar off, and Lazarus in his bosom.

Lu 16:28 For I have five brethren; that he may testify unto them, lest they also come into this place of torment.

Re 14:11 And the smoke of their torment ascendeth up for ever and ever: and they have no rest day nor night, who worship the beast and his image, and whosoever receiveth the mark of his name.

Re 16:10 And the fifth angel poured out his vial upon the seat of the beast; and his kingdom was full of darkness; and they gnawed their tongues for pain,

Re 18:10 Standing afar off for the fear of her torment, saying, Alas, alas, that great city Babylon, that mighty city! for in one hour is thy judgment come.

Re 20:10 And the devil that deceived them was cast into the lake of fire and brimstone, where the beast and the false prophet *are,* and shall be tormented day and night for ever and ever.

See **HELL, WICKED**

TORTOISES *See* **REPTILES**

TOWERS, *built for early sighting of approaching enemies*

Ge 11:5; 35:21; Jud 8:9, 17; 9:46–47; 2 K 9:17; 2 Chr 26:9; 32:5; Ne 3:11, 26; Eze 26:9; 27:11; Mt 21:33; Lu 13:4; 14:28

TRADE *See* **BUSINESS**

TRADING *See* **BUSINESS**

TRADITIONS

Is 29:13; Mt 15:3, 6; Mk 7:3, 5, 8; Ga 1:14; Col 2:8; Tit 1:14; 1 Pe 1:18

TRANCE, *mental state where senses are partially or completely suspended and the person is unconscious of physical surroundings*

Nu 24:4; Ac 10:10; 11:5; 22:17

TRANSFIGURATION *See* **CHRIST**

TRANSIENT, *things that are not enduring*

POWER

Ps 37:35–36 I have seen the wicked in great power, and spreading himself like a green bay tree.

Yet he passed away, and, lo, he *was* not: yea, I sought him, but he could not be found.

LIFE

Ps 90:10 The days of our years *are* threescore years and ten; and if by reason of strength *they be* fourscore years, yet *is* their strength labour and sorrow; for it is soon cut off, and we fly away.

MATERIAL THINGS

Ps 102:25–26 Of old hast thou laid the foundation of the earth: and the heavens *are* the work of thy hands.

They shall perish, but thou shalt endure: yea, all of them shall wax old like a garment; as a vesture shalt thou change them, and they shall be changed:

PLEASURE

Lu 12:19–20 And I will say to my soul, Soul, thou hast much goods laid up for many years; take thine ease, eat, drink, *and* be merry.

But God said unto him, *Thou fool,* this night thy soul shall be required of thee: then whose shall those things be, which thou hast provided?

KNOWLEDGE

1 Co 13:8 Charity never faileth: but whether *there be* prophecies, they shall fail; whether *there be* tongues, they shall cease; whether *there be* knowledge, it shall vanish away.

GLORY

1 Pe 1:24 For all flesh *is* as grass, and all the glory of man as the flower of grass. The grass withereth, and the flower thereof falleth away:

See **ENDURING**

TRAVELERS

Jud 5:6; 2 S 12:4; Je 14:8; Lu 11:6

TREACHERY, *treason, conspiracy*

Ge 34:25 And it came to pass on the third day, when they were sore, that two of the sons of Jacob, Simeon and Levi, Dinah's brethren, took each man his sword, and came upon the city boldly, and slew all the males.

Jud 4:18 And Jael went out to meet Sisera, and said unto him, Turn in, my lord, turn in to me; fear not. And when he had turned in unto her into the tent, she covered him with a mantle.

Jud 16:9 Now *there were* men lying in wait, abiding with her in the chamber. And she said unto him, The Philistines *be* upon thee, Samson. And he brake the withs, as a thread of tow is broken when it toucheth the fire. So his strength was not known.

Jud 16:19 And she made him sleep upon her knees; and she called for a man, and she caused him to shave off the seven locks of his head; and she began to afflict him, and his strength went from him.

1 S 18:17 And Saul said to David, Behold my elder daughter Merab, her will I give thee to wife: only be thou valiant for me, and fight the Lord's battles. For Saul said, Let not mine hand be upon him, but let the hand of the Philistines be upon him.

1 S 19:11 Saul also sent messengers unto David's house, to watch him, and to slay him in the morning: and Michal David's wife told him, saying, If thou save not thy life to night, to morrow thou shalt be slain.

2 S 3:27 And when Abner was returned to Hebron, Joab took him aside in the gate to speak with him quietly, and smote him there under the fifth *rib,* that he died, for the blood of Asahel his brother.

2 S 4:6 And they came thither into the midst of the house, *as though* they would have fetched wheat; and they smote him under the fifth *rib:* and Rechab and Baanah his brother escaped.

2 S 11:15 And he wrote in the letter, saying, Set ye Uriah in the forefront of the hottest battle, and retire ye from him, that he may be smitten, and die.

2 S 13:28 Now Absalom had commanded his servants, saying, Mark ye now when Amnon's heart is merry with wine, and when I say unto you, Smite Amnon; then kill him, fear not: have not I commanded you? be courageous and be valiant.

2 S 20:10 But Amasa took no heed to the sword that *was* in Joab's hand: so he smote him therewith in the fifth *rib*, and shed out his bowels to the ground, and struck him not again; and he died. So Joab and Abishai his brother pursued after Sheba the son of Bichri.

1 K 21:8 So she wrote letters in Ahab's name, and sealed *them* with his seal, and sent the letters unto the elders and to the nobles that *were* in his city, dwelling with Naboth.

2 K 9:23 And Joram turned his hands, and fled, and said to Ahaziah, *There is* treachery, O Ahaziah.

Ne 6:2 That Sanballat and Geshem sent unto me, saying, Come, let us meet together in *some one of* the villages in the plain of Ono. But they thought to do me mischief.

Est 3:8 And Haman said unto king Ahasuerus, There is a certain people scattered abroad and dispersed among the people in all the provinces of thy kingdom; and their laws *are* diverse from all people; neither keep they the king's laws: therefore it *is* not for the king's profit to suffer them.

Ps 55:20 He hath put forth his hands against such as be at peace with him: he hath broken his covenant.

Is 21:2 A grievous vision is declared unto me; the treacherous dealer dealeth treacherously, and the spoiler spoileth. Go up, O Elam: besiege, O Media; all the sighing thereof have I made to cease.

Is 24:16 From the uttermost part of the earth have we heard songs, *even* glory to the righteous. But I said, My leanness, my leanness, woe unto me! the treacherous dealers have dealt

treacherously; yea, the treacherous dealers have dealt very treacherously.

Is 33:1 Woe to thee that spoilest, and thou *wast* not spoiled; and dealest treacherously, and they dealt not treacherously with thee! when thou shalt cease to spoil, thou shalt be spoiled; *and* when thou shalt make an end to deal treacherously, they shall deal treacherously with thee.

Je 9:2 Oh that I had in the wilderness a lodging place of wayfaring men; that I might leave my people, and go from them! for they *be* all adulterers, an assembly of treacherous men.

Je 9:8 Their tongue *is as* an arrow shot out; it speaketh deceit: *one* speaketh peaceably to his neighbour with his mouth, but in heart he layeth his wait.

Je 12:6 For even thy brethren, and the house of thy father, even they have dealt treacherously with thee; yea, they have called a multitude after thee: believe them not, though they speak fair words unto thee.

Je 41:2 Then arose Ishmael the son of Nethaniah, and the ten men that were with him, and smote Gedaliah the son of Ahikam the son of Shaphan with the sword, and slew him, whom the king of Babylon had made governor over the land.

Da 11:26 Yea, they that feed of the portion of his meat shall destroy him, and his army shall overflow: and many shall fall down slain.

Obad 7 All the men of thy confederacy have brought thee *even* to the border: the men that were at peace with thee have deceived thee, *and* prevailed against thee; *they that eat* thy bread have laid a wound under thee: *there is* none understanding in him.

Mi 7:5 Trust ye not in a friend, put ye not confidence in a guide: keep the doors of thy mouth from her that lieth in thy bosom.

Mal 2:10 Have we not all one father? hath not one God created us? why do we deal treacherously every man against his brother, by profaning the covenant of our fathers?

Mt 26:16 And from that time he sought opportunity to betray him.

Mt 26:23 And he answered and said, He that dippeth *his* hand with me in the dish, the same shall betray me.

Mt 26:49 And forthwith he came to Jesus, and said, Hail, master; and kissed him.

Mk 14:20 And he answered and said unto them, *It is* one of the twelve, that dippeth with me in the dish.

Mk 14:44 And him had given them a token, saying, Whomsoever I shall kiss, that same is he; take him, and lead *him* away safely.

Lk 22:47 And while he yet spake, behold a multitude, and he that was called Judas, one of the twelve, went before them, and drew near unto Jesus to kiss him.

Jn 18:5 They answered him, Jesus of Nazareth. Jesus saith unto them, I am *he.* And Judas also, which betrayed him, stood with them.

2 Ti 3:4 Traitors, heady, highminded, lovers of pleasures more than lovers of God;

The Treacherous Kiss

2 S 15:5 And it was *so,* that when any man came nigh *to him* to do him obeisance, he put forth his hand, and took him, and kissed him.

2 S 20:9 And Joab said to Amasa, *Art* thou in health, my brother? And Joab took Amasa by the beard with the right hand to kiss him.

Pr 7:13 So she caught him, and kissed him, *and* with an impudent face said unto him,

Pr 27:6 Faithful *are* the wounds of a friend; but the kisses of an enemy *are* deceitful.

Mt 26:49 And forthwith he came to Jesus, and said, Hail, master; and kissed him.

Mk 14:45 And as soon as he was come, he goeth straightway to him, and saith, Master, master; and kissed him.

Lu 22:47 And while he yet spake, behold a multitude, and he that was called Judas, one of the twelve, went before them, and drew near unto Jesus to kiss him.

See **DECEPTION**

TREASON *See* **NATION**

TREASURIES, *places where valuables are kept*

1 Chr 9:26; 26:20; 28:12; 2 Chr 32:27; Ezr 7:20; Ne 10:38; 13:13; Mt 27:6; Mk 12:41; Lu 21:1; Jn 8:20

TREE OF LIFE, *located in the Garden of Eden; fruit gave immortality to the person who ate it*

Ge 2:9 And out of the ground made the LORD God to grow every tree that is pleasant to the sight, and good for food; the tree of life also in the midst of the garden, and the tree of knowledge of good and evil.

Ge 3:22 And the LORD God said, Behold, the man is become as one of us, to know good and evil: and now, lest he put forth his hand, and take also of the tree of life, and eat, and live for ever:

Ge 3:24 So he drove out the man; and he placed at the east of the garden of Eden Cherubims, and a flaming sword which turned every way, to keep the way of the tree of life.

Pr 3:18 She *is* a tree of life to them that lay hold upon her: and happy *is* every one that retaineth her.

Pr 11:30 The fruit of the righteous *is* a tree of life; and he that winneth souls *is* wise.

Eze 47:7 Now when I had returned, behold, at the bank of the river *were* very many trees on the one side and on the other.

Eze 47:12 And by the river upon the bank thereof, on this side and on that side, shall grow all trees for meat, whose leaf shall not fade, neither shall the fruit thereof be consumed: it shall bring forth new fruit according to his months, because their waters they issued out of the sanctuary: and the fruit thereof shall be for meat, and the leaf thereof for medicine.

Re 2:7 He that hath an ear, let him hear what the Spirit saith unto the churches; To him that overcometh will I give to eat of the tree of life, which is in the midst of the paradise of God.

Re 22:2 In the midst of the street of it, and on either side of the river, *was there* the tree of life, which bare twelve *manner* of fruits, *and* yielded her fruit every month: and the leaves of the tree *were* for the healing of the nations.

Re 22:14 Blessed *are* they that do his commandments, that they may have right to the tree of life, and may enter in through the gates into the city.

See **HEAVEN**

TREES

1. Laws
Le 19:23; 27:30; De 16:21; 20:19; Re 8:7

2. Evil, *sinners compared to*
Ps 37:35; Eze 17:24; 31:8, 14; Da 4:11, 20; Am 2:9; Mt 3:10; 7:18; 12:33; 15:13; Lu 3:9; Jude 12

3. Saints as
Nu 24:6; Ps 1:3; 52:8; 92:12; Is 61:3; 65:22; Je 11:16; 17:8; Eze 47:7, 12; Ho 14:6, 8; Mt 7:17; 12:33

4. Varieties

a. Almond
Ex 37:19; Nu 17:8; Ec 12:5; Je 1:11

b. Aloes
Ps 45:8; Pr 7:17; Song 4:14; Jn 19:39

c. Apple
Song 2:3; 8:5

d. Ash
Is 44:14

e. Bay
Ps 37:35

f. Box
Is 41:19

g. Cedar
Nu 24:6; Jud 9:15; 1 K 4:33; 5:6, 10; 9:11; 10:27; 2 K 14:9; 2 Chr 1:15; 2:3, 8; 9:27; 25:18; Ezr 3:7; Ps 29:5; 80:10; 104:16; 148:9; Song 5:15; Is 2:13; 37:24;

41:19; 44:14; Je 22:7; Eze 17:3, 22; 27:5; Zec 11:2

h. Cedar of Lebanon
2 K 14:9; 2 Chr 2:8; Ps 92:12; Is 40:16; Ho 14:5

i. Chestnut
Eze 31:8

j. Cypress
1 K 6:15, 34; 9:11; 2 Chr 2:8; 3:5; Is 14:8; 37:24; 41:19; 44:14; 55:13; 60:13; Ho 14:8; Zec 11:2

k. Fig
De 8:8; Jud 9:10; 1 K 4:25; 2 K 18:31; Ps 105:33; Pr 27:18; Song 2:13; Is 36:16; Je 8:13; Jl 1:12; 2:22; Na 3:12; Hab 3:17; Hag 2:19; Mt 21:19; 24:32; Mk 11:13, 21; 13:28; Lu 13:6; 21:29; Jn 1:48; Ja 3:12; Re 6:13

l. Fir
Ps 104:17; Song 1:17; Eze 27:5; 31:8

m. Juniper
1 K 19:4

n. Mulberry
2 S 5:23

o. Myrtle
Ne 8:15; Is 41:19; 55:13; Zec 1:8

p. Oak
Jos 24:26; 1 K 13:14; Is 6:13; 44:14; Eze 27:6; Ho 4:13; Zec 11:2

q. Oil
Is 41:19

r. Olive
Ge 8:11; De 28:40; Jud 9:9; 1 K 6:23, 31; 1 Chr 27:28; Ps 52:8; Je 11:16; Ho 14:6; Am 4:9; Hab 3:17; Hag 2:19; Zec 4:3, 11; Ro 11:17; Re 11:4

s. Palm
Ex 15:27; Nu 33:9; De 34:3; 1 K 6:29; 2 Chr 3:5; Ps 92:12; Song 7:7; Je 10:5; Eze 40:16, 34; 41:18, 26; Jl 1:12

t. Pine

Is 41:19

u. Pomegranate

1 S 14:2

v. Shittah

Is 41:19

w. Sycamore

1 K 10:27; 1 Chr 27:28; 2 Chr 1:15; 9:27; Ps 78:47; Am 7:14; Lu 19:4

x. Teil

Is 6:13

y. Willows

Le 23:40; Jb 40:22; Ps 137:2; Is 15:7; 44:4; Eze 17:5

TRENCHES, *ramparts, entrenchments; primarily for the protection from enemies*

1 K 18:32

TRESPASS *See* **OFFERINGS**

TRIALS

See **TEMPTATION, TESTS**

TRINITY, *the holy*

Mt 28:19 Go ye therefore, and teach all nations, baptizing them in the name of the Father, and of the Son, and of the Holy Ghost:

Jn 14:26 But the Comforter, *which is* the Holy Ghost, whom the Father will send in my name, he shall teach you all things, and bring all things to your remembrance, whatsoever I have said unto you.

Jn 15:26 But when the Comforter is come, whom I will send unto you from the Father, *even* the Spirit of truth, which proceedeth from the Father, he shall testify of me:

2 Co 13:14 The grace of the Lord Jesus Christ, and the love of God, and the communion of the Holy Ghost, *be* with you all. Amen.

1 Pe 1:2 Elect according to the foreknowledge of God the Father, through sanctification of the Spirit, unto obedience and sprinkling of the blood of Jesus Christ: Grace unto you, and peace, be multiplied.

1 Jn 5:7 For there are three that bear record in heaven, the Father, the Word, and the Holy Ghost: and these three are one.

See **CHRIST, GOD, HOLY SPIRIT**

TROAS, *a city of Asia Minor*

This is the city where, in a night vision, Paul saw the man of Macedonia (Ac 16:8–11). It lies just ten miles southwest of ancient Troy. It is mentioned three other times in the New Testament (Ac 20:6; 2 Co 2:12; 2 Ti 4:13).

See **CITIES, PAUL**

TROPHIMUS, *an Ephesian Christian*

Ac 20:4; 21:29; 2 Ti 4:20

TROUBLE, *common to all*

2 K 4:27 And when she came to the man of God to the hill, she caught him by the feet: but Gehazi came near to thrust her away. And the man of God said, Let her alone; for her soul *is* vexed within her: and the Lord hath hid *it* from me, and hath not told me.

Jb 1:16 While he *was* yet speaking, there came also another, and said, The fire of God is fallen from heaven, and hath burned up the sheep, and the servants, and consumed them; and I only am escaped alone to tell thee.

Jb 3:26 I was not in safety, neither had I rest, neither was I quiet; yet trouble came.

Jb 5:7 Yet man is born unto trouble, as the sparks fly upward.

Jb 14:1 Man *that is* born of a woman is of few days, and full of trouble.

Jb 14:22 But his flesh upon him shall have pain, and his soul within him shall mourn.

Jb 15:24 Trouble and anguish shall make him afraid; they shall prevail against him, as a king ready to the battle.

Ps 6:6 I am weary with my groaning; all the night make I my bed to swim; I water my couch with my tears.

Ps 9:9 The Lord also will be a refuge for the oppressed, a refuge in times of trouble.

Ps 9:13 Have mercy upon me, O Lord; consider my trouble *which I suffer* of them that hate me, thou that liftest me up from the gates of death:

Ps 13:2 How long shall I take counsel in my soul, *having* sorrow in my heart daily? how long shall mine enemy be exalted over me?

Ps 22:11 Be not far from me; for trouble *is* near; for *there is* none to help.

Ps 25:17 The troubles of my heart are enlarged: O bring thou me out of my distresses.

Ps 31:9 Have mercy upon me, O Lord, for I am in trouble: mine eye is consumed with grief, *yea,* my soul and my belly.

Ps 69:17 And hide not thy face from thy servant; for I am in trouble: hear me speedily.

Ps 71:20 *Thou,* which hast shewed me great and sore troubles, shalt quicken me again, and shalt bring me up again from the depths of the earth.

Ps 77:4 Thou holdest mine eyes waking: I am so troubled that I cannot speak.

Ps 88:3 For my soul is full of troubles: and my life draweth nigh unto the grave.

Ps 102:2 Hide not thy face from me in the day *when* I am in trouble; incline thine ear unto me: in the day *when* I call answer me speedily.

Ps 116:3 The sorrows of death compassed me, and the pains of hell gat hold upon me: I found trouble and sorrow.

Ps 119:143 Trouble and anguish have taken hold on me: *yet* thy commandments *are* my delights.

Ps 142:2 I poured out my complaint before him; I shewed before him my trouble.

Ecc 2:23 For all his days *are* sorrows, and his travail grief; yea, his heart taketh not rest in the night. This is also vanity.

Ecc 5:17 All his days also he eateth in darkness, and *he hath* much sorrow and wrath with his sickness.

Ecc 7:14 In the day of prosperity be joyful, but in the day of adversity consider: God also hath set the one over against the other, to the end that man should find nothing after him.

Ecc 11:8 But if a man live many years, *and* rejoice in them all; yet let him remember the days of darkness; for they shall be many. All that cometh *is* vanity.

Is 22:5 For *it is* a day of trouble, and of treading down, and of perplexity by the Lord God of hosts in the valley of vision, breaking down the walls, and of crying to the mountains.

Is 37:3 And they said unto him, Thus saith Hezekiah, This day *is* a day of trouble, and of rebuke, and of blasphemy: for the children are come to the birth, and *there is* not strength to bring forth.

Is 38:17 Behold, for peace I had great bitterness: but thou hast in love to my soul *delivered it* from the pit of corruption: for thou hast cast all my sins behind thy back.

Je 8:15 We looked for peace, but no good *came; and* for a time of health, and behold trouble!

Je 20:18 Wherefore came I forth out of the womb to see labour and sorrow, that my days should be consumed with shame?

2 Co 1:4 Who comforteth us in all our tribulation, that we may be able to comfort them which are in any trouble, by the comfort wherewith we ourselves are comforted of God.

2 Co 5:4 For we that are in *this* tabernacle do groan, being burdened: not for that we would be unclothed, but clothed upon, that mortality might be swallowed up of life.

2 Ti 3:11 Persecutions, afflictions, which came unto me at Antioch, at Iconium, at Lystra; what persecutions I endured: but out of *them* all the Lord delivered me.

TRUMPETS *See* **MUSIC**

TRUST

1. In God, belief, confidence, and reliance in the person and work of God

a. Exhortations

Jud 11:11 Then Jephthah went with the elders of Gilead, and the people made him head and captain over them: and Jephthah uttered all his words before the LORD in Mizpeh.

Ne 4:14 And I looked, and rose up, and said unto the nobles, and to the rulers, and to the rest of the people, Be not ye afraid of them: remember the Lord, *which is* great and terrible, and fight for your brethren, your sons, and your daughters, your wives, and your houses.

Jb 35:14 Although thou sayest thou shalt not see him, *yet* judgment *is* before him; therefore trust thou in him.

Ps 4:5 Offer the sacrifices of righteousness, and put your trust in the LORD.

Ps 5:11 But let all those that put their trust in thee rejoice: let them ever shout for joy, because thou defendest them: let them also that love thy name be joyful in thee.

Ps 34:8 O taste and see that the LORD *is* good: blessed *is* the man *that* trusteth in him.

Ps 37:3 Trust in the LORD, and do good; *so* shalt thou dwell in the land, and verily thou shalt be fed.

Ps 37:5 Commit thy way unto the LORD; trust also in him; and he shall bring *it* to pass.

Ps 40:4 Blessed is that man that maketh the LORD his trust, and respecteth not the proud, nor such as turn aside to lies.

Ps 62:8 Trust in him at all times; *ye* people, pour out your heart before him: God *is* a refuge for us. Selah.

Ps 115:11 Ye that fear the LORD, trust in the LORD: he *is* their help and their shield.

Ps 118:8 *It is* better to trust in the LORD than to put confidence in man.

Pr 3:5 Trust in the LORD with all thine heart; and lean not unto thine own understanding.

Pr 16:3 Commit thy works unto the LORD, and thy thoughts shall be established.

Pr 16:20 He that handleth a matter wisely shall find good: and whoso trusteth in the LORD, happy *is* he.

Pr 22:19 That thy trust may be in the LORD, I have made known to thee this day, even to thee.

Is 26:4 Trust ye in the LORD for ever: for in the LORD JEHOVAH *is* everlasting strength:

Is 36:7 But if thou say to me, We trust in the LORD our God: *is it* not he, whose high places and whose altars Hezekiah hath taken away, and said to Judah and to Jerusalem, Ye shall worship before this altar?

Is 50:10 Who *is* among you that feareth the LORD, that obeyeth the voice of his servant, that walketh *in* darkness, and hath no light? let him trust in the name of the LORD, and stay upon his God.

Je 49:11 Leave thy fatherless children, I will preserve *them* alive; and let thy widows trust in me.

Zec 9:12 Turn you to the strong hold, ye prisoners of hope: even to day do I declare *that* I will render double unto thee;

Mt 10:10 Nor scrip for *your* journey, neither two coats, neither shoes, nor yet staves: for the workman is worthy of his meat.

Mk 6:8 And commanded them that they should take nothing for *their* journey, save a staff only; no scrip, no bread, no money in *their* purse:

Lu 9:3 And he said unto them, Take nothing for *your* journey, neither staves, nor scrip, neither bread, neither money; neither have two coats apiece.

Lu 10:4 Carry neither purse, nor scrip, nor shoes: and salute no man by the way.

Lu 12:24 Consider the ravens: for they neither sow nor reap; which neither have storehouse nor barn; and God feedeth them: how much more are ye better than the fowls?

1 Ti 6:17 Charge them that are rich in this world, that they be not highminded, nor trust in uncertain riches, but in the living God, who giveth us richly all things to enjoy;

b. Special Promises

2 S 22:31 *As for* God, his way *is* perfect; the word of the LORD *is* tried: he *is* a buckler to all them that trust in him.

Ps 2:12 Kiss the Son, lest he be angry, and ye perish *from* the way, when his wrath is kindled but a little. Blessed *are* all they that put their trust in him.

Ps 9:10 And they that know thy name will put their trust in thee: for thou, LORD, hast not forsaken them that seek thee.

Ps 17:7 Shew thy marvellous lovingkindness, O thou that savest by thy right hand them which put their trust *in thee* from those that rise up *against them.*

Ps 31:19 Oh how great *is* thy goodness, which thou hast laid up for them that fear thee; *which* thou hast wrought for them that trust in thee before the sons of men!

Ps 32:10 Many sorrows *shall be* to the wicked: but he that trusteth in the LORD, mercy shall compass him about.

Ps 34:22 The LORD redeemeth the soul of his servants: and none of them that trust in him shall be desolate.

Ps 37:40 And the LORD shall help them and deliver them: he shall deliver them from the wicked, and save them, because they trust in him.

Ps 84:12 O LORD of hosts, blessed *is* the man that trusteth in thee.

Ps 125:1 They that trust in the LORD *shall be* as mount Zion, *which* cannot be removed, *but* abideth for ever.

Pr 28:25 He that is of a proud heart stirreth up strife: but he that putteth his trust in the LORD shall be made fat.

Pr 29:25 The fear of man bringeth a snare: but whoso putteth his trust in the LORD shall be safe.

Pr 30:5 Every word of God *is* pure: he *is* a shield unto them that put their trust in him.

Is 26:3 Thou wilt keep *him* in perfect peace, *whose* mind *is* stayed *on thee:* because he trusteth in thee.

Is 57:13 When thou criest, let thy companies deliver thee; but the wind shall carry them all away; vanity shall take *them:* but he that putteth his trust in me shall possess the land, and shall inherit my holy mountain;

Je 17:7 Blessed *is* the man that trusteth in the LORD, and whose hope the LORD is.

Na 1:7 The LORD *is* good, a strong hold in the day of trouble; and he knoweth them that trust in him.

1 Ti 5:5 Now she that is a widow indeed, and desolate, trusteth in God, and continueth in supplications and prayers night and day.

c. Examples

Ge 24:14 And let it come to pass, that the damsel to whom I shall say, Let down thy pitcher, I pray thee, that I may drink; and she shall say, Drink, and I will give thy camels drink also: *let the same be* she *that* thou hast appointed for thy servant Isaac; and thereby shall I know that thou hast shewed kindness unto my master.

Ge 31:42 Except the God of my father, the God of Abraham, and the fear of Isaac, had been with me, surely thou hadst sent me away now empty. God hath seen mine affliction and the labour of my hands, and rebuked *thee* yesternight.

Ge 32:12 And thou saidst, I will surely do thee good, and make thy seed as the sand of the sea, which cannot be numbered for multitude.

Ge 43:14 And God Almighty give you mercy before the man, that he may send away your other brother, and Benjamin. If I be bereaved *of my children,* I am bereaved.

Ex 17:9 And Moses said unto Joshua, Choose us out men, and go out, fight with Amalek: to morrow I will stand on the stand on the top of the hill with the rod of God in mine hand.

1 S 14:12 The men of the garrison answered Jonathan and his armourbearer, and said, Come up to us, and we will shew you a thing. And Jonathan said unto his armourbearer, Come up after me: for the LORD hath delivered them into the hand of Israel.

1 S 17:46 This day will the LORD deliver thee into mine hand; and I will smite thee, and take thine head from thee; and I will give the carcases of the host of the Philistines this day unto the fowls of the air, and to the wild beasts of the earth; that all the earth may know that there is a God in Israel.

1 S 26:24 And, behold, as thy life was much set by this day in mine eyes, so let my life be much set by in the eyes of the LORD, and let him deliver me out of all tribulation.

1 S 30:6 And David was greatly distressed; for the people spake of stoning him, because the soul of all the people was grieved, every man for his sons and for his daughters: but David encouraged himself in the LORD his God.

2 S 10:12 Be of good courage, and let us play the men for our people, and for the cities of our God: and the LORD do that which seemeth him good.

2 S 16:12 It may be that the LORD will look on mine affliction, and that the LORD will requite me good for his cursing this day.

2 S 22:3 The God of my rock; in him will I trust: *he is* my shield, and the horn of my salvation, my high tower, and my refuge, my saviour; thou savest me from violence.

2 K 3:11 But Jehoshaphat said, *Is there* not here a prophet of the LORD, that we may enquire of the LORD by him? And one of the king of Israel's servants answered and said, Here *is* Elisha the son of Shaphat, which poured water on the hands of Elijah.

2 K 6:16 And he answered, Fear not: for they that *be* with us *are* more than they that *be* with them.

2 K 18:5 He trusted in the LORD God of Israel; so that after him was none like him among all the kings of Judah, nor *any* that were before him.

2 K 19:4 It may be the LORD thy God will hear all the words of Rab-shakeh, whom the king of Assyria his master hath sent to reproach the living God; and will reprove the words which the LORD thy God hath heard: wherefore lift up *thy* prayer for the remnant that are left.

1 Chr 5:20 And they were helped against them, and the Hagarites were delivered into their hand, and all that *were* with them: for they cried to God in the battle, and he was intreated of them; because they put their trust in him.

1 Chr 19:13 Be of good courage, and let us behave ourselves valiantly for our people, and for the cities of our God: and let the LORD do *that which is* good in his sight.

2 Chr 14:11 And Asa cried unto the LORD his God, and said, LORD, *it is* nothing with thee to help, whether with many, or with them that have no power: help us, O LORD our God; for we rest on thee, and in thy name we go against this multitude. O LORD, thou *art* our God; let not man prevail against thee.

2 Chr 20:12 O our God, wilt thou not judge them? for we have no might against this great company that cometh against us; neither know we what to do: but our eyes *are* upon thee.

2 Chr 32:8 With him *is* an arm of flesh; but with us *is* the LORD our God to help us, and to fight our battles. And the people rested themselves upon the words of Hezekiah king of Judah.

Ne 2:4 Then the king said unto me, For what dost thou make request? So I prayed to the God of heaven.

Ne 4:4 Hear, O our God; for we are despised: and turn their reproach upon their own head, and give them for a prey in the land of captivity:

Ne 6:9 For they all made us afraid, saying, Their hands shall be weakened from the work, that it be not done. Now therefore, *O God*, strengthen my hands.

Jb 13:15 Though he slay me, yet will I trust in him: but I will maintain mine own ways before him.

Jb 23:6 Will he plead against me with *his* great power? No; but he would put *strength* in me.

Ps 4:8 I will both lay me down in peace, and sleep: for thou, LORD, only makest me dwell in safety.

Ps 7:1 O Lord my God, in thee do I put my trust: save me from all them that persecute me, and deliver me:

Ps 11:1 In the LORD put I my trust: How say ye to my soul, Flee *as* a bird to your mountain?

Ps 13:5 But I have trusted in thy mercy; my heart shall rejoice in thy salvation.

Ps 16:1 Preserve me, O God: for in thee do I put my trust.

Ps 18:2 The LORD *is* my rock, and my fortress, and my deliverer; my God, my strength, in whom I will trust; my buckler, and the horn of my salvation, *and* my high tower.

Ps 20:5 We will rejoice in thy salvation, and in the name of our God we will set up *our* banners: the LORD fulfil all thy petitions.

Ps 21:1 The king shall joy in thy strength, O LORD; and in thy salvation how greatly shall he rejoice!

Ps 21:7 For the king trusteth in the LORD, and through the mercy of the most High he shall not be moved.

Ps 22:4 Our fathers trusted in thee: they trusted, and thou didst deliver them.

Ps 25:2 O my God, I trust in thee: let me not be ashamed, let not mine enemies triumph over me.

Ps 25:20 O keep my soul, and deliver me: let me not be ashamed; for I put my trust in thee.

Ps 26:1 Judge me, O LORD; for I have walked in mine integrity: I have trusted also in the LORD; *therefore* I shall not slide.

Ps 27:1 The LORD *is* my light and my salvation; whom shall I fear? the LORD *is* the strength of my life; of whom shall I be afraid?

Ps 28:7 The LORD *is* my strength and my shield; my heart trusted in him, and I am helped: therefore my heart greatly rejoiceth; and with my song will I praise him.

Ps 31:1 In thee, O LORD, do I put my trust; let me never be ashamed: deliver me in thy righteousness.

Ps 31:14 But I trusted in thee, O LORD: I said, Thou *art* my God.

Ps 33:21 For our heart shall rejoice in him, because we have trusted in his holy name.

Ps 36:7 How excellent *is* thy lovingkindness, O God! therefore the children of men put their trust under the shadow of thy wings.

Ps 42:8 *Yet* the LORD will command his lovingkindness in the daytime, and in the night his song *shall be* with me, *and* my prayer unto the God of my life.

Ps 44:5 Through thee will we push down our enemies: through thy name will we tread them under that rise up against us.

Ps 52:8 But I *am* like a green olive tree in the house of God: I trust in the mercy of God for ever and ever.

Ps 55:16 As for me, I will call upon God; and the LORD shall save me.

Ps 56:3 What time I am afraid, I will trust in thee.

Ps 57:1 Be merciful unto me, O God, be merciful unto me: for my soul trusteth in thee: yea, in the shadow of thy wings will I make my refuge, until *these* calamities be overpast.

Ps 64:10 The righteous shall be glad in the LORD, and shall trust in him; and all the upright in heart shall glory.

Ps 71:5 For thou *art* my hope, O Lord GOD: *thou art* my trust from my youth.

Ps 73:28 But *it is* good for me to draw near to God: I have put my trust in the Lord GOD, that I may declare all thy works.

Ps 86:2 Preserve my soul; for I *am* holy: O thou my God, save thy servant that trusteth in thee.

Ps 91:2 I will say of the LORD, *He is* my refuge and my fortress: my God; in him will I trust.

Ps 112:7 He shall not be afraid of evil tidings: his heart is fixed, trusting in the LORD.

Ps 119:42 So shall I have wherewith to answer him that reproacheth me: for I trust in thy word.

Ps 141:8 But mine eyes *are* unto thee, O GOD the Lord: in thee is my trust; leave not my soul destitute.

Ps 143:8 Cause me to hear thy lovingkindness in the morning; for in thee do I trust: cause me to know the way wherein I should walk; for I lift up my soul unto thee.

Ps 144:2 My goodness, and my fortress; my high tower, and my deliverer; my shield, and *he* in whom I trust; who subdueth my people under me.

Is 10:20 And it shall come to pass in that day, *that* the remnant of Israel, and such as are escaped of the house of Jacob, shall no more again stay upon him that smote them; but shall stay upon the LORD, the Holy One of Israel, in truth.

Is 12:2 Behold, God *is* my salvation; I will trust, and not be afraid: for the LORD JEHOVAH *is* my strength and *my* song; he also is become my salvation.

Is 17:7 At that day shall a man look to his Maker, and his eyes shall have respect to the Holy One of Israel.

Is 38:14 Like a crane *or* a swallow, so did I chatter: I did mourn as a dove: mine eyes fail *with looking* upward: O LORD, I am oppressed; undertake for me.

Is 50:7 For the Lord GOD will help me; therefore shall I not be confounded: therefore have I set my face like a flint, and I know that I shall not be ashamed.

Je 11:20 But, O LORD of hosts, that judgest righteously, that triest the reins and the heart, let me see thy vengeance on them: for unto thee have I revealed my cause.

Je 14:22 Are there *any* among the vanities of the Gentiles that can cause rain? or can the heavens give showers? *art* not thou he, O LORD our God? therefore we will wait upon thee: for thou hast made all these *things*.

Je 18:19 Give heed to me, O LORD, and hearken to the voice of them that contend with me.

Je 39:18 For I will surely deliver thee, and thou shalt not fall by the sword, but thy life shall be for a prey unto thee: because thou hast put thy trust in me, saith the LORD.

Da 3:28 *Then* Nebuchadnezzar spake, and said, Blessed *be* the God of Shadrach, Meshach, and Abed-nego, who hath sent his angel, and delivered his servants that trusted in him, and have changed the king's word, and yielded their bodies, that they might not serve nor worship any god, except their own God.

Mi 7:7 Therefore I will look unto the LORD; I will wait for the God of my salvation: my God will hear me.

Hab 3:18 Yet I will rejoice in the LORD, I will joy in the God of my salvation.

Zep 3:12 I will also leave in the midst of thee an afflicted and poor people, and they shall trust in the name of the LORD.

Mk 14:36 And he said, Abba, Father, all things *are* possible unto thee; take away this cup from me: nevertheless not what I will, but what thou wilt.

2 Co 1:9 But we had the sentence of death in ourselves, that we should not trust in ourselves, but in God which raiseth the dead:

2 Co 5:6 Therefore *we are* always confident, knowing that, whilst we are at home in the body, we are absent from the Lord:

1 Ti 4:10 For therefore we both labour and suffer reproach, because we trust in the living God, who is the Saviour of all men, specially of those that believe.

2 Ti 1:12 For the which cause I also suffer these things: nevertheless I am not ashamed: for I know whom I have believed, and am persuaded that he is able to keep that which I have committed unto him against that day.

He 2:13 And again, I will put my trust in him. And again, Behold I and the children which God hath given me.

He 11:23 By faith Moses, when he was born, was hid three months of his parents, because they saw *he was* a proper child; and they were not afraid of the king's commandment.

d. By Committal into God's Hands

Jb 5:8; Ps 31:5; 37:5; Lu 23:46; Ac 7:59; 20:32; 2 Ti 1:12; 1 Pe 2:23; 4:19

2. In Works, *for salvation*

Lu 18:12 I fast twice in the week, I give tithes of all that I possess.

Ro 9:32 Wherefore? Because *they sought it* not by faith, but as it were by the works of the law. For they stumbled at that stumblingstone;

Ro 10:3 For they being ignorant of God's righteousness, and going about to establish their own righteousness, have not submitted themselves unto the righteousness of God.

Ga 2:21 I do not frustrate the grace of God: for if righteousness *come* by the law, then Christ is dead in vain.

Ga 3:10 For as many as are of the works of the law are under the curse: for it is written, Cursed *is* every one that continueth not in all things which are written in the book of the law to do them.

Ga 4:21 Tell me, ye that desire to be under the law, do ye not hear the law?

Ga 5:4 Christ is become of no effect unto you, whosoever of you are justified by the law; ye are fallen from grace

See **FAITH, FAITHFULNESS, STEADFASTNESS**

TRUTH, *that which is trustworthy, genuine, conforming to reality*

1. Its Preciousness

Jb 23:12 Neither have I gone back from the commandment of his lips; I have esteemed the words of his mouth more than my necessary *food.*

Ps 19:10 More to be desired *are they* than gold, yea, than much fine gold: sweeter also than honey and the honeycomb.

Ps 119:14 I have rejoiced in the way of thy testimonies, as *much as* in all riches.

Ps 119:72 The law of thy mouth *is* better unto me than thousands of gold and silver.

Ps 119:127 Therefore I love thy commandments above gold; yea, above fine gold.

Ps 119:162 I rejoice at thy word, as one that findeth great spoil.

Ps 139:17 How precious also are thy thoughts unto me, O God! how great is the sum of them!

Pr 3:15 She *is* more precious than rubies: and all the things thou canst desire are not to be compared unto her.

Pr 23:23 Buy the truth, and sell *it* not; *also* wisdom, and instruction, and understanding.

2 Ti 2:15 Study to shew thyself approved unto God, a workman that needeth not to be ashamed, rightly dividing the word of truth.

2. Attitude of the Wicked

Is 59:4 None calleth for justice, nor *any* pleadeth for truth: they trust in vanity, and speak lies; they conceive mischief, and bring forth iniquity.

Je 9:5 And they will deceive every one his neighbour, and will not speak the truth: they have taught their tongue to speak lies, *and* weary themselves to commit iniquity.

Ga 3:1 O foolish Galatians, who hath bewitched you, that ye should not obey the truth, before whose eyes Jesus Christ hath been evidently set forth, crucified among you?

2 Th 2:10 And with all deceivableness of unrighteousness in them that perish; because they received not the love of the truth, that they might be saved.

2 Ti 3:8 Now as Jannes and Jambres withstood Moses, so do these also resist the truth: men of corrupt minds, reprobate concerning the faith.

1 Ti 6:5 Perverse disputings of men of corrupt minds, and destitute of the truth, supposing that gain is godliness: from such withdraw thyself.

3. Found in Christ

Is 42:3 A bruised reed shall he not break, and the smoking flax shall he not quench: he shall bring forth judgment unto truth.

Mk 12:14 And when they were come, they say unto him, Master, we know that thou art true, and carest for no man: for thou regardest not the person of men, but teachest the way of God in truth: Is it lawful to give tribute to Caesar, or not?

Lu 20:21 And they asked him, saying, Master, we know that thou sayest and teachest rightly, neither acceptest thou the person *of any,* but teachest the way of God truly:

Jn 1:14 And the Word was made flesh, and dwelt among us, (and we beheld his glory, the glory as of the only begotten of the Father,) full of grace and truth.

Jn 1:17 For the law was given by Moses, *but* grace and truth came by Jesus Christ.

Jn 7:18 He that speaketh of himself seeketh his own glory: but he that seeketh his glory that sent him, the same is true, and no unrighteousness is in him.

Jn 8:14 Jesus answered and said unto them, Though I bear record of myself, *yet* my record is true: for I know whence I came, and whither I go; but ye cannot tell whence I come, and whither I go.

Jn 8:40 But now ye seek to kill me, a man that hath told you the truth, which I have heard of God: this did not Abraham.

Jn 8:45 And because I tell *you* the truth, ye believe me not.

Jn 14:6 Jesus saith unto him, I am the way, the truth, and the life: no man cometh unto the Father, but by me.

Jn 18:37 Pilate therefore said unto him, Art thou a king then? Jesus answered, Thou sayest that I am a king. To this end was I born, and for this cause came I into the world, that I should bear witness unto the truth. Every one that is of the truth heareth my voice.

2 Co 11:10 As the truth of Christ is in me, no man shall stop me of this boasting in the regions of Achaia.

Ep 4:21 If so be that ye have heard him, and have been taught by him, as the truth is in Jesus:

1 Jn 5:20 *And* we know that the Son of God is come, and hath given us an understanding, that we may know him that is true, and we are in him that is true, *even* in his Son Jesus Christ. This is the true God, and eternal life.

Re 3:7 And to the angel of the church in Philadelphia write; These things saith he that is holy, he that is true, he that hath the key of David, he that openeth, and no man shutteth; and shutteth, and no man openeth;

Re 3:14 And unto the angel of the church of the Laodiceans write; These things saith the Amen, the faithful and true witness, the beginning of the creation of God;

Re 19:11 And I saw heaven opened, and behold a white horse; and he that sat upon him *was* called Faithful and True, and in righteousness he doth judge and make war.

4. Found in God

Ex 34:6 And the LORD passed by before him, and proclaimed, The LORD, The LORD God, merciful and gracious, longsuffering, and abundant in goodness and truth,

Nu 23:19 God *is* not a man, that he should lie; neither the son of man, that he should repent: hath he said, and shall he not do *it?* or hath he spoken, and shall he not make it good?

De 32:4 *He is* the Rock, his work *is* perfect: for all his ways *are* judgment: a God of truth and without iniquity, just and right *is* he.

Jos 21:45 There failed not ought of any good thing which the LORD had spoken unto the house of Israel; all came to pass.

1 S 15:29 And also the Strength of Israel will not lie nor repent: for he *is* not a man, that he should repent.

2 S 7:28 And now, O Lord GOD, thou *art* that God, and thy words be true, and thou hast promised this goodness unto thy servant:

Ps 19:9 The fear of the LORD *is* clean, enduring for ever: the judgments of the LORD *are* true *and* righteous altogether.

Ps 31:5 Into thine hand I commit my spirit: thou hast redeemed me, O LORD God of truth.

Ps 33:4 For the word of the LORD *is* right; and all his works *are done* in truth.

Ps 40:11 Withhold not thou thy tender mercies from me, O LORD: let thy lovingkindness and thy truth continually preserve me.

Ps 57:10 For thy mercy is great unto the heavens, and thy truth unto the clouds.

Ps 86:15 But thou, O Lord, *art* a God full of compassion, and gracious, longsuffering, and plenteous in mercy and truth.

Ps 89:14 Justice and judgment *are* the habitation of thy throne: mercy and truth shall go before thy face.

Ps 89:35 Once have I sworn by my holiness that I will not lie unto David.

Ps 91:4 He shall cover thee with his feathers, and under his wings shalt thou trust: his truth *shall be thy* shield and buckler.

Ps 96:13 Before the LORD: for he cometh, for he cometh to judge the earth: he shall judge the world with righteousness, and the people with his truth.

Ps 100:5 For the LORD *is* good; his mercy *is* everlasting; and his truth *endureth* to all generations.

Ps 108:4 For thy mercy *is* great above the heavens: and thy truth *reacheth* unto the clouds.

Ps 111:7 The works of his hands *are* verity and judgment; all his commandments *are* sure.

Ps 115:1 Not unto us, O LORD, not unto us, but unto thy name give glory, for thy mercy, *and* for thy truth's sake.

Ps 117:2 For his merciful kindness is great toward us: and the truth of the LORD *endureth* for ever. Praise ye the LORD.

Ps 119:160 Thy word *is* true *from* the beginning: and every one of thy righteous judgments *endureth* for ever.

Ps 138:2 I will worship toward thy holy temple, and praise thy name for thy lovingkindness and for thy truth: for thou hast magnified thy word above all thy name.

Ps 146:6 Which made heaven, and earth, the sea, and all that therein *is:* which keepeth truth for ever:

Is 65:16 That he who blesseth himself in the earth shall bless himself in the God of truth; and he that sweareth in the earth shall swear by the God of truth; because the former troubles are forgotten, and because they are hid from mine eyes.

Je 10:10 But the LORD *is* the true God, he *is* the living God, and an everlasting king: at his wrath the earth shall tremble, and the nations shall not be able to abide his indignation.

Lam 2:17 The LORD hath done *that* which he had devised; he hath fulfilled his word that he had commanded in the days of old: he hath thrown down, and hath not pitied: and he hath caused *thine* enemy to rejoice over thee, he hath set up the horn of thine adversaries.

Da 4:37 Now I Nebuchadnezzar praise and extol and honour the King of heaven, all whose works *are* truth, and his ways judgment: and those that walk in pride he is able to abase.

Mi 7:20 Thou wilt perform the truth to Jacob, *and* the mercy to Abraham, which thou hast sworn unto our fathers from the days of old.

Jn 3:33 He that hath received his testimony hath set to his seal that God is true.

Jn 7:28 Then cried Jesus in the temple as he taught, saying, Ye both know me, and ye know whence I am: and I am not come of myself, but he that sent me is true, whom ye know not.

Jn 8:26 I have many things to say and to judge of you: but he that sent me is true; and I speak to the world those things which I have heard of him.

Ro 2:2 But we are sure that the judgment of God is according to truth against them which commit such things.

Ro 3:4 God forbid: yea, let God be true, but every man a liar; as it is written, That thou mightest be justified in thy sayings, and mightest overcome when thou art judged.

Ro 3:7 For if the truth of God hath more abounded through my lie unto his glory; why yet am I also judged as a sinner?

Tit 1:2 In hope of eternal life, which God, that cannot lie, promised before the world began;

He 6:18 That by two immutable things, in which *it was* impossible for God to lie, we might have a strong consolation, who have fled for refuge to lay hold upon the hope set before us:

1 Jn 5:20 *And* we know that the Son of God is come, and hath given us an understanding, that we may know him that is true, and we are in him that is true, *even* in his Son Jesus Christ. This is the true God, and eternal life.

Re 15:3 And they sing the song of Moses the servant of God, and the song of the Lamb, saying, Great and marvellous *are* thy works, Lord God Almighty; just and true *are* thy ways, thou King of saints.

5. Truthfulness

Ge 42:16 Send one of you, and let him fetch your brother, and ye shall be kept in prison, that your words may be proved, whether *there be any* truth in you: or else by the life of Pharaoh surely ye *are* spies.

Ex 23:7 Keep thee far from a false matter; and the innocent and righteous slay thou not: for I will not justify the wicked.

De 23:23 That which is gone out of thy lips thou shalt keep and perform; *even* a freewill offering, according as thou hast vowed unto the Lord thy God, which thou hast promised with thy mouth.

Jos 6:22 But Joshua had said unto the two men that had spied out the country, Go into the harlot's house, and bring out thence the woman, and all that she hath, as ye sware unto her.

Jos 9:18 And the children of Israel smote them not, because the princes of the congregation had sworn unto them by the Lord God of Israel. And all the congregation murmured against the princes.

1 K 17:24 And the woman said to Elijah, Now by this I know that thou *art* a man of God, *and* that the word of the Lord in thy mouth *is* truth.

1 K 22:16 And the king said unto him, How many times shall I adjure thee that thou tell me nothing but *that which is* true in the name of the Lord?

2 Chr 18:15 And the king said to him, How many times shall I adjure thee that thou say nothing but the truth to me in the name of the Lord?

Ne 5:13 Also I shook my lap, and said, So God shake out every man from his house, and from his labour, that performeth not this promise, even thus be he shaken out, and emptied. And all the congregation said, Amen, and praised the Lord. And the people did according to this promise.

Jb 6:28 Now therefore be content, look upon me; for *it is* evident unto you if I lie.

Jb 36:4 For truly my words *shall* not *be* false: he that is perfect in knowledge *is* with thee.

Ps 15:2 He that walketh uprightly, and worketh righteousness, and speaketh the truth in his heart.

Ps 24:4 He that hath clean hands, and a pure heart; who hath not lifted up his soul unto vanity, nor sworn deceitfully.

Ps 51:6 Behold, thou desirest truth in the inward parts: and in the hidden *part* thou shalt make me to know wisdom.

Ps 119:29 Remove from me the way of lying: and grant me thy law graciously.

Pr 3:3 Let not mercy and truth forsake thee: bind them about thy neck; write them upon the table of thine heart:

Pr 8:7 For my mouth shall speak truth; and wickedness *is* an abomination to my lips.

Pr 12:19 The lip of truth shall be established for ever: but a lying tongue *is* but for a moment.

Pr 14:5 A faithful witness will not lie: but a false witness will utter lies.

Pr 14:25 A true witness delivereth souls: but a deceitful *witness* speaketh lies.

Pr 16:13 Righteous lips *are* the delight of kings; and they love him that speaketh right.

Pr 30:8 Remove far from me vanity and lies: give me neither poverty nor riches; feed me with food convenient for me:

Is 63:8 For he said, Surely they *are* my people, children *that* will not lie: so he was their Saviour.

Je 4:2 And thou shalt swear, The Lord liveth, in truth, in judgment, and in righteousness; and the nations shall bless themselves in him, and in him shall they glory.

Je 5:1 Run ye to and fro through the streets of Jerusalem, and see now, and know, and seek in the broad places thereof, if ye can find a man, if there be *any* that executeth judgment, that seeketh the truth; and I will pardon it.

Zep 3:13 The remnant of Israel shall not do iniquity, nor speak lies; neither shall a deceitful tongue be found in their mouth: for they shall feed and lie down, and none shall make *them* afraid.

Zec 8:16 These *are* the things that ye shall do; Speak ye every man the truth to his neighbour; execute the judgment of truth and peace in your gates:

Mal 2:6 The law of truth was in his mouth, and iniquity was not found in his lips: he walked with me in peace and equity, and did turn many away from iniquity.

Mk 5:33 But the woman fearing and trembling, knowing what was done in her, came and fell down before him, and told him all the truth.

Jn 1:20 And he confessed, and denied not; but confessed, I am not the Christ.

Jn 10:41 And many resorted unto him, and said, John did no miracle: but all things that John spake of this man were true.

Jn 19:35 And he that saw *it* bare record, and his record is true: and he knoweth that he saith true, that ye might believe.

Jn 21:24 This is the disciple which testifieth of these things, and wrote these things: and we know that his testimony is true.

Ac 26:25 But he said, I am not mad, most noble Festus; but speak forth the words of truth and soberness.

Ro 9:1 I say the truth in Christ, I lie not, my conscience also bearing me witness in the Holy Ghost,

2 Co 1:18 But *as* God *is* true, our word toward you was not yea and nay.

2 Co 4:2 But have renounced the hidden things of dishonesty, not walking in craftiness, nor handling the word of God deceitfully; but by manifestation of the truth commending ourselves to every man's conscience in the sight of God.

2 Co 7:14 For if I have boasted any thing to him of you, I am not ashamed; but as we spake all things to you in truth, even so our boasting, which *I made* before Titus, is found a truth.

2 Co 11:10 As the truth of Christ is in me, no man shall stop me of this boasting in the regions of Achaia.

2 Co 11:31 The God and Father of our Lord Jesus Christ, which is blessed for evermore, knoweth that I lie not.

2 Co 12:6 For though I would desire to glory, I shall not be a fool; for I will say the truth: but *now* I forbear, lest any man should think of me above that which he seeth me *to be,* or *that* he heareth of me.

Ga 1:20 Now the things which I write unto you, behold, before God, I lie not.

Ga 4:16 Am I therefore become your enemy, because I tell you the truth?

Ep 4:15 But speaking the truth in love, may grow up into him in all things, which is the head, *even* Christ:

Ep 4:25 Wherefore putting away lying, speak every man truth with his neighbour: for we are members one of another.

Ep 5:9 (For the fruit of the Spirit is in all goodness and righteousness and truth;)

Ep 6:14 Stand therefore, having your loins girt about with truth, and having on the breastplate of righteousness;

Ph 4:8 Finally, brethren, whatsoever things are true, whatsoever things *are* honest, whatsoever things *are* just, whatsoever things *are* pure, whatsoever things *are* lovely, whatsoever things *are* of good report; if *there be* any virtue, and if *there be* any praise, think on these things.

1 Ti 2:7 Whereunto I am ordained a preacher, and an apostle, (I speak the truth in Christ, *and* lie not;) a teacher of the Gentiles in faith and verity.

Tit 1:13 This witness is true. Wherefore rebuke them sharply, that they may be sound in the faith;

Ja 5:12 But above all things, my brethren, swear not, neither by heaven, neither by the earth, neither by any other oath: but let your yea be yea; and *your* nay, nay; lest ye fall into condemnation.

2 Pe 1:16 For we have not followed cunningly devised fables, when we made known unto you the power and coming of our Lord Jesus Christ, but were eyewitnesses of his majesty.

3 Jn 12 Demetrius hath good report of all *men*, and of the truth itself: yea, and we *also* bear record; and ye know that our record is true.

6. Adaptation

THE USE OF PARABLES
Mk 4:33 And with many such parables spake he the word unto them, as they were able to hear *it*.

HUMAN WEAKNESS NECESSITATES
Jn 16:12 I have yet many things to say unto you, but ye cannot bear them now.

FEEDING THE LAMBS
Jn 21:15 So when they had dined, Jesus saith to Simon Peter, Simon, *son* of Jonas, lovest thou me more than these? He saith unto him, Yea, Lord; thou knowest that I love thee. He saith unto him, Feed my lambs.

SIMPLE TRUTH FOR THE IMMATURE
1 Co 3:2 I have fed you with milk, and not with meat: for hitherto ye were not able *to bear it*, neither yet now are ye able.

PAUL'S EXAMPLE
1 Co 9:22 To the weak became I as weak, that I might gain the weak: I am made all things to all *men*, that I might by all means save some.

SOME UNABLE TO RECEIVE DEEPER TRUTHS
He 5:12 For when for the time ye ought to be teachers, ye have need that one teach you again which *be* the first principles of the oracles of God; and are become such as have need of milk, and not of strong meat.

DIFFERENT MESSAGES TO DIFFERENT GROUPS
1 Jn 2:13 I write unto you, fathers, because ye have known him *that is* from the beginning. I write unto you, young men, because ye have overcome the wicked one. I write unto you, little children, because ye have known the Father.

7. Channels, *Holy Spirit speaks through believers*

Mt 10:20 For it is not ye that speak, but the Spirit of your Father which speaketh in you.

Mk 13:11 But when they shall lead *you,* and deliver you up, take no thought beforehand what ye shall speak, neither do ye premeditate: but whatsoever shall be given you in that hour, that speak ye: for it is not ye that speak, but the Holy Ghost.

Jn 1:23 He said, I *am* the voice of one crying in the wilderness, Make straight the way of the Lord, as said the prophet Esaias.

Jn 7:38 He that believeth on me, as the scripture hath said, out of his belly shall flow rivers of living water.

Ac 2:17 And it shall come to pass in the last days, saith God, I will pour out of my Spirit upon all flesh: and your sons and your daughters shall prophesy, and your young men shall see visions, and your old men shall dream dreams:

Ac 4:25 Who by the mouth of thy servant David hast said, Why did the heathen rage, and the people imagine vain things?

Ac 10:22 And they said, Cornelius the centurion, a just man, and one that feareth God, and of good report among all the nation of the Jews, was warned from God by an holy angel to send for thee into his house, and to hear words of thee.

1 Co 2:13 Which things also we speak, not in the words which man's wisdom teacheth, but which the Holy Ghost teacheth; comparing spiritual things with spiritual.

1 Pe 4:11 If any man speak, *let him speak* as the oracles of God; if any man minister, *let him do it* as of the ability which God giveth: that God in all things may be glorified through Jesus

Christ, to whom be praise and dominion for ever and ever. Amen.

2 Pe 1:21 For the prophecy came not in old time by the will of man: but holy men of God spake *as they were* moved by the Holy Ghost.

8. Eagerness

A JEWISH RULER

Mk 10:17 And when he was gone forth into the way, there came one running, and kneeled to him, and asked him, Good Master, what shall I do that I may inherit eternal life?

THE COMMON PEOPLE

Mk 12:37 David therefore himself calleth him Lord; and whence is he *then* his son? And the common people heard him gladly.

ATTENDANTS UPON THE TEMPLE

Lu 21:38 And all the people came early in the morning to him in the temple, for to hear him.

THE SAMARITANS

Jn 4:40 So when the Samaritans were come unto him, they besought him that he would tarry with them: and he abode there two days.

CORNELIUS AND HIS FAMILY

Ac 10:33 Immediately therefore I sent to thee; and thou hast well done that thou art come. Now therefore are we all here present before God, to hear all things that are commanded thee of God.

THE GENTILES AT ANTIOCH

Ac 13:42 And when the Jews were gone out of the synagogue, the Gentiles besought that these words might be preached to them the next sabbath.

THE BEREANS

Ac 17:11 These were more noble than those in Thessalonica, in that they received the word with all readiness of mind, and searched the scriptures daily, whether those things were so.

9. Misunderstood

CHRIST'S BODILY TEMPLE CONFUSED WITH THE EARTHLY TEMPLE

Jn 2:20 Then said the Jews, Forty and six years was this temple in building, and wilt thou rear it up in three days?

THE NEW BIRTH CONFUSED WITH THE PHYSICAL BIRTH

Jn 3:4 Nicodemus saith unto him, How can a man be born when he is old? can he enter the second time into his mother's womb, and be born?

THE WATER OF LIFE CONFUSED WITH PHYSICAL WATER

Jn 4:15 The woman saith unto him, Sir, give me this water, that I thirst not, neither come hither to draw.

SPIRITUAL NOURISHMENT CONFUSED WITH FOOD

Jn 4:33 Therefore said the disciples one to another, Hath any man brought him *ought* to eat?

ABSORBING CHRIST'S SPIRIT CONFUSED WITH EATING HIS BODY AND DRINKING HIS BLOOD

Jn 6:52 The Jews therefore strove among themselves, saying, How can this man give us *his* flesh to eat?

CHRIST'S DEPARTURE CONFUSED WITH SUICIDE

Jn 8:22 Then said the Jews, Will he kill himself? because he saith, Whither I go, ye cannot come.

SPIRITUAL BONDAGE CONFUSED WITH PHYSICAL SLAVERY

Jn 8:33 They answered him, We be Abraham's seed, and were never in bondage to any man: how sayest thou, Ye shall be made free?

See **DECEPTION, FALSEHOOD, SELF-DECEPTION**

TUBAL

1. Son of Japheth

Ge 10:2

2. Land
Is 66:19; Eze 27:13; 32:26; 38:2

TUMULTS, *a disorderly commotion or disturbance*
Ps 2:1; 74:23; 83:2; Is 37:29; Am 3:9; Mt 27:24; Mk 5:38; 14:2; Ac 17:5; 19:29, 34, 40; 21:30, 34; 23:9; 1 Co 14:33; 2 Co 6:5; 12:20; Ja 3:16

See **QUIETNESS**

TURTLEDOVES See **BIRDS**

TUTORS, *guardians, teachers*
2 K 10:1; Ac 22:3; Ga 4:2

See **TEACHER**

TWILIGHT, *the subdued light just after sunset, or just before sunrise*
1 S 30:17; 2 K 7:5; Jb 3:9; Eze 12:6

TWINS
Ge 25:24; 38:27

TYCHICUS, *one of Paul's companions*
Ac 20:4; Ep 6:21; Col 4:7; 2 Ti 4:12; Tit 3:12

TYPES AND SHADOWS, *Old Testament persons or events that anticipate Christ or a specific New Testament teaching*
He 8:5; 10:1

TYRE, *a city of Phoenicia*
Jos 19:29; 2 S 5:11; 24:7; 1 K 5:1; 7:13; 9:11; Ne 13:16; Ps 45:12; 87:4; Is 23:1, 5, 15; Eze 26:2, 15; 27:3, 8, 32; Jl 3:4; Am 1:9; Zec 9:3; Mt 11:21; 15:21; Mk 7:24, 31; Lu 6:17; 10:13; Ac 12:20; 21:3

See **CITIES**

U

ULAI *See* **RIVERS**

ULCERS *See* **DISEASE**

UNASHAMED, *the righteous*

Ps 69:6 Let not them that wait on thee, O Lord GOD of hosts, be ashamed for my sake: let not those that seek thee be confounded for my sake, O God of Israel.

Ps 71:1 In thee, O LORD, do I put my trust: let me never be put to confusion.

Ps 74:21 O let not the oppressed return ashamed: let the poor and needy praise thy name.

Ps 119:6 Then shall I not be ashamed, when I have respect unto all thy commandments.

Ps 119:31 I have stuck unto thy testimonies: O LORD, put me not to shame.

Is 50:7 For the Lord GOD will help me; therefore shall I not be confounded: therefore have I set my face like a flint, and I know that I shall not be ashamed.

Jl 2:26 And ye shall eat in plenty, and be satisfied, and praise the name of the LORD your God, that hath dealt wondrously with you: and my people shall never be ashamed.

Ro 9:33 As it is written, Behold, I lay in Sion a stumblingstone and rock of offence: and whosoever believeth on him shall not be ashamed.

Ph 1:20 According to my earnest expectation and *my* hope, that in nothing I shall be ashamed, but *that* with all boldness, as always, *so* now also Christ shall be magnified in my body, whether *it be* by life, or by death.

1 Pe 4:16 Yet if *any man suffer* as a Christian, let him not be ashamed; but let him glorify God on this behalf.

1 Jn 2:28 And now, little children, abide in him; that, when he shall appear, we may have confidence, and not be ashamed before him at his coming.

See **SHAME, SHAMELESSNESS**

UNBELIEF, *little or no trust, skeptical*

1. Of Religious Men

ABRAHAM, *when promised a child in old age*

Ge 17:17 Then Abraham fell upon his face, and laughed, and said in his heart, Shall *a child* be born unto him that is an hundred years old? and shall Sarah, that is ninety years old, bear?

MOSES, *when told the Israelites should be fed*

Nu 11:21 And Moses said, The people, among whom I *am, are* six hundred thousand footmen; and thou hast said, I will give them flesh, that they may eat a whole month.

Nu 20:12 And the LORD spake unto Moses and Aaron, Because ye believed me not, to sanctify me in the eyes of the children of Israel, therefore ye shall not bring this congregation into the land which I have given them.

THE DISCIPLES, *in failing to heal a demoniac*

Mt 17:19–20 Then came the disciples to Jesus apart, and said, Why could not we cast him out?

And Jesus said unto them, Because of your unbelief: for verily I say unto you, If ye have faith as a grain of mustard seed, ye shall say unto this mountain, Remove hence to yonder place; and it shall remove; and nothing shall be impossible unto you.

ZACHARIAS, *when promised that he should have a great son*

Lu 1:20 And, behold, thou shalt be dumb, and not able to speak, until the day that these things shall be performed, because thou believest not my words, which shall be fulfilled in their season.

THE DISCIPLES, *when told of the resurrection of Christ*

Lu 24:11 And their words seemed to them as idle tales, and they believed them not.

2. Examples

Ge 19:14 And Lot went out, and spake unto his sons in law, which married his daughters, and said, Up, get you out of this place; for the LORD will destroy this city. But he seemed as one that mocked unto his sons in law.

Ex 9:21 And he that regarded not the word of the LORD left his servants and his cattle in the field.

De 1:27 And ye murmured in your tents, and said, Because the LORD hated us, he hath brought us forth out of the land of Egypt, to deliver us into the hand of the Amorites, to destroy us.

2 K 7:2 Then a lord on whose hand the king leaned answered the man of God, and said, Behold, *if* the LORD would make windows in heaven, might this thing be? And he said, Behold, thou shalt see *it* with thine eyes, but shalt not eat thereof.

2 K 17:14 Notwithstanding they would not hear, but hardened their necks, like to the neck of their fathers, that did not believe in the LORD their God.

Ps 78:19 Yea, they spake against God; they said, Can God furnish a table in the wilderness?

Ps 78:32 For all this they sinned still, and believed not for his wondrous works.

Is 5:19 That say, Let him make speed, *and* hasten his work, that we may see it: and let the counsel of the Holy One of Israel draw nigh and come, that we may know *it!*

Is 53:1 Who hath believed our report? and to whom is the arm of the LORD revealed?

Je 5:12 They have belied the LORD, and said, *It is* not he; neither shall evil come upon us; neither shall we see sword nor famine:

Je 43:2 Then spake Azariah the son of Hoshaiah, and Johanan the son of Kareah, and all the proud men, saying unto Jeremiah, Thou speakest falsely: the LORD our God hath not sent thee to say, Go not into Egypt to sojourn there:

Eze 8:12 Then said he unto me, Son of man, hast thou seen what the ancients of the house of Israel do in the dark, every man in the chambers of his imagery? for they say, The LORD seeth us not; the LORD hath forsaken the earth.

Mt 13:58 And he did not many mighty works there because of their unbelief.

Mt 21:32 For John came unto you in the way of righteousness, and ye believed him not: but the publicans and the harlots believed him: and ye, when ye had seen *it,* repented not afterward, that ye might believe him.

Mt 27:64 Command therefore that the sepulchre be made sure until the third day, lest his disciples come by night, and steal him away, and say unto the people, He is risen from the dead: so the last error shall be worse than the first.

Mk 15:32 Let Christ the King of Israel descend now from the cross, that we may see and believe. And they that were crucified with him reviled him.

Lu 22:67 Art thou the Christ? tell us. And he said unto them, If I tell you, ye will not believe:

Lu 23:39 And one of the malefactors which were hanged railed on him, saying, If thou be Christ, save thyself and us.

Jn 3:11 Verily, verily, I say unto thee, We speak that we do know, and testify that we have seen; and ye receive not our witness.

Jn 4:48 Then said Jesus unto him, Except ye see signs and wonders, ye will not believe.

Jn 6:64 But there are some of you that believe not. For Jesus knew from the beginning who they were that believed not, and who should betray him.

Jn 7:5 For neither did his brethren believe in him.

Jn 10:25 Jesus answered them, I told you, and ye believed not: the works that I do in my Father's name, they bear witness of me.

Jn 12:37 But though he had done so many miracles before them, yet they believed not on him:

Ac 13:41 Behold, ye despisers, and wonder, and perish: for I work a work in your days, a work which ye shall in no wise believe, though a man declare it unto you.

Ac 19:9 But when divers were hardened, and believed not, but spake evil of that way before the multitude, he departed from them, and separated the disciples, disputing daily in the school of one Tyrannus.

Ac 23:8 For the Sadducees say that there is no resurrection, neither angel, nor spirit: but the Pharisees confess both.

Ro 10:16 But they have not all obeyed the gospel. For Esaias saith, Lord, who hath believed our report?

2 Pe 3:4 And saying, Where is the promise of his coming? for since the fathers fell asleep, all things continue as *they were* from the beginning of the creation.

3. Warnings

Ex 17:7 And he called the name of the place Massah, and Meribah, because of the chiding of the children of Israel, and because they tempted the LORD, saying, Is the LORD among us, or not?

Nu 14:11 And the LORD said unto Moses, How long will this people provoke me? and how long will it be ere they believe me, for all the signs which I have shewed among them?

De 1:32 Yet in this thing ye did not believe the LORD your God,

De 9:23 Likewise when the LORD sent you from Kadesh-barnea, saying, Go up and possess the land which I have given you; then ye rebelled against the commandment of the LORD your God, and ye believed him not, nor hearkened to his voice.

De 32:20 And he said, I will hide my face from them, I will see what their end *shall be:* for they *are* a very froward generation, children in whom *is* no faith.

2 Chr 16:7 And at that time Hanani the seer came to Asa king of Judah, and said unto him, Because thou hast relied on the king of Syria, and not relied on the LORD thy God, therefore is the host of the king of Syria escaped out of thine hand.

Ps 4:6 *There be* many that say, Who will shew us *any* good? LORD, lift thou up the light of thy countenance upon us.

Ps 78:22 Because they believed not in God, and trusted not in his salvation:

Ps 106:24 Yea, they despised the pleasant land, they believed not his word:

Is 7:9 And the head of Ephraim *is* Samaria, and the head of Samaria *is* Remaliah's son. If ye will not believe, surely ye shall not be established.

Eze 9:9 Then said he unto me, The iniquity of the house of Israel and Judah *is* exceeding great, and the land is full of blood, and the city full of perverseness: for they say, The LORD hath forsaken the earth, and the LORD seeth not.

Eze 11:2 Then said he unto me, Son of man, these *are* the men that devise mischief, and give wicked counsel in this city:

Eze 12:22 Son of man, what *is* that proverb *that* ye have in the land of Israel, saying, The days are prolonged, and every vision faileth?

Ho 8:12 I have written to him the great things of my law, *but* they were counted as a strange thing.

Hab 1:5 Behold ye among the heathen, and regard, and wonder marvellously: for *I* will work a work in your days, *which* ye will not believe, though it be told *you.*

Zep 3:2 She obeyed not the voice; she received not correction; she trusted not in the LORD; she drew not near to her God.

Mt 21:25 The baptism of John, whence was it? from heaven, or of men? And they reasoned with themselves, saying, If we shall say, From heaven; he will say unto us, Why did ye not then believe him?

Mt 27:42 He saved others; himself he cannot save. If he be the King of Israel, let him now come down from the cross, and we will believe him.

Mk 4:40 And he said unto them, Why are ye so fearful? how is it that ye have no faith?

Mk 6:6 And he marvelled because of their unbelief. And he went round about the villages, teaching.

Mk 16:14 Afterward he appeared unto the eleven as they sat at meat, and upbraided them with their unbelief and hardness of heart, because they believed not them which had seen him after he was risen.

Lu 9:41 And Jesus answering said, O faithless and perverse generation, how long shall I be with you, and suffer you? Bring thy son hither.

Lu 16:31 And he said unto him, If they hear not Moses and the prophets, neither will they be persuaded, though one rose from the dead.

Jn 3:18 He that believeth on him is not condemned: but he that believeth not is condemned already, because he hath not believed in the name of the only begotten Son of God.

Jn 3:36 He that believeth on the Son hath everlasting life: and he that believeth not the Son shall not see life; but the wrath of God abideth on him.

Jn 5:47 But if ye believe not his writings, how shall ye believe my words?

Jn 6:36 But I said unto you, That ye also have seen me, and believe not.

Jn 8:24 I said therefore unto you, that ye shall die in your sins: for if ye believe not that I am *he*, ye shall die in your sins.

Jn 12:38 That the saying of Esaias the prophet might be fulfilled, which he spake, Lord, who hath believed our report? and to whom hath the arm of the Lord been revealed?

Jn 16:8–9 And when he is come, he will reprove the world of sin, and of righteousness, and of judgment:

Of sin, because they believe not on me;

Ac 17:5 But the Jews which believed not, moved with envy, took unto them certain lewd fellows of the baser sort, and gathered a company, and set all the city on an uproar, and assaulted the house of Jason, and sought to bring them out to the people.

Ro 3:3 For what if some did not believe? shall their unbelief make the faith of God without effect?

Ro 11:20 Well; because of unbelief they were broken off, and thou standest by faith. Be not highminded, but fear:

Ro 11:30 For as ye in times past have not believed God, yet have now obtained mercy through their unbelief:

2 Th 2:12 That they all might be damned who believed not the truth, but had pleasure in unrighteousness.

2 Ti 2:13 If we believe not, *yet* he abideth faithful: he cannot deny himself.

He 3:12 Take heed, brethren, lest there be in any of you an evil heart of unbelief, in departing from the living God.

He 3:19 So we see that they could not enter in because of unbelief.

He 4:2 For unto us was the gospel preached, as well as unto them: but the word preached did not profit them, not being mixed with faith in them that heard *it*.

He 4:6 Seeing therefore it remaineth that some must enter therein, and they to whom it was first preached entered not in because of unbelief:

He 4:11 Let us labour therefore to enter into that rest, lest any man fall after the same example of unbelief.

He 11:6 But without faith *it is* impossible to please *him*: for he that cometh to God must believe that he is, and *that* he is a rewarder of them that diligently seek him.

1 Pe 2:7 Unto you therefore which believe *he is* precious: but unto them which be disobedient, the stone which the builders disallowed, the same is made the head of the corner,

1 Jn 5:10 He that believeth on the Son of God hath the witness in himself: he that believeth not God hath made him a liar; because he believeth not the record that God gave of his Son.

Jude 5 I will therefore put you in remembrance, though ye once knew this, how that the Lord, having saved the people out of the land of Egypt, afterward destroyed them that believed not.

See **FAITH, TRUST**

UNBELIEVERS

1. Exhortations

Ps 78:22 Because they believed not in God, and trusted not in his salvation:

Mk 2:7 Why doth this *man* thus speak blasphemies? who can forgive sins but God only?

Mk 5:35 While he yet spake, there came from the ruler of the synagogue's *house certain* which said, Thy daughter is dead: why troublest thou the Master any further?

Lu 8:12 Those by the way side are they that hear; then cometh the devil, and taketh away the word out of their hearts, lest they should believe and be saved.

Lu 8:53 And they laughed him to scorn, knowing that she was dead.

Lu 12:46 The lord of that servant will come in a day when he looketh not for *him,* and at an hour when he is not aware, and will cut him in sunder, and will appoint him his portion with the unbelievers.

Jn 3:18 He that believeth on him is not condemned: but he that believeth not is condemned already, because he hath not believed in the name of the only begotten Son of God.

Jn 4:48 Then said Jesus unto him, Except ye see signs and wonders, ye will not believe.

Jn 5:38 And ye have not his word abiding in you: for whom he hath sent, him ye believe not.

Jn 6:30 They said therefore unto him, What sign shewest thou then, that we may see, and believe thee? what dost thou work?

Jn 6:64 But there are some of you that believe not. For Jesus knew from the beginning who they were that be-

lieved not, and who should betray him.

Jn 8:45 And because I tell *you* the truth, ye believe me not.

Jn 9:18 But the Jews did not believe concerning him, that he had been blind, and received his sight, until they called the parents of him that had received his sight.

Jn 10:26 But ye believe not, because ye are not of my sheep, as I said unto you.

Jn 11:46 But some of them went their ways to the Pharisees, and told them what things Jesus had done.

Jn 12:47 And if any man hear my words, and believe not, I judge him not: for I came not to judge the world, but to save the world.

Jn 18:38 Pilate saith unto him, What is truth? And when he had said this, he went out again unto the Jews, and saith unto them, I find in him no fault *at all.*

Ac 14:2 But the unbelieving Jews stirred up the Gentiles, and made their minds evil affected against the brethren.

Ac 28:24 And some believed the things which were spoken, and some believed not.

Ro 15:31 That I may be delivered from them that do not believe in Judaea; and that my service which *I have* for Jerusalem may be accepted of the saints;

1 Co 6:6 But brother goeth to law with brother, and that before the unbelievers.

1 Co 7:12 But to the rest speak I, not the Lord: If any brother hath a wife that believeth not, and she be pleased to dwell with him, let him not put her away.

1 Co 14:22 Wherefore tongues are for a sign, not to them that believe, but to them that believe not: but prophesying *serveth* not for them that believe not, but for them which believe.

2 Co 4:4 In whom the god of this world hath blinded the minds of them which believe not, lest the light of the glorious gospel of Christ, who is the image of God, should shine unto them.

2 Co 6:14 Be ye not unequally yoked together with unbelievers: for what fellowship hath righteousness with unrighteousness? and what communion hath light with darkness?

2 Th 3:2 And that we may be delivered from unreasonable and wicked men: for all *men* have not faith.

1 Ti 5:8 But if any provide not for his own, and specially for those of his own house, he hath denied the faith, and is worse than an infidel.

2 Ti 3:8 Now as Jannes and Jambres withstood Moses, so do these also resist the truth: men of corrupt minds, reprobate concerning the faith.

Tit 1:15 Unto the pure all things *are* pure: but unto them that are defiled and unbelieving *is* nothing pure; but even their mind and conscience is defiled.

Tit 2:8 Sound speech, that cannot be condemned; that he that is of the contrary part may be ashamed, having no evil thing to say of you.

Jude 5 I will therefore put you in remembrance, though ye once knew this, how that the Lord, having saved the people out of the land of Egypt, afterward destroyed them that believed not.

Re 21:8 But the fearful, and unbelieving, and the abominable, and murderers, and whoremongers, and sorcerers, and idolaters, and all liars, shall have their part in the lake which burneth with fire and brimstone: which is the second death.

2. Described

THEIR LIFETIME SPENT IN VANITY

Ps 78:32-33 For all this they sinned still, and believed not for his wondrous works.

Therefore their days did he consume in vanity, and their years in trouble.

ALREADY CONDEMNED

Jn 3:18 He that believeth on him is not condemned: but he that believeth not is condemned already, because he hath not believed in the name of the only begotten Son of God.

DIE IN THEIR SINS

Jn 8:24 I said therefore unto you, that ye shall die in your sins: for if ye believe not that I am *he,* ye shall die in your sins.

SHALL BE JUDGED BY GOD'S WORD
IN THE LAST DAY

Jn 12:48 He that rejecteth me, and receiveth not my words, hath one that judgeth him: the word that I have spoken, the same shall judge him in the last day.

ARE BLINDED BY THE GOD OF THIS WORLD

2 Co 4:4 In whom the god of this world hath blinded the minds of them which believe not, lest the light of the glorious gospel of Christ, who is the image of God, should shine unto them.

WILL BE CLASSED WITH OTHER
SINNERS IN ETERNITY

Re 21:8 But the fearful, and unbelieving, and the abominable, and murderers, and whoremongers, and sorcerers, and idolaters, and all liars, shall have their part in the lake which burneth with fire and brimstone: which is the second death.

See **CONDEMNATION, HELL**

UNCERTAINTIES, *beliefs which are questionable, doubtful*

BEAUTY

Ps 39:11 When thou with rebukes dost correct man for iniquity, thou makest his beauty to consume away like a moth: surely every man *is* vanity. Selah.

Pr 31:30 Favour *is* deceitful, and beauty *is* vain: *but* a woman *that* feareth the LORD, she shall be praised.

MEN'S PROMISES

Ps 146:3 Put not your trust in princes, *nor* in the son of man, in whom *there is* no help.

RICHES

Pr 23:5 Wilt thou set thine eyes upon that which is not? for *riches* certainly make themselves wings; they fly away as an eagle toward heaven.

THE FUTURE

Pr 27:1 Boast not thyself of to morrow; for thou knowest not what a day may bring forth.

FRIENDSHIP

Jn 16:32 Behold, the hour cometh, yea, is now come, that ye shall be scattered, every man to his own, and shall leave me alone: and yet I am not alone, because the Father is with me.

LIFE

Ja 4:14 Whereas ye know not what *shall be* on the morrow. For what *is* your life? It is even a vapour, that appeareth for a little time, and then vanisheth away.

EARTHLY GLORY

1 Pe 1:24 For all flesh *is* as grass, and all the glory of man as the flower of grass. The grass withereth, and the flower thereof falleth away:

See **CERTAINTIES**

UNCHARITABLENESS *See* EVIL, LOVE

UNCIRCUMCISED, *figuratively, those whose hearts do not belong to God*

Ge 34:14; Ex 6:12; 12:48; Jud 14:3; 15:18; 1 S 14:6; 17:26, 36; 31:4; 2 S 1:20; Is 52:1; Je 9:26; Eze 28:10; 31:18; 32:19, 26, 32; 44:7; Ac 11:3; Ep 2:11

See **SEPARATION**

UNCLEANNESS, *ceremonial*

Le 7:20; 12:2, 5; 13:3, 8, 11, 14, 22, 25, 30, 36, 45, 55; 14:46; 15:3, 7, 10, 18, 25, 31; 16:16; 18:19; 22:3; Nu 9:10; 19:8, 13; De 23:10; 1 S 20:26; 2 Chr 30:18

See **CLEANSING, IMPURITY**

UNCLOTHED, *figurative*

Eze 16:7, 22; Ho 2:3, 9; Na 3:5; Mt 22:11; 2 Co 5:3; Re 3:17; 16:15

UNDERSTANDING

1. Spiritual Comprehension

Ex 31:3 And I have filled him with the spirit of God, in wisdom, and in understanding, and in knowledge, and in all manner of workmanship,

Ex 35:31 And he hath filled him with the spirit of God, in wisdom, in understanding, and in knowledge, and in all manner of workmanship;

Ex 36:1 Then wrought Bezaleel and Aholiab, and every wise hearted man, in whom the LORD put wisdom and understanding to know how to work all manner of work for the service of the sanctuary, according to all that the Lord had commanded.

De 4:6 Keep therefore and do *them;* for this *is* your wisdom and your understanding in the sight of the nations, which shall hear all these statutes, and say, Surely this great nation *is* a wise and understanding people.

1 K 3:9 Give therefore thy servant an understanding heart to judge thy people, that I may discern between good and bad: for who is able to judge this thy so great a people?

1 K 4:29 And God gave Solomon wisdom and understanding exceeding much, and largeness of heart, even as the sand that *is* on the sea shore.

1 Chr 12:32 And of the children of Issachar, *which were men* that had understanding of the times, to know what Israel ought to do; the heads of them *were* two hundred; and all their brethren *were* at their commandment.

1 Chr 22:12 Only the LORD give thee wisdom and understanding, and give thee charge concerning Israel, that thou mayest keep the law of the LORD thy God.

2 Chr 1:10 Give me now wisdom and knowledge, that I may go out and come in before this people: for who can judge this thy people, *that is so* great?

2 Chr 2:12 Huram said moreover, Blessed *be* the LORD God of Israel, that made heaven and earth, who hath given to David the king a wise son, endued with prudence and understanding, that might build an house for the LORD, and an house for his kingdom.

2 Chr 26:5 And he sought God in the days of Zechariah, who had understanding in the visions of God: and as long as he sought the LORD, God made him to prosper.

Ezr 8:16 Then sent I for Eliezer, for Ariel, for Shemaiah, and for Elnathan, and for Jarib, and for Elnathan, and for Nathan, and for Zechariah, and for Meshullam, chief men; also for Joiarib, and for Elnathan, men of understanding.

Ezr 8:18 And by the good hand of our God upon us they brought us a man of understanding, of the sons of Mahli, the son of Levi, the son of Israel; and Sherebiah, with his sons and his brethren, eighteen;

Ne 8:12 And all the people went their way to eat, and to drink, and to send portions, and to make great mirth, because they had understood the words that were declared unto them.

Ne 10:28 And the rest of the people, the priests, the Levites, the porters, the singers, the Nethinims, and all they that had separated themselves from the people of the lands unto the law of God, their wives, their sons, and their daughters, every one having knowledge, and having understanding;

Jb 12:3 But I have understanding as well as you; I *am* not inferior to you: yea, who knoweth not such things as these?

Jb 12:12 With the ancient *is* wisdom; and in length of days understanding.

Jb 13:1 Lo, mine eye hath seen all *this,* mine ear hath heard and understood it.

Jb 28:28 And unto man he said, Behold, the fear of the Lord, that *is* wisdom; and to depart from evil *is* understanding.

Jb 34:16 If now *thou hast* understanding, hear this: hearken to the voice of my words.

Ps 49:3 My mouth shall speak of wisdom; and the meditation of my heart *shall be* of understanding.

Ps 107:43 Whoso *is* wise, and will observe these *things,* even they shall understand the lovingkindness of the LORD.

Ps 111:10 The fear of the LORD *is* the beginning of wisdom: a good understanding have all they that do *his commandments:* his praise endureth for ever.

Ps 119:34 Give me understanding, and I shall keep thy law; yea, I shall observe it with *my* whole heart.

Ps 119:100 I understand more than the ancients, because I keep thy precepts.

Ps 119:104 Through thy precepts I get understanding: therefore I hate every false way.

Ps 119:125 I *am* thy servant; give me understanding, that I may know thy testimonies.

Ps 119:169 Let my cry come near before thee, O LORD: give me understanding according to thy word.

Pr 1:5 A wise *man* will hear, and will increase learning; and a man of understanding shall attain unto wise counsels:

Pr 2:2 So that thou incline thine ear unto wisdom, *and* apply thine heart to understanding;

Pr 2:6 For the LORD giveth wisdom: out of his mouth *cometh* knowledge and understanding.

Pr 3:13 Happy *is* the man *that* findeth wisdom, and the man *that* getteth understanding.

Pr 4:7 Wisdom *is* the principal thing; *therefore* get wisdom: and with all thy getting get understanding.

Pr 7:4 Say unto wisdom, Thou *art* my sister; and call understanding *thy* kinswoman:

Pr 8:14 Counsel *is* mine, and sound wisdom: I *am* understanding; I have strength.

Pr 11:12 He that is void of wisdom despiseth his neighbour: but a man of understanding holdeth his peace.

Pr 13:15 Good understanding giveth favour: but the way of transgressors *is* hard.

Pr 14:6 A scorner seeketh wisdom, and *findeth it* not: but knowledge *is* easy unto him that understandeth.

Pr 14:29 *He that is* slow to wrath *is* of great understanding: but *he that is* hasty of spirit exalteth folly.

Pr 14:33 Wisdom resteth in the heart of him that hath understanding: but *that which is* in the midst of fools is made known.

Pr 15:14 The heart of him that hath understanding seeketh knowledge: but the mouth of fools feedeth on foolishness.

Pr 16:16 How much better *is it* to get wisdom than gold! and to get understanding rather to be chosen than silver!

Pr 16:22 Understanding *is* a wellspring of life unto him that hath it: but the instruction of fools *is* folly.

Pr 17:24 Wisdom *is* before him that hath understanding; but the eyes of a fool *are* in the ends of the earth.

Pr 17:27 He that hath knowledge spareth his words: *and* a man of understanding is of an excellent spirit.

Pr 19:8 He that getteth wisdom loveth his own soul: *he that* keepeth understanding shall find good.

Pr 20:5 Counsel in the heart of man *is like* deep water; but a man of understanding will draw it out.

Pr 24:3 Through wisdom is an house builded; and by understanding it is established:

Pr 28:5 Evil men understand not judgment: but they that seek the LORD understand all *things*.

Pr 28:11 The rich man *is* wise in his own conceit; but the poor that hath understanding searcheth him out.

Is 32:4 The heart also of the rash shall understand knowledge, and the tongue of the stammerers shall be ready to speak plainly.

Is 43:10 Ye *are* my witnesses, saith the LORD, and my servant whom I have chosen: that ye may know and believe me, and understand that I *am* he: before me there was no God formed, neither shall there be after me.

Je 9:12 Who *is* the wise man, that may understand this? and *who is he* to whom the mouth of the LORD hath spoken, that he may declare it, for what the land perisheth *and* is burned up like a wilderness, that none passeth through?

Da 1:20 And in all matters of wisdom *and* understanding, that the king enquired of them, he found them ten times better than all the magicians *and* astrologers that *were* in all his realm.

Da 4:34 And at the end of the days I Nebuchadnezzar lifted up mine eyes unto heaven, and mine understanding returned unto me, and I blessed the most High, and I praised and honoured him that liveth for ever, whose dominion *is* an everlasting dominion, and his kingdom *is* from generation to generation:

Da 5:12 Forasmuch as an excellent spirit, and knowledge, and understanding, interpreting of dreams, and shewing of hard sentences, and dissolving of doubts, were found in the same Daniel, whom the king named Belteshazzar: now let Daniel be called, and he will shew the interpretation.

Da 5:14 I have even heard of thee, that the spirit of the gods *is* in thee, and *that* light and understanding and excellent wisdom is found in thee.

Da 10:1 In the third year of Cyrus king of Persia a thing was revealed unto Daniel, whose name was called Belteshazzar; and the thing *was* true, but the time appointed *was* long: and he understood the thing, and had understanding of the vision.

Da 11:33 And they that understand among the people shall instruct many: yet they shall fall by the sword, and by flame, by captivity, and by spoil, *many* days.

Ho 14:9 Who *is* wise, and he shall understand these *things?* prudent, and he shall know them? for the ways of the LORD *are* right, and the just shall walk in them: but the transgressors shall fall therein.

Mt 13:23 But he that received seed into the good ground is he that heareth the word, and understandeth *it;* which also beareth fruit, and bringeth forth, some an hundredfold, some sixty, some thirty.

Mt 13:51 Jesus saith unto them, Have ye understood all these things? They say unto him, Yea, Lord.

Mt 15:10 And he called the multitude, and said unto them, Hear, and understand:

Mt 16:12 Then understood they how that he bade *them* not beware of the leaven of bread, but of the doctrine of the Pharisees and of the Sadducees.

Mt 24:15 When ye therefore shall see the abomination of desolation, spoken of by Daniel the prophet, stand in the holy place, (whoso readeth, let him understand:)

Mk 12:34 And when Jesus saw that he answered discreetly, he said unto him, Thou art not far from the kingdom of God. And no man after that durst ask him *any question.*

Mk 13:29 So ye in like manner, when ye shall see these things come to pass, know that it is nigh, *even* at the doors.

Ac 13:7 Which was with the deputy of the country, Sergius Paulus, a prudent man; who called for Barnabas and Saul, and desired to hear the word of God.

1 Co 14:15 What is it then? I will pray with the spirit, and I will pray with the understanding also: I will sing with the spirit, and I will sing with the understanding also.

Ep 3:4 Whereby, when ye read, ye may understand my knowledge in the mystery of Christ)

Ep 3:18 May be able to comprehend with all saints what *is* the breadth, and length, and depth, and height;

Ep 5:17 Wherefore be ye not unwise, but understanding what the will of the Lord *is.*

Col 1:9 For this cause we also, since the day we heard *it,* do not cease to pray for you, and to desire that ye might be filled with the knowledge of his will in all wisdom and spiritual understanding;

2 Ti 2:7 Consider what I say; and the Lord give thee understanding in all things.

Ja 3:13 Who *is* a wise man and endued with knowledge among you? let him shew out of a good conversation his works with meekness of wisdom.

2. No Comprehension

De 32:28 For they *are* a nation void of counsel, neither *is there any* understanding in them.

Job 4:21 Doth not their excellency *which is* in them go away? they die, even without wisdom.

Job 11:12 For vain man would be wise, though man be born *like* a wild ass's colt.

Job 17:4 For thou hast hid their heart from understanding: therefore shalt thou not exalt *them.*

Job 32:9 Great men are not *always* wise: neither do the aged understand judgment.

Ps 14:4 Have all the workers of iniquity no knowledge? who eat up my people *as* they eat bread, and call not upon the LORD.

Ps 32:9 Be ye not as the horse, *or* as the mule, *which* have no understanding: whose mouth must be held in with bit and bridle, lest they come near unto thee.

Ps 49:20 Man *that is* in honour, and understandeth not, is like the beasts *that* perish.

Ps 82:5 They know not, neither will they understand; they walk on in darkness: all the foundations of the earth are out of course.

Ps 92:6 A brutish man knoweth not; neither doth a fool understand this.

Pr 7:7 And beheld among the simple ones, I discerned among the youths, a young man void of understanding,

Pr 9:16 Whoso *is* simple, let him turn in hither: and *as for* him that wanteth understanding, she saith to him,

Pr 10:13 In the lips of him that hath understanding wisdom is found: but a rod *is* for the back of him that is void of understanding.

Pr 10:21 The lips of the righteous feed many: but fools die for want of wisdom.

Pr 12:11 He that tilleth his land shall be satisfied with bread: but he that followeth vain *persons is* void of understanding.

Pr 17:18 A man void of understanding striketh hands, *and* becometh surety in the presence of his friend.

Pr 18:2 A fool hath no delight in understanding, but that his heart may discover itself.

Pr 24:30 I went by the field of the slothful, and by the vineyard of the man void of understanding;

Pr 28:5 Evil men understand not judgment: but they that seek the LORD understand all *things*.

Pr 28:16 The prince that wanteth understanding *is* also a great oppressor: *but* he that hateth covetousness shall prolong *his* days.

Pr 30:2 Surely I *am* more brutish than *any* man, and have not the understanding of a man.

Is 5:13 Therefore my people are gone into captivity, because *they have* no knowledge: and their honourable men *are* famished, and their multitude dried up with thirst.

Is 26:11 LORD, *when* thy hand is lifted up, they will not see: *but* they shall see, and be ashamed for *their* envy at the people; yea, the fire of thine enemies shall devour them.

Is 27:11 When the boughs thereof are withered, they shall be broken off: the women come, *and* set them on fire: for it *is* a people of no understanding: therefore he that made them will not have mercy on them, and he that formed them will shew them no favour.

Is 29:12 And the book is delivered to him that is not learned, saying, Read this, I pray thee: and he saith, I am not learned.

Is 44:19 And none considereth in his heart, neither *is there* knowledge nor understanding to say, I have burned part of it in the fire; yea, also I have baked bread upon the coals thereof; I have roasted flesh, and eaten *it:* and shall I make the residue thereof an abomination? shall I fall down to the stock of a tree?

Is 45:20 Assemble yourselves and come; draw near together, ye *that are* escaped of the nations: they have no knowledge that set up the wood of their graven image, and pray unto a god *that* cannot save.

Je 4:22 For my people *is* foolish, they have not known me; they *are* sottish children, and they have none understanding: they *are* wise to do evil, but to do good they have no knowledge.

Je 5:21 Hear now this, O foolish people, and without understanding; which have eyes, and see not; which have ears, and hear not:

Je 49:7 Concerning Edom, thus saith the LORD of hosts; *Is* wisdom no more in Teman? is counsel perished from the prudent? is their wisdom vanished?

Da 9:13 As *it is* written in the law of Moses, all this evil is come upon us: yet made we not our prayer before the LORD our God, that we might turn from our iniquities, and understand thy truth.

Ho 4:14 I will not punish your daughters when they commit whoredom, nor your spouses when they commit adultery: for themselves are separated with whores, and they sacrifice with harlots: therefore the people *that* doth not understand shall fall.

Ho 7:11 Ephraim also is like a silly dove without heart: they call to Egypt, they go to Assyria.

Mi 4:12 But they know not the thoughts of the LORD, neither understand they his counsel: for he shall gather them as the sheaves into the floor.

Mt 13:14 And in them is fulfilled the prophecy of Esaias, which saith, By hearing ye shall hear, and shall not understand; and seeing ye shall see, and shall not perceive:

Mt 13:19 When any one heareth the word of the kingdom, and understandeth *it* not, then cometh the wicked *one,* and catcheth away that which was sown in his heart. This is he which received seed by the way side.

Mt 15:17 Do not ye yet understand, that whatsoever entereth in at the mouth goeth into the belly, and is cast out into the draught?

Mt 16:9 Do ye not yet understand, neither remember the five loaves of the five thousand, and how many baskets ye took up?

Mt 16:22 Then Peter took him, and began to rebuke him, saying, Be it far from thee, Lord: this shall not be unto thee.

Mt 26:9 For this ointment might have been sold for much, and given to the poor.

Mt 26:61 And said, This *fellow* said, I am able to destroy the temple of God, and to build it in three days.

Mk 4:12 That seeing they may see, and not perceive; and hearing they may hear, and not understand; lest at any time they should be converted, and *their* sins should be forgiven them.

Mk 6:52 For they considered not *the miracle* of the loaves: for their heart was hardened.

Mk 8:17 And when Jesus knew *it,* he saith unto them, Why reason ye, because ye have no bread? perceive ye not yet, neither understand? have ye your heart yet hardened?

Mk 12:24 And Jesus answering said unto them, Do ye not therefore err, because ye know not the scriptures, neither the power of God?

Mk 14:5 For it might have been sold for more than three hundred pence, and have been given to the poor. And they murmured against her.

Mk 15:35 And some of them that stood by, when they heard *it,* said, Behold, he calleth Elias.

Lu 8:37 Then the whole multitude of the country of the Gadarenes round about besought him to depart from them; for they were taken with great fear: and he went up into the ship, and returned back again.

Lu 12:56 Ye hypocrites, ye can discern the face of the sky and of the earth; but how is it that ye do not discern this time?

Jn 4:11 The woman saith unto him, Sir, thou hast nothing to draw with, and the well is deep: from whence then hast thou that living water?

Jn 8:22 Then said the Jews, Will he kill himself? because he saith, Whither I go, ye cannot come.

Jn 10:6 This parable spake Jesus unto them: but they understood not what things they were which he spake unto them.

Jn 12:29 The people therefore, that stood by, and heard *it,* said that it thundered: others said, An angel spake to him.

Jn 12:40 He hath blinded their eyes, and hardened their heart; that they should not see with *their* eyes, nor understand with *their* heart, and be converted, and I should heal them.

Ac 8:31 And he said, How can I, except some man should guide me? And he desired Philip that he would come up and sit with him.

Ro 3:17 And the way of peace have they not known:

2 Co 10:12 For we dare not make ourselves of the number, or compare ourselves with some that commend themselves: but they measuring themselves by themselves, and comparing themselves among themselves, are not wise.

2 Pe 2:12 But these, as natural brute beasts, made to be taken and destroyed, speak evil of the things that they understand not; and shall utterly perish in their own corruption;

Jude 10 But these speak evil of those things which they know not: but what they know naturally, as brute beasts, in those things they corrupt themselves.

See **IGNORANCE, KNOWLEDGE, MIND, THOUGHTS**

UNFAITHFULNESS

1. Warnings

Song 1:6 Look not upon me, because I *am* black, because the sun hath looked upon me: my mother's children were angry with me; they made me the keeper of the vineyards; *but* mine own vineyard have I not kept.

Is 5:7 For the vineyard of the LORD of hosts *is* the house of Israel, and the men of Judah his pleasant plant: and he looked for judgment, but behold oppression; for righteousness, but behold a cry.

Is 43:23 Thou hast not brought me the small cattle of thy burnt offerings; neither hast thou honoured me with thy sacrifices. I have not caused thee to serve with an offering, nor wearied thee with incense.

Ho 10:1 Israel *is* an empty vine, he bringeth forth fruit unto himself: according to the multitude of his fruit he hath increased the altars; according to the goodness of his land they have made goodly images.

Mt 21:43 Therefore say I unto you, The kingdom of God shall be taken from you, and given to a nation bringing forth the fruits thereof.

Mt 25:24–25 Then he which had received the one talent came and said, Lord, I knew thee that thou art an hard man, reaping where thou hast not sown, and gathering where thou hast not strawed:

And I was afraid, and went and hid thy talent in the earth: lo, *there* thou hast *that is* thine.

Lu 16:12 And if ye have not been faithful in that which is another man's, who shall give you that which is your own?

Jn 10:12–13 But he that is an hireling, and not the shepherd, whose own the sheep are not, seeth the wolf coming, and leaveth the sheep, and fleeth: and the wolf catcheth them, and scattereth the sheep.

The hireling fleeth, because he is an hireling, and careth not for the sheep.

2. Covenant Breakers

Ge 17:14 And the uncircumcised man child whose flesh of his foreskin is not circumcised, that soul shall be cut off from his people; he hath broken my covenant.

Le 26:15 And if ye shall despise my statutes, or if your soul abhor my judgments, so that ye will not do all my commandments, *but* that ye break my covenant:

De 17:2 If there be found among you, within any of thy gates which the LORD thy God giveth thee, man or woman, that hath wrought wickedness in the sight of the LORD thy God, in transgressing his covenant,

De 29:25 Then men shall say, Because they have forsaken the covenant of the LORD God of their fathers, which he made with them when he brought them forth out of the land of Egypt:

De 31:16 And the LORD said unto Moses, Behold, thou shalt sleep with thy fathers; and this people will rise up, and go a whoring after the gods of the strangers of the land, whither they go *to be* among them, and will forsake me, and break my covenant which I have made with them.

De 31:20 For when I shall have brought them into the land which I sware unto their fathers, that floweth with milk and honey; and they shall have eaten and filled themselves, and waxen fat; then will they turn unto other gods, and serve them, and provoke me, and break my covenant.

Jos 7:11 Israel hath sinned, and they have also transgressed my covenant which I commanded them: for they have even taken of the accursed thing, and have also stolen, and dissembled also, and they have put *it* even among their own stuff.

Jos 7:15 And it shall be, *that* he that is taken with the accursed thing shall be burnt with fire, he and all that he hath: because he hath transgressed the covenant of the LORD, and because he hath wrought folly in Israel.

Jos 23:16 When ye have transgressed the covenant of the LORD your God, which he commanded you, and have gone and served other gods, and bowed yourselves to them; then shall the anger of the LORD be kindled against you, and ye shall perish quickly from off the good land which he hath given unto you.

Jud 2:20 And the anger of the LORD was hot against Israel; and he said, Because that this people hath transgressed my covenant which I commanded their fathers, and have not hearkened unto my voice;

Jud 16:17 That he told her all his heart, and said unto her, There hath not come a razor upon mine head; for I *have been* a Nazarite unto God from my mother's womb: if I be shaven, then my strength will go from me, and I shall become weak, and be like any *other* man.

1 K 2:43 Why then hast thou not kept the oath of the LORD, and the commandment that I have charged thee with?

1 K 11:11 Wherefore the LORD said unto Solomon, Forasmuch as this is done of thee, and thou hast not kept my covenant and my statutes, which I have commanded thee, I will surely rend the kingdom from thee, and will give it to thy servant.

1 K 19:10 And he said, I have been very jealous for the LORD God of hosts: for the children of Israel have forsaken thy covenant, thrown down thine altars, and slain thy prophets with the sword; and I, *even* I only, am left; and they seek my life, to take it away.

2 K 17:15 And they rejected his statutes, and his covenant that he made with their fathers, and his testimonies which he testified against them; and they followed vanity, and became vain, and went after the heathen that *were* round about them, *concerning* whom the LORD had charged them, that they should not do like them.

2 K 18:12 Because they obeyed not the voice of the LORD their God, but transgressed his covenant, *and* all that Moses the servant of the LORD commanded, and would not hear *them,* nor do *them.*

2 Chr 36:13 And he also rebelled against king Nebuchadnezzar, who had made him swear by God: but he stiffened his neck, and hardened his heart from turning unto the LORD God of Israel.

Ne 9:34 Neither have our kings, our princes, our priests, nor our fathers, kept thy law, nor hearkened unto thy commandments and thy testimonies, wherewith thou didst testify against them.

Ps 55:20 He hath put forth his hands against such as be at peace with him: he hath broken his covenant.

Ps 78:10 They kept not the covenant of God, and refused to walk in his law;

Ps 78:37 For their heart was not right with him, neither were they stedfast in his covenant.

Pr 2:17 Which forsaketh the guide of her youth, and forgetteth the covenant of her God.

Is 24:5 The earth also is defiled under the inhabitants thereof; because they have transgressed the laws, changed the ordinance, broken the everlasting covenant.

Is 33:8 The highways lie waste, the wayfaring man ceaseth: he hath broken the covenant, he hath despised the cities, he regardeth no man.

Je 2:20 For of old time I have broken thy yoke, *and* burst thy bands; and thou saidst, I will not transgress; when upon every high hill and under every green tree thou wanderest, playing the harlot.

Je 11:10 They are turned back to the iniquities of their forefathers, which refused to hear my words; and they went after other gods to serve them: the house of Israel and the house of Judah have broken my covenant which I made with their fathers.

Je 22:9 Then they shall answer, Because they have forsaken the covenant of the LORD their God, and worshipped other gods, and served them.

Je 31:32 Not according to the covenant that I made with their fathers in the day *that* I took them by the hand to bring them out of the land of Egypt; which my covenant they brake, although I was an husband unto them, saith the LORD:

Je 34:16 But ye turned and polluted my name, and caused every man his servant, and every man his handmaid, whom ye had set at liberty at their pleasure, to return, and brought them into subjection, to be unto you for servants and for handmaids.

Je 34:18 And I will give the men that have transgressed my covenant, which have not performed the words of the covenant which they had made before me, when they cut the calf in twain, and passed between the parts thereof,

Eze 16:59 For thus saith the Lord GOD; I will even deal with thee as thou hast done, which hast despised the oath in breaking the covenant.

Eze 17:15 But he rebelled against him in sending his ambassadors into Egypt, that they might give him horses and much people. Shall he prosper? shall he escape that doeth such *things?* or shall he break the covenant, and be delivered?

Eze 17:19 Therefore thus saith the Lord GOD; *As* I live, surely mine oath that he hath despised, and my covenant that he hath broken, even it will I recompense upon his own head.

Eze 44:7 In that ye have brought *into my sanctuary* strangers, uncircumcised in heart, and uncircumcised in flesh, to be in my sanctuary, to pollute it, *even* my house, when ye offer my bread, the fat and the blood, and they have broken my covenant because of all your abominations.

Da 11:30 For the ships of Chittim shall come against him: therefore he shall be grieved, and return, and have indignation against the holy covenant: so shall he do; he shall even return, and have intelligence with them that forsake the holy covenant.

Ho 6:7 But they like men have transgressed the covenant: there have they dealt treacherously against me.

Ho 8:1 *Set* the trumpet to thy mouth. *He shall come* as an eagle against the house of the LORD, because they have transgressed my covenant, and trespassed against my law.

Mal 2:8 But ye are departed out of the way; ye have caused many to stumble at the law; ye have corrupted the covenant of Levi, saith the LORD of hosts.

Mt 21:30 And he came to the second, and said likewise. And he answered and said, I *go,* sir: and went not.

Ro 1:31–32 Without understanding, covenantbreakers, without natural affection, implacable, unmerciful:

Who knowing the judgment of God, that they which commit such things are worthy of death, not only do the same, but have pleasure in them that do them.

Ro 2:23 Thou that makest thy boast of the law, through breaking the law dishonourest thou God?

He 8:9 Not according to the covenant that I made with their fathers in the day when I took them by the hand to lead them out of the land of Egypt; because they continued not in my covenant, and I regarded them not, saith the Lord.

See **FAITHFULNESS**

UNFRUITFULNESS

FAILURE TO INVEST LIFE'S RESOURCES

Lu 19:20 And another came, saying, Lord, behold, *here is* thy pound, which I have kept laid up in a napkin:

Jn 15:2 Every branch in me that beareth not fruit he taketh away: and every *branch* that beareth fruit, he purgeth it, that it may bring forth more fruit.

ENDS IN FINAL REJECTION

He 6:8 But that which beareth thorns and briers *is* rejected, and *is* nigh unto cursing; whose end *is* to be burned.

LEADS TO DIVINE JUDGMENT

Mt 3:10 And now also the axe is laid unto the root of the trees: therefore every tree which bringeth not forth good fruit is hewn down, and cast into the fire.

CAUSED BY WORLDLINESS

Mt 13:22 He also that received seed among the thorns is he that heareth the word; and the care of this world, and the deceitfulness of riches, choke the word, and he becometh unfruitful.

RESULTS IN THE MASTER'S DISAPPOINTMENT

Lu 13:6 He spake also this parable; A certain *man* had a fig tree planted in his vineyard; and he came and sought fruit thereon, and found none.

See **FRUITFULNESS**

UNGODLINESS, *sinfulness, wickedness*

Pr 16:27 An ungodly man diggeth up evil: and in his lips *there is* as a burning fire.

Ro 1:18 For the wrath of God is revealed from heaven against all ungodliness and unrighteousness of men, who hold the truth in unrighteousness;

2 Ti 2:16 But shun profane *and* vain babblings: for they will increase unto more ungodliness.

Tit 2:12 Teaching us that, denying ungodliness and worldly lusts, we should live soberly, righteously, and godly, in this present world;

Jude 18 How that they told you there should be mockers in the last time, who should walk after their own ungodly lusts.

See **GODLINESS**

UNGODLY, *those opposed to God and his desires*

1. Their Punishment

Ps 73:12 Behold, these *are* the ungodly, who prosper in the world; they increase *in* riches.

Ro 1:18 For the wrath of God is revealed from heaven against all ungodliness and unrighteousness of men, who hold the truth in unrighteousness;

1 Ti 1:9 Knowing this, that the law is not made for a righteous man, but for the lawless and disobedient, for the ungodly and for sinners, for unholy and profane, for murderers of fathers and murderers of mothers, for manslayers,

2 Pe 2:4-5 For if God spared not the angels that sinned, but cast *them* down to hell, and delivered *them* into chains of darkness, to be reserved unto judgment;

And spared not the old world, but saved Noah the eighth *person,* a preacher of righteousness, bringing in the flood upon the world of the ungodly;

2 Pe 3:7 But the heavens and the earth, which are now, by the same word are kept in store, reserved unto fire against the day of judgment and perdition of ungodly men.

Jude 4 For there are certain men crept in unawares, who were before of old ordained to this condemnation, ungodly men, turning the grace of our God into lasciviousness, and denying

the only Lord God, and our Lord Jesus Christ.

2. Gather against God's People

Jud 7:12 And the Midianites and the Amalekites and all the children of the east lay along in the valley like grasshoppers for multitude; and their camels *were* without number, as the sand by the sea side for multitude.

1 S 28:5 And when Saul saw the host of the Philistines, he was afraid, and his heart greatly trembled.

1 K 20:27 And the children of Israel were numbered, and were all present, and went against them: and the children of Israel pitched before them like two little flocks of kids; but the Syrians filled the country.

2 K 6:15 And when the servant of the man of God was risen early, and gone forth, behold, an host compassed the city both with horses and chariots. And his servant said unto him, Alas, my master! how shall we do?

2 K 6:24 And it came to pass after this, that Ben-hadad king of Syria gathered all his host, and went up, and besieged Samaria.

2 K 18:17 And the king of Assyria sent Tartan and Rabsaris and Rabshakeh from Lachish to king Hezekiah with a great host against Jerusalem. And they went up and came to Jerusalem. And when they were come up, they came and stood by the conduit of the upper pool, which is in the highway of the fuller's field.

2 Chr 12:3 With twelve hundred chariots, and threescore thousand horsemen: and the people *were* without number that came with him out of Egypt; the Lubim, the Sukkiims, and the Ethiopians.

2 Chr 13:8 And now ye think to withstand the kingdom of the LORD in the hand of the sons of David; and ye *be* a great multitude, and *there are* with you golden calves, which Jeroboam made you for gods.

2 Chr 14:9 And there came out against them Zerah the Ethiopian with an host of a thousand thousand, and three hundred chariots; and came unto Mareshah.

2 Chr 16:8 Were not the Ethiopians and the Lubims a huge host, with very many chariots and horsemen? yet, because thou didst rely on the LORD, he delivered them into thine hand.

2 Chr 20:2 Then there came some that told Jehoshaphat, saying, There cometh a great multitude against thee from beyond the sea on this side Syria; and, behold, they *be* Hazazon-tamar, which *is* En-gedi.

2 Chr 20:24 And when Judah came toward the watch tower in the wilderness, they looked unto the multitude, and, behold, they *were* dead bodies fallen to the earth, and none escaped.

2 Chr 32:7 Be strong and courageous, be not afraid nor dismayed for the king of Assyria, nor for all the multitude that *is* with him: for *there be* more with us than with him:

Ps 3:1 LORD, how are they increased that trouble me! many *are* they that rise up against me.

Ps 3:6 I will not be afraid of ten thousands of people, that have set *themselves* against me round about.

Ps 22:16 For dogs have compassed me: the assembly of the wicked have inclosed me: they pierced my hands and my feet.

Ps 27:3 Though an host should encamp against me, my heart shall not fear: though war should rise against me, in this *will* I *be* confident.

Ps 38:19 But mine enemies *are* lively, *and* they are strong: and they that hate me wrongfully are multiplied.

Ps 48:4 For, lo, the kings were assembled, they passed by together.

Ps 69:4 They that hate me without a cause are more than the hairs of mine head: they that would destroy me, *being* mine enemies wrongfully, are mighty: then I restored *that* which I took not away.

Ps 118:12 They compassed me about like bees; they are quenched as the fire of thorns: for in the name of the LORD I will destroy them.

Is 29:6 Thou shalt be visited of the LORD of hosts with thunder, and with earthquake, and great noise, with storm and tempest, and the flame of devouring fire.

Is 36:2 And the king of Assyria sent Rabshakeh from Lachish to Jerusalem unto king Hezekiah with a great army. And he stood by the conduit of the upper pool in the highway of the fuller's field.

Is 54:15 Behold, they shall surely gather together, *but* not by me: whosoever shall gather together against thee shall fall for thy sake.

Eze 23:12 She doted upon the Assyrians *her* neighbours, captains and rulers clothed most gorgeously, horsemen riding upon horses, all of them desirable young men.

Eze 31:2 Son of man, speak unto Pharaoh king of Egypt, and to his multitude; Whom art thou like in thy greatness?

Eze 31:18 To whom art thou thus like in glory and in greatness among the trees of Eden? yet shalt thou be brought down with the trees of Eden unto the nether parts of the earth: thou shalt lie in the midst of the uncircumcised with *them that be* slain by the sword. This *is* Pharaoh and all his multitude, saith the Lord GOD.

Eze 32:31 Pharaoh shall see them, and shall be comforted over all his multitude, *even* Pharaoh and all his army slain by the sword, saith the Lord GOD.

Eze 38:5 Persia, Ethiopia, and Libya with them; all of them with shield and helmet:

Eze 38:15 And thou shalt come from thy place out of the north parts, thou, and many people with thee, all of them riding upon horses, a great company, and a mighty army:

Eze 39:4 Thou shalt fall upon the mountains of Israel, thou, and all thy bands, and the people that *is* with thee: I will give thee unto the ravenous birds of every sort, and *to* the beasts of the field to be devoured.

Lu 22:47 And while he yet spake, behold a multitude, and he that was called Judas, one of the twelve, went before them, and drew near unto Jesus to kiss him.

Lu 23:1 And the whole multitude of them arose, and led him unto Pilate.

Re 17:15 And he saith unto me, The waters which thou sawest, where the whore sitteth, are peoples, and multitudes, and nations, and tongues.

3. Their Names

a. Children of the Devil

1 Chr 17:9 Also I will ordain a place for my people Israel, and will plant them, and they shall dwell in their place, and shall be moved no more; neither shall the children of wickedness waste them any more, as at the beginning,

Is 57:4 Against whom do ye sport yourselves? against whom make ye a wide mouth, *and* draw out the tongue? *are* ye not children of transgression, a seed of falsehood,

Eze 2:4 For *they are* impudent children and stiffhearted. I do send thee unto them; and thou shalt say unto them, Thus saith the Lord GOD.

Mt 13:38 The field is the world; the good seed are the children of the kingdom; but the tares are the children of the wicked *one;*

Mt 23:15 Woe unto you, scribes and Pharisees, hypocrites! for ye compass sea and land to make one proselyte, and when he is made, ye make him twofold more the child of hell than yourselves.

Jn 8:38 I speak that which I have seen with my Father: and ye do that which ye have seen with your father.

Jn 8:44 Ye are of your father the devil, and the lusts of *your* father ye will do. He was a murderer from the beginning, and abode not in the truth, because there is no truth in him. When he speaketh a lie, he speaketh of his own: for he is a liar, and the father of it.

Ac 13:10 And said, O full of all subtilty and all mischief, *thou* child of the devil, *thou* enemy of all righteousness, wilt thou not cease to pervert the right ways of the Lord?

Ep 2:2 Wherein in time past ye walked according to the course of this world, according to the prince of the power of the air, the spirit that now worketh in the children of disobedience:

Col 3:6 For which things' sake the wrath of God cometh on the children of disobedience:

2 Pe 2:14 Having eyes full of adultery, and that cannot cease from sin; beguiling unstable souls: an heart they have exercised with covetous practices; cursed children:

1 Jn 3:8 He that committeth sin is of the devil; for the devil sinneth from the beginning. For this purpose the Son of God was manifested, that he might destroy the works of the devil.

1 Jn 3:10 In this the children of God are manifest, and the children of the devil: whosoever doeth not righteousness is not of God, neither he that loveth not his brother.

Re 2:9 I know thy works, and tribulation, and poverty, (but thou art rich) and *I know* the blasphemy of them which say they are Jews, and are not, but *are* the synagogue of Satan.

Re 13:8 And all that dwell upon the earth shall worship him, whose names are not written in the book of life of the Lamb slain from the foundation of the world.

b. Children of the World

De 32:5 They have corrupted themselves, their spot *is* not *the spot* of his children: *they are* a perverse and crooked generation.

Ps 17:14 From men *which are* thy hand, O LORD, from men of the world, *which have* their portion in *this* life, and whose belly thou fillest with thy hid *treasure:* they are full of children, and leave the rest of their *substance* to their babes.

Lu 16:8 And the lord commended the unjust steward, because he had done wisely: for the children of this world are in their generation wiser than the children of light.

Lu 20:34 And Jesus answering said unto them, The children of this world marry, and are given in marriage:

Jn 8:23 And he said unto them, Ye are from beneath; I am from above: ye are of this world; I am not of this world.

Ep 2:3 Among whom also we all had our conversation in times past in the lusts of our flesh, fulfilling the desires of the flesh and of the mind; and were by nature the children of wrath, even as others.

Ep 5:6 Let no man deceive you with vain words: for because of these things cometh the wrath of God upon the children of disobedience.

Col 3:6 For which things' sake the wrath of God cometh on the children of disobedience:

1 Jn 4:5 They are of the world: therefore speak they of the world, and the world heareth them.

See **WICKED**

UNICORN *See* **ANIMALS**

UNITY, *of believers*

1. In Christ

Jn 11:52 And not for that nation only, but that also he should gather together in one the children of God that were scattered abroad.

Jn 17:11 And now I am no more in the world, but these are in the world, and I come to thee. Holy Father, keep through thine own name those whom thou hast given me, that they may be one, as we *are*.

Jn 17:22 And the glory which thou gavest me I have given them; that they may be one, even as we are one:

Ac 5:12 And by the hands of the apostles were many signs and wonders wrought among the people; (and they were all with one accord in Solomon's porch.

Ro 12:5 So we, *being* many, are one body in Christ, and every one members one of another.

1 Co 3:8 Now he that planteth and he that watereth are one: and every man shall receive his own reward according to his own labour.

1 Co 10:17 For we *being* many are one bread, *and* one body: for we are all partakers of that one bread.

1 Co 12:12 For as the body is one, and hath many members, and all the

members of that one body, being many, are one body: so also *is* Christ.

1 Co 12:20 But now *are they* many members, yet but one body.

2 Co 12:18 I desired Titus, and with *him* I sent a brother. Did Titus make a gain of you? walked we not in the same spirit? *walked we* not in the same steps?

Ga 3:28 There is neither Jew nor Greek, there is neither bond nor free, there is neither male nor female: for ye are all one in Christ Jesus.

Ep 1:10 That in the dispensation of the fulness of times he might gather together in one all things in Christ, both which are in heaven, and which are on earth; *even* in him:

Ep 2:14 For he is our peace, who hath made both one, and hath broken down the middle wall of partition *between us;*

Ep 2:22 In whom ye also are builded together for an habitation of God through the Spirit.

Ep 4:13 Till we all come in the unity of the faith, and of the knowledge of the Son of God, unto a perfect man, unto the measure of the stature of the fulness of Christ:

Ep 4:16 From whom the whole body fitly joined together and compacted by that which every joint supplieth, according to the effectual working in the measure of every part, maketh increase of the body unto the edifying of itself in love.

Ep 4:25 Wherefore putting away lying, speak every man truth with his neighbour: for we are members one of another.

Col 3:11 Where there is neither Greek nor Jew, circumcision nor uncircumcision, Barbarian, Scythian, bond *nor* free: but Christ *is* all, and in all.

Phm 16 Not now as a servant, but above a servant, a brother beloved, specially to me, but how much more unto thee, both in the flesh, and in the Lord?

2. Exhortations

Ge 13:8 And Abram said unto Lot, Let there be no strife, I pray thee, between me and thee, and between my herdmen and thy herdmen; for we *be* brethren.

Ps 133:1 Behold, how good and how pleasant *it is* for brethren to dwell together in unity!

Ec 4:12 And if one prevail against him, two shall withstand him; and a threefold cord is not quickly broken.

Mt 18:19 Again I say unto you, That if two of you shall agree on earth as touching any thing that they shall ask, it shall be done for them of my Father which is in heaven.

Ro 12:16 *Be* of the same mind one toward another. Mind not high things, but condescend to men of low estate. Be not wise in your own conceits.

Ro 15:6 That ye may with one mind *and* one mouth glorify God, even the Father of our Lord Jesus Christ.

1 Co 1:10 Now I beseech you, brethren, by the name of our Lord Jesus Christ, that ye all speak the same thing, and *that* there be no divisions among you; but *that* ye be perfectly joined together in the same mind and in the same judgment.

1 Co 12:25 That there should be no schism in the body; but *that* the members should have the same care one for another.

2 Co 13:11 Finally, brethren, farewell. Be perfect, be of good comfort, be of one mind, live in peace; and the God of love and peace shall be with you.

Ep 4:3 Endeavouring to keep the unity of the Spirit in the bond of peace.

Ph 1:27 Only let your conversation be as it becometh the gospel of Christ: that whether I come and see you, or else be absent, I may hear of your affairs, that ye stand fast in one spirit, with one mind striving together for the faith of the gospel;

Ph 2:2 Fulfil ye my joy, that ye be likeminded, having the same love, *being* of one accord, of one mind.

Ph 4:2 I beseech Euodias, and beseech Syntyche, that they be of the same mind in the Lord.

Col 2:2 That their hearts might be comforted, being knit together in love, and unto all riches of the full assurance of understanding, to the acknowledgement of the mystery of God, and of the Father, and of Christ;

Col 2:19 And not holding the Head, from which all the body by joints and bands having nourishment ministered, and knit together, increaseth with the increase of God.

1 Pe 3:8 Finally, *be ye* all of one mind, having compassion one of another, love as brethren, *be* pitiful, *be* courteous:

3. Examples

1 S 11:7 And he took a yoke of oxen, and hewed them in pieces, and sent *them* throughout all the coasts of Israel by the hands of messengers, saying, Whosoever cometh not forth after Saul and after Samuel, so shall it be done unto his oxen. And the fear of the LORD fell on the people, and they came out with one consent.

2 K 10:15 And when he was departed thence, he lighted on Jehonadab the son of Rechab *coming* to meet him: and he saluted him, and said to him, Is thine heart right, as my heart *is* with thy heart? And Jehonadab answered, It is. If it be, give *me* thine hand. And he gave *him* his hand; and he took him up to him into the chariot.

1 Chr 12:38 All these men of war, that could keep rank, came with a perfect heart to Hebron, to make David king over all Israel: and all the rest also of Israel *were* of one heart to make David king.

Ne 2:18 Then I told them of the hand of my God which was good upon me; as also the king's words that he had spoken unto me. And they said, Let us rise up and build. So they strengthened their hands for *this* good *work*.

Ne 10:29 They clave to their brethren, their nobles, and entered into a curse, and into an oath, to walk in God's law, which was given by Moses the servant of God, and to observe and do all the commandments of the LORD our Lord, and his judgments and his statutes;

Ac 1:14 These all continued with one accord in prayer and supplication, with the women, and Mary the mother of Jesus, and with his brethren.

Ac 2:1 And when the day of Pentecost was fully come, they were all with one accord in one place.

Ac 2:46 And they, continuing daily with one accord in the temple, and breaking bread from house to house, did eat their meat with gladness and singleness of heart,

Ac 4:32 And the multitude of them that believed were of one heart and of one soul: neither said any *of them* that ought of the things which he possessed was his own; but they had all things common.

Ac 5:12 And by the hands of the apostles were many signs and wonders wrought among the people; (and they were all with one accord in Solomon's porch.

Ac 15:25 It seemed good unto us, being assembled with one accord, to send chosen men unto you with our beloved Barnabas and Paul,

4. Prophesied

OLD DIFFERENCES FORGOTTEN

Is 11:13 The envy also of Ephraim shall depart, and the adversaries of Judah shall be cut off: Ephraim shall not envy Judah, and Judah shall not vex Ephraim.

HARMONY AMONG LEADERS

Is 52:8 Thy watchmen shall lift up the voice; with the voice together shall they sing: for they shall see eye to eye, when the LORD shall bring again Zion.

CONTRITION UNIFIES BELIEVERS

Je 3:18 In those days the house of Judah shall walk with the house of Israel, and they shall come together out of the land of the north to the land that I have given for an inheritance unto your fathers.

Je 50:4 In those days, and in that time, saith the LORD, the children of Israel shall come, they and the children of Judah together, going and

weeping: they shall go, and seek the LORD their God.

Ho 1:11 Then shall the children of Judah and the children of Israel be gathered together, and appoint themselves one head, and they shall come up out of the land: for great *shall be* the day of Jezreel.

ALL FINALLY GATHERED INTO ONE FOLD

Jn 10:16 And other sheep I have, which are not of this fold: them also I must bring, and they shall hear my voice; and there shall be one fold, *and* one shepherd.

THE SAVIOR PRAYS FOR A UNITED CHURCH

Jn 17:21 That they all may be one; as thou, Father, *art* in me, and I in thee, that they also may be one in us: that the world may believe that thou hast sent me.

ALL CAUSES OF SEPARATION
REMOVED IN CHRIST

Ep 2:14 For he is our peace, who hath made both one, and hath broken down the middle wall of partition *between us;*

See **FELLOWSHIP, STRIFE**

UNMERCIFULNESS, *having no compassion, pitiless*

IN FORGIVING INJURIES

Mt 6:15 But if ye forgive not men their trespasses, neither will your Father forgive your trespasses.

IN BUSINESS DEALING

Mt 18:28 But the same servant went out, and found one of his fellowservants, which owed him an hundred pence: and he laid hands on him, and took *him* by the throat, saying, Pay me that thou owest.

Mt 18:35 So likewise shall my heavenly Father do also unto you, if ye from your hearts forgive not every one his brother their trespasses.

IN SPIRIT

Ro 1:31 Without understanding, covenantbreakers, without natural affection, implacable, unmerciful:

IN EXERCISING JUDGMENT

Ja 2:13 For he shall have judgment without mercy, that hath shewed no mercy; and mercy rejoiceth against judgment.

See **FORGIVENESS, MERCY**

UNREADINESS, *for death and judgment*

Ec 9:12 For man also knoweth not his time: as the fishes that are taken in an evil net, and as the birds that are caught in the snare; so *are* the sons of men snared in an evil time, when it falleth suddenly upon them.

Mt 24:38–39 For as in the days that were before the flood they were eating and drinking, marrying and giving in marriage, until the day that Noe entered into the ark,

And knew not until the flood came, and took them all away; so shall also the coming of the Son of man be.

Mt 24:48–51 But and if that evil servant shall say in his heart, My lord delayeth his coming;

And shall begin to smite *his* fellowservants, and to eat and drink with the drunken;

The lord of that servant shall come in a day when he looketh not for *him,* and in an hour that he is not aware of,

And shall cut *him* asunder, and appoint *him* his portion with the hypocrites: there shall be weeping and gnashing of teeth.

Mt 25:6–10 And at midnight there was a cry made, Behold, the bridegroom cometh; go ye out to meet him.

Then all those virgins arose, and trimmed their lamps.

And the foolish said unto the wise, Give us of your oil; for our lamps are gone out.

But the wise answered, saying, *Not so;* lest there be not enough for us and you: but go ye rather to them that sell, and buy for yourselves.

And while they went to buy, the bridegroom came; and they that were ready went in with him to the marriage: and the door was shut.

Lu 21:34–35 And take heed to yourselves, lest at any time your hearts be overcharged with surfeiting, and drunkenness, and cares of this life, and so that day come upon you unawares.

For as a snare shall it come on all them that dwell on the face of the whole earth.

1 Th 5:3 For when they shall say, Peace and safety; then sudden destruction cometh upon them, as travail upon a woman with child; and they shall not escape.

See **READINESS**

UNREST, *uneasiness, disquiet*

1. The Result of the Sinful Life

Ge 41:8 And it came to pass in the morning that his spirit was troubled; and he sent and called for all the magicians of Egypt, and all the wise men thereof: and Pharaoh told them his dream; but *there was* none that could interpret them unto Pharaoh.

De 28:67 In the morning thou shalt say, Would God it were even! and at even thou shalt say, Would God it were morning! for the fear of thine heart wherewith thou shalt fear, and for the sight of thine eyes which thou shalt see.

2 Chr 15:5 And in those times *there was* no peace to him that went out, nor to him that came in, but great vexations *were* upon all the inhabitants of the countries.

Jb 3:26 I was not in safety, neither had I rest, neither was I quiet; yet trouble came.

Jb 7:3 So am I made to possess months of vanity, and wearisome nights are appointed to me.

Jb 20:20 Surely he shall not feel quietness in his belly, he shall not save of that which he desired.

Ps 32:4 For day and night thy hand was heavy upon me: my moisture is turned into the drought of summer. Selah.

Ps 38:3 *There is* no soundness in my flesh because of thine anger; neither *is there any* rest in my bones because of my sin.

Ps 38:8 I am feeble and sore broken: I have roared by reason of the disquietness of my heart.

Ps 39:6 Surely every man walketh in a vain shew: surely they are disquieted in vain: he heapeth up *riches,* and knoweth not who shall gather them.

Ps 109:23 I am gone like the shadow when it declineth: I am tossed up and down as the locust.

Ec 2:23 For all his days *are* sorrows, and his travail grief; yea, his heart taketh not rest in the night. This is also vanity.

Is 21:4 My heart panted, fearfulness affrighted me: the night of my pleasure hath he turned into fear unto me.

Is 23:12 And he said, Thou shalt no more rejoice, O thou oppressed virgin, daughter of Zidon: arise, pass over to Chittim; there also shalt thou have no rest.

Is 48:22 *There is* no peace, saith the LORD, unto the wicked.

Is 57:20 But the wicked *are* like the troubled sea, when it cannot rest, whose waters cast up mire and dirt.

Lam 5:5 Our necks *are* under persecution: we labour, *and* have no rest.

Da 2:3 And the king said unto them, I have dreamed a dream, and my spirit was troubled to know the dream.

Da 4:5 I saw a dream which made me afraid, and the thoughts upon my bed and the visions of my head troubled me.

Da 6:18 Then the king went to his palace, and passed the night fasting: neither were instruments of musick brought before him: and his sleep went from him.

Mt 2:3 When Herod the king had heard *these things,* he was troubled, and all Jerusalem with him.

Lu 8:29 (For he had commanded the unclean spirit to come out of the man. For oftentimes it had caught him: and he was kept bound with chains and in fetters; and he brake the bands, and

was driven of the devil into the wilderness.)

Jude 13 Raging waves of the sea, foaming out their own shame; wandering stars, to whom is reserved the blackness of darkness for ever.

Re 14:11 And the smoke of their torment ascendeth up for ever and ever: and they have no rest day nor night, who worship the beast and his image, and whosoever receiveth the mark of his name.

2. No Peace for the Wicked

De 28:65 And among these nations shalt thou find no ease, neither shall the sole of thy foot have rest: but the LORD shall give thee there a trembling heart, and failing of eyes, and sorrow of mind:

2 Chr 15:5 And in those times *there was* no peace to him that went out, nor to him that came in, but great vexations *were* upon all the inhabitants of the countries.

Is 23:12 And he said, Thou shalt no more rejoice, O thou oppressed virgin, daughter of Zidon: arise, pass over to Chittim; there also shalt thou have no rest.

Is 48:22 *There is* no peace, saith the LORD, unto the wicked.

Is 57:21 *There is* no peace, saith my God, to the wicked.

Is 59:8 The way of peace they know not; and *there is* no judgment in their goings: they have made them crooked paths: whosoever goeth therein shall not know peace.

Je 6:14 They have healed also the hurt *of the daughter* of my people slightly, saying, Peace, peace; when *there is* no peace.

Je 8:11 For they have healed the hurt of the daughter of my people slightly, saying, Peace, peace; when *there is* no peace.

Je 12:12 The spoilers are come upon all high places through the wilderness: for the sword of the LORD shall devour from the *one* end of the land even to the *other* end of the land: no flesh shall have peace.

Je 14:19 Hast thou utterly rejected Judah? hath thy soul lothed Zion?

why hast thou smitten us, and *there is* no healing for us? we looked for peace, and *there is* no good; and for the time of healing, and behold trouble!

Je 16:5 For thus saith the LORD, Enter not into the house of mourning, neither go to lament nor bemoan them: for I have taken away my peace from this people, saith the LORD, *even* lovingkindness and mercies.

Je 49:23 Concerning Damascus. Hamath is confounded, and Arpad: for they have heard evil tidings: they are fainthearted; there is sorrow on the sea; it cannot be quiet.

Lam 1:3 Judah is gone into captivity because of affliction, and because of great servitude: she dwelleth among the heathen, she findeth no rest: all her persecutors overtook her between the straits.

Lam 3:17 And thou hast removed my soul far off from peace: I forgat prosperity.

Eze 7:25 Destruction cometh; and they shall seek peace, and *there shall be* none.

Eze 13:10 Because, even because they have seduced my people, saying, Peace; and *there was* no peace; and one built up a wall, and, lo, others daubed it with untempered *morter:*

Eze 13:16 *To wit,* the prophets of Israel which prophesy concerning Jerusalem, and which see visions of peace for her, and *there is* no peace, saith the Lord GOD.

Da 5:9 Then was king Belshazzar greatly troubled, and his countenance was changed in him, and his lords were astonied.

Zec 8:10 For before these days there was no hire for man, nor any hire for beast; neither *was there any* peace to him that went out or came in because of the affliction: for I set all men every one against his neighbour.

Mt 2:3 When Herod the king had heard *these things,* he was troubled, and all Jerusalem with him.

Mk 5:5 And always, night and day, he was in the mountains, and in the tombs, crying, and cutting himself with stones.

Ro 3:17 And the way of peace have they not known:

3. Believers Need Not Fear

Ge 19:30 And Lot went up out of Zoar, and dwelt in the mountain, and his two daughters with him; for he feared to dwell in Zoar: and he dwelt in a cave, he and his two daughters.

Ex 4:3 And he said, Cast it on the ground. And he cast it on the ground, and it became a serpent; and Moses fled from before it.

Ex 14:10 And when Pharaoh drew nigh, the children of Israel lifted up their eyes, and, behold, the Egyptians marched after them; and they were sore afraid: and the children of Israel cried out unto the LORD.

Jud 6:22 And when Gideon perceived that he *was* an angel of the LORD, Gideon said, Alas, O Lord GOD! for because I have seen an angel of the LORD face to face.

Jud 13:22 And Manoah said unto his wife, We shall surely die, because we have seen God.

Da 8:17 So he came near where I stood: and when he came, I was afraid, and fell upon my face: but he said unto me, Understand, O son of man: for at the time of the end *shall be* the vision.

Mt 8:25 And his disciples came to *him,* and awoke him, saying, Lord, save us: we perish.

Mt 14:26 And when the disciples saw him walking on the sea, they were troubled, saying, It is a spirit; and they cried out for fear.

Mt 14:30 But when he saw the wind boisterous, he was afraid; and beginning to sink, he cried, saying, Lord, save me.

Mt 17:6 And when the disciples heard *it,* they fell on their face, and were sore afraid.

Mk 4:38 And he was in the hinder part of the ship, asleep on a pillow: and they awake him, and say unto him, Master, carest thou not that we perish?

Mk 5:33 But the woman fearing and trembling, knowing what was done in her, came and fell down before him, and told him all the truth.

Mk 6:50 For they all saw him, and were troubled. And immediately he talked with them, and saith unto them, Be of good cheer: it is I; be not afraid.

Mk 9:6 For he wist not what to say; for they were sore afraid.

Mk 16:3 And they said among themselves, Who shall roll us away the stone from the door of the sepulchre?

Mk 16:5 And entering into the sepulchre, they saw a young man sitting on the right side, clothed in a long white garment; and they were affrighted.

Mk 16:8 And they went out quickly, and fled from the sepulchre; for they trembled and were amazed: neither said they any thing to any *man;* for they were afraid.

Lu 1:12 And when Zacharias saw *him,* he was troubled, and fear fell upon him.

Lu 1:29 And when she saw *him,* she was troubled at his saying, and cast in her mind what manner of salutation this should be.

Lu 2:9 And, lo, the angel of the Lord came upon them, and the glory of the Lord shone round about them: and they were sore afraid.

Lu 8:24 And they came to him, and awoke him, saying, Master, master, we perish. Then he arose, and rebuked the wind and the raging of the water: and they ceased, and there was a calm.

Lu 9:34 While he thus spake, there came a cloud, and overshadowed them: and they feared as they entered into the cloud.

Lu 24:5 And as they were afraid, and bowed down *their* faces to the earth, they said unto them, Why seek ye the living among the dead?

Lu 24:37 But they were terrified and affrighted, and supposed that they had seen a spirit.

Jn 6:19 So when they had rowed about five and twenty or thirty furlongs, they see Jesus walking on the sea, and drawing nigh unto the ship: and they were afraid.

Ac 10:4 And when he looked on him, he was afraid, and said, What is it, Lord?

And he said unto him, Thy prayers and thine alms are come up for a memorial before God.

Re 5:4 And I wept much, because no man was found worthy to open and to read the book, neither to look thereon.

See **PEACE, REST**

UNRIGHTEOUSNESS, *wickedness*

De 25:16 For all that do such things, *and* all that do unrighteously, *are* an abomination unto the LORD thy God.

Ps 119:7 I will praise thee with uprightness of heart, when I shall have learned thy righteous judgments.

Is 46:12 Hearken unto me, ye stouthearted, that *are* far from righteousness:

Ro 1:18 For the wrath of God is revealed from heaven against all ungodliness and unrighteousness of men, who hold the truth in unrighteousness;

Ro 1:29 Being filled with all unrighteousness, fornication, wickedness, covetousness, maliciousness; full of envy, murder, debate, deceit, malignity; whisperers,

Ro 6:13 Neither yield ye your members *as* instruments of unrighteousness unto sin: but yield yourselves unto God, as those that are alive from the dead, and your members *as* instruments of righteousness unto God.

1 Co 6:9 Know ye not that the unrighteous shall not inherit the kingdom of God? Be not deceived: neither fornicators, nor idolaters, nor adulterers, nor effeminate, nor abusers of themselves with mankind,

2 Th 2:10 And with all deceivableness of unrighteousness in them that perish; because they received not the love of the truth, that they might be saved.

2 Pe 2:13 And shall receive the reward of unrighteousness, *as* they that count it pleasure to riot in the daytime. Spots *they are* and blemishes, sporting themselves with their own deceivings while they feast with you;

1 Jn 1:9 If we confess our sins, he is faithful and just to forgive us *our* sins, and to cleanse us from all un-righteousness.

1 Jn 3:10 In this the children of God are manifest, and the children of the devil: whosoever doeth not righteousness is not of God, neither he that loveth not his brother.

1 Jn 5:17 All unrighteousness is sin: and there is a sin not unto death.

See **GODLINESS, RIGHTEOUSNESS, WICKED**

UNSELFISHNESS

ABRAHAM

Ge 13:9 *Is* not the whole land before thee? separate thyself, I pray thee, from me: if *thou wilt take* the left hand, then I will go to the right; or if *thou depart* to the right hand, then I will go to the left.

Ge 14:23 That I will not *take* from a thread even to a shoelatchet, and that I will not take any thing that *is* thine, lest thou shouldest say, I have made Abram rich:

JOSEPH

Ge 50:21 Now therefore fear ye not: I will nourish you, and your little ones. And he comforted them, and spake kindly unto them.

MOSES

Nu 11:29 And Moses said unto him, Enviest thou for my sake? would God that all the LORD's people were prophets, *and* that the LORD would put his spirit upon them!

JONATHAN

1 S 18:4 And Jonathan stripped himself of the robe that *was* upon him, and gave it to David, and his garments, even to his sword, and to his bow, and to his girdle.

1 S 23:17 And he said unto him, Fear not: for the hand of Saul my father shall not find thee; and thou shalt be king over Israel, and I shall be next unto thee; and that also Saul my father knoweth.

DAVID

2 S 23:17 And he said, Be it far from me, O LORD, that I should do this: *is not this* the blood of the men that went in jeopardy of their lives? therefore he would not drink it. These things did these three mighty men.

DANIEL

Da 5:17 Then Daniel answered and said before the king, Let thy gifts be to thyself, and give thy rewards to another; yet I will read the writing unto the king, and make known to him the interpretation.

PAUL

1 Co 10:33 Even as I please all *men* in all *things,* not seeking mine own profit, but the *profit* of many, that they may be saved.

CHRIST

Ro 15:3 For even Christ pleased not himself; but, as it is written, The reproaches of them that reproached thee fell on me.

2 Co 8:9 For ye know the grace of our Lord Jesus Christ, that, though he was rich, yet for your sakes he became poor, that ye through his poverty might be rich.

2 Co 12:5 Of such an one will I glory: yet of myself I will not glory, but in mine infirmities.

See **SELF-EXALTATION, SELFISHNESS**

UNWORLDLINESS

De 17:14 When thou art come unto the land which the LORD thy God giveth thee, and shalt possess it, and shalt dwell therein, and shalt say, I will set a king over me, like as all the nations that *are* about me;

Ro 12:2 And be not conformed to this world: but be ye transformed by the renewing of your mind, that ye may prove what is that good, and acceptable, and perfect, will of God.

1 Co 7:31 And they that use this world, as not abusing *it:* for the fashion of this world passeth away.

Ga 6:14 But God forbid that I should glory, save in the cross of our Lord

Jesus Christ, by whom the world is crucified unto me, and I unto the world.

2 Ti 2:4 No man that warreth entangleth himself with the affairs of *this* life; that he may please him who hath chosen him to be a soldier.

He 11:24–25 By faith Moses, when he was come to years, refused to be called the son of Pharaoh's daughter;

Choosing rather to suffer affliction with the people of God, than to enjoy the pleasures of sin for a season;

1 Jn 2:15 Love not the world, neither the things *that are* in the world. If any man love the world, the love of the Father is not in him.

See **WORLDLINESS**

UNWORTHINESS

1. Examples

Mt 10:37; 22:8; Ac 13:46

2. Felt

BY JOHN THE BAPTIST

Mt 3:11 I indeed baptize you with water unto repentance: but he that cometh after me is mightier than I, whose shoes I am not worthy to bear: he shall baptize you with the Holy Ghost, and *with* fire:

BY THE CENTURION

Mt 8:8 The centurion answered and said, Lord, I am not worthy that thou shouldest come under my roof: but speak the word only, and my servant shall be healed.

BY THE RIGHTEOUS

Mt 25:37 Then shall the righteous answer him, saying, Lord, when saw we thee an hungred, and fed *thee*? or thirsty, and gave *thee* drink?

BY PETER

Lu 5:8 When Simon Peter saw *it*, he fell down at Jesus' knees, saying, Depart from me; for I am a sinful man, O Lord.

Jn 13:8 Peter saith unto him, Thou shalt never wash my feet. Jesus an-swered him, If I wash thee not, thou hast no part with me.

BY PAUL

1 Co 15:9 For I am the least of the apostles, that am not meet to be called an apostle, because I persecuted the church of God.

See **HUMILITY, WORTHINESS**

UPRIGHTNESS

Jb 4:6 *Is* not *this* thy fear, thy confidence, thy hope, and the uprightness of thy ways?

Jb 33:23 If there be a messenger with him, an interpreter, one among a thousand, to shew unto man his uprightness:

Ps 7:10 My defence *is* of God, which saveth the upright in heart.

Ps 32:11 Be glad in the LORD, and rejoice, ye righteous: and shout for joy, all *ye that are* upright in heart.

Ps 37:37 Mark the perfect *man,* and behold the upright: for the end of *that* man *is* peace.

Ps 49:14 Like sheep they are laid in the grave; death shall feed on them; and the upright shall have dominion over them in the morning; and their beauty shall consume in the grave from their dwelling.

Ps 64:10 The righteous shall be glad in the LORD, and shall trust in him; and all the upright in heart shall glory.

Ps 97:11 Light is sown for the righteous, and gladness for the upright in heart.

Ps 112:4 Unto the upright there ariseth light in the darkness: *he is* gracious, and full of compassion, and righteous.

Pr 2:7 He layeth up sound wisdom for the righteous: *he is* a buckler to them that walk uprightly.

Pr 2:21 For the upright shall dwell in the land, and the perfect shall remain in it.

Pr 10:9 He that walketh uprightly walketh surely: but he that perverteth his ways shall be known.

Pr 14:11 The house of the wicked shall be overthrown: but the tabernacle of the upright shall flourish.

Pr 28:6 Better *is* the poor that walketh in his uprightness, than *he that is* perverse *in his* ways, though he *be* rich.

Am 5:7 Ye who turn judgment to wormwood, and leave off righteousness in the earth,

Ro 1:18 For the wrath of God is revealed from heaven against all ungodliness and unrighteousness of men, who hold the truth in unrighteousness;

See **OBEDIENCE, PROSPERITY, REWARD**

UR, *a city of Chaldea*

Ge 11:28, 31; 15:7; Ne 9:7; Ac 7:4

URIAH, *the Hittite, husband of Bath-sheba*

2 S 11:6; 12:9; 23:39

URIJAH, *Yahweh is [my] light*

1. The Priest

2 K 16:10

2. The Prophet

Je 26:20

UZ, *land of*

Jb 1:1; Je 25:20; Lam 4:21

UZZAH, *or Uzza*

2 S 6:3; 1 Chr 13:7

UZZIAH, *or Azariah, king of Judah, son of Amaziah*

2 K 14:21; 15:1, 3, 7, 13, 17, 23, 27, 34; 2 Chr 26:1, 19, 23; Is 6:1; 7:1; Ho 1:1; Am 1:1; Zec 14:5; Mt 1:9

See **ISRAEL**

V

VAIL, *or veil*

1. A Covering for the Face

Ge 24:65; 38:14, 19; Ex 34:33; Ru 3:15; 1 Co 11:6; 2 Co 3:13

2. The Curtain, *separating the Holy Place from the Holy of Holies*

Ex 26:31, 33; 27:21; 30:6; 35:12; 36:35; 40:3, 21, 26; Le 4:6, 17; 16:2, 12, 15; 24:3; 2 Chr 3:14; Mt 27:51; Mk 15:38; Lu 23:45; He 6:19; 9:3; 10:20

VALLEYS

2 Chr 20:26; Ps 23:4; 84:6; Is 40:4; Eze 37:1; Jl 3:14

VANITY

De 32:21 They have moved me to jealousy with *that which is* not God; they have provoked me to anger with their vanities: and I will move them to jealousy with *those which are* not a people; I will provoke them to anger with a foolish nation.

1 S 12:21 And turn ye not aside: for *then should ye go* after vain *things,* which cannot profit nor deliver; for they *are* vain.

1 K 16:13 For all the sins of Baasha, and the sins of Elah his son, by which they sinned, and by which they made Israel to sin, in provoking the LORD God of Israel to anger with their vanities.

1 K 16:26 For he walked in all the way of Jeroboam the son of Nebat, and in his sin wherewith he made Israel to sin, to provoke the LORD God of Israel to anger with their vanities.

Ps 31:6 I have hated them that regard lying vanities: but I trust in the LORD.

Ecc 5:7 For in the multitude of dreams and many words *there are* also *divers* vanities: but fear thou God.

Je 2:5 Thus saith the LORD, What iniquity have your fathers found in me, that they are gone far from me, and have walked after vanity, and are become vain?

Je 8:19 Behold the voice of the cry of the daughter of my people because of them that dwell in a far country: *Is* not the LORD in Zion? *is* not her king in her? Why have they provoked me to anger with their graven images, *and* with strange vanities?

Je 10:8 But they are altogether brutish and foolish: the stock *is* a doctrine of vanities.

Je 16:19 O LORD, my strength, and my fortress, and my refuge in the day of affliction, the Gentiles shall come unto thee from the ends of the earth, and shall say, Surely our fathers have inherited lies, vanity, and *things wherein there is* no profit.

Ho 12:1 Ephraim feedeth on wind, and followeth after the east wind: he daily increaseth lies and desolation; and they do make a covenant with the Assyrians, and oil is carried into Egypt.

Ho 12:11 *Is there* iniquity *in* Gilead? surely they are vanity: they sacrifice bullocks in Gilgal; yea, their altars *are* as heaps in the furrows of the fields.

Am 6:13 Ye which rejoice in a thing of nought, which say, Have we not taken to us horns by our own strength?

Jona 2:8 They that observe lying vanities forsake their own mercy.

Hab 2:13 Behold, *is it* not of the LORD of hosts that the people shall labour in the very fire, and the people shall weary themselves for very vanity?

Ac 14:15 And saying, Sirs, why do ye these things? We also are men of like passions with you, and preach unto you that ye should turn from these vanities unto the living God, which made heaven, and earth, and the sea, and all things that are therein:

2 Pe 2:18 For when they speak great swelling *words* of vanity, they allure through the lusts of the flesh, *through much* wantonness, those that were clean escaped from them who live in error.

See **EMPTINESS, FOLLY**

VAPOR

See **WEATHER**

VASHTI, *wife of Ahasuerus*
Est 1:9, 17

VENGEANCE, *DIVINE, God's wrath, punishment, retribution*

Ex 22:24 And my wrath shall wax hot, and I will kill you with the sword; and your wives shall be widows, and your children fatherless.

Ex 32:10 Now therefore let me alone, that my wrath may wax hot against them, and that I may consume them: and I will make of thee a great nation.

Ex 32:27 And he said unto them, Thus saith the LORD God of Israel, Put every man his sword by his side, *and* go in and out from gate to gate throughout the camp, and slay every man his brother, and every man his companion, and every man his neighbour.

Le 20:5 Then I will set my face against that man, and against his family, and will cut him off, and all that go a whoring after him, to commit whoredom with Molech, from among their people.

Le 26:18 And if ye will not yet for all this hearken unto me, then I will punish you seven times more for your sins.

Nu 14:12 I will smite them with the pestilence, and disinherit them, and will make of thee a greater nation and mightier than they.

Nu 21:6 And the LORD sent fiery serpents among the people, and they bit the people; and much people of Israel died.

Nu 25:4 And the LORD said unto Moses, Take all the heads of the people, and hang them up before the LORD against the sun, that the fierce anger of the LORD may be turned away from Israel.

Nu 31:3 And Moses spake unto the people, saying, Arm some of your-selves unto the war, and let them go against the Midianites, and avenge the LORD of Midian.

De 7:10 And repayeth them that hate him to their face, to destroy them: he will not be slack to him that hateth him, he will repay him to his face.

De 29:27 And the anger of the LORD was kindled against this land, to bring upon it all the curses that are written in this book:

De 32:35 To me *belongeth* vengeance, and recompence; their foot shall slide in *due* time: for the day of their calamity *is* at hand, and the things that shall come upon them make haste.

De 32:41 If I whet my glittering sword, and mine hand take hold on judgment; I will render vengeance to mine enemies, and will reward them that hate me.

Jos 7:15 And it shall be, *that* he that is taken with the accursed thing shall be burnt with fire, he and all that he hath: because he hath transgressed the covenant of the LORD, and because he hath wrought folly in Israel.

1 S 2:25 If one man sin against another, the judge shall judge him: but if a man sin against the LORD, who shall intreat for him? Notwithstanding they hearkened not unto the voice of their father, because the LORD would slay them.

1 S 24:12 The LORD judge between me and thee, and the LORD avenge me of thee: but mine hand shall not be upon thee.

2 S 18:31 And, behold, Cushi came; and Cushi said, Tidings, my lord the king: for the LORD hath avenged thee this day of all them that rose up against thee.

2 S 22:48 It *is* God that avengeth me, and that bringeth down the people under me,

1 K 21:19 And thou shalt speak unto him, saying, Thus saith the LORD, Hast thou killed, and also taken possession? And thou shalt speak unto him, saying, Thus saith the LORD, In the place where dogs licked the blood of Naboth shall dogs lick thy blood, even thine.

2 K 9:7 And thou shalt smite the house of Ahab thy master, that I may avenge the blood of my servants the prophets, and the blood of all the servants of the LORD, at the hand of Jezebel.

2 Chr 36:17 Therefore he brought upon them the king of the Chaldees, who slew their young men with the sword in the house of their sanctuary, and had no compassion upon young man or maiden, old man, or him that stooped for age: he gave *them* all into his hand.

Jb 20:23 *When* he is about to fill his belly, *God* shall cast the fury of his wrath upon him, and shall rain *it* upon him while he is eating.

Ps 18:47 *It is* God that avengeth me, and subdueth the people under me.

Ps 21:9 Thou shalt make them as a fiery oven in the time of thine anger: the LORD shall swallow them up in his wrath, and the fire shall devour them.

Ps 56:7 Shall they escape by iniquity? in *thine* anger cast down the people, O God.

Ps 78:50 He made a way to his anger; he spared not their soul from death, but gave their life over to the pestilence;

Ps 79:10 Wherefore should the heathen say, Where *is* their God? let him be known among the heathen in our sight *by* the revenging of the blood of thy servants *which is* shed.

Ps 94:1 O LORD God, to whom vengeance belongeth; O God, to whom vengeance belongeth, shew thyself.

Ps 99:8 Thou answeredst them, O LORD our God: thou wast a God that forgavest them, though thou tookest vengeance of their inventions.

Ps 149:7 To execute vengeance upon the heathen, *and* punishments upon the people;

Pr 22:23 For the LORD will plead their cause, and spoil the soul of those that spoiled them.

Is 1:24 Therefore saith the Lord, the LORD of hosts, the mighty One of Israel, Ah, I will ease me of mine adversaries, and avenge me of mine enemies:

Is 9:17 Therefore the Lord shall have no joy in their young men, neither shall have mercy on their fatherless and widows: for every one is an hypocrite and an evildoer, and every mouth speaketh folly. For all this his anger is not turned away, but his hand *is* stretched out still.

Is 14:22 For I will rise up against them, saith the LORD of hosts, and cut off from Babylon the name, and remnant, and son, and nephew, saith the LORD.

Is 31:2 Yet he also *is* wise, and will bring evil, and will not call back his words: but will arise against the house of the evildoers, and against the help of them that work iniquity.

Is 34:2 For the indignation of the LORD *is* upon all nations, and *his* fury upon all their armies: he hath utterly destroyed them, he hath delivered them to the slaughter.

Is 34:8 For *it is* the day of the LORD's vengeance, *and* the year of recompences for the controversy of Zion.

Is 35:4 Say to them *that are* of a fearful heart, Be strong, fear not: behold, your God will come *with* vengeance, *even* God *with* a recompence; he will come and save you.

Is 47:3 Thy nakedness shall be uncovered, yea, thy shame shall be seen: I will take vengeance, and I will not meet *thee as* a man.

Is 49:26 And I will feed them that oppress thee with their own flesh; and they shall be drunken with their own blood, as with sweet wine: and all flesh shall know that I the LORD *am* thy Saviour and thy Redeemer, the mighty One of Jacob.

Is 59:17 For he put on righteousness as a breastplate, and an helmet of salvation upon his head; and he put on the garments of vengeance *for* clothing, and was clad with zeal as a cloke.

Is 61:2 To proclaim the acceptable year of the LORD, and the day of vengeance of our God; to comfort all that mourn;

Is 63:4 For the day of vengeance *is* in mine heart, and the year of my redeemed is come.

Je 5:9 Shall I not visit for these *things?* saith the LORD: and shall not my soul be avenged on such a nation as this?

Je 5:29 Shall I not visit for these *things?* saith the LORD: shall not my soul be avenged on such a nation as this?

Je 9:9 Shall I not visit them for these *things?* saith the LORD: shall not my soul be avenged on such a nation as this?

Je 14:16 And the people to whom they prophesy shall be cast out in the streets of Jerusalem because of the famine and the sword; and they shall have none to bury them, them, their wives, nor their sons, nor their daughters: for I will pour their wickedness upon them.

Je 20:12 But, O LORD of hosts, that triest the righteous, *and* seest the reins and the heart, let me see thy vengeance on them: for unto thee have I opened my cause.

Je 29:18 And I will persecute them with the sword, with the famine, and with the pestilence, and will deliver them to be removed to all the kingdoms of the earth, to be a curse, and an astonishment, and an hissing, and a reproach, among all the nations whither I have driven them:

Je 36:7 It may be they will present their supplication before the LORD, and will return every one from his evil way: for great *is* the anger and the fury that the LORD hath pronounced against this people.

Je 42:18 For thus saith the LORD of hosts, the God of Israel; As mine anger and my fury hath been poured forth upon the inhabitants of Jerusalem; so shall my fury be poured forth upon you, when ye shall enter into Egypt: and ye shall be an execration, and an astonishment, and a curse, and a reproach; and ye shall see this place no more.

Je 44:6 Wherefore my fury and mine anger was poured forth, and was kindled in the cities of Judah and in the streets of Jerusalem; and they are wasted *and* desolate, as at this day.

Je 46:10 For this *is* the day of the Lord GOD of hosts, a day of vengeance, that he may avenge him of his adversaries: and the sword shall devour, and it shall be satiate and made drunk with their blood: for the Lord GOD of hosts hath a sacrifice in the north country by the river Euphrates.

Je 50:15 Shout against her round about: she hath given her hand: her foundations are fallen, her walls are thrown down: for it *is* the vengeance of the LORD: take vengeance upon her; as she hath done, do unto her.

Je 50:28 The voice of them that flee and escape out of the land of Babylon, to declare in Zion the vengeance of the LORD our God, the vengeance of his temple.

Je 51:6 Flee out of the midst of Babylon, and deliver every man his soul: be not cut off in her iniquity; for this *is* the time of the LORD's vengeance; he will render unto her a recompence.

Je 51:11 Make bright the arrows; gather the shields: the LORD hath raised up the spirit of the kings of the Medes: for his device *is* against Babylon, to destroy it; because it *is* the vengeance of the LORD, the vengeance of his temple.

Je 51:36 Therefore thus saith the LORD; Behold, I will plead thy cause, and take vengeance for thee; and I will dry up her sea, and make her springs dry.

Lam 2:4 He hath bent his bow like an enemy: he stood with his right hand as an adversary, and slew all *that were* pleasant to the eye in the tabernacle of the daughter of Zion: he poured out his fury like fire.

Lam 4:11 The LORD hath accomplished his fury; he hath poured out his fierce anger, and hath kindled a fire in Zion, and it hath devoured the foundations thereof.

Eze 5:13 Thus shall mine anger be accomplished, and I will cause my fury to rest upon them, and I will be comforted: and they shall know that I the LORD have spoken *it* in my zeal, when I have accomplished my fury in them.

Eze 7:8 Now will I shortly pour out my fury upon thee, and accomplish mine anger upon thee: and I will judge thee according to thy ways, and will recompense thee for all thine abominations.

Eze 8:18 Therefore will I also deal in fury: mine eye shall not spare, neither will I have pity: and though they cry in mine ears with a loud voice, *yet* will I not hear them.

Eze 9:8 And it came to pass, while they were slaying them, and I was left, that I fell upon my face, and cried, and said, Ah Lord GOD! wilt thou destroy all the residue of Israel in thy pouring out of thy fury upon Jerusalem?

Eze 14:19 Or *if* I send a pestilence into that land, and pour out my fury upon it in blood, to cut off from it man and beast:

Eze 19:12 But she was plucked up in fury, she was cast down to the ground, and the east wind dried up her fruit: her strong rods were broken and withered; the fire consumed them.

Eze 20:8 But they rebelled against me, and would not hearken unto me: they did not every man cast away the abominations of their eyes, neither did they forsake the idols of Egypt: then I said, I will pour out my fury upon them to accomplish my anger against them in the midst of the land of Egypt.

Eze 20:33 *As* I live, saith the Lord GOD, surely with a mighty hand, and with a stretched out arm, and with fury poured out, will I rule over you:

Eze 22:22 As silver is melted in the midst of the furnace, so shall ye be melted in the midst thereof; and ye shall know that I the LORD have poured out my fury upon you.

Eze 25:14 And I will lay my vengeance upon Edom by the hand of my people Israel: and they shall do in Edom according to mine anger and according to my fury; and they shall know my vengeance, saith the Lord GOD.

Eze 25:17 And I will execute great vengeance upon them with furious rebukes; and they shall know that I *am* the LORD, when I shall lay my vengeance upon them.

Eze 38:18 And it shall come to pass at the same time when Gog shall come against the land of Israel, saith the Lord GOD, *that* my fury shall come up in my face.

Ho 2:3 Lest I strip her naked, and set her as in the day that she was born, and make her as a wilderness, and set her like a dry land, and slay her with thirst.

Ho 5:14 For I will *be* unto Ephraim as a lion, and as a young lion to the house of Judah: I, *even* I, will tear and go away; I will take away, and none shall rescue *him*.

Ho 13:8 I will meet them as a bear *that is* bereaved *of her whelps,* and will rend the caul of their heart, and there will I devour them like a lion: the wild beast shall tear them.

Am 9:4 And though they go into captivity before their enemies, thence will I command the sword, and it shall slay them: and I will set mine eyes upon them for evil, and not for good.

Mi 5:15 And I will execute vengeance in anger and fury upon the heathen, such as they have not heard.

Na 1:2 God *is* jealous, and the LORD revengeth; the LORD revengeth, and *is* furious; the LORD will take vengeance on his adversaries, and he reserveth *wrath* for his enemies.

Zep 2:11 The LORD *will be* terrible unto them: for he will famish all the gods of the earth; and *men* shall worship him, every one from his place, *even* all the isles of the heathen.

Zep 3:8 Therefore wait ye upon me, saith the LORD, until the day that I rise up to the prey: for my determination *is* to gather the nations, that I may assemble the kingdoms, to pour upon them mine indignation, *even* all my fierce anger: for all the earth shall be devoured with the fire of my jealousy.

Lu 21:22 For these be the days of vengeance, that all things which are written may be fulfilled.

Ro 3:5 But if our unrighteousness commend the righteousness of God, what shall we say? *Is* God unrighteous who taketh vengeance? (I speak as a man)

Ro 11:21 For if God spared not the natural branches, *take heed* lest he also spare not thee.

Ro 12:19 Dearly beloved, avenge not yourselves, but *rather* give place unto wrath: for it is written, Vengeance *is* mine; I will repay, saith the Lord.

1 Th 4:6 That no *man* go beyond and defraud his brother in *any* matter: because that the Lord *is* the avenger of all such, as we also have forewarned you and testified.

2 Th 1:8 In flaming fire taking vengeance on them that know not God, and that obey not the gospel of our Lord Jesus Christ:

He 10:30 For we know him that hath said, Vengeance *belongeth* unto me, I will recompense, saith the Lord. And again, The Lord shall judge his people.

Jude 7 Even as Sodom and Gomorrha, and the cities about them in like manner, giving themselves over to fornication, and going after strange flesh, are set forth for an example, suffering the vengeance of eternal fire.

Re 6:17 For the great day of his wrath is come; and who shall be able to stand?

Re 18:20 Rejoice over her, *thou* heaven, and *ye* holy apostles and prophets; for God hath avenged you on her.

Re 19:2 For true and righteous *are* his judgments: for he hath judged the great whore, which did corrupt the earth with her fornication, and hath avenged the blood of his servants at her hand.

See **GOD, RETALIATION, RETRIBUTION, RIGHTEOUSNESS**

VENISON, *wild game*

Ge 25:28; 27:3

VERILY, *assurances from Christ*

Mt 21:31 Whether of them twain did the will of *his* father? They say unto him, The first. Jesus saith unto them, Verily I say unto you, That the publicans and the harlots go into the kingdom of God before you.

Mk 11:23 For verily I say unto you, That whosoever shall say unto this mountain, Be thou removed, and be thou cast into the sea; and shall not doubt in his heart, but shall believe

that those things which he saith shall come to pass; he shall have whatsoever he saith.

Mk 13:30 Verily I say unto you, that this generation shall not pass, till all these things be done.

Mk 14:25 Verily I say unto you, I will drink no more of the fruit of the vine, until that day that I drink it new in the kingdom of God.

Jn 1:51 And he saith unto him, Verily, verily, I say unto you, Hereafter ye shall see heaven open, and the angels of God ascending and descending upon the Son of man.

Jn 3:3 Jesus answered and said unto him, Verily, verily, I say unto thee, Except a man be born again, he cannot see the kingdom of God.

Jn 5:19 Then answered Jesus and said unto them, Verily, verily, I say unto you, The Son can do nothing of himself, but what he seeth the Father do: for what things soever he doeth, these also doeth the Son likewise.

Jn 5:24 Verily, verily, I say unto you, He that heareth my word, and believeth on him that sent me, hath everlasting life, and shall not come into condemnation; but is passed from death unto life.

Jn 6:26 Jesus answered them and said, Verily, to you, Ye seek me, not because ye saw the miracles, but because ye did eat of the loaves, and were filled.

Jn 6:32 Then Jesus said unto them, Verily, verily, I say unto you, Moses gave you not that bread from heaven; but my Father giveth you the true bread from heaven.

Jn 6:47 Verily, verily, I say unto you, He that believeth on me hath everlasting life.

Jn 6:53 Then Jesus said unto them, Verily, verily, I say unto you, Except ye eat the flesh of the Son of man, and drink his blood, ye have no life in you.

Jn 8:34 Jesus answered them, Verily, verily, I say unto you, Whosoever committeth sin is the servant of sin.

Jn 8:51 Verily, verily, I say unto you, If a man keep my saying, he shall never see death.

Jn 8:58 Jesus said unto them, Verily, verily, I say unto you, Before Abraham was, I am.

Jn 10:1 Verily, verily, I say unto you, He that entereth not by the door into the sheepfold, but climbeth up some other way, the same is a thief and a robber.

Jn 10:7 Then said Jesus unto them again, Verily, verily, I say unto you, I am the door of the sheep.

Jn 12:24 Verily, verily, I say unto you, Except a corn of wheat fall into the ground and die, it abideth alone: but if it die, it bringeth forth much fruit.

Jn 13:16 Verily, verily, I say unto you, The servant is not greater than his lord; neither he that is sent greater than he that sent him.

Jn 13:20 Verily, verily, I say unto you, He that receiveth whomsoever I send receiveth me; and he that receiveth me receiveth him that sent me.

Jn 14:12 Verily, verily, I say unto you, He that believeth on me, the works that I do shall he do also; and greater *works* than these shall he do; because her.

Jn 16:20 Verily, verily, I say unto you, That ye shall weep and lament, but the world shall rejoice: and ye shall be sorrowful, but your sorrow shall be turned into joy.

Jn 16:23 And in that day ye shall ask me nothing. Verily, verily, I say unto you, Whatsoever ye shall ask the Father in my name, he will give *it* you.

Jn 21:18 Verily, verily, I say unto thee, When thou wast young, thou girdedst thyself, and walkedst whither thou wouldest: but when thou shalt be old, thou shalt stretch forth thy hands, and another shall gird thee, and carry *thee* whither thou wouldest not.

See **DECEPTION, TRUTH**

VESSELS, *HOLY, of the temple*

Ex 25:29; 37:16, 24; 39:37, 40; 40:9; Nu 3:31; 4:7, 16; 7:14, 26, 38, 44, 62, 80, 86; 1 K 7:45, 50–51; 8:4; 2 K 12:13; 14:14; 24:13; 25:14; 1 Chr 9:29; 22:19; 2 Chr 4:22; 5:5; 24:14; 25:24; 28:24; 29:19; 36:7, 18; Ezr 1:7; 5:14; 6:5; 7:19; Ne

13:9; Je 27:16, 21; 28:3; 52:18; Da 1:2; 5:2, 23

See **TEMPLE**

VESTURE, *garment*

Ge 41:42; De 22:12; Ps 22:18; 102:26; He 1:12; Re 19:13

See **APPAREL**

VIALS, *flasks*

1 S 10:1

VICTORY, *conquest, triumph, success*

1. Assurance from Christ

Ps 72:9 They that dwell in the wilderness shall bow before him; and his enemies shall lick the dust.

Is 53:12 Therefore will I divide him *a portion* with the great, and he shall divide the spoil with the strong; because he hath poured out his soul unto death: and he was numbered with the transgressors; and he bare the sin of many, and made intercession for the transgressors.

Da 2:34 Thou sawest till that a stone was cut out without hands, which smote the image upon his feet *that were* of iron and clay, and brake them to pieces.

Mt 12:20 A bruised reed shall he not break, and smoking flax shall he not quench, till he send forth judgment unto victory.

Jn 16:33 These things I have spoken unto you, that in me ye might have peace. In the world ye shall have tribulation: but be of good cheer; I have overcome the world.

1 Co 15:24 Then *cometh* the end, when he shall have delivered up the kingdom to God, even the Father; when he shall have put down all rule and all authority and power.

Re 3:21 To him that overcometh will I grant to sit with me in my throne, even as I also overcame, and am set down with my Father in his throne.

Re 5:5 And one of the elders saith unto me, Weep not: behold, the Lion of the tribe of Juda, the Root of David, hath prevailed to open the book, and to loose the seven seals thereof.

Re 6:2 And I saw, and behold a white horse: and he that sat on him had a bow; and a crown was given unto him: and he went forth conquering, and to conquer.

Re 17:14 These shall make war with the Lamb, and the Lamb shall overcome them: for he is LORD of lords, and King of kings: and they that are with him *are* called, and chosen, and faithful.

2. Promises of Ultimate Triumph

OVER EVIL INFLUENCES

Ps 44:5 Through thee will we push down our enemies: through thy name will we tread them under that rise up against us.

Mal 4:3 And ye shall tread down the wicked; for they shall be ashes under the soles of your feet in the day that I shall do *this*, saith the LORD of hosts.

OVER EVIL SPIRITUAL FORCES

Lu 10:19 Behold, I give unto you power to tread on serpents and scorpions, and over all the power of the enemy: and nothing shall by any means hurt you.

Ro 8:35 Who shall separate us from the love of Christ? *shall* tribulation, or distress, or persecution, or famine, or nakedness, or peril, or sword?

Ro 8:37 Nay, in all these things we are more than conquerors through him that loved us.

2 Co 10:4 (For the weapons of our warfare *are* not carnal, but mighty through God to the pulling down of strong holds;)

OVER WORLDLY ALLUREMENTS

1 Jn 5:4 For whatsoever is born of God overcometh the world: and this is the victory that overcometh the world, *even* our faith.

OVER SATANIC POWERS

Re 15:2 And I saw as it were a sea of glass mingled with fire: and them that had gotten the victory over the beast, and over his image, and over his mark, *and* over the number of his name, stand on the sea of glass, having the harps of God.

3. Rewards for Overcomers

SPIRITUAL FOOD

Re 2:7 He that hath an ear, let him hear what the Spirit saith unto the churches; To him that overcometh will I give to eat of the tree of life, which is in the midst of the paradise of God.

A NEW NAME

Re 2:17 He that hath an ear, let him hear what the Spirit saith unto the churches; To him that overcometh will I give to eat of the hidden manna, and will give him a white stone, and in the stone a new name written, which no man knoweth saving he that receiveth *it.*

AUTHORITY

Re 2:26 And he that overcometh, and keepeth my works unto the end, to him will I give power over the nations:

ROBES OF RIGHTEOUSNESS

Re 3:5 He that overcometh, the same shall be clothed in white raiment; and I will not blot out his name out of the book of life, but I will confess his name before my Father, and before his angels.

A MEMORIAL PILLAR

Re 3:12 Him that overcometh will I make a pillar in the temple of my God, and he shall go no more out: and I will write upon him the name of my God, and the name of the city of my God, *which is* new Jerusalem, which cometh down out of heaven from my God: and *I will write upon him* my new name.

ENTHRONEMENT

Re 3:21 To him that overcometh will I grant to sit with me in my throne, even as I also overcame, and am set down with my Father in his throne.

AN ETERNAL INHERITANCE

Re 21:7 He that overcometh shall inherit all things; and I will be his God, and he shall be my son.

See **FUTURE LIFE, INHERITANCE**

VINDICTIVENESS

2 K 6:21; 2 Chr 16:10; 18:26; 25:13; Est 3:6; Ps 137:9; Mk 6:19; Lu 9:54; 22:49; Jn 18:10; Ac 23:12

See **FORGIVENESS, MERCY, KINDNESS, RETALIATION, REVENGE, UNMERCIFULNESS, VENGEANCE**

VINEGAR, *sour wine*

Nu 6:3; Ru 2:14; Ps 69:21; Pr 10:26; Mt 27:48; Mk 15:36; Jn 19:29

VINEYARD

Song 8:12; Is 3:14; 5:1, 7; 27:2; Je 12:10; Mt 20:1; 21:28, 33; Mk 12:1; Lu 13:7; 20:9

See **AGRICULTURE**

VINTAGE, *grape harvest*

Le 26:5; Jud 8:2; Is 16:10; 24:13; 32:10; Je 48:32; Mi 7:1

VIOLS　*See* **MUSIC**

VIPERS　*See* **REPTILES**

VIRGIN BIRTH

1. Christ Not the Son Of Joseph

Is 7:14 Therefore the Lord himself shall give you a sign; Behold, a virgin shall conceive, and bear a son, and shall call his name Immanuel.

Mt 1:18 Now the birth of Jesus Christ was on this wise: When as his mother Mary was espoused to Joseph, before they came together, she was found with child of the Holy Ghost.

Mt 1:25 And knew her not till she had brought forth her firstborn son: and he called his name JESUS.

Lu 1:34–35 Then said Mary unto the angel, How shall this be, seeing I know not a man?

And the angel answered and said unto her, The Holy Ghost shall come upon thee, and the power of the Highest shall overshadow thee: therefore also that holy thing which shall be born of thee shall be called the Son of God.

2. The Only Begotten Son of God

Jn 1:14 And the Word was made flesh, and dwelt among us, (and we beheld his glory, the glory as of the only begotten of the Father,) full of grace and truth.

Jn 3:16 For God so loved the world, that he gave his only begotten Son, that whosoever believeth in him should not perish, but have everlasting life.

1 Jn 4:9 In this was manifested the love of God toward us, because that God sent his only begotten Son into the world, that we might live through him.

See **CHRIST**

VIRGIN, *a chaste unmarried woman*

Ge 24:16; Le 21:14; Nu 31:18, 35; Jud 11:37; 21:12; 2 S 13:2; 1 K 1:2; Est 2:2; Is 7:14; 62:5; Eze 44:22; Jl 1:8; Mt 1:23; 25:1; Lu 1:27; 1 Co 7:25, 34; 2 Co 11:2

See **WOMEN**

VISION

1. Earthly

a. A Source of Temptation

Ge 3:6 And when the woman saw that the tree *was* good for food, and that it *was* pleasant to the eyes, and a tree to be desired to make *one* wise, she took of the fruit thereof, and did eat, and gave also unto her husband with her; and he did eat.

Ge 13:10 And Lot lifted up his eyes, and beheld all the plain of Jordan, that it *was* well watered every where, before the LORD destroyed Sodom and Gomorrah, *even* as the garden of the LORD, like the land of Egypt, as thou comest unto Zoar.

Ge 13:12 Abram dwelled in the land of Canaan, and Lot dwelled in the cities of the plain, and pitched *his* tent toward Sodom.

Nu 15:39 And it shall be unto you for a fringe, that ye may look upon it, and remember all the commandments of the LORD, and do them; and that ye seek not after your own heart and your own eyes, after which ye use to go a whoring:

Jos 7:21 When I saw among the spoils a goodly Babylonish garment, and two hundred shekels of silver, and a wedge of gold of fifty shekels weight, then I coveted them, and took them; and, behold, they *are* hid in the earth in the midst of my tent, and the silver under it.

Jud 14:1 And Samson went down to Timnath, and saw a woman in Timnath of the daughters of the Philistines.

Job 31:7 If my step hath turned out of the way, and mine heart walked after mine eyes, and if any blot hath cleaved to mine hands;

Ps 119:37 Turn away mine eyes from beholding vanity; *and* quicken thou me in thy way.

Pr 23:5 Wilt thou set thine eyes upon that which is not? for *riches* certainly make themselves wings; they fly away as an eagle toward heaven.

Ec 2:9 So I was great, and increased more than all that were before me in Jerusalem: also my wisdom remained with me.

Ec 11:9 Rejoice, O young man, in thy youth; and let thy heart cheer thee in the days of thy youth, and walk in the ways of thine heart, and in the sight of thine eyes: but know thou, that for all these *things* God will bring thee into judgment.

Eze 6:9 And they that escape of you shall remember me among the nations whither they shall be carried captives, because I am broken with their whorish heart, which hath departed from me, and with their eyes, which go a whoring after their idols: and they shall lothe themselves for the evils which they have committed in all their abominations.

Eze 20:7 Then said I unto them, Cast ye away every man the abominations of his eyes, and defile not yourselves with the idols of Egypt: I *am* the LORD your God.

Eze 23:16 And as soon as she saw them with her eyes, she doted upon them, and sent messengers unto them into Chaldea.

Mt 4:8 Again, the devil taketh him up into an exceeding high mountain, and sheweth him all the kingdoms of the world, and the glory of them;

Lu 4:5 And the devil, taking him up into an high mountain, shewed unto him all the kingdoms of the world in a moment of time.

1 Jn 2:16 For all that *is* in the world, the lust of the flesh, and the lust of the eyes, and the pride of life, is not of the Father, but is of the world.

b. Focus

Ps 119:37 Turn away mine eyes from beholding vanity; *and* quicken thou me in thy way.

Pr 4:25 Let thine eyes look right on, and let thine eyelids look straight before thee.

Is 33:15 He that walketh righteously, and speaketh uprightly; he that despiseth the gain of oppressions, that shaketh his hands from holding of bribes, that stoppeth his ears from hearing of blood, and shutteth his eyes from seeing evil;

Mt 5:29 And if thy right eye offend thee, pluck it out, and cast *it* from thee: for it is profitable for thee that one of thy members should perish, and not *that* thy whole body should be cast into hell.

c. The Evil Eye

De 15:9 Beware that there be not a thought in thy wicked heart, saying, The seventh year, the year of release, is at hand; and thine eye be evil against thy poor brother, and thou givest him nought; and he cry unto the LORD against thee, and it be sin unto thee.

De 28:54 *So that* the man *that is* tender among you, and very delicate, his eye shall be evil toward his brother, and toward the wife of his bosom, and toward the remnant of his children which he shall leave:

1 S 18:9 And Saul eyed David from that day and forward.

Pr 23:6 Eat thou not the bread of *him that hath* an evil eye, neither desire thou his dainty meats:

Pr 28:22 He that hasteth to be rich *hath* an evil eye, and considereth not that poverty shall come upon him.

Mt 5:29 And if thy right eye offend thee, pluck it out, and cast *it* from thee: for it is profitable for thee that one of thy members should perish, and not *that* thy whole body should be cast into hell.

Mt 6:23 But if thine eye be evil, thy whole body shall be full of darkness. If therefore the light that is in thee be darkness, how great *is* that darkness!

Mk 7:22 Thefts, covetousness, wickedness, deceit, lasciviousness, an evil eye, blasphemy, pride, foolishness:

Mk 9:47 And if thine eye offend thee, pluck it out: it is better for thee to enter into the kingdom of God with one eye, than having two eyes to be cast into hell fire:

Lu 11:34 The light of the body is the eye: therefore when thine eye is single, thy whole body also is full of light; but when *thine eye* is evil, thy body also *is* full of darkness.

d. Dominates Life

LOOKING BACKWARD ARRESTS
PROGRESS

Ge 19:26 But his wife looked back from behind him, and she became a pillar of salt.

LOOKING CHRISTWARD SAVES

Nu 21:9 And Moses made a serpent of brass, and put it upon a pole, and it came to pass, that if a serpent had bitten any man, when he beheld the serpent of brass, he lived.

Jn 3:14–15 And as Moses lifted up the serpent in the wilderness, even so must the Son of man be lifted up:

That whosoever believeth in him should not perish, but have eternal life.

LOOKING AT DIFFICULTIES DEPRESSES

Mt 14:29–30 And he said, Come. And when Peter was come down out of the ship, he walked on the water, to go to Jesus.

But when he saw the wind boisterous, he was afraid; and beginning to sink, he cried, saying, Lord, save me.

LOOKING HEAVENWARD GLORIFIES

Ac 7:55 But he, being full of the Holy Ghost, looked up stedfastly into heaven, and saw the glory of God, and Jesus standing on the right hand of God,

2. Divine

a. Comprehends All Human Life

Ge 6:5 And God saw that the wickedness of man *was* great in the earth, and *that* every imagination of the thoughts of his heart *was* only evil continually.

Ge 11:5 And the LORD came down to see the city and the tower, which the children of men builded.

Ge 16:13 And she called the name of the LORD that spake unto her, Thou God seest me: for she said, Have I also here looked after him that seeth me?

Ex 3:9 Now therefore, behold, the cry of the children of Israel is come unto me: and I have also seen the oppression wherewith the Egyptians oppress them.

Ex 32:9 And the LORD said unto Moses, I have seen this people, and, behold, it *is* a stiffnecked people:

1 S 24:15 The LORD therefore be judge, and judge between me and thee, and see, and plead my cause, and deliver me out of thine hand.

2 S 22:28 And the afflicted people thou wilt save: but thine eyes *are* upon the haughty, *that* thou mayest bring *them* down.

2 K 13:4 And Jehoahaz besought the LORD, and the LORD hearkened unto him: for he saw the oppression of Israel, because the king of Syria oppressed them.

2 K 19:16 LORD, bow down thine ear, and hear: open, LORD, thine eyes, and see: and hear the words of Sennacherib, which hath sent him to reproach the living God.

2 Chr 6:20 That thine eyes may be open upon this house day and night, upon the place whereof thou hast said that thou wouldest put thy name there; to hearken unto the prayer which thy servant prayeth toward this place.

2 Chr 16:9 For the eyes of the LORD run to and fro throughout the whole earth, to shew himself strong in the behalf of *them* whose heart *is* perfect toward him. Herein thou hast done foolishly: therefore from henceforth thou shalt have wars.

Ezr 5:5 But the eye of their God was upon the elders of the Jews, that they could not cause them to cease, till the matter came to Darius: and then they returned answer by letter concerning this *matter.*

Ne 1:6 Let thine ear now be attentive, and thine eyes open, that thou mayest hear the prayer of thy servant, which I pray before thee now, day and night, for the children of Israel thy servants, and confess the sins of the children of Israel, which we have sinned against thee: both I and my father's house have sinned.

Jb 10:4 Hast thou eyes of flesh? or seest thou as man seeth?

Jb 22:14 Thick clouds *are* a covering to him, that he seeth not; and he walketh in the circuit of heaven.

Jb 24:23 *Though* it be given him *to be* in safety, whereon he resteth; yet his eyes *are* upon their ways.

Jb 28:24 For he looketh to the ends of the earth, *and* seeth under the whole heaven;

Jb 31:4 Doth not he see my ways, and count all my steps?

Jb 34:22 *There is* no darkness, nor shadow of death, where the workers of iniquity may hide themselves.

Jb 36:7 He withdraweth not his eyes from the righteous: but with kings *are* they on the throne; yea, he doth establish them for ever, and they are exalted.

Ps 10:11 He hath said in his heart, God hath forgotten: he hideth his face; he will never see *it.*

Ps 11:4 The LORD *is* in his holy temple, the LORD's throne *is* in heaven: his eyes behold, his eyelids try, the children of men.

Ps 14:2 The LORD looked down from heaven upon the children of men, to see if there were any that did understand, *and* seek God.

Ps 33:13 The LORD looketh from heaven; he beholdeth all the sons of men.

Ps 34:15 The eyes of the LORD *are* upon the righteous, and his ears *are open* unto their cry.

Ps 35:22 *This* thou hast seen, O LORD: keep not silence: O Lord, be not far from me.

Ps 53:2 God looked down from heaven upon the children of men, to see if there were *any* that did understand, that did seek God.

Ps 59:4 They run and prepare themselves without *my* fault: awake to help me, and behold.

Ps 66:7 He ruleth by his power for ever; his eyes behold the nations: let not the rebellious exalt themselves. Selah.

Ps 94:9 He that planted the ear, shall he not hear? he that formed the eye, shall he not see?

Ps 102:19 For he hath looked down from the height of his sanctuary; from heaven did the LORD behold the earth;

Ps 139:12 Yea, the darkness hideth not from thee; but the night shineth as the day: the darkness and the light *are* both alike *to thee.*

Ps 139:16 Thine eyes did see my substance, yet being unperfect; and in thy book all *my members* were written, *which* in continuance were fashioned, when *as yet there was* none of them.

Pr 5:21 For the ways of man *are* before the eyes of the LORD, and he pondereth all his goings.

Pr 15:3 The eyes of the LORD *are* in every place, beholding the evil and the good.

Pr 22:12 The eyes of the LORD preserve knowledge, and he overthroweth the words of the transgressor.

Pr 24:18 Lest the LORD see *it,* and it displease him, and he turn away his wrath from him.

Is 1:16 Wash you, make you clean; put away the evil of your doings from before mine eyes; cease to do evil;

Is 37:17 Incline thine ear, O LORD, and hear; open thine eyes, O LORD, and see: and hear all the words of Sennacherib, which hath sent to reproach the living God.

Is 59:15 Yea, truth faileth; and he *that* departeth from evil maketh himself a prey: and the LORD saw *it,* and it displeased him that *there was* no judgment.

Je 5:2 And though they say, The LORD liveth; surely they swear falsely.

Je 7:11 Is this house, which is called by my name, become a den of robbers in your eyes? Behold, even I have seen *it,* saith the LORD.

Je 13:27 I have seen thine adulteries, and thy neighings, the lewdness of thy whoredom, *and* thine abominations on the hills in the fields. Woe unto thee, O Jerusalem! wilt thou not be made clean? when *shall it* once *be?*

Je 16:17 For mine eyes *are* upon all their ways: they are not hid from my face, neither is their iniquity hid from mine eyes.

Je 23:24 Can any hide himself in secret places that I shall not see him? saith the LORD. Do not I fill heaven and earth? saith the LORD.

Je 32:19 Great in counsel, and mighty in work: for thine eyes *are* open upon all the ways of the sons of men: to give every one according to his ways, and according to the fruit of his doings:

Lam 3:60 Thou hast seen all their vengeance *and* all their imaginations against me.

Eze 8:12 Then said he unto me, Son of man, hast thou seen what the ancients of the house of Israel do in the dark, every man in the chambers of his imagery? for they say, The LORD seeth us not; the LORD hath forsaken the earth.

Am 9:8 Behold, the eyes of the Lord GOD *are* upon the sinful kingdom, and I will destroy it from off the face of the earth; saving that I will not utterly destroy the house of Jacob, saith the LORD.

Zec 4:10 For who hath despised the day of small things? for they shall rejoice, and shall see the plummet in the hand of Zerubbabel *with* those seven; they *are* the eyes of the LORD, which run to and fro through the whole earth.

Zec 9:8 And I will encamp about mine house because of the army, because of him that passeth by, and because of him that returneth: and no oppressor shall pass through them any more: for now have I seen with mine eyes.

Mt 6:6 But thou, when thou prayest, enter into thy closet, and when thou hast shut thy door, pray to thy Father which is in secret; and thy Father which seeth in secret shall reward thee openly.

Mt 9:9 And as Jesus passed forth from thence, he saw a man, named Matthew, sitting at the receipt of custom: and he saith unto him, Follow me. And he arose, and followed him.

Mk 6:48 And he saw them toiling in rowing; for the wind was contrary unto them: and about the fourth watch of the night he cometh unto them, walking upon the sea, and would have passed by them.

Jn 1:48 Nathanael saith unto him, Whence knowest thou me? Jesus answered and said unto him, Before that Philip called thee, when thou wast under the fig tree, I saw thee.

Ac 4:29 And now, Lord, behold their threatenings: and grant unto thy servants, that with all boldness they may speak thy word,

Ac 7:34 I have seen, I have seen the affliction of my people which is in Egypt, and I have heard their groaning, and am come down to deliver them. And now come, I will send thee into Egypt.

He 4:13 Neither is there any creature that is not manifest in his sight: but all things *are* naked and opened unto the eyes of him with whom we have to do.

1 Pe 3:12 For the eyes of the Lord *are* over the righteous, and his ears *are*

open unto their prayers: but the face of the Lord *is* against them that do evil.

Re 1:14 His head and *his* hairs *were* white like wool, as white as snow; and his eyes *were* as a flame of fire;

Re 2:18 And unto the angel of the church in Thyatira write; These things saith the Son of God, who hath his eyes like unto a flame of fire, and his feet *are* like fine brass;

Re 19:12 His eyes *were* as a flame of fire, and on his head *were* many crowns; and he had a name written, that no man knew, but he himself.

b. Of Christ

Lu 7:13 And when the Lord saw her, he had compassion on her, and said unto her, Weep not.

Lu 19:5 And when Jesus came to the place, he looked up, and saw him, and said unto him, Zacchaeus, make haste, and come down; for to day I must abide at thy house.

Jn 5:6 When Jesus saw him lie, and knew that he had been now a long time *in that case,* he saith unto him, Wilt thou be made whole?

Jn 11:33 When Jesus therefore saw her weeping, and the Jews also weeping which came with her, he groaned in the spirit, and was troubled,

c. Described

GIVEN IN ANSWER TO PRAYER

2 K 6:17 And Elisha prayed, and said, LORD, I pray thee, open his eyes, that he may see. And the LORD opened the eyes of the young man; and he saw: and, behold, the mountain *was* full of horses and chariots of fire round about Elisha.

SEEN IN AFFLICTIONS

Jb 42:5 I have heard of thee by the hearing of the ear, but now mine eye seeth thee.

SHOWN TO THE PURE IN HEART

Mt 5:8 Blessed *are* the pure in heart: for they shall see God.

POSSESSED BY BELIEVERS

Jn 14:19 Yet a little while, and the world seeth me no more; but ye see me: because I live, ye shall live also.

SHOWN BY THE HOLY SPIRIT

Jn 16:14–15 He shall glorify me: for he shall receive of mine, and shall shew *it* unto you.

All things that the Father hath are mine: therefore said I, that he shall take of mine, and shall shew *it* unto you.

SHOWN THROUGH THE TELESCOPE OF FAITH

He 11:27 By faith he forsook Egypt, not fearing the wrath of the king: for he endured, as seeing him who is invisible.

d. Looking Heavenward

2 Chr 20:12 O our God, wilt thou not judge them? for we have no might against this great company that cometh against us; neither know we what to do: but our eyes *are* upon thee.

Jb 22:26 For then shalt thou have thy delight in the Almighty, and shalt lift up thy face unto God.

Jb 35:5 Look unto the heavens, and see; and behold the clouds *which* are higher than thou.

Ps 5:3 My voice shalt thou hear in the morning, O LORD; in the morning will I direct *my prayer* unto thee, and will look up.

Ps 25:1 Unto thee, O LORD, do I lift up my soul.

Ps 25:15 Mine eyes *are* ever toward the LORD; for he shall pluck my feet out of the net.

Ps 34:5 They looked unto him, and were lightened: and their faces were not ashamed.

Ps 86:4 Rejoice the soul of thy servant: for unto thee, O Lord, do I lift up my soul.

Ps 121:1 I will lift up mine eyes unto the hills, from whence cometh my help.

Ps 123:1 Unto thee lift I up mine eyes, O thou that dwellest in the heavens.

Ps 141:8 But mine eyes *are* unto thee, O GOD the Lord: in thee is my trust; leave not my soul destitute.

Ps 143:8 Cause me to hear thy lovingkindness in the morning; for in thee do I trust: cause me to know the way wherein I should walk; for I lift up my soul unto thee.

Is 17:7 At that day shall a man look to his Maker, and his eyes shall have respect to the Holy One of Israel.

Is 38:14 Like a crane *or* a swallow, so did I chatter: I did mourn as a dove: mine eyes fail *with looking* upward: O LORD, I am oppressed; undertake for me.

Is 40:26 Lift up your eyes on high, and behold who hath created these *things,* that bringeth out their host by number: he calleth them all by names by the greatness of his might, for that *he is* strong in power; not one faileth.

Da 4:34 And at the end of the days I Nebuchadnezzar lifted up mine eyes unto heaven, and mine understanding returned unto me, and I blessed the most High, and I praised and honoured him that liveth for ever, whose dominion *is* an everlasting dominion, and his kingdom *is* from generation to generation:

Jona 2:4 Then I said, I am cast out of thy sight; yet I will look again toward thy holy temple.

Mi 7:7 Therefore I will look unto the LORD; I will wait for the God of my salvation: my God will hear me.

Zec 9:1 The burden of the word of the LORD in the land of Hadrach, and Damascus *shall be* the rest thereof: when the eyes of man, as of all the tribes of Israel, *shall be* toward the LORD.

Mt 14:19 And he commanded the multitude to sit down on the grass, and took the five loaves, and the two fishes, and looking up to heaven, he blessed, and brake, and gave the loaves to *his* disciples, and the disciples to the multitude.

Mk 6:41 And when he had taken the five loaves and the two fishes, he looked up to heaven, and blessed, and brake the loaves, and gave *them* to his

disciples to set before them; and the two fishes divided he among them all.

Lu 21:28 And when these things begin to come to pass, then look up, and lift up your heads; for your redemption draweth nigh.

Jn 11:41 Then they took away the stone *from the place* where the dead was laid. And Jesus lifted up *his* eyes, and said, Father, I thank thee that thou hast heard me.

Jn 17:1 These words spake Jesus, and lifted up his eyes to heaven, and said, Father, the hour is come; glorify thy Son, that thy Son also may glorify thee:

Ac 1:10 And while they looked stedfastly toward heaven as he went up, behold, two men stood by them in white apparel;

Ac 7:55 But he, being full of the Holy Ghost, looked up stedfastly into heaven, and saw the glory of God, and Jesus standing on the right hand of God,

e. Heavenly Vision

Ps 17:15 As for me, I will behold thy face in righteousness: I shall be satisfied, when I awake, with thy likeness.

Is 6:1 In the year that king Uzziah died I saw also the LORD sitting upon a throne, high and lifted up, and his train filled the temple.

Is 33:17 Thine eyes shall see the king in his beauty: they shall behold the land that is very far off.

Eze 1:1 Now it came to pass in the thirtieth year, in the fourth *month,* in the fifth *day* of the month, as I *was* among the captives by the river of Chebar, *that* the heavens were opened, and I saw visions of God.

Eze 8:3 And he put forth the form of an hand, and took me by a lock of mine head; and the spirit lifted me up between the earth and the heaven, and brought me in the visions of God to Jerusalem, to the door of the inner gate that looketh toward the north; where *was* the seat of the image of jealousy, which provoketh to jealousy.

Jn 17:24 Father, I will that they also, whom thou hast given me, be with me where I am; that they may behold my glory, which thou hast given me: for thou lovedst me before the foundation of the world.

1 Co 13:12 For now we see through a glass, darkly; but then face to face: now I know in part; but then shall I know even as also I am known.

1 Jn 3:2 Beloved, now are we the sons of God, and it doth not yet appear what we shall be: but we know that, when he shall appear, we shall be like him; for we shall see him as he is.

Re 22:4 And they shall see his face; and his name *shall be* in their foreheads.

See **BLINDNESS, FUTURE LIFE, IGNORANCE, KNOWLEDGE, LUST**

VISITATION

See **DAY OF THE LORD**

VOICE

1. God's

STRIKES TERROR INTO
HEARTS OF SINNERS

Ge 3:8 And they heard the voice of the LORD God walking in the garden in the cool of the day: and Adam and his wife hid themselves from the presence of the LORD God amongst the trees of the garden.

Ex 19:19 And when the voice of the trumpet sounded long, and waxed louder and louder, Moses spake, and God answered him by a voice.

A STILL SMALL VOICE

1 K 19:12 And after the earthquake a fire; *but* the LORD *was* not in the fire: and after the fire a still small voice.

FULL OF MAJESTY

Ps 29:4 The voice of the LORD *is* powerful; the voice of the LORD *is* full of majesty.

Is 30:30 And the LORD shall cause his glorious voice to be heard, and shall shew the lighting down of his arm, with the indignation of *his* anger, and *with* the flame of a devouring fire, *with* scattering, and tempest, and hailstones.

Eze 43:2 And, behold, the glory of the God of Israel came from the way of the east: and his voice *was* like a noise of many waters: and the earth shined with his glory.

WITNESSING TO CHRIST'S DIVINITY

Mt 17:5 While he yet spake, behold, a bright cloud overshadowed them: and behold a voice out of the cloud, which said, This is my beloved Son, in whom I am well pleased; hear ye him.

MISUNDERSTOOD

Jn 12:28–29 Father, glorify thy name. Then came there a voice from heaven, *saying,* I have both glorified *it,* and will glorify *it* again.

The people therefore, that stood by, and heard *it,* said that it thundered: others said, An angel spake to him.

2 Pe 1:17 For he received from God the Father honour and glory, when there came such a voice to him from the excellent glory, This is my beloved Son, in whom I am well pleased.

2. Christ's

PROVIDING JOY

John 3:29 He that hath the bride is the bridegroom: but the friend of the bridegroom, which standeth and heareth him, rejoiceth greatly because of the bridegroom's voice: this my joy therefore is fulfilled.

ASSURING FOLLOWERS

John 10:4 And when he putteth forth his own sheep, he goeth before them, and the sheep follow him: for they know his voice.

John 10:16 And other sheep I have, which are not of this fold: them also I must bring, and they shall hear my voice; and there shall be one fold, *and* one shepherd.

John 10:27 My sheep hear my voice, and I know them, and they follow me:

TESTING PEOPLE

John 18:37 Pilate therefore said unto him, Art thou a king then? Jesus answered, Thou sayest that I am a king. To this end was I born, and for this cause came I into the world, that I should bear witness unto the truth. Every one that is of the truth heareth my voice.

ARRESTING SINNERS

Acts 9:3-4 And as he journeyed, he came near Damascus: and suddenly there shined round about him a light from heaven:

And he fell to the earth, and heard a voice saying unto him, Saul, Saul, why persecutest thou me?

ASKING FOR ENTRANCE

Rev. 1:15 And his feet like unto fine brass, as if they burned in a furnace; and his voice as the sound of many waters.

ENTREATING UNBELIEVERS

Rev. 3:20 Behold, I stand at the door, and knock: if any man hear my voice, and open the door, I will come in to him, and will sup with him, and he with me.

See **HEARING, SPEECH**

VOWS, *solemn pledges*

1. Examples

Ge 28:20; 31:13; Nu 21:2; De 12:11, 17; Jud 11:30; 1 S 1:11; 2 S 15:8; Ps 56:12; 61:5; 66:13–14; 101:3; 132:2; Ec 5:4; Jona 1:16; Ac 18:18; 21:23

2. Sacred

Le 22:21; 27:2; Nu 6:21; 30:2, 9; De 23:21; Jud 11:35, 39; 21:18; 1 S 14:26; Jb 22:27; Ps 15:4; 22:25; 50:14; 65:1; 66:13; 76:11; 116:14; Pr 20:25; Ec 5:4; Is 19:21; Jona 2:9; Na 1:15; Mal 1:14; Mt 5:33

See **COVENANTS, CURSING, PROMISES**

VULTURES *See* **BIRDS**

W

WAFERS, *thin cakes*

Ex 16:31; 29:2, 23; Le 2:4; 7:12; 8:26; Nu 6:15

WAGES *See* **EMPLOYERS**

WAGONS, *used primarily to transport supplies*

Eze 23:24; 26:10

WAILING, *mourning, weeping*

Est 4:3; Je 9:10, 18; 48:20; Eze 27:32; 32:18; Am 5:17; 8:3; Mi 1:8; Zep 1:10; Mk 5:38; Lu 8:52

WAITING, *ON GOD*

Ps 25:5 Lead me in thy truth, and teach me: for thou *art* the God of my salvation; on thee do I wait all the day.

Ps 27:14 Wait on the LORD: be of good courage, and he shall strengthen thine heart: wait, I say, on the LORD.

Ps 37:9 For evildoers shall be cut off: but those that wait upon the LORD, they shall inherit the earth.

Ps 37:34 Wait on the LORD, and keep his way, and he shall exalt thee to inherit the land: when the wicked are cut off, thou shalt see *it*.

Ps 59:9 *Because of* his strength will I wait upon thee: for God *is* my defence.

Ps 62:1 Truly my soul waiteth upon God: from him *cometh* my salvation.

Ps 62:5 My soul, wait thou only upon God; for my expectation *is* from him.

Ps 123:2 Behold, as the eyes of servants *look* unto the hand of their masters, *and* as the eyes of a maiden unto the hand of her mistress; so our eyes *wait* upon the LORD our God, until that he have mercy upon us.

Pr 20:22 Say not thou, I will recompense evil; *but* wait on the LORD, and he shall save thee.

Is 8:17 And I will wait upon the LORD, that hideth his face from the house of Jacob, and I will look for him.

Is 40:31 But they that wait upon the LORD shall renew *their* strength; they shall mount up with wings as eagles; they shall run, and not be weary; *and* they shall walk, and not faint.

Ho 12:6 Therefore turn thou to thy God: keep mercy and judgment, and wait on thy God continually.

Zep 3:8 Therefore wait ye upon me, saith the LORD, until the day that I rise up to the prey: for my determination *is* to gather the nations, that I may assemble the kingdoms, to pour upon them mine indignation, *even* all my fierce anger: for all the earth shall be devoured with the fire of my jealousy.

See **IMPATIENCE, PATIENCE, PRAYER, QUIETNESS, SILENCE, SOLITUDE**

WALK, *lifestyle of Christians*

1. Its Characteristics

NEW LIFE

Ro 6:4 Therefore we are buried with him by baptism into death: that like as Christ was raised up from the dead by the glory of the Father, even so we also should walk in newness of life.

Ro 8:1 *There is* therefore now no condemnation to them which are in Christ Jesus, who walk not after the flesh, but after the Spirit.

FAITH

2 Co 5:7 (For we walk by faith, not by sight:)

SPIRITUALITY

Ga 5:16 *This* I say then, Walk in the Spirit, and ye shall not fulfil the lust of the flesh.

CONSISTENCY

Ep 4:1 I therefore, the prisoner of the Lord, beseech you that ye walk worthy of the vocation wherewith ye are called,

LOVE

Ep 5:2 And walk in love, as Christ also hath loved us, and hath given himself for us an offering and a sacrifice to God for a sweetsmelling savour.

CAUTION

Ep 5:15 See then that ye walk circumspectly, not as fools, but as wise,

ILLUMINATION

1 Jn 1:7 But if we walk in the light, as he is in the light, we have fellowship one with another, and the blood of Jesus Christ his Son cleanseth us from all sin.

CHRISTLIKENESS

Col 2:6 As ye have therefore received Christ Jesus the Lord, *so* walk ye in him:

1 Jn 2:6 He that saith he abideth in him ought himself also so to walk, even as he walked.

2. Before God

Ge 17:1 And when Abram was ninety years old and nine, the LORD appeared to Abram, and said unto him, I *am* the Almighty God; walk before me, and be thou perfect.

1 K 2:4 That the LORD may continue his word which he spake concerning me, saying, If thy children take heed to their way, to walk before me in truth with all their heart and with all their soul, there shall not fail thee (said he) a man on the throne of Israel.

2 K 20:3 I beseech thee, O LORD, remember now how I have walked before thee in truth and with a perfect heart, and have done *that which is* good in thy sight. And Hezekiah wept sore.

2 Chr 27:6 So Jotham became mighty, because he prepared his ways before the LORD his God.

Ps 56:13 For thou hast delivered my soul from death: *wilt* not *thou deliver* my feet from falling, that I may walk before God in the light of the living?

Ps 116:9 I will walk before the LORD in the land of the living.

3. In Truth

1 K 6:12 *Concerning* this house which thou art in building, if thou wilt walk in my statutes, and execute my judgments, and keep all my commandments to walk in them; then will I perform my word with thee, which I spake unto David thy father:

Ne 5:9 Also I said, It *is* not good that ye do: ought ye not to walk in the fear of our God because of the reproach of the heathen our enemies?

Ne 10:29 They clave to their brethren, their nobles, and entered into a curse, and into an oath, to walk in God's law, which was given by Moses the servant of God, and to observe and do all the commandments of the LORD our Lord, and his judgments and his statutes;

Ps 26:3 For thy lovingkindness *is* before mine eyes: and I have walked in thy truth.

Ps 86:11 Teach me thy way, O LORD; I will walk in thy truth: unite my heart to fear thy name.

Pr 10:9 He that walketh uprightly walketh surely: but he that perverteth his ways shall be known.

Is 2:5 O house of Jacob, come ye, and let us walk in the light of the LORD.

Mi 4:2 And many nations shall come, and say, Come, and let us go up to the mountain of the LORD, and to the house of the God of Jacob; and he will teach us of his ways, and we will walk in his paths: for the law shall go forth of Zion, and the word of the LORD from Jerusalem.

2 Jn 4 I rejoiced greatly that I found of thy children walking in truth, as we have received a commandment from the Father.

3 Jn 3 For I rejoiced greatly, when the brethren came and testified of the truth that is in thee, even as thou walkest in the truth.

See **DISCIPLESHIP, FAITH, LOVE, TRUTH**

WANDERERS

Ge 4:14 Behold, thou hast driven me out this day from the face of the earth; and from thy face shall I be hid; and I shall be a fugitive and a vagabond in the earth; and it shall come to pass, *that* every one that findeth me shall slay me.

Jb 31:7 If my step hath turned out of the way, and mine heart walked after mine eyes, and if any blot hath cleaved to mine hands;

Jb 34:27 Because they turned back from him, and would not consider any of his ways:

Ps 101:3 I will set no wicked thing before mine eyes: I hate the work of them that turn aside; *it* shall not cleave to me.

Ps 119:10 With my whole heart have I sought thee: O let me not wander from thy commandments.

Ps 119:176 I have gone astray like a lost sheep; seek thy servant; for I do not forget thy commandments.

Pr 1:32 For the turning away of the simple shall slay them, and the prosperity of fools shall destroy them.

Pr 5:23 He shall die without instruction; and in the greatness of his folly he shall go astray.

Pr 7:25 Let not thine heart decline to her ways, go not astray in her paths.

Pr 21:16 The man that wandereth out of the way of understanding shall remain in the congregation of the dead.

Pr 27:8 As a bird that wandereth from her nest, so *is* a man that wandereth from his place.

Is 53:6 All we like sheep have gone astray; we have turned every one to his own way; and the LORD hath laid on him the iniquity of us all.

Is 63:17 O LORD, why hast thou made us toys, *and* hardened our heart from thy fear? Return for thy servants' sake, the tribes of thine inheritance.

Je 2:36 Why gaddest thou about so much to change thy way? thou also shalt be ashamed of Egypt, as thou wast ashamed of Assyria.

Je 18:15 Because my people hath forgotten me, they have burned incense to vanity, and they have caused them to stumble in their ways *from* the ancient paths, to walk in paths, *in* a way not cast up;

Je 50:6 My people hath been lost sheep: their shepherds have caused them to go astray, they have turned them away *on* the mountains: they have gone from mountain to hill, they have forgotten their restingplace.

Lam 4:14 They have wandered *as* blind *men* in the streets, they have polluted themselves with blood, so that men could not touch their garments.

Eze 34:6 My sheep wandered through all the mountains, and upon every high hill: yea, my flock was scattered upon all the face of the earth, and none did search or seek *after them.*

1 Ti 1:6 From which some having swerved have turned aside unto vain jangling;

1 Pe 2:25 For ye were as sheep going astray; but are now returned unto the Shepherd and Bishop of your souls.

2 Pe 2:15 Which have forsaken the right way, and are gone astray, following the way of Balaam *the son* of Bosor, who loved the wages of unrighteousness;

Jude 13 Raging waves of the sea, foaming out their own shame; wandering stars, to whom is reserved the blackness of darkness for ever.

See **APOSTASY, BACKSLIDING, FORSAKING**

WANT, *the result of sin and slothfulness*

Ge 47:13 And *there was* no bread in all the land; for the famine *was* very sore, so that the land of Egypt and *all* the land of Canaan fainted by reason of the famine.

Le 26:16 I also will do this unto you; I will even appoint over you terror, consumption, and the burning ague, that shall consume the eyes, and cause sorrow of heart: and ye shall sow your seed in vain, for your enemies shall eat it.

Le 26:26 *And* when I have broken the staff of your bread, ten women shall bake your bread in one oven, and they shall deliver *you* your bread again by weight: and ye shall eat, and not be satisfied.

De 28:48 Therefore shalt thou serve thine enemies which the LORD shall send against thee, in hunger, and in thirst, and in nakedness, and in want of all *things:* and he shall put a yoke of iron upon thy neck, until he have destroyed thee.

De 28:55 So that he will not give to any of them of the flesh of his children whom he shall eat: because he hath nothing left him in the siege, and in the straitness, wherewith thine enemies shall distress thee in all thy gates.

Jud 6:4 And they encamped against them, and destroyed the increase of the earth, till thou come unto Gaza, and left no sustenance for Israel, neither sheep, nor ox, nor ass.

1 S 2:36 And it shall come to pass, *that* every one that is left in thine house shall come *and* crouch to him for a piece of silver and a morsel of bread, and shall say, Put me, I pray thee, into one of the priests' offices, that I may eat a piece of bread.

2 K 6:25 And there was a great famine in Samaria: and, behold, they besieged it, until an ass's head was *sold* for fourscore *pieces* of silver, and the fourth part of a cab of dove's dung for five *pieces* of silver.

Jb 5:5 Whose harvest the hungry eateth up, and taketh it even out of the thorns, and the robber swalloweth up their substance.

Jb 15:23 He wandereth abroad for bread, *saying,* Where *is it?* he knoweth that the day of darkness is ready at his hand.

Jb 18:12 His strength shall be hunger-bitten, and destruction *shall be* ready at his side.

Jb 20:22 In the fulness of his sufficiency he shall be in straits: every hand of the wicked shall come upon him.

Jb 27:14 If his children be multiplied, *it is* for the sword: and his offspring shall not be satisfied with bread.

Jb 30:3 For want and famine *they were* solitary; fleeing into the wilderness in former time desolate and waste.

Ps 59:15 Let them wander up and down for meat, and grudge if they be not satisfied.

Ps 107:5 Hungry and thirsty, their soul fainted in them.

Ps 109:10 Let his children be continually vagabonds, and beg: let them seek *their bread* also out of their desolate places.

Pr 6:11 So shall thy poverty come as one that travelleth, and thy want as an armed man.

Pr 10:3 The LORD will not suffer the soul of the righteous to famish: but he casteth away the substance of the wicked.

Pr 13:4 The soul of the sluggard desireth, and *hath* nothing: but the soul of the diligent shall be made fat.

Pr 13:25 The righteous eateth to the satisfying of his soul: but the belly of the wicked shall want.

Pr 19:15 Slothfulness casteth into a deep sleep; and an idle soul shall suffer hunger.

Pr 20:4 The sluggard will not plow by reason of the cold; *therefore* shall he beg in harvest, and *have* nothing.

Pr 22:16 He that oppresseth the poor to increase his *riches, and* he that giveth to the rich, *shall* surely *come* to want.

Pr 24:34 So shall thy poverty come as one that travelleth; and thy want as an armed man.

Pr 28:22 He that hasteth to be rich *hath* an evil eye, and considereth not that poverty shall come upon him.

Is 3:1 For, behold, the Lord, the LORD of hosts, doth take away from Jerusalem and from Judah the stay and the staff, the whole stay of bread, and the whole stay of water,

Is 5:13 Therefore my people are gone into captivity, because *they have* no knowledge: and their honourable men *are* famished, and their multitude dried up with thirst.

Is 8:21 And they shall pass through it, hardly bestead and hungry: and it shall come to pass, that when they shall be hungry, they shall fret themselves, and curse their king and their God, and look upward.

Is 9:20 And he shall snatch on the right hand, and be hungry; and he shall eat on the left hand, and they shall not be satisfied: they shall eat every man the flesh of his own arm:

Is 32:12 They shall lament for the teats, for the pleasant fields, for the fruitful vine.

Is 65:13 Therefore thus saith the Lord GOD, Behold, my servants shall eat, but ye shall be hungry: behold, my servants shall drink, but ye shall be thirsty: behold, my servants shall rejoice, but ye shall be ashamed:

Je 5:17 And they shall eat up thine harvest, and thy bread, *which* thy sons and thy daughters should eat: they shall eat up thy flocks and thine herds: they shall eat up thy vines and thy fig trees: they shall impoverish thy fenced cities, wherein thou trustedst, with the sword.

Lam 1:11 All her people sigh, they seek bread; they have given their pleasant things for meat to relieve the soul: see, O LORD, and consider; for I am become vile.

Lam 1:19 I called for my lovers, *but* they deceived me: my priests and mine elders gave up the ghost in the city, while they sought their meat to relieve their souls.

Lam 2:12 They say to their mothers, Where *is* corn and wine? when they swooned as the wounded in the streets of the city, when their soul was poured out into their mothers' bosom.

Lam 4:9 *They that be* slain with the sword are better than *they that be* slain with hunger: for these pine away, stricken through for *want of* the fruits of the field.

Lam 5:4 We have drunken our water for money; our wood is sold unto us.

Lam 5:9 We gat our bread with *the peril of* our lives because of the sword of the wilderness.

Eze 4:17 That they may want bread and water, and be astonied one with another, and consume away for their iniquity.

Eze 16:27 Behold, therefore I have stretched out my hand over thee, and have diminished thine ordinary *food,* and delivered thee unto the will of them that hate thee, the daughters of the Philistines, which are ashamed of thy lewd way.

Ho 9:2 The floor and the winepress shall not feed them, and the new wine shall fail in her.

Am 4:6 And I also have given you cleanness of teeth in all your cities, and want of bread in all your places: yet have ye not returned unto me, saith the LORD.

Hag 1:6 Ye have sown much, and bring in little; ye eat, but ye have not enough; ye drink, but ye are not filled with drink; ye clothe you, but there is none warm; and he that earneth wages earneth wages *to put it* into a bag with holes.

Lu 6:25 Woe unto you that are full! for ye shall hunger. Woe unto you that laugh now! for ye shall mourn and weep.

Lu 15:14 And when he had spent all, there arose a mighty famine in that land; and he began to be in want.

Re 6:6 And I heard a voice in the midst of the four beasts say, A measure of wheat for a penny, and three measures of barley for a penny; and *see* thou hurt not the oil and the wine.

See **ABUNDANCE, SATISFACTION**

WANTONNESS, *state of excessive and immoral living*

Ge 39:10 And it came to pass, as she spake to Joseph day by day, that he hearkened not unto her, to lie by her, *or* to be with her.

Pr 6:26 For by means of a whorish woman *a man is brought* to a piece of bread: and the adulteress will hunt for the precious life.

Pr 7:16 I have decked my bed with coverings of tapestry, with carved *works,* with fine linen of Egypt.

Pr 29:3 Whoso loveth wisdom rejoiceth his father: but he that keepeth company with harlots spendeth *his* substance.

Pr 31:3 Give not thy strength unto women, nor thy ways to that which destroyeth kings.

Is 3:16 Moreover the LORD saith, Because the daughters of Zion are haughty, and walk with stretched forth necks and wanton eyes, walking and mincing *as* they go, and making a tinkling with their feet:

Je 3:6 The LORD said also unto me in the days of Josiah the king, Hast thou seen *that* which backsliding Israel hath done? she is gone up upon every high mountain and under every green tree, and there hath played the harlot.

Je 5:8 They were *as* fed horses in the morning: every one neighed after his neighbour's wife.

Lu 15:30 But as soon as this thy son was come, which hath devoured thy living with harlots, thou hast killed for him the fatted calf.

Ro 13:13 Let us walk honestly, as in the day; not in rioting and drunkenness, not in chambering and wantonness, not in strife and envying.

Ja 5:5 Ye have lived in pleasure on the earth, and been wanton; ye have nourished your hearts, as in a day of slaughter.

2 Pe 2:18 For when they speak great swelling *words* of vanity, they allure through the lusts of the flesh, *through much* wantonness, those that were clean escaped from them who live in error.

See **LUST, HELL**

WAR, *prolonged conflict between nations, states, or parties*

Ge 14:2 That *these* made war with Bera king of Sodom, and with Birsha king of Gomorrah, Shinab king of Admah, and Shemeber king of Zeboiim, and the king of Bela, which is Zoar.

Jos 11:18 Joshua made war a long time with all those kings.

1 S 19:8 And there was war again: and David went out, and fought with the Philistines, and slew them with a great slaughter; and they fled from him.

2 S 3:1 Now there was long war between the house of Saul and the house of David: but David waxed stronger and stronger, and the house of Saul waxed weaker and weaker.

2 S 22:35 He teacheth my hands to war; so that a bow of steel is broken by mine arms.

1 K 14:30 And there was war between Rehoboam and Jeroboam all *their* days.

1 K 15:6 And there was war between Rehoboam and Jeroboam all the days of his life.

1 K 15:16 And there was war between Asa and Baasha king of Israel all their days.

1 K 15:32 And there was war between Asa and Baasha king of Israel all their days.

2 K 6:8 Then the king of Syria warred against Israel, and took counsel with his servants, saying, In such and such a place *shall be* my camp.

1 Chr 20:4 And it came to pass after this, that there arose war at Gezer with the Philistines; at which time Sibbechai the Hushathite slew Sippai, *that was* of the children of the giant: and they were subdued.

2 Chr 6:34 If thy people go out to war against their enemies by the way that thou shalt send them, and they pray unto thee toward this city which thou hast chosen, and the house which I have built for thy name;

Ps 27:3 Though an host should encamp against me, my heart shall not fear: though war should rise against me, in this *will* I *be* confident.

Ec 3:8 A time to love, and a time to hate; a time of war, and a time of peace.

Je 41:12 Then they took all the men, and went to fight with Ishmael the son of Nethaniah, and found him by the great waters that *are* in Gibeon.

Je 50:22 A sound of battle *is* in the land, and of great destruction.

Da 11:11 And the king of the south shall be moved with choler, and shall come forth and fight with him, *even* with the king of the north: and he shall set forth a great multitude; but the multitude shall be given into his hand.

Jl 3:10 Beat your plowshares into swords, and your pruninghooks into spears: let the weak say, I *am* strong.

Mt 24:6 And ye shall hear of wars and rumours of wars: see that ye be not troubled: for all *these things* must come to pass, but the end is not yet.

Lu 21:9 But when ye shall hear of wars and commotions, be not terrified: for these things must first come to pass; but the end *is* not by and by.

Re 6:4 And there went out another horse *that was* red: and *power* was given to him that sat thereon to take peace from the earth, and that they should kill one another: and there was given unto him a great sword.

Re 6:8 And I looked, and behold a pale horse: and his name that sat on him was Death, and Hell followed with him. And power was given unto them over the fourth part of the earth, to kill with sword, and with hunger, and with death, and with the beasts of the earth.

Re 19:19 And I saw the beast, and the kings of the earth, and their armies, gathered together to make war against him that sat on the horse, and against his army.

1. Jewish Laws

De 20:2 And it shall be, when ye are come nigh unto the battle, that the priest shall approach and speak unto the people,

De 20:12 And if it will make no peace with thee, but will make war against thee, then thou shalt besiege it:

De 20:20 Only the trees which thou knowest that they *be* not trees for meat, thou shalt destroy and cut them down; and thou shalt build bulwarks against the city that maketh war with thee, until it be subdued.

De 21:10 When thou goest forth to war against thine enemies, and the Lord thy God hath delivered them into thine hands, and thou hast taken them captive,

De 23:9 When the host goeth forth against thine enemies, then keep thee from every wicked thing.

De 24:5 When a man hath taken a new wife, he shall not go out to war, neither shall he be charged with any business: *but* he shall be free at home

one year, and shall cheer up his wife which he hath taken.

Lu 14:31 Or what king, going to make war against another king, sitteth not down first, and consulteth whether he be able with ten thousand to meet him that cometh against him with twenty thousand?

2. Peace Prophesied

Ps 46:9 He maketh wars to cease unto the end of the earth; he breaketh the bow, and cutteth the spear in sunder; he burneth the chariot in the fire.

Ps 65:7 Which stilleth the noise of the seas, the noise of their waves, and the tumult of the people.

Is 2:4 And he shall judge among the nations, and shall rebuke many people: and they shall beat their swords into plowshares, and their spears into pruninghooks: nation shall not lift up sword against nation, neither shall they learn war any more.

Is 65:25 The wolf and the lamb shall feed together, and the lion shall eat straw like the bullock: and dust *shall be* the serpent's meat. They shall not hurt nor destroy in all my holy mountain, saith the Lord.

Ho 2:18 And in that day will I make a covenant for them with the beasts of the field, and with the fowls of heaven, and *with* the creeping things of the ground: and I will break the bow and the sword and the battle out of the earth, and will make them to lie down safely.

Mi 4:3 And he shall judge among many people, and rebuke strong nations afar off; and they shall beat their swords into plowshares, and their spears into pruninghooks: nation shall not lift up a sword against nation, neither shall they learn war any more.

Zec 9:10 And I will cut off the chariot from Ephraim, and the horse from Jerusalem, and the battle bow shall be cut off: and he shall speak peace unto the heathen: and his dominion *shall be* from sea *even* to sea, and from river *even* to the ends of the earth.

3. Threatened as God's Judgment

Le 26:25 And I will bring a sword upon you, that shall avenge the quarrel of *my* covenant: and when ye are gathered together within your cities, I will send the pestilence among you; and ye shall be delivered into the hand of the enemy.

Le 26:33 And I will scatter you among the heathen, and will draw out a sword after you: and your land shall be desolate, and your cities waste.

De 28:22 The LORD shall smite thee with a consumption, and with a fever, and with an inflammation, and with an extreme burning, and with the sword, and with blasting, and with mildew; and they shall pursue thee until thou perish.

De 32:25 The sword without, and terror within, shall destroy both the young man and the virgin, the suckling *also* with the man of gray hairs.

2 Chr 12:15 Now the acts of Rehoboam, first and last, *are* they not written in the book of Shemaiah the prophet, and of Iddo the seer concerning genealogies? And *there were* wars between Rehoboam and Jeroboam continually.

2 Chr 15:6 And nation was destroyed of nation, and city of city: for God did vex them with all adversity.

2 Chr 16:9 For the eyes of the LORD run to and fro throughout the whole earth, to shew himself strong in the behalf of *them* whose heart *is* perfect toward him. Herein thou hast done foolishly: therefore from henceforth thou shalt have wars.

2 Chr 28:17 For again the Edomites had come and smitten Judah, and carried away captives.

Ps 78:62 He gave his people over also unto the sword; and was wroth with his inheritance.

Is 1:20 But if ye refuse and rebel, ye shall be devoured with the sword: for the mouth of the LORD hath spoken *it*.

Is 3:25 Thy men shall fall by the sword, and thy mighty in the war.

Is 7:24 With arrows and with bows shall *men* come thither; because all the land shall become briers and thorns.

Is 42:25 Therefore he hath poured upon him the fury of his anger, and the strength of battle: and it hath set him on fire round about, yet he knew not; and it burned him, yet he laid *it* not to heart.

Is 65:12 Therefore will I number you to the sword, and ye shall all bow down to the slaughter: because when I called, ye did not answer; when I spake, ye did not hear; but did evil before mine eyes, and did choose *that* wherein I delighted not.

Je 4:19 My bowels, my bowels! I am pained at my very heart; my heart maketh a noise in me; I cannot hold my peace, because thou hast heard, O my soul, the sound of the trump, the alarm of war.

Je 5:17 And they shall eat up thine harvest, and thy bread, *which* thy sons and thy daughters should eat: they shall eat up thy flocks and thine herds: they shall eat up thy vines and thy fig trees: they shall impoverish thy fenced cities, wherein thou trustedst, with the sword.

Je 6:4 Prepare ye war against her; arise, and let us go up at noon. Woe unto us! for the day goeth away, for the shadows of the evening are stretched out.

Je 6:25 Go not forth into the field, nor walk by the way; for the sword of the enemy *and* fear *is* on every side.

Je 9:16 I will scatter them also among the heathen, whom neither they nor their fathers have known: and I will send a sword after them, till I have consumed them.

Je 11:22 Therefore thus saith the LORD of hosts, Behold, I will punish them: the young men shall die by the sword; their sons and their daughters shall die by famine:

Je 14:12 When they fast, I will not hear their cry; and when they offer burnt offering and an oblation, I will not accept them: but I will consume them by the sword, and by the famine, and by the pestilence.

Je 15:3 And I will appoint over them four kinds, saith the LORD: the sword to slay, and the dogs to tear, and the fowls of the heaven, and the beasts of the earth, to devour and destroy.

Je 15:9 She that hath borne seven languisheth: she hath given up the ghost; her sun is gone down while *it was* yet day: she hath been ashamed and confounded: and the residue of them will I deliver to the sword before their enemies, saith the LORD.

Je 16:4 They shall die of grievous deaths; they shall not be lamented; neither shall they be buried; *but* they shall be as dung upon the face of the earth: and they shall be consumed by the sword, and by famine; and their carcases shall be meat for the fowls of heaven, and for the beasts of the earth.

Je 19:7 And I will make void the counsel of Judah and Jerusalem in this place; and I will cause them to fall by the sword before their enemies, and by the hands of them that seek their lives: and their carcases will I give to be meat for the fowls of the heaven, and for the beasts of the earth.

Je 20:4 For thus saith the LORD, Behold, I will make thee a terror to thyself, and to all thy friends: and they shall fall by the sword of their enemies, and thine eyes shall behold *it:* and I will give all Judah into the hand of the king of Babylon, and he shall carry them captive into Babylon, and shall slay them with the sword.

Je 21:7 And afterward, saith the LORD, I will deliver Zedekiah king of Judah, and his servants, and the people, and such as are left in this city from the pestilence, from the sword, and from the famine, into the hand of Nebuchadrezzar king of Babylon, and into the hand of their enemies, and into the hand of those that seek their life: and he shall smite them with the edge of the sword; he shall not spare them, neither have pity, nor have mercy.

Je 24:10 And I will send the sword, the famine, and the pestilence, among them, till they be consumed from off the land that I gave unto them and to their fathers.

Je 25:9 Behold, I will send and take all the families of the north, saith the LORD, and Nebuchadrezzar the king of Babylon, my servant, and will bring them against this land, and against the inhabitants thereof, and against all these nations round about, and will utterly destroy them, and make them an astonishment, and an hissing, and perpetual desolations.

Je 25:29 For, lo, I begin to bring evil on the city which is called by my name, and should ye be utterly unpunished? Ye shall not be unpunished: for I will call for a sword upon all the inhabitants of the earth, saith the LORD of hosts.

Je 27:8 And it shall come to pass, *that* the nation and kingdom which will not serve the same Nebuchadnezzar the king of Babylon, and that will not put their neck under the yoke of the king of Babylon, that nation will I punish, saith the LORD, with the sword, and with the famine, and with the pestilence, until I have consumed them by his hand.

Je 29:17 Thus saith the LORD of hosts; Behold, I will send upon them the sword, the famine, and the pestilence, and will make them like vile figs, that cannot be eaten, they are so evil.

Je 32:24 Behold the mounts, they are come unto the city to take it; and the city is given into the hand of the Chaldeans, that fight against it, because of the sword, and of the famine, and of the pestilence: and what thou hast spoken is come to pass; and, behold, thou seest *it.*

Je 32:36 And now therefore thus saith the LORD, the God of Israel, concerning this city, whereof ye say, It shall be delivered into the hand of the king of Babylon by the sword, and by the famine, and by the pestilence;

Je 34:17 Therefore thus saith the LORD; Ye have not hearkened unto me, in proclaiming liberty, every one to his brother, and every man to his neighbour: behold, I proclaim a liberty for you, saith the LORD, to the sword, to the pestilence, and to the famine; and I will make you to be removed into all the kingdoms of the earth.

Je 38:2 Thus saith the LORD, He that remaineth in this city shall die by the sword, by the famine, and by the pestilence: but he that goeth forth to the Chaldeans shall live; for he shall have his life for a prey, and shall live.

Je 42:16 Then it shall come to pass, *that* the sword, which ye feared, shall overtake you there in the land of Egypt, and the famine, whereof ye were afraid, shall follow close after you there in Egypt; and there ye shall die.

Je 46:14 Declare ye in Egypt, and publish in Migdol, and publish in Noph and in Tahpanhes: say ye, Stand fast, and prepare thee; for the sword shall devour round about thee.

Je 49:37 For I will cause Elam to be dismayed before their enemies, and before them that seek their life: and I will bring evil upon them *even* my fierce anger, saith the LORD; and I will send the sword after them, till I have consumed them:

Eze 5:2 Thou shalt burn with fire a third part in the midst of the city, when the days of the siege are fulfilled: and thou shalt take a third part, *and* smite about it with a knife: and a third part thou shalt scatter in the wind; and I will draw out a sword after them.

Eze 5:12 A third part of thee shall die with the pestilence, and with famine shall they be consumed in the midst of thee: and a third part shall fall by the sword round about thee and I will scatter a third part into all the winds, and I will draw out a sword after them.

Eze 5:17 So will I send upon you famine and evil beasts, and they shall bereave thee; and pestilence and blood shall pass through thee; and I will bring the sword upon thee. I the Lord have spoken *it*.

Eze 6:3 And say, Ye mountains of Israel, hear the word of the Lord GOD; Thus saith the Lord GOD to the mountains, and to the hills, to the rivers, and to the valleys; Behold, I, *even* I, will bring a sword upon you, and I will destroy your high places.

Eze 6:12 He that is far off shall die of the pestilence; and he that is near shall fall by the sword; and he that remaineth and is besieged shall die by the famine: thus will I accomplish my fury upon them.

Eze 11:8 Ye have feared the sword; and I will bring a sword upon you, saith the Lord GOD.

Eze 12:14 And I will scatter toward every wind all that *are* about him to help him, and all his bands; and I will draw out the sword after them.

Eze 14:17 Or *if* I bring a sword upon that land, and say, Sword, go through the land; so that I cut off man and beast from it:

Eze 21:9 Son of man, prophesy, and say, Thus saith the LORD; Say, A sword, a sword is sharpened, and also furbished:

Eze 21:12 Cry and howl, son of man: for it shall be upon my people, it *shall be* upon all the princes of Israel: terrors by reason of the sword shall be upon my people: smite therefore upon *thy* thigh.

Eze 24:21 Speak unto the house of Israel, Thus saith the Lord GOD; Behold, I will profane my sanctuary, the excellency of your strength, the desire of your eyes, and that which your soul pitieth; and your sons and your daughters whom ye have left shall fall by the sword.

Eze 25:13 Therefore thus saith the Lord GOD; I will also stretch out mine hand upon Edom, and will cut off man and beast from it; and I will make it desolate from Teman; and they of Dedan shall fall by the sword.

Eze 26:6 And her daughters which *are* in the field shall be slain by the sword; and they shall know that I *am* the LORD.

Eze 28:7 Behold, therefore I will bring strangers upon thee, the terrible of the nations: and they shall draw their swords against the beauty of thy wisdom, and they shall defile thy brightness.

Eze 28:23 For I will send into her pestilence, and blood into her street; and the wounded shall be judged in the midst of her by the sword upon her on every side; and they shall know that I *am* the LORD.

Eze 29:8 Therefore thus saith the Lord GOD; Behold, I will bring a sword upon thee, and cut off man and beast out of thee.

Eze 30:4 And the sword shall come upon Egypt, and great pain shall be in Ethiopia, when the slain shall fall in Egypt, and they shall take away her multitude, and her foundations shall be broken down.

Eze 30:17 The young men of Aven and of Pi-beseth shall fall by the sword: and these *cities* shall go into captivity.

Eze 32:11 For thus saith the Lord GOD; The sword of the king of Babylon shall come upon thee.

Eze 33:2 Son of man, speak to the children of thy people, and say unto them, When I bring the sword upon a land, if the people of the land take a man of their coasts, and set him for their watchman:

Eze 33:27 Say thou thus unto them, Thus saith the Lord GOD; *As* I live, surely they that *are* in the wastes shall fall by the sword, and him that *is* in the open field will I give to the beasts to be devoured, and they that be in the forts and in the caves shall die of the pestilence.

Eze 35:8 And I will fill his mountains with his slain *men:* in thy hills, and in thy valleys, and in all thy rivers, shall they fall that are slain with the sword.

Da 11:33 And they that understand among the people shall instruct many: yet they shall fall by the sword, and by flame, by captivity, and by spoil, *many* days.

Ho 11:6 And the sword shall abide on his cities, and shall consume his branches, and devour *them,* because of their own counsels.

Ho 13:16 Samaria shall become desolate; for she hath rebelled against her God: they shall fall by the sword: their infants shall be dashed in pieces, and their women with child shall be ripped up.

Mi 6:14 Thou shalt eat, but not be satisfied; and thy casting down *shall be* in the midst of thee; and thou shalt take hold, but shalt not deliver; and

that which thou deliverest will I give up to the sword.

Na 2:4 The chariots shall rage in the streets, they shall justle one against another in the broad ways: they shall seem like torches, they shall run like the lightnings.

Mt 24:7 For nation shall rise against nation, and kingdom against kingdom: and there shall be famines, and pestilences, and earthquakes, in divers places.

Mk 13:8 For nation shall rise against nation, and kingdom against kingdom: and there shall be earthquakes in divers places, and there shall be famines and troubles: these *are* the beginnings of sorrows.

Lu 21:10 Then said he unto them, Nation shall rise against nation, and kingdom against kingdom:

Lu 21:24 And they shall fall by the edge of the sword, and shall be led away captive into all nations: and Jerusalem shall be trodden down of the Gentiles, until the times of the Gentiles be fulfilled.

4. Its Horrors

Jud 12:6 Then said they unto him, Say now Shibboleth: and he said Sibboleth: for he could not frame to pronounce *it* right. Then they took him, and slew him at the passages of Jordan: and there fell at that time of the Ephraimites forty and two thousand.

Jud 20:48 And the men of Israel turned again upon the children of Benjamin, and smote them with the edge of the sword, as well the men of *every* city, as the beast, and all that came to hand: also they set on fire all the cities that they came to.

Jud 21:10 And the congregation sent thither twelve thousand men of the valiantest, and commanded them, saying, Go and smite the inhabitants of Jabesh-gilead with the edge of the sword, with the women and the children.

2 S 2:16 And they caught every one his fellow by the head, and *thrust* his sword in his fellow's side; so they fell down together: wherefore that place was called Helkath-hazzurim, which *is* in Gibeon.

2 S 12:31 And he brought forth the people that *were* therein, and put *them* under saws, and under harrows of iron, and under axes of iron, and made them pass through the brick-kiln: and thus did he unto all the cities of the children of Ammon. So David and all the people returned unto Jerusalem.

2 K 15:16 Then Menahem smote Tiphsah, and all that *were* therein, and the coasts thereof from Tirzah: because they opened not *to him*, therefore he smote *it; and* all the women therein that were with child he ripped up.

1 Chr 20:3 And he brought out the people that *were* in it, and cut *them* with saws, and with harrows of iron, and with axes. Even so dealt David with all the cities of the children of Ammon. And David and all the people returned to Jerusalem.

2 Chr 25:12 And *other* ten thousand *left* alive did the children of Judah carry away captive, and brought them unto the top of the rock, and cast them down from the top of the rock, that they all were broken in pieces.

Ps 79:3 Their blood have they shed like water round about Jerusalem; and *there was* none to bury *them*.

Is 9:5 For every battle of the warrior *is* with confused noise, and garments rolled in blood; but *this* shall be with burning *and* fuel of fire.

Is 13:16 Their children also shall be dashed to pieces before their eyes; their houses shall be spoiled, and their wives ravished.

Is 19:2 And I will set the Egyptians against the Egyptians: and they shall fight every one against his brother, and every one against his neighbour; city against city, *and* kingdom against kingdom.

Is 21:15 For they fled from the swords, from the drawn sword, and from the bent bow, and from the grievousness of war.

Lam 1:20 Behold, O LORD; for I *am* in distress: my bowels are troubled; mine heart is turned within me; for I have grievously rebelled: abroad the sword bereaveth, at home *there is* as death.

Lam 2:21 The young and the old lie on the ground in the streets: my virgins and my young men are fallen by the sword; thou hast slain *them* in the day of thine anger; thou hast killed, *and* not pitied.

Lam 5:11 They ravished the women in Zion, *and* the maids in the cities of Judah.

Eze 26:15 Thus saith the Lord GOD to Tyrus; Shall not the isles shake at the sound of thy fall, when the wounded cry, when the slaughter is made in the midst of thee?

Ho 10:14 Therefore shall a tumult arise among thy people, and all thy fortresses shall be spoiled, as Shalman spoiled Beth-arbel in the day of battle: the mother was dashed in pieces upon *her* children.

Ho 13:16 Samaria shall become desolate; for she hath rebelled against her God: they shall fall by the sword: their infants shall be dashed in pieces, and their women with child shall be ripped up.

Am 1:13 Thus saith the LORD; For three transgressions of the children of Ammon, and for four, I will not turn away *the punishment* thereof; because they have ripped up the women with child of Gilead, that they might enlarge their border:

Na 3:10 Yet *was* she carried away, she went into captivity: her young children also were dashed in pieces at the top of all the streets: and they cast lots for her honourable men, and all her great men were bound in chains.

Zec 14:2 For I will gather all nations against Jerusalem to battle; and the city shall be taken, and the houses rifled, and the women ravished; and half of the city shall go forth into captivity, and the residue of the people shall not be cut off from the city.

5. Its Spoils

Ge 14:11 And they took all the goods of Sodom and Gomorrah, and all their victuals, and went their way.

Ge 34:28 They took their sheep, and their oxen, and their asses, and that which *was* in the city, and that which *was* in the field,

Ex 12:36 And the Lord gave the people favour in the sight of the Egyptians, so that they lent unto them *such things as they required.* And they spoiled the Egyptians.

Nu 31:9 And the children of Israel took *all* the women of Midian captives, and their little ones, and took the spoil of all their cattle, and all their flocks, and all their goods.

Nu 31:32 And the booty, *being* the rest of the prey which the men of war had caught, was six hundred thousand and seventy thousand and five thousand sheep,

Nu 31:53 (*For* the men of war had taken spoil, every man for himself.)

De 2:35 Only the cattle we took for a prey unto ourselves, and the spoil of the cities which we took.

De 3:7 But all the cattle, and the spoil of the cities, we took for a prey to ourselves.

De 13:16 And thou shalt gather all the spoil of it into the midst of the street thereof, and shalt burn with fire the city, and all the spoil thereof every whit, for the Lord thy God: and it shall be an heap for ever; it shall not be built again.

De 20:14 But the women, and the little ones, and the cattle, and all that is in the city, *even* all the spoil thereof, shalt thou take unto thyself; and thou shalt eat the spoil of thine enemies, which the Lord thy God hath given thee.

Jos 8:2 And thou shalt do to Ai and her king as thou didst unto Jericho and her king: only the spoil thereof, and the cattle thereof, shall ye take for a prey unto yourselves: lay thee an ambush for the city behind it.

Jos 8:27 Only the cattle and the spoil of that city Israel took for a prey unto themselves, according unto the word of the Lord which he commanded Joshua.

Jos 11:14 And all the spoil of these cities, and the cattle, the children of Israel took for a prey unto themselves; but every man they smote with the edge of the sword, until they had de-stroyed them, neither left they any to breathe.

Jos 22:8 And he spake unto them, saying, Return with much riches unto your tents, and with very much cattle, with silver, and with gold, and with brass, and with iron, and with very much raiment: divide the spoil of your enemies with your brethren.

Jud 5:30 Have they not sped? have they *not* divided the prey; to every man a damsel *or* two; to Sisera a prey of divers colours, a prey of divers colours of needlework, of divers colours of needlework on both sides, *meet* for the necks of *them that take* the spoil?

Jud 8:21 Then Zebah and Zalmunna said, Rise thou, and fall upon us: for as the man *is,* so *is* his strength. And Gideon arose, and slew Zebah and Zalmunna, and took away the ornaments that *were* on their camels' necks.

Jud 8:26 And the weight of the golden earrings that he requested was a thousand and seven hundred *shekels* of gold; beside ornaments, and collars, and purple raiment that *was* on the kings of Midian, and beside the chains that *were* about their camels' necks.

Jud 14:19 And the Spirit of the Lord came upon him, and he went down to Ashkelon, and slew thirty men of them, and took their spoil, and gave change of garments unto them which expounded the riddle. And his anger was kindled, and he went up to his father's house.

1 S 14:32 And the people flew upon the spoil, and took sheep, and oxen, and calves, and slew *them* on the ground: and the people did eat *them* with the blood.

1 S 15:19 Wherefore then didst thou not obey the voice of the Lord, but didst fly upon the spoil, and didst evil in the sight of the Lord?

1 S 17:53 And the children of Israel returned from chasing after the Philistines, and they spoiled their tents.

1 S 23:5 So David and his men went to Keilah, and fought with the Philistines, and brought away their cattle, and smote them with a great slaughter. So David saved the inhabitants of Keilah.

1 S 27:9 And David smote the land, and left neither man nor woman alive, and took away the sheep, and the oxen, and the asses, and the camels, and the apparel, and returned, and came to Achish.

1 S 30:16 And when he had brought him down, behold, *they were* spread abroad upon all the earth, eating and drinking, and dancing, because of all the great spoil that they had taken out of the land of the Philistines, and out of the land of Judah.

1 S 30:20 And David took all the flocks and the herds, *which* they drave before those *other* cattle, and said, This *is* David's spoil.

2 S 3:22 And, Behold, the servants of David and Joab came from *pursuing* a troop, and brought in a great spoil with them: but Abner *was* not with David in Hebron; for he had sent him away, and he was gone in peace.

2 S 8:4 And David took from him a thousand *chariots,* and seven hundred horsemen, and twenty thousand footmen: and David houghed all the chariot *horses,* but reserved of them *for* an hundred chariots.

2 S 8:8 And from Betah, and from Berothai, cities of Hadadezer, king David took exceeding much brass.

2 S 12:30 And he took their king's crown from off his head, the weight whereof *was* a talent of gold with the precious stones: and it was *set* on David's head. And he brought forth the spoil of the city in great abundance.

2 S 23:10 He arose, and smote the Philistines until his hand was weary, and his hand clave unto the sword: and the LORD wrought a great victory that day; and the people returned after him only to spoil.

2 K 7:16 And the people went out, and spoiled the tents of the Syrians. So a measure of fine flour was *sold* for a shekel, and two measures of barley for a shekel, according to the word of the Lord.

1 Chr 5:21 And they took away their cattle; of their camels fifty thousand,

and of sheep two hundred and fifty thousand, and of asses two thousand, and of men an hundred thousand.

1 Chr 18:7 And David took the shields of gold that were on the servants of Hadarezer, and brought them to Jerusalem.

1 Chr 20:2 And David took the crown of their king from off his head, and found it to weigh a talent of gold, and *there were* precious stones in it; and it was set upon David's head: and he brought also exceeding much spoil out of the city.

1 Chr 26:27 Out of the spoils won in battles did they dedicate to maintain the house of the LORD.

2 Chr 14:13 And Asa and the people that *were* with him pursued them unto Gerar: and the Ethiopians were overthrown, that they could not recover themselves; for they were destroyed before the LORD, and before his host; and they carried away very much spoil.

2 Chr 15:11 And they offered unto the LORD the same time, of the spoil *which* they had brought, seven hundred oxen and seven thousand sheep.

2 Chr 20:25 And when Jehoshaphat and his people came to take away the spoil of them, they found among them in abundance both riches with the dead bodies, and precious jewels, which they stripped off for themselves, more than they could carry away: and they were three days in gathering of the spoil, it was so much.

2 Chr 28:8 And the children of Israel carried away captive of their brethren two hundred thousand, women, sons, and daughters, and took also away much spoil from them, and brought the spoil to Samaria.

Jb 29:17 And I brake the jaws of the wicked, and plucked the spoil out of his teeth.

Ps 68:12 Kings of armies did flee apace: and she that tarried at home divided the spoil.

Is 33:4 And your spoil shall be gathered *like* the gathering of the caterpiller: as the running to and fro of locusts shall he run upon them.

Je 49:32 And their camels shall be a booty, and the multitude of their cattle a spoil: and I will scatter into all winds them *that are* in the utmost corners; and I will bring their calamity from all sides thereof, saith the LORD.

Eze 26:12 And they shall make a spoil of thy riches, and make a prey of thy merchandise: and they shall break down thy walls, and destroy thy pleasant houses: and they shall lay thy stones and thy timber and thy dust in the midst of the water.

Eze 29:19 Therefore thus saith the Lord GOD; Behold, I will give the land of Egypt unto Nebuchadrezzar king of Babylon; and he shall take her multitude, and take her spoil, and take her prey; and it shall be the wages for his army.

Eze 38:12 To take a spoil, and to take a prey; to turn thine hand upon the desolate places *that are now* inhabited, and upon the people *that are* gathered out of the nations, which have gotten cattle and goods, that dwell in the midst of the land.

Da 11:24 He shall enter peaceably even upon the fattest places of the province; and he shall do *that* which his fathers have not done, nor his fathers' fathers; he shall scatter among them the prey, and spoil, and riches: *yea,* and he shall forecast his devices against the strong holds, even for a time.

Na 2:9 Take ye the spoil of silver, take the spoil of gold: for *there is* none end of the store *and* glory out of all the pleasant furniture.

Zec 14:14 And Judah also shall fight at Jerusalem; and the wealth of all the heathen round about shall be gathered together, gold, and silver, and apparel, in great abundance.

6. Strategy

Jos 8:5 And I, and all the people that *are* with me, will approach unto the city: and it shall come to pass, when they come out against us, as at the first, that we will flee before them,

Jos 8:15 And Joshua and all Israel made as if they were beaten before them, and fled by the way of the wilderness.

Jud 7:16 And he divided the three hundred men *into* three companies, and he put a trumpet in every man's hand, with empty pitchers, and lamps within the pitchers.

Jud 20:32 And the children of Benjamin said, They *are* smitten down before us, as at the first. But the children of Israel said, Let us flee, and draw them from the city unto the highways.

7. Mercenaries, *hired soldiers*

2 S 10:6 And when the children of Ammon saw that they stank before David, the children of Ammon sent and hired the Syrians of Beth-rehob, and the Syrians of Zoba, twenty thousand footmen, and of king Maacah a thousand men, and of Ish-tob twelve thousand men.

1 K 15:20 So Ben-hadad hearkened unto king Asa, and sent the captains of the hosts which he had against the cities of Israel, and smote Ijon, and Dan, and Abel-beth-maachah, and all Cinneroth, with all the land of Naphtali.

1 Chr 19:7 So they hired thirty and two thousand chariots, and the king of Maachah and his people; who came and pitched before Medeba. And the children of Ammon gathered themselves together from their cities, and came to battle.

2 Chr 16:3 *There is* a league between me and thee, as *there was* between my father and thy father: behold, I have sent thee silver and gold; go, break thy league with Baasha king of Israel, that he may depart from me.

2 Chr 25:6 He hired also an hundred thousand mighty men of valour out of Israel for an hundred talents of silver.

Is 7:20 In the same day shall the Lord shave with a razor that is hired, *namely,* by them beyond the river, by the king of Assyria, the head, and the hair of the feet: and it shall also consume the beard.

Je 46:21 Also her hired men *are* in the midst of her like fatted bullocks; for they also are turned back, *and* are fled away together: they did not stand, because the day of their calamity was come upon them, *and* the time of their visitation.

Eze 16:33 They give gifts to all whores: but thou givest thy gifts to all thy lovers, and hirest them, that they may come unto thee on every side for thy whoredom.

Eze 16:41 And they shall burn thine houses with fire, and execute judgments upon thee in the sight of many women: and I will cause thee to cease from playing the harlot, and thou also shalt give no hire any more.

Eze 29:18 Son of man, Nebuchadrezzar king of Babylon caused his army to serve a great service against Tyrus: every head *was* made bald, and every shoulder *was* peeled: yet had he no wages, nor his army, for Tyrus, for the service that he had served against it:

Ho 8:10 Yea, though they have hired among the nations, now will I gather them, and they shall sorrow a little for the burden of the king of princes.

Na 3:16 Thou hast multiplied thy merchants above the stars of heaven: the cankerworm spoileth, and fleeth away.

See **JUSTICE, PEACE, PEACEABLENESS, RIGHTEOUSNESS**

WAR MACHINES, *used for propelling stones, arrows, and darts*
2 Chr 26:15; Eze 26:9

WARNINGS, *cautions, admonitions*

1. Responsibilities
Ge 19:14 And Lot went out, and spake unto his sons in law, which married his daughters, and said, Up, get you out of this place; for the LORD will destroy this city. But he seemed as one that mocked unto his sons in law.

2 Chr 19:10 And what cause soever shall come to you of your brethren that dwell in their cities, between blood and blood, between law and commandment, statutes and judgments, ye shall even warn them that they trespass not against the LORD,

and so wrath come upon you, and upon your brethren: this do, and ye shall not trespass.

Is 58:1 Cry aloud, spare not, lift up thy voice like a trumpet, and shew my people their transgression, and the house of Jacob their sins.

Je 23:22 But if they had stood in my counsel, and had caused my people to hear my words, then they should have turned them from their evil way, and from the evil of their doings.

Je 36:3 It may be that the house of Judah will hear all the evil which I purpose to do unto them; that they may return every man from his evil way; that I may forgive their iniquity and their sin.

Eze 3:18 When I say unto the wicked, Thou shalt surely die; and thou givest him not warning, nor speakest to warn the wicked from his wicked way, to save his life; the same wicked *man* shall die in his iniquity; but his blood will I require at thine hand.

Eze 11:4 Therefore prophesy against them, prophesy, O son of man.

Eze 16:2 Son of man, cause Jerusalem to know her abominations,

Eze 33:9 Nevertheless, if thou warn the wicked of his way to turn from it; if he do not turn from his way, he shall die in his iniquity; but thou hast delivered thy soul.

Eze 43:10 Thou son of man, shew the house to the house of Israel, that they may be ashamed of their iniquities: and let them measure the pattern.

1 Th 5:14 Now we exhort you, brethren, warn them that are unruly, comfort the feebleminded, support the weak, be patient toward all *men*.

2. Examples
Ge 19:17 And it came to pass, when they had brought them forth abroad, that he said, Escape for thy life; look not behind thee, neither stay thou in all the plain; escape to the mountain, lest thou be consumed.

De 29:20 The LORD will not spare him, but then the anger of the LORD and his jealousy shall smoke against that man, and all the curses that are written in this book shall lie upon him, and the LORD shall blot out his name from under heaven.

Jos 24:20 If ye forsake the LORD, and serve strange gods, then he will turn and do you hurt, and consume you, after that he hath done you good.

1 S 12:15 But if ye will not obey the voice of the LORD, but rebel against the commandment of the LORD, then shall the hand of the LORD be against you, as *it was* against your fathers.

Is 28:14 Wherefore hear the word of the LORD, ye scornful men, that rule this people which *is* in Jerusalem.

Je 13:16 Give glory to the LORD your God, before he cause darkness, and before your feet stumble upon the dark mountains, and, while ye look for light, he turn it into the shadow of death, *and* make *it* gross darkness.

Je 37:9 Thus saith the LORD; Deceive not yourselves, saying, The Chaldeans shall surely depart from us: for they shall not depart.

Jona 3:4 And Jonah began to enter into the city a day's journey, and he cried, and said, Yet forty days, and Nineveh shall be overthrown.

He 12:25 See that ye refuse not him that speaketh. For if they escaped not who refused him that spake on earth, much more *shall not* we *escape,* if we turn away from him that *speaketh* from heaven:

2 Pe 3:17 Ye therefore, beloved, seeing ye know *these things* before, beware lest ye also, being led away with the error of the wicked, fall from your own stedfastness.

3. Admonitions

a. Be not deceived

Je 29:8 For thus saith the LORD of hosts, the God of Israel; Let not your prophets and your diviners, that *be* in the midst of you, deceive you, neither hearken to your dreams which ye cause to be dreamed.

Mt 24:4 And Jesus answered and said unto them, Take heed that no man deceive you.

1 Co 6:9 Know ye not that the unrighteous shall not inherit the kingdom of God? Be not deceived: neither fornicators, nor idolaters, nor adulterers, nor effeminate, nor abusers of themselves with mankind,

1 Co 15:33 Be not deceived: evil communications corrupt good manners.

Ga 6:7 Be not deceived; God is not mocked: for whatsoever a man soweth, that shall he also reap.

Ep 5:6 Let no man deceive you with vain words: for because of these things cometh the wrath of God upon the children of disobedience.

2 Th 2:3 Let no man deceive you by any means: for *that day shall not come,* except there come a falling away first, and that man of sin be revealed, the son of perdition;

1 Jn 3:7 Little children, let no man deceive you: he that doeth righteousness is righteous, even as he is righteous.

b. Beware of Evil

De 6:12 *Then* beware lest thou forget the LORD, which brought thee forth out of the land of Egypt, from the house of bondage.

Lu 12:1 In the mean time, when there were gathered together an innumerable multitude of people, insomuch that they trode one upon another, he began to say unto his disciples first of all, Beware ye of the leaven of the Pharisees, which is hypocrisy.

Lu 12:15 And he said unto them, Take heed, and beware of covetousness: for a man's life consisteth not in the abundance of the things which he possesseth.

Ac 13:40 Beware therefore, lest that come upon you, which is spoken of in the prophets;

Ph 3:2 Beware of dogs, beware of evil workers, beware of the concision.

Col 2:8 Beware lest any man spoil you through philosophy and vain deceit, after the tradition of men, after the rudiments of the world, and not after Christ.

2 Pe 3:17 Ye therefore, beloved, seeing ye know *these things* before, beware lest ye also, being led away with the error of the wicked, fall from your own stedfastness.

c. Shun evil

Jb 11:14 If iniquity *be* in thine hand, put it far away, and let not wickedness dwell in thy tabernacles.

Jb 28:28 And unto man he said, Behold, the fear of the Lord, that *is* wisdom; and to depart from evil *is* understanding.

Jb 36:21 Take heed, regard not iniquity: for this hast thou chosen rather than affliction.

Ps 34:14 Depart from evil, and do good; seek peace, and pursue it.

Ps 37:27 Depart from evil, and do good; and dwell for evermore.

Ps 97:10 Ye that love the LORD, hate evil: he preserveth the souls of his saints; he delivereth them out of the hand of the wicked.

Ps 119:101 I have refrained my feet from every evil way, that I might keep thy word.

Ps 125:3 For the rod of the wicked shall not rest upon the lot of the righteous hands unto iniquity.

Pr 1:15 My son, walk not thou in the way with them; refrain thy foot from their path:

Pr 3:7 Be not wise in thine own eyes: fear the LORD, and depart from evil.

Pr 4:15 Avoid it, pass not by it, turn from it, and pass away.

Pr 4:27 Turn not to the right hand nor to the left: remove thy foot from evil.

Pr 5:8 Remove thy way far from her, and come not nigh the door of her house:

Pr 14:16 A wise *man* feareth, and departeth from evil: but the fool rageth, and is confident.

Pr 16:17 The highway of the upright *is* to depart from evil: he that keepeth his way preserveth his soul.

Ecc 11:10 Therefore remove sorrow from thy heart, and put away evil from thy flesh: for childhood and youth *are* vanity.

Is 1:16 Wash you, make you clean; put away the evil of your doings from before mine eyes; cease to do evil;

Is 33:15 He that walketh righteously, and speaketh uprightly; he that despiseth the gain of oppressions, that shaketh his hands from holding of bribes, that stoppeth his ears from hearing of blood, and shutteth his eyes from seeing evil;

Is 56:2 Blessed *is* the man *that* doeth this, and the son of man *that* layeth hold on it; that keepeth the sabbath from polluting it, and keepeth his hand from doing any evil.

Zec 7:10 And oppress not the widow, nor the fatherless, the stranger, nor the poor; and let none of you imagine evil against his brother in your heart.

Ro 12:9 *Let* love be without dissimulation. Abhor that which is evil; cleave to that which is good.

1 Co 10:6 Now these things were our examples, to the intent we should not lust after evil things, as they also lusted.

2 Co 13:7 Now I pray to God that ye do no evil; not that we should appear approved, but that ye should do that which is honest, though we be as reprobates.

1 Th 5:22 Abstain from all appearance of evil.

2 Ti 2:19 Nevertheless the foundation of God standeth sure, having this seal, The Lord knoweth them that are his. And, Let every one that nameth the name of Christ depart from iniquity.

1 Pe 3:11 Let him eschew evil, and do good; let him seek peace, and ensue it.

3 Jn 11 Beloved, follow not that which is evil, but that which is good. He that doeth good is of God: but he that doeth evil hath not seen God.

d. Take Heed

De 4:9 Only take heed to thyself, and keep thy soul diligently, lest thou forget the things which thine eyes have seen, and lest they depart from thy heart all the days of thy life: but teach them thy sons, and thy sons' sons;

Mal 2:16 For the LORD, the God of Israel, saith that he hateth putting away: for *one* covereth violence with his garment, saith the LORD of hosts: therefore take heed to your spirit, that ye deal not treacherously.

Mt 6:1 Take heed that ye do not your alms before men, to be seen of them: otherwise ye have no reward of your Father which is in heaven.

Mt 18:10 Take heed that ye despise not one of these little ones; for I say unto you, That in heaven their angels do always behold the face of my Father which is in heaven.

Mt 24:4 And Jesus answered and said unto them, Take heed that no man deceive you.

Mk 4:24 And he said unto them, Take heed what ye hear: with what measure ye mete, it shall be measured to you: and unto you that hear shall more be given.

Mk 13:9 But take heed to yourselves: for they shall deliver you up to councils; and in the synagogues ye shall be beaten: and ye shall be brought before rulers and kings for my sake, for a testimony against them.

Mk 13:33 Take ye heed, watch and pray: for ye know not when the time is.

Lu 8:18 Take heed therefore how ye hear: for whosoever hath, to him shall be given; and whosoever hath not, from him shall be taken even that which he seemeth to have.

Lu 11:35 Take heed therefore that the light which is in thee be not darkness.

Lu 12:15 And he said unto them, Take heed, and beware of covetousness: for a man's life consisteth not in the abundance of the things which he possesseth.

Lu 21:8 And he said, Take heed that ye be not deceived: for many shall come in my name, saying, I am *Christ;* and the time draweth near: go ye not therefore after them.

1 Co 3:10 According to the grace of God which is given unto me, as a wise masterbuilder, I have laid the foundation, and another buildeth thereon. But let every man take heed how he buildeth thereupon.

1 Co 10:12 Wherefore let him that thinketh he standeth take heed lest he fall.

Col 4:17 And say to Archippus, Take heed to the ministry which thou hast received in the Lord, that thou fulfil it.

1 Ti 4:16 Take heed unto thyself, and unto the doctrine; continue in them: for in doing this thou shalt both save thyself, and them that hear thee.

2 Pe 1:19 We have also a more sure word of prophecy; whereunto ye do well that ye take heed, as unto a light that shineth in a dark place, until the day dawn, and the day star arise in your hearts:

See **EXHORTATIONS, CHOICE, INVITATIONS**

WARRIORS, *armed soldiers*

Nu 1:3, 20, 24; 26:2; 31:3; 32:17; De 3:18; Jos 1:14; 4:13; 6:3, 9; 8:3; 10:7; Jud 1:4; 21:10; 1 S 31:12; 2 S 17:10; 24:9; 2 K 24:16; 1 Chr 5:18; 7: 2, 11, 40; 8:40; 10:12; 12:2, 8, 21, 28, 35; 26:6, 30; 2 Chr 11:1; 13:3; 14:8; 17:13, 18; 25:5; 26:11, 13; Song 3:7; Is 3:2; Je 49:26; Eze 38:4; Ac 23:31

See **WAR**

WASHING, *ceremonial*

Ex 19:10; 29:4; Le 6:27; 8:21; 11:25, 40; 13:6, 34, 54, 58; 14:8, 47; 15:6, 10, 13, 22, 27; 16:28; 17:15; 22:6; Nu 8:7, 21; 19:7, 10, 19, 21; 31:24; 2 Chr 4:6; Mt 15:20

See **CLEANSING**

WASTE PLACES, *restored*

Jb 38:27 To satisfy the desolate and waste *ground;* and to cause the bud of the tender herb to spring forth?

Ps 74:3 Lift up thy feet unto the perpetual desolations; *even* all *that* the enemy hath done wickedly in the sanctuary.

Ps 107:35 He turneth the wilderness into a standing water, and dry ground into watersprings.

Is 32:15 Until the spirit be poured upon us from on high, and the wilderness be a fruitful field, and the fruitful field be counted for a forest.

Is 35:1 The wilderness and the solitary place shall be glad for them; and the desert shall rejoice, and blossom as the rose.

Is 35:7 And the parched ground shall become a pool, and the thirsty land springs of water: in the habitation of dragons, where each lay, *shall be* grass with reeds and rushes.

Is 41:19 I will plant in the wilderness the cedar, the shittah tree, and the myrtle, and the oil tree; I will set in the desert the fir tree, *and* the pine, and the box tree together:

Is 44:26 That confirmeth the word of his servant, and performeth the counsel of his messengers; that saith to Jerusalem, Thou shalt be inhabited; and to the cities of Judah, Ye shall be built, and I will raise up the decayed places thereof:

Is 49:8 Thus saith the Lord, In an acceptable time have I heard thee, and in a day of salvation have I helped thee: and I will preserve thee, and give thee for a covenant of the people, to establish the earth, to cause to inherit the desolate heritages;

Is 49:19 For thy waste and thy desolate places, and the land of thy destruction, shall even now be too narrow by reason of the inhabitants, and they that swallowed thee up shall be far away.

Is 51:3 For the Lord shall comfort Zion: he will comfort all her waste places; and he will make her wilderness like Eden, and her desert like the garden of the Lord; joy and gladness shall be found therein, thanksgiving, and the voice of melody.

Is 52:9 Break forth into joy, sing together, ye waste places of Jerusalem: for the Lord hath comforted his people, he hath redeemed Jerusalem.

Is 55:13 Instead of the thorn shall come up the fir tree, and instead of the brier shall come up the myrtle tree: and it shall be to the Lord for a name, for an everlasting sign *that* shall not be cut off.

Is 58:12 And *they that shall be* of thee shall build the old waste places: thou shalt raise up the foundations of many generations; and thou shalt be called, The repairer of the breach, The restorer of paths to dwell in.

See **RESTORATION**

WATCHES, *divisions of time*
2 K 11:7; Ne 4:9, 22; Mt 27:65; 28:11

WATCHING

1 S 18:9 And Saul eyed David from that day and forward.

Ps 10:8 He sitteth in the lurking places of the villages: in the secret places doth he murder the innocent: his eyes are privily set against the poor.

Ps 37:32 The wicked watcheth the righteous, and seeketh to slay him.

Is 29:20 For the terrible one is brought to nought, and the scorner is consumed, and all that watch for iniquity are cut off:

Je 20:10 For I heard the defaming of many, fear on every side. Report, *say they*, and we will report it. All my familiars watched for my halting, *saying*, Peradventure he will be enticed, and we shall prevail against him, and we shall take our revenge on him.

Da 6:11 Then these men assembled, and found Daniel praying and making supplication before his God.

Mk 3:2 And they watched him, whether he would heal him on the sabbath day; that they might accuse him.

Lu 6:7 And the scribes and Pharisees watched him, whether he would heal on the sabbath day; that they might find an accusation against him.

Lu 11:53 And as he said these things unto them, the scribes and the Pharisees began to urge *him* vehemently, and to provoke him to speak of many things:

Lu 14:1 And it came to pass, as he went into the house of one of the chief Pharisees to eat bread on the sabbath day, that they watched him.

Lu 20:20 And they watched *him*, and sent forth spies, which should feign themselves just men, that they might take hold of his words, that so they might deliver him unto the power and authority of the governor.

See **DECEPTION**

WATCHMAN

1. Of a City

1 S 14:16; 2 S 13:34; 18:25; 2 K 9:18; Ne 7:3; Ps 127:1; Song 3:3; 5:7; Is 21:6; 52:8; Je 31:6; Eze 33:2; Ho 9:8

2. Of Spiritual Events and Life

a. For the Coming of Christ

THE UNCERTAINTY OF THE TIME

Mt 25:13 Watch therefore, for ye know neither the day nor the hour wherein the Son of man cometh.

Mk 13:33 Take ye heed, watch and pray: for ye know not when the time is.

REWARD PROMISED THE VIGILANT

Lu 12:37 Blessed *are* those servants, whom the lord when he cometh shall find watching: verily I say unto you, that he shall gird himself, and make them to sit down to meat, and will come forth and serve them.

THE CHILDREN OF THE LIGHT WILL NOT SLEEP

1 Th 5:5–6 Ye are all the children of light, and the children of the day: we are not of the night, nor of darkness.

Therefore let us not sleep, as *do* others; but let us watch and be sober.

THE IMMINENCE OF THE ADVENT

Re 3:11 Behold, I come quickly: hold that fast which thou hast, that no man take thy crown.

HIS APPEARANCE WILL BE UNEXPECTED

Re 16:15 Behold, I come as a thief. Blessed *is* he that watcheth, and keepeth his garments, lest he walk naked, and they see his shame.

b. Against Sin and Temptation

De 4:9 Only take heed to thyself, and keep thy soul diligently, lest thou forget the things which thine eyes have seen, and lest they depart from thy heart all the days of thy life: but teach them thy sons, and thy sons' sons;

Ps 39:1 I said, I will take heed to my ways, that I sin not with my tongue: I will keep my mouth with a bridle, while the wicked is before me.

Mt 12:43 When the unclean spirit is gone out of a man, he walketh through dry places, seeking rest, and findeth none.

Mt 26:38 Then saith he unto them, My soul is exceeding sorrowful, even unto death: tarry ye here, and watch with me.

Mt 26:41 Watch and pray, that ye enter not into temptation: the spirit indeed *is* willing, but the flesh *is* weak.

Mk 14:34 And saith unto them, My soul is exceeding sorrowful unto death: tarry ye here, and watch.

Mk 14:38 Watch ye and pray, lest ye enter into temptation. The spirit truly *is* ready, but the flesh *is* weak.

Ac 20:31 Therefore watch, and remember, that by the space of three years I ceased not to warn every one night and day with tears.

1 Co 10:12 Wherefore let him that thinketh he standeth take heed lest he fall.

1 Co 16:13 Watch ye, stand fast in the faith, quit you like men, be strong.

Ep 6:18 Praying always with all prayer and supplication in the Spirit, and watching thereunto with all perseverance and supplication for all saints;

Col 4:2 Continue in prayer, and watch in the same with thanksgiving;

2 Ti 4:5 But watch thou in all things, endure afflictions, do the work of an evangelist, make full proof of thy ministry.

He 12:15 Looking diligently lest any man fail of the grace of God; lest any root of bitterness springing up trouble *you,* and thereby many be defiled;

1 Pe 5:8 Be sober, be vigilant; because your adversary the devil, as a roaring lion, walketh about, seeking whom he may devour:

2 Pe 3:17 Ye therefore, beloved, seeing ye know *these things* before, beware lest ye also, being led away with the error of the wicked, fall from your own stedfastness.

Re 3:2 Be watchful, and strengthen the things which remain, that are ready to die: for I have not found thy works perfect before God.

See **SECOND COMING**

WATER

1. For Physical Thirst

Ge 21:14; Ex 15:25; 17:6; Nu 20:8, 11, 17; 21:16; Jud 15:19; 1 K 13:19; 17:10; Ne 9:15; Ps 78:20; 114:8; Da 1:12; Am 4:8; Mk 9:41; Jn 2:7; 4:13

2. For Spiritual Thirst

ISSUING FROM GOD'S HOUSE

Eze 47:1 Afterward he brought me again unto the door of the house; and, behold, waters issued out from under the threshold of the house eastward: for the forefront of the house *stood toward* the east, and the waters came down from under from the right side of the house, at the south *side* of the altar.

Jl 3:18 And it shall come to pass in that day, *that* the mountains shall drop down new wine, and the hills shall flow with milk, and all the rivers of Judah shall flow with waters, and a fountain shall come forth of the house of the LORD, and shall water the valley of Shittim.

UNAFFECTED BY TIME AND SEASON

Zec 14:8 And it shall be in that day, *that* living waters shall go out from Jerusalem; half of them toward the former sea, and half of them toward the hinder sea: in summer and in winter shall it be.

UNIVERSAL CALL TO PARTAKE

Re 22:17 And the Spirit and the bride say, Come. And let him that heareth say, Come. And let him that is athirst come. And whosoever will, let him take the water of life freely.

CHRIST THE SOURCE

Jn 4:10 Jesus answered and said unto her, If thou knewest the gift of God, and who it is that saith to thee, Give me to drink; thou wouldest have asked of him, and he would have given thee living water.

EVER PRESENT SOURCE

Ps 110:7 He shall drink of the brook in the way: therefore shall he lift up the head.

REFRESHING SOURCE

Is 12:3 Therefore with joy shall ye draw water out of the wells of salvation.

LIFE-CHANGING SOURCE

Jn 4:14 But whosoever drinketh of the water that I shall give him shall never thirst; but the water that I shall give him shall be in him a well of water springing up into everlasting life.

OVERFLOWING SOURCE

Jn 7:38–39 He that believeth on me, as the scripture hath said, out of his belly shall flow rivers of living water.

(But this spake he of the Spirit, which they that believe on him should receive: for the Holy Ghost was not yet *given;* because that Jesus was not yet glorified.)

ALL-ENCOMPASSING SOURCE

Eze 47:9 And it shall come to pass, *that* every thing that liveth, which moveth, whithersoever the rivers shall come, shall live: and there shall be a very great multitude of fish, because these waters shall come thither: for they shall be healed; and every thing shall live whither the river cometh.

INEXHAUSTIBLE SOURCE

Re 7:17 For the Lamb which is in the midst of the throne shall feed them, and shall lead them unto living fountains of waters: and God shall wipe away all tears from their eyes.

Re 22:1–2 And he shewed me a pure river of water of life, clear as crystal, proceeding out of the throne of God and of the Lamb.

In the midst of the street of it, and on either side of the river, *was there* the tree of life, which bare twelve *manner* of fruits, *and* yielded her fruit every month: and the leaves of the tree *were* for the healing of the nations.

3. Comparisons

A BROOK

Ps 110:7 He shall drink of the brook in the way: therefore shall he lift up the head.

A WELL

Is 12:3 Therefore with joy shall ye draw water out of the wells of salvation.

A FOUNTAIN

Je 2:13 For my people have committed two evils; they have forsaken me the fountain of living waters, *and* hewed them out cisterns, broken cisterns, that can hold no water.

A RIVER

Eze 47:5 Afterward he measured a thousand; *and it was* a river that I could not pass over: for the waters were risen, waters to swim in, a river that could not be passed over.

See **CLEANSING, HOLY SPIRIT, SALVATION**

WATER SPOUTS

See **WEATHER**

WAVE OFFERINGS *See* **OFFERINGS**

WAVES, *of the sea*

Jb 38:11; Ps 65:7; 107:29; Is 51:15; Je 5:22; Zec 10:11

WAX, *easily melted*

Ps 22:14; 68:2; 97:5; Mi 1:4

WAY

1. Christ

Jn 10:1 Verily, verily, I say unto you, He that entereth not by the door into the sheepfold, but climbeth up some other way, the same is a thief and a robber.

Jn 10:7 Then said Jesus unto them again, Verily, verily, I say unto you, I am the door of the sheep.

Jn 14:4 And whither I go ye know, and the way ye know.

Jn 14:6 Jesus saith unto him, I am the way, the truth, and the life: no man cometh unto the Father, but by me.

He 9:8 The Holy Ghost this signifying, that the way into the holiest of all was not yet made manifest, while as the first tabernacle was yet standing:

He 10:20 By a new and living way, which he hath consecrated for us, through the veil, that is to say, his flesh;

2. Right

De 5:33 Ye shall walk in all the ways which the LORD your God hath commanded you, that ye may live, and *that it may be* well with you, and *that* ye may prolong *your* days in the land which ye shall possess.

1 S 12:23 Moreover as for me, God forbid that I should sin against the LORD in ceasing to pray for you: but I will teach you the good and the right way:

1 K 8:36 Then hear thou in heaven, and forgive the sin of thy servants, and of thy people Israel, that thou teach them the good way wherein they should walk, and give rain upon thy land, which thou hast given to thy people for an inheritance.

2 Chr 21:12 And there came a writing to him from Elijah the prophet, saying, Thus saith the LORD God of David thy father, Because thou hast not walked in the ways of Jehoshaphat thy father, nor in the ways of Asa king of Judah,

2 Chr 34:2 And he did *that which was* right in the sight of the LORD, and walked in the ways of David his father, and declined *neither* to the right hand, nor to the left.

Ps 50:23 Whoso offereth praise glorifieth me: and to him that ordereth *his* conversation *aright* will I shew the salvation of God.

Ps 85:13 Righteousness shall go before him; and shall set *us* in the way of his steps.

Ps 101:2 I will behave myself wisely in a perfect way. O when wilt thou come unto me? I will walk within my house with a perfect heart.

Ps 107:7 And he led them forth by the right way, that they might go to a city of habitation.

Ps 119:30 I have chosen the way of truth: thy judgments have I laid *before me.*

Ps 139:24 And see if *there be any* wicked way in me, and lead me in the way everlasting.

Pr 2:20 That thou mayest walk in the way of good *men,* and keep the paths of the righteous.

Pr 3:17 Her ways *are* ways of pleasantness, and all her paths *are* peace.

Pr 9:6 Forsake the foolish, and live; and go in the way of understanding.

Pr 10:17 He *is in* the way of life that keepeth instruction: but he that refuseth reproof erreth.

Pr 15:19 The way of the slothful *man* is as an hedge of thorns: but the way of the righteous *is* made plain.

Pr 15:24 The way of life *is* above to the wise, that he may depart from hell beneath.

Is 26:7 The way of the just *is* uprightness: thou, most upright, dost weigh the path of the just.

Is 30:21 And thine ears shall hear a word behind thee, saying, This *is* the way, walk ye in it, when ye turn to the right hand, and when ye turn to the left.

Is 35:8 And an highway shall be there, and a way, and it shall be called The way of holiness; the unclean shall not pass over it; but it *shall be* for those: the wayfaring men, though fools, shall not err *therein.*

Je 7:23 But this thing commanded I them, saying, Obey my voice, and I will be your God, and ye shall be my people: and walk ye in all the ways that I have commanded you, that it may be well unto you.

Je 42:3 That the LORD thy God may shew us the way wherein we may walk, and the thing that we may do.

Mt 7:14 Because strait *is* the gate, and narrow *is* the way, which leadeth unto life, and few there be that find it.

Lu 1:79 To give light to them that sit in darkness and *in* the shadow of death, to guide our feet into the way of peace.

Ac 16:17 The same followed Paul and us, and cried, saying, These men are the servants of the most high God, which shew unto us the way of salvation.

2 Pe 2:2 And many shall follow their pernicious ways; by reason of whom the way of truth shall be evil spoken of.

2 Pe 2:21 For it had been better for them not to have known the way of righteousness, than, after they have known *it,* to turn from the holy commandment delivered unto them.

See **PATHS**

WAYFARER, *traveler, especially on foot*
Jud 19:17; Is 33:8; 35:8; Je 9:2; 14:8

See **PILGRIMS**

WAYS, DIVINE, *perfect and upright*
Ex 13:18 But God led the people about, *through* the way of the wilderness of the Red sea: and the children of Israel went up harnessed out of the land of Egypt.

Ex 33:13 Now therefore, I pray thee, if I have found grace in thy sight, shew me now thy way, that I may know thee, that I may find grace in thy sight: and consider that this nation *is* thy people.

2 S 22:22 For I have kept the ways of the LORD, and have not wickedly departed from my God.

2 S 22:31 *As for* God, his way *is* perfect; the word of the LORD *is* tried: he *is* a buckler to all them that trust in him.

1 K 2:3 And keep the charge of the LORD thy God, to walk in his ways, to keep his statutes, and his commandments, and his judgments, and his testimonies, as it is written in the law of Moses, that thou mayest prosper in all that thou doest, and whithersoever thou turnest thyself:

1 K 3:14 And if thou wilt walk in my ways, to keep my statutes and my commandments, as thy father David did walk, then I will lengthen thy days.

1 K 8:58 That he may incline our hearts unto him, to walk in all his ways, and to keep his commandments, and his statutes, and his judgments, which he commanded our fathers.

1 K 11:38 And it shall be, if thou wilt hearken unto all that I command thee, and wilt walk in my ways, and do *that is* right in my sight, to keep my statutes and my commandments, as David my servant did; that I will be with thee, and build thee a sure house, as I built for David, and will give Israel unto thee.

2 K 21:22 And he forsook the LORD God of his fathers, and walked not in the way of the LORD.

2 Chr 17:6 And his heart was lifted up in the ways of the LORD: moreover he took away the high places and groves out of Judah.

Ps 5:9 For *there is* no faithfulness in their mouth; their inward part *is* very wickedness; their throat *is* an open sepulchre; they flatter with their tongue.

Ps 18:21 For I have kept the ways of the LORD, and have not wickedly departed from my God.

Ps 18:30 *As for* God, his way *is* perfect: the word of the LORD is tried: he *is* a buckler to all those that trust in him.

Ps 25:4 Shew me thy ways, O LORD; teach me thy paths.

Ps 25:9 The meek will he guide in judgment: and the meek will he teach his way.

Ps 37:34 Wait on the LORD, and keep his way, and he shall exalt thee to inherit the land: when the wicked are cut off, thou shalt see *it.*

Ps 67:2 That thy way may be known upon earth, thy saving health among all nations.

Ps 77:13 Thy way, O God, *is* in the sanctuary: who *is* so great a God as *our* God?

Ps 119:3 They also do no iniquity: they walk in his ways.

Ps 119:15 I will meditate in thy precepts, and have respect unto thy ways.

Ps 138:5 Yea, they shall sing in the ways of the LORD: for great *is* the glory of the LORD.

Ps 145:17 The LORD *is* righteous in all his ways, and holy in all his works.

Pr 10:29 The way of the LORD *is* strength to the upright: but destruction *shall be* to the workers of iniquity.

Is 55:9 For *as* the heavens are higher than the earth, so are my ways higher than your ways, and my thoughts than your thoughts.

Da 4:37 Now I Nebuchadnezzar praise and extol and honour the King of heaven, all whose works *are* truth, and his ways judgment: and those that walk in pride he is able to abase.

Ho 14:9 Who *is* wise, and he shall understand these *things?* prudent, and he shall know them? for the ways of the LORD *are* right, and the just shall walk in them: but the transgressors shall fall therein.

Hab 3:6 He stood, and measured the earth: he beheld, and drove asunder the nations; and the everlasting mountains were scattered, the perpetual hills did bow: his ways *are* everlasting.

Mt 11:26 Even so, Father: for so it seemed good in thy sight.

Ac 13:10 And said, O full of all subtilty and all mischief, *thou* child of the devil, *thou* enemy of all righteousness, wilt thou not cease to pervert the right ways of the Lord?

Ro 11:33 O the depth of the riches both of the wisdom and knowledge of God! how unsearchable *are* his judgments, and his ways past finding out!

He 3:10 Wherefore I was grieved with that generation, and said, They do alway err in *their* heart; and they have not known my ways.

Re 15:3 And they sing the song of Moses the servant of God, and the song of the Lamb, saying, Great and marvellous *are* thy works, Lord God Almighty; just and true *are* thy ways, thou King of saints.

See **GOD**

WEAKNESS, *frailty*

1. Manifested in All People

Ex 17:12 But Moses' hands *were* heavy; and they took a stone, and put *it* under him, and he sat thereon; and Aaron and Hur stayed up his hands, the one on the one side, and the other on the other side; and his hands were steady until the going down of the sun.

Nu 11:14 I am not able to bear all this people alone, because *it is* too heavy for me.

Mt 26:40 And he cometh unto the disciples, and findeth them asleep, and saith unto Peter, What, could ye not watch with me one hour?

Jn 16:12 I have yet many things to say unto you, but ye cannot bear them now.

1 Co 3:2 I have fed you with milk, and not with meat: for hitherto ye were not able *to bear it,* neither yet now are ye able.

2. People Dependent on God

Ge 41:16 And Joseph answered Pharaoh, saying, *It is* not in me: God shall give Pharaoh an answer of peace.

Ex 17:11 And it came to pass, when Moses held up his hand, that Israel prevailed: and when he let down his hand, Amalek prevailed.

Ex 33:15 And he said unto him, If thy presence go not *with me,* carry us not up hence.

1 K 17:4 And it shall be, *that* thou shalt drink of the brook; and I have commanded the ravens to feed thee there.

2 K 6:27 And he said, If the LORD do not help thee, whence shall I help thee? out of the barnfloor, or out of the winepress?

2 Chr 20:12 O our God, wilt thou not judge them? for we have no might against this great company that cometh against us; neither know we what to do: but our eyes *are* upon thee.

Ps 22:10 I was cast upon thee from the womb: thou *art* my God from my mother's belly.

Ps 127:1 Except the LORD build the house, they labour in vain that build it: except the LORD keep the city, the watchman waketh *but* in vain.

Je 10:23 O LORD, I know that the way of man *is* not in himself: *it is* not in man that walketh to direct his steps.

Mt 8:25 And his disciples came to *him,* and awoke him, saying, Lord, save us: we perish.

Mt 15:32 Then Jesus called his disciples *unto him,* and said, I have compassion on the multitude, because they continue with me now three days, and have nothing to eat: and I will not send them away fasting, lest they faint in the way.

Lu 9:3 And he said unto them, Take nothing for *your* journey, neither staves, nor scrip, neither bread, neither money; neither have two coats apiece.

Lu 11:3 Give us day by day our daily bread.

Jn 3:27 John answered and said, A man can receive nothing, except it be given him from heaven.

Jn 15:4–5 Abide in me, and I in you. As the branch cannot bear fruit of itself, except it abide in the vine; no more can ye, except ye abide in me.

I am the vine, ye *are* the branches: He that abideth in me, and I in him, the same bringeth forth much fruit: for without me ye can do nothing.

Ac 3:12 And when Peter saw *it,* he answered unto the people, Ye men of Israel, why marvel ye at this? or why look ye so earnestly on us, as though by our own power or holiness we had made this man to walk?

1 Co 4:7 For who maketh thee to differ *from another?* and what hast thou that thou didst not receive? now if thou didst receive *it,* why dost thou glory, as if thou hadst not received *it?*

2 Co 3:5 Not that we are sufficient of ourselves to think any thing as of ourselves; but our sufficiency *is* of God;

2 Co 4:7 But we have this treasure in earthen vessels, that the excellency of the power may be of God, and not of us.

3. Our Weakness Is God's Opportunity

THE PSALMIST

Ps 116:6 The LORD preserveth the simple: I was brought low, and he helped me.

THE DISCIPLES IN THE STORM

Mk 4:38 And he was in the hinder part of the ship, asleep on a pillow: and they awake him, and say unto him, Master, carest thou not that we perish?

Mk 6:48 And he saw them toiling in rowing; for the wind was contrary unto them: and about the fourth watch of the night he cometh unto them, walking upon the sea, and would have passed by them.

THE SICK WOMAN

Mk 5:25–26 And a certain woman, which had an issue of blood twelve years,

And had suffered many things of many physicians, and had spent all that she had, and was nothing bettered, but rather grew worse,

THE FATHER OF THE DEMONIAC

Mk 9:17–18 And one of the multitude answered and said, Master, I have brought unto thee my son, which hath a dumb spirit;

Then one of the crowd answered and said, "Teacher, I brought You my son, who has a mute spirit.

THE DISCIPLES FACING A HUNGRY MULTITUDE

Jn 6:9 There is a lad here, which hath five barley loaves, and two small fishes: but what are they among so many?

PETER IN PRISON

Ac 12:6 And when Herod would have brought him forth, the same night Peter was sleeping between two soldiers, bound with two chains: and the keepers before the door kept the prison.

PAUL AND HIS COMPANIONS ON THE SEA

Ac 27:20 And when neither sun nor stars in many days appeared, and no small tempest lay on *us,* all hope that we should be saved was then taken away.

See **DELIVERANCE, HELPLESSNESS, POWER**

WEAPONS AND ARMOR

1. Spiritual

1 S 17:45 Then said David to the Philistine, Thou comest to me with a sword, and with a spear, and with a shield: but I come to thee in the name of the LORD of hosts, the God of the armies of Israel, whom thou hast defied.

Is 59:17 For he put on righteousness as a breastplate, and an helmet of salvation upon his head; and he put on the garments of vengeance *for* clothing, and was clad with zeal as a cloke.

Mt 4:4 But he answered and said, It is written, Man shall not live by bread alone, but by every word that proceedeth out of the mouth of God.

2 Co 10:4 (For the weapons of our warfare *are* not carnal, but mighty through God to the pulling down of strong holds;)

Ep 6:17 And take the helmet of salvation, and the sword of the Spirit, which is the word of God:

1 Th 5:8 But let us, who are of the day, be sober, putting on the breastplate of faith and love; and for an helmet, the hope of salvation.

He 4:12 For the word of God *is* quick, and powerful, and sharper than any twoedged sword, piercing even to the dividing asunder of soul and spirit, and of the joints and marrow, and *is* a discerner of the thoughts and intents of the heart.

2. Provided

Ro 13:12 The night is far spent, the day is at hand: let us therefore cast off the works of darkness, and let us put on the armour of light.

2 Co 6:7 By the word of truth, by the power of God, by the armour of righteousness on the right hand and on the left,

Ep 6:11 Put on the whole armour of God, that ye may be able to stand against the wiles of the devil.

1 Th 5:8 But let us, who are of the day, be sober, putting on the breast-plate of faith and love; and for an helmet, the hope of salvation.

See **SATAN**

WEARINESS, *to the extent that one is wishful of death*

Ge 27:46; Jb 3:3, 20; 6:11; 7:6, 16; 10:1, 18; 16:7; Ec 2:17; 4:1–2; 7:1; 12:1; Je 8:3; 20:14; Jona 4:8

See **STRENGTH**

WEASEL *See* **ANIMALS**

WEATHER

1. Forecast

Mt 16:2; Lu 12:54–55; Ac 27:10

2. Affected by Prayer

1 S 12:16–18; 1 K 18:41–45; Ja 5:17–18

3. Clouds

Jud 5:4; Jb 26:8; 37:16; Ps 77:17; 148:8; Ec 11:3, 4; 12:2; Ac 27:20; 2 Pe 2:17

4. Dew

Ge 27:28; Ex 16:13; Nu 11:9; De 33:13, 28; Jud 6:40; 1 K 17:1; Ps 133:3; Pr 3:20; Is 26:19; Da 4:15, 25; Ho 14:5; Mi 5:7; Zec 8:12

5. Frost

Ge 31:40; Jb 37:10; Ps 78:47; 147:16

6. Drought

De 8:15; 11:17; 28:24; 1 K 8:35; 2 Chr 7:13; Jb 12:15; Is 5:6; 15:6; 19:5; 42:15; 50:2; Je 2:6; 14:1; 23:10; Ho 13:5; Zec 14:17

7. Heat

Ge 8:22; 18:1; Lu 12:55; Ja 1:11

8. Cold

Jb 37:9; Ps 147:17; Pr 20:4; Jn 18:18; Ac 28:2

9. Mist

Ge 2:6

10. Vapor

Ps 135:7; Ja 4:14; Je 10:13

11. Storms

a. Significant Storms

Ge 7:11; 19:24; Ex 9:23; Jos 10:11; 1 S 7:10; Ac 27:17–18

b. Hailstorms

Ex 9:18, 23; Jos 10:11; Jb 38:22; Ps 18:13; 78:47; 105:32; Is 28:2; 30:30; 32:19; Eze 13:11; 38:22; Hag 2:17; Re 8:7; 11:19; 16:21

c. Rain

Ge 7:12; 8:2; De 11:11; 28:12; 1 S 12:18; 1 K 18:1, 41, 45; 2 Chr 6:27; Ezr 10:9; Jb 5:10; 28:26; 36:27; 37:6; 38:26; Ps 65:10; 77:17; Ec 11:3; Is 55:10; Je 10:13; Jl 2:23; Am 5:8; Zec 10:1; Mt 5:45; 7:25; Lu 12:54; Ac 14:17; 28:2; Ja 5:7

d. Tempests

1 K 19:11; Jb 1:19; Ps 83:15; Is 28:2; 29:6; Eze 13:11; Jona 1:4, 11; Mt 8:24; Mk 4:37; Lu 8:23; Jn 6:18; Ac 27:14, 18, 27, 41; Ja 3:4; Re 6:13

e. Waterspouts

Ps 42:7

12. Thunder and Lightning

a. Sent as Punishment

Ex 9:23; 1 S 2:10; 7:10; 2 S 22:14; Jb 28:26; 40:9; Ps 18:13; 77:18; 104:7; Is 29:6

b. Sent as a Sign

Ex 19:16; 20:18; 1 S 12:18; Jb 37:4; Re 4:5; 16:18

c. Lightning

Ex 19:16; 20:18; 2 S 22:15; Jb 28:26; 37:3; 38:25, 35, Ps 18:14; 77:18; 78:48;

97:4; 135:7; 144:6; Je 10:13; 51:16; Eze 1:13; Na 2:4; Zec 9:14; Mt 24:27; Lu 17:24; Re 4:5; 8:5; 11:19; 16:18

13. Wind

a. Its Wonderful Effects

Ge 8:1; Ex 15:10; Nu 11:31; Eze 37:9; Jona 1:4

b. East Wind

Jb 27:21; Eze 17:10; Ho 13:15

c. North Wind

Song 4:16

d. South Wind

Jb 37:17; Lu 12:55; Ac 27:13

e. West Wind

Ex 10:19

14. Whirlwind

2 K 2:1, 11; Jb 37:9; 38:1; 40:6; Ps 58:9; Is 21:1; Eze 1:4; Na 1:3

Symbol of the Sudden Destruction of the Wicked

Pr 1:27; 10:25; Is 5:28; 17:13; 40:24; 41:16; 66:15; Je 4:13; 23:19; 25:32; 30:23; Da 11:40; Ho 4:19; 8:7; 13:3; Zec 7:14; 9:14

WEAVING *See* **ARTS AND CRAFTS**

WEEPING

1. In Grief

Ge 21:16 And she went, and sat her down over against *him* a good way off, as it were a bowshot: for she said, Let me not see the death of the child. And she sat over against *him,* and lift up her voice, and wept.

Ge 27:38 And Esau said unto his father, Hast thou but one blessing, my father? bless me, *even* me also, O my father. And Esau lifted up his voice, and wept.

Ge 37:35 And all his sons and all his daughters rose up to comfort him; but he refused to be comforted; and he said, For I will go down into the grave unto my son mourning. Thus his father wept for him.

1 S 1:7 And *as* he did so year by year, when she went up to the house of the LORD, so she provoked her; therefore she wept, and did not eat.

1 S 11:4 Then came the messengers to Gibeah of Saul, and told the tidings in the ears of the people: and all the people lifted up their voices, and wept.

2 S 3:16 And her husband went with her along weeping behind her to Bahurim. Then said Abner unto him, Go, return. And he returned.

2 S 3:32 And they buried Abner in Hebron: and the king lifted up his voice, and wept at the grave of Abner; and all the people wept.

2 S 15:30 And David went up by the ascent of *mount* Olivet, and wept as he went up, and had his head covered, and he went barefoot: and all the people that *was* with him covered every man his head, and they went up, weeping as they went up.

2 S 19:1 And it was told Joab, Behold, the king weepeth and mourneth for Absalom.

2 K 8:11 And he settled his countenance stedfastly, until he was ashamed: and the man of God wept.

2 K 13:14 Now Elisha was fallen sick of his sickness whereof he died. And Joash the king of Israel came down unto him, and wept over his face, and said, O my father, my father, the chariot of Israel, and the horsemen thereof.

2 K 20:3 I beseech thee, O LORD, remember now how I have walked before thee in truth and with a perfect heart, and have done *that which is* good in thy sight. And Hezekiah wept sore.

Ezr 3:12 But many of the priests and Levites and chief of the fathers, *who were* ancient men, that had seen the first house, when the foundation of this house was laid before their eyes, wept with a loud voice; and many shouted aloud for joy:

Jb 16:16 My face is foul with weeping, and my eyelids is the shadow of death;

Jb 17:7 Mine eye also is dim by reason of sorrow, and all my members *are* as a shadow.

Ps 6:8 Depart from me, all ye workers of iniquity; for the LORD hath heard the voice of my weeping.

Ps 137:1 By the rivers of Babylon, there we sat down, yea, we wept, when we remembered Zion.

Ec 3:4 A time to weep, and a time to laugh; a time to mourn, and a time to dance;

Is 38:3 And said, Remember now, O LORD, I beseech thee, how I have walked before thee in truth and with a perfect heart, and have done *that which is* good in thy sight. And Hezekiah wept sore.

Jn 11:33 When Jesus therefore saw her weeping, and the Jews also weeping which came with her, he groaned in the spirit, and was troubled,

Jn 20:11 But Mary stood without at the sepulchre weeping: and as she wept, she stooped down, *and looked* into the sepulchre,

Ac 9:39 Then Peter arose and went with them. When he was come, they brought him into the upper chamber: and all the widows stood by him weeping, and shewing the coats and garments which Dorcas made, while she was with them.

Ac 20:37 And they all wept sore, and fell on Paul's neck, and kissed him,

Ac 21:13 Then Paul answered, What mean ye to weep and to break mine heart? for I am ready not to be bound only, but also to die at Jerusalem for the name of the Lord Jesus.

Re 18:19 And they cast dust on their heads, and cried, weeping and wailing, saying, Alas, alas, that great city, wherein were made rich all that had ships in the sea by reason of her costliness! for in one hour is she made desolate.

2. Caused by Sin

Ge 27:34 And when Esau heard the words of his father, he cried with a great and exceeding bitter cry, and said unto his father, Bless me, *even* me also, O my father.

Nu 25:6 And, behold, one of the children of Israel came and brought unto his brethren a Midianitish woman in the sight of Moses, and in the sight of all the congregation of the children of Israel, who *were* weeping *before* the door of the tabernacle of the congregation.

De 1:45 And ye returned and wept before the LORD; but the LORD would not hearken to your voice, nor give ear unto you.

Jud 2:4 And it came to pass, when the angel of the LORD spake these words unto all the children of Israel, that the people lifted up their voice, and wept.

Ps 39:12 Hear my prayer, O LORD, and give ear unto my cry; hold not thy peace at my tears: for I *am* a stranger with thee, *and* a sojourner, as all my fathers *were.*

Is 15:3 In their streets they shall gird themselves with sackcloth: on the tops of their houses, and in their streets, every one shall howl, weeping abundantly.

Is 65:14 Behold, my servants shall sing for joy of heart, but ye shall cry for sorrow of heart, and shall howl for vexation of spirit.

Je 3:21 A voice was heard upon the high places, weeping *and* supplications of the children of Israel: for they have perverted their way, *and* they have forgotten the LORD their God.

Je 50:4 In those days, and in that time, saith the LORD, the children of Israel shall come, they and the children of Judah together, going and weeping: they shall go, and seek the LORD their God.

Lam 1:2 She weepeth sore in the night, and her tears *are* on her cheeks: among all her lovers she hath none to comfort *her:* all her friends have dealt treacherously with her, they are become her enemies.

Mt 26:75 And Peter remembered the word of Jesus, which said unto him, Before the cock crow, thou shalt deny me thrice. And he went out, and wept bitterly.

Mk 14:72 And the second time the cock crew. And Peter called to mind the word that Jesus said unto him,

Before the cock crow twice, thou shalt deny me thrice. And when he thought thereon, he wept.

Lu 6:21 Blessed *are ye* that hunger now: for ye shall be filled. Blessed *are ye* that weep now: for ye shall laugh.

Lu 6:25 Woe unto you that are full! for ye shall hunger. Woe unto you that laugh now! for ye shall mourn and weep.

Lu 7:38 And stood at his feet behind *him* weeping, and began to wash his feet with tears, and did wipe *them* with the hairs of her head, and kissed his feet, and anointed *them* with the ointment.

Lu 13:28 There shall be weeping and gnashing of teeth, when ye shall see Abraham, and Isaac, and Jacob, and all the prophets, in the kingdom of God, and you *yourselves* thrust out.

He 12:17 For ye know how that afterward, when he would have inherited the blessing, he was rejected: for he found no place of repentance, though he sought it carefully with tears.

Ja 4:9 Be afflicted, and mourn, and weep: let your laughter be turned to mourning, and *your* joy to heaviness.

Re 1:7 Behold, he cometh with clouds; and every eye shall see him, and they *also* which pierced him: and all kindreds of the earth shall wail because of him. Even so, Amen.

See **JOY, TEARS**

WEIGHING, *of money, a way of making payment*

Ge 23:16; Ezr 8:25, 33; Jb 28:15; Je 32:9; Zec 11:12

See **MONEY**

WEIGHTS AND MEASURES

See the chart on the following page.

WELLS, *natural water holes*

Ge 16:14; 21:19, 30; 24:11, 62; 25:11; 26:15, 18, 25, 32; 29:2, 8; Ex 2:15; 15:27; Nu 20:17; 21:16, 22; De 6:11; Jos 18:15; Jud 5:11; 7:1; 2 S 17:18; 23:15; 2 K 3:19; 1 Chr 11:17; Jn 4:6

See **WATER**

WHALES, *sea monsters*

Ge 1:21; Jb 7:12; Eze 32:2

WHEAT

1. A Grain

Ex 9:32; Nu 18:12; De 32:14; Jud 6:11; 1 K 5:11; 2 Chr 2:10, 15; Ezr 6:9; 7:22; Ps 147:14; Is 28:25; Je 31:12; 41:8; Eze 4:9; 27:17; 45:13; Jl 1:11; Mt 13:25; Lu 16:7; Jn 12:24; Ac 27:38; 1 Co 15:37; Re 6:6; 18:13

See **AGRICULTURE**

2. The Righteous Compared to

Je 23:28 The prophet that hath a dream, let him tell a dream; and he that hath my word, let him speak my word faithfully. What *is* the chaff to the wheat? saith the LORD.

Mt 3:12 Whose fan *is* in his hand, and he will throughly purge his floor, and gather his wheat into the garner; but he will burn up the chaff with unquenchable fire.

Mt 13:30 Let both grow together until the harvest: and in the time of harvest I will say to the reapers, Gather ye together first the tares, and bind them in bundles to burn them: but gather the wheat into my barn.

Lu 3:17 Whose fan *is* in his hand, and he will throughly purge his floor, and will gather the wheat into his garner; but the chaff he will burn with fire unquenchable.

See **JUSTICE, JUDGMENTS**

WHEELS

Je 18:3; Eze 1:15; 3:13; 10:9, 12

WHIPS, *scourges used to inflict punishment*

1 K 12:11; Pr 26:3; Na 3:2

WHIRLWIND　*See* **WEATHER**

WHITE, *a color symbolizing purity*

Da 12:10; Mt 28:3; Re 2:17; 3:4; 4:4; 6:2; 7:9; 19:8; 20:11

WEIGHTS

Unit	Weight	Equivalent
gerah	about 0.02 ounce (0.57 grams)	1/20 shekel
half-shekel (beka)	about 0.2 ounce (5.5 grams)	1/2 shekel; 10 gerahs
two-thirds of a shekel (pim)	0.33 ounce (7.6 grams)	2/3 shekel
shekel	about 0.4 ounce (11.5 grams) for common shek el; about 0.8 ounce for royal shekel	20 gerahs
pound (litra)	12 ounces	no equivalent
maneh, mina	1.25 pounds	50 shekels
talent	about 75 pounds for common talent; about 150 pounds for royal talent	60 minas; 3,000 shekels

LAND MEASURE AND LENGTH

Unit	Length	Equivalent
finger	0.75 inch	1/4 handbreadth
handbreadth	3 inches	1/3 span; 4 fingers
span	9 inches	1/2 cubit; 3 handbreadths
cubit, yards	18 inches	1/2 pace; 2 spans
pace	3 feet	1/3 rod; 2 cubits
fathom	6 feet	4 cubits
measuring rod	9 feet (10.5 feet in Ezekiel)	3 paces; 6 cubits
stadion, mile	about 600 feet	1/8 Roman mile
a Sabbath day's journey	about 3,000 feet	2,000 cubits
mile	about 4,800 feet	8 stadia
a day's journey	about 20 miles	no equivalent

LIQUID AND DRY MEASURES

Unit	Measure	Equivalent
log	1 pint	1/4 kab
kab	2 quarts	4 logs
hin	1 gallon	2 kabs
measure, bath	6 gallons	6 hins; (1 ephah)
gallon (metretes)	10.2 gallons	no equivalent
kor	60 gallons	10 baths
koros	1.03 gallons	no equivalent
pecks (saton)	1.5 pecks	1 1/2 modii
kab	1.16 quarts	4 logs
omer	2.08 quarts	1/10 ephah; 1 4/5 kab
measure, peck (seah)	7 quarts	1/3 ephah
ephah	.65 bushel, 20.8 quarts	1/10 homer
homer and a half (lethech)	3.26 bushels	1/2 kor; 1/2 homer
kor, measure	6.52 bushels	1 homer; 10 ephahs
homer	6.52 bushels	1 kor; 10 ephahs

MONEY

Unit	Equivalent
Hebrew Money	
gerah	1/20 shekel
beka	1/2 shekel; 10 gerahs
piece of money (qesitah)	about 3.2 pounds (1430 grams)
shekel	4 days' wages; 2 bekas; 20 gerahs
talent, one hundred pounds	3,000 shekels; 6,000 bekas
Persian Money	
daric, drachma	2 days' wages; 1/2 Hebrew silver shekel
Greek Money	
cents, small copper coin (lepton) (tetradrachma)	1/2 of a Roman kodrantes
coin, silver coins(drachma)	1 day's wage
two-drachma tax (didrachma)	2 drachmas
Stater	4 drachmas
Roman Money	
cent (kodrantes)	1/4 of an assarius
cent (assarius)	1/16 of a denarius
denarius	about 1 day's wage (for a laborer)

WHOLENESS, or health restored

Mt 9:12 But when Jesus heard *that,* he said unto them, They that be whole need not a physician, but they that are sick.

Mt 9:22 But Jesus turned him about, and when he saw her, he said, Daughter, be of good comfort; thy faith hath made thee whole. And the woman was made whole from that hour.

Mt 14:36 And besought him that they might only touch the hem of his garment: and as many as touched were made perfectly whole.

Mt 15:28 Then Jesus answered and said unto her, O woman, great *is* thy faith: be it unto thee even as thou wilt. And her daughter was made whole from that very hour.

Mk 5:28 For she said, If I may touch but his clothes, I shall be whole.

Mk 8:25 After that he put *his* hands again upon his eyes, and made him look up: and he was restored, and saw every man clearly.

Lu 7:10 And they that were sent, returning to the house, found the servant whole that had been sick.

Lu 8:49–50 While he yet spake, there cometh one from the ruler of the synagogue's *house,* saying to him, Thy daughter is dead; trouble not the Master.

But when Jesus heard *it,* he answered him, saying, Fear not: believe only, and she shall be made whole.

Jn 7:23 If a man on the sabbath day receive circumcision, that the law of Moses should not be broken; are ye angry at me, because I have made a man every whit whole on the sabbath day?

Ac 3:16 And his name through faith in his name hath made this man strong, whom ye see and know: yea, the faith which is by him hath given him this perfect soundness in the presence of you all.

Ac 4:9–10 If we this day be examined of the good deed done to the impotent man, by what means he is made whole;

Be it known unto you all, and to all the people of Israel, that by the name of Jesus Christ of Nazareth, whom ye crucified, whom God raised from the dead, *even* by him doth this man stand here before you whole.

Ac 9:34 And Peter said unto him, Aeneas, Jesus Christ maketh thee whole: arise, and make thy bed. And he arose immediately.

See **RESTORATION**

WHOSOEVER

1. Regarding Condemnation

Ex 32:33 And the LORD said unto Moses, Whosoever hath sinned against me, him will I blot out of my book.

De 18:19 And it shall come to pass, *that* whosoever will not hearken unto my words which he shall speak in my name, I will require *it* of him.

Mt 5:22 But I say unto you, That whosoever is angry with his brother without a cause shall be in danger of the judgment: and whosoever shall say to his brother, Raca, shall be in danger of the council: but whosoever shall say, Thou fool, shall be in danger of hell fire.

Jn 8:34 Jesus answered them, Verily, verily, I say unto you, Whosoever committeth sin is the servant of sin.

Ro 2:1 Therefore thou art inexcusable, O man, whosoever thou art that judgest: for wherein thou judgest another, thou condemnest thyself; for thou that judgest doest the same things.

1 Jn 2:23 Whosoever denieth the Son, the same hath not the Father: *[but] he that acknowledgeth the Son hath the Father also.*

1 Jn 3:4 Whosoever committeth sin transgresseth also the law: for sin is the transgression of the law.

1 Jn 3:10 In this the children of God are manifest, and the children of the devil: whosoever doeth not righteousness is not of God, neither he that loveth not his brother.

1 Jn 3:15 Whosoever hateth his brother is a murderer: and ye know that no murderer hath eternal life abiding in him.

2 Jn 9 Whosoever transgresseth, and abideth not in the doctrine of Christ, hath not God. He that abideth in the doctrine of Christ, he hath both the Father and the Son.

2. Regarding Salvation

Is 45:22 Look unto me, and be ye saved, all the ends of the earth: for I *am* God, and *there is* none else.

Jl 2:32 And it shall come to pass, *that* whosoever shall call on the name of the LORD shall be delivered: for in mount Zion and in Jerusalem shall be deliverance, as the LORD hath said, and in the remnant whom the LORD shall call.

Mt 22:9 Go ye therefore into the highways, and as many as ye shall find, bid to the marriage.

Lu 12:8 Also I say unto you, Whosoever shall confess me before men, him shall the Son of man also confess before the angels of God:

Jn 4:14 But whosoever drinketh of the water that I shall give him shall never thirst; but the water that I shall give him shall be in him a well of water springing up into everlasting life.

Ac 2:21 And it shall come to pass, *that* whosoever shall call on the name of the Lord shall be saved.

Ac 10:43 To him give all the prophets witness, that through his name whosoever believeth in him shall receive remission of sins.

Ro 10:13 For whosoever shall call upon the name of the Lord shall be saved.

1 Jn 5:1 Whosoever believeth that Jesus is the Christ is born of God: and every one that loveth him that begat loveth him also that is begotten of him.

Re 22:17 And the Spirit and the bride say, Come. And let him that heareth say, Come. And let him that is athirst come. And whosoever will, let him take the water of life freely.

See **INVITATIONS, WARNINGS**

WICKED, *sinful people*

1. Characteristics

Ps 5:9 For *there is* no faithfulness in their mouth; their inward part *is* very wickedness; their throat *is* an open sepulchre; they flatter with their tongue.

Ps 37:12 The wicked plotteth against the just, and gnasheth upon him with his teeth.

Ps 52:3 Thou lovest evil more than good; *and* lying rather than to speak righteousness. Selah.

Ps 64:3 Who whet their tongue like a sword, *and* bend *their bows to shoot* their arrows, *even* bitter words:

Pr 4:16 For they sleep not, except they have done mischief; and their sleep is taken away, unless they cause *some* to fall.

Is 1:4 Ah sinful nation, a people laden with iniquity, a seed of evildoers, children that are corrupters: they have forsaken the LORD, they have provoked the Holy One of Israel unto anger, they are gone away backward.

Is 57:20 But the wicked *are* like the troubled sea, when it cannot rest, whose waters cast up mire and dirt.

2 Ti 3:3 Without natural affection, trucebreakers, false accusers, incontinent, fierce, despisers of those that are good,

Jude 13 Raging waves of the sea, foaming out their own shame; wandering stars, to whom is reserved the blackness of darkness for ever.

2. Contrast with Righteous

Ps 11:5 The LORD trieth the righteous: but the wicked and him that loveth violence his soul hateth.

Ps 32:10 Many sorrows *shall be* to the wicked: but he that trusteth in the LORD, mercy shall compass him about.

Ps 37:17 For the arms of the wicked shall be broken: but the LORD upholdeth the righteous.

Ps 75:10 All the horns of the wicked also will I cut off; *but* the horns of the righteous shall be exalted.

Pr 28:1 The wicked flee when no man pursueth: but the righteous are bold as a lion.

Is 65:14 Behold, my servants shall sing for joy of heart, but ye shall cry for sorrow of heart, and shall howl for vexation of spirit.

Mal 3:18 Then shall ye return, and discern between the righteous and the wicked, between him that serveth God and him that serveth him not.

Ro 2:9 Tribulation and anguish, upon every soul of man that doeth evil, of the Jew first, and also of the Gentile;

3. Confounded

Ge 11:8 So the LORD scattered them abroad from thence upon the face of all the earth: and they left off to build the city.

Ge 19:11 And they smote the men that *were* at the door of the house with blindness, both small and great: so that they wearied themselves to find the door.

Ex 14:25 And took off their chariot wheels, that they drave them heavily: so that the Egyptians said, Let us flee from the face of Israel; for the LORD fighteth for them against the Egyptians.

Nu 24:10 And Balak's anger was kindled against Balaam, and he smote his hands together: and Balak said unto Balaam, I called thee to curse mine enemies, and, behold, thou hast altogether blessed *them* these three times.

Jos 8:20 And when the men of Ai looked behind them, they saw, and, behold, the smoke of the city ascended up to heaven, and they had no power to flee this way or that way: and the people that fled to the wilderness turned back upon the pursuers.

1 S 2:4 The bows of the mighty men *are* broken, and they that stumbled are girded with strength.

1 S 23:13 Then David and his men, *which were* about six hundred, arose and departed out of Keilah, and went whithersoever they could go. And it was told Saul that David was escaped from Keilah; and he forbare to go forth.

2 K 6:11 Therefore the heart of the king of Syria was sore troubled for this thing; and he called his servants, and said unto them, Will ye not shew me which of us *is* for the king of Israel?

2 K 19:26 Therefore their inhabitants were of small power, they were dismayed and confounded; they were *as* the grass of the field, and *as* the green herb, *as* the grass on the house tops, and *as corn* blasted before it be grown up.

2 K 19:32 Therefore thus saith the LORD concerning the king of Assyria, He shall not come into this city, nor shoot an arrow there, nor come before it with shield, nor cast a bank against it.

2 Chr 20:23 For the children of Ammon and Moab stood up against the inhabitants of mount Seir, utterly to slay and destroy *them:* and when they had made an end of the inhabitants of Seir, every one helped to destroy another.

Ne 4:15 And it came to pass, when our enemies heard that it was known unto us, and God had brought their counsel to nought, that we returned all of us to the wall, every one unto his work.

Ne 6:16 And it came to pass, that when all our enemies heard *thereof,* and all the heathen that *were* about us saw *these things,* they were much cast down in their own eyes: for they perceived that this work was wrought of our God.

Est 7:6 And Esther said, The adversary and enemy *is* this wicked Haman. Then Haman was afraid before the king and the queen.

Est 9:1 Now in the twelfth month, that *is,* the month Adar, on the thirteenth day of the same, when the king's commandment and his decree drew near to be put in execution, in the day that the enemies of the Jews hoped to have power over them, (though it was turned to the contrary, that the Jews had rule over them that hated them;)

Jb 5:12 He disappointeth the devices of the crafty, so that their hands cannot perform *their* enterprise.

Jb 12:17 He leadeth counsellors away spoiled, and maketh the judges fools.

Ps 33:10 The LORD bringeth the counsel of the heathen to nought: he maketh the devices of the people of none effect.

Ps 35:4 Let them be confounded and put to shame that seek after my soul: let them be turned back and brought to confusion that devise my hurt.

Ps 35:26 Let them be ashamed and brought to confusion together that rejoice at mine hurt: let them be clothed with shame and dishonour that magnify *themselves* against me.

Ps 40:14 Let them be ashamed and confounded together that seek after my soul to destroy it; let them be driven backward and put to shame that wish me evil.

Ps 55:9 Destroy, O Lord, *and* divide their tongues: for I have seen violence and strife in the city.

Ps 70:2 Let them be ashamed and confounded that seek after my soul: let them be turned backward, and put to confusion, that desire my hurt.

Ps 83:17 Let them be confounded and troubled for ever; yea, let them be put to shame, and perish:

Ps 109:29 Let mine adversaries be clothed with shame, and let them cover themselves with their own confusion, as with a mantle.

Ps 129:5 Let them all be confounded and turned back that hate Zion.

Ps 146:9 The LORD preserveth the strangers; he relieveth the fatherless and widow: but the way of the wicked he turneth upside down.

Pr 21:30 *There is* no wisdom nor understanding nor counsel against the LORD.

Pr 22:12 The eyes of the LORD preserve knowledge, and he overthroweth the words of the transgressor.

Is 1:29 For they shall be ashamed of the oaks which ye have desired, and ye shall be confounded for the gardens that ye have chosen.

Is 7:7 Thus saith the Lord GOD, It shall not stand, neither shall it come to pass.

Is 8:10 Take counsel together, and it shall come to nought; speak the word, and it shall not stand: for God *is* with us.

Is 19:3 And the spirit of Egypt shall fail in the midst thereof; and I will destroy the counsel thereof: and they shall seek to the idols, and to the charmers, and to them that have familiar spirits, and to the wizards.

Is 19:9 Moreover they that work in fine flax, and they that weave networks, shall be confounded.

Is 28:18 And your covenant with death shall be disannulled, and your agreement with hell shall not stand; when the overflowing scourge shall pass through, then ye shall be trodden down by it.

Is 37:27 Therefore their inhabitants *were* of small power, they were dismayed and confounded: they were *as* the grass of the field, and *as* the green herb, *as* the grass on the housetops, and *as corn* blasted before it be grown up.

Is 40:23 That bringeth the princes to nothing; he maketh the judges of the earth as vanity.

Is 41:11 Behold, all they that were incensed against thee shall be ashamed and confounded: they shall be as nothing; and they that strive with thee shall perish.

Is 44:25 That frustrateth the tokens of the liars, and maketh diviners mad; that turneth wise *men* backward, and maketh their knowledge foolish;

Is 45:16 They shall be ashamed, and also confounded, all of them: they shall go to confusion together *that are* makers of idols.

Je 9:19 For a voice of wailing is heard out of Zion, How are we spoiled! we are greatly confounded, because we have forsaken the land, because our dwellings have cast *us* out.

Je 19:7 And I will make void the counsel of Judah and Jerusalem in this place; and I will cause them to fall by the sword before their enemies, and by the hands of them that seek their lives: and their carcases will I give to be meat for the fowls of the heaven, and for the beasts of the earth.

Je 20:11 But the LORD *is* with me as a mighty terrible one: therefore my persecutors shall stumble, and they shall not prevail: they shall be greatly ashamed; for they shall not prosper: *their* everlasting confusion shall never be forgotten.

Je 22:22 The wind shall eat up all thy pastors, and thy lovers shall go into captivity: surely then shalt thou be ashamed and confounded for all thy wickedness.

Je 46:24 The daughter of Egypt shall be confounded; she shall be delivered into the hand of the people of the north.

Je 48:1 Against Moab thus saith the LORD of hosts, the God of Israel; Woe unto Nebo! for it is spoiled: Kiriathaim is confounded *and* taken: Misgab is confounded and dismayed.

Je 48:20 Moab is confounded; for it is broken down: howl and cry; and tell ye it in Arnon, that Moab is spoiled,

Eze 16:54 That thou mayest bear thine own shame, and mayest be confounded in all that thou hast done, in that thou art a comfort unto them.

Eze 16:63 That thou mayest remember, and be confounded, and never open thy mouth any more because of thy shame, when I am pacified toward thee for all that thou hast done, saith the Lord GOD.

Da 11:27 And both these kings' hearts *shall be* to do mischief, and they shall speak lies at one table; but it shall not prosper: for yet the end *shall be* at the time appointed.

Obad 8 Shall I not in that day, saith the LORD, even destroy the wise *men* out of Edom, and understanding out of the mount of Esau?

Mi 7:16 The nations shall see and be confounded at all their might: they shall lay *their* hand upon *their* mouth, their ears shall be deaf.

Zec 10:5 And they shall be as mighty *men,* which tread down *their enemies* in the mire of the streets in the battle: and they shall fight, because the LORD *is* with them, and the riders on horses shall be confounded.

Zec 12:4 In that day, saith the LORD, I will smite every horse with astonishment, and his rider with madness: and I will open mine eyes upon the house of Judah, and will smite every horse of the people with blindness.

Mal 1:4 Whereas Edom saith, We are impoverished, but we will return and build the desolate places; thus saith the LORD of hosts, They shall build, but I will throw down; and they shall call them, The border of wickedness, and, The people against whom the LORD hath indignation for ever.

Mt 2:14 When he arose, he took the young child and his mother by night, and departed into Egypt:

Mt 21:27 And they answered Jesus, and said, We cannot tell. And he said unto them, Neither tell I you by what authority I do these things.

Mt 22:46 And no man was able to answer him a word, neither durst any *man* from that day forth ask him any more *questions.*

Mt 28:2 And, behold, there was a great earthquake: for the angel of the Lord descended from heaven, and came and rolled back the stone from the door, and sat upon it.

Mk 11:33 And they answered and said unto Jesus, We cannot tell. And Jesus answering saith unto them, Neither do I tell you by what authority I do these things.

Lu 1:51 He hath shewed strength with his arm; he hath scattered the proud in the imagination of their hearts.

Lu 9:7 Now Herod the tetrarch heard of all that was done by him: and he was perplexed, because that it was said of some, that John was risen from the dead;

Lu 20:7 And they answered, that they could not tell whence *it was.*

Jn 8:9 And they which heard *it,* being convicted by *their own* conscience, went out one by one, beginning at the eldest, *even* unto the last: and Jesus was left alone, and the woman standing in the midst.

Jn 12:19 The Pharisees therefore said among themselves, Perceive ye how ye prevail nothing? behold, the world is gone after him.

Jn 18:6 As soon then as he had said unto them, I am *he,* they went backward, and fell to the ground.

Ac 4:16 Saying, What shall we do to these men? for that indeed a notable miracle hath been done by them *is* manifest to all them that dwell in Jerusalem; and we cannot deny *it*.

Ac 4:21 So when they had further threatened them, they let them go, finding nothing how they might punish them, because of the people: for all *men* glorified God for that which was done.

Ac 5:24 Now when the high priest and the captain of the temple and the chief priests heard these things, they doubted of them whereunto this would grow.

Ac 18:16 And he drave them from the judgment seat.

Ac 19:16 And the man in whom the evil spirit was leaped on them, and overcame them, and prevailed against them, so that they fled out of that house naked and wounded.

Ac 19:41 And when he had thus spoken, he dismissed the assembly.

1 Co 1:19 For it is written, I will destroy the wisdom of the wise, and will bring to nothing the understanding of the prudent.

4. Die before Their Time

Ge 38:7 And Er, Judah's firstborn, was wicked in the sight of the LORD; and the LORD slew him.

Ex 9:15 For now I will stretch out my hand, that I may smite thee and thy people with pestilence; and thou shalt be cut off from the earth.

Ex 15:1 Then sang Moses and the children of Israel this song unto the LORD, and spake, saying, I will sing unto the LORD, for he hath triumphed gloriously: the horse and his rider hath he thrown into the sea.

Ex 23:23 For mine Angel shall go before thee, and bring thee in unto the Amorites, and the Hittites, and the Perizzites, and the Canaanites, and the Hivites, and the Jebusites: and I will cut them off.

Ex 31:14 Ye shall keep the sabbath therefore; for it *is* holy unto you: every one that defileth it shall surely be put to death: for whosoever doeth *any* work therein, that soul shall be cut off from among his people.

Ex 32:28 And the children of Levi did according to the word of Moses: and there fell of the people that day about three thousand men.

Le 18:29 For whosoever shall commit any of these abominations, even the souls that commit *them* shall be cut off from among their people.

Le 19:8 Therefore *every one* that eateth it shall bear his iniquity, because he hath profaned the hallowed thing of the LORD: and that soul shall be cut off from among his people.

Le 20:3 And I will set my face against that man, and will cut him off from among his people; because he hath given of his seed unto Molech, to defile my sanctuary, and to profane my holy name.

Le 20:5 Then I will set my face against that man, and against his family, and will cut him off, and all that go a whoring after him, to commit whoredom with Molech, from among their people.

Le 20:17 And if a man shall take his sister, his father's daughter, or his mother's daughter, and see her nakedness, and she see his nakedness; it *is* a wicked thing; and they shall be cut off in the sight of their people: he hath uncovered his sister's nakedness; he shall bear his iniquity.

Le 26:38 And ye shall perish among the heathen, and the land of your enemies shall eat you up.

Nu 15:30 But the soul that doeth *ought* presumptuously, *whether he be* born in the land, or a stranger, the same reproacheth the LORD; and that soul shall be cut off from among his people.

De 2:14 And the space in which we came from Kadesh-barnea, until we were come over the brook Zered, *was* thirty and eight years; until all the generation of the men of war were wasted out from among the host, as the LORD sware unto them.

De 4:26 I call heaven and earth to witness against you this day, that ye shall soon utterly perish from off the land whereunto ye go over Jordan to possess it; ye shall not prolong *your* days upon it, but shall utterly be destroyed.

De 7:24 And he shall deliver their kings into thine hand, and thou shalt destroy their name from under heaven: there shall no man be able to stand before thee, until thou have destroyed them.

De 11:17 And *then* the LORD's wrath be kindled against you, and he shut up the heaven, that there be no rain, and that the land yield not her fruit; and *lest* ye perish quickly from off the good land which the LORD giveth you.

De 30:18 I denounce unto you this day, that ye shall surely perish, *and that* ye shall not prolong *your* days upon the land, whither thou passest over Jordan to go to possess it.

De 32:36 For the LORD shall judge his people, and repent himself for his servants, when he seeth that *their* power is gone, and *there is* none shut up, or left.

Jos 24:20 If ye forsake the LORD, and serve strange gods, then he will turn and do you hurt, and consume you, after that he hath done you good.

1 S 2:31 Behold, the days come, that I will cut off thine arm, and the arm of thy father's house, that there shall not be an old man in thine house.

1 S 4:17 And the messenger answered and said, Israel is fled before the Philistines, and there hath been also a great slaughter among the people, and thy two sons also, Hophni and Phinehas, are dead, and the ark of God is taken.

2 S 4:12 And David commanded his young men, and they slew them, and cut off their hands and their feet, and hanged *them* up over the pool in Hebron. But they took the head of Ishbosheth, and buried *it* in the sepulchre of Abner in Hebron.

1 K 13:34 And this thing became sin unto the house of Jeroboam, even to cut *it* off, and to destroy *it* from off the face of the earth.

1 K 14:10 Therefore, behold, I will bring evil upon the house of Jeroboam, and will cut off from Jeroboam him that pisseth against the wall, *and* him that is shut up and left

in Israel, and will take away the remnant of the house of Jeroboam, as a man taketh away dung, till it be all gone.

1 K 16:3 Behold, I will take away the posterity of Baasha, and the posterity of his house; and will make thy house like the house of Jeroboam the son of Nebat.

1 K 16:11 And it came to pass, when he began to reign, as soon as he sat on his throne, *that* he slew all the house of Baasha: he left him not one that pisseth against a wall, neither of his kinsfolks, nor of his friends.

1 K 18:40 And Elijah said unto them, Take the prophets of Baal; let not one of them escape. And they took them: and Elijah brought them down to the brook Kishon, and slew them there.

1 K 21:21 Behold, I will bring evil upon thee, and will take away thy posterity, and will cut off from Ahab him that pisseth against the wall, and him that is shut up and left in Israel,

2 K 7:20 And so it fell out unto him: for the people trode upon him in the gate, and he died.

2 K 9:8 For the whole house of Ahab shall perish: and I will cut off from Ahab him that pisseth against the wall, and him that is shut up and left in Israel:

2 K 9:33 And he said, Throw her down. So they threw her down: and *some* of her blood was sprinkled on the wall, and on the horses: and he trode her under foot.

2 K 10:11 So Jehu slew all that remained of the house of Ahab in Jezreel, and all his great men, and his kinsfolks, and his priests, until he left him none remaining.

2 K 10:14 And he said, Take them alive. And they took them alive, and slew them at the pit of the shearing house, *even* two and forty men; neither left he any of them.

2 K 11:20 And all the people of the land rejoiced, and the city was in quiet: and they slew Athaliah with the sword *beside* the king's house.

2 K 19:35 And it came to pass that night, that the angel of the LORD went out, and smote in the camp of the

Assyrians an hundred fourscore and five thousand: and when they arose early in the morning, behold, they *were* all dead corpses.

2 Chr 33:25 But the people of the land slew all them that had conspired against king Amon; and the people of the land made Josiah his son king in his stead.

Est 9:5 Thus the Jews smote all their enemies with the stroke of the sword, and slaughter, and destruction, and did what they would unto those that hated them.

Jb 4:10 The roaring of the lion, and the voice of the fierce lion, and the teeth of the young lions, are broken.

Jb 15:32 It shall be accomplished before his time, and his branch shall not be green.

Jb 18:16 His roots shall be dried up beneath, and above shall his branch be cut off.

Jb 20:5 That the triumphing of the wicked *is* short, and the joy of the hypocrite *but* for a moment?

Jb 21:21 For what pleasure *hath* he in his house after him, when the number of his months is cut off in the midst?

Jb 22:16 Which were cut down out of time, whose foundation was overflown with a flood:

Jb 24:19 Drought and heat consume the snow waters: *so doth* the grave *those which* have sinned.

Jb 36:6 He preserveth not the life of the wicked: but giveth right to the poor.

Jb 36:14 They die in youth, and their life *is* among the unclean.

Ps 12:3 The LORD shall cut off all flattering lips, *and* the tongue that speaketh proud things:

Ps 21:10 Their fruit shalt thou destroy from the earth, and their seed from among the children of men.

Ps 37:2 For they shall soon be cut down like the grass, and wither as the green herb.

Ps 37:9 For evildoers shall be cut off: but those that wait upon the LORD, they shall inherit the earth.

Ps 37:22 For *such as be* blessed of him shall inherit the earth; and *they that be* cursed of him shall be cut off.

Ps 37:34 Wait on the LORD, and keep his way, and he shall exalt thee to inherit the land: when the wicked are cut off, thou shalt see *it.*

Ps 37:38 But the transgressors shall be destroyed together: the end of the wicked shall be cut off.

Ps 54:5 He shall reward evil unto mine enemies: cut them off in thy truth.

Ps 55:23 But thou, O God, shalt bring them down into the pit of destruction: bloody and deceitful men shall not live out half their days; but I will trust in thee.

Ps 94:23 And he shall bring upon them their own iniquity, and shall cut them off in their own wickedness; *yea,* the LORD our God shall cut them off.

Ps 101:5 Whoso privily slandereth his neighbour, him will I cut off: him that hath an high look and a proud heart will not I suffer.

Ps 104:35 Let the sinners be consumed out of the earth, and let the wicked be no more. Bless thou the LORD, O my soul. Praise ye the LORD.

Ps 109:8 Let his days be few; *and* let another take his office.

Ps 109:13 Let his posterity be cut off; *and* in the generation following let their name be blotted out.

Pr 2:22 But the wicked shall be cut off from the earth, and the transgressors shall be rooted out of it.

Pr 10:27 The fear of the LORD prolongeth days: but the years of the wicked shall be shortened.

Ec 7:17 Be not over much wicked, neither be thou foolish: why shouldest thou die before thy time?

Ec 8:13 But it shall not be well with the wicked, neither shall he prolong *his* days, *which are* as a shadow; because he feareth not before God.

Is 1:30 For ye shall be as an oak whose leaf fadeth, and as a garden that hath no water.

Is 5:24 Therefore as the fire devoureth the stubble, and the flame consumeth the chaff, *so* their root shall be as rottenness, and their blossom shall go up as dust: because they have cast away the law of the LORD of hosts, and despised the word of the Holy One of Israel.

Is 10:23 For the Lord GOD of hosts shall make a consumption, even determined, in the midst of all the land.

Is 11:13 The envy also of Ephraim shall depart, and the adversaries of Judah shall be cut off: Ephraim shall not envy Judah, and Judah shall not vex Ephraim.

Is 13:22 And the wild beasts of the islands shall cry in their desolate houses, and dragons in *their* pleasant palaces: and her time *is* near to come, and her days shall not be prolonged.

Is 14:22 For I will rise up against them, saith the LORD of hosts, and cut off from Babylon the name, and remnant, and son, and nephew, saith the LORD.

Is 18:5 For afore the harvest, when the bud is perfect, and the sour grape is ripening in the flower, he shall both cut off the sprigs with pruninghooks, and take away *and* cut down the branches.

Is 24:6 Therefore hath the curse devoured the earth, and they that dwell therein are desolate: therefore the inhabitants of the earth are burned, and few men left.

Is 29:20 For the terrible one is brought to nought, and the scorner is consumed, and all that watch for iniquity are cut off:

Is 33:11 Ye shall conceive chaff, ye shall bring forth stubble: your breath, *as* fire, shall devour you.

Is 37:27 Therefore their inhabitants *were* of small power, they were dismayed and confounded: they were *as* the grass of the field, and *as* the green herb, *as* the grass on the housetops, and *as corn* blasted before it be grown up.

Is 40:24 Yea, they shall not be planted; yea, they shall not be sown: yea, their stock shall not take root in the earth: and he shall also blow upon them, and they shall wither, and the whirlwind shall take them away as stubble.

Je 15:9 She that hath borne seven languisheth: she hath given up the ghost; her sun is gone down while *it* was yet day: she hath been ashamed

and confounded: and the residue of them will I deliver to the sword before their enemies, saith the LORD.

Je 44:8 In that ye provoke me unto wrath with the works of your hands, burning incense unto other gods in the land of Egypt, whither ye be gone to dwell, that ye might cut yourselves off, and that ye might be a curse and a reproach among all the nations of the earth?

Je 47:5 Baldness is come upon Gaza; Ashkelon is cut off *with* the remnant of their valley: how long wilt thou cut thyself?

Je 48:2 *There shall be* no more praise of Moab: in Heshbon they have devised evil against it; come, and let us cut it off from *being* a nation. Also thou shalt be cut down, O Madmen; the sword shall pursue thee.

Je 50:30 Therefore shall her young men fall in the streets, and all her men of war shall be cut off in that day, saith the LORD.

Eze 7:11 Violence is risen up into a rod of wickedness: none of them *shall remain,* nor of their multitude, nor of any of theirs: neither *shall there be* wailing for them.

Eze 7:25 Destruction cometh; and they shall seek peace, and *there shall be* none.

Eze 14:8 And I will set my face against that man, and will make him a sign and a proverb, and I will cut him off from the midst of my people; and ye shall know that I *am* the LORD.

Eze 14:13 Son of man, when the land sinneth against me by trespassing grievously, then will I stretch out mine hand upon it, and will break the staff of the bread thereof, and will send famine upon it, and will cut off man and beast from it:

Eze 16:50 And they were haughty, and committed abomination before me: therefore I took them away as I saw *good.*

Eze 18:18 *As for* his father, because he cruelly oppressed, spoiled his brother by violence, and did *that* which *is* not good among his people, lo, even he shall die in his iniquity.

Eze 21:4 Seeing then that I will cut off from thee the righteous and the wicked, therefore shall my sword go forth out of his sheath against all flesh from the south to the north:

Eze 25:7 Behold, therefore I will stretch out mine hand upon thee, and will deliver thee for a spoil to the heathen; and I will cut thee off from the people, and I will cause thee to perish out of the countries: I will destroy thee; and thou shalt know that I *am* the LORD.

Eze 25:16 Therefore thus saith the Lord GOD; Behold, I will stretch out mine hand upon the Philistines, and I will cut off the Cherethims, and destroy the remnant of the sea coast.

Eze 29:8 Therefore thus saith the Lord GOD; Behold, I will bring a sword upon thee, and cut off man and beast out of thee.

Eze 31:12 And strangers, the terrible of the nations, have cut him off, and have left him: upon the mountains and in all the valleys his branches are fallen, and his boughs are broken by all the rivers of the land; and all the people of the earth are gone down from his shadow, and have left him.

Eze 35:7 Thus will I make mount Seir most desolate, and cut off from it him that passeth out and him that returneth.

Ho 10:7 *As for* Samaria, her king is cut off as the foam upon the water.

Ho 10:15 So shall Bethel do unto you because of your great wickedness: in a morning shall the king of Israel utterly be cut off.

Ho 13:3 Therefore they shall be as the morning cloud, and as the early dew that passeth away, as the chaff *that* is driven with the whirlwind out of the floor, and as the smoke out of the chimney.

Am 2:3 And I will cut off the judge from the midst thereof, and will slay all the princes thereof with him, saith the LORD.

Am 9:10 All the sinners of my people shall die by the sword, which say, The evil shall not overtake nor prevent us.

Obad 5 If thieves came to thee, if robbers by night, (how art thou cut off!)

would they not have stolen till they had enough? if the grapegatherers came to thee, would they not leave *some* grapes?

Obad 10 For *thy* violence against thy brother Jacob shame shall cover thee, and thou shalt be cut off for ever.

Mi 5:9 Thine hand shall be lifted up upon thine adversaries, and all thine enemies shall be cut off.

Na 1:12 Thus saith the LORD: Though *they be* quiet, and likewise many, yet thus shall they be cut down, when he shall pass through. Though I have afflicted thee, I will afflict thee no more.

Na 1:15 Behold upon the mountains the feet of him that bringeth good tidings, that publisheth peace! O Judah, keep thy solemn feasts, perform thy vows: for the wicked shall no more pass through thee; he is utterly cut off.

Na 3:15 There shall the fire devour thee; the sword shall cut thee off, it shall eat thee up like the cankerworm: make thyself many as the cankerworm, make thyself many as the locusts.

Zep 1:4 I will also stretch out mine hand upon Judah, and upon all the inhabitants of Jerusalem; and I will cut off the remnant of Baal from this place, *and* the name of the Chemarims with the priests;

Zep 1:11 Howl, ye inhabitants of Maktesh, for all the merchant people are cut down; all they that bear silver are cut off.

Zep 1:18 Neither their silver nor their gold shall be able to deliver them in the day of the LORD's wrath; but the whole land shall be devoured by the fire of his jealousy: for he shall make even a speedy riddance of all them that dwell in the land.

Zep 3:6 I have cut off the nations: their towers are desolate; I made their streets waste, that none passeth by: their cities are destroyed, so that there is no man, that there is none inhabitant.

Zec 5:3 Then said he unto me, This *is* the curse that goeth forth over the face of the whole earth: for every one that stealeth shall be cut off *as* on this side according to it; and every one that sweareth shall be cut off *as* on that side according to it.

Zec 9:6 And a bastard shall dwell in Ashdod, and I will cut off the pride of the Philistines.

Zec 11:8 Three shepherds also I cut off in one month; and my soul lothed them, and their soul also abhorred me.

Mal 2:12 The LORD will cut off the man that doeth this, the master and the scholar, out of the tabernacles of Jacob, and him that offereth an offering unto the LORD of hosts.

Lu 12:46 The lord of that servant will come in a day when he looketh not for *him,* and at an hour when he is not aware, and will cut him in sunder, and will appoint him his portion with the unbelievers.

Lu 13:9 And if it bear fruit, *well:* and if not, *then* after that thou shalt cut it down.

Lu 17:29 But the same day that Lot went out of Sodom it rained fire and brimstone from heaven, and destroyed *them* all.

Ac 3:23 And it shall come to pass, *that* every soul, which will not hear that prophet, shall be destroyed from among the people.

5. Their End

Ps 7:9 Oh let the wickedness of the wicked come to an end; but establish the just: for the righteous God trieth the hearts and reins.

Ps 37:20 But the wicked shall perish, and the enemies of the LORD *shall be* as the fat of lambs: they shall consume; into smoke shall they consume away.

Ps 37:38 But the transgressors shall be destroyed together: the end of the wicked shall be cut off.

Ps 73:17 Until I went into the sanctuary of God; *then* understood I their end.

Pr 14:12 There is a way which seemeth right unto a man, but the end thereof *are* the ways of death.

Is 31:8 Then shall the Assyrian fall with the sword, not of a mighty man; and the sword, not of a mean man,

shall devour him: but he shall flee from the sword, and his young men shall be discomfited.

Eze 9:5 And to the others he said in mine hearing, Go ye after him through the city, and smite: let not your eye spare, neither have ye pity:

Ro 6:21 What fruit had ye then in those things whereof ye are now ashamed? for the end of those things *is* death.

2 Co 11:15 Therefore *it is* no great thing if his ministers also be transformed as the ministers of righteousness; whose end shall be according to their works.

Ph 3:19 Whose end *is* destruction, whose God *is their* belly, and *whose* glory *is* in their shame, who mind earthly things.)

He 6:8 But that which beareth thorns and briers *is* rejected, and *is* nigh unto cursing; whose end *is* to be burned.

1 Pe 4:17 For the time *is come* that judgment must begin at the house of God: and if *it* first *begin* at us, what shall the end *be* of them that obey not the gospel of God?

Re 21:8 But the fearful, and unbelieving, and the abominable, and murderers, and whoremongers, and sorcerers, and idolaters, and all liars, shall have their part in the lake which burneth with fire and brimstone: which is the second death.

6. Their Fate

Ge 19:15 And when the morning arose, then the angels hastened Lot, saying, Arise, take thy wife, and thy two daughters, which are here; lest thou be consumed in the iniquity of the city.

De 9:5 Not for thy righteousness, or for the uprightness of thine heart, dost thou go to possess their land: but for the wickedness of these nations the LORD thy God doth drive them out from before thee, and that he may perform the word which the LORD sware unto thy fathers, Abraham, Isaac, and Jacob.

2 K 9:37 And the carcase of Jezebel shall be as dung upon the face of the field in the portion of Jezreel; *so* that they shall not say, This *is* Jezebel.

Ps 37:2 For they shall soon be cut down like the grass, and wither as the green herb.

Ps 37:10 For yet a little while, and the wicked *shall* not *be:* yea, thou shalt diligently consider his place, and it *shall* not *be.*

Ps 55:23 But thou, O God, shalt bring them down into the pit of destruction: bloody and deceitful men shall not live out half their days; but I will trust in thee.

Ps 75:8 For in the hand of the LORD *there is* a cup, and the wine is red; it is full of mixture; and he poureth out of the same: but the dregs thereof, all the wicked of the earth shall wring *them* out, *and* drink *them.*

Ps 92:7 When the wicked spring as the grass, and when all the workers of iniquity do flourish; *it is* that they shall be destroyed for ever:

Ps 112:10 The wicked shall see *it,* and be grieved; he shall gnash with his teeth, and melt away: the desire of the wicked shall perish.

Ps 139:19 Surely thou wilt slay the wicked, O God: depart from me therefore, ye bloody men.

Pr 5:22 His own iniquities shall take the wicked himself, and he shall be holden with the cords of his sins.

2 Pe 2:17 These are wells without water, clouds that are carried with a tempest; to whom the mist of darkness is reserved for ever.

Jude 13 Raging waves of the sea, foaming out their own shame; wandering stars, to whom is reserved the blackness of darkness for ever.

7. Their Portion

Jb 20:29 This *is* the portion of a wicked man from God, and the heritage appointed unto him by God.

Jb 24:18 He *is* swift as the waters; their portion is cursed in the earth: he beholdeth not the way of the vineyards.

Jb 27:13 This *is* the portion of a wicked man with God, and the heritage of oppressors, *which* they shall receive of the Almighty.

Ps 11:6 Upon the wicked he shall rain snares, fire and brimstone, and an horrible tempest: *this shall be* the portion of their cup.

Is 17:14 And behold at eveningtide trouble; *and* before the morning he *is* not. This *is* the portion of them that spoil us, and the lot of them that rob us.

Je 13:25 This *is* thy lot, the portion of thy measures from me, saith the LORD; because thou hast forgotten me, and trusted in falsehood.

Mt 24:51 And shall cut him asunder, and appoint *him* his portion with the hypocrites: there shall be weeping and gnashing of teeth.

Lu 12:46 The lord of that servant will come in a day when he looketh not for *him,* and at an hour when he is not aware, and will cut him in sunder, and will appoint him his portion with the unbelievers.

8. Their Rejection by God

De 1:45 And ye returned and wept before the LORD; but the LORD would not hearken to your voice, nor give ear unto you.

1 S 13:14 But now thy kingdom shall not continue: the LORD hath sought him a man after his own heart, and the LORD hath commanded him *to be* captain over his people, because thou hast not kept *that* which the LORD commanded thee.

1 S 15:23 For rebellion *is as* the sin of witchcraft, and stubbornness *is as* iniquity and idolatry. Because thou hast rejected the word of the LORD, he hath also rejected thee from *being* king.

1 S 16:1 And the LORD said unto Samuel, How long wilt thou mourn for Saul, seeing I have rejected him from reigning over Israel? fill thine horn with oil, and go, I will send thee to Jesse the Bethlehemite: for I have provided me a king among his sons.

2 K 17:20 And the LORD rejected all the seed of Israel, and afflicted them, and delivered them into the hand of spoilers, until he had cast them out of his sight.

2 K 24:3 Surely at the command-ment of the LORD came *this* upon Judah, to remove *them* out of his sight, for the sins of Manasseh, according to all that he did;

2 K 24:20 For through the anger of the LORD it came to pass in Jerusalem and Judah, until he had cast them out from his presence, that Zedekiah re-belled against the king of Babylon.

Ps 50:16 But unto the wicked God saith, What hast thou to do to declare my statutes, or *that* thou shouldest take my covenant in thy mouth?

Ps 53:5 There were they in great fear, *where* no fear was: for God hath scat-tered the bones of him that encam-peth *against* thee: thou hast put *them* to shame, because God hath despised them.

Is 1:15 And when ye spread forth your hands, I will hide mine eyes from you: yea, when ye make many prayers, I will not hear: your hands are full of blood.

Je 2:37 Yea, thou shalt go forth from him, and thine hands upon thine head: for the LORD hath rejected thy confidences, and thou shalt not pros-per in them.

Je 6:8 Be thou instructed, O Jerusa-lem, lest my soul depart from thee; lest I make thee desolate, a land not inhab-ited.

Je 6:30 Reprobate silver shall *men* call them, because the LORD hath rejected them.

Je 7:29 Cut off thine hair, *O Jerusa-lem,* and cast *it* away, and take up a lamentation on high places; for the LORD hath rejected and forsaken the generation of his wrath.

Je 14:10 Thus saith the LORD unto this people, Thus have they loved to wander, they have not refrained their feet, therefore the LORD doth not ac-cept them; he will now remember their iniquity, and visit their sins.

Je 14:19 Hast thou utterly rejected Judah? hath thy soul lothed Zion? why hast thou smitten us, and *there is* no healing for us? we looked for peace, and *there is* no good; and for the time of healing, and behold trouble!

Lam 5:22 But thou hast utterly re-jected us; thou art very wroth against us.

Ho 1:9 Then said *God,* Call his name Lo-ammi: for ye *are* not my people, and I will not be your *God.*

Ho 4:6 My people are destroyed for lack of knowledge: because thou hast rejected knowledge, I will also reject thee, that thou shalt be no priest to me: seeing thou hast forgotten the law of thy God, I will also forget thy chil-dren.

Ho 5:6 They shall go with their flocks and with their herds to seek the LORD; but they shall not find *him;* he hath withdrawn himself from them.

Ho 9:15 All their wickedness *is* in Gil-gal: for there I hated them: for the wickedness of their doings I will drive them out of mine house, I will love them no more: all their princes *are* revolters.

Mt 10:33 But whosoever shall deny me before men, him will I also deny before my Father which is in heaven.

Mt 13:48 Which, when it was full, they drew to shore, and sat down, and gathered the good into vessels, but cast the bad away.

Mt 25:12 But he answered and said, Verily I say unto you, I know you not.

Lu 12:9 But he that denieth me be-fore men shall be denied before the angels of God.

Lu 13:27 But he shall say, I tell you, I know you not whence ye are; depart from me, all *ye* workers of iniquity.

He 6:8 But that which beareth thorns and briers *is* rejected, and *is* nigh unto cursing; whose end *is* to be burned.

He 12:17 For ye know how that after-ward, when he would have inherited the blessing, he was rejected: for he found no place of repentance, though he sought it carefully with tears.

9. Rooted Up

De 29:28 And the LORD rooted them out of their land in anger, and in wrath, and in great indignation, and cast them into another land, as *it is* this day.

1 K 14:15 For the LORD shall smite Israel, as a reed is shaken in the water, and he shall root up Israel out of this good land, which he gave to their fathers, and shall scatter them beyond the river, because they have made their groves, provoking the LORD to anger.

1 K 22:46 And the remnant of the sodomites, which remained in the days of his father Asa, he took out of the land.

2 Chr 7:20 Then will I pluck them up by the roots out of my land which I have given them; and this house, which I have sanctified for my name, will I cast out of my sight, and will make it *to be* a proverb and a byword among all nations.

Jb 18:14 His confidence shall be rooted out of his tabernacle, and it shall bring him to the king of terrors.

Ps 52:5 God shall likewise destroy thee for ever, he shall take thee away, and pluck thee out of *thy* dwelling place, and root thee out of the land of the living. Selah.

Pr 2:22 But the wicked shall be cut off from the earth, and the transgressors shall be rooted out of it.

Is 16:4 Let mine outcasts dwell with thee, Moab; be thou a covert to them from the face of the spoiler: for the extortioner is at an end, the spoiler ceaseth, the oppressors are consumed out of the land.

Je 1:10 See, I have this day set thee over the nations and over the kingdoms, to root out, and to pull down, and to destroy, and to throw down, to build, and to plant.

Eze 17:9 Say thou, Thus saith the Lord GOD; Shall it prosper? shall he not pull up the roots thereof, and cut off the fruit thereof, that it wither? it shall wither in all the leaves of her spring, even without great power or many people to pluck it up by the roots thereof.

Eze 19:12 But she was plucked up in fury, she was cast down to the ground, and the east wind dried up her fruit: her strong rods were broken and withered; the fire consumed them.

Am 2:9 Yet destroyed I the Amorite before them, whose height *was* like the height of the cedars, and he *was*

strong as the oaks; yet I destroyed his fruit from above, and his roots from beneath.

Zep 2:4 For Gaza shall be forsaken, and Ashkelon a desolation: they shall drive out Ashdod at the noonday, and Ekron shall be rooted up.

Mt 15:13 But he answered and said, Every plant, which my heavenly Father hath not planted, shall be rooted up.

Jude 12 These are spots in your feasts of charity, when they feast with you, feeding themselves without fear: clouds *they are* without water, carried about of winds; trees whose fruit withereth, without fruit, twice dead, plucked up by the roots;

10. *Snared by Their Own Acts*

Ex 14:23 And the Egyptians pursued, and went in after them to the midst of the sea, *even* all Pharaoh's horses, his chariots, and his horsemen.

Jud 20:34 And there came against Gibeah ten thousand chosen men out of all Israel, and the battle was sore: but they knew not that evil *was* near them.

2 K 3:23 And they said, This *is* blood: the kings are surely slain, and they have smitten one another: now therefore, Moab, to the spoil.

2 K 6:20 And it came to pass, when they were come into Samaria, that Elisha said, LORD, open the eyes of these *men*, that they may see. And the LORD opened their eyes, and they saw; and, behold, *they were* in the midst of Samaria.

Est 5:14 Then said Zeresh his wife and all his friends unto him, Let a gallows be made of fifty cubits high, and to morrow speak thou unto the king that Mordecai may be hanged thereon: then go thou in merrily with the king unto the banquet. And the thing pleased Haman; and he caused the gallows to be made.

Jb 5:13 He taketh the wise in their own craftiness: and the counsel of the froward is carried headlong.

Jb 18:8 For he is cast into a net by his own feet, and he walketh upon a snare.

Jb 22:10 Therefore snares *are* round about thee, and sudden fear troubleth thee;

Ps 7:15 He made a pit, and digged it, and is fallen into the ditch *which* he made.

Ps 9:15 The heathen are sunk down in the pit *that* they made: in the net which they hid is their own foot taken.

Ps 10:2 The wicked in *his* pride doth persecute the poor: let them be taken in the devices that they have imagined.

Ps 35:8 Let destruction come upon him at unawares; and let his net that he hath hid catch himself: into that very destruction let him fall.

Ps 57:6 They have prepared a net for my steps; my soul is bowed down: they have digged a pit before me, into the midst whereof they are fallen *themselves*. Selah.

Ps 69:22 Let their table become a snare before them: and *that which should have been* for *their* welfare, *let it become* a trap.

Ps 94:23 And he shall bring upon them their own iniquity, and shall cut them off in their own wickedness; *yea*, the Lord our God shall cut them off.

Ps 140:10 Let burning coals fall upon them: let them be cast into the fire; into deep pits, that they rise not up again.

Ps 141:10 Let the wicked fall into their own nets, whilst that I withal escape.

Pr 7:23 Till a dart strike through his liver; as a bird hasteth to the snare, and knoweth not that it *is* for his life.

Pr 11:6 The righteousness of the upright shall deliver them: but transgressors shall be taken in their own naughtiness.

Pr 11:27 He that diligently seeketh good procureth favour: but he that seeketh mischief, it shall come unto him.

Pr 12:13 The wicked is snared by the transgression of *his* lips: but the just shall come out of trouble.

Pr 18:7 A fool's mouth *is* his destruction, and his lips *are* the snare of his soul.

Pr 22:5 Thorns *and* snares *are* in the way of the froward: he that doth keep his soul shall be far from them.

Pr 26:27 Whoso diggeth a pit shall fall therein: and he that rolleth a stone, it will return upon him.

Pr 28:10 Whoso causeth the righteous to go astray in an evil way, he shall fall himself into his own pit: but the upright shall have good *things* in possession.

Pr 29:6 In the transgression of an evil man *there is* a snare: but the righteous doth sing and rejoice.

Ec 7:26 And I find more bitter than death the woman, whose heart *is* snares and nets, *and* her hands *as* bands: whoso pleaseth God shall escape from her; but the sinner shall be taken by her.

Ec 9:12 For man also knoweth not his time: as the fishes that are taken in an evil net, and as the birds that are caught in the snare; so *are* the sons of men snared in an evil time, when it falleth suddenly upon them.

Ec 10:8 He that diggeth a pit shall fall into it; and whoso breaketh an hedge, a serpent shall bite him.

Is 8:15 And many among them shall stumble, and fall, and be broken, and be snared, and be taken.

Is 24:22 And they shall be gathered together, *as* prisoners are gathered in the pit, and shall be shut up in the prison, and after many days shall they be visited.

Is 28:13 But the word of the Lord was unto them precept upon precept, precept upon precept; line upon line, line upon line; here a little, *and* there a little; that they might go, and fall backward, and be broken, and snared, and taken.

Is 42:22 But this *is* a people robbed and spoiled; *they are* all of them snared in holes, and they are hid in prison houses: they are for a prey, and none delivereth; for a spoil, and none saith, Restore.

Is 51:20 Thy sons have fainted, they lie at the head of all the streets, as a wild bull in a net: they are full of the fury of the Lord, the rebuke of thy God.

Je 48:43 Fear, and the pit, and the snare, *shall be* upon thee, O inhabitant of Moab, saith the LORD.

Je 50:24 I have laid a snare for thee, and thou art also taken, O Babylon, and thou wast not aware: thou art found, and also caught, because thou hast striven against the LORD.

Eze 12:13 My net also will I spread upon him, and he shall be taken in my snare: and I will bring him to Babylon *to* the land of the Chaldeans; yet shall he not see it, though he shall die there.

Eze 17:20 And I will spread my net upon him, and he shall be taken in my snare, and I will bring him to Babylon, and will plead with him there for his trespass that he hath trespassed against me.

Eze 19:4 The nations also heard of him; he was taken in their pit, and they brought him with chains unto the land of Egypt.

Eze 19:8 Then the nations set against him on every side from the provinces, and spread their net over him: he was taken in their pit.

Eze 32:3 Thus saith the Lord GOD; I will therefore spread out my net over thee with a company of many people; and they shall bring thee up in my net.

Da 6:24 And the king commanded, and they brought those men which had accused Daniel, and they cast *them* into the den of lions, them, their children, and their wives; and the lions had the mastery of them, and brake all their bones in pieces or ever they came at the bottom of the den.

Da 11:32 And such as do wickedly against the covenant shall he corrupt by flatteries: but the people that do know their God shall be strong, and do *exploits*.

Ho 7:2 And they consider not in their hearts *that* I remember all their wickedness: now their own doings have beset them about; they are before my face.

Ho 7:12 When they shall go, I will spread my net upon them; I will bring them down as the fowls of the heaven; I will chastise them, as their congregation hath heard.

Mt 14:9 And the king was sorry: nevertheless for the oath's sake, and them which sat with him at meat, he commanded *it* to be given *her*.

Mt 26:70 But he denied before *them* all, saying, I know not what thou sayest.

Lu 21:35 For as a snare shall it come on all them that dwell on the face of the whole earth.

2 Ti 2:26 And *that* they may recover themselves out of the snare of the devil, who are taken captive by him at his will.

11. Pass Away Unlamented

2 Chr 21:20 Thirty and two years old was he when he began to reign, and he reigned in Jerusalem eight years, and departed without being desired. Howbeit they buried him in the city of David, but not in the sepulchres of the kings.

Jb 27:15 Those that remain of him shall be buried in death: and his widows shall not weep.

Ps 78:64 Their priests fell by the sword; and their widows made no lamentation.

Pr 11:10 When it goeth well with the righteous, the city rejoiceth: and when the wicked perish, *there is* shouting.

Je 16:4 They shall die of grievous deaths; they shall not be lamented; neither shall they be buried; *but* they shall be as dung upon the face of the earth: and they shall be consumed by the sword, and by famine; and their carcases shall be meat for the fowls of heaven, and for the beasts of the earth.

Je 16:6 Both the great and the small shall die in this land: they shall not be buried, neither shall *men* lament for them, nor cut themselves, nor make themselves bald for them:

Je 22:18 Therefore thus saith the LORD concerning Jehoiakim the son of Josiah king of Judah; They shall not lament for him, *saying*, Ah my brother! or, Ah sister! they shall not lament for him, *saying*, Ah lord! or, Ah his glory!

Je 25:33 And the slain of the LORD shall be at that day from *one* end of the earth even unto the *other* end of the earth: they shall not be lamented, neither gathered, nor buried; they shall be dung upon the ground.

Eze 7:11 Violence is risen up into a rod of wickedness: none of them *shall remain,* nor of their multitude, nor of any of theirs: neither *shall there be* wailing for them.

12. Compared to Chaff

Jb 21:18 They are as stubble before the wind, and as chaff that the storm carrieth away.

Ps 1:4 The ungodly *are* not so: but *are* like the chaff which the wind driveth away.

Ps 35:5 Let them be as chaff before the wind: and let the angel of the LORD chase *them.*

Ps 83:13 O my God, make them like a wheel; as the stubble before the wind.

Is 5:24 Therefore as the fire devoureth the stubble, and the flame consumeth the chaff, *so* their root shall be as rottenness, and their blossom shall go up as dust: because they have cast away the law of the LORD of hosts, and despised the word of the Holy One of Israel.

Is 17:13 The nations shall rush like the rushing of many waters: but *God* shall rebuke them, and they shall flee far off, and shall be chased as the chaff of the mountains before the wind, and like a rolling thing before the whirlwind.

Is 29:5 Moreover the multitude of thy strangers shall be like small dust, and the multitude of the terrible ones *shall be* as chaff that passeth away: yea, it shall be at an instant suddenly.

Is 33:11 Ye shall conceive chaff, ye shall bring forth stubble: your breath, *as* fire, shall devour you.

Da 2:35 Then was the iron, the clay, the brass, the silver, and the gold, broken to pieces together, and became like the chaff of the summer threshing-floors; and the wind carried them away, that no place was found for them: and the stone that smote the image became a great mountain, and filled the whole earth.

Ho 13:3 Therefore they shall be as the morning cloud, and as the early dew that passeth away, as the chaff *that* is driven with the whirlwind out of the floor, and as the smoke out of the chimney.

Zep 2:2 Before the decree bring forth, *before* the day pass as the chaff, before the fierce anger of the LORD come upon you, before the day of the LORD's anger come upon you.

Mt 3:12 Whose fan *is* in his hand, and he will throughly purge his floor, and gather his wheat into the garner; but he will burn up the chaff with unquenchable fire.

Lu 3:17 Whose fan *is* in his hand, and he will throughly purge his floor, and will gather the wheat into his garner; but the chaff he will burn with fire unquenchable.

13. Their Future State

a. Words of Christ

1). Banished from God

Mt 7:23 And then will I profess unto them, I never knew you: depart from me, ye that work iniquity.

Mt 8:12 But the children of the kingdom shall be cast out into outer darkness: there shall be weeping and gnashing of teeth.

Mt 13:50 And shall cast them into the furnace of fire: there shall be wailing and gnashing of teeth.

Mt 22:13 Then said the king to the servants, Bind him hand and foot, and take him away, and cast *him* into outer darkness; there shall be weeping and gnashing of teeth.

Mt 25:46 And these shall go away into everlasting punishment: but the righteous into life eternal.

2). Suffering Compared to Fire

Mt 5:22 But I say unto you, That whosoever is angry with his brother without a cause shall be in danger of the judgment: and whosoever shall say to his brother, Raca, shall be in danger of the council: but whosoever shall say, Thou fool, shall be in danger of hell fire.

Mt 13:42 And shall cast them into a furnace of fire: there shall be wailing and gnashing of teeth.

Mt 25:41 Then shall he say also unto them on the left hand, Depart from me, ye cursed, into everlasting fire, prepared for the devil and his angels:

Mk 9:43 And if thy hand offend thee, cut it off: it is better for thee to enter into life maimed, than having two hands to go into hell, into the fire that never shall be quenched:

Mk 9:45 And if thy foot offend thee, cut it off: it is better for thee to enter halt into life, than having two feet to be cast into hell, into the fire that never shall be quenched:

Mk 9:47 And if thine eye offend thee, pluck it out: it is better for thee to enter into the kingdom of God with one eye, than having two eyes to be cast into hell fire:

Mk 9:48 Where their worm dieth not, and the fire is not quenched.

Lu 16:22–24 And it came to pass, that the beggar died, and was carried by the angels into Abraham's bosom: the rich man also died, and was buried;

And in hell he lift up his eyes, being in torments, and seeth Abraham afar off, and Lazarus in his bosom.

And he cried and said, Father Abraham, have mercy on me, and send Lazarus, that he may dip the tip of his finger in water, and cool my tongue; for I am tormented in this flame.

3). Other References

Mt 10:28 And fear not them which kill the body, but are not able to kill the soul: but rather fear him which is able to destroy both soul and body in hell.

Mt 23:33 *Ye* serpents, *ye* generation of vipers, how can ye escape the damnation of hell?

Mt 24:51 And shall cut him asunder, and appoint *him* his portion with the hypocrites: there shall be weeping and gnashing of teeth.

Jn 5:28–29 Marvel not at this: for the hour is coming, in the which all that are in the graves shall hear his voice,

And shall come forth; they that have done good, unto the resurrection of life; and they that have done evil, unto the resurrection of damnation.

b. Words of the Apostles

Ro 2:8 But unto them that are contentious, and do not obey the truth, but obey unrighteousness, indignation and wrath,

1 Co 3:17 If any man defile the temple of God, him shall God destroy; for the temple of God is holy, which *temple* ye are.

2 Th 1:9 Who shall be punished with everlasting destruction from the presence of the Lord, and from the glory of his power;

He 2:2–3 For if the word spoken by angels was stedfast, and every transgression and disobedience received a just recompence of reward;

How shall we escape, if we neglect so great salvation; which at the first began to be spoken by the Lord, and was confirmed unto us by them that heard *him;*

He 10:29 Of how much sorer punishment, suppose ye, shall he be thought worthy, who hath trodden under foot the Son of God, and hath counted the blood of the covenant, wherewith he was sanctified, an unholy thing, and hath done despite unto the Spirit of grace?

2 Pe 2:4–5 For if God spared not the angels that sinned, but cast *them* down to hell, and delivered *them* into chains of darkness, to be reserved unto judgment;

And spared not the old world, but saved Noah the eighth *person,* a preacher of righteousness, bringing in the flood upon the world of the ungodly;

2 Pe 2:9 The Lord knoweth how to deliver the godly out of temptations, and to reserve the unjust unto the day of judgment to be punished:

Jude 13 Raging waves of the sea, foaming out their own shame; wandering stars, to whom is reserved the blackness of darkness for ever.

Re 11:8 And their dead bodies *shall lie* in the street of the great city, which spiritually is called Sodom and Egypt, where also our Lord was crucified.

Re 14:11 And the smoke of their torment ascendeth up for ever and ever: and they have no rest day nor night, who worship the beast and his image, and whosoever receiveth the mark of his name.

Re 20:15 And whosoever was not found written in the book of life was cast into the lake of fire.

Re 21:8 But the fearful, and unbelieving, and the abominable, and murderers, and whoremongers, and sorcerers, and idolaters, and all liars, shall have their part in the lake which burneth with fire and brimstone: which is the second death.

c. Other Allusions

Da 12:2 And many of them that sleep in the dust of the earth shall awake, some to everlasting life, and some to shame *and* everlasting contempt.

Mal 4:1 For, behold, the day cometh, that shall burn as an oven; and all the proud, yea, and all that do wickedly, shall be stubble: and the day that cometh shall burn them up, saith the LORD of hosts, that it shall leave them neither root nor branch.

Mt 3:12 Whose fan *is* in his hand, and he will throughly purge his floor, and gather his wheat into the garner; but he will burn up the chaff with unquenchable fire.

Jn 3:36 He that believeth on the Son hath everlasting life: and he that believeth not the Son shall not see life; but the wrath of God abideth on him.

Ac 1:25 That he may take part of this ministry and apostleship, from which Judas by transgression fell, that he might go to his own place.

1 Th 5:3 For when they shall say, Peace and safety; then sudden destruction cometh upon them, as travail upon a woman with child; and they shall not escape.

d. Eternal Fire

See **FIRE**

e. Hell

1). Gehenna (Greek), the Place of Punishment

2). Tartarus (Greek), the Place of Punishment

3). Sheol (Greek)

4). Tartarus (Greek), the Place of Punishment

See **EVIL, JUDGMENTS, JUSTICE, HELL, RIGHTEOUS, SALVATION, SIN, UNRIGHTEOUSNESS**

WIDOWS AND ORPHANS

1. Admonitions

Ex 22:22 Ye shall not afflict any widow or fatherless child.

De 14:29 And the Levite, (because he hath no part nor inheritance with thee,) and the stranger, and the fatherless, and the widow, which *are* within thy gates, shall come, and shall eat and be satisfied; that the LORD thy God may bless thee in all the work of thine hand which thou doest.

De 16:11 And thou shalt rejoice before the LORD thy God, thou, and thy son, and thy daughter, and thy manservant, and thy maidservant, and the Levite that *is* within thy gates, and the stranger, and the fatherless, and the widow, that *are* among you, in the place which the LORD thy God hath chosen to place his name there.

De 24:17 Thou shalt not pervert the judgment of the stranger, *nor* of the fatherless; nor take a widow's raiment to pledge:

De 24:19 When thou cuttest down thine harvest in thy field, and hast forgot a sheaf in the field, thou shalt not go again to fetch it: it shall be for the stranger, for the fatherless, and for the widow: that the LORD thy God may bless thee in all the work of thine hands.

De 26:12 When thou hast made an end of tithing all the tithes of thine increase the third year, *which is* the year of tithing, and hast given *it* unto the Levite, the stranger, the fatherless, and the widow, that they may eat within thy gates, and be filled;

De 27:19 Cursed *be* he that perverteth the judgment of the stranger, fatherless, and widow. And all the people shall say, Amen.

Ru 2:8 Then said Boaz unto Ruth, Hearest thou not, my daughter? Go not to glean in another field, neither go from hence, but abide here fast by my maidens:

Est 2:7 And he brought up Hadassah, that *is,* Esther, his uncle's daughter: for she had neither father nor mother, and the maid *was* fair and beautiful; whom Mordecai, when her father and mother were dead, took for his own daughter.

Jb 22:9 Thou hast sent widows away empty, and the arms of the fatherless have been broken.

Jb 24:3 They drive away the ass of the fatherless, they take the widow's ox for a pledge.

Jb 29:13 The blessing of him that was ready to perish came upon me: and I caused the widow's heart to sing for joy.

Jb 31:16 If I have withheld the poor from *their* desire, or have caused the eyes of the widow to fail;

Jb 31:21 If I have lifted up my hand against the fatherless, when I saw my help in the gate:

Ps 94:6 They slay the widow and the stranger, and murder the fatherless.

Pr 23:10 Remove not the old landmark; and enter not into the fields of the fatherless:

Is 1:17 Learn to do well; seek judgment, relieve the oppressed, judge the fatherless, plead for the widow.

Is 1:23 Thy princes *are* rebellious, and companions of thieves: every one loveth gifts, and followeth after rewards: they judge not the fatherless, neither doth the cause of the widow come unto them.

Is 10:2 To turn aside the needy from judgment, and to take away the right from the poor of my people, that widows may be their prey, and *that* they may rob the fatherless!

Je 5:28 They are waxen fat, they shine: yea, they overpass the deeds of the wicked: they judge not the cause, the cause of the fatherless, yet they prosper; and the right of the needy do they not judge.

Je 7:6 *If* ye oppress not the stranger, the fatherless, and the widow, and shed not innocent blood in this place, neither walk after other gods to your hurt:

Je 22:3 Thus saith the LORD; Execute ye judgment and righteousness, and deliver the spoiled out of the hand of the oppressor: and do violence to the stranger, the fatherless, nor the widow, neither shed innocent blood in this place.

Eze 22:7 In thee have they set light by father and mother: in the midst of thee have they dealt by oppression with the stranger: in thee have they vexed the fatherless and the widow.

Zec 7:10 And oppress not the widow, nor the fatherless, the stranger, nor the poor; and let none of you imagine evil against his brother in your heart.

Mt 23:14 Woe unto you, scribes and Pharisees, hypocrites! for ye devour widows' houses, and for a pretence make long prayer: therefore ye shall receive the greater damnation.

1 Ti 5:3 Honour widows that are widows indeed.

1 Ti 5:16 If any man or woman that believeth have widows, let them relieve them, and let not the church be charged; that it may relieve them that are widows indeed.

Ja 1:27 Pure religion and undefiled before God and the Father is this, To visit the fatherless and widows in their affliction, *and* to keep himself unspotted from the world.

2. God's Care

Ex 22:23 If thou afflict them in any wise, and they cry at all unto me, I will surely hear their cry;

De 10:18 He doth execute the judgment of the fatherless and widow, and loveth the stranger, in giving him food and raiment.

Ps 10:14 Thou hast seen *it;* for thou beholdest mischief and spite, to requite *it* with thy hand: the poor committeth himself unto thee; thou art the helper of the fatherless.

Ps 27:10 When my father and my mother forsake me, then the LORD will take me up.

Ps 68:5 A father of the fatherless, and a judge of the widows, *is* God in his holy habitation.

Ps 146:9 The LORD preserveth the strangers; he relieveth the fatherless and widow: but the way of the wicked he turneth upside down.

Pr 15:25 The LORD will destroy the house of the proud: but he will establish the border of the widow.

Je 49:11 Leave thy fatherless children, I will preserve *them* alive; and let thy widows trust in me.

Ho 14:3 Asshur shall not save us; we will not ride upon horses: neither will we say any more to the work of our hands, *Ye are* our gods: for in thee the fatherless findeth mercy.

Mal 3:5 And I will come near to you to judgment; and I will be a swift witness against the sorcerers, and against the adulterers, and against false swearers, and against those that oppress the hireling in *his* wages, the widow, and the fatherless, and that turn aside the stranger *from his right,* and fear not me, saith the LORD of hosts.

See **HELP, KINDNESS, LOVE**

WILDERNESS, *wild, uninhabited regions*

Ge 16:7; 21:14; Ex 3:18; 4:27; 15:22; 17:1; Le 16:10, 22; De 29:5; 1 K 19:4; Ps 55:7; 68:7; Je 9:10; Eze 20:23, 36; Am 2:10; 5:25; Mt 3:1; 4:1; Lu 3:2; 8:29; Jn 11:54; Re 12:6

WILL *See* **SURRENDER**

WILLOWS *See* **TREES**

WIND *See* **WEATHER**

WINDOWS

1. Of Houses

Ge 6:16; 26:8; Jos 2:15; Jud 5:28; 2 S 6:16; 1 K 6:4; 7:4; 2 K 9:30; 13:17; Pr 7:6;

Je 22:14; Eze 40:16, 29; 41:16, 26; 2 Co 11:33

2. Of Heaven, *floodgates of the sky*

Ge 7:11; Is 24:18; Mal 3:10

WINE

1. New

Nu 18:12; De 12:17; 14:23; 16:13; 18:4; 32:14; 2 Chr 31:5; Ne 10:37, 39; 13:5, 12; Is 24:7; 65:8; Ho 4:11; 9:2; Jl 1:5; 3:18; Hag 1:11; Zec 9:17; Mt 9:17; 26:29; Mk 2:22; Lu 5:37; Ac 2:13

2. Its Use

Ge 14:18 And Melchizedek king of Salem brought forth bread and wine: and he *was* the priest of the most high God.

Ex 29:40 And with the one lamb a tenth deal of flour mingled with the fourth part of an hin of beaten oil; and the fourth part of an hin of wine *for* a drink offering.

Nu 6:20 And the priest shall wave them *for* a wave offering before the LORD: this *is* holy for the priest, with the wave breast and heave shoulder: and after that the Nazarite may drink wine.

Nu 15:7 And for a drink offering thou shalt offer the third *part* of an hin of wine, *for* a sweet savour unto the LORD.

Nu 28:7 And the drink offering thereof *shall be* the fourth *part* of an hin for the one lamb: in the holy *place* shalt thou cause the strong wine to be poured unto the LORD *for* a drink offering.

De 14:26 And thou shalt bestow that money for whatsoever thy soul lusteth after, for oxen, or for sheep, or for wine, or for strong drink, or for whatsoever thy soul desireth: and thou shalt eat there before the LORD thy God, and thou shalt rejoice, thou, and thine household,

1 S 25:18 Then Abigail made haste, and took two hundred loaves, and two bottles of wine, and five sheep ready dressed, and five measures of parched *corn,* and an hundred clusters of raisins, and two hundred cakes of figs, and laid *them* on asses.

2 S 13:28 Now Absalom had commanded his servants, saying, Mark ye now when Amnon's heart is merry with wine, and when I say unto you, Smite Amnon; then kill him, fear not: have not I commanded you? be courageous and be valiant.

1 K 20:12 And it came to pass, when *Ben-hadad* heard this message, as he *was* drinking, he and the kings in the pavilions, that he said unto his servants, Set *yourselves in array*. And they set *themselves in array* against the city.

2 Chr 32:28 Storehouses also for the increase of corn, and wine, and oil; and stalls for all manner of beasts, and cotes for flocks.

Ne 2:1 And it came to pass in the month Nisan, in the twentieth year of Artaxerxes the king, *that* wine *was* before him: and I took up the wine, and gave *it* unto the king. Now I had not been *beforetime* sad in his presence.

Ne 5:18 Now *that* which was prepared *for me* daily *was* one ox *and* six choice sheep; also fowls were prepared for me, and once in ten days store of all sorts of wine: yet for all this required not I the bread of the governor, because the bondage was heavy upon this people.

Est 1:7 And they gave *them* drink in vessels of gold, (the vessels being diverse one from another,) and royal wine in abundance, according to the state of the king.

Est 5:6 And the king said unto Esther at the banquet of wine, What *is* thy petition? and it shall be granted thee: and what *is* thy request? even to the half of the kingdom it shall be performed.

Est 7:2 And the king said again unto Esther on the second day at the banquet of wine, What *is* thy petition, queen Esther? and it shall be granted thee: and what *is* thy request? and it shall be performed, *even* to the half of the kingdom.

Jb 1:13 And there was a day when his sons and his daughters *were* eating and drinking wine in their eldest brother's house:

Ps 104:15 And wine *that* maketh glad the heart of man, *and* oil to make *his* face to shine, and bread *which* strengtheneth man's heart.

Pr 31:6 Give strong drink unto him that is ready to perish, and wine unto those that be of heavy hearts.

Ec 2:3 I sought in mine heart to give myself unto wine, yet acquainting mine heart with wisdom; and to lay hold on folly, till I might see what *was* that good for the sons of men, which they should do under the heaven all the days of their life.

Ec 9:7 Go thy way, eat thy bread with joy, and drink thy wine with a merry heart; for God now accepteth thy works.

Ec 10:19 A feast is made for laughter, and wine maketh merry: but money answereth all *things*.

Is 62:8 The LORD hath sworn by his right hand, and by the arm of his strength, Surely I will no more give thy corn to be meat for thine enemies; and the sons of the stranger shall not drink thy wine, for the which thou hast laboured:

Je 40:12 Even all the Jews returned out of all places whither they were driven, and came to the land of Judah, to Gedaliah, unto Mizpah, and gathered wine and summer fruits very much.

Eze 27:18 Damascus *was* thy merchant in the multitude of the wares of thy making, for the multitude of all riches; in the wine of Helbon, and white wool.

Da 1:5 And the king appointed them a daily provision of the king's meat, and of the wine which he drank: so nourishing them three years, that at the end thereof they might stand before the king.

Ho 14:7 They that dwell under his shadow shall return; they shall revive *as* the corn, and grow as the vine: the scent thereof *shall be* as the wine of Lebanon.

Jl 2:19 Yea, the LORD will answer and say unto his people, Behold, I will send you corn, and wine, and oil, and ye shall be satisfied therewith: and I will no more make you a reproach among the heathen:

Am 9:14 And I will bring again the captivity of my people of Israel, and they shall build the waste cities, and inhabit *them;* and they shall plant vineyards, and drink the wine thereof; they shall also make gardens, and eat the fruit of them.

Mi 6:15 Thou shalt sow, but thou shalt not reap; thou shalt tread the olives, but thou shalt not anoint thee with oil; and sweet wine, but shalt not drink wine.

Lu 1:15 For he shall be great in the sight of the Lord, and shall drink neither wine nor strong drink; and he shall be filled with the Holy Ghost, even from his mother's womb.

Lu 5:39 No man also having drunk old *wine* straightway desireth new: for he saith, The old is better.

Jn 2:3 And when they wanted wine, the mother of Jesus saith unto him, They have no wine.

Jn 2:10 And saith unto him, Every man at the beginning doth set forth good wine; and when men have well drunk, then that which is worse: *but* thou hast kept the good wine until now.

1 Ti 5:23 Drink no longer water, but use a little wine for thy stomach's sake and thine often infirmities.

Re 6:6 And I heard a voice in the midst of the four beasts say, A measure of wheat for a penny, and three measures of barley for a penny; and *see* thou hurt not the oil and the wine.

3. Warnings

Ge 9:21 And he drank of the wine, and was drunken; and he was uncovered within his tent.

Ge 19:33 And they made their father drink wine that night: and the firstborn went in, and lay with her father; and he perceived not when she lay down, nor when she arose.

Ge 27:25 And he said, Bring *it* near to me, and I will eat of my son's venison, that my soul may bless thee. And he brought *it* near to him, and he did eat: and he brought him wine, and he drank.

Le 10:9 Do not drink wine nor strong drink, thou, nor thy sons with thee, when ye go into the tabernacle of the congregation, lest ye die: *it shall be* a statute for ever throughout your generations:

Nu 6:3 He shall separate *himself* from wine and strong drink, and shall drink no vinegar of wine, or vinegar of strong drink, neither shall he drink any liquor of grapes, nor eat moist grapes, or dried.

Est 3:15 The posts went out, being hastened by the king's commandment, and the decree was given in Shushan the palace. And the king and Haman sat down to drink; but the city Shushan was perplexed.

Pr 20:1 Wine *is* a mocker, strong drink *is* raging: and whosoever is deceived thereby is not wise.

Pr 21:17 He that loveth pleasure *shall be* a poor man: he that loveth wine and oil shall not be rich.

Pr 23:31 Look not thou upon the wine when it is red, when it giveth his colour in the cup, *when* it moveth itself aright.

Pr 31:4 *It is* not for kings, O Lemuel, *it is* not for kings to drink wine; nor for princes strong drink:

Is 5:11 Woe unto them that rise up early in the morning, *that* they may follow strong drink; that continue until night, *till* wine inflame them!

Is 5:22 Woe unto *them that are* mighty to drink wine, and men of strength to mingle strong drink:

Is 24:9 They shall not drink wine with a song; strong drink shall be bitter to them that drink it.

Is 28:1 Woe to the crown of pride, to the drunkards of Ephraim, whose glorious beauty is a fading flower, which *are* on the head of the fat valleys of them that are overcome with wine!

Is 28:7 But they also have erred through wine, and through strong drink are out of the way; the priest and the prophet have erred through strong drink, they are swallowed up of wine, they are out of the way through strong drink; they err in vision, they stumble *in* judgment.

Is 56:12 Come ye, *say they,* I will fetch wine, and we will fill ourselves with strong drink; and to morrow shall be as this day, *and* much more abundant.

Je 35:2 Go unto the house of the Rechabites, and speak unto them, and bring them into the house of the LORD, into one of the chambers, and give them wine to drink.

Eze 44:21 Neither shall any priest drink wine, when they enter into the inner court.

Da 5:2 Belshazzar, whiles he tasted the wine, commanded to bring the golden and silver vessels which his father Nebuchadnezzar had taken out of the temple which *was* in Jerusalem; that the king, and his princes, his wives, and his concubines, might drink therein.

Da 5:4 They drank wine, and praised the gods of gold, and of silver, of brass, of iron, of wood, and of stone.

Da 5:23 But hast lifted up thyself against the Lord of heaven; and they have brought the vessels of his house before thee, and thou, and thy lords, thy wives, and thy concubines, have drunk wine in them; and thou hast praised the gods of silver, and gold, of brass, iron, wood, and stone, which see not, nor hear, nor know: and the God in whose hand thy breath *is,* and whose *are* all thy ways, hast thou not glorified:

Da 10:3 I ate no pleasant bread, neither came flesh nor wine in my mouth, neither did I anoint myself at all, till three whole weeks were fulfilled.

Ho 4:11 Whoredom and wine and new wine take away the heart.

Jl 1:5 Awake, ye drunkards, and weep; and howl, all ye drinkers of wine, because of the new wine; for it is cut off from your mouth.

Jl 3:3 And they have cast lots for my people; and have given a boy for an harlot, and sold a girl for wine, that they might drink.

Am 2:8 And they lay *themselves* down upon clothes laid to pledge by every altar, and they drink the wine of the condemned in the house of their god.

Am 2:12 But ye gave the Nazarites wine to drink; and commanded the prophets, saying, Prophesy not.

Am 6:6 That drink wine in bowls, and anoint themselves with the chief ointments: but they are not grieved for the affliction of Joseph.

Mi 2:11 If a man walking in the spirit and falsehood do lie, *saying,* I will prophesy unto thee of wine and of strong drink; he shall even be the prophet of this people.

Hab 2:5 Yea also, because he transgresseth by wine, *he is* a proud man, neither keepeth at home, who enlargeth his desire as hell, and *is* as death, and cannot be satisfied, but gathereth unto him all nations, and heapeth unto him all people:

Ep 5:18 And be not drunk with wine, wherein is excess; but be filled with the Spirit;

See **DRUNKENNESS, TEMPERANCE**

WINEPRESS *See* **AGRICULTURE**

WINGS, *God's, figurative*

Ex 19:4; Ru 2:12; Ps 17:8; 36:7; 91:4; Mal 4:2

WINKING, *associated with the wicked*

Ps 35:19; Pr 6:13; 10:10

WINNOWING *See* **AGRICULTURE**

WINTER

Ps 74:17; Song 2:11; Mt 24:20; Mk 13:18; Jn 10:22; 2 Ti 4:21; Tit 3:12

WISDOM, *ability to discern between right and wrong*

1. Of Christ

Is 7:15 Butter and honey shall he eat, that he may know to refuse the evil, and choose the good.

Is 9:6 For unto us a child is born, unto us a son is given: and the government shall be upon his shoulder: and his name shall be called Wonderful, Counsellor, The mighty God, The everlasting Father, The Prince of Peace.

Is 11:2 And the spirit of the LORD shall rest upon him, the spirit of wisdom and understanding, the spirit of counsel and might, the spirit of knowledge and of the fear of the LORD;

Is 52:13 Behold, my servant shall deal prudently, he shall be exalted and extolled, and be very high.

Is 53:11 He shall see of the travail of his soul, *and* shall be satisfied: by his knowledge shall my righteous servant justify many; for he shall bear their iniquities.

Mt 12:11 And he said unto them, What man shall there be among you, that shall have one sheep, and if it fall into a pit on the sabbath day, will he not lay hold on it, and lift *it* out?

Mt 12:25 And Jesus knew their thoughts, and said unto them, Every kingdom divided against itself is brought to desolation; and every city or house divided against itself shall not stand:

Mt 13:54 And when he was come into his own country, he taught them in their synagogue, insomuch that they were astonished, and said, Whence hath this man this wisdom, and these mighty works?

Mt 21:24 And Jesus answered and said unto them, I also will ask you one thing, which if ye tell me, I in like wise will tell you by what authority I do these things.

Mt 22:21 They say unto him, Caesar's. Then saith he unto them, Render therefore unto Caesar the things which are Caesar's; and unto God the things that are God's.

Mt 22:46 And no man was able to answer him a word, neither durst any *man* from that day forth ask him any more *questions.*

Mk 6:2 And when the sabbath day was come, he began to teach in the synagogue: and many hearing *him* were astonished, saying, From whence hath this *man* these things? and what wisdom *is* this which is given unto him, that even such mighty works are wrought by his hands?

Mk 12:16 And they brought *it.* And he saith unto them, Whose *is* this image and superscription? And they said unto him, Caesar's.

Mk 12:28 And one of the scribes came, and having heard them reasoning together, and perceiving that he had answered them well, asked him, Which is the first commandment of all?

Lu 2:40 And the child grew, and waxed strong in spirit, filled with wisdom: and the grace of God was upon him.

Lu 2:47 And all that heard him were astonished at his understanding and answers.

Lu 5:31 And Jesus answering said unto them, They that are whole need not a physician; but they that are sick.

Lu 7:43 Simon answered and said, I suppose that *he,* to whom he forgave most. And he said unto him, Thou hast rightly judged.

Lu 20:3 And he answered and said unto them, I will also ask you one thing; and answer me:

Lu 20:25 And he said unto them, Render therefore unto Caesar the things which be Caesar's, and unto God the things which be God's.

Lu 20:39 Then certain of the scribes answering said, Master, thou hast well said.

Jn 3:32 And what he hath seen and heard, that he testifieth; and no man receiveth his testimony.

Jn 7:15 And the Jews marvelled, saying, How knoweth this man letters, having never learned?

Jn 8:14 Jesus answered and said unto them, Though I bear record of myself, *yet* my record is true: for I know whence I came, and whither I go; but ye cannot tell whence I come, and whither I go.

Jn 11:4 When Jesus heard *that,* he said, This sickness is not unto death, but for the glory of God, that the Son of God might be glorified thereby.

Jn 21:6 And he said unto them, Cast the net on the right side of the ship, and ye shall find. They cast therefore, and now they were not able to draw it for the multitude of fishes.

1 Co 1:24 But unto them which are called, both Jews and Greeks, Christ the power of God, and the wisdom of God.

Col 2:3 In whom are hid all the treasures of wisdom and knowledge.

Re 5:6 And I beheld, and, lo, in the midst of the throne and of the four beasts, and in the midst of the elders, stood a Lamb as it had been slain, having seven horns and seven eyes, which are the seven Spirits of God sent forth into all the earth.

2. Of God

Ge 1:31 And God saw every thing that he had made, and, behold, *it was* very good. And the evening and the morning were the sixth day.

Ge 41:16 And Joseph answered Pharaoh, saying, *It is* not in me: God shall give Pharaoh an answer of peace.

Jb 9:4 *He is* wise in heart, and mighty in strength: who hath hardened *himself* against him, and hath prospered?

Jb 12:13 With him *is* wisdom and strength, he hath counsel and understanding.

Jb 28:23 God understandeth the way thereof, and he knoweth the place thereof.

Jb 36:5 Behold, God *is* mighty, and despiseth not *any: he is* mighty in strength *and* wisdom.

Ps 104:24 O Lord, how manifold are thy works! in wisdom hast thou made them all: the earth is full of thy riches.

Ps 136:5 To him that by wisdom made the heavens: for his mercy *endureth* for ever.

Ps 147:4 He telleth the number of the stars; he calleth them all by *their* names.

Pr 3:19 The Lord by wisdom hath founded the earth; by understanding hath he established the heavens.

Pr 8:22 The Lord possessed me in the beginning of his way, before his works of old.

Is 28:29 This also cometh forth from the Lord of hosts, *which* is wonderful in counsel, *and* excellent in working.

Is 31:2 Yet he also *is* wise, and will bring evil, and will not call back his words: but will arise against the house of the evildoers, and against the help of them that work iniquity.

Is 40:13 Who hath directed the Spirit of the Lord, or *being* his counsellor hath taught him?

Je 10:7 Who would not fear thee, O King of nations? for to thee doth it appertain: forasmuch as among all the wise *men* of the nations, and in all their kingdoms, *there is* none like unto thee.

Je 10:12 He hath made the earth by his power, he hath established the world by his wisdom, and hath stretched out the heavens by his discretion.

Je 51:15 He hath made the earth by his power, he hath established the world by his wisdom, and hath stretched out the heaven by his understanding.

Da 2:20 Daniel answered and said, Blessed be the name of God for ever and ever: for wisdom and might are his:

Lu 10:21 In that hour Jesus rejoiced in spirit, and said, I thank thee, O Father, Lord of heaven and earth, that thou hast hid these things from the wise and prudent, and hast revealed them unto babes: even so, Father; for so it seemed good in thy sight.

Lu 11:49 Therefore also said the wisdom of God, I will send them prophets and apostles, and *some* of them they shall slay and persecute:

Ro 11:33 O the depth of the riches both of the wisdom and knowledge of God! how unsearchable *are* his judgments, and his ways past finding out!

Ro 16:27 To God only wise, *be* glory through Jesus Christ for ever. Amen.

1 Co 1:21 For after that in the wisdom of God the world by wisdom knew not God, it pleased God by the foolishness of preaching to save them that believe.

1 Co 1:25 Because the foolishness of God is wiser than men; and the weakness of God is stronger than men.

1 Co 2:7 But we speak the wisdom of God in a mystery, *even* the hidden *wisdom,* which God ordained before the world unto our glory:

Ep 1:8 Wherein he hath abounded toward us in all wisdom and prudence;

Ep 3:10 To the intent that now unto the principalities and powers in heavenly *places* might be known by the church the manifold wisdom of God,

3. True Wisdom

CANNOT EXIST WITHOUT THE FEAR OF GOD

Jb 28:28 And unto man he said, Behold, the fear of the Lord, that *is* wisdom; and to depart from evil *is* understanding.

CAN BE LEARNED

Jb 32:7 I said, Days should speak, and multitude of years should teach wisdom.

Ps 111:10 The fear of the LORD *is* the beginning of wisdom: a good understanding have all they that do *his commandments:* his praise endureth for ever.

Pr 1:20 Wisdom crieth without; she uttereth her voice in the streets:

THE SUPREME ACQUISITION

Pr 4:7 Wisdom *is* the principal thing; *therefore* get wisdom: and with all thy getting get understanding.

Pr 9:1 Wisdom hath builded her house, she hath hewn out her seven pillars:

APPREHENDS DIVINE TRUTH

Ho 14:9 Who *is* wise, and he shall understand these *things?* prudent, and he shall know them? for the ways of the LORD *are* right, and the just shall walk in them: but the transgressors shall fall therein.

LAYS AN IMMOVABLE FOUNDATION

Mt 7:24 Therefore whosoever heareth these sayings of mine, and doeth them, I will liken him unto a wise man, which built his house upon a rock:

1 Co 2:6 Howbeit we speak wisdom among them that are perfect: yet not the wisdom of this world, nor of the princes of this world, that come to nought:

1 Co 12:8 For to one is given by the Spirit the word of wisdom; to another the word of knowledge by the same Spirit;

SCRIPTURE IS THE SOURCE

2 Ti 3:15 And that from a child thou hast known the holy scriptures, which are able to make thee wise unto salvation through faith which is in Christ Jesus.

FULL OF SPIRITUAL FRUITS

Ja 3:17 But the wisdom that is from above is first pure, then peaceable, gentle, *and* easy to be intreated, full of mercy and good fruits, without partiality, and without hypocrisy.

1 Jn 2:20 But ye have an unction from the Holy One, and ye know all things.

4. Gained through Prayer

2 Chr 1:10 Give me now wisdom and knowledge, that I may go out and come in before this people: for who can judge this thy people, *that is so* great?

Ps 90:12 So teach *us* to number our days, that we may apply *our* hearts unto wisdom.

Pr 2:3 Yea, if thou criest after knowledge, *and* liftest up thy voice for understanding;

Ep 1:17 That the God of our Lord Jesus Christ, the Father of glory, may give unto you the spirit of wisdom and revelation in the knowledge of him:

Col 1:9 For this cause we also, since the day we heard *it,* do not cease to pray for you, and to desire that ye might be filled with the knowledge of his will in all wisdom and spiritual understanding;

Ja 1:5 If any of you lack wisdom, let him ask of God, that giveth to all *men* liberally, and upbraideth not; and it shall be given him.

5. Its Preciousness

Jb 28:16 It cannot be valued with the gold of Ophir, with the precious onyx, or the sapphire.

Ps 105:22 To bind his princes at his pleasure; and teach his senators wisdom.

Pr 3:13–14 Happy *is* the man *that* findeth wisdom, and the man *that* getteth understanding.

For the merchandise of it *is* better than the merchandise of silver, and the gain thereof than fine gold.

Pr 5:1 My son, attend unto my wisdom, *and* bow thine ear to my understanding:

Pr 7:4 Say unto wisdom, Thou *art* my sister; and call understanding *thy* kinswoman:

Pr 8:11 For wisdom *is* better than rubies; and all the things that may be desired are not to be compared to it.

Pr 14:24 The crown of the wise is their riches: *but* the foolishness of fools *is* folly.

Pr 16:16 How much better *is it* to get wisdom than gold! and to get understanding rather to be chosen than silver!

Pr 19:8 He that getteth wisdom loveth his own soul: *he that* keepeth understanding shall find good.

Pr 24:7 Wisdom *is* too high for a fool: he openeth not his mouth in the gate.

Pr 24:14 So *shall* the knowledge of wisdom *be* unto thy soul: when thou hast found *it,* then there shall be a reward, and thy expectation shall not be cut off.

Ec 2:13 Then I saw that wisdom excelleth folly, as far as light excelleth darkness.

Ec 7:11 Wisdom *is* good with an inheritance: and *by it there is* profit to them that see the sun.

Ec 7:19 Wisdom strengtheneth the wise more than ten mighty *men* which are in the city.

Ec 8:1 Who *is* as the wise *man?* and who knoweth the interpretation of a thing? a man's wisdom maketh his face to shine, and the boldness of his face shall be changed.

Ec 9:16 Then said I, Wisdom *is* better than strength: nevertheless the poor man's wisdom *is* despised, and his words are not heard.

Ec 9:18 Wisdom *is* better than weapons of war: but one sinner destroyeth much good.

Ec 10:10 If the iron be blunt, and he do not whet the edge, then must he put to more strength: but wisdom *is* profitable to direct.

6. Promised

2 Chr 1:12 Wisdom and knowledge *is* granted unto thee; and I will give thee riches, and wealth, and honour, such as none of the kings have had that *have been* before thee, neither shall there any after thee have the like.

Jb 35:11 Who teacheth us more than the beasts of the earth, and maketh us wiser than the fowls of heaven?

Jb 38:36 Who hath put wisdom in the inward parts? or who hath given understanding to the heart?

Ps 51:6 Behold, thou desirest truth in the inward parts: and in the hidden *part* thou shalt make me to know wisdom.

Pr 2:6 For the LORD giveth wisdom: out of his mouth *cometh* knowledge and understanding.

Pr 9:4 Whoso *is* simple, let him turn in hither: *as for* him that wanteth understanding, she saith to him,

Ec 2:26 For *God* giveth to a man that *is* good in his sight wisdom, and knowledge, and joy: but to the sinner he giveth travail, to gather and to heap up, that he may give to *him that is* good before God. This also *is* vanity and vexation of spirit.

Is 28:6 And for a spirit of judgment to him that sitteth in judgment, and for strength to them that turn the battle to the gate.

Is 33:6 And wisdom and knowledge shall be the stability of thy times, *and* strength of salvation: the fear of the LORD *is* his treasure.

Da 1:17 As for these four children, God gave them knowledge and skill in all learning and wisdom: and Daniel had understanding in all visions and dreams.

Da 2:21 And he changeth the times and the seasons: he removeth kings, and setteth up kings: he giveth wisdom unto the wise, and knowledge to them that know understanding:

Da 12:10 Many shall be purified, and made white, and tried; but the wicked shall do wickedly: and none of the wicked shall understand; but the wise shall understand.

Lu 21:15 For I will give you a mouth and wisdom, which all your adversaries shall not be able to gainsay nor resist.

Ja 1:5 If any of you lack wisdom, let him ask of God, that giveth to all *men* liberally, and upbraideth not; and it shall be given him.

7. Search for

1 K 3:9 Give therefore thy servant an understanding heart to judge thy people, that I may discern between good and bad: for who is able to judge this thy so great a people?

2 Chr 1:10 Give me now wisdom and knowledge, that I may go out and come in before this people: for who can judge this thy people, *that is so* great?

Jb 28:3 He setteth an end to darkness, and searcheth out all perfection: the stones of darkness, and the shadow of death.

Jb 28:12 But where shall wisdom be found? and where *is* the place of understanding?

Jb 28:20 Whence then cometh wisdom? and where *is* the place of understanding?

Ps 119:27 Make me to understand the way of thy precepts: so shall I talk of thy wondrous works.

Ps 119:34 Give me understanding, and I shall keep thy law; yea, I shall observe it with *my* whole heart.

Ps 119:73 Thy hands have made me and fashioned me: give me understanding, that I may learn thy commandments.

Ps 119:125 I *am* thy servant; give me understanding, that I may know thy testimonies.

Ps 119:144 The righteousness of thy testimonies *is* everlasting: give me understanding, and I shall live.

Ps 119:169 Let my cry come near before thee, O LORD: give me understanding according to thy word.

Pr 2:4 If thou seekest her as silver, and searchest for her as *for* hid treasures;

Pr 23:23 Buy the truth, and sell *it* not; *also* wisdom, and instruction, and understanding.

Pr 24:14 So *shall* the knowledge of wisdom *be* unto thy soul: when thou hast found *it,* then there shall be a reward, and thy expectation shall not be cut off.

Pr 29:3 Whoso loveth wisdom rejoiceth his father: but he that keepeth company with harlots spendeth *his* substance.

Ec 1:13 And I gave my heart to seek and search out by wisdom concerning all *things* that are done under heaven: this sore travail hath God given to the sons of man to be exercised therewith.

Ec 1:16 I communed with mine own heart, saying, Lo, I am come to great estate, and have gotten more wisdom than all *they* that have been before me in Jerusalem: yea, my heart had great experience of wisdom and knowledge.

Ec 2:12 And I turned myself to behold wisdom, and madness, and folly: for what *can* the man *do* that cometh after the king? *even* that which hath been already done.

Ec 7:25 I applied mine heart to know, and to search, and to seek out wisdom, and the reason *of things,* and to know the wickedness of folly, even of foolishness *and* madness:

Ec 8:16 When I applied mine heart to know wisdom, and to see the business that is done upon the earth: (for also *there is that* neither day nor night seeth sleep with his eyes:)

Mt 12:42 The queen of the south shall rise up in the judgment with this generation, and shall condemn it: for she came from the uttermost parts of the earth to hear the wisdom of Solomon; and, behold, a greater than Solomon *is* here.

Lu 11:31 The queen of the south shall rise up in the judgment with the men of this generation, and condemn them: for she came from the utmost parts of the earth to hear the wisdom of Solomon; and, behold, a greater than Solomon is here.

8. Its Call

Pr 1:20 Wisdom crieth without; she uttereth her voice in the streets:

Pr 8:1 Doth not wisdom cry? and understanding put forth her voice?

Pr 8:4 Unto you, O men, I call; and my voice *is* to the sons of man.

Pr 9:3 She hath sent forth her maidens: she crieth upon the highest places of the city,

Is 45:19 I have not spoken in secret, in a dark place of the earth: I said not unto the seed of Jacob, Seek ye me in vain: I the LORD speak righteousness, I declare things that are right.

9. Examples

Ex 31:6 And I, behold, I have given with him Aholiab, the son of Ahisamach, of the tribe of Dan: and in the hearts of all that are wise hearted I have put wisdom, that they may make all that I have commanded thee;

1 K 4:31 For he was wiser than all men; than Ethan the Ezrahite, and Heman, and Chalcol, and Darda, the sons of Mahol: and his fame was in all nations round about.

1 K 10:3 And Solomon told her all her questions: there was not *any* thing hid from the king, which he told her not.

Pr 21:22 A wise *man* scaleth the city of the mighty, and casteth down the strength of the confidence thereof.

Pr 28:2 For the transgression of a land many *are* the princes thereof: but by a man of understanding *and* knowledge the state *thereof* shall be prolonged.

Da 1:20 And in all matters of wisdom *and* understanding, that the king enquired of them, he found them ten times better than all the magicians *and* astrologers that *were* in all his realm.

Ac 6:10 And they were not able to resist the wisdom and the spirit by which he spake.

10. Wise Men

Ge 41:8 And it came to pass in the morning that his spirit was troubled; and he sent and called for all the magicians of Egypt, and all the wise men thereof: and Pharaoh told them his dream; but *there was* none that could interpret them unto Pharaoh.

1 S 6:2 And the Philistines called for the priests and the diviners, saying,

What shall we do to the ark of the LORD? tell us wherewith we shall send it to his place.

Est 1:13 Then the king said to the wise men, which knew the times, (for so *was* the king's manner toward all that knew law and judgment:

Ec 7:5 *It is* better to hear the rebuke of the wise, than for a man to hear the song of fools.

Da 2:13 And the decree went forth that the wise *men* should be slain; and they sought Daniel and his fellows to be slain.

Da 2:48 Then the king made Daniel a great man, and gave him many great gifts, and made him ruler over the whole province of Babylon, and chief of the governors over all the wise *men* of Babylon.

Mt 2:1 Now when Jesus was born in Bethlehem of Judaea in the days of Herod the king, behold, there came wise men from the east to Jerusalem,

11. Worldly, considered foolishness when compared to God's wisdom

Pr 26:12 Seest thou a man wise in his own conceit? *there is* more hope of a fool than of him.

Is 29:14 Therefore, behold, I will proceed to do a marvellous work among this people, *even* a marvellous work and a wonder: for the wisdom of their wise *men* shall perish, and the understanding of their prudent *men* shall be hid.

Is 47:10 For thou hast trusted in thy wickedness: thou hast said, None seeth me. Thy wisdom and thy knowledge, it hath perverted thee; and thou hast said in thine heart, I *am*, and none else beside me.

Je 4:22 For my people *is* foolish, they have not known me; they *are* sottish children, and they have none understanding: they *are* wise to do evil, but to do good they have no knowledge.

Je 8:9 The wise *men* are ashamed, they are dismayed and taken: lo, they have rejected the word of the LORD; and what wisdom *is* in them?

Je 18:18 Then said they, Come, and let us devise devices against Jeremiah;

for the law shall not perish from the priest, nor counsel from the wise, nor the word from the prophet. Come, and let us smite him with the tongue, and let us not give heed to any of his words.

Eze 28:4 With thy wisdom and with thine understanding thou hast gotten thee riches, and hast gotten gold and silver into thy treasures:

Ro 1:22 Professing themselves to be wise, they became fools,

1 Co 1:19 For it is written, I will destroy the wisdom of the wise, and will bring to nothing the understanding of the prudent.

1 Co 2:6 Howbeit we speak wisdom among them that are perfect: yet not the wisdom of this world, nor of the princes of this world, that come to nought:

1 Co 3:19–20 For the wisdom of this world is foolishness with God. For it is written, He taketh the wise in their own craftiness.

And again, The Lord knoweth the thoughts of the wise, that they are vain.

2 Co 1:12 For our rejoicing is this, the testimony of our conscience, that in simplicity and godly sincerity, not with fleshly wisdom, but by the grace of God, we have had our conversation in the world, and more abundantly to you-ward.

Col 2:23 Which things have indeed a shew of wisdom in will worship, and humility, and neglecting of the body; not in any honour to the satisfying of the flesh.

See **FOLLY, KNOWLEDGE, UNDERSTANDING**

WITCHCRAFT, *divination associated with idolatrous worship and demonic powers*

Ex 22:18 Thou shalt not suffer a witch to live.

Le 19:31 Regard not them that have familiar spirits, neither seek after wizards, to be defiled by them: I *am* the LORD your God.

Le 20:6 And the soul that turneth after such as have familiar spirits, and after wizards, to go a whoring after them, I will even set my face against that soul, and will cut him off from among his people.

Le 20:27 A man also or woman that hath a familiar spirit, or that is a wizard, shall surely be put to death: they shall stone them with stones: their blood *shall be* upon them.

De 18:10 There shall not be found among you *any one* that maketh his son or his daughter to pass through the fire, or that useth divination, *or* an observer of times, or an enchanter, or a witch,

1 S 15:23 For rebellion *is as* the sin of witchcraft, and stubbornness *is as* iniquity and idolatry. Because thou hast rejected the word of the LORD, he hath also rejected thee from *being* king.

1 S 28:3 Now Samuel was dead, and all Israel had lamented him, and buried him in Ramah, even in his own city. And Saul had put away those that had familiar spirits, and the wizards, out of the land.

1 S 28:7 Then said Saul unto his servants, Seek me a woman that hath a familiar spirit, that I may go to her, and enquire of her. And his servants said to him, Behold, *there is* a woman that hath a familiar spirit at Endor.

2 K 9:22 And it came to pass, when Joram saw Jehu, that he said, Is it peace, Jehu? And he answered, What peace, so long as the whoredoms of thy mother Jezebel and her witchcrafts *are so* many?

2 K 21:6 And he made his son pass through the fire, and observed times, and used enchantments, and dealt with familiar spirits and wizards: he wrought much wickedness in the sight of the LORD, to provoke *him* to anger.

2 K 23:24 Moreover the *workers with* familiar spirits, and the wizards, and the images, and the idols, and all the abominations that were spied in the land of Judah and in Jerusalem, did Josiah put away, that he might perform the words of the law which were written in the book that Hilkiah the priest found in the house of the LORD.

1 Chr 10:13 So Saul died for his transgression which he committed against the LORD, *even* against the word of the LORD, which he kept not, and also for asking *counsel* of *one that had* a familiar spirit, to enquire *of it;*

2 Chr 33:6 And he caused his children to pass through the fire in the valley of the son of Hinnom: also he observed times, and used enchantments, and used witchcraft, and dealt with a familiar spirit, and with wizards: he wrought much evil in the sight of the LORD, to provoke him to anger.

Is 8:19 And when they shall say unto you, Seek unto them that have familiar spirits, and unto wizards that peep, and that mutter: should not a people seek unto their God? for the living to the dead?

Is 19:3 And the spirit of Egypt shall fail in the midst thereof; and I will destroy the counsel thereof: and they shall seek to the idols, and to the charmers, and to them that have familiar spirits, and to the wizards.

Is 29:4 And thou shalt be brought down, *and* shalt speak out of the ground, and thy speech shall be low out of the dust, and thy voice shall be, as of one that hath a familiar spirit, out of the ground, and thy speech shall whisper out of the dust.

Mic 5:12 And I will cut off witchcrafts out of thine hand; and thou shalt have no *more* soothsayers:

Na 3:4 Because of the multitude of the whoredoms of the wellfavoured harlot, the mistress of witchcrafts, that selleth nations through her whoredoms, and families through her witchcrafts.

Ga 5:20 Idolatry, witchcraft, hatred, variance, emulations, wrath, strife, seditions, heresies,

See **MAGICIANS**

WITNESSES, *those who have seen or heard something*

1. Two or Three Required
Mt 18:16

2. Disciples and Early Christians
Is 43:12 I have declared, and have saved, and I have shewed, when *there was* no strange *god* among you: therefore ye *are* my witnesses, saith the LORD, that I *am* God.

Lu 1:2 Even as they delivered them unto us, which from the beginning were eyewitnesses, and ministers of the word;

Lu 24:48 And ye are witnesses of these things.

Jn 1:7 The same came for a witness, to bear witness of the Light, that all *men* through him might believe.

Jn 15:27 And ye also shall bear witness, because ye have been with me from the beginning.

Jn 19:35 And he that saw *it* bare record, and his record is true: and he knoweth that he saith true, that ye might believe.

Ac 1:22 Beginning from the baptism of John, unto that same day that he was taken up from us, must one be ordained to be a witness with us of his resurrection.

Ac 2:32 This Jesus hath God raised up, whereof we all are witnesses.

Ac 3:15 And killed the Prince of life, whom God hath raised from the dead; whereof we are witnesses.

Ac 5:32 And we are his witnesses of these things; and *so is* also the Holy Ghost, whom God hath given to them that obey him.

Ac 10:39 And we are witnesses of all things which he did both in the land of the Jews, and in Jerusalem; whom they slew and hanged on a tree:

Ac 10:41 Not to all the people, but unto witnesses chosen before of God, *even* to us, who did eat and drink with him after he rose from the dead.

Ac 13:31 And he was seen many days of them which came up with him from Galilee to Jerusalem, who are his witnesses unto the people.

Ac 22:15 For thou shalt be his witness unto all men of what thou hast seen and heard.

Ac 26:16 But rise, and stand upon thy feet: for I have appeared unto thee for this purpose, to make thee a minister and a witness both which thou hast seen, and of those things in the which I will appear unto thee;

3. False

a. Warnings

Ex 20:16 Thou shalt not bear false witness against thy neighbour.

Ex 23:1 Thou shalt not raise a false report: put not thine hand with the wicked to be an unrighteous witness.

De 19:16 If a false witness rise up against any man to testify against him *that which is* wrong;

Pr 6:19 A false witness *that* speaketh lies, and he that soweth discord among brethren.

Pr 12:17 *He that* speaketh truth sheweth forth righteousness: but a false witness deceit.

Pr 19:9 A false witness shall not be unpunished, and he that speaketh lies shall perish.

Pr 24:28 Be not a witness against thy neighbour without cause; and deceive *not* with thy lips.

Pr 25:18 A man that beareth false witness against his neighbour *is* a maul, and a sword, and a sharp arrow.

Mt 19:18 He saith unto him, Which? Jesus said, Thou shalt do no murder, Thou shalt not commit adultery, Thou shalt not steal, Thou shalt not bear false witness,

Ro 13:9 For this, Thou shalt not commit adultery, Thou shalt not kill, Thou shalt not steal, Thou shalt not bear false witness, Thou shalt not covet; and if *there be* any other commandment, it is briefly comprehended in this saying, namely, Thou shalt love thy neighbour as thyself.

b. Examples

1 K 21:13 And there came in two men, children of Belial, and sat before him: and the men of Belial witnessed against him, *even* against Naboth, in the presence of the people, saying, Naboth did blaspheme God and the king. Then they carried him forth out of the city, and stoned him with stones, that he died.

Ps 35:11 False witnesses did rise up; they laid to my charge *things* that I knew not.

Pr 29:12 If a ruler hearken to lies, all his servants *are* wicked.

Je 26:11 Then spake the priests and the prophets unto the princes and to all the people, saying, This man *is* worthy to die; for he hath prophesied against this city, as ye have heard with your ears.

Mt 27:13 Then said Pilate unto him, Hearest thou not how many things they witness against thee?

Mt 28:15 So they took the money, and did as they were taught: and this saying is commonly reported among the Jews until this day.

Mk 14:56 For many bare false witness against him, but their witness agreed not together.

Mk 15:4 And Pilate asked him again, saying, Answerest thou nothing? behold how many things they witness against thee.

Ac 6:11 Then they suborned men, which said, We have heard him speak blasphemous words against Moses, and *against* God.

Ac 17:6 And when they found them not, they drew Jason and certain brethren unto the rulers of the city, crying, These that have turned the world upside down are come hither also;

Ac 24:9 And the Jews also assented, saying that these things were so.

Ac 25:7 And when he was come, the Jews which came down from Jerusalem stood round about, and laid many and grievous complaints against Paul, which they could not prove.

See **EVANGELISM, TESTIMONY**

WIVES

1. Duty

Ge 31:14 And Rachel and Leah answered and said unto him, *Is there* yet any portion or inheritance for us in our father's house?

1 S 19:12 So Michal let David down through a window: and he went, and fled, and escaped.

Est 1:20 And when the king's decree which he shall make shall be published throughout all his empire, (for it is great,) all the wives shall give to their husbands honour, both to great and small.

Jb 19:17 My breath is strange to my wife, though I intreated for the children's *sake* of mine own body.

Pr 31:12 She will do him good and not evil all the days of her life.

Pr 31:27 She looketh well to the ways of her household, and eateth not the bread of idleness.

1 Co 7:3 Let the husband render unto the wife due benevolence: and likewise also the wife unto the husband.

1 Co 7:10 And unto the married I command, *yet* not I, but the Lord, Let not the wife depart from *her* husband:

1 Co 7:39 The wife is bound by the law as long as her husband liveth; but if her husband be dead, she is at liberty to be married to whom she will; only in the Lord.

1 Co 14:35 And if they will learn any thing, let them ask their husbands at home: for it is a shame for women to speak in the church.

Ep 5:22 Wives, submit yourselves unto your own husbands, as unto the Lord.

Ep 5:33 Nevertheless let every one of you in particular so love his wife even as himself; and the wife *see* that she reverence *her* husband.

Col 3:18 Wives, submit yourselves unto your own husbands, as it is fit in the Lord.

1 Ti 3:11 Even so *must their* wives be grave, not slanderers, sober, faithful in all things.

Tit 2:4 That they may teach the young women to be sober, to love their husbands, to love their children,

1 Pe 3:1 Likewise, ye wives, *be* in subjection to your own husbands; that, if any obey not the word, they also may without the word be won by the conversation of the wives;

2. Counsel

Jud 13:22–23; 2 K 4:8–10; Da 5:10–12; Mt 27:19

See **FAMILY, HUSBANDS**

WOES, *great sorrows, miseries, afflictions*

Nu 21:29 Woe to thee, Moab! thou art undone, O people of Chemosh: he hath given his sons that escaped, and his daughters, into captivity unto Sihon king of the Amorites.

Jb 10:15 If I be wicked, woe unto me; and *if* I be righteous, *yet* will I not lift up my head. *I am* full of confusion; therefore see thou mine affliction;

Is 3:9 The shew of their countenance doth witness against them; and they declare their sin as Sodom, they hide *it* not. Woe unto their soul! for they have rewarded evil unto themselves.

Is 5:8 Woe unto them that join house to house, *that* lay field to field, till *there be* no place, that they may be placed alone in the midst of the earth!

Is 5:20 Woe unto them that call evil good, and good evil; that put darkness for light, and light for darkness; that put bitter for sweet, and sweet for bitter!

Is 10:1 Woe unto them that decree unrighteous decrees, and that write grievousness *which* they have prescribed;

Is 18:1 Woe to the land shadowing with wings, which *is* beyond the rivers of Ethiopia:

Is 28:1 Woe to the crown of pride, to the drunkards of Ephraim, whose glorious beauty is a fading flower, which *are* on the head of the fat valleys of them that are overcome with wine!

Is 29:15 Woe unto them that seek deep to hide their counsel from the LORD, and their works are in the dark, and they say, Who seeth us? and who knoweth us?

Is 30:1 Woe to the rebellious children, saith the LORD, that take counsel, but not of me; and that cover with a covering, but not of my spirit, that they may add sin to sin:

Is 31:1 Woe to them that go down to Egypt for help; and stay on horses, and trust in chariots, because *they are*

many; and in horsemen, because they are very strong; but they look not unto the Holy One of Israel, neither seek the Lord!

Is 33:1 Woe to thee that spoilest, and thou *wast* not spoiled; and dealest treacherously, and they dealt not treacherously with thee! when thou shalt cease to spoil, thou shalt be spoiled; *and* when thou shalt make an end to deal treacherously, they shall deal treacherously with thee.

Je 4:13 Behold, he shall come up as clouds, and his chariots *shall be* as a whirlwind: his horses are swifter than eagles. Woe unto us! for we are spoiled.

Je 13:27 I have seen thine adulteries, and thy neighings, the lewdness of thy whoredom, *and* thine abominations on the hills in the fields. Woe unto thee, O Jerusalem! wilt thou not be made clean? when *shall it* once *be?*

Je 22:13 Woe unto him that buildeth his house by unrighteousness, and his chambers by wrong; *that* useth his neighbour's service without wages, and giveth him not for his work;

Je 23:1 Woe be unto the pastors that destroy and scatter the sheep of my pasture! saith the LORD.

Je 48:46 Woe be unto thee, O Moab! the people of Chemosh perisheth: for thy sons are taken captives, and thy daughters captives.

Eze 13:3 Thus saith the Lord GOD; Woe unto the foolish prophets, that follow their own spirit, and have seen nothing!

Eze 16:23 And it came to pass after all thy wickedness, (woe, woe unto thee! saith the Lord GOD;)

Eze 24:6 Wherefore thus saith the Lord GOD; Woe to the bloody city, to the pot whose scum is therein, and whose scum *is* not gone out of it! bring it out piece by piece; let no lot fall upon it.

Eze 24:9 Therefore thus saith the Lord GOD; Woe to the bloody city! I will even make the pile for fire great.

Eze 34:2 Son of man, prophesy against the shepherds of Israel, prophesy, and say unto them, Thus saith the Lord GOD unto the shepherds; Woe *be*

to the shepherds of Israel that do feed themselves! should not the shepherds feed the flocks?

Ho 7:13 Woe unto them! for they have fled from me: destruction unto them! because they have transgressed against me: though I have redeemed them, yet they have spoken lies against me.

Ho 9:12 Though they bring up their children, yet will I bereave them, *that there shall* not *be* a man *left:* yea, woe also to them when I depart from them!

Am 5:18 Woe unto you that desire the day of the LORD! to what end *is* it for you? the day of the LORD *is* darkness, and not light.

Am 6:1 Woe to them *that are* at ease in Zion, and trust in the mountain of Samaria, *which are* named chief of the nations, to whom the house of Israel came!

Mi 2:1 Woe to them that devise iniquity, and work evil upon their beds! when the morning is light, they practise it, because it is in the power of their hand.

Na 3:1 Woe to the bloody city! it is all full of lies *and* robbery; the prey departeth not;

Hab 2:6 Shall not all these take up a parable against him, and a taunting proverb against him, and say, Woe to him that increaseth *that which is* not his! how long? and to him that ladeth himself with thick clay!

Hab 2:12 Woe to him that buildeth a town with blood, and stablisheth a city by iniquity!

Hab 2:15 Woe unto him that giveth his neighbour drink, that puttest thy bottle to *him,* and makest *him* drunken also, that thou mayest look on their nakedness!

Zep 2:5 Woe unto the inhabitants of the sea coast, the nation of the Cherethites! the word of the LORD *is* against you; O Canaan, the land of the Philistines, I will even destroy thee, that there shall be no inhabitant.

Zep 3:1 Woe to her that is filthy and polluted, to the oppressing city!

Zec 11:17 Woe to the idol shepherd that leaveth the flock! the sword *shall be* upon his arm, and upon his right eye: his arm shall be clean dried up, and his right eye shall be utterly darkened.

Mt 11:21 Woe unto thee, Chorazin! woe unto thee, Bethsaida! for if the mighty works, which were done in you, had been done in Tyre and Sidon, they would have repented long ago in sackcloth and ashes.

Mt 18:7 Woe unto the world because of offences! for it must needs be that offences come; but woe to that man by whom the offence cometh!

Mt 23:23 Woe unto you, scribes and Pharisees, hypocrites! for ye pay tithe of mint and anise and cummin, and have omitted the weightier *matters* of the law, judgment, mercy, and faith: these ought ye to have done, and not to leave the other undone.

Mt 23:27 Woe unto you, scribes and Pharisees, hypocrites! for ye are like unto whited sepulchres, which indeed appear beautiful outward, but are within full of dead *men's* bones, and of all uncleanness.

Mt 26:24 The Son of man goeth as it is written of him: but woe unto that man by whom the Son of man is betrayed! it had been good for that man if he had not been born.

Mk 14:21 The Son of man indeed goeth, as it is written of him: but woe to that man by whom the Son of man is betrayed! good were it for that man if he had never been born.

Lu 6:24 But woe unto you that are rich! for ye have received your consolation.

Lu 11:42 But woe unto you, Pharisees! for ye tithe mint and rue and all manner of herbs, and pass over judgment and the love of God: these ought ye to have done, and not to leave the other undone.

Lu 17:1 Then said he unto the disciples, It is impossible but that offences will come: but woe *unto him,* through whom they come!

Jude 11 Woe unto them! for they have gone in the way of Cain, and ran greedily after the error of Balaam for reward, and perished in the gainsaying of Core.

Re 8:13 And I beheld, and heard an angel flying through the midst of heaven, saying with a loud voice, Woe, woe, woe, to the inhabiters of the earth by reason of the other voices of the trumpet of the three angels, which are yet to sound!

See **AFFLICTIONS, DELIVERANCE, HELPER, SORROW, SUFFERING**

WOLVES *See* ANIMALS

WOMEN

1. Creation and Temptation

Ge 1:27 So God created man in his *own* image, in the image of God created he him; male and female created he them.

Ge 2:22 And the rib, which the LORD God had taken from man, made he a woman, and brought her unto the man.

Ge 3:1 Now the serpent was more subtil than any beast of the field which the LORD God had made. And he said unto the woman, Yea, hath God said, Ye shall not eat of every tree of the garden?

Ge 3:5-6 For God doth know that in the day ye eat thereof, then your eyes shall be opened, and ye shall be as gods, knowing good and evil.

And when the woman saw that the tree *was* good for food, and that it *was* pleasant to the eyes, and a tree to be desired to make *one* wise, she took of the fruit thereof, and did eat, and gave also unto her husband with her; and he did eat.

Ge 3:13 And the LORD God said unto the woman, What *is* this *that* thou hast done? And the woman said, The serpent beguiled me, and I did eat.

2 Co 11:3 But I fear, lest by any means, as the serpent beguiled Eve through his subtilty, so your minds should be corrupted from the simplicity that is in Christ.

1 Ti 2:14 And Adam was not deceived, but the woman being deceived was in the transgression.

2. Rights

Nu 27:1–8 Then came the daughters of Zelophehad, the son of Hepher, the son of Gilead, the son of Machir, the son of Manasseh, of the families of Manasseh the son of Joseph: and these are the names of his daughters; Mahlah, Noah, and Hoglah, and Milcah, and Tirzah.

And they stood before Moses, and before Eleazar the priest, and before the princes and all the congregation, *by* the door of the tabernacle of the congregation, saying,

Our father died in the wilderness, and he was not in the company of them that gathered themselves together against the LORD in the company of Korah; but died in his own sin, and had no sons.

Why should the name of our father be done away from among his family, because he hath no son? Give unto us *therefore* a possession among the brethren of our father.

And Moses brought their cause before the LORD.

And the LORD spake unto Moses, saying,

The daughters of Zelophehad speak right: thou shalt surely give them a possession of an inheritance among their father's brethren; and thou shalt cause the inheritance of their father to pass unto them.

And thou shalt speak unto the children of Israel, saying, If a man die, and have no son, then ye shall cause his inheritance to pass unto his daughter.

3. Subjection

Ge 3:16 Unto the woman he said, I will greatly multiply thy sorrow and thy conception; in sorrow thou shalt bring forth children; and thy desire *shall be* to thy husband, and he shall rule over thee.

Ex 2:16 Now the priest of Midian had seven daughters: and they came and drew *water,* and filled the troughs to water their father's flock.

Est 1:22 For he sent letters into all the king's provinces, into every province according to the writing thereof, and to every people after their language, that every man should bear rule in his own house, and that *it* should be published according to the language of every people.

1 Co 11:3 But I would have you know, that the head of every man is Christ; and the head of the woman *is* the man; and the head of Christ *is* God.

1 Co 14:34 Let your women keep silence in the churches: for it is not permitted unto them to speak; but *they are commanded* to be under obedience, as also saith the law.

Ep 5:22 Wives, submit yourselves unto your own husbands, as unto the Lord.

1 Ti 2:11 Let the woman learn in silence with all subjection.

1 Pe 3:1 Likewise, ye wives, *be* in subjection to your own husbands; that, if any obey not the word, they also may without the word be won by the conversation of the wives;

1 Pe 3:5 For after this manner in the old time the holy women also, who trusted in God, adorned themselves, being in subjection unto their own husbands:

4. Wives

Ge 2:18 And the LORD God said, *It is* not good that the man should be alone; I will make him an help meet for him.

Ge 2:24 Therefore shall a man leave his father and his mother, and shall cleave unto his wife: and they shall be one flesh.

Ge 6:2 That the sons of God saw the daughters of men that they *were* fair; and they took them wives of all which they chose.

Ge 21:21 And he dwelt in the wilderness of Paran: and his mother took him a wife out of the land of Egypt.

Ge 24:4 But thou shalt go unto my country, and to my kindred, and take a wife unto my son Isaac.

Ge 29:21 And Jacob said unto Laban, Give *me* my wife, for my days are fulfilled, that I may go in unto her.

Ge 41:45 And Pharaoh called Joseph's name Zaphnath-paaneah;

and he gave him to wife Asenath the daughter of Poti-pherah priest of On. And Joseph went out over *all* the land of Egypt.

De 21:11 And seest among the captives a beautiful woman, and hast a desire unto her, that thou wouldest have her to thy wife;

De 24:5 When a man hath taken a new wife, he shall not go out to war, neither shall he be charged with any business: *but* he shall be free at home one year, and shall cheer up his wife which he hath taken.

De 28:54 *So that* the man *that is* tender among you, and very delicate, his eye shall be evil toward his brother, and toward the wife of his bosom, and toward the remnant of his children which he shall leave:

Jud 15:1 But it came to pass within a while after, in the time of wheat harvest, that Samson visited his wife with a kid; and he said, I will go in to my wife into the chamber. But her father would not suffer him to go in.

1 S 18:27 Wherefore David arose and went, he and his men, and slew of the Philistines two hundred men; and David brought their foreskins, and they gave them in full tale to the king, that he might be the king's son in law. And Saul gave him Michal his daughter to wife.

Ps 128:3 Thy wife *shall be* as a fruitful vine by the sides of thine house: thy children like olive plants round about thy table.

Pr 12:4 A virtuous woman *is* a crown to her husband: but she that maketh ashamed *is* as rottenness in his bones.

Pr 18:22 *Whoso* findeth a wife findeth a good *thing,* and obtaineth favour of the LORD.

Pr 19:14 House and riches *are* the inheritance of fathers and a prudent wife *is* from the LORD.

Pr 31:11 The heart of her husband doth safely trust in her, so that he shall have no need of spoil.

1 Co 7:34 There is difference *also* between a wife and a virgin. The unmarried woman careth for the things of the Lord, that she may be holy both in body and in spirit: but she that is

married careth for the things of the world, how she may please *her* husband.

5. Their Persistence

DELILAH

Jud 16:16 And it came to pass, when she pressed him daily with her words, and urged him, *so* that his soul was vexed unto death;

THE SHUNAMMITE

2 K 4:30 And the mother of the child said, *As* the LORD liveth, and *as* thy soul liveth, I will not leave thee. And he arose, and followed her.

THE SYROPHENICIAN

Mk 7:26 The woman was a Greek, a Syrophenician by nation; and she besought him that he would cast forth the devil out of her daughter.

THE WIDOW

Lu 18:5 Yet because this widow troubleth me, I will avenge her, lest by her continual coming she weary me.

6. Their Work

a. Manual Labor

Ex 35:25 And all the women that were wise hearted did spin with their hands, and brought that which they had spun, *both* of blue, and of purple, *and* of scarlet, and of fine linen.

Jud 4:4 And Deborah, a prophetess, the wife of Lapidoth, she judged Israel at that time.

Jud 5:7 *The inhabitants of* the villages ceased, they ceased in Israel, until that I Deborah arose, that I arose a mother in Israel.

Ru 2:7 And she said, I pray you, let me glean and gather after the reapers among the sheaves: so she came, and hath continued even from the morning until now, that she tarried a little in the house.

1 S 2:19 Moreover his mother made him a little coat, and brought *it* to him from year to year, when she came up with her husband to offer the yearly sacrifice.

1 S 8:13 And he will take your daughters *to be* confectionaries, and *to be* cooks, and *to be* bakers.

1 S 25:18 Then Abigail made haste, and took two hundred loaves, and two bottles of wine, and five sheep ready dressed, and five measures of parched *corn,* and an hundred clusters of raisins, and two hundred cakes of figs, and laid *them* on asses.

Ne 3:12 And next unto him repaired Shallum the son of Halohesh, the ruler of the half part of Jerusalem, he and his daughters.

Pr 31:13 She seeketh wool, and flax, and worketh willingly with her hands.

Pr 31:24 She maketh fine linen, and selleth *it;* and delivereth girdles unto the merchant.

Jn 4:7 There cometh a woman of Samaria to draw water: Jesus saith unto her, Give me to drink.

Ac 9:36 Now there was at Joppa a certain disciple named Tabitha, which by interpretation is called Dorcas: this woman was full of good works and almsdeeds which she did.

b. Housekeepers

Ge 27:9 Go now to the flock, and fetch me from thence two good kids of the goats; and I will make them savoury meat for thy father, such as he loveth:

1 S 8:13 And he will take your daughters *to be* confectionaries, and *to be* cooks, and *to be* bakers.

Pr 31:15 She riseth also while it is yet night, and giveth meat to her household, and a portion to her maidens.

Lu 10:40 But Martha was cumbered about much serving, and came to him, and said, Lord, dost thou not care that my sister hath left me to serve alone? bid her therefore that she help me.

7. Their Ministry

BEAUTIFYING THE TABERNACLE

Ex 35:25 And all the women that were wise hearted did spin with their hands, and brought that which they had spun, *both* of blue, and of purple, *and* of scarlet, and of fine linen.

JUDGING THE NATION

Jud 4:4 And Deborah, a prophetess, the wife of Lapidoth, she judged Israel at that time.

Jud 5:7 *The inhabitants of* the villages ceased, they ceased in Israel, until that I Deborah arose, that I arose a mother in Israel.

MOTHERLY DUTIES

1 S 2:19 Moreover his mother made him a little coat, and brought *it* to him from year to year, when she came up with her husband to offer the yearly sacrifice.

2 K 4:20 And when he had taken him, and brought him to his mother, he sat on her knees till noon, and *then* died.

MEETING AN EMERGENCY AND SAVING HER HOUSEHOLD

1 S 25:18 Then Abigail made haste, and took two hundred loaves, and two bottles of wine, and five sheep ready dressed, and five measures of parched *corn,* and an hundred clusters of raisins, and two hundred cakes of figs, and laid *them* on asses.

PHILANTHROPHY

Ac 9:36 Now there was at Joppa a certain disciple named Tabitha, which by interpretation is called Dorcas: this woman was full of good works and almsdeeds which she did.

SERVING THE CHURCH

Ro 16:1 I commend unto you Phebe our sister, which is a servant of the church which is at Cenchrea:

Ro 16:6 Greet Mary, who bestowed much labour on us.

Ph 4:3 And I intreat thee also, true yokefellow, help those women which laboured with me in the gospel, with Clement also, and *with* other my fellow-labourers, whose names *are* in the book of life.

8. Prophetesses

MIRIAM

Ex 15:20 And Miriam the prophetess, the sister of Aaron, took a timbrel in her hand; and all the women went out after her with timbrels and with dances.

DEBORAH

Jud 4:4 And Deborah, a prophetess, the wife of Lapidoth, she judged Israel at that time.

HULDAH

2 K 22:14 So Hilkiah the priest, and Ahikam, and Achbor, and Shaphan, and Asahiah, went unto Huldah the prophetess, the wife of Shallum the son of Tikvah, the son of Harhas, keeper of the wardrobe; (now she dwelt in Jerusalem in the college;) and they communed with her.

NOADIAH

Ne 6:14 My God, think thou upon Tobiah and Sanballat according to these their works, and on the prophetess Noadiah, and the rest of the prophets, that would have put me in fear.

ANNA

Lu 2:36 And there was one Anna, a prophetess, the daughter of Phanuel, of the tribe of Aser: she was of a great age, and had lived with an husband seven years from her virginity;

DAUGHTERS OF PHILIP

Ac 21:9 And the same man had four daughters, virgins, which did prophesy.

9. Church Workers

PRISCILLA

Ac 18:26 And he began to speak boldly in the synagogue: whom when Aquila and Priscilla had heard, they took him unto *them,* and expounded unto him the way of God more perfectly.
Ro 16:3 Greet Priscilla and Aquila my helpers in Christ Jesus:

PHEBE

Ro 16:1–2 I commend unto you Phebe our sister, which is a servant of the church which is at Cenchrea:

That ye receive her in the Lord, as becometh saints, and that ye assist her in whatsoever business she hath need of you: for she hath been a succourer of many, and of myself also.

OTHERS

Ph 4:3 And I intreat thee also, true yokefellow, help those women which laboured with me in the gospel, with Clement also, and *with* other my fellow-labourers, whose names *are* in the book of life.

10. Characteristics of Notable Women

EVE, THE WOMAN OF CURIOSITY

Ge 3:6 And when the woman saw that the tree *was* good for food, and that it *was* pleasant to the eyes, and a tree to be desired to make *one* wise, she took of the fruit thereof, and did eat, and gave also unto her husband with her; and he did eat.

HAGAR, THE DISCARDED WIFE

Ge 21:14–19 And Abraham rose up early in the morning, and took bread, and a bottle of water, and gave *it* unto Hagar, putting *it* on her shoulder, and the child, and sent her away: and she departed, and wandered in the wilderness of Beer-sheba.

And the water was spent in the bottle, and she cast the child under one of the shrubs.

And she went, and sat her down over against *him* a good way off, as it were a bowshot: for she said, Let me not see the death of the child. And she sat over against *him,* and lift up her voice, and wept.

And God heard the voice of the lad; and the angel of God called to Hagar out of heaven, and said unto her, What aileth thee, Hagar? fear not; for God hath heard the voice of the lad where he *is.*

Arise, lift up the lad, and hold him in thine hand; for I will make him a great nation.

And God opened her eyes, and she saw a well of water; and she went, and filled the bottle with water, and gave the lad drink.

MIRIAM, THE AMBITIOUS WOMAN

Nu 12:1–2 And Miriam and Aaron spake against Moses because of the Ethiopian woman whom he had married: for he had married an Ethiopian woman.

And they said, Hath the LORD indeed spoken only by Moses? hath he not spoken also by us? And the LORD heard *it*.

DEBORAH, THE PATRIOTIC WOMAN

Jud 4:4 And Deborah, a prophetess, the wife of Lapidoth, she judged Israel at that time.

RUTH, THE WOMAN OF CONSTANCY

Ru 1:16 And Ruth said, Intreat me not to leave thee, *or* to return from following after thee: for whither thou goest, I will go; and where thou lodgest, I will lodge: thy people *shall be* my people, and thy God my God:

HANNAH, THE IDEAL MOTHER

1 S 1:20 Wherefore it came to pass, when the time was come about after Hannah had conceived, that she bare a son, and called his name Samuel, *saying,* Because I have asked him of the LORD.

1 S 2:19 Moreover his mother made him a little coat, and brought *it* to him from year to year, when she came up with her husband to offer the yearly sacrifice.

ABIGAIL, THE CAPABLE WOMAN

1 S 25:3 Now the name of the man *was* Nabal; and the name of his wife Abigail: and *she was* a woman of good understanding, and of a beautiful countenance: but the man *was* churlish and evil in his doings; and he *was* of the house of Caleb.

1 S 25:18–19 Then Abigail made haste, and took two hundred loaves, and two bottles of wine, and five sheep ready dressed, and five measures of parched *corn,* and an hundred clusters of raisins, and two hundred cakes of figs, and laid *them* on asses.

And she said unto her servants, Go on before me; behold, I come after you. But she told not her husband Nabal.

THE SHUNAMMITE, THE HOSPITABLE WOMAN

2 K 4:8–10 And it fell on a day, that Elisha passed to Shunem, where *was* a great woman; and she constrained him to eat bread. And so it was, *that* as oft as he passed by, he turned in thither to eat bread.

And she said unto her husband, Behold now, I perceive that this *is* an holy man of God, which passeth by us continually.

Let us make a little chamber, I pray thee, on the wall; and let us set for him there a bed, and a table, and a stool, and a candlestick: and it shall be, when he cometh to us, that he shall turn in thither.

ESTHER, THE SELF-SACRIFICING WOMAN

Est 4:16 Go, gather together all the Jews that are present in Shushan, and fast ye for me, and neither eat nor drink three days, night or day: I also and my maidens will fast likewise; and so will I go in unto the king, which *is* not according to the law: and if I perish, I perish.

THE SYROPHENICIAN, THE WOMAN OF FAITH

Mt 15:28 Then Jesus answered and said unto her, O woman, great *is* thy faith: be it unto thee even as thou wilt. And her daughter was made whole from that very hour.

MARY MAGDALENE, THE TRANSFORMED WOMAN

Mk 16:1 And when the sabbath was past, Mary Magdalene, and Mary the *mother* of James, and Salome, had bought sweet spices, that they might come and anoint him.

Mk 16:9 Now when *Jesus* was risen early the first *day* of the week, he appeared first to Mary Magdalene, out of whom he had cast seven devils.

ELISABETH, THE HUMBLE WOMAN

Lu 1:43 And whence *is* this to me, that the mother of my Lord should come to me?

MARY, THE WOMAN CHOSEN OF GOD

Lu 1:30–38 And the angel said unto her, Fear not, Mary: for thou hast found favour with God.

And, behold, thou shalt conceive in thy womb, and bring forth a son, and shalt call his name JESUS.

He shall be great, and shall be called the Son of the Highest: and the Lord God shall give unto him the throne of his father David:

And he shall reign over the house of Jacob for ever; and of his kingdom there shall be no end.

Then said Mary unto the angel, How shall this be, seeing I know not a man?

And the angel answered and said unto her, The Holy Ghost shall come upon thee, and the power of the Highest shall overshadow thee: therefore also that holy thing which shall be born of thee shall be called the Son of God.

And, behold, thy cousin Elisabeth, she hath also conceived a son in her old age: and this is the sixth month with her, who was called barren.

For with God nothing shall be impossible.

And Mary said, Behold the handmaid of the Lord; be it unto me according to thy word. And the angel departed from her.

MARY OF BETHANY, THE WOMAN IMMORTALIZED BY CHRIST

Mt 26:13 Verily I say unto you, Wheresoever this gospel shall be preached in the whole world, *there* shall also this, that this woman hath done, be told for a memorial of her.

Lu 10:42 But one thing is needful: and Mary hath chosen that good part, which shall not be taken away from her.

MARTHA, THE WORRIED HOUSEKEEPER

Lu 10:40 But Martha was cumbered about much serving, and came to him, and said, Lord, dost thou not care that my sister hath left me to serve alone? bid her therefore that she help me.

THE WOMAN EVANGELIST

Jn 4:29 Come, see a man, which told me all things that ever I did: is not this the Christ?

DORCAS, THE BENEVOLENT SEAMSTRESS

Ac 9:36 Now there was at Joppa a certain disciple named Tabitha, which by interpretation is called Dorcas: this woman was full of good works and almsdeeds which she did.

LYDIA THE BUSINESS WOMAN

Ac 16:14–15 And a certain woman named Lydia, a seller of purple, of the city of Thyatira, which worshipped God, heard *us:* whose heart the Lord opened, that she attended unto the things which were spoken of Paul.

And when she was baptized, and her household, she besought *us,* saying, If ye have judged me to be faithful to the Lord, come into my house, and abide *there.* And she constrained us.

11. *Special Distinctions*

LAST AT THE CROSS

Mk 15:47 And Mary Magdalene and Mary *the mother* of Joses beheld where he was laid.

FIRST AT THE TOMB

Jn 20:1 The first *day* of the week cometh Mary Magdalene early, when it was yet dark, unto the sepulchre, and seeth the stone taken away from the sepulchre.

FIRST TO PROCLAIM THE RESURRECTION

Mt 28:8 And they departed quickly from the sepulchre with fear and great joy; and did run to bring his disciples word.

FIRST PREACHER TO THE JEWS

Lu 2:37 And she *was* a widow of about fourscore and four years, which departed not from the temple, but served *God* with fastings and prayers night and day.

Lu 2:38 And she coming in that instant gave thanks likewise unto the Lord, and spake of him to all them that looked for redemption in Jerusalem.

ATTENDED THE FIRST PRAYER MEETING

Ac 1:14 These all continued with one accord in prayer and supplication, with the women, and Mary the mother of Jesus, and with his brethren.

FIRST TO GREET CHRISTIAN MISSIONARIES
(PAUL AND SILAS) IN EUROPE

Ac 16:13 And on the sabbath we went out of the city by a river side, where prayer was wont to be made; and we sat down, and spake unto the women which resorted *thither.*

FIRST EUROPEAN CONVERT

Ac 16:14 And a certain woman named Lydia, a seller of purple, of the city of Thyatira, which worshipped God, heard *us:* whose heart the Lord opened, that she attended unto the things which were spoken of Paul.

12. Their Sufferings

a. As Mothers

Ge 3:16 Unto the woman he said, I will greatly multiply thy sorrow and thy conception; in sorrow thou shalt bring forth children; and thy desire *shall be* to thy husband, and he shall rule over thee.

Ge 35:16 And they journeyed from Bethel; and there was but a little way to come to Ephrath: and Rachel travailed, and she had hard labour.

Is 13:8 And they shall be afraid: pangs and sorrows shall take hold of them; they shall be in pain as a woman that travaileth: they shall be amazed one at another; their faces *shall be as* flames.

Is 42:14 I have long time holden my peace; I have been still, *and* refrained myself: *now* will I cry like a travailing

woman; I will destroy and devour at once.

Jn 16:21 A woman when she is in travail hath sorrow, because her hour is come: but as soon as she is delivered of the child, she remembereth no more the anguish, for joy that a man is born into the world.

1 Th 5:3 For when they shall say, Peace and safety; then sudden destruction cometh upon them, as travail upon a woman with child; and they shall not escape.

b. As Widows

Ru 1:3 And Elimelech Naomi's husband died; and she was left, and her two sons.

1 K 17:9 Arise, get thee to Zarephath, which *belongeth* to Zidon, and dwell there: behold, I have commanded a widow woman there to sustain thee.

2 K 4:1 Now there cried a certain woman of the wives of the sons of the prophets unto Elisha, saying, Thy servant my husband is dead; and thou knowest that thy servant did fear the LORD: and the creditor is come to take unto him my two sons to be bondmen.

Mk 12:42 And there came a certain poor widow, and she threw in two mites, which make a farthing.

Lu 2:37 And she *was* a widow of about fourscore and four years, which departed not from the temple, but served *God* with fastings and prayers night and day.

Lu 7:12 Now when he came nigh to the gate of the city, behold, there was a dead man carried out, the only son of his mother, and she was a widow: and much people of the city was with her.

Lu 18:3 And there was a widow in that city; and she came unto him, saying, Avenge me of mine adversary.

Ac 6:1 And in those days, when the number of the disciples was multiplied, there arose a murmuring of the Grecians against the Hebrews, because their widows were neglected in the daily ministration.

Ac 9:39 Then Peter arose and went with them. When he was come, they brought him into the upper chamber: and all the widows stood by him weeping, and shewing the coats and garments which Dorcas made, while she was with them.

13. Crowning Qualities

a. Devotional Spirit

Ge 25:22 And the children struggled together within her; and she said, If *it be* so, why *am* I thus? And she went to enquire of the LORD.

Ge 29:32 And Leah conceived, and bare a son, and she called his name Reuben: for she said, Surely the LORD hath looked upon my affliction; now therefore my husband will love me.

Ex 1:17 But the midwives feared God, and did not as the king of Egypt commanded them, but saved the men children alive.

Ex 15:20 And Miriam the prophetess, the sister of Aaron, took a timbrel in her hand; and all the women went out after her with timbrels and with dances.

Jud 11:36 And she said unto him, My father, *if* thou hast opened thy mouth unto the LORD, do to me according to that which hath proceeded out of thy mouth; forasmuch as the LORD hath taken vengeance for thee of thine enemies, *even* of the children of Ammon.

1 S 1:15 And Hannah answered and said, No, my lord, I *am* a woman of a sorrowful spirit: I have drunken neither wine nor strong drink, but have poured out my soul before the LORD.

1 S 1:26 And she said, Oh my lord, *as* thy soul liveth, my lord, I *am* the woman that stood by thee here, praying unto the LORD.

2 K 22:14 So Hilkiah the priest, and Ahikam, and Achbor, and Shaphan, and Asahiah, went unto Huldah the prophetess, the wife of Shallum the son of Tikvah, the son of Harhas, keeper of the wardrobe; (now she dwelt in Jerusalem in the college;) and they communed with her.

2 Chr 34:22 And Hilkiah, and *they* that the king *had appointed,* went to Huldah the prophetess, the wife of Shallum the son of Tikvath, the son of Hasrah, keeper of the wardrobe; (now she dwelt in Jerusalem in the college:) and they spake to her to that *effect.*

Est 4:16 Go, gather together all the Jews that are present in Shushan, and fast ye for me, and neither eat nor drink three days, night or day: I also and my maidens will fast likewise; and so will I go in unto the king, which *is* not according to the law: and if I perish, I perish.

Pr 31:30 Favour *is* deceitful, and beauty *is* vain: *but* a woman *that* feareth the LORD, she shall be praised.

Mk 15:40 There were also women looking on afar off: among whom was Mary Magdalene, and Mary the mother of James the less and of Joses, and Salome;

Lu 1:5 There was in the days of Herod, the king of Judaea, a certain priest named Zacharias, of the course of Abia: and his wife *was* of the daughters of Aaron, and her name *was* Elisabeth.

Lu 1:25 Thus hath the Lord dealt with me in the days wherein he looked on *me,* to take away my reproach among men.

Lu 1:30 And the angel said unto her, Fear not, Mary: for thou hast found favour with God.

Lu 1:38 And Mary said, Behold the handmaid of the Lord; be it unto me according to thy word. And the angel departed from her.

Lu 1:46 And Mary said, My soul doth magnify the Lord,

Lu 2:19 But Mary kept all these things, and pondered *them* in her heart.

Lu 2:36 And there was one Anna, a prophetess, the daughter of Phanuel, of the tribe of Aser: she was of a great age, and had lived with an husband seven years from her virginity;

Lu 10:42 But one thing is needful: and Mary hath chosen that good part, which shall not be taken away from her.

Ac 9:36 Now there was at Joppa a certain disciple named Tabitha, which by interpretation is called Dorcas: this woman was full of good works and almsdeeds which she did.

Ac 16:1 Then came he to Derbe and Lystra: and, behold, a certain disciple was there, named Timotheus, the son of a certain woman, which was a Jewess, and believed; but his father *was* a Greek:

Ac 16:14 And a certain woman named Lydia, a seller of purple, of the city of Thyatira, which worshipped God, heard *us:* whose heart the Lord opened, that she attended unto the things which were spoken of Paul.

Ac 17:4 And some of them believed, and consorted with Paul and Silas; and of the devout Greeks a great multitude, and of the chief women not a few.

Ac 21:9 And the same man had four daughters, virgins, which did prophesy.

Ro 16:1 I commend unto you Phebe our sister, which is a servant of the church which is at Cenchrea:

Ro 16:12 Salute Tryphena and Tryphosa, who labour in the Lord. Salute the beloved Persis, which laboured much in the Lord.

1 Ti 5:5 Now she that is a widow indeed, and desolate, trusteth in God, and continueth in supplications and prayers night and day.

1 Pe 3:5 For after this manner in the old time the holy women also, who trusted in God, adorned themselves, being in subjection unto their own husbands:

b. Modesty

Ge 24:65 For she *had* said unto the servant, What man *is* this that walketh in the field to meet us? And the servant *had* said, It *is* my master: therefore she took a vail, and covered herself.

Est 1:11–12 To bring Vashti the queen before the king with the crown royal, to shew the people and the princes her beauty: for she *was* fair to look on.

But the queen Vashti refused to come at the king's commandment by *his* chamberlains: therefore was the king very wroth, and his anger burned in him.

1 Ti 2:9–10 In like manner also, that women adorn themselves in modest apparel, with shamefacedness and sobriety; not with broided hair, or gold, or pearls, or costly array;

But (which becometh women professing godliness) with good works.

1 Pe 3:1–2 Likewise, ye wives, *be* in subjection to your own husbands; that, if any obey not the word, they also may without the word be won by the conversation of the wives;

While they behold your chaste conversation *coupled* with fear.

c. Generosity

Ex 35:25 And all the women that were wise hearted did spin with their hands, and brought that which they had spun, *both* of blue, and of purple, *and* of scarlet, and of fine linen.

Pr 31:20 She stretcheth out her hand to the poor; yea, she reacheth forth her hands to the needy.

Lu 8:2–3 And certain women, which had been healed of evil spirits and infirmities, Mary called Magdalene, out of whom went seven devils,

And Joanna the wife of Chuza Herod's steward, and Susanna, and many others, which ministered unto him of their substance.

Lu 21:2–4 And he saw also a certain poor widow casting in thither two mites.

And he said, Of a truth I say unto you, that this poor widow hath cast in more than they all:

For all these have of their abundance cast in unto the offerings of God: but she of her penury hath cast in all the living that she had.

Jn 12:3 Then took Mary a pound of ointment of spikenard, very costly, and anointed the feet of Jesus, and wiped his feet with her hair: and the house was filled with the odour of the ointment.

Ac 9:39 Then Peter arose and went with them. When he was come, they brought him into the upper chamber: and all the widows stood by him weeping, and shewing the coats and garments which Dorcas made, while she was with them.

d. Wisdom and Virtue

Nu 27:1 Then came the daughters of Zelophehad, the son of Hepher, the son of Gilead, the son of Machir, the son of Manasseh, of the families of Manasseh the son of Joseph: and these are the names of his daughters; Mahlah, Noah, and Hoglah, and Milcah, and Tirzah.

Ru 3:11 And now, my daughter, fear not; I will do to thee all that thou requirest: for all the city of my people doth know that thou *art* a virtuous woman.

1 S 25:18 Then Abigail made haste, and took two hundred loaves, and two bottles of wine, and five sheep ready dressed, and five measures of parched *corn,* and an hundred clusters of raisins, and two hundred cakes of figs, and laid *them* on asses.

Pr 11:16 A gracious woman retaineth honour: and strong *men* retain riches.

Pr 12:4 A virtuous woman *is* a crown to her husband: but she that maketh ashamed *is* as rottenness in his bones.

Pr 14:1 Every wise woman buildeth her house: but the foolish plucketh it down with her hands.

Pr 31:10 Who can find a virtuous woman? for her price *is* far above rubies.

Pr 31:30 Favour *is* deceitful, and beauty *is* vain: *but* a woman *that* feareth the LORD, she shall be praised.

Mt 27:19 When he was set down on the judgment seat, his wife sent unto him, saying, Have thou nothing to do with that just man: for I have suffered many things this day in a dream because of him.

14. Evil Women

Ge 19:32 Come, let us make our father drink wine, and we will lie with him, that we may preserve seed of our father.

Ge 39:7 And it came to pass after these things, that his master's wife cast her eyes upon Joseph; and she said, Lie with me.

Ge 39:18 And it came to pass, as I lifted up my voice and cried, that he left his garment with me, and fled out.

Jud 16:4 And it came to pass afterward, that he loved a woman in the valley of Sorek, whose name *was* Delilah.

1 K 16:31 And it came to pass, as if it had been a light thing for him to walk in the sins of Jeroboam the son of Nebat, that he took to wife Jezebel the daughter of Ethbaal king of the Zidonians, and went and served Baal, and worshipped him.

1 K 18:4 For it was *so,* when Jezebel cut off the prophets of the LORD, that Obadiah took an hundred prophets, and hid them by fifty in a cave, and fed them with bread and water.)

1 K 19:2 Then Jezebel sent a messenger unto Elijah, saying, So let the gods do *to me,* and more also, if I make not thy life as the life of one of them by to morrow about this time.

1 K 21:15 And it came to pass, when Jezebel heard that Naboth was stoned, and was dead, that Jezebel said to Ahab, Arise, take possession of the vineyard of Naboth the Jezreelite, which he refused to give thee for money: for Naboth is not alive, but dead.

2 K 8:18 And he walked in the way of the kings of Israel, as did the house of Ahab: for the daughter of Ahab was his wife: and he did evil in the sight of the LORD.

2 K 9:22 And it came to pass, when Joram saw Jehu, that he said, *Is it* peace, Jehu? And he answered, What peace, so long as the whoredoms of thy mother Jezebel and her witchcrafts *are so* many?

2 K 9:30 And when Jehu was come to Jezreel, Jezebel heard *of it;* and she painted her face, and tired her head, and looked out at a window.

2 K 9:34 And when he was come in, he did eat and drink, and said, Go, see now this cursed *woman,* and bury her: for she *is* a king's daughter.

2 K 11:1 And when Athaliah the mother of Ahaziah saw that her son was dead, she arose and destroyed all the seed royal.

2 Chr 15:16 And also concerning Maachah the mother of Asa the king, he removed her from being queen, because she had made an idol in a grove: and Asa cut down her idol, and stamped it, and burnt it at the brook Kidron.

2 Chr 22:3 He also walked in the ways of the house of Ahab: for his mother was his counsellor to do wickedly.

2 Chr 22:10 But when Athaliah the mother of Ahaziah saw that her son was dead, she arose and destroyed all the seed royal of the house of Judah.

2 Chr 24:7 For the sons of Athaliah, that wicked woman, had broken up the house of God; and also all the dedicated things of the house of the LORD did they bestow upon Baalim.

Ne 6:14 My God, think thou upon Tobiah and Sanballat according to these their works, and on the prophetess Noadiah, and the rest of the prophets, that would have put me in fear.

Ne 13:26 Did not Solomon king of Israel sin by these things? yet among many nations was there no king like him, who was beloved of his God, and God made him king over all Israel: nevertheless even him did outlandish women cause to sin.

Est 5:14 Then said Zeresh his wife and all his friends unto him, Let a gallows be made of fifty cubits high, and to morrow speak thou unto the king that Mordecai may be hanged thereon: then go thou in merrily with the king unto the banquet. And the thing pleased Haman; and he caused the gallows to be made.

Jb 2:9 Then said his wife unto him, Dost thou still retain thine integrity? curse God, and die.

Pr 2:16 To deliver thee from the strange woman, *even* from the stranger *which* flattereth with her words;

Pr 6:26 For by means of a whorish woman *a man is brought* to a piece of bread: and the adulteress will hunt for the precious life.

Pr 7:5 That they may keep thee from the strange woman, from the stranger *which* flattereth with her words.

Pr 7:26 For she hath cast down many wounded: yea, many strong *men* have been slain by her.

Pr 9:14 For she sitteth at the door of her house, on a seat in the high places of the city,

Pr 22:14 The mouth of strange women is a deep pit: he that is abhorred of the LORD shall fall therein.

Pr 30:20 Such *is* the way of an adulterous woman; she eateth, and wipeth her mouth, and saith, I have done no wickedness.

Ec 7:26 And I find more bitter than death the woman, whose heart *is* snares and nets, *and* her hands *as* bands: whoso pleaseth God shall escape from her; but the sinner shall be taken by her.

Is 3:16 Moreover the LORD saith, Because the daughters of Zion are haughty, and walk with stretched forth necks and wanton eyes, walking and mincing *as* they go, and making a tinkling with their feet:

Je 44:9 Have ye forgotten the wickedness of your fathers, and the wickedness of the kings of Judah, and the wickedness of their wives, and your own wickedness, and the wickedness of your wives, which they have committed in the land of Judah, and in the streets of Jerusalem?

Je 44:15 Then all the men which knew that their wives had burned incense unto other gods, and all the women that stood by, a great multitude, even all the people that dwelt in the land of Egypt, in Pathros, answered Jeremiah, saying,

Eze 8:14 Then he brought me to the door of the gate of the LORD's house which *was* toward the north; and, behold, there sat women weeping for Tammuz.

Eze 16:30 How weak is thine heart, saith the Lord GOD, seeing thou doest all these *things*, the work of an imperious whorish woman;

Mt 14:6 But when Herod's birthday was kept, the daughter of Herodias danced before them, and pleased Herod.

Mt 14:11 And his head was brought in a charger, and given to the damsel: and she brought it to her mother.

Ro 1:26 For this cause God gave them up unto vile affections: for even their women did change the natural use into that which is against nature:

Re 2:20 Notwithstanding I have a few things against thee, because thou sufferest that woman Jezebel, which calleth herself a prophetess, to teach and to seduce my servants to commit fornication, and to eat things sacrificed unto idols.

Stir up Strife

Pr 19:13 A foolish son is the calamity of his father: and the contentions of a wife are a continual dropping.

Pr 21:9 It is better to dwell in a corner of the housetop, than with a brawling woman in a wide house.

Pr 21:19 It is better to dwell in the wilderness, than with a contentious and an angry woman.

Pr 25:24 It is better to dwell in the corner of the housetop, than with a brawling woman and in a wide house.

Pr 27:15 A continual dropping in a very rainy day and a contentious woman are alike.

Pr 30:23 For an odious *woman* when she is married; and an handmaid that is heir to her mistress.

15. Temptresses

EVE

Ge 3:6 And when the woman saw that the tree was good for food, and that it was pleasant to the eyes, and a tree to be desired to make one wise, she took of the fruit thereof, and did eat, and gave also unto her husband with her; and he did eat.

DELILAH

Jud 16:6 And Delilah said to Samson, Tell me, I pray thee, wherein thy great strength lieth, and wherewith thou mightest be bound to afflict thee.

JEZEBEL

1 K 21:7 And Jezebel his wife said unto him, Dost thou now govern the kingdom of Israel? arise, *and* eat bread, and let thine heart be merry: I will give thee the vineyard of Naboth the Jezreelite.

1 K 21:25 But there was none like unto Ahab, which did sell himself to work wickedness in the sight of the LORD, whom Jezebel his wife stirred up.

ZERESH

Est 5:14 Then said Zeresh his wife and all his friends unto him, Let a gallows be made of fifty cubits high, and to morrow speak thou unto the king that Mordecai may be hanged thereon: then go thou in merrily with the king unto the banquet. And the thing pleased Haman; and he caused the gallows to be made.

JOB'S WIFE

Jb 2:9–10 Then said his wife unto him, Dost thou still retain thine integrity? curse God, and die.

But he said unto her, Thou speakest as one of the foolish women speaketh. What? shall we receive good at the hand of God, and shall we not receive evil? In all this did not Job sin with his lips.

STRANGE WOMEN

Pr 5:3–5 For the lips of a strange woman drop as an honeycomb, and her mouth is smoother than oil:

But her end is bitter as wormwood, sharp as a twoedged sword.

Her feet go down to death; her steps take hold on hell.

Eze 13:18–19 And say, Thus saith the Lord GOD; Woe to the *women* that sew pillows to all armholes, and make kerchiefs upon the head of every stature to hunt souls! Will ye hunt the souls of my people, and will ye save the souls alive *that come* unto you?

And will ye pollute me among my people for handfuls of barley and for pieces of bread, to slay the souls that should not die, and to save the souls alive that should not live, by your lying to my people that hear *your* lies?

HERODIAS AND SALOME

Mk 6:22 And when the daughter of the said Herodias came in, and danced, and pleased Herod and them that sat with him, the king said unto the damsel, Ask of me whatsoever thou wilt, and I will give *it* thee.

See **CHILDREN, FAMILY, HUSBANDS, MANKIND, WIVES**

WONDERS, *awe-inspiring acts of God*

Ex 3:20 And I will stretch out my hand, and smite Egypt with all my wonders which I will do in the midst thereof: and after that he will let you go.

Ex 4:3 And he said, Cast it on the ground. And he cast it on the ground, and it became a serpent; and Moses fled from before it.

Ex 4:21 And the LORD said unto Moses, When thou goest to return into Egypt, see that thou do all those wonders before Pharaoh, which I have put in thine hand: but I will harden his heart, that he shall not let the people go.

Ex 7:3 And I will harden Pharaoh's heart, and multiply my signs and my wonders in the land of Egypt.

Ex 11:9 And the LORD said unto Moses, Pharaoh shall not hearken unto you; that my wonders may be multiplied in the land of Egypt.

Ex 14:31 And Israel saw that great work which the LORD did upon the Egyptians: and the people feared the LORD, and believed the LORD, and his servant Moses.

Ex 15:11 Who *is* like unto thee, O LORD, among the gods? who *is* like thee, glorious in holiness, fearful *in* praises, doing wonders?

Ex 34:10 And he said, Behold, I make a covenant: before all thy people I will do marvels, such as have not been done in all the earth, nor in any nation: and all the people among which thou *art* shall see the work of the LORD: for it *is* a terrible thing that I will do with thee.

Nu 14:11 And the LORD said unto Moses, How long will this people provoke me? and how long will it be ere they believe me, for all the signs which I have shewed among them?

Nu 14:22 Because all those men which have seen my glory, and my miracles, which I did in Egypt and in the wilderness, and have tempted me now these ten times, and have not hearkened to my voice;

Nu 22:28 And the LORD opened the mouth of the ass, and she said unto Balaam, What have I done unto thee, that thou hast smitten me these three times?

De 4:34 Or hath God assayed to go *and* take him a nation from the midst of another *nation,* by temptations, by signs, and by wonders, and by war, and by a mighty hand, and by a stretched out arm, and by great terrors, according to all that the LORD your God did for you in Egypt before your eyes?

De 6:22 And the LORD shewed signs and wonders, great and sore, upon Egypt, upon Pharaoh, and upon all his household, before our eyes:

De 7:19 The great temptations which thine eyes saw, and the signs, and the wonders, and the mighty hand, and the stretched out arm, whereby the LORD thy God brought thee out: so shall the LORD thy God do unto all the people of whom thou art afraid.

De 11:3 And his miracles, and his acts, which he did in the midst of Egypt unto Pharaoh the king of Egypt, and unto all his land;

De 11:7 But your eyes have seen all the great acts of the LORD which he did.

De 26:8 And the LORD brought us forth out of Egypt with a mighty hand, and with an outstretched arm, and with great terribleness, and with signs, and with wonders:

De 29:3 The great temptations which thine eyes have seen, the signs, and those great miracles:

De 34:11 In all the signs and the wonders, which the LORD sent him to do in the land of Egypt to Pharaoh, and to all his servants, and to all his land,

Jos 3:5 And Joshua said unto the people, Sanctify yourselves: for to morrow the LORD will do wonders among you.

Jos 10:13 And the sun stood still, and the moon stayed, until the people had avenged themselves upon their enemies. *Is* not this written in the book of Jasher? So the sun stood still in the midst of heaven, and hasted not to go down about a whole day.

Jos 24:7 And when they cried unto the LORD, he put darkness between you and the Egyptians, and brought the sea upon them, and covered them; and your eyes have seen what I have done in Egypt: and ye dwelt in the wilderness a long season.

Jos 24:17 For the LORD our God, he *it is* that brought us up and our fathers out of the land of Egypt, from the house of bondage, and which did those great signs in our sight, and preserved us in all the way wherein we went, and among all the people through whom we passed:

Jos 24:31 And Israel served the LORD all the days of Joshua, and all the days of the elders that overlived Joshua, and which had known all the works of the LORD, that he had done for Israel.

Jud 2:7 And the people served the LORD all the days of Joshua, and all the days of the elders that outlived Joshua, who had seen all the great works of the LORD, that he did for Israel.

Jud 6:13 And Gideon said unto him, Oh my Lord, if the LORD be with us, why then is all this befallen us? and where *be* all his miracles which our fathers told us of, saying, Did not the LORD bring us up from Egypt? but now the LORD hath forsaken us, and delivered us into the hands of the Midianites.

Jud 6:21 Then the angel of the LORD put forth the end of the staff that *was* in his hand, and touched the flesh and the unleavened cakes; and there rose up fire out of the rock, and consumed the flesh and the unleavened cakes. Then the angel of the LORD departed out of his sight.

Jud 13:19 So Manoah took a kid with a meat offering, and offered *it* upon a rock unto the LORD: and *the angel* did wonderously; and Manoah and his wife looked on.

1 S 6:6 Wherefore then do ye harden your hearts, as the Egyptians and Pharaoh hardened their hearts? when he had wrought wonderfully among them, did they not let the people go, and they departed?

1 S 12:16 Now therefore stand and see this great thing, which the LORD will do before your eyes.

2 S 7:23 And what one nation in the earth *is* like thy people, *even* like Israel, whom God went to redeem for a people to himself, and to make him a name, and to do for you great things and terrible, for thy land, before thy people, which thou redeemedst to thee from Egypt, *from* the nations and their gods?

1 K 18:38 Then the fire of the LORD fell, and consumed the burnt sacrifice, and the wood, and the stones, and the dust, and licked up the water that *was* in the trench.

2 K 2:8 And Elijah took his mantle, and wrapped *it* together, and smote the waters, and they were divided hither and thither, so that they two went over on dry ground.

2 K 2:14 And he took the mantle of Elijah that fell from him, and smote the waters, and said, Where *is* the LORD God of Elijah? and when he also had smitten the waters, they parted hither and thither: and Elisha went over.

2 K 3:17 For thus saith the LORD, Ye shall not see wind, neither shall ye see rain; yet that valley shall be filled with water, that ye may drink, both ye, and your cattle, and your beasts.

1 Chr 16:12 Remember his marvellous works that he hath done, his wonders, and the judgments of his mouth;

Ne 9:10 And shewedst signs and wonders upon Pharaoh, and on all his servants, and on all the people of his land: for thou knewest that they dealt proudly against them. So didst thou get thee a name, as *it is* this day.

Ne 9:17 And refused to obey, neither were mindful of thy wonders that thou didst among them; but hardened their necks, and in their rebellion appointed a captain to return to their bondage: but thou *art* a God ready to pardon, gracious and merciful, slow to anger, and of great kindness, and forsookest them not.

Jb 5:10 Who giveth rain upon the earth, and sendeth waters upon the fields:

Jb 9:10 Which doeth great things past finding out; yea, and wonders without number.

Ps 9:1 I will praise *thee*, O LORD, with my whole heart; I will shew forth all thy marvellous works.

Ps 40:5 Many, O LORD my God, *are* thy wonderful works *which* thou hast done, and thy thoughts *which are* to us-ward: they cannot be reckoned up in order unto thee: *if* I would declare and speak *of them*, they are more than can be numbered.

Ps 44:1 We have heard with our ears, O God, our fathers have told us, *what* work thou didst in their days, in the times of old.

Ps 77:14 Thou *art* the God that doest wonders: thou hast declared thy strength among the people.

Ps 78:11 And forgat his works, and his wonders that he had shewed them.

Ps 78:43 How he had wrought his signs in Egypt, and his wonders in the field of Zoan:

Ps 86:10 For thou *art* great, and doest wondrous things: thou *art* God alone.

Ps 89:5 And the heavens shall praise thy wonders, O LORD: thy faithfulness also in the congregation of the saints.

Ps 96:3 Declare his glory among the heathen, his wonders among all people.

Ps 98:1 O sing unto the LORD a new song; for he hath done marvellous things: his right hand, and his holy arm, hath gotten him the victory.

Ps 105:5 Remember his marvellous works that he hath done; his wonders, and the judgments of his mouth;

Ps 105:27 They shewed his signs among them, and wonders in the land of Ham.

Ps 106:7 Our fathers understood not thy wonders in Egypt; they remembered not the multitude of thy mer-

cies; but provoked *him* at the sea, *even* at the Red sea.

Ps 106:22 Wondrous works in the land of Ham, *and* terrible things by the Red sea.

Ps 111:2 The works of the LORD *are* great, sought out of all them that have pleasure therein.

Ps 118:23 This is the LORD's doing; it *is* marvellous in our eyes.

Ps 135:9 *Who* sent tokens and wonders into the midst of thee, O Egypt, upon Pharaoh, and upon all his servants.

Ps 136:4 To him who alone doeth great wonders: for his mercy *endureth* for ever.

Is 25:1 O LORD, thou *art* my God; I will exalt thee, I will praise thy name; for thou hast done wonderful *things*; *thy* counsels of old *are* faithfulness *and* truth.

Is 29:14 Therefore, behold, I will proceed to do a marvellous work among this people, *even* a marvellous work and a wonder: for the wisdom of their wise *men* shall perish, and the understanding of their prudent *men* shall be hid.

Is 64:3 When thou didst terrible things *which* we looked not for, thou camest down, the mountains flowed down at thy presence.

Je 21:2 Enquire, I pray thee, of the LORD for us; for Nebuchadrezzar king of Babylon maketh war against us; if so be that the LORD will deal with us according to all his wondrous works, that he may go up from us.

Je 32:20 Which hast set signs and wonders in the land of Egypt, *even* unto this day, and in Israel, and among *other* men; and hast made thee a name, as at this day;

Je 33:3 Call unto me, and I will answer thee, and shew thee great and mighty things, which thou knowest not.

Da 4:3 How great *are* his signs! and how mighty *are* his wonders! his kingdom *is* an everlasting kingdom, and his dominion *is* from generation to generation.

Da 6:27 He delivereth and rescueth, and he worketh signs and wonders in heaven and in earth, who hath delivered Daniel from the power of the lions.

Jl 2:21 Fear not, O land; be glad and rejoice: for the LORD will do great things.

Jl 2:30 And I will shew wonders in the heavens and in the earth, blood, and fire, and pillars of smoke.

Mi 7:15 According to the days of thy coming out of the land of Egypt will I shew unto him marvellous *things.*

Mt 27:51 And, behold, the veil of the temple was rent in twain from the top to the bottom; and the earth did quake, and the rocks rent;

Mk 1:27 And they were all amazed, insomuch that they questioned among themselves, saying, What thing is this? what new doctrine *is* this? for with authority commandeth he even the unclean spirits, and they do obey him.

Lu 1:44 For, lo, as soon as the voice of thy salutation sounded in mine ears, the babe leaped in my womb for joy.

Lu 2:33 And Joseph and his mother marvelled at those things which were spoken of him.

Lu 5:26 And they were all amazed, and they glorified God, and were filled with fear, saying, We have seen strange things to day.

Ac 2:19 And I will shew wonders in heaven above, and signs in the earth beneath; blood, and fire, and vapour of smoke:

Ac 3:10 And they knew that it was he which sat for alms at the Beautiful gate of the temple: and they were filled with wonder and amazement at that which had happened unto him.

Ac 6:8 And Stephen, full of faith and power, did great wonders and miracles among the people.

Ac 7:31 When Moses saw *it,* he wondered at the sight: and as he drew near to behold *it,* the voice of the Lord came unto him,

Ac 7:36 He brought them out, after that he had shewed wonders and signs in the land of Egypt, and in the Red sea, and in the wilderness forty years.

Ac 13:41 Behold, ye despisers, and wonder, and perish: for I work a work

in your days, a work which ye shall in no wise believe, though a man declare it unto you.

Ac 14:3 Long time therefore abode they speaking boldly in the Lord, which gave testimony unto the word of his grace, and granted signs and wonders to be done by their hands.

He 3:9 When your fathers tempted me, proved me, and saw my works forty years.

Re 12:1 And there appeared a great wonder in heaven; a woman clothed with the sun, and the moon under her feet, and upon her head a crown of twelve stars:

See **DIVINATION, MAGICIANS, MIRACLES**

WOOL, *hair forming the coat of sheep and certain other animals; the material made from it*

Le 13:47; 19:19; De 18:4; Jud 6:37; Pr 27:26; 31:13; Eze 27:18; 34:3; 44:17; Ho 2:9

WORD OF GOD, *divine communication in written form*

1. Despised by the Foolish

See **REJECTION**

2. The Book of the Ages

2 S 22:31 *As for* God, his way *is* perfect; the word of the LORD *is* tried: he *is* a buckler to all them that trust in him.

Ps 12:6 The words of the LORD *are* pure words: *as* silver tried in a furnace of earth, purified seven times.

Ps 119:9 Wherewithal shall a young man cleanse his way? by taking heed *thereto* according to thy word.

Ps 119:50 This *is* my comfort in my affliction: for thy word hath quickened me.

Ps 147:15 He sendeth forth his commandment *upon* earth: his word runneth very swiftly.

Mk 12:24 And Jesus answering said unto them, Do ye not therefore err, because ye know not the scriptures, neither the power of God?

Lu 8:11 Now the parable is this: The seed is the word of God.

Ep 6:17 And take the helmet of salvation, and the sword of the Spirit, which is the word of God:

3. Food for the Soul

De 8:3 And he humbled thee, and suffered thee to hunger, and fed thee with manna, which thou knewest not, neither did thy fathers know; that he might make thee know that man doth not live by bread only, but by every *word* that proceedeth out of the mouth of the LORD doth man live.

Jb 23:12 Neither have I gone back from the commandment of his lips; I have esteemed the words of his mouth more than my necessary *food*.

Ps 19:10 More to be desired *are they* than gold, yea, than much fine gold: sweeter also than honey and the honeycomb.

Ps 119:103 How sweet are thy words unto my taste! *yea, sweeter* than honey to my mouth!

Je 15:16 Thy words were found, and I did eat them; and thy word was unto me the joy and rejoicing of mine heart: for I am called by thy name, O LORD God of hosts.

Eze 2:8 But thou, son of man, hear what I say unto thee; Be not thou rebellious like that rebellious house: open thy mouth, and eat that I give thee.

Eze 3:1 Moreover he said unto me, Son of man, eat that thou findest; eat this roll, and go speak unto the house of Israel.

Mt 4:4 But he answered and said, It is written, Man shall not live by bread alone, but by every word that proceedeth out of the mouth of God.

Lu 4:4 And Jesus answered him, saying, It is written, That man shall not live by bread alone, but by every word of God.

Ac 20:32 And now, brethren, I commend you to God, and to the word of his grace, which is able to build you up, and to give you an inheritance among all them which are sanctified.

1 Co 3:2 I have fed you with milk, and not with meat: for hitherto ye were not able *to bear it,* neither yet now are ye able.

1 Ti 4:6 If thou put the brethren in remembrance of these things, thou shalt be a good minister of Jesus Christ, nourished up in the words of faith and of good doctrine, whereunto thou hast attained.

He 5:13 For every one that useth milk *is* unskilful in the word of righteousness: for he is a babe.

He 6:5 And have tasted the good word of God, and the powers of the world to come,

1 Pe 2:2 As newborn babes, desire the sincere milk of the word, that ye may grow thereby:

Re 10:10 And I took the little book out of the angel's hand, and ate it up; and it was in my mouth sweet as honey: and as soon as I had eaten it, my belly was bitter.

4. Divinely Inspired

Je 25:3 From the thirteenth year of Josiah the son of Amon king of Judah, even unto this day, that *is* the three and twentieth year, the word of the LORD hath come unto me, and I have spoken unto you, rising early and speaking; but ye have not hearkened.

Je 34:12 Therefore the word of the LORD came to Jeremiah from the LORD, saying,

Je 36:2 Take thee a roll of a book, and write therein all the words that I have spoken unto thee against Israel, and against Judah, and against all the nations, from the day I spake unto thee, from the days of Josiah, even unto this day.

Je 36:28 Take thee again another roll, and write in it all the former words that were in the first roll, which Jehoiakim the king of Judah hath burned.

Eze 1:3 The word of the LORD came expressly unto Ezekiel the priest, the son of Buzi, in the land of the Chaldeans by the river Chebar; and the hand of the LORD was there upon him.

Eze 3:16 And it came to pass at the end of seven days, that the word of the LORD came unto me, saying,

Eze 22:1 Moreover the word of the LORD came unto me, saying,

Ho 1:2 The beginning of the word of the LORD by Hosea. And the LORD said to Hosea, Go, take unto thee a wife of whoredoms and children of whoredoms: for the land hath committed great whoredom, *departing* from the LORD.

Hag 1:1 In the second year of Darius the king, in the sixth month, in the first day of the month, came the word of the LORD by Haggai the prophet unto Zerubbabel the son of Shealtiel, governor of Judah, and to Joshua the son of Josedech, the high priest, saying,

Hag 2:1 In the seventh *month,* in the one and twentieth *day* of the month, came the word of the LORD by the prophet Haggai, saying,

Hag 2:10 In the four and twentieth *day* of the ninth *month,* in the second year of Darius, came the word of the LORD by Haggai the prophet, saying,

Zec 1:1 In the eighth month, in the second year of Darius, came the word of the LORD unto Zechariah, the son of Berechiah, the son of Iddo the prophet, saying,

Zec 4:6 Then he answered and spake unto me, saying, This *is* the word of the LORD unto Zerubbabel, saying, Not by might, nor by power, but by my spirit, saith the LORD of hosts.

Zec 7:4 Then came the word of the LORD of hosts unto me, saying,

Zec 7:12 Yea, they made their hearts *as* an adamant stone, lest they should hear the law, and the words which the LORD of hosts hath sent in his spirit by the former prophets: therefore came a great wrath from the LORD of hosts.

Zec 8:1 Again the word of the LORD of hosts came *to* me, saying,

Mal 1:1 The burden of the word of the LORD to Israel by Malachi.

Mt 22:31 But as touching the resurrection of the dead, have ye not read that which was spoken unto you by God, saying,

Ac 1:16 Men *and* brethren, this scripture must needs have been fulfilled, which the Holy Ghost by the mouth of David spake before concerning Judas, which was guide to them that took Jesus.

Ac 28:25 And when they agreed Paul had spoken one word, Well spake the Holy Ghost by Esaias the prophet unto our fathers,

2 Ti 3:16 All scripture *is* given by inspiration of God, and *is* profitable for doctrine, for reproof, for correction, for instruction in righteousness:

He 5:6 As he saith also in another *place,* Thou *art* a priest for ever after the order of Melchisedec.

2 Pe 1:21 For the prophecy came not in old time by the will of man: but holy men of God spake *as they were* moved by the Holy Ghost.

2 Pe 3:15 And account *that* the longsuffering of our Lord *is* salvation; even as our beloved brother Paul also according to the wisdom given unto him hath written unto you;

Re 1:1 The Revelation of Jesus Christ, which God gave unto him, to shew unto his servants things which must shortly come to pass; and he sent and signified *it* by his angel unto his servant John:

Re 1:11 Saying, I am Alpha and Omega, the first and the last: and, What thou seest, write in a book, and send *it* unto the seven churches which are in Asia; unto Ephesus, and unto Smyrna, and unto Pergamos, and unto Thyatira, and unto Sardis, and unto Philadelphia, and unto Laodicea.

Re 1:19 Write the things which thou hast seen, and the things which are, and the things which shall be hereafter;

Re 14:13 And I heard a voice from heaven saying unto me, Write, Blessed *are* the dead which die in the Lord from henceforth: Yea, saith the Spirit, that they may rest from their labours; and their works do follow them.

Re 21:5 And he that sat upon the throne said, Behold, I make all things new. And he said unto me, Write: for these words are true and faithful.

5. Precepts Written in the Heart

De 6:6 And these words, which I command thee this day, shall be in thine heart:

De 11:18 Therefore shall ye lay up these my words in your heart and in your soul, and bind them for a sign upon your hand, that they may be as frontlets between your eyes.

De 30:14 But the word *is* very nigh unto thee, in thy mouth, and in thy heart, that thou mayest do it.

Ps 119:11 Thy word have I hid in mine heart, that I might not sin against thee.

Eze 3: 10 Moreover he said unto me, Son of man, all my words that I shall speak unto thee receive in thine heart, and hear with thine ears.

Mk 4:15 And these are they by the way side, where the word is sown; but when they have heard, Satan cometh immediately, and taketh away the word that was sown in their hearts.

Lu 2:19 But Mary kept all these things, and pondered *them* in her heart.

Lu 2:51 And he went down with them, and came to Nazareth, and was subject unto them: but his mother kept all these sayings in her heart.

Ro 10:8 But what saith it? The word is nigh thee, *even* in thy mouth, and in thy heart: that is, the word of faith, which we preach;

Col 3:16 Let the word of Christ dwell in you richly in all wisdom; teaching and admonishing one another in psalms and hymns and spiritual songs, singing with grace in your hearts to the Lord.

1 Th 2:13 For this cause also thank we God without ceasing, because, when ye received the word of God which ye heard of us, ye received *it* not *as* the word of men, but as it is in truth, the word of God, which effectually worketh also in you that believe.

1 Jn 2:14 I have written unto you, fathers, because ye have known him *that is* from the beginning. I have written unto you, young men, because ye are strong, and the word of God abideth in you, and ye have overcome the wicked one.

1 Jn 2:24 Let that therefore abide in you, which ye have heard from the beginning. If that which ye have heard from the beginning shall remain in you, ye also shall continue in the Son, and in the Father.

6. Furnishes a Light in Darkness

Ps 19:8 The statutes of the LORD *are* right, rejoicing the heart: the commandment of the LORD *is* pure, enlightening the eyes.

Ps 119:105 Thy word *is* a lamp unto my feet, and a light unto my path.

Ps 119:130 The entrance of thy words giveth light; it giveth understanding unto the simple.

Pr 2:6 For the LORD giveth wisdom: out of his mouth *cometh* knowledge and understanding.

Pr 6:23 For the commandment *is* a lamp; and the law *is* light; and reproofs of instruction *are* the way of life:

Ro 15:4 For whatsoever things were written aforetime were written for our learning, that we through patience and comfort of the scriptures might have hope.

1 Co 10:11 Now all these things happened unto them for ensamples: and they are written for our admonition, upon whom the ends of the world are come.

2 Co 4:4 In whom the god of this world hath blinded the minds of them which believe not, lest the light of the glorious gospel of Christ, who is the image of God, should shine unto them.

2 Ti 3:15 And that from a child thou hast known the holy scriptures, which are able to make thee wise unto salvation through faith which is in Christ Jesus.

2 Pe 1:19 We have also a more sure word of prophecy; whereunto ye do well that ye take heed, as unto a light that shineth in a dark place, until the day dawn, and the day star arise in your hearts:

7. Loved by the Saints

Ps 1:2 But his delight *is* in the law of the LORD; and in his law doth he meditate day and night.

Ps 119:16 I will delight myself in thy statutes: I will not forget thy word.

Ps 119:24 Thy testimonies also *are* my delight *and* my counsellors.

Ps 119:47 And I will delight myself in thy commandments, which I have loved.

Ps 119:72 The law of thy mouth *is* better unto me than thousands of gold and silver.

Ps 119:82 Mine eyes fail for thy word, saying, When wilt thou comfort me?

Ps 119:97 O how love I thy law! it *is* my meditation all the day.

Ps 119:113 I hate *vain* thoughts: but thy law do I love.

Ps 119:127 Therefore I love thy commandments above gold; yea, above fine gold.

Ps 119:140 Thy word *is* very pure: therefore thy servant loveth it.

Ps 119:159 Consider how I love thy precepts: quicken me, O LORD, according to thy lovingkindness.

Ps 119:163 I hate and abhor lying: *but* thy law do I love.

Ps 119:167 My soul hath kept thy testimonies; and I love them exceedingly.

Ps 119:174 I have longed for thy salvation, O LORD; and thy law *is* my delight.

Je 15:16 Thy words were found, and I did eat them; and thy word was unto me the joy and rejoicing of mine heart: for I am called by thy name, O LORD God of hosts.

Eze 3:3 And he said unto me, Son of man, cause thy belly to eat, and fill thy bowels with this roll that I give thee. Then did I eat *it;* and it was in my mouth as honey for sweetness.

Tit 1:9 Holding fast the faithful word as he hath been taught, that he may be able by sound doctrine both to exhort and to convince the gainsayers.

8. Mighty in Its Influence

Ps 147:18 He sendeth out his word, and melteth them: he causeth his wind to blow, *and* the waters flow.

Je 1:18 For, behold, I have made thee this day a defenced city, and an iron pillar, and brasen walls ah, against the princes thereof, against the priests thereof, and against the people of the land.

Je 5:14 Wherefore thus saith the LORD God of hosts, Because ye speak this word, behold, I will make my words in thy mouth fire, and this people wood, and it shall devour them.

Je 23:29 *Is* not my word like as a fire? saith the LORD; and like a hammer *that* breaketh the rock in pieces?

Eze 37:7 So I prophesied as I was commanded: and as I prophesied, there was a noise, and behold a shaking, and the bones came together, bone to his bone.

Ho 6:5 Therefore have I hewed *them* by the prophets; I have slain them by the words of my mouth: and thy judgments *are as* the light *that* goeth forth.

Lu 4:4 And Jesus answered him, saying, It is written, That man shall not live by bread alone, but by every word of God.

Lu 4:8 And Jesus answered and said unto him, Get thee behind me, Satan: for it is written, Thou shalt worship the Lord thy God, and him only shalt thou serve.

Lu 4:32 And they were astonished at his doctrine: for his word was with power.

Ac 2:37 Now when they heard *this,* they were pricked in their heart, and said unto Peter and to the rest of the apostles, Men *and* brethren, what shall we do?

Ac 6:10 And they were not able to resist the wisdom and the spirit by which he spake.

Ac 18:24 And a certain Jew named Apollos, born at Alexandria, an eloquent man, *and* mighty in the scriptures, came to Ephesus.

Ac 19:20 So mightily grew the word of God and prevailed.

Ro 1:16 For I am not ashamed of the gospel of Christ: for it is the power of God unto salvation to every one that believeth; to the Jew first, and also to the Greek.

1 Co 1:18 For the preaching of the cross is to them that perish foolishness; but unto us which are saved it is the power of God.

Ep 6:17 And take the helmet of salvation, and the sword of the Spirit, which is the word of God:

1 Th 1:5 For our gospel came not unto you in word only, but also in power, and in the Holy Ghost, and in much assurance; as ye know what manner of men we were among you for your sake.

1 Th 2:13 For this cause also thank we God without ceasing, because, when ye received the word of God which ye heard of us, ye received *it* not *as* the word of men, but as it is in truth, the word of God, which effectually worketh also in you that believe.

2 Th 2:8 And then shall that Wicked be revealed, whom the Lord shall consume with the spirit of his mouth, and shall destroy with the brightness of his coming:

He 4:12 For the word of God *is* quick, and powerful, and sharper than any twoedged sword, piercing even to the dividing asunder of soul and spirit, and of the joints and marrow, and *is a* discerner of the thoughts and intents of the heart.

Re 1:16 And he had in his right hand seven stars: and out of his mouth went a sharp twoedged sword: and his countenance *was* as the sun shineth in his strength.

Re 11:10 And they that dwell upon the earth shall rejoice over them, and make merry, and shall send gifts one to another; because these two prophets tormented them that dwelt on the earth.

Re 19:15 And out of his mouth goeth a sharp sword, that with it he should smite the nations: and he shall rule them with a rod of iron: and he treadeth the winepress of the fierceness and wrath of Almighty God.

9. A Blessing to Those Who Reverence It

Jos 1:8 This book of the law shall not depart out of thy mouth; but thou shalt meditate therein day and night, that thou mayest observe to do according to all that is written therein: for then thou shalt make thy way

prosperous, and then thou shalt have good success.

Ps 19:11 Moreover by them is thy servant warned: *and* in keeping of them *there is* great reward.

Mt 7:24 Therefore whosoever heareth these sayings of mine, and doeth them, I will liken him unto a wise man, which built his house upon a rock:

Lu 11:28 But he said, Yea rather, blessed *are* they that hear the word of God, and keep it.

Jn 5:24 Verily, verily, I say unto you, He that heareth my word, and believeth on him that sent me, hath everlasting life, and shall not come into condemnation; but is passed from death unto life.

Jn 8:31 Then said Jesus to those Jews which believed on him, If ye continue in my word, *then* are ye my disciples indeed;

Re 1:3 Blessed *is* he that readeth, and they that hear the words of this prophecy, and keep those things which are written therein: for the time *is* at hand.

10. Purifies the Life

Ps 119:9 Wherewithal shall a young man cleanse his way? by taking heed *thereto* according to thy word.

Jn 15:3 Now ye are clean through the word which I have spoken unto you.

Jn 17:17 Sanctify them through thy truth: thy word is truth.

Ep 5:26 That he might sanctify and cleanse it with the washing of water by the word,

1 Ti 4:5 For it is sanctified by the word of God and prayer.

Ja 1:21 Wherefore lay apart all filthiness and superfluity of naughtiness, and receive with meekness the engrafted word, which is able to save your souls.

1 Pe 1:22 Seeing ye have purified your souls in obeying the truth through the Spirit unto unfeigned love of the brethren, *see that ye* love one another with a pure heart fervently:

11. Written with a Purpose

Jn 20:30 And many other signs truly did Jesus in the presence of his disciples, which are not written in this book:

Jn 20:31 But these are written, that ye might believe that Jesus is the Christ, the Son of God; and that believing ye might have life through his name.

Ro 15:4 For whatsoever things were written aforetime were written for our learning, that we through patience and comfort of the scriptures might have hope.

1 Co 10:11 Now all these things happened unto them for ensamples: and they are written for our admonition, upon whom the ends of the world are come.

1 Jn 1:4 And these things write we unto you, that your joy may be full.

1 Jn 2:1 My little children, these things write I unto you, that ye sin not. And if any man sin, we have an advocate with the Father, Jesus Christ the righteous:

1 Jn 5:13 These things have I written unto you that believe on the name of the Son of God; that ye may know that ye have eternal life, and that ye may believe on the name of the Son of God.

12. Read in the Great Congregation

Ex 24:7 And he took the book of the covenant, and read in the audience of the people: and they said, All that the LORD hath said will we do, and be obedient.

Jos 8:34 And afterward he read all the words of the law, the blessings and cursings, according to all that is written in the book of the law.

Je 36:8 And Baruch the son of Neriah did according to all that Jeremiah the prophet commanded him, reading in the book the words of the LORD in the LORD's house.

Je 36:15 And they said unto him, Sit down now, and read it in our ears. So Baruch read it in their ears.

Je 36:21 So the king sent Jehudi to fetch the roll: and he took it out of Elishama the scribe's chamber. And Jehudi read in the ears of all the princes which stood beside the king.

Je 51:61 And Jeremiah said to Seraiah, When thou comest to Babylon, and shalt see, and shalt read all these words;

Lu 4:16 And he came to Nazareth, where he had been brought up: and, as his custom was, he went into the synagogue on the sabbath day, and stood up for to read.

Ac 8:30 And Philip ran thither to him, and heard him read the prophet Esaias, and said, Understandest thou what thou readest?

Ac 13:27 For they that dwell at Jerusalem, and their rulers, because they knew him not, nor yet the voices of the prophets which are read every sabbath day, they have fulfilled them in condemning him.

Col 4:16 And when this epistle is read among you, cause that it be read also in the church of the Laodiceans; and that ye likewise read the epistle from Laodicea.

1 Th 5:27 I charge you by the Lord that this epistle be read unto all the holy brethren.

13. The Standard of Faith and Duty

Pr 29:18 Where there is no vision, the people perish: but he that keepeth the law, happy is he.

Is 8:20 To the law and to the testimony: if they speak not according to this word, it is because there is no light in them.

Jn 12:48 He that rejecteth me, and receiveth not my words, hath one that judgeth him: the word that I have spoken, the same shall judge him in the last day.

Ga 1:8 But though we, or an angel from heaven, preach any other gospel unto you than that which we have preached unto you, let him be accursed.

1 Th 2:13 For this cause also thank we God without ceasing, because, when ye received the word of God which ye heard of us, ye received it not as the word of men, but as it is in truth, the word of God, which effectually worketh also in you that believe.

14. Not to Be Altered

De 4:2 Ye shall not add unto the word which I command you, neither shall ye diminish *ought* from it, that ye may keep the commandments of the LORD your God which I command you.

De 12:32 What thing soever I command you, observe to do it: thou shalt not add thereto, nor diminish from it.

De 18:20 But the prophet, which shall presume to speak a word in my name, which I have not commanded him to speak, or that shall speak in the name of other gods, even that prophet shall die.

De 27:26 Cursed *be* he that confirmeth not *all* the words of this law to do them. And all the people shall say, Amen.

Ps 119:161 Princes have persecuted me without a cause: but my heart standeth in awe of thy word.

Pr 30:6 Add thou not unto his words, lest he reprove thee, and thou be found a liar.

Je 23:36 And the burden of the LORD shall ye mention no more: for every man's word shall be his burden; for ye have perverted the words of the living God, of the LORD of hosts our God.

Je 26:2 Thus saith the LORD; Stand in the court of the LORD's house, and speak unto all the cities of Judah, which come to worship in the LORD's house, all the words that I command thee to speak unto them; diminish not a word:

Je 36:23 And I came to pass, *that* when Jehudi had read three or four leaves, he cut it with the penknife, and cast *it* into the fire that *was* on the hearth, until all the roll was consumed in the fire that *was* on the hearth.

Zep 3:4 Her prophets *are* light *and* treacherous persons: her priests have polluted the sanctuary, they have done violence to the law.

Mt 5:19 Whosoever therefore shall break one of these least commandments, and shall teach men so, he shall be called the least in the kingdom of heaven: but whosoever shall do and teach *them,* the same shall be called great in the kingdom of heaven.

Mt 15:6 And honour not his father or his mother, *he shall be free.* Thus have ye made the commandment of God of none effect by your tradition.

2 Co 2:17 For we are not as many, which corrupt the word of God: but as of sincerity, but as of God, in the sight of God speak we in Christ.

2 Co 4:2 But have renounced the hidden things of dishonesty, not walking in craftiness, nor handling the word of God deceitfully; but by manifestation of the truth commending ourselves to every man's conscience in the sight of God.

Ga 1:8 But though we, or an angel from heaven, preach any other gospel unto you than that which we have preached unto you, let him be accursed.

1 Ti 6:14 That thou keep *this* commandment without spot, unrebukeable, until the appearing of our Lord Jesus Christ:

2 Pe 3:16 As also in all *his* epistles, speaking in them of these things; in which are some things hard to be understood, which they that are unlearned and unstable wrest, as *they do* also the other scriptures, unto their own destruction.

Re 22:19 And if any man shall take away from the words of the book of this prophecy, God shall take away his part out of the book of life, and out of the holy city, and *from* the things which are written in this book.

15. To Be Studied

De 17:19 And it shall be with him, and he shall read therein all the days of his life: that he may learn to fear the LORD his God, to keep all the words of this law and these statutes, to do them:

Is 8:20 To the law and to the testimony: if they speak not according to this word, *it is* because *there is* no light in them.

Is 34:16 Seek ye out of the book of the LORD, and read: no one of these shall fail, none shall want her mate: for my mouth it hath commanded, and his spirit it hath gathered them.

Da 9:2 In the first year of his reign I Daniel understood by books the number of the years, whereof the word of the LORD came to Jeremiah the prophet, that he would accomplish seventy years in the desolations of Jerusalem.

Mt 19:4 And he answered and said unto them, Have ye not read, that he which made *them* at the beginning made them male and female,

Mt 22:31 But as touching the resurrection of the dead, have ye not read that which was spoken unto you by God, saying,

Lu 10:26 He said unto him, What is written in the law? how readest thou?

Lu 16:29 Abraham saith unto him, They have Moses and the prophets; let them hear them.

Jn 5:39 Search the scriptures; for in them ye think ye have eternal life: and they are they which testify of me.

Ac 8:28 Was returning, and sitting in his chariot read Esaias the prophet.

Ac 17:11 These were more noble than those in Thessalonica, in that they received the word with all readiness of mind, and searched the scriptures daily, whether those things were so.

Ro 15:4 For whatsoever things were written aforetime were written for our learning, that we through patience and comfort of the scriptures might have hope.

1 Ti 4:13 Till I come, give attendance to reading, to exhortation, to doctrine.

16. Seed for the Sower

Ps 126:6 He that goeth forth and weepeth, bearing precious seed, shall doubtless come again with rejoicing, bringing his sheaves *with him*.

Is 55:11 So shall my word be that goeth forth out of my mouth: it shall not return unto me void, but it shall accomplish that which I please, and it shall prosper *in the thing* whereto I sent it.

Mt 13:20 But he that received the seed into stony places, the same is he that heareth the word, and anon with joy receiveth it;

Mt 13:22 He also that received seed among the thorns is he that heareth the word; and the care of this world, and the deceitfulness of riches, choke the word, and he becometh unfruitful.

Mt 13:24 Another parable put he forth unto them, saying, The kingdom of heaven is likened unto a man which sowed good seed in his field:

Mt 13:27 So the servants of the householder came and said unto him, Sir, didst not thou sow good seed in thy field? from whence then hath it tares?

Mk 4:4 And it came to pass, as he sowed, some fell by the way side, and the fowls of the air came and devoured it up.

Mk 4:14–15 The sower soweth the word.

And these are they by the way side, where the word is sown; but when they have heard, Satan cometh immediately, and taketh away the word that was sown in their hearts.

Mk 4:26 And he said, So is the kingdom of God, as if a man should cast seed into the ground;

Lu 8:11 Now the parable is this: The seed is the word of God.

Ac 12:24 But the word of God grew and multiplied.

2 Co 9:10 Now he that ministereth seed to the sower both minister bread for *your* food, and multiply your seed sown, and increase the fruits of your righteousness;)

1 Pe 1:23 Being born again, not of corruptible seed, but of incorruptible, by the word of God, which liveth and abideth for ever.

17. Absolutely Trustworthy

Ge 7:10 And it came to pass after seven days, that the waters of the flood were upon the earth.

Ge 21:1 And the LORD visited Sarah as he had said, and the LORD did unto Sarah as he had spoken.

Ge 41:54 And the seven years of dearth began to come, according as Joseph had said: and the dearth was in all lands; but in all the land of Egypt there was bread.

Ex 7:13 And he hardened Pharaoh's heart, that he hearkened not unto them; as the LORD had said.

Ex 7:22 And the magicians of Egypt did so with their enchantments: and Pharaoh's heart was hardened, neither did he hearken unto them; as the LORD had said.

Ex 9:6 And the LORD did that thing on the morrow, and all the cattle of Egypt died: but of the cattle of the children of Israel died not one.

Ex 13:19 And Moses took the bones of Joseph with him: for he had straitly sworn the children of Israel, saying, God will surely visit you; and ye shall carry up my bones away hence with you.

Ex 16:13 And it came to pass, that at even the quails came up, and covered the camp: and in the morning the dew lay round about the host.

Le 26:44 And yet for all that, when they be in the land of their enemies, I will not cast them away, neither will I abhor them, to destroy them utterly, and to break my covenant with them: for I *am* the LORD their God.

Nu 11:23 And the LORD said unto Moses, Is the LORD's hand waxed short? thou shalt see now whether my word shall come to pass unto thee or not.

Nu 14:35 I the LORD have said, I will surely do it unto all this evil congregation, that are gathered together against me: in this wilderness they shall be consumed, and there they shall die.

Nu 21:9 And Moses made a serpent of brass, and put it upon a pole, and it came to pass, that if a serpent had bitten any man, when he beheld the serpent of brass, he lived.

Nu 23:19 God *is* not a man, that he should lie; neither the son of man, that he should repent: hath he said, and shall he not do *it?* or hath he spoken, and shall he not make it good?

Nu 26:65 For the LORD had said of them, They shall surely die in the wilderness. And there was not left a man

of them, save Caleb the son of Jephunneh, and Joshua the son of Nun.

De 2:14 And the space in which we came from Kadesh-barnea, until we were come over the brook Zered, *was* thirty and eight years; until all the generation of the men of war were wasted out from among the host, as the LORD sware unto them.

De 34:5 So Moses the servant of the LORD died there in the land of Moab, according to the word of the LORD.

Jos 3:16 That the waters which came down from above stood *and* rose up upon an heap very far from the city Adam, that *is* beside Zaretan: and those that came down toward the sea of the plain, *even* the salt sea, failed, *and* were cut off: and the people passed over right against Jericho.

Jos 11:23 So Joshua took the whole land, according to all that the LORD said unto Moses; and Joshua gave it for an inheritance unto Israel according to their divisions by their tribes. And the land rested from war.

Jud 2:15 Whithersoever they went out, the hand of the LORD was against them for evil, as the LORD had said, and as the LORD had sworn unto them: and they were greatly distressed.

Jud 13:12 And Manoah said, Now let thy words come to pass. How shall we order the child, and *how* shall we do unto him?

1 S 1:23 And Elkanah her husband said unto her, Do what seemeth thee good; tarry until thou have weaned him; only the LORD establish his word. So the woman abode, and gave her son suck until she weaned him.

1 S 3:12 In that day I will perform against Eli all *things* which I have spoken concerning his house: when I begin, I will also make an end.

1 S 10:9 And it was *so*, that when he had turned his back to go from Samuel, God gave him another heart: and all those signs came to pass that day.

1 S 28:17 And the LORD hath done to him, as he spake by me: for the LORD hath rent the kingdom out of thine hand, and given it to thy neighbour, *even* to David:

1 S 30:19 And there was nothing lacking to them, neither small nor great, neither sons nor daughters, neither spoil, nor any *thing* that they had taken to them: David recovered all.

2 S 3:18 Now then do *it:* for the LORD hath spoken of David, saying, By the hand of my servant David I will save my people Israel out of the hand of the Philistines, and out of the hand of all their enemies.

2 S 7:25 And now, O LORD God, the word that thou hast spoken concerning thy servant, and concerning his house, establish *it* for ever, and do as thou hast said.

2 S 12:15 And Nathan departed unto his house. And the LORD struck the child that Uriah's wife bare unto David, and it was very sick.

2 S 23:5 Although my house *be* not so with God; yet he hath made with me an everlasting covenant, ordered in all *things,* and sure: for *this is* all my salvation, and all *my* desire, although he make *it* not to grow.

1 K 2:27 So Solomon thrust out Abiathar from being priest unto the LORD; that he might fulfil the word of the LORD, which he spake concerning the house of Eli in Shiloh.

1 K 6:12 *Concerning* this house which thou art in building, if thou wilt walk in my statutes, and execute my judgments, and keep all my commandments to walk in them; then will I perform my word with thee, which I spake unto David thy father:

1 K 8:15 And he said, Blessed *be* the LORD God of Israel, which spake with his mouth unto David my father, and hath with his hand fulfilled *it,* saying,

1 K 8:26 And now, O God of Israel, let thy word, I pray thee, be verified, which thou spakest unto thy servant David my father.

1 K 8:56 Blessed *be* the LORD, that hath given rest unto his people Israel, according to all that he promised: there hath not failed one word of all his good promise, which he promised by the hand of Moses his servant.

1 K 12:15 Wherefore the king hearkened not unto the people; for the cause was from the LORD, that he might perform his saying, which the LORD spake by Ahijah the Shilonite unto Jeroboam the son of Nebat.

1 K 13:5 The altar also was rent, and the ashes poured out from the altar, according to the sign which the man of God had given by the word of the LORD.

1 K 13:26 And when the prophet that brought him back from the way heard *thereof,* he said, It *is* the man of God, who was disobedient unto the word of the LORD: therefore the LORD hath delivered him unto the lion, which hath torn him, and slain him, according to the word of the LORD, which he spake unto him.

1 K 14:11 Him that dieth of Jeroboam in the city shall the dogs eat; and him that dieth in the field shall the fowls of the air eat: for the LORD hath spoken it.

1 K 14:17 And Jeroboam's wife arose, and departed, and came to Tirzah: *and* when she came to the threshold of the door, the child died;

1 K 15:29 And it came to pass, when he reigned, *that* he smote all the house of Jeroboam; he left not to Jeroboam any that breathed, until he had destroyed him, according unto the saying of the LORD, which he spake by his servant Ahijah the Shilonite:

1 K 16:12 Thus did Zimri destroy all the house of Baasha, according to the word of the LORD, which he spake against Baasha by Jehu the prophet,

1 K 16:34 In his days did Hiel the Bethelite build Jericho: he laid the foundation thereof in Abiram his firstborn, and set up the gates thereof in his youngest *son* Segub, according to the word of the LORD, which he spake by Joshua the son of Nun.

1 K 17:16 *And* the barrel of meal wasted not, neither did the cruse of oil fail, according to the word of the LORD, which he spake by Elijah.

1 K 22:38 And *one* washed the chariot in the pool of Samaria; and the dogs licked up his blood; and they washed his armour; according unto the word of the LORD which he spake.

2 K 1:17 So he died according to the word of the LORD which Elijah had spoken. And Jehoram reigned in his stead in the second year of Jehoram the son of Jehoshaphat king of Judah; because he had no son.

2 K 4:44 So he set it before them, and they did eat, and left thereof, according to the word of the LORD.

2 K 5:14 Then went he down, and dipped himself seven times in Jordan, according to the saying of the man of God: and his flesh came again like unto the flesh of a little child, and he was clean.

2 K 7:16 And the people went out, and spoiled the tents of the Syrians. So a measure of fine flour was sold for a shekel, and two measures of barley for a shekel, according to the word of the LORD.

2 K 9:26 Surely I have seen yesterday the blood of Naboth, and the blood of his sons, saith the LORD; and I will requite thee in this plat, saith the LORD. Now therefore take and cast him into the plat of ground, according to the word of the LORD.

2 K 9:36 Wherefore they came again, and told him. And he said, This is the word of the LORD, which he spake by his servant Elijah the Tishbite, saying, In the portion of Jezreel shall dogs eat the flesh of Jezebel:

2 K 10:10 Know now that there shall fall unto the earth nothing of the word of the LORD, which the LORD spake concerning the house of Ahab: for the LORD hath done that which he spake by his servant Elijah.

2 K 10:17 And when he came to Samaria, he slew all that remained unto Ahab in Samaria, till he had destroyed him, according to the saying of the LORD, which he spake to Elijah.

2 K 15:12 This was the word of the LORD which he spake unto Jehu, saying, Thy sons shall sit on the throne of Israel unto the fourth generation. And so it came to pass.

2 K 17:23 Until the LORD removed Israel out of his sight, as he had said by all his servants the prophets. So was Israel carried away out of their own land to Assyria unto this day.

2 K 22:16 Thus saith the LORD, Behold, I will bring evil upon this place,

and upon the inhabitants thereof, even all the words of the book which the king of Judah hath read:

2 K 23:16 And as Josiah turned himself, he spied the sepulchres that were there in the mount, and sent, and took the bones out of the sepulchres, and burned them upon the altar, and polluted it, according to the word of the LORD which the man of God proclaimed, who proclaimed these words.

2 K 24:2 And the LORD sent against him bands of the Chaldees, and bands of the Syrians, and bands of the Moabites, and bands of the children of Ammon, and sent them against Judah to destroy it, according to the word of the LORD, which he spake by his servants the prophets.

1 Chr 11:3 Therefore came all the elders of Israel to the king to Hebron; and David made a covenant with them in Hebron before the LORD; and they anointed David king over Israel, according to the word of the LORD by Samuel.

1 Chr 11:10 These also are the chief of the mighty men whom David had, who strengthened themselves with him in his kingdom, and with all Israel, to make him king, according to the word of the LORD concerning Israel.

1 Chr 12:23 And these are the numbers of the bands that were ready armed to the war, and came to David to Hebron, to turn the kingdom of Saul to him, according to the word of the LORD.

1 Chr 17:23 Therefore now, LORD, let the thing that thou hast spoken concerning thy servant and concerning his house be established for ever, and do as thou hast said.

2 Chr 6:4 And he said, Blessed be the LORD God of Israel, who hath with his hands fulfilled that which he spake with his mouth to my father David, saying,

2 Chr 6:10 The LORD therefore hath performed his word that he hath spoken: for I am risen up in the room of David my father, and am set on the throne of Israel, as the LORD promised, and have built the house for the name of the LORD God of Israel.

2 Chr 6:17 Now then, O LORD God of Israel, let thy word be verified, which thou hast spoken unto thy servant David.

2 Chr 10:15 So the king hearkened not unto the people: for the cause was of God, that the LORD might perform his word, which he spake by the hand of Ahijah the Shilonite to Jeroboam the son of Nebat.

2 Chr 23:3 And all the congregation made a covenant with the king in the house of God. And he said unto them, Behold, the king's son shall reign, as the LORD hath said of the sons of David.

2 Chr 36:21 To fulfil the word of the LORD by the mouth of Jeremiah, until the land had enjoyed her sabbaths: *for* as long as she lay desolate she kept sabbath, to fulfil threescore and ten years.

Ezr 1:1 Now in the first year of Cyrus king of Persia, that the word of the LORD by the mouth of Jeremiah might be fulfilled, the LORD stirred up the spirit of Cyrus king of Persia, that he made a proclamation throughout all his kingdom, and *put it* also in writing, saying,

Ps 89:34 My covenant will I not break, nor alter the thing that is gone out of my lips.

Ps 93:5 Thy testimonies are very sure: holiness becometh thine house, O LORD, for ever.

Ps 111:7 The works of his hands *are* verity and judgment; all his commandments *are* sure.

Ps 119:76 Let, I pray thee, thy merciful kindness be for my comfort, according to thy word unto thy servant.

Ps 119:86 All thy commandments *are* faithful: they persecute me wrongfully; help thou me.

Ps 148:6 He hath also stablished them for ever and ever: he hath made a decree which shall not pass.

Is 1:20 But if ye refuse and rebel, ye shall be devoured with the sword: for the mouth of the LORD hath spoken *it*.

Is 9:7 Of the increase of *his* government and peace *there shall be* no end,

upon the throne of David, and upon his kingdom, to order it, and to establish it with judgment and with justice from henceforth even for ever. The zeal of the LORD of hosts will perform this.

Is 21:17 And the residue of the number of archers, the mighty men of the children of Kedar, shall be diminished: for the LORD God of Israel hath spoken *it*.

Is 25:8 He will swallow up death in victory; and the Lord GOD will wipe away tears from off all faces; and the rebuke of his people shall he take away from off all the earth: for the LORD hath spoken *it*.

Is 31:2 Yet he also *is* wise, and will bring evil, and will not call back his words: but will arise against the house of the evildoers, and against the help of them that work iniquity.

Is 34:16 Seek ye out of the book of the LORD, and read: no one of these shall fail, none shall want her mate: for my mouth it hath commanded, and his spirit it hath gathered them.

Is 37:8 So Rabshakeh returned, and found the king of Assyria warring against Libnah: for he had heard that he was departed from Lachish.

Is 40:8 The grass withereth, the flower fadeth: but the word of our God shall stand for ever.

Is 44:26 That confirmeth the word of his servant, and performeth the counsel of his messengers; that saith to Jerusalem, Thou shalt be inhabited; and to the cities of Judah, Ye shall be built, and I will raise up the decayed places thereof:

Is 45:23 I have sworn by myself, the word is gone out of my mouth *in* righteousness, and shall not return, That unto me every knee shall bow, every tongue shall swear.

Is 46:11 Calling a ravenous bird from the east, the man that executeth my counsel from a far country: yea, I have spoken *it*, I will also bring it to pass; I have purposed *it*, I will also do it.

Is 48:3 I have declared the former things from the beginning; and they went forth out of my mouth, and I shewed them; I did *them* suddenly, and they came to pass.

Is 55:11 So shall my word be that goeth forth out of my mouth: it shall not return unto me void, but it shall accomplish that which I please, and it shall prosper *in the thing* whereto I sent it.

Is 58:14 Then shalt thou delight thyself in the LORD; and I will cause thee to ride upon the high places of the earth, and feed thee with the heritage of Jacob thy father: for the mouth of the LORD hath spoken *it.*

Je 1:12 Then said the LORD unto me, Thou hast well seen: for I will hasten my word to perform it.

Je 4:28 For this shall the earth mourn, and the heavens above be black: because I have spoken *it,* I have purposed *it,* and will not repent, neither will I turn back from it.

Je 25:13 And I will bring upon that land all my words which I have pronounced against it, *even* all that is written in this book, which Jeremiah hath prophesied against all the nations.

Je 28:17 So Hananiah the prophet died the same year in the seventh month.

Je 29:10 For thus saith the LORD, That after seventy years be accomplished at Babylon I will visit you, and perform my good word toward you, in causing you to return to this place.

Je 32:24 Behold the mounts, they are come unto the city to take it; and the city is given into the hand of the Chaldeans, that fight against it, because of the sword, and of the famine, and of the pestilence: and what thou hast spoken is come to pass; and, behold, thou seest *it.*

Je 34:5 *But* thou shalt die in peace: and with the burnings of thy fathers, the former kings which were before thee, so shall they burn *odours* for thee; and they will lament thee, *saying,* Ah lord! for I have pronounced the word, saith the LORD.

Je 39:16 Go and speak to Ebed-melech the Ethiopian, saying, Thus saith the LORD of hosts, the God of Israel; Behold, I will bring my words upon

this city for evil, and not for good; and they shall be *accomplished* in that day before thee.

Je 40:3 Now the LORD hath brought *it,* and done according as he hath said: because ye have sinned against the LORD, and have not obeyed his voice, therefore this thing is come upon you.

Je 48:8 And the spoiler shall come upon every city, and no city shall escape: the valley also shall perish, and the plain shall be destroyed, as the LORD hath spoken.

Je 51:12 Set up the standard upon the walls of Babylon, make the watch strong, set up the watchmen, prepare the ambushes: for the LORD hath both devised and done that which he spake against the inhabitants of Babylon.

Lam 2:17 The LORD hath done *that* which he had devised; he hath fulfilled his word that he had commanded in the days of old: he hath thrown down, and hath not pitied: and he hath caused *thine* enemy to rejoice over thee, he hath set up the horn of thine adversaries.

Eze 5:17 So will I send upon you famine and evil beasts, and they shall bereave thee; and pestilence and blood shall pass through thee; and I will bring the sword upon thee. I the LORD have spoken *it.*

Eze 6:10 And they shall know that I *am* the LORD, *and that* I have not said in vain that I would do this evil unto them.

Eze 12:25 For I *am* the LORD: I will speak, and the word that I shall speak shall come to pass; it shall be no more prolonged: for in your days, O rebellious house, will I say the word, and will perform it, saith the Lord GOD.

Eze 17:24 And all the trees of the field shall know that I the exalted the low tree, have dried up the green tree, and have made the dry tree to flourish: I the LORD have brought down the high tree, have exalted the low tree, have dried up the green tree, and have made the dry tree to flourish: I the LORD have spoken and have done *it.*

Eze 21:7 And it shall be, when they say unto thee, Wherefore sighest thou? that thou shalt answer, For the tidings; because it cometh: and every heart shall melt, and all hands shall be feeble, and every spirit shall faint, and all knees shall be weak *as* water: behold, it cometh, and shall be brought to pass, saith the Lord GOD.

Eze 22:14 Can thine heart endure, or can thine hands be strong, in the days that I shall deal with thee? I the LORD have spoken *it,* and will do *it.*

Eze 24:14 I the LORD have spoken *it:* it shall come to pass, and I will do *it;* I will not go back, neither will I spare, neither will I repent; according to thy ways, and according to thy doings, shall they judge thee, saith the LORD God.

Eze 26:5 It shall be *a place for* the spreading of nets in the midst of the sea: for I have spoken *it,* saith the Lord GOD: and it shall become a spoil to the nations.

Eze 26:14 And I will make thee like the top of a rock: thou shalt be *a place* to spread nets upon; thou shalt be built no more: for I the LORD have spoken *it,* saith the Lord GOD.

Eze 28:10 Thou shalt die the deaths of the uncircumcised by the hand of strangers: for I have spoken *it,* saith the Lord GOD.

Eze 39:5 Thou shalt fall upon the open field: for I have spoken *it,* saith the Lord GOD.

Eze 39:8 Behold, it is come, and it is done, saith the Lord GOD; this is the day whereof I have spoken.

Da 4:33 The same hour was the thing fulfilled upon Nebuchadnezzar: and he was driven from men, and did eat grass as oxen, and his body was wet with the dew of heaven, till his hairs were grown like eagles' *feathers,* and his nails like birds' *claws.*

Da 9:12 And he hath confirmed his words, which he spake against us, and against our judges that judged us, by bringing upon us a great evil: for under the whole heaven hath not been done as hath been done upon Jerusalem.

Ho 5:9 Ephraim shall be desolate in the day of rebuke: among the tribes of Israel have I made known that which shall surely be.

Jl 2:11 And the LORD shall utter his voice before his army: for his camp *is* very great: for *he is* strong that executeth his word: for the day of the LORD *is* great and very terrible; and who can abide it?

Jl 3:8 And I will sell your sons and your daughters into the hand of the children of Judah, and they shall sell them to the Sabeans, to a people far off: for the LORD hath spoken *it.*

Obad 18 And the house of Jacob shall be a fire, and the house of Joseph a flame, and the house of Esau for stubble, and they shall kindle in them, and devour them; and there shall not be *any* remaining of the house of Esau; for the LORD hath spoken *it.*

Mi 4:4 But they shall sit every man under his vine and under his fig tree; and none shall make *them* afraid: for the mouth of the LORD of hosts hath spoken *it.*

Hab 2:3 For the vision *is* yet for an appointed time, but at the end it shall speak, and not lie: though it tarry, wait for it; because it will surely come, it will not tarry.

Zec 1:6 But my words and my statutes, which I commanded my servants the prophets, did they not take hold of your fathers? and they returned and said, Like as the LORD of hosts thought to do unto us, according to our ways, and according to our doings, so hath he dealt with us.

Mt 1:22 Now all this was done, that it might be fulfilled which was spoken of the Lord by the prophet, saying,

Mt 2:5 And they said unto him, In Bethlehem of Judaea: for thus it is written by the prophet,

Mt 2:17 Then was fulfilled that which was spoken by Jeremy the prophet, saying,

Mt 5:18 For verily I say unto you, Till heaven and earth pass, one jot or one tittle shall in no wise pass from the law, till all be fulfilled.

Mt 13:14 And in them is fulfilled the prophecy of Esaias, which saith, By hearing ye shall hear, and shall not understand; and seeing ye shall see, and shall not perceive:

Mt 27:9 Then was fulfilled that which was spoken by Jeremy the prophet, saying, And they took the thirty pieces of silver, the price of him that was valued, whom they of the children of Israel did value;

Mk 7:30 And when she was come to her house, she found the devil gone out, and her daughter laid upon the bed.

Mk 11:4 And they went their way, and found the colt tied by the door without in a place where two ways met; and they loose him.

Mk 14:16 And his disciples went forth, and came into the city, and found as he had said unto them: and they made ready the passover.

Mk 16:7 But go your way, tell his disciples and Peter that he goeth before you into Galilee: there shall ye see him, as he said unto you.

Mk 16:20 And they went forth, and preached every where, the Lord working with *them,* and confirming the word with signs following. Amen.

Lu 1:20 And, behold, thou shalt be dumb, and not able to speak, until the day that these things be performed, because thou believest not my words, which shall be fulfilled in their season.

Lu 1:24 And after those days his wife Elisabeth conceived, and hid herself five months, saying,

Lu 1:45 And blessed *is* she that believed: for there shall be a performance of those things which were told her from the Lord.

Lu 1:57 Now Elisabeth's full time came that she should be delivered; and she brought forth a son.

Lu 1:72 To perform the mercy *promised* to our fathers, and to remember his holy covenant;

Lu 2:16 And they came with haste, and found Mary, and Joseph, and the babe lying in a manger.

Lu 2:29 Lord, now lettest thou thy servant depart in peace, according to thy word:

Lu 19:32 And they that were sent went their way, and found even as he had said unto them.

Lu 21:22 For these be the days of vengeance, that all things which are written may be fulfilled.

Lu 21:33 Heaven and earth shall pass away: but my words shall not pass away.

Lu 22:13 And they went, and found as he had said unto them: and they made ready the passover.

Lu 24:46 And said unto them, Thus it is written, and thus it behoved Christ to suffer, and to rise from the dead the third day:

Jn 2:22 When therefore he was risen from the dead, his disciples remembered that he had said this unto them; and they believed the scripture, and the word which Jesus had said.

Jn 4:51 And as he was now going down, his servants met him, and told *him,* saying, Thy son liveth.

Jn 10:35 If he called them gods, unto whom the word of God came, and the scripture cannot be broken;

Jn 12:38 That the saying of Esaias the prophet might be fulfilled, which he spake, Lord, who hath believed our report? and to whom hath the arm of the Lord been revealed?

Jn 19:24 They said therefore among themselves, Let us not rend it, but cast lots for it, whose it shall be: that the scripture might be fulfilled, which saith, They parted my raiment among them, and for my vesture they did cast lots. These things therefore the soldiers did.

Jn 19:36 For these things were done, that the scripture should be fulfilled, A bone of him shall not be broken.

Ac 1:16 Men *and* brethren, this scripture must needs have been fulfilled, which the Holy Ghost by the mouth of David spake before concerning Judas, which was guide to them that took Jesus.

Ac 7:17 But when the time of the promise drew nigh, which God had sworn to Abraham, the people grew and multiplied in Egypt,

Ac 11:28 And there stood up one of them named Agabus, and signified by the spirit that there should be great dearth throughout all the world:

which came to pass in the days of Claudius Caesar.

Ac 13:33 God hath fulfilled the same unto us their children, in that he hath raised up Jesus again; as it is also written in the second psalm, Thou art my Son, this day have I begotten thee.

Ac 25:13 And after certain days king Agrippa and Bernice came unto Caesarea to salute Festus.

Ac 27:44 And the rest, some on boards, and some on *broken pieces* of the ship. And so it came to pass, that they escaped all safe to land.

Ro 1:2 (Which he had promised afore by his prophets in the holy scriptures,)

Ro 4:16 Therefore *it is* of faith, that *it might be* by grace; to the end the promise might be sure to all the seed; not to that only which is of the law, but to that also which is of the faith of Abraham; who is the father of us all,

Ro 9:6 Not as though the word of God hath taken none effect. For they *are* not all Israel, which are of Israel:

Ro 15:8 Now I say that Jesus Christ was a minister of the circumcision for the truth of God, to confirm the promises *made* unto the fathers:

2 Co 1:20 For all the promises of God in him *are* yea, and in him Amen, unto the glory of God by us.

Ga 3:17 And this I say, *that* the covenant, that was confirmed before of God in Christ, the law, which was four hundred and thirty years after, cannot disannul, that it should make the promise of none effect.

Ga 4:28 Now we, brethren, as Isaac was, are the children of promise.

He 2:2 For if the word spoken by angels was stedfast, and every transgression and disobedience received a just recompence of reward;

He 6:15 And so, after he had patiently endured, he obtained the promise.

2 Pe 1:19 We have also a more sure word of prophecy; whereunto ye do well that ye take heed, as unto a light that shineth in a dark place, until the day dawn, and the day star arise in your hearts:

2 Pe 3:9 The Lord is not slack concerning his promise, as some men count slackness; but is longsuffering to us-ward, not willing that any should perish, but that all should come to repentance.

Re 17:17 For God hath put in their hearts to fulfil his will, and to agree, and give their kingdom unto the beast, until the words of God shall be fulfilled.

Re 21:5 And he that sat upon the throne said, Behold, I make all things new. And he said unto me, Write: for these words are true and faithful.

18. Profitable for Instruction

De 4:10 *Specially* the day that thou stoodest before the LORD thy God in Horeb, when the LORD said unto me, Gather me the people together, and I will make them hear my words, that they may learn to fear me all the days that they shall live upon the earth, and *that* they may teach their children.

De 5:5 (I stood between the LORD and you at that time, to shew you the word of the LORD: for ye were afraid by reason of the fire, and went not up into the mount;) saying,

De 11:19 And ye shall teach them your children, speaking of them when thou sittest in thine house, and when thou walkest by the way, when thou liest down, and when thou risest up.

De 31:12 Gather the people together, men, and women, and children, and thy stranger that *is* within thy gates, that they may hear, and that they may learn, and fear the LORD your God, and observe to do all the words of this law:

2 Chr 17:9 And they taught in Judah, and *had* the book of the law of the LORD with them, and went about throughout all the cities of Judah, and taught the people.

Ne 8:13 And on the second day were gathered together the chief of the fathers of all the people, the priests, and the Levites, unto Ezra the scribe, even to understand the words of the law.

Ps 40:9 I have preached righteousness in the great congregation: lo, I have not refrained my lips, O LORD, thou knowest.

Ps 68:11 The LORD gave the word: great *was* the company of those that published *it.*

Is 2:3 And many people shall go and say, Come ye, and let us go up to the mountain of the LORD, to the house of the God of Jacob; and he will teach us of his ways, and we will walk in his paths: for out of Zion shall go forth the law, and the word of the LORD from Jerusalem.

Ac 17:2 And Paul, as his manner was, went in unto them, and three sabbath days reasoned with them out of the scriptures,

Ac 18:11 And he continued *there* a year and six months, teaching the word of God among them.

Ac 18:28 For he mightily convinced the Jews, *and that* publickly, shewing by the scriptures that Jesus was Christ.

19. Ignorance of It Is Foolishness

Is 29:11 And the vision of all is become unto you as the words of a book that is sealed, which *men* deliver to one that is learned, saying, Read this, I pray thee: and he saith, I cannot; for it *is* sealed:

Mt 12:3 But he said unto them, Have ye not read what David did, when he was an hungred, and they that were with him;

Mt 19:4 And he answered and said unto them, Have ye not read, that he which made *them* at the beginning made them male and female,

Mt 21:16 And said unto him, Hearest thou what these say? And Jesus saith unto them, Yea; have ye never read, Out of the mouth of babes and sucklings thou hast perfected praise?

Mt 21:42 Jesus saith unto them, Did ye never read in the scriptures, The stone which the builders rejected, the same is become the head of the corner: this is the Lord's doing, and it is marvellous in our eyes?

Mt 22:29 Jesus answered and said unto them, Ye do err, not knowing the scriptures, nor the power of God.

Mk 2:25 And he said unto them, Have ye never read what David did, when he had need, and was an hungred, he, and they that were with him?

Mk 12:24 And Jesus answering said unto them, Do ye not therefore err, because ye know not the scriptures, neither the power of God?

Lu 6:3 And Jesus answering them said, Have ye not read so much as this, what David did, when himself was an hungred, and they which were with him;

Jn 7:52 They answered and said unto him, Art thou also of Galilee? Search, and look: for out of Galilee ariseth no prophet.

Jn 20:9 For as yet they knew not the scripture, that he must rise again from the dead.

Ac 13:27 For they that dwell at Jerusalem, and their rulers, because they knew him not, nor yet the voices of the prophets which are read every sabbath day, they have fulfilled *them* in condemning *him.*

2 Co 3:15 But even unto this day, when Moses is read, the vail is upon their heart.

1 Ti 1:7 Desiring to be teachers of the law; understanding neither what they say, nor whereof they affirm.

2 Ti 2:18 Who concerning the truth have erred, saying that the resurrection is past already; and overthrow the faith of some.

He 5:12 For when for the time ye ought to be teachers, ye have need that one teach you again which *be* the first principles of the oracles of God; and are become such as have need of milk, and not of strong meat.

20. The Message to Be Delivered

Nu 11:24 And Moses went out, and told the people the words of the LORD, and gathered the seventy men of the elders of the people, and set them round about the tabernacle.

Nu 22:35 And the angel of the LORD said unto Balaam, Go with the men: but only the word that I shall speak unto thee, that thou shalt speak. So Balaam went with the princes of Balak.

Nu 22:38 And Balaam said unto Balak, Lo, I am come unto thee: have I now any power at all to say any thing? the word that God putteth in my mouth, that shall I speak.

Nu 24:13 If Balak would give me his house full of silver and gold, I cannot go beyond the commandment of the LORD, to do *either* good or bad of mine own mind; *but* what the LORD saith, that will I speak?

1 K 21:19 And thou shalt speak unto him, saying, Thus saith the LORD, Hast thou killed, and also taken possession? And thou shalt speak unto him, saying, Thus saith the LORD, In the place where dogs licked the blood of Naboth shall dogs lick thy blood, even thine.

Ps 40:10 I have not hid thy righteousness within my heart; I have declared thy faithfulness and thy salvation: I have not concealed thy lovingkindness and thy truth from the great congregation.

Je 1:7 But the LORD said unto me, Say not, I *am* a child: for thou shalt go to all that I shall send thee, and whatsoever I command thee thou shalt speak.

Je 1:17 Thou therefore gird up thy loins, and arise, and speak unto them all that I command thee: be not dismayed at their faces, lest I confound thee before them.

Je 2:2 Go and cry in the ears of Jerusalem, saying, Thus saith the LORD; I remember thee, the kindness of thy youth, the love of thine espousals, when thou wentest after me in the wilderness, in a land *that was* not sown.

Je 7:27 Therefore thou shalt speak all these words unto them; but they will not hearken to thee: thou shalt also call unto them; but they will not answer thee.

Je 11:2 Hear ye the words of this covenant, and speak unto the men of Judah, and to the inhabitants of Jerusalem;

Je 18:11 Now therefore go to, speak to the men of Judah, and to the inhabitants of Jerusalem, saying, Thus saith the LORD; Behold, I frame evil against you, and devise a device against you: return ye now every one from his evil way, and make your ways and your doings good.

Je 19:2 And go forth unto the valley of the son of Hinnom, which *is* by the entry of the east gate, and proclaim there the words that I shall tell thee,

Je 22:1 Thus saith the LORD; Go down to the house of the king of Judah, and speak there this word,

Je 23:22 But if they had stood in my counsel, and had caused my people to hear my words, then they should have turned them from their evil way, and from the evil of their doings.

Je 26:2 Thus saith the LORD; Stand in the court of the LORD's house, and speak unto all the cities of Judah, which come to worship in the LORD's house, all the words that I command thee to speak unto them; diminish not a word:

Je 50:2 Declare ye among the nations, and publish, and set up a standard; publish, *and* conceal not: say, Babylon is taken, Bel is confounded, Merodach is broken in pieces; her idols are confounded, her images are broken in pieces.

Eze 2:7 And thou shalt speak my words unto them, whether they will hear, or whether they will forbear: for they *are* most rebellious.

Eze 3:17 Son of man, I have made thee a watchman unto the house of Israel: therefore hear the word at my mouth, and give them warning from me.

Eze 3:27 But when I speak with thee, I will open thy mouth, and thou shalt say unto them, Thus saith the Lord GOD; He that heareth, let him hear; and he that forbeareth, let him forbear: for they *are* a rebellious house.

Eze 24:21 Speak unto the house of Israel, Thus saith the Lord GOD; Behold, I will profane my sanctuary, the excellency of your strength, the desire of your eyes, and that which your soul pitieth; and your sons and your daughters whom ye have left shall fall by the sword.

Eze 33:2 Son of man, speak to the children of thy people, and say unto them, When I bring the sword upon a land, if the people of the land take a man of their coasts, and set him for their watchman:

Eze 33:10 Therefore, O thou son of man, speak unto the house of Israel; Thus ye speak, saying, If our transgressions and our sins *be* upon us, and we pine away in them, how should we then live?

Ac 4:29 And now, Lord, behold their threatenings: and grant unto thy servants, that with all boldness they may speak thy word,

Ac 5:20 Go, stand and speak in the temple to the people all the words of this life.

Ac 8:4 Therefore they that were scattered abroad went every where preaching the word.

Ac 18:9 Then spake the Lord to Paul in the night by a vision, Be not afraid, but speak, and hold not thy peace:

Ac 26:22 Having therefore obtained help of God, I continue unto this day, witnessing both to small and great, saying none other things than those which the prophets and Moses did say should come:

Col 1:25 Whereof I am made a minister, according to the dispensation of God which is given to me for you, to fulfill the word of God;

Tit 2:15 These things speak, and exhort, and rebuke with all authority. Let no man despise thee.

1 Pe 4:11 If any man speak, *let him speak* as the oracles of God; if any man minister, *let him do it* as of the ability which God giveth: that God in all things may be glorified through Jesus Christ, to whom be praise and dominion for ever and ever. Amen.

Re 10:11 And he said unto me, Thou must prophesy again before many peoples, and nations, and tongues, and kings.

21. Its Purity

Ps 12:6 The words of the LORD *are* pure words: *as* silver tried in a furnace of earth, purified seven times.

Ps 18:30 *As for* God, his way *is* perfect: the word of the LORD is tried: he *is* a buckler to all those that trust in him.

Ps 19:8 The statutes of the LORD *are* right, rejoicing the heart: the commandment of the LORD *is* pure, enlightening the eyes.

Ps 33:4 For the word of the LORD *is* right; and all his works *are done* in truth.

Ps 119:140 Thy word *is* very pure: therefore thy servant loveth it.

Pr 30:5 Every word of God *is* pure: he *is* a shield unto them that put their trust in him.

Is 39:8 Then said Hezekiah to Isaiah, Good *is* the word of the LORD which thou hast spoken. He said moreover, For there shall be peace and truth in my days.

Is 45:19 I have not spoken in secret, in a dark place of the earth: I said not unto the seed of Jacob, Seek ye me in vain: I the LORD speak righteousness, I declare things that are right.

Col 1:5 For the hope which is laid up for you in heaven, whereof ye heard before in the word of the truth of the gospel;

22. The Law

a. Ceremonial Abolished in Christ

Ac 15:10 Now therefore why tempt ye God, to put a yoke upon the neck of the disciples, which neither our fathers nor we were able to bear?

Ac 15:24 Forasmuch as we have heard, that certain which went out from us have troubled you with words, subverting your souls, saying, *Ye must* be circumcised, and keep the law: to whom we gave no *such* commandment:

Ro 14:3 Let not him that eateth despise him that eateth not; and let not him which eateth not judge him that eateth: for God hath received him.

2 Co 3:11 For if that which is done away *was* glorious, much more that which remaineth *is* glorious.

Ga 2:3 But neither Titus, who was with me, being a Greek, was compelled to be circumcised:

Ga 2:19 For I through the law am dead to the law, that I might live unto God.

Ga 5:6 For in Jesus Christ neither circumcision availeth any thing, nor uncircumcision; but faith which worketh by love.

Ga 6:15 For in Christ Jesus neither circumcision availeth any thing, nor uncircumcision, but a new creature.

Ep 2:15 Having abolished in his flesh the enmity, *even* the law of commandments *contained* in ordinances; for to make in himself of twain one new man, *so* making peace;

Col 2:14 Blotting out the handwriting of ordinances that was against us, which was contrary to us, and took it out of the way, nailing it to his cross;

He 7:18 For there is verily a disannulling of the commandment going before for the weakness and unprofitableness thereof.

He 8:13 In that he saith, A new *covenant,* he hath made the first old. Now that which decayeth and waxeth old *is* ready to vanish away.

He 10:1 For the law having a shadow of good things to come, *and* not the very image of the things, can never with those sacrifices which they offered year by year continually make the comers thereunto perfect.

He 12:27 And this *word,* Yet once more, signifieth the removing of those things that are shaken, as of things that are made, that those things which cannot be shaken may remain.

b. Perfection of the Divine

Ne 9:13 Thou camest down also upon mount Sinai, and spakest with them from heaven, and gavest them right judgments, and true laws, good statutes and commandments:

Ps 19:7 The law of the LORD *is* perfect, converting the soul: the testimony of the LORD *is* sure, making wise the simple.

Ps 119:142 Thy righteousness *is* an everlasting righteousness, and thy law *is* the truth.

Ps 119:172 My tongue shall speak of thy word: for all thy commandments *are* righteousness.

Is 42:21 The LORD is well pleased for his righteousness' sake; he will magnify the law, and make *it* honourable.

Ro 7:7 What shall we say then? *Is* the law sin? God forbid. Nay, I had not known sin, but by the law: for I had not known lust, except the law had said, Thou shalt not covet.

Ro 7:12 Wherefore the law *is* holy, and the commandment holy, and just, and good.

Ro 7:14 For we know that the law is spiritual: but I am carnal, sold under sin.

1 Ti 1:8 But we know that the law *is* good, if a man use it lawfully;

Ja 1:25 But whoso looketh into the perfect law of liberty, and continueth *therein,* he being not a forgetful hearer, but a doer of the work, this man shall be blessed in his deed.

1 Jn 5:3 For this is the love of God, that we keep his commandments: and his commandments are not grievous.

c. Instructions to Obey

De 17:19 And it shall be with him, and he shall read therein all the days of his life: that he may learn to fear the LORD his God, to keep all the words of this law and these statutes, to do them:

Jos 23:6 Be ye therefore very courageous to keep and to do all that is written in the book of the law of Moses, that ye turn not aside therefrom *to* the right hand or *to* the left;

2 K 23:24 Moreover the *workers with* familiar spirits, and the wizards, and the images, and the idols, and all the abominations that were spied in the land of Judah and in Jerusalem, did Josiah put away, that he might perform the words of the law which were written in the book that Hilkiah the priest found in the house of the LORD.

1 Chr 22:12 Only the LORD give thee wisdom and understanding, and give thee charge concerning Israel, that thou mayest keep the law of the LORD thy God.

2 Chr 14:4 And commanded Judah to seek the LORD God of their fathers, and to do the law and the commandment.

2 Chr 25:4 But he slew not their children, but *did as it is* written in the law in the book of Moses, where the LORD commanded, saying, The fathers shall not die for the children, neither shall the children die for the fathers, but every man shall die for his own sin.

2 Chr 35:6 So kill the passover, and sanctify yourselves, and prepare your brethren, that *they* may do according to the word of the LORD by the hand of Moses.

Ezr 10:3 Now therefore let us make a covenant with our God to put away all the wives, and such as are born of them, according to the counsel of my lord, and of those that tremble at the commandment of our God; and let it be done according to the law.

Ps 103:18 To such as keep his covenant, and to those that remember his commandments to do them.

Ps 119:34 Give me understanding, and I shall keep thy law; yea, I shall observe it with *my* whole heart.

Ps 119:44 So shall I keep thy law continually for ever and ever.

Ps 119:55 I have remembered thy name, O LORD, in the night, and have kept thy law.

Pr 7:2 Keep my commandments, and live; and my law as the apple of thine eye.

Pr 28:7 Whoso keepeth the law *is* a wise son: but he that is a companion of riotous *men* shameth his father.

Je 6:16 Thus saith the LORD, Stand ye in the ways, and see, and ask for the old paths, where is the good way, and walk therein, and ye shall find rest for your souls. But they said, We will not walk *therein*.

Je 11:6 Then the LORD said unto me, Proclaim all these words in the cities of Judah, and in the streets of Jerusalem, saying, Hear ye the words of this covenant, and do them.

Je 26:4 And thou shalt say unto them, Thus saith the LORD; If ye will not hearken to me, to walk in my law, which I have set before you,

Eze 44:24 And in controversy they shall stand in judgment; *and* they shall judge it according to my judgments: and they shall keep my laws and they shall hallow my sabbaths.

Mal 4:4 Remember ye the law of Moses my servant, which I commanded unto him in Horeb for all

Israel, *with* the statutes and judgments.

Mt 5:17 Think not that I am come to destroy the law, or the prophets: I am not come to destroy, but to fulfil.

Mt 8:4 And Jesus saith unto him, See thou tell no man; but go thy way, shew thyself to the priest, and offer the gift that Moses commanded, for a testimony unto them.

Mt 19:20 The young man saith unto him, All these things have I kept from my youth up: what lack I yet?

Mt 22:40 On these two commandments hang all the law and the prophets.

Mk 1:44 And saith unto him, See thou say nothing to any man: but go thy way, shew thyself to the priest, and offer for thy cleansing those things which Moses commanded, for a testimony unto them.

Mk 10:20 And he answered and said unto him, Master, all these have I observed from my youth.

Lu 1:59 And it came to pass, that on the eighth day they came to circumcise the child; and they called him Zacharias, after the name of his father.

Lu 2:21 And when eight days were accomplished for the circumcising of the child, his name was called Jesus, which was so named of the angel before he was conceived in the womb.

Lu 2:27 And he came by the Spirit into the temple: and when the parents brought in the child Jesus, to do for him after the custom of the law,

Lu 2:39 And when they had performed all things according to the law of the LORD, they returned into Galilee, to their own city Nazareth.

Lu 5:14 And he charged him to tell no man: but go, and shew thyself to the priest, and offer for thy cleansing, according as Moses commanded, for a testimony unto them.

Lu 10:26 He said unto him, What is written in the law? how readest thou?

Lu 11:28 But he said, Yea rather, blessed *are* they that hear the word of God, and keep it.

Lu 18:21 And he said, All these have I kept from my youth up.

Ro 2:25 For circumcision verily profiteth, if thou keep the law: but if thou be a breaker of the law, thy circumcision is made uncircumcision.

d. In the Heart

Ex 13:9 And it shall be for a sign unto thee upon thine hand, and for a memorial between thine eyes, that the LORD's law may be in thy mouth: for with a strong hand hath the LORD brought thee out of Egypt.

De 30:14 But the word *is* very nigh unto thee, in thy mouth, and in thy heart, that thou mayest do it.

Ps 1:2 But his delight *is* in the law of the LORD; and in his law doth he meditate day and night.

Ps 37:31 The law of his God *is* in his heart; none of his steps shall slide.

Ps 40:8 I delight to do thy will, O my God: yea, thy law *is* within my heart.

Ps 112:1 Praise ye the LORD. Blessed *is* the man *that* feareth the LORD, *that* delighteth greatly in his commandments.

Ps 119:29 Remove from me the way of lying: and grant me thy law graciously.

Ps 119:70 Their heart is as fat as grease; *but* I delight in thy law.

Ps 119:97 O how love I thy law! it *is* my meditation all the day.

Ps 119:165 Great peace have they which love thy law: and nothing shall offend them.

Pr 2:1 My son, if thou wilt receive my words, and hide my commandments with thee;

Pr 3:3 Let not mercy and truth forsake thee: bind them about thy neck; write them upon the table of thine heart:

Pr 4:4 He taught me also, and said unto me, Let thine heart retain my words: keep my commandments, and live.

Pr 4:21 Let them not depart from thine eyes; keep them in the midst of thine heart.

Pr 6:21 Bind them continually upon thine heart, *and* tie them about thy neck.

Pr 7:3 Bind them upon thy fingers, write them upon the table of thine heart.

Je 31:33 But this *shall be* the covenant that I will make with the house of Israel; After those days, saith the LORD, I will put my law in their hearts and will be their God, and they shall be my people.

Je 32:40 And I will make an everlasting covenant with them, that I will not turn away from them, to do them good; but I will put my fear in their hearts, that they shall not depart from me.

Ro 2:15 Which shew the work of the law written in their hearts, their conscience also bearing witness, and *their* thoughts the mean while accusing or else excusing one another;)

Ro 7:22 For I delight in the law of God after the inward man:

2 Co 3:3 *Forasmuch as ye are* manifestly declared to be the epistle of Christ ministered by us, written not with ink, but with the Spirit of the living God; not in tables of stone, but in fleshy tables of the heart.

He 8:10 For this *is* the covenant that I will make with the house of Israel after those days, saith the LORD; I will put my laws into their mind, and write them in their hearts: and I will be to them a God, and they shall be to me a people:

He 10:16 This *is* the covenant that I will make with them after those days, saith the LORD, I will put my laws into their hearts, and in their minds will I write them;

e. Despised

De 28:15 But it shall come to pass, if thou wilt not hearken unto the voice of the LORD thy God, to observe to do all his commandments and his statutes which I command thee this day; that all these curses shall come upon thee, and overtake thee:

1 K 12:31 And he made an house of high places, and made priests of the lowest of the people, which were not of the sons of Levi.

2 K 10:31 But Jehu took no heed to walk in the law of the LORD God of

Israel with all his heart: for he departed not from the sins of Jeroboam, which made Israel to sin.

2 K 17:34 Unto this day they do after the former manners: they fear not the LORD, neither do they after their statutes, or after their ordinances, or after the law and commandment which the LORD commanded the children of Jacob, whom he named Israel;

2 Chr 36:16 But they mocked the messengers of God, and despised his words, and misused his prophets, until the wrath of the LORD arose against his people, till *there was* no remedy.

Ne 9:26 Nevertheless they were disobedient, and rebelled against thee, and cast thy law behind their backs, and slew thy prophets which testified against them to turn them to thee, and they wrought great provocations.

Ne 9:34 Neither have our kings, our princes, our priests, nor our fathers, kept thy law, nor hearkened unto thy commandments and thy testimonies, wherewith thou didst testify against them.

Ps 78:10 They kept not the covenant of God, and refused to walk in his law;

Ps 78:56 Yet they tempted and provoked the most high God, and kept not his testimonies:

Ps 119:53 Horror hath taken hold upon me because of the wicked that forsake thy law.

Ps 119:126 *It is* time for *thee,* LORD, to work: *for* they have made void thy law.

Pr 28:4 They that forsake the law praise the wicked: but such as keep the law contend with them.

Pr 28:9 He that turneth away his ear from hearing the law, even his prayer *shall be* abomination.

Is 5:24 Therefore as the fire devoureth the stubble, and the flame consumeth the chaff, *so* their root shall be as rottenness, and their blossom shall go up as dust: because they have cast away the law of the LORD of hosts, and despised the word of the Holy One of Israel.

Is 30:9 That this *is* a rebellious people, lying children, children *that* will not hear the law of the LORD:

Is 42:24 Who gave Jacob for a spoil, and Israel to the robbers? did not the LORD, he against whom we have sinned? for they would not walk in his ways, neither were they obedient unto his law.

Je 6:19 Hear, O earth: behold, I will bring evil upon this people, *even* the fruit of their thoughts, because they have not hearkened unto my words, nor to my law, but rejected it.

Je 9:13 And the LORD saith, Because they have forsaken my law which I set before them, and have not obeyed my voice, neither walked therein;

Je 16:11 Then shalt thou say unto them, Because your fathers have forsaken me, saith the LORD, and have walked after other gods, and have served them, and have worshipped them, and have forsaken me, and have not kept my law;

Eze 5:6 And she hath changed my judgments into wickedness more than the nations, and my statutes more than the countries that *are* round about her: for they have refused my judgments and my statutes, they have not walked in them.

Eze 20:16 Because they despised my judgments, and walked not in my statutes, but polluted my sabbaths: for their heart went after their idols.

Eze 20:24 Because they had not executed my judgments, but had despised my statutes, eyes were after their fathers' idols.

Da 9:10 Neither have we obeyed the voice of the LORD our God, to walk in his laws, which he set before us by his servants the prophets.

Ho 4:6 My people are destroyed for lack of knowledge: because thou hast rejected knowledge, I will also reject thee, that thou shalt be no priest to me: seeing thou hast forgotten the law of thy God, I will also forget thy children.

Ho 4:10 For they shall eat, and not have enough: they shall commit whoredom, and shall not increase: because they have left off to take heed to the LORD.

Ho 8:1 *Set* the trumpet to thy mouth. *He shall come* as an eagle against the house of the LORD, because they have transgressed my covenant, and trespassed against my law.

Ho 8:12 I have written to him the great things of my law, *but* they were counted as a strange thing.

Am 2:4 Thus saith the LORD; For three transgressions of Judah, and for four, I will not turn away *the punishment* thereof; because they have despised the law of the LORD, and have not kept his commandments, and their lies caused them to err, after the which their fathers have walked:

Hab 1:4 Therefore the law is slacked, and judgment doth never go forth: for the wicked doth compass about the righteous; therefore wrong judgment proceedeth.

Zep 3:4 Her prophets *are* light *and* treacherous persons: her priests have polluted the sanctuary, they have done violence to the law.

Mt 15:6 And honour not his father or his mother, *he shall be free.* Thus have ye made the commandment of God of none effect by your tradition.

Mk 7:9 And he said unto them, Full well ye reject the commandment of God, that ye may keep your own tradition.

Ac 7:53 Who have received the law by the disposition of angels, and have not kept *it.*

Ga 6:13 For neither they themselves who are circumcised keep the law; but desire to have you circumcised, that they may glory in your flesh.

f. Public Readings

De 31:11 When all Israel is come to appear before the LORD thy God in the place which he shall choose, thou shalt read this law before all Israel in their hearing.

Jos 8:35 There was not a word of all that Moses commanded, which Joshua read not before all the congregation of Israel, with the women, and the little ones, and the strangers that were conversant among them.

2 K 22:10 And Shaphan the scribe shewed the king, saying, Hilkiah the priest hath delivered me a book. And Shaphan read it before the king.

2 K 23:2 And the king went up into the house of the LORD, and all the men of Judah and all the inhabitants of Jerusalem with him, and the priests, and the prophets, and all the people, both small and great: and he read in their ears all the words of the book of the covenant which was found in the house of the LORD.

2 Chr 34:18 Then Shaphan the scribe told the king, saying, Hilkiah the priest hath given me a book. And Shaphan read it before the king.

2 Chr 34:30 And the king went up into the house of the LORD, and all the men of Judah, and the inhabitants of Jerusalem, and the priests, and the Levites, and all the people, great and small: and he read in their ears all the words of the book of the covenant that was found in the house of the LORD.

Ne 8:3 And he read therein before the street that *was* before the water gate from the morning until midday, before the men and the women, and those that could understand; and the ears of all the people *were attentive* unto the book of the law.

Ne 8:8 So they read in the book in the law of God distinctly, and gave the sense, and caused *them* to understand the reading.

Ne 8:18 Also day by day, from the first day unto the last day, he read in the book of the law of God. And they kept the feast seven days; and on the eighth day *was* a solemn assembly, according unto the manner.

Ne 9:3 And they stood up in their place, and read in the book of the law of the LORD their God *one* fourth part of the day; and *another* fourth part they confessed, and worshipped the LORD their God.

Ne 13:1 On that day they read in the book of Moses in the audience of the people; and therein was found written, that the Ammonite and the Moabite should not come into the congregation of God for ever;

Je 36:6 Therefore go thou, and read in the roll, which thou hast written from my mouth, the words of the LORD in the ears of the people in the

LORD's house upon the fasting day: and also thou shalt read them in the ears of all Judah that come out of their cities.

Ac 13:15 And after the reading of the law and the prophets the rulers of the synagogue sent unto them, saying, *Ye* men *and* brethren, if ye have any word of exhortation for the people, say on.

Ac 15:21 For Moses of old time hath in every city them that preach him, being read in the synagogues every sabbath day.

g. Its Impartiality

Ex 12:49 One law shall be to him that is homeborn, and unto the stranger that sojourneth among you.

Le 24:22 Ye shall have one manner of law, as well for the stranger, as for one of your own country: for I *am* the LORD your God.

Nu 9:14 And if a stranger shall sojourn among you, and will keep the passover unto the LORD; according to the ordinance of the passover, and according to the manner thereof, so shall he do: ye shall have one ordinance, both for the stranger, and for him that was born in the land.

Nu 15:16 One law and one manner shall be for you, and for the stranger that sojourneth with you.

Nu 15:29 Ye shall have one law for him that sinneth through ignorance, *both for* him that is born among the children of Israel, and for the stranger that sojourneth among them.

Nu 19:10 And he that gathereth the ashes of the heifer shall wash his clothes, and be unclean until the even: and it shall be unto the children of Israel, and unto the stranger that sojourneth among them, for a statute for ever.

23. Its Statutes

a. Described

Ex 15:26 And said, If thou wilt diligently hearken to the voice of the LORD thy God, and wilt do that which is right in his sight, and wilt give ear to his commandments, and keep all his statutes, I will put none of these diseases upon thee, which I have brought upon the Egyptians: for I *am* the LORD that healeth thee.

Ex 18:16 When they have a matter, they come unto me; and I judge between one and another, and I do make *them* know the statutes of God, and his laws.

Le 10:11 And that ye may teach the children of Israel all the statutes which the LORD hath spoken unto them by the hand of Moses.

Le 18:5 Ye shall therefore keep my statutes, and my judgments: which if a man do, he shall live in them: I *am* the LORD.

Le 18:26 Ye shall therefore keep my statutes and my judgments, and shall not commit *any* of these abominations; *neither* any of your own nation, nor any stranger that sojourneth among you:

Le 19:37 Therefore shall ye observe all my statutes, and all my judgments, and do them: I *am* the LORD.

Le 20:8 And ye shall keep my statutes, and do them: I *am* the LORD which sanctify you.

Le 25:18 Wherefore ye shall do my statutes, and keep my judgments, and do them; and ye shall dwell in the land in safety.

Le 26:3 If ye walk in my statutes, and keep my commandments, and do them;

Le 26:46 These *are* the statutes and judgments and laws, which the LORD made between him and the children of Israel in mount Sinai by the hand of Moses.

Nu 27:11 And if his father have no brethren, then ye shall give his inheritance unto his kinsman that is next to him of his family, and he shall possess it: and it shall be unto the children of Israel a statute of judgment, as the LORD commanded Moses.

Nu 30:16 These *are* the statutes, which the LORD commanded Moses, between a man and his wife, between the father and his daughter, *being yet* in her youth in her father's house.

De 4:1 Now therefore hearken, O Israel, unto the statutes and unto the judgments, which I teach you, for to do *them*, that ye may live, and go in and possess the land which the LORD God of your fathers giveth you.

De 4:5 Behold, I have taught you statutes and judgments, even as the LORD my God commanded me, that ye should do so in the land whither ye go to possess it.

De 4:45 These *are* the testimonies, and the statutes, and the judgments, which Moses spake unto the children of Israel, after they came forth out of Egypt,

De 5:1 And Moses called all Israel, and said unto them, Hear, O Israel, the statutes and judgments which I speak in your ears this day, that ye may learn them, and keep, and do them.

De 5:31 But as for thee, stand thou here by me, and I will speak unto thee all the commandments, and the statutes, and the judgments, which thou shalt teach them, that they may do *them* in the land which I give them to possess it.

De 6:1 Now these *are* the commandments, the statutes, and the judgments, which the LORD your God commanded to teach you, that ye might do *them* in the land whither ye go to possess it:

De 6:17 Ye shall diligently keep the commandments of the LORD your God, and his testimonies, and his statutes, which he hath commanded thee.

De 6:24 And the LORD commanded us to do all these statutes, to fear the LORD our God, for our good always, that he might preserve us alive, as *it is* at this day.

De 7:11 Thou shalt therefore keep the commandments, and the statutes, and the judgments, which I command thee this day, to do them.

De 8:11 Beware that thou forget not the LORD thy God, in not keeping his commandments, and his judgments, and his statutes, which I command thee this day:

De 10:13 To keep the commandments of the LORD, and his statutes, which I command thee this day for thy good?

De 11:1 Therefore thou shalt love the LORD thy God, and keep his charge, and his statutes, and his judgments, and his commandments, alway.

De 11:32 And ye shall observe to do all the statutes and judgments which I set before you this day.

De 16:12 And thou shalt remember that thou wast a bondman in Egypt: and thou shalt observe and do these statutes.

De 26:16 This day the LORD thy God hath commanded thee to do these statutes and judgments: thou shalt therefore keep and do them with all thine heart, and with all thy soul.

De 27:10 Thou shalt therefore obey the voice of the LORD thy God, and do his commandments and his statutes, which I command thee this day.

De 30:10 If thou shalt hearken unto the voice of the LORD thy God, to keep his commandments and his statutes which are written in this book of the law, *and* if thou turn unto the LORD thy God with all thine heart, and with all thy soul.

Jos 24:25 So Joshua made a covenant with the people that day, and set them a statute and an ordinance in Shechem.

2 S 22:23 For all his judgments *were* before me: and *as for* his statutes, I did not depart from them.

1 K 2:3 And keep the charge of the LORD thy God, to walk in his ways, to keep his statutes, and his commandments, and his judgments, and his testimonies, as it is written in the law of Moses, that thou mayest prosper in all that thou doest, and whithersoever thou turnest thyself:

1 K 3:14 And if thou wilt walk in my ways, to keep my statutes and my commandments, as thy father David did walk, then I will lengthen thy days.

1 K 6:12 *Concerning* this house which thou art in building, if thou wilt walk in my statutes, and execute my judgments, and keep all my commandments to walk in them; then will I perform my word with thee, which I spake unto David thy father:

1 K 8:58 That he may incline our hearts unto him, to walk in all his ways, and to keep his commandments, and his statutes, and his judgments, which he commanded our fathers.

1 K 9:4 And if thou wilt walk before me, as David thy father walked, in integrity of heart, and in uprightness, to do according to all that I have commanded thee, *and* wilt keep my statutes and my judgments:

1 K 11:38 And it shall be, if thou wilt hearken unto all that I command thee, and wilt walk in my ways, and do *that is* right in my sight, to keep my statutes and my commandments, as David my servant did; that I will be with thee, and build thee a sure house, as I built for David, and will give Israel unto thee.

2 K 17:37 And the statutes, and the ordinances, and the law, and the commandment, which he wrote for you, ye shall observe to do for evermore; and ye shall not fear other gods.

1 Chr 29:19 And give unto Solomon my son a perfect heart, to keep thy commandments, thy testimonies, and thy statutes, and to do all *these things,* and to build the palace, for the which I have made provision.

2 Chr 7:17 And as for thee, if thou wilt walk before me, as David thy father walked, and do according to all that I have commanded thee, and shalt observe my statutes and my judgments;

2 Chr 33:8 Neither will I any more remove the foot of Israel from out of the land which I have appointed for your fathers; so that they will take heed to do all that I have commanded them, according to the whole law and the statutes and the ordinances by the hand of Moses.

Ezr 7:11 Now this *is* the copy of the letter that the king Artaxerxes gave unto Ezra the priest, the scribe, *even* a scribe of the words of the commandments of the LORD, and of his statutes to Israel.

Ne 9:14 And madest known unto them thy holy sabbath, and commandedst them precepts, statutes, and laws, by the hand of Moses thy servant:

Ne 10:29 They clave to their brethren, their nobles, and entered into a curse, and into an oath, to walk in God's law, which was given by Moses the servant of God, and to observe and do all the commandments of the LORD our LORD, and his judgments and his statutes;

Ps 18:22 For all his judgments *were* before me, and I did not put away his statutes from me.

Ps 19:8 The statutes of the LORD *are* right, rejoicing the heart: the commandment of the LORD *is* pure, enlightening the eyes.

Ps 81:4 For this *was* a statute for Israel, *and* a law of the God of Jacob.

Ps 105:45 That they might observe his statutes, and keep his laws. Praise ye the LORD.

Ps 119:5 O that my ways were directed to keep thy statutes!

Ps 119:12 Blessed *art* thou, O LORD: teach me thy statutes.

Ps 119:33 Teach me, O LORD, the way of thy statutes; and I shall keep it *unto* the end.

Ps 119:54 Thy statutes have been my songs in the house of my pilgrimage.

Ps 119:68 Thou *art* good, and doest good; teach me thy statutes.

Ps 119:135 Make thy face to shine upon thy servant; and teach me thy statutes.

Ps 119:145 I cried with *my* whole heart; hear me, O LORD: I will keep thy statutes.

Ps 147:19 He sheweth his word unto Jacob, his statutes and his judgments unto Israel.

Eze 20:11 And I gave them my statutes, and shewed them my judgments, which *if* a man do, he shall even live in them.

Mal 4:4 Remember ye the law of Moses my servant, which I commanded unto him in Horeb for all Israel, *with* the statutes and judgments.

Ro 10:5 For Moses describeth the righteousness which is of the law, That the man which doeth those things shall live by them.

b. Perpetual

Ex 12:17 And ye shall observe *the feast of* unleavened bread; for in this selfsame day have I brought your armies out of the land of Egypt: therefore shall ye observe this day in your generations by an ordinance for ever.

Ex 12:24 And ye shall observe this thing for an ordinance to thee and to thy sons for ever.

Ex 27:21 In the tabernacle of the congregation without the vail, which *is* before the testimony, Aaron and his sons shall order it from evening to morning before the LORD: *it shall be* a statute for ever unto their generations on the behalf of the children of Israel.

Ex 28:43 And they shall be upon Aaron, and upon his sons, when they come in unto the tabernacle of the congregation, or when they come near unto the altar to minister in the holy *place;* that they bear not iniquity, and die: *it shall be* a statute for ever unto him and his seed after him.

Ex 29:9 And thou shalt gird them with girdles, Aaron and his sons, and put the bonnets on them: and the priest's office shall be theirs for a perpetual statute: and thou shalt consecrate Aaron and his sons.

Ex 29:28 And it shall be Aaron's and his sons' by a statute for ever from the children of Israel: for it *is* an heave offering: and it shall be an heave offering from the children of Israel of the sacrifice of their peace offerings, *even* their heave offering unto the LORD.

Ex 30:8 And when Aaron lighteth the lamps at even, he shall burn incense upon it, a perpetual incense before the LORD throughout your generations.

Ex 30:21 So they shall wash their hands and their feet, that they die not: and it shall be a statute for ever to them, *even* to him and to his seed throughout their generations.

Le 3:17 *It shall be* a perpetual statute for your generations throughout all your dwellings, that ye eat neither fat nor blood.

Le 6:18 All the males among the children of Aaron shall eat of it. *It shall be* a statute for ever in your generations concerning the offerings of the LORD made by fire: every one that toucheth them shall be holy.

Le 6:22 And the priest of his sons that is anointed in his stead shall offer it: *it is* a statute for ever unto the LORD, it shall be wholly burnt.

Le 7:34 For the wave breast and the heave shoulder have I taken of the children of Israel from off the sacrifices of their peace offerings, and have given them unto Aaron the priest and unto his sons by a statute for ever from among the children of Israel.

Le 10:9 Do not drink wine nor strong drink, thou, nor thy sons with thee, when ye go into the tabernacle of the congregation, lest ye die: *it shall be* a statute for ever throughout your generations:

Le 10:15 The heave shoulder and the wave breast shall they bring with the offerings made by fire of the fat, to wave *it for* a wave offering before the LORD; and it shall be thine, and thy sons' with thee, by a statute for ever; as the LORD hath commanded.

Le 16:29 And *this* shall be a statute for ever unto you: *that* in the seventh month, on the tenth *day* of the month, ye shall afflict your souls, and do no work at all, *whether it be* one of your own country, or a stranger that sojourneth among you:

Le 16:34 And this shall be an everlasting statute unto you, to make an atonement for the children of Israel for all their sins once a year. And he did as the LORD commanded Moses.

Le 17:7 And they shall no more offer their sacrifices unto devils, after whom they have gone a whoring. This shall be a statute for ever unto them throughout their generations.

Le 23:14 And ye shall eat neither bread, nor parched corn, nor green ears, until the selfsame day that ye have brought an offering unto your God: *it shall be* a statute for ever throughout your generations in all your dwellings.

Le 23:21 And ye shall proclaim on the selfsame day, *that* it may be an holy convocation unto you: ye shall do no servile work *therein: it shall be* a statute for ever in all your dwellings throughout your generations.

Le 23:31 Ye shall do no manner of work: *it shall be* a statute for ever throughout your generations in all your dwellings.

Le 23:41 And ye shall keep it a feast unto the LORD seven days in the year. *It shall be* a statute for ever in your generations: ye shall celebrate it in the seventh month.

Le 24:3 Without the vail of the testimony, in the tabernacle of the congregation, shall Aaron order it from the evening unto the morning before the LORD continually: *it shall be* a statute for ever in your generations.

Le 24:9 And it shall be Aaron's and his sons'; and they shall eat it in the holy place: for it *is* most perpetual statute.

Nu 18:11 And this *is* thine; the heave offering of their gift, with all the wave offerings of the children of Israel: I have given them unto thee, and to thy sons and to thy daughters with thee, by a statute for ever: every one that is clean in thy house shall eat of it.

Nu 18:19 All the heave offerings of the holy things, which the children of Israel offer unto the LORD, have I given thee, and thy sons and thy daughters with thee, by a statute for ever: it is a covenant of salt for ever before the LORD unto thee and to thy seed with thee.

Nu 18:23 But the Levites shall do the service of the tabernacle of the congregation, and they shall bear their iniquity: *it shall be* a statute for ever throughout your generations, that among the children of Israel they have no inheritance.

Nu 19:10 And he that gathereth the ashes of the heifer shall wash his clothes, and be unclean until the even: and it shall be unto the children of Israel, and unto the stranger that sojourneth among them, for a statute for ever.

Nu 19:21 And it shall be a perpetual statute unto them, that he that sprinkleth the water of separation shall wash his clothes; and he that

toucheth the water of separation shall be unclean until even.

Nu 35:29 So these *things* shall be for a statute of judgment unto you throughout your generations in all your dwellings.

24. Its Commandments

a. Described

Ex 15:26 And said, If thou wilt diligently hearken to the voice of the LORD thy God, and wilt do that which is right in his sight, and wilt give ear to his commandments, and keep all his statutes, I will put none of these diseases upon thee, which I have brought upon the Egyptians: for I *am* the LORD that healeth thee.

Ex 20:1 And God spake all these words, saying,

Ex 24:12 And the LORD said unto Moses, Come up to me into the mount, and be there: and I will give thee tables of stone, and a law, and commandments which I have written; that thou mayest teach them.

Ex 35:1 And Moses gathered all the congregation of the children of Israel together, and said unto them, These *are* the words which the LORD hath commanded, that *ye* should do them.

Le 4:2 Speak unto the children of Israel, saying, If a soul shall sin through ignorance against any of the commandments of the LORD *concerning things* which ought not to be done, and shall do against any of them:

Le 4:13 And if the whole congregation of Israel sin through ignorance, and the thing be hid from the eyes of the assembly, and they have done *somewhat against* any of the commandments of the LORD *concerning things* which should not be done, and are guilty;

Le 4:22 When a ruler hath sinned, and done *somewhat* through ignorance *against* any of the commandments of the LORD his God *concerning things* which should not be done, and is guilty;

Le 4:27 And if any one of the common people sin through ignorance, while he doeth *somewhat against* any of the commandments of the LORD *concerning things* which ought not to be done, and be guilty;

Le 26:46 These *are* the statutes and judgments and laws, which the LORD made between him and the children of Israel in mount Sinai by the hand of Moses.

Le 27:34 These *are* the commandments, which the LORD commanded Moses for the children of Israel in mount Sinai.

Nu 15:22 And if ye have erred, and not observed all these commandments, which the LORD hath spoken unto Moses,

Nu 36:13 These *are* the commandments and the judgments, which the LORD commanded by the hand of Moses unto the children of Israel in the plains of Moab by Jordan *near* Jericho.

De 5:31 But as for thee, stand thou here by me, and I will speak unto thee all the commandments, and the statutes, and the judgments, which thou shalt teach them, that they may do *them* in the land which I give them to possess it.

De 6:1 Now these *are* the commandments, the statutes, and the judgments, which the LORD your God commanded to teach you, that ye might do *them* in the land whither ye go to possess it:

De 6:6 And these words, which I command thee this day, shall be in thine heart:

De 11:8 Therefore shall ye keep all the commandments which I command you this day, that ye may be strong, and go in and possess the land, whither ye go to possess it;

De 11:27 A blessing, if ye obey the commandments of the LORD your God, which I command you this day:

De 26:13 Then thou shalt say before the LORD thy God, I have brought away the hallowed things out of *mine* house, and also have given them unto the Levite, and unto the stranger, to the fatherless, and to the widow, according to all thy commandments which thou hast commanded me: I

have not transgressed thy commandments, neither have I forgotten *them:*

De 27:8 And thou shalt write upon the stones all the words of this law very plainly.

De 30:8 And thou shalt return and obey the voice of the LORD, and do all his commandments which I command thee this day.

Jud 3:4 And they were to prove Israel by them, to know whether they would hearken unto the commandments of the LORD, which he commanded their fathers by the hand of Moses.

Ne 9:13 Thou camest down also upon mount Sinai, and spakest with them from heaven, and gavest them right judgments, and true laws, good statutes and commandments:

Ps 19:8 The statutes of the LORD *are* right, rejoicing the heart: the commandment of the LORD *is* pure, enlightening the eyes.

Ps 103:20 Bless the LORD, ye his angels, that excel in strength, that do his commandments, hearkening unto the voice of his word.

Ps 119:6 Then shall I not be ashamed, when I have respect unto all thy commandments.

Ps 119:96 I have seen an end of all perfection: *but* thy commandment *is* exceeding broad.

Ps 119:151 Thou *art* near, O LORD; and all thy commandments *are* truth.

Ps 147:15 He sendeth forth his commandment *upon* earth: his word runneth very swiftly.

Is 48:18 O that thou hadst hearkened to my commandments! then had thy peace been as a river, and thy righteousness as the waves of the sea:

Ho 8:12 I have written to him the great things of my law, *but* they were counted as a strange thing.

Mt 15:3 But he answered and said unto them, Why do ye also transgress the commandment of God by your tradition?

Mt 22:38 This is the first and great commandment.

Mk 12:28 And one of the scribes came, and having heard them reasoning together, and perceiving that he had answered them well, asked him,

Which is the first commandment of all?

Ro 7:12 Wherefore the law *is* holy, and the commandment holy, and just, and good.

1 Co 7:19 Circumcision is nothing, and uncircumcision is nothing, but the keeping of the commandments of God.

1 Jn 2:7 Brethren, I write no new commandment unto you, but an old commandment which ye had from the beginning. The old commandment is the word which ye have heard from the beginning.

1 Jn 5:3 For this is the love of God, that we keep his commandments: and his commandments are not grievous.

2 Jn 4 I rejoiced greatly that I found of thy children walking in truth, as we have received a commandment from the Father.

b. To Be Kept

Ex 20:6 And shewing mercy unto thousands of them that love me, and keep my commandments.

Le 18:30 Therefore shall ye keep mine ordinance, that *ye* commit not *any one* of these abominable customs, which were committed before you, and that ye defile not yourselves therein: I *am* the LORD your God.

Le 19:19 Ye shall keep my statutes. Thou shalt not let thy cattle gender with a diverse kind: thou shalt not sow thy field with mingled seed: neither shall a garment mingled of linen and woollen come upon thee.

Le 20:8 And ye shall keep my statutes, and do them: I *am* the LORD which sanctify you.

Le 20:22 Ye shall therefore keep all my statutes, and all my judgments, and do them: that the land, whither I bring you to dwell therein, spue you not out.

Le 22:31 Therefore shall ye keep my commandments, and do them: I *am* the LORD.

Le 26:3 If ye walk in my statutes, and keep my commandments, and do them;

Nu 15:40 That ye may remember, and do all my commandments, and be holy unto your God.

De 4:2 Ye shall not add unto the word which I command you, neither shall ye diminish *ought* from it, that ye may keep the commandments of the LORD your God which I command you.

De 4:6 Keep therefore and do *them;* for this *is* your wisdom and your understanding in the sight of the nations, which shall hear all these statutes, and say, Surely this great nation *is* a wise and understanding people.

De 4:40 Thou shalt keep therefore his statutes, and his commandments, which I command thee this day, that it may go well with thee, and with thy children after thee, and that thou mayest prolong *thy* days upon the earth, which the LORD thy God giveth thee, for ever.

De 5:29 O that there were such an heart in them, that they would fear me, and keep all my commandments always, that it might be well with them, and with their children for ever!

De 6:2 That thou mightest fear the LORD thy God, to keep all his statutes and his commandments, which I command thee, thou, and thy son, and thy son's son, all the days of thy life; and that thy days may be prolonged.

De 6:17 Ye shall diligently keep the commandments of the LORD your God, and his testimonies, and his statutes, which he hath commanded thee.

De 7:11 Thou shalt therefore keep the commandments, and the statutes, and the judgments, which I command thee this day, to do them.

De 8:1 All the commandments which I command thee this day shall ye observe to do, that ye may live, and multiply, and go in and possess the land which the LORD sware unto your fathers.

De 8:6 Therefore thou shalt keep the commandments of the LORD thy God, to walk in his ways, and to fear him.

De 10:13 To keep the commandments of the LORD, and his statutes, which I command thee this day for thy good?

De 11:1 Therefore thou shalt love the Lord thy God, and keep his charge, and his statutes, and his judgments, and his commandments, alway.

De 11:22 For if ye shall diligently keep all these commandments which I command you, to do them, to love the Lord your God, to walk in all his ways, and to cleave unto him;

De 13:4 Ye shall walk after the Lord your God, and fear him, and keep his commandments, and obey his voice, and ye shall serve him and cleave unto him, and cleave unto him.

De 13:18 When thou shalt hearken to the voice of the Lord thy God, to keep all his commandments which I command thee this day, to do *that which is* right in the eyes of the Lord thy God.

De 15:5 Only if thou carefully hearken unto the voice of the Lord thy God, to observe to do all these commandments which I command thee this day.

De 19:9 If thou shalt keep all these commandments to do them, which I command thee this day, to love the Lord thy God, and to walk ever in his ways; then shalt thou add three cities more for thee, beside these three:

De 26:16 This day the Lord thy God hath commanded thee to do these statutes and judgments: thou shalt therefore keep and do them with all thine heart, and with all thy soul.

De 26:18 And the Lord hath avouched thee this day to be his peculiar people, as he hath promised thee, and that *thou* shouldest keep all his commandments;

De 27:1 And Moses with the elders of Israel commanded the people, saying, Keep all the commandments which I command you this day.

De 28:9 The Lord shall establish thee an holy people unto himself, as he hath sworn unto thee, if thou shalt keep the commandments of the Lord thy God, and walk in his ways.

De 30:10 If thou shalt hearken unto the voice of the Lord thy God, to keep his commandments and his statutes which are written in this book of the law, *and* if thou turn unto the Lord thy God with all thine heart, and with all thy soul.

De 30:16 In that I command thee this day to love the Lord thy God, to walk in his ways, and to keep his commandments and his statutes and his judgments, that thou mayest live and multiply: and the Lord thy God shall bless thee in the land whither thou goest to possess it.

Jos 1:7 Only be thou strong and very courageous, that thou mayest observe to do according to all the law, which Moses my servant commanded thee: turn not from it *to* the right hand or *to* the left, that thou mayest prosper whithersoever thou goest.

Jos 22:5 But take diligent heed to do the commandment and the law, which Moses the servant of the Lord charged you, to love the Lord your God, and to walk in all his ways, and to keep his commandments, and to cleave unto him, and to serve him with all your heart and with all your soul.

1 K 2:3 And keep the charge of the Lord thy God, to walk in his ways, to keep his statutes, and his commandments, and his judgments, and his testimonies, as it is written in the law of Moses, that thou mayest prosper in all that thou doest, and whithersoever thou turnest thyself:

1 K 6:12 *Concerning* this house which thou art in building, if thou wilt walk in my statutes, and execute my judgments, and keep all my commandments to walk in them; then will I perform my word with thee, which I spoke unto David thy father:

1 K 8:58 That he may incline our hearts unto him, to walk in all his ways, and to keep his commandments, and his statutes, and his judgments, which he commanded our fathers.

1 K 11:38 And it shall be, if thou wilt hearken unto all that I command thee, and wilt walk in my ways, and do *that is* right in my sight, to keep my statutes and my commandments, as David my servant did; that I will be with thee, and build thee a sure house, as I built for David, and will give Israel unto thee.

2 K 17:13 Yet the LORD testified against Israel, and against Judah, by all the prophets, *and by* all the seers, saying, Turn ye from your evil ways, and keep my commandments *and* my statutes, according to all the law which I commanded your fathers, and which I sent to you by my servants the prophets.

2 K 17:37 And the statutes, and the ordinances, and the law, and the commandment, which he wrote for you, ye shall observe to do for evermore; and ye shall not fear other gods.

2 K 21:8 Neither will I make the feet of Israel move any more out of the land which I gave their fathers; only if they will observe to do according to all that I have commanded them, and according to all the law that my servant Moses commanded them.

1 Chr 16:15 Be ye mindful always of his covenant; the word *which* he commanded to a thousand generations;

1 Chr 28:8 Now therefore in the sight of all Israel the congregation of the LORD, and in the audience of our God, keep and seek for all the commandments of the LORD your God: that ye may possess this good land, and leave *it* for an inheritance for your children after you for ever.

1 Chr 29:19 And give unto Solomon my son a perfect heart, to keep thy commandments, thy testimonies, and thy statutes, and to do all *these things,* and to build the palace, for the which I have made provision.

2 Chr 7:17 And as for thee, if thou wilt walk before me, as David thy father walked, and do according to all that I have commanded thee, and shalt observe my statutes and my judgments;

2 Chr 34:31 And the king stood in his place, and made a covenant before the LORD, to walk after the LORD, and to keep his commandments, and his testimonies, and his statutes, with all his heart, and with all his soul, to perform the words of the covenant which are written in this book.

Ps 19:11 Moreover by them is thy servant warned: *and* in keeping of them *there is* great reward.

Ps 25:10 All the paths of the LORD *are* mercy and truth unto such as keep his covenant and his testimonies.

Ps 78:7 That they might set their hope in God, and not forget the works of God, but keep his commandments:

Ps 105:45 That they might observe his statutes, and keep his laws. Praise ye the LORD.

Ps 119:4 Thou hast commanded *us* to keep thy precepts diligently.

Ps 119:101 I have refrained my feet from every evil way, that I might keep thy word.

Pr 3:1 My son, forget not my law; but let thine heart keep my commandments:

Pr 4:4 He taught me also, and said unto me, Let thine heart retain my words: Keep my commandments, and live.

Pr 7:2 Keep my commandments, and live; and my law as the apple of thine eye.

Pr 13:13 Whoso despiseth the word shall be destroyed: but he that feareth the commandment shall be rewarded.

Pr 19:16 He that keepeth the commandment keepeth his own soul; *but* he that despiseth his ways shall die.

Ec 8:5 Whoso keepeth the commandment shall feel no evil thing: and a wise man's heart discerneth both time and judgment.

Ec 12:13 Let us hear the conclusion of the whole matter: Fear God, and keep his commandments: for this *is* the whole *duty* of man.

Je 6:16 Thus saith the LORD, Stand ye in the ways, and see, and ask for the old paths, where is the good way, and walk therein, and ye shall find rest for your souls. But they said, We will not walk *therein.*

Je 17:22 Neither carry forth a burden out of your houses on the sabbath day, neither do ye any work, but hallow ye the sabbath day, as I commanded your fathers.

Eze 20:19 I *am* the LORD your God; walk in my statutes, and keep my judgments, and do them;

Eze 43:11 And if they be ashamed of all that they have done, shew them the form of the house, and the fashion thereof, and the goings out thereof, and the comings in thereof, and all the forms thereof, and all the ordinances thereof, and all the forms thereof, and all the laws thereof: and write *it* in their sight, that they may keep the whole form thereof, and all the ordinances thereof, and do them.

Eze 44:24 And in controversy they shall stand in judgment; *and* they shall judge it according to my judgments: and they shall keep my laws and my statutes in all mine assemblies; and they shall hallow my sabbaths.

Mt 19:17 And he said unto him, Why callest thou me good? *there is* none good but one, *that is,* God: but if thou wilt enter into life, keep the commandments.

Mk 10:19 Thou knowest the commandments, Do not commit adultery, Do not kill, Do not steal, Do not bear false witness, Defraud not, Honour thy father and mother.

1 Ti 6:14 That thou keep *this* commandment without spot, unrebukeable, until the appearing of our LORD Jesus Christ:

1 Jn 5:3 For this is the love of God, that we keep his commandments: and his commandments are not grievous.

2 Jn 6 And this is love, that we walk after his commandments. This is the commandment, That, as ye have heard from the beginning, ye should walk in it.

Re 14:12 Here is the patience of the saints: here *are* they that keep the commandments of God, and the faith of Jesus.

See **INSPIRATION, KNOWLEDGE, LAW, TRUTH, WISDOM**

WORDS OF CHRIST

1. *Characteristics*

IMPERISHABLE

Mk 13:31 Heaven and earth shall pass away: but my words shall not pass away.

GRACIOUS

Lu 4:22 And all bare him witness, and wondered at the gracious words which proceeded out of his mouth. And they said, Is not this Joseph's son?

MIGHTY

Lu 4:32 And they were astonished at his doctrine: for his word was with power.

SPIRITUAL

Jn 6:63 It is the spirit that quickeneth; the flesh profiteth nothing: the words that I speak unto you, *they* are spirit, and *they* are life.

LIFE-GIVING

Jn 6:68 Then Simon Peter answered him, Lord, to whom shall we go? thou hast the words of eternal life.

INCOMPARABLE

Jn 7:46 The officers answered, Never man spake like this man.

WORDS OF JUDGMENT

Jn 12:48 He that rejecteth me, and receiveth not my words, hath one that judgeth him: the word that I have spoken, the same shall judge him in the last day.

DIVINE

Jn 14:24 He that loveth me not keepeth not my sayings: and the word which ye hear is not mine, but the Father's which sent me.

1 Ti 6:3 If any man teach otherwise, and consent not to wholesome words, *even* the words of our Lord Jesus Christ, and to the doctrine which is according to godliness;

2. *Promises*

ETERNAL LIFE

Jn 8:51 Verily, verily, I say unto you, If a man keep my saying, he shall never see death.

THE ABIDING COMFORTER

Jn 14:15–16 If ye love me, keep my commandments.

And I will pray the Father, and he shall give you another Comforter, that he may abide with you for ever;

DIVINE FELLOWSHIP

Jn 14:23 Jesus answered and said unto him, If a man love me, he will keep my words: and my Father will love him, and we will come unto him, and make our abode with him.

DIVINE DISCLOSURE

Jn 17:6 I have manifested thy name unto the men which thou gavest me out of the world: thine they were, and thou gavest them me; and they have kept thy word.

ASSURANCE

1 Jn 2:3 And hereby we do know that we know him, if we keep his commandments.

ACCESS TO GOD

Re 3:8 I know thy works: behold, I have set before thee an open door, and no man can shut it: for thou hast a little strength, and hast kept my word, and hast not denied my name.

3. Remembered

Lu 24:8-9 And they remembered his words,

And returned from the sepulchre, and told all these things unto the eleven, and to all the rest.

Jn 2:22 When therefore he was risen from the dead, his disciples remembered that he had said this unto them; and they believed the scripture, and the word which Jesus had said.

Jn 12:16 These things understood not his disciples at the first: but when Jesus was glorified, then remembered they that these things were written of him, and *that* they had done these things unto him.

Jn 14:26 But the Comforter, *which is* the Holy Ghost, whom the Father will send in my name, he shall teach you all things, and bring all things to your remembrance, whatsoever I have said unto you.

Jn 16:4 But these things have I told you, that when the time shall come,

ye may remember that I told you of them. And these things I said not unto you at the beginning, because I was with you.

2 Pe 3:2 That ye may be mindful of the words which were spoken before by the holy prophets, and of the commandment of us the apostles of the Lord and Saviour:

See **CHRIST**

WORDS OF MEN

1. Evil

VAIN

Jb 16:3 Shall vain words have an end? or what emboldeneth thee that thou answerest?

IRRITATING

Pr 15:1 A soft answer turneth away wrath: but grievous words stir up anger.

HASTY

Pr 29:20 Seest thou a man *that is* hasty in his words? *there is* more hope of a fool than of him.

IRREVERENT

Mal 3:13 Your words have been stout against me, saith the LORD. Yet ye say, What have we spoken *so much* against thee?

ENTICING

Col 2:4 And this I say, lest any man should beguile you with enticing words.

FLATTERING

1 Th 2:5 For neither at any time used we flattering words, as ye know, nor a cloke of covetousness; God *is* witness:

INSINCERE

2 Pe 2:3 And through covetousness shall they with feigned words make merchandise of you: whose judgment now of a long time lingereth not, and their damnation slumbereth not.

PROUD

2 Pe 2:18 For when they speak great swelling *words* of vanity, they allure through the lusts of the flesh, *through much* wantonness, those that were clean escaped from them who live in error.

MALICIOUS

3 Jn 10 Wherefore, if I come, I will remember his deeds which he doeth, prating against us with malicious words: and not content therewith, neither doth he himself receive the brethren, and forbiddeth them that would, and casteth *them* out of the church.

2. Wise

FORCIBLE

Jb 6:25 How forcible are right words! but what doth your arguing reprove?
Pr 15:23 A man hath joy by the answer of his mouth: and a word *spoken* in due season, how good *is it!*

PLEASANT

Pr 16:24 Pleasant words *are as* an honeycomb, sweet to the soul, and health to the bones.

APPROPRIATE

Pr 25:11 A word fitly spoken *is like* apples of gold in pictures of silver.
Ec 9:17 The words of wise *men are* heard in quiet more than the cry of him that ruleth among fools.

GRACIOUS

Ec 10:12 The words of a wise man's mouth *are* gracious; but the lips of a fool will swallow up himself.

INSPIRING AND UNFORGETABLE

Ec 12:11 The words of the wise *are* as goads, and as nails fastened by the masters of assemblies, *which* are given from one shepherd.

COMFORTING

Is 50:4 The Lord GOD hath given me the tongue of the learned, that I should know how to speak a word in season to *him that is* weary: he wak-eneth morning by morning, he wak-eneth mine ear to hear as the learned.

3. Kind

Ge 50:21 Now therefore fear ye not: I will nourish you, and your little ones. And he comforted them, and spake kindly unto them.
2 Chr 10:7 And they spake unto him, saying, If thou be kind to this people, and please them, and speak good words to them, they will be thy servants for ever.
Jb 4:4 Thy words have upholden him that was falling, and thou hast strengthened the feeble knees.
Pr 12:25 Heaviness in the heart of man maketh it stoop: but a good word maketh it glad.
Pr 15:1 A soft answer turneth away wrath: but grievous words stir up anger.
Pr 25:15 By long forbearing is a prince persuaded, and a soft tongue breaketh the bone.
Pr 31:26 She openeth her mouth with wisdom; and in her tongue *is* the law of kindness.
Is 50:4 The Lord GOD hath given me the tongue of the learned, that I should know how to speak a word in season to *him that is* weary: he wak-eneth morning by morning, he wak-eneth mine ear to hear as the learned.
Je 52:32 And spake kindly unto him, and set his throne above the throne of the kings that *were* with him in Babylon,

See **SPEECH**

WORK

1. Commanded

Ge 2:15 And the LORD God took the man, and put him into the garden of Eden to dress it and to keep it.
Ge 3:19 In the sweat of thy face shalt thou eat bread, till thou return unto the ground; for out of it wast thou taken: for dust thou *art,* and unto dust shalt thou return.
Ge 3:23 Therefore the LORD God sent him forth from the garden of Eden, to

till the ground from whence he was taken.

Ex 20:9 Six days shalt thou labour, and do all thy work:

Ex 23:12 Six days thou shalt do thy work, and on the seventh day thou shalt rest: that thine ox and thine ass may rest, and the son of thy handmaid, and the stranger, may be refreshed.

Ex 34:21 Six days thou shalt work, but on the seventh day thou shalt rest: in earing time and in harvest thou shalt rest.

Ex 35:2 Six days shall work be done, but on the seventh day there shall be to you an holy day, a sabbath of rest to the LORD: whosoever doeth work therein shall be put to death.

Le 23:3 Six days shall work be done: but the seventh day *is* the sabbath of rest, an holy convocation; ye shall do no work *therein:* it *is* the sabbath of the LORD in all your dwellings.

De 5:13 Six days thou shalt labour, and do all thy work:

1 Chr 22:16 Of the gold, the silver, and the brass, and the iron, *there is* no number. Arise *therefore,* and be doing, and the LORD be with thee.

Job 24:5 Behold, *as* wild asses in the desert, go they forth to their work; rising betimes for a prey: the wilderness *yieldeth* food for them *and* for *their* children.

Ps 104:23 Man goeth forth unto his work and to his labour until the evening.

Pr 13:11 Wealth *gotten* by vanity shall be diminished: but he that gathereth by labour shall increase.

Pr 14:23 In all labour there is profit: but the talk of the lips *tendeth* only to penury.

Ec 9:10 Whatsoever thy hand findeth to do, do *it* with thy might; for *there is* no work, nor device, nor knowledge, nor wisdom, in the grave, whither thou goest.

Ep 4:28 Let him that stole steal no more: but rather let him labour, working with *his* hands the thing which is good, that he may have to give to him that needeth.

1 Th 4:11 And that ye study to be quiet, and to do your own business, and to work with your own hands, as we commanded you;

2 Th 3:12 Now them that are such we command and exhort by our Lord Jesus Christ, that with quietness they work, and eat their own bread.

2. Sometimes Disappointing

Nu 11:32 And the people stood up all that day, and all *that* night, and all the next day, and they gathered the quails: he that gathered least gathered ten homers: and they spread *them* all abroad for themselves round about the camp.

Ps 104:23 Man goeth forth unto his work and to his labour until the evening.

Ps 127:2 *It is* vain for you to rise up early, to sit up late, to eat the bread of sorrows: *for* so he giveth his beloved sleep.

Pr 23:4 Labour not to be rich: cease from thine own wisdom.

Ec 1:3 What profit hath a man of all his labour which he taketh under the sun?

Ec 1:14 I have seen all the works that are done under the sun; and, behold, all *is* vanity and vexation of spirit.

Ec 2:11 Then I looked on all the works that my hands had wrought, and on the labour that I had laboured to do: and, behold, all *was* vanity and vexation of spirit, and *there was* no profit under the sun.

Ec 2:22 For what hath man of all his labour, and of the vexation of his heart, wherein he hath laboured under the sun?

Ec 3:9 What profit hath he that worketh in that wherein he laboureth?

Ec 4:8 There is one *alone,* and *there is* not a second; yea, he hath neither child nor brother: yet *is there* no end of all his labour; neither is his eye satisfied with riches; neither *saith he,* For whom do I labour, and bereave my soul of good? This *is* also vanity, yea, it *is* a sore travail.

Ec 5:16 And this also *is* a sore evil, *that* in all points as he came, so shall he go: and what profit hath he that hath laboured for the wind?

Ec 8:16 When I applied mine heart to know wisdom, and to see the business that is done upon the earth: (for also *there is that* neither day nor night seeth sleep with his eyes:)

Is 55:2 Wherefore do ye spend money for *that which is* not bread? and your labour for *that which* satisfieth not? hearken diligently unto me, and eat ye *that which is* good, and let your soul delight itself in fatness.

Is 65:23 They shall not labour in vain, nor bring forth for trouble; for they *are* the seed of the blessed of the LORD, and their offspring with them.

Ho 12:8 And Ephraim said, Yet I am become rich, I have found me out substance: *in* all my labours they shall find none iniquity in me that *were* sin.

Hab 2:13 Behold, *is it* not of the LORD of hosts that the people shall labour in the very fire, and the people shall weary themselves for very vanity?

Hag 1:6 Ye have sown much, and bring in little; ye eat, but ye have not enough; ye drink, but ye are not filled with drink; ye clothe you, but there is none warm; and he that earneth wages earneth wages *to put it* into a bag with holes.

Hag 1:11 And I called for a drought upon the land, and upon the mountains, and upon the corn, and upon the new wine, and upon the oil, and upon *that* which the ground bringeth forth, and upon men, and upon cattle, and upon all the labour of the hands.

Lu 17:28 Likewise also as it was in the days of Lot; they did eat, they drank, they bought, they sold, they planted, they builded;

Jn 6:27 Labour not for the meat which perisheth, but for that meat which endureth unto everlasting life, which the Son of man shall give unto you: for him hath God the Father sealed.

Jn 21:3 Simon Peter saith unto them, I go a fishing. They say unto him, We also go with thee. They went forth, and entered into a ship immediately; and that night they caught nothing.

3. *Helpful*

Ge 24:18 And she said, Drink, my lord: and she hasted, and let down her pitcher upon her hand, and gave him drink.

Ex 2:17 And the shepherds came and drove them away: but Moses stood up and helped them, and watered their flock.

2 S 17:29 And honey, and butter, and sheep, and cheese of kine, for David, and for the people that *were* with him, to eat: for they said, The people *is* hungry, and weary, and thirsty, in the wilderness.

2 Chr 28:15 And the men which were expressed by name rose up, and took the captives, and with the spoil clothed all that were naked among them, and arrayed them, and shod them, and gave them to eat and to drink, and anointed them, and carried all the feeble of them upon asses, and brought them to Jericho, the city of palm trees, to their brethren: then they returned to Samaria.

Jb 4:3 Behold, thou hast instructed many, and thou hast strengthened the weak hands.

Jb 29:12 Because I delivered the poor that cried, and the fatherless, and *him that had* none to help him.

Jb 29:15–16 I was eyes to the blind, and feet *was* I to the lame.

I *was* a father to the poor: and the cause *which* I knew not I searched out.

Pr 29:7 The righteous considereth the cause of the poor: *but* the wicked regardeth not to know *it*.

Pr 31:20 She stretcheth out her hand to the poor; yea, she reacheth forth her hands to the needy.

Ec 4:10 For if they fall, the one will lift up his fellow: but woe to him *that is* alone when he falleth; for *he hath* not another to help him up.

Is 1:17 Learn to do well; seek judgment, relieve the oppressed, judge the fatherless, plead for the widow.

Is 16:3 Take counsel, execute judgment; make thy shadow as the night in the midst of the noonday; hide the outcasts; bewray not him that wandereth.

Is 21:14 The inhabitants of the land of Tema brought water to him that was thirsty, they prevented with their bread him that fled.

Is 35:3 Strengthen ye the weak hands, and confirm the feeble knees.

Is 50:4 The Lord GOD hath given me the tongue of the learned, that I should know how to speak a word in season to *him that is* weary: he wakeneth morning by morning, he wakeneth mine ear to hear as the learned.

Is 58:7 *Is it* not to deal thy bread to the hungry, and that thou bring the poor that are cast out to thy house? when thou seest the naked, that thou cover him; and that thou hide not thyself from thine own flesh?

Eze 18:7 And hath not oppressed any, *but* hath restored to the debtor his pledge, hath spoiled none by violence, hath given his bread to the hungry, and hath covered the naked with a garment;

Mt 10:42 And whosoever shall give to drink unto one of these little ones a cup of cold *water* only in the name of a disciple, verily I say unto you, he shall in no wise lose his reward.

Mt 25:35 For I was an hungred, and ye gave me meat: I was thirsty, and ye gave me drink: I was a stranger, and ye took me in:

Mk 1:32 And at even, when the sun did set, they brought unto him all that were diseased, and them that were possessed with devils.

Mk 2:3 And they come unto him, bringing one sick of the palsy, which was borne of four.

Mk 6:55 And ran through that whole region round about, and began to carry about in beds those that were sick, where they heard he was.

Lu 5:18 And, behold, men brought in a bed a man which was taken with a palsy: and they sought *means* to bring him in, and to lay *him* before him.

Lu 10:34 And went to *him,* and bound up his wounds, pouring in oil and wine, and set him on his own beast, and brought him to an inn, and took care of him.

Ac 3:7 And he took him by the right hand, and lifted *him* up: and immedi-

ately his feet and ancle bones received strength.

Ac 9:39 Then Peter arose and went with them. When he was come, they brought him into the upper chamber: and all the widows stood by him weeping, and shewing the coats and garments which Dorcas made, while she was with them.

Ro 16:2 That ye receive her in the Lord, as becometh saints, and that ye assist her in whatsoever business she hath need of you: for she hath been a succourer of many, and of myself also.

1 Co 16:15–16 I beseech you, brethren, (ye know the house of Stephanas, that it is the firstfruits of Achaia, and *that* they have addicted themselves to the ministry of the saints,)

That ye submit yourselves unto such, and to every one that helpeth with *us,* and laboureth.

1 Co 16:18 For they have refreshed my spirit and yours: therefore acknowledge ye them that are such.

2 Co 1:11 Ye also helping together by prayer for us, that for the gift *bestowed* upon us by the means of many persons thanks may be given by many on our behalf.

2 Co 8:16 But thanks *be* to God, which put the same earnest care into the heart of Titus for you.

Ph 2:30 Because for the work of Christ he was nigh unto death, not regarding his life, to supply your lack of service toward me.

Ph 4:3 And I intreat thee also, true yokefellow, help those women which laboured with me in the gospel, with Clement also, and *with* other my fellowlabourers, whose names *are* in the book of life.

Ph 4:10 But I rejoiced in the Lord greatly, that now at the last your care of me hath flourished again; wherein ye were also careful, but ye lacked opportunity.

1 Ti 5:10 Well reported of for good works; if she have brought up children, if she have lodged strangers, if she have washed the saints' feet, if she have relieved the afflicted, if she have diligently followed every good work.

2 Ti 1:16 The Lord give mercy unto the house of Onesiphorus; for he oft refreshed me, and was not ashamed of my chain:

Phm 7 For we have great joy and consolation in thy love, because the bowels of the saints are refreshed by thee, brother.

3 Jn 6 Which have borne witness of thy charity before the church: whom if thou bring forward on their journey after a godly sort, thou shalt do well:

4. Various Forms

WORKING WITH GOD

Hag 2:4 Yet now be strong, O Zerubbabel, saith the LORD; and be strong, O Joshua, son of Josedech, the high priest; and be strong, all ye people of the land, saith the LORD, and work: for *I am* with you, saith the LORD of hosts:

IMMEDIATE SERVICE

Mt 21:28 But what think ye? A *certain* man had two sons; and he came to the first, and said, Son, go work to day in my vineyard.

INDIVIDUAL TASKS

Mk 13:34 *For the Son of man is* as a man taking a far journey, who left his house, and gave authority to his servants, and to every man his work, and commanded the porter to watch.

ABUNDANT LABORS

1 Co 15:58 Therefore, my beloved brethren, be ye stedfast, unmovable, always abounding in the work of the Lord, forasmuch as ye know that your labour is not in vain in the Lord.

IN THE FIELD OF THEIR OWN LIVES

Ph 2:12 Wherefore, my beloved, as ye have always obeyed, not as in my presence only, but now much more in my absence, work out your own salvation with fear and trembling.

IN EVANGELIZING THE WORLD

2 Ti 4:5 But watch thou in all things, endure afflictions, do the work of an evangelist, make full proof of thy ministry.

5. Required

Mt 25:22-23 He also that had received two talents came and said, Lord, thou deliveredst unto me two talents: behold, I have gained two other talents beside them.

His lord said unto him, Well done, good and faithful servant; thou hast been faithful over a few things, I will make thee ruler over many things: enter thou into the joy of thy lord.

Mk 14:8 She hath done what she could: she is come aforehand to anoint my body to the burying.

Lu 12:48 But he that knew not, and did commit things worthy of stripes, shall be beaten with few *stripes*. For unto whomsoever much is given, of him shall be much required: and to whom men have committed much, of him they will ask the more.

1 Pe 4:11 If any man speak, *let him speak* as the oracles of God; if any man minister, *let him do it* as of the ability which God giveth: that God in all things may be glorified through Jesus Christ, to whom be praise and dominion for ever and ever. Amen.

6. In Cooperation with God

Ge 2:19 And out of the ground the LORD God formed every beast of the field, and every fowl of the air; and brought *them* unto Adam to see what he would call them: and whatsoever Adam called every living creature, that *was* the name thereof.

Ex 14:26 And the LORD said unto Moses, Stretch out thine hand over the sea, that the waters may come again upon the Egyptians, upon their chariots, and upon their horsemen.

Jos 8:18 And the LORD said unto Joshua, Stretch out the spear that *is* in thy hand toward Ai; for I will give it into thine hand. And Joshua stretched out the spear that *he had* in his hand toward the city.

1 S 14:45 And the people said unto Saul, Shall Jonathan die, who hath wrought this great salvation in Israel? God forbid: as the LORD liveth, there shall not one hair of his head fall to the ground; for he hath wrought with

God this day. So the people rescued Jonathan, that he died not.

2 S 5:24 And let it be, when thou hearest the sound of a going in the tops of the mulberry trees, that then thou shalt bestir thyself: for then shall the LORD go out before thee, to smite the host of the Philistines.

Ps 127:1 Except the LORD build the house, they labour in vain that build it: except the LORD keep the city, the watchman waketh *but* in vain.

Mt 14:19 And he commanded the multitude to sit down on the grass, and took the five loaves, and the two fishes, and looking up to heaven, he blessed, and brake, and gave the loaves to *his* disciples, and the disciples to the multitude.

Mt 15:36 And he took the seven loaves and the fishes, and gave thanks, and brake *them,* and gave to his disciples, and the disciples to the multitude.

Mk 6:41 And when he had taken the five loaves and the two fishes, he looked up to heaven, and blessed, and brake the loaves, and gave *them* to his disciples to set before them; and the two fishes divided he among them all.

Mk 8:6 And he commanded the people to sit down on the ground: and he took the seven loaves, and gave thanks, and brake, and gave to his disciples to set before *them;* and they did set *them* before the people.

Mk 16:20 And they went forth, and preached every where, the Lord working with *them,* and confirming the word with signs following. Amen.

Lu 9:16 Then he took the five loaves and the two fishes, and looking up to heaven, he blessed them, and brake, and gave to the disciples to set before the multitude.

Jn 6:11 And Jesus took the loaves; and when he had given thanks, he distributed to the disciples, and the disciples to them that were set down; and likewise of the fishes as much as they would.

1 Co 3:9 For we are labourers together with God: ye are God's husbandry, *ye are* God's building.

2 Co 6:1 We then, *as* workers together *with him,* beseech *you* also that ye receive not the grace of God in vain.

7. To Be Done Willingly

Ex 35:5 Take ye from among you an offering unto the LORD: whosoever *is* of a willing heart, let him bring it, an offering of the LORD; gold, and silver, and brass,

Ex 35:21 And they came, every one whose heart stirred him up, and every one whom his spirit made willing, *and* they brought the LORD's offering to the work of the tabernacle of the congregation, and for all his service, and for the holy garments.

Ex 35:29 The children of Israel brought a willing offering unto the LORD, every man and woman, whose heart made them willing to bring for all manner of work, which the LORD had commanded to be made by the hand of Moses.

Jud 5:2 Praise ye the LORD for the avenging of Israel, when the people willingly offered themselves.

Jud 5:9 My heart *is* toward the governors of Israel, that offered themselves willingly among the people. Bless ye the LORD.

Jud 8:25 And they answered, We will willingly give *them.* And they spread a garment, and did cast therein every man the earrings of his prey.

1 S 3:5 And he ran unto Eli, and said, Here *am* I; for thou calledst me. And he said, I called not; lie down again. And he went and lay down.

1 Chr 28:9 And thou, Solomon my son, know thou the God of thy father, and serve him with a perfect heart and with a willing mind: for the LORD searcheth all hearts, and understandeth all the imaginations of the thoughts: if thou seek him, he will be found of thee; but if thou forsake him, he will cast thee off for ever.

1 Chr 28:21 And, behold, the courses of the priests and the Levites, *even they shall be with thee* for all the service of the house of God: and *there shall be* with thee for all manner of workmanship every willing skilful man, for any manner of service: also the princes and all the people *will be* wholly at thy commandment.

1 Chr 29:6 Then the chief of the fathers and princes of the tribes of Israel, and the captains of thousands and of hundreds, with the rulers of the king's work, offered willingly,

1 Chr 29:17 I know also, my God, that thou triest the heart, and hast pleasure in uprightness. As for me, in the uprightness of mine heart I have willingly offered all these things: and now have I seen with joy thy people, which are present here, to offer willingly unto thee.

2 Chr 17:16 And next him *was* Amasiah the son of Zichri, who willingly offered himself unto the LORD; and with him two hundred thousand mighty men of valour.

Ezr 3:5 And afterward *offered* the continual burnt offering, both of the new moons, and of all the set feasts of the LORD that were consecrated, and of every one that willingly offered a freewill offering unto the LORD.

Ezr 7:13 I make a decree, that all they of the people of Israel, and *of* his priests and Levites, in my realm, which are minded of their own freewill to go up to Jerusalem, go with thee.

Ne 11:2 And the people blessed all the men, that willingly offered themselves to dwell at Jerusalem.

Ps 110:3 Thy people *shall be* willing in the day of thy power, in the beauties of holiness from the womb of the morning: thou hast the dew of thy youth.

Is 1:19 If ye be willing and obedient, ye shall eat the good of the land:

Is 6:8 Also I heard the voice of the Lord, saying, Whom shall I send, and who will go for us? Then said I, Here *am* I; send me.

1 Co 9:17 For if I do this thing willingly, I have a reward: but if against my will, a dispensation *of the gospel* is committed unto me.

2 Co 8:3 For to *their* power, I bear record, yea, and beyond *their* power *they were* willing of themselves;

2 Co 8:12 For if there be first a willing mind, *it is* accepted according to that a man hath, *and* not according to that he hath not.

1 Th 2:8 So being affectionately desirous of you, we were willing to have imparted unto you, not the gospel of God only, but also our own souls, because ye were dear unto us.

Phm 14 But without thy mind would I do nothing; that thy benefit should not be as it were of necessity, but willingly.

Phm 21 Having confidence in thy obedience I wrote unto thee, knowing that thou wilt also do more than I say.

1 Pe 5:2 Feed the flock of God which is among you, taking the oversight *thereof,* not by constraint, but willingly; not for filthy lucre, but of a ready mind;

8. Should Be Carried to Completion

Zec 4:9 The hands of Zerubbabel have laid the foundation of this house; his hands shall also finish it; and thou shalt know that the LORD of hosts hath sent me unto you.

Jn 4:34 Jesus saith unto them, My meat is to do the will of him that sent me, and to finish his work.

Jn 17:4 I have glorified thee on the earth: I have finished the work which thou gavest me to do.

Jn 19:30 When Jesus therefore had received the vinegar, he said, It is finished: and he bowed his head, and gave up the ghost.

Ac 20:24 But none of these things move me, neither count I my life dear unto myself, so that I might finish my course with joy, and the ministry, which I have received of the Lord Jesus, to testify the gospel of the grace of God.

2 Ti 4:7 I have fought a good fight, I have finished *my* course, I have kept the faith:

See **BUSINESS, EMPLOYEES, EMPLOYERS, OBEDIENCE, SUBMISSION**

WORKERS

BRINGING THE HELPLESS TO CHRIST

Mk 2:3 And they come unto him, bringing one sick of the palsy, which was borne of four.

WINNING MEMBERS OF THEIR OWN HOUSEHOLD

Jn 1:41–42 He first findeth his own brother Simon, and saith unto him, We have found the Messias, which is, being interpreted, the Christ.

And he brought him to Jesus. And when Jesus beheld him, he said, Thou art Simon the son of Jona: thou shalt be called Cephas, which is by interpretation, A stone.

RECOMMENDING CHRIST TO PERSONAL FRIENDS

Jn 1:45 Philip findeth Nathanael, and saith unto him, We have found him, of whom Moses in the law, and the prophets, did write, Jesus of Nazareth, the son of Joseph.

INSPIRING OTHER WORKERS

Ac 11:25–26 Then departed Barnabas to Tarsus, for to seek Saul:

And when he had found him, he brought him unto Antioch. And it came to pass, that a whole year they assembled themselves with the church, and taught much people. And the disciples were called Christians first in Antioch.

SAVING SOULS FROM DEATH

Ja 5:20 Let him know, that he which converteth the sinner from the error of his way shall save a soul from death, and shall hide a multitude of sins.

See **SERVANTS**

WORKS

1. Of God

Ge 1:16 And God made two great lights; the greater light to rule the day, and the lesser light to rule the night: *he made* the stars also.

Ge 1:31 And God saw every thing that he had made, and, behold, *it was* very good. And the evening and the morning were the sixth day.

Ex 34:10 And he said, Behold, I make a covenant: before all thy people I will do marvels, such as have not been done in all the earth, nor in any nation: and all the people among which thou *art* shall see the work of the LORD: for it *is* a terrible thing that I will do with thee.

Nu 23:23 Surely *there is* no enchantment against Jacob, neither *is there* any divination against Israel: according to this time it shall be said of Jacob and of Israel, What hath God wrought!

De 3:24 O Lord GOD, thou hast begun to shew thy servant thy greatness, and thy mighty hand: for what God *is there* in heaven or in earth, that can do according to thy works, and according to thy might?

1 Chr 16:9 Sing unto him, sing psalms unto him, talk ye of all his wondrous works.

Jb 36:24 Remember that thou magnify his work, which men behold.

Jb 37:14 Hearken unto this, O Job: stand still, and consider the wondrous works of God.

Ps 8:3 When I consider thy heavens, the work of thy fingers, the moon and the stars, which thou hast ordained;

Ps 19:1 The heavens declare the glory of God; and the firmament sheweth his handywork.

Ps 26:7 That I may publish with the voice of thanksgiving, and tell of all thy wondrous works.

Ps 40:5 Many, O LORD my God, *are* thy wonderful works *which* thou hast done, and thy thoughts *which are* to us-ward: they cannot be reckoned up in order unto thee: *if* I would declare and speak *of them,* they are more than can be numbered.

Ps 46:8 Come, behold the works of the LORD, what desolations he hath made in the earth.

Ps 66:5 Come and see the works of God: *he is* terrible *in his* doing toward the children of men.

Ps 71:17 O God, thou hast taught me from my youth: and hitherto have I declared thy wondrous works.

Ps 75:1 Unto thee, O God, do we give thanks, *unto thee* do we give thanks: for *that* thy name is near thy wondrous works declare.

Ps 77:11 I will remember the works of the LORD: surely I will remember thy wonders of old.

Ps 78:4 We will not hide *them* from their children, shewing to the generation to come the praises of the LORD, and his strength, and his wonderful works that he hath done.

Ps 86:8 Among the gods *there is* none like unto thee, O Lord; neither *are there any works* like unto thy works.

Ps 90:16 Let thy work appear unto thy servants, and thy glory unto their children.

Ps 92:5 O LORD, how great are thy works! *and* thy thoughts are very deep.

Ps 102:25 Of old hast thou laid the foundation of the earth: and the heavens *are* the work of thy hands.

Ps 103:22 Bless the LORD, all his works in all places of his dominion: bless the LORD, O my soul.

Ps 104:24 O LORD, how manifold are thy works! in wisdom hast thou made them all: the earth is full of thy riches.

Ps 104:31 The glory of the LORD shall endure for ever: the LORD shall rejoice in his works.

Ps 105:2 Sing unto him, sing psalms unto him: talk ye of all his wondrous works.

Ps 107:24 These see the works of the LORD, and his wonders in the deep.

Ps 111:4 He hath made his wonderful works to be remembered: the LORD *is* gracious and full of compassion.

Ps 119:27 Make me to understand the way of thy precepts: so shall I talk of thy wondrous works.

Ps 139:14 I will praise thee; for I am fearfully *and* wonderfully made: marvellous *are* thy works; and *that* my soul knoweth right well.

Ps 143:5 I remember the days of old; I meditate on all thy works; I muse on the work of thy hands.

Ps 145:5 I will speak of the glorious honour of thy majesty, and of thy wondrous works.

Pr 3:19 The LORD by wisdom hath founded the earth; by understanding hath he established the heavens.

Pr 8:22 The LORD possessed me in the beginning of his way, before his works of old.

Ec 3:11 He hath made every *thing* beautiful in his time: also he hath set the world in their heart, so that no man can find out the work that God maketh from the beginning to the end.

Ec 7:13 Consider the work of God: for who can make *that* straight, which he hath made crooked?

Ec 8:17 Then I beheld all the work of God, that a man cannot find out the work that is done under the sun: because though a man labour to seek *it* out, yet he shall not find *it;* yea further; though a wise *man* think to know *it,* yet shall he not be able to find *it.*

Ec 11:5 As thou knowest not what *is* the way of the spirit, *nor* how the bones *do grow* in the womb of her that is with child: even so thou knowest not the works of God who maketh all.

Is 28:21 For the LORD shall rise up as *in* mount Perazim, he shall be wroth as *in* the valley of Gibeon, that he may do his work, his strange work; and bring to pass his act, his strange act.

Is 29:14 Therefore, behold, I will proceed to do a marvellous work among this people, *even* a marvellous work and a wonder: for the wisdom of their wise *men* shall perish, and the understanding of their prudent *men* shall be hid.

Is 40:26 Lift up your eyes on high, and behold who hath created these *things,* that bringeth out their host by number: he calleth them all by names by the greatness of his might, for that *he is* strong in power; not one faileth.

Is 45:11 Thus saith the LORD, the Holy One of Israel, and his Maker, Ask me of things to come concerning my sons, and concerning the work of my hands command ye me.

Jn 5:17 But Jesus answered them, My Father worketh hitherto, and I work.

Jn 10:37 If I do not the works of my Father, believe me not.

Jn 14:10 Believest thou not that I am in the Father, and the Father in me? the words that I speak unto you I speak not of myself: but the Father that dwelleth in me, he doeth the works.

Ac 2:11 Cretes and Arabians, we do hear them speak in our tongues the wonderful works of God.

He 2:7 Thou madest him a little lower than the angels; thou crownedst him with glory and honour, and didst set him over the works of thy hands:

He 4:4 For he spake in a certain place of the seventh *day* on this wise, And God did rest the seventh day from all his works.

Re 15:3 And they sing the song of Moses the servant of God, and the song of the Lamb, saying, Great and marvellous *are* thy works, Lord God Almighty; just and true *are* thy ways, thou King of saints.

a. Spoken of as Great Things

De 10:21 He *is* thy praise, and he *is* thy God, that hath done for thee these great and terrible things, which thine eyes have seen.

1 S 12:24 Only fear the LORD, and serve him in truth with all your heart: for consider how great *things* he hath done for you.

2 S 7:21 For thy word's sake, and according to thine own heart, hast thou done all these great things, to make thy servant know *them.*

Jb 5:9 Which doeth great things and unsearchable; marvellous things without number:

Jb 9:10 Which doeth great things past finding out; yea, and wonders without number.

Jb 37:5 God thundereth marvellously with his voice; great things doeth he, which we cannot comprehend.

Ps 71:19 Thy righteousness also, O God, *is* very high, who hast done great things: O God, who *is* like unto thee!

Ps 72:18 Blessed *be* the LORD God, the God of Israel, who only doeth wondrous things.

Ps 106:21 They forgat God their saviour, which had done great things in Egypt;

Ps 126:2 Then was our mouth filled with laughter, and our tongue with singing: then said they among the heathen, The LORD hath done great things for them.

Jl 2:21 Fear not, O land; be glad and rejoice: for the LORD will do great things.

Mk 3:8 And from Jerusalem, and from Idumaea, and *from* beyond Jordan; and they about Tyre and Sidon, a great multitude, when they had heard what great things he did, came unto him.

Mk 5:19 Howbeit Jesus suffered him not, but saith unto him, Go home to thy friends, and tell them how great things the Lord hath done for thee, and hath had compassion on thee.

Lu 1:49 For he that is mighty hath done to me great things; and holy *is* his name.

Lu 8:39 Return to thine own house, and shew how great things God hath done unto thee. And he went his way, and published throughout the whole city how great things Jesus had done unto him.

b. Are "The Lord's Doings"

Ge 24:50 Then Laban and Bethuel answered and said, The thing proceedeth from the LORD: we cannot speak unto thee bad or good.

1 S 3:11 And the LORD said to Samuel, Behold, I will do a thing in Israel, at which both the ears of every one that heareth it shall tingle.

Ps 118:23 This is the LORD's doing; it *is* marvellous in our eyes.

Ps 126:3 The LORD hath done great things for us; *whereof* we are glad.

Is 28:21 For the LORD shall rise up as *in* mount Perazim, he shall be wroth as *in* the valley of Gibeon, that he may do his work, his strange work; and bring to pass his act, his strange act.

Is 29:14 Therefore, behold, I will proceed to do a marvellous work among this people, *even* a marvellous work and a wonder: for the wisdom of their wise *men* shall perish, and the understanding of their prudent *men* shall be hid.

Mt 21:42 Jesus saith unto them, Did ye never read in the scriptures, The stone which the builders rejected, the same is become the head of the corner: this is the Lord's doing, and it is marvellous in our eyes?

2. Of Christ

Mt 11:2 Now when John had heard in the prison the works of Christ, he sent two of his disciples,

Mt 11:20 Then began he to upbraid the cities wherein most of his mighty works were done, because they repented not:

Mt 11:23 And thou, Capernaum, which art exalted unto heaven, shalt be brought down to hell: for if the mighty works, which have been done in thee, had been done in Sodom, it would have remained until this day.

Mt 13:54 And when he was come into his own country, he taught them in their synagogue, insomuch that they were astonished, and said, Whence hath this *man* this wisdom, and *these* mighty works?

Mt 14:2 And said unto his servants, This is John the Baptist; he is risen from the dead; and therefore mighty works do shew forth themselves in him.

Mk 3:8 And from Jerusalem, and from Idumaea, and *from* beyond Jordan; and they about Tyre and Sidon, a great multitude, when they had heard what great things he did, came unto him.

Mk 6:2 And when the sabbath day was come, he began to teach in the synagogue: and many hearing *him* were astonished, saying, From whence hath this *man* these things? and what wisdom *is* this which is given unto him, that even such mighty works are wrought by his hands?

Mk 6:14 And king Herod heard *of him;* (for his name was spread abroad:) and he said, That John the Baptist was risen from the dead, and therefore mighty works do shew forth themselves in him.

Mk 7:37 And were beyond measure astonished, saying, He hath done all things well: he maketh both the deaf to hear, and the dumb to speak.

Lu 7:22 Then Jesus answering said unto them, Go your way, and tell John what things ye have seen and heard; how that the blind see, the lame walk, the lepers are cleansed, the deaf hear, the dead are raised, to the poor the gospel is preached.

Lu 9:7 Now Herod the tetrarch heard of all that was done by him: and he was perplexed, because that it was said of some, that John was risen from the dead;

Lu 9:43 And they were all amazed at the mighty power of God. But while they wondered every one at all things which Jesus did, he said unto his disciples,

Lu 13:17 And when he had said these things, all his adversaries were ashamed: and all the people rejoiced for all the glorious things that were done by him.

Lu 19:37 And when he was come nigh, even now at the descent of the mount of Olives, the whole multitude of the disciples began to rejoice and praise God with a loud voice for all the mighty works that they had seen;

Lu 24:19 And he said unto them, What things? And they said unto him, Concerning Jesus of Nazareth, which was a prophet mighty in deed and word before God and all the people:

Jn 2:23 Now when he was in Jerusalem at the passover, in the feast *day,* many believed in his name, when they saw the miracles which he did.

Jn 3:2 The same came to Jesus by night, and said unto him, Rabbi, we know that thou art a teacher come from God: for no man can do these miracles that thou doest, except God be with him.

Jn 4:45 Then when he was come into Galilee, the Galilaeans received him, having seen all the things that he did at Jerusalem at the feast: for they also went unto the feast.

Jn 5:17 But Jesus answered them, My Father worketh hitherto, and I work.

Jn 5:36 But I have greater witness than *that* of John: for the works which the Father *hath* given me to finish, the same works that I do, bear witness of me, that the Father hath sent me.

Jn 7:3 His brethren therefore said unto him, Depart hence, and go into Judaea, that thy disciples also may see the works that thou doest.

Jn 7:21 Jesus answered and said unto them, I have done one work, and ye all marvel.

Jn 7:31 And many of the people believed on him, and said, When Christ cometh, will he do more miracles than these which this *man* hath done?

Jn 9:4 I must work the works of him that sent me, while it is day: the night cometh, when no man can work.

Jn 9:16 Therefore said some of the Pharisees, This man is not of God, because he keepeth not the sabbath day. Others said, How can a man that is a sinner do such miracles? And there was a division among them.

Jn 10:25 Jesus answered them, I told you, and ye believed not: the works that I do in my Father's name, they bear witness of me.

Jn 10:32 Jesus answered them, Many good works have I shewed you from my Father; for which of those works do ye stone me?

Jn 10:38 But if I do, though ye believe not me, believe the works: that ye may know, and believe, that the Father is in me, and I in him.

Jn 14:11–12 Believe me that I *am* in the Father, and the Father in me: or else believe me for the very works' sake.

Verily, verily, I say unto you, He that believeth on me, the works that I do shall he do also; and greater *works* than these shall he do; because I go unto my Father.

Jn 15:24 If I had not done among them the works which none other man did, they had not had sin: but now have they both seen and hated both me and my Father.

Jn 21:25 And there are also many other things which Jesus did, the which, if they should be written every one, I suppose that even the world itself could not contain the books that should be written. Amen.

Ac 1:1 The former treatise have I made, O Theophilus, of all that Jesus began both to do and teach,

Ac 2:22 Ye men of Israel, hear these words; Jesus of Nazareth, a man approved of God among you by miracles and wonders and signs, which God did by him in the midst of you, as ye yourselves also know:

Ac 10:38 How God anointed Jesus of Nazareth with the Holy Ghost and with power: who went about doing good, and healing all that were oppressed of the devil; for God was with him.

3. Of Believers

a. Prescribed

GLORIFY GOD

Mt 5:16 Let your light so shine before men, that they may see your good works, and glorify your Father which is in heaven.

Col 1:10 That ye might walk worthy of the Lord unto all pleasing, being fruitful in every good work, and increasing in the knowledge of God;

ENRICH LIFE

1 Ti 6:18 That they do good, that they be rich in good works, ready to distribute, willing to communicate;

FURNISH A PATTERN FOR IMITATION

Tit 2:7 In all things shewing thyself a pattern of good works: in doctrine *shewing* uncorruptness, gravity, sincerity,

Tit 2:14 Who gave himself for us, that he might redeem us from all iniquity, and purify unto himself a peculiar people, zealous of good works.

Tit 3:8 *This is* a faithful saying, and these things I will that thou affirm constantly, that they which have believed in God might be careful to maintain good works. These things are good and profitable unto men.

TEND TO SUMMON OTHERS TO THEIR TASKS

He 10:24 And let us consider one another to provoke unto love and to good works:

DEMONSTRATE THE REALITY OF FAITH

Ja 2:17–18 Even so faith, if it hath not works, is dead, being alone.

Yea, a man may say, Thou hast faith, and I have works: shew me thy faith without thy works, and I will shew thee my faith by my works.

1 Pe 2:12 Having your conversation honest among the Gentiles: that, whereas they speak against you as evildoers, they may by *your* good works, which they shall behold, glorify God in the day of visitation.

b. Examples

2 Chr 24:16 And they buried him in the city of David among the kings, because he had done good in Israel, both toward God, and toward his house.

2 Chr 31:20 And thus did Hezekiah throughout all Judah, and wrought *that which was* good and right and truth before the LORD his God.

2 Chr 32:32 Now the rest of the acts of Hezekiah, and his goodness, behold, they *are* written in the vision of Isaiah the prophet, the son of Amoz, *and* in the book of the kings of Judah and Israel.

Ne 4:6 So built we the wall; and all the wall was joined together unto the half thereof: for the people had a mind to work.

Ne 4:21 So we laboured in the work: and half of them held the spears from the rising of the morning till the stars appeared.

Ne 6:3 And I sent messengers unto them, saying, I *am* doing a great work, so that I cannot come down: why should the work cease, whilst I leave it, and come down to you?

Ne 13:14 Remember me, O my God, concerning this, and wipe not out my good deeds that I have done for the house of my God, and for the offices thereof.

Hag 1:14 And the LORD stirred up the spirit of Zerubbabel the son of Shealtiel, governor of Judah, and the spirit of Joshua the son of Josedech, the high priest, and the spirit of all the remnant of the people; and they came

and did work in the house of the LORD of hosts, their God,

Mt 19:20 The young man saith unto him, All these things have I kept from my youth up: what lack I yet?

Mt 25:35–36 For I was an hungred, and ye gave me meat: I was thirsty, and ye gave me drink: I was a stranger, and ye took me in:

Naked, and ye clothed me: I was sick, and ye visited me: I was in prison, and ye came unto me.

Mt 26:7–8 There came unto him a woman having an alabaster box of very precious ointment, and poured it on his head, as he sat *at meat.*

But when his disciples saw *it,* they had indignation, saying, To what purpose *is* this waste?

Mt 26:10 When Jesus understood *it,* he said unto them, Why trouble ye the woman? for she hath wrought a good work upon me.

Lu 6:43 For a good tree bringeth not forth corrupt fruit; neither doth a corrupt tree bring forth good fruit.

Jn 3:21 But he that doeth truth cometh to the light, that his deeds may be made manifest, that they are wrought in God.

Ac 9:36 Now there was at Joppa a certain disciple named Tabitha, which by interpretation is called Dorcas: this woman was full of good works and almsdeeds which she did.

1 Co 16:10 Now if Timotheus come, see that he may be with you without fear: for he worketh the work of the Lord, as I also *do.*

Ph 2:30 Because for the work of Christ he was nigh unto death, not regarding his life, to supply your lack of service toward me.

1 Th 1:3 Remembering without ceasing your work of faith, and labour of love, and patience of hope in our Lord Jesus Christ, in the sight of God and our Father;

1 Th 5:13 And to esteem them very highly in love for their work's sake. *And* be at peace among yourselves.

2 Ti 3:17 That the man of God may be perfect, throughly furnished unto all good works.

He 6:10 For God *is* not unrighteous to forget your work and labour of love, which ye have shewed toward his name, in that ye have ministered to the saints, and do minister.

Ja 2:18 Yea, a man may say, Thou hast faith, and I have works: shew me thy faith without thy works, and I will shew thee my faith by my works.

Ja 2:24 Ye see then how that by works a man is justified, and not by faith only.

Re 2:2 I know thy works, and thy labour, and thy patience, and how thou canst not bear them which are evil: and thou hast tried them which say they are apostles, and are not, and hast found them liars:

Re 2:9 I know thy works, and tribulation, and poverty, (but thou art rich) and *I know* the blasphemy of them which say they are Jews, and are not, but *are* the synagogue of Satan.

Re 14:13 And I heard a voice from heaven saying unto me, Write, Blessed *are* the dead which die in the Lord from henceforth: Yea, saith the Spirit, that they may rest from their labours; and their works do follow them.

c. Insufficient for Salvation

De 9:5 Not for thy righteousness, or for the uprightness of thine heart, dost thou go to possess their land: but for the wickedness of these nations the LORD thy God doth drive them out from before thee, and that he may perform the word which the LORD sware unto thy fathers, Abraham, Isaac, and Jacob.

Is 57:12 I will declare thy righteousness, and thy works; for they shall not profit thee.

Eze 18:24 But when the righteous turneth away from his righteousness, and committeth iniquity, *and* doeth according to all the abominations that the wicked *man* doeth, shall he live? All his righteousness that he hath done shall not be mentioned: in his trespass that he hath trespassed, and in his sin that he hath sinned, in them shall he die.

Eze 33:12 Therefore, thou son of man, say unto the children of thy people, The righteousness of the righteous shall not deliver him in the day of his transgression: as for the wickedness of the wicked, he shall not fall thereby in the day that he turneth from his wickedness; neither shall the righteous be able to live for his *righteousness* in the day that he sinneth.

Mt 5:20 For I say unto you, That except your righteousness shall exceed *the righteousness* of the scribes and Pharisees, ye shall in no case enter into the kingdom of heaven.

Mt 7:22–23 Many will say to me in that day, Lord, Lord, have we not prophesied in thy name? and in thy name have cast out devils? and in thy name done many wonderful works?

And then will I profess unto them, I never knew you: depart from me, ye that work iniquity.

Mt 19:20 The young man saith unto him, All these things have I kept from my youth up: what lack I yet?

Mk 10:20 And he answered and said unto him, Master, all these have I observed from my youth.

Lu 18:22 Now when Jesus heard these things, he said unto him, Yet lackest thou one thing: sell all that thou hast, and distribute unto the poor, and thou shalt have treasure in heaven: and come, follow me.

Jn 6:28 Then said they unto him, What shall we do, that we might work the works of God?

Ro 3:20 Therefore by the deeds of the law there shall no flesh be justified in his sight: for by the law *is* the knowledge of sin.

Ro 4:2 For if Abraham were justified by works, he hath *whereof* to glory; but not before God.

Ro 9:32 Wherefore? Because they *sought* it not by faith, but as it were by the works of the law. For they stumbled at that stumblingstone;

Ro 11:6 And if by grace, then *is it* no more of works: otherwise grace is no more grace. But if *it be* of works, then is it no more grace: otherwise work is no more work.

Ga 2:16 Knowing that a man is not justified by the works of the law, but by the faith of Jesus Christ, even we have believed in Jesus Christ, that we might be justified by the faith of Christ, and not by the works of the law: for by the works of the law shall no flesh be justified.

Ga 5:4 Christ is become of no effect unto you, whosoever of you are justified by the law; ye are fallen from grace.

Ep 2:8–9 For by grace are ye saved through faith; and that not of yourselves: *it is* the gift of God:

Not of works, lest any man should boast.

2 Ti 1:9 Who hath saved us, and called *us* with an holy calling, not according to our works, but according to his own purpose and grace, which was given us in Christ Jesus before the world began,

Tit 3:4–5 But after that the kindness and love of God our Saviour toward man appeared,

Not by works of righteousness which we have done, but according to his mercy he saved us, by the washing of regeneration, and renewing of the Holy Ghost;

He 4:10 For he that is entered into his rest, he also hath ceased from his own works, as God *did* from his.

d. Special Commands about Doing Good

Ex 23:4 If thou meet thine enemy's ox or his ass going astray, thou shalt surely bring it back to him again.

Ps 34:14 Depart from evil, and do good; seek peace, and pursue it.

Ps 37:3 Trust in the LORD, and do good; *so* shalt thou dwell in the land, and verily thou shalt be fed.

Ps 37:27 Depart from evil, and do good; and dwell for evermore.

Ec 3:12 I know that *there is* no good in them, but for *a man* to rejoice, and to do good in his life.

Mt 7:12 Therefore all things whatsoever ye would that men should do to you, do ye even so to them: for this is the law and the prophets.

Mt 12:12 How much then is a man better than a sheep? Wherefore it is lawful to do well on the sabbath days.

Mk 14:7 For ye have the poor with you always, and whensoever ye will ye may do them good: but me ye have not always.

Lu 6:35 But love ye your enemies, and do good, and lend, hoping for nothing again; and your reward shall be great, and ye shall be the children of the Highest: for he is kind unto the unthankful and *to* the evil.

Ro 12:9 *Let* love be without dissimulation. Abhor that which is evil; cleave to that which is good.

Ro 13:3 For rulers are not a terror to good works, but to the evil. Wilt thou then not be afraid of the power? do that which is good, and thou shalt have praise of the same:

Ga 6:10 As we have therefore opportunity, let us do good unto all *men,* especially unto them who are of the household of faith.

Ep 6:8 Knowing that whatsoever good thing any man doeth, the same shall he receive of the Lord, whether *he be* bond or free.

1 Ti 6:18 That they do good, that they be rich in good works, ready to distribute, willing to communicate;

He 13:16 But to do good and to communicate forget not: for with such sacrifices God is well pleased.

Ja 4:17 Therefore to him that knoweth to do good, and doeth *it* not, to him it is sin.

1 Pe 2:15 For so is the will of God, that with well doing ye may put to silence the ignorance of foolish men:

1 Pe 3:11 Let him eschew evil, and do good; let him seek peace, and ensue it.

1 Pe 3:17 For *it is* better, if the will of God be so, that ye suffer for well doing, than for evil doing.

3 Jn 11 Beloved, follow not that which is evil, but that which is good. He that doeth good is of God: but he that doeth evil hath not seen God.

4. Of Evil People

2 Chr 34:25 Because they have forsaken me, and have burned incense unto other gods, that they might provoke me to anger with all the works of their hands; therefore my wrath shall be poured out upon this place, and shall not be quenched.

Ne 6:14 My God, think thou upon Tobiah and Sanballat according to these their works, and on the prophetess Noadiah, and the rest of the prophets, that would have put me in fear.

Jb 34:25 Therefore he knoweth their works, and he overturneth *them* in the night, so that they are destroyed.

Ps 14:1 The fool hath said in his heart, *There is* no God. They are corrupt, they have done abominable works, *there is* none that doeth good.

Ps 141:4 Incline not my heart to *any* evil thing, to practise wicked works with men that work iniquity: and let me not eat of their dainties.

Pr 12:6 The words of the wicked *are* to lie in wait for blood: but the mouth of the upright shall deliver them.

Ec 4:3 Yea, better *is he* than both they, which hath not yet been, who hath not seen the evil work that is done under the sun.

Is 41:29 Behold, they *are* all vanity; their works *are* nothing: their molten images *are* wind and confusion.

Is 57:12 I will declare thy righteousness, and thy works; for they shall not profit thee.

Is 59:6 Their webs shall not become garments, neither shall they cover themselves with their works: their works *are* works of iniquity, and the act of violence *is* in their hands.

Je 7:13 And now, because ye have done all these works, saith the LORD, and I spake unto you, rising up early and speaking, but ye heard not; and I called you, but ye answered not;

Eze 6:11 Thus saith the Lord GOD; Smite with thine hand, and stamp with thy foot, and say, Alas for all the evil abominations of the house of Israel! for they shall fall by the sword, by the famine, and by the pestilence.

Eze 7:3 Now *is* the end *come* upon thee, and I will send mine anger upon thee, and will judge thee according to thy ways, and will recompense upon thee all thine abominations.

Eze 16:30 How weak is thine heart, saith the Lord GOD, seeing thou doest all these *things,* the work of an imperious whorish woman;

Eze 20:43 And there shall ye remember your ways, and all your doings, wherein ye have been defiled; and ye shall lothe yourselves in your own sight for all your evils that ye have committed.

Eze 33:29 Then shall they know that I *am* the LORD, when I have laid the land most desolate because of all their abominations which they have committed.

Eze 36:17 Son of man, when the house of Israel dwelt in their own land, they defiled it by their own way and by their doings: their way was before me as the uncleanness of a removed woman.

Da 12:10 Many shall be purified, and made white, and tried; but the wicked shall do wickedly: and none of the wicked shall understand; but the wise shall understand.

Ho 10:13 Ye have plowed wickedness, ye have reaped iniquity; ye have eaten the fruit of lies: because thou didst trust in thy way, in the multitude of thy mighty men.

Mi 3:4 Then shall they cry unto the LORD, but he will not hear them: he will even hide his face from them at that time, as they have behaved themselves ill in their doings.

Mt 7:16 Ye shall know them by their fruits. Do men gather grapes of thorns, or figs of thistles?

Lu 3:19 But Herod the tetrarch, being reproved by him for Herodias his brother Philip's wife, and for all the evils which Herod had done,

Lu 6:43 For a good tree bringeth not forth corrupt fruit; neither doth a corrupt tree bring forth good fruit.

Jn 3:20 For every one that doeth evil hateth the light, neither cometh to the light, lest his deeds should be reproved.

Jn 7:7 The world cannot hate you; but me it hateth, because I testify of it, that the works thereof are evil.

Jn 8:41 Ye do the deeds of your father. Then said they to him, We be not born of fornication; we have one Father, *even* God.

Jn 8:44 Ye are of your father the devil, and the lusts of *your* father ye will do. He was a murderer from the beginning, and abode not in the truth, because there is no truth in him. When he speaketh a lie, he speaketh of his own: for he is a liar, and the father of it.

Ro 2:9 Tribulation and anguish, upon every soul of man that doeth evil, of the Jew first, and also of the Gentile;

Ro 3:10 As it is written, There is none righteous, no, not one:

1 Co 5:3 For I verily, as absent in body, but present in spirit, have judged already, as though I were present, *concerning* him that hath so done this deed,

Ga 5:19 Now the works of the flesh are manifest, which are *these;* Adultery, fornication, uncleanness, lasciviousness,

Col 1:21 And you, that were sometime alienated and enemies in *your* mind by wicked works, yet now hath he reconciled

Tit 1:16 They profess that they know God; but in works they deny *him,* being abominable, and disobedient, and unto every good work reprobate.

Ja 3:16 For where envying and strife *is,* there *is* confusion and every evil work.

2 Pe 2:8 (For that righteous man dwelling among them, in seeing and hearing, vexed *his* righteous soul from day to day with *their* unlawful deeds;)

1 Jn 3:12 Not as Cain, *who* was of that wicked one, and slew his brother. And wherefore slew he him? Because his own works were evil, and his brother's righteous.

Jude 15 To execute judgment upon all, and to convince all that are ungodly among them of all their ungodly deeds which they have ungodly committed, and of all their hard *speeches* which ungodly sinners have spoken against him.

Re 21:27 And there shall in no wise enter into it any thing that defileth, neither *whatsoever* worketh abomination, or *maketh* a lie: but they which are written in the Lamb's book of life.

See **CHRIST, EVIL, GOD, MANKIND, MIRACLES, WONDERS**

WORLD, *END OF*

Mt 13:39, 40, 49; 24:3, 14; 28:20; He 9:26

See **FUTURE LIFE, SECOND COMING**

WORLDLINESS, *ungodliness*

1. Warnings

Ps 17:14 From men *which are* thy hand, O LORD, from men of the world, *which have* their portion in *this* life, and whose belly thou fillest with thy hid *treasure:* they are full of children, and leave the rest of their *substance* to their babes.

Ec 5:16 And this also *is* a sore evil, *that* in all points as he came, so shall he go: and what profit hath he that hath laboured for the wind?

Mt 16:26 For what is a man profited, if he shall gain the whole world, and lose his own soul? or what shall a man give in exchange for his soul?

Lu 21:34 And take heed to yourselves, lest at any time your hearts be overcharged with surfeiting, and drunkenness, and cares of this life, and so that day come upon you unawares.

Ro 12:2 And be not conformed to this world: but be ye transformed by the renewing of your mind, that ye may prove what is that good, and acceptable, and perfect, will of God.

Col 3:2 Set your affection on things above, not on things on the earth.

Tit 2:12 Teaching us that, denying ungodliness and worldly lusts, we should live soberly, righteously, and godly, in this present world;

Ja 4:4 Ye adulterers and adulteresses, know ye not that the friendship of the world is enmity with God? whosoever therefore will be a friend of the world is the enemy of God.

1 Jn 2:15 Love not the world, neither the things *that are* in the world. If any man love the world, the love of the Father is not in him.

2. Evil Effects

DESTROYS THE INFLUENCE OF THE TRUTH

Mt 13:22 He also that received seed among the thorns is he that heareth the word; and the care of this world, and the deceitfulness of riches, choke the word, and he becometh unfruitful.

LEADS TO FALSE SECURITY

Mt 24:38–39 For as in the days that were before the flood they were eating and drinking, marrying and giving in marriage, until the day that Noe entered into the ark,

And knew not until the flood came, and took them all away; so shall also the coming of the Son of man be.

MAKES EARTHLY AFFECTIONS SUPREME

1 Co 7:32 But I would have you without carefulness. He that is unmarried careth for the things that belong to the Lord, how he may please the Lord:

MOLDS THE ACTIVITIES AND PLANS OF LIFE

Ep 2:2 Wherein in time past ye walked according to the course of this world, according to the prince of the power of the air, the spirit that now worketh in the children of disobedience:

LEADS TO RELIGIOUS APOSTASY

2 Ti 4:10 For Demas hath forsaken me, having loved this present world, and is departed unto Thessalonica; Crescens to Galatia, Titus unto Dalmatia.

Ja 5:5 Ye have lived in pleasure on the earth, and been wanton; ye have nourished your hearts, as in a day of slaughter.

3. Imitation Condemned

IN COMMITTING POPULAR SINS

Ex 23:2 Thou shalt not follow a multitude to *do* evil; neither shalt thou speak in a cause to decline after many to wrest *judgment:*

IN FALSE WORSHIP

De 12:30 Take heed to thyself that thou be not snared by following them, after that they be destroyed from before thee; and that thou enquire not after their gods, saying, How did these nations serve their gods? even so will I do likewise.

IN BAD GOVERNMENTAL POLICIES

1 S 8:19–20 Nevertheless the people refused to obey the voice of Samuel; and they said, Nay; but we will have a king over us;

That we also may be like all the nations; and that our king may judge us, and go out before us, and fight our battles.

IN HEATHENISH PRACTICES

2 K 17:15 And they rejected his statutes, and his covenant that he made with their fathers, and his testimonies which he testified against them; and they followed vanity, and became vain, and went after the heathen that *were* round about them, *concerning* whom the LORD had charged them, that they should not do like them.

IN FOLLOWING A BAD EXAMPLE

Mt 23:2–3 Saying, The scribes and the Pharisees sit in Moses' seat:

All therefore whatsoever they bid you observe, *that* observe and do; but do not ye after their works: for they say, and do not.

4. Examples

Jb 27:18; Je 22:14; Da 4:30; Mt 7:27; Lu 6:49; 12:18

5. Unprofitable

Ec 2:11 Then I looked on all the works that my hands had wrought, and on the labour that I had laboured to do: and, behold, all *was* vanity and vexation of spirit, and *there was* no profit under the sun.

Mt 6:19 Lay not up for yourselves treasures upon earth, where moth and rust doth corrupt, and where thieves break through and steal:

Lu 9:25 For what is a man advantaged, if he gain the whole world, and lose himself, or be cast away?

1 Jn 2:17 And the world passeth away, and the lust thereof: but he that doeth the will of God abideth for ever.

See **UNWORLDLINESS**

WORMS, *low forms of life*

Ex 16:20; Jb 25:6; Is 41:14; 51:8; Jona 4:7; Ac 12:23

WORMWOOD, *bitter plant growing in the wastelands*

De 29:18; Pr 5:4; Je 9:15; Re 8:11

See **AGRICULTURE**

WORSHIP, *act of honor, praise, and reverence of deity*

1. Of God

Ex 20:5 Thou shalt not bow down thyself to them, nor serve them: for I the LORD thy God *am* a jealous God, visiting the iniquity of the fathers upon the children unto the third and fourth *generation* of them that hate me;

Ex 23:17 Three times in the year all thy males shall appear before the Lord GOD.

Ex 24:1 And he said unto Moses, Come up unto the LORD, thou, and Aaron, Nadab, and Abihu, and seventy of the elders of Israel; and worship ye afar off.

De 5:9 Thou shalt not bow down thyself unto them, nor serve them: for I the LORD thy God *am* a jealous God, visiting the iniquity of the fathers upon the children unto the third and fourth *generation* of them that hate me,

De 26:10 And now, behold, I have brought the firstfruits of the land, which thou, O LORD, hast given me. And thou shalt set it before the LORD thy God, and worship before the LORD thy God:

2 K 17:36 But the LORD, who brought you up out of the land of Egypt with great power and a stretched out arm, him shall ye fear, and him shall ye worship, and to him shall ye do sacrifice.

1 Chr 16:29 Give unto the LORD the glory *due* unto his name: bring an offering, and come before him: worship the LORD in the beauty of holiness.

Ps 29:2 Give unto the LORD the glory due unto his name; worship the LORD in the beauty of holiness.

Ps 95:6 O come, let us worship and bow down: let us kneel before the LORD our maker.

Ps 96:9 O worship the LORD in the beauty of holiness: fear before him, all the earth.

Ps 97:7 Confounded be all they that serve graven images, that boast themselves of idols: worship him, all *ye* gods.

Ps 99:5 Exalt ye the LORD our God, and worship at his footstool; *for* he *is* holy.

Ps 99:9 Exalt the LORD our God, and worship at his holy hill; for the LORD our God *is* holy.

Eze 46:3 Likewise the people of the land shall worship at the door of this gate before the LORD in the sabbaths and in the new moons.

Zec 14:17 And it shall be, *that* whoso will not come up of *all* the families of the earth unto Jerusalem to worship the King, the LORD of hosts, even upon them shall be no rain.

Mt 4:10 Then saith Jesus unto him, Get thee hence, Satan: for it is written, Thou shalt worship the Lord thy God, and him only shalt thou serve.

Lu 4:8 And Jesus answered and said unto him, Get thee behind me, Satan: for it is written, Thou shalt worship the Lord thy God, and him only shalt thou serve.

Jn 4:24 God *is* a Spirit: and they that worship him must worship *him* in spirit and in truth.

Ac 24:14 But this I confess unto thee, that after the way which they call heresy, so worship I the God of my fathers, believing all things which are written in the law and in the prophets:

Re 14:7 Saying with a loud voice, Fear God, and give glory to him; for the hour of his judgment is come: and worship him that made heaven, and earth, and the sea, and the fountains of waters.

Re 15:4 Who shall not fear thee, O Lord, and glorify thy name? for *thou* only *art* holy: for all nations shall come and worship before thee; for thy judgments are made manifest.

Re 19:4 And the four and twenty elders and the four beasts fell down and worshipped God that sat on the throne, saying, Amen; Alleluia.

Re 19:10 And I fell at his feet to worship him. And he said unto me, See *thou do it* not: I am thy fellowservant, and of thy brethren that have the testimony of Jesus: worship God: for the testimony of Jesus is the spirit of prophecy.

Re 22:9 Then saith he unto me, See *thou do it* not: for I am thy fellowservant, and of thy brethren the prophets, and of them which keep the sayings of this book: worship God.

2. Of Christ

Mt 2:2 Saying, Where is he that is born King of the Jews? for we have seen his star in the east, and are come to worship him.

Mt 2:11 And when they were come into the house, they saw the young child with Mary his mother, and fell down, and worshipped him: and when they had opened their treasures, they presented unto him gifts; gold, and frankincense, and myrrh.

Mt 14:33 Then they that were in the ship came and worshipped him, saying, Of a truth thou art the Son of God.

Mt 28:9 And as they went to tell his disciples, behold, Jesus met them, saying, All hail. And they came and held him by the feet, and worshipped him.

Mt 28:17 And when they saw him, they worshipped him: but some doubted.

Lu 24:52 And they worshipped him, and returned to Jerusalem with great joy:

Ph 2:10 That at the name of Jesus every knee should bow, of *things* in heaven, and *things* in earth, and *things* under the earth;

He 1:6 And again, when he bringeth in the firstbegotten into the world, he saith, And let all the angels of God worship him.

Re 5:8 And when he had taken the book, the four beasts and four *and* twenty elders fell down before the Lamb, having every one of them harps, and golden vials full of odours, which are the prayers of saints.

See **MISSIONS**

3. Pure Attitude

Le 10:3 Then Moses said unto Aaron, This *is it* that the LORD spake, saying, I will be sanctified in them that come nigh me, and before all the people I will be glorified. And Aaron held his peace.

Ps 5:7 But as for me, I will come *into* thy house in the multitude of thy mercy: *and* in thy fear will I worship toward thy holy temple.

Ps 29:2 Give unto the LORD the glory due unto his name; worship the LORD in the beauty of holiness.

Ps 89:7 God is greatly to be feared in the assembly of the saints, and to be had in reverence of all *them that are* about him.

Ps 93:5 Thy testimonies are very sure: holiness becometh thine house, O LORD, for ever.

Ec 5:1 Keep thy foot when thou goest to the house of God, and be more ready to hear, than to give the sacrifice of fools: for they consider not that they do evil.

Hab 2:20 But the LORD *is* in his holy temple: let all the earth keep silence before him.

Jn 4:24 God *is* a Spirit: and they that worship him must worship *him* in spirit and in truth.

4. In the Sanctuary

2 Chr 30:1 And Hezekiah sent to all Israel and Judah, and wrote letters also to Ephraim and Manasseh, that they should come to the house of the LORD at Jerusalem, to keep the passover unto the LORD God of Israel.

Is 2:3 And many people shall go and say, Come ye, and let us go up to the mountain of the LORD, to the house of the God of Jacob; and he will teach us of his ways, and we will walk in his paths: for out of Zion shall go forth the law, and the word of the LORD from Jerusalem.

Je 31:6 For there shall be a day, *that* the watchmen upon the mount Ephraim shall cry, Arise ye, and let us go up to Zion unto the LORD our God.

Zec 8:21 And the inhabitants of one *city* shall go to another, saying, Let us go speedily to pray before the LORD, and to seek the LORD of hosts: I will go also.

See **MUSIC, REVERENCE, PRAISE TO GOD**

WORSHIPERS

Ge 22:5 And Abraham said unto his young men, Abide ye here with the ass; and I and the lad will go yonder and worship, and come again to you,

Ge 24:26 And the man bowed down his head, and worshipped the LORD.

Ge 28:18 And Jacob rose up early in the morning, and took the stone that he had put *for* his pillows, and set it up *for* a pillar, and poured oil upon the top of it.

Ex 34:8 And Moses made haste, and bowed his head toward the earth, and worshipped.

Jos 5:14 And he said, Nay; but *as* captain of the host of the LORD am I now come. And Joshua fell on his face to the earth, and did worship, and said unto him, What saith my lord unto his servant?

Jud 7:15 And it was *so,* when Gideon heard the telling of the dream, and the interpretation thereof, that he worshipped, and returned into the host of Israel, and said, Arise; for the LORD hath delivered into your hand the host of Midian.

1 S 1:28 Therefore also I have lent him to the LORD; as long as he liveth he shall be lent to the LORD. And he worshipped the LORD there.

2 S 12:20 Then David arose from the earth, and washed, and anointed *himself,* and changed his apparel, and came into the house of the LORD, and worshipped: then he came to his own house; and when he required, they set bread before him, and he did eat.

2 Chr 7:3 And when all the children of Israel saw how the fire came down, and the glory of the LORD upon the house, they bowed themselves with their faces to the ground upon the pavement, and worshipped, and praised the LORD, *saying,* For *he is* good; for his mercy *endureth* for ever.

Ne 8:6 And Ezra blessed the LORD, the great God. And all the people answered, Amen, Amen, with lifting up their hands: and they bowed their heads, and worshipped the LORD with *their* faces to the ground.

Jb 1:20 Then Job arose, and rent his mantle, and shaved his head, and fell down upon the ground, and worshipped,

Je 7:2 Stand in the gate of the LORD's house, and proclaim there this word, and say, Hear the word of the LORD, all *ye of* Judah, that enter in at these gates to worship the LORD.

Eze 46:2 And the prince shall enter by the way of the porch of *that* gate without, and shall stand by the post of the gate, and the priests shall prepare his burnt offering and his peace offerings, and he shall worship at the threshold of the gate: then he shall go forth; but the gate shall not be shut until the evening.

Jn 4:23 But the hour cometh, and now is, when the true worshippers shall worship the Father in spirit and in truth: for the Father seeketh such to worship him.

Re 4:10 The four and twenty elders fall down before him that sat on the throne, and worship him that liveth for ever and ever, and cast their crowns before the throne, saying,

Re 7:11 And all the angels stood round about the throne, and *about* the elders and the four beasts, and fell before the throne on their faces, and worshipped God,

Re 11:16 And the four and twenty elders, which sat before God on their seats, fell upon their faces, and worshipped God,

See **MUSIC, PRAISE TO GOD, PRAYER, REVERENCE**

WORTHINESS

2 S 22:4 I will call on the LORD, *who is* worthy to be praised: so shall I be saved from mine enemies.

Re 4:11 Thou art worthy, O Lord, to receive glory and honour and power: for thou hast created all things, and for thy pleasure they are and were created.

Re 5:12 Saying with a loud voice, Worthy is the Lamb that was slain to receive power, and riches, and wisdom, and strength, and honour, and glory, and blessing.

See **UNWORTHINESS**

WRATH

1. Of God, righteous anger against evil

2 K 22:13 Go ye, enquire of the LORD for me, and for the people, and for all Judah, concerning the words of this book that is found: for great is the wrath of the LORD that is kindled against us, because our fathers have not hearkened unto the words of this book, to do according unto all that which is written concerning us.

Ps 2:12 Kiss the Son, lest he be angry, and ye perish *from* the way, when his wrath is kindled but a little. Blessed *are* all they that put their trust in him.

Ec 5:6 Suffer not thy mouth to cause thy flesh to sin; neither say thou before the angel, that it *was* an error: wherefore should God be angry at thy voice, and destroy the work of thine hands?

Je 4:4 Circumcise yourselves to the LORD, and take away the foreskins of your heart, ye men of Judah and inhabitants of Jerusalem: lest my fury come forth like fire, and burn that none can quench *it*, because of the evil of your doings.

Jn 3:36 He that believeth on the Son hath everlasting life: and he that believeth not the Son shall not see life; but the wrath of God abideth on him.

Ro 1:18 For the wrath of God is revealed from heaven against all ungodliness and unrighteousness of men, who hold the truth in unrighteousness;

Ro 2:8 But unto them that are contentious, and do not obey the truth, but obey unrighteousness, indignation and wrath,

Ep 5:6 Let no man deceive you with vain words: for because of these things cometh the wrath of God upon the children of disobedience.

1 Th 2:16 Forbidding us to speak to the Gentiles that they might be saved, to fill up their sins alway: for the wrath is come upon them to the uttermost.

Re 15:7 And one of the four beasts gave unto the seven angels seven golden vials full of the wrath of God, who liveth for ever and ever.

2. Of Man

Ge 4:5 But unto Cain and to his offering he had not respect. And Cain was very wroth, and his countenance fell.

Ge 27:45 Until thy brother's anger turn away from thee, and he forget *that* which thou hast done to him: then I will send, and fetch thee from thence: why should I be deprived also of you both in one day?

Ge 30:2 And Jacob's anger was kindled against Rachel: and he said, *Am* I in God's stead, who hath withheld from thee the fruit of the womb?

Ge 31:36 And Jacob was wroth, and chode with Laban: and Jacob answered and said to Laban, What *is* my trespass? what *is* my sin, that thou hast so hotly pursued after me?

Ge 34:7 And the sons of Jacob came out of the field when they heard *it:* and the men were grieved, and they were very wroth, because he had wrought folly in Israel in lying with Jacob's daughter; which thing ought not to be done.

Ge 39:19 And it came to pass, when his master heard the words of his wife, which she spake unto him, saying, After this manner did thy servant to me; that his wrath was kindled.

Ge 49:6 O my soul, come not thou into their secret; unto their assembly, mine honour, be not thou united: for in their anger they slew a man, and in their selfwill they digged down a wall.

Nu 20:10 And Moses and Aaron gathered the congregation together before the rock, and he said unto them, Hear now, ye rebels; must we fetch you water out of this rock?

Nu 22:27 And when the ass saw the angel of the LORD, she fell down under Balaam: and Balaam's anger was kindled, and he smote the ass with a staff.

Nu 24:10 And Balak's anger was kindled against Balaam, and he smote his hands together: and Balak said unto Balaam, I called thee to curse mine enemies, and, behold, thou hast altogether blessed *them* these three times.

Jud 8:1 And the men of Ephraim said unto him, Why hast thou served us thus, that thou calledst us not, when thou wentest to fight with the Midianites? And they did chide with him sharply.

Jud 9:30 And when Zebul the ruler of the city heard the words of Gaal the son of Ebed, his anger was kindled.

Jud 14:19 And the Spirit of the LORD came upon him, and he went down to Ashkelon, and slew thirty men of them, and took their spoil, and gave change of garments unto them which expounded the riddle. And his anger was kindled, and he went up to his father's house.

1 S 18:8 And Saul was very wroth, and the saying displeased him; and he said, They have ascribed unto David ten thousands, and to me they have ascribed *but* thousands: and *what* can he have more but the kingdom?

1 S 29:4 And the princes of the Philistines were wroth with him; and the princes of the Philistines said unto him, Make this fellow return, that he may go again to his place which thou hast appointed him, and let him not go down with us to battle, lest in the battle he be an adversary to us: for wherewith should he reconcile himself unto his master? *should it* not *be* with the heads of these men?

2 S 3:8 Then was Abner very wroth for the words of Ish-bosheth, and said, *Am* I a dog's head, which against Judah do shew kindness this day unto the house of Saul thy father, to his brethren, and to his friends, and have not delivered thee into the hand of David, that thou chargest me to day with a fault concerning this woman?

2 K 5:12 *Are* not Abana and Pharpar, rivers of Damascus, better than all the waters of Israel? may I not wash in them, and be clean? So he turned and went away in a rage.

2 Chr 16:10 Then Asa was wroth with the seer, and put him in a prison house; for *he was* in a rage with him because of this *thing*. And Asa oppressed *some* of the people the same time.

2 Chr 25:10 Then Amaziah separated them, *to wit,* the army that was come to him out of Ephraim, to go home again: wherefore their anger was greatly kindled against Judah, and they returned home in great anger.

2 Chr 26:19 Then Uzziah was wroth, and *had* a censer in his hand to burn incense: and while he was wroth with the priests, the leprosy even rose up in his forehead before the priests in the house of the LORD, from beside the incense altar.

Ne 4:1 But it came to pass, that when Sanballat heard that we builded the wall, he was wroth, and took great indignation, and mocked the Jews.

Est 2:21 In those days, while Mordecai sat in the king's gate, two of the king's chamberlains, Bigthan and Teresh, of those which kept the door, were wroth, and sought to lay hand on the king Ahasuerus.

Est 3:5 And when Haman saw that Mordecai bowed not, nor did him reverence, then was Haman full of wrath.

Est 5:9 Then went Haman forth that day joyful and with a glad heart: but when Haman saw Mordecai in the king's gate, that he stood not up, nor moved for him, he was full of indignation against Mordecai.

Ps 124:3 Then they had swallowed us up quick, when their wrath was kindled against us:

Pr 19:19 A man of great wrath shall suffer punishment: for if thou deliver *him,* yet thou must do it again.

Pr 27:3 A stone *is* heavy, and the sand weighty; but a fool's wrath *is* heavier than them both.

Is 16:6 We have heard of the pride of Moab; *he is* very proud: *even* of his haughtiness, and his pride, and his wrath: *but* his lies *shall* not *be* so.

Je 48:30 I know his wrath, saith the Lord; but *it shall* not *be* so; his lies shall not so effect *it*.

Am 1:11 Thus saith the Lord; For three transgressions of Edom, and for four, I will not turn away *the punishment* thereof; because he did pursue his brother with the sword, and did cast off all pity, and his anger did tear perpetually, and he kept his wrath for ever:

Jona 4:1 But it displeased Jonah exceedingly, and he was very angry.

Mt 2:16 Then Herod, when he saw that he was mocked of the wise men, was exceeding wroth, and sent forth, and slew all the children that were in Bethlehem, and in all the coasts thereof, from two years old and under, according to the time which he had diligently enquired of the wise men.

Lu 4:28 And all they in the synagogue, when they heard these things, were filled with wrath,

Lu 6:11 And they were filled with madness; and communed one with another what they might do to Jesus.

Ac 5:17 Then the high priest rose up, and all they that were with him, (which is the sect of the Sadducees,) and were filled with indignation,

Ac 19:28 And when they heard *these sayings*, they were full of wrath, and cried out, saying, Great *is* Diana of the Ephesians.

Ep 4:31 Let all bitterness, and wrath, and anger, and clamour, and evil speaking, be put away from you, with all malice:

Col 3:8 But now ye also put off all these; anger, wrath, malice, blasphemy, filthy communication out of your mouth.

Ja 1:20 For the wrath of man worketh not the righteousness of God.

3. Of Kings

See **NATION**

4. The Wicked Will Drink It

Jb 21:20 His eyes shall see his destruction, and he shall drink of the wrath of the Almighty.

Ps 75:8 For in the hand of the Lord *there is* a cup, and the wine is red; it is full of mixture; and he poureth out of the same: but the dregs thereof, all the wicked of the earth shall wring *them* out, *and* drink *them*.

Is 29:9 Stay yourselves, and wonder; cry ye out, and cry: they are drunken, but not with wine; they stagger, but not with strong drink.

Is 51:17 Awake, awake, stand up, O Jerusalem, which hast drunk at the hand of the Lord the cup of his fury; thou hast drunken the dregs of the cup of trembling, *and* wrung *them* out.

Is 51:22 Thus saith thy Lord the Lord, and thy God *that* pleadeth the cause of his people, Behold, I have taken out of thine hand the cup of trembling, *even* the dregs of the cup of my fury; thou shalt no more drink it again:

Je 8:14 Why do we sit still? assemble yourselves, and let us enter into the defenced cities, and let us be silent there: for the Lord our God hath put us to silence, and given us water of gall to drink, because we have sinned against the Lord.

Je 9:15 Therefore thus saith the Lord of hosts, the God of Israel; Behold, I will feed them, *even* this people, with wormwood, and give them water of gall to drink.

Je 13:13 Then shalt thou say unto them, Thus saith the Lord, Behold, I will fill all the inhabitants of this land, even the kings that sit upon David's throne, and the priests, and the prophets, and all the inhabitants of Jerusalem, with drunkenness.

Je 23:15 Therefore thus saith the Lord of hosts concerning the prophets; Behold, I will feed them with wormwood, and make them drink the water of gall: for from the prophets of Jerusalem is profaneness gone forth into all the land.

Je 25:15 For thus saith the Lord God of Israel unto me; Take the wine cup of this fury at my hand, and cause all the nations, to whom I send thee, to drink it.

Je 25:28 And it shall be, if they refuse to take the cup at thine hand to drink, then shalt thou say unto them, Thus saith the Lord of hosts; Ye shall certainly drink.

Je 48:26 Make ye him drunken: for he magnified *himself* against the LORD: Moab also shall wallow in his vomit, and he also shall be in derision.

Je 49:12 For thus saith the LORD; Behold, they whose judgment *was* not to drink of the cup have assuredly drunken; and *art* thou he *that* shall altogether go unpunished? thou shalt not go unpunished, but thou shalt surely drink *of it.*

Je 51:7 Babylon *hath been* a golden cup in the LORD's hand, that made all the earth drunken: the nations have drunken of her wine; therefore the nations are mad.

Je 51:39 In their heat I will make their feasts, and I will make them drunken, that they may rejoice, and sleep a perpetual sleep, and not wake, saith the LORD.

Je 51:57 And I will make drunk her princes, and her wise *men,* her captains, and her rulers, and her mighty men: and they shall sleep a perpetual sleep, and not wake, saith the King, whose name *is* the LORD of hosts.

Lam 4:21 Rejoice and be glad, O daughter of Edom, that dwellest in the land of Uz; the cup also shall pass through unto thee: thou shalt be drunken, and shalt make thyself naked.

Eze 23:33 Thou shalt be filled with drunkenness and sorrow, with the cup of astonishment and desolation, with the cup of thy sister Samaria.

Obad 16 For as ye have drunk upon my holy mountain, *so* shall all the heathen drink continually, yea, they shall drink, and they shall swallow down, and they shall be as though they had not been.

Na 3:11 Thou also shalt be drunken: thou shalt be hid, thou also shalt seek strength because of the enemy.

Hab 2:16 Thou art filled with shame for glory: drink thou also, and let thy foreskin be uncovered: the cup of the LORD's right hand shall be turned unto thee, and shameful spewing *shall be* on thy glory.

Zec 12:2 Behold, I will make Jerusalem a cup of trembling unto all the people round about, when they shall be in the siege both against Judah *and* against Jerusalem.

Re 14:10 The same shall drink of the wine of the wrath of God, which is poured out without mixture into the cup of his indignation; and he shall be tormented with fire and brimstone in the presence of the holy angels, and in the presence of the Lamb:

Re 16:19 And the great city was divided into three parts, and the cities of the nations fell: and great Babylon came in remembrance before God, to give unto her the cup of the wine of the fierceness of his wrath.

Re 18:3 For all nations have drunk of the wine of the wrath of her fornication, and the kings of the earth have committed fornication with her, and the merchants of the earth are waxed rich through the abundance of her delicacies.

Re 18:6 Reward her even as she rewarded you, and double unto her double according to her works: in the cup which she hath filled fill to her double.

See **JUDGMENTS, JUSTICE, WICKED**

WREATHS, *woven chains used to decorate the tabernacle and the temple*

Ex 28:14; 1 K 7:17; 2 Chr 4:12

WRITING

Ex 24:4 And Moses wrote all the words of the LORD, and rose up early in the morning, and builded an altar under the hill, and twelve pillars, according to the twelve tribes of Israel.

Ex 31:18 And he gave unto Moses, when he had made an end of communing with him upon mount Sinai, two tables of testimony, tables of stone, written with the finger of God.

Ex 32:16 And the tables *were* the work of God, and the writing *was* the writing of God, graven upon the tables.

Ex 34:27 And the LORD said unto Moses, Write thou these words: for after the tenor of these words I have made a covenant with thee and with Israel.

Ex 39:30 And they made the plate of the holy crown *of* pure gold, and wrote upon it a writing, *like to* the engravings of a signet, HOLINESS TO THE LORD.

Nu 17:2 Speak unto the children of Israel, and take of every one of them a rod according to the house of *their* fathers, of all their princes according to the house of their fathers twelve rods: write thou every man's name upon his rod.

Nu 33:2 And Moses wrote their goings out according to their journeys by the commandment of the LORD: and these *are* their journeys according to their goings out.

De 6:9 And thou shalt write them upon the posts of thy house, and on thy gates.

De 10:4 And he wrote on the tables, according to the first writing, the ten commandments, which the LORD spake unto you in the mount out of the midst of the fire in the day of the assembly: and the LORD gave them unto me.

De. 11:20 And thou shalt write them upon the door posts of thine house, and upon thy gates:

De. 17:18 And it shall be, when he sitteth upon the throne of his kingdom, that he shall write him a copy of this law in a book out of *that which is* before the priests the Levites:

De 27:3 And thou shalt write upon them all the words of this law, when thou art passed over, that thou mayest go in unto the land which the LORD thy God giveth thee, a land that floweth with milk and honey; as the LORD God of thy fathers hath promised thee.

De 27:8 And thou shalt write upon the stones all the words of this law very plainly.

De 31:9 And Moses wrote this law, and delivered it unto the priests the sons of Levi, which bare the ark of the covenant of the LORD, and unto all the elders of Israel.

De 31:24 And it came to pass, when Moses had made an end of writing the words of this law in a book, until they were finished,

1 Chr 28:19 All *this, said David,* the LORD made me understand in writing by *his* hand upon me, *even* all the works of this pattern.

2 Chr 2:11 Then Huram the king of Tyre answered in writing, which he sent to Solomon, Because the LORD hath loved his people, he hath made thee king over them.

2 Chr 36:22 Now in the first year of Cyrus king of Persia, that the word of the LORD *spoken* by the mouth of Jeremiah might be accomplished, the LORD stirred up the spirit of Cyrus king of Persia, that he made a proclamation throughout all his kingdom, and *put it* also in writing, saying,

Ezr 1:1 Now in the first year of Cyrus king of Persia, that the word of the LORD by the mouth of Jeremiah might be fulfilled, the LORD stirred up the spirit of Cyrus king of Persia, that he made a proclamation throughout all his kingdom, and *put it* also in writing, saying,

Ezr 4:7 And in the days of Artaxerxes wrote Bishlam, Mithredath, Tabeel, and the rest of their companions, unto Artaxerxes king of Persia; and the writing of the letter *was* written in the Syrian tongue, and interpreted in the Syrian tongue.

Ezra 6:18 And they set the priests in their divisions, and the Levites in their courses, for the service of God, which *is* at Jerusalem; as it is written in the book of Moses.

Is 8:1 Moreover the LORD said unto me, Take thee a great roll, and write in it with a man's pen concerning Maher- shalal-hash-baz.

Is 38:9 The writing of Hezekiah king of Judah, when he had been sick, and was recovered of his sickness:

Je 30:2 Thus speaketh the LORD God of Israel, saying, Write thee all the words that I have spoken unto thee in a book.

Je 36:18 Then Baruch answered them, He pronounced all these words unto me with his mouth, and I wrote *them* with ink in the book.

Eze 43:11 And if they be ashamed of all that they have done, shew them the form of the house, and the fashion thereof, and the goings out thereof, and the comings in thereof, and all the forms thereof, and all the ordinances thereof, and all the forms thereof, and all the laws thereof: and write *it* in their sight, that they may keep the whole form thereof, and all the ordinances thereof, and do them.

Da 5:5 In the same hour came forth fingers of a man's hand, and wrote over against the candlestick upon the plaister of the wall of the king's palace: and the king saw the part of the hand that wrote.

Da 5:16 And I have heard of thee, that thou canst make interpretations, and dissolve doubts: now if thou canst read the writing, and make known to me the interpretation thereof, thou shalt be clothed with scarlet, and *have* a chain of gold about thy neck, and shalt be the third ruler in the kingdom.

Da 6:25 Then king Darius wrote unto all people, nations, and languages, that dwell in all the earth; Peace be multiplied unto you.

Lu 1:3 It seemed good to me also, having had perfect understanding of all things from the very first, to write unto thee in order, most excellent Theophilus,

Lu 1:63 And he asked for a writing table, and wrote, saying, His name is John. And they marvelled all.

Ph 3:1 Finally, my brethren, rejoice in the Lord. To write the same things to you, to me indeed *is* not grievous, but for you *it is* safe.

Re 1:11 Saying, I am Alpha and Omega, the first and the last: and, What thou seest, write in a book, and send *it* unto the seven churches which are in Asia; unto Ephesus, and unto Smyrna, and unto Pergamos, and unto Thyatira, and unto Sardis, and unto Philadelphia, and unto Laodicea.

On the Heart

Pr 3:3 Let not mercy and truth forsake thee: bind them about thy neck; write them upon the table of thine heart:

Pr 7:3 Bind them upon thy fingers, write them upon the table of thine heart.

Je 31:33 But this *shall be* the covenant that I will make with the house of Israel; After those days, saith the LORD, I will put my law in their inward parts, and write it in their hearts; and will be their God, and they shall be my people.

2 Co 3:2 Ye are our epistle written in our hearts, known and read of all men:

He 8:10 For this *is* the covenant that I will make with the house of Israel after those days, saith the Lord; I will put my laws into their mind, and write them in their hearts: and I will be to them a God, and they shall be to me a people:

See **BOOKS**

Y

YARN, *used to embroider the priestly garments*

1 K 10:28; 2 Chr 1:16;

YOUNG PEOPLE

1. Young Men

a. Truths to Be Kept in Mind

THE IDEAL OF A CLEAN LIFE

Ps 119:9 Wherewithal shall a young man cleanse his way? by taking heed *thereto* according to thy word.

THE CERTAINTY OF A DAY OF RECKONING

Ec 11:9 Rejoice, O young man, in thy youth; and let thy heart cheer thee in the days of thy youth, and walk in the ways of thine heart, and in the sight of thine eyes: but know thou, that for all these *things* God will bring thee into judgment.

THE VALUE OF RESTRAINT

Lam 3:27 *It is* good for a man that he bear the yoke in his youth.

THE POWER OF PERSONAL INFLUENCE

1 Ti 4:12 Let no man despise thy youth; but be thou an example of the believers, in word, in conversation, in charity, in spirit, in faith, in purity.

SOBERNESS IS BETTER THAN FRIVOLITY

Tit 2:6–7 Young men likewise exhort to be sober minded.

In all things shewing thyself a pattern of good works: in doctrine *shewing* uncorruptness, gravity, sincerity,

MORAL STRENGTH IS BETTER THAN PHYSICAL

1 Jn 2:13–14 I write unto you, fathers, because ye have known him *that is* from the beginning. I write unto you, young men, because ye have overcome the wicked one. I write unto you, little children, because ye have known the Father.

I have written unto you, fathers, because ye have known him *that is* from the beginning. I have written unto you, young men, because ye are strong, and the word of God abideth in you, and ye have overcome the wicked one.

b. Promoted to Leadership

Ge 41:46 And Joseph *was* thirty years old when he stood before Pharaoh king of Egypt. And Joseph went out from the presence of Pharaoh, and went throughout all the land of Egypt.

1 S 17:33 And Saul said to David, Thou art not able to go against this Philistine to fight with him: for thou *art but* a youth, and he a man of war from his youth.

2 S 5:4 David *was* thirty years old when he began to reign, *and* he reigned forty years.

2 Chr 24:1 Joash *was* seven years old when he began to reign, and he reigned forty years in Jerusalem. His mother's name also *was* Zibiah of Beer-sheba.

2 Chr 34:1 Josiah *was* eight years old when he began to reign, and he reigned in Jerusalem one and thirty years.

2 Chr 34:3 For in the eighth year of his reign, while he was yet young, he began to seek after the God of David his father: and in the twelfth year he began to purge Judah and Jerusalem from the high places, and the groves, and the carved images, and the molten images.

Lu 3:23 And Jesus himself began to be about thirty years of age, being (as was supposed) the son of Joseph, which was *the son* of Heli,

Lu 18:18 And a certain ruler asked him, saying, Good Master, what shall I do to inherit eternal life?

Ac 7:58 And cast *him* out of the city, and stoned *him:* and the witnesses laid down their clothes at a young man's feet, whose name was Saul.

Ac 9:6 And he trembling and astonished said, Lord, what wilt thou have me to do? And the Lord *said* unto him, Arise, and go into the city, and it shall be told thee what thou must do.

Ac 9:22 But Saul increased the more in strength, and confounded the Jews which dwelt at Damascus, proving that this is very Christ.

c. Godly Examples

JOSEPH

Ge 41:38 And Pharaoh said unto his servants, Can we find *such a one* as this *is,* a man in whom the Spirit of God is?

Ge 41:46 And Joseph *was* thirty years old when he stood before Pharaoh king of Egypt. And Joseph went out from the presence of Pharaoh, and went throughout all the land of Egypt.

SAMUEL

1 S 2:26 And the child Samuel grew on, and was in favour both with the LORD, and also with men.

1 S 3:1 And the child Samuel ministered unto the LORD before Eli. And the word of the LORD was precious in those days; *there was* no open vision.

DAVID

1 S 17:33 And Saul said to David, Thou art not able to go against this Philistine to fight with him: for thou *art but* a youth, and he a man of war from his youth.

1 S 17:37 David said moreover, The LORD that delivered me out of the paw of the lion, and out of the paw of the bear, he will deliver me out of the hand of this Philistine. And Saul said unto David, Go, and the LORD be with thee.

JEHOASH

2 K 12:2 And Jehoash did *that which was* right in the sight of the LORD all his days wherein Jehoiada the priest instructed him.

JOASH

2 Chr 24:1–2 Joash *was* seven years old when he began to reign, and he reigned forty years in Jerusalem. His mother's name also was Zibiah of Beer-sheba.

And Joash did *that which was* right in the sight of the LORD all the days of Jehoiada the priest.

JOSIAH

2 Chr 34:1–3 Josiah *was* eight years old when he began to reign, and he reigned in Jerusalem one and thirty years.

And he did *that which was* right in the sight of the LORD, and walked in the ways of David his father, and declined *neither* to the right hand, nor to the left.

For in the eighth year of his reign, while he was yet young, he began to seek after the God of David his father: and in the twelfth year he began to purge Judah and Jerusalem from the high places, and the groves, and the carved images, and the molten images.

JESUS

Lu 2:49 And he said unto them, How is it that ye sought me? wist ye not that I must be about my Father's business?

TIMOTHY

2 Ti 1:5 When I call to remembrance the unfeigned faith that is in thee, which dwelt first in thy grandmother Lois, and thy mother Eunice; and I am persuaded that in thee also.

2 Ti 3:15 And that from a child thou hast known the holy scriptures, which are able to make thee wise unto salvation through faith which is in Christ Jesus.

d. Sinful Examples

CAIN

Ge 4:8 And Cain talked with Abel his brother: and it came to pass, when they were in the field, that Cain rose up against Abel his brother, and slew him.

ESAU

Ge 25:33–34 And Jacob said, Swear to me this day; and he sware unto him: and he sold his birthright unto Jacob.

Then Jacob gave Esau bread and pottage of lentiles; and he did eat and drink, and rose up, and went his way: thus Esau despised his birthright.

SONS OF ELI

1 S 2:12 Now the sons of Eli *were* sons of Belial; they knew not the LORD.

SONS OF SAMUEL

1 S 8:3 And his sons walked not in his ways, but turned aside after lucre, and took bribes, and perverted judgment.

ABSALOM

2 S 15:6 And on this manner did Absalom to all Israel that came to the king for judgment: so Absalom stole the hearts of the men of Israel.

REHOBOAM

1 K 12:8 But he forsook the counsel of the old men, which they had given him, and consulted with the young men that were grown up with him, *and* which stood before him:

JEROBOAM

1 K 13:33–34 After this thing Jeroboam returned not from his evil way, but made again of the lowest of the people priests of the high places: whosoever would, he consecrated him, and he became *one* of the priests of the high places.

And this thing became sin unto the house of Jeroboam, even to cut *it* off, and to destroy *it* from off the face of the earth.

MANASSEH

2 K 21:1–2 Manasseh *was* twelve years old when he began to reign, and reigned fifty and five years in Jerusalem. And his mother's name was Hephzi-bah.

And he did *that which was* evil in the sight of the LORD, after the abominations of the heathen, whom the LORD cast out before the children of Israel.

THE PRODIGAL SON

Lu 15:13 And not many days after the younger son gathered all together, and took his journey into a far country, and there wasted his substance with riotous living.

2. Young Women

Godly Examples

JEPHTHAH'S DAUGHTER

Jud 11:36 And she said unto him, My father, *if* thou hast opened thy mouth unto the LORD, do to me according to that which hath proceeded out of thy mouth; forasmuch as the LORD hath taken vengeance for thee of thine enemies, *even* of the children of Ammon.

RUTH

Ru 1:16 And Ruth said, Intreat me not to leave thee, *or* to return from following after thee: for whither thou goest, I will go; and where thou lodgest, I will lodge: thy people *shall be* my people, and thy God my God:

ESTHER

Est 4:16 Go, gather together all the Jews that are present in Shushan, and fast ye for me, and neither eat nor drink three days, night or day: I also and my maidens will fast likewise; and so will I go in unto the king, which *is* not according to the law: and if I perish, I perish.

MARY MAGDALENE

Mk 16:1 And when the sabbath was past, Mary Magdalene, and Mary the *mother* of James, and Salome, had bought sweet spices, that they might come and anoint him.

THE VIRGIN MARY

Lu 1:38 And Mary said, Behold the handmaid of the Lord; be it unto me according to thy word. And the angel departed from her.

MARY OF BETHANY

Lu 10:39 And she had a sister called Mary, which also sat at Jesus' feet, and heard his word.

Jn 12:3 Then took Mary a pound of ointment of spikenard, very costly, and anointed the feet of Jesus, and wiped his feet with her hair: and the house was filled with the odour of the ointment.

MARTHA

Jn 11:24 Martha saith unto him, I know that he shall rise again in the resurrection at the last day.

DAUGHTERS OF PHILIP

Ac 21:9 And the same man had four daughters, virgins, which did prophesy.

3. Musicians

Jud 11:34; 1 S 16:18; Ps 68:25

4. Special Duties

a. Filial Honor and Obedience

See **HONOR, OBEDIENCE**

b. Honor for Old Age

Le 19:32 Thou shalt rise up before the hoary head, and honour the face of the old man, and fear thy God: I *am* the LORD.

Jb 30:1 But now *they that are* younger than I have me in derision, whose fathers I would have disdained to have set with the dogs of my flock.

Jb 32:6 And Elihu the son of Barachel the Buzite answered and said, I *am* young, and ye *are* very old; wherefore I was afraid, and durst not shew you mine opinion.

Pr 23:22 Hearken unto thy father that begat thee, and despise not thy mother when she is old.

Is 3:5 And the people shall be oppressed, every one by another, and every one by his neighbour: the child shall behave himself proudly against the ancient, and the base against the honourable.

Lam 5:12 Princes are hanged up by their hand: the faces of elders were not honoured.

1 Ti 5:1–2 Rebuke not an elder, but intreat *him* as a father; *and* the younger men as brethren;

The elder women as mothers; the younger as sisters, with all purity.

5. Sins of Youth

a. Results

A SAD INHERITANCE

Jb 13:26 For thou writest bitter things against me, and makest me to possess the iniquities of my youth.

DISEASE AND DEATH

Jb 20:11 His bones are full *of the sin* of his youth, which shall lie down with him in the dust.

BITTER MEMORIES

Ps 25:7 Remember not the sins of my youth, nor my transgressions: according to thy mercy remember thou me for thy goodness' sake, O LORD.

Ec 11:9 Rejoice, O young man, in thy youth; and let thy heart cheer thee in the days of thy youth, and walk in the ways of thine heart, and in the sight of thine eyes: but know thou, that for all these *things* God will bring thee into judgment.

SHAME AND REMORSE

Je 3:25 We lie down in our shame, and our confusion covereth us: for we have sinned against the LORD our God, we and our fathers, from our youth even unto this day, and have not obeyed the voice of the LORD our God.

Je 32:30 For the children of Israel and the children of Judah have only done evil before me from their youth: for the children of Israel have only provoked me to anger with the work of their hands, saith the LORD.

b. Disrespect for Old Age

2 K 2:23; Jb 30:1; Lam 5:12

See **AGE, FAMILY, HOME**

Z

ZACCHAEUS, *a publican*

Lu 19:2

See **HOSPITALITY**

ZACHARIAH, *king of Israel, son of Jeroboam II*

2 Kings 14:29; 15:8; 15:11; 18:2

ZACHARIAS

1. Slain by Jews

Mt 23:35; Lu 11:51

See **ISRAEL**

2. Father of John the Baptist

Luke 1:5, 12-13, 18, 21, 40, 59, 67; 3:2

See **JOHN THE BAPTIST**

ZADOK, *son of Ahitub*

2 S 8:17; 15:24, 35; 20:25; 1 K 1:8, 26, 32, 39; 2:35; 4:4; 1 Chr 6:8, 53; 12:28; 15:11; 16:39; 18:16; 24:3, 31; 29:22; 2 Chr 27:1; Ezr 7:2; Ne 11:11; Eze 40:46; 43:19; 44:15; 48:11

ZAREPHATH, *or Sarepta, a town in Phoenicia*

1 K 17:9; Obad 20; Lu 4:26

See **CITIES**

ZEAL

1. General

Ex 35:21; Nu 25:7, 11; 1 K 15:13; 2 K 10:16; 1 Chr 29:2; 2 Chr 29:34; 30:1, 23; 31:1; Ezr 1:5; Ne 4:6, 21; 13:21; Ps 69:9; 119:32, 60, 139; 132:4; Is 62:1; Je 20:9; Hag 1:14; Mk 2:4; 5:20; 16:20; Lu 5:18; 8:39; 24:33; Jn 2:17; Ac 5:28, 41; 8:40; 9:32; 17:17; 18:4; 20:31; 28:31; Ro 1:15; 15:20, 23; 16:12; 1 Co 15:10; 2 Co 5:13; 7:11; 8:17; 9:2; Col 1:29; 4:13; 1 Th 2:9; Tit 2:14

See **PAUL**

2. Commands

Jos 17:15; 2 K 13:19; 2 Chr 29:11; Ec 9:10; Zep 3:16; Hag 2:4; Lu 14:23; 1 Co 14:12; 15:58; Ga 4:18; 2 Ti 1:6; 4:2; He 6:12; 2 Pe 1:13; 3:14; Jude 3; Re 3:19

3. Of Christ, *focused discipline toward daily obedience to the will of his Father*

Mt 4:23 And Jesus went about all Galilee, teaching in their synagogues, and preaching the gospel of the kingdom, and healing all manner of sickness and all manner of disease among the people.

Mt 8:16 When the even was come, they brought unto him many that were possessed with devils: and he cast out the spirits with *his* word, and healed all that were sick:

Mt 9:35 And Jesus went about all the cities and villages, teaching in their synagogues, and preaching the gospel of the kingdom, and healing every sickness and every disease among the people.

Mt 21:12 And Jesus went into the temple of God, and cast out all them that sold and bought in the temple, and overthrew the tables of the money-changers, and the seats of them that sold doves,

Mk 1:38 And he said unto them, Let us go into the next towns, that I may preach there also: for therefore came I forth.

Mk 8:10 And straightway he entered into a ship with his disciples, and came into the parts of Dalmanutha.

Luke 2:49 And he said unto them, How is it that ye sought me? wist ye not that I must be about my Father's business?

Lu 8:1 And it came to pass afterward, that he went throughout every city and village, preaching and shewing the glad tidings of the kingdom of God: and the twelve *were* with him,

Lu 13:22 And he went through the cities and villages, teaching, and journeying toward Jerusalem.

Lu 15:4 What man of you, having an hundred sheep, if he lose one of them, doth not leave the ninety and nine in the wilderness, and go after that which is lost, until he find it?

Jn 2:17 And his disciples remembered that it was written, The zeal of thine house hath eaten me up.

Jn 4:34 Jesus saith unto them, My meat is to do the will of him that sent me, and to finish his work.

Jn 9:4 I must work the works of him that sent me, while it is day: the night cometh, when no man can work.

Ac 10:38 How God anointed Jesus of Nazareth with the Holy Ghost and with power: who went about doing good, and healing all that were oppressed of the devil; for God was with him.

a. For His Duty

TO BE ABOUT HIS FATHER'S BUSINESS

Lu 2:49 And he said unto them, How is it that ye sought me? wist ye not that I must be about my Father's business?

TO PREACH

Lu 4:43 And he said unto them, I must preach the kingdom of God to other cities also: for therefore am I sent.

TO ACCOMPLISH HIS WORK

Lu 12:50 But I have a baptism to be baptized with; and how am I straitened till it be accomplished!

TO WORK WHILE THE DAY LASTED

Jn 9:4 I must work the works of him that sent me, while it is day: the night cometh, when no man can work.

TO GO TO JERUSALEM TO SUFFER

Mt 16:21 From that time forth began Jesus to shew unto his disciples, how that he must go unto Jerusalem, and suffer many things of the elders and chief priests and scribes, and be killed, and be raised again the third day.

b. For Calling the Lost to Himself

Mt 18:11 For the Son of man is come to save that which was lost.

Jn 4:35 Say not ye, There are yet four months, and *then* cometh harvest? behold, I say unto you, Lift up your eyes, and look on the fields; for they are white already to harvest.

Ro 9:3 For I could wish that myself were accursed from Christ for my brethren, my kinsmen according to the flesh:

Ro 10:1 Brethren, my heart's desire and prayer to God for Israel is, that they might be saved.

Ro 11:14 If by any means I may provoke to emulation *them which are* my flesh, and might save some of them.

1 Co 9:22 To the weak became I as weak, that I might gain the weak: I am made all things to all *men*, that I might by all means save some.

4. Of the Unwise

Mt 9:31; 13:28; 26:51; Mk 1:45; 7:36; 14:47; Lu 22:50; Jn 6:15; 16:2; 18:10; Ro 10:2; Ga 4:17

ZEBEDEE, *Yahweh bestows, James and John were his sons*

Mt 4:21; Mk 1:20; Lu 5:10

ZEBULUN, *honor*

1. Son of Jacob

Ge 30:20; 35:23; 46:14; 49:13; Nu 1:9; 2:7; 10:16; 26:26; De 33:18; Jos 19:10, 16, 34; Eze 48:27, 33

2. Tribe

Nu 1:30; 13:10; 34:25; Jos 21:7, 34; Jud 1:30; 4:6; 6:35; 1 Chr 6:63, 77; 12:33; 27:19; 2 Chr 30:11, 18; Ps 68:27; Mt 4:15; Re 7:8

ZECHARIAH

1. Person, *a prophet*

Ezr 5:1; 6:14; Zec 1:1; 7:1

2. Book

Author: Zechariah, the son of Berechiah (1:1). Little is definitely known concerning this prophet. He was a contemporary of Haggai and joined him in arousing the Jews to rebuild the temple at Jerusalem (Ezr 6:14). Evidently he was a young man at the time of his prophecy (2:4). In the Septuagint version several psalms are accredited to Zechariah and Haggai.

Date Written: 520–519 B.C., two months after Haggai's prophecy (compare Hag 1:1 and Zec 1:1).

Purpose: To give hope to God's people during a time when circumstances were trying and promote spiritual revival so that people's hearts would turn again to the Lord.

To Whom Written: The remnant, especially those who had returned from exile in Babylon.

Main Theme: The future hope—"it shall be light" (14:7). Zechariah is known as the prophet of the long vision. His style was highly figurative. Like Haggai, he saw the sinful condition and religious indifference of his people and uttered stirring exhortations that aided in the rebuilding of the temple. But the prophecy had a broader scope—he looked down the ages and beheld the coming of the Messiah King and the dawning of a brighter day for Zion. Other themes are the divine presence (2:4), power (v. 6), glory (v. 7), and peace (v. 9).

Key Words: Your King is coming to you (9:9).

Key Verses: 1:3; 4:6.

ZEDEKIAH, *Yahweh is [my] righteousness*

1. Or Mattaniah, king of Judah, son of Josiah

2 K 24:17; 25:2; 1 Chr 3:15; 2 Chr 36:11; Je 1:3; 21:1; 24:8; 27:3, 12; 28:1; 32:3; 34:2; 37:1; 39:1; 49:34; 52:1

See **ISRAEL**

2. A False Prophet

1 K 22:11; 2 Chr 18:10; Je 29:22

ZEPHANIAH, *a priest in the reign of Zedekiah*

1. Person, *a priest in the reign of Zedekiah*

2 K 25:18; Je 21:1; 29:25; 52:24

2. Book

Author: Zephaniah is evidently a direct descendant of King Hezekiah (1:1). He prophesied during the reign of Josiah, King of Judah (1:1). Tradition says that Zephaniah was associated with Huldah, the prophetess, and Jeremiah in the initiation of the reformation of the kingdom.

Date Written: Probably shortly before 628 B.C. It is thought he uttered his prophecy near the beginning of Josiah's reign (640 B.C.), before the religious revival which swept over the kingdom in 628 B.C. See 2 Kings 22–23.

Purpose: To motivate God's people to repent and return to God.

To Whom Written: Judah and surrounding nations.

Main Theme: The searching judgments of God.

Key Words: Judgment ("The Day of the Lord") and Hope.

Key Verse: 1:12.

ZERESH See **WOMEN**

ZERUBBABEL, *or Sheshbazzar, leader of the Jews who returned from captivity*

Ezr 2:2; 3:2, 8; 4:2; 5:2; Ne 7:7; 12:1, 47; Hag 1:1, 12, 14; 2:2, 21, 23; Zec 4:6; Mt 1:12; Lu 3:27

ZERUIAH, *sister of David, mother of Joab, Abishai, and Asahel*

2 S 2:18; 3:39; 16:9; 17:25; 23:18; 1 Chr 2:16

ZIBA, *Saul's servant*

2 S 16:1; 19:26

ZIF See **MONTHS**

ZIKLAG, *a city of Judah*

Jos 15:31; 19:5; 1 S 27:6; 30:1, 14; 2 S
1:1; 1 Chr 4:30; 12:1, 20; Ne 11:28

ZIMRI See **ISRAEL**

ZIN, *wilderness*

Nu 13:21; 20:1; 27:14; 33:36; 34:3; De
1:19; 32:51; Jos 14:10; 15:1; 24:7

ZION, *or Sion*

Mount Zion originally referred to "the
city of David," which was the lower
eastern hill of Jerusalem known as
Ophel (2 Chr 27:3; 33:14). Later, when
Mount Moriah became the Temple Hill
and the ark of the covenant was
brought up out of the city of David to
the temple, the name was transferred
here (1 K 8:1; 2 Chr 5:2) and this became "Zion"—the most significant of
all sacred places to the prophets and
others of those centuries (Is 4:5;
Je 31:6; Zec 8:2–3). In certain poetic
writings Zion becomes the equivalent
of Jerusalem, the religious capital of the
people of God (Is 28:16; Ro 9:33). At
other points in the Old Testament it refers to the tribe or land of Judah or the
whole of Israel. By the fourth century
A.D., Zion referred to the southwest
ridge of Jerusalem instead of the original southeast ridge of David's time.

2 S 5:7; 1 K 8:1; 2 K 19:21; 1 Chr 11:5;
Ps 2:6; 9:11; 48:2, 12; 50:2; 51:18;
69:35; 74:2; 76:2; 87:2; 97:8; 102:13;
110:2; 132:13; 135:21; Is 1:27; 14:32;
24:23; 33:20; 40:9; 60:14; Je 50:5; Lam
5:18; Eze 48:15; Jl 2:1; 3:17, 21; Am 1:2;
Mi 4:8; Ro 11:26; He 12:22; Re 14:1

See **MOUNTAINS AND HILLS**

ZIPPORAH, *wife of Moses*

Ex 2:16; 4:25; 18:2; Nu 12:1

ZOAN, *a city of Egypt*

It was a royal Egyptian store city located
eighteen miles southeast of Damietta
near the mouth of the eastern branch
(Tanitic) of the Nile River (cf. Nu 13:22;
Ps 78:12; Eze 30:14).

See **CITIES**

ZOAR, *a small city of the Moabites near
Jordan*

Ge 13:10; 14:2; 19:22; De 34:3; Is 15:5;
Je 48:34

See **CITIES**

ZOPHAR, *Job's friend*

Jb 11:1; 2:11; 20:1

ZORAH, *a town of Dan*

It was the home of Samson the strong
man (Jud 13:2, 25; 16:31), is now called
Sara (Tel Zora) and is located fifteen
miles west of Jerusalem on a lofty hill
north of the Valley of Sorek. Muslims
have a strong, stone-built shrine here
dedicated to the memory of Samson.
Annexed to Judah (Jos 15:33), Zorah
was   fortified   by   Rehoboam
(2 Chr 11:10) and resettled by returning Judean exiles from Babylon
(Ne 11:29). The Danites collected their
forces here for their successful attack on
Laish (Jud 18).

Jos 19:41; Jud 13:2, 25; 16:31; 18:2;
2 Chr 11:10; Ne 11:29

See **CITIES, SAMSON**

ZUPH, *land of*

1 S 9:5